The Bible for
TODAY'S CHRISTIAN WOMAN

_____

is given to

_____

given by

_____

date

_____

occasion

THE BIBLE FOR

Today's

CHRISTIAN WOMAN

The Contemporary English Version

THOMAS NELSON PUBLISHERS
Nashville

Contents

Old Testament

New Testament

Alphabetical Listing with Abbreviations

Old Testament

New Testament

Other Abbreviations

Circa (around) . . . . c.
Old Testament . . . . OT
New Testament . . . . . . NT
Septuagint LXX

Publisher's Acknowledgment

The helps included in this Bible were created in collaboration with *Today's Christian Woman* magazine under the direction of Ramona Cramer Tucker and Carolyn Nystrom. The Publisher gratefully acknowledges the talents, energy, and enthusiasm they and their writers brought to the table to make this Bible possible.

Today's Christian Woman is a bi-monthly publication designed for women of all ages, single or married, who identify themselves as Christians and who seek to live out biblical values in their home, their workplace, and their community. To that end, TCW seeks to inform women as they face today's issues, to instruct them as they search for biblical answers, to encourage them as they meet new opportunities for growth, and to challenge them as they determine personal priorities in work, single/single again life, marriage, family, parenting, friendship, self life, health, and spiritual life. With sensitivity, humor, and candor, TCW provides depth and balance in lending perspective and insight to the issues that confront today's Christian woman. It affirms that the similar values held among today's Christian women far surpass the differences.

We pray that *The Bible for Today's Christian Woman* will likewise bless, uplift, and sustain the lives of all women who spend time within its pages.

Foreword

Life is filled with complex issues—and as women with busy, multifaceted lives, we're faced with unique challenges. For instance, we may wonder how to be a better friend (or how to find a close friend), how to balance home and work, how to not only survive but thrive in a difficult time, and how to grow closer to God.

If you find yourself asking questions like these and longing for realistic, "doable" advice, *The Bible for Today's Christian Woman* is uniquely suited for you. Its Bible book introductions, notes, character sketches, and quotes are crafted *by* women *for* women, with an easy reference system. Just look up your area of concern in the "Hope and Encouragement Index" pages under one of these seven important topics:

*friendship
*marriage
*parenting and family
*personal concerns
*single life
*spiritual life
*work

Scan the questions under that topic until you find one that's appropriate for your situation. Then look up one or more of the Bible verses noted under the question for a balanced and godly perspective.

What issues do you face today? In *The Bible for Today's Christian Woman,* you'll find answers. But most of all, you'll find irrefutable proof of God's love and care for you—a woman created by God after his own heart.

Ramona Cramer Tucker
Editor
Today's Christian Woman magazine

Introduction

I've always loved studying the Bible.

Some of my early memories of Bible study have to do with earnest (and sometimes loud) debates with my father. I remember attending a small group Bible study for families, led by a favorite high-school teacher. And now, as an adult, I've taken part in small group Bible studies composed of both men and women, representing a variety of ages and stages of belief (some mature Christians, others new believers or not-yet believers). I've found the diversity stimulating. So when *Today's Christian Woman* first approached me to work as general editor on this project, I naturally asked, "Why do a special Bible for women? Isn't the Bible for everyone?"

My answer came from a young woman who was leading a Bible study. "Sometimes when I read the Bible," she admitted to me, "I wonder if maybe God doesn't like women very much." She went on to describe the array of biblical prostitutes and evil queens and her confusion over the apostle Paul's words about women's roles and what that might mean as she turned her sights toward a career as a doctor.

Today, looking back on our conversation, I wish I had answered her gently with these words: *Although the Bible includes some wicked women (from whom we learn what not to do), it also portrays many women who were full of courage and faith, yet who, like us, are in need of God's love. God does love women—he demonstrates it all throughout Scripture!*

And that's why we've created *The Bible for Today's Christian Woman*—a Bible that shows God's specific working throughout history and in women's lives. The text, the Contemporary English Version, is the same as any CEV Bible. Its simple, straightforward language invites the reader to put aside any fears about entering foreign literary territory and just sit down and read. But the notes, book introductions, and character sketches of this Bible are written for women by women.

And what a collection of skills, stages, and interests these contributors represent! They range in age from twenty-something to sixty-seasoned. We have some full-time writers and editors; a couple of professional speakers; a youth pastor; ministry staff-workers; a corporate CEO; a college professor; several stay-at-home moms; two singles (one young, one retirement age); several seminary graduates; moms with newborns, elementary-school-age children, or teenagers; residents of Midwest, South, Far North, East Coast, West Coast, and one who moved from one coast to the other during the course of the project! But these eighteen contributors hold this in common: They're all students of the Bible, and they love the Lord.

But long before these writers began checking reference materials, putting down words, and clicking computer keys, others were gathering groups of women together to ask, "What kinds of questions do you have about the Bible and your life? What are some of the tension points in your relationships? What major areas do you and your friends struggle with?" Out of these discussions seven important topics for women emerged: friendship, marriage, parenting and family, personal concerns, single life, spiritual life, and work.

From these seven topics grew nearly ninety questions, such as: How can I repair a broken friendship? What does it really mean to "become one" with my husband? How can I know what's best for my elderly parents? How can I overcome my tendency to worry? Sometimes I really want to be married; how can I deal with those times? If I've turned away from God, is it possible to come back? How? What's a good way for me to share my faith at work?

The Bible for Today's Christian Woman addresses all these questions and more. After much digging and searching, we narrowed the field to 366 passages of Scripture that deal with these common questions and created notes for each one. (You could read one a day, if you wish.) As you let these passages speak to the important questions of your life you'll discover the amazing practicality of our God. And if you want to take away a nugget of each passage, you'll find the "Words To Remember" at the end of each note useful. You might even want to memorize these few words, so you can hold these truths in your heart long after you've closed the pages.

Besides the 366 notes, this Bible also provides inspirational quotes from well-known women and introductions to each of the Bible's sixty-six books. The book introductions set the stage in culture and history and help you look for ways the ancient events and teachings recorded there can impact your own life.

Also nestled in with the biblical text, sometimes in unexpected places, are character sketches of women who stand out in the pages of Scripture. Many are pictured as being faithful and heroic; others exhibit human weakness, failure, or outright wickedness. Consider Anna, an aging prophetess who knew God when she saw him—even in the form of a baby. Then there's Esther, who saved the life of many Jews in Persia. Gomer was a wayward wife. And Jezebel was so wickedly evil that today her name is still hissed as a term of spite! The Bible is a colorful book—and so are the women it portrays.

So settle into your favorite chair and take five minutes, or five hours, or a five-day retreat. Let the words of Scripture and the writings of other women bring you hope and encouragement for the relationships of your life. And invite the Lord himself to speak to you through the pages of his Word.

Carolyn Nystrom
General Editor
The Bible for Today's Christian Woman

Index to
Hope and Encouragement
for Today's Christian Woman

This easy-to-use index highlights seven major relationship areas that concern women at all ages and stages of life: friendship, marriage, parenting and family, personal concerns, single life, spiritual life, and work. Just scan through the questions in these main categories to zero in on the one that speaks to your immediate need. Underneath each question, you'll find several selections from the Bible—each followed by a one-sentence statement, giving the focus of the note found at that verse or Scripture passage. So set aside a few minutes, and see what God has to say about your particular situation.

✎ FRIENDSHIP ✐

What are the marks of a good friendship?
__ Ruth 1–4 It has staying power and commitment.
__ Proverbs 17.17; 18.24 It "hangs in there."
__ Proverbs 27.17-19 It shapes your character and reputation—for the good.
__ 1 Corinthians 13.4-8 That you love one another.
__ James 5.13-20 That you're able to lean on each other.

How can I have healthy friendships with men?
__ 1 Samuel 25 Focus on God's agenda.
__ 2 Kings 4.1-7 Don't be afraid to ask for appropriate help.
__ 1 Thessalonians 4.1-8 Remember that wrong use of sex cheats people—and God.

How can I tell if a friendship is unhealthy?
__ Psalm 1 By looking at character.
__ Proverbs 4.14,15 By looking at actions.
__ Proverbs 22.24,25 By looking at habits and attitudes.
__ 2 Corinthians 6.14-18 By looking at your commitment to Christ.

How can I repair a broken friendship?
__ Leviticus 19.17,18 Let go of grudges and build bridges instead.
__ Matthew 5.21-26 Ask yourself some difficult questions.
__ Matthew 18.15-20 If possible, keep the matter private between you.
__ Luke 6.37-42 See your own contribution to the rift in your relationship.

How can I keep from comparing myself with my friends?
__ Numbers 6.22-27 Learn to bless your friends.
__ 1 Samuel 16.1-13 Realize you don't know others the way God knows them.
__ Mark 10.29-31,35-45 Remember that earthly position is just that—earthly.

How can I speak the truth in love and still maintain a friendship?
__ Job 42.7-9 Don't give simple answers to hard problems.

__ Proverbs 27.6 Realize that a friendship without truth is not a true friendship.
__ Ephesians 4.25—5.2 Let go of your anger and resentment.
__ James 1.5-8 Ask God for wisdom.

How can I reach out to people who differ from me in habits, faith, culture, or race?

__ John 4.4-26 Be respectful, listen, and share yourself.
__ Romans 3.21-31 See the need for salvation as the great unifier.
__ 2 Corinthians 5.16-21 Focus on what you have in common—a need for Christ.
__ Galatians 3.26-29 Realize believers are all one in Christ.
__ Colossians 4.2-6 Remember that Christianity is about turning "outsiders" into insiders.

How can I encourage a friend who is going through a divorce?

__ Job 13.5-15 Listen, listen, listen.
__ Isaiah 43.2-4 Encourage her with God's words.
__ Isaiah 61.1-3 Point to the God of hope.
__ 2 Corinthians 1.3-7 Draw on the comfort God has given you.

What's the best way to find friends?

__ 1 Kings 19.1-21 Look toward God.
__ 2 Corinthians 2.14-17 Look for people who are "being saved."
__ Revelation 7.9-12 Enjoy the diversity of God's people.

If I'm naturally introverted and independent, why should I go out of my way to make friends?

__ Ecclesiastes 4.9-12 Life goes better with friends.
__ John 13.18-35 To live out God's command to "love each other."
__ Hebrews 13.1,2 Because God tells us to "welcome" others.

Sometimes I feel God is asking me to befriend someone I naturally dislike or who annoys me. How can I overcome my natural inclination to avoid that friendship?

__ Ezekiel 2.1-7 Remember that God doesn't limit himself to nice people.
__ Zechariah 4.1-10 Depend on God's Spirit, not your own strength.
__ Mark 2.13-17 Focus on that person's potential to follow Jesus.
__ 1 Corinthians 10.31—11.1 Follow the example of Christ.

How can I forgive a friend who has greatly wronged or disappointed me?

__ Romans 7.21—8.5 Make grace a state where you live.
__ Ephesians 2.1-10 Remember you, too, are a sinner saved by grace.
__ Colossians 3.12-14 Ask God to give you the power to forgive.

How can I show my friend that Christ is the only way to God?

__ Isaiah 7.10-17 Tell her Christ is the promised Savior.
__ Isaiah 53 Show her the straight path.
__ Mark 16.1-8 Point out that only Jesus rose from death never to die again.
__ John 14.1-14 Encourage her to get to know Jesus.

❧ MARRIAGE ☙

What does a healthy, successful marriage look like?

__ Genesis 2.18-23 It's a partnership.
__ Exodus 32.11-14 It forgives.
__ Song of Songs 8.5-7 It loves—forever.
__ Hosea 14.4-8 It mirrors the love of God.

__ Acts 18 It's a team effort.
__ Hebrews 13.4 It's focused and committed.

What does it really mean to "become one" with my husband?
__ Genesis 2.18-25 You realize becoming one requires both union and separation.
__ Ruth 1.15-18 You accept your husband's family as your own.
__ 1 Corinthians 12.12-31 You feel each other's pain and joy.

How does God define my role as a wife?
__ Proverbs 31.10-31 To be godly in attitude *and* actions.
__ Ecclesiastes 7.11-14 To be wise, godly, and cheerful—no matter what.
__ Colossians 3.15-19 To think of your husband before yourself.

How can we prevent financial issues from becoming stumbling blocks in our marriage?
__ Psalm 49.16-20 Grow a generous personality.
__ Malachi 3.8-12 Make giving to God your top priority.
__ Matthew 6.19-24 Treasure your husband.
__ 1 Timothy 6.6-10 Don't focus too much on finances.
__ Hebrews 13.5,6 Don't fall in love with money.

Why does the Bible talk about submission in marriage? What does God mean by it?
__ Proverbs 17.1 Mutual submission leads to a peaceful home life.
__ Ephesians 5.21-33 Submission is an issue for both husbands and wives.
__ Philippians 2.1-11 What's most important is doing what's best for each other.

How can my husband and I grow spiritually as a couple?
__ Galatians 6.1-3 Support each other as you grow together.
__ Hebrews 5.11—6.3 Learn to grow deeper.
__ 1 Peter 4.8-11 Enjoy and use your God-given differences.

How can I lead my unbelieving husband to Christ without offending him?
__ Genesis 39; 41.39 Keep doing what is right and leave the rest to God.
__ Song of Songs 2.16—3.4 Keep reaching for him.
__ John 13.1-17 Show your husband grace, humility, and unconditional love.
__ 1 Peter 3.1-6 Win him over by what you do.
__ Revelation 21.9—22.21 Show him your hope of eternity.

My husband doesn't share my passion for spiritual things. How can I deal with my frustration and sadness?
__ Job 6.14-21 Ask believing friends for help.
__ James 5.7-11 Practice patience.
__ Revelation 21.1-4 Remember that God himself will wipe away your tears.

What's essential for a healthy, rewarding sex life?
__ Genesis 1.27-31 Recognize that sex is a gift from God.
__ Song of Songs 5.10-16 Use passionate words.
__ 1 Corinthians 7.1-5 Keep practicing. Keep talking.

What does God think about divorce?
__ Malachi 2.13-16 Divorce is cruel.
__ Matthew 19.1-9 God's original design is for marriage—for a lifetime.
__ 1 Corinthians 7.10-16 God wants us to be at peace with each other.
__ Ephesians 4.1-6 God emphasizes unity.

How can I learn to forgive my husband even when he doesn't apologize?
__ Jeremiah 33.1-9 Choose to forgive.
__ Ephesians 2.14-18 Let Jesus help you tear down walls of discord.
__ 1 Peter 3.8-15 Remember that your feelings matter to God.

My husband is emotionally distant. How can I feel closer to him?
__ Proverbs 3.27-35 Resist closing yourself off.
__ Zephaniah 3.16,17 Keep trusting in God's power and goodness.
__ Ephesians 4.14-16 Tell him the truth with love.

PARENTING AND FAMILY

Sometimes I get upset and angry with my kids. How can I maintain a loving attitude when I'm about to explode?
__ Proverbs 15.1-4,18 Realize that anger only breeds more conflict.
__ Matthew 11.25-29 Set aside distractions.
__ Titus 3.3-8 Remember how much God's love and patience means to you.

How can I nurture my child's self-worth?
__ 1 Samuel 17.24-54 Invite questions.
__ Psalm 139 Create a sense of God-worth.
__ Luke 15.11-32 Show your children unconditional love.
__ Ephesians 1.3-14 Set an example of healthy self-worth.
__ 2 Thessalonians 3.6-15 Give your child age-appropriate work to do.

How can I effectively balance my roles as parent and wife?
__ Deuteronomy 8.1-10 Look to the example of God, the heavenly Father.
__ Job 38.1—40.5 Put everything in perspective.
__ 1 Peter 4.1-8 Love each other.

How can I raise a child to be kind and considerate of others?
__ Jonah 1 Remind your child that God cares about everyone.
__ Matthew 5.43-48 Pray for people you don't get along with.
__ Luke 10.25-37 Help your child see others in a new way.
__ 3 John 4-11 Be hospitable yourself.

How can I know what's best for my elderly parents?
__ Psalm 25 Keep communication lines open.
__ Proverbs 23.22-25 Show respect to your parents by living a godly life.
__ Joel 2.28-32 Respect their dreams.
__ 1 Corinthians 15.35-58 Accept the aging process—even death.
__ 1 Timothy 5.1-7 Take care of them.

How can I tell if I'm doing a good job as a mother?
__ Luke 2.41-52 Remember that God always knows what's best for your children.
__ Ephesians 6.1-4 Teach your children who they *really* belong to.
__ Hebrews 12.5-13 Practice the art of discipline.

How can I encourage my child's faith to grow?
__ Joshua 4 Draw attention to the many ways God is working in our lives.
__ 1 Chronicles 22 Remember that kids need prayers, too.
__ Ezra 3 Find a place to worship with God's people.
__ Proverbs 2.1-15 Be an example.
__ John 3.16-21 Explain the simple message of God's love.

How can I protect my kids from negative cultural influences?
__ Ezra 8.21-34 Ask God to guard them.
__ Psalm 119.97-105 Use proactive protection.
__ Proverbs 4.10-27 Model godly living in a fallen world.
__ Song of Songs 8.8,9 Protect, but don't smother.
__ 1 Peter 5.2-11 Be their shepherd.

What advice, if any, should I give to my twentysomething child?
__ Ecclesiastes 11.1—12.1 Enjoy youth; remember God.
__ Ezekiel 18.1-20 Remember that each of us is accountable to God.
__ Amos 5.6-27 Choose good instead of evil; see that justice is done.
__ Matthew 14.24-33 Aim for independence.
__ 1 Timothy 4.6-16 Keep the faith.

How can I best relate to my adult child?
__ Genesis 13,14 Be a resource, not a controller.
__ Ruth 3 Pass on your wisdom and experience, but let your child make final decisions.
__ John 3.1-21 Pray that your child will decide where he or she is heading—eternally.

How can I deal with the challenges of being a single parent?
__ 1 Kings 17.8-16 Trust God to meet your needs.
__ Psalm 71.1-6 Rely on past records of God's work in your life.
__ Psalm 138 Ask God—and others—for help.
__ Philippians 4.10-20 Invite help from people around you, and give your help to them.

~PERSONAL CONCERNS~

How can I learn to set priorities?
__ Genesis 22.1-19 Always put God first.
__ 1 Samuel 15.10-35 Practice zero-based prioritizing.
__ Haggai 2.6-9 Share the Lord's priority: his glory.
__ Luke 10.38-42 Make time to spend with God, no matter how busy you are.
__ Revelation 2.1-7 Don't put work ahead of love.

When a poor decision on my part has damaged my reputation as a Christian, what can I do?
__ Joel 2.12-17 Return to God with all your heart.
__ Jonah 2,3 Remember, God is a God of second chances.
__ Micah 7.18,19 Realize you can't change the past, but you can change the present.
__ Zechariah 10.6-12 Let God's forgiveness help you start afresh.
__ Luke 7.36-50 Serve others.
__ Galatians 1.11-24 Realize God can use even our failures for his good purposes.

How can I handle even difficult times positively?
__ Leviticus 26.1-13 Know that God is with you!
__ Job 23 Remember, God is always at work—even when you can't see him.
__ Micah 4.1-5 Realize your story's not over yet.
__ Nahum 1.2-7,15 Don't dwell on revenge.
__ Romans 8.18-30 Be confident about the future—even if you can't always smile.
__ Ephesians 1.7-23 Trust that God knows what he's doing in your life.

What can I do when I've hurt someone?
__ Psalm 51 Make a sincere apology.

___ Luke 19.1-10 Be willing to go the extra mile to make amends.

___ Luke 22.54-62 Let the other person see your genuine sorrow.

How can I forgive someone who has broken my trust?

___ Numbers 14.11-25 Forgive, but be careful where you place your trust the next time.

___ 1 Samuel 24 Trust God to look out for you.

___ Matthew 7.1-5 Use compassionate standards.

___ Matthew 18.21-35 Pass on God's love.

___ Luke 6.27-36 Model yourself on your heavenly Father.

How can I learn to be more content with my life?

___ Psalm 107 Blend the real with the ideal.

___ Ecclesiastes 6.1-9 Enjoy what you have.

___ Daniel 2.20,21 Realize God is in control of it.

___ 2 Peter 1.3-15 Fill up on more of the right things.

How can I overcome my tendency to worry and instead gain confidence about the future?

___ Joshua 23.14-16 Learn to rely on God's promises.

___ Psalm 91 See God as your Savior, not as a saboteur.

___ Micah 5.2-5 Know what's been and watch for what's coming.

___ Habakkuk 3.16-19 Trust God to give you strength.

___ Matthew 6.25-34 Do what you can in a single day.

___ Philippians 4.4-9 Turn your worries into conversation with God.

Sometimes I'm jealous of others. How can I get out of the jealousy/envy trap?

___ 1 Samuel 20 Nurture your friend's success.

___ Psalm 73.1-20 Believe that God knows you best.

___ Jonah 4 Practice contentment instead of anger.

___ James 3.1-12 Watch your mind—and your tongue.

How can I accept my body as it is?

___ Psalm 104 Don't judge yourself by magazine covers.

___ Psalm 139.13-16 Look in your mirror—and praise God.

___ Mark 14.3-9 Remember, beauty is more than skin deep.

When it comes to material things, how can I know what's enough and what's too much?

___ Leviticus 25.8-28 Remember that all our possessions belong to God.

___ Deuteronomy 24.19-22 Realize God gives us plenty so we can share with others.

___ Amos 6.1-7 Prayerfully consider what to buy and how to help others.

___ Philippians 3.7-16 Keep things in their proper perspective.

___ 1 Timothy 6.17-19 Focus your attention on God, instead of stuff.

Should I maintain friendships with non-Christians? If so, how can I keep from compromising my faith?

___ Obadiah 10-14 Be supportive, not condemning, when your non-Christian friends face hard times.

___ Matthew 22.34-40 Love your neighbor—but love God first.

___ Romans 3.9-20 Keep a balance of Christian and non-Christian friends.

How should I handle it when I feel rejected or excluded because of my faith?

___ Daniel 6 Face the lions—with God on your side.

___ John 15.18-27 Be comforted by the fact that Jesus was also hated.

___ Hebrews 10.32-39 Stand firm.
___ 1 Peter 4.12-19 Feel included—among the ranks of Christians.
___ Revelation 14.12,13 Learn to endure.

⮜ SINGLE LIFE ⮞

How can I resist the pressure to be sexually active?
___ Joshua 7 Determine to obey God completely—even when you are tempted.
___ Psalm 103 Ask for God's strength.
___ Ephesians 6.10-20 Be wise, and look for friends to support you.
___ James 1.12-18 Respect God's good gift.
___ 2 Peter 2.7-9 Remember that God rewards righteousness.

How can I feel whole when the world sees me as half?
___ Psalm 23 Let God stick up for you.
___ Isaiah 40.21-31 Remember, God gives you freedom to soar.
___ Philippians 1.12-30 Hang out with people who can manage bad press.

How can God use me as a single woman?
___ Exodus 15.19-21 Remember, he used Miriam as a prophet and worship leader.
___ Judges 6,7 Trust God's strength—not your own.
___ 2 Samuel 20.14-22 Be a clear thinker.
___ Malachi 3.16-18 Ask God how you can serve him!

How can I tell the difference between good ambition and self-centeredness?
___ Genesis 11.1-9 Look at your motives.
___ Mark 8.34-38 Shift your thinking to an eternal perspective.
___ Hebrews 4.12,13 Use Scripture as a check.

What should I look for in a future spouse?
___ Genesis 24 Look for qualities you could live with the rest of your life.
___ Song of Songs 1 Look for a man who treasures you.
___ 1 Corinthians 13 Look for someone who's able to give and receive love—long term.
___ Ephesians 5.21-33 Look for a man who's sacrificial.

Sometimes I really want to be married. How can I deal with those times?
___ Psalm 84 Find your heart's home.
___ Jeremiah 29.10-14 Remember that God holds your future in his hands.
___ 1 Peter 3.13-18 Consider your current status a sacrifice for your faith.

How can I overcome my feelings of loneliness?
___ Psalm 22 Take your pain to God.
___ Psalm 68.4-6 Ask God to provide family members.
___ Matthew 26.36-46 Realize that loneliness is common to *all* humans.
___ 2 Timothy 4.16-18 Focus on the one who never leaves us.
___ Revelation 3.20-22 Enjoy the company of Christ.

As a single mom, is it all right for me to date? Should I wait until my children are grown?
___ Isaiah 51.12-16 Put your fears in God's hand.
___ Daniel 12 Consider the end result.
___ 2 Thessalonians 2.13-17 Let love for God and your children determine your choices.

I like being single. Is that normal?
___ Numbers 11 God wants us to be content where he puts us.
___ Nehemiah 4; 6.15,16 God needs people who can give their all to their work.
___ Romans 14.1-12 God wants you to humbly enjoy your life.
___ 1 Corinthians 7.29-35 Sure, Paul liked it, too.

How can I best relate to my married friends?
___ Romans 15.1-6 Realize you have plenty to offer in any relationship.
___ Ephesians 5.1-5 Don't flirt with a friend's husband, for any reason.
___ 1 John 4.7-12 Remember that envy builds walls; love breaks them down.

What if I'm longing for children?
___ Jeremiah 20.7-18 God can handle your strongest emotions.
___ Daniel 10.2-19 God hears your prayers.
___ Matthew 18.5 For now, welcome and love the children you encounter.

☙ SPIRITUAL LIFE ❧

How should I pray?
___ 2 Samuel 7.18-29 Tell it like it is.
___ 2 Kings 19.14-19 Be specific when you present your requests.
___ 2 Chronicles 6,7 Pray for your nation.
___ Nehemiah 1 Praise God and confess your sins.
___ Psalm 85 Look beyond me, myself, and I.
___ Lamentations 5 Pour out your heart to God.
___ Matthew 6.5-15 Forget about appearances.
___ Acts 4.23-31 Ask God for courage.

What does God expect of me?
___ Exodus 20.1-17 Follow God's rules for loving him and others.
___ Judges 5.1-11 Give God praise for your victories.
___ Jeremiah 1.4-19 Speak up when he asks you to.
___ Micah 6.6-8 Be truly devoted, not outwardly religious.
___ Romans 8.1-17 Live by the power of his Spirit.
___ 1 Corinthians 6.12-20 Honor God with your body.

How can I make God's presence real in my life?
___ 2 Chronicles 29.20-36 Practice worship.
___ Ezekiel 10 Realize that even when you don't "feel" God's presence, he's there.
___ Romans 15.14-21 It's already real; just tune in!
___ Ephesians 3.14-21 Kneel before him.
___ Colossians 3.10,11 Treat others with respect and compassion.

How can I keep my life centered on God?
___ Genesis 12.1-7 Focus on the promises of God—and then do what he says.
___ Matthew 25.31-46 Serve others with your eye on God.
___ Acts 13.1-5 Invite help from other believers.
___ Galatians 5.16-26 Stay open to the presence and influence of the Holy Spirit.
___ 2 Timothy 2.14-26 Make the right choices along the way.
___ 2 John Get to know who Christ Jesus, his Son, really is.

Will God really condemn people who don't accept Christ as their Savior?
___ Deuteronomy 30 Rejecting God means choosing death.
___ Zephaniah 1.14-18 Only those who believe in him will be saved.

___ John 3.16-18 Those who don't receive Christ remain in the condemned state in which they were born.
___ John 6.60-69 God invites people to Christ, but they need to accept the invitation.
___ Romans 10.5-21 God condemns no one. People choose to reject God.

Is it okay to be angry at God?
___ Numbers 20.1-13 Don't let anger lead to active rebellion.
___ Job 19 Don't lose sight of who God is.
___ Psalm 10 Find the art of saying the "unsayable."
___ Habakkuk 1.2-5 Be angry at what angers God.

How can I learn to appreciate and use the talents and gifts God has given me?
___ 1 Samuel 16.14-23 Look for open doors.
___ 1 Chronicles 15.1—16.3 Don't underestimate your potential.
___ 1 Corinthians 14.1-25 Point others to God.

I'm so busy! How can I find time for God?
___ Mark 13.32-37 Make God the companion of your schedule.
___ 1 Thessalonians 4.13-18 Make every moment count.
___ Titus 3.4-7,14 Filter out activities that don't have lasting value.

How can I handle my doubts about God?
___ Job 1 Realize you can't see the big picture.
___ Psalm 136 Replay the events.
___ Jeremiah 23.16-32 Consider the source.
___ Romans 4.13-25 Let your doubts lead to deeper discovery.
___ Colossians 2.6-19 Plant your roots in Christ, and let them grow deeper.

Why is it important for me to go to church?
___ Ezekiel 43.1-5 You can see God's glory there.
___ Acts 2.1-13,41-47 The Christian faith is best practiced among other believers.
___ Romans 12.3-8 You need people; people need you.
___ 1 Corinthians 3.10-17 The people of a church make up God's temple.
___ Ephesians 2.11-22 The church shows Christ's transforming power to the world.

How can I reach out to a needy world?
___ 2 Samuel 9 Talk face-to-face.
___ Nehemiah 5.1-13 Do what you can to correct injustice.
___ Lamentations 2.11-13 Start with compassion.
___ Jonah 4.5-11 Try to see the world through God's eyes.
___ Zechariah 7.7-13 Give help to the powerless.
___ Matthew 6.1-4 Enjoy little secrets with God.
___ Luke 9.10-17 Realize Jesus has the power to use even our smallest efforts.

Does prayer really make a difference?
___ 2 Chronicles 20.1-30 Prayer gets us ready for God to act.
___ Jeremiah 21.1-10 Prayer prepares us for God's answer, even when it's a "no."
___ Matthew 7.7-12 Prayer cultivates a searching heart.
___ Luke 18.1-8 Prayer both demonstrates and strengthens our faith.
___ 2 Corinthians 12.6-10 God always responds to our requests.

How can I show my devotion to God?
___ 1 Kings 18 Speak up for God's truth.
___ 1 Chronicles 29.1-20 Let God decide who does what.
___ Haggai 1.1-11 Use some of your money for God's purposes.

__ Acts 4.32—5.11 Follow God's standards.
__ 1 Corinthians 13.11-13 Show faith, hope, and love.

How can I know good spiritual leaders?
__ 1 Kings 12.1-20 They are good listeners, wise, and discerning.
__ Ezra 7 They know God's law and follow it.
__ Matthew 17.1-13 They shine with the light of Jesus.
__ Jude 3-7 They preach God's righteousness.

How can I worship God as I should?
__ Nehemiah 8.1—9.6 Involve your whole being.
__ Nehemiah 12.27-43 Praise God with all kinds of music.
__ Job 42.1-6 Admit you cannot fully understand God.
__ Psalm 42 Worship with a thirsty heart.

If I've turned away from God, is it possible to come back? How?
__ Isaiah 55.6-13 Join the celebration.
__ Lamentations 3.31-40 Yes, because God always wants us back.
__ Ezekiel 37.1-14 Ask God, who can bring you back to life.
__ Hosea 3 Yes, because God keeps coming back.
__ Joel 2.25-27 God can make up for wasted years.
__ 1 John 1.8—2.2 Trust God to forgive you.

༄ WORK ༄

How can I balance the competing demands of home and work?
__ Exodus 23.10-13 Work during the week—but leave weekends for worship and recreation.
__ Deuteronomy 6.1-9 Put God first in every area of your life.
__ 2 Samuel 1 Focus your eyes on God.
__ Matthew 14.22,23 Plan a getaway.

How can I have healthy relationships with the men I work with?
__ Esther 4 Be someone your coworkers can count on.
__ Proverbs 5 Keep appropriate sexual boundaries.
__ Romans 12.9-18 Treat male coworkers as brothers.
__ Galatians 6.1-10 Help each other live by God's purposes.

How can I rise above office politics?
__ Deuteronomy 5.20,21 Hold yourself above gossip and jealousy.
__ Esther 7.1-6 Put yourself at risk if it will prevent harm to others.
__ Matthew 20.20-28 Remember who you are.
__ Galatians 5.13-16 Realize you're free—to respond with love.
__ Colossians 3.22—4.1 Recognize that your master is God.
__ James 3.5-18 Don't overrate the in-crowd.

Sometimes I think it's okay to work while my kids are young; other times I'm not sure. How can I be certain I'm making the best decision for my family?
__ Proverbs 16.1-3 Check the motives behind your decision.
__ Romans 14.13-23 Seek God's wisdom in your decision.
__ Titus 2.3-8 Make sure your priorities align with Scripture.

My husband is sometimes threatened by my career. How should I respond?
__ Numbers 12 Try these four steps for dealing with jealousy.
__ Luke 3.7-20 Focus on Christ's power, not your own.

__ 1 Corinthians 12.1-11 Respect your own and your husband's skills as gifts from God.

How can I find satisfaction with my life outside of work?
__ Deuteronomy 8.10-20 Realize your value doesn't depend on what you do but on who God is.
__ Ecclesiastes 3.1-14 Aim for balance in how you use time.
__ Isaiah 55.1-5 Accept God's invitation.

How can I deal with a dishonest coworker?
__ Psalm 26 Stay true to yourself—and don't doubt God's power.
__ Proverbs 28.11-26 Set an example by your own honesty and integrity.
__ Amos 2 Honor God in the way you do business.
__ Habakkuk 2.4-17 Remember, dishonesty often brings its own punishment.

Sometimes my male colleagues don't take me seriously. How can a Christian woman be assertive at work without being offensive?
__ Genesis 50.15-21 Trust God to bring good even from acts that are intended to harm.
__ Judges 4.4-15 When given opportunity to lead, do it well.
__ Isaiah 11.1-9 Learn to lead.
__ Ephesians 5.6-21 Demonstrate your talents with integrity and humility.

How can I be a good supervisor?
__ Exodus 18 Pick capable people and give them clearly defined responsibilities.
__ 1 Kings 3.5-15; 4.29-34 Listen to God.
__ Ezra 5.1—6.12 Manage conflicts by focusing on what's really important.
__ Jeremiah 32.26-44 Lead by example.
__ John 21.15-25 Be gracious about the imperfections of others.
__ 2 Timothy 1.1-7 Help other people flourish.
__ Philemon 8-16 Correct the mistake; forgive the person.
__ Philemon 15-25 Don't let position go to your head.

How can I be more confident about my work?
__ Deuteronomy 31.1-6 God always equips you to do what he calls you to do.
__ Joshua 1.1-9 God is always with you.
__ Psalm 73.21-28 God is your strength.
__ Psalm 108 God is your silent partner at work.
__ 1 John 3.19-24 Obedience to God leads to confidence.

Can I do the "Lord's work" in a secular job? If so, how?
__ 1 Samuel 14.1-15 Examine who you are at work.
__ Ecclesiastes 2.24-26 Try to enjoy the work you have or find work that you enjoy.
__ Matthew 4.18-22 Listen for God's voice.
__ Matthew 15.10-20 Let God work from the inside out.

What's a good way for me to share my faith at work?
__ 2 Corinthians 4.1-15 Remember you are a clay jar—with treasure inside.
__ 1 Thessalonians 4.9-12 Earn the respect of your coworkers.
__ 1 Timothy 5.17—6.2 Be honest, respectful, and fair—just as if you were in church.
__ 2 Timothy 1.6-14 Bring your faith up naturally when it's appropriate.

Index to
Women of the Bible
Character Sketches

Welcome to the Contemporary English Version

Languages are spoken before they are written. And far more communication is done through the spoken word than through the written word. In fact, more people *hear* the Bible read than read it for themselves. Traditional translations of the Bible count on the *reader's* ability to understand a *written* text. But the *Contemporary English Version* differs from all other English Bibles—past and present—in that it takes into consideration the needs of the *hearer*, as well as those of the reader, who may not be familiar with traditional biblical language.

The *Contemporary English Version* has been described as a "user-friendly" and a "mission-driven" translation that can be *read aloud* without stumbling, *heard* without misunderstanding, and *listened to* with enjoyment and appreciation, because the language is contemporary and the style is lucid and lyrical.

The *Contemporary English Version* invites you to *read*, to *hear*, to *understand* and to *share*

the Word of God now
as never before!

The Contemporary English Version

*Translation it is that opens the window, to let in the light; that breaks
the shell, that we may eat the kernel; that puts aside the curtain, that
we may look into the most holy place; that removes the cover of the
well, that we may come by the water* ("The Translators to the
Reader," King James Version, 1611).

The most important document in the history of the English language is the King
James Version of the Bible. To measure its spiritual impact on the English-speaking
world would be more impossible than counting the grains of sand along the ocean
shores. Historically, many Bible translators have attempted in some measure to
retain the form of the King James Version. But the translators of the Contemporary
English Version of the Bible have diligently sought to *capture the spirit* of the King
James Version by following certain principles set forth by its translators in the
document "The Translators to the Reader," which was printed in the earliest
editions.

This is the Word of God, which we translate

Accuracy, beauty, clarity, and dignity—all of these can and must be achieved in the
translation of the Bible. After all, as the translators of the King James Version
stated, "This is the Word of God, which we translate."

Every attempt has been made to produce a text that is faithful to the *meaning*
of the original. In order to assure the *accuracy* of the Contemporary English
Version, the Old Testament was translated directly from the Hebrew and Aramaic
texts published by the United Bible Societies (*Biblia Hebraica Stuttgartensia,* fourth
edition corrected). And the New Testament was translated directly from the Greek
text published by the United Bible Societies (third edition corrected and compared
with the fourth revised edition).

The drafts in their earliest stages were sent for review and comment to a
number of biblical scholars, theologians, and educators representing a wide variety
of church traditions. In addition, drafts were sent for review and comment to all
English-speaking Bible Societies and to more than forty United Bible Societies
translation consultants around the world. Final approval of the text was given by
the American Bible Society Board of Trustees on the recommendation of its
Translations Subcommittee.

We desire that the Scripture . . . may be understood

That the Scripture may be understood even by ordinary people was a primary goal
of the translators of the King James Version. And they raised the question, "What
can be more available thereto than to deliver God's book unto God's people in a
tongue which they understand?" Martin Luther also did his translation for the
common people, and he established the following guidelines:

We do not have to inquire of the literal Latin, how we are to
speak German . . . Rather we must inquire about this of the
mother in the home, the children on the street, the common

man in the marketplace. *We must be guided by their language, the way they speak, and do our translating accordingly.*

Today more people *hear* the Bible read aloud than read it for themselves! And statistics released by the National Center for Education indicate that "almost half of U.S. adults have very limited reading and writing skills." If this is the case, a contemporary translation must be a text that an inexperienced reader can *read aloud* without stumbling, that someone unfamiliar with traditional biblical terminology can *hear without misunderstanding,* and that everyone can *listen to with enjoyment* because the style is lucid and lyrical.

In order to attain these goals of clarity, beauty, and dignity, the translators of the Contemporary English Version carefully studied every word, phrase, clause, and paragraph of the original. Then, with equal care, they struggled to discover the best way to translate the text, so that it would be suitable both for *private* and *public* reading, and for *memorizing.* The result is an English text that is enjoyable and easily understood by the vast majority of English speakers, regardless of their religious or educational background.

In the *hearing* of a translation, even the inclusion of a simple word like "and" can make a significant difference. Matthew 2.9 of the Contemporary English Version reads as follows: "The wise men listened to what the king said and then left. *And* the star they had seen in the east went on ahead of them until it stopped over the place where the child was."

"And" at the beginning of the second sentence assists both the person who reads the text aloud and those who must depend upon hearing it read. Like all other punctuation marks, the period after "left" is silent, and so the text without "And" could possibly be *heard* as, "The wise men listened to what the king said and then left the star they had seen in the east." However, as the text now stands, the oral reader must pause briefly for a breath before "And," which will signal the hearer that a new sentence has begun.

As another example, try reading the following two sentences aloud: "You yourselves admit, then, that you agree with what your ancestors did" and "for it was better with me then than now." Both suffer from potential tongue twisters ("admit, then, that" and "then than"). But the first is doubly difficult because it consists of a lengthy series of unaccented syllables that do not allow the reader to take a breath. In the Contemporary English Version every attempt has been made to avoid these and other kinds of constructions that could possibly prove problematic for oral reading.

According to the rules of English grammar, the pronoun *he* must refer back to *God* in the following sentence: "The other, however, rebuked him saying, 'Don't you fear *God?* You received the same sentence *he* did.' " But the reference is actually to Jesus, who is mentioned earlier in the passage. Traditional translations assume that the reader can study the printed text and finally figure out the meaning, but the Contemporary English Version is concerned equally with the reader and the *hearer.* And in many situations, the hearer may have only *one* chance to understand what is read aloud.

In poetry, the *appearance of the text on the page* is important, since in oral reading there is a tendency to stress the last word on a line and to pause momentarily before going to the next line, especially if the second line is indented. Compare the three following examples, where the lines of the same text have been broken improperly (left column) and properly (right column):

He brought me out into a broad
    place.
	He brought me out
	    into a broad place.

With the loyal you show yourself
    loyal.
	With the loyal
	    you show yourself loyal.

The Lord my God lights up
    my darkness.
	The Lord my God
	    lights up my darkness.

No fault is to be found with the translation itself. Yet there is a significant difference in the *appearance* of the text on the page, because the lines on the right have been *measured,* in order to prevent unfortunate runovers. In this form, the text not only looks better on the page, but it is easier to read and memorize, and it avoids such disastrous combinations as "He brought me out into a broad" or "With the loyal you show yourself" or "The Lord my God lights up." Moreover, both formats require exactly the same amount of lines.

The first translation in the history of the English Bible to develop a text with measured poetry lines is the Contemporary English Version, in which the translators have consciously created a text that will not suffer from unfortunate line breaks when published in double columns. *Accuracy* is the main concern of translators, but it must be realized that in the translation of biblical poetry, what the reader *sees* is what will be *said,* and what others will *hear.* This means that lines improperly broken can easily lead to a misunderstanding of the text, especially for those who must depend upon *hearing* the Scriptures read.

Hebrew poetry has its own systems of sound, rhyme, and rhythm, as well as a *form* that involves much repetition. It is impossible in English to retain the sounds, rhymes, and rhythms of the Hebrew text, but traditional translations have attempted to reproduce the frequent repetition, in which a second line will repeat or expand, either negatively or positively, the thoughts of the previous line. However, this repetition is often ineffective for those English speakers, who are unaccustomed to the poetic style of the biblical authors. And so, the translators of the Contemporary English Version have followed the example of Martin Luther in the translation of poetry:

> Whoever would speak German *must not use Hebrew style.*
> Rather he must see to it—once he understands the Hebrew
> author—that he concentrates on the *sense* of the text, asking
> himself, "Pray tell, what do the Germans say in such a situa-
> tion?" Once he has the German words to serve his purpose, let
> him drop the Hebrew words and *express the meaning freely* in the
> best German he knows.

The qualities that many critics value most in modern poetry are effortless *economy* and *exactness* of language. It is hoped that readers will discover similar features in the poetry of the Contemporary English Version, which strives for beauty and dignity, as much as for accuracy and clarity. In this translation, the poetry often requires fewer lines than do traditional translations, but the *integrity, intent,* and *impact* of the original are consistently maintained. Note, for example, the rendering of Job 38.14,15:

> Early dawn outlines the hills
> like stitches on clothing
>   or sketches on clay.
> But its light is too much

for those who are evil,
and their power is broken.

Whenever the contents of two or more verses have been joined together and rearranged in the poetic sections of the Contemporary English Version, this is signaled by an asterisk (*) before the first verse number in the series.

In everyday speech, "gender generic" or "inclusive" language is used, because it sounds most natural to people today. This means that where the biblical languages require masculine nouns or pronouns when both men and women are intended, this intention must be reflected in translation, though the English *form* may be very different from that of the original. The Greek text of Matthew 16.24 is literally, "If anyone wants to follow me, *he* must deny *himself* and take up *his* cross and follow me." The Contemporary English Version shifts to a form which is still accurate, and at the same time more effective in English: "If any of *you* want to be my followers, *you* must forget about *yourself. You* must take up *your* cross and follow me."

Variety of translations is profitable

The translators of the King James Version said, ". . . variety of translations is profitable for the finding out of the sense of the Scriptures" and "We affirm and avow that the very meanest translation of the Bible in English, set forth by men of our profession . . . contains the Word of God, nay is the Word of God." They even stated, "No cause therefore why the Word translated should be denied to be the Word, or forbidden to be current, notwithstanding that some imperfections and blemishes may be noted in the setting forth of it."

Each English translation is, in its own right, the Word of God, yet each translation serves to meet the needs of a different audience. In this regard, the Contemporary English Version should be considered a *companion*—the *mission arm*—of traditional translations, because it takes seriously the words of the apostle Paul that "faith comes by *hearing.*"

It has pleased God in his divine providence

Translating the Bible may be compared to living the life of faith. God has not given us all the answers for our pilgrim journey, but we have been provided with all that we need to know in order to be saved. As the translators of the King James Version observed:

> . . . it has pleased God in His divine providence here and there to scatter those words and sentences of that difficulty and doubtfulness, not in doctrinal points that concern salvation (for in such it has been vouched that the Scriptures are plain), but in matters of less moment, that fearfulness would better beseem us than confidence . . .
>
> For as it is a fault of incredulity, to doubt of those things that are evident; so to determine of such things that the Spirit of God has left (even in the mind of the judicious) questionable, can be no less than presumption.

Bible translators do not have the privilege and luxury of working from the original manuscripts of either the Old or New Testament. Indeed, there are numerous difficult passages where decisions must be made concerning what word or words actually belong in the text, and what these words may, in fact, mean. At such places, the best a translator can do is to give what seems to be one possible meaning for the difficult text and to indicate this by a note, which was also what the King James translators did: ". . . so diversity of signification and sense in the margin, where the text is not clear, must needs be good; yea, is necessary, as we are persuaded." Fortunately, these "words and sentences of that difficulty and doubt-fulness" do not in any way leave unclear the central message of the Bible or any of its major doctrines.

Having and using as great helps as were needful

The translators of the Contemporary English Version have not created new or novel interpretations of the text. Rather, it was their goal to express mainstream interpre-tations of the text in current, everyday English. To do so required *listening* carefully to each word of the biblical text, to the way in which English is spoken today, to the remarks of their reviewers, and especially to the Spirit of God. Once again the comments of the translators of the King James Version are appropriate:

> Neither did we think much to consult the translators or
> commentators . . . but neither did we disdain to revise that
> which we had done, and to bring to the anvil that which we had
> hammered; but having and using as great helps as were needful,
> and fearing no reproach for slowness, nor coveting praise for
> expedition, we have at the length, through the good hand of the
> Lord upon us, brought forth the work to that pass that you see.

Accordingly, the translators of the Contemporary English Version are indebted to all translators and biblical scholars who have gone before them and have made it possible to understand something of the languages, cultures, and history of biblical times. And, together with the apostle Paul, they confess: *We don't have the right to claim that we have done anything on our own. God gives us what it takes to do all that we do.* (2 Corinthians 3.5)

Offer praise to God our Savior because of our Lord Jesus Christ! (Jude 24,25)

Old Testament

About the Old Testament

The Old Testament is a collection of 39 books written in Hebrew, with a few chapters written in Aramaic. These books are arranged in five groups in English Bibles:

(1) *The Pentateuch*. The name means "five books," and this group is made up of Genesis, Exodus, Leviticus, Numbers, and Deuteronomy. The group is sometimes called the "Law of Moses" or the "Torah," a Hebrew word referring to God's "law" or "teachings."

(2) *The Historical Books*. This group is made up of Joshua, Judges, Ruth, 1 and 2 Samuel, 1 and 2 Kings, 1 and 2 Chronicles, Ezra, Nehemiah, and Esther. Together, the Pentateuch and Historical books tell the history of Israel two times. The books of Genesis through 2 Kings tell the history the first time, while the books of 1 Chronicles through Nehemiah tell it the second time from a somewhat different point of view.

(3) *The Poetic Books*. This group is sometimes called the "Wisdom Books," and it contains Job, Psalms, Proverbs, Ecclesiastes, and the Song of Songs. Lamentations is also one of the poetic books, but in English Bibles it follows Jeremiah, because Jeremiah has often been thought to be its author.

(4) *The Major Prophets* are longer books that contain the messages of the prophets Isaiah, Jeremiah, Ezekiel, and Daniel.

(5) *The Minor Prophets* are the shorter books that contain the messages of the prophets Hosea, Joel, Amos, Obadiah, Jonah, Micah, Nahum, Habakkuk, Zephaniah, Haggai, Zechariah, and Malachi.

Genesis
A Book of Beginnings

"In the beginning God . . ." (1.1). What a comforting opening to God's holy book! Before there was anything (stars, sand, bugs, molecules), there was God. And he made it all. Not only that, when he had put on the last touches to each stage of his creation, he stood back, admired it, and said "it was good" (1.10). But after God had made the world, he added one more kind of being. This time he stooped down into the dust and with his own hands molded a shape. Then he did something he had not done with any other creature. He breathed into that shape his own breath—the breath of God. The breath that exhaled back into God's face was the breath of a person, a human being with a soul that could know God.

But creation was not the only beginning in Genesis. There was the first sin—and God's care for people who were no longer perfect. Then, the first family, and soon after, the first murder—coupled with a mother's grief—and God's comfort of a new child. When almost everyone refused to know God, he gave the world a fresh start through the family of Noah. Generations later Abraham (ancestor of the Jews and Arabs) gave God's people one more new beginning. Genesis traces the stories of Abraham's family for four generations. Here we see love, jealousy, loyalty, attempted murder, faithfulness, rape, and God's continued presence in their lives.

When we doubt our own worth, Genesis will help us remember God's care in creating us. When we struggle with family dysfunction, we can marvel at God's continued patience with the families here. When we feel "put down" as women, we can empathize with the women of this book and admire their strength. When we wonder if God has abandoned us to evil circumstances, we can imitate the integrity of Joseph—and know that God will continue to use us for good.

Genesis was probably written by Moses during the Hebrews' forty years of desert wanderings in about 1446–1406 B.C. Yet Genesis contains the oral history of God's people told from parent to child from the beginning of time.

Genesis at a Glance

1. Before there was anything, there was God (1.1)
2. Natural beauty comes from God; God made it all (1,2)
3. Why do we do wrong things? It started here (3)
4. The first family and the first murder (4)
5. God uses Noah to give the world a fresh start (5–9), and the world responds by building the Tower of Babel (10,11)
6. God calls Abram (Abraham) to form a new people who belong to God (12–20)

The Story of Creation

1 In the beginning God
created the heavens
and the earth.*

²The earth was barren,
with no form of life;*
it was under a roaring ocean
covered with darkness.
But the Spirit of God*
was moving over the water.

The First Day

³God said, "I command light to shine!" And light started shining. ⁴God looked at the light and saw that it was good. He separated light from darkness ⁵and named the light "Day" and the darkness "Night." Evening came and then morning—that was the first day.*

The Second Day

⁶God said, "I command a dome to separate the water above it from the water below it." ⁷And that's what happened. God made the dome ⁸and named it "Sky." Evening came and then morning—that was the second day.

The Third Day

⁹God said, "I command the water under the sky to come together in one place, so there will be dry ground." And that's what happened. ¹⁰God named the dry ground "Land," and he named the water "Ocean." God looked at what he had done and saw that it was good.

¹¹God said, "I command the earth to produce all kinds of plants, including fruit trees and grain." And that's what happened. ¹²The earth produced all kinds of vegetation. God looked at what he had done, and it was good. ¹³Evening came and then morning—that was the third day.

---

*1.1 *the heavens and the earth*: "The heavens and the earth" stood for the universe.   *1.1,2 *In . . . life*: Or "When God began to create the heavens and the earth, the earth was barren with no form of life."   *1.2 *the Spirit of God*: Or "a mighty wind."   *1.5 *the first day*: A day was measured from evening to evening.

MARRIAGE—What's essential for a healthy, rewarding sex life?
(Genesis 1.27-31)

Recognize that sex is a gift from God.

Is sex a duty? Is it dirty? Or is it just a bad joke? Sex doesn't need to be any of these. When God made the universe, he designed sex between husband and wife to be very good, to produce children, and to be treated as a gift from a loving Father to the people he had created. God made human beings (male and female) both in his image. This means that a woman can enjoy the body God has given her, and she can also appreciate the body God has given her husband. In some mysterious sense, men and women, so delightfully different yet complementary to each other, are both in the image of God.

God told his newly created man and woman, "Fill the earth with people" (1.28). This is God's invitation to participate in his creative work—through helping to give life to children. After God had finished his work of creation, he surveyed all he had made. He saw that "all of it was very good!" (1.31). And that includes sex. (See also Song of Songs 5.10-16; 1 Corinthians 7.1-5.)

Words To Remember: *So God created humans to be like himself; he made men and women.—Genesis 1.27*

The Fourth Day

[14]God said, "I command lights to appear in the sky and to separate day from night and to show the time for seasons, special days, and years. [15]I command them to shine on the earth." And that's what happened. [16]God made two powerful lights, the brighter one to rule the day and the other[e] to rule the night. He also made the stars. [17]Then God put these lights in the sky to shine on the earth, [18]to rule day and night, and to separate light from darkness. God looked at what he had done, and it was good. [19]Evening came and then morning—that was the fourth day.

The Fifth Day

[20]God said, "I command the ocean to be full of living creatures, and I command birds to fly above the earth." [21]So God made the giant sea monsters and all the living creatures that swim in the ocean. He also made every kind of bird. God looked at what he had done, and it was good. [22]Then he gave the living creatures his blessing—he told the ocean creatures to live everywhere in the ocean and the birds to live everywhere on earth. [23]Evening came and then morning—that was the fifth day.

The Sixth Day

[24]God said, "I command the earth to give life to all kinds of tame animals, wild animals, and reptiles." And that's what happened. [25]God made every one of them. Then he looked at what he had done, and it was good. [26]God said, "Now we will make humans, and they will be like us. We will let them rule the fish, the birds, and all other living creatures."

[27]So God created humans to be like himself; he made men and women. [28]God gave them his blessing and said:

Have a lot of children! Fill the earth with people and bring it under your control. Rule over the fish in the ocean, the birds in the sky, and every animal on the earth.

[29]I have provided all kinds of fruit and grain for you to eat. [30]And I have given the green plants as food for everything else that breathes. These will be food for animals, both wild and tame, and for birds.

[31]God looked at what he had done. All of it was very good! Evening came and then morning—that was the sixth day.

2 So the heavens and the earth and everything else were created.

The Seventh Day

[2]By the seventh day God had finished his work, and so he rested. [3]God blessed the seventh day and made it special because on that day he rested from his work.

[4]That's how God created the heavens and the earth.

The Garden of Eden

When the LORD God made the heavens and the earth, [5]no grass or plants were growing anywhere. God had not yet sent any rain, and there was no one to work the land. [6]But streams[f] came up from the ground and watered the earth.

[7]The LORD God took a handful of soil and made a man.[g] God breathed life into the man, and the man started breathing. [8]The LORD made a garden in a place called Eden, which was in the east, and he put the man there.

[9]The LORD God placed all kinds of beautiful trees and fruit trees in the garden. Two other trees were in the middle of the garden. One of the trees gave life—the other gave the power to know the difference between right and wrong.

[10]From Eden a river flowed out to water the garden, then it divided into four rivers. [11]The first one is the Pishon River that flows through the land of Havilah, [12]where pure gold, rare perfumes, and precious stones are found. [13]The second is the Gihon River that winds through Ethiopia.[h] [14]The Tigris River that flows east of Assyria is the third, and the fourth is the Euphrates River.

[15]The LORD God put the man in the Garden of Eden to take care of it and to look after it. [16]But the LORD told him, "You may

---

[e]1.16 *the brighter . . . the other*: The sun and the moon. But they are not called by their names, because in Old Testament times some people worshiped the sun and the moon as though they were gods.   [f]2.6 *streams*: Or "mist."   [g]2.7 *man*: In Hebrew "man" comes from the same word as "soil."   [h]2.13 *Ethiopia*: The Hebrew text has "Cush," which was a region south of Egypt that included parts of the present countries of Ethiopia and Sudan.

eat fruit from any tree in the garden, ¹⁷except the one that has the power to let you know the difference between right and wrong. If you eat any fruit from that tree, you will die before the day is over!"

¹⁸The LORD God said, "It isn't good for the man to live alone. I need to make a suitable partner for him." ¹⁹⁻²⁰So the LORD took some soil and made animals and birds. He brought them to the man to see what names he would give each of them. Then the man named the tame animals and the birds and the wild animals. That's how they got their names.

None of these was the right kind of partner for the man. ²¹So the LORD God made him fall into a deep sleep, and he took out one of the man's ribs. Then after closing the man's side, ²²the LORD made a woman out of the rib.

The LORD God brought her to the man, ²³and the man exclaimed,

> "Here is someone like me!
> She is part of my body,
>   my own flesh and bones.
> She came from me, a man.
>   So I will name her Woman!"ⁱ

²⁴That's why a man will leave his own father and mother. He marries a woman, and the two of them become like one person. ²⁵Although the man and his wife were both naked, they were not ashamed.

The First Sin

3 The snake was sneakier than any of the other wild animals that the LORD God had made. One day it came to the woman and asked, "Did God tell you not to eat fruit from any tree in the garden?"

²The woman answered, "God said we could eat fruit from any tree in the garden, ³except the one in the middle. He told us not to eat fruit from that tree or even to touch it. If we do, we will die."

⁴"No, you won't!" the snake replied. ⁵"God understands what will happen on the day you eat fruit from that tree. You will see what you have done, and you will know the difference between right and wrong, just as God does."

⁶The woman stared at the fruit. It looked beautiful and tasty. She wanted the wisdom

---

ⁱ2.23 *a man . . . woman*: In Hebrew the words "man" and "woman" are similar.

MARRIAGE—What does a healthy, successful marriage look like?
(Genesis 2.18-23)

It's a partnership.
Marriage links us to another person, but it's up to us to decide how we will use that link. If we choose, we can turn that link into a tug-of-war. All we need to do is face each other, dig our heels into the dirt, and pit all our strength against the other person. There isn't much forward motion, but what little motion there is will drag someone into the mud. The sad thing is, in the end the winner stands alone.

But marriage doesn't have to be that way. We can join hands across the link of marriage and form a partnership. We can march forward together and put our united strength into the job at hand. As a team, two strong people can do a powerful lot of work—and they finish together.

God made the first man and woman to be partners in marriage. Even the method he used to create them illustrated the link of partnership. We can put this concept to work by refusing to quibble over small things and by taking our husband's side whenever possible. On potentially divisive issues like financial planning, discipline of children, and use of free time, we can make every effort to create a two-person team—and finish together, as God intended. (See also Exodus 32.11-14; Song of Songs 8.5-7; Hosea 14.4-8; Acts 18; Hebrews 13.4.)

Words To Remember: The LORD God said, "It isn't good for the man to live alone. I need to make a suitable partner for him."—Genesis 2.18

that it would give her, and she ate some of the fruit. Her husband was there with her, so she gave some to him, and he ate it too. ⁷Right away they saw what they had done, and they realized they were naked. Then they sewed fig leaves together to make something to cover themselves.

⁸Late in the afternoon a breeze began to blow, and the man and woman heard the LORD God walking in the garden. They were frightened and hid behind some trees.

The Trouble with Sin

⁹The LORD called out to the man and asked, "Where are you?"

¹⁰The man answered, "I was naked, and when I heard you walking through the garden, I was frightened and hid!"

¹¹"How did you know you were naked?" God asked. "Did you eat any fruit from that tree in the middle of the garden?"

¹²"It was the woman you put here with me," the man said. "She gave me some of the fruit, and I ate it."

¹³The LORD God then asked the woman, "What have you done?"

"The snake tricked me," she answered. "And I ate some of that fruit."

¹⁴So the LORD God said to the snake:

"Because of what you have done,
you will be the only animal
to suffer this curse—

For as long as you live,
you will crawl on your stomach
and eat dirt.
¹⁵You and this woman
will hate each other;
your descendants and hers
will always be enemies.
One of hers will strike you
on the head,
and you will strike him
on the heel."

¹⁶Then the LORD said to the woman,

"You will suffer terribly
when you give birth.
But you will still desire your husband,
and he will rule over you."

¹⁷The LORD said to the man,

"You listened to your wife
and ate fruit from that tree.
And so, the ground
will be under a curse
because of what you did.
As long as you live,
you will have to struggle
to grow enough food.
¹⁸Your food will be plants,
but the ground will produce
thorns and thistles.
¹⁹You will have to sweat

MARRIAGE—What does it really mean to "become one" with my husband?
(*Genesis 2.18-25*)

You realize becoming one requires both union and separation.

You are an individual, so how could you possibly become *one* with any other person—even your husband? Marriage creates that seemingly impossible union—but not without work and sometimes a measure of pain. It all began when God looked at the then-perfect person he had made and said, "It isn't good for the man to live alone" (2.18). So God created woman and with her the concept of marriage.

But union also means separation. For many women, their most loving ties are with the family where they grew up. After marriage, we can still love that family, but we must put our husband first. Part of that union is sex. And guess what? Genesis shows that when the world was perfect, the first husband and wife ran around naked and felt no shame at all. That's something to remember when you worry about the way your body looks due to pregnancy or just the added pounds that years may bring. (See also Ruth 1.15-18; 1 Corinthians 12.12-31.)

Words To Remember: *That's why a man will leave his own father and mother. He marries a woman, and the two of them become like one person.—Genesis 2.24*

to earn a living;
you were made out of soil,
and you will once again
turn into soil."

[20]The man Adam[j] named his wife Eve[k] because she would become the mother of all who live.

[21]Then the LORD God made clothes out of animal skins for the man and his wife.

[22]The LORD said, "These people now know the difference between right and wrong, just as we do. But they must not be allowed to eat fruit from the tree that lets them live forever." [23]So the LORD God sent them out of the Garden of Eden, where they would have to work the ground from which the man had been made. [24]Then God put winged creatures at the entrance to the garden and a flaming, flashing sword to guard the way to the life-giving tree.

Cain Murders Abel

4 Adam[l] and Eve had a son. Then Eve said, "I'll name him Cain because I got[m] him with the help of the LORD." [2]Later she had another son and named him Abel.

Abel became a sheep farmer, but Cain farmed the land. [3]One day, Cain gave part of his harvest to the LORD, [4]and Abel also gave an offering to the LORD. He killed the firstborn lamb from one of his sheep and gave the LORD the best parts of it. The LORD was pleased with Abel and his offering, [5]but not with Cain and his offering. This made Cain so angry that he could not hide his feelings.

[6]The LORD said to Cain:

What's wrong with you? Why do you have such an angry look on your face? [7]If you had done the right thing, you would be smiling.[n] But you did the wrong thing, and now sin is waiting to attack you like a lion. Sin wants to destroy you, but don't let it!

[8]Cain said to his brother Abel, "Let's go for a walk."[o] And when they were out in a field, Cain killed him.

[9]Afterwards the LORD asked Cain, "Where is Abel?"

"How should I know?" he answered. "Am I supposed to look after my brother?"

[10]Then the LORD said:

Why have you done this terrible thing? You killed your own brother,

and his blood flowed onto the ground. Now his blood is calling out for me to punish you. [11]And so, I'll put you under a curse. Because you killed Abel and made his blood run out on the ground, you will never be able to farm the land again. [12]If you try to farm the land, it won't produce anything for you. From now on, you'll be without a home, and you'll spend the rest of your life wandering from place to place.

[13]"This punishment is too hard!" Cain said. [14]"You're making me leave my home and live far from you.[p] I will have to wander about without a home, and just anyone could kill me."

[15]"No!"[q] the LORD answered. "Anyone who kills you will be punished seven times worse than I am punishing you." So the LORD put a mark on Cain to warn everyone not to kill him. [16]But Cain had to go far from the LORD and live in the Land of Wandering,[r] which is east of Eden.

More and More People

[17]Later, Cain and his wife had a son named Enoch. At the time Cain was building a town, and so he named it Enoch after his son. [18]Then Enoch had a son named Irad, who had a son named Mehujael, who had a son named Methushael, who had a son named Lamech.

[19]Lamech married Adah, then Zillah. [20-21]Lamech and Adah had two sons, Jabal and Jubal. Their son Jabal was the first to live in tents and raise sheep and goats. Jubal was the first to play harps and flutes.

[22]Lamech and Zillah had a son named Tubal Cain who made tools out of bronze and iron. They also had a daughter, whose name was Naamah.

[23]One day, Lamech said to his two wives, "A young man wounded me, and I killed

---

[j]3.20 *The man Adam*: In Hebrew "man" and "Adam" are the same.   [k]3.20 *Eve*: In Hebrew "Eve" sounds like "living."   [l]4.1 *Adam*: See the note at 3.20.
[m]4.1 *Cain . . . got*: In Hebrew "Cain" sounds like "got."   [n]4.7 *you would be smiling*: Or "I would have accepted your offering."   [o]4.8 *Cain said to his brother Abel, "Let's . . . walk"*: Most ancient translations; Hebrew "Cain spoke to his brother Abel."   [p]4.14 *live . . . you*: At this time it was believed that the LORD was with his people only in their own land.   [q]4.15 *No*: Three ancient translations; Hebrew "Very well!"   [r]4.16 *Wandering*: The Hebrew text has "Nod," which means "wandering."

him. [24]Anyone who tries to get even with me will be punished ten times more than anyone who tries to get even with Cain."

[25]Adam and his wife had another son. They named him Seth, because they said, "God has given[s] us a son to take the place of Abel, who was killed by his brother Cain." [26]Later, Seth had a son and named him Enosh.

About this time people started worshiping the LORD.[t]

Descendants of Adam

5 [1-2]God created men and women to be like himself. He gave them his blessing and called them human beings. This is a list of the descendants of Adam, the first man:

[3-4]When Adam was one hundred thirty, he had a son who was just like him, and he named him Seth. Adam had more children [5]and died at the age of nine hundred thirty.

[6]When Seth was one hundred five, he had a son named Enosh. [7]Seth had more children [8]and died at the age of nine hundred twelve.

[9]When Enosh was ninety, he had a son named Kenan. [10]Enosh had more children [11]and died at the age of nine hundred five.

[12]When Kenan was seventy, he had a son named Mahalalel. [13]Kenan had more children [14]and died at the age of nine hundred ten.

[15]When Mahalalel was sixty-five, he had a son named Jared. [16]Mahalalel had more children [17]and died at the age of eight hundred ninety-five.

[18]When Jared was one hundred sixty-two, he had a son named Enoch. [19]Jared had more children [20]and died at the age of nine hundred sixty-two.

[21]When Enoch was sixty-five, he had a son named Methuselah, [22]and during the next three hundred years he had more children. Enoch truly loved God, [23-24]and God took him away at the age of three hundred sixty-five.

[25]When Methuselah was one hundred eighty-seven, he had a son named Lamech. [26]Methuselah had more children [27]and died at the age of nine hundred sixty-nine.

[28]When Lamech was one hundred eighty-two, he had a son. [29]Lamech said, "I'll name him Noah because he will give us comfort,[u] as we struggle hard to make a living on this land that the LORD has put under a curse." [30]Lamech had more children [31]and died at the age of seven hundred seventy-seven.

[32]After Noah was five hundred years old, he had three sons and named them Shem, Ham, and Japheth.

The LORD Will Send a Flood

6 [1-2]More and more people were born, until finally they spread all over the earth. Some of their daughters were so beautiful that supernatural beings[y] came down and married the ones they wanted. [3]Then the LORD said, "I won't let my life-giving breath remain in anyone forever.[w] No one will live for more than one hundred twenty years."[x]

[4]The children of the supernatural beings who had married these women became famous heroes and warriors. They were called Nephilim and lived on the earth at that time and even later.

[5]The LORD saw how bad the people on earth were and that everything they thought and planned was evil. [6]He was very sorry that he had made them, [7]and he said, "I'll destroy every living creature on earth! I'll wipe out people, animals, birds, and reptiles. I'm sorry I ever made them."

I want to delight God. I desire to be someone with whom he can consistently find comfort and pleasure when he thinks about me. I want to "make his day."

VALERIE BELL

---

[s]**4.25** *Seth . . . given:* In Hebrew "Seth" sounds like "given." [t]**4.26** *worshiping the LORD:* Or "worshiping in the name of the LORD." [u]**5.29** *Noah . . . comfort:* In Hebrew "Noah" sounds like "comfort." [v]**6.1,2** *supernatural beings:* Or "angels." [w]**6.3** *I won't . . . forever:* One possible meaning for the difficult Hebrew text. [x]**6.3** *No one . . . years:* Or "In fact, they will all be destroyed in about one hundred years" (that is, at the time of the flood).

⁸But the LORD was pleased with Noah, ⁹and this is the story about him. Noah was the only person who lived right and obeyed God. ¹⁰He had three sons: Shem, Ham, and Japheth.

¹¹⁻¹²God knew that everyone was terribly cruel and violent. ¹³So he told Noah:

Cruelty and violence have spread everywhere. Now I'm going to destroy the whole earth and all its people. ¹⁴Get some good lumber and build a boat. Put rooms in it and cover it with tar inside and out. ¹⁵Make it four hundred fifty feet long, seventy-five feet wide, and forty-five feet high. ¹⁶Build a roof[y] on the boat and leave a space of about eighteen inches between the roof and the sides.[z] Make the boat three stories high and put a door on one side.

¹⁷I'm going to send a flood that will destroy everything that breathes! Nothing will be left alive. ¹⁸But I solemnly promise that you, your wife, your sons, and your daughters-in-law will be kept safe in the boat.[a]

¹⁹⁻²⁰Bring into the boat with you a male and a female of every kind of animal and bird, as well as a male and a female of every reptile. I don't want them to be destroyed. ²¹Store up enough food both for yourself and for them.

²²Noah did everything the LORD told him to do.

The Flood

7 The LORD told Noah:

Take your whole family with you into the boat, because you are the only one on this earth who pleases me. ²Take seven pairs of every kind of animal that can be used for sacrifice[b] and one pair of all others. ³Also take seven pairs of every kind of bird with you. Do this so there will always be animals and birds on the earth. ⁴Seven days from now I will send rain that will last for forty days and nights, and I will destroy all other living creatures I have made.

⁵⁻⁷Noah was six hundred years old when he went into the boat to escape the flood, and he did everything the LORD had told him to do. His wife, his sons, and his daughters-in-law all went inside with him. ⁸⁻⁹He obeyed God and took a male and a female of each kind of animal and bird into the boat with him. ¹⁰Seven days later a flood began to cover the earth.

¹¹⁻¹²Noah was six hundred years old when the water under the earth started gushing out everywhere. The sky opened like windows, and rain poured down for forty days and nights. All this began on the seventeenth day of the second month of the year. ¹³On that day Noah and his wife went into the boat with their three sons, Shem, Ham, and Japheth, and their wives. ¹⁴They took along every kind of animal, tame and wild, including the birds. ¹⁵Noah took a male and a female of every living creature with him, ¹⁶just as God had told him to do. And when they were all in the boat, God closed the door.

> *The more time*
> *I spend on my knees*
> *with the Lord,*
> *the more petty my gripes—*
> *big and small—become.*
>
> JANE JOHNSON STRUCK

¹⁷⁻¹⁸For forty days the rain poured down without stopping. And the water became deeper and deeper, until the boat started floating high above the ground. ¹⁹⁻²⁰Finally, the mighty flood was so deep that even the highest mountain peaks were almost twenty-five feet below the surface of the water. ²¹Not a bird, animal, reptile, or human was left alive anywhere on earth. ²²⁻²³The LORD destroyed everything that breathed. Nothing was left alive except Noah and the

---

[y]6.16 *roof:* Or "window."   [z]6.16 *leave . . . sides:* One possible meaning for the difficult Hebrew text. [a]6.18 *boat:* One possible meaning for the difficult Hebrew text of verse 18.   [b]7.2 *animal . . . for sacrifice:* Hebrew "clean animals." Animals that could be used for sacrifice were called "clean," and animals that could not be used were called "unclean."

others in the boat. ²⁴A hundred fifty days later, the water started going down.

The Water Goes Down

8 God did not forget about Noah and the animals with him in the boat. So God made a wind blow, and the water started going down. ²God stopped up the places where the water had been gushing out from under the earth. He also closed up the sky, and the rain stopped. ³For one hundred fifty days the water slowly went down. ⁴Then on the seventeenth day of the seventh month of the year, the boat came to rest somewhere in the Ararat mountains. ⁵The water kept going down, and the mountain tops could be seen on the first day of the tenth month.

⁶⁻⁷Forty days later Noah opened a window to send out a raven, but it kept flying around until the water had dried up. ⁸Noah wanted to find out if the water had gone down, and he sent out a dove. ⁹Deep water was still everywhere, and the dove could not find a place to land. So it flew back to the boat. Noah held out his hand and helped it back in.

¹⁰Seven days later Noah sent the dove out again. ¹¹It returned in the evening, holding in its beak a green leaf from an olive tree. Noah knew that the water was finally going down. ¹²He waited seven more days before sending the dove out again, and this time it did not return.

¹³Noah was now six hundred one years old. And by the first day of that year, almost all the water had gone away. Noah made an opening in the roof of the boat* and saw that the ground was getting dry. ¹⁴By the twenty-seventh day of the second month, the earth was completely dry.

¹⁵God said to Noah, ¹⁶"You, your wife, your sons, and your daughters-in-law may now leave the boat. ¹⁷Let out the birds, animals, and reptiles, so they can mate and live all over the earth." ¹⁸After Noah and his family had gone out of the boat, ¹⁹the living creatures left in groups of their own kind.

The LORD's Promise for the Earth

²⁰Noah built an altar where he could offer sacrifices to the LORD. Then he offered on the altar one of each kind of animal and bird that could be used for a sacrifice.ᵈ ²¹The smell of the burning offering pleased God, and he said:

Never again will I punish the earth for the sinful things its people do. All of them have evil thoughts from the time they are young, but I will never destroy everything that breathes, as I did this time.

²²As long as the earth remains,
    there will be planting
        and harvest,
        cold and heat;
    winter and summer,
        day and night.

God's Promise to Noah

9 God said to Noah and his sons:
    I am giving you my blessing. Have a lot of children and grandchildren, so people will live everywhere on this earth. ²All animals, birds, reptiles, and fish will be afraid of you. I have placed them under your control, ³and I have given them to you for food. From now on, you may eat them, as well as the green plants that you have always eaten. ⁴But life is in the blood, and you must not eat any meat that still has blood in it. ⁵⁻⁶I created humans to be like me, and I will punish any animal or person that takes a human life. If an animal kills someone, that animal must die. And if a person takes the life of another, that person must be put to death.

⁷I want you and your descendants to have many children, so people will live everywhere on earth.

⁸Again, God said to Noah and his sons:
    ⁹I am going to make a solemn promise to you and to everyone who will live after you. ¹⁰This includes the birds and the animals that came out of the boat. ¹¹I promise every living creature that the earth and those living on it will never again be destroyed by a flood.

¹²⁻¹³The rainbow that I have put in the sky will be my sign to you and to every living creature on earth. It will

---

ᶜ**8.13** *made . . . boat:* One possible meaning for the difficult Hebrew text.   ᵈ**8.20** *animal . . . sacrifice:* See the note at 7.2.

remind you that I will keep this promise forever. [14]When I send clouds over the earth, and a rainbow appears in the sky, [15]I will remember my promise to you and to all other living creatures. Never again will I let floodwaters destroy all life. [16]When I see the rainbow in the sky, I will always remember the promise that I have made to every living creature. [17]The rainbow will be the sign of that solemn promise.

Noah and His Family

[18]Noah and his sons, Shem, Ham, and Japheth, came out of the boat. Ham later had a son named Canaan. [19]All people on earth are descendants of Noah's three sons. [20]Noah farmed the land and was the first to plant a vineyard. [21]One day he got drunk and was lying naked in his tent. [22]Ham entered the tent and saw him naked, then went back outside and told his brothers. [23]Shem and Japheth put a robe over their shoulders and walked backwards into the tent. Without looking at their father, they placed it over his body.

[24]When Noah woke up and learned what his youngest son had done, [25]he said,

"I now put a curse on Canaan!
He will be the lowest slave
    of his brothers.
[26]I ask the LORD my God
to bless Shem
    and make Canaan his slave.
[27]I pray that the LORD
will give Japheth
    more and more[c] land
and let him take over
    the territory of Shem.
May Canaan be his slave."

[28]Noah lived three hundred fifty years after the flood [29]and died at the age of nine hundred fifty.

The Descendants of Noah

10 After the flood Shem, Ham, and Japheth had many descendants.

The Descendants of Japheth

[2-5]Japheth's descendants had their own languages, tribes, and land. They were Gomer, Magog, Madai, Javan, Tubal, Meshech, and Tiras.

Gomer was the ancestor of Ashkenaz, Riphath, and Togarmah.

Javan was the ancestor of Elishah, Tarshish, Kittim, and Dodanim,[j] who settled along the coast.

The Descendants of Ham

[6-20]Ham's descendants had their own languages, tribes, and land. They were Ethiopia,[g] Egypt, Put, and Canaan.

Cush[h] was the ancestor of Seba, Havilah, Sabtah, Raamah, and Sabteca.

Raamah was the ancestor of Sheba and Dedan.

Cush was also the ancestor of Nimrod, a mighty warrior whose strength came from the LORD. Nimrod is the reason for the saying, "You hunt like Nimrod with the strength of the LORD!" Nimrod first ruled in Babylon, Erech, and Accad, all of[i] which were in Babylonia.[j] From there Nimrod went to Assyria and built the great city of Nineveh. He also built Rehoboth-Ir and Calah, as well as Resen, which is between Nineveh and Calah.

Egypt was the ancestor of Ludim, Anamim, Lehabim, Naphtuhim, Pathrusim, Casluhim, and Caphtorim, the ancestor of the Philistines.[k]

Canaan's sons were Sidon and Heth. He was also the ancestor of the Jebusites, the Amorites, the Girgashites, the Hivites, the Arkites, the Sinites, the Arvadites, the Zemarites, and the Hamathites.

Later the Canaanites spread from the territory of Sidon and went as far as Gaza in the direction of Gerar. They also went as far as Lasha in the direction of Sodom, Gomorrah, Admah, and Zeboiim.

---

[c]**9.27** *more and more*: In Hebrew "Japheth" sounds like "more and more." [j]**10.2-5** *Dodanim*: Most Hebrew manuscripts; some Hebrew manuscripts and one ancient translation have "Rodanim." [g]**10.6-20** *Ethiopia*: See the note at 2.13. [h]**10.6-20** *Cush*: See the note at 2.13. [i]**10.6-20** *and Accad, all of*: Or "Accad, and Calneh." [j]**10.6-20** *Babylonia*: The Hebrew text has "Shinar," another name for Babylonia. [k]**10.6-20** *Casluhim, and Caphtorim, the ancestor of the Philistines*: Hebrew "Caphtorim, and Casluhim, the ancestor of the Philistines." The Philistines were from Caphtor (see Jeremiah 47.4; Amos 9.7), better known as Crete.

The Descendants of Shem

²¹⁻³¹Shem's descendants had their own languages, tribes, and land. He was the older brother of Japheth and the ancestor of the tribes of Eber.

Shem was the ancestor of Elam, Asshur, Arpachshad, Lud, and Aram.

Aram was the ancestor of Uz, Hul, Gether, and Mash.

Arpachshad was the father of Shelah and the grandfather of Eber, whose first son was named Peleg,[l] because it was during his time that tribes divided up the earth. Eber's second son was Joktan.

Joktan was the ancestor of Almodad, Sheleph, Hazarmaveth, Jerah, Hadoram, Uzal, Diklah, Obal, Abimael, Sheba, Ophir, Havilah, and Jobab. Their land reached from Mesha in the direction of Sephar, the hill country in the east.

³²This completes the list of Noah's descendants. After the flood their descendants became nations and spread all over the world.

The Tower of Babel

11 At first everyone spoke the same language, ²but after some of them moved from the east[m] and settled in Babylonia,[n] ³⁻⁴they said:

Let's build a city with a tower that reaches to the sky! We'll use hard bricks and tar instead of stone and mortar. We'll become famous, and we won't be scattered all over the world.

⁵But when the LORD came down to look at the city and the tower, ⁶he said:

These people are working together because they all speak the same language. This is just the beginning. Soon they will be able to do anything they want. ⁷Come on! Let's go down and confuse them by making them speak different languages—then they won't be able to understand each other.

⁸⁻⁹So the people had to stop building the city, because the LORD confused their language and scattered them all over the earth. That's how the city of Babel[o] got its name.

The Descendants of Shem

¹⁰⁻¹¹Two years after the flood, when Shem was one hundred, he had a son named Arpachshad. He had more children and died at the age of six hundred. This is a list of his descendants:

¹²When Arpachshad was thirty-five, he had a son named Shelah. ¹³Arpachshad had

---

[l]10.21-31 *Peleg:* In Hebrew "Peleg" means "divided." [m]11.2 *from the east:* Or "to the east." [n]11.2 *Babylonia:* See the note at 10.6-20. [o]11.8,9 *Babel:* In Hebrew "Babel" sounds like "confused."

SingleLife—How can I tell the difference between good ambition and self-centeredness? *(Genesis 11.1-9)*

Look at your motives.

All human beings face many temptations to become self-centered—whether they are married, single, or single again. In particular, a single may worry that if she doesn't take care of herself, no one else will. Ambition is good—at least up to a point—because it keeps her from having to depend on others.

But ambition can also become self-centered. And self-centeredness can become dangerous. In the mysterious story of Genesis 11, a group of ambitious people decided to build "a tower that reaches to the sky!" (11.3). Their motive? "We'll become famous, and we won't be scattered all over the world" (11.4). For reasons not entirely understood by Bible scholars, God smashed their plans. They became famous all right. A famous failure.

It's not wrong for a woman to be ambitious. But a wise woman will recognize the dangers of ambition and look carefully at her motives. Are they selfish? Are they likely to hurt someone? Or are they guided by what she knows of God's will and character? A discerning woman evaluates first; then decides whether she should pull back or charge ahead. (See also Mark 8.34-38; Hebrews 4.12,13.)

Words To Remember: *They said: Let's build a city with a tower that reaches to the sky! . . . We'll become famous.—Genesis 11.3,4*

more children and died at the age of four hundred thirty-eight.

[14]When Shelah was thirty, he had a son named Eber. [15]Shelah had more children and died at the age of four hundred thirty-three.

[16]When Eber was thirty-four, he had a son named Peleg. [17]Eber had more children and died at the age of four hundred sixty-four.

[18]When Peleg was thirty, he had a son named Reu. [19]Peleg had more children and died at the age of two hundred thirty-nine.

[20]When Reu was thirty-two he had a son named Serug. [21]Reu had more children and died at the age of two hundred thirty-nine.

[22]When Serug was thirty, he had a son named Nahor. [23]Serug had more children and died at the age of two hundred thirty.

[24]When Nahor was twenty-nine, he had a son named Terah. [25]Nahor had more children and died at the age of one hundred forty-eight.

The Descendants of Terah

[26-28]After Terah was seventy years old, he had three sons: Abram, Nahor, and Haran, who became the father of Lot. Terah's sons were born in the city of Ur in Chaldea,[p] and Haran died there before the death of his father. The following is the story of Terah's descendants.

[29-30]Abram married Sarai, but she was not able to have any children. And Nahor married Milcah, who was the daughter of Haran and the sister of Iscah.

[31]Terah decided to move from Ur to the land of Canaan. He took along Abram and Sarai and his grandson Lot, the son of Haran. But when they came to the city of Haran,[q] they decided to settle there instead. [32]Terah lived to be two hundred five years old and died in Haran.

The LORD Chooses Abram

12 The LORD said to Abram:
Leave your country, your family, and your relatives and go to the land that I will show you. [2]I will bless you and make your descendants into a great nation. You will become famous and be a blessing to others. [3]I will bless anyone who blesses you, but I will put a curse on anyone who puts a curse on you. Everyone on earth will be blessed because of you.[r]

[4-5]Abram was seventy-five years old when the LORD told him to leave the city of Haran. He obeyed and left with his wife Sarai, his nephew Lot, and all the possessions and slaves they had gotten while in Haran.

---

[p]11.26-28 *Ur in Chaldea:* Chaldea was a region at the head of the Persian Gulf. Ur was on the main trade routes from Mesopotamia to the Mediterranean Sea.
[q]11.31 *Haran:* About 550 miles northwest of Ur.
[r]12.3 *Everyone . . . you:* Or "Everyone on earth will ask me to bless them as I have blessed you."

🐟

SpiritualLife—How can I keep my life centered on God? *(Genesis 12.1-7)*

Focus on the promises of God—and then do what he says.
How often in an hour, a day, or a week do you think about God? And when you think about God, what do you feel? Guilt, fear, challenge, worship, belonging, love? Being centered on God may bring out all of these responses at different times. But as we focus more on God, we will move toward worship, belonging, and love.

How can we become more centered on God? One way is to focus on his promises in Scripture. The Lord made some astounding promises to Abram in this passage, but with the promises came commands for immediate action. So what did Abram do? He packed up his belongings and did all that the Lord said.

Centering on God takes mental and physical work. We can discipline our minds to turn often to God. We can meditate on his promises to us. But then we need to get up and move—obeying all that Scripture commands us to do. (See also Matthew 25.31-46; Acts 13.1-5; Galatians 5.16-26; 2 Timothy 2.14-26; 2 John.)

🐟 **Words To Remember:** *The LORD said to Abram: . . . I will bless you and make your descendants into a great nation. You will become famous and be a blessing to others.*—Genesis 12.1,2

When they came to the land of Canaan, [6]Abram went as far as the sacred tree of Moreh in a place called Shechem. The Canaanites were still living in the land at that time, [7]but the LORD appeared to Abram and promised, "I will give this land to your family forever." Abram then built an altar there for the LORD.

[8]Abram traveled to the hill country east of Bethel and camped between Bethel and Ai, where he built another altar and worshiped the LORD. [9]Later, Abram started out toward the Southern Desert.

Abram in Egypt

[10-11]The crops failed, and there was no food anywhere in the land. So Abram and his wife Sarai went to live in Egypt for a while. But just before they got there, he said, "Sarai, you are really beautiful! [12]When the Egyptians see how lovely you are, they will murder me because I am your husband. But they won't kill you. [13]Please save my life by saying that you are my sister."

[14]As soon as Abram and Sarai arrived in Egypt, the Egyptians noticed how beautiful she was. [15]The king's[s] officials told him about her, and she was taken to his house. [16]The king was good to Abram because of

Sarai, and Abram was given sheep, cattle, donkeys, slaves, and camels.

[17]Because of Sarai, the LORD struck the king and everyone in his palace with terrible diseases. [18]Finally, the king sent for Abram and said to him, "What have you done to me? Why didn't you tell me Sarai was your wife? [19]Why did you make me believe she was your sister? Now I've married her. Take her and go! She's your wife."

[20]So the king told his men to let Abram and Sarai take their possessions and leave.

Abram and Lot Separate

13 Abram and Sarai took everything they owned and went to the Southern Desert. Lot went with them.

[2]Abram was very rich. He owned many cattle, sheep, and goats, and had a lot of silver and gold. [3]Abram moved from place to place in the Southern Desert. And finally, he went north and set up his tents between Bethel and Ai, [4]where he had earlier camped and built an altar. There he worshiped the LORD.

---

[s]12.15 *The king's*: The Hebrew text has "Pharaoh's," a Hebrew word sometimes used for the king of Egypt.

PARENTING&*family*—How can I best relate to my adult child?

(Genesis 13,14)

Be a resource, not a controller.

How much help should parents give an adult child? Pay overdue rent? Give money to a struggling business? Provide child care? Repair a junk car? Help sort out marriage problems? Assist with the downpayment for a house? Arrange for work? Let him move back home?

Abram became a "parent" to Lot, his adult nephew. When shortage of grazing space caused competition between their herds and workers, Abram insisted that they separate— and he offered Lot his choice of land. Not surprisingly, Lot chose a spot that looked good on the surface but had less obvious disadvantages. Abram accepted Lot's choice and moved away. But when Lot and his family became prisoners of war, Abram rode to the rescue with troops and battle gear.

Appropriate help for an adult child depends much on that person's age, need, responsibility, and ability to make appropriate use of parental resources. But parental help should not come with controlling strings attached. Like Abram, parents must encourage their adult children to make their own decisions. Parents must also consider their own strengths and limitations. And, like Abram, parents may (for the sake of peace) need to insist on separate places to live. (See also Ruth 3; John 3.1-21.)

Words To Remember: *Abram said to Lot, "We are close relatives. We shouldn't argue, and our men shouldn't be fighting one another. There is plenty of land for you to choose from. Let's separate. If you go north, I'll go south; if you go south, I'll go north."*—Genesis 13.8,9

[5]Lot, who was traveling with him, also had sheep, goats, and cattle, as well as his own family and slaves. [6-7]At this time the Canaanites and the Perizzites were living in the same area, and so there wasn't enough pastureland left for Abram and Lot with all of their animals. Besides this, the men who took care of Abram's animals and the ones who took care of Lot's animals started quarreling.

[8]Abram said to Lot, "We are close relatives. We shouldn't argue, and our men shouldn't be fighting one another. [9]There is plenty of land for you to choose from. Let's separate. If you go north, I'll go south; if you go south, I'll go north."

[10]This happened before the LORD had destroyed the cities of Sodom and Gomorrah. And when Lot looked around, he saw there was plenty of water in the Jordan Valley. All the way to Zoar the valley was as green as the garden of the LORD or the land of Egypt. [11]So Lot chose the whole Jordan Valley for himself, and as he started toward the east, he and Abram separated. [12]Abram stayed in the land of Canaan. But Lot settled near the cities of the valley and put up his tents not far from Sodom, [13]where the people were evil and sinned terribly against the LORD.

Abram Moves to Hebron

[14]After Abram and Lot had gone their separate ways, the LORD said to Abram:

Look around to the north, south, east, and west. [15]I will give you and your family all the land you can see. It will be theirs forever! [16]I will give you more descendants than there are specks of dust on the earth, and someday it will be easier to count the specks of dust than to count your descendants. [17]Now walk back and forth across the land, because I am giving it to you.

[18]Abram took down his tents and went to live near the sacred trees of Mamre at Hebron, where he built an altar in honor of the LORD.

Abram Rescues Lot

14 About this time, King Amraphel of Babylonia,[f] King Arioch of Ellasar, King Chedorlaomer of Elam, and King Tidal of Goiim [2]attacked King Bera of Sodom, King Birsha of Gomorrah, King Shinab of Admah, King Shemeber of Zeboiim, and the king of Bela, also known as the city of Zoar. [3-4]King Chedorlaomer and his allies had ruled these last five kings for twelve years, but in the thirteenth year the kings rebelled and came together in Siddim Valley, which is now covered by the southern part of the Dead Sea.

[5]A year later King Chedorlaomer and his allies attacked and defeated the Rephaites in Ashteroth-Karnaim, the Zuzites in Ham, and the Emites in Shaveh-Kiriathaim. [6]They also defeated the Horites in the hill country of Edom,[u] as far as El-Paran, near the desert. [7]They went back to the city of Enmishpat, better known as Kadesh. Then they captured all the land that belonged to the Amalekites, and they defeated the Amorites who were living in Hazazon-Tamar.

[8-9]At Siddim Valley, the armies of the kings of Sodom, Gomorrah, Admah, Zeboiim, and Bela fought the armies of King Chedorlaomer of Elam, King Tidal of Goiim, King Amraphel of Babylonia, and King Arioch of Ellasar. The valley [10]was full of tar pits, and when the troops from Sodom and Gomorrah started running away, some of them fell into the pits. Others escaped to the hill country. [11]Their enemies took everything of value from Sodom and Gomorrah, including their food supplies. [12]They also captured Abram's nephew Lot, who lived in Sodom. They took him and his possessions and then left.

[13]At this time Abram the Hebrew was living near the oaks that belonged to Mamre the Amorite. Mamre and his brothers Eshcol and Aner were Abram's friends. Someone who had escaped from the battle told Abram [14]that his nephew Lot had been taken away. Three hundred eighteen of Abram's servants were fighting men, so he took them and followed the enemy as far north as the city of Dan. [15]That night, Abram divided up his troops, attacked from all sides, and won a great victory. But some of the enemy escaped to the town of Hobah north of Damascus, [16]and Abram went after them. He brought back his nephew Lot, together with

---

[f]14.1 *Babylonia*: See the note at 10.6-20. [u]14.6 *Edom*: The Hebrew text has "Seir," another name for Edom.

Lot's possessions and the women and everyone else who had been captured.

Abram Is Blessed by Melchizedek

¹⁷Abram returned after he had defeated King Chedorlaomer and the other kings. Then the king of Sodom went to meet Abram in Shaveh Valley, which is also known as King's Valley.

¹⁸King Melchizedek of Salem was a priest of God Most High. He brought out some bread and wine ¹⁹and said to Abram:

"I bless you in the name
    of God Most High,
  Creator of heaven and earth.
²⁰All praise belongs
    to God Most High
  for helping you defeat
    your enemies."

Then Abram gave Melchizedek a tenth of everything.

²¹The king of Sodom said to Abram, "All I want are my people. You can keep everything else."

²²Abram answered:
    The LORD God Most High made the heavens and the earth. And I have promised him ²³that I won't keep anything of yours, not even a sandal strap or a piece of thread. Then you can never say that you are the one who made me rich. ²⁴Let my share be the food that my men have eaten. But Aner, Eshcol, and Mamre went with me, so give them their share of what we brought back.

The LORD's Promise to Abram

15 Later the LORD spoke to Abram in a vision, "Abram, don't be afraid! I will protect you and reward you greatly."

²But Abram answered, "LORD All-Powerful, you have given me everything I could ask for, except children. And when I die, Eliezer of Damascus will get all I own.ᵛ ³You have not given me any children, and this servant of mine will inherit everything."

⁴The LORD replied, "No, he won't! You will have a son of your own, and everything you have will be his." ⁵Then the LORD took Abram outside and said, "Look at the sky and see if you can count the stars. That's

how many descendants you will have." ⁶Abram believed the LORD, and the LORD was pleased with him.

The LORD Makes Another Promise to Abram

⁷The LORD said to Abram, "I brought you here from Ur in Chaldea, and I gave you this land."

⁸Abram asked, "LORD God, how can I know the land will be mine?"

⁹Then the LORD told him, "Bring me a three-year-old cow, a three-year-old female goat, a three-year-old ram, a dove, and a young pigeon."

> *If a situation is beyond our control, we should take neither credit nor blame for it.*
> HOLLY G. MILLER

¹⁰Abram obeyed the LORD. Then he cutʷ the animals in half and laid the two halves of each animal opposite each other on the ground. But he did not cut the doves and pigeons in half. ¹¹And when birds came down to eat the animals, Abram chased them away.

¹²As the sun was setting, Abram fell into a deep sleep, and everything became dark and frightening. ¹³⁻¹⁵Then the LORD said:
    Abram, you will live to an old age and die in peace.
    But I solemnly promise that your descendants will live as foreigners in a land that doesn't belong to them. They will be forced into slavery and abused for four hundred years. But I will terribly punish the nation that enslaves them, and they will leave with many possessions.
    ¹⁶Four generations later,ˣ your descendants will return here and take

---

ᵛ**15.2** *And . . . own:* One possible meaning for the difficult Hebrew text. ʷ**15.10** *cut:* In Hebrew "cut" sounds something like "agreement." What follows shows that the LORD is making an agreement with Abram. ˣ**15.16** *Four generations later:* This may refer to the "four hundred years" of verses 13-15.

Hagar

Genesis 16; 21.1-21; 25.1-18

Have you ever felt abused by God's people? It happens. It happened to Hagar. Hagar was a slave belonging to Sarai. Because Sarai was childless, she invited her husband to sleep with Hagar. "If she has a child," said Sarai, "it will be mine" (16.2). So Abram and Sarai, a God-fearing couple God called to begin a nation he would call his own, forced Hagar into surrogate motherhood. It's small wonder that Hagar did not think fondly of Sarai—or her God.

When Hagar, large with child, taunted her barren mistress, Sarai complained to her husband who absolved himself of responsibility with, "She's your slave . . . do whatever you want with her" (16.6). Sarai did. And Hagar protected herself and her child by running away. Since they were all nomads, Hagar's escape simply took her into the desert where she stopped to rest by a spring. We can only imagine her feelings of anger, abandonment, betrayal, and fear.

It was at this spring that God stepped in to make amends for the actions of his people. An angel of the Lord announced that God had heard her cry for help. He assured Hagar that she would have a son—even gave him a name and promises about his family. Then he told Hagar to go back home to her mistress. With all of the confidence of a person who has experienced God's presence in an emotional desert, Hagar named the place, "The God Who Sees Me" (16.13). Then Hagar went back home.

Hagar gave birth to Ishmael. Later, Sarai (whose name has now been changed to Sarah) had a son: Isaac. Shortly afterward, Abram (now called Abraham) sent Hagar away again—this time for good. Hagar and Ishmael nearly died of thirst in the desert. In fact, death was so close that Hagar placed her weakened son under a bush and moved away because she could not bear to watch him die. Once again God showed his care for Hagar. An angel said, "Hagar, why are you worried? Don't be afraid. I have heard your son crying. Help him up and hold his hand, because I will make him the father of a great nation" (21.17,18).

We don't hear much of Hagar and her son after that—except that after Sarah died, Abraham gave gifts to them. And when Abraham died, "his sons Isaac and Ishmael buried him" (25.9).

What can today's woman learn from Hagar? We can learn that life is not always fair—even among the people of God. Abraham became a hero and Sarah a heroine of the faith. But their dealings with Hagar were far from heroic or faithful. So we can expect limitations in God's people and not be shocked if we become the recipient of their failings. We do, however, need to protect ourselves from abuse. Sometimes running away is the only sensible thing to do. Even then, we can take comfort that no matter how alone we are, or how far we have to run, we are still in the presence of "The God Who Sees Me."

this land, because only then will the people who live here[y] be so sinful that they deserve to be punished.

[17]Sometime after sunset, when it was very dark, a smoking cooking pot[z] and a flaming fire went between the two halves of each animal. [18]At that time the LORD made an agreement with Abram and told him:

I will give your descendants the land east of the Shihor River[a] on the border of Egypt as far as the Euphrates River. [19]They will possess the land of the Kenites, the Kenizzites, the Kadmonites, [20]the Hittites, the Perizzites, the Rephaites, [21]the Amorites, the Canaanites, the Girgashites, and the Jebusites.

Hagar and Ishmael

16 Abram's wife Sarai had not been able to have any children. But she owned a young Egyptian slave woman named Hagar, [2]and Sarai said to Abram, "The LORD has not given me any children. Sleep with my slave, and if she has a child, it will be mine."[b] Abram agreed, [3]and Sarai gave him Hagar to be his wife. This happened after Abram had lived in the land of Canaan for ten years. [4]Later, when Hagar knew she was going to have a baby, she became proud and was hateful to Sarai.

[5]Then Sarai said to Abram, "It's all your fault![c] I gave you my slave woman, but she has been hateful to me ever since she found out she was pregnant. You have done me wrong, and you will have to answer to the LORD for this."

[6]Abram said, "All right! She's your slave, and you can do whatever you want with her." But Sarai began treating Hagar so harshly that she finally ran away.

[7]Hagar stopped to rest at a spring in the desert on the road to Shur. While she was there, the angel of the LORD came to her [8]and asked, "Hagar, where have you come from, and where are you going?"

She answered, "I'm running away from Sarai, my owner."

[9]The angel said, "Go back to Sarai and be her slave. [10-11]I will give you a son, who will be called Ishmael,[d] because I have heard your cry for help. And later I will give you so many descendants that no one will be able to count them all. [12]But your son will live far from his relatives; he will be like a wild don-

key, fighting everyone, and everyone fighting him."

[13]Hagar thought, "Have I really seen God and lived to tell about it?"[e] So from then on she called him, "The God Who Sees Me."[f] [14]That's why people call the well between Kadesh and Bered, "The Well of the Living One Who Sees Me."[g]

[15-16]Abram was eighty-six years old when Hagar gave birth to their son, and he named him Ishmael.

God's Promise to Abraham

17 Abram was ninety-nine years old when the LORD appeared to him again and said, "I am God All-Powerful. If you obey me and always do right, [2]I will keep my solemn promise to you and give you more descendants than can be counted." [3]Abram bowed with his face to the ground, and God said:

[4-5]I promise that you will be the father of many nations. That's why I now change your name from Abram to Abraham.[h] [6]I will give you a lot of descendants, and in the future they will become great nations. Some of them will even be kings.

[7]I will always keep the promise I have made to you and your descendants, because I am your God and their God. [8]I will give you and them the land in which you are now a foreigner. I will give the whole land of Canaan to your family forever, and I will be their God.

[9]Abraham, you and all future members of your family must promise to obey me. [10-11]As the sign that you are

---

[y]**15.16** *people who live here*: The Hebrew text has "Amorites," a name sometimes used of the people who lived in Palestine before the Israelites. [z]**15.17** *smoking cooking pot*: One possible meaning for the difficult Hebrew text. The smoke and fire represent the presence of the LORD. [a]**15.18** *Shihor River*: See Joshua 13.2-7. [b]**16.2** *Sleep . . . mine*: It was the custom for a wife who could not have children to let her husband sleep with one of her slave women. The children of the slave would belong to the wife. [c]**16.5** *It's . . . fault*: Or "I hope you'll be punished for what you did to me!" [d]**16.10,11** *Ishmael*: In Hebrew "Ishmael" sounds like "God hears." [e]**16.13** *Have . . . it*: One possible meaning for the difficult Hebrew text. [f]**16.13** *The God Who Sees Me*: Or "The God I Have Seen." [g]**16.14** *The Well . . . Me*: Or "Beer-Lahai-Roi" (see 25.11). [h]**17.4,5** *Abraham*: In Hebrew "Abraham" sounds like "father of many nations."

keeping this promise, you must circumcise every man and boy in your family. ¹²⁻¹³From now on, your family must circumcise every baby boy when he is eight days old. You must even circumcise any man or boy you have as a slave, both those born in your homes and those you buy from foreigners. This will be a sign that my promise to you will last forever. ¹⁴Any man who isn't circumcised hasn't kept his promise to me and cannot be one of my people.

¹⁵Abraham, your wife's name will now be Sarah instead of Sarai. ¹⁶I will bless her, and you will have a son by her. She will become the mother of nations, and some of her descendants will even be kings.

¹⁷Abraham bowed with his face to the ground and thought, "I am almost a hundred years old. How can I become a father? And Sarah is ninety. How can she have a child?" So he started laughing. ¹⁸Then he asked God, "Why not let Ishmael[i] inherit what you have promised me?"

¹⁹But God answered:

No! You and Sarah will have a son. His name will be Isaac,[j] and I will make an everlasting promise to him and his descendants.

²⁰I have heard what you asked me to do for Ishmael, and so I will also bless him with many descendants. He will be the father of twelve princes, and I will make his family a great nation. ²¹But your son Isaac will be born about this time next year, and the promise I am making to you and your family will be for him and his descendants forever.

²²God finished speaking to Abraham and then left.

²³⁻²⁷On that same day Abraham obeyed God by circumcising Ishmael. Abraham was also circumcised, and so were all other men and boys in his household, including his servants and slaves. He was ninety-nine years old at the time, and his son Ishmael was thirteen.

The LORD Promises Abraham a Son

18 One hot summer afternoon Abraham was sitting by the entrance to his tent near the sacred trees of Mamre, when the LORD appeared to him. ²Abraham looked up and saw three men standing nearby. He quickly ran to meet them, bowed with his face to the ground, ³and said, "Please come to my home where I can serve you. ⁴I'll have some water brought, so you can wash your feet, then you can rest under the tree. ⁵Let me get you some food to give you strength before you leave. I would be honored to serve you."

"Thank you very much," they answered. "We accept your offer."

⁶Abraham quickly went to his tent and said to Sarah, "Hurry! Get a large sack of flour and make some bread." ⁷After saying this, he rushed off to his herd of cattle and picked out one of the best calves, which his servant quickly prepared. ⁸He then served his guests some yogurt and milk together with the meat.

While they were eating, he stood near them under the trees, ⁹and they asked, "Where is your wife Sarah?"

"She is right there in the tent," Abraham answered.

¹⁰One of the guests was the LORD, and he said, "I'll come back about this time next year, and when I do, Sarah will already have a son."

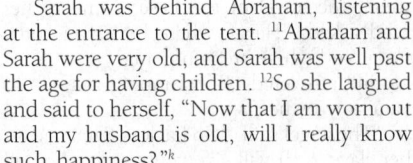

As human beings, we can't see the big picture. But the Lord can, and he's doing his work in his way in his time.

TWILA PARIS

Sarah was behind Abraham, listening at the entrance to the tent. ¹¹Abraham and Sarah were very old, and Sarah was well past the age for having children. ¹²So she laughed and said to herself, "Now that I am worn out and my husband is old, will I really know such happiness?"[k]

---

[i]**17.18** *Ishmael:* Ishmael was the son of Sarah's slave Hagar (see 16.1-16).   [j]**17.19** *Isaac:* In Hebrew "Isaac" sounds like "laugh."   [k]**18.12** *know such happiness:* Either the joy of making love or the joy of having children.

¹³The LORD asked Abraham, "Why did Sarah laugh? Does she doubt that she can have a child in her old age? ¹⁴I am the LORD! There is nothing too difficult for me. I'll come back next year at the time I promised, and Sarah will already have a son."

¹⁵Sarah was so frightened that she lied and said, "I didn't laugh."

"Yes, you did!" he answered.

Abraham Prays for Sodom

¹⁶When the three men got ready to leave, they looked down toward Sodom, and Abraham walked part of the way with them.

¹⁷The LORD said to himself, "I should tell Abraham what I am going to do, ¹⁸since his family will become a great and powerful nation that will be a blessing to all other nations on earth.^{l} ¹⁹I have chosen him to teach his family to obey me forever and to do what is right and fair. Then I will give Abraham many descendants, just as I promised."

²⁰The LORD said, "Abraham, I have heard that the people of Sodom and Gomorrah are doing all kinds of evil things. ²¹Now I am going down to see for myself if those people really are that bad. If they aren't, I want to know about it."

²²The men turned and started toward Sodom. But the LORD stayed with Abraham, ²³who asked, "LORD, when you destroy the evil people, are you also going to destroy those who are good? ²⁴Wouldn't you spare the city if there are only fifty good people in it? ²⁵You surely wouldn't let them be killed when you destroy the evil ones. You are the judge of all the earth, and you do what is right."

²⁶The LORD replied, "If I find fifty good people in Sodom, I will save the city to keep them from being killed."

²⁷Abraham answered, "I am nothing more than the dust of the earth. Please forgive me, LORD, for daring to speak to you like this. ²⁸But suppose there are only forty-five good people in Sodom. Would you still wipe out the whole city?"

"If I find forty-five good people," the LORD replied, "I won't destroy the city."

²⁹"Suppose there are just forty good people?" Abraham asked.

"Even for them," the LORD replied, "I won't destroy the city."

³⁰Abraham said, "Please don't be angry, LORD, if I ask you what you will do if there are only thirty good people in the city."

"If I find thirty," the LORD replied, "I still won't destroy it."

³¹Then Abraham said, "I don't have any right to ask you, LORD, but what would you do if you find only twenty?"

"Because of them, I won't destroy the city," was the LORD's answer.

³²Finally, Abraham said, "Please don't get angry, LORD, if I speak just once more. Suppose you find only ten good people there."

"For the sake of ten good people," the LORD told him, "I still won't destroy the city."

³³After speaking with Abraham, the LORD left, and Abraham went back home.

The Evil City of Sodom

19 That evening the two angels^m arrived in Sodom, while Lot was sitting near the city gate.^{n} When Lot saw them, he got up, bowed down low, ²and said, "Gentlemen, I am your servant. Please come to my home. You can wash your feet, spend the night, and be on your way in the morning."

They told him, "No, we'll spend the night in the city square." ³But Lot kept insisting, until they finally agreed and went home with him. He baked some bread,^{o} cooked a meal, and they ate.

⁴Before Lot and his guests could go to bed, every man in Sodom, young and old, came and stood outside his house ⁵and started shouting, "Where are your visitors? Send them out, so we can have sex with them!"

⁶Lot went outside and shut the door behind him. ⁷Then he said, "Friends, please don't do such a terrible thing! ⁸I have two daughters who have never been married. I'll bring them out, and you can do what you want with them. But don't harm these men. They are guests in my home."

⁹"Don't get in our way," the crowd answered. "You're an outsider. What right do

---

^{l}**18.18** *that will be . . . on earth:* Or "and all other nations on earth will ask me to bless them as I have blessed his family." ^{m}**19.1** *two angels:* The two men of 18.22. ^{n}**19.1** *near the city gate:* In a large area where the people would gather for community business and for meeting with friends. ^{o}**19.3** *bread:* The Hebrew text has "bread without yeast," which could be fixed quickly when guests came without warning.

you have to order us around? We'll do worse things to you than we're going to do to them."

The crowd kept arguing with Lot. Finally, they rushed toward the door to break it down. [10]But the two angels in the house reached out and pulled Lot safely inside. [11]Then they struck everyone in the crowd blind, and none of them could even find the door.

[12-13]The two angels said to Lot, "The LORD has heard many terrible things about the people of Sodom, and he has sent us here to destroy the city. Take your family and leave. Take every relative you have in the city, as well as the men your daughters are going to marry."

[14]Lot went to the men who were engaged to his daughters and said, "Hurry and get out of here! The LORD is going to destroy this city." But they thought he was joking, and they laughed at him.

[15]Early the next morning the two angels tried to make Lot hurry and leave. They said, "Take your wife and your two daughters and get out of here as fast as you can! If you don't, every one of you will be killed when the LORD destroys the city." [16]At first, Lot just stood there. But the LORD wanted to save him. So the angels took Lot, his wife, and his two daughters by the hand and led them out of the city. [17]When they were outside, one of the angels said, "Run for your lives! Don't even look back. And don't stop in the valley. Run to the hills, where you will be safe."

[18-19]Lot answered, "You have done us a great favor, sir. You have saved our lives, but please don't make us go to the hills. That's too far away. The city will be destroyed before we can get there, and we will be killed when it happens. [20]There's a town near here. It's only a small place, but my family and I will be safe, if you let us go there."

[21]"All right, go there," he answered. "I won't destroy that town. [22]Hurry! Run! I can't do anything until you are safely there."

The town was later called Zoar[p] because Lot had said it was small.

Sodom and Gomorrah Are Destroyed

[23]The sun was coming up as Lot reached the town of Zoar, [24]and the LORD sent burning sulfur down like rain on Sodom and Gomorrah. [25]He destroyed those cities and everyone who lived in them, as well as their land and the trees and grass that grew there.

[26]On the way, Lot's wife looked back and was turned into a block of salt.

[27]That same morning Abraham got up and went to the place where he had stood and spoken with the LORD. [28]He looked down toward Sodom and Gomorrah and saw smoke rising from all over the land—it was like a flaming furnace.

[29]When God destroyed the cities of the valley where Lot lived, he remembered his promise to Abraham and saved Lot from the terrible destruction.

Moab and Ammon

[30]Lot was afraid to stay on in Zoar. So he took his two daughters and moved to a cave in the hill country. [31]One day his older daughter said to her sister, "Our father is old, and there are no men anywhere for us to marry. [32]Let's get our father drunk! Then we can sleep with him and have children." [33]That night they got their father drunk, and the older daughter got in bed with him, but he was too drunk even to know she was there.

[34]The next day the older daughter said to her sister, "I slept with my father last night. We'll get him drunk again tonight, so you can go to bed with him, and we can each have a child." [35]That night they got their father drunk, and this time the younger sister slept with him. But once again he was too drunk even to know she was there.

[36]That's how Lot's two daughters had their children. [37]The older daughter named her son Moab,[q] and he is the ancestor of the Moabites. [38]The younger daughter named her son Benammi,[r] and he is the ancestor of the Ammonites.

Abraham and Sarah at Gerar

20 Abraham moved to the Southern Desert, where he settled between Kadesh and Shur. Later he went to Gerar, and while there [2]he told everyone that his wife Sarah was his sister. So King Abimelech of Gerar had Sarah brought to him. [3]But God came to Abime-

---

[p]19.22 *Zoar:* In Hebrew "Zoar" sounds like "small." [q]19.37 *Moab:* In Hebrew "Moab" sounds like "from (my) father." [r]19.38 *Benammi:* In Hebrew "Benammi" means "son of my relative."

lech in a dream and said, "You have taken a married woman, and for this you will die!"

⁴⁻⁵Abimelech said to the Lord, "Don't kill me! I haven't slept with Sarah. Didn't they say they were brother and sister? I am completely innocent."

⁶God spoke to Abimelech in another dream and said:

I know you are innocent. That's why I kept you from sleeping with Sarah and doing anything wrong. ⁷Her husband is a prophet. Let her go back to him, and his prayers will save you from death. But if you don't return her, you and all your people will die.

⁸Early the next morning Abimelech sent for his officials, and when he told them what had happened, they were frightened. ⁹Abimelech then called in Abraham and said:

Look what you've done to us! What have I ever done to you? Why did you make me and my nation guilty of such a terrible sin? ¹⁰What were you thinking when you did this?

¹¹Abraham answered:

I did it because I didn't think any of you respected God, and I was sure that someone would kill me to get my wife. ¹²Besides, she is my half sister. We have the same father, but different mothers. ¹³When God made us leave my father's home and start wandering, I told her, "If you really love me, you will tell everyone that I am your brother."

¹⁴Abimelech gave Abraham some sheep, cattle, and slaves. He sent Sarah back ¹⁵and told Abraham that he could settle anywhere in his country. ¹⁶Then he said to Sarah, "I have given your brother a thousand pieces of silver as proof to everyone that you have done nothing wrong."ˢ

¹⁷⁻¹⁸Meanwhile, God had kept Abimelech's wife and slaves from having children. But Abraham prayed, and God let them start having children again.

Sarah Has a Son

21 The LORD was good to Sarah and kept his promise. ²Although Abraham was very old, Sarah had a son exactly at the time God had said. ³Abraham named his son Isaac, ⁴and when the boy was eight days old, Abraham cir-

cumcised him, just as the LORD had commanded.

⁵Abraham was a hundred years old when Isaac was born, ⁶and Sarah said, "God has made me laugh.ᵗ Now everyone will laugh with me. ⁷Who would have dared to tell Abraham that someday I would have a child? But in his old age, I have given him a son."

⁸The time came when Sarah no longer had to nurse Isaac,ᵘ and on that day Abraham gave a big feast.

Hagar and Ishmael Are Sent Away

⁹⁻¹⁰One day, Sarah noticed Hagar's son Ishmaelᵛ playing,ʷ and she said to Abraham, "Get rid of that Egyptian slave woman and her son! I don't want him to inherit anything. It should all go to my son."ˣ

¹¹Abraham was worried about Ishmael. ¹²But God said, "Abraham, don't worry about your slave woman and the boy. Just do what Sarah tells you. Isaac will inherit your family name, ¹³but the son of the slave woman is also your son, and I will make his descendants into a great nation."

¹⁴Early the next morning Abraham gave Hagar an animal skin full of water and some bread. Then he put the boy on her shoulder and sent them away.

They wandered around in the desert near Beersheba, ¹⁵and after they had run out of water, Hagar put her son under a bush. ¹⁶Then she sat down a long way off, because she could not bear to watch him die. And she cried bitterly.

¹⁷When God heard the boy crying, the angel of God called out to Hagar from heaven and said, "Hagar, why are you worried? Don't be afraid. I have heard your son crying. ¹⁸Help him up and hold his hand, because I will make him the father of a great nation." ¹⁹Then God let her see a well. So

---

ˢ20.16 as proof . . . wrong: One possible meaning for the difficult Hebrew text. ᵗ21.6 God has made me laugh: In Hebrew "Isaac" sounds like "laugh." ᵘ21.8 no longer had to nurse Isaac: In ancient Israel mothers nursed their children until they were about three years old. Then there was a family celebration. ᵛ21.9,10 Ishmael: The son of Abraham and Hagar, who was Sarah's slave woman (see 16.1-16). ʷ21.9,10 playing: Hebrew; one ancient translation "playing with her son Isaac." ˣ21.9,10 Get rid . . . son: When Abraham accepted Ishmael as his son, it gave Ishmael the right to inherit part of what Abraham owned. But slaves who were given their freedom lost the right to inherit such property.

she went to the well and filled the skin with water, then gave some to her son.

²⁰⁻²¹God blessed Ishmael, and as the boy grew older, he became an expert with his bow and arrows. He lived in the Paran Desert, and his mother chose an Egyptian woman for him to marry.

A Peace Treaty

²²About this time Abimelech and his army commander Phicol said to Abraham, "God blesses everything you do! ²³Now I want you to promise in the name of God that you will always be loyal to me and my descendants, just as I have always been loyal to you in this land where you have lived as a foreigner." ²⁴And so, Abraham promised.

²⁵One day, Abraham told Abimelech, "Some of your servants have taken over one of my wells."

²⁶"This is the first I've heard about it," Abimelech replied. "Why haven't you said something before? I don't have any idea who did it." ²⁷Abraham gave Abimelech some sheep and cattle, and then the two men made a peace treaty.

²⁸Abraham separated seven female lambs from his flock of sheep, ²⁹and Abimelech asked, "Why have you done this?"

³⁰Abraham told him, "I want you to accept these seven lambs as proof that I dug this well." ³¹So they called the place Beersheba,ʸ because they made a treaty there.

³²When the treaty was completed, Abimelech and his army commander Phicol went back to the land of the Philistines. ³³Abraham planted a tamarisk treeᶻ in Beersheba and worshiped the eternal LORD God. ³⁴Then Abraham lived a long time as a foreigner in the land of the Philistines.

**The LORD Tells Abraham
To Offer Isaac as a Sacrifice**

22 Some years later God decided to test Abraham, so he spoke to him.

Abraham answered, "Here I am, LORD."

²The LORD said, "Go get Isaac, your only son, the one you dearly love! Take him to the land of Moriah, and I will show you a mountain where you must sacrifice him to

---

ʸ**21.31** *Beersheba*: Meaning "Well of Good Fortune" or "Peace Treaty Well."   ᶻ**21.33** *tamarisk tree*: A tall shade tree that has deep roots and needs little water.

Personal *Concerns*—How can I learn to set priorities? *(Genesis 22.1-19)*

Always put God first.

What are you most tempted to put ahead of God? For many women it is a person—perhaps a child, husband, or friend. God gives us these people as a kindness, to enrich our lives and bring us joy. But when it comes to priorities, God wants us to put him first.

Genesis 22 tells one of the most disturbing stories in the Bible. God commands Abraham to offer his son as a human sacrifice. Just in case Abraham might think God didn't understand the cost of that request, the Lord says, "Go get Isaac, your only son, the one you dearly love!" (22.2). So Abraham takes his son three days into the wilderness to do the job. We can only imagine the pain of each step. Because Abraham was living among the Canaanites, whose religious tradition was to sacrifice their first-born son, he may have seen other children sacrificed.

Did Abraham guess how it would end? We have clues. In verse 5, he tells his servants that "we" will return. In verse 8, he tells Isaac, "God will provide the lamb." And Hebrews tells us, "He was sure that God could raise people to life" (11.19). Even so, Abraham tied his son to the altar and raised the knife. God stopped him.

In the end, Abraham knew what God must have known all along. He would put God first—even above his beloved son. Today, God would never ask us to destroy a child. But he does test our priorities. Who, or what, is first in our lives? He wants us to answer, "God." (See also 1 Samuel 15.10-35; Haggai 2.6-9; Luke 10.38-42; Revelation 2.1-7.)

Words To Remember: *"Don't hurt the boy or harm him in any way!" the angel said. "Now I know that you truly obey God, because you were willing to offer him your only son."*—Genesis 22.12

me on the fires of an altar." [3]So Abraham got up early the next morning and chopped wood for the fire. He put a saddle on his donkey and left with Isaac and two servants for the place where God had told him to go.

[4]Three days later Abraham looked off in the distance and saw the place. [5]He told his servants, "Stay here with the donkey, while my son and I go over there to worship. We will come back."

[6]Abraham put the wood on Isaac's shoulder, but he carried the hot coals and the knife. As the two of them walked along, [7-8]Isaac said, "Father, we have the coals and the wood, but where is the lamb for the sacrifice?"

"My son," Abraham answered, "God will provide the lamb."

The two of them walked on, and [9]when they reached the place that God had told him about, Abraham built an altar and placed the wood on it. Next, he tied up his son and put him on the wood. [10]He then took the knife and got ready to kill his son. [11]But the LORD's angel shouted from heaven, "Abraham! Abraham!"

"Here I am!" he answered.

[12]"Don't hurt the boy or harm him in any way!" the angel said. "Now I know that you truly obey God, because you were willing to offer him your only son."

[13]Abraham looked up and saw a ram caught by its horns in the bushes. So he took the ram and sacrificed it in place of his son.

[14]Abraham named that place "The LORD Will Provide." And even now people say, "On the mountain of the LORD it will be provided."[a]

[15]The LORD's angel called out from heaven a second time:

[16]You were willing to offer the LORD your only son, and so he makes you this solemn promise, [17]"I will bless you and give you such a large family, that someday your descendants will be more numerous than the stars in the sky or the grains of sand along the beach. They will defeat their enemies and take over the cities where their enemies live. [18]You have obeyed me, and so you and your descendants will be a blessing to all nations on earth."

[19]Abraham and Isaac went back to the servants who had come with him, and they returned to Abraham's home in Beersheba.

The Children of Nahor

[20-23]Abraham's brother Nahor had married Milcah, and Abraham was later told that they had eight sons. Uz was their firstborn; Buz was next, and then there was Kemuel who became the father of Aram; their other five sons were: Chesed, Hazo, Pildash, Jidlaph, and Bethuel, who became the father of Rebekah. [24]Nahor also had another wife.[b] Her name was Reumah, and she had four sons: Tebah, Gaham, Tahash, and Maacah.

Sarah's Death and Burial

23 [1-2]When Sarah was one hundred twenty-seven years old, she died in Kiriath-Arba, better known as Hebron, in the land of Canaan. After Abraham had mourned for her, [3]he went to the Hittites and said, [4]"I live as a foreigner in your land, and I don't own any property where I can bury my wife. Please let me buy a piece of land."

[5-6]"Sir," they answered, "you are an important man. Choose the best place to bury your wife. None of us would refuse you a resting place for your dead."

[7]Abraham bowed down [8]and replied, "If you are willing to let me bury my wife here, please ask Zohar's son Ephron [9]to sell me Machpelah Cave at the end of his field. I'll pay what it's worth, and all of you can be witnesses."

[10]Ephron was sitting there near the city gate, when Abraham made this request, and he answered, [11]"Sir, the whole field, including the cave, is yours. With my own people as witnesses, I freely give it to you as a burial place for your dead."

[12]Once again, Abraham bowed down [13]and said to Ephron, "In front of these witnesses, I offer you the full price, so I can bury my wife. Please accept my offer."

[14-15]"But sir," the man replied, "the property is worth only four hundred pieces of

---

[a]22.14 *The LORD Will Provide . . . it will be provided:* Or "The LORD Will Be Seen . . . the LORD will be seen" or "It (a ram) Will Be Seen . . . it (a ram) will be seen."
[b]22.24 *another wife:* This translates a Hebrew word for a woman who was legally bound to a man, but without the full privileges of a wife.

silver. Why should we haggle over such a small amount? Take the land. It's yours."

¹⁶⁻¹⁸Abraham accepted Ephron's offer and paid him the four hundred pieces of silver in front of everyone at the city gate. That's how Abraham got Ephron's property east of Hebron,ᶜ which included the field with all of its trees, as well as Machpelah Cave at the end of the field. ¹⁹So Abraham buried his wife Sarah in Machpelah Cave that was in the field ²⁰he had bought from the Hittites.

A Wife for Isaac

24 Abraham was now a very old man. The LORD had made him rich, and he was successful in everything he did. ²One day, Abraham called in his most trusted servant and said to him, "Solemnly promise me ³in the name of the LORD, who rules heaven and earth, that you won't choose a wife for my son Isaac from the people here in the land of Canaan. ⁴Instead, go back to the land where I was born and find a wife for him from among my relatives."

⁵But the servant asked, "What if the young woman I choose refuses to leave home and come here with me? Should I send Isaac there to look for a wife?"

⁶"No!" Abraham answered. "Don't ever do that, no matter what. ⁷The LORD who rules heaven brought me here from the land where I was born and promised that he would give this land to my descendants forever. When you go back there, the LORD will send his angel ahead of you to help you find a wife for my son. ⁸If the woman refuses to come along, you don't have to keep this promise. But don't ever take my son back there." ⁹So the servant gave Abraham his word that he would do everything he had been told to do.

¹⁰Soon after that, the servant loaded ten of Abraham's camels with valuable gifts. Then he set out for the city in northern Syria,ᵈ where Abraham's brother Nahor lived.

¹¹When he got there, he let the camels rest near the well outside the city. It was late afternoon, the time when the women came out for water. ¹²The servant prayed:

You, LORD, are the God my master Abraham worships. Please keep your promise to him and let me find a wife

for Isaac today. ¹³The young women of the city will soon come to this well for water, ¹⁴and I'll ask one of them for a drink. If she gives me a drink and then offers to get some water for my camels, I'll know she is the one you have chosen and that you have kept your promise to my master.

¹⁵⁻¹⁶While he was still praying, a beautiful unmarried young woman came by with a water jar on her shoulder. She was Rebekah, the daughter of Bethuel, the son of Abraham's brother Nahor and his wife Milcah. Rebekah walked past Abraham's servant, then went over to the well, and filled her water jar. When she started back, ¹⁷Abraham's servant ran to her and said, "Please let me have a drink of water."

¹⁸"I'll be glad to," she answered. Then she quickly took the jar from her shoulder and held it while he drank. ¹⁹⁻²⁰After he had finished, she said, "Now I'll give your camels all the water they want." She quickly poured out water for them, and she kept going back for more, until his camels had drunk all they wanted. ²¹Abraham's servant did not say a word, but he watched everything Rebekah did, because he wanted to know for certain if this was the woman the LORD had chosen.

²²The servant had brought along an expensive gold ring and two large gold bracelets. When Rebekah had finished bringing the water, he gave her the ring for her noseᵉ and the bracelets for her arms. ²³Then he said, "Please tell me who your father is. Does he have room in his house for me and my men to spend the night?"

²⁴She answered, "My father is Bethuel, the son of Nahor and Milcah. ²⁵We have a place where you and your men can stay, and we also have enough straw and feed for your camels."

²⁶Then the servant bowed his head and prayed, ²⁷"I thank you, LORD God of my master Abraham! You have led me to his relatives and kept your promise to him."

ᶜ**23.16-18** *Hebron:* The Hebrew text has "Mamre," a place just north of Hebron. ᵈ**24.10** *northern Syria:* The Hebrew text has "Aram-Naharaim," probably referring to the land around the city of Haran (see also "Paddan-Aram" in 25.20; 28.2, 6; 31.18, 20; 33.18; 35.23-26; 46.8-15; and "Paddan" in 48.7). ᵉ**24.22** *ring for her nose:* Nose-rings were popular jewelry items, as were earrings.

²⁸Rebekah ran straight home and told her family everything. ²⁹⁻³⁰Her brother Laban heard her tell what the servant had said, and he saw the ring and the bracelets she was wearing. So Laban ran out to Abraham's servant, who was standing by his camels at the well. ³¹Then Laban said, "The LORD has brought you safely here. Come home with me. There's no need for you to keep on standing outside. I have a room ready for you in our house, and there's also a place for your camels."

³²Abraham's servant went home with Laban, where Laban's servants unloaded his camels and gave them straw and feed. Then they brought water into the house, so Abraham's servant and his men could wash their feet. ³³After that, they brought in food. But the servant said, "Before I eat, I must tell you why I have come."

"Go ahead and tell us," Laban answered.

³⁴The servant explained:

I am Abraham's servant. ³⁵The LORD has been good to my master and has made him very rich. He has given him many sheep, goats, cattle, camels, and donkeys, as well as a lot of silver and gold, and many slaves. ³⁶Sarah, my master's wife, didn't have any children until she was very old. Then she had a son, and my master has given him everything. ³⁷I solemnly promised my master that I would do what he said. And he told me, "Don't choose a wife for my son from the women in this land of Canaan. ³⁸Instead, go back to the land where I was born and find a wife for my son from among my relatives."

³⁹I asked my master, "What if the young woman refuses to come with me?"

⁴⁰My master answered, "I have always obeyed the LORD, and he will send his angel to help you find my son a wife from among my own relatives. ⁴¹But if they refuse to let her come back with you, then you are freed from your promise."

⁴²When I came to the well today, I silently prayed, "You, LORD, are the God my master Abraham worships, so please lead me to a wife for his son ⁴³while I am here at the well. When a young woman comes out to get water, I'll ask her to give me a drink. ⁴⁴If she

---

SingleLife—What should I look for in a future spouse? *(Genesis 24)*

Look for qualities you could live with the rest of your life.

Considering a future husband is hard work. Some women want the security and warmth of marriage so much that they overlook flaws that make security and warmth impossible. Other women are so satisfied with independence that they overlook a man who could bring new levels of joy. And some just "fall in love" and hope to solve any problems that emerge later. But marriage is so important that we must take a careful look at a potential partner.

Abraham's servant gives us some ideas about the process. First, he prayed often. He was also straightforward about faith. He said, "I . . . gave thanks to the God my master Abraham worships" (24.48), and he received a response showing common faith, "The LORD has done this" (24.50). The servant also observed character qualities. As he watched Rebekah, he could tell she was confident, kind, energetic, strong, generous, hospitable, willing to work beyond what was asked, and adventurous. These were qualities of a woman who might travel by camel more than five hundred miles and create a marriage with a nomad she had never met. She could and did—though the next two chapters show their marriage wasn't always easy.

In looking for a husband, you can follow some of this servant's pattern. Pray. Look in places likely to contain a godly man. Be honest about your potential spouse's faith—or lack of faith. Look for character qualities you could live with for a lifetime. (See also Song of Songs 1; 1 Corinthians 13; Ephesians 5.21-33.)

Words To Remember: *Isaac took Rebekah into the tent where his mother had lived before she died, and Rebekah became his wife. He loved her and was comforted over the loss of his mother.*—**Genesis 24.67**

gives me a drink and offers to get some water for my camels, I'll know she is the one you have chosen."

⁴⁵Even before I had finished praying, Rebekah came by with a water jar on her shoulder. When she had filled the jar, I asked her for a drink. ⁴⁶She quickly lowered the jar from her shoulder and said, "Have a drink. Then I'll get water for your camels." So I drank, and after that she got some water for my camels. ⁴⁷I asked her who her father was, and she answered, "My father is Bethuel the son of Nahor and Milcah." Right away I put the ring in her nose and the bracelets on her arms. ⁴⁸Then I bowed my head and gave thanks to the God my master Abraham worships. The LORD had led me straight to my master's relatives, and I had found a wife for his son.

⁴⁹Now please tell me if you are willing to do the right thing for my master. Will you treat him fairly, or do I have to look for another young woman?

⁵⁰Laban and Bethuel answered, "The LORD has done this. We have no choice in the matter. ⁵¹Take Rebekah with you; she can marry your master's son, just as the LORD has said." ⁵²Abraham's servant bowed down and thanked the LORD. ⁵³Then he gave clothing, as well as silver and gold jewelry, to Rebekah. He also gave expensive gifts to her brother and her mother.

⁵⁴Abraham's servant and the men with him ate and drank, then spent the night there. The next morning they got up, and the servant told Rebekah's mother and brother, "I would like to go back to my master now."

⁵⁵"Let Rebekah stay with us for a week or ten days," they answered. "Then she may go."

⁵⁶But he said, "Don't make me stay any longer. The LORD has already helped me find a wife for my master's son. Now let us return."

⁵⁷They answered, "Let's ask Rebekah what she wants to do." ⁵⁸They called her and asked, "Are you willing to leave with this man right now?"

"Yes," she answered.

⁵⁹So they agreed to let Rebekah and an old family servant woman[j] leave immediately with Abraham's servant and his men.

⁶⁰They gave Rebekah their blessing and said, "We pray that God will give you many children and grandchildren and that he will help them defeat their enemies." ⁶¹Afterwards, Rebekah and the young women who were to travel with her prepared to leave. Then they got on camels and left with Abraham's servant and his men.

⁶²At that time Isaac was living in the southern part of Canaan near a place called "The Well of the Living One Who Sees Me."[g] ⁶³⁻⁶⁵One evening he was walking out in the fields, when suddenly he saw a group of people approaching on camels. So he started toward them. Rebekah saw him coming; she got down from her camel, and asked, "Who is that man?"

"He is my master Isaac," the servant answered. Then Rebekah covered her face with her veil.[h]

⁶⁶The servant told Isaac everything that had happened.

⁶⁷Isaac took Rebekah into the tent[i] where his mother had lived before she died, and Rebekah became his wife. He loved her and was comforted over the loss of his mother.

Abraham Marries Keturah

25 Abraham married Keturah, ²and they had six sons: Zimran, Jokshan, Medan, Midian, Ishbak, and Shuah. ³Later, Jokshan became the father of Sheba and Dedan, and when Dedan grew up, he had three sons: Asshurim, Letushim, and Leummim. ⁴Midian also had five sons: Ephah, Epher, Hanoch, Abida, and Eldaah.

⁵⁻⁶While Abraham was still alive, he gave gifts to the sons of Hagar and Keturah. He also sent their sons to live in the east far from his son Isaac, and when Abraham died, he left everything to Isaac.

The Death of Abraham

⁷⁻⁸Abraham died at the ripe old age of one hundred seventy-five. ⁹⁻¹⁰His sons Isaac

---

*j*24.59 *old family servant woman:* Probably Deborah, who had taken care of Rebekah from the time she was born (see 35.8). *g*24.62 *Who Sees Me:* Or "I Have Seen." *h*24.63-65 *covered . . . veil:* Since the veiling of a bride was part of the wedding ceremony, this probably means that she was willing to become the wife of Isaac. *i*24.67 *took . . . tent:* This shows that Rebekah is now the wife of Isaac and the successor of Sarah as the leading woman in the tribe.

and Ishmael buried him east of Hebron[j] in Machpelah Cave that was part of the field Abraham had bought from Ephron son of Zohar the Hittite. Abraham was buried there beside his wife Sarah. [11]God blessed Isaac after this, and Isaac moved to a place called "The Well of the Living One Who Sees Me."[k]

Ishmael's Descendants

[12]Ishmael was the son of Abraham and Hagar, the slave woman of Sarah. [13]Ishmael had twelve sons, in this order: Nebaioth, Kedar, Adbeel, Mibsam, [14]Mishma, Dumah, Massa, [15]Hadad, Tema, Jetur, Naphish, and Kedemah. [16]Each of Ishmael's sons was a tribal chief, and a village was named after each of them.

[17-18]Ishmael had settled in the land east of his brothers, and his sons[l] settled everywhere from Havilah to Shur, east of Egypt on the way to Asshur.[m] Ishmael was one hundred thirty-seven when he died.

The Birth of Esau and Jacob

[19]Isaac was the son of Abraham, [20]and he was forty years old when he married Rebekah, the daughter of Bethuel. She was also the sister of Laban, the Aramean from northern Syria.[n]

Almost twenty years later, [21]Rebekah still had no children. So Isaac asked the LORD to let her have a child, and the LORD answered his prayer.

[22]Before Rebekah gave birth, she knew she was going to have twins, because she could feel them inside her, fighting each other. She thought, "Why is this happening to me?" Finally, she asked the LORD why her twins were fighting, [23]and he told her:

"Your two sons will become
    two separate nations.[o]
The younger of the two
    will be stronger,
and the older son
    will be his servant."

[24]When Rebekah gave birth, [25]the first baby was covered with red hair, so he was named Esau.[p] [26]The second baby grabbed on to his brother's heel, so they named him Jacob.[q] Isaac was sixty years old when they were born.

Esau Sells His Rights as the First-Born Son

[27]As Jacob and Esau grew older, Esau liked the outdoors and became a good hunter, while Jacob settled down and became a shepherd. [28]Esau would take the meat of wild animals to his father Isaac, and so Isaac loved him more, but Jacob was his mother's favorite son.

[29]One day, Jacob was cooking some stew, when Esau came home hungry [30]and said, "I'm starving to death! Give me some of that red stew right now!" That's how Esau got the name "Edom."[r]

> *A big part of Christian maturity is learning to be ruled less and less by your emotions.*
> TWILA PARIS

[31]Jacob replied, "Sell me your rights as the first-born son."[s]

[32]"I'm about to die," Esau answered. "What good will those rights do me?"

[33]But Jacob said, "Promise me your birthrights, here and now!" And that's what Esau did. [34]Jacob then gave Esau some bread and some of the bean stew, and when Esau had finished eating and drinking, he just got up and left, showing how little he thought of his rights as the first-born.

Isaac and Abimelech

26 Once during Abraham's lifetime, the fields had not produced enough grain, and now the same thing happened. So Isaac went to King

---

[j]25.9,10 *Hebron:* See the note at 23.16-18.
[k]25.11 *The Well . . . Sees Me:* Or "Beer-Lahai-Roi" (see 16.14). [l]25.17,18 *sons:* Or "descendants."
[m]25.17,18 *Havilah to Shur . . . Asshur:* The exact location of these places is not known. [n]25.20 *northern Syria:* See the note at 24.10. [o]25.23 *two separate nations:* Or "two nations always in conflict."
[p]25.25 *Esau:* In Hebrew "Esau" sounds like "hairy." [q]25.26 *Jacob:* In Hebrew "Jacob" sounds like "heel." [r]25.30 *Edom:* In Hebrew "Edom" sounds like "red." [s]25.31 *rights . . . son:* The first-born son inherited the largest amount of property, as well as the leadership of the family.

Abimelech of the Philistines in the land of Gerar, [2]because the LORD had appeared to Isaac and said:

Isaac, stay away from Egypt! I will show you where I want you to go. [3]You will live there as a foreigner, but I will be with you and bless you. I will keep my promise to your father Abraham by giving this land to you and your descendants.

[4]I will give you as many descendants as there are stars in the sky, and I will give your descendants all of this land. They will be a blessing to every nation on earth,[t] [5]because Abraham did everything I told him to do.

[6]Isaac moved to Gerar [7]with his beautiful wife Rebekah. He was afraid that someone might kill him to get her, and so he told everyone that Rebekah was his sister. [8]After Isaac had been there a long time, King Abimelech looked out a window and saw Isaac hugging and kissing Rebekah. [9]Abimelech called him in and said, "Rebekah must be your wife! Why did you say she is your sister?"

"Because I thought someone would kill me," Isaac answered.

[10]"Don't you know what you've done?" Abimelech exclaimed. "If someone had slept with her, you would have made our whole nation guilty!" [11]Then Abimelech warned his people that anyone who even touched Isaac or Rebekah would be put to death.

[12]Isaac planted grain and had a good harvest that same year. The LORD blessed him, [13]and Isaac was so successful that he became very rich. [14]In fact, the Philistines were jealous of the large number of sheep, goats, and slaves that Isaac owned, [15]and they stopped up the wells that Abraham's servants had dug before his death. [16]Finally, Abimelech said, "Isaac, I want you to leave our country. You have become too powerful to stay here."

[17]Isaac left and settled in Gerar Valley, [18]where he cleaned out those wells that the Philistines had stopped up. Isaac also gave each of the wells the same name[u] that Abraham had given to them. [19]While his servants were digging in the valley, they found a spring-fed well. [20]But the shepherds of Gerar Valley quarreled with Isaac's shepherds and claimed the water belonged to them. So

the well was named "Quarrel," because they had quarreled with Isaac.

[21]Isaac's servants dug another well, and the shepherds also quarreled about it. So that well was named "Jealous." [22]Finally, they dug one more well. There was no quarreling this time, and the well was named "Lots of Room," because the LORD had given them room and would make them very successful.

[23]Isaac went on to Beersheba, [24]where the LORD appeared to him that night and told him, "Don't be afraid! I am the God who was worshiped by your father Abraham, my servant. I will be with you and bless you, and because of Abraham I will give you many descendants." [25]Isaac built an altar there and worshiped the LORD. Then he set up camp, and his servants started digging a well.

[26]Meanwhile, Abimelech had left Gerar and was taking his advisor Ahuzzath and his army commander Phicol to see Isaac. [27]When they arrived, Isaac asked, "Why are you here? Didn't you send me away because you hated me?"

[28]They answered, "We now know for certain that the LORD is with you, and we have decided there needs to be a peace treaty between you and us. So let's make a solemn agreement [29]not to harm each other. Remember, we have never hurt you, and when we sent you away, we let you go in peace. The LORD has truly blessed you."

[30]Isaac gave a big feast for them, and everyone ate and drank. [31]Early the next morning Isaac and the others made a solemn agreement, then he let them go in peace.

[32]Later that same day Isaac's servants came and said, "We've struck water!" [33]So Isaac named the well Shibah,[v] and the town is still called Beersheba.[w]

Esau's Foreign Wives

[34]When Esau was forty, he married Judith the daughter of Beeri the Hittite and Basemath the daughter of Elon the Hittite.

---

[t]26.4 *They . . . on earth:* Or "All nations on earth will ask me to bless them." [u]26.18 *gave . . . same name:* By doing this Isaac claimed ownership of the wells. [v]26.33 *Shibah:* In Hebrew "Shibah" sounds something like "good luck" and "promise." [w]26.33 *Beersheba:* Meaning "Well of Good Fortune" or "Peace Treaty Well."

³⁵But these two women brought a lot of grief to his parents Isaac and Rebekah.

Isaac Blesses Jacob

27 After Isaac had become old and almost blind, he called in his first-born son Esau, who asked him, "Father, what can I do for you?"

²Isaac replied, "I am old and might die at any time. ³So take your bow and arrows, then go out in the fields, and kill a wild animal. ⁴Cook some of that tasty food that I love so much and bring it to me. I want to eat it once more and give you my blessing before I die."

⁵Rebekah had been listening, and as soon as Esau left to go hunting, ⁶she said to Jacob, "I heard your father tell Esau ⁷to kill a wild animal and cook some tasty food for your father before he dies. Your father said this because he wants to bless your brother with the LORD as his witness. ⁸Now, my son, listen carefully to what I want you to do. ⁹Go and kill two of your best young goats and bring them to me. I'll cook the tasty food that your father loves so much. ¹⁰Then you can take it to him, so he can eat it and give you his blessing before he dies."

¹¹"My brother Esau is a hairy man," Jacob reminded her. "And I am not. ¹²If my father touches me and realizes I am trying to trick him, he will put a curse on me instead of giving me a blessing."

¹³Rebekah insisted, "Let his curse fall on me! Just do what I say and bring me the meat." ¹⁴So Jacob brought the meat to his mother, and she cooked the tasty food that his father liked. ¹⁵Then she took Esau's best clothes and put them on Jacob. ¹⁶She also covered the smooth part of his hands and neck with goatskins ¹⁷and gave him some bread and the tasty food she had cooked.

¹⁸Jacob went to his father and said, "Father, here I am."

"Which one of my sons are you?" his father asked.

¹⁹Jacob replied, "I am Esau, your first-born, and I have done what you told me. Please sit up and eat the meat I have brought. Then you can give me your blessing."

²⁰Isaac asked, "My son, how did you find an animal so quickly?"

"The LORD your God was kind to me," Jacob answered.

²¹"My son," Isaac said, "come closer, where I can touch you and find out if you really are Esau." ²²Jacob went closer. His father touched him and said, "You sound like Jacob, but your hands feel hairy like Esau's." ²³And so Isaac blessed Jacob, thinking he was Esau.

²⁴Isaac asked, "Are you really my son Esau?"

"Yes, I am," Jacob answered.

²⁵So Isaac told him, "Serve me the wild meat, and I can give you my blessing."

Jacob gave him some meat, and he ate it. He also gave him some wine, and he drank it. ²⁶Then Isaac said, "Son, come over here and kiss me." ²⁷While Jacob was kissing him, Isaac caught the smell of his clothes and said:

"The smell of my son
  is like a field
    the LORD has blessed.
²⁸ God will bless you, my son,
    with dew from heaven
  and with fertile fields,
    rich with grain and grapes.
²⁹ Nations will be your servants
    and bow down to you.
  You will rule over your brothers,
    and they will kneel
      at your feet.
  Anyone who curses you
    will be cursed;
  anyone who blesses you
    will be blessed."

³⁰Right after Isaac had given Jacob his blessing and Jacob had gone, Esau came back from hunting. ³¹He cooked the tasty food, brought it to his father, and said, "Father, please sit up and eat the meat I have brought you, so you can give me your blessing."

³²"Who are you?" Isaac asked.

"I am Esau, your first-born son."

³³Isaac started trembling and said, "Then who brought me some wild meat right before you came in? I ate it and gave him a blessing that cannot be taken back."

³⁴Esau cried loudly and begged, "Father, give me a blessing too!"

³⁵Isaac answered, "Your brother tricked me and stole your blessing."

³⁶Esau replied, "My brother deserves the

name Jacob,[x] because he has already cheated me twice. The first time he cheated me out of my rights as the first-born son, and now he has cheated me out of my blessing." Then Esau asked his father, "Don't you still have any blessing left for me?"

[37]"My son," Isaac answered, "I have made Jacob the ruler over you and your brothers, and all of you will be his servants. I have also promised him all the grain and grapes that he needs. There's nothing left that I can do for you."

[38]"Father," Esau asked, "don't you have more than one blessing? You can surely give me a blessing too!" Then Esau started crying again.

[39]So his father said:

"Your home will be far
    from that fertile land,
where dew comes down
    from the heavens.
[40]You will live by the power
    of your sword
    and be your brother's slave.
But when you decide to be free,
    you will break loose."

[41]Esau hated his brother Jacob because he had stolen the blessing that was supposed to be his. So he said to himself, "Just as soon as my father dies, I'll kill Jacob."

[42]When Rebekah found out what Esau planned to do, she sent for Jacob and told him, "Son, your brother Esau is just waiting for the time when he can kill you. [43]Now listen carefully and do what I say. Go to the home of my brother Laban in Haran [44]and stay with him for a while. When Esau stops being angry [45]and forgets what you have done to him, I'll send for you to come home. Why should I lose both of my sons on the same day?"[y]

[46]Rebekah later told Isaac, "Those Hittite wives of Esau are making my life miserable! If Jacob marries a Hittite woman, I'd be better off dead."

Isaac's Instructions to Jacob

28 Isaac called in Jacob, then gave him a blessing, and said: Don't marry any of those Canaanite women. [2]Go at once to your mother's father Bethuel in northern Syria[z] and choose a wife from one of the daughters of Laban, your mother's brother. [3]I pray that God All-Powerful will bless you with many descendants and let you become a great nation. [4]May he bless you with the land he gave Abraham, so that you will take over this land where we now live as foreigners.

[5]Isaac then sent Jacob to stay with Rebekah's brother Laban, the son of Bethuel the Aramean.

Esau Marries the Daughter of Ishmael

[6]Esau found out that his father Isaac had blessed Jacob and had warned him not to marry any of the Canaanite women. He also learned that Jacob had been sent to find a wife in northern Syria[z] [7]and that he had obeyed his father and mother. [8]Esau already had several wives, but he realized at last how much his father hated the Canaanite women. [9]So he married Ishmael's daughter Mahalath, who was the sister of Nebaioth[a] and the granddaughter of Abraham.

Jacob's Dream at Bethel

[10]Jacob left the town of Beersheba and started out for Haran. [11]At sunset he stopped for the night and went to sleep, resting his head on a large rock. [12]In a dream he saw a ladder[b] that reached from earth to heaven, and God's angels were going up and down on it.

[13]The LORD was standing beside the ladder[c] and said:

I am the LORD God who was worshiped by Abraham and Isaac. I will give to you and your family the land on which you are now sleeping. [14]Your descendants will spread over the earth in all directions and will become as numerous as the specks of dust. Your family will be a blessing to all people.[d] [15]Wherever you go, I will watch over you, then later I will bring you back to

---

[x]**27.36** *Jacob:* In Hebrew "Jacob" sounds like "cheat." [y]**27.45** *lose . . . day:* Esau would be hunted down as a murderer if he killed Jacob, and so Rebekah would lose both of her sons. [z]**28.2,6** *northern Syria:* See the note at 24.10. [a]**28.9** *Nebaioth:* Ishmael's oldest son (see 25.13). [b]**28.12** *ladder:* Or "stairway." [c]**28.13** *the ladder:* Or "Jacob" or "the stairway" (see the note at 28.12). [d]**28.14** *Your family . . . people:* Or "All people will ask me to bless them as I have blessed your family."

this land. I won't leave you—I will do all I have promised.

¹⁶Jacob woke up suddenly and thought, "The LORD is in this place, and I didn't even know it." ¹⁷Then Jacob became frightened and said, "This is a fearsome place! It must be the house of God and the ladder*ᵉ* to heaven."

¹⁸When Jacob got up early the next morning, he took the rock that he had used for a pillow and stood it up for a place of worship. Then he poured olive oil on the rock to dedicate it to God, ¹⁹and he named the place Bethel.*ᶠ* Before that it had been named Luz.

²⁰Jacob solemnly promised God, "If you go with me and watch over me as I travel, and if you give me food and clothes ²¹and bring me safely home again, you will be my God. ²²This rock will be your house, and I will give back to you a tenth of everything you give me."

Jacob Arrives at Laban's Home

29 As Jacob continued on his way to the east, ²he looked out in a field and saw a well where shepherds took their sheep for water. Three flocks of sheep were lying around the well, which was covered with a large rock. ³Shepherds would roll the rock away when all their sheep had gathered there. Then after the sheep had been watered, the shepherds would roll the rock back over the mouth of the well.

⁴Jacob asked the shepherds, "Where are you from?"

"We're from Haran," they answered.

⁵Then he asked, "Do you know Nahor's grandson Laban?"

"Yes we do," they replied.

⁶"How is he?" Jacob asked.

"He's fine," they answered. "And here comes his daughter Rachel with the sheep."

⁷Jacob told them, "Look, the sun is still high up in the sky, and it's too early to bring in the rest of the flocks. Water your sheep and take them back to the pasture."

⁸But they replied, "We can't do that until they all get here, and the rock has been rolled away from the well."

⁹While Jacob was still talking with the men, his cousin Rachel came up with her father's sheep. ¹⁰When Jacob saw her and his uncle's sheep, he rolled the rock away

and watered the sheep. ¹¹He then kissed Rachel and started crying because he was so happy. ¹²He told her that he was the son of her aunt Rebekah, and she ran and told her father about him.

¹³As soon as Laban heard the news, he ran out to meet Jacob. He hugged and kissed him and brought him to his home, where Jacob told him everything that had happened. ¹⁴Laban said, "You are my nephew, and you are like one of my own family."

Jacob Marries Leah and Rachel

After Jacob had been there for a month, ¹⁵Laban said to him, "You shouldn't have to work without pay, just because you are a relative of mine. What do you want me to give you?"

¹⁶⁻¹⁷Laban had two daughters. Leah was older than Rachel, but her eyes didn't sparkle,*ᵍ* while Rachel was beautiful and had a good figure. ¹⁸Since Jacob was in love with Rachel, he answered, "If you will let me marry Rachel, I'll work seven years for you."

¹⁹Laban replied, "It's better for me to let you marry Rachel than for someone else to have her. So stay and work for me." ²⁰Jacob worked seven years for Laban, but the time seemed like only a few days, because he loved Rachel so much.

While the word love makes up the marriage painting, the ways we cherish each other add the beautiful strokes of color to the canvas.

CAROLE MAYHALL

²¹Jacob said to Laban, "The time is up, and I want to marry Rachel now!" ²²So Laban gave a big feast and invited all their neighbors. ²³But that evening he brought

---

ᵉ**28.17** *ladder:* See the note at 28.12. ᶠ**28.19** *Bethel:* In Hebrew "Bethel" means "House of God."
ᵍ**29.16,17** *but her eyes didn't sparkle:* Or "and her eyes sparkled."

Leah to Jacob, who married her and spent the night with her. [24]Laban also gave Zilpah to Leah as her servant woman.

[25]The next morning Jacob found out that he had married Leah, and he asked Laban, "Why did you do this to me? Didn't I work to get Rachel? Why did you trick me?"

[26]Laban replied, "In our country the older daughter must get married first. [27]After you spend this week[h] with Leah, you may also marry Rachel. But you will have to work for me another seven years."

[28-30]At the end of the week of celebration, Laban let Jacob marry Rachel, and he gave her his servant woman Bilhah. Jacob loved Rachel more than he did Leah, but he had to work another seven years for Laban.

[31]The LORD knew that Jacob loved Rachel more than he did Leah, and so he gave children to Leah, but not to Rachel. [32]Leah gave birth to a son and named him Reuben,[i] because she said, "The LORD has taken away my sorrow. Now my husband will love me more than he does Rachel." [33]She had a second son and named him Simeon,[j] because she said, "The LORD has heard that my husband doesn't love me." [34]When Leah's third son was born, she said, "Now my husband will hold me close." So this son was named Levi.[k] [35]She had one more son and named him Judah,[l] because she said, "I'll praise the LORD!"

Problems between Rachel and Leah

30 Rachel was very jealous of Leah for having children, and she said to Jacob, "I'll die if you don't give me some children!"

[2]But Jacob became upset with Rachel and answered, "Don't blame me! I'm not God."

[3]"Here, take my servant Bilhah," Rachel told him. "Have children by her, and I'll let them be born on my knees to show that they are mine."

[4]Then Rachel let Jacob marry Bilhah, [5]and they had a son. [6]Rachel named him Dan,[m] because she said, "God has answered my prayers. He has judged me and given me a son." [7]When Bilhah and Jacob had a second son, [8]Rachel said, "I've struggled hard with my sister, and I've won!" So she named the boy Naphtali.[n]

[9]When Leah realized she could not have

any more children, she let Jacob marry her servant Zilpah, [10]and they had a son. [11]"I'm really lucky," Leah said, and she named the boy Gad.[o] [12]When they had another son, [13]Leah exclaimed, "I'm happy now, and all the women will say how happy I am." So she named him Asher.[p]

Love Flowers

[14]During the time of the wheat harvest, Reuben found some love flowers[q] and took them to his mother Leah. Rachel asked Leah for some of them, [15]but Leah said, "It's bad enough that you stole my husband! Now you want my son's love flowers too."

"All right," Rachel answered. "Let me have the flowers, and you can sleep with Jacob tonight."

[16]That evening when Jacob came in from the fields, Leah told him, "You're sleeping with me tonight. I hired you with my son's love flowers."

They slept together that night, [17]and God answered Leah's prayers by giving her a fifth son. [18]Leah shouted, "God has rewarded me for letting Jacob marry my servant," and she named the boy Issachar.[r]

[19]When Leah had another son, [20]she exclaimed, "God has given me a wonderful gift, and my husband will praise me for giving him six sons." So she named the boy Zebulun.[s] [21]Later, Leah had a daughter and named her Dinah.

[22-23]Finally, God remembered Rachel—he answered her prayer by giving her a son. "God has taken away my disgrace," she said. [24]"I'll name the boy Joseph,[t] and I'll pray that the LORD will give me another son."

---

[h]**29.27** *this week*: The wedding feast lasted for seven days (see Judges 14.12, 17).   [i]**29.32** *Reuben*: In Hebrew "Reuben" means, "Look, a son!"
[j]**29.33** *Simeon*: In Hebrew "Simeon" sounds like "someone who hears."   [k]**29.34** *hold me close . . . Levi*: In Hebrew "Levi" sounds like "hold (someone) close."   [l]**29.35** *Judah*: In Hebrew "Judah" sounds like "praise."   [m]**30.6** *Dan*: In Hebrew "Dan" means "judge."   [n]**30.8** *Naphtali*: In Hebrew "Naphtali" means "struggle" or "contest."   [o]**30.11** *Gad*: In Hebrew "Gad" means "lucky."   [p]**30.13** *Asher*: In Hebrew "Asher" means "happy."   [q]**30.14** *love flowers*: Also called "mandrakes," a flowering plant that was thought to give sexual powers.   [r]**30.18** *Issachar*: In Hebrew "Issachar" sounds like "reward."   [s]**30.20** *Zebulun*: In Hebrew "Zebulun" sounds like "give" and "praise."   [t]**30.24** *Joseph*: In Hebrew "Joseph" sounds like "take away" and "add."

Jacob and Laban

²⁵After Joseph was born, Jacob said to Laban, "Release me from our agreement" and let me return to my own country. ²⁶You know how hard I've worked for you, so let me take my wives and children and leave."

²⁷⁻²⁸But Laban told him, "If you really are my friend, stay on, and I'll pay whatever you ask. I'm sureᵛ the LORD has blessed me because of you."

²⁹Jacob answered:

You've seen how hard I've worked for you, and you know how your flocks and herds have grown under my care. ³⁰You didn't have much before I came, but the LORD has blessed everything I have ever done for you. Now it's time for me to start looking out for my own family.

³¹"How much do you want me to pay you?" Laban asked.

Then Jacob told him:

I don't want you to pay me anything. Just do one thing, and I'll take care of your sheep and goats. ³²Let me go through your flocks and herds and take the sheep and goats that are either spotted or speckledʷ and the black lambs. That's all you need to give me. ³³In the future you can easily find out if I've been honest. Just look and see if my animals are either spotted or speckled, or if the lambs are black. If they aren't, they've been stolen from you.

³⁴"I agree to that," was Laban's response. ³⁵Before the end of the day, Laban had separated his spotted and speckled animals and the black lambs from the others and had put his sons in charge of them. ³⁶Then Laban made Jacob keep the rest of the sheep and goats at a distance of three days' journey.

³⁷Jacob cut branches from some poplar trees and from some almond and evergreen trees. He peeled off part of the bark and made the branches look spotted and speckled. ³⁸Then he put the branches where the sheep and goats would see themˣ while they were drinking from the water trough. The goats mated there ³⁹in front of the branches, and their young were spotted and speckled.

⁴⁰Some of the sheep that Jacob was keeping for Laban were already spotted. And when the others were ready to mate, he made sure that they faced in the direction of the spotted and black ones. In this way, Jacob built up a flock of sheep for himself and did not put them with the other sheep.

⁴¹When the stronger sheep were mating near the drinking place, Jacob made sure that the spotted branches were there. ⁴²But he would not put out the branches when the weaker animals were mating. So Jacob got all of the healthy animals, and Laban got what was left. ⁴³Jacob soon became rich and successful. He owned many sheep, goats, camels, and donkeys, as well as a lot of slaves.

Jacob Runs from Laban

31 Jacob heard that Laban's sons were complaining, "Jacob is now a rich man, and he got everything he owns from our father." ²Jacob also noticed that Laban was not as friendly as he had been before. ³One day the LORD said, "Jacob, go back to your relatives in the land of your ancestors, and I will bless you."

Sometimes God's grace is the hardest thing for me to grasp. He loves us not because we're good, but because he's good.

CINDY MORGAN

⁴Jacob sent for Rachel and Leah to meet him in the field where he kept his sheep, ⁵and he told them:

Your father isn't as friendly with me as he used to be, but the God my ancestors worshiped has been on my side. ⁶You know that I have worked

---

ᵘ**30.25** *Release . . . agreement:* Jacob had agreed to work seven years for each of Laban's two daughters (see 29.18). ᵛ**30.27,28** *I'm sure:* The Hebrew text means to find out by some kind of magic, such as fortunetelling. ʷ**30.32** *spotted or speckled:* In ancient times sheep were usually white, and goats were usually black or dark brown; only a few sheep would have black spots, and only a few goats would have white spots. ˣ**30.38** *would see them:* It was believed by some that what sheep and goats saw at the time of breeding would determine the color of their young.

hard for your father [7]and that he keeps cheating me by changing my wages time after time. But God has protected me. [8]When your father said the speckled sheep would be my wages, all of them were speckled. And when he said the spotted ones would be mine, all of them were spotted. [9]That's how God has taken sheep and goats from your father and given them to me.

[10]Once, when the flocks were mating, I dreamed that all the rams were either spotted or speckled. [11]Then God's angel called me by name. I answered, [12]and he said, "Notice that all the rams are either spotted or speckled. I know everything Laban is doing to you, [13]and I am the God you worshiped at Bethel,[y] when you poured olive oil on a rock and made a promise to me. Leave here right away and return to the land where you were born."

[14]Rachel and Leah said to Jacob:

There's nothing left for us to inherit from our father. [15]He treats us like foreigners and has even cheated us out of the bride price[z] that should have been ours. [16]Now do whatever God tells you to do. Even the property God took from our father and gave to you really belongs to us and our children.

[17]Then Jacob, his wives, and his children got on camels and left [18]for the home of his father Isaac in Canaan. Jacob took all of the flocks, herds, and other property that he had gotten in northern Syria.[a]

[19]Before Rachel left, she stole the household idols[b] while Laban was out shearing his sheep.

[20]Jacob tricked Laban the Aramean[c] by not saying that he intended to leave. [21]When Jacob crossed the Euphrates River and headed for the hill country of Gilead, he took with him everything he owned.

Laban Catches Up with Jacob

[22]Three days later Laban found out that Jacob had gone. [23]So he took some of his relatives along and chased after Jacob for seven days, before catching up with him in the hill country of Gilead. [24]But God appeared to Laban in a dream that night and warned, "Don't say a word to Jacob. Don't make a threat or a promise."

[25]Jacob had set up camp in the hill country of Gilead, when Laban and his relatives came and set up camp in another part of the hill country. Laban went to Jacob [26]and said:

Look what you've done! You've tricked me and run off with my daughters like a kidnapper. [27]Why did you sneak away without telling me? I would have given you a going-away party with singing and with music on tambourines and harps. [28]You didn't even give me a chance to kiss my own grandchildren and daughters good-by. That was really foolish. [29]I could easily hurt you, but the God your father worshiped has warned me not to make any threats or promises.

[30]I can understand why you were eager to return to your father, but why did you have to steal my idols?

[31]Jacob answered, "I left secretly because I was afraid you would take your daughters from me by force. [32]If you find that any one of us has taken your idols, I'll have that person killed. Let your relatives be witnesses. Show me what belongs to you, and you can take it back." Jacob did not realize that Rachel had stolen the household idols.

[33]Laban searched the tents of Jacob, Leah, and the two servant women,[d] but did not find the idols. Then he started for Rachel's tent. [34]She had already hidden them in the cushion she used as a saddle and was sitting on it. Laban searched everywhere and did not find them. [35]Rachel said, "Father, please don't be angry with me for not getting up; I am having my period." Laban kept on searching, but still did not find the idols.

[36]Jacob became very angry and said to Laban:

What have I done wrong? Have I

---

y[31.13] you . . . Bethel: Or "who appeared to you at Bethel." z[31.15] bride price: Usually the husband-to-be paid a bride price to the father of the bride. But Jacob didn't pay Laban a bride price for either Rachel or Leah. Instead he was tricked into working fourteen years to get the bride he loved. So there was no money for either of Laban's daughters. a[31.18] northern Syria: See the note at 24.10. b[31.19] household idols: These were thought to protect the household from danger. It is also possible that the person who had them would inherit the family property. c[31.20] the Aramean: Meaning someone from northern Syria (see the note at 24.10). d[31.33] two servant women: Bilhah and Zilpah (see 30.4, 9).

committed some crime? Is that why you hunted me down? ³⁷After searching through everything I have, did you find anything of yours? If so, put it here, where your relatives and mine can see it. Then we can decide what to do.

³⁸In all the twenty years that I've worked for you, not one of your sheep or goats has had a miscarriage, and I've never eaten even one of your rams. ³⁹If a wild animal killed one of your sheep or goats, I paid for it myself. In fact, you demanded the full price, whether the animal was killed during the day or at night.ᵉ ⁴⁰I sweated every day, and I couldn't sleep at night because of the cold.

⁴¹I had to work fourteen of these twenty long years to earn your two daughters and another six years to buy your sheep and goats. During that time you kept changing my wages. ⁴²If the fearsome Godᶠ worshiped by Abraham and my father Isaac had not been on my side, you would have sent me away without a thing. But God saw my hard work, and he knew the trouble I was in, so he helped me. Then last night he told you how wrong you were.

Jacob and Laban Make an Agreement

⁴³Laban said to Jacob, "Leah and Rachel are my daughters, and their children belong to me. All these sheep you are taking are really mine too. In fact, everything you have belongs to me. But there is nothing I can do to keep my daughters and their children. ⁴⁴So I am ready to make an agreement with you, and we will pile up some large rocks here to remind us of the agreement."

⁴⁵After Jacob had set up a large rock, ⁴⁶he told his men to get some more rocks and pile them up next to it. Then Jacob and Laban ate a meal together beside the rocks. ⁴⁷Laban named the pile of rocks Jegar Sahadutha.ᵍ But Jacob named it Galeed.ʰ ⁴⁸Laban said to Jacob, "This pile of rocks will remind us of our agreement." That's why the place was named Galeed. ⁴⁹Laban also said, "This pile of rocks means that the LORD will watch us both while we are apart from each other." So the place was also named Mizpah.ⁱ

⁵⁰Then Laban said:

If you mistreat my daughters or marry other women, I may not know about it, but remember, God is watching us! ⁵¹⁻⁵²Both this pile of rocks and this large rock have been set up between us as a reminder. I must never go beyond them to attack you, and you must never go beyond them to attack me. ⁵³My father Nahor, your grandfather Abraham, and their ancestors all worshiped the same God, and he will make sure that we each keep the agreement.

Then Jacob made a promise in the name of the fearsome Godʲ his father Isaac had worshiped. ⁵⁴Jacob killed an animal and offered it as a sacrifice there on the mountain, and he invited his men to eat with him. After the meal they spent the night on the mountain. ⁵⁵Early the next morning, Laban kissed his daughters and his grandchildren good-by, then he left to go back home.

Jacob Gets Ready To Meet Esau

32 As Jacob was on his way back home, some of God's angels came and met him. ²When Jacob saw them, he said, "This is God's camp." So he named the place Mahanaim.ᵏ

³Jacob sent messengers on ahead to Esau, who lived in the land of Seir, also known as Edom. ⁴Jacob told them to say to Esau, "Master, I am your servant! I have lived with Laban all this time, ⁵and now I own cattle, donkeys, and sheep, as well as many slaves. Master, I am sending these messengers in the hope that you will be kind to me."

⁶When the messengers returned, they told Jacob, "We went to your brother Esau, and now he is heading this way with four hundred men."

⁷Jacob was so frightened that he divided

ᵉ**31.39** *you demanded . . . night:* A shepherd was not responsible for sheep and goats killed by wild animals, if the shepherd could supply proof of how they were killed. ᶠ**31.42** *fearsome God:* One possible meaning for the difficult Hebrew text. ᵍ**31.47** *Jegar Sahadutha:* In Aramaic "Jegar Sahadutha" means "a pile of rocks to remind us." ʰ**31.47** *Galeed:* In Hebrew "Galeed" means "a pile of rocks to remind us." ⁱ**31.49** *Mizpah:* In Hebrew "Mizpah" sounds like "a place from which to watch." ʲ**31.53** *fearsome God:* See the note at 31.42. ᵏ**32.2** *Mahanaim:* In Hebrew "Mahanaim" means "two camps."

his people, sheep, cattle, and camels into two groups. [8]He thought, "If Esau attacks one group, perhaps the other can escape."

[9]Then Jacob prayed:

You, LORD, are the God who was worshiped by my grandfather Abraham and by my father Isaac. You told me to return home to my family, and you promised to be with me and make me successful. [10]I don't deserve all the good things you have done for me, your servant. When I first crossed the Jordan, I had only my walking stick, but now I have two large groups of people and animals. [11]Please rescue me from my brother. I am afraid he will come and attack not only me, but my wives and children as well. [12]But you have promised that I would be a success and that someday it will be as hard to count my descendants as it is to count the stars in the sky.

[13]After Jacob had spent the night there, he chose some animals as gifts for Esau: [14-15]two hundred female goats and twenty males, two hundred female sheep and twenty males, thirty female camels with their young, forty cows and ten bulls, and twenty female donkeys and ten males.

[16]Jacob put servants in charge of each herd and told them, "Go ahead of me and keep a space between each herd." [17]Then he said to the servant in charge of the first herd, "When Esau meets you, he will ask whose servant you are. He will want to know where you are going and who owns those animals in front of you. [18]So tell him, 'They belong to your servant Jacob, who is coming this way. He is sending them as a gift to his master Esau.' "

[19]Jacob also told the men in charge of the second and third herds and those who followed to say the same thing when they met Esau. [20]And Jacob told them to be sure to say that he was right behind them. Jacob hoped the gifts would make Esau friendly, so Esau would be glad to see him when they met. [21]Jacob's men took the gifts on ahead of him, but he spent the night in camp.

Jacob's Name Is Changed to Israel

[22-23]Jacob got up in the middle of the night and took his wives, his eleven children, and everything he owned across to the other side of the Jabbok River for safety. [24]Af-

terwards, Jacob went back and spent the rest of the night alone.

A man came and fought with Jacob until just before daybreak. [25]When the man saw that he could not win, he struck Jacob on the hip and threw it out of joint. [26]They kept on wrestling until the man said, "Let go of me! It's almost daylight."

"You can't go until you bless me," Jacob replied.

[27]Then the man asked, "What is your name?"

"Jacob," he answered.

[28]The man said, "Your name will no longer be Jacob. You have wrestled with God and with men, and you have won. That's why your name will be Israel."[l]

[29]Jacob said, "Now tell me your name."

"Don't you know who I am?" he asked. And he blessed Jacob.

[30]Jacob said, "I have seen God face to face, and I am still alive." So he named the place Peniel.[m] [31]The sun was coming up as Jacob was leaving Peniel. He was limping because he had been struck on the hip, [32]and the muscle on his hip joint had been injured. That's why even today the people of Israel don't eat the hip muscle of any animal.

Jacob Meets Esau

33 Later that day Jacob met Esau coming with his four hundred men. So Jacob had his children walk with their mothers. [2]The two servant women, Zilpah and Bilhah, together with their children went first, followed by Leah and her children, then by Rachel and Joseph. [3]Jacob himself walked in front of them all, bowing to the ground seven times as he came near his brother.

[4]But Esau ran toward Jacob and hugged and kissed him. Then the two brothers started crying.

[5]When Esau noticed the women and children he asked, "Whose children are these?"

Jacob answered, "These are the ones the LORD has been kind enough to give to me, your servant."

---

[l]32.28 *Israel*: In Hebrew one meaning of "Israel" is "a man who wrestles with God."   [m]32.30 *Peniel*: In Hebrew "Peniel" means "face of God."

[6]Then the two servant women and their children came and bowed down to Esau. [7]Next, Leah and her children came and bowed down; finally, Joseph and Rachel also came and bowed down.

Christ freely offers his strength and his hope. And his forgiveness is ours to extend to others.

ANGELA ELWELL HUNT

[8]Esau asked Jacob, "What did you mean by these herds I met along the road?"

"Master," Jacob answered, "I sent them so that you would be friendly to me."

[9]"But, brother, I already have plenty," Esau replied. "Keep them for yourself."

[10]"No!" Jacob said. "Please accept these gifts as a sign of your friendship for me. When you welcomed me and I saw your face, it was like seeing the face of God. [11]Please accept these gifts I brought to you. God has been good to me, and I have everything I need." Jacob kept insisting until Esau accepted the gifts.

[12]"Let's get ready to travel," Esau said. "I'll go along with you."

[13]But Jacob answered, "Master, you know traveling is hard on children, and I have to look after the sheep and goats that are nursing their young. If my animals travel too much in one day, they will all die. [14]Why don't you go on ahead and let me travel along slowly with the children, the herds, and the flocks. We can meet again in the country of Edom."

[15]Esau replied, "Let me leave some of my men with you."

"You don't have to do that," Jacob answered. "I am happy, simply knowing that you are friendly to me."

[16]So Esau left for Edom. [17]But Jacob went to Succoth,[n] where he built a house for himself and set up shelters for his animals. That's why the place is called Succoth.

Jacob Arrives at Shechem

[18]After leaving northern Syria,[o] Jacob arrived safely at Shechem in Canaan and set up camp outside the city. [19]The land where he camped was owned by the descendants of Hamor, the father of Shechem. So Jacob paid them one hundred pieces of silver[p] for the property, [20]then he set up his tents and built an altar there to honor the God of Israel.

Dinah Is Raped

34 Dinah, the daughter of Jacob and Leah, went to visit some of the women who lived there. [2]She was seen by Hamor's son Shechem, the leader of the Hivites, and he grabbed her and raped her. [3]But Shechem was attracted to Dinah, so he told her how much he loved her. [4]He even asked his father to get her for his wife.

[5]Meanwhile, Jacob heard what had happened. But his sons were out in the fields with the cattle, so he did not do anything at the time. [6]Hamor arrived at Jacob's home [7]just as Jacob's sons were coming in from work. When they learned that their sister had been raped, they became furiously angry. Nothing is more disgraceful than rape, and it should not be tolerated in Israel.

[8]Hamor said to Jacob and his sons:

My son Shechem really loves Dinah. Please let him marry her. [9]Why don't you start letting your families marry into our families and ours marry into yours? [10]You can share this land with us. Move freely about until you find the property you want; then buy it and settle down here.

[11]Shechem added, "Do this favor for me, and I'll give whatever you want. [12]Ask anything, no matter how expensive. I'll do anything, just let me marry Dinah."

[13]Jacob's sons wanted to get even with Shechem and his father because of what had happened to their sister. [14]So they tricked them by saying:

You're not circumcised![q] It would

[n]**33.17** *Succoth:* In Hebrew "Succoth" means "shelters."
[o]**33.18** *northern Syria:* See the note at 24.10.
[p]**33.19** *pieces of silver:* Or "lambs" or "cattle."
[q]**34.14** *You're not circumcised:* Israelite boys were circumcised when they were eight days old, and no uncircumcised man could be part of the people of Israel.

be a disgrace for us to let you marry Dinah now. ¹⁵But we will let you marry her, if you and the other men in your tribe get circumcised. ¹⁶Then your families can marry into ours, and ours can marry into yours, and we can live together like one nation. ¹⁷But if you don't agree to get circumcised, we'll take Dinah and leave this place.

¹⁸Hamor and Shechem liked what was said. ¹⁹Shechem was the most respected person in his family, and he was so in love with Dinah that he hurried off to get everything done. ²⁰The two men met with the other leaders of their city and told them:

²¹These people really are friendly. Why not let them move freely about until they find the property they want? There's enough land here for them and for us. Then our families can marry into theirs, and theirs can marry into ours.

²²We have to do only one thing before they will agree to stay here and become one nation with us. Our men will have to be circumcised like their men. ²³Just think! We'll get their property, as well as their flocks and herds. All we have to do is to agree, and they will live here with us.

²⁴Every grown man followed this advice and got circumcised.

Dinah's Brothers Take Revenge

²⁵Three days later the men who had been circumcised were still weak from pain. So Simeon and Levi,ʳ two of Dinah's brothers, attacked with their swords and killed every man in town, ²⁶including Hamor and Shechem. Then they took Dinah and left. ²⁷Jacob's other sons came and took everything they wanted. All this was done because of the horrible thing that had happened to their sister. ²⁸They took sheep, goats, donkeys, and everything else that was in the town or the fields. ²⁹After taking everything of value from the houses, they dragged away the wives and children of their victims.

³⁰Jacob said to Simeon and Levi, "Look what you've done! Now I'm in real trouble with the Canaanites and Perizzites who live around here. There aren't many of us, and if they attack, they'll kill everyone in my household."

³¹They answered, "Was it right to let our own sister be treated that way?"

Jacob Returns to Bethel

35 God told Jacob, "Return to Bethel, where I appeared to you when you were running from your brother Esau. Make your home there and build an altar for me."

²Jacob said to his family and to everyone else who was traveling with him:

Get rid of your foreign gods! Then make yourselves acceptable to worship God and put on clean clothes. ³Afterwards, we'll go to Bethel. I will build an altar there for God, who answered my prayers when I was in trouble and who has always been at my side.

⁴So everyone gave Jacob their idols and their earrings,ˢ and he buried them under the oak tree near Shechem.

⁵While Jacob and his family were traveling through Canaan, God terrified the people in the towns so much that no one dared bother them. ⁶Finally, they reached Bethel, also known as Luz. ⁷Jacob built an altar there and called it "God of Bethel," because that was the place where God had appeared to him when he was running from Esau. ⁸While they were there, Rebekah's personal servant Deborahᵗ died. They buried her under an oak tree and called it "Weeping Oak."

God Blesses Jacob at Bethel

⁹⁻¹¹After Jacob came back to the land of Canaan, God appeared to him again. This time he gave Jacob a new name and blessed him by saying:

I am God All-Powerful, and from now on your name will be Israelᵘ instead of Jacob. You will have many children. Your descendants will become nations, and some of the men in your family will even be kings. ¹²I will give you the land that I promised Abraham and Isaac, and it will belong to your family forever.

ʳ**34.25** *Simeon and Levi:* Dinah's full brothers.
ˢ**35.4** *earrings:* These would have had symbols of foreign gods on them. ᵗ**35.8** *Deborah:* See 24.59 and the note there. ᵘ**35.9-11** *Israel:* See the note at 32.28.

[13]After God had gone, [14]Jacob set up a large rock, so that he would remember what had happened there. Then he poured wine and olive oil on the rock to show that it was dedicated to God, [15]and he named the place Bethel.[v]

Benjamin Is Born

[16]Jacob and his family had left Bethel and were still a long way from Ephrath, when the time came for Rachel's baby to be born. [17]She was having a rough time, but the woman who was helping her said, "Don't worry! It's a boy." [18]Rachel was at the point of death, and right before dying, she said, "I'll name him Benoni."[w] But Jacob called him Benjamin.[x]

[19]Rachel was buried beside the road to Ephrath, which is also called Bethlehem. [20]Jacob set up a tombstone over her grave, and it is still there. [21]Jacob, also known as Israel, traveled to the south of Eder Tower, where he set up camp.

[22]During their time there, Jacob's oldest son Reuben slept with Bilhah, who was one of Jacob's other wives.[y] And Jacob found out about it.

Jacob's Twelve Sons

[23-26]Jacob had twelve sons while living in northern Syria.[z] His first-born Reuben was the son of Leah, who later gave birth to Simeon, Levi, Judah, Issachar, and Zebulun. Leah's servant Zilpah had two sons: Gad and Asher.

Jacob and his wife Rachel had Joseph and Benjamin. Rachel's servant woman Bilhah had two more sons: Dan and Naphtali.

Isaac Dies

[27]Jacob went to his father Isaac at Hebron, also called Mamre or Kiriath-Arba, where Isaac's father Abraham had lived as a foreigner. [28-29]Isaac died at the ripe old age of one hundred eighty, then his sons Esau and Jacob buried him.

Esau's Family

36 Esau, also known as Edom, had many descendants. [2]He married three Canaanite women: The first was Adah, the daughter of Elon the Hittite; the second was Oholibamah, the daughter of Anah and the granddaughter of Zibeon the Hivite; [3]the third was Basemath,

who was Ishmael's daughter and Nebaioth's sister.

[4-5]Esau and his three wives had five sons while in Canaan. Adah's son was Eliphaz; Basemath's son was Reuel; Oholibamah's three sons were Jeush, Jalam, and Korah.

[6]Esau took his children and wives, his relatives and servants, his animals and possessions he had gotten while in Canaan, and moved far from Jacob. [7]He did this because the land was too crowded and could not support him and his brother with their flocks and herds. [8]That's why Esau made his home in the hill country of Seir.

[9-14]Esau lived in the hill country of Seir and was the ancestor of the Edomites. Esau had three wives: Adah, Basemath, and Oholibamah. Here is a list of his descendants: Esau and Adah had a son named Eliphaz, whose sons were Teman, Omar, Zepho, Gatam, and Kenaz. Timna was the other wife[a] of Esau's son Eliphaz, and she had a son named Amalek.

Esau and Basemath had a son named Reuel, whose sons were Nahath, Zerah, Shammah, and Mizzah.

Esau and Oholibamah had three sons: Jeush, Jalam, and Korah.

Chiefs and Leaders in Edom

[15]Esau and Adah's oldest son was Eliphaz, and the clans that descended from him were Teman, Omar, Zepho, Kenaz, [16]Korah, Gatam, and Amalek. These and Esau's other descendants lived in the land of Edom.

[17]The clans that descended from Esau and Basemath's son Reuel were Nahath, Zerah, Shammah, and Mizzah.

[18]The clans that descended from Esau and Oholibamah the daughter of Anah were Jeush, Jalam, and Korah. [19]All of these clans descended from Esau, who was known as Edom.

[20]Seir was from the Horite tribe that had lived in Edom before the time of Esau. The clans that had descended from him were

---

[v]**35.15** *Bethel:* See the note at 28.19.　[w]**35.18** *Benoni:* In Hebrew "Benoni" means "Son of my Sorrow."　[x]**35.18** *Benjamin:* In Hebrew "Benjamin" can mean "Son at my Right Side" (the place of power).　[y]**35.22** *other wives:* See the note at 22.24. Bilhah had been Rachel's servant woman (see 29.28-30).　[z]**35.23-26** *northern Syria:* See the note at 24.10.　[a]**36.9-14** *other wife:* See the note at 22.24.

Lotan, Shobal, Zibeon, Anah, [21]Dishon, Ezer, and Dishan.

[22]Lotan's sons were Hori and Heman; his sister was Timna.

[23]Shobal's sons were Alvan, Manahath, Ebal, Shepho, and Onam.

[24]Zibeon's sons were Aiah and Anah— the same Anah who found an oasis[b] in the desert while taking the donkeys of his father out to pasture.

[25]Anah's children were Dishon and Oholibamah.

[26]Dishon's sons were Hemdan, Eshban, Ithran, and Cheran.

[27]Ezer's sons were Bilhan, Zaavan, and Akan.

[28]Dishan's sons were Uz and Aran.

[29]The clans of the Horites were Lotan, Shobal, Zibeon, Anah, [30]Dishon, Ezer, and Dishan, and they lived in the land of Seir.

[31-39]Before there were kings in Israel, the following kings ruled Edom one after another:

> Bela son of Beor from Dinhabah;
> Jobab son of Zerah from Bozrah;
> Husham from the land of Teman;
> Hadad son of Bedad from Avith
>   (Bedad had defeated the
>   Midianites in Moab);
> Samlah from Masrekah;
> Shaul from the city of Rehoboth
>   on the Euphrates River;
> Baalhanan son of Achbor;
> Hadar from the city of Pau (his
>   wife Mehetabel was the
>   daughter of Matred and the
>   granddaughter of Mezahab).

[40]The clans that descended from Esau took their names from their families and the places where they lived. They are Timna, Alvah, Jetheth, [41]Oholibamah, Elah, Pinon, [42]Kenaz, Teman, Mibzar, [43]Magdiel, and Iram. These clans descended from Esau, who was known as Edom, the father of the Edomites. They took their names from the places where they settled.

Joseph and His Brothers

37 Jacob lived in the land of Canaan, where his father Isaac had lived, [2]and this is the story of his family.

When Jacob's son Joseph was seventeen years old, he took care of the sheep with his brothers, the sons of Bilhah and Zilpah.[c] But he was always telling his father all sorts of bad things about his brothers.

[3]Jacob loved Joseph more than he did any of his other sons, because Joseph was born after Jacob was very old. Jacob had given Joseph a fancy coat[d] [4]to show that he was his favorite son, and so Joseph's brothers hated him and would not be friendly to him.

[5]One day, Joseph told his brothers what he had dreamed, and they hated him even more. [6]Joseph said, "Let me tell you about my dream. [7]We were out in the field, tying up bundles of wheat. Suddenly my bundle stood up, and your bundles gathered around and bowed down to it."

[8]His brothers asked, "Do you really think you are going to be king and rule over us?" Now they hated Joseph more than ever because of what he had said about his dream.

[9]Joseph later had another dream, and he told his brothers, "Listen to what else I dreamed. The sun, the moon, and eleven stars bowed down to me."

[10]When he told his father about this dream, his father became angry and said, "What's that supposed to mean? Are your mother and I and your brothers all going to come and bow down in front of you?" [11]Joseph's brothers were jealous of him, but his father kept wondering about the dream.

Joseph Is Sold and Taken to Egypt

[12]One day when Joseph's brothers had taken the sheep to a pasture near Shechem, [13]his father Jacob said to him, "I want you to go to your brothers. They are with the sheep near Shechem."

"Yes, sir," Joseph answered.

[14]His father said, "Go and find out how your brothers and the sheep are doing. Then come back and let me know." So he sent him from Hebron Valley.

Joseph was near Shechem [15]and wandering through the fields, when a man asked, "What are you looking for?"

---

[b]36.24 an oasis: One possible meaning for the difficult Hebrew text.   [c]37.2 Bilhah and Zilpah: See 30.1-13.   [d]37.3 fancy coat: Or "a coat of many colors" or "a coat with long sleeves."

¹⁶Joseph answered, "I'm looking for my brothers who are watching the sheep. Can you tell me where they are?"

¹⁷"They're not here anymore," the man replied. "I overheard them say they were going to Dothan."

Joseph left and found his brothers in Dothan. ¹⁸But before he got there, they saw him coming and made plans to kill him. ¹⁹They said to one another, "Look, here comes the hero of those dreams! ²⁰Let's kill him and throw him into a pit and say that some wild animal ate him. Then we'll see what happens to those dreams."

²¹Reuben heard this and tried to protect Joseph from them. "Let's not kill him," he said. ²²"Don't murder him or even harm him. Just throw him into a dry well out here in the desert." Reuben planned to rescue Joseph later and take him back to his father.

Pain has a purpose:
to sensitize us so God can
use us in great ways.

VALERIE BELL

---

²³When Joseph came to his brothers, they pulled off his fancy coat*ᵈ* ²⁴and threw him into a dry well.

²⁵As Joseph's brothers sat down to eat, they looked up and saw a caravan of Ishmaelites coming from Gilead. Their camels were loaded with all kinds of spices that they were taking to Egypt. ²⁶So Judah said, "What will we gain if we kill our brother and hide his body? ²⁷Let's sell him to the Ishmaelites and not harm him. After all, he is our brother." And the others agreed.

²⁸When the Midianite merchants came by, Joseph's brothers took him out of the well, and for twenty pieces of silver they sold him to the Ishmaelites*ᵉ* who took him to Egypt.

²⁹When Reuben returned to the well and did not find Joseph there, he tore his clothes in sorrow. ³⁰Then he went back to his brothers and said, "The boy is gone! What am I going to do?"

³¹Joseph's brothers killed a goat and dipped Joseph's fancy coat in its blood. ³²After this, they took the coat to their father and said, "We found this! Look at it carefully and see if it belongs to your son."

³³Jacob knew it was Joseph's coat and said, "It's my son's coat! Joseph has been torn to pieces and eaten by some wild animal."

³⁴Jacob mourned for Joseph a long time, and to show his sorrow he tore his clothes and wore sackcloth.*ᶠ* ³⁵All of Jacob's children came to comfort him, but he refused to be comforted. "No," he said, "I will go to my grave, mourning for my son." So Jacob kept on grieving.

³⁶Meanwhile, the Midianites had sold Joseph in Egypt to a man named Potiphar, who was the king's*ᵍ* official in charge of the palace guard.

Judah and Tamar

38 About that time Judah left his brothers in the hill country and went to live near his friend Hirah in the town of Adullam. ²While there he met the daughter of Shua, a Canaanite man. Judah married her, ³and they had three sons. He named the first one Er; ⁴she named the next one Onan. ⁵The third one was born when Judah was in Chezib, and she named him Shelah.

⁶Later, Judah chose Tamar as a wife for Er, his oldest son. ⁷But Er was very evil, and the LORD took his life. ⁸So Judah told Onan, "It's your duty to marry Tamar and have a child for your brother."*ʰ*

⁹Onan knew the child would not be his,*ⁱ*

---

*ᵈ***37.23** *fancy coat:* Or "a coat of many colors" or "a coat with long sleeves." *ᵉ***37.28** *Midianite . . . Ishmaelites:* According to 25.1, 2, 12 both the Midianites and the Ishmaelites were descendants of Abraham, and in Judges 8.22-24 the two names are used of the same people. It is possible that in this passage "Ishmaelite" has the meaning "nomadic traders," while "Midianite" refers to their ethnic origin. *ᶠ***37.34** *sackcloth:* A rough dark-colored cloth made from goat or camel hair and used to make grain sacks. It was worn in times of trouble or sorrow. *ᵍ***37.36** *the king's:* See the note at 12.15. *ʰ***38.8** *It's your duty . . . child . . . brother:* If a man died without having children, his brother was to marry the dead man's wife and have a child, who was to be considered the child of the dead brother (see Deuteronomy 25.5, 6). *ⁱ***38.9** *the child . . . not be his:* When Judah died, Onan would get his dead brother's share of the inheritance, but if his dead brother had a son, the inheritance would go to him instead.

Tamar

Genesis 38; Deuteronomy 25.5-10; Ruth 4.12; 1 Chronicles 2.3,4;
1 Chronicles 27.2,3; Nehemiah 11.4-6

*I*t's tough to be a young widow, and it takes toughness to survive widowhood. Tamar was a survivor. Through her, the whole tribe of Judah earned a place in history. Without her, it might have ended before it began.

Widowhood in Tamar's era was harsh. In order to survive, women needed land and children. Without them there would be no source of income and no one to care for them in old age. So being a young widow without children was especially tragic. The Hebrews had a custom, later described in Deuteronomy 25, that gave protection to young widows. In short, any brother of her dead husband was expected to impregnate her with a son. This had certain financial risks to the brother; it meant dividing property with the new heir. Tamar's brother-in-law didn't mind providing sexual service; he just made sure there would be no child. Because of that selfishness, God saw that he died.

Tamar waited several years. When she realized that Judah, her father-in-law, was not going to permit his remaining son to help her, she took matters into her own hands. She disguised herself as a prostitute and allowed Judah himself to produce a child—being careful to keep mementos of the occasion that would prove paternity. In the end Judah proclaimed, "She's a better person than I am" (Genesis 38.26). Tamar had merely pretended to be a prostitute. Judah had tried to deprive her of home and family.

Such an odd story, full of provincial customs that today's readers find appalling, would be just a minor interlude in Genesis, except for one fact. Tamar keeps coming up in other sections of the Bible—and never with any hint of judgment. Her son, Perez, appears in several genealogies including the line of King David and of Joseph, foster father to Jesus. Tamar is one of the few women (including Mary) mentioned in that list. Tamar even shows up in the blessing of a marriage. In the book of Ruth, the leaders of Bethlehem tell Boaz, "May the children you have by this young woman make your family as famous as the family of Perez, the son of Tamar and Judah" (Ruth 4.12).

What can today's woman learn from Tamar? We can see that God loves and cares for widows—and expects his people to do the same. We can see that widows need to be strong, but that they should not feel ashamed to ask help from their families. Although today's widows should not barter sexual favors, they can follow Tamar's example by using ingenuity to care for themselves—so as not to become an unnecessary burden to others. Once the worst grief is over, widows should move forward in life. (Tamar raised twin boys.) Most important, widows may expect God to take terrible circumstances and use them for his glory. Perhaps some present-day widow will have her name used generations later in prayers of blessing!

and when he had sex with Tamar, he made sure that she would not get pregnant. ¹⁰The LORD wasn't pleased with Onan and took his life too.

¹¹Judah did not want the same thing to happen to his son Shelah, and he told Tamar, "Go home to your father and live there as a widow until my son Shelah is grown." So Tamar went to live with her father.

¹²Some years later Judah's wife died, and he mourned for her. He then went with his friend Hirah to the town of Timnah, where his sheep were being sheared. ¹³Tamar found out that her father-in-law Judah was going to Timnah to shear his sheep. ¹⁴She also realized that Shelah was now a grown man, but she had not been allowed to marry him. So she decided to dress in something other than her widow's clothes and to cover her face with a veil. After this, she sat outside the town of Enaim on the road to Timnah.

¹⁵When Judah came along, he did not recognize her because of the veil. He thought she was a prostitute ¹⁶and asked her to sleep with him. She asked, "What will you give me if I do?"

¹⁷"One of my young goats," he answered.

"What will you give me to keep until you send the goat?" she asked.

¹⁸"What do you want?" he asked in return.

"The ring on that cord around your neck," was her reply. "I also want the special walking stick[j] you have with you." He gave them to her, they slept together, and she became pregnant.

¹⁹After returning home, Tamar took off the veil and dressed in her widow's clothes again.

²⁰Judah had his friend Hirah take a goat to the woman, so he could get back the ring and walking stick, but she wasn't there. ²¹Hirah asked the people of Enaim, "Where is the prostitute who sat along the road outside your town?"

"There's never been one here," they answered.

²²Hirah went back and told Judah, "I couldn't find the woman, and the people of Enaim said no prostitute had ever been there."

²³"If you couldn't find her, we'll just let her keep the things I gave her," Judah answered. "And we'd better forget about the goat, or else we'll look like fools."

²⁴About three months later someone told Judah, "Your daughter-in-law Tamar has behaved like a prostitute, and now she's pregnant!"

"Drag her out of town and burn her to death!" Judah shouted.

²⁵As Tamar was being dragged off, she sent someone to tell her father-in-law, "The man who gave me this ring, this cord, and this walking stick is the one who got me pregnant."

²⁶"Those are mine!" Judah admitted. "She's a better person than I am, because I broke my promise to let her marry my son Shelah." After this, Judah never slept with her again.

²⁷⁻²⁸Tamar later gave birth to twins. But before either of them was born, one of them stuck a hand out of her womb. The woman who was helping tied a red thread around the baby's hand and explained, "This one came out first."

²⁹Right away his hand went back in, and the other child was born first. The woman then said, "What an opening you've made for yourself!" So they named the baby Perez.[k] ³⁰When the brother with the red thread came out, they named him Zerah.[l]

Joseph and Potiphar's Wife

39 The Ishmaelites took Joseph to Egypt and sold him to Potiphar, the king's[m] official in charge of the palace guard. ²⁻³So Joseph lived in the home of Potiphar, his Egyptian owner.

Soon Potiphar realized that the LORD was helping Joseph to be successful in whatever he did. ⁴Potiphar liked Joseph and made him his personal assistant, putting him in charge of his house and all of his property. ⁵Because of Joseph, the LORD began to bless Potiphar's family and fields. ⁶Potiphar left everything up to Joseph, and with Joseph

---

[j]**38.18** ring . . . walking stick: The ring was shaped like a cylinder and could be rolled over soft clay as a way of sealing special documents. The walking stick was probably a symbol of power and the sign of leadership in the tribe, though it may have been a shepherd's rod. [k]**38.29** Perez: In Hebrew "Perez" sounds like "opening." [l]**38.30** Zerah: In Hebrew "Zerah" means "bright," probably referring to the red thread. [m]**39.1** the king's: See the note at 12.15.

there, the only decision he had to make was what he wanted to eat.

Joseph was well-built and handsome, [7]and Potiphar's wife soon noticed him. She asked him to make love to her, [8]but he refused and said, "My master isn't worried about anything in his house, because he has placed me in charge of everything he owns. [9]No one in my master's house is more important than I am. The only thing he hasn't given me is you, and that's because you are his wife. I won't sin against God by doing such a terrible thing as this." [10]She kept begging Joseph day after day, but he refused to do what she wanted or even to go near her.

[11]One day, Joseph went to Potiphar's house to do his work, and none of the other servants were there. [12]Potiphar's wife grabbed hold of his coat and said, "Make love to me!" Joseph ran out of the house, leaving her hanging onto his coat.

[13]When this happened, [14]she called in her servants and said, "Look! This Hebrew has come just to make fools of us. He tried to rape me, but I screamed for help. [15]And when he heard me scream, he ran out of the house, leaving his coat with me."

[16]Potiphar's wife kept Joseph's coat until her husband came home. [17]Then she said, "That Hebrew slave of yours tried to rape me! [18]But when I screamed for help, he left his coat and ran out of the house."

[19]Potiphar became very angry [20]and threw Joseph in the same prison where the king's prisoners were kept.

While Joseph was in prison, [21]the LORD helped him and was good to him. He even made the jailer like Joseph so much that [22]he put him in charge of the other prisoners and of everything that was done in the jail. [23]The jailer did not worry about anything, because the LORD was with Joseph and made him successful in all that he did.

Joseph Tells the Meaning of the Prisoners' Dreams

40 [1-3]While Joseph was in prison, both the king's[m] personal servant[n] and his chief cook made the king angry. So he had them thrown into the same prison with Joseph. [4]They spent a long time in prison, and Potiphar, the official in charge of the palace guard, made Joseph their servant.

---

[m]40.1-3 *the king's*: See the note at 12.15.   [n]40.1-3 *personal servant*: The Hebrew text has "cup bearer," an important and trusted official in the royal court, who personally served wine to the king.

MARRIAGE—How can I lead my unbelieving husband to Christ without offending him? *(Genesis 39; 41.39)*

Keep doing what is right and leave the rest to God.
Being married to an unbelieving husband is hard. The Christian wife feels that everything she does reflects on God. Besides, she and her husband have differing ideas about what is right and wrong—and how important all of that is anyway. And underneath is the constant hope that someday, somehow, her husband will join her in faith.

Joseph had a similar problem. Through no fault of his own, he got dumped into a pagan household and given a lot of responsibility. The problem was that the boss's wife had an eye for his body. Joseph refused and was careful to state his reasons. They had nothing to do with her, but he could not commit such a sin against God (39.9). In the short term, things got rapidly worse. She yelled, "Rape!" and Joseph went to jail. But God was still at work. Much later, the king admitted that Joseph was wise—and so was his God.

Like Joseph, a Christian wife should avoid unnecessary conflict. But when serious moral issues erupt, she must be firm. She should explain that she does not blame her husband, but that she has a responsibility to God. Remember, even after we have done all we can, God is still at work. (See also Song of Songs 2.16—3.4; John 13.1-17; 1 Peter 3.1-6; Revelation 21.9—22.21.)

Words To Remember: *The king told Joseph, "God is the one who has shown you these things. No one else is as wise as you are or knows as much as you do."*—Genesis 41.39

⁵One night each of the two men had a dream, but their dreams had different meanings. ⁶The next morning, when Joseph went to see the men, he could tell they were upset, ⁷and he asked, "Why are you so worried today?"

⁸"We each had a dream last night," they answered, "and there is no one to tell us what they mean."

Joseph replied, "Doesn't God know the meaning of dreams? Now tell me what you dreamed."

⁹The king's personal servant told Joseph, "In my dream I saw a vine ¹⁰with three branches. As soon as it budded, it blossomed, and its grapes became ripe. ¹¹I held the king's cup and squeezed the grapes into it, then I gave the cup to the king."

¹²Joseph said:

This is the meaning of your dream. The three branches stand for three days, ¹³and in three days the king will pardon you. He will make you his personal servant again, and you will serve him his wine, just as you used to do. ¹⁴But when these good things happen, please don't forget to tell the king about me, so I can get out of this place. ¹⁵I was kidnapped from the land of the Hebrews, and here in Egypt I haven't done anything to deserve being thrown in jail.

¹⁶When the chief cook saw that Joseph had given a good meaning to the dream, he told Joseph, "I also had a dream. In it I was carrying three breadbaskets stacked on top of my head. ¹⁷The top basket was full of all kinds of baked things for the king, but birds were eating them."

¹⁸Joseph said:

This is the meaning of your dream. The three baskets are three days, ¹⁹and in three days the king will cut off your head. He will hang your body on a pole, and birds will come and peck at it.

²⁰Three days later, while the king was celebrating his birthday with a dinner for his officials, he sent for his personal servant and the chief cook. ²¹He put the personal servant back in his old job ²²and had the cook put to death.

Everything happened just as Joseph had said it would, ²³but the king's personal servant completely forgot about Joseph.

Joseph Interprets the King's Dreams

41 Two years later the king⁰ of Egypt dreamed he was standing beside the Nile River. ²Suddenly, seven fat, healthy cows came up from the river and started eating grass along the bank. ³Then seven ugly, skinny cows came up out of the river and ⁴ate the fat, healthy cows. When this happened, the king woke up.

Spirituality is bringing the essence of Jesus Christ into the space that you occupy— and you can do that wherever you are.

CAROL KENT

⁵The king went back to sleep and had another dream. This time seven full heads of grain were growing on a single stalk. ⁶Later, seven other heads of grain appeared, but they were thin and scorched by the east wind. ⁷The thin heads of grain swallowed the seven full heads. Again the king woke up, and it had only been a dream.

⁸The next morning the king was upset. So he called in his magicians and wise men and told them what he had dreamed. None of them could tell him what the dreams meant.

⁹The king's personal servant said:

Now I remember what I was supposed to do. ¹⁰When you were angry with me and your chief cook, you threw us both in jail in the house of the captain of the guard. ¹¹One night we both had dreams, and each dream had a different meaning. ¹²A young Hebrew, who was a servant of the captain of the guard, was there with us at the time. When we told him our dreams, he explained what each of them meant, ¹³and everything happened just as he said it would. I got my job back, and the cook was put to death.

⁰**41.1** *the king*: See the note at 12.15.

¹⁴The king sent for Joseph, who was quickly brought out of jail. He shaved, changed his clothes, and went to the king.

¹⁵The king said to him, "I had a dream, yet no one can explain what it means. I am told that you can interpret dreams."

¹⁶"Your Majesty," Joseph answered, "I can't do it myself, but God can give a good meaning to your dreams."

¹⁷The king told Joseph:

I dreamed I was standing on the bank of the Nile River. ¹⁸I saw seven fat, healthy cows come up out of the river, and they began feeding on the grass. ¹⁹Next, seven skinny, bony cows came up out of the river. I have never seen such terrible looking cows anywhere in Egypt. ²⁰The skinny cows ate the fat ones. ²¹But you couldn't tell it, because these skinny cows were just as skinny as they were before. Right away, I woke up.

²²I also dreamed that I saw seven heads of grain growing on one stalk. The heads were full and ripe. ²³Then seven other heads of grain came up. They were thin and scorched by a wind from the desert. ²⁴These heads of grain swallowed the full ones. I told my dreams to the magicians, but none of them could tell me the meaning of the dreams.

²⁵Joseph replied:

Your Majesty, both of your dreams mean the same thing, and in them God has shown what he is going to do. ²⁶The seven good cows stand for seven years, and so do the seven good heads of grain. ²⁷The seven skinny, ugly cows that came up later also stand for seven years, as do the seven bad heads of grain that were scorched by the east wind. The dreams mean there will be seven years when there won't be enough grain.

²⁸It is just as I said—God has shown what he intends to do. ²⁹For seven years Egypt will have more than enough grain, ³⁰but that will be followed by seven years when there won't be enough. The good years of plenty will be forgotten, and everywhere in Egypt people will be starving. ³¹The famine will be so bad that no one will remember that once there had been

plenty. ³²God has given you two dreams to let you know that he has definitely decided to do this and that he will do it soon.

³³Your Majesty, you should find someone who is wise and will know what to do, so that you can put him in charge of all Egypt. ³⁴Then appoint some other officials to collect one-fifth of every crop harvested in Egypt during the seven years when there is plenty. ³⁵Give them the power to collect the grain during those good years and to store it in your cities. ³⁶It can be stored until it is needed during the seven years when there won't be enough grain in Egypt. This will keep the country from being destroyed because of the lack of food.

Joseph Is Made Governor over Egypt

³⁷The king° and his officials liked this plan. ³⁸So the king said to them, "No one could possibly handle this better than Joseph, since the Spirit of God is with him."

³⁹The king told Joseph, "God is the one who has shown you these things. No one else is as wise as you are or knows as much as you do. ⁴⁰I'm putting you in charge of my palace, and everybody will have to obey you. No one will be over you except me. ⁴¹You are now governor of all Egypt!"

⁴²Then the king took off his royal ring and put it on Joseph's finger. He gave him fine clothes to wear and placed a gold chain around his neck. ⁴³He also let him ride in the chariot next to his own, and people shouted, "Make way for Joseph!" So Joseph was governor of Egypt.

⁴⁴The king told Joseph, "Although I'm king, no one in Egypt is to do anything without your permission." ⁴⁵He gave Joseph the Egyptian name Zaphenath Paneah. And he let him marry Asenath, the daughter of Potiphera, a priest in the city of Heliopolis.ᵖ Joseph traveled all over Egypt.

⁴⁶Joseph was thirty when the king made him governor, and he went everywhere for the king. ⁴⁷For seven years there were big harvests of grain. ⁴⁸Joseph collected and stored up the extra grain in the cities of

---

ᵒ41.37 *The king*: See the note at 12.15.
ᵖ41.45 *Heliopolis*: The Hebrew text has "On," which is better known by its Greek name "Heliopolis."

Egypt near the fields where it was harvested. [49]In fact, there was so much grain that they stopped keeping record, because it was like counting the grains of sand along the beach.

[50]Joseph and his wife had two sons before the famine began. [51]Their first son was named Manasseh, which means, "God has let me forget all my troubles and my family back home." [52]His second son was named Ephraim, which means "God has made me a success[q] in the land where I suffered."[r]

[53]Egypt's seven years of plenty came to an end, [54]and the seven years of famine began, just as Joseph had said. There was not enough food in other countries, but all over Egypt there was plenty. [55]When the famine finally struck Egypt, the people asked the king for food, but he said, "Go to Joseph and do what he tells you to do."

[56]The famine became bad everywhere in Egypt, so Joseph opened the storehouses and sold the grain to the Egyptians. [57]People from all over the world came to Egypt, because the famine was severe in their countries.

Joseph's Brothers Go to Egypt To Buy Grain

42 When Jacob found out there was grain in Egypt, he said to his sons, "Why are you just sitting here, staring at one another? [2]I have heard there is grain in Egypt. Now go down and buy some, so we won't starve to death."

[3]Ten of Joseph's brothers went to Egypt to buy grain. [4]But Jacob did not send Joseph's younger brother Benjamin with them; he was afraid that something might happen to him. [5]So Jacob's sons joined others from Canaan who were going to Egypt because of the terrible famine.

[6]Since Joseph was governor of Egypt and in charge of selling grain, his brothers came to him and bowed with their faces to the ground. [7-8]They did not recognize Joseph, but right away he knew who they were, though he pretended not to know. Instead, he spoke harshly and asked, "Where do you come from?"

"From the land of Canaan," they answered. "We've come here to buy grain."

[9]Joseph remembered what he had dreamed about them and said, "You're spies! You've come here to find out where our country is weak."

[10]"No sir," they replied. "We're your servants, and we have only come to buy grain. [11]We're honest men, and we come from the same family—we're not spies."

[12]"That isn't so!" Joseph insisted. "You've come here to find out where our country is weak."

[13]But they explained, "Sir, we come from a family of twelve brothers. The youngest is still with our father in Canaan, and one of our brothers is dead."

[14]Joseph replied:

It's just like I said. You're spies, [15]and I'm going to find out who you really are. I swear by the life of the king that you won't leave this place until your youngest brother comes here. [16]Choose one of you to go after your brother, while the rest of you stay here in jail. That will show whether you are telling the truth. But if you are lying, I swear by the life of the king that you are spies!

[17]Joseph kept them all under guard for three days, [18]before saying to them:

Since I respect God, I'll give you a chance to save your lives. [19]If you are honest men, one of you must stay here in jail, and the rest of you can take the grain back to your starving families. [20]But you must bring your youngest brother to me. Then I'll know that you are telling the truth, and you won't be put to death.

Joseph's brothers agreed [21]and said to one another, "We're being punished because of Joseph. We saw the trouble he was in, but we refused to help him when he begged us. That's why these terrible things are happening."

[22]Reuben spoke up, "Didn't I tell you not to harm the boy? But you wouldn't listen, and now we have to pay the price for killing him."

[23]They did not know that Joseph could understand them, since he was speaking through an interpreter. [24]Joseph turned away from them and cried, but soon he turned back and spoke to them again. Then

q41.52 *God has made me a success*: Or "God has given me children." r41.52 *Ephraim . . . suffered*: In Hebrew "Ephraim" actually means either "fertile land" or "pastureland."

he had Simeon tied up and taken away while they watched.

Joseph's Brothers Return to Canaan

²⁵Joseph gave orders for his brothers' grain sacks to be filled with grain and for their money^s to be put in their sacks. He also gave orders for them to be given food for their journey home. After this was done, ²⁶they each loaded the grain on their donkeys and left.

²⁷When they stopped for the night, one of them opened his sack to get some grain for his donkey, and right away he saw his moneybag. ²⁸"Here's my money!" he told his brothers. "Right here in my sack."

They were trembling with fear as they stared at one another and asked themselves, "What has God done to us?"

²⁹When they returned to the land of Canaan, they told their father Jacob everything that had happened to them:

³⁰The governor of Egypt was rude and treated us like spies. ³¹But we told him, "We're honest men, not spies. ³²We come from a family of twelve brothers. The youngest is still with our father in Canaan, and the other is dead."

³³Then the governor of Egypt told us, "I'll find out if you really are honest. Leave one of your brothers here with me, while you take the grain to your starving families. ³⁴But bring your youngest brother to me, so I can be certain that you are honest men and not spies. After that, I'll let your other brother go free, and you can stay here and trade."

³⁵When the brothers started emptying their sacks of grain, they found their moneybags in them. They were frightened, and so was their father Jacob, ³⁶who said, "You have already taken my sons Joseph and Simeon from me. And now you want to take away Benjamin! Everything is against me."

³⁷Reuben spoke up, "Father, if I don't bring Benjamin back, you can kill both of my sons. Trust me with him, and I will bring him back."

³⁸But Jacob said, "I won't let my son Benjamin go down to Egypt with the rest of you. His brother is already dead, and he is the only son I have left.^t I am an old man,

and if anything happens to him on the way, I'll die from sorrow, and all of you will be to blame."

Joseph's Brothers Return to Egypt with Benjamin

43 The famine in Canaan got worse, ²until finally, Jacob's family had eaten all the grain they had bought in Egypt. So Jacob said to his sons, "Go back and buy some more grain."

³⁻⁵Judah replied, "The governor strictly warned us that we would not be allowed to see him unless we brought our youngest brother with us. If you let us take Benjamin along, we will go and buy grain. But we won't go without him!"

⁶Jacob asked, "Why did you cause me so much trouble by telling the governor you had another brother?"

⁷They answered, "He asked a lot of questions about us and our family. He wanted to know if you were still alive and if we had any more brothers. All we could do was answer his questions. How could we know he would tell us to bring along our brother?"

⁸Then Judah said to his father, "Let Benjamin go with me, and we will leave right away, so that none of us will starve to death. ⁹I promise to bring him back safely, and if I don't, you can blame me as long as I live. ¹⁰If we had not wasted all this time, we could already have been there and back twice."

¹¹Their father said:

If Benjamin must go with you, take the governor a gift of some of the best things from our own country, such as perfume, honey, spices, pistachio nuts, and almonds.^u ¹²Also take along twice the amount of money for the grain, because there must have been some mistake when the money was put back in your sacks. ¹³Take Benjamin with you and leave right away.

¹⁴When you go in to see the governor, I pray that God All-Powerful will be good to you and that the governor

---

^s42.25 *money*: Probably in the form of small pieces of silver and/or other precious or semi-precious metals; there were no coins or paper money at this time. ^t42.38 *only son I have left*: Jacob had only two sons by Rachel, his favorite wife. ^u43.11 *honey, spices, pistachio nuts, and almonds*: Some of these foods were still available in Canaan, but the main food was bread, and there was no grain to make bread.

will let your other brother and Benjamin come back home with you. If I must lose my children, I suppose I must.

¹⁵The brothers took the gifts, twice the amount of money, and Benjamin. Then they hurried off to Egypt. When they stood in front of Joseph, ¹⁶he saw Benjamin and told the servant in charge of his house, "Take these men to my house. Slaughter an animal and cook it, so they can eat with me at noon."

¹⁷The servant did as he was told and took the brothers to Joseph's house. ¹⁸But on the way they got worried and started thinking, "We are being taken there because of the money that was put back in our sacks last time. He will arrest us, make us his slaves, and take our donkeys."

¹⁹So when they arrived at Joseph's house, they said to the servant in charge, ²⁰"Sir, we came to Egypt once before to buy grain. ²¹But when we stopped for the night, we each found in our grain sacks the exact amount we had paid. We have brought that money back, ²²together with enough money to buy more grain. We don't know who put the money in our sacks."

> My car accident happened in a split second—but I'm still feeling the effects years later. However, this "thorn in the flesh" has prompted not only more compassion toward others who suffer, but my own spiritual growth.
>
> RAMONA CRAMER TUCKER

²³"It's all right," the servant replied. "Don't worry. The God you and your father worship must have put the money there, because I received your payment in full." Then he brought Simeon out to them.

²⁴The servant took them into Joseph's house and gave them water to wash their feet. He also tended their donkeys. ²⁵The brothers got their gifts ready to give to Joseph at noon, since they had heard they were going to eat there.

²⁶When Joseph came home, they gave him the gifts they had brought, and they bowed down to him. ²⁷After Joseph had asked how they were, he said, "What about your elderly father? Is he still alive?"

²⁸They answered, "Your servant our father is still alive and well." And again they bowed down to Joseph.

²⁹When Joseph looked around and saw his brother Benjamin, he said, "This must be your youngest brother, the one you told me about. God bless you, my son."

³⁰Right away he rushed off to his room and cried because of his love for Benjamin. ³¹After washing his face and returning, he was able to control himself and said, "Serve the meal!"

³²Joseph was served at a table by himself, and his brothers were served at another. The Egyptians sat at yet another table, because Egyptians felt it was disgusting to eat with Hebrews. ³³To the surprise of Joseph's brothers, they were seated in front of him according to their ages, from the oldest to the youngest. ³⁴They were served food from Joseph's table, and Benjamin was given five times as much as each of the others. So Joseph's brothers drank with him and had a good time.

The Missing Cup

44 ¹⁻²Later, Joseph told the servant in charge of his house, "Fill the men's grain sacks with as much as they can hold and put their money in the sacks. Also put my silver cup in the sack of the youngest brother." The servant did as he was told.

³Early the next morning, the men were sent on their way with their donkeys. ⁴But they had not gone far from the city when Joseph told the servant, "Go after those men! When you catch them, say, 'My master has been good to you. So why have you stolen his silver cup? ⁵Not only does he drink from his cup, but he also uses it to learn about the future. You have done a terrible thing.'"

⁶When the servant caught up with them, he said exactly what Joseph had told him to say. ⁷But they replied, "Sir, why do you say

such things? We would never do anything like that! [8]We even returned the money we found in our grain sacks when we got back to Canaan. So why would we want to steal any silver or gold from your master's house? [9]If you find that one of us has the cup, then kill him, and the rest of us will become your slaves."

[10]"Good!" the man replied, "I'll do what you have said. But only the one who has the cup will become my slave. The rest of you can go free."

[11]Each of the brothers quickly put his sack on the ground and opened it. [12]Joseph's servant started searching the sacks, beginning with the one that belonged to the oldest brother. When he came to Benjamin's sack, he found the cup. [13]This upset the brothers so much that they began tearing their clothes in sorrow. Then they loaded their donkeys and returned to the city.

[14]When Judah and his brothers got there, Joseph was still at home. So they bowed down to Joseph, [15]who asked them, "What have you done? Didn't you know I could find out?"

[16]"Sir, what can we say?" Judah replied. "How can we prove we are innocent? God has shown that we are guilty. And now all of us are your slaves, especially the one who had the cup."

[17]Joseph told them, "I would never punish all of you. Only the one who was caught with the cup will become my slave. The rest of you are free to go home to your father."

Judah Pleads for Benjamin

[18]Judah went over to Joseph and said:

Sir, you have as much power as the king[v] himself, and I am only your slave. Please don't get angry if I speak. [19]You asked us if our father was still alive and if we had any more brothers. [20]So we told you, "Our father is a very old man. In fact, he was already old when Benjamin was born. Benjamin's brother is dead. Now Benjamin is the only one of the two brothers who is still alive, and our father loves him very much."

[21]You ordered us to bring him here, so you could see him for yourself. [22]We told you that our father would die if Benjamin left him. [23]But you warned us that we could never see you again, unless our youngest brother came with us. [24]So we returned to our father and reported what you had said.

[25]Later our father told us to come back here and buy more grain. [26]But we answered, "We can't go back to Egypt without our youngest brother. We will never be let in to see the governor, unless he is with us."

[27]Sir, our father then reminded us that his favorite wife had given birth to two sons. [28]One of them was already missing and had not been seen for a long time. My father thinks the boy was torn to pieces by some wild animal, [29]and he said, "I am an old man. If you take Benjamin from me, and something happens to him, I will die of a broken heart."

[30]That's why Benjamin must be with us when I go back to my father. He loves him so much [31]that he will die if Benjamin doesn't come back with me. [32]I promised my father that I would bring him safely home. If I don't, I told my father he could blame me the rest of my life.

[33]Sir, I am your slave. Please let me stay here in place of Benjamin and let him return home with his brothers. [34]How can I face my father if Benjamin isn't with me? I couldn't bear to see my father in such sorrow.

Joseph Tells His Brothers Who He Is

45 Since Joseph could no longer control his feelings in front of his servants, he sent them out of the room. When he was alone with his brothers, he told them, "I am Joseph." [2]Then he cried so loudly that the Egyptians heard him and told about it in the king's[v] palace.

[3]Joseph asked his brothers if his father was still alive, but they were too frightened to answer. [4]Joseph told them to come closer to him, and when they did, he said:

Yes, I am your brother Joseph, the one you sold into Egypt. [5]Don't worry or blame yourselves for what you did. God is the one who sent me ahead of you to save lives.

---

[v]44.18 *the king*: See the note at 12.15. [v]45.2 *the king's*: See the note at 12.15.

[6]There has already been a famine for two years, and for five more years no one will plow fields or harvest grain. [7]But God sent me on ahead of you to keep your families alive and to save you in this wonderful way. [8]After all, you weren't really the ones who sent me here—it was God. He made me the highest official in the king's court and placed me over all Egypt.

[9]Now hurry back and tell my father that his son Joseph says, "God has made me ruler of Egypt. Come here as quickly as you can. [10]You will live near me in the region of Goshen with your children and grandchildren, as well as with your sheep, goats, cattle, and everything else you own. [11]I will take care of you there during the next five years of famine. But if you don't come, you and your family and your animals will starve to death."

[12]All of you, including my brother Benjamin, can tell by what I have said that I really am Joseph. [13]Tell my father about my great power here in Egypt and about everything you have seen. Hurry and bring him here.

[14]Joseph and Benjamin hugged each other and started crying. [15]Joseph was still crying as he kissed each of his other brothers. After this, they started talking with Joseph.

[16]When it was told in the palace that Joseph's brothers had come, the king and his officials were happy. [17]So the king said to Joseph:

Tell your brothers to load their donkeys and return to Canaan. [18]Have them bring their father and their families here. I will give them the best land in Egypt, and they can eat and enjoy everything that grows on it. [19]Also tell your brothers to take some wagons from Egypt for their wives and children to ride in. And be sure to have them bring their father. [20]They can leave their possessions behind, because they will be given the best of everything in Egypt.

[21]Jacob's sons agreed to do what the king had said. And Joseph gave them wagons and food for their trip home, just as the king had ordered. [22]Joseph gave some new clothes to each of his brothers, but to Benjamin he gave five new outfits and three hundred pieces of silver. [23]To his father he sent ten donkeys loaded with the best things in Egypt, and ten other donkeys loaded with grain and bread and other food for the return trip. [24]Then he sent his brothers off and told them, "Don't argue on the way home!"

[25]Joseph's brothers left Egypt, and when they arrived in Canaan, [26]they told their father that Joseph was still alive and was the ruler of Egypt. But their father was so surprised that he could not believe them. [27]Then they told him everything Joseph had said. When he saw the wagons Joseph had sent, he felt much better [28]and said, "Now I can believe you! My son Joseph must really be alive, and I will get to see him before I die."

Jacob and His Family Go to Egypt

46 Jacob packed up everything he owned and left for Egypt. On the way he stopped near the town of Beersheba and offered sacrifices to the God his father Isaac had worshiped. [2]That night, God spoke to him and said, "Jacob! Jacob!"

"Here I am," Jacob answered.

[3]God said, "I am God, the same God your father worshiped. Don't be afraid to go to Egypt. I will give you so many descendants that one day they will become a nation. [4]I will go with you to Egypt, and later I will bring your descendants back here. Your son Joseph will be at your side when you die."

[5-7]Jacob and his family set out from Beersheba and headed for Egypt. His sons put him in the wagon that the king[v] had sent for him, and they put their small children and their wives in the other wagons. Jacob's whole family went to Egypt, including his sons, his grandsons, his daughters, and his granddaughters. They took along their animals and everything else they owned.

[8-15]When Jacob went to Egypt, his children who were born in northern Syria[w] also went along with their families.

Jacob and his wife Leah had a total of thirty-three children, grandchildren, and great-grandchildren, but two of their grandchildren had died in Canaan.

Their oldest son Reuben took his

---

v[46.5-7] *the king:* See the note at 12.15.
w[46.8-15] *northern Syria:* See the note at 24.10.

sons Hanoch, Pallu, Hezron, and Carmi.

Their son Simeon took his sons Jemuel, Jamin, Ohad, Jachin, Zohar, and Shaul, whose mother was a Canaanite.

Their son Levi took his sons Gershon, Kohath, and Merari.

Their son Judah took his sons Shelah, Perez, and Zerah. Judah's sons Er and Onan had died in Canaan. Judah's son Perez took his sons Hezron and Hamul.

Their son Issachar took his sons Tola, Puvah, Jashub,[x] and Shimron.

Their son Zebulun took his sons Sered, Elon, and Jahleel.

Their daughter Dinah also went.

[16-18]Jacob and Zilpah, the servant woman Laban had given his daughter Leah, had a total of sixteen children, grandchildren, and great-grandchildren.

Their son Gad took his sons Ziphion, Haggi, Shuni, Ezbon, Eri, Arodi, and Areli.

Their son Asher took his sons Imnah, Ishvah, Ishvi, and Beriah, who took his sons, Heber and Malchiel.

Serah, the daughter of Asher, also went.

[19-22]Jacob and Rachel had fourteen children and grandchildren.

Their son Joseph was already in Egypt, where he had married Asenath, daughter of Potiphera, the priest of Heliopolis.[y] Joseph and Asenath had two sons, Manasseh and Ephraim.

Jacob and Rachel's son Benjamin took his sons Bela, Becher, Ashbel, Gera, Naaman, Ehi, Rosh, Muppim, Huppim, and Ard.

[23-25]Jacob and Bilhah, the servant woman Laban had given his daughter Rachel, had seven children and grandchildren.

Their son Dan took his son Hushim.

Their son Naphtali took his sons Jahzeel, Guni, Jezer, and Shillem.

[26]Sixty-six members of Jacob's family went to Egypt with him, not counting his daughters-in-law. [27]Jacob's two grandsons who were born there made it a total of seventy members of Jacob's family in Egypt.

[28]Jacob had sent his son Judah ahead of him to ask Joseph to meet them in Goshen.

[29]So Joseph got in his chariot and went to meet his father. When they met, Joseph hugged his father around the neck and cried for a long time. [30]Jacob said to Joseph, "Now that I have seen you and know you are still alive, I am ready to die."

[31]Then Joseph said to his brothers and to everyone who had come with them:

I must go and tell the king[z] that you have arrived from Canaan. [32]I will tell him that you are shepherds and that you have brought your sheep, goats, cattle, and everything else you own. [33]The king will call you in and ask what you do for a living. [34]When he does, be sure to say, "We are shepherds. Our families have always raised sheep." If you tell him this, he will let you settle in the region of Goshen.

Joseph wanted them to say this to the king, because the Egyptians did not like to be around anyone who raised sheep.

47

[1-2]Joseph took five of his brothers to the king and told him, "My father and my brothers have come from Canaan. They have brought their sheep, goats, cattle, and everything else they own to the region of Goshen."

Then he introduced his brothers to the king, [3]who asked them, "What do you do for a living?"

"Sir, we are shepherds," was their answer. "Our families have always raised sheep. [4]But in our country all the pastures are dried up, and our sheep have no grass to eat. So we, your servants, have come here. Please let us live in the region of Goshen."

[5]The king said to Joseph, "It's good that your father and brothers have arrived. [6]I will let them live anywhere they choose in the land of Egypt, but I suggest that they settle in Goshen, the best part of our land. I would also like for your finest shepherds to watch after my own sheep and goats."

[7]Then Joseph brought his father Jacob and introduced him to the king. Jacob gave the king his blessing, [8]and the king asked him, "How old are you?"

[9]Jacob answered, "I have lived only a hundred thirty years, and I have had to

---

x46.8-15 *Jashub*: The Samaritan Hebrew Text and one ancient translation; the Standard Hebrew Text "Iob."
y46.19-22 *Heliopolis*: See the note at 41.45.
z46.31 *the king*: See the note at 12.15.

move from place to place. My parents and my grandparents also had to move from place to place. But they lived much longer, and their life was not as hard as mine." [10]Then Jacob gave the king his blessing once again and left. [11]Joseph obeyed the king's orders and gave his father and brothers some of the best land in Egypt near the city of Rameses. [12]Joseph also provided food for their families.

A Famine in Egypt

[13]The famine was bad everywhere in Egypt and Canaan, and the people were suffering terribly. [14]So Joseph sold them the grain that had been stored up, and he put the money[a] in the king's treasury. [15]But when everyone had run out of money, the Egyptians came to Joseph and demanded, "Give us more grain! If you don't, we'll soon be dead, because our money's all gone."

[16]"If you don't have any money," Joseph answered, "give me your animals, and I'll let you have some grain." [17]From then on, they brought him their horses and donkeys and their sheep and goats in exchange for grain.

Within a year Joseph had collected every animal in Egypt. [18]Then the people came to him and said:

Sir, there's no way we can hide the truth from you. We are broke, and we don't have any more animals. We have nothing left except ourselves and our land. [19]Don't let us starve and our land be ruined. If you'll give us grain to eat and seed to plant, we'll sell ourselves and our land to the king.[b] We'll become his slaves.

[20]The famine became so severe that Joseph finally bought every piece of land in Egypt for the king [21]and made everyone the king's slaves,[c] [22]except the priests. The king gave the priests a regular food allowance, so they did not have to sell their land. [23]Then Joseph said to the people, "You and your land now belong to the king. I'm giving you seed to plant, [24]but one-fifth of your crops must go to the king. You can keep the rest as seed or as food for your families."

[25]"Sir, you have saved our lives!" they answered. "We are glad to be slaves of the king." [26]Then Joseph made a law that one-fifth of the harvest would always belong to the king. Only the priests did not lose their land.

Jacob Becomes an Old Man

[27]The people of Israel made their home in the land of Goshen, where they became prosperous and had large families. [28]Jacob himself lived there for seventeen years, before dying at the age of one hundred forty-seven. [29]When Jacob knew he did not have long to live, he called in Joseph and said, "If you really love me, you must make a solemn promise not to bury me in Egypt. [30]Instead, bury me in the place where my ancestors are buried."

"I will do what you have asked," Joseph answered.

[31]"Will you give me your word?" Jacob asked.

"Yes, I will," Joseph promised. After this, Jacob bowed down and prayed at the head of his bed.

Jacob Blesses Joseph's Two Sons

48 Joseph was told that his father Jacob had become very sick. So Joseph went to see him and took along his two sons, Manasseh and Ephraim. [2]When Joseph arrived, someone told Jacob, "Your son Joseph has come to see you." Jacob sat up in bed, but it took almost all his strength.

[3]Jacob told Joseph:

God All-Powerful appeared to me at Luz in the land of Canaan, where he gave me his blessing [4]and promised, "I will give you a large family with many descendants that will grow into a nation. And I am giving you this land that will belong to you and your family forever."

[5]Then Jacob went on to say:

Joseph, your two sons Ephraim and Manasseh were born in Egypt, but I accept them as my own, just as Reuben and Simeon are mine. [6]Any children you have later will be considered yours, but their inheritance will come from Ephraim and Manasseh. [7]Unfortunately, your mother Rachel died in Canaan after we had left northern Syria[d] and before we reached

---

[a]**47.14** *money*: See the note at 42.25. [b]**47.19** *the king*: See the note at 12.15. [c]**47.21** *made . . . slaves*: One ancient translation and the Samaritan Hebrew Text; the Standard Hebrew Text "made everyone move to the cities." [d]**48.7** *northern Syria*: See the note at 24.10.

Bethlehem.ᶜ And I had to bury her along the way.

⁸⁻¹⁰Jacob was very old and almost blind. He did not recognize the two boys, and so he asked Joseph, "Who are these boys?"

Joseph answered, "They are my sons. God has given them to me here in Egypt."

"Bring them to me," Jacob said. "I want to give them my blessing." Joseph brought the boys to him, and he hugged and kissed them.

> *You may be the only access many kids have to spiritual life. Be ready to help them see that God is active in their lives and that they matter to him.*
>
> VALERIE BELL

¹¹Jacob turned to Joseph and told him, "For many years I thought you were dead and that I would never see you again. But now God has even let me live to see your children." ¹²Then Joseph made his sons move away from Jacob's knees,ᶠ and Joseph bowed down in front of him with his face to the ground.

¹³After Joseph got up, he brought his two sons over to Jacob again. He led his younger son Ephraim to the left side of Jacob and his older son Manasseh to the right. ¹⁴But before Jacob gave them his blessing, he crossed his arms, putting his right hand on the head of Ephraim and his left hand on the head of Manasseh. ¹⁵Then he gave Joseph his blessing and said:

My grandfather Abraham and my father Isaac worshiped the LORD God. He has been with me all my life, ¹⁶and his angel has kept me safe. Now I pray that he will bless these boys and that my name and the names of Abraham and Isaac will live on because of them. I ask God to give them many children and many descendants as well.

¹⁷Joseph did not like it when he saw his father place his right hand on the head of the younger son. So he tried to move his father's right hand from Ephraim's head and place it on Manasseh. ¹⁸Joseph said, "Father, you have made a mistake. This is the older boy. Put your right hand on him."

¹⁹But his father said, "Son, I know what I am doing. It's true that Manasseh's family will someday become a great nation. But Ephraim will be even greater than Manasseh, because his descendants will become many great nations."

²⁰Jacob told him that in the future the people of Israel would ask God's blessings on one another by saying, "I pray for God to bless you as much as he blessed Ephraim and Manasseh." Jacob put Ephraim's name first to show that he would be greater than Manasseh. ²¹After that, Jacob said, "Joseph, you can see that I won't live much longer. But God will be with you and will lead you back to the land he promised our family long ago. ²²Meanwhile, I'm giving you the hillsideᵍ I captured from the Amorites."

Jacob Blesses His Sons

49 *¹Jacob called his sons together and said:

My sons, I am Jacob,
    your father Israel.
²Come, gather around,
    as I tell your future.

³Reuben, you are my oldest,
    born at the peak of my powers;
        you were an honored leader.
⁴Uncontrollable as a flood,
    you slept with my wife
        and disgraced my bed.
And so you no longer deserve
    the place of honor.

⁵Simeon and Levi, you are brothers,
    each a gruesome sword.
⁶I never want to take part
    in your plans or deeds.
You slaughtered people
    in your anger,

ᶜ**48.7** *Bethlehem:* The Hebrew text has "Ephrath, that is, Bethlehem." ᶠ**48.12** *move . . . Jacob's knees:* The two boys were placed either on or between Jacob's knees, as a sign that he had accepted them as his sons. ᵍ**48.22** *the hillside:* Or "a larger share than your brothers, the land."

and you crippled cattle
for no reason.
[7] Now I place a curse on you because of
your fierce anger.
Your descendants
will be scattered
among the tribes of Israel.

[8] Judah, you will be praised
by your brothers;
they will bow down to you,
as you defeat your enemies.
[9] My son, you are a lion
ready to eat your victim!
You are terribly fierce;
no one will bother you.
[10] You will have power and rule
until nations obey you[h]
and come bringing gifts.
[11] You will tie your donkey
to a choice grapevine
and wash your clothes
in wine from those grapes.
[12] Your eyes are darker than wine,
your teeth whiter than milk.

[13] Zebulun, you will settle
along the seashore
and provide safe harbors
as far north as Sidon.

[14] Issachar, you are a strong donkey
resting in the meadows.[i]
[15] You found them so pleasant
that you worked too hard
and became a slave.

[16] Dan,[j] you are the tribe
that will bring justice
to Israel.
[17] You are a snake that bites
the heel of a horse,
making its rider fall.

[18] Our LORD, I am waiting
for you to save us.

[19] Gad,[k] you will be attacked,
then attack your attackers.

[20] Asher, you will eat food
fancy enough for a king.

[21] Naphtali, you are a wild deer
with lovely fawns.[l]

[22] Joseph, you are a fruitful vine
growing near a stream
and climbing a wall.[m]
[23] Enemies attacked with arrows,
refusing to show mercy.
[24] But you stood your ground,
swiftly shooting back
with the help of Jacob's God,
the All-Powerful One—
his name is the Shepherd,
Israel's mighty rock.[n]
[25] Your help came from the God
your father worshiped,
from God All-Powerful.
God will bless you with rain
and streams from the earth;
he will bless you
with many descendants.
[26] My son, the blessings I give
are better than the promise
of ancient mountains
or eternal hills.[o]
Joseph, I pray these blessings
will come to you,
because you are the leader
of your brothers.

[27] Benjamin, you are a fierce wolf,
destroying your enemies
morning and evening.

[28] These are the twelve tribes of Israel,
and this is how Jacob gave each of them
their proper blessings.

Jacob's Death

[29-31] Jacob told his sons:
Soon I will die, and I want you to
bury me in Machpelah Cave. Abraham
bought this cave as a burial place from
Ephron the Hittite, and it is near the
town of Mamre in Canaan. Abraham
and Sarah are buried there, and so are

---

[h]**49.10** *until . . . you:* One possible meaning for the
difficult Hebrew text.   [i]**49.14** *resting . . . meadows:* One
possible meaning for the difficult Hebrew text.
[j]**49.16** *Dan:* In Hebrew "Dan" means "justice" or
"judgment."   [k]**49.19** *Gad:* In Hebrew "Gad" sounds
like "attack."   [l]**49.21** *with lovely fawns:* Or "speaking
lovely words."   [m]**49.22** *wall:* One possible meaning for
the difficult Hebrew text.   [n]**49.24** *mighty rock:* The
Hebrew text has "rock," which is sometimes used in
poetry to compare the LORD to a mountain where his
people can run for protection from their enemies.
[o]**49.26** *eternal hills:* One possible meaning for the
difficult Hebrew text.

Isaac and Rebekah. I buried Leah there
too. [32]Both the cave and the land that
goes with it were bought from the
Hittites.
[33]When Jacob had finished giving these
instructions to his sons, he lay down on his
50 bed and died. [1]Joseph started
crying, then leaned over to hug
and kiss his father.
[2]Joseph gave orders for Jacob's body to
be embalmed, [3]and it took the usual forty
days.

The Egyptians mourned seventy days for
Jacob. [4]When the time of mourning was
over, Joseph said to the Egyptian leaders, "If
you consider me your friend, please speak
to the king[p] for me. [5]Just before my father
died, he made me promise to bury him in
his burial cave in Canaan. If the king will
give me permission to go, I will come back
here."
[6]The king answered, "Go to Canaan and
keep your promise to your father."
[7-9]When Joseph left Goshen with his
brothers, his relatives, and his father's relatives
to bury Jacob, many of the king's highest
officials and even his military chariots
and cavalry went along. The Israelites left
behind only their children, their cattle, and
their sheep and goats.
[10]After crossing the Jordan River and
reaching Atad's threshing place, Joseph had
everyone mourn and weep seven days for
his father. [11]The Canaanites saw this and
said, "The Egyptians are in great sorrow."
Then they named the place "Egypt in
Sorrow."[q]
[12]So Jacob's sons did just as their father
had instructed. [13]They took him to Canaan
and buried him in Machpelah Cave, the
burial place Abraham had bought from
Ephron the Hittite.
[14]After the funeral, Joseph, his brothers,
and everyone else returned to Egypt.

Joseph's Promise to His Brothers

[15]After Jacob died, Joseph's brothers said
to each other, "What if Joseph still hates us
and wants to get even with us for all the
cruel things we did to him?"

---

[p]50.4 *the king*: See the note at 12.15.
[q]50.11 *Egypt in Sorrow*: Or "Abel-Mizraim."

WORK—Sometimes my male colleagues don't take me seriously. How can a Christian woman be assertive at work without being offensive?

(Genesis 50.15-21)

Trust God to bring good even from acts that are intended to harm.
On many jobs, it's still a man's world. Whether it's a condescending pat on the shoulder, a quick cutoff of your best idea, or an averted eye when it's time for important projects and promotions, gender discrimination happens. Often it's just habit and not intended to hurt anyone. But sometimes intent to harm is as real as if the offender took out a knife.

When you feel discriminated against, take a look at Joseph. His brothers hated him—and even shipped him off to another country. But in the end the brothers were forced to come to Joseph for help. They were scared—with good reason. It was payback time, and Joseph had all the power. Yet instead of retribution, Joseph gave his brothers comfort and protection.

During times of discrimination, a working woman can confront mild slights with mild admonition: "I know you didn't intend harm, but . . ." For major offenses, she may need to say, "If that happens again I must speak to . . ." Or when she's overlooked, "I know I could do good work on that project. Here's a sample I put together on my own time." But when all diplomacy fails, and real harm comes from real harmful intent, a working woman can turn to God. God is not limited by someone's intent. God can bring good anyway. (See also Judges 4.4-15; Isaiah 11.1-9; Ephesians 5.6-21.)

Words To Remember: ***"You tried to harm me, but God made it turn out for the best, so that he could save all these people, as he is now doing."*—Genesis 50.20**

¹⁶So they sent this message to Joseph:

Before our father died, ¹⁷he told us, "You did some cruel and terrible things to Joseph, but you must ask him to forgive you."

Now we ask you to please forgive the terrible things we did. After all, we serve the same God that your father worshiped.

When Joseph heard this, he started crying.

¹⁸Right then, Joseph's brothers came and bowed down to the ground in front of him and said, "We are your slaves."

¹⁹But Joseph told them, "Don't be afraid! I have no right to change what God has decided. ²⁰You tried to harm me, but God made it turn out for the best, so that he could save all these people, as he is now doing. ²¹Don't be afraid! I will take care of you and your children." After Joseph said this, his brothers felt much better.

Joseph's Death

²²Joseph lived in Egypt with his brothers until he died at the age of one hundred ten. ²³Joseph lived long enough to see Ephraim's children and grandchildren. He also lived to see the children of Manasseh's son Machir, and he welcomed them into his family. ²⁴Before Joseph died, he told his brothers, "I won't live much longer. But God will take care of you and lead you out of Egypt to the land he promised Abraham, Isaac, and Jacob. ²⁵Now promise me that you will take my body with you when God leads you to that land."

²⁶So Joseph died in Egypt at the age of one hundred ten; his body was embalmed and put in a coffin.

Exodus

God Saves His People

What happens when God deserts you? Enemies are everywhere, and he's nowhere in sight. All his promises seem to be forgotten. Your work seems meaningless and never-ending. And those who hate God are succeeding!

Even then, God is still powerful. That's what the people of Israel discovered. In Genesis, God miraculously created a nation and saved them from famine by bringing them to Egypt. By the time the book of Exodus began, these people (the descendants of Abraham) numbered more than a million—just as God had promised. There were so many Israelites that the king of Egypt became afraid of the people and made them into slaves. They thought God had forgotten them.

But God was busy preparing someone to deliver them: Moses, brought up by the Egyptians as one of their own princes. When the time was right, God did miracles to deliver his people from slavery. He punished their enemies by sending ten plagues on the Egyptians, then led them out of Egypt by parting the Red Sea in front of them. The story of the Exodus became a prime example of God's saving power.

But that's not the end of the story. God also wanted his people to have a relationship with him. He knew that it's impossible to please someone if you don't know what they want. So he took them into the desert, appeared to them at Sinai, and told them how to please him. He gave them a system of laws designed to keep the relationship with him healthy. Exodus contains the Decalogue (20.1-17) and the Book of the Covenant (20.22—23.19), which contains laws that flow from the more basic commands given in the Ten Commandments.

Now the Israelites knew they could trust God to save them. They also knew what he wanted. Then God told them to build a place for him to live, so he could be near them always. He gave them instructions for a tent where his presence could dwell.

The book of Exodus follows this three-fold pattern. First, God saved his people. Then God told them what he wanted. Finally, God came to live with them. The traditional author of the book is Moses. In three different chapters (17.14; 24.4; 34.4,27-29), Exodus tells us that Moses wrote an account of what happened.

Exodus at a Glance

1. The Israelites become slaves (1)
2. God sends Moses (2–6)
3. The ten plagues of Egypt (7.1—12.30)
4. Israel escapes from Egypt (12.31—15.21)
5. Israel in the desert (15.22—18.27)
6. God gives his law (19–24)
7. Instructions for building the sacred tent (25–27)
8. Instructions for priests and sacrifices (28–31)
9. The people disobey (32)
10. God forgives the people and gives new laws (33.1—35.3)
11. Further instructions for the tabernacle and priests (35.4—39.43)
12. God comes to live with his people (40)

The People of Israel Suffer

1 [1-5]When Jacob went to Egypt, his son Joseph was already there. So Jacob took his eleven other sons and their families. They were: Reuben, Simeon, Levi, Judah, Issachar, Zebulun, Benjamin, Dan, Naphtali, Gad, and Asher. Altogether, Jacob had seventy children, grandchildren, and great-grandchildren[a] who went with him.

[6]After Joseph, his brothers, and everyone else in that generation had died, [7]the people of Israel became so numerous that the whole region of Goshen was full of them.

[8]Many years later a new king came to power. He did not know what Joseph had done for Egypt, [9]and he told the Egyptians:

There are too many of those Israelites in our country, and they are becoming more powerful than we are. [10]If we don't outsmart them, their families will keep growing larger. And if our country goes to war, they could easily fight on the side of our enemies and escape from Egypt.

[11]The Egyptians put slave bosses in charge of the people of Israel and tried to wear them down with hard work. Those bosses forced them to build the cities of Pithom and Rameses,[b] where the king[c] could store his supplies. [12]But even though the Israelites were mistreated, their families grew larger, and they took over more land. Because of this, the Egyptians hated them worse than before [13]and made them work so hard [14]that their lives were miserable. The Egyptians were cruel to the people of Israel and forced them to make bricks and to mix mortar and to work in the fields.

[15]Finally, the king called in Shiphrah and Puah, the two women who helped the Hebrew[d] mothers when they gave birth. [16]He told them, "If a Hebrew woman gives birth to a girl, let the child live. If the baby is a boy, kill him!"

[17]But the two women were faithful to God and did not kill the boys, even though the king had told them to. [18]The king called them in again and asked, "Why are you letting those baby boys live?"

[19]They answered, "Hebrew women have their babies much quicker than Egyptian women. By the time we arrive, their babies are already born." [20-21]God was good to the two women because they truly respected him, and he blessed them with children of their own.

The Hebrews kept increasing [22]until finally, the king gave a command to everyone in the nation, "As soon as a Hebrew boy is born, throw him into the Nile River! But you can let the girls live."

Moses Is Born

2 A man from the Levi tribe married a woman from the same tribe, [2]and she later had a baby boy. He was a beautiful child, and she kept him inside for three months. [3]But when she could no longer keep him hidden, she made a basket out of reeds and covered it with tar. She put him in the basket and placed it in the tall grass along the edge of the Nile River. [4]The baby's older sister[e] stood off at a distance to see what would happen to him.

[5]About that time one of the king's[f] daughters came down to take a bath in the river, while her servant women walked along the river bank. She saw the basket in the tall grass and sent one of the young women to pull it out of the water. [6]When the king's daughter opened the basket, she saw the baby and felt sorry for him because he was crying. She said, "This must be one of the Hebrew babies."

[7]At once the baby's older sister came up and asked, "Do you want me to get a Hebrew woman to take care of the baby for you?"

[8]"Yes," the king's daughter answered.

So the girl brought the baby's mother, [9]and the king's daughter told her, "Take care of this child, and I will pay you."

The baby's mother carried him home and took care of him. [10]And when he was old enough, she took him to the king's

---

[a]1.1-5 seventy children . . . great-grandchildren: See Genesis 46.8-27. [b]1.11 Pithom and Rameses: This is the only mention of Pithom in the Bible; its exact location is unknown, though it was probably in the northern Delta of Egypt. Rameses is the famous Delta city that was the home of Rameses II; its exact location is also unknown. [c]1.11 the king: The Hebrew text has "Pharaoh," a Hebrew word sometimes used for the title of the king of Egypt. [d]1.15 Hebrew: An earlier term for "Israelite." [e]2.4 older sister: Miriam, the sister of Moses and Aaron. [f]2.5 the king's: See the note at 1.11.

Jochebed

Exodus 2.1-10; Numbers 26.59

What would you do if the government ordered you to kill your baby? For most of us, that's not a difficult question! We'd disobey at once, no matter what the cost. But one mother in the Old Testament, faced with such a command, chose to deal with it in a very inventive way.

Jochebed was a Hebrew slave in Egypt. She'd just had a baby—a beautiful boy. But she was a Hebrew slave, and the Egyptian king who ruled over her was afraid that the Hebrews were becoming too powerful. So he issued an order that all baby boys born to Hebrew mothers had to be thrown into the Nile River.

Jochebed kept her baby for several months. But when he became old enough to babble, she couldn't keep him quiet. She was afraid the Egyptian soldiers who prowled from house to house might hear her son and kill him. So she did something surprising: She obeyed the king's command and put her baby into the river! But instead of throwing the baby into the water, she made him a little boat and sent him floating into the Nile—just as the king's daughter came out to bathe. Jochebed also sent her older daughter, Miriam, to hide and see what would happen to the child. The king's daughter found the baby, adopted him, and hired his own mother as a nurse. Because of his mother's ingenuity, Moses' life was spared.

Jochebed serves as a wonderful example of how we should respond to ungodly orders. Jochebed refused to do evil; she would not kill her baby as the king of Egypt commanded. But she showed creativity in complying with the king's orders while still avoiding sin. She showed ingenuity in hiding her baby in a basket on the Nile. And she was rewarded with her baby's life.

We may not always be able to obey the laws of our own government. But, like Jochebed, we should do our best to comply without committing sin.

daughter, who adopted him. She named him Moses[g] because she said, "I pulled him out of the water."

Moses Escapes from Egypt

[11]After Moses had grown up, he went out to where his own people were hard at work, and he saw an Egyptian beating one of them. [12]Moses looked around to see if anyone was watching, then he killed the Egyptian and hid his body in the sand.

[13]When Moses went out the next day, he saw two Hebrews fighting. So he went to the man who had started the fight and asked, "Why are you beating up one of your own people?"

[14]The man answered, "Who put you in charge of us and made you our judge? Are you planning to kill me, just as you killed that Egyptian?"

This frightened Moses because he was sure that people must have found out what had happened. [15]When the king[h] heard what Moses had done, the king wanted to kill him. But Moses escaped and went to the land of Midian.

One day, Moses was sitting there by a well, [16]when the seven daughters of Jethro, the priest of Midian,[i] came up to water their father's sheep and goats. [17]Some shepherds tried to chase them away, but Moses came to their rescue and watered their animals. [18]When Jethro's daughters returned home, their father asked, "Why have you come back so early today?"

[19]They answered, "An Egyptian rescued us from the shepherds, and he even watered our sheep and goats."

[20]"Where is he?" Jethro asked. "Why did you leave him out there? Invite him to eat with us."

[21]Moses agreed to stay on with Jethro, who later let his daughter Zipporah marry Moses. [22]And when she had a son, Moses said, "I will name him Gershom,[j] since I am a foreigner in this country."

[23]After the death of the king of Egypt, the Israelites still complained because they were forced to be slaves. They cried out for help, [24]and God heard their loud cries. He did not forget the promise he had made to Abraham, Isaac, and Jacob, [25]and because he knew what was happening to his people, he felt sorry for them.

God Speaks to Moses

3 One day, Moses was taking care of the sheep and goats of his father-in-law Jethro, the priest of Midian, and Moses decided to lead them across the desert to Sinai,[k] the holy mountain. [2]There an angel of the LORD appeared to him from a burning bush. Moses saw that the bush was on fire, but it was not burning up. [3]"This is strange!" he said to himself. "I'll go over and see why the bush isn't burning up."

[4]When the LORD saw Moses coming near the bush, he called him by name, and Moses answered, "Here I am."

[5]God replied, "Don't come any closer. Take off your sandals—the ground where you are standing is holy. [6]I am the God who was worshiped by your ancestors Abraham, Isaac, and Jacob."

Moses was afraid to look at God, and so he hid his face.

[7]The LORD said:

I have seen how my people are suffering as slaves in Egypt, and I have heard them beg for my help because of the way they are being mistreated. I feel sorry for them, [8]and I have come down to rescue them from the Egyptians.

God is using the prayers you are praying today to open the curtain to the rest of your life.

EVELYN CHRISTENSON

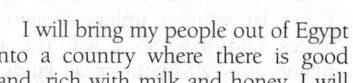

I will bring my people out of Egypt into a country where there is good land, rich with milk and honey. I will

---

[g]**2.10** *Moses:* In Hebrew "Moses" sounds like "pull out." [h]**2.15** *the king:* See the note at 1.11. [i]**2.16** *Jethro, the priest of Midian:* Hebrew "the priest of Midian." But see 3.1; 4.18; 18.1, 2-4 where his name is given. In the Hebrew of verse 18 he is spoken of as "Reuel," which may have been the name of the tribe to which Jethro belonged. [j]**2.22** *Gershom:* In Hebrew "Gershom" sounds like "foreigner." [k]**3.1** *Sinai:* The Hebrew text has "Horeb," another name for Sinai.

give them the land where the Canaanites, Hittites, Amorites, Perizzites, Hivites, and Jebusites now live. [9]My people have begged for my help, and I have seen how cruel the Egyptians are to them. [10]Now go to the king! I am sending you to lead my people out of his country.

[11]But Moses said, "Who am I to go to the king and lead your people out of Egypt?"

[12]God replied, "I will be with you. And you will know that I am the one who sent you, when you worship me on this mountain after you have led my people out of Egypt."[l]

[13]Moses answered, "I will tell the people of Israel that the God their ancestors worshiped has sent me to them. But what should I say, if they ask me your name?"

[14-15]God said to Moses:

I am the eternal God. So tell them that the LORD,[m] whose name is "I Am," has sent you. This is my name forever, and it is the name that people must use from now on.

[16]Call together the leaders of Israel and tell them that the God who was worshiped by Abraham, Isaac, and Jacob has appeared to you. Tell them I have seen how terribly they are being treated in Egypt, [17]and I promise to lead them out of their troubles. I will give them a land rich with milk and honey, where the Canaanites, Hittites, Amorites, Perizzites, Hivites, and Jebusites now live.

[18]The leaders of Israel will listen to you. Then you must take them to the king of Egypt and say, "The LORD God of the Hebrews has appeared to us. Let us walk three days into the desert, where we can offer a sacrifice to him."

[19]But I know that the king of Egypt won't let you go unless something forces him to. [20]So I will use my mighty power to perform all kinds of miracles and strike down the Egyptians. Then the king will send you away.

[21]After I punish the Egyptians, they will be so afraid of you that they will give you anything you want. You are my people, and I will let you take many things with you when you leave the land of Egypt. [22]Every Israelite woman will go to her Egyptian neighbors or to any Egyptian woman living in her house. She will ask them for gold and silver jewelry and for their finest clothes. The Egyptians will give them to you, and you will put these fine things on your sons and daughters. You will carry all this away when you leave Egypt.

The LORD Gives Great Power to Moses

4 Moses asked the LORD, "Suppose everyone refuses to listen to my message, and no one believes that you really appeared to me?"

[2]The LORD answered, "What's that in your hand?"

"A walking stick," Moses replied.

[3]"Throw it down!" the LORD commanded. So Moses threw the stick on the ground. It immediately turned into a snake, and Moses jumped back.

[4]"Pick it up by the tail!" the LORD told him. And when Moses did this, the snake turned back into a walking stick.

[5]"Do this," the LORD said, "and the Israelites will believe that you have seen me, the God who was worshiped by their ancestors Abraham, Isaac, and Jacob."

[6]Next, the LORD commanded Moses, "Put your hand inside your shirt." Moses obeyed, and when he took it out, his hand had turned white as snow—like someone with leprosy.[n]

[7]"Put your hand back inside your shirt," the LORD told him. Moses did so, and when he took it out again, it was as healthy as the rest of his body.

[8-9]Then the LORD said, "If no one believes either of these miracles, take some water from the Nile River and pour it on the ground. The water will immediately turn into blood."

[10]Moses replied, "I have never been a good speaker. I wasn't one before you spoke

---

[l]3.12 I will be with you . . . out of Egypt: Or "I will be with you. This bush is a sign that I am the one sending you, and it is a promise that you will worship me on this mountain after you have led my people out of Egypt." [m]3.14,15 LORD: The Hebrew text has "Yahweh," which is usually translated "LORD" in the CEV. Since it seems related to the word translated "I am," it may mean "I am the one who is" or "I will be what I will be" or "I am the one who brings into being." [n]4.6 leprosy: The word translated "leprosy" was used for many different kinds of skin diseases.

to me, and I'm not one now. I am slow at speaking, and I can never think of what to say."

My grandmother fixed her eyes on Jesus—nothing else. Throughout her life she held no political office or public position of influence. She accumulated no fortune to pass on, left no noticeable mark on the world at all, <u>except her faithfulness to God!</u>

MAYO MATHERS

[11]But the LORD answered, "Who makes people able to speak or makes them deaf or unable to speak? Who gives them sight or makes them blind? Don't you know that I am the one who does these things? [12]Now go! When you speak, I will be with you and give you the words to say."

[13]Moses begged, "LORD, please send someone else to do it."

[14]The LORD became irritated with Moses and said:

What about your brother Aaron, the Levite? I know he is a good speaker. He is already on his way here to visit you, and he will be happy to see you again. [15-16]Aaron will speak to the people for you, and you will be like me, telling Aaron what to say. I will be with both of you as you speak, and I will tell each of you what to do. [17]Now take this walking stick and use it to perform miracles.

Moses Returns to Egypt

[18]Moses went to his father-in-law Jethro and asked, "Please let me return to Egypt to see if any of my people are still alive."

"All right," Jethro replied. "I hope all goes well."

[19]But even before this, the LORD had told Moses, "Leave the land of Midian and return to Egypt. Everyone who wanted to kill you is dead." [20]So Moses put his wife and sons on donkeys and headed for Egypt, holding the walking stick that had the power of God.

[21]On the way the LORD said to Moses:

When you get to Egypt, go to the king and work the miracles I have shown you. But I will make him so stubborn that he will refuse to let my people go. [22]Then tell him that I have said, "Israel is my first-born son, [23]and I commanded you to release him, so he could worship me. But you refused, and now I will kill your first-born son."

Zipporah's Son Is Circumcised

[24]One night while Moses was in camp, the LORD was about to kill him. [25]But Zipporah[o] circumcised her son with a flint knife. She touched his[p] legs with the skin she had cut off and said, "My dear son, this blood will protect you."[q] [26]So the LORD did not harm Moses. Then Zipporah said, "Yes, my dear, you are safe because of this circumcision."[r]

Aaron Is Sent To Meet Moses

[27]The LORD sent Aaron to meet Moses in the desert. So Aaron met Moses at Mount Sinai[s] and greeted him with a kiss. [28]Moses told Aaron what God had sent him to say; he also told him about the miracles God had given him the power to perform.

[29]Later they brought together the leaders of Israel, [30]and Aaron told them what the LORD had sent Moses to say. Then Moses worked the miracles for the people, [31]and everyone believed. They bowed down and worshiped the LORD because they knew that he had seen their suffering and was going to help them.

Moses and Aaron Go to the King of Egypt

5 Moses and Aaron went to the king[t] of Egypt and told him, "The LORD God says, 'Let my people go into the desert, so they can honor me with a celebration there.'"

---

[o]4.25 *Zipporah:* The wife of Moses (see 2.16-21).
[p]4.25 *his:* Either Moses or the boy. [q]4.25 *My dear son . . . you:* Or "My dear husband, you are a man of blood" (meaning Moses). [r]4.26 *you are . . . circumcision:* Or "you are a man of blood."
[s]4.27 *Mount Sinai:* Hebrew "the mountain of God."
[t]5.1 *the king:* See the note at 1.11.

²"Who is this L ORD and why should I obey him?" the king replied. "I refuse to let you and your people go!"

³They answered, "The L ORD God of the Hebrews, has appeared to us. Please let us walk three days into the desert where we can offer sacrifices to him. If you don't, he may strike us down with terrible troubles or with war."

⁴⁻⁵The king said, "Moses and Aaron, why are you keeping these people from working? Look how many you are keeping from doing their work. Now everyone get back to work!"

⁶That same day the king gave orders to his slave bosses and to the men directly in charge of the Israelite slaves. He told them:

⁷Don't give the slaves any more straw ͧ to put in their bricks. Force them to find their own straw wherever they can, ⁸but they must make the same number of bricks as before. They are lazy, or else they would not beg me to let them go and sacrifice to their God. ⁹Make them work so hard that they won't have time to listen to these lies.

¹⁰The slave bosses and the men in charge of the slaves went out and told them, "The king says he will not give you any more straw. ¹¹Go and find your own straw wherever you can, but you must still make as many bricks as before."

¹²The slaves went all over Egypt, looking for straw. ¹³But the slave bosses were hard on them and kept saying, "Each day you have to make as many bricks as you did when you were given straw." ¹⁴The bosses beat the men in charge of the slaves and said, "Why didn't you force the slaves to make as many bricks yesterday and today as they did before?"

¹⁵Finally, the men in charge of the slaves went to the king and said, "Why are you treating us like this? ¹⁶No one brings us any straw, but we are still ordered to make the same number of bricks. We are beaten with whips, and your own people are to blame."

¹⁷The king replied, "You are lazy—nothing but lazy! That's why you keep asking me to let you go and sacrifice to your L ORD. ¹⁸Get back to work! You won't be given straw, but you must still make the same number of bricks."

¹⁹The men knew they were in deep trou-

ble when they were ordered to make the same number of bricks each day. ²⁰After they left the king, they went to see Moses and Aaron, who had been waiting for them. ²¹Then the men said, "We hope the L ORD will punish both of you for making the king and his officials hate us. Now they even have an excuse to kill us."

The L ORD's Promise to Moses

²²Moses left them and prayed, "Our L ORD, why have you brought so much trouble on your people? Is that why you sent me here? ²³Ever since you told me to speak to the king, ͮ he has caused nothing but trouble for these people. And you haven't done a thing to help."

6 The L ORD God told Moses:
    Soon you will see what I will do to the king. Because of my mighty power, he will let my people go, and he will even chase them out of his country.

²My name is the L ORD. ͩ ³But when I appeared to Abraham, Isaac, and Jacob, I came as God All-Powerful and did not use my name. ⁴I made an agreement and promised them the land of Canaan, where they were living as foreigners. ⁵Now I have seen how the people of Israel are suffering because of the Egyptians, and I will keep my promise.

Jesus does understand our struggles. He walked on earth as a human. He hurt as we hurt, and wept as we weep. His love and mercy are everlasting.

S USAN A SHTON

⁶Here is my message for Israel: "I am the L ORD! And with my mighty

---

ͧ**5.7** *straw:* The straw made the mud bricks stronger and kept them from shrinking, cracking, or losing their shape.   ͮ**5.23** *the king:* See the note at 1.11.   ͩ**6.2** *My name is the L ORD:* See the note at 3.14, 15.

power I will punish the Egyptians and free you from slavery. [7]I will accept you as my people, and I will be your God. Then you will know that I was the one who rescued you from the Egyptians. [8]I will bring you into the land that I solemnly promised Abraham, Isaac, and Jacob, and it will be yours. I am the LORD!"

[9]When Moses told this to the Israelites, they were too discouraged and mistreated to believe him.

[10]Then the LORD told Moses [11]to demand that the king of Egypt let the Israelites leave. [12]But Moses replied, "I'm not a powerful speaker. If the Israelites won't listen to me, why should the king of Egypt?" [13]But the LORD sent Aaron and Moses with a message for the Israelites and for the king; he also ordered Aaron and Moses to free the people from Egypt.

Family Record of Aaron and Moses

[14]The following men were the heads of their ancestral clans:

The sons of Reuben, Jacob's[x] oldest son, were Hanoch, Pallu, Hezron, and Carmi.

[15]The sons of Simeon were Jemuel, Jamin, Ohad, Jachin, Zohar, and Shaul, the son of a Canaanite woman.

[16]Levi lived to be one hundred thirty-seven; his sons were Gershon, Kohath, and Merari.

[17]Gershon's sons were Libni and Shimei.

[18]Kohath lived to be one hundred thirty-three; his sons were Amram, Izhar, Hebron, and Uzziel.

[19]Merari's sons were Mahli and Mushi. All of the above were from the Levi tribe.

[20]Amram lived to be one hundred thirty-seven. He married his father's sister Jochebed, and they had two sons, Aaron and Moses.

[21]Izhar's sons were Korah, Nepheg, and Zichri.

[22]Uzziel's sons were Mishael, Elzaphan, and Sithri.

[23]Aaron married Elisheba. She was the daughter of Amminadab and the sister of Nahshon; they had four sons, Nadab, Abihu, Eleazar, and Ithamar.

[24]Korah's sons were Assir, Elkanah, and Abiasaph.

[25]Aaron's son Eleazar married one of Putiel's daughters, and their son was Phinehas. This ends the list of those who were the heads of clans in the Levi tribe.

[26]The LORD had commanded Aaron and Moses to lead every family and tribe of Israel out of Egypt, [27]and so they ordered the king of Egypt to set the people of Israel free.

The LORD Commands Moses and Aaron To Speak to the King

[28]When the LORD spoke to Moses in the land of Egypt, [29]he said, "I am the LORD. Tell the king[y] of Egypt everything I say to you."

[30]But Moses answered, "You know I am a very poor speaker, and the king will never listen to me."

7 The LORD said:

I am going to let your brother Aaron speak for you. He will tell your message to the king, just as a prophet speaks my message to the people. [2]Tell Aaron everything I say to you, and he will order the king to let my people leave his country. [3-4]But I will make the king so stubborn that he won't listen to you. He won't listen even when I do many terrible things to him and his nation. Then I will bring a final punishment on Egypt, and the king will let Israel's families and tribes go. [5]When this happens, the Egyptians will know that I am the LORD.

[6]Moses and Aaron obeyed the LORD [7]and spoke to the king. At the time, Moses was eighty years old, and Aaron was eighty-three.

A Stick Turns into a Snake

[8-9]The LORD said, "Moses, when the king[y] asks you and Aaron to perform a miracle, command Aaron to throw his walking stick down in front of the king, and it will turn into a snake."

[10]Moses and Aaron went to the king and his officials and did exactly as the LORD had commanded—Aaron threw the stick down, and it turned into a snake. [11]Then the king

---

x6.14 *Jacob*: The Hebrew text has "Israel," Jacob's name after God renamed him.   y6.29; 7.8,9 *the king*: See the note at 1.11.

called in the wise men and the magicians, who used their secret powers to do the same thing—[12]they threw down sticks that turned into snakes. But Aaron's snake swallowed theirs. [13]The king behaved just as the LORD had said and stubbornly refused to listen.

> *I want my hunger for godliness
> to cause people to take
> a second look at Christianity
> and the God who longs to
> interact intimately with us.*
>
> KATHY TROCCOLI

The Nile River Turns into Blood

[14]The LORD said to Moses:

The Egyptian king[y] stubbornly refuses to change his mind and let the people go. [15]Tomorrow morning take the stick that turned into a snake, then wait beside the Nile River for the king. [16]Tell him, "The LORD God of the Hebrews sent me to order you to release his people, so they can worship him in the desert. But until now, you have paid no attention.

[17]"The LORD is going to do something to show you that he really is the LORD. I will strike the Nile with this stick, and the water will turn into blood. [18]The fish will die, the river will stink, and none of you Egyptians will be able to drink the water."

[19]Moses, then command Aaron to hold his stick over the water. And when he does, every drop of water in Egypt will turn into blood, including rivers, canals, ponds, and even the water in buckets and jars.

[20]Moses and Aaron obeyed the LORD. Aaron held out his stick, then struck the Nile, as the king and his officials watched. The river turned into blood, [21]the fish died, and the water smelled so bad that none of the Egyptians could drink it. Blood was everywhere in Egypt.

[22]But the Egyptian magicians used their secret powers to do the same thing. The king did just as the LORD had said—he stubbornly refused to listen. [23]Then he went back to his palace and never gave it a second thought. [24]The Egyptians had to dig holes along the banks of the Nile for drinking water, because water from the river was unfit to drink.

Frogs

[25]Seven days after the LORD had struck the Nile, [1]he said to Moses:

8 Go to the palace and tell the king[y] of Egypt that I order him to let my people go, so they can worship me. [2]If he refuses, I will cover his entire country with frogs. [3]Warn the king that the Nile will be full of frogs, and from there they will spread into the royal palace, including the king's bedroom and even his bed. Frogs will enter the homes of his officials and will find their way into ovens and into the bowls of bread dough. [4]Frogs will be crawling on everyone—the king, his officials, and every citizen of Egypt.

[5]Moses, now command Aaron to hold his stick over the water. Then frogs will come from all rivers, canals, and ponds in Egypt, and they will cover the land.

[6]Aaron obeyed, and suddenly frogs were everywhere in Egypt. [7]But the magicians used their secret powers to do the same thing.

[8]The king sent for Moses and Aaron and told them, "If you ask the LORD to take these frogs away from me and my people, I will let your people go and offer sacrifices to him."

[9]"All right," Moses answered. "You choose the time when I am to pray for the frogs to stop bothering you, your officials, and your people, and for them to leave your houses and be found only in the river."

[10]"Do it tomorrow!" the king replied.

"As you wish," Moses agreed. "Then everyone will discover that there is no god like the LORD, [11]and frogs will no longer be found anywhere, except in the Nile."

[12]After Moses and Aaron left the palace, Moses begged the LORD to do something

---

*y***7.14** *The Egyptian king:* See the note at 1.11.
*y***8.1** *the king:* See the note at 1.11.

about the frogs he had sent as punishment for the king. [13]The LORD listened to Moses, and frogs died everywhere—in houses, yards, and fields. [14]The dead frogs were placed in piles, and the whole country began to stink. [15]But when the king saw that things were now better, he again did just as the LORD had said and stubbornly refused to listen to Moses and Aaron.

Gnats

[16]The LORD said to Moses, "Command Aaron to strike the ground with his walking stick, and everywhere in Egypt the dust will turn into gnats." [17]They obeyed, and when Aaron struck the ground with the stick, gnats started swarming on people and animals. In fact, every speck of dust in Egypt turned into a gnat. [18]When the magicians tried to use their secret powers to do this,[z] they failed, and gnats stayed on people and animals.

[19]The magicians told the king,[a] "God has done this."

But, as the LORD had said, the king was too stubborn to listen.

Flies

[20]The LORD said to Moses:

Early tomorrow morning, while the king[a] is on his way to the river, go and say to him, "The LORD commands you to let his people go, so they can worship him. [21]If you don't, he will send swarms of flies to attack you, your officials, and every citizen of your country. Houses will be full of flies, and the ground will crawl with them.

[22-23]"The LORD's people in Goshen won't be bothered by flies, but your people in the rest of the country will be tormented by them. That's how you will know that the LORD is here in Egypt. This miracle will happen tomorrow."

[24]The LORD kept his promise—the palace and the homes of the royal officials swarmed with flies, and the rest of the country was infested with them as well. [25]Then the king sent for Moses and Aaron and told them, "Go sacrifice to your God, but stay here in Egypt."

[26]"That's impossible!" Moses replied. "Any sacrifices we offer to the LORD our God would disgust the Egyptians, and they would stone us to death. [27]No indeed! The LORD has ordered us to walk three days into the desert before offering sacrifices to him, and that's what we have to do."

[28]Then the king told him, "I'll let you go into the desert to offer sacrifices, if you don't go very far. But in the meantime, pray for me."

[29]"Your Majesty," Moses replied, "I'll pray for you as soon as I leave, and by tomorrow the flies will stop bothering you, your officials, and the citizens of your country. Only make sure that you're telling the truth this time and that you really intend to let our people offer sacrifices to the LORD."

[30]After leaving the palace, Moses prayed, [31]and the LORD answered his prayer. Not a fly was left to pester the king, his officials, or anyone else in Egypt. [32]But the king turned stubborn again and would not let the people go.

Dead Animals

9 The LORD sent Moses with this message for the king[a] of Egypt:

The LORD God of the Hebrews commands you to let his people go, so they can worship him. [2]If you keep refusing, [3]he will bring a terrible disease on your horses and donkeys, your camels and cattle, and your sheep and goats. [4]But the LORD will protect the animals that belong to the people of Israel, and none of theirs will die. [5]Tomorrow is the day the LORD has set to do this.

[6]It happened the next day—all of the animals belonging to the Egyptians died, but the Israelites did not lose even one. [7]When the king found out, he was still too stubborn to let the people go.

Sores

[8]The LORD said to Moses and Aaron:

Take a few handfuls of ashes from a stove and have Moses throw them into the air. Be sure the king is watching. [9]The ashes will blow across the land of Egypt, causing sores to break out on people and animals.

---

[z]**8.18** *to do this:* Or "to get rid of the gnats."
[a]**8.19,20; 9.1** *the king:* See the note at 1.11.

[10]So they took a few handfuls of ashes and went to the king.[a] Moses threw them into the air, and sores immediately broke out on the Egyptians and their animals. [11]The magicians were suffering so much from the sores, that they could not even come to Moses. [12]Everything happened just as the LORD had told Moses—he made the king too stubborn to listen to Moses and Aaron.

Hailstones

[13]The LORD told Moses to get up early the next morning and say to the king:[a]

The LORD God of the Hebrews commands you to let his people go, so they can worship him! [14]If you don't, he will send his worst plagues to strike you, your officials, and everyone else in your country. Then you will find out that no one can oppose the LORD. [15]In fact, he could already have sent a terrible disease and wiped you from the face of the earth. [16]But he has kept you alive, just to show you his power and to bring honor to himself everywhere in the world.

[17]You are still determined not to let the LORD's people go. [18]All right. At this time tomorrow, he will bring on Egypt the worst hailstorm in its history. [19]You had better give orders for every person and every animal in Egypt to take shelter. If they don't, they will die.

[20]Some of the king's officials were frightened by what the LORD had said, and they hurried off to make sure their slaves and animals were safe. [21]But others paid no attention to his threats and left their slaves and animals out in the open.

[22]Then the LORD told Moses, "Stretch your arm toward the sky, so that hailstones will fall on people, animals, and crops in the land of Egypt." [23-24]Moses pointed his walking stick toward the sky, and hailstones started falling everywhere. Thunder roared, and lightning flashed back and forth, striking the ground. This was the worst storm in the history of Egypt. [25]People, animals, and crops were pounded by the hailstones, and bark was stripped from trees. [26]Only Goshen, where the Israelites lived, was safe from the storm.

[27]The king sent for Moses and Aaron and told them, "Now I have really sinned! My people and I are guilty, and the LORD is right. [28]We can't stand any more of this thunder and hail. Please ask the LORD to make it stop. Your people can go—you don't have to stay in Egypt any longer."

[29]Moses answered, "As soon as I leave the city, I will lift my arms in prayer. When the thunder and hail stop, you will know that the earth belongs to the LORD. [30]But I am certain that neither you nor your officials really fear the LORD God."

[31]Meanwhile, the flax and barley crops had been destroyed by the storm because they were ready to ripen. [32]But the wheat crops[b] ripen later, and they were not damaged.

[33]After Moses left the royal palace and the city, he lifted his arms in prayer to the LORD, and the thunder, hail, and drenching rain stopped. [34]When the king realized that the storm was over, he disobeyed once more. He and his officials were so stubborn [35]that he refused to let the Israelites go. This was exactly what the LORD had said would happen.

Locusts

10 The LORD said to Moses:

Go back to the king.[c] I have made him and his officials stubborn, so that I could work these miracles. [2]I did this because I want you to tell your children and your grandchildren about my miracles and about my harsh treatment of the Egyptians. Then all of you will know that I am the LORD.

[3]Moses and Aaron went to the king and told him that the LORD God of the Hebrews had said:

How long will you stubbornly refuse to obey? Release my people so they can worship me. [4]Do this by tomorrow, or I will cover your country with so many locusts[d] [5]that you won't be able to see the ground. Most of your crops were ruined by the hailstones, but these locusts will destroy

---

[a]9.10,13 the king: See the note at 1.11.   [b]9.32 wheat crops: The Hebrew text mentions two kinds of wheat.   [c]10.1 the king: See the note at 1.11.   [d]10.4 locusts: A type of grasshopper that comes in swarms and causes great damage to crops.

what little is left, including the trees. [6]Your palace, the homes of your officials, and all other houses in Egypt will overflow with more locusts than have ever been seen in this country.

After Moses left the palace, [7]the king's officials asked, "Your Majesty, how much longer is this man going to be a troublemaker? Why don't you let the people leave, so they can worship the LORD their God? Don't you know that Egypt is a disaster?"

[8]The king had Moses and Aaron brought back, and he said, "All right, you may go and worship the LORD your God. But first tell me who will be going."

[9]"Everyone, young and old," Moses answered. "We will even take our sheep, goats, and cattle, because we want to hold a celebration in honor of the LORD."

[10]The king replied, "The LORD had better watch over you on the day I let you leave with your families! You're up to no good. [11]Do you want to worship the LORD? All right, take only the men and go." Then Moses and Aaron were chased out of the palace.

[12]The LORD told Moses, "Stretch your arm toward Egypt. Swarms of locusts will come and eat everything left by the hail."

[13]Moses held out his walking stick, and the LORD sent an east wind that blew across Egypt the rest of the day and all that night. By morning, locusts [14]were swarming everywhere. Never before had there been so many locusts in Egypt, and never again will there be so many. [15]The ground was black with locusts, and they ate everything left on the trees and in the fields. Nothing green remained in Egypt—not a tree or a plant.

[16]At once the king sent for Moses and Aaron. He told them, "I have sinned against the LORD your God and against you. [17]Forgive me one more time and ask the LORD to stop these insects from killing every living plant."

[18]Moses left the palace and prayed. [19]Then the LORD sent a strong west wind[c] that swept the locusts into the Red Sea.[f] Not one locust was left anywhere in Egypt, [20]but the LORD made the king so stubborn that he still refused to let the Israelites go.

Darkness

[21]The LORD said to Moses, "Stretch your arm toward the sky, and everything will be covered with darkness thick enough to touch." [22]Moses stretched his arm toward the sky, and Egypt was covered with darkness for three days. [23]During that time, the Egyptians could not see each other or leave their homes, but there was light where the Israelites lived.

[24]The king[g] sent for Moses and told him, "Go worship the LORD! And take your families with you. Just leave your sheep, goats, and cattle."

[25]"No!" Moses replied. "You must let us offer sacrifices to the LORD our God, [26]and we won't know which animals we will need until we get there. That's why we can't leave even one of them here."

[27]This time the LORD made the king so stubborn [28]that he said to Moses, "Get out and stay out! If you ever come back, you're dead!"

[29]"Have it your way," Moses answered. "You won't see me again."

Moses Warns the Egyptians That the LORD Will Kill Their First-Born Sons

11 The LORD said to Moses:

I am going to punish the king[g] of Egypt and his people one more time. Then the king will gladly let you leave his land, so that I will stop punishing the Egyptians. He will even chase you out. [2]Now go and tell my people to ask their Egyptian neighbors for gold and silver jewelry.

[3]So the LORD made the Egyptians greatly respect the Israelites, and everyone, including the king and his officials, considered Moses an important leader.

[4]Moses went to the king and said:

I have come to let you know what the LORD is going to do. About midnight he will go through the land of Egypt, [5]and wherever he goes, the first-born son in every family will die. Your own son will die, and so will the son of the lowest slave woman. Even the first-born males of cattle will die.

---

[c]10.19 *west wind*: The Hebrew text has "wind from the sea," referring to the Mediterranean Sea (see verse 13). [f]10.19 *Red Sea*: Hebrew *yam suph*, here referring to the Gulf of Suez, since the term is extended to include the northwestern arm of the Red Sea (see also the note at 13.18). [g]10.24 *The king*: See the note at 1.11. [g]11.1 *the king*: See the note at 1.11.

⁶Everywhere in Egypt there will be loud crying. Nothing like this has ever happened before or will ever happen again. ⁷But there won't be any need for the Israelites to cry. Things will be so quiet that not even a dog will be heard barking. Then you Egyptians will know that the LORD is good to the Israelites, even while he punishes you. ⁸Your leaders will come and bow down, begging me to take my people and leave your country. Then we will leave.

Moses was very angry; he turned and left the king.

⁹What the LORD had earlier said to Moses came true. He had said, "The king of Egypt won't listen. Then I will perform even more miracles." ¹⁰So the king of Egypt saw Moses and Aaron work miracles, but the LORD made him stubbornly refuse to let the Israelites leave his country.

The Passover

12 Some time later the LORD said to Moses and Aaron:
²This month[h] is to be the first month of the year for you. ³Tell the people of Israel that on the tenth day of this month the head of each family must choose a lamb or a young goat for his family to eat. ⁴⁻⁵If any family is too small to eat the whole animal, they must share it with their next-door neighbors. Choose either a sheep or a goat, but it must be a one-year-old male that has nothing wrong with it. And it must be large enough for everyone to have some of the meat.

⁶Each family must take care of its animal until the evening of the fourteenth day of the month, when the animals are to be killed. ⁷Some of the blood must be put on the two doorposts and above the door of each house where the animals are to be eaten. ⁸That night the animals are to be roasted and eaten, together with bitter herbs and thin bread made without yeast. ⁹Don't eat the meat raw or boiled. The entire animal, including its head, legs, and insides, must be roasted. ¹⁰Eat what you want that night, and the next morning burn

whatever is left. ¹¹When you eat the meal, be dressed and ready to travel. Have your sandals on, carry your walking stick in your hand, and eat quickly. This is the Passover Festival in honor of me, your LORD.

¹²That same night I will pass through Egypt and kill the first-born son in every family and the first-born male of all animals. I am the LORD, and I will punish the gods of Egypt. ¹³The blood on the houses will show me where you live, and when I see the blood, I will pass over you. Then you won't be bothered by the terrible disasters I will bring on Egypt.

¹⁴Remember this day and celebrate it each year as a festival in my honor. ¹⁵For seven days you must eat bread made without yeast. And on the first of these seven days, you must remove all yeast from your homes. If you eat anything made with yeast during this festival, you will no longer be part of Israel. ¹⁶Meet together for worship on the first and seventh days of the festival. The only work you are allowed to do on either of these two days is that of preparing the bread.

¹⁷Celebrate this Festival of Thin Bread as a way of remembering the day that I brought your families and tribes out of Egypt. And do this each year. ¹⁸Begin on the evening of the fourteenth day of the first month by eating bread made without yeast. Then continue this celebration until the evening of the twenty-first day. ¹⁹During these seven days no yeast is allowed in anyone's home, whether they are native Israelites or not. If you are caught eating anything made with yeast, you will no longer be part of Israel. ²⁰Stay away from yeast, no matter where you live. No one is allowed to eat anything made with yeast!

²¹Moses called the leaders of Israel together and said:

Each family is to pick out a sheep and kill it for Passover. ²²Make a brush from a few small branches of a hyssop

---

[h]12.2 *This month*: Abib (also called Nisan), the first month of the Hebrew calendar, from about mid-March to mid-April.

plant and dip the brush in the bowl that has the blood of the animal in it. Then brush some of the blood above the door and on the posts at each side of the door of your house. After this, everyone is to stay inside.

²³During that night the LORD will go through the country of Egypt and kill the first-born son in every Egyptian family. He will see where you have put the blood, and he will not come into your house. His angel that brings death will pass over and not kill your first-born sons.

I know Jesus is true, because he's the only one constant in life. He never changes; neither does the Bible.

CINDY MORGAN

²⁴⁻²⁵After you have entered the country promised to you by the LORD, you and your children must continue to celebrate Passover each year. ²⁶Your children will ask you, "What are we celebrating?" ²⁷And you will answer, "The Passover animal is killed to honor the LORD. We do these things because on that night long ago the LORD passed over the homes of our people in Egypt. He killed the first-born sons of the Egyptians, but he saved our children from death."

After Moses finished speaking, the people of Israel knelt down and worshiped the LORD. ²⁸Then they left and did what Moses and Aaron had told them to do.

Death for the First-Born Sons

²⁹At midnight the LORD killed the first-born son of every Egyptian family, from the son of the king*ⁱ* to the son of every prisoner in jail. He also killed the first-born male of every animal that belonged to the Egyptians.

³⁰That night the king, his officials, and everyone else in Egypt got up and started

crying bitterly. In every Egyptian home, someone was dead.

The People of Israel Escape from Egypt

³¹During the night the king*ⁱ* sent for Moses and Aaron and told them, "Get your people out of my country and leave us alone! Go and worship the LORD, as you have asked. ³²Take your sheep, goats, and cattle, and get out. But ask your God to be kind to me."

³³The Egyptians did everything they could to get the Israelites to leave their country fast. They said, "Please hurry and leave. If you don't, we will all be dead." ³⁴So the Israelites quickly made some bread dough and put it in pans. But they did not mix any yeast in the dough to make it rise. They wrapped cloth around the pans and carried them on their shoulders.

³⁵The Israelites had already done what Moses had told them to do. They had gone to their Egyptian neighbors and asked for gold and silver and for clothes. ³⁶The LORD had made the Egyptians friendly toward the people of Israel, and they gave them whatever they asked for. In this way they carried away the wealth of the Egyptians when they left Egypt.

³⁷The Israelites walked from the city of Rameses to the city of Succoth. There were about six hundred thousand of them, not counting women and children. ³⁸Many other people went with them as well, and there were also a lot of sheep, goats, and cattle. ³⁹They left Egypt in such a hurry that they did not have time to prepare any food except the bread dough made without yeast. So they baked it and made thin bread.

⁴⁰⁻⁴¹The LORD's people left Egypt exactly four hundred thirty years after they had arrived. ⁴²On that night the LORD kept watch for them, and on this same night each year Israel will always keep watch in honor of the LORD.

Instructions for Passover

⁴³The LORD gave Moses and Aaron the following instructions for celebrating Passover:

No one except Israelites may eat the Passover meal.

ⁱ12.29,31 *the king:* See the note at 1.11.

44Your slaves may eat the meal if they have been circumcised, 45but no foreigners who work for you are allowed to have any.

46The entire meal must be eaten inside, and no one may leave the house during the celebration.

No bones of the Passover lamb may be broken. 47And all Israelites must take part in the meal.

48If anyone who isn't an Israelite wants to celebrate Passover with you, every man and boy in that family must first be circumcised. Then they may join in the meal, just like native Israelites. No uncircumcised man or boy may eat the Passover meal! 49This law applies both to native Israelites and to those foreigners who live among you.

50The Israelites obeyed everything the LORD had commanded Moses and Aaron to tell them. 51And on that same day the LORD brought Israel's families and tribes out of Egypt.

Dedication of the First-Born

13 The LORD said to Moses, 2"Dedicate to me the first-born son of every family and the first-born males of your flocks and herds. These belong to me."

The Festival of Thin Bread

3-4Moses said to the people:

Remember this day in the month of Abib.j It is the day when the LORD's mighty power rescued you from Egypt, where you were slaves. Do not eat anything made with yeast. 5The LORD promised your ancestors that he would bring you into the land of the Canaanites, Hittites, Amorites, Hivites, and Jebusites. It is a land rich with milk and honey.

Each year during the month of Abib, celebrate these events in the following way: 6For seven days you are to eat bread made without yeast, and on the seventh day you are to celebrate a festival in honor of the LORD. 7During those seven days, you must not eat anything made with yeast or even have yeast anywhere near your homes. 8Then on the seventh day you must explain to your children that you do

this because the LORD brought you out of Egypt.

9This celebration will be like wearing a sign on your hand or on your forehead, because then you will pass on to others the teaching of the LORD, whose mighty power brought you out of Egypt. 10Celebrate this festival each year at the same time.

11The LORD will give you the land of the Canaanites, just as he promised you and your ancestors. 12From then on, you must give him every first-born son from your families and every first-born male from your animals, because these belong to him. 13You can save the life of a first-born donkeyk by sacrificing a lamb; if you don't, you must break the donkey's neck. You must save every first-born son.

14In the future your children will ask what this ceremony means. Explain it to them by saying, "The LORD used his mighty power to rescue us from slavery in Egypt. 15The kingl stubbornly refused to set us free, so the LORD killed the first-born male of every animal and the first-born son of every Egyptian family. This is why we sacrifice to the LORD every first-born male of every animal and save every first-born son."

16This ceremony will serve the same purpose as a sign on your hand or on your forehead to tell how the LORD's mighty power rescued us from Egypt.

The LORD Leads His People

17After the kingl had finally let the people go, the LORD did not lead them through Philistine territory,m though that was the shortest way. God had said, "If they are attacked, they may decide to return to Egypt."

---

j13.3,4 *Abib:* Or Nisan, the first month of the Hebrew calendar, from about mid-March to mid-April.
k13.13 *donkey:* This was the only "unclean" animal that had to be saved; the first-born of all "clean" animals (sheep, goats, cattle) had to be sacrificed. Donkeys were important because they were the basic means of transportation. l13.15 *The king:* See the note at 1.11. l13.17 *the king:* See the note at 1.11. m13.17 *Philistine territory:* The shortest land route from the Nile Delta to Canaan; it was the southern section of the major road that led to Megiddo and then on to Mesopotamia by way of Asia Minor.

[18]So he led them around through the desert and toward the Red Sea.[n]

The Israelites left Egypt, prepared for battle.

[19]Moses had them take along the bones of Joseph, whose dying words had been, "God will come to your rescue, and when he does, be sure to take along my bones."

[20]The people of Israel left Succoth and camped at Etham at the border of Egypt near the desert. [21-22]During the day the LORD went ahead of his people in a thick cloud, and during the night he went ahead of them in a flaming fire. That way the LORD could lead them at all times, whether day or night.

The Israelites Cross the Red Sea

14 At Etham the LORD said to Moses: [2]Tell the people of Israel to turn back and camp across from Pi-Hahiroth near Baal-Zephon, between Migdol and the Red Sea.[o] [3]The king[p] will think they were afraid to cross the desert and that they are wandering around, trying to find another way to leave the country. [4]I will make the king stubborn again, and he will try to catch you. Then I will destroy him and his army. People everywhere will praise me for my victory, and the Egyptians will know that I really am the LORD.

The Israelites obeyed the LORD and camped where he told them.

[5]When the king of Egypt heard that the Israelites had finally left, he and his officials changed their minds and said, "Look what we have done! We let them get away, and they will no longer be our slaves."

[6]The king got his war chariot and army ready. [7]He commanded his officers in charge of his six hundred best chariots and all his other chariots to start after the Israelites. [8]The LORD made the king so stubborn that he went after them, even though the Israelites proudly[q] went on their way. [9]But the king's horses and chariots and soldiers caught up with them while they were camping by the Red Sea near Pi-Hahiroth and Baal-Zephon.

[10]When the Israelites saw the king coming with his army, they were frightened and begged the LORD for help. [11]They also complained to Moses, "Wasn't there enough room in Egypt to bury us? Is that why you brought us out here to die in the desert? Why did you bring us out of Egypt anyway? [12]While we were there, didn't we tell you to leave us alone? We had rather be slaves in Egypt than die in this desert!"

[13]But Moses answered, "Don't be afraid! Be brave, and you will see the LORD save you today. These Egyptians will never bother you again. [14]The LORD will fight for you, and you won't have to do a thing."

[15]The LORD said to Moses, "Why do you keep calling out to me for help? Tell the Israelites to move forward. [16]Then hold your walking stick over the sea. The water will open up and make a road where they can walk through on dry ground. [17]I will make the Egyptians so stubborn that they will go after you. Then I will be praised because of what happens to the king and his chariots and cavalry. [18]The Egyptians will know for sure that I am the LORD."

[19]All this time God's angel had gone ahead of Israel's army, but now he moved behind them. A large cloud had also gone ahead of them, [20]but now it moved between the Egyptians and the Israelites. The cloud gave light to the Israelites, but made it dark for the Egyptians, and during the night they could not come any closer.

[21]Moses stretched his arm over the sea, and the LORD sent a strong east wind that blew all night until there was dry land where the water had been. The sea opened up, [22]and the Israelites walked through on dry land with a wall of water on each side.

[23]The Egyptian chariots and cavalry went after them. [24]But before daylight the LORD looked down at the Egyptian army from the fiery cloud and made them panic. [25]Their chariot wheels got stuck,[r] and it was hard for them to move. So the Egyptians said to one another, "Let's leave these people alone! The LORD is on their side and is fighting against us."

---

[n]13.18 *Red Sea*: Hebrew *yam suph* "Sea of Reeds," one of the marshes or fresh water lakes, near the eastern part of the Nile Delta. This identification is based on Exodus 13.17—14.9, which lists the towns on the route of the Israelites before crossing the sea. In the Greek translation of the Scriptures made about 200 B.C., the "Sea of Reeds" was named "Red Sea." [o]14.2 *Red Sea*: Hebrew *hayyam* "the Sea," understood as *yam suph*, "Sea of Reeds" (see also the note at 13.18). [p]14.3 *The king*: See the note at 1.11. [q]14.8 *proudly*: Or "victoriously." [r]14.25 *stuck*: The Samaritan Hebrew text and two ancient translations; Hebrew "came off."

²⁶The LORD told Moses, "Stretch your arm toward the sea—the water will cover the Egyptians and their cavalry and chariots." ²⁷Moses stretched out his arm, and at daybreak the water rushed toward the Egyptians. They tried to run away, but the LORD drowned them in the sea. ²⁸The water came and covered the chariots, the cavalry, and the whole Egyptian army that had followed the Israelites into the sea. Not one of them was left alive. ²⁹But the sea had made a wall of water on each side of the Israelites; so they walked through on dry land.

³⁰On that day, when the Israelites saw the bodies of the Egyptians washed up on the shore, they knew that the LORD had saved them. ³¹Because of the mighty power he had used against the Egyptians, the Israelites worshiped him and trusted him and his servant Moses.

The Song of Moses

15 Moses and the Israelites sang this song in praise of the LORD:

I sing praises to the LORD
for his great victory!
He has thrown the horses
and their riders
into the sea.
²The LORD is my strength,
the reason for my song,
because he has saved me.
I praise and honor the LORD—
he is my God and the God
of my ancestors.
³The LORD is his name,
and he is a warrior!
⁴He threw the chariots and army
of Egypt's king$
into the Red Sea,ᵗ
and he drowned the best
of the king's officers.
⁵They sank to the bottom
just like stones.

⁶With the tremendous force
of your right arm, our LORD,
you crushed your enemies.
⁷What a great victory was yours,
as you defeated everyone
who opposed you.
Your fiery anger wiped them out,
as though they were straw.
⁸You were so furious

that the sea piled up
like a wall,
and the ocean depths
curdled like cheese.

⁹Your enemies boasted
that they would
pursue and capture us,
divide up our possessions,
treat us as they wished,
then take out their swords
and kill us right there.
¹⁰But when you got furious,
they sank like lead,
swallowed by ocean waves.

¹¹Our LORD, no other gods
compare with you—
Majestic and holy!
Fearsome and glorious!
Miracle worker!
¹²When you signaled
with your right hand,
your enemies were swallowed
deep into the earth.

¹³The people you rescued
were led by your powerful love
to your holy place.
¹⁴Nations learned of this
and trembled—
Philistines shook with horror.
¹⁵The leaders of Edom and of Moab
were terrified.
Everyone in Canaan fainted,
¹⁶ struck down by fear.
Our LORD, your powerful arm
kept them still as a rock
until the people you rescued
for your very own
had marched by.

¹⁷You will let your people settle
on your chosen mountain,
where you built your home
and your temple.
¹⁸Our LORD, you will rule forever!

The Song of Miriam

¹⁹The LORD covered the royal Egyptian cavalry and chariots with the sea, after the Israelites had walked safely through on dry

---

$15.4 *Egypt's king*: See the note at 1.11. ᵗ15.4 *Red Sea*: See the note at 13.18.

ground. [20]Miriam the sister of Aaron was a prophet. So she took her tambourine and led the other women out to play their tambourines and to dance. [21]Then she sang to them:

"Sing praises to the LORD
    for his great victory!
He has thrown the horses
    and their riders into the sea."

Bitter Water at Marah

[22]After the Israelites left the Red Sea,[t] Moses led them through the Shur Desert for three days, before finding water. [23]They did find water at Marah, but it was bitter, which is how that place got its name.[u] [24]The people complained and said, "Moses, what are we going to drink?"

[25]Moses asked the LORD for help, and the LORD told him to throw a piece of wood into the water. Moses did so, and the water became fit to drink.

At Marah the LORD tested his people and also gave them some laws and teachings. [26]Then he said, "I am the LORD your God, and I cure your diseases. If you obey me by doing right and by following my laws and teachings, I won't punish you with the diseases I sent on the Egyptians."

[27]Later the Israelites came to Elim, where there were twelve springs and seventy palm trees. So they camped there.

The LORD Sends Food from Heaven

16 On the fifteenth day of the second month after the Israelites had escaped from Egypt, they left Elim and started through the western edge of the Sinai Desert[v] in the direction of Mount Sinai. [2]There in the desert they started complaining to Moses and Aaron, [3]"We wish the LORD had killed us in Egypt. When we lived there, we could at least sit down and eat all the bread and meat we wanted. But you have brought us out here into this desert, where we are going to starve."

[4]The LORD said to Moses, "I will send bread[w] down from heaven like rain. Each day the people can go out and gather only enough for that day. That's how I will see if they obey me. [5]But on the sixth day of each week they must gather and cook twice as much."

[6]Moses and Aaron told the people, "This evening you will know that the LORD was the one who rescued you from Egypt. [7]And in the morning you will see his glorious power, because he has heard your complaints against him. Why should you grumble to us? Who are we?"

[8]Then Moses continued, "You will know

---

[t]15.22 *Red Sea:* See the note at 13.18.
[u]15.23 *Marah . . . name:* In Hebrew "Marah" means "bitter." [v]16.1 *the western edge of the Sinai Desert:* Hebrew "the Sin Desert." [w]16.4 *bread:* This was something like a thin wafer, and it was called "manna," which in Hebrew means, "What is it?"

SingleLife—How can God use me as a single woman? *(Exodus 15.19-21)*

Remember, he used Miriam as a prophet and worship leader.

If you're single, chances are you've felt—or may currently be feeling—pressure from friends and family to marry. They might tell you the pressure is "for your own good." Or that you would be happier, more fulfilled, and a better servant of God if you had a husband.

Miriam, the sister of Moses and Aaron, shows that a single woman can act not only as God's servant, but as his minister. After God saved the Israelites from the Egyptian army that was chasing them, Miriam led them in inspired praise of God.

Miriam is spoken of as a prophet, which means she had a special gift for using words in God's service. As a servant of God, she praised him for his greatness. As a worship leader, she led the Israelites in singing and dancing before God's presence. Miriam also served as a role model for all the other women who followed her in praise.

Miriam used her prophetic gift as a single woman, even in a culture where single women were expected (and often required) to marry. Like Miriam, you can discover and use your gifts in God's service—and lead others to do the same. **(See also Judges 6,7; 2 Samuel 20.14-22; Malachi 3.16-18.)**

Words To Remember: *Miriam the sister of Aaron was a prophet.*—Exodus 15.20

it is the LORD when he gives you meat each evening and more than enough bread each morning. He is really the one you are complaining about, not us—we are nobodies—but the LORD has heard your complaints."

> *God can be trusted to provide what we need at the time we need it. That assurance will keep us looking for his options—and will help us live joyfully on whatever he provides.*
>
> SANDY LARSEN

⁹Moses turned to Aaron and said, "Bring the people together, because the LORD has heard their complaints."

¹⁰Aaron was speaking to them, when everyone looked out toward the desert and saw the bright glory of the LORD in a cloud. ¹¹The LORD said to Moses, ¹²"I have heard my people complain. Now tell them that each evening they will have meat and each morning they will have more than enough bread. Then they will know that I am the LORD their God."

¹³That evening a lot of quails came and landed everywhere in the camp, and the next morning dew covered the ground. ¹⁴After the dew had gone, the desert was covered with thin flakes that looked like frost. ¹⁵The people had never seen anything like this, and they started asking each other, "What is it?"ˣ

Moses answered, "This is the bread that the LORD has given you to eat. ¹⁶And he orders you to gather about two quarts for each person in your family—that should be more than enough."

¹⁷They did as they were told. Some gathered more and some gathered less, ¹⁸according to their needs, and none was left over.

¹⁹Moses told them not to keep any overnight. ²⁰Some of them disobeyed, but the next morning what they kept was stinking and full of worms, and Moses was angry.

²¹Each morning everyone gathered as much as they needed, and in the heat of the day the rest melted. ²²However, on the sixth day of the week, everyone gathered enough to have four quarts, instead of two. When the leaders reported this to Moses, ²³he told them that the LORD had said, "Tomorrow is the Sabbath, a sacred day of rest in honor of me. So gather all you want to bake or boil, and make sure you save enough for tomorrow."

²⁴The people obeyed, and the next morning the food smelled fine and had no worms. ²⁵"You may eat the food," Moses said. "Today is the Sabbath in honor of the LORD, and there won't be any of this food on the ground today. ²⁶You will find it there for the first six days of the week, but not on the Sabbath."

²⁷A few of the Israelites did go out to look for some, but there was none. ²⁸Then the LORD said, "Moses, how long will you people keep disobeying my laws and teachings? ²⁹Remember that I was the one who gave you the Sabbath. That's why on the sixth day I provide enough bread for two days. Everyone is to stay home and rest on the Sabbath." ³⁰And so they rested on the Sabbath.

³¹The Israelites called the bread manna.ʸ It was white like coriander seed and delicious as wafers made with honey. ³²Moses told the people that the LORD had said, "Store up two quarts of this manna, because I want future generations to see the food I gave you during the time you were in the desert after I rescued you from Egypt."

³³Then Moses told Aaron, "Put some manna in a jar and store it in the place of worship for future generations to see."

³⁴Aaron followed the LORD's instructions and put the manna in front of the sacred chest for safekeeping. ³⁵-³⁶The Israelites ate manna for forty years, before they came to the border of Canaan that was a settled land.ᶻ

The LORD Gives Water from a Rock
(Numbers 20.1-13)

17 The Israelites left the desert and moved from one place to another each time the LORD ordered them

---

ˣ**16.15** *What is it:* See the note at 16.4. ʸ**16.31** *manna:* See the note at 16.4. ᶻ**16.35,36** *land:* The Hebrew text adds, "An omer is one tenth of an ephah." In the CEV "omer" is usually translated "two quarts."

to. Once they camped at Rephidim,*a* but there was no water for them to drink.

²The people started complaining to Moses, "Give us some water!"

Moses replied, "Why are you complaining to me and trying to put the LORD to the test?"

³But the people were thirsty and kept on complaining, "Moses, did you bring us out of Egypt just to let us and our families and our animals die of thirst?"

⁴Then Moses prayed to the LORD, "What am I going to do with these people? They are about to stone me to death!"

⁵The LORD answered, "Take some of the leaders with you and go ahead of the rest of the people. Also take along the walking stick you used to strike the Nile River, ⁶and when you get to the rock at Mount Sinai,*b* I will be there with you. Strike the rock with the stick, and water will pour out for the people to drink." Moses did this while the leaders watched.

⁷The people had complained and tested the LORD by asking, "Is the LORD really with us?" So Moses named that place Massah, which means "testing" and Meribah, which means "complaining."

Israel Defeats the Amalekites

⁸When the Israelites were at Rephidim, they were attacked by the Amalekites. ⁹So Moses told Joshua, "Have some men ready to attack the Amalekites tomorrow. I will stand on a hilltop, holding this walking stick that has the power of God."

¹⁰Joshua led the attack as Moses had commanded, while Moses, Aaron, and Hur stood on the hilltop. ¹¹The Israelites outfought the Amalekites as long as Moses held up his arms, but they started losing whenever he had to lower them. ¹²Finally, Moses was so tired that Aaron and Hur got a rock for him to sit on. Then they stood beside him and supported his arms in the same position until sunset. ¹³That's how Joshua defeated the Amalekites.

¹⁴Afterwards, the LORD said to Moses, "Write an account of this victory and read it to Joshua. I want the Amalekites to be forgotten forever."

¹⁵Moses built an altar and named it "The LORD Gives Me Victory." ¹⁶Then Moses explained, "This is because I depended on the

LORD.*c* But in future generations, the LORD will have to fight the Amalekites again."

Jethro Visits Moses

18 Jethro was the priest of Midian and the father-in-law of Moses. And he heard what the LORD God had done for Moses and his people, after rescuing them from Egypt.

²⁻⁴In the meantime, Moses had sent his wife Zipporah and her two sons to stay with Jethro, and he had welcomed them. Moses was still a foreigner in Midian when his first son was born, and so Moses said, "I'll name him Gershom."*d*

When his second son was born, Moses said, "I'll name him Eliezer,*e* because the God my father worshiped has saved me from the king of Egypt."*f*

⁵⁻⁶While Israel was camped in the desert near Mount Sinai,*g* Jethro sent Moses this message: "I am coming to visit you, and I am bringing your wife and two sons."

⁷When they arrived, Moses went out and bowed down in front of Jethro, then kissed him. After they had greeted each other, they went into the tent, ⁸where Moses told him everything the LORD had done to protect Israel against the Egyptians and their king. He also told him how the LORD had helped them in all of their troubles.

⁹Jethro was so pleased to hear this good news about what the LORD had done, ¹⁰that he shouted, "Praise the LORD! He rescued you and the Israelites from the Egyptians and their king. ¹¹Now I know that the LORD is the greatest God, because he has rescued Israel from their arrogant enemies." ¹²Jethro offered sacrifices to God. Then Aaron and Israel's leaders came to eat with Jethro there at the place of worship.

Judges Are Appointed
(Deuteronomy 1.9-18)

¹³The next morning Moses sat down at the place where he decided legal cases for

---

*a*17.1 *Rephidim:* The last stopping place for the Israelites between the Red Sea and Mount Sinai; the exact location is not known. *b*17.6 *Sinai:* The Hebrew text has "Horeb," another name for Sinai. *c*17.16 *This . . . LORD:* One possible meaning for the difficult Hebrew text. *d*18.2-4 *Gershom:* See the note at 2.22. *e*18.2-4 *Eliezer:* In Hebrew "Eliezer" means "God has helped me." *f*18.2-4 *saved . . . Egypt:* See 2.1-15. *g*18.5,6 *Mount Sinai:* Hebrew "the mountain of God."

the people, and everyone crowded around him until evening. ¹⁴Jethro saw how much Moses had to do for the people, and he asked, "Why are you the only judge? Why do you let these people crowd around you from morning till evening?"

¹⁵Moses answered, "Because they come here to find out what God wants them to do. ¹⁶They bring their complaints to me, and I make decisions on the basis of God's laws."

¹⁷Jethro replied:

That isn't the best way to do it. ¹⁸You and the people who come to you will soon be worn out. The job is too much for one person; you can't do it alone. ¹⁹God will help you if you follow my advice. You should be the one to speak to God for the people, ²⁰and you should teach them God's laws and show them what they must do to live right.

²¹You will need to appoint some competent leaders who respect God and are trustworthy and honest. Then put them over groups of ten, fifty, a hundred, and a thousand. ²²These judges can handle the ordinary cases and bring the more difficult ones to you. Having them to share the load will make your work easier. ²³This is the way God wants it done. You won't be under nearly as much stress, and everyone else will return home feeling satisfied.

²⁴Moses followed Jethro's advice. ²⁵He chose some competent leaders from every tribe in Israel and put them over groups of ten, fifty, a hundred, and a thousand. ²⁶They served as judges, deciding the easy cases themselves, but bringing the more difficult ones to Moses.

²⁷After Moses and his father-in-law Jethro had said good-by to each other, Jethro returned home.

At Mount Sinai

19 ¹⁻²The Israelites left Rephidim.ʰ Then two months after leaving Egypt, they arrived at the desert near Mount Sinai, where they set up camp at the foot of the mountain.

³Moses went up the mountain to meet with the LORD God, who told him to say to the people:

⁴You saw what I did in Egypt, and you know how I brought you here to

---

ʰ**19.1,2** *Rephidim:* See the note at 17.1.

WORK—How can I be a good supervisor? *(Exodus 18)*

Pick capable people and give them clearly defined responsibilities.

Moses was exhausted. God had made him the leader of his people, and he was trying to do the job right. So he spent all day long, every day, hearing the people's problems and telling them God's will.

Moses faced the problem of any capable leader—too much work and not enough time! But Moses found a solution with the help of his father-in-law. He selected competent leaders—people who could be trusted, who loved God, and who weren't out to feather their own nests. Moses taught them all the laws God had given. He made each leader responsible for a small group of people and told them to come to him with any difficult decision.

Moses set a pattern all leaders should follow. First, pick subordinates you can trust—workers with a strong moral code who won't use their position for personal gain. Then teach them well. Set a good example for them, and give them all the information they need to carry out their jobs. Make sure your workers have limited, reasonable, clearly defined spheres of responsibility. Then give them the freedom to do their jobs. Only intrude into their space when they ask for help with a difficult challenge. (See also 1 Kings 3.5-15; 4.29-34; Ezra 5.1—6.12; Jeremiah 32.26-44; John 21.15-25; 2 Timothy 1.1-7; Philemon 8-16; Philemon 15-25.)

Words To Remember: *Having them to share the load will make your work easier.—Exodus 18.22*

me, just as a mighty eagle carries its young. ⁵Now if you will faithfully obey me, you will be my very own people. The whole world is mine, ⁶but you will be my holy nation and serve me as priests.

Moses, that is what you must tell the Israelites.

⁷After Moses went back, he reported to the leaders what the LORD had said, ⁸and they promised, "We will do everything the LORD has commanded." So Moses told the LORD about this.

⁹The LORD said to Moses, "I will come to you in a thick cloud and let the people hear me speak to you. Then they will always trust you." Again Moses reported to the people what the LORD had told him.

¹⁰Once more the LORD spoke to Moses:

Go back and tell the people that today and tomorrow they must get themselves ready to meet me. They must wash their clothes ¹¹and be ready by the day after tomorrow, when I will come down to Mount Sinai, where all of them can see me.

¹²Warn the people that they are forbidden to touch any part of the mountain. Anyone who does will be put to death, ¹³either with stones or arrows, and no one must touch the body of a person killed in this way. Even an animal that touches this mountain must be put to death. You may go up the mountain only after a signal is given on the trumpet.

¹⁴After Moses went down the mountain, he gave orders for the people to wash their clothes and make themselves acceptable to worship God. ¹⁵He told them to be ready in three days and not to have sex in the meantime.

The LORD Comes to Mount Sinai

¹⁶On the morning of the third day there was thunder and lightning. A thick cloud covered the mountain, a loud trumpet blast was heard, and everyone in camp trembled with fear. ¹⁷Moses led them out of the camp to meet God, and they stood at the foot of the mountain.

¹⁸Mount Sinai was covered with smoke because the LORD had come down in a flaming fire. Smoke poured out of the mountain just like a furnace, and the whole

mountain shook. ¹⁹The trumpet blew louder and louder. Moses spoke, and God answered him with thunder.

²⁰The LORD came down to the top of Mount Sinai and told Moses to meet him there. ²¹Then he said, "Moses, go and warn the people not to cross the boundary that you set at the foot of the mountain. They must not cross it to come and look at me, because if they do, many of them will die. ²²Only the priests may come near me, and they must obey strict rules before I let them. If they don't, they will be punished."

²³Moses replied, "The people cannot come up the mountain. You warned us to stay away because it is holy."

²⁴Then the LORD told Moses, "Go down and bring Aaron back here with you. But the priests and people must not try to push their way through, or I will rush at them like a flood!"

²⁵After Moses had gone back down, he told the people what the LORD had said.

The Ten Commandments

(Deuteronomy 5.1-21)

20 God said to the people of Israel: ²I am the LORD your God, the one who brought you out of Egypt where you were slaves.

³Do not worship any god except me.

⁴Do not make idols that look like anything in the sky or on earth or in the ocean under the earth. ⁵Don't bow down and worship idols. I am the LORD your God, and I demand all your love. If you reject me, I will punish your families for three or four generations. ⁶But if you love me and obey my laws, I will be kind to your families for thousands of generations.

⁷Do not misuse my name.ⁱ I am the LORD your God, and I will punish anyone who misuses my name.

⁸Remember that the Sabbath Day belongs to me. ⁹You have six days when you can do your work, ¹⁰but the seventh day of each week belongs to me, your God. No one is to work on

---

ⁱ**20.7** *misuse my name:* Probably includes breaking promises, telling lies after swearing to tell the truth, using the LORD's name as a curse word or a magic formula, and trying to control the LORD by using his name.

that day—not you, your children, your slaves, your animals, or the foreigners who live in your towns. ¹¹In six days I made the sky, the earth, the oceans, and everything in them, but on the seventh day I rested. That's why I made the Sabbath a special day that belongs to me.

¹²Respect your father and your mother, and you will live a long time in the land I am giving you.

¹³Do not murder.

¹⁴Be faithful in marriage.

¹⁵Do not steal.

¹⁶Do not tell lies about others.

¹⁷Do not want anything that belongs to someone else. Don't want anyone's house, wife or husband, slaves, oxen, donkeys or anything else.

The People Are Afraid
(Deuteronomy 5.23-33)

¹⁸The people trembled with fear when they heard the thunder and the trumpet and saw the lightning and the smoke coming from the mountain. They stood a long way off ¹⁹and said to Moses, "If you speak to us, we will listen. But don't let God speak to us, or we will die!"

²⁰"Don't be afraid!" Moses replied. "God has come only to test you, so that by obeying him you won't sin." ²¹But when Moses went near the thick cloud where God was, the people stayed a long way off.

Idols and Altars

²²The LORD told Moses to say to the people of Israel:

With your own eyes, you saw me speak to you from heaven. ²³So you must never make idols of silver or gold to worship in place of me.ʲ

²⁴Build an altar out of earth, and offer on it your sacrificesᵏ of sheep, goats, and cattle. Wherever I choose to be worshiped, I will come down to bless you. ²⁵If you ever build an altar for me out of stones, do not use any tools to chisel the stones, because that would make the altar unfit. ²⁶And don't build an altar that requires steps; you might expose yourself when you climb up.

Hebrew Slaves
(Deuteronomy 15.12-18)

21 The LORD gave Moses the following laws for his people:

²If you buy a Hebrew slave,

ʲ**20.23** *in place of me:* Or "together with me."
ᵏ**20.24** *sacrifices:* The Hebrew text mentions two types of sacrifices: Sacrifices to please the LORD (traditionally called "whole burnt offerings") and sacrifices to ask the LORD's blessing (traditionally called "peace offerings").

SpiritualLife—What does God expect of me? *(Exodus 20.1-17)*

Follow God's rules for loving him and others.
Did you ever try to have a relationship with someone who wouldn't tell you what he wanted? It's frustrating! You can try your hardest, but you're never sure you're doing exactly the right thing. And sometimes you might offend him—when you're just trying to be nice!

With God, we never have that problem. We don't have to guess what he wants. God tells us exactly what he expects us to do to have a healthy relationship with him. The Ten Commandments lay down the ground rules for our relationship with God—and with each other.

The first four commandments deal with how we treat God: He is to be the most important person in our life. We are not to worship anyone else, and we are to respect his name and his special day. This sets us apart from all other people on earth!

The last six commandments tell us how to behave toward each other. God's people must not lie, murder, commit adultery, steal, disrespect their parents, or covet each other's possessions. God commands us to follow these rules so we can demonstrate how much we love him by the way we act toward other people. (See also Judges 5.1-11; Jeremiah 1.4-19; Micah 6.6-8; Romans 8.1-17; 1 Corinthians 6.12-20.)

Words To Remember: *I am the LORD your God, and I demand all your love.*
—Exodus 20.5

he must remain your slave for six years. But in the seventh year you must set him free, without cost to him. [3]If he was single at the time you bought him, he alone must be set free. But if he was married at the time, both he and his wife must be given their freedom. [4]If you give him a wife, and they have children, only the man himself must be set free; his wife and children remain the property of his owner.

[5]But suppose the slave loves his wife and children so much that he won't leave without them. [6]Then he must stand beside either the door or the doorpost at the place of worship,[l] while his owner punches a small hole through one of his ears with a sharp metal rod. This makes him a slave for life.

[7]A young woman who was sold by her father doesn't gain her freedom in the same way that a man does. [8]If she doesn't please the man who bought her to be his wife, he must let her be bought back.[m] He cannot sell her to foreigners; this would break the contract he made with her. [9]If he selects her as a wife for his son, he must treat her as his own daughter.

[10]If the man later marries another woman, he must continue to provide food and clothing for the one he bought and to treat her as a wife. [11]If he fails to do any of these things, she must be given her freedom without cost.

Murder and Other Violent Crimes

The LORD said:

[12]Death is the punishment for murder. [13]But if you did not intend to kill someone, and I, the LORD, let it happen anyway, you may run for safety to a place that I have set aside. [14]If you plan in advance to murder someone, there's no escape, not even by holding on to my altar.[n] You will be dragged off and killed.

[15]Death is the punishment for attacking your father or mother.

[16]Death is the punishment for kidnapping. If you sell the person you kidnapped, or if you are caught with that person, the penalty is death.

[17]Death is the punishment for cursing your father or mother.

[18]Suppose two of you are arguing, and you hit the other with either a rock or your fist, without causing a fatal injury. If the victim has to stay in bed, [19]and later has to use a stick when walking outside, you must pay for the loss of time and do what you can to help until the injury is completely healed. That's your only responsibility.

[20]Death is the punishment for beating to death any of your slaves. [21]However, if the slave lives a few days after the beating, you are not to be punished. After all, you have already lost the services of that slave who was your property.

When I sought the Lord and looked outward to the needs of others, my own desires were met, too.

LIZ CURTIS HIGGS

[22]Suppose a pregnant woman suffers a miscarriage[o] as the result of an injury caused by someone who is fighting. If she isn't badly hurt, the one who injured her must pay whatever fine her husband demands and the judges approve. [23]But if she is seriously injured, the payment will be life for life, [24]eye for eye, tooth for tooth, hand for hand, foot for foot, [25]burn for burn, cut for cut, and bruise for bruise.

[26]If you hit one of your slaves and cause the loss of an eye, the slave must be set free. [27]The same law applies if you knock out a slave's tooth—the slave goes free.

[28]A bull that kills someone with its horns must be killed and its meat destroyed, but the owner of the bull isn't responsible for the death.

[29]Suppose you own a bull that has been in the habit of attacking people, but you have refused to keep it fenced in. If that bull kills someone, both you and the bull must

---

[l]**21.6** *at the place of worship*: The Hebrew text has "in the presence of God," which probably refers to the place where God was worshiped.   [m]**21.8** *bought back*: Either by her family or by another Israelite who wanted to marry her.   [n]**21.14** *altar*: As a rule, anyone who ran to the altar was safe from the death penalty, until proven guilty.   [o]**21.22** *suffers a miscarriage*: Or "gives birth before her time."

be put to death by stoning. [30]However, you may save your own life by paying whatever fine is demanded. [31]This same law applies if the bull gores someone's son or daughter. [32]If the bull kills a slave, you must pay the slave owner thirty pieces of silver for the loss of the slave, and the bull must be killed by stoning.

[33]Suppose someone's ox or donkey is killed by falling into an open pit that you dug or left uncovered on your property. [34]You must pay for the dead animal, and it becomes yours.

[35]If your bull kills someone else's, yours must be sold. Then the money from your bull and the meat from the dead bull must be divided equally between you and the other owner.

[36]If you refuse to fence in a bull that is known to attack others, you must pay for any animal it kills, but the dead animal will belong to you.

Property Laws

The LORD said:

22 If you steal an ox and slaughter or sell it, you must replace it with five oxen; if you steal a sheep and slaughter it or sell it, you must replace it with four sheep. [2-4]But if you cannot afford to replace the animals, you must be sold as a slave to pay for what you have stolen. If you steal an ox, donkey, or sheep, and are caught with it still alive, you must pay the owner double.

If you happen to kill a burglar who breaks into your home after dark, you are not guilty. But if you kill someone who breaks in during the day, you are guilty of murder.

[5]If you allow any of your animals to stray from your property and graze[p] in someone else's field or vineyard, you must repay the damage from the best part of your own harvest of grapes and grain.

[6]If you carelessly let a fire spread from your property to someone else's, you must pay the owner for any crops or fields destroyed by the fire.

[7]Suppose a neighbor asks you to keep some silver or other valuables, and they are stolen from your house. If the thief is caught, the thief must repay double. [8]But if

the thief isn't caught, some judges[q] will decide if you are the guilty one.

[9]Suppose two people claim to own the same ox or donkey or sheep or piece of clothing. Then the judges[r] must decide the case, and the guilty person will pay the owner double.

[10]Suppose a neighbor who is going to be away asks you to keep a donkey or an ox or a sheep or some other animal, and it dies or gets injured or is stolen while no one is looking. [11]If you swear with me as your witness that you did not harm the animal, you do not have to replace it. Your word is enough. [12]But if the animal was stolen while in your care, you must replace it. [13]If the animal was attacked and killed by a wild animal, and you can show the remains of the dead animal to its owner, you do not have to replace it.

[14]Suppose you borrow an animal from a neighbor, and it gets injured or dies while the neighbor isn't around. Then you must replace it. [15]But if something happens to the animal while the owner is present, you do not have to replace it. If you had leased the animal, the money you paid the owner will cover any harm done to it.

Laws for Everyday Life

The LORD said:

[16]Suppose a young woman has never been married and isn't engaged. If a man talks her into having sex, he must pay the bride price[s] and marry her. [17]But if her father refuses to let her marry the man, the bride price must still be paid.

[18]Death is the punishment for witchcraft.

[19]Death is the punishment for having sex with an animal.

[20]Death is the punishment for offering sacrifices to any god except me.

[21]Do not mistreat or abuse foreigners who live among you. Remember, you were foreigners in Egypt.

[22]Do not mistreat widows or orphans.

---

p**22.5** *graze:* Or "eat everything."   q**22.8** *some judges:* Or "I."   r**22.9** *the judges:* Or "I."   s**22.16** *bride price:* It was the custom for a man to pay his wife's family a bride price before the actual wedding ceremony took place.

[23]If you do, they will beg for my help, and I will come to their rescue. [24]In fact, I will get so angry that I will kill your men and make widows of their wives and orphans of their children.

[25]Don't charge interest when you lend money to any of my people who are in need. [26]Before sunset you must return any coat taken as security for a loan, [27]because that is the only cover the poor have when they sleep at night. I am a merciful God, and when they call out to me, I will come to help them.

[28]Don't speak evil of me[t] or of the ruler of your people.

[29]Don't fail to give me the offerings of grain and wine that belong to me.[u]

Dedicate to me your first-born sons [30]and the first-born of your cattle and sheep. Let the animals stay with their mothers for seven days, then on the eighth day give them to me, your God.

[31]You are my chosen people, so don't eat the meat of any of your livestock that was killed by a wild animal. Instead, feed the meat to dogs.

Equal Justice for All

The LORD said:

23 Don't spread harmful rumors or help a criminal by giving false evidence.

[2]Always tell the truth in court, even if everyone else is[v] dishonest and stands in the way of justice. [3]And don't favor the poor, simply because they are poor.

[4]If you find an ox or a donkey that has wandered off, take it back where it belongs, even if the owner is your enemy.

[5]If a donkey is overloaded and falls down, you must do what you can to help, even if it belongs to someone who doesn't like you.[w]

[6]Make sure that the poor are given equal justice in court. [7]Don't bring false charges against anyone or sentence an innocent person to death. I won't forgive you if you do.

[8]Don't accept bribes. Judges are blinded and justice is twisted by bribes.

[9]Don't mistreat foreigners. You were foreigners in Egypt, and you know what it is like.

Laws for the Sabbath

The LORD said:

[10]Plant and harvest your crops for six years, [11]but let the land rest during the seventh year. The poor are to eat what they want from your fields, vineyards, and olive trees during that year, and when they have all they want from your fields, leave the rest for wild animals.

[12]Work the first six days of the week, but rest and relax on the seventh day. This law is not only for you, but for your oxen, donkeys, and slaves, as well as for any foreigners among you.

[13]Make certain that you obey everything I have said. Don't pray to other gods or even mention their names.

Three Annual Festivals

(Exodus 34.18-26; Deuteronomy 16.1-17)

The LORD said:

[14]Celebrate three festivals each year in my honor.

[15]Celebrate the Festival of Thin Bread by eating bread made without yeast, just as I have commanded.[x] Do this at the proper time during the month of Abib,[y] because it is the month when you left Egypt. And make certain that everyone brings the proper offerings.

[16]Celebrate the Harvest Festival[z] each spring when you start harvesting your wheat, and celebrate the Festival of Shelters[a] each autumn when you pick your fruit.

[17]Your men must come to these three festivals each year to worship me.

[18]Do not offer bread made with yeast when you sacrifice an animal to me. And make sure that the fat of the animal is burned that same day.

---

[t]**22.28** *me*: Or "your judges."   [u]**22.29** *Don't fail . . . me*: One possible meaning for the difficult Hebrew text.
[v]**23.2** *everyone else is*: Or "the authorities are."
[w]**23.5** *you*: One possible meaning for the difficult Hebrew text of verse 5.   [x]**23.15** *as I have commanded*: See 12.14-20.   [y]**23.15** *Abib*: See the note at 12.2.
[z]**23.16** *Harvest Festival*: Traditionally called the "Festival of Weeks" and known in New Testament times as "Pentecost."   [a]**23.16** *Festival of Shelters*: The Hebrew text has "Festival of Ingathering" (so also in 34.22), which was the final harvesting of crops and fruits before the autumn rains began. But the usual name was "Festival of Shelters."

¹⁹Each year bring the best part of your first harvest to the place of worship.

Don't boil a young goat in its mother's milk.

A Promise and a Warning

The LORD said:

²⁰I am sending an angel to protect you and to lead you into the land I have ready for you. ²¹Carefully obey everything the angel says, because I am giving him complete authority, and he won't tolerate rebellion. ²²If you faithfully obey him, I will be a fierce enemy of your enemies. ²³My angel will lead you into the land of the Amorites, Hittites, Perizzites, Canaanites, Hivites, and Jebusites, and I will wipe them out. ²⁴Don't worship their gods or follow their customs. Instead, destroy their idols and shatter their stone images.

²⁵Worship only me, the LORD your God! I will bless you with plenty of food and water and keep you strong. ²⁶Your women will give birth to healthy children, and everyone will live a long life.

²⁷I will terrify those nations and make your enemies so confused that they will run from you. ²⁸I will make the Hivites, Canaanites, and Hittites panic as you approach. ²⁹But I won't do all this in the first year, because the land would become poor, and wild animals would be everywhere. ³⁰Instead, I will force out your enemies little by little and give your nation time to grow strong enough to take over the land.

³¹I will see that your borders reach from the Red Sea[b] to the Euphrates River and from the Mediterranean Sea to the desert. I will let you defeat the people who live there, and you will force them out of the land. ³²But you must not make any agreements with them or with their gods. ³³Don't let them stay in your land. They will trap you into sinning against me and worshiping their gods.

The People Agree To Obey God

24 The LORD said to Moses, "Come up to me on this mountain. Bring along Aaron, as well as his two sons Nadab and Abihu, and seventy of

---

[b]23.31 *Red Sea:* Hebrew *yam suph,* here referring to the Gulf of Aqaba, since the term is extended to include the northeastern arm of the Red Sea (see also the note at 13.18).

WORK—How can I balance the competing demands of home and work?
(Exodus 23.10-13)

Work during the week—but leave weekends for worship and recreation.
Phones, beepers, fax machines, e-mail—these days, work follows us home! There's always one more project, one more phone call, one more important contact to make. But work isn't all there is to life. We all try to balance our work with the rest of life: exercise, housework, grocery shopping, laundry. And those with families have an even more complicated juggling act, combining diapers, Little League, homework, and special nights out with all those other responsibilities.

Whew! With all that to do, how can you possibly justify taking a day off to picnic with the kids, soak in a bubble bath, or have a date with your husband?

It's helpful to know that both work and "free time" are important to God. In his laws, God affirmed the importance of work to the Israelites. As a matter of fact, he told them to work six days every week! But that's not all. One of God's sacred decrees was that his people take every seventh day off to rest, celebrate, and relax. As a matter of fact, rest is so important to God that he even ordered the Israelites to give their animals and fields time off. Our culture may push us to work until we drop, but that isn't God's command. In Exodus 23, he reminds us that work, worship, and family recreation are all important to him—and that we must not neglect them. (See also Deuteronomy 6.1-9; 2 Samuel 1; Matthew 14.22,23.)

Words To Remember: *Work the first six days of the week, but rest and relax on the seventh day.*—Exodus 23.12

Israel's leaders. They must worship me at a distance, ²but you are to come near. Don't let anyone else come up."

³Moses gave the LORD's instructions to the people, and they promised, "We will do everything the LORD has commanded!" ⁴Then Moses wrote down what the LORD had said.

The next morning Moses got up early. He built an altar at the foot of the mountain and set up a large stone for each of the twelve tribes of Israel. ⁵He also sent some young men to burn offerings and to sacrifice bulls as special offerings[c] to the LORD. ⁶Moses put half of the blood from the animals into bowls and sprinkled the rest on the altar. ⁷Then he read aloud the LORD's commands and promises, and the people shouted, "We will obey the LORD and do everything he has commanded!"

⁸Moses took the blood from the bowls and sprinkled it on the people. Next, he told them, "With this blood the LORD makes his agreement with you."

⁹Moses and Aaron, together with Nadab and Abihu and the seventy leaders, went up the mountain ¹⁰and saw the God of Israel. Under his feet was something that looked like a pavement made out of sapphire,[d] and it was as bright as the sky.

¹¹Even though these leaders of Israel saw God, he did not punish them. So they ate and drank.

Moses on Mount Sinai

¹²The LORD said to Moses, "Come up on the mountain and stay here for a while. I will give you the two flat stones on which I have written the laws that my people must obey." ¹³Moses and Joshua his assistant got ready, then Moses started up the mountain to meet with God.

¹⁴Moses had told the leaders, "Wait here until we come back. Aaron and Hur will be with you, and they can settle any arguments while we are away."

¹⁵When Moses went up on Mount Sinai, a cloud covered it, ¹⁶and the bright glory of the LORD came down and stayed there. The cloud covered the mountain for six days, and on the seventh day the LORD told Moses to come into the cloud. ¹⁷⁻¹⁸Moses did so and stayed there forty days and nights. To the people, the LORD's glory looked like a blazing fire on top of the mountain.

The Sacred Tent
(Exodus 35.4-9)

25 The LORD said to Moses:
²Tell everyone in Israel who wants to give gifts that they must bring them to you. ³Here is a list of what you are to collect: Gold, silver, and bronze; ⁴blue, purple, and red wool; fine linen; goat hair; ⁵tanned ram skins; fine leather; acacia wood; ⁶olive oil for the lamp; sweet-smelling spices to mix with the oil for dedicating the tent and ordaining the priests; ⁷and onyx[e] stones for the sacred vest and the breastpiece. ⁸I also want them to build a special place where I can live among my people. ⁹Make it and its furnishings exactly like the pattern I will show you.

The Sacred Chest
(Exodus 37.1-9)

The LORD said to Moses:

¹⁰Tell the people to build a chest of acacia wood forty-five inches long, twenty-seven inches wide, and twenty-seven inches high. ¹¹Cover it inside and out with pure gold and put a gold edging around the lid. ¹²Make four gold rings and fasten one of them to each of the four legs of the chest. ¹³Make two poles of acacia wood. Cover them with gold ¹⁴and put them through the rings, so the chest can be carried by the poles. ¹⁵Don't ever remove the poles from the rings. ¹⁶When I give you the Ten Commandments written on two flat stones, put them inside the chest.

¹⁷Cover the lid of the chest with pure gold. ¹⁸⁻¹⁹Then hammer out two winged creatures of pure gold and fasten them to the lid at the ends of the chest. ²⁰The creatures must face each other with their wings spread over the chest. ²¹Inside it place the two flat stones with the Ten Commandments and put the gold lid on top of the chest. ²²I will meet you there[f] between the two creatures and tell you what my people must do and what they must not do.

---

[c]**24.5** *special offerings:* Often translated "peace offerings," which were to make peace between God and his people, who ate certain parts of the sacrificed animal.
[d]**24.10** *sapphire:* A precious stone, blue in color.
[e]**25.7** *onyx:* A precious stone with bands of different colors. [f]**25.22** *I will meet you there:* It was believed that God had his earthly throne on the lid of the sacred chest.

The Table for the Sacred Bread
(Exodus 37.10-16)

The LORD said:

23Make a table of acacia wood thirty-six inches long, eighteen inches wide, and twenty-seven inches high. **24-25**Cover it with pure gold and put a gold edging around it with a border three inches wide.g **26**Make four gold rings and attach one to each of the legs **27-28**near the edging. The poles for carrying the table are to be placed through these rings and are to be made of acacia wood covered with gold. **29-30**The table is to be kept in the holy place, and the sacred loaves of bread must always be put on it. All bowls, plates, jars, and cups for wine offerings are to be made of pure gold and set on this table.

> *As a child of God,*
> *we have the awesome*
> *privilege of holding an*
> *audience with our*
> *Almighty Creator every time*
> *we worship him corporately—*
> *or individually.*
>
> JOSIE CRAMER

The Lampstand
(Exodus 37.17-24)

The LORD said:

31Make a lampstand of pure gold. The whole lampstand, including its decorative flowers, must be made from a single piece of hammered gold **32**with three branches on each of its two sides. **33**There are to be three decorative almond blossoms on each branch **34**and four on the stem. **35**There must also be a blossom where each pair of branches comes out from the stem. **36**The lampstand, including its branches and decorative flowers, must be made from a single piece of hammered pure gold. **37**The lamp on the top and those at the end of each of its six branches must be made so as to shine toward the front of the lampstand. **38**The tongs and trays for taking care of the lamps are to be made of pure gold. **39**The lampstand and its equipment will require seventy-five pounds of pure gold, **40**and they must be made according to the pattern I showed you on the mountain.

Curtains and Coverings for the Sacred Tent
(Exodus 36.8-19)

The LORD said to Moses:

26 Furnish the sacred tent with curtains made from ten pieces of the finest linen. They must be woven with blue, purple, and red wool and embroidered with figures of winged creatures. **2**Make each piece fourteen yards long and two yards wide **3**and sew them together into two curtains with five sections each. **4-6**Put fifty loops of blue cloth along one of the wider sides of each curtain, then fasten the two curtains at the loops with fifty gold hooks.

7-8 As the material for the tent, use goat hair to weave eleven sections fifteen yards by two yards each. **9**Sew five of the sections together to make one panel. Then sew the other six together to make a second panel, and fold the sixth section double over the front of the tent. **10**Put fifty loops along one of the wider sides of each panel **11**and fasten the two panels at the loops with fifty bronze hooks. **12-13**The panel of goat hair will be a yard longer than the tent itself, so fold half a yard of the material behind the tent and on each side as a protective covering. **14**Make two more coverings—one with ram skins dyed red and the other with fine leather.

The Framework for the Sacred Tent
(Exodus 36.20-34)

The LORD said:

15Build a framework of acacia wood for the walls of the sacred tent. **16**Each frame is to be fifteen feet high and twenty-seven inches wide **17**with two wooden pegs near the bottom. **18-21**Place two silver stands under each frame with sockets for the pegs, so the frames can be joined together. Twenty of

g**25.24,25** *a gold edging . . . wide:* Or "a gold edging around it three inches wide."

these frames are to be used along the south side and twenty more along the north. [22]For the back wall along the west side use six frames [23-24]with two more at the southwest and northwest corners. Make certain that these corner frames are joined from top to bottom. [25]Altogether, this back wall will have eight frames with two silver stands under each one.

[26-27]Make five crossbars for each of the wooden frames, [28]with the center crossbar running the full length of the wall. [29]Cover the frames and the crossbars with gold and attach gold rings to the frames to run the crossbars through. [30]Then set up the tent in the way I showed you on the mountain.

The Curtain inside the Sacred Tent
(Exodus 36.35-38)

The LORD said:

[31-33]Make a curtain to separate the holy place from the most holy place. Use fine linen woven with blue, purple, and red wool, and embroidered with figures of winged creatures. Cover four acacia wood posts with gold and set them each on a silver stand. Then fasten gold hooks to the posts and hang the curtain there.

[34]Inside the most holy place, you must put the sacred chest that has the place of mercy on its lid.[h] [35]Outside the curtain put the table for the sacred bread on the right side and the gold lampstand on the left.

[36]For the entrance to the tent, use a piece of fine linen woven with blue, purple, and red wool and embroidered with fancy needlework. [37]Cover five acacia wood posts with gold and set them each on a bronze stand. Then put gold hooks on the posts and hang the curtain there.

The Altar for Offering Sacrifices
(Exodus 38.1-7)

The LORD said to Moses:

27 Use acacia wood to build an altar seven and a half feet square and four and a half feet high, [2]and make each of the four top corners stick up like the horn of a bull. Then cover the whole altar with bronze, including the four horns. [3]All the equipment for the altar must also be made of bronze—the pans for the hot ashes, the shovels, the sprinkling bowls, the meat forks, and the fire pans. [4-5]Midway up the altar build a ledge around it, and cover the bottom half of the altar with a decorative bronze grating. Then attach a bronze ring beneath the ledge at the four corners of the altar. [6-7]Cover two acacia wood poles with bronze and put them through the rings for carrying the altar. [8]Construct the altar in the shape of an open box, just as you were shown on the mountain.

The Courtyard around the Sacred Tent
(Exodus 38.9-20)

The LORD said:

[9-15]Surround the sacred tent with a courtyard one hundred fifty feet long on the south and north and seventy-five feet wide on the east and west. Use twenty bronze posts on bronze stands for the south and north and ten for the west. Then hang a curtain of fine linen on the posts along each of these three sides by using silver hooks and rods.

Place three bronze posts on each side of the entrance at the east and hang a curtain seven and a half yards wide on each set of posts. [16]Use four more of these posts for the entrance way, then hang on them an embroidered curtain of fine linen ten yards long and woven with blue, purple, and red wool.

[17-18]The curtains that surround the courtyard must be two and a half yards high and are to be hung from the bronze posts with silver hooks and rods. [19]The rest of the equipment for the sacred tent must be made of bronze, including the pegs for the tent and for the curtain surrounding the courtyard.

The Oil for the Lamp in the Holy Place
(Leviticus 24.1-4)

The LORD said to Moses:

[20]Command the people of Israel to supply you with the purest olive oil. Do this so the lamp will keep burning [21]in front of the curtain that separates the holy place from the most holy place, where the sacred chest is kept. Aaron and his sons are responsible

---

[h]**26.34** *place of mercy on its lid:* It was believed that God had his earthly throne on the lid of the sacred chest, and from this place he showed mercy to his people.

for keeping the lamp burning every night in the sacred tent. The Israelites must always obey this command.

The Clothes for the High Priest
(Exodus 39.1-7)

The LORD said to Moses:

28 Send for your brother Aaron and his sons Nadab, Abihu, Eleazar, and Ithamar. They are the ones I have chosen from Israel to serve as my priests. [2]Make Aaron some beautiful clothes that are worthy of a high priest. [3]Aaron is to be dedicated as my high priest, and his clothes must be made only by persons who possess skills that I have given them. [4]Here are the items that need to be made: a breastpiece, a priestly vest, a robe, an embroidered shirt, a turban, and a sash. These sacred clothes are to be made for your brother Aaron and his sons who will be my priests. [5]Only gold and fine linen, woven with blue, purple, and red wool, are to be used for making these clothes.

The Vest for the High Priest
(Exodus 39.2-7)

The LORD said:

[6-8]The entire priestly vest must be made of fine linen skillfully woven with blue, purple, and red wool, and decorated with gold. It is to have two shoulder straps to support it and a sash that fastens around the waist. [9-12]Put two onyx[i] stones in gold settings, then attach one to each of the shoulder straps. On one of these stones engrave the names of Israel's first six sons in the order of their birth. And do the same with his remaining six sons on the other stone. In this way Aaron will always carry the names of the tribes of Israel when he enters the holy place, and I will never forget my people. [13-14]Attach two gold settings to the shoulder straps and fasten them with two braided chains of pure gold.

The Breastpiece for the High Priest
(Exodus 39.8-21)

The LORD said:

[15]From the same costly material make a breastpiece for the high priest to use in learning what I want my people to do. [16]It is

to be nine inches square and folded double [17]with four rows of three precious stones: In the first row put a carnelian, a chrysolite, and an emerald; [18]in the second row a turquoise, a sapphire, and a diamond; [19]in the third row a jacinth, an agate, and an amethyst; [20]and in the fourth row a beryl, an onyx, and a jasper.[j] Mount the stones in delicate gold settings [21]and engrave on each of them the name of one of the twelve tribes of Israel.

[22-25]Attach two gold rings to the upper front corners of the breastpiece and fasten them with two braided gold chains to gold settings on the shoulder straps. [26]Attach two other gold rings to the lower inside corners next to the vest [27]and two more near the bottom of the shoulder straps right above the sash. [28]Then take a blue cord and tie the two lower rings on the breastpiece to those on the vest. This will keep the breastpiece in place.

[29]In this way Aaron will have the names of the twelve tribes of Israel written on his heart each time he enters the holy place, and I will never forget my people. [30]He must also wear on his breastpiece the two small objects[k] that he uses to receive answers from me.

The Other High-Priestly Clothes
(Exodus 39.22-26, 30, 31)

The LORD said:

[31]Under his vest Aaron must wear a robe of blue wool [32]with an opening in the center for his head. Be sure to bind the material around the collar to keep it from raveling. [33-34]Along the hem of the robe weave pomegranates[l] of blue, purple, and red wool with a gold bell between each of them. [35]If Aaron wears these clothes when he enters the holy

---

[i]**28.9-12** *onyx:* See the note at 25.7. [j]**28.20** *jasper:* The stones mentioned in verses 17-20 are of different colors: *carnelian* is deep red or reddish white; *chrysolite* is olive green; *emerald* is green; *turquoise* is blue or blue green; *sapphire* is blue; *diamond* is colorless or white; *jacinth* is reddish orange; *agate* has circles of brown and white; *amethyst* is deep purple; *beryl* is green or bluish green; *onyx* has bands of different colors; and *jasper* is usually green or clear. [k]**28.30** *two small objects:* The Hebrew text has "urim and thummim," which may have been made of wood, stone, or metal, and were used in some way to receive answers from God. [l]**28.33,34** *pomegranates:* A bright red fruit that looks like an apple.

place as my high priest, the sound of the bells will be heard, and his life will not be in danger.

³⁶On a narrow strip of pure gold engrave the words: "Dedicated to the LORD." ³⁷Fasten it to the front of Aaron's turban with a blue cord, ³⁸so he can wear it on his forehead. This will show that he will take on himself the guilt for any sins the people of Israel commit in offering their gifts to me, and I will forgive them.

³⁹Make Aaron's robe and turban of fine linen and decorate his sash with fancy needlework.

The Clothes for the Other Priests
(Exodus 39.27-29)

⁴⁰Since Aaron's sons are priests, they should also look dignified. So make robes, sashes, and special caps for them. ⁴¹Then dress Aaron and his sons in these clothes, pour olive oil on their heads, and ordain them as my priests.

⁴²Make linen shorts for them that reach from the waist down to the thigh, so they won't expose themselves. ⁴³Whenever they enter the sacred tent or serve at the altar or enter the holy place, they must wear these shorts, or else they will be guilty and die. This same rule applies to any of their descendants who serve as priests.

Instructions for Ordaining Priests
(Leviticus 8.1-36)

The LORD said to Moses:

29 When you ordain one of Aaron's sons as my priest, choose a young bull and two rams that have nothing wrong with them. ²Then from your finest flour make three batches of dough without yeast. Shape some of it into larger loaves, some into smaller loaves mixed with olive oil, and the rest into thin wafers brushed with oil. ³Put all of this bread in a basket and bring it when you come to sacrifice the three animals to me.

⁴Bring Aaron and his sons to the entrance of the sacred tent and have them wash themselves. ⁵Dress Aaron in the priestly shirt, the robe that goes under the sacred vest, the vest itself, the breastpiece, and the sash. ⁶Put on his turban with its narrow strip of engraved gold ⁷and then ordain him by pouring olive oil on his head.

⁸Next, dress Aaron's sons in their special shirts ⁹and caps and their sashes,ᵐ then ordain them, because they and their descendants will always be priests.

¹⁰Lead the bull to the entrance of the sacred tent, where Aaron and his sons will lay their hands on its head. ¹¹Kill the bull near my altar in front of the tent. ¹²Use a finger to smear some of its blood on each of the four corners of the altar and pour out the rest of the blood on the ground next to the altar. ¹³Then take the fat from the animal's insides, as well as the lower part of the liver and the two kidneys with their fat, and send them up in smoke on the altar. ¹⁴But the meat, the skin, and the food still in the bull's stomach must be burned outside the camp as an offering to ask forgiveness for the sins of the priests.ⁿ

¹⁵Bring one of the rams to Aaron and his sons and have them lay their hands on its head. ¹⁶Kill the ram and splatter its blood against all four sides of the altar. ¹⁷Cut up the ram, wash its insides and legs, and lay all of its parts on the altar, including the head. ¹⁸Then make sure that the whole animal goes up in smoke with a smell that pleases me.

¹⁹Bring the other ram to Aaron and his sons and have them lay their hands on its head. ²⁰Kill the ram and place some of its blood on Aaron's right ear lobe, his right thumb, and the big toe of his right foot. Do the same for each of his sons and splatter the rest of the blood against the four sides of the altar. ²¹Then take some of the blood from the altar, mix it with the oil used for ordination, and sprinkle it on Aaron and his clothes, and also on his sons and their clothes. This will show that they and their clothes have been dedicated to me.

²²This ram is part of the ordination service. So remove its right hind leg,ᵒ its fat tail, the fat on its insides, as well as the lower part of the liver and the two kidneys with their fat. ²³Take one loaf of each kind of breadᵖ from the basket, ²⁴and put this bread,

---

ᵐ**29.9** *their sashes:* One ancient translation; Hebrew "the sashes of Aaron and his sons." ⁿ**29.14** *for the sins of the priests:* When a sacrifice for the forgiveness of sins was made for someone other than priests, the part that was not burned on the altar could be eaten by the priests (see Leviticus 5.13; 6.26). ᵒ**29.22** *right hind leg:* This was usually given to the officiating priest (see Leviticus 7.33). ᵖ**29.23** *each kind of bread:* See verses 2, 3.

together with the meat, into the hands of Aaron and his sons. Then they will lift it all up[q] to show that it is dedicated to me. ²⁵After this, the meat and bread are to be placed on the altar and sent up in smoke with a smell that pleases me.

²⁶You may eat the choice ribs from this second ram, but you must first lift them up[q] to show that this meat is dedicated to me.

²⁷⁻²⁸In the future, when anyone from Israel offers the ribs and a hind leg of a ram either to ordain a priest or to ask for my blessing, the meat belongs to me, but it may be eaten by the priests. This law will never change.

²⁹⁻³⁰After Aaron's death, his priestly clothes are to be handed down to each descendant who succeeds him as high priest, and these clothes must be worn during the seven-day ceremony of ordination.

³¹Boil the meat of the ordination ram in a sacred place, ³²then have Aaron and his sons eat it together with the three kinds of bread[r] at the entrance to the sacred tent. ³³At their ordination, a ceremony of forgiveness was performed for them with this sacred food, and only they have the right to eat it. ³⁴If any of the sacred food is left until morning, it must be burned up.

³⁵Repeat this ordination ceremony for Aaron and his sons seven days in a row, just as I have instructed you. ³⁶Each day you must offer a bull as a sacrifice for sin and as a way of purifying the altar. In addition, you must smear the altar with olive oil to make it completely holy. ³⁷Do this for seven days, and the altar will become so holy that anyone who touches it will become holy.

Daily Sacrifices
(Leviticus 6.8-13; Numbers 28.1-8)

The LORD said:

³⁸Each day you must sacrifice two lambs a year old, ³⁹one in the morning and one in the evening. ⁴⁰⁻⁴¹With each lamb offer two pounds of your finest flour mixed with a quart of pure olive oil, and also pour out a quart of wine as an offering. The smell of this sacrifice on the fires of the altar will be pleasing to me. ⁴²⁻⁴³You and your descendants must always offer this sacrifice on the altar at the entrance to the sacred tent.

People of Israel, I will meet and speak with you there, and my shining glory will

make the place holy. ⁴⁴Because of who I am, the tent will become sacred, and Aaron and his sons will become worthy to serve as my priests. ⁴⁵I will live among you as your God, ⁴⁶and you will know that I am the LORD your God, the one who rescued you from Egypt, so that I could live among you.

The Altar for Burning Incense
(Exodus 37.25-28)

The LORD said to Moses:

30 Build an altar of acacia wood where you can burn incense. ²Make it eighteen inches square and thirty-six inches high, and make each of its four corners stick up like the horn of a bull. ³Cover it with pure gold and put a gold edging around it. ⁴Then below the edging on opposite sides attach two gold rings through which you can put the poles for carrying the altar. ⁵These poles are also to be made of acacia wood covered with gold.

⁶Put the altar in front of the inside curtain of the sacred tent. The chest with the place of mercy[s] is kept behind that curtain, and I will talk with you there. ⁷⁻⁸From now on, when Aaron tends the lamp each morning and evening, he must burn sweet-smelling incense to me on the altar. ⁹Burn only the proper incense on the altar and never use it for grain sacrifices or animal sacrifices or drink offerings. ¹⁰Once a year Aaron must purify the altar by smearing on its four corners[t] the blood of an animal sacrificed for sin, and this practice must always be followed. The altar is sacred because it is dedicated to me.

The Money for the Sacred Tent

¹¹The LORD said to Moses:
¹²Find out how many grown men there are in Israel and require each of them to pay me to keep him safe from danger while you are counting them. ¹³⁻¹⁵Each man over nineteen, whether rich or poor, must pay me the same amount of money, weighed according to the official standards. ¹⁶This money is to be used for the upkeep of the sacred tent,

q29.24 lift it all up: Or "wave it all." q29.26 lift them up: Or "wave them." r29.32 three kinds of bread: See verses 2, 3. s30.6 place of mercy: See the note at 26.34. t30.10 four corners: See 27.2; 30.2.

and because of it, I will never forget my people.

The Large Bronze Bowl
(Exodus 38.8)

¹⁷The LORD said to Moses:

¹⁸⁻²¹Make a large bronze bowl and a bronze stand for it. Then put them between the altar for sacrifice and the sacred tent, so the priests can wash their hands and feet before entering the tent or offering a sacrifice on the altar. Each priest in every generation must wash himself in this way, or else he will die right there.

The Oil for Dedication and Ordination
(Exodus 37.29)

²²The LORD said to Moses:

²³⁻²⁵Mix a gallon of olive oil with the following costly spices: twelve pounds of myrrh, six pounds of cinnamon, six pounds of cane, and twelve pounds of cassia. Measure these according to the official standards. Then use this sacred mixture ²⁶for dedicating the tent and chest, ²⁷the table with its equipment, the lampstand with its equipment, the incense altar with all its utensils, ²⁸the altar for sacrifices, and the large bowl with its stand. ²⁹By dedicating them in this way, you will make them so holy that anyone who even touches them will become holy.

³⁰When you ordain Aaron and his sons as my priests, sprinkle them with some of this oil, ³¹and say to the people of Israel: "This oil must always be used in the ordination service of a priest. It is holy because it is dedicated to the LORD. ³²So treat it as holy! Don't ever use it for everyday purposes or mix any for yourselves. ³³If you do, you will no longer belong to the LORD's people."

The Sweet-Smelling Incense

³⁴⁻³⁵Mix equal amounts of the costly spices stacte, onycha, galbanum, and pure frankincense, then add salt to make the mixture pure and holy. ³⁶Pound some of it into powder and sprinkle it in front of the sacred chest, where I meet with you. Be sure to treat this incense as something very holy. ³⁷It is truly holy because it is dedicated to me, so don't ever make any for yourselves. ³⁸If you ever make any of it to use as perfume, you will no longer belong to my people.

The LORD Chooses Bezalel and Oholiab
(Exodus 35.30—36.1)

31 The LORD said to Moses: ²I have chosen Bezalel[u] from the Judah tribe to make the sacred tent and its furnishings. ³⁻⁵Not only have I filled him with my Spirit, but I have given him wisdom and made him a skilled craftsman who can create objects of art with gold, silver, bronze, stone, and wood. ⁶I have appointed Oholiab[v] from the tribe of Dan to work with him, and I have also given skills to those who will help them make everything exactly as I have commanded you: ⁷⁻¹¹the sacred tent with its furnishings, the sacred chest with its place of mercy, the table with all that is on it, the lamp with its equipment, the incense altar, the altar for sacrifices with its equipment, the bronze bowl with its stand, the beautiful priestly clothes for Aaron and his sons, the oil for dedication and ordination services, and the sweet-smelling incense for the holy place.

God gives us fifty-two Sabbaths, or seven-and-a-half weeks, of vacation time each year— time during which we are to do no work.
KAREN BURTON MAINS

Laws for the Sabbath

¹²⁻¹³Moses told the Israelites that the LORD had said:

The Sabbath belongs to me. Now I command you and your descendants to always obey the laws of the Sabbath. By doing this, you will know that I have chosen you as my own. ¹⁴⁻¹⁵Keep the Sabbath holy. You have six days to do your work, but the

---

[u]**31.2** *Bezalel*: Hebrew "Bezalel, son of Uri and grandson of Hur." [v]**31.6** *Oholiab*: Hebrew "Oholiab son of Ahisamach."

Sabbath is mine, and it must remain a day of rest. If you work on the Sabbath, you will no longer be part of my people, and you will be put to death.

¹⁶Every generation of Israelites must respect the Sabbath. ¹⁷This day will always serve as a reminder, both to me and to the Israelites, that I made the heavens and the earth in six days, then on the seventh day I rested and relaxed.

¹⁸When God had finished speaking to Moses on Mount Sinai, he gave him the two flat stones on which he had written all of his laws with his own hand.

The People Make an Idol To Worship
(Deuteronomy 9.6-29)

32 After the people saw that Moses had been on the mountain for a long time, they went to Aaron and said, "Make us an image of a god who will lead and protect us. Moses brought us out of Egypt, but nobody knows what has happened to him."

²Aaron told them, "Bring me the gold earrings that your wives and sons and daughters are wearing." ³Everybody took off their earrings and brought them to Aaron,

⁴then he melted them and made an idol in the shape of a young bull.

All the people said to one another, "This is the god who brought us out of Egypt!"

⁵When Aaron saw what was happening, he built an altar in front of the idol and said, "Tomorrow we will celebrate in honor of the LORD." ⁶The people got up early the next morning and killed some animals to be used for sacrifices and others to be eaten. Then everyone ate and drank so much that they began to carry on like wild people.

⁷The LORD said to Moses:

Hurry back down! Those people you led out of Egypt are acting like fools. ⁸They have already stopped obeying me and have made themselves an idol in the shape of a young bull. They have bowed down to it, offered sacrifices, and said that it is the god who brought them out of Egypt. ⁹Moses, I have seen how stubborn these people are, ¹⁰and I'm angry enough to destroy them, so don't try to stop me. But I will make your descendants into a great nation.

¹¹Moses tried to get the LORD God to change his mind:

Our LORD, you used your mighty

MARRIAGE—What does a healthy, successful marriage look like?
(Exodus 32.11-14)

It forgives.

Have you ever reached the point where you think, *Okay, that's enough! My husband blew it once too often. This time, I don't have to forgive him!*

That's exactly how God felt about his people, Israel. He'd brought them out of slavery. He'd parted the sea in front of them. He'd conquered their enemies. He'd given them food and water in the desert. They had promised to obey him forever. Then, as soon as Moses got out of their sight, the people forgot all about God and built an idol.

God said, "That's enough!" He threatened to destroy the people for their disobedience. But when Moses interceded for them, God displayed the unconditional love required by his covenant relationship with Israel. He forgave the unforgivable and gave them another chance because he had promised to make them his people forever.

Like God and Israel, you're in a covenant relationship with your husband—a relationship where you are sworn to be faithful and to love him unconditionally. God demonstrates to us that the center of a covenant relationship is the willingness to forgive over and over and over again—even when the other person doesn't deserve it. If we follow God's example in this, our own covenant relationship can weather many storms. (See also Genesis 2.18-23; Song of Songs 8.5-7; Hosea 14.4-8; Acts 18; Hebrews 13.4.)

Words To Remember: *So even though the LORD had threatened to destroy the people, he changed his mind and let them live.—Exodus 32.14*

power to bring these people out of Egypt. Now don't become angry and destroy them. ¹²If you do, the Egyptians will say that you brought your people out here into the mountains just to get rid of them. Please don't be angry with your people. Don't destroy them!

¹³Remember the solemn promise you made to Abraham, Isaac, and Jacob. You promised that someday they would have as many descendants as there are stars in the sky and that you would give them land.

¹⁴So even though the LORD had threatened to destroy the people, he changed his mind and let them live.

¹⁵⁻¹⁶Moses went back down the mountain with the two flat stones on which God had written all of his laws with his own hand, and he had used both sides of the stones.

¹⁷When Joshua heard the noisy shouts of the people, he said to Moses, "A battle must be going on down in the camp."

¹⁸But Moses replied, "It doesn't sound like they are shouting because they have won or lost a battle. They are singing wildly!"

¹⁹As Moses got closer to the camp, he saw the idol, and he also saw the people dancing around. This made him so angry that he threw down the stones and broke them to pieces at the foot of the mountain. ²⁰He melted the idol the people had made, and he ground it into powder. He scattered it in their water and made them drink it. ²¹Moses asked Aaron, "What did these people do to harm you? Why did you make them sin in this terrible way?"

²²Aaron answered:

Don't be angry with me. You know as well as I do that they are determined to do evil. ²³They even told me, "That man Moses led us out of Egypt, but now we don't know what has happened to him. Make us a god to lead us." ²⁴Then I asked them to bring me their gold earrings. They took them off and gave them to me. I threw the gold into a fire, and out came this bull.

²⁵Moses knew that the people were out of control and that it was Aaron's fault. And now they had made fools of themselves in front of their enemies. ²⁶So Moses stood at the gate of the camp and shouted, "Everyone who is on the LORD's side come over here!"

Then the men of the Levi tribe gathered around Moses, ²⁷and he said to them, "The LORD God of Israel commands you to strap on your swords and go through the camp, killing your relatives, your friends, and your neighbors."

²⁸The men of the Levi tribe followed his orders, and that day they killed about three thousand men. ²⁹Moses said to them, "You obeyed the LORD and did what was right, and so you will serve as his priests for the people of Israel. It was hard for you to kill your own sons and brothers, but the LORD has blessed you and made you his priests today."

³⁰The next day Moses told the people, "This is a terrible thing you have done. But I will go back to the LORD to see if I can do something to keep this sin from being held against you."

³¹Moses returned to the LORD and said, "The people have committed a terrible sin. They have made a gold idol to be their god. ³²But I beg you to forgive them. If you don't, please wipe my name out of your book."ʷ

³³The LORD replied, "I will wipe out of my book the name of everyone who has sinned against me. ³⁴Now take my people to the place I told you about, and my angel will lead you. But when the time comes, I will punish them for this sin."

³⁵So the LORD punished the people of Israel with a terrible disease for talking Aaron into making the gold idol.

The LORD Tells Israel To Leave Mount Sinai

33 The LORD said to Moses:
You led the people of Israel out of Egypt. Now get ready to lead them to the land I promised their ancestors Abraham, Isaac, and Jacob. ²⁻³It is a land rich with milk and honey, and I will send an angel to force out those people who live there—the Canaanites, the Amorites, the Hittites, the Perizzites, the Hivites, and the

---

ʷ32.32 your book: The people of Israel believed that the LORD kept a record of the names of his people, and anyone whose name was removed from that book no longer belonged to the LORD.

Jebusites. I would go with my people, but they are so rebellious that I would destroy them before they get there.

[4-5]Even before the LORD said these harsh things, he had told Moses, "These people really are rebellious, and I would kill them at once, if I went with them. But tell them to take off their fancy jewelry, then I'll decide what to do with them." So the people started mourning, [6]and after leaving Mount Sinai,[x] they stopped wearing fancy jewelry.

The LORD Is with His People

[7]Moses used to set up a tent far from camp. He called it the "meeting tent," and whoever needed some message from the LORD would go there. [8]Each time Moses went out to the tent, everyone would stand at the entrance to their own tents and watch him enter. [9-11]Then they would bow down because a thick cloud would come down in front of the tent, and the LORD would speak to Moses face to face, just like a friend. Afterwards, Moses would return to camp, but his young assistant Joshua[y] would stay at the tent.

The LORD Promises To Be with His People

[12]Moses said to the LORD, "I know that you have told me to lead these people to the land you promised them. But you have not told me who my assistant will be. You have said that you are my friend and that you are pleased with me. [13]If this is true, let me know what your plans are, then I can obey and continue to please you. And don't forget that you have chosen this nation to be your own."

> The Lord never promised us an easy road, but he did promise always to be with us on that road.
>
> SANDRA P. ALDRICH

[14]The LORD said, "I will go with you and give you peace."

[15]Then Moses replied, "If you aren't go-

ing with us, please don't make us leave this place. [16]But if you do go with us, everyone will know that you are pleased with your people and with me. That way, we will be different from the rest of the people on earth."

[17]So the LORD told him, "I will do what you have asked, because I am your friend and I am pleased with you."

[18]Then Moses said, "I pray that you will let me see you in all of your glory."

[19]The LORD answered:

All right. I am the LORD, and I show mercy and kindness to anyone I choose. I will let you see my glory and hear my holy name, [20]but I won't let you see my face, because anyone who sees my face will die. [21]There is a rock not far from me. Stand beside it, [22]and before I pass by in all of my shining glory, I will put you in a large crack in the rock. I will cover your eyes with my hand until I have passed by. [23]Then I will take my hand away, and you will see my back. You will not see my face.

The Second Set of Commandments
(Deuteronomy 10.1-5)

34 One day the LORD said to Moses, "Cut two flat stones like the first ones I made, and I will write on them the same commandments that were on the two you broke. [2]Be ready tomorrow morning to come up Mount Sinai and meet me at the top. [3]No one is to come with you or to be on the mountain at all. Don't even let the sheep and cattle graze at the foot of the mountain." [4]So Moses cut two flat stones like the first ones, and early the next morning he carried them to the top of Mount Sinai, just as the LORD had commanded.

[5]The LORD God came down in a cloud and stood beside Moses there on the mountain. God spoke his holy name, "the LORD."[z] [6]Then he passed in front of Moses and called out, "I am the LORD God. I am merciful and very patient with my people. I show great love, and I can be trusted. [7]I keep my promises to my people forever, but I also punish anyone who sins. When people

sin, I punish them and their children, and also their grandchildren and great-grandchildren."

[8]Moses quickly bowed down to the ground and worshiped the LORD. [9]He prayed, "LORD, if you really are pleased with me, I pray that you will go with us. It is true that these people are sinful and rebellious, but forgive our sin and let us be your people."

> *God is not just a faithful God but the faithful God. He is the same steadfast and good Father yesterday, today, and forever.*
>
> JONI EARECKSON TADA

A Promise and Its Demands
(Exodus 23.14-19; Deuteronomy 7.1-5; 16.1-17)

[10]The LORD said:

I promise to perform miracles for you that have never been seen anywhere on earth. Neighboring nations will stand in fear and know that I was the one who did these marvelous things. [11]I will force out the Amorites, the Canaanites, the Hittites, the Perizzites, the Hivites, and the Jebusites, but you must do what I command you today. [12]Don't make treaties with any of those people. If you do, it will be like falling into a trap. [13]Instead, you must destroy their altars and tear down the sacred poles[a] they use in the worship of the goddess Asherah. [14]I demand your complete loyalty—you must not worship any other god! [15]Don't make treaties with the people there, or you will soon find yourselves worshiping their gods and taking part in their sacrificial meals. [16]Your men will even marry their women and be influenced to worship their gods.

[17]Don't make metal images of gods.

[18]Don't fail to observe the Festival of Thin Bread in the month of Abib.[b] Obey me and eat bread without yeast for seven days during Abib, because that is the month you left Egypt.

[19]The first-born males of your families and of your flocks and herds belong to me.

[20]You can save the life of a first-born donkey[c] by sacrificing a lamb; if you don't, you must break the donkey's neck. You must save every first-born son.

Bring an offering every time you come to worship.

[21]Do your work in six days and rest on the seventh day, even during the seasons for plowing and harvesting. [22]Celebrate the Harvest Festival[d] each spring when you start harvesting your wheat, and celebrate the Festival of Shelters[e] each autumn when you pick your fruit.

[23]Your men must come to worship me three times a year, because I am the LORD God of Israel. [24]I will force the nations out of your land and enlarge your borders. Then no one will try to take your property when you come to worship me these three times each year.

[25]When you sacrifice an animal on the altar, don't offer bread made with yeast. And don't save any part of the Passover meal for the next day.

[26]I am the LORD your God, and you must bring the first part of your harvest to the place of worship.

Don't boil a young goat in its mother's milk.

[27]The LORD told Moses to put these laws in writing, as part of his agreement with Israel. [28]Moses stayed on the mountain with the LORD for forty days and nights, without eating or drinking. And he wrote down the Ten Commandments, the most important part of God's agreement with his people.

Moses Comes Down from Mount Sinai

[29]Moses came down from Mount Sinai, carrying the Ten Commandments. His face was shining brightly because the LORD had

---

[a]**34.13** *sacred poles:* Or "trees," used as symbols of Asherah, the goddess of fertility.   [b]**34.18** *Abib:* See the note at 12.2.   [c]**34.20** *donkey:* See the note at 13.13. [d]**34.22** *Harvest Festival:* See the note at 23.16. [e]**34.22** *Festival of Shelters:* See the note at 23.16.

been speaking to him. But Moses did not know at first that his face was shining. [30]When Aaron and the others looked at Moses, they saw that his face was shining, and they were afraid to go near him. [31]Moses called out for Aaron and the leaders to come to him, and he spoke with them. [32]Then the rest of the people of Israel gathered around Moses, and he gave them the laws that the LORD had given him on Mount Sinai.

[33]The face of Moses kept shining, and after he had spoken with the people, he covered his face with a veil. [34]Moses would always remove the veil when he went into the sacred tent to speak with the LORD. And when he came out, he would tell the people everything the LORD had told him to say. [35]They could see that his face was still shining. So after he had spoken with them, he would put the veil back on and leave it on until the next time he went to speak with the LORD.

Laws for the Sabbath

35 Moses called together the people of Israel and told them that the LORD had said:

[2]You have six days in which to do your work. But the seventh day must be dedicated to me, your LORD, as a day of rest. Whoever works on the Sabbath will be put to death. [3]Don't even build a cooking fire at home on the Sabbath.

Offerings for the Sacred Tent
(Exodus 25.1-9; 35.10-19)

[4]Moses told the people of Israel that the LORD had said:

[5]I would welcome an offering from anyone who wants to give something. You may bring gold, silver, or bronze; [6]blue, purple, or red wool; fine linen; goat hair; [7]tanned ram skin or fine leather; acacia wood; [8]olive oil for the lamp; sweet-smelling spices for the oil of dedication and for the incense; or [9]onyx[j] stones or other gems for the sacred vest and breastpiece.

[10]If you have any skills, you should use them to help make what I have commanded: [11]the sacred tent with its covering and hooks, its framework and crossbars, and its post and stands; [12]the sacred chest with its carrying poles, its place of mercy, and the curtain in front of it; [13]the table with all that goes on it, including the sacred bread; [14]the lamp with its equipment and oil; [15]the incense altar with its carrying poles and sweet-smelling incense; the ordination oil; the curtain for the entrance to the sacred tent; [16]the altar for sacrifices with its bronze grating, its carrying poles, and its equipment; the large bronze bowl with its stand; [17]the curtains with the posts and stands that go around the courtyard; [18]the pegs and ropes for the tent and the courtyard; [19]and the finely woven priestly clothes for Aaron and his sons.

Gifts for the LORD

[20]Moses finished speaking, and everyone left. [21]Then those who wanted to bring gifts to the LORD, brought them to be used for the sacred tent, the worship services, and the priestly clothes. [22]Men and women came willingly and gave all kinds of gold jewelry such as pins, earrings, rings, and necklaces. [23]Everyone brought their blue, purple, and red wool, their fine linen, and their cloth made of goat hair, as well as their ram skins dyed red and their fine leather. [24]Anyone who had silver or bronze or acacia wood brought it as a gift to the LORD. [25]The women who were good at weaving cloth brought the blue, purple, and red wool and the fine linen they had made. [26]And the women who knew how to make cloth from goat hair were glad to do so. [27]The leaders brought different kinds of jewels to be sewn on the special clothes and the breastpiece for the high priest. [28]They also brought sweet-smelling spices to be mixed with the incense and olive oil that were for the lamps and for ordaining the priests. [29]Moses had told the people what the LORD wanted them to do, and many of them decided to bring their gifts.

Bezalel and Oholiab
(Exodus 31.1-11)

[30]Moses said to the people of Israel:
The LORD has chosen Bezalel[g] of

---

[j]35.9 onyx: See the note at 25.7.   [g]35.30 Bezalel: See the note at 31.2.

the Judah tribe. [31-33]Not only has the LORD filled him with his Spirit, but he has given him wisdom and made him a skilled craftsman who can create objects of art with gold, silver, bronze, stone, and wood. [34]The LORD is urging him and Oholiab[h] from the tribe of Dan to teach others. [35]And he has given them all kinds of artistic skills, including the ability to design and embroider with blue, purple, and red wool and to weave fine linen.

36 The LORD has given to Bezalel, Oholiab, and others the skills needed for building a place of worship, and they will follow the LORD's instructions.

[2]Then Moses brought together these workers who were eager to work, [3]and he gave them the money that the people of Israel had donated for building the place of worship. In fact, so much money was being given each morning, [4]that finally everyone stopped working [5]and said, "Moses, there is already more money than we need for what the LORD has assigned us to do." [6]So Moses sent word for the people to stop giving, and they did. [7]But there was already more than enough to do what needed to be done.

> The place where you live is the place where you will have the most opportunities to serve the Lord by serving others.
> ANNETTE LAPLACA

The Curtains and Coverings for the Sacred Tent
(Exodus 26.1-14)

[8-9]The skilled workers got together to make the sacred tent and its linen curtains woven with blue, purple, and red wool and embroidered with figures of winged creatures. Each of the ten panels was fourteen yards long and two yards wide, [10]and they were sewn together to make two curtains with five panels each. [11-13]Then fifty loops of blue cloth were put along one of the wider

sides of each curtain, and the two curtains were fastened together at the loops with fifty gold hooks.

[14-15]As the material for the tent, goat hair was used to weave eleven sections fifteen yards by two yards each. [16]These eleven sections were joined to make two panels, one with five and the other with six sections. [17]Fifty loops were put along one of the wider sides of each panel, [18]and the two panels were fastened at the loops with fifty bronze hooks. [19]Two other coverings were made—one with fine leather and the other with ram skins dyed red.

The Framework for the Sacred Tent
(Exodus 26.15-30)

[20]Acacia wood was used to build the framework for the walls of the sacred tent. [21]Each frame was fifteen feet high and twenty-seven inches wide [22-26]with two wooden pegs near the bottom. Then two silver stands were placed under each frame with sockets for the pegs, so they could be joined together. Twenty of these frames were used along the south side and twenty more along the north. [27]Six frames were used for the back wall along the west side [28-29]with two more at the southwest and northwest corners. These corner frames were joined from top to bottom. [30]Altogether, along the back wall there were eight frames with two silver stands under each of them.

[31-33]Five crossbars were made for each of the wooden frames, with the center crossbar running the full length of the wall. [34]The frames and crossbars were covered with gold, and gold rings were attached to the frames to run the crossbars through.

The Inside Curtain for the Sacred Tent
(Exodus 26.31-37)

[35]They made the inside curtain[i] of fine linen woven with blue, purple, and red wool, and embroidered with figures of winged creatures. [36]They also made four acacia wood posts and covered them with gold. Then gold rings were fastened to the posts, which were set on silver stands. [37]For the entrance to the tent, they used a curtain of fine linen woven with blue,

[h]35.34 Oholiab: Hebrew "Oholiab son of Ahisamach." [i]36.35 inside curtain: Separating the holy place from the most holy place.

purple, and red wool and embroidered with fancy needlework. [38]They made five posts, covered them completely with gold, and set them each on a gold-covered bronze stand. Finally, they attached hooks for the curtain.

The Sacred Chest
(Exodus 25.10-22)

37 Bezalel built a chest of acacia wood forty-five inches long, twenty-seven inches wide, and twenty-seven inches high. [2]He covered it inside and out with pure gold and put a gold edging around the top. [3]He made four gold rings and fastened one of them to each of the four legs of the chest. [4]Then he made two poles of acacia wood, covered them with gold, [5]and put them through the rings, so the chest could be carried by the poles.

[6]The entire lid of the chest, which was also covered with pure gold, was the place of mercy.[J] [7-9]On each of the two ends of the chest he made a winged creature of hammered gold. They faced each other, and their wings covered the place of mercy.

The Table for the Sacred Bread
(Exodus 25.23-30)

[10]Bezalel built a table of acacia wood thirty-six inches long, eighteen inches wide, and twenty-seven inches high. [11-12]He covered it with pure gold and put a gold edging around it with a border three inches wide.[k] [13]He made four gold rings and attached one to each of the legs [14]near the edging. The poles for carrying the table were placed through these rings [15]and were made of acacia wood covered with gold. [16]Everything that was to be set on the table was made of pure gold—the bowls, plates, jars, and cups for wine offerings.

The Lampstand
(Exodus 25.31-40)

[17]Bezalel made a lampstand of pure gold. The whole lampstand, including its decorative flowers, was made from a single piece of hammered gold, [18]with three branches on each of its two sides. [19]There were three decorative almond blossoms on each branch [20]and four on the stem. [21]There was also a blossom where each pair of branches came out from the stem. [22]The lampstand, including its branches and decorative flowers, was made from a single

piece of hammered pure gold. [23-24]The lamp and its equipment, including the tongs and trays, were made of about seventy-five pounds of pure gold.

The Altar for Burning Incense
(Exodus 30.1-5)

[25]For burning incense, Bezalel made an altar of acacia wood. It was eighteen inches square and thirty-six inches high with each of its four corners sticking up like the horn of a bull. [26]He covered it with pure gold and put a gold edging around it. [27]Then below the edging on opposite sides he attached two gold rings through which he put the poles for carrying the altar. [28]These poles were also made of acacia wood and covered with gold.

The Oil for Dedication and the Incense
(Exodus 30.22-38)

[29]Bezalel mixed the oil for dedication and the sweet-smelling spices for the incense.

The Altar for Offering Sacrifices
(Exodus 27.1-8)

38 Bezalel built an altar of acacia wood for offering sacrifices. It was seven and a half feet square and four and a half feet high [2]with each of its four corners sticking up like the horn of a bull, and it was completely covered with bronze. [3]The equipment for the altar was also made of bronze—the pans for the hot ashes, the shovels, the meat forks, and the fire pans. [4]Midway up the altar he built a ledge around it and covered the bottom half of the altar with a decorative bronze grating. [5]Then he attached a bronze ring beneath the ledge at the four corners to put the poles through. [6]He covered two acacia wood poles with bronze and [7]put them through the rings for carrying the altar, which was shaped like an open box.

The Large Bronze Bowl
(Exodus 30.18-21)

[8]Bezalel made a large bowl and a stand out of bronze from the mirrors of the

---

J37.6 place of mercy: See the note at 26.34.
k37.11,12 a gold edging . . . wide: Or "a gold edging around it three inches wide."

women who helped at the entrance to the sacred tent.

The Courtyard around the Sacred Tent
(Exodus 27.9-19)

⁹⁻¹⁷Around the sacred tent Bezalel built a courtyard one hundred fifty feet long on the south and north and seventy-five feet wide on the east and west. He used twenty bronze posts on bronze stands for the south and north and ten for the west. Then he hung a curtain of fine linen on the posts along each of these three sides by using silver hooks and rods. He placed three bronze posts on each side of the entrance at the east and hung a curtain seven and a half yards wide on each set of posts.

> *For unto us, a child is born,*
> *a son is given!*
> *There is only one response:*
> *Worship and joyous praise!*
>
> JONI EARECKSON TADA

¹⁸⁻¹⁹For the entrance to the courtyard, Bezalel made a curtain ten yards long, which he hung on four bronze posts that were set on bronze stands. This curtain was the same height as the one for the rest of the courtyard and was made of fine linen embroidered and woven with blue, purple, and red wool. He hung the curtain on the four posts, using silver hooks and rods. ²⁰The pegs for the tent and for the curtain around the tent were made of bronze.

The Sacred Tent

²¹⁻²³Bezalel had worked closely with Oholiab,[l] who was an expert at designing and engraving, and at embroidering blue, purple, and red wool. The two of them completed the work that the LORD had commanded.

Moses made Aaron's son Ithamar responsible for keeping record of the metals used for the sacred tent. ²⁴According to the official weights, the amount of gold given was two thousand two hundred nine pounds, ²⁵and the silver that was collected when the people were counted[m] came to seven thousand five hundred fifty pounds. ²⁶Everyone who was counted paid the required amount, and there was a total of 603,550 men who were twenty years old or older.

²⁷Seventy-five pounds of the silver were used to make each of the one hundred stands for the sacred tent and the curtain. ²⁸The remaining fifty pounds of silver were used for the hooks and rods and for covering the tops of the posts.

²⁹Five thousand three hundred pounds of bronze were given. ³⁰And it was used to make the stands for the entrance to the tent, the altar and its grating, the equipment for the altar, ³¹the stands for the posts that surrounded the courtyard, including those at the entrance to the courtyard, and the pegs for the tent and the courtyard.

Making the Priestly Clothes
(Exodus 28.1-14)

39 Beautiful priestly clothes were made of blue, purple, and red wool for Aaron to wear when he performed his duties in the holy place. This was done exactly as the LORD had commanded Moses.

²⁻³The entire priestly vest was made of fine linen, woven with blue, purple, and red wool. Thin sheets of gold were hammered out and cut into threads that were skillfully woven into the vest. ⁴⁻⁵It had two shoulder straps to support it and a sash that fastened around the waist. ⁶Onyx[n] stones were placed in gold settings, and each one was engraved with the name of one of Israel's sons. ⁷Then these were attached to the shoulder straps of the vest, so the LORD would never forget his people. Everything was done exactly as the LORD had commanded Moses.

The Breastpiece
(Exodus 28.15-30)

⁸The breastpiece was made with the same materials and designs as the priestly vest. ⁹It was nine inches square and folded

---

*l*38.21-23 *Bezalel . . . Oholiab*: Hebrew "Bezalel son of Uri and grandson of Hur of the Judah tribe had worked closely with Oholiab son of Ahisamach from the tribe of Dan." *m*38.25 *counted*: See 30.11-16; Numbers 1. *n*39.6 *Onyx*: See the note at 25.7.

double ^{10}with four rows of three precious stones: A carnelian, a chrysolite, and an emerald were in the first row; ^{11}a turquoise, a sapphire, and a diamond were in the second row; ^{12}a jacinth, an agate, and an amethyst were in the third row; ^{13}and a beryl, an onyx, and a jasper^o were in the fourth row. They were mounted in a delicate gold setting, ^{14}and on each of them was engraved the name of one of the twelve tribes of Israel.

$^{15\text{-}18}$Two gold rings were attached to the upper front corners of the breastpiece and fastened with two braided gold chains to gold settings on the shoulder straps. ^{19}Two other gold rings were attached to the lower inside corners next to the vest, ^{20}and two more near the bottom of the shoulder straps right above the sash. ^{21}To keep the breastpiece in place, a blue cord was used to tie the two lower rings on the breastpiece to those on the vest. These things were done exactly as the LORD had commanded Moses.

The Clothes for the Priests
(Exodus 28.31-43)

^{22}The priestly robe was made of blue wool ^{23}with an opening in the center for the head. The material around the collar was bound so as to keep it from raveling. $^{24\text{-}26}$Along the hem of the robe were woven pomegranates^p of blue, purple, and red wool with a bell of pure gold between each of them. This robe was to be worn by Aaron when he performed his duties.

$^{27\text{-}29}$Everything that Aaron and his sons wore was made of fine linen woven with blue, purple, and red wool, including their robes and turbans, their fancy caps and underwear, and even their sashes that were embroidered with needlework.

^{30}"Dedicated to the LORD" was engraved on a narrow strip of pure gold, ^{31}which was fastened to Aaron's turban. These things were done exactly as the LORD had commanded Moses.

The Work Is Completed
(Exodus 35.10-19)

^{32}So the people of Israel finished making everything the LORD had told Moses to make. ^{33}Then they brought it all to Moses: the sacred tent and its equipment, including the hooks, the framework and crossbars, and its posts and stands; ^{34}the covering of tanned ram skins and fine leather; the inside curtain; ^{35}the sacred chest with its carrying poles and the place of mercy; ^{36}the table with all that goes on it, including the sacred bread; ^{37}the lampstand of pure gold, together with its equipment and oil; ^{38}the gold-covered incense altar; the ordination oil and the sweet-smelling incense; the curtain for the entrance to the tent; ^{39}the bronze altar for sacrifices with its bronze grating, its carrying poles, and its equipment; the large bronze bowl with its stand; ^{40}the curtain with its posts and cords, and its pegs and stands that go around the courtyard; everything needed for the sacred tent; ^{41}and the finely woven priestly clothes for Aaron and his sons.

$^{42\text{-}43}$When Moses saw that the people had done everything exactly as the LORD had commanded, he gave them his blessing.

The LORD's Tent Is Set Up

40 The LORD said to Moses: ^{2}Set up my tent on the first day of the year^q ^{3}and put the chest with the Ten Commandments behind the inside curtain^r of the tent. ^{4}Bring in the table and set on it those things that are made for it. Also bring in the lampstand and attach the lamps to it. ^{5}Then place the gold altar of incense in front of the sacred chest and hang a curtain at the entrance to the tent. ^{6}Set the altar for burning sacrifices in front of the entrance to my tent. ^{7}Put the large bronze bowl between the tent and the altar and fill the bowl with water. ^{8}Surround the tent and the altar with the wall of curtains and hang the curtain that was made for the entrance.

^{9}Use the sacred olive oil to dedicate the tent and everything in it to me. ^{10}Do the same thing with the altar for offering sacrifices and its equipment ^{11}and with the bowl and its stand. ^{12}Bring Aaron and his sons to the entrance of the tent and have them

---

^{o}**39.13** *jasper:* For the stones mentioned in verses 10-13, see the note at 28.20. ^{p}**39.24-26** *pomegranates:* See the note at 28.33, 34. ^{q}**40.2** *first day of the year:* See the note at 12.2. ^{r}**40.3** *inside curtain:* Separating the holy place from the most holy place.

wash themselves. [13]Dress Aaron in the priestly clothes, then use the sacred olive oil to ordain him and dedicate him to me as my priest. [14]Put the priestly robes on Aaron's sons [15]and ordain them in the same way, so they and their descendants will always be my priests.

Recognizing God's provision for both physical and emotional needs reassures me of his presence and gives me a peace only he offers.

MARIAN V. LIAUTAUD

[16]Moses followed the LORD's instructions. [17]And on the first day of the first month[s] of the second year, the sacred tent was set up. [18]The posts, stands, and framework were put in place, [19]then the two layers of coverings were hung over them. [20]The stones with the Ten Commandments written on them were stored in the sacred chest, the place of mercy[t] was put on top of it, and the carrying poles were attached. [21]The chest was brought into the tent and set behind the curtain in the most holy place. These things were done exactly as the LORD had commanded Moses.

[22]The table for the sacred bread was put along the north wall of the holy place, [23]after which the bread was set on the table. [24]The lampstand was put along the south wall, [25]then the lamps were attached to it there in the presence of the LORD. [26]The gold incense altar was set up in front of the curtain, [27]and sweet-smelling incense was burned on it. These things were done exactly as the LORD had commanded Moses.

[28]The curtain was hung at the entrance to the sacred tent. [29]Then the altar for offering sacrifices was put in front of the tent, and animal sacrifices and gifts of grain were offered there. [30]The large bronze bowl was placed between the altar and the entrance to the tent. It was filled with water, [31]then Moses and Aaron, together with Aaron's sons, washed their hands and feet. [32]In fact, they washed each time before entering the tent or offering sacrifices at the altar. These things were done exactly as the LORD had commanded Moses.

[33]Finally, Moses had the curtain hung around the courtyard.

The Glory of the LORD

[34]Suddenly the sacred tent was covered by a thick cloud and filled with the glory of the LORD. [35]And so, Moses could not enter the tent. [36]Whenever the cloud moved from the tent, the people would break camp and follow; [37]then they would set up camp and stay there, until it moved again. [38]No matter where the people traveled, the LORD was with them. Each day his cloud was over the tent, and each night a fire could be seen in the cloud.

---

[s]**40.17** *first month*: See the note at 12.2.   [t]**40.20** *place of mercy*: See the note at 26.34.

Leviticus

A Book about Paying for Sins

Why should you read a book that tells you the proper way to sacrifice a dove?

Although the book of Leviticus is filled with laws about sacrifices, each of these laws tells us something about our relationship to God. They demonstrate our need to be holy in God's eyes, our need for a payment for our sins, and our need to offer God sacrifices (after our sins have been paid for)—not because we *have* to, but because we *want* to.

Many of the laws in Leviticus have to do with "ritual cleanness." While they may seem strange and difficult to us, these laws were meant to remind the Israelites of God's holiness and how all who want to love him must keep themselves holy, too. All the laws about clothing, food, and cleanliness demonstrated to God's people that not only their bodies but their souls must be pure if they wanted to worship him.

Of course, none of us can keep ourselves perfectly holy! That's why the book of Leviticus recorded the many ways the Israelites could make sacrifices for their sins, showing God always makes a way for the unholy to be reconciled with him and with each other. The center of the book of Leviticus was the Great Day of Forgiveness. This celebration pictured how God forgives our sins—through the symbolism of the shedding of blood of one goat (our sins are forgiven) and the release of another goat into the wilderness (our sins are forgotten by God).

But that's not the only type of sacrifice in Leviticus! God also told his people to bring sacrifices as one would bring a present to someone you love. Our relationship with God isn't merely a matter of having our sins paid for. We're supposed to go beyond that—to show our love for God by bringing him presents because we love him.

The book of Leviticus also looks forward to the coming of Christ. The Great Day of Forgiveness foreshadows Christ's atonement for our sins. The laws about cleanness and uncleanness remind us that after we are saved, we can live holy lives. And the laws about gifts offered to God portray how we're supposed to give God gifts of praise, gratitude, and good works.

Leviticus at a Glance

1. Different kinds of sacrifices (1–7)
2. The priests offer sacrifices (8–10)
3. Laws about cleanness and uncleanness (11–15)
4. The Great Day of Forgiveness (16)
5. God's laws of morality (17–20)
6. More laws about sacrifices (21,22)
7. Laws about feasts (23–25)
8. Blessings and punishments (26)
9. Giving gifts to God (27)

1 ¹⁻³The LORD spoke to Moses from the sacred tent and gave him instructions for the community of Israel to follow when they offered sacrifices.

Sacrifices To Please the LORD

The LORD said:

Sacrifices to please me[a] must be completely burned on the bronze altar.[b]

Bulls or rams or goats[c] are the animals to be used for these sacrifices. If the animal is a bull, it must not have anything wrong with it. Lead it to the entrance of the sacred tent, and I will let you know if it is[d] acceptable to me. ⁴Lay your hand on its head, and I will accept the animal as a sacrifice for taking away your sins.

We don't know the meaning of worship until we praise God in the middle of a difficult situation, aware that he's still in control of the universe— even though we may not see it.

CAROL KENT

⁵After the bull is killed in my presence, some priests from Aaron's family will offer its blood to me by splattering it against the four sides of the altar.

⁶Skin the bull and cut it up, ⁷while the priests pile wood on the altar fire to make it start blazing. ⁸⁻⁹Wash the bull's insides and hind legs, so the priests can lay them on the altar with the head, the fat, and the rest of the animal. A priest will then send all of it up in smoke with a smell that pleases me.

¹⁰If you sacrifice a ram or a goat, it must not have anything wrong with it. ¹¹Lead the animal to the north side of the altar, where it is to be killed in my presence. Then some of the priests will splatter its blood against the four sides of the altar.

¹²⁻¹³Cut up the animal and wash its insides and hind legs. A priest will put these parts on the altar with the head, the fat,

and the rest of the animal. Then he will send all of it up in smoke with a smell that pleases me.

¹⁴If you offer a bird for this kind of sacrifice, it must be a dove or a pigeon. ¹⁵A priest will take the bird to the bronze altar, where he will wring its neck and put its head on the fire. Then he will drain out its blood on one side of the altar, ¹⁶remove the bird's craw with what is in it,[e] and throw them on the ash heap at the east side of the altar.[f] ¹⁷Finally, he will take the bird by its wings, tear it partially open,[g] and send it up in smoke with a smell that pleases me.

Sacrifices To Give Thanks to the LORD

The LORD said:

2 When you offer sacrifices to give thanks to me,[h] you must use only your finest flour. Put it in a dish, sprinkle olive oil and incense on the flour, ²and take it to the priests from Aaron's family. One of them will scoop up the incense together with a handful of the flour and oil. Then, to show that the whole offering belongs to me, the priest will lay this part on the bronze altar and send it up in smoke with a smell that pleases me. ³The rest of this sacrifice is for the priests; it is very holy because it was offered to me.

⁴If you bake bread in an oven for this sacrifice, use only your finest flour, but without any yeast. You may make the flour into a loaf mixed with olive oil, or you may make it into thin wafers and brush them with oil.

---

[a]**1.1-3** *Sacrifices to please me:* These sacrifices have traditionally been called "whole burnt offerings" because the whole animal was burned on the altar. A main purpose of such sacrifices was to please the LORD with the smell of the sacrifice, and so in the CEV they are often called "sacrifices to please the LORD." [b]**1.1-3** *bronze altar:* This altar for offering sacrifices was in front of the entrance to the sacred tent; it was made of acacia wood covered with bronze. A smaller altar for offering incense was inside the tent; it was made of acacia wood covered with gold. [c]**1.1-3** *goats:* Hebrew "male goats." [d]**1.1-3** *if it is:* Or "if you are." [e]**1.16** *with what is in it:* One possible meaning for the difficult Hebrew text. [f]**1.16** *ash heap at the east side of the altar:* Ashes were piled here, then once a day they were taken to the ash heap outside the camp (see 4.11, 12; 6.10, 11). [g]**1.17** *tear it partially open:* Or "tear it open without pulling off the wings." [h]**2.1** *sacrifices to give thanks to me:* These sacrifices have traditionally been called "grain offerings." A main purpose of such sacrifices was to thank the LORD with a gift of grain, and so in the CEV they are sometimes called "sacrifices to give thanks to the LORD."

⁵If you cook bread in a shallow pan for this sacrifice, use only your finest flour. Mix it with olive oil, but do not use any yeast. ⁶Then break the bread into small pieces and sprinkle them with oil. ⁷If you cook your bread in a pan with a lid on it, you must also use the finest flour mixed with oil.

> *Let thanksgiving be*
> *the habit of your life.*
> ELISABETH ELLIOT

⁸You may prepare sacrifices to give thanks in any of these three ways. Bring your sacrifice to a priest, and he will take it to the bronze altar. ⁹Then, to show that the whole offering belongs to me, the priest will lay part of it on the altar and send it up in smoke with a smell that pleases me. ¹⁰The rest of this sacrifice is for the priests; it is very holy because it was offered to me.

¹¹Yeast and honey must never be burned on the altar, so don't ever mix either of these in a grain sacrifice. ¹²You may offer either of them separately,ⁱ when you present the first part of your harvest to me, but they must never be burned on the altar.

¹³Salt is offered when you make an agreement with me, so sprinkle salt on these sacrifices.

¹⁴Freshly cut grain, either roasted or coarsely ground,ʲ must be used when you offer the first part of your grain harvest. ¹⁵You must mix in some olive oil and put incense on top, because this is a grain sacrifice. ¹⁶A priest will sprinkle all of the incense and some of the grain and oil on the altar and send them up in smoke to show that the whole offering belongs to me.

Sacrifices To Ask the LORD's Blessing

The LORD said:

3 When you offer sacrifices to ask my blessing,ᵏ you may offer either a bull or a cow, but there must be nothing wrong with the animal. ²Lead it to the entrance of the sacred tent, lay your hand on its head, and have it killed there. A priest from Aaron's family will splatter its blood against the four sides of the altar.

³Offer all of the fat on the animal's insides, ⁴as well as the lower part of the liver and the two kidneys with their fat. ⁵Some of the priests will lay these pieces on the altar and send them up in smoke with a smell that pleases me, together with the sacrifice that is offered to please me.ˡ

⁶Instead of a bull or a cow, you may offer any sheep or goat that has nothing wrong with it. ⁷If you offer a sheep, you must present it to me at the entrance to the sacred tent. ⁸Lay your hand on its head and have it killed there. A priest will then splatter its blood against the four sides of the altar. ⁹Offer the fat on the tail, the tailbone, and the insides, ¹⁰as well as the lower part of the liver and the two kidneys with their fat. ¹¹One of the priests will lay these pieces on the altar and send them up in smoke as a food offering for me.

¹²If you offer a goat, you must also present it to me ¹³at the entrance to the sacred tent. Lay your hand on its head and have it killed there. A priest will then splatter its blood against the four sides of the altar.

¹⁴Offer all of the fat on the animal's insides, ¹⁵as well as the lower part of the liver and the two kidneys with their fat. ¹⁶One of the priests will put these pieces on the altar and send them up in smoke as a food offering with a smell that pleases me.

All fat belongs to me. ¹⁷So you and your descendants must never eat any fat or any blood, not even in the privacy of your own homes.ᵐ This law will never change.

Sacrifices for Sin
(Leviticus 6.24-30)

4 The LORD told Moses ²to say to the community of Israel:

Offer a sacrifice to ask forgiveness when you sin by accidentally doing something I have told you not to do.

ⁱ**2.12** *You . . . separately:* One possible meaning for the difficult Hebrew text. ʲ**2.14** *either . . . ground:* Or "roasted and coarsely ground." ᵏ**3.1** *sacrifices to ask my blessing:* These sacrifices have traditionally been called "peace offerings" or "offerings of well-being." A main purpose was to ask for the LORD's blessing, and so in the CEV they are sometimes called "sacrifices to ask the LORD's blessing." ˡ**3.5** *sacrifice . . . to please me:* See the note at 1.1-3. ᵐ**3.17** *not even . . . homes:* Or "no matter where you live."

When the High Priest Sins

The LORD said:

[3]When the high priest sins, he makes everyone else guilty too. And so, he must sacrifice a young bull that has nothing wrong with it. [4]The priest will lead the bull to the entrance of the sacred tent, lay his hand on its head, and kill it there. [5]He will take a bowl of the blood inside the tent, [6]dip a finger in the blood, and sprinkle some of it seven times toward the sacred chest behind the curtain. [7]Then, in my presence, he will smear some of the blood on each of the four corners of the incense altar, before pouring out the rest at the foot of the bronze altar[n] near the entrance to the tent.

[8-10]The priest will remove the fat from the bull, just as he does when he sacrifices a bull to ask my blessing.[o] This includes the fat on the insides, as well as the lower part of the liver and the two kidneys with their fat. He will then send it all up in smoke.

What God has forgiven,
he has forgotten;
what he has forgotten
we need not remember.
JILL BRISCOE

[11-12]The skin and flesh of the bull, together with its legs, insides, and the food still in its stomach, are to be taken outside the camp and burned on a wood fire near the ash heap.[p]

When the Whole Nation Sins

The LORD said:

[13]When the nation of Israel disobeys me without meaning to, the whole nation is still guilty. [14]Once you realize what has happened, you must sacrifice a young bull to ask my forgiveness. Lead the bull to the entrance of the sacred tent, [15]where your tribal leaders will lay their hands on its head, before having it killed in my presence.

[16]The priest will take a bowl of the animal's blood inside the sacred tent, [17]dip a finger in the blood, and sprinkle some of it seven times toward the sacred chest behind the curtain. [18]Then, in my presence, he must smear some of the blood on each of the four corners of the incense altar, before pouring out the rest at the foot of the bronze altar[q] near the entrance to the tent. [19-21]After this, the priest will remove the fat from the bull and send it up in smoke on the altar. Finally, he will burn its remains outside the camp, just as he did with the other bull. By this sacrifice the sin of the whole nation will be forgiven.

When a Tribal Leader Sins

The LORD God said:

[22]Any tribal leader who disobeys me without meaning to is still guilty. [23]As soon as the leader realizes what has happened, he must sacrifice a goat[r] that has nothing wrong with it. [24]This is a sacrifice for sin. So he will lay his hand on the animal's head, before having it killed in my presence at the north side of the bronze altar. [25]The priest will dip a finger in the blood, smear some of it on each of the four corners of the altar, and pour out the rest at the foot of the altar. [26]Then he must send all of the fat up in smoke, just as he does when a sacrifice is offered to ask my blessing.[s] By this sacrifice the leader's sin will be forgiven.

When Ordinary People Sin

The LORD said:

[27]When any of you ordinary people disobey me without meaning to, you are still guilty. [28]As soon as you realize what you have done, you must sacrifice a female goat that has nothing wrong with it. [29]Lead the goat to the north side of the bronze altar and lay your hand on its head, before having it killed. [30]Then a priest will dip a finger in the blood; he will smear some of it on each of the four corners of the altar and pour out

---

[n]**4.7** *incense altar . . . bronze altar*: See the note at 1.1-3. [o]**4.8-10** *to ask my blessing*: See the note at 3.1. [p]**4.11,12** *ash heap*: See the note at 1.16. [q]**4.18** *incense altar . . . bronze altar*: See the note at 1.1-3. [r]**4.23** *goat*: See the note at 1.1-3. [s]**4.26** *sacrifice . . . blessing*: See the note at 3.1.

the rest at the foot of the altar. [31]After this, the priest will remove all of the fat, just as he does when an animal is sacrificed to ask my blessing.[s] The priest will then send the fat up in smoke with a smell that pleases me. This animal is sacrificed so that I will forgive you ordinary people when you sin.

[32]If you offer a lamb instead of a goat as a sacrifice for sin, it must be a female that has nothing wrong with it. [33]Lead the lamb to the altar and lay your hand on its head, before having it killed. [34]The priest will dip a finger in the blood, smear some of it on each of the four corners of the altar, and pour out the rest at the foot of the altar. [35]After this, all of the fat must be removed, just as when an animal is sacrificed to ask my blessing. Then the priest will send it up in smoke to me, together with a food offering, and your sin will be forgiven.

The LORD said:

5 If you refuse to testify in court about something you saw or know has happened, you have sinned and can be punished.

[2]You are guilty and unfit to worship me, if you accidentally touch the dead body of any kind of unclean animal.

[3]You are guilty if you find out that you have accidentally touched any waste that comes from a human body.

[4]You are guilty the moment you realize that you have made a hasty promise to do something good or bad.

[5]As soon as you discover that you have committed any of these sins, you must confess what you have done. [6]Then you must bring a female sheep or goat to me as the price for your sin. A priest will sacrifice the animal, and you will be forgiven.

[7]If you are poor and cannot afford to bring an animal, you may bring two doves or two pigeons. One of these will be a sacrifice to ask my forgiveness, and the other will be a sacrifice to please me.

[8]Give both birds to the priest, who will offer one as a sacrifice to ask my forgiveness. He will wring its neck without tearing off its head, [9]splatter some of its blood on one side of the bronze altar, and drain out the rest at the foot of the altar. [10]Then he will follow the proper rules for offering the other bird as a sacrifice to please me.

You will be forgiven when the priest offers these sacrifices as the price for your sin.

[11]If you are so poor that you cannot afford doves or pigeons, you may bring two pounds of your finest flour. This is a sacrifice to ask my forgiveness, so don't sprinkle olive oil or sweet-smelling incense on it. [12]Give the flour to a priest, who will scoop up a handful and send it up in smoke together with the other offerings. This is a reminder that all of the flour belongs to me. [13]By offering this sacrifice, the priest pays the price for any of these sins you may have committed. The priest gets the rest of the flour, just as he does with grain sacrifices.

Sacrifices To Make Things Right
(Leviticus 7.1-10)

[14-15]The LORD told Moses what the people must do to make things right when they find out they have cheated the LORD without meaning to:

If this happens, you must either sacrifice a ram that has nothing wrong with it or else pay the price of a ram with the official money used by the priests. [16]In addition, you must pay what you owe plus a fine of twenty percent. Then the priest will offer the ram as a sacrifice to make things right, and you will be forgiven.

All that I am not, he is;
all that I am and
should not be,
he forgives and covers.
RUTH BELL GRAHAM

[17-19]If you break any of my commands without meaning to, you are still guilty, and you can be punished. When you realize what you have done, you must either bring to the priest a ram that has nothing wrong with it or else pay him for one. The priest will then offer it as a sacrifice to make things right, and you will be forgiven.

[s]**4.31** *sacrificed to ask my blessing:* See the note at 3.1.

Other Sins That Need Sacrifices or Payments

(Numbers 5.5-10)

6 [1-3]The LORD told Moses what the people must do when they commit other sins against the LORD:

You have sinned if you rob or cheat someone, if you keep back money or valuables left in your care, or if you find something and claim not to have it.

[4]When this happens, you must return what doesn't belong to you [5]and pay the owner a fine of twenty percent. [6-7]In addition, you must either bring to the priest a ram that has nothing wrong with it or else pay him for one. The priest will then offer it as a sacrifice to make things right, and you will be forgiven for what you did wrong.

Daily Sacrifices

(Exodus 29.38-43; Numbers 28.1-8)

[8-9]The LORD told Moses to tell Aaron and his sons how to offer the daily sacrifices that are sent up in smoke to please the LORD:[t]

You must put the animal for the sacrifice on the altar in the evening and let it stay there all night. But make sure the fire keeps burning. [10]The next morning you will dress in your priestly clothes, including your linen underwear. Then clean away the ashes left by the sacrifices and pile them beside the altar. [11]Change into your everyday clothes, take the ashes outside the camp, and pile them in the special place.[u]

[12]The fire must never go out, so put wood on it each morning. After this, you are to lay an animal on the altar next to the fat that you sacrifice to ask my blessing.[v] Then send it all up in smoke to me. [13]The altar fire must always be kept burning—it must never go out.

Sacrifices To Give Thanks to the LORD

The LORD said:

[14]When someone offers a sacrifice to give thanks to me,[w] the priests from Aaron's family must bring it to the front of the bronze altar, [15]where one of them will scoop up a handful of the flour and oil, together with all the incense on it. Then, to show that the whole offering belongs to me, he will lay all of this on the altar and send it up in smoke with a smell that pleases me. [16-17]The rest of it is to be baked without yeast and eaten by the priests in the sacred courtyard of the sacred tent. This bread is very holy, just like the sacrifices for sin or for making things right, and I have given this part to the priests from what is offered to me on the altar.

[18]Only the men in Aaron's family are allowed to eat this bread, and they must go through a ceremony to be made holy before touching it.[x] This law will never change.

When Priests Are Ordained

[19]The LORD spoke to Moses [20]and told him what sacrifices the priests must offer on the morning and evening of the day they are ordained:

It is the same as the regular morning and evening sacrifices—a pound of flour [21]mixed with olive oil and cooked in a shallow pan. The bread must then be crumbled into small pieces[y] and sent up in smoke with a smell that pleases me. [22-23]Each of Aaron's descendants who is ordained as a priest must perform this ceremony and make sure that the bread is completely burned on the altar. None of it may be eaten!

Sacrifices for Sin

(Leviticus 4.1, 2)

[24]The LORD told Moses [25]how the priests from Aaron's family were to offer the sacrifice for sin:

This sacrifice is very sacred, and the animal must be killed in my presence at the north side of the bronze altar. [26]The priest who offers this sacrifice must eat it in the sacred courtyard of the sacred tent, [27]and anyone or anything that touches the meat will be holy.[z] If any of the animal's blood is splattered on the clothes of the priest, they must be washed in a holy place. [28]If the meat was cooked in a clay pot, the pot must be destroyed,[a] but if it was cooked in a

---

[t]**6.8,9** *to please the* LORD: See the note at 1.1-3.
[u]**6.11** *ashes . . . in the special place*: See the note at 1.16.
[v]**6.12** *sacrifice to ask my blessing*: See the note at 3.1.
[w]**6.14** *a sacrifice to give thanks to me*: See the note at 2.1.
[x]**6.18** *and they . . . touching it*: One possible meaning for the difficult Hebrew text. [y]**6.21** *crumbled . . . pieces*: One possible meaning for the difficult Hebrew text. [z]**6.27** *that touches . . . holy*: One possible meaning for the difficult Hebrew text. [a]**6.28** *clay pot . . . destroyed*: Juice from the meat cannot be completely cleaned from a clay pot.

bronze pot, the pot must be scrubbed and rinsed with water.

²⁹This sacrifice is very holy, and only the priests may have any part of it. ³⁰None of the meat may be eaten from the sacrifices for sin that require blood to be brought into the sacred tent.ᵇ These sacrifices must be completely burned.

Sacrifices To Make Things Right
(Leviticus 5.14-19)

The LORD said:

7 The sacrifice to make things right is very sacred. ²The animal must be killed in the same place where the sacrifice to please meᶜ is killed, and the animal's blood must be splattered against the four sides of the bronze altar. ³Offer all of the animal's fat, including the fat on its tail and on its insides, ⁴as well as the lower part of the liver and the two kidneys with their fat. ⁵One of the priests will lay these pieces on the altar and send them up in smoke to me. ⁶This sacrifice for making things right is very holy. Only the priests may eat it, and they must eat it in a holy place.ᵈ

⁷The ceremony for this sacrifice and the one for sin are just alike, and the meat may be eaten only by the priest who performs this ceremony of forgiveness.

⁸In fact, the priest who offers a sacrifice to please meᵉ may keep the skin of the animal, ⁹just as he may eat the bread from a sacrifice to give thanks to me.ᶠ ¹⁰All other grain sacrifices—with or without olive oil in them—are to be divided equally among the priests of Aaron's family.

Sacrifices To Ask the LORD's Blessing

The LORD said:

¹¹Here are the instructions for offering a sacrifice to ask my blessing:ᵍ ¹²If you offer it to give thanks, you must offer some bread together with it. Use the finest flour to make three kinds of bread without yeast—two in the form of loaves mixed with olive oil and one in the form of thin wafers brushed with oil. ¹³You must also make some bread with yeast. ¹⁴Give me one loaf or wafer from each of these four kinds of bread, after which they will belong to the priest who splattered the blood against the bronze altar.

¹⁵When you offer an animal to ask a

blessing from me or to thank me, the meat belongs to you, but it must be eaten the same day. ¹⁶It is different with the sacrifices you offer when you make me a promise or voluntarily give me something. The meat from those sacrifices may be kept and eaten the next day, ¹⁷⁻¹⁸but any that is left must be destroyed. If you eat any after the second day, your sacrifice will be useless and unacceptable, and you will be both disgusting and guilty.

¹⁹Don't eat any of the meat that touches something unclean. Instead, burn it. The rest of the meat may be eaten by anyone who is clean and acceptable to me. ²⁰⁻²¹But don't eat any of this meat if you have become unclean by touching something unclean from a human or an animal or from any other creature. If you do, you will no longer belong to the community of Israel.

²²The LORD told Moses ²³to say to the people:

Don't eat the fat of cattle, sheep, or goats. ²⁴If one of your animals dies or is killed by some wild animal, you may do anything with its fat except eat it. ²⁵If you eat the fat of an animal that can be used as a sacrifice to me, you will no longer belong to the community of Israel. ²⁶And no matter where you live, you must not eat the blood of any bird or animal, ²⁷or you will no longer belong to the community of Israel.

²⁸The LORD also told Moses ²⁹⁻³⁰to say to the people of Israel:

If you want to offer a sacrifice to ask my blessing, you must bring the part to be burned and lay it on the bronze altar. But you must first lift upʰ the choice ribs with their fat to show that the offering is dedicated to me. ³¹A priest from Aaron's family will then send the fat up in smoke, but the ribs belong to the priests. ³²⁻³³The upper joint of the right hind leg is for the priest who offers the blood and the fat of the animal. ³⁴I have decided that the people of Israel must always give the choice ribs and the upper joint of the right hind leg to Aaron's descendants ³⁵who have been ordained as priests to serve

---

ᵇ**6.30** *that require blood . . . tent:* See 4.1-21.
ᶜ**7.2** *sacrifice to please me:* See the note at 1.1-3.
ᵈ**7.6** *holy place:* The courtyard of the sacred tent (see 6.16, 17).   ᵉ**7.8** *sacrifice to please me:* See the note at 1.1-3.   ᶠ**7.9** *sacrifice to give thanks to me:* See the note at 2.1.   ᵍ**7.11** *sacrifice to ask my blessing:* See the note at 3.1.   ʰ**7.29,30** *lift up:* Or "wave."

me. ³⁶This law will never change. I am the
LORD!

³⁷These are the ceremonies for sacrifices
to please the LORD, to give him thanks, and
to ask his blessing or his forgiveness, as well
as the ceremonies for those sacrifices that
demand a payment and for the sacrifices
that are offered when priests are ordained.
³⁸While Moses and the people of Israel were
in the desert at Mount Sinai, the LORD commanded them to start offering these sacrifices.

The Ceremony for Ordaining Priests
(Exodus 29.1-37)

8 The LORD said to Moses: ²Send for Aaron and his sons, as
well as their priestly clothes, the oil
for ordination, the bull for the sin offering, the two rams, and a basket of
bread made without yeast. ³Then
bring the whole community of Israel
together at the entrance to the sacred
tent.

⁴Moses obeyed the LORD, and when
everyone had come together, ⁵he said, "We
are here to follow the LORD's instructions."

⁶After Moses told Aaron and his sons to
step forward, he had them wash themselves. ⁷He put the priestly shirt and robe on
Aaron and wrapped the sash around his
waist. Then he put the sacred vest on Aaron
and fastened it with the finely woven belt.
⁸Next, he put on Aaron the sacred breastpiece that was used in learning what the
LORD wanted his people to do. ⁹He placed
the turban on Aaron's head, and on the
front of the turban was the narrow strip of
thin gold as a sign of his dedication to the
LORD.

¹⁰Moses then dedicated the sacred tent
and everything in it to the LORD by sprinkling them with some of the oil for ordination. ¹¹He sprinkled the bronze altar seven
times, and he sprinkled its equipment, as
well as the large bronze bowl and its base.
¹²He also poured some of the oil on Aaron's
head to dedicate him to the LORD. ¹³At last,
Moses dressed Aaron's sons in their shirts,
then tied sashes around them and put
special caps on them, just as the LORD had
commanded.

¹⁴Moses led out the bull that was to be
sacrificed for sin, and Aaron and his sons
laid their hands on its head. ¹⁵After it was

killed, Moses dipped a finger in the blood
and smeared some of it on each of the four
corners of the bronze altar, before pouring
out the rest at the foot of the altar. This purified the altar and made it a fit place for offering the sacrifice for sin. ¹⁶Moses then took
the fat on the bull's insides, as well as the
lower part of the liver and the two kidneys
with their fat, and sent them up in smoke on
the altar fire. ¹⁷Finally, he took the skin and
the flesh of the bull, together with the food
still in its stomach, and burned them outside the camp, just as the LORD had commanded.

> *To be more joyful,*
> *I need to drink in*
> *God's presence. When*
> *I spend more time*
> *in his Word, he*
> *reveals more of what*
> *I need for joy.*
>
> CAROLE MAYHALL

¹⁸Moses led out the ram for the sacrifice
to please the LORD.ⁱ After Aaron and his
sons had laid their hands on its head, ¹⁹Moses killed the ram and splattered its blood
against the four sides of the altar. ²⁰⁻²¹Moses
had the animal cut up, and he washed its
insides and hind legs. Then he laid the
head, the fat, and the rest of the ram on the
altar and sent them up in smoke with a
smell that pleased the LORD. All this was
done just as the LORD had commanded.

²²Moses led out the ram for the ceremony of ordination. Aaron and his sons laid
their hands on its head, ²³and it was killed.
Moses smeared some of its blood on Aaron's
right earlobe, some on his right thumb, and
some on the big toe of his right foot. ²⁴Moses did the same thing for Aaron's sons, before splattering the rest of the blood against
the four sides of the altar. ²⁵He took the

ⁱ**8.18** *sacrifice to please the LORD:* See the note at 1.1-3.

animal's fat tail, the fat on its insides, and the lower part of the liver and the two kidneys with their fat, and the right hind leg. [26]Then he took from a basket some of each of the three kinds of bread[j] that had been made without yeast and had been dedicated to the LORD.

[27]Moses placed the bread on top of the meat and gave it all to Aaron and his sons, who lifted it up[k] to show that it was dedicated to the LORD. [28]After this, Moses placed it on the fires of the altar and sent it up in smoke with a smell that pleased the LORD. This was part of the ordination ceremony. [29]Moses lifted up[k] the choice ribs of the ram to show that they were dedicated to the LORD. This was the part that the LORD had said Moses could have.

[30]Finally, Moses sprinkled the priestly clothes of Aaron and his sons with some of the oil for ordination and with some of the blood from the altar. So Aaron and his sons, together with their priestly clothes, were dedicated to the LORD.

[31]Moses said to Aaron and his sons:

The LORD told me that you must boil this meat at the entrance to the sacred tent and eat it there with the bread. [32]Burn what is left over [33]and stay near the entrance to the sacred tent until the ordination ceremony ends seven days from now. [34]We have obeyed the LORD in everything that has been done today, so that your sins may be forgiven.[l] [35]The LORD has told me that you must stay near the entrance to the tent for seven days and nights, or else you will die.

[36]Aaron and his sons obeyed everything that the LORD had told Moses they must do.

The First Sacrifices Offered by Aaron and His Sons

9 Eight days later Moses called together Aaron, his sons, and Israel's leaders. [2]Then he said to Aaron:

Find a young bull and a ram that have nothing wrong with them. Offer the bull to the LORD as a sacrifice for sin and the ram as a sacrifice to please him.[m]

[3]Tell the people of Israel that they must offer sacrifices as well. They must offer a goat[n] as a sacrifice for sin, and a bull and a ram as a sacrifice to please the LORD. The bull and the ram must be a year old and have nothing wrong with them. [4]Then the people must offer a bull and a ram as a sacrifice to ask the LORD's blessing[o] and also a grain sacrifice[p] mixed with oil. Do this, because the LORD will appear to you today.

[5]After the animals and the grain had been brought to the front of the sacred tent, and the people were standing there in the presence of the LORD, [6]Moses said:

The LORD has ordered you to do this, so that he may appear to you in all of his glory. [7]Aaron, step up to the altar and offer the sacrifice to please the LORD, then offer the sacrifices for the forgiveness of your sins and for the sins of the people, just as the LORD has commanded.

[8]Aaron stepped up to the altar and killed the bull that was to be the sacrifice for his sins. [9]His sons brought him the blood. He dipped a finger in it, smeared some on the four corners of the bronze altar, and poured out the rest at its foot. [10]But he sent up in smoke the fat, the kidneys, and the lower part of the liver, just as the LORD had commanded Moses. [11]Then Aaron burned the skin and the flesh outside the camp.

[12]After Aaron had killed the ram that was sacrificed to please the LORD, Aaron's sons brought him the blood, and he splattered it against all four sides of the altar. [13]They brought him each piece of the animal, including the head, and he burned them all on the altar. [14]He washed the insides and the hind legs and also sent them up in smoke.

[15]Next, Aaron sacrificed the goat for the sins of the people, as he had done with the sacrifice for his own sins. [16]And so, he burned this sacrifice on the altar in the proper way. [17]He also presented the grain sacrifice and burned a handful of the flour on the altar as part of the morning sacrifice.

---

[j]8.26 three kinds of bread: Made from the finest wheat flour; olive oil was mixed into part of the dough, and some of it was made into thin wafers brushed with oil (see Exodus 29.2, 3).   [k]8.27 lifted it up: See the note at 7.29, 30.   [k]8.29 lifted up: See the note at 7.29, 30.   [l]8.34 forgiven: One possible meaning for the difficult Hebrew text of verse 34.   [m]9.2 sacrifice to please him: See the note at 1.1-3.   [n]9.3 goat: See the note at 1.1-3.   [o]9.4 to ask the LORD's blessing: See the note at 3.1.   [p]9.4 grain sacrifice: To give thanks to the LORD (see the note at 2.1).

18At last, he killed the bull and the ram as a sacrifice to ask the LORD's blessing on the people. Aaron's sons brought him the blood, and he splattered it against the four sides of the altar. 19His sons placed all the fat, as well as the kidneys and the lower part of the liver 20on top of the choice ribs. 21Then Aaron burned the fat on the altar and lifted up^q the ribs and the right hind leg to show that these were dedicated to the LORD. This was done just as the LORD had instructed Moses.

22Aaron held out his hand and gave the people his blessing, before coming down from the bronze altar where he had offered the sacrifices. 23He and Moses went into the sacred tent, and when they came out, they gave the people their blessing. Then the LORD appeared to the people in all of his glory. 24The LORD sent fiery flames that burned up everything on the altar, and when everyone saw this, they shouted and fell to their knees to worship the LORD.

Nadab and Abihu

10 Nadab and Abihu were two of Aaron's sons, but they disobeyed the LORD by burning incense to him on a fire pan, when they were not supposed to.^r 2Suddenly the LORD sent fiery flames and burned them to death. 3Then Moses told Aaron that this was exactly what the LORD had meant when he said:

> "I demand respect
>   from my priests,
> and I will be praised
>   by everyone!"

Aaron was speechless.

4Moses sent for Mishael and Elzaphan, the two sons of Aaron's uncle Uzziel. Then he told them, "Take these two dead relatives of yours outside the camp far from the entrance to the sacred tent." 5So they dragged the dead men away by their clothes.

6Then Moses told Aaron and his other two sons, Eleazar and Ithamar:

Don't show your sorrow by messing up your hair and tearing your priestly clothes, or the LORD will get angry. He will kill the three of you and punish everyone else. It's all right for your relatives, the people of Israel, to mourn for those he destroyed by fire.

7But you are the LORD's chosen priests, and you must not leave the sacred tent, or you will die.

Aaron and his two sons obeyed Moses.

8The LORD said to Aaron:

9When you or your sons enter the sacred tent, you must never drink beer or wine. If you do, you will die right there! This law will never change. 10You must learn the difference between what is holy and what isn't holy and between the clean and the unclean. 11You must also teach the people of Israel everything that I commanded Moses to say to them.

12Moses told Aaron and his two sons, Eleazar and Ithamar:

The grain sacrifice that was offered to give thanks to the LORD^s is very holy. So make bread without yeast from the part that wasn't sent up in smoke and eat it beside the altar. 13The LORD has said that this belongs to you and your sons, and that it must be eaten in a holy place. 14-15But the choice ribs and the hind leg that were lifted up^t may be eaten by your entire family, as long as you do so in an acceptable place.^u These parts are yours from the sacrifices that the people offer to ask the LORD's blessing.^v This is what the LORD has commanded, and it will never change.

16When Moses asked around and learned that the ram for the sin sacrifice had already been burned on the altar, he became angry with Eleazar and Ithamar and said, 17"Why didn't you eat the meat from this sacrifice in an acceptable place? It is very holy, and the LORD has given you this sacrifice to remove Israel's sin and guilt. 18Whenever an animal's blood isn't brought into the sacred tent, I commanded you to eat its meat in an acceptable place, but you burned it instead."

19Their father Aaron replied, "Today two of my sons offered the sacrifice for sin and the sacrifice to please the LORD, and look

---

^q9.21 lifted up: See the note at 7.29, 30. ^r10.1 when they . . . to: One possible meaning for the difficult Hebrew text. ^s10.12 grain sacrifice . . . to give thanks to the LORD: See the note at 2.1. ^t10.14,15 lifted up: See the note at 7.29, 30. ^u10.14,15 acceptable place: See 6.24-30. ^v10.14,15 to ask the LORD's blessing: See the note at 3.1.

what has happened to me! Would the LORD have approved if I had eaten the sacrifice for sin?"

²⁰Moses was satisfied with Aaron's reply.

Clean and Unclean Animals
(Deuteronomy 14.3-21)

11 The LORD told Moses and Aaron ²to say to the community of Israel:
You may eat ³any animal that has divided hoofs and chews the cud.ʷ ⁴⁻⁸But you must not eat animals such as camels, rock badgers, and rabbits that chew the cud but don't have divided hoofs. And you must not eat pigs—they have divided hoofs, but don't chew the cud. All of these animals are unclean,ˣ and you are forbidden even to touch their dead bodies.

⁹⁻¹²You may eat anything that lives in water and has fins and scales. But it would be disgusting for you to eat anything else that lives in water, and you must not even touch their dead bodies.

¹³⁻¹⁹Eagles, vultures, buzzards, crows, ostriches, hawks, sea gulls, owls, pelicans, storks, herons, hoopoes,ʸ and bats are also disgusting, and you are forbidden to eat any of them.

²⁰⁻²³The only winged insects you may eat are locusts, grasshoppers, and crickets. All other winged insects that crawl are too disgusting for you to eat.

²⁴⁻²⁸Don't even touch the dead bodies of animals that have divided hoofs but don't chew the cud. And don't touch the dead bodies of animals that have paws. If you do, you must wash your clothes, but you are still unclean until evening.

²⁹⁻³⁰Moles, rats, mice, and all kinds of lizards are unclean. ³¹Anyone who touches their dead bodies or anything touched by their dead bodies becomes unclean until evening. ³²If something made of wood, cloth, or leather touches one of their dead bodies, it must be washed, but it is still unclean until evening. ³³If any of these animals is found dead in a clay pot, the pot must be broken to pieces, and everything in it becomes unclean. ³⁴If you pour water from this pot on any food, that food becomes unclean, and anything drinkable in the pot becomes unclean. ³⁵If the dead body of one of these animals touches anything else, including ovens and stoves, that thing becomes unclean and must be destroyed. ³⁶A spring or a cistern where one of these dead animals is found is still clean, but anyone who touches the animal becomes unclean. ³⁷If the dead body of one of these animals is found lying on seeds that have been set aside for planting, the seeds remain clean. ³⁸But seeds that are soaking in water become unclean, if the dead animal is found in the water.

³⁹If an animal that may be eaten happens to die, and you touch it, you become unclean until evening. ⁴⁰If you eat any of its meat or carry its body away, you must wash your clothes, but you are still unclean until evening.

⁴¹⁻⁴²Don't eat any of those disgusting little creatures that crawl or walk close to the ground. ⁴³If you eat any of them, you will become just as disgusting and unclean as they are. ⁴⁴I am the LORD your God, and you must dedicate yourselves to me and be holy, just as I am holy. Don't become disgusting by eating any of these unclean creatures. ⁴⁵I brought you out of Egypt so that I could be your God. Now you must become holy, because I am holy!

> *Without a doubt,*
> *the most difficult place*
> *to live for Christ is not*
> *in the pulpit, it's at home.*
> ANNE GRAHAM LOTZ

⁴⁶⁻⁴⁷I have given these laws so that you will know what animals, birds, and fish are clean and may be eaten, and which ones are unclean and may not be eaten.

ʷ**11.3** *chews the cud*: Some animals that eat grass and leaves have more than one stomach and chew their food a second time after it has been partly digested in the first stomach. This partly digested food is called the "cud." ˣ**11.4-8** *unclean*: In the Old Testament "clean" and "unclean" refer to whatever makes a person, animal, or object acceptable or unacceptable to God. For example, a person became unclean by eating certain foods, touching certain objects, and having certain kinds of diseases or bodily discharges. ʸ**11.13-19** *Eagles . . . hoopoes*: Some of the birds in this list are difficult to identify.

What Women Must Do after Giving Birth

12 The LORD told Moses [2]to say to the community of Israel:

If a woman gives birth to a son, she is unclean for seven days, just as she is during her monthly period. [3]Her son must be circumcised on the eighth day, [4]but her loss of blood keeps her from being completely clean for another thirty-three days. During this time she must not touch anything holy or go to the place of worship. [5]Any woman who gives birth to a daughter is unclean for two weeks, just as she is during her period. And she won't be completely clean for another sixty-six days.

Children are a mother's dearest and most important responsibility next to her husband. Reserve your best for them and give to others whatever time and energy is left.

GRACE KETTERMAN

[6]When the mother has completed her time of cleansing, she must come to the front of the sacred tent and bring to the priest a year-old lamb as a sacrifice to please me[z] and a dove or a pigeon as a sacrifice for sin. [7]After the priest offers the sacrifices to me, the mother will become completely clean from her loss of blood, whether her child is a boy or a girl. [8]If she cannot afford a lamb, she can offer two doves or two pigeons, one as a sacrifice to please me and the other as a sacrifice for sin.

Skin Diseases

13 The LORD told Moses and Aaron to say to the people:

[2]If sores or boils or a skin rash should break out and start spreading on your body, you must be brought to Aaron or to one of the other priests. [3]If the priest discovers that the hair in the infected area has turned white and that the infection seems more than skin deep, he will say, "This is leprosy[a]—you are unclean."

[4]But if the infected area is white and only skin deep, and if the hair in it hasn't turned white, the priest will order you to stay away from everyone else for seven days. [5]If the disease hasn't spread by that time, he will order you to stay away from everyone else for another seven days. [6]Then if the disease hasn't gotten any worse or spread, the priest will say, "You are clean. It was only a sore. After you wash your clothes, you may go home."

[7]However, if the disease comes back, you must return to the priest. [8]If it is discovered that the disease has started spreading, he will say, "This is leprosy—you are unclean."

[9]Any of you with a skin disease must be brought to a priest. [10]If he discovers that the sore spot is white with pus and that the hair around it has also turned white, [11]he will say, "This is leprosy. You are unclean and must stay away from everyone else." [12-13]But if the disease has run its course and only the scars remain, he will say, "You are clean." [14-15]If the sores come back and turn white with pus, he will say, "This is leprosy—you are unclean."

[16-17]However, if the sores heal and only white spots remain, the priest will say, "You are now clean."

[18-19]If you have a sore that either swells or turns reddish-white after it has healed, then you must show it to a priest. [20]If he discovers that the hair in the infected area has turned white and that the infection seems more than skin deep, he will say, "This is leprosy—you are unclean." [21]But if the white area is only on the surface of the skin and hasn't gotten any worse, and if the hair in it hasn't turned white, he will have you stay away from everyone else for seven days.

[22]If the sore begins spreading during this time, the priest will say, "You are unclean because you have a disease." [23]But if it doesn't spread, and only a scar remains, he will say, "You are now clean."

[24]If you have a burn that gets infected and turns red or reddish-white, [25]a priest must examine it. Then if he discovers that the hair in the infected area has turned

---

[z]**12.6** *sacrifice to please me:* See the note at 1.1-3.
[a]**13.3** *leprosy:* The word translated "leprosy" was used for many different kinds of skin diseases.

white and that the infection seems more than skin deep, he will say, "The burn has turned into leprosy, and you are unclean." ²⁶But if the priest finds that the hair in the infected area hasn't turned white and that the sore is only skin deep and it is healing, he will have you stay away from everyone else for seven days. ²⁷On the seventh day the priest will examine you again, and if the infection is spreading, he will say, "This is leprosy—you are unclean." ²⁸However, if the infection hasn't spread and has begun to heal, and if only a scar remains, he will say, "Only a scar remains from the burn, and you are clean."

²⁹If you have a sore on your head or chin, ³⁰it must be examined by a priest. If the infection seems more than skin deep, and the hair in it has thinned out and lost its color, he will say, "This is leprosy—you are unclean." ³¹On the other hand, if he discovers that the itchy spot is only skin deep, but that the hair still isn't healthy, he will order you to stay away from everyone else for seven days. ³²By that time, if the itch hasn't spread, if the hairs seem healthy, and if the itch is only skin deep, ³³you must shave off the hairs around the infection, but not those on it. Then the priest will tell you to stay away from everyone else for another seven days. ³⁴By that time, if the itch hasn't spread and seems no more than skin deep, he will say, "You are clean; now you must wash your clothes."

³⁵⁻³⁶Later, if the itch starts spreading, even though the hair is still healthy, the priest will say, "You are unclean." ³⁷But if he thinks you are completely well, he will say, "You are clean."

³⁸If white spots break out on your skin, ³⁹but the priest discovers that it is only a rash, he will say, "You are clean."

⁴⁰⁻⁴¹If you become bald on any part of your head, you are still clean. ⁴²⁻⁴³But if a priest discovers that a reddish-white sore has broken out on the bald spot and looks like leprosy, he will say, ⁴⁴"This is leprosy—you are unclean."

⁴⁵If you ever have leprosy, you must tear your clothes, leave your hair uncombed, cover the lower part of your face, and go around shouting, "I'm unclean! I'm unclean!" ⁴⁶As long as you have the disease, you are unclean and must live alone outside the camp.

⁴⁷⁻⁵⁰If a greenish or reddish spot*ᵇ* appears anywhere on any of your clothing or on anything made of leather, you must let the priest examine the clothing or the leather. He will put it aside for seven days, ⁵¹and if the mildew has spread in that time, he will say, "This is unclean ⁵²because the mildew has spread." Then he will burn the clothing or the piece of leather.

⁵³If the priest discovers that the mildew hasn't spread, ⁵⁴he will tell you to wash the clothing or leather and put it aside for another seven days, ⁵⁵after which he will examine it again. If the spot hasn't spread, but is still greenish or reddish, the clothing or leather is unclean and must be burned. ⁵⁶But if the spot has faded after being washed, he will tear away the spot. ⁵⁷Later, if the spot reappears elsewhere on the clothing or the leather, you must burn it. ⁵⁸Even if the spot completely disappears after being washed, it must be washed again before it is clean.

⁵⁹These are the rules for deciding if clothing is clean or unclean after a spot appears on it.

The Ceremony for People Healed of Leprosy

14 The LORD told Moses to say to the people:

²⁻³After you think you are healed of leprosy,*ᶜ* you must ask for a priest to come outside the camp and examine you. And if you are well, ⁴he will have someone bring out two live birds that are acceptable for sacrifice, together with a stick of cedar wood, a piece of red yarn, and a branch from a hyssop plant. ⁵The priest will have someone kill one of the birds over a clay pot of spring water. ⁶Then he will dip the other bird, the cedar, the red yarn, and the hyssop in the blood of the dead bird. ⁷Next, he will sprinkle you seven times with the blood and say, "You are now clean." Finally, he will release the bird and let it fly away.

⁸After this you must wash your clothes, shave your entire body, and take a bath before you are completely clean. You may move back into camp, but you must not en-

---

*ᵇ*13.47-50 *spot:* The Hebrew word translated "spot" and "mildew" in verses 47-59 is the same one translated "leprosy" earlier in the chapter. *ᶜ*14.2,3 *leprosy:* See the note at 13.3.

ter your tent for seven days. ⁹Then you must once again shave your head, face, and eyebrows, as well as the hair on the rest of your body. Finally, wash your clothes and take a bath, and you will be completely clean.

> *Something liberating and healing happens when we relinquish our right to understand God's requests. Such joy can come over us that it's all we can do not to shout.*
>
> PATSY CLAIRMONT

¹⁰On the eighth day you must bring to the priest two rams and a year-old female lamb that have nothing wrong with them; also bring a half pint of olive oil and six pounds of your finest flour mixed with oil. ¹¹Then the priest will present you and your offerings to me at the entrance to my sacred tent. ¹²There he will offer one of the rams, together with the pint of oil, as a sacrifice to make things right.[d] He will also lift them up[e] to show that they are dedicated to me. ¹³This sacrifice is very holy. It belongs to the priest and must be killed in the same place where animals are killed as sacrifices for sins and as sacrifices to please me.[f]

¹⁴The priest will smear some of the blood from this sacrifice on your right ear lobe, some on your right thumb, and some on the big toe of your right foot. ¹⁵He will then pour some of the olive oil into the palm of his left hand, ¹⁶dip a finger of his right hand into the oil, and sprinkle some of it seven times toward the sacred tent. ¹⁷Next, he will smear some of the oil on your right ear lobe, some on your right thumb, and some on the big toe of your right foot, ¹⁸⁻²⁰and pour the rest of the oil from his palm on your head. Then he will offer the other two animals— one as a sacrifice for sin and the other as a sacrifice to please me, together with a grain sacrifice. After this you will be completely clean.

²¹If you are poor and cannot afford to of-fer this much, you may offer a ram as a sacrifice to make things right, together with a half pint of olive oil and two pounds of flour mixed with oil as a grain sacrifice. The priest will then lift these up[g] to dedicate them to me. ²²Depending on what you can afford, you must also offer either two doves or two pigeons, one as a sacrifice for sin and the other as a sacrifice to please me. ²³The priest will offer these to me in front of the sacred tent on the eighth day.

²⁴⁻²⁵The priest will kill this ram for the sacrifice to make things right, and he will lift it up[g] with the olive oil in dedication to me. Then he will smear some of the blood on your right ear lobe, some on your right thumb, and some on the big toe of your right foot.

²⁶The priest will pour some of the olive oil into the palm of his left hand, ²⁷then dip a finger of his right hand in the oil and sprinkle some of it seven times toward the sacred tent. ²⁸He will smear some of the oil on your right ear lobe, some on your right thumb, and some on the big toe of your right foot, just as he did with the blood of the sacrifice to make things right. ²⁹⁻³¹And he will pour the rest of the oil from his palm on your head.

Then, depending on what you can afford, he will offer either the doves or the pigeons together with the grain sacrifice. One of the birds is the sacrifice for sin, and the other is the sacrifice to please me. After this you will be completely clean.

³²These are the things you must do if you have leprosy and cannot afford the usual sacrifices to make you clean.

When Mildew Is in a House

³³The LORD told Moses and Aaron to say to the people:

³⁴After I have given you the land of Canaan as your permanent possession, here is what you must do, if I ever put mildew[h] on the walls of any of your homes. ³⁵First, you must say to a priest, "I think mildew is on the wall of my house."

---

[d]**14.12** *sacrifice to make things right:* See 7.1-10.
[e]**14.12** *lift them up:* See the note at 7.29, 30.
[f]**14.13** *sacrifices to please me:* See the note at 1.1-3.
[g]**14.21** *lift these up:* See the note at 7.29, 30.
[g]**14.24,25** *lift it up:* See the note at 7.29, 30.
[h]**14.34** *mildew:* The Hebrew word translated "mildew" is the same one translated "leprosy" and "spot" in chapter 13.

³⁶The priest will reply, "Empty the house before I inspect it, or else everything in it will be unclean."

³⁷If the priest discovers greenish or reddish spots that go deeper than the surface of the walls, ³⁸he will have the house closed for seven days. ³⁹Then he will return and check to see if the mildew has spread. ⁴⁰⁻⁴¹If so, he will have someone scrape the plaster from the walls, remove the filthy stones, then haul everything off and dump it in an unclean place outside the town. ⁴²Afterwards the wall must be repaired with new stones and fresh plaster.

⁴³If the mildew appears a second time, ⁴⁴the priest will come and say, "This house is unclean. It's covered with mildew that can't be removed." ⁴⁵Then he will have the house torn down and every bit of wood, stone, and plaster hauled off to an unclean place outside the town. ⁴⁶Meanwhile, if any of you entered the house while it was closed, you will be unclean until evening. ⁴⁷And if you either slept or ate in the house, you must wash your clothes.

⁴⁸On the other hand, if the priest discovers that mildew hasn't reappeared after the house was newly plastered, he will say, "This house is clean—the mildew has gone." ⁴⁹Then, to show that the house is now clean, he will get two birds, a stick of cedar wood, a piece of red yarn, and a branch from a hyssop plant and bring them to the house. ⁵⁰He will kill one of the birds over a clay pot of spring water ⁵¹⁻⁵²and let its blood drain into the pot. Then he will dip the cedar, the hyssop, the yarn, and the other bird into the mixture of blood and water. Next, he will sprinkle the house seven times with the mixture, then the house will be completely clean. ⁵³Finally, he will release the bird and let it fly away, ending the ceremony for purifying the house.

⁵⁴⁻⁵⁷These are the things you must do if you discover that you are unclean because of an itch or a sore, or that your clothing or house is unclean because of mildew.

Sexual Uncleanness

15 The LORD told Moses and Aaron ²to say to the community of Israel:

Any man with an infected penis is unclean, ³whether it is stopped up or keeps dripping. ⁴Anything that he rests on or sits on is also unclean, ⁵⁻⁷and if you touch either these or him, you must wash your clothes and take a bath, but you still remain unclean until evening.

⁸If you are spit on by the man, you must wash your clothes and take a bath, but you still remain unclean until evening. ⁹⁻¹⁰Any saddle or seat on which the man sits is unclean. And if you touch or carry either of these, you must wash your clothes and take a bath, but you still remain unclean until evening. ¹¹If the man touches you without first washing his hands, you must wash your clothes and take a bath, but you still remain unclean until evening. ¹²Any clay pot that he touches must be destroyed, and any wooden bowl that he touches must be washed.

¹³Seven days after the man gets well, he will be considered clean, if he washes his clothes and takes a bath in spring water. ¹⁴On the eighth day he must bring either two doves or two pigeons to the front of my sacred tent and give them to a priest. ¹⁵The priest will offer one of the birds as a sacrifice for sin and the other as a sacrifice to please me,ⁱ then I will consider the man completely clean.

¹⁶Any man who has a flow of semen must take a bath, but he still remains unclean until evening. ¹⁷If the semen touches anything made of cloth or leather, these must be washed, but they still remain unclean until evening. ¹⁸After having sex, both the man and the woman must take a bath, but they still remain unclean until evening.

¹⁹When a woman has her monthly period, she remains unclean for seven days, and if you touch her, you must take a bath, but you remain unclean until evening. ²⁰⁻²³Anything that she rests on or sits on is also unclean, and if you touch either of these, you must wash your clothes and take a bath, but you still remain unclean until evening. ²⁴Any man who has sex with her during this time becomes unclean for seven days, and anything he rests on is also unclean.

²⁵Any woman who has a flow of blood outside her regular monthly period is unclean until it stops, just as she is during her monthly period. ²⁶Anything that she rests on or sits on during this time is also un-

---

ⁱ**15.15** *sacrifice to please me*: See the note at 1.1-3.

clean, just as it would be during her period. [27]If you touch either of these, you must wash your clothes and take a bath, but you still remain unclean until evening.

[28]Seven days after the woman gets well, she will be considered clean. [29]On the eighth day, she must bring either two doves or two pigeons to the front of my sacred tent and give them to a priest. [30]He will offer one of the birds as a sacrifice for sin and the other as a sacrifice to please me; then I will consider the woman completely clean.

[31]When any of you are unclean, you must stay away from the rest of the community of Israel. Otherwise, my sacred tent will become unclean, and the whole nation will die.

[32-33]These are the things you men must do if you become unclean because of an infected penis or if you have a flow of semen. And these are the things you women must do when you become unclean either because of your monthly period or an unusual flow of blood. This is also what you men must do if you have sex with a woman who is unclean.

The Great Day of Forgiveness

16 [1-2]Two of Aaron's sons had already lost their lives for disobeying the LORD,[j] so the LORD told Moses to say to Aaron:

I, the LORD, appear in a cloud over the place of mercy on the sacred chest, which is behind the inside curtain[k] of the sacred tent. And I warn you not to go there except at the proper time. Otherwise, you will die!

[3]Before entering this most holy place, you must offer a bull as a sacrifice for your sins[l] and a ram as a sacrifice to please me.[m] [4]You will take a bath and put on the sacred linen clothes, including the underwear, the robe, the sash, and the turban. [5]Then the community of Israel will bring you a ram and two goats, both of them males. The goats are to be used as sacrifices for sin, and the ram is to be used as a sacrifice to please me.

[6]Aaron, you must offer the bull as a sacrifice of forgiveness for your own sins and for the sins of your family. [7]Then you will lead the two goats into my presence at the front of the sacred tent, [8]where I will show you[n] which goat will be sacrificed to me and which one will be sent into the desert to the

demon Azazel.[o] [9]After you offer the first goat as a sacrifice for sin, [10]the other one must be presented to me alive, before you send it into the desert to take away the sins of the people.

[11]You must offer the bull as a sacrifice to ask forgiveness for your own sins and for the sins of your family. [12]Then you will take a fire pan of live coals from the bronze altar, together with two handfuls of finely ground incense, into the most holy place. [13]There you will present them to me by placing the incense on the coals, so that the place of mercy will be covered with a cloud of smoke. Do this, or you will die right there! [14]Next, use a finger to sprinkle some of the blood on the place of mercy, which is on the lid of the sacred chest; then sprinkle blood seven times in front of the chest.

[15]Aaron, you must next sacrifice the goat for the sins of the people, and you must sprinkle its blood inside the most holy place, just as you did with the blood of the bull. [16]By doing this, you will take away the sins that make both the most holy place and the people of Israel unclean. Do the same for the sacred tent, which is here among the people. [17]Only you are allowed in the sacred tent from the time you enter until the time you come out. [18]After leaving the tent, you will purify the bronze altar by smearing each of its four corners with some of the blood from the bull and from the goat. [19]Use a finger to sprinkle the altar seven times with the blood, and it will be completely clean from the sins of the people.

[20]After you have purified the most holy place, the sacred tent, and the bronze altar, you must bring the live goat to the front of the tent. [21]There you will lay your hands on its head, while confessing every sin the people have committed, and you will appoint someone to lead the goat into the desert, so that it can take away their sins. [22]Finally, this goat that carries the heavy burden of Israel's sins must be released deep in the desert.

[23-24]Aaron, after this you must go inside

---

[j]16.1,2 lost . . . disobeying the LORD: See 10.1, 2. [k]16.1,2 inside curtain: That separated the holy place from the most holy place. [l]16.3 for your sins: See 4.3-12. [m]16.3 sacrifice to please me: See the note at 1.1-3. [n]16.8 I will show you: The Hebrew text has "you must cast lots to find out." Pieces of wood or stone (called "lots") were used to find out what God wanted his people to do. [o]16.8 Azazel: It was believed that a demon named Azazel lived in the desert.

the sacred tent, take a bath, put on your regular priestly clothes, and leave there the clothes you put on before entering the most holy place. Then you will come out and offer sacrifices to please me and sacrifices for your sins and for the sins of the people. [25]The fat from these sacrifices for sin must be sent up in smoke on the bronze altar.

> My whole life has been
> a process of understanding
> what grace means. It took me
> a long time to realize
> I don't have to be perfect
> for God to love me.
>
> ELISA MORGAN

[26]The one who led the goat into the desert and sent it off to the demon Azazel must take a bath and wash his clothes before coming back into camp. [27]The remains of the bull and the goat whose blood was taken into the most holy place must be taken outside the camp and burned. [28]And whoever does this must take a bath and change clothes before coming back into camp.

The LORD told Moses to say to the people:
[29]On the tenth day of the seventh month[p] of each year, you must go without eating to show sorrow for your sins, and no one, including foreigners who live among you, is allowed to work. [30]This is the day on which the sacrifice for the forgiveness of your sins will be made in my presence, [31]and from now on, it must be celebrated each year. Go without eating and make this a day of complete rest just like the Sabbath. [32]The high priest must offer the sacrifices for cleansing from sin, while wearing the sacred linen clothes. [33]He will offer these sacrifices for the most holy place, the sacred tent, the bronze altar, all the priests, and for the whole community. [34]You must celebrate this day each year—it is the Great Day of Forgiveness[q] for all the sins of the people of Israel.

Moses did exactly as the LORD had commanded.

Where To Offer Sacrifices

17 The LORD told Moses [2]to tell Aaron, his sons, and everyone else in Israel:
[3-4]Whenever you kill any of your cattle, sheep, or goats as sacrifices to me, you must do it at the entrance to the sacred tent. If you don't, you will be guilty of pouring out blood, and you will no longer belong to the community of Israel. [5]And so, when you sacrifice an animal to ask my blessing,[r] it must not be done out in a field, [6]but in front of the sacred tent. Then a priest can splatter its blood against the bronze altar and send its fat up in smoke with a smell that pleases me. [7]Don't ever turn from me again and offer sacrifices to goat-demons. This law will never change.

[8]Remember! No one in Israel, including foreigners, is to offer a sacrifice anywhere [9]except at the entrance to the sacred tent. If you do, you will no longer belong to my people.

Do Not Eat Blood

The LORD said:
[10]I will turn against any of my people who eat blood. This also includes any foreigners living among you. [11]Life is in the blood, and I have given you the blood of animals to sacrifice in place of your own. [12]That's also why I have forbidden you to eat blood. [13]Even if you should hunt and kill a bird or an animal, you must drain out the blood and cover it with soil.

[14]The life of every living creature is in its blood. That's why I have forbidden you to eat blood and why I have warned you that anyone who does will no longer belong to my people.

[15]If you happen to find a dead animal and eat it, you must take a bath and wash your clothes, but you are still unclean until evening. [16]If you don't take a bath, you will suffer for what you did wrong.

---

[p]16.29 *seventh month*: Tishri (also called Ethanim), the seventh month of the Hebrew calendar, from about mid-September to mid-October.   [q]16.34 *Great Day of Forgiveness*: Traditionally known as the Day of Atonement.   [r]17.5 *sacrifice . . . to ask my blessing*: See the note at 3.1.

Forbidden Sex

18 The LORD told Moses [2]to tell the people of Israel:

I am the LORD your God! [3]So don't follow the customs of Egypt where you used to live or those of Canaan where I am bringing you. [4]I am the LORD your God, and you must obey my teachings. [5]Obey them and you will live. I am the LORD.

[6]Don't have sex with any of your close relatives, [7]especially your own mother. This would disgrace your father. [8]And don't disgrace him by having sex with any of his other wives. [9]Don't have sex with your sister or stepsister, whether you grew up together or not. [10]Don't disgrace yourself by having sex with your granddaughter [11]or half sister [12-13]or a sister of your father or mother. [14]Don't disgrace your uncle by having sex with his wife. [15]Don't have sex with your daughter-in-law [16]or sister-in-law. [17]And don't have sex with the daughter or granddaughter of any woman that you have earlier had sex with. You may be having sex with a relative, and that would make you unclean. [18]As long as your wife is alive, don't cause trouble for her by taking one of her sisters as a second wife.

[19]When a woman is having her monthly period, she is unclean, so don't have sex with her.

> *A solid relationship requires commitment first and hard work second. But the payoff— a loving, lasting marriage— is worth the effort.*
>
> SANDRA P. ALDRICH

[20]Don't have sex with another man's wife—that would make you unclean.

[21]Don't sacrifice your children on the altar fires to the god Molech. I am the LORD your God, and that would disgrace me.

[22]It is disgusting for a man to have sex with another man.

[23]Anyone who has sex with an animal is unclean.

[24]Don't make yourselves unclean by any of these disgusting practices of those nations that I am forcing out of the land for you. They made themselves [25]and the land so unclean, that I punished the land because of their sins, and I made it vomit them up. [26-27]Now don't do these sickening things that make the land filthy. Instead, obey my laws and teachings. [28]Then the land won't become sick of you and vomit you up, just as it did them. [29-30]If any of you do these vulgar, disgusting things, you will be unclean and no longer belong to my people. I am the LORD your God, and I forbid you to follow their sickening way of life.

Moral and Religious Laws

19 The LORD told Moses [2]to say to the community of Israel:

I am the LORD your God. I am holy, and you must be holy too! [3-4]Respect your father and your mother, honor the Sabbath, and don't make idols or images. I am the LORD your God.

[5]When you offer a sacrifice to ask my blessing,[r] be sure to follow my instructions. [6]You may eat the meat either on the day of the sacrifice or on the next day, but you must burn anything left until the third day. [7]If you eat any of it on the third day, the sacrifice will be disgusting to me, and I will reject it. [8]In fact, you will be punished for not respecting what I say is holy, and you will no longer belong to the community of Israel.

[9]When you harvest your grain, always leave some of it standing along the edges of your fields and don't pick up what falls on the ground. [10]Don't strip your grapevines clean or gather the grapes that fall off the vines. Leave them for the poor and for those foreigners who live among you. I am the LORD your God.

[11]Do not steal or tell lies or cheat others.

[12]Do not misuse my name by making promises you don't intend to keep. I am the LORD your God.

[13]Do not steal anything or cheat anyone, and don't fail to pay your workers at the end of each day.[s]

[14]I am the LORD your God, and I

---

[r]**19.5** *to ask my blessing:* See the note at 3.1.
[s]**19.13** *to pay . . . end of each day:* Day laborers needed their wages to buy food for their evening meal, which was the main meal of the day.

command you not to make fun of the deaf or to cause a blind person to stumble.

¹⁵Be fair, no matter who is on trial—don't favor either the poor or the rich.

¹⁶Don't be a gossip, but never hesitate to speak up in court, especially if your testimony can save someone's life.ᵗ

¹⁷Don't hold grudges. On the other hand, it's wrong not to correct someone who needs correcting. ¹⁸Stop being angry and don't try to take revenge. I am the LORD, and I command you to love others as much as you love yourself.

¹⁹Breed your livestock animals only with animals of the same kind, and don't plant two kinds of seed in the same field or wear clothes made of different kinds of material.

²⁰If a man has sex with a slave woman who is promised in marriage to someone else, he must pay a fine, but they are not to be put to death. After all, she was still a slave at the time.ᵘ ²¹⁻²²The man must bring a ram to the entrance of the sacred tent and give it to a priest, who will then offer it as a sacrifice to me, so the man's sins will be forgiven.

²³After you enter the land, you will plant fruit trees, but you are not to eat any of their fruit for the first three years. ²⁴In the fourth year the fruit must be set apart, as an expression of thanks ²⁵to me, the LORD God. Do this, and in the fifth year, those trees will produce an abundant harvest of fruit for you to eat.

²⁶Don't eat the blood of any animal. Don't practice any kind of witchcraft.

²⁷⁻²⁸I forbid you to shave any part of your head or beard or to cut and tattoo yourself as a way of worshiping the dead.

²⁹Don't let your daughters serve as temple prostitutes—this would bring disgrace both to them and the land.

³⁰I command you to respect the Sabbath and the place where I am worshiped.

³¹Don't make yourselves disgusting to me by going to people who claim they can talk to the dead.

³²I command you to show respect for older people and to obey me with fear and trembling.

³³Don't mistreat any foreigners who live in your land. ³⁴Instead, treat them as well as you treat citizens and love them as much as you love yourself. Remember, you were once foreigners in the land of Egypt. I am the LORD your God.

³⁵⁻³⁶Use honest scales and don't cheat when you weigh or measure anything.

I am the LORD your God. I rescued you

ᵗ**19.16** *but never . . . someone's life:* One possible meaning for the difficult Hebrew text. ᵘ**19.20** *time:* One possible meaning for the difficult Hebrew text of verse 20.

Friendship—How can I repair a broken friendship? *(Leviticus 19.17,18)*

Let go of grudges and build bridges instead.

"I thought I could trust her, but she passed on my secret." "She ignored me when she got married—and now she wants to be friends again. I don't get it." If you faced these or any other situations where you've felt betrayed by a friend, you know that friendship isn't easy. It's risky to let someone get to know the real you. And when that person hurts you, the hurt can go down deep.

In such times, it's important to obey the biblical mandate from this passage: "Don't hold grudges. . . . Stop being angry and don't try to take revenge." When someone hurts us, it's only human to want to fight back—to hurt that person as much as he or she has hurt you. But a life of revenge is not the way God chooses for us to live. Instead, he commands, "Love others as much as you love yourself."

As startling as that statement sounds, it's right and true. When we seek revenge, revenge holds us in its bitter grip. But when we choose to forgive, and even reach out in love, revenge melts away. And who knows? We might gain an even deeper relationship with that friend—or, at the very least, we can rest in a clean conscience. (See also Matthew 5.21-26; Matthew 18.15-20; Luke 6.37-42.)

Words To Remember: *Stop being angry and don't try to take revenge. I am the LORD, and I command you to love others as much as you love yourself.—Leviticus 19.18*

from Egypt, ³⁷and I command you to obey my laws.

Penalties for Disobeying God's Laws

20 The LORD told Moses ²to say to the community of Israel:

Death by stoning is the penalty for any citizens or foreigners in the country who sacrifice their children to the god Molech. ³They have disgraced both the place where I am worshiped and my holy name, and so I will turn against them and no longer let them belong to my people. ⁴Some of you may let them get away with human sacrifice, ⁵but not me. If any of you worship Molech, I will turn against you and your entire family, and I will no longer let you belong to my people.

⁶I will be your enemy if you go to someone who claims to speak with the dead, and I will destroy you from among my people. ⁷Dedicate yourselves to me and be holy because I am the LORD your God. ⁸I have chosen you as my people, and I expect you to obey my laws.

⁹If you curse your father or mother, you will be put to death, and it will be your own fault.

¹⁰If any of you men have sex with another man's wife, both you and the woman will be put to death.

¹¹Having sex with one of your father's wives disgraces him. So both you and the woman will be put to death, just as you deserve. ¹²It isn't natural to have sex with your daughter-in-law, and both of you will be put to death, just as you deserve. ¹³It's disgusting for men to have sex with one another, and those who do will be put to death, just as they deserve. ¹⁴It isn't natural for a man to marry both a mother and her daughter, and so all three of them will be burned to death. ¹⁵⁻¹⁶If any of you have sex with an animal, both you and the animal will be put to death, just as you deserve.

¹⁷If you marry one of your sisters, you will be punished, and the two of you will be disgraced by being openly forced out of the community. ¹⁸If you have sex with a woman during her monthly period, both you and the woman will be cut off from the people of Israel. ¹⁹The sisters of your father and mother are your own relatives, and you will be punished for having sex with any of them. ²⁰If you have sex with your uncle's wife, neither

you nor she will ever have any children. ²¹And if you marry your sister-in-law, neither of you will ever have any children.^v

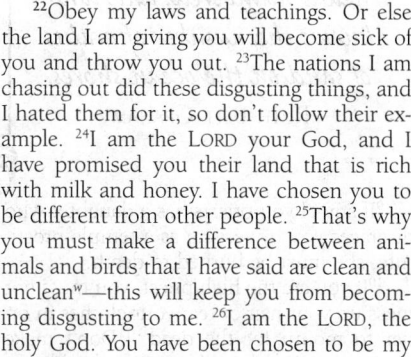

We must trust and obey God, then allow him to open his floodgates in our lives, pouring in more of his grace and peace than we could possibly contain.

JONI EARECKSON TADA

²²Obey my laws and teachings. Or else the land I am giving you will become sick of you and throw you out. ²³The nations I am chasing out did these disgusting things, and I hated them for it, so don't follow their example. ²⁴I am the LORD your God, and I have promised you their land that is rich with milk and honey. I have chosen you to be different from other people. ²⁵That's why you must make a difference between animals and birds that I have said are clean and unclean^w—this will keep you from becoming disgusting to me. ²⁶I am the LORD, the holy God. You have been chosen to be my people, and so you must be holy too.

²⁷If you claim to receive messages from the dead, you will be put to death by stoning, just as you deserve.

Instructions for Priests

21 The LORD gave Moses these instructions for Aaron's sons, the priests:

Touching a dead body will make you unclean. So don't go near a dead relative, ²except your mother, father, son, daughter, brother, ³or an unmarried sister, who has no husband to take care of her. ⁴Don't make yourself unclean by attending the funeral of

---

^v**20.21** *And . . . children:* According to Deuteronomy 25.5, 6 a man was supposed to marry his brother's widow if his brother had died without having children. Otherwise, such marriages were forbidden (see also Matthew 22.23-33; Mark 12.18-27; Luke 20.27-40). ^w**20.25** *clean and unclean:* See the note at 11.4-8.

someone related to you by marriage.[x] [5]Don't shave any part of your head or trim your beard or cut yourself to show that you are mourning. [6]I am the LORD your God, and I have chosen you alone to offer sacrifices of food to me on the altar. That's why you must keep yourselves holy. [7]Don't marry a divorced woman or a woman who has served as a temple prostitute. You are holy, [8]because I am holy. And so, you must be treated with proper respect, since you offer food sacrifices to me, the God of holiness.

> *Each person is special to him who calls every star by name, who has the hairs of our heads numbered, and who knows the number of grains of sand on the ocean shores.*
>
> RUTH BELL GRAHAM

[9]If any of you priests has a daughter who disgraces you by serving as a temple prostitute, she must be burned to death.

[10]If you are the high priest, you must not mess up your hair or tear your clothes in order to mourn for the dead. [11]Don't make yourself unclean by going near a dead body, not even that of your own father or mother. [12]If you leave the sacred place to attend a funeral, both you and the sacred place become unclean, because you are the high priest.

[13]If you are the high priest, you must marry only a virgin [14]from your own tribe. Don't marry a divorced woman or any other woman who has already had sex, including a temple prostitute. [15]In this way, your descendants will be qualified to serve me. Remember—I am the LORD, and I have chosen you.

[16]The LORD told Moses [17-18]to say to Aaron:

No descendant of yours can ever serve as my priest if he is blind or lame, if his face is disfigured, if one leg is shorter than the other, [19]if either a foot or a hand is crippled, [20]if he is a hunchback or a dwarf, if an eye or his skin is diseased, or if his testicles have been damaged. [21]These men may not serve as my priests and burn sacrifices to me. [22]They may eat the food offerings presented to me, [23]but they may not enter the sacred place or serve me at the altar. Remember—I am the LORD, the one who makes a priest holy.

[24]Moses told all of this to Aaron, his sons, and the people of Israel.

The Offerings Are Holy

22 The LORD told Moses [2]to say to Aaron and his sons:

I am the LORD God, and I demand that you honor my holy name by showing proper respect for the offerings brought to me by the people of Israel. [3]If any of you are unclean when you accept an offering for me, I will no longer let you serve as a priest. [4]None of you may take part in the sacred meals while you have a skin disease or an infected penis, or after you have been near a dead body or have had a flow of semen, [5]or if you have touched an unclean creature of any sort, including an unclean person. [6-7]Once you are unclean, you must take a bath, but you still cannot eat any of the sacred food until evening. [8]I command you not to eat anything that is killed by a wild animal or dies a natural death. This would make you unclean. [9]Obey me, or you will die on duty for disgracing the place of worship. Remember—I am the LORD, the one who makes a priest holy.

[10]Only you priests and your families may eat the food offerings; these are too sacred for any of your servants. [11]However, any slave that you own, including those born into your household, may eat this food. [12]If your daughter marries someone who isn't a priest, she can no longer have any of this food. [13]But if she returns to your home, either widowed or divorced, and has no children, she may join in the meal. Only members of a priestly family can eat this food, [14]and anyone else who accidentally does so, must pay for the food plus a fine of twenty percent.

[15]I warn you not to treat lightly the offerings that are brought by the people of Israel. [16]Don't let them become guilty of eating this

---

[x]21.4 *marriage*: One possible meaning for the difficult Hebrew text of verse 4.

sacred food. Remember—I am the LORD, the one who makes these offerings holy.

Acceptable Sacrifices

[17]The LORD told Moses [18]to tell Aaron and his sons and everyone else the rules for offering sacrifices. He said:

The animals that are to be completely burned on the altar [19-20]must have nothing wrong with them, or else I won't accept them. Bulls or rams or goats[y] are the animals to be used for these sacrifices.

[21]When you offer a sacrifice to ask my blessing,[z] there must be nothing wrong with the animal. This is true, whether the sacrifice is part of a promise or something you do voluntarily. [22]Don't offer an animal that is blind or injured or that has an infection or a skin disease. [23]If one of your cattle or lambs has a leg that is longer or shorter than the others, you may offer it voluntarily, but not as part of a promise. [24]As long as you live in this land, don't offer an animal with injured testicles. [25]And don't bring me animals you bought from a foreigner. I won't accept them, because they are no better than one that has something wrong with it.

> When God asks us
> to do something,
> he prepares the way—
> and gives us the
> tools to do it.
>
> EVANGELINE SCHOCK

[26]The LORD told Moses to say:
[27]Newborn cattle, sheep, or goats must remain with their mothers for seven days, but on the eighth day, you may send them up in smoke to me, and I will accept the offering. [28]Don't sacrifice a newborn animal and its mother on the same day.

[29]When you offer a sacrifice to give thanks[a] to me, you must do it in a way that is acceptable. [30]Eat all of the meat that same day and don't save any for the next day. I am the LORD your God!

[31]Obey my laws and teachings—I am the

LORD. [32-33]I demand respect from the people of Israel, so don't disgrace my holy name. Remember—I am the one who chose you to be priests and rescued all of you from Egypt, so that I would be your LORD.

Religious Festivals

23 The LORD told Moses [2]to say to the community of Israel:
I have chosen certain times for you to come together and worship me.

[3]You have six days when you can do your work, but the seventh day of each week is holy because it belongs to me. No matter where you live, you must rest on the Sabbath and come together for worship. This law will never change.

Passover and the Festival of Thin Bread
(Numbers 28.16-25)

The LORD said:

[4-5]Passover is another time when you must come together to worship me, and it must be celebrated on the evening of the fourteenth day of the first month[b] of each year.

[6]The Festival of Thin Bread begins on the fifteenth day of that same month; it lasts seven days, and during this time you must honor me by eating bread made without yeast. [7]On the first day of this festival you must rest from your work and come together for worship. [8]Each day of this festival you must offer sacrifices. Then on the final day you must once again rest from your work and come together for worship.

Offering the First Part of the Harvest

[9]The LORD told Moses [10]to say to the community of Israel:

After you enter the land I am giving you, the first bundle of wheat from each crop must be given to me. So bring it to a priest [11]on the day after the Sabbath. He will lift it up[c] in dedication to me, and I will accept you. [12]You must also offer a sacrifice to please me.[d] So bring the priest a one-year-

---

[y]22.19,20 goats: See the note at 1.1-3. [z]22.21 sacrifice to ask my blessing: See the note at 3.1. [a]22.29 sacrifice to give thanks: See 7.12. [b]23.4,5 first month: Abib (also called Nisan), the first month of the Hebrew calendar, from about mid-March to mid-April. [c]23.11 lift it up: See the note at 7.29, 30. [d]23.12 sacrifice to please me: See the note at 1.1-3.

old lamb that has nothing wrong with it
¹³and four pounds of your finest flour mixed
with olive oil. Then he will place these on
the bronze altar and send them up in smoke
with a smell that pleases me. Together with
these, you must bring a quart of wine as a
drink offering. ¹⁴I am your God, and I forbid
you to eat any new grain or anything made
from it until you have brought these offerings. This law will never change.

The Harvest Festival
(Numbers 28.26-31)

The LORD said:

¹⁵Seven weeks after you offer this bundle
of grain, each family must bring another offering of new grain. ¹⁶Do this exactly fifty
days later, which is the day following the
seventh Sabbath. ¹⁷Bring two loaves of bread
to be lifted up^e in dedication to me. Each
loaf is to be made with yeast and with four
pounds of the finest flour from the first part
of your harvest.
¹⁸At this same time, the entire community of Israel must bring seven lambs that are
a year old, a young bull, and two rams. These
animals must have nothing wrong with
them, and they must be offered as a sacrifice
to please me.^f You must also offer the proper
grain and wine sacrifices with each animal.^g
¹⁹Offer a goat^h as a sacrifice for sin, and two
rams a year old as a sacrifice to ask my
blessing.ⁱ ²⁰The priest will lift up^j the rams
together with the bread in dedication to me.
These offerings are holy and are my gift to the
priest. ²¹This is a day of celebration and worship, a time of rest from your work. You and
your descendants must obey this law.
²²When you harvest your grain, always
leave some of it standing around the edges
of your fields and don't pick up what falls on
the ground. Leave it for the poor and for
those foreigners who live among you. I am
the LORD your God!

The Festival of Trumpets
(Numbers 29.1-6)

²³The LORD told Moses ²⁴⁻²⁵to say to the
people of Israel:
The first day of the seventh month^k must
be a day of complete rest. Then at the sound
of the trumpets, you will come together to
worship and to offer sacrifices on the altar.

The Great Day of Forgiveness
(Numbers 29.7-11)

²⁶The LORD God said to Moses:
²⁷The tenth day of the seventh month^k is
the Great Day of Forgiveness.^l It is a solemn
day of worship; everyone must go without
eating to show sorrow for their sins, and sacrifices must be burned. ²⁸No one is to work
on that day—it is the Great Day of Forgiveness, when sacrifices will be offered to me,
so that I will forgive your sins. ²⁹I will destroy anyone who refuses to go without eating. ³⁰⁻³¹None of my people are ever to do
any work on that day—not now or in the
future. And I will wipe out those who do!
³²This is a time of complete rest just like the
Sabbath, and everyone must go without eating from the evening of the ninth to the evening of the tenth.

The Festival of Shelters
(Numbers 29.12-40)

³³The LORD told Moses ³⁴to say to the
community of Israel:
Beginning on the fifteenth day of the seventh month,^m and continuing for seven
days, everyone must celebrate the Festival of
Shelters in honor of me. ³⁵No one is to do
any work on the first day of the festival—it is
a time when everyone must come together
for worship. ³⁶For seven days, sacrifices
must be offered on the altar. The eighth day
is also to be a day of complete rest, as well as
a time of offering sacrifices on the altar and
of coming together for worship.
³⁷I have chosen these festivals as times
when my people must come together for
worship and when animals, grain, and wine
are to be offered on the proper days. ³⁸These
festivals must be celebrated in addition to
the Sabbaths and the times when you offer
special gifts or sacrifices to keep a promise
or as a voluntary offering.
³⁹Remember to begin the Festival of
Shelters on the fifteenth day of the seventh

e23.17 lifted up: See the note at 7.29, 30.
f23.18 sacrifice to please me: See the note at 1.1-3.
g23.18 proper grain . . . animal: See Numbers 15.1-16.
h23.19 goat: See the note at 1.1-3.   i23.19 sacrifice to
ask my blessing: See the note at 3.1.   j23.20 lift up: See
the note at 7.29, 30.   k23.24,25,27 seventh month:
See the note at 16.29.   l23.27 Great Day of
Forgiveness: See the note at 16.34.   m23.34 seventh
month: See the note at 16.29.

month after you have harvested your crops. Celebrate this festival for seven days in honor of me and don't do any work on the first day or on the day following the festival. [40]Pick the best fruit from your trees[n] and cut leafy branches to use during the time of this joyous celebration in my honor. [41]I command you and all of your descendants to celebrate this festival during the seventh month of each year. [42]For seven days every Israelite must live in a shelter, [43]so future generations will know that I made their ancestors live in shelters when I brought them out of Egypt. I am the LORD your God.

[44]This is how Moses instructed the people of Israel to celebrate the LORD's festivals.

Caring for the Lamps
(Exodus 27.20, 21)

24 The LORD told Moses [2]to say to the community of Israel:

You must supply the purest olive oil for the lamps in the sacred tent, so they will keep burning. [3-4]Aaron will set up the gold lampstand in the holy place of the sacred tent. Then he will light the seven lamps that must be kept burning there in my presence, every night from now on. This law will never change.

The Sacred Bread

The LORD said:

[5]Use your finest flour to bake twelve loaves of bread about four pounds each, [6]then take them into the sacred tent and lay them on the gold table in two rows of six loaves. [7]Alongside each row put some pure incense that will be sent up by fire in place of the bread as an offering to me. [8]Aaron must lay fresh loaves on the table each Sabbath, and priests in all generations must continue this practice as part of Israel's agreement with me. [9]This bread will always belong to Aaron and his family; it is very holy because it was offered to me, and it must be eaten in a holy place.[o]

Punishment for Cursing the LORD

[10-11]Shelomith, the daughter of Dibri from the tribe of Dan, had married an Egyptian, and they had a son. One day their son got into a fight with an Israelite man in camp and cursed the name of the LORD. So the young man was dragged off to Moses,

[12]who had him guarded while everyone waited for the LORD to tell them what to do. [13]Finally, the LORD said to Moses:

[14]This man has cursed me! Take him outside the camp and have the witnesses lay their hands on his head. Then command the whole community of Israel to stone him to death. [15-16]And warn the others that everyone else who curses me will die in the same way, whether they are Israelites by birth or foreigners living among you.

[17]Death is also the penalty for murder, [18]but the killing of an animal that belongs to someone else requires only that the animal be replaced. [19]Personal injuries to others must be dealt with in keeping with the crime—[20]a broken bone for a broken bone, an eye for an eye, or a tooth for a tooth. [21]It's possible to pay the owner for an animal that has been killed, but death is the penalty for murder. [22]I am the LORD your God, and I demand equal justice both for you Israelites and for those foreigners who live among you.

[23]When Moses finished speaking, the people did what the LORD had told Moses, and they stoned to death the man who had cursed the LORD.

The Seventh Year
(Deuteronomy 15.1-11)

25 When Moses was on Mount Sinai, the LORD told him [2]to say to the community of Israel:

After you enter the land that I am giving you, it must be allowed to rest one year out of every seven. [3]You may raise grain and grapes for six years, [4]but the seventh year you must let your fields and vineyards rest in honor of me, your LORD. [5]This is to be a time of complete rest for your fields and vineyards, so don't harvest anything they produce. [6-7]However, you and your slaves and your hired workers, as well as any domestic or wild animals, may eat whatever grows on its own.

---

[n]**23.40** *best fruit from your trees:* One possible meaning for the difficult Hebrew text.   [o]**24.9** *holy place:* The courtyard of the sacred tent (see 6.16, 17).

The Year of Celebration

The LORD said to his people:

[8]Once every forty-nine years [9]on the
tenth day of the seventh month,[p] which is
also the Great Day of Forgiveness,[q] trumpets
are to be blown everywhere in the land.
[10]This fiftieth year[r] is sacred—it is a time of
freedom and of celebration when everyone
will receive back their original property, and
slaves will return home to their families.
[11]This is a year of complete celebration, so
don't plant any seed or harvest what your
fields or vineyards produce. [12]In this time of
sacred celebration you may eat only what
grows on its own.

[13]During this year, all property must go
back to its original owner. [14-15]So when you
buy or sell farmland, the price is to be determined by the number of crops it can produce before the next Year of Celebration.
Don't try to cheat. [16]If it is a long time before
the next Year of Celebration, the price will
be higher, because what is really being sold
are the crops that the land can produce. [17]I
am the LORD your God, so obey me and
don't cheat anyone.

[18-19]If you obey my laws and teachings,
you will live safely in the land and enjoy its
abundant crops. [20]Don't ever worry about
what you will eat during the seventh year
when you are forbidden to plant or harvest.
[21]I will see to it that you harvest enough in
the sixth year to last for three years. [22]In the
eighth year you will live on what you harvested in the sixth year, but in the ninth year
you will eat what you plant and harvest in
the eighth year.

[23]No land may be permanently bought
or sold. It all belongs to me—it isn't your
land, and you only live there for a little
while.

[24]When property is being sold, the original owner must be given the first chance to
buy it.

[25]If any of you Israelites become so poor
that you are forced to sell your property,
your closest relative must buy it back, [26]if
that relative has the money. Later, if you can
afford to buy it, [27]you must pay enough to
make up for what the present owner will
lose on it before the next Year of Celebration, when the property would become
yours again. [28]But if you don't have the
money to pay the present owner a fair price,
you will have to wait until the Year of Celebration, when the property will once again
become yours.

[p]25.9 *seventh month*: See the note at 16.29.
[q]25.9 *Great Day of Forgiveness*: See the note at 16.34.
[r]25.10 *fiftieth year*: The year following seven periods of seven years.

Personal *Concerns*—When it comes to material things, how can I know what's enough and what's too much? *(Leviticus 25.8-28)*

Remember that all our possessions belong to God.

Think of everything you have. Can you remember where you bought it, or who gave it to you? Now imagine that all those possessions have to be given back to their original owners. Would you have anything left?

That's what happened in Israel every fifty years, on the Year of Celebration (also known as the Year of Jubilee). Every fiftieth year the people were supposed to return all land and houses to the person they'd bought them from. Why did they have to do this? Because God wanted them to remember that all property really belonged to him; the Israelites were merely using it with his permission.

What a wonderful reminder for us that all we have belongs to God! He's merely "leasing" it to us for a little while because he loves us and cares for us. And if all our possessions are really God's, we know he's capable of providing us with everything we need. If he provides us with plenty, that's wonderful. But we must remember that those material blessings don't really belong to us. God is simply allowing us to use his possessions for his glory. And when things get tight, remember: God is still in charge. (See also Deuteronomy 24.19-22; Amos 6.1-7; Philippians 3.7-16; 1 Timothy 6.17-19.)

Words To Remember: ***[The land] all belongs to me—it isn't your land, and you only live there for a little while.*—Leviticus 25.23**

[29]If you sell a house in a walled city, you have only one year in which to buy it back. [30]If you don't buy it back before that year is up, it becomes the permanent property of the one who bought it, and it will not be returned to you in the Year of Celebration. [31]But a house out in a village may be bought back at any time just like a field. And it must be returned to its original owner in the Year of Celebration. [32]If any Levites own houses inside a walled city, they will always have the right to buy them back. [33]And any houses that they do not buy back will be returned to them in the Year of Celebration, because these homes are their permanent property among the people of Israel. [34]No pastureland owned by the Levi tribe can ever be sold; it is their permanent possession.

Help for the Poor

The LORD said:

[35]If any of your people become poor and unable to support themselves, you must help them, just as you are supposed to help foreigners who live among you. [36-37]Don't take advantage of them by charging any kind of interest or selling them food for profit. Instead, honor me by letting them stay where they now live. [38]Remember—I am the LORD your God! I rescued you from Egypt and gave you the land of Canaan, so that I would be your God.

[39]Suppose some of your people become so poor that they have to sell themselves and become your slaves. [40]Then you must treat them as servants, rather than as slaves. And in the Year of Celebration they are to be set free, [41]so they and their children may return home to their families and property. [42]I brought them out of Egypt to be my servants, not to be sold as slaves. [43]So obey me, and don't be cruel to the poor.

[44]If you want slaves, buy them from other nations [45]or from the foreigners who live in your own country, and make them your property. [46]You can own them, and even leave them to your children when you die, but do not make slaves of your own people or be cruel to them.

[47]Even if some of you Israelites become so much in debt that you must sell yourselves to foreigners in your country, [48]you still have the right to be set free by a relative, such as a brother [49]or uncle or cousin, or some other family member. In fact, if you ever get enough money, you may buy your own freedom [50]by paying your owner for the number of years you would still be a slave before the next Year of Celebration. [51-52]The longer the time until then, the more you will have to pay. [53]And even while you are the slaves of foreigners in your own country, your people must make sure that you are not mistreated. [54]If you cannot gain your freedom in any of these ways, both you and your children will still be set free in the Year of Celebration. [55]People of Israel, I am the LORD your God, and I brought you out of Egypt to be my own servants.

Blessings for Obeying the LORD

The LORD said:

26 I am the LORD your God! So don't make or worship any sort of idols or images. [2]Respect the Sabbath and honor the place where I am worshiped, because I am the LORD.

[3]Faithfully obey my laws, [4]and I will send rain to make your crops grow and your trees produce fruit. [5]Your harvest of grain and grapes will be so abundant, that you won't know what to do with it all. You will eat and be satisfied, and you will live in safety. [6]I will bless your country with peace, and you will rest without fear. I will wipe out the dangerous animals and protect you from enemy attacks. [7]You will chase and destroy your enemies, [8]even if there are only five of you and a hundred of them, or only a hundred of you and ten thousand of them. [9]I will treat you with such kindness that your nation will grow strong, and I will also keep my promises to you. [10]Your barns will overflow with grain each year. [11]I will live among you and never again look on you with disgust. [12]I will walk with you—I will be your God, and you will be my people. [13]I am the LORD your God, and I rescued you from Egypt, so that you would never again be slaves. I have set you free; now walk with your heads held high.

Punishment for Disobeying the LORD

The LORD said:

[14-15]If you disobey me and my laws, and if you break our agreement, [16]I will punish you terribly, and you will be ruined. You will

be struck with incurable diseases and with fever that leads to blindness and depression. Your enemies will eat the crops you plant, [17]and I will turn from you and let you be destroyed by your attackers. You will even run at the very rumor of attack. [18]Then, if you still refuse to obey me, I will punish you seven times for each of your sins, [19]until your pride is completely crushed. I will hold back the rain, so the sky above you will be like iron, and the ground beneath your feet will be like copper. [20]All of your hard work will be for nothing—and there will be no harvest of grain or fruit.

[21]If you keep rebelling against me, I'll punish you seven times worse, just as your sins deserve! [22]I'll send wild animals to attack you, and they will gobble down your children and livestock. So few of you will be left that your roads will be deserted.

[23]If you remain my enemies after this, [24]I'll remain your enemy and punish you even worse. [25]War will break out because you broke our agreement, and if you escape to your walled cities, I'll punish you with horrible diseases, and you will be captured by your enemies. [26]You will have such a shortage of bread, that ten women will be able to bake their bread in the same oven. Each of you will get only a few crumbs, and you will go hungry.

[27]Then if you don't stop rebelling, [28]I'll really get furious and punish you terribly for your sins! [29]In fact, you will be so desperate for food that you will eat your own children. [30]I'll destroy your shrines and tear down your incense altars, leaving your dead bodies piled on top of your idols. And you will be disgusting to me. [31]I'll wipe out your towns and your places of worship and will no longer be pleased with the smell of your sacrifices. [32]Your land will become so desolate that even your enemies who settle there will be shocked when they see it. [33]After I destroy your towns and ruin your land with war, I'll scatter you among the nations.

[34-35]While you are prisoners in foreign lands, your own land will enjoy years of rest and refreshment, as it should have done each seventh year when you lived there. [36-37]In the land of your enemies, you will tremble at the rustle of a leaf, as though it were a sword. And you will become so weak that you will stumble and fall over each other, even when no one is chasing you. [38]Many of you will die in foreign lands, [39]and others of you will waste away in sorrow as the result of your sins and the sins of your ancestors.

[40-41]Then suppose you realize that I turned against you and brought you to the land of your enemies because both you and your ancestors had stubbornly sinned against me. If you humbly confess what you

---

Personal *Concerns*—How can I handle even difficult times positively?
(Leviticus 26.1-13)

Know that God is with you!
What if you had a personal line to the White House? You could call the president of the United States at any time with any problem. Troubles with your taxes? He'd straighten them out. Low on money? He'd arrange a transfer from the Federal Reserve. Worried about your teenagers? He'd assign a Secret Service man to keep an eye on them.

Think how easy it would be to have a positive attitude if you knew the president were on your side. Well, Leviticus tells us that we have someone even more powerful on our side—the God who rules the entire universe! God promises he will provide us with food; he will give us peace, even when troubles start to pile up against us; he will help us to grow spiritually strong. And most of all, God promises to "walk with us," which means he will go through every minute of every day with us.

God does give one command, though: Be obedient to me! This is the key to a positive attitude toward life—even when problems arise. Be obedient to God's commands, and you can be sure he will be with you, giving you strength and peace. (See also Job 23; Micah 4.1-5; Nahum 1.2-7,15; Romans 8.18-30; Ephesians 1.7-23.)

Words To Remember: *I have set you free; now walk with your heads held high.*—Leviticus 26.13

have done and start living right, ⁴²I'll keep the promise I made to your ancestors Abraham, Isaac, and Jacob. I will bless your land ⁴³and let it rest during the time that you are in a foreign country, paying for your rebellion against me and my laws.

⁴⁴No matter what you have done, I am still the LORD your God, and I will never completely reject you or become absolutely disgusted with you there in the land of your enemies. ⁴⁵While nations watched, I rescued your ancestors from Egypt so that I would be their God. Yes, I am your LORD, and I will never forget our agreement.

⁴⁶Moses was on Mount Sinai when the LORD gave him these laws and teachings for the people of Israel.

Making Promises to the LORD

27 The LORD told Moses ²to say to the community of Israel:

If you ever want to free someone who has been promised to me, ³⁻⁷you may do so by paying the following amounts, weighed according to the official standards:

> fifty pieces of silver for men
>   ages twenty to sixty,
> and thirty pieces for women;
> twenty pieces of silver
>   for young men
> ages five to twenty,
> and ten pieces
>   for young women;
> fifteen pieces of silver for men
> ages sixty and above
>   and ten pieces for women;
> five pieces of silver for boys
> ages one month to five years,
>   and three pieces for girls.

⁸If you have promised to give someone to me and can't afford to pay the full amount for that person's release, you will be taken to a priest, and he will decide how much you can afford.

⁹If you promise to sacrifice an animal to me, it becomes holy, and there is no way you can set it free. ¹⁰If you try to substitute any other animal, no matter how good, for the one you promised, they will both become holy and must be sacrificed. ¹¹Donkeys are unfit for sacrifice, so if you promise me a donkey,ˢ you must bring it to the priest, ¹²and let him determine its value.

¹³But if you want to buy it back, you must pay an additional twenty percent.

¹⁴If you promise a house to me, a priest will set the price, whatever the condition of the house. ¹⁵But if you decide to buy it back, you must pay an additional twenty percent.

¹⁶If you promise part of your family's land to me, its value must be determined by the bushels of seed needed to plant the land, and the rate will be ten pieces of silver for every bushel of seed. ¹⁷If this promise is made in the Year of Celebration,ᵗ the land will be valued at the full price. ¹⁸But any time after that, the price will be figured according to the number of years before the next Year of Celebration. ¹⁹If you decide to buy back the land, you must pay the price plus an additional twenty percent, ²⁰but you cannot buy it back once someone else has bought it. ²¹When the Year of Celebration comes, the land becomes holy because it belongs to me, and it will be given to the priests.

²²If you promise me a field that you have bought, ²³its value will be decided by a priest, according to the number of years before the next Year of Celebration, and the money you pay will be mine. ²⁴However, on the next Year of Celebration, the land will go back to the family of its original owner. ²⁵Every price will be set by the official standards.

Various Offerings

The LORD said:

²⁶All first-born animals of your flocks and herds are already mine, and so you cannot promise any of them to me. ²⁷If you promise me a donkey,ᵘ you may buy it back by adding an additional twenty percent to its value. If you don't buy it back, it can be sold to someone else for whatever a priest has said it is worth.

²⁸Anything that you completely dedicate to me must be completely destroyed.ᵛ It

---

ˢ**27.11** *Donkeys . . . donkey:* The Hebrew text has "If you promise me an unclean animal," which probably refers to a donkey (see Exodus 13.13; 34.20).   ᵗ**27.17** *Year of Celebration:* See 25.8-34.   ᵘ**27.27** *donkey:* See the note at verse 11.   ᵛ**27.28** *completely dedicate . . . completely destroyed:* In order to show that something belonged completely to the LORD and could not be used by anyone else, it was destroyed. This law most often applied to towns and people captured in war (see Joshua 6.16, 17).

cannot be bought back or sold. Every person, animal, and piece of property that you dedicate completely is only for me. [29]In fact, any humans who have been promised to me in this way must be put to death.

[30]Ten percent of everything you harvest is holy and belongs to me, whether it grows in your fields or on your fruit trees. [31]If you want to buy back this part of your harvest, you may do so by paying what it is worth plus an additional twenty percent. [32]When you count your flocks and herds, one out of ten of every newborn animal[w] is holy and belongs to me, [33]no matter how good or bad it is. If you substitute one animal for another, both of them become holy, and neither can be bought back.

[34]Moses was on Mount Sinai when the LORD gave him these laws for the people of Israel.

---

[w]**27.32** *one out of ten of every newborn animal:* Or "one out of every ten animals."

Numbers
A Story of Forgiveness

How many times does God forgive sin? The book of Numbers tells us the answer: over and over and over again.

Numbers tells the story of what God's people did after they left Mount Sinai and started wandering through the desert. They forgot about God's miracles and started to complain against God and against Moses. Even when God showed them the land he had promised them, they grumbled! Finally, they turned away from the God who had rescued them from slavery and worshiped other gods.

This was sin. And the message of Numbers is clear: Sin is judged! In Numbers, God told the people who rejected him that they wouldn't be allowed to enter the Promised Land.

But that wasn't the end of the story. God went on treating them as his chosen people. Even though they sinned against him, he gave them everything they needed to survive: food and water in the wilderness, and victory over their enemies. And he was willing to persevere with them, to always give another chance. He gave the next generation of Israelites a whole new opportunity to obey and to be blessed by him. The book of Numbers ends with the new generation of young Israelites preparing to cross over the Jordan and to receive the blessings God promised them.

The book of Numbers shows that even when one generation turns away from God, he gives their children an opportunity to reverse this. What a comfort for us today! No matter how corrupt our society appears, God will always give us a chance to repent, turn to him, and receive his blessing.

Numbers does contain lots of numbers in it! But there's much, much more. The book also has poetry (in the prophecies of Balaam), adventure (the twelve spies sneak into Canaan and find giants there!), deadly peril (poisonous snakes attack the rebellious people), and one of the most beautiful blessings found anywhere in Scripture (Aaron's blessing in 6.24-26).

Numbers at a Glance

1. The people get organized (1,2)
2. The duties of the Levites (3,4)
3. God gives various laws (5.1—9.14)
4. God's glory comes to the sacred tent (9.15-23)
5. The travels of the people begin (10)
6. The people complain (11,12)
7. The Promised Land comes into view (13,14)
8. God gives more laws (15)
9. The people complain and rebel (16,17)
10. More instructions (18,19)
11. God provides water and victory (20,21)
12. The story of Balaam (22—24)
13. The people worship false gods (25)
14. The people are counted (26)
15. Various laws and instructions (27–30)
16. The people get ready to enter the land (31–36)

The People of Israel Are Counted

1 The people of Israel had left Egypt and were living in the Sinai Desert. Then on the first day of the second month[a] of the second year, Moses was in the sacred tent when the LORD said:

2-3I want you and Aaron to find out how many people are in each of Israel's clans and families. And make a list of all the men twenty years and older who are able to fight in battle. 4-15The following twelve family leaders, one from each tribe, will help you:

Elizur son of Shedeur
from Reuben,
Shelumiel son of Zurishaddai
from Simeon,
Nahshon son of Amminadab
from Judah,
Nethanel son of Zuar
from Issachar,
Eliab son of Helon
from Zebulun,
Elishama son of Ammihud
from Ephraim,
Gamaliel son of Pedahzur
from Manasseh,
Abidan son of Gideoni
from Benjamin,
Ahiezer son of Ammishaddai
from Dan,
Pagiel son of Ochran
from Asher,
Eliasaph son of Deuel
from Gad,
and Ahira son of Enan
from Naphtali.

16-17Moses and Aaron, together with these twelve tribal leaders, 18called together the people that same day. They were counted according to their clans and families. Then Moses and the others listed the names of the men twenty years and older, 19just as the LORD had commanded. 20-46The number of men from each tribe who were at least twenty years old and strong enough to fight in Israel's army was as follows:

46,500 from Reuben,
the oldest son of Jacob,[b]
59,300 from Simeon,
45,650 from Gad,
74,600 from Judah,
54,400 from Issachar,
57,400 from Zebulun,
40,500 from Ephraim,
32,200 from Manasseh,
35,400 from Benjamin,
62,700 from Dan,
41,500 from Asher,
53,400 from Naphtali.

The total number of men registered by Moses, Aaron, and the twelve leaders was 603,550.

47But those from the Levi tribe were not included 48because the LORD had said to Moses:

49When you count the Israelites, do not include those from the Levi tribe. 50-51Instead, give them the job of caring for the sacred tent, its furnishings, and the objects used for worship. They will camp around the tent, and whenever you move, they will take it down, carry it to the new camp, and set it up again. Anyone else who tries to go near it must be put to death. 52The rest of the Israelites will camp in their own groups and under their own banners. 53But the Levites will camp around the sacred tent to make sure that no one goes near it and makes me furious with the Israelites. 54The people of Israel did everything the LORD had commanded.

Instructions for Setting Up Israel's Camp

2 The LORD told Moses and Aaron 2how the Israelites should arrange their camp:

Each tribe must set up camp under its own banner and under the flags of its ancestral families. These camps will be arranged around the sacred tent, but not close to it.

3-4Judah and the tribes that march with it must set up camp on the east side of the sacred tent, under their own banner. The 74,600 troops of the tribe of Judah will be arranged by divisions and led by Nahshon son of Amminadab. 5-6On one side of Judah will be the tribe of Issachar, with Nethanel

---

a1.1 *second month*: Ziv, the second month of the Hebrew calendar, from about mid-April to mid-May. b1.20-46 *Jacob*: The Hebrew text has "Israel," Jacob's name after God renamed him.

son of Zuar as the leader of its 54,400 troops. [7-8]On the other side will be the tribe of Zebulun, with Eliab son of Helon as the leader of its 57,400 troops. [9]These 186,400 troops will march into battle first.

[10-11]Reuben and the tribes that march with it must set up camp on the south side of the sacred tent, under their own banner. The 46,500 troops of the tribe of Reuben will be arranged by divisions and led by Elizur son of Shedeur. [12-13]On one side of Reuben will be the tribe of Simeon, with Shelumiel son of Zurishaddai as the leader of its 59,300 troops. [14-15]On the other side will be the tribe of Gad, with Eliasaph son of Deuel as the leader of its 45,650 troops. [16]These 151,450 troops will march into battle second.

Other than my relationship with Christ, friendship is the most important thing in my life. We only have so much time and energy, but friendship is worth it.

LUCI SWINDOLL

---

[17]Marching behind Reuben will be the Levites, arranged in groups, just as they are camped. They will carry the sacred tent and their own banners.

[18-19]Ephraim and the tribes that march with it must set up camp on the west side of the sacred tent, under their own banner. The 40,500 troops of the tribe of Ephraim will be arranged by divisions and led by Elishama son of Ammihud. [20-21]On one side of Ephraim will be the tribe of Manasseh, with Gamaliel son of Pedahzur as the leader of its 32,200 troops. [22-23]On the other side will be the tribe of Benjamin, with Abidan son of Gideoni as the leader of its 35,400 troops. [24]These 108,100 troops will march into battle third.

[25-26]Dan and the tribes that march with it must set up camp on the north side of the sacred tent, under their own banner. The 62,700 troops of the tribe of Dan will be arranged by divisions and led by Ahiezer son of Ammishaddai. [27-28]On one side of Dan

will be the tribe of Asher, with Pagiel son of Ochran as the leader of its 41,500 troops. [29-30]On the other side will be the tribe of Naphtali with Ahira son of Enan as the leader of its 53,400 troops. [31]These 157,600 troops will march into battle last.

[32]So all the Israelites in the camp were counted according to their ancestral families. The troops were arranged by divisions and totaled 603,550. [33]The only Israelites not included were the Levites, just as the LORD had commanded Moses.

[34]Israel did everything the LORD had told Moses. They arranged their camp according to clans and families, with each tribe under its own banner. And that was the order by which they marched into battle.

The Sons of Aaron

3 When the LORD talked with Moses on Mount Sinai, [2]Aaron's four sons, Nadab, Abihu, Eleazar, and Ithamar, [3]were the ones to be ordained as priests. [4]But the LORD killed Nadab and Abihu in the Sinai Desert when they used fire that was unacceptable[c] in their offering to the LORD.[d] And because Nadab and Abihu had no sons, only Eleazar and Ithamar served as priests with their father Aaron.

The Duties of the Levites

[5]The LORD said to Moses:
[6]Assign the Levi tribe to Aaron the priest. They will be his assistants [7]and will work at the sacred tent for him and for all the Israelites. [8]The Levites will serve the community by being responsible for the furnishings of the tent. [9]They are assigned to help Aaron and his sons, [10]who have been appointed to be priests. Anyone else who tries to perform the duties of a priest must be put to death.

[11-13]Moses, I have chosen these Levites from all Israel, and they will belong to me in a special way. When I killed the first-born sons of the Egyptians, I decided that the first-born sons in every Israelite family and the first-born males of their flocks and herds

---

[c]3.4 *fire that was unacceptable:* One possible meaning for the difficult Hebrew text. [d]3.4 *the LORD killed Nadab and Abihu . . . to the LORD:* See Leviticus 10.1, 2.

would be mine.*c* But now I accept these Levites in place of the first-born sons of the Israelites.

The Levites Are Counted

[14]In the Sinai Desert the LORD said to Moses, [15]"Now I want you to count the men and boys in the Levi tribe by families and by clans. Include every one at least a month old." [16]So Moses obeyed and counted them.

[17]Levi's three sons, Gershon, Kohath, and Merari, had become the heads of their own clans. [18]Gershon's sons were Libni and Shimei. [19]Kohath's sons were Amram, Izhar, Hebron, and Uzziel. [20]And Merari's sons were Mahli and Mushi. These were the sons and grandsons of Levi, and they had become the leaders of the Levite clans.

> *We're all looking for a harbor*
> *in this world — a place where*
> *we know we are safe, loved,*
> *appreciated, and yes,*
> *even adored a little.*
>
> SANDRA P. ALDRICH

[21]The two Gershon clans were the Libnites and Shimeites, [22]and they had seven thousand five hundred men and boys at least one month old. [23]The Gershonites were to camp on the west side of the sacred tent, [24]under the leadership of Eliasaph son of Lael. [25]Their duties at the tent included taking care of the tent itself, along with its outer covering, the curtain for the entrance, [26]the curtains hanging inside the courtyard around the tent, as well as the curtain and ropes for the entrance to the courtyard and its altar. The Gershonites were responsible for setting these things up and taking them down.

[27]The four Kohath clans were the Amramites, Izharites, Hebronites, and the Uzzielites, [28]and they had eight thousand six hundred*f* men and boys at least one month old. [29]The Kohathites were to camp on the south side of the sacred tent, [30]under the

leadership of Elizaphan son of Uzziel. [31]Their duties at the tent included taking care of the sacred chest, the table for the sacred bread, the lampstand, the altars, the objects used for worship, and the curtain in front of the most holy place. The Kohathites were responsible for setting these things up and taking them down.

[32]Eleazar son of Aaron was the head of the Levite leaders, and he made sure that the work at the sacred tent was done.

[33]The two Merari clans were the Mahlites and the Mushites, [34]and they had six thousand two hundred men and boys at least one month old. [35]The Merarites were to camp on the north side of the sacred tent, under the leadership of Zuriel son of Abihail. [36-37]Their duties included taking care of the tent frames and the pieces that held the tent up: the bars, the posts, the stands, and its other equipment. They were also in charge of the posts that supported the courtyard, as well as their stands, tent pegs, and ropes. The Merari clans were responsible for setting these things up and taking them down.

[38]Moses, Aaron, and his sons were to camp in front of the sacred tent, on the east side, and to make sure that the Israelites worshiped in the proper way. Anyone else who tried to do the work of Moses and Aaron was to be put to death.

[39]So Moses and Aaron obeyed the LORD and counted the Levites by their clans. The total number of Levites at least one month old was twenty-two thousand.

The Levites Are Accepted as Substitutes for the First-Born Sons

[40]The LORD said to Moses, "Make a list and count the first-born sons at least one month old in each of the Israelite families. [41]They belong to me, but I will accept the Levites as substitutes for them, and I will accept the Levites' livestock as substitutes for the Israelites' first-born livestock."

[42]Moses obeyed the LORD and counted the first-born sons; [43]there were 22,273 of them.

[44]Then the LORD said, [45]"The Levites will

---

*c*3.11-13 *When I killed . . . mine:* See Exodus 13.1, 2, 11-16. *f*3.28 *eight thousand six hundred:* Hebrew; some manuscripts of one ancient translation "eight thousand three hundred."

belong to me and will take the place of the first-born sons; their livestock will take the place of the Israelites' first-born livestock. [46]But since there are more first-born sons than Levites, the extra two hundred seventy-three men and boys must be bought back from me. [47]For each one, you are to collect five pieces of silver, weighed according to the official standards. [48]This money must then be given to Aaron and his sons."

[49]Moses collected the silver from the extra two hundred seventy-three first-born men and boys, [50]and it amounted to one thousand three hundred sixty-five pieces of silver, weighed according to the official standards. [51]Then he gave it to Aaron and his sons, just as the LORD had commanded.

The Duties of the Kohathite Clans

4 The LORD told Moses and Aaron: [2-3]Find out how many men between the ages of thirty and fifty are in the four Levite clans of Kohath. Count only those who are able to work at the sacred tent.

[4]The Kohathites will be responsible for carrying the sacred objects used in worship at the sacred tent. [5]When the Israelites are ready to move their camp, Aaron and his sons will enter the tent and take down the curtain that separates the sacred chest from the rest of the tent. They will cover the chest with this curtain, [6]and then with a piece of fine leather, and cover it all with a solid blue cloth. After this they will put the carrying poles in place.

[7]Next, Aaron and his sons will use another blue cloth to cover the table for the sacred bread.[g] On the cloth they will place the dishes, the bowls for incense, the cups, the jugs for wine, as well as the bread itself. [8]They are to cover all of this with a bright red cloth, and then with a piece of fine leather, before putting the carrying poles in place.

[9]With another blue cloth they will cover the lampstand, along with the lamps, the lamp snuffers, the fire pans, and the jars of oil for the lamps. [10]All of this will then be covered with a piece of fine leather and placed on a carrying frame.

[11]The gold incense altar[h] is to be covered with a blue cloth, and then with a piece of fine leather, before its carrying poles are put in place.

[12]Next, Aaron and his sons will take blue cloth and wrap all the objects used in worship at the sacred tent. These will need to be covered with a piece of fine leather, then placed on a carrying frame.

[13]They are to remove the ashes from the bronze altar and cover it with a purple cloth. [14]On that cloth will be placed the utensils used at the altar, including the fire pans, the meat forks, the shovels, and the sprinkling bowls. All of this will then be covered with a piece of fine leather, before the carrying poles are put in place.

[15]When the camp is ready to be moved, the Kohathites will be responsible for carrying the sacred objects and the furnishings of the sacred tent. But Aaron and his sons must have already covered those things so the Kohathites won't touch them and die.

[16]Eleazar son of Aaron the priest will be in charge of the oil for the lamps, the sweet-smelling incense, the grain for the sacrifices, and the olive oil used for dedications and ordinations. Eleazar is responsible for seeing that the sacred tent, its furnishings, and the sacred objects are taken care of.

[17-20]The Kohathites must not go near or even look at the sacred objects until Aaron and his sons have covered those objects. If they do, their entire clan will be wiped out. So make sure that Aaron and his sons go into the tent with them and tell them what to carry.

The Duties of the Gershonite Clans

[21]The LORD said to Moses: [22-23]Find out how many men between the ages of thirty and fifty are in the two Levite clans of Gershon. Count only those who are able to work at the sacred tent.

[24]The Gershonites will be responsible [25]for carrying the curtains of the sacred tent, its two outer coverings,[i] the curtain for the entrance to the tent, [26]the curtains hanging around the courtyard of the tent, and the curtain and ropes for the entrance to the

---

[g]4.7 sacred bread: This bread was offered to the LORD and was a symbol of his presence in the sacred tent. It was put out on a special table and was replaced with fresh bread each Sabbath (Leviticus 24.5-9).
[h]4.11 gold incense altar: This altar for offering incense was inside the sacred tent; it was made of acacia wood covered with gold. A large altar for offering sacrifices was in front of the entrance to the tent; it was made of acacia wood covered with bronze (see verse 13).
[i]4.25 two outer coverings: See Exodus 26.14.

courtyard. The Gershonites are to do whatever needs to be done to take care of these things, [27]and they will carry them wherever Aaron and his sons tell them to. [28]These are the duties of the Gershonites at the sacred tent, and Ithamar son of Aaron will make sure they do their work.

The Duties of the Merarite Clans

[29-30]The LORD said:

Moses, find out how many men between thirty and fifty are in the two Levite clans of Merari, but count only those who are able to work at the sacred tent. [31]The Merarites will be responsible for carrying the frames of the tent and its other pieces, including the bars, the posts, the stands, [32]as well as the posts that support the courtyard, together with their stands, tent pegs, and ropes. The Merarites are to be told exactly what objects they are to carry, [33]and Ithamar son of Aaron will make sure they do their work.

The Levites Are Counted Again

[34-49]Moses, Aaron, and the other Israelite leaders obeyed the LORD and counted the Levi tribe by families and clans, to find out how many men there were between the ages of thirty and fifty who could work at the sacred tent. There were two thousand seven hundred fifty Kohathites, two thousand six hundred thirty Gershonites, and three thousand two hundred Merarites, making a total of eight thousand five hundred eighty. Then they were all assigned their duties.

People Are Sent Outside the Camp

5 The LORD told Moses [2-3]to say to the people of Israel, "Put out of the camp everyone who has leprosy[j] or a bodily discharge or who has touched a dead body. Now that I live among my people, their camp must be kept clean."

[4]The Israelites obeyed the LORD's instructions.

The Penalty for Committing a Crime
(Leviticus 6.1-7)

[5]The LORD told Moses [6]to say to the community of Israel:

If any of you commit a crime against someone, you have sinned against me. [7]You must confess your guilt and pay the victim in full for whatever damage has been done,

plus a fine of twenty percent. [8]If the victim has no relative who can accept this money, it belongs to me and will be paid to the priest. In addition to that payment, you must take a ram for the priest to sacrifice so your sin will be forgiven.

[9-10]When you make a donation to the sacred tent, that money belongs only to the priest, and each priest will keep what is given to him.

A Suspicious Husband

[11]The LORD told Moses [12-14]to say to the people of Israel:

Suppose a man becomes jealous and suspects that his wife has been unfaithful, but he has no proof. [15]He must take his wife to the priest, together with two pounds of ground barley as an offering to find out if she is guilty. No olive oil or incense is to be put on that offering.

[16]The priest is to have the woman stand at my altar, [17]where he will pour sacred water into a clay jar and stir in some dust from the floor of the sacred tent. [18-22]Next, he will remove her veil, then hand her the barley offering, and say, "If you have been faithful to your husband, this water won't harm you. But if you have been unfaithful, it will bring down the LORD's curse—you will never be able to give birth to a child, and everyone will curse your name."

Then the woman will answer, "If I am guilty, let it happen just as you say."

[23]The priest will write these curses on special paper and wash them off into the bitter water, [24]so that when the woman drinks this water, the curses will enter her body. [25]He will take the barley offering from her and lift it up[k] in dedication to me, the LORD. Then he will place it on my altar [26]and burn part of it as a sacrifice. After that, the woman must drink the bitter water.

[27]If the woman has been unfaithful, the water will immediately make her unable to have children, and she will be a curse among her people. [28]But if she is innocent, her body will not be harmed, and she will still be able to have children.

[29-30]This is the ceremony that must take place at my altar when a husband suspects

---

[j]5.2,3 leprosy: The word translated "leprosy" was used for many different kinds of skin diseases.   [k]5.25 lift it up: Or "wave it."

that his wife has been unfaithful. The priest must have the woman stand in my presence and carefully follow these instructions. ³¹If the husband is wrong, he will not be punished; but if his wife is guilty, she will be punished.

Rules for Nazirites

6 The LORD told Moses ²to say to the people of Israel:
    If any of you want to dedicate yourself to me by vowing to become a Nazirite, ³you must no longer drink any wine or beer or use any kind of vinegar. Don't drink grape juice or eat grapes or raisins—⁴not even the seeds or skins.

⁵Even the hair of a Nazirite is sacred to me, and as long as you are a Nazirite, you must never cut your hair.

⁶During the time that you are a Nazirite, you must never go close to a dead body, ⁷⁻⁸not even that of your father, mother, brother, or sister. That would make you unclean. Your hair is the sign that you are dedicated to me, so remain holy.

⁹If someone suddenly dies near you, your hair is no longer sacred, and you must shave it seven days later during the ceremony to make you clean. ¹⁰Then on the next day, bring two doves or two pigeons to the priest at the sacred tent. ¹¹He will offer one of the birds as a sacrifice for sin and the other as a sacrifice to please me.ˡ You will then be forgiven for being too near a dead body, and your hair will again become sacred. ¹²But the dead body made you unacceptable, so you must make another vow to become a Nazirite and be dedicated once more. Finally, a year-old ram must be offered as the sacrifice to make things right.

¹³When you have completed your promised time of being a Nazirite, go to the sacred tent ¹⁴and offer three animals that have nothing wrong with them: a year-old ram as a sacrifice to please me, a year-old female lamb as a sacrifice for sin, and a full-grown ram as a sacrifice to ask my blessing.ᵐ ¹⁵Wine offerings and grain sacrifices must

---

ˡ6.11 *sacrifice to please me*: This sacrifice has traditionally been called a "whole burnt offering," because the whole animal was burned on the altar. A main purpose of such a sacrifice was to please the LORD with the smell of the sacrifice, and so in the CEV it is often called "a sacrifice to please the LORD." ᵐ6.14 *sacrifice to ask my blessing*: This sacrifice has traditionally been called a "peace offering" or an "offering of well-being." A main purpose of such a sacrifice was to ask the LORD's blessing, and so in the CEV it is often called a "sacrifice to ask the LORD's blessing."

Friendship—How can I keep from comparing myself with my friends?
(*Numbers 6.22-27*)

Learn to bless your friends.
Aaron and his sons had a big responsibility: They had to look out for the entire nation of Israel. So God gave them a special prayer—a blessing for all the people—to recite. And God promised that when Aaron and his sons blessed Israel, he would listen to them.

Like Aaron and his sons, we have the responsibility of praying for our friends. And Aaron's prayer is a wonderful model for us to use. When you pray for your friends, begin by asking God to protect them from spiritual danger, physical danger, illness, temptation, and other difficulties. Then ask God to show his kindness by actively blessing your friends with all that they need—food, clothing, shelter, spiritual wisdom and strength, healthy families and relationships. Pray that your friends will find peace. For your unsaved friends, ask that God will show them his salvation so they can be at peace with him. And for fellow believers, pray that God will protect them from spiritual discouragement and help them to grow in their knowledge of him.

When you spend time praying for your friends, your focus shifts from yourself and your own needs to their good. Follow the threefold pattern of Aaron's prayer, and you'll find you have a whole new perspective on friendship. (See also 1 Samuel 16.1-13; Mark 10.29-31, 35-45.)

Words To Remember: *I pray that the LORD will bless and protect you, and that he will show you mercy and kindness. May the LORD be good to you and give you peace.*—Numbers 6.24-26

also be brought with these animals. Finally, you are to bring a basket of bread made with your finest flour and olive oil, but without yeast. Also bring some thin wafers brushed with oil.

[16]The priest will take these gifts to my altar and offer them, so that I will be pleased and will forgive you. [17]Then he will sacrifice the ram and offer the wine, grain, and bread.

[18]After that, you will stand at the entrance to the sacred tent, shave your head, and put the hair in the fire where the priest has offered the sacrifice to ask my blessing.

[19]Once the meat from the ram's shoulder has been boiled, the priest will take it, along with one loaf of bread and one wafer brushed with oil, and give them to you. [20]You will hand them back to the priest, who will lift them up[n] in dedication to me. Then he can eat the meat from the ram's shoulder, its choice ribs, and its hind leg, because this is his share of the sacrifice. After this, you will no longer be a Nazirite and will be free to drink wine.

[21]These are the requirements for Nazirites. However, if you can afford to offer more, you must do so.

The Blessing for the People

[22]The LORD told Moses, [23]"When Aaron and his sons bless the people of Israel, they must say:

[24]I pray that the LORD
     will bless and protect you,
[25]and that he will show you mercy
     and kindness.
[26]May the LORD be good to you
     and give you peace."

[27]Then the LORD said, "If Aaron and his sons ask me to bless the Israelites, I will give them my blessing."

The Leaders Bring Gifts to the Sacred Tent

7 When Moses had finished setting up the sacred tent, he dedicated it to the LORD, together with its furnishings, the altar, and its equipment. [2]Then the twelve tribal leaders of Israel, the same men who had been in charge of counting the people,[o] came to the tent [3]with gifts for the LORD. They brought six strong carts and twelve oxen—one ox from each leader and a cart from every two.

[4]The LORD said to Moses, [5]"Accept these gifts, so the Levites can use them here at the sacred tent for carrying the sacred things."

[6]Then Moses took the carts and oxen and gave them to the Levites, [7-8]who were under the leadership of Ithamar son of Aaron. Moses gave two carts and four oxen to the Gershonites for their work, and four carts and eight oxen to the Merarites for their work. [9]But Moses did not give any to the Kohathites, because they were in charge of the sacred objects that had to be carried on their shoulders.

[10]On the day the altar was dedicated, the twelve leaders brought offerings for its dedication. [11]The LORD said to Moses, "Each day one leader is to give his offering for the dedication."

[12-83]So each leader brought the following gifts:

a silver bowl that weighed over three pounds and a silver sprinkling bowl weighing almost two pounds, both of them filled with flour and olive oil as grain sacrifices and weighed according to the official standards;

a small gold dish filled with incense;

a young bull, a full-grown ram, and a year-old ram as sacrifices to please the LORD;[p]

a goat[q] as a sacrifice for sin;

and two bulls, five full-grown rams, five goats, and five rams a year old as sacrifices to ask the LORD's blessing.[r]

The tribal leaders brought their gifts and offerings in the following order:

On the first day
     Nahshon from Judah,
on the second day
     Nethanel from Issachar,
on the third day
     Eliab from Zebulun,
on the fourth day
     Elizur from Reuben,
on the fifth day
     Shelumiel from Simeon,

---

[n]6.20 lift them up: See the note at 5.25. [o]7.2 the same men . . . the people: See 1.1-19. [p]7.12-83 sacrifices to please the LORD: See the note at 6.11. [q]7.12-83 goat: Hebrew "male goat." [r]7.12-83 sacrifices to ask the LORD's blessing: See the note at 6.14.

on the sixth day
    Eliasaph from Gad,
on the seventh day
    Elishama from Ephraim,
on the eighth day
    Gamaliel from Manasseh,
on the ninth day
    Abidan from Benjamin,
on the tenth day
    Ahiezer from Dan,
on the eleventh day
    Pagiel from Asher,
on the twelfth day
    Ahira from Naphtali.

[84-88]And so when the altar was dedicated to the LORD, these twelve leaders brought the following gifts:

twelve silver bowls and twelve silver sprinkling bowls, weighing a total of about sixty pounds, according to the official standards;

twelve gold dishes filled with incense and weighing about three pounds;

twelve bulls, twelve full-grown rams, and twelve rams a year old as sacrifices to please the LORD, along with the proper grain sacrifices;

twelve goats as sacrifices for sin;

and twenty-four bulls, sixty full-grown rams, sixty goats, and sixty rams a year old as sacrifices to ask the LORD's blessing.

[89]Whenever Moses needed to talk with the LORD, he went into the sacred tent, where he heard the LORD's voice coming from between the two winged creatures above the lid of the sacred chest.

Aaron Puts the Gold Lamps in Place

8 The LORD said to Moses, [2]"Tell Aaron to put the seven lamps on the lampstand so they shine toward the front."
[3]Aaron obeyed and placed the lamps as he was told. [4]The lampstand was made of hammered gold from its base to the decorative flowers on top, exactly like the pattern the LORD had described to Moses.

Instructions for Ordaining the Levites

[5]The LORD said to Moses:
[6]The Levites must be acceptable to me before they begin working at the sacred tent. So separate them from the rest of the Israelites [7]and sprinkle them with the water that

washes away their sins. Then have them shave their entire bodies and wash their clothes.

[8]They are to bring a bull and its proper grain sacrifice of flour mixed with olive oil. And they must bring a second bull as a sacrifice for sin.

[9]Then you, Moses, will call together all the people of Israel and have the Levites go to my sacred tent, [10]where the people will place their hands on them. [11]Aaron will present the Levites to me as a gift from the people, so that the Levites will do my work.

We can only achieve healthy self-acceptance and move on to love and serve others if we truly understand ourselves— our gifts, our quirks, and our deepest longings.
ELIZABETH CODY NEWENHUYSE

[12]After this, the Levites are to place their hands on the heads of the bulls. Then one of the bulls will be sacrificed for the forgiveness of sin, and the other to make sure that I am pleased. [13]The Levites will stand at my altar in front of Aaron and his sons, who will then dedicate the Levites to me.

[14]This ceremony will show that the Levites are different from the other Israelites and belong to me in a special way. [15]After they have been made acceptable and have been dedicated, they will be allowed to work at my sacred tent. [16]They are mine and will take the place of the first-born Israelite sons. [17]When I killed the oldest sons of the Egyptians, I decided that the first-born sons in each Israelite family would be mine, as well as every first-born male from their flocks and herds. [18]But now I have chosen these Levites as substitutes for the first-born sons, [19]and I have given them as gifts to Aaron and his sons to serve at the sacred tent. I will hold them responsible for what

happens to anyone who gets too close to the sacred tent.[s]

The Levites Are Dedicated to the LORD

[20]Moses, Aaron, and the other Israelites made sure that the Levites did everything the LORD had commanded. [21]The Levites sprinkled themselves with the water of forgiveness and washed their clothes. Then Aaron brought them to the altar and offered sacrifices to forgive their sins and make them acceptable to the LORD. [22]After this, the Levites worked at the sacred tent as assistants to Aaron and his sons, just as the LORD had commanded.

[23]The LORD also told Moses, [24-25]"Levites who are between the ages of twenty-five and fifty can work at my sacred tent. But once they turn fifty, they must retire. [26]They may help the other Levites in their duties, but they must no longer be responsible for any work themselves. Remember this when you assign their duties."

Regulations for Celebrating Passover

9 During the first month of Israel's second year in the Sinai Desert,[t] the LORD had told Moses [2]to say to the people, "Celebrate Passover [3]in the evening of the fourteenth day of this month[u] and do it by following all the regulations." [4-5]Moses told the people what the LORD had said, and they celebrated Passover there in the desert in the evening of the fourteenth day of the first month.

> As long as I remember to
> confess, rejoice, and lean on
> Christ, I can sing "To God Be
> the Glory"—and hit every note.
>
> LIZ CURTIS HIGGS

[6]Some people in Israel's camp had touched a dead body and had become unfit to worship the LORD, and they could not celebrate Passover. But they asked Moses and Aaron, [7]"Even though we have touched a dead body, why can't we celebrate Pass-

over and offer sacrifices to the LORD at the same time as everyone else?"

[8]Moses said, "Wait here while I go into the sacred tent and find out what the LORD says about this."

[9]The LORD then told Moses [10]to say to the community of Israel:

If any of you or your descendants touch a dead body and become unfit to worship me, or if you are away on a long journey, you may still celebrate Passover. [11]But it must be done in the second month,[v] in the evening of the fourteenth day. Eat the Passover lamb with thin bread and bitter herbs, [12]and don't leave any of it until morning or break any of the animal's bones. Be sure to follow these regulations.

[13]But if any of you refuse to celebrate Passover when you are not away on a journey, you will no longer belong to my people. You will be punished because you did not offer sacrifices to me at the proper time.

[14]Anyone, including foreigners who live among you, can celebrate Passover, if they follow all the regulations.

The Cloud over the Sacred Tent
(Exodus 40.34-38)

[15-16]As soon as the sacred tent was set up,[w] a thick cloud appeared and covered it. The cloud was there each day, and during the night, a fire could be seen in it. [17-19]The LORD used this cloud to tell the Israelites when to move their camp and where to set it up again. As long as the cloud covered the tent, the Israelites did not break camp. But when the cloud moved, they followed it, and wherever it stopped, they camped and stayed there, [20-22]whether it was only one night, a few days, a month, or even a year. As long as the cloud remained over the tent, the Israelites stayed where they were. But

---

[s]8.19 *I will hold . . . sacred tent*: One possible meaning for the difficult Hebrew text. [t]9.1 *first month . . . Sinai Desert*: The book of Numbers begins in the second month of the second year (see 1.1), so 9.1-5 refers to a Passover celebration that had already taken place. [u]9.3 *this month*: Abib (also called Nisan), the first month of the Hebrew calendar, from about mid-March to mid-April. [v]9.11 *second month*: See the note at 1.1. [w]9.15,16 *As soon as the sacred tent was set up*: According to Exodus 40.17, this took place "on the first day of the first month of the second year" of the Israelites' stay in the desert.

when the cloud moved, so did the Israelites. ²³They obeyed the LORD's commands and went wherever he directed Moses.

The Silver Trumpets

10 The LORD told Moses: ²Have someone make two trumpets out of hammered silver. These will be used to call the people together and to give the signal for moving your camp. ³If both trumpets are blown, everyone is to meet with you at the entrance to the sacred tent. ⁴But if just one is blown, only the twelve tribal leaders need to come together.

It is God to whom and with whom we travel, and while he is the end of our journey, he is also at every stopping place.
ELISABETH ELLIOT

⁵⁻⁶Give a signal on a trumpet when it is time to break camp. The first blast will be the signal for the tribes camped on the east side, and the second blast will be the signal for those on the south. ⁷But when you want everyone to come together, sound a different signal on the trumpet. ⁸The priests of Aaron's family will be the ones to blow the trumpets, and this law will never change.

⁹Whenever you go into battle against an enemy attacking your land, give a warning signal on the trumpets. Then I, the LORD, will hear it and rescue you. ¹⁰During the celebration of the New Moon Festival and other religious festivals, sound the trumpets while you offer sacrifices. This will be a reminder that I am the LORD your God.

The Israelites Begin Their Journey

¹¹On the twentieth day of the second month^x of that same year, the cloud over the sacred tent moved on. ¹²So the Israelites broke camp and left the Sinai Desert. And some time later, the cloud stopped in the Paran Desert.^y ¹³This was the first time the LORD had told Moses to command the people of Israel to move on.

¹⁴Judah and the tribes that camped alongside it marched out first, carrying their banner. Nahshon son of Amminadab was the leader of the Judah tribe, ¹⁵Nethanel son of Zuar was the leader of the Issachar tribe, ¹⁶and Eliab son of Helon was the leader of the Zebulun tribe.

¹⁷The sacred tent had been taken down, and the Gershonites and the Merarites carried it, marching behind the Judah camp.

¹⁸Reuben and the tribes that camped alongside it marched out second, carrying their banner. Elizur son of Shedeur was the leader of the Reuben tribe, ¹⁹Shelumiel son of Zurishaddai was the leader of the Simeon tribe, ²⁰and Eliasaph son of Deuel was the leader of the Gad tribe.

²¹Next were the Kohathites, carrying the objects for the sacred tent, which was to be set up before they arrived at the new camp.

²²Ephraim and the tribes that camped alongside it marched next, carrying their banner. Elishama son of Ammihud was the leader of the Ephraim tribe, ²³Gamaliel son of Pedahzur was the leader of the Manasseh tribe, ²⁴and Abidan son of Gideoni was the leader of the Benjamin tribe.

²⁵Dan and the tribes that camped alongside it were to protect the Israelites against an attack from behind, and so they marched last, carrying their banner. Ahiezer son of Ammishaddai was the leader of the tribe of Dan, ²⁶Pagiel son of Ochran was the leader of the Asher tribe, ²⁷and Ahira son of Enan was the leader of the Naphtali tribe.

²⁸This was the order in which the Israelites marched each time they moved their camp.

²⁹Hobab^z the Midianite, the father-in-law of Moses, was there. And Moses said to him, "We're leaving for the place the LORD has promised us. He has said that all will go well for us. So come along, and we will make sure that all goes well for you."

---

^x10.11 *second month*: See the note at 1.1.   ^y10.12 *the Paran Desert*: Probably a general name for the northernmost part of the Sinai Desert.   ^z10.29 *Hobab*: Hebrew "Hobab son of Reuel."

³⁰"No, I won't go," Hobab answered. "I'm returning home to be with my own people."

³¹"Please go with us!" Moses said. "You can be our guide because you know the places to camp in the desert. ³²Besides that, if you go, we will give you a share of the good things the LORD gives us."

³³The people of Israel began their journey from Mount Sinai.ᵃ They traveled three days, and the Levites who carried the sacred chest led the way, so the LORD could show them where to camp. ³⁴And the cloud always stayed with them.

³⁵Each day as the Israelites began their journey, Moses would pray, "Our LORD, defeat your enemies and make them run!" ³⁶And when they stopped to set up camp, he would pray, "Our LORD, stay close to Israel's thousands and thousands of people."

The Israelites Complain

11 One day the Israelites started complaining about their troubles. The LORD heard them and became so angry that he destroyed the outer edges of their camp with fire.

²When the people begged Moses to help, he prayed, and the fire went out. ³They named the place "Burning,"ᵇ because in his anger the LORD had set their camp on fire.

The People Grumble about Being Hungry

⁴One day some worthless foreigners among the Israelites became greedy for food, and even the Israelites themselves began moaning, "We don't have any meat! ⁵In Egypt we could eat all the fish we wanted, and there were cucumbers, melons, onions, and garlic. ⁶But we're starving out here, and the only food we have is this manna."

⁷The manna was like small whitish seeds ⁸⁻⁹and tasted like something baked with sweet olive oil. It appeared at night with the dew. In the morning the people would collect the manna, grind or crush it into flour, then boil it and make it into thin wafers.

¹⁰The Israelites stood around their tents complaining. Moses heard them and was upset that they had made the LORD angry. ¹¹He prayed:

I am your servant, LORD, so why are you doing this to me? What have I done to deserve this? You've made me responsible for all these people, ¹²but they're not my children. You told me to nurse them along and to carry them to the land you promised their ancestors. ¹³They keep whining for meat, but where can I get meat for them? ¹⁴This job is too much for me. How

---

ᵃ10.33 *Mount Sinai:* Hebrew "the LORD's mountain."
ᵇ11.3 *Burning:* Or "Taberah."

SingleLife—I like being single. Is that normal? *(Numbers 11)*

God wants us to be content where he puts us.
Our culture often breeds on discontent. Every TV ad we see, every how-to book we read, and every magazine we pick up tells us that we can't be happy unless we buy something, follow someone's diet or exercise plan, or get a new job. The list never ends!

If you're single, you may feel this pressure in a slightly different way. Even if you're perfectly content where you are, others may put pressure on you to marry because they assume you can't possibly be happy being on your own.

Be glad you are content with being single, for discontent should have no place in the life of the believer. In the Old Testament, God's judgment came on those who were discontented with their lot in life. God gave his people bread in the desert, but they refused to be happy with what they had. Instead, they complained and wished for the food that they had back in Egypt. What was God's response to this attitude? He sent them what they wanted—meat to eat—and many of them died from it.

God's message is clear: He wants us to be content with our life, whether we are married or single. (See also Nehemiah 4; 6.15,16; Romans 14.1-12; 1 Corinthians 7.29-35.)

Words To Remember: *The LORD answered, "I can do anything! Watch and you'll see my words come true."*—Numbers 11.23

can I take care of all these people by myself? ¹⁵If this is the way you're going to treat me, just kill me now and end my miserable life!

Seventy Leaders Are Chosen To Help Moses

¹⁶The LORD said to Moses:
Choose seventy of Israel's respected leaders and go with them to the sacred tent. ¹⁷While I am talking with you there, I will give them some of your authority, so they can share responsibility for my people. You will no longer have to care for them by yourself.
¹⁸As for the Israelites, I have heard them complaining about not having meat and about being better off in Egypt. So tell them to make themselves acceptable to me, because tomorrow they will have meat. ¹⁹⁻²⁰In fact, they will have meat day after day for a whole month—not just a few days, or even ten or twenty. They turned against me and wanted to return to Egypt. Now they will eat meat until they get sick of it.
²¹Moses replied, "At least six hundred thousand grown men are here with me. How can you say there will be enough meat to feed them and their families for a whole month? ²²Even if we butchered all of our sheep and cattle, or caught every fish in the sea, we wouldn't have enough to feed them."
²³The LORD answered, "I can do anything! Watch and you'll see my words come true."
²⁴Moses told the people what the LORD had said. Then he chose seventy respected leaders and went with them to the sacred tent. While the leaders stood in a circle around the tent, Moses went inside, ²⁵and the LORD spoke with him. Then the LORD took some authority^c from Moses and gave it to the seventy leaders. And when the LORD's Spirit took control of them, they started shouting like prophets. But they did it only this one time.
²⁶Eldad and Medad were two leaders who had not gone to the tent. But when the Spirit took control of them, they began shouting like prophets right there in camp. ²⁷A boy ran to Moses and told him about Eldad and Medad.

²⁸Joshua^d was there helping Moses, as he had done since he was young. And he said to Moses, "Sir, you must stop them!"
²⁹But Moses replied, "Are you concerned what this might do to me? I wish the LORD would give his Spirit to all his people so everyone could be a prophet." ³⁰Then Moses and the seventy leaders went back to camp.

The LORD Sends Quails

³¹Some time later the LORD sent a strong wind that blew quails in from the sea until Israel's camp was completely surrounded with birds, piled up about three feet high for miles in every direction. ³²The people picked up quails for two days—each person filled at least fifty bushels. Then they spread them out to dry. ³³But before the meat could be eaten, the LORD became angry and sent a disease through the camp.
³⁴After they had buried the people who had been so greedy for meat, they called the place "Graves for the Greedy."^e
³⁵Israel then broke camp and traveled to Hazeroth.

Miriam and Aaron Are Jealous of Moses

12 ¹⁻³Although Moses was the most humble person in all the world, Miriam and Aaron started complaining, "Moses had no right to marry that woman from Ethiopia!^f Who does he think he is? The LORD has spoken to us, not just to him."
The LORD heard their complaint ⁴and told Moses, Aaron, and Miriam to come to the entrance of the sacred tent. ⁵There the LORD appeared in a cloud and told Aaron and Miriam to come closer. ⁶Then after commanding them to listen carefully, he said:

"I, the LORD, speak to prophets
    in visions and dreams.
⁷But my servant Moses
    is the leader of my people.
⁸He sees me face to face,
    and everything I say to him

---

^c11.25 some authority: Or "some of the Spirit's power."
^d11.28 Joshua: Hebrew "Joshua son of Nun."
^e11.34 Graves for the Greedy: Or "Kibroth-Hattaavah."
^f12.1-3 Ethiopia: The Hebrew text has "Cush," which was a region south of Egypt that included parts of the present countries of Ethiopia and Sudan.

is perfectly clear.
You have no right to criticize
my servant Moses."

⁹The LORD became angry at Aaron and Miriam. And after the LORD left ¹⁰and the cloud disappeared from over the sacred tent, Miriam's skin turned white with leprosy.ᵍ When Aaron saw what had happened to her, ¹¹he said to Moses, "Sir, please don't punish us for doing such a foolish thing. ¹²Don't let Miriam's flesh rot away like a child born dead!"

¹³Moses prayed, "LORD God, please heal her."

¹⁴But the LORD replied, "Miriam would be disgraced for seven days if her father had punished her by spitting in her face. So make her stay outside the camp for seven days, before coming back."

¹⁵The people of Israel did not move their camp until Miriam returned seven days later. ¹⁶Then they left Hazeroth and set up camp in the Paran Desert.

Twelve Men Are Sent into Canaan
(Deuteronomy 1.19-33)

13 The LORD said to Moses, ²"Choose a leader from each tribe and send them into Canaan to explore the land I am giving you."

³So Moses sent twelve tribal leaders from Israel's camp in the Paran Desert ⁴⁻¹⁶with orders to explore the land of Canaan. And here are their names:

Shammua son of Zaccur
   from Reuben,
Shaphat son of Hori
   from Simeon,
Caleb son of Jephunneh
   from Judah,
Igal son of Joseph
   from Issachar,
Joshua son of Nun
   from Ephraim,ʰ

ᵍ**12.10** *leprosy:* See the note at 5.2, 3.
ʰ**13.4-16** *Joshua . . . Ephraim:* Hebrew "Hoshea son of Nun from Ephraim; Moses renamed him Joshua."

WORK—My husband is sometimes threatened by my career. How should I respond? *(Numbers 12)*

Try these four steps for dealing with jealousy.
Moses had an important job. As leader of the Israelites, his word was law, and God spoke to him as a friend. But his sister and brother complained about his importance. God judged their jealousy; he brought them into his presence and punished Miriam with leprosy. Then Moses prayed for his sister, and God healed her.

This story gives us four steps to deal with a husband who feels jealous of our success. First, check your attitude. The book of Numbers says that Moses was the most humble person in the world (12.1). That meant he didn't flaunt the importance of his job or let Aaron and Miriam know indirectly how indispensable he was. He kept his mouth shut and faithfully did his work. Examine yourself and make sure you aren't bragging about your job—either in words or in attitude!

Second, take the matter to God. When Miriam and Aaron complained about Moses, the matter was resolved in front of God himself. If your husband dislikes your work, make this a matter of private prayer.

Third, leave the resolution of his jealousy to God. Notice that Moses did nothing to correct his brother and sister! God is able to deal with jealous attitudes without your help. If your husband is jealous, your correction won't make matters better. Allow God to deal with your husband's heart problem in his own time.

Fourth, pray for your husband! Moses' only action in this entire story was to pray for Miriam's restoration. In the same way, pray for your husband's well-being. Ask God to give him satisfaction and success in his own work. (See also Luke 3.7-20; 1 Corinthians 12.1-11.)

Words To Remember: *He [the Lord] said, "My servant Moses is the leader of my people. He sees me face to face, and everything I say to him is perfectly clear. You have no right to criticize my servant Moses."—Numbers 12.6-8*

Palti son of Raphu
  from Benjamin,
Gaddiel son of Sodi
  from Zebulun,
Gaddi son of Susi
  from Manasseh,
Ammiel son of Gemalli
  from Dan,
Sethur son of Michael
  from Asher,
Nahbi son of Vophsi
  from Naphtali,
and Geuel son of Machi
  from Gad.

[17]Before Moses sent them into Canaan, he said:

After you go through the Southern Desert of Canaan, continue north into the hill country [18]and find out what those regions are like. Be sure to remember how many people live there, how strong they are, [19-20]and if they live in open towns or walled cities. See if the land is good for growing crops and find out what kinds of trees grow there. It's time for grapes to ripen, so try to bring back some of the fruit that grows there.

[21]The twelve men left to explore Canaan from the Zin Desert in the south all the way to the town of Rehob near Lebo-Hamath in the north. [22]As they went through the Southern Desert, they came to the town of Hebron, which was seven years older than the Egyptian town of Zoan. In Hebron, they saw the three Anakim[i] clans of Ahiman, Sheshai, and Talmai. [23-24]When they got to Bunch Valley,[j] they cut off a branch with such a huge bunch of grapes, that it took two men to carry it on a pole. That's why the place was called Bunch Valley. Along with the grapes, they also took back pomegranates[k] and figs.

The Men Report Back to the People

[25]After exploring the land of Canaan forty days, [26]the twelve men returned to Kadesh in the Paran Desert and told Moses, Aaron, and the people what they had seen. They showed them the fruit [27]and said:

Look at this fruit! The land we explored is rich with milk and honey. [28]But the people who live there are strong, and their cities are large and

walled. We even saw the three Anakim[i] clans. [29]Besides that, the Amalekites live in the Southern Desert; the Hittites, Jebusites, and Amorites are in the hill country; and the Canaanites[m] live along the Mediterranean Sea and the Jordan River.

> *Faith is what makes the uplook good, the outlook bright, the inlook favorable, and the future glorious!*
>
> BARBARA JOHNSON

[30]Caleb calmed down the crowd and said, "Let's go and take the land. I know we can do it!"

[31]But the other men replied, "Those people are much too strong for us." [32]Then they started spreading rumors and saying, "We won't be able to grow anything in that soil. And the people are like giants. [33]In fact, we saw the Nephilim who are the ancestors of the Anakim. They were so big that we felt as small as grasshoppers."

The Israelites Rebel against Moses

14 After the Israelites heard the report from the twelve men who had explored Canaan, the people cried all night [2]and complained to Moses and Aaron, "We wish we had died in Egypt or somewhere out here in the desert! [3]Is the LORD leading us into Canaan, just to have us killed and our women and children captured? We'd be better off in Egypt." [4]Then they said to one another, "Let's choose our own leader and go back."

[5]Moses and Aaron bowed down to pray

---

[i]**13.22** *Anakim:* Perhaps a group of very large people (see Deuteronomy 2.10, 11, 20, 21). [j]**13.23,24** *Bunch Valley:* Or "Eshcol Valley." [k]**13.23,24** *pomegranates:* A bright red fruit that looks like an apple. [l]**13.28** *Anakim:* See the note at verse 22. [m]**13.29** *Amalekites . . . Hittites . . . Jebusites . . . Amorites . . . Canaanites:* These people lived in Canaan before the Israelites.

in front of the crowd. ⁶Joshua and Caleb tore their clothes in sorrow ⁷and said:

We saw the land ourselves, and it's very good. ⁸If we obey the LORD, he will surely give us that land rich with milk and honey. ⁹So don't rebel. We have no reason to be afraid of the people who live there. The LORD is on our side, and they won't stand a chance against us!

¹⁰The crowd threatened to stone Moses and Aaron to death. But just then, the LORD appeared in a cloud at the sacred tent.

Moses Prays for the People

¹¹The LORD said to Moses, "I have done great things for these people, and they still reject me by refusing to believe in my power. ¹²So they will no longer be my people. I will destroy them, but I will make you the ancestor of a nation even stronger than theirs."

¹³⁻¹⁶Moses replied:

With your mighty power you rescued your people from Egypt, so please don't destroy us here in the desert. If you do, the Egyptians will hear about it and tell the people of Canaan. Those Canaanites already know that we are your people, and that we see you face to face. And they have heard how you lead us with a thick cloud during the day and flaming fire at night. But if you kill us, they will claim it was because you weren't powerful enough to lead us into Canaan as you promised.

¹⁷Show us your great power, LORD. You promised ¹⁸that you love to show mercy and kindness. And you said that you are very patient, but that you will punish everyone guilty of doing wrong—not only them but their children and grandchildren as well.

¹⁹You are merciful, and you treat people better than they deserve. So please forgive these people, just as you have forgiven them ever since they left Egypt.

²⁰Then the LORD said to Moses:

In answer to your prayer, I do forgive them. ²¹But as surely as I live and my power has no limit, ²²⁻²³I swear that not one of these Israelites will enter the land I promised to give their ancestors. These people have seen my power in Egypt and in the desert, but they will never see Canaan. They have disobeyed and tested me too many times.

Personal *Concerns*—How can I forgive someone who has broken my trust? *(Numbers 14.11-25)*

Forgive, but be careful where you place your trust the next time.
In his dealings with his people, God shows us his capacity for forgiveness over and over and over again. Israel continually rejected God, even after he had delivered them from slavery and provided for their needs. Each time, God forgave them.

But the ultimate rebellion came at the very edge of the Promised Land. Just as the people were getting ready to go into Canaan, the land God was giving them in his generosity and goodness, they rebelled again and tried to stone the leaders God had appointed. God threatened to destroy the people, but when Moses interceded for them, he forgave them once more.

As Christians we, too, are expected to forgive over and over and over again. People may continually violate our trust, but we must be willing to overlook their offenses. This doesn't mean, however, that we must trust them again! God forgave the Israelites who rejected him, but he also decreed that they would not enter the Promised Land. Only their children would be allowed to go in and claim God's promise.

In the same way, be wise about where you place your trust. You shouldn't nurse anger against someone who has broken her promise to you. But carefully consider whether or not you should give her another opportunity to violate your trust. (See also 1 Samuel 24; Matthew 7.1-5; Matthew 18.21-35; Luke 6.27-36.)

Words To Remember: *Show us your great power, LORD. You promised that you love to show mercy and kindness.—Numbers 14.17,18*

²⁴But my servant Caleb isn't like the others. So because he has faith in me, I will allow him to cross into Canaan, and his descendants will settle there.

²⁵Now listen, Moses! The Amalekites and the Canaanites live in the valleys of Canaan.ⁿ And tomorrow morning, you'll need to turn around and head back into the desert toward the Red Sea.ᵒ

The Israelites Are Punished for Complaining

²⁶The LORD told Moses and Aaron ²⁷⁻²⁸to give this message to the people of Israel:

You sinful people have complained against me too many times! Now I swear by my own life that I will give you exactly what you wanted.ᵖ ²⁹You will die right here in the desert, and your dead bodies will cover the ground. You have insulted me, and none of you men who are over twenty years old ³⁰will enter the land that I solemnly promised to give you as your own—only Caleb and Joshuaᵈ will go in.

³¹You were worried that your own children would be captured. But I, the LORD, will let them enter the land you have rejected. ³²You will die here in the desert! ³³Your children will wander around in this desert forty years, suffering because of your sins, until all of you are dead. ³⁴I will cruelly punish you every day for the next forty years—one year for each day that the land was explored. ³⁵You sinful people who ganged up against me will die here in the desert.

³⁶Ten of the men sent to explore the land had brought back bad news and had made the people complain against the LORD. ³⁷So he sent a deadly disease that killed those men, ³⁸but he let Joshua and Caleb live.

The Israelites Fail To Enter Canaan

(Deuteronomy 1.41-45)

³⁹The people of Israel were very sad after Moses gave them the LORD's message. ⁴⁰So they got up early the next morning and got ready to head toward the hill country of Canaan. They said, "We were wrong to complain about the LORD. Let's go into the land that he promised us."

⁴¹But Moses replied, "You're disobeying the LORD! Your plan won't work, ⁴²⁻⁴³so don't even try it. The LORD refuses to help you, because you turned your backs on him. The Amalekites and the Canaanites are your enemies, and they will attack and defeat you."

⁴⁴But the Israelites ignored Mosesʳ and marched toward the hill country, even though the sacred chest and Moses did not go with them. ⁴⁵The Amalekites and the Canaanites came down from the hill country, defeated the Israelites, and chased them as far as the town of Hormah.

Laws about Sacrifices

15 The LORD told Moses ²to give the Israelites the following laws about offering sacrifices:

³Bulls or rams or goatsˢ are the animals that you may burn on the altar as sacrifices to please me.ᵗ You may also offer sacrifices voluntarily or because you made a promise, or because they are part of your regular religious ceremonies. The smell of the smoke from these sacrifices is pleasing to me.

⁴⁻⁵If you sacrifice a young ram or goat, you must also offer two pounds of your finest flour mixed with a quart of olive oil as a grain sacrifice. A quart of wine must also be poured on the altar.

⁶⁻⁷And if the animal is a full-grown ram, you must offer four pounds of flour mixed with one and a half quarts of olive oil. One and a half quarts of wine must also be poured on the altar. The smell of this smoke is pleasing to me.

⁸If a bull is offered as a sacrifice to please me or to ask my blessing,ᵘ ⁹you must offer six pounds of flour mixed with two quarts of olive oil. ¹⁰Two quarts of wine must also be

ⁿ14.25 The Amalekites and the Canaanites . . . valleys of Canaan: That is, all possible ways into Canaan were blocked. ᵒ14.25 Red Sea: Hebrew yam suph, here referring to the Gulf of Aqaba, since the term is extended to include the northeastern arm of the Red Sea (see also the note at Exodus 13.18). ᵖ14.27,28 wanted: See verse 2. ᵈ14.30 Caleb and Joshua: Hebrew "Caleb son of Jephunneh and Joshua son of Nun." ʳ14.44 ignored Moses: One possible meaning for the difficult Hebrew text. ˢ15.3 goats: See the note at 7.12-83. ᵗ15.3 sacrifices to please me: See the note at 6.11. ᵘ15.8 to ask my blessing: See the note at 6.14.

poured on the altar. The smell of this smoke is pleasing to me.

¹¹⁻¹³If you are a native Israelite, you must obey these rules each time you offer a bull, a ram, or a goat as a sacrifice. ¹⁴And the foreigners who live among you must also follow these rules. ¹⁵⁻¹⁶This law will never change. I am the LORD, and I consider all people the same, whether they are Israelites or foreigners living among you.

¹⁷⁻¹⁹When you eat food in the land that I am giving you, remember to set aside some of it as an offering to me. ²⁰From the first batch of bread dough that you make after each new grain harvest, make a loaf of bread and offer it to me, just as you offer grain. ²¹All your descendants must follow this law and offer part of the first batch of bread dough.

²²⁻²³The LORD also told Moses to tell the people what must be done if they ever disobey his laws:

²⁴If all of you disobey one of my laws without meaning to, you must offer a bull as a sacrifice to please me, together with a grain sacrifice, a wine offering, and a goat as a sacrifice for sin. ²⁵Then the priest will pray and ask me to forgive you. And since you did not mean to do wrong, and you offered sacrifices, ²⁶the sin of everyone—both Israelites and foreigners among you—will be forgiven.

²⁷But if one of you does wrong without meaning to, you must sacrifice a year-old female goat as a sacrifice for sin. ²⁸The priest will then ask me to forgive you, and your sin will be forgiven.

²⁹The law will be the same for anyone who does wrong without meaning to, whether an Israelite or a foreigner living among you.

³⁰⁻³¹But if one of you does wrong on purpose, whether Israelite or foreigner, you have sinned against me by disobeying my laws. You will be sent away and will no longer live among the people of Israel.

A Man Put to Death for Gathering Firewood on the Sabbath

³²Once, while the Israelites were traveling through the desert, a man was caught gathering firewood on the Sabbath.ᵛ ³³He was taken to Moses, Aaron, and the rest of the community. ³⁴But no one knew what to do with him, so he was not allowed to leave.

³⁵Then the LORD said to Moses, "Tell the people to take that man outside the camp and stone him to death!" ³⁶So he was killed, just as the LORD had commanded Moses.

The Tassels on the People's Clothes

³⁷The LORD told Moses ³⁸to say to the people of Israel, "Sew tassels onto the bottom edge of your clothes and tie a purple string to each tassel. ³⁹⁻⁴⁰These will remind you that you must obey my laws and teachings. And when you do, you will be dedicated to me and won't follow your own sinful desires. ⁴¹I am the LORD your God who led you out of Egypt."

Korah, Dathan, and Abiram Lead a Rebellion

16 ¹⁻²Korah son of Izhar was a Levite from the Kohathite clan. One day he called together Dathan, Abiram, and Onʷ from the Reuben tribe, and the four of them decided to rebel against Moses. So they asked two hundred fifty respected Israelite leaders for their support, and together they went to Moses ³and Aaron and said, "Why do you think you're so much better than anyone else? We're part of the LORD's holy people, and he's with all of us. What makes you think you're the only ones in charge?"

⁴When Moses heard this, he knelt down to pray.ˣ ⁵Then he said to Korah and his followers:

Tomorrow morning the LORD will show us the person he has chosen to be his priest, and that man will faithfully serve him.

⁶⁻⁷Korah, now here is what you and your followers must do: Get some fire pans, fill them with coals and incense, and place them near the sacred tent. And the man the LORD chooses will be his priest.ʸ Korah, this time you Levites have gone too far!

⁸⁻⁹You know that the God of Israel

ᵛ15.32 *a man . . . Sabbath*: No work was to be done on the Sabbath (see Exodus 31.12-17). ʷ16.1,2 *Dathan, Abiram, and On*: Hebrew "Dathan and Abiram the sons of Eliab, and On son of Peleth." ˣ16.4 *he knelt down to pray*: Or "he fell to his knees in sorrow." ʸ16.6,7 *Get some fire pans . . . his priest*: Only priests could offer incense at the sacred altar; anyone else who tried would be killed. In this case, the man who lived would be the one the LORD had chosen.

has chosen you Levites from all Israel to serve him by being in charge of the sacred tent and by helping the community to worship in the proper way. What more do you want? [10]The LORD has given you a special responsibility, and now, Korah, you think you should also be his priest. [11]You and your followers have rebelled against the LORD, not against Aaron.

[12]Then Moses sent for Dathan and Abiram, but they sent back this message: "We won't come! [13]It's bad enough that you took us from our rich farmland in Egypt to let us die here in the desert. Now you also want to boss us around! [14]You keep promising us rich farmlands with fertile fields and vineyards—but where are they? Stop trying to trick these people. No, we won't come to see you."

[15]Moses was very angry and said to the LORD, "Don't listen to these men! I haven't done anything wrong to them. I haven't taken as much as a donkey."

[16]Then he said to Korah, "Tomorrow you and your followers must go with Aaron to the LORD's sacred tent. [17]Each of you take along your fire pan with incense in it and offer the incense to the LORD."

[18]The next day the men placed incense and coals in their fire pans and stood with Moses and Aaron at the entrance to the sacred tent. [19]Meanwhile, Korah had convinced the rest of the Israelites to rebel against their two leaders.

When that happened, the LORD appeared in all his glory [20]and said to Moses and Aaron, [21]"Get away from the rest of the Israelites so I can kill them right now!"

[22]But the two men bowed down and prayed, "Our God, you gave these people life. Why would you punish everyone here when only one man has sinned?"

[23]The LORD answered Moses, [24]"Tell the people to stay away from the tents of Korah, Dathan, and Abiram."

[25]Moses walked over to Dathan and Abiram, and the other leaders of Israel followed. [26]Then Moses warned the people, "Get away from the tents of these sinful men! Don't touch anything that belongs to them or you'll be wiped out." [27]So everyone moved away from those tents, except Korah, Dathan, Abiram, and their families.

[28]Moses said to the crowd, "The LORD has chosen me and told me to do these things—it wasn't my idea. And here's how you will know: [29]If these men die a natural death, it means the LORD hasn't chosen me. [30]But suppose the LORD does something that has never been done before. For example, what if a huge crack appears in the ground, and these men and their families fall into it and are buried alive, together with everything they own? Then you will know they have turned their backs on the LORD!"

[31]As soon as Moses said this, the ground under the men opened up [32-33]and swallowed them alive, together with their families and everything they owned. Then the ground closed back up, and they were gone.

[34]The rest of the Israelites heard their screams, so they ran off, shouting, "We don't want that to happen to us!"

[35]Suddenly the LORD sent a fire that burned up the two hundred fifty men who had offered incense to him.

[36]Then the LORD said to Moses, [37]"Tell Aaron's son Eleazar to take the fire pans from the smoldering fire and scatter the coals. The pans are now sacred, [38]because they were used for offering incense to me. Have them hammered into a thin layer of bronze as a covering for the altar. Those men died because of their sin, and now their fire pans will become a warning for the rest of the community."

[39]Eleazar collected the pans and had them hammered into a thin layer of bronze as a covering for the altar, [40]just as the LORD had told Moses. The pans were a warning to the Israelites that only Aaron's descendants would be allowed to offer incense to the LORD. Anyone else who tried would be punished like Korah and his followers.

The Israelites Rebel and Are Punished

[41]The next day the people of Israel again complained against Moses and Aaron, "The two of you killed some of the LORD's people!"

[42]As the people crowded around them, Moses and Aaron turned toward the sacred tent, and the LORD appeared in his glory in the cloud covering the tent. [43]So Moses and Aaron walked to the front of the tent, [44]where the LORD said to them, [45]"Stand back! I am going to wipe out these Israelites once and for all."

They immediately bowed down and

prayed. [46]Then Moses told Aaron, "Grab your fire pan and fill it with hot coals from the altar. Put incense in it, then quickly take it to where the people are and offer it to the LORD, so they can be forgiven. The LORD is very angry, and people have already started dying!"

[47-48]Aaron did exactly what he had been told. He ran over to the crowd of people and stood between the dead bodies and the people who were still alive. He placed the incense on the pan, then offered it to the LORD and asked him to forgive the people's sin. The disease immediately stopped spreading, and no one else died from it. [49]But fourteen thousand seven hundred Israelites were dead, not counting those who had died with Korah and his followers.

[50]Aaron walked back and stood with Moses at the sacred tent.

Aaron's Walking Stick Blooms and Produces Almonds

17 The LORD told Moses:
[2-3]Call together the twelve tribes of Israel and tell the leader of each tribe to write his name on the walking stick he carries as a symbol of his authority. Make sure Aaron's name is written on the one from the Levi tribe, then collect all the sticks.

[4]Place these sticks in the tent right in front of the sacred chest where I appear to you. [5]I will then choose a man to be my priest, and his stick will sprout. After that happens, I won't have to listen to any more complaints about you.

Remembering God's faithfulness in the past helps us trust him today.

KAY MARSHALL STROM

---

[6]Moses told the people what the LORD had commanded, and they gave him the walking sticks from the twelve tribal leaders, including Aaron's from the Levi tribe.

[7]Moses took them and placed them in the LORD's sacred tent.

[8]The next day when Moses went into the tent, flowers and almonds were already growing on Aaron's stick. [9]Moses brought the twelve sticks out of the tent and showed them to the people. Each of the leaders found his own and took it.

[10]But the LORD told Moses, "Put Aaron's stick back! Let it stay near the sacred chest as a warning to anyone who might think about rebelling. If these people don't stop their grumbling about me, I will wipe them out." [11]Moses did what he was told.

[12]The Israelites cried out to Moses, "We're done for [13]and doomed if we even get near the sacred tent!"

The Duties of the Priests and Levites

18 The LORD said to Aaron:
You, your sons, and the other Levites of the Kohath clan, are responsible for what happens at the sacred tent.[z] And you and your sons will be responsible for what the priests do. [2]The Levites are your relatives and are here to help you in your service at the tent. [3]You must see that they perform their duties. But if they go near any of the sacred objects or the altar, all of you will die. [4]No one else is allowed to take care of the sacred tent or to do anything connected with it. [5]Follow these instructions, so I won't become angry and punish the Israelites ever again.

[6]I alone chose the Levites from all the other tribes to belong to me, and I have given them to you as your helpers. [7]But only you and your sons can serve as priests at the altar and in the most holy place. Your work as priests is a gift from me, and anyone else who tries to do that work must be put to death.

The Priests' Share of Offerings Given to the LORD

(Deuteronomy 18.1-8)

[8-9]The LORD said to Aaron:
I have put you in charge of the sacred gifts and sacrifices that the Israelites bring to me. And from now on, you, your sons, and your descendants will receive part of the sacrifices for sin, as well as part of the grain

---

[z]18.1 *are responsible . . . sacred tent:* Or "are to make sure that no one gets near the sacred tent."

sacrifices, and the sacrifices to make things right. Your share of these sacrifices will be the parts not burned on the altar. [10]Since these things are sacred, they must be eaten near the sacred tent, but only men are allowed to eat them.

[11]You will also receive part of the special gifts and offerings that the Israelites bring to me. Any member of your family who is clean and acceptable for worship can eat these things. [12]For example, when the Israelites bring me the first batches of oil, wine, and grain, you can have the best parts of those gifts. [13]And the first part of the crops from their fields and vineyards also belongs to you. The people will offer this to me, then anyone in your family who is clean may have some of it.

[14]Everything in Israel that has been completely dedicated to me[a] will now belong to you.

[15]The first-born son in every Israelite family, as well as the first-born males of their flocks and herds, belong to me. But a first-born son and every first-born donkey[b] must be bought back from me. [16]The price for a first-born son who is at least one month old will be five pieces of silver, weighed according to the official standards. [17]However, all first-born cattle, sheep, and goats belong to me and cannot be bought back. Splatter their blood on the altar and send their fat up in smoke, so I can smell it and be pleased. [18]You are allowed to eat the meat of those animals, just as you can eat the choice ribs and the right hind leg of the special sacrifices.

[19]From now on, the sacred offerings that the Israelites give to me will belong to you, your sons, and your daughters. This is my promise to you and your descendants, and it will never change.

[20]You will not receive any land in Israel as your own. I am the LORD, and I will give you whatever you need.

What the Levites Receive

The LORD said to Aaron:

[21]Ten percent of the Israelites' crops and one out of every ten of their newborn animals belong to me. But I am giving all this to the Levites as their pay for the work they do at the sacred tent. [22-23]They are the only ones allowed to work at the tent, and they must

not let anyone else come near it. Those who do must be put to death, and the Levites will also be punished. This law will never change.

Since the Levites won't be given any land in Israel as their own, [24]they will be given the crops and newborn animals that the Israelites offer to me.

What the Levites Must Give

[25]The LORD told Moses [26]to say to the Levites:

When you receive from the people of Israel ten percent of their crops and newborn animals, you must offer a tenth of that to me. [27]Just as the Israelites give me part of their grain and wine, you must set aside part of what you receive [28]as an offering to me. That amount must then be given to Aaron, [29]so the best of what you receive will be mine.

[30]After you have dedicated the best parts to me, you can eat the rest, just as the Israelites eat part of their grain and wine after offering them to me.[c] [31]Your share may be eaten anywhere by anyone in your family, because it is your pay for working at the sacred tent. [32]You won't be punished for eating it, as long as you have already offered the best parts to me.

The gifts and sacrifices brought by the people must remain sacred, and if you eat any part of them before they are offered to me, you will be put to death.

The Ceremony To Wash Away Sin

19 [1-2]The LORD gave Moses and Aaron the following law:

The people of Israel must bring Moses a reddish-brown cow that has nothing wrong with it and that has never been used for plowing. [3]Moses will give it to Eleazar the priest, then it will be led outside the camp and killed while Eleazar watches. [4]He will dip his finger into the blood and sprinkle it seven times in the direction of the sacred tent. [5]Then the whole cow, including

---

[a]18.14 that has been completely dedicated to me: This translates a Hebrew word that describes property and things that were taken away from humans and given to God forever. Sometimes such things had to be completely destroyed (see Joshua 6.15-19). [b]18.15 donkey: The Hebrew text has "unclean animal," which probably refers to a donkey (see Exodus 13.13; 34.20). [c]18.30 just as the Israelites . . . to me: One possible meaning for the difficult Hebrew text.

its skin, meat, blood, and insides must be burned. [6]A priest[d] is to throw a stick of cedar wood, a hyssop[e] branch, and a piece of red yarn into the fire.

[7]After the ceremony, the priest is to take a bath and wash his clothes. Only then can he go back into the camp, but he remains unclean and unfit for worship until evening. [8]The man who burned the cow must also wash his clothes and take a bath, but he is also unclean until evening.

> *God's grace is not only*
> *sufficient—it is*
> *inexhaustible.*
>
> RUTH BELL GRAHAM

[9]A man who isn't unclean must collect the ashes of the burnt cow and store them outside the camp in a clean place. The people of Israel can mix these ashes with the water used in the ceremony to wash away sin. [10]The man who collects the ashes must wash his clothes, but will remain unclean until evening. This law must always be obeyed by the people of Israel and the foreigners living among them.

What Must Be Done after Touching a Dead Body

The LORD said:

[11]If you touch a dead body, you will be unclean for seven days. [12]But if you wash with the water mixed with the cow's ashes on the third day and again on the seventh day, you will be clean and acceptable for worship. You must wash yourself on those days; if you don't, you will remain unclean. [13]Suppose you touch a dead body, but refuse to be made clean by washing with the water mixed with ashes. You will be guilty of making my sacred tent unclean and will no longer belong to the people of Israel.

[14]If someone dies in a tent while you are there, you will be unclean for seven days. And anyone who later enters the tent will also be unclean. [15]Any open jar in the tent is unclean.

[16]If you touch the body of someone who was killed or who died of old age, or if you touch a human bone or a grave, you will be unclean for seven days.

[17-18]Before you can be made clean, someone who is clean must take some of the ashes from the burnt cow and stir them into a pot of spring water. That same person must dip a hyssop branch in the water and ashes, then sprinkle it on the tent and everything in it, including everyone who was inside. If you have touched a human bone, a grave, or a dead body, you must be sprinkled with that water. [19]If this is done on the third day and on the seventh day, you will be clean. Then after you take a bath and wash your clothes, you can worship that evening.

[20]If you are unclean and refuse to be made clean by washing with the water mixed with ashes, you will be guilty of making my sacred tent unclean, and you will no longer belong to the people of Israel. [21]These laws will never change.

The man who sprinkled the water and the ashes on you when you were unclean must also wash his clothes. And whoever touches this water is unclean until evening. [22]When you are unclean, everything you touch becomes unclean, and anyone who touches you will be unclean until evening.

Water from a Rock
(Exodus 17.1-7)

20 The people of Israel arrived at the Zin Desert during the first month[f] and set up camp near the town of Kadesh. It was there that Miriam died and was buried.

[2]The Israelites had no water, so they went to Moses and Aaron [3]and complained, "Moses, we'd be better off if we had died along with the others in front of the LORD's sacred tent.[g] [4]You brought us into this desert, and now we and our livestock are going to die! [5]Egypt was better than this horrible place. At least there we had grain and figs and grapevines and pomegranates.[h] But now we don't even have any water."

[6]Moses and Aaron went to the entrance

---

[d]19.6 *A priest*: Or "Eleazar." [e]19.6 *hyssop*: A plant with small clusters of blue flowers and sweet-smelling leaves. [f]20.1 *first month*: See the note at 9.3. [g]20.3 *if we had died . . . sacred tent*: See 16.41-49. [h]20.5 *pomegranates*: See the note at 13.23, 24.

to the sacred tent, where they bowed down. The LORD appeared to them in all of his glory [7-8] and said, "Moses, get your walking stick.[i] Then you and Aaron call the people together and command that rock to give you water. That's how you will provide water for the people of Israel and their livestock."

[9] Moses obeyed and took his stick from the sacred tent. [10] After he and Aaron had gathered the people around the rock, he said, "Look, you rebellious people, and you will see water flow from this rock!" [11] He raised his stick in the air and struck the rock two times. At once, water gushed from the rock, and the people and their livestock had water to drink.

[12] But the LORD said to Moses and Aaron, "Because you refused to believe in my power, these people did not respect me. And so, you will not be the ones to lead them into the land I have promised."

[13] The Israelites had complained against the LORD, and he had shown them his holy power by giving them water to drink. So they named the place Meribah, which means "Complaining."

Israel Isn't Allowed To Go through Edom

[14] Moses sent messengers from Israel's camp near Kadesh with this message for the king of Edom:

We are Israelites, your own relatives, and we're sure you have heard the terrible things that have happened to us. [15] Our ancestors settled in Egypt and lived there a long time. But later the Egyptians were cruel to us, [16] and when we begged our LORD for help, he answered our prayer and brought us out of that land.

Now we are camped at the border of your territory, near the town of Kadesh. [17] Please let us go through your country. We won't go near your fields and vineyards, and we won't drink any water from your wells. We will stay on the main road[j] until we leave your territory.

[18] But the Edomite king answered, "No, I won't let you go through our country! And if you try, we will attack you."

[19] Moses sent back this message: "We promise to stay on the main road, and if any of us or our livestock drink your water, we will pay for it. We just want to pass through."

---

[i] 20.7,8 *walking stick*: A symbol of his authority.
[j] 20.17 *the main road*: The Hebrew text has "the King's Highway," which was an important trade route through what is today the country of Jordan. It connected the city of Damascus in Syria with the Gulf of Aqaba in southern Jordan.

---

*Spiritual*Life—Is it okay to be angry at God? *(Numbers 20.1-13)*

Don't let anger lead to active rebellion.
It was hot and dry in the desert, and the people of Israel had no water to drink. They were sure God had finally deserted them. They were angry at him and at his servant Moses, and began complaining, as if to say, God has forgotten us! We're going to die out here in the desert! They even wanted to go back to Egypt. This showed that they had moved beyond merely registering a complaint with God and on to active rebellion against his design for them.

Of course, God hadn't forgotten his people—even in the desert. He provided water for them from a rock. But he was displeased with his people because they rebelled against him.

When do we feel angry with God? Often it's when we think he isn't meeting our needs. But this story shows us that God is always able to meet our needs, even when he has to do something as impossible as producing water from a rock! Even when we feel that God isn't giving us what we need, we aren't permitted to rebel against him.

God knows that we are human, that we sometimes feel the emotion of anger against him. But he warns us not to turn those feelings into action by rebelling out loud against what he is doing. Instead, we are to wait on his provision, trusting him to do what is right for us. (See also Job 19; Psalm 10; Habakkuk 1.2-5.)

Words To Remember: *The Israelites had complained against the* LORD, *and he had shown them his holy power by giving them water to drink.*—Numbers 20.13

²⁰But the Edomite king insisted, "You can't go through our land!"

Then Edom sent out its strongest troops ²¹to keep Israel from passing through its territory. So the Israelites had to go in another direction.

Aaron Dies

²²After the Israelites had left Kadesh and had gone as far as Mount Hor ²³on the Edomite border, the LORD said, ²⁴"Aaron, this is where you will die. You and Moses disobeyed me at Meribah, and so you will not enter the land I promised the Israelites. ²⁵Moses, go with Aaron and his son Eleazar to the top of the mountain. ²⁶Then take Aaron's priestly robe from him and place it on Eleazar. Aaron will die there."

²⁷Moses obeyed, and everyone watched as he and Aaron and Eleazar walked to the top of Mount Hor. ²⁸Moses then took the priestly robe from Aaron and placed it on Eleazar. Aaron died there.

When Moses and Eleazar came down, ²⁹the people knew that Aaron had died, and they mourned his death for thirty days.

Israel Defeats the Canaanites at Hormah

21 The Canaanite king of Arad lived in the Southern Desert of Canaan, and when he heard that the Israelites were on their way to the village of Atharim, he attacked and took some of them hostage.

²The Israelites prayed, "Our LORD, if you will help us defeat these Canaanites, we will completely destroy their towns and everything in them, to show that they belong to you."ᵏ

³The LORD answered their prayer and helped them wipe out the Canaanite army and completely destroy their towns. That's why one of the towns is named Hormah, which means "Destroyed Place."

Moses Makes a Bronze Snake

⁴The Israelites had to go around the territory of Edom, so when they left Mount Hor, they headed south toward the Red Sea.ˡ But along the way, the people became so impatient ⁵that they complained against God and said to Moses, "Did you bring us out of Egypt, just to let us die in the desert? There's no water out here, and we can't stand this awful food!"

⁶Then the LORD sent poisonous snakes that bit and killed many of them.

⁷Some of the people went to Moses and admitted, "It was wrong of us to insult you and the LORD. Now please ask him to make these snakes go away."

Faith is seeing clearly the all-sufficiency and strength of God.

CAROLE SANDERSON STREETER

Moses prayed, ⁸and the LORD answered, "Make a snake out of bronze and place it on top of a pole. Anyone who gets bitten can look at the snake and won't die."

⁹Moses obeyed the LORD. And all of those who looked at the bronze snake lived, even though they had been bitten by the poisonous snakes.

Israel's Journey to Moab

¹⁰As the Israelites continued their journey to Canaan, they camped at Oboth, ¹¹then at Iye-Abarim in the desert east of Moab, ¹²and then in the Zered Gorge. ¹³After that, they crossed the Arnon River gorge and camped in the Moabite desert bordering Amorite territory. The Arnon was the border between the Moabites and the Amorites. ¹⁴A song in *The Book of the LORD's Battles*ᵐ mentions the town of Waheb with its creeks in the territory of Suphah. It also mentions the Arnon River, ¹⁵with its valleys that lie alongside the Moabite border and extend to the town of Ar.

¹⁶From the Arnon, the Israelites went to the well near the town of Beer, where the LORD had said to Moses, "Call the people together, and I will give them water to drink."

¹⁷That's also the same well the Israelites sang about in this song:

ᵏ21.2 *completely destroy . . . belong to you:* The complete destruction of a town and everything in it, including its people and animals, showed that the town belonged to the LORD and could no longer be used by humans.
ˡ21.4 *Red Sea:* See the note at 14.25.   ᵐ21.14 *The Book of the LORD's Battles:* This may have been a collection of ancient war songs.

Let's celebrate!
The well has given us water.
[18] With their royal scepters,
our leaders pointed out
where to dig the well.

The Israelites left the desert and camped near the town of Mattanah, [19] then at Nahaliel, and then at Bamoth. [20] Finally, they reached Moabite territory, where they camped near Mount Pisgah[n] in a valley overlooking the desert north of the Dead Sea.

Israel Defeats King Sihon the Amorite
(Deuteronomy 2.26-37)

[21] The Israelites sent this message to King Sihon of the Amorites:
[22] Please let us pass through your territory. We promise to stay away from your fields and vineyards, and we won't drink any water from your wells. As long as we're in your land, we won't get off the main road.[o]
[23] But Sihon refused to let Israel travel through his land. Instead, he called together his entire army and marched into the desert to attack Israel near the town of Jahaz. [24] Israel defeated them and took over the Amorite territory from the Arnon River gorge in the south to the Jabbok River gorge in the north. Beyond the Jabbok was the territory of the Ammonites, who were much stronger than Israel.
[25] The Israelites settled in the Amorite towns, including the capital city of Heshbon with its surrounding villages. [26] King Sihon had ruled from Heshbon, after defeating the Moabites and taking over their land north of the Arnon River gorge. [27] That's why the Amorites had written this poem about Heshbon:

Come and rebuild Heshbon,
King Sihon's capital city!
[28] His armies marched out
like fiery flames,
burning down the town of Ar
and destroying[p] the hills
along the Arnon River.
[29] You Moabites are done for!
Your god Chemosh
deserted your people;
they were captured, taken away
by King Sihon the Amorite.
[30] We completely defeated Moab.

The towns of Heshbon and Dibon,
of Nophah and Medeba
are ruined and gone.[q]

[31] After the Israelites had settled in the Amorite territory, [32] Moses sent some men to explore the town of Jazer. Later, the Israelites captured the villages surrounding it and forced out the Amorites who lived there.

Israel Defeats King Og of Bashan
(Deuteronomy 3.1-11)

[33] The Israelites headed toward the region of Bashan, where King Og ruled, and he led his entire army to Edrei to meet Israel in battle.
[34] The LORD said to Moses, "Don't be afraid of Og. I will help you defeat him and his army, just as you did King Sihon who ruled in Heshbon. Og's territory will be yours."
[35] So the Israelites wiped out Og, his family, and his entire army—there were no survivors. Then Israel took over the land of Bashan.

22
Israel moved from there to the hills of Moab, where they camped across the Jordan River from the town of Jericho.

King Balak of Moab Hires Balaam To Curse Israel

[2-3] When King Balak[r] of Moab and his people heard how many Israelites there were and what they had done to the Amorites, he and the Moabites were terrified and panicked. [4] They said to the Midianite leaders, "That bunch of Israelites will wipe out everything in sight, like a bull eating grass in a field."
So King Balak [5] sent a message to Balaam son of Beor who lived among his relatives in the town of Pethor near the Euphrates River. It said:
I need your help. A huge group of people has come here from Egypt and settled near my territory. [6] They are too powerful for us to defeat, so would

---

[n]21.20 Mount Pisgah: This probably refers to the highest peak in the Abarim Mountains in Moab.   [o]21.22 the main road: See the note at 20.17.   [p]21.28 destroying: One ancient translation; Hebrew "the rulers of."   [q]21.30 gone: One possible meaning for the difficult Hebrew text of verse 30.   [r]22.2,3 Balak: Hebrew "Balak son of Zippor."

you come and place a curse on them? Maybe then we can run them off. I know that anyone you bless will be successful, but anyone you curse will fail.

⁷The leaders of Moab and Midian left and took along money to pay Balaam for his work. When they got to his house, they gave him Balak's message.

⁸"Spend the night here," Balaam replied, "and tomorrow I will tell you the LORD's answer." So the officials stayed at his house.

⁹During the night, God asked Balaam, "Who are these people at your house?"

¹⁰"They are messengers from King Balak of Moab," Balaam answered. "He sent them ¹¹to ask me to go to Moab and place a curse on the people who have come there from Egypt. They have settled everywhere around him, and he wants to run them off."

¹²But God replied, "Don't go with Balak's messengers. I have blessed those people who have come from Egypt, so don't curse them."

¹³The next morning, Balaam said to Balak's officials, "Go on back home. The LORD says I cannot go with you."

¹⁴The officials left and told Balak that Balaam refused to come.

¹⁵Then Balak sent a larger group of officials, who were even more important than the first ones. ¹⁶They went to Balaam and told him that Balak had said, "Balaam, if you come to Moab, ¹⁷I'll pay you very well and do whatever you ask. Just come and place a curse on these people."

¹⁸Balaam answered, "Even if Balak offered me a palace full of silver or gold, I wouldn't do anything to disobey the LORD my God. ¹⁹You are welcome to spend the night here, just as the others did. I will find out if the LORD has something else to say about this."

²⁰That night, God said, "Balaam, I'll let you go to Moab with Balak's messengers, but do only what I say."

²¹So Balaam got up the next morning and saddled his donkey, then left with the Moabite officials.

Balaam and His Donkey Meet an Angel

²²Balaam was riding his donkey to Moab, and two of his servants were with him. But God was angry that Balaam had gone, so one of the LORD's angels stood in the road

to stop him. ²³When Balaam's donkey saw the angel standing there with a sword, it walked off the road and into an open field. Balaam had to beat the donkey to get it back on the road.

²⁴Then the angel stood between two vineyards, in a narrow path with a stone wall on each side. ²⁵When the donkey saw the angel, it walked so close to one of the walls that Balaam's foot scraped against the wall. Balaam beat the donkey again.

> *God's part is to work—*
> *with all that divine,*
> *all-encompassing power. Our*
> *part is to trust him to do it.*
>
> ANNE ORTLUND

²⁶The angel moved once more and stood in a spot so narrow that there was no room for the donkey to go around. ²⁷So it just lay down. Balaam lost his temper, then picked up a stick and smacked the donkey.

²⁸When that happened, the LORD told the donkey to speak, and it asked Balaam, "What have I done to you that made you beat me three times?"

²⁹"You made me look stupid!" Balaam answered. "If I had a sword, I'd kill you here and now!"

³⁰"But you're my owner," replied the donkey, "and you've ridden me many times. Have I ever done anything like this before?"

"No," Balaam admitted.

³¹Just then, the LORD let Balaam see the angel standing in the road, holding a sword, and Balaam bowed down.

³²The angel said, "You had no right to treat your donkey like that! I was the one who blocked your way, because I don't think you should go to Moab.ˢ ³³If your donkey had not seen me and stopped those three times, I would have killed you and let the donkey live."

³⁴Balaam replied, "I was wrong. I didn't

ˢ**22.32** *I don't think you should go to Moab:* One possible meaning for the difficult Hebrew text.

know you were trying to stop me. If you don't think I should go, I'll return home right now."

[35]"It's all right for you to go," the LORD's angel answered. "But you must say only what I tell you." So Balaam went on with Balak's officials.

King Balak Meets Balaam

[36]When Balak heard that Balaam was coming, he went to meet him at the town of Ir, which is on the northern border of Moab. [37]Balak asked, "Why didn't you come when I invited you the first time? Did you think I wasn't going to pay you?"

[38]"I'm here now," Balaam answered. "But I will say only what God tells me to say."

[39]They left and went to the town of Kiriath-Huzoth, [40]where Balak sacrificed cattle and sheep and gave some of the meat to Balaam and the officials who were with him.

[41]The next morning, Balak took Balaam to the town of Bamoth-Baal. From there, Balaam could see some of the Israelites.[t]

Balaam's First Message

23 Balaam said to Balak, "Build seven altars here, then bring seven bulls and seven rams."

[2]After Balak had done this, they sacrificed a bull and a ram on each altar. [3]Then Balaam said, "Wait here beside your offerings, and I'll go somewhere to be alone. Maybe the LORD will appear to me. If he does, I will tell you everything he says." And he left.

[4]When God appeared to him, Balaam said, "I have built seven altars and have sacrificed a bull and a ram on each one."

[5]The LORD gave Balaam a message, then sent him back to tell Balak. [6]When Balaam returned, he found Balak and his officials standing beside the offerings.

[7]Balaam said:

"King Balak of Moab brought me
from the hills of Syria
to curse Israel
and announce its doom.
[8]But I can't go against God!
He did not curse
or condemn Israel.

*[9]"From the mountain peaks,
I look down and see Israel,

the obedient people of God.
[10]They are living alone in peace.
And though they are many,
they don't bother
the other nations.

"I hope to obey God
for as long as I live
and to die in such peace."

[11]Balak said, "What are you doing? I asked you to come and place a curse on my enemies. But you have blessed them instead!"

[12]Balaam answered, "I can say only what the LORD tells me."

Balaam's Second Message

[13]Balak said to Balaam, "Let's go somewhere else. Maybe if you see a smaller part of the Israelites, you will be able to curse them for me." [14]So he took Balaam to a field on top of Mount Pisgah where lookouts were stationed.[u] Then he built seven altars there and sacrificed a bull and a ram on each one.

[15]"Wait here beside your offerings," Balaam said. "The LORD will appear to me over there."

[16]The LORD appeared to Balaam and gave him another message, then he told him to go and tell Balak. [17]Balaam went back and saw him and his officials standing beside the offerings.

Balak asked, "What did the LORD say?"
[18]Balaam answered:

"Pay close attention
to my words—
[19]God is no mere human!
He doesn't tell lies
or change his mind.
God always keeps his promises.

[20]"My command from God
was to bless these people,
and there's nothing I can do
to change what he has done.
[21]Israel's king is the LORD God.
He lives there with them

---

[t]**22.41** *Balaam could see some of the Israelites:* For a curse to work, the people or thing being cursed had to be seen. [u]**23.14** *a field . . . where lookouts were stationed:* Or "Zophim Field on the top of Mount Pisgah."

and intends them no harm.
²²With the strength of a wild ox,
    God led Israel out of Egypt.
²³No magic charms can work
    against them—
    just look what God has done
      for his people.
²⁴They are like angry lions
    ready to attack;
    and they won't rest
    until their victim
      is gobbled down."

²⁵Balak shouted, "If you're not going to curse Israel, then at least don't bless them."

²⁶"I've already told you," Balaam answered. "I will say only what the LORD tells me."

Balaam's Third Message

²⁷Balak said to Balaam, "Come on, let's try another place. Maybe God will let you curse Israel from there." ²⁸So he took Balaam to Mount Peor overlooking the desert north of the Dead Sea.

²⁹Balaam said, "Build seven altars here, then bring me seven bulls and seven rams."

³⁰After Balak had done what Balaam asked, he sacrificed a bull and a ram on each altar.

24 Balaam was sure that the LORD would tell him to bless Israel again. So he did not use any magic to find out what the LORD wanted him to do, as he had the first two times. Instead, he looked out toward the desert ²and saw the tribes of Israel camped below. Just then, God's Spirit took control of him, ³and Balaam said:

"I am the son of Beor,
    and my words are true,ᵛ
      so listen to my message!
⁴It comes from the LORD,
    the God All-Powerful.
I bowed down to him
    and saw a vision of Israel.

⁵"People of Israel,
    your camp is lovely.
⁶It's like a grove of palm treesʷ
    or a garden beside a river.
You are like tall aloe trees
    that the LORD has planted,
or like cedars

growing near water.
⁷You and your descendants
    will prosper like an orchard
      beside a stream.
Your king will rule with power
    and be a greater king
      than Agag the Amalekite.ˣ
⁸With the strength of a wild ox,
    God led you out of Egypt.
You will defeat your enemies,
    shooting them with arrowsʸ
      and crushing their bones.
⁹Like a lion you lie down,
    resting after an attack.
Who would dare disturb you?

"Anyone who blesses you
    will be blessed;
anyone who curses you
    will be cursed."

> *God accepts and uses us just as we are.*
>
> DENISE TURNER

¹⁰When Balak heard this, he was so furious that he pounded his fist against his hand and said, "I called you here to place a curse on my enemies, and you've blessed them three times. ¹¹Leave now and go home! I told you I would pay you well, but since the LORD didn't let you do what I asked, you won't be paid."

¹²Balaam answered, "I told your messengers ¹³that even if you offered me a palace full of silver or gold, I would still obey the LORD. And I explained that I would say only what he told me. ¹⁴So I'm going back home, but I'm leaving you with a warning about what the Israelites will someday do to your nation."

ᵛ24.3 *my words are true:* One possible meaning for the difficult Hebrew text.   ʷ24.6 *grove of palm trees:* Or "green valley."   ˣ24.7 *Agag the Amalekite:* The Amalekites were long-time enemies of the Israelites (see Exodus 17.8-16), and Agag was one of their most powerful kings.   ʸ24.8 *shooting them with arrows:* One possible meaning for the difficult Hebrew text.

Balaam's Fourth Message

¹⁵Balaam said:

"I am the son of Beor,
and my words are true,ᶻ
so listen to my message!
¹⁶ My knowledge comes
from God Most High,
the LORD All-Powerful.
I bowed down to him
and saw a vision of Israel.

¹⁷ "What I saw in my vision
hasn't happened yet.
But someday, a king of Israel
will appear like a star.
He will wipe out you Moabitesᵃ
and destroyᵇ those tribes
who live in the desert.ᶜ
¹⁸ Israel will conquer Edom
and capture the land
of that enemy nation.
¹⁹ The king of Israel will rule
and destroy the survivors
of every town there.ᵈ

²⁰ "And I saw this vision
about the Amalekites:ᵉ
Their nation is now great,
but it will someday
disappear forever.ᶠ

²¹ "And this is what I saw
about the Kenites:ᵍ
They think they're safe,
living among the rocks,
²² but they will be wiped out
when Assyria conquers them.ʰ

²³ "No one can survive
if God plans destruction.ⁱ
²⁴ Ships will come from Cyprus,
bringing people who will invade
the lands of Assyria and Eber.
But finally, Cyprus itself
will be ruined."

²⁵After Balaam finished, he started home, and Balak also left.

The Israelites Worship Baal

25 While the Israelites were camped at Acacia, some of the men had sex with Moabite women. ²These women then invited the men to ceremonies where sacrifices were offered to their gods. The men ate the meat from the sacrifices and worshiped the Moabite gods.

³The LORD was angry with Israel because they had worshiped the god Baal Peor. ⁴So he said to Moses, "Take the Israelite leaders who are responsible for this and have them killed in front of my sacred tent where everyone can see. Maybe then I will stop being angry with the Israelites."

⁵Moses told Israel's officials,ʲ "Each of you must put to death any of your men who worshiped Baal."

⁶Later, Moses and the people were at the sacred tent, crying, when one of the Israelite men brought a Midianiteᵏ woman to meet his family. ⁷Phinehas, the grandson of Aaronˡ the priest, saw the couple and left the crowd. He found a spear ⁸and followed the man into his tent, where he ran the spear through the man and into the woman's stomach. The LORD immediately stopped punishing Israel with a deadly disease, ⁹but twenty-four thousand Israelites had already died.

¹⁰The LORD said to Moses, ¹¹"In my anger, I would have wiped out the Israelites if Phinehas had not been faithful to me. ¹²⁻¹³But instead of punishing them, I forgave them. So because of the loyalty that Phinehas showed, I solemnly promise that he and his descendants will always be my priests."

¹⁴The Israelite man that was killed was Zimri son of Salu, who was one of the leaders of the Simeon tribe. ¹⁵And the Midianite

<hr>

ᶻ**24.15** *my words are true:* One possible meaning for the difficult Hebrew text. ᵃ**24.17** *you Moabites:* Or "the territories of Moab." ᵇ**24.17** *destroy:* The Standard Hebrew Text; the Samaritan Hebrew Text "the skulls of." ᶜ**24.17** *those tribes . . . desert:* The Hebrew text has "the descendants of Sheth," which probably refers to the people who lived in the desert areas of Canaan before the Israelites. ᵈ**24.19** *every town there:* Or "Ir in Moab." ᵉ**24.20** *the Amalekites:* See the note at 24.7. ᶠ**24.20** *but . . . forever:* One possible meaning for the difficult Hebrew text. ᵍ**24.21** *the Kenites:* A group of people who lived in the desert south of Israel. ʰ**24.22** *them:* One possible meaning for the difficult Hebrew text of verse 22. ⁱ**24.23** *destruction:* One possible meaning for the difficult Hebrew text of verse 23. ʲ**25.5** *officials:* These were special leaders who were probably responsible for an entire tribe or part of a tribe. ᵏ**25.6** *Midianite:* Used here as a general term for various peoples who lived east of the Jordan River. Some of these people were probably ruled by the Moabite king (see Genesis 36.35). ˡ**25.7** *Phinehas . . . Aaron:* Hebrew "Phinehas, son of Eleazar and grandson of Aaron."

woman killed with him was Cozbi,
the daughter of a Midianite clan leader
named Zur.
16 The LORD told Moses, 17-18 "The Midianites are now enemies of Israel, so attack
and defeat them! They tricked the people of
Israel into worshiping their god at Peor, and
they are responsible for the death of Cozbi,
the daughter of one of their own leaders."

The Israelites Are Counted a Second Time

26 After the LORD had stopped the
deadly disease from killing the Israelites, he said to Moses and
Eleazar son of Aaron, 2 "I want you to find
out how many Israelites are in each family.
And list every man twenty years and older
who is able to serve in Israel's army."
3 Israel was now camped in the hills of
Moab across the Jordan River from the town
of Jericho. Moses and Eleazar told them
4 what the LORD had said about counting the
men twenty years and older, just as Moses
and their ancestors had done when they left
Egypt.[m]
5-7 There were 43,730 men from the tribe
of Reuben, the oldest son of Jacob.[n] These
men were from the clans of Hanoch, Pallu,
Hezron, and Carmi. 8 Pallu was the father of
Eliab 9 and the grandfather of Nemuel, Dathan, and Abiram. These are the same Dathan and Abiram who had been chosen by
the people, but who followed Korah and rebelled against Moses, Aaron, and the LORD.
10 That's when the LORD made the earth
open up and swallow Dathan, Abiram, and
Korah. At the same time, fire destroyed two
hundred fifty men as a warning to the other
Israelites.[o] 11 But the Korahite clan wasn't destroyed.
12-14 There were 22,200 men from the
tribe of Simeon; they were from the clans of
Nemuel, Jamin, Jachin, Zerah, and Shaul.
15-18 There were 40,500 men from the
tribe of Gad; they were from the clans of Ze-
phon, Haggi, Shuni, Ozni, Eri, Arod, and
Areli.
19-22 There were 76,500 men from the
tribe of Judah; they were from the clans of
Shelah, Perez, Zerah, Hezron, and Hamul.
Judah's sons Er and Onan had died in
Canaan.[p]
23-25 There were 64,300 men from the
tribe of Issachar; they were from the clans of
Tola, Puvah, Jashub, and Shimron.
26-27 There were 60,500 men from the
tribe of Zebulun; they were from the clans of
Sered, Elon, and Jahleel.
28-34 There were 52,700 men from the
tribe of Manasseh son of Joseph; they were
from the clan of Machir, the clan of Gilead
his son, and the clans of his six grandsons:
Iezer, Helek, Asriel, Shechem, Shemida, and
Hepher. Zelophehad son of Hepher had no
sons, but he had five daughters: Mahlah,
Noah, Hoglah, Milcah, and Tirzah.[q]
35-37 There were 32,500 men from the
tribe of Ephraim son of Joseph; they were
from the clans of Shuthelah, Becher, Tahan,
and Eran the son of Shuthelah.
38-41 There were 45,600 men from the
tribe of Benjamin; they were from the clans
of Bela, Ashbel, Ahiram, Shephupham, Hu-
pham, as well as from Ard and Naaman, the
two sons of Bela.
42-43 There were 64,400 men from the
tribe of Dan; they were all from the clan of
Shuham.
44-47 There were 53,400 men from the
tribe of Asher; they were from the clans of
Imnah, Ishvi, and Beriah, and from the two
clans of Heber and Malchiel, the sons of Beriah. Asher's daughter was Serah.
48-50 There were 45,400 men from the
tribe of Naphtali; they were from the clans
of Jahzeel, Guni, Jezer, and Shillem.
51 The total number of Israelite men listed
was 601,730.
52 The LORD said to Moses, 53 "Divide the
land of Canaan among these tribes, according to the number of people in each one,
54 so the larger tribes have more land than
the smaller ones. 55-56 I will show you[r] what
land to give each tribe, and they will receive
as much land as they need, according to the
number of people in it."
57 The tribe of Levi included the clans of
the Gershonites, Kohathites, Merarites, 58 as
well as the clans of Libni, Hebron, Mahli,
Mushi, and Korah. Kohath the Levite was

---

[m] **26.4** *just as . . . Egypt*: One possible meaning for the difficult Hebrew text. [n] **26.5-7** *Jacob*: The Hebrew text has "Israel," Jacob's name after God renamed him. [o] **26.10** *Israelites*: See 16.1-35. [p] **26.19-22** *Judah's sons . . . Canaan*: See Genesis 38.1-10.
[q] **26.28-34** *Zelophehad . . . Tirzah*: See also 27.1-11; 36.1-12. [r] **26.55,56** *I will show you*: The Hebrew text has "Cast lots to find out." Pieces of wood or stone (called "lots") were used to find out what the LORD wanted his people to do.

the father of Amram, ⁵⁹the husband of Levi's daughter Jochebed, who was born in Egypt. Amram and Jochebed's three children were Aaron, Moses, and Miriam. ⁶⁰Aaron was the father of Nadab, Abihu, Eleazar, and Ithamar. ⁶¹But Nadab and Abihu had died when they offered fire that was unacceptable to the LORD.ˢ

⁶²In the tribe of Levi there were 23,000 men and boys at least a month old. They were not listed with the other tribes, because they would not receive any land in Canaan.

⁶³Moses and Eleazar counted the Israelites while they were camped in the hills of Moab across the Jordan River from Jericho. ⁶⁴None of the people that Moses and Aaron had counted in the Sinai Desert were still alive, ⁶⁵except Caleb son of Jephunneh and Joshua son of Nun. The LORD had said that everyone else would die there in the desert.ᵗ

The Daughters of Zelophehad Are Given Land

27 Zelophehadᵘ was from the Manasseh tribe, and he had five daughters, whose names were Mahlah, Noah, Hoglah, Milcah, and Tirzah.

²One day his daughters went to the sacred tent, where they met with Moses, Eleazar, and some other leaders of Israel, as well as a large crowd of Israelites. The young women said:

³You know that our father died in the desert. But it was for something he did wrong, not for joining with Korah in rebelling against the LORD.

Our father left no sons ⁴to carry on his family name. But why should his name die out for that reason? Give us some land like the rest of his relatives in our clan, so our father's name can live on.

⁵Moses asked the LORD what should be done, ⁶and the LORD answered:

⁷Zelophehad's daughters are right. They should each be given part of the land their father would have received. ⁸Tell the Israelites that when a man dies without a son, his daughter will inherit his land. ⁹If he has no daughter, his brothers will inherit the land. ¹⁰But if he has no brothers, his father's brothers will inherit the land. ¹¹And if his father has no brothers, the land

must be given to his nearest relative in the clan. This is my law, and the Israelites must obey it.

Our earnest prayers waft
as incense up to
the heavenly Father
who knows our needs.

FLORENCE LITTAUER

Joshua Is Appointed Israel's Leader
(Deuteronomy 31.1-8)

¹²The LORD said to Moses, "One day you will go up into the Abarim Mountains, and from there you will see the land I am giving the Israelites. ¹³After you have seen it, you will die,ᵛ just like your brother Aaron, ¹⁴because both of you disobeyed me at Meribah near the town of Kadesh in the Zin Desert. When the Israelites insulted me there, you didn't believe in my holy power."ʷ

¹⁵Moses replied, ¹⁶"You are the LORD God, and you know what is in everyone's heart. So I ask you to appoint a leader for Israel. ¹⁷Your people need someone to lead them into battle, or else they will be like sheep wandering around without a shepherd."

¹⁸The LORD answered, "Joshua son of Nun can do the job. Place your hands on him to show that he is the one to take your place. ¹⁹Then go with him and have him stand in front of Eleazar the priest and the Israelites. Appoint Joshua as their new leader ²⁰and tell them they must now obey him, just as they obey you. ²¹But Joshua must depend on Eleazar to find out from meˣ what I want him to do as he leads Israel into battle."

ˢ**26.61** *Nadab and Abihu . . . the* LORD: See 3.1-4 and Leviticus 10.1, 2. ᵗ**26.64,65** *None of the people . . . the desert*: See 14.26-30. ᵘ**27.1** *Zelophehad*: Hebrew "Zelophehad son of Hepher son of Gilead son of Machir son of Manasseh son of Joseph." ᵛ**27.12,13** *One day . . . you will die*: The story of Moses' death is in Deuteronomy 34.1-8. ʷ**27.14** *both of you . . . my holy power*: See 20.1-13. ˣ**27.21** *from me*: The Hebrew text has "by the urim," something used by the priests to get answers from the LORD.

²²Moses followed the LORD's instructions and took Joshua to Eleazar and the people, ²³then he placed his hands on Joshua and appointed him Israel's leader.

Regular Daily Sacrifices
(Exodus 29.38-43; Leviticus 6.8-13)

28 The LORD told Moses ²to say to the people of Israel:

Offer sacrifices to me at the appointed times of worship, so that I will smell the smoke and be pleased.

³Each day offer two rams a year old as sacrifices to please me.ʸ The animals must have nothing wrong with them; ⁴one will be sacrificed in the morning, and the other in the evening. ⁵Along with each of them, two pounds of your finest flour mixed with a quart of olive oil must be offered as a grain sacrifice. ⁶This sacrifice to please me was first offered on Mount Sinai. ⁷Finally, along with each of these two sacrifices, a quart of wine must be poured on the altar as a drink offering. ⁸The second ram will be sacrificed that evening, along with the other offerings, just like the one sacrificed that morning. The smell of the smoke from these sacrifices will please me.

The Sacrifice on the Sabbath

The LORD said:

⁹⁻¹⁰On the Sabbath, in addition to the regular daily sacrifices,ᶻ you must sacrifice two rams a year old to please me.ᵃ These rams must have nothing wrong with them, and they will be sacrificed with a drink offering and four pounds of your finest flour mixed with olive oil.

The Sacrifices on the First Day of the Month

The LORD said:

¹¹On the first day of each month, bring to the altar two bulls, one full-grown ram, and seven rams a year old that have nothing wrong with them. Then offer these as sacrifices to please me.ᵃ ¹²Six pounds of your finest flour mixed with olive oil must be offered with each bull as a grain sacrifice. Four pounds of flour mixed with oil must be offered with the ram, ¹³and two pounds of flour mixed with oil must be offered with each of the young rams. The smell of

the smoke from these sacrifices will please me.

¹⁴⁻¹⁵Offer two quarts of wine as a drink offering with each bull, one and a half quarts with the ram, and one quart with each of the young rams.

Finally, you must offer a goatᵇ as a sacrifice for sin.

These sacrifices are to be offered on the first day of each month, in addition to the regular daily sacrifices.ᶜ

The Sacrifices during Passover and the Festival of Thin Bread
(Leviticus 23.4-8)

The LORD said:

¹⁶Celebrate Passover in honor of me on the fourteenth day of the first monthᵈ of each year. ¹⁷The following day will begin the Festival of Thin Bread, which will last for a week. During this time you must honor me by eating bread made without yeast.

God specializes in things fresh and firsthand. His plans for you this year may outshine those of the past. He's prepared to fill your days with reasons to give him praise!

JONI EARECKSON TADA

¹⁸On the first day of this festival, you must rest from your work and come together for worship. ¹⁹Bring to the altar two bulls, one full-grown ram, and seven rams a year old that have nothing wrong with them. And then offer these as sacrifices to please me.ᵉ ²⁰Six pounds of your finest flour mixed with olive oil must be offered with each bull

---

ʸ28.3 *sacrifices to please me*: See the note at 6.11.
ᶻ28.9,10 *regular daily sacrifices*: See 28.1-8.
ᵃ28.9,10 *sacrifice . . . to please me*: See the note at 6.11.
ᵃ28.11 *sacrifices to please me*: See the note at 6.11.
ᵇ28.14,15 *goat*: See the note at 7.12-83.
ᶜ28.14,15 *regular daily sacrifices*: See 28.1-8.
ᵈ28.16 *first month*: See the note at 9.3.
ᵉ28.19 *sacrifices to please me*: See the note at 6.11.

as a grain sacrifice. Four pounds of flour mixed with oil must be offered with the ram, [21]and two pounds of flour mixed with oil must be offered with each of the young rams. [22]Also offer a goat[f] as a sacrifice for the sins of the people. [23-24]All of these are to be offered in addition to the regular daily sacrifices,[g] and the smoke from them will please me. [25]Then on the last day of the festival, you must once again rest from work and come together for worship.

The Sacrifices during the Harvest Festival
(Leviticus 23.15-22)

The LORD said:

[26]On the first day of the Harvest Festival, you must rest from your work, come together for worship, and bring a sacrifice of new grain. [27]Offer two young bulls, one full-grown ram, and seven rams a year old as sacrifices to please me.[h] [28]Six pounds of your finest flour mixed with olive oil must be offered with each bull as a grain sacrifice. Four pounds of flour mixed with oil must be offered with the ram, [29]and two pounds of flour mixed with oil must be offered with each of the young rams. [30]Also offer a goat[i] as a sacrifice for sin. [31]The animals must have nothing wrong with them and are to be sacrificed along with the regular daily sacrifices.[j]

The Sacrifices at the Festival of Trumpets
(Leviticus 23.23-25)

The LORD said:

29 On the first day of the seventh month,[k] you must rest from your work and come together to celebrate at the sound of the trumpets. [2]Bring to the altar one bull, one full-grown ram, and seven rams a year old that have nothing wrong with them. And then offer these as sacrifices to please me.[l] [3]Six pounds of your finest flour mixed with olive oil must be offered with the bull as a grain sacrifice. Four pounds of flour mixed with oil must be offered with the ram, [4]and two pounds of flour mixed with oil must be offered with each of the young rams. [5]You must also offer a goat[m] as a sacrifice for sin. [6]These sacrifices will be made in addition to the regular daily sacrifices[n] and the sacrifices for the first day of the month.[o] The smoke from these sacrifices will please me.

The Sacrifices on the Great Day of Forgiveness
(Leviticus 23.26-32)

The LORD said:

[7]The tenth day of the seventh month[p] is the Great Day of Forgiveness.[q] On that day you must rest from all work and come together for worship. Show sorrow for your sins by going without food, [8]and bring to the altar one young bull, one full-grown ram, and seven rams a year old that have nothing wrong with them. Then offer these as sacrifices to please me.[r] [9]Six pounds of your finest flour mixed with olive oil must be offered with the bull as a grain sacrifice. Four pounds of flour mixed with oil must be offered with the ram, [10]and two pounds of flour mixed with oil must be offered with each of the young rams. [11]A goat[s] must also be sacrificed for the sins of the people. You will offer these sacrifices in addition to the sacrifice to ask forgiveness and the regular daily sacrifices.[t]

The Sacrifices during the Festival of Shelters
(Leviticus 23.33-44)

The LORD said:

[12]Beginning on the fifteenth day of the seventh month[u] and continuing for seven days, everyone must celebrate the Festival of Shelters in honor of me.

[13]On the first day, you must rest from your work and come together for worship. Bring to the altar thirteen bulls, two full-grown rams, and fourteen rams a year old that have nothing wrong with them. Then offer these as sacrifices to please me.[v] [14]Six

[f]**28.22** goat: See the note at 7.12-83.
[g]**28.23,24** regular daily sacrifices: See 28.1-8.
[h]**28.27** sacrifices to please me: See the note at 6.11.
[i]**28.30** goat: See the note at 7.12-83. [j]**28.31** regular daily sacrifices: See 28.1-8. [k]**29.1** seventh month: Tishri (also called Ethanim), the seventh month of the Hebrew calendar, from about mid-September to mid-October. [l]**29.2** sacrifices to please me: See the note at 6.11. [m]**29.5** goat: See the note at 7.12-83. [n]**29.6** regular daily sacrifices: See 28.1-8. [o]**29.6** sacrifices . . . month: See 28.11-15. [p]**29.7** seventh month: See the note at 29.1. [q]**29.7** Great Day of Forgiveness: Traditionally known as the Day of Atonement. [r]**29.8** sacrifices to please me: See the note at 6.11. [s]**29.11** goat: See the note at 7.12-83. [t]**29.11** regular daily sacrifices: See 28.1-8. [u]**29.12** seventh month: See the note at 29.1. [v]**29.13** sacrifices to please me: See the note at 6.11.

pounds of your finest flour mixed with olive oil must be offered with each bull as a grain sacrifice. Four pounds of flour mixed with oil must be offered with each of the rams, [15]and two pounds of flour mixed with oil must be offered with each of the young rams. [16]You must also offer a goat[w] as a sacrifice for sin. These are to be offered in addition to the regular daily sacrifices.[x]

[17-34]For the next six days of the festival, you will sacrifice one less bull than the day before, so that on the seventh day, seven bulls will be sacrificed. The other sacrifices and offerings must remain the same for each of these days.

[35]On the eighth day, you must once again rest from your work and come together for worship. [36]Bring to the altar one bull, one full-grown ram, and seven rams a year old that have nothing wrong with them. Then offer these as sacrifices to please me. [37]You must also offer the proper grain sacrifices and drink offerings of wine with each animal. [38]And offer a goat[y] as the sacrifice to ask forgiveness for the people. These sacrifices are made in addition to the regular daily sacrifices.[z]

[39]You must offer all these sacrifices to me at the appointed times of worship, together with any offerings that are voluntarily given or given because of a promise.

[40]Moses told the people of Israel everything the LORD had told him about the sacrifices.

Making Promises to the LORD

30 The LORD told Moses to say to Israel's tribal leaders:
[2]When one of you men makes a promise to the LORD,[a] you must keep your word.

[3]Suppose a young woman who is still living with her parents makes a promise to the LORD. [4]If her father hears about it and says nothing, she must keep her promise. [5]But if he hears about it and objects, then she no longer has to keep her promise. The LORD will forgive her, because her father did not agree with the promise.

[6-7]Suppose a woman makes a promise to the LORD and then gets married. If her husband later hears about the promise but says nothing, she must do what she said, whether she meant it or not. [8]But if her husband hears about the promise and objects, she no

longer has to keep it, and the LORD will forgive her.

[9]Widows and divorced women must keep every promise they make to the LORD.

> *How careful we should be with our words, when we consider the lasting power for good or evil of one hastily spoken sentence.*
>
> FLORENCE LITTAUER

[10]Suppose a married woman makes a promise to the LORD. [11]If her husband hears about the promise and says nothing, she must do what she said. [12]But if he hears about the promise and does object, she no longer has to keep it. The LORD will forgive her, because her husband would not allow her to keep the promise. [13]Her husband has the final say about any promises she makes to the LORD. [14]If her husband hears about a promise and says nothing about it for a whole day, she must do what she said— since he did not object, the promise must be kept. [15]But if he waits until the next day to stop her from keeping her promise, he is the one who must be punished.

[16]These are the laws that the LORD gave Moses about husbands and wives, and about young daughters who still live at home.

Israel's War against Midian

31 The LORD said to Moses, [2]"Before you die, make sure that the Midianites are punished for what they did to Israel."[b]

[3]Then Moses told the people, "The LORD wants to punish the Midianites. So have our men prepare for battle. [4]Each tribe will send a thousand men to fight."

---

[w]**29.16** *goat*: See the note at 7.12-83. [x]**29.16** *regular daily sacrifices*: See 28.1-8. [y]**29.38** *goat*: See the note at 7.12-83. [z]**29.38** *regular daily sacrifices*: See 28.1-8. [a]**30.2** *a promise to the LORD*: Either the promise of a gift or the promise to do something. [b]**31.2** *Midianites . . . to Israel*: See 25.1-18.

[5]Twelve thousand men were picked from the tribes of Israel, and after they were prepared for battle, [6]Moses sent them off to war. Phinehas the son of Eleazar went with them and took along some things from the sacred tent[c] and the trumpets for sounding the battle signal.

[7]The Israelites fought against the Midianites, just as the LORD had commanded Moses. They killed all the men, [8]including Balaam son of Beor and the five Midianite kings, Evi, Rekem, Zur, Hur, and Reba. [9]The Israelites captured every woman and child, then led away the Midianites' cattle and sheep, and took everything else that belonged to them. [10]They also burned down the Midianite towns and villages.

[11]Israel's soldiers gathered together everything they had taken from the Midianites, including the captives and the animals. [12-13]Then they returned to their own camp in the hills of Moab across the Jordan River from Jericho, where Moses, Eleazar, and the other Israelite leaders met the troops outside camp.

[14]Moses became angry with the army commanders [15]and said, "I can't believe you let the women live! [16]They are the ones who followed Balaam's advice and invited our people to worship the god Baal Peor. That's why the LORD punished us by killing so many of our people. [17]You must put to death every boy and all the women who have ever had sex. [18]But do not kill the young women who have never had sex. You may keep them for yourselves."

[19]Then Moses said to the soldiers, "If you killed anyone or touched a dead body, you are unclean and have to stay outside the camp for seven days. On the third and seventh days, you must go through a ceremony to make yourselves and your captives clean. [20]Then wash your clothes and anything made from animal skin, goat's hair, or wood."

[21-23]Eleazar then explained, "If you need to purify something that won't burn, such as gold, silver, bronze, iron, tin, or lead, you must first place it in a hot fire. After you take it out, sprinkle it with the water that purifies. Everything else should only be sprinkled with the water. Do all of this, just as the LORD commanded Moses. [24]Wash your clothes on the seventh day, and after that, you will be clean and may return to the camp."

Everything Taken from the Midianites Is Divided

[25]The LORD told Moses:

[26-27]Make a list of everything taken from the Midianites, including the captives and the animals. Then divide them between the soldiers and the rest of the people. Eleazar the priest and the family leaders will help you.

[28-29]From the half that belongs to the soldiers, set aside for the LORD one out of every five hundred people or animals and give these to Eleazar.

[30]From the half that belongs to the people, set aside one out of every fifty and give these to the Levites in charge of the sacred tent.

[31]Moses and Eleazar followed the LORD's instructions [32-35]and listed everything that had been taken from the Midianites. The list included 675,000 sheep and goats, 72,000 cattle, 61,000 donkeys, and 32,000 young women who had never had sex.

[36-47]Each half included 337,500 sheep and goats, 36,000 cattle, 30,500 donkeys, and 16,000 young women. From the half that belonged to the soldiers, Moses counted out 675 sheep and goats, 72 cattle, 61 donkeys, and 32 women and gave them to Eleazar to be dedicated to the LORD. Then from the half that belonged to the people, Moses set aside one out of every fifty animals and women, as the LORD had said, and gave them to the Levites.

[48]The army commanders went to Moses [49]and said, "Sir, we have counted our troops, and not one soldier is missing. [50]So we want to give the LORD all the gold jewelry we took from the Midianites. It's our gift to him for watching over us and our troops."

[51]Moses and Eleazar accepted the jewelry from the commanders, [52]and its total weight was over four hundred pounds. [53]This did not include the things that the soldiers had kept for themselves. [54]So Moses and Eleazar placed the gold in the LORD's sacred tent to remind Israel of what had happened.[d]

---

[c]31.6 *Phinehas . . . sacred tent*: Phinehas would serve as the priest during the battle, so he took along the things needed to ask God what he wanted done.
[d]31.54 *to remind . . . happened*: Or "so the LORD would continue to help Israel."

Land East of the Jordan River Is Settled
(Deuteronomy 3.12-22)

32 The tribes of Reuben and Gad owned a lot of cattle and sheep, and they saw that the regions of Jazer and Gilead had good pastureland. [2]So they went to Moses, Eleazar, and the other leaders of Israel and said, [3-4]"The LORD has helped us capture the land around the towns of Ataroth, Dibon, Jazer, Nimrah, Heshbon, Elealeh, Sebam, Nebo, and Beon. That's good pastureland, and since we own cattle and sheep, [5]would you let us stay here east of the Jordan River and have this land as our own?"

[6]Moses answered:

You mean you'd stay here while the rest of the Israelites go into battle? [7]If you did that, it would discourage the others from crossing over into the land the LORD promised them. [8]This is exactly what happened when I sent your ancestors from Kadesh-Barnea to explore the land. [9]They went as far as Eshcol Valley, then returned and told the people that we should not enter it. [10]The LORD became very angry. [11]And he said that no one who was twenty years or older when they left Egypt would enter the land he had promised to Abraham, Isaac, and Jacob. Not one of those people believed in the LORD's power, [12]except Caleb and Joshua.[c] They remained faithful to the LORD, [13]but he was so angry with the others that he forced them to wander around in the desert forty years. By that time everyone who had sinned against him had died.

[14]Now you people of Reuben and Gad are doing the same thing and making the LORD even angrier. [15]If you reject the LORD, he will once again abandon his people and leave them here in the desert. And you will be to blame!

[16]The men from Reuben and Gad replied:

Let us build places to keep our sheep and goats, and towns for our wives and children, [17]where they can stay and be safe. Then we'll prepare to fight and lead the other tribes into battle. [18]We will stay with them until they have settled in their own tribal lands. [19]The land on this side of the Jordan River will be ours, so we won't expect to receive any on the other side.

[20]Moses said:

You promised that you would be ready to fight for the LORD. [21]You also agreed to cross the Jordan and stay with the rest of the Israelites, until the LORD forces our enemies out of the land. If you do these things, [22]then after the LORD helps Israel capture the land, you can return to your own land. You will no longer have to stay with the others. [23]But if you don't keep your promise, you will sin against the LORD and be punished.

[24]Go ahead and build towns for your wives and children, and places for your sheep and goats. Just be sure to do what you have promised.

[25]The men from Reuben and Gad answered:

Sir, we will do just what you have said. [26]Our wives and children and sheep and cattle will stay here in the towns in Gilead. [27]But those of us who are prepared for battle will cross the Jordan and fight for the LORD.

[28]Then Moses said to Eleazar, Joshua, and the family leaders, [29]"Make sure that the tribes of Gad and Reuben prepare for battle and cross the Jordan River with you. If they do, then after the land is in your control, give them the region of Gilead as their tribal land. [30]But if they break their promise, they will receive land on the other side of the Jordan, like the rest of the tribes."

[31]The tribes of Gad and Reuben replied, "We are your servants and will do whatever the LORD has commanded. [32]We will cross the Jordan River, ready to fight for the LORD in Canaan. But the land we will inherit as our own will be on this side of the river."

[33]So Moses gave the tribes of Gad, Reuben, and half of Manasseh[f] the territory and towns that King Sihon the Amorite had ruled, as well as the territory and towns that King Og of Bashan had ruled.[g]

[34]The tribe of Gad rebuilt the towns of

---

[c]**32.12** *Caleb and Joshua:* See the note at 14.30.
[f]**32.33** *half of Manasseh:* Or "East Manasseh."
[g]**32.33** *ruled:* One possible meaning for the difficult Hebrew text of verse 33.

Dibon, Ataroth, Aroer, [35]Atroth-Shophan, Jazer, Jogbehah, [36]Beth-Nimrah, and Beth-Haran. They built walls around them and also built places to keep their sheep and goats.

[37]The tribe of Reuben rebuilt Heshbon, Elealeh, Kiriathaim, [38]Sibmah, as well as the towns that used to be known as Nebo and Baal-Meon. They renamed all those places.

[39]The clan of Machir from the tribe of East Manasseh went to the region of Gilead, captured its towns, and forced out the Amorites. [40]So Moses gave the Machirites the region of Gilead, and they settled there.

[41]Jair from the Manasseh tribe captured villages and renamed them "Villages of Jair."[h]

[42]Nobah captured the town of Kenath with its villages and renamed it Nobah.

Israel's Journey from Egypt to Moab

33 As Israel traveled from Egypt under the command of Moses and Aaron, [2]Moses kept a list of the places they camped, just as the LORD had instructed. Here is the record of their journey:

[3-4]Israel left the Egyptian city of Rameses on the fifteenth day of the first month.[i] This was the day after the LORD had punished Egypt's gods by killing the first-born sons in every Egyptian family. So while the Egyptians were burying the bodies, they watched the Israelites proudly[j] leave their country.

[5]After the Israelites left Rameses, they camped at Succoth, [6]and from there, they moved their camp to Etham on the edge of the desert. [7]Then they turned back toward Pi-Hahiroth, east of Baal-Zephon, and camped near Migdol. [8]They left Pi-Hahiroth,[k] crossed the Red Sea,[l] then walked three days into the Etham Desert and camped at Marah. [9]Next, they camped at Elim, where there were twelve springs of water and seventy palm trees. [10]They left Elim and camped near the Red Sea,[m] [11]then turned east and camped along the western edge of the Sinai Desert.[n] [12-14]From there they went to Dophkah, Alush, and Rephidim, where they had no water.[o] [15]They left Rephidim and finally reached the Sinai Desert.

[16-36]As Israel traveled from the Sinai Desert to Kadesh in the Zin Desert, they camped at Kibroth-Hattaavah, Hazeroth, Rithmah, Rimmon-Perez, Libnah, Rissah, Kehelathah, Mount Shepher, Haradah, Makheloth, Tahath, Terah, Mithkah, Hashmonah, Moseroth, Bene-Jaakan, Hor-Haggidgad, Jotbathah, Abronah, Ezion-Geber, and finally Kadesh. [37]When they left Kadesh, they came to Mount Hor, on the border of Edom.

[38]That's where the LORD commanded Aaron the priest to go to the top of the mountain. Aaron died there on the first day of the fifth month,[p] forty years after the Israelites left Egypt. [39]He was one hundred twenty-three years old at the time.

[40]It was then that the Canaanite king of Arad, who lived in the Southern Desert of Canaan, heard that Israel was headed that way.

[41-47]The Israelites left Mount Hor and headed toward Moab. Along the way, they camped at Zalmonah, Punon, Oboth, Iye-Abarim in the territory of Moab, Dibon-Gad, Almon-Diblathaim, at a place near Mount Nebo in the Abarim Mountains, [48]and finally in the lowlands of Moab across the Jordan River from Jericho. [49]Their camp stretched from Beth-Jeshimoth to Acacia.

The LORD's Command To Conquer Canaan

[50]While Israel was camped in the lowlands of Moab across the Jordan River from Jericho, the LORD told Moses [51]to give the people of Israel this message:

> When you cross the Jordan River and enter Canaan, [52]you must force out the people living there. Destroy their idols and tear down their altars. [53]Then settle in the land—I have given it to you as your own.
>
> [54]I will show you[q] how to divide the land among the tribes, according to

---

[h]**32.41** *Villages of Jair*: Or "Havvoth-Jair." [i]**33.3,4** *first month*: See the note at 9.3. [j]**33.3,4** *proudly*: Or "bravely." [k]**33.8** *Pi-Hahiroth*: Two ancient translations and the Samaritan Hebrew Text; the Standard Hebrew Text "a place near Hahiroth." [l]**33.8** *Red Sea*: Hebrew *hayyam* "the Sea," understood as *yam suph*, "Sea of Reeds" (see also the note at Exodus 13.18).
[m]**33.10** *Red Sea*: Hebrew *yam suph*, here referring to the Gulf of Suez, since the term is extended to include the northwestern arm of the Red Sea (see also the note at Exodus 13.18). [n]**33.11** *the western edge of the Sinai Desert*: Hebrew "the Sin Desert."
[o]**33.12-14** *Rephidim . . . no water*: See Exodus 17.1-7.
[p]**33.38** *fifth month*: Ab, the fifth month of the Hebrew calendar, from about mid-July to mid-August.
[q]**33.54** *I will show you*: See the note at 26.55, 56.

the number of clans in each one, so that the larger tribes will have more land than the smaller ones.

When I'm obedient to the Word and trust in the Lord, I have total faith that God will help me overcome anything and guide me where I need to go.

THELMA WELLS

⁵⁵If you don't force out all the people there, they will be like pointed sticks in your eyes and thorns in your back. They will always be trouble for you, ⁵⁶and I will treat you as cruelly as I planned on treating them.

Israel's Borders

34 The LORD told Moses ²to tell the people of Israel that their land in Canaan would have the following borders:

³The southern border will be the Zin Desert and the northwest part of Edom. This border will begin at the south end of the Dead Sea. ⁴It will go west from there, but will turn southward to include Scorpion Pass, the village of Zin, and the town of Kadesh-Barnea. From there, the border will continue to Hazar-Addar and on to Azmon. ⁵It will run along the Egyptian Gorge and end at the Mediterranean Sea.

⁶The western border will be the Mediterranean Sea.

⁷The northern border will begin at the Mediterranean, then continue eastward to Mount Hor.ʳ ⁸After that, it will run to Lebo-Hamath and across to Zedad, which is the northern edge of your land. ⁹From Zedad, the border will continue east to Ziphron and end at Hazar-Enan.

¹⁰The eastern border will begin at Hazar-Enan in the north, then run south to Shepham, ¹¹and on down to Riblah on the east side of Ain. From there, it will go south to the eastern hills of Lake Galilee,ˢ ¹²then follow the Jordan River down to the north end of the Dead Sea.

The land within those four borders will belong to you.

¹³Then Moses told the people, "You will receive the land inside these borders. It will be yours, but the LORD has commanded you to divide it among the nine and a half tribes. ¹⁴The tribes of Reuben, Gad, and East Manasseh have already been given their land ¹⁵across from Jericho, east of the Jordan River."

The Leaders Who Will Divide the Land

¹⁶The LORD said to Moses, ¹⁷"Eleazar the priest and Joshua son of Nun will divide the land for the Israelites. ¹⁸One leader from each tribe will help them, ¹⁹⁻²⁸and here is the list of their names:

Caleb son of Jephunneh
    from Judah,
Shemuel son of Ammihud
    from Simeon,
Elidad son of Chislon
    from Benjamin,
Bukki son of Jogli
    from Dan,
Hanniel son of Ephod
    from Manasseh,
Kemuel son of Shiphtan
    from Ephraim,
Elizaphan son of Parnach
    from Zebulun,
Paltiel son of Azzan
    from Issachar,
Ahihud son of Shelomi
    from Asher,
and Pedahel son of Ammihud
    from Naphtali."

²⁹These are the men the LORD commanded to help Eleazar and Joshua divide the land for the Israelites.

The Towns for the Levites

35 While the people of Israel were still camped in the lowlands of Moab across the Jordan River from Jericho, the LORD told Moses ²to say to them:

When you receive your tribal lands, you must give towns and pastures to the Levi tribe. ³That way, the Levites will have towns to live in and pastures for their animals. ⁴⁻⁵The pasture around each of these towns must be in the shape of a square, with the town itself in the center. The pasture is to measure three thousand feet on each side, with fifteen hundred feet of land outside each of the town walls. This will be the Levites' pastureland.

⁶Six of the towns you give them will be Safe Towns where a person who has accidentally killed someone can run for protection. But you will also give the Levites forty-two other towns, ⁷so they will have a total of forty-eight towns with their surrounding pastures.

⁸Since the towns for the Levites must come from Israel's own tribal lands, the larger tribes will give more towns than the smaller ones.

> When we go to the Lord with problems in our spiritual life only, and try to work out our physical needs and concerns on our own, we end up turning elsewhere for affirmation and validation.
>
> MARY ANN MAYO

The Safe Towns

(Deuteronomy 19.1-13; Joshua 20.1-9)

⁹The LORD then told Moses ¹⁰to tell the people of Israel:

After you have crossed the Jordan River and are settled in Canaan, ¹¹choose Safe Towns, where a person who has accidentally killed someone can run for protection. ¹²If the victim's relatives think it was murder, they might try to take revenge.ᶠ Anyone accused of murder can run to one of these Safe Towns for protection and not be killed before a trial is held.

¹³There are to be six of these Safe Towns, ¹⁴three on each side of the Jordan River. ¹⁵They will be places of protection for anyone who lives in Israel and accidentally kills someone.

Laws about Murder and Accidental Killing

The LORD said:

¹⁶⁻¹⁸Suppose you hit someone with a piece of iron or a large stone or a dangerous wooden tool. If that person dies, then you are a murderer and must be put to death ¹⁹by one of the victim's relatives.ᶠ He will take revenge for his relative's death as soon as he finds you.

²⁰⁻²¹Or suppose you get angry and kill someone by pushing or hitting or by throwing something. You are a murderer and must be put to death by one of the victim's relatives.

²²⁻²⁴But if you are not angry and accidentally kill someone in any of these ways, the townspeople must hold a trial and decide if you are guilty. ²⁵If they decide that you are innocent, you will be protected from the victim's relative and sent to stay in one of the Safe Towns until the high priest dies. ²⁶But if you ever leave the Safe Town ²⁷and are killed by the victim's relative, he cannot be punished for killing you. ²⁸You must stay inside the town until the high priest dies; only then can you go back home.

²⁹The community of Israel must always obey these laws.

³⁰Death is the penalty for murder. But no one accused of murder can be put to death unless there are at least two witnesses to the crime. ³¹You cannot give someone money to escape the death penalty; you must pay with your own life! ³²And if you have been proven

---

ᶠ**35.12** *the victim's relatives . . . revenge*: At this time in Israel's history, the clan would appoint the closest male relative to find and kill a person who had killed a member of their clan. ᶠ**35.19** *one of the victim's relatives*: At this time in Israel's history, the clan would appoint the closest male relative to find and kill a person who had killed a member of their clan.

innocent of murder and are living in a Safe Town, you cannot pay to go back home; you must stay there until the high priest dies.

33-34I, the LORD, live among you people of Israel, so your land must be kept pure. But when a murder takes place, blood pollutes the land, and it becomes unclean. If that happens, the murderer must be put to death, so the land will be clean again. Keep murder out of Israel!

The Laws about Married Women and Land

36 One day the family leaders from the Gilead clan of the Manasseh tribe went to Moses and the other family leaders of Israel 2and said, "Sir, the LORD has said that he will show*u* what land each tribe will receive as their own. And the LORD has commanded you to give the daughters of our relative Zelophehad the land that he would have received. 3But if they marry men from other tribes of Israel, the land they receive will become part of that tribe's inheritance and will no longer belong to us. 4Even when land is returned to its original owner in the Year of Celebration,v we will not get back Zelophehad's land—it will belong to the tribe into which his daughters married."

5So Moses told the people that the LORD had said:

These men from the Manasseh tribe are right. 6I will allow Zelophehad's daughters to marry anyone, as long as those men belong to one of the clans of the Manasseh tribe.

7Tribal land must not be given to another tribe—it will remain the property of the tribe that received it. 8-9In the future, any daughter who inherits land must marry someone from her own tribe. Israel's tribal land is never to be passed from one tribe to another.

10-11Mahlah, Tirzah, Hoglah, Milcah, and Noah the daughters of Zelophehad obeyed the LORD and married their uncles' sons 12and remained part of the Manasseh tribe. So their land stayed in their father's clan.

13These are the laws that the LORD gave to Moses and the Israelites while they were camped in the lowlands of Moab across the Jordan River from Jericho.

---

u36.2 *that he will show*: See the note at 26.55, 56.
v36.4 *Year of Celebration*: This was a sacred year for Israel, traditionally called the "Year of Jubilee." During this year, all property had to go back to its original owner. But here, the property was not sold; it became part of the other tribe's land when the daughter who owned it married into that tribe. So the property could not be returned even during this year.

Deuteronomy

How To Have a Relationship with God

Deuteronomy tells the story of how God forged a relationship with his people. This relationship, called a *covenant*, had two parts: First, God told the people how they had to act toward him. Then God promised to defend them and take care of them.

As the book opens, Moses is reminding the people of everything God has done for them. He wants them to realize something very important: They can trust God! He tells them that God has always been eager to protect and care for his people— and that God will continue to take care of them.

But there are conditions to this covenant. God doesn't want them to follow him just for what they can get out of it. He wants their hearts to be totally his. So he has given them directions to help them understand what it means to be truly his: the Ten Commandments (5.1-22) and the laws that follow it. All of God's instructions in Deuteronomy are summed up in the famous "Shema" in 6.5: "So love the LORD your God with all your heart, soul, and strength."

What happens when we give God our hearts? God promised his people that if they would love him and stay faithful to his laws, he would bless their work, their families, their country, and everything they did (11.27). But if they rebelled against God, he promised to bring judgment on them (11.28). The end of the book warns God's chosen people that, if they fell away,

God would punish them. The theme of Deuteronomy is clear: Obedience brings blessing, but disobedience brings destruction.

Deuteronomy at a Glance

The Final Speeches of Moses

1 [1-5]This book contains the speeches that Moses made while Israel was in the land of Moab, camped near the town of Suph in the desert east of the Jordan River. The town of Paran was in one direction from their camp, and the towns of Tophel, Laban, Hazeroth, and Dizahab[a] were in the opposite direction.

Earlier, Moses had defeated the Amorite King Sihon of Heshbon. Moses had also defeated King Og of Bashan, who used to live in Ashtaroth for part of the year and in Edrei for the rest of the year.

Although it takes only eleven days to walk from Mount Sinai[b] to Kadesh-Barnea by way of the Mount Seir Road, these speeches were not made until forty years after Israel left Egypt.[c]

THE FIRST SPEECH:
MOSES REVIEWS THE PAST

The LORD's Command at Mount Sinai

The LORD had given Moses his laws for the people of Israel. And on the first day of the eleventh month,[d] Moses began explaining those laws by saying:

[6]People of Israel, when we were in our camp at Mount Sinai,[e] the LORD our God told us:

You have stayed here long enough. [7]Leave this place and go into the land that belongs to the Amorites and their neighbors the Canaanites. This land includes the Jordan River valley, the hill country, the western foothills, the Southern Desert, the Mediterranean seacoast, the Lebanon Mountains, and all the territory as far as the Euphrates River. [8]I give you this land, just as I promised your ancestors Abraham, Isaac, and Jacob. Now you must go and take the land.

Leaders Were Appointed
(Exodus 18.13-27)

Moses said:

[9]Right after the LORD commanded us to leave Mount Sinai,[e] I told you:

Israel, being your leader is too big a job for one person. [10]The LORD our God has blessed us, and so now there are as many of us as there are stars in the sky. [11]God has even promised to bless us a thousand times more, and I pray that he will. [12]But I cannot take care of all your problems and settle all your arguments alone. [13]Each tribe must choose some experienced men who are known for their wisdom and understanding, and I will make those men the official leaders of their tribes.

[14]You answered, "That's a good idea!" [15]Then I took these men, who were already wise and respected leaders, and I appointed them as your official leaders. Some of them became military officers in charge of groups of a thousand, or a hundred, or fifty, or ten, [16]and others became judges. I gave these judges the following instructions:

When you settle legal cases, your decisions must be fair. It doesn't matter if the case is between two Israelites, or between an Israelite and a foreigner living in your community. [17]And it doesn't matter if one is helpless and the other is powerful. Don't be afraid of anyone! No matter who shows up in your court, God will help you make a fair decision.

If any case is too hard for you, bring the people to me, and I will make the decision.

[18]After I gave these instructions to the judges, I taught you the LORD's commands.

Men Were Sent To Explore the Hill Country
(Numbers 13.1-33)

Moses said to Israel:

[19]The LORD had commanded us to leave Mount Sinai[e] and go to the hill country that belonged to the Amorites, so we started out into the huge desert. You remember how frightening it was, but soon we were at Kadesh-Barnea, [20-21]and I told you, "We have

---

[a]1.1-5 Suph . . . Paran . . . Tophel, Laban, Hazeroth, and Dizahab: The exact location of these towns is not known. [b]1.1-5 Mount Sinai: The Hebrew text has "Horeb," another name for Mount Sinai. [c]1.1-5 Egypt: The Israelites would soon enter Canaan, but they would have entered the land of Canaan from Kadesh-Barnea forty years earlier if they had not rebelled against God (see verses 6-40). [d]1.1-5 eleventh month: Shebat, the eleventh month of the Hebrew calendar, from about mid-January to mid-February. [e]1.6,9,19 Mount Sinai: See the note at 1.1-5.

reached the hill country. It belongs to the Amorites now, but the LORD our God is giving it to us. He is the same God our ancestors worshiped, and he has told us to go in and take this land, so don't hesitate and be afraid."

²²Then all of you came to me and said, "Before we go into the land, let's send some men to explore it. When they come back, they can tell us about the towns we will find and what roads we should take to get there."

²³It seemed like a good idea, so I chose twelve men, one from each tribe. ²⁴They explored the hill country as far as Bunch Valley*ʲ* ²⁵and even brought back some of the fruit. They said, "The LORD our God is giving us good land."

Israel Refused To Obey the LORD
(Numbers 14.1-45)

Moses said to Israel:

²⁶You did not want to go into the land, and you refused to obey the LORD your God. ²⁷You stayed in your tents and grumbled, "The LORD must hate us—he brought us out of Egypt, just so he could hand us over to the Amorites and get rid of us. ²⁸We are afraid, because the men who explored the land told us that the cities are large, with walls that reach to the sky. The people who live there are taller and stronger than we are,*ᵍ* and some of them are Anakim.*ʰ* We have nowhere to go."

²⁹Then I said, "Don't worry! ³⁰The LORD our God will lead the way. He will fight on our side, just as he did when we saw him do all those things to the Egyptians. ³¹And you know that the LORD has taken care of us the whole time we've been in the desert, just as you might carry one of your children."

³²But you still would not trust the LORD, ³³even though he had always been with us in the desert. During the daytime, the LORD was in the cloud, leading us in the right direction and showing us where to camp. And at night, he was there in the fire.*ⁱ*

³⁴You had made the LORD angry, and he said:

³⁵You people of this generation are evil, and I refuse to let you go into the good land that I promised your ancestors. ³⁶Caleb son of Jephunneh is the only one of your generation that I

will allow to go in. He obeyed me completely, so I will give him and his descendants the land he explored.

³⁷The LORD was even angry with me because of you people, and he said, "Moses, I won't let you go into the land either. ³⁸Instead, I will let Joshua*ʲ* your assistant lead Israel to conquer the land. So encourage him."

³⁹Then the LORD spoke to you again:

People of Israel, you said that your innocent young children would be taken prisoner in the battle for the land. But someday I will let them go into the land, and with my help they will conquer it and live there.

⁴⁰Now, turn around and go back into the desert by way of Red Sea*ᵏ* Road.

⁴¹Then you told me, "We disobeyed the LORD our God, but now we want to obey him. We will go into the hill country and fight, just as he told us to do." So you picked up your weapons, thinking it would be easy to take over the hill country.

⁴²But the LORD said, "Moses, warn them not to go into the hill country. I won't help them fight, and their enemies will defeat them."

⁴³I told you what the LORD had said, but you paid no attention. You disobeyed him and went into the hill country anyway. You thought you were so great! ⁴⁴But when the Amorites in the hill country attacked from their towns, you ran from them as you would run from a swarm of bees. The Amorites chased your troops into Seir*ˡ* as far as Hormah, killing them as they went. ⁴⁵Then you came back to the place of worship at Kadesh-Barnea and wept, but the LORD would not listen to your prayers.

---

*ʲ***1.24** *Bunch Valley:* Or "Eshcol Valley," famous for its large bunches of grapes.　*ᵍ***1.28** *The people . . . we are:* Most Hebrew manuscripts; a few Hebrew manuscripts and one ancient translation "the people who live there are stronger than we are, and there are more of them than there are of us."　*ʰ***1.28** *Anakim:* Perhaps a group of very tall people that lived in or near Palestine before the Israelites. See also 2.10, 11, 20, 21; Numbers 13.33.　*ⁱ***1.33** *the cloud . . . the fire:* See Exodus 40.34-38; Numbers 9.15-23.　*ʲ***1.38** *Joshua:* Hebrew "Joshua son of Nun."　*ᵏ***1.40** *Red Sea:* Hebrew *yam suph,* here referring to the Gulf of Aqaba, since the term is extended to include the northeastern arm of the Red Sea (see also the note at 11.4).　*ˡ***1.44** *Seir:* An area of hills and mountains that was part of the territory of Edom.

Israel Spent Years in the Desert

Moses said to Israel:

⁴⁶After we had been in Kadesh for a few months, we obeyed the LORD and headed back into the desert by way of Red Sea*ᵐ* Road. ¹We spent many years wandering around outside the hill country of Seir,*ⁿ* ²until the LORD said:

Moses, ³Israel has wandered in these hills long enough. Turn and go north. ⁴And give the people these orders: "Be very careful, because you will soon go through the land that belongs to your relatives, the descendants of Esau.*ᵒ* They are afraid of you, ⁵but don't start a war with them. I have given them the hill country of Seir, so I won't give any of it to you, not even enough to set a foot on. ⁶And as you go through their land, you will have to buy food and water from them."

⁷The LORD has helped us and taken care of us during the past forty years that we have been in this huge desert. We've had everything we needed, and the LORD has blessed us and made us successful in whatever we have done.

⁸We went past the territory that belonged to our relatives, the descendants of Esau.*ᵖ* We followed Arabah Road that starts in the south at Elath and Ezion-Geber, then we turned onto the desert road that leads to Moab.

⁹The LORD told me, "Don't try to start a war with Moab. Leave them alone, because I gave the land of Ar*ᵈ* to them,*ʳ* and I will not let you have any of it."

Tribes That Lived near Canaan

¹⁰Before the LORD gave the Moabites their land, a large and powerful tribe lived there. They were the Emim, and they were as tall as the Anakim. ¹¹The Moabites called them Emim, though others sometimes used the name Rephaim*ˢ* for both the Anakim and the Emim.

¹²The Horites used to live in Seir, but the Edomites*ᵗ* took over that region. They killed many of the Horites and forced the rest of them to leave, just as Israel did to the people in the land that the LORD gave them.

Israel Crossed the Zered Gorge

Moses said to Israel:

¹³When we came to the Zered Gorge along the southern border of Moab, the LORD told us to cross the gorge into Moab, and we did. ¹⁴This was thirty-eight years after we left Kadesh-Barnea, and by that time all the men who had been in the army at Kadesh-Barnea had died, just as the LORD had said they would. ¹⁵⁻¹⁶The LORD kept getting rid of*ᵘ* them until finally none of them were left.

¹⁷Then the LORD told me, ¹⁸"Moses, now go past the town of Ar and cross Moab's northern border ¹⁹into Ammon. But don't start a war with the Ammonites. I gave them*ᵛ* their land, and I won't give any of it to Israel."

More Nations That Lived near Canaan

²⁰Before the Ammonites conquered the land that the LORD had given them, some of the Rephaim used to live there, although the Ammonites called them Zamzummim. ²¹The Zamzummim were a large and powerful tribe and were as tall as the Anakim.*ʷ* But the LORD helped the Ammonites, and they killed many of the Zamzummim and forced the rest to leave. Then the Ammonites settled there. ²²The LORD helped them as he had helped the Edomites,*ˣ* who killed many of the Horites in Seir and forced the rest to leave before settling there themselves.

²³A group called the Avvim used to live in

---

*ᵐ***1.46** *Red Sea:* See the notes at 1.40; 11.4.   *ⁿ***2.1** *hill country of Seir:* See the note at 1.44.   *ᵒ***2.4** *your relatives, the descendants of Esau:* Esau was the brother of Jacob, the ancestor of the nation of Israel. Esau's descendants were also known as the nation of Edom.   *ᵖ***2.8** *We went past . . . Esau:* According to Numbers 20.14-21, the king of Edom did not let the Israelites go through his land.   *ᵈ***2.9** *Ar:* One of the main cities of Moab (see Numbers 21.28); sometimes it may have stood for the whole territory of Moab.   *ʳ***2.9** *them:* The Hebrew text has "the descendants of Lot"; the nation of Moab descended from Moab, who was the son of Lot, the nephew of Abraham.   *ˢ***2.10,11** *Emim . . . Anakim . . . Rephaim:* These may refer to a group or groups of very tall people that lived in or near Palestine before the Israelites (see also Numbers 13.33).   *ᵗ***2.12** *Edomites:* The Hebrew text has "the descendants of Esau," who became the nation of Edom.   *ᵘ***2.15,16** *getting rid of:* Or "sending diseases on."   *ᵛ***2.19** *them:* The Hebrew text has "descendants of Lot"; the nation of Ammon descended from Benammi, who was the son of Lot, the nephew of Abraham.   *ʷ***2.21** *Anakim:* See the note at 2.10, 11.   *ˣ***2.22** *Edomites:* See the note at 2.12.

villages as far south as Gaza, but the Philistines[y] killed them and settled on their land.

Israel Crossed the Arnon Gorge

Moses said:

[24]After we went through Ammon, the LORD told us:

Israel, pack up your possessions, take down your tents, and cross the Arnon River gorge.[z] The territory of the Amorite King Sihon of Heshbon lies on the other side of the river, but I now give you his land. So attack and take it! [25]Today I will start making all other nations afraid of you. They will tremble with fear when anyone mentions you, and they will be terrified when you show up.

The Defeat of King Sihon of Heshbon
(Numbers 21.21-30)

Moses said to Israel:

[26]After we had crossed the Arnon and had set up camp in the Kedemoth Desert, I sent messengers to King Sihon of Heshbon, telling him that his nation and ours could be at peace. I said:

[27]Please let Israel go across your country. We will walk straight through, without turning off the road. [28-29]You can even sell us food and water, and we will pay with silver. We need to reach the Jordan River and cross it, because the LORD our God is giving us the land on the west side. The Edomites and Moabites[d] have already let us cross their land. Please let us cross your land as well.

[30-31]But Sihon refused to let us go across his country, because the LORD made him stubborn and eager to fight us. The LORD told me, "I am going to help you defeat Sihon and take his land, so attack him!"

[32]We met Sihon and his army in battle at Jahaz, [33]and the LORD our God helped us defeat them. We killed Sihon, his sons, and everyone else in his army. [34]Then we captured and destroyed every town in Sihon's kingdom, killing everyone, [35]but keeping the livestock and everything else of value. [36]The LORD helped us capture every town from the Arnon River gorge north to the boundary of Gilead, including the town of

Aroer on the edge of the gorge and the town in the middle of the gorge. [37]However, we stayed away from all the Ammonite towns, both in the hill country and near the Jabbok River, just as the LORD had commanded.

The Defeat of King Og of Bashan
(Numbers 21.31-35)

Moses said to Israel:

3 When we turned onto the road that leads to Bashan, King Og of Bashan led out his whole army to fight us at Edrei. [2]But the LORD told me, "Moses, don't be afraid of King Og. I am going to help you defeat him and his army and take over his land. Destroy him and his people, just as you did with the Amorite King Sihon of Heshbon."

[3-6]The LORD our God helped us destroy Og and his army and conquer his entire kingdom of Bashan, including the Argob region. His kingdom had lots of villages and sixty towns with high walls and gates that locked with bars. We completely destroyed[b] them all, killing everyone, [7]but keeping the livestock and everything else of value.

[8]Sihon and Og had ruled Amorite kingdoms east of the Jordan River. Their land stretched from the Arnon River gorge in the south to Mount Hermon in the north, and we captured it all. [9]Mount Hermon is called Mount Sirion by the people of Sidon, and it is called Mount Senir by the Amorites. [10]We captured all the towns in the highlands, all of Gilead, and all of Bashan as far as Salecah and Edrei, two of the towns that Og had ruled.

Og's Coffin

[11]King Og was the last of the Rephaim,[c] and his coffin[d] is in the town of Rabbah in

---

[y]2.23 *Philistines:* The Hebrew text has "the Caphtorim from Caphtor," probably referring to the Philistines who originally came from Crete.   [z]2.24 *Arnon River gorge:* The northern boundary of Moab's territory and the southern boundary of Sihon's kingdom.   [d]2.28,29 *Edomites and Moabites:* Hebrew "descendants of Esau, who live in Seir and Moabites who live in Ar."   [b]3.3-6 *completely destroyed:* The Hebrew word means that the town was given completely to the LORD, and since it could not be used for normal purposes any more, it had to be destroyed. Every person was killed and sometimes all the animals as well.   [c]3.11 *Rephaim:* See the note at 2.10, 11.   [d]3.11 *coffin:* Or "bed."

Ammon. It is made of hard black rock[c] and is thirteen and a half feet long and six feet wide.

The Land East of the Jordan River Is Divided

(Numbers 32.1-42)

Moses said to Israel:

[12-17]I gave some of the land and towns we captured to the tribes of Reuben and Gad. Their share started at the Arnon River gorge in the south, took in the town of Aroer on the edge of the gorge, and went far enough north to include the southern half of the Gilead region. The northern part of their land went as far east as the upper Jabbok River gorge, which formed their border with the Ammonites.[f] I also gave them the eastern side of the Jordan River valley, from Lake Galilee[g] south to the Dead Sea[h] below the slopes of Mount Pisgah.

I gave the northern half of Gilead and all of the Bashan region to half the tribe of Manasseh.[i] Bashan had belonged to King Og, and the Argob region in Bashan used to be called the Land of the Rephaim. Jair from the Manasseh tribe conquered the Argob region as far west as the kingdoms of Geshur and Maacah. The Israelites even started calling Bashan by the name "Villages of Jair,"[j] and that is still its name. I gave the northern half of Gilead to the Machir clan.[k]

[18-19]At that time I told the men of Reuben, Gad, and East Manasseh:

The LORD our God told me to give you this land with its towns, and that's what I have done. Now your wives and children can stay here with your large flocks of sheep and goats and your large herds of cattle. But all of you men that can serve in our army must cross the Jordan River and help the other tribes, because they are your relatives. [20]The LORD will let them defeat the enemy nations on the west side of the Jordan and take their land. Afterwards, you can come back here to the land I gave you.

[21-22]Then I told Joshua, "You saw how the LORD our God helped us destroy King Sihon and King Og. So don't be afraid! Wherever you go, the LORD will fight on your side and help you destroy your enemies."

God Refused To Let Moses Enter Canaan

Moses said to Israel:

[23]At that time I prayed and begged, [24]"Our LORD, it seems that you have just begun to show me your great power. No other god in the sky or on earth is able to do the mighty things that you do. [25]The land west of the Jordan is such good land. Please let me cross the Jordan and see the hills and the Lebanon Mountains."

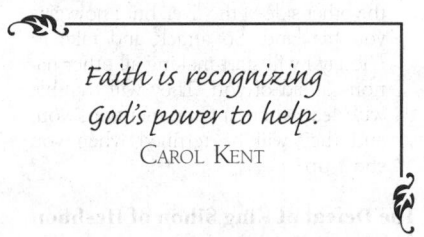

Faith is recognizing God's power to help.
CAROL KENT

[26]But the LORD was angry with me because of you people,[l] and he refused to listen. "That's enough!" he said. "I don't want to hear any more. [27]Climb to the top of Mount Pisgah and look north, south, east, and west. Take a good look, but you are not going to cross the Jordan River. [28]Joshua will lead Israel across the Jordan to take the land, so help him be strong and brave and tell him what he must do."

[29]After this we stayed in the valley at Beth-Peor.

Israel Must Obey God

Moses said:

4 Israel, listen to these laws and teachings! If you obey them, you will live, and you will go in and take the land

---

[c]3.11 *hard black rock*: The Hebrew text has "iron," which probably refers to basalt, a hard black rock.
[f]3.12-17 *The northern part . . . border with the Ammonites*: The Jabbok River flowed from south to north, then it turned west and formed the northern border of the land belonging to the Reuben and Gad tribes.
[g]3.12-17 *Lake Galilee*: The Hebrew text has "Lake Chinnereth," an earlier name. [h]3.12-17 *the Dead Sea*: Hebrew "the Sea of the Arabah, the Salt Sea."
[i]3.12-17 *half the tribe of Manasseh*: Or "East Manasseh." [j]3.12-17 *Villages of Jair*: Or "Havvoth-Jair." [k]3.12-17 *Machir clan*: One of the clans of the Manasseh tribe. [l]3.26 *But the LORD . . . people*: See 1.37.

that the LORD is giving you. He is the God your ancestors worshiped, [2]and now he is your God. I am telling you everything he has commanded, so don't add anything or take anything away.

[3]You saw how he killed everyone who worshiped the god Baal Peor.[m] [4]But all of you that were faithful to the LORD your God are still alive today.

[5-8]No other nation has laws that are as fair as the ones the Lord my God told me to give you. If you faithfully obey them when you enter the land, you will show other nations how wise you are. In fact, everyone that hears about your laws will say, "That great nation certainly is wise!" And what makes us greater than other nations? We have a God who is close to us and answers our prayers.

[9]You must be very careful not to forget the things you have seen God do for you. Keep reminding yourselves, and tell your children and grandchildren as well. [10]Do you remember the day you stood in the LORD's presence at Mount Sinai?[n] The LORD said, "Moses, bring the people of Israel here. I want to speak to them so they will obey me as long as they live, and so they will teach their children to obey me too."

[11]Mount Sinai[n] was surrounded by deep dark clouds, and fire went up to the sky. You came to the foot of the mountain, [12]and the LORD spoke to you from the fire. You could hear him and understand what he was saying, but you couldn't see him. [13]The LORD said he was making an agreement with you, and he told you that your part of the agreement is to obey the Ten Commandments. Then the LORD wrote these Commandments on two flat stones.

[14]That's when the LORD commanded me to give you the laws and teachings you must obey in the land that you will conquer west of the Jordan River.

Don't Worship Idols

Moses said to Israel:

[15]When God spoke to you from the fire, he was invisible. So be careful [16]not to commit the sin of worshiping idols. Don't make idols to be worshiped, whether they are shaped like men, women, [17]animals, birds, [18]reptiles, or fish. [19]And when you see the sun or moon or stars, don't be tempted to bow down and worship them. The LORD put them there for all the other nations to worship. [20]But you are the LORD's people, because he led you through fiery trials and rescued you from Egypt.

[21]The LORD was angry at me because of what you said,[o] and he told me that he would not let me cross the Jordan River into the good land that he is giving you.[p] [22]So I must stay here and die on this side of the Jordan, but you will cross the river and take the land.

[23]Always remember the agreement that the LORD your God made with you, and don't make an idol in any shape or form. [24]The LORD will be angry if you worship other gods, and he can be like a fire destroying everything in its path.

[25-26]Soon you will cross the Jordan River and settle down in the land. Then in the years to come, you will have children, and they will give you grandchildren. After many years, you might lose your sense of right and wrong and make idols, even though the LORD your God hates them. So I am giving you fair warning today, and I call the earth and the sky as witnesses. If you ever make idols, the LORD will be angry, and you won't have long to live, because the LORD will let you be wiped out. [27]Only a few of you will survive, and the LORD will force you to leave the land and will scatter you among the nations. [28]There you will have to worship gods made of wood and stone, and these are nothing but idols that can't see or hear or eat or smell.

[29-30]In all of your troubles, you may finally decide that you want to worship only the LORD. And if you turn back to him and obey him completely, he will again be your God. [31]The LORD your God will have mercy—he won't destroy you or desert you. The LORD will remember his promise, and he will keep the agreement he made with your ancestors.

[32-34]When the LORD your God brought you out of Egypt, you saw how he fought for you and showed his great power by performing terrifying miracles. You became his people, and at Mount Sinai you heard him talking to you out of fiery flames. And yet

---

[m]4.3 *Baal Peor*: See Numbers 25.1-9. [n]4.10,11 *Mount Sinai*: See the note at 1.1-5. [o]4.21 *what you said*: Or "you people." [p]4.21 *The LORD was angry . . . giving you*: See 1.37; 3.26.

you are still alive! Has anything like this ever happened since the time God created humans? No matter where you go or who you ask, you will get the same answer. No one has ever heard of another god even trying to do such things as the LORD your God has done for you.

35-36The LORD wants you to know he is the only true God, and he wants you to obey him. That's why he let you see his mighty miracles and his fierce fire on earth, and why you heard his voice from that fire and from the sky.

37The LORD loved your ancestors and decided that you would be his people. So the LORD used his great power to bring you out of Egypt. 38Now you face other nations more powerful than you are, but the LORD has already started forcing them out of their land and giving it to you.

39So remember that the LORD is the only true God, whether in the sky above or on the earth below. 40Today I am explaining his laws and teachings. And if you always obey them, you and your descendants will live long and be successful in the land the LORD is giving you.

Safe Towns

41-43Moses said, "People of Israel, you must set aside the following three towns east of the Jordan River as Safe Towns: Bezer in the desert highlands belonging to the Reuben tribe; Ramoth in Gilead, belonging to the Gad tribe; and Golan in Bashan, belonging to the Manasseh tribe. If you kill a neighbor without meaning to, and if you had not been angry with that person, you can run to one of these towns and find safety."[q]

THE SECOND SPEECH: MOSES TELLS WHAT THE LORD DEMANDS

Israel at Beth-Peor

44-46The Israelites had come from Egypt and were camped east of the Jordan River near Beth-Peor, when Moses gave these laws and teachings. The land around their camp had once belonged to King Sihon of Heshbon. But Moses and the Israelites defeated him 47and King Og of Bashan, and took their lands. These two Amorite kings had ruled the territory east of the Jordan River 48from the town of Aroer on the edge of the Arnon River gorge, north to Mount Hermon.[r] 49Their land included the eastern side of the Jordan River valley, as far south as the Dead Sea[s] below the slopes of Mount Pisgah.

The Ten Commandments

(Exodus 20.1-17)

5 Moses called together the people of Israel and said:

Today I am telling you the laws and teachings that you must follow, so listen carefully. 2The LORD our God made an agreement with our nation at Mount Sinai.[t] 3That agreement wasn't only with[u] our ancestors but with us, who are here today. 4The LORD himself spoke to you out of the fire, 5but you were afraid of the fire and refused to go up the mountain. So I spoke with the LORD for you, then I told you that he had said:

> 6I am the LORD your God, the one who brought you out of Egypt where you were slaves.
>
> 7Do not worship any god except me.
>
> 8Do not make idols that look like anything in the sky or on earth or in the ocean under the earth. 9Don't bow down and worship idols. I am the LORD your God, and I demand all your love. If you reject me and worship idols, I will punish your families for three or four generations. 10But if you love me and obey my laws, I will be kind to your families for thousands of generations.
>
> 11Do not misuse my name.[v] I am the LORD your God, and I will punish anyone who misuses my name.
>
> 12Show respect for the Sabbath Day—it belongs to me. 13You have six days when you can do your work,

---

[q]**4.41-43** *find safety*: From the victim's clan, who might appoint one of their men to track down and put to death the killer (see also 19.1-13). [r]**4.48** *Hermon*: The Hebrew text also includes the name "Sion," probably another form of "Sirion," the name used by the Sidonians. [s]**4.49** *the Dead Sea*: Hebrew "the Sea of the Arabah." [t]**5.2** *Mount Sinai*: See the note at 1.1-5. [u]**5.3** *wasn't only with*: Hebrew "wasn't with." [v]**5.11** *misuse my name*: Probably includes breaking promises, telling lies after swearing to tell the truth, using the LORD's name as a curse word or a magic formula, and trying to control the LORD by using his name.

¹⁴but the seventh day of the week belongs to me, your God. No one is to work on that day—not you, your children, your oxen or donkeys or any other animal, not even those foreigners who live in your towns. And don't make your slaves do any work. ¹⁵This special day of rest will remind you that I reached out my mighty arm and rescued you from slavery in Egypt.

¹⁶Respect your father and mother, and you will live a long and successful life in the land I am giving you.

¹⁷Do not murder.

¹⁸Be faithful in marriage.

¹⁹Do not steal.

²⁰Do not tell lies about others.

²¹Do not want anything that belongs to someone else. Don't want anyone's wife or husband, house, land, slaves, oxen, donkeys, or anything else.

²²When we were gathered on the mountain, the LORD spoke to us in a loud voice from the dark fiery cloud. The LORD gave us these commands, and only these. Then he wrote them on two flat stones and gave them to me.

The People Were Afraid
(Exodus 20.18-21)

Moses said to Israel:

²³When fire blazed from the mountain, and you heard the voice coming from the darkness, your tribal leaders came to me ²⁴and said:

Today the LORD our God has shown us how powerful and glorious he is. He spoke to us from the fire, and we learned that people can live, even though God speaks to them. ²⁵But we don't want to take a chance on being killed by that terrible fire, and if we keep on hearing the LORD's voice, we will die. ²⁶Has anyone else ever heard the only true God speaking from fire, as we have? And even if they have, would they live to tell about it? ²⁷Moses, go up close and listen to the LORD. Then come back and tell us, and we will do everything he says.

²⁸The LORD heard you and said:

Moses, I heard what the people said to you, and I approve. ²⁹I wish they would always worship me with fear and trembling and be this willing to obey me! Then they and their

---

WORK—How can I rise above office politics? *(Deuteronomy 5.20,21)*

Hold yourself above gossip and jealousy.

What makes an office uncomfortable? Rumors, circulating behind the backs of coworkers; jealousy that causes colleagues to distrust each other; theft of ideas, of credit, or even of paper clips! All these things can produce a terrible office atmosphere. And all of them are against God's law.

The Ten Commandments give us basic rules for how to behave toward each other. And the last two commandments, nine and ten, are particularly valuable in governing office relationships.

The ninth commandment orders us not to tell lies about each other. That means anything that's even slightly untrue—including half-truths, exaggerations, even stories that *might* be true, but you don't know for sure! If you follow the ninth commandment at work, you'll find yourself refusing to pass on juicy information about your coworkers. Instead, you'll spread kind, encouraging, complimentary words.

The tenth commandment tells us not to want what other people have. We often think of this in terms of possessions—big houses, fancy cars, nice clothes. But the commandment also tells us not to wish for a colleague's power, prestige, or job responsibilities. Instead of looking at what other people have, we're to examine our own responsibilities and fulfill them as well as we can. (See also Esther 7.1-6; Matthew 20.20-28; Galatians 5.13-16; Colossians 3.22—4.1; James 3.5-18.)

Words To Remember: *Do not tell lies about others. Do not want anything that belongs to someone else.*—Deuteronomy 5.20,21

children would always enjoy a successful life. ³⁰Now, tell them to return to their tents, ³¹but you come back here to me. After I tell you my laws and teachings, you will repeat them to the people, so they can obey these laws in the land I am giving them.

Moses said:

³²Israel, you must carefully obey the LORD's commands. ³³Follow them, because they make a path that will lead to a long successful life in the land the LORD your God is giving you.

The Most Important Commandment

Moses said to Israel:

6 The LORD told me to give you these laws and teachings,ʷ so you can obey them in the land he is giving you. Soon you will cross the Jordan River and take that land. ²And if you and your descendants want to live a long time, you must always worship the LORD and obey his laws. ³Pay attention, Israel! Our ancestors worshiped the LORD, and he promised to give us this land that is rich with milk and honey. Be careful to obey him, and you will become a successful and powerful nation.

⁴Listen, Israel! The LORD our God is the only true God!ˣ ⁵So love the LORD your God with all your heart, soul, and strength. ⁶Memorize his laws ⁷and tell them to your children over and over again. Talk about them all the time, whether you're at home or walking along the road or going to bed at night, or getting up in the morning. ⁸Write down copies and tie them to your wrists and foreheads to help you obey them. ⁹Write these laws on the door frames of your homes and on your town gates.

Worship Only the LORD

Moses said to Israel:

¹⁰The LORD promised your ancestors Abraham, Isaac, and Jacob that he would

---

ʷ**6.1** *these laws and teachings*: Or "the following commandment with its laws and teachings" (see 6.4, 5). ˣ**6.4** *The LORD . . . true God*: Or "Only the LORD is our God."

WORK—How can I balance the competing demands of home and work?
(Deuteronomy 6.1-9)

Put God first in every area of your life.
What can we do when work and family responsibilities seem to swallow every spare moment? God recognizes that we must take care of our children, spouse, and maybe even aging parents, as well as earn a living. But he warns us that we must put him first in everything we do.

When the people of Israel were preparing to enter the Promised Land, God gave them one command that was more important than all the others: "Love the LORD your God with all your heart, soul, and strength" (6.5). This may seem vague to us, but God followed it with several specific instructions that can also help us keep him first.

First, we are to memorize God's words. Make memorization of Scripture a priority. That way, God's instructions can always be in your mind, no matter what you are doing during the day.

Second, we are to tell our children about God's ways "over and over again" (6.7). Make God's Word a regular topic of conversation at home. That way, God can be at the center of your family life.

Third, we are to keep God's Word always in front of us—while we're at work and at home. Keep Scripture taped on your walls, to your car's dashboard, or beside your computer monitor. Listen to Scripture tapes as you drive. Read your Bible regularly. This way, God will be speaking to you daily, even as you fulfill your responsibilities. (See also Exodus. 23.10-13; 2 Samuel 1; Matthew 14.22,23.)

Words To Remember: *Listen, Israel! The LORD our God is the only true God! So love the LORD your God with all your heart, soul, and strength.—Deuteronomy 6.4,5*

give you this land. Now he will take you there and give you large towns, with good buildings that you didn't build, [11]and houses full of good things that you didn't put there. The LORD will give you wells[y] that you didn't have to dig, and vineyards and olive orchards that you didn't have to plant. But when you have eaten so much that you can't eat any more, [12]don't forget it was the LORD who set you free from slavery and brought you out of Egypt. [13]Worship and obey the LORD your God with fear and trembling, and promise that you will be loyal to him.

[14]Don't have anything to do with gods that are worshiped by the nations around you. [15]If you worship other gods, the LORD will be furious and wipe you off the face of the earth. The LORD your God is with you, [16]so don't try to make him prove that he can help you, as you did at Massah.[z] [17]Always obey the laws that the LORD has given you [18-19]and live in a way that pleases him. Then you will be able to go in and take this good land from your enemies, just as he promised your ancestors.

[20]Someday your children will ask, "Why did the LORD give us these laws and teachings?"

[21]Then you will answer:

We were slaves of the king of Egypt, but the LORD used his great power and set us free. [22]We saw him perform miracles and make horrible things happen to the king, his officials, and everyone else. [23]The LORD rescued us from Egypt, so he could bring us into this land, as he had promised our ancestors. [24-25]That's why the LORD our God demands that we obey his laws and worship him with fear and trembling. And if we do, he will protect us and help us be successful.

Force the Other Nations Out of the Land
(Exodus 34.11-16)

Moses said:

7 People of Israel, the LORD your God will help you take the land of the Hittites, the Girgashites, the Amorites, the Canaanites, the Perizzites, the Hivites, and the Jebusites. These seven nations have more people and are stronger than Israel,

but when you attack them, [2]the LORD will force them out of the land. Then you must destroy them without mercy. Don't make any peace treaties with them, [3]and don't let your sons and daughters marry any of them. [4]If you do, those people will lead your descendants to worship other gods and to turn their backs on the LORD. That will make him very angry, and he will quickly destroy Israel.

[5]So when you conquer these nations, tear down the altars where they worship their gods. Break up their sacred stones, cut down the poles that they use in worshiping the goddess Asherah, and throw their idols in the fire.

> *For the Christian there is a single source. It is God who is in charge of things, from stars to coins.*
> ELISABETH ELLIOT

The LORD's Chosen People

Moses said:

[6]Israel, you are the chosen people of the LORD your God. There are many nations on this earth, but he chose only Israel to be his very own. [7]You were the weakest of all nations, [8]but the LORD chose you because he loves you and because he had made a promise to your ancestors. Then with his mighty arm, he rescued you from the king of Egypt, who had made you his slaves.

[9]You know that the LORD your God is the only true God. So love him and obey his commands, and he will faithfully keep his agreement with you and your descendants for a thousand generations. [10]But if you turn against the LORD, he will quickly destroy you. [11]So be sure to obey his laws and teachings I am giving you today.

---

[y]6.11 *wells:* Cisterns cut into the rock to collect rainwater. [z]6.16 *Massah:* See Exodus 17.1-7; Numbers 20.2-13.

The LORD Will Bless You if You Obey
(Deuteronomy 28.1-14; Leviticus 26.3-13)

Moses said to Israel:

¹²If you completely obey these laws, the LORD your God will be loyal and keep the agreement he made with you, just as he promised our ancestors. ¹³The LORD will love you and bless you by giving you many children and plenty of food, wine, and olive oil. Your herds of cattle will have many calves, and your flocks of sheep will have many lambs. ¹⁴God will bless you more than any other nation—your families will grow and your livestock increase. ¹⁵You will no longer suffer with the same horrible diseases that you sometimes had in Egypt. You will be healthy, but the LORD will make your enemies suffer from those diseases.

Destroy the Nations and Their Gods

Moses said to Israel:

¹⁶When the LORD helps you defeat your enemies, you must destroy them without pity! And don't get trapped into worshiping their gods.

¹⁷You may be thinking, "How can we destroy these nations? They are more powerful than we are." ¹⁸But stop worrying! Just re-member what the LORD your God did to Egypt and its king. ¹⁹You saw how the LORD used his tremendous power to work great miracles and bring you out of Egypt. And he will again work miracles for you when you face these enemies you fear so much. ²⁰Some of them may try to survive by hiding from you, but the LORD will make them panic, and soon they will be dead.ᵃ ²¹So don't be frightened when you meet them in battle. The LORD your God is great and fear-some, and he will fight at your side.

²²As you attack these nations, the LORD will force them out little by little. He won't let you get rid of them all at once—if he did, there wouldn't be enough people living in the land to keep down the number of wild animals. ²³⁻²⁴But when you attack your enemies, the LORD will make them panic, and you will easily destroy them. You will defeat them one after another until they are gone, and no one will remember they ever lived.

²⁵After you conquer a nation, burn their idols. Don't get trapped into wanting the sil-ver or gold on an idol. Even the metal on an idol is disgusting to the LORD, ²⁶so destroy it. If you bring it home with you, both you

ᵃ7.20 *make them . . . dead*: Or "send hornets to kill them."

PARENTING&*family*—How can I effectively balance my roles as parent and wife? *(Deuteronomy 8.1-10)*

Look to the example of God, the heavenly Father.

Sometimes it seems that the demands of parenting never end. Kids always need some-thing—new shoes, help with homework, a story read, a ride to baseball practice, a listening ear. As a parent, you have to fill all sorts of roles: teacher, chauffeur, disciplinarian, love-giver, nurse, trainer, and treasurer.

All these demands create pressure! But when we look at the example of God, the heavenly Father, we see how pressure is the flipside of privilege. Yes, God found it frustrat-ing to take care of his children, the Israelites. They always wanted something from him! And most of the time they weren't even grateful.

But at the same time, God was delighted to give the Israelites the things they needed—not just food and clothing, but also discipline and nurture. He knew that children need attentive parenting more than anything else in the world.

When the pressures of parenting are wearing you out, try to remember the great privilege parents have! In a very real way, parents show their children what God is like. Let your children understand God's provision by providing for their needs. And train them in gratitude toward God by teaching them to be grateful for the things their earthly parents do for them. (See also Job 38.1—40.5; 1 Peter 4.1-8.)

Words To Remember: *After you eat and are full, give praise to the LORD your God.—Deuteronomy 8.10*

and your house will be destroyed. Stay away from those disgusting idols!

The LORD Takes Care of You

Moses said:

8 Israel, do you want to go into the land the LORD promised your ancestors? Do you want to capture it, live there, and become a powerful nation? Then be sure to obey every command I am giving you.

²Don't forget how the LORD your God has led you through the desert for the past forty years. He wanted to find out if you were truly willing to obey him and depend on him, ³so he made you go hungry. Then he gave you manna,ᵇ a kind of food that you and your ancestors had never even heard about. The LORD was teaching you that people need more than food to live—they need every word that the LORD has spoken.

⁴Over the past forty years, your clothing hasn't worn out, and your feet haven't swollen. ⁵So keep in mind that the LORD has been correcting you, just as parents correct their children. ⁶Obey the commands the LORD your God has given you and worship him with fear and trembling.

⁷The LORD your God is bringing you into a good land with streams that flow from springs in the valleys and hills. ⁸⁻⁹You can dig for copper in those hills, and the stones are made of iron ore. And you won't go hungry. Wheat and barley fields are everywhere, and so are vineyards and orchards full of fig, pomegranate,ᶜ and olive trees, and there is plenty of honey.

Don't Forget the LORD

Moses said to Israel:

¹⁰After you eat and are full, give praise to the LORD your God for the good land he gave you. ¹¹Make sure that you never forget the LORD or disobey his laws and teachings that I am giving you today. If you always obey them, ¹²you will have plenty to eat, and you will build good houses to live in. ¹³You will get more and more cattle, sheep, silver, gold, and other possessions.

¹⁴But when all this happens, don't be proud! Don't forget that you were once slaves in Egypt and that it was the LORD who set you free. ¹⁵Remember how he led you in that huge and frightening desert

---

ᵇ8.3 *manna:* See Exodus 16.1-36. ᶜ8.8,9 *pomegranate:* A bright red fruit that looks like an apple.

WORK—How can I find satisfaction with my life outside of work?
(Deuteronomy 8.10-20)

Realize your value doesn't depend on what you do but on who God is.
It's easy to get caught up in the demands of work. Sometimes you may feel that your job is the only activity that really rewards you—after all, your kids don't give you a paycheck. Sometimes you may think that your coworkers are the only people who really recognize your value—hey, your husband didn't even notice that you'd cleaned the bathroom, but your boss praised your last project to the skies.

This passage makes it clear that no matter what you're doing—or who is praising or not praising you—God values you. Your success at home or at work, as God reminds the Israelites, comes because of God's blessings on you. Ultimately, God is the one who gives you the energy to complete your tasks at work, and God is in control of your home and all the to-dos awaiting you there.

Once you know this, you can relax a bit. You don't have to let work consume all your energies. You can leave the workplace (or shut the door on your at-home office) on time, knowing you've done a good day's work.

So do your best on the job; then leave and enjoy your off-work hours! Remember that, whether on the job or off, God is your partner. He is the one who gives you the strength you need daily. (See also Ecclesiastes 3.1-14; Isaiah 55.1-5.)

Words To Remember: *When you become successful, don't say, "I'm rich, and I've earned it all myself." Instead, remember that the LORD your God gives you the strength to make a living.—Deuteronomy 8.17,18*

where poisonous snakes and scorpions live. There was no water, but the LORD split open a rock, and water poured out so you could drink. [16]He also gave you manna,[d] a kind of food your ancestors had never even heard about. The LORD was testing you to make you trust him, so that later on he could be good to you.

[17]When you become successful, don't say, "I'm rich, and I've earned it all myself." [18]Instead, remember that the LORD your God gives you the strength to make a living. That's how he keeps the promise he made to your ancestors.

[19-20]But I'm warning you—if you forget the LORD your God and worship other gods, the LORD will destroy you, just as he destroyed the nations you fought.

Why the LORD Will Help Israel

Moses said:

9 Israel, listen to me! You will soon cross the Jordan River and go into the land to force out the nations that live there. They are more powerful than you are, and the walls around their cities reach to the sky. [2]Some of these nations are descendants of the Anakim.[e] You know how tall and strong they are, and you've heard that no one can defeat them in battle. [3]But the LORD your God has promised to go ahead of you, like a raging fire burning everything in its path. So when you attack your enemies, it will be easy for you to destroy them and take their land.

> *Getting an emotional makeover doesn't involve denying your problems; it welcomes trials full-strength all the time, saying, "Lord, I accept each day as it comes, filtered through your love. In these troubles I choose joy."*
>
> BARBARA JOHNSON

[4-6]After the LORD helps you wipe out these nations and conquer their land, don't think he did it because you are such good people. You aren't good—you are stubborn! No, the LORD is going to help you, because the nations that live there are evil, and because he wants to keep the promise he made to your ancestors Abraham, Isaac, and Jacob.

When Israel Made an Idol
(Exodus 32)

Moses said to Israel:

[7]Don't ever forget how you kept rebelling and making the LORD angry the whole time you were in the desert. You rebelled from the day you left Egypt until the day you arrived here.

[8]At Mount Sinai[f] you made the LORD so angry that he was going to destroy you. [9-11]It happened during those forty days and nights that I was on the mountain, without anything to eat or drink. He had told me to come up there so he could give me the agreement he made with us. And this agreement was actually the same Ten Commandments[g] he had announced to you when he spoke from the fire on the mountain. The LORD had written them on two flat stones with his own hand. But after giving me the two stones, [12]he said:

Moses, hurry down the mountain to those people you led out of Egypt. They have already disobeyed me and committed the terrible sin of making an idol.

[13]I've been watching the Israelites, and I've seen how stubborn and rebellious they are. [14]So don't try to stop me! I am going to wipe them out, and no one on earth will remember they ever lived. Then I will let your descendants become an even bigger and more powerful nation than Israel.

Moses said:

[15]Fire was raging on the mountaintop as I went back down, carrying the two stones with the commandments on them. [16]I saw how quickly you had sinned and disobeyed the LORD your God. There you were, worshiping the metal idol you had made in the shape of a calf. [17]So I threw down the two

---

[d]**8.16** *manna:* See the note at 8.3. [e]**9.2** *Anakim:* See the note at 2.10, 11. [f]**9.8** *Mount Sinai:* See the note at 1.1-5. [g]**9.9-11** *Ten Commandments:* Hebrew "commandments."

stones and smashed them before your very eyes.

¹⁸⁻²⁰I bowed down at the place of worship and prayed to the LORD, without eating or drinking for forty days and nights. You had committed a terrible sin by making that idol, and the LORD hated what you had done. He was angry enough to destroy all of you and Aaron as well. So I prayed for you and Aaron as I had done before, and this time the LORD answered my prayers.ʰ

²¹It was a sin for you to make that idol, so I threw it into the fire to melt it down. Then I took the lump of gold, ground it into powder, and threw the powder into the stream flowing down the mountain.

²²You also made the LORD angry when you were staying at Taberah,ⁱ at Massah,ʲ and at Kibroth-Hattaavah.ᵏ ²³Then at Kadesh-Barnea the LORD said, "I am giving you the land, so go ahead and take it!" But since you didn't trust the LORD, you rebelled and disobeyed his command.ˡ ²⁴In fact, you've rebelled against the LORD for as long as he hasᵐ known you.

²⁵After you had made the idol in the shape of a calf, the LORD said he was going to destroy you. So I bowed down in front of the sacred tent for forty days and nights, ²⁶and I prayed:

Our LORD, please don't wipe out your people. You used your great power to rescue them from Egypt and to make them your very own. ²⁷Israel's ancestors Abraham, Isaac, and Jacob obeyed you faithfully. Think about them, and not about Israel's stubbornness, evil, and sin. ²⁸If you destroy your people, the Egyptians will say, "The LORD promised to give Israel land, but he wasn't powerful enough to keep his promise. In fact, he hated them so much that he took them into the desert and killed them." ²⁹But you, our LORD, chose the people of Israel to be your own, and with your mighty power you rescued them from Egypt.

The Second Set of Commandments
(Exodus 34.1-10)

Moses said to the people:

10 The LORD told me to chisel out two flat stones, just like the ones he had given me earlier. He also commanded me to make a wooden chest, then come up the mountain and meet with him. ²He told me that he would write the same words on the new stones that he had written on the ones I broke, and that I could put these stones in this sacred chest.

³So I made a chest out of acacia wood, and I chiseled two flat stones like the ones I broke. Then I carried the stones up the mountain, ⁴where the LORD wrote the Ten Commandments on them, just as he had done the first time. The commandments were exactly what he had announced from the fire, when you were gathered at the mountain.

After the LORD returned the stones to me, ⁵I took them down the mountainside and put them in the chest, just as he had commanded. And they are still there.

Aaron Died
(Numbers 20.22-29)

Moses said to Israel:

⁶Later we set up camp at the wells belonging to the descendants of Jaakan.ⁿ Then we moved on and camped at Moserah, where Aaron died and was buried, and his son Eleazar became the priest. ⁷Next, we camped at Gudgodah and then at Jotbathah, where there are flowing streams.

The Levites Were Appointed To Carry the Chest

Moses said to Israel:

⁸After I put the two stones in the sacred chest,ᵒ the LORD chose the tribe of Levi, not only to carry the chest, but also to serve as his priests at the place of worship and to bless the other tribes in his name. And they still do these things. ⁹The LORD promised that he would always provide for the tribe of Levi, and that's why he won't give them any

ʰ**9.18-20** as I had done before . . . prayers: This may refer to Moses' praying for Israel before he came down from the mountain (see Exodus 32.11-14). ⁱ**9.22** Taberah: See Numbers 11.1-3. ʲ**9.22** Massah: See the note at 6.16. ᵏ**9.22** Kibroth-Hattaavah: See Numbers 11.31-34. ˡ**9.23** Kadesh-Barnea . . . you rebelled and disobeyed his command: See Numbers 13, 14. ᵐ**9.24** he has: The Samaritan Hebrew Text and one ancient translation; the Standard Hebrew Text "I have." ⁿ**10.6** the wells . . . Jaakan: Or "Beeroth Bene-Jaakan." ᵒ**10.8** After . . . chest: Or "After Israel reached Jotbathah."

land, when he divides it among the other tribes.

The LORD Answered the Prayers of Moses
(Exodus 34.9, 10, 27-29)

Moses said to Israel:

[10]When I had taken the second set of stones up the mountain, I spent forty days and nights there, just as I had done before. Once again, the LORD answered my prayer and did not destroy you. [11]Instead, he told me, "Moses, get ready to lead the people into the land that I promised their ancestors."[p]

What the LORD Wants

Moses said:

[12]People of Israel, what does the LORD your God want from you? The LORD wants you to respect and follow him, to love and serve him with all your heart and soul, [13]and to obey his laws and teachings that I am giving you today. Do this, and all will go well for you.

God's ideal design is for a mother, father, and children to live and love together under one roof. But God is sufficient to provide whatever single parents need to raise their children—whether it's financial, emotional, or physical.

PATRICIA FUNDERBURK WARE

[14]Everything belongs to the LORD your God, not only the earth and everything on it, but also the sky and the highest heavens. [15]Yet the LORD loved your ancestors and wanted them to belong to him. So he chose them and their descendants rather than any other nation, and today you are still his people.

[16]Remember your agreement with the LORD and stop being so stubborn. [17]The LORD your God is more powerful than all other gods and lords, and his tremendous power is to be feared. His decisions are always fair, and you cannot bribe him to change his mind. [18]The LORD defends the rights of orphans and widows. He cares for foreigners and gives them food and clothing. [19]And you should also care for them, because you were foreigners in Egypt.

[20]Respect the LORD your God, serve only him, and make promises in his name alone. [21]Offer your praises to him, because you have seen him work such terrifying miracles for you.

[22]When your ancestors went to live in Egypt, there were only seventy of them. But the LORD has blessed you, and now there are more of you than there are stars in the sky.

If You Are Loyal to the LORD, He Will Bless You

Moses said to Israel:

11 The LORD is your God, so you must always love him and obey his laws and teachings. [2]Remember, he corrected you and not your children. You are the ones who saw the LORD use his great power [3]when he worked miracles in Egypt, making terrible things happen to the king and all his people. [4]And when the Egyptian army chased you in their chariots, you saw the LORD drown them and their horses in the Red Sea.[q] Egypt still suffers from that defeat!

[5]You saw what the LORD did for you while you were in the desert, right up to the time you arrived here. [6]And you saw how the LORD made the ground open up in the middle of our camp underneath the tents of Dathan and Abiram,[r] who were swallowed up along with their families, their animals, and their tents.

---

[p]**10.11** *lead . . . ancestors:* The LORD would later tell Moses that he would not be allowed to enter the land (see 1.37; 3.23-28; Numbers 20.10-12). [q]**11.4** *Red Sea:* Hebrew *yam suph* "Sea of Reeds," one of the marshes or fresh water lakes near the eastern part of the Nile Delta. This identification is based on Exodus 13.7—14.9, which lists towns on the route of the Israelites before crossing the sea. In the Greek translation of the Scriptures made about 200 B.C., the "Sea of Reeds," was named "Red Sea." [r]**11.6** *Dathan and Abiram:* Hebrew "Dathan and Abiram, the sons of Eliab from the Reuben tribe."

[7]With your own eyes, you saw the LORD's mighty power do all these things.

[8]Soon you will cross the Jordan River, and if you obey the laws and teachings I'm giving you today, you will be strong enough to conquer the land [9]that the LORD promised your ancestors and their descendants. It's rich with milk and honey, and you will live there and enjoy it for a long time. [10]It's better land than you had in Egypt, where you had to struggle just to water your crops.[s] [11]But the hills and valleys in the promised land are watered by rain from heaven,[t] [12]because the LORD your God keeps his eye on this land and takes care of it all year long.

[13]The LORD your God commands you to love him and to serve him with all your heart and soul. If you obey him, [14-15]he will send rain at the right seasons,[u] so you will have more than enough food, wine, and olive oil, and there will be plenty of grass for your cattle.

[16]But watch out! You will be tempted to turn your backs on the LORD. And if you worship other gods, [17]the LORD will become angry and keep the rain from falling. Nothing will grow in your fields, and you will die and disappear from the good land that the LORD is giving you.

> *The way you treat your children gives them a picture of the way God, their heavenly Father, feels about them.*
>
> EVANGELINE SCHOCK

[18]Memorize these laws and think about them. Write down copies and tie them to your wrists and your foreheads to help you obey them. [19]Teach them to your children. Talk about them all the time—whether you're at home or walking along the road or going to bed at night, or getting up in the morning. [20]Write them on the door frames of your homes and on your town gates. [21]Then you and your descendants will live a long time in the land that the LORD prom-

ised your ancestors. Your families will live there as long as the sky is above the earth.

[22]Love the LORD your God and obey all the laws and teachings that I'm giving you today. If you live the way the LORD wants, [23]he will help you take the land. And even though the nations there are more powerful than you, the LORD will force them to leave when you attack. [24]You will capture the land everywhere you go, from the Southern Desert to the Lebanon Mountains, and from the Euphrates River west to the Mediterranean Sea. [25]No one will be able to stand up to you. The LORD will make everyone terrified of you, just as he promised.

[26]You have a choice—do you want the LORD to bless you, or do you want him to put a curse on you? [27]Today I am giving you his laws, and if you obey him, he will bless you. [28]But if you disobey him and worship those gods that have never done anything for you, the LORD will put a curse on you.

[29]After the LORD your God helps you take the land, you must have a ceremony where you announce his blessings from Mount Gerizim and his curses from Mount Ebal. [30]You know that these two mountains are west of the Jordan River in land now controlled by the Canaanites living in the Jordan River valley. The mountains are west of the road near the sacred trees of Moreh on the other side of Gilgal.

[31]Soon you will cross the Jordan River to conquer the land that the LORD your God is giving you. And when you have settled there, [32]be careful to obey his laws and teachings that I am giving you today.

Only One Place To Worship the LORD

Moses said to Israel:

12 Now I'll tell you the laws and teachings that you have to obey as long as you live. Your ancestors worshiped the LORD, and he is giving you this land. [2]But the nations that live there worship other gods. So after you capture the land, you must completely destroy

---

[s]**11.10** *where . . . crops:* One possible meaning for the difficult Hebrew text. [t]**11.10,11** *to water your crops . . . rain from heaven:* Egypt was flat and had very little rain. All water for crops had to come from the Nile River. [u]**11.14,15** *rain . . . seasons:* In Palestine, almost all the rain for the year comes during the months from October through April.

their places of worship—on mountains and hills or in the shade of large trees. ³Wherever these nations worship their gods, you must tear down their altars, break their sacred stones, burn the sacred poles^v used in worshiping the goddess Asherah, and smash their idols to pieces. Destroy these places of worship so completely that no one will remember they were ever there. ⁴Don't worship the LORD your God in the way those nations worship their gods.

⁵⁻¹⁹Soon you will cross the Jordan, and the LORD will help you conquer your enemies and let you live in peace, there in the land he has given you. But after you are settled, life will be different. You must not offer sacrifices just anywhere you want to. Instead, the LORD will choose a place somewhere in Israel where you must go to worship him. All of your sacrifices and offerings must be taken there, including sacrifices to please the LORD^w and any gift you promise or voluntarily give him. That's where you must also take one tenth of your grain, wine, and olive oil,^x as well as the firstborn of your cattle, sheep, and goats.^y You and your family and servants will eat your gifts and sacrifices^z and celebrate there at the place of worship, because the LORD your God has made you successful in everything you have done. And since Levites will not have any land of their own, you must ask some of them to come along and celebrate with you.

Sometimes you may want to kill an animal for food and not as a sacrifice. If the LORD has blessed you and given you enough cows or sheep or goats, then you can butcher one of them where you live. You can eat it just like the meat from a deer or gazelle that you kill when you go hunting. And even those people who are unclean and unfit for worship can have some of the meat. But you must not eat the blood of any animal—let the blood drain out on the ground.

²⁰⁻²¹The LORD has promised that later on he will give Israel more land, and some of you may not be able to travel all the way from your homes to the place of worship each time you are hungry for meat.^a But the LORD will give you cattle, sheep, and goats, and you can butcher any of those animals at home and eat as much as you want. ²²It is the same as eating the meat from a deer or a gazelle that you kill when you go hunting.

And in this way, anyone who is unclean and unfit for worship can have some of the meat.^b

²³⁻²⁴But don't eat the blood. It is the life of the animal, so let it drain out on the ground before you eat the meat. ²⁵Do you want the LORD to make you successful? Do you want your children to be successful even after you are gone? Then do what pleases the LORD and don't eat blood.

²⁶⁻²⁷All sacrifices and offerings to the LORD must be taken to the place where he chooses to be worshiped. If you offer a sacrifice to please the LORD, all of its meat must be burned on the altar. You can eat the meat from certain kinds of sacrifices, but you must always pour out the animal's blood on the altar.

²⁸If you obey these laws, you will be doing what the LORD your God says is right and good. Then he will help you and your descendants be successful.

Worship the LORD in the Right Way

Moses said:

²⁹Israel, as you go into the land and attack the nations that are there, the LORD will get rid of them, and you can have their land.

³⁰But that's when you must be especially careful not to ask, "How did those nations worship their gods? Shouldn't we worship the LORD in the same way?" ³¹No, you should not! The LORD hates the disgusting way those nations worship their gods, be-

---

^v**12.3** *sacred poles:* Or "trees," used as symbols of Asherah, the goddess of fertility. ^w**12.5-19** *sacrifices to please the LORD:* These sacrifices have traditionally been called "whole burnt offerings" because the whole animal was burned on the altar. A main purpose of such sacrifices was to please the LORD with the smell of the sacrifice, and so in the CEV they are often called "sacrifices to please the LORD." ^x**12.5-19** *one tenth of your grain, wine, and olive oil:* The Israelites had to give one tenth of their harvest of these products to the LORD each year (see 14.22-29; 26.12, 13; Leviticus 27.30-33). ^y**12.5-19** *the first-born of your cattle, sheep, and goats:* The Israelites had to sacrifice these to the LORD (see 15.19-22). ^z**12.5-19** *sacrifices:* Some sacrifices were completely burned on the altar; in other sacrifices, part of the animal was burned and part was given to the priests, but most of the meat was eaten by the worshipers as a sacred meal. ^a**12.20,21** *meat:* Usually eaten only on special occasions, such as during a sacred meal when sacrifices were offered to the LORD. ^b**12.22** *anyone . . . the meat:* Only those who were properly prepared for worship, or "clean," could eat a sacred meal, but anyone could eat this kind of meat.

cause they even burn their sons and daughters as sacrifices.

³²Obey all the laws and teachings I am giving you. Don't add any, and don't take any away.

Don't Worship Other Gods

Moses said to Israel:

13 ¹⁻²Someday a prophet° may come along who is able to perform miracles or tell what will happen in the future. Then the prophet may say, "Let's start worshiping some new gods—some gods that we know nothing about." ³If the prophet says this, don't listen! The LORD your God will be watching to find out whether or not you love him with all your heart and soul. ⁴You must be completely faithful to the LORD. Worship and obey only the LORD and do this with fear and trembling, ⁵because he rescued you from slavery in Egypt.

If a prophet tells you to disobey the LORD your God and to stop worshiping him, then that prophet is evil and must be put to death.

⁶⁻¹⁰Someone else may say to you, "Let's worship other gods." That person may be your best friend, your brother or sister, your son or daughter, or your own dear wife or husband. But you must not listen to people who say such things. Instead, you must stone them to death. You must be the first to throw the stones, then others from the community will finish the job. Don't show any pity.

The gods worshiped by other nations have never done anything for you or your ancestors. People who ask you to worship other gods are trying to get you to stop worshiping the LORD, who rescued you from slavery in Egypt. So put to death anyone who asks you to worship another god. ¹¹And when the rest of Israel hears about it, they will be afraid, and no one else will ever do such an evil thing again.

¹²After the LORD your God gives you towns to live in, you may hear a rumor about one of the towns. ¹³You may hear that some worthless people have talked everyone there into worshiping other gods, even though these gods had never done anything for them. ¹⁴You must carefully find out if the rumor is true. Then if the people of that

town have actually done such a disgusting thing in your own country, ¹⁵you must take your swords and kill every one of them, and their livestock too. ¹⁶⁻¹⁷Gather all the possessions of the people who lived there, and pile them up in the marketplace, without keeping anything for yourself. Set the pile and the whole town on fire, and don't ever rebuild the town. The whole town will be a sacrifice to the LORD your God. Then he won't be angry anymore, and he will have mercy on you and make you successful, just as he promised your ancestors. ¹⁸That's why you must do what the LORD your God says is right. I am giving you his laws and teachings today, and you must obey them.

Don't Mourn like Other Nations

Moses said:

14 People of Israel, you are the LORD's children, so when you mourn for the dead, you must not cut yourselves or shave your forehead.ᵈ ²Out of all the nations on this earth, the LORD your God chose you to be his own. You belong to the LORD, so don't behave like those who worship other gods.

Animals That Can Be Eaten
(Leviticus 11.1-47)

³Don't eat any disgusting animals.

⁴⁻⁵You may eat the meat of cattle, sheep, and goats; wild sheep and goats; and gazelles, antelopes, and all kinds of deer. ⁶It is all right to eat meat from any animals that have divided hoofs and also chew the cud.ᵉ

⁷But don't eat camels, rabbits, and rock badgers. These animals chew the cud but do not have divided hoofs. You must treat them as unclean. ⁸And don't eat pork, since pigs have divided hoofs, but they do not chew their cud. Don't even touch a dead pig!

⁹You can eat any fish that has fins and scales. But there are other creatures that live in the water, ¹⁰and if they do not have fins

---

ᶜ**13.1,2** *a prophet*: Hebrew adds "or a dreamer of dreams," another name for a prophet.   ᵈ**14.1** *when you mourn . . . forehead*: Or "you must not worship Baal, cutting yourselves and shaving your forehead."
ᵉ**14.6** *chew the cud*: Some animals that eat grass and leaves have more than one stomach, and they chew their food a second time, after it has been partly digested in the first stomach. This partly digested food is called "cud."

and scales, you must not eat them. Treat them as unclean.

[11]You can eat any clean bird. [12-18]But don't eat the meat of any of the following birds: eagles, vultures, falcons, kites, ravens, ostriches, owls, sea gulls, hawks, pelicans, ospreys, cormorants, storks, herons, and hoopoes.[f] You must not eat bats. [19]Swarming insects are unclean, so don't eat them. [20]However, you are allowed to eat certain kinds of winged insects.[g]

[21]You belong to the LORD your God, so if you happen to find a dead animal, don't eat its meat. You may give it to foreigners who live in your town or sell it to foreigners who are visiting your town.

Don't boil a young goat in its mother's milk.

Either God is in charge, or he is not. Either he loves us, or he does not. If he is in charge and loves us, then whatever is given is subject to his control and is meant ultimately for our joy.

ELISABETH ELLIOT

Give the LORD Ten Percent of Your Harvest

Moses said:

[22]People of Israel, every year you must set aside ten percent of your grain harvest. [23]Also set aside ten percent of your wine and olive oil, and the first-born of every cow, sheep, and goat. Take these to the place where the LORD chooses to be worshiped, and eat them there. This will teach you to always respect the LORD your God.

[24]But suppose you can't carry that ten percent of your harvest to the place where the LORD chooses to be worshiped. If you live too far away, or if the LORD gives you a big harvest, [25]then sell this part and take the money there instead. [26]When you and your family arrive, spend the money on food for a

big celebration. Buy cattle, sheep, goats, wine, beer, and if there are any other kinds of food that you want, buy those too. [27]And since people of the Levi tribe won't own any land for growing crops, remember to ask the Levites to celebrate with you.

[28]Every third year, instead of using the ten percent of your harvest for a big celebration, bring it into town and put it in a community storehouse. [29]The Levites have no land of their own, so you must give them food from the storehouse. You must also give food to the poor who live in your town, including orphans, widows, and foreigners. If they have enough to eat, then the LORD your God will be pleased and make you successful in everything you do.

Loans
(Leviticus 25.1-7)

Moses said:

15 [1-2]Every seven years you must announce, "The LORD says loans do not need to be paid back." Then if you have loaned money to another Israelite, you can no longer ask for payment.[h] [3]This law applies only to loans you have made to other Israelites. Foreigners will still have to pay back what you have loaned them.

[4-6]No one in Israel should ever be poor. The LORD your God is giving you this land, and he has promised to make you very successful, if you obey his laws and teachings that I'm giving you today. You will lend money to many nations, but you won't have to borrow. You will rule many nations, but they won't rule you.

[7]After the LORD your God gives land to each of you, there may be poor Israelites in the town where you live. If there are, then don't be mean and selfish with your money. [8]Instead, be kind and lend them what they need. [9]Be careful! Don't say to yourself, "Soon it will be the seventh year, and then I won't be able to get my money back." It

---

[f]**14.12-18** *eagles . . . hoopoes:* Some of the birds in this list are difficult to identify.   [g]**14.20** *certain kinds of winged insects:* These were locusts, crickets, and grasshoppers; see Leviticus 11.21, 22.   [h]**15.1,2** *The LORD says . . . no longer ask for payment:* Or " 'The LORD says loans do not need to be paid back this year.' Then if you have loaned money to another Israelite, you cannot ask for payment until the next year."

would be horrible for you to think that way and to be so selfish that you refuse to help the poor. They are your relatives, and if you don't help them, they may ask the LORD to decide whether you have done wrong. And he will say that you are guilty. ¹⁰You should be happy to give the poor what they need, because then the LORD will make you successful in everything you do.

Dear God,
Whose very nature is to love,
So fan the flames of our
relationship that it may be
a warm place where we live
to give each other room to
breathe and space to grow.

JILL BRISCOE

¹¹There will always be some Israelites who are poor and needy. That's why I am commanding you to be generous with them.

Setting Slaves Free
(Exodus 21.1-11)

Moses said to Israel:

¹²If any of you buy Israelites as slaves, you must set them free after six years. ¹³And don't just tell them they are free to leave—¹⁴give them sheep and goats and a good supply of grain and wine. The more the LORD has given you, the more you should give them. ¹⁵I am commanding you to obey the LORD as a reminder that you were slaves in Egypt before he set you free. ¹⁶But one of your slaves may say, "I love you and your family, and I would be better off staying with you, so please don't make me leave." ¹⁷Take the slave to the door of your house and push a sharp metal rod through one earlobe and into the door. Such slaves will belong to you for life, whether they are men or women.

¹⁸Don't complain when you have to set a slave free. After all, you got six years of service at half the cost of hiring someone to do the work.ⁱ

First-Born Animals
(Leviticus 27.26, 27; Numbers 18.15-18)

Moses said to Israel:

¹⁹If the first-born animal of a cow or sheep or goat is a male, it must be given to the LORD. Don't put first-born cattle to work or cut wool from first-born sheep. ²⁰Instead, each year you must take the first-born of these animals to the place where the LORD your God chooses to be worshiped. You and your family will sacrifice them to the LORD and then eat them as part of a sacred meal.

²¹But if the animal is lame or blind or has something else wrong with it, you must not sacrifice it to the LORD your God. ²²You can butcher it where you live, and eat it just like the meat of a deer or gazelle that you kill while hunting. Even those people who are unclean and unfit for worship can have some. ²³But you must never eat the blood of an animal—let it drain out on the ground.

Passover
(Exodus 12.1-20; Leviticus 23.4-8)

Moses said:

16 People of Israel, you must celebrate Passover in the month of Abib,ʲ because one night in that month years ago, the LORD your God rescued you from Egypt. ²The Passover sacrifice must be a cow, a sheep, or a goat, and you must offer it at the place where the LORD chooses to be worshiped. ³⁻⁴Eat all of the meat of the Passover sacrifice that same night. But don't serve bread made with yeast at the Passover meal. Serve the same kind of thin bread that you ate when you were slaves suffering in Egyptᵏ and when you had to leave Egypt quickly. As long as you live, this thin bread will remind you of the day you left Egypt.

For seven days following Passover,ˡ don't

ⁱ**15.18** *six years . . . work:* Or "six years of service, and it cost you no more than if you had hired someone to do the work"; or "six years of service, for what you would have had to pay a worker for two years." ʲ**16.1** *in the month of Abib:* Abib (also called Nisan), the first month of the Hebrew calendar, from about mid-March to mid-April. Passover was celebrated on the evening of the fourteenth of Abib (see Exodus 12.6; Leviticus 23.4, 5). ᵏ**16.3,4** *the same kind . . . in Egypt:* One possible meaning for the difficult Hebrew text. ˡ**16.3,4** *seven days following Passover:* This period was called the Festival of Thin Bread (see also verse 16).

make any bread with yeast. In fact, there should be no yeast anywhere in Israel.

[5]Don't offer the Passover sacrifice in just any town where you happen to live. [6]It must be offered at the place where the LORD chooses to be worshiped. Kill the sacrifice at sunset, the time of day when you left Egypt.[m] [7]Then cook it and eat it there at the place of worship, returning to your tents the next morning.

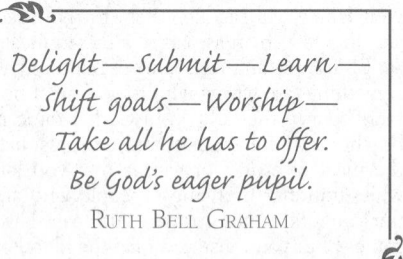

> *Delight—Submit—Learn—*
> *Shift goals—Worship—*
> *Take all he has to offer.*
> *Be God's eager pupil.*
> RUTH BELL GRAHAM

[8]Eat thin bread for the next six days. Then on the seventh day, don't do any work. Instead, come together and worship the LORD.

The Harvest Festival

(Exodus 34.22; Leviticus 23.15-21)

Moses said to Israel:

[9]Seven weeks after you start your grain harvest, [10-11]go to the place where the LORD chooses to be worshiped and celebrate the Harvest Festival[n] in honor of the LORD your God. Bring him an offering as large as you can afford, depending on how big a harvest he has given you. Be sure to take along your sons and daughters and all your servants. Also invite the poor, including Levites, foreigners, orphans, and widows. [12]Remember that you used to be slaves in Egypt, so obey these laws.

The Festival of Shelters

(Leviticus 23.33-43; Numbers 29.12-38)

Moses said to Israel:

[13-15]After you have finished the grain harvest and the grape harvest,[o] take your sons and daughters and all your servants to the place where the LORD chooses to be worshiped. Celebrate the Festival of Shelters for seven days. Also invite the poor, including Levites, foreigners, orphans, and widows.

The LORD will give you big harvests and make you successful in everything you do. You will be completely happy, so celebrate this festival in honor of the LORD your God.

Three Festivals at the Place of Worship

(Exodus 23.14-17)

Moses said:

[16]Each year there are three festivals when all Israelite men must go to the place where the LORD chooses to be worshiped. These are the Festival of Thin Bread, the Harvest Festival,[p] and the Festival of Shelters. And don't forget to take along a gift for the LORD. [17]The bigger the harvest the LORD gives you, the bigger your gift should be.

Treat Everyone with Justice

Moses said to Israel:

[18-19]After you are settled in the towns that you will receive from the LORD your God, the people in each town must appoint judges and other officers. Those of you that become judges must be completely fair when you make legal decisions, even if someone important is involved. Don't take bribes to give unfair decisions. Bribes keep people who are wise from seeing the truth and turn honest people into liars.[q]

[20]People of Israel, if you want to enjoy a long and successful life, make sure that everyone is treated with justice in the land the LORD is giving you.

Don't Set Up Sacred Poles or Stones

Moses said to Israel:

[21]When you build the altar for offering sacrifices to the LORD your God, don't set up a sacred pole[r] for the worship of the god-

---

[m]**16.6** *sunset, the time of day when you left Egypt*: Or "sunset on the same date as when you left Egypt." [n]**16.10,11** *Harvest Festival*: Traditionally called the "Festival of Weeks," and known in New Testament times as "Pentecost." [o]**16.13-15** *After you . . . harvest*: Leviticus 23.34 gives the exact date as the fifteenth day of the seventh month of the Hebrew calendar, which would be early in October. [p]**16.16** *Harvest Festival*: See the note at 16.10, 11. [q]**16.18,19** *turn . . . liars*: Or "keep innocent people from getting justice." [r]**16.21** *sacred pole*: See the note at 12.3.

dess Asherah. ²²And don't set up a sacred stone! The LORD hates these things.

Sacrifices That Have Something Wrong with Them

Moses said to Israel:

17 If an ox or a sheep has something wrong with it, don't offer it as a sacrifice to the LORD your God—he will be disgusted!

Put To Death People Who Worship Idols

Moses said to Israel:

²⁻³The LORD your God is giving you towns to live in. But later, a man or a woman in your town may start worshiping other gods, or even the sun, moon, or stars.^s I have warned you not to worship other gods, because whoever worships them is disobeying the LORD and breaking the agreement he made with you. ⁴So when you hear that someone in your town is committing this disgusting sin, you must carefully find out if that person really is guilty. ⁵⁻⁷But you will need two or three witnesses—one witness isn't enough to prove a person guilty.

Get rid of those who are guilty of such evil. Take them outside your town gates and have everyone stone them to death. But the witnesses must be the first to throw stones.

Difficult Cases

Moses said to Israel:

⁸⁻¹²It may be difficult to find out the truth in some legal cases in your town. You may not be able to decide if someone was killed accidentally or murdered. Or you may not be able to tell whether an injury or some property damage was done by accident or on purpose. If the case is too difficult, take it to the court at the place where the LORD your God chooses to be worshiped.

This court will be made up of one judge and several priests^t who serve at the LORD's altar. They will explain the law to you and give you their decision about the case. Do exactly what they tell you, or you will be put to death. ¹³When other Israelites hear about it, they will be afraid and obey the decisions of the court.

The King

Moses said:

¹⁴People of Israel, after you capture the land the LORD your God is giving you, and after you settle on it, you will say, "We want a king, just like the nations around us."

¹⁵Go ahead and appoint a king, but make sure that he is an Israelite and that he is the one the LORD has chosen.

¹⁶The king should not have many horses, especially those from Egypt. The LORD has said never to go back there again. ¹⁷And the king must not have a lot of wives—they might tempt him to be unfaithful to the LORD.^u Finally, the king must not try to get huge amounts of silver and gold.

¹⁸The official copy of God's laws^v will be kept by the priests of the Levi tribe. So, as soon as anyone becomes king, he must go to the priests and write out a copy of these laws while they watch. ¹⁹Each day the king must read and obey these laws, so that he will learn to worship the LORD with fear and trembling ²⁰and not think that he's better than everyone else.

If the king completely obeys the LORD's commands, he and his descendants will rule Israel for many years.

Special Privileges for Priests and Levites
(Numbers 18.8-32)

Moses said to Israel:

18 The people of the Levi tribe, including the priests, will not receive any land. Instead, they will receive part of the sacrifices that are offered to the LORD, ²because he has promised to provide for them in this way.

³When you sacrifice a bull or sheep, the priests will be given the shoulder, the jaws, and the stomach.^w ⁴In addition, they will receive the first part of your grain harvest and part of your first batches of wine and olive

---

^s**17.2,3** *sun, moon, or stars:* Some people thought these were gods and worshiped them. ^t**17.8-12** *several priests:* The Hebrew text has "the priests, the Levites"; priests belonged to the Levi tribe. ^u**17.17** *a lot of wives . . . unfaithful to the LORD:* A king would often marry the daughter of another king that he was making a treaty with. These foreign women would naturally want to worship their own gods, and would want their husband the king to do so as well. ^v**17.18** *God's laws:* Or "God's laws for the king." ^w**18.3** *stomach:* Certain portions of the stomach were considered a delicacy.

oil.[x] You must also give them the first wool that is cut from your sheep each year. [5]Give these gifts to the priests, because the LORD has chosen them and their descendants out of all the tribes of Israel to be his special servants at the place of worship.

[6]Any Levite can leave his hometown, and go to the place where the LORD chooses to be worshiped, [7]and then be a special servant of the LORD[y] there, just like all the other Levites. [8]Some Levites may have money from selling family possessions, and others may not. But all Levites serving at the place of worship will receive the same amount of food from the sacrifices and gifts brought by the people.

Don't Do Disgusting Things

Moses said to Israel:

[9]Soon you will go into the land that the LORD your God is giving you. The nations that live there do things that are disgusting to the LORD, and you must not follow their example. [10-11]Don't sacrifice your son or daughter. And don't try to use any kind of magic or witchcraft to tell fortunes[z] or to cast spells or to talk with spirits of the dead. [12]The LORD is disgusted with anyone who does these things, and that's why he will help you destroy the nations that are in the land. [13]Never be guilty of doing any of these disgusting things!

A Prophet like Moses

Moses said to Israel:

[14]You will go in and take the land from nations that practice magic and witchcraft. But the LORD your God won't allow you to do those things. [15]Instead, he will choose one of your own people to be a prophet just like me, and you must do what that prophet says. [16]You were asking for a prophet the day you were gathered at Mount Sinai[a] and said to the LORD, "Please don't let us hear your voice or see this terrible fire again—if we do, we will die!"

[17]Then the LORD told me:

Moses, they have said the right thing. [18]So when I want to speak to them, I will choose one of them to be a prophet like you. I will give my message to that prophet, who will tell the people exactly what I have said.

[19]Since the message comes from me, anyone who doesn't obey the message will have to answer to me.

[20]But if I haven't spoken, and a prophet claims to have a message from me, you must kill that prophet, and you must also kill any prophet who claims to have a message from another god.

Moses said to Israel:

[21]You may be asking yourselves, "How can we tell if a prophet's message really comes from the LORD?" [22]You will know, because if the LORD says something will happen, it will happen. And if it doesn't, you will know that the prophet was falsely claiming to speak for the LORD. Don't be afraid of any prophet whose message doesn't come from the LORD.

Safe Towns
(Numbers 35.9-28; Joshua 20.1-9)

Moses said to Israel:

19 Soon you will go into the land and attack the nations. The LORD your God will destroy them and give you their lands, towns, and homes. Then after you are settled, [2-4]you must choose three of your towns to be Safe Towns. Divide the land into three regions with one Safe Town near the middle of each, so that a Safe Town can be easily reached from anywhere in your land.

Then, if one of you accidentally kills someone, you can run to a Safe Town and find protection from being put to death. But you must not have been angry with the person you killed.

[5]For example, suppose you and a friend go into the forest to cut wood. You are chopping down a tree with an ax, when the ax head slips off the handle, hits your friend, and kills him. You can run to one of the Safe Towns and save your life. [6]You don't deserve

---

[x]**18.4** *grain . . . olive oil:* An Israelite was supposed to offer the first part of the harvest as a gift to the LORD (see Leviticus 23.10, 11). [y]**18.7** *a special servant of the LORD:* Or "one of the LORD's priests." [z]**18.10,11** *tell fortunes:* Fortunetellers thought they could learn secrets or learn about the future by watching the flight of birds or looking at the livers of animals or in many other ways. [a]**18.16** *Mount Sinai:* See the note at 1.1-5.

to die, since you did not mean to harm your friend. But he did get killed, and his relatives might be very angry. They might even choose one of the men from their family to track you down and kill you. If it is too far to one of the Safe Towns, the victim's relative might be able to catch you and kill you. ⁷That's why I said there must be three Safe Towns.

⁸⁻⁹Israel, the LORD your God has promised that if you obey his laws and teachings I'm giving you, and if you always love him, then he will give you the land he promised your ancestors. When that happens, you must name three more Safe Towns in the new territory. ¹⁰You will need them, so innocent people won't be killed on your land while they are trying to reach a Safe Town that is too far away. You will be guilty of murder, if innocent people lose their lives because you didn't name enough Safe Towns in the land the LORD your God will give you.

> *Comforting a friend may not mean drying her tears but giving her the freedom to let her tears flow.*
>
> VICKI HUFFMAN

¹¹But what if you really do commit murder? Suppose one of you hates a neighbor. So you wait in a deserted place, kill the neighbor, and run to a Safe Town. ¹²If that happens, the leaders of your town must send messengers to bring you back from the Safe Town. They will hand you over to one of the victim's relatives, who will put you to death. ¹³Israel, for the good of the whole country, you must kill anyone who murders an innocent person. Never show mercy to a murderer!

Property Lines

Moses said to Israel:

¹⁴In the land the LORD is giving you, there are already stones set up to mark the property lines between fields. So don't move those stones.

Witnesses Must Tell the Truth

Moses said to Israel:

¹⁵Before you are convicted of a crime, at least two witnesses must be able to testify that you did it.

¹⁶If you accuse someone of a crime, but seem to be lying, ¹⁷⁻¹⁸then both you and the accused must be taken to the court at the place where the LORD is worshiped. There the priests and judges will find out if you are lying or telling the truth.

If you are lying and the accused is innocent, ¹⁹⁻²¹then you will be punished without mercy. You will receive the same punishment the accused would have received if found guilty, whether it means losing an eye, a tooth, a hand, a foot, or even your life.

Israel, the crime of telling lies in court must be punished. And when people hear what happens to witnesses that lie, everyone else who testifies in court will tell the truth.

Laws for Going to War

Moses said to Israel:

20 If you have to go to war, you may find yourselves facing an enemy army that is bigger than yours and that has horses and chariots. But don't be afraid! The LORD your God rescued you from Egypt, and he will help you fight. ²Before you march into battle, a priest will go to the front of the army ³and say, "Soldiers of Israel, listen to me! Today when you go into battle, don't be afraid of the enemy, and when you see them, don't panic. ⁴The LORD your God will fight alongside you and help you win the battle."

⁵Then the tribal officials will say to the troops:

If any of you have built a new house, but haven't yet moved in, you may go home. It isn't right for you to die in battle and for somebody else to live in your new house.

⁶If any of you have planted a vineyard but haven't had your first grape harvest, you may go home. It isn't right for you to die in battle and for somebody else to enjoy your grapes.

⁷If any of you are engaged to be married, you may go back home and get married. It isn't right for you to die in battle and for somebody else to marry the woman you are engaged to.

⁸Finally, if any of you are afraid, you may go home. We don't want you to discourage the other soldiers.

⁹When the officials are finished giving these orders, they will appoint officers to be in command of the army.

¹⁰⁻¹⁵Before you attack a town that is far from your land, offer peace to the people who live there. If they surrender and open their town gates, they will become your slaves. But if they reject your offer of peace and try to fight, surround their town and attack. Then, after the LORD helps you capture it, kill all the men. Take the women and children as slaves and keep the livestock and everything else of value.

¹⁶Whenever you capture towns in the land the LORD your God is giving you, be sure to kill all the people and animals. ¹⁷He has commanded you to completely wipe out the Hittites, the Amorites, the Canaanites, the Perizzites, the Hivites, and the Jebusites. ¹⁸If you allow them to live, they will persuade you to worship their disgusting gods, and you will be unfaithful to the LORD.

¹⁹When you are attacking a town, don't chop down its fruit trees, not even if you have had the town surrounded for a long time. Fruit trees aren't your enemies, and they produce food that you can eat, so don't cut them down. ²⁰You may need wood to make ladders and towers to help you get over the walls and capture the town. But use only trees that you know are not fruit trees.

Unsolved Murder

Moses said to Israel:

21 Suppose the body of a murder victim is found in a field in the land the LORD your God is giving you, and no one knows who the murderer is. ²The judges and other leaders from the towns around there must find out what town is the closest to where the body was found. ³The leaders from that town will go to their cattle herds and choose a young cow that has never been put to work.*ᵇ* ⁴⁻⁵They and some of the priests will take this cow to

a nearby valley where there is a stream, but no crops. Once they reach the valley, the leaders will break the cow's neck.

The priests must be there, because the LORD your God has chosen them to be his special servants at the place of worship. The LORD has chosen them to bless the people in his name and to be judges in all legal cases, whether property or injury is involved. ⁶The town leaders will wash their hands over the body of the dead cow ⁷and say, "We had no part in this murder, and we don't know who did it. ⁸⁻⁹But since an innocent person was murdered, we beg you, our LORD, to accept this sacrifice and forgive Israel. We are your people, and you rescued us. Please don't hold this crime against us."

If you obey the LORD and do these things, he will forgive Israel.

Marrying a Woman Taken Prisoner in War

Moses said to Israel:

¹⁰From time to time, you men will serve as soldiers and go off to war. The LORD your God will help you defeat your enemies, and you will take many prisoners. ¹¹⁻¹³One of these prisoners may be a beautiful woman, and you may want to marry her. But first you must bring her into your home, and have her shave her head, cut her nails, get rid of her foreign clothes, and start wearing Israelite clothes. She will mourn a month for her father and mother, then you can marry her.

¹⁴Later on, if you are not happy with the woman, you can divorce her, and she can go free. But you have slept with her as your wife, so you cannot sell her as a slave or make her into your own slave.

Rights of a First-Born Son

Moses said to Israel:

¹⁵⁻¹⁷Suppose a man has two wives and loves one more than the other. The first son of either wife is the man's first-born son, even if the boy's mother is the wife the man doesn't love. Later, when the man is near death and is dividing up his property, he

---

*ᵇ***21.3** *young cow . . . work*: Cows and oxen pulled plows and wagons.

must give a double share to his first-born son, simply because he was the first to be born.

A Son Who Rebels

Moses said to Israel:

[18]A father and a mother may have a stubborn and rebellious son who refuses to obey them even after he has been punished. [19]If a son is like that, his parents must drag him to the town gate, where the leaders of the town hold their meetings. [20]The parents will tell the leaders, "This son of ours is stubborn and never obeys. He spends all his time drinking and partying."

[21]The men of the town will stone that son to death, because they must get rid of the evil he brought into the community. Everyone in Israel will be afraid when they hear how he was punished.

The Body of a Criminal

Moses said to Israel:

[22]If a criminal is put to death, and you hang the dead body on a tree, [23]you must not let it hang there overnight. Bury it the same day, because the dead body of a criminal will bring God's curse on the land. The LORD your God is giving this land to you, so don't make it unclean by leaving the bodies of executed criminals on display.

Helping Others

Moses said to Israel:

22 If you see a cow or sheep wandering around lost, take the animal back to its owner. [2]If the owner lives too far away, or if you don't know who the owner is, take the animal home with you and take care of it. The owner will come looking for the animal, and then you can give it back. [3]That's what you should do if you find anything that belongs to someone else. Do whatever you can to help, whether you find a cow or sheep or donkey or some clothing.

[4]Oxen and donkeys that carry heavy loads can stumble and fall, and be unable to get up by themselves. So as you walk along the road, help anyone who is trying to get an ox or donkey back on its feet.

Don't Pretend To Be the Opposite Sex

Moses said to Israel:

[5]Women must not pretend to be men, and men must not pretend to be women.[c] The LORD your God is disgusted with people who do that.

Don't Take a Mother Bird

Moses said to Israel:

[6-7]As you walk along the road, you might see a bird's nest in a tree or on the ground. If the mother bird is in the nest with either her eggs or her baby birds, you are allowed to take the baby birds or the eggs, but not the mother bird. Let her go free, and the LORD will bless you with a long and successful life.

Put a Wall around Your Flat Roof

[8]If you build a house, make sure to put a low wall around the edge of the flat roof.[d] Then if someone falls off the roof and is killed, it won't be your fault.

Laws against Mixing Different Things

Moses said to Israel:

[9]If you plant a vineyard, don't plant any other fruit tree or crop in it. If you do plant something else there, you must bring to the place of worship everything you harvest from the vineyard.

[10]Don't hitch an ox and a donkey to your plow at the same time.

[11]When you weave cloth for clothing, you can use thread made of flax[e] or wool, but not both together. [12]And when you make a coat, sew a tassel on each of the four corners.

When a Husband Accuses His Wife

Moses said to Israel:

[13]Suppose a man starts hating his wife soon after they are married. [14]He might tell

---

[c]22.5 *pretend to be men . . . pretend to be women:* Or "wear men's clothing . . . wear women's clothing."
[d]22.8 *flat roof:* Houses usually had flat roofs. In hot dry weather, it was cooler on the roof than in the house, and so roofs were used for sleeping and living quarters, and for entertaining guests. [e]22.11 *flax:* The stalks of flax plants were harvested, soaked in water, and dried, then their fibers were separated and spun into thread, which was woven into linen cloth.

ugly lies about her, and say, "I married this woman, but when we slept together, I found out she wasn't a virgin."

¹⁵If this happens, the bride's father and mother must go to the town gate to show the town leaders the proof that the woman was a virgin. ¹⁶Her father will say, "I let my daughter marry this man, but he started hating her ¹⁷and accusing her of not being a virgin. But he is wrong, because here is proof that she was a virgin!" Then the bride's parents will show them the bed sheet from the woman's wedding night.

¹⁸The town leaders will beat the man with a whip ¹⁹because he accused his bride of not being a virgin. He will have to pay her father one hundred pieces of silver and will never be allowed to divorce her.

²⁰But if the man was right and there is no proof that his bride was a virgin, ²¹the men of the town will take the woman to the door of her father's house and stone her to death. This woman brought evil into your community by sleeping with someone before she got married, and you must get rid of that evil by killing her.

Laws about Illegal Sex

Moses said:

²²People of Israel, if a man is caught having sex with someone else's wife, you must put them both to death. That way, you will get rid of the evil they have done in Israel.

²³⁻²⁴If a man is caught in town having sex with an engaged woman who isn't screaming for help, they both must be put to death. The man is guilty of having sex with a married woman.ʲ And the woman is guilty because she didn't call for help, even though she was inside a town and people were nearby. Take them both to the town gate and stone them to death. You must get rid of the evil they brought into your community.

²⁵If an engaged woman is raped out in the country, only the man will be put to death. ²⁶Do not punish the woman at all; she has done nothing wrong, and certainly nothing deserving death. This crime is like murder, ²⁷because the woman was alone out in the country when the man attacked her. She screamed, but there was no one to help her.

²⁸Suppose a woman isn't engaged to be married, and a man talks her into sleeping with him. If they are caught, ²⁹they will be forced to get married. He must give her father fifty pieces of silver as a bride-price andᵍ can never divorce her.

³⁰A man must not marry a woman who was married to his father. This would be a disgrace to his father.

Who Cannot Become One of the LORD's People

Moses said to Israel:

23 If a man's private parts have been crushed or cut off,ʰ he cannot fully belong to the LORD's people. ²No one born outside of a legal marriage, or any of their descendants for ten generations, can fully belong to the LORD's people.

³No Ammonites or Moabites, or any of their descendants for ten generations, can become part of Israel, the LORD's people. ⁴This is because when you came out of Egypt, they refused to provide you with food and water. And besides, they hired Balaamⁱ to put a curse on you. ⁵But the LORD your God loves you, so he refused to listen to Balaam and turned Balaam's curse into a blessing. ⁶Don't even think of signing a peace treaty with Moab or Ammon.

⁷But Edomites are your relatives, and you lived as foreigners in the country of Egypt. Now you must be kind to Edomites and Egyptians ⁸and let their great-grandchildren become part of Israel, the LORD's people.

Keep the Army Camp Acceptable

Moses said to Israel:

⁹When you men go off to fight your enemies, make sure your camp is acceptable to the LORD. ¹⁰For example, if something happens at night that makes a man unclean and unfit for worship, heʲ must go outside the camp

---

ʲ**22.23,24** *engaged woman . . . married woman:* An engaged woman was legally married, but had not yet slept with her husband or started living with him. ᵍ**22.28,29** *talks her into sleeping with him . . . bride-price and:* Or "forces her to have sex. ²⁹Then if they are caught, he will have to marry her. He must give her father fifty pieces of silver as a bride-price and." ʰ**23.1** *a man's private parts have been crushed or cut off:* This was sometimes done to show devotion to pagan gods. ⁱ**23.4** *Balaam:* Hebrew "Balaam son of Beor from Pethor." ʲ**23.10** *if something . . . worship, he:* Or "if a man has a flow of semen at night, he is unclean and unfit for worship, and he."

and stay there [11]until late afternoon. Then he must take a bath, and at sunset he can go back into camp.

[12]Set up a place outside the camp to be used as a toilet area. [13]And make sure that you have a small shovel in your equipment. When you go out to the toilet area, use the shovel to dig a hole. Then, after you relieve yourself, bury the waste in the hole. [14]You must keep your camp clean of filthy and disgusting things. The LORD is always present in your camp, ready to rescue you and give you victory over your enemies. But if he sees something disgusting in your camp, he may turn around and leave.

I'm convinced God's character is always loving and good, even when circumstances appear otherwise.

VIRELLE KIDDER

Runaway Slaves from Other Countries

Moses said:

[15]When runaway slaves from other countries come to Israel and ask for protection, you must not hand them back to their owners. [16]Instead, you must let them choose which one of your towns they want to live in. Don't be cruel to runaway slaves.

Temple Prostitutes

Moses said:

[17]People of Israel, don't any of you ever be temple prostitutes.[k] [18]The LORD your God is disgusted with men and women who are prostitutes of any kind, and he will not accept a gift from them, even if it had been promised to him.

Interest on Loans

Moses said:

[19]When you lend money, food, or anything else to another Israelite, you are not allowed to charge interest. [20]You can charge a foreigner interest. But if you charge other Israelites interest, the LORD your God will not let you be successful in the land you are about to take.

Sacred Promises to the LORD

Moses said:

[21]People of Israel, if you make a sacred promise to give a gift to the LORD, then do it as soon as you can. If the LORD has to come looking for the gift you promised, you will be guilty of breaking that promise. [22]On the other hand, if you never make a sacred promise, you can't be guilty of breaking it. [23]You must keep whatever promises you make to the LORD. After all, you are the one who chose to make the promises.

Eating Someone Else's Produce

[24]If you go into a vineyard that belongs to someone else, you are allowed to eat as many grapes as you want while you are there. But don't take any with you when you leave. [25]In the same way, if you are in a grain field that belongs to someone else, you can pick heads of grain and eat the kernels. But don't cut down the stalks of grain and take them with you.

A Law about Divorce

Moses said to Israel:

24 Suppose a woman was divorced by her first husband because he found something disgraceful about her.[l] He wrote out divorce papers, gave them to her, and sent her away. [2]Later she married another man, [3]who then either divorced her in the same way or died. [4]Since she has slept with her second husband, she cannot marry her first husband again. Their marriage would pollute the land that the LORD your God is giving you, and he would be disgusted.

---

[k]23.17 *temple prostitutes*: Some Canaanites worshiped by going to their temples and having sex with prostitutes that represented their gods.   [l]24.1 *something disgraceful about her*: One possible meaning for the difficult Hebrew text.

Newlyweds

Moses said to Israel:

⁵If a man and a woman have been married less than one year, he must not be sent off to war or sent away to do forced labor. He must be allowed to stay home for a year and be happy with his wife.

Loans

Moses said to Israel:

⁶When you lend money to people, you are allowed to keep something of theirs as a guarantee that they will pay back the loan. But don't take one or both of their millstones, or else they may starve. They need these stones for grinding grain into flour to make bread.

Kidnapping

Moses said to Israel:

⁷If you are guilty of kidnapping Israelites and forcing them into slavery, you will be put to death to remove this evil from the community.

Skin Diseases

Moses said to Israel:

⁸I have told the priests^m what to do if any of you have leprosy,^n so do exactly what they say. ⁹And remember what the LORD your God did to Miriam° after you left Egypt.

Loans

Moses said to Israel:

¹⁰When you lend money to people, you are allowed to keep something of theirs as a guarantee that the money will be paid back. But you must not go into their house to get it. ¹¹Wait outside, and they will bring out the item you have agreed on.

¹²Suppose someone is so poor that a coat is the only thing that can be offered as a guarantee on a loan. Don't keep the coat overnight. ¹³Instead, give it back before sunset, so the owner can keep warm and sleep and ask the LORD to bless you. Then the

---

^m24.8 *the priests:* See the note at 17.8-12.
^n24.8 *leprosy:* The word "leprosy" was used for many different kinds of skin diseases. °24.9 *what the LORD your God did to Miriam:* See Numbers 12.1-16.

Personal *Concerns*—When it comes to material things, how can I know what's enough and what's too much? *(Deuteronomy 24.19-22)*

Realize God gives us plenty so we can share with others.

One of God's promises to his people was the blessing of good crops. When Israel obeyed him, God sent rain and sunshine on the fields and protected the wheat from destruction. Good harvests were a gift from God to those he loved.

But the recipients of these blessings were not to keep all the grain for themselves. God gave them specific rules about harvesting. When farmers brought wheat in from the fields, they were to leave plenty out there for the poor to pick up and eat. After all, orphans and widows didn't have fields. In the same way, growers of olives and grapes were to leave some fruit on the vines so those with no source of food could pick and eat them.

Today, God still often chooses to meet the needs of the poor indirectly. Instead of providing directly to those who are hungry, he may give extra to us, so we can take from our abundance and share with them.

Has God blessed you with material things? Take the opportunity to give food, clothing, and other possessions to those who have less. (See also Leviticus 25.8-28; Amos 6.1-7; Philippians 3.7-16; 1 Timothy 6.17-19.)

Words To Remember: *If you forget to bring in a stack of harvested grain, don't go back in the field to get it. Leave it for the poor, including foreigners, orphans, and widows, and the LORD will make you successful in everything you do.*
—Deuteronomy 24.19

LORD your God will notice that you have done the right thing.

Poor People's Wages

Moses said:

[14]If you hire poor people to work for you, don't hold back their pay,[p] whether they are Israelites or foreigners who live in your town. [15]Pay them their wages at the end of each day, because they live in poverty and need the money to survive. If you don't pay them on time, they will complain about you to the LORD, and he will punish you.

The Death Penalty

Moses said to Israel:

[16]Parents must not be put to death for crimes committed by their children, and children must not be put to death for crimes committed by their parents. Don't put anyone to death for someone else's crime.

Don't Mistreat the Powerless

Moses said to Israel:

[17]Make sure that orphans and foreigners are treated fairly. And if you lend money to a widow and want to keep something of hers to guarantee that she will pay you back, don't take any of her clothes. [18]You were slaves in Egypt until the LORD your God rescued you. That's why I am giving you these laws.

Leave Some of Your Harvest for the Poor

Moses said to Israel:

[19]If you forget to bring in a stack of harvested grain, don't go back in the field to get it. Leave it for the poor, including foreigners, orphans, and widows, and the LORD will make you successful in everything you do. [20]When you harvest your olives, don't try to get them all for yourself, but leave some for the poor. [21]And when you pick your grapes, go over the vines only once, then let the poor have what is left. [22]You lived in poverty as slaves in Egypt until the LORD your God rescued you. That's why I am giving you these laws.

Whipping as Punishment for a Crime

Moses said to Israel:

25 [1-2]Suppose you and someone else each accuse the other of doing something wrong, and you go to court, where the judges decide you are guilty. If your punishment is to be beaten with a whip,[q] one of the judges will order you to lie down, and you will receive the number of lashes you deserve. [3]Forty lashes is the most that you can be given, because more than that might make other Israelites think you are worthless.

Don't Muzzle an Ox

Moses said to Israel:

[4]Don't muzzle an ox while it is threshing grain.[r]

A Son for a Dead Brother

Moses said to Israel:

[5-6]Suppose two brothers are living on the same property, when one of them dies without having a son to carry on his name. If this happens, his widow must not marry anyone outside the family. Instead, she must marry her late husband's brother, and their first son will be the legal son of the dead man. [7]But suppose the brother refuses to marry the widow. She must go to a meeting of the town leaders at the town gate and say, "My husband died without having a son to carry on his name. And my husband's brother refuses to marry me so I can have a son." [8]The leaders will call the living brother to the town gate and try to persuade him to marry the widow. But if he doesn't change his mind and marry her, [9]she must go over to him while the town leaders watch. She will pull off one of his sandals and spit in his face, while saying, "That's what happens to a man who won't help provide descendants for his dead brother." [10]From then on, that man's family will be known as "the family of the man whose sandal was pulled off."

---

p**24.14** *don't hold back their pay:* The Dead Sea Scrolls; the Standard Hebrew Text "treat them right." q**25.1,2** *whip:* Or "rod." r**25.4** *threshing grain:* Oxen were used at the threshing place to walk on heads of grain, or pull heavy slabs of wood over it, to separate the kernels from the husks.

When Two Men Fight

Moses said to Israel:

[11]If two men are fighting, and the wife of one man tries to rescue her husband by grabbing the other man's private parts, [12]you must cut off her hand. Don't have any mercy.

Be Honest in Business

Moses said to Israel:

[13-14]Don't try to cheat people by having two sets of weights or measures, one to get more when you are buying, and the other to give less when you are selling. [15]If you weigh and measure things honestly, the LORD your God will let you enjoy a long life in the land he is giving you. [16]But the LORD is disgusted with anyone who cheats or is dishonest.

Wipe Out Amalek

Moses said:

[17]People of Israel, do you remember what the Amalekites did to you after you came out of Egypt? [18]You were tired, and they followed along behind, attacking those who could not keep up with the others. This showed that the Amalekites have no respect for God.
[19]The LORD your God will help you capture the land, and he will give you peace. But when that day comes, you must wipe out Amalek so completely that no one will remember they ever lived.

Give the LORD the First Part of Your Harvest

Moses said to Israel:

26 The LORD is giving you the land, and soon you will conquer it, settle down, [2]and plant crops. And when you begin harvesting each of your crops, the very first things you pick must be put in a basket. Take them to the place where the LORD your God chooses to be worshiped, [3]and tell the priest, "Long ago the LORD our God promised our ancestors that he would give us this land. And today, I thank him for keeping his promise and giving me a share of the land."
[4]The priest will take the basket and set it in front of the LORD's altar. [5]Then, standing there in front of the place of worship, you must pray:

My ancestor was homeless,
an Aramean who went to live
     in Egypt.
There were only a few
     in his family then,
but they became great
and powerful,
     a nation of many people.

[6]The Egyptians were cruel
     and had no pity on us.
They mistreated our people
     and forced us into slavery.
[7]We called out for help
to you, the LORD God
     of our ancestors.
You heard our cries;
you knew we were in trouble
     and abused.
[8]Then you terrified the Egyptians
with your mighty miracles
     and rescued us from Egypt.
[9]You brought us here
and gave us this land
     rich with milk and honey.
[10]Now, LORD, I bring to you
the best of the crops
     that you have given me.

Give to God your time, thought, and commitment. And then you will find peace, joy, and fulfillment far beyond your dreams.

MRS. NORMAN VINCENT PEALE

After you say these things, place the basket in front of the LORD's altar and bow down to worship him.
[11]Then you and your family must celebrate by eating a meal at the place of worship to thank the LORD your God for giving you such a good harvest. And remember to invite the Levites and the foreigners who live in your town.

Ten Percent of the Harvest

Moses said to Israel:

[12]Every year you are to give ten percent of your harvest to the LORD.[s] But every third year,[t] this ten percent must be given to the poor who live in your town, including Levites, foreigners, orphans, and widows. That way, they will have enough to eat. [13]Then you must pray:

Our LORD and our God, you have said that ten percent of my harvest is sacred. I have obeyed your command and given this to the poor, including the Levites, foreigners, orphans, and widows. [14]I have not eaten any of this sacred food while I was in mourning; in fact, I never touched it when I was unclean.[u] And none of it has been offered as a sacrifice to the spirits of the dead. I have done everything exactly as you commanded.

[15]Our LORD, look down from your temple in heaven and bless your people Israel. You promised our ancestors that you would give us this land rich with milk and honey, and you have kept your promise.

The LORD Is Your God, and You Are His People

Moses said to Israel:

[16]Today the LORD your God has commanded you to obey these laws and teachings with all your heart and soul.

[17]In response, you have agreed that the LORD will be your God, that you will obey all his laws and teachings, and that you will listen when he speaks to you.

[18]Since you have agreed to obey the LORD, he has agreed that you will be his people and that you will belong to him, just as he promised. [19]The LORD created all nations, but he will make you more famous than any of them, and you will receive more praise and honor. You will belong only to the LORD your God, just as he promised.

Build an Altar on Mount Ebal

27 Moses stood together with the leaders and told the people of Israel:

Obey all the laws and teachings that I am giving you today. [2-4]Soon you will enter the land that the LORD your God is giving to you. He is the God your ancestors worshiped, and he has promised that this land is rich with milk and honey.

After you cross the Jordan River, go to Mount Ebal. Set up large slabs of stone, then cover them with white plaster and write on them a copy of these laws.

[5]At this same place, build an altar for offering sacrifices to the LORD your God. But don't use stones that have been cut with iron tools. [6]Look for stones that can be used without being cut. Then offer sacrifices to please the LORD,[v] burning them completely on the altar. [7]Next, offer sacrifices to ask the LORD's blessing,[w] and serve the meat at a sacred meal where you will celebrate in honor of the LORD.

[8]Don't forget to write out a copy of these laws on the stone slabs that you are going to set up. Make sure that the writing is easy to read.

Curses on Those Who Disobey

[9]Moses stood together with the priests[x] and said, "Israel, be quiet and listen to me! Today you have become the people of the LORD your God.[y] [10]So you must obey his laws and teachings that I am giving you."

[11]That same day, Moses gave them the following instructions:

[12-13]After you cross the Jordan River, you will go to Mount Gerizim and Mount Ebal.[z] The tribes of Simeon, Levi, Judah, Issachar, Ephraim, Manasseh,[a] and Benjamin will go

---

[s]**26.12** *Every year . . . LORD:* See 14.22-29.
[t]**26.12** *every third year:* Probably the third and sixth years of the seven-year cycle described in 15.1-11 and Leviticus 25.1-7.   [u]**26.14** *in mourning . . . unclean:* Touching a dead body made a person unclean and unfit to worship God. Ten percent of the harvest belonged to God, and was not to be touched by an unclean person.
[v]**27.6** *sacrifices to please the LORD:* See the note at 12.5-19.   [w]**27.7** *sacrifices to ask the LORD's blessing:* These sacrifices have traditionally been called "peace offerings" or "offerings of well-being." A main purpose was to ask for the LORD's blessing, and so in the CEV they are sometimes called "sacrifices to ask the LORD's blessing."   [x]**27.9** *priests:* See the note at 17.8-12.
[y]**27.9** *Today you have become the people of the LORD your God:* As a result of the agreement that the LORD had made with them, recorded in 26.16-19.
[z]**27.12,13** *Mount Gerizim and Mount Ebal:* These mountains were separated by a valley.
[a]**27.12,13** *Ephraim, Manasseh:* The Hebrew text has "Joseph"; the descendants of Joseph formed the two tribes of Ephraim and Manasseh.

up on Mount Gerizim, where they will bless the people of Israel. The tribes of Reuben, Gad, Asher, Zebulun, Dan, and Naphtali will go up on Mount Ebal where they will agree to the curses.

14-26The people of the Levi tribe will speak each curse in a loud voice, then the rest of the people[b] will agree to that curse by saying, "Amen!" Here are the curses:

We ask the LORD to put a curse on anyone who makes an idol or worships idols, even secretly. The LORD is disgusted with idols.

We ask the LORD to put a curse on all who do not show respect for their father and mother.

We ask the LORD to put a curse on anyone who moves the rocks that mark property lines.

We ask the LORD to put a curse on anyone who tells blind people to go the wrong way.

We ask the LORD to put a curse on anyone who keeps the poor from getting justice, whether these poor are foreigners, widows, or orphans.

We ask the LORD to put a curse on any man who sleeps with his father's wife; that man has shown no respect for his father's marriage.

We ask the LORD to put a curse on anyone who has sex with an animal.

We ask the LORD to put a curse on any man who sleeps with his sister or his half sister or his mother-in-law.

We ask the LORD to put a curse on anyone who commits murder, even when there are no witnesses to the crime.

We ask the LORD to put a curse on anyone who accepts money to murder an innocent victim.

We ask the LORD to put a curse on anyone who refuses to obey his laws.

And so, to each of these curses, the people will answer, "Amen!"

The LORD Will Bless You if You Obey

Moses said to Israel:

28 1-2Today I am giving you the laws and teachings of the LORD your God. Always obey them, and the LORD will make Israel the most famous and important nation on earth, and he will bless you in many ways.

3The LORD will make your businesses and your farms successful.

4You will have many children. You will harvest large crops, and your herds of cattle and flocks of sheep and goats will produce many young.

5You will have plenty of bread[c] to eat.

6The LORD will make you successful in your daily work.

7The LORD will help you defeat your enemies and make them scatter in all directions.

8The LORD your God is giving you the land, and he will make sure you are successful in everything you do. Your harvests will be so large that your storehouses will be full.

9If you follow and obey the LORD, he will make you his own special people, just as he promised. 10Then everyone on earth will know that you belong to the LORD, and they will be afraid of you.

11The LORD will give you a lot of children and make sure that your animals give birth to many young. The LORD promised your ancestors that this land would be yours, and he will make it produce large crops for you.

12The LORD will open the storehouses of the skies where he keeps the rain, and he will send rain on your land at just the right times. He will make you successful in everything you do. You will have plenty of money to lend to other nations, but you won't need to borrow any yourself.

13Obey the laws and teachings that I'm giving you today, and the LORD your God will make Israel a leader among the nations, and not a follower. Israel will be wealthy and powerful, not poor and weak. 14But you must not reject any of his laws and teachings or worship other gods.

The LORD Will Put Curses on You if You Disobey
(*Leviticus 26.14-46*)

Moses said:

15Israel, today I am giving you the laws and teachings of the LORD your God. And if you don't obey them all, he will put many curses on you.

16Your businesses and farms will fail.

---

[b]**27.14-26** *the rest of the people:* Or "all the people who are standing on Mount Ebal." [c]**28.5** *bread:* The main food of the Israelites.

¹⁷You won't have enough bread^c to eat.
¹⁸You'll have only a few children, your crops will be small, and your herds of cattle and flocks of sheep and goats won't produce many young.
¹⁹The LORD will make you fail in everything you do.
²⁰No matter what you try to accomplish, the LORD will confuse you, and you will feel his anger. You won't last long, and you may even meet with disaster, all because you rejected the LORD.
²¹⁻²³The LORD will send terrible diseases to attack you, and you will never be well again. You will suffer with burning fever and swelling and pain until you die somewhere in the land that you captured.

The LORD will make the sky overhead seem like a bronze roof that keeps out the rain, and the ground under your feet will become as hard as iron. Your crops will be scorched by the hot east wind or ruined by mildew. ²⁴He will send dust and sandstorms instead of rain, and you will be wiped out.
²⁵The LORD will let you be defeated by your enemies, and you will scatter in all directions. You will be a horrible sight for the other nations to see, ²⁶and no one will disturb the birds and wild animals while they eat your dead bodies.
²⁷The LORD will make you suffer with diseases that will cause oozing sores or crusty itchy patches on your skin or boils like the ones that are common in Egypt. And there will be no cure for you! ²⁸You will become insane and go blind. The LORD will make you so confused, ²⁹that even in bright sunshine you will have to feel your way around like a blind person, who cannot tell day from night. For the rest of your life, people will beat and rob you, and no one will be able to stop them.
³⁰A man will be engaged to a woman, but before they can get married, she will be raped by enemy soldiers. Some of you will build houses, but never get to live in them. If you plant a vineyard, you won't be around long enough to enjoy the first harvest. ³¹Your cattle will be killed while you watch, but you won't get to eat any of the meat. Your donkeys and sheep will be stolen from you, and no one will be around to force your enemies to give them back. ³²Your sons and daughters will be dragged off to a foreign country, while you stand there helpless.

And even if you watch for them until you go blind, you will never see them again.
³³You will work hard on your farms, but everything you harvest will be eaten by foreigners, who will mistreat you and abuse you for the rest of your life.
³⁴What you see will be so horrible that you will go insane, ³⁵and the LORD will punish you from head to toe with boils that never heal.
³⁶The LORD will let you and your king be taken captive to a country that you and your ancestors have never even heard of, and there you will have to worship idols^d made of wood and stone. ³⁷People of nearby countries will shudder when they see your terrible troubles, but they will still make fun of you.
³⁸You will plant a lot of seed, but gather a small harvest, because locusts^e will eat your crops. ³⁹You will plant vineyards and work hard at taking care of them, but you won't gather any grapes, much less get any wine, and the vines themselves will be eaten by worms. ⁴⁰Even if your olive trees grow everywhere in your country, the olives will fall off before they are ready, and there won't be enough olive oil for combing your hair.^f
⁴¹Even your infant sons and daughters will be taken as prisoners of war.
⁴²Locusts^g will eat your crops and strip your trees of leaves and fruit.
⁴³Foreigners in your towns will become wealthy and powerful, while you become poor and powerless. ⁴⁴You will be so short of money that you will have to borrow from those foreigners. They will be the leaders in the community, and you will be the followers.

More Curses for Disobedience

Moses said:

⁴⁵Israel, if you don't obey the laws and teachings that the LORD your God is giving you, he will send these curses to chase, attack, and destroy you. ⁴⁶Then everyone will

---

^c28.17 *bread:* The main food of the Israelites.
^d28.36 *have to worship idols:* It was sometimes thought that only the gods of a country could be worshiped within the borders of that country.   ^e28.38 *locusts:* A type of grasshopper that comes in swarms and causes great damage to plant life.   ^f28.40 *olive oil . . . hair:* Olive oil was used for combing the hair.
^g28.42 *Locusts:* See the note at 28.38.

look at you and your descendants and realize that the LORD has placed you under a curse.

⁴⁷If the LORD makes you wealthy, but you don't joyfully worship and honor him, ⁴⁸he will send enemies to attack you and make them their slaves. Then you will live in poverty with nothing to eat, drink, or wear, and your owners will work you to death.

⁴⁹Foreigners who speak a strange language will be sent to attack you without warning, just like an eagle swooping down. ⁵⁰They won't show any mercy, and they will have no respect for old people or pity for children. ⁵¹They will take your cattle, sheep, goats, grain, wine, and olive oil, then leave you to starve.

⁵²All over the land that the LORD your God gave you, the enemy army will surround your towns. You may feel safe inside your town walls, but the enemy will tear them down, ⁵³while you wait in horror. Finally, you will get so hungry that you will eat the sons and daughters that the LORD gave you. ⁵⁴⁻⁵⁵Because of hunger, a man who had been gentle and kind will eat his own children and refuse to share the meal with his brother or wife or with his other children. ⁵⁶⁻⁵⁷A woman may have grown up in such luxury that she never had to put a foot on the ground. But times will be so bad that she will secretly eat both her newborn baby and the afterbirth, without sharing any with her husband or her other children.

Disobedience Brings Destruction

Moses said to Israel:

⁵⁸You must obey everything in *The Book of God's Law*. Because if you don't respect the LORD, ⁵⁹he will punish you and your descendants with incurable diseases, ⁶⁰like those you were so afraid of in Egypt. ⁶¹Remember! If the LORD decides to destroy your nation, he can use any disease or disaster, not just the ones written in *The Book of God's Law*.

⁶²There are as many of you now as the stars in the sky, but if you disobey the LORD your God, only a few of you will be left. ⁶³The LORD is happy to make you successful and to help your nation grow while you conquer the land. But if you disobey him, he will be just as happy to pull you up by your roots.

⁶⁴Those of you that survive will be scattered to every nation on earth, and you will have to worship stone and wood idols[h] that never helped you or your ancestors. ⁶⁵You will be restless—always longing for home, but never able to return. ⁶⁶You will live in constant fear of death. ⁶⁷Each morning you will wake up to such terrible sights that you will say, "I wish it were night!" But at night you will be terrified and say, "I wish it were day!"

⁶⁸I told you never to go back to Egypt. But now the LORD himself will load you on ships and send you back. Then you will even try to sell yourselves as slaves, but no one will be interested.

The Agreement in Moab

29 So Moses finished telling the Israelites what they had to do in order to keep the agreement the LORD was making with them in Moab, which was in addition to the one the LORD had made with them at Mount Sinai.[i]

THE THIRD SPEECH:
ISRAEL MUST KEEP ITS AGREEMENT WITH THE LORD

The LORD Is Your God

²⁻³Moses called the nation of Israel together and told them:

When you were in Egypt, you saw the LORD perform great miracles that caused trouble for the king, his officials, and everyone else in the country. ⁴⁻⁶He has even told you, "For forty years I, the LORD, led you through the desert, but your clothes and your sandals didn't wear out, and I gave you special food.[j] I did these things so you would realize that I am your God."

But the LORD must give you a change of heart before you truly understand what you have seen and heard.

⁷When we first camped here, King Sihon of Heshbon and King Og of Bashan attacked, but we defeated them. ⁸Then we captured their land and divided it among the tribes of Reuben, Gad, and East Manasseh.

---

[h]**28.64** *have to worship . . . idols:* See the note at 28.36.
[i]**29.1** *Mount Sinai:* See the note at 1.1-5.
[j]**29.4-6** *I gave . . . food:* Hebrew "you didn't eat bread or drink any wine or beer."

Keep the Agreement

Moses said:

⁹Israel, the LORD has made an agreement with you, and if you keep your part, you will be successful in everything you do. ¹⁰⁻¹²To-day everyone in our nation is standing here in the LORD's presence, including leaders and officials, parents and children, and even those foreigners who cut wood and carry water for us. We are at this place of worship to promise that we will keep our part of the agreement with the LORD our God.

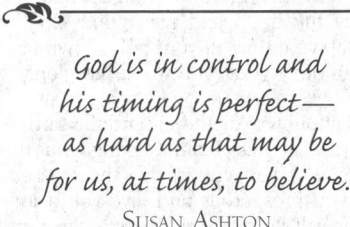

God is in control and
his timing is perfect—
as hard as that may be
for us, at times, to believe.

SUSAN ASHTON

¹³⁻¹⁵In this agreement, the LORD promised that you would be his people and that he would be your God. He first made this promise to your ancestors Abraham, Isaac, and Jacob, and today the LORD is making this same promise to you. But it isn't just for you; it is also for your descendants.

¹⁶⁻¹⁷When we lived in Egypt, you saw the Egyptians worship disgusting idols of wood, stone, silver, and gold. Then as we traveled through other nations, you saw those people worship other disgusting idols. ¹⁸So make sure that everyone in your tribe remains faithful to the LORD and never starts worshiping gods of other nations.

If even one of you worships idols, you will be like the root of a plant that produces bitter, poisonous fruit. ¹⁹You may be an Israelite and know all about the LORD's agreement with us, but he won't bless you if you rebel against him. You may think you can get away with it, but you will cause the rest of Israel to be punished along with you.ᵏ

²⁰⁻²¹The LORD will be furious, and instead of forgiving you, he will separate you from the other tribes. Then he will destroy you, by piling on you all the curses in *The Book of God's Law*, and you will be forgotten forever.

²²The LORD will strike your country with diseases and disasters. Your descendants and foreigners from distant countries will see that your land ²³has become a scorching desert of salt and sulfur, where nothing is planted, nothing sprouts, and nothing grows. It will be as lifeless as the land around the cities of Sodom, Gomorrah, Admah, and Zeboiim, after the LORD became angry and destroyed them.ˡ

²⁴People from other nations will ask, "Why did the LORD destroy this country? Why was he so furious?"

²⁵And they will be given this answer:

Our ancestors worshiped the LORD, but after he brought them out of Egypt and made an agreement with them, they rejected the agreement ²⁶and decided to worship gods that had never helped them. The LORD had forbidden Israel to worship these gods, ²⁷⁻²⁸and so he became furious and punished the land with all the curses in *The Book of God's Law*. Then he pulled up Israel by the roots and tossed them into a foreign country, where they still are today.

²⁹The LORD our God hasn't explained the present or the future, but he has commanded us to obey the laws he gave to us and our descendants.

The LORD Will Bring You Back

Moses said to Israel:

30 I have told you everything the LORD your God will do for you, and I've also told you the curses he will put on you if you reject him. He will scatter you in faraway countries, but when you realize that he is punishing you, ²return to him with all your heart and soul and start obeying the commands I have given to you today. ³⁻⁴Then he will stop punishing you and treat you with kindness. He may have scattered you to the farthest countries on earth, but he will bring you back ⁵to the land that had belonged to your ancestors and make you even more successful and powerful than they ever were.

ᵏ**29.19** *you will cause the rest of Israel to be punished along with you:* Hebrew "The mud will be swept away as well as the dust." ˡ**29.23** *Sodom . . . destroyed them:* See Genesis 18.16-28.

⁶You and your descendants are stubborn, but the LORD will make you willing to obey him and love him with all your heart and soul, and you will enjoy a long life.

⁷Then the LORD your God will remove the curses from you and put them on those enemies who hate and attack you.

⁸You will again obey the laws and teachings of the LORD, ⁹and he will bless you with many children, large herds and flocks, and abundant crops. The LORD will be happy to do good things for you, just as he did for your ancestors. ¹⁰But you must decide once and for all to worship him with all your heart and soul and to obey everything in *The Book of God's Law*.

Choose Life, Not Death

Moses said to Israel:

¹¹You know God's laws, and it isn't impossible to obey them. ¹²His commands aren't in heaven, so you can't excuse yourselves by saying, "How can we obey the LORD's commands? They are in heaven, and no one can go up to get them, then bring them down and explain them to us." ¹³And you can't say, "How can we obey the LORD's commands? They are across the sea, and someone must go across, then bring them back and explain them to us." ¹⁴No, these commands are nearby and you know them by heart. All you have to do is obey!

¹⁵Today I am giving you a choice. You can choose life and success or death and disaster. ¹⁶⁻¹⁸I am commanding you to be loyal to the LORD, to live the way he has told you, and to obey his laws and teachings. You are about to cross the Jordan River and take the land that he is giving you. If you obey him, you will live and become successful and powerful.

On the other hand, you might choose to disobey the LORD and reject him. So I'm warning you that if you bow down and worship other gods, you won't have long to live.

¹⁹Right now I call the sky and the earth to be witnesses that I am offering you this choice. Will you choose for the LORD to make you prosperous and give you a long life? Or will he put you under a curse and kill you? Choose life! ²⁰Be completely faithful to the LORD your God, love him, and do whatever he tells you. The LORD is the only one who can give life, and he will let you live a long time in the land that he promised to your ancestors Abraham, Isaac, and Jacob.

---

*Spiritual*Life—**Will God really condemn people who don't accept Christ as their Savior?** *(Deuteronomy 30)*

Rejecting God means choosing death.

God made some wonderful promises in the book of Deuteronomy. He promised his people that if they chose to follow him, they chose life. If they were obedient, he would treat them with kindness; he would bless them, their work, and their children. Throughout the Bible, God reminds us that he is the only one who can give life. And he will give it to those who love him.

But there's a flip side to this. God also warns us that to reject him is to choose death and disaster. Those who refuse to worship God bring death on themselves—even though God is anxious to give them life instead.

The New Testament is clear—Jesus Christ is God himself in human form. So those who reject Christ are doing exactly what God warned against: rejecting the only one who can give life. Christ repeated God's words to the Israelites in the Old Testament when he told his followers he came to bring life "in its fullest" (John 10.10). Yet not all choose this life. Some will suffer the judgment God outlines in Deuteronomy 30. Because they refuse to worship the one true God, they will be placed under a curse. Every person has a choice—for "life and success" or "death and disaster." What have you chosen? (See also Zephaniah 1.14-18; John 3.16-18; John 6.60-69; Romans 10.5-21.)

Words To Remember: *Be completely faithful to the LORD your God, love him, and do whatever he tells you. The LORD is the only one who can give life.—Deuteronomy 30.20*

FINAL SPEECHES AND THE DEATH OF MOSES

Joshua Is Appointed the Leader of Israel

31 Moses again spoke to the whole nation of Israel:
²I am a hundred twenty years old, and I am no longer able to be your leader. And besides that, the LORD your God has told me that he won't let me cross the Jordan River. ³⁻⁵But he has promised that he and Joshua will lead you across the Jordan to attack the nations that live on the other side. The LORD will destroy those nations just as he destroyed Sihon and Og, those two Amorite kings. Just remember—whenever you capture a place, kill everyone who lives there.

⁶Be brave and strong! Don't be afraid of the nations on the other side of the Jordan. The LORD your God will always be at your side, and he will never abandon you.

⁷Then Moses called Joshua up in front of the crowd and said:

Joshua, be brave and strong as you lead these people into their land. The LORD made a promise long ago to Israel's ancestors that this land would someday belong to Israel. That time has now come, and you must divide up the land among the people. ⁸The

LORD will lead you into the land. He will always be with you and help you, so don't ever be afraid of your enemies.

Read These Laws

⁹Moses wrote down all of these laws and teachings and gave them to the priests and the leaders of Israel. The priests were from the Levi tribe, and they carried the sacred chest that belonged to the LORD. ¹⁰⁻¹¹Moses told these priests and leaders:

Each year the Israelites must come together to celebrate the Festival of Shelters at the place where the LORD chooses to be worshiped. You must read these laws and teachings to the people at the festival every seventh year, the year when loans do not need to be repaid.ᵐ ¹²⁻¹³Everyone must come—men, women, children, and even the foreigners who live in your towns. And each new generation will listen and learn to worship the LORD their God with fear and trembling and to do exactly what is said in God's Law.

ᵐ31.10,11 *every seventh year . . . repaid:* See 15.1, 2 and the note there.

WORK—How can I be more confident about my work? *(Deuteronomy 31.1-6)*

God always equips you to do what he calls you to do.

Talk about filling big shoes! Moses, the leader of Israel, had turned water into blood and seen the sea divide in front of him. He'd watched God write the Ten Commandments, and had seen and spoken to God repeatedly. He'd faced down rebellious Israelites, led the people in battle, and settled their disputes.

But now, Moses was one hundred and twenty years old. It was time for him to appoint a successor. He chose Joshua, his second in command. Joshua, not Moses, would lead the people across the Jordan River and into the Promised Land.

Joshua must have been nervous. After all, God had assigned him a big job. But as the story of the conquest tells us, Joshua wasn't alone. Moses promised the people that God and Joshua together would lead them across the Jordan.

When God calls us to do a job, he doesn't abandon us. Instead, he stays beside us and works with us—just as he went with Joshua and the people of Israel, fighting beside them until the Promised Land was theirs. God gave Joshua the wisdom and strength to lead Israel. But most important of all, he gave Joshua his presence. He will do the same for us as we do the work he has given us to do. (See also Joshua 1.1-9; Psalm 73.21-28; Psalm 108; 1 John 3.19-24.)

Words To Remember: *Be brave and strong! Don't be afraid of the nations on the other side of the Jordan. The LORD your God will always be at your side, and he will never abandon you.—Deuteronomy 31.6*

Israel Will Reject the LORD

[14]The LORD told Moses, "You will soon die, so bring Joshua to the sacred tent, and I will appoint him the leader of Israel."

Moses and Joshua went to the sacred tent, [15]and the LORD appeared in a thick cloud right over the entrance to the tent. [16]The LORD said:

Moses, you will soon die. But Israel is going into a land where other gods are worshiped, and Israel will reject me and start worshiping these gods. The people will break the agreement I made with them, [17]and I will be so furious that I will abandon them and ignore their prayers. I will send disasters and suffering that will nearly wipe them out. Finally, they will realize that the disasters happened because I abandoned them. [18]They will pray to me, but I will ignore them because they were evil and started worshiping other gods.

[19]Moses and Joshua, I am going to give you the words to a new song. Write them down and teach the song to the Israelites. If they learn it, they will know what I want them to do, and so they will have no excuse for not obeying me. [20]I am bringing them into the land that I promised their ancestors. It is a land rich with milk and honey, and the Israelites will have more than enough food to eat. But they will get fat and turn their backs on me and start worshiping other gods. The Israelites will reject me and break the agreement that I made with them.

[21]When I punish the Israelites and their descendants with suffering and disasters, I will remind them that they know the words to this song, so they have no excuse for not obeying me. I will give them the land that I promised, but I know the way they are going to live later on.

[22]Moses wrote down the words to the song[n] right away, and he taught it to the Israelites.

[23]The LORD told Joshua, "Be brave and strong! I will help you lead the people of Israel into the land that I have promised them."

[24]Moses wrote down all these laws and teachings in a book, [25]then he went to the Levites who carried the sacred chest and said:

[26]This is *The Book of God's Law*. Keep it beside the sacred chest that holds the agreement the LORD your God made with Israel. This book is proof that you know what the LORD wants you to do. [27]I know how stubborn and rebellious you and the rest of the Israelites are. You have rebelled against the LORD while I have been alive, and it will only get worse after I am gone. [28]So call together the leaders and officials of the tribes of Israel. I will bring this book and read every word of it to you, and I will call the sky and the earth as witnesses that all of you know what you are supposed to do.

[29]I am going to die soon, and I know that in the future you will stop caring about what is right and what is wrong, and so you will disobey the LORD and stop living the way I told you to live. The LORD will be angry, and terrible things will happen to you.

The Song of Moses

[30]Moses called a meeting of all the people of Israel, so he could teach them the words to the song that the LORD had given him. And here are the words:

32

Earth and Sky,
    listen to what I say!
[2]Israel, I will teach you.
My words will be like gentle rain
    on tender young plants,
    or like dew on the grass.

[3]Join with me in praising
    the wonderful name
        of the LORD our God.
[4]The LORD is a mighty rock,[o]
    and he never does wrong.
God can always be trusted
    to bring justice.

---

[n]**31.22** *the words to the song:* See 32.1-43.
[o]**32.4** *mighty rock:* The Hebrew text has "rock," which is sometimes used in poetry to compare the LORD to a mountain where his people can run for protection from their enemies.

5 But you lie and cheat
and are unfaithful to him.
You have disgraced yourselves
and are no longer worthy
to be his children.[p]
6 Israel, the LORD is your Father,
the one who created you,
but you repaid him
by being foolish.
7 Think about past generations.
Ask your parents
or any of your elders.
They will tell you
8 that God Most High
gave land to every nation.
He assigned a guardian angel
to each of them,[q]
9 but the LORD himself
takes care of Israel.[r]

If we put our complete trust in God we can transcend tragedy—not reacting out of fear, anger, etc., but responding in unconditional love as we rest in the assurance of God's faithfulness.

BARBARA JOHNSON

10 Israel, the LORD discovered you
in a barren desert
filled with howling winds.
God became your fortress,
protecting you as though
you were his own eyes.
11 The LORD was like an eagle
teaching its young to fly,
always ready to swoop down
and catch them on its back.
12 Israel, the LORD led you,
and without the aid
of a foreign god,
13 he helped you
capture the land.
Your fields were rich
with grain.
Olive trees grew
in your stony soil,
and honey was found
among the rocks.
14 Your flocks and herds
produced milk and yogurt,
and you got choice meat
from your sheep and goats
that grazed in Bashan.
Your wheat was the finest,
and you drank the best wine.

15 Israel,[s] you grew fat and rebelled
against God, your Creator;
you rejected the Mighty Rock,[t]
your only place of safety.
16 You made God jealous and angry
by worshiping disgusting idols
and foreign gods.
17 You offered sacrifices
to demons, those useless gods[u]
that never helped you,
new gods that your ancestors
never worshiped.
18 You turned away
from God, your Creator;
you forgot the Mighty Rock,[v]
the source of your life.
19 You were the LORD's children,
but you made him angry.
Then he rejected you 20 and said,
"You are unfaithful
and can't be trusted.
So I won't answer your prayers;
I'll just watch and see
what happens to you.
21 You worshiped worthless idols,
and made me jealous
and angry!
Now I will send a cruel[w]

---

[p] **32.5** *and are unfaithful . . . children*: One possible meaning for the difficult Hebrew text. [q] **32.8** *He assigned . . . them*: The Dead Sea Scrolls and one ancient translation; the Standard Hebrew Text "So there were as many nations as Israel (that is, Jacob) had children." [r] **32.9** *Israel*: The Hebrew text has "Jacob," another name for Israel's ancestor. [s] **32.15** *Israel*: The Standard Hebrew Text has "Jeshurun," a rare name for Israel related to a word meaning "honest." The Samaritan Hebrew Text and one ancient translation also use "Jacob," another name for the ancestor of the nation of Israel. [t] **32.15** *Mighty Rock*: See the note at 32.4. [u] **32.16,17** *disgusting idols . . . foreign gods . . . demons . . . those useless gods*: Different ways of referring to gods of other nations. [v] **32.18** *Mighty Rock*: See the note at 32.4. [w] **32.21** *cruel*: One possible meaning for the difficult Hebrew text.

and worthless nation
to make you jealous and angry.

22 "My people, I will breathe out fire
that sends you down
to the world of the dead.
It will scorch your farmlands
and burn deep down
under the mountains.
23 I'll send disaster after disaster
to strike you like arrows.
24 You'll be struck by starvation
and deadly diseases,
by the fangs of wild animals
and poisonous snakes.
25 Young and old alike
will be killed in the streets
and terrified at home.

26 "I wanted to scatter you,
so no one would remember
that you had ever lived.
27 But I dreaded the sound
of your enemies saying,
'We defeated Israel with no help
from the LORD.' "

28 People of Israel,
that's what the LORD
has said to you.
But you don't have good sense,
and you never listen
to advice.
29 If you did, you could see
where you are headed.
30 How could one enemy soldier
chase a thousand
of Israel's troops?
Or how could two of theirs
pursue ten thousand of ours?
It can only happen if the LORD
stops protecting Israel
and lets the enemy win.
31 Even our enemies know
that only our God
is a Mighty Rock.ˣ

32 Our enemies are grapevines
rooted in the fields
of Sodom and Gomorrah.ʸ
The grapes they produce
are full of bitter poison;
33 their wine is more deadly
than cobra venom.
34 But the LORD has written

a list of their sins
and locked it in his vault.
35 Soon our enemies will get
what they deserveᶻ—
suddenly they will slip,
and total disaster
will quickly follow.

36 When only a few
of the LORD's people remain,
when their strength is gone,
and some of them are slaves,
the LORD will feel sorry for them
and give them justice.

37 But first the LORD will say,
"You ran for safety to other gods—
couldn't they help you?
38 You offered them wine
and your best sacrifices.
Can't those gods help you now
or give you protection?
39 Don't you understand?
I am the only God;
there are no others.
I am the one who takes life
and gives it again.
I punished you with suffering.
But now I will heal you,
and nothing can stop me!

40 "I make this solemn promise:
Just as I live forever,
41 I will take revenge
on my hateful enemies.
I will sharpen my sword
and let it flash
like lightning.
42 My arrows will get drunk
on enemy blood;
my sword will taste the flesh
and the blood of the enemy.
It will kill prisoners,
and cut off the heads
of their leaders."ᵃ

ˣ**32.31** *Mighty Rock:* See the note at 32.4.
ʸ**32.32** *Sodom and Gomorrah:* Two cities that the LORD destroyed because their people were so evil (see Genesis 18.16—19.28). ᶻ**32.35** *our enemies . . . deserve:* The Samaritan Hebrew Text and one ancient translation; the Standard Hebrew Text "I will pay them back." ᵃ**32.42** *leaders:* Or "long-haired warriors," who let their hair grow to show that they had made sacred promises to their gods.

⁴³Tell the heavens to celebrate
and all gods to bow down
to the LORD,*ᵇ*
because he will take revenge
on those hateful enemies
who killed his people.
He will forgive the sins of Israel
and purify their land.*ᶜ*

⁴⁴⁻⁴⁵Moses spoke the words of the song
so that all the Israelites could hear, and
Joshua*ᵈ* helped him. When Moses had finished, ⁴⁶he said, "Always remember this
song I have taught you today. And let it be a
warning that you must teach your children
to obey everything written in The Book of
God's Law. ⁴⁷The Law isn't empty words. It
can give you a long life in the land that you
are going to take."

Moses Will See the Land

⁴⁸Later that day the LORD said to Moses:
⁴⁹Go up into the Abarim Mountain
range here in Moab across the Jordan
River valley from Jericho. And when
you reach the top of Mount Nebo, you
will be able to see the land of Canaan,
which I am giving to Israel. ⁵⁰Then you
will die and be buried on the mountaintop, just as your brother Aaron
died and was buried on Mount Hor.
⁵¹Both of you were unfaithful to me at
Meribah Spring near Kadesh in the Zin
Desert.*ᵉ* I am God, but there in front of
the Israelites, you did not treat me
with the honor and respect I deserve.
⁵²So I will give the land to the people
of Israel, but you will only get to see it
from a distance.

Moses Blesses the Tribes of Israel

33
Moses was a prophet, and before
he died, he blessed the tribes of
Israel by saying:

²The LORD came from Mount Sinai.
From Edom, he gave light
to his people,
and his glory was shining
from Mount Paran.
Thousands of his warriors
were with him, and fire
was at his right hand.*ᶠ*
³The LORD loves the tribes
of Israel,*ᵍ*

and he protects his people.
They listen to his words
and worship at his feet.
*⁴I called a meeting
of the tribes of Israel*ʰ*
and gave you God's Law.
*⁵Then you and your leaders
made the LORD your king.

> God's creative power is so
> beyond our ability to make
> something that it is
> mind-boggling. His love
> for us is so beyond our
> capacity for love that it
> should utterly astound us.
>
> JILL BRISCOE

⁶Tribe of Reuben, you will live,
even though your tribe
will always be small.*ⁱ*

⁷The LORD will listen to you,
tribe of Judah, as you beg
to come safely home.
You fought your enemies alone;*ʲ*
now the LORD will help you.

⁸At Massah and Meribah Spring,*ᵏ*
the LORD tested you,
tribe of Levi.

---

*ᵇ***32.43** *Tell . . . LORD:* The Dead Sea Scrolls and one
ancient translation; the Standard Hebrew Text "Let the
nations, his people, celebrate." *ᶜ***32.43** *because he
will . . . land:* One possible meaning for the difficult
Hebrew text. *ᵈ***32.44,45** *Joshua:* The Hebrew text
has "Hoshea," another form of Joshua's name.
*ᵉ***32.51** *Both of you were unfaithful . . . the Zin Desert:*
See Numbers 20.1-13. *ᶠ***33.2** *Thousands . . . right hand:*
One possible meaning for the difficult Hebrew text.
*ᵍ***33.3** *the tribes of Israel:* Or "the nations." *ʰ***33.4** *Israel:*
The Hebrew text also uses the name "Jeshurun," a rare
name for "Israel." *ⁱ***33.6** *even though . . . small:* One
possible meaning for the difficult Hebrew text.
*ʲ***33.7** *beg . . . alone:* One possible meaning for the
difficult Hebrew text. *ᵏ***33.8** *Massah and Meribah
Spring:* See Exodus 17.1-7; Numbers 20.1-13.

You were faithful,[l]
and so the priesthood[m] belongs
    to the Levi tribe.
[9] Protecting Israel's agreement
    with the LORD
was more important to you
than the life of your father
    or mother,
or brothers or sisters,
    or your own children.[n]

[10] You teach God's laws to Israel,[o]
and at the place of worship
you offer sacrifices
    and burn incense.
[11] I pray that the LORD will bless
    everything you do,
and make you strong enough
    to crush your enemies.

[12] The LORD Most High[p] loves you,
    tribe of Benjamin.
He will live among your hills
    and protect you.

[13] Descendants of Joseph,
    the LORD will bless you
with precious water
from deep wells
    and with dew from the sky.
[14] Month by month, your fruit
    will ripen in the sunshine.
[15] You will have a rich harvest
from the slopes
    of the ancient hills.
[16] The LORD who appeared
    in the burning bush
wants to give you the best
    the land can produce,
and it will be a princely crown
    on Joseph's head.

[17] The armies of Ephraim
    and Manasseh
are majestic and fierce
    like a bull or a wild ox.
They will run their spears
    through faraway nations.

[18] Be happy, Zebulun,
    as your boats set sail;
be happy, Issachar,
    in your tents.
[19] The sea will make you wealthy,
and from the sandy beach

you will get treasure.[q]
So invite the other tribes[r]
to celebrate with you
    and offer sacrifices to God.

[20] Tribe of Gad,
    the LORD will bless you
    with more land.
So shout his praises!
Your tribe is like a lion
    ripping up its victim.
[21] Your leaders met together
and chose the best land
    for your tribe,
but you obeyed the LORD
    and helped the other tribes.[s]

[22] Tribe of Dan,
you are like a lion cub,
    startled by a snake.[t]

[23] The LORD is pleased with you,
    people of Naphtali.
He will bless you
and give you the land
    to the west and the south.[u]

[24] The LORD's greatest blessing
    is for you, tribe of Asher.
You will be the favorite
    of all the other tribes.
You will be rich with olive oil
[25] and have strong town gates
    with bronze and iron bolts.
Your people will be powerful
    for as long as they live.

---

[l]**33.8** *the LORD tested you, tribe of Levi. You were faithful*:
Or "the LORD tested me. I was faithful" or "the LORD
tested Aaron and me. We were faithful."
[m]**33.8** *priesthood*: The Hebrew text has "your thummim
and your urim," objects that were used by priests to
get answers from God.   [n]**33.9** *Protecting Israel's
agreement . . . your own children*: See Exodus 32.25-29.
[o]**33.10** *Israel*: See the note at 32.9.   [p]**33.12** *Most High*:
One possible meaning for the difficult Hebrew text.
[q]**33.19** *sandy beach . . . treasure*: Possibly a reference to
glass made from sand; glass was rare and very
valuable.   [r]**33.19** *other tribes*: Or "nations."
[s]**33.21** *tribes*: One possible meaning for the difficult
Hebrew text of verse 21. The Gad tribe asked for some
of the land east of the Jordan River, but promised that
their warriors would cross the Jordan and help the
other tribes take over the land west of the Jordan
(see Numbers 32.1-33; Joshua 4.10-13).
[t]**33.22** *startled by a snake*: Or "jumping out from the
forest of Bashan."   [u]**33.23** *land to the west and the south*:
Or "land south as far as Lake Galilee."

²⁶Israel,ᵛ no other god
    is like ours—
the clouds are his chariot
as he rides across the skies
    to come and help us.
²⁷The eternal God
    is our hiding place;
    he carries us in his arms.
When God tells you
    to destroy your enemies,
    he will make them run.
²⁸Israel, you will live in safety;
    your enemies will be gone.ʷ
The dew will fall from the sky,
and you will have plenty
    of grain and wine.
²⁹The LORD has rescued you
and given you more blessings
    than any other nation.
He protects you like a shield
    and is your majestic sword.
Your enemies will bow in fear,
and you will trample
    on their backs.

The Death of Moses

34 Sometime later, Moses left the lowlands of Moab. He went up Mount Pisgah to the peak of Mount Nebo,ˣ which is across the Jordan River from Jericho. The LORD showed him all the land as far north as Gilead and the town of Dan. ²He let Moses see the territories that would soon belong to the tribes of Naphtali, Ephraim, Manasseh, and Judah, as far west as the Mediterranean Sea. ³The LORD also showed him the land in the south, from the valley near the town of Jericho, known as The City of Palm Trees, down to the town of Zoar.

⁴The LORD said, "Moses, this is the land I was talking about when I solemnly promised Abraham, Isaac, and Jacob that I would give land to their descendants. I have let you see it, but you will not cross the Jordan and go in."

⁵And so, Moses the LORD's servant died there in Moab, just as the LORD had said. ⁶The LORD buried him in a valley near the town of Beth-Peor, but even today no one knows exactly where. ⁷Moses was a hundred twenty years old when he died, yet his eyesight was still good, and his body was strong. ⁸The people of Israel stayed in the lowlands of Moab, where they mourned and grieved thirty days for Moses, as was their custom.

Joshua Becomes the Leader of Israel

⁹Before Moses died, he had placed his hands on Joshua, and the LORD had given Joshua wisdom. The Israelites paid attention to what Joshua said and obeyed the commands that the LORD had given Moses.

Moses Was a Great Prophet

¹⁰There has never again been a prophet in Israel like Moses. The LORD spoke face to face with him ¹¹and sent him to perform powerful miracles in the presence of the king of Egypt and his entire nation. ¹²No one else has ever had the power to do such great things as Moses did for everyone to see.

ᵛ**33.26** *Israel:* See the note at 33.4.   ʷ**33.28** *your enemies will be gone:* One possible meaning for the difficult Hebrew text.   ˣ**34.1** *Mount Pisgah . . . Mount Nebo:* Mount Nebo was probably one peak of the ridge known as Mount Pisgah.

Joshua

Moving Beyond Our Fears

Have you ever agreed to take on a position of responsibility that not only challenged your capabilities but also involved taking over for someone who had been successful and highly respected? Can you remember the fears you faced?

Joshua experienced similar feelings when it came time for him to lead the people of Israel into the Promised Land. The book of Joshua opens with God communicating personally with Joshua about his calling to take over where Moses—the most powerful spiritual leader Israel had ever known—had left off. Joshua must have struggled with fear and inadequacy, because God went to great lengths to reassure him of his presence and power, instructing him to move beyond fear to courageous action (1.8,9).

The Greek form of the name "Joshua" is "Jesus." Many commentators understand Joshua to be an early example of the leadership Christ would provide in rescuing us from sin and death and leading us into spiritual rest.

As Joshua led the Israelites to victory and possession of the Promised Land, they faced many of the same challenges we face today. Although the loss of Moses had been a great one, the Israelites grew to love and respect their new leader. They became aware of their own weaknesses as they frequently vacillated between fear of their enemies and faith in God. The Israelites learned to receive God's help even when it came from unlikely sources. They discovered that one individual's sin could hurt the entire community. And they were intent upon remembering the mighty ways in which God had led them and cared for them.

The book of Joshua records the fulfillment of God's promise that he would establish a great nation through Abraham and lead them into their own land (Genesis 12.1,2). Although God had already given the parameters of the land to Abraham, and Moses had led them through the wilderness to the Promised Land, much of it still needed to be claimed. As God's chosen leader for the last leg of the Israelites' journey, Joshua is an inspiring example of what is possible for each of us—if we remain faithful to God in moving beyond our fears and answering his call upon our life.

Joshua at a Glance

1. Joshua becomes the leader of Israel and receives encouragement from God (1)
2. The Israelites cross the Jordan River and conquer Jericho with help from an unlikely source (2–6)
3. One person's sin hurts the entire community (7)
4. Victory at Ai (8)
5. Gibeonites deceive the Israelites (9)
6. God fights on Israel's side (10–12)
7. Israelite leaders work together to divide up the land fairly (13–22)
8. Joshua gives the Israelites a reminder and a challenge (23.1—24.15)
9. A renewed commitment (24.16-28)
10. The death of Joshua (24.29-33)

Joshua Becomes the Leader of Israel

1 Moses, the LORD's servant, was dead. So the LORD spoke to Joshua son of Nun, who had been the assistant of Moses. The LORD said:

²My servant Moses is dead. Now you must lead Israel across the Jordan River into the land I'm giving to all of you. ³Wherever you go, I'll give you that land, as I promised Moses. ⁴It will reach from the Southern Desert to the Lebanon Mountains in the north, and to the northeast as far as the great Euphrates River. It will include the land of the Hittites,ᵃ and the land from here at the Jordan River to the Mediterranean Sea on the west. ⁵Joshua, I will always be with you and help you as I helped Moses, and no one will ever be able to defeat you.

⁶⁻⁸Long ago I promised the ancestors of Israel that I would give this land to their descendants. So be strong and brave! Be careful to do everything my servant Moses taught you. Never stop reading *The Book of the Law*ᵇ he gave you. Day and night you must think about what it says. If you obey it completely, you and Israel will be able to take this land.

⁹I've commanded you to be strong and brave. Don't ever be afraid or discouraged! I am the LORD your God, and I will be there to help you wherever you go.

> *When you pour out God's love on others, it will boomerang right back to you, flooding you with peace and joy!*
>
> BARBARA JOHNSON

The Eastern Tribes Promise To Help

¹⁰Joshua ordered the tribal leaders ¹¹to go through the camp and tell everyone:

In a few days we will cross the Jordan River to take the land that the LORD our God is giving us. So fix as much food as you'll need for the march into the land.

¹²Joshua told the men of the tribes of Reuben, Gad, and East Manasseh:ᶜ

ᵃ1.4 *the land . . . Hittites*: This refers to the northern part of Syria, which had been the southernmost part of the Hittite empire.   ᵇ1.6-8 *the Law*: Or "Teachings."   ᶜ1.12 *East Manasseh*: The half of Manasseh that settled east of the Jordan River.

WORK—How can I be more confident about my work? *(Joshua 1.1-9)*

God is always with you.

Have you ever been handed a task you weren't sure you could do? a job you don't think you have the necessary skills or personality for? Most of us have—at one time or another—and Joshua was no exception.

When Moses, the leader of the Israelites died, the Lord told Joshua that he was now in charge. The Lord gave him specific instructions about where to lead the people, then reiterated his promise to give the land to the Israelites. He also reminded Joshua of the importance of reading and obeying the law.

But the Lord didn't stop there. He knew that Joshua, as a new leader, needed confidence and strength. So he told Joshua, "Joshua, I will always be with you and help you as I helped Moses, and no one will ever be able to defeat you" (1.5).

What a wonderful promise this is for us today, as we seek to be godly in our work! When you don't feel equal to the task before you, meditate on these words. Let God give you the confidence you need to complete your task. (See also Deuteronomy 31.1-6; Psalm 73.21-28; Psalm 108; 1 John 3.19-24.)

Words To Remember: *Be strong and brave. Don't ever be afraid or discouraged! I am the LORD your God, and I will be there to help you wherever you go.* —Joshua 1.9

Rahab

Joshua 2,6; Hebrews 11.30,31; James 2.24-26

*H*ave you ever felt that you just weren't good enough to serve God or help others in any significant way? If your answer is yes, you are not alone; feeling "less than" is a common human experience.

If any woman had reason to feel she had nothing of value to offer to God or to the world, it would have been Rahab—a prostitute who lived in the town of Jericho. We don't know what caused her to choose this dubious line of work; perhaps she felt she had no other options. Nevertheless, even though the outward circumstances of her life were less than ideal, Rahab did not allow them to completely harden her heart. She possessed a great deal of faith and wisdom. Intuitively, she understood that the one true God was on the side of the Israelites and she chose to align herself with him.

When Israelite spies came to her in desperate need of a place to hide, Rahab was wise enough to offer a classic win-win solution: she would help them escape if they would promise to spare her and her family when the Israelites came to destroy the city (Joshua 2.8-13). Considering what might have happened to her if she was discovered harboring spies, Rahab took a great risk. Her trust was well placed, however. When the walls of Jericho fell, her house still stood; Rahab and her relatives were led to safety. Because of her faith, Rahab helped the Israelites win victory over Jericho, and she saved herself and her family.

Eventually Rahab and her family became a part of the Israelite community. Rahab married Salmon, and their son Boaz married Ruth. It was through this ancestral line that David and eventually Jesus himself were born (Matthew 1.5).

Because of the risk she took in welcoming the spies, Rahab is put forward as an example of one who had great faith (Hebrews 11.31). In fact, the apostle James used Rahab as an example of one who demonstrated the reality of her faith through courageous action in a way that was pleasing to God (James 2.24-26).

Do you ever look back on some of the lifestyle choices you made and feel inadequate as a mother, wife, or member of the community of faith? Are you struggling in areas of your life right now that cause you to question whether you are valuable to God and to the people around you? Rahab's story reminds us that no matter what our circumstances, mistakes, or inadequacies, God will honor whatever steps of faith we take. God can turn even our mistakes and character flaws into great good for ourselves and for those we love.

¹³⁻¹⁴The LORD's servant Moses said that the LORD our God has given you land here on the east side of the Jordan River, where you could live in peace. Your wives and children and your animals can stay here in the land Moses gave you. But all of you that can serve in our army must pick up your weapons and lead the men of the other tribes across the Jordan River. They are your relatives, so you must help them ¹⁵conquer the land that the LORD is giving them. The LORD will give peace to them as he has given peace to you, and then you can come back and settle here in the land that Moses promised you.

¹⁶The men answered:

We'll cross the Jordan River and help our relatives. We'll fight anywhere you send us. ¹⁷⁻¹⁸If the LORD our God will help you as he helped Moses, and if you are strong and brave, we will obey you as we obeyed Moses. We'll even put to death anyone who rebels against you or refuses to obey you.

Rahab Helps the Israelite Spies

2 Joshua chose two men as spies and sent them from their camp at Acacia with these instructions: "Go across the river and find out as much as you can about the whole region, especially about the town of Jericho."

The two spies left the Israelite camp at Acacia and went to Jericho, where they decided to spend the night at the house of a prostitute[d] named Rahab.

²But someone found out about them and told the king of Jericho, "Some Israelite men came here tonight, and they are spies." ³⁻⁷So the king sent soldiers to Rahab's house to arrest the spies.

Meanwhile, Rahab had taken the men up to the flat roof of her house and had hidden them under some piles of flax plants[e] that she had put there to dry.

The soldiers came to her door and demanded, "Let us have the men who are staying at your house. They are spies."

She answered, "Some men did come to my house, but I didn't know where they had come from. They left about sunset, just before it was time to close the town gate.[f] I don't know where they were going,

but if you hurry, maybe you can catch them."

The guards at the town gate let the soldiers leave Jericho, but they closed the gate again as soon as the soldiers went through. Then the soldiers headed toward the Jordan River to look for the spies at the place where people cross the river.

⁸Rahab went back up to her roof. The spies were still awake, so she told them:

⁹I know that the LORD has given Israel this land. Everyone shakes with fear because of you. ¹⁰We heard how the LORD dried up the Red Sea[g] so you could leave Egypt. And we heard how you destroyed Sihon and Og, those two Amorite kings east of the Jordan River. ¹¹We know that the LORD your God rules heaven and earth, and we've lost our courage and our will to fight.

¹²Please promise me in the LORD's name that you will be as kind to my family as I have been to you. Do something to show ¹³that you won't let your people kill my father and mother and my brothers and sisters and their families.

¹⁴"Rahab," the spies answered, "if you keep quiet about what we're doing, we promise to be kind to you when the LORD gives us this land. We pray that the LORD will kill us if we don't keep our promise!"[h]

¹⁵Rahab's house was built into the town wall,[i] and one of the windows in her house faced outside the wall. She gave the spies a rope, showed them the window, and said, "Use this rope to let yourselves down to the ground outside the wall. ¹⁶Then hide in the hills. The men who are looking for you

---

[d]2.1 prostitute: Rahab was possibly an innkeeper.
[e]2.3-7 flax plants: The stalks of flax plants were harvested, soaked in water, and dried, then their fibers were separated and spun into thread, which was woven into linen cloth. [f]2.3-7 gate: Many towns and cities had walls with heavy gates that were closed at night for protection. [g]2.10 Red Sea: Hebrew yam suph "Sea of Reeds," one of the marshes or fresh water lakes near the eastern part of the Nile Delta. This identification is based on Exodus 13.17—14.9, which lists the towns on the route of the Israelites before crossing the sea. In the Greek translation of the Scriptures made about 200 B.C., the "Sea of Reeds" was named "Red Sea." [h]2.14 We pray . . . promise: Or "If you save our lives, we will save yours!" [i]2.15 wall: In ancient times, cities and larger towns had high walls around them to protect them against attack. Sometimes houses were built against the wall so that the city wall formed one wall of the house. This added strength to the city wall.

won't be able to find you there. They'll give up and come back after a few days, and you can be on your way."

¹⁷⁻²⁰The spies said:

You made us promise to let you and your family live. We will keep our promise, but you can't tell anyone why we were here. You must tie this red rope on your window when we attack, and your father and mother, your brothers, and everyone else in your family must be here with you. We'll take the blame if anyone who stays in this house gets hurt. But anyone who leaves your house will be killed, and it won't be our fault.

²¹"I'll do exactly what you said," Rahab promised. Then she sent them on their way and tied the red rope to the window.

²²The spies hid in the hills for three days while the king's soldiers looked for them along the roads. As soon as the soldiers gave up and returned to Jericho, ²³the two spies went down into the Jordan valley and crossed the river. They reported to Joshua and told him everything that had happened. ²⁴"We're sure the LORD has given us the whole country," they said. "The people there shake with fear every time they think of us."

Israel Crosses the Jordan River

3 Early the next morning, Joshua and the Israelites packed up and left Acacia. They went to the Jordan River and camped there that night. ²Two days later^j their leaders went through the camp, ³⁻⁴shouting, "When you see some of the priests^k carrying the sacred chest, you'll know it is time to cross to the other side. You've never been there before, and you won't know the way, unless you follow the chest. But don't get too close! Stay about half a mile back."

⁵Joshua told the people, "Make yourselves acceptable^l to worship the LORD, because he is going to do some amazing things for us."

⁶Then Joshua turned to the priests and said, "Take the chest and cross the Jordan River ahead of us." So the priests picked up the chest by its carrying poles and went on ahead.

⁷The LORD told Joshua, "Beginning today I will show the people that you are their leader, and they will know that I am helping

you as I helped Moses. ⁸Now, tell the priests who are carrying the chest to go a little way into the river and stand there."

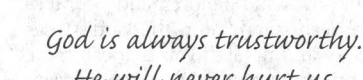

God is always trustworthy. He will never hurt us.

PATSY CLAIRMONT

⁹Joshua spoke to the people:

Come here and listen to what the LORD our God said he will do! ¹⁰The Canaanites, the Hittites, the Hivites, the Perizzites, the Girgashites, the Amorites, and the Jebusites control the land on the other side of the river. But the living God will be with you and will force them out of the land when you attack. And now, God is going to prove that he's powerful enough to force them out. ¹¹⁻¹³Just watch the sacred chest that belongs to the LORD, the ruler of the whole earth. As soon as the priests carrying the chest step into the Jordan, the water will stop flowing and pile up as if someone had built a dam across the river.

The LORD has also said that each of the twelve tribes should choose one man to represent it.

¹⁴The Israelites packed up and left camp. The priests carrying the chest walked in front, ¹⁵until they came to the Jordan River. The water in the river had risen over its banks, as it often does in springtime.^m But as soon as the feet of the priests touched the water, ¹⁶⁻¹⁷the river stopped flowing, and the water started piling up at the town of Adam near Zarethan. No water flowed toward the Dead Sea, and the priests stood in the middle of the dry riverbed near Jericho while everyone else crossed over.

---

^j**3.2** *Two days later*: The Hebrew text has "At the end of three days," two days after they had set up camp. ^k**3.3,4** *the priests*: The Hebrew text has "the priests, the Levites"; priests belonged to the tribe of Levi. ^l**3.5** *Make yourselves acceptable*: People had to do certain things to make themselves acceptable to worship the LORD (see Leviticus 7.20, 21; 15.2, 33; 22.4-8; Deuteronomy 23.10, 11). ^m**3.15** *springtime*: Or "harvest time"; the grain harvest was in late spring.

The People Set Up a Monument

4 After Israel had crossed the Jordan, the LORD said to Joshua: [n]2-3Tell[n] one man from each of the twelve tribes to pick up a large rock from where the priests are standing. Then have the men set up those rocks as a monument at the place where you camp tonight.

4Joshua chose twelve men; he called them together, 5and told them:

Go to the middle of the riverbed where the sacred chest is, and pick up a large rock. Carry it on your shoulder to our camp. There are twelve of you, so there will be one rock for each tribe. 6-7Someday your children will ask, "Why are these rocks here?" Then you can tell them how the water stopped flowing when the chest was being carried across the river. These rocks will always remind our people of what happened here today.

8The men followed the instructions that the LORD had given Joshua. They picked up twelve rocks, one for each tribe, and carried them to the camp, where they put them down.

9Joshua had some other men set up a monument next to the place where the priests were standing. This monument was also made of twelve large rocks, and it is still there in the middle of the river.

The People of Israel Set Up Camp at Gilgal

10-13The army got ready for battle and crossed the Jordan. They marched quickly past the sacred chest[o] and into the desert near Jericho. Forty thousand soldiers from the tribes of Reuben, Gad, and East Manasseh[p] led the way, as Moses had ordered.[q]

The priests stayed right where they were until the army had followed the orders that the LORD had given Moses and Joshua. Then the army watched as the priests carried the chest the rest of the way across.

14-18"Joshua," the LORD said, "have the priests come up from the Jordan and bring the chest with them." So Joshua went over

---

[n]4.1-3 Joshua . . . Tell: Or "Joshua, you and the other leaders must tell." [o]4.10-13 the sacred chest: The Hebrew text has "the LORD." The army was marching past the sacred chest, which was a symbol of God's throne on earth (see 1 Samuel 4.4 and Exodus 25.10-22; 37.1-9). [p]4.10-13 Forty thousand soldiers from the tribes of Reuben, Gad, and East Manasseh: Or "There were forty thousand soldiers altogether, and those from the tribes of Reuben, Gad, and East Manasseh." [q]4.10-13 Moses . . . ordered: See Numbers 32.16-32; Joshua 1.12-16.

PARENTING&family—How can I encourage my child's faith to grow?
(Joshua 4)

Draw attention to the many ways God is working in our lives.
Before we become parents, it's easy to think sharing our faith with our children will be effortless. But it isn't always as easy as it sounds, especially as children get older and more distracted by the world around them.

Here's a practical idea for cultivating a child's faith. As the people of Israel conquered their enemies and settled into Canaan, God wanted to be sure that future generations were aware of how he had worked in their lives. He instructed them to build monuments that would give parents and other adults the opportunity to tell children what God had done. Because children are naturally curious and ask a lot of questions, the monuments would provide natural "conversation starters" about spiritual things.

We, too, can nurture our children's faith by creating physical signs and symbols that have spiritual significance. A plaque with a life verse or poem, artwork that portrays a spiritual truth, a tree planted at a significant moment in a family's life, a grouping or collection of special objects that represent moments when God intervened in a miraculous way: all these can trigger opportunities to discuss the many ways we experience God's presence in our lives as we journey with him. (See also 1 Chronicles 22; Ezra 3; Proverbs 2.1-15; John 3.16-21.)

Words To Remember: Someday your children will ask, "Why are these rocks here?" Then you can tell them . . . what happened here today.—Joshua 4.6,7

to the priests and told them what the LORD had said. And as soon as the priests carried the chest past the highest place that the floodwaters of the Jordan had reached, the river flooded its banks again.

That's how the LORD showed the Israelites that Joshua was their leader.[r] For the rest of Joshua's life, they respected him as they had respected Moses.

[19]It was the tenth day of the first month[s] of the year when Israel crossed the Jordan River. They set up camp at Gilgal, which was east of the land controlled by Jericho. [20]The men who had carried the twelve rocks from the Jordan brought them to Joshua, and they made them into a monument. [21]Then Joshua told the people:

Years from now your children will ask you why these rocks are here. [22-23]Tell them, "The LORD our God dried up the Jordan River so we could walk across. He did the same thing here for us that he did for our people at the Red Sea,[t] [24]because he wants everyone on earth to know how powerful he is. And he wants us to worship only him."

5 The Amorite kings west of the Jordan River and the Canaanite kings along the Mediterranean Sea lost their courage and their will to fight, when they heard how the LORD had dried up the Jordan River to let Israel go across.

**Israel Gets Ready
To Celebrate Passover**

[2]While Israel was camped at Gilgal, the LORD said, "Joshua, make some flint knives[u] and circumcise the rest of the Israelite men and boys."[v]

[3]Joshua made the knives, then circumcised those men and boys at Haaraloth Hill.[w] [4-7]This had to be done, because none of Israel's baby boys had been circumcised during the forty years that Israel had wandered through the desert after leaving Egypt.

And why had they wandered for forty years? It was because right after they left Egypt, the men in the army had disobeyed the LORD. And the LORD had said, "None of you men will ever live to see the land that I promised Israel. It is a land rich with milk and honey, and someday your children will live there, but not before you die here in the desert."

[8]Everyone who had been circumcised needed time to heal, and they stayed in camp.

[9]The LORD told Joshua, "It was a disgrace for my people to be slaves in Egypt, but now I have taken away that disgrace." So the Israelites named the place Gilgal,[x] and it still has that name.

[10]Israel continued to camp at Gilgal in the desert near Jericho, and on the fourteenth day of the same month,[y] they celebrated Passover.

[11-12]The next day, God stopped sending the Israelites manna[z] to eat each morning, and they started eating food grown in the land of Canaan. They ate roasted grain[a] and thin bread[b] made of the barley they had gathered from nearby fields.

Israel Captures Jericho

[13]One day, Joshua was near Jericho when he saw a man standing some distance in front of him. The man was holding a sword, so Joshua walked up to him and asked, "Are you on our side or on our enemies' side?"

[14]"Neither," he answered. "I am here because I am the commander of the LORD's army."

Joshua fell to his knees and bowed down to the ground. "I am your servant," he said. "Tell me what to do."

[15]"Take off your sandals," the commander answered. "This is a holy place."

So Joshua took off his sandals.

---

[r]4.14-18 *leader*: See 3.7. [s]4.19 *first month*: Abib (also called Nisan), the first month of the Hebrew calendar, from about mid-March to mid-April. [t]4.22,23 *Red Sea*: See the note at 2.10. [u]5.2 *flint knives*: Flint is a stone that can be chipped until it forms a very sharp edge. [v]5.2 *circumcise . . . men and boys*: They could not celebrate Passover unless they were circumcised (see Exodus 12.43-49). [w]5.3 *Haaraloth Hill*: Or "Foreskin Hill." [x]5.9 *Gilgal*: In Hebrew "Gilgal" sounds like "take away." [y]5.10 *the same month*: See the note at 4.19. [z]5.11,12 *manna*: The special food that God provided for the Israelites while they were in the desert for forty years. It was about the size of a small seed, and it appeared on the ground during the night, except on the Sabbath. It was gathered early in the morning, ground up, and then baked or boiled (see Exodus 16.13-35; Numbers 11.4-9). [a]5.11,12 *roasted grain*: Roasted grain was made by cooking the grain in a dry pan or on a flat rock, or by holding a bunch of grain stalks over a fire. [b]5.11,12 *thin bread*: Bread made without yeast. Israelites were not supposed to eat bread made with yeast for the week following Passover. That week is called the Festival of Thin Bread (see Exodus 12.14-20; 13.3-7).

6 Meanwhile, the people of Jericho had been locking the gates in their town wall because they were afraid of the Israelites. No one could go out or come in.

²⁻³The LORD said to Joshua:

With my help, you and your army will defeat the king of Jericho and his army, and you will capture the town. Here is how to do it: March slowly around Jericho once a day for six days. ⁴Take along the sacred chest and have seven priests walk in front of it, carrying trumpets.ᶜ

But on the seventh day, march slowly around the town seven times while the priests blow their trumpets. ⁵Then the priests will blast on their trumpets, and everyone else will shout. The wall will fall down, and your soldiers can go straight in from every side.

⁶Joshua called the priests together and said, "Take the chest and have seven priests carry trumpets and march ahead of it."

⁷⁻¹⁰Next, he gave the army their orders: "March slowly around Jericho. A few of you will go ahead of the chest to guard it, but most of you will follow it. Don't shout the battle cry or yell or even talk until the day I tell you to. Then let out a shout!"

As soon as Joshua finished giving the orders, the army started marching. One group of soldiers led the way, with seven priests marching behind them and blowing trumpets. Then came the priests carrying the chest, followed by the rest of the soldiers. ¹¹They obeyed Joshua's orders and carried the chest once around the town before returning to camp for the night.

¹²⁻¹⁴Early the next morning, Joshua and everyone else started marching around Jericho in the same order as the day before. One group of soldiers was in front, followed by the seven priests with trumpets and the priests who carried the chest. The rest of the army came next. The seven priests blew their trumpets while everyone marched slowly around Jericho and back to camp. They did this once a day for six days.

¹⁵On the seventh day, the army got up at daybreak. They marched slowly around Jericho the same as they had done for the past six days, except on this day they went around seven times. ¹⁶Then the priests blew the trumpets, and Joshua yelled:

Get ready to shout! The LORD will let you capture this town. ¹⁷But you must destroy it and everything in it, to show that it now belongs to the LORD.ᵈ The woman Rahab helped the spies we sent,ᵉ so protect her and the others who are inside her house. But kill everyone else in the town. ¹⁸⁻¹⁹The silver and gold and everything made of bronze and iron belong to the LORD and must be put in his treasury. Be careful to follow these instructions, because if you see something you want and take it, the LORD will destroy Israel. And it will be all your fault.ᶠ

²⁰The priests blew their trumpets again, and the soldiers shouted as loud as they could. The walls of Jericho fell flat. Then the soldiers rushed up the hill, went straight into the town, and captured it. ²¹⁻²⁵They killed everyone, men and women, young and old, everyone except Rahab and the others in her house. They even killed every cow, sheep, and donkey.

Joshua said to the two men who had been spies, "Rahab kept you safe when I sent you to Jericho. We promised to protect her and her family, and we will keep that promise. Now go into her house and bring them out."

The two men went into Rahab's house and brought her out, along with her father and mother, her brothers, and her other relatives. Rahab and her family had to stay in a place just outside the Israelite army camp.ᵍ But later they were allowed to live among the Israelites, and her descendants still do.

The Israelites took the silver and gold and the things made of bronze and iron and put them with the rest of the treasure that was kept at the LORD's house.ʰ Finally, they set fire to Jericho and everything in it.

ᶜ**6.4** *trumpets:* These were hollowed-out ram's horns. ᵈ**6.17** *destroy . . . now belongs to the LORD:* Destroying a city and everything in it, including its people and animals, showed that it belonged to the LORD and could no longer be used by humans. ᵉ**6.17** *sent:* See 2.1, 21. ᶠ**6.18,19** *Be careful . . . fault:* One ancient translation; Hebrew "Don't keep any of it for yourself. If you do, the LORD will destroy both you and Israel." ᵍ**6.21-25** *camp:* Rahab and her family were Canaanites and were considered unclean. If they stayed in the Israelite army camp, the Lord would not help the Israelite army in battle (see Deuteronomy 23.9-14). However, Rahab and her family later became part of Israel. ʰ**6.21-25** *the LORD's house:* A name for the place of worship, which at that time was the sacred tent.

²⁶After Jericho was destroyed, Joshua warned the people, "Someday a man will rebuild Jericho, but the LORD will put a curse on him, and the man's oldest son will die when he starts to build the town wall. And by the time he finishes the wall and puts gates in it, all his children will be dead."ⁱ

²⁷The LORD helped Joshua in everything he did, and Joshua was famous everywhere in Canaan.

Achan Is Punished for Stealing from the LORD

7 The LORD had said that everything in Jericho belonged to him.ʲ But Achanᵏ from the Judah tribe took some of the things from Jericho for himself. And so the LORD was angry with the Israelites, because one of them had disobeyed him.ˡ

²While Israel was still camped near Jericho, Joshua sent some spies with these instructions: "Go to the town of Aiᵐ and find out whatever you can about the region around the town."

The spies left and went to Ai, which is east of Bethel and near Beth-Aven. ³They went back to Joshua and reported, "You don't need to send the whole army to attack Ai—two or three thousand troops will be enough. Why bother the whole army for a town that small?"

⁴⁻⁵Joshua sent about three thousand soldiers to attack Ai. But the men of Ai fought back and chased the Israelite soldiers away from the town gate and down the hill to the stone quarries.ⁿ Thirty-six Israelite soldiers were killed, and the Israelite army felt discouraged.

⁶Joshua and the leaders of Israel tore their clothes and put dirt on their heads to show their sorrow. They lay facedown on the ground in front of the sacred chest until sunset. ⁷Then Joshua said:

Our LORD, did you bring us across the Jordan River just so the Amorites could destroy us? This wouldn't have happened if we had agreed to stay on the other side of the Jordan. ⁸I don't even know what to say to you, since Israel's army has turned and run from the enemy. ⁹Everyone will think you weren't strong enough to protect your

---

ⁱ6.26 *by the time . . . dead*: Or "when he puts gates into the town wall, his youngest son will die." ʲ7.1 *belonged to him*: See the note at 6.17. ᵏ7.1 *Achan*: The Hebrew text has "Achan, son of Carmi, grandson of Abdi, and great-grandson of Zerah." ˡ7.1 *the LORD was angry . . . disobeyed him*: Even though only one person had disobeyed, it meant that the LORD's instructions to the people of Israel had not been followed, and the whole nation was held responsible. ᵐ7.2 *of Ai*: Or "called The Ruins." ⁿ7.4,5 *stone quarries*: Or "Shebarim."

SingleLife—How can I resist the pressure to be sexually active? (*Joshua 7*)

Determine to obey God completely—even when you are tempted.
We live in an individualistic society where people often believe that their actions won't affect anyone else: you do your thing, I'll do mine, and we'll all be fine. Achan thought he could sin without hurting anyone else. He succumbed to the temptation to take clothing and money from the ruins of Jericho even though God had instructed the Israelites not to keep anything from the conquered cities for themselves. Achan thought he could keep his sin private by hiding the loot under his tent, but he couldn't have been more wrong. God knew and punished the entire community with a terrible defeat at Ai.

Today we also need to understand that our actions do affect each other. This is especially true in the area of sexuality. When we fail to save the fullest expression of our sexuality for the marriage relationship, not only do we rob sexuality of its God-given meaning as the culminating expression of complete commitment to another person, but we hurt our partner and our families as well. When we have sex outside the context of marriage, we're taking something that doesn't belong to us; and trying to cover up the results does not undo the damage. God wants us to obey him completely, and the first step is to believe that he really does know what's best for us—even in this most personal area. (**See also** Psalm 103; Ephesians 6.10-20; James 1.12-18; 2 Peter 2.7-9.)

Words To Remember: *I cannot help you anymore until you do exactly what I have said.—Joshua 7.12* people. Now the Canaanites and everyone else who lives in the land will surround us and wipe us out.

[10]The LORD answered:

Stop lying there on the ground! Get up! [11]I said everything in Jericho belonged to me and had to be destroyed. But the Israelites have kept some of the things for themselves. They stole from me and hid what they took. Then they lied about it. [12]What they stole was supposed to be destroyed, and now Israel itself must be destroyed. I cannot help you anymore until you do exactly what I have said. That's why Israel turns and runs from its enemies instead of standing up to them.

[13]Tell the people of Israel, "Tomorrow you will meet with the LORD your God, so make yourselves acceptable to worship him. The LORD says that you have taken things that should have been destroyed. You won't be able to stand up to your enemies until you get rid of those things.

[14]"Tomorrow morning everyone must gather near the place of worship. You will come forward tribe by tribe, and the LORD will show which tribe is guilty. Next, the clans in that tribe must come forward, and the LORD will show which clan is guilty. The families in that clan must come, and the LORD will point out the guilty family. Finally, the men in that family must come, [15]and the LORD will show who stole what should have been destroyed. That man must be put to death, his body burned, and his possessions thrown into the fire. He has done a terrible thing by breaking the sacred agreement that the LORD made with Israel."

[16]Joshua got up early the next morning and brought each tribe to the place of worship, where the LORD showed that the Judah tribe was guilty. [17]Then Joshua brought the clans of Judah to the LORD, and the LORD showed that the Zerah clan was guilty. One by one he brought the leader of each family in the Zerah clan to the LORD, and the LORD showed that Zabdi's family was guilty. [18]Finally, Joshua brought each man in Zabdi's family to the LORD, and the LORD showed that Achan was the guilty one.

[19]"Achan," Joshua said, "the LORD God of Israel has decided that you are guilty. Is this true? Tell me what you did, and don't try to hide anything."

[20]"It's true," Achan answered. "I sinned and disobeyed the LORD God of Israel. [21-22]While we were in Jericho, I saw a beautiful Babylonian robe, two hundred pieces of silver, and a gold bar that weighed the same as fifty pieces of gold. I wanted them for myself, so I took them. I dug a hole under my tent and hid the silver, the gold, and the robe."

Joshua had some people run to Achan's tent, where they found the silver, the gold, and the robe. [23]They brought them back and put them in front of the sacred chest, so Joshua and the rest of the Israelites could see them. [24]Then everyone took Achan and the things he had stolen to Trouble Valley.[o] They also took along his sons and daughters, his cattle, donkeys, and sheep, his tent, and everything else that belonged to him.

[25]Joshua said, "Achan, you caused us a lot of trouble. Now the LORD is paying you back with the same kind of trouble."

The people of Israel then stoned to death Achan and his family. They made a fire and burned the bodies, together with what Achan had stolen, and all his possessions. [26]They covered the remains with a big pile of rocks, which is still there. Then the LORD stopped being angry with Israel.

That's how the place came to be called Trouble Valley.

Israel Destroys the Town of Ai

8 [1-2]The LORD told Joshua:

Don't be afraid, and don't be discouraged by what happened at the town of Ai. Take the army and attack again. But first, have part of the army set up an ambush on the other side of the town. I will help you defeat the king of Ai and his army, and you will capture the town and the land around it. Destroy Ai and kill its king as you did at Jericho. But you may keep the livestock and everything else you want.

[3-4]Joshua quickly got the army ready to attack Ai. He chose thirty thousand of his best soldiers and gave them these orders:

---

[o]7.24 *Trouble Valley:* Or "Achor Valley."

Tonight, while it is dark, march to
Ai and take up a position behind the
town. Get as close to the town as you
can without being seen, but be ready
to attack.

> *We must trust in God*
> *and learn of his ways—*
> *herein lies wisdom.*
> BARBARA JOHNSON

[5-6]The rest of the army will come
with me and attack near the gate.
When the people of Ai come out to
fight, we'll run away and let them
chase us. They will think we are running from them just like the first time.
But when we've let them chase us far
enough away, [7]you come out of hiding. The LORD our God will help you
capture the town. [8]Then set it on fire,
as the LORD has told us to do. Those
are your orders, [9]now go!

The thirty thousand soldiers went to a
place on the west side of Ai, between Ai and
Bethel, where they could hide and wait to
attack.

That night, Joshua stayed in camp with
the rest of the army. [10]Early the next morning he got his troops ready to move out, and
he and the other leaders of Israel led them
to Ai. [11]They set up camp in full view of
the town, across the valley to the north.
[12]Joshua had already sent five thousand soldiers to the west side of the town to hide
and wait to attack. [13]Now all his troops were
in place. Part of the army was in the camp to
the north of Ai, and the others were hiding
to the west, ready to make a surprise attack.
That night, Joshua went into the valley.[p]

[14-15]The king of Ai saw Joshua's army, so
the king and his troops hurried out early the
next morning to fight them. Joshua and his
army pretended to be beaten, and they let
the men of Ai chase them toward the desert.
The king and his army were facing the Jordan valley as Joshua had planned.

The king did not realize that some Israelite soldiers were hiding behind the town.
[16-17]So he called out every man in Ai to go
after Joshua's troops. They all rushed out to
chase the Israelite army, and they left the
town gates wide open. Not one man was left
in Ai or in Bethel.[q]

Joshua let the men of Ai chase him and
his army farther and farther away from Ai.
[18]Finally, the LORD told Joshua, "Point your
sword[r] at the town of Ai, because now I am
going to help you defeat it!"

As soon as Joshua pointed his sword at
the town, [19]the soldiers who had been hiding got up and ran into the town. They captured it and set it on fire.

[20-21]When Joshua and his troops saw
smoke rising from the town, they knew that
the other part of their army had captured it.
So they turned and attacked.

The men of Ai looked back and saw
smoke rising from their town. But they
could not escape, because the soldiers they
had been chasing had suddenly turned and
started fighting. [22-24]Meanwhile, the other
Israelite soldiers had come from the town
and attacked the men of Ai from the rear.
The Israelites captured the king of Ai and
brought him to Joshua. They also chased
the rest of the men of Ai into the desert and
killed them.[s]

The Israelite army went back to Ai and
killed everyone there. [25-26]Joshua kept his
sword pointed at the town of Ai until every
last one of Ai's twelve thousand people was
dead. [27]But the Israelites took the animals
and the other possessions of the people of
Ai, because this was what the LORD had told
Joshua to do.

[28-29]Joshua made sure every building in
Ai was burned to the ground. He told his
men to kill the king of Ai and hang his body
on a tree. Then at sunset he told the Israelites to take down the body,[t] throw it in the
gateway of the town, and cover it with a big
pile of rocks. Those rocks are still there, and
the town itself has never been rebuilt.

---

[p]**8.13** *valley*: This may refer either to the Jordan River valley or to the valley between the Israelite camp and Ai. [q]**8.16,17** *Ai or in Bethel*: Hebrew; one ancient translation "Ai." [r]**8.18** *sword*: Or "spear." [s]**8.22-24** *Joshua. They also chased . . . them*: Or "Joshua. The men of Ai had chased the Israelites into the desert, but the Israelites killed them there." [t]**8.28,29** *take down the body*: See Deuteronomy 21.22, 23.

Joshua Reads the Blessings and Curses
(Deuteronomy 27.1-26)

³⁰⁻³²One day, Joshua led the people of Israel to Mount Ebal, where he told some of his men, "Build an altar for offering sacrifices to the LORD. And use stones that have never been cut with iron tools,ᵘ because that is what Moses taught in *The Book of the Law*."ᵛ

Joshua offered sacrifices to please the LORDʷ and to ask his blessing.ˣ Then with the Israelites still watching, he copied parts of *The Book of the Law*ʸ of Moses onto stones.

³³⁻³⁵Moses had said that everyone in Israel was to go to the valley between Mount Ebal and Mount Gerizim, where they were to be blessed. So everyone went there, including the foreigners, the leaders, officials, and judges. Half of the people stood on one side of the valley, and half on the other side, with the priests from the Levi tribe standing in the middle with the sacred chest. Then in a loud voice, Joshua read the blessings and curses from *The Book of the Law*ʸ of Moses.ᶻ

The People of Gibeon Trick the Leaders of Israel

9 ¹⁻²The kings west of the Jordan River heard about Joshua's victories, and so they got together and decided to attack Joshua and Israel. These kings were from the hill country and from the foothills to the west, as well as from the Mediterranean seacoast as far north as the Lebanon Mountains. Some of them were Hittites, others were Amorites or Canaanites, and still others were Perizzites, Hivites, or Jebusites.

³The people of Gibeon had also heard what Joshua had done to Jericho and Ai. ⁴So they decided that some of their men should pretend to be messengers to Israel from a faraway country.ᵃ The men put worn-out bags on their donkeys and found some old wineskins that had cracked and had been sewn back together. ⁵Their sandals were old and patched, and their clothes were worn out. They even took along some dry and crumbly bread. ⁶Then they went to the Israelite camp at Gilgal, where they said to Joshua and the men of Israel, "We have come from a country that is far from here. Please make a peace treaty with us."

⁷⁻⁸The Israelites replied, "But maybe you really live near us. We can't make a peace treaty with you if you live nearby."ᵇ

The Gibeonitesᶜ said, "If you make a peace treaty with us, we will be your servants."

"Who are you?" Joshua asked. "Where do you come from?"

They answered:

⁹We are your servants, and we live far from here. We came because the LORD your God is so famous. We heard what the LORD did in Egypt ¹⁰and what he did to those two Amorite kings on the other side of the Jordan: King Og of Bashan, who lived in Ashtaroth, and King Sihon of Heshbon.

¹¹Our leaders and everyone who lives in our country told us to meet with you and tell you that all of us are your servants. They said to ask you to make a peace treaty with our people. They told us to be sure and take along enough food for our journey. ¹²See this dry, crumbly bread of ours? It was hot out of the oven when we packed the food on the day we left our homes. ¹³These cracked wineskins were new when we filled them, and our clothes and sandals are worn out because we have traveled so far.

¹⁴The Israelites tried some of the food,ᵈ but they did not ask the LORD if he wanted them to make a treaty. ¹⁵So Joshua made a peace treaty with the messengers and promised that Israel would not kill their people.

ᵘ**8.30-32** *use stones . . . iron tools:* See Exodus 20.25. ᵛ**8.30-32** *taught . . . Law:* Or "commanded . . . Teachings." ʷ**8.30-32** *sacrifices to please the LORD:* These sacrifices have been traditionally called "whole burnt offerings" because the whole animal was burned on the altar. A main purpose of such sacrifices was to please the LORD with the smell of the sacrifice, and so in the CEV they are often called "sacrifices to please the LORD." ˣ**8.30-32** *to ask his blessing:* These sacrifices have traditionally been called "peace offerings," or "offerings of well-being." A main purpose was to ask for the LORD's blessing, and so in the CEV they are often called "sacrifices to ask the LORD's blessing." ʸ**8.30-32,33-35** *Law:* Or "Teachings." ᶻ**8.33-35** *the blessings . . . Moses:* Or "all of *The Book of the Law of Moses*, including the blessings and the curses." ᵃ**9.4** *So . . . country:* One possible meaning for the difficult Hebrew text. ᵇ**9.7,8** *nearby:* See Deuteronomy 20.10-18. ᶜ**9.7,8** *Gibeonites:* Hebrew "Hivites." ᵈ**9.14** *tried . . . food:* Probably to see if it really was old or to show that they wanted peace.

Israel's leaders swore that Israel would keep this promise.

[16-17]A couple of days later,[e] the Israelites found out that these people actually lived in the nearby towns of Gibeon, Chephirah, Beeroth, and Kiriath-Jearim.[f] So the Israelites left the place where they had camped and arrived at the four towns two days later.[g] [18]But they did not attack the towns, because the Israelite leaders had sworn in the name of the LORD that they would let these people live.

The Israelites complained about their leaders' decision not to attack, [19-21]but the leaders reminded them, "We promised these people in the name of the LORD God of Israel that we would let them live, so we must not harm them. If we break our promise, God will punish us. We'll let them live, but we'll make them cut wood and carry water for our people."

[22]Joshua told some of his soldiers, "I want to meet with the Gibeonite leaders. Bring them here."

When the Gibeonites came, Joshua said, "You live close to us. Why did you lie by claiming you lived far away? [23]Now you are under a curse, and your people will have to send workers to cut wood and carry water for the place of worship."[h]

[24]The Gibeonites answered, "The LORD your God told his servant Moses that you were to kill everyone who lives here and take their land for yourselves. We were afraid you would kill us, and so we tricked you into making a peace treaty. But we agreed to be your servants, [25]and you are strong enough to do anything to us that you want. We just ask you to do what seems right."

[26]Joshua did not let the Israelites kill the Gibeonites, [27]but he did tell the Gibeonites that they would have to be servants of the nation of Israel. They would have to cut firewood and bring it for the priests to use for burning sacrifices on the LORD's altar, wherever the LORD decided the altar would be. The Gibeonites would also have to carry water for the priests. And that is still the work of the Gibeonites.

Joshua Commands the Sun To Stand Still

10 King Adonizedek of Jerusalem[i] heard that Joshua had captured and destroyed the town of Ai, and then killed its king as he had done at Jericho. He also learned that the Gibeonites had signed a peace treaty with Israel. [2]This frightened Adonizedek and his people. They knew that Gibeon was a large town, as big as the towns that had kings, and even bigger than the town of Ai had been. And all of the men of Gibeon were warriors. [3]So Adonizedek sent messages to the kings of four other towns: King Hoham of Hebron, King Piram of Jarmuth, King Japhia of Lachish, and King Debir of Eglon. The messages said, [4]"The Gibeonites have signed a peace treaty with Joshua and the Israelites. Come and help me attack Gibeon!"

> *Open your eyes, my friend, and fill all your life with the brightness of the splendor of God! Live all your life seeing your powerful, loving Lord at work everywhere, in everything, in all your circumstances, in all your moments.*
>
> ANNE ORTLUND

[5]When these five Amorite kings called their armies together and attacked Gibeon, [6]the Gibeonites sent a message to the Israelite camp at Gilgal: "Joshua, please come and rescue us! The Amorite kings from the hill country have joined together and are attacking us. We are your servants, so don't let us down. Please hurry!"

[e]**9.16,17** *A couple . . . later:* The Hebrew text has "At the end of three days," meaning two days after the day the treaty was made.   [f]**9.16,17** *Gibeon, Chephirah, Beeroth, and Kiriath-Jearim:* These towns were twenty to thirty miles west of the Israelite camp at Gilgal.   [g]**9.16,17** *A couple of days . . . later:* Or "A couple of days later, the Israelites moved their camp to the area near the towns of Gibeon, Chephirah, Beeroth, and Kiriath-Jearim. When they arrived, they realized that they had made a peace treaty with the people of these nearby towns!"   [h]**9.23** *the place of worship:* The Hebrew text has "God's house," which at that time was the sacred tent.   [i]**10.1** *Jerusalem:* Jerusalem was not an Israelite city at this time.

[7]Joshua and his army, including his best warriors, left Gilgal. [8]"Joshua," the LORD said, "don't be afraid of the Amorites. They will run away when you attack, and I will help you defeat them."

[9]Joshua marched all night from Gilgal to Gibeon and made a surprise attack on the Amorite camp. [10]The LORD made the enemy panic, and the Israelites started killing them right and left. They[j] chased the Amorite troops up the road to Beth-Horon and kept on killing them, until they reached the towns of Azekah and Makkedah.[k] [11]And while these troops were going down through Beth-Horon Pass,[l] the LORD made huge hailstones fall on them all the way to Azekah. More of the enemy soldiers died from the hail than from the Israelite weapons.

[12-13]The LORD was helping the Israelites defeat the Amorites that day. So about noon, Joshua prayed to the LORD loud enough for the Israelites to hear:

> "Our LORD, make the sun stop
>   in the sky over Gibeon,
> and the moon stand still
>   over Aijalon Valley."[m]
> So the sun and the moon
>   stopped and stood still
> until Israel defeated its enemies.

This poem can be found in *The Book of Jashar*.[n] The sun stood still and didn't go down for about a whole day. [14]Never before and never since has the LORD done anything like that for someone who prayed. The LORD was really fighting for Israel.

[15]After the battle, Joshua and the Israelites went back to their camp at Gilgal.

Joshua Kills the Five Enemy Kings

[16]While the enemy soldiers were running from the Israelites, the five enemy kings ran away and hid in a cave near Makkedah. [17]Joshua's soldiers told him, "The five kings have been found in a cave near Makkedah." [18]Joshua answered, "Roll some big stones over the mouth of the cave and leave a few soldiers to guard it. [19]But you and everyone else must keep after the enemy troops, because they will be safe if they reach their walled towns. Don't let them get away! The LORD our God is helping us get rid of them." [20]So Joshua and the Israelites

almost wiped out the enemy soldiers. Only a few safely reached their walled towns.

[21]The Israelite army returned to their camp at Makkedah, where Joshua was waiting for them. No one around there dared say anything bad about the Israelites. [22]Joshua told his soldiers, "Now, move the rocks from the entrance to the cave and bring those five kings to me."

[23]The soldiers opened the entrance to the cave and brought out the kings of Jerusalem, Hebron, Jarmuth, Lachish, and Eglon. [24]After Joshua had called the army together, he forced the five kings to lie down on the ground. Then he called his officers forward and told them, "You fought these kings along with me, so put your feet on their necks." The officers did, [25]and Joshua continued, "Don't ever be afraid or discouraged. Be brave and strong. This is what the LORD will do to all your enemies."

[26]Joshua killed the five kings and told his men to hang each body on a tree. Then at sunset [27]he told some of his troops, "Take the bodies down and throw them into the cave where the kings were found. Cover the entrance to the cave with big rocks."

Joshua's troops obeyed his orders, and those rocks are still there.

Joshua Continues the Fighting

[28]Later that day, Joshua captured Makkedah and killed its king and everyone else in the town, just as he had done at Jericho.

[29]Joshua and his army left Makkedah and attacked the town of Libnah. [30]The LORD let them capture the town and its king, and they killed the king and everyone else, just as they had done at Jericho.

[31]Joshua then led his army to Lachish, and they set up camp around the town. They attacked, [32]and the next day the LORD let them capture the town. They killed everyone, as they had done at Libnah. [33]King Horam of Gezer arrived to help Lachish, but Joshua and his troops attacked and destroyed him and his army.

---

[j]**10.10** *They:* Or "The LORD." [k]**10.10** *Makkedah:* A total distance of about twenty-five miles.
[l]**10.11** *Beth-Horon Pass:* A two-mile long, steeply-sloping valley between the towns of Upper Beth-Horon and Lower Beth-Horon. [m]**10.12,13** *Aijalon Valley:* A valley southwest of Beth-Horon Pass. [n]**10.12,13** *Book of Jashar:* This book may have been a collection of ancient war songs.

[34]From Lachish, Joshua took his troops to Eglon, where they set up camp surrounding the town. They attacked, [35]captured it that same day, then killed everyone, as they had done at Lachish.

[36]Joshua and his army left Eglon and attacked Hebron. [37]They captured the town and the nearby villages, then killed everyone, including the king. They destroyed Hebron in the same way they had destroyed Eglon.

[38]Joshua and the Israelite army turned and attacked Debir. [39]They captured the town, and its nearby villages. Then they destroyed Debir and killed its king, together with everyone else, just as they had done with Hebron and Libnah.

[40]Joshua captured towns everywhere in the land: In the central hill country and the foothills to the west, in the Southern Desert and the region that slopes down toward the Dead Sea. Whenever he captured a town, he would kill the king and everyone else, as the LORD God of Israel had commanded. [41]Joshua wiped out towns from Kadesh-Barnea to Gaza, everywhere in the region of Goshen,[o] and as far north as Gibeon. [42-43]The LORD fought on Israel's side, so Joshua and the Israelite army were able to capture these kings and take their land. They fought one battle after another, then they went back to their camp at Gilgal after capturing all that land.

Joshua Captures Towns in the North

11 King Jabin of Hazor heard about Joshua's victories, so he sent messages to many nearby kings and asked them to join him in fighting Israel. He sent these messages to King Jobab of Madon, the kings of Shimron and Achshaph, [2]the kings in the northern hill country and in the Jordan River valley south of Lake Galilee,[p] and the kings in the foothills and in Naphath-Dor to the west. [3]He sent messages to the Canaanite kings in the east and the west, to the Amorite, Hittite, Perizzite, and Jebusite kings in the hill country, and to the Hivite kings in the region of Mizpah, near the foot of Mount Hermon.[q]

[4-5]The kings and their armies went to Merom Pond,[r] where they set up camp, and got ready to fight Israel. It seemed as though there were more soldiers and horses and chariots than there are grains of sand on a beach.

[6]The LORD told Joshua:

Don't let them frighten you! I'll help you defeat them, and by this time tomorrow they will be dead.

When you attack, the first thing you have to do is to cripple their horses. Then after the battle is over,[s] burn their chariots.

> *We need to surrender our will to God's will and choose to trust God so we can begin making faith-filled decisions.*
>
> CAROL KENT

[7]Joshua and his army made a surprise attack against the enemy camp at Merom Pond[t] [8-9]and crippled the enemies' horses.[u] Joshua followed the LORD's instructions, and the LORD helped Israel defeat the enemy. The Israelite army even chased enemy soldiers as far as Misrephoth-Maim to the northwest,[v] the city of Sidon to the north, and Mizpeh Valley to the northeast.[w] None of the enemy soldiers escaped alive. The Israelites came back after the battle and burned the enemy's chariots.

[10]Up to this time, the king of Hazor had controlled the kingdoms that had joined to-

---

[o]10.41 *Goshen*: A region between the hill country of Judah and the desert further south. Not the same Goshen as in Genesis 47.4-6. [p]11.2 *Lake Galilee*: The Hebrew text has "Lake Chinnereth," an earlier name. [q]11.3 *Mizpah, near the foot of Mount Hermon*: Probably the same region as Mizpeh Valley in verses 8, 9, but different from the two other places named Mizpeh in 15.37-41; 18.25-28, and also different from the Mizpah mentioned in Genesis 31.49 and Judges 10.17. [r]11.4,5 *Pond*: Or "Gorge." [s]11.6 *When . . . over*: Or "After the battle is over, cripple their horses and burn their chariots." [t]11.7 *Pond*: See the note at 11.4, 5. [u]11.8,9 *and crippled the enemies' horses*: It is also possible that the Israelites crippled the enemies' horses after the battle at the same time they burned the enemies' chariots; see the note at 11.6. [v]11.8,9 *Misrephoth-Maim . . . northwest*: Or "the town of Misrephoth to the northwest" or "the Misrephoth River." [w]11.8,9 *northeast*: These three areas were twenty to thirty-five miles north of Merom.

gether to attack Israel, so Joshua led his army back and captured Hazor. They killed its king [11]and everyone else, then they set the town on fire.

[12-15]Joshua captured all the towns where the enemy kings had ruled. These towns were built on small hills,[x] and Joshua did not set fire to any of these towns, except Hazor. The Israelites kept the animals and everything of value from these towns, but they killed everyone who lived in them, including their kings. That's what the LORD had told his servant Moses to do, that's what Moses had told Joshua to do, and that's exactly what Joshua did.

[16]Joshua and his army took control of the northern and southern hill country, the foothills to the west, the Southern Desert, the whole region of Goshen,[y] and the Jordan River valley. [17-18]They took control of the land from Mount Halak near the country of Edom in the south to Baal-Gad in Lebanon Valley at the foot of Mount Hermon in the north. Joshua and his army were at war with the kings in this region for a long time, but finally they captured and put to death the last king.

[19-20]The LORD had told Moses that he wanted the towns in this region destroyed and their people killed without mercy. That's why the LORD made the people in the towns stubborn and determined to fight Israel. The only town that signed a peace treaty with Israel was the Hivite town of Gibeon. The Israelite army captured the rest of the towns in battle.

[21]During this same time, Joshua and his army killed the Anakim[z] from the northern and southern hill country. They also destroyed the towns where the Anakim had lived, including Hebron, Debir, and Anab. [22]There were not any Anakim left in the regions where the Israelites lived, although there were still some in Gaza, Gath, and Ashdod.[a]

[23]That's how Joshua captured the land, just as the LORD had commanded Moses, and Joshua divided it up among the tribes. Finally, there was peace in the land.

The Kings Defeated by the Israelites

12 Before Moses died, he and the people of Israel had defeated two kings east of the Jordan River. These kings had ruled the region from the Arnon River gorge in the south to Mount Hermon in the north, including the eastern side of the Jordan River valley.

[2]The first king that Moses and the Israelites defeated was an Amorite, King Sihon of Heshbon.[b] The southern border of his kingdom ran down the middle of the Arnon River gorge, taking in the town of Aroer on the northern edge of the gorge. The Jabbok River separated Sihon's kingdom from the Ammonites on the east. Then the Jabbok turned west and became his northern border, so his kingdom included the southern half of the region of Gilead. [3]Sihon also controlled the eastern side of the Jordan River valley from Lake Galilee[c] south to Beth-Jeshimoth and the Dead Sea. In addition to these regions, he ruled the town called Slopes of Mount Pisgah[d] and the land south of there at the foot of the hill.

[4]Next, Moses and the Israelites defeated King Og of Bashan,[e] who lived in the town of Ashtaroth part of each year and in Edrei the rest of the year. Og was one of the last of the Rephaim.[f] [5]His kingdom stretched north to Mount Hermon, east to the town of Salecah, and included the land of Bashan as far west as the borders of the kingdoms of Geshur and Maacah. He also ruled the northern half of Gilead.

[6]Moses, the LORD's servant, had led the people of Israel in defeating Sihon and Og. Then Moses gave their land to the tribes of Reuben, Gad, and East Manasseh.

[7-8]Later, Joshua and the Israelites defeated many kings west of the Jordan River, from Baal-Gad in Lebanon Valley in the north to Mount Halak near the country of Edom in the south. This region included the hill country and the foothills, the Jordan River valley and its western slopes, and the Southern Desert. Joshua and the Israelites

---

[x]**11.12-15** *small hills:* Towns were often built on top of the ruins of a previous town that had been destroyed. When this happened many times at one place, a hill was formed. [y]**11.16** *Goshen:* See the note at 10.41.
[z]**11.21** *Anakim:* Perhaps a group of very large people that lived in Palestine before the Israelites (see Numbers 13.33 and Deuteronomy 2.10, 11, 20, 21).
[a]**11.22** *Gaza, Gath, and Ashdod:* Towns in Philistia.
[b]**12.2** *King Sihon of Heshbon:* See Numbers 21.21-31.
[c]**12.3** *Lake Galilee:* See the note at 11.2. [d]**12.3** *the town called Slopes of Mount Pisgah:* Or "the slopes of Mount Pisgah." [e]**12.4** *King Og of Bashan:* See Numbers 21.33-35. [f]**12.4** *Rephaim:* Perhaps a group of very large people that lived in Palestine before the Israelites (see Deuteronomy 2.10, 11, 20, 21).

took this land from the Hittites, the Amorites, the Canaanites, the Perizzites, the Hivites, and the Jebusites. Joshua divided up the land among the tribes of Israel.

The Israelites defeated the kings of the following towns west of the Jordan River: [9-24]Jericho, Ai near Bethel, Jerusalem, Hebron, Jarmuth, Lachish, Eglon, Gezer, Debir, Geder, Hormah, Arad, Libnah, Adullam, Makkedah, Bethel, Tappuah, Hepher, Aphek, Lasharon,[g] Madon, Hazor, Shimron-Meron, Achshaph, Taanach, Megiddo, Kedesh, Jokneam on Mount Carmel, Dor in Naphath-Dor, Goiim in Galilee,[h] and Tirzah.[i]

There were thirty-one of these kings in all.

The Land Israel Had Not Yet Taken

13 Many years later, the LORD told Joshua:

Now you are very old, but there is still a lot of land that Israel has not yet taken. [2-7]First, there is the Canaanite territory that starts at the Shihor River just east of Egypt and goes north to Ekron. The southern part of this region belongs to the Avvites and the Geshurites,[j] and the land around Gaza, Ashdod, Ashkelon, Gath, and Ekron belongs to the five Philistine rulers.

God is out in front of you preparing, planning, going before, leading, and guiding you every step of the way.

JONI EARECKSON TADA

The other Canaanite territory is in the north. Its northern border starts at the town of Arah, which belongs to the Sidonians. From there, it goes to Aphek,[k] then along the Amorite border[l] to Hamath Pass.[m] The eastern border starts at Hamath Pass and goes south to Baal-Gad at the foot of Mount Hermon, and its southern boundary

runs west from there to Misrephoth-Maim.[n] This northern region includes the Lebanon Mountains and the land that belongs to the Gebalites[o] and the Sidonians who live in the hill country from the Lebanon Mountains to Misrephoth-Maim.

With my help, Israel will capture these Canaanite territories and force out the people who live there. But you must divide up the land from the Jordan River to the Mediterranean Sea[p] among the nine tribes and the half of Manasseh that don't have any land yet. Then each tribe will have its own land.

The Land East of the Jordan River

[8]Moses had already given land east of the Jordan River to the tribes of Reuben, Gad, and half of Manasseh. [9]This region stretched north from the town in the middle of the Arnon River valley, and included the town of Aroer on the northern edge of the valley. It covered the flatlands of Medeba north of Dibon, [10]and took in the towns that had belonged to Sihon, the Amorite king of Heshbon. Some of these towns were as far east as the Ammonite border.

[11-12]Geshur and Maacah were part of this region, and so was the whole territory that King Og had ruled, that is, Gilead, Mount Hermon, and all of Bashan as far east as Salecah. Og had lived in Ashtaroth part of each year, and he had lived in Edrei the rest of the year. Og had been one of the last of the Rephaim,[q] but Moses had defeated Sihon and Og and their people[r] and had forced them to leave their land. [13]However, the Isra-

[g]12.9-24 *Aphek, Lasharon:* Or "Aphek in the Sharon Plain."   [h]12.9-24 *Galilee:* One ancient translation; Hebrew "Gilgal."   [i]12.9-24 *Jericho . . . Tirzah:* There are some differences in this list between the Hebrew and several ancient translations.   [j]13.2-7 *Geshurites:* Not the same Geshur as in 12.5 and 13.11. One ancient translation has "Gezerites." Gezer was a town north of Ekron that the Israelites did not capture (see Judges 1.29).   [k]13.2-7 *Aphek:* Not the same Aphek as in 12.9-24.   [l]13.2-7 *Amorite border:* What had been the southern border of the old Amorite kingdom of Amurru.   [m]13.2-7 *Hamath Pass:* Or "Lebo-Hamath."   [n]13.2-7 *Misrephoth-Maim:* Or "Misrephoth" or "the Misrephoth River."   [o]13.2-7 *Gebalites:* Gebal was another name for Byblos.   [p]13.2-7 *from . . . Sea:* One ancient translation; the Hebrew text does not have these words.   [q]13.11,12 *Rephaim:* See the note at 12.4.   [r]13.11,12 *Sihon . . . people:* Or "the Rephaim."

elites did not force the people of Geshur and Maacah to leave, and they still live there among the Israelites.

Moses Did Not Give Land to the Levi Tribe

[14]Moses did not give any land to the Levi tribe, because the LORD God of Israel had told them, "Instead of land, you will receive the sacrifices offered at my altar."

Moses Gives Land to the Reuben Tribe

[15]Moses gave land to each of the clans in the Reuben tribe. [16]Their land started in the south at the town in the middle of the Arnon River valley, took in the town of Aroer on the northern edge of the valley, and went as far north as the flatlands around Medeba. [17-21]The Amorite King Sihon had lived in Heshbon and had ruled the towns in the flatlands. Now Heshbon belonged to Reuben, and so did the following towns in the flatlands: Dibon, Bamoth-Baal, Beth-Baal-Meon, Jahaz, Kedemoth, Mephaath, Kiriathaim, Sibmah, Zereth-Shahar on the hill in the valley, Beth-Peor, Slopes of Mount Pisgah, and Beth-Jeshimoth.

Moses defeated Sihon and killed him and the Midianite chiefs who ruled parts of his kingdom for him. Their names were Evi, Rekem, Zur, Hur, and Reba. [22]The Israelites also killed Balaam the son of Beor, who had been a fortuneteller.

[23]This region with its towns and villages was the land for the Reuben tribe, and the Jordan River was its western border.

Moses Gives Land to the Gad Tribe

[24]Moses also gave land to each of the clans in the Gad tribe. [25]It included the town of Jazer, and in the Gilead region their territory took in the land and towns as far east as the town of Aroer[s] just west of Rabbah.[t] This was about half of the land that had once belonged to the Ammonites. [26]The land given to Gad stretched from Heshbon in the south to Ramath-Mizpeh and Betonim in the north, and even further north to Mahanaim and Lidebor.[u] [27]Gad also received the eastern half of the Jordan River valley, which had been ruled by King Sihon of Heshbon. This territory stretched as far north as Lake Galilee,[v] and included the towns of Beth-Haram, Beth-Nimrah, Succoth, and Zaphon. [28]These regions with

their towns and villages were given to the Gad tribe.

Moses Gives Land to Half of the Manasseh Tribe

[29]Moses gave land east of the Jordan River to half of the clans from the Manasseh tribe. [30-31]Their land started at Mahanaim and took in the region that King Og of Bashan had ruled, including Ashtaroth and Edrei, the two towns where he had lived. The villages where the Jair clan settled were part of Manasseh's land, and so was the northern half of the region of Gilead. The clans of this half of Manasseh had sixty towns in all.

The Manasseh tribe is sometimes called the Machir tribe, after Manasseh's son Machir.

[32]That was how Moses divided up the Moab Plains to the east of Jericho on the other side of the Jordan River, so these two and a half tribes would have land of their own. [33]But Moses did not give any land to the Levi tribe, because the LORD had promised that he would always provide for them.

The Land West of the Jordan River

[14] [1-5]Nine and a half tribes still did not have any land, although two and a half tribes had already received land east of the Jordan River. Moses had divided that land among them, and he had also said that the Levi tribe would not receive a large region like the other tribes. Instead, the people of Levi would receive towns and the nearby pastures for their sheep, goats, and cattle. And since the descendants of Joseph had become the two tribes of Ephraim and Manasseh, there were still nine and a half tribes that needed land. The LORD had told Moses that he would show those tribes[w] how to divide up the land of Canaan.

When the priest Eleazar, Joshua, and the leaders of the families and tribes of Israel

---

[s]**13.25** *Aroer:* Not the same town as the Aroer in verse 16. [t]**13.25** *Rabbah:* The capital city of Ammon. [u]**13.26** *Lidebor:* This may be another name for Lodebar, a town a few miles east of the Jordan River and about ten miles south of Lake Galilee. [v]**13.27** *Lake Galilee:* See the note at 11.2. [w]**14.1-5** *he would show those tribes:* The Hebrew text has "those tribes must cast lots to find out." Pieces of wood or stone (called "lots") were used to find out what God wanted his people to do.

met to divide up the land of Canaan, the LORD showed them how to do it.

Joshua Gives Hebron to Caleb

[6]One day while the Israelites were still camped at Gilgal, Caleb the son of Jephunneh went to talk with Joshua. Caleb belonged to the Kenaz clan, and many other people from the Judah tribe went with Caleb. He told Joshua:

You know that back in Kadesh-Barnea the LORD talked to his prophet Moses about you and me. [7]I was forty years old at the time Moses sent me from Kadesh-Barnea into Canaan as a spy. When I came back and told him about the land, everything I said was true. [8]The other spies said things that made our people afraid, but I completely trusted the LORD God. [9]The same day I came back, Moses told me, "Since you were faithful to the LORD God, I promise that the places where you went as a spy will belong to you and your descendants forever."

[10]Joshua, it was forty-five years ago that the LORD told Moses to make that promise, and now I am eighty-five. Even though Israel has moved from place to place in the desert, the LORD has kept me alive all this time as he said he would. [11]I'm just as strong today as I was then, and I can still fight as well in battle.

> *The more we are faithful,*
> *the more we observe*
> *God's faithfulness to us.*
> GIGI GRAHAM TCHIVIDJIAN

[12]So I'm asking you for the hill country that the LORD promised me that day. You were there. You heard the other spies talk about that part of the hill country and the large, walled towns where the Anakim[x] live. But maybe the LORD will help me take their land, just as he promised.

[13]Joshua prayed that God would help Caleb, then he gave Hebron to Caleb and his descendants. [14]And Hebron still belongs to Caleb's descendants, because he was faithful to the LORD God of Israel.

[15]Hebron used to be called Arba's Town,[y] because Arba had been one of the greatest[z] of the Anakim.

There was peace in the land.

Judah's Land

15 The clans of the Judah tribe were given land that went south along the border of Edom, and at its farthest point south it even reached the Zin Desert. [2]Judah's southern border started at the south end of the Dead Sea. [3]As it went west from there, it ran south of Scorpion Pass[a] to Zin, and then came up from the south to Kadesh-Barnea. It continued past Hezron up to Addar, turned toward Karka, [4]and ran along to Azmon. After that, it followed the Egyptian Gorge and ended at the Mediterranean Sea. This was also Israel's southern border.

[5]Judah's eastern border ran the full length of the Dead Sea.

The northern border started at the northern end of the Dead Sea.[b] [6]From there it went west up to Beth-Hoglah, continued north of Beth-Arabah, and went up to the Monument of Bohan,[c] who belonged to the Reuben tribe. [7]From there, it went to Trouble Valley[d] and Debir,[e] then turned north and went to Gilgal,[f] which is on the north side of the valley across from Adummim Pass. It continued on to Enshemesh, Enrogel, [8]and up through Hinnom Valley on the land sloping south from Jerusalem. The city of Jerusalem itself belonged to the Jebusites.

Next, the border went up to the top of the mountain on the west side of Hinnom Valley and at the north end of Rephaim Valley. [9]At the top of the mountain it turned

---

[x]**14.12** *Anakim:* See the note at 11.21.   [y]**14.15** *Arba's Town:* Or "Kiriath-Arba."   [z]**14.15** *Arba's Town, because . . . greatest:* Hebrew; one ancient translation "Arba's Town. It was one of the main towns."   [a]**15.3** *Scorpion Pass:* Or "Akrabbim Pass."   [b]**15.5** *at . . . Dead Sea:* One possible meaning for the difficult Hebrew text.   [c]**15.6** *Monument of Bohan:* Or "Bohan Rock," possibly a natural rock formation.   [d]**15.7** *Trouble Valley:* Or "Achor Valley."   [e]**15.7** *Debir:* Not the same town as in 10.38, 39.   [f]**15.7** *Gilgal:* Not the same "Gilgal" as in 4.19.

and went to Nephtoah Spring and then to the ruins[g] on Mount Ephron. From there, it went to Baalah, which is now called Kiriath-Jearim.

[10]From Baalah the northern border curved west to Mount Seir and then ran along the northern ridge of Mount Jearim, where Chesalon is located. Then it went down to Beth-Shemesh[h] and over to Timnah. [11]It continued along to the hillside north of Ekron, curved around to Shikkeron, and then went to Mount Baalah. After going to Jabneel, the border finally ended at the Mediterranean Sea, [12]which was Judah's western border.

The clans of Judah lived within these borders.

Caleb's Land
(Judges 1.12-15)

[13]Joshua gave Caleb some land among the people of Judah, as God had told him to do. Caleb's share was Hebron, which at that time was known as Arba's Town,[i] because Arba was the famous ancestor of the Anakim.[j]

[14]Caleb attacked Hebron and forced the three Anakim clans of[k] Sheshai, Ahiman, and Talmai to leave. [15]Next, Caleb started a war with the town of Debir, which at that time was called Kiriath-Sepher. [16]He told his men, "The man who captures Kiriath-Sepher can marry my daughter Achsah."

[17]Caleb's nephew Othniel[l] captured Kiriath-Sepher, and Caleb let him marry Achsah. [18]Right after the wedding, Achsah started telling Othniel that he[m] ought to ask her father for a field. She went to see her father, and while she was getting down from[n] her donkey, Caleb asked her, "What's bothering you?"

[19]She answered, "I need your help. The land you gave me is in the Southern Desert, so I really need some spring-fed ponds[o] for a water supply."

Caleb gave her a couple of small ponds, named Higher Pond and Lower Pond.[p]

Towns in Judah's Land

[20]The following is a list of the towns in each region given to the Judah clans:

[21-32]The first region was located in the Southern Desert along the border with Edom, and it had the following twenty-nine towns with their surrounding villages:

Kabzeel, Eder, Jagur, Kinah, Dimonah, Aradah,[q] Kedesh, Hazor of Ithnan,[r] Ziph, Telem, Bealoth, Hazor-Hadattah, Kerioth-Hezron, which is also called Hazor, Amam, Shema, Moladah, Hazar-Gaddah, Heshmon, Beth-Pelet, Hazar-Shual, Beersheba and its surrounding villages,[s] Baalah, Iim, Ezem, Eltolad, Chesil, Hormah, Ziklag, Madmannah, Sansannah, Lebaoth, Shilhim, and Enrimmon.[t]

[33-36]The second region was located in the northern part of the lower foothills, and it had the following fourteen towns with their surrounding villages:

Eshtaol, Zorah, Ashnah, Zanoah, En-Gannim, Tappuah, Enam, Jarmuth, Adullam, Socoh, Azekah, Shaaraim, Adithaim, Gederah, and Gederothaim.

[37-41]The third region was located in the southern part of the lower foothills, and it had the following sixteen towns with their surrounding villages:

Zenan, Hadashah, Migdalgad, Dilan, Mizpeh, Joktheel, Lachish, Bozkath, Eglon, Cabbon, Lahmas,[u] Chitlish, Gederoth, Beth-Dagon, Naamah, and Makkedah.

[42-44]The fourth region was located in the central part of the lower foothills, and it had the following nine towns with their surrounding villages:

Libnah, Ether, Ashan, Iphtah, Ashnah, Nezib, Keilah, Achzib, and Mareshah.

---

[g]15.9 *ruins:* Hebrew; one ancient translation "towns."
[h]15.10 *Beth-Shemesh:* Probably the same town as the Ir-Shemesh of 19.41-46. Two other towns were also named Beth-Shemesh (see 19.17-23 and 19.35-39).
[i]15.13 *Arba's Town:* See the note at 14.15.
[j]15.13 *Anakim:* See the note at 11.21.   [k]15.14 *clans of:* Or "warriors."   [l]15.17 *Caleb's nephew Othniel:* Hebrew "Othniel the son of Caleb's brother Kenaz."
[m]15.18 *Achsah . . . Othniel . . . he:* Hebrew; one manuscript of one ancient translation and two ancient translations of the parallel in Judges 1.14 "Othniel . . . Achsah . . . she."   [n]15.18 *getting down from:* One possible meaning for the difficult Hebrew text.
[o]15.19 *spring-fed ponds:* Or "wells."   [p]15.19 *small ponds . . . Pond . . . Pond:* Or "wells . . . Well . . . Well."
[q]15.21-32 *Aradah:* One possible meaning for the difficult Hebrew text.   [r]15.21-32 *Hazor of Ithnan:* One ancient translation; Hebrew "Hazor and Ithnan."
[s]15.21-32 *its . . . villages:* One ancient translation; Hebrew "Biziothiah."   [t]15.21-32 *Enrimmon:* One ancient translation; Hebrew "Ain and Rimmon."   [u]15.37-41 *Lahmas:* Most Hebrew manuscripts; many other Hebrew manuscripts and one manuscript of one ancient translation "Lahmam."

45-47 The fifth region was located along the Mediterranean seacoast, and it had the following towns with their surrounding settlements and villages:

Ekron and the towns between there and the coast, Ashdod and the larger towns nearby, Gaza, the towns from Gaza to the Egyptian Gorge, and the towns along the coast of the Mediterranean Sea.

48-51 The sixth region was in the southwestern part of the hill country, and it had the following eleven towns with their surrounding villages:

Shamir, Jattir, Socoh, Dannah, Kiriath-Sannah, which is now called Debir, Anab, Eshtemoh,[v] Anim, Goshen, Holon, and Giloh.

52-54 The seventh region was located in the south-central part of Judah's hill country, and it had the following nine towns with their surrounding villages:

Arab, Dumah,[w] Eshan, Janim, Beth-Tappuah, Aphekah, Humtah, Kiriath-Arba, which is now called Hebron, and Zior.

55-57 The eighth region was located in the southeastern part of the hill country, and it had the following ten towns with their surrounding villages:

Maon, Carmel, Ziph, Juttah, Jezreel,[x] Jokdeam,[y] Zanoah, Kain, Gibeah,[z] and Timnah.

58-59 The ninth region was located in the central part of Judah's hill country, and it had the following six towns with their surrounding villages:

Halhul, Beth-Zur, Gedor, Maarath, Beth-Anoth, and Eltekon.

The tenth region was located in the north-central part of Judah's hill country, and it had the following eleven towns with their surrounding villages:

Tekoa, Ephrath, which is also called Bethlehem, Peor, Etam, Culon, Tatam, Shoresh, Kerem, Gallim, Bether, and Manahath.[a]

60The eleventh region was located in the northern part of Judah's hill country, and it had the following two towns with their surrounding villages:

Rabbah, and Kiriath-Baal, which is also called Kiriath-Jearim.

61-62 The twelfth region was located in the desert along the Dead Sea, and it had the following six towns with their surrounding villages:

Beth-Arabah, Middin, Secacah, Nibshan, Salt Town, and En-Gedi.

The Jebusites

63The Jebusites lived in Jerusalem, and the people of the Judah tribe could not capture the city and get rid of them. That's why Jebusites still live in Jerusalem along with the people of Judah.[b]

Ephraim's Land

16 **1-4**Ephraim and Manasseh are the two tribes descended from Joseph, and the following is a description of the land they received. The southern border of their land started at the Jordan River east of the spring at Jericho. From there it went west through the desert up to the hill country around Bethel. From Bethel it went to Luz and then[c] to the border of the Archites in Ataroth.[d] It continued west down to the land that belonged to the Japhlet clan, then went on to Lower Beth-Horon, Gezer, and the Mediterranean Sea.

5The following is a description of the land that was divided among the clans of the Ephraim tribe. Their southern border started at Ataroth-Addar and went west to Upper Beth-Horon **6-8**and the Mediterranean Sea. Their northern border started on the east at Janoah, curved a little to the north, then came back south to Michmethath and Tappuah, where it followed the Kanah Gorge west to the Mediterranean Sea.

The eastern border started on the north near Janoah and went between Janoah on the southwest and Taanath-Shiloh on the northeast. Then it went south to Ataroth,

---

[v]**15.48-51** *Eshtemoh:* Another spelling for the name Eshtemoa (see 21.9-19). [w]**15.52-54** *Dumah:* Most Hebrew manuscripts; some Hebrew manuscripts and one ancient translation "Rumah." [x]**15.55-57** *Jezreel:* Not the same Jezreel as in 19.17-23. [y]**15.55-57** *Jokdeam:* Hebrew; one ancient translation "Jorkeam." [z]**15.55-57** *Gibeah:* Not the same Gibeah as in 18.25-28. [a]**15.58,59** *The tenth region . . . Manahath:* One ancient translation; the Hebrew text does not have these words. [b]**15.63** *Jebusites . . . Judah:* Israel captured Jerusalem in King David's time, but even then the Jebusites were not forced to leave. [c]**16.1-4** *it . . . then:* Or "which is also called Luz, it went." [d]**16.1-4** *Ataroth:* This is the same Ataroth as Ataroth-Addar in verse 5, but a different Ataroth from the one in verses 6-8.

Naarah, and on as far as the edge of the land that belonged to Jericho. At that point it turned east and went to the Jordan River. The clans of Ephraim received this region as their tribal land. ⁹Ephraim also had some towns and villages that were inside Manasseh's tribal land.

¹⁰Ephraim could not force the Canaanites out of Gezer, so there are still some Canaanites who live there among the Israelites. But now these Canaanites have to work as slaves for the Israelites.

Manasseh's Land West of the Jordan River

17 ¹⁻⁶Manasseh was Joseph's oldest son, and Machir was Manasseh's oldest son. Machir had a son named Gilead, and some of his descendants had already received the regions of Gilead and Bashan because they were good warriors. The other clans of the Manasseh tribe descended from Gilead's sons Abiezer, Helek, Asriel, Shechem, Hepher, and Shemida. The following is a description of the land they received.

Hepher's son Zelophehad did not have any sons, but he did have five daughters: Mahlah, Noah, Hoglah, Milcah, and Tirzah. One day the clans that were descendants of Zelophehad's five daughters went to the priest Eleazar, Joshua, and the leaders of Israel. The people of these clans said, "The LORD told Moses to give us land just as he gave land to our relatives."ᵉ

Joshua followed the LORD's instructions and gave land to these five clans, as he had given land to the five clans that had descended from Hepher's brothers.ᶠ So Manasseh's land west of the Jordan River was divided into ten parts.

⁷The land of the Manasseh tribe went from its northern border with the Asher tribe south to Michmethath, which is to the east of Shechem. The southern border started there, but curved even farther south to include the people who lived around Tappuah Spring.ᵍ ⁸The town of Tappuah was on Manasseh's border with Ephraim. Although the land around Tappuah belonged to Manasseh, the town itself belonged to Ephraim.

⁹⁻¹⁰Then the border went west to the Kanah Gorge and ran along the northern edge of the gorge to the Mediterranean Sea. The land south of the gorge belonged to Ephraim. And even though there were a few towns that belonged to Ephraim north of the gorge, the land north of the gorge belonged to Manasseh.

The western border of Manasseh was the Mediterranean Sea, and the tribe shared a border with the Asher tribe on the northwest and with the Issachar tribe on the northeast.

¹¹Manasseh was supposed to have the following towns with their surrounding villages inside the borders of Issachar's and Asher's tribal lands:

Beth-Shan, Ibleam, Endor, Taanach, Megiddo, and Dor, which is also called Naphath.ʰ

> *No matter where we women live, we're all sisters in Christ. And we have a lot to offer each other—our time, our talents, our resources, our compassion, and our desire to make the world better.*
>
> RAMONA CRAMER TUCKER

¹²But the people of Manasseh could not capture these towns, so the Canaanites kept on living in them. ¹³When the Israelites grew stronger, they made the Canaanites in these towns work as their slaves, though they never did force them to leave.

ᵉ**17.1-6** *The LORD told Moses . . . relatives:* See Numbers 27.1-11; 36.1-12. ᶠ**17.1-6** *the clans that were descendants of Zelophehad's five daughters . . . Hepher's brothers:* Or "Zelophehad's five daughters went to the priest Eleazar, Joshua, and the leaders of Israel. The five sisters said, 'The LORD told Moses to give us land just as he gave land to our relatives.' Joshua followed the LORD's instructions and gave land to these five sisters, as he had given land to Hepher's brothers."
ᵍ**17.7** *to include . . . Tappuah Spring:* Hebrew; one ancient translation "to Jassiben-Tappuah" or "and turns toward Tappuah Spring." ʰ**17.11** *Dor . . . Naphath:* One possible meaning for the difficult Hebrew text.

Joseph's Descendants Ask for More Land

[14]One day the Joseph tribes[i] came to Joshua and asked, "Why didn't you give us more land? The LORD has always been kind to us, and we have too many people for this small region."

[15]Joshua replied, "If you have so many people that you don't have enough room in the hill country of Ephraim, then go into the forest that belonged to the Perizzites and the Rephaim.[j] Clear out the trees and make more room for yourselves there."

[16]"Even if we do that," they answered, "there still won't be enough land for us in the hill country. And we can't move down into Jezreel Valley, because the Canaanites who live in Beth-Shan and in other parts of the valley have iron chariots."

[17]"Your tribes do have a lot of people," Joshua admitted. "I'll give you more land. Your tribes are powerful, [18]so you can have the rest of the hill country, but it's a forest, and you'll have to cut down the trees and clear the land. You can also have Jezreel Valley. Even though the Canaanites there are strong and have iron chariots, you can force them to leave the valley."

Joshua Gives Out the Rest of the Land

18 After Israel had captured the land, they met at Shiloh and set up the sacred tent.[k] [2]There were still seven tribes without any land, [3-7]so Joshua told the people:

The Judah tribe has already settled in its land in the south, and the Joseph tribes[l] have settled in their land in the north. The tribes of Gad, Reuben, and East Manasseh already have the land that the LORD's servant Moses gave them east of the Jordan River. And the people of Levi won't get a single large region of the land like the other tribes. Instead, they will serve the LORD as priests.

But the rest of you haven't done a thing to take over any land. The LORD God who was worshiped by your ancestors has given you the land, and now it's time to go ahead and settle there.

Seven tribes still don't have any land. Each of these tribes should choose three men, and I'll send them to explore the remaining land. They will divide it into seven regions, write a description of each region, and bring these descriptions back to me. I will find out[m] from the LORD our God what region each tribe should get.

[8]Just before the men left camp, Joshua repeated their orders: "Explore the land and write a description of it. Then come back to Shiloh, and I will find out from the LORD how to divide the land."

[9]The men left and went across the land, dividing it into seven regions. They wrote down a description of each region, town by town, and returned to Joshua at the camp at Shiloh. [10]Joshua found out from the LORD how to divide the land, and he told the tribes what the LORD had decided.

Benjamin's Land

[11]Benjamin was the first tribe chosen to receive land. The region for its clans lay between the Judah tribe on the south and the Joseph tribes[n] on the north. [12]Benjamin's northern border started at the Jordan River and went up the ridge north of Jericho, then on west into the hill country as far as the Beth-Aven Desert. [13-14]From there it went to Luz, which is now called Bethel. The border ran along the ridge south of Luz, then went to Ataroth-Orech[o] and on as far as the mountain south of Lower Beth-Horon. At that point it turned south and became the western border. It went as far south as Kiriath-Baal, a town in Judah now called Kiriath-Jearim.

[15]Benjamin's southern border started at the edge of Kiriath-Jearim and went east to the ruins[p] and on to Nephtoah Spring. [16]From there it went to the bottom of the hill at the northern end of Rephaim Valley. The other side of this hill faces Hinnom Valley, which is on the land that slopes south from Jerusalem.[q] The border went down through Hinnom Valley until it reached Enrogel.

---

[i]17.14 *Joseph tribes:* Ephraim and the half of Manasseh that lived west of the Jordan River. [j]17.15 *Rephaim:* See the note at 12.4. [k]18.1 *sacred tent:* Or "meeting tent." [l]18.3-7 *Joseph tribes:* See the note at 17.14. [m]18.3-7 *find out:* Hebrew "cast lots to find out" (see the note at 14.1-5). [n]18.11 *Joseph tribes:* See the note at 17.14. [o]18.13,14 *Ataroth-Orech:* One ancient translation; Hebrew "Ataroth-Addar." [p]18.15 *the ruins:* One possible meaning for the difficult Hebrew text. [q]18.16 *Jerusalem:* Hebrew "the Jebusite town."

[17]At Enrogel the border curved north and went to Enshemesh and on east to Geliloth,[r] which is across the valley from Adummim Pass. Then it went down to the Monument of Bohan,[s] who belonged to the Reuben tribe. [18]The border ran along the hillside north of Beth-Arabah,[t] then down into the Jordan River valley. [19]Inside the valley it went south as far as the northern hillside of Beth-Hoglah. The last section of the border went from there to the northern end of the Dead Sea,[u] at the mouth of the Jordan River. [20]The Jordan River itself was Benjamin's eastern border.

These were the borders of Benjamin's tribal land, where the clans of Benjamin lived.

[21-24]One region of Benjamin's tribal land had twelve towns with their surrounding villages. Those towns were Jericho, Beth-Hoglah, Emek-Keziz, Beth-Arabah, Zemaraim, Bethel, Avvim, Parah, Ophrah, Chephar-Ammoni, Ophni, and Geba.

[25-28]In the other region there were the following fourteen towns with their surrounding villages: Gibeon, Ramah, Beeroth, Mizpeh, Chephirah, Mozah, Rekem, Irpeel, Taralah, Zelah, Haeleph, Gibeah, Kiriath-Jearim,[v] and Jerusalem, which is also called Jebusite Town.

These regions are the tribal lands of Benjamin.

Simeon's Land

19 Simeon was the second tribe chosen to receive land, and the region for its clans was inside Judah's borders. [2-6]In one region of Simeon's tribal land there were the following thirteen towns with their surrounding villages:

Beersheba, Shema,[w] Moladah, Hazar-Shual, Balah, Ezem, Eltolad, Bethul, Hormah, Ziklag, Beth-Marcaboth, Hazar-Susah, Beth-Lebaoth, and Sha-ruhen.

[7]In another region, Simeon had the following four towns with their surrounding villages:

Enrimmon,[x] Tachan,[y] Ether, and Ashan.

[8]Simeon's land also included all the other towns and villages as far south as Baalath-Beer, which is also called Ramah of the South.

[9]Simeon's tribal land was actually inside Judah's territory. Judah had received too much land for the number of people in its tribe, so part of Judah's land was given to Simeon.

Zebulun's Land

[10-12]Zebulun was the third tribe chosen to receive land. The southern border for its clans started in the west at the edge of the gorge near Jokneam. It went east to the edge of the land that belongs to the town of Dabbesheth, and continued on to Maralah and Sarid. It took in the land that belongs to Chislothtabor, then ended at Daberath.

The eastern border went up to Japhia [13]and continued north to Gath-Hepher, Ethkazin, and Rimmonah,[z] where it curved[d] toward Neah [14]and became the northern border. Then it curved south around Hannathon and went as far west as Iphtahel Valley.

[15]Zebulun had twelve towns with their surrounding villages. Some of these were Kattath, Nahalal, Shimron, Jiralah,[b] and Bethlehem.[c]

[16]This is the tribal land, and these are the towns and villages of the Zebulun clans.

Issachar's Land

[17-23]Issachar was the fourth tribe chosen to receive land. The northern border for its clans went from Mount Tabor east to the Jordan River. Their land included the following

---

[r]18.17 Geliloth: Probably another name for Gilgal.
[s]18.17 Monument of Bohan: See the note at 15.6.
[t]18.18 hillside north of Beth-Arabah: One ancient translation (see also the border description in 15.6); Hebrew "the northern hillside overlooking the Jordan River valley." [u]18.19 northern . . . Dead Sea: One possible meaning for the difficult Hebrew text.
[v]18.25-28 Kiriath-Jearim: One ancient translation; Hebrew "Kiriath." [w]19.2-6 Shema: One ancient translation and some manuscripts of another ancient translation (see also the list at 15.21-32); Hebrew and some manuscripts of one ancient translation "Sheba." The list in 1 Chronicles 4.28 does not have either "Shema" or "Sheba." [x]19.7 Enrimmon: Some Hebrew manuscripts and one ancient translation; most Hebrew manuscripts "Ain, Rimmon." [y]19.7 Tachan: Some manuscripts of one ancient translation; the Hebrew text does not have this word. [z]19.13 Rimmonah: Or "Rimmon." [d]19.13 Rimmonah . . . curved: One possible meaning for the difficult Hebrew text.
[b]19.15 Jiralah: Some Hebrew manuscripts and two ancient translations; most Hebrew manuscripts "Idalah." [c]19.15 Bethlehem: This town is different from the Bethlehem in 15.58, 59.

sixteen towns with their surrounding villages:

Jezreel, Chesulloth, Shunem, Hapharaim, Shion, Anaharath, Debirath,[d] Kishion, Ebez, Remeth, En-Gannim, Enhaddah, Beth-Pazzez, Tabor,[e] Shahazumah and Beth-Shemesh.[f]

Asher's Land

24-26Asher was the fifth tribe chosen to receive land, and the region for its clans included the following towns:

Helkath, Hali, Beten, Achshaph, Allammelech, Amad, and Mishal.

Asher's southern border ran from the Mediterranean Sea southeast along the Shihor-Libnath River at the foot of Mount Carmel, 27then east to Beth-Dagon. On the southeast, Asher shared a border with Zebulun along the Iphtahel Valley. On the eastern side their border ran north to Beth-Emek, went east of Cabul, and then on to Neiel, 28Abdon,[g] Rehob, Hammon, Kanah, and as far north as the city of Sidon. 29-31Then it turned west to become the northern border and went to Ramah[h] and the fortress-city of Tyre.[i] Near Tyre it turned toward Hosah and ended at the Mediterranean Sea.

Asher had a total of twenty-two towns with their surrounding villages, including Mahalab,[j] Achzib, Acco,[k] Aphek, and Rehob.

Naphtali's Land

32-34Naphtali was the sixth tribe chosen to receive land. The southern border for its clans started in the west, where the tribal lands of Asher and Zebulun meet near Hukkok. From that point it ran east and southeast along the border with Zebulun as far as Aznoth-Tabor. From there the border went east to Heleph, Adami-Nekeb, Jabneel,[l] then to the town called Oak in Zaanannim,[m] and Lakkum. The southern border ended at the Jordan River, at the edge of the town named Jehudah.[n] Naphtali shared a border with Asher on the west.

35-39The Naphtali clans received this region as their tribal land, and it included nineteen towns with their surrounding villages. The following towns had walls around them:

Ziddim, Zer, Hammath, Rakkath, Chinnereth, Adamah, Ramah,[o] Hazor, Kedesh, Edrei,[p] Enhazor, Iron, Mig-

dalel, Horem, Beth-Anath, and Beth-Shemesh.[q]

Dan's Land

40-46Dan was the seventh tribe chosen to receive land, and the region for its clans included the following towns:

Zorah, Eshtaol, Ir-Shemesh,[r] Shaalabbin, Aijalon, Ithlah, Elon, Timnah, Ekron, Eltekeh, Gibbethon, Baalath, Jehud, Azor,[s] Beneberak, Gath-Rimmon, Mejarkon, and Rakkon.

Dan's tribal land[t] went almost as far as Joppa. 47-48Its clans received this land and these towns with their surrounding villages. Later, when enemies[u] forced them to leave their tribal land, they went to the town of Leshem. They attacked the town, captured it, and killed the people who lived there. Then they settled there themselves and renamed the town Dan after their ancestor.

Joshua's Land

49-51The Israelites were still gathered in Shiloh in front of the sacred tent,[v] when Ele-

---

[d]19.17-23 Debirath: One ancient translation; Hebrew "Rabbith." Debirath is probably the same place as Daberath in verse 12.   [e]19.17-23 Mount Tabor . . . Tabor: In Hebrew the name "Tabor" is used only once. It was probably intended as the name of a town located at the foot of Mount Tabor and which formed one point on the northern border of Issachar. [f]19.17-23 Beth-Shemesh: Not the same Beth-Shemesh as in 15.10 or 19.35-39.   [g]19.28 Abdon: A few Hebrew manuscripts and one ancient translation; most Hebrew manuscripts "Ebron."   [h]19.29-31 Ramah: Not the same "Ramah" as in 18.25-28 or 19.35-39. [i]19.29-31 fortress-city of Tyre: Tyre was a walled city built on an island about half a mile from shore. [j]19.29-31 Mahalab: One possible meaning for the difficult Hebrew text.   [k]19.29-31 Acco: One ancient translation; Hebrew "Ummah."   [l]19.32-34 Jabneel: This town is not the same Jabneel as in 15.11. [m]19.32-34 the town . . . Zaanannim: Or "the oak tree in the town of Zaanannim."   [n]19.32-34 at . . . Jehudah: One possible meaning for the difficult Hebrew text. [o]19.35-39 Ramah: Not the same "Ramah" as in 18.25-28 or 19.29-31.   [p]19.35-39 Edrei: Not the same Edrei as the town in Bashan east of the Jordan River where King Og had lived (see 12.4; 13.11, 12, 30, 31).   [q]19.35-39 Beth-Shemesh: Not the same Beth-Shemesh as in 15.10 or 19.17-23. [r]19.40-46 Ir-Shemesh: Possibly the same town as the Beth-Shemesh of 15.10.   [s]19.40-46 Azor: Some manuscripts of one ancient translation; the Hebrew text does not have this word. [t]19.40-46 Gath-Rimmon, Mejarkon, and Rakkon. Dan's tribal land: Or "Gath-Rimmon, and Rakkon. Dan's tribal land also included the Yarkon River and."   [u]19.47,48 enemies: Probably the Philistines. [v]19.49-51 sacred tent: Or "meeting tent."

azar the priest, Joshua, and the family leaders of Israel finished giving out the land to the tribes. The LORD had told the people to give Joshua whatever town he wanted. So Joshua chose Timnath-Serah in the hill country of Ephraim, and the people gave it to him. Joshua went to Timnath-Serah, rebuilt it, and lived there.

The Safe Towns
(Numbers 35.9-15; Deuteronomy 19.1-13)

20 One day the LORD told Joshua: [2]When Moses was still alive, I had him tell the Israelites about the Safe Towns. Now you tell them that it is time to set up these towns. [3-4]If a person accidentally kills someone and the victim's relatives say it was murder, they might try to take revenge.[w] Anyone accused of murder can run to one of the Safe Towns and be safe from the victim's relatives. The one needing protection will stand at the entrance to the town gate and explain to the town leaders what happened. Then the leaders will bring that person in and provide a place to live in their town.

[5]One of the victim's relatives might come to the town, looking for revenge. But the town leaders must not simply hand over the person accused of murder. After all, the accused and the victim had been neighbors, not enemies. [6]The citizens of that Safe Town must come together and hold a trial. They may decide that the victim was killed accidentally and that the accused is not guilty of murder.

Everyone found not guilty[x] must still live in the Safe Town until the high priest dies. Then they can go back to their own towns and their homes that they had to leave behind.
[7]The Israelites decided that the following three towns west of the Jordan River would be Safe Towns:
Kedesh in Galilee in Naphtali's hill country, Shechem in Ephraim's hill country, and Kiriath-Arba in Judah's hill country. Kiriath-Arba is now called Hebron.
[8]The Israelites had already decided on the following three towns east of the Jordan River:

Bezer in the desert flatlands of Reuben, Ramoth in Gilead, which was a town that belonged to Gad, and Golan in Bashan, which belonged to Manasseh.
[9]These Safe Towns were set up, so that if Israelites or even foreigners who lived in Israel accidentally killed someone, they could run to one of these towns. There they would be safe until a trial could be held, even if one of the victim's relatives came looking for revenge.

Levi's Towns

21 [1-2]While the Israelites were still camped at Shiloh in the land of Canaan, the family leaders of the Levi tribe went to speak to the priest Eleazar, Joshua, and the family leaders of the other Israelite tribes. The leaders of Levi said, "The LORD told Moses that you have to give us towns and provide pastures for our animals."[y]

[3]Since the LORD had said this, the leaders of the other Israelite tribes agreed to give some of the towns and pastures from their tribal lands to Levi. [4]The leaders asked the LORD to show them[z] in what order the clans of Levi would be given towns, and which towns each clan would receive.

The Kohath clans were first. The descendants of Aaron, Israel's first priest,[a] were given thirteen towns from the tribes of Judah, Simeon, and Benjamin. [5]The other members of the Kohath clans received ten towns from the tribes of Ephraim, Dan, and West Manasseh. [6]The clans that were descendants of Gershon were given thirteen towns from the tribes of Issachar, Asher, Naphtali, and East Manasseh. [7]The clans that were descendants of Merari[b] received

---

[w]**20.3,4** *revenge:* At this time in Israel's history, the clan could appoint a close male relative to find and kill a person who had killed a member of their clan.
[x]**20.6** *not guilty:* If the person was found to be guilty of murder, the citizens of the Safe Town were to let the victim's relatives kill the murderer (see Deuteronomy 19.11-13). [y]**21.1,2** *The LORD told Moses . . . animals:* See Numbers 35.1-8. [z]**21.4** *asked the LORD to show them:* Hebrew "cast lots to find out." See the note at 14.1-5. [a]**21.4** *The descendants . . . priest:* Hebrew text; three ancient translations "The priests, the descendants of Aaron." The male descendants of Aaron would also be priests. [b]**21.4-7** *Kohath . . . Gershon . . . Merari:* Sons of Levi, the ancestor of the tribe of Levi.

twelve towns from the tribes of Reuben, Gad, and Zebulun.

⁸The LORD had told Moses that he would show the Israelites which towns and pastures to give to the clans of Levi, and he did.

Towns from Judah, Simeon, Benjamin

⁹⁻¹⁹The descendants of Aaron from the Kohath clans of Levi were priests, and they were chosen to receive towns first. They were given thirteen towns and the pastureland around them. Nine of these towns were from the tribes of Judah and Simeon and four from Benjamin.

Hebron, Libnah, Jattir, Eshtemoa, Holon, Debir, Ashan,ᶜ Juttah, and Beth-Shemesh were from Judah and Simeon. Hebron, located in the hill country of Judah, was earlier called Arba's Town.ᵈ It had been named after Arba, the ancestor of the Anakim.ᵉ Hebron's pasturelands went along with the town, but its farmlands and the villages around it had been given to Caleb.ᶠ Hebron was also one of the Safe Towns for people who had accidentally killed someone.

Gibeon, Geba, Anathoth, and Almon were from Benjamin.

Towns from Ephraim, Dan, West Manasseh

²⁰⁻²⁶The rest of the Kohath clans of the Levi tribe received ten towns and the pastureland around them. Four of these towns were from the tribe of Ephraim, four from Dan, and two from West Manasseh.

Shechem, Gezer, Kibzaim, and Beth-Horon were from Ephraim. Shechem was located in the hill country, and it was also one of the Safe Towns for people who had accidentally killed someone.

Elteke, Gibbethon, Aijalon, and Gath-Rimmon were from Dan.

Taanach and Jibleamᵍ were from West Manasseh.

Towns from East Manasseh, Issachar, Asher, Naphtali

²⁷⁻³³The clans of Levi that were descendants of Gershon received thirteen towns and the pastureland around them. Two of these towns were from the tribe of East Manasseh, four from Issachar, four from Asher, and three from Naphtali.

Golan in Bashan and Beeshterah were from East Manasseh.

Kishion, Daberath, Jarmuth, and En-Gannim were from Issachar.

Mishal, Abdon, Helkath, and Rehob were from Asher.

Kedesh in Galilee, Hammothdor, and Kartan were from Naphtali. Golan in Bashan and Kedesh in Galilee were also Safe Towns for people who had accidentally killed someone.

Towns from Zebulun, Reuben, Gad

³⁴⁻⁴⁰The rest of the Levi clans were descendants of Merari, and they received twelve towns with the pastureland around them. Four towns were from the tribe of Zebulun, four from Reuben, and four from Gad.

> *It's hard to open ourselves to the peace that passes understanding when we're constantly on the run. Part of contentment is a sort of spiritual sitting still that says, I'm here and it is good and God is good.*
>
> ELIZABETH CODY NEWENHUYSE

Jokneam, Kartah, Rimmonah,ʰ and Nahalal were from Zebulun.

Bezer, Jazah, Kedemoth, and Mephaath were from Reuben. Bezer was located in the desert flatlands east of the Jordan River across from Jericho.ⁱ

Ramoth in Gilead, Mahanaim, Heshbon, and Jazer were from Gad.

Bezer and Ramoth in Gilead were Safe

ᶜ**21.9-19** *Ashan:* One ancient translation and the parallel in 1 Chronicles 6.59; Hebrew "Ain."   ᵈ**21.9-19** *Arba's Town:* See the note at 14.15.   ᵉ**21.9-19** *Anakim:* See the note at 11.21.   ᶠ**21.9-19** *Caleb:* See 14.6-14.   ᵍ**21.20-26** *Jibleam:* One ancient translation and the parallel in 1 Chronicles 6.70; Hebrew "Gath-Rimmon."   ʰ**21.34-40** *Rimmonah:* One possible meaning for the difficult Hebrew text.   ⁱ**21.34-40** *Bezer . . . Jericho:* One possible meaning for the difficult Hebrew text.

Towns[j] for people who had accidentally killed someone.

[41-42]The people of the Levi tribe had a total of forty-eight towns within Israel, and they had pastures around each one of their towns.

Israel Settles in the Land

[43]The LORD gave the Israelites the land he had promised their ancestors, and they captured it and settled in it. [44]There still were enemies around Israel, but the LORD kept his promise to let his people live in peace. And whenever the Israelites did have to go to war, no enemy could defeat them. The LORD always helped Israel win. [45]The LORD promised to do many good things for Israel, and he kept his promise every time.

The Two and a Half Tribes Return Home

22 Joshua had the men of the tribes of Reuben, Gad, and East Manasseh come for a meeting, and he told them:

[2-3]You have obeyed every command of the LORD your God and of his servant Moses. And you have done everything I've told you to do. It's taken a long time, but you have stayed and helped your relatives. [4]The LORD promised to give peace to your relatives, and that's what he has done. Now it's time for you to go back to your own homes in the land that Moses gave you east of the Jordan River.

[5]Moses taught you to love the LORD your God, to be faithful to him, and to worship and obey him with your whole heart and with all your strength. So be very careful to do everything Moses commanded.

[6-9]You've become rich from what you've taken from your enemies. You have big herds of cattle, lots of silver, gold, bronze, and iron, and plenty of clothes. Take everything home with you and share with the people of your tribe.

I pray that God will be kind to you. You are now free to go home.

The tribes of Reuben and Gad started back to Gilead, their own land. Moses had given the land of Bashan to the East Manasseh tribe, so they started back along with Reuben and Gad. God had told Moses that

these two and a half tribes should conquer Gilead and Bashan, and they had done so.

Joshua had given land west of the Jordan River to the other half of the Manasseh tribe, so they stayed at Shiloh in the land of Canaan with the rest of the Israelites.

> *Mother taught me by her example that there's nothing more satisfying than a personal love relationship with the Lord. It's what made her strong. When Daddy would come home exhausted from ministry, my mother's unflagging faith consistently encouraged him.*
>
> ANNE GRAHAM LOTZ

[10-11]The tribes of Reuben, Gad, and East Manasseh reached the western side of the Jordan River valley[k] and built a huge altar there beside the river.

When the rest of the Israelites heard what these tribes had done,[l] [12]the Israelite men met at Shiloh to get ready to attack the two and a half tribes. [13]But first they sent a priest, Phinehas the son of Eleazar, to talk with the two and a half tribes. [14]Each of the tribes at Shiloh sent the leader of one of its families along with Phinehas.

[15]Phinehas and these leaders went to Gilead and met with the tribes of Reuben, Gad, and East Manasseh. They said:

[16]All of the LORD's people have gathered together and have sent us to find out why you are unfaithful to our God. You have turned your backs on

---

[j]21.34-40 *Bezer and Ramoth in Gilead were Safe Towns*: One ancient translation; Hebrew "Ramoth in Gilead was a Safe Town." [k]22.10,11 *western . . . valley*: Or "the town of Geliloth, which is in the land of Canaan near the Jordan River." [l]22.10,11 *built a huge altar . . . tribes had done*: According to Deuteronomy 12.5-14, the LORD wanted the Israelites to have only one altar for offering sacrifices. To build another altar would be to disobey the LORD.

the LORD by building that altar. Why are you rebelling against him? [17]Wasn't our people's sin at Peor[m] terrible enough for you? The LORD punished us by sending a horrible sickness that killed many of us, and we still suffer because of that sin.[n] [18]Now you are turning your backs on the LORD again.

If you don't stop rebelling against the LORD right now, he will be angry at the whole nation. [19]If you don't think your land is a fit place to serve God, then move across the Jordan and live with us in the LORD's own land, where his sacred tent is located. But don't rebel against the LORD our God or against us by building another altar besides the LORD's own altar.[o] [20]Don't you remember what happened when Achan was unfaithful[p] and took some of the things that belonged to God? This made God angry with the entire nation. Achan died because he sinned, but he also caused the death of many others.

[21]The tribes of Reuben, Gad, and East Manasseh answered:

[22]The LORD is the greatest God! We ask him to be our witness, because he knows whether or not we were rebellious or unfaithful when we built that altar. If we were unfaithful, then we pray that God won't rescue us today. Let us tell you why we built that altar, [23]and we ask the LORD to punish us if we are lying. We didn't build it so we could turn our backs on the LORD. We didn't even build it so we could offer animal or grain sacrifices to please the LORD or ask his blessing.[q]

[24-25]We built that altar because we were worried. Someday your descendants might tell our descendants, "The LORD made the Jordan River the boundary between us Israelites and you people of Reuben and Gad. The LORD is Israel's God, but you're not part of Israel, so you can't take part in worshiping the LORD."

Your descendants might say that and try to make our descendants stop worshiping and obeying the LORD. [26]That's why we decided to build the altar. It isn't for offering sacrifices, not even sacrifices to please the LORD.[q]

[27-29]To build another altar for offering sacrifices would be the same as turning our backs on the LORD and rebelling against him. We could never do that! No, we built the altar to remind us and you and the generations to come that we will worship the LORD. And so we will keep bringing our sacrifices to the LORD's altar, there in front of his sacred tent. Now your descendants will never be able to say to our descendants, "You can't worship the LORD."

But if they do say this, our descendants can answer back, "Look at this altar our ancestors built! It's like the LORD's altar, but it isn't for offering sacrifices. It's here to remind us and you that we belong to the LORD, just as much as you do."

[30-31]Phinehas and the clan leaders were pleased when they heard the tribes of Reuben, Gad, and East Manasseh explain why they had built the altar. Then Phinehas told them, "Today we know that the LORD is helping us. You have not been unfaithful to him, and this means that the LORD will not be angry with us."

[32]Phinehas and the clan leaders left Gilead and went back to Canaan to tell the Israelites about their meeting with the Reuben and Gad tribes. [33]The Israelites were happy and praised God. There was no more talk about going to war and wiping out the tribes of Reuben and Gad.

[34]The people of Reuben and Gad named the altar "A Reminder to Us All That the LORD Is Our God."[r]

Joshua's Farewell Speech

23 The LORD let Israel live in peace with its neighbors for a long time, and Joshua lived to a ripe

---

[m]**22.17** *our people's sin at Peor:* See Numbers 25. [n]**22.17** *we still . . . sin:* Or "There are still people in Israel who want to worship other gods." [o]**22.19** *or against . . . altar:* Or "by building another altar besides the LORD's own altar. That would even make us into rebels along with you." [p]**22.20** *Achan was unfaithful:* See 7.1, 26. [q]**22.26** *sacrifices to please the LORD:* See the note at 8.30-32. [r]**22.34** *named . . . God:* Or "gave a name to the altar. They explained, 'This altar is here to remind us all that the LORD is our God' "; most Hebrew manuscripts. A few Hebrew manuscripts and one ancient translation "named the altar 'Reminder.' They explained, 'This altar is here to remind us all that the LORD is our God.' "

old age. ²One day he called a meeting of the leaders of the tribes of Israel, including the old men, the judges, and the officials. Then he told them:

I am now very old. ³You have seen how the LORD your God fought for you and helped you defeat the nations who lived in this land. ⁴⁻⁵There are still some nations left, but the LORD has promised you their land. So when you attack them, he will make them run away. I have already divided their land among your tribes, as I did with the land of the nations I defeated between the Jordan River and the Mediterranean Sea.

⁶Be sure that you carefully obey everything written in *The Book of the Law*ˢ of Moses and do exactly what it says.

⁷Don't have anything to do with the nations that live around you. Don't worship their gods or pray to their idols or make promises in the names of their gods. ⁸Be as faithful to the LORD as you have always been.

⁹When you attacked powerful nations, the LORD made them run away, and no one has ever been able to stand

up to you. ¹⁰Any one of you can defeat a thousand enemy soldiers, because the LORD God fights for you, just as he promised. ¹¹Be sure to always love the LORD your God. ¹²⁻¹³Don't ever turn your backs on him by marrying people from the nations that are left in the land. Don't even make friends with them. I tell you that if you are friendly with those nations, the LORD won't chase them away when you attack. Instead, they'll be like a trap for your feet, a whip on your back, and thorns in your eyes. And finally, none of you will be left in this good land that the LORD has given you.

¹⁴I will soon die, as everyone must. But deep in your hearts you know that the LORD has kept every promise he ever made to you. Not one of them has been broken. ¹⁵⁻¹⁶Yes, when the LORD makes a promise, he does what he has promised. But when he makes a threat, he will also do what he has threatened. The LORD is our God. He gave us this wonderful land and made

---

ˢ**23.6** *Law*: See the note at 8.30-32.

Personal *Concerns*—How can I overcome my tendency to worry and instead gain confidence about the future? *(Joshua 23.14-16)*

Learn to rely on God's promises.

Joshua could have spent a lot of time worrying. With enemies to conquer, rivers to cross, in-house problems to solve, and land to divide fairly, many people depended on him for their safety and well-being. But before Joshua had embarked on the task of leading the Israelites into the Promised Land, God had spoken to him in the strongest possible way about ridding his life of fear and worry. He said, "Joshua, I will always be with you and help you as I helped Moses, and no one will ever be able to defeat you. . . . Be strong and brave. Don't ever be afraid or discouraged! I am the LORD your God, and I will be there to help you wherever you go" (1.5,9).

By the end of his life, Joshua was able to talk about overcoming worry by believing in God's faithfulness to his promises. Every time Joshua acted on faith rather than fear, God came through with everything Joshua needed to accomplish God's purposes.

God has made the same promise to us that he made to Joshua—and more (see Hebrews 13.5). As we familiarize ourselves with the promises of God found in Scripture, allowing them to sink into our souls so that they become our deepest reality, we will increasingly respond to circumstances of our lives with faith rather than fear. We will begin to recognize more and more ways that God has come through for us—and our faith will grow. (See also Psalm 91; Micah 5.2-5; Habakkuk 3.16-19; Matthew 6.25-34; Philippians 4.4-9.)

Words To Remember: *Yes, when the LORD makes a promise, he does what he has promised.—Joshua 23.15,16*

an agreement with us that we would worship only him. But if you worship other gods, it will make the LORD furious. He will start getting rid of them, and soon not one of you will be left in this good land that he has given you.

We Will Worship and Obey the LORD

24 Joshua called the tribes of Israel together for a meeting at Shechem. He had the leaders, including the old men, the judges, and the officials, come up and stand near the sacred tent.[t] [2]Then Joshua told everyone to listen to this message from the LORD, the God of Israel:

Long ago your ancestors lived on the other side of the Euphrates River, and they worshiped other gods. This continued until the time of your ancestor Terah and his two sons, Abraham and Nahor. [3]But I brought Abraham across the Euphrates River and led him through the land of Canaan. I blessed him by giving him Isaac, the first in a line of many descendants. [4]Then I gave Isaac two sons, Jacob and Esau. I had Esau live in the hill country of Mount Seir, but your ancestor Jacob and his children went to live in Egypt.

[5-6]Later I sent Moses and his brother Aaron to help your people, and I made all those horrible things happen to the Egyptians. I brought your ancestors out of Egypt, but the Egyptians got in their chariots and on their horses and chased your ancestors, catching up with them at the Red Sea.[u] [7]Your people cried to me for help, so I put a dark cloud between them and the Egyptians. Then I opened up the sea and let your people walk across on dry ground. But when the Egyptians tried to follow, I commanded the sea to swallow them, and they drowned while you watched.

You lived in the desert for a long time, [8]then I brought you into the land east of the Jordan River. The Amorites were living there, and they fought you. But with my help, you defeated them, wiped them out, and took their land. [9]King Balak decided that his nation Moab would go to war against you,

so he asked Balaam[v] to come and put a curse on you. [10]But I wouldn't listen to Balaam, and I rescued you by making him bless you instead of curse you.

[11]You crossed the Jordan River and came to Jericho. The rulers of Jericho fought you, and so did the Amorites, the Perizzites, the Canaanites, the Hittites, the Girgashites, the Hivites, and the Jebusites. I helped you defeat them all. [12]Your enemies ran from you, but not because you had swords and bows and arrows. I made your enemies panic and run away, as I had done with the two Amorite kings east of the Jordan River.

[13]You didn't have to work for this land—I gave it to you. Now you live in towns you didn't build, and you eat grapes and olives from vineyards and trees you didn't plant.

[14]Then Joshua told the people:

Worship the LORD, obey him, and always be faithful. Get rid of the idols your ancestors worshiped when they lived on the other side of the Euphrates River and in Egypt. [15]But if you don't want to worship the LORD, then choose right now! Will you worship the same idols your ancestors did? Or since you're living on land that once belonged to the Amorites, maybe you'll worship their gods. I won't. My family and I are going to worship and obey the LORD!

[16]The people answered:

We could never worship other gods or stop worshiping the LORD. [17]The LORD is our God. We were slaves in Egypt as our ancestors had been, but we saw the LORD work miracles to set our people free and to bring us out of Egypt. Even though other nations were all around us, the LORD protected us wherever we went. [18]And when we fought the Amorites and the other nations that lived in this land, the LORD made them run away. Yes, we

---

[t]24.1 near . . . tent: Or "in front of the sacred chest"; Hebrew "in the presence of God."   [u]24.5,6 Red Sea: See the note at 2.10.   [v]24.9 King Balak . . . Balaam: The Hebrew text has "King Balak the son of Zippor . . . Balaam the son of Beor."

will worship and obey the LORD, because the LORD is our God.

> *Home is where we pray together and remember God's blessings to us.*
>
> KAY MARSHALL STROM

¹⁹Joshua said:

The LORD is fearsome; he is the one true God, and I don't think you are able to worship and obey him in the ways he demands. You would have to be completely faithful, and if you sin or rebel, he won't let you get away with it. ²⁰If you turn your backs on the LORD and worship the gods of other nations, the LORD will turn against you. He will make terrible things happen to you and wipe you out, even though he had been good to you before.

²¹But the people shouted, "We won't worship any other gods. We will worship and obey only the LORD!"

²²Joshua said, "You have heard yourselves say that you will worship and obey the LORD. Isn't that true?"

"Yes, it's true," they answered.

²³Joshua said, "But you still have some idols, like those the other nations worship. Get rid of your idols! You must decide once and for all that you really want to obey the LORD God of Israel."

²⁴The people said, "The LORD is our God, and we will worship and obey only him."

²⁵Joshua helped Israel make an agreement with the LORD that day at Shechem. Joshua made laws for Israel ²⁶and wrote them down in *The Book of the Law*ʷ *of God.* Then he set up a large stone under the oak tree at the place of worship in Shechem ²⁷and told the people, "Look at this stone. It has heard everything that the LORD has said to us. Our God can call this stone as a witness if we ever reject him."

²⁸Joshua sent everyone back to their homes.

Joshua, Joseph, and Eleazar Are Buried

²⁹Not long afterwards, the LORD's servant Joshua died at the age of one hundred ten. ³⁰The Israelites buried him in his own land at Timnath-Serah, north of Mount Gaash in the hill country of Ephraim.

³¹As long as Joshua lived, Israel worshiped and obeyed the LORD. There were other leaders old enough to remember everything that the LORD had done for Israel. And for as long as these men lived, Israel continued to worship and obey the LORD.

³²When the people of Israel left Egypt, they brought the bones of Joseph along with them. They took the bones to the town of Shechem and buried them in the field that Jacob had bought for one hundred pieces of silverˣ from Hamor, the founder of Shechem. The town and the field bothʸ became part of the land belonging to the descendants of Joseph.

³³When Eleazar the priestᶻ died, he was buried in the hill country of Ephraim on a hill that belonged to his son Phinehas.

ʷ24.26 *Law:* See the note at 8.30-32.   ˣ24.32 *pieces of silver:* One possible meaning for the difficult Hebrew word.   ʸ24.32 *town . . . both:* One possible meaning for the difficult Hebrew text.   ᶻ24.33 *Eleazar the priest:* Hebrew "Eleazar the son of Aaron."

Judges — Haunted by Violence

Most women worry (at least a little) about violence. There's that uncomfortable tingle along your spine as you reach for your keys in a dark parking lot. There's the quickened pace and uneasy glance as you pass an alley or a cluster of overhanging trees. Even home is not always safe. Some women live in constant fear of an angry husband or son.

The era of the Judges is one of the most violent eras recorded in Scripture. As in any period of instability, women were frequent victims of the bloodshed that caused them to lose husbands in warfare and the lawlessness that frequently prevailed. Consider the Levite's wife, who was raped and abused to death by strangers as she and her husband traveled to Ephraim.

Undergirding these outbursts of violence is a rhythmic theme. The people of Israel stray away from the true God and worship idols. God allows their enemies to overcome them. The people turn from their idols (briefly), then cry to God for help. God sends them a judge who defeats their enemies, and the land has a time of peace. The people stop worshiping God and return to idols. And so the cycle repeats for centuries.

One other theme is a closing litany after each episode of more repugnant violence: "In those days Israel wasn't ruled by a king, and everyone did what they thought was right" (21.25). Politically, that statement is simply an advertisement for government by monarchy—which Israel had next. But theologically and morally, it's a statement of what happens when people turn from God and follow their own designs. It appears that "our own eyes" don't give us an accurate picture of what is right—or even safe.

But despite the violence, Judges also brings comfort—especially for women who fear. It is not a comfort in people—but in God himself. Over and over God rescues and forgives his people. He will do the same for us.

Judges at a Glance

1. Israel conquers only part of Canaan (1.1—2.5)
2. Joshua dies; the people serve idols; God allows enemies to live among them (2.6—3.6)
3. Othniel, Ehud, and Shamgar win battles (3.7-31)
4. Deborah defeats an army and sings a song (4,5)
5. Gideon fights Midian with 300 men—and the help of God (6–8)
6. Abimelech kills his 70 brothers and tries to be king (9)
7. Tola and Jair rescue Israel, but the people turn to other gods (10)
8. Jephthah wins a battle—but loses his daughter (11,12)

9. Samson smashes enemies but falls to Delilah (13–16)

10. Micah makes an idol and hires a priest, but the tribe of Dan takes them (17,18)

11. A Levite saves his skin by letting men gang-rape his wife (19.1—20.19)

12. Civil war breaks out, creating war brides by kidnapping and murder (20.20—21.25)

The Tribes of Judah and Simeon Fight the Canaanites

1 After the death of Joshua, the Israelites asked the LORD, "Which of our tribes should attack the Canaanites first?"

²"Judah!" the LORD answered. "I'll help them take the land."

³The people of Judah went to their relatives, the Simeon tribe, and said, "Canaanites live in the land God gave us. Help us fight them, and we will help you."

Troops from Simeon came to help Judah. ⁴⁻⁵Together they attacked an army of ten thousand Canaanites and Perizzites at Bezek, and the LORD helped Judah defeat them. During the battle, Judah's army found out where the king of Bezek^d was, and they attacked there. ⁶Bezek tried to escape, but soldiers from Judah caught him. They cut off his thumbs and big toes, ⁷and he said, "I've cut off the thumbs and big toes of seventy kings and made those kings crawl around under my table for scraps of food. Now God is paying me back."

The army of Judah took the king of Bezek along with them to Jerusalem, where he died. ⁸They attacked Jerusalem,^{b} captured it, killed everyone who lived there, and then burned it to the ground.

⁹Judah's army fought the Canaanites who lived in the hill country, the Southern Desert, and the foothills to the west. ¹⁰After that, they attacked the Canaanites who lived at Hebron, defeating the three clans called^c Sheshai, Ahiman, and Talmai. At that time, Hebron was called Kiriath-Arba.

¹¹From Hebron, Judah's army went to attack Debir, which at that time was called Kiriath-Sepher. ¹²Caleb^d told his troops, "The man who captures Kiriath-Sepher can marry my daughter Achsah."

¹³Caleb's nephew Othniel captured Kiriath-Sepher, so Caleb let him marry Achsah. Othniel was the son of Caleb's younger brother Kenaz.^{e} ¹⁴Right after the wedding, Achsah started telling Othniel that he^f ought to ask her father for a field. She went to see her father, and while she was getting down from^g her donkey, Caleb asked, "What's bothering you?"

¹⁵She answered, "I need your help. The land you gave me is in the Southern Desert, so please give me some spring-fed ponds for a water supply."

Caleb gave her a couple of small ponds named Higher Pond and Lower Pond.^{h}

¹⁶The people who belonged to the Kenite clan were the descendants of the father-in-law of Moses. They left Jericho^i with the people of Judah and settled near Arad in the Southern Desert of Judah not far from the Amalekites.^{j}

¹⁷Judah's army helped Simeon's army attack the Canaanites who lived at Zephath. They completely destroyed^k the town and renamed it Hormah.^{l}

¹⁸⁻¹⁹The LORD helped the army of Judah capture Gaza, Ashkelon, Ekron, and the land near those towns. They also took the hill country. But the people who lived in the valleys had iron chariots, so Judah was not able to make them leave or to take their land.

---

^{a}**1.4,5** *king of Bezek:* Or "Adoni-Bezek." ^{b}**1.8** *Jerusalem:* This probably refers to towns and villages belonging to Jerusalem but lying in Judah's territory south of the city wall. Jerusalem itself was just inside Benjamin's territory, but was not captured by Israel at this time (see verse 21; Joshua 15.5-9; 18.15-18). ^{c}**1.10** *clans called:* Or "warriors." ^{d}**1.12** *Caleb:* One of the leaders of Judah; see Joshua 14.6-14 and Numbers 13.6, 30; 14.6, 10, 20-24. For verses 12-15, see Joshua 15.13-19. ^{e}**1.13** *Othniel was the son of . . . Kenaz:* Or "Othniel and Caleb both belonged to the Kenaz clan, but Othniel was younger than Caleb." ^{f}**1.14** *Achsah . . . Othniel . . . he:* Hebrew; two ancient translations "Othniel . . . Achsah . . . she." ^{g}**1.14** *getting down from:* One possible meaning for the difficult Hebrew text. ^{h}**1.15** *spring-fed ponds . . . small ponds . . . Higher Pond and Lower Pond:* Or "wells . . . wells . . . Higher Well and Lower Well." ^{i}**1.16** *Jericho:* The Hebrew text has "Town of Palm Trees," another name for Jericho. ^{j}**1.16** *not far . . . Amalekites:* One possible meaning for the difficult Hebrew text. ^{k}**1.17** *completely destroyed:* The Hebrew word means that the town was given completely to the LORD, and since it could not be used for normal purposes anymore, it had to be destroyed. ^{l}**1.17** *Hormah:* In Hebrew "Hormah" sounds like "completely destroyed."

[20]The tribe of Judah gave the town of Hebron to Caleb, as Moses had told them to do. Caleb defeated the three Anakim[m] clans[n] and took over the town.

The Benjamin Tribe
Does Not Capture Jerusalem

[21]The Jebusites were living in Jerusalem, and the Benjamin tribe did not defeat them or capture the town. That's why Jebusites still live in Jerusalem along with the people of Benjamin.

The Ephraim and Manasseh
Tribes Capture Bethel

[22-23]The Ephraim and Manasseh tribes[o] were getting ready to attack Bethel, which at that time was called Luz. And the LORD helped them when they sent spies to find out as much as they could about Bethel. [24]While the spies were watching the town, a man came out, and they told him, "If you show us how our army can get into the town,[p] we will make sure that you aren't harmed." [25]The man showed them, and the two Israelite tribes attacked Bethel, killing everyone except the man and his family. The two tribes made the man and his family leave, [26]so they went to the land of the Hittites,[q] where he built a town. He named the town Luz, and that is still its name.

Israel Does Not Get Rid of All
the Canaanites

[27-28]Canaanites lived in the towns of Beth-Shan, Taanach, Dor, Ibleam, Megiddo, and all the villages nearby. The Canaanites were determined to stay, and the Manasseh tribe never did get rid of them. But later on, when the Israelites grew more powerful, they made slaves of the Canaanites.
[29]The Ephraim tribe did not get rid of the Canaanites who lived in Gezer, so the Canaanites lived there with Israelites all around them.
[30]The Zebulun tribe did not get rid of the Canaanites who lived in Kitron and Nahalol, and the Canaanites stayed there with Israelites around them. But the people of Zebulun did force the Canaanites into slave labor.
[31-32]The Asher tribe did not get rid of the Canaanites who lived in Acco, Sidon, Ahlab, Achzib, Helbah, Aphik, and Rehob, and the Asher tribe lived with Canaanites all around them.

[33]The Naphtali tribe did not get rid of the Canaanites who lived in Beth-Shemesh and Beth-Anath, but they did force the Canaanites into slave labor. The Naphtali tribe lived with Canaanites around them.
[34]The Amorites[r] were strong enough to keep the tribe of Dan from settling in the valleys, so Dan had to stay in the hill country.
[35]The Amorites on Mount Heres and in Aijalon and Shaalbim were also determined to stay. Later on, as Ephraim and Manasseh grew more powerful, they forced those Amorites into slave labor.

The Amorite-Edomite Border

[36]The old Amorite-Edomite border used to go from Sela through Scorpion Pass[s] into the hill country.[t]

The LORD's Angel Speaks to Israel

2 The LORD's angel went from Gilgal to Bochim[u] and gave the Israelites this message from the LORD:
I promised your ancestors that I would give this land to their families, and I brought your people here from Egypt. We made an agreement that I promised never to break, [2]and you promised not to make any peace treaties with the other nations that live in the land. Besides that, you agreed to tear down the altars where they sacrifice to their idols. But you didn't keep your promise.
[3]And so, I'll stop helping you defeat your enemies. Instead, they will be there to trap[v] you into worshiping their idols.

---

[m]1.20 Anakim: Perhaps a group of very large people that lived in Palestine before the Israelites (see Numbers 13.33 and Deuteronomy 2.10, 11, 20, 21).
[n]1.20 clans: See the note at 1.10.   [o]1.22,23 The Ephraim and Manasseh tribes: The Hebrew text has "The Joseph family," which was divided into these two tribes named after Joseph's sons.   [p]1.24 If you . . . town: Sometimes there were small doors in the town wall that could be opened from the inside even when the main town gates were shut and locked.   [q]1.26 land of the Hittites: The Hittites had an empire centered in what is now Turkey. At one time their empire reached south into Syria, north of Israel.   [r]1.34 Amorites: Used in the general sense of nations that lived in Canaan before the Israelites.   [s]1.36 Scorpion Pass: Or "Akrabbim Pass."
[t]1.36 country: One possible meaning for the difficult Hebrew text of verse 36.   [u]2.1 Bochim: In Hebrew "Bochim" means "crying" (see verse 5).   [v]2.3 trap: One possible meaning for the difficult Hebrew text.

[4]The Israelites started crying loudly, [5]and they offered sacrifices to the LORD. From then on, they called that place "Crying."[w]

Israel Stops Worshiping the LORD

[6-9]Joshua had been faithful to the LORD. And after Joshua sent the Israelites to take the land they had been promised, they remained faithful to the LORD until Joshua died at the age of one hundred ten. He was buried on his land in Timnath-Heres, in the hill country of Ephraim north of Mount Gaash. Even though Joshua was gone, the Israelites were faithful to the LORD during the lifetime of those men who had been leaders with Joshua and who had seen the wonderful things the LORD had done for Israel.

[10]After a while the people of Joshua's generation died, and the next generation did not know the LORD or any of the things he had done for Israel. [11-13]The LORD had brought their ancestors out of Egypt, and they had worshiped him. But now the Israelites stopped worshiping the LORD and worshiped the idols of Baal and Astarte, as well as the idols of other gods from nearby nations.

The LORD was so angry [14-15]at the Israelites that he let other nations raid Israel and steal their crops and other possessions. Enemies were everywhere, and the LORD always let them defeat Israel in battle. The LORD had warned Israel he would do this, and now the Israelites were miserable.

The LORD Chooses Leaders for Israel

[16]From time to time, the LORD would choose special leaders known as judges.[x] These judges would lead the Israelites into battle and defeat the enemies that made raids on them. [17]In years gone by, the Israelites had been faithful to the LORD, but now they were quick to be unfaithful and to refuse even to listen to these judges. The Israelites would disobey the LORD, and instead of worshiping him, they would worship other gods.

[18]When enemies made life miserable for the Israelites, the LORD would feel sorry for them. He would choose a judge and help that judge rescue Israel from its enemies. The LORD would be kind to Israel as long as that judge lived. [19]But afterwards, the Israelites would become even more sinful than their ancestors had been. The Israelites were

stubborn—they simply would not stop worshiping other gods or following the teachings of other religions.

> *Over the past seven-plus decades I've become utterly convinced of this reality: that God is the only solid Rock we can count on in this life.*
>
> JOSIE CRAMER

The LORD Lets Enemies Test Israel

[20]The LORD was angry with Israel and said:

The Israelites have broken the agreement I made with their ancestors. They won't obey me, [21]so I'll stop helping them defeat their enemies. Israel still had a lot of enemies when Joshua died, [22]and I'm going to let those enemies stay. I'll use them to test Israel, because then I can find out if Israel will worship and obey me as their ancestors did.

[23]That's why the LORD had not let Joshua get rid of all those enemy nations right away.

3 [1-2]And the LORD had another reason for letting these enemies stay. The Israelites needed to learn how to fight in war, just as their ancestors had done. Each new generation would have to learn by fighting [3]the Philistines and their five rulers, as well as the Canaanites, the Sidonians, and the Hivites that lived in the Lebanon Mountains from Mount Baal-Hermon to Hamath Pass.[y]

[4]Moses had told the Israelites what the LORD had commanded them to do, and now the LORD was using these nations to find out if Israel would obey. [5-6]But they refused. And it was because of the Canaanites,

---

[w]2.5 *Crying:* Or "Bochim." [x]2.16 *special leaders known as judges:* The Hebrew text has "judges." In addition to leading Israelites in battle, these special leaders also decided legal cases and sometimes performed religious duties. [y]3.3 *Hamath Pass:* Or "Lebo-Hamath."

Hittites, Amorites, Perizzites, Hivites, and Jebusites who lived all around them. Some of the Israelites married the people of these nations, and that's how they started worshiping foreign gods.

Othniel

[7]The Israelites sinned against the LORD by forgetting him and worshiping idols of Baal and Astarte. [8]This made the LORD angry, so he let Israel be defeated by King Cushan Rishathaim of northern Syria,[z] who ruled Israel eight years and made everyone pay taxes. [9]The Israelites begged the LORD for help, and he chose Othniel to rescue them. Othniel was the son of Caleb's younger brother Kenaz.[a] [10]The Spirit of the LORD took control of Othniel, and he led Israel in a war against Cushan Rishathaim. The LORD gave Othniel victory, [11]and Israel was at peace until Othniel died about forty years later.

Ehud

[12]Once more the Israelites started disobeying the LORD. So he let them be defeated by King Eglon of Moab, [13]who had joined forces with the Ammonites and the Amalekites to attack Israel. Eglon and his army captured Jericho.[b] [14]Then he ruled Israel for eighteen years and forced the Israelites to pay heavy taxes.

God clearly says when we admit our neediness, he is able to meet us. God can turn our point of need into our area of supernatural spiritual strength!

ELISA MORGAN

[15-16]The Israelites begged the LORD for help, and the LORD chose Ehud[c] from the Benjamin tribe to rescue them. They put Ehud in charge of taking the taxes to King Eglon, but before Ehud went, he made a double-edged dagger. Ehud was left-handed,

so he strapped the dagger to his right thigh, where it would be hidden under his robes.

[17-18]Ehud and some other Israelites took the taxes to Eglon, who was a very fat man. As soon as they gave the taxes to Eglon, Ehud said it was time to go home.

[19-20]Ehud went with the other Israelites as far as the statues[d] at Gilgal.[e] Then he turned back and went upstairs to the cool room[f] where Eglon had his throne. Ehud said, "Your Majesty, I need to talk with you in private."

Eglon replied, "Don't say anything yet!" His officials left the room, and Eglon stood up as Ehud came closer.

"Yes," Ehud said, "I have a message for you from God!" [21]Ehud pulled out the dagger with his left hand and shoved it so far into Eglon's stomach [22-23]that even the handle was buried in his fat. Ehud left the dagger there. Then after closing and locking the doors to the room, he climbed through a window onto the porch[g] [24]and left.

When the king's officials came back and saw that the doors were locked, they said, "The king is probably inside relieving himself." [25]They stood there waiting until they felt foolish, but Eglon never opened the doors. Finally, they unlocked the doors and found King Eglon lying dead on the floor. [26]But by that time, Ehud had already escaped past the statues.[h]

Ehud went to the town of Seirah [27-28]in the hill country of Ephraim and started blowing a signal on a trumpet. The Israelites came together, and he shouted, "Follow me! The LORD will help us defeat the Moabites."

The Israelites followed Ehud down to the Jordan valley, and they captured the

---

[z]**3.8** *northern Syria:* The Hebrew text has "Aram-Naharaim," probably referring to the land around the city of Haran (see Genesis 24.10; 25.20; 28.2, 6; 31.18, 20; 33.18; 35.23-26; 46.8-15; 48.7). [a]**3.9** *Othniel was the son of . . . Kenaz:* See the note at 1.13. [b]**3.13** *Jericho:* See the note at 1.16. [c]**3.15,16** *Ehud:* Hebrew "Ehud the son of Gera." [d]**3.19,20** *statues:* Or "stone idols" or "stone monuments." [e]**3.19,20** *Gilgal:* About a mile and a half from Jericho, where Eglon probably was (see verse 13). [f]**3.19,20** *upstairs . . . cool room:* Houses usually had flat roofs, and sometimes a room was built on one corner of the roof where it could best catch the breeze and be kept cooler than the rest of the house. [g]**3.22,23** *he climbed . . . porch:* One possible meaning for the difficult Hebrew text. [h]**3.26** *statues:* See the note at 3.19, 20.

places where people cross the river on the way to Moab. They would not let anyone go across, ²⁹and before the fighting was over, they killed about ten thousand Moabite warriors—not one escaped alive.

³⁰Moab was so badly defeated that it was a long time before they were strong enough to attack Israel again. And Israel was at peace for eighty years.

Shamgar

³¹Shamgar the son of Anath was the next to rescue Israel. In one battle, he used a sharp wooden pole^i to kill six hundred Philistines.

Deborah and Barak

4 After the death of Ehud, the Israelites again started disobeying the LORD. ²So the LORD let the Canaanite King Jabin of Hazor conquer Israel. Sisera, the commander of Jabin's army, lived in Harosheth-Ha-Goiim. ³Jabin's army had nine hundred iron chariots, and for twenty years he made life miserable for the Israelites, until finally they begged the LORD for help.

⁴Deborah the wife of Lappidoth was a prophet and a leader^j of Israel during those days. ⁵She would sit under Deborah's Palm Tree between Ramah and Bethel in the hill

country of Ephraim, where Israelites would come and ask her to settle their legal cases.

⁶One day, Barak the son of Abinoam was in Kedesh in Naphtali, and Deborah sent word for him to come and talk with her. When he arrived, she said:

I have a message for you from the LORD God of Israel! You are to get together an army of ten thousand men from the Naphtali and Zebulun tribes and lead them to Mount Tabor. ⁷The LORD will trick Sisera into coming out to fight you at the Kishon River. Sisera will be leading King Jabin's army as usual, and they will have their chariots, but the LORD has promised to help you defeat them.

⁸"I'm not going unless you go!" Barak told her.

⁹"All right, I'll go!" she replied. "But I'm warning you that the LORD is going to let a woman defeat Sisera, and no one will honor you for winning the battle."

Deborah and Barak left for Kedesh, ¹⁰where Barak called together the troops from Zebulun and Naphtali. Ten thousand

---

^i**3.31** *sharp wooden pole:* The Hebrew text has "cattle-prod," a pole with a sharpened tip or metal point at one end. ^j**4.4** *leader:* See 2.16 and the note there.

WORK—Sometimes my male colleagues don't take me seriously. How can a Christian woman be assertive at work without being offensive? *(Judges 4.4-15)*

When given opportunity to lead, do it well.

Some women rarely have a chance to take charge at work. But an opportunity will come at some point—whether it's organizing Christmas decorations, arranging food for the company picnic, or plotting your company's next marketing campaign. Whether the leadership task is large or small, give it all you've got.

Deborah was already a respected leader of Israel. Then came a battle so fearsome that the military leader Barak refused to go without Deborah. She didn't say, "My job is to be a prophet and a judge. I don't do battles." Instead she marched to the head of the troops and took charge. She did not brush Barak away, but she offered him wise advice and told him the consequences of his actions. Then they did the job together. In the end, they sang a victory song—also together. (But people remember it as Deborah's song.)

As a working woman today, you can follow suit. Don't push male colleagues aside or try to make them look bad. Instead, when asked to take charge, don't hesitate to do so. Inspire confidence by being confident. Encourage people to work together. Afterwards, express appreciation to your coworkers. Deborah did. **(See also Genesis 50.15-21; Isaiah 11.1-9; Ephesians 5.6-21.)**

Words To Remember: *Deborah the wife of Lappidoth was a prophet and a leader of Israel.—Judges 4.4*

Deborah

Judges 4,5

Women in the military are not exactly new. But it takes a unique woman to lead combat; Deborah was that kind of woman. Yet long before she became a military leader, Deborah learned leadership in other settings. Most important, Deborah knew how to receive leadership from God.

Our first view of Deborah finds her sitting under a palm—pointedly known as Deborah's Palm Tree. There she improvised a legal court room, where people from all over the hill country of Ephraim came to her to settle their disputes. She was, in a very practical sense, their judge.

Deborah was also a prophet. God revealed to Deborah his plans for the people. God even sent messages to military commanders through her. Once, Barak was so lacking in confidence that he refused to lead his men out unless Deborah went with him. During the battle she shouted, "Barak, it's time to attack Sisera! . . . The LORD has already gone on ahead to fight for you" (4.14). Deborah was matching foot soldiers against iron chariots, but she knew who was really leading this battle: the Lord himself. When the battle was won, Deborah and Barak led their people in a song that was part praise to the Lord, part retelling the event, part thanks to the tribes who sent soldiers (and scolding to those who didn't), and part a most uncompassionate taunt to the losing side. We can almost hear Hebrew mothers singing Deborah's song to their children as a home-taught lesson in national history.

Almost as an aside to Deborah's other roles is the introductory phrase to her story, "Deborah the wife of Lappidoth" (4.4). So this great prophet, judge, and military leader also did the ordinary wifely chores of homemaking. She shared her life with a husband.

Deborah's prayer that all the Lord's enemies would die like Sisera may seem harsh to the modern reader, but her first loyalty was to the Lord—and that was admirable.

Today's woman can draw much from Deborah's character. Deborah was a leader. We can regard her strength—and not cover up our own. We can respect her wise ability to resolve differences, and we can use the wisdom God gives us to help people resolve conflict. We can honor Deborah's willingness to listen to God and develop similar listening skills as we study Scripture and "tune in" to God's work around us. Deborah opened and closed her victory song with praise to God. We, too, when we tell the stories of our lives, can point to God. Then we can invite our listeners to praise God with us.

soldiers gathered there, and Barak led them out from Kedesh. Deborah went too.

[11]At this time, Heber of the Kenite clan was living near the village of Oak in Zaanannim,[k] not far from Kedesh. The Kenites were descendants of Hobab, the father-in-law of Moses, but Heber had moved and had set up his tents away from the rest of the clan.

[12]When Sisera learned that Barak had led an army to Mount Tabor, [13]he called his troops together and got all nine hundred iron chariots ready. Then he led his army away from Harosheth-Ha-Goiim to the Kishon River.

[14]Deborah shouted, "Barak, it's time to attack Sisera! Because today the LORD is going to help you defeat him. In fact, the LORD has already gone on ahead to fight for you."

Barak led his ten thousand troops down from Mount Tabor. [15]And during the battle, the LORD confused Sisera, his chariot drivers, and his whole army. Everyone was so afraid of Barak and his army, that even Sisera jumped down from his chariot and tried to escape. [16]Barak's forces went after Sisera's chariots and army as far as Harosheth-Ha-Goiim.

Sisera's entire army was wiped out. [17]Only Sisera escaped. He ran to Heber's camp, because Heber and his family had a peace treaty with the king of Hazor. Sisera went to the tent that belonged to Jael, Heber's wife. [18]She came out to greet him and said, "Come in, sir! Please come on in. Don't be afraid."

After they had gone inside, Sisera lay down, and Jael covered him with a blanket. [19]"Could I have a little water?" he asked. "I'm thirsty."

Jael opened a leather bottle and poured him some milk, then she covered him back up.

[20]"Stand at the entrance to the tent," Sisera told her. "If someone comes by and asks if anyone is inside, tell them 'No.' "

[21]Sisera was exhausted and soon fell fast asleep. Jael took a hammer and drove a tentpeg through his head into the ground, and he died.

[22]Meanwhile, Barak had been following Sisera, and Jael went out to meet him. "The man you're looking for is inside," she said. "Come in and I'll show him to you."

They went inside, and there was Sisera—dead and stretched out with a tent-peg through his skull.

[23]That same day the Israelites defeated the Canaanite King Jabin, and his army was no longer powerful enough to attack the Israelites. [24]Jabin grew weaker while the Israelites kept growing stronger, and at last the Israelites destroyed him.

Deborah and Barak Sing for the LORD

5 After the battle was over that day, Deborah and Barak sang this song:

[2]We praise you, LORD!
Our soldiers volunteered,
 ready to follow you.
[3]Listen, kings and rulers,
while I sing for the LORD,
 the God of Israel.

*[4]Our LORD, God of Israel,
when you came from Seir,
 where the Edomites live,
[5]rain poured from the sky,
the earth trembled,
 and mountains shook.

[6]In the time of Shamgar
 son of Anath,
and now again in Jael's time,
roads were too dangerous
 for caravans.
Travelers had to take
 the back roads,
[7]and villagers couldn't work
 in their fields.[l]
Then Deborah[m] took command,
protecting Israel as a mother
 protects her children.

[8]The Israelites worshiped
 other gods,
and the gates of their towns
 were then attacked.[n]
But they had no shields
 or spears to fight with.
[9]I praise you, LORD,
 and I am grateful
for those leaders and soldiers

---

[k]**4.11** *the village . . . Zaanannim:* Or "the oak tree in the town of Zaanannim." [l]**5.7** *villagers . . . fields:* One possible meaning for the difficult Hebrew text.
[m]**5.7** *Deborah:* Or "I, Deborah." [n]**5.8** *The Israelites . . . attacked:* One possible meaning for the difficult Hebrew text.

who volunteered.
10 Listen, everyone!
Whether you ride a donkey
with a padded saddle
or have to walk.
11 Even those who carry water[o]
to the animals will tell you,
"The LORD has won victories,
and so has Israel."

Then the LORD's people marched
down to the town gates
12 and said, "Deborah, let's go!
Let's sing as we march.
Barak, capture our enemies."

13 The LORD's people who were left
joined with their leaders
and fought at my side.[p]
14 Troops came from Ephraim,
where Amalekites once lived.
Others came from Benjamin;
officers and leaders came
from Machir and Zebulun.
15 The rulers of Issachar
came along with Deborah,
and Issachar followed Barak
into the valley.

But the tribe of Reuben
was no help at all![q]
16 Reuben, why did you stay
among your sheep pens?[r]
Was it to listen to shepherds
whistling for their sheep?
No one could figure out
why Reuben wouldn't come.[s]
17 The people of Gilead stayed
across the Jordan.
Why did the tribe of Dan
remain on their ships
and the tribe of Asher
stay along the coast
near the harbors?

18 But soldiers of Zebulun
and Naphtali
risked their lives
to attack the enemy.[t]
19 Canaanite kings fought us
at Taanach by the stream
near Megiddo[u]—
but they couldn't rob us
of our silver.[v]

[o]**5.11** *Even . . . water*: One possible meaning for the difficult Hebrew text. [p]**5.13** *side*: One possible meaning for the difficult Hebrew text of verse 13. [q]**5.15** *But . . . at all*: Or "But the people of Reuben couldn't make up their minds." [r]**5.16** *sheep pens*: Or "campfires." [s]**5.16** *No . . . come*: Or "The people of Reuben couldn't make up their minds." [t]**5.18** *to attack the enemy*: One possible meaning for the difficult Hebrew text. [u]**5.19** *stream near Megiddo*: Probably refers to one of the streams that flow into the Kishon River. [v]**5.19** *rob us of our silver*: The army that won a battle would take everything of value from the dead enemy soldiers.

*Spiritual*Life—What does God expect of me? *(Judges 5.1-11)*

Give God praise for your victories.

Victories are hard to come by. Whether it's the last ten pounds you've been trying to lose, a long anticipated promotion, or winning the war against addiction, victories are hard earned. We want to stand up and shout, "I did it!" And sometimes we should.

Deborah's song does not minimize her role in victorious battle. She sang, "Then Deborah took command, protecting Israel as a mother protects her children" (5.7). But she also acknowledged that the Lord was their leader: "We praise you, LORD! Our soldiers volunteered, ready to follow you" (5.2).

We need to remember our victories are not ours alone. A Christian woman fights her battles with the strength of her Lord. And when she wins, it's only fair (and worshipful) to give praise where it belongs—with God. We can do that with a simple phrase like "God helped me." We can pour our creative talent (as Deborah did) into a song, essay, or art piece of praise. Or we can whisper a simple *thanks* to our Lord, who has given us the victory. (See also Exodus 20.1-17; Jeremiah 1.4-19; Micah 6.6-8; Romans 8.1-17; 1 Corinthians 6.12-20.)

Words To Remember: ***Even those who carry water to the animals will tell you, "The LORD has won victories, and so has Israel."*—Judges 5.11**

²⁰From their pathways in the sky
   the stars^w fought Sisera,
²¹and his soldiers were swept away
   by the ancient Kishon River.

I will march on and be brave.

²²Sisera's horses galloped off,
   their hoofs thundering
      in retreat.

²³The LORD's angel said,
    "Put a curse on Meroz Town!
Its people refused
to help the LORD fight
   his powerful enemies."
²⁴But honor Jael,
   the wife of Heber
      from the Kenite clan.
Give more honor to her
than to any other woman
   who lives in tents.
Yes, give more honor to her
   than to any other woman.
²⁵Sisera asked for water,
   but Jael gave him milk—
      cream in a fancy cup.
²⁶She reached for a tent-peg
   and held a hammer
      in her right hand.
And with a blow to the head,
   she crushed his skull.
²⁷Sisera sank to his knees
   and fell dead at her feet.

²⁸Sisera's mother looked out
   through her window.
"Why is he taking so long?"
   she asked.
"Why haven't we heard
   his chariots coming?"
²⁹She and her wisest women
   gave the same answer:
³⁰"Sisera and his troops
are finding treasures
   to bring back—
a woman, or maybe two,
   for each man,
and beautiful dresses
   for those women to wear."^x

³¹Our LORD, we pray
   that all your enemies
      will die like Sisera.
But let everyone who loves you

shine brightly like the sun
   at dawn.

Midian Steals Everything from Israel

6 There was peace in Israel for about forty years. ¹Then once again the Israelites started disobeying the LORD, so he let the nation of Midian control Israel for seven years. ²The Midianites were so cruel that many Israelites ran to the mountains and hid in caves.

³Every time the Israelites would plant crops, the Midianites invaded Israel together with the Amalekites and other eastern nations. ⁴⁻⁵They rode in on their camels, set up their tents, and then let their livestock eat the crops as far as the town of Gaza. The Midianites stole food, sheep, cattle, and donkeys. Like a swarm of locusts,^y they could not be counted, and they ruined the land wherever they went.

⁶⁻⁷The Midianites took almost everything that belonged to the Israelites, and the Israelites begged the LORD for help. ⁸⁻⁹Then the LORD sent a prophet to them with this message:

I am the LORD God of Israel, so listen to what I say. You were slaves in Egypt, but I set you free and led you out of Egypt into this land. And when nations here made life miserable for you, I rescued you and helped you get rid of them and take their land. ¹⁰I am your God, and I told you not to worship Amorite gods, even though you are living in the land of the Amorites. But you refused to listen.

The LORD Chooses Gideon

¹¹One day an angel from the LORD went to the town of Ophrah and sat down under the big tree that belonged to Joash, a member of the Abiezer clan. Joash's son Gideon was nearby, threshing grain in a shallow pit, where he could not be seen by the Midianites.

¹²The angel appeared and spoke to Gideon, "The LORD is helping you, and you are a strong warrior."

---

^w**5.20** *stars*: In ancient times, the stars were sometimes regarded as supernatural beings.   ^x**5.30** *and beautiful . . . wear*: One possible meaning for the difficult Hebrew text.   ^y**6.4,5** *locusts*: Insects like grasshoppers that travel in swarms and cause great damage to crops.

¹³Gideon answered, "Please don't take this wrong, but if the LORD is helping us, then why have all of these awful things happened? We've heard how the LORD performed miracles and rescued our ancestors from Egypt. But those things happened long ago. Now the LORD has abandoned us to the Midianites."

¹⁴Then the LORD himself said, "Gideon, you will be strong, because I am giving you the power to rescue Israel from the Midianites."

¹⁵Gideon replied, "But how can I rescue Israel? My clan is the weakest one in Manasseh, and everyone else in my family is more important than I am."

¹⁶"Gideon," the LORD answered, "you can rescue Israel because I am going to help you! Defeating the Midianites will be as easy as beating up one man."

¹⁷Gideon said, "It's hard to believe that I'm actually talking to the LORD. Please do something so I'll know that you really are the LORD. ¹⁸And wait here until I bring you an offering."

"All right, I'll wait," the LORD answered.

¹⁹Gideon went home and killed a young goat, then started boiling the meat. Next, he opened a big sack of flour and made it into thin bread.ᶻ When the meat was done, he put it in a basket and poured the broth into a clay cooking pot. He took the meat, the broth, and the bread and placed them under the big tree.

²⁰God's angel said, "Gideon, put the meat and the bread on this rock, and pour the broth over them." Gideon did as he was told. ²¹The angel was holding a walking stick, and he touched the meat and the bread with the end of the stick. Flames jumped from the rock and burned up the meat and the bread.

When Gideon looked, the angel was gone. ²²Gideon realized that he had seen one of the LORD's angels. "Oh!" he moaned. "Now I'm going to die,"ᵃ

²³"Calm down!" the LORD told Gideon. "There's nothing to be afraid of. You're not going to die."

²⁴Gideon built an altar for worshiping the LORD and called it "The LORD Calms Our Fears." It still stands there in Ophrah, a town in the territory of the Abiezer clan.

ᶻ6.19 *thin bread*: Bread made without yeast, since there was no time for the dough to rise.   ᵃ6.22 *Now I'm going to die*: The Hebrew text has "I have seen an angel of the LORD face to face." Some people believed that if they saw one of the LORD's angels, they would die (see 13.22).

SingleLife—How can God use me as a single woman? *(Judges 6,7)*

Trust God's strength—not your own.

Do you ever think that if God wanted to get anything big done, he'd choose someone with a lot more resources than yours? Single women sometimes feel that they have half of what everyone else has: half the income, half the family, half the living space—and twice the responsibility of most women. So if God wants a big job done, he should give it to someone else. Right?

Wrong. Gideon's resources were so meager that when an angel appeared and said, "The LORD is helping you, and you are a strong warrior," Gideon answered, "Please don't take this wrong, but if the LORD is helping us, then why have all of these awful things happened?" (6.12,13). In order to find Gideon, the angel had to go down into a pit—which is where Gideon was hiding while he threshed his small harvest of grain. Otherwise, the Midianite raiders would have stolen the grain from him.

After debating with God about his capabilities and resources, Gideon put together an army of 32,000 soldiers—except God wouldn't let him keep that many. God reduced their numbers to 300, then put the whole Midianite army on the run with hardly more deadly weapons than torches, trumpets, and God-inspired fear.

Sometimes God uses our lack of resources to reveal his strength—and to do very large jobs indeed. (See also Exodus 15.19-21; 2 Samuel 20.14-22; Malachi 3.16-18.)

Words To Remember: *Then the LORD himself said, "Gideon, you will be strong, because I am giving you the power to rescue Israel from the Midianites."—Judges 6.14*

Gideon Tears Down Baal's Altar

[25]That night the LORD spoke to Gideon again:

Get your father's second-best bull, the one that's seven years old. Use it to pull down the altar where your father worships Baal and cut down the sacred pole[b] next to the altar. [26]Then build an altar for worshiping me on the highest part of the hill where your town is built. Use layers of stones for my altar, not just a pile of rocks. Cut up the wood from the pole, make a fire, kill the bull, and burn it as a sacrifice to me.

[27]Gideon chose ten of his servants to help him, and they did everything God had said. But since Gideon was afraid of his family and the other people in town, he did it all at night.

[28]When the people of the town got up the next morning, they saw that Baal's altar had been knocked over, and the sacred pole next to it had been cut down. Then they noticed the new altar covered with the remains of the sacrificed bull.

[29]"Who could have done such a thing?" they asked. And they kept on asking, until finally someone told them, "Gideon the son of Joash did it."

[30]The men of the town went to Joash and said, "Your son Gideon knocked over Baal's altar and cut down the sacred pole next to it. Hand him over, so we can kill him!"

[31]The crowd pushed closer and closer, but Joash replied, "Are you trying to take revenge for Baal? Are you trying to rescue Baal? If you are, you will be the ones who are put to death, and it will happen before another day dawns. If Baal really is a god, let him take his own revenge on someone who tears down his altar."

[32]That same day, Joash changed Gideon's name to Jerubbaal, explaining, "He tore down Baal's altar, so let Baal take revenge himself."[c]

Gideon Defeats the Midianites

[33]All the Midianites, Amalekites, and other eastern nations got together and crossed the Jordan River. Then they invaded the land of Israel and set up camp in Jezreel Valley.

[34]The LORD's Spirit took control of Gideon, and Gideon blew a signal on a trumpet to tell the men in the Abiezer clan to follow him. [35]He also sent messengers to the tribes of Manasseh, Asher, Zebulun, and Naphtali, telling the men of these tribes to come and join his army. Then they set out toward the enemy camp.

[36-37]Gideon prayed to God, "I know that you promised to help me rescue Israel, but I need proof. Tonight I'll put some wool on the stone floor of that threshing-place over there. If you really will help me rescue Israel, then tomorrow morning let there be dew on the wool, but let the stone floor be dry."

[38]And that's just what happened. Early the next morning, Gideon got up and checked the wool. He squeezed out enough water to fill a bowl. [39]But Gideon prayed to God again. "Don't be angry at me," Gideon said. "Let me try this just one more time, so I'll really be sure you'll help me. Only this time, let the wool be dry and the stone floor be wet with dew."

[40]That night, God made the stone floor wet with dew, but he kept the wool dry.

7 Early the next morning, Gideon and his army got up and moved their camp to Fear Spring.[d] The Midianite camp was to the north, in the valley at the foot of Moreh Hill.[e]

[2]The LORD said, "Gideon, your army is too big. I can't let you win with this many soldiers. The Israelites would think that they had won the battle all by themselves and that I didn't have anything to do with it. [3]So call your troops together and tell them that anyone who is really afraid can leave Mount Gilead[f] and go home."

Twenty-two thousand men returned home, leaving Gideon with only ten thousand soldiers.

[4]"Gideon," the LORD said, "you still have too many soldiers. Take them down to the spring and I'll test them. I'll tell you which ones can go along with you and which ones must go back home."

---

[b]**6.25** *sacred pole*: Or "sacred tree," used as a symbol of Asherah, the Canaanite goddess of fertility.
[c]**6.32** *Jerubbaal . . . take revenge himself*: In Hebrew, "Jerubbaal" means "Let Baal take revenge."
[d]**7.1** *Fear Spring*: Or "Harod Spring."   [e]**7.1** *Moreh Hill*: About 5 miles north of Fear Spring.   [f]**7.3** *Mount Gilead*: Usually "Gilead" refers to an area east of the Jordan River, but in this verse it refers to a place near Jezreel Valley west of the Jordan.

[5]When Gideon led his army down to the spring, the LORD told him, "Watch how each man gets a drink of water. Then divide them into two groups—those who lap the water like a dog and those who kneel down to drink."

[6]Three hundred men scooped up water in their hands and lapped it, and the rest knelt to get a drink. [7]The LORD said, "Gideon, your army will be made up of everyone who lapped the water from their hands. Send the others home. I'm going to rescue Israel by helping you and your army of three hundred defeat the Midianites."

[8]Then Gideon gave these orders, "You three hundred men stay here. The rest of you may go home, but leave your food and trumpets with us."

Gideon's army camp was on top of a hill overlooking the Midianite camp in the valley,

---

God can teach us. We all have something to give. The secret is finding where God wants to use us.

ELIZABETH MITTELSTAEDT

---

[9]That night, the LORD said to Gideon, "Get up! Attack the Midianite camp. I am going to let you defeat them, [10]but if you're still afraid, you and your servant Purah should sneak down to their camp. [11]When you hear what the Midianites are saying, you'll be brave enough to attack."

Gideon and Purah worked their way to the edge of the enemy camp, where soldiers were on guard duty. [12]The camp was huge. The Midianites, Amalekites, and other eastern nations covered the valley like a swarm of locusts.[g] And it would be easier to count the grains of sand on a beach than to count their camels. [13]Gideon overheard one enemy guard telling another, "I had a dream about a flat[h] loaf of barley bread that came tumbling into our camp. It hit the headquarters tent,[i] and the tent flipped over and fell down."

[14]The other soldier answered, "Your dream must have been about Gideon, the Israelite commander. It means God will let him and his army defeat the Midianite army and everyone else in our camp."

[15]As soon as Gideon heard about the dream and what it meant, he bowed down to praise God. Then he went back to the Israelite camp and shouted, "Let's go! The LORD is going to let us defeat the Midianite army."

[16]Gideon divided his little army into three groups of one hundred men, and he gave each soldier a trumpet and a large clay jar with a burning torch inside. [17-18]Gideon said, "When we get to the enemy camp, spread out and surround it. Then wait for me to blow a signal on my trumpet. As soon as you hear it, blow your trumpets and shout, 'Fight for the LORD! Fight for Gideon!' "

[19]Gideon and his group reached the edge of the enemy camp a few hours after dark, just after the new guards had come on duty.[j] Gideon and his soldiers blew their trumpets and smashed the clay jars that were hiding the torches. [20]The rest of Gideon's soldiers blew the trumpets they were holding in their right hands. Then they smashed the jars and held the burning torches in their left hands. Everyone shouted, "Fight with your swords for the LORD and for Gideon!"

[21]The enemy soldiers started yelling and tried to run away. Gideon's troops stayed in their positions surrounding the camp [22]and blew their trumpets again. As they did, the LORD made the enemy soldiers pull out their swords and start fighting each other.

The enemy army tried to escape from the camp. They ran to Acacia Tree Town, toward Zeredah,[k] and as far as the edge of the land that belonged to the town of Abel-Meholah near Tabbath.[l]

---

[g]**7.12** *locusts:* See the note at 6.4, 5.   [h]**7.13** *flat:* Or "moldy."   [i]**7.13** *the headquarters tent:* Or "a tent."   [j]**7.19** *a few hours after dark, just . . . duty:* The Hebrew text has "at the beginning of the second watch, just . . . duty." The night was divided into three periods called "watches," each about four hours long, and different guards would come on duty at the beginning of each watch. The first watch began at sunset, so the beginning of the second watch would have been shortly after 10:00 P.M.   [k]**7.22** *Zeredah:* Some Hebrew manuscripts; most Hebrew manuscripts "Zererah"; these may be different names for the town of Zarethan in the Jordan River valley.   [l]**7.22** *Acacia Tree Town . . . Zeredah . . . Abel-Meholah near Tabbath:* These were places east of the Jordan River.

[23]Gideon sent word for more Israelite soldiers to come from the tribes of Naphtali, Asher, and both halves of Manasseh[m] to help fight the Midianites. [24]He also sent messengers to tell all the men who lived in the hill country of Ephraim, "Come and help us fight the Midianites! Put guards at every spring, stream, and well, as far as Beth-Barah before the Midianites can get to them. And guard the Jordan River."

Troops from Ephraim did exactly what Gideon had asked, [25]and they even helped chase the Midianites on the east side of the Jordan River. These troops captured Raven and Wolf,[n] the two Midianite leaders. They killed Raven at a large rock that has come to be known as Raven Rock, and they killed Wolf near a wine-pit that has come to be called Wolf Wine-Pit.[o]

The men of Ephraim brought the heads of the two Midianite leaders to Gideon.

8 [1]But the men were really upset with Gideon and complained, "When you went to war with Midian, you didn't ask us to help! Why did you treat us like that?"

[2]Gideon answered:

> Don't be upset! Even though you came later, you were able to do much more than I did. It's just like the grape harvest: The grapes your tribe doesn't even bother to pick are better than the best grapes my family can grow. [3]Besides, God chose you to capture Raven and Wolf. I didn't do a thing compared to you.

By the time Gideon had finished talking, the men of Ephraim had calmed down and were no longer angry at him.

Gideon Finishes Destroying the Midianite Army

[4]After Gideon and his three hundred troops had chased the Midianites as far as the Jordan River, they were exhausted. [5]The town of Succoth was nearby, so he went there and asked, "Please give my troops some food. They are worn out, but we have to keep chasing Zebah and Zalmunna, the two Midianite kings."

[6]The town leaders of Succoth answered, "Why should we feed your army? We don't know if you really will defeat Zebah and Zalmunna."

[7]"Just wait!" Gideon said. "After the LORD helps me defeat them, I'm coming back here. I'll make a whip out of thorns and rip the flesh from your bones."

[8]After leaving Succoth, Gideon went to Penuel and asked the leaders there for some food. But he got the same answer as he had gotten at Succoth. [9]"I'll come back safe and sound," Gideon said, "but when I do, I'm going to tear down your tower!"[p]

[10]Zebah and Zalmunna were in Karkor[q] with an army of fifteen thousand troops. They were all that was left of the army of the eastern nations, because one hundred twenty thousand of their warriors had been killed in the battle.

[11]Gideon reached the enemy camp by going east along Nomad[r] Road past Nobah and Jogbehah. He made a surprise attack, [12]and the enemy panicked. Zebah and Zalmunna tried to escape, but Gideon chased and captured them.

[13]After the battle, Gideon set out for home. As he was going through Heres Pass, [14]he caught a young man who lived in Succoth. Gideon asked him who the town officials of Succoth were, and the young man wrote down seventy-seven names.

[15]Gideon went to the town officials and said, "Here are Zebah and Zalmunna. Remember how you made fun of me? You said, 'We don't know if you really will defeat those two Midianite kings. So why should we feed your worn-out army?' "

[16]Gideon made a whip from thorn plants and used it to beat the town officials. [17]Afterwards he went to Penuel, where he tore down the tower and killed all the town officials[s] there.

[18]Then Gideon said, "Zebah and Zalmunna, tell me about the men you killed at Tabor."

"They were a lot like you," the two kings answered. "They were dignified, almost like royalty."

[19]"They were my very own brothers!" Gideon said. "I swear by the living LORD

---

[m]**7.23** *both halves of Manasseh*: Half of Manasseh lived east of the Jordan River, and the other half lived on the west. [n]**7.25** *Raven and Wolf*: Or "Oreb and Zeeb." [o]**7.25** *Raven Rock . . . Wolf Wine-Pit*: Or "Oreb Rock . . . Zeeb Wine-Pit." [p]**8.9** *tower*: Towers were often part of a town wall. [q]**8.10** *Karkor*: A little over 100 miles east of the Dead Sea. [r]**8.11** *Nomad*: A person who lives in a tent and moves from place to place. [s]**8.17** *all . . . officials*: Or "every man in town."

that if you had let them live, I would let you live."

²⁰Gideon turned to Jether, his oldest son. "Kill them!" Gideon said.

But Jether was young,ᵗ and he was too afraid to even pull out his sword.

²¹"What's the matter, Gideon?" Zebah and Zalmunna asked. "Do it yourself, if you're not too much of a coward!"

Gideon jumped up and killed them both. Then he took the fancy gold ornaments from the necks of their camels.

The Israelites Ask Gideon To Be Their King

²²After the battle with the Midianites, the Israelites said, "Gideon, you rescued us! Now we want you to be our king. Then after your death, your son and then your grandson will rule."

²³"No," Gideon replied, "I won't be your king, and my son won't be king either. Only the LORD is your ruler. ²⁴But I will ask you to do one thing: Give me all the earrings you took from the enemy."

The enemy soldiers had been Ishmaelites,ᵘ and they wore gold earrings.

²⁵The Israelite soldiers replied, "Of course we will give you the earrings." Then they spread out a robe on the ground and tossed the earrings on it. ²⁶The total weight of this gold was over forty pounds. In addition, there was the gold from the camels' ornaments and from the beautiful jewelry worn by the Midianite kings. Gideon also took their purple robes.

²⁷⁻²⁹Gideon returned to his home in Ophrah and had the gold made into a statue, which the Israelites soon started worshiping. They became unfaithful to God, and even Gideon and his family were trapped into worshiping the statue.ᵛ

The Midianites had been defeated so badly that they were no longer strong enough to attack Israel. And so Israel was at peace for the remaining forty years of Gideon's life.

Gideon Dies

³⁰Gideon had many wives and seventy sons. ³¹He even had a wifeʷ who lived at Shechem.ˣ They had a son, and Gideon named him Abimelech.

³²Gideon lived to be an old man. And when he died, he was buried in the family tomb in his hometown of Ophrah, which belonged to the Abiezer clan.

³³Soon after Gideon's death, the Israelites turned their backs on God again. They set up idols of Baal and worshiped Baal Berithʸ as their god. ³⁴The Israelites forgot that the LORD was their God, and that he had rescued them from the enemies who lived around them. ³⁵Besides all that, the Israelites were unkind to Gideon's family, even though Gideon had done so much for Israel.

Abimelech Tries To Be King

9 Abimelech the son of Gideonᶻ went to Shechem. While there, he met with his mother's relatives ²and told them to say to the leaders of Shechem, "Do you think it would be good to have all seventy of Gideon's sons ruling us? Wouldn't you rather have just one man be king? Abimelech would make a good king, and he's related to us."

³Abimelech's uncles talked it over with the leaders of Shechem who agreed, "Yes, it would be better for one of our relatives to be king." ⁴Then they gave Abimelech seventy piecesᵃ of silver from the temple of their god Baal Berith.ᵇ

Abimelech used the silver to hire a gang of rough soldiers who would do anything for money. ⁵Abimelech and his soldiers went to his father's home in Ophrah and brought out Gideon's other sons to a large rock, where they murdered all seventy. Gideon's youngest son Jotham hid from the soldiers, but he was the only one who escaped.

⁶The leaders of Shechem, including the

ᵗ8.20 *young*: Gideon wanted to insult the kings by having a young boy kill them.   ᵘ8.24 *Ishmaelites*: According to Genesis 25.1, 2, 12, both Ishmaelites and Midianites were descendants of Abraham. It is possible that in this passage "Ishmaelites" has the meaning "nomadic traders," while "Midianites" (verses 22, 26-29) refers to their ethnic origin.   ᵛ8.27-29 *statue . . . statue*: Or "sacred priestly vest . . . vest."   ʷ8.31 *wife*: This translates a Hebrew word for a woman who was legally bound to a man, but without the full privileges of a wife.   ˣ8.31 *who lived at Shechem*: Sometimes marriages were arranged so that the wife lived with her parents, and the husband visited her from time to time.   ʸ8.33 *Baal Berith*: Or "Baal of the Agreement" or "the Lord of the Agreement."   ᶻ9.1 *Gideon*: The Hebrew text has "Jerubbaal," another name for Gideon (see 6.32).   ᵃ9.4 *seventy pieces*: About 28 ounces.   ᵇ9.4 *Baal Berith*: See the note at 8.33.

priests and the military officers,[c] met at the tree next to the sacred rock[d] in Shechem to crown Abimelech king. [7]Jotham heard what they were doing. So he climbed to the top of Mount Gerizim and shouted down to the people who were there at the meeting:

Leaders of Shechem,
    listen to me,
and maybe God
    will listen to you.

[8]Once the trees searched
    for someone to be king;
they asked the olive tree,
    "Will you be our king?"
[9]But the olive tree replied,
    "My oil brings honor
      to people and gods.
I won't stop making oil,
    just to have my branches wave
      above the other trees."

[10]Then they asked the fig tree,
    "Will you be our king?"
[11]But the fig tree replied,
    "I won't stop growing
      my delicious fruit,
just to have my branches wave
    above the other trees."

[12]Next they asked the grape vine,
    "Will you be our king?"
[13]But the grape vine replied,
    "My wine brings cheer
      to people and gods.
I won't stop making wine,
    just to have my branches wave
      above the other trees."

[14]Finally, they went
    to the thornbush and asked,
      "Will you be our king?"
[15]The thornbush replied,
    "If you really want me
      to be your king,
then come into my shade
    and I will protect you.
But if you're deceiving me,
    I'll start a fire
that will spread out and destroy
    the cedars of Lebanon."[e]

After Jotham had finished telling this story, he said:

[16-18]My father Gideon risked his life for you when he fought to rescue you from the Midianites. Did you reward Gideon by being kind to his family? No, you did not! You attacked his family and killed all seventy of his sons on that rock.

And was it right to make Abimelech your king? He's merely the son of my father's slave girl.[f] But just because he's your relative, you made him king of Shechem.

[19]So, you leaders of Shechem, if you treated Gideon and his family the way you should have, then I hope you and Abimelech will make each other very happy. [20]But if it was wrong to treat Gideon and his family the way you did, then I pray that Abimelech will destroy you with fire, and I pray that you will do the same to him.

[21]Jotham ran off and went to live in the town of Beer, where he could be safe from his brother Abimelech.

Abimelech Destroys Shechem

[22]Abimelech had been a military commander of Israel for three years, [23-24]when God decided to punish him and the leaders of Shechem for killing Gideon's seventy sons.

So God turned the leaders of Shechem against Abimelech. [25]Then they sent some men to hide on the hilltops and watch for Abimelech and his troops, while they sent others to rob everyone that went by on the road. But Abimelech found out what they were doing.

[26]One day, Gaal son of Ebed went to live in Shechem. His brothers moved there too, and soon the leaders of Shechem started trusting him.

[27]The time came for the grape harvest, and the people of Shechem went into their vineyards and picked the grapes. They put the grapes in their wine-pits and walked on

---

[c]**9.6** *including the priests and the military officers:* The Hebrew text has "and the Millo house," another name for the temple of Baal Berith. It probably also served as a military fortress. [d]**9.6** *tree . . . rock:* One ancient translation; Hebrew "propped-up sacred tree." [e]**9.15** *cedars of Lebanon:* The cedars that grew in the Lebanon mountains were some of the largest trees in that part of the world. [f]**9.16-18** *son of . . . slave girl:* See 8.31.

them to squeeze out the juice in order to make wine. Then they went into the temple of their god and threw a big party. There was a lot of eating and drinking, and before long they were cursing Abimelech.

²⁸Gaal said:

Hamor was the founder of Shechem, and one of his descendants should be our ruler. But Abimelech's father was Gideon, so Abimelech isn't really one of us. He shouldn't be our king, and we shouldn't have to obey him or Zebul, who rules Shechem for him. ²⁹If I were the ruler of Shechem, I'd get rid of that Abimelech. I'd tell him, "Get yourself an even bigger army, and we will still defeat you."

³⁰Zebul was angry when he found out what Gaal had said. ³¹And so he sent some messengers to Abimelech. But they had to pretend to be doing something else, or they would not have been allowed to leave Shechem.ᵍ Zebul told the messengers to say:

Gaal the son of Ebed has come to Shechem along with his brothers, and they have persuaded the people to let Gaal rule Shechem instead of you. ³²This is what I think you should do. Lead your army here during the night and hide in the fields. ³³Get up the next morning at sunrise and rush out of your hiding places to attack the town. Gaal and his followers will come out to fight you, but you will easily defeat them.

³⁴So one night, Abimelech led his soldiers to Shechem. He divided them into four groups, and they all hid near the town. ³⁵The next morning, Gaal went out and stood in the opening of the town gate. Abimelech and his soldiers left their hiding places, ³⁶and Gaal saw them. Zebul was standing there with Gaal, and Gaal remarked, "Zebul, that looks like a crowd of people coming down from the mountaintops."

"No," Zebul answered, "it's just the shadows of the mountains. It only looks like people moving."

³⁷"But Zebul, look over there," Gaal said. "There's a crowd coming down from the sacred mountain,ʰ and another group is coming along the road from the tree where people talk with the spirits of the dead."

³⁸Then Zebul replied, "What good is all of your bragging now? You were the one who said Abimelech shouldn't be the ruler of Shechem. Out there is the army that you made fun of. So go out and fight them!"

³⁹Gaal and the leaders of Shechem went out and fought Abimelech. ⁴⁰Soon the people of Shechem turned and ran back into the town. However, Abimelech and his troops were close behind and killed many of them along the way.

⁴¹Abimelech stayed at Arumah,ⁱ and Zebul forced Gaal and his brothers out of Shechem.

⁴²The next morning, the people of Shechem were getting ready to work in their fields as usual, but someone told Abimelech about it. ⁴³Abimelech divided his army into three groups and set up an ambush in the fields near Shechem. When the people came out of the town, he and his army rushed out from their hiding places and attacked. ⁴⁴Abimelech and the troops with him ran to the town gate and took control of it, while two other groups attacked and killed the people who were in the fields. ⁴⁵He and his troops fought in Shechem all day, until they had killed everyone in town. Then he and his men tore down the houses and buildings and scattered saltʲ everywhere.

⁴⁶Earlier that day, the leaders of the temple of El Berithᵏ at Shechem had heard about the attack. So they went into the temple fortress, ⁴⁷but Abimelech found out where they were. ⁴⁸He led his troops to Mount Zalmon, where he took an ax and chopped off a tree branch. He lifted the branch onto his shoulder and shouted, "Hurry! Cut off a branch just as I did."

⁴⁹When they all had branches, they followed Abimelech back to Shechem. They piled the branches against the fortress and set them on fire, burning down the fortress

---

ᵍ9.31 *But . . . Shechem:* One possible meaning for the difficult Hebrew text.   ʰ9.37 *sacred mountain:* The Hebrew text has "the navel of the land," which probably refers to Mount Gerizim as a sacred mountain linking heaven and earth.   ⁱ9.41 *Arumah:* About five miles from Shechem.   ʲ9.45 *scattered salt:* This may have been part of a ceremony to place a curse on the town.   ᵏ9.46 *temple of El Berith:* The Hebrew text also calls all or part of this temple the "Fortress of Shechem." El Berith, "the God of the Agreement," was also known as Baal Berith, "the Lord of the Agreement" (see also 8.33; 9.4).

and killing about one thousand men and women.

⁵⁰After destroying Shechem, Abimelech went to Thebez. He surrounded the town and captured it. ⁵¹But there was a tall fortress in the middle of the town, and the town leaders and everyone else went inside. Then they barred the gates and went up to the flat roof.

⁵²Abimelech and his army rushed to the fortress and tried to force their way inside. Abimelech himself was about to set the heavy wooden doors on fire, ⁵³when a woman on the roof dropped a large rock[l] on his head and cracked his skull. ⁵⁴The soldier who carried his weapons was nearby, and Abimelech told him, "Take out your sword and kill me. I don't want people to say that I was killed by a woman!"

So the soldier ran his sword through Abimelech. ⁵⁵And when the Israelite soldiers saw that their leader was dead, they went back home.

⁵⁶That's how God punished Abimelech for killing his brothers and bringing shame on his father's family. ⁵⁷God also punished the people of Shechem for helping Abimelech.[m] Everything happened just as Jotham's curse said it would.

Tola

10 Tola was the next person to rescue Israel. He belonged to the Issachar tribe, but he lived in Shamir, a town in the hill country of Ephraim. His father was Puah, and his grandfather was Dodo. ²Tola was a leader[n] of Israel for twenty-three years, then he died and was buried in Shamir.

Jair

³The next leader[n] of Israel was Jair, who lived in Gilead. He was a leader for twenty-two years. ⁴He had thirty sons, and each son had his own mule[o] and was in charge of one town in Gilead. Those thirty towns are still called The Settlements of Jair.[p] ⁵When he died, he was buried in the town of Kamon.

Israel Is Unfaithful Again

⁶Before long, the Israelites began disobeying the LORD by worshiping Baal, Astarte, and gods from Syria, Sidon, Moab, Ammon, and Philistia.

⁷The LORD was angry at Israel and decided to let Philistia and Ammon conquer them. ⁸So the same year that Jair died, Israel's army was crushed by these two nations. For eighteen years, Ammon was cruel to the Israelites who lived in Gilead, the region east of the Jordan River that had once belonged to the Amorites. ⁹Then the Ammonites began crossing the Jordan and attacking the tribes of Judah, Benjamin, and Ephraim. Life was miserable for the Israelites. ¹⁰They begged the LORD for help and confessed, "We were unfaithful to you, our LORD. We stopped worshiping you and started worshiping idols of Baal."

> *Our God, the great God of the universe, is for us.*
> CAROLE MAYHALL

¹¹⁻¹²The LORD answered:

In the past when you came crying to me for help, I rescued you. At one time or another I've rescued you from the Egyptians, the Amorites, the Ammonites, the Philistines, the Sidonians, the Amalekites, and the Maonites.[q] ¹³⁻¹⁴But I'm not going to rescue you any more! You've left me and gone off to worship other gods. If you're in such big trouble, go cry to them for help!

¹⁵"We have been unfaithful," the Israelites admitted. "If we must be punished, do it yourself, but please rescue us from the Ammonites."

¹⁶Then the Israelites got rid of the idols of the foreign gods, and they began worshiping only the LORD. Finally, there came a time when the LORD could no longer stand to see them suffer.

---

l9.53 *large rock:* One that was used in the grinding of grain. m9.57 *helping Abimelech:* Hebrew "their evil" (see 9.3, 4). n10.2,3 *leader:* See 2.16 and the note there. o10.4 *each son had his own mule:* A sign that the family was wealthy. p10.4 *The Settlements of Jair:* Or "Havvoth-Jair." q10.11,12 *Maonites:* Hebrew; one ancient translation "Midianites."

The Ammonites Invade Gilead

¹⁷The rulers of Ammon called their soldiers together and led them to Gilead, where they set up camp.

The Israelites gathered at Mizpah* and set up camp there. ¹⁸The leaders of Gilead asked each other, "Who can lead an attack on the Ammonites?" Then they agreed, "If we can find someone who can lead the attack, we'll make him the ruler of Gilead."

Jephthah

11 ¹⁻⁵The leaders of the Gilead clan decided to ask a brave warrior named Jephthah son of Gilead to lead the attack against the Ammonites.

Even though Jephthah belonged to the Gilead clan, he had earlier been forced to leave the region where they had lived. Jephthah was the son of a prostitute, but his half-brothers were the sons of his father's wife.

One day his half-brothers told him, "You don't really belong to our family, so you can't have any of the family property." Then they forced Jephthah to leave home.

Jephthah went to the country of Tob, where he was joined by a number of men who would do anything for money.

So the leaders of Gilead went to Jephthah and said, ⁶"Please come back to Gilead! If you lead our army, we will be able to fight off the Ammonites."

⁷"Didn't you hate me?" Jephthah replied. "Weren't you the ones who forced me to leave my family? You're coming to me now, just because you're in trouble."

⁸"But we do want you to come back," the leaders said. "And if you lead us in battle against the Ammonites, we will make you the ruler of Gilead."

⁹"All right," Jephthah said. "If I go back with you and the LORD lets me defeat the Ammonites, will you really make me your ruler?"

¹⁰"You have our word," the leaders answered. "And the LORD is a witness to what we have said."

¹¹So Jephthah went back to Mizpah* with the leaders of Gilead. The people of Gilead gathered at the place of worship and made Jephthah their ruler. Jephthah also made promises to them.

¹²After the ceremony, Jephthah sent messengers to say to the king of Ammon, "Are you trying to start a war? You have invaded my country, and I want to know why!"

¹³The king of Ammon replied, "Tell Jephthah that the land really belongs to me, all the way from the Arnon River in the south, to the Jabbok River in the north, and west to the Jordan River. When the Israelites came out of Egypt, they stole it. Tell Jephthah to return it to me, and there won't be any war."

Our Father God is love, essential love, and therefore cannot possibly desire for his child anything but what is best. He is all-wise and therefore knows just what that best is. He is all-powerful and therefore can give what he wants to give.

ELISABETH ELLIOT

¹⁴Jephthah sent the messengers back to the king of Ammon, ¹⁵and they told him that Jephthah had said:

Israel hasn't taken any territory from Moab or Ammon. ¹⁶When the Israelites came from Egypt, they traveled in the desert to the Red Sea⁵ and then to Kadesh. ¹⁷They sent messengers to the king of Edom and said, "Please, let us go through your country." But the king of Edom refused. They also sent messengers to the king of Moab, but he wouldn't let them cross his country either. And so the Israelites stayed at Kadesh.

¹⁸A little later, the Israelites set out into the desert, going east of Edom

---

*10.17; 11.11 *Mizpah:* In chapters 10–12, Mizpah is the name of a town in Gilead (see 11.29), not the same town as the Mizpah of chapters 20, 21.
⁵11.16 *Red Sea:* Hebrew *yam suph,* here referring to the Gulf of Aqaba, since the term is extended to include the northeastern arm of the Red Sea (see also the note at Exodus 13.18).

and Moab, and camping on the eastern side of the Arnon River gorge. The Arnon is the eastern border of Moab, and since the Israelites didn't cross it, they didn't even set foot in Moab.

¹⁹The Israelites sent messengers to the Amorite King Sihon of Heshbon. "Please," they said, "let our people go through your country to get to our own land."

²⁰Sihon didn't think the Israelites could be trusted, so he called his army together. They set up camp at Jahaz, then they attacked the Israelite camp. ²¹But the LORD God helped Israel defeat Sihon and his army. Israel took over all of the Amorite land where Sihon's people had lived, ²²from the Arnon River in the south to the Jabbok River in the north, and from the desert in the east to the Jordan River in the west.

²³The messengers also told the king of Ammon that Jephthah had said:

The LORD God of Israel helped his nation get rid of the Amorites and take their land. Now do you think you're going to take over that same territory? ²⁴If Chemosh your god^t takes over a country and gives it to you, don't you have a right to it? And if the LORD takes over a country and gives it to us, the land is ours!

²⁵Are you better than Balak the son of Zippor? He was the king of Moab, but he didn't quarrel with Israel or start a war with us.

²⁶For three hundred years, Israelites have been living in Heshbon and Aroer and the nearby villages, and in the towns along the Arnon River gorge. If the land really belonged to you Ammonites, you wouldn't have waited until now to try to get it back.

²⁷I haven't done anything to you, but it's certainly wrong of you to start a war. I pray that the LORD will show whether Israel or Ammon is in the right.

²⁸But the king of Ammon paid no attention to Jephthah's message.

²⁹Then the LORD's Spirit took control of Jephthah, and Jephthah went through Gilead and Manasseh, raising an army. Finally, he arrived at Mizpah in Gilead, where ³⁰he

promised the LORD, "If you will let me defeat the Ammonites ³¹and come home safely, I will sacrifice to you whoever comes out to meet me first."

³²From Mizpah, Jephthah attacked the Ammonites, and the LORD helped him defeat them.

³³Jephthah and his army destroyed the twenty towns between Aroer and Minnith, and others as far as Abel-Keramim. After that, the Ammonites could not invade Israel any more.

Jephthah's Daughter

³⁴When Jephthah returned to his home in Mizpah, the first one to meet him was his daughter. She was playing a tambourine and dancing to celebrate his victory, and she was his only child.

³⁵"Oh!" Jephthah cried. Then he tore his clothes in sorrow and said to his daughter, "I made a sacred promise to the LORD, and I must keep it. Your coming out to meet me has broken my heart."

³⁶"Father," she said, "you made a sacred promise to the LORD, and he let you defeat the Ammonites. Now, you must do what you promised, even if it means I must die. ³⁷But first, please let me spend two months, wandering in the hill country with my friends. We will cry together, because I can never get married and have children."

³⁸"Yes, you may have two months," Jephthah said.

She and some other girls left, and for two months they wandered in the hill country, crying because she could never get married and have children. ³⁹Then she went back to her father. He did what he had promised, and she never got married.

That's why ⁴⁰every year, Israelite girls walk around for four days, weeping for^u Jephthah's daughter.

The Ephraim Tribe Fights Jephthah's Army

12 The men of the Ephraim tribe got together an army and went across the Jordan River to Zaphon to

---

^t11.24 *Chemosh your god:* Chemosh was actually the national god of Moab, not Ammon. The land that Ammon was trying to take over had belonged to the Moabites before belonging to the Amorites (see Numbers 21.26). So the Ammonites may have thought that Chemosh controlled it. ^u11.40 *weeping for:* Or "remembering."

Samson's Mother/ Manoah's Wife

Judges 13–16

D o you ever feel that you are best known by your relationship to someone else? That was true for this woman. Scripture doesn't even record her name. But it describes her faith and her character in a way that leaves no doubt about her importance—and her value to her family. But her life was not easy. At first she was unable to have children—a terrible handicap to women of her culture. Who would carry on her husband's name? Who would support them in their old age?

Then a crisis came. An angel of the Lord spoke, not to her husband, but to her. The angel announced that she'd give birth to a son. She could have kept this message secret. Or she could have doubted her sanity. Instead she told her husband. Manoah wanted his own personal conference with the angel—and said so. God granted his request. But when Manoah saw the angel disappear into heaven in the blaze of fire that consumed his sacrifice, he was terrified and convinced that the Lord would kill them both.

But his wife knew the Lord better than that. So she calmed her husband with a reasoned faith anchored in the character of God. "The LORD isn't going to kill us. The LORD accepted our sacrifice and grain offering. . . . Besides, he told us that we're going to have a son" (13.23).

Manoah's wife gave birth to Samson—one of the most difficult children in all of Scripture. He gave her continued opportunity to exercise her confidence in God! Not much is said about this woman after that. We never learn her name. But through her we see how a woman of God acts in a crisis. She acts in faith rather than reacts in fear. She steps back from circumstances and focuses on the character of God. (In this case, Manoah's wife knew that God is just, God is constantly with us, and God does not contradict himself.) With this faith, she could calm her husband and focus on the child to come.

meet with Jephthah. They said, "Why did you go to war with the Ammonites without asking us to help? Just for that, we're going to burn down your house with you inside!"

²"But I did ask for your help," Jephthah answered. "That was back when the people of Gilead and I were having trouble with the Ammonites, and you wouldn't do a thing to help us. ³So when we realized you weren't coming, we risked our lives and attacked the Ammonites. And the LORD let us defeat them. There's no reason for you to come here today to attack me."

⁴But the men from Ephraim said, "You people of Gilead are nothing more than refugees from Ephraim. You even live on land that belongs to the tribes of Ephraim and Manasseh."ᵛ

So Jephthah called together the army of Gilead, then they attacked and defeated the army from Ephraim. ⁵The army of Gilead also posted guards at all the places where the soldiers from Ephraim could cross the Jordan River to return to their own land.

Whenever one of the men from Ephraim would try to cross the river, the guards would say, "Are you from Ephraim?"

"No," the man would answer, "I'm not from Ephraim."

⁶The guards would then tell them to say "Shiboleth," because they knew that people of Ephraim could say "Sibboleth," but not "Shiboleth."

If the man said "Sibboleth," the guards would grab him and kill him right there. Altogether, forty-two thousand men from Ephraim were killed in the battle and at the Jordan.

⁷Jephthah was a leaderʷ of Israel for six years, before he died and was buried in his hometown Mizpahˣ in Gilead.

Ibzan

⁸Ibzan, the next leaderʸ of Israel, came from Bethlehem. ⁹He had thirty daughters and thirty sons, and he let them all marry outside his clan.

Ibzan was a leader for seven years, ¹⁰before he died and was buried in Bethlehem.

Elon

¹¹Elon from the Zebulun tribe was the next leaderʸ of Israel. He was a leader for ten years, ¹²before he died and was buried in Aijalon that belonged to the Zebulun tribe.

Abdon

¹³⁻¹⁵Abdon the son of Hillel was the next leaderʸ of Israel. He had forty sons and thirty grandsons, and each one of them had his own donkey.ᶻ Abdon was a leader for eight years, before he died and was buried in his hometown of Pirathon, which is located in the part of the hill country of Ephraim where Amalekites used to live.

Samson Is Born

13 Once again the Israelites started disobeying the LORD. So he let the Philistines take control of Israel for forty years.

²Manoah from the tribe of Dan lived in the town of Zorah. His wife was not able to have children, ³⁻⁵but one day an angel from the LORD appeared to her and said:

You have never been able to have any children, but very soon you will be pregnant and have a son. He will belong to Godᵃ from the day he is born, so his hair must never be cut. And even before he is born, you must not drink any wine or beer or eat any food forbidden by God's laws.

Your son will begin to set Israel free from the Philistines.

⁶She went to Manoah and said, "A prophet who looked like an angel of God came and talked to me. I was so frightened, that I didn't even ask where he was from. He didn't tell me his name, ⁷but he did say that I'm going to have a baby boy. I'm not supposed to drink any wine or beer or eat any food forbidden by God's laws. Our son will belong to God for as long as he lives."

⁸Then Manoah prayed, "Our LORD, please send that prophet again and let him tell us what to do for the son we are going to have."

⁹God answered Manoah's prayer, and the angel went back to Manoah's wife while she was resting in the fields. Manoah wasn't

ᵛ12.4 You people of Gilead . . . Ephraim and Manasseh: One possible meaning for the difficult Hebrew text. ʷ12.7 leader: See 2.16 and the note there. ˣ12.7 his hometown Mizpah: One possible meaning for the difficult Hebrew text. ʸ12.8,11,13-15 leader: See 2.16 and the note there. ᶻ12.13-15 each . . . donkey: A sign that the family was wealthy. ᵃ13.3-5 belong to God: The Hebrew text has "be a Nazirite of God." Nazirites were dedicated to God and had to follow special rules to stay that way (see Numbers 6.1, 21).

there at the time, [10]so she found him and said, "That same man is here again! He's the one I saw the other day."

[11]Manoah went with his wife and asked the man, "Are you the one who spoke to my wife?"

"Yes, I am," he answered.

[12]Manoah then asked, "When your promise comes true, what rules must he obey and what will be his work?"

[13]"Your wife must be careful to do everything I told her," the LORD's angel answered. [14]"She must not eat or drink anything made from grapes. She must not drink wine or beer or eat anything forbidden by God's laws. I told her exactly what to do."

[15]"Please," Manoah said, "stay here with us for just a little while, and we'll fix a young goat for you to eat." [16]Manoah didn't realize that he was really talking to one of the LORD's angels.

The angel answered, "I can stay for a little while, although I won't eat any of your food. But if you would like to offer the goat as a sacrifice to the LORD, that would be fine."

[17]Manoah said, "Tell us your name, so we can honor you after our son is born."

[18]"No," the angel replied. "You don't need to know my name. And if you did, you couldn't understand it."

[19]So Manoah took a young goat over to a large rock he had chosen for an altar, and he built a fire on the rock. Then he killed the goat, and offered it with some grain as a sacrifice to the LORD. But then an amazing thing happened. [20]The fire blazed up toward the sky, and the LORD's angel went up toward heaven in the fire. Manoah and his wife bowed down low when they saw what happened.

[21]The angel was gone, but Manoah and his wife realized that he was one of the LORD's angels. [22]Manoah said, "We have seen an angel.[b] Now we're going to die."[c]

[23]"The LORD isn't going to kill us," Manoah's wife responded. "The LORD accepted our sacrifice and grain offering, and he let us see something amazing. Besides, he told us that we're going to have a son."

[24]Later, Manoah's wife did give birth to a son, and she named him Samson. As the boy grew, the LORD blessed him. [25]Then, while Samson was staying at Dan's Camp[d] between the towns of Zorah and Eshtaol, the Spirit of the LORD took control of him.

Samson Gets Married

14 One day, Samson went to Timnah, where he saw a Philistine woman. [2]When he got back home, he told his parents, "I saw a Philistine woman in Timnah, and I want to marry her. Get her for me!"[e]

[3]His parents answered, "There are a lot of women in our clan and even more in the rest of Israel. Those Philistines are pagans. Why would you want to marry one of their women?"

"She looks good to me," Samson answered. "Get her for me!"

[4]At that time, the Philistines were in control of Israel, and the LORD wanted to stir up trouble for them. That's why he made Samson desire that woman.

[5]As Samson and his parents reached the vineyards near Timnah, a fierce young lion suddenly roared and attacked Samson. [6]But the LORD's Spirit took control of Samson, and with his bare hands he tore the lion apart, as though it had been a young goat. His parents didn't know what he had done, and he didn't tell them.

[7]When they got to Timnah, Samson talked to the woman, and he was sure that she was the one for him.

[8]Later,[f] Samson returned to Timnah for the wedding. And when he came near the place where the lion had attacked, he left the road to see what was left of the lion. He was surprised to see that bees were living in the lion's skeleton, and that they had made some honey. [9]He scooped up the honey in his hands and ate some of it as he walked along. When he got back to his parents, he gave them some of the honey, and they ate it too. But he didn't tell them he had found the honey in the skeleton of a lion.[g]

[10]While Samson's father went to make the final arrangements with the bride and her family, Samson threw a big party,[h] as

---

[b]13.22 angel: The Hebrew text has "god," which can be used of God or of other supernatural beings. [c]13.22 We have seen an angel. Now we're going to die: Some people believed that if they saw the LORD or one of the LORD's angels, they would die. [d]13.25 Dan's Camp: Or "Mahaneh-Dan." [e]14.2 Get her for me: At that time, parents arranged marriages for their children. [f]14.8 Later: Or "The following year." [g]14.9 But he didn't tell them . . . skeleton of a lion: To eat anything that had touched a skeleton was against God's laws (see Leviticus 11.27-40). [h]14.10 party: The Hebrew term means a party that involved a lot of drinking.

grooms[i] usually did. [11]When the Philistines saw what Samson was like, they told thirty of their young men to stay with him at the party.

[12]Samson told the thirty young men, "This party will last for seven days. Let's make a bet: I'll tell you a riddle, and if you can tell me the right answer before the party is over, I'll give each one of you a shirt and a full change of clothing. [13]But if you can't tell me the answer, then each of you will have to give me a shirt and a full change of clothing."

"It's a bet!" the Philistines said. "Tell us the riddle."

[14]Samson said:

Once so strong and mighty—
now so sweet and tasty!

Three days went by, and the Philistine young men had not come up with the right answer. [15]Finally, on the seventh[j] day of the party they went to Samson's bride and said, "You had better trick your husband into telling you the answer to his riddle. Have you invited us here just to rob us? If you don't find out the answer, we will burn you and your family to death."

[16]Samson's bride went to him and started crying in his arms. "You must really hate me," she sobbed. "If you loved me at all, you would have told me the answer to your riddle."

"But I haven't even told my parents the answer!" Samson replied. "Why should I tell you?"

[17]For the entire seven days of the party, she had been whining and trying to get the answer from him. But that seventh day she put so much pressure on Samson that he finally gave in and told her the answer. She went straight to the young men and told them.

[18]Before sunset that day, the men of the town went to Samson with this answer:

A lion is the strongest—
honey is the sweetest!

Samson replied,

This answer you have given me
doubtless came
from my bride-to-be.

[19]Then the LORD's Spirit took control of Samson. He went to Ashkelon,[k] where he killed thirty men and took their clothing. Samson then gave it to the thirty young men at Timnah and stormed back home to his own family.

[20]The father of the bride had Samson's wife marry one of the thirty young men that had been at Samson's party.[l]

15 Later, during the wheat harvest, Samson went to visit the young woman he thought was still his wife.[m] He brought along a young goat as a gift and said to her father, "I want to go into my wife's bedroom."

"You can't do that," he replied. [2]"When you left the way you did, I thought you were divorcing[n] her. So I arranged for her to marry one of the young men who were at your party. But my younger daughter is even prettier, and you can have her as your wife."

[3]"This time," Samson answered, "I have a good reason for really hurting some Philistines."

Samson Takes Revenge

[4]Samson went out and caught three hundred foxes and tied them together in pairs with oil-soaked rags around their tails. [5]Then Samson took the foxes into the Philistine wheat fields that were ready to be harvested. He set the rags on fire and let the foxes go. The wheat fields went up in flames, and so did the stacks of wheat that had already been cut. Even the Philistine vineyards and olive orchards burned.

[6]Some of the Philistines started asking around, "Who could have done such a thing?"

"It was Samson," someone told them. "He married the daughter of that man in Timnah, but then the man gave Samson's wife to one of the men at the wedding."

The Philistine leaders went to Timnah and burned to death Samson's wife and her father.[o]

---

[i]14.10 grooms: Or "warriors." [j]14.15 Finally, on the seventh: Hebrew; three ancient translations "on the fourth." [k]14.19 Ashkelon: Another Philistine town. [l]14.20 one . . . at Samson's party: One possible meaning for the difficult Hebrew text. [m]15.1 Samson went to visit . . . his wife: See the note at 8.31. [n]15.2 divorcing: It was often very easy for a husband to divorce his wife. [o]15.6 and her father: Most Hebrew manuscripts; many Hebrew manuscripts and two ancient translations "and her family."

[7]When Samson found out what they had done, he went to them and said, "You killed them! And I won't rest until I get even with you." [8]Then Samson started hacking them to pieces with his sword.[p]

Samson left Philistia and went to live in the cave at Etam Rock. [9]But it wasn't long before the Philistines invaded Judah[q] and set up a huge army camp at Jawbone.[r]

[10]The people of Judah asked, "Why have you invaded our land?"

The Philistines answered, "We've come to get Samson. We're going to do the same things to him that he did to our people."

[11]Three thousand men from Judah went to the cave at Etam Rock and said to Samson, "Don't you know that the Philistines rule us, and they will punish us for what you did?"

"I was only getting even with them," Samson replied. "They did the same things to me first."

[12]"We came here to tie you up and turn you over to them," said the men of Judah.

"I won't put up a fight," Samson answered, "but you have to promise not to hurt me yourselves."

[13-14]"We promise," the men said. "We will only tie you up and turn you over to the Philistines. We won't kill you." Then they tied up his hands and arms with two brand-new ropes and led him away from Etam Rock.

When the Philistines saw that Samson was being brought to their camp at Jawbone, they started shouting and ran toward him. But the LORD's Spirit took control of Samson, and Samson broke the ropes, as though they were pieces of burnt cloth. [15]Samson glanced around and spotted the jawbone of a donkey. The jawbone had not yet dried out, so it was still hard and heavy. Samson grabbed it and started hitting Philistines—he killed a thousand of them! [16]After the fighting was over, he made up this poem about what he had done to the Philistines:

> I used a donkey's jawbone
>   to kill a thousand men;
> I beat them with this jawbone
>   over and over again.[s]

[17]Samson tossed the jawbone on the ground and decided to call the place Jawbone Hill.[t] It is still called that today.

[18]Samson was so thirsty that he prayed, "Our LORD, you helped me win a battle against a whole army. Please don't let me die of thirst now. Those heathen Philistines will carry off my dead body."

[19]Samson was tired and weary, but God sent water gushing from a rock.[u] Samson drank some and felt strong again.

Samson named the place Caller Spring,[v] because he had called out to God for help. The spring is still there at Jawbone.

[20]Samson was a leader[w] of Israel for twenty years, but the Philistines were still the rulers of Israel.

Samson Carries Off the Gates of Gaza

16 One day while Samson was in Gaza, he saw a prostitute and went to her house to spend the night. [2]The people who lived in Gaza found out he was there, and they decided to kill him at sunrise. So they went to the city gate and waited all night in the guardrooms on each side of the gate.[x]

[3]But Samson got up in the middle of the night and went to the town gate. He pulled the gate doors and doorposts out of the wall and put them on his shoulders. Then he carried them all the way to the top of the hill that overlooks Hebron,[y] where he set the doors down, still closed and locked.

Delilah Tricks Samson

[4]Some time later, Samson fell in love with a woman named Delilah, who lived in Sorek Valley. [5]The Philistine rulers[z] went to Delilah and said, "Trick Samson into telling you what makes him so strong and what can make him weak. Then we can tie him up so he can't get away. If you find out his secret,

---

[p]15.8 *hacking . . . sword*: One possible meaning for the difficult Hebrew text.   [q]15.9 *Judah*: Samson belonged to the Dan tribe, but his hideout in the cave at Etam Rock was in Judah, a few miles southwest of Bethlehem.   [r]15.9 *Jawbone*: Or "Lehi" (see verse 17).   [s]15.16 *I beat . . . again*: One possible meaning for the difficult Hebrew text.   [t]15.17 *Jawbone Hill*: Or "Ramath-Lehi."   [u]15.19 *God sent . . . a rock*: One possible meaning for the difficult Hebrew text.   [v]15.19 *Caller Spring*: Or "Enhakkore."   [w]15.20 *leader*: See 2.16 and the note there.   [x]16.2 *guardrooms . . . gate*: The gate was often in a part of the town wall that was thicker and taller than the rest of the wall, and that had rooms where guards stayed when they were on duty.   [y]16.3 *Hebron*: About forty miles from Gaza.   [z]16.5 *Philistine rulers*: There were five rulers, each one controlling part of Philistia.

we will each give you eleven hundred pieces of silver."[a]

[6]The next time Samson was at Delilah's house, she asked, "Samson, what makes you so strong? How can I tie you up so you can't get away? Come on, you can tell me."

[7]Samson answered, "If someone ties me up with seven new bowstrings that have never been dried,[b] it will make me just as weak as anyone else."

[8-9]The Philistine rulers gave seven new bowstrings to Delilah. They also told some of their soldiers to go to Delilah's house and hide in the room where Samson and Delilah were. If the bowstrings made Samson weak, they would be able to capture him.

Delilah tied up Samson with the bowstrings and shouted, "Samson, the Philistines are attacking!"

Samson snapped the bowstrings, as though they were pieces of scorched string. The Philistines had not found out why Samson was so strong.

[10]"You lied and made me look like a fool," Delilah said. "Now tell me. How can I really tie you up?"

[11]Samson answered, "Use some new ropes. If I'm tied up with ropes that have never been used, I'll be just as weak as anyone else."

[12]Delilah got new ropes and again had some Philistines hide in the room. Then she tied up Samson's arms and shouted, "Samson, the Philistines are attacking!"

Samson snapped the ropes as if they were threads.

[13]"You're still lying and making a fool of me," Delilah said. "Tell me how I can tie you up!"

"My hair is in seven braids," Samson replied. "If you weave my braids into the threads on a loom and nail the loom[c] to a wall, then I will be as weak as anyone else."

[14]While Samson was asleep, Delilah wove his braids into the threads on a loom and nailed the loom to a wall.[d] Then she shouted, "Samson, the Philistines are attacking!"

Samson woke up and pulled the loom free from its posts in the ground and from the nails in the wall. Then he pulled his hair free from the woven cloth.

[15]"Samson," Delilah said, "you claim to love me, but you don't mean it! You've made me look like a fool three times now,

and you still haven't told me why you are so strong." [16]Delilah started nagging and pestering him day after day, until he couldn't stand it any longer.

[17]Finally, Samson told her the truth. "I have belonged to God[e] ever since I was born, so my hair has never been cut. If it were ever cut off, my strength would leave me, and I would be as weak as anyone else."

[18]Delilah realized that he was telling the truth. So she sent someone to tell the Philistine rulers, "Come to my house one more time. Samson has finally told me the truth."

The Philistine rulers went to Delilah's house, and they brought along the silver they had promised her. [19]Delilah had lulled Samson to sleep with his head resting in her lap. She signaled to one of the Philistine men as she began cutting off Samson's seven braids. And by the time she was finished, Samson's strength was gone. Delilah tied him up [20]and shouted, "Samson, the Philistines are attacking!"

Samson woke up and thought, "I'll break loose and escape, just as I always do." He did not realize that the LORD had stopped helping him.

[21]The Philistines grabbed Samson and poked out his eyes. They took him to the prison in Gaza and chained him up. Then they put him to work, turning a millstone to grind grain. [22]But they didn't cut his hair any more, so it started growing back.

[23]The Philistine rulers threw a big party and sacrificed a lot of animals to their god Dagon. The rulers said:

> Samson was our enemy,
>   but our god Dagon
>   helped us capture him!

[24-25]Everyone there was having a good time, and they shouted, "Bring out Samson—he's still good for a few more laughs!" The rulers had Samson brought from the

---

[a]16.5 *silver:* About 140 pounds of silver altogether.
[b]16.7 *new bowstrings . . . dried:* The string for a bow was often made from sinews or internal organs of animals. These strings were made while the animal tissues were still moist, and they became much stronger, once they were dry. [c]16.13 *loom:* A large wooden frame on which cloth is woven. [d]16.13,14 *If you weave . . . to a wall:* Some manuscripts of one ancient translation; Hebrew "Weave my braids into the threads on a loom. She nailed the loom to a wall." [e]16.17 *belonged to God:* See the note at 13.3-5.

prison, and when the people saw him, this is how they praised their god:

> Samson ruined our crops
> and killed our people.
> He was our enemy,
> but our god helped us
> capture him.

They made fun of Samson for a while, then they told him to stand near the columns that supported the roof. [26]A young man was leading Samson by the hand, and Samson said to him, "I need to lean against something. Take me over to the columns that hold up the roof."

[27]The Philistine rulers were celebrating in a temple packed with people and with three thousand[f] more on the flat roof. They had all been watching Samson and making fun of him.[g]

[28]Samson prayed, "Please remember me, LORD God. The Philistines poked out my eyes, but make me strong one last time, so I can take revenge for at least one of my eyes!"[h]

[29]Samson was standing between the two middle columns that held up the roof. He felt around and found one column with his right hand, and the other with his left hand. [30]Then he shouted, "Let me die with the Philistines!" He pushed against the columns as hard as he could, and the temple collapsed with the Philistine rulers and everyone else still inside. Samson killed more Philistines when he died than he had killed during his entire life.

[31]His brothers and the rest of his family went to Gaza and took his body back home. They buried him in his father's tomb,[i] which was located between Zorah and Eshtaol.

Samson was a leader[j] of Israel for twenty years.

Micah Makes Idols and Hires a Priest

17 Micah[k] belonged to the Ephraim tribe and lived in the hill country. [2]One day he told his mother, "Do you remember those eleven hundred pieces of silver[l] that were stolen from you? I was there when you put a curse on whoever stole them. Well, I'm the one who did it."

His mother answered, "I pray that the LORD will bless[m] you, my son."

[3-4]Micah returned the silver to his mother, and she said, "I give this silver to the LORD, so my son can use it to make an idol." Turning to her son, she said, "Micah, now the silver belongs to you."

But Micah handed it back to his mother. She took two hundred pieces[n] of the silver and gave them to a silver worker, who made them into an idol.[o] They kept the idol in Micah's house. [5]He had a shrine for worshiping God there at his home, and he had made some idols and a sacred priestly vest. Micah chose one of his own sons to be the priest for his shrine.

[6]This was before kings ruled Israel, so all the Israelites did whatever they thought was right.

[7-8]One day a young Levite came to Micah's house in the hill country of Ephraim. He had been staying with one of the clans of Judah in Bethlehem, but he had left Bethlehem to find a new place to live[p] where he could be a priest.[q]

[9]"Where are you from?" Micah asked.

"I am a Levite from Bethlehem in Judah," the man answered, "and I'm on my way to find a new place to live."

[10]Micah said, "Why don't you stay here with me? You can be my priest and tell me what God wants me to do. Every year I'll give you ten pieces of silver and one complete set of clothes, and I'll provide all your food."

The young man went for a walk, [11-12]then he agreed to stay with Micah and be his priest. He lived in Micah's house, and Micah treated him like one of his own sons. [13]Micah said, "I have a Levite as my own priest. Now I know that the LORD will be kind to me."

[f]16.27 *three thousand*: Hebrew; some manuscripts of one ancient translation "seven hundred."
[g]16.27 *They . . . him*: Samson may have been in a courtyard visible from the roof.   [h]16.28 *one of my eyes*: Or "my eyes."   [i]16.31 *buried him in his father's tomb*: Several family members were often buried in one tomb.   [j]16.31 *leader*: See 2.16 and the note there.
[k]17.1 *Micah*: The Hebrew also uses the longer form "Micaiah."   [l]17.2 *eleven hundred . . . silver*: About 28 pounds.   [m]17.2 *curse . . . bless*: A curse could not be taken back, but it could be made powerless by a blessing.   [n]17.3,4 *two hundred pieces*: About 5 pounds.   [o]17.3,4 *idol*: Probably carved from wood and covered with the silver.   [p]17.7,8 *place to live*: The people of the Levi tribe did not have a large area of land like the other tribes.   [q]17.7,8 *to find . . . priest*: Or "and was on his way to find a new place to live."

18

These things happened before kings ruled Israel.

The Tribe of Dan
Takes Micah's Priest and Idols

About this time, the tribe of Dan was looking for a place to live. The other tribes had land, but the people of Dan did not really have any to call their own. ²The tribe chose five warriors to represent their clans and told them, "Go and find some land where we can live."

The warriors left the area of Zorah and Eshtaol and went into the hill country of Ephraim. One night they stayed at Micah's house, ³because they heard the young Levite talking, and they knew from his accent that he was from the south. They asked him, "What are you doing here? Who brought you here?"

⁴The Levite replied, "Micah hired me as his priest." Then he told them how well Micah had treated him.

⁵"Please talk to God for us," the men said. "Ask God if we will be successful in what we are trying to do."

⁶"Don't worry," answered the priest. "The LORD is pleased with what you are doing."

⁷The five men left and went to the town of Laish, whose people were from Sidon,ʳ but Sidon was too far away to protect them. Even though their town had no walls, the people thought they were safe from attack. So they had not asked anyone elseˢ for protection, which meant that the tribe of Dan could easily take over Laish.ᵗ

⁸The five men went back to Zorah and Eshtaol, where their relatives asked, "Did you find any land?"

⁹⁻¹⁰"Let's go!" the five men said. "We saw some very good land with enough room for all of us, and it has everything we will ever need. What are you waiting for? Let's attack and take it. You'll find that the people think they're safe, but God is giving the land to us."

¹¹Six hundred men from the tribe of Dan strapped on their weapons and left Zorah and Eshtaol with their families.ᵘ ¹²One night they camped near Kiriath-Jearim in the territory of Judah, and that's why the place just west of Kiriath-Jearim is still known as Dan's Camp.ᵛ ¹³Then they went into the hill country of Ephraim.

When they came close to Micah's house, ¹⁴the five men who had been spies asked the other warriors, "Did you know that someone in this village has several idols and a sacred priestly vest? What do you think we should do about it?"

¹⁵⁻¹⁸The six hundred warriors left the road and went to the house on Micah's property where the young Levite priest lived. They stood at the gate and greeted the priest. Meanwhile, the five men who had been there before went into Micah's house and took the sacred priestly vest and the idols.

"Hey!" the priest shouted. "What do you think you're doing?"

¹⁹"Quiet!" the men said. "Keep your mouth shut and listen. Why don't you come with us and be our priest, so you can tell us what God wants us to do? You could stay here and be a priest for one man's family, but wouldn't you rather be the priest for a clan or even a whole tribe of Israel?"

²⁰The priest really liked that idea. So he took the vest and the idols and joined the others ²¹from the tribe of Dan. Then they turned and left, after putting their children, their cattle, and the rest of their other possessions in front.

²²They had traveled for some time, before Micah asked his neighbors to help him get his things back. He and his men caught up with the people of Dan ²³and shouted for them to stop.

They turned to face him and asked, "What's wrong? Why did you bring all these men?"

²⁴Micah answered, "You know what's wrong. You stole the godsʷ I made, and you took my priest. I don't have anything left."

²⁵"We don't want to hear any more about it," the people of Dan said. "And if you make us angry, you'll only get yourself and your family killed." ²⁶After saying this, they turned and left.

ʳ18.7 *whose people . . . Sidon:* One possible meaning for the difficult Hebrew text. ˢ18.7 *anyone else:* Hebrew; one ancient translation has "the Arameans," who were a short distance to the north. ᵗ18.7 *which . . . Laish:* One possible meaning for the difficult Hebrew text. ᵘ18.11 *Eshtaol with their families:* Hebrew "Eshtaol" (see verse 21). ᵛ18.12 *Dan's Camp:* See the note at 13.25. ʷ18.24 *gods:* Or "god."

Micah realized there was no way he could win a fight with them, and so he went back home.

The Tribe of Dan Captures Laish

27-28The tribe of Dan took Micah's priest and the things Micah had made, and headed for Laish, which was located in a valley controlled by the town of Beth-Rehob. Laish was defenseless, because it had no walls and was too far from Sidon for the Sidonians to help defend it. The leaders of Laish had not even asked nearby towns to help them in case of an attack.

The warriors from Dan made a surprise attack on Laish, killing everyone and burning it down. Then they rebuilt the town and settled there themselves. 29But they named it Dan, after one of Israel's[x] sons, who was the ancestor of their tribe.

30-31Even though the place of worship[y] was in Shiloh, the people of Dan set up the idol Micah had made. They worshiped the idol, and the Levite was their priest. His name was Jonathan, and he was a descendant of Gershom the son of Moses.[z] His descendants served as priests for the tribe of Dan, until the people of Israel were taken away as prisoners by their enemies.

A Woman Is Murdered

19 Before kings ruled Israel, a Levite[a] was living deep in the hill country of the Ephraim tribe. He married[b] a woman from Bethlehem in Judah, 2but she was unfaithful and went back to live with her family in Bethlehem.

Four months later 3her husband decided to try and talk her into coming back. So he went to Bethlehem, taking along a servant and two donkeys. He talked with his wife, and she invited him into her family's home. Her father was glad to see him 4and did not want him to leave. So the man stayed three days, eating and drinking with his father-in-law.

5When everyone got up on the fourth day, the Levite started getting ready to go home. But his father-in-law said, "Don't leave until you have a bite to eat. You'll need strength for your journey."

6The two men sat down together and ate a big meal. "Come on," the man's father-in-law said. "Stay tonight and have a good time."

7The Levite tried to leave, but his father-in-law insisted, and he spent one more night. 8The fifth day, the man got up early to leave, but his wife's father said, "You need to keep up your strength! Why don't you leave right after lunch?" So the two of them started eating.

9Finally, the Levite got up from the meal, so he and his wife and servant could leave. "Look," his father-in-law said, "it's already late afternoon, and if you leave now, you won't get very far before dark. Stay with us one more night and enjoy yourself. Then you can get up early tomorrow morning and start home."

10But the Levite decided not to spend the night there again. He had the saddles put on his two donkeys, then he and his wife and servant traveled as far as Jebus, which is now called Jerusalem. 11It was beginning to get dark, and the man's servant said, "Let's stop and spend the night in this town where the Jebusites live."

12"No," the Levite answered. "They aren't Israelites, and I refuse to spend the night there. We'll stop for the night at Gibeah, 13because we can make it to Gibeah or maybe even to Ramah[c] before dark."

14They walked on and reached Gibeah in the territory of Benjamin just after sunset. 15They left the road and went into Gibeah. But the Levite couldn't find a house where anyone would let them spend the night, and they sat down in the open area just inside the town gates.

16Soon an old man came in through the gates on his way home from working in the fields. Most of the people who lived in Gibeah belonged to the tribe of Benjamin, but this man was originally from the hill country of Ephraim. 17He noticed that the Levite was

---

[x]18.29 Israel's: Israel was another name for Jacob, the father of the twelve ancestors of the tribes of Israel. [y]18.30,31 place of worship: The Hebrew text has "house of God," which at this time was probably the sacred tent. [z]18.30,31 Moses: Some manuscripts of two ancient translations; the Standard Hebrew Text has "Manasseh," but written in a special way that tells the reader "Moses" had been changed to "Manasseh." [a]19.1 a Levite: Someone from the Levi tribe, which had no tribal lands of its own. [b]19.1 married: See the note at 8.31. [c]19.13 Gibeah . . . Ramah: It was about three miles from Jerusalem to Gibeah, and another three miles to Ramah.

just in town to spend the night. "Where are you going?" the old man asked. "Where did you come from?"

¹⁸"We've come from Bethlehem in Judah," the Levite answered. "We went there on a visit. Now we're going to the place where the LORD is worshiped, and later we will return to our home in the hill country of Ephraim. But no one here will let us spend the night*d* in their home. ¹⁹We brought food for our donkeys and bread and wine for ourselves, so we don't need anything except a place to sleep."

²⁰The old man said, "You are welcome to spend the night in my home and to be my guest, but don't stay out here!"

²¹The old man brought them into his house and fed their donkeys. Then he and his guests washed their feet*e* and began eating and drinking. ²²They were having a good time, when some worthless men of that town surrounded the house and started banging on the door and shouting, "A man came to your house tonight. Send him out, so we can have sex with him!"

²³The old man went outside and said, "My friends, please don't commit such a horrible crime against a man who is a guest in my house. ²⁴Let me send out my daughter instead. She's a virgin. And I'll even send out the man's wife.*f* You can rape them or do whatever else you want, but please don't do such a horrible thing to this man."

²⁵The men refused to listen, so the Levite grabbed his wife and shoved her outside. The men raped her and abused her all night long. Finally, they let her go just before sunrise, ²⁶and it was almost daybreak when she went back to the house where her husband*g* was staying. She collapsed at the door and lay there until sunrise.

²⁷About that time, her husband woke up and got ready to leave. He opened the door and went outside, where he found his wife lying at the door with her hands on the doorstep. ²⁸"Get up!" he said. "It's time to leave."

But his wife didn't move.*h*

He lifted her body onto his donkey and left. ²⁹When he got home, he took a butcher knife and cut her body into twelve pieces. Then he told some messengers, "Take one piece to each tribe of Israel ³⁰and ask everyone if anything like this has ever happened since Israel left Egypt. Tell them to think

about it, talk it over, and tell us what should be done."

Everyone who saw a piece of the body said, "This is horrible! Nothing like this has ever happened since the day Israel left Egypt."*i*

Israel Gets Ready for War

20 ¹⁻³The Israelites called a meeting of the nation. And since they were God's people, the meeting was held at the place of worship in Mizpah. Men who could serve as soldiers came from everywhere in Israel—from Dan in the north, Beersheba in the south, and Gilead east of the Jordan River. Four hundred thousand of them came to Mizpah, and they each felt the same about what those men from the tribe of Benjamin had done.

News about the meeting at Mizpah reached the tribe of Benjamin.

As soon as the leaders of the tribes of Israel took their places, the Israelites said, "How could such a horrible thing happen?"

⁴The husband of the murdered woman answered:

My wife*j* and I went into the town of Gibeah in Benjamin to spend the night. ⁵Later that night, the men of Gibeah surrounded the house. They wanted to kill me, but instead they raped and killed my wife. ⁶It was a terrible thing for Israelites to do! So I cut up her body and sent pieces everywhere in Israel.

⁷You are the people of Israel, and you must decide today what to do about the men of Gibeah.

⁸The whole army was in agreement, and they said, "None of us will go home. ⁹⁻¹⁰We'll

---

*d*19.18 *spend the night:* People usually considered it a duty to ask travelers to spend the night in their homes, since there were often no other places to stay.
*e*19.21 *washed their feet:* This was a custom, since people wore open sandals and their feet would be dirty after walking on the dirt roads or working in the fields.
*f*19.24 *wife:* See the note at 8.31. *g*19.26 *husband:* Or "owner"; the Hebrew word may mean that she was his slave and had no legal rights. *h*19.28 *move:* Hebrew; one ancient translation "move. She was dead."
*i*19.29,30 *he told some messengers . . . since Israel left Egypt:* One ancient translation; Hebrew "he told some messengers, 'Take one piece to each tribe of Israel.' Everyone who saw a piece of the body said, 'This is horrible! Nothing like this has ever happened since Israel left Egypt. Think of it! Let's talk it over and decide what to do.' " *j*20.4 *wife:* See the note at 8.31.

send one tenth of the men from each tribe to get food for the army. And we'll ask God[k] who should attack Gibeah, because those men[l] deserve to be punished for committing such a horrible crime in Israel."

[11]Everyone agreed that Gibeah had to be punished.

[12]The tribes of Israel sent messengers to every town and village in Benjamin. And wherever the messengers went, they said, "How could those worthless men in Gibeah do such a disgusting thing? [13]We can't allow such a terrible crime to go unpunished in Israel! Hand the men over to us, and we will put them to death."

But the people of Benjamin refused to listen to the other Israelites. [14]Men from towns all over Benjamin's territory went to Gibeah and got ready to fight Israel. [15]The Benjamin tribe had twenty-six thousand soldiers, not counting the seven hundred who were Gibeah's best warriors. [16]In this army there were seven hundred left-handed experts who could sling a rock[m] at a target the size of a hair and hit it every time.

[17]The other Israelite tribes organized their army and found they had four hundred thousand experienced soldiers. [18]So they went to the place of worship at Bethel[n] and asked God, "Which tribe should be the first to attack the people of Benjamin?"

"Judah," the LORD answered.

[19]The next morning the Israelite army moved its camp to a place near Gibeah. [20]Then they left their camp and got into position to attack the army of Benjamin.

The War Between Israel and Benjamin

[21]Benjamin's soldiers came out of Gibeah and attacked, and when the day was over, twenty-two thousand Israelite soldiers lay dead on the ground.

[22-24]The people of Israel went to the place of worship and cried until sunset. Then they asked the LORD, "Should we attack the people of Benjamin again, even though they are our relatives?"

"Yes," the LORD replied, "attack them again!"

The Israelite soldiers encouraged each other to be brave and to fight hard. Then the next day they went back to Gibeah and took up the same positions as they had before.

[25]That same day, Benjamin's soldiers came out of Gibeah and attacked, leaving another eighteen thousand Israelite soldiers dead on the battlefield.

[26-28]The people of Israel went to the place of worship at Bethel,[n] where the sacred chest was being kept. They sat on the ground, crying and not eating for the rest of the day. Then about sunset, they offered sacrifices to please the LORD and to ask his blessing.[o] Phinehas[p] the priest then prayed, "Our LORD, the people of Benjamin are our relatives. Should we stop fighting or attack them again?"

"Attack!" the LORD answered. "Tomorrow I will let you defeat them."

[29]The Israelites surrounded Gibeah, but stayed where they could not be seen. [30]Then the next day, they took the same positions as twice before, [31-41]but this time they had a different plan. They said, "When the men of Benjamin attack, we will run off and let them chase us away from the town and into the country roads."

The soldiers of Benjamin attacked the Israelite army and started pushing it back from the town. They killed about thirty Israelites in the fields and along the road between Gibeah and Bethel. The men of Benjamin were thinking, "We're mowing them down like we did before."

The Israelites were running away, but they headed for Baal-Tamar, where they regrouped. They had set an ambush, and they were sure it would work. Ten thousand of Israel's best soldiers had been hiding west of Gibeah,[q] and as soon as the men of Benjamin chased the Israelites into the countryside, these ten thousand soldiers made a surprise attack on the town gates. They dashed in and captured Gibeah, killing everyone there. Then they set the town on fire, because the smoke would be the signal

---

[k]**20.9,10** *ask God*: The Hebrew text has "use lots to decide"; small pieces of wood or stone called "lots" were used to find out what God wanted his people to do. [l]**20.9,10** *those men*: One Hebrew manuscript and one ancient translation; The Standard Hebrew text "the men of Geba." [m]**20.16** *sling a rock*: By using a sling made from a leather strap. [n]**20.18,26-28** *place . . . Bethel*: The Hebrew text has "beth-el," which means "house of God." This could refer to the town of Bethel, to the place of worship at Mizpah, or to the sacred tent at Shiloh (see 18.30, 31). [o]**20.26-28** *sacrifices . . . blessing*: See Leviticus 1–3. [p]**20.26-28** *Phinehas*: Hebrew "Phinehas the son of Eleazar the son of Aaron." [q]**20.31-41** *west of Gibeah*: three ancient translations; Hebrew "in a field at Geba."

for the other Israelite soldiers to turn and attack the soldiers of Benjamin.

The fighting had been so heavy around the soldiers of Benjamin, that they did not know the trouble they were in. But then they looked back and saw clouds of smoke rising from the town. They looked in front and saw the soldiers of Israel turning to attack. This terrified them, because they realized that something horrible was happening. And it was horrible—over twenty-five thousand[r] soldiers of Benjamin died that day, and those who were left alive knew that the LORD had given Israel the victory.

⁴²The men of Benjamin headed down the road toward the desert, trying to escape from the Israelites. But the Israelites stayed right behind them, keeping up their attack. Men even came out of the nearby towns to help kill the men of Benjamin, ⁴³who were having to fight on all sides. The Israelite soldiers never let up their attack.[s] They chased and killed the warriors of Benjamin as far as a place directly east of Gibeah,[t] ⁴⁴until eighteen thousand of these warriors lay dead.

⁴⁵Some other warriors of Benjamin turned and ran down the road toward Rimmon Rock in the desert. The Israelites killed five thousand of them on the road, then chased the rest until they had killed[u] two thousand more. ⁴⁶Twenty-five thousand soldiers of Benjamin died that day, all of them experienced warriors. ⁴⁷Only six hundred of them finally made it into the desert to Rimmon Rock, where they stayed for four months.

⁴⁸The Israelites turned back and went to every town in Benjamin's territory, killing all the people and animals, and setting the towns on fire.

Wives for the Men of Benjamin

21 When the Israelites had met at Mizpah before the war with Benjamin,[v] they had made this sacred promise: "None of us will ever let our daughters marry any man from Benjamin."

²After the war with Benjamin, the Israelites went to the place of worship at Bethel and sat there until sunset. They cried loudly and bitterly ³and prayed, "Our LORD, you are the God of Israel. Why did you let this happen? Now one of our tribes is almost gone."

⁴Early the next morning, the Israelites

built an altar and offered sacrifices to please the LORD and to ask his blessing.[w] ⁵Then they asked each other, "Did any of the tribes of Israel fail to come to the place of worship? We made a sacred promise that anyone who didn't come to the meeting at Mizpah would be put to death."

⁶The Israelites were sad about what had happened to the Benjamin tribe, and they said, "One of our tribes was almost wiped out. ⁷Only a few men of Benjamin weren't killed in the war. We need to get wives for them, so the tribe won't completely disappear. But how can we do that, after promising in the LORD's name that we wouldn't let them marry any of our daughters?"

⁸⁻⁹Again the Israelites asked, "Did any of the tribes stay away from the meeting at Mizpah?"

After asking around, they discovered that no one had come from Jabesh in Gilead. ¹⁰⁻¹¹So they sent twelve thousand warriors with these orders: "Attack Jabesh in Gilead and kill everyone, except the women who have never been married."

¹²The warriors attacked Jabesh in Gilead, and returned to their camp in Canaan[x] with four hundred young women.

¹³The Israelites met and sent messengers to the men of Benjamin at Rimmon Rock, telling them that the Israelites were willing to make peace with them. ¹⁴So the men of Benjamin came back from Rimmon Rock, and the Israelites let them marry the young women from Jabesh. But there weren't enough women.

¹⁵The Israelites were very sad, because the LORD had almost wiped out one of their tribes. ¹⁶Then their national leaders said:

All the women of the Benjamin tribe were killed. How can we get wives for the men of Benjamin who are left? ¹⁷If they don't have children, one of the Israelite tribes will die out. ¹⁸But we can't let the men of Benjamin marry any of our daughters. We made

---

[r]**20.31-41** *over twenty-five thousand*: Hebrew "twenty-five thousand one hundred." [s]**20.42,43** *Men even came out . . . their attack*: One possible meaning for the difficult Hebrew text. [t]**20.43** *Gibeah*: Or "Geba." [u]**20.45** *until . . . killed*: Or "as far as Gidom, killing." [v]**21.1** *the Israelites . . . Benjamin*: See 20.1-3. [w]**21.4** *sacrifices . . . blessing*: See the note at 20.26-28. [x]**21.12** *in Canaan*: Jabesh was in Gilead, across the Jordan River from the land of Canaan.

a sacred promise not to do that, and if we break our promise, we will be under our own curse.

¹⁹Then someone suggested, "What about the LORD's Festival that takes place each year in Shiloh? It's held north of Bethel, south of Lebonah, and just east of the road that goes from Bethel to Shechem."

²⁰The leaders told the men of Benjamin who still did not have wives:

Go to Shiloh and hide in the vineyards near the festival. ²¹Wait there for the young women of Shiloh to come out and perform their dances. Then rush out and grab one of the young women, then take her home as your wife. ²²If the fathers or brothers of these women complain about this, we'll say, "Be kind enough to let those men keep your daughter. After all, we couldn't get enough wives for all the men of Benjamin in the battle at Jabesh. And because you didn't give them permission to marry your daughters, you won't be under the curse we earlier agreed on.ʸ

²³The men of Benjamin went to Shiloh and hid in the vineyards. The young women soon started dancing, and each man grabbed one of them and carried her off. Then the men of Benjamin went back to their own land and rebuilt their towns and started living in them again.

²⁴Afterwards, the rest of the Israelites returned to their homes and families.

Israel Was Not Ruled by a King

²⁵In those days Israel wasn't ruled by a king, and everyone did what they thought was right.

ʸ21.22 *on*: One possible meaning for the difficult Hebrew text of verse 22.

Ruth — Friends and Family

Ruth was an in-law, a widow, an alien. She lived in the violent era of the judges—first in Moab, and then in Bethlehem. Yet Ruth's story contrasts with her personal and political setting. This book is as quiet, kind, and peaceful as Judges is violent. The only hint to national chaos comes in Boaz's protective suggestion: "I think it would be best for you not to pick up grain in anyone else's field. Stay here with the women. . . . I have warned the men not to bother you" (2.8,9). In Ruth, we see what happened when ordinary people worshiped and obeyed God.

One of the most beautiful qualities of the book of Ruth is its picture of Ruth's relationship with her mother-in-law. Ruth's vow of commitment to the also-widowed Naomi is so poetic and so intense that it appears today in many wedding ceremonies. Ruth said,

"I will go where you go, I will live where you live; your people will be my people, your God will be my God. I will die where you die and be buried beside you" (1.16,17). In the end, the women of Bethlehem said to Naomi, "She [Ruth] loves you more than seven sons of your own would love you" (4.15).

But the love between these women wasn't one-sided or overly possessive. When Naomi decided to return to her homeland, she left Ruth perfectly free to remain in Moab—even begged her to do so. However, Ruth determined to stay with Naomi, so once they arrived in Bethlehem, Naomi made great effort to arrange a marriage with Boaz for Ruth—for the security of both women.

Today's woman can gain much from Ruth and Naomi. We can admire their faithful, unselfish commitment to friend-ship—and follow its pattern in our own. We can imitate their self-reliance and concern for each other. We can be thankful for the gentle integrity of Boaz who, in spite of the brutality of his era, insisted on doing what was kind and right. And above all, we can worship their God, the God whom they chose to serve, the God who cared for them in the arms of his people.

Ruth at a Glance

1. Tragedy after tragedy strikes Naomi's family (1.1-5)
2. Ruth promises commitment to Naomi; they travel to Bethlehem (1.6-22)
3. Ruth picks grain from a field belonging to Boaz; he offers her protection (2)
4. Naomi instructs Ruth on how to propose marriage (3)
5. Boaz settles a business deal and an engagement (4.1-10)
6. Town leaders pray a blessing (4.11,12)
7. "Naomi's Boy" is born (4.13-22)

Ruth Is Loyal to Naomi

1 1-2Before Israel was ruled by kings, Elimelech from the tribe of Ephrath lived in the town of Bethlehem. His wife was named Naomi, and their two sons were Mahlon and Chilion. But when their crops failed, they moved to the country of Moab.*ᵈ* And while they were there, ³Elimelech died, leaving Naomi with only her two sons.

⁴Later, Naomi's sons married Moabite women. One was named Orpah and the other Ruth. About ten years later, ⁵Mahlon and Chilion also died. Now Naomi had no husband or sons.

⁶⁻⁷When Naomi heard that the LORD had given his people a good harvest, she and her two daughters-in-law got ready to leave Moab and go to Judah. As they were on their way there, ⁸Naomi said to them, "Don't you want to go back home to your own mothers? You were kind to my husband and sons, and you have always been kind to me. I pray that the LORD will be just as kind to you. ⁹May he give each of you another husband and a home of your own."

Naomi kissed them. They cried ¹⁰and said, "We want to go with you and live among your people."

¹¹But she replied, "My daughters, why don't you return home? What good will it do you to go with me? Do you think I could have more sons for you to marry?*ᵇ* ¹²You must go back home, because I am too old to marry again. Even if I got married tonight and later had more sons, ¹³would you wait for them to become old enough to marry? No, my daughters! Life is harder for me than it is for you, because the LORD has turned against me."*ᶜ*

¹⁴They cried again. Orpah kissed her mother-in-law good-by, but Ruth held on to her. ¹⁵Naomi then said to Ruth, "Look, your sister-in-law is going back to her people and to her gods! Why don't you go with her?"

¹⁶Ruth answered,

"Please don't tell me
to leave you
     and return home!
I will go where you go,
     I will live where you live;

---

*ᵃ***1.1,2** *Moab:* The people of Moab worshiped idols and were usually enemies of the people of Israel. *ᵇ***1.11** *for you to marry:* When a married man died and left no children, it was the custom for one of his brothers to marry his widow. Any children they had would then be thought of as those of the dead man, so that his family name would live on. *ᶜ***1.13** *Life . . . me:* Or "I'm sorry that the LORD has turned against me and made life so hard for you."

Friendship—What are the marks of a good friendship? *(Ruth 1–4)*

It has staying power and commitment.

The friendship between Ruth and Naomi had much against it. They were in-laws. They were from different generations, cultures, and religions. They each had been weakened by tragedy. Yet they also had bonds that held them together. Their understanding of each other's intense pain united them in ways more gentle forces could not.

But even after their fresh grief eased, Ruth and Naomi remained committed to each other. When Naomi returned to Bethlehem, Ruth left her own culture and returned with Naomi. She also adopted Naomi's Hebrew faith. Naomi, in turn, integrated Ruth into her culture by employing the ancient rights of levirate marriage and the privileges of gleaning. Their friendship became well known in the community. Boaz said, "I've heard how you've helped your mother-in-law ever since your husband died" (2.11). Naomi's neighbors remarked, "And she [Ruth] loves you more than seven sons of your own would love you" (4.15).

Friendship takes work, time, endurance, and sometimes sacrifice. But the best friendships are worth it. As we overcome our differences with another person, we'll see our own character refined. God can use this softening toward each other to make us both more like himself. (See also Proverbs 17.17; 18.24; Proverbs 27.17-19; 1 Corinthians 13.4-8; James 5.13-20.)

Words To Remember: *He will make you happy and take care of you in your old age, because he is the son of your daughter-in-law. And she loves you more than seven sons of your own would love you.—Ruth 4.15*

your people will be my people,
    your God will be my God.
¹⁷I will die where you die
    and be buried beside you.
May the LORD punish me
    if we are ever separated,
        even by death!"ᵈ

¹⁸When Naomi saw that Ruth had made up her mind to go with her, she stopped urging her to go back.

¹⁹They reached Bethlehem, and the whole town was excited to see them. The women who lived there asked, "Can this really be Naomi?"

²⁰Then she told them, "Don't call me Naomi any longer! Call me Mara,ᵉ because God has made my life bitter. ²¹I had everything when I left, but the LORD has brought me back with nothing. How can you still call me Naomi, when God has turned against me and made my life so hard?"

²²The barley harvest was just beginning when Naomi and Ruth, her Moabite daughter-in-law, arrived in Bethlehem.

Ruth Meets Boaz

2 ¹⁻³One day, Ruth said to Naomi, "Let me see if I can find someone who will let me pick up the grain left in the fields by the harvest workers."ᶠ

Naomi answered, "Go ahead, my daughter." So right away, Ruth went out to pick up grain in a field owned by Boaz. He was a relative of Naomi's husband Elimelech, as well as a rich and important man.

⁴When Boaz left Bethlehem and went out to his field, he said to the harvest workers, "The LORD bless you!"

They replied, "And may the LORD bless you!"

⁵Then Boaz asked the man in charge of the harvest workers, "Who is that young woman?"

⁶The man answered, "She is the one who came back from Moab with Naomi. ⁷She asked if she could pick up grain left by the harvest workers, and she has been working all morning without a moment's rest."ᵍ

⁸Boaz went over to Ruth and said, "I think it would be best for you not to pick up grain in anyone else's field. Stay here with the women ⁹and follow along behind them, as they gather up what the men have cut. I have warned the men not to bother you,

---

ᵈ1.17 *even by death*: Or "by anything but death."
ᵉ1.20 *Mara*: In Hebrew "Naomi" means "pleasant," and "Mara" means "bitter." ᶠ2.1-3 *grain left . . . workers*: It was the custom at harvest time to leave some grain in the field for the poor to pick up (see Leviticus 19.10; 23.22). ᵍ2.7 *she has . . . rest*: One possible meaning for the difficult Hebrew text.

MARRIAGE—What does it really mean to "become one" with my husband?
(Ruth 1.15-18)

You accept your husband's family as your own.
"I'm not marrying your family; I'm marrying you," some couples say when they first encounter the specter of in-laws. It's a statement that can get them into trouble. While it's true that a wife's first priority is to her husband (before either set of parents), it is also true that she is indeed marrying her in-laws. The family that nurtured her husband becomes her own. Likewise, her family is now his. Husband and wife each have a responsibility to honor both sets of parents and (if necessary) to care for them in old age. In many families this is a happy bonus for all involved.

But when it comes to holidays, visits with grandchildren, and financial arrangements, practicality becomes a factor. Naturally, as they make these decisions, all couples must weigh the needs of their parents, geographical logistics, and the well-being of their own family. But unity is more likely if each considers both sets of parents his or her own.

It may seem strange to draw an example for "becoming one" in marriage from two women who happened to be in-laws. Most of us will reserve words of such strong commitment for our husband alone. But Ruth reminds us that we marry our in-laws as well. (See also Genesis 2.18-25; 1 Corinthians 12.12-31.)

Words To Remember: *Ruth answered, "I will go where you go, I will live where you live; your people will be my people, your God will be my God."—Ruth 1.16*

and whenever you are thirsty, you can drink from the water jars they have filled."

[10]Ruth bowed down to the ground and said, "You know I come from another country. Why are you so good to me?"

[11]Boaz answered, "I've heard how you've helped your mother-in-law ever since your husband died. You even left your own father and mother to come and live in a foreign land among people you don't know. [12]I pray that the LORD God of Israel will reward you for what you have done. And now that you have come to him for protection, I pray that he will bless you."

[13]Ruth replied, "Sir, it's good of you to speak kindly to me and make me feel so welcome. I'm not even one of your servants."

[14]At mealtime Boaz said to Ruth, "Come, eat with us. Have some bread and dip it in the sauce." Right away she sat down with the workers, and Boaz handed her some roasted grain. Ruth ate all she wanted and had some left over.

[15]When Ruth got up to start picking up grain, Boaz told his men, "Don't stop her, even if she picks up grain from where it is stacked. [16]Be sure to pull out some stalks of grain from the bundles and leave them on the ground for her. And don't speak harshly to her!"

[17]Ruth worked in the field until evening. Then after she had pounded the grain off the stalks, she had a large basket full of grain. [18]She took the grain to town and showed Naomi how much she had picked up. Ruth also gave her the food left over from her lunch.

[19]Naomi said, "Where did you work today? Whose field was it? God bless the man who treated you so well!" Then Ruth told her that she had worked in the field of a man named Boaz.

[20]"The LORD bless Boaz!" Naomi replied. "He[h] has shown that he is still loyal to the living and to the dead. Boaz is a close relative, one of those who is supposed to look after us."

[21]Ruth told her, "Boaz even said I could stay in the field with his workers until they had finished gathering all his grain."

[22]Naomi replied, "My daughter, it's good that you can pick up grain alongside the women who work in his field. Who knows what might happen to you in someone else's

---

[h]2.20 He: Or "The LORD."

PARENTING&*family*—How can I best relate to my adult child? *(Ruth 3)*

Pass on your wisdom and experience, but let your child make final decisions.
Parents of adult children often err in two directions. We *underestimate* what experience has taught us, and we *overestimate* what our adult children can absorb from our experience, or even fully "hear" what we say about it. Our children, like us, learn best from events in their own lives.

Naomi passed to Ruth practical instructions on how she might propose marriage to Boaz without public embarrassment to either of them. The process had risks, even danger. But Ruth knew that this was Naomi's area of expertise—and so far Naomi had been right about Boaz. So Ruth took those risks. Instead of rape, she received a blessing (3.10). Instead of rejection, she received a gift (3.15-18).

Passing on our wisdom is worth the effort. Whether it is how to make grandmother's lemon pie, gauge the long-term trends of the stock market, or keep a growing relationship with God, we owe our children the heritage of our experience. But we also owe them the freedom to use or ignore that information (fresh-squeezed lemon might not be practical in their time-crunched microwave world). Even if our adult children do not follow our counsel exactly, a relationship of trust and respect allows them to draw on our wisdom in unexpected ways. Ruth and Naomi trusted and respected each other. This kind of relationship will aid the process of parents deciding what to share—and children deciding what to use. (See also Genesis 13,14; John 3.1-21.)

Words To Remember: *Ruth answered, "I'll do whatever you say." She went out to the place where Boaz was working and did what Naomi had told her.—Ruth 3.5,6*

field!" ²³And so, Ruth stayed close to the women, while picking up grain in his field.

Ruth worked in the fields until the barley and wheat were harvested. And all this time she lived with Naomi.

Naomi Makes Plans for Ruth

3 One day, Naomi said to Ruth:
It's time I found you a husband, who will give you a home and take care of you.

²You have been picking up grain alongside the women who work for Boaz, and you know he is a relative of ours. Tonight he will be threshing the grain. ³Now take a bath and put on some perfume, then dress in your best clothes. Go where he is working, but don't let him see you until he has finished eating and drinking. ⁴Watch where he goes to spend the night, then when he is asleep, lift the cover and lie down at his feet.ⁱ He will tell you what to do.

⁵Ruth answered, "I'll do whatever you say." ⁶She went out to the place where Boaz was working and did what Naomi had told her.

⁷After Boaz finished eating and drinking and was feeling happy, he went over and fell asleep near the pile of grain. Ruth slipped over quietly. She lifted the cover and lay down near his feet.

⁸In the middle of the night, Boaz suddenly woke up and was shocked to see a woman lying at his feet. ⁹"Who are you?" he asked.

"Sir, I am Ruth," she answered, "and you are the relative who is supposed to take care of me. So spread the edge of your cover over me."ʲ

¹⁰Boaz replied:
The LORD bless you! This shows how truly loyal you are to your family. You could have looked for a younger man, either rich or poor, but you didn't. ¹¹Don't worry, I'll do what you have asked. You are respected by everyone in town.

¹²It's true that I am one of the relatives who is supposed to take care of you, but there is someone who is an even closer relative. ¹³Stay here until morning, then I will find out if he is willing to look after you. If he isn't,

I promise by the living God to do it myself. Now go back to sleep until morning.

¹⁴Ruth lay down again, but she got up before daylight, because Boaz did not want anyone to know she had been there. ¹⁵Then he told her to spread out her cape. And he filled it with a lot of grain and placed it on her shoulder.

When Ruth got back to town, ¹⁶Naomi asked herᵏ what had happened, and Ruth told her everything. ¹⁷She also said, "Boaz gave me this grain, because he didn't want me to come back without something for you."

¹⁸Naomi replied, "Just be patient and don't worry about what will happen. He won't rest until everything is settled today!"

Ruth and Boaz Get Married

4 In the meanwhile, Boaz had gone to the meeting place at the town gate and was sitting there when the other close relative came by. So Boaz invited him to come over and sit down, and he did. ²Then Boaz got ten of the town leaders and also asked them to sit down. After they had sat down, ³he said to the man:

Naomi has come back from Moab and is selling the land that belonged to her husband Elimelech. ⁴I am telling you about this, since you are his closest relative and have the right to buy the property. If you want it, you can buy it now. These ten men and the others standing here can be witnesses. But if you don't want the property, let me know, because I am next in line.

The man replied, "I will buy it!"

⁵"If you do buy it from Naomi," Boaz told him, "you must also marry Ruth. Then if you have a son by her, the property will stay in the family of Ruth's first husband."

⁶The man answered, "If that's the case, I don't want to buy it! That would make problems with the property I already own.ˡ You may buy it yourself, because I cannot."

ⁱ**3.4** *lift the cover . . . feet:* To ask for protection and possibly for marriage. ʲ**3.9** *So . . . me:* To show that he would protect and take care of her. ᵏ**3.15,16** *When . . . her:* Some Hebrew manuscripts and two ancient translations; most Hebrew manuscripts "Boaz went back to town. ¹⁶Naomi asked Ruth." ˡ**4.6** *property . . . own:* This property would then have to be shared with Ruth and her children as well as with his own family.

Naomi

Ruth 1–4

How do you feel about God when your circumstances are awful? A discomforting sense of anger, a hint of mistrust? But what if the circumstances are beyond awful? What if life crashes upon you with repeated tragedy—job loss, followed by a forced move, followed by the death of a much-loved family member, followed by a second and third death, followed by poverty—with no good end in sight? At times like these, even the most sturdy among us begins to question God: "Where is God? Has he lost his power? Is God really good? Does he care about me? Does God hate me?" And we wonder, "Why me?"

Naomi suffered these losses. It's small wonder that when she returned to her former home in Bethlehem she greeted her friends with, "Don't call me Naomi any longer! Call me Mara, because God has made my life bitter. I had everything when I left, but the LORD has brought me back with nothing" (1.20,21).

But despite tragedies and questions, Naomi remained soft toward God. Even her return to Bethlehem speaks of an openness to his work in her life. She knew that people there worshiped the true God. A few days later when Ruth came home with a basket full of grain, Naomi's first words pointed toward God: "The LORD bless Boaz!" (2.20).

Naomi then set about following the ancient religious customs of her people. Years earlier, God had given instructions about how to provide for the poor. At harvest, landowners were to leave some grain in the fields so those without property might pick up enough to eat. Naomi followed this practice when she sent Ruth to the fields. And Boaz followed it when he left grain for Ruth to glean. And the law also provided for widows by instructing a brother-in-law or other close relative to offer marriage, children, and property (see Deuteronomy 24.19-22; 25.5-10; and Leviticus 25.25). Naomi began to invoke these old religious customs not for herself but for Ruth. In all of this she took great care to allow dignity and personal choice for both Ruth and Boaz.

In time, Naomi was able once again to experience the kindness of God. By the end of the story, we see the old and wise Naomi rocking her grandchild, encircled by neighboring women who pray God's blessing on the baby and invite Naomi to "praise the LORD!" (4.14).

Naomi's life encourages us to endure in faith. During tragedy, we can surround ourselves with God's people—as Naomi did. And we can allow them to fan to life the weakened embers of our faith. We can nurture healthy friendships, being careful to allow these friends dignity and independence. We can remember God's kindness and mercy and look for it again. When praise sticks in our throat, we can know that these painful days will pass and that someday we will once again offer our praise to God.

[7]To make a sale legal in those days, one person would take off a sandal and give it to the other. [8]So after the man had agreed to let Boaz buy the property, he took off one of his sandals and handed it to Boaz.

[9]Boaz told the town leaders and everyone else:

All of you are witnesses that today I have bought from Naomi the property that belonged to Elimelech and his two sons, Chilion and Mahlon. [10]You are also witnesses that I have agreed to marry Mahlon's widow Ruth, the Moabite woman. This will keep the property in his family's name, and he will be remembered in this town.

[11]The town leaders and the others standing there said:

We are witnesses to this. And we pray that the LORD will give your wife many children, just as he did Leah and Rachel, the wives of Jacob. May you be a rich man in the tribe of Ephrath and an important man in Bethlehem. [12]May the children you have by this young woman make your family as famous as the family of Perez,[m] the son of Tamar and Judah.

[13]Boaz married Ruth, and the LORD blessed her with a son. [14]After his birth, the women said to Naomi:

Praise the LORD! Today he has given you a grandson to take care of you. We pray that the boy will grow up to be famous everywhere in Israel. [15]He will[n] make you happy and take care of you in your old age, because he is the son of your daughter-in-law. And she loves you more than seven sons of your own would love you.

[16]Naomi loved the boy and took good care of him. [17]The neighborhood women named him Obed, but they called him "Naomi's Boy."

When Obed grew up he had a son named Jesse, who later became the father of King David. [18-22]Here is a list of the ancestors of David: Jesse, Obed, Boaz, Salmon, Nahshon, Amminadab, Ram, Hezron, and Perez.

---

[m]**4.12** *Perez:* One of the sons of Judah; he was an ancestor of Boaz and of many others who lived in Bethlehem. [n]**4.14,15** *We pray that . . . famous . . .* [15] *He will:* Or "We pray that the LORD will be praised everywhere in Israel. [15]Your grandson will."

1 Samuel
What It Means To Choose God

What does it mean to keep choosing God in the midst of successes and failures? When it's easy and when it's not?

As one of Israel's history books, 1 Samuel presents us with accounts of people who did and did not choose God. It begins during the rule of the judges—sporadic leaders, mostly for military purposes, but the government was a theocracy (with God as the only leader). One of the first people we meet is Hannah who, after a struggle with infertility, gave birth to Samuel. Samuel later became a priest, judge, and prophet, guiding Israel wisely.

Samuel got upset, however, when the people of Israel wanted an earthly king. But because of their insistence, God gave in and guided Samuel in selecting Saul as Israel's first king. Unfortunately, Saul ignored God and did things his own way, so God asked Samuel to anoint David as a replacement.

The focus of the book then changes to the interaction between King Saul and David, the slayer of Goliath. Saul became increasingly jealous of David's popularity. In the meantime, Saul's son Jonathan befriended David when he had every reason to hate him as a rival for the throne. Saul's spiritual life deteriorated, and he repeatedly tried to kill David, chasing him throughout Israel. David's renegade but skillful army could have killed Saul, but instead spared him. Eventually, Saul became his own worst enemy through sorcery, witchcraft, and suicide.

These two characters present a fascinating study in what happens when we choose to follow God (David) and when we choose not to (Saul). At any point, Saul could have turned around, but he chose to do his own thing. David's frantic life on the run refined his integrity and zeal for God. He understood what Saul didn't: "[The LORD] doesn't want your sacrifices. He wants you to obey him" (15.22). David managed to obey in tough places—showing mercy to enemies, being loyal to friends, and choosing God no matter what.

1 Samuel at a Glance

1. Samuel's birth, growth, and background (1–3)
2. Samuel guides Israel with God as its only leader (4–7)
3. Israel demands a king, and Saul is appointed (8–10)
4. King Saul fights the Philistines with his son, Jonathan, at his side (11,13,14)
5. Samuel's farewell speech (12)
6. Saul disobeys; God rejects him and chooses David to be king (15,16)
7. David kills Goliath (17)
8. David and Jonathan become friends while Saul tries to kill David (17–23)
9. David spares Saul's life twice and meets Abigail (24–26)
10. Saul's defeat and death (27–31)

Hannah Asks the Lord for a Child

1 Elkanah lived in Ramah,[a] a town in the hill country of Ephraim. His great-great-grandfather was Zuph, so Elkanah was a member of the Zuph clan of the Ephraim tribe. Elkanah's father was Jeroham, his grandfather was Elihu, and his great-grandfather was Tohu.

[2]Elkanah had two wives,[b] Hannah and Peninnah. Although Peninnah had children, Hannah did not have any.

[3]Once a year Elkanah traveled from his hometown to Shiloh, where he worshiped the Lord All-Powerful and offered sacrifices. Eli was the Lord's priest there, and his two sons Hophni and Phinehas served with him as priests.[c]

[4]Whenever Elkanah offered a sacrifice, he gave some of the meat[d] to Peninnah and some to each of her sons and daughters. [5]But he gave Hannah even more, because he loved Hannah very much, even though the Lord had kept her from having children of her own.

[6]Peninnah liked to make Hannah feel miserable about not having any children, [7]especially when the family went to the house of the Lord[e] each year.

One day, Elkanah was there offering a sacrifice, when Hannah began crying and refused to eat. [8]So Elkanah asked, "Hannah, why are you crying? Why won't you eat? Why do you feel so bad? Don't I mean more to you than ten sons?"

[9]When the sacrifice had been offered, and they had eaten the meal, Hannah got up and went to pray. Eli was sitting in his chair near the door to the place of worship. [10]Hannah was brokenhearted and was crying as she prayed, [11]"Lord All-Powerful, I am your servant, but I am so miserable! Please let me have a son. I will give him to you for as long as he lives, and his hair will never be cut."[f]

[12-13]Hannah prayed silently to the Lord for a long time. But her lips were moving, and Eli thought she was drunk. [14]"How long are you going to stay drunk?" he asked. "Sober up!"

[15-16]"Sir, please don't think I'm no good!" Hannah answered. "I'm not drunk, and I haven't been drinking. But I do feel miserable and terribly upset. I've been praying all this time, telling the Lord about my problems."

[17]Eli replied, "You may go home now and stop worrying. I'm sure the God of Israel will answer your prayer."

[18]"Sir, thank you for being so kind to me," Hannah said. Then she left, and after eating something, she felt much better.

Samuel Is Born

[19]Elkanah and his family got up early the next morning and worshiped the Lord. Then they went back home to Ramah. Later the Lord blessed Elkanah and Hannah [20]with a son. She named him Samuel because she had asked the Lord for him.[g]

Hannah Gives Samuel to the Lord

[21]The next time Elkanah and his family went to offer their yearly sacrifice, he took along a gift that he had promised to give to the Lord. [22]But Hannah stayed home, because she had told Elkanah, "Samuel and I won't go until he's old enough for me to stop nursing him. Then I'll give him to the Lord, and he can stay there at Shiloh for the rest of his life."

[23]"You know what's best," Elkanah said. "Stay here until it's time to stop nursing him. I'm sure the Lord will help you do what you have promised."[h] Hannah did not go to Shiloh until she stopped nursing Samuel.

[24-25]When it was the time of year to go to Shiloh again, Hannah and Elkanah[i] took Samuel to the Lord's house. They brought

---

[a]1.1 *Ramah:* The Hebrew has "Ramathaim," a longer form of "Ramah" (see verse 19).   [b]1.2 *two wives:* Having more than one wife was allowed in those times.   [c]1.3 *Eli . . . priests:* One ancient translation; Hebrew "Hophni and Phinehas, the two sons of Eli, served the Lord as priests."   [d]1.4 *meat:* For some sacrifices, like this one, only part of the meat was burned. Some was given to the priest, and the rest was eaten by the family and guests of the worshiper (see Leviticus 3.1-17; 7.11-18).   [e]1.7 *house of the Lord:* Another name for the place of worship at Shiloh, which still may have been the sacred tent at this time.   [f]1.11 *his hair . . . cut:* Never cutting the child's hair would be a sign that he would belong to the Lord (see Numbers 6.1, 21, especially verse 5).   [g]1.20 *him:* In Hebrew "Samuel" sounds something like "Someone from God" or "The name of God" or "His name is God."   [h]1.23 *the Lord . . . promised:* The Dead Sea Scrolls and two ancient translations; the Standard Hebrew Text "the Lord will do what he said."   [i]1.24,25 *When it was the time of year to go to Shiloh again, Hannah and Elkanah:* The Dead Sea Scrolls and one ancient translation; the Standard Hebrew Text "she."

Hannah

1 Samuel 1.1—2.21

*T*he annual journey to worship at Shiloh must have been an arduous trip for Hannah. She was the favorite wife of her husband, Elkanah; but his other wife, Peninnah, had children. In addition to the agony of infertility, Hannah lived with the despair that childless women in her culture faced because having sons determined a woman's worth. Having no son meant she was cursed by God and worthless. And, without a son, she would become a pauper when widowed.

Where was God? she may have wondered as her prayers went unanswered year after year. On these journeys to Shiloh, Peninnah liked to make Hannah feel miserable. Imagine how Peninnah taunted her over the voices of her sons and daughters.

Hannah's husband, Elkanah, meant well, no doubt, when he asked, "Why are you crying? Why won't you eat? Why do you feel so bad? Don't I mean more to you than ten sons?" (1.8). How could she explain?

Hannah found herself praying with such emotion in the presence of Eli the priest, that he assumed she was drunk and told her to "sober up!" (1.14). Can you imagine how Hannah must have felt? First, Peninnah taunted her; next her husband offered mindless comfort; and then the priest accused her of being drunk. Add this to her struggle with infertility, and you wonder how she explained herself to Eli without exploding. But she did, and Eli assured her God would answer her prayer. Not giving into cynicism, she felt much better.

Sure enough, Samuel was born. A few years later, she brought this boy—her only child—to Eli to be "the LORD's servant for as long as he lives" (1.28). Was it tempting to hold on to this boy she had prayed for? We can only imagine the strength of character and cultivated skill of gratitude she must have had to relinquish this child she wanted so badly.

Hannah then offered a song that became well known in Israel (2.1-10). The song shows her ability to see beyond herself to the struggles of people around her. It shows her understanding of God's ways. She sang not only about how God benefited her ("A woman did not have a child, and you gave her seven"—2.5), but also about God's work ("You set the world on foundations, and they belong to you"—2.8) and God's ways in the world ("You lift the poor and homeless out of the garbage dump and give them places of honor in royal palaces"—2.8). After a few more years, Hannah and Elkanah went on to have three sons and two daughters, but Hannah never forgot Samuel. She made him a special linen garment every year.

In personal struggles such as these—infertility, jealousy, child-related heartaches—it is easy to become self-focused and bitter. Hannah had an intriguing strength of character that compelled her to devote herself to God and to see beyond herself.

along a three-year-old bull,[j] a twenty-pound sack of flour, and a clay jar full of wine. Hannah and Elkanah offered the bull as a sacrifice, then brought the little boy to Eli.

[26]"Sir," Hannah said, "a few years ago I stood here beside you and asked the LORD [27]to give me a child. Here he is! The LORD gave me just what I asked for. [28]Now I am giving him to the LORD, and he will be the LORD's servant for as long as he lives."

Hannah Prays

2 Elkanah[k] worshiped the LORD there at Shiloh, and [1]Hannah prayed:

You make me strong
    and happy, LORD.
You rescued me.
Now I can be glad
    and laugh at my enemies.
[2]No other god[l] is like you.
We're safer with you
    than on a high mountain.[m]
[3]I can tell those proud people,
    "Stop your boasting!
Nothing is hidden from the LORD,
    and he judges what we do."

[4]Our LORD, you break
    the bows of warriors,
but you give strength
    to everyone who stumbles.
[5]People who once
    had plenty to eat
must now hire themselves out
    for only a piece of bread.
But you give the hungry more
    than enough to eat.
A woman did not have a child,
    and you gave her seven,
but a woman who had many
    was left with none.
[6]You take away life,
    and you give life.
You send people down
to the world of the dead
    and bring them back again.

[7]Our LORD, you are the one
    who makes us rich or poor.
You put some in high positions
    and bring disgrace on others.
[8]You lift the poor and homeless
    out of the garbage dump

and give them places of honor
    in royal palaces.

You set the world on foundations,
    and they belong to you.
[9]You protect your loyal people,
    but everyone who is evil
    will die in darkness.

We cannot win a victory
    by our own strength.
[10]Our LORD, those who attack you
    will be broken in pieces
when you fight back
    with thunder from heaven.
You will judge the whole earth
    and give power and strength
    to your chosen king.

Samuel Stays with Eli

[11]Elkanah and Hannah went back home to Ramah, but the boy Samuel stayed to help Eli serve the LORD.

Eli's Sons

[12-13]Eli's sons were priests, but they were dishonest and refused to obey the LORD. So, while people were boiling the meat from their sacrifices, these priests would send over a servant with a large, three-pronged fork. [14]The servant would stick the fork into the cooking pot, and whatever meat came out on the fork was taken back to the priests. That is how these two priests treated every Israelite who came to offer sacrifices in Shiloh. [15]Sometimes, when people were offering sacrifices, the servant would come over, even before the fat had been cut off and sacrificed to the LORD.[n]

Then the servant would tell them, "The priest doesn't want his meat boiled! Give him some raw meat that he can roast!"

[16]Usually the people answered, "Take what you want. But first, let us sacrifice the fat to the LORD."

---

[j]**1.24,25** *a three-year-old bull:* The Dead Sea Scrolls and two ancient translations; the Standard Hebrew Text "three bulls."   [k]**1.28** *Elkanah:* Or "They" or "Samuel."   [l]**2.2** *god:* The Hebrew text has "holy one," a term for supernatural beings or gods.   [m]**2.2** *mountain:* One possible meaning for the difficult Hebrew text of verse 2.   [n]**2.15** *sacrificed to the LORD:* The fat belonged to the LORD and was supposed to be burned as a sacrifice before the rest of the animal was cooked and eaten (see Leviticus 3.3, 4, 9, 10, 14, 15).

"No," the servant would reply. "If you don't give it to me now, I'll take it by force."

[17]Eli's sons did not show any respect for the sacrifices that the people offered. This was a terrible sin, and it made the LORD very angry.

Hannah Visits Samuel

[18]The boy Samuel served the LORD and wore a special linen garment[p] [19]and the clothes[p] his mother made for him. She would bring new clothes every year, when she and her husband came to offer sacrifices at Shiloh.

[20]Eli would always bless Elkanah and his wife and say, "Samuel was born in answer to your prayers. Now you have given him to the LORD. I pray that the LORD will bless you with more children to take his place." After Eli had blessed them, Elkanah and Hannah would return home.

[21]The LORD was kind to Hannah, and she had three more sons and two daughters. But Samuel grew up at the LORD's house in Shiloh.

Eli Warns His Sons

[22]Eli was now very old, and he heard what his sons were doing to the people of Israel.[q] [23-24]"Why are you doing these awful things?" he asked them. "I've been hearing nothing but complaints about you from all of the LORD's people. [25]If you harm another person, God can help make things right between the two of you. But if you commit a crime against the LORD, no one can help you!"

But the LORD had already decided to kill them. So he kept them from listening to their father.

A Prophet Speaks to Eli

[26]Each day the LORD and his people liked Samuel more and more.

[27]One day a prophet came to Eli and gave him this message from the LORD:

When your ancestors were slaves of the king of Egypt, I came and showed them who I am. [28-29]Out of all the tribes of Israel, I chose your family to be my priests. I wanted them to offer sacrifices and burn incense to me and to find out from me what I want my people to do. I commanded everyone to bring their sacrifices here where I live, and I allowed you and your family to keep those that were not offered to me on the altar.

But you honor your sons instead of me! You don't respect[r] the sacrifices and offerings that are brought to me, and you've all gotten fat from eating the best parts.

[30]I am the LORD, the God of Israel. I promised to always let your family serve me as priests, but now I tell you that I cannot do this any longer! I honor anyone who honors me, but I put a curse on anyone who hates me. [31]The time will come when I will kill you and everyone else in your family. Not one of you will live to an old age.

[32]Your family[s] will have a lot of trouble. I will be kind to Israel,[t] but everyone in your family will die young. [33]If I let anyone from your family be a priest, his[u] life will be full of sadness and sorrow. But most of the men in your family will die a violent death![v]
[34]To prove to you that I will do these things, your two sons, Hophni and Phinehas, will die on the same day.

[35]I have chosen someone else to be my priest, someone who will be faithful and obey me. I will always let his family serve as priests and help my chosen king. [36]But if anyone is left from your family, he will come to my priest and beg for money or a little bread. He may even say to my priest, "Please let me be a priest, so I will at least have something to eat."

---

[p]2.18 *a special linen garment:* Either a loin cloth or a jacket or a vest worn only by priests.   [p]2.19 *clothes:* The Hebrew word means a sleeveless coat or robe that was worn by priests. Samuel was a small child, but his mother made him clothes just like those worn by priests.   [q]2.22 *Israel:* The Dead Sea Scrolls and one ancient translation; the Standard Hebrew Text adds "He heard that his sons were even sleeping with the women who worked at the entrance to the sacred tent."   [r]2.28,29 *don't respect:* The Standard Hebrew Text; the Dead Sea Scrolls and one ancient translation "are greedy for."   [s]2.32 *Your family:* Or "My house of worship."   [t]2.31,32 *Not one . . . to Israel:* The Standard Hebrew Text; the Dead Sea Scrolls and one ancient translation do not have these words.   [u]2.33 *his:* The Dead Sea Scrolls and one ancient translation; the Standard Hebrew Text "your."   [v]2.33 *die a violent death:* The Dead Sea Scrolls and one ancient translation; the Standard Hebrew Text "die."

The LORD Speaks to Samuel

3 [1-2]Samuel served the LORD by helping Eli the priest, who was by that time almost blind. In those days, the LORD hardly ever spoke directly to people, and he did not appear to them in dreams very often. But one night, Eli was asleep in his room, [3]and Samuel was sleeping on a mat near the sacred chest in the LORD's house. They had not been asleep very long[w] [4]when the LORD called out Samuel's name.

"Here I am!" Samuel answered. [5]Then he ran to Eli and said, "Here I am. What do you want?"

"I didn't call you," Eli answered. "Go back to bed."

Samuel went back.

[6]Again the LORD called out Samuel's name. Samuel got up and went to Eli. "Here I am," he said. "What do you want?"

Eli told him, "Son, I didn't call you. Go back to sleep."

[7]The LORD had not spoken to Samuel before, and Samuel did not recognize the voice. [8]When the LORD called out his name for the third time, Samuel went to Eli again and said, "Here I am. What do you want?"

Eli finally realized that it was the LORD who was speaking to Samuel. [9]So he said, "Go back and lie down! If someone speaks to you again, answer, 'I'm listening, LORD. What do you want me to do?' "

Once again Samuel went back and lay down. [10]The LORD then stood beside Samuel and called out as he had done before, "Samuel! Samuel!"

"I'm listening," Samuel answered. "What do you want me to do?"

[11]The LORD said:

Samuel, I am going to do something in Israel that will shock everyone who hears about it! [12]I will punish Eli and his family, just as I promised. [13]He knew that his sons refused to respect me,[x] and he let them get away with it, even though I said I would punish his family forever. [14]I warned Eli that sacrifices or offerings could never make things right! His family has done too many disgusting things.

[15]The next morning, Samuel got up and opened the doors to the LORD's house. He was afraid to tell Eli what the LORD had said.

[16]But Eli told him, "Samuel, my boy, come here!"

"Here I am," Samuel answered.

[17]Eli said, "What did God say to you? Tell me everything. I pray that God will punish you terribly if you don't tell me every word he said!"

[18]Samuel told Eli everything. Then Eli said, "He is the LORD, and he will do what's right."

> *Through my study of God's Word, I'm constantly reminded that my life on earth is just a brief blip on God's timeline. Yet living my life to please God, through service for him and a personal relationship with him, has eternal significance.*
>
> ANNE GRAHAM LOTZ

The LORD Helps Samuel

[19]As Samuel grew up, the LORD helped him and made everything Samuel said come true. [20]From the town of Dan in the north to the town of Beersheba in the south, everyone in the country knew that Samuel was truly the LORD's prophet. [21]The LORD often appeared to Samuel at Shiloh and told him

4 what to say. [1]Then Samuel would speak to the whole nation of Israel.

The Philistines Capture the Sacred Chest

One day the Israelites went out to fight the Philistines. They set up camp near Ebenezer, and the Philistines camped at Aphek. [2]The Philistines made a fierce attack. They defeated the Israelites and killed about four thousand of them.

[3]The Israelite army returned to their camp, and the leaders said, "Why did the

---

[w]3.3 *They . . . long*: The Hebrew text has "The lamp was still burning." An olive oil lamp would go out after a few hours if the wick was not adjusted.
[x]3.13 *refused . . . me*: Or "were insulting everyone."

LORD let us lose to the Philistines today? Let's get the sacred chest where the LORD's agreement with Israel is kept. Then the LORD[y] will help us and rescue us from our enemies."

⁴The army sent some soldiers to bring back the sacred chest from Shiloh, because the LORD All-Powerful has his throne on the winged creatures on top of the chest.

As Eli's two sons, Hophni and Phinehas, ⁵brought the chest into camp, the army cheered so loudly that the ground shook. ⁶The Philistines heard the noise and said, "What are those Hebrews shouting about?"

When the Philistines learned that the sacred chest had been brought into the camp, ⁷they were scared to death and said:

The gods have come into their camp. Now we're in real trouble! Nothing like this has ever happened to us before. ⁸We're in big trouble! Who can save us from these powerful gods? They're the same gods who made all those horrible things happen to the Egyptians in the desert.

⁹Philistines, be brave and fight hard! If you don't, those Hebrews will rule us, just as we've been ruling them. Fight and don't be afraid.

¹⁰The Philistines did fight. They killed thirty thousand Israelite soldiers, and all the rest ran off to their homes. ¹¹Hophni and Phinehas were killed, and the sacred chest was captured.

Eli Dies

¹²That same day a soldier from the tribe of Benjamin ran from the battlefront to Shiloh. He had torn his clothes and put dirt on his head to show his sorrow. ¹³He went into town and told the news about the battle, and everyone started crying.

Eli was afraid that something might happen to the sacred chest. So he was sitting on his chair beside the road, just waiting. ¹⁴⁻¹⁵He was ninety-eight years old and blind, but he could hear everyone crying, and he asked, "What's all that noise?"

The soldier hurried over and told Eli, ¹⁶"I escaped from the fighting today and ran here."

"Young man, what happened?" Eli asked.

¹⁷"Israel ran away from the Philistines," the soldier answered. "Many of our people

were killed, including your two sons, Hophni and Phinehas. But worst of all, the sacred chest was captured."

I know that unless I keep up my relationship with God, I could easily fall flat on my face. But with him, I can walk forward in confidence.

KATHY PEEL

¹⁸Eli was still sitting on a chair beside the wall of the town gate. And when the man said that the Philistines had taken the sacred chest, Eli fell backwards. He was a very heavy old man, and the fall broke his neck and killed him. He had been a leader[z] of Israel for forty years.

¹⁹The wife of Phinehas was about to give birth. And soon after she heard that the sacred chest had been captured and that her husband and his father had died, her baby came. The birth was very hard, ²⁰and she was dying. But the women taking care of her said, "Don't be afraid—it's a boy!"

She didn't pay any attention to them. ²¹⁻²²Instead she kept thinking about losing her husband and her father-in-law. So she said, "My son will be named Ichabod,[a] because the glory of Israel left our country when the sacred chest was captured."

God Causes Trouble for the Philistines

5 The Philistines took the sacred chest from near Ebenezer to the town of Ashdod. ²They brought it into the temple of their god Dagon and put it next to the statue of Dagon, which they worshiped.

³When the people of Ashdod got up early the next morning, they found the statue lying facedown on the floor in front of the sacred chest. They put the statue back

---

where it belonged. [4]But early the next morning, it had fallen over again and was lying facedown on the floor in front of the chest. The body of the statue was still in one piece, but its head and both hands had broken off and were lying on the stone floor in the doorway. [5]This is the reason the priests and everyone else step over that part of the doorway when they enter the temple of Dagon in Ashdod.

[6]The LORD caused a lot of trouble for the people of Ashdod and their neighbors. He made sores break out all over their bodies,[b] and everyone was in a panic.[c] [7]Finally, they said, "The God of Israel did this. He is the one who caused all this trouble for us and our god Dagon. We've got to get rid of this chest."

[8]The people of Ashdod had all the Philistine rulers come to Ashdod, and they asked them, "What can we do with the sacred chest that belongs to the God of Israel?"

"Send it to Gath," the rulers answered. But after they took it there, [9]the LORD made sores break out on everyone in town. The people of Gath were frightened, [10]so they sent the sacred chest to Ekron. But before they could take it through the town gates, the people of Ekron started screaming, "They've brought the sacred chest that belongs to the God of Israel! It will kill us and our families too!"

The Philistines Send Back the Sacred Chest

[11]The people of Ekron called for another meeting of the Philistine rulers and told them, "Send this chest back where it belongs. Then it won't kill us."

Everyone was in a panic, because God was causing a lot of people to die, [12]and those who had survived were suffering from the sores. They all cried to their gods for help.

6 After the sacred chest had been in Philistia for seven months,[d] [2]the Philistines called in their priests and fortunetellers, and asked, "What should we do with this sacred chest? Tell us how to send it back where it belongs!"

[3]"Don't send it back without a gift," the priests and fortunetellers answered. "Send along something to Israel's God to make up for taking the chest in the first place. Then you will be healed, and you will find out why the LORD was causing you so much trouble."

[4]"What should we send?" the Philistines asked.

The priests and fortunetellers answered:

There are five Philistine rulers, and they all have the same disease that you have. [5]So make five gold models of the sores and five gold models of the rats that are wiping out your crops. If you honor the God of Israel with this gift, maybe he will stop causing trouble for you and your gods and your crops. [6]Don't be like the Egyptians and their king. They were stubborn, but when Israel's God was finished with them, they had to let Israel go.

[7]Get a new cart and two cows that have young calves and that have never pulled a cart. Hitch the cows to the cart, but take the calves back to their barn. [8]Then put the chest on the cart. Put the gold rats and sores into a bag and put it on the cart next to the chest. Then send it on its way.

[9]Watch to see if the chest goes on up the road to the Israelite town of Beth-Shemesh. If it goes back to its own country, you will know that it was the LORD who made us suffer so badly. But if the chest doesn't go back to its own country, then the LORD had nothing to do with the disease that hit us—it was simply bad luck.

[10]The Philistines followed their advice. They hitched up the two cows to the cart, but they kept their calves in a barn. [11]Then they put the chest on the cart, along with the bag that had the gold rats and sores in it.

[12]The cows went straight up the road toward Beth-Shemesh, mooing as they went. The Philistine rulers followed them until they got close to Beth-Shemesh.

[13]The people of Beth-Shemesh were harvesting their wheat[e] in the valley. When they looked up and saw the chest, they were so happy that they stopped working and started celebrating.

---

[b]5.6 *sores . . . bodies*: Or "He struck them with bubonic plague." [c]5.6 *panic*: Two ancient translations add "Rats came from their ships, and people were dying right and left." [d]6.1 *months*: One ancient translation adds "and rats were everywhere" or "and rats ate the crops." [e]6.13 *wheat*: The wheat harvest took place in May and June.

¹⁴⁻¹⁵The cows left the road and pulled the cart into a field that belonged to Joshua from Beth-Shemesh, and they stopped beside a huge rock. Some men from the tribe of Levi were there. So they took the chest off the cart and placed it on the rock, and then they did the same thing with the bag of gold rats and sores. A few other people chopped up the cart and made a fire. They killed the cows and burned them as sacrifices to the LORD. After that, they offered more sacrifices.

¹⁶When the five rulers of the Philistines saw what had happened, they went back to Ekron that same day.

¹⁷That is how the Philistines sent gifts to the LORD to make up for taking the sacred chest. They sent five gold sores, one each for their towns of Ashdod, Gaza, Ashkelon, Gath, and Ekron. ¹⁸They also sent one gold rat for each walled town and for every village that the five Philistine rulers controlled. The huge stone*ʲ* where the Levites set the chest is still there in Joshua's field as a reminder of what happened.

The Sacred Chest Is Sent to Kiriath-Jearim

¹⁹Some of the men of Beth-Shemesh looked inside the sacred chest, and the LORD God killed seventy*ᵍ* of them. This made the people of Beth-Shemesh very sad, ²⁰and they started saying, "No other God is like the LORD! Who can go near him and still live? We'll have to send the chest away from here. But where can we send it?"

²¹They sent messengers to tell the people of Kiriath-Jearim, "The Philistines have sent back the sacred chest. Why don't you take it and keep it there with you?"

7 The people of Kiriath-Jearim got the chest and took it to Abinadab's house, which was on a hill in their town. They chose his son Eleazar to take care of it, ²and it stayed there for twenty years.

During this time everyone in Israel was very sad and begged the LORD for help.*ʰ*

The People of Israel Turn Back to the LORD

³One day, Samuel told all the people of Israel, "If you really want to turn back to the LORD, then prove it. Get rid of your foreign idols, including the ones of the goddess Astarte. Turn to the LORD with all your heart and worship only him. Then he will rescue you from the Philistines."

⁴The people got rid of their idols of Baal and Astarte and began worshiping only the LORD.

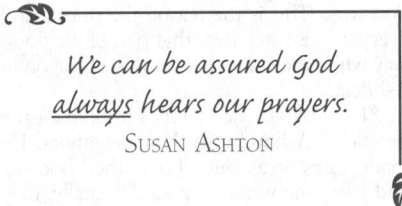

We can be assured God always hears our prayers.
SUSAN ASHTON

⁵Then Samuel said, "Tell everyone in Israel to meet together at Mizpah, and I will pray to the LORD for you."

⁶The Israelites met together at Mizpah with Samuel as their leader. They drew water from the well and poured it out as an offering to the LORD. On that same day they went without eating to show their sorrow, and they confessed they had been unfaithful to the LORD.

The Philistines Attack Israel

⁷When the Philistine rulers found out about the meeting at Mizpah, they sent an army there to attack the people of Israel.

The Israelites were afraid when they heard that the Philistines were coming. ⁸"Don't stop praying!" they told Samuel. "Ask the LORD our God to rescue us."

⁹⁻¹⁰Samuel begged the LORD to rescue Israel, then he sacrificed a young lamb to the LORD. Samuel had not even finished offering the sacrifice when the Philistines started to attack. But the LORD answered his prayer and made thunder crash all around them. The Philistines panicked and ran away. ¹¹The men of Israel left Mizpah and went after them as far as the hillside below Beth-Car, killing every enemy soldier they caught.

¹²⁻¹³The Philistines were so badly beaten that it was quite a while before they attacked Israel again. After the battle, Samuel set up a monument between Mizpah and the rocky

---

*ʲ***6.18** *stone:* A few Hebrew manuscripts; most Hebrew manuscripts "meadow" or "stream." *ᵍ***6.19** *seventy:* A few Hebrew manuscripts; most Hebrew manuscripts "seventy men, fifty thousand men." *ʰ***7.2** *Israel . . . help:* Or "Israel turned to the LORD and begged him for help."

cliffs. He named it "Help Monument"[i] to remind Israel how much the LORD had helped them.

For as long as Samuel lived, the LORD helped Israel fight the Philistines. [14]The Israelites were even able to recapture their towns and territory between Ekron and Gath.

Israel was also at peace with the Amorites.[j]

Samuel Is a Leader in Israel

[15]Samuel was a leader[k] in Israel all his life. [16]Every year he would go around to the towns of Bethel, Gilgal, and Mizpah where he served as judge for the people. [17]Then he would go back to his home in Ramah and do the same thing there. He also had an altar built for the LORD at Ramah.

The People of Israel Want a King

8 [1-2]Samuel had two sons. The older one was Joel, and the younger one was Abijah. When Samuel was getting old, he let them be leaders[k] at Beersheba. [3]But they were not like their father. They were dishonest and accepted bribes to give unfair decisions.

[4]One day the nation's leaders came to Samuel at Ramah [5]and said, "You are an old man. You set a good example for your sons, but they haven't followed it. Now we want a king to be our leader,[k] just like all the other nations. Choose one for us!"

[6]Samuel was upset to hear the leaders say they wanted a king, so he prayed about it. [7]The LORD answered:

Samuel, do everything they want you to do. I am really the one they have rejected as their king. [8]Ever since the day I rescued my people from Egypt, they have turned from me to worship idols. Now they are turning away from you. [9]Do everything they ask, but warn them and tell them how a king will treat them.

[10]Samuel told the people who were asking for a king what the LORD had said:

[11]If you have a king, this is how he will treat you. He will force your sons to join his army. Some of them will ride in his chariots, some will serve in the cavalry, and others will run ahead of his own chariot.[l] [12]Some of them will be officers in charge of a thousand soldiers, and others will be in charge of fifty. Still others will have to farm the king's land and harvest his crops, or make weapons and parts for his chariots. [13]Your daughters will have to make perfume or do his cooking and baking.

[14]The king will take your best fields, as well as your vineyards, and olive orchards and give them to his own officials. [15]He will also take a tenth of your grain and grapes and give it to his officers and officials.

[16]The king will take your slaves and your best young men and your donkeys and make them do his work. [17]He will also take a tenth of your sheep and goats. You will become the king's slaves, [18]and you will finally cry out for the LORD to save you from the king you wanted. But the LORD won't answer your prayers.

[19-20]The people would not listen to Samuel. "No!" they said. "We want to be like other nations. We want a king to rule us and lead us in battle."

[21]Samuel listened to them and then told the LORD exactly what they had said. [22]"Do what they want," the LORD answered. "Give them a king."

Samuel told the people to go back to their homes.

Saul Meets Samuel

9 Kish was a wealthy man who belonged to the tribe of Benjamin. His father was Abiel, his grandfather was Zeror, his great-grandfather was Becorath, and his great-great-grandfather was Aphiah. [2]Kish had a son named Saul, who was better looking and more than a head taller than anyone else in all Israel.

[3]Kish owned some donkeys, but they had run off. So he told Saul, "Take one of the servants and go look for the donkeys."

[4]Saul and the servant went through the hill country of Ephraim and the territory of Shalishah, but they could not find the donkeys. Then they went through the territories of Shaalim and Benjamin, but still there was

---

[i]**7.12,13** *Help Monument:* Or "Ebenezer."
[j]**7.14** *Amorites:* In this verse, the non-Israelite peoples of Canaan. [k]**7.15; 8.1,2,5** *leader(s):* The Hebrew word could mean an army commander, a judge, and a religious leader. [l]**8.11** *others . . . chariot:* These men were probably his bodyguards.

no sign of the donkeys. [5]Finally they came to the territory where the clan of Zuph[m] lived. "Let's go back home," Saul told his servant. "If we don't go back soon, my father will stop worrying about the donkeys and start worrying about us!"

[6]"Wait!" the servant answered. "There's a man of God who lives in a town near here. He's amazing! Everything he says comes true. Let's talk to him. Maybe he can tell us where to look."

[7]Saul said, "How can we talk to the prophet when I don't have anything to give him? We don't even have any bread left in our sacks. What can we give him?"

[8]"I have a small piece of silver," the servant answered. "We can give him that, and then he will tell us where to look for the donkeys."

[9-10]"Great!" Saul replied. "Let's go to the man who can see visions!" He said this because in those days God would answer questions by giving visions to prophets.

Saul and his servant went to the town where the prophet lived. [11]As they were going up the hill to the town, they met some young women coming out to get water,[n] and the two men said to them, "We're looking for the man who can see visions. Is he in town?"

[12]"Yes, he is," they replied. "He's in town today because there's going to be a sacrifice and a sacred meal at the place of worship. In fact, he's just ahead of you. Hurry [13]and you should find him right inside the town gate. He's on his way out to the place of worship to eat with the invited guests. They can't start eating until he blesses the sacrifice. If you go now, you should find him."

[14]They went to the town, and just as they were going through the gate, Samuel was coming out on his way to the place of worship.

[15]The day before Saul came, the LORD had told Samuel, [16]"I've seen how my people are suffering, and I've heard their call for help. About this time tomorrow I'll send you a man from the tribe of Benjamin, who will rescue my people from the Philistines. I want you to pour olive oil[o] on his head to show that he will be their leader."

[17]Samuel looked at Saul, and the LORD told Samuel, "This is the man I told you about. He's the one who will rule Israel."

[18]Saul went over to Samuel in the gateway and said, "A man who can see visions lives here in town. Could you tell me the way to his house?"

[19]"I am the one who sees visions!" Samuel answered. "Go on up to the place of worship. You will eat with me today, and in the morning I'll answer your questions. [20]Don't worry about your donkeys that ran off three days ago. They've already been found. Everything of value in Israel now belongs to you and your family."[p]

[21]"Why are you telling me this?" Saul asked. "I'm from Benjamin, the smallest tribe in Israel, and my clan is the least important in the tribe."

Saul Eats with Samuel and Stays at His House

[22]Samuel took Saul and his servant into the dining room at the place of worship. About thirty people were there for the dinner, but Samuel gave Saul and his servant the places of honor. [23-24]Then Samuel told the cook, "I gave you the best piece of meat and told you to set it aside. Bring it here now."

The cook brought the meat over and set it down in front of Saul. "This is for you," Samuel told him. "Go ahead and eat it. I had this piece saved especially for you, and I invited these guests to eat with you."

After Saul and Samuel had finished eating, [25]they went down from the place of worship and back into town. A bed was set up for Saul on the flat roof[q] of Samuel's house, [26]and Saul slept there.

About sunrise the next morning,[r] Samuel called up to Saul on the roof, "Time to get up! I'll help you get started on your way."

Saul got up. He and Samuel left together [27]and had almost reached the edge of town

---

[m]9.5 *Zuph:* Samuel's father Elkanah was from the Zuph clan.   [n]9.11 *water:* Towns were often built on a hill near a source of water, which would often be down in the valley outside of the town. It was usually the job of women to get water for their family.   [o]9.16 *olive oil:* Olive oil was poured on the head of someone who was chosen to be a priest, a prophet, or a king.
[p]9.20 *Everything . . . family:* Or "You and your family are what all Israel wants."   [q]9.25 *roof:* Guests often slept on the flat roof of their host's house, where it was cool and breezy.   [r]9.25,26 *was set . . . morning:* One ancient translation; Hebrew "Samuel spoke with Saul on the flat roof of his house. They got up early the next morning, around sunrise, and . . . "

when Samuel stopped and said, "Have your servant go on. Stay here with me for a few minutes, and I'll tell you what God has told me."

Samuel Tells Saul He Will Be King

10 After the servant had gone, [1]Samuel took a small jar of olive oil and poured it on Saul's head. Then he kissed[s] Saul and told him:

The LORD has chosen you to be the leader and ruler of his people.[t] [2]When you leave me today, you'll meet two men near Rachel's tomb at Zelzah in the territory of Benjamin. They'll tell you, "The donkeys you've been looking for have been found. Your father has forgotten about them, and now he's worrying about you! He's wondering how he can find you."

> *Faith grows richer and more abundant as you feel God's Spirit guiding and enhancing your life.*
> MRS. NORMAN VINCENT PEALE

[3]Go on from there until you reach the big oak tree at Tabor, where you'll meet three men on their way to worship God at Bethel. One of them will be leading three young goats, another will be carrying three round loaves of bread, and the last one will be carrying a clay jar of wine. [4]After they greet you, they'll give you two loaves of bread.

[5]Next, go to Gibeah,[u] where the Philistines have an army camp. As you're going into the town, you'll meet a group of prophets coming down from the place of worship. They'll be going along prophesying while others are walking in front of them, playing small harps, small drums, and flutes. [6]The Spirit of the LORD will suddenly take control of you.[v] You'll become a different person and start prophesying right along with them. [7]After these things happen, do whatever you think is right! God will help you.

[8]Then you should go to Gilgal. I'll come a little later, so wait for me. It may even take a week for me to get there, but when I come, I'll offer sacrifices and offerings to the LORD. I'll also tell you what to do next.

Saul Goes Back Home

[9]As Saul turned around to leave Samuel, God made Saul feel like a different person. That same day, everything happened just as Samuel had said. [10]When Saul arrived at Gibeah, a group of prophets met him. The Spirit of God suddenly took control of him,[w] and right there in the middle of the group he began prophesying.

[11]Some people who had known Saul for a long time saw that he was speaking and behaving like a prophet. They said to each other, "What's happened? How can Saul be a prophet?"

[12]"Why not?" one of them answered. "Saul has as much right to be a prophet as anyone else!"[x] That's why everyone started saying, "How can Saul be a prophet?"

[13]After Saul stopped prophesying, he went to the place of worship.

[14]Later, Saul's uncle asked him, "Where have you been?"

Saul answered, "Looking for the donkeys. We couldn't find them, so we went to talk with Samuel."

[15]"And what did he tell you?" Saul's uncle asked.

[16]Saul answered, "He told us the donkeys had been found." But Saul didn't mention that Samuel had chosen him to be king.

---

[s]10.1 *kissed:* Relatives or close friends often greeted one another with a kiss. But this may have been a ceremonial kiss after Samuel poured oil on Saul's head to show that he was to be the king. [t]10.1 *people:* One ancient translation adds "You will rule the LORD's people and save them from their enemies who are all around them. These things will prove that what I say is true." [u]10.5 *Gibeah:* The Hebrew text has "Gibeah of God," which may or may not have been the same Gibeah as Saul's hometown. [v]10.6 *take . . . you:* Or "will take control of you in a powerful way." [w]10.10 *suddenly . . . him:* Or "came over him in a powerful way." [x]10.12 *Why not . . . anyone else:* Or "Sure he is! He's probably the leader of the prophets!" or "How can he be? Those prophets are nobodies!"

The LORD Shows Israel that Saul Will Be King

¹⁷Samuel sent messengers to tell the Israelites to come to Mizpah and meet with the LORD. ¹⁸When everyone had arrived, Samuel said:

The LORD God of Israel told me to remind you that he had rescued you from the Egyptians and from the other nations that abused you.

¹⁹God has rescued you from your troubles and hard times. But you have rejected your God and have asked for a king. Now each tribe and clan must come near the place of worship so the LORD can choose a king.

²⁰Samuel brought each tribe, one after the other, to the altar, and the LORD chose the Benjamin tribe. ²¹Next, Samuel brought each clan of Benjamin there, and the LORD chose the Matri clan. Finally, Saul the son of Kish was chosen. But when they looked for him, he was nowhere to be found.

²²The people prayed, "Our LORD, is Saul here?"

"Yes," the LORD answered, "he is hiding behind the baggage."

²³The people ran and got Saul and brought him into the middle of the crowd. He was more than a head taller than anyone else. ²⁴"Look closely at the man the LORD has chosen!" Samuel told the crowd. "There is no one like him!"

The crowd shouted, "Long live the king!"

²⁵Samuel explained the rights and duties of a king and wrote them all in a book. He put the book in a temple building at one of the places where the LORD was worshiped. Then Samuel sent everyone home.

²⁶God had encouraged some young men to become followers of Saul, and when he returned to his hometown of Gibeah, they went with him. ²⁷But some worthless fools said, "How can someone like Saul rescue us from our enemies?" They did not want Saul to be their king, and so they didn't bring him any gifts. But Saul kept calm.

Saul Rescues the Town of Jabesh in Gilead

11 About this time,^y King Nahash of Ammon came with his army and surrounded the town of Jabesh in Gilead. The people who lived there told Na-

hash, "If you will sign a peace treaty with us, you can be our ruler, and we will pay taxes to you."

²Nahash answered, "Sure, I'll sign a treaty! But not before I insult Israel by poking out the right eye of every man who lives in Jabesh."

³The town leaders said, "Give us seven days so we can send messengers everywhere in Israel to ask for help. If no one comes here to save us, we will surrender to you."

⁴Some of the messengers went to Gibeah, Saul's hometown. They told what was happening at Jabesh, and everyone in Gibeah started crying. ⁵Just then, Saul came in from the fields, walking behind his oxen.

"Why is everyone crying?" Saul asked.

They told him what the men from Jabesh had said. ⁶Then the Spirit of God suddenly took control of Saul and made him furious. ⁷Saul killed two of his oxen, cut them up in pieces, and gave the pieces to the^z messengers. He told them to show the pieces to everyone in Israel and say, "Saul and Samuel are getting an army together. Come and join them. If you don't, this is what will happen to your oxen!"

The LORD made the people of Israel terribly afraid. So all the men came together ⁸at Bezek. Saul had them organized and counted. There were three hundred thousand from Israel and thirty thousand^a from Judah.

⁹Saul and his officers sent the messengers back to Jabesh with this promise: "We will rescue you tomorrow afternoon." The messengers went back to the people at Jabesh and told them that they were going to be rescued.

Everyone was encouraged! ¹⁰So they told the Ammonites, "We will surrender to you tomorrow, and then you can do whatever you want to."

¹¹The next day, Saul divided his army into three groups and attacked before day-

---

^y10.27—11.1 *But Saul . . . time:* The Standard Hebrew Text; the Dead Sea Scrolls add "King Nahash of Ammon was making the people of Gad and Reuben miserable. He was poking out everyone's right eye, and no one in Israel could stop him. He had poked out the right eye of every Israelite man who lived east of the Jordan River. Only seven thousand men had escaped from the Ammonites, and they had gone into the town of Jabesh in Gilead. About a month later . . . ," ^z11.7 *the:* Or "some other." ^a11.8 *three hundred thousand . . . thirty thousand:* The Dead Sea Scrolls and some ancient translations have different numbers.

light. They started killing Ammonites and kept it up until afternoon. A few Ammonites managed to escape, but they were scattered far from each other.

¹²The Israelite soldiers went to Samuel and demanded, "Where are the men who said they didn't want Saul to be king? Bring them to us, and we will put them to death!"

¹³"No you won't!" Saul told them. "The LORD rescued Israel today, and no one will be put to death."

Saul Is Accepted as King

¹⁴"Come on!" Samuel said. "Let's go to Gilgal and make an agreement that Saul will continue to be our king."

¹⁵Everyone went to the place of worship at Gilgal, where they agreed that Saul would be their king. Saul and the people sacrificed animals to ask for the LORD's blessing,ᵇ and they had a big celebration.

Samuel's Farewell Speech

12 Samuel told the Israelites: I have given you a king, just as you asked. ²You have seen how I have led you ever since I was a young man. I'm already old. My hair is gray, and my own sons are grown. Now you must see how well your king will lead you.

³Let me ask this. Have I ever taken anyone's ox or donkey or forced you to give me anything? Have I ever hurt anyone or taken a bribe to give an unfair decision? Answer me so the LORD and his chosen king can hear you. And if I have done any of these things, I will give it all back.

⁴"No," the Israelites answered. "You've never cheated us in any way!"

⁵Samuel said, "The LORD and his chosen king are witnesses to what you have said."

"That's true," they replied.

⁶Then Samuel told them:

The LORD brought your ancestors out of Egypt and chose Moses and Aaron to be your leaders. ⁷Now the LORD will be your judge. So stand here and listen, while I remind you how often the LORD has saved you and your ancestors from your enemies.

⁸After Jacob went to Egypt, your ancestors cried out to the LORD for

help, and he sent Moses and Aaron. They led your ancestors out of Egypt and had them settle in this land. ⁹But your ancestors forgot the LORD, so he let them be defeated by the Philistines, the king of Moab, and Sisera, the commander of Hazor's army.

¹⁰Again your ancestors cried out to the LORD for help. They said, "We have sinned! We stopped worshiping you, our LORD, and started worshiping Baal and Astarte. But now, if you rescue us from our enemies, we will worship you."

God proves his faithfulness to us, over and over.
CAROL KENT

¹¹The LORD sent Gideon,ᶜ Bedan, Jephthah, and Samuel to rescue you from your enemies, and you didn't have to worry about being attacked. ¹²Then you saw that King Nahash of Ammon was going to attack you. And even though the LORD your God is your king, you told me, "This time it's different. We want a king to rule us!"

¹³You asked for a king, and you chose one. Now he stands here where all of you can see him. But it was really the LORD who made him your king. ¹⁴If you and your king want to be followers of the LORD, you must worship himᵈ and do what he says. Don't be stubborn! ¹⁵If you're stubborn and refuse to obey the LORD, he will turn against you and your king.ᵉ

¹⁶Just stand here and watch the

ᵇ11.15 *sacrificed . . . blessing:* This kind of sacrifice is described in Leviticus 3; 7.11-36; 19.5-8. People who offered these sacrifices were allowed to eat most of the meat, and they could invite others to share it with them. ᶜ12.11 *Gideon:* The Hebrew text has "Jerubbaal," another name for "Gideon." ᵈ12.14 *If . . . him:* Or "If you and your king want things to go well for you, then you must worship the LORD." ᵉ12.15 *and your king:* One ancient translation; Hebrew "and your ancestors" or "as he was against your ancestors."

LORD show his mighty power. [17]Isn't this the dry season?[j] I'm going to ask the LORD to send a thunderstorm. When you see it, you will realize how wrong you were to ask for a king.

[18]Samuel prayed, and that same day the LORD sent a thunderstorm. Everyone was afraid of the LORD and of Samuel. [19]They told Samuel, "Please, pray to the LORD your God for us! We don't want to die. We have sinned many times in the past, and we were very wrong to ask for a king."

[20]Samuel answered:

Even though what you did was wrong, you don't need to be afraid. But you must always follow the LORD and worship him with all your heart. [21]Don't worship idols! They don't have any power, and they can't help you or save you when you're in trouble. [22]But the LORD has chosen you to be his own people. He will always take care of you so that everyone will know how great he is.

[23]I would be disobeying the LORD if I stopped praying for you! I will always teach you how to live right. [24]You also must obey the LORD—you must worship him with all your heart and remember the great things he has done for you. [25]But if you and your king do evil, the LORD will wipe you out.

Saul Disobeys the LORD

13 Saul was a young man[g] when he became king, and he ruled Israel for two years. [2]Then[h] he chose three thousand men from Israel to be full-time soldiers and sent everyone else[i] home. Two thousand of these troops stayed with him in the hills around Michmash and Bethel. The other thousand were stationed with Jonathan[j] at Gibeah[k] in the territory of Benjamin.

[3]Jonathan led an attack on the Philistine army camp at Geba.[l] The Philistine camp was destroyed, but[m] the other Philistines heard what had happened. Then Saul told his messengers, "Go to every village in the country. Give a signal with the trumpet, and when the people come together, tell them what has happened."

[4]The messengers then said to the people of Israel, "Saul has destroyed the Philistine army camp at Geba."[n] Now the Philistines really hate Israel, so every town and village must send men to join Saul's army at Gilgal."

[5]The Philistines called their army together to fight Israel. They had three thousand[o] chariots, six thousand cavalry, and as many foot soldiers as there are grains of sand on the beach. They went to Michmash and set up camp there east of Beth-Aven.[p]

[6]The Israelite army realized that they were outnumbered and were going to lose the battle. Some of the Israelite men hid in caves or in clumps of bushes,[q] and some ran to places where they could hide among large rocks. Others hid in tombs[r] or in deep dry pits. [7]Still others[s] went to Gad and Gilead on the other side of the Jordan River.

Saul stayed at Gilgal. His soldiers were shaking with fear, [8]and they were starting to run off and leave him. Saul waited there seven days, just as Samuel had ordered him to do,[t] but Samuel did not come. [9]Finally, Saul commanded, "Bring me some animals, so we can offer sacrifices to please the LORD and ask for his help."

Saul killed one of the animals, [10]and just as he was placing it on the altar, Samuel arrived. Saul went out to welcome him.

[11]"What have you done?" Samuel asked.

Saul answered, "My soldiers were leaving in all directions, and you didn't come when

---

[j]12.17 *the dry season*: The Hebrew text has "time for wheat harvest," which was usually in the spring, the beginning of the dry season.   [g]13.1 *a young man*: One possible meaning for the difficult Hebrew text; several manuscripts of one ancient translation have "thirty years old."   [h]13.1,2 *for . . . Then*: One possible meaning for the difficult Hebrew text.   [i]13.2 *everyone else*: People who were not full-time soldiers, but fought together with the army when the nation was in danger.   [j]13.2 *Jonathan*: Saul's son (see verse 16).   [k]13.2 *Michmash . . . Bethel . . . Gibeah*: These three towns form a triangle, with Bethel to the north.   [l]13.3 *Geba*: Geba was between Gibeah and Michmash.   [m]13.3 *led an attack . . . destroyed, but*: Or "killed the Philistine military governor who lived at Geba, and . . ."   [n]13.4 *destroyed . . . Geba*: Or "killed the Philistine military governor who lived at Geba."   [o]13.5 *three thousand*: Some ancient translations; Hebrew "thirty thousand."   [p]13.5 *Beth-Aven*: This Beth-Aven was probably located about a mile southwest of Michmash, between Michmash and Geba.   [q]13.6 *in . . . bushes*: Or "in cracks in the rocks."   [r]13.6 *tombs*: The Hebrew word may mean a room cut into solid rock and used as a burial place, or it may mean a cellar.   [s]13.7 *Still others*: This translates a Hebrew word which may be used of wandering groups of people who sometimes became outlaws or hired soldiers (see also 14.21).   [t]13.8 *Samuel . . . to do*: See 10.8.

you were supposed to. The Philistines were gathering at Michmash, [12]and I was worried that they would attack me here at Gilgal. I hadn't offered a sacrifice to ask for the LORD's help, so I forced myself to offer a sacrifice on the altar fire."

[13]"That was stupid!" Samuel said. "You didn't obey the LORD your God. If you had obeyed him, someone from your family would always have been king of Israel. [14]But no, you disobeyed, and so the LORD won't choose anyone else from your family to be king. In fact, he has already chosen the one he wants to be the next leader of his people." [15]Then Samuel left Gilgal.

> *If I choose to follow Jesus through the pain and stand on his promises, I'll have hope — even when I don't know what's ahead.*
>
> KATHY TROCCOLI

Part of Saul's army had not deserted him, and he led them to Gibeah in Benjamin to join his other troops. Then he counted them[u] and found that he still had six hundred men. [16]Saul, Jonathan, and their army set up camp at Geba in Benjamin.

Jonathan Attacks the Philistines

The Philistine army was camped at Michmash. [17]Each day they sent out patrols to attack and rob villages and then destroy them. One patrol would go north along the road to Ophrah in the region of Shual. [18]Another patrol would go west along the road to Beth-Horon. A third patrol would go east toward the desert on the road to the ridge that overlooks Zeboim Valley.

[19]The Philistines would not allow any Israelites to learn how to make iron tools. "If we allowed that," they said, "those worthless Israelites would make swords and spears."

[20-21]Whenever the Israelites wanted to get an iron point put on a cattle prod,[v] they had to go to the Philistines. Even if they wanted to sharpen plow-blades, picks, axes,

sickles,[w] and pitchforks[x] they still had to go to them. And the Philistines charged high prices. [22]So, whenever the Israelite soldiers had to go into battle, none of them had a sword or a spear except Saul and his son Jonathan.

[23]The Philistines moved their camp to the pass at Michmash, [1-3]and Saul was in Geba[y] with his six hundred men. Saul's own tent was set up under a fruit tree[z] by the threshing place[a] at the edge of town. Ahijah was serving as priest, and one of his jobs was to get answers from the LORD for Saul. Ahijah's father was Ahitub, and his father's brother was Ichabod. Ahijah's grandfather was Phinehas, and his great-grandfather Eli had been the LORD's priest at Shiloh.

One day, Jonathan told the soldier who carried his weapons that he wanted to attack the Philistine camp on the other side of the valley. So they slipped out of the Israelite camp without anyone knowing it. Jonathan didn't even tell his father he was leaving.

[4-5]Jonathan decided to get to the Philistine camp by going through the pass that led between Shiny Cliff and Michmash to the north and Thornbush Cliff[b] and Geba to the south.

[6]Jonathan and the soldier who carried his weapons talked as they went toward the Philistine camp. "It's just the two of us against all those godless men," Jonathan said. "But the LORD can help a few soldiers win a battle just as easily as he can help a whole army. Maybe the LORD will help us win this battle."

[7]"Do whatever you want," the soldier answered. "I'll be right there with you."

[8]"This is what we will do," Jonathan said. "We will go across and let them see us.

[u]13.15 *Then Samuel . . . counted them*: Two ancient translations; Hebrew "Then Samuel left Gilgal and went to Gibeah in Benjamin. Saul counted his army."
[v]13.20,21 *cattle prod*: A pole used to poke cattle and make them move. [w]13.20,21 *sickles*: One ancient translation; Hebrew "plow-blades."
[x]13.20,21 *pitchforks*: One possible meaning for the difficult Hebrew text. [y]14.1-3 *Geba*: Or "Gibeah." In 13.16 and 14.5 the name "Geba" is used, while 14.2,16 have "Gibeah." In ancient Hebrew writing there is only one letter different between the two words. [z]14.1-3 *fruit tree*: Hebrew "pomegranate tree." A pomegranate is a bright red fruit that looks like an apple. [a]14.1-3 *threshing place*: Or "in Migron."
[b]14.4,5 *Shiny Cliff . . . Thornbush Cliff*: Or "Bozez Cliff . . . Seneh Cliff."

⁹If they agree to come down the hill and fight where we are, then we won't climb up to their camp. ¹⁰But we will go if they tell us to come up the hill and fight. That will mean the LORD is going to help us win."

¹¹⁻¹²Jonathan and the soldier stood at the bottom of the hill where the Philistines could see them. The Philistines said, "Look! Those worthless Israelites have crawled out of the holes where they've been hiding." Then they yelled down to Jonathan and the soldier, "Come up here, and we will teach you a thing or two!"

Jonathan turned to the soldier and said, "Follow me! The LORD is going to let us win."

¹³Jonathan crawled up the hillside with the soldier right behind him. When they got to the top, Jonathan killed the Philistines who attacked from the front, and the soldier killed those who attacked from behind.ᶜ ¹⁴Before they had gone a hundred feet,ᵈ they had killed about twenty Philistines.

¹⁵The whole Philistine army panicked—those in camp, those on guard duty, those in the fields, and those on raiding patrols. All of them were afraid and confused. Then God sent an earthquake, and the ground began to tremble.ᵉ

Israel Defeats the Philistines

¹⁶Saul's lookouts at Gebaᶠ saw that the Philistine army was running in every direction, like melted wax. ¹⁷Saul told his officers, "Call the roll and find out who left our camp." When they had finished, they found out that Jonathan and the soldier who carried his weapons were missing.

¹⁸At that time, Ahijah was serving as priest for the army of Israel, and Saul told him, "Come over here! Let's ask God what we should do."ᵍ ¹⁹Just as Saul finished saying this, he could see that the Philistine army camp was getting more and more confused, and he said, "Ahijah, never mind!"

²⁰Saul quickly called his army together, then led them to the Philistine camp. By this time the Philistines were so confused that they were killing each other.

²¹There were also some hired soldiersʰ in the Philistine camp, who now switched to Israel's side and fought for Saul and Jonathan.

ᶜ**14.13** *Jonathan killed . . . from behind*: Or "Jonathan attacked the Philistines with his sword, and the soldier killed those who fell to the ground wounded."
ᵈ**14.14** *a hundred feet*: One possible meaning for the difficult Hebrew text. ᵉ**14.15** *Then . . . tremble*: Or "Then the ground began to tremble, and everyone was in a terrible panic." Or "Then the ground began to tremble, and God made them all panic." ᶠ**14.16** *Geba*: See the note at 14.1-3. ᵍ**14.18** *At that time . . . should do*: One ancient translation; Hebrew "Saul told Ahijah, 'Bring the sacred chest,' because at that time it was with the army of Israel." ʰ**14.21** *hired soldiers*: See the note at 13.7.

WORK—Can I do the "Lord's work" in a secular job? If so, how?
(1 Samuel 14.1-15)

Examine who you are at work.
What is it that makes work the "Lord's work"? It's not the specific task itself, but the character of the person doing the work. Work that is supposedly the "Lord's work" can be done with a selfish heart that is laced with perfectionism, that doesn't care about others. And a "secular job" can be done with a heart for God—one that works hard, responds to those in need, and strives to bring God's presence in the workplace. Look at Jonathan, for example. His courage and character as a soldier inspired the loyalty of the soldiers who attended him.

Ask yourself: Who am I at work? Is God's presence obvious in me? Am I cooperative, or do I insist on my own way? Am I a team player rather than someone who looks for recognition? When someone asks me to do a difficult task, do I pray and give it a try instead of insisting the task is impossible?

As we learn to connect with God in the mundane moments of life, everything we do becomes the "Lord's work." (See also Ecclesiastes 2.24-26; Matthew 4.18-22; Matthew 15.10-20.)

Words To Remember: *"Follow me! The LORD is going to let us win."*—1 Samuel 14.11,12

[22]Many Israelites had been hiding in the hill country of Ephraim. And when they heard that the Philistines were running away, they came out of hiding and joined in chasing the Philistines.

[23-24]So the LORD helped Israel win the battle that day.

Saul's Curse on Anyone Who Eats

Saul had earlier told his soldiers, "I want to get even with those Philistines by sunset. If any of you eat before then, you will be under a curse!" So he made them swear not to eat.

By the time the fighting moved past Beth-Aven,[i] the Israelite troops were weak from hunger. [25-26]The army and the people who lived nearby had gone into a forest, and they came to a place where honey was dripping on the ground.[j] But no one ate any of it, because they were afraid of being put under the curse.

[27]Jonathan did not know about Saul's warning to the soldiers. So he dipped the end of his walking stick in the honey and ate some with his fingers. He felt stronger and more alert. [28]Then a soldier told him, "Your father swore that anyone who ate food today would be put under a curse, and we agreed not to eat. That's why we're so weak."

[29]Jonathan said, "My father has caused you a lot of trouble. Look at me! I had only a little of this honey, but already I feel strong and alert. [30]I wish you had eaten some of the food the Philistines left behind. We would have been able to kill a lot more of them."

[31]By evening the Israelite army was exhausted from killing Philistines all the way from Michmash to Aijalon.[k] [32]They grabbed the food they had captured from the Philistines and started eating. They even killed sheep and cows and calves right on the ground and ate the meat without draining the blood.[l] [33]Someone told Saul, "Look! The army is disobeying the LORD by eating meat before the blood drains out."

"You're right," Saul answered. "They are being unfaithful to the LORD! Hurry! Roll a big rock over here."[m] [34]Then tell everyone in camp to bring their cattle and lambs to me. They can kill the animals on this rock,[n] then eat the meat. That way no one will disobey the LORD by eating meat with blood still in it."

That night the soldiers brought their cat-

tle over to the big rock and killed them there. [35]It was the first altar Saul had built for offering sacrifices to the LORD.[o]

The Army Rescues Jonathan

[36]Saul said, "Let's attack the Philistines again while it's still dark. We can fight them all night. Let's kill them and take everything they own!"

The people answered, "We will do whatever you want."

"Wait!" Ahijah the priest said. "Let's ask God what we should do."

[37]Saul asked God, "Should I attack the Philistines? Will you help us win?"

This time God did not answer. [38]Saul called his army officers together and said, "We have to find out what sin has kept God from answering. [39]I swear by the living LORD that whoever sinned must die, even if it turns out to be my own son Jonathan."

No one said a word.

[40]Saul told his army, "You stand on that side of the priest, and Jonathan and I will stand on the other side."

Everyone agreed.

[41]Then Saul prayed, "Our LORD, God of Israel, why haven't you answered me today? Please show us who sinned. Was it my son Jonathan and I, or was it your people Israel?"[p]

The answer came back that Jonathan or Saul had sinned, not the army. [42]Saul told Ahijah, "Now ask the LORD to decide between Jonathan and me."

The answer came back that Jonathan had sinned. [43]"Jonathan," Saul exclaimed, "tell me what you did!"

"I dipped the end of my walking stick in some honey and ate a little. Now you say I have to die!"

[44]"Yes, Jonathan. I swear to God that you must die."

---

[i]14.23,24 *Beth-Aven*: See the note at 13.5.
[j]14.25,26 *The army . . . ground*: One possible meaning for the difficult Hebrew text. [k]14.31 *Aijalon*: About 20 miles west of Michmash. [l]14.32 *blood*: The Israelites were supposed to drain the blood from a butchered animal before the meat was cooked and eaten (see Genesis 9.4; Leviticus 17.11; Deuteronomy 12.23).
[m]14.33 *over here*: One ancient translation; Hebrew "today." [n]14.34 *kill . . . rock*: That is, up off the ground so the blood could drain out. [o]14.35 *offering sacrifices to the LORD*: Even when animals were killed for food, it was often done as a sacrifice to the LORD.
[p]14.41 *why . . . Israel*: One ancient translation; Hebrew "give me an answer."

45“No!” the soldiers shouted. “God helped Jonathan win the battle for us. We won’t let you kill him. We swear to the LORD that we won’t let you kill him or even lay a hand on him!” So the army kept Saul from killing Jonathan.

46Saul stopped hunting down the Philistines, and they went home.

Saul Fights His Enemies

47-48When Saul became king, the Moabites, the Ammonites, the Edomites, the kings of Zobah, the Philistines, and the Amalekites had all been robbing the Israelites. Saul fought back against these enemies and stopped them from robbing Israel. He was a brave commander and always won his battles.[q]

Saul’s Family

49-51Saul’s wife was Ahinoam, the daughter of Ahimaaz. They had three sons: Jonathan, Ishvi,[r] and Malchishua. They also had two daughters: The older one was Merab, and the younger one was Michal.

Abner, Saul’s cousin, was the commander of the army. Saul’s father Kish and Abner’s father Ner were sons of Abiel.

War with the Philistines

52Saul was at war with the Philistines for as long as he lived. Whenever he found a good warrior or a brave man, Saul made him join his army.

Saul Disobeys the LORD

15 One day, Samuel told Saul: The LORD had me choose you to be king of his people, Israel. Now listen to this message from the LORD: 2“When the Israelites were on their way out of Egypt, the nation of Amalek attacked them. I am the LORD All-Powerful, and now I am going to make Amalek pay!

3“Go and attack the Amalekites! Destroy them and all their possessions. Don’t have any pity. Kill their men, women, children, and even their babies. Slaughter their cattle, sheep, camels, and donkeys.”

4Saul sent messengers who told every town and village to send men to join the army at Telaim. There were two hundred ten thousand troops in all, and ten thousand of these were from Judah. Saul organized them, 5then led them to a valley near one of the towns in[s] Amalek, where they got ready to make a surprise attack. 6Some Kenites lived nearby, and Saul told them, “Your people were kind to our nation when we left Egypt, and I don’t want you to get killed when I wipe out the Amalekites. Leave here and stay away from them.”

The Kenites left, 7and Saul attacked the Amalekites from Havilah[t] to Shur, which is just east of Egypt. 8Every Amalekite was killed except King Agag. 9Saul and his army let Agag live, and they also spared the best sheep and cattle. They didn’t want to destroy anything of value, so they only killed the animals that were worthless or weak.[u]

The LORD Rejects Saul

10The LORD told Samuel, 11“Saul has stopped obeying me, and I’m sorry that I made him king.”

Samuel was angry, and he cried out in prayer to the LORD all night. 12Early the next morning he went to talk with Saul. Someone told him, “Saul went to Carmel, where he had a monument built so everyone would remember his victory. Then he left for Gilgal.”

13Samuel finally caught up with Saul,[v] and Saul told him, “I hope the LORD will bless you! I have done what the LORD told me.”

14“Then why,” Samuel asked, “do I hear sheep and cattle?”

15“The army took them from the Amalekites,” Saul explained. “They kept the best sheep and cattle, so they could sacrifice them to the LORD your God. But we destroyed everything else.”

16“Stop!” Samuel said. “Let me tell you what the LORD told me last night.”

---

[q]**14.47,48** *won his battles*: One ancient translation; Hebrew “hurt them.” [r]**14.49-51** *Ishvi*: Also known as Eshbaal (see 1 Chronicles 8.33; 9.39) and Ishbosheth (see 2 Samuel 2.8-13; 3.8-15; 4.5-12). [s]**15.5** *one . . . in*: Or “the town of.” [t]**15.7** *from Havilah*: Or “from the valley” (see 15.5). [u]**15.9** *animals . . . weak*: One possible meaning for the difficult Hebrew text.
[v]**15.13** *Saul*: One ancient translation adds “Saul had sacrificed to the LORD the best animals they had taken from Amalek, when Samuel came up to him . . .”

"All right," Saul answered.

[17]Samuel continued, "You may not think you're very important, but the LORD chose you to be king, and you are in charge of the tribes of Israel. [18]When the LORD sent you on this mission, he told you to wipe out those worthless Amalekites. [19]Why didn't you listen to the LORD? Why did you keep the animals and make him angry?"

[20]"But I did listen to the LORD!" Saul answered. "He sent me on a mission, and I went. I captured King Agag and destroyed his nation. [21]All the animals were going to be destroyed[w] anyway. That's why the army brought the best sheep and cattle to Gilgal as sacrifices to the LORD your God."

[22]"Tell me," Samuel said. "Does the LORD really want sacrifices and offerings? No! He doesn't want your sacrifices. He wants you to obey him. [23]Rebelling against God or disobeying him because you are proud is just as bad as worshiping idols or asking them for advice. You refused to do what God told you, so God has decided that you can't be king."

[24]"I have sinned," Saul admitted. "I disobeyed both you and the LORD. I was afraid of the army, and I listened to them instead. [25]Please forgive me and come back with me so I can worship the LORD."

[26]"No!" Samuel replied, "You disobeyed the LORD, and I won't go back with you. Now the LORD has said that you can't be king of Israel any longer."

[27]As Samuel turned to go, Saul grabbed the edge of Samuel's robe. It tore! [28]Samuel said, "The LORD has torn the kingdom of Israel away from you today, and he will give it to someone who is better than you. [29]Besides, the eternal[x] God of Israel isn't a human being. He doesn't tell lies or change his mind."

[30]Saul said, "I did sin, but please honor me in front of the leaders of the army and the people of Israel. Come back with me, so I can worship the LORD your God."

[31]Samuel followed Saul back, and Saul worshiped the LORD. [32]Then Samuel shouted, "Bring me King Agag of Amalek!"

Agag came in chains,[y] and he was saying to himself, "Surely they won't kill me now."[z]

[33]But Samuel said, "Agag, you have snatched children from their mothers' arms and killed them. Now your mother will be without children." Then Samuel chopped Agag to pieces at the place of worship in Gilgal.

[34]Samuel went home to Ramah, and Saul returned to his home in Gibeah. [35]Even though Samuel felt sad about Saul, Samuel never saw him again.

---

[w]15.21 *animals . . . destroyed*: The Hebrew means things that were set aside for God. They could not be used for anything else, so they had to be destroyed. [x]15.29 *eternal*: Or "glorious." [y]15.32 *in chains*: One possible meaning for the difficult Hebrew text. [z]15.32 *Surely . . . now*: Hebrew; one ancient translation "It would have been better to die in battle!"

Personal *Concerns*—How can I learn to set priorities? *(1 Samuel 15.10-35)*

Practice zero-based prioritizing.
Life is so overwhelming that sometimes it helps to start from zero—to cut out everything and then ask yourself, *What must I do? What is God absolutely urging me to do?*

Pretend for a moment that you are looking at your calendar or datebook. In your imagination, erase every single thing you should do. Look at that empty space and ask God to make it clear what you need to do to fulfill his purpose for you. Ask him, "What one or two tasks do you want me to do?" (Consider the simplest commands: to love God with all your self and to love others.)

Then review each of the other items. With rigorous honesty examine your motives. Ask yourself, *Why do I do this? To please others? Because I want to be admired?* (The latter one was one of King Saul's driving motivations, 15.30.) Which tasks do you carry out because God has convinced you that they are important? If you can't tell, put all those items on hold and ask God to reveal your motives and his priorities to you. (See also Genesis 22.1-19; Haggai 2.6-9; Luke 10.38-42; Revelation 2.1-7.)

Words To Remember: *"Does the LORD really want sacrifices and offerings? No! He doesn't want your sacrifices. He wants you to obey him."*—1 Samuel 15.22

The LORD Chooses David To Be King

16 The LORD was sorry he had made Saul the king of Israel. ¹One day he said, "Samuel, I've rejected Saul, and I refuse to let him be king any longer. Stop feeling sad about him. Put some olive oil*ᵃ* in a small container*ᵇ* and go visit a man named Jesse, who lives in Bethlehem. I've chosen one of his sons to be my king."

²Samuel answered, "If I do that, Saul will find out and have me killed."

"Take a calf with you," the LORD replied. "Tell everyone that you've come to offer it as a sacrifice to me, ³then invite Jesse to the sacrifice.*ᶜ* When I show you which one of his sons I have chosen, pour the olive oil on his head."

⁴Samuel did what the LORD told him and went to Bethlehem. The town leaders went to meet him, but they were terribly afraid and asked, "Is this a friendly visit?"

⁵"Yes, it is!" Samuel answered. "I've come to offer a sacrifice to the LORD. Get yourselves ready*ᵈ* to take part in the sacrifice and come with me." Samuel also invited Jesse and his sons to come to the sacrifice, and he got them ready to take part.

⁶When Jesse and his sons arrived, Samuel noticed Jesse's oldest son, Eliab. "He has to be the one the LORD has chosen," Samuel said to himself.

⁷But the LORD told him, "Samuel, don't think Eliab is the one just because he's tall and handsome. He isn't the one I've chosen. People judge others by what they look like, but I judge people by what is in their hearts."

⁸Jesse told his son Abinadab to go over to Samuel, but Samuel said, "No, the LORD hasn't chosen him."

⁹Next, Jesse sent his son Shammah to him, and Samuel said, "The LORD hasn't chosen him either."

¹⁰Jesse had all seven of his sons go over to Samuel. Finally, Samuel said, "Jesse, the LORD hasn't chosen any of these young men. ¹¹Do you have any more sons?"

---

*ᵃ*16.1 *olive oil:* See the note at 9.16. *ᵇ*16.1 *small container:* Hebrew "horn"; animal horns were sometimes hollowed out and used as containers. *ᶜ*16.3 *sacrifice:* A sacrifice often involved a dinner where the meat from the sacrificed animal would be served. *ᵈ*16.5 *Get yourselves ready:* The people of Israel sometimes had to perform certain ceremonies to make themselves acceptable to God.

Friendship—How can I keep from comparing myself with my friends?
(1 Samuel 16.1-13)

Realize you don't know others the way God knows them.
As you look around at your group of friends, you may notice one has a great body or personality, another has a great job, still another has a great family. One may be categorized by others as a "winner" and another as a "loser."

But society's standards are confusing. The "best" person is the one who makes the most, who has a spouse who treats her like a queen, or whose kids are on the honor roll. Our culture does not value what's most important: the quiet simplicity of knowing God, and the strength and peace such a relationship gives us.

Imagine the surprise of David's family when Samuel wanted to see the runt who had been out in the fields singing to himself (we now call those songs *psalms*). Who, him? Apparently, no one would have guessed David was a candidate because they didn't even bring him in to meet Samuel.

Outwardly, David may have seemed like an unlikely choice, but God saw much deeper than David's relatives and friends could. We can't read someone else's motives; we can't know her pain or imagine her dreams. There is so much we don't know about others—or God's plans for them—that it makes no sense for us to compare ourselves to them. Instead, we need to focus on purifying our own motives and giving God our dreams. Then who knows what glorious things God may bring into our lives! (See also Numbers 6.22-27; Mark 10.29-31,35-45.)

Words To Remember: *"People judge others by what they look like, but I judge people by what is in their hearts."*—1 Samuel 16.7

"Yes," Jesse answered. "My youngest son David is out taking care of the sheep."

"Send for him!" Samuel said. "We won't start the ceremony until he gets here."

¹²Jesse sent for David. He was a healthy, good-looking boy with a sparkle in his eyes. As soon as David came, the LORD told Samuel, "He's the one! Get up and pour the olive oil on his head."ᵉ

¹³Samuel poured the oil on David's head while his brothers watched. At that moment, the Spirit of the LORD took control of David and stayed with him from then on.

Samuel returned home to Ramah.

David Plays the Harp for Saul

¹⁴The Spirit of the LORD had left Saul, and an evil spirit from the LORD was terrifying him. ¹⁵"It's an evil spirit from God that's frightening you," Saul's officials told him. ¹⁶"Your Majesty, let us go and look for someone who is good at playing the harp. He can play for you whenever the evil spirit from God bothers you, and you'll feel better."

¹⁷"All right," Saul answered. "Find me someone who is good at playing the harp and bring him here."

¹⁸"A man named Jesse who lives in Bethlehem has a son who can play the harp," one official said. "He's a brave warrior, he's

good-looking, he can speak well, and the LORD is with him."

¹⁹Saul sent a message to Jesse: "Tell your son David to leave your sheep and come here to me."

²⁰Jesse loaded a donkey with bread and a goatskin full of wine,ᶠ then he told David to take the donkey and a young goat to Saul. ²¹David went to Saul and started working for him. Saul liked him so much that he put David in charge of carrying his weapons. ²²Not long after this, Saul sent another message to Jesse: "I really like David. Please let him stay with me."

²³Whenever the evil spirit from God bothered Saul, David would play his harp. Saul would relax and feel better, and the evil spirit would go away.

Goliath Challenges Israel's Army

17 The Philistines got ready for war and brought their troops together to attack the town of Socoh in Judah. They set up camp at Ephes-Dammim, between Socoh and Azekah.ᵍ ²⁻³King Saul

---

ᵉ**16.12** *olive oil on his head:* See the note at 9.16.
ᶠ**16.20** *wine:* Wine was sometimes kept in bottles made of goatskin sewn up with the fur on the outside.
ᵍ**17.1** *Socoh and Azekah:* Socoh was controlled by the Israelites, while Azekah was in Philistine hands.

---

*Spiritual*Life—**How can I learn to appreciate and use the talents and gifts God has given me?** (1 Samuel 16.14-23)

Look for open doors.

After David was anointed king, you would have expected him to enter the royal court in some executive capacity, right? No, he gained entrance as a harp player! Who would have guessed God would use his harp-playing skills that way? In the same way, we can look at our knack for gardening, our love for small children, or our ability to argue a court case, and wonder how God can use it.

But our gifts and talents *can* open doors. Picture the frustrated neighbor who asks you to help her pick out perennials for her backyard. Seeing you as a fair, caring woman who understands how living things thrive and what makes a garden take shape can give real texture to the compassion and truth of the gospel. Or a haggard mother may notice how you deal with her children so affectionately at preschool. Or a vengeful plaintiff may notice you argue the case fairly and to his benefit, but you don't leave the defendant destitute. The use of your gifts can show the gospel at work in a genuine way.

When we lay our talents and gifts before God, we need to ask: *Show me how to use this talent simply for the love of you!* Then we must wait with alert eyes to see what God will do. In time, someone will say, "Find me someone who is good at . . ." (16.17) and that will be your open door. (See also 1 Chronicles 15.1—16.3; 1 Corinthians 14.1-25.)

Words To Remember: *"Find me someone who is good at playing the harp and bring him here. . . . The LORD is with him."*—1 Samuel 16.17,18

and the Israelite army set up camp on a hill overlooking Elah Valley, and they got ready to fight the Philistine army that was on a hill on the other side of the valley.

⁴The Philistine army had a hero named Goliath who was from the town of Gath and was over nine feet[h] tall. ⁵⁻⁶He wore a bronze helmet and had bronze armor to protect his chest and legs. The chest armor alone weighed about one hundred twenty-five pounds. He carried a bronze sword strapped on his back, ⁷and his spear was so big that the iron spearhead alone weighed more than fifteen pounds. A soldier always walked in front of Goliath to carry his shield.

⁸Goliath went out and shouted to the army of Israel:

Why are you lining up for battle? I'm the best soldier in our army, and all of you are in Saul's army. Choose your best soldier to come out and fight me! ⁹If he can kill me, our people will be your slaves. But if I kill him, your people will be our slaves. ¹⁰Here and now I challenge Israel's whole army! Choose someone to fight me!

¹¹Saul and his men heard what Goliath said, but they were so frightened of Goliath that they couldn't do a thing.

David Meets King Saul

¹²David's father Jesse was an old man, who belonged to the Ephrath clan and lived in Bethlehem in Judah. Jesse had eight sons: ¹³⁻¹⁴the oldest was Eliab, the next was Abinadab, and Shammah was the third. The three of them had gone off to fight in Saul's army.

David was Jesse's youngest son. ¹⁵He took care of his father's sheep, and he went back and forth between Bethlehem and Saul's camp.

¹⁶Goliath came out and gave his challenge every morning and every evening for forty days.

¹⁷One day, Jesse told David, "Hurry and take this sack of roasted grain and these ten loaves of bread to your brothers at the army camp. ¹⁸And here are ten large chunks of cheese to take to their commanding officer. Find out how your brothers are doing and bring back something that shows that they're all right. ¹⁹They're with Saul's army, fighting the Philistines in Elah Valley."

²⁰David obeyed his father. He got up early the next morning and left someone else in charge of the sheep; then he loaded the sup-

---

[h]17.4 *over nine feet:* The Standard Hebrew Text; the Dead Sea Scrolls and some manuscripts of one ancient translation have "almost seven feet."

PARENTING&*family*—How can I nurture my child's self-worth?
(1 Samuel 17.24-54)

Invite questions.
Have you ever been in a heated discussion when a quiet child who has gone unnoticed pipes up and asks, "But what about . . . ?" or, "Why can't we just . . . ?" This child, uncluttered with all the nuances that overwhelm adults, has seen the big picture and has the courage to speak up.

Children can simplify things by asking cut-to-the-chase questions. Sometimes it's even good to approach a child and ask, "What do you think about . . . ?" Whether or not they say something profound, we are letting them know we value their opinions, that we believe they have something to contribute to the discussion.

We know we have forgotten these truths when a child asks, as David did, "Can't I even ask a question?" (17.29). As parents we need to do our best to encourage their questioning, then honor them with attention and thoughtfulness—even when there's a Goliath or two of a problem waiting to be solved. (See also Psalm 139; Luke 15.11-32; Ephesians 1.3-14; 2 Thessalonians 3.6-15.)

Words To Remember: *David answered [Goliath], "You've come out to fight me with a sword and a spear and a dagger. But I've come out to fight you in the name of the LORD All-Powerful. . . . The LORD always wins his battles, and he will help us defeat you."*—1 Samuel 17.45,47

plies and started off. He reached the army camp just as the soldiers were taking their places and shouting the battle cry. ²¹The army of Israel and the Philistine army stood there facing each other.

²²David left his things with the man in charge of supplies and ran up to the battle line to ask his brothers if they were well. ²³While David was talking with them, Goliath came out from the line of Philistines and started boasting as usual. David heard him.

²⁴When the Israelite soldiers saw Goliath, they were scared and ran off. ²⁵They said to each other, "Look how he keeps coming out to insult us. The king is offering a big reward to the man who kills Goliath. That man will even get to marry the king's daughter, and no one in his family will ever have to pay taxes again."

²⁶David asked some soldiers standing nearby, "What will a man get for killing this Philistine and stopping him from insulting our people? Who does that worthless Philistine think he is? He's making fun of the army of the living God!"

²⁷The soldiers told David what the king would give the man who killed Goliath.

²⁸David's oldest brother Eliab heard him talking with the soldiers. Eliab was angry at him and said, "What are you doing here, anyway? Who's taking care of that little flock of sheep out in the desert? You spoiled brat! You came here just to watch the fighting, didn't you?"

²⁹"Now what have I done?" David answered. "Can't I even ask a question?" ³⁰Then he turned and asked another soldier the same thing he had asked the others, and he got the same answer.

³¹Some soldiers overheard David talking, so they told Saul what David had said. Saul sent for David, and David came. ³²"Your Majesty," he said, "this Philistine shouldn't turn us into cowards. I'll go out and fight him myself!"

³³"You don't have a chance against him," Saul replied. "You're only a boy, and he's been a soldier all his life."

³⁴But David told him:

Your Majesty, I take care of my father's sheep. And when one of them is dragged off by a lion or a bear, ³⁵I go after it and beat the wild animal until it lets the sheep go. If the wild animal

turns and attacks me, I grab it by the throat and kill it.

³⁶Sir, I have killed lions and bears that way, and I can kill this worthless Philistine. He shouldn't have made fun of the army of the living God! ³⁷The LORD has rescued me from the claws of lions and bears, and he will keep me safe from the hands of this Philistine.

"All right," Saul answered, "go ahead and fight him. And I hope the LORD will help you."

³⁸Saul had his own military clothes and armor put on David, and he gave David a bronze helmet to wear. ³⁹David strapped on a sword and tried to walk around, but he was not used to wearing those things.

"I can't move with all this stuff on," David said. "I'm just not used to it."

David took off the armor ⁴⁰and picked up his shepherd's stick. He went out to a stream and picked up five smooth rocks and put them in his leather bag. Then with his sling in his hand, he went straight toward Goliath.

David Kills Goliath

⁴¹Goliath came toward David, walking behind the soldier who was carrying his shield. ⁴²When Goliath saw that David was just a healthy, good-looking boy, he made fun of him. ⁴³"Do you think I'm a dog?" Goliath asked. "Is that why you've come after me with a stick?" He cursed David in the name of the Philistine gods ⁴⁴and shouted, "Come on! When I'm finished with you, I'll feed you to the birds and wild animals!"

⁴⁵David answered:

You've come out to fight me with a sword and a spear and a dagger. But I've come out to fight you in the name of the LORD All-Powerful. He is the God of Israel's army, and you have insulted him too!

⁴⁶Today the LORD will help me defeat you. I'll knock you down and cut off your head, and I'll feed the bodies of the other Philistine soldiers to the birds and wild animals. Then the whole world will know that Israel has a real God. ⁴⁷Everybody here will see that the LORD doesn't need swords or spears to save his people. The LORD

always wins his battles, and he will help us defeat you.

[48]When Goliath started forward, David ran toward him. [49]He put a rock in his sling and swung the sling around by its straps. When he let go of one strap, the rock flew out and hit Goliath on the forehead. It cracked his skull, and he fell facedown on the ground. [50]David defeated Goliath with a sling and a rock. He killed him without even using a sword.

[51]David ran over and pulled out Goliath's sword. Then he used it to cut off Goliath's head.

When the Philistines saw what had happened to their hero, they started running away. [52]But the soldiers of Israel and Judah let out a battle cry and went after them as far as Gath[i] and Ekron. The bodies of the Philistines were scattered all along the road from Shaaraim to Gath and Ekron.

[53]When the Israelite army returned from chasing the Philistines, they took what they wanted from the enemy camp. [54]David took Goliath's head to Jerusalem, but he kept Goliath's weapons in his own tent.

David Becomes One of Saul's Officers

[55]After King Saul had watched David go out to fight Goliath, Saul turned to the commander of his army and said, "Abner, who is that young man?"

"Your Majesty," Abner answered, "I swear by your life that I don't know."

[56]"Then find out!" Saul told him.

[57]When David came back from fighting Goliath, he was still carrying Goliath's head. Abner took David to Saul, [58]and Saul asked, "Who are you?"

"I am David the son of Jesse, a loyal Israelite from Bethlehem."

18 David and Saul finished talking, and soon David and Jonathan[j] became best friends. Jonathan thought as much of David as he did of himself. [2]From that time on, Saul kept David in his service and would not let David go back to his own family.

[3]Jonathan liked David so much that they promised to always be loyal friends. [4]Jonathan took off the robe that he was wearing and gave it to David. He also gave him his military clothes,[k] his sword, his bow and arrows, and his belt.

[5]David was a success in everything that Saul sent him to do, and Saul made him a high officer in his army. That pleased everyone, including Saul's other officers.

Friends whom we allow to share our grief also share in our joy when God answers.

VIRELLE KIDDER

Saul Becomes David's Enemy

[6]David had killed Goliath, the battle was over, and the Israelite army set out for home. As the army went along, women came out of each Israelite town to welcome King Saul. They were singing happy songs and dancing to the music of tambourines and harps. [7]They sang:

> Saul has killed
>   a thousand enemies;
> David has killed
>   ten thousand enemies!

[8]This song made Saul very angry, and he thought, "They are saying that David has killed ten times more enemies than I ever did. Next they will want to make him king." [9]Saul never again trusted David.

[10]The next day the LORD let an evil spirit take control of Saul, and he began acting like a crazy man inside his house. David came to play the harp for Saul as usual, but this time Saul had a spear in his hand. [11]Saul thought, "I'll pin David to the wall." He threw the spear at David twice, but David dodged and got away both times.

[12]Saul was afraid of David, because the LORD was helping David and was no longer helping him. [13]Saul put David in charge of a thousand soldiers and sent him out to fight. [14]The LORD helped David, and he and his soldiers always won their battles. [15]This made Saul even more afraid of David. [16]But everyone else in Judah and Israel was

---

[i]**17.52** *Gath:* One ancient translation; Hebrew "a valley." [j]**18.1** *Jonathan:* Saul's oldest son (see chapter 14). [k]**18.4** *military clothes:* Or "armor."

loyal to[l] David, because he led the army in battle.

[17]One day, Saul told David, "If you'll be brave and fight the LORD's battles for me, I'll let you marry my oldest daughter Merab." But Saul was really thinking, "I don't want to kill David myself, so I'll let the Philistines do it for me."

[18]David answered, "How could I possibly marry your daughter? I'm not very important, and neither is my family."

[19]But when the time came for David to marry Saul's daughter Merab, Saul told her to marry Adriel from the town of Meholah.

[20]Saul had another daughter. Her name was Michal, and Saul found out that she was in love with David. This made Saul happy, [21]and he thought, "I'll tell David he can marry Michal, but I'll set it up so that the Philistines will kill him." He told David, "I'm going to give you a second chance to marry one of my daughters."

[22-23]Saul ordered his officials to speak to David in private, so they went to David and said, "Look, the king likes you, and all of his officials are loyal to you. Why not ask the king if you can marry his daughter Michal?"

"I'm not rich[m] or famous enough to marry princess Michal!" David answered.

[24]The officials went back to Saul and told him exactly what David had said. [25]Saul was hoping that the Philistines would kill David, and he told his officials to tell David, "The king doesn't want any silver or gold. He only wants to get even with his enemies. All you have to do is to bring back proof that you have killed a hundred Philistines!"[n] [26]The officials told David, and David wanted to marry the princess.

King Saul had set a time limit, and before it ran out, [27]David and his men left and killed two hundred Philistines. He brought back the proof and showed it to Saul, so he could marry Michal. Saul agreed to let David marry Michal. [28]Saul knew that she loved David,[o] and he also realized that the LORD was helping David. [29]But knowing those things made Saul even more afraid of David, and he was David's enemy for the rest of his life.

[30]The Philistine rulers kept coming to fight Israel, but whenever David fought them, he won. He was famous because he won more battles against the Philistines than any of Saul's other officers.

Saul Tries To Have David Killed

19 One day, Saul told his son Jonathan and his officers to kill David. But Jonathan liked David a lot, [2-3]and he warned David, "My father is trying to have you killed, so be very careful. Hide in a field tomorrow morning, and I'll bring him there. Then I'll talk to him about you, and if I find out anything, I'll let you know."

[4-5]The next morning, Jonathan reminded Saul about the many good things David had done for him. Then he said, "Why do you want to kill David? He hasn't done anything to you. He has served in your army and has always done what's best for you. He even risked his life to kill Goliath. The LORD helped Israel win a great victory that day, and it made you happy."

[6]Saul agreed and promised, "I swear by the living LORD that I won't have David killed!"

[7]Jonathan called to David and told him what Saul had said. Then he brought David to Saul, and David served in Saul's army just as he had done before.

[8]The next time there was a war with the Philistines, David fought hard and forced them to retreat.

Michal Helps David Escape

[9-10]One night, David was in Saul's home, playing the harp for him. Saul was sitting there, holding a spear, when an evil spirit from the LORD took control of him. Saul tried to pin David to the wall with the spear, but David dodged, and it stuck in the wall. David ran out of the house and escaped.

[11]Saul sent guards to watch David's house all night and then to kill him in the morning.

Michal, David's wife, told him, "If you don't escape tonight, they'll kill you tomorrow!" [12]She helped David go through a window and climb down to the ground.[p] As

[l]18.16 was loyal to: Or "loved." [m]18.22,23 not rich: It was the custom for a man to give the bride's father some silver or gold in order to marry his daughter, and it would take a large amount to marry the daughter of the king. [n]18.25 proof . . . Philistines: Hebrew "one hundred Philistine foreskins." In ancient times soldiers would sometimes cut off body parts of their dead enemies to prove how many they had killed. [o]18.28 she . . . David: Hebrew; one ancient translation "all Israel was loyal to David." [p]19.12 ground: The house was probably built into the town wall, allowing David to come down outside the wall.

David ran off, ¹³Michal put a statue in his bed. She put goat hair on its head and dressed it in some of David's clothes.

¹⁴The next morning, Saul sent guards to arrest David. But Michal told them, "David is sick."

¹⁵Saul sent the guards back and told them, "Get David out of his bed and bring him to me, so I can have him killed."

¹⁶When the guards went in, all they found in the bed was the statue with the goat hair on its head.

¹⁷"Why have you tricked me this way?" Saul asked Michal. "You helped my enemy get away!"

She answered, "He said he would kill me if I didn't help him escape!"

Samuel Helps David Escape

¹⁸Meanwhile, David went to Samuel at Ramah and told him what Saul had done. Then Samuel and David went to Prophets Village[q] and stayed there.

¹⁹Someone told Saul, "David is at Prophets Village in Ramah."

²⁰Saul sent a few soldiers to bring David back. They went to Ramah and found Samuel in charge of a group of prophets who were all prophesying. Then the Spirit of God took control of the soldiers and they started prophesying too.

> *Faith is authentic in everyday living, not just through some huge trial or mountaintop spiritual experience.*
>
> CAROLE MAYHALL

²¹When Saul heard what had happened, he sent another group of soldiers, but they prophesied the same way. He sent a third group of soldiers, but the same thing happened to them. ²²Finally, Saul left for Ramah himself. He went as far as the deep pit[r] at the town of Secu, and he asked, "Where are Samuel and David?"

"At Prophets Village in Ramah," the people answered.

²³Saul left for Ramah. But as he walked along, the Spirit of God took control of him, and he started prophesying. Then, when he reached Prophets Village, ²⁴he stripped off his clothes and prophesied in front of Samuel. He dropped to the ground and lay there naked all day and night. That's how the saying started, "Is Saul now a prophet?"

Jonathan Helps David Escape

20 David escaped from Prophets Village. Then he ran to see Jonathan and asked, "Why does your father Saul want to kill me? What have I done wrong?"

²"My father can't be trying to kill you! He never does anything without telling me about it. Why would he hide this from me? It can't be true!"

³"Jonathan, I swear it's true! But your father knows how much you like me, and he didn't want to break your heart. That's why he didn't tell you. I swear by the living LORD and by your own life that I'm only one step ahead of death."

⁴Then Jonathan said, "Tell me what to do, and I'll do it."

⁵David answered:

Tomorrow is the New Moon Festival,[s] and I'm supposed to eat dinner with your father. But instead, I'll hide in a field until the evening of the next day. ⁶If Saul wonders where I am, tell him, "David asked me to let him go to his hometown of Bethlehem, so he could take part in a sacrifice his family makes there every year."

⁷If your father says it's all right, then I'm safe. But if he gets angry, you'll know he wants to harm me. ⁸Be kind to me. After all, it was your idea to promise the LORD that we would always be loyal friends. If I've done anything wrong, kill me yourself, but don't hand me over to your father.

⁹"Don't worry," Jonathan said. "If I find out that my father wants to kill you, I'll certainly let you know."

¹⁰"How will you do that?" David asked.

---

q19.18 *Prophets Village:* Or "Naioth." r19.22 *pit:* A cistern, a large pit dug down into the rock and used for storing rainwater. s20.5 *New Moon Festival:* The first day of the month, when Israelites offered special sacrifices to the LORD and had special sacred meals.

¹¹"Let's go out to this field, and I'll tell you," Jonathan answered.

When they got there, ¹²Jonathan said:

I swear by the LORD God of Israel, that two days from now I'll know what my father is planning. Of course I'll let you know if he's friendly toward you. ¹³But if he wants to harm you, I promise to tell you and help you escape. And I ask the LORD to punish me severely if I don't keep my promise.

I pray that the LORD will bless you, just as he used to bless my father. ¹⁴⁻¹⁵Someday the LORD will wipe out all of your enemies. Then if I'm still alive, please be as kind to me as the LORD has been. But if I'm dead, be kind to my family.

¹⁶Jonathan and David made an agreement that even David's descendants would have to keep.ᵗ Then Jonathan said, "I pray that the LORD will take revenge on your descendants if they break our promise."ᵘ

¹⁷Jonathan thought as much of David as he did of himself, so he asked David to promise once more that he would be a loyal friend. ¹⁸After this Jonathan said:

Tomorrow is the New Moon Festival, and people will wonder where you are, because your place will be empty. ¹⁹By the day after tomorrow, everyone will think you've been gone a long time.ᵛ Then go to the place where you hid before and stay beside Going-Away Rock.ʷ ²⁰I'll shoot three arrows at a target off to the side of the rock, ²¹and send my servant to find the arrows.

You'll know if it's safe to come out by what I tell him. If it is safe, I swear by the living LORD that I'll say, "The arrows are on this side of you! Pick them up!" ²²But if it isn't safe, I'll say to the boy, "The arrows are farther away!" This will mean that the LORD wants you to leave, and you must go. ²³But he will always watch us to make sure that we keep the promise we made to each other.

²⁴So David hid there in the field.

During the New Moon Festival, Saul sat down to eat ²⁵by the wall, just as he always did. Jonathan sat across from him,ˣ and Abner sat next to him. But David's place was empty. ²⁶Saul didn't say anything that day, because he was thinking, "Something must have happened to make David unfit to be at

---

ᵗ20.16 Jonathan . . . keep: Or, continuing Jonathan's statement to David, "You and your descendants must not kill off my descendants."   ᵘ20.16 I pray . . . promise: Or "I pray that the LORD take revenge on you if you break our promise!"   ᵛ20.19 By . . . time: One possible meaning for the difficult Hebrew text.   ʷ20.19 Going-Away Rock: Or "Ezel Rock"; one ancient translation "that mound" (see 20.41).   ˣ20.25 sat . . . him: One ancient translation; Hebrew "stood up."

Personal *Concerns*—Sometimes I'm jealous of others. How can I get out of the jealousy/envy trap? *(1 Samuel 20)*

Nurture your friend's success.

We usually make friends with people with whom we have a lot in common, but sometimes those common interests can split us up because of competition.

Jonathan and David had a lot in common; both were fearless warriors. They could have been competitive, but instead they were "best friends" (18.1). Jonathan loved his friend David and knew the worth of true friendship—something our transient culture does not always value over advancement or accomplishments.

Don't let envy rob you of a treasured friendship—particularly if you have known each other a long time. If your friend is successful, she needs you more than ever. Others may feel jealous of her too, and try to undercut her. Jonathan remained a supportive, caring friend, willing to sacrifice his life for David. Imagine how much this must have meant to David as he was hunted by King Saul. Your successful friend needs someone she can be truly honest with, who keeps confidences, who does not want to grab anything from her, who does not set her on a pedestal. You have an opportunity to be a friend to someone who may value you as others do not. (See also Psalm 73.1-20; Jonah 4; James 3.1-12.)

Words To Remember: *I pray that the LORD will bless you.*—1 Samuel 20.13

the Festival.[y] Yes, something must have happened."

[27]The day after the New Moon Festival, when David's place was still empty, Saul asked Jonathan, "Why hasn't that son of Jesse come to eat with us? He wasn't here yesterday, and he still isn't here today!"

[28-29]Jonathan answered, "The reason David hasn't come to eat with you is that he begged me to let him go to Bethlehem. He said, 'Please let me go. My family is offering a sacrifice, and my brother told me I have to be there. Do me this favor and let me slip away to see my brothers.'"

[30]Saul was furious with Jonathan and yelled, "You're no son of mine, you traitor! I know you've chosen to be loyal to that son of Jesse. You should be ashamed of yourself! And your own mother should be ashamed that you were ever born. [31]You'll never be safe, and your kingdom will be in danger as long as that son of Jesse is alive. Turn him over to me now! He deserves to die!"

[32]"Why do you want to kill David?" Jonathan asked. "What has he done?"

[33]Saul threw his spear at Jonathan and tried to kill him. Then Jonathan was sure that his father really did want to kill David. [34]Jonathan was angry that his father had insulted David[z] so terribly. He got up, left the table, and didn't eat anything all that day.

[35]In the morning, Jonathan went out to the field to meet David. He took a servant boy along [36]and told him, "When I shoot the arrows, you run and find them for me."

The boy started running, and Jonathan shot an arrow so that it would go beyond him. [37]When the boy got near the place where the arrow had landed, Jonathan shouted, "Isn't the arrow on past you?" [38]Jonathan shouted to him again, "Hurry up! Don't stop!"

The boy picked up the arrows and brought them back to Jonathan, [39]but he had no idea about what was going on. Only Jonathan and David knew. [40]Jonathan gave his weapons to the boy and told him, "Take these back into town."

[41]After the boy had gone, David got up from beside the mound[a] and bowed very low three times. Then he and Jonathan kissed[b] each other and cried, but David cried louder. [42]Jonathan said, "Take care of yourself. And remember, we each have asked the LORD to watch and make sure that we and our descendants keep our promise forever."

David left and Jonathan went back to town.

Ahimelech Helps David

21 David went to see Ahimelech, a priest who lived in the town of Nob. Ahimelech was trembling with fear as he came out to meet David. "Why are you alone?" Ahimelech asked. "Why isn't anyone else with you?"

[2]"I'm on a mission for King Saul," David answered. "He ordered me not to tell anyone what the mission is all about, so I had my soldiers stay somewhere else. [3]Do you have any food you can give me? Could you spare five loaves of bread?"

[4]"The only bread I have is the sacred bread," the priest told David. "You can have it if your soldiers didn't sleep with women last night."[c]

> *If you always stay with what's safe, in a sense you dictate what God can do with you—he can only move you as far as you're willing to go.*
>
> MARGARET BECKER

[5]"Of course we didn't sleep with women," David answered. "I never let my men do that when we're on a mission. They have to be acceptable to worship God even when we're on a regular mission, and today we're on a special mission."

---

[y]20.26 unfit . . . Festival: During the New Moon Festival a sacred meal was served that could only be eaten by people who were properly prepared. Some of the things that could make a person unfit are listed in Leviticus 7.20, 21; 15.2, 31; 22.4-8; Deuteronomy 23.10, 11. [z]20.34 insulted David: Or "insulted him" (that is, Jonathan). [a]20.41 the mound: One ancient translation; Hebrew "from the south side." [b]20.41 kissed: A common way of greeting or saying good-by in biblical times (see Mark 14.44). [c]21.4 night: Having sex was one of the things that would make someone temporarily unfit to take part in worship or a sacred meal (see Exodus 19.15; Leviticus 15.18).

⁶The only bread the priest had was the sacred bread that he had taken from the place of worship after putting out the fresh loaves. So he gave it to David.

⁷It so happened that one of Saul's officers was there, worshiping the LORD that day. His name was Doeg the Edomite,ᵈ and he was the strongest ofᵉ Saul's shepherds.

⁸David asked Ahimelech, "Do you have a spear or a sword? I had to leave so quickly on this mission for the king that I didn't bring along my sword or any other weapons."

⁹The priest answered, "The only sword here is the one that belonged to Goliath the Philistine. You were the one who killed him in Elah Valley, and so you can take his sword if you want to. It's wrapped in a cloth behind the statue."

"It's the best sword there is," David said. "I'll take it!"

David Tries To Find Safety in Gath

¹⁰David kept on running from Saul that day until he came to Gath,ᶠ where he met with King Achish. ¹¹The officers of King Achish were also there, and they asked Achish, "Isn't David a king back in his own country? Don't the Israelites dance and sing,

> 'Saul has killed
> a thousand enemies;
> David has killed
> ten thousand enemies'?"

¹²David thought about what they were saying, and it made him afraid of Achish. ¹³So right there in front of everyone, he pretended to be insane. He acted confused and scratched up the doors of the town gate, while drooling in his beard.

¹⁴"Look at him!" Achish said to his officers. "You can see he's crazy. Why did you bring him to me? ¹⁵I have enough crazy people without your bringing another one here. Keep him away from my palace!"

People Join David

22 When David escaped from the town of Gath, he went to Adullam Cave. His brothers and the rest of his family found out where he was, and they followed him there. ²A lot of other people joined him too. Some were in trouble, others were angry or in debt, and David was soon the leader of four hundred men.

³David left Adullam Cave and went to the town of Mizpeh in Moab, where he talked with the king of Moab. "Please," David said, "let my father and mother stay with you until I find out what God will do with me." ⁴So he brought his parents to the king of Moab, and they stayed with him while David was in hiding.

⁵One day the prophet Gad told David, "Don't stay here! Go back to Judah." David then left and went to Hereth Forest.

Saul Kills the Priests of the LORD

⁶Saul was sitting under a small tree on top of the hill at Gibeah when he heard that David and his men had been seen. Saul was holding his spear, and his officers were standing in front of him. ⁷He told them:

All of us need a support system (a wise friend, a competent counselor) to help us hear what we are feeling, to hold us accountable to change, and to initially validate us as we grow.

PATSY CLAIRMONT

Listen to me! You belong to the Benjamin tribe,ᵍ so if that son of Jesse ever becomes king, he won't give you fields or vineyards. He won't make you officers in charge of thousands or hundreds as I have done. ⁸But you're all plotting against me! Not one of you told me that my own son Jonathan had made an agreement with him. Not one of you cared enough to tell me

---

ᵈ21.7 *Edomite*: A person from the country of Edom, to the south of Israel. ᵉ21.7 *the strongest of*: Or "in charge of." ᶠ21.10 *Gath*: One of the five main Philistine towns. ᵍ22.7 *You . . . Benjamin tribe*: David was from the Judah tribe and would have given special privileges to the people of his own tribe rather than to those of Benjamin.

that Jonathan had helped one of my officers[h] rebel. Now that son of Jesse is trying to ambush me.

[9]Doeg the Edomite was standing with the other officers and spoke up, "When I was in the town of Nob, I saw that son of Jesse. He was visiting the priest Ahimelech the son of Ahitub. [10]Ahimelech talked to the LORD for him, then gave him food and the sword that had belonged to Goliath the Philistine."

[11]Saul sent a message to Ahimelech and his whole family of priests at Nob, ordering them to come to him. When they came, [12]Saul told them, "Listen to me, you son of Ahitub."

"Certainly, Your Majesty," Ahimelech answered.

[13]Saul demanded, "Why did you plot against me with that son of Jesse? You helped him rebel against me by giving him food and a sword, and by talking with God for him. Now he's trying to ambush me!"

[14]"Your Majesty, none of your officers is more loyal than David!" Ahimelech replied. "He's your son-in-law and the captain of your bodyguard. Everyone in your family respects him. [15]This isn't the first time I've talked with God for David, and it's never made you angry before! Please don't accuse me or my family like this. I have no idea what's going on!"

[16]"Ahimelech," Saul said, "you and your whole family are going to die."

[17]Saul shouted to his bodyguards, "These priests of the LORD helped David! They knew he was running away, but they didn't tell me. Kill them!"

But the king's officers would not attack the priests of the LORD.

[18]Saul turned to Doeg, who was from Edom, and said, "Kill the priests!"

On that same day, Doeg killed eighty-five priests. [19]Then he attacked the town of Nob, where the priests had lived, and he killed everyone there—men, women, children, and babies. He even killed their cattle, donkeys, and sheep.

Only Abiathar Escapes from Nob

[20]Ahimelech's son Abiathar was the only one who escaped. He ran to David [21]and told him, "Saul has murdered the priests at Nob!"

[22]David answered, "That day when I saw Doeg, I knew he would tell Saul! Your family died because of me. [23]Stay here. Isn't the same person trying to kill both of us? Don't worry! You'll be safe here with me."

David Rescues the Town of Keilah

23 One day some people told David, "The Philistines keep attacking the town of Keilah and stealing grain from the threshing place."

[2]David asked the LORD, "Should I attack these Philistines?"

"Yes," the LORD answered. "Attack them and rescue Keilah."

[3]But David's men said, "Look, even here in Judah we're afraid of the Philistines. We will be terrified if we try to fight them at Keilah!"[i]

[4]David asked the LORD about it again. "Leave right now," the LORD answered. "I will give you victory over the Philistines at Keilah."

[5]David and his men went there and fiercely attacked the Philistines. They killed many of them, then led away their cattle, and rescued the people of Keilah.

[6-8]Meanwhile, Saul heard that David was in Keilah. "God has let me catch David," Saul said. "David is trapped inside a walled town where the gates can be locked." Saul decided to go there and surround the town, in order to trap David and his men. He sent messengers who told the towns and villages, "Send men to serve in Saul's army!"

By this time, Abiathar had joined David in Keilah and had brought along everything he needed to get answers from God.

[9]David heard about Saul's plan to capture him, and he told Abiathar, "Let's ask God what we should do."

[10]David prayed, "LORD God of Israel, I was told that Saul is planning to come here. What should I do? Suppose he threatens to destroy the town because of me. [11]Would the leaders of Keilah turn me over to Saul? Or is he really coming? Please tell me, LORD."

"Yes, he will come," the LORD answered.

[12]David asked, "Would the leaders of Keilah hand me and my soldiers over to Saul?"

"Yes, they would," the LORD answered.

---

[h]22.7,8 son of Jesse . . . officers: That is, David. Saul avoids even saying David's name. [i]23.3 Keilah: Keilah was probably not controlled by Israelites at this time.

[13]David and his six hundred men got out of there fast and started moving from place to place. Saul heard that David had left Keilah, and he decided not to go after him.

> *My parents lived out their faith in very visible, practical ways. We'd pray constantly—and sing songs to Jesus all day!*
>
> PAM THUM

Jonathan Says David Will Be King

[14]David stayed in hideouts in the hill country of Ziph Desert. Saul kept searching, but God never let Saul catch him.

[15]One time, David was at Horesh in Ziph Desert. He was afraid because[j] Saul had come to the area to kill him. [16]But Jonathan went to see David, and God helped him encourage David. [17]"Don't be afraid," Jonathan said. "My father Saul will never get his hands on you. In fact, you're going to be the next king of Israel, and I'll be your highest official. Even my father knows it's true."

[18]They both promised the LORD that they would always be loyal to each other. Then Jonathan went home, but David stayed at Horesh.

David Escapes from Saul

[19]Some people from the town of Ziph went to Saul at Gibeah and said, "Your Majesty, David has a hideout not far from us! It's near Horesh, somewhere on Mount Hachilah south of Jeshimon.[k] [20]If you come, we will help you catch him."

[21]Saul told them:

You've done me a big favor, and I pray that the LORD will bless you. [22]Now please do just a little more for me. Find out exactly where David is, as well as where he goes, and who has seen him there. I've been told that he's very tricky. [23]Find out where all his hiding places are and come back when you're sure. Then I'll go with you. If he

is still in the area, or anywhere among the clans of Judah, I'll find him.

[24]The people from Ziph went back ahead of Saul, and they found out that David and his men were still south of Jeshimon in the Maon Desert. [25]Saul and his army set out to find David. But David heard that Saul was coming, and he went to a place called The Rock, one of his hideouts in Maon Desert.

Saul found out where David was and started closing in on him. [26]Saul was going around a hill on one side, and David and his men were on the other side, trying to get away. Saul and his soldiers were just about to capture David and his men, [27]when a messenger came to Saul and said, "Come quickly! The Philistines are attacking Israel and taking everything."

[28]Saul stopped going after David and went back to fight the Philistines. That's why the place is called "Escape Rock."

[29]David left and went to live in the hideouts at En-Gedi.

David Lets Saul Live

24 When Saul got back from fighting off the Philistines, he heard that David was in the desert around En-Gedi. [2]Saul led three thousand of Israel's best soldiers out to look for David and his men near Wild Goat Rocks at En-Gedi. [3]There were some sheep pens along the side of the road, and one of them was built around the entrance to a cave. Saul went into the cave to relieve himself.

David and his men were hiding at the back of the cave. [4]They whispered to David, "The LORD told you he was going to let you defeat your enemies and do whatever you want with them. This must be the day the LORD was talking about."

David sneaked over and cut off a small piece[l] of Saul's robe, but Saul didn't notice a thing. [5]Afterwards, David was sorry that he had even done that, [6-7]and he told his men, "Stop talking foolishly. We're not going to attack Saul. He's my king, and I pray that the LORD will keep me from doing anything to harm his chosen king."

Saul left the cave and started down the

---

[j]23.15 *He . . . because:* Or "He saw that."
[k]23.19 *Jeshimon:* A place in the desert near the southern border of Judah. [l]24.4 *small piece:* Hebrew "corner" or "lower hem."

road. [8]Soon, David also got up and left the cave. "Your Majesty!" he shouted from a distance.

Saul turned around to look. David bowed down very low [9]and said:

Your Majesty, why do you listen to people who say that I'm trying to harm you? [10]You can see for yourself that the LORD gave me the chance to catch you in the cave today. Some of my men wanted to kill you, but I wouldn't let them do it. I told them, "I will not harm the LORD's chosen king!" [11]Your Majesty, look at what I'm holding. You can see that it's a piece of your robe. If I could cut off a piece of your robe, I could have killed you. But I let you live, and that should prove I'm not trying to harm you or to rebel. I haven't done anything to you, and yet you keep trying to ambush and kill me.

[12]I'll let the LORD decide which one of us has done right. I pray that the LORD will punish you for what you're doing to me, but I won't do anything to you. [13]An old proverb says, "Only evil people do evil things," and so I won't harm you.

[14]Why should the king of Israel be out chasing me, anyway? I'm as worthless as a dead dog or a flea. [15]I pray that the LORD will help me escape and show that I am in the right.

[16]"David, my son—is that you?" Saul asked. Then he started crying [17]and said:

David, you're a better person than I am. You treated me with kindness, even though I've been cruel to you. [18]You've told me how you were kind enough not to kill me when the LORD gave you the chance. [19]If you really were my enemy, you wouldn't have let me leave here alive. I pray that the LORD will give you a big reward for what you did today.

[20]I realize now that you will be the next king, and a powerful king at that. [21]Promise me with the LORD as your witness, that you won't wipe out my descendants. Let them live to keep my family name alive.

[22]So David promised, and Saul went home. David and his men returned to their hideout.

Samuel Dies

25 Samuel died, and people from all over Israel gathered to mourn for him when he was buried at his home[m] in Ramah. Meanwhile, David moved his camp to Paran Desert.[n]

Abigail Keeps David from Killing Innocent People

[2-3]Nabal was a very rich man who lived in Maon. He owned three thousand sheep and a thousand goats, which he kept at Carmel.[o] His wife Abigail was sensible and beautiful, but he was from the Caleb clan[p] and was rough and mean.

[4]One day, Nabal was in Carmel, having his servants cut the wool from his sheep. David was in the desert when he heard about it. [5-6]So he sent ten men to Carmel with this message for Nabal:

I hope that you and your family are healthy and that all is going well for you. [7]I've heard that you are cutting the wool from your sheep.

When your shepherds were with us in Carmel, we didn't harm them, and nothing was ever stolen from them. [8]Ask your shepherds, and they'll tell you the same thing.

My servants are your servants, and you are like a father to me. This is a day for celebrating,[q] so please be kind and share some of your food with us.

[9]David's men went to Nabal and gave him David's message, then they waited for Nabal's answer.

[10]This is what he said:

Who does this David think he is? That son of Jesse is just one more slave on the run from his master, and there are too many of them these days. [11]What makes you think I would take my bread, my water, and the meat that I've had cooked for my own servants[r]

---

[m]**25.1** *at his home:* Hebrew "in his house." Family tombs were sometimes underneath the house or in the courtyard of the home.   [n]**25.1** *Paran Desert:* Hebrew; some manuscripts of one ancient translation "Maon Desert."   [o]**25.2,3** *Carmel:* About one mile north of Maon in the Southern Desert of Judah.   [p]**25.2,3** *from the Caleb clan:* Or "behaved like a dog."   [q]**25.8** *celebrating:* Cutting the wool from the sheep was a time for celebrating as well as for working.   [r]**25.11** *servants:* Hebrew "shearers," the servants who cut the wool from the sheep.

and give it to you? Besides, I'm not sure that David sent you!⁵
¹²The men returned to their camp and told David everything Nabal had said.
¹³"Everybody get your swords!" David ordered.

They all strapped on their swords. Two hundred men stayed behind to guard the camp, but the other four hundred followed David.

¹⁴⁻¹⁶Meanwhile, one of Nabal's servants told Abigail:

David's men were often nearby while we were taking care of the sheep in the fields. They were very good to us, they never hurt us, and nothing was ever stolen from us while they were nearby. With them around day or night, we were as safe as we would have been inside a walled city.

David sent some messengers from the desert to wish our master well, but he shouted insults at them. ¹⁷He's a bully who won't listen to anyone.

Isn't there something you can do? Please think of something! Or else our master and his family and everyone who works for him are all doomed.

¹⁸Abigail quickly got together two hundred loaves of bread, two large clay jars of wine, the meat from five sheep, a large sack of roasted grain, a hundred handfuls of raisins, and two hundred handfuls of dried figs. She loaded all the food on donkeys ¹⁹and told her servants, "Take this on ahead, and I'll catch up with you." She didn't tell her husband Nabal what she was doing.

²⁰Abigail was riding her donkey on the path that led around the hillside, when suddenly she met David and his men heading straight at her.

²¹David had just been saying, "I surely wasted my time guarding Nabal's things in the desert and keeping them from being stolen! I was good to him, and now he pays me back with insults. ²²I swear that by morning, there won't be a man or boy left from his family or his servants' families. I pray that God will punish meᵗ if I don't do it!"

²³Abigail quickly got off her donkey and bowed down in front of David. ²⁴Then she said:

Sir, please let me explain! ²⁵Don't pay any attention to that good-for-nothing Nabal. His name means "fool," and it really fits him!

I didn't see the men you sent, ²⁶⁻²⁷but please take this gift of food that

---

⁵25.11 *I'm not sure . . . sent you:* Or "I don't know where you come from." ᵗ25.22 *me:* One ancient translation; Hebrew "my enemies."

Personal *Concerns*—How can I forgive someone who has broken my trust? (1 Samuel 24)

Trust God to look out for you.
When you ask yourself the above question, ask it gently. When someone offends you or works against you, it is foolish to force yourself to say you have forgiven him or her. Especially if that person is anything like King Saul, your reticence may be merited. Even after their relationship appeared to be ironed out, David and his men returned to their hideout (24.22) to keep themselves from further danger.

The first step is to trust God to work with this person. David did that in two ways. He assumed God was in charge of the situation. If Saul was still king, then that must have been God's will. Also, David did not assume he was right and Saul was wrong—even when it sure looked like it. Although Saul had tried to murder David, David responded by not murdering Saul when he had the chance, refusing to pay evil for evil. When we leave the judgment and consequences in God's hands we indicate that in the face of grievous error, we believe in God's ability to rescue us and bring about justice. Under that umbrella of God's protection, we can afford to see our enemy as a person with heartbreaks and problems, in need of God's love, perhaps even from us. (See also Numbers 14.11-25; Matthew 7.1-5; Matthew 18.21-35; Luke 6.27-36.)

Words To Remember: *I'll let the LORD decide which one of us has done right.*
—1 Samuel 24.12

Abigail

1 Samuel 25.2-44

*H*ow do you cope when you're hooked up with someone who has no concern for godly ways? who is not compassionate or faithful? who makes life miserable for everyone around him (and maybe even endangers your safety)?

Even though Abigail was a "sensible and beautiful" woman, her husband Nabal "was rough and mean" (25.3). Some women probably envied her for her money—imagine being able to quickly gather two hundred loaves of bread, meat from five sheep, a sack of roasted grain, and hundreds of handfuls of raisins and figs! But other women, especially those who knew Nabal, must have pitied her for having to live with such a bully.

No doubt she was used to unpleasantness, but this time disaster loomed. After assisting Nabal's shepherds in sizable ways, David and his men asked for food. Instead of being grateful, Nabal insulted them. Abigail had her hands full with being a peacemaker in a potentially violent situation.

Just as David was planning a bloodthirsty revenge, Abigail intervened. She could have viewed this situation as a handy way to dispose of her bully husband, but she respected human life and saw her chance to promote harmony.

First, Abigail responded to David's gracious request (sent to Nabal, not to her) and sent David food. Then she approached him. While her speech was somewhat disrespectful of Nabal ("that good-for-nothing," 25.25), we can credit her for not pretending Nabal was a kind person. She suggested that God was guiding David to avoid shedding innocent blood; she hoped he never did evil for the rest of his life; she reminded him that he was a future king (Nabal had called him a runaway slave of Saul's in 25.10!). In so doing, Abigail appealed to David's integrity and saved him from a ruinous, barbaric decision.

In this chaotic situation, Abigail wisely adopted God's causes as her own: mercy for a cantankerous Nabal, peace among the hundreds of men, and integrity for the future king. No wonder David accepted her hospitality. This savvy woman was also up-front with Nabal. When he finished partying, she did not hide her actions, but told him everything.

Difficult people (a hard-to-get-along-with spouse, a grouchy co-worker, a disgruntled parent, a hormone-ridden teen) make us want to argue or run the other way. We get sidetracked by frustration or maybe even revenge. Abigail shows us that it is possible to resolve unjust situations with compassion and graciousness. She did not cringe and grovel before David—she spoke up, appealing to his integrity. Her sensible, caring approach in the midst of wild and crazy rantings saved lives, showed compassion, and made her attractive. When Nabal died of a heart attack and Abigail was free, David asked her to marry him.

I've brought and share it with your followers. The LORD has kept you from taking revenge and from killing innocent people. But I hope your enemies and anyone else who wants to harm you will end up like Nabal. I swear this by the living LORD and by your life.

²⁸Please forgive me if I say a little more. The LORD will always protect you and your family, because you fight for him. I pray that you won't ever do anything evil as long as you live. ²⁹The LORD your God will keep you safe when your enemies try to kill you. But he will snatch away their lives quicker than you can throw a rock from a sling.

³⁰The LORD has promised to do many good things for you, even to make you the ruler of Israel. The LORD will keep his promises to you, ³¹and now your conscience will be clear, because you won't be guilty of taking revenge and killing innocent people.

When the LORD does all those good things for you, please remember me.

³²David told her:

I praise the LORD God of Israel! He must have sent you to meet me today. ³³And you should also be praised. Your good sense kept me from taking revenge and killing innocent people. ³⁴If you hadn't come to meet me so quickly, every man and boy in Nabal's family and in his servants' families would have been killed by morning. I swear by the living LORD God of Israel who protected you that this is the truth.

³⁵David accepted the food Abigail had brought. "Don't worry," he said. "You can go home now. I'll do what you asked."

³⁶Abigail went back home and found Nabal throwing a party fit for a king. He was very drunk and feeling good, so she didn't tell him anything that night. ³⁷But when he sobered up the next morning, Abigail told him everything that had happened. Nabal had a heart attack, and he lay in bed as still as a stone. ³⁸Ten days later, the LORD took his life.

³⁹⁻⁴⁰David heard that Nabal had died. "I praise the LORD!" David said. "He has judged Nabal guilty for insulting me. The LORD kept me from doing anything wrong, and he made sure that Nabal hurt only himself with his own evil."

Friendship—How can I have healthy friendships with men? (1 Samuel 25)

Focus on God's agenda.
Male-female friendships are ripe for all kinds of pitfalls—sexual attraction, male-bashing or female-bashing, even competition. It is a miracle that Abigail, a "sensible and beautiful" (25.3) woman with the financial, personal, and spiritual resources to help a promising man, became David's friend instead of manipulating him.

The key is that Abigail stayed focused on God's agenda. She did not flatter this future king or become subservient to him. Her respectful appeal, in fact, urged him to obey God in peaceful, helpful ways. Even though she was a rich woman who held the power and purse strings, she didn't talk down to him but offered reasonable, wise solutions.

In the same way, we can stay focused on God's agenda in our friendships with men. We can pray for God's best in our male friend's life—that our friend will behave with integrity, will seek God's will in his work, will see temptation coming and resist it.

If an inappropriate attraction begins to glimmer at all, fight it immediately. Even a platonic "affair of the heart" can cause trouble. Stay out of situations in which you are alone together; and if either of you is married, meet each other's spouse and children and befriend them. This emphasizes reality instead of fantasy. If you have a female friend you can trust, confess your struggle to her and be accountable for your thoughts and behavior. The prayer support and accountability your women friends provide can get you through temptations. (See also 2 Kings 4.1-7; 1 Thessalonians 4.1-8.)

Words To Remember: *I pray that you won't ever do anything evil as long as you live. The LORD your God will keep you safe.*—1 Samuel 25.28,29

David and Abigail Are Married

Abigail was still at Carmel. So David sent messengers to ask her if she would marry him.

⁴¹She bowed down and said, "I would willingly be David's slave and wash his servants' feet."

⁴²Abigail quickly got ready and went back with David's messengers. She rode on her donkey, while five of her servant women walked alongside. She and David were married as soon as she arrived.

⁴³David had earlier married Ahinoam from the town of Jezreel, so both she and Abigail were now David's wives.ᵘ ⁴⁴Meanwhile, Saul had arranged for Michalᵛ to marry Palti the son of Laish, who came from the town of Gallim.

David Again Lets Saul Live

26 Once again,ʷ some people from Ziph went to Gibeah to talk with Saul. "David has a hideout on Mount Hachilah near Jeshimon out in the desert," they told him.

²Saul took three thousand of Israel's best soldiers and went to look for David there in Ziph Desert. ³Saul set up camp on Mount Hachilah, which is across the road from Jeshimon. But David was hiding out in the desert.

When David heard that Saul was following him, ⁴he sent some spies to find out if it was true. ⁵Then he sneaked up to Saul's camp. He noticed that Saul and his army commander Abner the son of Ner were sleeping in the middle of the camp, with soldiers sleeping all around them. ⁶David asked Ahimelech the Hittite and Joab's brother Abishai,ˣ "Which one of you will go with me into Saul's camp?"

"I will!" Abishai answered.

⁷That same night, David and Abishai crept into the camp. Saul was sleeping, and his spear was stuck in the ground not far from his head. Abner and the soldiers were sound asleep all around him.

⁸Abishai whispered, "This time God has let you get your hands on your enemy! I'll pin him to the ground with one thrust of his own spear."

⁹"Don't kill him!" David whispered back. "The LORD will punish anyone who kills his chosen king. ¹⁰As surely as the LORD

lives, the LORD will kill Saul, or Saul will die a natural death or be killed in battle. ¹¹But I pray that the LORD will keep me from harming his chosen king. Let's grab his spear and his water jar and get out of here!"

> *God uses pain to open you up to other people and to give you a heart of mercy.*
>
> BODIE THOENE

¹²David took the spear and the water jar, then left the camp. None of Saul's soldiers knew what had happened or even woke up—the LORD had made all of them fall sound asleep. ¹³David and Abishai crossed the valley and went to the top of the next hill, where they were at a safe distance. ¹⁴"Abner!" David shouted toward Saul's army. "Can you hear me?"

Abner shouted back. "Who dares disturb the king?"

¹⁵"Abner, what kind of a man are you?" David replied. "Aren't you supposed to be the best soldier in Israel? Then why didn't you protect your king? Anyone who went into your camp could have killed him tonight.ʸ ¹⁶You're a complete failure! I swear by the living LORD that you and your men deserve to die for not protecting the LORD's chosen king. Look and see if you can find the king's spear and the water jar that were near his head."

¹⁷Saul could tell it was David's voice, and he called out, "David, my son! Is that you?"

"Yes it is, Your Majesty. ¹⁸Why are you after me? Have I done something wrong, or have I committed a crime? ¹⁹Please listen to what I have to say. If the LORD has turned you against me, maybe a sacrifice will make him

---

ᵘ25.43 *wives:* Having more than one wife was allowed in those times. ᵛ**25.44** *Michal:* David's first wife (see 18.20—19.17). ʷ**26.1** *again:* See 23.19.
ˣ**26.6** *Abishai:* Hebrew "Abishai the son of Zeruiah." Zeruiah was David's older sister, so Abishai and Joab were David's nephews (see 1 Chronicles 2.12-17; 2 Samuel 17.25 and the note there).
ʸ**26.15** *Anyone . . . tonight:* Or "Someone went into your camp to kill him tonight."

change his mind. But if some people have turned you against me, I hope the LORD will punish them! They have forced me to leave the land that belongs to the LORD and have told me to worship foreign gods.[z] [20]Don't let me die in a land far away from the LORD. I'm no more important than a flea! Why should the king of Israel hunt me down as if I were a bird in the mountains?"

[21]"David, you had the chance to kill me today. But you didn't. I was very wrong about you. It was a terrible mistake for me to try to kill you. I've acted like a fool, but I'll never try to harm you again. You're like a son to me, so please come back."

[22]"Your Majesty, here's your spear! Have one of your soldiers come and get it. [23]The LORD put you in my power today, but you are his chosen king and I wouldn't harm you. The LORD rewards people who are faithful and live right. [24]I saved your life today, and I pray that the LORD will protect me and keep me safe."

[25]"David, my son, I pray that the Lord will bless you and make you successful!"

David in Philistia

27 Saul went back home. David also left, [1]but he thought to himself, "One of these days, Saul is going to kill me. The only way to escape from him is to go to Philistia. Then I'll be outside of Israel, and Saul will give up trying to catch me."

[2-3]David and his six hundred men went across the border to stay in Gath with King Achish the son of Maoch. His men brought their families with them. David brought his wife Ahinoam whose hometown was Jezreel, and he also brought his wife Abigail who had been married to Nabal from Carmel. [4]When Saul found out that David had run off to Gath, he stopped trying to catch him.

[5]One day, David was talking with Achish and said, "If you are happy with me, then let me live in one of the towns in the countryside. I'm not important enough to live here with you in the royal city."

[6]Achish gave David the town of Ziklag that same day, and Ziklag has belonged to the kings of Judah ever since.

[7]David was in Philistia for a year and four months. [8]The Geshurites, the Girzites, and the Amalekites lived in the area from Telam to Shur[d] and on as far as Egypt, and David often

attacked their towns. [9]Whenever David and his men attacked a town, they took the sheep, cattle, donkeys, camels, and the clothing, and killed everyone who lived there.

After he returned from a raid, David always went to see Achish, [10]who would ask, "Where did you attack today?"[b]

David would answer, "Oh, we attacked some desert town that belonged to the Judah tribe." Sometimes David would say, "Oh, we attacked a town in the desert where the Jerahmeel clan lives" or "We attacked a town in the desert where the Kenites[c] live." [11]That's why David killed everyone in the towns he attacked. He thought, "If I let any of them live, they might come to Gath and tell what I've really been doing."

David made these raids all the time he was in Philistia. [12]But Achish trusted David and thought, "David's people must be furious with him. From now on he will have to take orders from me."

Saul Talks
with Samuel's Ghost

28 [1-3]Samuel had died some time earlier,[d] and people from all over Israel had attended his funeral in his hometown of Ramah.

Meanwhile, Saul had been trying to get rid of everyone who spoke with the spirits of the dead.[e] But one day the Philistines brought their soldiers together to attack Israel.

Achish told David, "Of course, you know that you and your men must fight as part of our Philistine army."

David answered, "That will give you a chance to see for yourself just how well we can fight!"

"In that case," Achish said, "you and your men will always be my bodyguards."

---

[z]26.19 gods: In ancient times it was often believed that gods (even the God of Israel) could only be properly worshiped in their own countries, and only a country's gods should be worshiped in that country. [a]27.8 lived . . . Shur: One ancient translation; Hebrew "had lived for a long time in Shur." [b]27.10 Where . . . today: A few Hebrew manuscripts, the Dead Sea Scrolls, and three ancient translations; most Hebrew manuscripts "Didn't you make a raid today?" [c]27.10 Jerahmeel . . . Kenites: These were clans of the Judah tribe. [d]28.1-3 earlier: See 25.1. [e]28.1-3 dead: Many people believed that it was possible to talk to spirits of the dead, and that these spirits could tell the future.

⁴The Philistines went to Shunem and set up camp. Saul called the army of Israel together, and they set up their camp in Gilboa. ⁵Saul took one look at the Philistine army and started shaking with fear. ⁶So he asked the LORD what to do. But the LORD would not answer, either in a dream or by a priest or a prophet. ⁷Then Saul told his officers, "Find me a woman who can talk to the spirits of the dead. I'll go to her and find out what's going to happen."

His servants told him, "There's a woman at Endor who can talk to spirits of the dead."

⁸That night, Saul put on different clothing so nobody would recognize him. Then he and two of his men went to the woman, and asked, "Will you bring up the ghost of someone for us?"

⁹The woman said, "Why are you trying to trick me and get me killed? You know King Saul has gotten rid of everyone who talks to the spirits of the dead!"

¹⁰Saul replied, "I swear by the living LORD that nothing will happen to you because of this."

¹¹"Who do you want me to bring up?" she asked.

"Bring up the ghost of Samuel," he answered.

¹²When the woman saw Samuel, she screamed. Then she turned to Saul and said, "You've tricked me! You're the king!"

¹³"Don't be afraid," Saul replied. "Just tell me what you see."

She answered, "I see a spirit rising up out of the ground."

¹⁴"What does it look like?"

"It looks like an old man wearing a robe."

Saul knew it was Samuel, so he bowed down low.

¹⁵"Why are you bothering me by bringing me up like this?" Samuel asked.

"I'm terribly worried," Saul answered. "The Philistines are about to attack me. God has turned his back on me and won't answer any more by prophets or by dreams. What should I do?"

¹⁶Samuel said:

If the LORD has turned away from you and is now your enemy, don't ask me what to do. ¹⁷I've already told you: The LORD has sworn to take the kingdom from Saul and give it to David.

And that's just what he's doing! ¹⁸When the LORD was angry with the Amalekites, he told you to destroy them, but you didn't do it. That's why the LORD is doing this to you. ¹⁹Tomorrow the LORD will let the Philistines defeat Israel's army, then you and your sons will join me down here in the world of the dead.

> *We cannot have joy without staying in contact with the __source__ of all joy, without being connected to his power, to his love, to his strength.*
>
> CAROLE MAYHALL

²⁰At once, Saul collapsed and lay stretched out on the floor, terrified at what Samuel had said. He was weak because he had not eaten anything since the day before. ²¹The woman came over to Saul, and when she saw that he was completely terrified, she said, "Your Majesty, I listened to you and risked my life to do what you asked. ²²Now please listen to me. Let me get you a little something to eat. It will give you strength for your walk back to camp."

²³"No, I won't eat!"

But his officers and the woman kept on urging Saul, until he finally agreed. He got up off the floor and sat on the bed. ²⁴Right away the woman killed a calf that she had been fattening up. She cooked part of the meat and baked some thin bread.ᶠ ²⁵Then she served the food to Saul and his officers, who ate and left before daylight.

The Philistines Send David Back

29 The Philistines had brought their whole army to Aphek,ᵍ while Israel's army was camping near

---

ᶠ**28.24** *thin bread*: Bread made without yeast, since there was no time for the bread to rise.   ᵍ**29.1** *Aphek*: The events of chapter 29 probably took place as the Philistine army was on its way to Shunem, which they reached in 28.4.

Jezreel Spring. [2-3]The Philistine rulers and their troops were marching past the Philistine army commanders in groups of a hundred and a thousand. When David and his men marched by at the end with Achish, the commanders said, "What are these worthless Israelites doing here?"

"They are David's men," Achish answered. "David used to be one of Saul's officers, but he left Saul and joined my army a long time ago. I've never had even one complaint about him."

[4]The Philistine army commanders were angry and shouted:

Send David back to the town you gave him. We won't have him going into the battle with us. He could turn and fight against us! Saul would take David back as an officer if David brought him the heads of our soldiers.

[5]The Israelites even dance and sing,

"Saul has killed
    a thousand enemies;
David has killed
    ten thousand enemies!"

[6]Achish called David over and said:

I swear by the living LORD that you've been honest with me, and I want you to fight by my side. I don't think you've done anything wrong from the day you joined me until this very moment. But the other Philistine rulers don't want you to come along. [7]Go on back home and try not to upset them.

[8]"But what have I done?" David asked. "Do you know of anything I've ever done that would keep me from fighting the enemies of my king?"[h]

[9]Achish said:

I believe that you're as good as an angel of God, but our army commanders have decided that you can't fight in this battle. [10]You and your troops will have to go back to the town I gave you.[i] Get up and leave tomorrow morning as soon as it's light. I am pleased with you, so don't let any of this bother you.[j]

[11]David and his men got up early in the morning and headed back toward Philistia, while the Philistines left for Jezreel.

David Rescues His Soldiers' Families

30 It took David and his men three days to reach Ziklag. But while they had been away, the Amalekites had been raiding in the desert around there. They had attacked Ziklag, burned it to the ground, [2]and had taken away the women and children. [3]When David and his men came to Ziklag, they saw the burned-out ruins and learned that their families had been taken captive. [4]They started crying and kept it up until they were too weak to cry any more. [5]David's two wives, Ahinoam and Abigail, had been taken captive with everyone else.

The heavier your burdens grow, the more of grace, strength, and comfort God will give you.

KAY MARSHALL STROM

[6]David was desperate. His soldiers were so upset over what had happened to their sons and daughters that they were thinking about stoning David to death. But he felt the LORD God giving him strength, [7]and he said to the priest, "Abiathar, let's ask God what to do."

Abiathar brought everything he needed to get answers from God, and he went over to David. [8]Then David asked the LORD, "Should I go after the people who raided our town? Can I catch up with them?"

"Go after them," the LORD answered. "You will catch up with them, and you will rescue your families."

[9-10]David led his six hundred men to Besor Gorge, but two hundred of them were too tired to go across. So they stayed behind, while David and the other four hundred men crossed the gorge.

[11]Some of David's men found an

---

[h]29.8 *my king:* David may be referring to either Saul or Achish.   [i]29.10 *go . . . you:* One ancient translation; these words are not in the Hebrew text.   [j]29.10 *I am . . . bother you:* One ancient translation; these words are not in the Hebrew text.

Egyptian out in a field and took him to David. They gave the Egyptian some bread, and he ate it. Then they gave him a drink of water, [12]some dried figs, and two handfuls of raisins. This was the first time in three days he had tasted food or water. Now he felt much better.

[13]"Who is your master?" David asked. "And where do you come from?"

"I'm from Egypt," the young man answered. "I'm the servant of an Amalekite, but he left me here three days ago because I was sick. [14]We had attacked some towns in the desert where the Cherethites live, in the area that belongs to Judah, and in the desert where the Caleb clan lives. And we burned down Ziklag."

[15]"Will you take me to those Amalekites?" David asked.

"Yes, I will, if you promise with God as a witness that you won't kill me or hand me over to my master."

[16]He led David to the Amalekites. They were eating and drinking everywhere, celebrating because of what they had taken from Philistia and Judah. [17]David attacked just before sunrise the next day and fought until sunset.[k] Four hundred Amalekites rode away on camels, but they were the only ones who escaped.

[18]David rescued his two wives and everyone else the Amalekites had taken from Ziklag. [19]No one was missing—young or old, sons or daughters. David brought back everything that had been stolen, [20]including their livestock.

David also took the sheep and cattle that the Amalekites had with them, but he kept these separate from the others. Everyone agreed that these would be David's reward.

[21]On the way back, David went to the two hundred men he had left at Besor Gorge, because they had been too tired to keep up with him. They came toward David and the people who were with him. When David was close enough, he greeted the two hundred men and asked how they were doing.

[22]Some of David's men were good-for-nothings, and they said, "Those men didn't go with us to the battle, so they don't get any of the things we took back from the Amalekites. Let them take their wives and children and go!"

[23]But David said:

My friends, don't be so greedy with what the LORD has given us! The LORD protected us and gave us victory over the people who attacked. [24]Who would pay attention to you, anyway? Soldiers who stay behind to guard the camp get as much as those who go into battle.

[25]David made this a law for Israel, and it has been the same ever since.

[26]David went back to Ziklag with everything they had taken from the Amalekites. He sent some of these things as gifts to his friends who were leaders of Judah, and he told them, "We took these things from the LORD's enemies. Please accept them as a gift."

[27-31]This is a list of the towns where David sent gifts: Bethel,[l] Ramoth in the Southern Desert, Jattir, Aroer, Siphmoth, Eshtemoa, Racal, the towns belonging to the Jerahmeelites and the Kenites, Hormah, Bor-Ashan, Athach, and Hebron. He also sent gifts to the other towns where he and his men had traveled.

Saul and His Sons Die

31 Meanwhile, the Philistines were fighting Israel at Mount Gilboa. Israel's soldiers ran from the Philistines, and many of them were killed. [2]The Philistines closed in on Saul and his sons, and they killed his sons Jonathan, Abinadab, and Malchishua. [3]The fighting was fierce around Saul, and he was badly wounded by enemy arrows.

[4]Saul told the soldier who carried his weapons, "Kill me with your sword! I don't want those worthless Philistines to torture me and make fun." But the soldier was afraid to kill him.

Saul then took out his own sword; he stuck the blade into his stomach, and fell on it. [5]When the soldier knew that Saul was dead, he killed himself in the same way.

[6]Saul was dead, his three sons were dead, and the soldier who carried his weapons was dead. They and all his soldiers died on that same day. [7]The Israelites on the other side of Jezreel Valley[m] and the other

---

[k]30.17 *just . . . sunset*: Or "at dusk, and fought until sunset on the next day." [l]30.27-31 *Bethel*: Or "Bethuel" (see Joshua 19.4). [m]31.7 *Jezreel Valley*: Hebrew "valley." Shunem (see 28.4) and Gilboa (see verse 1) were across the Jezreel Valley from each other.

side of the Jordan learned that Saul and his sons were dead. They saw that the Israelite army had run away. So they ran away too, and the Philistines moved into the towns the Israelites had left behind.

⁸The day after the battle, when the Philistines returned to the battlefield to take the weapons of the dead Israelite soldiers, they found Saul and his three sons lying dead on Mount Gilboa. ⁹⁻¹⁰The Philistines cut off Saul's head and pulled off his armor. Then they put his armor in the temple of the goddess Astarte, and they nailed his body to the city wall of Beth-Shan. They also sent messengers everywhere in Philistia to spread the good news in the temples of their idols and among their people.

¹¹The people who lived in Jabesh in Gilead heard what the Philistines had done to Saul's body. ¹²So one night, some brave men from Jabesh went to Beth-Shan. They took down the bodies of Saul and his sons, then brought them back to Jabesh and burned them. ¹³They buried the bones under a small tree in Jabesh, and for seven days, they went without eating to show their sorrow.

2 Samuel

A Life after God's Own Heart

One great feature of the Old Testament is its biographical nature. We are able to observe people for many years of their lives and see what their relationships with God were like. In 2 Samuel, we view David from head to toe. We see his successes and struggles, his personal greatness and vulnerabilities, his relationships with his friends, enemies, and children.

Because of David's God-seeking character, he became Israel's greatest king. Yet his rule was always tied up in God's will for Israel. He worked hard and played hard for God—leading the armies to make Canaan a home for Israel (8–10) and praising God with dance as the sacred chest was brought back to the tent David had set up for it (6.1-23).

David's character included a careful sense of justice. He showed mercy and fairness to Saul's family even when they were not gracious to him. He went out of his way to make good decisions about his enemies, rebels, allies, and close friends.

But a good biography also chronicles its hero's humanness, and 2 Samuel does that. David got involved in adultery, which led to a cover-up that involved murder. Watching David come clean before God is as riveting to us fallen creatures as watching him rise to power. David showed us what repentance looks like: confession, mourning, restitution. What a relief to know that when a person after God's own heart sinned, he could still connect with God. There is hope for us!

Perhaps David's greatest grief was caused by his troubles with his grown children, one of whom incited a national rebellion against him. Yet even in this, David exhibited faithfulness, patience, courage, generosity, and commitment. His darkest moments are full of shining light for us when we fail with our children, marriage, or work, and want to live in God's grace and truth in the midst of that failure.

2 Samuel at a Glance

1. David becomes king over the tribe of Judah while Abner, Joab, Ishbosheth, and others engage in power plays (1–4)
2. David is made king of all Israel (5,6)
3. David wants to build a temple for God (7)
4. David's military victories and kindness to Mephibosheth (8–10)
5. David's sin of adultery (11,12)
6. David's troubles with his children and Saul's children (13–17; 21.1-14)
7. David is chased by his son Absalom and then restored (18–20)
8. David's psalm of praise and record of valiant men (21.15—23.39)
9. David's census of the people and the punishment that results (24)

David Finds Out about Saul's Death

1 Saul was dead. Meanwhile, David had defeated the Amalekites and returned to Ziklag. ²Three days later, a soldier came from Saul's army. His clothes were torn, and dirt was on his head.*a* He went to David and knelt down in front of him.

³David asked, "Where did you come from?"

The man answered, "From Israel's army. I barely escaped with my life."

⁴"Who won the battle?" David asked.

The man said, "Our army turned and ran, but many were wounded and died. Even King Saul and his son Jonathan are dead."

⁵David asked, "How do you know Saul and Jonathan are dead?"

⁶The young man replied:

I was on Mount Gilboa and saw King Saul leaning on his spear. The enemy's war chariots and cavalry were closing in on him. ⁷When he turned around and saw me, he called me over. I went and asked what he wanted.

⁸Saul asked me, "Who are you?"

"An Amalekite," I answered.

⁹Then he said, "Kill me! I'm dying, and I'm in terrible pain."*b*

¹⁰So I killed him. I knew he was too badly wounded to live much longer. Then I took his crown and his armband, and I brought them to you, Your Majesty. Here they are.

¹¹Right away, David and his soldiers tore their clothes in sorrow. ¹²They cried all day long and would not eat anything. Everyone was sad because Saul, his son Jonathan, and many of the LORD's people had been killed in the battle.

¹³David asked the young man, "Where is your home?"

The man replied, "My father is an Amalekite, but we live in Israel."

¹⁴⁻¹⁶David said to him, "Why weren't you afraid to kill the LORD's chosen king? And you even told what you did. It's your own fault that you're going to die!"

Then David told one of his soldiers, "Come here and kill this man!"

---

*a*1.2 *His clothes . . . his head:* People tore their clothes and put dirt on their heads to show they were sad because someone had died.   *b*1.9 *in terrible pain:* Or "very weak."

WORK—How can I balance the competing demands of home and work?
(2 Samuel 1)

Focus your eyes on God.

How easy it is to forget to look into the eyes of the people we love! Children beg us to go on a bike ride, and we barely glance up from the project we brought home from work. Our husband tries to explain a new investment plan, but our eyes never leave the vegetables we are chopping for tonight's dinner. A friend drops by to plan a surprise party for another friend, but, to be honest, we are exhausted and our eyes are focused on the television while she talks.

If you've made commitments to your employer, it's important to honor them. If you let your child's needs keep you from meeting obligations you've agreed to, you need to find a way to avoid that conflict. Perhaps someone can babysit for you while you complete your task.

But it's important to open your eyes and focus on the people you love—and that requires discipline. It takes wisdom to realize that those you love are a feast for the eyes—one of the most crucial elements of your life.

David was in the midst of delight over a successful military campaign when the death of Saul and Jonathan told him it was time to change his focus. He turned his time of celebration to mourning and honored them with a song. David seemed to have a good sense of when it was time to work hard and when it was time to focus on people. (See also Exodus 23.10-13; Deuteronomy 6.1-9; Matthew 14.22,23.)

Words To Remember: *Jonathan, I miss you most! I loved you like a brother.*
—2 Samuel 1.26

David Sings in Memory of Saul

¹⁷David sang a song in memory of Saul and Jonathan, ¹⁸and he ordered his men to teach the song to everyone in Judah. He called it "The Song of the Bow," and it can be found in *The Book of Jashar.*ᶜ This is the song:

¹⁹Israel, your famous hero
  lies dead on the hills,
and your mighty warriors
  have fallen!
²⁰Don't tell it in Gath
  or spread the news
  on the streets of Ashkelon.
The godless Philistine women
  will be happy
  and jump for joy.
²¹Don't let dew or rain fall
  on the hills of Gilboa.
Don't let its fields
  grow offerings for God.
There the warriors' shields
  were smeared with mud,
and Saul's own shield
  was left unpolished.ᵈ

²²The arrows of Jonathan struck,
  and warriors died.
The sword of Saul cut
  the enemy apart.

²³It was easy to love Saul
  and Jonathan.
Together in life,
  together in death,
they were faster than eagles
  and stronger than lions.

²⁴Women of Israel, cry for Saul.
He brought you fine red cloth
  and jewelry made of gold.
²⁵Our warriors have fallen
  in the heat of battle,
and Jonathan lies dead
  on the hills of Gilboa.

²⁶Jonathan, I miss you most!
I loved you
  like a brother.
You were truly loyal to me,
  more faithful than a wife
  to her husband.ᵉ

²⁷Our warriors have fallen,
  and their weaponsᶠ
  are destroyed.

David Becomes King of Judah

2 Later, David asked the LORD, "Should I go back to one of the towns of Judah?"

The LORD answered, "Yes."

David asked, "Which town should I go to?"

"Go to Hebron," the LORD replied.

²David went to Hebron with his two wives, Ahinoam and Abigail. Ahinoam was from Jezreel, and Abigail was the widow of Nabal from Carmel. ³David also had his men and their families come and live in the villages near Hebron.

⁴The people of Judah met with David at Hebron and poured olive oil on his head to show that he was their new king. Then they told David, "The people from Jabesh in Gilead buried Saul."

⁵David sent messengers to tell them:

The LORD bless you! You were kind enough to bury Saul your ruler, ⁶and I pray that the LORD will be kind and faithful to you. I will be your friend because of what you have done. ⁷Saul is dead, but the tribe of Judah has made me their king. So be strong and have courage.

Ishbosheth Becomes King of Israel

⁸Abner the son of Nerᵍ had been the general of Saul's army. He took Saul's son Ishboshethʰ across the Jordan River to Mahanaim ⁹and made him king of Israel,ⁱ in-

---

ᶜ**1.18** *The Book of Jashar*: This book may have been a collection of ancient war songs. ᵈ**1.21** *unpolished*: Some shields were made of leather and were polished with olive oil. ᵉ**1.26** *You . . . husband*: Or "You loved me more than a wife could possibly love her husband." ᶠ**1.27** *weapons*: This may refer to Saul and Jonathan. ᵍ**2.8** *son of Ner*: Abner was Saul's cousin (see 1 Samuel 14.50). ʰ**2.8** *Ishbosheth*: One ancient translation has "Ishbaal" (see also 1 Chronicles 8.33). In Hebrew "baal" means "lord" and was used as the name of a Canaanite god. The people of Israel often changed "baal" to "bosheth" (which means "shame") in personal names. Ishbosheth was probably called Ishvi or Ishyo in 1 Samuel 14.49. ⁱ**2.9** *Israel*: Sometimes "Israel" means the northern tribes and does not include the tribes of Judah and Simeon. That is how it is used in this verse.

cluding the areas of Gilead, Asher,[j] Jezreel, Ephraim, and Benjamin. [10]Ishbosheth was forty years old at the time, and he ruled for two years. But the tribe of Judah made David their king, [11]and he ruled from Hebron for seven and a half years.

The War between David and Ishbosheth

[12]One day, Abner and the soldiers of Ishbosheth[k] left Mahanaim and went to Gibeon. [13]Meanwhile, Joab the son of Zeruiah[l] was leading David's soldiers, and the two groups met at the pool in Gibeon.[m] Abner and his men sat down on one side of the pool, while Joab and his men sat on the other side. [14]Abner yelled to Joab, "Let's have some of our best soldiers get up and fight each other!"

> When I make
> my time alone with
> God and his Word a daily
> priority, I find my choices
> about wants vs. needs
> amazingly easy.
>
> LIZ CURTIS HIGGS

Joab agreed, [15]and twelve of Ishbosheth's men from the tribe of Benjamin got up to fight twelve of David's men. [16]They grabbed each other by the hair and stabbed each other in the side with their daggers. They all died right there! That's why the place in Gibeon is called "Field of Daggers."[n] [17]Then everyone started fighting. Both sides fought very hard, but David's soldiers defeated Abner and the soldiers of Israel.

[18]Zeruiah's three sons were there: Joab, Abishai, and Asahel. Asahel could run as fast as a deer in an open field, [19]and he ran straight after Abner, without looking to the right or to the left. [20]When Abner turned and saw him, he said, "Is that you, Asahel?"

Asahel answered, "Yes it is."

[21]Abner said, "There are soldiers all around. Stop chasing me and fight one of them! Kill him and take his clothes and weapons for yourself."

But Asahel refused to stop.

[22]Abner said, "If you don't turn back, I'll have to kill you! Then I could never face your brother Joab again."

[23]But Asahel would not turn back, so Abner struck him in the stomach with the back end of his spear. The spear went all the way through and came out of his back. Asahel fell down and died. Everyone who saw Asahel lying dead just stopped and stood still. [24]But Joab and Abishai went after Abner. Finally, about sunset, they came to the hill of Ammah, not far from Giah on the road to Gibeon Desert. [25]Abner brought the men of Benjamin together in one group on top of a hill, and they got ready to fight.

[26]Abner shouted to Joab, "Aren't we ever going to stop killing each other? Don't you know that the longer we keep on doing this, the worse it's going to be when it's all over? When are you going to order your men to stop chasing their own relatives?"

[27]Joab shouted back, "I swear by the living God, if you hadn't spoken, my men would have chased their relatives all night!" [28]Joab took his trumpet and blew the signal for his soldiers to stop chasing the soldiers of Israel. Right away, the fighting stopped.

[29]Abner and his troops marched through the Jordan River valley all that night. Then they crossed the river and marched all morning[o] until they arrived back at Mahanaim.

[30]As soon as Joab stopped chasing Abner, he got David's troops together and counted them. There were nineteen missing besides Asahel. [31]But David's soldiers had killed 360 of Abner's men from the tribe of Benjamin. [32]Joab and his troops carried

---

[j]**2.9** *Asher:* The Hebrew text has "Ashur," which is the Hebrew name for the Assyrians. It may be another spelling for Asher (one of the tribes of Israel) or it may refer to Geshur (a small area between Gilead and Jezreel, east of Lake Galilee). [k]**2.12** *Ishbosheth:* See the note at 2.8. [l]**2.13** *the son of Zeruiah:* Zeruiah was David's older sister, so Joab was David's nephew (see 1 Chronicles 2.12-17 and the note at 2 Samuel 17.25). [m]**2.13** *pool in Gibeon:* This pool was located just inside the city wall and was used for storing water. It was in the shape of a circle and was 36 feet wide and 36 feet deep. [n]**2.16** *Field of Daggers:* Or "Field of Opponents" or "Battlefield." [o]**2.29** *all morning:* One possible meaning for the difficult Hebrew text.

Asahel's body to Bethlehem and buried him in the family burial place. Then they marched all night and reached Hebron before sunrise.

3 This battle was the beginning of a long war between the followers of Saul and the followers of David. Saul's power grew weaker, but David's grew stronger.

David's Sons Born in Hebron
(1 Chronicles 3.1-4)

2-5Several of David's sons were born while he was living in Hebron. His oldest son was Amnon, whose mother was Ahinoam from Jezreel. David's second son was Chileab, whose mother was Abigail, who had been married to Nabal from Carmel. Absalom was the third. His mother was Maacah, the daughter of King Talmai of Geshur. The fourth was Adonijah, whose mother was Haggith. The fifth was Shephatiah, whose mother was Abital. The sixth was Ithream, whose mother was Eglah, another one of David's wives.

Abner Decides To Help David

6As the war went on between the families of David and Saul, Abner was gaining more power than ever in Saul's family. 7He had even slept with a wife[p] of Saul by the name of Rizpah the daughter of Aiah. But Saul's son Ishbosheth[q] told Abner, "You shouldn't have slept with one of my father's wives!"

8Abner was very angry at what Ishbosheth had said, and he told Ishbosheth:

Am I some kind of worthless dog from Judah? I've always been loyal to your father's family and to his relatives and friends. I haven't turned you over to David. And yet you talk to me as if I've committed a crime with this woman.

9I ask God to punish me if I don't help David get what the LORD promised him! 10God said that he wouldn't let anyone in Saul's family ever be king again and that David would be king instead. He also said that David would rule both Israel and Judah, all the way from Dan in the north to Beersheba in the south.[r]

11Ishbosheth was so afraid of Abner that he could not even answer.

12Abner sent some of his men to David with this message: "You should be the ruler of the whole nation.[s] If you make an agreement with me, I will persuade everyone in Israel to make you their king."

> *God is waiting to reveal to you his heavenly agenda and his plans for you.*
> PATSY CLAIRMONT

13David sent this message back: "Good! I'll make an agreement with you. But before I will even talk with you about it, you must get Saul's daughter Michal back for me."

14David sent a few of his officials to Ishbosheth to give him this message: "Give me back my wife Michal! I killed a hundred Philistines so I could marry her."[t]

15Ishbosheth sent some of his men to take Michal away from her new husband, Paltiel the son of Laish. 16Paltiel followed Michal and the men all the way to Bahurim, crying as he walked. But he went back home after Abner ordered him to leave.

17Abner talked with the leaders of the tribes of Israel and told them, "You've wanted to make David your king for a long time now. 18So do it! After all, God said he would use his servant David to rescue his people Israel from their enemies, especially from the Philistines."

19Finally, Abner talked with the tribe of Benjamin. Then he left for Hebron to tell David everything that the tribe of Benjamin and the rest of the people of Israel wanted to do. 20Abner took twenty soldiers with him, and when they got to Hebron, David gave a big feast for them.

21After the feast, Abner said, "Your Majesty, let me leave now and bring Israel here to make an agreement with you. You'll be

---

p3.7 *wife:* This translates a Hebrew word for a woman who was legally bound to a man, but without the full privileges of a wife. q3.7 *Ishbosheth:* See the note at 2.8. r3.10 *from . . . south:* Hebrew "from Dan to Beersheba." This was one way of describing all of the Israelite land, from north to south. s3.12 *You . . . nation:* Or "I like you." t3.14 *I killed . . . marry her:* See 1 Samuel 18.20-27.

king of the whole nation, just as you've been wanting."

David told Abner he could leave, and he left without causing any trouble.

Joab Kills Abner

²²Soon after Abner had left Hebron, Joab and some of David's soldiers came back, bringing a lot of things they had taken from an enemy village. ²³Right after they arrived, someone told Joab, "Abner visited the king, and the king let him go. Abner even left without causing any trouble."

²⁴Joab went to David and said, "What have you done? Abner came to you, and you let him go. Now he's long gone! ²⁵You know Abner—he came to trick you. He wants to find out how strong your army is and to know everything you're doing."

²⁶Joab left David, then he sent some messengers to catch up with Abner. They brought him back from the well at Sirah,ᵘ but David did not know anything about it. ²⁷When Abner returned to Hebron, Joab pretended he wanted to talk privately with him. So he took Abner into one of the small rooms that were part of the town gate and stabbed him in the stomach. Joab killed him because Abner had killed Joab's brother Asahel.

Abner's Funeral

²⁸David heard how Joab had killed Abner, and he said, "I swear to the LORD that I am completely innocent of Abner's death! ²⁹Joab and his family are the guilty ones. I pray that Joab's family will always be sick with sores and other skin diseases. May they all be cowards,ᵛ and may they die in war or starve to death."

³⁰Joab and his brother Abishai killed Abner because he had killed their brother Asahel in the battle at Gibeon.

³¹David told Joab and everyone with him, "Show your sorrow by tearing your clothes and wearing sackcloth!ʷ Walk in front of Abner's body and cry!"

David walked behind the stretcher on which Abner's body was being carried. ³²Abner was buried in Hebron, while David and everyone else stood at the tomb and cried loudly. ³³Then the king sang a funeral song about Abner:

Abner, why should you
    have died like an outlaw?ˣ
³⁴No one tied your hands
    or chained your feet,
yet you died as a victim
    of murderers.

Everyone started crying again. ³⁵Then they brought some food to David and told him he would feel better if he had something to eat. It was still daytime, and David said, "I swear to God that I'll not take a bite of bread or anything else until sunset!"

³⁶Everyone noticed what David did, and they liked it, just as they always liked what he did. ³⁷Now the people of Judah and Israel were certain that David had nothing to do with killing Abner.

³⁸David said to his officials, "Don't you realize that today one of Israel's great leaders has died? ³⁹I am the chosen king, but Joab and Abishai have more power than I do. So God will have to pay them backʸ for the evil thing they did."

Ishbosheth Is Killed

4 Ishboshethᶻ felt like giving up after he heard that Abner had died in Hebron. Everyone in Israel was terrified.

²Ishbosheth had put the two brothers Baanah and Rechab in charge of the soldiers who raided enemy villages. Rimmon was their father, and they were from the town of Beeroth, which belonged to the tribe of Benjamin. ³The people who used to live in Beeroth had run away to Gittaim, and they still liveᵃ there.

⁴Saul's son Jonathan had a son named Mephibosheth,ᵇ who had not been able to walk since he was five years old. It happened when someone from Jezreel told his nurse that Saul and Jonathan had died.ᶜ She

---

ᵘ3.26 *well at Sirah:* Or "oasis of Sirah" or "cistern at Sirah." ᵛ3.29 *cowards:* One possible meaning for the difficult Hebrew text. ʷ3.31 *sackcloth:* Sackcloth was a rough, dark-colored cloth made from goat or camel hair and was used to make grain sacks. People wore sackcloth or tore their clothes in times of trouble or sorrow. ˣ3.33 *outlaw:* Or "fool." ʸ3.39 *God . . . back:* Or "I pray that God will pay them back." ᶻ4.1 *Ishbosheth:* Hebrew "The Son of Saul." ᵃ4.3 *live:* The Hebrew word means that they did not have the full legal rights of citizens. ᵇ4.4 *Mephibosheth:* Some manuscripts of one ancient translation have "Mephibaal." In 1 Chronicles 8.34 and 9.40 he is called "Meribbaal." See the note on "baal" and "bosheth" at 2.8. ᶜ4.4 *Saul . . . died:* See 1 Samuel 31.1-6.

hurried off with the boy in her arms, but he fell and injured his legs.

⁵One day about noon, Rechab and Baanah went in to Ishbosheth's house. It was a hot day, and he was resting ⁶⁻⁷in his bedroom. The two brothers went into the house, pretending to get some flour. But once they were inside, they stabbed Ishbosheth in the stomach and killed him. Then they cut off his head and took it with them.

Rechab and Baanah walked through the Jordan River valley all night long. ⁸Finally they turned west and went to Hebron. They went in to see David and told him, "Your Majesty, here is the head of Ishbosheth, the son of your enemy Saul who tried to kill you! The LORD has let you get even with Saul and his family."

⁹David answered:

I swear that only the LORD rescues me when I'm in trouble! ¹⁰When a man came to Ziklag and told me that Saul was dead, he thought he deserved a reward for bringing good news. But I grabbed him and killed him.

¹¹You evil men have done something much worse than he did. You've killed an innocent man in his own house and on his own bed. I'll make you pay for that. I'll wipe you from the face of the earth!

¹²Then David said to his troops, "Kill these two brothers! Cut off their hands and feet and hang their bodies by the pool in Hebron. But bury Ishbosheth's head in Abner's tomb near Hebron." And they did.

David Becomes King of Israel
(1 Chronicles 11.1-3)

5 Israel's leaders met with David at Hebron and said, "We are your relatives. ²Even when Saul was king, you led our nation in battle. And the LORD promised that someday you would rule Israel and take care of us like a shepherd."

³During the meeting, David made an agreement with the leaders and asked the LORD to be their witness. Then the leaders poured olive oil on David's head to show that he was now the king of Israel.

⁴David was thirty years old when he became king, and he ruled for forty years. ⁵He lived in Hebron for the first seven and a half

years and ruled only Judah. Then he moved to Jerusalem, where he ruled both Israel and Judah for thirty-three years.

How David Captured Jerusalem
(1 Chronicles 11.4-9; 14.1-2)

⁶The Jebusites lived in Jerusalem, and David led his army there to attack them. The Jebusites did not think he could get in, so they told him, "You can't get in here! We could run you off, even if we couldn't see or walk!"

⁷⁻⁹David told his troops, "You will have to go up through the water tunnel to get those Jebusites. I hate people like them who can't walk or see."ᵈ

That's why there is still a rule that says, "Only people who can walk and see are allowed in the temple."ᵉ

David captured the fortress on Mount Zion, then he moved there and named it David's City. He had the city rebuilt, starting with the landfill to the east. ¹⁰David became a great and strong ruler, because the LORD All-Powerful was on his side.

¹¹King Hiram of Tyre sent some officials to David. Carpenters and stone workers came with them, and they brought cedar logs so they could build David a palace.

¹²David knew that the LORD had made him king of Israel and that he had made him a powerful ruler for the good of his people.

David's Sons Born in Jerusalem
(1 Chronicles 14.3-7)

¹³After David left Hebron and moved to Jerusalem, he married many womenᶠ from Jerusalem,ᵍ and he had a lot of children. ¹⁴His sons who were born there were Shammua, Shobab, Nathan, Solomon, ¹⁵Ibhar, Elishua, Nepheg, Japhia, ¹⁶Elishama, Eliada,ʰ and Eliphelet.

David Fights the Philistines
(1 Chronicles 14.8-17)

¹⁷The Philistines heard that David was now king of Israel, and they came into the hill country to try and capture him. But

ᵈ**5.7-9** *You will . . . or see*: One possible meaning for the difficult Hebrew text.   ᵉ**5.7-9** *temple*: Or "palace."
ᶠ**5.13** *married many women*: Some of these women were second-class wives (see the note at 3.7).   ᵍ**5.13** *from Jerusalem*: Or "in Jerusalem."   ʰ**5.16** *Eliada*: See 1 Chronicles 3.8. First Chronicles 14.7 has "Baalyada."

David found out and went into his fortress.[i] [18]So the Philistines camped in Rephaim Valley.[j]

[19]David asked the LORD, "Should I attack the Philistines? Will you let me win?"

The LORD told David, "Attack! I will let you win."

[20]David attacked the Philistines and defeated them. Then he said, "I watched the LORD break through my enemies like a mighty flood." So he named the place "The Lord Broke Through."[k] [21]David and his troops also carried away the idols that the Philistines had left behind.

[22]Some time later, the Philistines came back into the hill country and camped in Rephaim Valley. [23]David asked the LORD what he should do, and the LORD answered:

Don't attack them from the front. Circle around behind and attack from among the balsam[l] trees. [24]Wait until you hear a sound like troops marching through the tops of the trees. Then attack quickly! That sound will mean I have marched out ahead of you to fight the Philistine army.

[25]David obeyed the LORD and defeated the Philistines. He even chased them all the way from Geba to the entrance to Gezer.

David Brings the Sacred Chest Back to Jerusalem
(1 Chronicles 13.1-14; 15.1—16.3, 43)

6 David brought together thirty thousand of Israel's best soldiers and [2]led them to Baalah in Judah, which was also called Kiriath-Jearim. They were going there[m] to get the sacred chest and bring it back to Jerusalem. The throne of the LORD All-Powerful is above the winged creatures[n] on top of this chest, and he is worshiped there.[o]

[3]They put the sacred chest on a new ox cart and started bringing it down the hill from Abinadab's house. Abinadab's sons Uzzah and Ahio were guiding the ox cart, [4]with Ahio[p] walking in front of it. [5]Some of the people of Israel were playing music on small harps and other stringed instruments, and on tambourines, castanets, and cymbals. David and the others were happy, and they danced for the LORD with all their might.

[6]But when they came to Nacon's threshing-floor, the oxen stumbled, so Uzzah reached out and took hold of the sacred chest. [7]The LORD God was very angry at Uzzah for doing this, and he killed Uzzah right there beside the chest.

[8]David got angry at God for killing Uzzah. He named that place "Bursting Out Against Uzzah,"[q] and that's what it's still called.

[9]David was afraid of the LORD and thought, "Should I really take the sacred chest to my city?" [10]He decided not to take it there. Instead, he turned off the road and took it to the home of Obed Edom, who was from Gath.[r]

[11-12]The chest stayed there for three months, and the LORD greatly blessed Obed Edom, his family, and everything he owned. Then someone told King David, "The LORD has done this because the sacred chest is in Obed Edom's house."

Right away, David went to Obed Edom's house to get the chest and bring it to David's City. Everyone was celebrating. [13]The people carrying the chest walked six steps, then David sacrificed an ox and a choice cow. [14]He was dancing for the LORD with all his might, but he wore only a linen cloth.[s] [15]He and everyone else were celebrating by shouting and blowing horns while the chest was being carried along.

[16]Saul's daughter Michal looked out her window and watched the chest being brought into David's City. But when she saw David jumping and dancing for the LORD, she was disgusted.

[17]They put the chest inside a tent that

---

[i]5.17 fortress: Probably the fortress of Adullam, which was David's former hideout (see 1 Samuel 22.1, 4; 24.22). Or it could refer to the older walled city of Jerusalem, called the "fortress on Mount Zion" in verses 7-9.   [j]5.18 Rephaim Valley: A few miles southwest of Jerusalem.   [k]5.20 The Lord Broke Through: Or "Baal-Perazim."   [l]5.23 balsam: One possible meaning for the difficult Hebrew text.   [m]6.2 to Baalah . . . there: The Dead Sea Scrolls and 1 Chronicles 13.6; the Standard Hebrew Text "from Baalah in Judah. They had gone there."   [n]6.2 winged creatures: Two golden statues of winged creatures were on top of the sacred chest and were symbols of the LORD's throne on earth (see Exodus 25.18).   [o]6.2 he is worshiped there: Or "the chest belongs to him."   [p]6.3,4 Ahio . . . Ahio: Or "his brother . . . his brother."   [q]6.8 Bursting . . . Uzzah: Or "Perez-Uzzah."   [r]6.10 Gath: Or perhaps, "Gittaim."   [s]6.14 only a linen cloth: The Hebrew word is "ephod," which can mean either a piece of clothing like a skirt that went from the waist to the knee or a garment like a vest or a jacket that only the priests wore.

David had set up for it. David worshiped the LORD by sacrificing animals and burning them on an altar,[f] [18]then he blessed the people in the name of the LORD All-Powerful. [19]He gave all the men and women in the crowd a small loaf of bread, some meat, and a handful of raisins, and everyone went home.

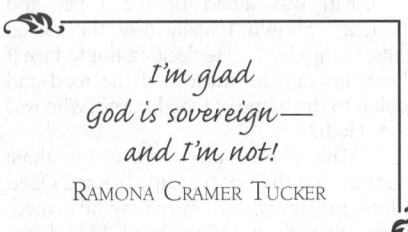

I'm glad
God is sovereign—
and I'm not!

RAMONA CRAMER TUCKER

Michal Talks to David

[20]David went home so he could ask the LORD to bless his family. But Saul's daughter Michal went out and started yelling at him. "You were really great today!" she said. "You acted like a dirty old man, dancing around half-naked in front of your servants' slave-girls."

[21]David told her, "The LORD didn't choose your father or anyone else in your family to be the leader of his people. The LORD chose me, and I was celebrating in honor of him. [22]I'll show you just how great I can be! I'll even be disgusting to myself. But those slave-girls you talked about will still honor me!"

[23]Michal never had any children.

The LORD's Message to David
(1 Chronicles 17.1-15)

7 King David moved into his new palace, and the LORD let his kingdom be at peace. [2]Then one day, as David was talking with Nathan the prophet, David said, "Look around! I live in a palace made of cedar, but the sacred chest has to stay in a tent."

[3]Nathan replied, "The LORD is with you, so do what you want!"

[4]That night, the LORD told Nathan [5]to go to David and give him this message:

David, you are my servant, so listen to what I say. Why should you build a temple for me? [6]I didn't live in a temple when I brought my people out of Egypt, and I don't live in one now. A tent has always been my home wherever I have gone with them. [7]I chose leaders and told them to be like shepherds for my people Israel. But did I ever say anything to even one of them about building a cedar temple for me?

[8]David, this is what I, the LORD All-Powerful, say to you. I brought you in from the fields where you took care of sheep, and I made you the leader of my people. [9]Wherever you went, I helped you and destroyed your enemies right in front of your eyes. I have made you one of the most famous people in the world.

[10]I have given my people Israel a land of their own where they can live in peace, and they won't have to tremble with fear any more. Evil nations won't bother them, as they did [11]when I let judges rule my people. And I have kept your enemies from attacking you.

Now I promise that you and your descendants will be kings. [12]I'll choose one of your sons to be king when you reach the end of your life and are buried in the tomb of your ancestors. I'll make him a strong ruler, [13]and no one will be able to take his kingdom away from him. He will be the one to build a temple for me. [14]I will be his father, and he will be my son.

When he does wrong, I'll see that he is corrected, just as children are corrected by their parents. [15]But I will never put an end to my agreement with him, as I put an end to my agreement with Saul, who was king before you. [16]I will make sure that one of your descendants will always be king.

[17]Nathan told David exactly what he had heard in the vision.

David Gives Thanks to the LORD
(1 Chronicles 17.16-27)

[18]David went into the tent he had set up for the sacred chest. Then he sat there and prayed:

---

[f]6.17 *sacrificing . . . altar:* The Hebrew mentions two kinds of sacrifices. In one kind of sacrifice, the whole animal was burned on the altar. In the other kind, only part was burned, and the worshipers ate the rest, as in verse 19 (see Leviticus 1.2-17; 3.1-17).

LORD All-Powerful, my family and I don't deserve what you have already done for us, [19]and yet you have promised to do even more. Is this the way you usually treat people?[u] [20]I am your servant, and you know my thoughts, so there is nothing more that I need to say. [21]You have done this wonderful thing, and you have let me know about it, because you wanted to keep your promise.

[22]LORD All-Powerful, you are greater than all others. No one is like you, and you alone are God. Everything we have heard about you is true. [23]And there is no other nation on earth like Israel, the nation you rescued from slavery in Egypt to be your own. You became famous by using great and wonderful miracles to force other nations and their gods out of your land, so your people could live here.[v] [24]You have chosen Israel to be your people forever, and you have become their God.

[25]And now, LORD God, please do what you have promised me and my descendants. [26]Then you will be famous forever, and everyone will say, "The LORD God All-Powerful rules Israel, and David's descendants are his chosen kings." [27]After all, you really are Israel's God, the LORD All-Powerful. You've told me that you will let my descendants be kings. That's why I have the courage to pray to you like this, even though I am only your servant.

[28]LORD All-Powerful, you are God. You have promised me some very good things, and you can be trusted to do what you promise. [29]Please bless my descendants and let them always be your chosen kings. You have already promised, and I'm sure that you will bless my family forever.

A List of David's Victories in War
(1 Chronicles 18.1-13)

8 Later, David attacked and badly defeated the Philistines. Israel was now free from their control.[w]
[2]David also defeated the Moabites. Then he made their soldiers lie down on the ground, and he measured them off with a rope. He would measure off two lengths of

---

[u]**7.19** *Is this . . . people:* One possible meaning for the difficult Hebrew text. [v]**7.23** *You . . . here:* One possible meaning for the difficult Hebrew text. [w]**8.1** *Israel . . . control:* Or "David also took the town of Metheg-Ammah away from them."

---

*Spiritual*Life—How should I pray? *(2 Samuel 7.18-29)*

Tell it like it is.
Prayer is a mysterious communication between the All-Powerful Lord and a limited human being, but at its core it's a conversation. Although God knows you and your thoughts (7.20), he made you to worship him and to commune with him.

So when you pray, sound like yourself. Tell God what you think you need and why it seems important. Don't submit a wish list, but share your heart's desires as you would in any good conversation.

Then explore God's agenda. What do you know from God's Word regarding his intentions in this matter? What are his promises in relation to what you have asked? (For example, did he promise a fun car and new vertical blinds to faithful believers?) As we consider who God is and what we know about him, we may or may not adjust our requests. We always have to ask, *What do my requests have to do with God's primary concern of bringing the people of the world into relationship with him?*

Putting together our desires and God's will takes quiet time. So don't be afraid to bring up the same topic to God many times. It isn't a sign of weakness, but of openness for more input and wisdom from God. (See also 2 Kings 19.14-19; 2 Chronicles 6,7; Nehemiah 1; Psalm 85; Lamentations 5; Matthew 6.5-15; Acts 4.23-31.)

Words To Remember: *LORD All-Powerful, you are God. You have promised me some very good things, and you can be trusted to do what you promise.—2 Samuel 7.28*

the rope and have those men killed, then he would measure off one length and let those men live. The people of Moab had to accept David as their ruler and pay taxes to him.

³David set out for the Euphrates River to build a monument[x] there. On his way,[y] he defeated the king of Zobah, whose name was Hadadezer the son of Rehob. ⁴In the battle, David captured seventeen hundred cavalry[z] and twenty thousand foot soldiers. He also captured war chariots, but he destroyed all but one hundred of them.[a] ⁵When troops from the Aramean kingdom of Damascus came to help Hadadezer, David killed twenty thousand of them. ⁶He left some of his soldiers in Damascus, and the Arameans had to accept David as their ruler and pay taxes to him.

Everywhere David went, the LORD helped him win battles.

⁷Hadadezer's officers had carried their arrows in gold cases hung over their shoulders, but David took these cases[b] and brought them to Jerusalem. ⁸He also took a lot of bronze from the cities of Betah and Berothai, which had belonged to Hadadezer.

Simple obedience. Joyful, eager, unquestioning obedience is the height of training for the Christian. For it is this that gives God the greatest pleasure.

RUTH BELL GRAHAM

---

⁹⁻¹⁰King Toi of Hamath and King Hadadezer had been enemies. So when Toi heard that David had attacked and defeated[c] Hadadezer's whole army, he sent his son Joram to praise and congratulate David. Joram also brought him gifts made of silver, gold, and bronze. ¹¹David gave these to the LORD, just as he had done with the silver and gold that he had captured from ¹²Edom,[d] Moab, Ammon, Philistia, and from King Hadadezer of Zobah.

¹³David fought the Edomite[e] army in Salt Valley and killed eighteen thousand of their

soldiers. When he returned, he built a monument.[f] ¹⁴David left soldiers all through Edom, and the people of Edom had to accept him as their ruler.

Wherever David went, the LORD helped him.

A List of David's Officials

(1 Chronicles 18.14-17)

¹⁵David ruled all Israel with fairness and justice.

¹⁶Joab the son of Zeruiah was the commander in chief of the army.

Jehoshaphat the son of Ahilud kept the government records.

¹⁷Zadok the son of Ahitub, and Abiathar the son of Ahimelech,[g] were the priests.

Seraiah was the secretary.

¹⁸Benaiah the son of Jehoiada was the commander of[h] David's bodyguard.[i]

David's sons were priests.

David Is Kind to Mephibosheth

9 One day, David thought, "I wonder if any of Saul's family are still alive. If they are, I will be kind to them, because I made a promise to Jonathan." ²David called in Ziba, one of the servants of Saul's family. David said, "So you are Ziba."

"Yes, Your Majesty, I am."

³David asked, "Are any of Saul's family

---

[x]**8.3** *monument*: Kings sometimes set up monuments in lands they had conquered. [y]**8.3** *David . . . way*: One possible meaning for the difficult Hebrew text. It may have been Hadadezer who was going to the Euphrates River. And he may have gone there either to build a monument or to put down a rebellion. [z]**8.4** *seventeen hundred cavalry*: Hebrew; one ancient translation and 1 Chronicles 18.4 "a thousand chariots and seven thousand cavalry." [a]**8.4** *He also captured . . . them*: Or "He crippled all but one hundred of the horses." [b]**8.7** *Hadadezer's . . . cases*: Or "Hadadezer's soldiers carried gold shields, but David took these shields." [c]**8.9,10** *defeated*: Or "killed." [d]**8.12** *Edom*: Some Hebrew manuscripts and two ancient translations (see also 1 Chronicles 18.11); most Hebrew manuscripts "Aram." In Hebrew the words for "Edom" and "Aram" look almost alike. [e]**8.13** *Edomite*: Some Hebrew manuscripts and two ancient translations (see also 1 Chronicles 18.12); most Hebrew manuscripts "Aramean." In Hebrew the words for "Edomite" and "Aramean" look almost alike. [f]**8.13** *built a monument*: Or "was famous." [g]**8.17** *Abiathar the son of Ahimelech*: One ancient translation and 1 Samuel 22.11-23; Hebrew "Ahimelech the son of Abiathar." [h]**8.18** *was the commander of*: Not in the Hebrew text of this verse, but see 1 Chronicles 18.17. [i]**8.18** *David's bodyguard*: The Hebrew text has "the Cherethites and the Pelethites," who were foreign soldiers hired by David to be his bodyguard.

still alive? If there are, I want to be kind to them."

Ziba answered, "One of Jonathan's sons is still alive, but he can't walk."

[4]"Where is he?" David asked.

Ziba replied, "He lives in Lo-Debar with Machir the son of Ammiel."

[5-6]David sent some servants to bring Jonathan's son from Lo-Debar. His name was Mephibosheth,[j] and he was the grandson of Saul. He came to David and knelt down.

David asked, "Are you Mephibosheth?"

"Yes, I am, Your Majesty."

[7]David said, "Don't be afraid. I'll be kind to you because Jonathan was your father. I'm going to give you back the land that belonged to your grandfather Saul. Besides that, you will always eat with me at my table."

[8]Mephibosheth knelt down again and said, "Why should you care about me? I'm worth no more than a dead dog."

[9]David called in Ziba, Saul's chief servant, and told him, "Since Mephibosheth is Saul's grandson, I've given him back everything that belonged to your master Saul and his family. [10]You and your fifteen sons and twenty servants will work for Mephibosheth. You will farm his land and bring in his crops, so that Saul's family and servants[k] will have food. But Mephibosheth will always eat with me at my table."

[11-13]Ziba replied, "Your Majesty, I will do exactly what you tell me to do." So Ziba's

family and servants worked for Mephibosheth.

Mephibosheth was lame, but he lived in Jerusalem and ate at David's[l] table, just like one of David's own sons. And he had a young son of his own, named Mica.

Israel Fights Ammon
(1 Chronicles 19.1-19)

10 Some time later, King Nahash of Ammon died, and his son Hanun became king. [2]David said, "Nahash was kind to me, and I will be kind to his son." So he sent some officials to the country of Ammon to tell Hanun how sorry he was that his father had died.

[3]But Hanun's officials told him, "Do you really believe David is honoring your father by sending these people to comfort you? He probably sent them to spy on our city, so he can destroy it." [4]Hanun arrested David's officials and had their beards shaved off on one side of their faces. He had their robes cut off just below the waist, and then he sent them away. [5]They were terribly ashamed.

When David found out what had happened to his officials, he sent a message and told them, "Stay in Jericho until your beards grow back. Then you can come home."

[6]The Ammonites realized that they had

---

[j]9.5,6 *Mephibosheth*: Or "Mephibaal" (see the note at 4.4).   [k]9.10 *Saul's family and servants*: Some manuscripts of one ancient translation; Hebrew "the son of your master."   [l]9.11-13 *David's*: Hebrew "my."

---

*Spiritual*Life—How can I reach out to a needy world? *(2 Samuel 9)*

Talk face-to-face.
There's a difference between giving that makes us feel good and giving that makes others feel good. The first soothes our conscience, and the latter is personal and well researched.

David researched how he could help Saul's relatives. Were they alive? Yes. Then he talked with Saul's grandson, Mephibosheth, and gave him a gift that had personal as well as monetary value: the property that had belonged to Saul. David could have given him the land through his servant, Ziba, but instead he spoke personally to Mephibosheth about his father, Jonathan, and how much Jonathan had meant to him.

Sometimes, when we are not sure what to do to help someone, we need a face-to-face, person-to-person conversation with them. Researched giving helps us respect the person's feelings and dignity, and connect with someone God loves. And one of the things the world needs most is healing, caring relationships. (See also Nehemiah 5.1-13; Lamentations 2.11-13; Jonah 4.5-11; Zechariah 7.7-13; Matthew 6.1-4; Luke 9.10-17.)

Words To Remember: *David said, "Don't be afraid. I'll be kind to you."*
—2 Samuel 9.7

made David very angry, so they hired more foreign soldiers. Twenty thousand of them were foot soldiers from the Aramean cities of Beth-Rehob and Zobah, one thousand were from the king of Maacah, and twelve thousand were from the region of Tob. [7]David heard what they had done, and he sent out Joab with all of his well-trained soldiers.

[8]The Ammonite troops came out and got ready to fight in front of the gate to their city. The Arameans from Zobah and Rehob and the soldiers from Tob and Maacah formed a separate group in the nearby fields.

[9]Joab saw that he had to fight in front and behind at the same time, and he picked some of the best Israelite soldiers to fight the Arameans. [10]He put his brother Abishai in command of the rest of the army and had them fight the Ammonites. [11]Joab told his brother, "If the Arameans are too much for me to handle, you can come and help me. If the Ammonites are too strong for you, I'll come and help you. [12]Be brave and fight hard to protect our people and the cities of our God. I pray that the LORD will do whatever pleases him."

[13]Joab and his soldiers attacked the Arameans, and the Arameans ran from them. [14]When the Ammonite soldiers saw that the Arameans had run away, they ran from Abishai's soldiers and went back into their own city. Joab stopped fighting the Ammonites and returned to Jerusalem.

[15]The Arameans realized they had lost the battle, so they brought all their troops together again. [16]Hadadezer sent messengers to call in the Arameans who were on the other side of the Euphrates River. Then Shobach, the commander of Hadadezer's army, led them to the town of Helam. [17]David found out what the Arameans were doing, and he brought Israel's whole army together. They crossed the Jordan River and went to Helam, where the Arameans were ready to meet them. [18]The Arameans attacked, but then they ran from Israel. David killed seven hundred chariot drivers and forty thousand cavalry.[m] He also killed Shobach, their commander.

[19]When the kings who had been under Hadadezer's rule saw that Israel had beaten them, they made peace with Israel and accepted David as their ruler. The Arameans were afraid to help Ammon any more.

David and Bathsheba
(1 Chronicles 20.1a)

11 It was now spring, the time when kings go to war.[n] David sent out the whole Israelite army under the command of Joab and his officers. They destroyed the Ammonite army and surrounded the capital city of Rabbah, but David stayed in Jerusalem.

[2-4]Late one afternoon, David got up from a nap and was walking around on the flat roof of his palace. A beautiful young woman was down below in her courtyard, bathing as her religion required.[o] David happened to see her, and he sent one of his servants to find out who she was.

The servant came back and told David, "Her name is Bathsheba. She is the daughter of Eliam, and she is the wife of Uriah the Hittite."

David sent some messengers to bring her to his palace. She came to him, and he slept with her. Then she returned home. [5]But later, when she found out that she was going to have a baby, she sent someone to David with this message: "I'm pregnant!"

[6]David sent a message to Joab: "Send Uriah the Hittite to me."

Joab sent Uriah [7]to David's palace, and David asked him, "Is Joab well? How is the army doing? And how about the war?" [8]Then David told Uriah, "Go home and clean up."[p] Uriah left the king's palace, and David had dinner sent to Uriah's house. [9]But Uriah didn't go home. Instead, he slept outside the entrance to the royal palace, where the king's guards slept.

[10]Someone told David that Uriah had not gone home. So the next morning David asked him, "Why didn't you go home? Haven't you been away for a long time?"

[11]Uriah answered, "The sacred chest and the armies of Israel and Judah are camping out somewhere in the fields[q] with our commander Joab and his officers and troops. Do you really think I would go home to eat and

---

[m]**10.18** *cavalry:* The Hebrew manuscripts and ancient translations differ as to how many and what kind of soldiers were killed. [n]**11.1** *when . . . war:* Or "when the messengers had gone to Ammon" (see 10.2) or "the time when the kings had gone to war" (see 10.6-8). [o]**11.2-4** *as . . . required:* This bathing was often a requirement for worshiping God. [p]**11.8** *and clean up:* Or "and sleep with your wife." [q]**11.11** *somewhere in the fields:* Or "at Succoth."

drink and sleep with my wife? I swear by your life that I would not!"

¹²Then David said, "Stay here in Jerusalem today, and I will send you back tomorrow."

Uriah stayed in Jerusalem that day. Then the next day, ¹³David invited him for dinner. Uriah ate with David and drank so much that he got drunk, but he still did not go home. He went out and slept on his mat near the palace guards. ¹⁴Early the next morning, David wrote a letter and told Uriah to deliver it to Joab. ¹⁵The letter said: "Put Uriah on the front line where the fighting is the worst. Then pull the troops back from him, so that he will be wounded and die."

> *The media tells us that romance and sex are what count, not relationship. But what we really need is Jesus' love and a relationship with him. Only then can our deepest needs be satisfied.*
>
> FRANCINE RIVERS

¹⁶Joab had been carefully watching the city of Rabbah, and he put Uriah in a place where he knew there were some of the enemy's best soldiers. ¹⁷When the men of the city came out, they fought and killed some of David's soldiers—Uriah the Hittite was one of them.

¹⁸Joab sent a messenger to tell David everything that was happening in the war. ¹⁹He gave the messenger these orders:

When you finish telling the king everything that has happened, ²⁰he may get angry and ask, "Why did you go so near the city to fight? Didn't you know they would shoot arrows from the wall? ²¹Don't you know how Abimelech the son of Gideon[r] was killed at Thebez? Didn't a woman kill him by dropping a large rock from the top of the city wall? Why did you go so close to the city walls?"

Then you tell him, "One of your soldiers who was killed was Uriah the Hittite."

²²The messenger went to David and reported everything Joab had told him. ²³He added, "The enemy chased us from the wall and out into the open fields. But we pushed them back as far as the city gate. ²⁴Then they shot arrows at us from the top of the wall. Some of your soldiers were killed, and one of them was Uriah the Hittite."

²⁵David replied, "Tell Joab to cheer up and not to be upset about what happened. You never know who will be killed in a war. Tell him to strengthen his attack against the city and break through its walls."[s]

²⁶When Bathsheba heard that her husband was dead, she mourned for him. ²⁷Then after the time for mourning was over, David sent someone to bring her to the palace. She became David's wife, and they had a son.

The LORD's Message for David

12 The LORD was angry at what David had done, ¹and he sent Nathan the prophet to tell this story to David:

A rich man and a poor man lived in the same town. ²The rich man owned a lot of sheep and cattle, ³but the poor man had only one little lamb that he had bought and raised. The lamb became a pet for him and his children. He even let it eat from his plate and drink from his cup and sleep on his lap. The lamb was like one of his own children.

⁴One day someone came to visit the rich man, but the rich man didn't want to kill any of his own sheep or cattle and serve it to the visitor. So he stole the poor man's little lamb and served it instead.

⁵David was furious with the rich man and said to Nathan, "I swear by the living LORD that the man who did this deserves to

---

r**11.21** *Gideon:* The Hebrew text has Jerubbesheth, which stands for "Jerubbaal," another name for Gideon. See Judges 6.32 and the note on "bosheth" at 2.8 ("besheth" means the same as "bosheth").
s**11.25** *break . . . walls:* Or "destroy it."

die! [6]And because he didn't have any pity on the poor man, he will have to pay four times what the lamb was worth."

[7]Then Nathan told David:

You are that rich man! Now listen to what the LORD God of Israel says to you: "I chose you to be the king of Israel. I kept you safe from Saul [8]and even gave you his house and his wives. I let you rule Israel and Judah, and if that had not been enough, I would have given you much more. [9]Why did you disobey me and do such a horrible thing? You murdered Uriah the Hittite by having the Ammonites kill him, so you could take his wife.

[10]"Because you wouldn't obey me and took Uriah's wife for yourself, your family will never live in peace. [11]Someone from your own family will cause you a lot of trouble, and I will take your wives and give them to another man before your very eyes. He will go to bed with them while everyone looks on. [12]What you did was in secret, but I will do this in the open for everyone in Israel to see."

[13-14]David said, "I have disobeyed the LORD."

"Yes, you have!" Nathan answered. "You showed you didn't care what the LORD wanted.[t] He has forgiven you, and you won't die. But your newborn son will." [15]Then Nathan went back home.

David's Young Son Dies

The LORD made David's young son very sick.

[16]So David went without eating to show his sorrow, and he begged God to make the boy well. David would not sleep on his bed, but spent each night lying on the floor. [17]His officials stood beside him and tried to talk him into getting up. But he would not get up or eat with them.

[18]After the child had been sick for seven days, he died, but the officials were afraid to tell David. They said to each other, "Even when the boy was alive, David wouldn't listen to us. How can we tell him his son is dead? He might do something terrible!"

[19]David noticed his servants whispering, and he knew the boy was dead. "Did my son die?" he asked his servants.

"Yes, he did," they answered.

[20]David got up off the floor; he took a bath, combed his hair, and dressed. He went into the LORD's tent and worshiped, then he went back home. David asked for something to eat, and when his servants brought him some food, he ate it.

sex should always be presented as something good: sex isn't the enemy; it's the abuse of sex that causes harm. We want young people to see that sex within marriage is a wonderful thing worth waiting for.

PATRICIA FUNDERBURK WARE

[21]His officials said, "What are you doing? You went without eating and cried for your son while he was alive! But now that he's dead, you're up and eating."

[22]David answered:

While he was still alive, I went without food and cried because there was still hope. I said to myself, "Who knows? Maybe the LORD will have pity on me and let the child live." [23]But now that he's dead, why should I go without eating? I can't bring him back! Someday I will join him in death, but he can't return to me.

Solomon Is Born

[24]David comforted his wife Bathsheba and slept with her. Later on, she gave birth to another son and named him Solomon. The LORD loved Solomon [25]and sent Nathan the prophet to tell David, "The LORD will call him Jedidiah."[u]

---

[t]**12.13,14** *what . . . wanted:* One manuscript of one ancient translation; one Hebrew manuscript "what the LORD had said"; most Hebrew manuscripts "what the enemies of the LORD would think." [u]**12.25** *Jedidiah:* In Hebrew this name means "Loved by the LORD."

The End of the War with Ammon
(1 Chronicles 20.1b-3)

²⁶Meanwhile, Joab had been in the country of Ammon, attacking the city of Rabbah. He captured the royal fortress ²⁷and sent a messenger to tell David:

I have attacked Rabbah and captured the fortress guarding the city water supply. ²⁸Call the rest of the army together. Then surround the city, and capture it yourself. If you don't, everyone will remember that I captured the city.

²⁹David called the rest of the army together and attacked Rabbah. He captured the city ³⁰and took the crown from the statue of their god Milcom.^v The crown was made of seventy-five pounds of gold, and there was a valuable jewel on it. David put the jewel on his own crown.^w He also carried off everything else of value. ³¹David made the people of Rabbah tear down the city walls^x with iron picks and axes, and then he put them to work making bricks. He did the same thing with all the other Ammonite cities.

David went back to Jerusalem, and the people of Israel returned to their homes.

Amnon Disgraces Tamar

13 David had a beautiful daughter named Tamar, who was the sister of Absalom. She was also the half sister of Amnon,^y who fell in love with her. ²But Tamar was a virgin, and Amnon could not think of a way to be alone with her. He was so upset about it that he made himself sick.

³Amnon had a friend named Jonadab, who was the son of David's brother Shimeah. Jonadab always knew how to get what he wanted, ⁴and he said to Amnon, "What's the matter? You're the king's son! You shouldn't have to go around feeling sorry for yourself every morning."

Amnon said, "I'm in love with Tamar, my brother Absalom's sister."

⁵Jonadab told him, "Lie down on your bed and pretend to be sick. When your father comes to see you, ask him to send Tamar, so you can watch her cook something for you. Then she can serve you the food."

⁶So Amnon went to bed and pretended to be sick. When the king came to see him,

Amnon said, "Please, ask Tamar to come over. She can make some special bread^z while I watch, and then she can serve me the bread."

⁷David told Tamar, "Go over to Amnon's house and fix him some food." ⁸When she got there, he was lying in bed. She mixed the dough, made the loaves, and baked them while he watched. ⁹Then she took the bread out of the pan and put it on his plate, but he refused to eat it.

Amnon said, "Send the servants out of the house." After they had gone, ¹⁰he said to Tamar, "Serve the food in my bedroom."

Tamar picked up the bread that she had made and brought it into Amnon's bedroom. ¹¹But as she was taking it over to him, he grabbed her and said, "Come to bed with me!"

¹²She answered, "No! Please don't force me! This sort of thing isn't done in Israel. It's too disgusting! ¹³Think of me. I'll be disgraced forever! And think of yourself. Everyone in Israel will say you're nothing but trash! Just ask the king, and he will let you marry me."

¹⁴But Amnon would not listen to what she said. He was stronger than she was, so he overpowered her and raped her. ¹⁵Then Amnon hated her even more than he had loved her before. So he told her, "Get up and get out!"

¹⁶She said, "Don't send me away! That would be worse than what you have already done."

But Amnon would not listen. ¹⁷He called in his servant and said, "Throw this woman out and lock the door!"

¹⁸The servant made her leave, and he locked the door behind her.

The king's unmarried daughters used to wear long robes with sleeves.^a ¹⁹Tamar tore the robe she was wearing and put ashes on her head. Then she covered her face with her hands and cried loudly as she walked away.

---

^v**12.30** *the statue of their god Milcom:* Or "their king."
^w**12.30** *David . . . crown:* Or "and David wore the crown."   ^x**12.31** *tear . . . walls:* One possible meaning for the difficult Hebrew text.   ^y**13.1** *Tamar . . . Absalom . . . Amnon:* David was their father, but Amnon had a different mother.   ^z**13.6** *special bread:* Or "heart-shaped bread" or "dumplings."   ^a**13.18** *long . . . sleeves:* One possible meaning for the difficult Hebrew text.

Absalom Kills Amnon

²⁰Tamar's brother Absalom said to her, "How could Amnon have done such a terrible thing to you! But since he's your brother, don't tell anyone what happened. Just try not to think about it."

> *It is in the home that the child learns the basic principle of accountability for actions: first to those around him, and ultimately to God.*
>
> MAXINE HANCOCK

Tamar soon moved into Absalom's house, but she was always sad and lonely. ²¹When David heard what had happened to Tamar, he was very angry. But Amnon was his oldest son and also his favorite, and David would not do anything to make Amnon unhappy.ᵇ

²²Absalom treated Amnon as though nothing had happened, but he hated Amnon for what he had done to his sister Tamar.

²³Two years later, Absalom's servants were cutting wool from his sheep in Baal-Hazor near the town of Ephraim, and Absalom invited all of the king's sons to be there.ᶜ ²⁴Then he went to David and said, "My servants are cutting the wool from my sheep. Please come and join us!"

²⁵David answered, "No, my son, we won't go. It would be too expensive for you." Absalom tried to get him to change his mind, but David did not want to go. He only said that he hoped they would have a good time.

²⁶Absalom said, "If you won't go, at least let my brother Amnon come with us."

David asked, "Why should he go with you?" ²⁷But Absalom kept on insisting, and finally David let Amnon and all his other sons go with Absalom.

Absalom prepared a banquet fit for a king.ᵈ ²⁸But he told his servants, "Keep an eye on Amnon. When he gets a little drunk from the wine and is feeling good, I'll give the signal. Then kill him! I've commanded you to do it, so don't be afraid. Be strong and brave."

²⁹Absalom's servants killed Amnon, just as Absalom had told them. The rest of the king's sons quickly rode away on their mules to escape from Absalom.

³⁰While they were on their way to Jerusalem, someone told David, "Absalom has killed all of your sons! Not even one is left." ³¹David got up, and in his sorrow he tore his clothes and lay down on the ground. His servants remained standing, but they tore their clothes too.

³²Then David's nephewᵉ Jonadab said, "Your Majesty, not all of your sons were killed! Only Amnon is dead. On the day that Amnon raped Tamar, Absalom decided to kill him. ³³Don't worry about the report that all your sons were killed. Only Amnon is dead, ³⁴and Absalom has run away."

One of the guards noticed a lot of people coming along the hillside on the road to Horonaim.ᶠ He went and told the king, "I saw some men coming along Horonaim Road."ᵍ

³⁵Jonadab said, "Your Majesty, look! Here come your sons now, just as I told you."

³⁶No sooner had he said it, than David's sons came in. They were weeping out loud, and David and all his officials cried just as loudly. ³⁷⁻³⁸David was sad for a long time because Amnon was dead.

David Lets Absalom Come Home

Absalom had run away to Geshur, where he stayed for three years with King Talmaiʰ the son of Ammihud. ³⁹David still felt so sad over the loss of Amnon that he wanted to take his army there and capture Absalom.ⁱ

ᵇ13.21 *But Amnon . . . unhappy:* The Dead Sea Scrolls and one ancient translation; these words are not in the Standard Hebrew Text. ᶜ13.23 *invited . . . there:* Cutting the wool from sheep was a time for celebrating as well as working. ᵈ13.27 *Absalom prepared . . . king:* One ancient translation; these words are not in the Hebrew text. ᵉ13.32 *David's nephew:* The Hebrew text has "the son of David's brother Shimeah." ᶠ13.34 *the road to Horonaim:* Or "the road behind him" or "the road to the west." ᵍ13.34 *He . . . Road:* One ancient translation; these words are not in the Hebrew text. ʰ13.37,38 *King Talmai:* Absalom's grandfather (see 3.3). ⁱ13.39 *David . . . Absalom:* Or "David was comforted over the loss of Amnon, and he no longer wanted to take his army there to capture Absalom."

14

Joab knew that David couldn't stop thinking about Absalom, [2-3]and he sent someone to bring in the wise woman who lived in Tekoa. Joab told her, "Put on funeral clothes and don't use any makeup. Go to the king and pretend you have spent a long time mourning the death of a loved one." Then he told her what to say.

[4]The woman from Tekoa went to David. She bowed very low and said, "Your Majesty, please help me!"

[5]David asked, "What's the matter?"

She replied:

My husband is dead, and I'm a widow. [6]I had two sons, but they got into a fight out in a field where there was no one to pull them apart, and one of them killed the other. [7]Now all of my relatives have come to me and said, "Hand over your son! We're going to put him to death for killing his brother." But what they really want is to get rid of him, so they can take over our land.

God doesn't expect us—
or our children—to be
finished products now.

COLLEEN TOWNSEND EVANS

Please don't let them put out my only flame of hope! There won't be anyone left on this earth to carry on my husband's name.

[8]"Go on home," David told her. "I'll take care of this matter for you."

[9]The woman said, "I hope your decision doesn't cause any problems for you. But if it does, you can blame me."[j]

[10]He said, "If anyone gives you any trouble, bring them to me, and it won't happen again!"

[11]"Please," she replied, "swear by the LORD your God that no one will be allowed to kill my son!"

He said, "I swear by the living LORD that no one will touch even a hair on his head!"

[12]Then she asked, "Your Majesty, may I say something?"

"Yes," he answered.

[13]The woman said:

Haven't you been hurting God's people? Your own son had to leave the country. And when you judged in my favor, it was the same as admitting that you should have let him come back. [14]We each must die and disappear like water poured out on the ground. But God doesn't take our lives.[k] Instead, he figures out ways of bringing us back when we run away.

[15]Your Majesty, I came here to tell you about my problem, because I was afraid of what someone might do to me. I decided to come to you, because I thought you could help. [16]In fact, I knew that you would listen and save my son and me from those who want to take the land that God gave us.[l]

[17]I can rest easy now that you have given your decision. You know the difference between right and wrong just like an angel of God, and I pray that the LORD your God will be with you.

[18]Then David said to the woman, "Now I'm going to ask you a question, and don't try to hide the truth!"

The woman replied, "Please go ahead, Your Majesty."

[19]David asked, "Did Joab put you up to this?"

The woman answered, "Your Majesty, I swear by your life that no one can hide the truth from you. Yes, Joab did tell me what to say, [20]but only to show you the other side of this problem. You must be as wise as the angel of God to know everything that goes on in this country."

[21]David turned to Joab and said, "It seems that I have already given my decision. Go and bring Absalom back."

[22]Joab bowed very low and said, "Your Majesty, I thank you for giving your permission. It shows that you approve of me."

[23]Joab went to Geshur to get Absalom. But when they came back to Jerusalem, [24]David told Joab, "I don't want to see my

---

[j]14.9 *I hope . . . me:* Or "May I speak some more?"
[k]14.14 *take our lives:* Or "make any exceptions."
[l]14.16 *take . . . us:* Or "make sure we have no part in God's people."

son Absalom. Tell him to stay away from me." So Absalom went to his own house without seeing his father.

Absalom Was Handsome

[25]No one in all Israel was as handsome and well-built as Absalom. [26]He got his hair cut once a year, and when the hair was weighed, it came to about five pounds. [27]Absalom had three sons. He also had a daughter named Tamar, who grew up to be very beautiful.

Absalom Finally Sees David

[28]Absalom lived in Jerusalem for two years without seeing his father. [29]He wanted Joab to talk to David for him. So one day he sent a message asking Joab to come over, but Joab refused. Absalom sent another message, but Joab still refused. [30]Finally, Absalom told his servants, "Joab's barley field is right next to mine. Go set it on fire!" And they did.

[31]Joab went to Absalom's house and demanded, "Why did your servants set my field on fire?"

[32]Absalom answered, "You didn't pay any attention when I sent for you. I want you to ask my father why he told me to come back from Geshur. I was better off there. I want to see my father now! If I'm guilty, let him kill me."

[33]Joab went to David and told him what Absalom had said. David sent for Absalom, and Absalom came. He bowed very low, and David leaned over and kissed him.

Absalom Rebels against David

15 Some time later, Absalom got himself a chariot with horses to pull it, and he had fifty men run in front. [2]He would get up early each morning and wait by the side of the road that led to the city gate.[m] Anyone who had a complaint to bring to King David would have to go that way, and Absalom would ask each of them, "Where are you from?"

If they said, "I'm from a tribe in the north," [3]Absalom would say, "You deserve to win your case. It's too bad the king doesn't have anyone to hear complaints like yours. [4]I wish someone would make me the judge around here! I would be fair to everyone."

[5]Whenever anyone would come to Absa-

lom and start bowing down, he would reach out and hug and kiss them. [6]That's how he treated everyone from Israel who brought a complaint to the king. Soon everyone in Israel liked Absalom better than they liked David.

[7]Four years[n] later, Absalom said to David, "Please, let me go to Hebron. I have to keep a promise that I made to the LORD, [8]when I was living with the Arameans in Geshur. I promised that if the LORD would bring me back to live in Jerusalem, I would worship him in Hebron."[o]

[9]David gave his permission, and Absalom went to Hebron. [10-12]He took two hundred men from Jerusalem with him, but they had no idea what he was going to do. Absalom offered sacrifices in Hebron and sent someone to Gilo to tell David's advisor Ahithophel to come.

More and more people were joining Absalom and supporting his plot. Meanwhile, Absalom had secretly sent some messengers to the northern tribes of Israel. The messengers told everyone, "When you hear the sound of the trumpets, you must shout, 'Absalom now rules as king in Hebron!' "

David Has To Leave Jerusalem

[13]A messenger came and told David, "Everyone in Israel is on Absalom's side!"

[14]David's officials were in Jerusalem with him, and he told them, "Let's get out of here! We'll have to leave soon, or none of us will escape from Absalom. Hurry! If he moves fast, he could catch us while we're still here. Then he will kill us and everyone else in the city."

[15]The officials said, "Your Majesty, we'll do whatever you say."

[16-17]David left behind ten of his wives[p] to take care of the palace, but the rest of his family and his officials and soldiers went with him.

They stopped at the last house at the edge of the city. [18]Then David stood there and watched while his regular troops and his bodyguards[q] marched past. The last group was the six hundred soldiers who had

---

m15.2 *the city gate:* Or "the entrance to the king's palace."   n15.7 *Four years:* The Hebrew text has "forty years."   o15.8 *in Hebron:* Some manuscripts of one ancient translation; these words are not in the Hebrew text.   P15.16,17 *wives:* See the note at 3.7.   q15.18 *bodyguards:* See the note at 8.18.

followed him from Gath.^r Their commander was Ittai.

¹⁹David spoke to Ittai and said, "You're a foreigner from the town of Gath. You don't have to leave with us. Go back and join the new king! ²⁰You haven't been with me very long, so why should you have to follow me, when I don't even know where I'm going? Take your soldiers and go back. I pray that the Lord will be^s kind and faithful to you."

There's a purpose in our pain, and we don't suffer alone. God is with us, and through the pain reveals who we really are and what our place is in his kingdom.

LEE EZELL

²¹Ittai answered, "Your Majesty, just as surely as you and the LORD live, I will go where you go, no matter if it costs me my life."

²²"Then come on!" David said.

So Ittai and all his men and their families walked on past David.

David Sends the Sacred Chest Back to Jerusalem

²³The people of Jerusalem were crying and moaning as David and everyone with him passed by. He led them across Kidron Valley^t and along the road toward the desert.

²⁴Zadok and Abiathar the priests were there along with several men from the tribe of Levi who were carrying the sacred chest. They set the chest down, and left it there until David and his followers had gone out of the city.

²⁵Then David said:

Zadok, take the sacred chest back to Jerusalem. If the LORD is pleased with me, he will bring me back and let me see it and his tent again. ²⁶But if he says he isn't pleased with me, then let him do what he knows is best.

²⁷Zadok, you are a good judge of things,^u so return to the city and don't cause any trouble. Take your son Ahimaaz with you. Abiathar and his son Jonathan will also go back. ²⁸I'll wait at the river crossing in the desert until I hear from you.

²⁹Zadok and Abiathar took the sacred chest back into Jerusalem and stayed there. ³⁰David went on up the slope of the Mount of Olives. He was barefoot and crying, and he covered his head to show his sorrow. Everyone with him was crying, and they covered their heads too.

³¹Someone told David, "Ahithophel is helping Absalom plot against you!"

David said, "Please, LORD, keep Ahithophel's plans from working!"

David Sends Hushai Back as a Spy

³²When David reached the top of the Mount of Olives, he met Hushai the Archite^v at a place of worship. Hushai's robe was torn, and dust was on his head.^w ³³David told him:

If you come with me, you might slow us down.^x ³⁴Go back into the city and tell Absalom, "Your Majesty, I am your servant. I will serve you now, just as I served your father in the past."

Hushai, if you do that, you can help me ruin Ahithophel's plans. ³⁵Zadok and Abiathar the priests will be there with you, and you can tell them everything you hear in the palace. ³⁶Then have them send their sons Ahimaaz and Jonathan to tell me what you've heard.

³⁷David's advisor Hushai slipped back into Jerusalem, just about the same time that Absalom was coming in.

Ziba Gives Food to David

16 David had started down the other side of the Mount of Olives, when he was met by Ziba, the chief

---

^r15.18 *the six . . . Gath:* These were Philistine soldiers who were loyal to David. ^s15.20 *I pray . . . be:* One ancient translation; these words are not in the Hebrew text. ^t15.23 *Kidron Valley:* This was considered the eastern boundary of Jerusalem. ^u15.27 *you . . . things:* Or "You are a prophet" or "You are not a prophet." ^v15.32 *Archite:* The Archites were part of the tribe of Benjamin (see Joshua 16.2). ^w15.32 *Hushai's . . . head:* See the note at 1.2. ^x15.33 *you might slow us down:* Hushai was probably very old.

servant of Mephibosheth.[y] Ziba had two donkeys that were carrying two hundred loaves of bread, a hundred handfuls of raisins, a hundred figs,[z] and some wine.

[2]"What's all this?" David asked.

Ziba said, "The donkeys are for your family to ride. The bread and fruit are for the people to eat, and the wine is for them to drink in the desert when they are tired out."

[3]"And where is Mephibosheth?" David asked.

Ziba answered, "He stayed in Jerusalem, because he thinks the people of Israel want him to rule the kingdom of his grandfather Saul."

[4]David then told him, "Everything that used to belong to Mephibosheth is now yours."

Ziba said, "Your Majesty, I am your humble servant, and I hope you will be pleased with me."

Shimei Curses David

[5]David was near the town of Bahurim when a man came out and started cursing him. The man was Shimei the son of Gera, and he was one of Saul's distant relatives. [6]He threw stones at David, at his soldiers, and at everyone else, including the bodyguards who walked on each side of David. [7]Shimei was yelling at David, "Get out of here, you murderer! You good-for-nothing, [8]the LORD is paying you back for killing so many in Saul's family. You stole his kingdom, but now the LORD has given it to your son Absalom. You're a murderer, and that's why you're in such big trouble!"

[9]Abishai said, "Your Majesty, this man is as useless as a dead dog! He shouldn't be allowed to curse you. Let me go over and chop off his head."

[10]David replied, "What will I ever do with you and your brother Joab? If Shimei is cursing me because the LORD has told him to, then who are you to tell him to stop?"

[11]Then David said to Abishai and all his soldiers:

My own son is trying to kill me! Why shouldn't this man from the tribe of Benjamin want me dead even more? Let him curse all he wants. Maybe the LORD did tell him to curse me. [12]But if the LORD hears these curses and sees the trouble I'm in, maybe he will have pity on me instead.

[13]David and the others went on down the road. Shimei went along the hillside by the road, cursing and throwing rocks and dirt at them. [14]When David and those with him came to the Jordan River, they were tired out. But after they rested, they[a] felt much better.

Hushai Meets Absalom

[15]By this time, Absalom, Ahithophel, and the others had reached Jerusalem. [16]David's friend Hushai came to Absalom and said, "Long live the king! Long live the king!"

I continually examine myself to see where my sense of worth is coming from: my accomplishments, other people's opinions—or God. No matter what challenges come my way next, I want to exhibit God's love. That's my life goal.

KATHY TROCCOLI

[17]But Absalom asked Hushai, "Is this how you show loyalty to your friend David? Why didn't you go with him?"

[18]Hushai answered, "The LORD and the people of Israel have chosen you to be king. I can't leave. I have to stay and serve the one they've chosen. [19]Besides, it seems right for me to serve you, just as I served your father."

Ahithophel's Advice

[20]Absalom turned to Ahithophel and said, "Give us your advice! What should we do?"

[21]Ahithophel answered, "Some of your

---

[y]16.1 *chief servant of Mephibosheth:* See 9.1-13.
[z]16.1 *figs:* Or "pomegranates," a bright red fruit that looks like an apple.   [a]16.14 *they:* Hebrew "he."

father's wives[b] were left here to take care of the palace. You should have sex with them. Then everyone will find out that you have publicly disgraced your father. This will make you and your followers even more powerful."

²²Absalom had a tent set up on the flat roof of the palace, and everyone watched as he went into the tent with his father's wives.

²³Ahithophel gave such good advice in those days that both Absalom and David thought it came straight from God.

17 Ahithophel said to Absalom: Let me choose twelve thousand men and attack David tonight, ²while he is tired and discouraged. He will panic, and everyone with him will run away. I won't kill anyone except David, ³since he's the one you want to get rid of. Then I'll bring the whole nation back to you like a bride coming home to her husband.[c] This way there won't be a civil war.

Hushai Fools Absalom

⁴Absalom and all the leaders of the tribes of Israel agreed that Ahithophel had a good plan. ⁵Then Absalom said, "Bring in Hushai the Archite. Let's hear what he has to say."

⁶Hushai came in, and Absalom told him what Ahithophel had planned. Then Absalom said, "Should we do what he says? And if we shouldn't, can you come up with anything better?"

⁷Hushai said:

This time Ahithophel's advice isn't so good. ⁸You know that your father and his followers are real warriors. Right now they are as fierce as a mother bear whose cubs have just been killed. Besides, your father has a lot of experience in fighting wars, and he won't be spending the night with the others. ⁹He has probably already found a hiding place in a cave or somewhere else.

As soon as anyone hears that some of your soldiers have been killed, everyone will think your whole army has been destroyed. ¹⁰Then even those who are as brave as a lion will lose their courage. All Israel knows what a great warrior your father is and what brave soldiers he has.

¹¹My advice is to gather all the fighting men of Israel from the town of Dan in the north down to the town of Beersheba in the south. You will have more soldiers than there are grains of sand on the seashore. Absalom, you should lead them yourself, ¹²and we will all go to fight David wherever he is. We will fall on him just as dew falls and covers the ground. He and all his soldiers will die! ¹³If they go into a walled town, we will put ropes around that town and drag it into the river. We won't leave even one small piece of a stone.

¹⁴Absalom and the others liked Hushai's plan better than Ahithophel's plan. This was because the LORD had decided to keep Ahithophel's plan from working and to cause trouble for Absalom.

Jonathan and Ahimaaz Tell David the News

¹⁵Right away, Hushai went to Zadok and Abiathar. He told them what advice Ahithophel had given to Absalom and to the leaders of Israel. He also told them about the advice he had given. ¹⁶Then he said, "Hurry! Send someone to warn David not to spend the night on this side of the river. He must get across the river, so he and the others won't be wiped out!"

¹⁷Jonathan and Ahimaaz[d] had been waiting at Rogel Spring[e] because they did not want to be seen in Jerusalem. A servant girl went to the spring and gave them the message for David. ¹⁸But a young man saw them and went to tell Absalom. So Jonathan and Ahimaaz left and hurried to the house of a man who lived in Bahurim. Then they climbed down into a well in the courtyard. ¹⁹The man's wife put the cover on the well and poured grain on top of it, so the well could not be seen.[f]

²⁰Absalom's soldiers came to the woman and demanded, "Where are Ahimaaz and Jonathan?"

---

[b]16.21 *wives:* See the note at 3.7. [c]17.3 *back to you . . . husband:* One ancient translation; Hebrew "back to you. The man you are chasing is like bringing back the whole nation." [d]17.17 *Jonathan and Ahimaaz:* See 15.27. [e]17.17 *Rogel Spring:* South of Jerusalem in Kidron Valley. [f]17.19 *The man's wife . . . seen:* Everyone would have thought that the woman was drying grain on a mat that she had spread on the ground.

The woman answered, "They went across the stream."

The soldiers went off to look for the two men. But when they did not find the men, they went back to Jerusalem.

²¹After the soldiers had gone, Jonathan and Ahimaaz climbed out of the well. They went to David and said, "Hurry! Get ready to cross the river!" Then they told him about Ahithophel's plan.

²²David and the others got ready and started crossing the Jordan River. By sunrise all of them were on the other side.

My friends are an oasis to me, encouraging me to go on. They are essential to my well-being.

DEE BRESTIN

Ahithophel Kills Himself

²³When Ahithophel saw that Absalom and the leaders of Israel were not going to follow his advice, he saddled his donkey and rode back to his home in Gilo. He told his family and servants what to do. Then he hanged himself, and they buried him in his family's burial place.

Absalom Puts Amasa in Charge of the Army

²⁴David went to the town of Mahanaim, and Absalom crossed the Jordan River with the army of Israel. ²⁵Absalom put Amasa in Joab's place as commander of the army. Amasa's father was Ithra*ᵍ* from the family of Ishmael,*ʰ* and his mother was Abigal,*ⁱ* the daughter of Nahash and the sister of Joab's mother Zeruiah. ²⁶The Israelites under Absalom's command set up camp in the region of Gilead.

Friends Bring Supplies to David

²⁷After David came to the town of Mahanaim, Shobi the son of Nahash came from Rabbah in Ammon,*ʲ* Machir the son of Ammiel came from Lo-Debar, and Barzillai the Gileadite came from Rogelim. ²⁸⁻²⁹Here is a list of what they brought:

sleeping mats, blankets, bowls, pottery jars, wheat, barley, flour, roasted grain, beans, lentils, honey, yogurt, sheep, and cheese.

They brought the food for David and the others because they knew that everyone would be hungry, tired, and thirsty from being out in the desert.

David Gets Ready for Battle

18 David divided his soldiers into groups of a hundred and groups of a thousand. Then he chose officers to be in command of each group. ²He sent out one-third of his army under the command of Joab, another third under the command of Abishai the son of Zeruiah, and the rest under the command of Ittai from Gath. He told the soldiers, "I'm going into battle with you."

³But the soldiers said, "No, don't go into battle with us! It won't matter to our enemies if they make us all run away, or even if they kill half of us. But you are worth ten thousand of us. It would be better for you to stay in town and send help if we need it."

⁴⁻⁶David said, "All right, if you think I should."

Then in a voice loud enough for everyone to hear, he said, "Joab! Abishai! Ittai! For my sake, be sure that Absalom comes back unharmed."

David stood beside the town gate as his army marched past in groups of a hundred and in groups of a thousand.

Joab Kills Absalom

The war with Israel took place in Ephraim Forest. ⁷⁻⁸Battles were being fought all over the forest, and David's soldiers were winning. Twenty thousand soldiers were killed*ᵏ* that day, and more of them died from

---

ᵍ17.25 Ithra: Or "Jether." *ʰ17.25 the family of Ishmael:* Some manuscripts of one ancient translation; other manuscripts of the same translation "the town of Jezreel"; Hebrew "the people of Israel." *ⁱ17.25 Amasa . . . Abigal:* Abigal and Zeruiah (Joab's mother) were full sisters, and David was evidently their half brother with the same mother, but a different father. This made Amasa one of David's nephews (see 1 Chronicles 2.12-17). *ʲ17.27 Shobi . . . Ammon:* Shobi was probably the new king of the Ammonites that David had appointed after he captured Rabbah (see 2 Samuel 10.1-3; 12.26-31). *ᵏ18.7,8 Twenty . . . killed:* This may refer to the total number or to the number of Absalom's soldiers who were killed.

the dangers of the forest than from the fighting itself.

⁹Absalom was riding his mule under a huge tree when his head*l* caught in the branches. The mule ran off and left Absalom hanging in midair. Some of David's soldiers happened by, ¹⁰and one of them went and told Joab, "I saw Absalom hanging in a tree!"

¹¹Joab said, "You saw Absalom? Why didn't you kill him? I would have given you ten pieces of silver and a special belt."

¹²The man answered, "Even if you paid me a thousand pieces of silver here and now, I still wouldn't touch the king's son. We all heard King David tell you and Abishai and Ittai not to harm Absalom. ¹³He always finds out what's going on. I would have been risking my life to kill Absalom, because you would have let me take the blame."

¹⁴Joab said, "I'm not going to waste any more time on you!"

Absalom was still alive, so Joab took three spears and stuck them through Absalom's chest. ¹⁵Ten of Joab's bodyguards came over and finished him off. ¹⁶Then Joab blew a trumpet to signal his troops to stop chasing Israel's soldiers. ¹⁷They threw Absalom's body into a deep pit in the forest and put a big pile of rocks over it.

Meanwhile, the people of Israel had all run back to their own homes.

¹⁸When Absalom was alive, he had set up a stone monument for himself in King's Valley. He explained, "I don't have any sons*m* to keep my name alive." He called it Absalom's Monument, and that is the name it still has today.*n*

Ahimaaz Wants To Tell David

¹⁹Ahimaaz the son of Zadok said, "Joab, let me run and tell King David that the LORD has rescued him from his enemies."

²⁰Joab answered, "You're not the one to tell the king that his son is dead. You can take him a message some other time, but not today."

²¹Someone from Ethiopia*o* was standing there, and Joab told him, "Go and tell the king what you have seen." The man knelt down in front of Joab and then got up and started running.

²²Ahimaaz spoke to Joab again, "No matter what happens, I still want to run. And besides, the Ethiopian has already left."

Joab said, "Why should you run? You won't get a reward for the news you have!"

²³"I'll run no matter what!" Ahimaaz insisted.

"All right then, run!" Joab said.

Ahimaaz took the road through the Jordan Valley and outran the Ethiopian.

²⁴Meanwhile, David was sitting between the inner and outer gates*p* in the city wall. One of his soldiers was watching from the roof of the gate-tower. He saw a man running toward the town ²⁵and shouted down to tell David.

David answered, "If he's alone, he must have some news."

The runner was getting closer, ²⁶when the soldier saw someone else running. He shouted down to the gate, "Look! There's another runner!"

David said, "He must have some news too."

²⁷The soldier on the roof shouted, "The first one runs just like Ahimaaz the son of Zadok."

This time David said, "He's a good man. He must have some good news."

²⁸Ahimaaz called out, "We won! We won!" Then he bowed low to David and said, "Your Majesty, praise the LORD your God! He has given you victory over your enemies."

²⁹"Is my son Absalom all right?" David asked.

Ahimaaz said, "When Joab sent your personal servant and me, I saw a noisy crowd. But I don't know what it was all about."

³⁰David told him, "Stand over there and wait."

Ahimaaz went over and stood there. ³¹The Ethiopian came and said, "Your Majesty, today I have good news! The LORD has rescued you from all your enemies!"

---

*l*18.9 *head:* Or "hair." *m*18.18 *I don't have any sons:* According to 14.27, Absalom had three sons. But they could have died young or been put to death for Absalom's murder of Amnon. *n*18.18 *today:* That is, at the time of writing. This monument is not the same as the structure now known as "Absalom's Tomb," which was built at least 600 years later. *o*18.21 *Ethiopia:* The Hebrew text has "Cush," which was a region south of Egypt that included parts of the present countries of Ethiopia and Sudan. *p*18.24 *between . . . gates:* The city gate was often like a tower in the city wall, with one gate on the outside of the wall and another gate on the inside of the wall.

³²"Is my son Absalom all right?" David asked.

The Ethiopian replied, "I wish that all Your Majesty's enemies and everyone who tries to harm you would end up like him!"

David Cries for Absalom

³³David started trembling. Then he went up to the room above the city gate to cry. As he went, he kept saying, "My son Absalom! My son, my son Absalom! I wish I could have died instead of you! Absalom, my son, my son!"^q

19 Someone told Joab, "The king is crying because Absalom is dead."

²David's army found out he was crying because his son had died, and their day of victory suddenly turned into a day of sadness. ³The troops were sneaking into Mahanaim, just as if they had run away from a battle and were ashamed.

⁴David held his hands over his face and kept on crying loudly, "My son, Absalom! Absalom, my son, my son!"

⁵Joab went to the house where David was staying and told him:

Emotional healing can happen for anyone. We just need to be honest with God and patient with ourselves and those who are trying to help us.

KATHY TROCCOLI

You've made your soldiers ashamed! Not only did they save your life, they saved your sons and daughters and wives as well. ⁶You're more loyal to your enemies than to your friends. What you've done today has shown your officers and soldiers that they don't mean a thing to you. You would be happy if Absalom was still alive, even if the rest of us were dead. ⁷Now get up! Go out there and thank them for what they did. If you

don't, I swear by the LORD that you won't even have one man left on your side tomorrow morning. You may have had a lot of troubles in the past, but this will be the worst thing that has ever happened to you!

⁸David got up and went to the town gate and sat down. When the people heard that he was sitting there, they came to see him.

Israel and Judah Want David Back

After Israel's soldiers had all returned home, ⁹⁻¹⁰everyone in Israel started arguing. They were saying to each other, "King David rescued us from the Philistines and from our other enemies. But then we chose Absalom to be our new leader, and David had to leave the country to get away. Absalom died in battle, so why hasn't something been done to bring David back?"

¹¹When David found out what they were saying, he sent a message to Zadok and Abiathar the priests. It said:

Say to the leaders of Judah, "Why are you the last tribe to think about bringing King David back home? ¹²He is your brother, your own relative! Why haven't you done anything to bring him back?"

¹³And tell Amasa, "You're my nephew, and with God as a witness, I swear I'll make you commander of my army instead of Joab."

¹⁴Soon the tribe of Judah again became followers of David, and they sent him this message: "Come back, and bring your soldiers with you."

David Starts Back for Jerusalem

¹⁵David started back and had gone as far as the Jordan River when he met the people of Judah. They had gathered at Gilgal and had come to help him cross the river.

¹⁶Shimei^r the son of Gera was there with them. He had hurried from Bahurim to meet David. Shimei was from the tribe of Benjamin, and ¹⁷a thousand others from Benjamin had come with him.

Ziba, the chief servant of Saul's family, also came to the Jordan River. He and his fifteen sons and twenty servants waded

---

^q**18.33** *son:* In Hebrew, this verse is 19.1.
^r**19.16** *Shimei:* See 16.5-13.

across[s] to meet David. [18]Then they brought David's family and servants back across the river, and they did everything he wanted them to do.

Shimei Meets with David

Shimei crossed the Jordan River and bowed down in front of David. [19]He said, "Your Majesty, I beg you not to punish me! Please, forget what I did when you were leaving Jerusalem. Don't even think about it. [20]I know I was wrong. That's why I wanted to be the first one from the northern tribes to meet you."

[21]But Abishai shouted, "You should be killed for cursing the LORD's chosen king!"

[22]David said, "Abishai, what will I ever do with you and your brother Joab? Is it your job to tell me who has done wrong? I've been made king of all Israel today, and no one will be put to death!" [23]Then David promised Shimei that he would not be killed.

Mephibosheth Meets with David

[24]Mephibosheth, the grandson of Saul, also came to meet David. He had missed David so much that he had not taken a bath or trimmed his beard or washed his clothes the whole time David was gone.

[25]After they had gone back to Jerusalem, Mephibosheth came to see David, who asked him, "Why didn't you go with me?"

[26]He answered, "Your Majesty, you know I can't walk. I told my servant to saddle a donkey for me[t] so I could go with you. But my servant left without me, and [27]then he lied about me. You're as wise as an angel of God, so do what you think is right. [28]After all, you could have killed my whole family and me. But instead, you let me eat at your own table. Your Majesty, what more could I ask?"

[29]David answered, "You've said enough! I've decided to divide the property[u] between you and Ziba."

[30]Mephibosheth replied, "He can have it all! I'm just glad you've come home safely."

Barzillai Returns Home

[31]Barzillai came from Rogelim in Gilead to meet David at the Jordan River and go across with him. [32]Barzillai was eighty years old. He was very rich and had sent food to David in Mahanaim.

[33]David said to him, "Cross the river and go to Jerusalem with me. I will take care of you."

[34]Barzillai answered:

Your Majesty, why should I go to Jerusalem? I don't have much longer to live. [35]I'm already eighty years old, and my body is almost numb. I can't taste my food or hear the sound of singing, and I would be nothing but a burden. [36]I'll cross the river with you, but I'll only go a little way on the other side. You don't have to be so kind to me. [37]Just let me return to my hometown, where I can someday be buried near my father and mother. My servant Chimham[v] can go with you, and you can treat him as your own.

[38]David said, "I'll take Chimham with me, and whatever you ask me to do for him, I'll do. And if there's anything else you want, I'll also do that."

[39]David's soldiers went on across the river, while he stayed behind to tell Barzillai good-by and to wish him well. Barzillai returned home, but [40]Chimham crossed the river with David.

Israel and Judah Argue

All of Judah's army and half of Israel's army were there to help David cross the river. [41]The soldiers from Israel came to him and said, "Why did our relatives from Judah sneak you and your family and your soldiers across the Jordan?"

[42]The people of Judah answered, "Why are you so angry? We are the king's relatives. He didn't give us any food, and we didn't take anything for ourselves!"

[43]Those from Israel said, "King David belongs to us ten times more than he belongs to you.[w] Why didn't you think we were good enough to help you? After all, we were the first ones to think of bringing him back!"

The people of Judah spoke more harshly than the people of Israel.

[s]19.17 waded across: Or "rushed." [t]19.26 I told ... me: Two ancient translations; Hebrew, "I said, 'I will saddle a donkey for myself.'" [u]19.29 the property: The property that had belonged to Saul (see 9.7; 16.4). [v]19.37 My servant Chimham: Or "My son Chimham." [w]19.43 King David ... you: In this verse "Israel" stands for the ten northern tribes and does not include the tribe of Judah in the south.

Sheba Rebels against David

20 A troublemaker from the tribe of Benjamin was there. His name was Sheba the son of Bichri, and he blew a trumpet to get everyone's attention. Then he said, "People of Israel, David the son of Jesse doesn't belong to us! Let's go home."

²So they stopped following David and went off with Sheba. But the people of Judah stayed close to David all the way from the Jordan to Jerusalem.

David's Ten Wives

³David had left ten of his wives in Jerusalem to take care of his palace. But when he came back, he had them taken to another house, and he placed soldiers there to guard them. He gave them whatever they needed, but he never slept with any of them again.ˣ They had to live there for the rest of their lives as if they were widows.

The Army Goes after Sheba

⁴David said to Amasa, "Three days from now I want you and all of Judah's army to be here!"

⁵Amasa started bringing the army together, but it was taking him more than three days. ⁶So David said to Abishai, "Sheba will hurt us more than Absalom ever did. Take my best soldiers and go after him. We don't want him to take over any walled cities and get away from us."ʸ

Joab Kills Amasa

⁷Abishai left Jerusalem to try and capture Sheba. He took along Joab and his soldiers, as well as David's bodyguardᶻ and best troops. ⁸They had gone as far as the big rock at Gibeon when Amasa caught up with them. Joab had a dagger strapped around his waist over his military uniform, but it fell out as he started toward Amasa.

⁹Joab said, "Amasa, my cousin, how are you?" Then Joab took hold of Amasa's beard with his right hand, so that he could greet him with a kiss. ¹⁰Amasa did not see the dagger in Joab's other hand. Joab stuck it in Amasa's stomach, and his insides spilled out on the ground. Joab only struck him once, but Amasa was dying.

Joab and his brother Abishai went off to chase Sheba. ¹¹One of Joab's soldiers stood by Amasa and shouted, "If any of you like Joab, and if you are for David, then follow Joab!"

¹²Amasa was still rolling in his own blood in the middle of the road. The soldier who had shouted noticed that everyone who passed by would stop, so he dragged Amasa off the road and covered him with a blanket. ¹³After this, no one else stopped. They all walked straight past him on their way to help Joab capture Sheba.

ˣ20.3 he . . . again: Because of what Absalom had done (see 16.21, 22).   ʸ20.6 get . . . us: One possible meaning for the difficult Hebrew text.   ᶻ20.7 bodyguard: See the note at 8.18.

SingleLife—How can God use me as a single woman? *(2 Samuel 20.14-22)*

Be a clear thinker.
Imagine talking back to a battering ram (20.15)! That's what one wise, courageous woman did—without the backup of a father, husband, brother, or town leader. Even if these men were available to her, it appears that God used her with great effectiveness. She found out what those attacking her town wanted (a leader of the rebellion), and was able to negotiate peace by meeting their demands. As a result, her town was saved.

Clear thinkers come in all shapes and sizes, male and female, single and married. In the midst of puzzling situations, God can use a person who seeks him. He will most likely use a person who has acquired a little wisdom from him along the way and has the courage to use that wisdom. He doesn't give certain tasks to certain people based on their marital status. His qualifications are different: a heart that seeks after God's wisdom and courage. (See also Exodus 15.19-21; Judges 6,7; Malachi 3.16-18.)

Words To Remember: *A wise woman shouted from the top of the wall, "Listen to me! Listen to me!"*—2 Samuel 20.16

Sheba Hides Out in the Town of Abel

[14]Sheba had gone through all of the tribes of Israel when he came to the town of Abel Beth-Maacah. All of his best soldiers[a] met him there and followed him into the town.

[15]Joab and his troops came and surrounded Abel, so that no one could go in or come out. They made a dirt ramp up to the town wall and then started to use a battering ram to knock the wall down.

A Wise Woman Saves the Town

[16]A wise woman shouted from the top of the wall,[b] "Listen to me! Listen to me! I have to talk to Joab! Tell him to come here!" [17]When he came, the woman said, "Are you Joab?"

"Yes, I am," he answered.

She said, "Please, listen to what I have to say."

"All right," he said. "I'll listen."

[18]She said, "Long ago people used to say, 'If you want good advice, go to the town of Abel to get it.' The answers they got here were all that was needed to settle any problem. [19]We are Israelites, and we want peace! You can trust us. Why are you trying to destroy a town that's like a mother in Israel? Why do you want to wipe out the LORD's people?"

[20]Joab answered, "No, no! I'm not trying to wipe you out or destroy your town! [21]That's not it at all. There's a man in your town from the hill country of Ephraim. His name is Sheba, and he is the leader of a rebellion against King David. Turn him over to me, and we will leave your town alone."

The woman told Joab, "We will throw his head over the wall."

[22]She went to the people of the town and talked them into doing it. They cut off Sheba's head and threw it to Joab.

Joab blew a signal on his trumpet, and the soldiers returned to their homes. Joab went back to David in Jerusalem.

Another List of David's Officials[c]

[23]Joab was the commander of Israel's entire army.

Benaiah the son of Jehoiada was in command of David's bodyguard.[d]

[24]Adoram[e] was in charge of the slave-labor force.

Jehoshaphat the son of Ahilud kept government records.

[25]Sheva was the secretary.

Zadok and Abiathar were the priests. [26]Ira from Jair was David's priest.

The Gibeonites Hang Saul's Descendants

21 While David was king, there were three years in a row when the nation of Israel could not grow enough food. So David asked the LORD for help, and the LORD answered, "Saul and his family are guilty of murder, because he had the Gibeonites killed."

[2]The Gibeonites were not Israelites; they were descendants of the Amorites. The people of Israel had promised not to kill them,[f] but Saul had tried to kill them because he wanted Israel and Judah to control all the land.

David had the Gibeonites come, and he talked with them. [3]He said, "What can I do to make up for what Saul did, so that you'll ask the LORD to be kind to his people again?"[g]

[4]The Gibeonites answered, "Silver and gold from Saul and his family are not enough. On the other hand, we don't have the right to put any Israelite to death."

David said, "I'll do whatever you ask."[h]

[5]They replied, "Saul tried to kill all our people so that none of us would be left in the land of Israel. [6]Give us seven of his descendants. We will hang[i] these men near the place where the LORD is worshiped in Gibeah, the hometown of Saul, the LORD's chosen king."

"I'll give them to you," David said.

[7]David had made a promise to Jonathan with the LORD as his witness, so he spared Jonathan's son Mephibosheth, the grandson of Saul. [8]But Saul and Rizpah the daughter

---

[a]20.14 best soldiers: One ancient translation; the difficult Hebrew text may mean either "Berites" or "Bichrites," Sheba's relatives.　[b]20.16 the top of the wall: Or "the town."　[c]20.23 Another List of David's Officials: See also the list in 8.16, 17.　[d]20.23 David's bodyguard: See the note at 8.18.　[e]20.24 Adoram: One ancient translation "Adoniram" (see 1 Kings 4.6; 5.14).　[f]21.2 promised . . . them: See Joshua 9.3-27.　[g]21.3 ask . . . again: Saul's guilt had become a curse on Israel that had resulted in famine. For the effects of this curse to be removed, the Gibeonites would have to ask the LORD to be kind to Israel.　[h]21.4 I'll . . . ask: Or "What are you asking me to do for you?"　[i]21.6 hang: One possible meaning for the difficult Hebrew text.

of Aiah had two sons named Armoni and Mephibosheth. Saul's daughter Merab[j] had five sons whose father was Adriel the son of Barzillai from Meholah.[k] David took Rizpah's two sons and Merab's five sons and [9]turned them over to the Gibeonites, who hanged[l] all seven of them on the mountain near the place where the LORD was worshiped. This happened right at the beginning of the barley harvest.[m]

Rizpah Takes Care of the Bodies

[10]Rizpah spread out some sackcloth[n] on a nearby rock. She wouldn't let the birds land on the bodies during the day, and she kept the wild animals away at night. She stayed there from the beginning of the harvest until it started to rain.[o]

The Burial of Saul and His Descendants

[11-12]Earlier the Philistines had killed Saul and Jonathan on Mount Gilboa and had hung their bodies in the town square at Beth-Shan. The people of Jabesh in Gilead had secretly taken the bodies away, but David found out what Saul's wife[p] Rizpah had done, and he went to the leaders of Jabesh to get the bones of Saul and his son Jonathan. [13-14]David had their bones taken to the land of Benjamin and buried in a side room in Saul's family burial place. Then he gave orders for the bones of the men who had been hanged[q] to be buried there. It was done, and God answered prayers to bless the land.

The Descendants of the Rephaim
(1 Chronicles 20.4-8)

[15]One time David got very tired when he and his soldiers were fighting the Philistines. [16]One of the Philistine warriors was Ishbibenob, who was a descendant of the Rephaim,[r] and he tried to kill David. Ishbibenob was armed with a new sword,[s] and his bronze spearhead[t] alone weighed seven and a half pounds. [17]But Abishai[u] came to the rescue and killed the Philistine.

David's soldiers told him, "We can't let you risk your life in battle anymore! You give light to our nation, and we want that flame to keep burning."

[18]There was another battle with the Philistines at Gob, where Sibbecai from Hushah killed a descendant of the Rephaim named Saph.

[19]There was still another battle with the Philistines at Gob. A soldier named Elhanan killed Goliath[v] from Gath, whose spear shaft was like a weaver's beam.[w] Elhanan's father was Jari[x] from Bethlehem. [20]There was another war, this time in Gath. One of the enemy soldiers was a descendant of the Rephaim. He was as big as a giant and had six fingers on each hand and six toes on each foot. [21]But when he made fun of Israel, David's nephew Jonathan killed him. Jonathan was the son of David's brother Shimei. [22]David and his soldiers killed these four men who were descendants of the Rephaim from Gath.

David Sings to the LORD
(Psalm 18.1-50)

22 David sang a song to the LORD after the LORD had rescued him from his enemies, especially Saul. These are the words to David's song:

[2]Our LORD and our God,
   you are my mighty rock,[y]
      my fortress, my protector.
[3]You are the rock
      where I am safe.
   You are my shield,

---

[j]**21.8** *Merab*: Some Hebrew manuscripts and some manuscripts of one ancient translation. Most other manuscripts have "Michal," Saul's daughter who was one of David's wives, but she never had any children (see 2 Samuel 6.23). According to 1 Samuel 18.19, Merab was Saul's daughter, and she married Adriel from Meholah. [k]**21.8** *Meholah*: Also known as Abel-Meholah. [l]**21.9** *hanged*: One possible meaning for the difficult Hebrew text. [m]**21.9** *This . . . harvest*: This would have been late in April. [n]**21.10** *sackcloth*: See the note at 3.31. [o]**21.10** *started to rain*: This may have been the beginning of the rainy season in September or October. It usually didn't rain from May to September. Or, it may have been a sign that now there would be enough rain again. [p]**21.11,12** *wife*: See the note at 3.7. [q]**21.13,14** *hanged*: One possible meaning for the difficult Hebrew text. [r]**21.16** *Rephaim*: This may refer to a group of people that lived in Palestine before the Israelites and who were famous for their large size. [s]**21.16** *new sword*: One possible meaning for the difficult Hebrew text. [t]**21.16** *spearhead*: Or "helmet." [u]**21.17** *Abishai*: David's nephew, the brother of Joab. [v]**21.19** *Goliath*: According to 1 Chronicles 20.5, Elhanan killed the brother of Goliath. [w]**21.19** *weaver's beam*: A large wooden rod used by a weaver when making cloth. [x]**21.19** *Jari*: Or "Jaare." [y]**22.2** *mighty rock*: The Hebrew text has "rock," which is sometimes used in poetry to compare the LORD to a mountain where his people can run for protection from their enemies.

my powerful weapon,^z
  and my place of shelter.

You rescue me and keep me
  from being hurt.
⁴I praise you, our LORD!
  I prayed to you,
and you rescued me
  from my enemies.
⁵Death, like ocean waves,
  surrounded me,
and I was almost swallowed
  by its flooding waters.

⁶Ropes from the world
of the dead
  had coiled around me,
and death had set a trap
  in my path.
⁷I was in terrible trouble
  when I called out to you,
but from your temple
you heard me
  and answered my prayer.
⁸Earth shook and shivered!
The columns supporting the sky^a
  rocked back and forth.
You were angry
⁹   and breathed out smoke.
Scorching heat and fiery flames
  spewed from your mouth.

> *In order to do everything*
> *for God, I must do*
> *everything with him.*
> CAROLE MAYHALL

¹⁰You opened the heavens
  like curtains,
and you came down
with storm clouds
under your feet.
¹¹You rode on the backs
  of flying creatures.^b
You appeared^c
  with the wind as wings.
¹²Darkness was your tent!
  Thunderclouds filled the sky,
  hiding you from sight.

¹³Fiery coals lit up the sky
  in front of you.

¹⁴LORD Most High, your voice
  thundered from the heavens.
¹⁵You scattered your enemies
  with arrows of lightning.
¹⁶You roared at the sea,
  and its deepest channels
  could be seen.
You snorted,
and the earth shook
  to its foundations.

¹⁷You reached down from heaven,
  and you lifted me
  from deep in the ocean.
¹⁸You rescued me from enemies
who were hateful
  and too powerful for me.
¹⁹On the day disaster struck,
they came and attacked,
  but you defended me.
²⁰When I was fenced in,
you freed and rescued me
  because you love me.
²¹You are good to me, LORD,
  because I do right,
and you reward me
  because I am innocent.
²²I do what you want
  and never turn to do evil.
²³I keep your laws in mind
and never turn away
  from your teachings.
²⁴I obey you completely
  and guard against sin.
²⁵You have been good to me
  because I do right;
you have rewarded me
for being innocent
  by your standards.

²⁶You are always loyal
  to your loyal people,
and you are faithful

---

^z**22.3** *powerful weapon:* The Hebrew has "the horn,"
which refers to the horn of a bull, one of the most
powerful animals in ancient Palestine.
^a**22.8** *columns . . . sky:* The sky was sometimes described
as a dome that was held up by a foundation or pillars.
^b**22.11** *flying creatures:* These were supernatural beings
(see the note at 6.2).   ^c**22.11** *appeared:* Most Hebrew
manuscripts; some Hebrew manuscripts "swooped
down" (see Psalm 18.10).

to the faithful.
²⁷ With all who are sincere
   you are sincere,
but you treat the unfaithful
   as their deeds deserve.
²⁸ You rescue the humble,
   but you look for ways
      to put down the proud.

²⁹ Our LORD and God,
   you are my lamp.
You turn darkness to light.
³⁰ You help me defeat armies
   and capture cities.

³¹ Your way is perfect, LORD,
   and your word is correct.
You are a shield for those
   who run to you for help.
³² You alone are God!
   Only you are a mighty rock.ᵈ
³³ You are my strong fortress,
   and you set me free.
³⁴ You make my feet run as fast
   as those of a deer,
and you help me stand
   on the mountains.

³⁵ You teach my hands to fight
   and my arms to use
      a bow of bronze.
³⁶ You alone are my shield,
   and by coming to help me,
      you have made me famous.
³⁷ You clear the way for me,
   and now I won't stumble.

³⁸ I kept chasing my enemies
   until I caught them
      and destroyed them.
³⁹ I destroyed them!
   I stuck my sword
      through my enemies,
and they were crushed
   under my feet.
⁴⁰ You helped me win victories
   and forced my attackers
      to fall victim to me.

⁴¹ You made my enemies run,
   and I killed them.
⁴² They cried out for help,
   but no one saved them;
they called out to you,
   but there was no answer.

⁴³ I ground them to dust,
   and I squashed them
      like mud in the streets.

God can use anyone who's dependent on him since the responsibility for the work is his—he just wants our availability.

ANNE GRAHAM LOTZ

⁴⁴ You rescued me
   from my stubborn people
and made me the leader
   of foreign nations,
who are now my slaves.
⁴⁵ They obey and come crawling.
⁴⁶   They have lost all courage
and from their fortresses
   they come trembling.

⁴⁷ You are the living LORD!
   I will praise you!
You are a mighty rock.ᵈ
   I will honor you
      for keeping me safe.
⁴⁸ You took revenge for me,
   and you put nations
      in my power.
⁴⁹ You protected me
   from violent enemies,
and you made me much greater
   than all of them.

⁵⁰ I will praise you, LORD,
   and I will honor you
      among the nations.
⁵¹ You give glorious victories
   to your chosen king.
Your faithful love for David
   and for his descendants
      will never end.

David's Last Words

23 These are the last words
of David the son of Jesse.
The God of Jacob chose David

ᵈ**22.32,47** *mighty rock:* See the note at 22.2.

and made him a great king.
  The Mighty God of Israel
  loved him.[e]
When God told him to speak,
  David said:
[2] The Spirit of the LORD
  has told me what to say.
[3] Our Mighty Rock,[f]
  the God of Jacob, told me,
"A ruler who obeys God
  and does right
[4] is like the sunrise
  on a cloudless day,
or like rain that sparkles
  on the grass."[g]

[5] I have ruled this way,
  and God will never break
  his promise to me.
God's promise is complete
  and unchanging;
he will always help me
  and give me what I hope for.
[6] But evil people are pulled up
  like thornbushes.
They are not dug up by hand,
[7] but with a sharp spear
  and are burned on the spot.

The Three Warriors
(1 Chronicles 11.10-19)

[8] These are the names of David's warriors:

Ishbosheth[h] the son of Hachmon[i] was the leader of the Three Warriors.[j] In one battle, he killed eight hundred men with his spear.[k]

[9] The next one of the Three Warriors was Eleazar the son of Dodo the Ahohite. One time when the Philistines were at war with Israel, he and David dared the Philistines to fight them. Every one of the Israelite soldiers turned and ran, [10] except Eleazar. He killed Philistines until his hand was cramped, and he couldn't let go of his sword. When Eleazar finished, all the Israelite troops had to do was come back and take the enemies' weapons and armor. The LORD gave Israel a great victory that day.

[11] Next was Shammah the son of Agee the Hararite. One time the Philistines brought their army together to destroy a crop of peas growing in a field near Lehi. The rest of Israel's soldiers ran away from the Philistines, [12] but Shammah stood in the middle of the field and killed the Philistines. The crops were saved, and the LORD gave Israel a great victory.

[13] One year at harvest time, the Three Warriors[l] went to meet David at Adullam Cave.[m] The Philistine army had set up camp in Rephaim Valley [14] and had taken over Bethlehem. David was in his fortress, [15] and he was very thirsty. He said, "I wish I had a drink from the well by the gate at Bethlehem."

[16] The Three Warriors[n] sneaked into the Philistine camp and got some water from the well near Bethlehem's gate. But after they brought the water back to David, he refused to drink it. Instead, he poured it out as a sacrifice [17] and said to the LORD, "I can't drink this water! It's like the blood of these men who risked their lives to get it for me."

The Three Warriors did these brave deeds.

The Thirty Warriors
(1 Chronicles 11.20-47)

[18] Joab's brother Abishai was the leader of the Thirty Warriors,[o] and in one battle he killed three hundred men with his spear. He was as famous as the Three Warriors [19] and certainly just as famous as the rest of the Thirty Warriors. He was the commander of the Thirty Warriors, but he still did not become one of the Three Warriors.

[20] Benaiah the son of Jehoiada was a brave man from Kabzeel who did some amazing things. He killed two of Moab's

---

[e]**23.1** *The Mighty . . . him*: Or "He wrote Israel's favorite songs." [f]**23.3** *Mighty Rock*: See the note at 22.2. [g]**23.4** *sparkles . . . grass*: Or "makes the grass grow." [h]**23.8** *Ishbosheth*: Hebrew "Josheb Bashebeth," which seems to be another spelling of Ishbosheth. See the note at 2.8, although this is a different Ishbosheth. [i]**23.8** *the son of Hachmon*: Or "the Tahchemonite" (see 1 Chronicles 11.11). [j]**23.8** *the Three Warriors*: The most honored group of warriors. They may have been part of the Thirty Warriors. "Three" and "thirty" are spelled almost the same in Hebrew, so there is some confusion in the manuscripts as to which group is being talked about in some places in the following lists. [k]**23.8** *with . . . spear*: One possible meaning for the difficult Hebrew text (see 1 Chronicles 11.11). [l]**23.13** *the Three Warriors*: Or "three warriors." Hebrew "three of the thirty most important." [m]**23.13** *Adullam Cave*: This may have happened during the time that David was an outlaw (see 1 Samuel 22.1-6). [n]**23.16** *The Three Warriors*: Or "three warriors." [o]**23.18** *the Thirty Warriors*: The second most honored group of warriors. They may have also been officers in the army (see the note at 23.8).

best fighters,[p] and on a snowy day he went down into a pit and killed a lion. [21]Another time, he killed an Egyptian, as big as a giant.[q] The Egyptian was armed with a spear, but Benaiah only had a club. Benaiah grabbed the spear from the Egyptian and killed him with it. [22-23]Benaiah did these things. He never became one of the Three Warriors, but he was just as famous as they were and certainly just as famous as the rest of the Thirty Warriors. David made him the leader of his bodyguard.

We do not pray answers; we pray requests.

EVELYN CHRISTENSON

[24-39]Some of the Thirty Warriors were:

Asahel the brother of Joab
Elhanan the son of Dodo from Beth-lehem
Shammah from Harod
Elika from Harod
Helez the Paltite
Ira the son of Ikkesh from Tekoa
Abiezer from Anathoth
Mebunnai[r] the Hushathite
Zalmon the Ahohite
Maharai from Netophah
Heleb the son of Baanah from Netophah
Ittai the son of Ribai from Gibeah of the tribe of Benjamin
Benaiah from Pirathon
Hiddai from the streams on Mount Gaash
Abialbon from Beth-Arabah
Azmaveth from Bahurim[s]
Eliahba from Shaalbon
Jashen[t]
Jonathan the son of Shammah the Hara-rite[u]
Ahiam the son of Sharar the Hararite
Eliphelet the son of Ahasbai from Maa-cah
Eliam the son of Ahithophel from Gilo
Hezro from Carmel
Paarai the Arbite
Igal the son of Nathan from Zobah

Bani the Gadite
Zelek from Ammon
Naharai from Beeroth, who carried the weapons of Joab the son of Zeruiah
Ira the Ithrite
Gareb the Ithrite
Uriah the Hittite
There were thirty-seven in all.

David Counts the People
(1 Chronicles 21.1-6)

24 The LORD was angry at Israel again, and he made David think it would be a good idea to count the people in Israel and Judah. [2]So David told Joab and the army officers,[v] "Go to every tribe in Israel, from the town of Dan in the north all the way south to Beersheba, and count everyone who can serve in the army. I want to know how many there are."

[3]Joab answered, "I hope the LORD your God will give you a hundred times more soldiers than you already have. I hope you will live to see that day! But why do you want to do a thing like this?"

[4]But when David refused to change his mind, Joab and the army officers went out and started counting the people. [5]They crossed the Jordan River and began with[w] Aroer and the town in the middle of the river valley. From there they went toward Gad and on as far as Jazer. [6]They went to Gilead and to Kadesh in Syria.[x] Then they went to Dan, Ijon,[y] and on toward Sidon. [7]They came to the fortress of Tyre, then went through every town of the Hivites and the Canaanites. Finally, they went to Beersheba in the Southern Desert of Judah. [8]After they had gone through the whole land, they went

---

[p]23.20 *Moab's best fighters*: Or "big lions in Moab;" one ancient translation "sons of Ariel from Moab." [q]23.21 *Egyptian . . . giant*: First Chronicles 11.23; in this verse the Hebrew text has "good-looking Egyptian." [r]23.24-39 *Mebunnai*: Or "Sibbecai" (see 1 Chronicles 11.26-47). [s]23.24-39 *Bahurim*: Or "Barhum." [t]23.24-39 *Jashen*: Hebrew "sons of Jashen." [u]23.24-39 *Jonathan . . . Hararite*: Some manuscripts of one ancient translation (see 1 Chronicles 26-47). In the Hebrew text Jonathan and Shamah are separate members of the list. [v]24.2 *Joab . . . officers*: Some manuscripts of one ancient translation (see 24.4); 1 Chronicles 21.2; Hebrew "Joab, the officer of the army." [w]24.5 *began with*: Some manuscripts of one ancient translation; Hebrew "set up camp in." [x]24.6 *Kadesh in Syria*: Or "the lower slopes of Mount Hermon." [y]24.6 *Dan, Ijon*: Or "Danjaan," an unknown place.

back to Jerusalem. It had taken them nine months and twenty days.

⁹Joab came and told David, "In Israel there are eight hundred thousand who can serve in the army, and in Judah there are five hundred thousand."

The LORD Punishes David
(1 Chronicles 21.7-17)

¹⁰After David had everyone counted, he felt guilty and told the LORD, "What I did was stupid and terribly wrong. LORD, please forgive me."

¹¹Before David even got up the next morning, the LORD had told David's prophet Gad ¹²⁻¹³to take a message to David. Gad went to David and told him:

You must choose one of three ways for the LORD to punish you: Will there be seven² years when the land won't grow enough food for your people? Or will your enemies chase you and make you run from them for three months? Or will there be three days of horrible disease in your land? Think about it and decide, because I have to give your answer to God, who sent me.

¹⁴David was really frightened and said, "It's a terrible choice to make! But the LORD is kind, and I'd rather have him punish us than for anyone else to do it."

¹⁵⁻¹⁶So that morning, the LORD sent an angel to spread a horrible disease everywhere in Israel, from Dan to Beersheba. And before it was over, seventy thousand people had died.

When the angel was about to destroy Jerusalem, the LORD felt sorry for all the suffering he had caused and told the angel, "That's enough! Don't touch them." This happened at the threshing place that belonged to Araunah the Jebusite.

¹⁷David saw the angel killing everyone and told the LORD, "These people are like sheep with me as their shepherd.ᵃ I have

sinned terribly, but they have done nothing wrong. Please, punish me and my family instead of them!"

David Buys Araunah's Threshing Place
(1 Chronicles 21.18—22.1)

¹⁸⁻¹⁹That same day the prophet Gad came and told David, "Go to the threshing place that belongs to Araunah and build an altar there for the LORD."

So David went.

²⁰Araunah looked and saw David and his soldiers coming up toward him. He went over to David, bowed down low, ²¹and said, "Your Majesty! Why have you come to see me?"

David answered, "I've come to buy your threshing place. I have to build the LORD an altar here, so this disease will stop killing the people."

²²Araunah said, "Take whatever you want and offer your sacrifice. Here are some oxen for the sacrifice. You can use the threshing-boardsᵇ and the wooden yokes for the fire. ²³Take them—they're yours! I hope the LORD your God will be pleased with you."

²⁴But David answered, "No! I have to pay you what they're worth. I can't offer the LORD my God a sacrifice that I got for nothing." So David bought the threshing place and the oxen for fifty pieces of silver. ²⁵Then he built an altar for the LORD. He sacrificed animals and burned them on the altar.

The LORD answered the prayers of the people, and no one else died from the terrible disease.

ᶻ**24.12,13** *seven*: Hebrew; some manuscripts of one ancient translation "three" (see 1 Chronicles 21.12). ᵃ**24.17** *as their shepherd*: The Dead Sea Scrolls, and some manuscripts of two ancient translations (see 1 Chronicles 21.17); these words are not in the Standard Hebrew Text of this verse. ᵇ**24.22** *threshing-boards*: Heavy boards with bits of rock or metal on the bottom. They were dragged across the grain to separate the husks from the kernels.

1 Kings
A House Divided Tries To Stand without God

It can be fun to go through a family album with your relatives and listen to their stories: "This relative was a hero, but this other one"—your relatives roll their eyes and snicker. Or, "She could have amounted to more." Then there are family members they don't talk about. Finally, someone gives you the whole scoop. Gulp!

First Kings is like that—full of heroes, less-than heroes, and downright villains. You begin with the death of David, the hero of 2 Samuel, and then his son, Solomon. A seeker of wisdom, Solomon built God's temple and carried Israel to great glory. Although godly in some ways, Solomon showed us how easy it is to become self-indulgent when things go well.

Wise Solomon's son and successor, Rehoboam, listened to foolish advice and chose to be harsh with God's people. As a result, a revolt broke out and God's kingdom of Israel split. The ten northern tribes (called Israel) named Jeroboam as their king. All that was left to Rehoboam was the southern nation of Judah, which included the tribes of Judah and Benjamin. Throughout 1 Kings, you meet the kings of these two nations. Some did what was right; others did not. One of the worst was Israel's King Ahab and his queen, Jezebel. God responded to their idolatry, thievery, and murder by creating a powerful opponent in Elijah, his prophet.

Elijah's exploits with Ahab and Jezebel highlight what it means to trust God and move in his will when everything is

moving against you. Ahab and Jezebel openly hunted Elijah, but Elijah's relationship with God throughout persecution shows us what it takes to survive tough times and to work to advance God's kingdom.

1 Kings at a Glance

1. Solomon becomes king when David dies (1,2)
2. Solomon's wisdom (3,4)
3. Solomon builds the temple and palace (5–7)
4. Solomon dedicates the temple and renews the covenant with God (8,9)
5. Solomon's splendor as the Queen of Sheba visits and his downfall of marrying foreign wives (10,11)
6. Jeroboam and the northern tribes revolt against Rehoboam (12–14)
7. Various kings of Israel and Judah (15,16)
8. Elijah confronts Ahab (17–19; 20.35-43)
9. Kings of Israel and Judah (20.1-34; 21,22)

David in His Old Age

1 King David was now an old man, and he always felt cold, even under a lot of blankets. [2]His officials said, "Your Majesty, we will look for a young woman to take care of you. She can lie down beside you and keep you warm." [3-4]They looked everywhere in Israel until they found a very beautiful young woman named Abishag, who lived in the town of Shunem.[a] They brought her to David, and she took care of him. But David did not have sex with her.

Adonijah Tries To Become King

[5-6]Adonijah was the son of David and Haggith. He was Absalom's younger brother[b] and was very handsome. One day, Adonijah started bragging, "I'm going to make myself king!" So he got some chariots and horses, and he hired fifty men as bodyguards. David did not want to hurt his feelings, so he never asked Adonijah why he was doing these things.

[7]Adonijah met with Joab the son of Zeruiah and Abiathar the priest and asked them if they would help him become king. Both of them agreed to help. [8]But Zadok the priest, Benaiah the son of Jehoiada, Nathan the prophet, Shimei, Rei,[c] and David's bodyguards all refused.

[9]Adonijah invited his brothers and David's officials from Judah to go with him to Crawling Rock[d] near Rogel Spring, where he sacrificed some sheep, cattle, and fat calves.[e] [10]But he did not invite Nathan, Benaiah, David's bodyguards, or his own brother Solomon.

[11]When Nathan heard what had happened, he asked Bathsheba, Solomon's mother:

Have you heard that Adonijah the son of Haggith has made himself king? But David doesn't know a thing about it. [12]You and your son Solomon will be killed, unless you do what I tell you. [13]Go say to David, "You promised me that Solomon would be the next king. So why is Adonijah now king?"

[14]While you are still talking to David, I'll come in and tell him that everything you said is true.

[15]Meanwhile, David was in his bedroom where Abishag was taking care of him be-cause he was so old. Bathsheba went in [16]and bowed down.

"What can I do for you?" David asked. [17]Bathsheba answered:

Your Majesty, you promised me in the name of the LORD your God that my son Solomon would be the next king. [18]But Adonijah has already been made king, and you didn't know anything about it. [19]He sacrificed a lot of cattle, calves, and sheep. And he invited Abiathar the priest, Joab your army commander, and all your sons to be there, except Solomon, your loyal servant.

Jesus is the hub of my life. I am here to serve. And when I do, I don't have enough hours in the day.

LUCI SWINDOLL

[20]Your Majesty, everyone in Israel is waiting for you to announce who will be the next king. [21]If you don't, they will say that Solomon and I have rebelled. They will treat us like criminals and kill us as soon as you die.

[22]Just then, Nathan the prophet arrived. [23]Someone told David that he was there, and Nathan came in. He bowed with his face to the ground [24]and said:

Your Majesty, did you say that Adonijah would be king? [25]Earlier today, he sacrificed a lot of cattle, calves, and sheep. He invited the army commanders, Abiathar, and all your sons to be there. Right now they are eating and

---

[a]**1.3,4** *Shunem:* A town in northern Israel, just north of Jezreel Valley.   [b]**1.5,6** *brother:* Since Absalom was dead, Adonijah was now David's oldest living son and would be next in line to be king.   [c]**1.8** *Shimei, Rei:* Or "Shimei his advisor."   [d]**1.9** *Crawling Rock:* Or "Zoheleth Rock."   [e]**1.9** *sacrificed . . . calves:* This was part of a ceremony where Adonijah was made the new king.

drinking and shouting, "Long live King Adonijah!" [26]But he didn't invite me or Zadok the priest or Benaiah or Solomon. [27]Did you say they could do this without telling the rest of us who would be the next king?

Solomon Becomes King

[28]David said, "Tell Bathsheba to come here." She came and stood in front of him. [29-30]Then he said, "The living LORD God of Israel has kept me safe. And so today, I will keep the promise I made to you in his name: Solomon will be the next king!"

[31]Bathsheba bowed with her face to the ground and said, "Your Majesty, I pray that you will live a long time!"

[32]Then David said, "Tell Zadok, Nathan, and Benaiah to come here."

When they arrived, [33]he told them:

Take along some of my officials and have Solomon ride my own mule to Gihon Spring. [34]When you get there, Zadok and Nathan will make Solomon the new king of Israel. Then after the ceremony[j] is over, have someone blow a trumpet and tell everyone to shout, "Long live King Solomon!" [35]Bring him back here, and he will take my place as king. He is the one I have chosen to rule Israel and Judah.

[36]Benaiah answered, "We will do it, Your Majesty. I pray that the LORD your God will let it happen. [37]The LORD has always watched over you, and I pray that he will now watch over Solomon. May the LORD help Solomon to be an even greater king than you."

[38]Zadok, Nathan, and Benaiah left and took along the two groups of David's special bodyguards.[g] Solomon rode on David's mule as they led him to Gihon Spring. [39]Zadok the priest brought some olive oil from the sacred tent and poured it on Solomon's head to show that he was now king. A trumpet was blown and everyone shouted, "Long live King Solomon!" [40]Then they played flutes and celebrated as they followed Solomon back to Jerusalem. They made so much noise that the ground shook.

[41]Adonijah and his guests had almost finished eating when they heard the noise. Joab also heard the trumpet and asked, "What's all that noise about in the city?"

[42]Just then, Jonathan son of Abiathar came running up. "Come in," Adonijah said. "An important man like you must have some good news."

[43]Jonathan answered:

No, I don't! David has just announced that Solomon will be king. [44-45]Solomon rode David's own mule to Gihon Spring, and Zadok, Nathan, Benaiah, and David's special bodyguards[h] went with him. When they got there, Zadok and Nathan made Solomon king. Then everyone celebrated all the way back to Jerusalem. That's the noise you hear in the city. [46]Solomon is now king.

[47]And listen to this! David's officials told him, "We pray that your God will help Solomon to be an even greater king!"

David was in his bed at the time, but he bowed [48]and prayed, "I praise you, LORD God of Israel. You have made my son Solomon king and have let me live to see it."

[49]Adonijah's guests shook with fear when they heard this news, and they left as fast as they could. [50]Adonijah himself was afraid of what Solomon might do to him, so he ran to the sacred tent and grabbed hold of the corners of the altar for protection.[i]

[51]Someone told Solomon, "Adonijah is afraid of you and is holding onto the corners of the altar. He wants you to promise that you won't kill him."

[52]Solomon answered, "If Adonijah doesn't cause any trouble, I won't hurt him. But if he does, I'll have him killed." [53]Then he sent someone to the altar to get Adonijah.

After Adonijah came and bowed down, Solomon said, "Adonijah, go home."

David's Instructions to Solomon

2 Not long before David died, he told Solomon:

[2]My son, I will soon die, as everyone must. But I want you to be

---

[j]1.34 the ceremony: Part of this ceremony was pouring olive oil on Solomon's head to show that he was now king. [g]1.38 the two . . . bodyguards: The Hebrew text has "the Cherethites and the Pelethites," who were foreign soldiers hired by David to be part of his bodyguard. [h]1.44,45 David's special bodyguards: See the note at 1.38. [i]1.50 the corners . . . for protection: The four corners of some ancient altars looked like animal horns. Since the entire altar was sacred, anyone holding on to its corners was supposed to be safe from being killed.

strong and brave. [3]Do what the LORD your God commands and follow his teachings. Obey everything written in the Law of Moses. Then you will be a success, no matter what you do or where you go. [4]You and your descendants must always faithfully obey the LORD. If you do, he will keep the solemn promise he made to me that someone from our family will always be king of Israel.

> To us as parents is entrusted the vital task of character development—of helping our children develop the distinctive stamp of godliness upon their lives.
>
> MAXINE HANCOCK

[5]Solomon, don't forget what Joab did to me by killing Abner son of Ner and Amasa son of Jether, the two commanders of Israel's army. He killed them as if they were his enemies in a war, but he did it when there was no war.[j] He is guilty, and now it's up to you to punish him [6]in the way you think best. Whatever you do, don't let him die peacefully in his old age. [7]The sons of Barzillai from Gilead helped me when I was running from your brother Absalom.[k] Be kind to them and let them eat at your table.

[8]Be sure to do something about Shimei son of Gera from Bahurim in the territory of Benjamin. He cursed and insulted me the day I went to Mahanaim. But later, when he came to meet me at the Jordan River, I promised that I wouldn't kill him.[l] [9]Now you must punish him. He's an old man, but you're wise enough to know that you must have him killed.

David Dies

[10-11]David was king of Israel forty years. He ruled seven years from Hebron and thirty-three years from Jerusalem. Then he died and was buried in Jerusalem.[m] [12]His son Solomon became king and took control of David's kingdom.

Adonijah Is Killed

[13]One day, Adonijah went to see Bathsheba, Solomon's mother, and she asked, "Is this a friendly visit?"

"Yes. [14]I just want to talk with you."

"All right," she told him, "go ahead."

[15]"You know that I was king for a little while," Adonijah replied. "And everyone in Israel accepted me as their ruler. But the LORD wanted my brother to be king, so now things have changed. [16]Would you do me a favor?"

"What do you want?" Bathsheba asked.

[17]"Please ask Solomon to let me marry Abishag. He won't say no to you."

[18]"All right," she said. "I'll ask him."

[19]When Bathsheba went to see Solomon, he stood up to meet her, then bowed low. He sat back down and had another throne brought in, so his mother could sit at his right side.[n] [20]Bathsheba sat down and then asked, "Would you do me a small favor?"

Solomon replied, "Mother, just tell me what you want, and I will do it."

[21]"Allow your brother Adonijah to marry Abishag," she answered.

[22]Solomon said:

What? Let my older brother marry Abishag? You may as well ask me to let him rule the kingdom! And why don't you ask such favors for Abiathar and Joab?[o]

[23]I swear in the name of the LORD that Adonijah will die because he asked for this! If he doesn't, I pray that God will severely punish me. [24]The LORD made me king in my father's place and promised that the kings of Israel would come from my family. Yes, I swear by the living LORD that Adonijah will die today.

[25]"Benaiah," Solomon shouted, "go kill Adonijah." So Adonijah died.

---

[j]2.5 *war:* See 2 Samuel 3.22-27 and 20.7-10. [k]2.7 *Absalom:* See 2 Samuel 17.27-29. [l]2.8 *him:* See 2 Samuel 16.5-14 and 19.16-23. [m]2.10,11 *Jerusalem:* Hebrew "the city of David." [n]2.19 *at his right side:* The place of honor. [o]2.22 *And why . . . Joab:* One possible meaning for the difficult Hebrew text.

Abiathar Is Sent Back Home

[26]Solomon sent for Abiathar the priest and said:

Abiathar, go back home to Anathoth! You ought to be killed too, but I won't do it now. When my father David was king, you were in charge of the sacred chest, and you went through a lot of hard times with my father. [27]But I won't let you be a priest of the LORD anymore.

And so the promise that the LORD had made at Shiloh about the family of Eli came true.[p]

Joab Is Killed

[28]Joab had not helped Absalom try to become king, but he had helped Adonijah. So when Joab learned that Adonijah had been killed, he ran to the sacred tent and grabbed hold of the corners of the altar for protection.[q] [29]When Solomon heard about this, he sent someone to ask Joab, "Why did you run to the altar?"

Joab sent back his answer, "I was afraid of you, and I ran to the LORD for protection."[r]

Then Solomon shouted, "Benaiah, go kill Joab!"

[30]Benaiah went to the sacred tent and yelled, "Joab, the king orders you to come out!"

"No!" Joab answered. "Kill me right here."

Benaiah went back and told Solomon what Joab had said.

[31-32]Solomon replied:

Do what Joab said. Kill him and bury him! Then my family and I won't be responsible for what he did to Abner the commander of Israel's army and to Amasa the commander of Judah's army. He killed those innocent men without my father knowing about it. Both of them were better men than Joab. Now the LORD will make him pay for those murders. [33]Joab's family will always suffer because of what he did, but the LORD will always bless David's family and his kingdom with peace.

[34]Benaiah went back and killed Joab. His body was taken away and buried near his home in the desert.

[35]Solomon put Benaiah in Joab's place as army commander, and he put Zadok in Abiathar's place as priest.

Shimei Is Killed

[36]Solomon sent for Shimei and said, "Build a house here in Jerusalem and live in it. But whatever you do, don't leave the city! [37]If you ever cross Kidron Valley and leave Jerusalem, you will be killed. And it will be your own fault."

[38]"That's fair, Your Majesty," Shimei answered. "I'll do that." So Shimei lived in Jerusalem from then on.

[39]About three years later, two of Shimei's servants ran off to King Achish in Gath. When Shimei found out where they were, [40]he saddled his donkey and went after them. He found them and brought them back to Jerusalem.

[41]Someone told Solomon that Shimei had gone to Gath and was back. [42]Solomon sent for him and said:

Shimei, you promised in the name of the LORD that you would never leave Jerusalem. I warned you that you would die if you did. You agreed that this was fair, didn't you? [43]You have disobeyed me and have broken the promise you made to the LORD.

[44]I know you remember all the cruel things you did to my father David. Now the LORD is going to punish you for what you did. [45]But the LORD will bless me and make my father's kingdom strong forever.

[46]"Benaiah," Solomon shouted, "kill Shimei." So Shimei died.

Solomon was now in complete control of his kingdom.

The LORD Makes Solomon Wise
(2 Chronicles 1.1-13)

3 Solomon signed a treaty with the king of Egypt and married his daughter. She lived in the older part of Jerusalem[s] until the palace, the LORD's temple, and the wall around Jerusalem were completed.

---

[p]2.27 the promise . . . came true: See 1 Samuel 2.27-34.
[q]2.28 the corners . . . for protection: See the note at 1.50.
[r]2.29 he sent someone . . . for protection: One ancient translation; these words are not in the Hebrew text.
[s]3.1 the older . . . Jerusalem: Hebrew "the city of David."

²At that time, there was no temple for worshiping the LORD, and everyone offered sacrifices at the local shrines.ᵗ ³Solomon loved the LORD and followed his father David's instructions, but Solomon also offered sacrifices and burned incense at the shrines.

⁴The most important shrine was in Gibeon, and Solomon had offered more than a thousand sacrifices on that altar.

⁵One night while Solomon was in Gibeon, the LORD God appeared to him in a dream and said, "Solomon, ask for anything you want, and I will give it to you."

⁶Solomon answered:

My father David, your servant, was honest and did what you commanded. You were always loyal to him, and you gave him a son who is now king. ⁷LORD God, I'm your servant, and you've made me king in my father's place. But I'm very young and know so little about being a leader. ⁸And now I must rule your chosen people, even though there are too many of them to count.

⁹Please make me wise and teach me the difference between right and wrong. Then I will know how to rule your people. If you don't, there is no way I could rule this great nation of yours.

¹⁰⁻¹¹God said:

Solomon, I'm pleased that you asked for this. You could have asked to live a long time or to be rich. Or you could have asked for your enemies to be destroyed. Instead, you asked for wisdom to make right decisions. ¹²So I'll make you wiser than anyone who has ever lived or ever will live.

¹³I'll also give you what you didn't ask for. You'll be rich and respected as long as you live, and you'll be greater than any other king. ¹⁴If you obey me and follow my commands, as your father David did, I'll let you live a long time.

¹⁵Solomon woke up and realized that God had spoken to him in the dream. He went back to Jerusalem and stood in front of the sacred chest, where he offered sacrifices to please the Lordᵘ and sacrifices to ask his blessing.ᵛ Then Solomon gave a feast for his officials.

ᵗ3.2 *local shrines*: The Hebrew text has "high places," which were local places to worship God or foreign gods.　ᵘ3.15 *sacrifices to please the Lord*: See Leviticus 1.1-17.　ᵛ3.15 *sacrifices to ask his blessing*: See Leviticus 3.1-17.

WORK—How can I be a good supervisor? *(1 Kings 3.5-15; 4.29-34)*

Listen to God.

It's fascinating to be in a situation where it looks as if everyone is going to lose what they want, but some wise person comes up with an idea and suddenly, it's a win-win situation.

That wise person often has not been part of the commotion, but somehow has maintained neutrality and distance. Supervisors need that objectivity, and one of the best ways to get it is to suspend decisions until you have consulted God. People may pressure you to make important decisions on the spot, but it's important not to act hastily.

In quiet and solitude, deliberately put your decisions on hold. Ask God to show you what is truly right and wrong in the situation (3.9). Ask God to help you see a just and fair path that exceeds common sense. Treating everyone the same is not always fair; it takes wisdom to know what is best for everyone. Then go about your routine. Don't be surprised if incredible insights come to you, especially in quiet moments in the car or as you pick up the clutter in your house.

Between these crises, ask God to store principles of wisdom within you. Like Solomon, study the ways of plants and animals, and look at the wisdom to be found in the instinct God gave these creations (4.33). There's enough wisdom to go around—even for you and the people you supervise. (See also Exodus 18; Ezra 5.1—6.12; Jeremiah 32.26-44; John 21.15-25; 2 Timothy 1.1-7; Philemon 8-16, Philemon 15-25.)

Words To Remember: *Please make me wise and teach me the difference between right and wrong.—1 Kings 3.9*

Solomon Makes a Difficult Decision

[16]One day two women[w] came to King Solomon, [17]and one of them said:

Your Majesty, this woman and I live in the same house. Not long ago my baby was born at home, [18]and three days later her baby was born. Nobody else was there with us.

[19]One night while we were all asleep, she rolled over on her baby, and he died. [20]Then while I was still asleep, she got up and took my son out of my bed. She put him in her bed, then she put her dead baby next to me.

[21]In the morning when I got up to feed my son, I saw that he was dead. But when I looked at him in the light, I knew he wasn't my son.

[22]"No!" the other woman shouted. "He was your son. My baby is alive!"

"The dead baby is yours," the first woman yelled. "Mine is alive!"

They argued back and forth in front of Solomon, [23]until finally he said, "Both of you say this live baby is yours. [24]Someone bring me a sword."

A sword was brought, and Solomon ordered, [25]"Cut the baby in half! That way each of you can have part of him."

[26]"Please don't kill my son," the baby's mother screamed. "Your Majesty, I love him very much, but give him to her. Just don't kill him."

The other woman shouted, "Go ahead and cut him in half. Then neither of us will have the baby."

[27]Solomon said, "Don't kill the baby." Then he pointed to the first woman, "She is his real mother. Give the baby to her."

[28]Everyone in Israel was amazed when they heard how Solomon had made his decision. They realized that God had given him wisdom to judge fairly.

Solomon's Officials

4 [1-6]Here is a list of Solomon's highest officials while he was king of Israel:

Azariah son of Zadok was the priest;
Elihoreph and Ahijah sons of Shisha were the secretaries;
Jehoshaphat son of Ahilud kept the government records;
Benaiah son of Jehoiada was the army commander;
Zadok and Abiathar were priests;
Azariah son of Nathan was in charge of the regional officers;
Zabud son of Nathan was a priest and the king's advisor;
Ahishar was the prime minister;
Adoniram son of Abda was in charge of the forced labor.

[7]Solomon chose twelve regional officers, who took turns bringing food for him and his household. Each officer provided food from his region for one month of the year. [8]These were the twelve officers:

The son of Hur was in charge of the hill country of Ephraim.

[9]The son of Deker was in charge of the towns of Makaz, Shaalbim, Beth-Shemesh, and Elon-Beth-Hanan.

[10]The son of Hesed was in charge of the towns of Arubboth and Socoh, and the region of Hepher.

[11]The son of Abinadab was in charge of Naphath-Dor and was married to Solomon's daughter Taphath.

[12]Baana son of Ahilud was in charge of the towns of Taanach and Megiddo. He was also in charge of the whole region of Beth-Shan near the town of Zarethan, south of Jezreel from Beth-Shan to Abel-Meholah to the other side of Jokmeam.

[13]The son of Geber was in charge of the town of Ramoth in Gilead and the villages in Gilead belonging to the family of Jair, a descendant of Manasseh. He was also in charge of the region of Argob in Bashan, which had sixty walled towns with bronze bars on their gates.

[14]Ahinadab son of Iddo was in charge of the territory of Mahanaim.

[15]Ahimaaz was in charge of the territory of Naphtali and was married to Solomon's daughter Basemath.

[16]Baana son of Hushai was in charge of the territory of Asher and the town of Bealoth.

[17]Jehoshaphat son of Paruah was in charge of the territory of Issachar.

[18]Shimei son of Ela was in charge of the territory of Benjamin.

---

[w]**3.16** *women:* Hebrew "prostitutes."

¹⁹Geber son of Uri was in charge of Gilead, where King Sihon of the Amorites and King Og of Bashan had lived.

And one officer was in charge of the territory of Judah.ˣ

The Size of Solomon's Kingdom

²⁰There were so many people living in Judah and Israel while Solomon was king that they seemed like grains of sand on a beach. Everyone had enough to eat and drink, and they were happy.

²¹Solomon ruled every kingdom between the Euphrates River and the land of the Philistines down to Egypt. These kingdoms paid him taxes as long as he lived. ²²Every day, Solomon needed one hundred fifty bushels of fine flour, three hundred bushels of coarsely-ground flour, ²³ten grain-fed cattle, twenty pasture-fed cattle, one hundred sheep, as well as deer, gazelles, and geese.

²⁴Solomon ruled the whole region west of the Euphrates River, from Tiphsah to Gaza, and he was at peace with all of the countries around him. ²⁵Everyone living in Israel, from the town of Dan in the north to Beersheba in the south, was safe as long as Solomon lived. Each family sat undisturbed beneath its own grape vines and fig trees.

²⁶Solomon had forty thousand stalls of chariot horses and twelve thousand chariot soldiers.

²⁷Each of the twelve regional officers brought food to Solomon and his household for one month of the year. They provided everything he needed, ²⁸as well as barley and straw for the horses.

Solomon's Wisdom

²⁹Solomon was brilliant. God had blessed him with insight and understanding. ³⁰⁻³¹He was wiser than anyone else in the world, including the wisest people of the east and of Egypt. He was even wiser than Ethan the Ezrahite, and Mahol's three sons, Heman, Calcol, and Darda. Solomon became famous in every country around Judah and Israel. ³²Solomon wrote three thousand wise sayings and composed more than one thousand songs. ³³He could talk about all kinds of plants, from large trees to small bushes, and he taught about animals, birds, reptiles, and fish. ³⁴Kings all over the world heard about Solomon's wisdom and sent people to listen to him teach.

Solomon Asks Hiram
To Help Build the Temple
(2 Chronicles 2.1-16)

5 King Hiram of Tyreʸ had always been friends with Solomon's father David. When Hiram learned that Solomon was king, he sent some of his officials to meet with Solomon.

²Solomon sent a message back to Hiram: ³Remember how my father David wanted to build a temple where the LORD his God could be worshiped? But enemies kept attacking my father's kingdom, and he never had the chance. ⁴Now, thanks to the LORD God, there is peace in my kingdom and no trouble or threat of war anywhere.

> *Life is full of subtle,*
> *unsuspected, hidden*
> *perks, ready to make their*
> *presence known at the turn*
> *of a corner to cheer us, to*
> *lift us, to change our*
> *attitudes, to give our souls*
> *a reason to celebrate.*
>
> LUCI SWINDOLL

⁵The LORD God promised my father that when his son became king, he would build a temple for worshiping the LORD. So I've decided to do that.

⁶I'd like you to have your workers cut down cedar trees in Lebanon for me. I will pay them whatever you say and will even have my workers help

---

ˣ4.19 *of Judah*: One ancient translation; these words are not in the Hebrew text. ʸ5.1 *Tyre*: The most important city in Phoenicia. It was located on the coast of the Mediterranean Sea north of Israel, in what is today southern Lebanon.

them. We both know that your workers are more experienced than anyone else at cutting lumber.

[7]Hiram was so happy when he heard Solomon's request that he said, "I am grateful that the LORD gave David such a wise son to be king of that great nation!" [8]Then he sent back his answer:

I received your message and will give you all the cedar and pine logs you need. [9]My workers will carry them down from Lebanon to the Mediterranean Sea. They will tie the logs together and float them along the coast to wherever you want them. Then they will untie the logs, and your workers can take them from there.

To pay for the logs, you can provide the grain I need for my household.

[10]Hiram gave Solomon all the cedar and pine logs he needed. [11]In return, Solomon gave Hiram about one hundred twenty-five thousand bushels of wheat and about one thousand one hundred gallons of pure olive oil each year.

[12]The LORD kept his promise and made Solomon wise. Hiram and Solomon signed a treaty and never went to war against each other.

Solomon's Workers

[13]Solomon ordered thirty thousand people from all over Israel to cut logs for the temple, [14]and he put Adoniram in charge of these workers. Solomon divided them into three groups of ten thousand. Each group worked one month in Lebanon and had two months off at home.

[15]He also had eighty thousand workers to cut stone in the hill country of Israel, seventy thousand workers to carry the stones, [16]and over three thousand assistants to keep track of the work and to supervise the workers. [17]He ordered the workers to cut and shape large blocks of good stone for the foundation of the temple.

[18]Solomon's and Hiram's men worked with men from the city of Gebal,[z] and together they got the stones and logs ready for the temple.

The Outside of the Temple Is Completed

6 Solomon's workers started building the temple during Ziv,[a] the second month of the year. It had been four

years since Solomon became king of Israel, and four hundred eighty years since the people of Israel left Egypt.

[2]The inside of the LORD's temple was ninety feet long, thirty feet wide, and forty-five feet high. [3]A fifteen-foot porch went all the way across the front of the temple. [4]The windows were narrow on the outside but wide on the inside.

[5-6]Along the sides and back of the temple, there were three levels of storage rooms. The rooms on the bottom level were seven and a half feet wide, the rooms on the middle level were nine feet wide, and those on the top level were ten and a half feet wide. There were ledges on the outside of the temple that supported the beams of the storage rooms, so that nothing was built into the temple walls.

[7]Solomon did not want the noise of hammers and axes to be heard at the place where the temple was being built. So he had the workers shape the blocks of stone at the quarry.

[8]The entrance to the bottom storage rooms was on the south side of the building, and stairs to the other rooms were also there. [9]The roof of the temple was made out of beams and cedar boards.

The workers finished building the outside of the temple. [10]Storage rooms seven and a half feet high were all around the temple, and they were attached to the temple by cedar beams.

[11]The LORD told Solomon:

[12-13]If you obey my commands and do what I say, I will keep the promise I made to your father David. I will live among my people Israel in this temple you are building, and I will not desert them.

[14]So Solomon's workers finished building the temple.

The Inside of the Temple Is Furnished
(2 Chronicles 3.8-14)

[15]The floor of the temple was made out of pine, and the walls were lined with cedar from floor to ceiling.[b]

[16]The most holy place was in the back of

---

[z]5.18 *Gebal*: Later known as Byblos. [a]6.1 *Ziv*: The second month of the Hebrew calendar, from about mid-April to mid-May. [b]6.15 *from floor to ceiling*: One possible meaning for the difficult Hebrew text.

the temple, and it was thirty feet square. Cedar boards standing from floor to ceiling[c] separated it from the rest of the temple. [17]The temple's main room was sixty feet long, and it was in front of the most holy place.

[18]The inside walls were lined with cedar to hide the stones, and the cedar was decorated with carvings of gourds and flowers.

[19]The sacred chest was kept in the most holy place. [20-22]This room was thirty feet long, thirty feet wide, and thirty feet high, and it was lined with pure gold. There were also gold chains across the front of the most holy place. The inside of the temple, as well as the cedar altar in the most holy place, was covered with gold.

> *It's when I spend private time with God that I'm truly renewed and grounded.*
>
> MAYO MATHERS

[23]Solomon had two statues of winged creatures[d] made from olive wood to put in the most holy place. Each creature was fifteen feet tall [24-26]and fifteen feet across. They had two wings, and the wings were seven and a half feet long. [27]Solomon put them next to each other in the most holy place. Their wings were spread out and reached across the room. [28]The creatures were also covered with gold.

[29]The walls of the two rooms were decorated with carvings of palm trees, flowers, and winged creatures. [30]Even the floor was covered with gold.

[31-32]The two doors to the most holy place were made out of olive wood and were decorated with carvings of palm trees, flowers, and winged creatures. The doors and the carvings were covered with gold. The door frame came to a point at the top.

[33-34]The two doors to the main room of the temple were made out of pine, and each one had two sections[e] so they could fold open. The door frame was shaped like a rectangle and was made out of olive wood.

[35]The doors were covered with gold and were decorated with carvings of palm trees, flowers, and winged creatures.

[36]The inner courtyard of the temple had walls made out of three layers of cut stones with one layer of cedar beams.

[37]Work began on the temple during Ziv,[f] the second month of the year, four years after Solomon became king of Israel. [38]Seven years later the workers finished building it during Bul,[g] the eighth month of the year. It was built exactly as it had been planned.

Solomon's Palace Is Built

7 Solomon's palace took thirteen years to build.

[2-3]Forest Hall was the largest room in the palace. It was one hundred fifty feet long, seventy-five feet wide, and forty-five feet high, and was lined with cedar from Lebanon. It had four rows of cedar pillars, fifteen in a row, and they held up forty-five cedar beams. The ceiling was covered with cedar. [4]Three rows of windows on each side faced each other, [5]and there were three doors on each side near the front of the hall.

[6]Pillar Hall was seventy-five feet long and forty-five feet wide. A covered porch supported by pillars went all the way across the front of the hall.

[7]Solomon's throne was in Justice Hall, where he judged cases. This hall was completely lined with cedar.

[8]The section of the palace where Solomon lived was behind Justice Hall and looked exactly like it. He had a similar place built for his wife, the daughter of the king of Egypt.

[9]From the foundation all the way to the top, these buildings and the courtyard were made out of the best stones[h] carefully cut to size, then smoothed on every side with saws. [10]The foundation stones were huge, good stones—some of them fifteen feet long and others twelve feet long. [11]The cedar beams and other stones that had been cut to

---

[c]**6.16** *standing . . . ceiling:* One possible meaning for the difficult Hebrew text. [d]**6.23** *statues of winged creatures:* These were symbols of the LORD's throne on earth (see Exodus 25.18-22). [e]**6.33,34** *two sections:* One possible meaning for the difficult Hebrew text. [f]**6.37** *Ziv:* See the note at 6.1. [g]**6.38** *Bul:* The eighth month of the Hebrew calendar, from about mid-October to mid-November. [h]**7.9** *From . . . best stones:* One possible meaning for the difficult Hebrew text.

size were on top of these foundation stones. ¹²The walls around the palace courtyard were made out of three layers of cut stones with one layer of cedar beams, just like the front porch and the inner courtyard of the temple.

Hiram Makes the Bronze Furnishings
(2 Chronicles 3.15-17; 4.1-10)

¹³⁻¹⁴Hiram was a skilled bronze worker from the city of Tyre.ⁱ His father was now dead, but he also had been a bronze worker from Tyre, and his mother was from the tribe of Naphtali.

King Solomon asked Hiram to come to Jerusalem and make the bronze furnishings to use for worship in the LORD's temple, and he agreed to do it.

¹⁵Hiram made two bronze columns twenty-seven feet tall and about six feet across. ¹⁶For the top of each column, he also made a bronze cap seven and a half feet high. ¹⁷The caps were decorated with seven rows of designs that looked like chains,ʲ ¹⁸with two rows of designs that looked like pomegranates.ᵏ

¹⁹The caps for the columns of the porch were six feet high and were shaped like lilies.ˡ

²⁰The chain designs on the caps were right above the rounded tops of the two columns, and there were two hundred pomegranates in rows around each cap. ²¹Hiram placed the two columns on each side of the main door of the temple. The column on the south side was called Jachin,ᵐ and the one on the north was called Boaz.ⁿ

²²The lily-shaped caps were on top of the columns.

This completed the work on the columns.

²³Hiram also made a large bowl called the Sea. It was seven and a half feet deep, about fifteen feet across, and forty-five feet around. ²⁴Two rows of bronze gourds were around the outer edge of the bowl, ten gourds to every eighteen inches. ²⁵The bowl itself sat on top of twelve bronze bulls with three bulls facing outward in each of four directions. ²⁶The sides of the bowl were four inches thick, and its rim was like a cup that curved outward like flower petals. The bowl held about eleven thousand gallons.

²⁷Hiram made ten movable bronze stands, each one four and a half feet high,

six feet long, and six feet wide. ²⁸⁻²⁹The sides were made with panels attached to frames decorated with flower designs. The panels themselves were decorated with figures of lions, bulls, and winged creatures. ³⁰⁻³¹Each stand had four bronze wheels and axles and a round frame twenty-seven inches across, held up by four supports eighteen inches high. A small bowl rested in the frame. The supports were decorated with flower designs, and the frame with carvings.

The side panels of the stands were square, ³²and the wheels and axles were underneath them. The wheels were about twenty-seven inches high ³³and looked like chariot wheels. The axles, rims, spokes, and hubs were made out of bronze.

³⁴⁻³⁵Around the top of each stand was a nine-inch strip, and there were four bracesᵒ attached to the corners of each stand. The panels and the supports were attached to the stands, ³⁶and the stands were decorated with flower designs and figures of lions, palm trees, and winged creatures. ³⁷Hiram made the ten bronze stands from the same mold, so they were exactly the same size and shape.

³⁸Hiram also made ten small bronze bowls, one for each stand. The bowls were six feet across and could hold about two hundred thirty gallons.

³⁹He put five stands on the south side of the temple, five stands on the north side, and the large bowl at the southeast corner of the temple.

⁴⁰Hiram made pans for hot ashes, and also shovels and sprinkling bowls.

A List of Everything inside the Temple
(2 Chronicles 4.11—5.1)

This is a list of the bronze items that Hiram made for the LORD's temple: ⁴¹two columns; two bowl-shaped caps for the tops of the columns; two chain designs on the caps; ⁴²four hundred pomegranatesᵖ for the

---

ⁱ7.13,14 *Hiram . . . city of Tyre*: This is not the same person as "King Hiram of Tyre" (see 5.1).   ʲ7.17 *seven rows . . . chains*: One possible meaning for the difficult Hebrew text.   ᵏ7.18 *pomegranates*: One possible meaning for the difficult Hebrew text of verse 18. A pomegranate is a bright red fruit that looks like an apple. In ancient times, it was a symbol of life.   ˡ7.19 *lilies*: One possible meaning for the difficult Hebrew text of verse 19.   ᵐ7.21 *Jachin*: Or "He makes secure."   ⁿ7.21 *Boaz*: Or "He is strong."   ᵒ7.34,35 *braces*: Or "handles."   ᵖ7.42 *pomegranates*: See the note at 7.18.

chain designs; [43]ten movable stands; ten small bowls for the stands; [44]a large bowl; twelve bulls that held up the bowl; [45]pans for hot ashes, and also shovels and sprinkling bowls.

Hiram made these bronze things for Solomon [46]near the Jordan River between Succoth and Zarethan by pouring melted bronze into clay molds.

[47]There were so many bronze things that Solomon never bothered to weigh them, and no one ever knew how much bronze was used.

[48]Solomon gave orders to make the following temple furnishings out of gold: the altar; the table that held the sacred loaves of bread;[q] [49]ten lampstands that went in front of the most holy place; flower designs; lamps and tongs; [50]cups, lamp snuffers, and small sprinkling bowls; dishes for incense; fire pans; and the hinges for the doors to the most holy place and the main room of the temple.

[51]After the LORD's temple was finished, Solomon put into its storage rooms everything that his father David had dedicated to the LORD, including the gold and the silver.

Solomon Brings the Sacred Chest to the Temple
(2 Chronicles 5.2—6.2)

8 [1-2]The sacred chest had been kept on Mount Zion, also known as the city of David. But Solomon decided to have the chest moved to the temple while everyone was in Jerusalem, celebrating the Festival of Shelters during Ethanim,[r] the seventh month of the year.

Solomon called together the important leaders of Israel. [3-4]Then the priests and the Levites carried to the temple the sacred chest, the sacred tent, and the objects used for worship. [5]Solomon and a crowd of people walked in front of the chest, and along the way they sacrificed more sheep and cattle than could be counted.

[6]The priests carried the chest into the most holy place and put it under the winged creatures, [7]whose wings covered the chest and the poles used for carrying it. [8]The poles were so long that they could be seen from right outside the most holy place, but not from anywhere else. And they stayed there from then on.

[9]The only things kept in the chest were the two flat stones Moses had put there when the LORD made his agreement with the people of Israel at Mount Sinai,[s] after bringing them out of Egypt.

[10]Suddenly a cloud filled the temple as the priests were leaving the most holy place. [11]The LORD's glory was in the cloud, and the light from it was so bright that the priests could not stay inside to do their work. [12]Then Solomon prayed:

"Our LORD, you said that you
    would live in a dark cloud.
[13] Now I have built a glorious temple
    where you can live forever."

Solomon Speaks to the People
(2 Chronicles 6.3-11)

[14]Solomon turned toward the people standing there. Then he blessed them [15-16]and said:

Praise the LORD God of Israel! Long ago he brought his people out of Egypt. He later kept his promise to make my father David the king of Israel. The LORD also said that he had not chosen the city where his temple would be built.

[17]So when David wanted to build a temple for the LORD God of Israel, [18]the LORD said, "It's good that you want to build a temple where I can be worshiped. [19]But you're not the one to do it. Your son will build a temple to honor me."

[20]The LORD has done what he promised. I am the king of Israel like my father, and I've built a temple for the LORD our God. [21]I've also made a place in the temple for the sacred chest. And in that chest are the two flat stones on which is written the solemn agreement the LORD made with our ancestors when he led them out of Egypt.

---

[q]**7.48** *sacred loaves of bread*: This bread was offered to the LORD and was a symbol of the LORD's presence in the temple. It was put out on a special table, and was replaced with fresh bread each week (see Leviticus 24.5-9).   [r]**8.1,2** *Ethanim*: The seventh month of the Hebrew calendar, from about mid-September to mid-October.   [s]**8.9** *Sinai*: Hebrew "Horeb."

Solomon Prays at the Temple

(2 Chronicles 6.12-42)

²²Solomon stood facing the altar with everyone standing behind him. Then he lifted his arms toward heaven ²³and prayed:

LORD God of Israel, no other god in heaven or on earth is like you!

You never forget the agreement you made with your people, and you are loyal to anyone who faithfully obeys your teachings. ²⁴My father David was your servant, and today you have kept every promise you made to him.

²⁵LORD God of Israel, you promised my father that someone from his family would always be king of Israel, if they do their best to obey you, just as he did. ²⁶Please keep this promise you made to your servant David.

²⁷There's not enough room in all of heaven for you, LORD God. How could you possibly live on earth in this temple I have built? ²⁸But I ask you to answer my prayer. ²⁹This is the temple where you have chosen to be worshiped. Please watch over it day and night and listen when I turn toward it and pray. ³⁰I am your servant, and the people of Israel belong to you. So whenever any of us look toward this temple and pray, answer from your home in heaven and forgive our sins.

³¹Suppose someone accuses a person of a crime, and the accused has to stand in front of the altar in your temple and say, "I swear I am innocent!" ³²Listen from heaven and decide who is right. Then punish the guilty person and let the innocent one go free.

³³Suppose your people Israel sin against you, and then an enemy defeats them. If they come to this temple and beg for forgiveness, ³⁴listen from your home in heaven. Forgive them and bring them back to the land you gave their ancestors.

³⁵Suppose your people sin against you, and you punish them by holding back the rain. If they turn toward this temple and pray in your name and stop sinning, ³⁶listen from your home in heaven and forgive them. The people of Israel are your servants, so teach them to live right. And please send rain on the land you promised them forever.

³⁷Sometimes the crops may dry up or rot or be eaten by locusts[t] or grasshoppers, and your people will be starving. Sometimes enemies may surround their towns, or your people will become sick with deadly diseases. ³⁸Listen when anyone in Israel truly feels sorry and sincerely prays with arms lifted toward your temple. ³⁹You know what is in everyone's heart. So from your home in heaven answer their prayers, according to the way they live and what is in their hearts. ⁴⁰Then your people will worship and obey you for as long as they live in the land you gave their ancestors.

⁴¹⁻⁴²Foreigners will hear about you and your mighty power, and some of them will come to live among your people Israel. If any of them pray toward this temple, ⁴³listen from your home in heaven and answer their prayers. Then everyone on earth will worship you, just like your people Israel, and they will know that I have built this temple to honor you.

⁴⁴Our LORD, sometimes you will order your people to attack their enemies. Then your people will turn toward this temple I have built for you in your chosen city, and they will pray to you. ⁴⁵Answer their prayers from heaven and give them victory.

⁴⁶Everyone sins. But when your people sin against you, suppose you get angry enough to let their enemies drag them away to foreign countries. ⁴⁷⁻⁴⁹Later, they may feel sorry for what they did and ask your forgiveness. Answer them when they pray toward this temple I have built for you in your chosen city, here in this land you gave their ancestors. From your home in heaven, listen to their sincere prayers and do what they ask. ⁵⁰Forgive your people no matter how much they have sinned against you. Make the enemies who defeated them be kind to them. ⁵¹Remember, they are the people you

---

[t]8.37 *locusts:* A type of grasshopper that comes in swarms and causes great damage to plant life.

chose and rescued from Egypt that was like a blazing fire to them.

⁵²I am your servant, and the people of Israel belong to you. So listen when any of us pray and cry out for your help. ⁵³When you brought our ancestors out of Egypt, you told your servant Moses to say to them, "From all people on earth, the LORD God has chosen you to be his very own."

Solomon Blesses the People

⁵⁴When Solomon finished his prayer at the altar, he was kneeling with his arms lifted toward heaven. He stood up, ⁵⁵turned toward the people, blessed them, and said loudly:

> *After seeing the way*
> *God's worked in our lives,*
> *I have no doubt God is*
> *100 percent faithful.*
> LEE EZELL

⁵⁶Praise the LORD! He has kept his promise and given us peace. Every good thing he promised to his servant Moses has happened.

⁵⁷The LORD our God was with our ancestors to help them, and I pray that he will be with us and never abandon us. ⁵⁸May the LORD help us obey him and follow all the laws and teachings he gave our ancestors.

⁵⁹I pray that the LORD our God will remember my prayer day and night. May he help everyone in Israel each day, in whatever way we need it. ⁶⁰Then every nation will know that the LORD is the only true God.

⁶¹Obey the LORD our God and follow his commands with all your heart, just as you are doing today.

Solomon Dedicates the Temple
(2 Chronicles 7.4-10)

⁶²⁻⁶³Solomon and the people dedicated the temple to the LORD by offering twenty-two thousand cattle and one hundred twenty thousand sheep as sacrifices to ask the LORD's blessing.ᵘ ⁶⁴On that day, Solomon dedicated the courtyard in front of the temple and made it acceptable for worship. He offered the sacrifices there because the bronze altar in front of the temple was too small.

⁶⁵Solomon and the huge crowd celebrated the Festival of Shelters at the temple for seven days.ᵛ There were people from as far away as the Egyptian Gorge in the south and Lebo-Hamath in the north. ⁶⁶Then on the eighth day, he sent everyone home. They said good-by and left, very happy, because of all the good things the LORD had done for his servant David and his people Israel.

The LORD Appears to Solomon Again
(2 Chronicles 7.11-22)

9 The LORD's temple and Solomon's palace were now finished, and Solomon had built everything he wanted. ²Some time later the LORD appeared to him again in a dream, just as he had done at Gibeon. ³The LORD said:

I heard your prayer and what you asked me to do. This temple you have built is where I will be worshiped forever. It belongs to me, and I will never stop watching over it.

⁴You must obey me, as your father David did, and be honest and fair. Obey my laws and teachings, ⁵and I will keep my promise to David that someone from your family will always be king of Israel.

⁶But if you or any of your descendants disobey my commands or start worshiping foreign gods, ⁷I will no longer let my people Israel live in this land I gave them. I will desert this temple where I said I would be worshiped. Then people everywhere will think this nation is only a joke and will make fun of it. ⁸This temple will become a pile of rocks!ʷ Everyone who walks by will be shocked, and they will ask,

---

ᵘ8.62,63 *sacrifices to ask the LORD's blessing*: See Leviticus 3.1-17. ᵛ8.65 *seven days*: One ancient translation; Hebrew "seven days and seven more days, fourteen days in all." ʷ9.8 *a pile of rocks*: Some ancient translations; Hebrew "high."

"Why did the LORD do such a terrible thing to his people and to this temple?" ⁹Then they will answer, "We know why the LORD did this. The people of Israel rejected the LORD their God, who rescued their ancestors from Egypt, and they started worshiping other gods."

Other Things Solomon Did
(2 Chronicles 8.1-18)

¹⁰It took twenty years for the LORD's temple and Solomon's palace to be built. ¹¹Later, Solomon gave King Hiram of Tyre twenty towns in the region of Galilee to repay him for the cedar, pine, and gold he had given Solomon.

¹²When Hiram went to see the towns, he did not like them. ¹³He said, "Solomon, my friend, are these the kind of towns you want to give me?" So Hiram called the region Cabul because he thought it was worthless.ˣ ¹⁴He sent Solomon only five tons of gold in return.

¹⁵After Solomon's workers had finished the temple and the palace, he ordered them to fill in the land on the east side of Jerusalem,ʸ to build a wall around the city, and to rebuild the towns of Hazor, Megiddo, and Gezer.

¹⁶Earlier, the king of Egypt had captured the town of Gezer; he burned it to the ground and killed the Canaanite people living there. Then he gave it to his daughter as a wedding present when she married Solomon. ¹⁷So Solomon had the town rebuilt.

Solomon had his workers rebuild Lower Beth-Horon, ¹⁸Baalath, and Tamar in the desert of Judah. ¹⁹They also built towns where he could keep his supplies and his chariots and horses. Solomon had them build whatever he wanted in Jerusalem, Lebanon, and anywhere in his kingdom.

²⁰⁻²²Solomon did not force the Israelites to do his work. They were his soldiers, officials, leaders, commanders, chariot captains, and chariot drivers. But he did make slaves of the Amorites, Hittites, Perizzites, Hivites, and Jebusites who were living in Israel. These were the descendants of those foreigners the Israelites could not destroy, and they remained Israel's slaves.

²³Solomon appointed five hundred fifty officers to be in charge of his workers and to watch over his building projects.

²⁴Solomon's wife, the daughter of the king of Egypt, moved from the older part of Jerusalemᶻ to her new palace. Then Solomon had the land on the east side of Jerusalem filled in.ᵃ

²⁵Three times a year, Solomon burned incense and offered sacrifices to the LORD on the altar he had built.

Solomon had now finished building the LORD's temple.

²⁶He also had a lot of ships at Ezion-Geber, a town in Edom near Eloth on the Red Sea.ᵇ ²⁷⁻²⁸King Hiram let some of his experienced sailors go to the country of Ophirᶜ with Solomon's own sailors, and they brought back about sixteen tons of gold for Solomon.

The Queen of Sheba Visits Solomon
(2 Chronicles 9.1-12)

10 The Queen of Sheba heard how famous Solomon was, so she went to Jerusalem to test him with difficult questions. ²She took along several of her officials, and she loaded her camels with gifts of spices, jewels, and gold. When she arrived, she and Solomon talked about everything she could think of. ³He answered every question, no matter how difficult it was.

⁴⁻⁵The Queen was amazed at Solomon's wisdom. She was breathless when she saw his palace, the food on his table, his officials, his servants in their uniforms, the people who served his food, and the sacrifices he offered at the LORD's temple. ⁶She said:

Solomon, in my own country I had heard about your wisdom and all you've done. ⁷But I didn't believe it until I saw it with my own eyes! And there's so much I didn't hear about. You are wiser and richer than I was told. ⁸Your wivesᵈ and officials are

---

ˣ9.13 *Cabul . . . worthless:* Cabul sounds like the Hebrew word for "worthless."   ʸ9.15 *fill . . . Jerusalem:* The Hebrew text has "build the Millo," which probably refers to a landfill to strengthen and extend the hill where the city was built.   ᶻ9.24 *the older . . . Jerusalem:* See the note at 3.1.   ᵃ9.24 *the land . . . filled in:* See the note at 9.15.   ᵇ9.26 *Red Sea:* Hebrew *yam suph,* here referring to the Gulf of Aqaba, since the term is extended to include the northeastern arm of the Red Sea (see also the note at Exodus 13.11).   ᶜ9.27,28 *Ophir:* The location of this place is not known.   ᵈ10.8 *wives:* Two ancient translations; Hebrew "men."

lucky to be here where they can listen to the wise things you say.

⁹I praise the LORD your God. He is pleased with you and has made you king of Israel. The LORD loves Israel, so he has given them a king who will rule fairly and honestly.

¹⁰The Queen of Sheba gave Solomon almost five tons of gold, many jewels, and more spices than anyone had ever brought into Israel.

¹¹⁻¹³In return, Solomon gave her the gifts he would have given any other ruler, but he also gave her everything else she wanted. Then she and her officials went back to their own country.

Solomon's Wealth
(2 Chronicles 9.13-28)

King Hiram's ships brought gold, juniper wood, and jewels from the country of Ophir. Solomon used the wood to make stepsᵉ for the temple and palace, and harps and other stringed instruments for the musicians. It was the best juniper wood anyone in Israel had ever seen.

¹⁴Solomon received about twenty-five tons of gold a year. ¹⁵The merchants and traders, as well as the kings of Arabia and rulers from Israel, also gave him gold.

Solomon talks of having everything but finally concludes that the only thing of value is having God in your life. He alone gives meaning to life.

MARY ANN MAYO

---

¹⁶Solomon made two hundred gold shields and used about seven and a half pounds of gold for each one. ¹⁷He also made three hundred smaller gold shields, using almost four pounds for each one, and he put the shields in his palace in Forest Hall. ¹⁸His throne was made of ivory and covered with pure gold. ¹⁹⁻²⁰The back of the throne was rounded at the top, and it had armrests on each side. There was a statue of a lion on both sides of the throne, and there was a statue of a lion at both ends of each of the six steps leading up to the throne. No other throne in the world was like Solomon's.

²¹Since silver was almost worthless in those days, everything was made of gold, even the cups and dishes used in Forest Hall.

²²Solomon had a lot of seagoing ships.ᶠ Every three years he sent them out with Hiram's ships to bring back gold, silver, and ivory, as well as monkeys and peacocks.ᵍ

²³He was the richest and wisest king in the world. ²⁴People from every nation wanted to hear the wisdom God had given him. ²⁵Year after year people came and brought gifts of silver and gold, as well as clothes, weapons, spices, horses, or mules.

²⁶Solomon had one thousand four hundred chariots and twelve thousand horses that he kept in Jerusalem and other towns. ²⁷While he was king, there was silver everywhere in Jerusalem, and cedar was as common as ordinary sycamore trees in the foothills.

²⁸⁻²⁹Solomon's merchants bought his horses and chariots in the regions of Musri and Kue.ʰ They paid about fifteen pounds of silver for a chariot and almost four pounds of silver for a horse. They also sold horses and chariots to the Hittite and Syrian kings.

Solomon Disobeys the LORD

11 ¹⁻²The LORD did not want the Israelites to worship foreign gods, so he had warned them not to marry anyone who was not from Israel.

Solomon loved his wife, the daughter of the king of Egypt. But he also loved some women from Moab, Ammon, and Edom, and others from Sidon and the land of the Hittites. ³⁻⁴Seven hundred of his wives were daughters of kings, but he also married three hundred other women.ⁱ

ᵉ**10.11-13** *steps:* Or "stools" or "railings."
ᶠ**10.22** *seagoing ships:* The Hebrew text has "ships of Tarshish," which may have been a Phoenician city in Spain. "Ships of Tarshish" probably means large, seagoing ships. ᵍ**10.22** *peacocks:* Or "baboons."
ʰ**10.28,29** *Musri and Kue:* Hebrew "Egypt and Kue." Musri and Kue were regions located in what is today southeast Turkey. ⁱ**11.3,4** *other women:* This translates a Hebrew word for a woman who was legally bound to a man, but without the full privileges of a wife.

As Solomon got older, some of his wives led him to worship their gods. He wasn't like his father David, who had worshiped only the LORD God. ⁵Solomon also worshiped Astarte the goddess of Sidon, and Milcom the disgusting god of Ammon. ⁶Solomon's father had obeyed the LORD with all his heart, but Solomon disobeyed and did what the LORD hated.

⁷Solomon built shrines on a hill east of Jerusalem to worship Chemosh the disgusting god of Moab, and Molech the disgusting god of Ammon. ⁸In fact, he built a shrine for each of his foreign wives, so all of them could burn incense and offer sacrifices to their own gods.

⁹⁻¹⁰The LORD God of Israel had appeared to Solomon two times and warned him not to worship foreign gods. But Solomon disobeyed and did it anyway. This made the LORD very angry, ¹¹and he said to Solomon:

You did what you wanted and not what I told you to do. Now I'm going to take your kingdom from you and give it to one of your officials. ¹²But because David was your father, you will remain king as long as you live. I will wait until your son becomes king, then I will take the kingdom from him. ¹³When I do, I will still let him rule one tribe, because I have not forgotten that David was my servant and Jerusalem is my city.

Hadad Becomes an Enemy of Solomon

¹⁴Hadad was from the royal family of Edom, and here is how the LORD made him Solomon's enemy:

¹⁵⁻¹⁶Some time earlier, when David conquered the nation of Edom,ʲ Joab his army commander went there to bury those who had died in battle. Joab and his soldiers stayed in Edom six months, and during that time they killed every man and boy who lived there.

¹⁷⁻¹⁹Hadad was a boy at the time, but he escaped to Midian with some of his father's officials. At Paran some other men joined them, and they went to the king of Egypt. The king liked Hadad and gave him food, some land, and a house, and even let him marry the sister of Queen Tahpenes. ²⁰Hadad and his wife had a son named Genubath, and the queen let the boy grow up in the palace with her own children.

²¹When Hadad heard that David and Joab were dead, he said to the king, "Your Majesty, please let me go back to my own country."

²²"Why?" asked the king. "Do you want something I haven't given you?"

"No, I just want to go home."

Rezon Becomes an Enemy of Solomon

²³Here is how God made Rezon son of Eliada an enemy of Solomon:

Rezon had run away from his master, King Hadadezer of Zobah. ²⁴⁻²⁵He formed his own small army and became its leader after David had defeated Hadadezer's troops.ᵏ Then Rezon and his army went to Damascus, where he became the ruler of Syria and an enemy of Israel.

Both Hadad and Rezon were enemies of Israel while Solomon was king, and they caused him a lot of trouble.

The LORD Makes a Promise to Jeroboam

²⁶Jeroboam was from the town of Zeredah in Ephraim. His father Nebat had died, but his mother Zeruah was still alive. Jeroboam was one of Solomon's officials, but even he rebelled against Solomon. ²⁷Here is how it happened:

While Solomon's workers were filling in the land on the east side of Jerusalemˡ and repairing the city walls, ²⁸Solomon noticed that Jeroboam was a hard worker. So he put Jeroboam in charge of the work force from Manasseh and Ephraim.

²⁹⁻³⁰One day when Jeroboam was leaving Jerusalem, he met Ahijah, a prophet from Shiloh. No one else was anywhere around. Suddenly, Ahijah took off his new coat and ripped it into twelve pieces. ³¹Then he said:

Jeroboam, take ten pieces of this coat and listen to what the LORD God of Israel says to you. "Jeroboam, I am the LORD God, and I am about to take Solomon's kingdom from him and give you ten tribes to rule. ³²But Solomon will still rule one tribe,ᵐ since he

---

ʲ11.15,16 *Edom:* See 2 Samuel 8.13, 14.
ᵏ11.24,25 *troops:* See 2 Samuel 8.3-6.
ˡ11.27 *filling . . . Jerusalem:* See the note at 9.15.
ᵐ11.31,32 *ten tribes . . . one tribe:* By this time the tribe of Simeon had become part of the tribe of Judah. "One tribe" refers to Judah. Instead of "one tribe," one ancient translation has "two tribes."

is the son of David my servant, and Jerusalem is my chosen city.
³³"Solomon and the Israelites are not like their ancestor David. They will not listen to me, obey me, or do what is right. They have turned from me to worship Astarte the goddess of Sidon, Chemosh the god of Moab, and Milcom the god of Ammon.
³⁴"Solomon is David's son, and David was my chosen leader, who did what I commanded. So I will let Solomon be king until he dies. ³⁵Then I will give you ten tribes to rule, ³⁶but Solomon's son will still rule one tribe. This way, my servant David will always have a descendant ruling in Jerusalem, the city where I have chosen to be worshiped.
³⁷"You will be king of Israel and will rule every nation you want. ³⁸I'll help you if you obey me. And if you do what I say, as my servant David did, I will always let someone from your family rule in Israel, just as someone from David's family will always rule in Judah. The nation of Israel will be yours.
³⁹"I will punish the descendants of David, but not forever."
⁴⁰When Solomon learned what the LORD had told Jeroboam, Solomon tried to kill Jer-

oboam. But he escaped to King Shishak of Egypt and stayed there until Solomon died.

Solomon Dies
(2 Chronicles 9.29-31)

⁴¹Everything else Solomon did while he was king is written in the book about him and his wisdom. ⁴²After he had ruled forty years from Jerusalem, ⁴³he died and was buried in the city of his father David. His son Rehoboam then became king.

Some of the People Rebel against Rehoboam
(2 Chronicles 10.1-19)

12 Rehoboam went to Shechem where everyone was waiting to crown him king.
²Jeroboam son of Nebat heard what was happening, and he stayed in Egypt,ⁿ where he had gone to hide from Solomon. ³But the people from the northern tribes of Israel sent for him. Then together they went to Rehoboam and said, ⁴"Your father Solomon forced us to work very hard. But if you make our work easier, we will serve you and do whatever you ask."

ⁿ12.2 *he stayed in Egypt:* Hebrew; two ancient translations "he returned from Egypt" (see also 2 Chronicles 10.2).

---

*Spiritual*Life—**How can I know good spiritual leaders?** *(1 Kings 12.1-20)*

They are good listeners, wise, and discerning.
If you had to make a big decision (who to marry or not marry; whether to change jobs or move to another country), to whom would you go for advice? You'd probably ask friends who know you well, family members you trust, a church leader you look up to. But most of all, you'd want someone who's a good listener, who can help you examine wisely all possible angles of your decision, and then leave the final decision up to you.

It's important to surround yourself with godly advisors so that you'll have a ready resource for such times. In this passage, Solomon's son, Rehoboam, *did* ask his father's senior officials what he should do. But when he didn't like their advice, he ignored it. Instead he asked his group of friends (who weren't very wise) what to do—and followed their instructions. Because of Rehoboam's action, the country of Israel became a divided kingdom, with Rehoboam only able to rule over Judah.

In contrast, a good spiritual leader is interested in serving you, not in personal gain or in looking good. A good spiritual leader also is a prayer warrior who's always in communion with God through his Word. (See also Ezra 7; Matthew 17.1-13; Jude 3-7.)

Words To Remember: *When the people [of Israel] realized that Rehoboam would not listen to them, they shouted: ". . . Let's go home! Rehoboam can rule his own people."*—1 Kings 12.15

5“Give me three days to think about it,” Rehoboam replied, “then come back for my answer.” So the people left.

6Rehoboam went to some leaders who had been his father’s senior officials, and he asked them, “What should I tell these people?”

7They answered, “If you want them to serve and obey you, then you should do what they ask today. Tell them you will make their work easier.”

8But Rehoboam refused their advice and went to the younger men who had grown up with him and were now his officials. 9He asked, “What do you think I should say to these people who asked me to make their work easier?”

10His younger advisors said:

> Here’s what we think you should say to them: “Compared to me, my father was weak.[o] 11He made you work hard, but I’ll make you work even harder. He punished you with whips, but I’ll use whips with pieces of sharp metal!”

12Three days later, Jeroboam and the others came back. 13Rehoboam ignored the advice of the older advisors. 14He spoke bluntly and told them exactly what his own advisors had suggested: “My father made you work hard, but I’ll make you work even harder. He punished you with whips, but I’ll use whips with pieces of sharp metal!”

15-19When the people realized that Rehoboam would not listen to them, they shouted: “We don’t have to be loyal to David’s family. We can do what we want. Come on, people of Israel, let’s go home! Rehoboam can rule his own people.”

Adoniram[p] was in charge of the forced labor, and Rehoboam sent him to talk to the people. But they stoned him to death. Then Rehoboam ran to his chariot and hurried back to Jerusalem.

So the people from the northern tribes of Israel went home, leaving Rehoboam to rule only the people from the towns in Judah. Ever since that day, the people of Israel have opposed David’s family in Judah. All of this happened just as the LORD’s prophet Ahijah had told Jeroboam.

20When the Israelites heard that Jeroboam was back, they called everyone together. Then they sent for Jeroboam and made him king of Israel. Only the people from the tribe of Judah[q] remained loyal to David’s family.

Shemaiah Warns Rehoboam

(2 Chronicles 11.1-4)

21After Rehoboam returned to Jerusalem, he decided to attack Israel and take control of the whole country. So he called together one hundred eighty thousand soldiers from the tribes of Judah and Benjamin.

22Meanwhile, God told Shemaiah the prophet 23to give Rehoboam and everyone from Judah and Benjamin this warning: 24“Don’t go to war against the people from Israel—they are your relatives. Go home! I am the LORD, and I made these things happen.”

Rehoboam and his army obeyed the LORD and went home.

Jeroboam Makes Religious Changes

25Jeroboam rebuilt Shechem in Ephraim and made it a stronger town, then he moved there. He also fortified the town of Penuel.

26-27One day, Jeroboam started thinking, “Everyone in Israel still goes to the temple in Jerusalem to offer sacrifices to the LORD. What if they become loyal to David’s family again? They will kill me and accept Rehoboam as their king.”

28Jeroboam asked for advice and then made two gold statues of calves. He showed them to the people and said, “Listen everyone! You won’t have to go to Jerusalem to worship anymore. Here are your gods[r] who rescued you from Egypt.” 29-30Then he put one of the gold calves in the town of Bethel. He put the other one in the town of Dan, and the crowd walked out in front as the calf was taken there.[s] What Jeroboam did was a terrible sin.

31Jeroboam built small places of worship at the shrines[t] and appointed men who were not from the tribe of Levi to serve as priests. 32-33He also decided to start a new festival for

---

[o] **12.10** *Compared . . . weak*: Hebrew “My little finger is bigger than my father’s waist.” [p] **12.15-19** *Adoniram*: Two ancient translations (see also 4.6 and 5.14); Hebrew “Adoram.” [q] **12.20** *Israelites . . . Israel . . . Judah*: From this time on, “Israel” usually refers to the northern kingdom, and “Israelites” refers to the people who lived there. The southern kingdom is called “Judah.” [r] **12.28** *Here are your gods*: Or “Here is your God.” [s] **12.29,30** *the crowd . . . taken there*: One possible meaning for the difficult Hebrew text. [t] **12.31** *shrines*: See the note at 3.2.

the Israelites on the fifteenth day of the eighth month, just like the one in Judah.ᵘ On that day, Jeroboam went to Bethel and offered sacrifices on the altar to the gold calf he had put there. Then he assigned the priests their duties.

A Prophet Condemns the Altar at Bethel

13 ¹⁻²One day, Jeroboam was standing at the altar in Bethel, ready to make an offering. Suddenly one of God's prophetsᵛ arrived from Judah and shouted:

The LORD sent me with a message about this altar. A child named Josiah will be born into David's family. He will sacrifice on this altar the priests who make offerings here, and human bones will be burned on it.

³You will know that the LORD has said these things when the altar splits in half, and the ashes on it fall to the ground.

Faith is what comes out of knowing to whom you belong and knowing that he is in control.

BARBARA JOHNSON

---

⁴Jeroboam pointed at the prophet and shouted, "Grab him!" But right away, Jeroboam's hand became stiff, and he could not move it. ⁵The altar split in half, and the ashes fell to the ground, just as the prophet had warned.

⁶"Please pray to the LORD your God and ask him to heal my hand," Jeroboam begged.

The prophet prayed, and Jeroboam's hand was healed.

⁷"Come home with me and eat something," Jeroboam said. "I want to give you a gift for what you have done."

⁸"No, I wouldn't go with you, even if you offered me half of your kingdom. I won't eat or drink here either. ⁹The LORD said I can't eat or drink anything and that I can't go home the same way I came." ¹⁰Then he started home down a different road.

An Old Prophet from Bethel

¹¹At that time an old prophet lived in Bethel, and one of his sons told him what the prophet from Judah had said and done. ¹²"Show me which way he went," the old prophet said, and his sons pointed out the road. ¹³"Put a saddle on my donkey," he told them. After they did, he got on the donkey ¹⁴and rode off to look for the prophet from Judah.

The old prophet found him sitting under an oak tree and asked, "Are you the prophet from Judah?"

"Yes, I am."

¹⁵"Come home with me," the old prophet said, "and have something to eat."

¹⁶"I can't go back with you," the prophet replied, "and I can't eat or drink anything with you. ¹⁷The LORD warned me not to eat or drink or to go home the same way I came."

¹⁸The old prophet said, "I'm a prophet too. One of the LORD's angels told me to take you to my house and give you something to eat and drink."

The prophet from Judah did not know that the old prophet was lying, ¹⁹so he went home with him and ate and drank.

²⁰During the meal the LORD gave the old prophet ²¹a message for the prophet from Judah:

Listen to the LORD's message. You have disobeyed the LORD your God. ²²He told you not to eat or drink anything here, but you came home and ate with me. And so, when you die, your body won't be buried in your family tomb.

²³After the meal the old prophet got a donkey ready, ²⁴and the prophet from Judah left. Along the way, a lion attacked and killed him, and the donkey and the lion stood there beside his dead body. ²⁵Some people walked by and saw the body with the lion standing there. They ran into Bethel, telling everyone what they had seen.

²⁶When the old prophet heard the news, he said, "That must be the prophet from Judah. The LORD warned him, but he disobeyed. So the LORD sent a lion to kill him."

ᵘ**12.32,33** *the one in Judah*: This probably refers to the Festival of Shelters.   ᵛ**13.1,2** *one of God's prophets*: Hebrew "a man of God."

²⁷The old prophet told his sons to saddle his donkey, and when it was ready, ²⁸he left. He found the body lying on the road, with the donkey and lion standing there. The lion had not eaten the body or attacked the donkey. ²⁹The old prophet picked up the body, put it on his own donkey, and took it back to Bethel, so he could bury it and mourn for the prophet from Judah.

³⁰He buried the body in his own family tomb and cried for the prophet. ³¹He said to his sons, "When I die, bury my body next to this prophet. ³²I'm sure that everything he said about the altar in Bethel and the shrines in Samaria will happen."

³³But Jeroboam kept on doing evil things. He appointed men to be priests at the local shrines, even if they were not Levites. In fact, anyone who wanted to be a priest could be one. ³⁴This sinful thing led to the downfall of his kingdom.

Jeroboam's Son Dies

14 About the same time, Abijah son of Jeroboam got sick. ²⁻³Jeroboam told his wife:

Disguise yourself so no one will know you're my wife, then go to Shiloh, where the prophet Ahijah lives. Take him ten loaves of bread, some small cakes, and honey, and ask him what will happen to our son. He can tell you, because he's the one who told me I would become king.

⁴She got ready and left for Ahijah's house in Shiloh.

Ahijah was now old and blind, ⁵but the LORD told him, "Jeroboam's wife is coming to ask about her son. I will tell you what to say to her."

Jeroboam's wife came to Ahijah's house, pretending to be someone else. ⁶But when Ahijah heard her walking up to the door, he said:

Come in! I know you're Jeroboam's wife—why are you pretending to be someone else? I have some bad news for you. ⁷Give your husband this message from the LORD God of Israel: "Jeroboam, you know that I, the LORD, chose you over anyone else to be the leader of my people Israel. ⁸I even took David's kingdom away from his family and gave it to you. But you are not like my servant David. He always obeyed me and did what was right.

⁹"You have made me very angry by rejecting me and making idols out of gold. Jeroboam, you have done more evil things than any king before you.

¹⁰"Because of this, I will destroy your family by killing every man and boy in it, whether slave or free. I will wipe out your family, just as fire burns up trash. ¹¹Dogs will eat the bodies of your relatives who die in town, and vultures will eat the bodies of those who die in the country. I, the LORD, have spoken and will not change my mind!"

¹²That's the LORD's message to your husband. As for you, go back home, and right after you get there, your son will die. ¹³Everyone in Israel will mourn at his funeral. But he will be the last one from Jeroboam's family to receive a proper burial, because he's the only one the LORD God of Israel is pleased with.

¹⁴The LORD will soon choose a new king of Israel, who will destroy Jeroboam's family. And I mean very soon.ʷ ¹⁵The people of Israel have made the LORD angry by setting up sacred polesˣ for worshiping the goddess Asherah. So the LORD will punish them until they shake like grass in a stream. He will take them out of the land he gave to their ancestors, then scatter them as far away as the Euphrates River. ¹⁶Jeroboam sinned and caused the Israelites to sin. Now the LORD will desert Israel.

¹⁷Jeroboam's wife left and went back home to the town of Tirzah. As soon as she set foot in her house, her son died. ¹⁸Everyone in Israel came and mourned at his funeral, just as the LORD's servant Ahijah had said.

Jeroboam Dies

¹⁹Everything else Jeroboam did while he was king, including the battles he won, is written in *The History of the Kings of Israel*.

ʷ**14.14** *And I mean very soon*: One possible meaning for the difficult Hebrew text.   ˣ**14.15** *sacred poles*: Or "trees," used as symbols of Asherah, the goddess of fertility.

[20]He was king of Israel for twenty-two years, then he died, and his son Nadab became king.

King Rehoboam of Judah
(2 Chronicles 11.5—12.16)

[21]Rehoboam son of Solomon was forty-one years old when he became king of Judah, and he ruled seventeen years from Jerusalem, the city where the LORD had chosen to be worshiped. His mother Naamah was from Ammon.

[22]The people of Judah disobeyed the LORD and made him even angrier than their ancestors had. [23]They also built their own local shrines[y] and stone images of foreign gods, and they set up sacred poles[z] for worshiping the goddess Asherah on every hill and in the shade of large trees. [24]Even worse, they allowed prostitutes[a] at the shrines, and followed the disgusting customs of the foreign nations that the LORD had forced out of Canaan.

[25]After Rehoboam had been king for four years, King Shishak of Egypt attacked Jerusalem. [26]He took everything of value from the temple and the palace, including Solomon's gold shields.

[27]Rehoboam had bronze shields made to replace the gold ones, and he ordered the guards at the city gates to keep them safe. [28]Whenever Rehoboam went to the LORD's temple, the guards carried the shields. But they always took them back to the guardroom as soon as he was finished.

[29]Everything else Rehoboam did while he was king is written in *The History of the Kings of Judah*. [30]He and Jeroboam were constantly at war. [31]Rehoboam's mother Naamah was from Ammon, but when Rehoboam died, he was buried beside his ancestors in Jerusalem.[b] His son Abijam then became king.

King Abijam of Judah
(2 Chronicles 13.1-22)

15 Abijam became king of Judah in Jeroboam's eighteenth year as king of Israel, [2]and he ruled from Jerusalem for three years. His mother was Maacah the daughter of Abishalom.

[3]Abijam did not truly obey the LORD his God as his ancestor David had done. Instead, he was sinful just like his father Rehoboam. [4-5]David had always obeyed the LORD's commands by doing right, except in the case of Uriah.[c] And since Abijam was David's great-grandson, the LORD kept Jerusalem safe and let Abijam have a son who would be the next king.

[6-7]The war that had broken out between Rehoboam and Jeroboam continued during the time that Abijam was king.

Everything else Abijam did while he was king is written in *The History of the Kings of Judah*. [8]Abijam died and was buried in Jerusalem,[d] and his son Asa became king.

King Asa of Judah
(2 Chronicles 15.16—16.6, 11-13)

[9]Asa became king of Judah in the twentieth year of Jeroboam's rule in Israel, [10]and he ruled forty-one years from Jerusalem. His grandmother was Maacah the daughter of Abishalom.

There are some things we can't do, change, or understand, and those are God's parts to take care of.
PATSY CLAIRMONT

[11]Asa obeyed the LORD, as David had done. [12]He forced the prostitutes[e] at the shrines to leave the country, and he got rid of the idols his ancestors had made. [13]His own grandmother Maacah had made an idol of Asherah, and Asa took it and burned it in Kidron Valley. Then he removed Maacah from her position as queen mother.[f]

[14]As long as Asa lived, he was completely faithful to the LORD, even though he did not

[y]14.23 *local shrines*: See the note at 3.2. [z]14.23 *sacred poles*: See the note at 14.15. [a]14.24 *prostitutes*: Men and women sometimes served at the local shrines as prostitutes in the worship of Canaanite gods, but the LORD had forbidden the people of Israel to worship in this way (see Deuteronomy 23.17, 18). [b]14.31 *Jerusalem*: See the note at 2.10, 11. [c]15.4,5 *Uriah*: A Hittite who served in David's army; David had him killed so he could marry his wife Bathsheba (see 2 Samuel 11.1-27). [d]15.8 *Jerusalem*: See the note at 2.10, 11. [e]15.12 *prostitutes*: See the note at 14.24. [f]15.13 *queen mother*: Or "the mother of the king," an important position in biblical times (see 2.19).

destroy the local shrines. [15]He placed in the temple all the silver and gold objects that he and his father had dedicated to the LORD.

[16]Asa was always at war with King Baasha of Israel. [17]One time, Baasha invaded Judah and captured the town of Ramah. He started making the town stronger, so he could put troops there to stop people from going in and out of Judah.

[18]When Asa heard about this, he took the silver and gold from his palace and from the LORD's temple. He gave it to some of his officials and sent them to Damascus with this message for King Benhadad[g] of Syria: [19]"Our fathers signed a peace treaty. Why don't we do the same thing? This silver and gold is a present for you. So, would you please break your treaty with Baasha and force him to leave my country?"

[20]Benhadad did what Asa asked and sent the Syrian army into Israel. They captured the towns of Ijon, Dan, and Abel-Bethmaacah, and the territories of Chinneroth and Naphtali. [21]When Baasha heard about it, he left Ramah and went back to Tirzah.

[22]Asa ordered everyone in Judah to carry away the stones and wood Baasha had used to strengthen the town of Ramah. Then he used these same stones and wood to fortify the town of Geba in the territory of Benjamin and the town of Mizpah.

[23]Everything else Asa did while he was king, including his victories and the towns he rebuilt, is written in *The History of the Kings of Judah*. When he got older, he had a foot disease. [24]Asa died and was buried in the tomb of his ancestors in Jerusalem.[h] His son Jehoshaphat then became king.

King Nadab of Israel

[25]Nadab son of Jeroboam became king of Israel in Asa's second year as king of Judah, and he ruled two years. [26]Nadab disobeyed the LORD by following the evil example of his father, who had caused the Israelites to sin.

[27-28]Baasha son of Ahijah was from the tribe of Issachar, and he made plans to kill Nadab. When Nadab and his army went to attack the town of Gibbethon in Philistia, Baasha killed Nadab there. So in the third year of Asa's rule, Baasha became king of Israel.

[29]The LORD's prophet Ahijah had earlier said, "Not one man or boy in Jeroboam's family will be left alive." And, as soon as Baasha became king, he killed everyone in Jeroboam's family, [30]because Jeroboam had made the LORD God of Israel angry by sinning and causing the Israelites to sin.

[31]Everything else Nadab did while he was king is written in *The History of the Kings of Israel*.

[32]King Asa of Judah and King Baasha of Israel were always at war.

King Baasha of Israel

[33]Baasha son of Ahijah became king of Israel in Asa's third year as king of Judah, and he ruled twenty-four years from Tirzah. [34]Baasha also disobeyed the LORD by acting like Jeroboam, who had caused the Israelites to sin.

16 The LORD sent Jehu son of Hanani to say to Baasha: [2]Nobody knew who you were until I, the LORD, chose you[i] to be the leader of my people Israel. And now you're acting exactly like Jeroboam by causing the Israelites to sin. What you've done has made me so angry [3]that I will destroy you and your family, just as I did the family of Jeroboam. [4]Dogs will eat the bodies of your relatives who die in town, and vultures will eat the bodies of those who die in the country.

[5-7]Baasha made the LORD very angry, and that's why the LORD gave Jehu this message for Baasha and his family. Baasha constantly disobeyed the LORD by following Jeroboam's sinful example—but even worse, he killed everyone in Jeroboam's family!

Everything else Baasha did while he was king, including his brave deeds, is written in *The History of the Kings of Israel*. Baasha died and was buried in Tirzah, and his son Elah became king.

King Elah of Israel

[8]Elah son of Baasha became king of Israel after Asa had been king of Judah for twenty-five years, and he ruled from Tirzah for two years.

---

[g]15.18 *Benhadad:* Hebrew "Benhadad son of Tabrimmon son of Hezion." [h]15.24 *Jerusalem:* Hebrew "the city of David his ancestor." [i]16.2 *Nobody . . . you:* Hebrew "I pulled you up out of the dust."

⁹Zimri commanded half of Elah's chariots, and he made plans to kill Elah.

One day, Elah was in Tirzah, getting drunk at the home of Arza, his prime minister, ¹⁰when Zimri went there and killed Elah. So Zimri became king in the twenty-seventh year of Asa's rule in Judah.

¹¹As soon as Zimri became king, he killed everyone in Baasha's family. Not one man or boy in his family was left alive—even his close friends were killed. ¹²Baasha's family was completely wiped out, just as the LORD's prophet Jehu had warned. ¹³Baasha and Elah sinned and caused the Israelites to sin, and they made the LORD angry by worshiping idols.

¹⁴Everything else Elah did while he was king is written in *The History of the Kings of Israel*.

King Zimri of Israel

¹⁵⁻¹⁶Zimri became king of Israel in Asa's twenty-seventh year as king of Judah, but he ruled only seven days from Tirzah.

Israel's army was camped near Gibbethon in Philistia under the command of Omri. The soldiers heard that Zimri had killed Elah, and they made Omri their king that same day. ¹⁷At once, Omri and his army marched to Tirzah and attacked. ¹⁸When Zimri saw that the town was captured, he ran into the strongest part of the palace and killed himself by setting it on fire. ¹⁹Zimri had disobeyed the LORD by following the evil example of Jeroboam, who had caused the Israelites to sin.

²⁰Everything else Zimri did while he was king, including his rebellion against Elah, is written in *The History of the Kings of Israel*.

King Omri of Israel

²¹After Zimri died, some of the Israelites wanted Tibni son of Ginath to be king, but others wanted Omri. ²²Omri's followers were stronger than Tibni's, so Tibni was killed, and Omri became king of Israel ²³in the thirty-first year of Asa's rule in Judah.

Omri ruled Israel for twelve years. The first six years he ruled from Tirzah, ²⁴then he bought the hill of Samaria from Shemer for about one hundred fifty pounds of silver. He built a town there and named it Samaria, after Shemer who had owned the hill.

²⁵Omri did more evil things than any king before him. ²⁶He acted just like Jeroboam and made the LORD God of Israel angry by causing the Israelites to sin and to worship idols.

²⁷Everything else Omri did while he was king, including his brave deeds, is written in *The History of the Kings of Israel*. ²⁸Omri died and was buried in Samaria, and his son Ahab became king.

King Ahab of Israel

²⁹Ahab son of Omri became king of Israel in the thirty-eighth year of Asa's rule in Judah, and he ruled twenty-two years from Samaria.

³⁰Ahab did more things to disobey the LORD than any king before him. ³¹He acted just like Jeroboam. Even worse, he married Jezebel the daughter of King Ethbaal of Sidonʲ and started worshiping Baal. ³²Ahab built an altar and temple for Baal in Samaria ³³and set up a sacred poleᵏ for worshiping the goddess Asherah. Ahab did more to make the LORD God of Israel angry than any king of Israel before him.

³⁴While Ahab was king, a man from Bethel named Hiel rebuilt the town of Jericho. But while Hiel was laying the foundation for the town wall, his oldest son Abiram died. And while he was finishing the gates, his youngest son Segub died. This happened just as the LORD had told Joshua to say many years ago.ˡ

Elijah Stops the Rain

17 Elijah was a prophet from Tishbe in Gilead.ᵐ One day he went to King Ahab and said, "I'm a servant of the living LORD, the God of Israel. And I swear in his name that it won't rain until I say so. There won't even be any dew on the ground."

²Later, the LORD said to Elijah, ³"Leave and go across the Jordan River so you can hide near Cherith Creek. ⁴You can drink water from the creek, and eat the food I've told the ravens to bring you."

⁵Elijah obeyed the LORD and went to live near Cherith Creek. ⁶Ravens brought him

---

ʲ**16.31** *Sidon:* One of the most important cities in Phoenicia. It was located on the coast of the Mediterranean Sea, north of Israel, in what is today southern Lebanon. ᵏ**16.33** *sacred pole:* See the note at 14.15. ˡ**16.34** *a man from Bethel . . . ago:* See Joshua 6.26. ᵐ**17.1** *from Tishbe in Gilead:* Or "from the settlers in Gilead."

Jezebel

1 Kings 16.29-34; 18.1—19.18; 21; 2 Kings 9

Although Queen Jezebel was well dressed and well groomed (2 Kings 9.30), on the inside she was ugly with hate. Not only was she a wicked influence on her husband, King Ahab, who "did more things to disobey the LORD than any king before him" (1 Kings 16.30), but she herself did evil deeds, even participating in witchcraft (2 Kings 9.22).

Jezebel grew up as the daughter of Ethbaal, king of the Sidonians (1 Kings 16.31), and worshiped Baal. Under her pro-Baal influence, Ahab built an altar and temple for Baal. Jezebel herself housed and fed 850 prophets for pagan religions (1 Kings 18.19). Then she started killing as many prophets of the Lord God as she could find. You have to wonder about her conscience—did she really believe she was doing the decent thing by obliterating God's prophets, or was she cold-blooded?

Soon the murdering became personal. After Elijah defeated the prophets of Baal on Mount Carmel, Jezebel wrote Elijah this message: "You killed my prophets. Now I'm going to kill you! I pray that the gods will punish me even more severely if I don't do it by this time tomorrow" (1 Kings 19.2). Her reference to the gods punishing her if she did not kill Elijah makes you think that she was still on a holy crusade.

But murdering people seemed to have become a habit. After Ahab pouted and refused to eat because Naboth would not sell him his vineyard, Jezebel ordered the town officials to execute their hapless neighbor. People did what Jezebel told them to do—except for Elijah. She scared him, however, so after her death threat, he ran hundreds of miles to Mount Sinai, where God took care of him. With God's help, Elijah then stood up to Jezebel, predicting that she, Ahab, and their family would be wiped out. Dogs, Elijah said, would eat Jezebel's body in the town where Naboth was murdered. Twenty years later, Jehu drove over her body with a chariot, splattering the walls with her blood (2 Kings 9.33). Elijah's prophecy was fulfilled. Nothing of all that she had accumulated was left: power, luxury, money, family.

Jezebel's focus on promoting Baal worship turned her into a destructive woman. Whenever we have to deal with someone like Jezebel (self-absorbed, manipulative, backstabbing), we would like to run two hundred miles away—fast. But God can give us, as he did Elijah, intimacy with him and courage to face a Jezebel when no one else will.

bread and meat twice a day, and he drank water from the creek. ⁷But after a while, it dried up because there was no rain.

Elijah Helps a Widow in Zarephath

⁸The LORD told Elijah, ⁹"Go to the town of Zarephath in Sidon and live there. I've told a widow in that town to give you food."

¹⁰When Elijah came near the town gate of Zarephath, he saw a widow gathering sticks for a fire. "Would you please bring me a cup of water?" he asked. ¹¹As she left to get it, he asked, "Would you also please bring me a piece of bread?"

¹²The widow answered, "In the name of the living LORD your God, I swear that I don't have any bread. All I have is a handful of flour and a little olive oil. I'm on my way home now with these few sticks to cook what I have for my son and me. After that, we will starve to death."

¹³Elijah said, "Everything will be fine. Do what you said. Go home and fix something for you and your son. But first, please make a small piece of bread and bring it to me. ¹⁴The LORD God of Israel has promised that your jar of flour won't run out and your bottle of oil won't dry up before he sends rain for the crops."

¹⁵The widow went home and did exactly what Elijah had told her. She and Elijah and her family had enough food for a long time. ¹⁶The LORD kept the promise that his prophet Elijah had made, and she did not run out of flour or oil.

Elijah Brings a Boy Back to Life

¹⁷Several days later, the son of the woman who owned the house[n] got sick, and he kept getting worse, until finally he died.

¹⁸The woman shouted at Elijah, "What have I done to you? I thought you were God's prophet. Did you come here to cause the death of my son as a reminder that I've sinned against God?"[o]

¹⁹"Bring me your son," Elijah said. Then he took the boy from her arms and carried him upstairs to the room where he was staying. Elijah laid the boy on his bed ²⁰and prayed, "LORD God, why did you do such a terrible thing to this woman? She's letting me stay here, and now you've let her son

---

[n]**17.17** *the woman who owned the house:* This may or may not be the same woman as the widow in verses 8-16.
[o]**17.18** *Did you . . . God:* In ancient times people sometimes thought that if they sinned, something terrible would happen to them.

PARENTING&*family*—How can I deal with the challenges of being a single parent? *(1 Kings 17.8-16)*

Trust God to meet your needs.
Raising a child alone is difficult enough. When you're the only breadwinner as well as the only parent, things can get sticky.

But there's proof that God has his eye on the struggling single mom! Back in Old Testament days, single women with children were at the bottom of the social ladder. They had no voice in the courts, no way to make a living. But the Lord God sent his busy prophet Elijah—fresh from speaking with kings and performing great miracles—to help a single mom in distress. A great famine had covered the land, and the widow of Zarephath had no food. She and her son were about to starve when Elijah came to her and asked her for a meal in the name of the Lord. He promised her that if she fed him, the Lord would protect her from starvation. She trusted the Lord's promise to provide for her and gave the prophet her last meal. What happened? The Lord miraculously provided her and her son with food until the famine was over.

There may be times when you feel as powerless as the widow of Zarephath—down to your last box of cereal and wondering where the next rent payment will come from! Like the widow in the story, believe in God's promise of provision, day by day. Trust God to meet your basic needs, and he will provide for you and your children. (See also Psalm 71.1-6; Psalm 138; Philippians 4.10-20.)

Words To Remember: *The LORD kept the promise that his prophet Elijah had made, and she did not run out of flour or oil.*—1 Kings 17.16

Widow of Zarephath

1 Kings 17.8-24

*H*ave you ever wondered, <u>Where has my faith gotten me?</u> An unnamed, courageous single mother seems to have wondered just that. It all started when God spoke to her. We don't know what God said, only that God told the prophet Elijah: "I've told a widow in that town [Zarephath] to give you food" (17.9). When Elijah arrived and asked for food, the woman gave him what she had "in the name of the living LORD your God" (17.12). <u>Your God?</u> Yes, Elijah's God. The woman lived in the Gentile town of Zarephath, a city in Sidon, and probably was not schooled in the ways of God. But she listened to this God, went out on a limb, and trusted the miracles of a foreign holy man.

What an incredible risk she took—after all, Elijah was hiding out from his own king! At the end of her rope, without resources, she agreed to share what little she had instead of hoarding it. Each time she peeked into her jar of flour and bottle of oil, miraculously there was a little more. She ended up letting this renegade prophet stay in her upstairs room. She had shown great faith and Elijah had turned out to be a man of God after all.

But when her son died, that faith was tested to the limit—as it would be for any of us. She blamed Elijah for her son's death, "What have I done to you? I thought you were God's prophet" (17.18). She was understandably upset; they had survived the worst times of famine and drought, so how could her son, her only child, die now?

It didn't occur to her that God had saved her son's life and her own once through Elijah—and that he might do it again. But to give her some credit, Elijah got upset, too. Agitated, yet obedient, Elijah carried the boy upstairs and railed at God. "LORD God, why did you do such a terrible thing to this woman?" (17.20). Answering Elijah's prayers, God brought the boy back to life.

God met this woman at the rawest edges of life. When she was near starvation, God asked her to give away food. Then when her son died, he asked her to have faith in his love and mercy, as shown through a bewildered prophet. God met her needs—even when she was sure he would not. What a reminder that our faith will never match God's goodness! When we doubt, God's grace picks us up. And when we go out to the edge, we'll find miracles waiting for us.

die." ²¹Elijah stretched himself out over the boy three times, while praying, "LORD God, bring this boy back to life!"

²²The LORD answered Elijah's prayer, and the boy started breathing again. ²³Elijah picked him up and carried him downstairs. He gave the boy to his mother and said, "Look, your son is alive."

²⁴"You are God's prophet!" the woman replied. "Now I know that you really do speak for the LORD."

Elijah Proves He Is the LORD's Prophet

18 ¹⁻²For three years no rain fell in Samaria, and there was almost nothing to eat anywhere. The LORD said to Elijah, "Go and meet with King Ahab. I will soon make it rain." So Elijah went to see Ahab.

³⁻⁴At that time Obadiah was in charge of Ahab's palace, but he faithfully worshiped the LORD. In fact, when Jezebel was trying to kill the LORD's prophets, Obadiah hid one hundred of them in two caves and gave them food and water.

Ahab sent for Obadiah ⁵and said, "We have to find something for our horses and mules to eat. If we don't, we will have to kill them. Let's look around every creek and spring in the country for some grass. ⁶You go one way, and I'll go the other." Then they left in separate directions.

⁷As Obadiah was walking along, he met Elijah. Obadiah recognized him, bowed down, and asked, "Elijah, is it really you?"

⁸"Yes. Go tell Ahab I'm here."

⁹Obadiah replied:

King Ahab would kill me if I told him that. And I haven't even done anything wrong. ¹⁰I swear to you in the name of the living LORD your God that the king has looked everywhere for you. He sent people to look in every country, and when they couldn't find you, he made the leader of each country swear that you were not in that country. ¹¹Do you really want me to tell him you're here?

¹²What if the LORD's Spirit takes you away as soon as I leave? When Ahab comes to get you, he won't find you. Then he will surely kill me.

I have worshiped the LORD since I was a boy. ¹³I even hid one hundred of the LORD's prophets in caves when Jezebel was trying to kill them. I also gave them food and water. ¹⁴Do you really want me to tell Ahab you're here? He will kill me!

¹⁵Elijah said, "I'm a servant of the living LORD All-Powerful, and I swear in his name that I will meet with Ahab today."

¹⁶Obadiah left and told Ahab where to find Elijah.

Ahab went to meet Elijah, ¹⁷and when he

---

*Spiritual*Life—**How can I show my devotion to God?** *(1 Kings 18)*

Speak up for God's truth.
Sometimes you think you will burst if someone does not speak up. A bunch of kids are watching an inappropriate video, a newspaper editorial challenges the Christian faith and invites letters in response, or an important person takes advantage of a needy person. God has a way of taking care of this himself, but sometimes, as in the case of Elijah and Ahab, God directs his servant (you) to speak up.

If you do this, you may be called a "troublemaker" (18.17). Be prepared with prayer and self-examination to state briefly but clearly what the problem is. Be prepared to show through examples what God wants and how well it works. Ask God to equip you with words that confront and clarify.

But also be sure you care more about God's message than about yourself. Set aside your own agenda. Personal injuries and hurt feelings are not the issue. Having people look up to you or at you is not important. You, the messenger, will do better to remain the humble servant, as Elijah did.   (See also 1 Chronicles 29.1-20; Haggai 1.1-11; Acts 4.32—5.11; 1 Corinthians 13.11-13.)

Words To Remember: *Elijah said, "I'm a servant of the living LORD All-Powerful, and I swear in his name that I will meet with Ahab today."—1 Kings 18.15*

saw him, Ahab shouted, "There you are, the biggest troublemaker in Israel!"

[18]Elijah answered:

You're the troublemaker—not me! You and your family have disobeyed the LORD's commands by worshiping Baal.

[19]Call together everyone from Israel and have them meet me on Mount Carmel. Be sure to bring along the four hundred fifty prophets of Baal and the four hundred prophets of Asherah who eat at Jezebel's table.

[20]Ahab got everyone together, then they went to meet Elijah on Mount Carmel. [21]Elijah stood in front of them and said, "How much longer will you try to have things both ways? If the LORD is God, worship him! But if Baal is God, worship him!"

The people did not say a word.

[22]Then Elijah continued:

I am the LORD's only prophet, but Baal has four hundred fifty prophets.

[23]Bring us two bulls. Baal's prophets can take one of them, kill it, and cut it into pieces. Then they can put the meat on the wood without lighting the fire. I will do the same thing with the other bull, and I won't light a fire under it either.

[24]The prophets of Baal will pray to their god, and I will pray to the LORD. The one who answers by starting the fire is God.

"That's a good idea," everyone agreed.

[25]Elijah said to Baal's prophets, "There are more of you, so you go first. Pick out a bull and get it ready, but don't light the fire. Then pray to your god."

[26]They chose their bull, then they got it ready and prayed to Baal all morning, asking him to start the fire. They danced around the altar and shouted, "Answer us, Baal!" But there was no answer.

[27]At noon, Elijah began making fun of them. "Pray louder!" he said. "Baal must be a god. Maybe he's day-dreaming or using the toilet or traveling somewhere. Or maybe he's asleep, and you have to wake him up."

[28]The prophets kept shouting louder and louder, and they cut themselves with swords and knives until they were bleeding. This was the way they worshiped, [29]and they kept it up all afternoon. But there was no answer of any kind.

[30]Elijah told everyone to gather around him while he repaired the LORD's altar. [31-32]Then he used twelve stones to build an altar in honor of the LORD. Each stone stood for one of the tribes of Israel, which was the name the LORD had given to their ancestor Jacob. Elijah dug a ditch around the altar, large enough to hold about thirteen quarts. [33]He placed the wood on the altar, then they cut the bull into pieces and laid the meat on the wood.

He told the people, "Fill four large jars with water and pour it over the meat and the wood." After they did this, [34]he told them to do it two more times. They did exactly as he said [35]until finally, the water ran down the altar and filled the ditch.

[36]When it was time for the evening sacrifice, Elijah prayed:

Our LORD, you are the God of Abraham, Isaac, and Israel. Now, prove that you are the God of this nation,[p] and that I, your servant, have done this at your command. [37]Please answer me, so these people will know that you are the LORD God, and that you will turn their hearts back to you.[q]

[38]The LORD immediately sent fire, and it burned up the sacrifice, the wood, and the stones. It scorched the ground everywhere around the altar and dried up every drop of water in the ditch. [39]When the crowd saw what had happened, they all bowed down and shouted, "The LORD is God! The LORD is God!"

[40]Just then, Elijah said, "Grab the prophets of Baal! Don't let any of them get away."

So the people captured the prophets and took them to Kishon River, where Elijah killed every one of them.

It Starts To Rain

[41]Elijah told Ahab, "Get something to eat and drink. I hear a heavy rain coming."

[42]Ahab left, but Elijah climbed back to the top of Mount Carmel. Then he stooped down with his face almost to the ground [43]and said to his servant, "Look toward the sea."

The servant left. And when he came back, he said, "I looked, but I didn't see

p18.36 *this nation:* Hebrew "Israel."   q18.37 *will turn . . . to you:* One possible meaning for the difficult Hebrew text.

anything." Elijah told him to look seven more times.

⁴⁴After the seventh time the servant replied, "I see a small cloud coming this way. But it's no bigger than a fist."

Elijah told him, "Tell Ahab to get his chariot ready and start home now. Otherwise, the rain will stop him."

⁴⁵⁻⁴⁶A few minutes later, it got very cloudy and windy, and rain started pouring down. So Elijah wrapped his coat around himself, and the LORD gave him strength to run all the way to Jezreel. Ahab followed him.

Elijah Runs Away from Ahab and Jezebel

19 Ahab told his wife Jezebel what Elijah had done and that he had killed the prophets. ²She sent a message to Elijah: "You killed my prophets. Now I'm going to kill you! I pray that the gods will punish me even more severely if I don't do it by this time tomorrow."

³Elijah was afraid when he got her message, and he ran to the town of Beersheba in Judah. He left his servant there, ⁴then walked another whole day into the desert. Finally, he came to a large bush and sat down in its shade. He begged the LORD, "I've had enough. Just let me die! I'm no better off than my ancestors." ⁵Then he lay down in the shade and fell asleep.

Suddenly an angel woke him up and said, "Get up and eat." ⁶Elijah looked around, and by his head was a jar of water and some baked bread. He sat up, ate and drank, then lay down and went back to sleep.

⁷Soon the LORD's angel woke him again and said, "Get up and eat, or else you'll get too tired to travel." ⁸So Elijah sat up and ate and drank.

The food and water made him strong enough to walk forty more days. At last, he reached Mount Sinai,ʳ the mountain of God, ⁹and he spent the night there in a cave.

The LORD Appears to Elijah

While Elijah was on Mount Sinai, the LORD asked, "Elijah, why are you here?"

¹⁰He answered, "LORD God All-Powerful, I've always done my best to obey you. But your people have broken their solemn promise to you. They have torn down your altars and killed all your prophets, except me. And now they are even trying to kill me!"

¹¹"Go out and stand on the mountain," the LORD replied. "I want you to see me when I pass by."

All at once, a strong wind shook the mountain and shattered the rocks. But the

---

ʳ19.8 *Sinai:* Hebrew "Horeb."

Friendship—What's the best way to find friends? *(1 Kings 19.1-21)*

Look toward God.

It can be lonely when you move and leave friends behind, or a friend at work gets a different job. Or perhaps your small group changes, or your PTA group moves on. While you maintain contact, it's never quite the same.

Elijah was led to a friend in one of the worst moments of his life. He was running scared and wanted to die. God ministered to him in several ways, giving him food, rest, an intimate encounter with himself, and a few jobs to do. Elijah found his friend in the most unusual place—within one of those jobs. His friend was, in fact, Elisha, his replacement.

We can do the same thing—lay our loneliness out before God. What is going on that you don't understand? What do you need to get through rough times? God may lead you to a group or person to help you. Or he may ask you to serve within a cause or a ministry that needs you. There, you will most likely find people you have something in common with. They may be different in some ways (Elijah was much older than Elisha), but nevertheless, a camaraderie can grow that becomes vital in your life. (See also 2 Corinthians 2.14-17; Revelation 7.9-12.)

Words To Remember: *The LORD asked, "Elijah, why are you here?" Elijah answered, "LORD God All-Powerful, I've always done my best to obey you."*
—1 Kings 19.13,14

LORD was not in the wind. Next, there was an earthquake, but the LORD was not in the earthquake. ¹²Then there was a fire, but the LORD was not in the fire.

Finally, there was a gentle breeze,ˢ ¹³and when Elijah heard it, he covered his face with his coat. He went out and stood at the entrance to the cave.

The LORDᵗ asked, "Elijah, why are you here?"

¹⁴Elijah answered, "LORD God All-Powerful, I've always done my best to obey you. But your people have broken their solemn promise to you. They have torn down your altars and killed all your prophets, except me. And now they are even trying to kill me!"

¹⁵The LORD said:

Elijah, you can go back to the desert near Damascus. And when you get there, appointᵘ Hazael to be king of Syria. ¹⁶Then appoint Jehu son of Nimshi to be king of Israel, and Elisha son of Shaphatᵛ to take your place as my prophet.

¹⁷Hazael will start killing the people who worship Baal. Jehu will kill those who escape from Hazael, and Elisha will kill those who escape from Jehu.

¹⁸But seven thousand Israelites have refused to worship Baal, and they will live.

Elisha Becomes Elijah's Assistant

¹⁹Elijah left and found Elisha plowing a field with a pair of oxen. There were eleven other men in front of him, and each one was also plowing with a pair of oxen. Elijah went over and put his own coat on Elisha.ʷ

²⁰Elisha stopped plowing and ran after him. "Let me kiss my parents good-by, then I'll go with you," he said.

"You can go," Elijah said. "But remember what I've done for you."

²¹Elisha left and took his oxen with him. He killed them and boiled them over a fire he had made with the wood from his plow. He gave the meat to the people who were with him, and they ate it. Then he left with Elijah and became his assistant.

Syria Attacks Israel

20 King Benhadad of Syriaˣ called his army together. He was joined by thirty-two other kings with their horses and chariots, and together they marched to Samaria and attacked. ²Benhadad sent a messenger to tell King Ahab of Israel, ³"Ahab, give me your silver and gold, your wives,ʸ and your strongest sons!"

⁴"Your Majesty," Ahab replied, "everything I have is yours, including me."

⁵Later, Benhadad sent another messenger to say to Ahab, "I already told you to give me your silver and gold, your wives, and your children. ⁶But tomorrow at this time, I will send my officials into your city to search your palace and the houses of your officials. They will take everything else that youᶻ own."

⁷Ahab called a meeting with the leaders of Israel and said, "Benhadad is causing real trouble. He told me to give him my wives and children, as well as my silver and gold. And I agreed."

⁸"Don't listen to him!" they answered. "You don't have to do what he says."

⁹So Ahab sent someone to tell Benhadad, "Your Majesty, I'll give you my silver and gold, and even my wives and children. But I won't let you have anything else."

When Benhadad got his answer, ¹⁰he replied, "I'll completely destroy Samaria! There won't even be enough of it left for my soldiers to carry back in their hands. If I don't do it, I pray that the gods will punish me terribly."

¹¹Ahab then answered, "Benhadad, don't brag before the fighting even begins. Wait and see if you live through it."

¹²Meanwhile, Benhadad and the other kings had been drinking in their tents. But when Ahab's reply came, he ordered his soldiers to prepare to attack Samaria, and they all got ready.

¹³At that very moment, a prophet ran up to Ahab and said, "You can see that Benhadad's army is very strong. But the LORD has promised to help you defeat them

---

ˢ**19.12** *a gentle breeze:* Or "a soft whisper" or "hardly a sound." ᵗ**19.13** *The LORD:* Hebrew "A voice." ᵘ**19.15** *appoint:* This would have included a ceremony in which olive oil would be poured on his head to show that he was now king. ᵛ**19.16** *Shaphat:* Hebrew "Shaphat from Abel-Meholah." ʷ**19.19** *put . . . Elisha:* This was a sign that Elijah wanted Elisha to follow him and become a prophet. ˣ**20.1** *King Benhadad of Syria:* This is probably not the same Benhadad mentioned in 15.18-21. ʸ**20.3** *wives:* Having more than one wife was allowed in those times. ᶻ**20.6** *you:* Hebrew; three ancient translations "they."

today. Then you will know that the LORD is in control."

[14]"Who will fight the battle?" Ahab asked.

The prophet answered, "The young bodyguards who serve the district officials."

"But who will lead them into battle?" Ahab asked.

"You will!" the prophet replied.

[15]So Ahab called together the two hundred thirty-two young soldiers and the seven thousand troops in Israel's army, and he got them ready to fight the Syrians.

Israel Defeats the Syrians

[16-17]At noon, King Ahab and his Israelite army marched out of Samaria, with the young soldiers in front.

King Benhadad of Syria and the thirty-two kings with him were drunk when the scouts he had sent out ran up to his tent, shouting, "We just now saw soldiers marching out of Samaria!"

[18]"Take them alive!" Benhadad ordered. "I don't care if they have come out to fight or to surrender."

[19]The young soldiers led Israel's troops into battle, [20]and each of them attacked and killed an enemy soldier. The rest of the Syrian army turned and ran, and the Israelites went after them. Benhadad and some others escaped on horses, [21]but Ahab and his soldiers followed them and captured[a] their horses and chariots.

Ahab and Israel's army crushed the Syrians.

[22]Later, the prophet[b] went back and warned Ahab, "Benhadad will attack you again next spring. Build up your troops and make sure you have some good plans."

Syria Attacks Israel Again

[23]Meanwhile, Benhadad's officials went to him and explained:

Israel's gods are mountain gods. We fought Israel's army in the hills, and that's why they defeated us. But if we fight them on flat land, there's no way we can lose.

[24]Here's what you should do. First, get rid of those thirty-two kings and put army commanders in their places. [25]Then get more soldiers, horses, and chariots, so your army will be as strong

as it was before. We'll fight Israel's army on flat land and wipe them out.

Benhadad agreed and did what they suggested.

[26]In the spring, Benhadad got his army together, and they marched to the town of Aphek to attack Israel. [27]The Israelites also prepared to fight. They marched out to meet the Syrians, and the two armies camped across from each other. The Syrians covered the whole area, but the Israelites looked like two little flocks of goats.

[28]The prophet went to Ahab and said, "The Syrians think the LORD is a god of the hills and not of the valleys. So he has promised to help you defeat their powerful army. Then you will know that the LORD is in control."

[29]For seven days the two armies stayed in their camps, facing each other. Then on the seventh day the fighting broke out, and before sunset the Israelites had killed one hundred thousand Syrian troops. [30]The rest of the Syrian army ran back to Aphek, but the town wall fell and crushed twenty-seven thousand of them.

Benhadad also escaped to Aphek and hid in the back room of a house. [31]His officials said, "Your Majesty, we've heard that Israel's kings keep their agreements. We will wrap sackcloth around our waists, put ropes around our heads, and ask Ahab to let you live."

[32]They dressed in sackcloth and put ropes on their heads, then they went to Ahab and said, "Your servant Benhadad asks you to let him live."

"Is he still alive?" Ahab asked. "Benhadad is like a brother to me."

[33]Benhadad's officials were trying to figure out what Ahab was thinking, and when he said "brother," they quickly replied, "You're right! You and Benhadad are like brothers."

"Go get him," Ahab said.

When Benhadad came out, Ahab had him climb up into his chariot.

[34]Benhadad said, "I'll give back the towns my father took from your father. And you can have shops in Damascus, just as my father had in Samaria."

Ahab replied, "If you do these things, I'll

---

[a]20.21 *captured*: One ancient translation; Hebrew "attacked." [b]20.22 *the prophet*: See verse 13.

let you go free." Then they signed a peace treaty, and Ahab let Benhadad go.

A Prophet Condemns Ahab

³⁵About this time the LORD commanded a prophet to say to a friend, "Hit me!" But the friend refused, ³⁶and the prophet told him, "You disobeyed the LORD, and as soon as you walk away, a lion will kill you." The friend left, and suddenly a lion killed him. ³⁷The prophet found someone else and said, "Hit me!" So this man beat him up. ³⁸The prophet left and put a bandage over his face to disguise himself. Then he went and stood beside the road, waiting for Ahab to pass by.

³⁹When Ahab went by, the prophet shouted, "Your Majesty, right in the heat of battle, someone brought a prisoner to me and told me to guard him. He said if the prisoner got away, I would either be killed or forced to pay seventy-five pounds of silver. ⁴⁰But I got busy doing other things, and the prisoner escaped."

Ahab answered, "You will be punished just as you have said."

⁴¹The man quickly tore the bandage off his face, and Ahab saw that he was one of the prophets. ⁴²The prophet said, "The LORD told you to kill Benhadad, but you let him go. Now you will die in his place, and your people will die in place of his people."

⁴³Ahab went back to Samaria, angry and depressed.

Jezebel Has Naboth Killed

21 Naboth owned a vineyard in Jezreel near King Ahab's palace. ²One day, Ahab said, "Naboth, your vineyard is near my palace. Give it to me so I can turn it into a vegetable garden. I'll give you a better vineyard or pay whatever you want for yours."

³Naboth answered, "This vineyard has always been in my family. I won't let you have it."

⁴So Ahab went home, angry and depressed because of what Naboth had told him. He lay on his bed, just staring at the wall and refusing to eat a thing.

⁵Jezebel his wife came in and asked, "What's wrong? Why won't you eat?"

⁶"I asked Naboth to sell me his vineyard or to let me give him a better one," Ahab replied. "And he told me I couldn't have it."

⁷"Aren't you the king of Israel?" Jezebel asked. "Get out of bed and eat something! Don't worry, I'll get Naboth's vineyard for you."

⁸⁻¹⁰Jezebel wrote a letter to each of the leaders of the town where Naboth lived. In the letters she said:

Call everyone together and tell them to go without eating*ᶜ* today. When they come together, give Naboth a seat at the front. Have two liars sit across from him and swear that Naboth has cursed God and the king. Then take Naboth outside and stone him to death!

She signed Ahab's name to the letters and sealed them with his seal. Then she sent them to the town leaders.

¹¹After receiving her letters, they did exactly what she had asked. ¹²They told the people that it was a day to go without eating, and when they all came together, they seated Naboth at the front. ¹³The two liars came in and sat across from Naboth. Then they accused him of cursing God and the king, so the people dragged Naboth outside and stoned him to death.

¹⁴The leaders of Jezreel sent a message back to Jezebel that said, "Naboth is dead."

¹⁵As soon as Jezebel got their message, she told Ahab, "Now you can have the vineyard Naboth refused to sell. He's dead." ¹⁶Ahab got up and went to take over the vineyard.

Elijah Condemns Ahab

¹⁷The LORD said to Elijah the prophet, ¹⁸"King Ahab of Israel is in Naboth's vineyard right now, taking it over. ¹⁹Go tell him that I say, 'Ahab, you murdered Naboth and took his property. And so, in the very spot where dogs licked up Naboth's blood, they will lick up your blood.' "

When Elijah found him, ²⁰Ahab said, "So, my enemy, you found me at last."

Elijah answered:

Yes, I did! Ahab, you have managed to do everything the LORD hates. ²¹Now you will be punished. You and every man and boy in your family will die, whether slave or free. ²²Your whole

---

ᶜ21.8-10 *to go without eating:* People sometimes came together to worship and to go without eating to show that they were sorry for their sins.

family will be wiped out, just like the families of King Jeroboam and King Baasha. You've made the LORD very angry by sinning and causing the Israelites to sin.

²³And as for Jezebel, dogs will eat her body there in Jezreel. ²⁴Dogs will also eat the bodies of your relatives who die in town, and vultures will eat the bodies of those who die in the country.

²⁵⁻²⁹When Ahab heard this, he tore his clothes and wore sackcloth day and night. He was depressed and refused to eat.

Some time later, the LORD said, "Elijah, do you see how sorry Ahab is for what he did? I won't punish his family while he is still alive. I'll wait until his son is king."

No one was more determined than Ahab to disobey the LORD. And Jezebel encouraged him. Worst of all, he had worshiped idols, just as the Amorites[d] had done before the LORD forced them out of the land and gave it to Israel.

Micaiah Warns Ahab about Disaster
(2 Chronicles 18.2-27)

22 For the next three years there was peace between Israel and Syria. ²During the third year King Jehoshaphat of Judah went to visit King Ahab of Israel.

³Ahab asked his officials, "Why haven't we tried to get Ramoth in Gilead back from the Syrians? It belongs to us." ⁴Then he asked Jehoshaphat, "Would you go to Ramoth with me and attack the Syrians?"

"Just tell me what to do," Jehoshaphat answered. "My army and horses are at your command. ⁵But first, let's ask the LORD."

⁶Ahab sent for about four hundred prophets and asked, "Should I attack the Syrians at Ramoth?"

"Yes!" the prophets answered. "The Lord will help you defeat them."

⁷But Jehoshaphat said, "Just to make sure, is there another of the LORD's prophets we can ask?"

⁸"We could ask Micaiah son of Imlah," Ahab said. "But I hate Micaiah. He always has bad news for me."

"Don't say that!" Jehoshaphat replied.

⁹Then Ahab sent someone to bring Micaiah as soon as possible.

¹⁰All this time, Ahab and Jehoshaphat were dressed in their royal robes and were seated on their thrones at the threshing place near the gate of Samaria. They were listening to the prophets tell them what the LORD had said.

¹¹Zedekiah son of Chenaanah was one of the prophets. He had made some horns out of iron and shouted, "Ahab, the LORD says you will attack the Syrians like a bull with iron horns and wipe them out!"

¹²All the prophets agreed that Ahab should attack the Syrians at Ramoth, and they promised that the LORD would help him defeat them.

¹³Meanwhile, the messenger who went to get Micaiah whispered, "Micaiah, all the prophets have good news for Ahab. Now go and say the same thing."

¹⁴"I'll say whatever the living LORD tells me to say," Micaiah replied.

¹⁵Then Micaiah went to Ahab, and Ahab asked, "Micaiah, should I attack the Syrians at Ramoth?"

"Yes!" Micaiah answered. "The LORD will help you defeat them."

¹⁶"Micaiah, I've told you over and over to tell me the truth!" Ahab shouted. "What does the LORD really say?"

¹⁷He answered, "In a vision[e] I saw Israelite soldiers walking around in the hills like sheep without a shepherd to guide them. The LORD said, 'This army has no leader. They should go home and not fight.' "

¹⁸Ahab turned to Jehoshaphat and said, "I told you he would bring bad news!"

¹⁹Micaiah replied:

Listen to this! I also saw the LORD seated on his throne with every creature in heaven gathered around him. ²⁰The LORD asked, "Who can trick Ahab and make him go to Ramoth where he will be killed?"

They talked about it for a while, ²¹then finally a spirit came forward and said to the LORD, "I can trick Ahab."

"How?" the LORD asked.

²²"I'll make Ahab's prophets lie to him."

"Good!" the LORD replied. "Now go and do it."

---

[d]21.25-29 *Amorites:* A name sometimes used of the people who lived in Palestine before the Israelites.
[e]22.17 *vision:* In ancient times, prophets often told about future events from what they had seen in visions or dreams.

²³This is exactly what has happened, Ahab. The LORD made all your prophets lie to you, and he knows you will soon be destroyed.

> *You can control three things: your choice of a foundation on which you can build your life, the structure or purpose you give to your life, and your day-to-day behavior.*
>
> CAROLE SANDERSON STREETER

²⁴Zedekiah walked up to Micaiah and slapped him on the face. Then he asked, "Do you really think the LORD would speak to you and not to me?"

²⁵Micaiah answered, "You'll find out on the day you have to hide in the back room of some house."

²⁶Ahab shouted, "Arrest Micaiah! Take him to Prince Joash and Governor Amon of Samaria. ²⁷Tell them to put him in prison and to give him nothing but bread and water until I come back safely."

²⁸Micaiah said, "If you do come back, I was wrong about what the LORD wanted me to say." Then he told the crowd, "Don't forget what I said!"

Ahab Dies at Ramoth
(2 Chronicles 18.28-34)

²⁹Ahab and Jehoshaphat led their armies to Ramoth in Gilead. ³⁰Before they went into battle, Ahab said, "Jehoshaphat, I'll disguise myself, but you wear your royal robe." Then Ahab disguised himself and went into battle.

³¹The king of Syria had ordered his thirty-two chariot commanders to attack only Ahab. ³²So when they saw Jehoshaphat in his robe, they thought he was Ahab and started to attack him. But when Jehoshaphat shouted out to them, ³³they realized he wasn't Ahab, and they left him alone.

³⁴However, during the fighting a soldier shot an arrow without even aiming, and it hit Ahab where two pieces of his armor joined. He shouted to his chariot driver, "I've been hit! Get me out of here!"

³⁵The fighting lasted all day, with Ahab propped up in his chariot so he could see the Syrian troops. He bled so much that the bottom of the chariot was covered with blood, and by evening he was dead. ³⁶As the sun was going down, someone in Israel's army shouted to the others, "Retreat! Go back home!"

³⁷Ahab's body was taken to Samaria and buried there. ³⁸Some workers washed his chariot near a spring in Samaria, and prostitutes washed themselves in his blood.ʲ Dogs licked Ahab's blood off the ground, just as the LORD had warned.

³⁹Everything else Ahab did while he was king, including the towns he strengthened and the palace he built and furnished with ivory, is written in *The History of the Kings of Israel*. ⁴⁰Ahab died, and his son Ahaziah became king.

King Jehoshaphat of Judah
(2 Chronicles 20.31—21.1)

⁴¹Jehoshaphat son of Asa became king of Judah in Ahab's fourth year as king of Israel. ⁴²Jehoshaphat was thirty-five years old when he became king, and he ruled from Jerusalem for twenty-five years. His mother was Azubah daughter of Shilhi.

⁴³⁻⁴⁶Jehoshaphat obeyed the LORD, just as his father Asa had done, and during his rule he was at peace with the king of Israel.

He got rid of the rest of the prostitutesᵍ from the local shrines, but he did not destroy the shrines, and they were still used as places for offering sacrifices.

Everything else Jehoshaphat did while he was king, including his brave deeds and military victories, is written in *The History of the Kings of Judah*. ⁴⁷The country of Edom had no king at the time, so a lower official ruled the land.

⁴⁸Jehoshaphat had seagoing shipsʰ built to sail to Ophir for gold. But they were wrecked at Ezion-Geber and never sailed.

ʲ22.38 *prostitutes . . . blood:* Or "they cleaned his weapons." ᵍ22.43-46 *prostitutes:* See the note at 14.24. ʰ22.48 *seagoing ships:* See the note at 10.22.

⁴⁹Ahaziah son of Ahab offered to let his sailors go with Jehoshaphat's sailors, but Jehoshaphat refused.

⁵⁰Jehoshaphat died and was buried beside his ancestors in Jerusalem,ⁱ and his son Jehoram became king.

King Ahaziah of Israel

⁵¹Ahaziah son of Ahab became king of Israel in the seventeenth year of Jehoshaphat's rule in Judah, and he ruled two years from Samaria.

⁵²Ahaziah disobeyed the LORD, just as his father, his mother, and Jeroboam had done. They all led Israel to sin. ⁵³Ahaziah worshiped Baal and made the LORD God of Israel very angry, just as his father had done.

ⁱ**22.50** *Jerusalem:* Hebrew "the city of his ancestor David."

2 Kings
The Penalties of Disobedience

God's people were in chaos! David's family was supposed to be sitting on the throne, but the descendants of David only ruled the two tribes known as the nation of "Judah." The other ten northern tribes, called "Israel," underwent centuries of unrest and civil war as different kings struggled for the throne.

Unfortunately, neither Israel nor Judah consistently worshiped the true God. Under the rulers of 2 Kings, the people continued to disobey the laws God had handed down to them through Moses. Instead, they followed false gods and built altars to idols; the kings married pagan women and oppressed the poor.

These years weren't completely dark, however. God sent the prophet Elisha to remind his people of his laws. Some kings such as Joash remained faithful to God, while others such as Josiah called the people back to the law of God.

But then Israel rebelled one final time, and God sent the judgments he had threatened back in Deuteronomy. Israel was dragged into exile in 722 B.C. by cruel, merciless Assyrians. These ten tribes of Israel were scattered throughout the Assyrian Empire.

Even then, God showed great patience. He spared the two southern tribes for over a century. He even sent an angel of God to kill an army that was attacking them! But Judah didn't learn from Israel's example. Judah too rejected God. In 586 B.C., the Babylonians conquered Judah, destroyed Jerusalem, and took many of the people into captivity.

Second Kings ends with Judah in exile. But there's still a note of hope. At the end of the book, the last king of Judah has just been set free from thirty-five years of imprisonment and made an honored guest of the new king of Babylon. The implication is clear: If God's people turn to him, even now, he will still protect and defend them!

2 Kings at a Glance

The LORD Condemns Ahaziah

1 [1,2]Soon after King Ahab of Israel died, the country of Moab rebelled against his son King Ahaziah.[a]

One day, Ahaziah fell through the wooden slats around the porch on the flat roof of his palace in Samaria, and he was badly injured. So he sent some messengers to the town of Ekron[b] with orders to ask the god Baalzebub if he would get well.

[3]About the same time, an angel from the LORD sent Elijah the prophet from Tishbe to say to the king's messengers, "Ahaziah has rejected Israel's own God by sending you to ask Baalzebub about his injury. [4]Tell him that because he has done this, he's on his deathbed!" And Elijah did what he was told.

[5]When the messengers returned to Ahaziah, he asked, "Why are you back so soon?"

[6]"A man met us along the road with a message for you from the LORD," they answered. "The LORD wants to know why you sent us to ask Baalzebub about your injury and why you don't believe there's a God in Israel. The man also told us that the LORD says you're going to die."

[7]"What did the man look like?" Ahaziah asked.

God's always there, always available.
MAYO MATHERS

[8]"He was hairy[c] and had a leather belt around his waist," they answered.

"It must be Elijah!" replied Ahaziah. [9]So at once he sent an army officer and fifty soldiers to meet Elijah.

Elijah was sitting on top of a hill[d] at the time. The officer went up to him and said, "Man of God,[e] the king orders you to come down and talk with him."

[10]"If I am a man of God," Elijah answered, "God will send down fire on you and your fifty soldiers." Fire immediately came down from heaven and burned up the officer and his men.

[11]Ahaziah sent another officer and fifty more soldiers to Elijah. The officer said,

"Man of God, the king orders you to come see him right now."

[12]"If I am a man of God," Elijah answered, "fire will destroy you and your fifty soldiers." And God sent down fire[f] from heaven on the officer and his men.

[13]Ahaziah sent a third army officer and fifty more soldiers. This officer went up to Elijah, then he got down on his knees and begged, "Man of God, please be kind to me and these fifty servants of yours. Let us live! [14]Fire has already wiped out the other officers and their soldiers. Please don't let it happen to me."

[15]The angel from the LORD said to Elijah, "Go with him and don't be afraid." So Elijah got up and went with the officer.

[16]When Elijah arrived, he told Ahaziah, "The LORD wants to know why you sent messengers to Ekron to ask Baalzebub about your injury. Don't you believe there's a God in Israel? Ahaziah, because you did that, the LORD says you will die."

[17]Ahaziah died, just as the LORD had said. But since Ahaziah had no sons, Joram[g] his brother[h] then became king. This happened in the second year that Jehoram son of Jehoshaphat was king of Judah.[i] [18]Everything else Ahaziah did while he was king is written in *The History of the Kings of Israel.*

The LORD Takes Elijah Away

2 Not long before the LORD took Elijah up into heaven in a strong wind, Elijah and Elisha were leaving Gilgal. [2]Elijah said to Elisha, "The LORD wants me to go to Bethel, but you must stay here."

Elisha replied, "I swear by the living LORD and by your own life that I will stay with you no matter what!" And he went with Elijah to Bethel.

[a]**1.1,2** *the country . . . King Ahaziah:* The story of Moab's rebellion is in 3.4-27. [b]**1.1,2** *Ekron:* An important Philistine town about forty miles southwest of Samaria. [c]**1.8** *hairy:* Or "wearing a furry coat." [d]**1.9** *a hill:* Probably Mount Carmel. [e]**1.9** *Man of God:* Another name for a prophet of the LORD. [f]**1.12** *God sent down fire:* Or "A mighty fire came down." [g]**1.17** *Joram:* The Hebrew text has "Jehoram," another spelling of the name. [h]**1.17** *his brother:* Some ancient translations (see also 3.1); these words are not in the Hebrew text. [i]**1.17** *This happened . . . Judah:* According to 3.1, this was also the eighteenth year of Jehoshaphat's rule in Judah. In biblical times, a father and son sometimes rule as kings at the same time. This way, when the father died, the son would already have control of the kingdom (see also 8.16).

³A group of prophets who lived there asked Elisha, "Do you know that today the LORD is going to take away your master?"

"Yes, I do," Elisha answered. "But don't remind me of it."

⁴Elijah then said, "Elisha, now the LORD wants me to go to Jericho, but you must stay here."

Elisha replied, "I swear by the living LORD and by your own life, that I will stay with you no matter what!" And he went with Elijah to Jericho.

⁵A group of prophets who lived there asked Elisha, "Do you know that today the LORD is going to take away your master?"

"Yes, I do," Elisha answered. "But don't remind me of it."

⁶Elijah then said to Elisha, "Now the LORD wants me to go to the Jordan River, but you must stay here."

Elisha replied, "I swear by the living LORD and by your own life that I will never leave you!" So the two of them walked on together.

⁷Fifty prophets followed Elijah and Elisha from Jericho, then stood at a distance and watched as the two men walked toward the river. ⁸When they got there, Elijah took off his coat, then he rolled it up and struck the water with it. At once a path opened up through the river, and the two of them walked across on dry ground.

⁹After they had reached the other side, Elijah said, "Elisha, the LORD will soon take me away. What can I do for you before that happens?"

Elisha answered, "Please give me twice as much of your power as you give the other prophets, so I can be the one who takes your place as their leader."

¹⁰"It won't be easy," Elijah answered. "It can happen only if you see me as I am being taken away."

¹¹Elijah and Elisha were walking along and talking, when suddenly there appeared between them a flaming chariot pulled by fiery horses. Right away, a strong wind took Elijah up into heaven. ¹²Elisha saw this and shouted, "Israel's cavalry and chariots have taken my master away!"ʲ After Elijah had gone, Elisha tore his clothes in sorrow.

¹³Elijah's coat had fallen off, so Elisha picked it up and walked back to the Jordan River. ¹⁴He struck the water with the coat and wondered, "Will the LORD perform miracles for me as he did for Elijah?" As soon as Elisha did this, a dry path opened up through the water, and he walked across.

¹⁵When the prophets from Jericho saw what happened, they said to each other, "Elisha now has Elijah's power."

They walked over to him, bowed down, ¹⁶and said, "There are fifty strong men here with us. Please let them go look for your master. Maybe the Spirit of the LORD carried him off to some mountain or valley."

"No," Elisha replied, "they won't find him."

¹⁷They kept begging until he was embarrassed to say no. He finally agreed, and the prophets sent the men out. They looked three days for Elijah but never found him. ¹⁸They returned to Jericho, and Elisha said, "I told you that you wouldn't find him."

Elisha Makes the Water Pure at Jericho

¹⁹One day the people of Jericho said, "Elisha, you can see that our city is in a good spot. But the water from our spring is so bad that it even keeps our crops from growing."

²⁰He replied, "Put some salt in a new bowl and bring it to me."

They brought him the bowl of salt, ²¹and he carried it to the spring. He threw the salt into the water and said, "The LORD has made this water pure again. From now on you'll be able to grow crops, and no one will starve."

²²The water has been fine ever since, just as Elisha said.

Some Boys Make Fun of Elisha

²³Elisha left and headed toward Bethel. Along the way some boys started making fun of him by shouting, "Go away, baldy! Get out of here!"

²⁴Elisha turned around and stared at the boys. Then he cursed them in the name of the LORD. Right away two bears ran out of the woods and ripped to pieces forty-two of the boys.

²⁵Elisha went up to Mount Carmel, then returned to Samaria.

ʲ2.12 Israel's . . . away: Or "Master, you were like cavalry and chariots for the people of Israel!"

King Joram of Israel

3 Joram[k] son of Ahab became king of Israel in Jehoshaphat's eighteenth year as king of Judah.[l] Joram ruled twelve years from Samaria ²and disobeyed the LORD by doing wrong. He tore down the stone image his father had made to honor Baal, and so he wasn't as sinful as his parents. ³But he kept doing the sinful things that Jeroboam son of Nebat had led Israel to do.[m]

The Country of Moab Rebels against Israel

⁴For many years the country of Moab had been controlled by Israel and was forced to pay taxes to the kings of Israel. King Mesha of Moab raised sheep, so he paid the king of Israel one hundred thousand lambs and the wool from one hundred thousand rams. ⁵But soon after the death of Ahab, Mesha rebelled against Israel.

⁶One day, Joram left Samaria and called together Israel's army. ⁷He sent this message to King Jehoshaphat of Judah, "The king of Moab has rebelled. Will you go with me to attack him?"

"Yes, I will," Jehoshaphat answered. "I'm on your side, and my soldiers and horses are at your command. ⁸But which way should we go?"

"We will march through Edom Desert," Joram replied.

⁹So Joram, Jehoshaphat, and the king of Edom led their troops out. But seven days later, there was no drinking water left for them or their animals. ¹⁰Joram cried out, "This is terrible! The LORD must have led us out here to be captured by Moab's army."

¹¹Jehoshaphat said, "Which of the LORD's prophets is with us? We can find out from him what the LORD wants us to do."

One of Joram's officers answered, "Elisha son of Shaphat is here. He was one of Elijah's closest followers."

¹²Jehoshaphat replied, "He can give us the LORD's message."

The three kings went over to Elisha, ¹³and he asked Joram, "Why did you come to me? Go talk to the prophets of the foreign gods your parents worshiped."[n]

"No," Joram answered. "It was the LORD who led us out here, so that Moab's army could capture us."

¹⁴Elisha said to him, "I serve the LORD All-Powerful, and as surely as he lives, I swear I wouldn't even look at you if I didn't respect King Jehoshaphat." ¹⁵Then Elisha said, "Send for someone who can play the harp."

The harpist began playing, and the LORD gave Elisha this message for Joram:

¹⁶The LORD says that this dry riverbed will be filled with water.[o] ¹⁷You won't feel any wind or see any rain, but there will be plenty of water for you and your animals.

¹⁸That simple thing isn't all the LORD is going to do. He will also help you defeat Moab's army. ¹⁹You will capture all their walled cities and important towns. You will chop down every good tree and stop up every spring of water, then ruin their fertile fields by covering them with rocks.

²⁰The next morning, while the sacrifice was being offered, water suddenly started flowing from the direction of Edom, and it flooded the land.

²¹Meanwhile, the people of Moab had heard that the three kings were coming to attack them. They had called together all of their fighting men, from the youngest to the oldest, and these troops were now standing at their border, ready for battle. ²²When they got up that morning, the sun was shining across the water, making it look red. The Moabite troops took one look ²³and shouted, "Look at that blood! The armies of those kings must have fought and killed each other. Come on, let's go take what's left in their camp."

²⁴But when they arrived at Israel's camp, the Israelite soldiers came out and attacked them, until they turned and ran away. Israel's army chased them all the way back to Moab, and even there they kept up the attack.[p] ²⁵The Israelites destroyed the Moab-

---

[k]3.1 *Joram:* See the note at 1.17. [l]3.1 *Joram . . . Judah:* See 1.17 and 8.16 and the notes there. [m]3.3 *the sinful things . . . to do:* When Jeroboam became king of Israel, he made two gold statues of calves and put them in the towns of Bethel and Dan, so the people of Israel could worship there (see 1 Kings 12.26-30). [n]3.13 *the prophets . . . worshiped:* These were prophets of the Canaanite god Baal and the goddess Asherah (see 1 Kings 16.30-33; 18.19). [o]3.16 *that . . . water:* Or "to dig holes everywhere in this riverbed." [p]3.24 *chased . . . attack:* One possible meaning for the difficult Hebrew text.

ite towns. They chopped down the good trees and stopped up the springs of water, then covered the fertile fields with rocks.

Finally, the only city left standing was Kir-Hareseth, but soldiers armed with slings surrounded and attacked it. ²⁶King Mesha of Moab saw that he was about to be defeated. So he took along seven hundred soldiers with swords and tried to break through the front line where the Edomite troops were positioned. But he failed. ²⁷He then grabbed his oldest son who was to be the next king and sacrificed him as an offering on the city wall. The Israelite troops were so horrified that*ᵈ* they left the city and went back home.

Elisha Helps a Poor Widow

4 One day the widow of one of the LORD's prophets said to Elisha, "You know that before my husband died, he was a follower of yours and a worshiper of the LORD. But he owed a man some money, and now that man is on his way to take my two sons as his slaves."

²"Maybe there's something I can do to help," Elisha said. "What do you have in your house?"

"Sir, I have nothing but a small bottle of olive oil."

³Elisha told her, "Ask your neighbors for their empty jars. And after you've borrowed as many as you can, ⁴go home and shut the door behind you and your sons. Then begin filling the jars with oil and set each one aside as you fill it." ⁵The woman left.

Later, when she and her sons were back inside their house, the two sons brought her the jars, and she began filling them.

⁶At last, she said to one of her sons, "Bring me another jar."

"We don't have any more," he answered, and the oil stopped flowing from the small bottle.

⁷After she told Elisha what had happened, he said, "Sell the oil and use part of the money to pay what you owe the man. You and your sons can live on what is left."

Elisha Brings a Rich Woman's Son Back to Life

⁸Once, while Elisha was in the town of Shunem,ʳ he met a rich woman who invited him to her home for dinner. After that, whenever he was in Shunem, he would have a meal there with her and her husband.

⁹Some time later the woman said to her husband, "I'm sure the man who comes here so often is a prophet of God. ¹⁰Why don't we build him a small room on the flat roof of our house? We can put a bed, a table and chair, and an oil lamp in it. Then whenever he comes, he can stay with us."

ᵈ3.27 *The Israelite . . . that:* One possible meaning for the difficult Hebrew text. ʳ4.8 *Shunem:* A town in Israel, about twenty-five miles north of Samaria.

Friendship—How can I have healthy friendships with men? *(2 Kings 4.1-7)*

Don't be afraid to ask for appropriate help.
Elisha was a great prophet and teacher. Other prophets, young men who loved and served God, followed him around to learn from him. Some of these men had wives and children—like the widow in this story. Her husband had been one of Elisha's followers, but when he died, he left her with debts to pay and two sons to raise. Finally her creditors decided to take her children as slaves in repayment for her debts. This widow appealed to Elisha for help. Elisha performed a miracle by multiplying a small amount of oil so she could sell it and earn the money to pay her creditors.

The widow's friendship with her husband's teacher enabled her to save her children from slavery. Through Elisha, God delivered this widow. And when we're in difficulty, God can use our friends, too!

One important point to remember: Never ask a male friend for help until you've first asked your husband. Your spouse should always be given that opportunity. But if you are single, or your husband is unable to help, male friends can be a gift from God for your protection and assistance. (See also 1 Samuel 25; 1 Thessalonians 4.1-8.)

Words To Remember: *"Maybe there's something I can do to help,"* Elisha said.—2 Kings 4.2

¹¹The next time Elisha was in Shunem, he stopped at their house and went up to his room to rest. ¹²⁻¹³He said to his servant Gehazi, "This woman has been very helpful. Have her come up here to the roof for a moment." She came, and Elisha told Gehazi to say to her, "You've gone to a lot of trouble for us, and we want to help you. Is there something we can request the king or army commander to do?"ˢ

> *God keeps his promises.*
> *My Father responds*
> *to my spiritual needs*
> *and provides for me*
> *as no one else can.*
>
> MAYO MATHERS

The woman answered, "With my relatives nearby, I have everything I need."
¹⁴"Then what can we do for her?" Elisha asked Gehazi.
Gehazi replied, "I do know that her husband is old, and that she doesn't have a son."
¹⁵"Ask her to come here again," Elisha told his servant. He called for her, and she came and stood in the doorway of Elisha's room.
¹⁶Elisha said to her, "Next year at this time, you'll be holding your own baby son in your arms."
"You're a man of God," the woman replied. "Please don't lie to me."
¹⁷But a few months later, the woman got pregnant. She gave birth to a son, just as Elisha had promised.
¹⁸One day while the boy was still young, he was out in the fields with his father, where the workers were harvesting the crops. ¹⁹Suddenly he shouted, "My head hurts. It hurts a lot!"
"Carry him back to his mother," the father said to his servant. ²⁰The servant picked up the boy and carried him to his mother. The boy lay on her lap all morning, and by noon he was dead. ²¹She carried him upstairs to Elisha's room and laid him across

the bed. Then she walked out and shut the door behind her.
²²The woman called to her husband, "I need to see the prophet. Let me use one of the donkeys. Send a servant along with me, and let me leave now, so I can get back quickly."
²³"Why do you need to see him today?" her husband asked. "It's not the Sabbath or time for the New Moon Festival."
"That's all right," she answered. ²⁴She saddled the donkey and said to her servant, "Let's go. And don't slow down unless I tell you to." ²⁵She left at once for Mount Carmel to talk with Elisha.ᵗ
When Elisha saw her coming, he said, "Gehazi, look! It's the woman from Shunem. ²⁶Run and meet her. And ask her if everything is all right with her and her family."
"Everything is fine," she answered Gehazi. ²⁷But as soon as she got to the top of the mountain, she went over and grabbed Elisha by the feet.
Gehazi started toward her to push her away, when Elisha said, "Leave her alone! Don't you see how sad she is? But the LORD hasn't told me why."
²⁸The woman said, "Sir, I begged you not to get my hopes up, and I didn't even ask you for a son."
²⁹"Gehazi, get ready and go to her house," Elisha said. "Take along my walking stick, and when you get there, lay it on the boy's face. Don't stop to talk to anyone, even if they try to talk to you."
³⁰But the boy's mother said to Elisha, "I swear by the living LORD and by your own life that I won't leave without you." So Elisha got up and went with them.
³¹Gehazi ran on ahead and laid Elisha's walking stick on the boy's face, but the boy didn't move or make a sound. Gehazi ran back to Elisha and said, "The boy didn't wake up."
³²Elisha arrived at the woman's house and went straight to his room, where he saw the boy's body on his bed. ³³He walked in, shut the door, and prayed to the LORD. ³⁴Then he got on the bed and stretched out

---

ˢ**4.12,13** *request the king . . . do:* Elisha may have meant that he could ask these leaders to lower her taxes.
ᵗ**4.25** *Elisha:* Mount Carmel is about twenty-five miles from Shunem.

over the dead body, with his mouth on the boy's mouth, his eyes on his eyes, and his hand on his hands. As he lay there, the boy's body became warm. [35]Elisha got up and walked back and forth in the room, then he went back and leaned over the boy's body. The boy sneezed seven times and opened his eyes.

[36]Elisha called out to Gehazi, "Have the boy's mother come here." Gehazi did, and when she was at the door, Elisha said, "You can take your son."

[37]She came in and bowed down at Elisha's feet. Then she picked up her son and left.

Elisha Makes Some Stew Taste Better

[38]Later, Elisha went back to Gilgal, where there was almost nothing to eat, because the crops had failed.

One day while the prophets who lived there were meeting with Elisha, he said to his servant, "Fix a big pot of stew for these prophets."

[39]One of them went out into the woods to gather some herbs. He found a wild vine and picked as much of its fruit as he could carry, but he didn't know that the fruit was very sour. When he got back, he cut up the fruit and put it in the stew.

[40]The stew was served, and when the prophets started eating it, they shouted, "Elisha, this stew tastes terrible! We can't eat it."

[41]"Bring me some flour," Elisha said. He sprinkled the flour in the stew and said, "Now serve it to them." And the stew tasted fine.

Elisha Feeds One Hundred People

[42]A man from the town of Baal-Shalishah[u] brought Elisha some freshly cut grain and twenty loaves of bread made from the first barley that was harvested. Elisha said, "Give it to the people so they can eat."

[43]"There's not enough here for a hundred people," his servant said.

"Just give it to them," Elisha replied. "The LORD has promised there will be more than enough."

[44]So the servant served the bread and grain to the people. They ate and still had some left over, just as the LORD had promised.

Elisha Heals Naaman

5 Naaman was the commander of the Syrian army. The LORD had helped him and his troops defeat their enemies, so the king of Syria respected Naaman very much. Naaman was a brave soldier, but he had leprosy.[v]

[2]One day while the Syrian troops were raiding Israel, they captured a girl, and she became a servant of Naaman's wife. [3]Some time later the girl said, "If your husband Naaman would go to the prophet in Samaria, he would be cured of his leprosy."

[4]When Naaman told the king what the girl had said, [5]the king replied, "Go ahead! I will give you a letter to take to the king of Israel."

Naaman left and took along seven hundred fifty pounds of silver, one hundred fifty pounds of gold, and ten new outfits. [6]He also carried the letter to the king of Israel. It said, "I am sending my servant Naaman to you. Would you cure him of his leprosy?"

[7]When the king of Israel read the letter, he tore his clothes in fear and shouted, "That Syrian king believes I can cure this man of leprosy! Does he think I'm God with power over life and death? He must be trying to pick a fight with me."

[8]As soon as Elisha the prophet[w] heard what had happened, he sent the Israelite king this message: "Why are you so afraid? Send the man to me, so that he will know there is a prophet in Israel."

[9]Naaman left with his horses and chariots and stopped at the door of Elisha's house. [10]Elisha sent someone outside to say to him, "Go wash seven times in the Jordan River. Then you'll be completely cured."

[11]But Naaman stormed off, grumbling, "Why couldn't he come out and talk to me? I thought for sure he would stand in front of me and pray to the LORD his God, then wave his hand over my skin and cure me. [12]What about the Abana River[x] or the Pharpar River? Those rivers in Damascus are just

---

[u]4.42 Baal-Shalishah: The exact location of this town is not known, but it was probably somewhere near Shechem. [v]5.1 leprosy: The word translated "leprosy" was used for many different kinds of skin diseases. [w]5.8 the prophet: Hebrew "the man of God." [x]5.12 Abana River: Most Hebrew manuscripts; some Hebrew manuscripts and two ancient translations "Amana River."

as good as any river in Israel. I could have washed in them and been cured."

[13]His servants went over to him and said, "Sir, if the prophet had told you to do something difficult, you would have done it. So why don't you do what he said? Go wash and be cured."

[14]Naaman walked down to the Jordan; he waded out into the water and stooped down in it seven times, just as Elisha had told him. Right away, he was cured, and his skin became as smooth as a child's.

[15]Naaman and his officials went back to Elisha. Naaman stood in front of him and announced, "Now I know that the God of Israel is the only God in the whole world. Sir, would you please accept a gift from me?"

[16]"I am a servant of the living LORD," Elisha answered, "and I swear that I will not take anything from you."

Naaman kept begging, but Elisha kept refusing. [17]Finally Naaman said, "If you won't accept a gift, then please let me take home as much soil as two mules can pull in a wagon. Sir, from now on I will offer sacrifices only to the LORD.[y] [18]But I pray that the LORD will forgive me when I go into the temple of the god Rimmon and bow down there with the king of Syria."

[19]"Go on home, and don't worry about that," Elisha replied. Then Naaman left.

Elisha Places a Curse on Gehazi

After Naaman had gone only a short distance, [20]Gehazi said to himself, "Elisha let that Syrian off too easy. He should have taken Naaman's gift. I swear by the living LORD that I will talk to Naaman myself and get something from him." [21]So he hurried after Naaman.

When Naaman saw Gehazi running after him, he got out of his chariot to meet him. Naaman asked, "Is everything all right?"

[22]"Yes," Gehazi answered. "But my master has sent me to tell you about two young prophets from the hills of Ephraim. They came asking for help, and now Elisha wants to know if you would give them about seventy-five pounds of silver and some new clothes?"

[23]"Sure," Naaman replied. "But why don't you take twice that amount of silver?" He convinced Gehazi to take it all, then put the silver in two bags. He handed the bags

and the clothes to his two servants, and they carried them for Gehazi.

[24]When they reached the hill where Gehazi lived, he took the bags from the servants and placed them in his house, then sent the men away. After they had gone, [25]Gehazi went in and stood in front of Elisha, who asked, "Gehazi, where have you been?"

"Nowhere, sir," Gehazi answered.

[26]Elisha asked, "Don't you know that my spirit was there when Naaman got out of his chariot to talk with you? Gehazi, you have no right to accept money or clothes, olive orchards or vineyards, sheep or cattle, or servants. [27]Because of what you've done, Naaman's leprosy[z] will now be on you and your descendants forever!"

Suddenly, Gehazi's skin became white with leprosy, and he left.

Elisha Makes an Ax Head Float

6 One day the prophets said to Elisha, "The place where we meet with you is too small. [2]Why don't we build a new meeting place near the Jordan River? Each of us could get some wood, then we could build it."

"That's a good idea," Elisha replied, "get started."

[3]"Aren't you going with us?" one of the prophets asked.

"Yes, I'll go," Elisha answered, [4]and he left with them.

They went to the Jordan River and began chopping down trees. [5]While one of the prophets was working, his ax head fell off and dropped into the water. "Oh!" he shouted. "Sir, I borrowed this ax."

[6]"Where did it fall in?" Elisha asked. The prophet pointed to the place, and Elisha cut a stick and threw it into the water at that spot. The ax head floated to the top of the water.

[7]"Now get it," Elisha told him. And the prophet reached in and grabbed it.

Elisha Stops an Invasion of the Syrian Army

[8]Time after time, when the king of Syria was at war against the Israelites, he met with

---

[y]5.17 *let me take . . . the LORD:* It was believed that the LORD had to be worshiped in Israel or on soil taken from Israel. [z]5.27 *leprosy:* See the note at 5.1.

his officers and announced, "I've decided where we will set up camp."

⁹Each time, Elisha[a] would send this warning to the king of Israel: "Don't go near there. That's where the Syrian troops have set up camp."[b] ¹⁰So the king would warn the Israelite troops in that place to be on guard.

¹¹The king of Syria was furious when he found out what was happening. He called in his officers and asked, "Which one of you has been telling the king of Israel our plans?"

¹²"None of us, Your Majesty," one of them answered. "It's an Israelite named Elisha. He's a prophet, so he can tell his king everything—even what you say in your own room."

¹³"Find out where he is!" the king ordered. "I'll send soldiers to bring him here."

They learned that Elisha was in the town of Dothan[c] and reported it to the king. ¹⁴He ordered his best troops to go there with horses and chariots. They marched out during the night and surrounded the town.

¹⁵When Elisha's servant got up the next morning, he saw that Syrian troops had the town surrounded. "Sir, what are we going to do?" he asked.

> *Be content to know that God is at work in his world, even when you do not see how he is at work.*
>
> RUTH SENTER

¹⁶"Don't be afraid," Elisha answered. "There are more troops on our side than on theirs." ¹⁷Then he prayed, "LORD, please help him to see." And the LORD let the servant see that the hill[d] was covered with fiery horses and flaming chariots all around Elisha.

¹⁸As the Syrian army came closer, Elisha prayed, "LORD, make those soldiers blind!" And the LORD blinded them with a bright light.

¹⁹Elisha told the enemy troops, "You've taken the wrong road and are in the wrong town. Follow me. I'll lead you to the man

you're looking for." Elisha led them straight to the capital city of Samaria.

²⁰When all the soldiers were inside the city, Elisha prayed, "LORD, now let them see again." The LORD let them see that they were standing in the middle of Samaria.

²¹The king of Israel saw them and asked Elisha, "Should I kill them, sir?"

²²"No!" Elisha answered. "You didn't capture these troops in battle, so you have no right to kill them. Instead, give them something to eat and drink and let them return to their leader."

²³The king ordered a huge meal to be prepared for Syria's army, and when they finished eating, he let them go.

For a while, the Syrian troops stopped invading Israel's territory.

King Benhadad of Syria Attacks Samaria

²⁴Some time later, King Benhadad of Syria[e] called his entire army together, then they marched to Samaria and attacked. ²⁵They kept up the attack until there was nothing to eat in the city. In fact, a donkey's head cost about two pounds of silver, and a small bowl of pigeon droppings[f] cost about two ounces of silver.

²⁶One day as the king of Israel[g] was walking along the top of the city wall, a woman shouted to him, "Please, Your Majesty, help me!"

²⁷"Let the LORD help you!" the king said. "Do you think I have grain or wine to give you?" ²⁸Then he asked, "What's the matter anyway?"

The woman answered, "Another woman and I were so hungry that we agreed to eat our sons. She said if we ate my son one day, we could eat hers the next day. ²⁹So yesterday we cooked my son and ate him. But today when I went to her house to eat her son, she had hidden him."

---

[a]6.9 *Elisha*: Hebrew "the man of God." [b]6.9 *have set up camp*: Or "are going." [c]6.13 *Dothan*: About ten miles north of Samaria. [d]6.17 *the hill*: The hill on which the town was built. [e]6.24 *King Benhadad of Syria*: This may or may not be the same Benhadad mentioned in 1 Kings 20.1. Several of the Syrian kings were named Benhadad. [f]6.25 *pigeon droppings*: This may have been used for food or to burn for fuel. It also may have been a popular name for roasted beans or the shells of certain seeds. [g]6.26 *the king of Israel*: Probably either Jehoahaz or Jehoash, but possibly even Joram.

³⁰The king tore off his clothes in sorrow, and since he was on top of the city wall, the people saw that he was wearing sackcloth underneath. ³¹He said, "I pray that God will punish me terribly, if Elisha's head is still on his shoulders by this time tomorrow." ³²Then he sent a messenger to Elisha.

Elisha was home at the time, and the important leaders of Israel were meeting with him. Even before the king's messenger arrived, Elisha told the leaders, "That murderer[h] is sending someone to cut off my head. When you see him coming, shut the door and don't let him in. I'm sure the king himself will be right behind him."

³³Before Elisha finished talking, the messenger[i] came up and said, "The LORD has made all these terrible things happen to us. Why should I think he will help us now?"

7 Elisha answered, "I have a message for you. The LORD promises that tomorrow here in Samaria, you will be able to buy a large sack of flour or two large sacks of barley for almost nothing."

²The chief officer there with the king replied, "I don't believe it! Even if the LORD sent a rainstorm, it couldn't produce that much grain by tomorrow."

"You will see it happen, but you won't eat any of the food," Elisha warned him.

The Syrian Army Stops Its Attack

³About the same time, four men with leprosy[j] were just outside the gate of Samaria. They said to each other, "Why should we sit here, waiting to die? ⁴There's nothing to eat in the city, so we would starve if we went inside. But if we stay out here, we will die for sure. Let's sneak over to the Syrian army camp and surrender. They might kill us, but they might not." ⁵⁻⁸That evening the four men got up and left for the Syrian camp.

As they walked toward the camp, the Lord caused the Syrian troops to hear what sounded like the roar of a huge cavalry. The soldiers said to each other, "Listen! The king of Israel must have hired Hittite and Egyptian troops to attack us. Let's get out of here!" So they ran out of their camp that night, leaving their tents and horses and donkeys.

When the four men with leprosy reached the edge of the Syrian camp, no one was there. They walked into one of the tents, where they ate and drank, before carrying off clothes, as well as silver and gold. They hid all this, then walked into another tent; they took what they wanted and hid it too.

⁹They said to each other, "This isn't right. Today is a day to celebrate, and we haven't told anyone else what has happened. If we wait until morning, we will be punished. Let's go to the king's palace right now and tell the good news."

¹⁰They went back to Samaria and shouted up to the guards at the gate, "We've just come from the Syrian army camp, and all the soldiers are gone! The tents are empty, and the horses and donkeys are still tied up. We didn't see or hear anybody."

¹¹The guards reported the news to the king's palace. ¹²The king got out of bed and said to his officers, "I know what those Syrians are doing. They know we're starving, so they're hiding in the fields, hoping we will go out to look for food. When we do, they can capture us and take over our city."

¹³One of his officers replied, "We have a few horses left—why don't we let some men take five of them and go to the Syrian camp and see what's happening? We're going to die anyway like those who have already died."[k] ¹⁴They found two chariots, and the king commanded the men to find out what had happened to the Syrian troops.

¹⁵The men rode as far as the Jordan River. All along the way they saw clothes and equipment that the Syrians had thrown away as they escaped. Then they went back to the king and told him what they had seen.

¹⁶At once the people went to the Syrian camp and carried off what was left. They took so much that a large sack of flour and two large sacks of barley sold for almost nothing, just as the LORD had promised.

¹⁷The king of Israel had put his chief officer in charge of the gate, but he died when the people trampled him as they rushed out of the city. ¹⁸Earlier, when the king was at Elisha's house, Elisha had told him that flour or barley would sell for almost nothing. ¹⁹But the officer refused to believe that even the LORD could do that. So Elisha

---

[h]**6.32** *That murderer:* Hebrew "That murderer's son."
[i]**6.33** *messenger:* Or "king" (see 7.2, 18); the two Hebrew words are very similar.   [j]**7.3** *leprosy:* See the note at 5.1.   [k]**7.13** *We're going . . . died:* One possible meaning for the difficult Hebrew text.

warned him that he would see it happen, but would not eat any of the food. [20]And that's exactly what happened—the officer was trampled to death.

The Woman from Shunem Is Given Back Her Land

8 Elisha told the woman whose son he had brought back to life,[l] "The LORD has warned that there will be no food here for seven years. Take your family and go live somewhere else for a while." [2]The woman did exactly what Elisha had said and went to live in Philistine territory.

She and her family lived there seven years. [3]Then she returned to Israel and immediately begged the king to give back her house and property.

[4]Meanwhile, the king was asking Gehazi the servant of Elisha about the amazing things Elisha had been doing. [5]While Gehazi was telling him that Elisha had brought a dead boy back to life, the woman and her son arrived.

"Here's the boy, Your Majesty," Gehazi said. "And this is his mother."

[6]The king asked the woman to tell her story, and she told him everything that had happened. He then said to one of his officials, "I want you to make sure that this woman gets back everything that belonged to her, including the money her crops have made since the day she left Israel."

Hazael Kills Benhadad

[7]Some time later Elisha went to the capital city of Damascus to visit King Benhadad of Syria, who was sick. And when Benhadad was told he was there, [8]he said to Hazael,[m] "Go meet with Elisha the man of God and have him ask the LORD if I will get well. And take along a gift for him."

[9]Hazael left with forty camel loads of the best things made in Damascus as a gift for Elisha. He found the prophet and said, "Your servant, King Benhadad, wants to know if he will get well."

[10]"Tell him he will," Elisha said to Hazael. "But the LORD has already told me that Benhadad will definitely die." [11]Elisha stared at him until Hazael was embarrassed, then Elisha began crying.[n]

[12]"Sir, why are you crying?" Hazael asked.

Elisha answered, "Because I know the terrible things you will do to the people of Israel. You will burn down their walled cities and slaughter their young men. You will even crush the heads of their babies and rip open their pregnant women."

[13]"How could I ever do anything like that?" Hazael replied. "I'm only a servant and don't have that kind of power."

"Hazael, the LORD has told me that you will be the next king of Syria."

[14]Hazael went back to Benhadad and told him, "Elisha said that you will get well." [15]But the very next day, Hazael got a thick blanket; he soaked it in water and held it over Benhadad's face until he died. Hazael then became king.

King Jehoram of Judah

(2 Chronicles 21.2-20)

[16]Jehoram son of Jehoshaphat became king of Judah in Joram's fifth year as king of Israel, while Jehoshaphat was still king of Judah.[o] [17]Jehoram was thirty-two years old when he became king, and he ruled eight years from Jerusalem.

[18]Jehoram disobeyed the LORD by doing wrong. He married Ahab's daughter and was as sinful as Ahab's family and the kings of Israel. [19]But the LORD refused to destroy Judah, because he had promised his servant David that someone from his family would always rule in Judah.

[20]While Jehoram was king, the people of Edom rebelled and chose their own king. [21]So Jehoram[p] and his cavalry marched to Zair, where the Edomite army surrounded him and his commanders. During the night he attacked the Edomites, but he was defeated, and his troops escaped to their homes.[q] [22]Judah was never able to regain control of Edom. Even the town of Libnah[r] rebelled at that time.

---

[l]**8.1** *Elisha . . . life*: See 4.8-37. [m]**8.8** *Hazael*: Probably one of Benhadad's officials. [n]**8.11** *Elisha stared . . . crying*: Or "Hazael stared at him until Elisha was embarrassed and began to cry." [o]**8.16** *while Jehoshaphat . . . Judah*: In biblical times, a father and son would sometimes rule as kings at the same time. That way, when the father died, his son would already have control of the kingdom. [p]**8.21** *Jehoram*: The Hebrew text has "Joram," another spelling of the name. [q]**8.21** *he attacked . . . homes*: One possible meaning for the difficult Hebrew text. [r]**8.22** *Even the town of Libnah*: This was a town on the border between Philistia and Judah, which means that Jehoram was facing rebellion on two sides of his kingdom.

²³Everything else Jehoram did while he was king is written in *The History of the Kings of Judah.* ²⁴Jehoram died and was buried beside his ancestors in Jerusalem.ˢ His son Ahaziah then became king.

King Ahaziah of Judah
(2 Chronicles 22.1-6)

²⁵Ahaziah son of Jehoram became king of Judah in the twelfth year of Joram's rule in Israel. ²⁶Ahaziah was twenty-two years old when he became king, and he ruled from Jerusalem for only one year. His mother was Athaliah, a granddaughter of King Omri of Israel. ²⁷Since Ahaziah was related to Ahab's family,ᵗ he acted just like them and disobeyed the LORD by doing wrong.

²⁸Ahaziah went with King Joram of Israel to attack King Hazael and the Syrian troops at Ramoth in Gilead. Joram was wounded in that battle, ²⁹so he went to the town of Jezreel to recover. Ahaziah went there to visit him.

Jehu Becomes King of Israel

9 One day, Elisha called for one of the other prophets and said:

Take this bottle of olive oil and get ready to go to the town of Ramoth in Gilead. ²When you get there, find Jehu son of Jehoshaphat and grandson of Nimshi. Take him to a place where the two of you can be alone, ³then pour olive oil on his head to show that he is the new king. Say to him, "The LORD has chosen you to be king of Israel." Then leave quickly—don't wait around for anything!

⁴The young prophet left for Ramoth. ⁵When he arrived, the army officers were meeting together. "Sir, I have a message for you," he said.

"For which one of us?" Jehu asked.

"You, sir," the prophet answered. ⁶So Jehu got up and went inside.ᵘ The prophet poured olive oil on Jehu's head and told him:

The LORD God of Israel has this message for you: "I am the LORD, and I have chosen you to be king of my people Israel. ⁷I want you to wipe out the family of Ahab, so Jezebel will be punished for killing the prophets and my other servants. ⁸Every man and boy in Ahab's family must die, whether slave

or free. ⁹His whole family must be destroyed, just like the families of Jeroboam son of Nebat and Baasha son of Ahijah. ¹⁰As for Jezebel, her body will be eaten by dogs in the town of Jezreel. There won't be enough left of her to bury."

Then the young prophet opened the door and ran out.

¹¹Jehu went back to his officers, and one of them asked, "What did that crazy prophet want? Is everything all right?"

"You know him and how he talks," Jehu answered.

True freedom comes when you surrender all and say, "God, you are who you say you are. Nothing happens to me that you don't allow."

JAN DRAVECKY

¹²"No, we don't. What did he say?" they asked.

"He had a message from the LORD," Jehu replied. "He said that the LORD has chosen me to be the next king of Israel."

¹³They quickly grabbed their coats and spread them out on the steps where Jehu was standing. Someone blew a trumpet, and everyone shouted, "Jehu is king!"

Jehu Kills Joram and Ahaziah

¹⁴⁻¹⁶King Joramᵛ of Israel had been badly wounded in the battle at Ramoth, trying to defend it against King Hazael and the Syrian army. Joram was now recovering in Jezreel, and King Ahaziah of Judah was there, visiting him.

Meanwhile, Jehu was in Ramoth, making plans to kill Joram. He said to his officers, "If you want me to be king, then don't

ˢ**8.24** *Jerusalem:* Hebrew "the city of David." ᵗ**8.27** *Since . . . family:* Ahaziah's mother was Ahab's daughter (see verse 18). ᵘ**9.6** *went inside:* The officers were probably meeting outside in an open courtyard of some building. ᵛ**9.14-16** *Joram:* The Hebrew text has "Jehoram," another spelling of the name.

let anyone leave this town. They might go to Jezreel and tell Joram." Then Jehu got in his chariot and rode to Jezreel.

¹⁷When the guard in the watchtower at Jezreel saw Jehu and his men riding up, he shouted to the king, "I see a bunch of men coming this way."

Joram ordered, "Send someone out to ask them if this is a friendly visit."

¹⁸One of the soldiers rode out and said to Jehu, "King Joram wants to know if this is a friendly visit."

"What's it to you?" Jehu asked. "Just stay behind me with the rest of my troops!"

About the same time the guard in the watchtower said, "Your Majesty, the rider got there, but he isn't coming back."

¹⁹So Joram sent out another rider, who rode up to Jehu and said, "The king wants to know if this is a friendly visit."

"What's it to you?" Jehu asked. "Just get behind me with the rest of my troops!"

²⁰The guard in the watchtower said, "Your Majesty, the rider got there, but he isn't coming back either. Wait a minute! That one man is a reckless chariot driver—it must be Jehu!"

²¹Joram commanded, "Get my chariot ready." Then he and Ahaziah got in their chariots and rode out to meet Jehu. They all met on the land that had belonged to Naboth.ʷ ²²Joram asked, "Jehu, is this a peaceful visit?"

"How can there be peace?" Jehu asked. "Your mother Jezebel has caused everyone to worship idols and practice witchcraft."

²³"Ahaziah, let's get out of here!" Joram yelled. "It's a trap!" As Joram tried to escape, ²⁴Jehu shot an arrow. It hit Joram between his shoulders, then it went through his heart and came out his chest. He fell over dead in his chariot.

²⁵⁻²⁶Jehu commanded his assistant Bidkar, "Get Joram's body and throw it in the field that Naboth once owned. Do you remember when you and I used to ride side by side behind Joram's father Ahab? It was then that the LORD swore to Ahab that he would be punished in the same field where he had killed Naboth and his sons. So throw Joram's body there, just as the LORD said."

²⁷Ahaziah saw all of this happen and tried to escape to the town of Beth-Haggan, but Jehu caught up with him and shouted, "Kill him too!" So his troops shot Ahaziah

with an arrow while he was on the road to Gur near Ibleam. He went as far as Megiddo, where he died. ²⁸Ahaziah's officers put his body in a chariot and took it back to Jerusalem, where they buried him beside his ancestors.

²⁹Ahaziah had become king of Judah in the eleventh year of the rule of Ahab's son Joram.

Jehu Kills Jezebel

³⁰Jehu headed toward Jezreel, and when Jezebel heard he was coming, she put on eye shadow and brushed her hair. Then she stood at the window, waiting for him to arrive. ³¹As he walked through the city gate, she shouted down to him, "Why did you come here, you murderer? To kill the king? You're no better than Zimri!"ˣ

³²He looked up toward the window and asked, "Is anyone up there on my side?" A few palace workers stuck their heads out of a window, ³³and Jehu shouted, "Throw her out the window!" They threw her down, and her blood splattered on the walls and on the horses that trampled her body.ʸ

³⁴Jehu left to get something to eat and drink. Then he told some workers, "Even though she was evil, she was a king's daughter,ᶻ so make sure she has a proper burial."

³⁵But when they went out to bury her body, they found only her skull, her hands, and her feet. ³⁶They reported this to Jehu, and he said, "The LORD told Elijah the prophet that Jezebel's body would be eaten by dogs right here in Jezreel. ³⁷And he warned that her bones would be spread all over the ground like manure, so that no one could tell who it was."

Jehu Kills All of Ahab's Descendants

10

Ahab still had seventy descendants living in Samaria. So Jehu wrote a letter to each of the important leaders and officials of the town,ᵃ

ʷ**9.21** *the land . . . Naboth:* See 1 Kings 21.
ˣ**9.31** *Zimri:* An Israelite king who killed King Elah and his family so he could become king, but who ruled only seven days (see 1 Kings 16.8-20). ʸ**9.33** *horses . . . her body:* Two ancient translations; Hebrew "horses. Then Jehu trampled her body." ᶻ**9.34** *she . . . daughter:* Her father was King Ethbaal of Sidon (see 1 Kings 16.31). ᵃ**10.1** *the town:* Two ancient translations; Hebrew "Jezreel."

and to those who supported Ahab. In the letters he wrote:

²Your town is strong, and you're protected by chariots and an armed cavalry. And I know that King Ahab's descendants live there with you. So as soon as you read this letter, ³choose the best person for the job and make him the next king. Then be prepared to defend Ahab's family.

⁴The officials and leaders read the letters and were very frightened. They said to each other, "Jehu has already killed King Joram and King Ahaziah! We have to do what he says." ⁵The prime minister, the mayor of the city, as well as the other leaders and Ahab's supporters, sent this answer to Jehu, "We are your servants, Your Majesty, and we will do whatever you tell us. But it's not our place to choose someone to be king. You do what you think is best."

⁶Jehu then wrote another letter which said, "If you are on my side and will obey me, then prove it. Bring me the heads of the descendants of Ahab! And be here in Jezreel by this time tomorrow."

The seventy descendants of King Ahab were living with some of the most important people of the city. ⁷And when these people read Jehu's second letter, they called together all seventy of Ahab's descendants. They killed them, put their heads in baskets, and sent them to Jezreel.

⁸When Jehu was told what had happened, he said, "Put the heads in two piles at the city gate, and leave them there until morning."

⁹The next morning, Jehu went out and stood where everyone could hear him, and he said, "You people are not guilty of anything. I'm the one who plotted against Joram and had him killed. But who killed all these men? ¹⁰Listen to me. Everything the LORD's servant Elijah promised about Ahab's family will come true."ᵇ

¹¹Then Jehu killed the rest of Ahab's relatives living in Jezreel, as well as his highest officials, his priests, and his closest friends. No one in Ahab's family was left alive in Jezreel.

¹²⁻¹³Jehu left for Samaria, and along the way, he met some relatives of King Ahaziah of Judah at a place where shepherds meet.ᶜ He asked, "Who are you?"

"We are relatives of Ahaziah," they answered. "We're going to visit his family."

¹⁴"Take them alive!" Jehu said to his officers. So they grabbed them and led them to the well near the shepherds' meeting place, where they killed all forty-two of them.

¹⁵As Jehu went on, he saw Jehonadab son of Rechabᵈ coming to meet him. Jehu greeted him, then said, "Jehonadab, I'm on your side. Are you on mine?"

"Yes, I am."

"Then give me your hand," Jehu answered. He helped Jehonadab into his chariot ¹⁶and said, "Come with me and see how faithful I am to the LORD."

They rode together in Jehu's chariot ¹⁷to Samaria. Jehu killed everyone there who belonged to Ahab's family, as well as all his officials. Everyone in his family was now dead, just as the LORD had promised Elijah.

Jehu Kills All the Worshipers of Baal

¹⁸Jehu called together the people in Samaria and said:

King Ahab sometimes worshiped Baal, but I will be completely faithful to Baal. ¹⁹I'm going to offer a huge sacrifice to him. So invite his prophets and priests, and be sure everyone who worships him is there. Anyone who doesn't come will be killed.

But this was a trick—Jehu was really planning to kill the worshipers of Baal. ²⁰He said, "Announce a day of worship for Baal!" After the day had been announced, ²¹Jehu sent an invitation to everyone in Israel. All the worshipers of Baal came, and the temple was filled from one end to the other. ²²Jehu told the official in charge of the sacred robes to make sure that everyone had a robe to wear.

²³Jehu and Jehonadab went into the temple, and Jehu said to the crowd, "Look around and make sure that only the worshipers of Baal are here. No one who worships the LORD is allowed in." ²⁴Then they began to offer sacrifices to Baal.

Earlier, Jehu had ordered eighty soldiers to wait outside the temple. He had warned them, "I will get all these worshipers here, and if any of you let even one of them escape, you will be killed instead!"

ᵇ10.10 *Everything . . . come true*: See 1 Kings 21.17-24. ᶜ10.12,13 *at a place where shepherds meet*: Or "at Betheked of the Shepherds." ᵈ10.15 *Jehonadab son of Rechab*: Or "Jehonadab the chariot driver."

²⁵As soon as Jehu finished offering the sacrifice, he told the guards and soldiers, "Come in and kill them! Don't let anyone escape." They slaughtered everyone in the crowd and threw the bodies outside. Then they went back into the temple ²⁶and carried out the image of Baal. They burned it ²⁷and broke it into pieces, then they completely destroyed Baal's temple. And since that time, it's been nothing but a public toilet.ᵉ ²⁸That's how Jehu stopped the worship of Baal in Israel. ²⁹But he did not stop the worship of the gold statues of calves at Dan and Bethel that Jeroboam had made for the people to worship.ᶠ ³⁰Later the LORD said, "Jehu, you have done right by destroying Ahab's entire family, just as I had planned. So I will make sure that the next four kings of Israel will come from your own family."

³¹But Jehu did not completely obey the commands of the LORD God of Israel. Instead, he kept doing the sinful things that Jeroboam had caused the Israelites to do.

Jehu Dies

³²In those days the LORD began to reduce the size of Israel's territory. King Hazael of Syria defeated the Israelites and took control ³³of the regions of Gilead and Bashan east of the Jordan River and north of the town of Aroer near the Arnon River. This was the land where the tribes of Gad, Reuben, and Manasseh had once lived. ³⁴Everything else Jehu did while he was king, including his brave deeds, is written in *The History of the Kings of Israel.* ³⁵Jehu died and was buried in Samaria, and his son Jehoahaz became king. ³⁶Jehu had ruled Israel twenty-eight years from Samaria.

Queen Athaliah of Judah
(2 Chronicles 22.10-12)

11 As soon as Athaliah heard that her son King Ahaziah was dead, she decided to kill any relative who could possibly become king. She would have done that, ²but Jehosheba rescued Joash son of Ahaziah just as he was about to be murdered. Jehosheba, who was Jehoram'sᵍ daughter and Ahaziah's half sister, hid her nephew Joash and his personal servant in a bedroom in the LORD's temple where he was safe from Athaliah. ³Joash hid in the temple with Jehoshebaʰ for six years while Athaliah ruled as queen of Judah.

Jehoiada Makes Joash King of Judah
(2 Chronicles 23.1-21)

⁴Joash son of Ahaziah had hidden in the LORD's temple six years. Then in the seventh year, Jehoiada the priest sent for the commanders of the king's special bodyguardsⁱ and the commanders of the palace guards. They met him at the temple, and he asked them to make a promise in the name of the LORD. Then he brought out Joash ⁵and said to them:

Here's what I want you to do. Three of your guard units will be on duty on the Sabbath. I want one unit to guard the palace. ⁶Another unit will guard Sur Gate, and the third unit will guard the palace gate and relieve the palace guards.

I've found that praise and obedience to the Lord keeps the devil from destroying my peace of mind, no matter the problem.

THELMA WELLS

⁷The other two guard units are supposed to be off duty on the Sabbath. But I want both of them to stay here at the temple and protect King Joash. ⁸Make sure they follow him wherever he goes, and have them keep their swords ready to kill anyone who tries to get near him.

⁹The commanders followed Jehoiada's orders. Each one called together his guards—those coming on duty and those going off duty. ¹⁰Jehoiada brought out the

---

ᵉ10.27 *public toilet:* Or "garbage dump." ᶠ10.29 *gold statues . . . to worship:* See 1 Kings 12.26-30. ᵍ11.2 *Jehoram's:* The Hebrew text has "Joram's," another spelling of the name. ʰ11.3 *Jehosheba:* Jehosheba was the wife of Jehoiada the priest (see 2 Chronicles 22.11), which is why she could hide Joash in one of the private bedrooms used only by the priests. ⁱ11.4 *the king's special bodyguards:* The Hebrew text has "the Carites," who were probably foreign soldiers hired to serve as royal bodyguards.

swords and shields that had belonged to King David and gave them to the commanders. [11]Then they gave the weapons to their guards, who took their positions around the temple and the altar to protect Joash on every side.

[12]Jehoiada brought Joash outside, where he placed the crown on his head and gave him a copy of instructions for ruling the nation. Olive oil was poured on his head to show that he was now king, while the crowd clapped and shouted, "Long live the king!"

[13]Queen Athaliah heard the crowd and went to the temple. [14]There she saw Joash standing by one of the columns, which was the usual place for the king. The singers[j] and the trumpet players were standing next to him, and the people were celebrating and blowing trumpets. Athaliah tore her clothes in anger and shouted, "You betrayed me, you traitors!"

[15]Right away, Jehoiada said to the army commanders, "Kill her! But don't do it anywhere near the LORD's temple. Take her out in front of the troops and kill anyone who is with her!" [16]So the commanders dragged her to the gate where horses are led into the palace, and they killed her there.

[17]Jehoiada the priest asked King Joash and the people to promise that they would be faithful to each other and to the LORD. [18]Then the crowd went to the temple built to honor Baal and tore it down. They smashed the altars and idols and killed Mattan the priest of Baal right in front of the altars.

After Jehoiada had placed guards around the LORD's temple, [19]he called together all the commanders, the king's special bodyguards,[k] the palace guards, and the people. They led Joash from the temple, through the Guards' Gate, and into the palace. He took his place on the throne and became king of Judah. [20]Everyone celebrated because Athaliah had been killed and Jerusalem was peaceful again. [21]Joash was only seven years old when this happened.

King Joash of Judah
(2 Chronicles 24.1-16)

12 Joash[l] became king of Judah in Jehu's seventh year as king of Israel, and he ruled forty years from Jerusalem. His mother Zibiah was from the town of Beersheba.

[2]Jehoiada the priest taught Joash what was right, and so for the rest of his life Joash obeyed the LORD. [3]But even Joash did not destroy the local shrines,[m] and they were still used as places for offering sacrifices.

[4]One day, Joash said to the priests, "Collect all the money that has been given to the LORD's temple, whether from taxes or gifts, [5]and use it to repair the temple. You priests can contribute your own money too."[n]

[6]But the priests never started repairing the temple. So in the twenty-third year of his rule, [7]Joash called for Jehoiada and the other priests and said, "Why aren't you using the money to repair the temple? Don't take any more money for yourselves. It is only to be used to pay for the repairs." [8]The priests agreed that they would not collect any more money or be in charge of the temple repairs.

[9]Jehoiada found a wooden box; he cut a hole in the top of it and set it on the right side of the altar where people went into the temple. Whenever someone gave money to the temple, the priests guarding the entrance would put it into this box. [10]When the box was full of money, the king's secretary and the chief priest would count the money and put it in bags. [11]Then they would give it to the men supervising the repairs to the temple. Some of the money was used to pay the builders, the woodworkers, [12]the stonecutters, and the men who built the walls. And some was used to buy wood and stone and to pay any other costs for repairing the temple.

[13]While the repairs were being made, the money that was given to the temple was not used to make silver bowls, lamp snuffers, small sprinkling bowls, trumpets, or anything gold or silver for the temple. [14]It went only to pay for repairs. [15]The men in charge were honest, so no one had to keep track of the money.

[16]The fines that had to be paid along with the sacrifices to make things right and the sacrifices for sin did not go to the temple. This money belonged only to the priests.

---

[j]11.14 singers: Two ancient translations; Hebrew "commanders." [k]11.19 the king's special bodyguards: See the note at verse 4. [l]12.1 Joash: The Hebrew text has "Jehoash," another spelling of the name. [m]12.3 local shrines: The Hebrew text has "high places," which were local places to worship God or foreign gods. [n]12.5 You priests . . . money too: One possible meaning for the difficult Hebrew text.

¹⁷About the same time, King Hazael of Syria attacked the town of Gath and captured it. Next, he decided to attack Jerusalem. ¹⁸So Joash collected everything he and his ancestors Jehoshaphat, Jehoram, and Ahaziah had dedicated to the LORD, as well as the gold in the storage rooms in the temple and palace. He sent it all to Hazael as a gift, and when Hazael received it, he ordered his troops to leave Jerusalem.

¹⁹Everything else Joash did while he was king is written in *The History of the Kings of Judah*. ²⁰⁻²¹At the end of his rule, some of his officers rebelled against him. Jozabad[o] son of Shimeath and Jehozabad son of Shomer murdered him in a building where the land was filled in on the east side of Jerusalem,[p] near the road to Silla. Joash was buried beside his ancestors in Jerusalem,[q] and his son Amaziah became king.

King Jehoahaz of Israel

13 Jehoahaz son of Jehu became king of Israel in the twenty-third year of Joash's rule in Judah. Jehoahaz ruled seventeen years from Samaria ²and disobeyed the LORD by doing wrong. He never stopped following the example of Jeroboam, who had caused the Israelites to sin.

³The LORD was angry at the Israelites, so he let King Hazael of Syria and his son Benhadad rule over them for a long time. ⁴Jehoahaz prayed to the LORD for help, and the LORD saw how terribly Hazael was treating the Israelites. He answered Jehoahaz ⁵by sending Israel a leader who rescued them from the Syrians,[r] and the Israelites lived in peace as they had before. ⁶⁻⁷But Hazael had defeated Israel's army so badly that Jehoahaz had only ten chariots, fifty cavalry troops, and ten thousand regular soldiers left in his army.

The Israelites kept sinning and following the example of Jeroboam's family. They did not tear down the sacred poles[s] that had been set up in Samaria for the worship of the goddess Asherah.

⁸Everything else Jehoahaz did while he was king, including his brave deeds, is written in *The History of the Kings of Israel*. ⁹Jehoahaz died and was buried in Samaria, and his son Jehoash became king.

King Jehoash of Israel

¹⁰Jehoash became king of Israel in the thirty-seventh year of Joash's rule in Judah, and he ruled sixteen years from Samaria. ¹¹He disobeyed the LORD by doing just like Jeroboam, who had caused the Israelites to sin.

¹²Everything else Jehoash did while he was king, including his war against King Amaziah of Judah, is written in *The History of the Kings of Israel*. ¹³Jehoash died and was buried in Samaria beside the other Israelite kings. His son Jeroboam then became king.

Elisha the Prophet Dies

¹⁴Some time before the death of King Jehoash, Elisha the prophet was very sick and about to die. Jehoash went in and stood beside him, crying. He said, "Master, what will Israel's chariots and cavalry be able to do without you?"[t]

¹⁵⁻¹⁶"Grab a bow and some arrows," Elisha told him, "and hold them in your hand." Jehoash grabbed the bow and arrows and held them. Elisha placed his hand on the king's hand ¹⁷and said, "Open the window facing east." When it was open, Elisha shouted, "Now shoot!" Jehoash shot an arrow and Elisha said, "That arrow is a sign that the LORD will help you completely defeat the Syrian army at Aphek."

¹⁸Elisha said, "Pick up the arrows and hit the ground with them." Jehoash grabbed the arrows and hit the ground three times, then stopped. ¹⁹Elisha became angry at the king and exclaimed, "If you had struck it five or six times, you would completely wipe out the Syrians. Now you will defeat them only three times."

²⁰Elisha died and was buried.

Every year in the spring, Moab's leaders sent raiding parties into Israel. ²¹Once, while some Israelites were burying a man's

---

o**12.20,21** *Jozabad:* Some manuscripts of the Hebrew text; other manuscripts "Jozacar." p**12.20,21** *where . . . Jerusalem:* The Hebrew text has "on the Millo," which probably refers to a landfill to strengthen and extend the hill where the city was built. q**12.20,21** *Jerusalem:* See the note at 8.24. r**13.5** *by sending . . . the Syrians:* The name of this leader is not given, but it may refer to Elisha the prophet, King Jehoash of Israel, or his son King Jeroboam. s**13.6,7** *sacred poles:* Or "trees," used as symbols of Asherah, the goddess of fertility. t**13.14** *Master . . . without you:* Or "Master, you were like chariots and cavalry for Israel!"

body, they saw a group of Moabites. The Israelites quickly threw the body into Elisha's tomb and ran away. As soon as the man's body touched the bones of Elisha, the man came back to life and stood up.

We need to educate ourselves by looking at what God says about life. He tells us clearly in the Bible that he's the author of life.

CAROL EVERETT

Israel Defeats Syria

²²Israel was under the power of King Hazael of Syria during the entire rule of Jehoahaz. ²³But the LORD was kind to the Israelites and showed them mercy because of his solemn agreement with their ancestors Abraham, Isaac, and Jacob. In fact, he has never turned his back on them or let them be completely destroyed.

²⁴Hazael died, and his son Benhadad then became king of Syria. ²⁵King Jehoash of Israel attacked and defeated the Syrian army three times. He took back from Benhadad all the towns Hazael had captured in battle from his father Jehoahaz.

King Amaziah of Judah
(2 Chronicles 25.1-24)

14 Amaziah son of Joash became king of Judah in the second year of Jehoash's rule in Israel. ²Amaziah was twenty-five years old when he became king, and he ruled twenty-nine years from Jerusalem, which was also the hometown of his mother Jehoaddin.

³Amaziah followed the example of his father Joash by obeying the LORD and doing right. But he was not as faithful as his ancestor David. ⁴Amaziah did not destroy the local shrines, and they were still used as places for offering sacrifices.

⁵As soon as Amaziah had control of Judah, he arrested and killed the officers who had murdered his father. ⁶But the children of those officers were not killed. The LORD

had commanded in the Law of Moses that only the people who sinned were to be punished, not their parents or children.ᵘ

⁷While Amaziah was king, he killed ten thousand Edomite soldiers in Salt Valley. He captured the town of Sela and renamed it Joktheel, which is still its name.

⁸One day, Amaziah sent a message to King Jehoash of Israel: "Come out and face me in battle!"

⁹Jehoash sent back this reply:

Once upon a time, a small thornbush in Lebanon announced that his son was going to marry the daughter of a large cedar tree. But a wild animal came along and trampled the small bush.

¹⁰Amaziah, you think you're so powerful because you defeated Edom. Go ahead and celebrate—but stay at home. If you cause any trouble, both you and your kingdom of Judah will be destroyed.

¹¹But Amaziah refused to listen. So Jehoash and his troops marched to the town of Beth-Shemesh in Judah to attack Amaziah and his troops. ¹²During the battle, Judah's army was crushed. Every soldier from Judah ran back home, ¹³and Jehoash captured Amaziah.

Jehoash then marched to Jerusalem and broke down the city wall from Ephraim Gate to Corner Gate, a section about six hundred feet long. ¹⁴He took the gold and silver, as well as everything of value from the LORD's temple and the king's treasury. He took hostages, then returned to Samaria.

¹⁵Everything else Jehoash did while he was king, including his brave deeds and how he defeated King Amaziah of Judah, is written in *The History of the Kings of Israel.* ¹⁶Jehoash died and was buried in Samaria beside the other Israelite kings. His son Jeroboam then became king.

¹⁷Fifteen years after Jehoash died, ¹⁸⁻²⁰some people in Jerusalem plotted against Amaziah. He was able to escape to the town of Lachish, but another group of people caught him and killed him there. His body was taken back to Jerusalem on horseback and buried beside his ancestors.

Everything else Amaziah did while he

ᵘ**14.6** *The LORD had commanded . . . children:* See Deuteronomy 24.16.

was king is written in *The History of the Kings of Judah*. [21]After his death the people of Judah made his son Azariah king, even though he was only sixteen at the time. [22]Azariah was the one who later recaptured and rebuilt the town of Elath.

King Jeroboam the Second of Israel

[23]Jeroboam son of Jehoash became king of Israel in the fifteenth year of Amaziah's rule in Judah. Jeroboam ruled forty-one years from Samaria. [24]He disobeyed the LORD by following the evil example of Jeroboam son of Nebat, who had caused the Israelites to sin.

[25]Jeroboam extended the boundaries of Israel from Lebo-Hamath in the north to the Dead Sea in the south, just as the LORD had promised his servant Jonah son of Amittai, who was a prophet from Gath-Hepher. [26]The LORD helped Jeroboam do this because he had seen how terribly the Israelites were suffering, whether slave or free, and no one was left to help them. [27]And since the LORD had promised that he would not let Israel be completely destroyed, he helped Jeroboam rescue them.

[28]Everything else Jeroboam did while he was king, including his brave deeds and how he recaptured the towns of Damascus and Hamath,[v] is written in *The History of the Kings of Israel*. [29]Jeroboam died and was buried, and his son Zechariah became king.

King Azariah of Judah
(2 Chronicles 26.1-23)

15 Azariah son of Amaziah became king of Judah in Jeroboam's twenty-seventh year as king of Israel. [2]He was only sixteen years old when he became king, and he ruled fifty-two years from Jerusalem, which was also the hometown of his mother Jecoliah.

[3]Azariah obeyed the LORD by doing right, as his father Amaziah had done. [4]But Azariah did not destroy the local shrines,[w] and they were still used as places for offering sacrifices.

[5]The LORD punished Azariah with leprosy[x] for the rest of his life. He wasn't allowed to live in the royal palace, so his son Jotham lived there and ruled in his place.

[6]Everything else Azariah did while he was king is written in *The History of the Kings of Judah*. [7]Azariah died and was buried be-

side his ancestors in Jerusalem. His son Jotham then became king.

King Zechariah of Israel

[8]Zechariah son of Jeroboam became king of Israel in the thirty-eighth year of Azariah's rule in Judah, but he ruled only six months from Samaria. [9]Like his ancestors, Zechariah disobeyed the LORD by following the evil ways of Jeroboam son of Nebat, who had caused the Israelites to sin.

[10]Shallum son of Jabesh plotted against Zechariah and killed him in public.[y] Shallum then became king. [11-12]So the LORD had kept his promise to Jehu that the next four kings of Israel would come from his family.[z]

Everything else Zechariah did while he was king is written in *The History of the Kings of Israel*.

King Shallum of Israel

[13]Shallum became king of Israel in the thirty-ninth year of Azariah's[a] rule in Judah. But only one month after Shallum became king, [14-16]Menahem son of Gadi came to Samaria from Tirzah and killed him. Menahem then became king. The town of Tiphsah would not surrender to him, so he destroyed it and all the surrounding towns as far as Tirzah. He killed everyone living in Tiphsah, and with his sword he even ripped open pregnant women.

Everything else Shallum did while he was king, including his plot against Zechariah, is written in *The History of the Kings of Israel*.

King Menahem of Israel

[17]Menahem became king of Israel in Azariah's thirty-ninth year as king of Judah, and he ruled Israel ten years from Samaria. [18]He constantly disobeyed the LORD by following the example of Jeroboam son of Nebat, who had caused the Israelites to sin.

[19]During Menahem's rule, King Tiglath

---

[v]14.28 *how he recaptured . . . Hamath*: One possible meaning for the difficult Hebrew text.
[w]15.4 *local shrines*: See the note at 12.3.
[x]15.5 *leprosy*: See the note at 5.1. [y]15.10 *in public*: Hebrew; some manuscripts of one ancient translation "in Ibleam." [z]15.11,12 *So the LORD . . . family*: See 10.28-31. [a]15.13 *Azariah's*: The Hebrew text has "Uzziah's," another spelling of the name.

Pileser[b] of Assyria invaded Israel. He agreed to help Menahem keep control of his kingdom, if Menahem would pay him over thirty tons of silver. [20]So Menahem ordered every rich person in Israel to give him at least one pound of silver, and he gave it all to Tiglath Pileser, who stopped his attack and left Israel.

[21]Everything else Menahem did while he was king is written in *The History of the Kings of Israel.* [22]Menahem died, and his son Pekahiah became king.

King Pekahiah of Israel

[23]Pekahiah became king of Israel in the fiftieth year of Azariah's rule in Judah, and he ruled two years from Samaria. [24]He disobeyed the LORD and caused the Israelites to sin, just as Jeroboam son of Nebat had done.

[25]Pekah son of Remaliah was Pekahiah's chief officer, but he made plans to kill the king. So he and fifty men from Gilead broke into the strongest part of the palace in Samaria and murdered Pekahiah, together with Argob and Arieh.[c] Pekah then became king.

[26]Everything else Pekahiah did while he was king is written in *The History of the Kings of Israel.*

King Pekah of Israel

[27]Pekah son of Remaliah became king of Israel in Azariah's fifty-second year as king of Judah, and he ruled twenty years from Samaria. [28]He disobeyed the LORD and followed the evil example of Jeroboam son of Nebat, who had caused the Israelites to sin.

[29]During Pekah's rule, King Tiglath Pileser of Assyria marched into Israel. He captured the territories of Gilead and Galilee, including the towns of Ijon, Abel-Bethmaachah, Janoah, Kedesh, and Hazor, as well as the entire territory of Naphtali. Then he took Israelites from those regions to Assyria as prisoners.[d]

[30]In the twentieth year of Jotham's rule in Judah, Hoshea son of Elah plotted against Pekah and murdered him. Hoshea then became king of Israel.

[31]Everything else Pekah did while he was king is written in *The History of the Kings of Israel.*

King Jotham of Judah
(2 Chronicles 27.1-9)

[32]Jotham son of Azariah[e] became king of Judah in the second year of Pekah's rule in Israel. [33]Jotham was twenty-five years old when he became king, and he ruled sixteen years from Jerusalem. His mother Jerusha was the daughter of Zadok.

> *Successful parenting means:*
> *One, becoming what you*
> *should be. And two,*
> *staying close enough to the*
> *children for it to rub off.*
> ANNE ORTLUND

[34]Jotham followed the example of his father by obeying the LORD and doing right. [35]It was Jotham who rebuilt the Upper Gate that led into the court around the LORD's temple. But the local shrines were not destroyed, and they were still used as places for offering sacrifices.

[36]Everything else Jotham did while he was king is written in *The History of the Kings of Judah.* [37]During his rule, the LORD let King Rezin of Syria and King Pekah of Israel start attacking Judah. [38]Jotham died and was buried beside his ancestors in Jerusalem, and his son Ahaz became king.

King Ahaz of Judah
(2 Chronicles 28.1-27)

16 Ahaz son of Jotham became king of Judah in the seventeenth year of Pekah's rule in Israel. [2]He was twenty years old at the time, and he ruled from Jerusalem for sixteen years.

Ahaz wasn't like his ancestor David. Instead, he disobeyed the LORD [3]and was even more sinful than the kings of Israel. He sac-

---

[b]15.19 *Tiglath Pileser:* The Hebrew text has "Pul," another name for Tiglath Pileser, who ruled Assyria from 745 to 727 B.C.   [c]15.25 *together with Argob and Arieh:* One possible meaning for the difficult Hebrew text.
[d]15.29 *prisoners:* The events in this verse probably took place around 733 B.C.   [e]15.32 *Azariah:* See the note at 15.13.

rificed his own son, which was a disgusting custom of the nations that the LORD had forced out of Israel. ⁴Ahaz offered sacrifices at the local shrines, as well as on every hill and in the shade of large trees.

⁵⁻⁶While Ahaz was ruling Judah, the king of Edom recaptured the town of Elath from Judah and forced out the people of Judah. Edomitesʲ then moved into Elath, and they still live there.

About the same time, King Rezin of Syria and King Pekah of Israel marched to Jerusalem and attacked, but they could not capture it.

⁷Ahaz sent a message to King Tiglath Pileser of Assyria that said, "Your Majesty, King Rezin and King Pekah are attacking me, your loyal servant. Please come and rescue me." ⁸Along with the message, Ahaz sent silver and gold from the LORD's temple and from the palace treasury as a gift for the Assyrian king.

⁹As soon as Tiglath Pileser received the message, he and his troops marched to Syria. He captured the capital city of Damascus, then he took the people living there to the town of Kir as prisoners and killed King Rezin.ᵍ

¹⁰Later, Ahaz went to Damascus to meet Tiglath Pileser. And while Ahaz was there, he saw an altar and sent a model of it back to Uriah the priest, along with the plans for building one. ¹¹Uriah followed the plans and built an altar exactly like the one in Damascus, finishing it just before Ahaz came back.

¹²When Ahaz returned, he went to see the altar and to offer sacrifices on it. He walked up to the altar ¹³and poured wine over it. Then he offered sacrifices to please the LORD, to give him thanks, and to ask for his blessings.ʰ ¹⁴After that, he had the bronze altar moved aside,ⁱ so his new altar would be right in front of the LORD's temple. ¹⁵He told Uriah the priest:

From now on, the morning and evening sacrifices as well as all gifts of grain and wine are to be offered on this altar. The sacrifices for the people and for the king must also be offered here. Sprinkle the blood from all the sacrifices on it, but leave the bronze altar for me to use for prayer and finding out what God wants me to do.

¹⁶Uriah did everything Ahaz told him.

¹⁷Ahaz also had the side panels and the small bowls taken off the movable stands in the LORD's temple. He had the large bronze bowl, called the Sea, removed from the bronze bulls on which it rested and had it placed on a stand made of stone. ¹⁸He took down the special tent that was used for worship on the Sabbathʲ and closed up the private entrance that the kings of Judah used for going into the temple. He did all these things to please Tiglath Pileser.

¹⁹Everything else Ahaz did while he was king is written in *The History of the Kings of Judah*. ²⁰Ahaz died and was buried beside his ancestors in Jerusalem,ᵏ and his son Hezekiah became king.

King Hoshea of Israel

17 Hoshea son of Elah became king of Israel in the twelfth year of Ahaz's rule in Judah, and he ruled nine years from Samaria. ²Hoshea disobeyed the LORD and sinned, but not as much as the earlier Israelite kings had done.

³During Hoshea's rule, King Shalmaneser of Assyriaˡ invaded Israel; he took control of the country and made Hoshea pay taxes. ⁴But later, Hoshea refused to pay the taxes and asked King So of Egypt to help him rebel. When Shalmaneser found out, he arrested Hoshea and put him in prison.

Samaria Is Destroyed and the Israelites Are Taken to Assyria

⁵Shalmaneser invaded Israel and attacked the city of Samaria for three years, ⁶before capturing it in the ninth year of Hoshea's rule. The Assyrian kingᵐ took the

---

ʲ16.5,6 *the king of Edom . . . Edomites*: The Hebrew text has "King Rezin of Syria . . . Syrians"; in Hebrew, there is only one letter difference between "Edom" and "Aram," which is the usual Hebrew name for Syria in the Bible (see also 2 Chronicles 28.17). ᵍ16.9 *King Rezin*: This probably took place around 734 B.C., before the events in 15.29. ʰ16.13 *offered . . . blessings*: In traditional translations, these sacrifices are usually called "whole burnt offerings," "grain offerings," and "peace offerings." These are described in Leviticus 1–3. ⁱ16.14 *aside*: Hebrew "to the north." ʲ16.18 *the special tent . . . Sabbath*: One possible meaning for the difficult Hebrew text. ᵏ16.20 *Jerusalem*: See the note at 8.24. ˡ17.3 *King Shalmaneser of Assyria*: The son of Tiglath Pileser, who ruled Assyria from 727 to 722 B.C. ᵐ17.6 *The Assyrian king*: Probably Sargon, Shalmaneser's successor. Shalmaneser died after the city of Samaria was captured (722 B.C.) but before the people were taken away as prisoners (720 B.C.). Sargon ruled Assyria from 721 to 705 B.C.

Israelites away to Assyria as prisoners. He forced some of them to live in the town of Halah, others to live near the Habor River in the territory of Gozan, and still others to live in towns where the Median people lived.

⁷All of this happened because the people of Israel had sinned against the LORD their God, who had rescued them from Egypt, where they had been slaves. They worshiped foreign gods, ⁸followed the customs of the nations that the LORD had forced out of Israel, and were just as sinful as the Israelite kings. ⁹Even worse, the Israelites tried to hide their sins from the LORD their God. They built their own local shrines everywhere in Israel—from small towns to large, walled cities. ¹⁰They also built stone images of foreign gods and set up sacred poles[n] for the worship of Asherah on every hill and under every shady tree. ¹¹They offered sacrifices at the shrines,[o] just as the foreign nations had done before the LORD forced them out of Israel. They did sinful things that made the LORD very angry.

¹²Even though the LORD had commanded the Israelites not to worship idols,[p] they did it anyway. ¹³So the LORD made sure that every prophet warned Israel and Judah with these words: "I, the LORD, command you to stop doing sinful things and start obeying my laws and teachings! I gave them to your ancestors, and I told my servants the prophets to repeat them to you."

¹⁴But the Israelites would not listen; they were as stubborn as their ancestors who had refused to worship the LORD their God. ¹⁵They ignored the LORD's warnings and commands, and they rejected the solemn agreement he had made with their ancestors. They worshiped worthless idols and became worthless themselves. The LORD had told the Israelites not to do the things that the foreign nations around them were doing, but Israel became just like them.

¹⁶The people of Israel disobeyed all the commands of the LORD their God. They made two gold statues of calves and set up a sacred pole for Asherah; they also worshiped the stars and the god Baal. ¹⁷They used magic and witchcraft and even sacrificed their own children. The Israelites were determined to do whatever the LORD hated. ¹⁸The LORD became so furious with the people of Israel that he allowed them to be carried away as prisoners.

Only the people living in Judah were left, ¹⁹but they also disobeyed the LORD's commands and acted like the Israelites. ²⁰So the LORD turned his back on everyone in Israel and Judah[q] and let them be punished and defeated until no one was left.

²¹Earlier, when the LORD took the northern tribes away from David's family,[r] the people living in northern Israel chose Jeroboam son of Nebat as their king. Jeroboam caused the Israelites to sin and to stop worshiping the LORD. ²²The people kept on sinning like Jeroboam, ²³until the LORD got rid of them, just as he had warned his servants the prophets.

That's why the people of Israel were taken away as prisoners to Assyria, and that's where they remained.

Foreigners Are Resettled in Israel

²⁴The king of Assyria took people who were living in the cities of Babylon, Cuthah, Avva, Hamath, and Sepharvaim, and forced them to move to Israel. They took over the towns where the Israelites had lived, including the capital city of Samaria.

²⁵At first these people did not worship the LORD, so he sent lions to attack them, and the lions killed some of them. ²⁶A messenger told the king of Assyria, "The people you moved to Israel don't know how to worship the god of that country. So he sent lions that have attacked and killed some of them."

²⁷The king replied, "Get one of the Israelite priests we brought here and send him back to Israel. He can live there and teach them about the god of that country." ²⁸One of the Israelite priests was chosen to go back to Israel. He lived in Bethel and taught the people how to worship the LORD.

²⁹But in towns all over Israel, the different groups of people made statues of their own gods, then they placed these idols in local Israelite[s] shrines. ³⁰The people from Babylonia made the god Succoth-Benoth; those from Cuthah made the god Nergal;

---

[n]**17.10** *sacred poles*: See the note at 13.6, 7. [o]**17.11** *shrines*: See the note at 12.3. [p]**17.12** *the LORD . . . idols*: See Exodus 20.4, 5. [q]**17.20** *Israel and Judah*: Or "Israel," that is, the northern kingdom only. [r]**17.21** *when the LORD . . . family*: See 1 Kings 11.29-39. [s]**17.29** *Israelite*: The Hebrew text has "Samaritan," which is a later word to describe the people who lived in northern Israel at this time.

those from Hamath made Ashima; [31]those from Avva made Nibhaz and Tartak; and the people from Sepharvaim sacrificed their children to their own gods Adrammelech and Anammelech. [32-33]They worshiped their own gods, just as they had before they were taken away to Israel. They also worshiped the LORD, but they chose their own people to be priests at the shrines. [34]Everyone followed their old customs. None of them worshiped only the LORD, and they refused to obey the laws and commands that the LORD had given to the descendants of Jacob, the man he named Israel. [35]At the time when the LORD had made his solemn agreement with the people of Israel, he told them:

Do not worship any other gods! Do not bow down to them or offer them a sacrifice. [36]Worship only me! I am the one who rescued you from Egypt with my mighty power. Bow down to me and offer sacrifices. [37]Never worship any other god, always obey my laws and teachings, [38]and remember the solemn agreement between us.

I will say it again: Do not worship any god [39]except me. I am the LORD your God, and I will rescue you from all your enemies.

[40]But the people living in Israel ignored that command and kept on following their old customs. [41]They did worship the LORD, but they also worshiped their own idols. Their descendants did the same thing.

King Hezekiah of Judah

(2 Chronicles 29.1, 2; 31.1)

18 Hezekiah son of Ahaz became king of Judah in the third year of Hoshea's rule in Israel. [2]Hezekiah was twenty-five years old when he became king, and he ruled twenty-nine years from Jerusalem. His mother Abi was the daughter of Zechariah.

[3]Hezekiah obeyed the LORD, just as his ancestor David had done. [4]He destroyed the local shrines, then tore down the images of foreign gods and cut down the sacred pole for worshiping the goddess Asherah. He also smashed the bronze snake Moses had made. The people had named it Nehushtan[t] and had been offering sacrifices to it.

[5]Hezekiah trusted the LORD God of Israel. No other king of Judah was like Hezekiah, either before or after him. [6]He was completely faithful to the LORD and obeyed the laws the LORD had given to Moses for the people. [7]The LORD helped Hezekiah, so he was successful in everything he did. He even rebelled against the king of Assyria, refusing to be his servant. [8]Hezekiah defeated the Philistine towns as far away as Gaza—from the smallest towns to the large, walled cities.

How comforting it is to rely on God—who is omniscient—to supply me with wisdom. I habitually pray, "Father, you see what I don't; you follow where I can't. Make me aware of what I need to be aware of."

MAYO MATHERS

[9]During the fourth year of Hezekiah's rule, which was the seventh year of Hoshea's rule in Israel, King Shalmaneser of Assyria led his troops to Samaria, the capital city of Israel. They attacked [10]and captured it three years later,[u] in the sixth year of Hezekiah's rule and the ninth year of Hoshea's rule. [11]The king of Assyria[v] took the Israelites away as prisoners; he forced some of them to live in the town of Halah, others to live near the Habor River in the territory of Gozan, and still others to live in towns where the Median people lived. [12]All of that happened because the people of Israel had not obeyed the LORD their God. They rejected the solemn agreement he had made with them, and they ignored everything that the LORD's servant Moses had told them.

---

[t]**18.4** *the bronze snake . . . Nehushtan:* See Numbers 21.8, 9. "Nehushtan" is a nickname that sounds like the Hebrew words for "snake" and "bronze."

[u]**18.10** *three years later:* When the Israelites measured time, part of a year could be counted as a whole year. [v]**18.11** *The king of Assyria:* Probably Sargon, Shalmaneser's successor (see the note at 17.6).

King Sennacherib of Assyria Invades Judah

(2 Chronicles 32.1-19; Isaiah 36.1-22)

¹³In the fourteenth year of Hezekiah's rule in Judah, King Sennacherib of Assyria invaded the country and captured every walled city,ʷ except Jerusalem. ¹⁴Hezekiah sent this message to Sennacherib, who was in the town of Lachish: "I know I am guilty of rebellion. But I will pay you whatever you want, if you stop your attack."

Sennacherib told Hezekiah to pay about eleven tons of silver and almost a ton of gold. ¹⁵So Hezekiah collected all the silver from the LORD's temple and the royal treasury. ¹⁶He even stripped the gold that he had used to cover the doors and doorpostsˣ in the temple. He gave it all to Sennacherib.

¹⁷The king of Assyria ordered his three highest military officers to leave Lachish and take a large army to Jerusalem. When they arrived, the officers stood on the road near the cloth makers' shops along the canal from the upper pool. ¹⁸They called out to Hezekiah, and three of his highest officials came out to meet them. One of them was Hilkiah's son Eliakim, who was the prime minister. The other two were Shebna, assistant to the prime minister, and Joah son of Asaph, keeper of the government records.

¹⁹One of the Assyrian commanders told them:

I have a message for Hezekiah from the great king of Assyria. Ask Hezekiah why he feels so sure of himself. ²⁰Does he think he can plan and win a war with nothing but words? Who is going to help him, now that he has turned against the king of Assyria? ²¹Is he depending on Egypt and its king? That's the same as leaning on a broken stick, and it will go right through his hand.

²²Is Hezekiah now depending on the LORD your God? Didn't Hezekiah tear down all except one of the LORD's altars and places of worship?ʸ Didn't he tell the people of Jerusalem and Judah to worship at that one place?

²³The king of Assyria wants to make a bet with you people. He will give you two thousand horses, if you have enough troops to ride them. ²⁴How could you even defeat our lowest ranking officer, when you have to depend on Egypt for chariots and cavalry? ²⁵Don't forget that it was the LORD who sent me here with orders to destroy your nation!

²⁶Eliakim, Shebna, and Joah said, "Sir, we don't want the people listening from the city wall to understand what you are saying. So please speak to us in Aramaic instead of Hebrew."

²⁷The Assyrian army commander answered, "My king sent me to speak to everyone, not just to you leaders. These people will soon have to eat their own body waste and drink their own urine! And so will the three of you."

²⁸Then, in a voice loud enough for everyone to hear, he shouted in Hebrew:

Listen to what the great king of Assyria says! ²⁹Don't be fooled by Hezekiah. He can't save you. ³⁰Don't trust him when he tells you that the LORD will protect you from the king of Assyria. ³¹Stop listening to Hezekiah! Pay attention to my king. Surrender to him. He will let you keep your own vineyards, fig trees, and cisterns ³²for a while. Then he will come and take you away to a country just like yours, where you can plant vineyards, raise your own grain, and have plenty of olive oil and honey. Believe me, you won't starve there.

Hezekiah claims the LORD will save you. But don't be fooled by him. ³³Were any other gods able to defend their land against the king of Assyria? ³⁴What happened to the gods of Hamath and Arpad? What about the gods of Sepharvaim, Hena, and Ivvah? Were the gods of Samaria able to protect their land against the Assyrian forces? ³⁵None of these gods kept their people safe from the king of Assyria. Do you think the LORD your God can do any better?

ʷ**18.13** *King Sennacherib . . . walled city*: Sennacherib ruled Assyria 705-681 B.C., and this event probably took place in 701 B.C. ˣ**18.16** *doorposts*: One possible meaning for the difficult Hebrew text. ʸ**18.22** *worship*: Hezekiah actually had torn down the places where idols were worshiped, and he had told the people to worship the LORD at the one place of worship in Jerusalem. But the Assyrian leader was confused and thought these were also places where the LORD was supposed to be worshiped.

³⁶⁻³⁷Eliakim, Shebna, and Joah had been warned by King Hezekiah not to answer the Assyrian commander. So they tore their clothes in sorrow and reported to Hezekiah everything the commander had said.

Hezekiah Asks Isaiah the Prophet for Advice
(Isaiah 37.1-13)

19 As soon as Hezekiah heard the news, he tore off his clothes in sorrow and put on sackcloth. Then he went into the temple of the LORD. ²He told Prime Minister Eliakim, Assistant Prime Minister Shebna, and the senior priests to dress in sackcloth and tell the prophet Isaiah:

³These are difficult and disgraceful times. Our nation is like a woman too weak to give birth, when it's time for her baby to be born. ⁴Please pray for those of us who are left alive. The king of Assyria sent his army commander to insult the living God. Perhaps the LORD heard what he said and will do something, if you will pray.

⁵When these leaders went to Isaiah, ⁶he told them that the LORD had this message for Hezekiah:

I am the LORD. Don't worry about the insulting things that have been said about me by these messengers from the king of Assyria. ⁷I will upset him with rumors about what's happening in his own country. He will go back, and there I will make him die a violent death.

⁸Meanwhile, the commander of the Assyrian forces heard that his king had left the town of Lachish and was now attacking Libnah. So he went there.

⁹About this same time the king of Assyria learned that King Tirhakah of Ethiopia^z was on his way to attack him. Then the king of Assyria sent some messengers with this note for Hezekiah:

¹⁰Don't trust your God or be fooled by his promise to defend Jerusalem against me. ¹¹You have heard how we Assyrian kings have completely wiped out other nations. What makes you feel so safe? ¹²The Assyrian kings before me destroyed the towns of Gozan, Haran, Rezeph, and everyone from

^z**19.9** *Ethiopia:* The Hebrew text has "Cush," which was a region south of Egypt that included parts of the present countries of Ethiopia and Sudan.

SpiritualLife—How should I pray? (2 Kings 19.14-19)

Be specific when you present your requests.
Hezekiah was in trouble. He was the king of the nation of Judah (the two southern tribes). The other ten tribes had been conquered by the vicious Assyrians. Now, twenty years later, the Assyrian king was camped just outside the walls of Hezekiah's capital city, Jerusalem, threatening to destroy the city and take all its people captive. He even sent Hezekiah a letter warning him that God wouldn't be able to help.

Hezekiah was greatly distressed. So he took the Assyrian king's letter into the temple, into God's presence. Then he asked the Lord to deliver Judah so the nations all around them would be able to see God's greatness. God answered his prayer and saved Judah from the Assyrians.

This story reveals two important things about prayer.

First, God wants to hear your specific requests. Don't be afraid to ask God to take care of each trouble or difficulty that seems to be attacking you. Then ask God to take care of each one.

Second, God will always protect his reputation. Instead of praying for your own selfish desires, ask God to show others how great he is. Pray that his acts on your behalf will display his power and righteousness to those who don't know him. (See also 2 Samuel 7.18-29; 2 Chronicles 6,7; Nehemiah 1; Psalm 85; Lamentations 5; Matthew 6.5-15; Acts 4.23-31.)

Words To Remember: *Then everyone in every kingdom on earth will know that you are the only God.—2 Kings 19.19*

Eden who lived in Telassar. What good did their gods do them? ¹³The kings of Hamath, Arpad, Sepharvaim, Hena, and Ivvah have all disappeared.

Hezekiah Prays
(Isaiah 37.14-20)

¹⁴After Hezekiah had read the note from the king of Assyria, he took it to the temple and spread it out for the LORD to see. ¹⁵He prayed:

LORD God of Israel, your throne is above the winged creatures.^a You created the heavens and the earth, and you alone rule the kingdoms of this world. ¹⁶But just look how Sennacherib has insulted you, the living God.

¹⁷It is true, our LORD, that Assyrian kings have turned nations into deserts. ¹⁸They destroyed the idols of wood and stone that the people of those nations had made and worshiped. ¹⁹But you are our LORD and our God! We ask you to keep us safe from the Assyrian king. Then everyone in every kingdom on earth will know that you are the only God.

The LORD's Answer to Hezekiah
(Isaiah 37.21-35)

²⁰Isaiah went to Hezekiah and told him that the LORD God of Israel had said:

Hezekiah, I heard your prayer about King Sennacherib of Assyria. ²¹Now this is what I say to that king:

The people of Jerusalem
hate and make fun of you;
   they laugh
   behind your back.

²²Sennacherib, you cursed,
   shouted, and sneered at me,
      the holy God of Israel.
²³You let your officials
      insult me, the Lord.
And here is what you
      have said about yourself,
"I led my chariots
   to the highest heights
      of Lebanon's mountains.
I went deep into its forest,
   cutting down the best cedar
      and cypress trees.
²⁴I dried up every stream

in the land of Egypt,
   and I drank water
      from wells I had dug."

²⁵Sennacherib, now listen
      to me, the Lord.
I planned all this long ago.
And you don't even realize
      that I alone am the one
who decided that you
      would do these things.
I let you make ruins
      of fortified cities.
²⁶Their people became weak,
      terribly confused.
They were like wild flowers
   or tender young grass
      growing on a flat roof,
scorched before it matures.^b

²⁷I know all about you,
   even how fiercely angry
      you are with me.
²⁸I have seen your pride
   and the tremendous hatred
      you have for me.
Now I will put a hook
   in your nose,
      a bit in your mouth,^c
then I will send you back
      to where you came from.

²⁹Hezekiah, I will tell you what's going to happen. This year you will eat crops that grow on their own, and the next year you will eat whatever springs up where those crops grew. But the third year you will plant grain and vineyards, and you will eat what you harvest. ³⁰Those who survive in Judah will be like a vine that puts down deep roots and bears fruit. ³¹I, the LORD All-Powerful, will see to it that some who live in Jerusalem will survive.

³²I promise that the king of Assyria won't get into Jerusalem, or shoot an

---

^a**19.15** *winged creatures:* Two winged creatures made of gold were on the top of the sacred chest and were symbols of the LORD's throne on earth (see Exodus 25.18; 2 Samuel 6.2).   ^b**19.26** *tender young grass . . . matures:* Many of the houses had roofs made of packed earth. Grass would sometimes grow out of the roof, but would die quickly because of the sun and hot winds.   ^c**19.28** *I will put . . . your mouth:* This is how the Assyrians treated their prisoners, and now the LORD will treat Sennacherib the same way.

arrow into the city, or even surround it and prepare to attack. ³³As surely as I am the LORD, he will return by the way he came and will never enter Jerusalem. ³⁴I will protect it for myself and for my servant David.

The Death of King Sennacherib
(Isaiah 37.36-38)

³⁵That same night the LORD sent an angel to the camp of the Assyrians, and he killed one hundred eighty-five thousand of them. And so the next morning, the camp was full of dead bodies. ³⁶After this King Sennacherib went back to Assyria and lived in the city of Nineveh. ³⁷One day he was worshiping in the temple of his god Nisroch, when his sons, Adrammelech and Sharezer, killed him with their swords. They escaped to the land of Ararat, and his son Esarhaddon became king.*ᵈ*

Hezekiah Gets Sick and Almost Dies
(2 Chronicles 32.24-26; Isaiah 38.1-8, 21, 22)

20 About this time, Hezekiah got sick and was almost dead. Isaiah the prophet went in and told him, "The LORD says you won't ever get well. You are going to die, so you had better start doing what needs to be done."

²Hezekiah turned toward the wall and prayed, ³"Don't forget that I have been faithful to you, LORD. I have obeyed you with all my heart, and I do whatever you say is right." After this, he cried hard.

god is working in our lives!

RACHAEL CRABB

⁴Before Isaiah got to the middle court of the palace, ⁵the LORD sent him back to Hezekiah with this message:

Hezekiah, you are the ruler of my people, and I am the LORD God, who was worshiped by your ancestor David. I heard you pray, and I saw you cry. I will heal you, so that three days from now you will be able to worship

in my temple. ⁶I will let you live fifteen years more, while I protect you and your city from the king of Assyria. I will defend this city as an honor to me and to my servant David.

⁷Then Isaiah said to the king's servants, "Bring some mashed figs and place them on the king's open sore. He will then get well."

⁸Hezekiah asked Isaiah, "Can you prove that the LORD will heal me, so that I can worship in his temple in three days?"

⁹Isaiah replied, "The LORD will prove to you that he will keep his promise. Will the shadow made by the setting sun on the stairway go forward ten steps or back ten steps?"*ᵉ*

¹⁰"It's normal for the sun to go forward," Hezekiah answered. "But how can it go back?"

¹¹Isaiah prayed, and the LORD made the shadow go back ten steps on the stairway built for King Ahaz.*ᶠ*

The LORD Is Still with Hezekiah
(Isaiah 39.1-8)

¹²Merodach*ᵍ* Baladan, the son of Baladan, was now king of Babylonia.*ʰ* And when he learned that Hezekiah had been sick, he sent messengers with letters and a gift for him. ¹³Hezekiah welcomed*ⁱ* the messengers and showed them all the silver, the gold, the spices, and the fine oils that were in his storehouse. He even showed them where he kept his weapons. Nothing in his palace or in his entire kingdom was kept hidden from them.

¹⁴Isaiah asked Hezekiah, "Where did these men come from? What did they want?"

"They came all the way from Babylonia," Hezekiah answered.

¹⁵"What did you show them?" Isaiah asked.

Hezekiah answered, "I showed them everything in my kingdom."

¹⁶Then Isaiah told Hezekiah:
    I have a message for you from the

---

*ᵈ*19.37 *Esarhaddon became king:* Ruled Assyria 681-669 B.C.   *ᵉ*20.9 *Will . . . steps:* One possible meaning for the difficult Hebrew text.   *ᶠ*20.11 *the shadow . . . Ahaz:* One possible meaning for the difficult Hebrew text.   *ᵍ*20.12 *Merodach:* The Hebrew text has "Berodach," another spelling of the name.   *ʰ*20.12 *Merodach Baladan . . . Babylonia:* Ruled Babylonia 722-710 and 704-703 B.C.   *ⁱ*20.13 *welcomed:* Or "listened to."

LORD. [17]One day everything you and your ancestors have stored up will be taken to Babylonia. The LORD has promised that nothing will be left. [18]Some of your own sons will be taken to Babylonia, where they will be disgraced and made to serve in the king's palace. [19]Hezekiah thought, "At least our nation will be at peace for a while." So he told Isaiah, "The message you brought me from the LORD is good."

Hezekiah Dies
(2 Chronicles 32.32, 33)

[20]Everything else Hezekiah did while he was king, including how he made the upper pool and tunnel to bring water into Jerusalem, is written in The History of the Kings of Judah. [21]Hezekiah died, and his son Manasseh became king.

King Manasseh of Judah
(2 Chronicles 33.1-20)

21 Manasseh was twelve years old when he became king of Judah, and he ruled fifty-five years from Jerusalem. His mother was Hephzibah. [2]Manasseh disobeyed the LORD by following the disgusting customs of the nations that the LORD had forced out of Israel. [3]He rebuilt the local shrines that his father Hezekiah had torn down. He built altars for the god Baal and set up a sacred pole for worshiping the goddess Asherah, just as King Ahab of Israel had done. And he faithfully worshiped the stars in heaven.

[4]In the temple, where only the LORD was supposed to be worshiped, Manasseh built altars for pagan gods [5]and for the stars. He placed these altars in both courts of the temple, [6-7]and even set up the pole for Asherah there. Manasseh practiced magic and witchcraft; he asked fortunetellers for advice and sacrificed his own son. He did many sinful things and made the LORD very angry.

Years ago the LORD had told David and his son Solomon:

Jerusalem is the place I prefer above all others in Israel. It belongs to me, and there I will be worshiped forever. [8]If my people will faithfully obey all the commands in the Law of my servant Moses, I will never make them leave the land I gave to their ancestors.

[9]But the people of Judah disobeyed the LORD. They listened to Manasseh and did even more sinful things than the nations the LORD had wiped out.

[10]One day the LORD said to some of his prophets:

[11]King Manasseh has done more disgusting things than the Amorites,[j] and he has led my people to sin by forcing them to worship his idols. [12]Now I, the LORD God of Israel, will destroy both Jerusalem and Judah! People will hear about it but won't believe it. [13]Jerusalem is as sinful as Ahab and the people of Samaria were. So I will wipe out Jerusalem and be done with it, just as someone wipes water off a plate and turns it over to dry.

[14]I will even get rid of my people who survive. They will be defeated and robbed by their enemies. [15]My people have done what I hate and have not stopped making me angry since their ancestors left Egypt.

[16]Manasseh was guilty of causing the people of Judah to sin and disobey the LORD. He also refused to protect innocent people—he even let so many of them be killed[k] that their blood filled the streets of Jerusalem.

[17]Everything else Manasseh did while he was king, including his terrible sins, is written in The History of the Kings of Judah. [18]He died and was buried in Uzza Garden near his palace, and his son Amon became king.

King Amon of Judah
(2 Chronicles 33.21-25)

[19]Amon was twenty-two years old when he became king of Judah, and he ruled from Jerusalem for two years. His mother Meshullemeth was the daughter of Haruz from Jotbah. [20]Amon disobeyed the LORD, just as his father Manasseh had done. [21]Amon worshiped the idols Manasseh had made and [22]refused to be faithful to the LORD, the God his ancestors had worshiped.

[23]Some of Amon's officials plotted against him and killed him in his palace. [24-26]He was buried in Uzza Garden. Soon

---

[j]21.11 Amorites: Here used in the general sense of nations that lived in Canaan before the Israelites.
[k]21.16 He also refused . . . killed: Or "He killed so many innocent people."

after that, the people of Judah killed the murderers of Amon, then they made his son Josiah king.

Everything else Amon did while he was king is written in *The History of the Kings of Judah*.

King Josiah of Judah
(2 Chronicles 34.1, 2)

22 Josiah was eight years old when he became king of Judah, and he ruled thirty-one years from Jerusalem. His mother Jedidah was the daughter of Adaiah from Bozkath. [2]Josiah always obeyed the LORD, just as his ancestor David had done.

Hilkiah Finds *The Book of God's Law*
(2 Chronicles 34.8-28)

[3]After Josiah had been king for eighteen years, he told Shaphan,[*l*] one of his highest officials:

Go to the LORD's temple [4]and ask Hilkiah the high priest to collect from the guards all the money that the people have donated. [5]Have Hilkiah give it to the men supervising the repairs to the temple. They can use some of the money to pay [6]the workers, and with the rest of it they can buy wood and stone for the repair work. [7]They are honest, so we won't ask them to keep track of the money.

[8]While Shaphan was at the temple, Hilkiah handed him a book and said, "Look what I found here in the temple—*The Book of God's Law*."

Shaphan read it, [9]then went back to Josiah and reported, "Your officials collected the money in the temple and gave it to the men supervising the repairs. [10]But there's something else, Your Majesty. The priest Hilkiah gave me this book." Then Shaphan read it out loud.

[11]When Josiah heard what was in *The Book of God's Law*, he tore his clothes in sorrow. [12]At once he called together Hilkiah, Shaphan, Ahikam son of Shaphan, Achbor son of Micaiah, and his own servant Asaiah. He said, [13]"The LORD must be furious with me and everyone else in Judah, because our ancestors did not obey the laws written in this book. Go find out what the LORD wants us to do."

[14]The five men left right away and went to talk with Huldah the prophet. Her husband was Shallum,[*m*] who was in charge of the king's clothes. Huldah lived in the northern part of Jerusalem, and when they met in her home, [15]she said:

> *Pass on godly legacies in your own home and in the community around you. What a joy it would be to have someone say to you, down the road, "I learned about God through your love and belief in me!"*
>
> TWILA PARIS

You were sent here by King Josiah, and this is what the LORD God of Israel says to him: [16]"Josiah, I am the LORD! And I will see to it that this country and everyone living in it will be destroyed. It will happen just as this book says. [17]The people of Judah have rejected me. They have offered sacrifices to foreign gods and have worshiped their own idols. I cannot stand it any longer. I am furious.

[18]"Josiah, listen to what I am going to do. [19]I noticed how sad you were when you read that this country and its people would be completely wiped out. You even tore your clothes in sorrow, and I heard you cry. [20]So I will let you die in peace, before I destroy this place."

The men left and took Huldah's answer back to Josiah.

Josiah Reads *The Book of God's Law*
(2 Chronicles 34.29-33)

23 King Josiah called together the older leaders of Judah and Jerusalem. [2]Then he went to the

---

[*l*]**22.3** *Shaphan:* Hebrew "Shaphan son of Azaliah son of Meshullam."   [*m*]**22.14** *Shallum:* Hebrew "Shallum son of Tikvah son of Harhas."

LORD's temple, together with the people of Judah and Jerusalem, the priests, and the prophets. Finally, when everybody was there, he read aloud *The Book of God's Law*[n] that had been found in the temple.

³After Josiah had finished reading, he stood by one of the columns. He asked the people to promise in the LORD's name to faithfully obey the LORD and to follow his commands. The people agreed to do everything written in the book.

Josiah Follows the Teachings of God's Law
(2 Chronicles 34.3-7)

⁴Josiah told Hilkiah the priest, the assistant priests, and the guards at the temple door to go into the temple and bring out the things used to worship Baal, Asherah, and the stars. Josiah had these things burned in Kidron Valley just outside Jerusalem, and he had the ashes carried away to the town of Bethel.

⁵Josiah also got rid of the pagan priests at the local shrines in Judah and around Jerusalem. These were the men that the kings of Judah had appointed to offer sacrifices to Baal and to the sun, moon, and stars. ⁶Josiah had the sacred pole[o] for Asherah brought out of the temple and taken to Kidron Valley, where it was burned. He then had its ashes ground into dust and scattered over the public cemetery there. ⁷He had the buildings torn down where the male prostitutes[p] lived next to the temple, and where the women wove sacred robes[q] for the idol of Asherah.

⁸In almost every town in Judah, priests had been offering sacrifices to the LORD at local shrines.[r] Josiah brought these priests to Jerusalem and had their shrines made unfit for worship—every shrine from Geba just north of Jerusalem to Beersheba in the south. He even tore down the shrine at Beersheba that was just to the left of Joshua Gate, which was named after the highest official of the city. ⁹Those local priests could not serve at the LORD's altar in Jerusalem, but they were allowed to eat sacred bread,[s] just like the priests from Jerusalem.

¹⁰Josiah sent some men to Hinnom Valley just outside Jerusalem with orders to make the altar there unfit for worship. That way, people could no longer use it for sacrificing their children to the god Molech. ¹¹He

also got rid of the horses that the kings of Judah used in their ceremonies to worship the sun, and he destroyed the chariots along with them. The horses had been kept near the entrance to the LORD's temple, in a courtyard[t] close to where an official named Nathan-Melech lived.

> *God's Word acts like a time-release vitamin. When we put it into our mind, we may not immediately feel it working, but one day we realize we have the ability to overcome a temptation or the answer to a problem.*
>
> KATHY PEEL

¹²Some of the kings of Judah, especially Manasseh, had built altars in the two courts of the temple and in the room that Ahaz had built on the palace roof. Josiah had these altars torn down and smashed to pieces, and he had the pieces thrown into Kidron Valley, just outside Jerusalem. ¹³After that, he closed down the shrines that Solomon had built east of Jerusalem and south of Spoil Hill to honor Astarte the disgusting goddess of Sidon, Chemosh the disgusting god of Moab, and Milcom the disgusting god of

---

[n]**23.2** *The Book of God's Law:* The Hebrew text has "The Book of God's Agreement," which is the same as "The Book of God's Law" in 22.8, 11. In traditional translations this is called "The Book of the Covenant." [o]**23.6** *sacred pole:* See the note at 13.6, 7. [p]**23.7** *male prostitutes:* Young men or boys sometimes served as prostitutes in the worship of Canaanite gods, but the LORD had forbidden the people of Israel and Judah to worship in this way (see Deuteronomy 23.17, 18). [q]**23.7** *sacred robes:* Or "coverings." [r]**23.8** *local shrines:* See the note at 12.3. [s]**23.9** *sacred bread:* The Hebrew text has "thin bread," which may be either the pieces of thin bread made without yeast to be eaten during the Passover Festival (see verses 21-23) or the baked flour used in sacrifices to give thanks to the LORD (see Leviticus 2.4, 5). [t]**23.11** *in a courtyard:* One possible meaning for the difficult Hebrew text.

Ammon.[u] [14]He tore down the stone images of foreign gods and cut down the sacred pole used in the worship of Asherah. Then he had the whole area covered with human bones.[v]

[15]But Josiah was not finished yet. At Bethel he destroyed the shrine and the altar that Jeroboam son of Nebat had built and that had caused the Israelites to sin. Josiah had the shrine and the Asherah pole burned and ground into dust. [16]As he looked around, he saw graves on the hillside. He had the bones in them dug up and burned on the altar, so that it could no longer be used. This happened just as God's prophet had said when Jeroboam was standing at the altar, celebrating a festival.[w]

Then Josiah saw the grave of the prophet who had said this would happen [17]and he asked,[x] "Whose grave is that?"

Some people who lived nearby answered, "It belongs to the prophet from Judah who told what would happen to this altar."

[18]Josiah replied, "Then leave it alone. Don't dig up his bones." So they did not disturb his bones or the bones of the old prophet from Israel who had also been buried there.[y]

[19]Some of the Israelite kings had made the LORD angry by building pagan shrines all over Israel. So Josiah sent troops to destroy these shrines just as he had done to the one in Bethel. [20]He killed the priests who served at them and burned their bones on the altars.

After all that, Josiah went back to Jerusalem.

Josiah and the People of Judah Celebrate Passover
(2 Chronicles 35.1-19)

[21]Josiah told the people of Judah, "Celebrate Passover in honor of the LORD your God, just as it says in *The Book of God's Law*."[z]
[22]This festival had not been celebrated in this way since kings ruled Israel and Judah. [23]But in Josiah's eighteenth year as king of Judah, everyone came to Jerusalem to celebrate Passover.

The LORD Is Still Angry at the People of Judah

[24]Josiah got rid of every disgusting person and thing in Judah and Jerusalem—in-

cluding magicians, fortunetellers, and idols. He did his best to obey every law written in the book that the priest Hilkiah found in the LORD's temple. [25]No other king before or after Josiah tried as hard as he did to obey the Law of Moses.

[26]But the LORD was still furious with the people of Judah because Manasseh had done so many things to make him angry. [27]The LORD said, "I will desert the people of Judah, just as I deserted the people of Israel. I will reject Jerusalem, even though I chose it to be mine. And I will abandon this temple built to honor me."

Josiah Dies in Battle
(2 Chronicles 35.20—36.1)

[28]Everything else Josiah did while he was king is written in *The History of the Kings of Judah*. [29]During Josiah's rule, King Neco of Egypt led his army north to the Euphrates River to help the king of Assyria. Josiah led his troops north to fight Neco, but when they met in battle at Megiddo, Josiah was killed.[a] [30]A few of Josiah's servants put his body in a chariot and took it back to Jerusalem, where they buried it in his own tomb. Then the people of Judah found his son Jehoahaz and poured olive oil on his head to show that he was their new king.

King Jehoahaz of Judah
(2 Chronicles 36.2-4)

[31]Jehoahaz was twenty-three years old when he became king of Judah, and he ruled from Jerusalem only three months. His mother Hamutal was the daughter of Jeremiah from Libnah. [32]Jehoahaz disobeyed the LORD, just as some of his ancestors had done.

[33]King Neco of Egypt had Jehoahaz arrested and put in prison at Riblah[b] near Ha-

---

[u]**23.13** *the shrines . . . Ammon:* See 1 Kings 11.5-7.
[v]**23.14** *Then he . . . human bones:* This made the whole area unfit for the worship of any god.   [w]**23.16** *just . . . festival:* See 1 Kings 13.1, 2.   [x]**23.16,17** *said when Jeroboam . . . asked:* One ancient translation; Hebrew "said. [17]Then Josiah asked."   [y]**23.18** *old prophet . . . there:* See 1 Kings 13.11-32.   [z]**23.21** *The Book of God's Law:* See the note at verse 2.   [a]**23.29** *killed:* At this time, King Neco of Egypt (609-595 B.C.) was fighting on the side of the Assyrians. He marched north to fight the Babylonian army and help Assyria keep control of its land. Since Josiah considered Assyria an enemy, he set out to stop Neco and the Egyptian troops. [b]**23.33** *Riblah:* An important town in Syria on the Orontes River.

math. Then he forced the people of Judah to pay him almost four tons of silver and about seventy-five pounds of gold as taxes. ³⁴Neco appointed Josiah's son Eliakim king of Judah, and changed his name to Jehoiakim. He took Jehoahaz as a prisoner to Egypt, where he died.

³⁵Jehoiakim forced the people of Judah to pay higher taxes, so he could give Neco the silver and gold he demanded.

King Jehoiakim of Judah
(2 Chronicles 36.5-8)

³⁶Jehoiakim was twenty-five years old when he was appointed king, and he ruled eleven years from Jerusalem. His mother Zebidah was the daughter of Pedaiah from Rumah. ³⁷Jehoiakim disobeyed the LORD by following the example of his ancestors.

24 During Jehoiakim's rule, King Nebuchadnezzar of Babylonia^c invaded and took control of Judah. Jehoiakim obeyed Nebuchadnezzar for three years, but then he rebelled.

²At that time, the LORD started sending troops to rob and destroy towns in Judah. Some of these troops were from Babylonia, and others were from Syria, Moab, and Ammon. The LORD had sent his servants the prophets to warn Judah about this, ³and now he was making it happen. The country of Judah was going to be wiped out, because Manasseh had sinned ⁴and caused many innocent people to die. The LORD would not forgive this.

⁵Everything else Jehoiakim did while he was king is written in *The History of the Kings of Judah*. ⁶Jehoiakim died, and his son Jehoiachin became king.

⁷King Nebuchadnezzar defeated King Neco of Egypt and took control of his land from the Egyptian Gorge all the way north to the Euphrates River. So Neco never invaded Judah again.^d

King Jehoiachin of Judah
Is Taken to Babylon
(2 Chronicles 36.9, 10)

⁸Jehoiachin was eighteen years old when he became king of Judah, and he ruled only three months from Jerusalem. His mother Nehushta was the daughter of Elnathan from Jerusalem. ⁹Jehoiachin disobeyed the LORD, just as his father Jehoiakim had done.

¹⁰King Nebuchadnezzar of Babylonia sent troops to attack Jerusalem soon after Jehoiachin became king. ¹¹During the attack, Nebuchadnezzar himself arrived at the city. ¹²Jehoiachin immediately surrendered, together with his mother and his servants, as well as his army officers and officials. Then Nebuchadnezzar had Jehoiachin arrested. These things took place in the eighth year of Nebuchadnezzar's rule in Babylonia.^e

¹³The LORD had warned^f that someday the treasures would be taken from the royal palace and from the temple, including the gold objects that Solomon had made for the temple. And that's exactly what Nebuchadnezzar ordered his soldiers to do. ¹⁴He also led away as prisoners the Jerusalem officials, the military leaders, and the skilled workers—ten thousand in all. Only the very poorest people were left in Judah.

¹⁵Nebuchadnezzar took Jehoiachin to Babylon, along with his mother, his wives, his officials, and the most important leaders of Judah. ¹⁶He also led away seven thousand soldiers, one thousand skilled workers, and anyone who would be useful in battle.

¹⁷Then Nebuchadnezzar appointed Jehoiachin's uncle Mattaniah king of Judah and changed his name to Zedekiah.

King Zedekiah of Judah
(2 Chronicles 36.11-16; Jeremiah 52.1-3)

¹⁸Zedekiah was twenty-one years old when he was appointed king of Judah, and he ruled from Jerusalem for eleven years. His mother Hamutal was the daughter of Jeremiah from Libnah. ¹⁹Zedekiah disobeyed the LORD, just as Jehoiakim had done. ²⁰It was Zedekiah who finally rebelled against Nebuchadnezzar.

The people of Judah and Jerusalem had made the LORD so angry that he finally turned his back on them. That's why these horrible things were happening.

---

^c**24.1** *King Nebuchadnezzar of Babylonia*: Ruled Babylonia 605-562 B.C. ^d**24.7** *again*: Nebuchadnezzar defeated the Egyptian army in 605 B.C. at the town of Carchemish. But a few years later, he was forced to retreat all the way back to Babylonia, which allowed Jehoiakim to rebel (see verse 1). ^e**24.12** *Babylonia*: These events took place in 597 B.C. ^f**24.13** *warned*: See 20.16-18.

Jerusalem Is Captured and Destroyed
(2 Chronicles 36.17-21; Jeremiah 52.3-30)

25 In Zedekiah's ninth year as king, on the tenth day of the tenth month,[g] King Nebuchadnezzar of Babylonia led his entire army to attack Jerusalem. The troops set up camp outside the city and built ramps up to the city walls. [2-3]After a year and a half, all the food in Jerusalem was gone. Then on the ninth day of the fourth[h] month, [4]the Babylonian troops broke through the city wall.[i] That same night, Zedekiah and his soldiers tried to escape through the gate near the royal garden, even though they knew the enemy had the city surrounded. They headed toward the desert, [5]but the Babylonian troops caught up with them near Jericho. They arrested Zedekiah, but his soldiers scattered in every direction.

[6]Zedekiah was taken to Riblah, where Nebuchadnezzar put him on trial and found him guilty. [7]Zedekiah's sons were killed right in front of him. His eyes were then poked out, and he was put in chains and dragged off to Babylon.

[8]About a month later,[j] in Nebuchadnezzar's nineteenth year as king, Nebuzaradan, who was his official in charge of the guards, arrived in Jerusalem. [9]Nebuzaradan burned down the LORD's temple, the king's palace, and every important building in the city, as well as all the houses. [10]Then he ordered the Babylonian soldiers to break down the walls around Jerusalem. [11]He led away as prisoners the people left in the city, including those who had become loyal to Nebuchadnezzar. [12]Only some of the poorest people were left behind to work the vineyards and the fields.

[13]The Babylonian soldiers took the two bronze columns that stood in front of the temple, the ten movable bronze stands, and the large bronze bowl called the Sea. They broke them into pieces so they could take the bronze to Babylonia. [14]They carried off the bronze things used for worship at the temple, including the pans for hot ashes, and the shovels, snuffers, and also the dishes for incense, [15]as well as the fire pans and the sprinkling bowls. Nebuzaradan ordered his soldiers to take everything made of gold or silver.

[16]The pile of bronze from the columns, the stands, and the large bowl that Solomon had made for the temple was too large to be weighed. [17]Each column had been twenty-seven feet tall with a bronze cap four and a half feet high. These caps were decorated with bronze designs—some of them like chains and others like pomegranates.[k]

[18]Next, Nebuzaradan arrested Seraiah the chief priest, Zephaniah his assistant, and three temple officials. [19]Then he arrested one of the army commanders, the king's five personal advisors, and the officer in charge of gathering the troops for battle. He also found sixty more soldiers who were still in Jerusalem. [20]Nebuzaradan led them all to Riblah [21]near Hamath, where Nebuchadnezzar had them killed.

The people of Judah no longer lived in their own country.

Gedaliah Is Made Ruler of the People Left in Judah
(Jeremiah 40.7-9; 41.1-3)

[22]King Nebuchadnezzar appointed Gedaliah son of Ahikam[l] to rule the few people still living in Judah. [23]When the army officers and troops heard that Gedaliah was their ruler, the officers met with him at Mizpah. These men were Ishmael son of Nethaniah, Johanan son of Kareah, Seraiah son of Tanhumeth from Netophah, and Jaazaniah from Maacah.

[24]Gedaliah said to them, "Everything will be fine, I promise. We don't need to be afraid of the Babylonian rulers, if we live here peacefully and do what Nebuchadnezzar says."

[25]Ishmael[m] was from the royal family. And about two months after Gedaliah began his rule,[n] Ishmael and ten other men went to Mizpah. They killed Gedaliah and his officials, including those from Judah and those from Babylonia. [26]After that, the army officers and all the people in Mizpah, whether

---

[g]25.1 *tenth month:* Tebeth, the tenth month of the Hebrew calendar, from about mid-December to mid-January. [h]25.2,3 *fourth:* This word is not in the Hebrew text here, but see the parallel in Jeremiah 52.5, 6. [i]25.4 *wall:* Jerusalem was destroyed in 586 B.C. [j]25.8 *About a month later:* Hebrew "On the seventh day of the fifth month." [k]25.17 *pomegranates:* A bright red fruit that looks like an apple. [l]25.22 *Ahikam:* Hebrew "Ahikam son of Shaphan." [m]25.25 *Ishmael:* Hebrew "Ishmael son of Nethaniah son of Elishama." [n]25.25 *about two months . . . his rule:* Hebrew "in the seventh month."

important or not, were afraid of what the Babylonians might do. So they left Judah and went to Egypt.

Jehoiachin Is Set Free

(Jeremiah 52.31-34)

²⁷Jehoiachin was a prisoner in Babylon for thirty-seven years. Then Evil-Merodach became king of Babylonia,° and in the first year of his rule, on the twenty-seventh day of the twelfth month,ᵖ he let Jehoiachin out of prison. ²⁸Evil-Merodach was kind to Je-hoiachin and honored him more than any of the other kings held prisoner there. ²⁹Jehoia-chin was even allowed to wear regular clothes, and he ate at the king's table every day. ³⁰As long as Jehoiachin lived, he was paid a daily allowance to buy whatever he needed.

°25.27 Evil-Merodach . . . Babylonia: The son of Nebuchadnezzar, who ruled Babylonia from 562 to 560 B.C. *ᵖ25.27 twelfth month:* Adar, the twelfth month of the Hebrew calendar, from about mid-February to mid-March.

1 Chronicles

The History of God's People

First and 2 Chronicles relate the long history of God's people from the reign of David to the exile of the nation of Judah to Babylonia, over four hundred years (that's twice the length of the U.S. as a nation!). Thus, these two books deal with many events noted in 2 Samuel and 1 and 2 Kings.

The center of attention is King David, his royal descendants, and the nation of Judah. David was from the tribe of Judah, the predominant tribe in that nation, which also included the tribe of Benjamin. Any references to the northern ten tribes (Israel) are viewed in light of the history of Judah.

The purpose of 1 Chronicles is similar to an event in U.S. history. In 1976, the United States' bicentennial year, numerous speeches, books, and magazine articles (about the Constitution, the presidents, and other issues) evaluated those two hundred years. The books of 1 and 2 Chronicles do the same about the twelve tribes—except the focus is religious, centered on God's choice of David, who becomes the second king of Israel and whose reign becomes the ideal for the messianic kingdom.

Besides the kingship, these two books' chief interest is the Solomonic temple and its attendant worship, including the priests, Levites, and musicians. At the end, the temple has been completely destroyed—but the story doesn't end there. There's also the promise of a new one when the people return from captivity.

First Chronicles opens with nine chapters of detailed genealogies, giving the source for their ancestry (starting with Adam!) and of the tribes (ruled over by David). A brief chapter (10) describes the death of King Saul, the first king of the twelve tribes. Then the focus turns to David: all Israel "met with David at Hebron" (11.1). (See 2 Samuel 1–5 for more details on his becoming king.)

David captured the city, later called Jerusalem, and it became his political capital. He brings in the long-forsaken sacred chest, places it in a temporary tent, and starts worship services. But his desire to build a permanent temple was denied (28.3). The end of 1 Chronicles tells of David's death.

Why read 1 Chronicles today? If you want proof of God's love and care for his people, you'll find it here.

1 Chronicles at a Glance

1. A family tree (1–9)
2. The tragic death of Saul, Israel's first king (10)
3. David receives the kingdom (11,12)
4. David brings the sacred chest to Jerusalem (13–16)
5. God promises that Solomon will build the temple (17)
6. King David at war (18–20)
7. A disastrous census (21)
8. Preparing for the future temple (22–28)
9. The kingdom passes to Solomon (29)

The Descendants of Adam
(Genesis 5.1-32; 10.1-32; 11.10-32)

1 [superscript]1-4[/superscript]Adam was the father of Seth, and his descendants were Enosh, Kenan, Mahalalel, Jared, Enoch, Methuselah, Lamech, and Noah, who had three sons: Shem, Ham, and Japheth.

[superscript]5[/superscript]Japheth was the father of Gomer, Magog, Madai, Javan, Tubal, Meshech, and Tiras, and they were the ancestors of the kingdoms named after them. [superscript]6[/superscript]Gomer was the ancestor of Ashkenaz, Riphath,[superscript]a[/superscript] and Togarmah. [superscript]7[/superscript]Javan was the ancestor of Elishah, Tarshish, Kittim, and Dodanim.[superscript]b[/superscript]

[superscript]8[/superscript]Ham was the father of Ethiopia,[superscript]c[/superscript] Egypt, Put, and Canaan, and they were the ancestors of the kingdoms named after them. [superscript]9[/superscript]Ethiopia was the ancestor of Seba, Havilah, Sabta, Raamah, and Sabteca. Raamah was the ancestor of Sheba and Dedan. [superscript]10[/superscript]Ethiopia was also the father of Nimrod, the world's first mighty warrior. [superscript]11[/superscript]Egypt was the ancestor of Ludim, Anamim, Lehabim, Naphtuhim, [superscript]12[/superscript]Pathrusim, Casluhim, and Caphtorim, the ancestor of the Philistines.[superscript]d[/superscript] [superscript]13[/superscript]Canaan's oldest son was Sidon; his other son was Heth. [superscript]14-16[/superscript]Canaan was also the ancestor of the Jebusites, the Amorites, the Girgashites, the Hivites, and Arkites, the Sinites, the Arvadites, the Zemarites, and the Hamathites.

[superscript]17[/superscript]Shem was the ancestor of Elam, Asshur, Arpachshad, Lud, Aram, Uz, Hul, Gether, and Meshech;[superscript]e[/superscript] they were the ancestors of the kingdoms named after them. [superscript]18[/superscript]Arpachshad was Shelah's father and Eber's grandfather. [superscript]19[/superscript]Eber named his first son Peleg,[superscript]f[/superscript] because in his time the earth was divided into tribal regions. Eber's second son was Joktan, [superscript]20-23[/superscript]the ancestor of Almodad, Sheleph, Hazarmaveth, Jerah, Hadoram, Uzal, Diklah, Ebal, Abimael, Sheba, Ophir, Havilah, and Jobab.

[superscript]24-27[/superscript]Shem's descendants included Arpachshad, Shelah, Eber, Peleg, Reu, Serug, Nahor, Terah, and Abram, later renamed Abraham.

Abraham's Family
(Genesis 25.1-4, 12-16)

[superscript]28[/superscript]Abraham was the father of Isaac and Ishmael.

[superscript]29-31[/superscript]Ishmael had twelve sons, who were born in the following order: Nebaioth, Kedar, Adbeel, Mibsam, Mishma, Dumah, Massa, Hadad, Tema, Jetur, Naphish, and Kedemah.

[superscript]32[/superscript]Abraham and his slave woman Keturah had six sons: Zimran, Jokshan, Medan, Midian, Ishbak, and Shuah. Jokshan was the father of Sheba and Dedan. [superscript]33[/superscript]Midian was the father of Ephah, Epher, Hanoch, Abida, and Eldaah.

> *Your family is a mystery, a marvel, a wonder. God has put you together, and things are happening in you and between you from day to day, from moment to moment.*
>
> ANNE ORTLUND

Esau's Family
(Genesis 36.1-14)

[superscript]34[/superscript]Abraham's son Isaac was the father of Esau and Jacob.[superscript]g[/superscript] [superscript]35[/superscript]Esau was the father of Eliphaz, Reuel, Jeush, Jalam, and Korah. [superscript]36[/superscript]Eliphaz was the father of Teman, Omar, Zephi, Gatam, Kenaz, Timna, and Amalek. [superscript]37[/superscript]Reuel was the father of Nahath, Zerah, Shammah, and Mizzah.

The First Edomites and Their Kings
(Genesis 36.20-43)

[superscript]38[/superscript]Seir was the father of Lotan, Shobal, Zibeon, Anah, Dishon, Ezer, and Dishan.

[superscript]a[/superscript]**1.6** *Riphath*: Most Hebrew manuscripts and two ancient translations (see also Genesis 10.2-5); some Hebrew manuscripts "Diphath." In Hebrew the letters "d" and "r" look almost exactly the same. [superscript]b[/superscript]**1.7** *Dodanim*: Most Hebrew manuscripts and one ancient translation (see also Genesis 10.2-5); some Hebrew manuscripts "Rodanim." In Hebrew the letters "d" and "r" look almost exactly the same. [superscript]c[/superscript]**1.8** *Ethiopia*: The Hebrew text has "Cush," which was a region south of Egypt that included parts of the present countries of Ethiopia and Sudan. [superscript]d[/superscript]**1.12** *Casluhim, and Caphtorim, the ancestor of the Philistines*: The Hebrew text has "Casluhim, the ancestor of the Philistines, and Caphtorim"; but see Jeremiah 47.4 and Amos 9.7. [superscript]e[/superscript]**1.17** *Meshech*: Most Hebrew manuscripts; a few Hebrew manuscripts and some manuscripts of one ancient translation "Mash" (see also Genesis 10.21-31). [superscript]f[/superscript]**1.19** *Peleg*: In Hebrew "Peleg" means "divided." [superscript]g[/superscript]**1.34** *Jacob*: The Hebrew text has "Israel," which was Jacob's name after God renamed him.

[39]Lotan was the father of Hori and Homam; Lotan's sister was Timna. [40]Shobal was the father of Alvan,[h] Manahath, Ebal, Shephi, and Onam. Zibeon was the father of Aiah and Anah. [41]Anah was the father of Dishon and the grandfather of Hemdan,[i] Eshban, Ithran, and Cheran. [42]Ezer was the father of Bilhan, Zaavan, and Jaakan.[j] Dishan[k] was the father of Uz and Aran.

[43]Before kings ruled in Israel, Bela son of Beor ruled the country of Edom from its capital of Dinhabah. [44]After Bela's death, Jobab son of Zerah from Bozrah became king. [45]After Jobab's death, Husham from the land of Teman became king. [46]After Husham's death, Hadad son of Bedad became king and ruled from Avith. Earlier, Bedad had defeated the Midianites in the territory of Moab. [47]After Hadad's death, Samlah from Masrekah became king; [48]after Samlah's death, Shaul from the town of Rehoboth on the Euphrates River became king; [49]and after Shaul's death, Baal Hanan son of Achbor became king. [50]After Baal Hanan's death, Hadad ruled from Pai. His wife was Mehetabel, the daughter of Matred and granddaughter of Mezahab. [51]The Edomite clans[l] were Timna, Alvah,[m] Jetheth, [52]Oholibamah, Elah, Pinon, [53]Kenaz, Teman, Mibzar, [54]Magdiel, and Iram.

The Descendants of Judah

2 [1-2]Jacob[n] was the father of twelve sons: Reuben, Simeon, Levi, Judah, Issachar, Zebulun, Dan, Joseph, Benjamin, Naphtali, Gad, and Asher.

[3]Judah and his Canaanite wife Bathshua had three sons: Er, Onan, and Shelah. But the LORD had Er put to death, because he disobeyed and did what the LORD hated. [4]Judah and his daughter-in-law Tamar also had two sons: Perez and Zerah.

[5]Perez was the father of Hezron and Hamul. [6]Zerah was the father of Zimri, Ethan, Heman, Calcol, and Darda.[o] [7]Achan,[p] who was a descendant of Zerah and the son of Carmi, caused trouble for Israel, because he kept for himself things that belonged only to the LORD.[q] [8]Ethan's son was Azariah.

The Ancestors of King David

[9]Hezron was the father of Jerahmeel, Ram, and Caleb.[r] [10]Ram was the father of Amminadab and the grandfather of Nahshon, a tribal leader of Judah. [11]Nahshon's descendants included Salma, Boaz, [12]Obed, and Jesse. [13-15]Jesse had seven sons, who were born in the following order: Eliab, Abinadab, Shimea, Nethanel, Raddai, Ozem, and David. [16]Jesse also had two daughters: Zeruiah and Abigail. Zeruiah was the mother of Abishai, Joab, and Asahel. [17]Abigail's husband was Jether, who was a descendant of Ishmael, and their son was Amasa.

The Descendants of Hezron

[18]Hezron's son Caleb married Azubah, and their daughter was Jerioth,[s] the mother of Jesher, Shobab, and Ardon. [19]After the death of Azubah, Caleb married Ephrath. Their son Hur [20]was the father of Uri and the grandfather of Bezalel.

[21]When Hezron was sixty years old, he married the daughter of Machir, who settled the region of Gilead. Their son Segub [22]was the father of Jair, who ruled twenty-three villages in the region of Gilead. [23]Some time later the nations of Geshur and Aram captured sixty towns in that region, including the villages that belonged to Jair, as well as the town of Kenath and the nearby villages. Everyone from the region of Gilead was a descendant of Machir.

[24]After the death of Hezron, Caleb married Ephrath, his father's wife. Their son was Ashhur,[t] who later settled the town of Tekoa.

The Descendants of Jerahmeel

[25]Jerahmeel, Hezron's oldest son, was the father of Ram, Bunah, Oren, Ozem, and

[h]1.40 Alvan: Or "Alian." [i]1.41 Hemdan: Most Hebrew manuscripts and some manuscripts of one ancient translation (see also Genesis 36.26); other Hebrew manuscripts "Hamran." [j]1.42 Jaakan: Or "Akan" (see Genesis 36.27). [k]1.42 Dishan: The Hebrew text has "Dishon," another spelling of the name (see Genesis 36.28). [l]1.51 The Edomite clans: Or "The leaders of the Edomite clans." [m]1.51 Alvah: Or "Aliah." [n]2.1,2 Jacob: See the note at 1.34. [o]2.6 Darda: Most Hebrew manuscripts and two ancient translations (see also 1 Kings 4.30, 31); some Hebrew manuscripts "Dara." [p]2.7 Achan: The Hebrew text has "Achar," which means "trouble." [q]2.7 Achan . . . the LORD: See Joshua 7.1-26. [r]2.9 Caleb: The Hebrew text has "Chelubai," another form of the name. [s]2.18 married Azubah . . . Jerioth: One possible meaning for the difficult Hebrew text. [t]2.24 After the death of Hezron . . . Ashhur: Two ancient translations; Hebrew "After Hezron died in Caleb-Ephrathah, Abijah his wife gave birth to Ashhur."

Ahijah. ²⁶Jerahmeel had a second wife, Atarah, who gave birth to Onam. ²⁷Ram was the father of Maaz, Jamin, and Eker. ²⁸Onam was the father of Shammai and Jada.

Shammai was the father of Nadab and Abishur. ²⁹Abishur married Abihail, and their two sons were Ahban and Molid. ³⁰Nadab was the father of Seled and Appaim. Seled had no children; ³¹Appaim's son was Ishi, the father of Sheshan and the grandfather of Ahlai.

> *God placed you and your*
> *sister in the same family.*
> *No one shares your history*
> *as intimately as she does.*
> *The unity that God desires*
> *for all believers is what*
> *he desires for you.*
>
> Dr. Diane Mandt Langberg

³²Jada was the father of Jether and Jonathan. Jether had no children, ³³but Jonathan had two sons: Peleth and Zaza.

³⁴⁻³⁵Sheshan had no sons, and so he let one of his daughters marry Jarha, his Egyptian slave. Their son was Attai, ³⁶the father of Nathan and the grandfather of Zabad. ³⁷⁻⁴¹Zabad's descendants included Ephlal, Obed, Jehu, Azariah, Helez, Eleasah, Sismai, Shallum, Jekamiah, and Elishama.

The Descendants of Caleb

⁴²Caleb, Jerahmeel's brother, had the following descendants: Mesha,ᵘ Ziph, Mareshah,ᵛ Hebron, ⁴³and Hebron's four sons, Korah, Tappuah, Rekem, and Shema. ⁴⁴Shema was the father of Raham and the grandfather of Jorkeam. Rekem was the father of Shammai, ⁴⁵the grandfather of Maon, and the great-grandfather of Bethzur.

⁴⁶Ephah was one of Caleb's wives,ʷ and their sons were Haran, Moza, and Gazez. Haran named his son after his brother Gazez. ⁴⁷Ephah was the daughter of Jahdai, who was also the father of Regem, Jotham, Geshan, Pelet, and Shaaph.ˣ

⁴⁸Maacah was another of Caleb's wives,ʸ and their sons were Sheber and Tirhanah. ⁴⁹Later, they had two more sons: Shaaph the father of Madmannah, and Sheva the father of Machbenah and Gibea. Caleb's daughter was Achsah. ⁵⁰⁻⁵¹All of these were Caleb's descendants.

Hur, the oldest son of Caleb and Ephrath, had three sons: Shobal, Salma, and Hareph, who settled the town of Beth-Gader. ⁵²Shobal, who settled the town of Kiriath-Jearim, was the ancestor of Haroeh, half of the Menuhoth clan, ⁵³and the clans that lived near Kiriath-Jearim; they were the Ithrites, the Puthites, the Shumathites, and the Mishraites. The Zorathites and the Eshtaolites were descendants of the Mishraites.

⁵⁴Salma settled the town of Bethlehem and was the ancestor of the Netophathites, the people of Atroth-Bethjoab, half of the Manahathite clan, and the Zorites. ⁵⁵Salma was also the ancestor of the clans in Jabez that kept the court and government records; they were the Tirathites, the Shimeathites, and the Sucathites. These clans were the descendants of Hammath the Kenite, who was also the ancestor of the Rechabites.

The Descendants of King David

3 ¹⁻⁴King David ruled from Hebron for seven years and six months, and during that time he had six sons, who were born in the following order: Amnon, Daniel, Absalom, Adonijah, Shephatiah, and Ithream. Ahinoam from Jezreel was the mother of Amnon; Abigail from Carmel was the mother of Daniel; Maacah daughter of King Talmai of Geshur was the mother of Absalom; Haggith was the mother of Adonijah; Abital was the mother of Shephatiah; and Eglah was the mother of Ithream.

David then ruled from Jerusalem for thirty-three years, ⁵and during that time, he had thirteen more sons. His wife Bathshebaᶻ daughter of Ammiel gave birth to Shimea, Shobab, Nathan, and Solomon. ⁶⁻⁸David's

---

ᵘ**2.42** *Mesha*: Hebrew; one ancient translation "Mareshah." ᵛ**2.42** *following descendants . . . Mareshah*: One possible meaning for the difficult Hebrew text. ʷ**2.46** *wives*: See the note at 3.9. ˣ**2.47** *Shaaph*: One possible meaning for the difficult Hebrew text of verse 47. ʸ**2.48** *wives*: See the note at 3.9. ᶻ**3.5** *Bathsheba*: Two ancient translations (see also 2 Samuel 11); Hebrew "Bathshua."

other sons included Ibhar, Elishua,[a] Eliphelet, Nogah, Nepheg, Japhia, Elishama, Eliada, and Eliphelet. [9]David's other wives[b] also gave birth to sons. Tamar was his daughter.

The Descendants of King Solomon

[10-15]Solomon's descendants included the following kings: Rehoboam, Abijah, Asa, Jehoshaphat, Jehoram,[c] Ahaziah, Joash, Amaziah, Azariah, Jotham, Ahaz, Hezekiah, Manasseh, Amon, and Josiah and his four sons, Johanan, Jehoiakim, Zedekiah, and Jehoahaz.[d] [16]Jehoiakim was the father of Jehoiachin and Zedekiah.

[17]Jehoiachin, who was taken to Babylon as a prisoner, had seven sons: Shealtiel, [18]Malchiram, Pedaiah, Shenazzar, Jekamiah, Hoshama, and Nedabiah. [19]Pedaiah had two sons: Zerubbabel and Shimei. Zerubbabel was the father of Meshullam, Hananiah, and Shelomith their sister. [20]He also had five other sons: Hashubah, Ohel, Berechiah, Hasadiah, and Jushabhesed. [21]Hananiah's descendants were Pelatiah, Jeshaiah, Rephaiah, Arnan, Obadiah, and Shecaniah,[e] [22]the father of Shemaiah and the grandfather of Hattush, Igal, Bariah, Neariah, and Shaphat. [23]Neariah was the father of Elioenai, Hizkiah, and Azrikam. [24]Elioenai was the father of Hodaviah, Eliashib, Pelaiah, Akkub, Johanan, Delaiah, and Anani.

The Descendants of Judah

4 Judah was the father of five sons: Perez, Hezron, Carmi, Hur, and Shobal. [2]Shobal was the father of Reaiah, the grandfather of Jahath, and the great-grandfather of Ahumai and Lahad. These men all belonged to the Zorathite clan.

[3-4]Hur was the oldest son of Caleb and Ephrath. Some of his descendants settled the town of Bethlehem. Hur's other descendants included Etam, Penuel, and Ezer. Etam's sons[f] were Jezreel, Ishma, and Idbash, and his daughter was Hazzelelponi. Penuel settled the town of Gedor, and Ezer settled the town of Hushah.

[5]Ashhur, who settled the town of Tekoa, had two wives: Helah and Naarah. [6]Ashhur and Naarah were the parents of Ahuzzam, Hepher, Temeni, and Haahashtari. [7]Ashhur and Helah were the parents of Zereth, Izhar, and Ethnan.

[8]Koz, the father of Anub and Zobebah,

was also the ancestor of the clans of Aharhel, the son of Harum.

[9]Jabez was a man who got his name because of the pain he caused his mother during birth.[g] But he was still the most respected son in his family. [10]One day he prayed to Israel's God, "Please bless me and give me a lot of land. Be with me so I will be safe from harm."[h] And God did just what Jabez had asked.

[11]Chelub was the brother of Shuhah and the father of Mehir. Later, Mehir had a son, Eshton, [12]whose three sons were Bethrapha, Paseah, and Tehinnah. It was Tehinnah who settled the town of Nahash.[i] These men and their families lived in the town of Recah.

The family is God's idea, part of his loving plan for human well-being and joy.

MAXINE HANCOCK

[13]Kenaz was the father of Othniel and Seraiah. Othniel had two sons: Hathath and Meonothai,[j] [14]who was the father of Ophrah. Seraiah was the father of Joab, who settled a place called "Valley of Crafts"[k] because the people who lived there were experts in making things.

[15]Caleb son of Jephunneh had three sons: Iru, Elah, and Naam. Elah was the father of Kenaz.

---

[a]**3.6-8** *Elishua:* Some Hebrew manuscripts and some manuscripts of one ancient translation (see also 2 Samuel 5.14, 15); most Hebrew manuscripts "Elishama." [b]**3.9** *other wives:* This translates a Hebrew word for women who were legally bound to a man, but without the full privileges of a wife. [c]**3.10-15** *Jehoram:* The Hebrew text has "Joram," another spelling of the name. [d]**3.10-15** *Jehoahaz:* The Hebrew text has "Shallum," probably another name for Jehoahaz (see also 2 Kings 23.30). [e]**3.21** *Shecaniah:* One possible meaning for the difficult Hebrew text of verse 21. [f]**4.3,4** *Etam's sons:* Some manuscripts of one ancient translation; Hebrew "Etam's ancestors." [g]**4.9** *Jabez . . . pain . . . birth:* In Hebrew "Jabez" sounds like "pain." [h]**4.10** *I . . . harm:* Or "keep me from harm, so I won't cause any pain." [i]**4.12** *who settled the town of Nahash:* Or "who was the father of Irnahash." [j]**4.13** *and Meonothai:* Two ancient translations; these words are not in the Hebrew text. [k]**4.14** *Valley of Crafts:* Hebrew "Geharashim."

¹⁶Jehallelel was the father of Ziph, Ziphah, Tiria, and Asarel.

¹⁷⁻¹⁸Ezrah was the father of Jether, Mered, Epher, and Jalon. Mered was married to Bithiah the daughter of the king of Egypt. They had a daughter named Miriam and two sons: Shammai and Ishbah. It was Ishbah who settled the town of Eshtemoa. Mered was also married to a woman from the tribe of Judah, and their sons were Jered, Heber, and Jekuthiel. Jered settled the town of Gedor; Heber settled the town of Soco; and Jekuthiel settled the town of Zanoah.

¹⁹A man named Hodiah was married to the sister of Naham. Hodiah's descendants included Keilah of the Garmite clan and Eshtemoa of the Maacathite clan.

²⁰Shimon was the father of Amnon, Rinnah, Benhanan, and Tilon.

Ishi was the father of Zoheth and Benzoheth.

²¹⁻²²Judah also had a son named Shelah, whose descendants included Jokim and the people of the town of Cozeba, as well as Er who settled the town of Lecah and Laadah who settled the town of Mareshah. The people who lived in Beth-Ashbea were also descendants of Shelah, and they were experts in weaving cloth. Shelah was the ancestor of Joash and Saraph, two men who married Moabite women and then settled near Bethlehem[l]—but these family records are very old. ²³The members of these clans were the potters who lived in the towns of Netaim and Gederah and worked for the king.

The Descendants of Simeon

²⁴Simeon had five sons: Nemuel, Jamin, Jarib, Zerah, and Shaul. ²⁵The descendants of Shaul included his son Shallum, his grandson Mibsam, and his great-grandson Mishma. ²⁶The descendants of Mishma included his son Hammuel, his grandson Zaccur, and his great-grandson Shimei. ²⁷Shimei had sixteen sons and six daughters. But his brothers did not have as many children, so the Simeon tribe was smaller than the Judah tribe.

²⁸⁻³¹Before David became king, the people of the Simeon tribe lived in the following towns: Beersheba, Moladah, Hazar-Shual, Bilhah, Ezem, Tolad, Bethuel, Hormah, Ziklag, Beth-Marcaboth, Hazarsusim, Bethbiri, and Shaaraim. ³²They also lived in the five villages of Etam, Ain, Rimmon, Tochen, and Ashan, ³³as well as in the nearby villages as far as the town of Baal. These are the places where Simeon's descendants had settled, according to their own family records.

³⁴⁻³⁸As their families and clans became larger, the people of Simeon had the following leaders: Meshobab, Jamlech, Joshah son of Amaziah, Joel, Jehu,[m] Elioenai, Jaakobah, Jeshohaiah, Asaiah, Adiel, Jesimiel, Benaiah, and Ziza.[n] ³⁹When the people needed more pastureland for their flocks and herds, they looked as far as the eastern side of the valley where the town of Gerar[o] is located, ⁴⁰and they found a lot of good pastureland that was quiet and undisturbed. This had once belonged to the Hamites, ⁴¹but when Hezekiah was king of Judah, the descendants of Simeon attacked and forced the Hamites and Meunites off the land, then settled there.

⁴²Some time later, five hundred men from the Simeon tribe went into Edom[p] under the command of Pelatiah, Neariah, Rephaiah, and Uzziel the sons of Ishi. ⁴³They killed the last of the Amalekites and lived there from then on.

The Descendants of Reuben

5 Reuben was the oldest son of Jacob,[q] but he lost his rights as the first-born son[r] because he slept with one of his father's wives.[s] The honor of the first-born son was then given to Joseph, ²even though it was the Judah tribe that became the most powerful and produced a leader.

³Reuben had four sons: Hanoch, Pallu, Hezron, and Carmi.

⁴⁻⁶The descendants of Joel included Shemaiah, Gog, Shimei, Micah, Reaiah, Baal, and Beerah, a leader of the Reuben tribe. Later, King Tiglath Pileser of Assyria took Beerah away as prisoner.

---

[l]**4.21,22** *who married Moabite women and then settled near Bethlehem*: Or "who ruled in Moab and Jashubi-Lahem" or "who ruled in Moab but then returned to Lahem." [m]**4.34-38** *Jehu*: Hebrew "Jehu son of Joshibiah son of Seraiah son of Asiel." [n]**4.34-38** *Ziza*: Hebrew "Ziza son of Shiphi son of Allon son of Jedaiah son of Shimri son of Shemaiah." [o]**4.39** *Gerar*: One ancient translation; Hebrew "Gedor." [p]**4.42** *Edom*: The Hebrew text has "Mount Seir," a common name for the nation of Edom. [q]**5.1** *Jacob*: See the note at 1.34. [r]**5.1** *rights as the first-born son*: The first-born son inherited the largest amount of property, as well as the leadership of the family. [s]**5.1** *wives*: See Genesis 35.22; 49.3, 4.

7-8The family records also include Jeiel, who was a clan leader, Zechariah, and Bela son of Azaz and grandson of Shema of the Joel clan. They lived in the territory around the town of Aroer, as far north as Nebo and Baal-Meon, 9and as far east as the desert just west of the Euphrates River. They needed this much land because they owned too many cattle to keep them all in Gilead.

10When Saul was king, the Reuben tribe attacked and defeated the Hagrites, then took over their land east of Gilead.

The Descendants of Gad

11The tribe of Gad lived in the region of Bashan, north of the Reuben tribe. Gad's territory extended all the way to the town of Salecah. 12Some of the clan leaders were Joel, Shapham, Janai, and Shaphat. 13Their relatives included Michael, Meshullam, Sheba, Jorai, Jacan, Zia, and Eber.

14They were all descendants of Abihail, whose family line went back through Huri, Jaroah, Gilead, Michael, Jeshishai, Jahdo, and Buz. 15Ahi, the son of Abdiel and the grandson of Guni, was the leader of their clan.

16The people of Gad lived in the towns in the regions of Bashan and Gilead, as well as in the pastureland of Sharon. 17Their family records were written when Jotham was king of Judah and Jeroboam was king of Israel.

18The tribes of Reuben, Gad, and East Manasseh had 44,760 soldiers trained to fight in battle with shields, swords, bows, and arrows. 19They fought against the Hagrites and the tribes of Jetur, Naphish, and Nodab. 20Whenever these soldiers went to war against their enemies, they prayed to God and trusted him to help. That's why the tribes of Reuben, Gad, and East Manasseh defeated the Hagrites and their allies. 21These Israelite tribes captured fifty thousand camels, two hundred fifty thousand sheep, two thousand donkeys, and one hundred thousand people. 22Many of the Hagrites died in battle, because God was fighting this battle against them. The tribes of Reuben, Gad, and East Manasseh lived in that territory until they were taken as prisoners to Assyria.t

The Tribe of East Manasseh

23East Manasseh was a large tribe, so its people settled in the northern region of Ba-

shan, as far north as Baal-Hermon,u Senir, and Mount Hermon. 24Epher, Ishi, Eliel, Azriel, Jeremiah, Hodaviah, and Jahdiel were their clan leaders; they were well-known leaders and brave soldiers.

The Tribes of Reuben, Gad, and East Manasseh Are Defeated

25The people of the tribes of Reuben, Gad, and East Manasseh were unfaithful to the God their ancestors had worshiped, and they started worshiping the gods of the nations that God had forced out of Canaan. 26So God sent King Tiglath Pileserv of Assyria to attack these Israelite tribes. The king led them away as prisoners to Assyria, and from then on, he forced them to live in Halah, Habor, Hara, and near the Gozan River.

The Descendants of Levi

6 Levi was the father of Gershon, Kohath, and Merari.

2Kohath was the father of Amram, Izhar, Hebron, and Uzziel. 3Amram was the father of Aaron, Moses, and Miriam.

Aaron had four sons: Nadab, Abihu, Eleazar, and Ithamar.

4-14Eleazar's descendants included Phinehas, Abishua, Bukki, Uzzi, Zerahiah, Meraioth, Amariah, Ahitub, Zadok, Ahimaaz, Azariah, Johanan, Azariah the priest who served in the temple built by King Solomon, Amariah, Ahitub, Zadok, Shallum, Hilkiah, Azariah, Seraiah, and Jehozadak. 15King Nebuchadnezzar of Babylonia took Jehozadak to Babylon as prisoner when the LORD let the people of Judah and Jerusalem be dragged from their land.w

16Levi's three sons had sons of their own. 17Gershon was the father of Libni and Shimei. 18Kohath was the father of Amram, Izhar, Hebron, and Uzziel. 19Merari was the father of Mahli and Mushi. These descendants of Levi each became leaders of their own clans.

20-21Gershon's descendants included Libni, Jahath, Zimmah, Joah, Iddo, Zerah, and Jeatherai.

22-24Kohath's descendants included Am-

---

t5.22 they were taken as prisoners to Assyria: See 2 Kings 15.29; 17.5-23. u5.23 Baal-Hermon: The location of this place is unknown. v5.26 King Tiglath Pileser: The Hebrew text also includes "King Pul," another name by which he was known. w6.15 King Nebuchadnezzar . . . dragged from their land: See 2 Kings 24.8-17; 25.1-21.

minadab, Korah, Assir, Elkanah, Ebiasaph, Assir, Tahath, Uriel, Uzziah, and Shaul. [25]Elkanah was the father of Amasai and Ahimoth. [26-27]Ahimoth's descendants included Elkanah, Zophai, Nahath, Eliab, Jeroham, and Elkanah.

[28]Samuel was the father of Joel[x] and Abijah, born in that order.

[29-30]Merari's descendants included Mahli, Libni, Shimei, Uzzah, Shimea, Haggiah, and Asaiah.

The Temple Musicians

[31]After King David had the sacred chest moved to Jerusalem, he appointed musicians from the Levi tribe to be in charge of the music at the place of worship. [32]These musicians served at the sacred tent and later at the LORD's temple that King Solomon built.

[33-38]Here is a list of these musicians and their family lines:

Heman from the Kohathite clan was the director. His ancestors went all the way back to Jacob and included Joel, Samuel, Elkanah, Jeroham, Eliel, Toah, Zuph, Elkanah, Mahath, Amasai, Elkanah, Joel, Azariah, Zephaniah, Tahath, Assir, Ebiasaph, Korah, Izhar, Kohath, Levi.

[39-43]Asaph was Heman's relative and served as his assistant. Asaph's ancestors included Berechiah, Shimea, Michael, Baaseiah, Malchijah, Ethni, Zerah, Adaiah, Ethan, Zimmah, Shimei, Jahath, Gershon, and Levi.

[44-47]Ethan was also Heman's relative and served as his assistant. Ethan belonged to the Merari clan, and his ancestors included Kishi, Abdi, Malluch, Hashabiah, Amaziah, Hilkiah, Amzi, Bani, Shemer, Mahli, Mushi, Merari, and Levi.

[48]The rest of the Levites were appointed to work at the sacred tent.

The Descendants of Aaron

[49]Only Aaron and his descendants were allowed to offer sacrifices and incense on the two altars at the sacred tent.[y] They were in charge of the most holy place and the ceremonies to forgive sins, just as God's servant Moses had commanded.

[50-53]Aaron's descendants included his son Eleazar, Phinehas, Abishua, Bukki, Uzzi, Zerahiah, Meraioth, Amariah, Ahitub, Zadok, and Ahimaaz.

The Towns for the Levites

(*Joshua 21.1-42*)

[54]Aaron's descendants belonged to the Levite clan of Kohath, and they were the first group chosen to receive towns to live in. [55]They received the town of Hebron in the territory of Judah and the pastureland around it. [56]But the farmland and villages around Hebron were given to Caleb son of Jephunneh. [57-59]So Aaron's descendants received the following Safe Towns[z] and the pastureland around them: Hebron, Libnah, Jattir, Eshtemoa, Hilen, Debir, Ashan, and Beth-Shemesh. [60]From the Benjamin tribe they were given the towns of Geba, Alemeth, and Anathoth and the pastureland around them. Thirteen towns were given to Aaron's descendants.

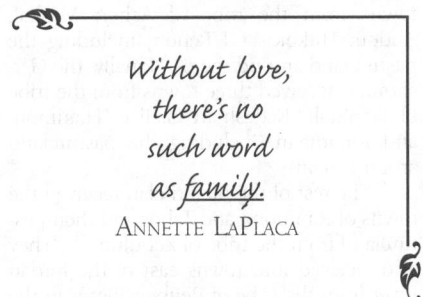

Without love, there's no such word as family.

ANNETTE LAPLACA

[61]The rest of the Levite clan of Kohath received ten towns from West Manasseh.

[62]The Levite clan of Gershon received thirteen towns from the tribes of Issachar, Asher, Naphtali, and East Manasseh in Bashan.

[63]The Levite clan of Merari received twelve towns from the tribes of Reuben, Gad, and Zebulun.

[64]So the people of Israel gave the Levites towns to live in and the pastureland around them. [65]All the towns were chosen with the

---

[x]**6.28** *Joel:* Two ancient translations (see also verse 33 and 1 Samuel 8.1, 2); this name is not in the Hebrew text. [y]**6.49** *the two altars at the sacred tent:* The Hebrew text mentions two different altars: A large altar for offering sacrifices, and a smaller altar for offering incense. [z]**6.57-59** *Safe Towns:* These were special towns set aside where a person who had accidentally killed someone could run for protection from the victim's relatives (see Numbers 35.9-15; Deuteronomy 19.1-13; Joshua 20.1-9).

LORD's help,[a] including those towns from the tribes of Judah, Simeon, and Benjamin.

[66]Some of the families of the Kohath clan received their towns from the tribe of Ephraim. [67-69]These families received the following Safe Towns and the pastureland around them: Shechem in the hill country, Gezer, Jokmeam, Beth-Horon, Aijalon, and Gath-Rimmon. [70]And from West Manasseh they received Aner and Bileam, together with their pastureland.

[71]The Gershonite clan received two towns from the tribe of East Manasseh: Golan in Bashan and Ashtaroth, including the pastureland around them. [72-73]The Gershonites also received four towns from the tribe of Issachar: Kedesh, Daberath, Ramoth, and Anem, including the pastureland around them. [74-75]The Gershonites received four towns from the tribe of Asher: Mashal, Abdon, Hukok, and Rehob, including the pastureland around them. [76]Finally, the Gershonites received three towns from the tribe of Naphtali: Kedesh in Galilee, Hammon, and Kiriathaim, including the pastureland around them.

[77]The rest of the Merari clan received the towns of Rimmono and Tabor and their pastureland from the tribe of Zebulun. [78-79]They also received four towns east of the Jordan River from the tribe of Reuben: Bezer in the flatlands, Jahzah, Kedemoth, and Mephaath, including the pastures around them. [80-81]And from the tribe of Gad the Merarites received the towns of Ramoth in Gilead, Mahanaim, Heshbon, and Jazer, including the pastureland around them.

The Descendants of Issachar

7 Issachar was the father of four sons: Tola, Puah, Jashub, and Shimron. [2]Tola was the father of Uzzi, Rephaiah, Jeriel, Jahmai, Ibsam, and Shemuel, who were all brave soldiers and family leaders in their clan. There were 22,600 people in Tola's family by the time David became king.

[3]Uzzi was the father of Izrahiah and the grandfather of Michael, Obadiah, Joel, and Isshiah, who were also family leaders. [4]Their families were so large that they had 36,000 soldiers in their clans. [5]In fact, according to family records, the tribe of Issachar had a total of 87,000 warriors.

The Descendants of Benjamin and Dan

[6]Benjamin was the father of three sons: Bela, Becher, and Jediael. [7]Bela was the father of Ezbon, Uzzi, Uzziel, Jerimoth, and Iri. They were all brave soldiers and family leaders in their father's clan. The number of soldiers in their clan was 22,034.

[8]Becher was the father of Zemirah, Joash, Eliezer, Elioenai, Omri, Jeremoth, Abijah, Anathoth, and Alemeth. [9]The official family records listed 20,200 soldiers in the families of this clan, as well as their family leaders.

[10]Jediael was the father of Bilhan and the grandfather of Jeush, Benjamin, Ehud, Chenaanah, Zethan, Tarshish, and Ahishahar. [11]They were family leaders in their clan, which had 17,200 soldiers prepared to fight in battle. [12]Ir was the father of Shuppim and Huppim, who also belonged to this clan.

Dan[b] was the father of Hushim.

The Descendants of Naphtali

[13]Naphtali's mother was Bilhah,[c] and he was the father of Jahziel, Guni, Jezer, and Shallum.

The Descendants of Manasseh

[14]Manasseh and his Syrian wife[d] were the parents of Asriel and Machir the father of Gilead. [15]Machir found a wife for Huppim and one for Shuppim. Machir had a sister named Maacah.

Zelophehad was also a descendant of Manasseh, and he had five daughters.[e]

[16]Machir and his wife Maacah were the parents of Peresh and Sheresh. Peresh was the father of Ulam and Rekem. [17]Ulam was the father of Bedan. These were all descendants of Gilead, the son of Machir and the grandson of Manasseh.

[18]Gilead's sister Hammolecheth was the mother of Ishhod, Abiezer, and Mahlah. [19]Shemida, another descendant of Ma-

---

[a]**6.65** *with the LORD's help*: The Hebrew text has "by lot." Pieces of wood or stone (called "lots") were used to find out what God wanted his people to do. [b]**7.12** *Dan*: The Hebrew text has "Aher," which can mean "someone else" (see Genesis 46.23-25). [c]**7.13** *Bilhah*: One of Jacob's wives and the mother of Dan and Naphtali (see Genesis 46.23-25). [d]**7.14** *wife*: See the note at 3.9. [e]**7.15** *Zelophehad . . . daughters*: One possible meaning for the difficult Hebrew text (see also Numbers 26.28-33).

nasseh, was the father of Ahian, Shechem, Likhi, and Aniam.

The Descendants of Ephraim

²⁰Ephraim was the father of Shuthelah and the ancestor of Bered, Tahath, Eleadah, Tahath, ²¹Zabad, and Shuthelah.

Ephraim had two other sons, Ezer and Elead. But they were killed when they tried to steal livestock from the people who lived in the territory of Gath. ²²Ephraim mourned for his sons a long time, and his relatives came to comfort him. ²³Some time later his wife gave birth to another son, and Ephraim named him Beriah, because he was born during a time of misery.^j

²⁴Ephraim's daughter was Sheerah. She built the towns of Lower Beth-Horon, Upper Beth-Horon, and Uzzen-Sheerah.

²⁵Ephraim also had a son named Rephah, and his descendants included Resheph, Telah, Tahan, ²⁶Ladan, Ammihud, Elishama, ²⁷Nun, and Joshua.

²⁸The descendants of Ephraim took over the territory as far south as Bethel, as far east as Naaran, and as far west as Gezer. Their territory included all the villages around these towns, as well as Shechem, Ayyah, and the nearby villages.

²⁹The descendants of Manasseh settled in the territory that included Beth-Shan, Taanach, Megiddo, Dor, and the nearby villages.

The descendants of Joseph^g lived in these towns and villages.

The Descendants of Asher

³⁰Asher had four sons, Imnah, Ishvah, Ishvi, and Beriah, and one daughter, Serah. ³¹Beriah was the father of Heber and Malchiel the father of Birzaith. ³²Heber was the father of three sons, Japhlet, Shomer, and Hotham, and one daughter, Shua. ³³Japhlet was the father of Pasach, Bimhal, and Ashvath. ³⁴Shomer was the father of Ahi, Rohgah, Hubbah, and Aram. ³⁵And Japhlet's brother Hotham^h was the father of Zophah, Imna, Shelesh, and Amal. ³⁶Zophah was the father of Suah, Harnepher, Shual, Beri, Imrah, ³⁷Bezer, Hod, Shamma, Shilshah, Ithran, and Beera. ³⁸Jether was the father of Jephunneh, Pispa, and Ara. ³⁹Ulla was the father of Arah, Hanniel, and Rizia.

⁴⁰These were the descendants of Asher, and they were all respected family leaders and brave soldiers. The tribe of Asher had a total of 26,000 soldiers.

More Descendants of Benjamin

8 Benjamin had five sons, who were born in the following order: Bela, Ashbel, Aharah, ²Nohah, and Rapha. ³Bela was the father of Addar, Gera, Abihud, ⁴Abishua, Naaman, Ahoah, ⁵Gera, Shephuphan, and Huram.

⁶⁻⁷Ehud was the father of Naaman, Ahijah, and Gera. They were clan leaders in the town of Geba, but were later forced to move to the town of Manahath, and Gera led the way. He had two sons: Uzza and Ahihud.

⁸⁻¹¹Shaharaim and his wife Hushim had two sons: Abitub and Elpaal. But Shaharaim later divorced her and his other wife, Baara. Then he moved to the country of Moab and married Hodesh, and they had seven sons: Jobab, Zibia, Mesha, Malcam, Jeuz, Sachia, and Mirmah. They were all family leaders in his clan. ¹²Elpaal was the father of Eber, Misham, and Shemed, who settled the towns of Ono and Lod, as well as the nearby villages.

¹³Beriah and Shema were family leaders in the clan that lived in the town of Aijalon and that forced out the people of Gath. ¹⁴⁻¹⁶Beriah's descendants included Ahio, Shashak, Jeremoth, Zebadiah, Arad, Eder, Michael, Ishpah, and Joha. ¹⁷⁻¹⁸Elpaal's descendants included Zebadiah, Meshullam, Hizki, Heber, Ishmerai, Izliah, and Jobab. ¹⁹⁻²¹Shimei's descendants included Jakim, Zichri, Zabdi, Elienai, Zillethai, Eliel, Adaiah, Beraiah, and Shimrath. ²²⁻²⁵Shashak's descendants included Ishpan, Eber, Eliel, Abdon, Zichri, Hanan, Hananiah, Elam, Anthothijah, Iphdeiah, and Penuel. ²⁶⁻²⁷Jeroham's descendants included Shamsherai, Shehariah, Athaliah, Jaareshiah, Elijah, and Zichri. ²⁸These were the family leaders in their ancestor's clan, and they and their descendants lived in Jerusalem.

²⁹Jeielⁱ settled the town of Gibeon. He and his wife Maacah lived there ³⁰along with their sons, who were born in the following

---

^j7.23 Beriah . . . misery: In Hebrew "Beriah" sounds like "in misery." ^g7.29 Joseph: Hebrew "Joseph son of Israel." ^h7.35 Hotham: The Hebrew text has "Helem," another spelling of the name. ⁱ8.29 Jeiel: One ancient translation and 9.35; the Hebrew text does not have this name.

order: Abdon, Zur, Kish, Baal, Ner,[j] Nadab, [31]Gedor, Ahio, Zecher, [32]and Mikloth the father of Shimeah. Some of them went to live in Jerusalem near their relatives.

The Descendants of King Saul

[33]Ner was the father of Kish and the grandfather of King Saul.

Saul had four sons: Jonathan, Malchishua, Abinadab, and Eshbaal.[k] [34]Jonathan was the father of Meribbaal,[l] the grandfather of Micah, [35]and the great-grandfather of Pithon, Melech, Tarea, and Ahaz. [36]Saul's other descendants were Jehoaddah, Alemeth, Azmaveth, Zimri, Moza, [37]Binea, Raphah, Eleasah, Azel, [38]as well as Azel's six sons: Azrikam, Bocheru, Ishmael, Sheariah, Obadiah, and Hanan. [39]Azel's brother Eshek was the father of Ulam, Jeush, and Eliphelet. [40]Ulam's sons were brave soldiers who were experts at using a bow and arrows. They had a total of one hundred fifty children and grandchildren.

All of these belonged to the tribe of Benjamin.

The People Who Returned from Babylonia and Settled in Jerusalem

9 Everyone in Israel was listed in the official family records that were included in the history of Israel's kings. The people of Judah were taken to Babylonia as prisoners because they sinned against the LORD. [2]And the first people to return to their towns included priests, Levites, temple workers, and other Israelites. [3]People from the tribes of Judah, Benjamin, Ephraim, and Manasseh settled in Jerusalem.

[4-6]There were six hundred ninety people from the Judah tribe who settled in Jerusalem. They were all descendants of Judah's three sons: Perez, Shelah, and Zerah. Their leaders were Uthai, Asaiah, and Jeuel. Uthai was the son of Ammihud and a descendant of Omri, Imri, Bani, and Perez. Asaiah was a descendant of Shelah; Jeuel was a descendant of Zerah.

[7-9]There were also nine hundred fifty-six family leaders from the Benjamin tribe who settled in Jerusalem. They included: Sallu son of Meshullam, grandson of Hodaviah, and great-grandson of Hassenuah; Ibneiah son of Jeroham; Elah son of Uzzi and grand-

son of Michri; Meshullam son of Shephatiah, grandson of Reuel, and great-grandson of Ibnijah.

The Priests Who Settled in Jerusalem

[10-12]Here is a list of priests who settled in Jerusalem: Jedaiah; Jehoiarib; Jachin; Azariah, who was a temple official, and whose ancestors included Hilkiah, Meshullam, Zadok, Meraioth, and Ahitub; Adaiah son of Jeroham, whose ancestors included Pashhur and Malchijah; Maasai son of Adiel, whose ancestors included Jahzerah, Meshullam, Meshillemith, and Immer. [13]There was a total of 1,760 priests, all of them family leaders in their clan and trained in the work at the temple.

The Levites Who Settled in Jerusalem

[14-16]Here is a list of Levites who settled in Jerusalem: Shemaiah from the Merari clan, whose ancestors included Hasshub, Azrikam, and Hashabiah; Bakbakkar; Heresh; Galal; Mattaniah son of Mica, whose ancestors included Zichri and Asaph; Obadiah son of Shemaiah, whose ancestors included Galal and Jeduthun; Berechiah son of Asa and grandson of Elkanah, who had lived in the villages near the town of Netophah.

The Temple Guards Who Settled in Jerusalem

[17]Shallum, Akkub, Talmon, Ahiman, and their relatives were the guards at the temple gates. Shallum was the leader of this clan, [18]and for a long time they had been the guards at the King's Gate on the east side of the city. Before that, their ancestors guarded the entrance to the Levite camp.

[19]Shallum son of Kore,[m] as well as the other men in the Korahite clan, guarded the entrance to the temple, just as their ancestors had guarded the entrance to the sacred tent. [20]Phinehas son of Eleazar had supervised their work because the LORD was with him.

---

[j]**8.30** *Ner*: One ancient translation and 9.36; the Hebrew text does not have this name. [k]**8.33** *Eshbaal*: Also called "Ishbosheth" (see 2 Samuel 2.8 and the note there). [l]**8.34** *Meribbaal*: Also called "Mephibosheth" (see 2 Samuel 4.4 and the note there). [m]**9.19** *Shallum son of Kore*: Hebrew "Shallum son of Kore, grandson of Ebiasaph, and great-grandson of Korah."

[21]Zechariah son of Meshelemiah was also one of the guards at the temple.

[22]There was a total of two hundred twelve guards, all of them listed in the family records in their towns. Their ancestors had been chosen by King David and by Samuel the prophet to be responsible for this work, [23]and now they guarded the temple gates.

[24]There was one full-time guard appointed to each of the four sides of the temple. [25]Their assistants lived in the villages outside the city, and every seven days a group of them would come into the city and take their turn at guard duty. [26]The four full-time guards were Levites, and they supervised the other guards and were responsible for the rooms in the temple and the supplies kept there. [27]They guarded the temple day and night and opened its doors every morning.

Always allow God the privilege of working in another's life differently from the way he has in your own.

SUSAN ALEXANDER YATES

The Duties of the Levites

[28]Some of the Levites were responsible for the equipment used in worship at the temple, and they had to count everything before and after it was used. [29]Others were responsible for the temple furnishings and its sacred objects, as well as the flour, wine, olive oil, incense, and spices. [30]But only the priests could mix the spices. [31]Mattithiah, Shallum's oldest son, was a member of the Levite clan of Korah, and he was in charge of baking the bread used for offerings.[n] [32]The Levites from the Kohath clan were in charge of baking the sacred loaves of bread for each Sabbath.[o]

[33]The Levite family leaders who were the musicians also lived at the temple. They had no other responsibilities, because they were on duty day and night.

[34]All of these men were family leaders in the Levi tribe and were listed that way in their family records. They lived in Jerusalem.

King Saul's Family

(1 Chronicles 8.29-38)

[35]Jeiel had settled the town of Gibeon, where he and his wife Maacah lived. [36]They had ten sons, who were born in the following order: Abdon, Zur, Kish, Baal, Ner, Nadab, [37]Gedor, Ahio, Zechariah, and Mikloth [38]the father of Shimeam. Some of them went to live in Jerusalem near their relatives.

[39]Ner was the father of Kish and the grandfather of King Saul.

Saul had four sons: Jonathan, Malchishua, Abinadab, and Eshbaal.[p] [40-41]Jonathan was the father of Meribbaal,[q] the grandfather of Micah, and the great-grandfather of Pithon, Melech, Tahrea, and Ahaz.[r] [42-44]The descendants of Ahaz included Jarah, Alemeth, Azmaveth, Zimri, Moza, Binea, Rephaiah, Eleasah, and Azel and his six sons: Azrikam, Bocheru, Ishmael, Sheariah, Obadiah, and Hanan.

King Saul and His Sons Die

(1 Samuel 31.1-13)

10 The Philistines fought against Israel in a battle at Mount Gilboa. Israel's soldiers ran from the Philistines, and many of them were killed. [2]The Philistines closed in on Saul and his sons and killed three of them: Jonathan, Abinadab, and Malchishua. [3]The fighting was fierce around Saul, and he was badly wounded by enemy arrows.

[4]Saul told the soldier who carried his weapons, "Kill me with your sword! I don't want those godless Philistines to torture and make fun of me."

But the soldier was afraid to kill him. Then Saul stuck himself in the stomach with his own sword and fell on the blade. [5]When the soldier realized that Saul was dead, he killed himself in the same way.

[6]Saul, three of his sons, and all his male relatives were dead. [7]The Israelites who lived

---

[n]9.31 *the bread used for offerings*: See Leviticus 2.4-7. [o]9.32 *the sacred loaves of bread for each Sabbath*: See Leviticus 24.5-9. [p]9.39 *Eshbaal*: See the note at 8.33. [q]9.40,41 *Meribbaal*: See the note at 8.34. [r]9.40,41 *and Ahaz*: Most ancient translations and 8.35; the Hebrew text does not have this name.

in Jezreel Valley[s] learned that their army had run away and that Saul and his sons were dead. They ran away too, and the Philistines moved into the towns the Israelites left behind.

[8]The next day the Philistines came back to the battlefield to carry away the weapons of the dead Israelite soldiers. When they found the bodies of Saul and his sons on Mount Gilboa, [9]they took Saul's weapons, pulled off his armor, and cut off his head. Then they sent messengers everywhere in Philistia to spread the news among their people and to thank the idols of their gods. [10]They put Saul's armor in the temple of their gods and hung his head in the temple of their god Dagon.

[11]When the people who lived in Jabesh in Gilead heard what the Philistines had done to Saul, [12]some brave men went to get his body and the bodies of his three sons. The men brought the bodies back to Jabesh, where they buried them under an oak tree. Then for seven days, they went without eating to show their sorrow.

[13]Saul died because he was unfaithful and disobeyed the LORD. He even asked advice from a woman who talked to spirits of the dead, [14]instead of asking the LORD. So the LORD had Saul killed and gave his kingdom to David, the son of Jesse.

David Becomes King of Israel
(2 Samuel 5.1-3)

11 Israel's leaders met with David at Hebron and said, "We are your relatives, [2]and we know that you have led our army into battle, even when Saul was still our king. The LORD God has promised that you would rule our country and take care of us like a shepherd. [3]So we have come to crown you king of Israel."

David made an agreement with the leaders and asked the LORD to be their witness. Then the leaders poured olive oil on David's head to show that he was now king of Israel. This happened just as the LORD's prophet Samuel had said.

David Captures Jerusalem
(2 Samuel 5.6-10)

[4]Jerusalem was called Jebus at the time, and David led Israel's army to attack the town. [5]The Jebusites said, "You won't be able to get in here!" But David captured the

fortress of Mount Zion, which is now called the City of David.

[6]David had told his troops, "The first soldier to kill a Jebusite will become my army commander." And since Joab son of Zeruiah attacked first, he became commander.

> *Commit your soul to a faithful Creator and ask him to keep you securely attached to that Rock, which is Christ, the only adequate foundation.*
>
> CAROLE SANDERSON STREETER

[7]Later, David moved to the fortress—that's why it's called the City of David. [8]He had the city rebuilt, starting at the landfill on the east side.[t] Meanwhile, Joab supervised the repairs to the rest of the city.

[9]David became a great and strong ruler, because the LORD All-Powerful was on his side.

The Three Warriors
(2 Samuel 23.8-17)

[10]The LORD had promised that David would become king, and so everyone in Israel gave David their support. Certain warriors also helped keep his kingdom strong.

[11]The first of these warriors was Jashobeam the son of Hachmoni, the leader of the Three Warriors.[u] In one battle he killed three hundred men with his spear.

[12]Another one of the Three Warriors was Eleazar son of Dodo the Ahohite. [13]During a battle against the Philistines at Pas-

---

[s]10.7 *Jezreel Valley*: Hebrew "the valley."
[t]11.8 *the landfill on the east side*: The Hebrew text has "the Millo," which probably refers to a landfill to strengthen and extend the hill where the city was built.
[u]11.11 *the Three Warriors*: One ancient translation and 2 Samuel 23.8; Hebrew "the Thirty Warriors." The "Three Warriors" was the most honored group of warriors and may have been part of the "Thirty Warriors." "Three" and "thirty" are spelled almost the same in Hebrew, so there is some confusion in the manuscripts as to which group is being talked about in some places in the following lists.

Dammim, all the Israelite soldiers ran away, [14]except Eleazar, who stayed with David. They took their positions in a nearby barley field and defeated the Philistines! The LORD gave Israel a great victory that day.

[15]One time the Three Warriors[v] went to meet David among the rocks at Adullam Cave. The Philistine army had set up camp in Rephaim Valley [16]and had taken over Bethlehem. David was in a fortress, [17]and he said, "I'm very thirsty. I wish I had a drink of water from the well by the gate to Bethlehem."

[18]The Three Warriors sneaked through the Philistine camp and got some water from the well near Bethlehem's gate. They took it back to David, but he refused to drink it. Instead, he poured out the water as a sacrifice to the LORD [19]and said, "Drinking this water would be like drinking the blood of these men who risked their lives to get it for me."

The Three Warriors did these brave deeds.

The Thirty Warriors
(2 Samuel 23.18-39)

[20]Joab's brother Abishai was the leader of the Thirty Warriors,[w] and in one battle he killed three hundred men with his spear. He was just as famous as the Three Warriors [21]and was more famous than the rest of the Thirty Warriors. He was their commander, but he never became one of the Three Warriors.[x]

[22]Benaiah the son of Jehoiada was a brave man from Kabzeel who did some amazing things. One time he killed two of Moab's best fighters, and one snowy day he went into a pit and killed a lion. [23]Another time he killed an Egyptian who was seven and a half feet tall and was armed with a spear. Benaiah only had a club, so he grabbed the spear from the Egyptian and killed him with it. [24]Benaiah did things like that; he was just as brave as the Three Warriors, [25]even though he never became one of them. And he was certainly as famous as the rest of the Thirty Warriors. So David made him the leader of his own bodyguard.

[26-47]Here is a list of the other famous warriors:

Asahel the brother of Joab; Elhanan the son of Dodo from Bethlehem; Shammoth from Haror; Helez from Pelon; Ira the son of Ikkesh from Tekoa; Abiezer from Anathoth; Sibbecai the Hushathite; Ilai[y] the Ahohite; Maharai from Netophah; Heled the son of Baanah from Netophah; Ithai the son of Ribai from Gibeah in Benjamin; Benaiah from Pirathon; Hurai[z] from near the streams on Mount Gaash; Abiel from Arbah; Azmaveth from Baharum; Eliahba from Shaalbon; Hashem[a] the Gizonite; Jonathan the son of Shagee from Harar; Ahiam the son of Sachar the Hararite; Eliphal the son of Ur; Hepher from Mecherah; Ahijah from Pelon; Hezro from Carmel; Naarai the son of Ezbai; Joel the brother of Nathan; Mibhar the son of Hagri; Zelek from Ammon; Naharai from Beeroth who carried Joab's weapons; Ira the Ithrite; Gareb the Ithrite; Uriah the Hittite; Zabad the son of Ahlai; Adina the son of Shiza, a leader in the Reuben tribe, and thirty of his soldiers; Hanan the son of Maacah; Joshaphat from Mithan; Uzzia from Ashterah; Shama and Jeiel the sons of Hotham from Aroer; Jediael and Joha the sons of Shimri from Tiz; Eliel from Mahavah; Jeribai and Joshaviah the sons of Elnaam; Ithmah from Moab; Eliel, Obed, and Jaasiel from Mezobah.

David's Men at Ziklag

12 Some time earlier, David had gone to live in the town of Ziklag to escape from King Saul. While David was there, several brave warriors joined him to help fight his battles.[b]

Warriors from the Benjamin tribe

[2]Several of these warriors were from King Saul's own tribe of Benjamin. They were experts at using a bow and arrows, and they could shoot an arrow or sling a stone with

---

[v]11.15 *the Three Warriors:* Hebrew "three of the thirty most important warriors." [w]11.20 *the Thirty Warriors:* One ancient translation; Hebrew "the Three Warriors." The "Thirty Warriors" was the second most honored group of warriors and may have been officers in the army. [x]11.20,21 *Warriors:* One possible meaning for the difficult Hebrew text of these verses. [y]11.26-47 *Ilai:* Or "Zalmon" (see 2 Samuel 23.24-39). [z]11.26-47 *Hurai:* Or "Hiddai" (see 2 Samuel 23.24-39). [a]11.26-47 *Hashem:* One ancient translation; Hebrew "the sons of Hashem." [b]12.1 *David had gone . . . battles:* Ziklag was the Philistine town that King Achish of Gath gave David in return for his loyalty (see 1 Samuel 27.6). This happened during the time that David was living as an outlaw, so the events in this chapter actually took place before chapter 11 when David became king of Israel.

either hand. ³⁻⁷Their leaders were Ahiezer and Joash, the sons of Shemaah from Gibeah. Here is a list of those men from Benjamin: Jeziel and Pelet the sons of Azmaveth; Beracah and Jehu from Anathoth; Ishmaiah from Gibeon, who was the leader of the Thirty Warriors; Jeremiah, Jahaziel, Johanan, and Jozabad from Gederah; Eluzai, Jerimoth, Bealiah, Shemariah, and Shephatiah from Haruph; Elkanah, Isshiah, Azarel, Joezer, and Jashobeam from the Korah clan; Joelah and Zebadiah the sons of Jeroham from Gedor.

Warriors from the Gad tribe

⁸Men from the tribe of Gad also joined David at his fortress in the desert and served as his warriors. They were also brave soldiers—fierce as lions and quick as gazelles. They were always prepared to fight with shields and spears. ⁹⁻¹³There were eleven of them, ranked in the following order: Ezer the leader, then Obadiah, Eliab, Mishmannah, Jeremiah, Attai, Eliel, Johanan, Elzabad, Jeremiah, and Machbannai.

¹⁴All these men were army officers; some were high-ranking officers over a thousand troops, and others were officers over a hundred troops. ¹⁵Earlier, they had crossed the Jordan River when it flooded, and they chased out the people who lived in the valleys on each side of the river.

Warriors from the Benjamin and Judah tribes

¹⁶One time a group of men from the tribes of Benjamin and Judah went to the fortress where David was staying. ¹⁷David met them outside and said, "If you are coming as friends to fight on my side, then stay and join us. But if you try to turn me over to my enemies, the God our ancestors worshiped will punish you, because I have done nothing wrong."

¹⁸Amasai, who later became the leader of the Thirty Warriors, was one of these men who went to David. God's Spirit took control of him, and he said, "We will join you, David son of Jesse! You and your followers will always be successful, because God fights on your side."

So David agreed to let them stay, and he even put them in charge of his soldiers who raided enemy villages.

Warriors from the Manasseh tribe

¹⁹Some of the warriors who joined David were from the tribe of Manasseh. They had earlier gone with David when he agreed to fight on the side of the Philistines against King Saul. But as soon as the Philistine rulers realized that David might turn against them and rejoin Saul, they sent David away to the town of Ziklag. ²⁰That's when the following men from Manasseh joined him: Adnah, Jozabad, Jediael, Michael, Jozabad, Elihu, and Zillethai. They had all been commanders in Saul's army ²¹and brave soldiers, and so David made them officers in his army. They fought on his side when enemy troops attacked.

²²Day after day, new men came to join David, and soon he had a large, powerful army.

David's Men at Hebron

²³⁻³⁷The kingdom of Israel had been taken away from Saul, and it now belonged to David. He was ruling from Hebron, and thousands of well-trained soldiers from each tribe went there to crown David king of all Israel, just as the LORD had promised. These soldiers, who were always prepared for battle, included: 6,800 from Judah, who were armed with shields and spears; 7,100 from Simeon; 4,600 from Levi, including Jehoiada, who was a leader from Aaron's descendants, and his 3,700 men, as well as Zadok, who was a brave soldier, and 22 of his relatives, who were also officers; 3,000 from Benjamin, because this was Saul's own tribe and most of the men had remained loyal to him; 20,800 from Ephraim, who were not only brave, but also famous in their clans; 18,000 from West Manasseh, who had been chosen to help make David king; 200 leaders from Issachar, along with troops under their command—these leaders knew the right time to do what needed to be done; 50,000 from Zebulun, who were not only loyal, but also trained to use any weapon; 1,000 officers from Naphtali and 37,000 soldiers armed with shields and spears; 28,600 from Dan; 40,000 from Asher; and 120,000 from the tribes of Reuben, Gad, and East Manasseh, who were armed with all kinds of weapons.

³⁸All of these soldiers voluntarily came to Hebron because they wanted David to become king of Israel. In fact, everyone in Is-

rael wanted the same thing. [39]The soldiers stayed in Hebron three days, eating and drinking what their relatives had prepared for them. [40]Other Israelites from as far away as the territories of Issachar, Zebulun, and Naphtali brought cattle and sheep to slaughter for food. They also brought donkeys, camels, mules, and oxen that were loaded down with flour, dried figs, wine, and olive oil.

Everyone in Israel was very happy.

David Moves the Sacred Chest to Jerusalem
(2 Samuel 6.1-12a)

13 Some time later, David talked with his army commanders, [2-3]and then announced to the people of Israel:

While Saul was king, the sacred chest was ignored. But now it's time to bring the chest to Jerusalem. We will invite everyone in Israel to come here, including the priests and the Levites in the towns surrounded by pastureland. But we will do these things only if you agree, and if the LORD our God wants us to.

[4]The people agreed this was the right thing to do.

[5]David gathered everyone from the Shihor River in Egypt to Lebo-Hamath in the north. [6]Then he led them to Baalah in Judah, which was also called Kiriath-Jearim. They went there to get the sacred chest and bring it to Jerusalem, because it belonged to the LORD God, whose throne is above the winged creatures[c] on the lid of the chest.

[7]The sacred chest was still at Abinadab's house,[d] and when David and the crowd arrived there, they brought the chest outside and placed it on a new ox cart. Abinadab's sons[e] Uzzah and Ahio guided the cart, [8]while David and the crowd danced and sang praises to the LORD with all their might. They played music on small harps and other stringed instruments, and on tambourines, cymbals, and trumpets.

[9]But when they came to Chidon's threshing place, the oxen stumbled, and Uzzah reached out and took hold of the chest to stop it from falling. [10]The LORD God was very angry at Uzzah for doing this, and he killed Uzzah right there beside the chest. [11]David then got angry at God for killing

Uzzah. So he named that place "Attack on Uzzah,"[f] and it's been called that ever since.

[12]David was afraid what the LORD might do to him, and he asked himself, "Should I really be the one to take care of the sacred chest?" [13]So instead of taking it to Jerusalem, David decided to take it to the home of Obed-Edom, who lived in the town of Gath.

[14]The chest stayed there for three months, and the LORD blessed Obed-Edom, his family, and everything he owned.

David's Palace in Jerusalem
(2 Samuel 5.11-16)

14 King Hiram of Tyre sent some officials to David. They brought along carpenters and stone workers, and enough cedar logs to build David a palace. [2]David now knew that the LORD had made him a powerful king of Israel for the good of his people.

[3]After David moved to Jerusalem, he married more women and had more sons and daughters. [4-7]His children born there were Shammua, Shobab, Nathan, Solomon, Ibhar, Elishua, Elpelet, Nogah, Nepheg, Japhia, Elishama, Beeliada,[g] and Eliphelet.

David Defeats the Philistines
(2 Samuel 5.17-25)

[8]When the Philistines heard that David had become king of Israel, they came to capture him. But David heard about their plan and marched out to meet them in battle. [9]The Philistines had already camped in Rephaim Valley and were raiding the nearby villages.

[10]David asked God, "Should I attack the Philistines? Will you help me win?"

The LORD told David, "Yes, attack them! I will give you victory."

[11]David and his army marched to Baal-Perazim, where they attacked and defeated the Philistines. He said, "I defeated my enemies because God broke through them like a mighty flood." So he named the place

---

[c]13.6 winged creatures: Two golden statues of winged creatures were on top of the sacred chest and were symbols of the LORD's throne on earth (see Exodus 25.18). [d]13.7 The sacred chest . . . Abinadab's house: See 1 Samuel 6.19—7.2. [e]13.7 Abinadab's sons: These words are not in the Hebrew text, but see 2 Samuel 6.3. [f]13.11 Attack on Uzzah: Or "Perez-Uzzah." [g]14.4-7 Beeliada: Or "Eliada" (see 3.6-8).

"The Lord Broke Through."[h] [12]Then David ordered his troops to burn the idols that the Philistines had left behind.

> *Talking with God about daily joys, expressing our praise and gratitude, interceding for others; in these ways we can grow spiritually through prayer.*
>
> MAXINE HANCOCK

[13]Some time later, the Philistines came back into the hill country and camped in Rephaim Valley. [14]David asked God what he should do, and God answered, "Don't attack them from the front. Circle around behind them where the balsam[i] trees are. [15]Wait there until you hear the treetops making the sound of marching troops. That sound will mean I have marched out ahead of you to fight the Philistine army. So you must then attack quickly!"

[16]David obeyed God and he defeated the Philistines. He even chased them all the way from Gibeon to the entrance to Gezer.

[17]From then on, David became even more famous, and the LORD made all the nations afraid of him.

David Gets Ready To Bring the Sacred Chest to Jerusalem

15 David had several buildings built in Jerusalem, and he had a tent set up where the sacred chest would be kept. [2]He said, "Only Levites will be allowed to carry the chest, because the LORD has chosen them to do that work and to serve him forever."

[3]Next, David invited everyone to come to Jerusalem and watch the sacred chest being carried to the place he had set up for it. [4]He also sent for Aaron's descendants and for the Levites. The Levites that came were: [5]Uriel, the leader of the Kohath clan, and one hundred twenty of his relatives; [6]Asaiah, the leader of the Merari clan, and two hundred twenty of his relatives; [7]Joel, the leader of the Gershon clan, and one hundred thirty of his relatives; [8]Shemaiah, the leader of the Elizaphan clan, and two

---

[h]**14.11** *The Lord Broke Through:* Or "Baal-Perazim."
[i]**14.14** *balsam:* One possible meaning for the difficult Hebrew text.

---

*Spiritual*Life—How can I learn to appreciate and use the talents and gifts God has given me? *(1 Chronicles 15.1—16.3)*

Don't underestimate your potential.
When we think of the talents and gifts God has given us, it's easy to fall into one of two extremes: we envy the abilities of other people and belittle our own strengths, or we resent the fact nobody gives us credit for our skills and feel underappreciated.

But what looks to us like the smallest talent may be exactly what God wants to use in a certain situation. God is a God of possibility, and he can use any gift we have for his glory and others' good.

For years God's sacred chest had sat neglected. It belonged in the worship tent that King David had recently set up in Jerusalem. Now it was time to bring the chest home. The occasion called for a celebration.

David gave people various roles in the worship procession based on the skills God had given them. His role was of unbridled worship—he jumped and danced in honor of the Lord! Despite the fact he was a king, musician, and warrior, God called him to put his whole self into praising God—and he did! (See also 1 Samuel 16.14-23; 1 Corinthians 14.1-25.)

Words To Remember: *While the sacred chest was being carried into Jerusalem, everyone was celebrating by shouting and playing music on horns, trumpets, cymbals, harps, and other stringed instruments.*—1 Chronicles 15.28

hundred of his relatives; [9]Eliel, the leader of the Hebron clan, and eighty of his relatives; and [10]Amminadab, the leader of the Uzziel clan, with one hundred twelve of his relatives.

[11]David called together these six Levites and the two priests, Zadok and Abiathar. [12]He said to them, "You are the leaders of the clans in the Levi tribe. You and your relatives must first go through the ceremony to make yourselves clean and acceptable to the LORD. Then you may carry the sacred chest that belongs to the LORD God of Israel and bring it to the place I have prepared for it. [13]The first time we tried to bring the chest to Jerusalem, we didn't ask the LORD what he wanted us to do. He was angry at us, because you Levites weren't there to carry the chest."

[14]The priests and the Levites made themselves clean. They were now ready to carry the sacred chest [15]on poles that rested on their shoulders, just as the LORD had told Moses to do.

[16]David then told the leaders to choose some Levites to sing and play music on small harps, other stringed instruments, and cymbals. [17-21]The men chosen to play the cymbals were Heman the son of Joel, his relative Asaph the son of Berechiah, and Ethan the son of Kushaiah from the Merari clan. Some of their assistants played the smaller harps; they were Zechariah, Aziel, Shemiramoth, Jehiel, Unni, Eliab, Maaseiah, and Benaiah. Others played the larger harps: they were Mattithiah, Eliphelehu, Mikneiah, Azaziah, and two of the temple guards, Obed-Edom and Jeiel.

[22]Chenaniah was chosen to be the music director, because he was a skilled musician. [23-24]Four Levites were then appointed to guard the sacred chest. They were Berechiah, Elkanah, Obed-Edom, and Jehiah.

Finally, David chose priests to walk in front of the sacred chest and blow trumpets. They were Shebaniah, Joshaphat, Nethanel, Amasai, Zechariah, Benaiah, and Eliezer.

The Sacred Chest Is Brought to Jerusalem
(2 Samuel 6.12-22)

[25]David, the leaders of Israel, and the army commanders were very happy as they went to Obed-Edom's house to get the sacred chest. [26]God gave the Levites the strength they needed to carry the chest, and so they sacrificed seven bulls and seven rams.

[27]David, the Levites, Chenaniah the music director, and all the musicians were wearing linen robes, and David was also wearing a linen cloth.[j] [28]While the sacred chest was being carried into Jerusalem, everyone was celebrating by shouting and playing music on horns, trumpets, cymbals, harps, and other stringed instruments.

[29]Saul's daughter Michal[k] looked out her window and watched the chest being brought into David's City. But when she saw David jumping and dancing in honor of the LORD, she was disgusted.

16 They put the sacred chest inside the tent that David had set up for it, then they offered sacrifices to please the LORD[l] and sacrifices to ask his blessing.[m] [2]After David had finished, he blessed the people in the name of the LORD [3]and gave every person in the crowd a small loaf of bread, some meat, and a handful of raisins.

[4]David appointed some of the Levites to serve at the sacred chest; they were to play music and sing praises to the LORD God of Israel. [5]Asaph was their leader, and Zechariah was his assistant. Jeiel, Shemiramoth, Jehiel, Mattithiah, Eliab, Benaiah, Obed-Edom, and another man named Jeiel were appointed to play small harps and stringed instruments. Asaph himself played the cymbals, [6]and the two priests Benaiah and Jahaziel were to blow trumpets every day in front of the sacred chest.

David's Song of Praise
(Psalms 105.1-15; 96.1-3; 106.1, 47, 48)

[7]That same day, David instructed Asaph and his relatives for the first time to sing these praises to the LORD:

---

[j]15.27 a linen cloth: The Hebrew word is "ephod," which can mean either a piece of clothing like a skirt that went from the waist to the knee or a garment like a vest or jacket that only the priests wore. [k]15.29 Michal: One of David's wives. [l]16.1 sacrifices to please the LORD: These sacrifices have traditionally been called "whole burnt offerings" because the whole animal was burned on the altar. A main purpose of such sacrifices was to please the LORD with the smell of the sacrifice, and so in the CEV they are often called "sacrifices to please the LORD." [m]16.1 sacrifices to ask his blessing: These sacrifices have traditionally been called "peace offerings" or "offerings of well-being." A main purpose was to ask for the LORD's blessing, and so in the CEV they are sometimes called "sacrifices to ask the LORD's blessing."

⁸ Praise the LORD
  and pray in his name!
Tell everyone
  what he has done.
⁹ Sing praises to the LORD!
  Tell about his miracles.
¹⁰ Celebrate and worship
  his holy name
    with all your heart.

¹¹ Trust the LORD
  and his mighty power.
    Worship him always.
¹² Remember his miracles
  and all his wonders
    and his fair decisions.
¹³ You belong to the family
  of Israel, his servant;
  you are his chosen ones,
    the descendants of Jacob.

¹⁴ The LORD is our God,
  bringing justice
    everywhere on earth.
¹⁵ We must never forget
  his agreement and his promises,
    not in thousands of years.
*¹⁶ God made an eternal promise
¹⁷   to Abraham, Isaac, and Jacob
¹⁸ when he said, "I'll give you
    the land of Canaan."

¹⁹ At the time there were
  only a few of us,
    and we were homeless.
²⁰ We wandered from nation
  to nation, from one country
    to another.
²¹ God did not let anyone
    mistreat our people.
  Instead he protected us
    by punishing rulers
²² and telling them,
  "Don't touch my chosen leaders
    or harm my prophets!"

²³ Everyone on this earth,
    sing praises to the LORD.
  Day after day announce,
    "The LORD has saved us!"
²⁴ Tell every nation on earth,
    "The LORD is wonderful
      and does marvelous things!
²⁵ The LORD is great and deserves
    our greatest praise!

He is the only God
    worthy of our worship.
²⁶ Other nations worship idols,
  but the LORD created
    the heavens.
²⁷ Give honor and praise
    to the LORD,
  whose power and beauty
    fill his holy temple."

²⁸ Tell everyone of every nation,
  "Praise the glorious power
    of the LORD.
²⁹ He is wonderful! Praise him
  and bring an offering
    into his temple.
  Worship the LORD,
    majestic and holy.
³⁰ Everyone on earth, now tremble!"

The world stands firm,
    never to be shaken.
³¹ Tell the heavens and the earth
    to be glad and celebrate!
  And announce to the nations,
    "The LORD is King!"
³² Command the ocean to roar
    with all of its creatures
  and the fields to rejoice
    with all of their crops.
³³ Then every tree in the forest
  will sing joyful songs
    to the LORD.
  He is coming to judge
    all people on earth.

³⁴ Praise the LORD
  because he is good to us,
    and his love never fails.
³⁵ Say to him, "Save us, LORD God!
  Bring us back
    from among the nations.
  Let us celebrate and shout
    in praise of your holy name.
³⁶ LORD God of Israel,
  you deserve to be praised
    forever and ever."

After David finished, the people
shouted, "Amen! Praise the LORD!"

David Appoints Worship Leaders at Jerusalem and Gibeon

³⁷ David chose Asaph and the Levites in
his clan to be in charge of the daily worship

at the place where the sacred chest was kept. ³⁸Obed-Edom and sixty-eight of his relatives were their assistants, and Hosah and Obed-Edom the son of Jeduthun were the guards.

³⁹David also chose Zadok the priest and his relatives who were priests to serve at the LORD's sacred tent at Gibeon. ⁴⁰They were to offer sacrifices on the altar every morning and evening, just as the LORD had commanded in the Law he gave Israel. ⁴¹Heman and Jeduthun were their assistants, as well as the other men who had been chosen to praise the LORD for his never-ending love. ⁴²Heman and Jeduthun were also responsible for blowing the trumpets, and for playing the cymbals and other instruments during worship at the tent. The Levites in Jeduthun's clan were the guards at Gibeon.

⁴³After that, everyone went home, and David went home to his family.

The LORD's Message to David
(2 Samuel 7.1-17)

17 Soon after David moved into his new palace, he said to Nathan the prophet, "Look around! I live in a palace made of cedar, but the sacred chest is kept in a tent."

²Nathan replied, "The LORD is with you—do what you want."

³That night, the LORD told Nathan ⁴to go to David and tell him:

David, you are my servant, so listen carefully: You are not the one to build a temple for me. ⁵I didn't live in a temple when I brought my people out of Egypt, and I don't live in one now. A tent has always been my home wherever I have gone with them. ⁶I chose special leaders and told them to be like shepherds for my people Israel. But did I ever say anything to even one of them about building a cedar temple for me?

⁷David, this is what I, the LORD All-Powerful, say to you. I brought you in from the fields where you took care of sheep, and I made you the leader of my people. ⁸Wherever you went, I helped you and destroyed your enemies right in front of your eyes. I have made you one of the most famous people in the world.

⁹I have given my people Israel a land of their own where they can live in peace. They will no longer have to tremble with fear—evil nations won't bother them, as they did ¹⁰when I let judges rule my people, and I will keep your enemies from attacking you.

> *Surrender to God. Relax; sink down into his arms. Let him create in your spirit beauty and peace and rest.*
>
> ANNE ORTLUND

Now I promise that like you, your descendants will be kings. ¹¹I'll choose one of your sons to be king when you reach the end of your life and are buried beside your ancestors. I'll make him a strong ruler, ¹²and no one will be able to take his kingdom away from him. He will be the one to build a temple for me. ¹³I will be like a father to him, and he will be like a son to me. I will never put an end to my agreement with him, as I put an end to my agreement with Saul, who was king before you. ¹⁴I will make sure that your son and his descendants will rule my people and my kingdom forever.

¹⁵Nathan told David exactly what the LORD had said.

David Gives Thanks to the LORD
(2 Samuel 7.18-29)

¹⁶David went into the tent he had set up for the sacred chest. He sat there and prayed:

LORD God, my family and I don't deserve what you have already done for us, ¹⁷and yet you have promised to do even more for my descendants. You are treating me as if I am a very important person.[n] ¹⁸I am your servant, and you know my thoughts. What else can

---

[n]17.17 *You are treating me . . . person*: One possible meaning for the difficult Hebrew text.

I say, except that you have honored me? [19]It was your choice to do these wonderful things for me and to make these promises.

[20]No other god is like you, LORD— you alone are God. Everything we have heard about you is true. [21]And there is no other nation on earth like Israel, the nation you rescued from slavery in Egypt to be your own. You became famous by using great and wonderful miracles to force other nations and their gods out of your land, so that your people could live here. [22]You have chosen Israel to be your people forever, and you have become their God.

[23]LORD God, please do what you promised me and my descendants. [24]Then you will be famous forever, and everyone will say, "The LORD All-Powerful rules Israel and is their God."

My kingdom will be strong, [25]because you are my God, and you have promised that my descendants will be kings. That's why I have the courage to pray to you like this, even though I am only your servant. [26]You are the LORD God, and you have made this good promise to me. [27]Now please bless my descendants forever, and let them always be your chosen kings. You have already blessed my family, and I know you will bless us forever.

A List of David's Victories in War
(2 Samuel 8.1-14)

18 Later, David attacked and defeated the Philistines. He captured their town of Gath and the nearby villages. [2]David also defeated the Moabites, and so they had to accept him as their ruler and pay taxes to him. [3]While King Hadadezer of Zobah was trying to gain control of the territory near the Euphrates River, David met him in battle at Hamath and defeated him. [4]David captured one thousand chariots, seven thousand chariot drivers, and twenty thousand soldiers. And he crippled all but one hundred of the horses.

[5]When troops from the Syrian kingdom of Damascus came to help Hadadezer, David killed twenty-two thousand of them. [6]Then David stationed some of his troops in Damascus, and the people there had to accept David as their ruler and pay taxes to him.

Everywhere David went, the LORD helped him win battles.

[7]Hadadezer's officers had carried gold shields, but David took these shields and brought them back to Jerusalem. [8]He also took a lot of bronze from the cities of Tibhath and Cun, which had belonged to Hadadezer. Later, Solomon used this bronze to make the large bowl called the Sea, and to make the pillars and other furnishings for the temple.

[9-10]King Tou of Hamath and King Hadadezer had been enemies. So when Tou heard that David had defeated Hadadezer's whole army, he sent his son Hadoram to congratulate David on his victory. Hadoram also brought him gifts made of gold, silver, and bronze. [11]David gave these gifts to the LORD, just as he had done with the silver and gold he had captured from Edom, Moab, Ammon, Philistia, and Amalek.

[12]Abishai the son of Zeruiah defeated the Edomite army in Salt Valley and killed eighteen thousand of their troops. [13]Then he stationed troops in Edom, and the people there had to accept David as their ruler.

Everywhere David went, the LORD gave him victory in war.

A List of David's Officials
(2 Samuel 8.15-18)

[14]David ruled all Israel with fairness and justice.

[15]Joab the son of Zeruiah was the commander in chief of the army.

Jehoshaphat the son of Ahilud kept the government records.

[16]Zadok the son of Ahitub and Ahimelech the son of Abiathar were the priests.

Shavsha was the secretary.

[17]Benaiah the son of Jehoiada was the commander of David's bodyguard.[o]

David's sons were his highest-ranking officials.

---

[o]18.17 David's bodyguard: The Hebrew text has "the Cherethites and the Pelethites," who were foreign soldiers hired by David to be his bodyguard.

Israel Fights Ammon and Syria
(2 Samuel 10.1-19)

19 Some time later, King Nahash of Ammon died, and his son Hanun became king. ²David said, "Nahash was kind to me, so I will be kind to his son." He sent some officials to Ammon to tell Hanun how sorry he was that his father had died.

But when David's officials arrived at Ammon, ³the Ammonite leaders said to Hanun, "Do you really believe King David is honoring your father by sending these men to comfort you? He probably sent them to spy on our country, so he can come and destroy it."

⁴Hanun arrested David's officials and had their beards shaved off and their robes cut off just below the waist, and then he sent them away. ⁵They were terribly ashamed.

When David found out what had happened to his officials, he sent a message that told them, "Stay in Jericho until your beards grow back. Then you can come home."

⁶The Ammonites realized they had made David furious. So they paid over thirty tons of silver to hire chariot troops from Mesopotamia and from the Syrian kingdoms of Maacah and Zobah. ⁷Thirty-two thousand troops, as well as the king of Maacah and his army, came and camped near Medeba. The Ammonite troops also left their towns and came to prepare for battle.

⁸David heard what was happening, and he sent out Joab with his army. ⁹The Ammonite troops marched to the entrance of the city*p* and prepared for battle, while the Syrian troops took their positions in the open fields.

¹⁰Joab saw that the enemy troops were lined up on both sides of him. So he picked some of the best Israelite soldiers to fight the Syrians. ¹¹Then he put his brother Abishai in command of the rest of the army and told them to fight against the Ammonites. ¹²Joab told his brother, "If the Syrians are too much for me to handle, come and help me. And if the Ammonites are too strong for you, I'll come and help you. ¹³Be brave and fight hard to protect our people and the towns of our LORD God. I pray he will do whatever pleases him."

¹⁴Joab and his soldiers attacked the Syrians, and the Syrians ran from them. ¹⁵When the Ammonite troops saw that the Syrians had run away, they ran from Abishai's soldiers and went back into their own city. Joab then returned to Jerusalem.

¹⁶As soon as the Syrians realized they had been defeated, they sent for their troops that were stationed on the other side of the Euphrates River. Shophach, the commander of Hadadezer's army, led these troops to Ammon.

¹⁷David found out what the Syrians were doing, and he brought Israel's entire army together. They crossed the Jordan River, and he commanded them to take their positions facing the Syrian troops.

Soon after the fighting began, ¹⁸the Syrians ran from Israel. David killed seven thousand chariot troops and forty thousand regular soldiers. He also killed Shophach, their commander.

¹⁹When the kings who had been under Hadadezer's rule saw that Israel had defeated them, they made peace with David and accepted him as their new ruler. The Syrians never helped the Ammonites again.

The End of the War with Ammon
(2 Samuel 11.1; 12.26-31)

20 The next spring, the time when kings go to war, Joab marched out in command of the Israelite army and destroyed towns all over the country of Ammon. He attacked the capital city of Rabbah and left it in ruins. But David stayed in Jerusalem.

²Later, David himself went to Rabbah, where he took the crown from the statue of their god Milcom.*q* The crown was made of seventy-five pounds of gold, and there was a valuable jewel on it. David put the jewel on his crown,*r* then carried off everything else of value. ³He forced the people of Rabbah to work with saws, iron picks, and axes. He also did the same thing with the people in all the other Ammonite towns.

David then led Israel's army back to Jerusalem.

---

*p***19.9** *the city*: Probably Rabbah, the capital city of Ammon. *q***20.2** *the statue of their god Milcom*: Or "their king." *r***20.2** *David put the jewel on his crown*: Or "David put the crown on his head."

The Descendants of the Rephaim
(2 Samuel 21.15-22)

⁴Some time later, Israel fought a battle against the Philistines at Gezer. During this battle, Sibbecai from Hushah killed Sippai, a descendant of the Rephaim,⁵ and the Philistines were defeated.

⁵In another battle against the Philistines, Elhanan the son of Jair killed Lahmi the brother of Goliath from Gath, whose spear shaft was like a weaver's beam.ᵗ

⁶Another one of the Philistine soldiers who was a descendant of the Rephaim was as big as a giant and had six fingers on each hand and six toes on each foot. During a battle at Gath, ⁷he made fun of Israel, so David's nephew Jonathanᵘ killed him.

⁸David and his soldiers killed these three men from Gath who were descendants of the Rephaim.

David Counts the People
(2 Samuel 24.1-9)

21 Satan decided to cause trouble for Israel by making David think it was a good idea to find out how many people there were in Israel and Judah. ²David told Joab and the army commanders, "Count everyone in Israel, from the town of Beersheba in the south all the way north to Dan. Then I will know how many people can serve in my army."

³Joab answered, "Your Majesty, even if the LORD made your kingdom a hundred times larger, you would still rule everyone in it. Why do you need to know how many soldiers there are? Don't you think that would make the whole nation angry?"

⁴But David would not change his mind. And so Joab went everywhere in Israel and Judah and counted the people. He returned to Jerusalem ⁵and told David that the total number of men who could serve in the army was one million one hundred thousand in Israel and four hundred seventy thousand in Judah. ⁶Joab refused to include anyone from the tribes of Levi and Benjamin, because he still disagreed with David's orders.

God Punishes Israel
(2 Samuel 24.10-17)

⁷David's order to count the people made God angry, and he punished Israel. ⁸David prayed, "I am your servant. But what I did was stupid and terribly wrong. Please forgive me."

⁹The LORD said to Gad, one of David's prophets, ¹⁰"Tell David that I will punish him in one of three ways. But he will have to choose which one it will be."

¹¹Gad went to David and told him:

You must choose how the LORD will punish you: ¹²Will there be three years when the land won't grow enough food for its people? Or will your enemies constantly defeat you for three months? Or will the LORD send a horrible disease to strike your land for three days? Think about it and decide, because I have to give your answer to God who sent me.

> *Whatever your lifestyle, your situation, your connections—first of all, most of all, fix your eyes on God. Then all your relationships will fall into place.*
> ANNE ORTLUND

¹³David was miserable and said, "It's a terrible choice to make! But the LORD is kind, and I'd rather have him punish me than for anyone else to do it."

¹⁴So the LORD sent a horrible disease on Israel, and seventy thousand Israelites died. ¹⁵Then he sent an angel to destroy the city of Jerusalem. But just as the angel was about to do that, the LORD felt sorry for all the suffering he had caused the people, and he told the angel, "Stop! They have suffered enough." This happened at the threshing place that belonged to Araunahᵛ the Jebusite.

ˢ**20.4** *Rephaim*: This may refer to a group of people that lived in Palestine before the Israelites and who were famous for their large size.   ᵗ**20.5** *weaver's beam*: When a weaver made cloth, one set of threads was tied onto a large wooden rod that was known as a weaver's beam. ᵘ**20.7** *David's nephew Jonathan*: Hebrew "Jonathan son of Shimea, David's brother."   ᵛ**21.15** *Araunah*: The Hebrew text has "Ornan," another spelling of Araunah (see 2 Samuel 24.16).

[16]David saw the LORD's angel in the air, holding a sword over Jerusalem. He and the leaders of Israel, who were all wearing sackcloth,[w] bowed with their faces to the ground, [17]and David prayed, "It's my fault! I sinned by ordering the people to be counted. They have done nothing wrong—they are innocent sheep. LORD God, please punish me and my family. Don't let the disease wipe out your people."

David Buys Araunah's Threshing Place
(2 Samuel 24.18-25)

[18]The LORD's angel told the prophet Gad to tell David that he must go to Araunah's threshing place and build an altar in honor of the LORD. [19]David followed the LORD's instructions.

[20]Araunah and his four sons were threshing wheat at the time, and when they saw the angel, the four sons ran to hide. [21]Just then, David arrived, and when Araunah saw him, he stopped his work and bowed down. [22]David said, "Would you sell me your threshing place, so I can build an altar on it to the LORD? Then this disease will stop killing the people. I'm willing to pay whatever you say it's worth."

[23]Araunah answered, "Take it, Your Majesty, and do whatever you want with it. I'll even give you the oxen for the sacrifice and the wheat for the grain sacrifice. And you can use the threshing-boards[x] for the fire. It's all yours!"

[24]But David replied, "No! I want to pay you what they're worth. I can't just take something from you and then offer the LORD a sacrifice that cost me nothing."

[25]So David paid Araunah six hundred gold coins for his threshing place. [26]David built an altar and offered sacrifices to please the LORD[y] and sacrifices to ask his blessing.[z] David prayed, and the LORD answered him by sending fire down on the altar. [27]Then the LORD commanded the angel to put the sword away.[a]

[28]When David saw that the LORD had answered his prayer, he offered more sacrifices there at the threshing place, [29-30]because he was afraid of the angel's sword and did not want to go all the way to Gibeon. That's where the sacred tent that Moses had made in the desert was kept, as well as the altar where sacrifices were offered to the LORD.

22

David said, "The temple of the LORD God must be built right here at this threshing place. And the altar for offering sacrifices will also be here."

David Prepares To Build the Temple

[2]David ordered the foreigners living in Israel to come to Jerusalem. Then he assigned some to cut blocks of stone for building the temple. [3]He got a large supply of iron to make into nails and hinges for the doors, and he provided so much bronze that it could not be weighed. [4]He also had cedar logs brought in from the cities of Sidon and Tyre.

[5]He said, "The temple for the LORD must be great, so that everyone in the world will know about it. But since my son Solomon is young and has no experience, I will make sure that everything is ready for the temple to be built."

That's why David did all these things before he died.

David Instructs Solomon To Build the Temple

[6]David sent for his son Solomon and told him to build a temple for the LORD God of Israel. [7]He said:

My son, I wanted to build a temple where the LORD my God would be worshiped. [8]But some time ago, he told me, "David, you have killed too many people and have fought too many battles. That's why you are not the one to build my temple. [9]But when your son becomes king, I will give him peace throughout his kingdom. His name will be Solomon, because during his rule I will keep Israel safe and peaceful.[b] [10]Solomon will build my temple. He will be like a son to me, and I will be like a father to him. In fact, one of his descendants will always rule in Israel."

---

[w]21.16 sackcloth: A rough, dark-colored cloth made from goat or camel hair and used to make grain sacks. It was worn in times of trouble or sorrow.
[x]21.23 threshing-boards: Heavy boards with bits of rock or metal on the bottom. They were dragged across the grain to separate the husks from the kernels.
[y]21.26 sacrifices to please the LORD: See the note at 16.1.
[z]21.26 sacrifices to ask his blessing: See the note at 16.1.
[a]21.27 the LORD commanded the angel to put the sword away: See verse 16. [b]22.9 Solomon . . . safe and peaceful: In Hebrew "Solomon" sounds like "peace."

¹¹Solomon, my son, I now pray that the LORD your God will be with you and keep his promise to help you build a temple for him. ¹²May he give you wisdom and knowledge, so that you can rule Israel according to his Law. ¹³If you obey the laws and teachings that the LORD gave Moses, you will be successful. Be strong and brave and don't get discouraged or be afraid of anything.

¹⁴I have all the supplies you'll need to build the temple: You have four thousand tons of gold and forty thousand tons of silver. There's also plenty of wood, stone, and more bronze and iron than I could weigh. Ask for anything else you need. ¹⁵I have also assigned men who will cut and lay the stone. And there are carpenters and people who are experts in working with ¹⁶gold, silver, bronze, and iron. You have plenty of workers to do the job. Now get started, and I pray that the LORD will be with you in your work.

¹⁷David then gave orders for the leaders of Israel to help Solomon. ¹⁸David said:

The LORD our God has helped me defeat all the people who lived here before us, and he has given you peace from all your enemies. Now this land belongs to the LORD and his people. ¹⁹Obey the LORD your God with your heart and soul. Begin work on the temple to honor him, so that the sa-cred chest and the things used for wor-ship can be kept there.

David Assigns the Levites Their Duties

23 David was old when he chose his son Solomon to be king of Israel. ²Some time later, David called together all of Israel's leaders, priests, and Levites. ³He then counted the Levite men who were at least thirty years old, and the total was thirty-eight thousand. ⁴He said, "Twenty-four thousand of the Levites will be in charge of the temple, six thousand will be temple officials and judges, ⁵four thousand will be guards at the temple, and four thousand will praise the LORD by playing the musical instruments I have given them."

⁶David then divided the Levites into three groups according to the clans of Levi's sons, Gershon, Kohath, and Merari.

⁷Gershon had two sons: Ladan and Shimei. ⁸Ladan was the father of Jehiel, Ze-tham, and Joel. ⁹They were all family leaders among their father's descendants. Shimei was the father of Shelomoth, Haziel, and Haran. ¹⁰⁻¹¹Later, Shimei had four more sons, in the following order: Jahath, Zina, Jeush, and Beriah. But Jeush and Beriah didn't have many children, so their descendants were counted as one family.

¹²Kohath had four sons: Amram, Izhar, Hebron, and Uzziel. ¹³Amram was the father of Aaron and Moses. Aaron and his descendants were chosen to be in charge of all the sacred things. They served the LORD by offering sacrifices to him and by blessing the

---

PARENTING&family—How can I encourage my child's faith to grow?
(1 Chronicles 22)

Remember that kids need prayers, too.
King David's son Solomon was still young, and people still thought of David as king. But God let David know that power was already passing to the next generation. Naturally, David had lots of instructions to pass along. But before he made any pronouncements from on high, David prayed for his son—and let his son know he was praying for him.

If the children in your life make you hold your breath at times with anxiety, remember you were once a child. Sometimes you didn't look very promising, either! Maybe at that age you had nobody to pray for you. Or you were surrounded by prayers but too caught up in other things to be interested in the Lord. In any case, God stayed faithful to you, and he will stay faithful to your children as well. You can do your part by continuing to pray for them—and not giving up. (See also Joshua 4; Ezra 3; Proverbs 2.1-15; John 3.16-21.)

Words To Remember: Solomon, my son, I now pray that the LORD your God will be with you. . . . May he give you wisdom and knowledge.—1 Chronicles 22.11,12

people in his name. [14-15]Moses, the man of God, was the father of Gershom and Eliezer, and their descendants were considered Levites. [16]Gershom's oldest son was Shebuel. [17]Rehabiah, who was Eliezer's only son, had many children. [18]The second son born to Kohath was Izhar, and his oldest son was Shelomith. [19]Hebron, the third son of Kohath, was the father of Jeriah, Amariah, Jahaziel, and Jekameam. [20]Kohath's youngest son, Uzziel, was the father of Micah and Isshiah.

[21]Merari had two sons: Mahli and Mushi. Mahli was the father of Eleazar and Kish. [22]Eleazar had no sons, only daughters, and they married their uncle's sons. [23]Mushi the second son of Merari, was the father of Mahli, Eder, and Jeremoth.

[24]These were the clans and families of the tribe of Levi. Those who were twenty years and older were assigned to work at the LORD's temple.

[25]David said:

The LORD God of Israel has given his people peace, and he will live in Jerusalem forever. [26]And so, the Levites won't need to move the sacred tent and the things used for worship from place to place. [27]From now on, all Levites at least twenty years old [28]will serve the LORD by helping Aaron's descendants do their work at the temple, by keeping the courtyards and rooms of the temple clean, and by making sure that everything used in worship stays pure. [29]They will also be in charge of the sacred loaves of bread, the flour for the grain sacrifices, the thin wafers, any offerings to be baked, and the flour mixed with olive oil. These Levites will weigh and measure these offerings.

[30]Every morning and evening, the Levites are to give thanks to the LORD and sing praises to him. [31]They must also give thanks and sing praises when sacrifices are offered on each Sabbath, as well as during New Moon Festivals and other religious feasts. There must always be enough Levites on duty at the temple to do everything that needs to be done. [32]They were once in charge of taking care of the sacred tent; now they are responsible for the temple and for helping Aaron's descendants.

David Assigns the Priests Their Duties

24 Aaron's descendants were then divided into work groups. Aaron had four sons: Nadab, Abihu, Eleazar, and Ithamar. [2]But Nadab and Abihu died long before their father, without having any sons. That's why Eleazar and Ithamar served as priests.

[3]David divided Aaron's descendants into groups, according to their assigned work. Zadok, one of Eleazar's descendants, and Ahimelech, one of Ithamar's descendants, helped David.

[4]Eleazar's descendants were divided into sixteen groups, and Ithamar's were divided into eight groups, because Eleazar's family included more family leaders. [5]However, both families included temple officials and priests, and so to make sure the work was divided fairly, David asked God what to do.[c]

[6]As each group was assigned their duties, Shemaiah the son of Nethanel the Levite wrote down the name of the family leader in charge of that group. The witnesses were David and his officials, as well as Zadok the priest, Ahimelech the son of Abiathar, and the family leaders from the clans of the priests and the Levites.

[7-18]Each group of priests went by the name of its family leader, and they were assigned their duties in the following order: Jehoiarib, Jedaiah, Harim, Seorim, Malchijah, Mijamin, Hakkoz, Abijah, Jeshua, Shecaniah, Eliashib, Jakim, Huppah, Jeshebeab, Bilgah, Immer, Hezir, Happizzez, Pethahiah, Jehezkel, Jachin, Gamul, Delaiah, Maaziah. [19]These men were assigned their duties at the temple, just as the LORD God of Israel had commanded their ancestor Aaron.

The Rest of the Levites Are Assigned Their Duties

[20]Here is a list of the other descendants of Levi:

Amram was the ancestor of Shubael and Jehdeiah.
[21]Rehabiah was the ancestor of Isshiah, the oldest son in his family.
[22]Izhar was the father of Shelomoth and the grandfather of Jahath.

---

[c]**24.5** *asked God what to do*: The Hebrew text has "cast lots" (see the note at 6.65).

²³Hebron had four sons, in the following order: Jeriah, Amariah, Jahaziel, and Jekameam. ²⁴Uzziel was the father of Micah and the grandfather of Shamir. ²⁵Isshiah, Micah's brother, was the father of Zechariah. ²⁶Merari was the father of Mahli, Mushi, and Jaaziah.

²⁷Jaaziah had three sons: Shoham, Zaccur, and Ibri.ᵈ ²⁸⁻²⁹Mahli was the father of Eleazar and Kish. Eleazar had no sons, but Kish was the father of Jerahmeel. ³⁰Mushi had three sons: Mahli, Eder, and Jerimoth.

Your investment of yourself in the lives of other people is treasure laid up in heaven.

ANNETTE LAPLACA

These were the descendants of Levi, according to their clans. ³¹Each one was assigned his duties in the same way that their relatives the priests had been assigned their duties. David, Zadok, Ahimelech, and the family leaders of the priests and Levites were the witnesses.

David Assigns the Temple Musicians Their Duties

25 David and the temple officials chose the descendants of Asaph, Heman, and Jeduthun to be in charge of music. They were to praise the LORD by playing cymbals, harps and other stringed instruments. Here is a list of the musicians and their duties:

²Asaph's four sons, Zaccur, Joseph, Nethaniah, and Asarelah, were under the direction of their father and played music whenever the king told them to.

³Jeduthun's six sons, Gedaliah, Zeri, Jeshaiah, Shimei,ᵉ Hashabiah, and Mattithiah, were under the direction of their father and played harps and sang praises to the LORD.

⁴Heman had fourteen sons: Bukkiah, Mattaniah, Uzziel, Shebuel, Jerimoth, Hananiah, Hanani, Eliathah, Giddalti, Romamtiezer, Joshbekashah, Mallothi, Hothir, Mahazioth. ⁵Heman was one of the king's prophets, and God honored Heman by giving him fourteen sons and three daughters. ⁶His sons were under his direction and played cymbals, harps, and other stringed instruments during times of worship at the temple.

Asaph, Jeduthun, and Heman took their orders directly from the king.

⁷There were two hundred eighty-eight of these men, and all of them were skilled musicians. ⁸David assigned them their duties by asking the LORD what he wanted.ʲ Everyone was responsible for something, whether young or old, teacher or student.

⁹⁻³¹The musicians were divided into twenty-four groups of twelve, and each group went by the name of their family leader. They were assigned their duties in the following order: Joseph, Gedaliah, Zaccur, Zeri, Nethaniah, Bukkiah, Asarelah, Jeshaiah, Mattaniah, Shimei, Uzziel, Hashabiah, Shebuel, Mattithiah, Jerimoth, Hananiah, Joshbekashah, Hanani, Mallothi, Eliathah, Hothir, Giddalti, Mahazioth, and Romamtiezer.

The Temple Guards Are Assigned Their Duties

26 The temple guards were also divided into groups according to clans.

Meshelemiah son of Kore was from the Korah clan and was a descendant of Asaph. ²He had seven sons, who were born in the following order: Zechariah, Jediael, Zebadiah, Jathniel, ³Elam, Jehohanan, and Eliehoenai.

⁴⁻⁵Obed-Edom had been blessed with eight sons: Shemaiah, Jehozabad, Joah, Sachar, Nethanel, Ammiel, Issachar, and Peullethai.

⁶⁻⁷Shemaiah was the father of Othni, Rephael, Obed, Elzabad, Elihu, and Semachiah. They were all respected leaders in their clan. ⁸There were sixty-two descendants of Obed-Edom who were strong enough to be guards at the temple.

ᵈ24.26,27 *Ibri:* One possible meaning for the difficult Hebrew text of verses 26, 27. ᵉ25.3 *Shimei:* One Hebrew manuscript and two ancient translations; other Hebrew manuscripts do not have this name. ʲ25.8 *asking the LORD what he wanted:* The Hebrew text has "casting lots" (see the note at 6.65).

[9]Eighteen descendants of Meshelemiah were chosen for this work.

[10-11]Hosah, from the Merari clan, was the father of Shimri, Hilkiah, Tebaliah, and Zechariah. Hosah had made Shimri the family leader, even though he was not the oldest son. Thirteen men from Hosah's family were chosen to be temple guards.

[12]The guards were divided into groups, according to their family leaders, and they were assigned duties at the temple, just like the other Levites. [13]Each group, no matter how large or small, was assigned a gate to guard, and they let the LORD show them what he wanted done.[g]

[14]Shelemiah[h] was chosen to guard the East Gate. Zechariah his son was a wise man and was chosen to guard the North Gate. [15]Obed-Edom was then chosen to guard the South Gate, and his sons were chosen to guard the storerooms. [16]Shuppim and Hosah were chosen to guard the West Gate and the Shallecheth Gate on the upper road.

The guards were assigned the following work schedule: [17]Each day six guards were on duty on the east side of the temple, four were on duty on the north side, and four were on duty on the south side. Two guards were stationed at each of the two storerooms, [18]four were stationed along the road leading to the west courtyard,[i] and two guards stayed in the court itself.

[19]These were the guard duties assigned to the men from the clans of Korah and Merari.

Guards Are Assigned to the Treasury

[20]The Levites who were relatives of the Korahites and the Merarites were[j] in charge of guarding the temple treasury and the gifts that had been dedicated to God.

[21]Ladan was from the Gershon clan and was the father of Jehieli. Many of his other descendants were family leaders in the clan.[k] [22]Jehieli was the father of Zetham and Joel, and they were responsible for guarding the treasury.

[23]Other guards at the treasury were from the Kohathite clans of Amram, Izhar, Hebron, and Uzziel.

[24]Shebuel was a descendant of Gershom the son of Moses. He was the chief official in charge of the temple treasury. [25]The descendants of Gershom's brother Eliezer included Rehabiah, Jeshaiah, Joram, Zichri, and Shelomoth.

[26]Shelomoth and his relatives were in charge of all the gifts that were dedicated to the LORD. These included the gifts that King David had dedicated, as well as those dedicated by the family leaders, army officers, and army commanders. [27]And whenever valuable things were captured in battle, these men brought some of them to the temple. [28]Shelomoth and his relatives were responsible for any gifts that had been given to the temple, including those from Samuel the prophet, King Saul the son of Kish, Abner the son of Ner,[l] and Joab the son of Zeruiah.

Other Officers Are Assigned Their Duties

[29]Chenaniah from the Izhar clan and his sons were government officials and judges. They did not work at the temple.

[30]Hashabiah from the Hebron clan and one thousand seven hundred of his skilled relatives were the officials in charge of all religious and government business in the Israelite territories west of the Jordan River.

[31-32]Jerijah was the leader of the Hebron clan. David assigned him and two thousand seven hundred of his relatives, who were all respected family leaders, to be the officials in charge of all religious and government business in the tribes of Reuben, Gad, and East Manasseh. David found out about these men during the fortieth year of his rule, when he had a list made of all the families in the Hebron clan. They were from the town of Jazer in the territory of Gilead.

David Assigns Army Commanders

27 Each month a group of twenty-four thousand men served as soldiers in Israel's army. These men, which included the family leaders, army commanders, and officials of the king, were under the command of the following men, arranged by the month of their service:

---

[g]26.13 they let the LORD show them what he wanted done: The Hebrew text has "they cast lots to find out what the LORD wanted done" (see the note at 6.65).
[h]26.14 Shelemiah: Another spelling for Meshelemiah.
[i]26.18 courtyard: One possible meaning for the difficult Hebrew text. [j]26.20 The Levites . . . were: One ancient translation; Hebrew "Ahijah the Levite was."
[k]26.21 Many of his other . . . clan: One possible meaning for the difficult Hebrew text. [l]26.28 Abner the son of Ner: Abner was King Saul's uncle (see 9.39).

[2]In the first month, Jashobeam the son of Zabdiel, [3]a descendant of Perez;

[4]in the second month, Dodai the Ahohite, whose assistant was Mikloth;[m]

[5]in the third month, Benaiah the son of Jehoiada the priest, [6]who was the leader of the Thirty Warriors, and whose son Ammizabad was also an army commander;[n]

[7]in the fourth month, Asahel the brother of Joab, whose son Zebadiah took over command after him;

[8]in the fifth month, Shamhuth from the Izrah clan;

[9]in the sixth month, Ira the son of Ikkesh from Tekoa;

[10]in the seventh month, Helez from Pelon in the territory of Ephraim;

[11]in the eighth month, Sibbecai from Hushah of the Zerah clan;

[12]in the ninth month, Abiezer from Anathoth in the territory of Benjamin;

[13]in the tenth month, Maharai from Netophah of the Zerah clan;

[14]in the eleventh month, Benaiah from Pirathon in the territory of Ephraim;

[15]in the twelfth month, Heldai from Netophah, who was a descendant of Othniel.

David Assigns Tribal Leaders

[16-22]Here is a list of the leaders of each tribe in Israel:

Eliezer son of Zichri was over Reuben; Shephatiah son of Maacah was over Simeon; Hashabiah son of Kemuel was over the Levites, and Zadok the priest was over the descendants of Aaron; Elihu the brother of David was over Judah; Omri son of Michael was over Issachar; Ishmaiah son of Obadiah was over Zebulun; Jerimoth son of Azriel was over Naphtali; Hoshea son of Azaziah was over Ephraim; Joel son of Pedaiah was over West Manasseh; Iddo son of Zechariah was over East Manasseh; Jaasiel son of Abner was over Benjamin; Azarel son of Jeroham was over Dan.

[23]When David decided to count the people of Israel, he gave orders not to count anyone under twenty years of age, because the LORD had promised long ago that Israel would have as many people as there are stars in the sky. [24]Joab the son of Zeruiah had begun to count the people, but he stopped when the LORD began punishing Israel. So the total number was never included in David's official records.

Officials in Charge of the King's Property

[25]Azmaveth the son of Adiel was in charge of the king's personal storage rooms. Jonathan the son of Uzziah was in charge of the king's other storerooms that were in the towns, the villages, and the defense towers in Israel.

[26]Ezri the son of Chelub was in charge of the workers who farmed the king's land.

[27]Shimei from Ramah was in charge of the vineyards, and Zabdi from Shepham was in charge of storing the wine.

[28]Baal Hanan from Geder was in charge of the olive and sycamore trees in the western foothills, and Joash was in charge of storing the olive oil.

[29]Shitrai from Sharon was responsible for the cattle that were kept in Sharon Plain, and Shaphat son of Adlai was responsible for those kept in the valleys.

[30]Obil the Ishmaelite was in charge of the camels, Jehdeiah from Meronoth was in charge of the donkeys, and Jaziz the Hagrite was in charge of the sheep and goats.

[31]These were the men in charge of David's royal property.

David's Personal Advisors

[32]David's uncle Jonathan was a wise and intelligent advisor. He and Jehiel the son of Hachmoni taught David's sons.

[33]Ahithophel and Hushai the Archite were two of David's advisors. [34]Jehoiada the son of Benaiah was the king's advisor after Ahithophel, and later, Abiathar was his advisor.

Joab was commander of Israel's army.

David Gives Solomon the Plans for the Temple

28 David called a meeting in Jerusalem for all of Israel's leaders, including the tribal leaders, the government officials, the army commanders, the officials in charge of the royal property and livestock, the palace officials, and the brave warriors.

[2]After everyone was there, David stood up and said:

Listen to me, my people. I wanted

---

to build a place where the sacred chest would be kept, so we could go there and worship the LORD our God. I have prepared all the supplies for building a temple, ³but the LORD has refused to let me build it, because he said I have killed too many people in battle.

A home is a place where we find direction.

GIGI GRAHAM TCHIVIDJIAN

⁴The LORD God chose Judah to be the leading tribe in Israel. Then from Judah, he chose my father's family, and from that family, he chose me to be the king of Israel, and he promised that my descendants will also rule as kings. ⁵The LORD has blessed me with many sons, but he chose my son Solomon to be the next king of Israel. ⁶The LORD said to me, "Your son Solomon will build my temple, and it will honor me. Solomon will be like a son to me, and I will be like a father to him. ⁷If he continues to obey my laws and commands, his kingdom will never end."

⁸My friends, you are the LORD's people. And now, with God as your witness, I want you to promise that you will do your best to obey everything the LORD God has commanded us. Then this land will always belong to you and your descendants.

⁹Solomon, my son, worship God and obey him with all your heart and mind, just as I have done. He knows all your thoughts and your reasons for doing things, and so if you turn to him, he will hear your prayers. But if you ignore him, he will reject you forever. ¹⁰The LORD has chosen you to build a temple for worshiping him. Be confident and do the work you have been assigned.

¹¹After David finished speaking, he gave Solomon the plans for building the main rooms of the temple, including the porch, the storerooms, the rooms upstairs and downstairs, as well as the most holy place. ¹²He gave Solomon his plans for the courtyards and the open areas around the temple, and for the rooms to store the temple treasures and gifts that had been dedicated to God.

¹³David also gave Solomon his plans for dividing the priests and the Levites into groups, as well as for the work that needed to be done at the temple and for taking care of the objects used for worship. ¹⁴He told Solomon how much gold and silver was to be used in making the sacred objects, ¹⁵including the lampstands and lamps, ¹⁶the gold table which held the sacred loaves of bread, the tables made of silver, ¹⁷the meat forks, the bowls and cups, ¹⁸the gold incense altar, and the gold statue of a chariot for the winged creatures which were on the lid of the sacred chest.

¹⁹David then said to Solomon:

The LORD showed me how his temple is to be built. ²⁰But you must see that everything is done according to these plans. Be confident, and never be afraid of anything or get discouraged. The LORD my God will help you do everything needed to finish the temple, so it can be used for worshiping him. ²¹The priests and Levites have been assigned their duties, and all the skilled workers are prepared to do their work. The people and their leaders will do anything you tell them.

Gifts for Building the Temple

29 David told the crowd:

God chose my son Solomon to build the temple, but Solomon is young and has no experience. This is not just any building—this is the temple for the LORD God! ²That's why I have done my best to get everything Solomon will need to build it—gold, silver, bronze, iron, wood, onyx, turquoise, colored gems, all kinds of precious stones, and marble.

³Besides doing all that, I have promised to give part of my own gold and silver as a way of showing my love for God's temple. ⁴Almost one hundred twenty tons of my finest gold and over two hundred fifty tons of my silver will be used to decorate its walls ⁵and to make the gold and silver

objects. Now, who else will show their dedication to the LORD by giving gifts for building his temple?

⁶After David finished speaking, the family leaders, the tribal leaders, the army commanders, and the government officials voluntarily gave gifts ⁷for the temple. These gifts included almost two hundred tons of gold, three hundred eighty tons of silver, almost seven hundred tons of bronze, and three thousand seven hundred fifty tons of iron. ⁸Everyone who owned precious stones also donated them to the temple treasury, where Jehiel from the Levite clan of Gershon guarded them.

⁹David and the people were very happy that so much had been given to the LORD, and they all celebrated.

David Praises the LORD

¹⁰Then, in front of everyone, David sang praises to the LORD:

I praise you forever, LORD! You are the God our ancestor Jacob° worshiped. ¹¹Your power is great, and your glory is seen everywhere in heaven and on earth. You are king of the entire world, ¹²and you rule with strength and power. You make people rich and powerful and famous. ¹³We thank you, our God, and praise you.

¹⁴But why should we be happy that we have given you these gifts? They belong to you, and we have only given back what is already yours. ¹⁵We are only foreigners living here on earth for a while, just as our ancestors were. And we will soon be gone, like a shadow that suddenly disappears.

¹⁶Our LORD God, we have brought all these things for building a temple to honor you. They belong to you, and you gave them to us. ¹⁷But we are happy, because everyone has voluntarily given you these things. You know what is in everyone's heart, and you are pleased when people are honest. ¹⁸Always make us eager to give, and help us be faithful to you, just as our ancestors Abraham, Isaac, and Jacob faithfully worshiped you. ¹⁹And give Solomon the desire to completely obey your laws and teachings, and the

---

°**29.10** *Jacob:* See the note at 1.34.

*Spiritual*Life—How can I show my devotion to God? *(1 Chronicles 29.1-20)*

Let God decide who does what.

The program you carefully planned gets put into someone else's hands at the last minute. It goes great, and that person gets credit for the success.

You jump into a new enterprise with every hope that it will succeed, and it flops. All your best efforts can't make it work.

Where is God at those times? He is closer than we think. And often he gives us certain responsibilities but doesn't expect us to do everything. Sometimes he chooses someone else for a job we'd like to do. Sometimes he lets us take a project only so far, then hands it over to someone else. Sometimes he lets us find out the hard way that we can't do everything.

In each of those difficult circumstances, we can find reasons to worship him for his wisdom. King David did that after he realized God's plans were different from his own. David wanted to build a permanent temple in Jerusalem to replace the movable tent of worship. God said no; the building of the temple would be left to David's son Solomon. In fact, David would never see it.

David's response to disappointment was to make sure Solomon had everything he needed for the future task—and to lead a huge crowd of people in public worship. His prayers pointed everyone's attention away from himself and toward the Lord. (See also 1 Kings 18; Haggai 1.1-11; Acts 4.32—5.11; 1 Corinthians 13.11-13.)

Words To Remember: *But why should we be happy that we have given you these gifts? They belong to you, and we have only given back what is already yours.*
—1 Chronicles 29.14

desire to build the temple for which I have provided these gifts.

²⁰David then said to the people, "Now it's your turn to praise the LORD, the God your ancestors worshiped!" So everyone praised the LORD, and they bowed down to honor him and David their king.

Solomon Is Crowned King

²¹The next day, the Israelites slaughtered a thousand bulls, a thousand rams, and a thousand lambs, and they offered them as sacrifices to please the LORD,ᵖ along with offerings of wine. ²²The people were very happy, and they ate and drank there at the LORD's altar.

That same day, Solomon was crowned king. The people celebrated and poured olive oil on Solomon's head to show that he would be their next king. They also poured oil on Zadok's head to show that he was their priest.

²³So Solomon became king after David his father. Solomon was successful, and everyone in Israel obeyed him. ²⁴Every official and every soldier, as well as all of David's other sons, were loyal to him. ²⁵The LORD made Solomon a great king, and the whole nation was amazed at how famous he was. In fact, no other king of Israel was as great as Solomon.

David Dies

²⁶David the son of Jesse was king of Israel ²⁷for forty years. He ruled from Hebron for seven years and from Jerusalem for thirty-three years. ²⁸David was rich and respected and lived to be an old man. Then he died, and his son Solomon became king.

²⁹Everything David did while he was king is included in the history written by the prophets Samuel, Nathan, and Gad. ³⁰They wrote about his powerful rule and about the things that happened not only to him, but also to Israel and the other nations.

ᵖ**29.21** *sacrifices to please the* LORD: See the note at 16.1.

2 Chronicles

History with Hindsight

Second Chronicles opens with the wise Solomon on the throne (but see 1 Kings 1,2 for the rough road in securing it!). A relative period of peace in that geographical area allowed Solomon to have one key point in his agenda—the temple—desired by his father but denied because of his military battles (1 Chronicles 22.8; 28.3). With the help of David's planning (materials, money, men) and verbal encouragement, Solomon oversees the temple's completion in seven years.

Then this magnificent temple and its furnishings was dedicated. First the sacred chest (left in a tent in Zion to the south in Jerusalem) was brought to the sound of vocal and instrumental music. It was a grand day for singing! Then the Lord showed his acceptance—the temple was filled with a cloud: the Lord's glory (5.13,14). After Solomon gives a prayer of dedication, there's a national festival, and the people are joyful when they return home. They know that the Lord has done a great and good thing for David, Solomon, and the people of Israel.

During the temple's construction, Solomon was involved in extensive trade, including revenues rivaling Fort Knox's gold bars. (The Queen of Sheba's mission was undoubtedly one involving commerce between the two kingdoms.) Solomon also increased his army, especially with chariots, but apparently never used them in battle.

However, the push for Solomon's immense and precise construction (including the temple and palaces he built for his many wives) had its human cost. Many foreigners in the land (possibly attracted by its economic prosperity and as a place of safety in earlier wars) were drafted into being stonecutters and carriers. Israelites, too, were forced into labor.

There was heavy taxation, and unrest was rampant.

Soon after Solomon's death, revolution broke out, led by Jeroboam, a foreman in the building of the temple. Civil war split the nation. Two tribes (Judah and Benjamin) followed Solomon's son, and the other ten in the more northern area crowned Jeroboam. But unlike the book of 2 Kings, 2 Chronicles emphasizes the nation of Judah and its kings as the royal descendants of David.

Idolatry, social injustice, and military confrontations with the nation of Israel and other countries weakened Judah. God militarily saved them (701 B.C.) from the Assyrian siege of Jerusalem (2 Chronicles 32), and there were great revivals under Hezekiah and Josiah.

But the sin was too deep, the idolatry too rampant. After Josiah's untimely death in the battle of Megiddo, his four successors could not stem the tide of ultimate defeat. In 586 B.C. Jerusalem as a city with its temple of grandeur was destroyed by the Babylonians. Most of the survivors became exiles. They and their descendants were in Babylon for seventy years.

What can we learn from 2 Chronicles? That we need to survey our own past, looking for the hand of God. Then we should make whatever adjustments are needed in our current priorities and relationship with him—before he has to call them to our attention.

2 Chronicles at a Glance

The LORD Makes Solomon Wise

(1 Kings 3.1-15)

1 King Solomon, the son of David, was now in complete control of his kingdom, because the LORD God had blessed him and made him a powerful king. ²⁻⁵At that time, the sacred tent that Moses the servant of the LORD had made in the desert was still kept at Gibeon, and in front of the tent was the bronze altar that Bezalel[a] had made.

One day, Solomon told the people of Israel, the army commanders, the officials, and the family leaders, to go with him to the place of worship at Gibeon, even though his father King David had already moved the sacred chest from Kiriath-Jearim to the tent that he had set up for it in Jerusalem. Solomon and the others went to Gibeon to worship the LORD, ⁶and there at the bronze altar, Solomon offered a thousand animals as sacrifices to please the LORD.[b]

⁷God appeared to Solomon that night in a dream and said, "Solomon, ask for anything you want, and I will give it to you."

⁸Solomon answered:

LORD God, you were always loyal to my father David, and now you have made me king of Israel. ⁹I am supposed to rule these people, but there are as many of them as there are specks of dust on the ground. So keep the promise you made to my father ¹⁰and make me wise. Give me the knowledge I'll need to be the king of this great nation of yours.

¹¹God replied:

Solomon, you could have asked me to make you rich or famous or to let you live a long time. Or you could have asked for your enemies to be destroyed. Instead, you asked for wisdom and knowledge to rule my people. ¹²So I will make you wise and intelligent. But I will also make you richer and more famous than any king before or after you.

---

[a]1.2-5 *Bezalel*: Hebrew "Bezalel son of Uri son of Hur."
[b]1.6 *sacrifices to please the LORD*: These sacrifices have traditionally been called "whole burnt offerings," because the whole animal was burned on the altar. A main purpose of such sacrifices was to please the LORD with the smell of the sacrifice, and so in the CEV they are often called "sacrifices to please the LORD."

¹³Solomon then left Gibeon and returned to Jerusalem, the capital city of Israel.

God is not impressed with sophisticated words, but with sincere hearts.

PAMELA PEARSON WONG
AND KELSEY D. MENEHAN

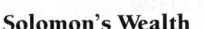

Solomon's Wealth
(1 Kings 10.26-29)

¹⁴Solomon had a force of one thousand four hundred chariots and twelve thousand horses that he kept in Jerusalem and other towns.

¹⁵While Solomon was king of Israel, there was silver and gold everywhere in Jerusalem, and cedar was as common as ordinary sycamore trees in the foothills.

¹⁶⁻¹⁷Solomon's merchants bought his horses and chariots in the regions of Musri and Kue.ᶜ They paid about fifteen pounds of silver for a chariot and almost four pounds of silver for a horse. They also sold horses and chariots to the Hittite and Syrian kings.

Solomon Asks Hiram
To Help Build the Temple
(1 Kings 5.1-12)

2 Solomon decided to build a temple where the LORD would be worshiped, and also to build a palace for himself. ²He assigned seventy thousand men to carry building supplies and eighty thousand to cut stone from the hills. And he chose three thousand six hundred men to supervise these workers.

³Solomon sent the following message to King Hiram of Tyre:

Years ago, when my father David was building his palace, you supplied him with cedar logs. Now will you send me supplies? ⁴I am building a temple where the LORD my God will be worshiped. Sweet-smelling incense will be burned there, and sacred bread will be offered to him. Worshipers will offer sacrifices to the LORD every morning and evening, every Sabbath, and on the first day of each month, as well as during all our religious festivals. These things will be done for all time, just as the LORD has commanded.

⁵This will be a great temple, because our God is greater than all other gods. ⁶No one can ever build a temple large enough for God—even the heavens are too small a place for him to live in! All I can do is build a place where we can offer sacrifices to him.

⁷Send me a worker who can not only carve, but who can work with gold, silver, bronze, and iron, as well as make brightly colored cloth. The person you send will work here in Judah and Jerusalem with the skilled workers that my father has already hired.

⁸I know that you have workers who are experts at cutting lumber in Lebanon. So would you please send me some cedar, pine, and juniper logs? My workers will be there to help them, ⁹because I'll need a lot of lumber to build such a large and glorious temple. ¹⁰I will pay your woodcutters one hundred twenty-five thousand bushels of wheat, the same amount of barley, one hundred fifteen thousand gallons of wine, and that same amount of olive oil.

¹¹Hiram sent his answer back to Solomon:

I know that the LORD must love his people, because he has chosen you to be their king. ¹²Praise the LORD God of Israel who made heaven and earth! He has given David a son who isn't only wise and smart, but who has the knowledge to build a temple for the LORD and a palace for himself.

¹³I am sending Huram Abi to you. He is very bright. ¹⁴His mother was from the Israelite tribe of Dan, and his father was from Tyre. Not only is Huram an expert at working with gold, silver, bronze, iron, stone, and wood, but he can also make colored cloth

---

ᶜ1.16,17 *Musri and Kue:* Hebrew "Egypt and Kue." Musri and Kue were regions located in what is today southeast Turkey.

and fine linen. And he can carve anything if you give him a pattern to follow. He can help your workers and those hired by your father King David.

[15]Go ahead and send the wheat, barley, olive oil, and wine you promised to pay my workers. [16]I will tell them to start cutting down trees in Lebanon. They will cut as many as you need, then tie them together into rafts, and float them down along the coast to Joppa. Your workers can take them to Jerusalem from there.

Solomon's Work Force

[17]Solomon counted all the foreigners who were living in Israel, just as his father David had done when he was king, and the total was 153,600. [18]He assigned 70,000 of them to carry building supplies and 80,000 of them to cut stone from the hills. He chose 3,600 others to supervise the workers and to make sure the work was completed.

The Temple Is Built
(1 Kings 6.1-38)

3 [1-2]Solomon's workers began building the temple in Jerusalem on the second day of the second month,[d] four years after Solomon had become king of Israel. It was built on Mount Moriah where the LORD had appeared to David at the threshing place that had belonged to Araunah[e] from Jebus.

[3]The inside of the temple was ninety feet long and thirty feet wide, according to the older standards.[f] [4]Across the front of the temple was a porch thirty feet wide and thirty feet[g] high. The inside walls of the porch were covered with pure gold.

[5]Solomon had the inside walls of the temple's main room paneled first with pine and then with a layer of gold, and he had them decorated with carvings of palm trees and designs that looked like chains. [6]He used precious stones to decorate the temple, and he used gold imported from Parvaim[h] [7]to decorate the ceiling beams, the doors, the door frames, and the walls. Solomon also had the workers carve designs of winged creatures into the walls.

[8]The most holy place was thirty feet square, and its walls were covered with almost twenty-five tons of fine gold. [9]More than a pound of gold was used to cover the

heads of the nails. The walls of the small storage rooms were also covered with gold.[i]

[10]Solomon had two statues of winged creatures[j] made to put in the most holy place, and he covered them with gold. [11-13]Each creature had two wings and was fifteen feet from the tip of one wing to the tip of the other wing. Solomon set them next to each other in the most holy place, facing the doorway. Their wings were spread out and reached all the way across the thirty foot room.

[14]A curtain[k] was made of fine linen woven with blue, purple, and red wool, and embroidered with designs of winged creatures.

The Two Columns
(1 Kings 7.15-22)

[15]Two columns were made for the entrance to the temple. Each one was fifty-two feet tall and had a cap on top that was seven and a half feet high. [16]The top of each column was decorated with designs that looked like chains[l] and with a hundred carvings of pomegranates.[m] [17]Solomon had one of the columns placed on the south side of the temple's entrance; it was called Jachin.[n] The other one was placed on the north side of the entrance; it was called Boaz.[o]

The Furnishings for the Temple
(1 Kings 7.23-51)

4 Solomon had a bronze altar made that was thirty feet square and fifteen feet high. [2]He also gave orders to make a large metal bowl called the Sea. It was fifteen feet across, about seven and a half feet deep,

---

[d]**3.1,2** second month: Ziv, the second month of the Hebrew calendar, from about mid-April to mid-May. [e]**3.1,2** Araunah: The Hebrew text has "Ornan," another spelling of the name (see 2 Samuel 24.18-25; 1 Chronicles 21.18—22.1). [f]**3.3** according to the older standards: There were possibly two different standards of measurement during Israel's history. [g]**3.4** thirty feet: Some manuscripts of two ancient translations; Hebrew "one hundred eighty feet." [h]**3.6** Parvaim: An unknown place. [i]**3.9** The walls . . . gold: One possible meaning for the difficult Hebrew text. [j]**3.10** statues of winged creatures: These were symbols of the LORD's throne on earth (see Exodus 25.18-22). [k]**3.14** A curtain: To separate the most holy place from the main room of the temple. [l]**3.16** designs that looked like chains: One possible meaning for the difficult Hebrew text. [m]**3.16** pomegranates: A pomegranate is a small red fruit that looks like an apple. In ancient times, it was a symbol of life. [n]**3.17** Jachin: Or "He (God) makes secure." [o]**3.17** Boaz: Or "He (God) is strong."

and forty-five feet around. ³Its outer edge was decorated with two rows of carvings of bulls, ten bulls to every eighteen inches, all made from the same piece of metal as the bowl. ⁴The bowl itself sat on top of twelve bronze bulls, with three bulls facing outward in each of four directions. ⁵The sides of the bowl were four inches thick, and its rim was in the shape of a cup that curved outward like flower petals. The bowl held about fifteen thousand gallons.

⁶He also made ten small bowls and put five on each side of the large bowl. The small bowls were used to wash the animals that were burned on the altar as sacrifices, and the priests used the water in the large bowl to wash their hands.

⁷Ten gold lampstands were also made according to the plans. Solomon placed these lampstands inside the temple, five on each side of the main room. ⁸He also made ten tables and placed them in the main room, five on each side. And he made a hundred small gold sprinkling bowls.

⁹Solomon gave orders to build two courtyards: a smaller one that only priests could use and a larger one. The doors to these courtyards were covered with bronze. ¹⁰The large bowl called the Sea was placed near the southeast corner of the temple.

¹¹Huram made shovels, sprinkling bowls, and pans for hot ashes. Here is a list of the other furnishings he made for God's temple: ¹²two columns, two bowl-shaped caps for the tops of these columns, two chain designs on the caps, ¹³four hundred pomegranates^p for the chain designs, ¹⁴the stands and the small bowls, ¹⁵the large bowl and the twelve bulls that held it up, ¹⁶pans for hot ashes, as well as shovels and meat forks.

Huram made all these things out of polished bronze ¹⁷by pouring melted bronze into the clay molds he had set up near the Jordan River, between Succoth and Zeredah.

¹⁸There were so many bronze furnishings that no one ever knew how much bronze it took to make them.

¹⁹Solomon also gave orders to make the following temple furnishings out of gold: the altar, the tables that held the sacred loaves of bread,^q ²⁰the lampstands and the lamps that burned in front of the most holy place, ²¹flower designs, lamps and tongs, ²²lamp snuffers, small sprinkling bowls,

ladles, fire pans, and the doors to the most holy place and the main room of the temple.

5 After the LORD's temple was finished, Solomon put in its storage rooms everything that his father David had dedicated to the LORD, including the gold and silver, and the objects used in worship.

Solomon Brings the Sacred Chest to the Temple
(1 Kings 8.1-13)

²⁻³The sacred chest had been kept on Mount Zion, also known as the city of David. But Solomon decided to have the chest moved to the temple while everyone was in Jerusalem to celebrate the Festival of Shelters during the seventh month.^r

We can allow inevitable disappointments to gnaw at our marital contentment, or use them to grow closer to each other and to God.

CLAUDIA ARP

Solomon called together all the important leaders of Israel. ⁴⁻⁵Then the priests and the Levites picked up the sacred chest, the sacred tent, and the objects used for worship, and they carried them to the temple. ⁶Solomon and a crowd of people walked in front of the chest, and along the way they sacrificed more sheep and cattle than could be counted.

⁷The priests carried the chest into the most holy place and put it under the winged creatures, ⁸whose wings covered the chest and the poles used for carrying it. ⁹The poles were so long that they could be seen from just outside the most holy place, but

not from anywhere else. And they stayed there from then on.

[10]The only things kept in the chest were the two flat stones Moses had put there when the LORD made his agreement with the people of Israel at Mount Sinai,[s] after bringing them out of Egypt.

[11-13]The priests of every group had gone through the ceremony to make themselves clean and acceptable to the LORD. The Levite musicians, including Asaph, Heman, Jeduthun, and their sons and relatives, were wearing robes of fine linen. They were standing on the east side of the altar, playing cymbals, small harps, and other stringed instruments. One hundred twenty priests were with these musicians, and they were blowing trumpets.

They were praising the LORD by playing music and singing:

"The LORD is good,
    and his love never ends."

Suddenly a cloud filled the temple as the priests were leaving the holy place. [14]The LORD's glory was in that cloud, and the light from it was so bright that the priests could not stay inside to do their work.

6 Solomon prayed:

"Our LORD, you said that you
    would live in a dark cloud.
[2]Now I've built a glorious temple
    where you can live forever."

Solomon Speaks to the People
(1 Kings 8.14-21)

[3]Solomon turned toward the people standing there. Then he blessed them [4-6]and said:

Praise the LORD God of Israel! He brought his people out of Egypt long ago and later kept his promise to make my father David the king of Israel. The LORD also promised him that Jerusalem would be the city where his temple will be built, and now that promise has come true.

[7]When my father wanted to build a temple for the LORD God of Israel, [8]the LORD said, "It's good that you want to build a temple where I can be worshiped. [9]But you're not the one to do

it. Your son will build the temple to honor me."

[10]The LORD has done what he promised. I am now the king of Israel, and I've built a temple for the LORD our God. [11]I've also put the sacred chest in the temple. And in that chest are the two flat stones on which is written the solemn agreement the LORD made with our ancestors when he rescued them from Egypt.

Solomon Prays at the Temple
(1 Kings 8.22-53)

[12-13]Earlier, Solomon had a bronze platform made that was about eight feet square and five feet high, and he put it in the center of the outer courtyard near the altar. Solomon stood on the platform facing the altar with everyone standing behind him. Then he lifted his arms toward heaven; he knelt down [14]and prayed:

LORD God of Israel, no other god in heaven or on earth is like you!

You never forget the agreement you made with your people, and you are loyal to anyone who faithfully obeys your teachings. [15]My father David was your servant, and today you have kept every promise you made to him.

[16]You promised that someone from his family would always be king of Israel, if they do their best to obey you, just as he did. [17]Please keep this promise you made to your servant David. [18]There's not enough room in all of heaven for you, LORD God. How could you possibly live on earth in this temple I have built? [19]But I ask you to answer my prayer. [20]This is the temple where you have chosen to be worshiped. Please watch over it day and night and listen when I turn toward it and pray. [21]I am your servant, and the people of Israel belong to you, and so whenever any of us look toward this temple and pray, answer from your home in heaven and forgive our sins.

[22]Suppose someone accuses a person of a crime, and the accused has to stand in front of the altar in your temple and say, "I swear I am innocent!"

---

[s]5.10 *Sinai*: Hebrew "Horeb."

²³Listen from heaven and decide who is right. Then punish the guilty person and let the innocent one go free.

²⁴Suppose your people Israel sin against you, and then an enemy defeats them. If they come to this temple and beg for forgiveness, ²⁵listen from your home in heaven. Forgive them and bring them back to the land you gave their ancestors.

²⁶Suppose your people sin against you, and you punish them by holding back the rain. If they stop sinning and turn toward this temple to pray in your name, ²⁷listen from your home in heaven and forgive them. The people of Israel are your servants, so teach them to live right. And send rain on the land you promised them forever.

²⁸Sometimes the crops may dry up or rot or be eaten by locusts[t] or grasshoppers, and your people will be starving. Sometimes enemies may surround their towns, or your people will become sick with deadly diseases. ²⁹Please listen when anyone in Israel truly feels sorry and sincerely prays with arms lifted toward your temple.

³⁰You know what is in everyone's heart. So from your home in heaven answer their prayers, according to what they do and what is in their hearts. ³¹Then your people will worship you and obey you for as long as they live in the land you gave their ancestors.

³²Foreigners will hear about you and your mighty power, and some of them will come to live among your people Israel. If any of them pray toward this temple, ³³listen from your home in heaven and answer their prayers. Then everyone on earth will worship you, just as your own people Israel do, and they will know that I have built this temple in your honor.

³⁴Sometimes you will order your people to attack their enemies. Then your people will turn toward this temple I have built for you in your chosen city, and they will pray to you. ³⁵Answer their prayers from heaven and give them victory.

---

[t]6.28 *locusts*: A type of grasshopper that comes in swarms and causes great damage to crops.

---

*Spiritual*Life—How should I pray? *(2 Chronicles 6,7)*

Pray for your nation.
While prayer for our nation is not high on most prayer lists, maybe it should be. When King Solomon dedicated the temple, he offered one of the most lofty prayers in Scripture. First, Solomon assembled the people as if the dedication were a grand affair of State—which it was. He stood in front of them and lifted his arms toward heaven. Then he knelt down.

Solomon prayed for his people, not just those present on that day, but for those who would worship in that temple for the nearly four hundred years it would stand. His prayer was full of praise: "No other god in heaven or on earth is like you!" (6.14). But Solomon also had a realistic view of his people. Over and over he said, "Suppose your people sin" (6.26). Suppose someone committed a crime, suppose they sinned and the Lord brought sickness, suppose he became angry enough to let enemies drag them away. In the event of each offense, Solomon begged that if his people repented, that the Lord would hear their prayers and forgive.

Solomon's prayer provides a model for our own praying. We can kneel, as he did, and follow his prayer paragraph by paragraph. At each point we can insert descriptions, needs, and temptations of our own particular nation. God answered Solomon's prayer with a beautiful promise. Perhaps he will do the same for us. (See also 2 Samuel 7.18-29; 2 Kings 19.14-19; Nehemiah 1; Psalm 85; Lamentations 5; Matthew 6.5-15; Acts 4.23-31.)

Words To Remember: *If my own people will humbly pray and turn back to me and stop sinning, then I will answer them from heaven. I will forgive them and make their land fertile once again.—2 Chronicles 7.14*

³⁶Everyone sins. But when your people sin against you, suppose you get angry enough to let their enemies drag them away to foreign countries. ³⁷⁻³⁹Later, they may feel sorry for what they did and ask your forgiveness. Answer them when they pray toward this temple I have built for you in your chosen city, here in this land you gave their ancestors. From your home in heaven, listen to their sincere prayers and forgive your people who have sinned against you.

⁴⁰LORD God, hear us when we pray in this temple. ⁴¹Come to your new home, where we have already placed the sacred chest, which is the symbol of your strength. I pray that when the priests announce your power to save people, those who are faithful to you will celebrate what you've done for them. ⁴²Always remember the love you had for your servant David,ᵘ so that you will not reject your chosen kings.

Solomon Dedicates the Temple
(1 Kings 8.62-66)

7 As soon as Solomon finished praying, fire came down from heaven and burned up the offerings. The LORD's dazzling glory then filled the temple, ²and the priests could not go in.

³When the crowd of people saw the fire and the LORD's glory, they knelt down and worshiped the LORD. They prayed:

"The LORD is good,
    and his love never ends."

⁴⁻⁵Solomon and the people dedicated the temple to the LORD by sacrificing twenty-two thousand cattle and one hundred twenty thousand sheep. ⁶Everybody stood up during the ceremony. The priests were in their assigned places, blowing their trumpets. And the Levites faced them, playing the musical instruments that David had made for them to use when they praised the LORD for his never-ending love.

⁷On that same day, Solomon dedicated the courtyard in front of the temple and got it ready to be used for worship. The bronze altar he had made was too small, so he used the courtyard to offer sacrifices to please the

LORDᵛ and grain sacrifices, and also to send up in smoke the fat from the other offerings.

⁸For seven days, Solomon and the crowd celebrated the Festival of Shelters, and people came from as far away as the Egyptian Gorge in the south and Lebo-Hamath in the north. ⁹Then on the next day, everyone came together for worship. They had celebrated a total of fourteen days, seven days for the dedication of the altar and seven more days for the festival. ¹⁰Then on the twenty-third day of the seventh month,ʷ Solomon sent everyone home. They left very happy because of all the good things the LORD had done for David and Solomon, and for his people Israel.

The LORD Appears to Solomon Again
(1 Kings 9.1-9)

¹¹The LORD's temple and Solomon's palace were now finished. In fact, everything Solomon had planned to do was completed. ¹²Some time later, the LORD appeared to Solomon in a dream and said:

I heard your prayer, and I have chosen this temple as the place where sacrifices will be offered to me.

¹³Suppose I hold back the rain or send locustsˣ to eat the crops or make my people suffer with deadly diseases. ¹⁴If my own people will humbly pray and turn back to me and stop sinning, then I will answer them from heaven. I will forgive them and make their land fertile once again. ¹⁵I will hear the prayers made in this temple, ¹⁶because it belongs to me, and this is where I will be worshiped forever. I will never stop watching over it.

¹⁷Your father David obeyed me, and now, Solomon, you must do the same. Obey my laws and teachings, ¹⁸and I will keep my solemn promise to him that someone from your family will always be king of Israel.

¹⁹But if you or any of the people of Israel disobey my laws or start worshiping foreign gods, ²⁰I will pull you out of this land I gave you. I will desert

---

ᵘ**6.42** *the love you had for your servant David*: Or "how loyal your servant David was to you."
ᵛ**7.7** *sacrifices to please the LORD*: See the note at 1.6.
ʷ**7.10** *seventh month*: See the note at 5.2, 3.
ˣ**7.13** *locusts*: See the note at 6.28.

this temple where I said I would be worshiped, so that people everywhere will think it is only a joke and will make fun of it. ²¹This temple is now magnificent. But when these things happen, everyone who walks by it will be shocked and will ask, "Why did the LORD do such a terrible thing to his people and to this temple?" ²²Then they will answer, "It was because the people of Israel rejected the LORD their God, who rescued their ancestors from Egypt, and they started worshiping other gods."

Other Things Solomon Did
(1 Kings 9.10-28)

8 It took twenty years for the LORD's temple and Solomon's palace to be built. ²After that, Solomon had his workers rebuild the towns that Hiram had given him. Then Solomon sent Israelites to live in those towns.

³Solomon attacked and captured the town of Hamath-Zobah. ⁴He had his workers build the town of Tadmor in the desert and some towns in Hamath where he could keep his supplies. ⁵He strengthened Upper Beth-Horon and Lower Beth-Horon by adding walls and gates that could be locked. ⁶He did the same thing to the town of Baalath and to the cities where he kept supplies, chariots, and horses. Solomon had his workers build whatever he wanted in Jerusalem, Lebanon, and anywhere else in his kingdom.

⁷⁻⁹Solomon did not force the Israelites to do his work. Instead, they were his soldiers, officers, army commanders, and cavalry troops. But he did make slaves of the Hittites, Amorites, Perizzites, Hivites, and Jebusites who were living in Israel. These were the descendants of those foreigners the Israelites did not destroy, and they remained Israel's slaves.

¹⁰Solomon appointed two hundred fifty officers to be in charge of his workers.

¹¹Solomon's wife, the daughter of the king of Egypt, moved from the part of Jerusalem called David's City to her new palace that Solomon had built. The sacred chest had been kept in David's City, which made his palace sacred, and so Solomon's wife could no longer live there.

¹²Solomon offered sacrifices to the LORD on the altar he had built in front of the temple. ¹³He followed the requirements that Moses had given for sacrifices offered on the Sabbath, on the first day of each month, the Festival of Thin Bread, the Harvest Festival, and the Festival of Shelters.

¹⁴Solomon then assigned the priests and the Levites their duties at the temple, and he followed the instructions that his father David had given him. Some of the Levites were to lead music and help the priests in their duties, and others were to guard the temple gates ¹⁵and the storage rooms. The priests and Levites followed these instructions exactly.

¹⁶Everything Solomon had planned to do was now finished—from the laying of the temple's foundation to its completion.

¹⁷Solomon went to Ezion-Geber and Eloth, two Edomite towns on the Red Sea.ʸ ¹⁸Hiram sent him ships and some of his experienced sailors. They went with Solomon's own sailors to the country of Ophirᶻ and brought back about seventeen tons of gold for Solomon.

The Queen of Sheba Visits Solomon
(1 Kings 10.1-13)

9 The Queen of Sheba heard how famous Solomon was, so she went to Jerusalem to test him with difficult questions. She took along several of her officials, and she loaded her camels with gifts of spices, jewels, and gold. When she arrived, she and Solomon talked about everything she could think of. ²He answered every question, no matter how difficult it was.

³⁻⁴The Queen was amazed at Solomon's wisdom. She was breathless when she saw his palace,ᵃ the food on his table, his officials, all his servants in their uniforms, and the sacrifices he offered at the LORD's temple. ⁵She said:

Solomon, in my own country I had heard about your wisdom and all you've done. ⁶But I didn't believe it until I saw it with my own eyes! And there's so much I didn't hear about. You are greater than I was told. ⁷Your

---

ʸ8.17 *Red Sea*: Hebrew *yam suph*, here referring to the Gulf of Aqaba, since the term is extended to include the northeastern arm of the Red Sea (see also the note at Exodus 13.18). ᶻ8.18 *Ophir*: The location of this place is not known. ᵃ9.3,4 *his palace*: Or "the temple."

people and officials are lucky to be here where they can listen to the wise things you say.

> *When I look back on trials,*
> *I see the tracing of*
> *God's ways, the wisdom*
> *of his design.*
> VIRELLE KIDDER

⁸I praise the LORD your God. He is pleased with you and has made you king of Israel. God loves the people of this country and will never desert them, so he has given them a king who will rule fairly and honestly.

⁹The Queen of Sheba gave Solomon almost five tons of gold, a large amount of jewels, and the best spices anyone had ever seen.

¹⁰⁻¹²In return, Solomon gave her everything she wanted—even more than she had given him. Then she and her officials went back to their own country.

Solomon's Wealth
(1 Kings 10.14-29)

Hiram's and Solomon's sailors brought gold, juniper wood, and jewels from the country of Ophir. Solomon used the wood to make steps[b] for the temple and palace, and harps and other stringed instruments for the musicians. Nothing like these had ever been made in Judah.

¹³Solomon received about twenty-five tons of gold each year, ¹⁴not counting what the merchants and traders brought him. The kings of Arabia and the leaders of Israel also gave him gold and silver.

¹⁵Solomon made two hundred gold shields that weighed about seven and a half pounds each. ¹⁶He also made three hundred smaller gold shields that weighed almost four pounds, and he put these shields in his palace in Forest Hall.

¹⁷His throne was made of ivory and covered with pure gold. ¹⁸It had a gold footstool attached to it and armrests on each side. There was a statue of a lion on each side of the throne, ¹⁹and there were two lion statues on each of the six steps leading up to the throne. No other throne in the world was like Solomon's.

²⁰Solomon's cups and dishes in Forest Hall were made of pure gold, because silver was almost worthless in those days.

²¹Solomon had a lot of seagoing ships.[c] Every three years he sent them out with Hiram's ships to bring back gold, silver, and ivory, as well as monkeys and peacocks.[d]

²²Solomon was the richest and wisest king in the world. ²³⁻²⁴Year after year, other kings came to hear the wisdom God had given him. And they brought gifts of silver and gold, as well as clothes, weapons, spices, horses, and mules.

²⁵Solomon had four thousand stalls for his horses and chariots, and he owned twelve thousand horses that he kept in Jerusalem and other towns.

²⁶He ruled all the nations from the Euphrates River in the north to the land of Philistia in the south, as far as the border of Egypt.

²⁷While Solomon was king, there was silver everywhere in Jerusalem, and cedar was as common as the sycamore trees in the western foothills. ²⁸Solomon's horses were brought in from other countries, including Musri.[e]

Solomon Dies
(1 Kings 11.41-43)

²⁹Everything else Solomon did while he was king is written in the records of Nathan the prophet, Ahijah the prophet from Shiloh, and Iddo the prophet who wrote about Jeroboam son of Nebat. ³⁰After Solomon had ruled forty years from Jerusalem, ³¹he died and was buried in the city of his father David. His son Rehoboam then became king.

Some of the People Rebel against Rehoboam
(1 Kings 12.1-20)

10 Rehoboam went to Shechem where everyone was waiting to crown him king.

---

[b]**9.10-12** *steps*: Or "stools" or "railings."
[c]**9.21** *seagoing ships*: The Hebrew text has "ships of Tarshish," which may have been a Phoenician city in Spain. "Ships of Tarshish" probably means large, seagoing ships.   [d]**9.21** *peacocks*: Or "baboons."
[e]**9.28** *Musri*: See the note at 1.16, 17.

²Jeroboam son of Nebat heard what was happening, and he returned from Egypt, where he had gone to hide from Solomon. ³The people from the northern tribes of Israel sent for him. Then together they went to Rehoboam and said, ⁴"Your father Solomon forced us to work very hard. But if you make our work easier, we will serve you and do whatever you ask."

⁵Rehoboam replied, "Come back in three days for my answer." So the people left.

⁶Rehoboam went to some leaders who had been his father's senior officials, and he asked them, "What should I tell these people?"

⁷They answered, "If you want them to serve and obey you, then you should be kind and promise to make their work easier."

⁸But Rehoboam refused their advice and went to the younger men who had grown up with him and were now his officials. ⁹He asked, "What do you think I should say to these people who asked me to make their work easier?"

¹⁰His younger advisors said:

Here's what we think you should say to them: "Compared to me, my father was weak.ʲ ¹¹He made you work hard, but I'll make you work even harder. He punished you with whips, but I'll use whips with pieces of sharp metal!"

¹²Three days later, Jeroboam and the others came back. ¹³Rehoboam ignored the advice of the older advisors. He spoke bluntly ¹⁴and told them exactly what his own advisors had suggested. He said: "My father made you work hard, but I'll make you work even harder. He punished you with whips, but I'll use whips with pieces of sharp metal!"

¹⁵⁻¹⁹When the people realized that Rehoboam would not listen to them, they shouted: "We don't have to be loyal to David's family. We can do what we want. Come on, people of Israel, let's go home! Rehoboam can rule his own people."

Adoniramᵍ was in charge of the work force, and Rehoboam sent him to talk to the people. But they stoned him to death. Then Rehoboam ran to his chariot and hurried back to Jerusalem.

Everyone from Israel's northern tribes went home, leaving Rehoboam to rule only the people from Judah. And since that day, the people of Israel have been opposed to David's descendants in Judah.ʰ All of this happened just as Ahijah the LORD's prophet from Shiloh had told Jeroboam.

Shemaiah the Prophet Warns Rehoboam
(1 Kings 12.21-24)

11 After Rehoboam returned to Jerusalem, he decided to attack Israel and regain control of the whole country. So he called together one hundred eighty thousand soldiers from the tribes of Judah and Benjamin.

²Meanwhile, the LORD had told Shemaiah the prophet ³to tell Rehoboam and everyone from Judah and Benjamin, ⁴"The LORD warns you not to go to war against the people from the northern tribes—they are your relatives. Go home! The LORD is the one who made these things happen."

God is the one who has his hands on the steering wheel of the universe. That's a great comfort to me.

BARBARA JOHNSON

Rehoboam and his army obeyed the LORD's message and did not attack Jeroboam and his troops.

Rehoboam Fortifies Cities in Judah

⁵Rehoboam ruled from Jerusalem, and he had several cities in Judah turned into fortresses so he could use them to defend his country. These cities included ⁶Bethlehem, Etam, Tekoa, ⁷Beth-Zur, Soco, Adullam, ⁸Gath, Mareshah, Ziph, ⁹Adoraim,

---

ʲ**10.10** *Compared . . . weak:* Hebrew "My little finger is bigger than my father's waist." ᵍ**10.15-19** *Adoniram:* The Hebrew text has "Hadoram," another spelling of the name. ʰ**10.15-19** *the people of Israel have been opposed . . . Judah:* From this time on, "Israel" usually refers only to the northern kingdom. The southern kingdom is called "Judah."

Lachish, Azekah, [10]Zorah, Aijalon, and Hebron. After he had fortified these cities in the territories of Judah and Benjamin, [11]he assigned an army commander to each of them and stocked them with supplies of food, olive oil, and wine, [12]as well as with shields and spears. He used these fortified cities to keep control of Judah and Benjamin.

The Priests and the Levites Support Rehoboam

[13]The priests and Levites from the northern tribes of Israel gave their support to King Rehoboam. [14]And since Jeroboam and the kings of Israel that followed him would not allow any Levites to serve as priests, most Levites left their towns and pasturelands in Israel and moved to Jerusalem and other towns in Judah. [15]Jeroboam chose his own priests to serve at the local shrines[i] in Israel and at the places of worship where he had set up statues of goat-demons and of calves.

[16]But some of the people from Israel wanted to worship the LORD God, just as their ancestors had done. So they followed the priests and Levites to Jerusalem, where they could offer sacrifices to the LORD. [17]For the next three years, they lived in Judah and were loyal to Rehoboam and his kingdom, just as they had been loyal to David and Solomon.

Rehoboam's Family

[18]Rehoboam married Mahalath, whose father was Jerimoth son of David, and whose mother was Abihail the daughter of Eliab and granddaughter of Jesse. [19]Rehoboam and Mahalath had three sons: Jeush, Shemariah, and Zaham. [20]Then Rehoboam married Maacah the daughter of Absalom. Their sons were Abijah, Attai, Ziza, and Shelomith. [21]Rehoboam had eighteen wives, but he also married sixty other women,[j] and he was the father of twenty-eight sons and sixty daughters. Rehoboam loved his wife Maacah the most, [22]so he chose their oldest son Abijah to be the next king. [23]Rehoboam was wise enough to put one of his sons in charge of each fortified city in his kingdom. He gave them all the supplies they needed and found wives for every one of them.

King Shishak of Egypt Invades Judah
(1 Kings 14.25-28)

12 Soon after Rehoboam had control of his kingdom, he and everyone in Judah stopped obeying the LORD. [2]So in the fifth year of Rehoboam's rule, the LORD punished them for their unfaithfulness and allowed King Shishak of Egypt to invade Judah. [3]Shishak attacked with his army of one thousand two hundred chariots and sixty thousand cavalry troops, as well as Egyptian soldiers from Libya, Sukkoth, and Ethiopia.[k] [4]He captured every one of the fortified cities in Judah and then marched to Jerusalem.

[5]Rehoboam and the leaders of Judah had gone to Jerusalem to escape Shishak's invasion. And while they were there, Shemaiah the prophet told them, "The LORD says that because you have disobeyed him, he has now abandoned you. The LORD will not help you against Shishak!"

> God loves me not because I'm a good wife or mom, but just because I'm his. He isn't shocked when I fail. He knows I'm weak and is waiting to forgive me.
> SUSAN ALEXANDER YATES

[6]Rehoboam and the leaders were sorry for what they had done and admitted, "The LORD is right. We have deserted him."
[7]When the LORD heard this, he told Shemaiah:

The people of Judah are truly sorry for their sins, and so I won't let

---

[i]11.15 *local shrines:* The Hebrew text has "high places," which were local places to worship foreign gods.
[j]11.21 *other women:* This translates a Hebrew word for women who were legally bound to a man, but without the full privileges of a wife. [k]12.3 *Ethiopia:* The Hebrew text has "Cush," which was a region south of Egypt that included parts of the present countries of Ethiopia and Sudan.

Shishak completely destroy them. But because I am still angry, [8]he will conquer and rule them.

Then my people will know what it's like to serve a foreign king instead of serving me.

[9]Shishak attacked Jerusalem and took all the valuable things from the temple and from the palace, including Solomon's gold shields.

[10]Rehoboam had bronze shields made to replace the gold ones, and he ordered the guards at the city gates to keep them safe. [11]Whenever Rehoboam went to the LORD's temple, the guards carried the shields. But they always took them back to the guardroom as soon as he had finished worshiping.

[12]Rehoboam turned back to the LORD, and so the LORD did not let Judah be completely destroyed, and Judah was prosperous again.

Rehoboam's Rule in Judah
(1 Kings 14.21, 29-31)

[13]Rehoboam was forty-one years old when he became king, and he ruled seventeen years from Jerusalem, the city where the LORD had chosen to be worshiped. His mother Naamah was from Ammon. Rehoboam was a powerful king, [14]but he still did wrong and refused to obey the LORD.

[15]Everything else Rehoboam did while he was king, including a history of his family, is written in the records of the two prophets, Shemaiah and Iddo. During Rehoboam's rule, he and King Jeroboam of Israel were constantly at war. [16]When Rehoboam died, he was buried beside his ancestors in Jerusalem, and his son Abijah became king.

King Abijah of Judah
(1 Kings 15.1-8)

13 Abijah[l] became king of Judah in Jeroboam's eighteenth year as king of Israel, [2]and he ruled from Jerusalem for three years. His mother was Micaiah the daughter of Uriel from Gibeah.

Some time later, Abijah and King Jeroboam of Israel went to war against each other. [3]Abijah's army had four hundred thousand troops, and Jeroboam met him in battle with eight hundred thousand troops.

[4]Abijah went to the top of Mount Zemaraim[m] in the hills of Ephraim and shouted:

Listen, Jeroboam and all you Israelites! [5]The LORD God of Israel has made a solemn promise that every king of Israel will be from David's family. [6]But Jeroboam, you were King Solomon's official, and you rebelled. [7]Then right after Rehoboam became king, you and your bunch of worthless followers challenged Rehoboam, who was too young to know how to stop you.

[8]Now you and your powerful army think you can stand up to the kingdom that the LORD has given to David's descendants. The only gods you have are those gold statues of calves that Jeroboam made for you. [9]You don't even have descendants of Aaron on your side, because you forced out the LORD's priests and Levites. In their place, you appoint ordinary people to be priests, just as the foreign nations do. In fact, anyone who brings a bull and seven rams to the altar can become a priest of your so-called gods.

[10]But we have not turned our backs on the LORD God! Aaron's own descendants serve as our priests, and the Levites are their assistants. [11]Two times every day they offer sacrifices and burn incense to the LORD. They set out the sacred loaves of bread on a table that has been purified, and they light the lamps in the gold lampstand every day at sunset. We follow the commands of the LORD our God—you have rejected him! [12]That's why God is on our side and will lead us into battle when the priests sound the signal on the trumpets. It's no use, Israelites. You might as well give up. There's no way you can defeat the LORD, the God your ancestors worshiped.

[13]But while Abijah was talking, Jeroboam had sent some of his troops to attack Judah's army from behind, while the rest attacked from the front. [14]Judah's army realized they were trapped, and so they prayed

---

[l]13.1 *Abijah:* In 1 Kings 15.1-8 his name is spelled "Abijam." [m]13.4 *Mount Zemaraim:* Probably located on the northern border of the territory of Benjamin.

to the LORD. The priests blew the signal on the trumpet, [15]and the troops let out a battle cry. Then with Abijah leading them into battle, God defeated Jeroboam and Israel's army. [16]The Israelites ran away, and God helped Judah's soldiers slaughter [17]five hundred thousand enemy troops. [18]Judah's army won because they had trusted the LORD God of their ancestors.

[19]Abijah kept up his attack on Jeroboam's army and captured the Israelite towns of Bethel, Jeshanah, and Ephron, as well as the villages around them.

[20]Jeroboam never regained his power during the rest of Abijah's rule. The LORD punished Jeroboam, and he died, but Abijah became more powerful.

[21]Abijah had a total of fourteen wives, twenty-two sons, and sixteen daughters. [22]Everything Abijah said and did while he was king is written in the records of Iddo the prophet.

King Asa of Judah

14 Abijah died and was buried in Jerusalem. Then his son Asa became king, and Judah had ten years of peace.

[2]Asa obeyed the LORD his God and did right. [3]He destroyed the local shrines[n] and the altars to foreign gods. He smashed the stone images of gods and cut down the sacred poles[o] used in worshiping the goddess Asherah. [4]Then he told everyone in Judah to worship the LORD God, just as their ancestors had done, and to obey his laws and teachings. [5]He destroyed every local shrine and incense altar in Judah.

[6]The LORD blessed Judah with peace while Asa was king, and so during that time, Asa fortified many of the towns. [7]He said to the people, "Let's build walls and defense towers for these towns, and put in gates that can be locked with bars. This land still belongs to us, because we have obeyed the LORD our God. He has given us peace from all our enemies." The people did everything Asa had suggested.

[8]Asa had a large army of brave soldiers: Three hundred thousand of them were from the tribe of Judah and were armed with shields and spears; two hundred eighty thousand were from Benjamin and were armed with bows and arrows.

Judah Defeats Ethiopia's Army

[9]Zerah from Ethiopia[p] led an army of a million soldiers and three hundred chariots to the town of Mareshah[q] in Judah. [10]Asa met him there, and the two armies prepared for battle in Zephathah Valley.

God is amazingly creative in the way he can fashion a ministry from the deficits in your life.

ELISA MORGAN

[11]Asa prayed:

LORD God, only you can help a powerless army defeat a stronger one. So we depend on you to help us. We will fight against this powerful army to honor your name, and we know that you won't be defeated. You are the LORD our God.

[12]The LORD helped Asa and his army defeat the Ethiopians. The enemy soldiers ran away, [13]but Asa and his troops chased them as far as Gerar. It was a total defeat—the Ethiopians could not even fight back![r]

The soldiers from Judah took everything that had belonged to the Ethiopians. [14]The people who lived in the villages around Gerar learned what had happened and were afraid of the LORD. So Judah's army easily defeated them and carried off everything of value that they wanted from these towns. [15]They also attacked the camps where the shepherds lived and took a lot of sheep, goats, and camels. Then they went back to Jerusalem.

Asa Destroys the Idols in Judah

15 Some time later, God spoke to Azariah son of Oded. [2]At once, Azariah went to Asa and said:

---

[n]14.3 *local shrines:* See the note at 11.15.
[o]14.3 *sacred poles:* Or "trees," used as symbols of Asherah, the goddess of fertility.   [p]14.9 *Ethiopia:* See the note at 12.3.   [q]14.9 *Mareshah:* About twenty-five miles southwest of Jerusalem.   [r]14.13 *the Ethiopians could not even fight back:* Or "not one of the Ethiopians survived!"

Listen to me, King Asa and you people of Judah and Benjamin. The LORD will be with you and help you, as long as you obey and worship him. But if you disobey him, he will desert you.

As I've struggled to deal with my loneliness, I've come to realize that the "solution" doesn't lie in increased activity, but in facing the reality of loneliness and seeking the presence of God within it.

BONNIE BUDZOWSKI

---

³For a long time, the people of Israel did not worship the true God or listen to priests who could teach them about God. They refused to obey God's Law. ⁴But whenever trouble came, Israel turned back to the LORD their God and worshiped him.

⁵There was so much confusion in those days that it wasn't safe to go anywhere in Israel. ⁶Nations were destroying each other, and cities were wiping out other cities, because God was causing trouble and unrest everywhere.

⁷So you must be brave. Don't give up! God will honor you for obeying him.

⁸As soon as Asa heard what Azariah the prophet said, he gave orders for all the idols in Judah and Benjamin to be destroyed, including those in the towns he had captured in the territory of Ephraim. He also repaired the LORD's altar that was in front of the temple porch.

⁹Asa called together the people from Judah and Benjamin, as well as the people from the territories of Ephraim, West Manasseh, and Simeon who were living in Judah. Many of these people were now loyal to Asa, because they had seen that the LORD was with him.

¹⁰In the third month of the fifteenth year of Asa's rule, they all met in Jerusalem. ¹¹That same day, they took seven hundred bulls and seven thousand sheep and goats from what they had brought back from Gerar and sacrificed them as offerings to the LORD. ¹²They made a solemn promise to faithfully worship the LORD God their ancestors had worshiped, ¹³and to put to death anyone who refused to obey him. ¹⁴The crowd solemnly agreed to keep their promise to the LORD, then they celebrated by shouting and blowing trumpets and horns. ¹⁵Everyone was happy because they had made this solemn promise, and in return, the LORD blessed them with peace from all their enemies.

¹⁶Asa's grandmother Maacah had made a disgusting idol of the goddess Asherah, so he cut it down, crushed it, and burned it in Kidron Valley. Then he removed Maacah from her position as queen mother.ˢ ¹⁷As long as Asa lived, he was faithful to the LORD, even though he did not destroy the local shrinesᵗ in Israel. ¹⁸He placed in the temple all the silver and gold objects that he and his father had dedicated to God.

¹⁹There was peace in Judah until the thirty-fifth year of Asa's rule.

King Baasha of Israel Invades Judah
(1 Kings 15.16-22)

16 In the thirty-sixth year of Asa's rule, King Baasha of Israel invaded Judah and captured the town of Ramah. He started making the town stronger, and he put troops there to stop people from going in and out of Judah.

²When Asa heard about this, he took the silver and gold from his palace and from the LORD's temple. Then he sent it to Damascus with this message for King Benhadad of Syria: ³"I think we should sign a peace treaty, just as our fathers did. This silver and gold is a present for you. Would you please break your treaty with King Baasha of Israel and force him to leave my country?"

⁴Benhadad did what Asa asked and sent the Syrian army into Israel. They captured the towns of Ijon, Dan, Abel-Maim,ᵘ and all

---

ˢ15.16 *queen mother*: Or "the mother of the king," which was an important position in biblical times (see 1 Kings 2.19). ᵗ15.17 *local shrines*: See the note at 11.15. ᵘ16.4 *Abel-Maim*: Also called "Abel-Bethmaacah" (see 1 Kings 15.20).

the towns in Naphtali where supplies were kept. ⁵When Baasha heard about it, he stopped his work on the town of Ramah.

⁶Asa ordered everyone in Judah to carry away the stones and wood Baasha had used to fortify Ramah. Then he fortified the towns of Geba and Mizpah with these same stones and wood.

Hanani the Prophet Condemns Asa

⁷Soon after that happened, Hanani the prophet went to Asa and said:

You depended on the king of Syria instead of depending on the LORD your God. And so, you will never defeat the Syrian army. ⁸Remember how powerful the Ethiopianᵛ and Libyan army was, with all their chariots and cavalry troops! You trusted the LORD to help you then, and you defeated them. ⁹The LORD is constantly watching everyone, and he gives strength to those who faithfully obey him. But you have done a foolish thing, and your kingdom will never be at peace again.

¹⁰When Asa heard this, he was so angry that he put Hanani in prison. Asa was also cruel to some of his people.ʷ

Asa Dies
(1 Kings 15.23, 24)

¹¹Everything Asa did while he was king is written in *The History of the Kings of Judah and Israel.* ¹²In the thirty-ninth year of his rule, he got a very bad foot disease, but he relied on doctors and refused to ask the LORD for help. ¹³He died two years later.

¹⁴Earlier, Asa had his own tomb cut out of a rock hill in Jerusalem. So he was buried there, and the tomb was filled with spices and sweet-smelling oils. Then the people built a bonfire in his honor.

King Jehoshaphat of Judah

17 Jehoshaphat son of Asa became king and strengthened his defenses against Israel. ²He assigned troops to the fortified cities in Judah, as well as to other towns in Judah and to those towns in Ephraim that his father Asa had captured.

³⁻⁴When Jehoshaphat's father had first become king of Judah, he was faithful to the LORD and refused to worship the god Baal as the kings of Israel did. Jehoshaphat followed his father's example and obeyed and worshiped the LORD. And so the LORD blessed Jehoshaphat ⁵and helped him keep firm control of his kingdom. The people of Judah brought gifts to Jehoshaphat, but even after he became very rich and respected, ⁶he remained completely faithful to the LORD. He destroyed all the local shrinesˣ in Judah, including the places where the goddess Asherah was worshiped.

> *Of all the gifts that a parent can give a child, the gift of learning to make good choices is the most valuable and long-lasting.*
>
> GRACE KETTERMAN

⁷In the third year of Jehoshaphat's rule, he chose five officials and gave them orders to teach the LORD's Law in every city and town in Judah. They were Benhail, Obadiah, Zechariah, Nethanel, and Micaiah. ⁸Their assistants were the following nine Levites: Shemaiah, Nethaniah, Zebadiah, Asahel, Shemiramoth, Jehonathan, Adonijah, Tobijah, and Tob-Adonijah. Two priests, Elishama and Jehoram, also went along. ⁹They carried with them a copy of the LORD's Law wherever they went and taught the people from it.

¹⁰The nations around Judah were afraid of the LORD's power, so none of them attacked Jehoshaphat. ¹¹Philistines brought him silver and other gifts to keep peace. Some of the Arab people brought him seventy-seven hundred rams and the same number of goats.

¹²As Jehoshaphat became more powerful, he built fortresses and cities ¹³where he stored supplies. He also kept in Jerusalem some experienced soldiers ¹⁴from the Judah

---

ᵛ**16.8** *Ethiopian:* See the note at 12.3.   ʷ**16.10** *Asa was also cruel . . . people:* Or "Asa also started being cruel to some of his people."   ˣ**17.6** *local shrines:* See the note at 11.15.

and Benjamin tribes. These soldiers were grouped according to their clans.

Adnah was the commander of the troops from Judah, and he had three hundred thousand soldiers under his command. [15]Jehohanan was second in command, with two hundred eighty thousand soldiers under him. [16]Amasiah son of Zichri, who had volunteered to serve the LORD, was third in command, with two hundred thousand soldiers under him.

[17]Eliada was a brave warrior who commanded the troops from Benjamin. He had two hundred thousand soldiers under his command, all of them armed with bows and shields. [18]Jehozabad was second in command, with one hundred eighty thousand soldiers under him. [19]These were the troops who protected the king in Jerusalem, not counting those he had assigned to the fortified cities throughout the country.

Micaiah Warns King Ahab of Israel
(1 Kings 22.1-28)

18 Jehoshaphat was now very rich and famous. He signed a treaty with King Ahab of Israel by arranging the marriage of his son and Ahab's daughter.

[2]One day, Jehoshaphat went to visit Ahab in his capital city of Samaria. Ahab slaughtered sheep and cattle and prepared a big feast to honor Jehoshaphat and the officials with him. Ahab talked about attacking the city of Ramoth in Gilead,[y] [3]and finally asked, "Jehoshaphat, would you go with me to attack Ramoth?"

"Yes," Jehoshaphat answered. "My army is at your command. [4]But first let's ask the LORD what to do."

[5]Ahab sent for four hundred prophets and asked, "Should I attack the city of Ramoth?"

"Yes!" the prophets answered. "God will help you capture the city."

[6]But Jehoshaphat said, "Just to make sure, is there another of the LORD's prophets we can ask?"

[7]"We could ask Micaiah son of Imlah," Ahab said. "But I hate Micaiah. He always has bad news for me."

"Don't say that!" Jehoshaphat replied. [8]Then Ahab sent someone to bring Micaiah as soon as possible.

[9]All this time, Ahab and Jehoshaphat were dressed in their royal robes and were seated on their thrones at the threshing place near the gate of Samaria, listening to the prophets tell them what the LORD had said.

[10]Zedekiah son of Chenaanah was one of the prophets. He had made some horns out of iron and shouted, "Ahab, the LORD says you will attack the Syrians like a bull with iron horns and wipe them out!"

[11]All the prophets agreed that Ahab should attack the Syrians at Ramoth and promised that the LORD would help him defeat them.

[12]Meanwhile, the messenger who went to get Micaiah whispered, "Micaiah, all the prophets have good news for Ahab. Now go and say the same thing."

[13]"I'll say whatever the living LORD my God tells me to say," Micaiah replied.

[14]Then Micaiah went up to Ahab, who asked, "Micaiah, should we attack Ramoth?"

"Yes!" Micaiah answered. "The LORD will help you capture the city."

[15]Ahab shouted, "Micaiah, I've told you over and over to tell me the truth! What does the LORD really say?"

[16]Micaiah answered, "In a vision[z] I saw Israelite soldiers wandering around, lost in the hills like sheep without a shepherd. The LORD said, 'These troops have no leader. They should go home and not fight.' "

[17]Ahab turned to Jehoshaphat and said, "I told you he would bring me bad news!"

[18]Micaiah replied:

I then saw the LORD seated on his throne with every creature in heaven gathered around him. [19]The LORD asked, "Who can trick Ahab and make him go to Ramoth where he will be killed?"

They talked about it for a while, [20]then finally a spirit came forward and said to the LORD, "I can trick Ahab."

"How?" the LORD asked.

[21]"I'll make Ahab's prophets lie to him."

---

[y]18.2 *attacking the city of Ramoth in Gilead*: The Syrians had taken control of Ramoth (see 1 Kings 22.3, 4).
[z]18.16 *vision*: In ancient times, prophets often told about future events from what they had seen in visions or dreams.

"Good!" the LORD replied. "Now go and do it. You will be successful."

²²Ahab, this is exactly what has happened. The LORD made all your prophets lie to you, and he knows you will soon be destroyed.

²³Zedekiah walked over and slapped Micaiah on the face. Then he asked, "Do you really think the LORD would speak to you and not to me?"

²⁴Micaiah answered, "You'll find out on the day you have to hide in the back room of some house."

²⁵Ahab shouted, "Arrest Micaiah! Take him to Prince Joash and Governor Amon of Samaria. ²⁶Tell them to put him in prison and to give him nothing but bread and water until I come back safely."

²⁷Micaiah said, "If you do come back, I was wrong about what the LORD wanted me to say." Then he told the crowd, "Don't forget what I said!"

Ahab Dies at Ramoth
(1 Kings 22.29-35)

²⁸Ahab and Jehoshaphat led their armies to Ramoth in Gilead. ²⁹Before they went into battle, Ahab said, "Jehoshaphat, I'll disguise myself, but you wear your royal robe." Ahab disguised himself and went into battle.

³⁰The king of Syria had ordered his chariot commanders to attack only Ahab. ³¹So when they saw Jehoshaphat in his robe, they thought he was Ahab and started to attack him. But Jehoshaphat prayed, and the LORD made the Syrian soldiers stop. ³²And when they realized he wasn't Ahab, they left him alone.

³³However, during the fighting a soldier shot an arrow without even aiming, and it hit Ahab between two pieces of his armor. He shouted to his chariot driver, "I've been hit! Get me out of here!"

³⁴The fighting lasted all day, with Ahab propped up in his chariot so he could see the Syrian troops. He stayed there until evening, and by sundown he was dead.

19 Jehoshaphat returned safely to his palace in Jerusalem. ²But the prophet Jehu son of Hanani met him and said:

By helping that wicked Ahab, you have made friends with someone who hates the LORD. Now the LORD God is angry at you! ³But not everything about you is bad. You destroyed the sacred poles[a] used in worshiping the goddess Asherah—that shows you have tried to obey the LORD.

Jehoshaphat Appoints Judges To Settle Cases

⁴Jehoshaphat lived in Jerusalem, but he often traveled through his kingdom, from Beersheba in the south to the edge of the hill country of Ephraim in the north. He talked with the people and convinced them to turn back to the LORD God and worship him, just as their ancestors had done.

⁵He assigned judges to each of the fortified cities in Judah ⁶and told them:

Be careful when you make your decisions in court, because these are the LORD's people, and he will know what you decide. ⁷So do your work in honor of him and know that he won't allow you to be unfair to anyone or to take bribes.

⁸Jehoshaphat also chose some Levites, some priests, and some of the family leaders, and he appointed them to serve as judges in Jerusalem. ⁹He told them:

Faithfully serve the LORD! ¹⁰The people of Judah will bring you legal cases that involve every type of crime, including murder. You must settle these cases and warn the people to stop sinning against the LORD, so that he won't get angry and punish Judah. Remember, if you follow these instructions, you won't be held responsible for anything that happens.

¹¹Amariah the high priest will have the final say in any religious case. And Zebadiah, the leader[b] of the Judah tribe, will have the final say in all other cases. The rest of the Levites will serve as your assistants. Be brave, and I pray that the LORD will help you do right.

Moab and Ammon Are Defeated

20 Some time later, the armies of Moab and Ammon, together with the Meunites,[c] went to war

[a]19.3 *sacred poles*: See the note at 14.3.
[b]19.11 *Zebadiah, the leader*: Hebrew "Zebadiah son of Ishmael, who is the leader." [c]20.1 *Meunites*: One ancient translation (see also 26.7); Hebrew "Ammonites."

against Jehoshaphat. [2]Messengers told Jehoshaphat, "A large army from Edom[d] east of the Dead Sea has invaded our country. They have already reached En-Gedi."[e]

[3]Jehoshaphat was afraid, so he asked the LORD what to do. He then told the people of Judah to go without eating to show their sorrow. [4]They immediately left for Jerusalem to ask for the LORD's help.

[5]After everyone from Judah and Jerusalem had come together at the LORD's temple, Jehoshaphat stood in front of the new courtyard [6]and prayed:

You, LORD, are the God our ancestors worshiped, and from heaven you rule every nation in the world. You are so powerful that no one can defeat you. [7]Our God, you forced out the nations who lived in this land before your people Israel came here, and you gave it to the descendants of your friend Abraham forever. [8]Our ancestors lived in this land and built a temple to honor you. [9]They believed that whenever this land is struck by war or disease or famine, your people can pray to you at the temple, and you will hear their prayer and save them.

[10]You can see that the armies of Ammon, Moab, and Edom are attacking us! Those are the nations you would not let our ancestors invade on their way from Egypt, so these nations were not destroyed. [11]Now they are coming to take back the land you gave us. [12]Aren't you going to punish them? We won't stand a chance when this army attacks. We don't know what to do—we are begging for your help.

[13]While every man, woman, and child of Judah was standing there at the temple, [14]the LORD's Spirit suddenly spoke to Jahaziel, a Levite from the Asaph clan.[f] [15]Then Jahaziel said:

Your Majesty and everyone from Judah and Jerusalem, the LORD says that you don't need to be afraid or let this powerful army discourage you. God will fight on your side! [16]So here's what you must do. Tomorrow the enemy armies will march through the

---

[d]20.2 *Edom*: The Hebrew text has "Syria"; in Hebrew there is only one letter difference between "Edom" and "Aram," which is the usual Hebrew name for Syria in the Bible. [e]20.2 *En-Gedi*: The Hebrew text has "Hazazon-Tamar, also known as En-Gedi," a city on the west shore of the Dead Sea, about twenty-five miles southeast of Jerusalem. [f]20.14 *Jahaziel, a Levite from the Asaph clan*: Hebrew "Jahaziel son of Zechariah son of Benaiah son of Jeiel son of Mattaniah, who was a Levite from the Asaph clan."

---

*Spiritual*Life—Does prayer really make a difference? (*2 Chronicles 20.1-30*)

Prayer gets us ready for God to act.

King Jehoshaphat was in trouble. He was a good king. He had torn down idols throughout his kingdom. He had chosen officials to read the Lord's Law to the people of every city of Judah. He had appointed civil judges and instructed them to "be careful when you make your decisions in court, because these are the LORD's people" (19.6). He had made a few mistakes, such as forming an alliance with wicked King Ahab and giving his son to marry Ahab's daughter. But, for the most part, Jehoshaphat had followed God and led his people to do the same. Yet now he was surrounded by three armies. What could he do?

Pray. Jehoshaphat stood in the courtyard and worshiped God. He recounted for God their history together. Then he ended with, "We don't know what to do—we are begging for your help" (20.12). God did help. In fact, Jehoshaphat's soldiers never had to lift a weapon.

Did Jehoshaphat change God's mind? Probably not. Did his prayer prepare him to see the power of God? Certainly. Jehoshaphat learned that he had a battle partner more powerful than even King Ahab. The Lord himself would fight for him.

So why pray? Prayer admits our own limitations. Prayer opens our eyes to the power of God. (See also Jeremiah 21.1-10; Matthew 7.7-12; Luke 18.1-8; 2 Corinthians 12.6-10.)

Words To Remember: *You won't even have to fight. Just take your positions and watch the LORD rescue you from your enemy. Don't be afraid. Just do as you're told. And as you march out tomorrow, the LORD will be there with you.*—2 Chronicles 20.17

desert around the town of Jeruel. March down and meet them at the town of Ziz as they come up the valley. [17]You won't even have to fight. Just take your positions and watch the LORD rescue you from your enemy. Don't be afraid. Just do as you're told. And as you march out tomorrow, the LORD will be there with you.

[18]Jehoshaphat bowed low to the ground and everyone worshiped the LORD. [19]Then some Levites from the Kohath and Korah clans stood up and shouted praises to the LORD God of Israel.

[20]Early the next morning, as everyone got ready to leave for the desert near Tekoa, Jehoshaphat stood up and said, "Listen my friends, if we trust the LORD God and believe what these prophets have told us, the LORD will help us, and we will be successful." [21]Then he explained his plan and appointed men to march in front of the army and praise the LORD for his holy power by singing:[g]

"Praise the LORD!
His love never ends."

[22]As soon as they began singing, the LORD confused the enemy camp, [23]so that the Ammonite and Moabite troops attacked and completely destroyed those from Edom. Then they turned against each other and fought until the entire camp was wiped out! [24]When Judah's army reached the tower that overlooked the desert, they saw that every soldier in the enemy's army was lying dead on the ground. [25]So Jehoshaphat and his troops went into the camp to carry away everything of value. They found a large herd of livestock,[h] a lot of equipment, clothes,[i] and other valuable things. It took them three days to carry it all away, and there was still some left over.

[26]Then on the fourth day, everyone came together in Beracah Valley and sang praises to the LORD. That's why that place was called Praise Valley.[j]

[27-28]Jehoshaphat led the crowd back to Jerusalem. And as they marched, they played harps and blew trumpets. They were very happy because the LORD had given them victory over their enemies, so when they reached the city, they went straight to the temple.

[29]When the other nations heard how the LORD had fought against Judah's enemies, they were too afraid [30]to invade Judah. The LORD let Jehoshaphat's kingdom be at peace.

Jehoshaphat Dies
(1 Kings 22.41-50)

[31]Jehoshaphat was thirty-five years old when he became king of Judah, and he ruled from Jerusalem for twenty-five years. His mother was Azubah daughter of Shilhi. [32]Jehoshaphat obeyed the LORD, just as his father Asa had done, [33]but he did not destroy the local shrines.[k] So the people still worshiped foreign gods, instead of faithfully serving the God their ancestors had worshiped.

[34]Everything else Jehoshaphat did while he was king is written in the records of Jehu son of Hanani that are included in The History of the Kings of Israel.

[35]While Jehoshaphat was king, he signed a peace treaty with Ahaziah the wicked king of Israel. [36]They agreed to build several seagoing ships[l] at Ezion-Geber. [37]But the prophet Eliezer[m] warned Jehoshaphat, "The LORD will destroy these ships because you have supported Ahaziah." The ships were wrecked and never sailed.

21 Jehoshaphat died and was buried beside his ancestors in Jerusalem, and his son Jehoram became king.

King Jehoram of Judah
(2 Kings 8.16-24)

[2]King Jehoshaphat had seven sons: Jehoram, Azariah, Jehiel, Zechariah, Azariah, Michael, and Shephatiah. [3]Jehoshaphat gave each of them silver and gold, as well as other valuable gifts. He also put them in charge of the fortified cities in Judah, but he had chosen his oldest son Jehoram to succeed him as king.

---

[g]20.21 to march in front . . . singing: Or "to put on their sacred robes, lead the army into battle, and praise the LORD by singing."   [h]20.25 a large herd of livestock: One ancient translation; Hebrew "among the bodies a large herd of."   [i]20.25 clothes: One ancient translation; Hebrew "dead bodies."   [j]20.26 Beracah Valley . . . sang praises . . . Praise Valley: In Hebrew the name "Beracah" means "praise."   [k]20.33 local shrines: See the note at 11.15.   [l]20.36 seagoing ships: See the note at 9.21.   [m]20.37 Eliezer: Hebrew "Eliezer son of Dodavahu from Mareshah."

⁴After Jehoram had taken control of Judah, he had his brothers killed, as well as some of the nation's leaders. ⁵He was thirty-two years old when he became king, and he ruled eight years from Jerusalem.

⁶Jehoram married Ahab's daughter and followed the sinful example of Ahab's family and the other kings of Israel. He disobeyed the LORD by doing wrong, ⁷but because the LORD had made a solemn promise to King David that someone from his family would always rule in Judah, he refused to wipe out David's descendants.

⁸While Jehoram was king, the people of Edom rebelled and chose their own king. ⁹Jehoram, his officers, and his cavalry marched to Edom, where the Edomite army surrounded them. He escaped during the night, ¹⁰but Judah was never able to regain control of Edom. Even the town of Libnah[n] rebelled at that time.

Those things happened because Jehoram had turned away from the LORD, the God his ancestors had worshiped. ¹¹Jehoram even built local shrines[o] in the hills of Judah and let the people sin against the LORD by worshiping foreign gods.

¹²One day, Jehoram received a letter from Elijah the prophet that said:

I have a message for you from the LORD God your ancestor David worshiped. He knows that you have not followed the example of Jehoshaphat your father or Asa your grandfather. ¹³Instead you have acted like those sinful kings of Israel and have encouraged the people of Judah to stop worshiping the LORD, just as Ahab and his descendants did. You even murdered your own brothers, who were better men than you.

¹⁴Because you have done these terrible things, the LORD will severely punish the people in your kingdom, including your own family, and he will destroy everything you own. ¹⁵You will be struck with a painful stomach disease and suffer until you die.

¹⁶The LORD later caused the Philistines and the Arabs who lived near the Ethiopians[p] to become angry at Jehoram. ¹⁷They invaded Judah and stole the royal property from the palace, and they led Jehoram's wives and sons away as prisoners. The only one left behind was Ahaziah,[q] his youngest son.

¹⁸After this happened, the LORD struck Jehoram with an incurable stomach disease. ¹⁹About two years later, Jehoram died in terrible pain. No bonfire was built to honor him, even though the people had done this for his ancestors.

²⁰Jehoram was thirty-two years old when he became king, and he ruled eight years from Jerusalem. He died, and no one even felt sad. He was buried in Jerusalem, but not in the royal tombs.

King Ahaziah of Judah
(2 Kings 8.25-29; 9.21, 27, 28)

22 Earlier, when the Arabs led a raid against Judah, they killed all of Jehoram's sons, except Ahaziah, the youngest one. So the people of Jerusalem crowned him their king. ²He was twenty-two[r] years old at the time, and he ruled only one year from Jerusalem.

Ahaziah's mother was Athaliah, a granddaughter of King Omri of Israel, ³and she encouraged her son to sin against the LORD. He followed the evil example of King Ahab and his descendants. ⁴In fact, after his father's death, Ahaziah sinned against the LORD by appointing some of Ahab's relatives to be his advisors.

Their advice led to his downfall. ⁵He listened to them and went with King Joram of Israel to attack King Hazael and the Syrian troops at Ramoth in Gilead. Joram was wounded in that battle, ⁶and he went to the town of Jezreel to recover. And Ahaziah later went there to visit him. ⁷It was during that visit that God had Ahaziah put to death.

When Ahaziah arrived at Jezreel, he and Joram went to meet with Jehu grandson of Nimshi. The LORD had already told Jehu to kill every male in Ahab's family, ⁸and while Jehu was doing that, he saw some of Judah's leaders and Ahaziah's nephews who had come with Ahaziah. Jehu killed them on the spot, ⁹then gave orders to find Ahaziah. Jehu's officers found him hiding in Samaria.

---

[n]21.10 *Even the town of Libnah*: This was a town on the border between Philistia and Judah, which means that Jehoram was facing rebellion on both sides of his kingdom. [o]21.11 *local shrines*: See the note at 11.15. [p]21.16 *Ethiopians*: See the note at 12.3. [q]21.17 *Ahaziah*: The Hebrew text has "Jehoahaz," another spelling of the name. [r]22.2 *twenty-two*: One ancient translation (see also 2 Kings 8.26); Hebrew "forty-two."

They brought Ahaziah to Jehu, who immediately put him to death. They buried Ahaziah only because they respected Jehoshaphat his grandfather, who had done his best to obey the LORD.

There was no one from Ahaziah's family left to become king of Judah.

Queen Athaliah of Judah
(2 Kings 11.1-3)

¹⁰As soon as Athaliah heard that her son King Ahaziah was dead, she decided to kill any relative who could possibly become king. She would have done just that, ¹¹but Jehosheba⁵ rescued Joash son of Ahaziah just as the others were about to be murdered. Jehosheba, who was Jehoram's daughter and Ahaziah's half sister, was married to Jehoiada the priest. So she was able to hide her nephew Joash and his personal servant in a bedroom in the LORD's temple where he was safe from Athaliah. ¹²Joash hid in the temple with them for six years while Athaliah ruled as queen of Judah.

Jehoiada Makes Joash King of Judah
(2 Kings 11.4-21)

23 After Ahaziah's son Joash had hidden in the temple for six years, Jehoiada the priest knew that something had to be done. So he made sure he had the support of several army officers. They were Azariah son of Jeroham, Ishmael son of Jehohanan, Azariah son of Obed, Maaseiah son of Adaiah, and Elishaphat son of Zichri. ²These five men went to the towns in Judah and called together the Levites and the clan leaders. They all came to Jerusalem ³and gathered at the temple, where they agreed to help Joash.

Jehoiada said to them:

Joash will be our next king, because long ago the LORD promised that one of David's descendants would always be king. ⁴Here is what we will do. Three groups of priests and Levites will be on guard duty on the Sabbath—one group will guard the gates of the temple, ⁵one will guard the palace, and the other will guard Foundation Gate. The rest of you will stand guard in the temple courtyards. ⁶Only the priests and Levites who are on duty will be able to enter the temple, because they will be the only ones

who have gone through the ceremony to make themselves clean and acceptable. The others must stay outside in the courtyards, just as the LORD has commanded. ⁷You Levites must protect King Joash. Don't let him out of your sight! And keep your swords ready to kill anyone who comes into the temple.

Satisfaction comes from having a lasting, positive impact on the lives of others.
JANET BLY

⁸The Levites and the people of Judah followed Jehoiada's orders. The guards going off duty were not allowed to go home, and so each commander had all his guards available—those going off duty as well as those coming on duty. ⁹Jehoiada went into the temple and brought out the swords and shields that had belonged to King David, and he gave them to the commanders. ¹⁰They gave the weapons to the guards, and Jehoiada then made sure that the guards took their positions around the temple and the altar to protect the king on every side.

¹¹Jehoiada and his sons brought Joash outside, where they placed the crown on his head and gave him a copy of the instructions for ruling the nation. Olive oil was poured on his head to show that he was now king, and the crowd cheered and shouted, "Long live the king!"

¹²As soon as Queen Athaliah heard the crowd cheering for Joash, she went to the temple. ¹³There she saw Joash standing by one of the columns near the entrance, which was the usual place for the king. The commanders and the trumpet players were standing next to him, and the musicians were playing instruments and leading the people as they celebrated and blew trumpets. Athaliah tore her clothes in anger and shouted, "You betrayed me, you traitors!"

---

⁵22.11 *Jehosheba*: The Hebrew text has "Jehoshabeath," another spelling of the name.

¹⁴Right away, Jehoiada said to the army commanders, "Don't kill her near the LORD's temple. Take her out in front of the troops, and be sure to kill all of her followers!" ¹⁵She tried to escape, but the commanders caught and killed her near the gate where horses are led into the palace.

¹⁶Jehoiada asked King Joash and the people to join with him in being faithful to the LORD. They agreed, ¹⁷then rushed to the temple of the god Baal and tore it down. They smashed the altars and the idols and killed Mattan the priest of Baal in front of the altars.

¹⁸Jehoiada assigned the priests and Levites their duties at the temple, just as David had done. They were in charge of offering sacrifices to the LORD according to the Law of Moses, and they were responsible for leading the celebrations with singing. ¹⁹Jehoiada ordered the guards at the temple gates to keep out anyone who was unclean.

²⁰Finally, Jehoiada called together the army commanders, the most important citizens of Judah, and the government officials. The crowd of people followed them as they led Joash from the temple, through the Upper Gate, and into the palace, where he took his place as king of Judah. ²¹Everyone celebrated because Athaliah had been killed and Jerusalem was peaceful again.

King Joash of Judah
(2 Kings 12.1-16)

24 Joash was only seven years old when he became king of Judah, and he ruled forty years from Jerusalem. His mother Zibiah was from the town of Beersheba.

²While Jehoiada the priest was alive, Joash obeyed the LORD by doing right. ³Jehoiada even chose two women for Joash to marry so he could have a family.

⁴Some time later, Joash decided it was time to repair the temple. ⁵He called together the priests and Levites and said, "Go everywhere in Judah and collect the annual tax from the people. I want this done right away—we need that money to repair the temple."

But the Levites were in no hurry to follow the king's orders. ⁶So he sent for Jehoiada the high priest and asked, "Why didn't you send the Levites to collect the taxes? The LORD's servant Moses and the people agreed long ago that this tax would be collected and used to pay for the upkeep of the sacred tent. ⁷And now we need it to repair the temple because the sons of that evil woman Athaliah came in and wrecked it. They even used some of the sacred objects to worship the god Baal."

⁸Joash gave orders for a wooden box to be made and had it placed outside, near the gate of the temple. ⁹He then sent letters everywhere in Judah and Jerusalem, asking everyone to bring their taxes to the temple, just as Moses had required their ancestors to do.

¹⁰The people and their leaders agreed, and they brought their money to Jerusalem and placed it in the box. ¹¹Each day, after the Levites took the box into the temple, the king's secretary and the high priest's assistant would dump out the money and count it. Then the empty box would be taken back outside.

This happened day after day, and soon a large amount of money was collected. ¹²Joash and Jehoiada turned the money over to the men who were supervising the repairs to the temple. They used the money to hire stonecutters, carpenters, and experts in working with iron and bronze.

¹³These workers went right to work repairing the temple, and when they were finished, it looked as good as new. ¹⁴They did not use all the tax money for the repairs, so the rest of it was handed over to Joash and Jehoiada, who then used it to make dishes and other gold and silver objects for the temple.

Sacrifices to please the LORD[t] were offered regularly in the temple for as long as Jehoiada lived. ¹⁵He died at the ripe old age of one hundred thirty years, ¹⁶and he was buried in the royal tombs in Jerusalem, because he had done so much good for the people of Israel, for God, and for the temple.

Joash Turns Away from the LORD

¹⁷After the death of Jehoiada the priest, the leaders of Judah went to Joash and talked him into doing what they wanted. ¹⁸Right away, the people of Judah stopped worshiping in the temple of the LORD God, and they started worshiping idols and the

---

ᵗ**24.14** *Sacrifices to please the* LORD: See the note at 1.6.

symbols of the goddess Asherah. These sinful things made the LORD God angry at the people of Judah and Jerusalem, [19]but he still sent prophets who warned them to turn back to him. The people refused to listen.

[20]God's Spirit spoke to Zechariah son of Jehoiada the priest, and Zechariah told everyone that God was saying: "Why are you disobeying me and my laws? This will only bring punishment! You have deserted me, so now I will desert you."

[21-22]King Joash forgot that Zechariah's father had always been a loyal friend. So when the people of Judah plotted to kill Zechariah, Joash joined them and gave orders for them to stone him to death in the courtyard of the temple. As Zechariah was dying, he said, "I pray that the LORD will see this and punish all of you."

Joash Is Killed

[23]In the spring of the following year, the Syrian army invaded Judah and Jerusalem, killing all of the nation's leaders. They collected everything of value that belonged to the people and took it back to their king in Damascus. [24]The Syrian army was very small, but the LORD let them defeat Judah's large army, because he was punishing Joash and the people of Judah for turning away from him.

[25-26]Joash was severely wounded during the battle, and as soon as the Syrians left Judah, two of his officials, Zabad and Jehozabad,[u] decided to revenge the death of Zechariah. They plotted and killed Joash while he was in bed, recovering from his wounds. Joash was buried in Jerusalem, but not in the royal tombs. [27]The History of the Kings also tells more about the sons of Joash, what the prophets said about him, and how he repaired the temple. Amaziah son of Joash became king after his father's death.

King Amaziah of Judah
(2 Kings 14.1-6)

25 Amaziah was twenty-five years old when he became king, and he ruled twenty-nine years from Jerusalem, the hometown of his mother Jehoaddin.[v]

[2]Even though Amaziah obeyed the LORD by doing right, he refused to be completely faithful. [3]For example, as soon as he had

control of Judah, he arrested and killed the officers who had murdered his father. [4]But the children of those officers were not killed; the LORD had commanded in the Law of Moses that only the people who sinned were to be punished.[w]

Edom Is Defeated
(2 Kings 14.7)

[5]Amaziah sent a message to the tribes of Judah and Benjamin and called together all the men who were twenty years old and older. Three hundred thousand men went to Jerusalem, all of them ready for battle and able to fight with spears and shields. Amaziah grouped these soldiers according to their clans and put them under the command of his army officers. [6]Amaziah also paid almost four tons of silver to hire one hundred thousand soldiers from Israel.

[7]One of God's prophets said, "Your Majesty, don't let these Israelite soldiers march into battle with you. The LORD has refused to help anyone from the northern kingdom of Israel, [8]and so he will let your enemies defeat you, even if you fight hard. He is the one who brings both victory and defeat."

[9]Amaziah replied, "What am I supposed to do about all the silver I paid those troops?"

"The LORD will give you back even more than you paid," the prophet answered.

[10]Amaziah ordered the troops from Israel to go home, but when they left, they were furious with the people of Judah.

[11]After Amaziah got his courage back, he led his troops to Salt Valley, where he killed ten thousand Edomite soldiers in battle. [12]He captured ten thousand more soldiers and dragged them to the top of a high cliff. Then he pushed them over the side, and they all were killed on the rocks below.

[13]Meanwhile, the Israelite troops that Amaziah had sent home, raided the towns in Judah between Samaria and Beth-Horon. They killed three thousand people and carried off their possessions.

[14]After Amaziah had defeated the Edomite army, he returned to Jerusalem. He took

u24.25,26 Zabad and Jehozabad: Hebrew "Zabad son of Shimeath from Ammon and Jehozabad son of Shimrith from Moab." v25.1 Jehoaddin: The Hebrew text has "Jehoaddan," another spelling of the name. w25.4 the LORD had commanded . . . punished: See Deuteronomy 24.16.

with him the idols of the Edomite gods and set them up. Then he bowed down and offered them sacrifices. [15]This made the LORD very angry, and he sent a prophet to ask Amaziah, "Why would you worship these foreign gods that couldn't even save their own people from your attack?"

[16]But before the prophet finished speaking, Amaziah interrupted and said, "You're not one of my advisors! Don't say another word, or I'll have you killed."

The prophet stopped. But then he added, "First you sinned and now you've ignored my warning. It's clear that God has decided to punish you!"

Israel Defeats Judah
(2 Kings 14.8-14)

[17]King Amaziah of Judah talked with his officials, then sent a message to King Jehoash[x] of Israel: "Come out and face me in battle!"

[18]Jehoash sent back a reply that said:

Once upon a time, a small thornbush in Lebanon arranged the marriage between his son and the daughter of a large cedar tree. But a wild animal came along and trampled the small bush.

[19]Amaziah, you think you're so powerful because you defeated Edom. But stay at home and do your celebrating. If you cause any trouble, both you and your kingdom of Judah will be destroyed.

[20]God made Amaziah stubborn because he was planning to punish him for worshiping the Edomite gods. Amaziah refused to listen to Jehoash's warning, [21]so Jehoash led his army to the town of Beth-Shemesh in Judah to attack Amaziah and his troops. [22]During the battle, Judah's army was crushed. Every soldier from Judah ran back home, [23]and Jehoash captured Amaziah.

Jehoash took Amaziah with him when he went to attack Jerusalem. Jehoash broke down the city wall from Ephraim Gate to Corner Gate, a section about six hundred feet long. [24]He carried away the gold, the silver, and all the valuable furnishings from God's temple where the descendants of Obed-Edom stood guard. He robbed the king's treasury, took hostages, then returned to Samaria.

Amaziah Is Killed
(2 Kings 14.15-20)

[25]Amaziah lived fifteen years after Jehoash died. [26]Everything else Amaziah did while he was king is written in *The History of the Kings of Judah and Israel.*

[27]As soon as Amaziah started disobeying the LORD, some people in Jerusalem plotted against Amaziah. He was able to escape to the town of Lachish, but another group of people caught him and killed him there. [28]His body was taken to Jerusalem on horseback and buried beside his ancestors.

King Uzziah of Judah
(2 Kings 14.21, 22; 15.1-7)

26 [1-3]After the death of King Amaziah, the people of Judah crowned his son Uzziah[y] king, even though he was only sixteen at the time. Uzziah ruled fifty-two years from Jerusalem, the hometown of his mother Jecoliah. During his rule, he recaptured and rebuilt the town of Elath.

Kids are great. They are exciting. Their potential is simply phenomenal. And in any given family there is the potential to change this world for God.

MAXINE HANCOCK

[4]He obeyed the LORD by doing right, as his father Amaziah had done. [5]Zechariah was Uzziah's advisor and taught him to obey God. And so, as long as Zechariah was alive, Uzziah was faithful to God, and God made him successful.

[6]While Uzziah was king, he started a war

x25.17 King Jehoash: The Hebrew text has "King Joash son of Jehoahaz son of Jehu"; Jehoash is another spelling for the name Joash. y26.1-3 Uzziah: In the parallel passages in 2 Kings, he is called "Azariah" (see also 1 Chronicles 3.10-15). He is also called "Uzziah" in 2 Kings 15.13; Isaiah 1.1; Hosea 1.1; and Amos 1.1. One of these names was probably his birth name, while the other was his name after he became king.

against the Philistines. He smashed the walls of the cities of Gath, Jabneh, and Ashdod, then rebuilt towns around Ashdod and in other parts of Philistia. [7]God helped him defeat the Philistines, the Arabs living in Gur-Baal, and the Meunites. [8]Even the Ammonites paid taxes to Uzziah. He became very powerful, and people who lived as far away as Egypt heard about him.

[9]In Jerusalem, Uzziah built fortified towers at the Corner Gate, the Valley Gate, and the place where the city wall turned inward.[z] [10]He also built defense towers out in the desert.

He owned such a large herd of livestock in the western foothills and in the flatlands, that he had cisterns dug there to catch the rainwater. He loved farming, so he had crops and vineyards planted in the hill country wherever there was fertile soil, and he hired farmers to take care of them.

[11]Uzziah's army was always ready for battle. Jeiel and Maaseiah were the officers who kept track of the number of soldiers, and these two men were under the command of Hananiah, one of Uzziah's officials. [12-13]There were 307,500 trained soldiers, all under the command of 2,600 clan leaders. These powerful troops protected the king against any enemy. [14]Uzziah supplied his army with shields, spears, helmets, armor, bows, and stones used for slinging. [15]Some of his skilled workers invented machines that could shoot arrows and sling large stones. Uzziah set these up in Jerusalem at his defense towers and at the corners of the city wall.

God helped Uzziah become more and more powerful, and he was famous all over the world.

Uzziah Becomes Too Proud

[16]Uzziah became proud of his power, and this led to his downfall.

One day, Uzziah disobeyed the LORD his God by going into the temple and burning incense as an offering to him.[a] [17]Azariah the priest and eighty other brave priests followed Uzziah into the temple [18]and said, "Your Majesty, this isn't right! You are not allowed to burn incense to the LORD. That must be done only by priests who are descendants of Aaron. You will have to leave! You have sinned against the LORD, and so he will no longer bless you."

[19]Uzziah, who was standing next to the incense altar at the time, was holding the incense burner, ready to offer incense to the LORD. He became very angry when he heard Azariah's warning, and leprosy[b] suddenly appeared on his forehead! [20]Azariah and the other priests saw it and immediately told him to leave the temple. Uzziah realized that the LORD had punished him, so he hurried to get outside.

[21]Uzziah had leprosy the rest of his life. He was no longer allowed in the temple or in his own palace. That's why his son Jotham lived there and ruled in his place. [22]Everything else Uzziah did while he was king is in the records written by the prophet Isaiah son of Amoz. [23]Since Uzziah had leprosy, he could not be buried in the royal tombs. Instead, he was buried in a nearby cemetery that the kings owned. His son Jotham then became king.

King Jotham of Judah
(2 Kings 15.32-38)

27 Jotham was twenty-five years old when he became king of Judah, and he ruled from Jerusalem for sixteen years. Jerushah his mother was the daughter of Zadok.

[2]Jotham obeyed the LORD and did right. He followed the example of his father Uzziah, except he never burned incense in the temple as his father had done. But the people of Judah kept sinning against the LORD.

[3]Jotham rebuilt the Upper Gate of the temple and did a lot of work to repair the wall near Mount Ophel. [4]He built towns in the mountains of Judah and built fortresses and defense towers in the forests.

[5]During his rule he attacked and defeated the Ammonites. Then every year for the next three years, he forced them to pay four tons of silver, sixty thousand bushels of wheat, and sixty thousand bushels of barley.

[6]Jotham remained faithful to the LORD his God and became a very powerful king.

[7]Everything else Jotham did while he was king, including the wars he fought, is

---

[z]**26.9** *the place where the city wall turned inward:* One possible meaning for the difficult Hebrew text.
[a]**26.16** *going into the temple and burning incense as an offering to him:* This was to be done only by priests (see Exodus 30.1-10; Numbers 16.39, 40). [b]**26.19** *leprosy:* The word translated "leprosy" was used for many different kinds of skin diseases.

written in *The History of the Kings of Israel and Judah*. [8]After he had ruled Judah sixteen years, he died at the age of forty-one. [9]He was buried in Jerusalem, and his son Ahaz became king.

King Ahaz of Judah
(2 Kings 16.1-4)

28 Ahaz was twenty years old when he became king of Judah, and he ruled from Jerusalem for sixteen years.

Ahaz was nothing like his ancestor David. Ahaz disobeyed the LORD [2]and was as sinful as the kings of Israel. He made idols of the god Baal, [3]and he offered sacrifices in Hinnom Valley. Worst of all, Ahaz sacrificed his own sons, which was a disgusting custom of the nations that the LORD had forced out of Israel. [4]Ahaz offered sacrifices at the local shrines,[c] as well as on every hill and in the shade of large trees.

Syria and Israel Attack Judah
(2 Kings 16.5, 6)

[5-6]Ahaz and the people of Judah sinned and turned away from the LORD, the God their ancestors had worshiped. So the LORD punished them by letting their enemies defeat them.

The king of Syria attacked Judah and took many of its people to Damascus as prisoners. King Pekah[d] of Israel later defeated Judah and killed one hundred twenty thousand of its bravest soldiers in one day. [7]During that battle, an Israelite soldier named Zichri killed three men from Judah: Maaseiah the king's son; Azrikam, the official in charge of the palace; and Elkanah, the king's second in command. [8]The Israelite troops captured two hundred thousand women and children and took them back to their capital city of Samaria, along with a large amount of their possessions. They did these things even though the people of Judah were their own relatives.

Oded the Prophet Condemns Israel

[9]Oded lived in Samaria and was one of the LORD's prophets. He met Israel's army on their way back from Judah and said to them:

The LORD God of your ancestors let you defeat Judah's army only because he was angry with them. But you

should not have been so cruel! [10]If you make slaves of the people of Judah and Jerusalem, you will be as guilty as they are of sinning against the LORD.

> *I need God's help to have the kind of desire it takes to do whatever I do for him . . . alone.*
>
> CAROLE MAYHALL

[11]Send these prisoners back home—they are your own relatives. If you don't, the LORD will punish you in his anger. [12]About the same time, four of Israel's leaders arrived. They were Azariah son of Johanan, Berechiah son of Meshillemoth, Jehizkiah son of Shallum, and Amasa son of Hadlai. They agreed with Oded that the Israelite troops were wrong, [13]and they said:

If you bring these prisoners into Samaria, that will be one more thing we've done to sin against the LORD. And he is already angry enough at us.

[14]So in front of the leaders and the crowd, the troops handed over their prisoners and the property they had taken from Judah. [15]The four leaders took some of the stolen clothes and gave them to the prisoners who needed something to wear. They later gave them all a new change of clothes and shoes, then fixed them something to eat and drink, and cleaned their wounds with olive oil. They gave donkeys to those who were too weak to walk, and led all of them back to Jericho, the city known for its palm trees. The leaders then returned to Samaria.

Ahaz Asks the King of Assyria for Help
(2 Kings 16.7-9)

[16-18]Some time later, the Edomites attacked the eastern part of Judah again and carried away prisoners. And at the same

---

[c]**28.4** *local shrines*: See the note at 11.15.
[d]**28.5,6** *Pekah*: Hebrew "Pekah son of Remaliah."

time, the Philistines raided towns in the western foothills and in the Southern Desert. They conquered the towns of Beth-Shemesh, Aijalon, Gederoth, Soco, Timnah, and Gimzo, including the villages around them. Then some of the Philistines went to live in these places.

Ahaz sent a message to King Tiglath Pileser of Assyria and begged for help. [19]But God was punishing Judah with these disasters, because Ahaz had disobeyed him and refused to stop Judah from sinning. [20]So Tiglath Pileser came to Judah, but instead of helping, he made things worse. [21]Ahaz gave him gifts from the LORD's temple and the king's palace, as well as from the homes of Israel's other leaders. The Assyrian king still refused to help Ahaz.

The Final Sin of Ahaz and His Death

[22]Even after all these terrible things happened to Ahaz, he sinned against the LORD even worse than before. [23]He said to himself, "The Syrian gods must have helped their kings defeat me. Maybe if I offer sacrifices to those gods, they will help me." That was the sin that finally led to the downfall of Ahaz, as well as to the destruction of Judah. [24]Ahaz collected all the furnishings of the temple and smashed them to pieces. Then he locked the doors to the temple and set up altars to foreign gods on every street corner in Jerusalem. [25]In every city and town in Judah he built local shrines[c] to worship foreign gods. All of this made the LORD God of his ancestors very angry.

[26]Everything else Ahaz did while he was king is written in *The History of the Kings of Judah and Israel.* [27]Ahaz died and was buried in Jerusalem, but not in the royal tombs. His son Hezekiah then became king.

King Hezekiah of Judah

(2 Kings 18.1-3)

29 Hezekiah was twenty-five years old when he became king of Judah, and he ruled twenty-nine years from Jerusalem. His mother was Abijah daughter of Zechariah. [2]Hezekiah obeyed the LORD by doing right, just as his ancestor David had done.

The Temple Is Purified

[3]In the first month[f] of the first year of Hezekiah's rule, he unlocked the doors to

the LORD's temple and had them repaired.[g] [4]Then he called the priests and Levites to the east courtyard of the temple [5]and said:

It's time to purify the temple of the LORD God of our ancestors. You Levites must first go through the ceremony to make yourselves clean, then go into the temple and bring out everything that is unclean and unacceptable to the LORD. [6]Some of our ancestors were unfaithful and disobeyed the LORD our God. Not only did they turn their backs on the LORD, but they also completely ignored his temple. [7]They locked the doors, then let the lamps go out and stopped burning incense and offering sacrifices to him. [8]The LORD became terribly angry at the people of Judah and Jerusalem, and everyone was shocked and horrified at what he did to punish them. Not only were [9]our ancestors killed in battle, but our own children and wives were taken captive.

[10]So I have decided to renew our agreement with the LORD God of Israel. Maybe then he will stop being so angry at us. [11]Let's not waste any time, my friends. You are the ones who were chosen to be the LORD's priests and to offer him sacrifices.

[12-14]When Hezekiah finished talking, the following Levite leaders went to work:

Mahath son of Amasai and Joel son of Azariah from the Kohath clan; Kish son of Abdi and Azariah son of Jehallel from the Merari clan; Joah son of Zimmah and Eden son of Joah from the Gershon clan; Shimri and Jeuel from the Elizaphan clan; Zechariah and Mattaniah from the Asaph clan; Jehuel and Shimei from the Heman clan; Shemaiah and Uzziel from the Jeduthun clan.

[15]These leaders gathered together the rest of the Levites, and they all went through the ceremony to make themselves clean. Then they began to purify the temple according to the Law of the LORD, just as Hezekiah had commanded.

---

c28.25 *local shrines:* See the note at 11.15. f29.3 *first month:* Abib (also called Nisan), the first month of the Hebrew calendar, from about mid-March to mid-April. g29.3 *he unlocked the doors . . . repaired:* King Ahaz had locked the doors and stopped everyone from worshiping the LORD (see 28.24, 25).

¹⁶The priests went into the temple and carried out everything that was unclean. They put these things in the courtyard, and from there, the Levites carried them outside the city to Kidron Valley.

¹⁷The priests and Levites began their work on the first day of the first month.ʰ It took them one week to purify the courtyards of the temple and another week to purify the temple. So on the sixteenth day of that same month ¹⁸they went back to Hezekiah and said:

Your Majesty, we have finished our work. The entire temple is now pure again, and so is the altar and its utensils, as well as the table for the sacred loaves of bread and its utensils. ¹⁹And we have brought back all the things that King Ahaz took from the temple during the time he was unfaithful to God. We purified them and put them back in front of the altar.

Worship in the Temple

²⁰Right away, Hezekiah called together the officials of Jerusalem, and they went to the temple. ²¹They brought with them seven bulls, seven rams, seven lambs, and seven goatsⁱ as sacrifices to take away the sins of Hezekiah's family and of the people of Ju-

dah, as well as to purify the temple. Hezekiah told the priests, who were descendants of Aaron, to sacrifice these animals on the altar.

²²The priests killed the bulls, the rams, and the lambs, then splattered the blood on the altar. ²³They took the goats to Hezekiah and the worshipers, and they laid their hands on the animals. ²⁴The priests then killed the goats and splattered the blood on the altar as a sacrifice to take away the sins of everyone in Israel, because Hezekiah had commanded that these sacrifices be made for all the people of Israel.

²⁵Next, Hezekiah assigned the Levites to their places in the temple. He gave them cymbals, harps, and other stringed instruments, according to the instructions that the LORD had given King David and the two prophets, Gad and Nathan. ²⁶The Levites were ready to play the instruments that had belonged to David; the priests were ready to blow the trumpets.

²⁷As soon as Hezekiah gave the signal for the sacrifices to be burned on the altar, the musicians began singing praises to the LORD and playing their instruments, ²⁸and every-

---

ʰ**29.17** *first month*: See the note at 29.3.
ⁱ**29.21** *goats*: Hebrew "male goats."

*Spiritual*Life—How can I make God's presence real in my life?
(2 Chronicles 29.20-36)

Practice worship.

Sometimes we tramp through our days hoping that God will announce that he is with us. While we aren't looking for bright lights or a thundering voice from heaven, we'd like at least some sense of his presence—an inner warmth that says, *I am with you*; a small symbol that whispers, *I am a gift from God*. Sometimes, in God's kindness, that is exactly what happens. We *know* God is here. But other times, when we feel the greatest need, God seems totally absent. What can we do then?

King Hezekiah provides an excellent model. Look through this passage for examples of worship. The people gathered at their place of worship and confessed their sin, asking for God's forgiveness. They made music with instruments, knelt down and prayed, repeated the writings of great spiritual leaders from the past, brought offerings, sang joyful praises to God, thanked him, and asked his blessing.

It's hard to worship when God seems distant, but God invites us to worship him anyway. When we discipline ourselves to worship (even when we don't feel like it), we sometimes become aware of something we didn't notice before—that our Lord has been with us all the time. (See also Ezekiel 10; Romans 15.14-21; Ephesians 3.14-21; Colossians 3.10,11.)

Words To Remember: *They bowed down and joyfully sang praises to the LORD.*
—2 Chronicles 29.30

one worshiped the LORD. This continued until the last animal was sacrificed.

²⁹After that, Hezekiah and the crowd of worshipers knelt down and worshiped the LORD. ³⁰Then Hezekiah and his officials ordered the Levites to sing the songs of praise that David and Asaph the prophet had written. And so they bowed down and joyfully sang praises to the LORD.

³¹Hezekiah said to the crowd, "Now that you are once again acceptable to the LORD, bring sacrifices and offerings to give him thanks."

The people did this, and some of them voluntarily brought animals to be offered as sacrifices. ³²Seventy bulls, one hundred rams, and two hundred lambs were brought as sacrifices to please the LORD;ʲ ³³six hundred bulls and three thousand sheep were brought as sacrifices to ask the LORD's blessing.ᵏ ³⁴There were not enough priests to skin all these animals, because many of the priests had not taken the time to go through the ceremony to make themselves clean. However, since all the Levites had made themselves clean, they helped the priests until the last animal was skinned. ³⁵Besides all the sacrifices that were burned on the altar, the fat from the other animal sacrifices was burned, and the offerings of wine were poured over the altar.

So the temple was once again used for worshiping the LORD. ³⁶Hezekiah and the people of Judah celebrated, because God had helped them make this happen so quickly.

Hezekiah Prepares To Celebrate Passover

30 ¹⁻⁴Passover wasn't celebrated in the first month,ʲ which was the usual time, because many of the priests were still unclean and unacceptable to serve, and because not everyone in Judah had come to Jerusalem for the festival. So Hezekiah, his officials, and the people agreed to celebrate Passover in the second month.ᵐ

Hezekiah sent a message to everyone in Israel and Judah, including those in the territories of Ephraim and West Manasseh, inviting them to the temple in Jerusalem for the celebration of Passover in honor of the LORD God of Israel. ⁵Everyone from Beersheba in the south to Dan in the north was invited. This was the largest crowd of people

that had ever celebrated Passover, according to the official records.

⁶Hezekiah's messengers went everywhere in Israel and Judah with the following letter:

I'm glad God doesn't announce upfront what we'll be doing in the future—it could be overwhelming. But knowing God himself holds the past, present, and future should put our minds at ease.

RAMONA CRAMER TUCKER

People of Israel, now that you have survived the invasion of the Assyrian kings,ⁿ it's time for you to turn back to the LORD God our ancestors Abraham, Isaac, and Jacob worshiped. If you do this, he will stop being angry. ⁷Don't follow the example of your ancestors and your Israelite relatives in the north. They were unfaithful to the LORD, and he punished them horribly. ⁸Don't be stubborn like your ancestors. Decide now to obey the LORD our God! Come to Jerusalem and worship him in the temple that will belong to him forever. Then he will stop being angry, ⁹and the enemies that have captured your families will show pity and send them back home. The LORD God is kind and merciful, and if you turn back to him, he will no longer turn his back on you.

¹⁰The messengers went to every town in Ephraim and West Manasseh as far north as the territory of Zebulun, but everyone laughed and insulted them. ¹¹Only a few

---

ʲ**29.32** *sacrifices to please the LORD:* See the note at 1.6.   ᵏ**29.33** *sacrifices to ask the LORD's blessing:* These sacrifices have traditionally been called "peace offerings" or "offerings of well-being." A main purpose was to ask for the LORD's blessing, and so in the CEV they are sometimes called "sacrifices to ask the LORD's blessing."   ʲ**30.1-4** *first month:* See the note at 29.3.   ᵐ**30.1-4** *second month:* See the note at 3.1, 2.   ⁿ**30.6** *the invasion of the Assyrian kings:* See 2 Kings 17.1-22.

people from the tribes of Asher, West Manasseh, and Zebulun were humble and went to Jerusalem. [12]God also made everyone in Judah eager to do what Hezekiah and his officials had commanded.

Passover Is Celebrated

[13]In the second month,[o] a large crowd of people gathered in Jerusalem to celebrate the Festival of Thin Bread.[p] [14]They took all the foreign altars and incense altars in Jerusalem and threw them into Kidron Valley.

[15-17]Then, on the fourteenth day of that same month, the Levites began killing the lambs for Passover, because many of the worshipers were unclean and were not allowed to kill their own lambs. Meanwhile, some of the priests and Levites felt ashamed because they had not gone through the ceremony to make themselves clean. They immediately went through that ceremony and went to the temple, where they offered sacrifices to please the LORD.[q] Then the priests and Levites took their positions, according to the Law of Moses, the servant of God.

As the Levites killed the lambs, they handed some of the blood to the priests, who splattered it on the altar.

[18-19]Most of the people that came from Ephraim, West Manasseh, Issachar, and Zebulun had not made themselves clean, but they ignored God's Law and ate the Passover lambs anyway. Hezekiah found out what they had done and prayed, "LORD God, these people are unclean according to the laws of holiness. But they are worshiping you, just as their ancestors did. So, please be kind and forgive them." [20]The LORD answered Hezekiah's prayer and did not punish them.

[21]The worshipers in Jerusalem were very happy and celebrated the Festival for seven days. The Levites and priests sang praises to the LORD every day and played their instruments. [22]Hezekiah thanked the Levites for doing such a good job, leading the celebration.

The worshipers celebrated for seven days by offering sacrifices, by eating the sacred meals, and by praising the LORD God of their ancestors. [23]Everyone was so excited that they agreed to celebrate seven more days.

[24]So Hezekiah gave the people one thousand bulls and seven thousand sheep to be offered as sacrifices and to be used as food for the sacred meals. His officials gave one thousand bulls and ten thousand sheep, and many more priests agreed to go through the ceremony to make themselves clean. [25]Everyone was very happy, including those from Judah and Israel, the priests and Levites, and the foreigners living in Judah and Israel. [26]It was the biggest celebration in Jerusalem since the days of King Solomon, the son of David. [27]The priests and Levites asked God to bless the people, and from his home in heaven, he did.

The People Destroy the Local Shrines
(2 Kings 18.4)

31 After the Festival, the people went to every town in Judah and smashed the stone images of foreign gods and cut down the sacred poles[r] for worshiping the goddess Asherah. They destroyed all the local shrines[s] and foreign altars in Judah, as well as those in the territories of Benjamin, Ephraim, and West Manasseh. Then everyone went home.

Offerings for the Priests and Levites

[2]Hezekiah divided the priests and Levites into groups, according to their duties. Then he assigned them the responsibilities of offering sacrifices to please the LORD[t] and sacrifices to ask his blessing.[u] He also appointed people to serve at the temple and to sing praises at the temple gates. [3]Hezekiah provided animals from his own herds and flocks to use for the morning and evening sacrifices, as well as for the sacrifices during the Sabbath celebrations, the New Moon Festivals, and the other religious feasts required by the Law of the LORD.

[4]He told the people of Jerusalem to bring the offerings that were to be given to the priests and Levites, so that they would have time to serve the LORD with their work. [5]As soon as the people heard what the king wanted, they brought a tenth of everything

---

[o]**30.13** *second month*: See the note at 3.1, 2.   [p]**30.13** *the Festival of Thin Bread*: The celebration of this Festival began one day after Passover. And so these two festivals were often referred to as one.   [q]**30.15-17** *sacrifices to please the LORD*: See the note at 1.6.   [r]**31.1** *sacred poles*: See the note at 14.3.   [s]**31.1** *local shrines*: See the note at 11.15.   [t]**31.2** *sacrifices to please the LORD*: See the note at 1.6.   [u]**31.2** *sacrifices to ask his blessing*: See the note at 29.33.

they owned, including their best grain, wine, olive oil, honey, and other crops. ⁶The people from the other towns of Judah brought a tenth of their herds and flocks, as well as a tenth of anything they had dedicated to the LORD. ⁷The people started bringing their offerings to Jerusalem in the third month,ᵛ and the last ones arrived four months later. ⁸When Hezekiah and his officials saw these offerings, they thanked the LORD and the people.

⁹Hezekiah asked the priests and Levites about the large amount of offerings. ¹⁰The high priest at the time was Azariah, a descendant of Zadok, and he replied, "Ever since the people have been bringing us their offerings, we have had more than enough food and supplies. The LORD has certainly blessed his people. Look at how much is left over!"

¹¹So the king gave orders for storerooms to be built in the temple, and when they were completed, ¹²⁻¹³all the extra offerings were taken there. Hezekiah and Azariah then appointed Conaniah the Levite to be in charge of these storerooms. His brother Shimei was his assistant, and the following Levites worked with them: Jehiel, Azaziah, Nahath, Asahel, Jerimoth, Jozabad, Eliel, Ismachiah, Mahath, and Benaiah. ¹⁴Kore son of Imnah was assigned to guard the East Gate, and he was put in charge of receiving the offerings voluntarily given to God and of dividing them among the priests and Levites. ¹⁵⁻¹⁶He had six assistants who were responsible for seeing that all the priests in the other towns of Judah also got their share of these offerings. They were Eden, Miniamin, Jeshua, Shemaiah, Amariah, and Shecaniah.

Every priest and every Levite over thirtyʷ years old who worked daily in the temple received part of these offerings, according to their duties. ¹⁷The priests were listed in the official records by clans, and the Levites twenty years old and older were listed by their duties. ¹⁸The official records also included their wives and children, because they had also been faithful in keeping themselves clean and acceptable to serve the LORD.

¹⁹Hezekiah also appointed other men to take food and supplies to the priests and Levites whose homes were in the pastureland around the towns of Judah. But the priests had to be descendants of Aaron, and the Levites had to be listed in the official records.

²⁰⁻²¹Everything Hezekiah did while he was king of Judah, including what he did for the temple in Jerusalem, was right and good. He was a successful king, because he obeyed the LORD God with all his heart.

King Sennacherib of Assyria Invades Judah

(2 Kings 18.13-37; Isaiah 36.1-22)

32 After King Hezekiah had faithfully obeyed the LORD's instructions by doing these things, King Sennacherib of Assyria invaded Judah. He attacked the fortified cities and thought he would capture every one of them.

²As soon as Hezekiah learned that Sennacherib was planning to attack Jerusalem, ³⁻⁴he and his officials worked out a plan to cut off the supply of water outside the city, so that the Assyrians would have no water when they came to attack. The officials got together a large work force that stopped up the springs and streams near Jerusalem.

⁵Hezekiah also had workers repair the broken sections of the city wall. Then they built defense towers and an outer wall to help protect the one already there. The landfill on the east side of David's City was also strengthened.

He gave orders to make a large supply of weapons and shields, ⁶and he appointed army commanders over the troops. Then he gathered the troops together in the open area in front of the city gate and said to them:

⁷Be brave and confident! There's no reason to be afraid of King Sennacherib and his powerful army. We are much more powerful, ⁸because the LORD our God fights on our side. The Assyrians must rely on human power alone.

These words encouraged the army of Judah.

⁹When Sennacherib and his troops were camped at the town of Lachish, he sent a

---

ᵛ**31.7** *third month*: Sivan, the third month of the Hebrew calendar, from about mid-May to mid-June. ʷ**31.15,16** *thirty*: The Hebrew text has "three" instead of "thirty"; in Hebrew, these two words look almost exactly the same (see also Numbers 4.3; 1 Chronicles 23.3).

message to Hezekiah and the people in Jerusalem. It said:

> *Do you worry a lot?*
> *Is your life frantic?*
> *Perfect peace comes by fixing*
> *your mind on Jesus Christ.*
> *Once you try peace on,*
> *you'll wear it constantly.*
>
> MARY WHELCHEL

[10]I am King Sennacherib of Assyria, and I have Jerusalem surrounded. Do you think you can survive my attack? [11]Hezekiah your king is telling you that the LORD your God will save you from me. But he is lying, and you'll die of hunger and thirst. [12]Didn't Hezekiah tear down all except one of the LORD's altars and places of worship?[x] And didn't he tell you people of Jerusalem and Judah to worship at that one place?

[13]You've heard what my ancestors and I have done to other nations. Were the gods of those nations able to defend their land against us? [14]None of those gods kept their people safe from the kings of Assyria. Do you really think your God can do any better? [15]Don't be fooled by Hezekiah! No god of any nation has ever been able to stand up to Assyria. Believe me, your God cannot keep you safe!

[16]The Assyrian officials said terrible things about the LORD God and his servant Hezekiah. [17]Sennacherib's letter even made fun of the LORD. It said, "The gods of other nations could not save their people from Assyria's army, and neither will the God that Hezekiah worships." [18]The officials said all these things in Hebrew, so that everyone listening from the city wall would understand and be terrified and surrender. [19]The officials talked about the LORD God as if he were nothing but an ordinary god or an idol that someone had made.

The Death of King Sennacherib
(2 Kings 19.14-19, 35-37; Isaiah 37.14-20; 37.36-38)

[20]Hezekiah and the prophet Isaiah son of Amoz asked the LORD for help, [21]and he sent an angel that killed every soldier and commander in the Assyrian camp.

Sennacherib returned to Assyria, completely disgraced. Then one day he went into the temple of his god where some of his sons killed him.

[22]The LORD rescued Hezekiah and the people of Jerusalem from Sennacherib and also protected them from other enemies. [23]People brought offerings to Jerusalem for the LORD and expensive gifts for Hezekiah, and from that day on, every nation on earth respected Hezekiah.

Hezekiah Gets Sick and Almost Dies
(2 Kings 20.1-11; Isaiah 38.1-8)

[24]About this same time, Hezekiah got sick and was almost dead. He prayed, and the LORD gave him a sign that he would recover. [25]But Hezekiah was so proud that he refused to thank the LORD for everything he had done for him. This made the LORD angry, and he punished Hezekiah and the people of Judah and Jerusalem. [26]Hezekiah and the people later felt sorry and asked the LORD to forgive them. So the LORD did not punish them as long as Hezekiah was king.

Hezekiah's Wealth
(2 Kings 20.12-19; Isaiah 39.1-8)

[27]Hezekiah was very rich, and everyone respected him. He built special rooms to store the silver, the gold, the precious stones and spices, the shields, and the other valuable possessions. [28]Storehouses were also built for his supply of grain, wine, and olive oil; barns were built for his cattle, and pens were put up for his sheep. [29]God made Hezekiah extremely rich, so he bought even more sheep, goats, and cattle. And he built towns where he could keep all these animals.

[30]It was Hezekiah who built a tunnel that

---

[x]**32.12** *worship:* Hezekiah actually had torn down the places where idols were worshiped, and he had told the people to worship the LORD at the one place of worship in Jerusalem. But the Assyrian leader was confused and thought these were also places where the LORD was supposed to be worshiped.

carried the water from Gihon Spring into the city of Jerusalem. In fact, everything he did was successful! [31]Even when the leaders of Babylonia sent messengers to ask Hezekiah about the sign God had given him, God let Hezekiah give his own answer to test him and to see if he would remain faithful.

Hezekiah Dies
(2 Kings 20.20, 21)

[32]Everything else Hezekiah did while he was king, including how faithful he was to the LORD, is included in the records kept by Isaiah the prophet. These are written in *The History of the Kings of Judah and Israel*. [33]When Hezekiah died, he was buried in the section of the royal tombs that was reserved for the most respected kings,[y] and everyone in Judah and Jerusalem honored him. His son Manasseh then became king.

King Manasseh of Judah
(2 Kings 21.1-9, 17, 18)

33 Manasseh was twelve years old when he became king of Judah, and he ruled fifty-five years from Jerusalem. [2]Manasseh disobeyed the LORD by following the disgusting customs of the nations that the LORD had forced out of Israel. [3]He rebuilt the local shrines[z] that his father Hezekiah had torn down. He built altars for the god Baal and set up sacred poles[a] for worshiping the goddess Asherah. And he faithfully worshiped the stars in the sky.

[4]In the temple, where only the LORD was supposed to be worshiped, Manasseh built altars for pagan gods [5]and for the stars. He placed these altars in both courtyards of the temple [6-7]and even set up a stone image of a foreign god. Manasseh practiced magic and witchcraft; he asked fortunetellers for advice and sacrificed his own sons in Hinnom Valley. He did many other sinful things and made the LORD very angry.

Years ago, God had told David and Solomon:

Jerusalem is the place I prefer above all others in Israel. It belongs to me, and there in the temple I will be worshiped forever. [8]If my people will faithfully obey all the laws and teaching I gave to my servant Moses, I will never again force them to leave the land I gave to their ancestors. [9]But the people of Judah and Jerusalem

listened to Manasseh and did even more sinful things than the nations the LORD had wiped out.

[10]The LORD tried to warn Manasseh and the people about their sins, but they ignored the warning. [11]So he let Assyrian army commanders invade Judah and capture Manasseh. They put a hook in his nose and tied him up in chains, and they took him to Babylon. [12]While Manasseh was held captive there, he asked the LORD God to forgive him and to help him. [13]The LORD listened to Manasseh's prayer and saw how sorry he was, and so he let him go back to Jerusalem and rule as king. Manasseh knew from then on that the LORD was God.

[14]Later, Manasseh rebuilt the eastern section of Jerusalem's outer wall and made it taller. This section went from Gihon Valley north to Fish Gate and around the part of the city called Mount Ophel. He also assigned army officers to each of the fortified cities in Judah.[b]

[15]Manasseh also removed the idols and the stone image of the foreign god from the temple, and he gathered the altars he had built near the temple and in other parts of Jerusalem. He threw all these things outside the city. [16]Then he repaired the LORD's altar and offered sacrifices to thank him and sacrifices to ask his blessing.[c] He gave orders that everyone in Judah must worship the LORD God of Israel. [17]The people obeyed Manasseh, but they worshiped the LORD at their own shrines.

[18]Everything else Manasseh did while he was king, including his prayer to the LORD God and the warnings from his prophets, is written in *The History of the Kings of Israel*. [19]Hozai[d] wrote a lot about Manasseh, including his prayer and God's answer. But Hozai also recorded the evil things Manasseh did before turning back to God, as well as a list of places where Manasseh set up idols, and where he built local shrines and

---

[y]**32.33** *in the section . . . reserved for the most respected kings:* One possible meaning for the difficult Hebrew text. [z]**33.3** *local shrines:* See the note at 11.15. [a]**33.3** *sacred poles:* See the note at 14.3. [b]**33.14** *fortified cities in Judah:* At this time, Judah was under the control of Assyria. The fortifications mentioned in this verse may have been done under orders from Assyrian officials, hoping to strengthen their southern border against the rising power of Egypt. [c]**33.16** *sacrifices to ask his blessing:* See the note at 29.33. [d]**33.19** *Hozai:* Or "The prophets."

places to worship Asherah. [20]Manasseh died and was buried near the palace, and his son Amon became king.

King Amon of Judah
(2 Kings 21.19-26)

[21]Amon was twenty-two years old when he became king of Judah, and he ruled from Jerusalem for two years. [22]Amon disobeyed the LORD, just as his father Manasseh had done, and he worshiped and offered sacrifices to the idols his father had made. [23]Manasseh had turned back to the LORD, but Amon refused to do that. Instead, he sinned even more than his father.

[24]Some of Amon's officials plotted against him and killed him in his palace. [25]But the people of Judah killed the murderers of Amon and made his son Josiah king.

King Josiah of Judah
(2 Kings 22.1, 2)

34 Josiah was eight years old when he became king of Judah, and he ruled thirty-one years from Jerusalem. [2]He followed the example of his ancestor David and always obeyed the LORD.

> *God is the Author of all things perfect—yet he loves me, warts and all.*
>
> JEANNE ZORNES

Josiah Stops the Worship of Foreign Gods
(2 Kings 23.4-20)

[3]When Josiah was only sixteen years old he began worshiping God, just as his ancestor David had done. Then, four years later, he decided to destroy the local shrines[e] in Judah and Jerusalem, as well as the sacred poles[f] for worshiping the goddess Asherah and the idols of foreign gods. [4]He watched as the altars for the worship of the god Baal were torn down, and as the nearby incense altars were smashed. The Asherah poles, the idols, and the stone images were also

smashed, and the pieces were scattered over the graves of their worshipers. [5]Josiah then had the bones of the pagan priests burned on the altars.[g]

And so Josiah got rid of the worship of foreign gods in Judah and Jerusalem. [6]He did the same things in the towns and ruined villages[h] in the territories of West Manasseh, Ephraim, and Simeon, as far as the border of Naphtali. [7]Everywhere in the northern kingdom of Israel, Josiah tore down pagan altars and Asherah poles; he crushed idols to dust and smashed incense altars.

Then Josiah went back to Jerusalem.

Hilkiah Finds *The Book of God's Law*
(2 Kings 22.3-20)

[8]In the eighteenth year of Josiah's rule in Judah, after he had gotten rid of all the sinful things from the land and from the LORD's temple, he sent three of his officials to repair the temple. They were Shaphan son of Azaliah, Governor Maaseiah of Jerusalem, and Joah son of Joahaz, who kept the government records.

[9]These three men went to Hilkiah the high priest. They gave him the money that the Levite guards had collected from the people of West Manasseh, Ephraim, and the rest of Israel, as well as those living in Judah, Benjamin, and Jerusalem. [10]Then the money was turned over to the men who supervised the repairs to the temple. They used some of it to pay the workers, [11]and they gave the rest of it to the carpenters and builders, who used it to buy the stone and wood they needed to repair the other buildings that Judah's kings had not taken care of.

[12]The workers were honest, and their supervisors were Jahath and Obadiah from the Levite clan of Merari, and Zechariah and Meshullam from the Levite clan of Kohath. Other Levites, who were all skilled musicians, [13]were in charge of carrying supplies and supervising the workers. Other Levites were appointed to stand guard around the temple.

[14]While the money was being given to these supervisors, Hilkiah found the book

---

[e]**34.3** *local shrines*: See the note at 11.15.   [f]**34.3** *sacred poles*: See the note at 14.3.   [g]**34.5** *the bones of the pagan priests burned on the altars*: This made the altars unclean, so that they could not be used in worshiping any god. [h]**34.6** *ruined villages*: One possible meaning for the difficult Hebrew text.

that contained the laws that the LORD had given to Moses. [15]Hilkiah handed the book to Shaphan the official and said, "Look what I found here in the temple—*The Book of God's Law.*"

[16]Shaphan took the book to Josiah and reported, "Your officials are doing everything you wanted. [17]They have collected the money from the temple and have given it to the men supervising the repairs. [18]But there's something else, Your Majesty. The priest Hilkiah gave me this book." Then Shaphan read it aloud.

[19]When Josiah heard what was in *The Book of God's Law,* he tore his clothes in sorrow. [20]At once he called together Hilkiah, Shaphan, Ahikam son of Shaphan, Abdon son of Micah,[i] and his own servant Asaiah. He said, [21]"The LORD must be furious with me and everyone else in Israel and Judah, because our ancestors did not obey the laws written in this book. Go find out what the LORD wants us to do."

[22]Hilkiah and the four other men left right away and went to talk with Huldah the prophet. Her husband was Shallum,[j] who was in charge of the king's clothes. Huldah lived in the northern part of Jerusalem, and when they met in her home, [23]she said:

You were sent here by King Josiah, and this is what the LORD God of Israel says to him: [24]"Josiah, I am the LORD! And I intend to punish this country and everyone in it, just as this book says. [25]The people of Judah and Israel have rejected me. They have offered sacrifices to foreign gods and have worshiped their own idols. I can't stand it any longer. I am furious.

[26-27]"Josiah, listen to what I am going to do. I noticed how sad you were when you heard that this country and its people would be completely wiped out. You even tore your clothes in sorrow, and I heard you cry. [28]So before I destroy this place, I will let you die in peace."

The men left and reported to Josiah what Huldah had said.

Josiah Reads *The Book of God's Law*
(2 Kings 23.1-3)

[29]King Josiah called together the leaders of Judah and Jerusalem. [30]Then he went to the LORD's temple, together with all the people of Judah and Jerusalem, the priests, and the Levites.

Finally, when everybody was there, he read aloud *The Book of God's Law*[k] that had been found in the temple. [31]After Josiah had finished reading, he stood in the place reserved for the king. He promised in the LORD's name to faithfully obey the LORD and to follow his laws and teachings that were written in the book. [32]Then he asked the people of Jerusalem and Benjamin to make that same promise and to obey the God their ancestors had worshiped.

[33]Josiah destroyed all the idols in the territories of Israel, and he commanded everyone in Israel to worship only the LORD God. The people did not turn away from the LORD God of their ancestors for the rest of Josiah's rule as king.

Passover Is Celebrated
(2 Kings 23.21-23)

35 Josiah commanded that Passover be celebrated in Jerusalem to honor the LORD. So, on the fourteenth day of the first month,[l] the lambs were killed for the Passover celebration.

[2]On that day, Josiah made sure the priests knew what duties they were to do in the temple. [3]He called together the Levites who served the LORD and who taught the people his laws, and he said:

No longer will you have to carry the sacred chest from place to place. It will stay in the temple built by King Solomon son of David, where you will serve the LORD and his people Israel. [4]Get ready to do the work that David and Solomon assigned to you, according to your clans. [5]Divide yourselves into groups, then arrange yourselves throughout the temple so that each family of worshipers will be able to get help from one of you.[m] [6]When the

---

[i]**34.20** *Abdon son of Micah*: Also called "Achbor son of Micaiah" (see 2 Kings 22.12). [j]**34.22** *Shallum*: Hebrew "Shallum son of Tokhath son of Hasrah." [k]**34.30** *The Book of God's Law*: The Hebrew text has "The Book of God's Agreement," which is the same as "The Book of God's Law" in verses 15 and 19. In traditional translations this is called "The Book of the Covenant." [l]**35.1** *first month*: See the note at 29.3. [m]**35.5** *each family of worshipers . . . you*: One possible meaning for the difficult Hebrew text.

people bring you their Passover lamb, you must kill it and prepare it to be sacrificed to the LORD. Make sure the people celebrate according to the instructions that the LORD gave Moses, and don't do anything to make yourselves unclean and unacceptable.

[7]Josiah donated thirty thousand sheep and goats, and three thousand bulls from his own flocks and herds for the people to offer as sacrifices. [8]Josiah's officials also voluntarily gave some of their animals to the people, the priests, and the Levites as sacrifices. Hilkiah, Zechariah, and Jehiel, who were the officials in charge of the temple, gave the priests twenty-six hundred sheep and lambs and three hundred bulls to sacrifice during the Passover celebration. [9]Conaniah, his two brothers Shemaiah and Nethanel, as well as Hashabiah, Jeiel, and Jozabad were leaders of the Levites, and they gave the other Levites five thousand sheep and goats, and five hundred bulls to offer as sacrifices.

[10]When everything was ready to celebrate Passover, the priests and the Levites stood where Josiah had told them. [11]Then the Levites killed and skinned the Passover lambs, and they handed some of the blood to the priests, who splattered it on the altar. [12]The Levites set aside the parts of the animal that the worshipers needed for their sacrifices to please the LORD,[n] just as the Law of Moses required. They also did the same thing with the bulls. [13]They sacrificed the Passover animals on the altar and boiled the meat for the other offerings in pots, kettles, and pans. Then they quickly handed the meat to the people so they could eat it.

[14]All day long, the priests were busy offering sacrifices and burning the animals' fat on the altar. And when everyone had finished, the Levites prepared Passover animals for themselves and for the priests.

[15]During the celebration some of the Levites prepared Passover animals for the musicians and the guards, so that the Levite musicians would not have to leave their places, which had been assigned to them according to the instructions of David, Asaph, Heman, and Jeduthun the king's prophet. Even the guards at the temple gates did not have to leave their posts.

[16]So on that day, Passover was celebrated to honor the LORD, and sacrifices were offered on the altar to him, just as Josiah had commanded. [17]The worshipers then celebrated the Festival of Thin Bread for the next seven days.

[18]People from Jerusalem and from towns all over Judah and Israel were there. Passover had not been observed like this since the days of Samuel the prophet. In fact, this was the greatest Passover celebration in Israel's history! [19]All these things happened in the eighteenth year of Josiah's rule in Judah.

Josiah Dies in Battle
(2 Kings 23.28-30)

[20]Some time later, King Neco of Egypt led his army to the city of Carchemish on the Euphrates River. And Josiah led his troops north to meet the Egyptians in battle.[o]

[21]Neco sent the following message to Josiah:

> I'm not attacking you, king of Judah! We're not even at war. But God has told me to quickly attack my enemy. God is on my side, so if you try to stop me, he will punish you.

[22]But Josiah ignored Neco's warning, even though it came from God! Instead, he disguised himself and marched into battle against Neco in the valley near Megiddo. [23]During the battle an Egyptian soldier shot Josiah with an arrow. Josiah told his servants, "Get me out of here! I've been hit." [24]They carried Josiah out of his chariot, then put him in the other chariot he had there and took him back to Jerusalem, where he soon died. He was buried beside his ancestors, and everyone in Judah and Jerusalem mourned his death.

[25]Jeremiah the prophet wrote a funeral song in honor of Josiah. And since then, anyone in Judah who mourns the death of Josiah sings that song. It is included in the collection of funeral songs.

[26]Everything else Josiah did while he was king, including how he faithfully obeyed the

---

[n]**35.12** *sacrifices to please the* LORD: See the note at 1.6.   [o]**35.20** *battle*: At this time, King Neco of Egypt (609-595 B.C.) was fighting on the side of the Assyrians. He marched north to fight the Babylonian army and help Assyria keep control of its land. Since Josiah considered Assyria an enemy, he set out to stop Neco and the Egyptian troops.

LORD, [27]is written in *The History of the Kings of Israel and Judah.*

King Jehoahaz of Judah
(2 Kings 23.30-35)

36 After the death of Josiah, the people of Judah crowned his son Jehoahaz their new king. [2]He was twenty-three years old at the time, and he ruled only three months from Jerusalem. [3]King Neco of Egypt captured Jehoahaz and forced Judah to pay almost four tons of silver and seventy-five pounds of gold as taxes. [4]Then Neco appointed Jehoahaz's brother Eliakim king of Judah and changed his name to Jehoiakim. He led Jehoahaz away to Egypt as his prisoner.

King Jehoiakim of Judah
(2 Kings 23.36—24.7)

[5]Jehoiakim was twenty-five years old when he was appointed king, and he ruled eleven years from Jerusalem. Jehoiakim disobeyed the LORD his God by doing evil. [6]During Jehoiakim's rule, King Nebuchadnezzar of Babylonia invaded Judah. He arrested Jehoiakim and put him in chains, and he sent him to the capital city of Babylon. [7]Nebuchadnezzar also carried off many of the valuable things in the LORD's temple, and he put them in his palace in Babylon. [8]Everything else Jehoiakim did while he was king, including all the disgusting and evil things, is written in *The History of the Kings of Israel and Judah.* His son Jehoiachin then became king.

King Jehoiachin of Judah
(2 Kings 24.8-17)

[9]Jehoiachin was eighteen[p] years old when he became king of Judah, and he ruled only three months and ten days from Jerusalem. Jehoiachin also disobeyed the LORD by doing evil. [10]In the spring of the year, King Nebuchadnezzar of Babylonia had Jehoiachin arrested and taken to Babylon, along with more of the valuable items in the temple. Then Nebuchadnezzar appointed Zedekiah king of Judah.

King Zedekiah of Judah
(2 Kings 24.18-20; Jeremiah 52.1-3)

[11]Zedekiah was twenty-one years old when he was appointed king of Judah, and he ruled from Jerusalem for eleven years.

[12]He disobeyed the LORD his God and refused to change his ways, even after a warning from Jeremiah, the LORD's prophet.

[13]King Nebuchadnezzar of Babylonia had forced Zedekiah to promise in God's name that he would be loyal. Zedekiah was stubborn and refused to turn back to the LORD God of Israel, so he rebelled against Nebuchadnezzar. [14]The people of Judah and even the priests who were their leaders became more unfaithful. They followed the disgusting example of the nations around them and made the LORD's holy temple unfit for worship. [15]But the LORD God felt sorry for his people, and instead of destroying the temple, he sent prophets who warned the people over and about their sins. [16]But the people only laughed and insulted these prophets. They ignored what the LORD God was trying to tell them, until he finally became so angry that nothing could stop him from punishing Judah and Jerusalem.

Jerusalem Is Destroyed
(2 Kings 25.1-21; Jeremiah 52.3-30)

[17]The LORD sent King Nebuchadnezzar of Babylonia to attack Jerusalem. Nebuchadnezzar killed the young men who were in the temple, and he showed no mercy to anyone, whether man or woman, young or old. God let him kill everyone in the city. [18]Nebuchadnezzar carried off everything that was left in the temple; he robbed the treasury and the personal storerooms of the king and his officials. He took everything back to Babylon.

[19]Nebuchadnezzar's troops burned down the temple and destroyed every important building in the city. Then they broke down the city wall. [20]The survivors were taken to Babylonia as prisoners, where they were slaves of the king and his sons, until Persia became a powerful nation.

[21]Judah was an empty desert, and it stayed that way for seventy years, to make up for all the years it was not allowed to rest.[q] These things happened just as Jeremiah the LORD's prophet had said.[r]

---

*p*36.9 *eighteen*: Some manuscripts of one ancient translation (see also 2 Kings 24.8); Hebrew "eight." *q*36.21 *rest*: According to Leviticus 25.1-7, the land was supposed to rest every seventh year. *r*36.21 *Jeremiah . . . said*: Jeremiah 25.11, 12; 29.10. According to the Law, the people had to allow the land to rest one out of every seven years (see Leviticus 25.1-7).

Cyrus Lets the Jews Return Home
(Ezra 1.1-4)

²²In the first year that Cyrus was king of Persia,ˢ the LORD had Cyrus send a message to all parts of his kingdom. This happened just as Jeremiah the LORD's prophet had promised. ²³The message said:

I am King Cyrus of Persia.

The LORD God of heaven has made me the ruler of every nation on earth. He has also chosen me to build a temple for him in Jerusalem, which is in Judah. The LORD God will watch over any of his people who want to go back to Judah.

ˢ**36.22** *the first year that Cyrus was king of Persia:* Probably 538 B.C., when Cyrus captured Babylonia. He had actually ruled Persia since 549 B.C.

Ezra
Starting Over

"Years ago the LORD sent Jeremiah with a message about a promise. . . . Then in the first year that Cyrus was king of Persia, the LORD kept his promise" (1.1).

For seventy years God's people had been living as captives and exiles under the rule of the Babylonian Empire—waiting for God to fulfill his promise to bring them back to Jerusalem (see Jeremiah 29.10-14). Imagine being part of the generation to see the Lord's faithfulness proven! What a marvelous new start to a new life!

At first the people seemed to have their priorities right as they resettled their old homeland. They celebrated and worshiped according to the laws God had given through Moses long ago (3.1-6). They began rebuilding God's temple (3.7-13). But almost immediately they faced the challenges of being a God-fearing people among godless people (4). Ultimately, many of them, even the leaders, forgot they were to be set apart as God's distinct people. So they threw in their lot with the unbelieving nations around them.

The final chapters of the book of Ezra are a shocking ending to a story that began with proof of God's faithfulness. What are we to make of a godly leader like Ezra who commands men to divorce their wives and drive away their children? Are we to believe that God is a God who endorses divorce and cares little for women and children? Surely not! Jesus himself taught the very opposite later in the New Testament (see Matthew 19.3-9). But God does take seriously the spiritual and moral compromises that too often resulted when the Jewish people joined themselves in marriage with the idolatrous people around them.

Rather than devaluing women, the book of Ezra demonstrates with shocking clarity the important role wives and mothers play in their marriages and families—it was so critical that the only way to limit the influence of ungodly women was to send them away.

Ezra at a Glance

1. The Jewish people go back to their homeland after being in exile (1,2)
2. Renewing worship and rebuilding the temple (3.1—4.5)
3. Facing and overcoming opposition in rebuilding the temple (4.6—6.22)
4. Ezra leads many families from Babylonia to Jerusalem (7,8)
5. Ezra insists that men marry wives who worship the true God (9,10)

Cyrus Lets the Jews Return Home

1 Years ago the LORD sent Jeremiah with a message about a promise[a] for the people of Israel. Then in the first year that Cyrus was king of Persia,[b] the LORD kept his promise by having Cyrus send this official message to all parts of his kingdom:

2-3I am King Cyrus of Persia.

The LORD God of heaven, who is also the God of Israel, has made me the ruler of all nations on earth. And he has chosen me to build a temple for him in Jerusalem, which is in Judah. The LORD God will watch over and encourage any of his people who want to go back to Jerusalem and help build the temple.

4Everyone else must provide what is needed. They must give money, supplies, and animals, as well as gifts for rebuilding God's temple.

5Many people felt that the LORD God wanted them to help rebuild his temple, and they made plans to go to Jerusalem. Among them were priests, Levites, and leaders of the tribes of Judah and Benjamin. 6The others helped by giving silver articles, gold, personal possessions, cattle, and other valuable gifts, as well as offerings for the temple.

7King Cyrus gave back the things that Nebuchadnezzar[c] had taken from the LORD's temple in Jerusalem and had put in the temple of his own gods. 8Cyrus placed Mithredath, his chief treasurer, in charge of these things. Mithredath counted them and gave a list to Sheshbazzar, the governor of Judah. 9-10Included among them were: 30 large gold dishes; 1,000 large silver dishes; 29 other dishes;[d] 30 gold bowls; 410 silver bowls; and 1,000 other articles. 11Altogether, there were 5,400 gold and silver dishes, bowls, and other articles. Sheshbazzar took them with him when he and the others returned to Jerusalem from Babylonia.

A List of People Who Returned from Exile
(Nehemiah 7.4-73)

2 King Nebuchadnezzar[e] of Babylonia had captured many of the people of Judah and had taken them as prisoners to Babylonia. Now they were on their way back to Jerusalem and to their own towns everywhere in Judah.

2-20Zerubbabel, Joshua,[f] Nehemiah, Seraiah, Reelaiah, Mordecai, Bilshan, Mispar, Bigvai, Rehum, and Baanah were in charge of the ones who were coming back. And here is a list of how many returned from each family group: 2,172 from the family of Parosh; 372 from the family of Shephatiah; 775 from the family of Arah; 2,812 descendants of Jeshua and Joab[g] from the family of Pahath Moab; 1,254 from the family of Elam; 945 from the family of Zattu; 760 from the family of Zaccai; 642 from the family of Bani; 623 from the family of Bebai; 1,222 from the family of Azgad; 666 from the family of Adonikam; 2,056 from the family of Bigvai; 454 from the family of Adin; 98 from the family of Ater, also known as Hezekiah; 323 from the family of Bezai; 112 from the family of Jorah; 223 from the family of Hashum; and 95 from the family of Gibbar.

21-35Here is how many people returned whose ancestors had come from the following towns: 123 from Bethlehem; 56 from Netophah; 128 from Anathoth; 42 from Azmaveth; 743 from Kiriatharim, Chephirah, and Beeroth; 621 from Ramah and Geba; 122 from Michmas; 223 from Bethel and Ai; 52 from Nebo; 156 from Magbish; 1,254 from the other Elam; 320 from Harim; 725 from Lod, Hadid, and Ono; 345 from Jericho; and 3,630 from Senaah.

36-39Here is a list of how many returned from each family of priests: 973 descendants of Jeshua from the family of Jedaiah; 1,052 from the family of Immer; 1,247 from the family of Pashhur; and 1,017 from the family of Harim.

40-42And here is a list of how many re-

a1.1 a promise: That the people of Israel would be set free from Babylonia after seventy years (see Jeremiah 25.11; 29.10). b1.1 the first year that Cyrus was king of Persia: Probably 539 B.C., when Cyrus captured Babylonia. He had actually ruled Persia since 549 B.C. c1.7 Nebuchadnezzar: Known as Nebuchadnezzar II, who ruled Babylonia from 605 to 562 B.C. In 586 B.C. he destroyed Jerusalem and took many of its people to Babylonia. d1.9,10 other dishes: One possible meaning for the difficult Hebrew text. e2.1 Nebuchadnezzar: See the note at 1.7. f2.2-20 Joshua: Hebrew "Jeshua." In this translation the name "Joshua" is used of the descendant of Jozadak, the last chief priest before the exile; this same Joshua is often mentioned together with Zerubbabel (2.2-20; 3.2, 8, 9; 4.3; 5.2; 10.18, 19). In other places the name "Jeshua" is used (2.2-20, 36-39, 40-42; 8.33). g2.2-20 Jeshua and Joab: Hebrew "Jeshua Joab."

turned from the families of Levites: 74 descendants of Hodaviah from the families of Jeshua and Kadmiel; 128 descendants of Asaph from the temple musicians; and 139 descendants of Shallum, Ater, Talmon, Akkub, Hatita, and Shobai from the temple guards.

43-54Here is a list of the families of temple workers whose descendants returned: Ziha, Hasupha, Tabbaoth, Keros, Siaha, Padon, Lebanah, Hagabah, Akkub, Hagab, Shamlai, Hanan, Giddel, Gahar, Reaiah, Rezin, Nekoda, Gazzam, Uzza, Paseah, Besai, Asnah, Meunim, Nephisim, Bakbuk, Hakupha, Harhur, Bazluth, Mehida, Harsha, Barkos, Sisera, Temah, Neziah, and Hatipha.

55-57Here is a list of Solomon's servants whose descendants returned: Sotai, Hassophereth, Peruda, Jaalah, Darkon, Giddel, Shephatiah, Hattil, Pochereth Hazzebaim, and Ami.

58A total of 392 descendants of temple workers and of Solomon's servants returned.

59-60There were 652 who returned from the families of Delaiah, Tobiah, and Nekoda, though they could not prove that they were Israelites. They had lived in the Babylonian towns of Tel-Melah, Tel-Harsha, Cherub, Addan, and Immer.

61-62The families of Habaiah, Hakkoz, and Barzillai could not prove that they were priests. The ancestor of the family of Barzillai had married the daughter of Barzillai from Gilead and had taken his wife's family name. But the records of these three families could not be found, and none of them were allowed to serve as priests. 63In fact, the governor[h] told them, "You cannot eat the food offered to God until we find out if you really are priests."

64-67There were 42,360 who returned, in addition to 7,337 servants and 200 musicians, both women and men. They brought with them 736 horses, 245 mules, 435 camels, and 6,720 donkeys.

68When the people came to where the LORD's temple had been in Jerusalem, some of the family leaders gave gifts so it could be rebuilt in the same place. 69They gave all they could, and it came to a total of 1,030 pounds of gold, 5,740 pounds of silver, and 100 robes for the priests.

70Everyone returned to the towns from which their families had come, including the priests, the Levites, the musicians, the temple guards, and the workers.[i]

The First Offering on the New Altar

3 During the seventh month[j] of the year, the Israelites who had settled in their towns went to Jerusalem. 2The priest Joshua son of Jozadak, together with the other priests, and Zerubbabel son of Shealtiel and his relatives rebuilt the altar of Israel's God. Then they were able to offer sacrifices there by following the instructions God had given to Moses. 3And they built the altar where it had stood before,[k] even though they were afraid of the people who were already living around there. Then every morning and evening they burned sacrifices and offerings to the LORD.

4The people followed the rules for celebrating the Festival of Shelters and offered the proper sacrifices each day. 5They offered sacrifices to please the LORD,[l] sacrifices at each New Moon Festival, and sacrifices at the rest of the LORD's festivals. Every offering the people had brought was presented to the LORD.

6Although work on the temple itself had not yet begun, the people started offering sacrifices on the LORD's altar on the first day of the seventh month of that year.

The Rebuilding of the Temple Begins

7King Cyrus of Persia had said the Israelites could have cedar trees brought from Lebanon to Joppa by sea. So they sent grain, wine, and olive oil to the cities of Tyre and Sidon as payment for these trees, and they gave money to the stoneworkers and carpenters.

8During the second month[m] of the second year after the people had returned from Babylonia, they started rebuilding the LORD's temple. Zerubbabel son of Shealtiel,

---

h2.63 governor: In Nehemiah 8.9; 10.1, this same title is used of Nehemiah, though it is doubtful if he is the one referred to here.   i2.70 workers: One possible meaning for the difficult Hebrew text of verse 70.   j3.1 seventh month: Tishri (also called Ethanim), the seventh month of the Hebrew calendar, from about mid-September to mid-October.   k3.3 where it had stood before: One possible meaning for the difficult Hebrew text.   l3.5 sacrifices to please the LORD: In traditional translations these sacrifices are usually called "whole burnt offerings" (see Leviticus 1.1-16).   m3.8 second month: Ziv, the second month of the Hebrew calendar, from about mid-April to mid-May.

Joshua son of Jozadak, the priests, the Levites, and everyone else who had returned
started working. Every Levite over twenty
years of age was put in charge of some part
of the work. 9The Levites in charge of the
whole project were Joshua and his sons and
relatives and Kadmiel and his sons from the
family of Hodaviah.[n] The family of Henadad
worked along with them.

10When the builders had finished laying
the foundation of the temple, the priests put
on their robes and blew trumpets in honor
of the LORD, while the Levites from the family of Asaph praised God with cymbals. All
of them followed the instructions given
years before by King David.[o] 11They praised
the LORD and gave thanks as they took turns
singing:

> "The LORD is good!
> His faithful love for Israel
> will last forever."

Everyone started shouting and praising
the LORD because work on the foundation
of the temple had begun. 12Many of the
older priests and Levites and the heads of
families cried aloud because they remembered seeing the first temple years before.
But others were so happy that they celebrated with joyful shouts. 13Their shouting
and crying were so noisy that it all sounded
alike and could be heard a long way off.

Foreigners[p] Want To Help Rebuild the Temple

4 The enemies of the tribes of Judah
and Benjamin heard that the people
had come back to rebuild the temple
of the LORD God of Israel. 2So they went to
Zerubbabel and to the family leaders and
said, "Let us help! Ever since King Esarhaddon of Assyria[q] brought us here, we have
worshiped your God and offered sacrifices
to him."

3But Zerubbabel, Joshua, and the family
leaders answered, "You cannot take part in
building a temple for the LORD our God! We
will build it ourselves, just as King Cyrus of
Persia commanded us."

---

[n]3.9 *Hodaviah*: Or "Yehudah" or "Hodiah."
[o]3.10 *King David*: Ruled from about 1010 to 970 B.C.
[p]4.1 *Foreigners*: People from foreign countries who had been captured by Assyrian and Babylonian kings and forced to settle in Palestine. [q]4.2 *King Esarhaddon of Assyria*: Ruled from 681 to 669 B.C. These people may have been brought to Palestine in 677 or 676 B.C., when Esarhaddon invaded Syria.

PARENTING&*family*—How can I encourage my child's faith to grow?

(Ezra 3)

Find a place to worship with God's people.

If you've ever moved, you know how much work it is to settle your family in a new community. Besides locating everything you need for running your household—finding the best grocery store, selecting new doctors—you want to make the transition healthy for your children. You visit their school and help them make new friends.

The women who moved to Judah didn't have schools and shopping malls to choose from, but they did have one priority that all godly mothers should share: They did whatever it took to bring their families to worship with the Lord's people.

For the women of Judah, finding a place of worship meant traveling to Jerusalem. The facilities were far from perfect; at first there wasn't even a building (3.6)—and they probably didn't have a youth group. But that didn't keep the people away. Imagine what this told the children about the priorities of their parents!

We can show our children that worshiping with God's people is a priority in our life, too. Whether we're freshly transplanted into a new community, or living in the same home we've had for years, it's never too early—or too late—to find a place of worship with others who believe in God. When we worship with our children, we nurture their faith both by our example and their own experience. (See also Joshua 4; 1 Chronicles 22; Proverbs 2.1-15; John 3.16-21.)

Words To Remember: ***They praised the LORD and gave thanks as they took turns singing: "The LORD is good! His faithful love for Israel will last forever."*—Ezra 3.11**

[4]Then the neighboring people began to do everything possible to frighten the Jews[r] and to make them stop building. [5]During the time that Cyrus was king and even until Darius[s] became king, they kept bribing government officials to slow down the work.

*Sometimes my expectations
lead to discouragement or
exhaustion, but God's
expectations bring
rest and balance.*

MAYO MATHERS

Trouble Rebuilding Jerusalem[t]

[6]In the first year that Xerxes was king,[u] the neighboring people brought written charges against the people of Judah and Jerusalem.

[7]Later, Bishlam, Mithredath, Tabeel, and their advisors got together and wrote a letter to Artaxerxes when he was king of Persia.[v] It was written in Aramaic and had to be translated.[w]

[8-10]A letter was also written to Artaxerxes about Jerusalem by Governor Rehum, Secretary Shimshai, and their advisors, including the judges, the governors, the officials, and the local leaders. They were joined in writing this letter by people from Erech and Babylonia, the Elamites from Susa,[x] and people from other foreign nations that the great and famous Ashurbanipal[y] had forced to settle in Samaria and other parts of Western Province.[z]

[11]This letter said:

Your Majesty King Artaxerxes, we are your servants from everywhere in Western Province, and we send you our greetings.

[12]You should know that the Jews who left your country have moved back to Jerusalem and are now rebuilding that terrible city. In fact, they have almost finished rebuilding the walls and repairing the foundations. [13]You should also know that if the walls are completed and the city is re-built, the Jews won't pay any kind of taxes, and there will be less money in your treasury.

[14]We are telling you this, because you have done so much for us, and we want everyone to respect you. [15]If you look up the official records of your ancestors, you will find that Jerusalem has constantly rebelled and has led others to rebel against kings and provinces. That's why the city was destroyed in the first place. [16]If Jerusalem is rebuilt and its walls completed, you will no longer have control over Western Province.

[17]King Artaxerxes answered:

Greetings to Governor Rehum, Secretary Shimshai, and to your advisors in Samaria and other parts of Western Province.

[18]After your letter was translated and read to me, [19]I had the old records checked. It is true that for years Jerusalem has rebelled and caused trouble for other kings and nations. [20]And powerful kings have ruled Western Province from Jerusalem and have collected all kinds of taxes.

[21]I want you to command the people to stop rebuilding the city until I give further notice. [22]Do this right now, so that no harm will come to the kingdom.

[23]As soon as this letter was read, Governor Rehum, Secretary Shimshai, and their

---

[r]**4.4** *Jews:* This was the name given to those Israelites who settled in Judah after returning from Babylonia.
[s]**4.5** *Cyrus . . . Darius:* Cyrus ruled 539-530 B.C. (see the note at 1.1); Darius I, known as Darius the Great, ruled 522-486 B.C.   [t]**4.6** *Jerusalem:* Verses 6-23, which tell about the events of a later period, are placed here because they are also concerned with the problem of stopping or slowing down work on the temple.
[u]**4.6** *first year that Xerxes was king:* Either the end of 486 or the beginning of 485 B.C. The Hebrew has the king's Persian name "Ahasuerus," but he is better known as "Xerxes," the Greek form of the name.
[v]**4.7** *Artaxerxes . . . Persia:* Artaxerxes I (465-425 B.C.).
[w]**4.7** *It was . . . translated:* One possible meaning for the difficult Hebrew text. Ezra 4.8—6.18 is written in Aramaic, instead of in Hebrew like most of the Old Testament.   [x]**4.8-10** *the judges . . . Susa:* One possible translation for the names and titles.
[y]**4.8-10** *Ashurbanipal:* King of Assyria 669-633 (or possibly 627) B.C. In Aramaic the king's name is "Osnapper," but he is better known as Ashurbanipal.
[z]**4.8-10** *Western Province:* The land from the Euphrates River west to the Mediterranean Sea.

advisors went to Jerusalem and forced everyone to stop rebuilding the city.

Work on the Temple Starts Again

²⁴The Jews were forced to stop work on the temple and were not able to do any more building until the year after Darius became king of Persia.ᵃ ¹Then the LORD God of Israel told the prophets Haggai and Zechariahᵇ to speak in his name to the people of Judah and Jerusalem. And they did. ²So Zerubbabel the governor and Joshua the priest urged the people to start working on the temple again, and God's prophets encouraged them.

³Governor Tattenai of Western Province and his assistant Shethar Bozenai got together with some of their officials. Then they went to Jerusalem and said to the people, "Who told you to rebuild this temple? ⁴Give us the names of the workers!"

⁵But God was looking after the Jewish leaders. So the governor and his group decided not to make the people stop working on the temple until they could report to Darius and get his advice.

⁶Governor Tattenai, Shethar Bozenai, and their advisors sent a report to Darius, ⁷which said:

King Darius, we wish you the best! ⁸We went to Judah, where the temple of the great God is being built with huge stones and wooden beams set in the walls. Everyone is working hard, and the building is going up fast. ⁹We asked those in charge to tell us who gave them permission to rebuild the temple. ¹⁰We also asked for the names of their leaders, so that we could write them down for you.

¹¹They claimed to be servants of the God who rules heaven and earth. And they said they were rebuilding the temple that was built many years ago by one of Israel's greatest kings.ᶜ

¹²We were told that their people had made God angry, and he let them be captured by Nebuchadnezzar,ᵈ the Babylonian kingᵉ who took them away as captives to Babylonia. Nebuchadnezzar tore down their temple, ¹³⁻¹⁵took its gold and silver articles, and put them in the temple of his own god in Babylon.

They also said that during the first year Cyrus was king of Babylonia,ᶠ he gave orders for God's temple to be

---

ᵃ**4.24** *year after . . . king of Persia:* 520 B.C. ᵇ**5.1** *Zechariah:* Aramaic "Zechariah son of Iddo." ᶜ**5.11** *one of Israel's greatest kings:* Solomon (ruled from about 970 to 931 B.C.). ᵈ**5.12** *Nebuchadnezzar:* See the note at 1.7. ᵉ**5.12** *the Babylonian king:* Aramaic "the Babylonian king from Chaldea," but Chaldea is another name for Babylonia. ᶠ**5.13-15** *Cyrus was king of Babylonia:* King Cyrus of Persia became king of Babylonia when the Persians conquered the city of Babylon in 539 B.C.

WORK—How can I be a good supervisor? *(Ezra 5.1—6.12)*

Manage conflicts by focusing on what's really important.

If you've ever had your authority questioned at work, you can identify with Zerubbabel. He was giving his all to an important job—and not only was he not getting any appreciation, he was being attacked! Leaders from other provinces were undermining the morale of Zerubbabel's workers and challenging Zerubbabel's right to do his job.

The book of Ezra wasn't written to provide management principles. But we can learn from Zerubbabel's example as a godly supervisor. He encouraged his people to stick to the task (5.2) because he knew that the record would confirm his authority (6.2,3). He didn't waste his time or energy in counterattack; he focused on the job he was called to do.

Of course, doing your job well doesn't guarantee that you'll be immune from office politics. But when you refuse to be lured into spending your energy on conflicts instead of on your work, you'll have the confidence that comes from knowing you are being faithful to the work God has given you. (See also Exodus 18; 1 Kings 3.5-15; 4.29-34; Jeremiah 32.26-44; John 21.15-25; 2 Timothy 1.1-7; Philemon 8-16; Philemon 15-25.)

Words To Remember: *So Zerubbabel the governor and Joshua the priest urged the people to start working on the temple again.—Ezra 5.2*

rebuilt in Jerusalem where it had stood before. So Cyrus appointed Shesh-bazzar governor of Judah and sent these gold and silver articles for him to put in the temple. [16]Sheshbazzar then went to Jerusalem and laid the foundation for the temple, and the work is still going on.

[17]Your Majesty, please have someone look up the old records in Babylonia and find out if King Cyrus really did give orders to rebuild God's temple in Jerusalem. We will do whatever you think we should.

King Cyrus' Order Is Rediscovered

6 King Darius ordered someone to go through the old records kept in Babylonia. [2]Finally, a scroll[g] was found in Ecbatana, the capital of Media Province, and it said:

This official record will show [3]that in the first year Cyrus was king, he gave orders to rebuild God's temple in Jerusalem, so that sacrifices and offerings could be presented there.[h] It is to be built ninety feet high and ninety feet wide, [4]with one[i] row of wooden beams for each three rows of large stones. The royal treasury will pay for everything. [5]Then return to their proper places the gold and silver things that Nebuchadnezzar took from the temple and brought to Babylonia.

King Darius Orders the Work To Continue

[6]King Darius sent this message:

Governor Tattenai of Western Province and Shethar Bozenai, you and your advisors must stay away from the temple. [7]Let the Jewish governor and leaders rebuild it where it stood before. And stop slowing them down!

[8]Starting right now, I am ordering you to help the leaders by paying their expenses from the tax money collected in Western Province. [9]And don't fail to let the priests in Jerusalem have whatever they need each day so they can offer sacrifices to the God of heaven. Give them young bulls, rams, sheep, as well as wheat, salt, wine, and olive oil. [10]I want them to be able to offer pleasing sacrifices to God and to pray for me and my family.

[11]If any of you don't obey this order, a wooden beam will be taken from your house and sharpened on one end. Then it will be driven through your body,[j] and your house will be torn down and turned into a garbage dump. [12]I ask the God who is worshiped in Jerusalem to destroy any king or nation who tries either to change what I have said or to tear down his temple. I, Darius, give these orders, and I expect them to be followed carefully.

The Temple Is Dedicated

[13]Governor Tattenai, Shethar Bozenai, and their advisors carefully obeyed King Darius. [14]With great success the Jewish leaders continued working on the temple, while Haggai and Zechariah encouraged them by their preaching. And so, the temple was completed at the command of the God of Israel and by the orders of kings Cyrus, Darius, and Artaxerxes of Persia.[k] [15]On the third day of the month of Adar[l] in the sixth year of the rule of Darius,[m] the temple was finished.

[16]The people of Israel, the priests, the Levites, and everyone else who had returned from exile were happy and celebrated as they dedicated God's temple. [17]One hundred bulls, two hundred rams, and four hundred lambs were offered as sacrifices at the dedication. Also twelve goats were sacrificed as sin offerings for the twelve tribes of Israel. [18]Then the priests and Levites were assigned their duties in God's temple in Jerusalem, according to the instructions Moses had written.

The Passover

[19]Everyone who had returned from exile celebrated Passover on the fourteenth day of the first month.[n] [20]The priests and Levites

---

[g]**6.2** *scroll:* A roll of paper or special leather used for writing on. [h]**6.3** *so that . . . there:* One possible meaning for the difficult Aramaic text. [i]**6.4** *one:* One possible meaning for the difficult Aramaic text. [j]**6.11** *driven through your body:* A well-known punishment in the ancient Near East. [k]**6.14** *Artaxerxes of Persia:* See the note at 4.7. [l]**6.15** *Adar:* The twelfth month of the Hebrew calendar, from about mid-February to about mid-March. [m]**6.15** *sixth year . . . Darius:* 515 B.C. [n]**6.19** *the first month:* Nisan, the first month of the Hebrew calendar, from about mid-March to mid-April.

had gone through a ceremony to make themselves acceptable to lead in worship. Then some of them killed Passover lambs for those who had returned, including the other priests and themselves.

²¹The sacrifices were eaten by the Israelites who had returned and by the neighboring people who had given up the sinful customs of other nations in order to worship the LORD God of Israel. ²²For seven days they celebrated the Festival of Thin Bread. Everyone was happy because the LORD God of Israel had made sure that the king of Assyria° would be kind to them and help them build the temple.

> *Doing things for Christ—*
> *and no other person or*
> *reason—indeed helps*
> *me to overflow with joy.*
> CAROLE MAYHALL

Ezra Comes to Jerusalem

7 ¹⁻⁶Much later, when Artaxerxes^p was king of Persia, Ezra came to Jerusalem from Babylonia. Ezra was the son of Seraiah and the grandson of Azariah. His other ancestors were Hilkiah, Shallum, Zadok, Ahitub, Amariah, Azariah, Meraioth, Zerahiah, Uzzi, Bukki, Abishua, Phinehas, Eleazar, and Aaron, the high priest.

Ezra was an expert in the Law that the LORD God of Israel had given to Moses, and the LORD made sure that the king gave Ezra everything he asked for.

⁷Other Jews, including priests, Levites, musicians, the temple guards, and servants, came to Jerusalem with Ezra. This happened during the seventh year that Artaxerxes^q was king.

⁸⁻⁹God helped Ezra, and he arrived in Jerusalem on the first day of the fifth month^r of that seventh year, after leaving Babylonia on the first day of the first month.^s ¹⁰Ezra had spent his entire life studying and obeying the Law of the LORD and teaching it to others.

Artaxerxes Gives a Letter to Ezra

¹¹Ezra was a priest and an expert in the laws and commands that the LORD had given to Israel. One day King Artaxerxes gave Ezra a letter which said:

¹²Greetings from the great King Artaxerxes to Ezra the priest and expert in the teachings of the God of heaven.

¹³⁻¹⁴Any of the people of Israel or their priests or Levites in my kingdom may go with you to Jerusalem if they want to. My seven advisors and I agree that you may go to Jerusalem and Judah to find out if^t the laws of your God are being obeyed.

¹⁵When you go, take the silver and gold that I and my advisors are freely giving to the God of Israel, whose temple is in Jerusalem. ¹⁶Take the silver and gold that you collect from everywhere in Babylonia. Also take the gifts that your own people and priests have so willingly contributed for the temple of your God in Jerusalem.

¹⁷Use the money carefully to buy the best bulls, rams, lambs, grain, and wine. Then sacrifice them on the altar at God's temple in Jerusalem. ¹⁸If any silver or gold is left, you and your people may use it for whatever pleases your God. ¹⁹Give your God the other articles that have been contributed for use in his temple. ²⁰If you need to get anything else for the temple, you may have the money you need from the royal treasury.

²¹Ezra, you are a priest and an expert in the laws of the God of heaven, and I order all treasurers in Western Province to do their very best to help you. ²²They will be allowed to give as much as 7,500 pounds of silver, 500 bushels of wheat, 550 gallons of wine, 550 gallons of olive oil, and all the salt you need.

°6.22 *king of Assyria*: Meaning the king of Persia, because Assyria was now part of the Persian Empire. ^p7.1-6 *Artaxerxes*: Either Artaxerxes I (ruled from 465 to 425 B.C.) or Artaxerxes II (ruled from 405-358 B.C.). ^q7.7 *seventh year . . . Artaxerxes*: 458 B.C. if this is Artaxerxes I; 398 B.C., if this is Artaxerxes II (see the note at 7.1-6). ^r7.8,9 *fifth month*: Ab, the fifth month of the Hebrew calendar, from about mid-July to mid-August. ^s7.8,9 *first month*: See the note at 6.19. ^t7.13,14 *find out if*: Or "make sure that."

²³They must provide whatever the God of heaven demands for his temple, so that he won't be angry with me and with the kings who rule after me. ²⁴We want you to know that no priests, Levites, musicians, guards, temple servants, or any other temple workers will have to pay any kind of taxes.

²⁵Ezra, use the wisdom God has given you and choose officials and leaders to govern the people of Western Province. These leaders should know God's laws and have them taught to anyone who doesn't know them. ²⁶Everyone who fails to obey God's Law or the king's law will be punished without pity. They will either be executed or put in prison or forced to leave their country, or have all they own taken away.

Ezra Praises God

²⁷Because King Artaxerxes was so kind, Ezra said:

Praise the LORD God of our ancestors! He made sure that the king honored the LORD's temple in Jerusalem. ²⁸God has told the king, his advisors, and his powerful officials to treat me with kindness. The LORD God has helped me, and I have been able to bring many Jewish leaders back to Jerusalem.

The Families Who Came Back with Ezra

8 Artaxerxes was king of Persia when Iᵘ led the following chiefs of the family groups from Babylonia to Jerusalem:

²⁻¹⁴Gershom of the Phinehas family;
Daniel of the Ithamar family;
Hattush son of Shecaniah of the David family;
Zechariah and 150 other men of the Parosh family, who had family records;
Eliehoenai son of Zerahiah with 200 men of the Pahath Moab family;
Shecaniah son of Jahaziel with 300 men of the Zattu family;ᵛ
Ebed son of Jonathan with 50 men of the Adin family;
Jeshaiah son of Athaliah with 70 men of the Elam family;
Zebadiah son of Michael with 80 men of the Shephatiah family;
Obadiah son of Jehiel with 218 men of the Joab family;
Shelomith son of Josiphiah with 160 men of the Bani family;ʷ
Zechariah son of Bebai with 28 men of the Bebai family;

ᵘ**8.1** *I:* Ezra. ᵛ**8.2-14** *of the Zattu family*: One ancient translation; these words are not in the Hebrew text, but see 2.2-20, where Zattu is mentioned. ʷ**8.2-14** *of the Bani family*: One ancient translation; these words are not in the Hebrew text, but see 2.2-20.

---

*Spiritual*Life—How can I know good spiritual leaders? *(Ezra 7)*

They know God's law and follow it.
Christian leaders cannot simply be well-intentioned, morally upright people. They must be students of the Bible, continually returning to God's Word to understand God's work in the world and his will for our lives. Until a person has scoured the Bible, he or she isn't ready to be a spiritual leader.

But it isn't enough simply to know what God wants. Leaders must also be followers—followers of God's law and God's will. Too many tragic scandals have rocked the Christian church because of leaders who *knew* but did not *do*.

"Ezra was a priest and an expert in the laws and commands that the LORD had given to Israel" (7.11). But Ezra's qualifications went beyond scholarship. He proved himself trustworthy and honest as he distributed the wealth entrusted to him for the rebuilding of the temple. His wisdom and ethical standards enabled him to be a leader of leaders (7.28). (See also 1 Kings 12.1-20; Matthew 17.1-13; Jude 3-7.)

Words To Remember: *Ezra had spent his entire life studying and obeying the Law of the LORD and teaching it to others.—Ezra 7.10*

Johanan son of Hakkatan with
110 men of the Azgad family;
Eliphelet, Jeuel, and Shemaiah
who returned sometime later
with 60 men of the Adonikam
family;
Uthai and Zaccur with 70 men of
the Bigvai family.

Ezra Finds Levites for the Temple

¹⁵I[x] brought everyone together by the river[y] that flows to the town of Ahava[z] where we camped for three days. Not one Levite could be found among the people and priests. ¹⁶So I sent for the leaders Eliezer, Ariel, Shemaiah, Elnathan, Jarib, Elnathan, Nathan, Zechariah, and Meshullam. I also sent for Joiarib and Elnathan, who were very wise. ¹⁷Then I sent them to Iddo, the leader at Casiphia,[a] and I told them to ask him and his temple workers to send people to serve in God's temple.

¹⁸God was kind to us and had them send a skillful man named Sherebiah, who was a Levite from the family of Mahli. Eighteen of his relatives came with him. ¹⁹We were also sent Hashabiah and Jeshaiah from the family of Merari along with twenty of their relatives. ²⁰In addition, 220 others came to help the Levites in the temple. The ancestors of these workers had been chosen years ago by King David[b] and his officials, and they were all listed by name.

Ezra Asks the People
To Go without Eating and To Pray

²¹Beside the Ahava River,[c] I[d] asked the people to go without eating[e] and to pray. We humbled ourselves and asked God to bring us and our children safely to Jerusalem with all of our possessions. ²²I was ashamed to ask the king to send soldiers and cavalry to protect us against enemies along the way. After all, we had told the king that our God takes care of everyone who truly worships him, but that he gets very angry and punishes anyone who refuses to obey. ²³So we went without food and asked God himself to protect us, and he answered our prayers.

The Gifts for the Temple

²⁴I[f] chose twelve of the leading priests— Sherebiah, Hashabiah and ten of their relatives. ²⁵⁻²⁷Then I weighed the gifts that had been given for God's temple, and I divided them among the twelve priests I had chosen. There were gifts of silver and gold, as well as the articles that the king, his advisors and officials, and the people of Israel had

---

[x]**8.15** *I:* See the note at 8.1.   [y]**8.15** *river:* Or "canal." [z]**8.15** *town of Ahava:* A town (or place) in Babylonia, but the exact location is unknown.   [a]**8.17** *Casiphia:* The location is not known.   [b]**8.20** *King David:* See the note at 3.10.   [c]**8.21** *River:* See the note at 8.15.   [d]**8.21** *I:* See the note at 8.1.   [e]**8.21** *to go without eating:* The Jews often went without eating as a way of worshiping God. This is sometimes called "fasting."   [f]**8.24** *I:* See the note at 8.1.

PARENTING&*family*—How can I protect my kids from negative cultural influences? *(Ezra 8.21-34)*

Ask God to guard them.

When Ezra and the people prayed for safety for themselves and their children, they had in mind more than simply physical well-being. If ever a band of believers were surrounded by negative cultural influences, this group was it. The great fear of these Israelite parents was that their children would become ensnared in the pagan practices of the people around them (9.1).

Children today grow up in a culture rife with negative influences. Television, videos, and the Internet have opened the doors of our homes to materialism, sensualism, and a host of harmful forces. Christian parents can and must take many steps to guard our children and help them discern what is good and what is dangerous. But we cannot win the fight on our own. Our first step must be to ask God's help. (See also Psalm 119.97-105; Proverbs 4.10-27; Song of Songs 8.8,9; 1 Peter 5.2-11.)

Words To Remember: *We humbled ourselves and asked God to bring us and our children safely to Jerusalem with all of our possessions.—Ezra 8.21*

contributed. In all there were: 25 tons of silver; 100 silver articles weighing 150 pounds; 7,500 pounds of gold; 20 gold bowls weighing 270 ounces; and 2 polished bronze articles as valuable as gold.

[28]I said to the priests:

You belong to the LORD, the God of your ancestors, and these things also belong to him. The silver and gold were willingly given as gifts to the LORD. [29]Be sure to guard them and keep them safe until you reach Jerusalem. Then weigh them inside God's temple in the presence of the chief priests, the Levites, and the heads of the Israelite families.

[30]The priests and Levites then took charge of the gifts that had been weighed, so they could take them to the temple of our God in Jerusalem.

The Return to Jerusalem

[31]On the twelfth day of the first month,[g] we left the Ahava River[h] and started for Jerusalem. Our God watched over us, and as we traveled along, he kept our enemies from ambushing us.

[32]After arriving in Jerusalem, we rested for three days. [33]Then on the fourth day we went to God's temple, where the silver, the gold, and the other things were weighed and given to the priest Meremoth son of Uriah. With him were Eleazar son of Phinehas and the two Levites, Jozabad son of Jeshua and Noadiah son of Binnui. [34]Everything was counted, weighed, and recorded.

[35]Those who had returned from exile offered sacrifices on the altar to the God of Israel. Twelve bulls were offered for all Israel. Ninety-six rams and seventy-seven[i] lambs were offered on the altar. And twelve goats were sacrificed for the sins of the people. [36]Some of those who had returned took the king's orders to the governors and officials in Western Province. Then the officials did what they could for the people and for the temple of God.

Ezra Condemns Mixed Marriages

9 Later the Jewish leaders came to me[j] and said:

Many Israelites, including priests and Levites, are living just like the people around them. They are even guilty of some of the horrible sins of the Ca-naanites, the Hittites, the Perizzites, the Jebusites, the Ammonites, the Moabites, the Egyptians, and the Amorites. [2]Some Israelite men have married foreign women and have let their sons do the same thing. Our own officials and leaders were the first to commit this disgusting sin, and now God's holy people are mixed with foreigners. [3]This news made me so angry that I ripped my clothes and tore hair from my head and beard. Then I just sat in shock [4]until time for the evening sacrifice. Many of our people were greatly concerned and gathered around me, because the God of Israel had warned us to stay away from foreigners.

Ezra's Prayer

[5]At the time of the evening sacrifice, I was still sitting there in sorrow with my clothes all torn. So I got down on my knees, then lifted my arms, [6]and prayed:

The reason people are so guilt-ridden in Christ is because they have unconfessed sin. They may have confessed it to God, but it's very difficult, humanly, to get beyond the guilt unless you tell someone you trust, "I messed up!"

STAR PARKER

I am much too ashamed to face you, LORD God. Our sins and our guilt have swept over us like a flood that reaches up to the heavens. [7]Since the time of our ancestors, all of us have sinned. That's why we, our kings, and our priests have often been defeated by other kings. They have killed some of us and made slaves of others; they

---

[g]8.31 *first month*: See the note at 6.19. [h]8.31 *River*: See the note at 8.15. [i]8.35 *seventy-seven*: Or "seventy-two." [j]9.1 *me*: Ezra.

have taken our possessions and made us ashamed, just as we are today.

⁸But for now, LORD God, you have shown great kindness to us. You made us truly happy by letting some of us settle in this sacred place and by helping us in our time of slavery. ⁹We are slaves, but you have never turned your back on us. You love us, and because of you, the kings of Persia have helped us. It's as though you have given us new life! You let us rebuild your temple and live safely in Judah and Jerusalem.

¹⁰Our God, what can we say now? Even after all this, we have disobeyed the commands ¹¹that were given to us by your servants the prophets. They said the land you are giving us is full of sinful and wicked people, who never stop doing disgusting things.ᵏ ¹²And we were warned not to let our daughters and sons marry their sons and daughters.

Your prophets also told us never to help those foreigners or even let them live in peace. You wanted us to become strong and to enjoy the good things in the land, then someday to leave it to our children forever. ¹³You punished us because of our terrible sins. But you did not punish us nearly as much as we deserve, and you have brought some of us back home. ¹⁴Why should we disobey your commands again by letting our sons and daughters marry these foreigners who do such disgusting things? That would make you angry enough to destroy us all! ¹⁵LORD God of Israel, you have been more than fair by letting a few of us survive. But once again, our sins have made us ashamed to face you.

The Plan for Ending Mixed Marriages

10 While Ezra was down on his knees in front of God's temple, praying with tears in his eyes, and confessing the sins of the people of Israel, a large number of men, women, and children gathered around him and cried bitterly. ²Shecaniah son of Jehiel from the family of Elam said:

Ezra, we have disobeyed God by marrying these foreign women. But there is still hope for the people of Israel, ³if we follow your advice and the advice of others who truly respect the laws of God. We must promise God that we will divorce our foreign wives and send them away, together with their children.

⁴Ezra, it's up to you to do something! We will support whatever you do. So be brave!

⁵Ezra stood up and made the chief priests, the Levites, and everyone else in Israel swear that they would follow the advice of Shecaniah. ⁶Then Ezra left God's temple and went to spend the night in the living quarters of Jehohanan son of Eliashib. He felt sorry for what the people had done, and he did not eat or drink a thing.

⁷⁻⁸The officials and leaders sent a message to all who had returned from Babylonia and were now living in Jerusalem and Judah. It told them to meet in Jerusalem within three days, or else they would lose everything they owned and would no longer be considered part of the people that had returned from Babylonia.

⁹Three days later, on the twentieth day of the ninth month,ˡ everyone from Judah and Benjamin came to Jerusalem and sat in the temple courtyard. It was a serious meeting, and they sat there, trembling in the rain.

¹⁰Ezra the priest stood up and said:

You have broken God's Law by marrying foreign women, and you have made the whole nation guilty! ¹¹Now you must confess your sins to the LORD God of your ancestors and obey him. Divorce your foreign wives and don't have anything to do with the rest of the foreigners who live around here.

¹²Everyone in the crowd shouted:

You're right! We will do what you say. ¹³But there are so many of us, and we can't just stay out here in this downpour. A lot of us have sinned by marrying foreign women, and the matter can't be settled in only a day or two.

ᵏ9.11 *doing disgusting things*: Probably worshiping idols. ˡ10.9 *ninth month*: Chislev, the ninth month of the Hebrew calendar, from about mid-November to mid-December.

[14]Why can't our officials stay on in Jerusalem and take care of this for us? Let everyone who has sinned in this way meet here at a certain time with leaders and judges from their own towns. If we take care of this problem, God will surely stop being so terribly angry with us.

[15]Jonathan son of Asahel and Jahzeiah son of Tikvah were the only ones who objected, except for the two Levites, Meshullam and Shabbethai.

[16]Everyone else who had returned from exile agreed with the plan. So Ezra the priest chose men[m] who were heads of the families, and he listed their names. They started looking into the matter on the first day of the tenth month,[n] [17]and they did not finish until the first day of the first month[o] of the next year.

The Men Who Had Foreign Wives

[18-19]Here is a list of the priests who had agreed to divorce their foreign wives and to sacrifice a ram as a sin offering:

Maaseiah, Eliezer, Jarib, and Gedaliah from the family of Joshua son of Jozadak and his brothers; [20]Hanani and Zebadiah from the family of Immer; [21]Maaseiah, Elijah, Shemaiah, Jehiel, and Uzziah from the family of Harim; [22]Elioenai, Maaseiah, Ishmael, Nethanel, Jozabad, and Elasah from the family of Pashhur.

[23]Those Levites who had foreign wives were: Jozabad, Shimei, Kelaiah (also known as Kelita), Pethahiah, Judah, and Eliezer.

[24]Eliashib, the musician, had a foreign wife.

These temple guards had foreign wives: Shallum, Telem, and Uri.

[25]Here is a list of the others from Israel who had foreign wives:

Ramiah, Izziah, Malchijah, Mijamin, Eleazar, Hashabiah,[p] and Benaiah from the family of Parosh;

[26]Mattaniah, Zechariah, Jehiel, Abdi, Jeremoth, and Elijah from the family of Elam;

[27]Elioenai, Eliashib, Mattaniah, Jeremoth, Zabad, and Aziza from the family of Zattu;

[28]Jehohanan, Hananiah, Zabbai, and Athlai from the family of Bebai;

[29]Meshullam, Malluch, Adaiah, Jashub, Sheal, and Jeremoth from the family of Bani;

[30]Adna, Chelal, Benaiah, Maaseiah, Mattaniah, Bezalel, Binnui, and Manasseh from the family of Pahath Moab;

[31-32]Eliezer, Isshijah, Malchijah, Shemaiah, Shimeon, Benjamin, Malluch, and Shemariah from the family of Harim;

[33]Mattenai, Mattattah, Zabad, Eliphelet, Jeremai, Manasseh, and Shimei from the family of Hashum;

[34-37]Maadai, Amram, Uel, Benaiah, Bedeiah, Cheluhi, Vaniah, Meremoth, Eliashib, Mattaniah, Mattenai, and Jaasu from the family of Bani;

[38-42]Shimei, Shelemiah, Nathan, Adaiah, Machnadebai, Shashai, Sharai, Azarel, Shelemiah, Shemariah, Shallum, Amariah, and Joseph from the family of Binnui;[q]

[43]Jeiel, Mattithiah, Zabad, Zebina, Jaddai, Joel, and Benaiah from the family of Nebo.

[44]These men divorced their foreign wives, then sent them and their children away.[r]

---

[m]**10.16** *So . . . men:* One possible meaning for the difficult Hebrew text. [n]**10.16** *tenth month:* Tebeth, the tenth month of the Hebrew calendar, from about mid-December to mid-January. [o]**10.17** *first month:* See the note at 6.19. [p]**10.25** *Hashabiah:* One ancient translation; Hebrew "Malchijah." [q]**10.38-42** *from the family of Binnui:* One possible meaning for the difficult Hebrew text. [r]**10.44** *away:* One possible meaning for the difficult Hebrew text of verse 44.

Nehemiah
Building the Walls of Jerusalem

The book of Nehemiah picks up the story that started so hopefully in the book of Ezra—with the fulfillment of God's promise to bring his people to their homeland. But this installment starts with bad news. Nearly one hundred years after the Jewish people began returning to Jerusalem, the rebuilding of the city walls was still incomplete.

In the face of opposition from outsiders and discouragement among his own people, Nehemiah combined faith and action in practical ways to get a big job done: "We kept on praying to our God, and we also stationed guards day and night" (4.9).

On first reading, the opposition to "foreigners" that Nehemiah preached and that Jerusalem's wall represented seems politically incorrect today. But God's ultimate purpose was not to erect barriers based on race or nationality; instead, God used the wall around Jerusalem to protect his children from the dangers and wicked influences around them—just as mothers today do for their children.

For Christians today, Christ has broken down the walls that divide us from one another. But he still calls us to be noticeably different from the culture around us. Like Nehemiah, as we face ungodly influences we need to keep on praying and stay on guard.

Nehemiah at a Glance

1. Bad news about the disrepair of Jerusalem (1)
2. Nehemiah goes to Jerusalem to supervise rebuilding the wall (2–4)
3. Nehemiah teaches the people to show generosity to poor families (5)
4. In spite of enemy plots, the wall is finished (6.1—7.3)
5. A list of the exiles who returned to Jerusalem (7.4-73)
6. The people hear God's Law, confess their sins, and promise to be faithful (8–10)
7. Lists of families who settled in Jerusalem and other towns (11.1—12.26)
8. Dedication of the wall and rededication of the people (12.27—13.31)

Nehemiah's Prayer

1 I am Nehemiah son of Hacaliah, and in this book I tell what I have done.

During the month of Chislev[a] in the twentieth year that Artaxerxes[b] ruled Persia, I was in his fortress city of Susa,[c] ²when my brother Hanani came with some men from Judah. So I asked them about the Jews who had escaped[d] from being captives in Babylonia. I also asked them about the city of Jerusalem.

³They told me, "Those captives who have come back are having all kinds of troubles. They are terribly disgraced, Jerusalem's walls are broken down, and its gates have been burned."

⁴When I heard this, I sat down and cried. Then for several days, I mourned; I went without eating to show my sorrow, and I prayed:

⁵LORD God of heaven, you are great and fearsome. And you faithfully keep your promises to everyone who loves you and obeys your commands. ⁶I am your servant, so please have mercy on me and answer the prayer that I make day and night for these people of Israel who serve you. I, my family, and the rest of your people have sinned ⁷by choosing to disobey you and the laws and teachings you gave to your servant Moses.

⁸Please remember the promise you made to Moses. You told him that if we were unfaithful, you would scatter us among foreign nations. ⁹But you also said that no matter how far away we were, we could turn to you and start obeying your laws. Then you would bring us back to the place where you have chosen to be worshiped.

¹⁰Our LORD, I am praying for your servants—those you rescued by your great strength and mighty power. ¹¹Please answer my prayer and the prayer of your other servants who gladly honor your name. When I serve the king his wine today, make him pleased with me and have him do what I ask.

Nehemiah Goes to Jerusalem

2 During the month of Nisan[e] in the twentieth year that Artaxerxes was king, I served him his wine, as I had done before. But this was the first time I had ever looked depressed. ²So the king said, "Why do you look so sad? You're not sick. Something must be bothering you."

Even though I was frightened, ³I answered, "Your Majesty, I hope you live forever! I feel sad because the city where my ancestors is buried is in ruins, and its gates have been burned down."

⁴The king asked, "What do you want me to do?"

---

[a]1.1 Chislev: The ninth month of the Hebrew calendar, from about mid-November to mid-December. [b]1.1 Artaxerxes: Probably Artaxerxes I, who ruled Persia 465-425 B.C. [c]1.1 Susa: Capital of Elam Province, the winter home of Persian kings. [d]1.2 escaped: Or "returned." [e]2.1 Nisan: Or Abib, the first month of the Hebrew calendar, from about mid-March to mid-April.

---

*Spiritual*Life—How should I pray? *(Nehemiah 1)*

Praise God and confess your sins.

God wants to hear our needs. But when we pour out nothing but requests to God, we miss the point of prayer. Prayer is not meant to be like placing a celestial catalog order; it's communication between us and God. That communication falls short of all it could be when we forget to acknowledge who God is—the great, fearsome, faithful, and loving Lord of heaven, worthy of our praise (1.5)—and who we are—weak people who have chosen to disobey and need to confess our sins (1.6,7). Amazingly, despite the enormous gap between who God is and who we are, God promises to hear our prayers! (See also 2 Samuel 7.18-29; 2 Kings 19.14-19; 2 Chronicles 6,7; Psalm 85; Lamentations 5; Matthew 6.5-15; Acts 4.23-31.)

Words To Remember: *LORD God of heaven, you are great and fearsome. And you faithfully keep your promises to everyone who loves you and obeys your commands.—Nehemiah 1.5*

I prayed to the God who rules from heaven. ⁵Then I told the king, "Sir, if it's all right with you, please send me back to Judah, so that I can rebuild the city where my ancestors are buried."

⁶The queen was sitting beside the king when he asked me, "How long will it take, and when will you be back?" The king agreed to let me go, and I told him when I would return.

⁷Then I asked, "Your Majesty, would you be willing to give me letters to the governors of the provinces west of the Euphrates River, so that I can travel safely to Judah? ⁸I will need timber to rebuild the gates of the fortress near the temple and more timber to construct the city wall and to build a place for me to live. And so, I would appreciate a letter to Asaph, who is in charge of the royal forest." God was good to me, and the king did everything I asked.

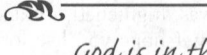

God is in the business of encouragement.

ELIZABETH MITTELSTAEDT

⁹The king sent some army officers and cavalry troops along with me, and as I traveled through the Western Provinces, I gave the letters to the governors. ¹⁰But when Sanballat from Horon*f* and Tobiah the Ammonite official heard about what had happened, they became very angry, because they didn't want anyone to help the people of Israel.

Nehemiah Inspects the Wall of Jerusalem

¹¹Three days after arriving in Jerusalem, ¹²I got up during the night and left my house. I took some men with me, without telling anyone what I thought God wanted me to do for the city. The only animal I took was the donkey I rode on. ¹³I went through Valley Gate on the west, then south past Dragon Spring, before coming to Garbage Gate. As I rode along, I took a good look at the crumbled walls of the city and the gates that had been torn down and burned. ¹⁴On the east side of the city, I headed north to Fountain Gate and King's Pool, but then the trail became too narrow for my donkey. ¹⁵So

I went down to Kidron Valley and looked at the wall from there. Then before daylight I returned to the city through Valley Gate.

¹⁶None of the city officials knew what I had in mind. And I had not even told any of the Jews—not the priests, the leaders, the officials, or any other Jews who would be helping in the work. ¹⁷But when I got back, I said to them, "Jerusalem is truly in a mess! The gates have been torn down and burned, and everything is in ruins. We must rebuild the city wall so that we can again take pride in our city."

¹⁸Then I told them how kind God had been and what the king had said.

Immediately, they replied, "Let's start building now!" So they got everything ready.

¹⁹When Sanballat, Tobiah, and Geshem the Arab heard about our plans, they started insulting us and saying, "Just look at you! Do you plan to rebuild the walls of the city and rebel against the king?"

²⁰I answered, "We are servants of the God who rules from heaven, and he will make our work succeed. So we will start rebuilding Jerusalem, but you have no right to any of its property, because you have had no part in its history."

Rebuilding the Wall of Jerusalem

3 These are the people who helped rebuild the wall and gates of Jerusalem: The high priest Eliashib and the other priests rebuilt Sheep Gate and hung its doors. Then they dedicated Sheep Gate and the section of the wall as far as Hundred Tower and Hananel Tower.

²The people of Jericho rebuilt the next section of the wall, and Zaccur son of Imri rebuilt the section after that.

³The family of Hassenaah built Fish Gate. They put the beams in place and hung the doors, then they added metal bolts and wooden beams as locks.

⁴Meremoth, son of Uriah and grandson of Hakkoz, completed the next section of the wall.

---

*f*2.10 *Horon:* Possibly meaning that Sanballat was the official in charge of Beth-Horon, an important town on the road from Jerusalem to Lydda and the Mediterranean Sea.

Meshullam, son of Berechiah and grandson of Meshezabel, rebuilt the next section, and Zadok son of Baana rebuilt the section beside that.

[5]The next section was to be repaired by the men of Tekoa, but their town leaders refused to do the hard work they were assigned.[g]

[6]Joiada son of Paseah and Meshullam son of Besodeiah restored Ancient Gate. They put the beams in place, hung the doors, and added metal bolts and wooden beams as locks. [7]Melatiah from Gibeon, Jadon from Meronoth, and the men from Gibeon and Mizpah rebuilt the next section of the wall. This section reached as far as the house of the governor of West Euphrates Province.[h]

[8]Uzziel son of Harhaiah the goldsmith rebuilt the next section.

Hananiah the perfume maker rebuilt the section next after that, and it went as far as Broad Wall.

[9]Rephaiah son of Hur ruled half of the Jerusalem District, and he rebuilt the next section of the wall.

[10]The section after that was close to the home of Jedaiah son of Harumaph, and he rebuilt it.

Hattush son of Hashabneiah constructed the next section of the wall.

[11]Malchijah son of Harim and Hasshub son of Pahath Moab rebuilt the section after that, and they also built Oven Tower.

[12]Shallum son of Hallohesh ruled the other half of the Jerusalem District, and he rebuilt the next section of the wall. Shallum's daughters also worked with him.

[13]Hanun and the people who lived in the town of Zanoah rebuilt Valley Gate. They hung the doors and added metal bolts and wooden beams as locks. They also rebuilt the wall for fifteen hundred feet, all the way to Garbage Gate.

[14]Malchijah son of Rechab ruled the district of Beth-Haccherem, and he rebuilt Garbage Gate. He hung the doors and added metal bolts and wooden beams as locks.

[15]Shallum[i] son of Colhozeh ruled the district of Mizpah, and he rebuilt

Fountain Gate. He put a cover over the gateway, then hung the doors and added metal bolts and wooden beams as locks. He also rebuilt the wall at Shelah Pool. This section was next to the king's garden and went as far as the stairs leading down from David's City.

[16]Nehemiah son of Azbuk ruled half of the district of Beth-Zur, and he rebuilt the next section of the wall. It went as far as the royal cemetery,[j] the artificial pool, and the army barracks.

Levites Who Worked on the Wall

[17]The Levites who worked on the next sections of the wall were Rehum son of Bani; Hashabiah, who ruled half of the district of Keilah and did this work for his district; [18]Binnui[k] son of Henadad, who ruled the other half of the district of Keilah; [19]Ezer son of Jeshua, who ruled Mizpah, rebuilt the section of the wall that was in front of the armory and reached to the corner of the wall; [20]Baruch son of Zabbai eagerly rebuilt the section of the wall that went all the way to the door of the house of Eliashib the high priest; [21]Meremoth, son of Uriah and grandson of Hakkoz, built up to the far end of Eliashib's house.

Priests Who Worked on the Wall

[22]Here is a list of the priests who worked on the wall:

Priests from the region around Jerusalem rebuilt the next section of the wall.

[23]Benjamin and Hasshub rebuilt the wall in front of their own houses.

Azariah, who was the son of Maaseiah and the grandson of Ananiah, rebuilt the section in front of his house.

[24]Binnui son of Henadad rebuilt the section of the wall from Azariah's house to the corner of the wall.

[25]Palal son of Uzai rebuilt the next

---

[g]3.5 refused . . . assigned: One possible meaning for the difficult Hebrew text. [h]3.7 as far as . . . Province: One possible meaning for the difficult Hebrew text. [i]3.15 Shallum: A few Hebrew manuscripts and one ancient translation; most Hebrew manuscripts "Shallun"; one ancient translation "Solomon." [j]3.16 royal cemetery: Hebrew "David's tombs." [k]3.18 Binnui: Two ancient translations; Hebrew "Bavvai."

section, which began at the corner of the wall and the tower of the upper palace near the court of the guard.

Pedaiah son of Parosh rebuilt the next section of the wall. [26]He stopped at a place near the Water Gate on the east and the tower guarding the temple. This was close to a section in the city called Ophel, where the temple workers lived.[l]

Other Builders Who Worked on the Wall

[27]The men from Tekoa rebuilt the next section of the wall, and it was their second section.[m] It started at a place across from the large tower that guarded the Temple, and it went all the way to the wall near Ophel.

[28]Some priests rebuilt the next section of the wall. They began working north of Horse Gate, and each one worked on a section in front of his own house.

[29]Zadok son of Immer rebuilt the wall in front of his house.

Shemaiah son of Shecaniah, who looked after the East Gate, rebuilt the section after that.

[30]Hananiah and Hanun[n] rebuilt the next section, which was the second section[o] for them.

Meshullam son of Berechiah rebuilt the next section, which happened to be in front of his house.

[31]Malchijah, a goldsmith, rebuilt the next section, as far as the house used by the temple workers and merchants. This area was across from Gathering Gate, near the room on top of the wall at the northeast corner.

[32]The goldsmiths and merchants rebuilt the last section of the wall, which went from the corner room all the way to Sheep Gate.

Nehemiah's Enemies

4 When Sanballat, the governor of Samaria, heard that we were rebuilding the walls of Jerusalem, he became angry and started insulting our people. [2]In front of his friends and the Samaritan army he said, "What is this feeble bunch of Jews trying to do? Are they going to rebuild the wall and offer sacrifices all in one day? Do they think they can make something out of this pile of scorched stones?"

[3]Tobiah from Ammon was standing beside Sanballat and said, "Look at the wall they are building! Why, even a fox could knock over this pile of stones."

[4]But I prayed, "Our God, these people hate us and have wished horrible things for us. Please answer our prayers and make their insults fall on them! Let them be the ones to be dragged away as prisoners of war. [5]Don't forgive the mean and evil way they have insulted the builders."

[6]The people worked hard, and we built the walls of Jerusalem halfway up again. [7]But Sanballat, Tobiah, the Arabs, the Ammonites, and the people from the city of Ashdod saw the walls going up and the holes being repaired. So they became angry [8]and decided to stir up trouble, and to fight against the people of Jerusalem. [9]But we kept on praying to our God, and we also stationed guards day and night.

[10]Meanwhile, the people of Judah were singing a sorrowful song:

> "So much rubble for us to haul!
>   Worn out and weary,
>   will we ever finish this wall?"

[11]Our enemies were saying, "Before those Jews know what has happened, we will sneak up and kill them and put an end to their work."

[12]On at least ten different occasions, the Jews living near our enemies warned us against attacks from every side,[p] [13]and so I sent people to guard the wall at its lowest places and where there were still holes in it. I placed them according to families, and they stood guard with swords and spears and with bows and arrows. [14]Then I looked things over and told the leaders, the officials, and the rest of the people, "Don't be afraid of your enemies! The Lord is great and fearsome. So think of him and fight for your relatives and children, your wives and homes!"

---

[l]3.26 This . . . lived: One possible meaning for the difficult Hebrew text.   [m]3.27 second section: See verse 5.   [n]3.30 Hananiah and Hanun: Hebrew "Hananiah son of Shelemiah and Hanun, Zalaph's sixth son."   [o]3.30 second section: See verses 8, 13.   [p]4.12 against . . . side: One possible meaning for the difficult Hebrew text.

15 Our enemies found out that we knew
about their plot against us, but God kept
them from doing what they had planned. So
we went back to work on the wall.
16 From then on, I let half of the young
men work while the other half stood guard.
They wore armor and had spears and
shields, as well as bows and arrows. The
leaders helped the workers
17 who were rebuilding the wall. Everyone who hauled
building materials kept one hand free to
carry a weapon.
18 Even the workers who
were rebuilding the wall strapped on a
sword. The worker who was to blow the signal trumpet stayed with me.
19 I told the people and their officials and
leaders, "Our work is so spread out, that we
are a long way from one another.
20 If you
hear the sound of the trumpet, come
quickly and gather around me. Our God
will help us fight."
21 Every day from dawn to dark, half of
the workers rebuilt the walls, while the rest
stood guard with their spears.
22 I asked the men in charge and their
workers to stay inside Jerusalem and stand
guard at night. So they guarded the city at
night and worked during the day.
23 I even
slept in my work clothes at night; my children, the workers, and the guards slept in
theirs as well. And we always kept our weapons close by.[q]

Nehemiah's Concern for the Poor

5 Some of the men and their wives complained about the Jews in power
2 and
said, "We have large families, and it
takes a lot of grain merely to keep them
alive."
3 Others said, "During the famine we
even had to mortgage our fields, vineyards,
and homes to them in order to buy grain."
4 Then others said, "We had to borrow
money from those in power to pay the
government tax on our fields and vineyards.
5 We are Jews just as they are, and our
children are as good as theirs. But we
still have to sell our children as slaves, and
some of our daughters have already been
raped. We are completely helpless; our
fields and vineyards have even been taken
from us."
6 When I heard their complaints and
their charges, I became very angry.
7 So I
thought it over and said to the leaders and
officials, "How can you charge your own
people interest?"
Then I called a public meeting and accused the leaders
8 by saying, "We have tried
to buy back all of our people who were sold
into exile. But here you are, selling more of
them for us to buy back!" The officials and
leaders did not say a word, because they
knew this was true.
9 I continued, "What you have done is
wrong! We must honor our God by the way
we live, so the Gentiles can't find fault with
us.
10 My relatives, my friends, and I are also
lending money and grain, but we must
no longer demand payment in return.
11 Now give back the fields, vineyards, olive

[q] **4.23** *And . . . by*: One possible meaning for the difficult Hebrew text.

SingleLife—I like being single. Is that normal? *(Nehemiah 4; 6.15,16)*

God needs people who can give their all to their work.
Some jobs require more effort than you can fit into a "9 to 5" day. Other jobs—whether they're paying jobs, volunteer work, or something else—are worth all the effort and energy that you have. As a single woman, you can give it all you've got!

The work of building up the walls of Jerusalem was so important and so dangerous that it required high-commitment prayer and effort. This was no "9 to 5" job. Workers were on duty day and night (4.9).

God still calls workers to build up his kingdom. Sometimes the work calls for more time and energy than a woman busy with husband or family can give. As you enjoy your singleness, enjoy your freedom to serve God to the hilt! (See also Numbers 11; Romans 14.1-12; 1 Corinthians 7.29-35.)

Words To Remember: ***But we kept on praying to our God, and we also stationed guards day and night.*—Nehemiah 4.9**

orchards, and houses you have taken and also the interest you have been paid."

¹²The leaders answered, "We will do whatever you say and return their property, without asking to be repaid."

So I made the leaders promise in front of the priests to give back the property. ¹³Then I emptied my pockets and said, "If you don't keep your promise, that's what God will do to you. He will empty out everything you own, even taking away your houses."

The people answered, "We will keep our promise." Then they praised the LORD and did as they had promised.

Nehemiah Is Generous

¹⁴I was governor of Judah from the twentieth year that Artaxerxes* was king until the thirty-second year. And during these entire twelve years, my relatives and I refused to accept the food that I was allowed. ¹⁵Each governor before me had been a burden to the people by making them pay for his food and wine and by demanding forty silver coins a day. Even their officials had been a burden to the people. But I respected God, and I didn't think it was right to be so hard on them. ¹⁶I spent all my time getting the wall rebuilt and did not buy any property. Everyone working for me did the same thing. ¹⁷I usually fed a hundred fifty of our

own Jewish people and their leaders, as well as foreign visitors from surrounding lands. ¹⁸Each day one ox, six of the best sheep, and lots of chickens were prepared. Then every ten days, a large supply of wine was brought in. I knew what a heavy burden this would have been for the people, and so I did not ask for my food allowance as governor.

¹⁹I pray that God will bless me for everything I have done for my people.

Plots against Nehemiah

6 Sanballat, Tobiah, Geshem, and our other enemies learned that I had completely rebuilt the wall. All I lacked was hanging the doors in the gates. ²Then Sanballat and Geshem sent a message, asking me to meet with them in one of the villages in Ono Valley. I knew they were planning to harm me in some way. ³So I sent messengers to tell them, "My work is too important to stop now and go there. I can't afford to slow down the work just to visit with you." ⁴They invited me four times, but each time I refused to go.

⁵Finally, Sanballat sent an official to me with an unsealed letter, ⁶which said:

A rumor is going around among the nations that you and the other

---

*5.14 *Artaxerxes*: See the note at 1.1.

*Spiritual*Life—How can I reach out to a needy world? *(Nehemiah 5.1-13)*

Do what you can to correct injustice.
Even after watching just one nightly news broadcast, it would be easy to conclude that this world is too full of injustice for any one of us to make a difference. That would be an easy conclusion—but it would be wrong.

Consider Nehemiah's situation. Although he was on temporary leave from his day job, in the middle of an enormous construction project, and surrounded by hostile enemies, when he learned of injustice among his workers he confronted the problem immediately. Did Nehemiah's attempt to restore justice make more than a dent in the problems engulfing the people? Probably not, but Nehemiah didn't care. His goal was to be part of the solution, no matter how many problems existed. He knew that as one of God's people, he had to live in a way that represented God's justice.

How can you work to restore justice? Start where you see a need. Perhaps you can become more politically active, donate money to a charitable cause, or volunteer at a homeless shelter. Whatever you do, try to show God's love to people who desperately need it. (See also 2 Samuel 9; Lamentations 2.11-13; Jonah 4.5-11; Zechariah 7.7-13; Matthew 6.1-4; Luke 9.10-17.)

Words To Remember: *I continued, "What you have done is wrong! We must honor our God by the way we live, so the Gentiles can't find fault with us."*
—Nehemiah 5.9

Jews are rebuilding the wall and planning to rebel, because you want to be their king. And Geshem[s] says it's true! [7]You even have prophets in Jerusalem, claiming you are now the king of Judah. You know the Persian king will hear about this, so let's get together and talk it over.

[8]I sent a message back to Sanballat, saying, "None of this is true! You are making it all up."

> *We need to be rooted and built up in the person of Christ— safe, secure, nurtured in Jesus as our steadfast shelter.*
>
> INGRID TROBISCH

[9]Our enemies were trying to frighten us and to keep us from our work. But I asked God to give me strength.

[10]One day I went to visit Shemaiah.[t] He was looking very worried, and[u] he said, "Let's hurry to the holy place of the temple and hide there.[v] We will lock the temple doors, because your enemies are planning to kill you tonight."

[11]I answered, "Why should someone like me have to run and hide in the temple to save my life? I won't go!"

[12]Suddenly I realized that God had not given Shemaiah this message. But Tobiah and Sanballat had paid him to trick me [13]and to frighten me into doing something wrong, because they wanted to ruin my good name.

[14]Then I asked God to punish Tobiah and Sanballat for what they had done. I prayed that God would punish the prophet Noadiah and the other prophets who, together with her, had tried to frighten me.

The Work Is Finished

[15]On the twenty-fifth day of the month Elul,[w] the wall was completely rebuilt. It had taken fifty-two days. [16]When our enemies in the surrounding nations learned that the work was finished, they felt helpless, because they knew that our God had helped us rebuild the wall.

[17]All this time the Jewish leaders and Tobiah had been writing letters back and forth. [18]Many people in Judah were loyal to Tobiah for two reasons: Shecaniah son of Arah was his father-in-law, and Tobiah's son Jehohanan had married the daughter of Meshullam son of Berechiah.[x] [19]The people would always tell me about the good things Tobiah had done, and then they would tell Tobiah everything I had said. So Tobiah kept sending letters, trying to frighten me.

7 After the wall had been rebuilt and the gates hung, then the temple guards, the singers, and the other Levites were assigned their work. [2]I put my brother Hanani in charge of Jerusalem, along with Hananiah, the commander of the fortress, because Hananiah could be trusted, and he respected God more than most people did. [3]I said to them, "Don't let the gates to the city be opened until the sun has been up for a while. And make sure that they are closed and barred before the guards go off duty at sunset. Choose people from Jerusalem to stand guard at different places around the wall and others to stand guard near their own houses."

A List of Exiles Who Returned
(Ezra 2.1-70)

[4]Although Jerusalem covered a large area, not many people lived there, and no new houses had been built. [5-6]So God gave me the idea to bring together the people, their leaders, and officials and to check the family records of those who had returned from captivity in Babylonia, after having been taken there by King Nebuchadnezzar.[y] About this same time, I found records of those who had been the first to return to

---

[s]6.6 *Geshem:* Hebrew "Gashmu" (see verse 1 and 2.19).   [t]6.10 *Shemaiah:* Hebrew "Shemaiah son of Delaiah son of Mehetabel."   [u]6.10 *was . . . worried, and:* Or "wasn't supposed to leave his house, but."   [v]6.10 *holy place . . . hide there:* Only priests were allowed to enter the holy place; anyone else could be put to death.   [w]6.15 *Elul:* The sixth month of the Hebrew calendar, from about mid-August to mid-September.   [x]6.18 *Shecaniah . . . Berechiah:* Jews who had helped rebuild the Jerusalem wall (see 3.4, 29, 30).   [y]7.5,6 *Nebuchadnezzar:* Known as Nebuchadnezzar II, who ruled Babylonia from 605 to 562 B.C. In 586 B.C. he destroyed Jerusalem and took many of its people to Babylonia.

Jerusalem from Babylon Province.[z] By reading these records, I learned that they settled in their own hometowns, [7]and that they had come with Zerubbabel, Joshua, Nehemiah, Azariah, Raamiah, Nahamani, Mordecai, Bilshan, Mispereth, Bigvai, Nehum, and Baanah.

[8-25]Here is how many had returned from each family group: 2,172 from Parosh; 372 from Shephatiah; 652 from Arah; 2,818 from Pahath Moab, who were all descendants of Jeshua and Joab; 1,254 from Elam; 845 from Zattu; 760 from Zaccai; 648 from Binnui; 628 from Bebai; 2,322 from Azgad; 667 from Adonikam; 2,067 from Bigvai; 655 from Adin; 98 from Ater, also known as Hezekiah; 328 from Hashum; 324 from Bezai; 112 from Hariph; and 95 from Gibeon.

[26-38]Here is how many people returned whose ancestors had come from the following towns: 188 from Bethlehem and Netophah; 128 from Anathoth; 42 from Beth-Azmaveth; 743 from Kiriath-Jearim, Chephirah, and Beeroth; 621 from Ramah and Geba; 122 from Michmas; 123 from Bethel and Ai; 52 from Nebo;[a] 1,254 from Elam;[b] 320 from Harim; 345 from Jericho; 721 from Lod, Hadid, and Ono; and 3,930 from Senaah.

[39-42]Here is how many returned from each family of priests: 973 descendants of Jeshua from Jedaiah; 1,052 from Immer; 1,247 from Pashhur; and 1,017 from Harim.

[43-45]Here is how many returned from the families of Levites: 74 descendants of Hodevah from the families of Jeshua and Kadmiel; 148 descendants of Asaph from the temple musicians; and 138 descendants of Shallum, Ater, Talmon, Akkub, Hatita, and Shobai from the temple guards.

[46-56]Here are the names of the families of temple workers whose descendants returned: Ziha, Hasupha, Tabbaoth, Keros, Sia, Padon, Lebana, Hagaba, Shalmai, Hanan, Giddel, Gahar, Reaiah, Rezin, Nekoda, Gazzam, Uzza, Paseah, Besai, Meunim, Nephushesim, Bakbuk, Hakupha, Harhur, Bazlith, Mehida, Harsha, Barkos, Sisera, Temah, Neziah, and Hatipha.

[57-59]Here are the names of Solomon's servants whose descendants returned: Sotai, Sophereth, Perida, Jaala, Darkon, Giddel, Shephatiah, Hattil, Pochereth Hazzebaim, and Amon.

[60]A total of 392 descendants of temple workers and of Solomon's servants returned.

[61-62]There were 642 who returned from the families of Delaiah, Tobiah, and Nekoda, though they could not prove they were Israelites. They had lived in the Babylonian towns of Tel-Melah, Tel-Harsha, Cherub, Addon, and Immer.

[63-64]The families of Hobaiah, Hakkoz, and Barzillai could not prove they were priests. The ancestor of the family of Barzillai had married the daughter of Barzillai from Gilead and had taken his wife's family name. But the records of these three families could not be found, and none of them were allowed to serve as priests. [65]In fact, the governor told them, "You cannot eat the food offered to God until he lets us know if you really are priests."[c]

[66-69]There were 42,360 who returned, in addition to 7,337 servants, and 245 musicians. Altogether, they brought with them 736 horses, 245 mules,[d] 435 camels, and 6,720 donkeys.

[70-72]Many people gave gifts to help pay for the materials to rebuild the temple. The governor himself gave 17 pounds of gold, 50 bowls to be used in the temple, and 530 robes for the priests. Family leaders gave 337 pounds of gold and 3,215 pounds of silver. The rest of the people gave 337 pounds of gold, 2,923 pounds of silver, and 67 robes for the priests.

[73]And so, by the seventh month,[e] priests, Levites, temple guards, musicians, workers, and many of the ordinary people had settled in the towns of Judah.

Ezra Reads God's Law to the People

8 [1-2]On the first day of the seventh month,[e] the people came together in the open area in front of the Water

---

[z]**7.5,6** *first to return . . . Province:* Probably 539 B.C., when Cyrus, the ruler of Persia, captured the city of Babylon.   [a]**7.26-38** *Nebo:* Hebrew "the other Nebo."
[b]**7.26-38** *Elam:* Hebrew "the other Elam."
[c]**7.65** *until . . . priests:* The Hebrew text has "until a priest comes with the urim and thummim," sacred objects which were used in some way to receive answers from God.   [d]**7.66-69** *736 horses, 245 mules:* A few Hebrew manuscripts; this is not found in most Hebrew manuscripts of verse 68.
[e]**7.73; 8.1,2** *seventh month:* Tishri (also called Ethanim), the seventh month of the Hebrew calendar, from about mid-September to mid-October.

Gate. Then they asked Ezra, who was a teacher of the Law of Moses, to read to them from this Law that the LORD had given his people. Ezra the priest came with the Law and stood before the crowd of men, women, and the children who were old enough to understand. ³From early morning till noon, he read the Law of Moses to them, and they listened carefully. ⁴Ezra stood on a high wooden platform that had been built for this occasion. Mattithiah, Shema, Anaiah, Uriah, Hilkiah, and Maaseiah were standing to his right, while Pedaiah, Mishael, Malchijah, Hashum, Hash Baddanah, Zechariah, and Meshullam were standing to his left.

⁵Ezra was up on the high platform, where he could be seen by everyone, and when he opened the book, they all stood up. ⁶Ezra praised the great LORD God, and the people shouted, "Amen! Amen!" Then they bowed with their faces to the ground and worshiped the LORD.

⁷⁻⁸After this, the Levites Jeshua, Bani, Sherebiah, Jamin, Akkub, Shabbethai, Hodiah, Maaseiah, Kelita, Azariah, Jozabad, Hanan, and Pelaiah went among the people, explaining the meaning of what Ezra had read.

⁹The people started crying when God's Law was read to them. Then Nehemiah the governor, Ezra the priest and teacher, and the Levites who had been teaching the people all said, "This is a special day for the LORD your God. So don't be sad and don't cry!"

¹⁰Nehemiah told the people, "Enjoy your good food and wine and share some with those who didn't have anything to bring. Don't be sad! This is a special day for the LORD, and he will make you happy and strong."

¹¹The Levites encouraged the people by saying, "This is a sacred day, so don't worry or mourn!" ¹²When the people returned to their homes, they celebrated by eating and drinking and by sharing their food with those in need, because they had understood what had been read to them.

Celebrating the Festival of Shelters

¹³On the second day of the seventh month,ᶠ the leaders of all the family groups came together with the priests and the Levites, so Ezra could teach them the Law ¹⁴that the LORD had given to Moses. They learned from the Law that the people of Israel were to live in shelters when they celebrated the festival in the seventh month of the year. ¹⁵They also learned that they were to go into the woods and gather branches of leafy trees such as olives, myrtles, and palms for making these shelters.

ᶠ8.13 *seventh month:* Hebrew "same month."

---

*Spiritual*Life—How can I worship God as I should? (*Nehemiah 8.1—9.6*)

Involve your whole being.
It has been said that "all of life is worship." When Ezra read and explained God's Law to the people, they caught this vision. They listened to God's Word (8.3), then responded with their bodies (8.5,6), their voices (8.6), and their tears (8.9). Their worship included confession (9.3), prayer (9.4,6), and praise (9.5). As the Old Testament rituals involved entire families to instruct children in the story of God's great salvation, their worship extended into their homes. And their worship extended to their neighborhoods as they "celebrated by eating and drinking and by sharing their food with those in need, because they had understood what had been read to them" (8.12).

The shape of our worship today will differ from that of Ezra's day. While we may not throw dirt on our heads to show sorrow for our sins or build shelters out of branches on our roofs, we still must allow God's Word to capture all our being and infect all our living—because our God is greater than mere words can express! (See also Nehemiah 12.27-43; Job 42.1-6; Psalm 42.)

Words To Remember: *"Stand and shout praises to your LORD, the eternal God! Praise his wonderful name, though he is greater than words can express."*
—Nehemiah 9.5

[16]So the people gathered branches and made shelters on the flat roofs of their houses, in their yards, in the courtyard of the temple, and in the open areas around the Water Gate and Ephraim Gate. [17]Everyone who had returned from Babylonia built shelters. They lived in them and joyfully celebrated the Festival of Shelters for the first time since the days of Joshua son of Nun. [18]On each of the first seven days of the festival, Ezra read to the people from God's Law. Then on the eighth day, everyone gathered for worship, just as the Law had said they must.

The People Confess Their Sins

9 On the twenty-fourth day of the seventh month,[f] the people of Israel went without eating, and they dressed in sackcloth and threw dirt on their heads to show their sorrow. [2]They refused to let foreigners join them, as they met to confess their sins and the sins of their ancestors. [3]For three hours they stood and listened to the Law of the LORD their God, and then for the next three hours they confessed their sins and worshiped the LORD.

[4]Jeshua, Bani, Kadmiel, Shebaniah, Bunni, Sherebiah, Bani, and Chenani stood on the special platform for the Levites and prayed aloud to the LORD their God. [5]Then the Levites Jeshua, Kadmiel, Bani, Hashabneiah, Sherebiah, Hodiah, Shebaniah, and Pethahiah said:

"Stand and shout praises
  to your LORD,
    the eternal God![g]
Praise his wonderful name,
though he is greater
  than words can express."

The People Pray

[6]You alone are the LORD,
  Creator of the heavens
    and all the stars,
  Creator of the earth
    and those who live on it,
  Creator of the ocean
    and all its creatures.
You are the source of life,
  praised by the stars
    that fill the heavens.
[7]You are the LORD our God,
  the one who chose Abram—

you brought him from Ur
  in Babylonia
    and named him Abraham.
[8]Because he was faithful,
  you made an agreement
    to give his descendants
  the land of the Canaanites
    and Hittites,
  of the Amorites and Perizzites,
  and of the Jebusites
    and Girgashites.
Now you have kept your promise,
  just as you always do.

[9]When our ancestors
  were in Egypt,
    you saw their suffering;
when they were at the Red Sea,[h]
  you heard their cry for help.
[10]You knew that the King of Egypt
  and his officials and his nation
    had mistreated your people.
So you worked fearsome miracles
  against the Egyptians
and earned a reputation
  that still remains.
[11]You divided the deep sea,
  and your people walked through
    on dry land.
But you tossed their enemies in,
  and they sank down
    like a heavy stone.
[12]Each day you led your people
  with a thick cloud,
and at night you showed the way
  with a flaming fire.
[13]At Sinai you came down
  from heaven,
and you gave your people
  good laws and teachings
    that are fair and honest.
[14]You commanded them to respect
  your holy Sabbath,
and you instructed
  your servant Moses
    to teach them your laws.

---

[f]9.1 *seventh month*: Hebrew "same month." [g]9.5 *shout . . . God*: Or "shout eternal praises to the LORD your God." [h]9.9 *Red Sea*: Hebrew *yam suph* "Sea of Reeds," one of the marshes of fresh water lakes near the eastern part of the Nile Delta. This identification is based on Exodus 13.17—14.9, which lists the towns on the route of the Israelites before crossing the sea. In the Greek translation of the Scriptures made about 200 B.C., the "Sea of Reeds" was named "Red Sea."

¹⁵When they were hungry,
you sent bread from heaven,
and when they were thirsty,
you let water flow
from a rock.
Then you commanded them
to capture the land
that you had solemnly promised.

*¹⁶Our stubborn ancestors
refused to obey—
they forgot about the miracles
you had worked for them,
and they were determined
to return to Egypt
and become slaves again.
¹⁷But, our God, you are merciful
and quick to forgive;
you are loving, kind,
and very patient.
So you never turned away
from them—
¹⁸not even when they made
an idol shaped like a calf
and insulted you by claiming,
"This is the god who rescued us
from Egypt."

¹⁹Because of your great mercy,
you never abandoned them
in the desert.
And you always guided them
with a cloud by day
and a fire at night.
²⁰Your gentle Spirit
instructed them,ⁱ
and you gave them mannaʲ to eat
and water to drink.
²¹You took good care of them,
and for forty years
they never lacked a thing.
Their shoes didn't wear out,
and their feet were never swollen.

²²You let them conquer kings
and take their land,
including King Sihon of Heshbon
and King Og of Bashan.ᵏ
²³You brought them into the land
that you had promised
their ancestors,
and you blessed their nation
with people that outnumbered
the stars in the sky.

²⁴Then their descendants
conquered the land.
You helped them defeat
the kings and nations
and treat their enemies
however they wished.
²⁵They captured strong cities
and rich farmland;
they took furnished houses,
as well as cisterns,ˡ
vineyards, olive orchards,
and numerous fruit trees.
They ate till they were satisfied,
and they celebrated
your abundant blessings.

²⁶In spite of this, they rebelled
and disobeyed your laws.
They killed your prophets,
who warned them
to turn back to you,
and they cursed your name.
²⁷So you handed them over
to their enemies,
who treated them terribly.
But in their sufferings,
they begged you to help.
From heaven you listened
to their prayers
and because of your great mercy,
you sent leaders to rescue them.

²⁸But when they were at peace,
they would turn against you,
and you would hand them over
to their enemies.
Then they would beg for help,
and because you are merciful,
you rescued them
over and over again.
²⁹You warned them to turn back
and discover true life
by obeying your laws.
But they stubbornly refused
and continued to sin.
³⁰For years, you were patient,
and your Spiritᵐ warned them
with messages spoken
by your prophets.

ⁱ9.20 *Your gentle Spirit instructed them:* Or "You gently instructed them."   ʲ9.20 *manna:* This was something like a thin wafer (see Exodus 16.1-36).   ᵏ9.22 *Bashan:* One possible meaning for the difficult Hebrew text of verse 22.   ˡ9.25 *cisterns:* Pits dug into the ground to hold water.   ᵐ9.30 *your Spirit:* Or "you."

Still they refused to listen,
and you handed them over
to their enemies.
[31] But you are merciful and kind,
and so you never forgot them
or let them be destroyed.

[32] Our God, you are powerful,
fearsome, and faithful,
always true to your word.
So please keep in mind
the terrible sufferings
of our people, kings, leaders,
priests, and prophets,
from the time Assyria ruled
until this very day.
[33] You have always been fair
when you punished us
for our sins.

[34] Our kings, leaders, and priests
have never obeyed your commands
or heeded your warnings.
[35] You blessed them with a kingdom
and with an abundance
of rich, fertile land,
but they refused to worship you
or turn from their evil.
[36] Now we are slaves
in this fruitful land
you gave to our ancestors.
[37] Its plentiful harvest is taken
by kings you placed over us
because of our sins.
Our suffering is unbearable,
because they do as they wish
to us and our livestock.

The People Make an Agreement

[38] And so, a firm agreement was made that had the official approval of the leaders, the Levites, and priests. **10** [1] As governor, I[n] signed the agreement together with Zedekiah and the following priests: [2-8] Seraiah, Azariah, Jeremiah, Pashhur, Amariah, Malchijah, Hattush, Shebaniah, Malluch, Harim, Meremoth, Obadiah, Daniel, Ginnethon, Baruch, Meshullam, Abijah, Mijamin, Maaziah, Bilgai, and Shemaiah.

[9] The Levites who signed were: Jeshua son of Azaniah, Binnui from the clan of Henadad, Kadmiel, [10] Shebaniah, Hodiah, Kelita, Pelaiah, Hanan, [11] Mica, Rehob, Hashabiah, [12] Zaccur, Sherebiah, Shebaniah, [13] Hodiah, Bani, and Beninu.

[14] The leaders who signed were: Parosh, Pahath Moab, Elam, Zattu, Bani, [15] Bunni, Azgad, Bebai, [16] Adonijah, Bigvai, Adin, [17] Ater, Hezekiah, Azzur, [18] Hodiah, Hashum, Bezai, [19] Hariph, Anathoth, Nebai, [20] Magpiash, Meshullam, Hezir, [21] Meshezabel, Zadok, Jaddua, [22] Pelatiah, Hanan, Anaiah, [23] Hoshea, Hananiah, Hasshub, [24] Hallohesh, Pilha, Shobek, [25] Rehum, Hashabnah, Maaseiah, [26] Ahiah, Hanan, Anan, [27] Malluch, Harim, and Baanah.

*Has God put before you
an open door? Oh, answer him,
"Lord, here I am. I am ready
to do your will."*
EVELYN CHRISTENSON

The Agreement

[28-29] All of us, including priests, Levites, temple guards, singers, temple workers and leaders, together with our wives and children, have separated ourselves from the foreigners in this land and now enter into an agreement with a complete understanding of what we are doing. And so, we now place ourselves under the curse of the LORD our God, if we fail to obey his laws and teachings that were given to us by his servant Moses.

[30] We won't let our sons and daughters marry foreigners.

[31] We won't buy goods or grain on the Sabbath or on any other sacred day, not even from foreigners.

Every seven years we will let our fields rest, and we will cancel all debts.

[32] Once a year we will each donate a small amount of silver to the temple of our God. [33] This is to pay for the sacred bread, as well as for the daily sacrifices and special sacrifices such as those offered on the Sabbath and during the

---

[n]10.1 *I:* Hebrew "Nehemiah son of Hacaliah."

New Moon Festival and the other festivals. It will also pay for the sacrifices to forgive our sins and for all expenses connected with the worship of God in the temple.

[34]We have decided that the families[o] of priests, Levites, and ordinary people will supply firewood for the temple each year, so that sacrifices can be offered on the altar, just as the LORD our God has commanded.

[35]Each year we will bring to the temple the first part of our harvest of grain and fruit.

[36]We will bring our first-born sons and the first-born males of our herds and flocks and offer them to the priests who serve in the temple, because this is what is written in God's Law.[p]

[37]To the priests in the temple of our God, we will bring the bread dough from the first harvest, together with our best fruit, and an offering of new wine and olive oil.

We will bring ten percent of our grain harvest to those Levites who are responsible for collecting it in our towns. [38]A priest from the family of Aaron must be there when we give this to the Levites. Then the Levites will put one tenth of this part in the temple storeroom, [39]which is also the place for the sacred objects used by the priests, the temple guards, and the singers.

Levites and everyone else must bring their gifts of grain, wine, and olive oil to this room.

We will not neglect the temple of our God.

People Who Settled in Jerusalem

11 The nation's leaders and their families settled in Jerusalem. But there was room for only one out of every ten of the remaining families, and so they asked God to show them[q] who would live there. [2]Then everyone else asked God to bless those who were willing to live in Jerusalem.

[3]Some of the people of Israel, the priests, the Levites, the temple workers, and the descendants of Solomon's servants lived on their own property in the towns of Judah.

But the leaders of the province lived in Jerusalem with their families.

The Judah Tribe

[4-6]From the Judah tribe, two leaders settled in Jerusalem with their relatives. One of them was Athaiah son of Uzziah. His ancestors were Zechariah, Amariah, Shephatiah, Mahalalel, and Perez, the son of Judah. From the descendants of Perez, four hundred sixty-eight of the best men lived in Jerusalem.

The other leader from Judah was Maaseiah the son of Baruch. His ancestors were Colhozeh, Hazaiah, Adaiah, Joiarib, Zechariah, and Shelah, the son of Judah.

The Benjamin Tribe

[7-8]From the Benjamin tribe, three leaders settled in Jerusalem. The first was Sallu son of Meshullam, and the others were Gabbai and Sallai. Sallu's ancestors were Joed, Pedaiah, Kolaiah, Maaseiah, Ithiel, and Jeshaiah. Altogether, there were nine hundred twenty-eight men of the Benjamin tribe living in Jerusalem. [9]Joel son of Zichri was their leader, and Judah son of Hassenuah was second in command.

Priests

[10]Four priests settled in Jerusalem. The first was Jedaiah; he was the son of Joiarib and the uncle of Jachin.[r]

[11]The second priest to settle there was Seraiah son of Hilkiah. His ancestors were Meshullam, Zadok, Meraioth, and Ahitub, who had been a high priest. [12]Altogether, there were eight hundred twenty-two from his clan who served in the temple.

The third priest to settle there was Adaiah son of Jeroham. His ancestors were Pelaliah, Amzi, Zechariah, Pashhur, and Malchijah. [13]Altogether, there were two hundred forty-two clan leaders among his relatives.

The fourth priest to settle there was Amashsai son of Azarel. His ancestors were

---

o[11.34] *that the families:* Or "which families."
p[11.36] *first-born sons . . . God's Law:* See Exodus 13.2, 12-15; 34.19, 20. q[11.1] *asked God to show them:* The Hebrew text has "cast lots." These were made of wood or stone and were thrown on the ground by a priest or official to find out how and when to do something.
r[11.10] *son of Joiarib and the uncle of Jachin:* See 1 Chronicles 9.10; the Hebrew text has "son of Joiarib, Jachin."

Ahzai, Meshillemoth, and Immer. [14]Altogether, there were one hundred twenty-eight brave warriors from their clans, and their leader was Zabdiel son of Haggedolim.

Levites

[15]Several Levites settled in Jerusalem. First, there was Shemaiah son of Hasshub. His ancestors were Azrikam, Hashabiah, and Bunni.

[16]Next, there were Shabbethai and Jozabad, who were in charge of the work outside the temple.

[17]Then there was Mattaniah son of Mica. His ancestors were Zabdi and Asaph. Mattaniah led the temple choir in the prayer of praise. Bakbukiah, who also settled in Jerusalem, was his assistant.

Finally, there was Abda son of Shammua; his grandfather was Galal, and his great-grandfather was Jeduthun.

[18]Altogether, two hundred eighty-four Levites settled in the holy city.

Temple Guards and Others

[19]One hundred seventy-two temple guards settled in Jerusalem; their leaders were Akkub and Talmon.

[20]The rest of the Israelites, including priests and Levites, lived on their own property in the other towns of Judah. [21]But the temple workers lived in the section of Jerusalem known as Ophel, and the two men in charge of them were Ziha and Gishpa.

[22]Uzzi son of Bani was the leader of the Levites in Jerusalem. His grandfather was Hashabiah, his great-grandfather was Mattaniah, and his great-great-grandfather was Mica. He belonged to the Asaph clan that was in charge of the music for the temple services, [23]though the daily choice of music and musicians was decided by royal decree of the Persian king.

[24]The people of Israel were represented at the Persian court by Pethahiah son of Meshezabel from the Zerah clan of the Judah tribe.

The People in the Other Towns and Villages

[25]Some of the people of Judah lived in the following towns near their farms: Kiriath-Arba, Dibon, Jekabzeel, [26]Jeshua, Moladah, Beth-Pelet, [27]Hazar-Shual, Beersheba, [28]Ziklag, Meconah, [29]Enrimmon, Zo-

rah, Jarmuth, [30]Zanoah, Adullam, Lachish, and Azekah. In fact, they settled the towns from Beersheba in the south to Hinnom Valley in the north.

[31]The people of Benjamin lived in the towns of Geba, Michmash, Aija, Bethel with its nearby villages, [32]Anathoth, Nob, Ananiah, [33]Hazor, Ramah, Gittaim, [34]Hadid, Zeboim, Neballat, [35]Lod, and Ono, as well as in Craft Valley. [36]Several groups of Levites from the territory of Judah were sent to live among the people of Benjamin.

A List of Priests and Levites

12 Many priests and Levites had returned from Babylonia with Zerubbabel[s] and Joshua as their leaders. Those priests were Seraiah, Jeremiah, Ezra, [2]Amariah, Malluch, Hattush, [3]Shecaniah, Rehum, Meremoth, [4]Iddo, Ginnethoi, Abijah, [5]Mijamin, Maadiah, Bilgah, [6]Shemaiah, Joiarib, Jedaiah, [7]Sallu, Amok, Hilkiah, and another Jedaiah. These were the leading priests and their assistants during the time of Joshua.[t]

[8]The Levites who returned were Jeshua, Binnui, Kadmiel, Sherebiah, Judah, and Mattaniah. They and their assistants were responsible for the songs of praise, [9]while Bakbukiah and Unno, together with their assistants, were responsible for the choral responses.

Descendants of Joshua the High Priest

[10]Joshua was the father of Joiakim, the grandfather of Eliashib, and the great-grandfather of Joiada. [11]Joiada was the father of Jonathan and the grandfather of Jaddua.

Leaders of the Priestly Clans

[12]When Joiakim was high priest, the following priests were leaders of their clans: Meraiah of the Seraiah clan, Hananiah of Jeremiah, [13]Meshullam of Ezra, Jehohanan of Amariah, [14]Jonathan of Malluchi, Joseph of Shebaniah, [15]Adna of Harim, Helkai of Meraioth, [16]Zechariah of Iddo, Meshullam of Ginnethon, [17]Zichri of Abijah,[u] Piltai of Moadiah, [18]Shammua of Bilgah, Jehonathan of

---

[s]12.1 *Zerubbabel*: Hebrew "Zerubbabel son of Shealtiel." [t]12.7 *Joshua*: Joshua the high priest and friend of Zerubbabel (see verse 1 and Haggai 1.1; 2.2). [u]12.17 *of Abijah*: The Hebrew text adds ". . . of Miniamin."

Shemaiah, [19]Mattenai of Joiarib, Uzzi of Jedaiah, [20]Kallai of Sallai, Eber of Amok, [21]Hashabiah of Hilkiah, and Nethanel of Jedaiah.

The Priestly and Levite Families

[22]During the time of the high priests Eliashib, Joiada, Johanan, and Jaddua, and including the time that Darius was king of Persia, a record was kept of the heads of the Levite and priestly families. [23]However, no official record was kept of the heads of the Levite clans after the death of Johanan,[v] the grandson of Eliashib.

[24]Hashabiah, Sherebiah, Jeshua son of Kadmiel,[w] and their assistants organized two choirs of Levites to offer praises to God, just as King David, the man of God, had commanded.

[25]Mattaniah, Bakbukiah, Obadiah, Meshullam, Talmon, and Akkub were responsible for guarding the storerooms near the temple gates.

[26]All of these men lived during the time of Joiakim[x] and during the time that I was governor and Ezra, a teacher of the Law of Moses, was priest.

Nehemiah Dedicates the City Wall

[27]When the city wall was dedicated, Levites from everywhere in Judah were invited to join in the celebration with songs of praise and with the music of cymbals, small harps, and other stringed instruments. [28-29]The Levite singers lived in villages around Jerusalem, and so they came from there, as well as from the villages around Netophah, Beth-Gilgal, Geba, and Azmaveth. [30]The priests and Levites held special ceremonies to make themselves holy, and then they did the same for the rest of the people and for the gates and walls of the city.

[31]I brought the leaders of Judah to the top of the city wall and put them in charge of the two groups that were to march around on top of the wall, singing praises to God. One group marched to the right in the direction of Garbage Gate. [32]Hoshaiah and half of the leaders followed them. [33]Then came the priests Azariah, Ezra, Meshullam, [34]Judah, Benjamin, Shemaiah, and Jeremiah, [35]all of them blowing trumpets. Next, there was Zechariah of the Asaph clan[y] [36]and his relatives, Shemaiah, Azarel, Milalai, Gilalai, Maai, Nethanel, Judah, and Hanani. They played musical instruments like those that had been played by David, the man of God. And they marched behind Ezra, the teacher of the Law. [37]When they reached Fountain Gate, they climbed the steps to David's City and went past his palace, before stopping at the Water Gate near the eastern wall of the city.

[v]12.23 *death of Johanan:* Probably between 408 and 405 B.C., when Darius II died. [w]12.24 *son of Kadmiel:* Or possibly "Binnui, Kadmiel" (see 10.9; 12.8).
[x]12.26 *Joiakim:* Hebrew "Joiakim son of Joshua son of Jozadak." [y]12.35 *Zechariah of the Asaph clan:* Hebrew "Zechariah son of Jonathan son of Shemaiah son of Mattaniah son of Micaiah son of Zaccur son of Asaph."

*Spiritual*Life—How can I worship God as I should? *(Nehemiah 12.27-43)*

Praise God with all kinds of music.

Singing, cymbals, harps, strings, trumpets, even a marching band—what a joyful noise must have risen at the dedication of the city wall! Apparently some of the singers were especially trained for this task (12.28), but the focus wasn't on the performance or the performers; it was all on God, for "God had made the people very happy" (12.43). What a contrast to just a short time earlier; when the Babylonians, who had deported the Jews, taunted their prisoners to sing about Jerusalem, all they could do was cry (Psalm 137).

As former prisoners of sin who are now set free from our old ways of living, we can relate to the joy these released prisoners felt. We, too, can worship with "joyful shouts" (12.43) when we celebrate what God has done for us. **(See also Nehemiah 8.1—9.6; Job 42.1-6; Psalm 42.)**

Words To Remember: *God had made the people very happy, and so on that day they celebrated and offered many sacrifices. The women and children joined in the festivities, and joyful shouts could be heard far from the city of Jerusalem.*
—Nehemiah 12.43

[38]The second group of singers marched along the wall in the opposite direction, and I followed them, together with the other half of the leaders of Judah. We went past Oven Tower, Broad Wall, [39]Ephraim Gate, Old Gate, Fish Gate, Hananel Tower, Hundred Tower, and on to Sheep Gate. Finally, we stopped at Gate of the Guard, [40]where we stood in front of the temple with the other group, praising God. In the group with me were half of the leaders, [41]as well as the priests Eliakim, Maaseiah, Miniamin, Micaiah, Elioenai, Zechariah, and Hananiah, who were blowing trumpets. [42]Maaseiah, Shemaiah, Eleazar, Uzzi, Jehohanan, Malchijah, Elam, and Ezer also stood there, as Jezrahiah led the singers. [43]God had made the people very happy, and so on that day they celebrated and offered many sacrifices. The women and children joined in the festivities, and joyful shouts could be heard far from the city of Jerusalem.

Preparation for Worship

[44]On that same day, some leaders were appointed to be responsible for the safekeeping of gifts for the temple and to be in charge of receiving the first part of the harvest and the ten percent of the crops and livestock that was offered to God. These same leaders also collected the part of crops that the Law of Moses taught was to be given to the Levites.

Everyone was pleased with the work of the priests and Levites, [45]when they performed the ceremonies to make people acceptable to worship God. And the singers and the temple guards did their jobs according to the instructions given by David and his son Solomon. [46]In fact, ever since the days of David and Asaph, there had been song leaders and songs of praise and worship. [47]During the time that Zerubbabel and I were in charge, everyone in Israel gave what they were supposed to give for the daily needs of the singers and temple guards from the Levi tribe. Then the Levites would give the priests their share from what they had received.

Foreigners Are Sent Away

13

On that day when the Law of Moses was read aloud to everyone, it was discovered that Ammonites and Moabites were forbidden to belong to the people of God. [2]This was because they had refused to give food and water to Israel and had hired Balaam[z] to call down a curse on them. However, our God turned the curse into a blessing. [3]Following the reading of the Law of Moses, the people of Israel started sending away anyone who had any foreign ancestors.

Nehemiah Makes Other Changes

[4]The priest Eliashib was a relative of Tobiah and had earlier been put in charge of the temple storerooms. [5]So he let Tobiah live in one of these rooms, where all kinds of things had been stored—the grain offerings, incense, utensils for the temple, as well as the tenth of the grain, wine, and olive oil that had been given for the use of the Levites, singers, and temple guards, and the gifts for the priests.

[6]This happened in the thirty-second year that Artaxerxes[a] ruled Babylonia. I was away from Jerusalem at the time, because I was visiting him. Later I received permission from the king [7]to return to Jerusalem. Only then did I find out that Eliashib had done this terrible thing of letting Tobiah have a room in the temple. [8]It upset me so much that I threw out every bit of Tobiah's furniture. [9]Then I ordered the room to be cleaned and the temple utensils, the grain offerings, and the incense to be brought back into the room.

[10]I also found out that the temple singers and several other Levites had returned to work on their farms, because they had not been given their share of the harvest. [11]I called the leaders together and angrily asked them, "Why is the temple neglected?" Then I told them to start doing their jobs. [12]After this, everyone in Judah brought a tenth of their grain, wine, and olive oil to the temple storeroom. [13]Finally, I appointed three men with good reputations to be in charge of what was brought there and to distribute it to the others. They were Shelemiah the priest, Zadok the teacher of the Law, and Pedaiah the Levite. Their assistant was Hanan, the son of Zaccur and the grandson of Mattaniah.

[14]I pray that my God will remember

---

[z]13.2 *Balaam*: See Numbers 22.1-6.   [a]13.6 *Artaxerxes*: See the note at 1.1.

these good things that I have done for his temple and for those who worship there.

The Sabbath

[15]I also noticed what the people of Judah were doing on the Sabbath. Not only were they trampling grapes to make wine, but they were harvesting their grain, grapes, figs, and other crops, and then loading these on donkeys to sell in Jerusalem. So I warned them not to sell food on the Sabbath. [16]People who had moved to Jerusalem from the city of Tyre were bringing in fish and other things to sell there on the Sabbath. [17]I got angry and said to the leaders of Judah, "This evil you are doing is an insult to the Sabbath! [18]Didn't God punish us and this city because our ancestors did these very same things? And here you are, about to make God furious again by disgracing the Sabbath!"

[19]I ordered the gates of Jerusalem to be closed on the eve of the Sabbath[b] and not to be opened until after the Sabbath had ended. Then I put some of my own men in charge of the gates to make certain that nothing was brought in on the Sabbath. [20]Once or twice some merchants spent the night outside Jerusalem with their goods. [21]But I warned them, "If you do this again, I'll have you arrested." From then on, they did not come on the Sabbath. [22]I ordered the Levites to make themselves holy and to guard the gates on the Sabbath, so that it would be kept holy.

God is truly merciful, and I pray that he will treat me with kindness and bless me for doing this.

Mixed Marriages

[23]I discovered that some Jewish men had married women from Ashdod, Ammon, and Moab. [24]About half of their children could not speak Hebrew—they spoke only the language of Ashdod or some other foreign language. [25]So in my anger, I called down curses on those men. I had them beaten and even pulled out the hair of some of them.

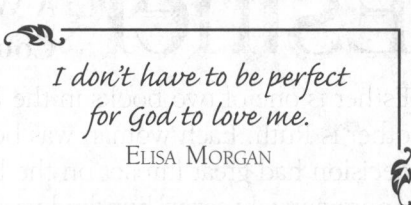

I don't have to be perfect for God to love me.
ELISA MORGAN

Then I made them promise:

In the name of God we solemnly promise not to let our sons and daughters marry foreigners. [26]God dearly loved King Solomon of Israel and made him the greatest king on earth, but Solomon's foreign wives led him into sin. [27]So we will obey you and not rebel against our God by marrying foreign women.

[28]Jehoiada, the son of the high priest Eliashib, had a son who had married a daughter of Sanballat from Horon,[c] and I forced his son to leave.

[29]I pray that God will punish them for breaking their priestly vows and disgracing the Levi tribe.

[30]Then I made sure that the people were free from every foreign influence, and I assigned duties for the priests and Levites. [31]I also arranged for the people to bring firewood to the altar each day and for them to bring the first part of their harvest to the temple.

I pray that God will bless me for the good I have done.

---

[b]**13.19** *eve of the Sabbath*: The Jewish day began at sunset.   [c]**13.28** *Horon*: See the note at 2.10.

Esther

A Woman of Courage

Esther is one of two books in the Bible named after a woman; the other is Ruth. Each woman was beautiful, loyal to her family, and her decision had great impact on the history of God's chosen people. Approximately seven hundred years separated these two. Ruth lived in the time of the judges; Esther lived long after the Babylon exile was only a memory (her ancestors remained in Babylon of their own choice). Ruth was a peasant in an obscure Israelite town; Esther was the queen in the capital of Persia, the world's most powerful empire. As one of the poor, Ruth gleaned in the fields; Esther graced the royal court in costly robes. Ruth became David's great-grandmother; Esther later saved the lives of countless descendants of David's tribe and people—the Jews.

Events in this book occur in the context of the crucial Persian-Greek War. The Persian king (Xerxes I) was planning an invasion of Greece, with a massive banquet for officials and military leaders following the decisive planning stage. His queen Vashti refused his command to appear at the celebration and consequently was deprived of her position.

After the unsuccessful invasion of Greece, the king's interest turned homeward—and toward the need for a new queen. Esther won the beauty contest. She truly was a "star" (the meaning of her name).

Most of the book deals with Esther as queen and her dramatic, faithful decision to save and benefit her own people—the Jews. The Jews still celebrate the Festival of Purim (9.17-32), a memorial to the main event of this book: the preservation of the Jewish people in Persia.

May we, in times of difficulty, have the courage of Esther to do whatever it takes—for God.

Esther at a Glance

1. Queen Vashti refuses to appear at King Xerxes' party (1)
2. Esther is abducted into the king's harem and later chosen as the new queen (2.1-18)
3. Esther's cousin Mordecai foils a plot to kill the king (2.19-23)
4. Mordecai refuses to bow to Haman, so Haman plots to kill all Jews (3)
5. Mordecai asks Esther to reveal that she is a Jew and ask the king for help (4)
6. Esther invites Haman and Xerxes to dinner twice (5–8)
7. Haman plans to kill Mordecai but has to honor him instead (5,6)
8. Esther asks the king to spare her people; Xerxes hangs Haman on the tower he built for Mordecai (7)
9. Xerxes allows Jews to defend themselves (8.1—9.19)
10. Esther and Mordecai set up the Festival of Purim (9.20—10.3)

Queen Vashti Disobeys King Xerxes

1 [1-2]King Xerxes[a] of Persia lived in his capital city of Susa[b] and ruled one hundred twenty-seven provinces from India to Ethiopia.[c] [3]During the third year of his rule, Xerxes gave a big dinner for all his officials and officers. The governors and leaders of the provinces were also invited, and even the commanders of the Persian and Median armies came. [4]For one hundred eighty days he showed off his wealth and spent a lot of money to impress his guests with the greatness of his kingdom.

[5]King Xerxes soon gave another dinner and invited everyone in the city of Susa, no matter who they were. The eating and drinking lasted seven days in the beautiful palace gardens. [6]The area was decorated with blue and white cotton curtains tied back with purple linen cords that ran through silver rings fastened to marble columns. Couches of gold and silver rested on pavement that had all kinds of designs made from costly bright-colored stones and marble and mother-of-pearl.

[7]The guests drank from gold cups, and each cup had a different design. The king was generous [8]and said to them, "Drink all you want!" Then he told his servants, "Keep their cups full."

[9]While the men were enjoying themselves, Queen Vashti gave the women a big dinner inside the royal palace.

[10]By the seventh day, King Xerxes was feeling happy because of so much wine. And he asked his seven personal servants, Mehuman, Biztha, Harbona, Bigtha, Abagtha, Zethar, and Carkas, [11]to bring Queen Vashti to him. The king wanted her to wear her crown and let his people and his officials see how beautiful she was. [12]The king's servants told Queen Vashti what he had said, but she refused to go to him, and this made him terribly angry.

[13-14]The king called in the seven highest officials of Persia and Media. They were Carshena, Shethar, Admatha, Tarshish, Meres, Marsena, and Memucan. These men were very wise and understood all the laws and customs of the country, and the king always asked them what they thought about such matters.

[15]The king said to them, "Queen Vashti refused to come to me when I sent my servants for her. What does the law say I should do about that?"

[16]Then Memucan told the king and the officials:

Your Majesty, Queen Vashti has not only embarrassed you, but she has insulted your officials and everyone else in all the provinces. [17]The women in the kingdom will hear about this, and they will refuse to respect their husbands. They will say, "If Queen Vashti doesn't obey her husband, why should we?" [18]Before this day is over, the wives of the officials of Persia and Media will find out what Queen Vashti has done, and they will refuse to obey their husbands. They won't respect their husbands, and their husbands will be angry with them.

[19]Your Majesty, if you agree, you should write for the Medes and Persians a law that can never be changed. This law would keep Queen Vashti from ever seeing you again. Then you could let someone who respects you be queen in her place. [20]When the women in your great kingdom hear about this new law, they will respect their husbands, no matter if they are rich or poor.

[21]King Xerxes and his officials liked what Memucan had said, [22]and he sent letters to all of his provinces. Each letter was written in the language of the province to which it was sent, and it said that husbands should have complete control over their wives and children.

Esther Becomes Queen

2 After a while, King Xerxes got over being angry. But he kept thinking about what Vashti had done and the law that he had written because of her. [2]Then the king's personal servants said:

Your Majesty, a search must be made to find you some beautiful

---

[a]1.1,2 *Xerxes*: The Hebrew text has "Ahasuerus," who was better known as King Xerxes I (485-465 B.C.). [b]1.1,2 *in his capital city of Susa*: Or "in his royal fortress in the city of Susa." Susa was a city east of Babylon and a winter home for Persian kings. [c]1.1,2 *Ethiopia*: The Hebrew text has "Cush," which was a region south of Egypt that included parts of the present countries of Ethiopia and Sudan.

young women. ³You can select officers in every province to bring them to the place where you keep your wives in the capital city of Susa. Put your servant Hegai in charge of them since that is his job. He can see to it that they are given the proper beauty treatments. ⁴Then let the young woman who pleases you most take Vashti's place as queen.

King Xerxes liked these suggestions, and he followed them.

⁵At this time a Jew named Mordecai was living in Susa. His father was Jair, and his grandfather Shimei was the son of Kish from the tribe of Benjamin. ⁶Kish^d was one of the people that Nebuchadnezzar had taken from Jerusalem, when he took King Jeconiah of Judah to Babylonia.

⁷Mordecai had a very beautiful cousin named Esther, whose Hebrew name was Hadassah. He had raised her as his own daughter, after her father and mother died. ⁸When the king ordered the search for beautiful women, many were taken to the king's palace in Susa, and Esther was one of them.

Hegai was put in charge of all the women, ⁹and from the first day, Esther was his favorite. He began her beauty treatments at once. He also gave her plenty of food and seven special maids from the king's palace, and they had the best rooms.

¹⁰Mordecai had warned Esther not to tell anyone that she was a Jew, and she obeyed him. ¹¹He was anxious to see how Esther was getting along and to learn what had happened to her. So each day he would walk back and forth in front of the court where the women lived.

¹²The young women were given beauty treatments for one whole year. The first six months their skin was rubbed with olive oil and myrrh, and the last six months it was treated with perfumes and cosmetics. Then each of them spent the night alone with King Xerxes. ¹³When a young woman went to the king, she could wear whatever clothes or jewelry she chose from the women's living quarters. ¹⁴In the evening she would go to the king, and the following morning she would go to the place where his wives stayed after being with him. There a man named Shaashgaz was in charge of the king's wives.^{e} Only the ones the king wanted and

asked for by name could go back to the king.

¹⁵⁻¹⁶Xerxes had been king for seven years when Esther's turn came to go to him during Tebeth,^{f} the tenth month of the year. Everyone liked Esther. The king's personal servant Hegai was in charge of the women, and Esther trusted Hegai and asked him what she ought to take with her.^{g}

¹⁷Xerxes liked Esther more than he did any of the other young women. None of them pleased him as much as she did, and right away he fell in love with her and crowned her queen in place of Vashti. ¹⁸In honor of Esther he gave a big dinner for his leaders and officials. Then he declared a holiday everywhere in his kingdom and gave expensive gifts.

Mordecai Saves the King's Life

¹⁹When the young women were brought together again, Esther's cousin Mordecai had become a palace official. ²⁰He had told Esther never to tell anyone that she was a Jew, and she obeyed him, just as she had always done.

²¹Bigthana and Teresh were the two men who guarded King Xerxes' rooms, but they got angry with the king and decided to kill him. ²²Mordecai found out about their plans and asked Queen Esther to tell the king what he had found out. ²³King Xerxes learned that Mordecai's report was true, and he had the two men hanged. Then the king had all of this written down in his record book as he watched.

Haman Plans To Destroy the Jews

3 Later, King Xerxes promoted Haman the son of Hammedatha to the highest position in his kingdom. Haman was a descendant of Agag,^{h} ²and the king had given orders for his officials at the royal gate to honor Haman by kneeling down to him.

---

^{d}**2.6** *Kish:* Or "Mordecai." The Hebrew text has "He."
^{e}**2.14** *wives:* This translates a Hebrew word for women who were legally married to a man, but without the full privileges of a wife. ^{f}**2.15,16** *Tebeth:* The tenth month of the Hebrew calendar, from about mid-December to mid-January. ^{g}**2.15,16** *her:* The Hebrew text adds, "Esther was the daughter of Abihail and was the cousin of Mordecai, who had adopted her after her parents died" (see verse 7). ^{h}**3.1** *Agag:* Agag was a king who had fought against the Jews long before the time of Esther (see 1 Samuel 15.1-33).

All of them obeyed except Mordecai. ³When the other officials asked Mordecai why he disobeyed the king's command, ⁴he said, "Because I am a Jew." They spoke to him for several days about kneeling down, but he still refused to obey. Finally, they reported this to Haman, to find out if he would let Mordecai get away with it.

⁵Haman was furious to learn that Mordecai refused to kneel down and honor him. ⁶And when he found out that Mordecai was a Jew, he knew that killing only Mordecai was not enough. Every Jew in the whole kingdom had to be killed.

⁷It was now the twelfth year of the rule of King Xerxes. During Nisan,ⁱ the first month of the year, Haman said, "Find out the best time for me to do this."ʲ The time chosen was Adar,ᵏ the twelfth month.

⁸Then Haman went to the king and said:

Your Majesty, there are some people who live all over your kingdom and won't have a thing to do with anyone else. They have customs that are different from everyone else's, and they refuse to obey your laws. We would be better off to get rid of them! ⁹Why not give orders for all of them to be killed? I can promise that you will get tons of silver for your treasury.

¹⁰The king handed his official ring to Haman, who hated the Jews, and the king told

him, ¹¹"Do what you want with those people! You can keep their money."

¹²On the thirteenth day of Nisan, Haman called in the king's secretaries and ordered them to write letters in every language used in the kingdom. The letters were written in the name of the king and sealed by using the king's own ring.ˡ At once they were sent to the king's highest officials, the governors of each province, and the leaders of the different nations in the kingdom of Xerxes.

¹³The letters were taken by messengers to every part of the kingdom, and this is what was said in the letters:

On the thirteenth day of Adar, the twelfth month, all Jewish men, women, and children are to be killed. And their property is to be taken.

¹⁴⁻¹⁵King Xerxes gave orders for these letters to be posted where they could be seen by everyone all over the kingdom. The king's command was obeyed, and one of

---

ⁱ**3.7** *Nisan:* The first month of the Hebrew calendar, from about mid-March to mid-April.   ʲ**3.7** *Find out . . . do this:* The Hebrew text has "cast lots," which were pieces of wood or stone used to find out how and when to do something. For "lots" the Hebrew text uses the Babylonian word "purim."   ᵏ**3.7** *Adar:* The twelfth month of the Hebrew calendar, from about mid-February to mid-March.   ˡ**3.12** *king's own ring:* Melted wax was used to seal a letter, and while the wax was still soft, the king's ring was pressed in the wax to show that the letter was official.

WORK—How can I have healthy relationships with the men I work with?
(Esther 4)

Be someone your coworkers can count on.

Relationships at work are often based on *work*. If we want a healthy relationship with the men we work with, we should expect to make our deadline, sell our quota, tighten all the bolts, present a professional proposal, treat our clients with courtesy, or type our letters without mistakes. Our coworkers should be able to count on us not to let them or our company look bad.

But sometimes being counted on involves unusual effort and risk. Esther carried the fate of the Jewish people in her hands. If she failed, she would die and so would they. But if she succeeded, she might save them all. Esther took the risk. She listened to her wise relative Mordecai, and asked him to join her in a fast (a sign of asking God's help). Then she observed all the customs she had learned from her years in the palace and approached the king. Esther succeeded, and Jewish people tell her story to this day.

To enjoy healthy relationships with men at work, use all your skills to do the best job that you can. Be a person they can count on—and be innovative and courageous. (See also Proverbs 5; Romans 12.9-18; Galatians 6.1-10.)

Words To Remember: *[Mordecai said to Esther,] "It could be that you were made queen for a time like this!"—Esther 4.14*

Esther

Esther 2–9

Do you ever wonder just why God created you? Why he's led you to a particular job? Why you were born into a certain family? What your real purpose on earth is?

All of us have those days. As human beings created by God, we long for purpose and meaning in our lives—whether we're single, married, married again, or in the workplace or at home. It's the times when a child says, "I love you," or a friend shares, "You're really special and important to me. And here's why," that we feel that purpose—to share God's love with the people we meet and interact with on a daily basis. Even so, at times we question the impact our actions will have.

That's when it's good to turn to the book of Esther. Because she won King Xerxes' beauty contest and became his new queen, we know that she must have been beautiful. But she was still just one of his many wives. She couldn't even go in to see him "without being invited by him"; in fact, she would be put to death unless the king held out his gold scepter to her (4.11).

But it's clear that, even in her position as one woman among many, Esther didn't let her status stop her from doing what she knew was right. When her relative Mordecai told her that Haman was plotting the death of the Jews, she not only listened, she got up and did what Mordecai asked her to do: speak to the king. She knew even trying to speak to the king could mean death. But she determined to do what was right even if she died.

She was also smart in the way she handled the king. First, she invited him to dinner not only once—but twice. With his stomach happily full, the king was ready to grant her almost any request: "What can I do for you? Just ask, and I will give you as much as half of my kingdom" (5.6). When Esther finally revealed her request at the second dinner (7.3), she spoke wisely and truthfully. She revealed that she was a Jew, and that a reward had been promised to anyone who killed her people.

Through her wise and courageous actions, Esther saved not only herself and her relative Mordecai, but a large number of the Jews in Persia. And for this reason, Esther is still remembered today, every year, at the Festival of Purim.

The next time you wonder if God created you with a special purpose, reread Esther's story. God had placed her in a unique position (as one of the king's wives in Persia, a great kingdom) at the right time (when the Jews in Persia needed to be saved) and the right place (where Mordecai could get to her to tell her the news, and where she was near the king) to protect his people.

Esther's life reveals God's special purpose for her (4.14)—and he has a special purpose for each of us. What is God asking you to do today? Will you be confident and courageous?

the letters was read aloud to the people in the walled city of Susa. Then the king and Haman sat down to drink together, but no one in the city[m] could figure out what was going on.

Mordecai Asks for Esther's Help

4 When Mordecai heard about the letter, he tore his clothes in sorrow and put on sackcloth. Then he covered his head with ashes and went through the city, crying and weeping. [2]But he could go only as far as the palace gate, because no one wearing sackcloth was allowed inside the palace. [3]In every province where the king's orders were read, the Jews cried and mourned, and they went without eating.[n] Many of them even put on sackcloth and sat in ashes.

[4]When Esther's servant girls and her other servants told her what Mordecai was doing, she became very upset and sent Mordecai some clothes to wear in place of the sackcloth. But he refused to take them. [5]Esther had a servant named Hathach, who had been given to her by the king. So she called him in and said, "Find out what's wrong with Mordecai and why he's acting this way."

[6]Hathach went to Mordecai in the city square in front of the palace gate, [7]and Mordecai told him everything that had happened. He also told him how much money Haman had promised to add to the king's treasury, if all the Jews were killed.

[8]Mordecai gave Hathach a copy of the orders for the murder of the Jews and told him that these had been read in Susa. He said, "Show this to Esther and explain what it means. Ask her to go to the king and beg him to have pity on her people, the Jews!"

[9]Hathach went back to Esther and told her what Mordecai had said. [10]She answered, "Tell Mordecai [11]there is a law about going in to see the king, and all his officials and his people know about this law. Anyone who goes in to see the king without being invited by him will be put to death. The only way that anyone can be saved is for the king to hold out the gold scepter to that person. And it's been thirty days since he has asked for me."

[12]When Mordecai was told what Esther had said, [13]he sent back this reply, "Don't think that you will escape being killed with the rest of the Jews, just because you live in the king's palace. [14]If you don't speak up now, we will somehow get help, but you and your family will be killed. It could be that you were made queen for a time like this!"

[15]Esther sent a message to Mordecai, saying, [16]"Bring together all the Jews in Susa and tell them to go without eating for my sake! Don't eat or drink for three days and nights. My servant girls and I will do the same. Then I will go in to see the king, even if it means I must die." [17]Mordecai did everything Esther told him to do.

Esther Invites the King and Haman to a Dinner

5 Three days later, Esther dressed in her royal robes and went to the inner court of the palace in front of the throne. The king was sitting there, facing the open doorway. [2]He was happy to see Esther, and he held out the gold scepter to her.

> *The next time you wonder what you should be doing for God, remember this: God doesn't ask us to do everything, but he does ask us to be faithful in doing what he's called us to do—and to keep our priorities in line with his Word and his will.*
>
> RAMONA CRAMER TUCKER

When Esther came up and touched the tip of the scepter, [3]the king said, "Esther, what brings you here? Just ask, and I will give you as much as half of my kingdom." [4]Esther answered, "Your Majesty, please

---

[m]**3.14,15** *walled city . . . city:* Or "royal fortress . . . rest of the city." [n]**4.3** *went without eating:* The Israelites would sometimes go without eating (also called "fasting") in times of great sorrow or danger.

come with Haman to a dinner I will prepare for you later today."

⁵The king said to his servants, "Hurry and get Haman, so we can accept Esther's invitation."

The king and Haman went to Esther's dinner, ⁶and while they were drinking wine, the king asked her, "What can I do for you? Just ask, and I will give you as much as half of my kingdom."

⁷⁻⁸Esther replied, "Your Majesty, if you really care for me and are willing to do what I want, please come again tomorrow with Haman to the dinner I will prepare for you. At that time I will answer Your Majesty's question."

Haman Plans To Kill Mordecai

⁹Haman was feeling great as he left. But when he saw Mordecai at the palace gate, he noticed that Mordecai did not stand up or show him any respect. This made Haman really angry, ¹⁰but he did not say a thing.

When Haman got home, he called together his friends and his wife Zeresh ¹¹and started bragging about his great wealth and all his sons. He told them the many ways that the king had honored him and how all the other officials and leaders had to respect him. ¹²Haman added, "That's not all! Besides the king himself, I'm the only person Queen Esther invited for dinner. She has also invited the king and me to dinner tomorrow. ¹³But none of this makes me happy, as long as I see that Jew Mordecai sitting at the palace gate."

¹⁴Haman's wife and friends said to him, "Have a tower built about seventy-five feet high, and tomorrow morning ask the king to hang Mordecai there. Then later, you can have dinner with the king and enjoy yourself."

This seemed like a good idea to Haman, and he had the tower built.

The King Honors Mordecai

6 That night the king could not sleep, and he had a servant read him the records of what had happened since he had been king. ²When the servant read how Mordecai had kept Bigthana and Teresh from killing the king, ³the king asked, "What has been done to reward Mordecai for this?"

"Nothing, Your Majesty!" the king's servants replied.

⁴About this time, Haman came in to ask the king to have Mordecai hanged on the tower he had built. The king saw him and asked, "Who is that man waiting in front of the throne room?"

> *We all have to get to the point where we have our "Esther experience," when we decide to go before the king with what is right, no matter the consequences.*
>
> KAY COLES JAMES

⁵The king's servants answered, "Your Majesty, it is Haman."

"Have him come in," the king commanded.

⁶When Haman entered the room, the king asked him, "What should I do for a man I want to honor?"

Haman was sure that he was the one the king wanted to honor. ⁷So he replied, "Your Majesty, if you wish to honor a man, ⁸have someone bring him one of your own robes and one of your own horses with a fancy headdress. ⁹Have one of your highest officials place your robe on this man and lead him through the streets on your horse, while someone shouts, 'This is how the king honors a man!' "

¹⁰The king replied, "Hurry and do just what you have said! Don't forget a thing. Get the robe and the horse for Mordecai the Jew, who is on duty at the palace gate!"

¹¹Haman got the king's robe and put it on Mordecai. He led him through the city on the horse and shouted as he went, "This is how the king honors a man!"

¹²Afterwards, Mordecai returned to his duties at the palace gate, and Haman hurried home, hiding his face in shame. ¹³Haman told his wife and friends what happened. Then his wife and his advisors said, "If Mordecai is a Jew, this is just the beginning of your troubles! You will end up

a ruined man." ¹⁴They were still talking, when the king's servants came and quickly took Haman to the dinner that Esther had prepared.

Haman Is Punished

7 The king and Haman were dining with Esther ²and drinking wine during the second dinner, when the king again said, "Esther, what can I do for you? Just ask, and I will give you as much as half of my kingdom!"

³Esther answered, "Your Majesty, if you really care for me and are willing to help, you can save me and my people. That's what I really want, ⁴because a reward has been promised to anyone who kills my people. Your Majesty, if we were merely going to be sold as slaves, I would not have bothered you."ᵒ

⁵"Who would dare to do such a thing?" the king asked.

⁶Esther replied, "That evil Haman is the one out to get us!"

Haman was terrified, as he looked at the king and the queen.

⁷The king was so angry that he got up, left his wine, and went out into the palace garden.

Haman realized that the king had already decided what to do with him, and he stayed and begged Esther to save his life.

⁸Just as the king came back into the room, Haman got down on his knees beside Esther, who was lying on the couch. The king shouted, "Now you're even trying to rape my queen here in my own palace!"

As soon as the king said this, his servants covered Haman's head. ⁹Then Harbona, one of the king's personal servants, said, "Your Majesty, Haman built a tower seventy-five feet high beside his house, so he could hang Mordecai on it. And Mordecai is the very one who spoke up and saved your life."

"Hang Haman from his own tower!" the king commanded. ¹⁰Right away, Haman was hanged on the tower he had built to hang Mordecai, and the king calmed down.

A Happy Ending for the Jews

8 Before the end of the day, King Xerxes gave Esther everything that had belonged to Haman, the enemy of the

---

ᵒ7.4 *I would . . . bothered you*: One possible meaning for the difficult Hebrew text.

WORK—How can I rise above office politics? *(Esther 7.1-6)*

Put yourself at risk if it will prevent harm to others.
In today's climate of corporate downsizing and high job turnover, we women who work must guard our jobs as carefully as we guard our bank accounts. So when a dangerous problem erupts, should we hope someone else steps forward to solve it? Or should we confront it ourselves and risk losing our job?

One factor to consider is the impact of a particular problem on other people. When Esther was forced into a harem, she didn't resist. (It probably would have done her no good.) But when the conflict between Mordecai and Haman became a threat to the life of all Jews, Esther took action. For years, Mordecai had warned her never to reveal that she was a Jew. But now, after careful preparation, she took that risk. Even though Xerxes had offered her half his kingdom, she asked for mere safety for "me and my people" (7.3).

Esther could have died for her efforts. Xerxes could have executed her for simply entering his court without his summons. Or he could have backed his powerful official Haman and sent Esther to the streets to be slaughtered with the rest of the Jews. But he did neither.

Office politics says, "Manipulate others to get what's best for me." But Esther's example tells us to put ourselves at risk for the sake of others. Sure, it may mean losing a promotion, or even a job. But it's the godly way. (See also Deuteronomy 5.20,21; Matthew 20.20-28; Galatians 5.13-16; Colossians 3.22—4.1; James 3.5-18.)

Words To Remember: *Esther answered, "Your Majesty, if you really care for me and are willing to help, you can save me and my people."—Esther 7.3*

Jews. Esther told the king that Mordecai was her cousin. So the king made Mordecai one of his highest officials [2]and gave him the royal ring that Haman had worn. Then Esther put Mordecai in charge of Haman's property.

[3]Once again Esther went to speak to the king. This time she fell down at his feet, crying and begging, "Please stop Haman's evil plan to have the Jews killed!" [4]King Xerxes held out the golden scepter to Esther, [5]and she got up and said, "Your Majesty, I know that you will do the right thing and that you really love me. Please stop what Haman has planned. He has already sent letters demanding that the Jews in all your provinces be killed, [6]and I can't bear to see my people and my own relatives destroyed."

[7]King Xerxes then said to Esther and Mordecai, "I have already ordered Haman to be hanged and his house given to Esther, because of his evil plans to kill the Jews. [8]I now give you permission to make a law that will save the lives of your people. You may use my ring to seal the law, so that it can never be changed."

[9]On the twenty-third day of Sivan,[p] the third month, the king's secretaries wrote the law. They obeyed Mordecai and wrote to the Jews, the rulers, the governors, and the officials of all one hundred twenty-seven provinces from India to Ethiopia.[q] The letters were written in every language used in the kingdom, including the Jewish language. [10]They were written in the name of King Xerxes and sealed with his ring. Then they were taken by messengers who rode the king's finest and fastest horses.

[11-13]In these letters the king said:

On the thirteenth day of Adar,[r] the twelfth month, the Jews in every city and province will be allowed to get together and defend themselves. They may destroy any army that attacks them, and they may kill all of their enemies, including women and children. They may also take everything that belongs to their enemies.

A copy of this law is to be posted in every province and read by everyone.

[14-15]Then the king ordered his messengers to take their fastest horses and deliver the law as quickly as possible to every province. When Mordecai left, he was wearing clothes fit for a king. He wore blue and

white robes, a large gold crown, and a cape made of fine linen and purple cloth.

After the law was announced in Susa, everyone shouted and cheered, [16]and the Jews were no longer afraid. In fact, they were very happy and felt that they had won a victory.

[17]In every province and city where the law was sent, the Jews had parties and celebrated. Many of the people in the provinces accepted the Jewish religion, because they were now afraid of the Jews.

> *When we focus on others'*
> *good instead of thinking*
> *about our own well-being,*
> *we are following the*
> *way of the Cross.*
>
> JOSIE CRAMER

The Jews Destroy Their Enemies

9 The first law that the king had made was to be followed on the thirteenth day of Adar,[r] the twelfth month. This was the very day that the enemies of the Jews had hoped to do away with them. But the Jews turned things around, [2]and in the cities of every province they came together to attack their enemies. Everyone was afraid of the Jews, and no one could do anything to oppose them.

[3]The leaders of the provinces, the rulers, the governors, and the court officials were afraid of Mordecai and took sides with the Jews. [4]Everyone in the provinces knew that the king had promoted him and had given him a lot of power.

[5]The Jews took their swords and did away with their enemies, without showing any mercy. [6-10]They killed five hundred people in Susa,[s] but they did not take anything

---

[p]**8.9** *Sivan:* The third month of the Hebrew calendar, from about mid-May to mid-June.   [q]**8.9** *Ethiopia:* See the note at 1.1, 2.   [r]**8.11-13; 9.1** *Adar:* See the note at 3.7.   [s]**9.6-10** *in Susa:* Or "in the royal fortress in Susa."

that belonged to the ones they killed. Haman had been one of the worst enemies of the Jews, and ten of his sons were among those who were killed. Their names were Parshandatha, Dalphon, Aspatha, Poratha, Adalia, Aridatha, Parmashta, Arisai, Aridai, and Vaizatha.

[11]Later that day, someone told the king how many people had been killed in Susa.[s] [12]Then he told Esther, "Five hundred people, including Haman's ten sons, have been killed in Susa alone. If that many were killed here, what must have happened in the provinces? Is there anything else you want done? Just tell me, and it will be done."

[13]Esther answered, "Your Majesty, please let the Jews in Susa fight to defend themselves tomorrow, just as they did today. And order the bodies of Haman's ten sons to be hanged in public."

[14]King Xerxes did what Esther had requested, and the bodies of Haman's sons were hung in Susa. [15]Then on the fourteenth day of Adar the Jews of the city got together and killed three hundred more people. But they still did not take anything that belonged to their enemies.

[16-17]On the thirteenth day of Adar, the Jews in the provinces had come together to defend themselves. They killed seventy-five thousand of their enemies, but the Jews did not take anything that belonged to the ones they killed. Then on the fourteenth day of the month the Jews celebrated with a feast.

[18]On the fifteenth day of the month the Jews in Susa held a holiday and celebrated, after killing their enemies on the thirteenth and the fourteenth. [19]This is why the Jews in the villages now celebrate on the fourteenth day of the month. It is a joyful holiday that they celebrate by feasting and sending gifts of food to each other.

The Festival of Purim

[20]Mordecai wrote down everything that had happened. Then he sent letters to the Jews everywhere in the provinces [21]and told them:

Each year you must celebrate on both the fourteenth and the fifteenth of Adar, [22]the days when we Jews defeated our enemies. Remember this month as a time when our sorrow was turned to joy, and celebration took the place of crying. Celebrate by having parties and by giving to the poor and by sharing gifts of food with each other.

[23]They followed Mordecai's instructions and set aside these two days every year as a time of celebration.

The Reason for the Festival of Purim

[24]Haman was the son of Hammedatha and a descendant of Agag. He hated the Jews so much that he planned to destroy them, but he wanted to find out the best time to do it. So he cast lots.[t]

[25]Esther went to King Xerxes and asked him to save her people. Then the king gave written orders for Haman and his sons to be punished in the same terrible way that Haman had in mind for the Jews. So they were hanged. [26]Mordecai's letter had said that the Jews must celebrate for two days because of what had happened to them. This time of celebration is called Purim,[u] which is the Hebrew word for the lots that were cast. [27]Now every year the Jews set aside these two days for having parties and celebrating, just as they were told to do. [28]From now on, all Jewish families must remember to celebrate Purim on these two days each year.

[29]Queen Esther, daughter of Abihail, wanted to give full authority to Mordecai's letter about the Festival of Purim, and with his help she wrote a letter about the feast. [30]Copies of this letter were sent to Jews in the one hundred twenty-seven provinces of King Xerxes. In the letter they said:

We pray that all of you will live in peace and safety.

[31]You and your descendants must always remember to celebrate Purim at the time and in the way that we have said. You must also follow the instructions that we have given you about mourning and going without eating.[v]

---

[s]**9.11** *in Susa:* Or "in the royal fortress in Susa."
[t]**9.24** *cast lots:* See the note at 3.7. [u]**9.26** *Purim:* The Jewish festival of Purim got its name from "purim," which is the Babylonian name for the lots that Haman used. Purim is celebrated each year on the 14th and 15th of Adar, which is about the first of March.
[v]**9.31** *going without eating:* See the note at 4.3.

³²These laws about Purim are written by the authority of Queen Esther.

The Greatness of Xerxes and Mordecai

10 King Xerxes made everyone in his kingdom pay taxes, even those in lands across the sea. ²All the great and famous things that King Xerxes did are written in the record books of the kings of Media and Persia. These records also tell about the honors that the king gave to Mordecai. ³Next to the king himself, Mordecai was the highest official in the kingdom. He was a popular leader of the Jews, because he helped them in many ways and would even speak to the king for them.

Job
Why Suffering?

What can you offer a friend who is suffering? The causes of pain are legion: divorce, death of a child, cancer, bankruptcy, betrayal. But whatever the cause, you may find your friend stammering (or thinking) words like: "Why me?" "Why is God doing this?" Or even, "Where is God?"

The book of Job raises the same questions. Job was a righteous man, not perfect, but "a truly good person, who respected God and refused to do evil" (1.1). Yet in a single day, Job lost all his belongings and all his family except his wife. Shortly afterward he lost his health. His friends came and sat with him in silence for a whole week, which is probably the most compassionate act they could do.

Then they began to talk. For thirty-five chapters they argued with Job, trying to explain God's actions. They gave some explanations we might give: You sinned; just confess and God will be kind to you again. Or, your problems are not so bad; just smile, you'll feel better after awhile. Or even, God is so far away that he doesn't care much about what is going on with you.

Neither Job nor his friends knew about what had gone on behind the scenes in heaven: that God and Satan had argued about Job's motives. Job begged to see God, begged God to explain his suffering. When God did appear to Job and his friends, he didn't answer their questions. Instead, he displayed his creation as if to say, "Look at *all* I have done. Look at who I am. How could you think you can understand all that I do?"

In Job, we can learn how to comfort a suffering friend and how to endure our own suffering. We can see that silence is sometimes more comforting than talk, that

suffering is not necessarily the result of sin, that we cannot expect answers to all our "whys," and that we find stability by focusing on God himself.

Job at a Glance

1. God and Satan argue about Job; Job loses everything (1,2)
2. Job laments that he was ever born (3)
3. First debate: Job's three friends try to explain his trouble; Job answers each (4–14)
4. Second debate: Job's friends offer new explanations; Job denies each (15–21)
5. Third debate: Eliphaz and Bildad try again to explain Job's trouble; Job answers (22–27)
6. A poem about wisdom (28)
7. Job examines himself and begs God to do the same (29–31)
8. Elihu enters the scene and argues that God will do whatever he wants, but that he is beyond our reach (32–37)
9. God speaks; he introduces Job to all his creation (38–41)
10. Job repents to God (42.1-6)
11. God tells the three friends that they were wrong, that they must ask Job to pray for them (42.7-9)
12. God restores what Job lost (42.10-17)

Job and His Family

1 Many years ago, a man named Job lived in the land of Uz.[a] He was a truly good person, who respected God and refused to do evil.

[2]Job had seven sons and three daughters. [3]He owned seven thousand sheep, three thousand camels, five hundred pair of oxen, five hundred donkeys, and a large number of servants. He was the richest person in the East.

[4]Job's sons took turns having feasts in their homes, and they always invited their three sisters to join in the eating and drinking. [5]After each feast, Job would send for his children and perform a ceremony, as a way of asking God to forgive them of any wrongs they may have done. He would get up early the next morning and offer a sacrifice for each of them, just in case they had sinned or silently cursed God.

Angels, the LORD, and Satan

[6]One day, when the angels[b] had gathered around the LORD, and Satan[c] was there with them, [7]the LORD asked, "Satan, where have you been?"

Satan replied, "I have been going all over the earth."

[8]Then the LORD asked, "What do you think of my servant Job? No one on earth is like him—he is a truly good person, who respects me and refuses to do evil."

[9]"Why shouldn't he respect you?" Satan remarked. [10]"You are like a wall protecting not only him, but his entire family and all his property. You make him successful in whatever he does, and his flocks and herds are everywhere. [11]Try taking away everything he owns, and he will curse you to your face."

[12]The LORD replied, "All right, Satan, do what you want with anything that belongs to him, but don't harm Job."

Then Satan left.

Job Loses Everything

[13]Job's sons and daughters were having a feast in the home of his oldest son, [14]when someone rushed up to Job and said, "While your servants were plowing with your oxen, and your donkeys were nearby eating grass, [15]a gang of Sabeans[d] attacked and stole the

---

[a]1.1 *Uz:* The exact location of this place is unknown, though it was possibly somewhere in northwest Arabia. [b]1.6 *angels:* See the note at 15.8. [c]1.6 *Satan:* Hebrew "the accuser." [d]1.15 *Sabeans:* Perhaps the people of Sheba in what is now southwest Arabia (see Isaiah 60.6).

*Spiritual*Life—How can I handle my doubts about God? *(Job 1)*

Realize you can't see the big picture.

Our mind is naturally curious. So when we have a question about God, we want to be able to fill in the blank with the right answer, then move on to the next question and finish with an "A" for a perfect grade.

But we can't grade our knowledge of God that way. Walking with God is part knowledge and part faith. (If we could *know* everything, we wouldn't need faith.) The book of Job shows us an example of what we can't know: a scene in heaven. In this strange picture, Satan came to God and complained that Job's supposed righteousness was mere selfishness, that Job was serving God just because of what he could get (wealth, family, success, protection).

God proved Satan wrong. But to do so, God removed Job's protection and allowed Satan to put Job through horrible suffering. Job never saw that scene in heaven. Even when God talked with him at the end of the book, God didn't explain the reason behind Job's suffering. But God allowed Job to glimpse how powerful he is and how little Job could know of him. Satan is still at work in the world. There are many scenes we don't know about, and much about God we cannot understand. But even when we can't fill in the blanks, we can keep on believing. (See also Psalm 136; Jeremiah 23.16-32; Romans 4.13-25; Colossians 2.6-19.)

Words To Remember: *[Job] said: "We bring nothing at birth; we take nothing with us at death. The LORD alone gives and takes. Praise the name of the LORD!"* —Job 1.21

oxen and donkeys! Your other servants were killed, and I was the only one who escaped to tell you."

¹⁶That servant was still speaking, when a second one came running up and saying, "God sent down a fire that killed your sheep and your servants. I am the only one who escaped to tell you."

¹⁷Before that servant finished speaking, a third one raced up and said, "Three gangs of Chaldeans*e* attacked and stole your camels! All of your other servants were killed, and I am the only one who escaped to tell you."

¹⁸That servant was still speaking, when a fourth one dashed up and said, "Your children were having a feast and drinking wine at the home of your oldest son, ¹⁹when suddenly a windstorm from the desert blew the house down, crushing all of your children. I am the only one who escaped to tell you."

²⁰When Job heard this, he tore his clothes and shaved his head because of his great sorrow. He knelt on the ground, then worshiped God ²¹and said:

"We bring nothing at birth;
    we take nothing
        with us at death.
The LORD alone gives and takes.
Praise the name of the LORD!"

²²In spite of everything, Job did not sin or accuse God of doing wrong.

Job Loses His Health

2 When the angels*f* gathered around the LORD again, Satan*g* was there with them, ²and the LORD asked, "Satan, where have you been?"

Satan replied, "I have been going all over the earth."

³Then the LORD asked, "What do you think of my servant Job? No one on earth is like him—he is a truly good person, who respects me and refuses to do evil. And he hasn't changed, even though you persuaded me to destroy him for no reason."

⁴Satan answered, "There's no pain like your own.*h* People will do anything to stay alive. ⁵Try striking Job's own body with pain, and he will curse you to your face."

⁶"All right!" the LORD replied. "Make Job suffer as much as you want, but just don't kill him." ⁷Satan left and caused painful sores to break out all over Job's body—from head to toe.

⁸Then Job sat on the ash-heap to show his sorrow. And while he was scraping his sores with a broken piece of pottery, ⁹his wife asked, "Why do you still trust God? Why don't you curse him and die?"

If you and your spouse are to grow in faith, love, and compassion, it's important to make good choices during all times—whether joyful or difficult.

LUCI SWINDOLL

¹⁰Job replied, "Don't talk like a fool! If we accept blessings from God, we must accept trouble as well." In all that happened, Job never once said anything against God.

Job's Three Friends

¹¹Eliphaz from Teman, Bildad from Shuah, and Zophar from Naamah*i* were three of Job's friends, and they heard about his troubles. So they agreed to visit Job and comfort him. ¹²When they came near enough to see Job, they could hardly recognize him. And in their great sorrow, they tore their clothes, then sprinkled dust on their heads and cried bitterly. ¹³For seven days and nights, they sat silently on the ground beside him, because they realized what terrible pain he was in.

---

*e*1.17 *Chaldeans:* People from the region of Babylonia, northeast of Palestine. *f*2.1 *angels:* See the note at 15.8. *g*2.1 *Satan:* See the note at 1.6. *h*2.4 *There's no pain like your own:* The Hebrew text has "Skin for skin," which was probably a popular saying. *i*2.11 *Teman . . . Shuah . . . Naamah:* Teman was a place in northern Edom; Shuah may have been a town on the Euphrates River or else further south, near the towns of Dedan and Sheba; Naamah may have been located on the road between Beirut and Damascus, though its exact location is unknown.

Job's First Speech

Blot Out the Day of My Birth

3 Finally, Job cursed the day
of his birth
² by saying to God:
³ Blot out the day of my birth
and the night when my parents
created a son.
⁴ Forget about that day,
cover it with darkness,
⁵ and send thick, gloomy shadows
to fill it with dread.
⁶ Erase that night from the calendar
and conceal it with darkness.
⁷ Don't let children be created
or joyful shouts be heard
ever again in that night.
⁸ Let those with magic powers *j*
place a curse on that day.
⁹ Darken its morning stars
and remove all hope of light,
¹⁰ because it let me be born
into a world of trouble.

While you're suffering, you can't see the "why." It's only after the fact that you see that God makes true his promises—he works all things together for good.

JAN DRAVECKY

Why Didn't I Die at Birth?

¹¹ Why didn't I die at birth?
¹² Why was I accepted *k*
and allowed to nurse
at my mother's breast?
¹³ Now I would be at peace
in the silent world below
¹⁴ with kings and their advisors
whose palaces lie in ruins,
¹⁵ and with rulers once rich
with silver and gold.
¹⁶ I wish I had been born dead
and then buried, never to see
the light of day.
¹⁷ In the world of the dead,

the wicked and the weary rest
without a worry.
*¹⁸ Everyone is there—
¹⁹ where captives and slaves
are free at last.

Why Does God Let Me Live?

²⁰ Why does God let me live
when life is miserable
and so bitter?
²¹ I keep longing for death
more than I would seek
a valuable treasure.
²² Nothing could make me happier
than to be in the grave.
²³ Why do I go on living
when God has me surrounded,
and I can't see the road?
²⁴ Moaning and groaning
are my food and drink,
²⁵ and my worst fears
have all come true.
²⁶ I have no peace or rest—
only troubles and worries.

Eliphaz's First Speech

Please Be Patient and Listen

4 Eliphaz from Teman *l* said:
² Please be patient and listen
to what I have to say.
*³ Remember how your words
⁴ have guided and encouraged
many in need.
⁵ But now you feel discouraged
when struck by trouble.
⁶ You respect God and live right,
so don't lose hope!
⁷ No truly innocent person
has ever died young.
⁸ In my experience, only those
who plant seeds of evil
harvest trouble,
⁹ and then they are swept away

---

*j***3.8** *those with magic powers:* The Hebrew text has "those
who can place a curse on the day and rouse up
Leviathan," which was some kind of sea monster. God's
victory over this monster sometimes stood for God's
power over all creation and sometimes for his defeat of his
enemies (see Isaiah 27.1). In Job 41.1, Leviathan is either
a sea monster or a crocodile with almost supernatural
powers. *k***3.12** *Why was I accepted:* The Hebrew text has
"Why were there knees to receive me," which may refer
either to Job's mother or to his father, who would have
placed Job on his knees to show that he had accepted
him as his child. *l***4.1** *Teman:* See the note at 2.11.

by the angry breath of God.
¹⁰ They may roar and growl
   like powerful lions.
   But when God breaks their teeth,
¹¹ they starve, and their children
   are scattered.

A Secret Was Told to Me

¹² A secret was told to me
   in a faint whisper—
¹³ I was overcome by sleep,
   but disturbed by dreams;
¹⁴ I trembled with fear,
¹⁵ and my hair stood on end,
   as a wind blew past my face.
¹⁶ It stopped and stood still.
   Then a form appeared—
   a shapeless form.
   And from the silence,
   I heard a voice say,
¹⁷ "No humans are innocent
   in the eyes of God
   their Creator.
¹⁸ He finds fault with his servants
   and even with his angels.
¹⁹ Humans are formed from clay
   and are fragile as moths,
   so what chance do you have?
²⁰ Born after daybreak,
   you die before nightfall
   and disappear forever.
²¹ Your tent pegs are pulled up,
   and you leave this life,
   having gained no wisdom."

Eliphaz Continues

Call Out for Help

5 Job, call out for help
   and see if an angel comes!

² Envy and jealousy
   will kill a stupid fool.
³ I have seen fools take root.
   But God sends a curse,
   suddenly uprooting them
⁴ and leaving their children
   helpless in court.
⁵ Then hungry and greedy people
   gobble down their crops
   and grab up their wealth.^m
⁶ Our suffering isn't caused
   by the failure of crops;
⁷ it's all part of life,
   like sparks shooting skyward.

⁸ Job, if I were you,
   I would ask God for help.
⁹ His miracles are marvelous,
   more than we can count.
¹⁰ God sends showers on earth
   and waters the fields.
¹¹ He protects the sorrowful
   and lifts up those
   who have been disgraced.
*¹² God swiftly traps the wicked
¹³ in their own evil schemes,
   and their wisdom fails.
¹⁴ Darkness is their only companion,
   hiding their path at noon.
¹⁵ God rescues the needy
   from the words of the wicked
   and the fist of the mighty.
¹⁶ The poor are filled with hope,
   and injustice is silenced.

Consider Yourself Fortunate

¹⁷ Consider yourself fortunate
   if God All-Powerful
   chooses to correct you.
¹⁸ He may cause injury and pain,
   but he will bandage and heal
   your cuts and bruises.
¹⁹ God will protect you from harm,
   no matter how often
   trouble may strike.

²⁰ In times of war and famine,
   God will keep you safe.
²¹ You will be sheltered,
   without fear of hurtful words
   or any other weapon.
²² You will laugh at the threat
   of destruction and famine.
   And you won't be afraid
   of wild animals—
²³ they will no longer be fierce,
   and your rocky fields
   will become friendly.
²⁴ Your home will be secure,
   and your sheep will be safe.
²⁵ You will have more descendants
   than there are blades of grass
   on the face of the earth.
²⁶ You will live a long life,
   and your body will be strong
   until the day you die.
²⁷ Our experience has proven

---

*m***5.5** *wealth*: One possible meaning for the difficult
Hebrew text of verse 5.

these things to be true,
so listen and learn.

Job's Reply to Eliphaz

It's Impossible

6 Job said:
² It's impossible to weigh
my misery and grief!
³ They outweigh the sand
along the beach,
and that's why I have spoken
without thinking first.
⁴ The fearsome arrows
of God All-Powerful
have filled my soul
with their poison.
⁵ Do oxen and wild donkeys
cry out in distress
unless they are hungry?
⁶ What is food without salt?
What is more tasteless
than the white of an egg?ⁿ
⁷ That's how my food tastes,
and my appetite is gone.

*⁸ How I wish that God
would answer my prayer
⁹   and do away with me.
¹⁰ Then I would be comforted,
knowing that in all of my pain
I have never disobeyed God.

¹¹ Why should I patiently hope
when my strength is gone?
¹² I am not strong as stone
or bronze,
¹³ and I have finally reached
the end of my rope.

My Friends, I Am Desperate

¹⁴ My friends, I am desperate,
and you should help me,
even if I no longer respect
God All-Powerful.ᵒ
*¹⁵ But you are treacherous
¹⁶ as streams that swell
with melting snow,
¹⁷ then suddenly disappear
in the summer heat.
¹⁸ I am like a caravan,
lost in the desert
while searching for water.
¹⁹ Caravans from Tema and Shebaᵖ
²⁰   thought they would find water.
But they were disappointed,
²¹   just as I am with you.ᑫ

ⁿ**6.6** *What is more tasteless . . . egg:* One possible
meaning for the difficult Hebrew text.   ᵒ**6.14** *and you
should help me . . . God All-Powerful:* Or "and if you don't
help me, you no longer respect God All-Powerful."
ᵖ**6.19** *Tema and Sheba:* Tema was a region in northwest
Arabia, and Sheba was probably a region in southwest
Arabia.   ᑫ**6.21** *just . . . you:* One possible meaning for
the difficult Hebrew text.

MARRIAGE—**My husband doesn't share my passion for spiritual things. How
can I deal with my frustration and sadness?** *(Job 6.14-21)*

Ask believing friends for help.
If you're married to an unbeliever, you probably experience loneliness, because even though
you may share much of your life, the one most important area is missing—your walk with
God. But you don't have to walk entirely alone.

God can give you believing friends to share that walk. That's why if you're married to an
unbeliever, it's important to nurture supportive relationships with other women. Find two
or three women who will pray with you for your husband, encourage you to keep on living
by the teachings of Scripture, and help you to keep on believing in your Lord—even when
your faith is weak. Friendships with fellow believers can help you be the best wife you can,
and avoid the temptation of building a close friendship with a Christian man to meet your
unfulfilled spiritual needs.

Job called on his friends for help. He told them how desperate he was, that he was even
having trouble respecting his All-Powerful God. Unfortunately, Job's friends weren't much
help—but you can do differently by working at your relationships and keeping your eyes
open for the godly women out there. (See also James 5.7-11; Revelation 21.1-4.)

 Words To Remember: *My friends, I am desperate, and you should help me. . . .
I am like a caravan, lost in the desert while searching for water.*—Job 6.14,18

Only one look at my suffering,
and you run away scared.

What Have I Done Wrong?

²² Have I ever asked any of you
to give me a gift
²³ or to purchase my freedom
from brutal enemies?
²⁴ What have I done wrong?
Show me,
and I will keep quiet.
²⁵ The truth is always painful,
but your arguments
prove nothing.
²⁶ Here I am desperate,
and you consider my words
as worthless as wind.
²⁷ Why, you would sell an orphan
or your own neighbor!
²⁸ Look me straight in the eye;
I won't lie to you.
²⁹ Stop accusing me falsely;
my reputation is at stake.
³⁰ I know right from wrong,
and I am not telling lies.

Job Continues

Why Is Life So Hard?

7 Why is life so hard?
Why do we suffer?
² We are slaves in search of shade;
we are laborers longing
for our wages.
³ God has made my days drag on
and my nights miserable.
⁴ I pray for night to end,
but it stretches out
while I toss and turn.
⁵ My parched skin is covered
with worms, dirt, and sores,
⁶ and my days are running out
quicker than the thread
of a fast-moving needle.

Don't Forget!

⁷ I beg you, God, don't forget!
My life is just a breath,
and trouble lies ahead.
⁸ I will vanish from sight,
and no one, including you,
will ever see me again.
⁹ I will disappear in the grave
or vanish from sight
like a passing cloud.

¹⁰ Never will I return home;
soon I will be forgotten.

¹¹ And so, I cry out to you
in agony and distress.
¹² Am I the sea or a sea monster?
Is that why you imprison me?ʳ

*God is smart enough to
figure out what's best for me.*
MADALENE HARRIS

¹³ I go to bed, hoping for rest,
¹⁴ but you torture me
with terrible dreams.
*¹⁵ I'd rather choke to death
than live in this body.
¹⁶ Leave me alone and let me die;
my life has no meaning.
¹⁷ What makes you so concerned
about us humans?
¹⁸ Why do you test us
from sunrise to sunset?
¹⁹ Won't you look away
just long enough
for me to swallow?
²⁰ Why do you watch us so closely?
What's it to you, if I sin?
Why am I your target
and such a heavy burden?
²¹ Why do you refuse to forgive?
Soon you won't find me,
because I'll be dead.

Bildad's First Speech

How Long Will You Talk?

8 Bildad from Shuahˢ said:
² How long will you talk
and keep saying nothing?
³ Does God All-Powerful
stand in the way of justice?
⁴ He made your children pay

ʳ**7.12** *sea monster . . . imprison me:* "Sea monster"
translates the Hebrew word "Tannin," which was
possibly a sea monster similar to Leviathan (3.8), Rahab
(9.13), and Behemoth (40.15). According to 38.8-11,
God makes the sea his prisoner by setting its
boundaries.   ˢ**8.1** *Shuah:* See the note at 2.11.

for their sins.
⁵So why don't you turn to him
⁶   and start living right?
Then he will decide
to rescue and restore you
    to your place of honor.
⁷Your future will be brighter
    by far than your past.

Our Ancestors Were Wise

⁸Our ancestors were wise,
    so learn from them.
⁹Our own time has been short,
    like a fading shadow,
    and we know very little.
¹⁰But they will instruct you
    with great understanding.

¹¹Papyrus reeds grow healthy
    only in a swamp,
¹²and if the water dries up,
    they die sooner than grass.
¹³Such is the hopeless future
    of all who turn from God
¹⁴and trust in something as frail
    as a spider's web—
¹⁵they take hold and fall
    because it's so flimsy.
¹⁶Sinful people are like plants
    with spreading roots and plenty
    of sun and water.
¹⁷They wrap their roots tightly
    around rocks.ᵗ
¹⁸But once they are pulled up,
    they have no more place;
¹⁹their life slips away,ᵘ
    and other plants grow there.

> *Laughter puts the world
> into perspective. And it
> keeps us from taking
> ourselves too seriously.*
>
> SUSAN ALEXANDER YATES

²⁰We know God doesn't reject
    an innocent person
    or help a sinner.
²¹And so, he will make you happy
    and give you something

to smile about.
²²But your evil enemies
    will be put to shame
    and disappear forever.

Job's Reply to Bildad

What You Say Is True

9 Job said:
²What you say is true.
No human is innocent
    in the sight of God.
³Not once in a thousand times
    could we win our case
    if we took him to court.
⁴God is wise and powerful—
    who could possibly
    oppose him and win?
⁵When God becomes angry,
    he can move mountains
    before they even know it.
⁶God can shake the earth loose
    from its foundations
⁷or command the sun and stars
    to hold back their light.
⁸God alone stretched out the sky,
    stepped on the sea,ᵛ
⁹and set the stars in place—
    the Big Dipper and Orion,
    the Pleiades and the stars
    in the southern sky.
¹⁰Of all the miracles God works,
    we cannot understand a one.
¹¹God walks right past me,
    without making a sound.
¹²And if he grabs something,
    who can stop him
    or raise a question?

¹³When God showed his anger,
    the servants of the sea monsterʷ
    fell at his feet.
¹⁴How, then, could I possibly
    argue my case with God?

Though I Am Innocent

¹⁵Even though I am innocent,
    I can only beg for mercy.

ᵗ**8.17** *rocks:* One possible meaning for the difficult Hebrew text of verse 17.   ᵘ**8.19** *their . . . away:* One possible meaning for the difficult Hebrew text. ᵛ**9.8** *sea:* Or "sea monster" (see verse 13 and the note there).   ʷ**9.13** *the sea monster:* The Hebrew text has "Rahab," which was some kind of sea monster with supernatural powers (see the notes at 3.8 and 26.12).

¹⁶ And if God came into court
when I called him,
  he would not hear my case.
¹⁷ He would strike me with a storm^x
and increase my injuries
  for no reason at all.
¹⁸ Before I could get my breath,
  my miseries would multiply.
¹⁹ God is much stronger than I am,
and who would call me into court
  to give me justice?

²⁰ Even if I were innocent,
  God would prove me wrong.^y
²¹ I am not guilty,
but I no longer care
  what happens to me.
²² What difference does it make?
God destroys the innocent
  along with the guilty.
²³ When a good person dies
a sudden death,
  God sits back and laughs.
²⁴ And who else but God
blindfolds the judges,
  then lets the wicked
  take over the earth?

My Life Is Speeding By

²⁵ My life is speeding by,
  without a hope of happiness.
²⁶ Each day passes swifter
than a sailing ship
  or an eagle swooping down.
²⁷ Sometimes I try to be cheerful
and to stop complaining,
²⁸ but my sufferings frighten me,
because I know that God
  still considers me guilty.
²⁹ So what's the use of trying
  to prove my innocence?
³⁰ Even if I washed myself
  with the strongest soap,
³¹ God would throw me into a pit
of stinking slime, leaving me
  disgusting to my clothes.

³² God isn't a mere human like me.
  I can't put him on trial.
³³ Who could possibly judge
  between the two of us?
³⁴ Can someone snatch away
the stick God carries
  to frighten me?
³⁵ Then I could speak up

without fear of him,
  but for now, I cannot speak.^z

Job Complains to God

I Am Sick of Life!

10 I am sick of life!
And from my deep despair,
  I complain to you, my God.
² Don't just condemn me!
  Point out my sin.
³ Why do you take such delight
in destroying those you created
  and in smiling on sinners?
⁴ Do you look at things
  the way we humans do?
⁵ Is your life as short as ours?
⁶ Is that why you are so quick
  to find fault with me?
⁷ You know I am innocent,
but who can defend me
  against you?
⁸ Will you now destroy
  someone you created?
⁹ Remember that you molded me
like a piece of clay.
So don't turn me back
  into dust once again.
¹⁰ As cheese is made from milk,
you created my body
  from a tiny drop.
¹¹ Then you tied my bones together
with muscles and covered them
  with flesh and skin.
¹² You, the source of my life,
showered me with kindness
  and watched over me.

You Have Not Explained

¹³ You have not explained
  all of your mysteries,
¹⁴ but you catch and punish me
  each time I sin.
¹⁵ Guilty or innocent,
I am condemned and ashamed
  because of my troubles.
¹⁶ No matter how hard I try,
you keep hunting me down
  like a powerful lion.^a

---

^x**9.17** *strike . . . storm*: One possible meaning for
the difficult Hebrew text.   ^y**9.20** *God . . . wrong*:
Or "my own words would prove me wrong."
^z**9.35** *but . . . speak*: One possible meaning for the
difficult Hebrew text.   ^a**10.16** *lion*: One possible
meaning for the difficult Hebrew text of verse 16.

¹⁷You never stop accusing me;
you become furious and attack
over and over again.

¹⁸Why did you let me be born?
I would rather have died
before birth
¹⁹and been carried to the grave
without ever breathing.
²⁰I have only a few days left.
Why don't you leave me alone?^b
Let me find some relief,
*²¹before I travel to the land
²²of darkness and despair,
the place of no return.

Zophar's First Speech

So Much Foolish Talk

11 Zophar from Naamah^c said:
²So much foolish talk
cannot go unanswered.
³Your words have silenced others
and made them ashamed;
now it is only right for you
to be put to shame.
⁴You claim to be innocent
and argue that your beliefs
are acceptable to God.
⁵But I wish he would speak
⁶and let you know that wisdom
has many different sides.
You would then discover
that God has punished you
less than you deserve.

⁷Can you understand the mysteries
surrounding God All-Powerful?
⁸They are higher than the heavens
and deeper than the grave.
So what can you do
when you know so little,
⁹and these mysteries outreach
the earth and the ocean?

¹⁰If God puts you in prison
or drags you to court,
what can you do?
¹¹God has the wisdom to know
when someone is worthless
and sinful,
¹²but it's easier to tame
a wild donkey
than to make a fool wise.^d

Surrender Your Heart to God

¹³Surrender your heart to God,
turn to him in prayer,
¹⁴and give up your sins—
even those you do in secret.
¹⁵Then you won't be ashamed;
you will be confident
and fearless.
¹⁶Your troubles will go away
like water beneath a bridge,
¹⁷and your darkest night
will be brighter than noon.

*Earthly things don't bring
long-term satisfaction—
only God does.*

MARY HUNT

¹⁸You will rest safe and secure,
filled with hope
and emptied of worry.
¹⁹You will sleep without fear
and be greatly respected.
²⁰But those who are evil
will go blind and lose their way.
Their only escape is death!

Job's Reply to Zophar

You Think You Are So Great

12 *¹Job said to his friends:
²You think you are so great,
with all the answers.
³But I know as much as you do,
and so does everyone else.
⁴I have always lived right,
and God answered my prayers;
now friends make fun of me.
⁵It's easy to condemn
those who are suffering,
when you have no troubles.
⁶Robbers and other godless people
live safely at home and say,
"God is in our hands!"^e

---

^b10.20 *I have only . . . alone*: One possible meaning for
the difficult Hebrew text.   ^c11.1 *Naamah*: See the note
at 2.11.   ^d11.12 *it's . . . wise*: One possible meaning for
the difficult Hebrew text.   ^e12.6 *God is in our hands*:
One possible meaning for the difficult Hebrew text.

If You Want To Learn

⁷ If you want to learn,
     then go and ask
the wild animals and the birds,
⁸   the flowers and the fish.
⁹ Any of them can tell you
     what the LORD has done.ʲ
¹⁰ Every living creature
     is in the hands of God.

¹¹ We hear with our ears,
     taste with our tongues,
¹² and gain some wisdom from those
     who have lived a long time.
¹³ But God is the real source
     of wisdom and strength.
¹⁴ No one can rebuild
     what he destroys, or release
       those he has imprisoned.
¹⁵ God can hold back the rain
     or send a flood,
¹⁶ just as he rules over liars
     and those they lie to.

¹⁷ God destroys counselors,
     turns judges into fools,
¹⁸   and makes slaves of kings.
¹⁹ God removes priests and others
     who have great power—
²⁰ he confuses wise,
     experienced advisors,
²¹ puts mighty kings to shame,
     and takes away their power.
²² God turns darkness to light;
²³ he makes nations strong,
     then shatters their strength.
²⁴ God strikes their rulers senseless,
     then leaves them to roam
       through barren deserts,
²⁵ lost in the dark, staggering
     like someone drunk.

Job Continues

I Know and Understand

13 I know and understand
     every bit of this.
² None of you are smarter
     than I am;
there's nothing you know
     that I don't.
³ But I prefer to argue my case
     with God All-Powerful—
⁴ you are merely useless doctors,

who treat me with lies.
⁵ The wisest thing you can do
is to keep quiet ⁶ and listen
     to my argument.
⁷ Are you telling lies for God
⁸ and not telling the whole truth
     when you argue his case?
⁹ If he took you to court,
     could you fool him,
       just as you fool others?
¹⁰ If you were secretly unfair,
     he would correct you,
¹¹ and his glorious splendor
     would make you terrified.
¹² Your wisdom and arguments
     are as delicate as dust.

Be Quiet While I Speak

¹³ Be quiet while I speak,
     then say what you will.
¹⁴ I will be responsible
     for what happens to me.
¹⁵ God may kill me, but still
     I will trust himᵍ
     and offer my defense.
¹⁶ This may be what saves me,
     because no guilty person
       would come to his court.
¹⁷ Listen carefully to my words!
¹⁸ I have prepared my case well,
     and I am certain to win.
¹⁹ If you can prove me guilty,
     I will give up and die.

I'm grateful for a loving, merciful Father who doesn't hang up on me no matter how long I keep him waiting.

MAYO MATHERS

Job Prays

I Ask Only Two Things

²⁰ I ask only two things
     of you, my God,
and I will no longer
     hide from you—

ʲ **12.9** *Any . . . done:* One possible meaning for the difficult Hebrew text. ᵍ **13.15** *God . . . trust him:* Or "God will surely kill me; I have lost all hope."

²¹stop punishing
and terrifying me!

²²Then speak, and I will reply;
or else let me speak,
and you reply.
²³Please point out my sins,
so I will know them.
²⁴Why have you turned your back
and count me your enemy?
²⁵Do you really enjoy
frightening a fallen leaf?
²⁶Why do you accuse me
of horrible crimes
and make me pay for sins
I did in my youth?
²⁷You have tied my feet down
and keep me surrounded;
²⁸I am rotting away like cloth
eaten by worms.

Job Continues His Prayer

Life Is Short and Sorrowful

14 Life is short and sorrowful
for every living soul.
²We are flowers that fade
and shadows that vanish.
³And so, I ask you, God,
why pick on me?
⁴There's no way a human
can be completely pure.
⁵Our time on earth is brief;

the number of our days
is already decided by you.
⁶Why don't you leave us alone
and let us find some happiness
while we toil and labor?

When a Tree Is Chopped Down

⁷When a tree is chopped down,
there is always the hope
that it will sprout again.
⁸Its roots and stump may rot,
⁹but at the touch of water,
fresh twigs shoot up.
¹⁰Humans are different—
we die, and that's the end.
¹¹We are like streams and lakes
after the water has gone;
¹²we fall into the sleep of death,
never to rise again,
until the sky disappears.
¹³Please hide me, God,
deep in the ground—
and when you are angry no more,
remember to rescue me.

Will We Humans Live Again?

¹⁴Will we humans live again?
I would gladly suffer
and wait for my time.
¹⁵My Creator, you would want me;
you would call out,
and I would answer.
¹⁶You would take care of me,

Friendship—How can I encourage a friend who is going through a divorce?
(Job 13.5-15)

Listen, listen, listen.
Divorce is one of life's most painful experiences. Many women cry for months, lose (or gain) thirty pounds, and generally feel their life has ended. During this acute stage of grief, it doesn't do much good to rehash the mistakes of the marriage or to offer hollow hopes of reconciliation. Just listen and take cues from your friend about what she wants to talk about. She probably won't remember much of what you say anyway. But she *will* remember the comfort of your presence and perhaps a bowl of hot homemade soup.

Job wasn't getting a divorce, but he must have felt that God had "divorced" or abandoned him. Although his friends tried to help by explaining God, their ill-informed advice was less than comforting for Job. But even though Job didn't understand God, he didn't separate from him. In the end Job was able to say, "God may kill me, but still I will trust him and offer my defense" (13.15). Offer your divorcing friend a quiet example of your own faith. In time she may be able to trust God, too. (See also Isaiah 43.2-4; Isaiah 61.1-3; 2 Corinthians 1.3-7.)

Words To Remember: *The wisest thing you can do is to keep quiet and listen to my argument.—Job 13.5,6*

but not count my sins—
¹⁷ you would put them in a bag,
tie it tight,
and toss them away.
¹⁸ But in the real world,
mountains tumble,
and rocks crumble;
¹⁹ streams wear away stones
and wash away soil.
And you destroy our hopes!
²⁰ You change the way we look,
then send us away,
wiped out forever.
²¹ We never live to know
if our children are praised
or disgraced.
²² We feel no pain but our own,
and when we mourn,
it's only for ourselves.

Eliphaz's Second Speech

If You Had Any Sense

15 Eliphaz from Teman^h said:
*² Job, if you had any sense,
³ you would stop spreading
all of this hot air.
⁴ Your words are enough
to make others turn from God
and lead them to doubt.
⁵ And your sinful, scheming mind
is the source of all you say.
⁶ I am not here as your judge;
your own words are witnesses
against you.

⁷ Were you the first human?
Are you older than the hills?
⁸ Have you ever been present
when God's councilⁱ meets?
Do you alone have wisdom?
⁹ Do you know and understand
something we don't?
¹⁰ We have the benefit of wisdom
older than your father.
¹¹ And you have been offered
comforting words from God.
Isn't this enough?

¹² Your emotions are out of control,
making you look fierce;
¹³ that's why you attack God
with everything you say.
¹⁴ No human is pure and innocent,
¹⁵ and neither are angels—

not in the sight of God.
If God doesn't trust his angels,
¹⁶ what chance do humans have?
We are so terribly evil
that we thirst for sin.

Just Listen to What I Know

¹⁷ Just listen to what I know,
and you will learn
¹⁸ wisdom known by others
since ancient times.
¹⁹ Those who gained such insights
also gained the land,
and they were not influenced
by foreign teachings.
²⁰ But suffering is in store
each day for those who sin.
²¹ Even in times of success,
they constantly hear
the threat of doom.
²² Darkness, despair, and death
are their destiny.
²³ They scrounge around for food,
all the while dreading
the approaching darkness.
²⁴ They are overcome with despair,
like a terrified king
about to go into battle.
²⁵ This is because they rebelled
against God All-Powerful
²⁶ and have attacked him
with their weapons.

²⁷ They may be rich and fat,
²⁸ but they will live in the ruins
of deserted towns.
²⁹ Their property and wealth
will shrink and disappear.
³⁰ They won't escape the darkness,
and the blazing breath of God
will set their future aflame.
*³¹ They have put their trust
in something worthless;
now they will become worthless
³² like a date palm tree
without a leaf.^j
³³ Or like vineyards or orchards
whose blossoms and unripe fruit
drop to the ground.
³⁴ Yes, the godless and the greedy
will have nothing but flames

---

^h**15.1** *Teman:* See the note at 2.11.   ⁱ**15.8** *God's council:*
The angels and others who gather to discuss matters
with God (see 1.6; 2.1).   ^j**15.32** *leaf:* One possible
meaning for the difficult Hebrew text of verse 32.

feasting on their homes,
³⁵ because they are the parents
of trouble and vicious lies.

Job's Reply to Eliphaz

I Have Often Heard This

16 Job said:
² I have often heard this,
and it offers no comfort.
³ So why don't you keep quiet?
What's bothering you?
⁴ If I were in your place,
it would be easy to criticize
or to give advice.
⁵ But I would offer hope
and comfort instead.

*Part of godliness is learning
to give and receive love.*

MARTHA REAPSOME

⁶ If I speak, or if I don't,
I hurt all the same.
My torment continues.
⁷ God has worn me down
and destroyed my family;
⁸ my shriveled up skin proves
that I am his prisoner.
⁹ God is my hateful enemy,
glaring at me and attacking
with his sharp teeth.
¹⁰ Everyone is against me;
they sneer and slap my face.
¹¹ And God is the one
who handed me over
to this merciless mob.

Everything Was Going Well

¹² Everything was going well,
until God grabbed my neck
and shook me to pieces.
God set me up as the target
¹³   for his arrows,
and without showing mercy,
he slashed my stomach open,
spilling out my insides.
¹⁴ God never stops attacking,
¹⁵   and so, in my sorrow
I dress in sackcloth*ᵏ*

and sit in the dust.
¹⁶ My face is red with tears,
and dark shadows
circle my eyes,
¹⁷ though I am not violent,
and my prayers are sincere.

¹⁸ If I should die,
I beg the earth not to cover
my cry for justice.
¹⁹ Even now, God in heaven
is both my witness
and my protector.
²⁰ My friends have rejected me,
but God is the one I beg*ˡ*
²¹ to show that I am right,
just as a friend should.
²² Because in only a few years,
I will be dead and gone.

Job Complains to God

My Hopes Have Died

17 My hopes have died,
my time is up,
and the grave is ready.
² All I can see are angry crowds,
making fun of me.
³ If you, LORD, don't help,
who will pay the price
for my release?
⁴ My friends won't really listen,
all because of you,
and so you must be the one
to prove them wrong.
⁵ They have condemned me,
just to benefit themselves;
now blind their children.

⁶ You, God, are the reason
I am insulted and spit on.
⁷ I am almost blind with grief;
my body is a mere shadow.

⁸ People who are truly good
would feel so alarmed,
that they would become angry
at my worthless friends.
⁹ They would do the right thing

---

*ᵏ*16.15 *sackcloth:* A rough, dark-colored cloth made
from goat hair and used to make grain sacks. It was
worn in times of trouble or sorrow. *ˡ*16.20 *My
friends . . . beg:* Or "God is my friend, and he is the
one I beg."

and because they did,
    they would grow stronger.[m]
[10] But none of my friends
    show any sense.

[11] My life is drawing to an end;
    hope has disappeared.
[12] But all my friends can do
    is offer empty hopes.[n]
[13] I could tell the world below
    to prepare me a bed.
[14] Then I could greet the grave
    as my father
    and say to the worms,
    "Hello, mother and sisters!"

[15] But what kind of hope is that?
[16] Will it keep me company
    in the world of the dead?

Bildad's Second Speech

How Long Will You Talk?

18 Bildad from Shuah[o] said:
[2] How long will you talk?
    Be sensible! Let us speak.
[3] Or do you think that we
    are dumb animals?
[4] You cut yourself in anger.
    Will that shake the earth
    or even move the rocks?

*[5] The lamps of sinful people
    soon are snuffed out,
[6]   leaving their tents dark.
[7] Their powerful legs become weak,
    and they stumble on schemes
    of their own doing.
*[8] Before they know it,
[9] they are trapped in a net,
[10]   hidden along the path.
[11] Terror strikes and pursues
    from every side.
[12] Starving, they run,
    only to meet disaster,
[13] then afterwards to be eaten alive
    by death itself.

[14] Those sinners are dragged
    from the safety of their tents
    to die a gruesome death.
[15] Then their tents and possessions
    are burned to ashes,
[16] and they are left like trees,
    dried up from the roots.

[17] They are gone and forgotten,
[18] thrown far from the light
    into a world of darkness,
[19] without any children
    to carry on their name.
[20] Everyone, from east to west,
    is overwhelmed with horror.
[21] Such is the fate of sinners
    and their families
    who don't know God.

Job's Reply to Bildad

How Long Will You Torture Me?

19 Job said:
[2] How long will you torture me
    with your words?
[3] Isn't ten times enough
    for you to accuse me?
    Aren't you ashamed?
[4] Even if I have sinned,
    you haven't been harmed.
[5] You boast of your goodness,
    claiming I am suffering
    because I am guilty.
[6] But God is the one at fault
    for finding fault with me.

[7] Though I pray to be rescued
    from this torment,
    no whisper of justice
    answers me.
[8] God has me trapped
    with a wall of darkness
[9]   and stripped of respect.
[10] God rips me apart,
    uproots my hopes,
[11] and attacks with fierce anger,
    as though I were his enemy.
[12] His entire army advances,
    then surrounds my tent.

I Am Forgotten

*[13] God has turned relatives
    and friends against me,
[14]   and I am forgotten.
[15] My guests and my servants
    consider me a stranger,
[16] and when I call my servants,
    they pay no attention.

---

[m]**17.9** *stronger*: One possible meaning for the difficult Hebrew text of verses 8, 9.   [n]**17.12** *hopes*: One possible meaning for the difficult Hebrew text of verse 12.   [o]**18.1** *Shuah*: See the note at 2.11.

17 My breath disgusts my wife;
everyone in my family
turns away.
18 Young children can't stand me,
and when I come near,
they make fun.
19 My best friends and loved ones
have turned from me.
20 I am skin and bones—
just barely alive.
21 My friends, I beg you for pity!
God has made me his target.
22 Hasn't he already done enough?
Why do you join the attack?

23 I wish that my words
could be written down
24 or chiseled into rock.
25 I know that my Savior[p] lives,
and at the end
he will stand on this earth.
26 My flesh may be destroyed,
yet from this body
I will see God.[q]
27 Yes, I will see him for myself,
and I long for that moment.

28 My friends, you think up ways
to blame and torment me, saying
I brought it on myself.
29 But watch out for the judgment,
when God will punish you!

Zophar's Second Speech

Your Words Are Disturbing

20 Zophar from Naamah[r] said:
2 Your words are disturbing;
now I must speak.
3 You have accused
and insulted me,
and reason requires a reply.
4 Since the time of creation,
everyone has known
5 that sinful people are happy
for only a while.
6 Though their pride and power
may reach to the sky,
7 they will disappear like dust,
and those who knew them
will wonder what happened.
8 They will be forgotten
like a dream
9 and vanish from the sight
of family and friends.
10 Their children will have to repay
what the parents took
from the poor.
11 Indeed, the wicked will die
and go to their graves
in the prime of life.

---

p19.25 *Savior*: Or "Defender." q19.26 *God*: One possible meaning for the difficult Hebrew text of verses 25, 26. r20.1 *Naamah*: See the note at 2.11.

---

*Spiritual*Life—Is it okay to be angry at God? (*Job 19*)

Don't lose sight of who God is.

Job was angry, and he had a right to be. God had allowed him almost every loss possible on this earth. Job was poor, sick, and in deep grief, yet his friends sat around for days, accusing him of sin and pretending they themselves were without fault. Job finally said, "God has made me his target" (19.21). He complained that even "my breath disgusts my wife" (19.17). In fact, this whole chapter is one long complaint, except for five verses. In those verses we find one of the most lofty statements of hope in all the Old Testament—the hope of seeing God face to face.

So yes, be angry at God if you must. Tell him what you are angry about. Use all the poetic language you want. God is not injured by your anger. But don't forget who he is. One day you will see God face to face—despite your anger—so "long for that moment" when everything, even life's suffering, will be erased by his presence. (See also Numbers 20.1-13; Psalm 10; Habakkuk 1.2-5.)

Words To Remember: ***I wish that my words could be written down or chiseled into rock. I know that my Savior lives, and at the end he will stand on this earth. My flesh may be destroyed, yet from this body I will see God. Yes, I will see him for myself, and I long for that moment.—Job 19.23-27***

Sinners Love the Taste of Sin

¹² Sinners love the taste of sin;
   they relish every bite
¹³   and swallow it slowly.
¹⁴ But their food will turn sour
   and poison their stomachs.
¹⁵ Then God will make them lose
   the wealth they gobbled down.
¹⁶ They will die from the fangs
   of poisonous snakes
¹⁷ and never enjoy rivers flowing
   with milk and honey.
¹⁸ Their hard work will result
   in nothing gained,
¹⁹ because they cheated the poor
   and took their homes.

²⁰ Greedy people want everything
   and are never satisfied.ˢ
²¹ But when nothing remains
   for them to grab,
   they will be nothing.
²² Once they have everything,
   distress and despair
   will strike them down,
²³ and God will make them swallow
   his blazing anger.ᵗ

²⁴ While running from iron spears,
   they will be killed
   by arrows of bronze,
²⁵ whose shining tips go straight
   through their bodies.
   They will be trapped by terror,
²⁶ and what they treasure most
   will be lost in the dark.
   God will send flames
   to destroy them in their tents
   with all their property.
²⁷ The heavens and the earth
   will testify against them,
²⁸ and all their possessions
   will be dragged off
   when God becomes angry.
²⁹ This is what God has decided
   for those who are evil.

Job's Reply to Zophar

If You Want To Offer Comfort

21 Job said:
   ² If you want to offer comfort,
      then listen to me.
   ³ And when I have finished,

you can start your insults
   all over again.
⁴ My complaint is against God;
   that's why I am impatient.
⁵ Just looking at me is enough
   to make you sick,
⁶ and the very thought of myself
   fills me with disgust.

*When we desire to serve God in
all arenas and relationships,
we can experience a renewed
joy in each other.*

JANE JOHNSON STRUCK

⁷ Why do evil people live so long
   and gain such power?
⁸ Why are they allowed to see
   their children grow up?ᵘ
⁹ They have no worries at home,
   and God never punishes them.
¹⁰ Their cattle have lots of calves
   without ever losing one;
¹¹ their children play and dance
   safely by themselves.
¹² These people sing and celebrate
   to the sound of tambourines,
   small harps, and flutes,
¹³ and they are successful,
   without a worry,
   until the day they die.

Leave Us Alone!

¹⁴ Those who are evil say
   to God All-Powerful,
   "Leave us alone! Don't bother us
   with your teachings.
¹⁵ What do we gain from praying
   and worshiping you?
¹⁶ We succeeded all on our own."
   And so, I keep away from them
   and their evil schemes.

¹⁷ How often does God become angry
   and send disaster and darkness

ˢ20.20 *are never satisfied:* One possible meaning for the difficult Hebrew text. ᵗ20.23 *anger:* One possible meaning for the difficult Hebrew text of verse 23. ᵘ21.8 *up:* One possible meaning for the difficult Hebrew text of verse 8.

to punish sinners?

¹⁸How often does he strike them
like a windstorm
that scatters straw?

¹⁹You say, "God will punish
those sinners' children
in place of those sinners."
But I say, "Let him punish
those sinners themselves
until they really feel it.
²⁰Let God All-Powerful force them
to drink their own destruction
from the cup of his anger.
²¹Because after they are dead,
they won't care what happens
to their children."

Who Can Tell God What To Do?

²²Who can tell God what to do?
He judges powerful rulers.
*²³Some of us die prosperous,
²⁴   enjoying good health,
²⁵while others die in poverty,
having known only pain.
²⁶But we all end up dead,
beneath a blanket of worms.

²⁷My friends, I know that you
are plotting against me.
²⁸You ask, "Where is the home
of that important person
who does so much evil?"

²⁹Everyone, near and far, agrees
³⁰   that those who do wrong
never suffer disaster,
when God becomes angry.
³¹No one points out their sin
or punishes them.
³²Then at their funerals,
they are highly praised;
³³the earth welcomes them home,
while crowds mourn.

³⁴But empty, meaningless words
are the comfort you offer me.

Eliphaz's Third Speech

What Use Are We Humans to God?

22 Eliphaz from Teman^v said:
²What use are we humans
to God,
even the wisest of us?

³If you were completely sinless,
that would still mean nothing
to God All-Powerful.
⁴Is he correcting you
for worshiping him?
⁵No! It's because
of your terrible sins.
⁶To guarantee payment of a debt,
you have taken clothes
from the poor.
⁷And you refused bread and water
to the hungry and thirsty,
⁸although you were rich,
respected, and powerful.
⁹You have turned away widows
and have broken the arms
of orphans.
¹⁰That's why you were suddenly
trapped by terror,
¹¹blinded by darkness,
and drowned in a flood.

God Lives in the Heavens

¹²God lives in the heavens
above the highest stars,
where he sees everything.
¹³Do you think the deep darkness
hides you from God?
¹⁴Do thick clouds cover his eyes,
as he walks around heaven's dome
high above the earth?
¹⁵Give up those ancient ideas
believed by sinners,
¹⁶who were swept away
without warning.
¹⁷They rejected God All-Powerful,
feeling he was helpless,
¹⁸although he had been kind
to their families.
The beliefs of these sinners
are truly disgusting.
¹⁹When God's people see
the godless swept away,
they celebrate, ²⁰saying,
"Our enemies are gone,
and fire has destroyed
their possessions."

Surrender to God All-Powerful

²¹Surrender to God All-Powerful!
You will find peace
and prosperity.

---

^v**22.1** *Teman:* See the note at 2.11.

22 Listen to his teachings
   and take them to heart.
23 If you return to God
   and turn from sin,
   all will go well for you.
24 So get rid of your finest gold,
   as though it were sand.
25 Let God All-Powerful
   be your silver and gold,
26 and you will find happiness
   by worshiping him.
27 God will answer your prayers,
   and you will keep the promises
   you made to him.
28 He will do whatever you ask,
   and life will be bright.
29 When others are disgraced,
   God will clear their names
   in answer to your prayers.
30 Even those who are guilty
   will be forgiven,
   because you obey God.ʷ

Job's Reply to Eliphaz

Today I Complain Bitterly

23 Job said:
   2 Today I complain bitterly,
   because God has been cruel

and made me suffer.
3 If I knew where to find God,
   I would go there
4   and argue my case.
5 Then I would discover
   what he wanted to say.
6 Would he overwhelm me
   with his greatness?
   No! He would listen
7   because I am innocent,
   and he would say,
   "I now set you free!"

8 I cannot find God anywhere—
   in front or back of me,
9   to my left or my right.
   God is always at work,
   though I never see him.
10 But he knows what I am doing,
   and when he tests me,
   I will be pure as gold.
*11 I have never refused to follow
   any of his commands,
12 and I have always treasured
   his teachings.ˣ

ʷ**22.30** *God:* One possible meaning for the difficult Hebrew text of verses 29, 30.   ˣ**23.12** *treasured his teachings:* One possible meaning for the difficult Hebrew text.

Personal *Concerns*—How can I handle even difficult times positively?
(Job 23)

Remember, God is always at work—even when you can't see him.
Some of us tend to be a little gloomy. We may even imagine "worst-case scenarios" so we are prepared for any dreaded possibility. And sometimes "worst-case" actually does happen. It did for Job. He lost everything: children, possessions, even his health. Besides that, his three friends lectured him endlessly, demanding he confess some hidden sin that had brought on God's anger. Three times they gave him some variation of that lecture. Even God seemed to ignore him. Job said, "If I knew where to find God, I would go there and argue my case" (23.3).

Despite his pain, frustration, and confusion, Job was absolutely sure God was still at work—even in him. He believed that when God was finished testing him, he would be as pure as gold. So Job didn't give up. In the end, God proved him right. Not sinless, but right.

Sometimes it's our natural disposition to be gloomy. But sometimes it's because all that's important in life has gone wrong. Even when that happens, we can agree with Job: "God is always at work." God will continue his work in us, especially during the painful times, so that when he is finished we will be "pure as gold." If we remember that, we may even smile more often. (See also Leviticus 26.1-13; Micah 4.1-5; Nahum 1.2-7,15; Romans 8.18-30; Ephesians 1.7-23.)

Words To Remember: *God is always at work, though I never see him. But he knows what I am doing, and when he tests me, I will be pure as gold.*—Job 23.9,10

¹³ But he alone is God,
and who can oppose him?
God does as he pleases,
¹⁴ and he will do exactly
what he intends with me.
*¹⁵ Merely the thought
of God All-Powerful
¹⁶   makes me tremble with fear.
¹⁷ God has covered me
with darkness,
but I refuse to be silent.^y

Job Continues

Why Doesn't God Set a Time?

24 Why doesn't God
set a time for court?
Why don't his people know
where he can be found?
² Sinners remove boundary markers
and take care of sheep
they have stolen.
³ They cheat orphans and widows
by taking their donkeys
and oxen.
⁴ The poor are trampled
and forced to hide
⁵   in the desert,
where they and their children
must live like wild donkeys
and search for food.
⁶ If they want grain or grapes,^z
they must go to the property
of these sinners.
⁷ They sleep naked in the cold,
because they have no cover,
⁸ and during a storm
their only shelters are caves
among the rocky cliffs.

⁹ Children whose fathers have died
are taken from their mothers
as payment for a debt.
¹⁰ Then they are forced to work
naked in the grain fields
because they have no clothes,
and they go hungry.
¹¹ They crush olives to make oil
and grapes to make wine—
but still they go thirsty.
¹² And along the city streets,
the wounded and dying cry out,
yet God does nothing.

Some Reject the Light

¹³ Some rebel and refuse
to follow the light.
¹⁴ Soon after sunset they murder
the poor and the needy,
and at night they steal.

¹⁵ Others wait for the dark,
thinking they won't be seen
if they sleep with the wife
or husband of someone else.
¹⁶ Robbers hide during the day,
then break in after dark
because they reject the light.
¹⁷ They prefer night to day,
since the terrors of the night
are their friends.

Sinners Are Filthy Foam

¹⁸ Those sinners are filthy foam
on the surface of the water.
And so, their fields and vineyards
will fall under a curse
and won't produce.
¹⁹ Just as the heat of summer
swallows the snow,
the world of the dead
swallows those who sin.
²⁰ Forgotten here on earth,
and with their power broken,
they taste sweet to worms.

²¹ Sinners take advantage of widows
and other helpless women.^a
²² But God's mighty strength
destroys those in power.
Even if they seem successful,
they are doomed to fail.
²³ God may let them feel secure,
but they are never
out of his sight.
²⁴ Great for a while; gone forever!
Sinners are mowed down
like weeds,
then they wither and die.
²⁵ If I haven't spoken the truth,
then prove me wrong.

---

^y**23.17** *silent:* One possible meaning for the difficult
Hebrew text of verse 17.   ^z**24.6** *If they want grain or
grapes:* Poor people were allowed to gather what was
left in the fields and vineyards after the harvest.
^a**24.21** *women:* One possible meaning for the difficult
Hebrew text of verse 21.

Bildad's Third Speech

God Is the One To Fear

25 Bildad from Shuah[b] said:
2 God is the one to fear,
because God is in control
and rules the heavens.
3 Who can count his army of stars?
Isn't God the source of light?
4 How can anyone be innocent
in the sight of God?
5 To him, not even the light
of the moon and stars
can ever be pure.
6 So how can we humans,
when we are merely worms?

Job's Reply to Bildad

You Have Really Been Helpful

26 Job said:
2 You have really been helpful
to someone weak and weary.
3 You have given great advice
and wonderful wisdom
to someone truly in need.
4 How can anyone possibly speak
with such understanding?

> *Loving acceptance, both*
> *demonstrated and spoken,*
> *can lay the foundation*
> *for trusting confidence*
> *and self-acceptance.*
>
> MAXINE HANCOCK

5 Remember the terrible trembling
of those in the world of the dead
below the mighty ocean.
6 Nothing in that land
of death and destruction
is hidden from God,
7 who hung the northern sky
and suspended the earth
on empty space.
8 God stores water in clouds,
but they don't burst,
9 and he wraps them around

the face of the moon.
10 On the surface of the ocean,
God has drawn a boundary line
between light and darkness.
11 And columns supporting the sky
tremble at his command.

12 By his power and wisdom,
God conquered the force
of the mighty ocean.[c]
13 The heavens became bright
when he breathed,
and the escaping sea monster[d]
died at the hands of God.
14 These things are merely a whisper
of God's power at work.
How little we would understand
if this whisper
ever turned into thunder!

Job Continues

I Am Desperate

27 Job said:
2 I am desperate because
God All-Powerful refuses
to do what is right.
As surely as God lives,
3 and while he gives me breath,
4   I will tell only the truth.
5 Until the day I die,
I will refuse to do wrong
by saying you are right,
6 because each day my conscience
agrees that I am innocent.

7 I pray that my enemies
will suffer no less
than the wicked.
8 Such people are hopeless,
and God All-Powerful
will cut them down,
9 without listening
when they beg for mercy.
10 And that is what God should do,
because they don't like him
or ever pray.

[b]**25.1** *Shuah:* See the note at 2.11. [c]**26.12** *the force of the mighty ocean:* The Hebrew text has "the ocean . . . Rahab." In this passage the sea monster Rahab stands for the fearsome power of the ocean (see the notes at 3.8 and 9.13). [d]**26.13** *sea monster:* The Hebrew text has "snake," which probably stands for some kind of fearsome sea monster, such as Leviathan (see Isaiah 27.1).

¹¹Now I will explain in detail
    what God All-Powerful does.
¹²All of you have seen these things
for yourselves.
    So you have no excuse.

How God Treats the Wicked

¹³Here is how God All-Powerful
    treats those who are wicked
    and brutal.
¹⁴They may have many children,
    but most of them will go hungry
    or suffer a violent death.
¹⁵Others will die of disease,
    and their widows
    won't be able to weep.
¹⁶The wicked may collect riches
    and clothes in abundance
    as easily as clay.
¹⁷But God's people will wear
    clothes taken from them
    and divide up their riches.
¹⁸No homes built by the wicked
    will outlast a cocoon
    or a shack.
¹⁹Those sinners may go to bed rich,
    but they will wake up poor.^e
²⁰Terror will strike at night
    like a flood or a storm.
²¹Then a scorching wind
    will sweep them away
²²without showing mercy,
    as they try to escape.
²³At last, the wind will celebrate
    because they are gone.

Job Continues

Gold and Silver Are Mined

28

Gold and silver are mined,
    then purified;
²the same is done
    with iron and copper.
³Miners carry lanterns
deep into the darkness
    to search for these metals.
⁴They dig tunnels
    in distant, unknown places,
    where they dangle by ropes.
⁵Far beneath the grain fields,
    fires are built
    to break loose those rocks
⁶   that have jewels or gold.^f

⁷Miners go to places unseen
    by the eyes of hawks;
⁸they walk on soil unknown
    to the proudest lions.
⁹With their own hands
    they remove sharp rocks
    and uproot mountains.
¹⁰They dig through the rocks
    in search of jewels
    and precious metals.
¹¹They also uncover
    the sources of^g rivers
    and discover secret places.

Where Is Wisdom Found?

¹²But where is wisdom found?
¹³   No human knows the way.^h
¹⁴Nor can it be discovered
    in the deepest sea.
*¹⁵It is worth much more
    than silver or pure gold
¹⁶   or precious stones.
¹⁷Nothing is its equal—
    not gold or costly glass.ⁱ
¹⁸Wisdom is worth much more than
    coral, jasper,^j or rubies.
¹⁹All the topaz^k of Ethiopia^l
    and the finest gold
    cannot compare with it.
²⁰Where then is wisdom?
²¹It is hidden from human eyes
    and even from birds.
²²Death and destruction
    have merely heard rumors
    about where it is found.
²³God is the only one who knows
    the way to wisdom,
²⁴because he sees everything
    beneath the heavens.
²⁵When God divided out
    the wind and the water,
²⁶and when he decided the path
    for rain and lightning,
²⁷he also determined the truth

---

^e**27.19** *poor:* Or "dead." ^f**28.6** *gold:* One possible
meaning for the difficult Hebrew text of verses 5, 6.
^g**28.11** *uncover the sources of:* Two ancient translations;
Hebrew "dam up." ^h**28.13** *the way:* Or "its worth."
ⁱ**28.17** *costly glass:* In the ancient world, objects made
of glass were costly. ^j**28.18** *jasper:* A valuable stone,
usually green or clear. ^k**28.19** *topaz:* A valuable, yellow
stone. ^l**28.19** *Ethiopia:* The Hebrew text has "Cush,"
which was a region south of Egypt that included parts
of the present countries of Ethiopia and Sudan.

and defined wisdom.
²⁸God told us, "Wisdom means
that you respect me, the Lord,
and turn from sin."

Job Continues

I Long for the Past

29 Job said:
²I long for the past,
when God took care of me,
³and the light from his lamp
showed me the way
through the dark.
⁴I was in the prime of life,
God All-Powerful
was my closest friend,
⁵and all of my children
were nearby.
⁶My herds gave enough milk
to bathe my feet,
and from my olive harvest
flowed rivers of oil.
*⁷When I sat down at the meeting
of the city council,
⁸the young leaders stepped aside,
*⁹while the older ones stood
¹⁰   and remained silent.

Everyone Was Pleased

¹¹Everyone was pleased
with what I said and did.
¹²When poor people or orphans
cried out for help,
I came to their rescue.
¹³And I was highly praised
for my generosity to widows
and others in poverty.
¹⁴Kindness and justice
were my coat and hat;
¹⁵I was good to the blind
and to the lame.
¹⁶I was a father to the needy,
and I defended them in court,
even if they were strangers.
¹⁷When criminals attacked,
I broke their teeth
and set their victims free.

¹⁸I felt certain that I would live
a long and happy life,
then die in my own bed.

¹⁹In those days I was strong
like a tree with deep roots
and with plenty of water,
²⁰   or like an archer's new bow.
²¹Everyone listened in silence
to my welcome advice,
²²and when I finished speaking,
nothing needed to be said.
²³My words were eagerly accepted
like the showers of spring,
²⁴and the smile on my face
renewed everyone's hopes.
²⁵My advice was followed
as though I were a king
leading my troops,
or someone comforting
those in sorrow.

Job Continues

Young People Now Insult Me

30 Young people now insult me,
although their fathers
would have been a disgrace
to my sheep dogs.
²And those who insult me
are helpless themselves.
³They must claw the desert sand
in the dark for something
to satisfy their hunger.^m
⁴They gather tasteless shrubs
for food and firewood,
⁵and they are run out of towns,
as though they were thieves.
⁶Their only homes are ditches
or holes between rocks,
⁷where they bray like donkeys
gathering around shrubs.
⁸And like senseless donkeys,
they are chased away.

Those Worthless Nobodies

⁹Those worthless nobodies
make up jokes and songs
to disgrace me.
¹⁰They are hateful
and keep their distance,
even while spitting
in my direction.
¹¹God has destroyed me,

---

^m**30.3** *hunger*: One possible meaning for the difficult
Hebrew text of verse 3.

and so they don't care
  what they do.ⁿ
¹²Their attacks never stop,
  though I am defenseless,
  and my feet are trapped.ᵒ
¹³Without any help,
  they prevent my escape,
destroying me completelyᵖ
¹⁴   and leaving me crushed.
¹⁵Terror has me surrounded;
  my reputation and my riches
  have vanished like a cloud.

I Am Sick at Heart

¹⁶I am sick at heart!
  Pain has taken its toll.
¹⁷Night chews on my bones,
  causing endless torment,
¹⁸and God has shrunk my skin,
  choking me to death.
¹⁹I have been thrown in the dirt
  and now am dirt myself.
²⁰I beg God for help,
  but there is no answer;
  and when I stand up,
  he simply stares.
²¹God has turned brutal,
²²stirring up a windstorm
  to toss me about.
²³Soon he will send me home
  to the world of the dead,
  where we all must go.

²⁴No one refuses help to others,
  when disaster strikes.𐞥
²⁵I mourned for the poor
  and those who suffered.
²⁶But when I beg for relief
  and light,
  all I receive are disaster
  and darkness.
²⁷My stomach is tied in knots;
  pain is my daily companion.
²⁸Suffering has scorched my skin,
  and in the city council
  I stand and cry out,
²⁹making mournful sounds
  like jackalsʳ and owls.
³⁰My skin is so parched,
  that it peels right off,
  and my bones are burning.
³¹My only songs are sorrow
  and sadness.

Job Continues

I Promised Myself

31 I promised myself
  never to stare with desire
    at a young woman.
²God All-Powerful punishes
  men who do that.
³In fact, God sends disaster
  on all who sin,
⁴and he keeps a close watch
  on everything I do.

⁵I am not dishonest or deceitful,
⁶and I beg God to prove
  my innocence.
⁷If I have disobeyed him
  or even wanted to,
⁸then others can eat my harvest
  and uproot my crops.
⁹If I have desired someone's wife
  and chased after her,
¹⁰then let some stranger
  steal my wife from me.
¹¹If I took someone's wife,
  it would be a horrible crime,
¹²sending me to destruction
  and my crops to the flames.ˢ

¹³When my servants
  complained against me,
  I was fair to them.
¹⁴Otherwise, what answer
  would I give to God
  when he judges me?
¹⁵After all, God is the one
  who gave life to each of us
  before we were born.

I Have Never Cheated Anyone

¹⁶I have never cheated widows
  or others in need,
¹⁷and I have always shared
  my food with orphans.
¹⁸Since the time I was young,

ⁿ**30.11** *God . . . do:* Or "They have destroyed me, and so they don't care what else they do." ᵒ**30.12** *trapped:* One possible meaning for the difficult Hebrew text of verse 12. ᵖ**30.13** *destroying . . . completely:* One possible meaning for the difficult Hebrew text. 𐞥**30.24** *strikes:* One possible meaning for the difficult Hebrew text of verse 24. ʳ**30.29** *jackals:* Desert animals related to wolves, but smaller. ˢ**31.12** *flames:* One possible meaning for the difficult Hebrew text of verse 12.

I have cared for orphans
and helped widows.[t]
¹⁹I provided clothes for the poor,
²⁰   and I was praised
for supplying woolen garments
to keep them warm.
²¹If I have ever raised my arm
to threaten an orphan
when the power was mine,
²²I hope that arm will fall
from its socket.
²³I could not have been abusive;
I was terrified at the thought
that God might punish me.
²⁴I have never trusted
the power of wealth,
²⁵or taken pride in owning
many possessions.
*²⁶I have never openly or secretly
²⁷   worshiped the sun or moon.
²⁸Such horrible sins
would have deserved
punishment from God.
²⁹I have never laughed
when my enemies
were struck by disaster.
³⁰Neither have I sinned
by asking God
to send down on them
the curse of death.
³¹No one ever went hungry[u]
at my house,
³²and travelers
were always welcome.
³³Many have attempted to hide
their sins from others—
but I refused.
³⁴And the fear of public disgrace
never forced me to keep silent
about what I had done.

Why Doesn't God Listen?

³⁵Why doesn't God All-Powerful
listen and answer?
If God has something against me,
let him speak up
or put it in writing!
³⁶Then I would wear his charges
on my clothes and forehead.
³⁷And with my head held high,
I would tell him everything
I have ever done.

³⁸I have never mistreated
the land I farmed

and made it mourn.[v]
³⁹Nor have I cheated
my workers
and caused them pain.[w]
⁴⁰If I had, I would pray
for weeds instead of wheat
to grow in my fields.
After saying these things,
Job was silent.

Elihu Is Upset with Job's Friends

32 Finally, these three men stopped
arguing with Job, because he refused to admit that he was guilty.
²Elihu from Buz[x] was there, and he had
become upset with Job for blaming God instead of himself. ³He was also angry with
Job's three friends for not being able to
prove that Job was wrong. ⁴Elihu was younger than these three, and he let them speak
first. ⁵But he became irritated when they
could not answer Job, ⁶and he said to them:

I am much younger than you,
so I have shown respect
by keeping silent.
⁷I once believed age
was the source of wisdom;
⁸now I truly realize
wisdom comes from God.
⁹Age is no guarantee of wisdom
and understanding.
¹⁰That's why I ask you
to listen to me.

I Eagerly Listened

*¹¹I eagerly listened
to each of your arguments,
¹²but not one of you proved
Job to be wrong.
¹³You shouldn't say,
"We know what's right!

---

[t]**31.18** *widows:* One possible meaning for the difficult
Hebrew text of verse 18.   [u]**31.31** *ever went hungry:* Or
"was ever sexually abused" (see Genesis 19.1-11; Judges
17.22-30). In ancient Israel, the lives of one's guests
were sacred and had to be protected at any cost.
[v]**31.38** *mourn:* In biblical times there were strict
regulations for proper use of the land, and land that was
abused was said to "mourn" and become no longer
productive.   [w]**31.39** *pain:* One possible meaning for
the difficult Hebrew text of verse 39.   [x]**32.2** *Elihu from
Buz:* The Hebrew text has "Elihu son of Barachel from
Buz of the family of Ram." Buz may have been
somewhere in the territory of Edom; in Jeremiah 25.23
it is mentioned along with Dedan and Tema (see 6.19).

Let God punish him."
¹⁴Job hasn't spoken against me,
and so I won't answer him
with your arguments.

¹⁵All of you are shocked;
you don't know what to say.
¹⁶But am I to remain silent,
just because you
have stopped speaking?
¹⁷No! I will give my opinion,
¹⁸because I have so much to say,
that I can't keep quiet.
¹⁹I am like a swollen wineskin,
and I will burstʸ
²⁰   if I don't speak.

> *God has never had a*
> *prejudiced thought. The*
> *more time we spend alone*
> *with him, the more his*
> *attitude will rub off on us.*
>
> JILL BRISCOE

*²¹I don't know how to be unfair
or to flatter anyone—
²²if I did, my Creator
would quickly destroy me!

Elihu Speaks

Job, Listen to Me!

33 Job, listen to me!
Pay close attention.
*²Everything I will say
³   is true and sincere,
⁴just as surely as the Spirit
of God All-Powerfulᶻ
gave me the breath of life.
⁵Now line up your arguments
and prepare to face me.
⁶We each were made from clay,
and God has no favorites,
⁷so don't be afraid of me
or what I might do.

I Have Heard You Argue

⁸I have heard you argue
⁹that you are innocent,
guilty of nothing.
¹⁰You claim that God
has made you his enemy,
¹¹that he has bound your feet
and blocked your path.
¹²But, Job, you're wrong—
God is greater
than any human.
¹³So why do you challenge God
to answer you?ᵃ
¹⁴God speaks in different ways,
and we don't always
recognize his voice.
*¹⁵Sometimes in the night,
he uses terrifying dreams
¹⁶   to give us warnings.
¹⁷God does this to make us turn
from sin and pride
¹⁸and to protect us
from being swept away
to the world of the dead.

¹⁹Sometimes we are punished
with a serious illness
and aching joints.
²⁰Merely the thought
of our favorite food
makes our stomachs sick,
²¹and we become so skinny
that our bones stick out.
²²We feel death and the grave
taking us in their grip.

²³One of a thousand angels
then comes to our rescue
by saying we are innocent.
²⁴The angel shows kindness,
commanding death to release us,
because the price was paid.
²⁵Our health is restored,
we feel young again,
²⁶   and we ask God to accept us.
Then we joyfully worship God,
and we are rewarded
because we are innocent.
²⁷When that happens,
we tell everyone,
"I sinned and did wrong,

ʸ32.19 *swollen wineskin . . . burst:* While the juice from
grapes was becoming wine, it would swell and stretch
the skins in which it had been stored; sometimes the
swelling would burst the wineskins.   ᶻ33.4 *the Spirit
of God All-Powerful:* Or "God All-Powerful."
ᵃ33.13 *answer you:* One possible meaning for the
difficult Hebrew text of verse 13.

but God forgave me
²⁸ and rescued me from death!
Now I will see the light."

²⁹ God gives each of us
chance after chance
³⁰ to be saved from death
and brought into the light
that gives life.
³¹ So, Job, pay attention
and don't interrupt,
³² though I would gladly listen
to anything you say
that proves you are right.
³³ Otherwise, listen in silence
to my wisdom.

Elihu Continues

You Men Think You Are Wise

34 Elihu said:
²You men think you are wise,
but just listen to me!
³ Think about my words,
as you would taste food.
⁴ Then we can decide the case
and give a just verdict.
⁵ Job claims he is innocent
and God is guilty
of mistreating him.
⁶ Job also argues that God
considers him a liar
and that he is suffering severely
in spite of his innocence.
⁷ But to tell the truth,
Job is shameless!
⁸ He spends his time with sinners,
⁹ because he has said,
"It doesn't pay to please God."

If Any of You Are Smart

¹⁰ If any of you are smart,
you will listen and learn
that God All-Powerful
does what is right.
¹¹ God always treats everyone
the way they deserve,
¹² and he is never unfair.
¹³ From the very beginning,
God has been in control
of all the world.

¹⁴ If God took back the breath
that he breathed into us,
¹⁵ we humans would die

and return to the soil.
¹⁶ So be smart and listen!
¹⁷ The mighty God is the one
who brings about justice,
and you are condemning him.
¹⁸ Indeed, God is the one
who condemns unfair rulers.
¹⁹ And God created us all;
he has no favorites,
whether rich or poor.
²⁰ Even powerful rulers die
in the darkness of night
when they least expect it,
just like the rest of us.

God Watches Everything We Do

²¹ God watches everything we do.
²² No evil person can hide
in the deepest darkness.
²³ And so, God doesn't need
to set a time for judgment.
²⁴ Without asking for advice,
God removes mighty leaders
and puts others in their place.
²⁵ He knows what they are like,
and he wipes them out
in the middle of the night.
²⁶ And while others look on,
he punishes them
because they were evil
²⁷ and refused to obey him.
²⁸ The persons they mistreated
had prayed for help,
until God answered
their prayers.
²⁹ When God does nothing,
can any person or nation
find fault with him?
³⁰ But still, he punishes rulers
who abuse their people.*ᵇ*

³¹ Job, you should tell God
that you are guilty
and promise to do better.
³² Then ask him to point out
what you did wrong,
so you won't do it again.
³³ Do you make the rules,
or does God?
You have to decide—
I can't do it for you;
now make up your mind.

---

*ᵇ***34.30** *people:* One possible meaning for the difficult
Hebrew text of verses 29, 30.

³⁴Job, anyone with good sense
    can easily see
³⁵that you are speaking nonsense
    and lack good judgment.
³⁶So I pray for you to suffer
    as much as possible
    for talking like a sinner.
³⁷You have rebelled against God,
    time after time,
    and have even insulted us.

Elihu Continues

Are You Really Innocent?

35 Elihu said:
    ²Job, are you really innocent
        in the sight of God?ᶜ
³Don't you honestly believe
    it pays to obey him?
⁴I will give the answers
    to you and your friends.
*⁵Look up to the heavens
⁶   and think!
Do your sins hurt God?
⁷Is any good you may have done
    at all helpful to him?
⁸The evil or good you do
    only affects other humans.

⁹In times of trouble,
    everyone begs the mighty God
    to have mercy.
¹⁰But after their Creator
    helps them through hard times,
    they forget about him,
¹¹though he makes us wiser
    than animals or birds.
¹²God won't listen to the prayers
    of proud and evil people.
¹³If God All-Powerful refuses
    to answer their empty prayers,
¹⁴   he will surely deny
    your impatient request
    to face him in court.
¹⁵Job, you were wrong to say
    God doesn't punish sin.
¹⁶Everything you have said
    adds up to nonsense.

Elihu Continues

Be Patient a While Longer

36 Elihu said:
    ²Be patient a while longer;
    I have something else to say

in God's defense.
³God always does right—
    and this knowledge
    comes straight from God.ᵈ
⁴You can rest assured
    that what I say is true.
⁵Although God is mighty,
    he cares about everyone
    and makes fair decisions.

⁶The wicked are cut down,
    and those who are wronged
    receive justice.
⁷God watches over good people
    and places them in positions
    of power and honor forever.
⁸But when people are prisoners
    of suffering and pain,
*⁹God points out their sin
    and their pride,
¹⁰then he warns them
    to turn back to him.
¹¹And if they obey,
    they will be successful
    and happy from then on.
¹²But if they foolishly refuse,
    they will be rewarded
    with a violent death.

Godless People Are Too Angry

¹³Godless people are too angry
    to ask God for help
    when he punishes them.
¹⁴So they die young
    in shameful disgrace.
¹⁵Hard times and trouble
    are God's way
    of getting our attention!
¹⁶And at this very moment,
    God deeply desires
    to lead you from trouble
    and to spread your table
    with your favorite food.

¹⁷Now that the judgment
    for your sins
    has fallen upon you,

ᶜ**35.2** *are . . . God:* Or "is it right for you to accuse God?" ᵈ**36.3** *comes straight from God:* The Hebrew text has "comes from a distant place," which refers to the place where God lives; Elihu is claiming that he learned this from God.

¹⁸ don't let your anger
  and the pain you endured
    make you sneer at God.
¹⁹ Your reputation and riches
  cannot protect you
    from distress,

---

*God is the great healer of
memories, who can turn scars
into something beautiful.*

KATHY PEEL

---

²⁰ nor can you find safety
  in the dark world below.^e
²¹ Be on guard! Don't turn to evil
  as a way of escape.
²² God's power is unlimited.
  He needs no teachers
²³   to guide or correct him.

Others Have Praised God

²⁴ Others have praised God
  for what he has done,
    so join with them.
²⁵ From down here on earth,
  everyone has looked up and seen
²⁶   how great God is—
  God is more than we imagine;
  no one can count the years
    he has lived.
*²⁷ God gathers moisture
  into the clouds
²⁸   and supplies us with rain.
²⁹ Who can understand
  how God scatters the clouds
  and speaks from his home
    in the thunderstorm?
³⁰ And when God sends lightning,
  it can be seen
    at the bottom of the sea.
³¹ By producing such rainstorms,
  God rules the world
    and provides us with food.
³² Each flash of lightning
  is one of his arrows
    striking its target,
³³ and the thunder tells
  of his anger against sin.^f

Elihu Continues

I Am Frightened

37 I am frightened
  and tremble all over,
² when I hear the roaring voice
  of God in the thunder,
³ and when I see his lightning
  flash across the sky.
⁴ God's majestic voice
  thunders his commands,^g
⁵ creating miracles too marvelous
  for us to understand.
⁶ Snow and heavy rainstorms
⁷ make us stop and think
  about God's power,
⁸ and they force animals
  to seek shelter.
⁹ The windstorms of winter strike,
¹⁰ and the breath of God
  freezes streams and rivers.
¹¹ Rain clouds filled with lightning
  appear at God's command,
¹² traveling across the sky
¹³   to release their cargo—
  sometimes as punishment for sin,
  sometimes as kindness.

Consider Carefully

¹⁴ Job, consider carefully
  the many wonders of God.
¹⁵ Can you explain why lightning
  flashes at the orders
¹⁶   of God who knows all things?
  Or how he hangs the clouds
    in empty space?
¹⁷ You almost melt in the heat
  of fierce desert winds
    when the sky is like brass.
¹⁸ God can spread out the clouds
  to get relief from the heat,
    but can you?

¹⁹ Tell us what to say to God!
  Our minds are in the dark,
  and we don't know how
    to argue our case.
²⁰ Should I risk my life
  by telling God

---

^e**36.20** *below:* One possible meaning for the difficult
Hebrew text of verses 18-20.   ^f**36.33** *sin:* One possible
meaning for the difficult Hebrew text of verse 33.
^g**37.4** *commands:* One possible meaning for the difficult
Hebrew text of verse 4.

that I want to speak?
²¹No one can stare at the sun
after a breeze has blown
the clouds from the sky.
²²Yet the glorious splendor
of God All-Powerful
is brighter by far.
²³God cannot be seen—
but his power is great,
and he is always fair.
²⁴And so we humans fear God,
because he shows no respect
for those who are proud
and think they know so much.

The LORD Speaks

From Out of a Storm

38

From out of a storm,
the LORD said to Job:
²Why do you talk so much
when you know so little?
³Now get ready to face me!
Can you answer
the questions I ask?
⁴How did I lay the foundation
for the earth?
Were you there?
⁵Doubtless you know who decided
its length and width.
⁶What supports the foundation?

Who placed the cornerstone,
⁷   while morning stars sang,
and angels rejoiced?

⁸When the ocean was born,
I set its boundaries
⁹and wrapped it in blankets
of thickest fog.
¹⁰Then I built a wall around it,
locked the gates, ¹¹and said,
"Your powerful waves stop here!
They can go no farther."

Did You Ever Tell the Sun To Rise?

¹²Did you ever tell the sun to rise?
And did it obey?
¹³Did it take hold of the earth
and shake out the wicked
like dust from a rug?
¹⁴Early dawn outlines the hills
like stitches on clothing
or sketches on clay.
¹⁵But its light is too much
for those who are evil,
and their power is broken.

¹⁶Job, have you ever walked
on the ocean floor?
¹⁷Have you seen the gate
to the world of the dead?

PARENTING&*family*—How can I effectively balance my roles as parent and wife? *(Job 38.1—40.5)*

Put everything in perspective.
Car pools. Demanding schedules at home and at work. Mounting laundry. School lunches to make. A house to clean. A husband and kids who all need a listening ear—at once—after a long, hard day.

It's no wonder that sometimes we women just want to cry, "Stop the world! I want to get off!" (Even if it's just for a fifteen-minute walk around the block or a treasured half-hour soak in the tub.)

It's during those times that we need to read this passage again to help us gain perspective. Job had lost everything that mattered to him; his world had literally fallen apart. But he discovered that all was not lost: No matter what, God is still God, and he's in control of our life.

When you're having one of "those days," think of God's response to Job. After all, a God who tells the sun when to rise, walks the ocean floor, tells the wind where to blow, and arranges the stars in order can certainly handle whatever happens to us—even on our very worst days! (See also Deuteronomy 8.1-10; 1 Peter 4.1-8.)

Words To Remember: *When the ocean was born, I set its boundaries and wrapped it in blankets of thickest fog. . . . I am the LORD All-Powerful.—Job 38.8,9; 40.1*

¹⁸ And how large is the earth?
    Tell me, if you know!

¹⁹ Where is the home of light,
    and where does darkness live?
²⁰   Can you lead them home?
²¹ I'm certain you must be able to,
    since you were already born
        when I created everything.

²² Have you been to the places
    where I keep snow and hail,
²³ until I use them to punish
    and conquer nations?
²⁴ From where does lightning leap,
    or the east wind blow?
²⁵ Who carves out a path
    for thunderstorms?
    Who sends torrents of rain
²⁶ on empty deserts
    where no one lives?
²⁷ Rain that changes barren land
    to meadows green with grass.
²⁸ Who is the father of the dew
    and of the rain?
²⁹ Who gives birth to the sleet
    and the frost
³⁰ that fall in winter,
    when streams and lakes
        freeze solid as a rock?

Can You Arrange Stars?

³¹ Can you arrange stars in groups
    such as Orion
        and the Pleiades?
³² Do you control the stars
    or set in place the Big Dipper
        and the Little Dipper?
³³ Do you know the laws
    that govern the heavens,
    and can you make them rule
        the earth?
³⁴ Can you order the clouds
    to send a downpour,
³⁵ or will lightning flash
    at your command?
³⁶ Did you teach birds to know
    that rain or floods
        are on their way?ʰ
³⁷ Can you count the clouds
    or pour out their water
³⁸   on the dry, lumpy soil?

³⁹ When lions are hungry,
    do you help them hunt?

⁴⁰ Do you send an animal
    into their den?
⁴¹ And when starving young ravens
    cry out to me for food,
        do you satisfy their hunger?

The LORD Continues

When Do Mountain Goats Give Birth?

39 When do mountain goats
        and deer give birth?
    Have you been there
        when their young are born?
*²How long are they pregnant
³   before they deliver?
⁴ Soon their young grow strong
    and then leave
        to be on their own.

⁵ Who set wild donkeys free?
⁶ I alone help them survive
    in salty desert sand.
⁷ They stay far from crowded cities
    and refuse to be tamed.
⁸ Instead, they roam the hills,
    searching for pastureland.

⁹ Would a wild ox agree
    to live in your barn
        and labor for you?
¹⁰ Could you force him to plow
    or to drag a heavy log
        to smooth out the soil?
¹¹ Can you depend on him
    to use his great strength
        and do your heavy work?
¹² Can you trust him
    to harvest your grain
    or take it to your barn
        from the threshing place?

An Ostrich Proudly Flaps Her Wings

¹³ An ostrich proudly
        flaps her wings,
    but not because
        she loves her young.
¹⁴ She abandons her eggs
    and lets the dusty ground
        keep them warm.
¹⁵ And she doesn't seem to worry
    that the feet of an animal

ʰ**38.36** *way:* One possible meaning for the difficult
Hebrew text of verse 36.

could crush them all.
¹⁶ She treats her eggs as though
they were not her own,
unconcerned that her work
might be for nothing.
¹⁷ I myself made her foolish
and without common sense.
¹⁸ But once she starts running,ⁱ
she laughs at a rider
on the fastest horse.

Did You Give Horses Their Strength?

¹⁹ Did you give horses their strength
and the flowing hair
along their necks?
²⁰ Did you make them able
to jump like grasshoppers
or to frighten people
with their snorting?

²¹ Before horses are ridden
into battle,
they paw at the ground,
proud of their strength.
²² Laughing at fear, they rush
toward the fighting,
²³ while the weapons of their riders
rattle and flash in the sun.
²⁴ Unable to stand still,
they gallop eagerly into battle
when trumpets blast.
²⁵ Stirred by the distant smells
and sounds of war, they snort
in reply to the trumpet.

²⁶ Did you teach hawks to fly south
for the winter?
*²⁷ Did you train eaglesʲ to build
²⁸   their nests on rocky cliffs,
²⁹ where they can look down
to spot their next meal?
³⁰ Then their young gather to feast
wherever the victim lies.

The LORD Continues

I Am the LORD All-Powerful

40 *¹ I am the LORD All-Powerful,
² but you have argued
that I am wrong.
Now you must answer me.

³ Job said to the LORD:
⁴ Who am I to answer you?

⁵ I did speak once or twice,
but never again.

⁶ Then out of the storm
the LORD said to Job:
⁷ Face me and answer
the questions I ask!
⁸ Are you trying to prove
that you are innocent
by accusing me of injustice?
⁹ Do you have a powerful arm
and a thundering voice
that compare with mine?
¹⁰ If so, then surround yourself
with glory and majesty.
*¹¹ Show your furious anger!
Throw down and crush
¹²   all who are proud and evil.
¹³ Wrap them in grave clothes
and bury them together
in the dusty soil.
¹⁴ Do this, and I will agree
that you have won
this argument.

I Created You

¹⁵ I created both you
and the hippopotamus.ᵏ
It eats only grass like an ox,
¹⁶ but look at the mighty muscles
in its body ¹⁷ and legs.
Its tail is like a cedar tree,
and its thighs are thick.
¹⁸ The bones in its legs
are like bronze or iron.

¹⁹ I made it more powerful
than any other creature,
yet I am stronger still.
²⁰ Undisturbed, it eats grass
while the other animals
play nearby.ˡ
*²¹ It rests in the shade of trees
along the riverbank
²² or hides among reeds
in the swamp.
²³ It remains calm and unafraid

ⁱ**39.18** *starts running*: One possible meaning for the difficult Hebrew text. ʲ**39.27** *eagles*: Or "vultures." ᵏ**40.15** *the hippopotamus*: The Hebrew text has "Behemoth," which was sometimes understood to be a sea monster like Rahab (9.13; 26.12), Leviathan (3.8; 41.1), and Tannin (7.12). ˡ**40.20** *nearby*: One possible meaning for the difficult Hebrew text of verse 20.

with the Jordan River rushing
and splashing in its face.
24 There is no way to capture
a hippopotamus—
not even by hooking its nose
or blinding its eyes.

The LORD Continues

Can You Catch a Sea Monster?

41 Can you catch a sea monster[m]
by using a fishhook?
Can you tie its mouth shut
with a rope?
2 Can it be led around
by a ring in its nose
or a hook in its jaw?
3 Will it beg for mercy?
4 Will it surrender
as a slave for life?
5 Can it be tied by the leg
like a pet bird
for little girls?
6 Is it ever chopped up
and its pieces bargained for
in the fish-market?
7 Can it be killed
with harpoons or spears?
8 Wrestle it just once—
that will be the end.
9 Merely a glimpse of this monster

makes all courage melt.
10 And if it is too fierce
for anyone to attack,
who would dare oppose me?
11 I am in command of the world
and in debt to no one.

12 What powerful legs,
what a stout body
this monster possesses!
13 Who could strip off its armor
or bring it under control
with a harness?
14 Who would try to open its jaws,
full of fearsome teeth?
*15 Its back[n] is covered
with shield after shield,
16 firmly bound and closer together
17   than breath to breath.

When This Monster Sneezes

18 When this monster sneezes,
lightning flashes, and its eyes
glow like the dawn.
19 Sparks and fiery flames
explode from its mouth.

---

[m]41.1 *sea monster*: The Hebrew text has "Leviathan," which may refer to a sea monster or possibly to a crocodile in this verse (see the note at 3.8).
[n]41.15 *back*: Two ancient translations; Hebrew "pride."

---

*Spiritual*Life—How can I worship God as I should? *(Job 42.1-6)*

Admit you cannot fully understand God.

Our prayers of praise usually grow out of what we know about God's attributes: God is holy, God is wise, God is compassionate, God is merciful, God knows all things, God has all power, God is pure, God is love, God is a friend, God rules over all. When we worship God, we praise him for who he is and what he has done.

But worship isn't limited to what we know about God; it also springs from admitting that God is beyond what our mind can grasp.

One of the knotty questions of the book of Job is, "Why did Job repent?" God had allowed unprecedented disaster to fall on Job. Quite opposite to the explanations posed by Job's friends, God did not condemn Job of sinful actions. Instead God asked him why he talked so much when he knew so little (38.2). God said, "I am the LORD All-Powerful, but you have argued that I am wrong. . . . Are you trying to prove that you are innocent by accusing me of injustice?" (40.1,2,8).

And Job repented—not for sinful deeds, but for assuming that he knew more about God than he did. True worship stems from our knowledge of God, but also from admitting what we do not know. (See also Nehemiah 8.1—9.6; Nehemiah 12.27-43; Psalm 42.)

Words To Remember: *Job said: "No one can oppose you, because you have the power to do what you want. . . . I have talked about things that are far beyond my understanding.—Job 42.1-3*

²⁰ And smoke spews from its nose
like steam
from a boiling pot,
²¹ while its blazing breath
scorches everything in sight.

²² Its neck is so tremendous
that everyone trembles,
²³ the weakest parts of its body
are harder than iron,
²⁴   and its heart is stone.
²⁵ When this noisy monster appears,
even the most powerful^o
turn and run in fear.
²⁶ No sword or spear can harm it,
²⁷ and weapons of bronze or iron
are as useless as straw
or rotten wood.
²⁸ Rocks thrown from a sling
cause it no more harm
than husks of grain.
This monster fears no arrows,
²⁹   it simply smiles at spears,
and striking it with a stick
is like slapping it with straw.

³⁰ As it crawls through the mud,
its sharp and spiny hide

tears the ground apart.
³¹ And when it swims down deep,
the sea starts churning
like boiling oil,
³² and it leaves behind a trail
of shining white foam.
³³ No other creature on earth
is so fearless.
³⁴ It is king of all proud creatures,
and it looks upon the others
as nothing.

Job's Reply to the LORD

No One Can Oppose You

42 Job said:
² No one can oppose you,
because you have the power
to do what you want.
³ You asked why I talk so much
when I know so little.
I have talked about things
that are far beyond
my understanding.
⁴ You told me to listen

---

^o**41.25** *most powerful:* Or "gods."

Friendship—How can I speak the truth in love and still maintain a friendship? *(Job 42.7-9)*

Don't give simple answers to hard problems.
A friend has a problem. The solution seems simple to you. Should you share your insight with your friend?

Maybe. But first ask yourself a few questions. Does your friend want advice, or does she just want you to listen to her feelings? Are you sure your solution will work? Maybe your friend has already tried it and found that it failed. Maybe she has considered it and rejected it for reasons you don't know. Will your advice actually solve her problem, or will it just get you off the hook because "you've done all you could"?

Many of us are born fixers. We are convinced that if people would only listen to us we could make everything right. Job's friends were like that. They *knew* why Job was suffering, and they *knew* what he should do about it. They were certain Job was suffering because he had sinned. In their minds, the solution was perfectly obvious—he needed to confess, and God would relieve his suffering. No matter how much Job objected to their explanation, they *knew* he was wrong. But God said *they* were wrong. He demanded repentance *from them.*

So don't be too quick to advise your friend. Listen first, and respect what she says. Most solutions are not as simple as *they* seem. (See also Proverbs 27.6; Ephesians 4.25—5.2; James 1.5-8.)

    Words To Remember: *The* LORD *said to Eliphaz: What my servant Job has said about me is true, but I am angry at you and your two friends for not telling the truth.* —**Job 42.7**

and answer your questions.[p]
[5] I heard about you from others;
now I have seen you
with my own eyes.
[6] That's why I hate myself
and sit here in dust and ashes
to show my sorrow.

The LORD Corrects Job's Friends

[7] The LORD said to Eliphaz:
What my servant Job has said
about me is true, but I am angry at you
and your two friends for not telling the
truth. [8] So I want you to go over to Job
and offer seven bulls and seven goats
on an altar as a sacrifice to please me.[q]
After this, Job will pray, and I will agree
not to punish you for your foolishness.
[9] Eliphaz, Bildad, and Zophar obeyed the
LORD, and he answered Job's prayer.

A Happy Ending

[10] After Job had prayed for his three
friends, the LORD made Job twice as rich as
he had been before. [11] Then Job gave a feast
for his brothers and sisters and for his old
friends. They expressed their sorrow for the
suffering the LORD had brought on him, and
they each gave Job some silver and a gold
ring.

[12] The LORD now blessed Job more than
ever; he gave him fourteen thousand sheep,
six thousand camels, a thousand pair of
oxen, and a thousand donkeys.

[13] In addition to seven sons, Job had
three daughters, [14] whose names were Jemi-
mah, Keziah, and Keren Happuch. [15] They
were the most beautiful women in that part
of the world, and Job gave them shares of
his property, along with their brothers.

[16] Job lived for another one hundred forty
years—long enough to see his great-grandchildren have children of their own—[17] and
when he finally died, he was very old.

---

[p]**42.4** *questions:* One possible meaning for the difficult
Hebrew text of verse 4.   [q]**42.8** *sacrifice to please me:*
These sacrifices have traditionally been called "whole
burnt offerings" because the whole animal was burned
on the altar. A main purpose of such sacrifices was to
please the LORD with the smell of the sacrifice, and so
in the CEV they are often called "sacrifices to please
the LORD."

Psalms

Real Prayers for Real People

Stumped about how to pray? The book of Psalms doesn't tell you how to pray; the psalmists just do it—and you can join in any time.

The psalms give voice to all kinds of emotions. By reading them, we learn how to express them to God: shouting for joy when you get out of a jam; crying out when you feel abandoned; expressing doubt and despair when life is overwhelming; thanking God for the ways he never forgets us. Yet the psalm writers wrapped these feelings and experiences in and around God and his presence.

Enjoy the different types of psalms: praise hymns, complaints, records of past rescue, special occasion songs, and royal refrains about the king or Messiah. Still others retell important historical events or extol God's glory through the wonders of his creation.

Because the psalms are poetry, they are filled with metaphors. They frequently compare feelings to something else in a picturesque way that identifies exactly how you feel. Have you ever felt so far away from God, it was as though you were living in a foreign country, trying to find him? With David you may pray: "Please listen, God, and answer my prayer! I feel hopeless, and I cry out to you from a faraway land" (61.1,2). The psalms are also full of poetic devices such as repetition and hyperbole (exaggeration), which portray feelings in a colorful way: "There are more people who hate me for no reason than there are hairs on my head" (69.4). Although it is not literally true, sometimes it feels that way.

Other times, the psalms express majestic feelings you may have had but perhaps could not put into words: "You spread out the sky like a tent, and you built your home over the mighty ocean. The clouds are your chariot with the wind as its wings" (104.2,3).

Some of the complaint psalms sound downright vengeful: "Let the people he [my enemy] owes take everything he owns. Give it all to strangers. Don't let anyone be kind to him or have pity on the children he leaves behind" (109.11,12). Yet they also show a passion for righteousness and justice. When we are upset that justice isn't done, it's better to complain to God (the One who can do something, after all) rather than take matters into our own hands. And many of us have not experienced the persecution the people of Israel went through, so we may not understand their hurt and rage.

Nearly half the psalms were written by David, while Asaph, Solomon, Moses, and some anonymous authors wrote the rest over several centuries. They became important in Jewish worship services.

Psalms at a Glance
(The Psalms were not arranged thematically, but were compiled into books.)
1. Book One (Psalms 1–41)
2. Book Two (Psalms 42–72)
3. Book Three (Psalms 73–89)
4. Book Four (Psalms 90–106)
5. Book Five (Psalms 107–150)

BOOK I
(Psalms 1–41)

Psalm 1

The Way to Happiness

[1] God blesses those people
who refuse evil advice
and won't follow sinners
or join in sneering at God.
[2] Instead, the Law of the LORD
makes them happy,
and they think about it
day and night.

[3] They are like trees
growing beside a stream,
trees that produce
fruit in season
and always have leaves.
Those people succeed
in everything they do.

[4] That isn't true of those
who are evil,
because they are like straw
blown by the wind.
[5] Sinners won't have an excuse
on the day of judgment,

and they won't have a place
with the people of God.
[6] The LORD protects everyone
who follows him,
but the wicked follow a road
that leads to ruin.

Psalm 2

The LORD's Chosen King

[1] Why do the nations plot,[a]
and why do their people
make useless plans?[b]
[2] The kings of this earth
have all joined together
to turn against the LORD
and his chosen one.
[3] They say, "Let's cut the ropes
and set ourselves free!"

[4] In heaven the LORD laughs
as he sits on his throne,
making fun of the nations.
[5] The LORD becomes furious
and threatens them.
His anger terrifies them
as he says,

---

[a]**2.1** *Why... plot:* Or "Why are the nations restless?"
[b]**2.1** *make useless plans:* Or "grumble uselessly."

Friendship—How can I tell if a friendship is unhealthy? *(Psalm 1)*

By looking at character.
When you and your friend share different values it's easy to feel as if your friendship is unhealthy. Yet having a friend with different standards and morals isn't necessarily wrong— if you stand up for what you believe and refuse to compromise your standards. You can respect your friend for the godly qualities she shows, but pray she will find the truth and love of God through Jesus Christ. Love her with a genuine, humble heart and stay away from an attitude of superiority.

If, however, any friend—no matter what her beliefs—offers evil advice or sneers at God, put some distance between you and that person for a while. Don't let yourself fall into cynical, scoffing ways, but be grateful to God in all things. Ask God to guide you in the details of this friendship.

In any case, nourish yourself with God's Word and delight yourself in God's love. Watch those at your church who reflect God's love and pick up their gentleness and kindness. When your roots go down deep with God, you are better equipped to let him use you to salt the earth and light the world. (See also Proverbs 4.14,15; 22.24,25; 2 Corinthians 6.14-18.)

Words To Remember: *They are like trees growing beside a stream, trees that produce fruit in season and always have leaves. Those people succeed in everything they do.*—Psalm 1.3

6 "I've put my king on Zion,
   my sacred hill."

7 I will tell the promise
   that the LORD made to me:
   "You are my son, because today
   I have become your father.
8 Ask me for the nations,
   and every nation on earth
   will belong to you.
9 You will smash them
   with an iron rod
   and shatter them
   like dishes of clay."

10 Be smart, all you rulers,
   and pay close attention.
11 Serve and honor the LORD;
   be glad and tremble.
12 Show respect to his son
   because if you don't,
   the LORD might become furious
   and suddenly destroy you.*c*
   But he blesses and protects
   everyone who runs to him.

Psalm 3

*[Written by David when he was running
from his son Absalom.]*

An Early Morning Prayer

1 I have a lot of enemies, LORD.
   Many fight against 2me and say,
   "God won't rescue you!"

3 But you are my shield,
   and you give me victory
   and great honor.
4 I pray to you, and you answer
   from your sacred hill.

5 I sleep and wake up refreshed
   because you, LORD,
      protect me.
6 Ten thousand enemies attack
   from every side,
      but I am not afraid.

7 Come and save me, LORD God!
   Break my enemies' jaws
   and shatter their teeth,

8 because you protect
   and bless your people.

Psalm 4

*[A psalm by David for the music leader.
Use stringed instruments.]*

An Evening Prayer

1 You are my God and protector.
   Please answer my prayer.
   I was in terrible distress,
   but you set me free.
   Now have pity and listen
   as I pray.

2 How long will you people
   refuse to respect me?*d*
   You love foolish things,
   and you run after
   what is worthless.*e*

3 The LORD has chosen
   everyone who is faithful
   to be his very own,*f*
   and he answers my prayers.
4 But each of you
   had better tremble
   and turn from your sins.
   Silently search your heart
   as you lie in bed.
5 Offer the proper sacrifices
   and trust the LORD.

6 There are some who ask,
   "Who will be good to us?"
   Let your kindness, LORD,
   shine brightly on us.
7 You brought me more happiness
   than a rich harvest
   of grain and grapes.
8 I can lie down
   and sleep soundly
   because you, LORD,
   will keep me safe.

---

*c*2.11,12 *Serve . . . you:* One possible meaning for the
difficult Hebrew text of verses 11, 12.   *d*4.2 *me:* Or
"my God."   *e*4.2 *foolish . . . worthless:* This may refer to
idols and false gods.   *f*4.3 *has chosen . . . very own:*
Some Hebrew manuscripts have "work miracles for his
faithful people."

Psalm 5

[A psalm by David for the music leader. Use flutes.]

A Prayer for Help

[1] Listen, LORD, as I pray!
Pay attention when I groan.[g]
[2] You are my King and my God.
Answer my cry for help
because I pray to you.
[3] Each morning you listen
to my prayer,
as I bring my requests[h] to you
and wait for your reply.

[4] You are not the kind of God
who is pleased with evil.
Sinners can't stay with you.
[5] No one who boasts can stand
in your presence, LORD,
and you hate evil people.
[6] You destroy every liar,
and you despise violence
and deceit.

[7] Because of your great mercy,
I come to your house, LORD,
and I am filled with wonder
as I bow down to worship
at your holy temple.
[8] You do what is right,
and I ask you to guide me.
Make your teaching clear
because of my enemies.

[9] Nothing they say is true!
They just want to destroy.
Their words are deceitful
like a hidden pit,
and their tongues are good
only for telling lies.
[10] Punish them, God,
and let their own plans
bring their downfall.
Get rid of them!
They keep committing crimes
and turning against you.

[11] Let all who run to you
for protection
always sing joyful songs.
Provide shelter for those
who truly love you
and let them rejoice.

[12] Our LORD, you bless those
who live right,
and you shield them
with your kindness.

When we worship together, we grow together—not only spiritually, but as a community.
RAMONA CRAMER TUCKER

Psalm 6

[A psalm by David for the music leader. Use stringed instruments.[i]]

A Prayer in Time of Trouble

[1] Don't punish me, LORD,
or even correct me
when you are angry!
[2] Have pity on me and heal
my feeble body.
My bones tremble with fear,
[3] and I am in deep distress.
How long will it be?

[4] Turn and come to my rescue.
Show your wonderful love
and save me, LORD.
[5] If I die, I cannot praise you
or even remember you.
[6] My groaning has worn me out.
At night my bed and pillow
are soaked with tears.
[7] Sorrow has made my eyes dim,
and my sight has failed
because of my enemies.

[8] You, LORD, heard my crying,
and those hateful people
had better leave me alone.
[9] You have answered my prayer

---

[g]**5.1** *when I groan*: Or "to my thoughts" or "to my words." [h]**5.3** *requests*: Or "sacrifices."
[i]**Psalm 6** *instruments*: The Hebrew text adds "according to the sheminith," which may refer to a musical instrument with eight strings.

and my plea for mercy.
¹⁰ My enemies will be ashamed
and terrified,
as they quickly run away
in complete disgrace.

Psalm 7

[Written by David.^j
He sang this to the LORD because
of Cush from the tribe of Benjamin.]

The LORD Always Does Right

¹ You, LORD God,
are my protector.
Rescue me and keep me safe
from all who chase me.
² Or else they will rip me apart
like lions attacking a victim,
and no one will save me.

³ I am innocent, LORD God!
⁴ I have not betrayed a friend
or had pity on an enemy^k
who attacks for no reason.
⁵ If I have done any of this,
then let my enemies
chase and capture me.
Let them stomp me to death
and leave me in the dirt.

⁶ Get angry, LORD God!
Do something!
Attack my furious enemies.
See that justice is done.
⁷ Make the nations come to you,
as you sit on your throne^l
above them all.

⁸ Our LORD, judge the nations!
Judge me and show that I
am honest and innocent.
⁹ You know every heart and mind,
and you always do right.
Now make violent people stop,
but protect all of us
who obey you.

¹⁰ You, God, are my shield,
the protector of everyone
whose heart is right.
¹¹ You see that justice is done,
and each day
you take revenge.

¹² Whenever your enemies refuse
to change their ways,
you sharpen your sword
and string your bow.
¹³ Your deadly arrows are ready
with flaming tips.

¹⁴ An evil person is like a woman
about to give birth
to a hateful, deceitful,
and rebellious child.
¹⁵ Such people dig a deep hole,
then fall in it themselves.
¹⁶ The trouble they cause
comes back on them,
and their heads are crushed
by their own evil deeds.

¹⁷ I will praise you, LORD!
You always do right.
I will sing about you,
the LORD Most High.

Psalm 8

[A psalm by David for the music leader.^m*]*

The Wonderful Name of the LORD

¹ Our LORD and Ruler,
your name is wonderful
everywhere on earth!
You let your glory be seenⁿ
in the heavens above.
² With praises from children
and from tiny infants,
you have built a fortress.
It makes your enemies silent,
and all who turn against you
are left speechless.

³ I often think of the heavens
your hands have made,
and of the moon and stars
you put in place.
⁴ Then I ask, "Why do you care
about us humans?

---

^j**Psalm 7** *Written by David:* The Hebrew text has "a
shiggaion by David," which may refer to a psalm of
mourning. ^k**7.4** *had pity on an enemy:* Or "failed to
have pity on an enemy." ^l**7.7** *sit . . . throne:* Or "return
to your place." ^m**Psalm 8** *leader:* The Hebrew text
adds "according to the gittith," which may refer to
either a musical instrument or a tune.
ⁿ**8.1** *You . . . seen:* Or "I will worship your glory."

Why are you concerned
   for us weaklings?"
⁵You made us a little lower
   than you yourself,ᵒ
and you have crowned us
   with glory and honor.

⁶You let us rule everything
   your hands have made.
And you put all of it
   under our power—
⁷the sheep and the cattle,
   and every wild animal,
⁸the birds in the sky,
   the fish in the sea,
   and all ocean creatures.

⁹Our LORD and Ruler,
   your name is wonderful
   everywhere on earth!

Psalm 9

[*A psalm by David for the music leader.
To the tune "The Death of the Son."*]

Sing Praises to the LORD

¹I will praise you, LORD,
   with all my heart
and tell about the wonders
   you have worked.
²God Most High, I will rejoice;
   I will celebrate and sing
   because of you.

³When my enemies face you,
   they run away and stumble
   and are destroyed.
⁴You take your seat as judge,
   and your fair decisions prove
   that I was in the right.
⁵You warn the nations
   and destroy evil people;
you wipe out their names
   forever and ever.
⁶Our enemies are destroyed
   completely for all time.
Their cities are torn down,
   and they will never
   be remembered again.

⁷You rule forever, LORD,
   and you are on your throne,
   ready for judgment.

⁸You judge the world fairly
   and treat all nations
   with justice.
⁹The poor can run to you
   because you are a fortress
   in times of trouble.
¹⁰Everyone who honors your name
   can trust you,
because you are faithful
   to all who depend on you.

¹¹You rule from Zion, LORD,
   and we sing about you
to let the nations know
   everything you have done.
¹²You did not forget
   to punish the guilty
or listen to the cries
   of those in need.

¹³Please have mercy, LORD!
   My enemies mistreat me.
Keep me from the gates
   that lead to death,
¹⁴and I will sing about you
   at the gate to Zion.
I will be happy there
   because you rescued me.

¹⁵Our LORD, the nations fell
   into their own pits,
and their feet were caught
   in their own traps.
¹⁶You showed what you are like,
   and you made certain
   that justice is done,
but evil people are trapped
   by their own evil deeds.
¹⁷The wicked will go down
   to the world of the dead
to be with those nations
   that forgot about you.

¹⁸The poor and the homeless
   won't always be forgotten
   and without hope.

¹⁹Do something, LORD!
   Don't let the nations win.
Make them stand trial
   in your court of law.
²⁰Make the nations afraid

ᵒ**8.5** *you yourself*: Or "the angels" or "the beings in heaven."

and let them all discover
   just how weak they are.

Psalm 10

A Prayer for Help

[1] Why are you far away, LORD?
Why do you hide yourself
   when I am in trouble?
[2] Proud and brutal people
   hunt down the poor.
But let them get caught
   by their own evil plans!

[3] The wicked brag about
   their deepest desires.
Those greedy people hate
   and curse you, LORD.
[4] The wicked are too proud
   to turn to you
   or even think about you.
[5] They are always successful,
   though they can't understand
   your teachings,
and they keep sneering
   at their enemies.

[6] In their hearts they say,
   "Nothing can hurt us!
We'll always be happy
   and free from trouble."

[7] They curse and tell lies,
and all they talk about
   is how to be cruel
   or how to do wrong.

[8] They hide outside villages,
   waiting to strike and murder
   some innocent victim.
[9] They are hungry lions
   hiding in the bushes,
   hoping to catch
   some helpless passerby.
They trap the poor in nets
   and drag them away.
[10] They crouch down and wait
   to grab a victim.
[11] They say, "God can't see!
   He's got on a blindfold."

[12] Do something, LORD God,
   and use your powerful arm
   to help those in need.
[13] The wicked don't respect you.
In their hearts they say,
   "God won't punish us!"

[14] But you see the trouble
   and the distress,
   and you will do something.
The poor can count on you,
   and so can orphans.
[15] Now break the arms
   of all merciless people.

---

*Spiritual*Life—Is it okay to be angry at God? *(Psalm 10)*

Find the art of saying the "unsayable."
Putting your anger into words and pouring it forth is a bad idea—right? Yes, it usually is, especially when it spills on other people and they have to defend themselves or wade through hostile words.

But God isn't fragile. As long as you maintain a respectful tone, God is willing and more than able to be the recipient of your anger. For example, the psalmist, in great frustration, asked hard questions (10.1) and brooded over people's wickedness (10.2-5), but he also cared deeply for God's causes: These enemies of God could not understand his teachings (10.5). Yearning for truth, the psalmist became upset with the wicked who said that God couldn't see (10.11). But by the end he expressed confidence in God's faithfulness.

The next time you're angry, consider turning to this psalm and paraphrasing it to fit your situation. What good would that do? You would be addressing your anger to the one who is most capable of doing something constructive about your situation—God. Pouring forth these emotions builds intimacy with God and transforms your raw emotion into faith. (See also Numbers 20.1-13; Job 19; Habakkuk 1.2-5.)

Words To Remember: *You listen to the longings of those who suffer. You offer them hope, and you pay attention to their cries for help.—Psalm 10.17*

Punish them for doing wrong
   and make them stop.

[16] Our LORD, you will always rule,
   but nations will vanish
      from the earth.
[17] You listen to the longings
   of those who suffer.
You offer them hope,
   and you pay attention
      to their cries for help.
[18] You defend orphans
      and everyone else in need,
so that no one on earth
   can terrify others again.

Psalm 11

[A psalm by David for the music leader.]

Trusting the LORD

[1] The LORD is my fortress!
   Don't say to me,
"Escape like a bird
   to the mountains!"
[2] You tell me, "Watch out!
Those evil people have put
   their arrows on their bows,
and they are standing
in the shadows,
   aiming at good people.
[3] What can an honest person do
   when everything crumbles?"

[4] The LORD is sitting
in his sacred temple
   on his throne in heaven.
He knows everything we do
   because he sees us all.
[5] The LORD tests honest people,
but despises those
   who are cruel
   and love violence.
[6] He will send fiery coals[p]
and flaming sulfur
   down on the wicked,
and they will drink nothing
   but a scorching wind.

[7] The LORD always does right
   and wants justice done.
Everyone who does right
   will see his face.

Psalm 12

[A psalm by David for the music leader.[q]]

A Prayer for Help

[1] Please help me, LORD!
All who were faithful
and all who were loyal
   have disappeared.
[2] Everyone tells lies,
   and no one is sincere.
[3] Won't you chop off
all flattering tongues
   that brag so loudly?
[4] They say to themselves,
"We are great speakers.
   No one else has a chance."

[5] But you, LORD, tell them,
   "I will do something!
The poor are mistreated
and helpless people moan.
   I'll rescue all who suffer."

[6] Our LORD, you are true
   to your promises,
and your word is like silver
heated seven times
   in a fiery furnace.[r]
[7] You will protect us
and always keep us safe
   from those people.
[8] But all who are wicked
   will keep on strutting,
while everyone praises
   their shameless deeds.[s]

Psalm 13

[A psalm by David for the music leader.]

A Prayer for the LORD's Help

[1] How much longer, LORD,
   will you forget about me?
Will it be forever?
   How long will you hide?

---

[p]**11.6** *fiery coals:* Or "trouble, fire."   [q]**Psalm 12** *leader:*
The Hebrew text adds "according to the sheminith,"
which may be a musical instrument with eight strings.
[r]**12.6** *in a fiery furnace:* The Hebrew text has "in a
furnace to the ground," which may describe part of a
process for refining silver in Old Testament times.
[s]**12.8** *while . . . deeds:* One possible meaning for the
difficult Hebrew text.

2 How long must I be confused
    and miserable all day?
How long will my enemies
    keep beating me down?

3 Please listen, LORD God,
    and answer my prayers.
Make my eyes sparkle again,
    or else I will fall
        into the sleep of death.
4 My enemies will say,
    "Now we've won!"
They will be greatly pleased
    when I am defeated.

5 I trust your love,
    and I feel like celebrating
        because you rescued me.
6 You have been good to me, LORD,
    and I will sing about you.

Psalm 14

[*A psalm by David for the music leader.*]

No One Can Ignore the LORD

1 Only a fool would say,
    "There is no God!"
People like that are worthless;
    they are heartless and cruel
        and never do right.

2 From heaven the LORD
    looks down to see
if anyone is wise enough
    to search for him.
3 But all of them are corrupt;
    no one does right.

4 Won't you evil people learn?
    You refuse to pray,
and you gobble down
    the LORD's people.
5 But you will be frightened,
    because God is on the side
        of every good person.
6 You may spoil the plans
    of the poor,
        but the LORD protects them.

7 I long for someone from Zion
    to come and save Israel!
Our LORD, when you bless

your people again,
Jacob's family will be glad,
    and Israel will celebrate.

Psalm 15

[*A psalm by David.*]

Who May Worship the LORD?

1 Who may stay in God's temple
or live on the holy mountain
    of the LORD?

2 Only those who obey God
    and do as they should.
They speak the truth
3   and don't spread gossip;
they treat others fairly
    and don't say cruel things.

4 They hate worthless people,
    but show respect for all
        who worship the LORD.
And they keep their promises,
    no matter what the cost.
5 They lend their money
    without charging interest,
and they don't take bribes
    to hurt the innocent.

Those who do these things
    will always stand firm.

Psalm 16

[*A special psalm by David.*]

The Best Choice

1 Protect me, LORD God!
    I run to you for safety,
2 and I have said,
    "Only you are my Lord!
Every good thing I have
    is a gift from you."

3 Your people are wonderful,
    and they make me happy,[t]
4 but worshipers of other gods
    will have much sorrow.[u]

---

[t]**16.3** *Your people . . . happy:* Or "I was happy worshiping gods I thought were powerful." [u]**16.4** *but . . . sorrow:* One possible meaning for the difficult Hebrew text.

I refuse to offer sacrifices
of blood to those gods
or worship in their name.

⁵You, LORD, are all I want!
You are my choice,
and you keep me safe.
⁶You make my life pleasant,
and my future is bright.

⁷I praise you, LORD,
for being my guide.
Even in the darkest night,
your teachings fill my mind.

> My mother has said, "You can't teach your children to enjoy spinach if every time they see you eating it, you gag." My mother had such a joyous love for the Lord that I wanted a relationship with him like she had.
>
> ANNE GRAHAM LOTZ

⁸I will always look to you,
as you stand beside me
and protect me from fear.
⁹With all my heart,
I will celebrate,
and I can safely rest.

¹⁰I am your chosen one.
You won't leave me in the grave
or let my body decay.
¹¹You have shown me
the path to life,
and you make me glad
by being near to me.
Sitting at your right side,ᵛ
I will always be joyful.

Psalm 17

[A prayer by David.]

The Prayer of an Innocent Person

¹I am innocent, LORD!
Won't you listen as I pray
and beg for help?
I am honest!
Please hear my prayer.
²Only you can say
that I am innocent,
because only your eyes
can see the truth.

³You know my heart,
and even during the night
you have tested me
and found me innocent.
I have made up my mind
never to tell a lie.
⁴I don't do like others.
I obey your teachings
and am not cruel.
⁵I have followed you,
without ever stumbling.

⁶I pray to you, God,
because you will help me.
Listen and answer my prayer!
⁷   Show your wonderful love.
Your mighty arm protects those
who run to you for safety
from their enemies.
⁸Protect me as you would
your very own eyes;
hide me in the shadow
of your wings.

⁹Don't let my brutal enemies
attack from all sides
and kill me.
¹⁰They refuse to show mercy,
and they keep bragging.

¹¹They have caught up with me!
My enemies are everywhere,
eagerly hoping to smear me
in the dirt.
¹²They are like hungry lions
hunting for food,

ᵛ**16.11** *right side*: The place of power and honor.

or like young lions
    hiding in ambush.

¹³ Do something, LORD!
    Attack and defeat them.
Take your sword and save me
    from those evil people.
¹⁴ Use your powerful arm
    and rescue me
from the hands of mere humans
    whose world won't last.ʷ

You provide food
    for those you love.
Their children have plenty,
    and their grandchildren
    will have more than enough.

¹⁵ I am innocent, LORD,
    and I will see your face!
When I awake, all I want
    is to see you as you are.

Psalm 18

*[For the music leader. A psalm by David,
the LORD's servant. David sang this to the LORD
after the LORD had rescued him from his enemies,
but especially from Saul.]*

David's Song of Thanks

¹ I love you, LORD God,
    and you make me strong.

> *We are held together by a
> God who does not change.*
> RUTH SENTER

² You are my mighty rock,ˣ
    my fortress, my protector,
the rock where I am safe,
my shield, my powerful weapon,ʸ
    and my place of shelter.

³ I praise you, LORD!
I prayed, and you rescued me
    from my enemies.

⁴ Death had wrapped
    its ropes around me,
and I was almost swallowed
    by its flooding waters.

⁵ Ropes from the world
    of the dead
    had coiled around me,
and death had set a trap
    in my path.
⁶ I was in terrible trouble
    when I called out to you,
but from your temple
you heard me
    and answered my prayer.
⁷ The earth shook and shivered,
and the mountains trembled
    down to their roots.
You were angry
⁸   and breathed out smoke.
Scorching heat and fiery flames
    spewed from your mouth.

⁹ You opened the heavens
    like curtains,
and you came down
with storm clouds
    under your feet.
¹⁰ You rode on the backs
    of flying creatures
and swooped down
    with the wind as wings.
¹¹ Darkness was your robe;
thunderclouds filled the sky,
    hiding you from sight.
¹² Hailstones and fiery coals
    lit up the sky
    in front of you.

¹³ LORD Most High, your voice
    thundered from the heavens,
as hailstones and fiery coals
    poured down like rain.
¹⁴ You scattered your enemies
    with arrows of lightning.
¹⁵ You roared at the sea,
    and its deepest channels

ʷ**17.14** *last:* One possible meaning for the difficult
Hebrew text of verse 14.   ˣ**18.2** *mighty rock:* The
Hebrew text has "rock," which is sometimes used in
poetry to compare the Lord to a mountain where his
people can run for protection from their enemies.
ʸ**18.2** *my powerful weapon:* The Hebrew text has "the
horn," which refers to the horn of a bull, one of the
most powerful animals in ancient Palestine.

could be seen.
You snorted,
and the earth shook
   to its foundations.

16 You reached down from heaven,
   and you lifted me
   from deep in the ocean.
17 You rescued me from enemies,
   who were hateful
   and too powerful for me.
18 On the day disaster struck,
   they came and attacked,
   but you defended me.
19 When I was fenced in,
   you freed and rescued me
   because you love me.

20 You are good to me, LORD,
   because I do right,
   and you reward me
   because I am innocent.
21 I do what you want
   and never turn to do evil.
22 I keep your laws in mind
   and never look away
   from your teachings.
23 I obey you completely
   and guard against sin.
24 You have been good to me
   because I do right;
   you have rewarded me
   for being innocent
   by your standards.

25 You are always loyal
   to your loyal people,
   and you are faithful
   to the faithful.
26 With all who are sincere,
   you are sincere,
   but you treat the unfaithful
   as their deeds deserve.
27 You rescue the humble,
   but you put down all
   who are proud.

28 You, the LORD God,
   keep my lamp burning
   and turn darkness to light.
29 You help me defeat armies
   and capture cities.

30 Your way is perfect, LORD,
   and your word is correct.

You are a shield for those
   who run to you for help.
31 You alone are God!
   Only you are a mighty rock.ᶻ
32 You give me strength
   and guide me right.
33 You make my feet run as fast
   as those of a deer,
   and you help me stand
   on the mountains.

34 You teach my hands to fight
   and my arms to use
   a bow of bronze.
35 You alone are my shield.
   Your right hand supports me,
   and by coming to help me,
   you have made me famous.
36 You clear the way for me,
   and now I won't stumble.

37 I kept chasing my enemies,
   until I caught them
   and destroyed them.
38 I stuck my sword
   through my enemies,
   and they were crushed
   under my feet.
39 You helped me win victories,
   and you forced my attackers
   to fall victim to me.

40 You made my enemies run,
   and I killed them.
41 They cried out for help,
   but no one saved them;
   they called out to you,
   but there was no answer.
42 I ground them to dust
   blown by the wind,
   and I poured them out
   like mud in the streets.

43 You rescued me
   from stubborn people,
   and you made me the leader
   of foreign nations,
   who are now my slaves.
44 They obey and come crawling.
45   They have lost all courage,
   and from their fortresses,
   they come trembling.

ᶻ18.31 *mighty rock:* See the note at 18.2.

⁴⁶You are the living LORD!
  I will praise you.
  You are a mighty rock.ᶻ
  I will honor you
    for keeping me safe.
⁴⁷You took revenge for me,
  and you put nations
    in my power.
⁴⁸You protected me
    from violent enemies
  and made me much greater
    than all of them.

⁴⁹I will praise you, LORD,
  and I will honor you
    among the nations.
⁵⁰You give glorious victories
    to your chosen king.
  Your faithful love for David
  and for his descendants
    will never end.

Psalm 19

[*A psalm by David for the music leader.*]

The Wonders of God and the Goodness of His Law

¹The heavens keep telling
    the wonders of God,
  and the skies declare
    what he has done.
²Each day informs
    the following day;
  each night announces
    to the next.
³They don't speak a word,
  and there is never
    the sound of a voice.
⁴Yet their message reaches
    all the earth,
  and it travels
    around the world.

In the heavens a tent
    is set up for the sun.
⁵It rises like a bridegroom
  and gets ready like a hero
    eager to run a race.
⁶It travels all the way
  across the sky.
    Nothing hides from its heat.

⁷The Law of the LORD is perfect;
    it gives us new life.
  His teachings last forever,
  and they give wisdom
    to ordinary people.
⁸The LORD's instruction is right;
    it makes our hearts glad.
  His commands shine brightly,
    and they give us light.

⁹Worshiping the LORD is sacred;
    he will always be worshiped.
  All of his decisions
    are correct and fair.
¹⁰They are worth more
    than the finest gold
  and are sweeter than honey
    from a honeycomb.

¹¹By your teachings, Lord,
    I am warned;
  by obeying them,
    I am greatly rewarded.
¹²None of us know our faults.
  Forgive me when I sin
    without knowing it.
¹³Don't let me do wrong
    on purpose, Lord,
  or let sin have control
    over my life.
  Then I will be innocent,
  and not guilty
    of some terrible fault.

¹⁴Let my words and my thoughts
    be pleasing to you, LORD,
  because you are my mighty rockᶻ
    and my protector.

Psalm 20

[*A psalm by David for the music leader.*]

A Prayer for Victory

¹I pray that the LORD
  will listen when you
    are in trouble,
  and that the God of Jacob
    will keep you safe.
²May the LORD send help
    from his temple

ᶻ**18.46; 19.14** *mighty rock:* See the note at 18.2.

and come to your rescue
 from Mount Zion.
³May he remember your gifts
and be pleased
 with what you bring.

⁴May God do what you want most
 and let all go well for you.
⁵Then you will win victories,
 and we will celebrate,
while raising our banners
 in the name of our God.
May the LORD answer
 all of your prayers!

⁶I am certain, LORD,
that you will help
 your chosen king.
You will answer my prayers
from your holy place
 in heaven,
and you will save me
 with your mighty arm.

⁷Some people trust the power
of chariots or horses,
 but we trust you, LORD God.
⁸Others will stumble and fall,
but we will be strong
 and stand firm.

⁹Give the king victory, LORD,
 and answer our prayers.ᵃ

Psalm 21

[*A psalm by David for the music leader.*]

Thanking the LORD for Victory

¹Our LORD, your mighty power
 makes the king glad,
and he celebrates victories
 that you have given him.
²You did what he wanted most
 and never told him "No."
³You truly blessed the king,
and you placed on him
 a crown of finest gold.
⁴He asked to live a long time,
and you promised him life
 that never ends.

⁵The king is highly honored.
You have let him win victories

that have made him famous.
⁶You have given him blessings
 that will last forever,
and you have made him glad
 by being so near to him.
⁷LORD Most High,
 the king trusts you,
and your kindness
 keeps him from defeat.

⁸With your mighty arm, LORD,
you will strike down all
 of your hateful enemies.
⁹They will be destroyed by fire
 once you are here,
and because of your anger,
 flames will swallow them.
¹⁰You will wipe their families
from the earth,
 and they will disappear.
¹¹All their plans to harm you
 will come to nothing.
¹²You will make them run away
by shooting your arrows
 at their faces.

¹³Show your strength, LORD,
so that we may sing
 and praise your power.

Psalm 22

[*A psalm by David for the music leader.
To the tune "A Deer at Dawn."*]

Suffering and Praise

¹My God, my God, why have you
 deserted me?
Why are you so far away?
Won't you listen to my groans
 and come to my rescue?
²I cry out day and night,
but you don't answer,
 and I can never rest.

³Yet you are the holy God,
ruling from your throne
 and praised by Israel.
⁴Our ancestors trusted you,
 and you rescued them.

ᵃ20.9 *victory . . . prayers:* Or "victory. He (God or the king) answers us."

⁵When they cried out for help,
  you saved them,
and you did not let them down
  when they depended on you.

⁶But I am merely a worm,
    far less than human,
and I am hated and rejected
    by people everywhere.
⁷Everyone who sees me
    makes fun and sneers.
They shake their heads,
⁸   and say, "Trust the LORD!
If you are his favorite,
let him protect you
and keep you safe."

⁹You, LORD, brought me
    safely through birth,
and you protected me
  when I was a baby
    at my mother's breast.
¹⁰From the day I was born,
    I have been in your care,
and from the time of my birth,
    you have been my God.

¹¹Don't stay far off
  when I am in trouble
    with no one to help me.
¹²Enemies are all around
    like a herd of wild bulls.

Powerful bulls from Bashan[b]
    are everywhere.
¹³My enemies are like lions
  roaring and attacking
    with jaws open wide.

¹⁴I have no more strength
    than a few drops of water.
All my bones are out of joint;
    my heart is like melted wax.
¹⁵My strength has dried up
    like a broken clay pot,
and my tongue sticks
    to the roof of my mouth.
You, God, have left me
    to die in the dirt.

¹⁶Brutal enemies attack me
    like a pack of dogs,
tearing at[c] my hands
    and my feet.
¹⁷I can count all my bones,
    and my enemies just stare
    and sneer at me.
¹⁸They took my clothes
    and gambled for them.

---

[b]22.12 *Bashan*: A land east of the Jordan River, where there were pastures suitable for raising fine cattle.
[c]22.16 *tearing at*: One possible meaning for the difficult Hebrew text.

SingleLife—How can I overcome my feelings of loneliness? *(Psalm 22)*

Take your pain to God.
Can God possibly understand loneliness? Scripture doesn't say that God gets lonely, but he did create humankind, then watched us reject him. He longs for us to have continual fellowship with him, because that's the way he designed us.

The pain of loneliness, then, is not foreign to the one who made us to be like himself (Genesis 1.27). This psalm, in fact, describes that pain: the author felt like an earthworm, something to be stepped on and squashed; he felt cornered by wild bulls and open-mouthed lions, weak as a dried-up piece of "broken clay pot" with a heart like "melted wax" (22.6,12-15). Which, if any, of those pictures describe how you have felt when you are lonely?

Notice also how the last nine verses of the psalm emphasize worshiping the Lord: "When your people meet, you will fill my heart with your praises, LORD, and everyone will see me keep my promises to you" (22.25). What an appropriate antidote to loneliness—to enjoy God's presence, to live in an intense awareness that the one who created you for a love relationship with him does protect you and keep you safe. (See also Psalm 68.4-6; Matthew 26.36-46; 2 Timothy 4.16-18; Revelation 3.20-22.)

Words To Remember: *When I cried out, he listened and did not turn away.*
—Psalm 22.24

¹⁹ Don't stay far away, LORD!
My strength comes from you,
so hurry and help.
²⁰ Rescue me from enemy swords
and save me from those dogs.
²¹   Don't let lions eat me.

You rescued me from the horns
of wild bulls,
²² and when your people meet,
I will praise you, LORD.

²³ All who worship the LORD,
now praise him!
You belong to Jacob's family
and to the people of Israel,
so fear and honor the LORD!
²⁴ The LORD doesn't hate
or despise the helpless
in all of their troubles.
When I cried out, he listened
and did not turn away.

²⁵ When your people meet,
you will fill my heart
with your praises, LORD,
and everyone will see me
keep my promises to you.
²⁶ The poor will eat and be full,
and all who worship you
will be thankful
and live in hope.

²⁷ Everyone on this earth
will remember you, LORD.
People all over the world
will turn and worship you,
²⁸ because you are in control,
the ruler of all nations.

²⁹ All who are rich
and have more than enough
will bow down to you, Lord.
Even those who are dying
and almost in the grave
will come and bow down.
³⁰ In the future, everyone
will worship and learn
about you, our Lord.
³¹ People not yet born
will be told,
"The Lord has saved us!"

Psalm 23
.
[A psalm by David.]

The Good Shepherd

¹ You, LORD, are my shepherd.
I will never be in need.
² You let me rest in fields
of green grass.
You lead me to streams
of peaceful water,
³   and you refresh my life.

SingleLife—How can I feel whole when the world sees me as half? *(Psalm 23)*

Let God stick up for you.
Imagine you're in a room where people are thinking you are *only half*. Then Jesus shows up beside you and responds, "You mean her? Not a chance. I've filled her with an overflowing life. I've done special things for her."

Is that far-fetched? No, David imagined the Lord was right beside him as he wrote Psalm 23. He portrayed himself sitting at a table enjoying a feast God prepared especially for him, while his enemies watched. Then God honored David as a guest until his cup was filled to the brim and then some (23.5).

Meditating on this scene comes in handy when we get into situations in which we might feel inadequate. With this in mind, we can socialize with the confidence of a woman who has received special treatment from an important figure. We don't have to defend ourselves against comments and looks, but we can rely on God to do the enlightening. While people can make us feel we need something more (specifically, a man) to be better off, we can realize that God has already given us all we need—himself! **(See also Isaiah 40.21-31; Philippians 1.12-30.)**

Words To Remember: *You treat me to a feast, while my enemies watch. You honor me as your guest, and you fill my cup until it overflows.—Psalm 23.5*

You are true to your name,
and you lead me
   along the right paths.
⁴I may walk through valleys
as dark as death,
   but I won't be afraid.
You are with me,
and your shepherd's rod*ᵈ*
   makes me feel safe.

⁵You treat me to a feast,
   while my enemies watch.
You honor me as your guest,
and you fill my cup
   until it overflows.
⁶Your kindness and love
will always be with me
   each day of my life,
and I will live forever
   in your house, LORD.

Psalm 24

[A psalm by David.]

Who Can Enter the LORD's Temple?

¹The earth and everything on it
   belong to the LORD.
The world and its people
   belong to him.
²The LORD placed it all
   on the oceans and rivers.

³Who may climb the LORD's hill*ᵉ*
   or stand in his holy temple?
⁴Only those who do right
   for the right reasons,
and don't worship idols
   or tell lies under oath.
⁵The LORD God, who saves them,
   will bless and reward them,
⁶because they worship and serve
   the God of Jacob.*ᶠ*
⁷Open the ancient gates,
so that the glorious king
   may come in.

⁸Who is this glorious king?
He is our LORD, a strong
   and mighty warrior.

⁹Open the ancient gates,
so that the glorious king
   may come in.

¹⁰Who is this glorious king?
He is our LORD,
   the All-Powerful!

Psalm 25

[By David.]

A Prayer for Guidance and Help

¹I offer you my heart, LORD God,
²   and I trust you.
Don't make me ashamed
   or let enemies defeat me.
³Don't disappoint any
   of your worshipers,
but disappoint all
   deceitful liars.
⁴Show me your paths
   and teach me to follow;
⁵guide me by your truth
   and instruct me.
You keep me safe,
   and I always trust you.

⁶Please, LORD, remember,
you have always
   been patient and kind.
⁷Forget each wrong I did
   when I was young.
Show how truly kind you are
   and remember me.
⁸You are honest and merciful,
and you teach sinners
   how to follow your path.

⁹You lead humble people
to do what is right
   and to stay on your path.
¹⁰In everything you do,
   you are kind and faithful
to everyone who keeps
   our agreement with you.

¹¹Be true to your name, LORD,
   by forgiving each one
   of my terrible sins.

ᵈ23.4 shepherd's rod: The Hebrew text mentions two objects carried by the shepherd: a club to defend against wild animals and a long pole to guide and control the sheep. *ᵉ24.3 the LORD's hill:* The hill in Jerusalem where the temple was built. *ᶠ24.6 worship . . . Jacob:* Two ancient translations; Hebrew "worship God and serve the descendants of Jacob."

¹²You will show the right path
    to all who worship you.
¹³They will have plenty,
    and then their children
        will receive the land.

¹⁴Our LORD, you are the friend
    of your worshipers,
    and you make an agreement
        with all of us.
¹⁵I always look to you,
    because you rescue me
        from every trap.
¹⁶I am lonely and troubled.
    Show that you care
        and have pity on me.
¹⁷My awful worries keep growing.
    Rescue me from sadness.
¹⁸See my troubles and misery
    and forgive my sins.

¹⁹Look at all my enemies!
    See how much they hate me.
²⁰I come to you for shelter.
    Protect me, keep me safe,
        and don't disappoint me.
²¹I obey you with all my heart,
    and I trust you, knowing
        that you will save me.

²²Our God, please save Israel
    from all of its troubles.

Psalm 26

[*By David.*]

The Prayer of an Innocent Person

¹Show that I am right, LORD!
    I stay true to myself,
    and I have trusted you
        without doubting.
²Test my thoughts and find out
    what I am like.
³I never forget your kindness,
    and I am always faithful
        to you.ᵍ
⁴I don't spend my time
    with worthless liars
⁵   or go with evil crowds.

⁶I wash my hands, LORD,
    to show my innocence,
    and I worship at your altar,
⁷while gratefully singing
    about your wonders.
⁸I love the temple
    where you live, and where
        your glory shines.
⁹Don't sweep me away,
    as you do sinners.
    Don't punish me with death
    as you do those people
        who are brutal

ᵍ**26.3** *I am . . . to you:* Or "I trust your faithfulness."

⌐℞

PARENTING&*family*—How can I know what's best for my elderly parents?
(*Psalm 25*)

Keep communication lines open.
What's good for aging parents one month may not be best the next month. Forget finding the perfect answer, and don't stop seeking God.

Even after the most difficult questions are answered (Should Mom stay in her house? Should Dad have that surgery?), other issues return. Does she feel loved? Is he taking his medicine? The same dilemmas occur in different ways: Should I hover or step back? Should I do what I think is best or try to second-guess my parents' desires? When your parents don't seem to know what to do, ask God to show you cues in their behavior and offhand comments. Ask God to lead you in ways that are both honest and merciful (25.8).

What if you make a wrong decision? Take the situation to God in prayer because God rescues us "from every trap" (25.15). Just as your parents watched and prayed over you as a child (and felt uncertain and inadequate), you now do the same. You are offering a steady hand to your parents as they once did to you. (See also Proverbs 23.22-25; Joel 2.28-32; 1 Corinthians 15.35-58; 1 Timothy 5.1-7.)

⌐℞ Words To Remember: *You will show the right path to all who worship you.*
—Psalm 25.12

10   or full of meanness
      or who bribe others.
11 I stay true to myself.
      Be kind and rescue me.

12 Now I stand on solid ground!
   And when your people meet,
      I will praise you, LORD.

Psalm 27

[By David.]

A Prayer of Praise

1 You, LORD, are the light
      that keeps me safe.
   I am not afraid of anyone.
   You protect me,
      and I have no fears.
2 Brutal people may attack
   and try to kill me,
      but they will stumble.
   Fierce enemies may attack,
      but they will fall.
3 Armies may surround me,
      but I won't be afraid;
   war may break out,
      but I will trust you.

4 I ask only one thing, LORD:
   Let me live in your house
      every day of my life

to see how wonderful you are
   and to pray in your temple.

5 In times of trouble,
      you will protect me.
   You will hide me in your tent
   and keep me safe
      on top of a mighty rock.*h*
6 You will let me defeat
      all of my enemies.
   Then I will celebrate,
      as I enter your tent
   with animal sacrifices
      and songs of praise.

7 Please listen when I pray!
      Have pity. Answer my prayer.
8 My heart tells me to pray.
   I am eager to see your face,
9   so don't hide from me.
   I am your servant,
      and you have helped me.
         Don't turn from me in anger.
   You alone keep me safe.
         Don't reject or desert me.
10 Even if my father and mother
   should desert me,
      you will take care of me.

11 Teach me to follow, LORD,
   and lead me on the right path

---

*h*27.5 *mighty rock:* See the note at 18.2.

WORK—How can I deal with a dishonest coworker? *(Psalm 26)*

Stay true to yourself—and don't doubt God's power.
Let's face it. Not everyone you work with will always be honest. Maybe you've worked long hours to come up with a winning slogan. Then just before you're ready to present it to your supervisor, a coworker who snoops through your desk claims credit for your concept. Or you discover some money missing from the cash register at the end of the day. When you bring it to the store owner's attention, you get blamed (even though you know the store owner's son had his hand in the till).

When life isn't fair, remember this psalm, David's plea to God to defend him: "Show that I am right, LORD!" Although it may look like dishonest people not only survive but thrive, they'll have to undergo a reckoning someday.

The next time you're blamed for something someone else does, stay true to yourself and trust God without doubting, like David did in this psalm. God always has the upper hand. (See also Proverbs 28.11-26; Amos 2; Habakkuk 2.4-17.)

Words To Remember: *Show that I am right, LORD! I stay true to myself, and I have trusted you without doubting. Test my thoughts and find out what I am like. I never forget your kindness, and I am always faithful to you.—Psalm 26.1-3*

because of my enemies.
¹² Don't let them do to me
   what they want.
People tell lies about me
   and make terrible threats,

*Real life is sometimes hard,
scary, tragic. But it's also filled
with hope and God's grace.*

JANE JOHNSON STRUCK

¹³ but I know I will live
   to see how kind you are.

¹⁴ Trust the LORD!
Be brave and strong
   and trust the LORD.

Psalm 28

[By David.]

A Prayer for Help

¹ Only you, LORD,
   are a mighty rock!ʰ
Don't refuse to help me
   when I pray.
If you don't answer me,
   I will soon be dead.
² Please listen to my prayer
   and my cry for help,
as I lift my hands
   toward your holy temple.

³ Don't drag me away, LORD,
   with those cruel people,
who speak kind words,
   while planning trouble.
⁴ Treat them as they deserve!
   Punish them for their sins.
⁵ They don't pay any attention
   to your wonderful deeds.
Now you will destroy them
   and leave them in ruin.

⁶ I praise you, LORD,
   for answering my prayers.

⁷ You are my strong shield,
   and I trust you completely.
You have helped me,
   and I will celebrate
   and thank you in song.

⁸ You give strength
   to your people, LORD,
and you save and protect
   your chosen ones.
⁹ Come save us and bless us.
Be our shepherd and always
   carry us in your arms.

Psalm 29

[A psalm by David.]

The Voice of the LORD in a Storm

¹ All of you angelsⁱ in heaven,
   honor the glory and power
      of the LORD!
² Honor the wonderful name
      of the LORD,
and worship the LORD
   most holy and glorious.ʲ

³ The voice of the LORD
   echoes over the oceans.
The glorious LORD God
   thunders above the roar
      of the raging sea,
⁴ and his voice is mighty
   and marvelous.
⁵ The voice of the LORD
   destroys the cedar trees;
the LORD shatters cedars
   on Mount Lebanon.
⁶ God makes Mount Lebanon
   skip like a calf
and Mount Hermon
   jump like a wild ox.

⁷ The voice of the LORD
   makes lightning flash
⁸   and the desert tremble.
And because of the LORD,
   the desert near Kadesh
   shivers and shakes.

ʰ**28.1** *mighty rock*: See the note at 18.2.   ⁱ**29.1** *angels*:
Or "supernatural beings" or "gods."   ʲ**29.2** *most . . .
glorious*: Or "in his holy place" or "and wear your
glorious clothes."

[9] The voice of the LORD
makes deer give birth
before their time.[k]
Forests are stripped of leaves,
and the temple is filled
with shouts of praise.

[10] The LORD rules on his throne,
king of the flood[l] forever.
[11] Pray that our LORD
will make us strong
and give us peace.

Psalm 30

[A psalm by David for the dedication of the temple.]

A Prayer of Thanks

[1] I will praise you, LORD!
You saved me from the grave
and kept my enemies
from celebrating my death.
[2] I prayed to you, LORD God,
and you healed me,
[3] saving me from death
and the grave.

[4] Your faithful people, LORD,
will praise you with songs
and honor your holy name.
[5] Your anger lasts a little while,
but your kindness lasts
for a lifetime.
At night we may cry,
but when morning comes
we will celebrate.

[6] I was carefree and thought,
"I'll never be shaken!"
[7] You, LORD, were my friend,
and you made me strong
as a mighty mountain.
But when you hid your face,
I was crushed.

[8] I prayed to you, LORD,
and in my prayer I said,
[9] "What good will it do you
if I am in the grave?
Once I have turned to dust,
how can I praise you
or tell how loyal you are?
[10] Have pity, LORD! Help!"

[11] You have turned my sorrow
into joyful dancing.
No longer am I sad
and wearing sackcloth.[m]
[12] I thank you from my heart,
and I will never stop
singing your praises,
my LORD and my God.

Psalm 31

[A psalm by David for the music leader.]

A Prayer for Protection

[1] I come to you, LORD,
for protection.
Don't let me be ashamed.
Do as you have promised
and rescue me.
[2] Listen to my prayer
and hurry to save me.
Be my mighty rock[n]
and the fortress
where I am safe.

[3] You, LORD God,
are my mighty rock
and my fortress.
Lead me and guide me,
so that your name
will be honored.
[4] Protect me from hidden traps
and keep me safe.
[5] You are faithful,
and I trust you
because you rescued me.

[6] I hate the worshipers
of worthless idols,
but I trust you, LORD.
[7] I celebrate and shout
because you are kind.
You saw all my suffering,
and you cared for me.
[8] You kept me from the hands

---

[k]**29.9** *makes . . . time*: Or "twists the oak trees around."
[l]**29.10** *king of the flood*: In ancient times the people of
Israel believed that a mighty ocean surrounded all of
creation, and that God could release the water to flood
the earth. [m]**30.11** *sackcloth*: A rough, dark-colored
cloth made from goat or camel hair and used to make
grain sacks. It was worn in times of trouble or
sorrow. [n]**31.2** *mighty rock*: See the note at 18.2.

of my enemies,
and you set me free.

⁹Have pity, LORD!
I am hurting and almost blind.
My whole body aches.
¹⁰I have known only sorrow
all my life long, and I suffer
year after year.
I am weak from sin,
and my bones are limp.

¹¹My enemies insult me.
Neighbors are even worse,
and I disgust my friends.
People meet me on the street,
and they turn and run.

> *Discovering I was weak
> enough to stumble and repeat
> my mistakes kept me running
> back to God for help. I was
> humbled by knowing that
> although Christ is perfect, he
> suffered far worse things than I
> ever will. He died so I might
> accept his love and forgiveness
> and have eternal life.*
>
> DONNA RICE HUGHES

¹²I am completely forgotten
like someone dead.
I am merely a broken dish.
¹³I hear the crowds whisper,
"Everyone is afraid!"
They are plotting and scheming
to murder me.

¹⁴But I trust you, LORD,
and I claim you as my God.
¹⁵My life is in your hands.
Save me from enemies
who hunt me down.
¹⁶Smile on me, your servant.
Have pity and rescue me.

¹⁷I pray only to you.
Don't disappoint me.
Disappoint my cruel enemies
until they lie silent
in their graves.
¹⁸Silence those proud liars!
Make them stop bragging
and insulting your people.

¹⁹You are wonderful,
and while everyone watches,
you store up blessings for all
who honor and trust you.
²⁰You are their shelter
from harmful plots,
and you are their protection
from vicious gossip.

²¹I will praise you, LORD,
for showing great kindness
when I was like a city
under attack.
²²I was terrified and thought,
"They've chased me
far away from you!"
But you answered my prayer
when I shouted for help.

²³All who belong to the LORD,
show how you love him.
The LORD protects the faithful,
but he severely punishes
everyone who is proud.
²⁴All who trust the LORD,
be cheerful and strong.

Psalm 32

[A special psalm by David.]

The Joy of Forgiveness

¹Our God, you bless everyone
whose sins you forgive
and wipe away.
²You bless them by saying,
"You told me your sins,
without trying to hide them,
and now I forgive you."

³Before I confessed my sins,
my bones felt limp,
and I groaned all day long.
⁴Night and day your hand
weighed heavily on me,

and my strength was gone
  as in the summer heat.

⁵ So I confessed my sins
  and told them all to you.
I said, "I'll tell the LORD
  each one of my sins."
Then you forgave me
  and took away my guilt.

⁶ We worship you, Lord,
  and we should always pray
whenever we find out
  that we have sinned.ᵒ
Then we won't be swept away
  by a raging flood.
⁷ You are my hiding place!
  You protect me from trouble,
and you put songs in my heart
  because you have saved me.

⁸ You said to me,
"I will point out the road
  that you should follow.
I will be your teacher
  and watch over you.
⁹ Don't be stupid
  like horses and mules
that must be led with ropes
  to make them obey."

¹⁰ All kinds of troubles
  will strike the wicked,
but your kindness shields those
  who trust you, LORD.
¹¹ And so your good people
  should celebrate and shout.

Psalm 33

Sing Praises to the LORD

¹ You are the LORD's people.
Obey him and celebrate!
  He deserves your praise.
² Praise the LORD with harps!
Use harps with ten strings
  to make music for him.
³ Sing a new song. Shout!
  Play beautiful music.

⁴ The LORD is truthful;
  he can be trusted.
⁵ He loves justice and fairness,

and he is kind to everyone
  everywhere on earth.

⁶ The LORD made the heavens
  and everything in them
    by his word.
⁷ He scooped up the ocean
  and stored the water.
⁸ Everyone in this world
  should worship and honor
    the LORD!
⁹ As soon as he spoke
  the world was created;
at his command,
  the earth was formed.

> *Most of us believe that faith in Christ brings contentment, peace, and joy. So when we still experience fear, we feel like a spiritual failure! However, we can continue to respond with fearful emotions—or recognize God's power to help.*
>
> CAROL KENT

¹⁰ The LORD destroys the plans
  and spoils the schemes
    of the nations.
¹¹ But what the LORD has planned
  will stand forever.
    His thoughts never change.
¹² The LORD blesses each nation
  that worships only him.
    He blesses his chosen ones.
¹³ The LORD looks at the world
¹⁴ from his throne in heaven,
  and he watches us all.
¹⁵ The LORD gave us each a mind,
  and nothing we do
    can be hidden from him.

ᵒ**32.6** *whenever . . . sinned:* Hebrew "at a time of finding only."

¹⁶Mighty armies alone
    cannot win wars for a king;
great strength by itself
    cannot keep a soldier safe.
¹⁷In war the strength of a horse
  cannot be trusted
    to take you to safety.
¹⁸But the LORD watches over
  all who honor him
    and trust his kindness.
¹⁹He protects them from death
  and starvation.

²⁰We depend on you, LORD,
    to help and protect us.
²¹You make our hearts glad
  because we trust you,
    the only God.
²²Be kind and bless us!
    We depend on you.

Psalm 34

[Written by David when he pretended to be crazy in front of Abimelech, so that Abimelech would send him away, and David could leave.]

Honor the LORD

¹I will always praise the LORD.
²With all my heart,
    I will praise the LORD.
Let all who are helpless,
    listen and be glad.
³Honor the LORD with me!
    Celebrate his great name.

⁴I asked the LORD for help,
  and he saved me
    from all my fears.
⁵Keep your eyes on the LORD!
You will shine like the sun
    and never blush with shame.
⁶I was a nobody, but I prayed,
  and the LORD saved me
    from all my troubles.

⁷If you honor the LORD,
    his angel will protect you.
⁸Discover for yourself
    that the LORD is kind.
Come to him for protection,
    and you will be glad.

⁹Honor the LORD!
    You are his special people.
No one who honors the LORD
    will ever be in need.
¹⁰Young lions^p may go hungry
  or even starve,
but if you trust the LORD,
  you will never miss out
    on anything good.

¹¹Come, my children, listen
  as I teach you
    to respect the LORD.
¹²Do you want to live
    and enjoy a long life?

No matter what kind of thrill we get from its conspiratorial camaraderie, no matter what kind of secret power we feel, gossip undermines our relationship to God and others.

JANE JOHNSON STRUCK

¹³Then don't say cruel things
    and don't tell lies.
¹⁴Do good instead of evil
    and try to live at peace.

¹⁵If you obey the LORD,
  he will watch over you
    and answer your prayers.
¹⁶But God despises evil people,
  and he will wipe them all
from the earth,
    till they are forgotten.
¹⁷When his people pray for help,
  he listens and rescues them
    from their troubles.
¹⁸The LORD is there to rescue
  all who are discouraged
    and have given up hope.

---

*p*34.10 *Young lions:* In the Psalms wild animals often stand for God's enemies.

¹⁹ The LORD's people
  may suffer a lot,
but he will always
  bring them safely through.
²⁰ Not one of their bones
  will ever be broken.

²¹ Wicked people are killed
  by their own evil deeds,
and if you hate God's people
  you will be punished.
²² The LORD saves the lives
  of his servants.
Run to him for protection,
  and you won't be punished.

Psalm 35

[A psalm by David.]

A Prayer for Protection from Enemies

¹ Fight my enemies, LORD!
  Attack my attackers!
²   Shield me and help me.
³ Aim your spear at everyone
  who hunts me down,
    but promise to save me.

⁴ Let all who want to kill me
  be disappointed
    and disgraced.
Chase away and confuse
  all who plan to harm me.
⁵ Send your angel after them
  and let them be like straw
    in the wind.
⁶ Make them run in the dark
  on a slippery road,
    as your angel chases them.
⁷ I did them no harm,
  but they hid a net
    to trap me,
  and they dug a deep pit
    to catch and kill me.
⁸ Surprise them with disaster!
  Trap them in their own nets
and let them fall and rot
  in the pits they have dug.

⁹ I will celebrate and be joyful
  because you, LORD,
    have saved me.
¹⁰ Every bone in my body
  will shout:

"No one is like the LORD!"
You protect the helpless
  from those in power;
you save the poor and needy
  from those who hurt them.

¹¹ Liars accuse me of crimes
  I know nothing about.
¹² They repay evil for good,
  and I feel all alone.
¹³ When they were sick,
  I wore sackcloth^q
    and went without food.^r
  I truly prayed for them,^s
¹⁴ as I would for a friend
  or a relative.
  I was in sorrow and mourned,
    as I would for my mother.

¹⁵ I have stumbled,
  and worthless liars
I don't even know
  surround me and sneer.
¹⁶ Worthless people make fun^t
  and never stop laughing.
¹⁷ But all you do is watch!
  When will you do something?
Save me from the attack
  of those vicious lions.
¹⁸ And when your people meet,
  I will praise you
and thank you, Lord,
  in front of them all.

¹⁹ Don't let my brutal enemies
  be glad because of me.
They hate me for no reason.
Don't let them wink
  behind my back.
²⁰ They say hurtful things,
  and they lie to people
    who want to live in peace.
²¹ They are quick to accuse me.
They say, "You did it!
  We saw you ourselves."

²² You see everything, LORD!
  Please don't keep silent
    or stay so far away.

---

²³ Fight to defend me, Lord God,
²⁴ and prove that I am right
      by your standards.
   Don't let them laugh at me
²⁵   or say to each other,
   "Now we've got what we want!
      We'll gobble him down!"

²⁶ Disappoint and confuse
   all who are glad
      to see me in trouble,
   but disgrace and embarrass
   my proud enemies who say to me,
      "You are nothing!"

²⁷ Let all who want me to win
      be happy and joyful.
   From now on let them say,
      "The LORD is wonderful!
   God is glad when all goes well
      for his servant."
²⁸ Then I will shout all day,
   "Praise the LORD God!
      He did what was right."

Psalm 36

*[For the music leader by David,
the LORD's servant.]*

Human Sin and God's Goodness

¹ Sinners don't respect God;
      sin is all they think about.
² They like themselves too much
   to hate their own sins
      or even to see them.
³ They tell deceitful lies,
   and they don't have the sense
      to live right.
⁴ Those people stay awake,
      thinking up mischief,
   and they follow the wrong road,
      refusing to turn from sin.

⁵ Your love is faithful, LORD,
   and even the clouds in the sky
      can depend on you.
⁶ Your decisions are always fair.
   They are firm like mountains,
      deep like the sea,
   and all people and animals
      are under your care.

⁷ Your love is a treasure,
   and everyone finds shelter
      in the shadow of your wings.
⁸ You give your guests a feast
      in your house,
   and you serve a tasty drink
      that flows like a river.
⁹ The life-giving fountain
      belongs to you,
   and your light gives light
      to each of us.

¹⁰ Our LORD, keep showing love
      to everyone who knows you,
   and use your power to save all
      whose thoughts please you.
¹¹ Don't let those proud
      and merciless people
   kick me around
      or chase me away.

¹² Look at those wicked people!
   They are knocked down,
      never to get up again.

Psalm 37

[By David.]

Trust the LORD

¹ Don't be annoyed by anyone
   who does wrong,
      and don't envy them.
² They will soon disappear
      like grass without rain.

³ Trust the LORD and live right!
   The land will be yours,
      and you will be safe.
⁴ Do what the LORD wants,
   and he will give you
      your heart's desire.

⁵ Let the LORD lead you
      and trust him to help.
⁶ Then it will be as clear
   as the noonday sun
      that you were right.

⁷ Be patient and trust the LORD.
      Don't let it bother you
   when all goes well for those
      who do sinful things.
⁸ Don't be angry or furious.

Anger can lead to sin.
⁹ All sinners will disappear,
but if you trust the LORD,
the land will be yours.

¹⁰ Sinners will soon disappear,
never to be found,
¹¹ but the poor will take the land
and enjoy a big harvest.

¹² Merciless people make plots
against good people
and snarl like animals,
¹³ but the Lord laughs and knows
their time is coming soon.
¹⁴ The wicked kill with swords
and shoot arrows to murder
the poor and the needy
and all who do right.
¹⁵ But they will be killed
by their own swords,
and their arrows
will be broken.

¹⁶ It is better to live right
and be poor
than to be sinful and rich.
¹⁷ The wicked will lose all
of their power,
but the LORD gives strength
to everyone who is good.

¹⁸ Those who obey the LORD
are daily in his care,
and what he has given them
will be theirs forever.
¹⁹ They won't be in trouble
when times are bad,
and they will have plenty
when food is scarce.

²⁰ Wicked people are enemies
of the LORD
and will vanish like smoke
from a field on fire.

²¹ An evil person borrows
and never pays back;
a good person is generous
and never stops giving.
²² Everyone the LORD blesses
will receive the land;
everyone the LORD curses
will be destroyed.

²³ If you do what the LORD wants,
he will make certain
each step you take is sure.
²⁴ The LORD will hold your hand,
and if you stumble,
you still won't fall.

²⁵ As long as I can remember,
good people have never
been left helpless,
and their children have never
gone begging for food.
²⁶ They gladly give and lend,
and their children
turn out good.

²⁷ If you stop sinning
and start doing right,
you will keep living
and be secure forever.
²⁸ The LORD loves justice,
and he won't ever desert
his faithful people.
He always protects them,
but destroys the children
of the wicked.
²⁹ God's people will own the land
and live here forever.

³⁰ Words of wisdom come
when good people speak
for justice.
³¹ They remember God's teachings,
and they never take
a wrong step.

³² The wicked try to trap
and kill good people,
³³ but the LORD is on their side,
and he will defend them
when they are on trial.

³⁴ Trust the LORD and follow him.
He will give you the land,
and you will see
the wicked destroyed.

³⁵ I have seen brutal people
abuse others and grow strong
like trees in rich soil.ᵘ
³⁶ Suddenly they disappeared!

ᵘ37.35 like . . . soil: One possible meaning for the
difficult Hebrew text.

I looked, but they were gone
and no longer there.

37 Think of the bright future
waiting for all the families
of honest and innocent
and peace-loving people.
38 But not a trace will be left
of the wicked
or their families.

39 The LORD protects his people,
and they can come to him
in times of trouble.
40 The LORD helps them
and saves them from the wicked
because they run to him.

Psalm 38

*[A psalm by David to be used
when an offering is made.]*

A Prayer in Times of Trouble

1 When you are angry, LORD,
please don't punish me
or even correct me.
2 You shot me with your arrows,
and you struck me
with your hand.

3 My body hurts all over
because of your anger.
Even my bones are in pain,
and my sins 4 are so heavy
that I am crushed.

5 Because of my foolishness,
I am covered with sores
that stink and spread.
6 My body is twisted and bent,
and I groan all day long.
7 Fever has my back in flames,
and I hurt all over.
8 I am worn out and weak,
moaning and in distress.

9 You, Lord, know every one
of my deepest desires,
and my noisy groans
are no secret to you.
10 My heart is beating fast.
I feel weak all over,
and my eyes are red.

11 Because of my sickness,
no friends or neighbors
will come near me.

*It's God who gives us the
desire for children, the desire
for motherhood. Where else
would we get a yearning to
serve, to love unconditionally,
to give unselfish care? We
can always answer God's
call for spiritual motherhood,
a powerful and fulfilling
role in its own right.*

DANDI DALEY MACKALL

12 All who want me dead
set traps to catch me,
and those who want
to harm and destroy me
plan and plot all day.

13 I am not able to hear
or speak a word;
14 I am completely deaf
and can't make a sound.

15 I trust you, LORD God,
and you will do something.
16 I said, "Don't let them laugh
or brag because I slip."

17 I am about to collapse
from constant pain.
18 I told you my sins,
and I am sorry for them.
19 Many deadly and powerful
enemies hate me,
20 and they repay evil for good
because I try to do right.

21 You are the LORD God!
Stay nearby
and don't desert me.
22 You are the one who saves me.
Please hurry and help.

Psalm 39

[A psalm by David for Jeduthun, the music leader.]

A Prayer for Forgiveness

¹ I told myself, "I'll be careful
    not to sin by what I say,
and I'll muzzle my mouth
    when evil people are near."
² I kept completely silent,
but it did no good,ᵛ
    and I hurt even worse.

³ I felt a fire burning inside,
    and the more I thought,
the more it burned,
    until at last I said:
⁴ "Please, LORD,
show me my future.
    Will I soon be gone?
⁵ You made my life short,
so brief that the time
    means nothing to you.

"Human life is but a breath,
⁶ and it disappears
    like a shadow.
Our struggles are senseless;
we store up more and more,
    without ever knowing
    who will get it all.

⁷ "What am I waiting for?
    I depend on you, Lord!
⁸ Save me from my sins.
    Don't let fools sneer at me.
⁹ You treated me like this,
and I kept silent,
    not saying a word.

¹⁰ "Won't you stop punishing me?
    You have worn me down.
¹¹ You punish us severely
    because of our sins.
Like a moth, you destroy
what we treasure most.
    We are as frail as a breath.

¹² "Listen, LORD, to my prayer!
My eyes are flooded with tears,
    as I pray to you.
I am merely a stranger
visiting in your home
    as my ancestors did.
¹³ Stop being angry with me
and let me smile again
    before I am dead and gone."

Psalm 40

[A psalm by David for the music leader.]

A Prayer for Help

¹ I patiently waited, LORD,
    for you to hear my prayer.
You listened ²and pulled me
from a lonely pit
    full of mud and mire.
You let me stand on a rock
    with my feet firm,
³ and you gave me a new song,
    a song of praise to you.
Many will see this,
and they will honor and trust
    you, the LORD God.

⁴ You bless all of those
    who trust you, LORD,
and refuse to worship idols
    or follow false gods.
⁵ You, LORD God, have done
    many wonderful things,
and you have planned
    marvelous things for us.
No one is like you!
I would never be able to tell
    all you have done.

⁶ Sacrifices and offerings
    are not what please you;
gifts and payment for sin
    are not what you demand.
But you made me willing
    to listen and obey.
⁷ And so, I said, "I am here
    to do what is written
about me in the book,
    where it says,
⁸ 'I enjoy pleasing you.
    Your Law is in my heart.' "

⁹ When your people worshiped,
    you know I told them,
    "Our LORD always helps!"
¹⁰ When all your people met,
    I did not keep silent.

ᵛ**39.2** *but . . . good:* One possible meaning for the
difficult Hebrew text.

I said, "Our LORD is kind.
He is faithful and caring,
and he saves us."

[11] You, LORD, never fail
to have pity on me;
your love and faithfulness
always keep me secure.

[12] I have more troubles
than I can count.
My sins are all around me,
and I can't find my way.
My sins outnumber
the hairs on my head,
and I feel weak.
[13] Please show that you care
and come to my rescue.
Hurry and help me!

[14] Disappoint and confuse
all who want me dead;
turn away and disgrace
all who want to hurt me.
[15] Embarrass and shame
all of those who say,
"Just look at you now!"
[16] Our LORD, let your worshipers
rejoice and be glad.
They love you for saving them,
so let them always say,
"The LORD is wonderful!"

[17] I am poor and needy,
but, LORD God,
you care about me,
and you come to my rescue.
Please hurry and help.

Psalm 41

[*A psalm by David for the music leader.*]

A Prayer in Time of Sickness

[1] You, LORD God, bless everyone
who cares for the poor,
and you rescue those people
in times of trouble.
[2] You protect them
and keep them alive.
You make them happy here
in this land,
and you don't hand them over
to their enemies.

[3] You always heal them
and restore their strength
when they are sick.

*When God blesses your efforts
and you see people being
helped, you become more
confident in your work.*

CAROL KENT

[4] I prayed, "Have pity, LORD!
Heal me, though I have sinned
against you."

[5] My vicious enemies ask me,
"When will you die
and be forgotten?"
[6] When visitors come,
all they ever bring
are worthless words,
and when they leave,
they spread gossip.

[7] My enemies whisper about me.
They think the worst,
[8]   and they say,
"You have some fatal disease!
You'll never get well."
[9] My most trusted friend
has turned against me,
though he ate at my table.

[10] Have pity, LORD! Heal me,
so I can pay them back.
[11] Then my enemies
won't defeat me,
and I will know
that you really care.
[12] You have helped me
because I am innocent,
and you will always
be close to my side.

[13] You, the LORD God of Israel,
will be praised forever!
Amen and amen.

BOOK II
(Psalms 42–72)

Psalm 42

*[A special psalm for the people of Korah
and for the music leader.]*

Longing for God

¹As a deer gets thirsty
   for streams of water,
I truly am thirsty
   for you, my God.
²In my heart, I am thirsty
for you, the living God.
   When will I see your face?
³Day and night my tears
   are my only food,
as everyone keeps asking,
   "Where is your God?"

⁴Sorrow floods my heart,
   when I remember
leading the worshipers
   to your house.ʷ
I can still hear them shout
   their joyful praises.
⁵Why am I discouraged?
Why am I restless?
   I trust you!
And I will praise you again

because you help me,
⁶   and you are my God.

I am deeply discouraged
   as I think about you
from where the Jordan begins
at Mount Hermon
   and from Mount Mizar.ˣ
⁷Your vicious waves
   have swept over me
like an angry ocean
   or a roaring waterfall.

⁸Every day, you are kind,
   and at night
you give me a song
as my prayer to you,
   the living LORD God.

⁹You are my mighty rock.ʸ
   Why have you forgotten me?
Why must enemies mistreat me
   and make me sad?
¹⁰Even my bones are in pain,
   while all day long
my enemies sneer and ask,
   "Where is your God?"

ʷ**42.4** *leading . . . house*: One possible meaning for the
difficult Hebrew text. ˣ**42.6** *Mount Mizar*: The location
is not known. ʸ**42.9** *mighty rock*: See the note at 18.2.

---

*Spiritual*Life—How can I worship God as I should? *(Psalm 42)*

Worship with a thirsty heart.
Worship as I should? As I'm obligated to? Despite whatever worship techniques you follow,
let worship become a matter of the heart. But how does that occur? It happens when your
heart longs for God, when you become thirsty for his companionship.

Let the words of the Psalms become familiar one-liners in your life; carry a songsheet in
your car so you can sing out a worship song in the midst of your routine; peek out the
window each evening for a short "Yea, God" to each beautiful sunset. As you become more
experienced in your life with God, worship can move out of its religious settings and
happen anywhere.

While emotions play a part in worship, what's more important is the recognition that
you are missing—and craving—intimacy with God.

So recall the songs, Scripture verses, or settings that help you stay aware of God's
presence and make them a regular part of your life. Ponder the times you've tasted and seen
that the Lord is good. If you let God draw you to himself rather than worship only because
you "should," you will find that in the in-between moments of life, you are thirsting for
God. (See also Nehemiah 8.1—9.6; Nehemiah 12.27-43; Job 42.1-6.)

Words To Remember: *In my heart, I am thirsty for you, the living God. When
will I see your face?—Psalm 42.2*

¹¹ Why am I discouraged?
Why am I restless?
    I trust you!
And I will praise you again
because you help me,
    and you are my God.

Psalm 43

A Prayer in Times of Trouble

¹ Show that I am right, God!
Defend me against everyone
    who doesn't know you;
rescue me from each
    of those deceitful liars.
² I run to you
    for protection.
Why have you turned me away?
Why must enemies mistreat me
    and make me sad?

³ Send your light and your truth
    to guide me.
Let them lead me to your house
    on your sacred mountain.
⁴ Then I will worship
at your altar because you
    make me joyful.
You are my God,
    and I will praise you.
Yes, I will praise you
    as I play my harp.

*If we remember we are
God's creation, we'll welcome
the opportunity to use our
God-given talents.*
HOLLY MILLER

⁵ Why am I discouraged?
Why am I restless?
    I trust you!
And I will praise you again
because you help me,
    and you are my God.

Psalm 44

*[A special psalm for the people of Korah
and for the music leader.]*

A Prayer for Help

¹ Our God, our ancestors told us
what wonders you worked
    and we listened carefully.
² You chased off the nations
by causing them trouble
    with your powerful arm.
Then you let our ancestors
    take over their land.
³ Their strength and weapons
were not what won the land
    and gave them victory!
You loved them and fought
with your powerful arm
    and your shining glory.

⁴ You are my God and King,
and you give victory^z
    to the people of Jacob.
⁵ By your great power,
we knocked our enemies down
    and stomped on them.
⁶ I don't depend on my arrows
    or my sword to save me.
⁷ But you saved us
from our hateful enemies,
    and you put them to shame.
⁸ We boast about you, our God,
    and we are always grateful.

⁹ But now you have rejected us;
you don't lead us into battle,
    and we look foolish.
¹⁰ You made us retreat,
and our enemies have taken
    everything we own.
¹¹ You let us be slaughtered
    like sheep,
and you scattered us
    among the nations.
¹² You sold your people
for little or nothing,
    and you earned no profit.

¹³ You made us look foolish
    to our neighbors,

^z**44.4** *and . . . victory*: One ancient translation; Hebrew "please give victory."

and people who live nearby
    insult us and sneer.
14 Foreigners joke about us
    and shake their heads.
15 I am embarrassed every day,
    and I blush with shame.
16 But others mock and sneer,
    as they watch my enemies
    take revenge on me.

17 All of this has happened to us,
    though we didn't forget you
    or break our agreement.
18 We always kept you in mind
    and followed your teaching.
19 But you crushed us,
    and you covered us
    with deepest darkness
    where wild animals live.

20 We did not forget you
    or lift our hands in prayer
    to foreign gods.
21 You would have known it
    because you discover
    every secret thought.
22 We face death all day for you.
    We are like sheep on their way
    to be slaughtered.

23 Wake up! Do something, Lord!
    Why are you sleeping?
    Don't desert us forever.
24 Why do you keep looking away?
    Don't forget our sufferings
    and all of our troubles.
25 We are flat on the ground,
    holding on to the dust.
26 Do something! Help us!
    Show how kind you are
    and come to our rescue.

Psalm 45

*[A special psalm for the people of Korah and for the
music leader. To the tune "Lilies." A love song.]*

For a Royal Wedding

1 My thoughts are filled
    with beautiful words
    for the king,
    and I will use my voice
    as a writer would use
    pen and ink.

2 No one is as handsome as you!
    Your words are always kind.
That is why God
    will always bless you.
3 Mighty king, glorious ruler,
    strap on your sword
4   and ride out in splendor!
Win victories for truth
    and mercy and justice.
Do fearsome things
    with your powerful arm.
5 Send your sharp arrows
    through enemy hearts
and make all nations fall
    at your feet.

6 You are God, and you will rule
    forever as king.[a]
Your royal power
    brings about justice.
7 You love justice and hate evil.
    And so, your God chose you
    and made you happier
    than any of your friends.
8 The sweet aroma of the spices
    myrrh, aloes, and cassia,
    covers your royal robes.
You enjoy the music of harps
    in palaces decorated
    with ivory.
9 Daughters of kings are here,
    and your bride stands
    at your right side,
    wearing a wedding gown
    trimmed with pure gold.[b]

10 Bride of the king,
    listen carefully to me.
Forget your own people
    and your father's family.
11 The king is your husband,
    so do what he desires.
12 All of the richest people
    from the city of Tyre
will try to influence you
13   with precious treasures.

Your bride, my king,
    has inward beauty,[c]

---

[a]**45.6** *You . . . king:* Or "God has made you king, and
you will rule forever."   [b]**45.9** *trimmed with pure gold:*
Hebrew has "with gold from Ophir," which may have
been in Africa or India. Gold from there was considered
the very best.   [c]**45.13** *has inward beauty:* Or "is dressed
in her room."

and her wedding gown is woven
    with threads of gold.
¹⁴Wearing the finest garments,
    she is brought to you,
followed by her young friends,
    the bridesmaids.
¹⁵Everyone is excited,
    as they follow you
        to the royal palace.

¹⁶Your sons and your grandsons
    will also be kings
        as your ancestors were.
You will make them the rulers
    everywhere on earth.

¹⁷I will make your name famous
    from now on,
and you will be praised
    forever and ever.

Psalm 46

*[A special song for the people of Korah
    and for the music leader.]*

God Is Our Mighty Fortress

¹God is our mighty fortress,
    always ready to help
        in times of trouble.
²And so, we won't be afraid!
        Let the earth tremble
and the mountains tumble
        into the deepest sea.
³Let the ocean roar and foam,
    and its raging waves
        shake the mountains.

⁴A river and its streams
        bring joy to the city,
    which is the sacred home
        of God Most High.
⁵God is in that city,
    and it won't be shaken.
        He will help it at dawn.

⁶Nations rage! Kingdoms fall!
    But at the voice of God
        the earth itself melts.
⁷The LORD All-Powerful
    is with us.
The God of Jacob
    is our fortress.

⁸Come! See the fearsome things
    the LORD has done on earth.
⁹God brings wars to an end
    all over the world.
He breaks the arrows,
    shatters the spears,
    and burns the shields.ᵈ
¹⁰Our God says, "Calm down,
    and learn that I am God!
All nations on earth
    will honor me."

¹¹The LORD All-Powerful
    is with us.
The God of Jacob
    is our fortress.

Psalm 47

*[A psalm for the people of Korah and
    for the music leader.]*

God Rules the Nations

¹All of you nations,
    clap your hands and shout
        joyful praises to God.
²The LORD Most High is fearsome,
    the ruler of all the earth.
³God has put every nation
    under our power,
⁴and he chose for us the land
    that was the pride of Jacob,
        his favorite.

⁵God goes up to his throne,
    as people shout
        and trumpets blast.
⁶Sing praises to God our King,
⁷the ruler of all the earth!
        Praise God with songs.

⁸God rules the nations
    from his sacred throne.
⁹Their leaders come together
    and are now the people
        of Abraham's God.
All rulers on earth
    surrender their weapons,
        and God is greatly praised!

ᵈ**46.9** *shields*: Or "chariots."

Psalm 48

[A song and a psalm for the people of Korah.]

The City of God

¹ The LORD God is wonderful!
He deserves all praise
　in the city where he lives.
His holy mountain,
² beautiful and majestic,
　brings joy to all on earth.
Mount Zion, truly sacred,
　is home for the Great King.
³ God is there to defend it
and has proved to be
　its protector.

⁴ Kings joined forces
　to attack the city,
⁵ but when they saw it,
they were terrified
　and ran away.
⁶ They trembled all over
　like women giving birth
⁷ or like seagoing ships*ᵉ*
　wrecked by eastern winds.
⁸ We had heard about it,
and now we have seen it
　in the city of our God,
　the LORD All-Powerful.
This is the city that God
　will let stand forever.

*I don't like it when God
confines me in difficult
circumstances, but I've
found he holds me close
there and makes the trial
at least bearable.*

VIRELLE KIDDER

⁹ Our God, here in your temple
　we think about your love.
¹⁰ You are famous and praised
　everywhere on earth,
as you win victories
　with your powerful arm.

¹¹ Mount Zion will celebrate,
and all Judah will be glad,
　because you bring justice.

¹² Let's walk around Zion
　and count its towers.
¹³ We will see its strong walls
　and visit each fortress.
Then you can say
　to future generations,
¹⁴ "Our God is like this forever
　and will always*ᶠ* guide us."

Psalm 49

*[A psalm for the people of Korah
and for the music leader.]*

Don't Depend on Wealth

¹ Everyone on this earth,
　now listen to what I say!
² Listen, no matter who you are,
　rich or poor.
³ I speak words of wisdom,
　and my thoughts make sense.
⁴ I have in mind a mystery
that I will explain
　while playing my harp.

⁵ Why should I be afraid
　in times of trouble,
when I am surrounded
　by vicious enemies?
⁶ They trust in their riches
and brag about
　all of their wealth.
⁷ You cannot buy back your life
　or pay off God!
⁸ It costs far too much
　to buy back your life.
You can never pay God enough
⁹ to stay alive forever
　and safe from death.

¹⁰ We see that wise people die,
　and so do stupid fools.
Then their money is left
　for someone else.

---

*ᵉ***48.7** *seagoing ships:* The Hebrew text has "ships of
Tarshish," which probably means large, seagoing ships.
*ᶠ***48.14** *always:* One possible meaning for the difficult
Hebrew text.

¹¹The grave^g will be their home
forever and ever,
although they once had land
of their own.
¹²Our human glory disappears,
and, like animals, we die.

¹³Here is what happens to fools
and to those who trust
the words of fools:
¹⁴They are like sheep
with death as their shepherd,
leading them to the grave.^h
In the morning God's people
will walk all over them,
as their bodies lie rotting
in their home, the grave.
¹⁵But God will rescue me
from the power of death.

¹⁶Don't let it bother you
when others get rich
and live in luxury.
¹⁷Soon they will die
and all of their wealth
will be left behind.

¹⁸We humans are praised
when we do well,

and all of us are glad
to be alive.
¹⁹But we each will go down
to our ancestors,
never again to see
the light of day.
²⁰Our human glory disappears,
and, like animals, we die.

Psalm 50

[*A psalm by Asaph.*]

What Pleases God

¹From east to west,
the powerful LORD God
has been calling together
everyone on earth.
²God shines brightly from Zion,
the most beautiful city.

³Our God approaches,
but not silently;

---

^g**49.11** *The grave*: Some ancient translations; Hebrew "Their inward thoughts." ^h**49.14** *as their . . . grave*: One possible meaning for the difficult Hebrew text.

MARRIAGE—How can we prevent financial issues from becoming stumbling blocks in our marriage? *(Psalm 49.16-20)*

Grow a generous personality.
There are a few really hot cars in the church parking lot, and one of them is not yours, right? And even if they were, someone else would show up next month with a better car.

The truth is that if you or your husband have a full-time job in an English-speaking country, globally you are already among "the rich people of this world" (see 1 Timothy 6.17). Your income is higher than most of the people in this world. Two-thirds of the world eat mostly rice and beans, so if you had chicken last night, you are doing pretty well. Yet you probably are not too impressed with your "riches" because money is tricky stuff, and we always seem to have one eye on achieving the next level.

Yet this attitude can poison a marriage. When moving up or having more than your neighbors or friends becomes your focus, your bonding is based on acquiring possessions rather than outgiving each other in love. Joyful moments revolve around buying a new piece of furniture rather than around building memories together.

But when you focus on giving money instead of making it, you cultivate a generous personality. Generosity and largeness of heart create character and make you more accepting of each other's mistakes and foibles, more appreciative of each other's growth and increasing wisdom. (See also Malachi 3.8-12; Matthew 6.19-24; 1 Timothy 6.6-10; Hebrews 13.5,6.)

Words To Remember: *Don't let it bother you when others get rich and live in luxury.*—Psalm 49.16

a flaming fire comes first,
and a storm surrounds him.
⁴God comes to judge his people.
He shouts to the heavens
and to the earth,
⁵"Call my followers together!
They offered me a sacrifice,
and we made an agreement."

⁶The heavens announce,
"God is the judge,
and he is always honest."

⁷My people, I am God!
Israel, I am your God.
Listen to my charges
against you.
⁸Although you offer sacrifices
and always bring gifts,
⁹I won't accept your offerings
of bulls and goats.

¹⁰Every animal in the forest
belongs to me,
and so do the cattle
on a thousand hills.
¹¹I know all the birds
in the mountains,
and every wild creature
is in my care.

¹²If I were hungry,
I wouldn't tell you,
because I own the world
and everything in it.
¹³I don't eat the meat of bulls
or drink the blood of goats.
¹⁴I am God Most High!
The only sacrifice I want
is for you to be thankful
and to keep your word.
¹⁵Pray to me in time of trouble.
I will rescue you,
and you will honor me.

¹⁶But to the wicked I say:
"You don't have the right
to mention my laws or claim
to keep our agreement!
¹⁷You refused correction
and rejected my commands.
¹⁸You made friends
with every crook you met,
and you liked people who break
their wedding vows.

¹⁹You talked only about violence
and told nothing but lies;
²⁰you sat around gossiping,
ruining the reputation
of your own relatives."

²¹When you did all of this,
I didn't say a word,
and you thought,
"God is just like us!"
But now I will accuse you.
²²You have ignored me!
So pay close attention
or I will tear you apart,
and no one can help you.

²³The sacrifice that honors me
is a thankful heart.
Obey me,ⁱ and I, your God,
will show my power to save.

Psalm 51

*[For the music leader. A psalm by David when
the prophet Nathan came to him
after David had been with Bathsheba.]*

A Prayer for Forgiveness

¹You are kind, God!
Please have pity on me.
You are always merciful!
Please wipe away my sins.
²Wash me clean from all
of my sin and guilt.
³I know about my sins,
and I cannot forget
my terrible guilt.
⁴You are really the one
I have sinned against;
I have disobeyed you
and have done wrong.
So it is right and fair for you
to correct and punish me.

⁵I have sinned and done wrong
since the day I was born.
⁶But you want complete honesty,
so teach me true wisdom.
⁷Wash me with hyssopʲ

ⁱ**50.23** *Obey me:* One possible meaning for the difficult
Hebrew text.   ʲ**51.7** *hyssop:* A small bush with bunches
of small, white flowers. It was sometimes used as a
symbol for making a person clean from sin.

until I am clean
and whiter than snow.
⁸ Let me be happy and joyful!
You crushed my bones,
now let them celebrate.
⁹ Turn your eyes from my sin
and cover my guilt.
¹⁰ Create pure thoughts in me
and make me faithful again.
¹¹ Don't chase me away from you
or take your Holy Spirit
away from me.

¹² Make me as happy as you did
when you saved me;
make me want to obey!
¹³ I will teach sinners your Law,
and they will return to you.
¹⁴ Keep me from any deadly sin.
Only you can save me!
Then I will shout and sing
about your power to save.

¹⁵ Help me to speak,
and I will praise you, Lord.
¹⁶ Offerings and sacrifices
are not what you want.
¹⁷ The way to please you
is to feel sorrow
deep in our hearts.

This is the kind of sacrifice
you won't refuse.

¹⁸ Please be willing, Lord,
to help the city of Zion
and to rebuild its walls.
¹⁹ Then you will be pleased
with the proper sacrifices,
and we will offer bulls
on your altar once again.

Psalm 52

[*A special psalm by David for the music leader.
He wrote this when Doeg from Edom went to Saul
and said, "David has gone to Ahimelech's house."*]

God Is in Control

¹ You people may be strong
and brag about your sins,
but God can be trusted
day after day.
² You plan brutal crimes,
and your lying words cut
like a sharp razor.
³ You would rather do evil
than good, and tell lies
than speak the truth.
⁴ You love to say cruel things,
and your words are a trap.

Personal *Concerns*—What can I do when I've hurt someone? (Psalm 51)

Make a sincere apology.
Theoretically, we learned to say "I'm sorry" in kindergarten, but those words don't come easy to us as adults.

Before we apologize, it helps to go before God, as the psalmist did, and ponder our mistake. Yes, I blew it, but why? Was I jealous? Was I afraid? Was I angry? In the safety of God's presence, we can admit our true but often repulsive motives. We then can ask for forgiveness and the strength to admit these faults to the person we hurt.

What makes a difference in our apology is a sincere desire to mend the situation. If we only want to get ourselves out of a sticky situation without owning up to what we've done, it won't work. The psalmist wanted to be washed clean, so he freely admitted his sin and guilt (51.2-7). Because he wanted to improve the situation, he asked specifically for pure thoughts and a faithful heart (51.10). The person we've hurt needs to hear from us what our plans are to make amends. We're not only looking for pardon, but for restoration.

But what if we think the person we hurt is carrying this too far, so we don't feel truly sorry? Once again, it becomes a matter between God and us. If we are truly sorry we've sinned against God, we then can ask him to give us a desire to seek forgiveness and reconciliation with the other person. (See also Luke 19.1-10; Luke 22.54-62.)

Words To Remember: *You are kind, God! Please have pity on me. You are always merciful! Please wipe away my sins.*—Psalm 51.1

⁵ God will destroy you forever!
He will grab you and drag you
    from your homes.
You will be uprooted
    and left to die.
⁶ When good people see
    this fearsome sight,
they will laugh and say,
⁷   "Just look at them now!
Instead of trusting God,
    they trusted their wealth
    and their cruelty."

⁸ But I am like an olive tree
    growing in God's house,
and I can count on his love
    forever and ever.
⁹ I will always thank God
    for what he has done;
I will praise his good name
    when his people meet.

Psalm 53

*[A special psalm by David for the music leader.
To the tune "Mahalath."ᵏ]*

No One Can Ignore God

¹ Only a fool would say,
    "There is no God!"
People like that are worthless!
They are heartless and cruel
    and never do right.

² From heaven God
    looks down to see
if anyone is wise enough
    to search for him.
³ But all of them
    are crooked and corrupt.
    Not one of them does right.

⁴ Won't you lawbreakers learn?
    You refuse to pray,
and you gobble down
    the people of God.
⁵ But you will be terrified
    worse than ever before.
God will scatter the bones
    of his enemies,
and you will be ashamed
    when God rejects you.

⁶ I long for someone from Zion
    to come and save Israel!
Our God, when you bless
    your people again,
Jacob's family will be glad,
    and Israel will celebrate.

Psalm 54

*[For the music leader. Use with stringed
instruments. A special psalm that David wrote
when the people of Ziph went to Saul and said,
"David is hiding here with us."]*

Trusting God in Times of Trouble

¹ Save me, God, by your power
    and prove that I am right.
² Listen to my prayer
    and hear what I say.
³ Cruel strangers have attacked
    and want me dead.
Not one of them cares
    about you.

⁴ You will help me, Lord God,
    and keep me from falling;
⁵ you will punish my enemies
    for their evil deeds.
Be my faithful friend
    and destroy them.

⁶ I will bring a gift
    and offer a sacrifice
    to you, LORD.
I will praise your name
    because you are good.
⁷ You have rescued me
    from all of my troubles,
and my own eyes have seen
    my enemies fall.

Psalm 55

*[A special psalm by David for the music leader.
Use with stringed instruments.]*

Betrayed by a Friend

¹ Listen, God, to my prayer!
    Don't reject my request.

ᵏ**Psalm 53** *Mahalath:* Or "For flutes," one possible
meaning for the difficult Hebrew text.

² Please listen and help me.
My thoughts are troubled,
    and I keep groaning
³ because my loud enemies
    shout and attack.
They treat me terribly
    and hold angry grudges.
⁴ My heart is racing fast,
    and I am afraid of dying.
⁵ I am trembling with fear,
    completely terrified.

⁶ I wish I had wings
    like a dove,
so I could fly far away
    and be at peace.
⁷ I would go and live
    in some distant desert.
⁸ I would quickly find shelter
from howling winds
    and raging storms.

*Each day I must make
choices and set priorities.
Until daily time alone
with God becomes the one
non-negotiable activity of
my life, he will never be
the power in my life
he wants to be.*

MAYO MATHERS

⁹ Confuse my enemies, Lord!
    Upset their plans.
Cruelty and violence
    are all I see in the city,
¹⁰ and they are like guards
    on patrol day and night.
The city is full of trouble,
    evil, ¹¹ and corruption.

Troublemakers and liars
    freely roam the streets.

¹² My enemies are not the ones
    who sneer and make fun.
I could put up with that
    or even hide from them.
¹³ But it was my closest friend,
    the one I trusted most.
¹⁴ We enjoyed being together,
    and we went with others
    to your house, our God.

¹⁵ All who hate me are controlled
    by the power of evil.
Sentence them to death
and send them down alive
    to the world of the dead.

¹⁶ I ask for your help, LORD God,
    and you will keep me safe.
¹⁷ Morning, noon, and night
    you hear my concerns
    and my complaints.
¹⁸ I am attacked from all sides,
    but you will rescue me
    unharmed by the battle.
¹⁹ You have always ruled,
    and you will hear me.
You will defeat my enemies
because they won't turn
    and worship you.

²⁰ My friend turned against me
    and broke his promise.
²¹ His words were smoother
    than butter, and softer
        than olive oil.
But hatred filled his heart,
    and he was ready to attack
        with a sword.

²² Our LORD, we belong to you.
    We tell you what worries us,
        and you won't let us fall.
²³ But what about those people
    who are cruel and brutal?
You will throw them down
    into the deepest pit
long before their time.
    I trust you, LORD!

Psalm 56

[*For the music leader. To the tune "A Silent Dove in the Distance."* [1] *A special psalm by David when the Philistines captured him in Gath.*]

A Prayer of Trust in God

[1] Have pity, God Most High!
My enemies chase me all day.
[2] Many of them are pursuing
and attacking me,
[3] but even when I am afraid,
I keep on trusting you.
[4] I praise your promises!
I trust you and am not afraid.
No one can harm me.

[5] Enemies spend the whole day
finding fault with me;
all they think about
is how to do me harm.
[6] They attack from ambush,
watching my every step
and hoping to kill me.
[7] They won't get away[m]
with these crimes, God,
because when you get angry,
you destroy people.

[8] You have kept record
of my days of wandering.
You have stored my tears
in your bottle
and counted each of them.

[9] When I pray, LORD God,
my enemies will retreat,
because I know for certain
that you are with me.
[10] I praise your promises!
[11] I trust you and am not afraid.
No one can harm me.

[12] I will keep my promises
to you, my God,
and bring you gifts.
[13] You protected me from death
and kept me from stumbling,
so that I would please you
and follow the light
that leads to life.

Psalm 57

[*For the music leader. To the tune "Don't Destroy."* [n] *A special psalm by David when he was in the cave while running from Saul.*]

Praise and Trust in Times of Trouble

[1] God Most High, have pity on me!
Have mercy. I run to you
for safety.
In the shadow of your wings,
I seek protection
till danger dies down.
[2] I pray to you, my protector.
[3] You will send help from heaven
and save me,
but you will bring trouble
on my attackers.
You are faithful,
and you can be trusted.

[4] I live among lions,
who gobble down people!
They have spears and arrows
instead of teeth,
and they have sharp swords
instead of tongues.

[5] May you, my God, be honored
above the heavens;
may your glory be seen
everywhere on earth.

[6] Enemies set traps for my feet
and struck me down.
They dug a pit in my path,
but fell in it themselves.
[7] I am faithful to you,
and you can trust me.
I will sing and play music
for you, my God.
[8] I feel wide awake!
I will wake up my harp
and wake up the sun.
[9] I will praise you, Lord,
for everyone to hear,
and I will sing hymns to you
in every nation.

---

[l] **Psalm 56** *A Silent . . . Distance*: One possible meaning for the difficult Hebrew text. [m] **56.7** *They . . . away*: One possible meaning for the difficult Hebrew text. [n] **Psalm 57** *Don't Destroy*: One possible meaning for the difficult Hebrew text.

[10] Your love reaches higher
   than the heavens;
 your loyalty extends
   beyond the clouds.

[11] May you, my God, be honored
   above the heavens;
 may your glory be seen
   everywhere on earth.

Psalm 58

*[A special psalm by David for the music leader.
To the tune "Don't Destroy."[n]]*

A Prayer When All Goes Wrong

[1] Do you mighty people[o] talk
   only to oppose justice?[p]
   Don't you ever judge fairly?
[2] You are always planning evil,
   and you are brutal.
[3] You have done wrong and lied
   from the day you were born.
[4] Your words spread poison
   like the bite of a cobra
[5] that refuses to listen
   to the snake charmer.

[6] My enemies are fierce
   as lions, LORD God!
 Shatter their teeth.
   Snatch out their fangs.
[7] Make them disappear
 like leaking water,
   and make their arrows miss.
[8] Let them dry up like snails
 or be like a child that dies
   before seeing the sun.
[9] Wipe them out quicker
 than a pot can be heated
   by setting thorns on fire.[q]

[10] Good people will be glad
   when they see the wicked
     getting what they deserve,
 and they will wash their feet
   in their enemies' blood.
[11] Everyone will say, "It's true!
   Good people are rewarded.
 God does rule the earth
   with justice."

Psalm 59

*[For the music leader. To the tune "Don't Destroy."[r]
A special psalm by David when Saul had David's
house watched so that he could kill him.]*

A Prayer for Protection

[1] Save me, God! Protect me
   from enemy attacks!
[2] Keep me safe from brutal people
   who want to kill me.

[3] Merciless enemies, LORD,
 are hiding and plotting,
   hoping to kill me.
 I have not hurt them
   in any way at all.
[4] But they are ready to attack.
 Do something! Help me!
   Look at what's happening.
[5] LORD God All-Powerful,
   you are the God of Israel.
 Punish the other nations
 and don't pity those terrible
   and rebellious people.

[6] My enemies return at evening,
 growling like dogs
   roaming the city.
[7] They curse and their words
   cut like swords,
 as they say to themselves,
   "No one can hear us!"

[8] You, LORD, laugh at them
   and sneer at the nations.
[9] You are my mighty fortress,
   and I depend on you.
[10] You love me and will let me
   see my enemies defeated.
[11] Don't kill them,
   or everyone may forget!
 Just use your mighty power
   to make them tremble
     and fall.

 You are a shield
   for your people.

---

[n]**Psalm 58** *Don't Destroy:* One possible meaning for the
difficult Hebrew text.   [o]**58.1** *mighty people:* Or
"mighty rulers" or "mighty gods."   [p]**58.1** *Do . . . justice:*
One possible meaning for the difficult Hebrew text.
[q]**58.9** *Wipe . . . fire:* See the note at Psalm 57.
[r]**Psalm 59** *Don't Destroy:* See the note at Psalm 57.

¹² My enemies are liars!
So let them be trapped
by their boastful lies.
¹³ Get angry and destroy them.
Leave them in ruin.
Then all the nations will know
that you rule in Israel.

¹⁴ Those liars return at evening,
growling like dogs
roaming the city.
¹⁵ They search for scraps of food,
and they snarl
until they are stuffed.

¹⁶ But I will sing about
your strength, my God,
and I will celebrate
because of your love.
You are my fortress,
my place of protection
in times of trouble.
¹⁷ I will sing your praises!
You are my mighty fortress,
and you love me.

Psalm 60

[*For the music leader. To the tune "Lily of the Promise." A special psalm by David for teaching. He wrote it during his wars with the Arameans of northern Syria,^s when Joab came back and killed twelve thousand Edomites^t in Salt Valley.*]

You Can Depend on God

¹ You, God, are angry with us!
We are rejected and crushed.
Make us strong again!
² You made the earth shake
and split wide open;
now heal its wounds
and stop its trembling.
³ You brought hard times
on your people,
and you gave us wine
that made us stagger.

⁴ You gave a signal to those
who worship you,
so they could escape
from enemy arrows.^u
⁵ Answer our prayers!
Use your powerful arm
and give us victory.

Then the people you love
will be safe.

⁶ Our God, you solemnly promised,
"I would gladly divide up
the city of Shechem
and give away Succoth Valley
piece by piece.
⁷ The lands of Gilead
and Manasseh are mine.
Ephraim is my war helmet,
and Judah is the symbol
of my royal power.
⁸ Moab is merely my washbasin.
Edom belongs to me,
and I shout in triumph
over the Philistines."

⁹ Our God, who will bring me
to the fortress,
or lead me to Edom?
¹⁰ Have you rejected us
and deserted our armies?
¹¹ Help us defeat our enemies!
No one else can rescue us.
¹² You will give us victory
and crush our enemies.

Psalm 61

[*A psalm by David for the music leader. Use with stringed instruments.*]

Under the Protection of God

¹ Please listen, God,
and answer my prayer!
² I feel hopeless,
and I cry out to you
from a faraway land.

Lead me to the mighty rock^v
high above me.
³ You are a strong tower,
where I am safe
from my enemies.

⁴ Let me live with you forever
and find protection
under your wings, my God.

---

^s**Psalm 60** *wars . . . Syria:* See 2 Samuel 8.3-8; 10.16-18; 1 Chronicles 18.3-11; 19.6-19. ^t**Psalm 60** *killed . . . Edomites:* See 2 Samuel 8.13; 1 Chronicles 18.12. ^u**60.4** *so . . . arrows:* Some ancient translations and one possible meaning for the difficult Hebrew text. ^v**61.2** *mighty rock:* See the note at 18.2.

⁵You heard my promises,
   and you have blessed me,
just as you bless everyone
   who worships you.

⁶Let the king have a long
   and healthy life.
⁷May he always rule
   with you, God, at his side;
may your love and loyalty
   watch over him.

⁸I will sing your praises
   forever and will always
   keep my promises.

Psalm 62

[A psalm by David for Jeduthun, the music leader.]

God Is Powerful and Kind

¹Only God can save me,
   and I calmly wait for[w] him.
²God alone is the mighty rock[x]
   that keeps me safe
and the fortress
   where I am secure.

³I feel like a shaky fence
   or a sagging wall.
How long will all of you
   attack and assault me?
⁴You want to bring me down
   from my place of honor.

*You're not a bad wife,
friend, mother, or employee
for taking alone time.
Friends and family will
appreciate a rejuvenated you.*

JUDITH COUCHMAN

You love to tell lies,
   and when your words are kind,
      hatred hides in your heart.
⁵Only God gives inward peace,
   and I depend on him.

⁶God alone is the mighty rock
   that keeps me safe,
and he is the fortress
   where I feel secure.
⁷God saves me and honors me.
He is that mighty rock
   where I find safety.

⁸Trust God, my friends,
   and always tell him
each one of your concerns.
   God is our place of safety.

⁹We humans are only a breath;
   none of us are truly great.
All of us together weigh less
   than a puff of air.
¹⁰Don't trust in violence
   or depend on dishonesty
   or rely on great wealth.

¹¹I heard God say two things:
   "I am powerful,
¹²   and I am very kind."
The Lord rewards each of us
   according to what we do.

Psalm 63

*[A psalm by David when he was
in the desert of Judah.]*

God's Love Means More than Life

¹You are my God. I worship you.
   In my heart, I long for you,
as I would long for a stream
   in a scorching desert.

²I have seen your power
   and your glory
      in the place of worship.
³Your love means more
   than life to me,
      and I praise you.
⁴As long as I live,
   I will pray to you.
⁵I will sing joyful praises
   and be filled with excitement
      like a guest at a banquet.

[w]**62.1** *calmly wait for*: Or "am at peace with."
[x]**62.2** *mighty rock*: See the note at 18.2.

⁶I think about you
  before I go to sleep,
and my thoughts turn to you
  during the night.
⁷You have helped me,
  and I sing happy songs
  in the shadow of your wings.
⁸I stay close to you,
  and your powerful arm
  supports me.

⁹All who want to kill me
  will end up in the ground.
¹⁰Swords will run them through,
  and wild dogs will eat them.

¹¹Because of you, our God,
  the king will celebrate
with your faithful followers,
  but liars will be silent.

Psalm 64

[*A psalm by David for the music leader.*]

Celebrate because of the LORD

¹Listen to my concerns, God,
and protect me
  from my terrible enemies.
²Keep me safe from secret plots
  of corrupt and evil gangs.
³Their words cut like swords,
  and their cruel remarks
  sting like sharp arrows.
⁴They fearlessly ambush
  and shoot innocent people.

⁵They are determined to do evil,
  and they tell themselves,
"Let's set traps!
  No one can see us."^y
⁶They make evil plans and say,
"We'll commit a perfect crime.
  No one knows our thoughts."^z

⁷But God will shoot his arrows
  and quickly wound them.
⁸They will be destroyed
  by their own words,
and everyone who sees them
  will tremble with fear.^a
⁹They will be afraid and say,
"Look at what God has done
  and keep it all in mind."

¹⁰May the LORD bless his people
with peace and happiness
  and let them celebrate.

Psalm 65

[*A psalm by David
and a song for the music leader.*]

God Answers Prayer

¹Our God, you deserve^b praise
in Zion, where we keep
  our promises to you.
²Everyone will come to you
  because you answer prayer.
³Our terrible sins get us down,
  but you forgive us.
⁴You bless your chosen ones,
  and you invite them
to live near you
  in your temple.
We will enjoy your house,
  the sacred temple.

⁵Our God, you save us,
  and your fearsome deeds answer
  our prayers for justice!
You give hope to people
everywhere on earth,
  even those across the sea.
⁶You are strong,
  and your mighty power
  put the mountains in place.
⁷You silence the roaring waves
and the noisy shouts
  of the nations.
⁸People far away marvel
  at your fearsome deeds,
and all who live under the sun
celebrate and sing
  because of you.

⁹You take care of the earth
and send rain to help the soil
  grow all kinds of crops.
Your rivers never run dry,
and you prepare the earth
  to produce much grain.

---

^y**64.5** *us:* One ancient translation; Hebrew "them."
^z**64.6** *thoughts:* One possible meaning for the difficult
Hebrew text of verse 6. ^a**64.8** *tremble with fear:* Or
"turn and run." ^b**65.1** *deserve:* One possible meaning
for the difficult Hebrew text.

¹⁰You water all of its fields
    and level the lumpy ground.
You send showers of rain
to soften the soil
    and help the plants sprout.
¹¹Wherever your footsteps
touch the earth,
    a rich harvest is gathered.
¹²Desert pastures blossom,
    and mountains celebrate.
¹³Meadows are filled
    with sheep and goats;
valleys overflow with grain
    and echo with joyful songs.

We traveled through fire
    and through floods,
but you brought us
    to a land of plenty.

*Looking back over the years,
I'm not sure I'd trade in my
hard times because they are
what pushed me toward God.*

ELIZABETH MITTELSTAEDT

Psalm 66

[A song and a psalm for the music leader.]

Shout Praises to God

¹Tell everyone on this earth
    to shout praises to God!
²Sing about his glorious name.
    Honor him with praises.
³Say to God, "Everything you do
    is fearsome,
and your mighty power makes
    your enemies come crawling.
⁴You are worshiped by everyone!
    We all sing praises to you."

⁵Come and see the fearsome things
    our God has done!
⁶When God made the sea dry up,
    our people walked across,
and because of him,
    we celebrated there.
⁷His mighty power rules forever,
    and nothing the nations do
can be hidden from him.
    So don't turn against God.

⁸All of you people,
    come praise our God!
    Let his praises be heard.
⁹God protects us from death
    and keeps us steady.

¹⁰Our God, you tested us,
    just as silver is tested.
¹¹You trapped us in a net
    and gave us heavy burdens.
¹²You sent war chariots
    to crush our skulls.

¹³I will bring sacrifices
    into your house, my God,
and I will do what I promised
¹⁴   when I was in trouble.
¹⁵I will sacrifice my best sheep
    and offer bulls and goats
    on your altar.

¹⁶All who worship God,
    come here and listen;
I will tell you everything
    God has done for me.
¹⁷I prayed to the Lord,
    and I praised him.
¹⁸If my thoughts had been sinful,
    he would have refused
    to hear me.
¹⁹But God did listen
    and answered my prayer.
²⁰Let's praise God!
    He listened when I prayed,
    and he is always kind.

Psalm 67

*[A psalm and a song for the music leader.
Use with stringed instruments.]*

Tell the Nations To Praise God

¹Our God, be kind and bless us!
    Be pleased and smile.
²Then everyone on earth
    will learn to follow you,
and all nations will see
    your power to save us.

³Make everyone praise you
  and shout your praises.
⁴Let the nations celebrate
  with joyful songs,
because you judge fairly
  and guide all nations.
⁵Make everyone praise you
  and shout your praises.

⁶Our God has blessed the earth
  with a wonderful harvest!
⁷Pray for his blessings
  to continue
and for everyone on earth
  to worship our God.

Psalm 68

*[A psalm and a song by David
for the music leader.]*

God Will Win the Battle

¹Do something, God!
Scatter your hateful enemies.
  Make them turn and run.
²Scatter them like smoke!
  When you come near,
make them melt
  like wax in a fire.
³But let your people be happy
  and celebrate because of you.

⁴Our God, you are the one
who rides on the clouds,
  and we praise you.
Your name is the LORD,
and we celebrate
  as we worship you.

⁵Our God, from your sacred home
you take care of orphans
  and protect widows.
⁶You find families
  for those who are lonely.
You set prisoners free
  and let them prosper,^c
but all who rebel will live
  in a scorching desert.

⁷You set your people free,
and you led them
  through the desert.
⁸God of Israel,
  the earth trembled,
  and rain poured down.
You alone are the God
  who rules from Mount Sinai.
⁹When your land was thirsty,
you sent showers
  to refresh it.
¹⁰Your people settled there,

---

^c**68.6** *and let them prosper*: Or "and give them a song."

SingleLife—How can I overcome my feelings of loneliness? *(Psalm 68.4-6)*

Ask God to provide family members.

Maybe you feel lonely because a friend has moved away, or because there is no one with whom you can truly connect among all the people you know. Alone or in a crowd, you long for attachment.

God has a way of bringing people into our lives who can become family to us. At first we may not see them that way because they are people we might never choose: people we volunteer with, people who become our boss, even people who annoy us when we first meet them. But time passes, and something brings us together—most often working side by side at a job or service project, or going through similar horrific experiences. Out of that side-by-side experience is forged a strong bond, one that's difficult to find even in families.

Does it sound like a fairy tale that God would provide a friend for you? God puts in a special category those who experience an intense sort of loneliness—orphans and widows. He promises to champion their cause and locate other people to provide what they need. He seems to understand that we might miss certain relationships in life. So until we get to heaven and know him fully, he provides pieces of himself with skin on for us to know and love. (See also Psalm 22; Matthew 26.36-46; 2 Timothy 4.16-18; Revelation 3.20-22.)

Words To Remember: *You find families for those who are lonely.—Psalm 68.6*

and you were generous
  to everyone in need.

[11] You gave the command,
  and a chorus of women told
    what had happened:
[12] "Kings and their armies
  retreated and ran,
  and everything they left
    is now being divided.
[13] And for those who stayed back
  to guard the sheep,
there are metal doves
  with silver-coated wings
  and shiny gold feathers."

[14] God All-Powerful, you scattered
  the kings like snow falling
  on Mount Zalmon.[d]

[15] Our LORD and our God,
  Bashan is a mighty mountain
  covered with peaks.
[16] Why is it jealous of Zion,
  the mountain you chose
    as your home forever?

[17] When you, LORD God, appeared
  to your people[e] at Sinai,
you came with thousands
  of mighty chariots.
[18] When you climbed
  the high mountain,
you took prisoners with you
  and were given gifts.
Your enemies didn't want you
  to live there,
  but they gave you gifts.

[19] We praise you, Lord God!
  You treat us with kindness
    day after day,
  and you rescue us.
[20] You always protect us
  and save us from death.

[21] Our Lord and our God,
  your terrible enemies
    are ready for war,[f]
but you will crush
  their skulls.
[22] You promised to bring them
  from Bashan
    and from the deepest sea.
[23] Then we could stomp

on their blood,
  and our dogs could chew
  on their bones.

[24] We have seen crowds marching
  to your place of worship,
  our God and King.
[25] The singers come first,
  and then the musicians,
surrounded by young women
  playing tambourines.
[26] They come shouting,
  "People of Israel,
  praise the LORD God!"
[27] The small tribe of Benjamin
  leads the way,
followed by the leaders
  from Judah.
Then come the leaders
  from Zebulun and Naphtali.

[28] Our God, show your strength!
  Show us once again.
[29] Then kings will bring gifts
  to your temple
  in Jerusalem.[g]

[30] Punish that animal
  that lives in the swamp![h]
Punish that nation
  whose leaders and people
  are like wild bulls.
Make them come crawling
  with gifts of silver.
Scatter those nations
  that enjoy making war.[i]
[31] Force the Egyptians to bring
  gifts of bronze;
make the Ethiopians[j] hurry
  to offer presents.[k]

---

[d] **68.14** *Mount Zalmon:* The location of this mountain is not known. [e] **68.17** *to your people:* Or "in all your holiness" or "in your holy place." [f] **68.21** *are ready for war:* The Hebrew text has "have long hair," which probably refers to the ancient custom of wearing long hair on special occasions, such as a "holy war." [g] **68.28,29** *Our God . . . Jerusalem:* One possible meaning for the difficult Hebrew text of verses 28, 29. [h] **68.30** *animal . . . swamp:* Probably Egypt. [i] **68.30** *war:* One possible meaning for the difficult Hebrew text of verse 30. [j] **68.31** *the Ethiopians:* The Hebrew text has "the people of Cush," which was a region south of Egypt that included parts of the present countries of Ethiopia and Sudan. [k] **68.31** *presents:* One possible meaning for the difficult Hebrew text of verse 31.

³²Now sing praises to God!
Every kingdom on earth,
sing to the Lord!
³³Praise the one who rides
across the ancient skies;
listen as he speaks
with a mighty voice.

³⁴Tell about God's power!
He is honored in Israel,
and he rules the skies.
³⁵The God of Israel is fearsome
in his temple,
and he makes us strong.
Let's praise our God!

Psalm 69

[By David for the music leader.
To the tune "Lilies."]

God Can Be Trusted

¹Save me, God!
I am about to drown.
²I am sinking deep in the mud,
and my feet are slipping.
I am about to be swept under
by a mighty flood.
³I am worn out from crying,
and my throat is dry.
I have waited for you
till my eyes are blurred.

⁴There are more people
who hate me for no reason
than there are hairs
on my head.
Many terrible enemies
want to destroy me, God.
Am I supposed to give back
something I didn't steal?
⁵You know my foolish sins.
Not one is hidden from you.

⁶LORD God All-Powerful,
ruler of Israel,
don't let me embarrass anyone
who trusts and worships you.
⁷It is for your sake alone
that I am insulted
and blush with shame.
⁸I am like a stranger
to my relatives

and like a foreigner
to my own family.

⁹My love for your house
burns in me like a fire,
and when others insulted you,
they insulted me as well.
¹⁰I cried and went without food,ˡ
but they still insulted me.
¹¹They sneered at me
for wearing sackclothᵐ
to show my sorrow.
¹²Rulers and judges gossip
about me,
and drunkards make up songs
to mock me.

¹³But I pray to you, LORD.
So when the time is right,
answer me and help me
with your wonderful love.
¹⁴Don't let me sink in the mud,
but save me from my enemies
and from the deep water.
¹⁵Don't let me be
swept away by a flood
or drowned in the ocean
or swallowed by death.

¹⁶Answer me, LORD!
You are kind and good.
Pay attention to me!
You are truly merciful.
¹⁷Don't turn away from me.
I am your servant,
and I am in trouble.
Please hurry and help!
¹⁸Come and save me
from my enemies.

¹⁹You know how I am insulted,
mocked, and disgraced;
you know every one
of my enemies.
²⁰I am crushed by insults,
and I feel sick.
I had hoped for mercy and pity,
but there was none.
²¹Enemies poisoned my food,
and when I was thirsty,
they gave me vinegar.

ˡ**69.10** *went without food*: See the note at 35.13.
ᵐ**69.11** *sackcloth*: See the note at 30.11.

22 Make their table a trap
 for them and their friends.
23 Blind them with darkness
 and make them tremble.
24 Show them how angry you are!
 Be furious and catch them.
25 Destroy their camp
 and don't let anyone live
 in their tents.

26 They cause trouble for people
 you have already punished;
 their gossip hurts those
 you have wounded.
27 Make them guiltier than ever
 and don't forgive them.
28 Wipe their names from the book
 of the living;
 remove them from the list
 of the innocent.
29 I am mistreated and in pain.
 Protect me, God,
 and keep me safe!

30 I will praise the LORD God
 with a song
 and a thankful heart.
31 This will please the LORD
 better than offering an ox
 or a full-grown bull.
32 When those in need see this,
 they will be happy,
 and the LORD's worshipers
 will be encouraged.
33 The LORD will listen
 when the homeless cry out,
 and he will never forget
 his people in prison.

34 Heaven and earth
 will praise our God,
 and so will the oceans
 and everything in them.
35 God will rescue Jerusalem,
 and he will rebuild
 the towns of Judah.
 His people will live there
 on their own land,
36 and when the time comes,
 their children will inherit
 the land.
 Then everyone who loves God
 will also settle there.

Psalm 70

*[By David for the music leader.
To be used when an offering is made.]*

God Is Wonderful

1 Save me, LORD God!
 Hurry and help.
2 Disappoint and confuse
 all who want to kill me.
 Turn away and disgrace
 all who want to hurt me.
3 Embarrass and shame those
 who say, "We told you so!"

4 Let your worshipers celebrate
 and be glad because of you.
 They love your saving power,
 so let them always say,
 "God is wonderful!"
5 I am poor and needy,
 but you, the LORD God,
 care about me.

You are the one who saves me.
 Please hurry and help!

Psalm 71

A Prayer for God's Protection

1 I run to you, LORD,
 for protection.
 Don't disappoint me.
2 You do what is right,
 so come to my rescue.
 Listen to my prayer
 and keep me safe.
3 Be my mighty rock,[n] the place
 where I can always run
 for protection.
 Save me by your command!
 You are my mighty rock
 and my fortress.

4 Come and save me, LORD God,
 from vicious and cruel
 and brutal enemies!
5 I depend on you,
 and I have trusted you
 since I was young.

---

[n]71.3 *mighty rock:* See the note at 18.2.

⁶I have relied on you°
  from the day I was born.
You brought me safely
  through birth,
    and I always praise you.

⁷Many people think of me
  as something evil.
But you are my mighty protector,
⁸and I praise and honor you
  all day long.
⁹Don't throw me aside
  when I am old;
don't desert me
  when my strength is gone.
¹⁰My enemies are plotting
  because they want me dead.
¹¹They say, "Now we'll catch you!
God has deserted you,
  and no one can save you."
¹²Come closer, God!
  Please hurry and help.
¹³Embarrass and destroy
  all who want me dead;
disgrace and confuse
  all who want to hurt me.
¹⁴I will never give up hope
  or stop praising you.
¹⁵All day long I will tell
  the wonderful things you do

to save your people.
But you have done much more
  than I could possibly know.
¹⁶I will praise you, LORD God,
  for your mighty deeds
    and your power to save.

¹⁷You have taught me
  since I was a child,
and I never stop telling about
  your marvelous deeds.
¹⁸Don't leave me when I am old
  and my hair turns gray.
Let me tell future generations
  about your mighty power.
¹⁹Your deeds of kindness
  are known in the heavens.
  No one is like you!

²⁰You made me suffer a lot,
  but you will bring me
back from this deep pit
  and give me new life.
²¹You will make me truly great
  and take my sorrow away.

°71.6 *I . . . you:* One possible meaning for the difficult
Hebrew text.

PARENTING&*family*—How can I deal with the challenges of being a single parent? *(Psalm 71.1-6)*

Rely on past records of God's work in your life.

As human beings, we all struggle with feeling overwhelmed at times—and single parents are no exception! After long hours of work in order to pay for housing, clothing, and so on, making dinners, reading books, doing laundry, and helping with homework, you may have little emotional or physical energy left. When you're feeling discouraged with all the hats you wear, do what the psalmist did: Remember how God has helped you since you were born (71.4-6). Maybe you can even start a record of the jams God has rescued you from—financial dilemmas, child-care fiascos, legal decisions—to read in future dark moments.

Or look at how God has provided basic blessings, such as getting you through child-birth (71.6). Some simple blessings are actually quite complex: air to breathe, water to revive your body, sleep to give you strength, hope to look ahead. God is always amazingly and wonderfully at work in our lives, and we can rely on him for all our needs. As the psalmist pens, "Listen to my prayer and keep me safe. Be my mighty rock, the place where I can always run for protection" (71.2,3). (See also 1 Kings 17.8-16; Psalm 138; Philippians 4.10-20.)

Words To Remember: *I have relied on you from the day I was born. . . . Let me tell future generations about your mighty power. Your deeds of kindness are known in the heavens. No one is like you!—Psalm 71.6,18,19*

22 I will praise you, God,
the Holy One of Israel.
You are faithful.
I will play the harp
and sing your praises.
23 You have rescued me!
I will celebrate and shout,
singing praises to you
with all my heart.
24 All day long I will announce
your power to save.
I will tell how you disgraced
and disappointed those
who wanted to hurt me.

Psalm 72

[*By Solomon.*]

A Prayer for God To Guide and Help the King

1 Please help the king
to be honest and fair
just like you, our God.
2 Let him be honest and fair
with all your people,
especially the poor.
3 Let peace and justice rule
every mountain and hill.
4 Let the king defend the poor,
rescue the homeless, and crush
everyone who hurts them.
5 Let the king live[p] forever
like the sun and the moon.
6 Let him be as helpful as rain
that refreshes the meadows
and the ground.
7 Let the king be fair
with everyone,
and let there be peace
until the moon
falls from the sky.

8 Let his kingdom reach
from sea to sea,
from the Euphrates River
across all the earth.
9 Force the desert tribes
to accept his rule,
and make his enemies
crawl in the dirt.
10 Force the rulers of Tarshish[q]
and of the islands
to pay taxes to him.
Make the kings of Sheba
and of Seba[r] bring gifts.
11 Make other rulers bow down
and all nations serve him.

12 Do this because the king
rescues the homeless
when they cry out,
and he helps everyone
who is poor and in need.
13 The king has pity
on the weak and the helpless
and protects those in need.
14 He cares when they hurt,
and he saves them from cruel
and violent deaths.

15 Long live the king!
Give him gold from Sheba.
Always pray for the king
and praise him each day.
16 Let cities overflow with food
and hills be covered with grain,
just like Mount Lebanon.
Let the people in the cities
prosper like wild flowers.
17 May the glory of the king
shine brightly forever
like the sun in the sky.
Let him make nations prosper
and learn to praise him.

18 LORD God of Israel,
we praise you.
Only you can work miracles.
19 We will always praise
your glorious name.
Let your glory be seen
everywhere on earth.
Amen and amen.

20 This ends the prayers
of David, the son of Jesse.

---

[p] **72.5** *Let the king live*: One ancient translation; Hebrew "Let them worship you." [q] **72.10** *Tarshish*: Possibly a city in Spain. [r] **72.10** *Sheba . . . Seba*: Sheba may have been a place in what is now southwest Arabia, and Seba may have been in southern Arabia.

BOOK III
(Psalms 73–89)

Psalm 73

[A psalm by Asaph.]

God Is Good

¹ God is truly good to Israel,ˢ
especially to everyone
with a pure heart.
² But I almost stumbled and fell,
³   because it made me jealous
to see proud and evil people
and to watch them prosper.
⁴ They never have to suffer,ᵗ
they stay healthy,
⁵ and they don't have troubles
like everyone else.

⁶ Their pride is like a necklace,
and they commit sin more often
than they dress themselves.
⁷ Their eyes poke out with fat,
and their minds are flooded
with foolish thoughts.
⁸ They sneer and say cruel things,
and because of their pride,
they make violent threats.
⁹ They dare to speak against God
and to order others around.

¹⁰ God will bring his people back,
and they will drink the water
he so freely gives.ᵘ

¹¹ Only evil people would say,
"God Most High cannot
know everything!"
¹² Yet all goes well for them,
and they live in peace.
¹³ What good did it do me
to keep my thoughts pure
and refuse to do wrong?
¹⁴ I am sick all day,
and I am punished
each morning.
¹⁵ If I had said evil things,
I would not have been loyal
to your people.

¹⁶ It was hard for me
to understand all this!
¹⁷ Then I went to your temple,
and there I understood
what will happen
to my enemies.
¹⁸ You will make them stumble,
never to get up again.
¹⁹ They will be terrified,

ˢ**73.1** *to Israel*: Or "to those who do right."
ᵗ**73.4** *They . . . suffer*: Or "They die a painless death."
ᵘ**73.10** *gives*: One possible meaning for the difficult Hebrew text of verse 10.

Personal *Concerns*—Sometimes I'm jealous of others. How can I get out of the jealousy/envy trap? *(Psalm 73.1-20)*

Believe that God knows you best.
People around us seem to have what we don't—better work situations, better families, better homes. It is difficult to watch others move ahead in life and then be truly happy for them.

The trick is to believe that God knows us through and through, and that he's watching out for us, despite how other people's lives look. When we become jealous, it's as if we were giving God advice: *You should give me this, God. You should make sure that happens to me, too!* While something may look exactly like what we want, only God sees the future and knows what we need. Only he is equipped to know whether the things we demand will fit.

Second-guessing God through jealousy is like saying God doesn't see into our hearts or bring us what we need to be satisfied in life. God, who can be known and loved, can also be trusted. He will not disappoint. (See also 1 Samuel 20; Jonah 4; James 3.1-12.)

Words To Remember: *God is truly good to Israel, especially to everyone with a pure heart.—Psalm 73.1*

suddenly swept away
and no longer there.
²⁰ They will disappear, Lord,
despised like a bad dream
the morning after.

²¹ Once I was bitter
and brokenhearted.
²² I was stupid and ignorant,
and I treated you
as a wild animal would.
²³ But I never really left you,
and you hold my right hand.
²⁴ Your advice has been my guide,
and later you will welcome me
in glory.ᵛ
²⁵ In heaven I have only you,
and on this earth
you are all I want.
²⁶ My body and mind may fail,
but you are my strength
and my choice forever.

²⁷ Powerful LORD God,
all who stay far from you
will be lost,
and you will destroy those
who are unfaithful.
²⁸ It is good for me
to be near you.
I choose you as my protector,
and I will tell about
your wonderful deeds.

Psalm 74

[*A special psalm by Asaph.*]

A Prayer for the Nation in Times of Trouble

¹ Our God, why have you
completely rejected us?
Why are you so angry
with the ones you care for?
² Remember the people
you rescued long ago,
the tribe you chose
to be your very own.
Think of Mount Zion,
your home;
³ walk over to the temple
left in ruins forever
by those who hate us.

⁴ Your enemies roared like lions
in your holy temple,
and they have placed
their banners there.
⁵ It looks like a forest
chopped to pieces.ʷ
⁶ They used axes and hatchets
to smash the carvings.
⁷ They burned down your temple
and badly disgraced it.

ᵛ**73.24** *in glory*: Or "with honor." ʷ**74.5** *pieces*: One
meaning for the difficult Hebrew text of verse 5.

WORK—How can I be more confident about my work? *(Psalm 73.21-28)*

God is your strength.
If your job is threatening to overwhelm you, you may be wondering, *How can they ask me to do a job I'm not trained for? How am I supposed to work this much overtime? Should I just quit?* How can you keep listening for God to speak and watching for him to work when you feel like you can't keep going? It doesn't help to keep asking yourself, *Can I go on?* Consider the issue settled and the question answered: *Yes, I can go on.*

Remember, your constant companion here on earth is God, who will help you with difficult relationships and assist you in difficult tasks. Even during doubt and frustration, God can be the strength of your heart. Staying near to the heart of God helps you focus on God's strength and how he equips you for the job.

Even when you're in the middle of columns of figures that don't add up, puzzling personalities that won't blend, or obscure pieces that don't seem to fit together, God can give you a quiet strength you never could have imagined. (See also Deuteronomy 31.1-6; Joshua 1.1-9; Psalm 108; 1 John 3.19-24.)

Words To Remember: *My body and mind may fail, but you are my strength and my choice forever.—Psalm 73.26*

⁸ They said to themselves,
    "We'll crush them!"
Then they burned every one
of your meeting places
    all over the country.
⁹ There are no more miracles
    and no more prophets.
Who knows how long
    it will be like this?

¹⁰ Our God, how much longer
    will our enemies sneer?
Won't they ever stop
    insulting you?
¹¹ Why don't you punish them?
    Why are you holding back?

¹² Our God and King,
you have ruled
    since ancient times;
you have won victories
    everywhere on this earth.
¹³ By your power you made a path
    through the sea,
and you smashed the heads
    of sea monsters.
¹⁴ You crushed the heads
    of the monster Leviathan,ˣ
then fed him to wild creatures
    in the desert.
¹⁵ You opened the ground
    for streams and springs
and dried up mighty rivers.
¹⁶ You rule the day and the night,
and you put the moon
    and the sun in place.
¹⁷ You made summer and winter
    and gave them to the earth.ʸ

¹⁸ Remember your enemies, LORD!
They foolishly sneer
    and won't respect you.
¹⁹ You treat us like pet doves,
    but they mistreat us.
Don't keep forgetting us
and letting us be fed
    to those wild animals.
²⁰ Remember the agreement
    you made with us.
Violent enemies are hiding
in every dark corner
    of the earth.
²¹ Don't disappoint those in need
    or make them turn from you,

but help the poor and homeless
    to shout your praises.
²² Do something, God!
    Defend yourself.
Remember how those fools
    sneer at you all day long.
²³ Don't forget the loud shouts
    of your enemies.

Psalm 75

[*A psalm and a song by Asaph for the music leader. To the tune "Don't Destroy."*ᶻ]

Praise God for All He Has Done

¹ Our God, we thank you
    for being so near to us!
Everyone celebrates
    your wonderful deeds.

² You have set a time
    to judge with fairness.
³ The earth trembles,
    and its people shake;
you alone keep
    its foundations firm.
⁴ You tell every bragger,
    "Stop bragging!"
And to the wicked you say,
    "Don't boast of your power!
⁵ Stop bragging! Quit telling me
    how great you are."

⁶ Our LORD and our God,
    victory doesn't come
from the east or the west
    or from the desert.
⁷ You are the one who judges.
You can take away power
    and give it to others.
⁸ You hold in your hand
a cup filled with wine,ᵃ
    strong and foaming.
You will pour out some
for every sinful person
    on this earth,

ˣ**74.14** *Leviathan:* God's victory over this monster sometimes stands for his power over all creation and sometimes for his defeat of Egypt. ʸ**74.17** *gave . . . earth:* Or "made boundaries for the earth."
ᶻ**Psalm 75** *Don't Destroy:* See the note at Psalm 57.
ᵃ**75.8** *a cup . . . wine:* In the Old Testament "a cup filled with wine" sometimes stands for God's anger.

and they will have to drink
until it is gone.
9 But I will always tell about
you, the God of Jacob,
and I will sing your praise.

10 Our Lord, you will destroy
the power of evil people,
but you will give strength
to those who are good.

Psalm 76

[A song and a psalm for the music leader.
Use stringed instruments.]

God Always Wins

1 You, our God,
are famous in Judah
and honored in Israel.
2 Your home is on Mount Zion
in the city of peace.
3 There you destroyed
fiery arrows, shields, swords,
and all the other weapons.

4 You are more glorious than
the eternal mountains.*b*
5 Brave warriors were robbed
of what they had taken,
and now they lie dead,
unable to lift an arm.
6 God of Jacob, when you roar,
enemy chariots and horses
drop dead in their tracks.

7 Our God, you are fearsome,
and no one can oppose you
when you are angry.
8 From heaven you announced
your decisions as judge!
And all who live on this earth
were terrified and silent
9 when you took over as judge,
ready to rescue
everyone in need.
10 Even the most angry people
will praise you
when you are furious.*c*

11 Everyone, make your promises
to the LORD your God
and do what you promise.

The LORD is fearsome,
and all of his servants
should bring him gifts.
12 God destroys the courage
of rulers and kings
and makes cowards of them.

Psalm 77

[A psalm by Asaph for Jeduthun, the music leader.]

In Times of Trouble
God Is with His People

1 I pray to you, Lord God,
and I beg you to listen.
2 In days filled with trouble,
I search for you.
And at night I tirelessly
lift my hands in prayer,
refusing comfort.
3 When I think of you,
I feel restless and weak.

4 Because of you, Lord God,
I can't sleep.
I am restless
and can't even talk.
5 I think of times gone by,
of those years long ago.
6 Each night my mind
is flooded with questions:*d*
7 "Have you rejected me forever?
Won't you be kind again?
8 Is this the end of your love
and your promises?
9 Have you forgotten
how to have pity?
Do you refuse to show mercy
because of your anger?"
10 Then I said, "God Most High,
what hurts me most
is that you no longer help us
with your mighty arm."

11 Our LORD, I will remember
the things you have done,
your miracles of long ago.

---

*b*76.4 *the eternal mountains:* One ancient translation;
Hebrew "the mountains of victims (of wild animals)."
*c*76.10 *furious:* One possible meaning for the difficult
Hebrew text of verse 10. *d*77.6 *my mind . . . questions:*
One ancient translation; Hebrew "I remember
my music."

¹² I will think about each one
      of your mighty deeds.
¹³ Everything you do is right,
   and no other god
      compares with you.
¹⁴ You alone work miracles,
   and you have let nations
      see your mighty power.
¹⁵ With your own arm you rescued
   your people, the descendants
      of Jacob and Joseph.

¹⁶ The ocean looked at you, God,
   and it trembled deep down
      with fear.
¹⁷ Water flowed from the clouds.
      Thunder was heard above
   as your arrows of lightning
      flashed about.
¹⁸ Your thunder roared
      like chariot wheels.
   The world was made bright
   by lightning,
      and all the earth trembled.

> *Taking time out to
> remember the past—
> in all its sorrow and joy—
> is crucial. For reliving
> our memories is like
> looking through a window
> and seeing life's pieces
> fitting together in glory.*
> RAMONA CRAMER TUCKER

¹⁹ You walked through the water
      of the mighty sea,
   but your footprints
      were never seen.
²⁰ You guided your people
      like a flock of sheep,
   and you chose Moses and Aaron
      to be their leaders.

Psalm 78

[A special psalm by Asaph.]

What God Has Done for His People

¹ My friends, I beg you
      to listen as I teach.
² I will give instruction
   and explain the mystery
      of what happened long ago.
³ These are things we learned
      from our ancestors,
⁴ and we will tell them
      to the next generation.
   We won't keep secret
      the glorious deeds
   and the mighty miracles
      of the LORD.

⁵ God gave his Law
   to Jacob's descendants,
      the people of Israel.
   And he told our ancestors
      to teach their children,
⁶ so that each new generation
   would know his Law
      and tell it to the next.
⁷ Then they would trust God
      and obey his teachings,
   without forgetting anything
      God had done.
⁸ They would be different
      from their ancestors,
   who were stubborn, rebellious,
      and unfaithful to God.

⁹ The warriors from Ephraim
      were armed with arrows,
   but they ran away
      when the battle began.
¹⁰ They broke their agreement
      with God,
   and they turned their backs
      on his teaching.
¹¹ They forgot all he had done,
      even the mighty miracles
¹² he did for their ancestors
      near Zoanᵉ in Egypt.

¹³ God made a path in the sea
   and piled up the water
      as he led them across.

ᵉ**78.12** *Zoan:* A city in the eastern part of the Nile Delta.

14 He guided them during the day
  with a cloud,
and each night he led them
  with a flaming fire.
15 God made water flow
  from rocks he split open
  in the desert,
and his people drank freely,
  as though from a lake.
16 He made streams gush out
  like rivers from rocks.

17 But in the desert,
  the people of God Most High
  kept sinning and rebelling.
18 They stubbornly tested God
and demanded from him
  what they wanted to eat.
19 They challenged God by saying,
  "Can God provide food
  out here in the desert?
20 It's true God struck the rock
and water gushed out
  like a river,
but can he give his people
  bread and meat?"

---

*We all have busy schedules.
However, I've discovered that
when we take time to play
with our kids, we give them
a sense of value and worth.
That's what makes a
home kid-friendly!*

KARYN HENLEY

---

21 When the LORD heard this,
  he was angry and furious
with Jacob's descendants,
  the people of Israel.
22 They had refused to trust him,
and they had doubted
  his saving power.

23 But God gave a command
  to the clouds,
and he opened the doors
  in the skies.
24 From heaven he sent grain
  that they called manna.ʲ
25 He gave them more than enough,
  and each one of them ate
  this special food.

26 God's mighty power
  brought a strong wind
  from the southeast,
27 and it brought birds
  that covered the ground,
  like sand on the beach.
28 Then God made the birds fall
in the camp of his people
  near their tents.

29 God gave his people
  all they wanted,
and each of them ate
  until they were full.
30 But before they had swallowed
  the last bite,
31 God became angry and killed
  the strongest and best
  from the families of Israel.

32 But the rest kept on sinning
and would not trust
  God's miracles.
33 So he cut their lives short
  and made them terrified.
34 After he killed some of them,
  the others turned to him
  with all their hearts.
35 They remembered God Most High,
  the mighty rockᵍ
  that kept them safe.
36 But they tried to flatter God,
  and they told him lies;
37 they were unfaithful
  and broke their promises.

38 Yet God was kind.
He kept forgiving their sins
  and didn't destroy them.
He often became angry,
  but never lost his temper.

ʲ**78.24** *manna*: When the people of Israel were
wandering through the desert, the Lord gave them a
special kind of food to eat. It tasted like a wafer and
was called "manna," which in Hebrew means, "What
is this?" ᵍ**78.35** *mighty rock*: See the note at 18.2.

³⁹ God remembered that they
were made of flesh
and were like a wind
that blows once
and then dies down.

⁴⁰ While they were in the desert,
they often rebelled
and made God sad.
⁴¹ They kept testing him
and caused terrible pain
for the Holy One of Israel.
⁴² They forgot about his power
and how he had rescued them
from their enemies.
⁴³ God showed them all kinds
of wonderful miracles
near Zoan^h in Egypt.
⁴⁴ He turned the rivers of Egypt
into blood,
and no one could drink
from the streams.
⁴⁵ He sent swarms of flies
to pester the Egyptians,
and he sent frogs
to cause them trouble.

⁴⁶ God let worms and grasshoppers
eat their crops.
⁴⁷ He destroyed their grapevines
and their fig trees
with hail and floods.ⁱ
⁴⁸ Then he killed their cattle
with hail
and their other animals
with lightning.

⁴⁹ God was so angry and furious
that he went into a rage
and caused them great trouble
by sending swarms
of destroying angels.
⁵⁰ God gave in to his anger
and slaughtered them
in a terrible way.
⁵¹ He killed the first-born son
of each Egyptian family.

⁵² Then God led his people
out of Egypt
and guided them in the desert
like a flock of sheep.
⁵³ He led them safely along,
and they were not afraid,

but their enemies drowned
in the sea.

⁵⁴ God brought his people
to the sacred mountain
that he had taken
by his own power.
⁵⁵ He made nations run
from the tribes of Israel,
and he let the tribes
take over their land.

⁵⁶ But the people tested
God Most High,
and they refused
to obey his laws.
⁵⁷ They were as unfaithful
as their ancestors,
and they were as crooked
as a twisted arrow.
⁵⁸ God demanded all their love,
but they made him angry
by worshiping idols.

⁵⁹ So God became furious
and completely rejected
the people of Israel.
⁶⁰ Then he deserted his home
at Shiloh, where he lived
here on earth.
⁶¹ He let enemies capture
the sacred chest^j
and let them dishonor him.

⁶² God took out his anger
on his chosen ones
and let them be killed
by enemy swords.
⁶³ Fire destroyed the young men,
and the young women were left
with no one to marry.
⁶⁴ Priests died violent deaths,
but their widows
were not allowed to mourn.

⁶⁵ Finally the Lord woke up,
and he shouted
like a drunken soldier.
⁶⁶ God scattered his enemies

---

^h**78.43** *Zoan:* See the note at 78.12. ⁱ**78.47** *floods:* Or
"frost." ^j**78.61** *sacred chest:* The Hebrew text has "his
power," which refers to the sacred chest. In Psalm 132.8
it is called "powerful."

and made them ashamed
forever.

⁶⁷ Then the Lord decided
not to make his home
with Joseph's descendants
in Ephraim.ᵏ
⁶⁸ Instead he chose the tribe
of Judah,
and he chose Mount Zion,
the place he loves.
⁶⁹ There he built his temple
as lofty as the mountains
and as solid as the earth
that he had made
to last forever.

⁷⁰ The Lord God chose David
to be his servant and took him
from tending sheep
⁷¹   and from caring for lambs.
Then God made him the leader
of Israel, his own nation.
⁷² David treated the people fairly
and guided them with wisdom.

Psalm 79

[A psalm by Asaph.]

Have Pity on Jerusalem

¹ Our God, foreign nations
have taken your land,
disgraced your temple,
and left Jerusalem in ruins.
² They have fed the bodies
of your servants
to flesh-eating birds;
your loyal people are food
for savage animals.
³ All Jerusalem is covered
with their blood,
and there is no one left
to bury them.
⁴ Every nation around us
sneers and makes fun.

⁵ Our LORD, will you keep on
being angry?
Will your angry feelings
keep flaming up like fire?
⁶ Get angry with those nations
that don't know you
and won't worship you!

⁷ They have gobbled down
Jacob's descendants
and left the land in ruins.

⁸ Don't make us pay for the sins
of our ancestors.
Have pity and come quickly!
We are completely helpless.
⁹ Our God, you keep us safe.
Now help us! Rescue us.
Forgive our sins
and bring honor to yourself.

¹⁰ Why should nations ask us,
"Where is your God?"
Let us and the other nations
see you take revenge
for your servants who died
a violent death.

¹¹ Listen to the prisoners groan!
Let your mighty power save all
who are sentenced to die.
¹² Each of those nations sneered
at you, our Lord.
Now let others sneer at them,
seven times as much.
¹³ Then we, your people,
will always thank you.
We are like sheep
with you as our shepherd,
and all generations
will hear us praise you.

Psalm 80

[A psalm by Asaph for the music leader.
To the tune "Lilies of the Agreement."]

Help Our Nation

¹ Shepherd of Israel, you lead
the descendants of Joseph,
and you sit on your throne
above the winged creatures.ˡ

ᵏ78.67 with . . . Ephraim: Ephraim was Joseph's
youngest son. One of the twelve tribes was named after
him, and sometimes the northern kingdom of Israel was
also known as Ephraim. The town of Shiloh was in the
territory of Ephraim, but the place where God was
worshiped was moved from there to Zion (Jerusalem) in
the territory of Judah.   ˡ80.1 winged creatures: Two
winged creatures made of gold were on the top of the
sacred chest and were symbols of the LORD's throne on
earth (see Exodus 25.18).

Listen to our prayer
    and let your light shine
2 for the tribes of Ephraim,
Benjamin, and Manasseh.
    Save us by your power.

3 Our God, make us strong again!
    Smile on us and save us.

4 LORD God All-Powerful,
    how much longer
will the prayers of your people
    make you angry?
5 You gave us tears for food,
and you made us drink them
    by the bowlful.
6 Because of you,
our enemies who live nearby
    laugh and joke about us.
7 But if you smile on us,
    we will be saved.

8 We were like a grapevine
    you brought out of Egypt.
You chased other nations away
    and planted us here.
9 Then you cleared the ground,
and we put our roots deep,
    spreading over the land.
10 Shade from this vine covered
    the mountains.
Its branches climbed
    the mighty cedars
11   and stretched to the sea;
its new growth reached
    to the river.ᵐ

12 Our Lord, why have you
torn down the wall
    from around the vineyard?
You let everyone who walks by
    pick the grapes.
13 Now the vine is gobbled down
by pigs from the forest
    and other wild animals.

14 God All-Powerful,
    please do something!
Look down from heaven
and see what's happening
    to this vine.
15 With your own hands
    you planted its roots,
and you raised it
    as your very own.

16 Enemies chopped the vine down
    and set it on fire.
Now show your anger
    and destroy them.
17 But help the one who sits
    at your right side,ⁿ
the one you raised
    to be your own.
18 Then we will never turn away.
Put new life into us,
    and we will worship you.

19 LORD God All-Powerful,
make us strong again!
    Smile on us and save us.

Psalm 81

[By Asaph for the music leader.ᵒ]

God Makes Us Strong

1 Be happy and shout to God
    who makes us strong!
Shout praises to the God
    of Jacob.
2 Sing as you play tambourines
and the lovely sounding
    stringed instruments.
3 Sound the trumpets and start
    the New Moon Festival.ᵖ
We must also celebrate
    when the moon is full.
4 This is the law in Israel,
and it was given to us
    by the God of Jacob.
5 The descendants of Joseph
    were told to obey it,
when God led them out
    from the land of Egypt.

In a language unknown to me,
    I heard someone say:
6 "I lifted the burden
    from your shoulder
and took the heavy basket
    from your hands.

ᵐ80.11 *the sea . . . the river*: The Mediterranean Sea and
the Euphrates River were part of the ideal boundaries
for Israel.   ⁿ80.17 *right side*: See the note at 16.11.
ᵒ**Psalm 81** *leader*: See the note at Psalm 8.
ᵖ81.3 *New Moon Festival*: Celebrated on the first day of
each new moon, which was the beginning of the
month. But this may refer to either the New Year
celebration or the Harvest Festival. "The moon is full"
suggests a festival in the middle of the month.

7 When you were in trouble,
  I rescued you,
and from the thunderclouds,
  I answered your prayers.
Later I tested you
  at Meribah Spring.*q*

8 "Listen, my people,
  while I, the Lord,
    correct you!
Israel, if you would only
  pay attention to me!
9 Don't worship foreign gods
  or bow down to gods
    you know nothing about.
10 I am the LORD your God.
  I rescued you from Egypt.
Just ask, and I will give you
  whatever you need.

11 "But, my people, Israel,
  you refused to listen,
and you would have nothing
  to do with me!
12 So I let you be stubborn
  and keep on following
    your own advice.

13 "My people, Israel,
  if only you would listen
    and do as I say!
14 I, the LORD, would quickly
  defeat your enemies
    with my mighty power.
15 Everyone who hates me
  would come crawling,
and that would be the end
  of them.
16 But I would feed you
  with the finest bread
and with the best honey*r*
  until you were full."

Psalm 82

[A psalm by Asaph.]

Please Do Something, God!

1 When all of the other gods*s*
  have come together,
the Lord God judges them
  and says:
2 "How long will you

keep judging unfairly
  and favoring evil people?
3 Be fair to the poor
  and to orphans.
Defend the helpless
  and everyone in need.
4 Rescue the weak and homeless
  from the powerful hands
    of heartless people.

5 "None of you know
  or understand a thing.
You live in darkness,
  while the foundations
    of the earth tremble.*t*

6 "I, the Most High God, say
  that all of you are gods*u*
    and also my own children.
7 But you will die,
  just like everyone else,
    including powerful rulers."

8 Do something, God!
Judge the nations of the earth;
  they belong to you.

Psalm 83

[A song and a psalm by Asaph.]

God Rules All the Earth

1 Our God, don't just sit there,
  silently doing nothing!
2 Your hateful enemies
  are turning against you
    and rebelling.
3 They are sly, and they plot
  against those you treasure.
4 They say, "Let's wipe out
  the nation of Israel

and make sure that no one
remembers its name!"

⁵All of them fully agree
in their plans against you,
and among them are
⁶Edom and the Ishmaelites;
Moab and the Hagrites;
⁷Gebal, Ammon, and Amalek;
Philistia and Phoenicia.ᵛ
⁸Even Assyria has joined forces
with Moab and Ammon.ʷ

⁹Our Lord, punish all of them
as you punished Midian.
Destroy them, as you destroyed
Sisera and Jabin
at Kishon Creek ¹⁰near Endor,
and let their bodies rot.
¹¹Treat their leaders as you did
Oreb and Zeeb,
Zebah and Zalmunna.
¹²All of them said, "We'll take
God's valuable land!"

¹³Our God, scatter them around
like dust in a whirlwind.
¹⁴Just as flames destroy forests
on the mountains,
¹⁵pursue and terrify them

with storms of your own.
¹⁶Make them blush with shame,
until they turn and worship
you, our LORD.
¹⁷Let them be forever ashamed
and confused.
Let them die in disgrace.
¹⁸Make them realize that you
are the LORD Most High,
the only ruler of earth!

Psalm 84

[*For the music leader.ˣ A psalm
for the people of Korah.*]

The Joy of Worship

¹LORD God All-Powerful,
your temple is so lovely!
²Deep in my heart I long
for your temple,
and with all that I am
I sing joyful songs to you.

ᵛ**83.7** *Phoenicia:* The Hebrew text has "Tyre," the main city in Phoenicia. ʷ**83.8** *Moab and Ammon:* The Hebrew text has "the descendants of Lot," whose older daughter was the mother of the Moabites and whose younger daughter was the mother of the Ammonites (see Genesis 19.30-38). ˣ**Psalm 84** *leader:* See the note at Psalm 8.

SingleLife—Sometimes I really want to be married. How can I deal with those times? *(Psalm 84)*

Find your heart's home.

If God is all-powerful, he can do anything, right? Well, then, why doesn't he take care of the dilemmas I face because I'm single—loneliness, fewer financial resources, unexpressed sexuality, invisibility in a couple-oriented world?

The Lord God is so all-powerful that he can address those needs whether or not you have a spouse. He can create a climate and surroundings that enable you to feel at home—relaxed, safe, attended to.

It's easy to get off-track when your goal becomes finding a spouse instead of building a home. Yet, every woman, single or married, struggles to find her heart's home in God and to feel comfortable here on earth. God can show you what's required for you to feel at home with yourself in this world. When you allow him to do this, your heart will be peaceful and content. Whether or not a spouse joins along the way, your heart will be satisfied, you'll feel valuable because you're walking in God's will, and you'll have joy! (See also Jeremiah 29.10-14; 1 Peter 3.13-18.)

Words To Remember: LORD God All-Powerful, my King and my God, . . . you bless everyone who lives in your house, and they sing your praises.—Psalm 84.3,4

³LORD God All-Powerful,
  my King and my God,
  sparrows find a home
    near your altars;
  swallows build nests there
    to raise their young.

⁴You bless everyone
  who lives in your house,
    and they sing your praises.
⁵You bless all who depend
    on you for their strength
  and all who deeply desire
    to visit your temple.
⁶When they reach Dry Valley,ʸ
    springs start flowing,
  and the autumn rain fills it
    with pools of water.ᶻ
⁷Your people grow stronger,
  and you, the God of gods,
    will be seen in Zion.

⁸LORD God All-Powerful,
  the God of Jacob,
    please answer my prayer!
⁹You are the shield
    that protects your people,

and I am your chosen one.
  Won't you smile on me?

¹⁰One day in your temple
  is better than a thousand
    anywhere else.
I would rather serve
    in your house,
  than live in the homes
    of the wicked.

¹¹Our LORD and our God,
  you are like the sun
    and also like a shield.
You treat us with kindness
    and with honor,
  never denying any good thing
    to those who live right.

¹²LORD God All-Powerful,
  you bless everyone
    who trusts you.

ʸ84.6 *Dry Valley*: Or "Balsam Tree Valley." The exact location is not known.   ᶻ84.6 *and . . . water*: One possible meaning for the difficult Hebrew text.

*Spiritual*Life—How should I pray? (*Psalm 85*)

Look beyond me, myself, and I.
When you have a friend who is a foster parent, it's amazing how foster-care issues take on a new importance for you. You become familiar with related laws, you understand the concerns of the biological and foster parents, you see the value in people (like your foster-parent friend) with giving hearts.

As we grow to love God, his concerns take on new meaning for us. We see how he works for goodness and peace in the world, and we want to be a part of that work. As we experience the compassionate heart of the Father, *we* become more compassionate. Our prayer life takes on new proportions as we pray for loyalty, love, and peace to come alive in the world. As we see the world through God's eyes, current events give us many reasons to pray. While people may irritate us, when we see them through God's perspective, we can at least pray for them.

We begin to view ourselves as part of a larger group—a family, a church, a neighborhood, a nation. As a representative of that group, we seek God's will, asking him how we can be more obedient, asking forgiveness for our group's mistakes. We discover reasons to be thankful for how God works in the lives of other people here on earth. (See also 2 Samuel 7.18-29; 2 Kings 19.14-19; 2 Chronicles 6,7; Nehemiah 1; Lamentations 5; Matthew 6.5-15; Acts 4.23-31.)

Words To Remember: *You are ready to rescue everyone who worships you, so that you will live with us in all of your glory. Love and loyalty will come together; goodness and peace will unite.—Psalm 85.9,10*

Psalm 85

[A psalm by the people of Korah for the music leader.]

A Prayer for Peace

¹ Our LORD, you have blessed
your land
and made all go well
for Jacob's descendants.
² You have forgiven the sin
and taken away the guilt
of your people.
³ Your fierce anger is no longer
aimed at us.

⁴ Our LORD and our God,
you save us!
Please bring us back home
and don't be angry.
⁵ Will you always be angry
with us and our families?
⁶ Won't you give us fresh life
and let your people be glad
because of you?
⁷ Show us your love
and save us!

⁸ I will listen to you, LORD God,
because you promise peace
to those who are faithful
and no longer foolish.
⁹ You are ready to rescue
everyone who worships you,
so that you will live with us
in all of your glory.

¹⁰ Love and loyalty
will come together;
goodness and peace
will unite.
¹¹ Loyalty will sprout
from the ground;
justice will look down
from the sky above.

¹² Our LORD, you will bless us;
our land will produce
wonderful crops.
¹³ Justice will march in front,
making a path
for you to follow.

Psalm 86

[A prayer by David.]

A Prayer for Help

¹ Please listen, LORD,
and answer my prayer!
I am poor and helpless.
² Protect me and save me
because you are my God.
I am your faithful servant,
and I trust you.
³ Be kind to me!
I pray to you all day.
⁴ Make my heart glad!
I serve you,
and my prayer is sincere.
⁵ You willingly forgive,
and your love is always there
for those who pray to you.
⁶ Please listen, LORD!
Answer my prayer for help.
⁷ When I am in trouble, I pray,
knowing you will listen.

When we wait in faith on God's promise and offer our pain to him, it's never wasted.

ELIZABETH MITTELSTAEDT

⁸ No other gods are like you;
only you work miracles.
⁹ You created each nation,
and they will all bow down
to worship and honor you.
¹⁰ You perform great wonders
because you alone are God.

¹¹ Teach me to follow you,
and I will obey your truth.
Always keep me faithful.
¹² With all my heart I thank you.
I praise you, LORD God.
¹³ Your love for me is so great
that you protected me
from death and the grave.

¹⁴ Proud and violent enemies,
who don't care about you,
have ganged up to attack
and kill me.
¹⁵ But you, the Lord God,
are kind and merciful.
You don't easily get angry,
and your love
can always be trusted.
¹⁶ I serve you, LORD,
and I am the child
of one of your servants.
Look on me with kindness.
Make me strong and save me.
¹⁷ Show that you approve of me!
Then my hateful enemies
will feel like fools,
because you have helped
and comforted me.

Psalm 87

[A psalm and a song by the people of Korah.]

The Glory of Mount Zion

¹ Zion was built by the LORD
on the holy mountain,
² and he loves that city
more than any other place
in all of Israel.
³ Zion, you are the city of God,
and wonderful things
are told about you.

⁴ Egypt,ᵃ Babylonia, Philistia,
Phoenicia,ᵇ and Ethiopiaᶜ
are some of those nations
that know you,
and their people all say,
"I was born in Zion."

⁵ God Most High will strengthen
the city of Zion.
Then everyone will say,
"We were born here too."
⁶ The LORD will make a list
of his people,
and all who were born here
will be included.

⁷ All who sing or dance will say,
"I too am from Zion."

Psalm 88

[A song and a psalm by the people of Korah
for the music leader. To the tune "Mahalath
Leannoth."ᵈ A special psalm by
Heman the Ezrahite.]

A Prayer When You Can't Find the Way

¹ You keep me safe, LORD God.
So when I pray at night,
²   please listen carefully
to each of my concerns.

³ I am deeply troubled
and close to death;
⁴ I am as good as dead
and completely helpless.
⁵ I am no better off
than those in the grave,
those you have forgotten
and no longer help.

⁶ You have put me in the deepest
and darkest grave;
⁷ your anger rolls over me
like ocean waves.
⁸ You have made my friends turn
in horror from me.
I am a prisoner
who cannot escape,
⁹ and I am almost blind
because of my sorrow.

Each day I lift my hands
in prayer to you, LORD.
¹⁰ Do you work miracles
for the dead?
Do they stand up
and praise you?
¹¹ Are your love and loyalty
announced in the world
of the dead?
¹² Do they know of your miracles
or your saving power
in the dark world below
where all is forgotten?

¹³ Each morning I pray
to you, LORD.

ᵃ**87.4** *Egypt:* The Hebrew text has "Rahab," the name of
a monster that stands for Egypt (see Isaiah 30.7).
ᵇ**87.4** *Phoenicia:* See the note at 83.7.   ᶜ**87.4** *Ethiopia:*
See the note at 68.31.   ᵈ**Psalm 88** *To . . . Leannoth:* Or
"For the flutes," one possible meaning for the difficult
Hebrew text.

¹⁴Why do you reject me?
  Why do you turn from me?
¹⁵Ever since I was a child,
  I have been sick
    and close to death.
  You have terrified me
    and made me helpless.ᵉ

¹⁶Your anger is like a flood!
  And I am shattered
    by your furious attacks
¹⁷that strike each day
    and from every side.
¹⁸My friends and neighbors
  have turned against me
    because of you,
  and now darkness
    is my only companion.

Psalm 89

[A special psalm by Ethan the Ezrahite.]

The LORD's Agreement with David

¹Our LORD, I will sing
    of your love forever.
  Everyone yet to be born
  will hear me praise
    your faithfulness.
²I will tell them, "God's love
    can always be trusted,
  and his faithfulness lasts
    as long as the heavens."

³You said, "David, my servant,
    is my chosen one,
  and this is the agreement
    I made with him:
⁴David, one of your descendants
  will always be king."

⁵Our LORD, let the heavens
    now praise your miracles,
  and let all of your angels
    praise your faithfulness.

⁶None who live in the heavens
    can compare with you.
⁷You are the most fearsome
    of all who live in heaven;
  all the others fear
    and greatly honor you.
⁸You are LORD God All-Powerful!
  No one is as loving

  and faithful as you are.
⁹You rule the roaring sea
    and calm its waves.
¹⁰You crushed the monster Rahab,ᶠ
  and with your powerful arm
    you scattered your enemies.
¹¹The heavens and the earth
    belong to you.
  And so does the world
    with all its people
  because you created them
¹²   and everything else.ᵍ

Mount Tabor and Mount Hermon
    gladly praise you.
¹³You are strong and mighty!
¹⁴Your kingdom is ruled
    by justice and fairness
  with love and faithfulness
    leading the way.

¹⁵Our LORD, you bless those
    who join in the festival
  and walk in the brightness
    of your presence.
¹⁶We are happy all day
    because of you,
  and your saving power
    brings honor to us.
¹⁷Your own glorious power
    makes us strong,
  and because of your kindness,
    our strength increases.
¹⁸Our LORD and our King,
    the Holy One of Israel,
  you are truly our shield.

¹⁹In a vision, you once said
    to your faithful followers:
  "I have helped a mighty hero.
  I chose him from my people
    and made him famous.
²⁰David, my servant, is the one
    I chose to be king,
²¹and I will always be there
    to help and strengthen him.

ᵉ**88.15** *and made me helpless:* One possible meaning for the difficult Hebrew text. ᶠ**89.10** *Rahab:* Many people in the ancient world thought that the world was controlled by this sea monster that the Lord destroyed at the time of creation (see Isaiah 51.9). ᵍ**89.12** *and everything else:* The Hebrew text has "Zaphon and Yamin," which may either be the names of mountains or refer to the directions "north and south," with the meaning "everything from north to south."

22 "No enemy will outsmart David,
and he won't be defeated
by any hateful people.
23 I will strike down and crush
his troublesome enemies.
24 He will always be able
to depend on my love,
and I will make him strong
with my own power.
25 I will let him rule the lands
across the rivers and seas.
26 He will say to me,
'You are my Father
and my God,
as well as the mighty rock[h]
where I am safe.'

27 "I have chosen David
as my first-born son,
and he will be the ruler
of all kings on earth.
28 My love for him will last,
and my agreement with him
will never be broken.

29 "One of David's descendants
will always be king,
and his family will rule
until the sky disappears.
30 Suppose some of his children
should reject my Law
and refuse my instructions.
31 Or suppose they should disobey
all of my teachings.
32 Then I will correct
and punish them
because of their sins.
33 But I will always love David
and faithfully keep all
of my promises to him.

34 "I won't break my agreement
or go back on my word.
35 I have sworn once and for all
by my own holy name,
and I won't lie to David.
36 His family will always rule.
I will let his kingdom last
as long as the sun 37 and moon
appear in the sky."

38 You are now angry, God,
and you have turned your back
on your chosen king.
39 You broke off your agreement
with your servant, the king,
and you completely destroyed
his kingdom.
40 The walls of his city
have been broken through,
and every fortress
now lies in ruin.
41 All who pass by
take what they want,
and nations everywhere
joke about the king.

42 You made his enemies powerful
and let them celebrate.
43 But you forced him to retreat
because you did not fight
on his side.
44 You took his crown[i]
and threw his throne
in the dirt.
45 You made an old man of him
and put him to shame.

46 How much longer, LORD?
Will you hide forever?
How long will your anger
keep burning like fire?
47 Remember, life is short![j]
Why did you empty our lives
of all meaning?
48 No one can escape the power
of death and the grave.

49 Our Lord, where is the love
you have always shown
and that you promised
so faithfully to David?
50 Remember your servant, Lord!
People make jokes about me,
and I suffer many insults.
51 I am your chosen one,
but your enemies chase
and make fun of me.

52 Our LORD, we praise you
forever. Amen and amen.

---

h**89.26** *mighty rock*: See the note at 18.2.   i**89.44** *You took ... crown*: One possible meaning for the difficult Hebrew text.   j**89.47** *Remember ... short*: One possible meaning for the difficult Hebrew text.

BOOK IV
(Psalms 90–106)

Psalm 90

[A prayer by Moses, the man of God.]

God Is Eternal

¹ Our Lord, in all generations
  you have been our home.
² You have always been God—
long before the birth
  of the mountains,
even before you created
  the earth and the world.

³ At your command we die
  and turn back to dust,
⁴ but a thousand years
  mean nothing to you!
They are merely a day gone by
  or a few hours in the night.

⁵ You bring our lives to an end
  just like a dream.
We are merely tender grass
⁶   that sprouts and grows
in the morning,
  but dries up by evening.
⁷ Your furious anger frightens
  and destroys us,
⁸ and you know all of our sins,
  even those we do in secret.

⁹ Your anger is a burden
each day we live,
  then life ends like a sigh.
¹⁰ We can expect seventy years,
  or maybe eighty,
  if we are healthy,
but even our best years
  bring trouble and sorrow.
Suddenly our time is up,
  and we disappear.
¹¹ No one knows the full power
  of your furious anger,
but it is as great as the fear
  that we owe to you.
¹² Teach us to use wisely
  all the time we have.

¹³ Help us, LORD! Don't wait!
  Pity your servants.

¹⁴ When morning comes,
  let your love satisfy
  all our needs.
Then we can celebrate
and be glad for what time
  we have left.
¹⁵ Make us happy for as long
  as you caused us trouble
  and sorrow.
¹⁶ Do wonderful things for us,
  your servants,
and show your mighty power
  to our children.
¹⁷ Our Lord and our God,
  treat us with kindness
and let all go well for us.
  Please let all go well!

Psalm 91

The LORD Is My Fortress

¹ Live under the protection
  of God Most High
and stay in the shadow
  of God All-Powerful.
² Then you will say to the LORD,
"You are my fortress,
  my place of safety;
you are my God,
  and I trust you."

³ The Lord will keep you safe
from secret traps
  and deadly diseases.
⁴ He will spread his wings
over you
  and keep you secure.
His faithfulness is like
  a shield or a city wall.ᵏ

⁵ You won't need to worry
  about dangers at night
  or arrows during the day.
⁶ And you won't fear diseases
that strike in the dark
  or sudden disaster at noon.

⁷ You will not be harmed,
  though thousands fall

ᵏ**91.4** *city wall*: One possible meaning for a difficult
Hebrew word; it may possibly mean some kind of shield
or weapon.

all around you.
⁸ And with your own eyes
  you will see the punishment
    of the wicked.
⁹ The LORD Most High
  is your fortress.
  Run to him for safety,
¹⁰ and no terrible disasters
  will strike you
  or your home.

¹¹ God will command his angels
  to protect you
    wherever you go.
¹² They will carry you
  in their arms,
  and you won't hurt your feet
    on the stones.
¹³ You will overpower
  the strongest lions
  and the most deadly snakes.

¹⁴ The Lord says, "If you love me
  and truly know who I am,
  I will rescue you
    and keep you safe.
¹⁵ When you are in trouble,
  call out to me.
  I will answer and be there
    to protect and honor you.
¹⁶ You will live a long life
  and see my saving power."

Psalm 92

[A psalm and a song for the Sabbath.]

Sing Praises to the LORD

¹ It is wonderful to be grateful
  and to sing your praises,
    LORD Most High!
² It is wonderful each morning
  to tell about your love
  and at night to announce
    how faithful you are.
³ I enjoy praising your name
  to the music of harps,
⁴ because everything you do
  makes me happy,
  and I sing joyful songs.

⁵ You do great things, LORD.
  Your thoughts are too deep
⁶ for an ignorant fool
  to know or understand.
⁷ Though the wicked sprout
  and spread like grass,
  they will be pulled up
    by their roots.
⁸ But you will rule
  over all of us forever,
⁹ and your hateful enemies
  will be scattered
  and then destroyed.

¹⁰ You have given me
  the strength of a wild ox,

Personal *Concerns*—How can I overcome my tendency to worry and instead gain confidence about the future? *(Psalm 91)*

See God as your Savior, not as a saboteur.
How do you view God? Is he out to get you or out to save you?

Sometimes we develop wrong ideas about God. We see God as a sleeping giant (distant and inattentive), a grouch (ruining a good time), an occasional visitor (nice when he comes), a cosmic cop (walks around pouncing on people), or a dirty trickster (changing the rules all the time).

None of those images represent God. Instead, God can be compared to a powerful bird spreading his wings to shield us, a strong city wall, or a dispatcher of angels (91.4,11). With this kind of God, we don't have to fear weapons, diseases, darkness, disasters, or wild animals. He offers protection. Our part is to understand who God is and to accept him as the guarantor of our safety. (See also Joshua 23.14-16; Micah 5.2-5; Habakkuk 3.16-19; Matthew 6.25-34; Philippians 4.4-9.)

Words To Remember: *Live under the protection of God Most High and stay in the shadow of God All-Powerful.*—Psalm 91.1

and you have chosen me
  to be your very own.
[11] My eyes have seen,
  and my ears have heard
the doom and destruction
  of my terrible enemies.

[12] Good people will prosper
  like palm trees,
and they will grow strong
  like the cedars of Lebanon.
[13] They will take root
  in your house, LORD God,
  and they will do well.
[14] They will be like trees
  that stay healthy and fruitful,
  even when they are old.
[15] And they will say about you,
  "The LORD always does right!
  God is our mighty rock."[l]

Psalm 93

The LORD Is King

[1] Our LORD, you are King!
Majesty and power
  are your royal robes.
You put the world in place,
  and it will never be moved.
[2] You have always ruled,
  and you are eternal.

[3] The ocean is roaring, LORD!
  The sea is pounding hard.
[4] Its mighty waves are majestic,
but you are more majestic,
  and you rule over all.
[5] Your decisions are firm,
and your temple will always
  be beautiful and holy.

Psalm 94

The LORD Punishes the Guilty

[1] LORD God, you punish
  the guilty.
Show what you are like
  and punish them now.
[2] You judge the earth.
  Come and help us!
Pay back those proud people
  for what they have done.

[3] How long will the wicked
  celebrate and be glad?

[4] All of those cruel people
  strut and boast,
[5] and they crush and wound
  your chosen nation, LORD.
[6] They murder widows,
  foreigners, and orphans.
[7] Then they say,
  "The LORD God of Jacob
  doesn't see or know."

[8] Can't you fools see?
  Won't you ever learn?
[9] God gave us ears and eyes!
  Can't he hear and see?
[10] God instructs the nations
  and gives knowledge to us all.
  Won't he also correct us?
[11] The LORD knows how useless
  our plans really are.

[12] Our LORD, you bless everyone
  that you instruct and teach
  by using your Law.
[13] You give them rest
  from their troubles,
until a pit can be dug
  for the wicked.
[14] You won't turn your back
  on your chosen nation.
[15] Justice and fairness
  will go hand in hand,
and all who do right
  will follow along.

[16] Who will stand up for me
  against those cruel people?
[17] If you had not helped me, LORD,
  I would soon have gone
  to the land of silence.[m]
[18] When I felt my feet slipping,
  you came with your love
  and kept me steady.
[19] And when I was burdened
  with worries,
  you comforted me
  and made me feel secure.
[20] But you are opposed
  to dishonest lawmakers

---

[l]92.15 *mighty rock*: See the note at 18.2. [m]94.17 *land of silence*: The grave or the world of the dead.

21 who gang up to murder
   innocent victims.

22 You, LORD God, are my fortress,
   that mighty rock[n]
      where I am safe.
23 You will pay back my enemies,
   and you will wipe them out
      for the evil they did.

Psalm 95

Worship and Obey the LORD

1 Sing joyful songs to the LORD!
   Praise the mighty rock[n]
      where we are safe.
2 Come to worship him
   with thankful hearts
      and songs of praise.

3 The LORD is the greatest God,
   king over all other gods.
4 He holds the deepest part
   of the earth in his hands,
   and the mountain peaks
      belong to him.
5 The ocean is the Lord's
   because he made it,
   and with his own hands
      he formed the dry land.

*When I find myself getting
weary from life's pressures,
I put on praise music and
begin to thank the Lord.*

THELMA WELLS

6 Bow down and worship
   the LORD our Creator!
7 The LORD is our God,
   and we are his people,
   the sheep he takes care of
      in his own pasture.

Listen to God's voice today!
8 Don't be stubborn and rebel

as your ancestors did
at Meribah and Massah[o]
   out in the desert.
9 For forty years
   they tested God and saw
      the things he did.
10 Then God got tired of them
   and said,
   "You never show good sense,
   and you don't understand
      what I want you to do."
11 In his anger, God told them,
   "You people will never enter
      my place of rest."

Psalm 96

Sing a New Song to the LORD

1 Sing a new song to the LORD!
   Everyone on this earth,
      sing praises to the LORD,
2   sing and praise his name.

   Day after day announce,
      "The LORD has saved us!"
3 Tell every nation on earth,
   "The LORD is wonderful
      and does marvelous things!
4 The LORD is great and deserves
      our greatest praise!
   He is the only God
      worthy of our worship.
5 Other nations worship idols,
   but the LORD created
      the heavens.
6 Give honor and praise
   to the LORD,
   whose power and beauty
      fill his holy temple."

7 Tell everyone of every nation,
   "Praise the glorious power
      of the LORD.
8 He is wonderful! Praise him
   and bring an offering
      into his temple.
9 Everyone on earth, now tremble
   and worship the LORD,
      majestic and holy."

---

¹⁰ Announce to the nations,
    "The LORD is King!
The world stands firm,
    never to be shaken,
and he will judge its people
    with fairness."

¹¹ Tell the heavens and the earth
        to be glad and celebrate!
    Command the ocean to roar
        with all of its creatures
¹² and the fields to rejoice
        with all of their crops.
    Then every tree in the forest
    will sing joyful songs
¹³   to the LORD.
    He is coming to judge
    all people on earth
        with fairness and truth.

Psalm 97

The LORD Brings Justice

¹ The LORD is King!
Tell the earth to celebrate
    and all islands to shout.
² Dark clouds surround him,
    and his throne is supported
        by justice and fairness.
³ Fire leaps from his throne,
    destroying his enemies,
⁴ and his lightning is so bright
    that the earth sees it
        and trembles.
⁵ Mountains melt away like wax
    in the presence of the LORD
        of all the earth.

⁶ The heavens announce,
    "The LORD brings justice!"
    Everyone sees God's glory.
⁷ Those who brag about
    the useless idols they worship
        are terribly ashamed,
and all the false gods
    bow down to the LORD.

⁸ When the people of Zion
        and of the towns of Judah
    hear that God brings justice,
        they will celebrate.
⁹ The LORD rules the whole earth,

and he is more glorious
    than all the false gods.

¹⁰ Love the LORD
    and hate evil!
God protects his loyal people
and rescues them
    from violence.
¹¹ If you obey and do right,
    a light will show you the way
    and fill you with happiness.
¹² You are the LORD's people!
    So celebrate and praise
        the only God.

Psalm 98

The LORD Works Miracles

¹ Sing a new song to the LORD!
    He has worked miracles,
and with his own powerful arm,
    he has won the victory.
² The LORD has shown the nations
    that he has the power to save
        and to bring justice.
³ God has been faithful
        in his love for Israel,
and his saving power is seen
        everywhere on earth.

⁴ Tell everyone on this earth
    to sing happy songs
        in praise of the LORD.
⁵ Make music for him on harps.
    Play beautiful melodies!
⁶ Sound the trumpets and horns
    and celebrate with joyful songs
        for our LORD and King!

⁷ Command the ocean to roar
        with all of its creatures,
    and the earth to shout
        with all of its people.
⁸ Order the rivers
        to clap their hands,
    and all of the hills
        to sing together.
⁹ Let them worship the LORD!
    He is coming to judge
        everyone on the earth,
    and he will be honest
        and fair.

Psalm 99

Our LORD Is King

[1] Our LORD, you are King!
You rule from your throne
above the winged creatures,[p]
as people tremble
and the earth shakes.
[2] You are praised in Zion,
and you control all nations.
[3] Only you are God!
And your power alone,
so great and fearsome,
is worthy of praise.
[4] You are our mighty King,[q]
a lover of fairness,
who sees that justice is done
everywhere in Israel.
[5] Our LORD and our God,
we praise you
and kneel down to worship you,
the God of holiness!

[6] Moses and Aaron were two
of your priests.
Samuel was also one of those
who prayed in your name,
and you, our LORD,
answered their prayers.
[7] You spoke to them
from a thick cloud,
and they obeyed your laws.

[8] Our LORD and our God,
you answered their prayers
and forgave their sins,
but when they did wrong,
you punished them.
[9] We praise you, LORD God,
and we worship you
at your sacred mountain.
Only you are God!

Psalm 100

[A psalm of praise.]

The LORD Is God

[1] Shout praises to the LORD,
everyone on this earth.
[2] Be joyful and sing
as you come in
to worship the LORD!

[3] You know the LORD is God!
He created us,
and we belong to him;
we are his people,
the sheep in his pasture.

You and I are children of the King, the Creator of the universe! No matter what family we're born into— or not born into— it isn't possible to have a better lineage than that! Just knowing that helps me face every day and new situation with confidence.

RAMONA CRAMER TUCKER

[4] Be thankful and praise the LORD
as you enter his temple.
[5] The LORD is good!
His love and faithfulness
will last forever.

Psalm 101

[A psalm by David.]

A King and His Promises

[1] I will sing to you, LORD!
I will celebrate your kindness
and your justice.
[2] Please help me learn
to do the right thing,
and I will be honest and fair
in my own kingdom.
[3] I refuse to be corrupt
or to take part
in anything crooked,

---

[p]**99.1** *winged creatures*: See the note at 80.1.
[q]**99.4** *You . . . King*: One possible meaning for the difficult Hebrew text.

⁴and I won't be dishonest
  or deceitful.

⁵Anyone who spreads gossip
    will be silenced,
and no one who is conceited
    will be my friend.

⁶I will find trustworthy people
    to serve as my advisors,
and only an honest person
    will serve as an official.

⁷No one who cheats or lies
  will have a position
    in my royal court.
⁸Each morning I will silence
    any lawbreakers I find
  in the countryside
    or in the city of the LORD.

Psalm 102

*[A prayer for someone who hurts and needs
to ask the LORD for help.]*

A Prayer in Time of Trouble

¹I pray to you, LORD!
    Please listen.
²Don't hide from me
    in my time of trouble.
Pay attention to my prayer
    and quickly give an answer.

³My days disappear like smoke,
  and my bones are burning
    as though in a furnace.
⁴I am wasting away like grass,
    and my appetite is gone.
⁵My groaning never stops,
  and my bones can be seen
    through my skin.
⁶I am like a lonely owl
    in the desert
⁷or a restless sparrow
    alone on a roof.

⁸My enemies insult me all day,
  and they use my name
    for a curse word.
⁹Instead of food,
  I have ashes to eat
    and tears to drink,

¹⁰because you are furious
    and have thrown me aside.
¹¹My life fades like a shadow
  at the end of day
    and withers like grass.

¹²Our LORD, you are King forever
    and will always be famous.
¹³You will show pity to Zion
    because the time has come.
¹⁴We, your servants,
    love each stone in the city,
  and we are sad to see them
    lying in the dirt.

¹⁵Our LORD, the nations
    will honor you,
  and all kings on earth
    will praise your glory.
¹⁶You will rebuild
    the city of Zion.
  Your glory will be seen,
¹⁷and the prayers of the homeless
    will be answered.

¹⁸Future generations must also
  praise the LORD,
    so write this for them:
¹⁹"From his holy temple,
  the LORD looked down
    at the earth.
²⁰He listened to the groans
    of prisoners,
  and he rescued everyone
    who was doomed to die."

²¹All Jerusalem should praise
    you, our LORD,
²²when people from every nation
    meet to worship you.

²³I should still be strong,
  but you, LORD, have made
    an old person of me.
²⁴You will live forever!
  Years mean nothing to you.
    Don't cut my life in half!

²⁵In the beginning, LORD,
  you laid the earth's foundation
    and created the heavens.
²⁶They will all disappear
    and wear out like clothes.

You change them,
as you would a coat,
but you last forever.
²⁷You are always the same.
Years cannot change you.
²⁸Every generation of those
who serve you
will live in your presence.

Psalm 103

[*By David.*]

The LORD's Wonderful Love

¹With all my heart
I praise the LORD,
and with all that I am
I praise his holy name!
²With all my heart
I praise the LORD!
I will never forget
how kind he has been.

³The LORD forgives our sins,
heals us when we are sick,
⁴   and protects us from death.
His kindness and love
are a crown on our heads.
⁵Each day that we live,ʳ
he provides for our needs
and gives us the strength
of a young eagle.

⁶For all who are mistreated,
the LORD brings justice.
⁷He taught his Law to Moses
and showed all Israel
what he could do.

⁸The LORD is merciful!
He is kind and patient,
and his love never fails.
⁹The LORD won't always be angry
and point out our sins;
¹⁰he doesn't punish us
as our sins deserve.

¹¹How great is God's love for all
who worship him?
Greater than the distance
between heaven and earth!
¹²How far has the LORD taken
our sins from us?
Farther than the distance
from east to west!

¹³Just as parents are kind
to their children,
the LORD is kind
to all who worship him,
¹⁴because he knows
we are made of dust.
¹⁵We humans are like grass

ʳ**103.5** *Each . . . live:* One possible meaning for the
difficult Hebrew text.

SingleLife—How can I resist the pressure to be sexually active? (*Psalm 103*)

Ask for God's strength.

It doesn't matter because . . . This rationalization often trips us up morally. We think, *It doesn't matter if I become sexually active because I've gone too far anyway;* or, *I'm just not the kind of person who can stand up to others.* Giving in to sexual sin is often preceded by a put-down: *After all, I'm not perfect—so why bother?*

But God knows about our lack of perfection better than we do. He made us and is well acquainted with the fact that we are dust (103.14). God comes to an opposite conclusion from the one above: Obedience matters—even if we're not perfect. He desires our obedience, yet doesn't treat us "as our sins deserve" (103.10) because of his patience and mercy.

Although God forgives our sins and heals our wounds when we confess our disobedience, this is Plan B. Plan A is to obey God. And he promises to give us the strength to do just that—instead of giving in to our lesser possibilities. (**See also Joshua 7; Ephesians 6.10-20; James 1.12-18; 2 Peter 2.7-9.**)

Words To Remember: *Each day that we live, he provides for our needs and gives us the strength of a young eagle.—Psalm 103.5*

or wild flowers
    that quickly bloom.
¹⁶But a scorching wind blows,
    and they quickly wither
        to be forever forgotten.

¹⁷The LORD is always kind
    to those who worship him,
  and he keeps his promises
  to their descendants
¹⁸   who faithfully obey him.

¹⁹God has set up his kingdom
  in heaven, and he rules
    the whole creation.
²⁰All of you mighty angels,
  who obey God's commands,
    come and praise your LORD!
²¹All of you thousands
  who serve and obey God,
    come and praise your LORD!
²²All of God's creation
  and all that he rules,
    come and praise your LORD!
  With all my heart
    I praise the LORD!

Psalm 104

The LORD Takes Care of His Creation

¹I praise you, LORD God,
  with all my heart.
  You are glorious and majestic,
  dressed in royal robes
²   and surrounded by light.
  You spread out the sky
    like a tent,
³and you built your home
    over the mighty ocean.
  The clouds are your chariot
    with the wind as its wings.
⁴The winds are your messengers,
  and flames of fire
    are your servants.

⁵You built foundations
  for the earth, and it
    will never be shaken.
⁶You covered the earth
  with the ocean that rose
    above the mountains.
⁷Then your voice thundered!
  And the water flowed

⁸   down the mountains
  and through the valleys
    to the place you prepared.
⁹Now you have set boundaries,
  so that the water will never
    flood the earth again.

¹⁰You provide streams of water
  in the hills and valleys,
¹¹so that the donkeys
  and other wild animals
    can satisfy their thirst.
¹²Birds build their nests nearby
  and sing in the trees.
¹³From your home above
  you send rain on the hills
    and water the earth.
¹⁴You let the earth produce
    grass for cattle,
    plants for our food,
¹⁵   wine to cheer us up,
    olive oil for our skin,
    and grain for our health.

¹⁶Our LORD, your trees
    always have water,
  and so do the cedars
    you planted in Lebanon.
¹⁷Birds nest in those trees,
  and storks make their home
    in the fir trees.
¹⁸Wild goats find a home
    in the tall mountains,
  and small animals can hide
    between the rocks.

¹⁹You created the moon
    to tell us the seasons.
  The sun knows when to set,
²⁰   and you made the darkness,
  so the animals in the forest
    could come out at night.
²¹Lions roar as they hunt
    for the food you provide.
²²But when morning comes,
  they return to their dens,
²³then we go out to work
    until the end of day.

²⁴Our LORD, by your wisdom
  you made so many things;
  the whole earth is covered
    with your living creatures.
²⁵But what about the ocean
    so big and wide?

It is alive with creatures,
    large and small.
²⁶And there are the ships,
    as well as Leviathan,ˢ
the monster you created
    to splash in the sea.

²⁷All of these depend on you
    to provide them with food,
²⁸and you feed each one
    with your own hand,
        until they are full.
²⁹But when you turn away,
    they are terrified;
when you end their life,
    they die and rot.
³⁰You created all of them
    by your Spirit,
and you give new life
    to the earth.

³¹Our LORD, we pray
    that your glory
        will last forever
and that you will be pleased
    with what you have done.
³²You look at the earth,
    and it trembles.
You touch the mountains,
    and smoke goes up.
³³As long as I live,

I will sing and praise you,
    the LORD God.
³⁴I hope my thoughts
    will please you,
because you are the one
    who makes me glad.

³⁵Destroy all wicked sinners
from the earth
    once and for all.
With all my heart
I praise you, LORD!
    I praise you!

Psalm 105

The LORD Can Be Trusted

¹Praise the LORD
    and pray in his name!
Tell everyone
    what he has done.
²Sing praises to the LORD!
    Tell about his miracles.
³Celebrate and worship
    his holy name
        with all your heart.

ˢ**104.26** *Leviathan*: See the note at 74.14.

Personal *Concerns*—How can I accept my body as it is? *(Psalm 104)*

Don't judge yourself by magazine covers.
So . . . your body doesn't look like the fashion models who grace the front covers of magazines? Neither did their predecessors. Forty years ago, the women in magazine cover photos were not waiflike but more robust. Why? Because beauty standards are constantly changing, and back then, thin wasn't "in." And when the artist Rembrandt and his contemporaries painted, the standards for the beautiful feminine body were even larger and rounder. Imagine how inadequate thin women must have felt then!

Standards of beauty are subjective. Is a mole on the face dramatically beautiful, or unsightly and distracting? Is a heart-shaped face cute or babyish? Is height in a woman an asset or a liability?

Whose standards do we accept? God's standards. He knows beauty when he creates it—a well-watered earth, a sun and moon that take turns appearing in the sky, animals that create homes on the earth (104.16-23). We, too, are one of his creations—in fact, the pinnacle of his creation. Our waist size, hip size, bust size, and shoe size are known to God. When we view ourselves from God's perspective, our thoughts please him, for he is the one who makes us glad. (See also Psalm 139.13-16; Mark 14.3-9.)

Words To Remember: *I hope my thoughts will please you, because you are the one who makes me glad.*—Psalm 104.34

⁴Trust the LORD
and his mighty power.
⁵Remember his miracles
and all his wonders
and his fair decisions.
⁶You belong to the family
of Abraham, his servant;
you are his chosen ones,
the descendants of Jacob.

⁷The LORD is our God,
bringing justice
everywhere on earth.
⁸He will never forget
his agreement or his promises,
not in thousands of years.
*⁹God made an eternal promise
¹⁰   to Abraham, Isaac, and Jacob,
¹¹when he said, "I'll give you
the land of Canaan."

¹²At the time there were
only a few of us,
and we were homeless.
¹³We wandered from nation
to nation, from one country
to another.
¹⁴God did not let anyone
mistreat our people.
Instead he protected us
by punishing rulers
¹⁵and telling them,
"Don't touch my chosen leaders
or harm my prophets!"

¹⁶God kept crops from growing
until food was scarce
everywhere in the land.
¹⁷But he had already sent Joseph,
sold as a slave into Egypt,
¹⁸with chains of iron
around his legs and neck.

¹⁹Joseph remained a slave
until his own words
had come true,
and the LORD had finished
testing him.
²⁰Then the king of Egypt
set Joseph free
²¹and put him in charge
of everything he owned.
²²Joseph was in command
of the officials,

and he taught the leaders
how to use wisdom.

²³Jacob and his family
came and settled in Egypt
as foreigners.
²⁴They were the LORD's people,
so he let them grow stronger
than their enemies.
²⁵They served the LORD,
and he made the Egyptians plan
hateful things against them.
²⁶God sent his servant Moses.
He also chose and sent Aaron
²⁷   to his people in Egypt,
and they worked miracles
and wonders there.
²⁸Moses and Aaron obeyed God,
and he sent darkness
to cover Egypt.
²⁹God turned their rivers
into streams of blood,
and the fish all died.
³⁰Frogs were everywhere,
even in the royal palace.
³¹When God gave the command,
flies and gnats
swarmed all around.

³²In place of rain,
God sent hailstones
and flashes of lightning.
³³He destroyed their grapevines
and their fig trees,
and he made splinters
of all the other trees.
³⁴God gave the command,
and more grasshoppers came
than could be counted.
³⁵They ate every green plant
and all the crops that grew
in the land of Egypt.
³⁶Then God took the life
of every first-born son.

³⁷When God led Israel from Egypt,
they took silver and gold,
and no one was left behind.
³⁸The Egyptians were afraid
and gladly let them go.
³⁹God hid them under a cloud
and guided them by fire
during the night.

⁴⁰ When they asked for food,
    he sent more birds
        than they could eat.
⁴¹ God even split open a rock,
    and streams of water
        gushed into the desert.
⁴² God never forgot
    his sacred promise
        to his servant Abraham.

⁴³ When the Lord rescued
    his chosen people from Egypt,
        they celebrated with songs.
⁴⁴ The Lord gave them the land
    and everything else
        the nations had worked for.
⁴⁵ He did this so that his people
    would obey all of his laws.
        Shout praises to the LORD!

Psalm 106

A Nation Asks for Forgiveness

¹ We will celebrate
    and praise you, LORD!
You are good to us,
    and your love never fails.
² No one can praise you enough
    for all of the mighty things
        you have done.
³ You bless those people
    who are honest and fair
        in everything they do.

⁴ Remember me, LORD,
    when you show kindness
        by saving your people.
⁵ Let me prosper with the rest
    of your chosen ones,
as they celebrate with pride
    because they belong to you.

⁶ We and our ancestors
    have sinned terribly.
⁷ When they were in Egypt,
    they paid no attention
to your marvelous deeds
    or your wonderful love.
And they turned against you
    at the Red Sea.ᶦ

⁸ But you were true to your name,
    and you rescued them to prove
        how mighty you are.

⁹ You said to the Red Sea,ᶦ
    "Dry up!"
Then you led your people across
    on land as dry as a desert.
¹⁰ You saved all of them
¹¹ and drowned every one
    of their enemies.
¹² Then your people trusted you
    and sang your praises.

¹³ But they soon forgot
    what you had done
        and rejected your advice.
¹⁴ They became greedy for food
    and tested you there
        in the desert.
¹⁵ So you gave them
    what they wanted,
but later you destroyed them
    with a horrible disease.

¹⁶ Everyone in camp was jealous
    of Moses and of Aaron,
        your chosen priest.
¹⁷ Dathan and Abiram rebelled,
    and the earth opened up
        and swallowed them.
¹⁸ Then fire broke out
    and destroyed all
        of their followers.

¹⁹ At Horeb your people
    made and worshiped the statue
²⁰   of a bull, instead of you,
        their glorious God.
²¹ You worked powerful miracles
    to save them from Egypt,
but they forgot about you
²² and the fearsome things
    you did at the Red Sea.ᶦ
²³ You were angry and started
    to destroy them,
but Moses, your chosen leader,
    begged you not to do it.

²⁴ They would not trust
    you, LORD,

ᶦ**106.7,9,22** *Red Sea:* Hebrew *yam suph* "Sea of Reeds,"
one of the marshes or fresh water lakes near the eastern
part of the Nile Delta. This identification is based on
Exodus 13.17—14.9, which lists the towns on the
route of the Israelites before crossing the sea. In the
Greek translation of the Scriptures made about
200 B.C., the "Sea of Reeds" was named "Red Sea."

and they did not like
the promised land.
25 They would not obey you,
and they grumbled
in their tents.
26 So you threatened them
by saying, "I'll kill you
out here in the desert!
27 I'll scatter your children
everywhere in the world."

28 Your people became followers
of a god named Baal Peor,
and they ate sacrifices
offered to the dead.[u]
29 They did such terrible things
that you punished them
with a deadly disease.
30 But Phinehas[v] helped them,
and the sickness stopped.
31 Now he will always
be highly honored.

32 At Meribah Spring[w]
they turned against you
and made you furious.
33 Then Moses got into trouble
for speaking in anger.

34 Our LORD, they disobeyed you
by refusing to destroy
the nations.
35 Instead they were friendly
with those foreigners
and followed their customs.
36 Then they fell into the trap
of worshiping idols.
37 They sacrificed their sons
and their daughters to demons
38   and to the gods of Canaan.
Then they poured out the blood
of these innocent children
and made the land filthy.
39 By doing such gruesome things,
they also became filthy.

40 Finally, LORD, you were angry
and terribly disgusted
with your people.
41 So you put them in the power
of nations that hated them.
42 They were mistreated and abused
by their enemies,
43 but you saved them
time after time.

They were determined to rebel,
and their sins caused
their downfall.

44 You answered their prayers
when they were in trouble.
45 You kept your agreement
and were so merciful
46 that their enemies
had pity on them.

47 Save us, LORD God!
Bring us back
from among the nations.
Let us celebrate and shout
in praise of your holy name.

48 LORD God of Israel,
you deserve to be praised
forever and ever.
Let everyone say, "Amen!
Shout praises to the LORD!"

BOOK V
(Psalms 107–150)

Psalm 107

The LORD Is Good to His People

1 Shout praises to the LORD!
He is good to us,
and his love never fails.
2 Everyone the LORD has rescued
from trouble
should praise him,
3 everyone he has brought
from the east and the west,
the north and the south.[x]

4 Some of you were lost
in the scorching desert,
far from a town.
5 You were hungry and thirsty
and about to give up.
6 You were in serious trouble,

---

u106.28 *the dead*: Or "lifeless idols."
v106.30 *Phinehas*: The grandson of Aaron, who put two
people to death and kept the Lord from being angry
with the rest of his people (see Numbers 25.1-13).
w106.32 *Meribah Spring*: See the note at 81.7.
x107.3 *south*: The Hebrew text has "sea," probably
referring to the Mediterranean Sea.

but you prayed to the LORD,
and he rescued you.
⁷ Right away he brought you
to a town.
⁸ You should praise the LORD
for his love
and for the wonderful things
he does for all of us.
⁹ To everyone who is thirsty,
he gives something to drink;
to everyone who is hungry,
he gives good things to eat.

¹⁰ Some of you were prisoners
suffering in deepest darkness
and bound by chains,
¹¹ because you had rebelled
against God Most High
and refused his advice.
¹² You were worn out
from working like slaves,
and no one came to help.
¹³ You were in serious trouble,
but you prayed to the LORD,
and he rescued you.
¹⁴ He brought you out
of the deepest darkness
and broke your chains.

¹⁵ You should praise the LORD
for his love
and for the wonderful things
he does for all of us.

¹⁶ He breaks down bronze gates
and shatters iron locks.

¹⁷ Some of you had foolishly
committed a lot of sins
and were in terrible pain.
¹⁸ The very thought of food
was disgusting to you,
and you were almost dead.
¹⁹ You were in serious trouble,
but you prayed to the LORD,
and he rescued you.
²⁰ By the power of his own word,
he healed you and saved you
from destruction.

²¹ You should praise the LORD
for his love
and for the wonderful things
he does for all of us.
²² You should celebrate
by offering sacrifices
and singing joyful songs
to tell what he has done.

²³ Some of you made a living
by sailing the mighty sea,
²⁴ and you saw the miracles
the LORD performed there.
²⁵ At his command a storm arose,
and waves covered the sea.
²⁶ You were tossed to the sky
and to the ocean depths,

Personal *Concerns*—How can I learn to be more content with my life?
(Psalm 107)

Blend the real with the ideal.

Being content does not mean wearing rose-colored glasses—it means viewing life through God's perspective and accepting his grip on reality. Throughout Scripture, God shows us what's *real* (especially in prophecy and narrative!), yet challenges us with what's *ideal*.

Life this side of heaven is full of detours and problems, and realistically we can expect our share. But we can be content even though they exist. God encourages us to ask him to rescue us, and he often provides a way out—whether it's through a person who knows what to do, a thought that occurs to us, or an unexpected opportunity.

But because real life is often trying, we also need to focus on the ideal. The psalmist repeatedly says how we should praise God for his love (107.2,15,21,31), remembering that he's in charge. God's love is the mightiest force on this earth, able to deliver and change circumstances quickly. As we keep our minds on this truth and praise him for it, we'll fill ourselves with hope—even when life is difficult. (See also Ecclesiastes 6.1-9; Daniel 2.20,21; 2 Peter 1.3-15.)

Words To Remember: *You should praise the LORD for his love and for the wonderful things he does for all of us.—Psalm 107.8*

until things looked so bad
    that you lost your courage.
²⁷You staggered like drunkards
    and gave up all hope.
²⁸You were in serious trouble,
    but you prayed to the LORD,
    and he rescued you.
²⁹He made the storm stop
    and the sea be quiet.
³⁰You were happy because of this,
    and he brought you to the port
    where you wanted to go.

³¹You should praise the LORD
    for his love
and for the wonderful things
    he does for all of us.
³²Honor the LORD
when you and your leaders
    meet to worship.

³³If you start doing wrong,
    the LORD will turn rivers
        into deserts,
³⁴flowing streams
    into scorched land,
and fruitful fields
    into beds of salt.

³⁵But the LORD can also turn
    deserts into lakes
and scorched land
    into flowing streams.
³⁶If you are hungry,
you can settle there
    and build a town.
³⁷You can plant fields
and vineyards that produce
    a good harvest.
³⁸The LORD will bless you
with many children
    and with herds of cattle.

³⁹Sometimes you may be crushed
    by troubles and sorrows,
until only a few of you
    are left to survive.
⁴⁰But the LORD will take revenge
    on those who conquer you,
and he will make them wander
    across desert sands.
⁴¹When you are suffering
    and in need,
he will come to your rescue,

and your families will grow
    as fast as a herd of sheep.
⁴²You will see this because
    you obey the LORD,
but everyone who is wicked
    will be silenced.

⁴³Be wise! Remember this
and think about the kindness
    of the LORD.

Psalm 108

[A song and a psalm by David.]

With God on Our Side

¹Our God, I am faithful to you
with all my heart,
    and you can trust me.
I will sing
and play music for you
    with all that I am.
²I will start playing my harps
    before the sun rises.
³I will praise you, LORD,
    for everyone to hear;
I will sing hymns to you
    in every nation.
⁴Your love reaches higher
    than the heavens,
and your loyalty extends
    beyond the clouds.

⁵Our God, may you be honored
    above the heavens;
may your glory be seen
    everywhere on earth.
⁶Answer my prayers
and use your powerful arm
    to give us victory.
Then the people you love
    will be safe.

⁷Our God, from your holy place
    you made this promise:
"I will gladly divide up
    the city of Shechem
and give away Succoth Valley
    piece by piece.
⁸The lands of Gilead
    and Manasseh are mine.
Ephraim is my war helmet,
and Judah is my symbol
    of royal power.

⁹Moab is merely my washbasin,
and Edom belongs to me.
I shout with victory
over the Philistines."

¹⁰Our God, who will bring me
to the fortress
or lead me to Edom?
¹¹Have you rejected us?
You don't lead our armies.
¹²Help us defeat our enemies!
No one else can rescue us.
¹³You are the one
who gives us victory
and crushes our enemies.

Psalm 109

[*A psalm by David for the music leader.*]

A Prayer for the LORD's Help

¹I praise you, God!
Don't keep silent.
²Destructive and deceitful lies
are told about me,
³and hateful things are said
for no reason.

⁴I had pity and prayed*ʸ*
for my enemies,
but their words to me
were harsh and cruel.
⁵For being friendly and kind,
they paid me back
with meanness and hatred.
⁶My enemies said,
"Find some worthless fools
to accuse him of a crime.
⁷Try him and find him guilty!
Consider his prayers a lie.
⁸Cut his life short
and let someone else
have his job.
⁹Make orphans of his children
and a widow of his wife;
¹⁰make his children beg for food
and live in the slums.

¹¹"Let the people he owes
take everything he owns.
Give it all to strangers.
¹²Don't let anyone be kind to him
or have pity on the children
he leaves behind.

---

*ʸ***109.4** *and prayed*: One possible meaning for the
difficult Hebrew text.

WORK—How can I be more confident about my work? (*Psalm 108*)

God is your silent partner at work.

It may appear that you are alone as you sit at your computer keyboard, stand as a solitary adult in a roomful of children, perch at the head of the table calling a meeting to order, or wait at your cash register, but that's an illusion. In reality, God is beside you at your workplace—in stuffy meetings, on windy playgrounds, at cluttered sales counters. In all these places, you talk, listen, and offer assistance with the watchful companionship of the Holy Spirit.

God, your constant partner, provides what you need and opens your eyes to the people around you: Who is hurting? Who is distracted? Who is greedy for power? This kind of guidance can help you work through the land mines of office politics and childish power plays. Others can make up self-promoting rules and play by them, but your partnership with God reminds you that you work with a different heart. You cannot use a coworker to advance your causes, and you cannot force your opinion on others, but you *can* rely on God to advance your causes as needed. He will defend you from those who oppose you. You are not left alone.

If possible, keep some physical object at your workplace to remind you that God is your partner—a card, a candle, a tiny rock. Your silent partner is alive and active where you work, waiting for you to acknowledge him. (See also Deuteronomy 31.1-6; Joshua 1.1-9; Psalm 73.21-28; 1 John 3.19-24.)

Words To Remember: *Your love reaches higher than the heavens, and your loyalty extends beyond the clouds.*—Psalm 108.4

¹³ Bring an end to his family,
and from now on let him be
a forgotten man.

¹⁴ "Don't let the LORD forgive
the sins of his parents
and his ancestors.
¹⁵ Don't let the LORD forget
the sins of his family,
or let anyone remember
his family ever lived.
¹⁶ He was so cruel to the poor,
homeless, and discouraged
that they died young.

¹⁷ "He cursed others.
Now place a curse on him!
He never wished others well.
Wish only trouble for him!
¹⁸ He cursed others more often
than he dressed himself.
Let his curses strike him deep,
just as water and olive oil
soak through to our bones.
¹⁹ Let his curses surround him,
just like the clothes
he wears each day."

²⁰ Those are the cruel things
my enemies wish for me.
Let it all happen to them!
²¹ Be true to your name, LORD God!
Show your great kindness
and rescue me.

²² I am poor and helpless,
and I have lost all hope.
²³ I am fading away
like an evening shadow;
I am tossed aside
like a crawling insect.
²⁴ I have gone without eating,ᶻ
until my knees are weak,
and my body is bony.
²⁵ When my enemies see me,
they say cruel things
and shake their heads.

²⁶ Please help me, LORD God!
Come and save me
because of your love.
²⁷ Let others know that you alone
have saved me.

²⁸ I don't care if they curse me,
as long as you bless me.
You will make my enemies fail
when they attack,
and you will make me glad
to be your servant.
²⁹ You will cover them with shame,
just as their bodies
are covered with clothes.

³⁰ I will sing your praises
and thank you, LORD,
when your people meet.
³¹ You help everyone in need,
and you defend them
when they are on trial.

Psalm 110

[A psalm by David.]

The LORD Gives Victory

¹ The LORD said to my Lord,
"Sit at my right side,ᵃ
until I make your enemies
into a footstool for you."

² The LORD will let your power
reach out from Zion,
and you will rule
over your enemies.
³ Your glorious power
will be seen on the day
you begin to rule.
You will wear the sacred robes
and shine like the morning sun
in all of your strength.ᵇ
⁴ The LORD has made a promise
that will never be broken:
"You will be a priest forever,
just like Melchizedek."

⁵ My Lord is at your right side,
and when he gets angry
he will crush
the other kings.
⁶ He will judge the nations
and crack their skulls,

ᶻ109.24 *without eating*: See the note at 35.13.
ᵃ110.1 *right side*: See the note at 16.11.   ᵇ110.3 *You will . . . strength*: One possible meaning for the difficult Hebrew text.

leaving piles of dead bodies
  all over the earth.
[7] He will drink from any stream
  that he chooses, while winning
    victory after victory.[c]

Psalm 111

Praise the LORD for All He Has Done

[1] Shout praises to the LORD!
  With all my heart
  I will thank the LORD
    when his people meet.
[2] The LORD has done
    many wonderful things!
  Everyone who is pleased
  with God's marvelous deeds
    will keep them in mind.
[3] Everything the LORD does
    is glorious and majestic,
  and his power to bring justice
    will never end.

[4] The LORD God is famous
  for his wonderful deeds,
    and he is kind and merciful.
[5] He gives food to his worshipers
  and always keeps his agreement
    with them.
[6] He has shown his mighty power
    to his people
  and has given them the lands
    of other nations.

[7] God is always honest and fair,
    and his laws can be trusted.
[8] They are true and right
    and will stand forever.
[9] God rescued his people,
    and he will never break
  his agreement with them.
    He is fearsome and holy.

[10] Respect and obey the LORD!
  This is the first step
    to wisdom and good sense.[d]
  God will always be respected.

Psalm 112

God Blesses His Worshipers

[1] Shout praises to the LORD!
  The LORD blesses everyone

who worships him and gladly
  obeys his teachings.
[2] Their descendants will have
    great power in the land,
  because the LORD blesses
    all who do right.
[3] They will get rich and prosper
  and will always be remembered
    for their fairness.
[4] They will be so kind
    and merciful and good,
  that they will be a light
  in the dark for others
    who do the right thing.

[5] Life will go well for those
  who freely lend
    and are honest in business.
[6] They won't ever be troubled,
  and the kind things they do
    will never be forgotten.
[7] Bad news won't bother them;
  they have decided
    to trust the LORD.
[8] They are dependable
    and not afraid,
  and they will live to see
    their enemies defeated.
[9] They will always be remembered
    and greatly praised,
  because they were kind
    and freely gave to the poor.
[10] When evil people see this,
  they angrily bite their tongues
    and disappear.
  They will never get
    what they really want.

Psalm 113

The LORD Helps People in Need

[1] Shout praises to the LORD!
  Everyone who serves him,
    come and praise his name.

[2] Let the name of the LORD
    be praised now and forever.
[3] From dawn until sunset
  the name of the LORD
    deserves to be praised.

---

[c]**110.7** *while . . . victory*: Or "God will give him victory
after victory." [d]**111.10** *This . . . sense*: Or "This is what
wisdom and good sense are all about."

⁴The LORD is far above
all of the nations;
he is more glorious
than the heavens.

*Racism is something we
must change one heart at
a time—by deciding to
love each other as people
for whom Christ died, and
to treat those in the church
as sisters and brothers in
Christ, regardless of color.*

STAR PARKER

⁵No one can compare
with the LORD our God.
His throne is high above,
⁶and he looks down to see
the heavens and the earth.
⁷God lifts the poor and needy
from dust and ashes,
⁸and he lets them take part
in ruling his people.
⁹When a wife has no children,
he blesses her with some,
and she is happy.
Shout praises to the LORD!

Psalm 114

The LORD Works Wonders

¹God brought his people
out of Egypt, that land
with a strange language.
²He made Judah his holy place
and ruled over Israel.

³When the sea looked at God,
it ran away,
and the Jordan River
flowed upstream.
⁴The mountains and the hills
skipped around like goats.

⁵Ask the sea why it ran away
or ask the Jordan
why it flowed upstream.
⁶Ask the mountains and the hills
why they skipped like goats!

⁷Earth, you will tremble,
when the Lord God of Jacob
comes near,
⁸because he turns solid rock
into flowing streams
and pools of water.

Psalm 115

The LORD Deserves To Be Praised

¹We don't deserve praise!
The LORD alone deserves
all of the praise,
because of his love
and faithfulness.
²Why should the nations ask,
"Where is your God?"

³Our God is in the heavens,
doing as he chooses.
⁴The idols of the nations
are made of silver and gold.
⁵They have a mouth and eyes,
but they can't speak or see.
⁶Their ears can't hear,
and their noses can't smell.
⁷Their hands have no feeling,
their legs don't move,
and they can't make a sound.
⁸Everyone who made the idols
and all who trust them
are just as helpless
as those useless gods.

⁹People of Israel,
you must trust the LORD
to help and protect you.
¹⁰Family of Aaron the priest,
you must trust the LORD
to help and protect you.
¹¹All of you worship the LORD,
so you must trust him
to help and protect you.

¹²The LORD will not forget
to give us his blessing;
he will bless all of Israel
and the family of Aaron.

¹³ All who worship the LORD,
   no matter who they are,
    will receive his blessing.

*Giving the outcome to God
means laying down our
cherished hopes and dreams
if our son or daughter doesn't
turn around. It hurts, but
God hurts with us. He'll
always watch over our
children when we fully give
them to him in prayer.*

VIRELLE KIDDER

¹⁴ I pray that the LORD
   will let your family
   and your descendants
    always grow strong.
¹⁵ May the LORD who created
   the heavens and the earth
    give you his blessing.

¹⁶ The LORD has kept the heavens
   for himself,
   but he has given the earth
    to us humans.
¹⁷ The dead are silent
   and cannot praise the LORD,
¹⁸ but we will praise him
   now and forevermore.
    Shout praises to the LORD!

Psalm 116

When the LORD Saves You from Death

¹ I love you, LORD!
   You answered my prayers.
² You paid attention to me,
   and so I will pray to you
    as long as I live.
³ Death attacked from all sides,
   and I was captured
    by its painful chains.
   But when I was really hurting,

⁴ I prayed and said, "LORD,
   please don't let me die!"

⁵ You are kind, LORD,
   so good and merciful.
⁶ You protect ordinary people,
   and when I was helpless,
    you saved me
⁷ and treated me so kindly
   that I don't need
    to worry anymore.

⁸ You, LORD, have saved
   my life from death,
   my eyes from tears,
   my feet from stumbling.
⁹ Now I will walk at your side
   in this land of the living.
¹⁰ I was faithful to you
   when I was suffering,
¹¹ though in my confusion I said,
   "I can't trust anyone!"

¹² What must I give you, LORD,
   for being so good to me?
¹³ I will pour out an offering
   of wine to you,
   and I will pray in your name
   because you
    have saved me.
¹⁴ I will keep my promise to you
   when your people meet.
¹⁵ You are deeply concerned
   when one of your loyal people
    faces death.

*Although God loves us, he
doesn't grant us immunity
from the consequences of
our choices. However, when
we mess up, if we ask his
forgiveness he'll redeem those
choices, using our mistakes as a
"door of hope" for other people.*

DONNA RICE HUGHES

¹⁶ I worship you, LORD,
just as my mother did,
and you have rescued me
from the chains of death.
¹⁷ I will offer you a sacrifice
to show how grateful I am,
and I will pray.
¹⁸ I will keep my promise to you
when your people
¹⁹ gather at your temple
in Jerusalem.
Shout praises to the LORD!

Psalm 117

Come Praise the LORD

¹ All of you nations,
come praise the LORD!
Let everyone praise him.
² His love for us is wonderful;
his faithfulness never ends.
Shout praises to the LORD!

Psalm 118

The LORD Is Always Merciful

¹ Tell the LORD
how thankful you are,
because he is kind
and always merciful.

² Let Israel shout,
"God is always merciful!"
³ Let the family of Aaron
the priest shout,
"God is always merciful!"
⁴ Let every true worshiper
of the LORD shout,
"God is always merciful!"

⁵ When I was really hurting,
I prayed to the LORD.
He answered my prayer,
and took my worries away.
⁶ The LORD is on my side,
and I am not afraid
of what others can do to me.
⁷ With the LORD on my side,
I will defeat all
of my hateful enemies.
⁸ It is better to trust the LORD
for protection
than to trust anyone else,

⁹   including strong leaders.
¹⁰ Nations surrounded me,
but I got rid of them
by the power of the LORD.
¹¹ They attacked from all sides,
but I got rid of them
by the power of the LORD.
¹² They swarmed around like bees,
but by the power of the LORD,
I got rid of them
and their fiery sting.
¹³ Their attacks were so fierce
that I nearly fell,
but the LORD helped me.
¹⁴ My power and my strength
come from the LORD,
and he has saved me.

¹⁵ From the tents of God's people
come shouts of victory:
"The LORD is powerful!"
¹⁶ With his mighty arm
the LORD wins victories!
The LORD is powerful!"

¹⁷ And so my life is safe,
and I will live to tell
what the LORD has done.
¹⁸ He punished me terribly,
but he did not let death
lay its hands on me.
¹⁹ Open the gates of justice!
I will enter and tell the LORD
how thankful I am.

²⁰ Here is the gate of the LORD!
Everyone who does right
may enter this gate.

²¹ I praise the LORD
for answering my prayers
and saving me.
²² The stone that the builders
tossed aside
has now become
the most important stone.

²³ The LORD has done this,
and it is amazing to us.
²⁴ This day belongs to the LORD!
Let's celebrate
and be glad today.
²⁵ We'll ask the LORD to save us!
We'll sincerely ask the LORD
to let us win.

²⁶ God bless the one who comes
in the name of the LORD!
We praise you from here
in the house of the LORD.

> *To experience happiness we*
> *must train ourselves to live*
> *in this moment, to savor it*
> *for what it is, not running*
> *ahead in anticipation of*
> *some future date nor*
> *lagging behind in the*
> *paralysis of the past.*
>
> LUCI SWINDOLL

²⁷ The LORD is our God,
and he has given us light!
Start the celebration!
March with palm branches
all the way to the altar.^e

²⁸ The LORD is my God!
I will praise him and tell him
how thankful I am.

²⁹ Tell the LORD
how thankful you are,
because he is kind
and always merciful.

Psalm 119

In Praise of the Law of the LORD

¹ Our LORD, you bless everyone
who lives right
and obeys your Law.
² You bless all of those
who follow your commands
from deep in their hearts
³ and who never do wrong
or turn from you.
⁴ You have ordered us always
to obey your teachings;
⁵ I don't ever want to stray
from your laws.

⁶ Thinking about your commands
will keep me from doing
some foolish thing.
⁷ I will do right and praise you
by learning to respect
your perfect laws.
⁸ I will obey all of them!
Don't turn your back on me.

⁹ Young people can live
a clean life
by obeying your word.
¹⁰ I worship you
with all my heart.
Don't let me walk away
from your commands.
¹¹ I treasure your word
above all else;
it keeps me from sinning
against you.
¹² I praise you, LORD!
Teach me your laws.
¹³ With my own mouth,
I tell others the laws
that you have spoken.
¹⁴ Obeying your instructions
brings as much happiness
as being rich.
¹⁵ I will study your teachings
and follow your footsteps.
¹⁶ I will take pleasure
in your laws
and remember your words.

¹⁷ Treat me with kindness, LORD,
so that I may live
and do what you say.
¹⁸ Open my mind
and let me discover
the wonders of your Law.
¹⁹ I live here as a stranger.
Don't keep me from knowing
your commands.
²⁰ What I want most of all
and at all times
is to honor your laws.
²¹ You punish those boastful,
worthless nobodies who turn
from your commands.
²² Don't let them sneer
and insult me
for following you.

---

^e**118.27** *Start . . . altar*: One possible meaning for the
difficult Hebrew text.

²³ I keep thinking about
    your teachings, LORD,
  even if rulers plot
    against me.
²⁴ Your laws are my greatest joy!
    I follow their advice.

²⁵ I am at the point of death.
  Let your teachings
    breathe new life into me.
²⁶ When I told you my troubles,
  you answered my prayers.
    Now teach me your laws.
²⁷ Help me to understand
    your teachings,
  and I will think about
    your marvelous deeds.
²⁸ I am overcome with sorrow.
  Encourage me,
    as you have promised to do.
²⁹ Keep me from being deceitful,
  and be kind enough
    to teach me your Law.
³⁰ I am determined to be faithful
    and to respect your laws.
³¹ I follow your rules, LORD.
    Don't let me be ashamed.
³² I am eager to learn all
    that you want me to do;
  help me to understand
    more and more.

³³ Point out your rules to me,
  and I won't disobey
    even one of them.
³⁴ Help me to understand your Law;
  I promise to obey it
    with all my heart.
³⁵ Direct me by your commands!
    I love to do what you say.
³⁶ Make me want to obey you,
    rather than to be rich.
³⁷ Take away my foolish desires,
  and let me find life
    by walking with you.
³⁸ I am your servant!
  Do for me what you promised
    to those who worship you.
³⁹ Your wonderful teachings
  protect me from the insults
    that I hate so much.
⁴⁰ I long for your teachings.
  Be true to yourself
    and let me live.

⁴¹ Show me your love
  and save me, LORD,
    as you have promised.
⁴² Then I will have an answer
  for everyone who insults me
    for trusting your word.
⁴³ I rely on your laws!
  Don't take away my chance
    to speak your truth.
⁴⁴ I will keep obeying your Law
    forever and ever.
⁴⁵ I have gained perfect freedom
    by following your teachings,
⁴⁶ and I trust them so much
    that I tell them to kings.
⁴⁷ I love your commands!
    They bring me happiness.
⁴⁸ I love and respect them
    and will keep them in mind.

⁴⁹ Don't forget your promise
  to me, your servant.
    I depend on it.
⁵⁰ When I am hurting,
  I find comfort in your promise
    that leads to life.
⁵¹ Conceited people sneer at me,
    but I obey your Law.
⁵² I find true comfort, LORD,
  because your laws have stood
    the test of time.
⁵³ I get furious when evil people
    turn against your Law.
⁵⁴ No matter where I am,
  your teachings
    fill me with songs.
⁵⁵ Even in the night
  I think about you, LORD,
    and I obey your Law.
⁵⁶ You have blessed me
  because I have always followed
    your teachings.

⁵⁷ You, LORD, are my choice,
    and I will obey you.
⁵⁸ With all my heart
  I beg you to be kind to me,
    just as you have promised.
⁵⁹ I pay careful attention
  as you lead me,
    and I follow closely.
⁶⁰ As soon as you command,
    I do what you say.
⁶¹ Evil people may set a trap,
    but I obey your Law.

⁶²Your laws are so fair
that I wake up and praise you
in the middle of the night.
⁶³I choose as my friends
everyone who worships you
and follows your teachings.
⁶⁴Our LORD, your love is seen
all over the world.
Teach me your laws.

⁶⁵I am your servant, LORD,
and you have kept your promise
to treat me with kindness.
⁶⁶Give me wisdom and good sense.
I trust your commands.
⁶⁷Once you corrected me
for not obeying you,
but now I obey.
⁶⁸You are kindhearted,
and you do good things,
so teach me your laws.
⁶⁹My reputation is being ruined
by conceited liars,
but with all my heart
I follow your teachings.
⁷⁰Those liars have no sense,
but I find happiness
in your Law.
⁷¹When you corrected me,
it did me good
because it taught me
to study your laws.
⁷²I would rather obey you
than to have a thousand pieces
of silver and gold.

⁷³You created me
and put me together.
Make me wise enough to learn
what you have commanded.
⁷⁴Your worshipers will see me,
and they will be glad
that I trust your word.
⁷⁵Your decisions are correct,
and you were right
to punish me.
⁷⁶I serve you, LORD.
Comfort me with your love,
just as you have promised.
⁷⁷I love to obey your Law!
Have mercy and let me live.
⁷⁸Put down those proud people
who hurt me with their lies,
because I have chosen
to study your teachings.

⁷⁹Let your worshipers come to me,
so they will learn
to obey your rules.
⁸⁰Let me truly respect your laws,
so I won't be ashamed.

⁸¹I long for you to rescue me!
Your word is my only hope.
⁸²I am worn out from waiting
for you to keep your word.
When will you have mercy?
⁸³My life is wasting away
like a dried-up wineskin,ᶠ
but I have not forgotten
your teachings.
⁸⁴I am your servant!
How long must I suffer?
When will you punish
those troublemakers?
⁸⁵Those proud people reject
your teachings,
and they dig pits
for me to fall in.
⁸⁶Your laws can be trusted!
Protect me from cruel liars.
⁸⁷They have almost killed me,
but I have been faithful
to your teachings.
⁸⁸Show that you love me
and let me live,
so that I may obey all
of your commands.

⁸⁹Our LORD, you are eternal!
Your word will last as long
as the heavens.ᵍ
⁹⁰You remain faithful
in every generation,
and the earth you created
will keep standing firm.
⁹¹All things are your servants,
and the laws you made
are still in effect today.
⁹²If I had not found happiness
in obeying your Law,
I would have died in misery.
⁹³I won't ever forget
your teachings,

ᶠ**119.83** *a dried-up wineskin*: The Hebrew text has "a
wineskin in the smoke." In ancient times bags were
made from animal skins to hold wine, but when the
bags dried up they cracked and could no longer
be used.   ᵍ**119.89** *Our . . . heavens*: Or "Our LORD,
your word is eternal. It will last as long as the heavens."

because you give me new life
   by following them.
⁹⁴ I belong to you,
   and I have respected your laws,
      so keep me safe.
⁹⁵ Brutal enemies are waiting
   to ambush and destroy me,
      but I obey your rules.
⁹⁶ Nothing is completely perfect,
   except your teachings.

⁹⁷ I deeply love your Law!
   I think about it all day.
⁹⁸ Your laws never leave my mind,
   and they make me much wiser
      than my enemies.
⁹⁹ Thinking about your teachings
   gives me better understanding
      than my teachers,
¹⁰⁰ and obeying your laws
   makes me wiser than those
      who have lived a long time.
¹⁰¹ I obey your word
   instead of following a way
      that leads to trouble.
¹⁰² You have been my teacher,
   and I won't reject
      your instructions.
¹⁰³ Your teachings are sweeter
   than honey.
¹⁰⁴ They give me understanding
   and make me hate all lies.

¹⁰⁵ Your word is a lamp
   that gives light
      wherever I walk.
¹⁰⁶ Your laws are fair,
   and I have given my word
      to respect them all.
¹⁰⁷ I am in terrible pain!
   Save me, LORD,
      as you said you would.
¹⁰⁸ Accept my offerings of praise
   and teach me your laws.
¹⁰⁹ I never forget your teachings,
   although my life is always
      in danger.
¹¹⁰ Some merciless people
   are trying to trap me,
      but I never turn my back
         on your teachings.
¹¹¹ They will always be
   my most prized possession
      and my source of joy.
¹¹² I have made up my mind
   to obey your laws forever,
      no matter what.

¹¹³ I hate anyone
   whose loyalty is divided,
      but I love your Law.
¹¹⁴ You are my place of safety
   and my shield.
      Your word is my only hope.

PARENTING&*family*—How can I protect my kids from negative cultural influences? (*Psalm 119.97-105*)

Use proactive protection.

Ever get tired of being a no-no-no parent? Wouldn't it be nice to say "yes" more often? The best protection from negative cultural influences is helping our children live a life that says "yes" to God.

Kids like and appreciate people who walk according to God's laws. Kids want parents they can *trust* to tell them the *truth*. Kids appreciate parents who are *grateful* to God every day and find things to be joyful and positive about. Kids admire parents who *stand up for the underdog,* maybe a child who's being bullied. Kids like being around parents who *don't disrespect* others by talking down to them, assuming they don't know anything, or interrupting them while they talk.

The psalmist loved obeying God's laws. And loving—and following—God's ways has an attractiveness that wins children over. They can sense that if our desire is to love God and love others, they can trust our judgments about negative cultural influences. (See also Ezra 8.21-34; Proverbs 4.10-27; Song of Songs 8.8,9; 1 Peter 5.2-11.)

Words To Remember: *Your word is a lamp that gives light wherever I walk.*
—Psalm 119.105

¹¹⁵All of you worthless people,
    get away from me!
I am determined to obey
    the commands of my God.

¹¹⁶Be true to your word, LORD.
    Keep me alive and strong;
don't let me be ashamed
    because of my hope.
¹¹⁷Keep me safe and secure,
so that I will always
    respect your laws.
¹¹⁸You reject all deceitful liars
because they refuse
    your teachings.
¹¹⁹As far as you are concerned,
all evil people are[h] garbage,
    and so I follow your rules.
¹²⁰I tremble all over
when I think of you
    and the way you judge.

¹²¹I did what was fair and right!
    Don't hand me over to those
        who want to mistreat me.
¹²²Take good care of me,
        your servant,
    and don't let me be harmed
        by those conceited people.
¹²³My eyes are weary from waiting
    to see you keep your promise
        to come and save me.
¹²⁴Show your love for me,
    your servant,
        and teach me your laws.
¹²⁵I serve you,
    so let me understand
        your teachings.
¹²⁶Do something, LORD!
    They have broken your Law.
¹²⁷Your laws mean more to me
    than the finest gold.
¹²⁸I follow all of your commands,[i]
    but I hate anyone
        who leads me astray.

¹²⁹Your teachings are wonderful,
    and I respect them all.
¹³⁰Understanding your word
    brings light to the minds
        of ordinary people.
¹³¹I honestly want to know
    everything you teach.
¹³²Think about me and be kind,

just as you are to everyone
    who loves your name.
¹³³Keep your promise
    and don't let me stumble
        or let sin control my life.
¹³⁴Protect me from abuse,
    so I can obey your laws.
¹³⁵Smile on me, your servant,
    and teach me your laws.
¹³⁶When anyone disobeys you,
    my eyes overflow with tears.

¹³⁷Our LORD, you always do right,
    and your decisions are fair.
¹³⁸All of your teachings are true
    and trustworthy.
¹³⁹It upsets me greatly
    when my enemies neglect
        your teachings.
¹⁴⁰Your word to me, your servant,
    is like pure gold;
        I treasure what you say.
¹⁴¹Everyone calls me a nobody,
    but I remember your laws.
¹⁴²You will always do right,
    and your teachings are true.
¹⁴³I am in deep distress,
    but I love your teachings.
¹⁴⁴Your rules are always fair.
    Help me to understand them
        and live.

¹⁴⁵I pray to you, LORD!
    Please answer me.
        I promise to obey your laws.
¹⁴⁶I beg you to save me,
    so I can follow your rules.
¹⁴⁷Even before sunrise,
    I pray for your help,
and I put my hope
    in what you have said.
¹⁴⁸I lie awake at night,
    thinking of your promises.
¹⁴⁹Show that you love me, LORD,
    and answer my prayer.
Please do the right thing
    and save my life.
¹⁵⁰People who disobey your Law

---

[h]119.119 As far as . . . are: A few Hebrew manuscripts
and ancient translations. Most Hebrew manuscripts
have "You get rid of evil people as if they were."
[i]119.128 I . . . commands: One possible meaning for the
difficult Hebrew text.

have made evil plans
and want to hurt me,
¹⁵¹ but you are with me,
and all of your commands
can be trusted.
¹⁵² From studying your laws,
I found out long ago
that you made them
to last forever.

¹⁵³ I have not forgotten your Law!
Look at the trouble I am in,
and rescue me.
¹⁵⁴ Be my defender and protector!
Keep your promise
and save my life.
¹⁵⁵ Evil people won't obey you,
and so they have no hope
of being saved.
¹⁵⁶ You are merciful, LORD!
Please do the right thing
and save my life.
¹⁵⁷ I have a lot of brutal enemies,
but still I never turn
from your laws.
¹⁵⁸ All of those unfaithful people
who refuse to obey you
are disgusting to me.
¹⁵⁹ Remember how I love your laws,
and show your love for me
by keeping me safe.
¹⁶⁰ All you say can be trusted;
your teachings are true
and will last forever.

¹⁶¹ Rulers are cruel to me
for no reason.
But with all my heart
I respect your words,
¹⁶² because they bring happiness
like treasures taken in war.
¹⁶³ I can't stand liars,
but I love your Law.
¹⁶⁴ I praise you seven times a day
because your laws are fair.
¹⁶⁵ You give peace of mind
to all who love your Law.
Nothing can make them fall.
¹⁶⁶ You are my only hope
for being saved, LORD,
and I do all you command.
¹⁶⁷ I love and obey your laws
with all my heart.
¹⁶⁸ You know everything I do.

You know I respect every law
you have given.

¹⁶⁹ Please, LORD, hear my prayer
and give me the understanding
that comes from your word.
¹⁷⁰ Listen to my concerns
and keep me safe,
just as you have promised.
¹⁷¹ If you will teach me your laws,
I will praise you ¹⁷² and sing
about your promise,
because all of your teachings
are what they ought to be.
¹⁷³ Be ready to protect me
because I have chosen
to obey your laws.
¹⁷⁴ I am waiting for you
to save me, LORD.
Your Law makes me happy.
¹⁷⁵ Keep me alive,
so I can praise you,
and let me find help
in your teachings.
¹⁷⁶ I am your servant,
but I have wandered away
like a lost sheep.
Please come after me,
because I have not forgotten
your teachings.

Psalm 120

[A song for worship.]

A Prayer for the LORD's Help

¹ When I am in trouble, I pray,
² "Come and save me, LORD,
from deceitful liars!"

³ What punishment is fitting
for you deceitful liars?
⁴ Your reward should be
sharp and flaming arrows!

⁵ But I must live as a foreigner
among the people of Meshech
and in the tents of Kedar.^J
⁶ I have spent too much time

---

^J120.5 *Meshech . . . Kedar:* Meshech was a country near the Black Sea, and Kedar was a tribe of the Syrian desert.

living among people
who hate peace.
⁷ I am in favor of peace,
but when I speak of it,
all they want is war.

Psalm 121

[A song for worship.]

The LORD Will Protect His People

¹ I look to the hills!
Where will I find help?
² It will come from the LORD,
who created the heavens
and the earth.

³ The LORD is your protector,
and he won't go to sleep
or let you stumble.
⁴ The protector of Israel
doesn't doze
or ever get drowsy.

⁵ The LORD is your protector,
there at your right side
to shade you from the sun.
⁶ You won't be harmed
by the sun during the day
or by the moon*ᵏ* at night.

⁷ The LORD will protect you
and keep you safe
from all dangers.
⁸ The LORD will protect you
now and always
wherever you go.

Psalm 122

[A song by David for worship.]

A Song of Praise

¹ It made me glad
to hear them say,
"Let's go to the house
of the LORD!"
² Jerusalem, we are standing
inside your gates.

³ Jerusalem, what a strong
and beautiful city you are!
⁴ Every tribe of the LORD

obeys him and comes to you
to praise his name.
⁵ David's royal throne is here
where justice rules.

⁶ Jerusalem, we pray
that you will have peace,
and that all will go well
for those who love you.
⁷ May there be peace
inside your city walls
and in your palaces.
⁸ Because of my friends
and my relatives,
I will pray for peace.
⁹ And because of the house
of the LORD our God,
I will work for your good.

Psalm 123

[A song for worship.]

A Prayer for Mercy

¹ Our LORD and our God,
I turn my eyes to you,
on your throne in heaven.

> *God is ultimately
> faithful—and so should
> we be, as his children.*
>
> ANNE ORTLUND

² Servants look to their master,
but we will look to you,
until you have mercy on us.

³ Please have mercy, LORD!
We have been insulted
more than we can stand,
⁴ and we can't take more abuse
from those proud,
conceited people.

ᵏ**121.6** *harmed . . . sun . . . moon:* In ancient times
people saw the harmful effects of the rays of the sun,
and they thought that certain illnesses (especially
mental disorders) were also caused by the rays of
the moon.

Psalm 124

[A song by David for worship.]

Thanking the LORD for Victory

[1] The LORD was on our side!
Let everyone in Israel say:
[2]   "The LORD was on our side!
Otherwise, the enemy attack
[3] would have killed us all,
    because it was furious.
[4] We would have been swept away
in a violent flood
[5]   of high and roaring waves."

[6] Let's praise the LORD!
He protected us from enemies
    who were like wild animals,
[7] and we escaped like birds
    from a hunter's torn net.

[8] The LORD made heaven and earth,
and he is the one
    who sends us help.

Psalm 125

[A song for worship.]

The LORD's People Are Safe

[1] Everyone who trusts the LORD
    is like Mount Zion
that cannot be shaken
    and will stand forever.
[2] Just as Jerusalem is protected
    by mountains on every side,
the LORD protects his people
by holding them in his arms
    now and forever.
[3] He won't let the wicked
rule his people
    or lead them to do wrong.
[4] Let's ask the LORD to be kind
to everyone who is good
    and completely obeys him.

[5] When the LORD punishes
    the wicked,
he will punish everyone else
who lives a crooked life.
    Pray for peace in Israel!

Psalm 126

[A song for worship.]

Celebrating the Harvest

[1] It seemed like a dream
when the LORD brought us back
    to the city of Zion.[1]
[2] We celebrated with laughter
    and joyful songs.
In foreign nations it was said,
    "The LORD has worked miracles
    for his people."
[3] And so we celebrated
because the LORD had indeed
    worked miracles for us.

*A friend once told me,
"Blessed are those who can
laugh at themselves—
for they shall never cease
to be amused."
Humor used correctly
can heal and restore.*

SUSAN ALEXANDER YATES

[4] Our LORD, we ask you to bless
    our people again,
and let us be like streams
    in the Southern Desert.
[5] We cried as we went out
    to plant our seeds.
Now let us celebrate
    as we bring in the crops.
[6] We cried on the way
    to plant our seeds,
but we will celebrate and shout
    as we bring in the crops.

---

[1] **126.1** *brought . . . Zion:* Or "made the city of Zion prosperous again."

Psalm 127

[A song by Solomon for worship.]

Only the LORD Can Bless a Home

¹ Without the help of the LORD
it is useless to build a home
  or to guard a city.
² It is useless to get up early
and stay up late
  in order to earn a living.
God takes care of his own,
  even while they sleep.ᵐ

³ Children are a blessing
  and a gift from the LORD.
⁴ Having a lot of children
to take care of you
  in your old age
is like a warrior
  with a lot of arrows.
⁵ The more you have,
  the better off you will be,
because they will protect you
when your enemies attack
  with arguments.

Psalm 128

[A song for worship.]

The LORD Rewards His Faithful People

¹ The LORD will bless you
if you respect him
  and obey his laws.
² Your fields will produce,
and you will be happy
  and all will go well.
³ Your wife will be as fruitful
  as a grapevine,
and just as an olive tree
  is rich with olives,
your home will be rich
  with healthy children.
⁴ That is how the LORD will bless
  everyone who respects him.

⁵ I pray that the LORD
  will bless you from Zion
and let Jerusalem prosper
  as long as you live.
⁶ May you live long enough
  to see your grandchildren.
Let's pray for peace in Israel!

Psalm 129

[A song for worship.]

A Prayer for Protection

¹ Since the time I was young,
  enemies have often attacked!
Let everyone in Israel say:
² "Since the time I was young,
  enemies have often attacked!
But they have not defeated me,
³ though my back is like a field
  that has just been plowed."

⁴ The LORD always does right,
  and he has set me free
from the ropes
  of those cruel people.
⁵ I pray that all who hate
  the city of Zion
will be made ashamed
  and forced to turn and run.
⁶ May they be like grass
  on the flat roof of a house,
grass that dries up
  as soon as it sprouts.
⁷ Don't let them be like wheat
  gathered in bundles.
⁸ And don't let anyone
who passes by say to them,
  "The LORD bless you!
I give you my blessing
  in the name of the LORD."

Psalm 130

[A song for worship.]

Trusting the LORD in Times of Trouble

¹ From a sea of troubles
  I call out to you, LORD.
² Won't you please listen
  as I beg for mercy?

³ If you kept record of our sins,
  no one could last long.
⁴ But you forgive us,
  and so we will worship you.

⁵ With all my heart,
  I am waiting, LORD, for you!

ᵐ**127.2** *God . . . sleep:* One possible meaning for the difficult Hebrew text.

I trust your promises.
[6] I wait for you more eagerly
than a soldier on guard duty
waits for the dawn.
Yes, I wait more eagerly
than a soldier on guard duty
waits for the dawn.

[7] Israel, trust the LORD!
He is always merciful,
and he has the power
to save you.
[8] Israel, the LORD will save you
from all of your sins.

Psalm 131

[A song by David for worship.]

Trust the LORD!

[1] I am not conceited, LORD,
and I don't waste my time
on impossible schemes.
[2] But I have learned to feel safe
and satisfied,
just like a young child
on its mother's lap.

[3] People of Israel,
you must trust the LORD
now and forever.

Psalm 132

[A song for worship.]

The LORD Is Always with His People

[1] Our LORD, don't forget David
and how he suffered.
[2] Mighty God of Jacob,
remember how he promised:
[3] "I won't go home
or crawl into bed
[4]   or close my eyelids,
[5] until I find a home for you,
the mighty LORD God of Jacob."

[6] When we were in Ephrath,
we heard that the sacred chest
was somewhere near Jaar.
[7] Then we said, "Let's go
to the throne of the LORD
and worship at his feet."

[8] Come to your new home, LORD,
you and the sacred chest
with all of its power.
[9] Let victory be like robes
for the priests;
let your faithful people
celebrate and shout.
[10] David is your chosen one,
so don't reject him.
[11] You made a solemn promise
to David, when you said,
"I, the LORD, promise
that someone in your family
will always be king.
[12] If they keep our agreement
and follow my teachings,
then someone in your family
will rule forever."

[13] You have gladly chosen Zion
as your home, our LORD.
[14] You said, "This is my home!
I will live here forever.
[15] I will bless Zion with food,
and even the poor will eat
until they are full.
[16] Victory will be like robes
for the priests,
and its faithful people
will celebrate and shout.
[17] I will give mighty power
to the kingdom of David.
Each one of my chosen kings
will shine like a lamp
[18]   and wear a sparkling crown.
But I will disgrace
their enemies."

Psalm 133

[A song for worship.]

Living Together in Peace

[1] It is truly wonderful
when relatives live together
in peace.
[2] It is as beautiful as olive oil
poured on Aaron's head[n]
and running down his beard

---

[n]133.2 *head*: Olive oil was poured on Aaron's head to
show that God had chosen him to be the high priest.

and the collar of his robe.
³ It is like the dew
from Mount Hermon,
   falling on Zion's mountains,
where the LORD has promised
to bless his people
   with life forevermore.

Psalm 134

[A song for worship.]

Praising the LORD at Night

¹ Everyone who serves the LORD,
   come and offer praises.
Everyone who has gathered
   in his temple tonight,
² lift your hands in prayer
toward his holy place
   and praise the LORD.

³ The LORD is the Creator
   of heaven and earth,
and I pray that the LORD
   will bless you from Zion.

Psalm 135

In Praise of the LORD's Kindness

¹ Shout praises to the LORD!
You are his servants,
   so praise his name.
² All who serve in the temple
of the LORD our God,
³   come and shout praises.
Praise the name of the LORD!
   He is kind and good.
⁴ He chose the family of Jacob
and the people of Israel
   for his very own.

⁵ The LORD is much greater
   than any other god.
⁶ He does as he chooses
in heaven and on earth
   and deep in the sea.
⁷ The LORD makes the clouds rise
   from far across the earth,
and he makes lightning
   to go with the rain.

Then from his secret place
   he sends out the wind.

⁸ The LORD killed the first-born
of people and animals
   in the land of Egypt.
⁹ God used miracles and wonders
to fight the king of Egypt
   and all of his officials.
¹⁰ He destroyed many nations
   and killed powerful kings,
¹¹ including King Sihon
of the Amorites
   and King Og of Bashan.
He conquered every kingdom
   in the land of Canaan
¹² and gave their property
   to his people Israel.

¹³ The name of the LORD
   will be remembered forever,
and he will be famous
   for all time to come.
¹⁴ The LORD will bring justice
and show mercy to all
   who serve him.

¹⁵ Idols of silver and gold
are made and worshiped
   in other nations.
¹⁶ They have a mouth and eyes,
   but they can't speak or see.
¹⁷ They are completely deaf,
   and they can't breathe.
¹⁸ Everyone who makes idols
and all who trust them
will end up as helpless
   as their idols.

¹⁹ Everyone in Israel,
   come praise the LORD!
All the family of Aaron
²⁰ and all the tribe of Levi,ᵒ
   come praise the LORD!
All of his worshipers,
   come praise the LORD.
²¹ Praise the LORD from Zion!
   He lives here in Jerusalem.
   Shout praises to the LORD!

ᵒ**135.19,20** *Aaron . . . Levi:* Aaron was from the
tribe of Levi, and all priests were from his family.
The temple helpers, singers, and musicians were
also from the tribe of Levi.

Psalm 136

God's Love Never Fails

1 Praise the LORD! He is good.
God's love never fails.
2 Praise the God of all gods.
God's love never fails.
3 Praise the Lord of lords.
God's love never fails.

4 Only God works great miracles.[p]
God's love never fails.
5 With wisdom he made the sky.
God's love never fails.
6 The Lord stretched the earth
over the ocean.
God's love never fails.
7 He made the bright lights
in the sky.
God's love never fails.
8 He lets the sun rule each day.
God's love never fails.
9 He lets the moon and the stars
rule each night.
God's love never fails.

10 God struck down the first-born
in every Egyptian family.
God's love never fails.
11 He rescued Israel from Egypt.
God's love never fails.
12 God used his great strength
and his powerful arm.
God's love never fails.
13 He split the Red Sea[q] apart.
God's love never fails.

14 The Lord brought Israel safely
through the sea.
God's love never fails.
15 He destroyed the Egyptian king
and his army there.
God's love never fails.
16 The Lord led his people
through the desert.
God's love never fails.

17 Our God defeated mighty kings.
God's love never fails.
18 And he killed famous kings.
God's love never fails.
19 One of them was Sihon,
king of the Amorites.
God's love never fails.
20 Another was King Og of Bashan.
God's love never fails.
21 God took away their land.
God's love never fails.

[p]136.4 *great miracles*: One Hebrew manuscript and one ancient translation have "miracles." [q]136.13 *Red Sea*: See the note at 106.7, 9, 22.

*Spiritual*Life—How can I handle my doubts about God? *(Psalm 136)*

Replay the events.

Tempted to skip this entry because you don't have doubts? Or is it that when you do have doubts, you simply dismiss them?

Most people have doubts about God now and then. It works better to face them than to ignore them. In fact, you can prepare ahead for doubts by developing a catalog of reasons for believing in God's faithfulness.

The simplest reason is recounting God's faithfulness. The psalmist did this by listing the ways that God's love came through. He broke down the events of each familiar Bible story and cited God's providential care—often in the form of a miracle (136.10-22).

We, too, can look at the different ways God has delivered us throughout life. What almost happened? What did I think should have happened? Why might that have been disastrous? Where did that person come from who helped me? How did she know what I needed? What if she had come sooner or later?

God is not always showy about his grace. His favor moves quietly into our life so we need to pay attention to it. Each detail gives us a reason to be thankful and more reasons to believe. (See also Job 1; Jeremiah 23.16-32; Romans 4.13-25; Colossians 2.6-19.)

Words To Remember: ***Only God works great miracles. God's love never fails.*** **—Psalm 136.4**

²² He gave their land to Israel,
the people who serve him.
God's love never fails.

²³ God saw the trouble we were in.
God's love never fails.
²⁴ He rescued us from our enemies.
God's love never fails.
²⁵ He gives food to all who live.
God's love never fails.

²⁶ Praise God in heaven!
God's love never fails.

Psalm 137

A Prayer for Revenge

¹ Beside the rivers of Babylon
we thought about Jerusalem,
and we sat down and cried.
² We hung our small harps
on the willow^r trees.
³ Our enemies had brought us here
as their prisoners,
and now they wanted us to sing
and entertain them.
They insulted us and shouted,
"Sing about Zion!"

⁴ Here in a foreign land,
how can we sing
about the LORD?
⁵ Jerusalem, if I forget you,
let my right hand go limp.
⁶ Let my tongue stick
to the roof of my mouth,
if I don't think about you
above all else.

⁷ Our LORD, punish the Edomites!
Because the day Jerusalem fell,
they shouted,
"Completely destroy the city!
Tear down every building!"

⁸ Babylon, you are doomed!
I pray the Lord's blessings
on anyone who punishes you
for what you did to us.
⁹ May the Lord bless everyone
who beats your children
against the rocks!

Psalm 138

[By David.]

Praise the LORD with All Your Heart

¹ With all my heart
I praise you, LORD.
In the presence of angels^s
I sing your praises.
² I worship at your holy temple
and praise you for your love
and your faithfulness.
You were true to your word
and made yourself more famous
than ever before.^t

> *To pray in Jesus' name is
> to ask to be selfless.*
>
> JONI EARECKSON TADA

³ When I asked for your help,
you answered my prayer
and gave me courage.^u

⁴ All kings on this earth
have heard your promises, LORD,
and they will praise you.
⁵ You are so famous
that they will sing about
the things you have done.
⁶ Though you are above us all,
you care for humble people,
and you keep a close watch
on everyone who is proud.

⁷ I am surrounded by trouble,
but you protect me
against my angry enemies.
With your own powerful arm
you keep me safe.

---

^r**137.2** *willow:* Or "poplar." ^s**138.1** *angels:* Or
"gods" or "supernatural beings" who worship and
serve God in heaven or "rulers" or "leaders."
^t**138.2** *You were . . . before:* One possible meaning
for the difficult Hebrew text. ^u**138.3** *and gave me
courage:* One possible meaning for the difficult
Hebrew text.

⁸You, LORD, will always
  treat me with kindness.
    Your love never fails.
  You have made us what we are.
    Don't give up on us now!^v

                Psalm 139

[*A psalm by David for the music leader.*]

The LORD Is Always Near

¹You have looked deep
  into my heart, LORD,
    and you know all about me.
²You know when I am resting
  or when I am working,
and from heaven
  you discover my thoughts.

³You notice everything I do
  and everywhere I go.
⁴Before I even speak a word,
  you know what I will say,
⁵and with your powerful arm
you protect me
  from every side.
⁶I can't understand all of this!
  Such wonderful knowledge
    is far above me.

⁷Where could I go to escape
  from your Spirit
    or from your sight?
⁸If I were to climb up
  to the highest heavens,
    you would be there.
If I were to dig down
  to the world of the dead
    you would also be there.

⁹Suppose I had wings
  like the dawning day
    and flew across the ocean.
¹⁰Even then your powerful arm
  would guide and protect me.
¹¹Or suppose I said, "I'll hide
  in the dark until night comes
    to cover me over."
¹²But you see in the dark
  because daylight and dark
    are all the same to you.

¹³You are the one
  who put me together
    inside my mother's body,
¹⁴and I praise you because of

---

^v**138.8** *You have . . . now:* Or "Please don't desert
your people."

PARENTING&*family*—How can I deal with the challenges of being a single parent? *(Psalm 138)*

Ask God—and others—for help.
If you find yourself in the position of raising your children alone, the Lord can give you the strength and resources you need (138.3). The Lord is still our husband, and he has promised not to put you in situations that are more than you can handle. He is true to his word (138.2), he keeps you safe (138.7), and he always treats you with kindness (138.8). So if you're overwhelmed by pressure to pay the bills and still spend quality time with your kids, the Lord will make a way for you. Continue to teach your children by your loving example and wise words that the Lord's love never fails (138.8).

Remember, too, that you are part of the body of Christ, which means you need the other parts in order to function well. If you're trying to juggle all your responsibilities alone because you're uncomfortable asking for help or you don't think anyone cares, be realistic about your limits. Let a few people in your church or Bible study group know some specific ways they can help. You'll be amazed at how people who have received much, love much. Think of asking for help as a way to give people a chance to show their thanks to the Lord! With their help, you can have more time and energy to raise your little ones to know and love the Lord. (See also 1 Kings 17.8-16; Psalm 71.1-6; Philippians 4.10-20.)

Words To Remember: *When I asked for your help, you answered my prayer and gave me courage. . . . You, LORD, will always treat me with kindness. Your love never fails.*—Psalm 138.3,8

the wonderful way
    you created me.
Everything you do is marvelous!
    Of this I have no doubt.

¹⁵Nothing about me
    is hidden from you!
I was secretly woven together
    deep in the earth below,
¹⁶but with your own eyes you saw
    my body being formed.
Even before I was born,
you had written in your book
everything I would do.

¹⁷Your thoughts are far beyond
    my understanding,
much more than I
    could ever imagine.
¹⁸I try to count your thoughts,
but they outnumber the grains
    of sand on the beach.
And when I awake,
    I will find you nearby.

¹⁹How I wish that you would kill
all cruel and heartless people
and protect me from them!
²⁰They are always rebelling
and speaking evil of you.ʷ
²¹You know I hate anyone
who hates you, LORD,
    and refuses to obey.

²²They are my enemies too,
    and I truly hate them.

²³Look deep into my heart, God,
    and find out everything
        I am thinking.
²⁴Don't let me follow evil ways,
    but lead me in the way
        that time has proven true.

Psalm 140

[A psalm by David for the music leader.]

A Prayer for the LORD's Help

¹Rescue me from cruel
    and violent enemies, LORD!
²They think up evil plans
    and always cause trouble.
³Their words bite deep
like the poisonous fangs
    of a snake.

⁴Protect me, LORD, from cruel
and brutal enemies,
    who want to destroy me.
⁵Those proud people have hidden
traps and nets
    to catch me as I walk.

ʷ**139.20** *you*: One possible meaning for the difficult Hebrew text of verse 20.

PARENTING&*family*—How can I nurture my child's self-worth? *(Psalm 139)*

Create a sense of God-worth.
Kids somehow get the impression that God is concerned only about doing right and wrong. They think, *Sure, God loves me, but it's a lot easier for him to love me if I behave.*

True security comes from knowing God loves us no matter what. That's evidenced by the fact that God stays with us all the time (139.7-12). We can never get away from him—and when we understand what God is really like, we wouldn't want to. Our God created us to be with him and to be protected by him. He never stays at a distance.

Another reason God loves us is that he created us (139.13-17). The things other kids make fun of (thin hair or big feet) are things God thought were a good idea. If God thinks our physical appearance is good, who should criticize?

The truth is, God can't take his eyes off us! He has kept a record of what we do as if it were a huge baby book (139.16) written in advance. Our God is fascinated with us and delights in us. Not only does this make us feel better about ourselves, but it pulls us toward a fascination with God. (See also 1 Samuel 17.24-54; Luke 15.11-32; Ephesians 1.3-14; 2 Thessalonians 3.6-15.)

Words To Remember: *You are the one who put me together inside my mother's body, and I praise you because of the wonderful way you created me.—Psalm 139.13,14*

⁶You, LORD, are my God!
  Please listen to my prayer.
⁷You have the power to save me,
  and you keep me safe
    in every battle.

⁸Don't let the wicked succeed
  in doing what they want,
  or else they might never
    stop planning evil.
⁹They have me surrounded,
  but make them the victims
    of their own vicious lies.ˣ
¹⁰Dump flaming coals on them
  and throw them into pits
    where they can't climb out.
¹¹Chase those cruel liars away!
  Let trouble hunt them down.

¹²Our LORD, I know that you
  defend the homeless
  and see that the poor
    are given justice.
¹³Your people will praise you
  and will live with you
    because they do right.

Psalm 141

[A psalm by David.]

A Prayer for the LORD's Protection

¹I pray to you, LORD!
  Please listen when I pray
    and hurry to help me.

²Think of my prayer
  as sweet-smelling incense,
  and think of my lifted hands
    as an evening sacrifice.

³Help me to guard my words
  whenever I say something.
⁴Don't let me want to do evil
  or waste my time doing wrong
    with wicked people.
  Don't let me even taste
    the good things they offer.

⁵Let your faithful people
  correct and punish me.
  My prayers condemn the deeds
    of those who do wrong,
  so don't let me be friends
    with any of them.
⁶Everyone will admit
  that I was right
  when their rulers are thrown
    down a rocky cliff,
⁷and their bones lie scattered
  like broken rocks
    on top of a grave.ʸ

⁸You are my LORD and God,
  and I look to you for safety.
  Don't let me be harmed.

ˣ140.8,9 or else . . . lies: One possible meaning for the
difficult Hebrew text.   ʸ141.5-7 Let . . . grave: One
possible meaning for the difficul· Hebrew text of
verses 5-7.

Personal *Concerns*—How can I accept my body as it is? *(Psalm 139.13-16)*

Look in your mirror—and praise God.
Your body is God's idea—and he physically put you together. The things you may dislike about yourself (maybe you have a big nose or you're not good at reading or socializing) are part of the package God assembled. God created you special and unique: body, intellect, temperament.

It can be fun—and almost mind-bending—to look at yourself in the mirror on a bad-hair day and say to God, "Everything you do is marvelous!" (139.14). Or, when you put on a swimsuit or summer clothes for the first time in late spring, to praise God for the wonderful way he created you (139.14). Sure, your body isn't the same as the moment God created you—it has bulges and droops. But it has also developed more muscles, feminine features, and stronger bones to get your body where it needs to go. You had none of those things at your creation; God has continued his marvelous work on you, and it's *his* opinion that counts. (See also Psalm 104; Mark 14.3-9.)

Words To Remember: *I was secretly woven together deep in the earth below, but with your own eyes you saw my body being formed.—Psalm 139.15,16*

⁹Protect me from the traps
  of those violent people,
¹⁰and make them fall
  into their own traps
    while you help me escape.

Psalm 142

*[A special psalm and a prayer by David
when he was in the cave.]*

A Prayer for Help

¹I pray to you, LORD.
  I beg for mercy.
²I tell you all of my worries
  and my troubles,
³and whenever I feel low,
  you are there to guide me.

A trap has been hidden
  along my pathway.
⁴Even if you look,
  you won't see anyone
who cares enough
  to walk beside me.
There is no place to hide,
  and no one who really cares.

⁵I pray to you, LORD!
  You are my place of safety,
and you are my choice
  in the land of the living.
Please answer my prayer.
  I am completely helpless.

⁶Help! They are chasing me,
  and they are too strong.
⁷Rescue me from this prison,
  so I can praise your name.
And when your people notice
your wonderful kindness to me,
  they will rush to my side.

Psalm 143

[A psalm by David.]

A Prayer in Time of Danger

¹Listen, LORD, as I pray!
You are faithful and honest
  and will answer my prayer.
²I am your servant.
  Don't try me in your court,

because no one is innocent
  by your standards.
³My enemies are chasing me,
  crushing me in the ground.
I am in total darkness,
  like someone long dead.
⁴I have given up all hope,
  and I feel numb all over.

⁵I remember to think about
the many things you did
  in years gone by.
⁶Then I lift my hands in prayer,
because my soul is a desert,
  thirsty for water from you.

⁷Please hurry, LORD,
and answer my prayer.
  I feel hopeless.
Don't turn away
  and leave me here to die.
⁸Each morning let me learn
more about your love
  because I trust you.
I come to you in prayer,
  asking for your guidance.

⁹Please rescue me
from my enemies, LORD!
  I come to you for safety.ᶻ
¹⁰You are my God. Show me
  what you want me to do,
and let your gentle Spirit
  lead me in the right path.

¹¹Be true to your name, LORD,
  and keep my life safe.
Use your saving power
  to protect me from trouble.
¹²I am your servant.
Show how much you love me
  by destroying my enemies.

Psalm 144

[By David.]

A Prayer for the Nation

¹I praise you, LORD!
  You are my mighty rock,ᵃ

ᶻ**143.9** *I . . . safety:* Or "You are my hiding place."
ᵃ**144.1** *mighty rock:* See the note at 18.2.

and you teach me
　　how to fight my battles.
[2] You are my friend,
　and you are my fortress
　　where I am safe.
You are my shield,
　and you made me the ruler
　　of our people.[b]

[3] Why do we humans mean anything
to you, our LORD?
　Why do you care about us?
[4] We disappear like a breath;
we last no longer
　than a faint shadow.

[5] Open the heavens like a curtain
　and come down, LORD.
Touch the mountains
　and make them send up smoke.
[6] Use your lightning as arrows
　to scatter my enemies
　　and make them run away.
[7] Reach down from heaven
　and set me free.
Save me from the mighty flood
[8] of those lying foreigners
　who can't tell the truth.

[9] In praise of you, our God,
　I will sing a new song,
　　while playing my harp.
[10] By your power, kings win wars,
　and your servant David is saved
　　from deadly swords.
[11] Won't you keep me safe
　from those lying foreigners
　　who can't tell the truth?

[12] Let's pray that our young sons
　will grow like strong plants
and that our daughters
will be as lovely as columns
　in the corner of a palace.
[13] May our barns be filled
　with all kinds of crops.
May our fields be covered
with sheep by the thousands,
[14]　　and every cow have calves.[c]
Don't let our city be captured
　or any of us be taken away,
and don't let cries of sorrow
　be heard in our streets.

[15] Our LORD and our God,
you give these blessings
　to all who worship you.

Psalm 145

[By David for praise.]

The LORD Is Kind and Merciful

[1] I will praise you,
　my God and King,
　　and always honor your name.
[2] I will praise you each day
　and always honor your name.
[3] You are wonderful, LORD,
　and you deserve all praise,
because you are much greater
　than anyone can understand.

[4] Each generation will announce
to the next your wonderful
　and powerful deeds.
[5] I will keep thinking about
your marvelous glory
　and your mighty miracles.[d]
[6] Everyone will talk about
　your fearsome deeds,
and I will tell all nations
　how great you are.
[7] They will celebrate and sing
about your matchless mercy
　and your power to save.

[8] You are merciful, LORD!
You are kind and patient
　and always loving.
[9] You are good to everyone,
and you take care
　of all your creation.

[10] All creation will thank you,
　and your loyal people
　　will praise you.
[11] They will tell about
your marvelous kingdom
　and your power.
[12] Then everyone will know about

---

[b]144.2 *of our people*: Some Hebrew manuscripts and ancient translations have "of the nations."
[c]144.14 *have calves*: Or "grow fat." [d]145.5 *and . . . miracles*: One Hebrew manuscript and two ancient translations have "as others tell about your mighty miracles."

the mighty things you do
and your glorious kingdom.
¹³ Your kingdom will never end,
and you will rule forever.

Our LORD, you keep your word
and do everything you say.ᵉ
¹⁴ When someone stumbles or falls,
you give a helping hand.
¹⁵ Everyone depends on you,
and when the time is right,
you provide them with food.
¹⁶ By your own hand you satisfy
the desires of all who live.

¹⁷ Our LORD, everything you do
is kind and thoughtful,
¹⁸ and you are near to everyone
whose prayers are sincere.
¹⁹ You satisfy the desires
of all your worshipers,
and you come to save them
when they ask for help.
²⁰ You take care of everyone
who loves you,
but you destroy the wicked.

²¹ I will praise you, LORD,
and everyone will respect
your holy name forever.

Psalm 146

Shout Praises to the LORD

¹ Shout praises to the LORD!
With all that I am,
I will shout his praises.
² I will sing and praise
the LORD God
for as long as I live.

³ You can't depend on anyone,
not even a great leader.
⁴ Once they die and are buried,
that will be the end
of all their plans.

⁵ The LORD God of Jacob blesses
everyone who trusts him
and depends on him.
⁶ God made heaven and earth;
he created the sea
and everything else.
God always keeps his word.

⁷ He gives justice to the poor
and food to the hungry.

The LORD sets prisoners free
⁸   and heals blind eyes.
He gives a helping hand
to everyone who falls.
The LORD loves good people

> *Beware of letting your*
> *feelings dictate what is*
> *truth. Rather, allow truth*
> *to dictate your feelings.*
>
> JILL BRISCOE

⁹   and looks after strangers.
He defends the rights
of orphans and widows,
but destroys the wicked.

¹⁰ The LORD God of Zion
will rule forever!
Shout praises to the LORD!

Psalm 147

Sing and Praise the LORD

¹ Shout praises to the LORD!
Our God is kind,
and it is right and good
to sing praises to him.
² The LORD rebuilds Jerusalem
and brings the people of Israel
back home again.
³ He renews our hopes
and heals our bodies.
⁴ He decided how many stars
there would be in the sky
and gave each one a name.
⁵ Our LORD is great and powerful!
He understands everything.
⁶ The LORD helps the poor,
but he smears the wicked
in the dirt.

ᵉ**145.13** *Our . . . say:* These words are found in one
Hebrew manuscript and two ancient translations.

⁷ Celebrate and sing!
Play your harps
   for the LORD our God.
⁸ He fills the sky with clouds
and sends rain to the earth,
so that the hills
   will be green with grass.
⁹ He provides food for cattle
and for the young ravens,
   when they cry out.
¹⁰ The LORD doesn't care about
the strength of horses
   or powerful armies.
¹¹ The LORD is pleased only
with those who worship him
   and trust his love.

¹² Everyone in Jerusalem,
come and praise
   the LORD your God!
¹³ He makes your city gates strong
and blesses your people
   by giving them children.
¹⁴ God lets you live in peace,
and he gives you
   the very best wheat.
¹⁵ As soon as God speaks,
   the earth obeys.
¹⁶ He covers the ground with snow
like a blanket of wool,
and he scatters frost
   like ashes on the ground.
¹⁷ God sends down hailstones
like chips of rocks.
   Who can stand the cold?
¹⁸ At his command the ice melts,
the wind blows,
   and streams begin to flow.

¹⁹ God gave his laws and teachings
to the descendants of Jacob,
   the nation of Israel.
²⁰ But he has not given his laws
to any other nation.
   Shout praises to the LORD!

Psalm 148

Come Praise the LORD

¹ Shout praises to the LORD!
Shout the LORD's praises
   in the highest heavens.
² All of you angels,
and all who serve him above,
   come and offer praise.

³ Sun and moon,
and all of you bright stars,
   come and offer praise.
⁴ Highest heavens, and the water
above the highest heavens,^f
   come and offer praise.

⁵ Let all things praise
the name of the LORD,
because they were created
   at his command.
⁶ He made them to last forever,
and nothing can change
   what he has done.^g

⁷ All creatures on earth,
you obey his commands,
   so come praise the LORD!

⁸ Sea monsters and the deep sea,
fire and hail, snow and frost,
and every stormy wind,
   come praise the LORD!

⁹ All mountains and hills,
fruit trees and cedars,
¹⁰ every wild and tame animal,
all reptiles and birds,
   come praise the LORD!
¹¹ Every king and every ruler,
all nations on earth,
¹² every man and every woman,
young people and old,
   come praise the LORD!

¹³ All creation, come praise
the name of the LORD.
Praise his name alone.
The glory of God is greater
   than heaven and earth.

¹⁴ Like a bull with mighty horns,
the LORD protects
his faithful nation Israel,
because they belong to him.
   Shout praises to the LORD!

---

^f148.4 *the water . . . heavens:* It was believed that the earth and the heavens were surrounded by water. ^g148.6 *nothing . . . done:* Or "his laws will never change."

Psalm 149

A New Song of Praise

[1] Shout praises to the LORD!
Sing him a new song of praise
when his loyal people meet.
[2] People of Israel, rejoice
because of your Creator.
People of Zion, celebrate
because of your King.
[3] Praise his name by dancing
and playing music on harps
and tambourines.
[4] The LORD is pleased
with his people,
and he gives victory
to those who are humble.
[5] All of you faithful people,
praise our glorious Lord!
Celebrate and worship.
[6] Praise God with songs
on your lips
and a sword in your hand.
[7] Take revenge and punish
the nations.
[8] Put chains of iron
on their kings and rulers.
[9] Punish them as they deserve;

this is the privilege
of God's faithful people.
Shout praises to the LORD!

Psalm 150

The LORD Is Good to His People

[1] Shout praises to the LORD!
Praise God in his temple.
Praise him in heaven,
his mighty fortress.
[2] Praise our God!
His deeds are wonderful,
too marvelous to describe.

[3] Praise God with trumpets
and all kinds of harps.
[4] Praise him with tambourines
and dancing,
with stringed instruments
and woodwinds.
[5] Praise God with cymbals,
with clashing cymbals.
[6] Let every living creature
praise the LORD.
Shout praises to the LORD!

Proverbs

A Book of Wise Sayings

The book of Proverbs isn't like any other book in the Bible. That's what makes it so interesting and sometimes humorous. These brief, pithy truisms that teach a lesson in one or two verses are easy to memorize and apply to everyday life. The theme for the book is: "Respect and obey the LORD! This is the beginning of knowledge. Only a fool rejects wisdom and good advice" (1.7).

Wisdom literature (which includes proverbs, riddles, and more extensive writings such as the book of Job and the Song of Songs) was a style of thinking and writing that emphasized practical counsel for everyday life. Why? Because every area of life is of interest to God. Thus, in Proverbs, God's wisdom touches every department of life: work, marriage, family, friendship, money, honesty, integrity, attitudes. Furthermore, it says that the person who refuses to be guided by these principles is a fool.

In the New Testament, Jesus used the concepts and methods of proverbs in his teachings, especially in the parables he told and in his interaction with his listeners. The apostle Peter showed his knowledge of proverbs in his first epistle; the apostle Paul also used them in his writings.

The very nature of the book of Proverbs suggests that, unlike more cohesive books, these proverbs be read or meditated on separately. Yet they are part of a whole perspective on living life wisely under the hand of God. (Interestingly enough, it was during Hezekiah's revival

that this collection of Solomon's proverbs was made, more than two hundred years after his death, indicating great honor and respect for Solomon's wisdom.)

Is there an area of your life in which you need counsel? There's a proverb for you! So don't hurry. Take your time and enjoy this practical book. When you find a wise saying that's just what you need, maybe you'll even want to write it on a card to carry with you!

Proverbs at a Glance

1. An introduction to the theme of the book (1.1-7)
2. Poems teaching the nature and value of wisdom (1.8—9.18)
3. Solomon's wise sayings (10.1—22.16)
4. Sayings of wise men (22.17—24.34)
5. Hezekiah's collection of Solomon's wise sayings (25–29)
6. Wise sayings of Agur and King Lemuel's mother (30.1—31.9)
7. Praise of a good wife (31.10-31)

How Proverbs Can Be Used

1 These are the proverbs
of King Solomon of Israel,
    the son of David.
[2] Proverbs will teach you
    wisdom and self-control
and how to understand
    sayings with deep meanings.
[3] You will learn what is right
    and honest and fair.
[4] From these, an ordinary person
    can learn to be smart,
and young people can gain
    knowledge and good sense.

[5] If you are already wise,
    you will become even wiser.
And if you are smart,
you will learn to understand
[6]   proverbs and sayings,
as well as words of wisdom
    and all kinds of riddles.

*It's not how
much you make;
it's what you do with
what you get.*

MARY HUNT

[7] Respect and obey the LORD!
This is the beginning
    of knowledge.[a]
Only a fool rejects wisdom
    and good advice.

Warnings against Bad Friends

[8] My child, obey the teachings
    of your parents,
[9] and wear their teachings
    as you would a lovely hat
    or a pretty necklace.
[10] Don't be tempted by sinners
    or listen [11] when they say,
"Come on! Let's gang up
    and kill somebody,
    just for the fun of it!
[12] They're well and healthy now,

but we'll finish them off
    once and for all.
[13] We'll take their valuables
    and fill our homes
    with stolen goods.
[14] If you join our gang,
    you'll get your share."

[15] Don't follow anyone like that
    or do what they do.
[16] They are in a big hurry
    to commit some crime,
    perhaps even murder.
[17] They are like a bird
    that sees the bait,
    but ignores the trap.[b]
[18] They gang up to murder someone,
    but they are the victims.
[19] The wealth you get from crime
    robs you of your life.

Wisdom Speaks

[20] Wisdom[c] shouts in the streets
    wherever crowds gather.
[21] She shouts in the marketplaces
    and near the city gates
    as she says to the people,
[22] "How much longer
    will you enjoy
    being stupid fools?
Won't you ever stop sneering
    and laughing at knowledge?
[23] Listen as I correct you
    and tell you what I think.
[24] You completely ignored me
    and refused to listen;
[25] you rejected my advice
    and paid no attention
    when I warned you.

[26] "So when you are struck
    by some terrible disaster,
[27] or when trouble and distress
    surround you like a whirlwind,
    I will laugh and make fun.
[28] You will ask for my help,
    but I won't listen;

---

[a] **1.7** *the beginning of knowledge:* Or "what knowledge
is all about." [b] **1.17** *They are . . . trap:* Or "Be like a
bird that won't go for the bait, if it sees the trap."
[c] **1.20** *Wisdom:* In the book of Proverbs the word
"wisdom" is sometimes used as though wisdom were
a supernatural being who was with God at the time
of creation.

you will search,
  but you won't find me.
²⁹ No, you would not learn,
  and you refused
    to respect the LORD.
³⁰ You rejected my advice
  and paid no attention
    when I warned you.

³¹ "Now you will eat the fruit
  of what you have done,
until you are stuffed full
  with your own schemes.
³² Sin and self-satisfaction
  bring destruction and death
    to stupid fools.
³³ But if you listen to me,
you will be safe and secure
  without fear of disaster."

Wisdom and Bad Friends

2 My child, you must follow
  and treasure my teachings
    and my instructions.
² Keep in tune with wisdom
  and think what it means
    to have common sense.
³ Beg as loud as you can
  for good common sense.
⁴ Search for wisdom
  as you would search for silver
    or hidden treasure.
⁵ Then you will understand
  what it means to respect
    and to know the LORD God.

⁶ All wisdom comes from the LORD,
  and so do common sense
    and understanding.
⁷ God gives helpful advice[d]
  to everyone who obeys him
and protects all of those
  who live as they should.
⁸ God sees that justice is done,
  and he watches over everyone
    who is faithful to him.
⁹ With wisdom you will learn
  what is right
    and honest and fair.

¹⁰ Wisdom will control your mind,
  and you will be pleased
    with knowledge.
¹¹ Sound judgment and good sense
  will watch over you.
¹² Wisdom will protect you
  from evil schemes
and from those liars
¹³ who turned from doing good
  to live in the darkness.
¹⁴ Most of all they enjoy
  being mean and deceitful.
¹⁵ They are dishonest themselves,
  and all they do is crooked.

Wisdom and Sexual Purity

¹⁶ Wisdom will protect you
  from the smooth talk
    of a sinful woman,

---

[d]2.7 *helpful advice*: Or "wisdom."

PARENTING&*family*—How can I encourage my child's faith to grow?
(Proverbs 2.1-15)

Be an example.

Your practice of faith is one of the greatest influences in developing your child's faith. If you pray, your child will take note. If you read the Bible, your child will see its importance to you—and often copy your practice. If you explain a difficult decision by saying that you want to "follow God's rules," your child will begin to recognize right and wrong.

Young children love to be like their parents. The habits and attitudes they learn from you will influence them their entire lives. Proverbs 2.4 says that we are to search for wisdom as we would for treasure. Teaching biblical lessons is important. But the old adage "Children learn more by what you do than by what you say" is still true. So love God and love your children. You will lead them toward loving you and loving God in return. (See also Joshua 4; 1 Chronicles 22; Ezra 3; John 3.16-21.)

Words To Remember: *My child, you must follow and treasure my teachings and my instructions.—Proverbs 2.1*

¹⁷who breaks her wedding vows
and leaves the man she married
when she was young.
¹⁸The road to her house leads
down to the dark world
of the dead.
¹⁹Visit her, and you will never
find the road to life again.

²⁰Follow the example
of good people
and live an honest life.
²¹If you are honest and innocent,
you will keep your land;
²²if you do wrong
and can never be trusted,
you will be rooted out.

Trust God

3 My child, remember
my teachings and instructions
and obey them completely.
²They will help you live
a long and prosperous life.
³Let love and loyalty
always show like a necklace,
and write them in your mind.
⁴God and people will like you
and consider you a success.

⁵With all your heart
you must trust the LORD
and not your own judgment.
⁶Always let him lead you,
and he will clear the road
for you to follow.
⁷Don't ever think that you
are wise enough,
but respect the LORD
and stay away from evil.
⁸This will make you healthy,
and you will feel strong.
⁹Honor the LORD by giving him
your money and the first part
of all your crops.
¹⁰Then you will have
more grain and grapes
than you will ever need.

¹¹My child, don't turn away
or become bitter
when the LORD
corrects you.
¹²The LORD corrects
everyone he loves,

just as parents correct
their favorite child.

The Value of Wisdom

¹³God blesses everyone
who has wisdom
and common sense.
¹⁴Wisdom is worth more
than silver;
it makes you much richer
than gold.
¹⁵Wisdom is more valuable
than precious jewels;
nothing you want
compares with her.

¹⁶In her right hand
Wisdom holds a long life,
and in her left hand
are wealth and honor.
¹⁷Wisdom makes life pleasant
and leads us safely along.
¹⁸Wisdom is a life-giving tree,
the source of happiness
for all who hold on to her.

¹⁹By his wisdom and knowledge
the LORD created
heaven and earth.
²⁰By his understanding
he let the ocean break loose
and clouds release the rain.
²¹My child, use common sense
and sound judgment!
Always keep them in mind.
²²They will help you to live
a long and beautiful life.
²³You will walk safely
and never stumble;
²⁴you will rest without a worry
and sleep soundly.
²⁵So don't be afraid
of sudden disasters
or storms that strike
those who are evil.
²⁶You can be sure that the LORD
will protect you from harm.

²⁷Do all you can for everyone
who deserves your help.
²⁸Don't tell your neighbor
to come back tomorrow,
if you can help today.
²⁹Don't try to be mean
to neighbors who trust you.

³⁰ Don't argue just to be arguing,
  when you haven't been hurt.
³¹ Don't be jealous
  of cruel people
  or follow their example.

³² The LORD doesn't like
  anyone who is dishonest,
but he lets good people
  be his friends.
³³ He places a curse on the home
  of everyone who is evil,
but he blesses the home
  of every good person.
³⁴ The LORD sneers at those
  who sneer at him,
but he is kind to everyone
  who is humble.
³⁵ You will be praised
  if you are wise,
but you will be disgraced
  if you are a stubborn fool.

Advice to Young People

4 My child, listen closely
  to my teachings
    and learn common sense.
² My advice is useful,
  so don't turn away.
³ When I was still very young
and my mother's favorite child,
  my father ⁴said to me:
"If you follow my teachings
and keep them in mind,
  you will live.

⁵ Be wise and learn good sense;
  remember my teachings
  and do what I say.

⁶ If you love Wisdom
  and don't reject her,
    she will watch over you.
⁷ The best thing about Wisdom
    is Wisdom herself;
good sense is more important
    than anything else.
⁸ If you value Wisdom
  and hold tightly to her,
    great honors will be yours.
⁹ It will be like wearing
  a glorious crown
    of beautiful flowers.

The Right Way and the Wrong Way

¹⁰ My child, if you listen
  and obey my teachings,
    you will live a long time.
¹¹ I have shown you the way
    that makes sense;
I have guided you
    along the right path.
¹² Your road won't be blocked,
  and you won't stumble
    when you run.
¹³ Hold firmly to my teaching
  and never let go.
    It will mean life for you.
¹⁴ Don't follow the bad example
    of cruel and evil people.

MARRIAGE—My husband is emotionally distant. How can I feel closer to him? *(Proverbs 3.27-35)*

Resist closing yourself off.
When a spouse is distant, we usually respond in one of two ways. Some of us tend to withdraw, thereby creating an even larger distance. Others keep pestering their husband to open up—usually resulting in an annoyed or angry mate.

Instead of responding these ways, try this technique from Proverbs: Continue to serve him with genuine love and kindness. Perhaps your husband needs time and space to sort through something that's troubling him. Try to be physically and emotionally present without being pushy. The proverb "Do all you can for everyone who deserves your help" (3.27) applies to those in your family, too.

When we're helpful to our neighbors and to those in our home, God calls us his friends and he blesses our home. Those are valuable promises for a marriage relationship. (See also Zephaniah 3.16,17; Ephesians 4.14-16.)

Words To Remember: *Do all you can for everyone who deserves your help. . . . You will be praised if you are wise.*—Proverbs 3.27,35

¹⁵ Turn aside and keep going.
   Stay away from them.
¹⁶ They can't sleep or rest
until they do wrong or harm
   some innocent victim.
¹⁷ Their food and drink
   are violence and cruelty.

¹⁸ The lifestyle of good people
   is like sunlight at dawn
that keeps getting brighter
   until broad daylight.
¹⁹ The lifestyle of the wicked
   is like total darkness,
and they will never know
   what makes them stumble.

²⁰ My child, listen carefully
   to everything I say.
²¹ Don't forget a single word,
   but think about it all.
²² Knowing these teachings
will mean true life
   and good health for you.
²³ Carefully guard your thoughts
because they are the source
   of true life.
²⁴ Never tell lies or be deceitful
   in what you say.
²⁵ Keep looking straight ahead,
   without turning aside.
²⁶ Know where you are headed,
   and you will stay
      on solid ground.
²⁷ Don't make a mistake by turning
   to the right or the left.

Be Faithful to Your Wife

5 My son, if you listen closely
      to my wisdom and good sense,
² you will have sound judgment,
and you will always know
   the right thing to say.
³ The words of an immoral woman
   may be as sweet as honey
      and as smooth as olive oil.
⁴ But all that you really get
   from being with her
      is bitter poison and pain.
⁵ If you follow her,
   she will lead you down
      to the world of the dead.
⁶ She has missed the path
   that leads to life
      and doesn't even know it.

⁷ My son, listen to me
   and do everything I say.
⁸ Stay away from a bad woman!
   Don't even go near the door
      of her house.
⁹ You will lose your self-respect
   and end up in debt
to some cruel person
   for the rest of your life.
¹⁰ Strangers will get your money
   and everything else
      you have worked for.
¹¹ When it's all over,
   your body will waste away,
      as you groan ¹²and shout,
   "I hated advice and correction!
¹³ I paid no attention

Friendship—How can I tell if a friendship is unhealthy? *(Proverbs 4.14,15)*

By looking at actions.
The closer we are to a friend, the more difficult it is not to be influenced by her example. That's why we need to cultivate friendships that are mutually supportive in doing what's right. This doesn't mean we can't be friends with people who don't hold the same biblical values we hold. But if a friend persists in trying to lead us away from these values, Proverbs recommends that we not only turn aside but that we stay away from this person.

If you find you are in an unhealthy friendship, put these verses on a card to memorize as a reminder of God's word about friendships. And ask a godly friend to pray with you about what to do. It may be that God wants to use you to help change the other person, but you must also consider the possibility that he wants you to move away from that friendship. If we put ourselves in healthy situations, God will provide the healthy friendships we need. (See also Psalm 1; Proverbs 22.24,25; 2 Corinthians 6.14-18.)

Words To Remember: *Don't follow the bad example of cruel and evil people. Turn aside and keep going. Stay away from them.—Proverbs 4.14,15*

to my teachers,
[14] and now I am disgraced
in front of everyone."

[15] You should be faithful
to your wife,
just as you take water
from your own well.[e]
[16] And don't be like a stream
from which just any woman
may take a drink.
[17] Save yourself for your wife
and don't have sex
with other women.
[18] Be happy with the wife
you married
when you were young.
[19] She is beautiful and graceful,
just like a deer;
you should be attracted to her
and stay deeply in love.

[20] Don't go crazy over a woman
who is unfaithful
to her own husband!
[21] The LORD sees everything,
and he watches us closely.
[22] Sinners are trapped and caught
by their own evil deeds.
[23] They get lost and die
because of their foolishness
and lack of self-control.

Don't Be Foolish

6 My child, suppose you agree
to pay the debt of someone,
who cannot repay a loan.
[2] Then you are trapped
by your own words,
[3] and you are now in the power
of someone else.
Here is what you should do:
Go and beg for permission
to call off the agreement.
[4] Do this before you fall asleep
or even get sleepy.
[5] Save yourself, just as a deer
or a bird tries to escape
from a hunter.

[6] You lazy people can learn
by watching an anthill.
[7] Ants don't have leaders,
[8] but they store up food
during harvest season.
[9] How long will you lie there
doing nothing at all?
When are you going to get up
and stop sleeping?
[10] Sleep a little. Doze a little.
Fold your hands
and twiddle your thumbs.

---

[e]5.15 *own well*: In biblical times water was scarce and wells were carefully guarded.

PARENTING&*family*—How can I protect my kids from negative cultural influences? *(Proverbs 4.10-27)*

Model godly living in a fallen world.

This passage from Proverbs gives guidance about the *right* way to live. There are many descriptions of the *right* way: "the way that makes sense" (4.11); "the right path" (4.11); "life for you" (4.13); "like sunlight at dawn" (4.18); "true life and good health" (4.22); and "solid ground" (4.26). What comforting and encouraging phrases!

In order to teach our children, we must study what God says and apply it to our lifestyle. The way we live must acknowledge that God has shown us the sensible way and that he has guided us along it (4.11). What we think, what we say, and how we say it all influence what our children think and say. Just read through verses 20-27 again. "Listen carefully to everything I say" (4.20). "Carefully guard your thoughts" (4.23). "Never tell lies or be deceitful" (4.24). Parents have a far greater influence than anyone else on the values of their children. If we live as godly examples in our family, our children will have our influence as an armor against the negative cultural influences around them. (See also Ezra 8.21-34; Psalm 119.97-105; Song of Songs 8.8,9; 1 Peter 5.2-11.)

Words To Remember: *The lifestyle of good people is like sunlight at dawn that keeps getting brighter until broad daylight.—Proverbs 4.18*

¹¹ Suddenly, everything is gone,
    as though it had been taken
        by an armed robber.

¹² Worthless liars go around
¹³ winking and giving signals
        to deceive others.
¹⁴ They are always thinking up
    something cruel and evil,
        and they stir up trouble.
¹⁵ But they will be struck
    by sudden disaster
        and left without a hope.

> *While my thoughts are*
> *private, sooner or later*
> *they go public. As I*
> *think, so I act.*
>
> RUTH SENTER

¹⁶ There are six or seven
    kinds of people
        the LORD doesn't like:
¹⁷ Those who are too proud
    or tell lies or murder,
¹⁸ those who make evil plans
    or are quick to do wrong,

¹⁹ those who tell lies in court
    or stir up trouble
        in a family.

²⁰ Obey the teaching
    of your parents—
²¹ always keep it in mind
    and never forget it.
²² Their teaching will guide you
    when you walk,
protect you when you sleep,
and talk to you
    when you are awake.

²³ The Law of the Lord is a lamp,
    and its teachings
        shine brightly.
Correction and self-control
    will lead you through life.
²⁴ They will protect you
    from the flattering words
        of someone else's wife.ᶠ
²⁵ Don't let yourself be attracted
    by the charm and lovely eyes
        of someone like that.
²⁶ A woman who sells her love
    can be bought for as little
        as the price of a meal.
But making love

ᶠ**6.24** *someone else's wife:* Or "an evil woman."

WORK—How can I have healthy relationships with the men I work with?
(Proverbs 5)

Keep appropriate sexual boundaries.
Too many sad women and men could tell you that the "thrill" of adultery only leads to destruction. But a healthy view of marriage contributes to keeping appropriate sexual boundaries. If you believe that marriage is a sacred covenant before God between two people, this will help you respect the marriage of your colleague as an enduring relationship. Belief in the sanctity of marriage will help you to set safe boundaries—such as being wise about having meals out alone with a male colleague or holding private meetings behind closed doors with only one person.

Remember, whenever there is a scandal, the woman is often blamed. That's been the pattern since the book of Genesis (Genesis 3.12) when Adam and Eve ate the forbidden fruit. It's still true today. So guard your reputation diligently. Ask God to make you keenly aware of his presence in every relationship and every communication so that you exercise great integrity with all coworkers—whether they are men or women. (See also Esther 4; Romans 12.9-18; Galatians 6.1-10.)

Words To Remember: *The LORD sees everything, and he watches us closely.*
—**Proverbs 5.21**

to another man's wife
　　will cost you everything.
[27] If you carry burning coals,
　　you burn your clothes;
[28] if you step on hot coals,
　　you burn your feet.
[29] And if you go to bed
　　with another man's wife,
　　you pay the price.

[30] We don't put up with thieves,
　　not even[g] with one who steals
　　　for something to eat.
[31] And thieves who get caught
　　must pay back
　　seven times what was stolen
　　　and lose everything.
[32] But if you go to bed
　　with another man's wife,
　　you will destroy yourself
　　　by your own stupidity.
[33] You will be beaten
　　and forever disgraced,
[34] because a jealous husband
　　can be furious and merciless
　　　when he takes revenge.
[35] He won't let you pay him off,
　　no matter what you offer.

The Foolishness of Unfaithfulness

7 My son, pay close attention
　　and don't forget
　　　what I tell you to do.
[2] Obey me, and you will live!
　　Let my instructions be
　　　your greatest treasure.
[3] Keep them at your fingertips
　　and write them
　　　in your mind.
[4] Let wisdom be your sister
　　and make common sense
　　　your closest friend.
[5] They will protect you
　　from the flattering words
　　　of someone else's wife.

[6] From the window of my house,
　　I once happened to see
[7] 　some foolish young men.
[8] It was late in the evening,
　　sometime after dark.
[9] One of these young men
　　turned the corner
　　and was walking by the house
　　　of an unfaithful wife.

[10] She was dressed fancy
　　like a woman of the street
　　　with only one thing in mind.
[11] She was one of those women
　　who are loud and restless
　　　and never stay at home,
[12] who walk street after street,
　　waiting to trap a man.

[13] She grabbed him and kissed him,
　　and with no sense of shame,
　　　she said:
[14] "I had to offer a sacrifice,
　　and there is enough meat
　　　left over for a feast.
[15] So I came looking for you,
　　and here you are!
[16] The sheets on my bed
　　are bright-colored cloth
　　　from Egypt.
[17] And I have covered it
　　with perfume made of myrrh,
　　　aloes, and cinnamon.

[18] "Let's go there
　　and make love all night.
[19] My husband is traveling,
　　and he's far away.
[20] He took a lot of money along,
　　and he won't be back home
　　before the middle
　　　of the month."

[21] And so, she tricked him
　　with all of her sweet talk
　　　and her flattery.
[22] Right away he followed her
　　like an ox on the way
　　　to be slaughtered,
　　or like a fool on the way
　　to be punished[h]
[23] 　　and killed with arrows.
　　He was no more than a bird
　　　rushing into a trap,
　　without knowing
　　　it would cost him his life.

[24] My son, pay close attention
　　to what I have said.
[25] Don't even think about
　　that kind of woman

---

[g] 6.30 *not even*: Or "except."　[h] 7.22 *a fool . . . punished*:
One possible meaning for the difficult Hebrew text.

or let yourself be misled
   by someone like her.
²⁶ Such a woman has caused
   the downfall and destruction
     of a lot of men.
²⁷ Her house is a one-way street
   leading straight down
     to the world of the dead.

In Praise of Wisdom

8 With great understanding,
     Wisdom[i] is calling out
     ² as she stands at the crossroads
     and on every hill.
³ She stands by the city gate
   where everyone enters the city,
   and she shouts:
⁴ "I am calling out
   to each one of you!
⁵ Good sense and sound judgment
   can be yours.
⁶ Listen, because what I say
   is worthwhile and right.
⁷ I always speak the truth
   and refuse to tell a lie.
⁸ Every word I speak is honest,
   not one is misleading
     or deceptive.

⁹ "If you have understanding,
   you will see that my words
     are just what you need.
¹⁰ Let instruction and knowledge
   mean more to you than silver
     or the finest gold.
¹¹ Wisdom is worth much more
   than precious jewels
     or anything else you desire."

Wisdom Speaks

¹² I am Wisdom[i]—Common Sense
   is my closest friend;
   I possess knowledge
     and sound judgment.
¹³ If you respect the LORD,
   you will hate evil.
   I hate pride and conceit
     and deceitful lies.
¹⁴ I am strong, and I offer
   sensible advice
     and sound judgment.
¹⁵ By my power kings govern,
   and rulers make laws
     that are fair.

¹⁶ Every honest leader rules
   with help from me.

¹⁷ I love everyone who loves me,
   and I will be found by all
     who honestly search.
¹⁸ I can make you rich and famous,
   important and successful.

*My parents carried Jesus
into every aspect of their
lives. Because of this,
I knew Jesus was real and
always with me.*

PAM THUM

¹⁹ What you receive from me
   is more valuable
   than even the finest gold
     or the purest silver.
²⁰ I always do what is right,
²¹ and I give great riches
     to everyone who loves me.

²² From the beginning,
   I was with the LORD.[j]
   I was there before he began
²³   to create the earth.
   At the very first,
     the LORD gave life to[k] me.
²⁴ When I was born,
   there were no oceans
     or springs of water.
²⁵ My birth was before
   mountains were formed
     or hills were put in place.
²⁶ It happened long before God
   had made the earth
   or any of its fields
     or even the dust.
²⁷ I was there when the LORD
   put the heavens in place

---

[i]**8.1,12** *Wisdom:* See the note at 1.20.
[j]**8.22** *From the beginning . . . with the* LORD:
Or "In the very beginning, the LORD created me."
[k]**8.23** *gave life to:* Or "formed."

and stretched the sky
over the surface of the sea.
[28] I was with him when he placed
the clouds in the sky
and created the springs
that fill the ocean.
[29] I was there when he set
boundaries for the sea
to make it obey him,
and when he laid foundations
to support the earth.

[30] I was right beside the LORD,
helping him plan and build.[l]
I made him happy each day,
and I was happy at his side.
[31] I was pleased with his world
and pleased with its people.

[32] Pay attention, my children!
Follow my advice,
and you will be happy.
[33] Listen carefully
to my instructions,
and you will be wise.

[34] Come to my home each day
and listen to me.
You will find happiness.
[35] By finding me, you find life,
and the LORD will be pleased
with you.
[36] But if you don't find me,
you hurt only yourself,
and if you hate me,
you are in love with death.

Wisdom Gives a Feast

9 Wisdom has built her house
with its seven columns.
[2] She has prepared the meat
and set out the wine.
Her feast is ready.

[3] She has sent her servant women
to announce her invitation
from the highest hills:
[4] "Everyone who is ignorant
or foolish is invited!
[5] All of you are welcome
to my meat and wine.
[6] If you want to live,
give up your foolishness
and let understanding
guide your steps."

True Wisdom

[7] Correct a worthless bragger,
and all you will get
are insults and injuries.
[8] Any bragger you correct
will only hate you.
But if you correct someone
who has common sense,
you will be loved.
[9] If you have good sense,
instruction will help you
to have even better sense.
And if you live right,
education will help you
to know even more.

[10] Respect and obey the LORD!
This is the beginning
of wisdom.[m]
To have understanding,
you must know the Holy God.
[11] I am Wisdom. If you follow me,
you will live a long time.
[12] Good sense is good for you,
but if you brag,
you hurt yourself.

A Foolish Invitation

[13] Stupidity[n] is reckless,
senseless, and foolish.
[14] She sits in front of her house
and on the highest hills
in the town.
[15] She shouts to everyone
who passes by,
[16] "If you are stupid,
come on inside!"
And to every fool she says,
[17]   "Stolen water tastes best,
and the food you eat in secret
tastes best of all."
[18] None who listen to Stupidity
understand that her guests
are as good as dead.

Solomon's Wise Sayings

10 Here are some proverbs
of Solomon:
Children with good sense
make their parents happy,

---

[l]**8.30** *helping . . . build:* Or "like his own child."
[m]**9.10** *the beginning of wisdom:* Or "what wisdom is all about."   [n]**9.13** *Stupidity:* Or "A foolish woman."

but foolish children
      make them sad.
² What you gain by doing evil
      won't help you at all,
but being good°
      can save you from death.

³ If you obey the LORD,
      you won't go hungry;
if you are wicked,
God won't let you have
      what you want.
⁴ Laziness leads to poverty;
      hard work makes you rich.
⁵ At harvest season
      it's smart to work hard,
      but stupid to sleep.

⁶ Everyone praises good people,
but evil hides behind
      the words of the wicked.
⁷ Good people are remembered
      long after they are gone,
but the wicked
      are soon forgotten.

⁸ If you have good sense,
      you will listen and obey;
if all you do is talk,
      you will destroy yourself.
⁹ You will be safe,
      if you always do right,
but you will get caught,
      if you are dishonest.
¹⁰ Deceit causes trouble,
and foolish talk
      will bring you to ruin.ᵖ
¹¹ The words of good people
      are a source of life,
but evil hides behind
      the words of the wicked.

¹² Hatred stirs up trouble;
love overlooks the wrongs
      that others do.
¹³ If you have good sense,
      it will show when you speak.
But if you are stupid,
you will be beaten
      with a stick.
¹⁴ If you have good sense,
      you will learn all you can,
but foolish talk
      will soon destroy you.

¹⁵ Great wealth can be a fortress,
but poverty
      is no protection at all.
¹⁶ If you live right,
      the reward is a good life;
if you are evil,
      all you have is sin.

¹⁷ Accept correction,
      and you will find life;
reject correction,
      and you will miss the road.
¹⁸ You can hide your hatred
      by telling lies,
but you are a fool
      to spread lies.
¹⁹ You will say the wrong thing
      if you talk too much—
so be sensible and watch
      what you say.
²⁰ The words of a good person
      are like pure silver,
but the thoughts
of an evil person
      are almost worthless.
²¹ Many are helped
      by useful instruction,
but fools are killed
      by their own stupidity.

²² When the LORD blesses you
with riches,
      you have nothing to regret. q
²³ Fools enjoy doing wrong,
but anyone with good sense
      enjoys acting wisely.
²⁴ What evil people dread most
      will happen to them,
but good people will get
      what they want most.
²⁵ Those crooks will disappear
      when a storm strikes,
but God will keep safe
      all who obey him.
²⁶ Having a lazy person on the job
      is like a mouth full of vinegar
      or smoke in your eyes.

°10.2 good: Or "generous." ᵖ10.10 and foolish . . .
ruin: One ancient translation "but you can help people
by correcting them." q10.22 When . . . regret: Or "No
matter how hard you work, your riches really come from
the LORD."

²⁷If you respect the LORD,
　　you will live longer;
　if you keep doing wrong,
　　your life will be cut short.
²⁸If you obey the Lord,
　　you will be happy,
　but there is no future
　　for the wicked.
²⁹The LORD protects everyone
　　who lives right,
　but he destroys anyone
　　who does wrong.
³⁰Good people will stand firm,
　but the wicked
　　will lose their land.
³¹Honest people speak sensibly,
　but deceitful liars
　　will be silenced.
³²If you obey the Lord,
　you will always know
　　the right thing to say.
　But no one will trust you
　　if you tell lies.

Watch What You Say and Do

11 The LORD hates anyone
　　who cheats,
　but he likes everyone
　　who is honest.
²Too much pride
　can put you to shame.
　　It's wiser to be humble.
³If you do the right thing,
　　honesty will be your guide.
　But if you are crooked,
　you will be trapped
　　by your own dishonesty.

⁴When God is angry,
　　money won't help you.
　Obeying God is the only way
　　to be saved from death.
⁵If you are truly good,
　　you will do right;
　if you are wicked,
　you will be destroyed
　　by your own sin.
⁶Honesty can keep you safe,
　but if you can't be trusted,
　　you trap yourself.
⁷When the wicked die,
　　their hopes die with them.
⁸Trouble goes right past
　the LORD's people
　　and strikes the wicked.

⁹Dishonest people use gossip
　　to destroy their neighbors;
　good people are protected
　　by their own good sense.
¹⁰When honest people prosper
　and the wicked disappear,
　　the whole city celebrates.
¹¹When God blesses his people,
　　their city prospers,
　but deceitful liars
　　can destroy a city.

¹²It's stupid to say bad things
　　about your neighbors.
　If you are sensible,
　　you will keep quiet.
¹³A gossip tells everything,
　but a true friend
　　will keep a secret.
¹⁴A city without wise leaders
　　will end up in ruin;
　a city with many wise leaders
　　will be kept safe.

¹⁵It's a dangerous thing
　　to guarantee payment
　for someone's debts.
　　Don't do it!
¹⁶A gracious woman
　　will be respected,
　but a man must work hard
　　to get rich.ʳ
¹⁷Kindness is rewarded—
　but if you are cruel,
　　you hurt yourself.
¹⁸Meanness gets you nowhere,
　　but goodness is rewarded.
¹⁹Always do the right thing,
　　and you will live;
　keep on doing wrong,
　　and you will die.

²⁰The LORD hates sneaky people,
　but he likes everyone
　　who lives right.
²¹You can be sure of this:
　All crooks will be punished,
　　but God's people won't.
²²A beautiful woman
　　who acts foolishly

ʳ**11.16** *but . . . rich*: Or "a ruthless man will only get rich."

is like a gold ring
  on the snout of a pig.
²³ Good people want what is best,
  but troublemakers
    hope to stir up trouble.ˢ

²⁴ Sometimes you can become rich
  by being generous
  or poor by being greedy.
²⁵ Generosity will be rewarded:
  Give a cup of water,
  and you will receive
    a cup of water in return.
²⁶ Charge too much for grain,
  and you will be cursed;
  sell it at a fair price,
    and you will be praised.
²⁷ Try hard to do right,
  and you will win friends;
  go looking for trouble,
    and you will find it.
²⁸ Trust in your wealth,
  and you will be a failure,
  but God's people will prosper
    like healthy plants.

²⁹ Fools who cause trouble
  in the family
    won't inherit a thing.
  They will end up as slaves
    of someone with good sense.

> We all have been carried to Christ by someone. If we want our friends to become part of God's family, we need to be persistent.
>
> ELISA MORGAN

³⁰ Live right, and you will eat
  from the life-giving tree.
  And if you act wisely,
    others will follow.ᵗ
³¹ If good people are rewardedᵘ
  here on this earth,
  all who are cruel and mean
    will surely be punished.

You Can't Hide behind Evil

12 To accept correction is wise,
  to reject it is stupid.
² The LORD likes everyone
  who lives right,
  but he punishes everyone
    who makes evil plans.
³ Sin cannot offer security!
  But if you live right,
  you will be as secure
    as a tree with deep roots.
⁴ A helpful wife is a jewel
  for her husband,
  but a shameless wife
    will make his bones rot.

⁵ Good people have kind thoughts,
  but you should never trust
    the advice of someone evil.
⁶ Bad advice is a deadly trap,
  but good advice
    is like a shield.
⁷ Once the wicked are defeated,
  they are gone forever,
  but no one who obeys God
    will ever be thrown down.
⁸ Good sense is worthy of praise,
  but stupidity is a curse.
⁹ It's better to be ordinary
  and have only one servantᵛ
  than to think you are somebody
    and starve to death.
¹⁰ Good people are kind
  to their animals,
  but a mean person is cruel.

¹¹ Hard working farmers have more
  than enough food;
  daydreamers are nothing more
    than stupid fools.
¹² An evil person tries to hide
  behind evil;ʷ
  good people are like trees
    with deep roots.
¹³ We trap ourselves
  by telling lies,

ˢ**11.23** *Good people . . . trouble:* Or "Good people do what is best, but troublemakers just stir up trouble." ᵗ**11.30** *act . . . follow:* Hebrew; one ancient translation "but violence leads to death." ᵘ**11.31** *rewarded:* Or "punished." ᵛ**12.9** *It's . . . servant:* Or "It is better just to have an ordinary job." ʷ**12.12** *An evil . . . evil:* Or "Evil people love what they get from being evil."

but we stay out of trouble
by living right.
¹⁴ We are rewarded or punished
for what we say and do.
¹⁵ Fools think they know
what is best,
but a sensible person
listens to advice.

¹⁶ Losing your temper is foolish;
ignoring an insult is smart.
¹⁷ An honest person
tells the truth in court,
but a dishonest person
tells nothing but lies.
¹⁸ Sharp words cut like a sword,
but words of wisdom heal.
¹⁹ Truth will last forever;
lies are soon found out.
²⁰ An evil mind is deceitful,
but gentle thoughts
bring happiness.
²¹ Good people never have trouble,
but troublemakers
have more than enough.
²² The LORD hates every liar,
but he is the friend of all
who can be trusted.
²³ Be sensible and don't tell
everything you know—
only fools spread
foolishness everywhere.

²⁴ Work hard, and you
will be a leader;
be lazy, and you
will end up a slave.
²⁵ Worry is a heavy burden,
but a kind word
always brings cheer.
²⁶ You are better off to do right,
than to lose your way
by doing wrong.ˣ
²⁷ Anyone too lazy to cook
will starve,
but a hard worker
is a valuable treasure.ʸ
²⁸ Follow the road to life,
and you won't be bothered
by death.

Wise Friends Make You Wise

13 Children with good sense
accept correction
from their parents,

but stubborn children
ignore it completely.
² You will be well rewarded
for saying something kind,
but all some people think about
is how to be cruel and mean.
³ Keep what you know to yourself,
and you will be safe;
talk too much,
and you are done for.
⁴ No matter how much you want,
laziness won't help a bit,
but hard work will reward you
with more than enough.
⁵ A good person hates deceit,
but those who are evil
cause shame and disgrace.
⁶ Live right, and you are safe!
But sin will destroy you.

⁷ Some who have nothing
may pretend to be rich,
and some who have everything
may pretend to be poor.

Take time to pray, and seek counsel from others and from Scripture. By doing so, all the comfort and strength in God's promises will be yours.

VIRELLE KIDDER

⁸ The rich may have
to pay a ransom,
but the poor don't have
that problem.
⁹ The lamp of a good person
keeps on shining;
the lamp of an evil person
soon goes out.
¹⁰ Too much pride causes trouble.
Be sensible and take advice.

ˣ**12.26** *wrong:* One possible meaning for the difficult Hebrew text of verse 26. ʸ**12.27** *but . . . treasure:* One possible meaning for the difficult Hebrew text.

[11] Money wrongly gotten
        will disappear bit by bit;
    money earned little by little
        will grow and grow.
[12] Not getting what you want
        can make you feel sick,
    but a wish that comes true
        is a life-giving tree.
[13] If you reject God's teaching,
        you will pay the price;
    if you obey his commands,
        you will be rewarded.

[14] Sensible instruction
        is a life-giving fountain
    that helps you escape
        all deadly traps.
[15] Sound judgment is praised,
    but people without good sense
        are on the way to disaster.[z]
[16] If you have good sense,
        you will act sensibly,
        but fools act like fools.
[17] Whoever delivers your message
    can make things better
        or worse for you.

[18] All who refuse correction
        will be poor and disgraced;
    all who accept correction
        will be praised.
[19] It's a good feeling
        to get what you want,
    but only a stupid fool
        hates to turn from evil.
[20] Wise friends make you wise,
    but you hurt yourself
        by going around with fools.
[21] You are in for trouble
        if you sin,
    but you will be rewarded
        if you live right.
[22] If you obey God,
    you will have something
        to leave your grandchildren.
    If you don't obey God,
    those who live right
        will get what you leave.

[23] Even when the land of the poor
        produces good crops,
    they get cheated
        out of what they grow.[a]
[24] If you love your children,
    you will correct them;

if you don't love them,
    you won't correct them.
[25] If you live right,
    you will have plenty to eat;
if you don't live right,
    you will go away empty.

Wisdom Makes Good Sense

14 A woman's family
        is held together
            by her wisdom,
    but it can be destroyed
        by her foolishness.
[2] By living right, you show
        that you respect the LORD;
    by being deceitful, you show
        that you despise him.
[3] Proud fools are punished
        for their stupid talk,
    but sensible talk
        can save your life.
[4] Without the help of an ox
        there can be no crop,
    but with a strong ox
        a big crop is possible.
[5] An honest witness
        tells the truth;
    a dishonest witness
        tells nothing but lies.

[6] Make fun of wisdom,
        and you will never find it.
    But if you have understanding,
        knowledge comes easily.
[7] Stay away from fools,
        or you won't learn a thing.
[8] Wise people have enough sense
        to find their way,
        but stupid fools get lost.
[9] Fools don't care
        if they are wrong,[b]
    but God is pleased
        when people do right.

[10] No one else can really know
        how sad or happy you are.
[11] The tent of a good person
    stands longer than the house
        of someone evil.

---

[z]13.15 *people . . . disaster*: One possible meaning for the
difficult Hebrew text.   [a]13.23 *grow*: One possible
meaning for the difficult Hebrew text of verse 23.
[b]14.9 *Fools . . . wrong*: One possible meaning for the
difficult Hebrew text.

¹²You may think you are
on the right road
and still end up dead.
¹³Sorrow may hide
behind laughter,
and happiness may end
in sorrow.
¹⁴You harvest what you plant,
whether good or bad.

¹⁵Don't be stupid
and believe all you hear;
be smart and know
where you are headed.
¹⁶Only a stupid fool
is never cautious—
so be extra careful
and stay out of trouble.
¹⁷Fools have quick tempers,
and no one likes you
if you can't be trusted.
¹⁸Stupidity leads to foolishness;
be smart and learn.

¹⁹The wicked will come crawling
to those who obey God.
²⁰You have no friends
if you are poor,
but you have lots of friends
if you are rich.
²¹It's wrong to hate others,
but God blesses everyone
who is kind to the poor.
²²It's a mistake
to make evil plans,
but you will have loyal friends
if you want to do right.
²³Hard work is worthwhile,
but empty talk
will make you poor.
²⁴Wisdom can make you rich,
but foolishness leads
to more foolishness.
²⁵An honest witness
can save your life,
but liars can't be trusted.

²⁶If you respect the LORD,
you and your children
have a strong fortress
²⁷and a life-giving fountain
that keeps you safe
from deadly traps.

²⁸Rulers of powerful nations
are held in honor;
rulers of weak nations
are nothing at all.
²⁹It's smart to be patient,
but it's stupid
to lose your temper.
³⁰It's healthy to be content,
but envy can eat you up.
³¹If you mistreat the poor,
you insult your Creator;
if you are kind to them,
you show him respect.
³²In times of trouble
the wicked are destroyed,
but even at death
the innocent have faith.ᶜ

³³Wisdom is found in the minds
of people with good sense,
but fools don't know it.ᵈ
³⁴Doing right brings honor
to a nation,
but sin brings disgrace.
³⁵Kings reward servants
who act wisely,
but they punish those
who act foolishly.

The LORD Sees Everything

15 A kind answer
soothes angry feelings,
but harsh words
stir them up.
²Words of wisdom
come from the wise,
but fools speak foolishness.

³The LORD sees everything,
whether good or bad.
⁴Kind words are good medicine,
but deceitful words
can really hurt.
⁵Don't be a fool
and disobey your parents.
Be smart! Accept correction.
⁶Good people become wealthy,

ᶜ14.32 *but even . . . faith*: One possible meaning for the difficult Hebrew text. Some ancient translations "but good people trust their innocence."   ᵈ14.33 *but . . . it*: One possible meaning for the difficult Hebrew text; some ancient translations "but not in the mind of a fool."

but those who are evil
will lose what they have.
⁷Words of wisdom
make good sense;
the thoughts of a fool
make no sense at all.

⁸The LORD is disgusted
by gifts from the wicked,
but it makes him happy
when his people pray.
⁹The LORD is disgusted
with all who do wrong,
but he loves everyone
who does right.
¹⁰If you turn from the right way,
you will be punished;
if you refuse correction,
you will die.

¹¹If the LORD can see everything
in the world of the dead,
he can see in our hearts.
¹²Those who sneer at others
don't like to be corrected,
and they won't ask help
from someone with sense.
¹³Happiness makes you smile;
sorrow can crush you.
¹⁴Anyone with good sense
is eager to learn more,
but fools are hungry
for foolishness.

¹⁵The poor have a hard life,
but being content is as good

as an endless feast.
¹⁶It's better to obey the LORD
and have only a little,
than to be very rich
and terribly confused.
¹⁷A simple meal with love
is better than a feast
where there is hatred.

¹⁸Losing your temper
causes a lot of trouble,
but staying calm
settles arguments.
¹⁹Being lazy is like walking
in a thorn patch,
but everyone who does right
walks on a smooth road.
²⁰Children with good sense
make their parents happy,
but foolish children
are hateful to them.
²¹Stupidity brings happiness
to senseless fools,
but everyone with good sense
follows the straight path.

²²Without good advice
everything goes wrong—
it takes careful planning
for things to go right.
²³Giving the right answer
at the right time
makes everyone happy.
²⁴All who are wise follow a road

PARENTING&*family*—Sometimes I get upset and angry with my kids. How can I maintain a loving attitude when I'm about to explode?

(*Proverbs 15.1-4,18*)

Realize that anger only breeds more conflict.

It's best to withdraw from an explosive situation until you have control of your anger. Everyone gets upset and angry, but problems come when you rush to speak out of anger. Once "harsh words" are spoken, they can't be recalled. But "a kind answer soothes angry feelings" (15.1; see also verse 18).

With your anger under control, you can talk with your children about what's upsetting you. In that setting, it's okay to admit your anger. Focusing on inappropriate behavior rather than blaming your children helps them know exactly how they need to change. If you use kind words rather than harsh ones, they are more likely to *want* to change. And by focusing on behavior, you can reassure your children of your unconditional love for them as persons. (See also Matthew 11.25-29; Titus 3.3-8.)

Words To Remember: *Kind words are good medicine.*—**Proverbs 15.4**

that leads upward to life
and away from death.

²⁵The LORD destroys the homes
of those who are proud,
but he protects the property
of widows.
²⁶The LORD hates evil thoughts,
but kind words please him.
²⁷Being greedy causes trouble
for your family,
but you protect yourself
by refusing bribes.
²⁸Good people think
before they answer,
but the wicked speak evil
without ever thinking.

²⁹The LORD never even hears
the prayers of the wicked,
but he answers the prayers
of all who obey him.
³⁰A friendly smile
makes you happy,
and good news
makes you feel strong.
³¹Healthy correction is good,
and if you accept it,
you will be wise.
³²You hurt only yourself
by rejecting instruction,
but it makes good sense
to accept it.
³³Showing respect to the LORD
will make you wise,

and being humble
will bring honor to you.

The LORD Has the Final Word

16 We humans make plans,
but the LORD
has the final word.
²We may think we know
what is right,
but the LORD is the judge
of our motives.
³Share your plans with the LORD,
and you will succeed.

⁴The LORD has a reason
for everything he does,
and he lets evil people live
only to be punished.
⁵The LORD doesn't like
anyone who is conceited—
you can be sure
they will be punished.
⁶If we truly love God,
our sins will be forgiven;
if we show him respect,
we will keep away from sin.
⁷When we please the LORD,
even our enemies
make friends with us.
⁸It's better to be honest
and poor
than to be dishonest
and rich.

⁹We make our own plans,
but the LORD decides

WORK—Sometimes I think it's okay to work while my kids are young; other times I'm not sure. How can I be certain I'm making the best decision for my family? *(Proverbs 16.1-3)*

Check the motives behind your decision.
Do you truly want what's best for everyone concerned? Or do your motives lean more toward your own self-interest? These verses remind us that "the LORD is the judge of our motives" (16.2) and that we should share our plans with the Lord in order to succeed (16.3). Talking your concerns over with your family and praying about them together is the first step. If you are still uncertain about your decision, ask some friends from your Christian community to pray with you for guidance.

Once you and your family agree on what seems best for you, move ahead with your plans. You can be confident that "the LORD has the final word" (16.1) with the plans we humans make. (See also Romans 14.13-23; Titus 2.3-8.)

Words To Remember: *Share your plans with the LORD, and you will succeed.* —**Proverbs 16.3**

where we will go.
¹⁰ Rulers speak with authority
and are never wrong.
¹¹ The LORD doesn't like it
when we cheat in business.
¹² Justice makes rulers powerful.
They should hate evil
¹³ and like honesty and truth.
¹⁴ An angry ruler
can put you to death.
So be wise!
Don't make one angry.
¹⁵ When a ruler is happy
and pleased with you,
it's like refreshing rain,
and you will live.

¹⁶ It's much better to be wise
and sensible
than to be rich.
¹⁷ God's people avoid evil ways,
and they protect themselves
by watching where they go.
¹⁸ Too much pride
will destroy you.
¹⁹ You are better off
to be humble and poor
than to get rich
from what you take by force.
²⁰ If you know what you're doing,ᵉ
you will prosper.
God blesses everyone
who trusts him.
²¹ Good judgment proves
that you are wise,
and if you speak kindly,
you can teach others.
²² Good sense is a fountain
that gives life,
but fools are punished
by their foolishness.
²³ You can persuade others
if you are wise
and speak sensibly.

²⁴ Kind words are like honey—
they cheer you up
and make you feel strong.
²⁵ Sometimes what seems right
is really a road to death.
²⁶ The hungrier you are,
the harder you work.
²⁷ Worthless people plan trouble.
Even their words burn
like a flaming fire.

²⁸ Gossip is no good!
It causes hard feelings
and comes between friends.

²⁹ Don't trust violent people.
They will mislead you
to do the wrong thing.
³⁰ When someone winks
or grins behind your back,
trouble is on the way.
³¹ Gray hair is a glorious crown
worn by those
who have lived right.
³² Controlling your temper
is better than being a hero
who captures a city.
³³ We make our own decisions,
but the LORD alone
determines what happens.

Our Thoughts Are Tested by the LORD

17 A dry crust of bread eaten
in peace and quiet
is better than a feast eaten
where everyone argues.
² A hard-working slave
will be placed in charge
of a no-good child,
and that slave will be given
the same inheritance
that each child receives.
³ Silver and gold are tested
by flames of fire;
our thoughts are tested
by the LORD.
⁴ Troublemakers listen
to troublemakers,
and liars listen to liars.
⁵ By insulting the poor,
you insult your Creator.
You will be punished
if you make fun
of someone in trouble.
⁶ Grandparents are proud
of their grandchildren,
and children should be proud
of their parents.

⁷ It sounds strange for a fool
to talk sensibly,
but it's even worse
for a ruler to tell lies.

ᵉ**16.20** *know what . . . doing*: Or "do what you're taught."

⁸A bribe works miracles
  like a magic charm
    that brings good luck.
⁹You will keep your friends
    if you forgive them,
  but you will lose your friends
  if you keep talking about
    what they did wrong.
¹⁰A sensible person
    accepts correction,
  but you can't beat sense
    into a fool.

¹¹Cruel people want to rebel,
  and so vicious attackers
    will be sent against them.
¹²A bear robbed of her cubs
  is far less dangerous
    than a stubborn fool.
¹³You will always have trouble
  if you are mean to those
    who are good to you.
¹⁴The start of an argument
  is like a water leak—
  so stop it before
    real trouble breaks out.
¹⁵The LORD doesn't like those
  who defend the guilty
    or condemn the innocent.
¹⁶Why should fools have money
  for an education
    when they refuse
    to learn?

¹⁷A friend is always a friend,
  and relatives are born
    to share our troubles.

*Friends demonstrate their
love for each other freely.*

DEE BRESTIN

¹⁸It's stupid to guarantee
    someone else's loan.
¹⁹The wicked and the proud
  love trouble and keep begging
    to be hurt.
²⁰Dishonesty does you no good,
  and telling lies
    will get you in trouble.
²¹It's never pleasant
  to be the parent of a fool
    and have nothing but pain.
²²If you are cheerful,
    you feel good;
  if you are sad,
    you hurt all over.

²³Crooks accept secret bribes
  to keep justice
    from being done.
²⁴Anyone with wisdom knows
    what makes good sense,

MARRIAGE—Why does the Bible talk about submission in marriage? What does God mean by it? *(Proverbs 17.1)*

Mutual submission leads to a peaceful home life.
If you've ever been around a couple who argues a lot, you know that you can feel the tension in the air—from the time you walk in their front door. It isn't fun to visit them, is it?

But when a husband and wife submit to one another, always looking for the best in each other and respecting one another, they are a witness to outsiders about God's love (especially in a day when many marriages are breaking apart). Whether they have much (a feast) or little (a dry crust—or maybe today's version, macaroni-and-cheese!) isn't the point. What's important is how people treat each other.

If our apartment, dorm room, or home is filled with "peace and quiet," people will *want* to be there. And we may have a chance to introduce them not only to what a healthy marriage looks like, but to the Ultimate Healer, Jesus Christ! (See also Ephesians 5.21-33; Philippians 2.1-11.)

Words To Remember: *A dry crust of bread eaten in peace and quiet is better than a feast eaten where everyone argues.—Proverbs 17.1*

but fools can never
   make up their minds.
²⁵ Foolish children bring sorrow
  to their father
   and pain to their mother.
²⁶ It isn't fair
  to punish the innocent
   and those who do right.
²⁷ It makes a lot of sense
  to be a person of few words
   and to stay calm.
²⁸ Even fools seem smart
  when they are quiet.

It's Wrong to Favor the Guilty

18 It's selfish and stupid
   to think only of yourself
  and to sneer at people
   who have sense.ʲ
² Fools have no desire to learn;
they would much rather
  give their own opinion.
³ Wrongdoing leads to shame
  and disgrace.
⁴ Words of wisdom
are a stream that flows
  from a deep fountain.
⁵ It's wrong to favor the guilty
and keep the innocent
  from getting justice.

⁶ Foolish talk will get you
  into a lot of trouble.
⁷ Saying foolish things
is like setting a trap
  to destroy yourself.
⁸ There's nothing so delicious
as the taste of gossip!
  It melts in your mouth.
⁹ Being lazy is no different
  from being a troublemaker.

¹⁰ The LORD is a mighty tower
where his people can run
  for safety—
¹¹ the rich think their money
  is a wall of protection.

¹² Pride leads to destruction;
  humility leads to honor.
¹³ It's stupid and embarrassing
to give an answer
  before you listen.

¹⁴ Being cheerful helps
  when we are sick,
but nothing helps
  when we give up.
¹⁵ Everyone with good sense
  wants to learn.
¹⁶ A gift will get you in
  to see anyone.
¹⁷ You may think you have won
your case in court,
  until your opponent speaks.
¹⁸ Drawing straws is one way
  to settle a difficult case.
¹⁹ Making up with a friend
you have offendedᵍ
is harder than breaking
  through a city wall.

²⁰ Make your words good—
  you will be glad you did.
²¹ Words can bring death or life!
Talk too much, and you will eat
  everything you say.
²² A man's greatest treasure
is his wife—
  she is a gift from the LORD.
²³ The poor must beg for help,
but the rich can give
  a harsh reply.

*It is only when we appreciate
what a gift our women friends
are that we'll make the effort
to overcome the obstacles that
threaten friendship's survival.*

DEE BRESTIN

²⁴ Some friends don't help,ʰ
but a true friend is closer
  than your own family.

ʲ**18.1** *sense:* One possible meaning for the difficult
Hebrew text of verse 1.   ᵍ**18.19** *Making . . . offended:*
One possible meaning for the difficult Hebrew text.
ʰ**18.24** *Some . . . help:* One possible meaning for the
difficult Hebrew text.

It's Wise To Be Patient

19 It's better to be poor
and live right
than to be a stupid liar.
² Willingness and stupidity
don't go well together.
If you are too eager,
you will miss the road.
³ We are ruined
by our own stupidity,
though we blame the LORD.

⁴ The rich have many friends;
the poor have none.
⁵ Dishonest witnesses and liars
won't escape punishment.
⁶ Everyone tries to be friends
of those who can help them.
⁷ If you are poor,
your own relatives reject you,
and your friends are worse.
When you really need them,
they are not there.ⁱ

⁸ Do yourself a favor
by having good sense—
you will be glad you did.
⁹ Dishonest witnesses and liars
will be destroyed.
¹⁰ It isn't right for a fool
to live in luxury
or for a slave to rule
in place of a king.
¹¹ It's wise to be patient

and show what you are like
by forgiving others.
¹² An angry king roars
like a lion,
but when a king is pleased,
it's like dew on the crops.

*Wisdom is the ability
to apply God's truth
to everyday living.*
KAREN DOCKREY

¹³ A foolish son brings disgrace
to his father.
A nagging wife goes on and on
like the drip, drip, drip
of the rain.
¹⁴ You may inherit all you own
from your parents,
but a sensible wife
is a gift from the LORD.
¹⁵ If you are lazy
and sleep your time away,
you will starve.

ⁱ**19.7** *When . . . there:* One possible meaning for the difficult Hebrew text.

Friendship—What are the marks of a good friendship? *(Proverbs 17.17; 18.24)*

It "hangs in there."

Loyalty is a primary mark of friendship. A true friend is someone who has been through fun times and hard times with you and is there when you need her. While some people claim to be friends, when they have to give as well as receive, they look for other friends. Proverbs 18.24 uses direct language: "Some friends don't help," and helping each other is what friendship is all about.

Both proverbs speak of family. Family members are obligated to share each other's troubles because they are family, yet often that sense of obligation stands in the way of our experiencing the closeness with family that we do with true friends. It can be a real challenge—but a real blessing—to develop meaningful friendships with extended family members.

These proverbs show us what to look for in friendship. But they also show that we need to evaluate our own loyalty in friendships. Are we being the kind of friend Proverbs talks about? (See also Ruth 1–4; Proverbs 27.17-19; 1 Corinthians 13.4-8; James 5.13-20.)

Words To Remember: *A friend is always a friend.—Proverbs 17.17*

¹⁶ Obey the Lord's teachings
and you will live—
   disobey and you will die.
¹⁷ Caring for the poor
is lending to the LORD,
   and you will be well repaid.
¹⁸ Correct your children
   before it's too late;
if you don't punish them,
   you are destroying them.
¹⁹ People with bad tempers
   are always in trouble,
and they need help
   over and over again.^j
²⁰ Pay attention to advice
and accept correction,
   so you can live sensibly.

²¹ We may make a lot of plans,
but the LORD will do
   what he has decided.
²² What matters most is loyalty.
It's better to be poor
   than to be a liar.
²³ Showing respect to the LORD
   brings true life—
if you do it, you can relax
   without fear of danger.

²⁴ Some people are too lazy
to lift a hand
   to feed themselves.
²⁵ Stupid fools learn good sense
   by seeing others punished;
a sensible person learns
   by being corrected.
²⁶ Children who bring disgrace
rob their father
   and chase their mother away.
²⁷ If you stop learning,
you will forget
   what you already know.
²⁸ A lying witness makes fun
of the court system,
and criminals think crime
   is really delicious.
²⁹ Every stupid fool
is just waiting
   to be punished.

Words of Wisdom Are Better than Gold

20 It isn't smart to get drunk!
Drinking makes a fool of you
   and leads to fights.

² An angry ruler
   is like a roaring lion—
make either one angry,
   and you are dead.
³ It makes you look good
when you avoid a fight—
   only fools love to quarrel.
⁴ If you are too lazy to plow,
   don't expect a harvest.
⁵ Someone's thoughts may be
   as deep as the ocean,
but if you are smart,
   you will discover them.

⁶ There are many who say,
"You can trust me!"
   But can they be trusted?
⁷ Good people live right,
and God blesses the children
   who follow their example.
⁸ When rulers decide cases,
   they weigh the evidence.
⁹ Can any of us really say,
"My thoughts are pure,
   and my sins are gone"?

¹⁰ Two things the LORD hates
are dishonest scales
   and dishonest measures.
¹¹ The good or bad
that children do
   shows what they are like.
¹² Hearing and seeing
are gifts from the LORD.
¹³ If you sleep all the time,
   you will starve;
if you get up and work,
   you will have enough food.
¹⁴ Everyone likes to brag
   about getting a bargain.
¹⁵ Sensible words are better
   than gold or jewels.

¹⁶ You deserve to lose your coat
   if you loan it to someone
to guarantee payment
   for the debt of a stranger.
¹⁷ The food you get by cheating
may taste delicious,
   but it turns to gravel.
¹⁸ Be sure you have sound advice

---

^j**19.19** *and they . . . again:* One possible meaning for the difficult Hebrew text.

before making plans
or starting a war.
¹⁹ Stay away from gossips—
they tell everything.
²⁰ Children who curse their parents
will go to the land of darkness
long before their time.
²¹ Getting rich quick[k]
may turn out to be a curse.
²² Don't try to get even.
Trust the LORD,
and he will help you.

²³ The LORD hates dishonest scales
and dishonest weights.
So don't cheat!
²⁴ How can we know
what will happen to us
when the LORD alone decides?
²⁵ Don't fall into the trap
of making promises to God
before you think!
²⁶ A wise ruler severely punishes
every criminal.
²⁷ Our inner thoughts are a lamp
from the LORD,
and they search our hearts.
²⁸ Rulers are protected
by God's mercy and loyalty,
but[l] they must be merciful
for their kingdoms to last.
²⁹ Young people take pride
in their strength,
but the gray hairs of wisdom
are even more beautiful.
³⁰ A severe beating can knock all
of the evil out of you!

The LORD Is In Charge

21 The LORD controls rulers,
just as he determines
the course of rivers.
² We may think we are doing
the right thing,
but the LORD always knows
what is in our hearts.
³ Doing what is right and fair
pleases the LORD
more than an offering.
⁴ Evil people are proud
and arrogant,
but sin is the only crop
they produce.[m]
⁵ If you plan and work hard,
you will have plenty;

if you get in a hurry,
you will end up poor.

⁶ Cheating to get rich
is a foolish dream
and no less than suicide.[n]
⁷ You destroy yourself
by being cruel and violent
and refusing to live right.
⁸ All crooks are liars,
but anyone who is innocent
will do right.
⁹ It's better to stay outside
on the roof of your house
than to live inside
with a nagging wife.
¹⁰ Evil people want to do wrong,
even to their friends.
¹¹ An ignorant fool learns
by seeing others punished;
a sensible person learns
by being instructed.

¹² God is always fair!
He knows what the wicked do
and will punish them.
¹³ If you won't help the poor,
don't expect to be heard
when you cry out for help.
¹⁴ A secret bribe will save you
from someone's fierce anger.
¹⁵ When justice is done,
good citizens are glad
and crooks are terrified.
¹⁶ If you stop using good sense,
you will find yourself
in the grave.

---

[k]20.21 *quick*: Or "the wrong way."   [l]20.28 *by God's
mercy . . . but*: Or "by their mercy . . . and."
[m]21.4 *but sin . . . produce*: Or "but sin is the only light
they ever follow."   [n]21.6 *and . . . suicide*: One possible
meaning for the difficult Hebrew text.

¹⁷ Heavy drinkers and others
who live only for pleasure
will lose all they have.

¹⁸ God's people will escape,
but all who are wicked
will pay the price.
¹⁹ It's better out in the desert
than at home with a nagging,
complaining wife.
²⁰ Be sensible and store up
precious treasures—
don't waste them
like a fool.
²¹ If you try to be kind and good,
you will be blessed with life
and goodness and honor.
²² One wise person can defeat
a city full of soldiers
and capture their fortress.
²³ Watching what you say
can save you
a lot of trouble.
²⁴ If you are proud and conceited,
everyone will say,
"You're a snob!"

²⁵ If you want too much
and are too lazy to work,
it could be fatal.
²⁶ But people who obey God
are always generous.

²⁷ The Lord despises the offerings
of wicked people
with evil motives.
²⁸ If you tell lies in court,
you are done for;
only a reliable witness
can do the job.
²⁹ Wicked people bluff their way,
but God's people think
before they take a step.

³⁰ No matter how much you know
or what plans you make,
you can't defeat the LORD.
³¹ Even if your army has horses
ready for battle,
the LORD will always win.

The Value of a Good Reputation

22 A good reputation and respect
are worth much more
than silver and gold.

² The rich and the poor
are all created
by the LORD.
³ When you see trouble coming,
don't be stupid
and walk right into it—
be smart and hide.

⁴ Respect and serve the LORD!
Your reward will be wealth,
a long life, and honor.
⁵ Crooks walk down a road
full of thorny traps.
Stay away from there!
⁶ Teach your children
right from wrong,
and when they are grown
they will still do right.
⁷ The poor are ruled by the rich,
and those who borrow
are slaves of moneylenders.
⁸ Troublemakers get in trouble,
and their terrible anger
will get them nowhere.

⁹ The LORD blesses everyone
who freely gives food
to the poor.
¹⁰ Arguments and fights
will come to an end,
if you chase away those
who insult others.
¹¹ The king is the friend of all
who are sincere
and speak with kindness.

¹² The LORD watches over everyone
who shows good sense,
but he frustrates the plans
of deceitful liars.
¹³ Don't be so lazy that you say,
"If I go to work,
a lion will eat me!"
¹⁴ The words of a bad woman
are like a deep pit;
if you make the LORD angry,
you will fall right in.
¹⁵ All children are foolish,
but firm correction
will make them change.
¹⁶ Cheat the poor to make profit
or give gifts to the rich—
either way you lose.

Thirty Wise Sayings

17 Here are some sayings
    of people with wisdom,
so listen carefully
    as I teach.
18 You will be glad
    that you know these sayings
    and can recite them.
19 I am teaching them today,
    so that you
        may trust the LORD.
20 I have written thirty sayings
    filled with sound advice.
21 You can trust them completely
    to give you the right words
        for those in charge of you.

–1–

22 Don't take advantage
    of the poor
        or cheat them in court.
23 The LORD is their defender,
    and what you do to them,
        he will do to you.

–2–

24 Don't make friends with anyone
    who has a bad temper.
25 You might turn out like them
    and get caught in a trap.

–3–

26 Don't guarantee to pay
    someone else's debt.

27 If you don't have the money,
    you might lose your bed.

–4–

28 Don't move a boundary marker[o]
    set up by your ancestors.

–5–

29 If you do your job well,
    you will work for a ruler
        and never be a slave.

–6–

23 When you are invited
    to eat with a king,
        use your best manners.
2 Don't go and stuff yourself!
    That would be just the same
        as cutting your throat.
3 Don't be greedy for all
    of that fancy food!
        It may not be so tasty.

–7–

4 Give up trying so hard
    to get rich.
5 Your money flies away
    before you know it,

---

o**22.28** *marker*: In ancient Israel boundary lines were sacred because all property was a gift from the Lord (see Deuteronomy 19.14).

Friendship—How can I tell if a friendship is unhealthy? *(Proverbs 22.24,25)*

By looking at habits and attitudes.

We tend to become like the people we stay around. This tendency is particularly noticeable in children. They readily pick up the language and behavior of their playmates. But it's also true of adults. That's why we need to choose friends whose conduct we'd like to model.

You know the kind of person described in verse 24. She mutters bitterly in stalled traffic. She complains at each new set of instructions from the boss. She gripes about her husband's lack of attention. She snaps at her children. She even complains about the music in church. If you're not careful, before long you'll find that the same things that irritate her also irritate you.

The Bible has a lot to say about anger and controlling our temper. Perhaps that's because anger often leads to violence—a trap we want to avoid. Healthy friendships are those that encourage us to please God in all our habits and attitudes, including the way we handle our anger. (See also Psalm 1; Proverbs 4.14,15; 2 Corinthians 6.14-18.)

Words To Remember: *Don't make friends with anyone who has a bad temper. You might turn out like them and get caught in a trap.—Proverbs 22.24,25*

just like an eagle
   suddenly taking off.

–8–

6 Don't accept an invitation
to eat a selfish person's food,
   no matter how good it is.
7 People like that take note
of how much you eat.[p]
They say, "Take all you want!"
But they don't mean it.
8 Each bite will come back up,
and all your kind words
   will be wasted.

–9–

9 Don't talk to fools—
   they will just make fun.

–10–

10 Don't move a boundary marker[q]
or take the land
   that belongs to orphans.
11 God All-Powerful is there
   to defend them against you.

–11–

12 Listen to instruction
   and do your best to learn.

–12–

13 Don't fail to correct
   your children.
You won't kill them
   by being firm,
14 and it may even
   save their lives.

–13–

15 My children,
if you show good sense,
   I will be happy,
16 and if you are truthful,
   I will really be glad.

–14–

17 Don't be jealous of sinners,
   but always honor the LORD.
18 Then you will truly have hope
   for the future.

–15–

19 Listen to me, my children!
Be wise and have enough sense

to follow the right path.
20 Don't be a heavy drinker
   or stuff yourself with food.
21 It will make you feel drowsy,
and you will end up poor
   with only rags to wear.

–16–

22 Pay attention to your father,
and don't neglect your mother
   when she grows old.
23 Invest in truth and wisdom,
discipline and good sense,
   and don't part with them.
24 Make your father truly happy
by living right and showing
   sound judgment.
25 Make your parents proud,
   especially your mother.

–17–

26 My son, pay close attention,
and gladly follow
   my example.
27 Bad women and unfaithful wives
   are like a deep pit—
28 they are waiting to attack you
like a gang of robbers
   with victim after victim.

–18–

29 Who is always in trouble?
   Who argues and fights?
Who has cuts and bruises?
   Whose eyes are red?
30 Everyone who stays up late,
   having just one more drink.
31 Don't even look
at that colorful stuff
   bubbling up in the glass!
It goes down so easily,
32 but later it bites
   like a poisonous snake.
33 You will see weird things,
and your mind
   will play tricks on you.
34 You will feel tossed about
like someone trying to sleep
   on a ship in a storm.
35 You will be bruised all over,

---

p 23.7 *People . . . eat*: One possible meaning for the
difficult Hebrew text. q 23.10 *marker*: See the note
at 22.28.

without even remembering
  how it all happened.
And you will lie awake asking,
"When will morning come,
  so I can drink some more?"

–19–

24 Don't be jealous of crooks
    or want to be their friends.
² All they think about
and talk about
  is violence and cruelty.

–20–

³ Use wisdom and understanding
  to establish your home;
⁴ let good sense fill the rooms
  with priceless treasures.

–21–

⁵ Wisdom brings strength,
  and knowledge gives power.
⁶ Battles are won
  by listening to advice
  and making a lot of plans.

–22–

⁷ Wisdom is too much for fools!
  Their advice is no good.

–23–

⁸ No one but troublemakers
  think up trouble.

⁹ Everyone hates senseless fools
  who think up ways to sin.

–24–

¹⁰ Don't give up and be helpless
  in times of trouble.

–25–

¹¹ Don't fail to rescue those
  who are doomed to die.
¹² Don't say, "I didn't know it!"
  God can read your mind.
He watches each of us
  and knows our thoughts.
And God will pay us back
  for what we do.

–26–

¹³ Honey is good for you,
  my children,
    and it tastes sweet.
¹⁴ Wisdom is like honey
  for your life—
if you find it,
  your future is bright.

–27–

¹⁵ Don't be a cruel person
  who attacks good people
    and hurts their families.
¹⁶ Even if good people
  fall seven times,
    they will get back up.
But when trouble strikes

PARENTING&*family*—How can I know what's best for my elderly parents? *(Proverbs 23.22-25)*

Show respect to your parents by living a godly life.

These verses from Proverbs remind us of the commandment "Respect your father and your mother, and you will live a long time in the land I am giving you" (Exodus 20.12). The proverbs here reflect the ideals of that day. Since the father was responsible for spiritual guidance in the Hebrew religious culture, the best way to honor him was to live in the light of his teaching. Mothers were the primary caregivers, so they took great pride in their children. In short, the best way to honor parents was to live a godly life. In an age without social security, part of that godly life was for children to care for their elderly parents.

Although our society offers a variety of ways to care for aging parents, one thing hasn't changed: The Bible is unequivocable in stating its expectation that we care for our parents and make them proud. Reflecting God's character in all we do for them and others will bring them joy. (See also Psalm 25; Joel 2.28-32; 1 Corinthians 15.35-58; 1 Timothy 5.1-7.)

Words To Remember: *Pay attention to your father, and don't neglect your mother when she grows old.—Proverbs 23.22*

the wicked,
  that's the end of them.

I've found that when I'm
worn out, envy not only gets
a foothold, it takes hold
of my mouth as well.

LIZ CURTIS HIGGS

–28–

17 Don't be happy
  to see your enemies trip
    and fall down.
18 The LORD will find out
  and be unhappy.
Then he will stop
  being angry with them.

–29–

19 Don't let evil people
  worry you
    or make you jealous.
20 They will soon be gone
  like the flame of a lamp
    that burns out.

–30–

21 My children, you must respect
  the LORD and the king,
and you must not make friends
with anyone who rebels
  against either of them.
22 Who knows what sudden disaster
  the LORD or a ruler
    might bring?

More Sayings That Make Good Sense

23 Here are some more sayings
  that make good sense:
When you judge,
  you must be fair.
24 If you let the guilty
  go free,
people of all nations
  will hate and curse you.
25 But if you punish the guilty,
  things will go well for you,
    and you will prosper.

26 Giving an honest answer
  is a sign
    of true friendship.
27 Get your fields ready
  and plant your crops
    before starting a home.
28 Don't accuse anyone
  who isn't guilty.
Don't ever tell a lie
29 or say to someone,
  "I'll get even with you!"

30 I once walked by the field
  and the vineyard
    of a lazy fool.
31 Thorns and weeds
  were everywhere,
and the stone wall
  had fallen down.
32 When I saw this,
  it taught me a lesson:
33 Sleep a little. Doze a little.
Fold your hands
  and twiddle your thumbs.
34 Suddenly poverty hits you
  and everything is gone!

More of Solomon's Wise Sayings

25 Here are more
of Solomon's proverbs.
They were copied by the officials
  of King Hezekiah of Judah.
2 God is praised
  for being mysterious;
rulers are praised
  for explaining mysteries.
3 Who can fully understand
  the thoughts of a ruler?
They reach beyond the sky
  and go deep in the earth.

4 Silver must be purified
  before it can be used
    to make something of value.
5 Evil people must be removed
  before anyone can rule
    with justice.

6 Don't try to seem important
  in the court of a ruler.
7 It's better for the ruler
  to give you a high position
than for you to be embarrassed
  in front of royal officials.
Be sure you are right

8 before you sue someone,
or you might lose your case
and be embarrassed.

9 When you and someone else
can't get along,
don't gossip about it.*r*
10 Others will find out,
and your reputation
will then be ruined.

11 The right word
at the right time
is like precious gold
set in silver.
12 Listening to good advice
is worth much more
than jewelry made of gold.
13 A messenger you can trust
is just as refreshing
as cool water in summer.
14 Broken promises
are worse than rain clouds
that don't bring rain.
15 Patience and gentle talk
can convince a ruler
and overcome any problem.

16 Eating too much honey
can make you sick.
17 Don't visit friends too often,
or they will get tired of it
and start hating you.
18 Telling lies about friends
is like attacking them
with clubs and swords
and sharp arrows.
19 A friend you can't trust
in times of trouble
is like having a toothache
or a sore foot.
20 Singing to someone
in deep sorrow
is like pouring vinegar
in an open cut.*s*

21 If your enemies are hungry,
give them something to eat.
And if they are thirsty,
give them something
to drink.
22 This will be the same
as piling burning coals
on their heads.

And the LORD
will reward you.
23 As surely as rain blows in
from the north,
anger is caused
by cruel words.
24 It's better to stay outside
on the roof of your house
than to live inside
with a nagging wife.

25 Good news from far away
refreshes like cold water
when you are thirsty.
26 When a good person gives in
to the wicked,
it's like dumping garbage
in a stream of clear water.
27 Don't eat too much honey
or always want praise.*t*
28 Losing self-control
leaves you as helpless
as a city without a wall.

Don't Be a Fool

26 Expecting snow in summer
and rain in the dry season
makes more sense
than honoring a fool.
2 A curse you don't deserve
will take wings and fly away
like a sparrow or a swallow.
3 Horses and donkeys
must be beaten and bridled—
and so must fools.
4 Don't make a fool of yourself
by answering a fool.
5 But if you answer any fools,
show how foolish they are,
so they won't feel smart.

6 Sending a message by a fool
is like chopping off your foot
and drinking poison.
7 A fool with words of wisdom
is like an athlete
with legs that can't move.*u*
8 Are you going to honor a fool?

---

r **25.9** *When . . . it:* Or "Settle a problem privately
between you and your neighbor and don't involve
others." *s* **25.20** *cut:* One possible meaning for the
difficult Hebrew text of verse 20. *t* **25.27** *or . . .
praise:* One possible meaning for the difficult
Hebrew text. *u* **26.7** *with . . . move:* One possible
meaning for the difficult Hebrew text.

Why not shoot a slingshot
   with the rock tied tight?
⁹A thornbush waved around
   in the hand of a drunkard
is no worse than a proverb
   in the mouth of a fool.

¹⁰It's no smarter to shoot arrows
   at every passerby
than it is to hire a bunch
   of worthless nobodies.ᵛ
¹¹Dogs return to eat their vomit,
   just as fools repeat
   their foolishness.
¹²There is more hope for a fool
   than for someone who says,
   "I'm really smart!"

¹³Don't be lazy and keep saying,
   "There's a lion outside!"
¹⁴A door turns on its hinges,
   but a lazy person
   just turns over in bed.
¹⁵Some of us are so lazy
   that we won't lift a hand
   to feed ourselves.
¹⁶A lazy person says,
   "I am smarter
   than everyone else."

¹⁷It's better to take hold
   of a mad dog by the ears
than to take part
   in someone else's argument.

¹⁸It's no crazier to shoot
   sharp and flaming arrows
¹⁹than to cheat someone and say,
   "I was only fooling!"

²⁰Where there is no fuel
   a fire goes out;
where there is no gossip
   arguments come to an end.
²¹Troublemakers start trouble,
   just as sparks and fuel
   start a fire.
²²There is nothing so delicious
   as the taste of gossip!
   It melts in your mouth.

²³Hiding hateful thoughts
   behind smoothʷ talk
is like coating a clay pot
   with a cheap glaze.
²⁴The pleasant talk
   of an enemy
   hides more evil plans
²⁵than can be counted—
   so don't believe a word!
²⁶Everyone will see through
   those evil plans.
²⁷If you dig a pit,
   you will fall in;
if you start a stone rolling,
   it will roll back on you.

ᵛ**26.10** *nobodies:* One possible meaning for the difficult Hebrew text of verse 10. ʷ**26.23** *smooth:* One ancient translation; Hebrew "hateful."

Friendship—How can I speak the truth in love and still maintain a friendship? *(Proverbs 27.6)*

Realize that a friendship without truth is not a true friendship.
When you care about someone, it's tempting to avoid telling the truth—especially if that truth might hurt. You might be tempted to shade the truth about yourself because you want to look as good as you possibly can. And you may even be tempted to speak less than the truth to your friend because you don't want to hurt or offend her or (even worse) be accused of being a "control freak."

But a faithful friend must sometimes speak words that bring pain. If your words hurt, are they spoken lovingly? And are they offered as "faithful wounds," the kind that are necessary for your friend's best interests? Speaking the truth can be done without love—even with a friend. But speaking the "truth in love" means you speak with respect, gentleness, and kindness—maintaining your friend's dignity. (See also Job 42.7-9; Ephesians 4.25—5.2; James 1.5-8.)

Words To Remember: *You can trust a friend who corrects you, but kisses from an enemy are nothing but lies.*—Proverbs 27.6

²⁸Watch out for anyone
  who tells lies and flatters—
    they are out to get you.

Don't Brag about Tomorrow

27 Don't brag about tomorrow!
  Each day brings
    its own surprises.
²Don't brag about yourself—
  let others praise you.
³Stones and sand are heavy,
  but trouble caused by a fool
    is a much heavier load.
⁴An angry person is dangerous,
  but a jealous person
    is even worse.

⁵A truly good friend
  will openly correct you.
⁶You can trust a friend
  who corrects you,
but kisses from an enemy
  are nothing but lies.
⁷If you have had enough to eat,
  honey doesn't taste good,
but if you are really hungry,
  you will eat anything.

⁸When you are far from home,
  you feel like a bird
    without a nest.
⁹The sweet smell of incense
  can make you feel good,
but true friendship
  is better still.ˣ
¹⁰Don't desert an old friend
  of your family
or visit your relatives
  when you are in trouble.
A friend nearby is better
  than relatives far away.

¹¹My child, show good sense!
  Then I will be happy
and able to answer anyone
  who criticizes me.
¹²Be cautious and hide
  when you see danger—
don't be stupid and walk
  right into trouble.
¹³Don't loan money to a stranger
  unless you are given something
    to guarantee payment.

ˣ**27.9** *still:* One possible meaning for the difficult Hebrew text of verse 9.

Friendship—What are the marks of a good friendship? (*Proverbs 27.17-19*)

It shapes your character and reputation—for the good.

"Just as iron sharpens iron" (27.17), a good friend will challenge what we think and even who we are. As we test ourselves against each other, we rub away those qualities that are loose and weak. What's left is even stronger than when we began. We sharpen each other in thought and in character.

A second image this proverb supplies about friendship is the mirror. When you look in your mirror, you expect to see your own face. As you look close into your own eyes, you can almost read your thoughts. But how startling it would be to look in your mirror some sleepy morning and see instead the thoughts of your friend. That's how influential friendship is! For good or for bad, we rub off on each other.

The best friendships are those where both persons are strong in their faith and they encourage each other to grow stronger in it. This takes work, but when we nurture friendships, we benefit from having someone to share with and receive helpful correction from. The key to good friendships is mutuality—mutual respect, mutual independence, mutual caring, and mutual submission.

Choose friends who sharpen you in good ways, instead of cutting you to pieces. And provide the same service for your friends. (See also Ruth 1–4; Proverbs 17.17; 18.24; 1 Corinthians 13.4-8; James 5.13-20.)

Words To Remember: *Just as iron sharpens iron, friends sharpen the minds of each other. . . . You see your face in a mirror and your thoughts in the minds of others.*
—**Proverbs 27.17,19**

¹⁴A loud greeting
   early in the morning
      is the same as a curse.
¹⁵The steady dripping of rain
   and the nagging of a wife
      are one and the same.
¹⁶It's easier to catch the wind
   or hold olive oil in your hand
      than to stop a nagging wife.

¹⁷Just as iron sharpens iron,
   friends sharpen the minds
      of each other.
¹⁸Take care of a tree,
      and you will eat its fruit;
   look after your master,
      and you will be praised.
¹⁹You see your face in a mirror
   and your thoughts
      in the minds of others.
²⁰Death and the grave
   are never satisfied,
      and neither are we.
²¹Gold and silver are tested
   in a red-hot furnace,
      but we are tested by praise.
²²No matter how hard
      you beat a fool,
   you can't pound out
      the foolishness.

²³You should take good care
   of your sheep and goats,
²⁴because wealth and honor
   don't last forever.
²⁵After the hay is cut
   and the new growth appears

and the harvest is over,
²⁶you can sell lambs and goats
   to buy clothes and land.
²⁷From the milk of the goats,
   you can make enough cheese
to feed your family
   and all your servants.

The Law of God Makes Sense

28 Wicked people run away
         when no one chases them,
      but those who live right
         are as brave as lions.
²In time of civil war
      there are many leaders,
   but a sensible leader
      restores law and order.ʸ
³When someone poor takes over
      and mistreats the poor,
   it's like a heavy rain
      destroying the crops.

⁴Lawbreakers praise criminals,
   but law-abiding citizens
      always oppose them.
⁵Criminals don't know
      what justice means,
   but all who respect the LORD
      understand it completely.
⁶It's better to be poor
      and live right,
   than to be rich
      and dishonest.

ʸ28.2 *but . . . order*: One possible meaning for the difficult Hebrew text.

WORK—How can I deal with a dishonest coworker? *(Proverbs 28.11-26)*

Set an example by your own honesty and integrity.
These verses give good advice about how to maintain one's integrity before dishonest coworkers. Celebrate honesty, yours and that of others! Be willing to admit when you're wrong and change your shortcomings. Refuse to mistreat, be unfair to, or cheat anyone. Work hard and don't waste time. Be loyal to your company and leaders. Be generous and trust the Lord for your needs. Seek wisdom and advice from your coworkers.

But being a positive example may not be enough. You also need to point out the dishonesty once you have evidence to prove it. This is hard for all of us to do, but remember, "Honest correction is appreciated more than flattery" (28.23). (See also Psalm 26; Amos 2; Habakkuk 2.4-17.)

Words To Remember: *Honest correction is appreciated more than flattery.*
—Proverbs 28.23

⁷It makes good sense
   to obey the Law of God,
but you disgrace your parents
if you make friends
   with worthless nobodies.
⁸If you make money by charging
   high interest rates,
you will lose it all to someone
   who cares for the poor.
⁹God cannot stand the prayers
of anyone who disobeys
   his Law.
¹⁰By leading good people to sin,
   you dig a pit for yourself,
but all who live right
   will have a bright future.

¹¹The rich think highly
   of themselves,
but anyone poor and sensible
   sees right through them.
¹²When an honest person wins,
   it's time to celebrate;
when crooks are in control,
   it's best to hide.
¹³If you don't confess your sins,
   you will be a failure.
But God will be merciful
if you confess your sins
   and give them up.
¹⁴The LORD blesses everyone
   who is afraid to do evil,
but if you are cruel,
   you will end up in trouble.

¹⁵A ruler who mistreats the poor
is like a roaring lion
   or a bear hunting for food.
¹⁶A heartless leader is a fool,
   but anyone who refuses
to get rich by cheating others
   will live a long time.
¹⁷Don't give help to murderers!
Make them stay on the run
   for as long as they live.ᶻ

¹⁸Honesty will keep you safe,
   but everyone who is crooked
   will suddenly fall.
¹⁹Work hard, and you will have
   a lot of food;
waste time, and you will have
   a lot of trouble.

²⁰God blesses his loyal people,
   but punishes all who want
      to get rich quick.
²¹It isn't right to be unfair,
   but some people can be bribed
      with only a piece of bread.
²²Don't be selfish
   and eager to get rich—
you will end up worse off
   than you can imagine.

²³Honest correction
   is appreciated
      more than flattery.
²⁴If you cheat your parents
   and don't think it's wrong,
      you are a common thief.
²⁵Selfish people cause trouble,
   but you will live a full life
      if you trust the LORD.
²⁶Only fools would trust
   what they alone think,
but if you live by wisdom,
   you will do all right.

²⁷Giving to the poor
   will keep you from poverty,
but if you close your eyes
   to their needs,
      everyone will curse you.
²⁸When crooks are in control,
   everyone tries to hide,
but when they lose power,
   good people are everywhere.

Use Good Sense

29 If you keep being stubborn
   after many warnings,
you will suddenly discover
   you have gone too far.
²When justice rules a nation,
   everyone is glad;
when injustice rules,
   everyone groans.
³If you love wisdom
   your parents will be glad,
but chasing after bad women
   will cost you everything.
⁴An honest ruler
   makes the nation strong;
a ruler who takes bribes
   will bring it to ruin.

ᶻ**28.17** *live*: One possible meaning for the difficult
Hebrew text of verse 17.

⁵Flattery is nothing less
    than setting a trap.
⁶Your sins will catch you,
  but everyone who lives right
    will sing and celebrate.
⁷The wicked don't care
  about the rights of the poor,
    but good people do.
⁸Sneering at others is a spark
    that sets a city on fire;
using good sense can put out
    the flames of anger.

⁹Be wise and don't sue a fool.
    You won't get satisfaction,
because all the fool will do
  is sneer and shout.
¹⁰A murderer hates everyone
  who is honest
    and lives right.*a*
¹¹Don't be a fool
  and quickly lose your temper—
    be sensible and patient.

¹²A ruler who listens to lies
    will have corrupt officials.
¹³The poor and all who abuse them
  must each depend on God
    for light.
¹⁴Kings who are fair to the poor
    will rule forever.

¹⁵Correct your children,
    and they will be wise;
children out of control
    disgrace their mothers.
¹⁶Crime increases
    when crooks are in power,
but law-abiding citizens
    will see them fall.
¹⁷If you correct your children,
  they will bring you peace
    and happiness.

¹⁸Without guidance from God
    law and order disappear,
but God blesses everyone
    who obeys his Law.
¹⁹Even when servants are smart,
  it takes more than words
    to make them obey.
²⁰There is more hope for a fool
  than for someone who speaks
    without thinking.
²¹Slaves that you treat kindly

from their childhood
    will cause you sorrow.*b*
²²A person with a quick temper
  stirs up arguments
    and commits a lot of sins.

*When you ask God to give
you his perspective, your
husband's small flaws and
foibles will become miniscule
compared to the breathtaking
scope of a God's-eye-view.*

KAREN SCALF LINAMEN

²³Too much pride brings disgrace;
    humility leads to honor.
²⁴If you take part in a crime
    you are your worst enemy,
because even under oath
    you can't tell the truth.
²⁵Don't fall into the trap
    of being a coward—
trust the LORD,
    and you will be safe.
²⁶Many try to make friends
  with a ruler,
but justice comes
    from the LORD.
²⁷Good people and criminals
    can't stand each other.

The Sayings of Agur

30 These are the sayings
and the message
of Agur son of Jakeh.
Someone cries out to God,
"I am completely worn out!
    How can I last?*c*
²I am far too stupid
    to be considered human.
³I never was wise,

---

*a***29.10** *and lives right:* Or "and those who live right are
friends of honest people." *b***29.21** *will . . . sorrow:*
One possible meaning for the difficult Hebrew text.
*c***30.1** *last:* One possible meaning for the difficult
Hebrew text of verse 1.

and I don't understand
    what God is like."

⁴Has anyone gone up to heaven
    and come back down?
Has anyone grabbed hold
    of the wind?
Has anyone wrapped up the sea
or marked out boundaries
    for the earth?
If you know of any
    who have done such things,
then tell me their names
    and their children's names.

⁵Everything God says is true—
and it's a shield for all
    who come to him for safety.
⁶Don't change what God has said!
He will correct you and show
    that you are a liar.

⁷There are two things, Lord,
I want you to do for me
    before I die:
⁸Make me absolutely honest
and don't let me be too poor
    or too rich.
Give me just what I need.
⁹If I have too much to eat,
    I might forget about you;
if I don't have enough,
I might steal
    and disgrace your name.

¹⁰Don't tell a slave owner
something bad
    about one of the slaves.
That slave will curse you,
    and you will be in trouble.

¹¹Some people curse their father
    and even their mother;
¹²others think they are perfect,
    but they are stained by sin.
¹³Some people are stuck-up
    and act like snobs;
¹⁴others are so greedy
that they gobble down
    the poor and homeless.

¹⁵Greed^d has twins,
    each named "Give me!"
There are three or four things

that are never satisfied:
¹⁶The world of the dead
    and a childless wife,
the thirsty earth
    and a flaming fire.

¹⁷Don't make fun of your father
    or disobey your mother—
crows will peck out your eyes,
and buzzards will eat
    the rest of you.

¹⁸There are three or four things
    I cannot understand:
¹⁹How eagles fly so high
    or snakes crawl on rocks,
how ships sail the ocean
    or people fall in love.

²⁰An unfaithful wife says,
    "Sleeping with another man
    is as natural as eating."

²¹There are three or four things
    that make the earth tremble
    and are unbearable:
²²A slave who becomes king,
    a fool who eats too much,
²³a hateful woman
    who finds a husband,
and a slave who takes the place
    of the woman who owns her.

²⁴On this earth four things
    are small but very wise:
²⁵Ants, who seem to be feeble,
    but store up food
    all summer long;
²⁶badgers, who seem to be weak,
    but live among the rocks;
²⁷locusts, who have no king,
    but march like an army;
²⁸lizards,^e which can be caught
in your hand,
    but sneak into palaces.

²⁹Three or four creatures
    really strut around:
³⁰Those fearless lions
    who rule the jungle,
³¹those proud roosters,
    those mountain goats,

---

^d30.15 *Greed*: Or "A leech."   ^e30.28 *lizards*:
Or "spiders."

and those rulers
  who have no enemies.[f]

32 If you are foolishly bragging
  or planning something evil,
    then stop it now!
33 If you churn milk
  you get butter;
  if you pound on your nose,
    you get blood—
  and if you stay angry,
    you get in trouble.

What King Lemuel's Mother Taught Him

31 These are the sayings
   that King Lemuel of Massa
     was taught by his mother.
2 My son Lemuel, you were born
  in answer to my prayers,
    so listen carefully.
3 Don't waste your life
  chasing after women!
    This has ruined many kings.

4 Kings and leaders
  should not get drunk
    or even want to drink.
5 Drinking makes you forget
  your responsibilities,
    and you mistreat the poor.
6 Beer and wine are only
  for the dying or for those
    who have lost all hope.
7 Let them drink and forget
  how poor and miserable
    they feel.

8 But you must defend
  those who are helpless
    and have no hope.
9 Be fair and give justice
  to the poor and homeless.

In Praise of a Good Wife

10 A truly good wife
  is the most precious treasure
    a man can find!
11 Her husband depends on her,
  and she never
    lets him down.
12 She is good to him
  every day of her life,
13 and with her own hands
  she gladly makes clothes.

14 She is like a sailing ship
  that brings food
    from across the sea.
15 She gets up before daylight
  to prepare food for her family
    and for her servants.[g]
16 She knows how to buy land
  and how to plant a vineyard,
17   and she always works hard.
18 She knows when to buy or sell,
  and she stays busy
    until late at night.
19 She spins her own cloth,
20 and she helps the poor
  and the needy.

---

[f]30.31 *enemies:* One possible meaning for the difficult Hebrew text of verse 31.   [g]31.15 *and . . . servants:* Or "and to tell her servants what to do."

MARRIAGE—How does God define my role as a wife? *(Proverbs 31.10-31)*

To be godly in attitude *and* actions.

This "good wife" of Proverbs 31 was compassionate, competent, dependable, industrious, skillful, and an astute business woman. God had given her skills in many areas, and her family encouraged her abilities. Her children praised her, and her husband took great pride in her accomplishments. Far from being a hindrance to her husband, she contributed to his position of honor in the community. He even praised her publicly for what she'd done.

It appears that this ideal couple recognized each other's talents and encouraged each other in their use. This relationship was quite a contrast to what was generally practiced in the religious culture of that day. By using this example to help determine what your role should be as a wife, you and your husband have the freedom to recognize the gifts and skills God has given you, to use them to support each other, and to glorify God. (See also Ecclesiastes 7.11-14; Colossians 3.15-19.)

Words To Remember: *Charm can be deceiving, and beauty fades away, but a woman who honors the LORD deserves to be praised.—Proverbs 31.30*

The Ideal Woman

Proverbs 31.10-31

*M*any women let out a groan of frustration whenever they hear about the ideal woman of Proverbs 31. We feel exhausted just reading about all that she does! One explanation for her outstanding abilities is that she may not have been one woman but a composite portrait of ideal womanhood. Whether she was real or a composite, her virtuous principles are worth emulating today. Industrious, skillful, compassionate, sensible, cheerful, and loving, she exercised sound judgment and good business sense, respected her husband, and honored God. In short, the ideal woman portrayed traits that Proverbs advocates throughout the book.

One wonders if all women in that day had as much freedom as this woman, or if she had this freedom because of her wealth. Many clues tell us that she was a woman of wealth. She had servants, owned land, wore beautiful clothes, and had a husband who was a leader in the city. Because she and her husband were respected by the community, we can assume her freedom was not unusual, that other women also had this kind of freedom. They were not censured by the community for their roles; they were respected.

What does God want us to learn from this example of a godly marriage? Even though most of us don't have the kind of wealth described here or perhaps this kind of freedom, we can still emulate the ideal woman's strength of character. If someone wrote a "praise tribute" about you, what would you want it to say? You may want to select two or three traits you'd like to build into your life and then work on them.

It's interesting that Proverbs opens by telling us how to gain knowledge and wisdom: "Respect and obey the LORD! This is the beginning of knowledge. Only a fool rejects wisdom and good advice" (1.7). Appropriately, Proverbs ends with the example of a woman who honored the Lord—and the results that brought to her life. "Charm can be deceiving, and beauty fades away, but a woman who honors the LORD deserves to be praised" (31.30). That's the kind of woman I want to be. How about you?

²¹ Her family has warm clothing,
and so she doesn't worry
when it snows.
²² She does her own sewing,
and everything she wears
is beautiful.

²³ Her husband is a well-known
and respected leader
in the city.
²⁴ She makes clothes to sell
to the shop owners.
²⁵ She is strong and graceful,ʰ
as well as cheerful
about the future.
²⁶ Her words are sensible,
and her advice
is thoughtful.
²⁷ She takes good care

of her family
and is never lazy.
²⁸ Her children praise her,
and with great pride
her husband says,
²⁹ "There are many good women,
but you are the best!"

³⁰ Charm can be deceiving,
and beauty fades away,
but a woman
who honors the LORD
deserves to be praised.
³¹ Show her respect—
praise her in public
for what she has done.

ʰ**31.25** *She . . . graceful*: Or "The clothes she makes are attractive and of good quality."

Ecclesiastes

Is Anything in Life Worthwhile?

"Why am I here?"

"Why should I bother to get up in the morning?"

"Is there any way to find joy in this life?"

"Will I leave behind a legacy when I die?"

Most of us ask these questions at some point in our life. Some of us ask them almost every day. When we are searching for real meaning in a world that feels meaningless, what we don't need is someone with a forced smile saying, "Put on a happy face."

Ecclesiastes offers no such platitude. King Solomon probably authored the book late in his life. The most wealthy king in the history of Israel, he inherited from his father a nation with more expansive borders than any time since then. He was also the last king to rule a united kingdom. In that setting, Solomon could have and do almost anything he wished. Yet he searched for meaning to his life—and had a hard time finding it.

Solomon looked in all the usual places: knowledge, wealth, fun, power. But he kept coming up empty. He said things like, "Our eyes and our ears are never satisfied" (1.8). And "Everything that happens has happened before; nothing is new, nothing under the sun" (1.9). Sometimes his words turned dark and empty like the thoughts we don't quite dare put into words, even to ourselves: "Like animals we breathe and die, and we are no better off than they are" (3.19). And "The dead are better off than the living" (4.2).

Oddly, during our own times of grief and emptiness, Ecclesiastes is a good place to turn. It's a book that doesn't pretend. Ecclesiastes takes our sorrows seriously; it doesn't try to push them aside. We sense that the writer knew the meaning of disappointment.

But Ecclesiastes isn't all bleak. Although the writer rejected many avenues to meaning, he did find contentment in ordinary places that we can share. He discovered that wisdom is better than foolishness, that we can be thankful for the common grace of food and drink, that enjoying our work is a gift from God, that friendship has great value, and that we should respect and obey our Creator.

Ecclesiastes at a Glance

1. Is anything in life worthwhile? (1,2)
2. A poem about time and complaints about the future (3.1—4.8)
3. Friends bring comfort to life (4.9-16)
4. Respect and obey God (5)
5. Money can't buy joy (6)
6. Proverbs and questions (7)
7. Life is short and unpredictable, so enjoy everyday things like food and work (8.1—9.12)
8. Wise proverbs for down-to-earth living (9.13—11.6)
9. Prepare to grow old (11.7—12.8)
10. Respect and obey God; only this brings meaning to life (12.9-14)

Nothing Makes Sense

1 When the son of David was king in Jerusalem, he was known to be very wise,[a] and he said:

2 Nothing makes sense!
   Everything is nonsense.
   I have seen it all—
   nothing makes sense!
3 What is there to show
   for all of our hard work
   here on this earth?
4 People come, and people go,
   but still the world
   never changes.

5 The sun comes up,
   the sun goes down;
   it hurries right back
   to where it started from.
6 The wind blows south,
   the wind blows north;
   round and round it blows
   over and over again.
7 All rivers empty into the sea,
   but it never spills over;
   one by one the rivers return
   to their source.[b]

*There's power in what you say—
and what you don't. Fasting
from criticism for a week will
impact your relationships.*

JANE JOHNSON STRUCK

8 All of life is far more boring
   than words could ever say.
   Our eyes and our ears
   are never satisfied
   with what we see and hear.
9 Everything that happens
   has happened before;
   nothing is new,
   nothing under the sun.
10 Someone might say,
   "Here is something new!"
   But it happened before,
   long before we were born.

11 No one who lived in the past
   is remembered anymore,
   and everyone yet to be born
   will be forgotten too.

It Is Senseless To Be Wise

12 I said these things when I lived in Jerusalem as king of Israel. 13 With all my wisdom I tried to understand everything that happens here on earth. And God has made this so hard for us humans to do. 14 I have seen it all, and everything is just as senseless as chasing the wind.[c]

15 If something is crooked,
   it can't be made straight;
   if something isn't there,
   it can't be counted.

16 I said to myself, "You are by far the wisest person who has ever lived in Jerusalem. You are eager to learn, and you have learned a lot." 17 Then I decided to find out all I could about wisdom and foolishness. Soon I realized that this too was as senseless as chasing the wind.[c]

18 The more you know,
   the more you hurt;
   the more you understand,
   the more you suffer.

It Is Senseless To Be Selfish

2 I said to myself, "Have fun and enjoy yourself!" But this didn't make sense. 2 Laughing and having fun is crazy. What good does it do? 3 I wanted to find out what was best for us during the short time we have on this earth. So I decided to make myself happy with wine and find out what it means to be foolish, without really being foolish myself.

4 I did some great things. I built houses and planted vineyards. 5 I had flower gardens and orchards full of fruit trees. 6 And I had pools where I could get water for the trees. 7 I owned slaves, and their sons and daughters became my slaves. I had more sheep and

---

[a]1.1 *known to be very wise*: This stands for the Hebrew word often translated "preacher" or "teacher." The word may refer to someone who was a very wise leader or to someone who had become wise from collecting sayings about wisdom. [b]1.7 *return to their source*: Or "flow into the sea." [c]1.14,17 *chasing the wind*: Or "eating the wind."

goats than anyone who had ever lived in Jerusalem. ⁸Foreign rulers brought me silver, gold, and precious treasures. Men and women sang for me, and I had many wives*d* who gave me great pleasure.

⁹I was the most famous person who had ever lived in Jerusalem, and I was very wise. ¹⁰I got whatever I wanted and did whatever made me happy. But most of all, I enjoyed my work. ¹¹Then I thought about everything I had done, including the hard work, and it was simply chasing the wind.*e* Nothing on earth is worth the trouble.

Wisdom Makes Sense

¹²I asked myself, "What can the next king do that I haven't done?" Then I decided to compare wisdom with foolishness and stupidity. ¹³And I discovered that wisdom is better than foolishness, just as light is better than darkness. ¹⁴Wisdom is like having two good eyes; foolishness leaves you in the dark. But wise or foolish, we all end up the same.

¹⁵Finally, I said to myself, "Being wise got me nowhere! The same thing will happen to me that happens to fools. Nothing makes sense. ¹⁶Wise or foolish, we all die and are soon forgotten." ¹⁷This made me hate life. Everything we do is painful; it's just as senseless as chasing the wind.*e*

¹⁸Suddenly I realized that others would someday get everything I had worked for so hard, then I started hating it all. ¹⁹Who knows if those people will be sensible or stupid? Either way, they will own everything I have earned by hard work and wisdom. It doesn't make sense.

²⁰I thought about all my hard work, and I felt depressed. ²¹When we use our wisdom, knowledge, and skill to get what we own, why do we have to leave it to someone who didn't work for it? This is senseless and wrong. ²²What do we really gain from all of our hard work? ²³Our bodies ache during the day, and work is torture. Then at night our thoughts are troubled. It just doesn't make sense.

²⁴The best thing we can do is to enjoy eating, drinking, and working.*f* I believe these are God's gifts to us, ²⁵and no one enjoys eating and living more than I do. ²⁶If we please God, he will make us wise, understanding, and happy. But if we sin, God will make us struggle for a living, then he will give all we own to someone who pleases

---

*d***2.8** *many wives:* One possible meaning for the difficult Hebrew text. *e***2.11,17** *chasing the wind:* See the note at 1.14, 17. *f***2.24** *The best . . . working:* One possible meaning for the difficult Hebrew text.

WORK—Can I do the "Lord's work" in a secular job? If so, how?
(*Ecclesiastes 2.24-26*)

Try to enjoy the work you have or find work that you enjoy.
Enjoy *work?* Those words might bring a loud burst of laughter. You picture the most disagreeable part of your job—whether it's scrubbing toilets, typing letters, or practicing diplomacy with the boss—and say, "Enjoy work? Not with my job."

Yet, after the writer of Ecclesiastes had searched in all the obvious places for meaning in life (and met with disappointment), he began to look at everyday things like work. To enjoy work, he declared, is not only possible, it's a gift from God.

Even in boring jobs, we can set small goals and feel personal satisfaction when we achieve them. We can also refuse to get caught up in gossip about coworkers and petty criticism of the boss. We can nurture friendships by celebrating a coworker's birthday or sharing a joke, building a bond that enables us to talk about our faith. While we may not enjoy every moment on the job, we can take pleasure in much of the work and thank God for that.

But some jobs are just not well matched to your skills and interests. In that case, consider a change. Perhaps God will grant you the gift of enjoying your work in some new setting. We can serve God, even in a secular job, with our enjoyment of his gift. (See also 1 Samuel 14.1-15; Matthew 4.18-22; Matthew 15.10-20.)

Words To Remember: *The best thing we can do is to enjoy eating, drinking, and working. I believe these are God's gifts to us.*—Ecclesiastes 2.24

him. This makes no more sense than chasing the wind.[g]

Everything Has Its Time

3 Everything on earth
has its own time
and its own season.
[2] There is a time
for birth and death,
planting and reaping,
[3] for killing and healing,
destroying and building,
[4] for crying and laughing,
weeping and dancing,
[5] for throwing stones
and gathering stones,
embracing and parting.
[6] There is a time
for finding and losing,
keeping and giving,
[7] for tearing and sewing,
listening and speaking.
[8] There is also a time
for love and hate,
for war and peace.

What God Has Given Us To Do

[9] What do we gain by all of our hard work? [10] I have seen what difficult things God demands of us. [11] God makes everything happen at the right time. Yet none of us can ever fully understand all he has done, and he puts questions in our minds about the past and the future. [12] I know the best thing we can do is to always enjoy life, [13] because God's gift to us is the happiness we get from our food and drink and from the work we do. [14] Everything God has done will last forever; nothing he does can ever be changed. God has done all this, so that we will worship him.

[15] Everything that happens
has happened before,
and all that will be
has already been—
God does everything
over and over again.[h]

The Future Is Known Only to God

[16] Everywhere on earth I saw violence and injustice instead of fairness and justice. [17] So I told myself that God has set a time and a place for everything. He will judge everyone, both the wicked and the good. [18] I know that God is testing us to show us that we are merely animals. [19] Like animals we breathe and die, and we are no better off

---

[g]2.26 *chasing the wind*: See the note at 1.14, 17.
[h]3.15 *God does . . . again*: One possible meaning for the difficult Hebrew text.

WORK—How can I find satisfaction with my life outside of work?

(*Ecclesiastes 3.1-14*)

Aim for balance in how you use time.

Work has a way of infecting our whole life. If you hate your job, or even have a tense day, you may come home feeling as though you want to shake your husband, yell at the kids, and kick the cat. But if you love your job, you may work late at night and on the weekends, then come home with just enough energy to "veg out" in front of TV. Even your most casual conversation will be filled with talk of work.

Enjoying work is a gift from God, but joy at work does not necessarily equal enjoyment of life. Early in his book, the author tucks in a poem about time. It is a poem of opposites: birth/death, crying/laughing, keeping/giving. The point of the poem is balance. "There is a time" for all of these (3.2). Finding satisfaction outside your work has something to do with that balance.

Use your time away from work to do something totally different. Take a night-school course in literature, or sign up for an aerobics class. Cultivate relationships outside of work. And if you work for a company that "works 'em till they drop," make up for long days by taking blocks of time away to deliberately clear your head of work issues. (See also Deuteronomy 8.10-20; Isaiah 55.1-5.)

Words To Remember: *Everything on earth has its own time and its own season.*
—Ecclesiastes 3.1

than they are. It just doesn't make sense. [20]All living creatures go to the same place. We are made from earth, and we return to the earth. [21]Who really knows if our spirits go up and the spirits of animals go down into the earth? [22]We were meant to enjoy our work, and that's the best thing we can do. We can never know the future.

4 I looked again and saw people being mistreated everywhere on earth. They were crying, but no one was there to offer comfort, and those who mistreated them were powerful. [2]I said to myself, "The dead are better off than the living. [3]But those who have never been born are better off than anyone else, because they have never seen the terrible things that happen on this earth."

[4]Then I realized that we work and do wonderful things just because we are jealous of others. This makes no more sense than chasing the wind.[i]

[5]Fools will fold their hands
   and starve to death.
[6]Yet a very little food
   eaten in peace

is better than twice as much
earned from overwork
   and chasing the wind.[i]

[7]Once again I saw that nothing on earth makes sense. [8]For example, some people don't have friends or family. But they are never satisfied with what they own, and they never stop working to get more. They should ask themselves, "Why am I always working to have more? Who will get what I leave behind?" What a senseless and miserable life!

It Is Better To Have a Friend

[9]You are better off to have a friend than to be all alone, because then you will get more enjoyment out of what you earn. [10]If you fall, your friend can help you up. But if you fall without having a friend nearby, you are really in trouble. [11]If you sleep alone, you won't have anyone to keep you warm on a cold night. [12]Someone might be able to beat up one of you, but not both of you. As the

---

[i]4.4,6 *chasing the wind*: See the note at 1.14, 17.

Friendship—If I'm naturally introverted and independent, why should I go out of my way to make friends? *(Ecclesiastes 4.9-12)*

Life goes better with friends.

It's tempting to be independent: You don't have anybody asking you for favors when it's inconvenient. You don't have to wonder what other people think of you because they rarely think of you at all. You don't have to worry about anybody's problems but your own.

Exactly. Friends are a little like insurance. You don't notice it most of the time—except to pay the bills. But when disaster strikes, you're mighty glad you have it. At times of illness, emotional loss, or minor crisis, such as a broken lawn mower or a flat tire, friends come to the rescue. The author describes needs as they'd appear in his setting: "If you fall, your friend can help you up" (4.10); "Someone might be able to beat up one of you, but not both of you" (4.12).

But friendship is not just for trouble. Friends enrich our life even during ordinary times. Ecclesiastes says that a friend will help you "get more enjoyment out of what you earn" (4.9) and "keep you warm on a cold night" (4.11). But the most interesting picture is the illustration of a strong rope, "three strands of cord" (4.12). Even today this metaphor appears in many weddings. The bride and groom invite into their friendship with each other the friendship of one more person: God. It's the strength of this three-stranded cord (friend, friend, and God) that isn't easily broken.

A woman who enjoys privacy may chose fewer friends than average. But don't leave out friendship altogether. Friends are worth the effort. (See also John 13.18-35; Hebrews 13.1,2.)

Words To Remember: *A rope made from three strands of cord is hard to break.*
—Ecclesiastes 4.12

saying goes, "A rope made from three strands of cord is hard to break."

[13]You may be poor and young. But if you are wise, you are better off than a foolish old king who won't listen to advice. [14]Even if you were not born into the royal family and have been a prisoner and poor, you can still be king. [15]I once saw everyone in the world follow a young leader who came to power after the king was gone. [16]His followers could not even be counted. But years from now, no one will praise him—this makes no more sense than chasing the wind.[i]

Be Careful How You Worship

5 Be careful what you do when you enter the house of God. Some fools go there to offer sacrifices, even though they haven't sinned.[j] But it's best just to listen when you go to worship. [2]Don't talk before you think or make promises to God without thinking them through. God is in heaven, and you are on earth, so don't talk too much. [3]If you keep thinking about something, you will dream about it. If you talk too much, you will say the wrong thing.

[4]God doesn't like fools. So don't be slow to keep your promises to God. [5]It's better not to make a promise at all than to make one and not keep it. [6]Don't let your mouth get you in trouble! And don't say to the worship leader,[k] "I didn't mean what I said." God can destroy everything you have worked for, so don't say something that makes God angry.

[7]Respect and obey God! Daydreaming leads to a lot of senseless talk.[l]

[8]Don't be surprised if the poor of your country are abused, and injustice takes the place of justice. After all, the lower officials must do what the higher ones order them to do. [9]And since the king is the highest official, he benefits most from the taxes paid on the land.[m]

[10]If you love money and wealth, you will never be satisfied with what you have. This doesn't make sense either. [11]The more you have, the more everyone expects from you. Your money won't do you any good—others will just spend it for you. [12]If you have to work hard for a living, you can rest well at night, even if you don't have much to eat. But if you are rich, you can't even sleep.

[13]I have seen something terribly unfair. People get rich, but it does them no good.

[14]Suddenly they lose everything in a bad business deal, then have nothing to leave for their children. [15]They came into this world naked, and when they die, they will be just as naked. They can't take anything with them, and they won't have anything to show for all their work. [16]That's terribly unfair. They leave the world just as they came into it. They gained nothing from running after the wind. [17]Besides all this, they are always gloomy at mealtime, and they are troubled, sick, and bitter.[n]

[18]What is the best thing to do in the short life that God has given us? I think we should enjoy eating, drinking, and working hard. This is what God intends for us to do. [19]Suppose you are very rich and able to enjoy everything you own. Then go ahead and enjoy working hard—this is God's gift to you. [20]God will keep you so happy that you won't have time to worry about each day.

Don't Depend on Wealth

6 There is something else terribly unfair, and it troubles everyone on earth. [2]God may give you everything you want—money, property, and wealth. Then God doesn't let you enjoy it, and someone you don't even know gets it all. That's senseless and terribly unfair!

[3]You may live a long time and have a hundred children. But a child born dead is better off than you, unless you enjoy life and have a decent burial. [4-5]That child will never live to see the sun or to have a name, and it will go straight to the world of darkness. But it will still find more rest than you, [6]even if you live two thousand years and don't enjoy life. As you know, we all end up in the same place.

[7]We struggle just to have enough to eat, but we are never satisfied. [8]We may be sensible, yet we are no better off than a fool. And if we are poor, it still doesn't do us any good to try to live right. [9]It's better to enjoy what we have than to always want something

---

[i]**4.16** *chasing the wind:* See the note at 1.14, 17.
[j]**5.1** *even . . . sinned:* One possible meaning for the difficult Hebrew text.　[k]**5.6** *worship leader:* Or "messenger."　[l]**5.7** *Daydreaming . . . talk:* One possible meaning for the difficult Hebrew text.
[m]**5.9** *land:* One possible meaning for the difficult Hebrew text of verse 9.　[n]**5.17** *bitter:* One possible meaning for the difficult Hebrew text of verse 17.

else, because that makes no more sense than chasing the wind.*

¹⁰Everything that happens was decided long ago. We humans know what we are like, and we can't argue with God, because he is* too strong for us. ¹¹The more we talk, the less sense we make, so what good does it do to talk? ¹²Life is short and meaningless, and it fades away like a shadow. Who knows what is best for us? Who knows what will happen after we are gone?

The Best in Life

7 A good reputation
    at the time of death
  is better than loving care
    at the time of birth.*
² It's better to go to a funeral
    than to attend a feast;
  funerals remind us
    that we all must die.
³ Choose sorrow over laughter
  because a sad face
    may hide a happy heart.
⁴ A sensible person mourns,
    but fools always laugh.
⁵ Harsh correction is better
    than the songs of a fool.

⁶ Foolish laughter is stupid.
  It sounds like thorns
    crackling in a fire.
⁷ Corruption* makes fools
  of sensible people,
    and bribes can ruin you.
⁸ Something completed is better
    than something just begun;
  patience is better
    than too much pride.
⁹ Only fools get angry quickly
    and hold a grudge.
¹⁰ It isn't wise to ask,
  "Why is everything worse
    than it used to be?"
¹¹ Having wisdom is better
    than an inheritance.
¹² Wisdom will protect you
    just like money;
  knowledge with good sense
    will lead you to life.
¹³ Think of what God has done!

---

*6.9 *chasing the wind*: See the note at 1.14, 17. *6.10 *with God, because he is*: Or "with anyone who is." *7.1 *birth*: One possible meaning for the difficult Hebrew text of verse 1. *7.7 *Corruption*: Or "Oppression."

Personal *Concerns*—How can I learn to be more content with my life?
(*Ecclesiastes* 6.1-9)

Enjoy what you have.
Stuff. It fills our closets, our cupboards, our file drawers. Yet something inside us nags for more. *Shouldn't I dump that rug for a more current color? Those drapes are old and dusty. Should I bother to clean them, or just get new ones? And isn't it time I got a new set of dishes? Nothing matches anymore. Who says china is only for brides?* There's a restlessness about us that says whatever we have isn't quite enough. We want more and better.

In one of the more bleak sections of Ecclesiastes, the author complains, "God may give you everything you want. . . . Then God doesn't let you enjoy it. . . . That's senseless and terribly unfair!" (6.2). Then he adds that it would be better to be born dead than to be plagued with this endless dissatisfaction.

We don't have to let ourselves sink into this whirlpool of greed. We can combat it by practicing appreciation for what we have—especially those things that have no monetary cost. Enjoy art in a museum, books from a library, and walks in a park. Set aside one day a month as "dump day." On that day, empty a drawer, shelf, or cupboard and give away anything you don't need. When you buy something, give away two items in a similar category. (Homeless shelters, garage sales, and resale stores are great places to recycle.) Then ask God for the gift of contentment. (See also Psalm 107; Daniel 2.20,21; 2 Peter 1.3-15.)

Words To Remember: *It's better to enjoy what we have than to always want something else, because that makes no more sense than chasing the wind.*
—Ecclesiastes 6.9

If God makes something crooked,
   can you make it straight?

¹⁴When times are good,
      you should be cheerful;
   when times are bad,
      think what it means.
   God makes them both
      to keep us from knowing
         what will happen next.

Some of Life's Questions

¹⁵I have seen everything during this senseless life of mine. I have seen good citizens die for doing the right thing, and I have seen criminals live to a ripe old age. ¹⁶So don't destroy yourself by being too good or acting too smart! ¹⁷Don't die before your time by being too evil or acting like a fool. ¹⁸Keep to the middle of the road. You can do this if you truly respect God.

¹⁹Wisdom will make you stronger than the ten most powerful leaders in your city.

²⁰No one in this world always does right.

²¹Don't listen to everything that everyone says, or you might hear your servant cursing you. ²²Haven't you cursed many others?

²³I told myself that I would be smart and try to understand all of this, but it was too much for me. ²⁴The truth is beyond us. It's far too deep. ²⁵So I decided to learn everything I could and become wise enough to discover what life is all about. At the same time, I wanted to understand why it's stupid and senseless to be an evil fool.

²⁶Here is what I discovered: A bad woman is worse than death. She is a trap, reaching out with body and soul to catch you. But if you obey God, you can escape. If you don't obey, you are done for. ²⁷With all my wisdom I have tried to find out how everything fits together, ²⁸but so far I have not been able to. I do know there is one good man in a thousand, but never have I found a good woman. ²⁹I did learn one thing: We were completely honest when God created us, but now we have twisted minds.

8 Who is smart enough
      to explain everything?
   Wisdom makes you cheerful
      and gives you a smile.

Obey the King

²If you promised God that you would be loyal to the king, I advise you to keep that promise. ³Don't quickly oppose the king or argue when he has already made up his mind. ⁴The king's word is law. No one can ask him, "Why are you doing this?" ⁵If you obey the king, you will stay out of trouble. So be smart and learn what to do and when to do it. ⁶Life is hard, but there is a time and a place for everything, ⁷though no one can

---

MARRIAGE—How does God define my role as a wife? *(Ecclesiastes 7.11-14)*

To be wise, godly, and cheerful—no matter what.
Not many passages of Scripture (other than Proverbs 31) specifically define the role of a wife, or even the role of a woman. But much of Scripture tells how God's people as a whole ought to think and live. These general passages hold valuable principles a wife can use to create a healthy marriage and a happy home.

Ecclesiastes 7.11-14 is one such passage. When you're stirring up a macaroni-and-cheese dinner for the third night in a row due to tight finances, reading "Having wisdom is better than an inheritance" can bring laughter to life. (It'll also give you some needed long-range perspective for when your husband spends money on an expensive hobby instead of purchasing the new kitchen sink you'd talked about!)

Above all, the writer of Ecclesiastes shows that we need to trust God, no matter the circumstances of our home, finances, or marriage. It's clear that God is in control—in good times and bad. And we can rest easy in the future because "of what God has done" in the past! (See also Proverbs 31.10-31; Colossians 3.15-19.)

   Words To Remember: *Having wisdom is better than an inheritance. Wisdom will protect you just like money; knowledge with good sense will lead you to life. Think of what God has done!—Ecclesiastes 7.11-13*

tell the future. [8]We cannot control the wind[s] or determine the day of our death. There is no escape in time of war, and no one can hide behind evil. [9]I noticed all this and thought seriously about what goes on in the world. Why does one person have the power to hurt another?

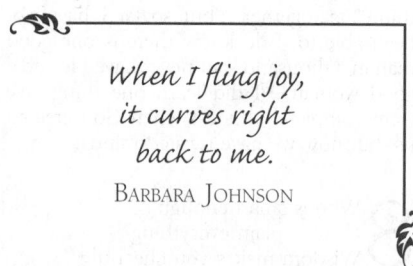

When I fling joy,
it curves right
back to me.

BARBARA JOHNSON

Who Can Understand the Ways of God?

[10]I saw the wicked buried with honor, but God's people had to leave the holy city and were forgotten.[t] None of this makes sense. [11]When we see criminals commit crime after crime without being punished, it makes us want to start a life of crime. [12]They commit hundreds of crimes and live to a ripe old age, in spite of the saying:

Everyone who lives right
and respects God
will prosper,
[13]but no one who sins
and rejects God
will prosper or live very long.

[14]There is something else that doesn't make sense to me. Good citizens are treated as criminals, while criminals are honored as though they were good citizens. [15]So I think we should get as much out of life as we possibly can. There is nothing better than to enjoy our food and drink and to have a good time. Then we can make it through this troublesome life that God has given us here on earth.

[16]Day and night I went without sleep, trying to understand what goes on in this world. [17]I saw everything God does, and I realized that no one can really understand what happens. We may be very wise, but no matter how much we try or how much we claim to know, we cannot understand it all.

One Day at a Time

9 I thought about these things. Then I understood that God has power over everyone, even those of us who are wise and live right. Anything can happen to any of us, and so we never know if life will be good or bad.[u] [2]But exactly[v] the same thing will finally happen to all of us, whether we live right and respect God or sin and don't respect God. Yes, the same thing will happen if we offer sacrifices to God or if we don't, if we keep our promises or break them.

[3]It's terribly unfair for the same thing to happen to each of us. We are mean and foolish while we live, and then we die. [4]As long as we are alive, we still have hope, just as a live dog is better off than a dead lion. [5]We know that we will die, but the dead don't know a thing. Nothing good will happen to them—they are gone and forgotten. [6]Their loves, their hates, and their jealous feelings have all disappeared with them. They will never again take part in anything that happens on this earth.

[7]Be happy and enjoy eating and drinking! God decided long ago that this is what you should do. [8]Dress up, comb your hair, and look your best. [9]Life is short, and you love your wife, so enjoy being with her. This is what you are supposed to do as you struggle through life on this earth. [10]Work hard at whatever you do. You will soon go to the world of the dead, where no one works or thinks or reasons or knows anything.

[11]Here is something else I have learned:

The fastest runners
and the greatest heroes
don't always win races
and battles.
Wisdom, intelligence, and skill
don't always make you healthy,
rich, or popular.
We each have our share
of bad luck.

---

[s]**8.8** *control the wind:* Or "escape from death." [t]**8.10** *but . . . forgotten:* One possible meaning for the difficult Hebrew text. [u]**9.1** *or bad:* Three ancient translations; the Hebrew text does not have these words. [v]**9.2** *exactly:* One possible meaning for the difficult Hebrew text.

> *Even after twenty-two years of marriage, we're still learning each other's strengths and weaknesses and how we complement each other. But the Lord does bless you when you commit to each other—for life.*
>
> KARYN HENLEY

they have no sense.
[4]Don't give up your job
  when your boss gets angry.
If you stay calm,
  you'll be forgiven.

[5]Some things rulers do are terribly unfair: [6]They honor fools, but dishonor the rich; [7]they let slaves ride on horses, but force slave owners to walk.

[8]If you dig a pit,
  you might fall in;
if you break down a wall,
  a snake might bite you.[w]
[9]You could even get hurt
by chiseling a stone
  or chopping a log.
[10]If you don't sharpen your ax,
  it will be harder to use;
if you are smart,
  you'll know what to do.[x]
[11]The power to charm a snake
does you no good
  if it bites you anyway.

[12]If you talk sensibly,
  you will have friends;
if you talk foolishly,
  you will destroy yourself.
[13]Fools begin with nonsense,
  and their stupid chatter
    ends with disaster.
[14]They never tire of talking,
  but none of us really know
    what the future will bring.
[15]Fools wear themselves out—
  they don't know enough
    to find their way home.[y]

[16]A country is in for trouble
  when its ruler is childish,
and its leaders
  party all day long.
[17]But a nation will prosper
  when its ruler is mature,
and its leaders
  don't party too much.

[12]None of us know when we might fall victim to a sudden disaster and find ourselves like fish in a net or birds in a trap.

Better To Be Wise than Foolish

[13]Once I saw what people really think of wisdom. [14]It happened when a powerful ruler surrounded and attacked a small city where only a few people lived. The enemy army was getting ready to break through the city walls. [15]But the city was saved by the wisdom of a poor person who was soon forgotten. [16]So I decided that wisdom is better than strength. Yet if you are poor, no one pays any attention to you, no matter how smart you are.

[17]Words of wisdom spoken softly
  make much more sense
than the shouts of a ruler
  to a crowd of fools.
[18]Wisdom is more powerful
  than weapons,
yet one mistake can destroy
  all the good you have done.

10 A few dead flies in perfume
  make all of it stink,
and a little foolishness
  outweighs a lot of wisdom.
[2]Sensible thoughts lead you
  to do right;
foolish thoughts lead you
  to do wrong.
[3]Fools show their stupidity
  by the way they live;
  it's easy to see

---

[w]**10.8** *a snake might bite you:* Walls of houses were often made of stones with mud to fill in the cracks between them. If some of the mud washed out, a snake could be living inside the wall.   [x]**10.10** *do:* One possible meaning for the difficult Hebrew text of verse 10. [y]**10.15** *home:* One possible meaning for the difficult Hebrew text of verse 15.

¹⁸ Some people are too lazy
     to fix a leaky roof—
         then the house falls in.
¹⁹ Eating and drinking
       make you feel happy,
     and bribes can buy
         everything you need.
²⁰ Don't even think
         about cursing the king;
     don't curse the rich,
         not even in secret.
     A little bird might hear
         and tell everything.

It Pays To Work Hard

11 Be generous, and someday
       you will be rewarded.ᶻ
     ² Share what you have
       with seven or eight others,
because you never know
     when disaster may strike.
³ Rain clouds always bring rain;
trees always stay
     wherever they fall.
⁴ If you worry about the weather
     and don't plant seeds,
       you won't harvest a crop.

⁵ No one can explain how a baby breathes before it is born.ᵃ So how can anyone explain what God does? After all, he created everything.

⁶ Plant your seeds early in the morning and keep working in the field until dark. Who knows? Your work might pay off, and your seeds might produce.

*Life is celebrating
each day as special.*

LUCI SWINDOLL

Youth and Old Age

⁷ Nothing on earth is more beautiful than the morning sun. ⁸ Even if you live to a ripe old age, you should try to enjoy each day,

---

ᶻ**11.1** *Be generous . . . rewarded*: Or "Don't be afraid to invest. Someday it will pay off." ᵃ**11.5** *how . . . born*: Or "what makes the wind blow or how a baby grows inside its mother."

PARENTING&*family*—What advice, if any, should I give to my twentysomething child? *(Ecclesiastes 11.1—12.1)*

Enjoy youth; remember God.

It's hard to be a parent to young adults. While much of our parenting job is finished, our parent/child relationship continues. We know how important it is for our grown children to exercise independence, get careers and families started, and take responsibility for their lives. So we worry, *Has my daughter studied that career choice carefully? Does my son know how important saving is at this stage? Why aren't they working harder?* And, *I really wish I could see them in church more often.*

The final sections of Ecclesiastes are the words of an old, wise man looking back on a life that was far from satisfying. For a few moments he speaks to young adults. He voices some of the concerns common among today's parents, but he also shows that early adulthood is far more than gaining financial stability. He says things like: "Be generous" (11.1). "Share" (11.2). "Enjoy each day" (11.8). "Be cheerful . . . find pleasure in what you see" (11.9). But lest we think he advocates perpetual childhood, he also advises, "Plant your seeds early . . . keep working . . . until dark" (11.6). "Nothing on earth is more beautiful than the morning sun" (11.7). And, "Keep your Creator in mind while you are young!" (12.1).

Probably the less often we voice our concerns, the better. And the more often twentysomethings heed them, the better yet. **(See also Ezekiel 18.1-20; Amos 5.6-27; Matthew 14.24-33; 1 Timothy 4.6-16.)**

Words To Remember: *Keep your Creator in mind while you are young!*
—Ecclesiastes 12.1

because darkness will come and will last a long time. Nothing makes sense.[b]

[9]Be cheerful and enjoy life while you are young! Do what you want and find pleasure in what you see. But don't forget that God will judge you for everything you do.

[10]Rid yourself of all worry and pain, because the wonderful moments of youth quickly disappear.

12 Keep your Creator in mind while you are young! In years to come, you will be burdened down with troubles and say, "I don't enjoy life anymore."

[2]Someday the light of the sun
and the moon and the stars
  will all seem dim to you.
Rain clouds will remain
  over your head.
[3]Your body will grow feeble,
your teeth will decay,
  and your eyesight fail.
[4]The noisy grinding of grain
will be shut out
  by your deaf ears,
but even the song of a bird
  will keep you awake.

[5]You will be afraid
to climb up a hill
  or walk down a road.
Your hair will turn as white
  as almond blossoms.
You will feel lifeless
and drag along
  like an old grasshopper.

We each go to our eternal home,
and the streets are filled
  with those who mourn.
[6]The silver cord snaps,
  the golden bowl breaks;
the water pitcher is smashed,
and the pulley at the well
  is shattered.
[7]So our bodies return
to the earth,
and the life-giving breath[c]
  returns to God.
[8]Nothing makes sense.

I have seen it all—
  nothing makes sense.

Respect and Obey God

[9]I was a wise teacher with much understanding, and I collected a number of proverbs that I had carefully studied. [10]Then I tried to explain these things in the best and most accurate way.

> *I learned—the hard way—that God blesses those who obey him. How could I demand that he meet my needs if I wasn't willing to obey him?*
>
> MARY HUNT

[11]Words of wisdom are like the stick a farmer uses to make animals move. These sayings come from God, our only shepherd, and they are like nails that fasten things together.[d] [12]My child, I warn you to stay away from any teachings except these.

There is no end to books,
and too much study
  will wear you out.

[13]Everything you were taught can be put into a few words:

Respect and obey God!
This is what life
  is all about.
[14]God will judge
everything we do,
even what is done in secret,
  whether good or bad.

[b]**11.8** *Nothing makes sense:* Or "There's nothing to look forward to!" [c]**12.7** *life-giving breath:* Or "spirit." [d]**12.11** *These sayings . . . together:* One possible meaning for the difficult Hebrew text.

Song of Songs

A Poem of Love

Passionate words. Erotic imagery. Extravagant statements of how physically attractive and desirable that "special someone" is. This powerful, romantically and sexually charged writing isn't out of some romance novel. It's from a book right in the middle of the Holy Bible.

What is this mysterious Song of Songs (otherwise known as the Song of Solomon) doing in the Bible? In the past several thousand years, a lot of people have puzzled over that question. It may have been written for the wedding of King Solomon; it may be the story of a young woman Solomon wanted to marry but who returned to her shepherd lover—teaching the king the meaning of true, pure love.

While readers speculate about the lovers' identity, Song of Songs makes no apologies for its subject matter or its candor. It simply continues to fascinate, excite, embarrass, and captivate its readers.

Many of us like to make a clear division between spirit and flesh, but Song of Songs merges the two inseparably. Its language is sensuous and ethereal at the same time. First of all, it celebrates sexual love between a woman and a man. Some Christians also interpret this book as an expression of the love between Christ and the church (all believers); other Christians note that Song of Songs is never quoted in the New Testament.

This beautiful book can be liberating for a woman in any stage of life or any marital status. If you feel inhibited about your sexuality, this book's joyous honesty can free you. If you regret your past sexual behavior, this book affirms purity and commitment to one life partner. If your marriage is full of criticism, this book exemplifies the tender words that breathe life into a relationship. If you are single, this book reminds you of a love worth waiting for. If you have lost your life's partner, this book floods your heart with memories and gratitude for human love.

No matter what your situation, read Song of Songs with pleasure and without shame, rejoicing in its physical and spiritual richness.

Song of Songs at a Glance

1. Two lovers approach each other (1)
2. They anticipate the pleasures of being together (2,3)
3. The man praises the woman (4.1-15)
4. The woman praises the man (4.16—5.16)
5. The desire of the lovers is only for each other (6,7)
6. Love is stronger than anything else (8)

Love Is Better than Wine

1 This is Solomon's
most beautiful song.

She Speaks:

²Kiss me tenderly!
Your love is better than wine,
³   and you smell so sweet.
All the young women adore you;
the very mention of your name
    is like spreading perfume.
**⁴Hurry, my king! Let's hurry.
⁵   Take me to your home.

The Young Women Speak:

We are happy for you!
And we praise your love
    even more than wine.

She Speaks:

Young women of Jerusalem,
it is only right
    that you should adore him.
My skin is dark and beautiful,
like a tent in the desert
    or like Solomon's curtains.
⁶Don't stare at me
just because the sun
    has darkened my skin.
My brothers were angry with me;

they made me work in the vineyard,
and so I neglected
my complexion.

Don't let the other shepherds
    think badly of me.*ᵃ*
⁷I'm not one of those women
who shamelessly follow
    after shepherds.*ᵇ*
My darling, I love you!
Where do you feed your sheep
    and let them rest at noon?

He Speaks:

⁸My dearest, if you don't know,
just follow the path
    of the sheep.
Then feed your young goats
    near the shepherds' tents.
⁹You move as gracefully
as the pony that leads
    the chariot of the king.
¹⁰Earrings add to your beauty,
and you wear a necklace
    of precious stones.
¹¹Let's make you some jewelry
    of gold, woven with silver.

---

*ᵃ*1.6 *Don't . . . me:* One possible meaning for the difficult Hebrew text.   *ᵇ*1.7 *I'm . . . shepherds:* One possible meaning for the difficult Hebrew text.

SingleLife—What should I look for in a future spouse? *(Song of Songs 1)*

Look for a man who treasures you.
Perhaps you're dating a man who values you. But why does he think you're valuable? Where does he think your worth comes from? Is it because you're a person God created, with your own unique history and abilities? Or is it because you laugh at his jokes and make an attractive addition to him when he goes out in public? While it's fine to laugh at his jokes and be attractive, things like that shouldn't be the main reason he holds you in high regard.

A man to live with for a lifetime should be someone who values you because you are a unique creation of God. He should remember God created you for other purposes besides what you can do for him—although you'll do much for him. And he should think you're worthwhile not only because you add to his life, but simply because you exist.

In this opening passage of Song of Songs, the woman apologized for flaws in her physical beauty. Her lover not only overlooked her flaws, but lavished intense praise on her. She was valuable not for how she looked but for who she was.

A man like that is worth waiting for. **(See also Genesis 24; 1 Corinthians 13; Ephesians 5.21-33.)**

Words To Remember: *My darling, you are lovely, so very lovely—your eyes are those of a dove.*—Song of Songs 1.15

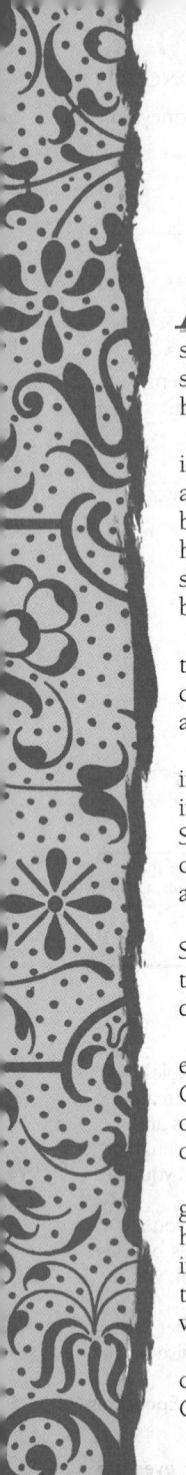

Beloved

Song of Songs 1–8

A woman in love. Where can we find anyone with a more explosive combination of idealism and earthiness?

In Song of Songs, we find a woman in love who also knows she's a woman loved. She's never identified by name. We could assume she is a fictional character or a symbol—if it weren't for the fact the historical person King Solomon is identified as visiting her.

This woman's very anonymity makes her a someone we can all identify with. We will call her "Beloved" because in the poem she is always seen in relation to her lover. She says that her skin was darkened by working in the sun, but otherwise the only physical descriptions we have of her are lavishly exaggerated. So we are left to focus where we should focus: on her inner character. We must search for her identity beneath the skin.

Throughout the poem, Beloved's full attention is on her lover. She thinks and talks of him constantly. She idealizes him, praising his every characteristic in the most extravagant language. She fully enjoys his attentions and draws strength from his love.

Yet we do not get the impression that this woman is about to fade into the shadow of her husband and become invisible. She is no fluttering, defenseless, shrinking violet. Beloved has a strong sense of herself. She makes plans for the life she and her husband will share. She's confident she will be the sexual mate he needs and wants. She isn't shy about expressing her desire for him (7.12).

Beloved insists that her lover is hers, but she isn't overly possessive. She enjoys her friends' wholesome appreciation of him. And she's willing to make a lifetime commitment to him in a love that's stronger than death.

The woman in Song of Songs would be a powerful example to us even if she were only a character in an ancient love poem. But some Christians for centuries have also interpreted Song of Songs as an allegory of the love between Christ and his people. In that case we are the character Beloved! She stands for all believers, not only women.

The allegory fits—or should fit! Christ's love should energize us and give us the confidence to be the people he made us to be. We should give him our full attention and praise everything about him. We should introduce others to him rather than be exclusive. Christ promises himself to us eternally, and we, too, can respond with a commitment to him that will outlast this earthly life.

Beloved still stands as our example. She shows us the earthy love we can give our husband—but also the committed love we can give Jesus Christ.

She Speaks:

¹²My king, while you
   were on your couch,
      my love was a magic charm.ᶜ
¹³My darling, you are perfume
   between my breasts;
¹⁴you are flower blossoms
   from the gardens of En-Gedi.ᵈ

He Speaks:

¹⁵My darling, you are lovely,
   so very lovely—
      your eyes are those of a dove.

She Speaks:

¹⁶My love, you are handsome,
   truly handsome—
      the fresh green grass
      will be our wedding bed
¹⁷in the shade of cedar
   and cypress trees.

Love Makes Everything Beautiful

She Speaks:

2 I am merely a roseᵉ
   from the land of Sharon,
      a lily from the valley.

He Speaks:

²My darling, when compared

with other young women,
   you are a lily among thorns.

She Speaks:

³And you, my love,
   are an apple tree
      among trees of the forest.
Your shade brought me pleasure;
   your fruit was sweet.
⁴You led me to your banquet room
   and showered me with love.
⁵Refresh and strengthen me
   with raisins and apples.
      I am hungry for love!
⁶Put your left hand under my head
   and embrace me
      with your right arm.

⁷Young women of Jerusalem,
   promise me by the power
      of deer and gazellesᶠ
   never to awaken love
      before it is ready.

ᶜ**1.12** *magic charm*: The Hebrew text has "spikenard" (or "nard"), a sweet-smelling ointment made from a plant that comes from India. The ointment was sometimes used as a love charm. ᵈ**1.14** *En-Gedi*: An oasis west of the Dead Sea. ᵉ**2.1** *rose*: The traditional translation. The exact variety of the flower is not known, though it may have been a crocus. ᶠ**2.7** *deer and gazelles*: Deer and gazelles were sacred animals in some religions of Old Testament times, and they were thought to have special powers.

MARRIAGE—How can I lead my unbelieving husband to Christ without offending him? *(Song of Songs 2.16—3.4)*

Keep reaching for him.

In this passage, often interpreted as a dream, the woman reached out for her lover but her hands found nothing. He wasn't there. She didn't simply shrug and say, "Oh, well." She went out searching for him and didn't give up until she found him.

If your husband doesn't share your faith in Christ, you know all about those yearnings. You often experience the bewilderment of reaching but not touching. He is there physically but not "there," where he should be, spiritually.

You still love him—or you want to love him again. You still see so much good in him. You want him to have the best gift possible, the gift of God's life and forgiveness.

Keep reaching out for him physically and spiritually. Don't build walls that puzzle or frustrate him. Enjoy him for all the reasons you married him, and keep looking for new reasons. Continue saying, as this woman did, "My darling, I am yours, and you are mine" (2.16). Let him know that you accept him, and let God love him through you. (See also Genesis 39; 41.39; John 13.1-17; 1 Peter 3.1-6; Revelation 21.9—22.21.)

Words To Remember: *While in bed at night, I reached for the one I love with heart and soul.*—Song of Songs 3.1

Winter Is Past

She Speaks:

⁸I hear the voice
  of the one I love,
as he comes leaping
over mountains and hills
⁹   like a deer or a gazelle.
Now he stands outside our wall,
looking through the window
¹⁰   and speaking to me.

He Speaks:

My darling, I love you!
  Let's go away together.
¹¹Winter is past,
  the rain has stopped;
¹²flowers cover the earth,
  it's time to sing.ᵍ
The cooing of doves
  is heard in our land.
¹³Fig trees are bearing fruit,
while blossoms on grapevines
  fill the air with perfume.
My darling, I love you!
  Let's go away together.
¹⁴You are my dove
hiding among the rocks
  on the side of a cliff.
Let me see how lovely you are!
Let me hear the sound
  of your melodious voice.
¹⁵Our vineyards are in blossom;
we must catch the little foxes
  that destroy the vineyards.ʰ

She Speaks:

¹⁶My darling, I am yours,
  and you are mine,
as you feed your sheep
  among the lilies.
¹⁷Pretend to be a young deer
dancing on mountain slopesⁱ
  until daylight comes
  and shadows fade away.

Beautiful Dreams

She Speaks:

3 While in bed at night,
  I reached for the one I love
    with heart and soul.
I looked for him,
  but he wasn't there.
²So I searched through the town

for the one I love.
I looked on every street,
  but he wasn't there.
³I even asked the guards
  patrolling the town,
"Have you seen the one
  I love so much?"
⁴Right after that, I found him.
I held him and would not let go
  until I had taken him
  to the home of my mother.
⁵Young women of Jerusalem,
promise me by the power
  of deer and gazelles,ʲ
never to awaken love
  before it is ready.

Cleaving to each other illustrates a commitment that goes beyond just sticking together. It means being the one person the other can always count on, being best friends, sharing life on the deepest, most intimate levels—and giving each other permission to be less than perfect.

CLAUDIA ARP

The Groom and the Wedding Party

Their Friends Speak:

⁶What do we see approaching
from the desert
  like a cloud of smoke?
With it comes the sweet smell
of spices, including myrrh
  and frankincense.
⁷It is King Solomon
  carried on a throne,

ᵍ**2.12** *sing:* Or "trim the vines." ʰ**2.15** *vineyards:* One possible meaning for the difficult Hebrew text of verse 15. ⁱ**2.17** *mountain slopes:* One possible meaning for the difficult Hebrew text. ʲ**3.5** *deer and gazelles:* See the note at 2.7.

surrounded by sixty
   of Israel's best soldiers.
[8] Each of them wears a sword.
   They are experts at fighting,
      even in the dark.
[9] The throne is made of trees
   from Lebanon.
[10] Its posts are silver,
   the back is gold,
   and the seat is covered
      with purple cloth.
You women of Jerusalem
have taken great care
   to furnish the inside.[k]
[11] Now come and see the crown
given to Solomon by his mother
   on his happy wedding day.

What a Beautiful Bride

He Speaks:

4 My darling, you are lovely,
   so very lovely—
   as you look through your veil,
      your eyes are those of a dove.
Your hair tosses about
as gracefully as goats
   coming down from Gilead.
[2] Your teeth are whiter
   than sheep freshly washed;
they match perfectly,
   not one is missing.
[3] Your lips are crimson cords,
   your mouth is shapely;
behind your veil are hidden
   beautiful rosy cheeks.[l]
[4] Your neck is more graceful
   than the tower of David,
decorated with thousands
   of warriors' shields.

[5] Your breasts are perfect;
   they are twin deer
      feeding among lilies.
[6] I will hasten to those hills
   sprinkled with sweet perfume
   and stay there till sunrise.
[7] My darling, you are lovely
   in every way.
[8] My bride, together
   we will leave Lebanon!
We will say good-by
   to the peaks of Mount Amana,
   Senir, and Hermon,

where lions and leopards
   live in the caves.
[9] My bride, my very own,
   you have stolen my heart!
With one glance from your eyes
and the glow of your necklace,
   you have stolen my heart.

*Prayer and sex are words
seldom used in the same
sentence. But they should be.*

KATHY PEEL

[10] Your love is sweeter than wine;
   the smell of your perfume
      is more fragrant than spices.
[11] Your lips are a honeycomb;
   milk and honey
      flow from your tongue.
Your dress has the aroma
   of cedar trees from Lebanon.

[12] My bride, my very own,
   you are a garden, a fountain
      closed off to all others.
[13] Your arms[m] are vines,
   covered with delicious fruits
      and all sorts of spices—
   henna, nard, [14] saffron,
      calamus, cinnamon,
frankincense, myrrh, and aloes
   —all the finest spices.
[15] You are a spring in the garden,
   a fountain of pure water,
and a refreshing stream
   from Mount Lebanon.

She Speaks:

[16] Let the north wind blow,
   the south wind too!
Let them spread the aroma
   of my garden,
so the one I love

---

[k] *3.10 inside:* One possible meaning for the difficult
Hebrew text. [l] *4.3 beautiful rosy cheeks:* One possible
meaning for the difficult Hebrew text. [m] *4.13 Your
arms:* One possible meaning for the difficult
Hebrew text.

may enter and taste
   its delicious fruits.

He Speaks:

5 My bride, my very own,
   I come to my garden
     and enjoy its spices.
I eat my honeycomb and honey;
   I drink my wine and milk.

Their Friends Speak:

Eat and drink until
   you are drunk with love.

Another Dream

She Speaks:

² I was asleep, but dreaming:
The one I love was at the door,
   knocking and saying,
"My darling, my very own,
my flawless dove,
   open the door for me!
My head is drenched
   with evening dew."

³ But I had already undressed
   and bathed my feet.
Should I dress again
   and get my feet dirty?
⁴ Then my darling's hand
reached to open the latch,
   and my heart stood still.
⁵ When I rose to open the door,

my hands and my fingers
   dripped with perfume.

⁶ My heart stood still
   while he spoke to me,
but when I opened the door,
   my darling had disappeared.
I searched and shouted,
   but I could not find him—
   there was no answer.
⁷ Then I was found by the guards
patrolling the town
   and guarding the wall.
They beat me up
   and stripped off my robe.

⁸ Young women of Jerusalem,
   if you find the one I love,
please say to him,
   "She is weak with desire."

Their Friends Speak:

⁹ Most beautiful of women,
   why is the one you love
     more special than others?
Why do you ask us
   to tell him how you feel?

She Speaks:

¹⁰ He is handsome and healthy,
   the most outstanding
     among ten thousand.
¹¹ His head is purest gold;
   his hair is wavy,

MARRIAGE—What's essential for a healthy, rewarding sex life?
(Song of Songs 5.10-16)

Use passionate words.

Song of Songs gives us an example of the sort of lavish, intimate praise that comes naturally from the lips of people who love each other deeply.

In this passage the woman extols her lover's physical attributes. If taken literally, this passage would be absurd—a man with a garden growing on his face, birds taking a bath in his eyes, legs that belong in front of a courthouse. But these are the lavish statements of love. She can't say strongly enough how he affects her.

Sexual love involves words as well as actions. Just as you are free to say anything to God in prayer, you can let go of any verbal inhibitions with your husband. Tell him how he looks and feels to you and how his body stirs you. Don't worry about overstating your case, because if you love him completely, there's no way to overstate that love. (See also Genesis 1.27-31; 1 Corinthians 7.1-5.)

Words To Remember: *His kisses are sweet. I desire him so much! . . . He is my lover and friend.*—Song of Songs 5.16

black as a raven.
¹²His eyes are a pair of doves
bathing in a stream
flowing with milk.ⁿ
¹³His face is a garden
of sweet-smelling spices;
his lips are lilies
dripping with perfume.

¹⁴His arms are branches of gold
covered with jewels;
his body is ivoryᵒ
decorated with sapphires.
¹⁵His legs are columns of marble
on feet of gold.
He stands there majestic
like Mount Lebanon
and its choice cedar trees.
¹⁶His kisses are sweet.
I desire him so much!
Young women of Jerusalem,
he is my lover and friend.

Their Friends Speak:

6 Most beautiful of women,
tell us where he has gone.
Let us help you find him.

She Speaks:

²My darling has gone down
to his garden of spices,
where he will feed his sheep
and gather lilies.
³I am his, and he is mine,
as he feeds his sheep
among the lilies.

He Speaks:

⁴My dearest, the cities of Tirzah
and Jerusalem
are not as lovely as you.
Your charms are more powerful
than all of the stars
in the heavens.ᵖ
⁵Turn away your eyes—
they make me melt.
Your hair tosses about
as gracefully as goats
coming down from Gilead.
⁶Your teeth are whiter
than sheep freshly washed;
they match perfectly,
not one is missing.

⁷Behind your veil are hidden
beautiful rosy cheeks.ᑫ

⁸What if I could have
sixty queens, eighty wives,
and thousands of others!

*Romance is an element of
fascination and delight
that culminates in a deep
desire to experience all of
life with the one we love.*
COLLEEN TOWNSEND EVANS

⁹You would be my only choice,
my flawless dove,
the favorite child
of your mother.
The young women, the queens,
and all the others
tell how excited you are
as they sing your praises:
¹⁰"You are as majestic
as the morning sky—
glorious as the moon—
blinding as the sun!
Your charms are more powerful
than all the stars above."ʳ

She Speaks:

¹¹I went down to see if blossoms
were on the walnut trees,
grapevines, and fruit trees.
¹²But in my imagination
I was suddenly riding
on a glorious chariot.ˢ

Their Friends Speak:

¹³Dance! Dance!
Beautiful woman from Shulam,
let us see you dance!

ⁿ**5.12** *milk:* One possible meaning for the difficult Hebrew text of verse 12. ᵒ**5.14** *his . . . ivory:* One possible meaning for the difficult Hebrew text. ᵖ**6.4** *all . . . heavens:* Or "a mighty army ready for war." ᑫ**6.7** *cheeks:* One possible meaning for the difficult Hebrew text of verse 7. ʳ**6.10** *all . . . above:* Or "a mighty army ready for war." ˢ**6.12** *chariot:* One possible meaning for the difficult Hebrew text of verse 12.

She Speaks:

Why do you want to see
this woman from Shulam
dancing with the others?ᵗ

The Wedding Dance

He Speaks:

7 You are a princess,
  and your feet are graceful
    in their sandals.
Your thighs are works of art,
  each one a jewel;

*Marriage is one
of the best testing
grounds for living
out our faith.*

CLAUDIA ARP

²your navel is a wine glass
  filled to overflowing.
Your body is full and slender
like a bundle of wheat
  bound together by lilies.
³Your breasts are like twins
  of a deer.
⁴Your neck is like ivory,

and your eyes sparkle
like the pools of Heshbon
  by the gate of Bath-Rabbim.
Your nose is beautiful
like Mount Lebanon
  above the city of Damascus.
⁵Your head is held high
  like Mount Carmel;
your hair is so lovely
  it holds a king prisoner.ᵘ

⁶You are beautiful,
  so very desirable!
⁷You are tall and slender
  like a palm tree,
  and your breasts are full.
⁸I will climb that tree
  and cling to its branches.
I will discover that your breasts
  are clusters of grapes,
and that your breath
  is the aroma of apples.
⁹Kissing you is more delicious
  than drinking the finest wine.
  How wonderful and tasty!ᵛ

She Speaks:

¹⁰My darling, I am yours,
  and you desire me.

ᵗ**6.13** *dancing . . . others:* One possible meaning for the difficult Hebrew text. ᵘ**7.5** *it . . . prisoner:* One possible meaning for the difficult Hebrew text. ᵛ**7.9** *How . . . tasty:* One possible meaning for the difficult Hebrew text.

MARRIAGE—What does a healthy, successful marriage look like?
(Song of Songs 8.5-7)

It loves—forever.
Soap operas and certain popular songs make it sound as though love is nothing more than a fleeting feeling. Passion flares up, burns hotly for a short time, then it fades, only to be replaced by another temporary flare-up that also burns out.

But think about a truly great love story. If it's fictional, it outlives its author. If it's historical, it outlives the lovers themselves. The sort of love it describes is literally stronger than death—and that's the sort of love we all long for.

What makes love so lasting that it can be called "more powerful than death, stronger than the grave" (8.6)? Love lasts when it's rooted in the eternal God. When we understand God's eternal commitment to us, and when we make an eternal commitment to him, we can better understand strong and lasting human commitments. Then we can willingly promise to love forever and never trade our love for anything, because our love "cannot be bought, no matter what is offered" (8.7). (See also Genesis 2.18-23; Exodus 32.11-14; Hosea 14.4-8; Acts 18; Hebrews 13.4.)

Words To Remember: *The passion of love bursting into flame is more powerful than death, stronger than the grave.*—Song of Songs 8.6

¹¹ Let's stroll through the fields
    and sleep in the villages.
¹² At dawn let's slip out and see
    if grapevines and fruit trees
        are covered with blossoms.
When we are there,
    I will give you my love.
¹³ Perfume from the magic flower[w]
    fills the air, my darling.
Right at our doorstep
I have stored up for you
    all kinds of tasty fruits.

If Only You and I . . .

She Speaks:

8 If you were my brother,
    I could kiss you
whenever we happen to meet,
and no one would say
    I did wrong.
² I could take you to the home
of my mother,
    who taught me all I know.[x]
I would give you delicious wine
    and fruit juice as well.
³ Put your left hand under my head
and embrace me
    with your right arm.

⁴ Young women of Jerusalem,
promise me by the power

of deer and gazelles[y]
never to awaken love
    before it is ready.

Their Friends Speak:

⁵ Who is this young woman
    coming in from the desert
and leaning on the shoulder
    of the one she loves?

She Speaks:

I stirred up your passions
    under the apple tree
        where you were born.
⁶ Always keep me in your heart
    and wear this bracelet
        to remember me by.
The passion of love
    bursting into flame
is more powerful than death,
    stronger than the grave.
⁷ Love cannot be drowned
    by oceans or floods;
it cannot be bought,
    no matter what is offered.

---

[w]**7.13** *magic flower:* The Hebrew text has "mandrake," a plant that was thought to give sexual powers. [x]**8.2** *who . . . know:* One possible meaning for the difficult Hebrew text. [y]**8.4** *deer and gazelles:* See the note at 2.7.

PARENTING&*family*—How can I protect my kids from negative cultural influences? *(Song of Songs 8.8,9)*

Protect, but don't smother.
We want to protect our kids from negative cultural influences, but in this world there are no guarantees of safety. The only way to totally insulate our children from the world's values would be to shut them up in a soundproof room with no communication devices linked to the outside. What an ugly prospect! It's not only cruel, it's impractical—and it wouldn't work in the long run.

Still, we have a responsibility to act as our children's loving protectors. God gives parents a good sense of what children can handle emotionally. As much as possible, we should shelter them from early and inappropriate sexual knowledge, and certainly we must protect them from sexual contact. That's difficult when sexual imagery is used commercially to sell products and keep people watching the screen.

Children's natural curiosity is healthy, but they don't have to have immediate answers to everything they're curious about. We shield them not because we are repressed or inhibited about sexuality, but because we know that sex is for marriage partners and not children. (See also Ezra 8.21-34; Psalm 119.97-105; Proverbs 4.10-27; 1 Peter 5.2-11.)

Words To Remember: *She isn't a wall that we can defend behind a silver shield. Neither is she a room that we can protect behind a wooden door.*—Song of Songs 8.9

Their Friends Speak:

[8] We have a little sister
   whose breasts
      are not yet formed.
   If someone asks to marry her,
      what should we do?
[9] She isn't a wall
   that we can defend
      behind a silver shield.
   Neither is she a room
   that we can protect
      behind a wooden door.

She Speaks:

[10] I am a wall around a city,
      my breasts are towers,
   and just looking at me
      brings him great pleasure.
[11] Solomon has a vineyard

at Baal-Hamon,
   which he rents to others
   for a thousand pieces
      of silver each.
[12] My vineyard is mine alone!
   Solomon can keep his silver
   and the others can keep
      their share of the profits.

He Speaks:

[13] You are in the garden
   with friends all around.
      Let me hear your voice!

She Speaks:

[14] Hurry to me, my darling!
   Run faster than a deer
      to mountains of spices.

Isaiah
God's Care for His Rebellious Children

Sometimes the Christian life feels like a battle of wills: God's versus ours. We butt heads with God, trying to get our own way, asking (make that *telling*) God to lay out the future we desire. When God persists with his own plans, we cry out in frustration, anger, and pain. We wonder why God won't give us what we want.

Throughout history, God's children have pushed against, argued with, and flat out rejected God's plans for them. Despite God's repeated promise of a glorious future, the nation of Israel pursued its own path, only to be consistently reminded that God's path was much better.

It's this battle of wills that the prophet Isaiah recounts. Yet far from serving up a historical narrative detailing the many times the nation of Israel failed to follow God's plan for them, Isaiah offers a kind of free-form flashback, pointing out the patterns in Israel's behavior. In some ways, Isaiah's visions tell of God's history with Israel from God's eternal point of view. The book of Isaiah points to the tragic failures of the people of Israel (who are now reduced to the two southern tribes—the nation of Judah). But more important, Isaiah also points to God's unfailing mercy.

We can read Isaiah as a kind of reverse road map that shows us where we've been and helps us rethink where we're going. We can see that God's path has remained straight and his plans unchanged, no matter how far off the path his people have strayed. And because we can see evidence of God's faithfulness in the past, we can trust him to be just as faithful in the future.

Isaiah's prophetic visions came to him while he served four separate kings (1.1). His prophecies are directed primarily to Judah, but by the end of the book, his vision of God's grace grows to include people of all nations.

Isaiah at a Glance

1. A call to attention (1)
2. Big trouble for Judah and Israel (2–5)
3. High points in Isaiah's ministry (6.1—9.7)
4. Bad news and good news (9.8—12.6)
5. God's punishment (13–23)
6. A message of hope (24–27)
7. Punishment for those who rebel (28–31)
8. Punishment for Edom, blessings for Jerusalem (32–35)
9. Assyria enters the picture (36–39)
10. God rescues his people (40–48)
11. Isaiah's mission (49–53)
12. God's unfailing promises (54,55)
13. God welcomes his people back (56.1-8)
14. Leaders are especially guilty (56.9—59.21)
15. A glorious future (60–62)
16. God's wonderful new creation (63–66)

1 I am Isaiah, the son of Amoz. And this is the message*a* that I was given about Judah and Jerusalem when Uzziah, Jotham, Ahaz, and Hezekiah were the kings of Judah:*b*

A Guilty Nation

²The LORD has said,
"Listen, heaven and earth!
The children I raised
have turned against me.
³Oxen and donkeys know
who owns and feeds them,
but my people won't ever learn."

⁴Israel, you are a sinful nation
loaded down with guilt.
You are wicked and corrupt
and have turned from the LORD,
the holy God of Israel.
⁵Why be punished more?
Why not give up your sin?
Your head is badly bruised,
and you are weak all over.
⁶From your head to your toes
there isn't a healthy spot.
Bruises, cuts, and open sores
go without care
or oil to ease the pain.

A Country in Ruins

⁷Your country lies in ruins;
your towns are in ashes.
Foreigners and strangers
take and destroy your land
while you watch.
⁸Enemies surround Jerusalem,
alone like a hut in a vineyard*c*
or in a cucumber field.
⁹Zion would have disappeared
like Sodom and Gomorrah,*d*
if the LORD All-Powerful
had not let a few
of its people survive.

Justice, Not Sacrifices

¹⁰You are no better
than the leaders and people
of Sodom and Gomorrah!
So listen to the LORD God:
¹¹"Your sacrifices
mean nothing to me.
I am sick of your offerings
of rams and choice cattle;

I don't like the blood
of bulls or lambs or goats.
¹²"Who asked you to bring all this
when you come to worship me?
Stay out of my temple!
¹³Your sacrifices are worthless,
and incense is disgusting.
I can't stand the evil you do
on your New Moon Festivals
or on your Sabbaths
and other times of worship.
¹⁴I hate your New Moon Festivals
and all others as well.
They are a heavy burden
I am tired of carrying.

*While adding the word
<u>please</u> may be polite,
and ending my request with
"in Jesus' name" may sound
pious—neither phrase helps
if the thing I'm praying
for is less than divine.*

LIZ CURTIS HIGGS

¹⁵"No matter how much you pray,
I won't listen.
You are too violent.
¹⁶Wash yourselves clean!
I am disgusted
with your filthy deeds.
Stop doing wrong
¹⁷ and learn to live right.
See that justice is done.
Defend widows and orphans
and help those in need."*e*

---

*a*1.1 *message:* Or "vision."   *b*1.1 *kings of Judah:* Uzziah (783-742 B.C.); Jotham (742-735 B.C.); Ahaz (735-715 B.C.); Hezekiah (715-687 B.C.).   *c*1.8 *a hut in a vineyard:* When it was almost time for grapes to ripen, farmers would put up a temporary shelter or hut in the field or vineyard and stay there to keep thieves and wild animals away.   *d*1.9 *Sodom and Gomorrah:* Two ancient cities of Palestine that God destroyed because the people were so wicked (see Genesis 19.1-29).   *e*1.17 *and help those in need:* Or "and punish cruel people."

An Invitation from the LORD

¹⁸ I, the LORD, invite you
  to come and talk it over.
Your sins are scarlet red,
but they will be whiter
  than snow or wool.
¹⁹ If you willingly obey me,
  the best crops in the land
  will be yours.
²⁰ But if you turn against me,
  your enemies will kill you.
  I, the LORD, have spoken.

The LORD Condemns Jerusalem

²¹ Jerusalem, you are like
  an unfaithful wife.
Once your judges were honest
  and your people lived right;
now you are a city
  full of murderers.
²² Your silver is fake,
  and your wine
  is watered down.
²³ Your leaders have rejected me
  to become friends of crooks;
your rulers are looking
  for gifts and bribes.
Widows and orphans
  never get a fair trial.

²⁴ I am the LORD All-Powerful,
  the mighty ruler of Israel,
  and I make you a promise:
You are now my enemy,
and I will show my anger
  by taking revenge on you.
²⁵ I will punish you terribly
  and burn away everything
that makes you unfit
  to worship me.
²⁶ Jerusalem, I will choose
  judges and advisors
  like those you had before.
Your new name will be
  "Justice and Faithfulness."

The LORD Will Save Jerusalem

²⁷ Jerusalem, you will be saved
  by showing justice;^f
Zion's people who turn to me
  will be saved
by doing right.
²⁸ But those rebellious sinners
  who turn against me, the LORD,
  will all disappear.

²⁹ You will be made ashamed
  of those groves of trees
  where you worshiped idols.
³⁰ You will be like a grove of trees
  dying in a drought.
³¹ Your strongest leaders
  will be like dry wood
  set on fire by their idols.^g
No one will be able to help,
  as they all go up in flames.

Peace That Lasts Forever

2 This is the message^h that I was given
about Judah and Jerusalem:

² In the future, the mountain
with the LORD's temple
  will be the highest of all.
It will reach above the hills;
  every nation will rush to it.
³ Many people will come and say,
  "Let's go to the mountain
of the LORD God of Jacob
  and worship in his temple."

---

*As we seek God's peace
and ask his help in setting
our mind on "things above"—
no matter what the world
may be throwing at us—
we may be able to say,
echoing the apostle Paul,
"I am learning to be content
in every circumstance."*

ELIZABETH CODY NEWENHUYSE

The LORD will teach us his Law
from Jerusalem,
  and we will obey him.
⁴ He will settle arguments
  between nations.

---

^f**1.27** *by showing justice:* Or "by my saving power."
^g**1.31** *Your . . . idols:* Or "Your wealth will be like dry
wood, set on fire by its owners."   ^h**2.1** *message:* See the
note at 1.1.

They will pound their swords
and their spears
    into rakes and shovels;
they will never make war
    or attack one another.
⁵People of Israel, let's live
    by the light of the LORD.

Following Sinful Customs

⁶Our LORD, you have deserted
    your people, Israel,
because they follow customs
    of nations from the east.
They worship Philistine gods
and are close friends
    of foreigners.ⁱ
⁷They have endless treasures
    of silver and gold;
they have countless horses
    and war chariots.
⁸Everywhere in the country
they worship the idols
    they have made.
⁹And so, all of them
will be ashamed and disgraced.
    Don't help them!

A Day of Judgment

¹⁰Every one of you,
    go hide among the rocks
    and in the ground,
because the LORD is fearsome,
    marvelous, and glorious.
¹¹When the LORD comes,
everyone who is proud
    will be made humble,
and the LORD alone
    will be honored.
¹²The LORD All-Powerful
    has chosen a day
when those who are proud
and conceited
    will be put down.

¹³The tall and towering
cedars of Lebanon
    will be destroyed.
So will the oak trees of Bashan,
¹⁴all high mountains and hills,
¹⁵   every strong fortress,
¹⁶all the seagoing ships,ʲ
    and every beautiful boat.
¹⁷When that day comes,
everyone who is proud
    will be put down.

Only the LORD will be honored.
¹⁸   Idols will be gone for good.

¹⁹You had better hide
    in caves and holes—
the LORD will be fearsome,
    marvelous, and glorious
when he comes to terrify
    people on earth.

²⁰On that day everyone will throw
    to the rats and bats
their idols of silver and gold
    they made to worship.
²¹The LORD will be fearsome,
    marvelous, and glorious
when he comes to terrify
    people on earth—
they will hide in caves
    and in the hills.

²²Stop trusting the power
    of humans.
They are all going to die,
    so how can they help?

Judgment on Jerusalem and Judah

3 The mighty LORD All-Powerful
is going to take away
    from Jerusalem and Judah
everything you need—
    your bread and water,
²soldiers and heroes,
    judges and prophets,
    leaders and army officers,
³officials and advisors,
fortunetellers and others
    who tell the future.
⁴He will let children and babiesᵏ
    become your rulers.
⁵You will each be cruel
    to friends and neighbors.
Young people will insult
    their elders;
no one will show respect
    to those who deserve it.

⁶Some of you will grab hold
    of a relative and say,

ⁱ**2.6** *because . . . foreigners*: One possible meaning for the difficult Hebrew text. ʲ**2.16** *seagoing ships*: The Hebrew text has "ships of Tarshish," which may have been a Phoenician city in Spain. "Ships of Tarshish" probably means large, seagoing ships. ᵏ**3.4** *babies*: Or "worthless nobodies."

"You still have a coat.
Be our leader and rule
　this pile of ruins."
7 But the answer will be,
"I can't do you any good.
　Don't make me your leader.
There's no food or clothing
left in my house."

8 Jerusalem and Judah,
you rebelled against
　your glorious LORD—
your words and your actions,
　made you stumble and fall.
9 The look on your faces shows
that you are sinful as Sodom,
　and you don't try to hide it.
You are in for trouble,
and you have brought it all
on yourselves.

The Wrong Kind of Leaders

10 Tell those who obey God,
"You're very fortunate—
　you will be rewarded
　for what you have done."
11 Tell those who disobey,
"You're in big trouble—
　what you did to others
　will come back to you."
12 Though you are God's people,
you are ruled and abused
　by women and children.
You are confused by leaders
who guide you
　down the wrong path.

13 The LORD is ready to accuse
and judge all nations.
14 He will even judge
you rulers and leaders
of his own nation.
You destroyed his vineyard[l]
and filled your houses
by robbing the poor.
15 The LORD All-Powerful says,
"You have crushed my people
and rubbed in the dirt
the faces of the poor."

The Women of Jerusalem

16 The LORD says:
The women of Jerusalem
are proud and strut around,
winking shamelessly.

They wear anklets that jingle
and call attention
to the way they walk.
17 But I, the LORD, will cover
their heads with sores,
and I will uncover
their private parts.

18-23 When that day comes, I will take away from those women all the fine jewelry they wear on their ankles, heads, necks, ears, arms, noses, fingers, and on their clothes. I will remove their veils, their belts, their perfume, their magic charms, their royal robes, and all their fancy dresses, hats, and purses.

24 In place of perfume,
there will be a stink;
in place of belts,
there will be ropes;
in place of fancy hairdos,
they will have bald heads.
Instead of expensive clothes,
they will wear sackcloth;
instead of beauty,
they will have ugly scars.
25 The fighting men of Jerusalem
will be killed in battle.
26 The city will mourn
and sit in the dirt,
emptied of its people.

4 When this happens, seven women will grab the same man, and each of them will say, "I'll buy my own food and clothes! Just marry me and take away my disgrace."[m]

The LORD Will Bless His People Who Survive

2 The time is coming when the LORD will make his land fruitful and glorious again, and the people of Israel who survive will take great pride in what the land produces. 3 Everyone who is left alive in Jerusalem will be called special, 4 after the LORD sends a fiery judgment to clean the city and its people of their violent deeds. 5 Then the LORD will cover the whole city

---

l 3.14 his vineyard: The nation Israel (see 5.1-7).
m 4.1 take away my disgrace: If a woman did not have a husband or children, it was thought that God was punishing her.

and its meeting places with a thick cloud each day and with a flaming fire[n] each night. God's own glory will be like a huge tent that covers everything. [6]It will provide shade from the heat of the sun and a place of shelter and protection from storms and rain.

Nothing slows things down more than spending time with the Author of Peace.

SARA DuBOSE AND
DENISE TURNER

A Song about a Vineyard

The LORD said:

5 I will sing a song
about my friend's vineyard
that was on the side
of a fertile hill.
[2] My friend dug the ground,
removed the stones,
and planted the best vines.
He built a watchtower
and dug a pit in rocky ground
for pressing the grapes.
He hoped they would be sweet,
but bitter grapes
were all it produced.

[3] Listen, people of Jerusalem
and of Judah!
You be the judge of me
and my vineyard.
[4] What more could I have done
for my vineyard?
I hoped for sweet grapes,
but bitter grapes
were all that grew.

[5] Now I will let you know
what I am going to do.
I will cut down the hedge
and tear down the wall.
My vineyard will be trampled
and left in ruins.
[6] It will turn into a desert,
neither pruned nor hoed;

it will be covered
with thorns and briars.
I will command the clouds
not to send rain.

[7] I am the LORD All-Powerful!
Israel is the vineyard,
and Judah is the garden
I tended with care.
I had hoped for honesty
and for justice,
but dishonesty
and cries for mercy
were all I found.

Isaiah Condemns Social Injustice

[8]You are in for trouble! You take over house after house and field after field, until there is no room left for anyone else in all the land. [9]But the LORD All-Powerful has made this promise to me:
Those large and beautiful homes will be left empty, with no one to take care of them. [10]Ten acres of grapevines will produce only six gallons of juice, and five bushels of seed will produce merely a half-bushel of grain.
[11]You are in for trouble! You get up early to start drinking, and you keep it up late into the night. [12]At your drinking parties you have the music of stringed instruments, tambourines, and flutes. But you never even think about all the LORD has done, [13]and so his people know nothing about him. That's why many of you will be dragged off to foreign lands. Your leaders will starve to death, and everyone else will suffer from thirst.
[14]The world of the dead has opened its mouth wide and is eagerly waiting for the leaders of Jerusalem and for its noisy crowds, especially for those who take pride in that city. [15]Its citizens have been put down, and its proud people have been brought to shame. [16]But the holy LORD God All-Powerful is praised, because he has shown who he is by bringing justice. [17]His people will be like sheep grazing in their own pasture, and they will take off what was left by others.[o]

---

[n]4.5 *thick . . . fire*: This is how the LORD led the people of Israel during the forty years they were in the desert (see Exodus 13.20-22; 40.36-38). [o]5.17 *and they . . . others*: One possible meaning for the difficult Hebrew text.

¹⁸You are in for trouble! The lies you tell are like ropes by which you drag along sin and evil. ¹⁹And you say, "Let the holy God of Israel hurry up and do what he has promised, so we can see it for ourselves." ²⁰You are headed for trouble! You say wrong is right, darkness is light, and bitter is sweet. ²¹You think you are clever and smart. ²²And you are great at drinking and mixing drinks. But you are in for trouble. ²³You accept bribes to let the guilty go free, and you cheat the innocent out of a fair trial.

²⁴You will go up in flames like straw and hay! You have rejected the teaching of the holy LORD God All-Powerful of Israel. Now your roots will rot, and your blossoms will turn to dust.

²⁵You are the LORD's people, but you made him terribly angry, and he struck you with his mighty arm. Mountains shook, and dead bodies covered the streets like garbage. The LORD is still angry, and he is ready to strike you again.ᵖ

Foreign Nations Will Attack

²⁶The LORD has signaled for the foreign nations to come and attack you. He has already whistled, and they are coming as fast as they can. ²⁷None of them are tired. They don't sleep or get drowsy, and they run without stumbling. Their belts don't come loose; their sandal straps don't break. ²⁸Their arrows are sharp, and their bows are ready. The hoofs of their horses are hard as flint; the wheels of their war chariots turn as fast as a whirlwind.

²⁹They roar and growl like fierce young lions as they grab their victims and drag them off where no one can rescue them. ³⁰On the day they attack, they will roar like the ocean. And across the land you will see nothing but darkness and trouble, because the light of day will be covered by thick clouds.

A Vision of the LORD in the Temple

6 In the year that King Uzziah died,�q I had a vision of the LORD. He was on his throne high above, and his robe filled the temple. ²Flaming creatures with six wings each were flying over him. They covered their faces with two of their wings and their bodies with two more. They used the other two wings for flying, ³as they shouted,

"Holy, holy, holy,
   LORD All-Powerful!
The earth is filled
   with your glory."

⁴As they shouted, the doorposts of the temple shook, and the temple was filled with smoke. ⁵Then I cried out, "I'm doomed! Everything I say is sinful, and so are the words of everyone around me. Yet I have seen the King, the LORD All-Powerful."

> *God has done, and is doing, awesome things, and I want to inspire people to open their life to him and say, "Lord, I'm your servant. Just take me wherever you want me to go." I know he'll do it.*
>
> KARYN HENLEY

⁶One of the flaming creatures flew over to me with a burning coal that it had taken from the altar with a pair of metal tongs. ⁷It touched my lips with the hot coal and said, "This has touched your lips. Your sins are forgiven, and you are no longer guilty."

⁸After this, I heard the LORD ask, "Is there anyone I can send? Will someone go for us?"

"I'll go," I answered. "Send me!"

⁹Then the LORD told me to go and speak this message to the people:

"You will listen and listen,
   but never understand.
You will look and look,
   but never see."

The LORD also said,

¹⁰ "Make these people stubborn!
   Make them stop up
      their ears,

ᵖ**5.25** *is ready . . . again:* Or "hasn't given up on you yet."
�q**6.1** *the year that King Uzziah died:* Probably 742 B.C.

cover their eyes,
  and fail to understand.
Don't let them turn to me
  and be healed."

[11]Then I asked the LORD, "How long will this last?"

The LORD answered:

Until their towns are destroyed and their houses are deserted, until their fields are empty, [12]and I have sent them far away, leaving their land in ruins. [13]If only a tenth of the people are left, even they will be destroyed. But just as stumps remain after trees have been cut down,[r] some of my chosen ones will be left.

Isaiah Offers Hope to King Ahaz

7 Ahaz, the son of Jotham and the grandson of Uzziah, was king of Judah when King Rezin of Syria and King Pekah son of Remaliah of Israel went to attack Jerusalem. But they were not able to do what they had planned.[s] [2]When news reached the royal palace that Syria had joined forces with Israel, King Ahaz and everyone in Judah were so terrified that they shook like trees in a windstorm.

[3]Then the LORD said to me:

Take your son Shearjashub[t] and go see King Ahaz. You will find him on the road near the cloth makers' shops at the end of the canal that brings wa-

ter from the upper pool. [4]Tell Ahaz to stop worrying. There's no need for him to be afraid of King Rezin and King Pekah. They are very angry, but they are nothing more than a dying fire. Ahaz doesn't need to fear [5]their evil threats [6]to invade and defeat Judah and Jerusalem and to let the son of Tabeel be king in his place.

[7]I, the LORD, promise that this will never happen. [8-9]Damascus is just the capital of Syria, and King Rezin rules only in Damascus. Samaria is just the capital of Israel, and King Pekah rules only in Samaria. But in less than sixty-five years, Israel will be destroyed. And if Ahaz and his officials don't trust me, they will be defeated.

A Son Named Immanuel

[10]Once again the LORD God spoke to King Ahaz. This time he said, [11]"Ask me for proof that my promise will come true. Ask for something to happen deep in the world of the dead or high in the heavens above."

[12]"No, LORD," Ahaz answered. "I won't test you!"

[13]Then I said:

---

[r]6.13 *But just . . . down*: One possible meaning for the difficult Hebrew text.   [s]7.1 *went . . . had planned*: Or "attacked Jerusalem, but could not capture it."   [t]7.3 *Shearjashub*: In Hebrew "Shearjashub" means "a few will return."

Friendship—How can I show my friend that Christ is the only way to God?
(Isaiah 7.10-17)

Tell her Christ is the promised Savior.

We can read the Old Testament in a lot of different ways. We can see it as a history lesson, a collection of amazing adventure stories, or a warning of just how bad things can get when we ignore God and do our own thing. But every once in a while, the Old Testament points to something else, something far in the future of that time: the birth of Jesus Christ.

Hundreds, even thousands of years before Mary and Joseph wandered into that cold stable in Bethlehem, God hinted through prophecies at the arrival of the Savior. As he watched his people reject him again and again, God knew he'd need to take a dramatic step to convince them that he, and he alone, was their God, their only hope for eternal life. So in Isaiah he told them about the greatest miracle the world would ever see: A virgin would give birth to the Son of God who would save the people from their sins. This amazing prophecy—unique to Christianity alone—was fulfilled in the birth and death of Christ. (See also Isaiah 53; Mark 16.1-8; John 14.1-14.)

Words To Remember: *But the LORD will still give you proof. A virgin is pregnant; she will have a son and will name him Immanuel.*—Isaiah 7.14

Listen, every one of you in the royal family of David. You have already tried my patience. Now you are trying God's patience by refusing to ask for proof. [14]But the LORD will still give you proof. A virgin[u] is pregnant; she will have a son and will name him Immanuel.[v] [15-16]Even before the boy is old enough to know how to choose between right and wrong, he will eat yogurt and honey,[w] and the countries of the two kings you fear will be destroyed. [17]But the LORD will make more trouble for your people and your kingdom than any of you have known since Israel broke away from Judah. He will even bring the king of Assyria to attack you.

The Threat of an Invasion

[18]When that time comes, the LORD will whistle, and armies will come from Egypt like flies and from Assyria like bees. [19]They will settle everywhere—in the deep valleys and between the rocks, on every bush and all over the pastureland.

[20]The Lord will pay the king of Assyria to bring a razor from across the Euphrates River and shave your head and every hair on your body, including your beard.[x]

[21]No one will have more than one young cow and two sheep, [22]but those who do will have enough milk to make yogurt. In fact, everyone left in the land will eat yogurt and honey.[y]

[23]Vineyards that had a thousand vines and were worth a thousand pieces of silver will turn into thorn patches. [24]You will go there to hunt with your bow and arrows, because the whole country will be covered with thornbushes. [25]The hills where you once planted crops will be overgrown with thorns and thistles. You will be afraid to go there, and your cattle, sheep, and goats will be turned loose on those hills.

A Warning and a Hope

8 The LORD said, "Isaiah, get something to write on. Then write in big clear letters[z] the name, MAHER-SHALAL-HASH-BAZ.[a] [2]I will have Uriah the priest

and Zechariah son of Jeberechiah serve as witnesses to this."

[3]Sometime later, my wife and I had a son, and the LORD said, "Name him Maher-Shalal-Hash-Baz. [4]Because before he can say 'Mommy' or 'Daddy', the king of Assyria will attack and take everything of value from Damascus and Samaria."

[5]The LORD spoke to me again and said:

[6]These people have refused the gentle waters of Shiloah[b] and have gladly gone over to the side of King Rezin and King Pekah. [7]Now I will send the king of Assyria against them with his powerful army, which will attack like the mighty Euphrates River overflowing its banks. [8]Enemy soldiers will cover Judah like a flood reaching up to your neck.

But God is with us.[c]
He will spread his wings
    and protect our land.[d]
[9]All of you foreign nations,
    go ahead and prepare for war,
        but you will be crushed.
[10]Get together and make plans,
    but you will fail
        because God is with us.

[11]The LORD took hold of me with his powerful hand and said:

I'm warning you! Don't act like these people. [12]Don't call something a rebellious plot, just because they do,

---

[u]**7.14** *virgin*: Or "young woman." In this context the difficult Hebrew word did not imply a virgin birth. However, in the Greek translation made about 200 B.C. and used by the early Christians, the word *parthenos* had a double meaning. While the translator took it to mean "young woman," Matthew understood it to mean "virgin" and quoted the passage (Matthew 1.23) because it was the appropriate description of Mary, the mother of Jesus. [v]**7.14** *Immanuel*: In Hebrew "Immanuel" means "God is with us." [w]**7.15,16** *yogurt and honey*: This may refer either to expensive foods eaten in a time of plenty or to a limited diet eaten in times of a food shortage. [x]**7.20** *shave . . . head . . . body . . . beard*: This would have been a terrible insult. [y]**7.22** *yogurt and honey*: See the note at 7.15, 16. [z]**8.1** *in big clear letters*: One possible meaning for the difficult Hebrew text. [a]**8.1** *MAHER-SHALAL-HASH-BAZ*: In Hebrew "Maher-Shalal-Hash-Baz" means "suddenly attacked, quickly taken." [b]**8.6** *Shiloah*: The canal that brought water from Gihon Spring to Jerusalem. [c]**8.8** *God is with us*: Here and in verse 10 this translates the Hebrew word "Immanuel" (see 7.14). [d]**8.8** *But . . . land*: One possible meaning for the difficult Hebrew text.

and don't be afraid of something, just because they are. [13]I am the one you should fear and respect. I am the holy God, the LORD All-Powerful! [14-15]Run to me for protection. I am a rock that will make both Judah and Israel stumble and break their bones. I am a trap that will catch the people of Jerusalem—they will be captured and dragged away.

Isaiah and His Followers

[16]My message and my teachings are to be sealed and given to my followers. [17]Meanwhile, I patiently trust the LORD, even though he is no longer pleased with Israel. [18]My children and I are warning signs to Israel from the LORD All-Powerful, who lives on Mount Zion.

[19]Someone may say to you, "Go to the fortunetellers who make soft chirping sounds or ask the spirits of the dead. After all, a nation ought to be able to ask its own gods [20]what it should do."

None of those who talk like that will live to see the light of day! [21]They will go around in great pain and will become so hungry that they will angrily curse their king and their gods. And when they try to find help in heaven [22]and on earth, they will find only trouble and darkness, terrible trouble and deepest darkness.

9 But those who have suffered will no longer be in pain.[e] The territories of Zebulun and Naphtali in Galilee were once hated. But this land of the Gentiles across the Jordan River and along the Mediterranean Sea will be greatly respected.

War Is Over

[2]Those who walked in the dark
have seen a bright light.
And it shines upon everyone
who lives in the land
of darkest shadows.
[3]Our LORD, you have made
your nation stronger.[f]
Because of you, its people
are glad and celebrate
like workers at harvest time
or like soldiers dividing up
what they have taken.

[4]You have broken the power
of those who abused
and enslaved your people.

You have rescued them
just as you saved your people
from Midian.[g]
[5]The boots of marching warriors
and the blood-stained uniforms
have been fed to flames
and eaten by fire.

A Child Has Been Born

[6]A child has been born for us.
We have been given a son
who will be our ruler.
His names will be
Wonderful Advisor
and Mighty God,
Eternal Father
and Prince of Peace.

Because of what Jesus did on the cross for us, we can talk to our heavenly Father as naturally as we talk to a good friend.

SANDRA P. ALDRICH

[7]His power will never end;
peace will last forever.
He will rule David's kingdom
and make it grow strong.
He will always rule
with honesty and justice.
The LORD All-Powerful
will make certain
that all of this is done.

God Will Punish Israel

[8]The Lord had warned the people of Israel, [9]and all of them knew it, including everyone in the capital city of Samaria. But they were proud and stubborn and said,

[10] "Houses of brick and sycamore
have fallen to the ground,

---

[e]**9.1** *will . . . pain:* One possible meaning for the difficult Hebrew text. [f]**9.3** *stronger:* Or "happy" or "larger." [g]**9.4** *rescued . . . from Midian:* The time when Gideon defeated the people of Midian in Jezreel Valley (see Judges 6–8).

but we will build houses
with stones and cedar."

[11]The LORD made their enemies[h] attack them. [12]He sent the Arameans from the east and the Philistines from the west, and they swallowed up Israel. But even this did not stop him from being angry, so he kept on punishing them.[i] [13]The people of Israel still did not turn back to the LORD All-Powerful and worship him.

[14]In one day he cut off their head and tail, their leaves and branches. [15]Their rulers and leaders were the head, and the lying prophets were the tail. [16]They had led the nation down the wrong path, and the people were confused. [17]The Lord was angry with his people and kept punishing them, because they had turned against him.[j] They were evil and spoke foolishly. That's why he did not have pity on their young people or on their widows and orphans.

[18]Evil had spread like a raging forest fire sending thornbushes up in smoke. [19]The LORD All-Powerful was angry and used the people as fuel for a fire that scorched the land. They turned against each other [20]like wild animals attacking and eating everyone around them, even their own relatives.[k] But still they were not satisfied. [21]The tribes of Ephraim and Manasseh turned against each other, then joined forces to attack Judah. But the LORD was still angry and ready to punish the nation even more.

10 You people are in for trouble! You have made cruel and unfair laws [2]that let you cheat the poor and needy and rob widows and orphans. [3]But what will you do when you are fiercely attacked and punished by foreigners? Where will you run for help? Where will you hide your valuables? [4]How will you escape being captured[l] or killed? The Lord is still angry, and he isn't through with you yet![m]

The Lord's Purpose and the King of Assyria

[5]The Lord says:
I am furious! And I will use the king of Assyria[n] as a club [6]to beat down you godless people. I am angry with you, and I will send him to attack you. He will take what he wants and walk on you like mud in the streets. [7]He has even bigger plans in mind, because he wants to destroy many nations.

[8]The king of Assyria says:
My army commanders are kings! [9]They have already captured[o] the cities of Calno, Carchemish, Hamath, Arpad, Samaria, and Damascus. [10-11]The gods of Jerusalem and Samaria are weaker than the gods of those powerful nations. And I will destroy Jerusalem, together with its gods and idols, just as I did Samaria.

[12]The Lord will do what he has planned against Jerusalem and Mount Zion. Then he will punish the proud and boastful king of Assyria, [13]who says:
I did these things by my own power because I am smart and clever. I attacked kings like a wild bull, and I took the land and the treasures of their nations. [14]I have conquered the whole world! And it was easier than taking eggs from an unguarded nest. No one even flapped a wing or made a peep.

[15]King of Assyria, can an ax or a saw overpower the one who uses it? Can a wooden pole lift whoever holds it? [16]The mighty LORD All-Powerful will send a terrible disease to strike down your army, and you will burn with fever under your royal robes. [17]The holy God, who is the light of Israel, will turn into a fire, and in one day you will go up in flames, just like a thornbush. [18]The Lord will make your beautiful forests and fertile fields slowly rot. [19]There will be so few trees that even a young child can count them.

Only a Few Will Come Back

[20]A time is coming when the survivors from Israel and Judah will completely depend on the holy LORD of Israel, instead of the nation[p] that defeated them. [21-22]There

---

[h]**9.11** *their enemies*: Hebrew "the enemies of Rezin." [i]**9.12** *so . . . them*: Or "but he hasn't given up on them yet." [j]**9.17** *and kept . . . against him*: Or "but even though they had turned against him, he still had not given up on them." [k]**9.20** *their own relatives*: One possible meaning for the difficult Hebrew text. [l]**10.4** *escape being captured*: One possible meaning for the difficult Hebrew text. [m]**10.4** *and he . . . yet*: Or "but he hasn't given up on you yet!" [n]**10.5** *king of Assyria*: Probably King Sennacherib who invaded Israel in 701 B.C. [o]**10.9** *already captured*: Calno (in northern Syria), Carchemish (on the Euphrates River), Hamath (on the Orontes River), Arpad (near Aleppo in northern Syria), Samaria, and Damascus had already been captured by Assyrian kings (738-717 B.C.). [p]**10.20** *nation*: That is, Assyria.

were as many people as there are grains of sand along the seashore, but only a few will survive to come back to Israel's mighty God. This is because he has threatened to destroy their nation, just as they deserve. [23]The LORD All-Powerful has promised that everyone on this earth[q] will be punished.

[24]Now the LORD God All-Powerful says to his people in Jerusalem:

The Assyrians will beat you with sticks and abuse you, just as the Egyptians did. But don't be afraid of them. [25]Soon I will stop being angry with you, and I will punish them for their crimes.[r] [26]I will beat the Assyrians with a whip, as I did the people of Midian near the rock at Oreb. And I will show the same mighty power that I used when I made a path through the sea in Egypt. [27]Then they will no longer rule your nation. All will go well for you,[s] and your burden will be lifted.

[28]Enemy troops have reached the town of Aiath.[t] They have gone through Migron, and they stored their supplies at Michmash, [29]before crossing the valley and spending the night at Geba.[u] The people of Ramah are terrified; everyone in Gibeah, the hometown of Saul, has run away. [30]Loud crying can be heard in the towns of Gallim, Laishah, and sorrowful Anathoth. [31]No one is left in Madmenah or Gebim. [32]Today the enemy will camp at Nob[v] and shake a threatening fist at Mount Zion in Jerusalem.

[33]But the LORD All-Powerful
will use his fearsome might
to bring down the tallest trees
and chop off every branch.
[34]With an ax, the glorious Lord
will destroy every tree
in the forests of Lebanon.[w]

Peace at Last

11 Like a branch that sprouts
from a stump,
someone from David's family[x]
will someday be king.

---

[q]10.23 *on this earth:* Or "in this land."
[r]10.25 *punish . . . crimes:* Or "completely destroy them." [s]10.27 *All . . . you:* One possible meaning for the difficult Hebrew text. [t]10.28 *Aiath:* Probably Ai (Joshua 7.2). [u]10.29 *Geba:* Only six miles from Jerusalem. [v]10.32 *Nob:* Perhaps within two miles of Jerusalem. [w]10.34 *Lebanon:* One possible meaning for the difficult Hebrew text of verse 34. [x]11.1 *David's family:* Hebrew "Jesse's family." Jesse was the father of King David.

WORK—Sometimes my male colleagues don't take me seriously. How can a Christian woman be assertive at work without being offensive? *(Isaiah 11.1-9)*

Learn to lead.

It's not easy being a Christian woman in the workplace. We get so many messages: *Be strong. Be soft. Be tough. Be tender. Be aggressive. Be passive.* Ironically, we sometimes use our faith as an excuse for sitting quietly on the sidelines while letting the men around us make all the "important" decisions. No wonder we have a hard time finding a comfortable niche in the working world!

But the Bible doesn't ask women to be doormats. Instead, the Bible paints a picture of a future world where enemies are friends and the weak and the strong live together peacefully (11.6,7). We can model that kind of world right now in the way we live. By standing apart from the competitive hierarchy common in business, we are free to be truly equal, showing integrity and courage in everything we do. As working women that means we don't have to hide our talents or keep our great ideas to ourselves. In fact, this passage in Isaiah pictures a kind of leadership based on "understanding, wisdom, and insight" (11.2)—traits that come naturally for many women.

So let your gifts shine through. Not only will you surprise your male colleagues, you might just surprise yourself. (See also Genesis 50.15-21; Judges 4.4-15; Ephesians 5.6-21.)

Words To Remember: *The Spirit of the LORD will be with him to give him understanding, wisdom, and insight. He will be powerful, and he will know and honor the LORD.*—Isaiah 11.2

² The Spirit of the LORD
    will be with him
to give him understanding,
    wisdom, and insight.
He will be powerful,
    and he will know
    and honor the LORD.
³ His greatest joy will be
    to obey the LORD.

This king won't judge
by appearances
    or listen to rumors.
⁴ The poor and the needy
will be treated with fairness
    and with justice.
His word will be law
    everywhere in the land,
and criminals
    will be put to death.
⁵ Honesty and fairness
    will be his royal robes.

⁶ Leopards will lie down
    with young goats,
and wolves will rest
    with lambs.
Calves and lions
    will eat together
and be cared for
    by little children.
⁷ Cows and bears will share
    the same pasture;
their young will rest
    side by side.
Lions and oxen
    will both eat straw.

⁸ Little children will play
    near snake holes.
They will stick their hands
into dens of poisonous snakes
    and never be hurt.

⁹ Nothing harmful will take place
    on the LORD's holy mountain.
Just as water fills the sea,
    the land will be filled
with people who know
    and honor the LORD.

God's People Will Come Back Home

¹⁰ The time is coming when one of David's descendants[y] will be the signal for the people of all nations to come together.

They will follow his advice, and his own nation will become famous.

¹¹ When that day comes, the Lord will again reach out his mighty arm and bring home his people who have survived in Assyria, Egypt, Pathros, Ethiopia,[z] Elam, Shinar, Hamath, and the land along the coast.[a] ¹²He will give a signal to the nations, and he will bring together the refugees from Judah and Israel, who have been scattered all over the earth. ¹³Israel will stop being jealous of Judah, and Judah will no longer be the enemy of Israel. ¹⁴Instead, they will get together and attack the Philistines in the west. Then they will defeat the Edomites, the Moabites, and the Ammonites in the east. They will rule those people and take from them whatever they want.

¹⁵The Lord will dry up the arm of the Red Sea near Egypt,[b] and he will send a scorching wind to divide the Euphrates River into seven streams that anyone can step across. ¹⁶Then for his people who survive, there will be a good road from Assyria, just as there was a good road for their ancestors when they left Egypt.

A Song of Praise

12 At that time you will say,
    "I thank you, LORD!
    You were angry with me,
but you stopped being angry
    and gave me comfort.
² I trust you to save me,
LORD God,
    and I won't be afraid.
My power and my strength[c]
come from you,
    and you have saved me."

³ With great joy, you people
will get water
    from the well of victory.
⁴ At that time you will say,
"Our LORD, we are thankful,
    and we worship only you.
We will tell the nations

---

how glorious you are
and what you have done.
⁵Because of your wonderful deeds
we will sing your praises
everywhere on earth."

*Blessed are the glad-hearted
servants who shine with the
Master's joy and praise him!*

BARBARA JOHNSON

⁶Sing, people of Zion!
Celebrate the greatness
of the holy LORD of Israel.
God is here to help you.

Babylon Will Be Punished

13 This is the message*d* that I was
given about Babylon:

²From high on a barren hill
give a signal, shout the orders,
and point the way
to enter the gates
of Babylon's proud rulers.
³The LORD has commanded
his very best warriors
and his proud heroes
to show how angry he is.

⁴Listen to the noisy crowds
on the mountains!
Kingdoms and nations
are joining forces.
The LORD All-Powerful
is bringing together
an army for battle.
⁵From a distant land
the LORD is coming
fierce and furious—
he brings his weapons
to destroy the earth.

⁶Cry and weep!
The day is coming
when the mighty LORD
will bring destruction.
*⁷All people will be terrified.

Hands will grow limp;
courage will melt away.
⁸Everyone will tremble with pain
like a woman giving birth;
they will stare at each other
with horror on their faces.

There Will Be No Mercy

⁹I, the LORD,
will show no mercy or pity
when that time comes.
In my anger I will destroy
the earth and every sinner
who lives on it.
¹⁰Light will disappear
from the stars in the sky;
the dawning sun will turn dark,
and the moon
will lose its glow.

¹¹I will punish this evil world
and its people
because of their sins.
I will crush the horrible pride
of those who are cruel.
¹²Survivors will be harder to find
than the purest gold.
¹³I, the LORD All-Powerful,
am terribly angry—
I will make the sky tremble
and the earth shake loose.

¹⁴Everyone will run
to their homelands,
just as hunted deer run,
and sheep scatter
when they have no shepherd.
¹⁵Those who are captured
will be killed by a sword.
¹⁶They will see their children
beaten against rocks,
their homes robbed,
and their wives abused.

¹⁷The Medes*e* can't be bought off
with silver or gold,
and I'm sending them
to attack Babylonia.
¹⁸Their arrows will slaughter
the young men;

---

*d*13.1 *message:* See the note at 1.1.   *e*13.17 *Medes:*
People of a nation northeast of Babylonia, which
became part of the Persian Empire.

no pity will be shown
    to babies and children.

The LORD Will Destroy Babylon

19 The city of Babylon
  is glorious and powerful,
    the pride of the nation.
But it will be like the cities
  of Sodom and Gomorrah
after I, the Lord,
    destroyed them.
20 No one will live in Babylon.
Even nomads won't camp nearby,
  and shepherds won't let
    their sheep rest there.
21 Only desert creatures,
  hoot owls, and ostriches
will live in its ruins,
    and goats[j] will leap about.
22 Hyenas and wolves will howl
from Babylon's fortresses
  and beautiful palaces.
Its time is almost up!

The LORD's People Will Come Home

14 The LORD will have mercy on Israel and will let them be his chosen people once again. He will bring them back to their own land, and foreigners will join them as part of Israel. 2 Other nations will lead them home, and Israel will make slaves of them in the land that belongs to the Lord. Israel will rule over those who once governed and mistreated them.

Death to the King of Babylonia!

3 The LORD will set you free from your sorrow, suffering, and slavery. 4 Then you will make fun of the King of Babylonia by singing this song:

That cruel monster is done for!
  He won't attack us again.[g]
5 The LORD has crushed the power
  of those evil kings,
6 who were furious
and never stopped abusing
  the people of other nations.

7 Now all the world is at peace;
  its people are celebrating
    with joyful songs.
8 King of Babylonia,
  even the cypress trees

and the cedars of Lebanon
  celebrate and say,
"Since you were put down,
  no one comes along
    to chop us down."

9 The world of the dead
  eagerly waits for you.
With great excitement,
  the spirits of ancient rulers
    hear about your coming.
10 Each one of them will say,
  "Now you are just as weak
    as any of us!
11 Your pride and your music
have ended here
  in the world of the dead.
Worms are your blanket,
  maggots are your bed."

12 You, the bright morning star,
  have fallen from the sky!
You brought down other nations;
  now you are brought down.
13 You said to yourself,
  "I'll climb to heaven
and place my throne
  above the highest stars.
I'll sit there with the gods
  far away in the north.
14 I'll be above the clouds,
  just like God Most High."

15 But now you are deep
  in the world of the dead.
16 Those who see you will stare
  and wonder, "Is this the man
who made the world tremble
  and shook up kingdoms?
17 Did he capture every city
  and make earth a desert?
Is he the one who refused
  to let prisoners go home?"

18 When kings die, they are buried
  in glorious tombs.
19 But you will be left unburied,
  just another dead body
    lying underfoot
    like a broken branch.
You will be one of many

---

[j] 13.21 *goats:* Or "demons."   [g] 14.4 *He . . . again:* One possible meaning for the difficult Hebrew text.

killed in battle and gone down
to the deep rocky pit.[h]
²⁰ You won't be buried with kings;
you ruined your country
and murdered your people.

You evil monster!
We hope that your family
will be forgotten forever.
²¹ We will slaughter your sons
to make them pay for the crimes
of their ancestors.
They won't take over the world
or build cities
anywhere on this earth.

²² The LORD All-Powerful has promised to
attack Babylonia and destroy everyone
there, so that none of them will ever be remembered again. ²³ The LORD will sweep out
the people, and the land will become a
swamp for wild animals.

Assyria Will Be Punished

²⁴ The LORD All-Powerful
has made this promise:
Everything I have planned
will happen just as I said.
²⁵ I will wipe out every Assyrian
in my country,
and I will crush those
on my mountains.
I will free my people
from slavery
to the Assyrians.
²⁶ I have planned this
for the whole world,
and my mighty arm
controls every nation.
²⁷ I, the LORD All-Powerful,
have made these plans.
No one can stop me now!

The Philistines Will Be Punished

²⁸ This message came from the LORD
in the year King Ahaz died:[i]
²⁹ Philistines, don't be happy
just because the rod
that punished you
is broken.
That rod will become
a poisonous snake, and then
a flying fiery dragon.

³⁰ The poor and needy will find
pastures for their sheep
and will live in safety.
But I will starve some of you,
and others will be killed.

³¹ Cry and weep in the gates
of your towns,
you Philistines!
Smoke blows in from the north,[j]
and every soldier is ready.
³² If a messenger comes
from a distant nation,
you must say:
"The LORD built Zion.
Even the poorest of his people
will find safety there."

Moab Will Be Punished

15 This is a message
about Moab:
The towns of Ar and Kir
were destroyed in a night.
Moab is left in ruins!
² Everyone in Dibon has gone up
to the temple[k] and the shrines
to cry and weep.
All of Moab is crying.
Heads and beards are shaved[l]
because of what happened
at Nebo and Medeba.
³ In the towns and at home,
everyone wears sackcloth
and cries loud and long.
⁴ From Heshbon and Elealeh,
weeping is heard in Jahaz;
Moab's warriors scream
while trembling with fear.

Pity Moab

⁵ I pity Moab!
Its people are running to Zoar
and to Eglath-Shelishiyah.
They cry on their way up
to the town of Luhith;
on the road to Horonaim
they tell of disasters.
⁶ The streams of Nimrim

---

[h]**14.19** *deep rocky pit*: The world of the dead.
[i]**14.28** *King Ahaz died*: 715 B.C. [j]**14.31** *north*: The
Assyrian and Babylonian attacks came from the north.
[k]**15.2** *Everyone . . . temple*: One possible meaning for the
difficult Hebrew text. [l]**15.2** *Heads . . . shaved*: As a sign
of sorrow and mourning.

6 17 6 17 6 17 6 17 6 17 6 17 6 17 6 17

and the grasslands
   have dried up.
Every plant is parched.

[7] The people of Moab are leaving,
   crossing over Willow Creek,
taking everything they own
   and have worked for.
[8] In the towns of Eglaim
   and of Beerelim
and everywhere else in Moab
   mournful cries are heard.
[9] The streams near Dimon
   are flowing with blood.
But the Lord will bring
   even worse trouble to Dimon,[m]
because all in Moab who escape
   will be attacked by lions.

More Troubles for Moab

16 Send lambs[n] as gifts
   to the ruler of the land.
Send them across the desert
   from Sela[o] to Mount Zion.
[2] The women of Moab
   crossing the Arnon River
are like a flock of birds
   scattered from their nests.
[3] Moab's messengers say
   to the people of Judah,
"Be kind and help us!
Shade us from the heat
   of the noonday sun.
Hide our refugees!
   Don't turn them away.
[4] Let our people live
in your country
   and find safety here."

Moab, your cruel enemies
   will disappear;
they will no longer attack
   and destroy your land.
[5] Then a kingdom of love
   will be set up,
and someone from David's family
   will rule with fairness.
He will do what is right
   and quickly bring justice.

Moab's Pride Is Destroyed

[6] We have heard of Moab's pride.
   Its people strut and boast,

but without reason.
[7] Tell everyone in Moab
   to mourn for their nation.
Tell them to cry and weep
for those fancy raisins[p]
   of Kir-Hareseth.

[8] Vineyards near Heshbon
and Sibmah
   have turned brown.
The rulers of nations
   used to get drunk
on wine from those vineyards[q]
   that spread to Jazer,
then across the desert
   and beyond the sea.

[9] Now I mourn like Jazer
for the vineyards
   of Sibmah.
I shed tears for Heshbon
   and for Elealeh.
There will be no more
   harvest celebrations
[10] or joyful and happy times,
   while bringing in the crops.
Singing and shouting are gone
   from the vineyards.
There are no joyful shouts
   where grapes were pressed.
   God has silenced them all.

[11] Deep in my heart I hurt
   for Moab and Kir-Heres.
[12] It's useless for Moab's people
   to wear themselves out
by going to their altars
   to worship and pray.

[13] The LORD has already said all of this about Moab. [14] Now he says, "The contract of a hired worker is good for three years, but Moab's glory and greatness won't last any longer than that. Only a few of its people will survive, and they will be left helpless."

---

[m]15.9 *Dimon . . . Dimon:* The Standard Hebrew Text; the Dead Sea Scrolls and one ancient translation have *Dibon . . . Dibon.* [n]16.1 *lambs:* The main product of Moab. [o]16.1 *Sela:* A town in Edom. [p]16.7 *fancy raisins:* The Hebrew text has "raisin-cakes," which could mean either the rich produce or the prosperous farmers. [q]16.8 *The rulers . . . vineyards:* Or "The rulers of nations have destroyed those vineyards."

Damascus Will Be Punished

17 This is a message
about Damascus:
Damascus is doomed!
It will end up in ruins.
² The villages around Aroer^r
will be deserted,
with only sheep living there
and no one to bother them.
³ Israel^s will lose its fortresses.
The kingdom of Damascus
will be destroyed;
its survivors will suffer
the same fate as Israel.
The LORD All-Powerful
has promised this.

Sin and Suffering

⁴When that time comes,
the glorious nation of Israel
will be brought down;
its prosperous people
will be skin and bones.
⁵ Israel will be like wheat fields
in Rephaim Valley
picked clean of grain.
⁶ It will be like an olive tree
beaten with a stick,
leaving two or three olives
or maybe four or five
on the highest
or most fruitful branches.
The LORD God of Israel
has promised this.

⁷At that time the people will turn and
trust their Creator, the holy God of Israel.
⁸They have built altars and places for burning incense to their goddess Asherah, and
they have set up sacred poles^t for her. But
they will stop worshiping at these places.
⁹Israel captured powerful cities and
chased out the people who lived there. But
these cities will lie in ruins, covered over
with weeds and underbrush.^u

¹⁰ Israel, you have forgotten
the God who saves you,
the one who is the mighty rock^v
where you find protection.
You plant the finest flowers
to honor a foreign god.
¹¹ The plants may sprout
and blossom

that very same morning,
but it will do you no good,
because you will suffer
endless agony.

God Defends His People

¹² The nations are a noisy,
thunderous sea.
¹³ But even if they roar
like a fearsome flood,
God will give the command
to turn them back.
They will be like dust,
or like a tumbleweed
blowing across the hills
in a windstorm.
¹⁴ In the evening
their attack is fierce,
but by morning
they are destroyed.
This is what happens to those
who raid and rob us.

Ethiopia Will Be Punished

18 Downstream from Ethiopia^w
lies the country of Egypt,
swarming with insects.^x
² Egypt sends messengers
up the Nile River
on ships made of reeds.^y
Send them fast to Ethiopia,
whose people are tall
and have smooth skin.
Their land is divided by rivers;
they are strong and brutal,
feared all over the world.^z

³ Everyone on this earth,
listen with care!
A signal will be given

^r**17.2** *Aroer:* Either a city near Damascus with the same
name as the Moabite city or the Moabite city itself, here
used as an example of what will happen to Damascus.
^s**17.3** *Israel:* The Hebrew text has "Ephraim," another
name for the northern kingdom.   ^t**17.8** *sacred poles:* Or
"trees," used as symbols of Asherah, the goddess of
fertility.   ^u**17.9** *covered . . . underbrush:* Hebrew; one
ancient translation "like the cities of the Hivites and the
Amorites."   ^v**17.10** *mighty rock:* The Hebrew text has
"rock," which is sometimes used in poetry to compare
the Lord to a mountain where his people can run for
protection from their enemies.   ^w**18.1** *Ethiopia:* See the
note at 11.11.   ^x**18.1** *insects:* Or "sailing ships."
^y**18.2** *reeds:* Ancient Egypt was famous for the papyrus
reeds that grew in the Nile Delta.   ^z**18.2** *world:* One
possible meaning for the difficult Hebrew text of verse 2.

on the mountains,
    and you will hear a trumpet.
[4] The LORD said to me,
"I will calmly look down
    from my home above—
as calmly as the sun at noon
or clouds in the heat
    of harvest season."

[5] Before the blossoms
    can turn into grapes,
God will cut off the sprouts
    and hack off the branches.
[6] Ethiopians will be food
for mountain buzzards
    during the summer
and for wild animals
    during the winter.

[7] Those Ethiopians are tall and their skin is smooth. They are feared all over the world, because they are strong and brutal. But at that time they will come from their land divided by rivers, and they will bring gifts to the LORD All-Powerful, who is worshiped on Mount Zion.

Egypt Will Be Punished

19 This is a message
    about Egypt:
The LORD comes to Egypt,
    riding swiftly on a cloud.
The people are weak from fear.
Their idols tremble
    as he approaches and says,
[2] "I will punish Egypt
    with civil war—
neighbors, cities, and kingdoms
    will fight each other.

[3] "Egypt will be discouraged
    when I confuse their plans.
They will try to get advice
    from their idols,
from the spirits of the dead,
    and from fortunetellers.
[4] I will put the Egyptians
under the power of a cruel,
    heartless king.
I, the LORD All-Powerful,
    have promised this."

Trouble along the Nile

[5] The Nile River will dry up
    and become parched land.

[6] Its streams will stink,
Egypt will have no water,
and the reeds and tall grass
    will dry up.
[7] Fields along the Nile
will be completely barren;
    every plant will disappear.

[8] Those who fish in the Nile
will be discouraged
    and mourn.
[9] None of the cloth makers[a]
will know what to do,
    and they will turn pale.[b]
[10] Weavers will be confused;
paid workers will cry and mourn.

Egypt's Helpless Leaders

[11] The king's officials in Zoan[c]
are foolish themselves
    and give stupid advice.
How can they say to him,
"We are very wise,
and our families go back
    to kings of long ago?"
[12] Where are those wise men now?
If they can, let them say
what the LORD All-Powerful
    intends for Egypt.

[13] The royal officials in Zoan
and in Memphis
    are foolish and deceived.
The leaders in every state
have given bad advice
    to the nation.
[14] The LORD has confused Egypt;
its leaders have made it stagger
    and vomit like a drunkard.
[15] No one in Egypt can do a thing,
    no matter who they are.

[16] When the LORD All-Powerful punishes Egypt with his mighty arm, the Egyptians will become terribly weak and will tremble with fear. [17] They will be so terrified of Judah that they will be frightened by the very mention of its name. This will happen because of what the LORD All-Powerful is planning against Egypt.

---

[a] **19.9** *cloth makers:* Cloth was made from several kinds of plants that grew in the fields along the Nile. [b] **19.9** *turn pale:* One possible meaning for the difficult Hebrew text. [c] **19.11** *Zoan:* The city of Tanis in the Nile delta.

The LORD Will Bless Egypt, Assyria, and Israel

[18]The time is coming when Hebrew will be spoken in five Egyptian cities, and their people will become followers of the LORD. One of these cities will be called City of the Sun.[d]

[19]In the heart of Egypt an altar will be set up for the LORD; at its border a shrine will be built to honor him. [20]These will remind the Egyptians that the LORD All-Powerful is with them. And when they are in trouble and ask for help, he will send someone to rescue them from their enemies. [21]The LORD will show the Egyptians who he is, and they will know and worship the LORD. They will bring him sacrifices and offerings, and they will keep their promises to him. [22]After the LORD has punished Egypt, the people will turn to him. Then he will answer their prayers, and the Egyptians will be healed.

[23]At that time a good road will run from Egypt to Assyria. The Egyptians and the Assyrians will travel back and forth from Egypt to Assyria, and they will worship together. [24]Israel will join with these two countries. They will be a blessing to everyone on earth, [25]then the LORD All-Powerful will bless them by saying,

> "The Egyptians are my people.
> I created the Assyrians
>   and chose the Israelites."

Isaiah Acts Out the Defeat of Egypt and Ethiopia

20 King Sargon of Assyria gave orders for his army commander to capture the city of Ashdod.[e] [2]About this same time the LORD had told me, "Isaiah, take off everything, including your sandals!" I did this and went around naked and barefoot [3]for three years.

Then the LORD said:

What Isaiah has done is a warning to Egypt and Ethiopia.[f] [4]Everyone in these two countries will be led away naked and barefoot by the king of Assyria. Young or old, they will be taken prisoner, and Egypt will be disgraced. [5]They will be confused and frustrated, because they depended on Ethiopia and bragged about Egypt. [6]When this happens, the people who live along the coast[g] will say, "Look what happened to them! We ran to them for safety, hoping they would protect us from the king of Assyria. But now, there is no escape for us."

The Fall of Babylonia[h]

21 This is a message about
        a desert beside the sea:[i]
    Enemies from a hostile nation
attack like a whirlwind
    from the Southern Desert.
[2]What a horrible vision
        was shown to me—
a vision of betrayal
    and destruction.
Tell Elam and Media[j]
to surround and attack
    the Babylonians.
The LORD has sworn to end
    the suffering they caused.

[3]I'm in terrible pain
    like a woman giving birth.
I'm shocked and hurt so much
    that I can't hear or see.
[4]My head spins; I'm horrified!
Early evening, my favorite time,
    has become a nightmare.

[5]In Babylon the high officials
    were having a feast.
They were eating and drinking,
    when someone shouted,
"Officers, take your places!
    Grab your shields."

[6]The LORD said to me,
    "Send guards to find out

---

[d]**19.18** *City of the Sun:* Some manuscripts of the Standard Hebrew Text, the Dead Sea Scrolls, and one ancient translation; most manuscripts of the Standard Hebrew Text have "City of Destruction." This probably refers to Heliopolis which means "City of the Sun" (see Jeremiah 43.13).   [e]**20.1** *Ashdod:* King Sargon II of Assyria captured this Philistine city in 711 B.C.   [f]**20.3** *Ethiopia:* See the note at 11.11.   [g]**20.6** *people . . . coast:* Probably the Philistines.   [h]**21.1** *Babylonia:* King Cyrus and his army of Medes and Persians captured the city of Babylon in 539 B.C.   [i]**21.1** *This . . . sea:* One possible meaning for the difficult Hebrew text. The prophet may be speaking of Babylonia as a desert, because of the terrible punishment God will bring on it. The southern part of Babylonia on the Persian Gulf was sometimes called "the land beside the sea."   [j]**21.2** *Elam and Media:* People from the Iranian highlands; the capital of Elam was Susa, in the hill country east of Babylon.

what's going on.
[7] When they see cavalry troops
and columns of soldiers
on donkeys and camels,
tell them to be ready!"

[8] Then a guard[k] said,
"I have stood day and night
on this watchtower, Lord.
[9] Now I see column after column
of cavalry troops."

Right away someone shouted,
"Babylon has fallen!
Every idol in the city
lies broken on the ground."

[10] Then I said, "My people,
you have suffered terribly,
but I have a message for you
from the LORD All-Powerful,
the God of Israel."

How Much Longer?

[11] This is a message about Dumah:
From the country of Seir,[l]
someone shouts to me,
"Guard, how much longer
before daylight?"

[12] From my guard post, I answered,
"Morning will soon be here,
but night will return.
If you want to know more,
come back later."

[13] This is a message for Arabs
who live in the barren desert
in the region of Dedan:[m]
You must order your caravans
[14] to bring water for those
who are thirsty.
You people of Tema[n]
must bring food
for the hungry refugees.
[15] They are worn out and weary
from being chased by enemies
with swords and arrows.

[16] The Lord said to me:
A year from now the glory of the
people of Kedar[o] will all come to an
end, just as a worker's contract ends
after a year. [17] Only a few of their warriors will be left with bows and arrows.

This is a promise that I, the LORD God
of Israel, have made.

Trouble in Vision Valley

22 This is a message
about Vision Valley:[p]
Why are you celebrating
on the flat roofs[q]
of your houses?
[2] Your city is filled
with noisy shouts.
Those who lie drunk
in your streets
were not killed in battle.
[3] Your leaders ran away,
but they were captured
without a fight.
No matter how far they ran,
they were found and caught.[r]

[4] Then I said, "Leave me alone!
Let me cry bitter tears.
My people have been destroyed,
so don't try to comfort me."

[5] The LORD All-Powerful
had chosen a time
for noisy shouts and confusion
to fill Vision Valley,
and for everyone to beg
the mountains for help.[s]
[6] The people of Elam and Kir[t]
attacked with chariots[u]
and carried shields.
[7] Your most beautiful valleys
were covered with chariots;

---

[k]21.8 *guard*: The Dead Sea Scrolls and one ancient
translation; the Standard Hebrew Text has "lion."
[l]21.11 *Dumah . . . Seir*: Dumah was an oasis in the Arabian
desert. One ancient translation has "Edom," which may be
what is meant. Seir is a mountainous region of Edom
southwest of the Dead Sea. [m]21.13 *Dedan*: A region in
northwest Arabia. [n]21.14 *Tema*: A region in north
Arabia. [o]21.16 *Kedar*: A region in the Arabian desert.
[p]22.1 *Vision Valley*: The exact location is not known. In
Hebrew the name sounds something like "Hinnom
Valley," where the people of Jerusalem sometimes
offered human sacrifices to the gods of Canaan.
[q]22.1 *flat roofs*: In Palestine the houses usually had a
flat roof. Stairs on the outside led up to the roof, which
was made of beams and boards covered with packed
earth. [r]22.3 *No matter . . . caught*: One possible
meaning for the difficult Hebrew text. [s]22.5 *and
for . . . help*: One possible meaning for the difficult
Hebrew text. [t]22.6 *Elam and Kir*: Regions in the
Iranian highlands. [u]22.6 *chariots*: One possible
meaning for the difficult Hebrew text.

your cities were surrounded
  by cavalry troops.
⁸   Judah was left defenseless.

At that time you trusted in the weapons you had stored in Forest Palace.^v ⁹You saw the holes in the outer wall of Jerusalem, and you brought water from the lower pool.^w ¹⁰You counted the houses in Jerusalem and tore down some of them, so you could get stones to repair the city wall. ¹¹Then you built a large tank between the walls^x to store the water. But you refused to trust the God who planned this long ago and made it happen.

A Time To Weep

¹²When all of this happened,
  the LORD All-Powerful told you
    to weep and mourn,
    to shave your heads,
    and wear sackcloth.
¹³But instead, you celebrated
  by feasting on beef and lamb
    and by drinking wine,
  because you said,
    "Let's eat and drink!
    Tomorrow we may die."

¹⁴The LORD All-Powerful
  has spoken to me
  this solemn promise:
    "I won't forgive them for this,
    not as long as they live."

Selfish Officials Are Doomed

¹⁵The LORD All-Powerful is sending you with this message for Shebna, the prime minister:
¹⁶Shebna, what gives you the right to have a tomb carved out of rock in this burial place of royalty? None of your relatives are buried here. ¹⁷You may be powerful, but the LORD is about to snatch you up and throw you away. ¹⁸He will roll you into a ball and throw you into a wide open country, where you will die and your chariots will be destroyed. You're a disgrace to those you serve.

¹⁹The LORD is going to take away your job! ²⁰⁻²¹He will give your official robes and your authority to his servant Eliakim son of Hilkiah.

Eliakim will be like a father to the people of Jerusalem and to the royal family of Judah. ²²The LORD will put him in charge of the key that belongs to King David's family. No one will be able to unlock what he locks, and no one will be able to lock what he unlocks. ²³The LORD will make him as firm in his position as a tent peg hammered in the ground, and Eliakim will bring honor to his family.

²⁴His children and relatives will be supported by him, like pans hanging from a peg on the wall. ²⁵That peg is fastened firmly now, but someday it will be shaken loose and fall down. Then everything that was hanging on it will be destroyed. This is what the LORD All-Powerful has promised.

The City of Tyre Will Be Punished

23 This is a message
  from distant islands
    about the city of Tyre:^y
Cry, you seagoing ships!^z
Tyre and its houses
  lie in ruins.^a
²Mourn in silence,
  you shop owners of Sidon,^b
    you people on the coast.
Your sailors crossed oceans,
  making your city rich.
³Your merchants sailed the seas,
  making you wealthy by trading
    with nation after nation.
They brought back grain
  that grew along the Nile.^c
⁴Sidon, you are a mighty fortress
  built along the sea.
But you will be disgraced

---

^v**22.8** *Forest Palace:* Built by Solomon (1 Kings 7.2) and used as a place for storing weapons. ^w**22.9** *the lower pool:* Mentioned only here; probably in the southern part of the Central Valley (Tyropoean Valley) of Jerusalem. ^x**22.11** *between the walls:* Some cities had two walls with a space between them. If the enemy broke through the outer wall, the city was still protected by the inner wall. The houses that were torn down to repair the outer wall were probably squatters' huts that had been built between the two walls. ^y**23.1** *Tyre:* A fortress city built on an island in the Mediterranean Sea off the coast of what is now Lebanon. ^z**23.1** *seagoing ships:* See the note at 2.16. ^a**23.1** *Tyre . . . ruins:* One possible meaning for the difficult Hebrew text. ^b**23.2** *Sidon:* A coastal city just north of Tyre. ^c**23.3** *along the Nile:* The Hebrew text has "grain of Shihor, the harvest of the Nile," but Shihor is probably a name for a region near the lower part of the Nile.

like a married woman
who never had children.*d*

⁵When Egypt hears about Tyre,
it will tremble.
⁶All of you along the coast
had better cry and sail
far across the ocean.*e*
⁷Can this be the happy city
that has stood for centuries?
Its people have spread
to distant lands;
⁸its merchants were kings
honored all over the world.
Who planned to destroy Tyre?
⁹The LORD All-Powerful planned it
to bring shame and disgrace
to those who are honored
by everyone on earth.
¹⁰People of Tyre,*f*
your harbor is destroyed!
You will have to become farmers
just like the Egyptians.*g*

Tyre Will Be Forgotten

¹¹The LORD's hand has reached
across the sea,
upsetting the nations.
He has given a command
to destroy fortresses
in the land of Canaan.
¹²The LORD has said
to the people of Sidon,
"Your celebrating is over—
you are crushed.
Even if you escape to Cyprus,
you won't find peace."

¹³Look what the Assyrians have done to Babylonia! They have attacked, destroying every palace in the land. Now wild animals live among the ruins.*h* ¹⁴Not a fortress will be left standing, so tell all the seagoing ships*i* to mourn.

¹⁵The city of Tyre will be forgotten for seventy years, which is the lifetime of a king. Then Tyre will be like that evil woman in the song:

¹⁶You're gone and forgotten,
you evil woman!
So strut through the town,
singing and playing
your favorite tune
to be remembered again.

¹⁷At the end of those seventy years, the LORD will let Tyre get back into business. The city will be like a woman who sells her body to everyone of every nation on earth, ¹⁸but none of what is earned will be kept in the city. That money will belong to the LORD, and it will be used to buy more than enough food and good clothes for those who worship the LORD.

The Earth Will Be Punished

24 The LORD is going to twist the earth out of shape and turn it into a desert. Everyone will be scattered, ²including ordinary people and priests, slaves and slave owners, buyers and sellers, lenders and borrowers, the rich and the poor. ³The earth will be stripped bare and left that way. This is what the LORD has promised.

⁴The earth wilts away;
its mighty leaders melt
to nothing.*j*
⁵The earth is polluted
because its people
disobeyed the laws of God,
breaking their agreement
that was to last forever.

⁶The earth is under a curse;
its people are dying out
because of their sins.
⁷Grapevines have dried up;
wine is almost gone—
mournful sounds are heard
instead of joyful shouts.

⁸No one plays tambourines
or stringed instruments;
all noisy celebrating
has come to an end.
⁹They no longer sing
as they drink their wine,
and it tastes sour.

*d*23.4 *children:* One possible meaning for the difficult Hebrew text. *e*23.6 *far across the ocean:* The Hebrew text has "to Tarshish," probably meaning a long distance. *f*23.10 *People of Tyre:* The Hebrew text has "the people of Tarshish," which stands for the colonies of Tyre. *g*23.10 *Egyptians:* One possible meaning for the difficult Hebrew text of verse 10. *h*23.13 *ruins:* One possible meaning for the difficult Hebrew text of verse 13. *i*23.14 *seagoing ships:* See the note at 2.16. *j*24.4 *its . . . to nothing:* One possible meaning for the difficult Hebrew text.

¹⁰Towns are crushed and in chaos;
  houses are locked tight.
¹¹Happy times have disappeared
    from the earth,
  and people shout in the streets,
    "We're out of wine!"
¹²Cities are destroyed;
    their gates are torn down.
¹³Nations will be stripped bare,
  like olive trees or vineyards
    after the harvest season.

Praise the God of Justice

¹⁴People in the west shout;
  they joyfully praise
    the majesty of the LORD.
¹⁵And so, everyone in the east
    and those on the islands
  should praise the LORD,
    the God of Israel.
¹⁶From all over the world
  songs of praise are heard
    for the God of justice.ᵏ
  But I feel awful,
    terribly miserable.
  Can anyone be trusted?
    So many are treacherous!

There's No Escape

¹⁷Terror, traps, and pits
    are waiting for everyone.
¹⁸If you are terrified and run,
    you will fall into a pit;
  if you crawl out of the pit,
    you will get caught in a trap.

  The sky has split apart
    like a window thrown open.
  The foundations of the earth
    have been shaken;
¹⁹the earth is shattered,
    ripped to pieces.
²⁰It staggers and shakes
  like a drunkard
    or a hut in a windstorm.
  It is burdened down with sin;
  the earth will fall,
    never again to get up.

²¹On that day the LORD
  will punish the powers
  in the heavensˡ
    and the kings of the earth.
²²He will put them in a pit
    and keep them prisoner.

Then later on,
  he will punish them.
²³The moon and sun will both
  be embarrassed and ashamed.
The LORD All-Powerful will rule
  on Mount Zion in Jerusalem,
where he will show its rulers
  his wonderful glory.

A Prayer of Thanks to God

25 You, LORD, are my God!
    I will praise you
  for doing the wonderful things
you had planned and promised
  since ancient times.
²You have destroyed the fortress
of our enemies,
  leaving their city in ruins.
Nothing in that foreign city
  will ever be rebuilt.
³Now strong and cruel nations
  will fear and honor you.

*God asks us to give thanks
in advance—before we see
or know the consequences.*

MADALENE HARRIS

⁴You have been a place of safety
  for the poor and needy
    in times of trouble.
Brutal enemies pounded us
  like a heavy rain
or the heat of the sun at noon,
  but you were our shelter.
⁵Those wild foreigners struck
  like scorching desert heat.
But you were like a cloud,
  protecting us from the sun.
You kept our enemies from singing
  songs of victory.

ᵏ**24.16** *God of justice:* Or "people who do right."
ˡ**24.21** *the powers in the heavens:* In ancient times the
stars were thought of as powerful spiritual beings, and
sometimes they stood for pagan gods.

The LORD Has Saved Us

⁶ On this mountain
   the LORD All-Powerful
will prepare for all nations
   a feast of the finest foods.
Choice wines and the best meats
   will be served.
⁷ Here the LORD will strip away
   the burial clothes
   that cover the nations.
⁸ The LORD All-Powerful
will destroy the power of death
   and wipe away all tears.
No longer will his people
be insulted everywhere.
   The LORD has spoken!

⁹ At that time, people will say,
   "The LORD has saved us!
   Let's celebrate.
We waited and hoped—
   now our God is here."
¹⁰ The powerful arm of the LORD
   will protect this mountain.

The Moabites will be put down
and trampled on like straw
   in a pit of manure.
¹¹ They will struggle to get out,
   but God will humiliate them
   no matter how hard they try.ᵐ
¹² The walls of their fortresses
will be knocked down
   and scattered in the dirt.

A Song of Victory

26 The time is coming
   when the people of Judah
   will sing this song:
"Our cityⁿ is protected.
The LORD is our fortress,
   and he gives us victory.
² Open the city gates
for a law-abiding nation
   that is faithful to God.
³ The LORD gives perfect peace
   to those whose faith is firm.
⁴ So always trust the LORD
because he is forever
   our mighty rock.ᵒ
⁵ God has put down our enemies
in their mountain cityᵖ
   and rubbed it in the dirt.

⁶ Now the poor and abused
   stomp all over that city."

The LORD Can Be Trusted

⁷ Our LORD, you always do right,
   and you make the path smooth
   for those who obey you.
⁸ You are the one we trust
   to bring about justice;
above all else we want
   your name to be honored.

*Real answers help us keep
our perspective in a world
where desire is out of control.
Real answers take us deeper
into the relationship for which
we were created. And it's only
then that we'll be satisfied.*

RUTH HALEY BARTON

⁹ Throughout the night,
   my heart searches for you,
because your decisions
show everyone on this earth
   how to live right.

¹⁰ Even when the wicked
   are treated with mercy
   in this land of justice,
they do wrong and are blind
   to your glory, our LORD.
¹¹ Your hand is raised and ready
   to punish them,
   but they don't see it.
   Put them to shame!
Show how much you care for us
and throw them into the fire
   intended for your enemies.

¹² You will give us peace, LORD,
   because everything we have done

ᵐ**25.11** *no matter . . . try:* One possible meaning for
the difficult Hebrew text.   ⁿ**26.1** *city:* Probably
Jerusalem.   ᵒ**26.4** *mighty rock:* See the note at 17.10.
ᵖ**26.5** *our enemies . . . city:* One possible meaning for the
difficult Hebrew text.

was by your power.
¹³ Others have ruled over us
besides you, our LORD God,
but we obey only you.
¹⁴ Those enemies are now dead
and can never live again.
You have punished them—
they are destroyed,
completely forgotten.
¹⁵ Our nation has grown
because of you, our LORD.
We have more land than before,
and you are honored.

The LORD Gives Life to the Dead

¹⁶ When you punished our people,
they turned and prayed
to you, our LORD.^q
¹⁷ Because of what you did to us,
we suffered like a woman
about to give birth.
¹⁸ But instead of having a child,
our terrible pain
produced only wind.
We have won no victories,
and we have no descendants
to take over the earth.

¹⁹ Your people will rise to life!
Tell them to leave their graves
and celebrate with shouts.
You refresh the earth
like morning dew;
you give life to the dead.

²⁰ Go inside and lock the doors,
my people.
Hide there for a little while,
until the LORD
is no longer angry.

The Earth and the Sea Will Be Punished

²¹ The LORD will come out
to punish everyone on earth
for their sins.
And when he does,
those who did violent crimes
will be known and punished.

27

On that day, Leviathan,^r
the sea monster,
will squirm and try to escape,
but the LORD will kill him
with a cruel, sharp sword.

Protection and Forgiveness

The LORD said:

² At that time you must sing
about a fruitful^s vineyard.
³ I, the LORD, will protect it
and always keep it watered.
I will guard it day and night
to keep it from harm.
⁴ I am no longer angry.
But if it produces thorns,
I will go to war against it
and burn it to the ground.
⁵ Yet if the vineyard depends
on me for protection,
it will become my friend
and be at peace with me.

*God wants
the first part
of everything.*
MARY HUNT

⁶ Someday Israel will take root
like a vine.
It will blossom and bear fruit
that covers the earth.

⁷ I, the LORD, didn't punish and kill
the people of Israel
as fiercely as I punished
and killed their enemies.
⁸ I carefully measured out
Israel's punishment^t
and sent the scorching heat
to chase them far away.

⁹ There's only one way
that Israel's sin and guilt
can be completely forgiven:

---

^q**26.16** LORD: One possible meaning for the difficult Hebrew text of verse 16. ^r**27.1** *Leviathan:* God's victory over this monster sometimes stands for God's power over all creation and sometimes for his defeat of his enemies, especially Egypt. ^s**27.2** *fruitful:* Some Hebrew manuscripts have "lovely." ^t**27.8** *I . . . punishment:* One possible meaning for the difficult Hebrew text.

They must crush the stones
of every pagan altar
and place of worship.

The LORD Will Bring His People Together

¹⁰ Fortress cities are left
like a desert
where no one lives.
Cattle walk through the ruins,
stripping the trees bare.
¹¹ When broken branches
fall to the ground,
women pick them up
to feed the fire.
But these people are so stupid
that the God who created them
will show them no mercy.

¹²The time is coming when the LORD will
shake the land between the Euphrates River
and the border of Egypt, and one by one he
will bring all of his people together. ¹³A loud
trumpet will be heard. Then the people of
Israel who were dragged away to Assyria and
Egypt will return to worship the LORD on
his holy mountain in Jerusalem.

Samaria Will Be Punished

28 The city of Samaria
above a fertile valley
is in for trouble!
Its leaders are drunkards,
who stuff themselves
with food and wine.
But they will be like flowers
that dry up and wilt.
² Only the Lord is strong
and powerful!
His mighty hand
will strike them down
with the force of a hailstorm
or a mighty whirlwind
or an overwhelming flood.

³ Every drunkard in Ephraim ᵘ
takes pride in Samaria,
but it will be crushed.
⁴ Samaria above a fertile valley
will quickly lose its glory.
It will be gobbled down
like the first ripe fig
at harvest season.

⁵ When this time comes,
the LORD All-Powerful

will be a glorious crown
for his people who survive.
⁶ He will see that justice rules
and that his people are able
to defend their cities.

Corrupt Leaders Will Be Punished

⁷ Priests and prophets stumble
because they are drunk.
Their minds are too confused
to receive God's messages
or give honest decisions.
⁸ Their tables are covered,
completely covered,
with their stinking vomit.

⁹ You drunken leaders
are like babies!
How can you possibly understand
or teach the LORD's message?
¹⁰ You don't even listen—
all you hear is senseless sound
after senseless sound.ᵛ

¹¹ So, the Lord will speak
to his people
in strange sounds
and foreign languages.ʷ
¹² He promised you
perfect peace and rest,
but you refused to listen.
¹³ Now his message to you
will be senseless sound
after senseless sound.ˣ
Then you will fall backwards,
injured and trapped.

False Security Is Fatal

¹⁴ You rulers of Jerusalem
do nothing but sneer;
now you must listen
to what the LORD says.
¹⁵ Do you think you have
an agreement with death
and the world of the dead?
Why do you trust in your lies
to keep you safe from danger
and the mighty flood?

ᵘ**28.3** *Ephraim:* The northern kingdom of Israel; Samaria
was its capital.   ᵛ**28.10** *sound:* One possible meaning
for the difficult Hebrew text of verses 9, 10.
ʷ**28.11** *in . . . foreign languages:* This probably refers to
the language of the Assyrians.   ˣ**28.13** *Now . . . sound:*
One possible meaning for the difficult Hebrew text.

16 And so the LORD says,
"I'm laying a firm foundation
for the city of Zion.
It's a valuable cornerstone
proven to be trustworthy;
no one who trusts it
will ever be disappointed.
17 Justice and fairness
will be the measuring lines
that help me build."

Hailstones and floods
will destroy and wash away
your shelter of lies.
18 Your agreement with death
and the world of the dead
will be broken.
Then angry, roaring waves
will sweep over you.
19 Morning, noon, and night
an overwhelming flood
will wash you away.
The terrible things that happen
will teach you this lesson:
20 Your bed is too short,
your blanket too skimpy.ʸ

21 The LORD will fiercely attack
as he did at Mount Perazimᶻ
and in Gibeon Valley.ᵃ
But this time the LORD
will do something surprising,
not what you expect.
22 So you had better stop sneering
or you will be in worse shape
than ever before.
I heard the LORD All-Powerful
threaten the whole country
with destruction.

All Wisdom Comes from the LORD

23 Pay close attention
to what I am saying.
24 Farmers don't just plow
and break up the ground.
25 When a field is ready,
they scatter the seeds
of dill and cumin;
they plant the seeds
of wheat and barley
in the proper places.
26 They learn this from their God.

27 After dill and cumin
have been harvested,

the stalks are pounded,
not run over with a wagon.
28 Wheat and barley are pounded,
but not beaten to pulp;
they are run over with a wagon,
but not ground to dust.
29 This wonderful knowledge comes
from the LORD All-Powerful,
who has such great wisdom.

Jerusalem Will Suffer

The LORD said:

29 Jerusalem, city of David,
the place of my altar,ᵇ
you are in for trouble!
Celebrate your festivals
year after year.
2 I will still make you suffer,
and your people will cry
when I make an altar of you.ᶜ
3 I will surround you and prepare
to attack from all sides.ᵈ
4 From deep in the earth,
you will call out for help
with only a faint whisper.

5 Then your cruel enemies
will suddenly be swept away
like dust in a windstorm.
6 I, the LORD All-Powerful,
will come to your rescue
with a thundering earthquake
and a fiery whirlwind.

7 Every brutal nation
that attacks Jerusalem
and makes it suffer
will disappear like a dream
when night is over.
8 Those nations that attack
Mount Zion

ʸ28.20 *Your bed . . . skimpy*: Isaiah quotes a popular saying to teach that the treaty made with Egypt (verse 18) cannot give the nation security from its enemies. ᶻ28.21 *Mount Perazim*: This may refer to David's defeat of the Philistines at Baal Perazim (2 Samuel 5.17-21). ᵃ28.21 *Gibeon Valley*: This refers to Joshua's victory at Gibeon (Joshua 10.1-11). ᵇ29.1 *the place of my altar*: One possible meaning for "ariel, ariel" of the Hebrew text. In Hebrew "ariel" can mean "God's hero" or "God's lion" or "God's altar." ᶜ29.2 *when . . . you*: One possible meaning for the difficult Hebrew text. ᵈ29.3 *from all sides*: One possible meaning for the difficult Hebrew text. One ancient translation has "like David."

will suffer from hunger
    and thirst.
They will dream of food and drink
    but wake up weary and hungry
    and thirsty as ever.

Prophets Who Fool Themselves

[9] Be shocked and stunned,
    you prophets!
Refuse to see.
Get drunk and stagger,
    but not from wine.
[10] The LORD has made you drowsy;
    he put you into a deep sleep
    and covered your head.

[11] Now his message is like a sealed letter to you. Some of you say, "We can't read it, because it's sealed." [12] Others say, "We can't read it, because we don't know how to read."
    [13] The Lord has said:

"These people praise me
    with their words,
but they never really
    think about me.
They worship me by repeating
    rules made up by humans.
[14] So once again I will do things
    that shock and amaze them,
and I will destroy the wisdom
    of those who claim to know
    and understand."

[15] You are in for trouble,
    if you try to hide your plans
        from the LORD!
Or if you think what you do
    in the dark can't be seen.
[16] You have it all backwards.
A clay dish doesn't say
    to the potter,
"You didn't make me.
    You don't even know how."

Hope for the Future

[17] Soon the forest of Lebanon
    will become a field with crops,
        thick as a forest.[e]
[18] The deaf will be able to hear
    whatever is read to them;
the blind will be freed
    from a life of darkness.

[19] The poor and the needy
    will celebrate and shout
because of the LORD,
    the holy God of Israel.

[20] All who are cruel and arrogant
    will be gone forever.
Those who live by crime
    will disappear,
[21] together with everyone
    who tells lies in court
and keeps innocent people
    from getting a fair trial.

[22] The LORD who rescued Abraham
    has this to say
        about Jacob's descendants:
"They will no longer
    be ashamed and disgraced.
[23] When they see how great
    I have made their nation,
they will praise and honor me,
    the holy God of Israel.
[24] Everyone who is confused
    will understand,
and all who have complained
    will obey my teaching."

Don't Expect Help from Egypt

30 This is the LORD's message
    for his rebellious people:
"You follow your own plans
    instead of mine;
you make treaties
    without asking me,
    and you keep on sinning.
[2] You trust Egypt for protection.
    So you refuse my advice
and send messengers to Egypt
    to beg their king for help.

[3] You will be disappointed,
    completely disgraced
        for trusting Egypt.
[4] The king's power reaches
    from the city of Zoan
        as far south as Hanes.[f]
[5] But Egypt can't protect you,

---

[e] **29.17** with . . . forest: Or "and Mount Carmel will be covered with forests." [f] **30.4** Zoan . . . Hanes: Or "Your messengers have reached the city of Zoan and gone as far as Hanes." Zoan was in northeast Egypt; Hanes was to the south.

and to trust that nation
  is useless and foolish.

⁶ This is a message
  about the animals
    of the Southern Desert:
You people carry treasures
  on donkeys and camels.
You travel to a feeble nation
through a troublesome desert
  filled with lions
  and flying fiery dragons.
⁷ Egypt can't help you!
That's why I call that nation
  a helpless monster.[g]

Israel Refuses To Listen

⁸The LORD told me to write down his message for his people, so that it would be there forever. ⁹They have turned against the LORD and can't be trusted. They have refused his teaching ¹⁰and have said to his messengers and prophets:

Don't tell us what God has shown you and don't preach the truth. Just say what we want to hear, even if it's false. ¹¹Stop telling us what God has said! We don't want to hear any more about the holy God of Israel.

¹² Now this is the answer
  of the holy God of Israel:
"You rejected my message,
and you trust in violence
  and lies.
¹³ This sin is like a crack
  that makes a high wall
quickly crumble ¹⁴and shatter
  like a crushed bowl.
There's not a piece left
big enough to carry hot coals
  or to dip out water."

Trust the LORD

¹⁵ The holy LORD God of Israel
  had told all of you,
"I will keep you safe
if you turn back to me
  and calm down.
I will make you strong
  if you quietly trust me."

Then you stubbornly ¹⁶said,
"No! We will safely escape
  on speedy horses."

But those who chase you
  will be even faster.
¹⁷ As few as five of them,
or even one, will be enough
  to chase a thousand of you.
Finally, all that will be left
  will be a few survivors
as lonely as a flag pole
  on a barren hill.

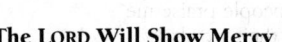

When the world is silent,
without breath of wind,
or bark of dog, or call of bird,
that's when God feeds into
me his deep thoughts.
LUCI SHAW

The LORD Will Show Mercy

¹⁸ The LORD God is waiting
  to show how kind he is
    and to have pity on you.
The LORD always does right;
  he blesses those who trust him.

¹⁹People of Jerusalem, you don't need to cry anymore. The Lord is kind, and as soon as he hears your cries for help, he will come. ²⁰The Lord has given you trouble and sorrow as your food and drink. But now you will again see the Lord, your teacher, and he will guide you. ²¹Whether you turn to the right or to the left, you will hear a voice saying, "This is the road! Now follow it." ²²Then you will treat your idols of silver and gold like garbage; you will throw them away like filthy rags.

²³The Lord will send rain to water the seeds you have planted—your fields will produce more crops than you need, and your cattle will graze in open pastures. ²⁴Even the oxen and donkeys that plow your fields will be fed the finest grain.[h] ²⁵On that day people will be slaughtered

---

[g]30.7 *a helpless monster*: One possible meaning for the difficult Hebrew text.   [h]30.24 *the finest grain*: The Hebrew text refers to grain with the husks removed.

and towers destroyed, but streams of water will flow from high hills and towering mountains. ²⁶Then the LORD will bandage his people's injuries and heal the wounds he has caused. The moon will shine as bright as the sun, and the sun will shine seven times brighter than usual. It will be like the light of seven days all at once.

Assyria Will Be Punished

²⁷The LORD is coming
    from far away
with his fiery anger
    and thick clouds of smoke.ⁱ
His angry words flame up
    like a destructive fire;
²⁸he breathes out a flood
    that comes up to the neck.
He sifts the nations
    and destroys them.
Then he puts a bridle
    in every foreigner's mouth
    and leads them to doom.

²⁹The LORD's people will sing as they do when they celebrate a religious festival^j at night. The LORD is Israel's mighty rock,^k and his people will be as happy as they are when they follow the sound of flutes to the mountain where he is worshiped. ³⁰The LORD will get furious. His fearsome voice will be heard, his arm will be seen ready to strike, and his anger will be like a destructive fire, followed by thunderstorms and hailstones. ³¹When the Assyrians hear the LORD's voice and see him striking with his iron rod, they will be terrified. ³²He will attack them in battle, and each time he strikes them, it will be to the music of tambourines and harps. ³³Long ago the LORD got a place ready for burning the body of the dead king.^l The place for the fire is deep and wide, the wood is piled high, and the LORD will start the fire by breathing out flaming sulfur.

Don't Trust the Power of Egypt

31 You are in for trouble
        if you go to Egypt for help,
    or if you depend on
an army of chariots
    or a powerful cavalry.
Instead you should depend on
and trust the holy LORD God
    of Israel.

²The LORD isn't stupid!
He does what he promises,
    and he can bring doom.
If you are cruel yourself,
    or help those who are evil,
        you will be destroyed.

³The Egyptians are mere humans.
    They aren't God.
Their horses are made of flesh;
    they can't live forever.
When the LORD shows his power,
he will destroy the Egyptians
    and all who depend on them.
Together they will fall.

⁴The LORD All-Powerful
    said to me,
"I will roar and attack
    like a fearless lion
not frightened by the shouts
of shepherds trying to protect
    their sheep.
That's how I will come down
    and fight on Mount Zion.
⁵I, the LORD All-Powerful,
    will protect Jerusalem
like a mother bird circling
    over her nest."

Come Back to the LORD

⁶People of Israel, come back!
You have completely turned
    from the LORD.
⁷The time is coming
    when you will throw away
your idols of silver and gold,
    made by your sinful hands.

⁸The Assyrians will be killed,
    but not by the swords
        of humans.
Their young men will try
    to escape,
but they will be captured
    and forced into slavery.

ⁱ**30.27** *with . . . smoke:* One possible meaning for the difficult Hebrew text. ^j**30.29** *a religious festival:* Probably Passover. ^k**30.29** *mighty rock:* See the note at 17.10. ^l**30.33** *burning . . . king:* Or "sacrificing the king" or "sacrificing to Molech." Human sacrifices were sometimes offered to Molech, a god whose name sounds like the Hebrew word for "king" (see 2 Kings 23.10; Jeremiah 32.35).

⁹Their fortress*ᵐ* will fall
  when terror strikes;
their army officers
will be frightened
  and run from the battle.
This is what the LORD has said,
the LORD whose fiery furnace
  is built on Mount Zion.

Justice Will Rule

32 A king and his leaders
  will rule with justice.
²They will be a place of safety
  from stormy winds,
a stream in the desert,
and a rock that gives shade
  from the heat of the sun.
³Then everyone who has eyes
  will open them and see,
and those who have ears
  will pay attention.
⁴All who are impatient
  will take time to think;
everyone who stutters
  will talk clearly.

⁵Fools will no longer
  be highly respected,
and crooks won't be given
  positions of honor.
⁶Fools talk foolishness.
They always make plans
  to do sinful things,
  to lie about the LORD,
  to let the hungry starve,
and to keep water from those
  who are thirsty.
⁷Cruel people tell lies—
they do evil things,
  and make cruel plans
  to destroy the poor and needy,
even when they beg
  for justice.
⁸But helpful people
can always be trusted
  to make helpful plans.

Punishment for the Women of Jerusalem

⁹Listen to what I say,
  you women who are carefree
  and careless!
¹⁰You may not have worries now,
  but in about a year,
the grape harvest will fail,
  and you will tremble.

¹¹Shake and shudder,
  you women without a care!
  Strip off your clothes—
  put on sackcloth.
¹²Slap your breasts in sorrow
  because of what happened
to the fruitful fields
  and vineyards,
¹³and to the happy homes
  in Jerusalem.
The land of my people
  is covered with thorns.

¹⁴The palace will be deserted,
  the crowded city empty.
Fortresses and towers
  will forever become
playgrounds for wild donkeys
  and pastures for sheep.

God's Spirit Makes the Difference

¹⁵When the Spirit is given to us
  from heaven,
deserts will become orchards
  thick as fertile forests.
¹⁶Honesty and justice
  will prosper there,
¹⁷and justice will produce
  lasting peace and security.

¹⁸You, the LORD's people,
  will live in peace,
  calm and secure,
¹⁹even if hailstones flatten
  forests and cities.
²⁰You will have God's blessing,
  as you plant your crops
  beside streams,
while your donkeys and cattle
  roam freely about.

Jerusalem Will Be Safe

33 You defeated my people.
  Now you're in for trouble!
  You've never been destroyed,
  but you will be destroyed;
you've never been betrayed,
  but you will be betrayed.
When you have finished
  destroying and betraying,
you will be destroyed
  and betrayed in return.

---

*ᵐ*31.9 *fortress:* The Hebrew text has "rock," which may
refer to the Assyrian god or king, or to their army.

² Please, LORD, be kind to us!
We depend on you.
Make us strong each morning,
and come to save us
when we are in trouble.
³ Nations scatter when you roar
and show your greatness.ⁿ
⁴ We attack our enemies
like swarms of locusts;^o
we take everything
that belongs to them.^p

---

*I've learned my
circumstances have
absolutely nothing to
do with God's ability
to fulfill his Word.*

KATHY TROCCOLI

---

⁵ You, LORD, are above all others,
and you live in the heavens.
You have brought justice
and fairness to Jerusalem;
⁶ you are the foundation
on which we stand today.
You always save us and give
true wisdom and knowledge.
Nothing means more to us^q
than obeying you.

The LORD Will Do Something

⁷ Listen! Our bravest soldiers
are running through the streets,
screaming for help.^r
Our messengers hoped for peace,
but came home crying.
⁸ No one travels anymore;
every road is empty.
Treaties are broken,
and no respect is shown
to any who keep promises.^s
⁹ Fields are dry and barren;
Mount Lebanon wilts
with shame.
Sharon Valley is a desert;
the forests of Bashan and Carmel
have lost their leaves.

¹⁰ But the LORD says,
"Now I will do something
and be greatly praised.
¹¹ Your deeds are straw
that will be set on fire
by your very own breath.
¹² You will be burned to ashes
like thorns in a fire.
¹³ Everyone, both far and near,
come look at what I have done.
See my mighty power!"

Punishment and Rewards

¹⁴ Those terrible sinners
on Mount Zion tremble
as they ask in fear,
"How can we possibly live
where a raging fire
never stops burning?"

¹⁵ But there will be rewards
for those who live right
and tell the truth,
for those who refuse
to take money by force
or accept bribes,
for all who hate murder
and violent crimes.
¹⁶ They will live in a fortress
high on a rocky cliff,
where they will have food
and plenty of water.

The LORD Is Our King

¹⁷ With your own eyes
you will see the glorious King;
you will see his kingdom
reaching far and wide.
¹⁸ Then you will ask yourself,
"Where are those officials
who terrified us and forced us
to pay such heavy taxes?"
¹⁹ You will never again have to see
the proud people who spoke
a strange and foreign language
you could not understand.

---

n33.3 *greatness*: One possible meaning for the difficult Hebrew text of verse 3.   **o33.4** *locusts*: Insects like grasshoppers that travel in swarms and cause great damage to crops.   **p33.4** *them*: One possible meaning for the difficult Hebrew text of verse 4. **q33.6** *Nothing . . . us*: One possible meaning for the difficult Hebrew text.   **r33.7** *Listen . . . help*: Or "The LORD heard our shouts and will come to help us." **s33.8** *to any . . . promises*: The Dead Sea Scrolls; the Standard Hebrew Text "to those in the cities."

²⁰ Look to Mount Zion
where we celebrate
our religious festivals.
You will see Jerusalem,
secure as a tent with pegs
that cannot be pulled up
and fastened with ropes
that can never be broken.
²¹ Our wonderful LORD
will be with us!
There will be deep rivers
and wide streams
safe from enemy ships.ᵗ

The LORD Is Our Judge

²² The LORD is our judge
and our ruler;
the LORD is our king
and will keep us safe.
²³ But your nationᵘ is a ship
with its rigging loose,
its mast shaky,
and its sail not spread.

Someday even you that are lame
will take everything you want
from your enemies.
²⁴ The LORD will forgive your sins,
and none of you will say,
"I feel sick."

The Nations Will Be Judged

34 Everyone of every nation,
the entire earth,
and all of its creatures,
come here and listen!
² The LORD is terribly angry
with the nations;
he has condemned them
to be slaughtered.
³ Their dead bodies will be left
to rot and stink;
their blood will flow
down the mountains.
⁴ Each starᵛ will disappear—
the sky will roll up
like a scroll.ʷ
Everything in the sky
will dry up and wilt
like leaves on a vine
or fruit on a tree.

Trouble for Edom

⁵ After the sword of the LORD
has done what it wants

to the skies above,ˣ
it will come down on Edom,
the nation that the LORD
has doomed for destruction.

⁶ The sword of the LORD
is covered with blood
from lambs and goats,
together with fat
from kidneys of rams.
This is because the LORD
will slaughter many people
and make a sacrifice of them
in the city of Bozrah
and everywhere else
in Edom.
⁷ Edom's leaders are wild oxen.
They are powerful bulls,
but they will die
with the others.
Their country will be soaked
with their blood,
and its soil made fertile
with their fat.

⁸ The LORD has chosen
the year and the day,
when he will take revenge
and come to Zion's defense.
⁹ Edom's streams will turn into tar
and its soil into sulfur—
then the whole country
will go up in flames.
¹⁰ It will burn night and day
and never stop smoking.
Edom will be a desert,
generation after generation;
no one will ever travel
through that land.
¹¹ Owls, hawks, and wild animalsʸ
will make it their home.
God will leave it in ruins,
merely a pile of rocks.

ᵗ33.21 *safe . . . ships:* This probably means that
Jerusalem will have a lot of water, without the danger of
attacks from enemy ships. ᵘ33.23 *your nation:* Possibly
Judah or Assyria. ᵛ34.4 *star:* Stars were worshiped
as gods. ʷ34.4 *scroll:* A roll of paper or specially
prepared leather used for writing on. ˣ34.5 *has
done . . . above:* The Standard Hebrew Text; the Dead Sea
Scrolls "appears in the skies above." ʸ34.11 *Owls . . .
animals:* One possible meaning for the difficult
Hebrew text.

The End of Edom

[12] Edom will be called
"Kingdom of Nothing."
Its rulers will also be nothing.
[13] Its palaces and fortresses
will be covered with thorns;
only wolves and ostriches
will make their home there.
[14] Wildcats and hyenas
will hunt together,
demons will scream to demons,
and creatures of the night
will live among the ruins.
[15] Owls will nest there
to raise their young
among its shadows,[z]
while families of buzzards
circle around.

[16] In *The Book of the LORD*[a]
you can search and find
where it is written,
"The LORD brought together
all of his creatures
by the power of his Spirit.
Not one is missing."
[17] The LORD has decided
where they each should live;
they will be there forever,
generation after generation.

God's Splendor Will Be Seen

35 Thirsty deserts will be glad;
barren lands will celebrate
and blossom with flowers.
[2] Deserts will bloom everywhere
and sing joyful songs.
They will be as majestic
as Mount Lebanon,
as glorious as Mount Carmel
or Sharon Valley.
Everyone will see
the wonderful splendor
of the LORD our God.

God Changes Everything

*[3] Here is a message for all
who are weak, trembling,
and worried:
[4] "Cheer up! Don't be afraid.
Your God is coming
to punish your enemies.
God will take revenge on them
and rescue you."

[5] The blind will see,
and the ears of the deaf
will be healed.
[6] Those who were lame
will leap around like deer;
tongues once silent
will begin to shout.
Water will rush
through the desert.
[7] Scorching sand
will turn into a lake,
and thirsty ground
will flow with fountains.
Grass will grow in wetlands,
where packs of wild dogs
once made their home.[b]

*When God restores, he restores
beyond our dreams. I'm
learning not to be surprised
at the amazing things he does,
just very thankful. I now
look toward the future with
excitement and enthusiasm.
By faith, you can, too.*
VIRELLE KIDDER

God's Sacred Highway

[8] A good road will be there,
and it will be named
"God's Sacred Highway."
It will be for God's people;
no one unfit to worship God
will walk on that road.
And no fools can travel
on that highway.[c]
[9] No lions or other wild animals
will come near that road;
only those the LORD has saved
will travel there.

---

[z]**34.15** *Owls . . . shadows:* One possible meaning for the
difficult Hebrew text.   [a]**34.16** *The Book of the LORD:*
The book that Isaiah refers to is unknown.
[b]**35.7** *where . . . home:* One possible meaning for the
difficult Hebrew text.   [c]**35.8** *And . . . highway:* Or "And
not even a fool can miss that highway."

¹⁰The people the LORD has rescued
will come back singing
   as they enter Zion.
Happiness will be a crown
   they will always wear.
They will celebrate and shout
because all sorrows and worries
   will be gone far away.

The Assyrians Surround Jerusalem
(2 Kings 18.13-37; 2 Chronicles 32.1-19)

36 Hezekiah had been king of Judah for fourteen years when King Sennacherib of Assyria invaded the country and captured every walled city ²except Jerusalem. The Assyrian king ordered his army commander to leave the city of Lachish and to take a large army to Jerusalem.

The commander went there and stood on the road near the cloth makers' shops along the canal from the upper pool. ³Three of the king's highest officials came out of Jerusalem to meet him. One of them was Hilkiah's son Eliakim, who was the prime minister. The other two were Shebna, assistant to the prime minister, and Joah son of Asaph, keeper of the government records.

⁴The Assyrian commander told them:

I have a message for Hezekiah from the great king of Assyria. Ask Hezekiah why he feels so sure of himself. ⁵Does he think he can plan and win a war with nothing but words? Who is going to help him, now that he has turned against the king of Assyria? ⁶Is he depending on Egypt and its king? That's the same as leaning on a broken stick, and it will go right through his hand.

⁷Is Hezekiah now depending on the LORD, your God? Didn't Hezekiah tear down all except one of the LORD's altars and places of worship?^d Didn't he tell the people of Jerusalem and Judah to worship at that one place?

⁸The king of Assyria wants to make a bet with you people! He will give you two thousand horses, if you have enough troops to ride them. ⁹How could you even defeat our lowest ranking officer, when you have to depend on Egypt for chariots and cavalry? ¹⁰Don't forget that it was the LORD who sent me here with orders to destroy your nation!

¹¹Eliakim, Shebna, and Joah said, "Sir, we don't want the people listening from the city wall to understand what you are saying. So please speak to us in Aramaic instead of Hebrew."

¹²The Assyrian army commander answered, "My king sent me to speak to everyone, not just to you leaders. These people will soon have to eat their own body waste and drink their own urine! And so will the three of you!"

¹³Then, in a voice loud enough for everyone to hear, he shouted out in Hebrew:

Listen to what the great king of Assyria says! ¹⁴Don't be fooled by Hezekiah. He can't save you. ¹⁵Don't trust him when he tells you that the LORD will protect you from the king of Assyria. ¹⁶Stop listening to Hezekiah. Pay attention to my king. Surrender to him. He will let you keep your own vineyards, fig trees, and cisterns ¹⁷for a while. Then he will come and take you away to a country just like yours, where you can plant vineyards and raise your own grain.

¹⁸Hezekiah claims the LORD will save you. But don't be fooled by him. Were any other gods able to defend their land against the king of Assyria? ¹⁹What happened to the gods of Hamath, Arpad, and Sepharvaim? Were the gods of Samaria able to protect their land against the Assyrian forces? ²⁰None of these gods kept their people safe from the king of Assyria. Do you think the LORD, your God, can do any better?

²¹⁻²²Eliakim, Shebna, and Joah had been warned by King Hezekiah not to answer the Assyrian commander. So they tore their clothes in sorrow and reported to Hezekiah everything the commander had said.

Hezekiah Asks Isaiah for Advice
(2 Kings 19.1-13)

37 As soon as Hezekiah heard the news, he tore off his clothes in sorrow and put on sackcloth.

---

^d**36.7** *worship:* Hezekiah actually had torn down the places where idols were worshiped, and he had told the people to worship the LORD at the one place of worship in Jerusalem. But the Assyrian leader was confused and thought these were also places where the LORD was supposed to be worshiped.

Then he went into the temple of the LORD. [2]He told Prime Minister Eliakim, Assistant Prime Minister Shebna, and the senior priests to dress in sackcloth and tell me: [3]Isaiah, these are difficult and disgraceful times. Our nation is like a woman too weak to give birth, when it's time for her baby to be born. [4]Please pray for those of us who are left alive. The king of Assyria sent his army commander to insult the living God. Perhaps the LORD heard what he said and will do something, if you will pray.

[5]When these leaders came to me, [6]I told them that the LORD had this message for Hezekiah:

I am the LORD. Don't worry about the insulting things that have been said about me by these messengers from the king of Assyria. [7]I will upset him with rumors about what's happening in his own country. He will go back, and there I will make him die a violent death.

[8]Meanwhile the commander of the Assyrian forces heard that his king had left the town of Lachish and was now attacking Libnah. So he went there.

[9]About this same time, the king of Assyria learned that King Tirhakah of Ethiopia[e] was on his way to attack him. Then the king of Assyria sent some messengers with this note for Hezekiah:

[10]Don't trust your God or be fooled by his promise to defend Jerusalem against me. [11]You have heard how we Assyrian kings have completely wiped out other nations. What makes you feel so safe? [12]The Assyrian kings before me destroyed the towns of Gozan, Haran, Rezeph, and everyone from Eden who lived in Telassar. What good did their gods do them? [13]The kings of Hamath, Arpad, Sepharvaim, Hena, and Ivvah have all disappeared.

Hezekiah Prays
(2 Kings 19.14-19)

[14]After Hezekiah had read the note from the king of Assyria, he took it to the temple and spread it out for the LORD to see. [15]Then he prayed:

[16]LORD God All-Powerful of Israel, your throne is above the winged creatures.[f] You created the heavens and the earth, and you alone rule the kingdoms of this world. [17]Just look and see how Sennacherib has insulted you, the living God.

[18]It is true, our LORD, that Assyrian kings have turned nations into deserts. [19]They destroyed the idols of wood and stone that the people of those nations had made and worshiped. [20]But you are our LORD and our God! We ask you to keep us safe from the Assyrian king. Then everyone in every kingdom on earth will know that you are the only LORD.

Isaiah Gives the LORD's Answer to Hezekiah
(2 Kings 19.20-34)

[21-22]I went to Hezekiah and told him that the LORD God of Israel had said:

Hezekiah, you prayed to me about King Sennacherib of Assyria.[g] Now this is what I say to that king:

The people of Jerusalem
hate and make fun of you;
    they laugh behind your back.

[23]Sennacherib, you cursed,
    shouted, and sneered at me,
        the holy God of Israel.
[24]You let your officials
    insult me, the Lord.
And here is what you
    have said about yourself,
"I led my chariots
to the highest heights
    of Lebanon's mountains.
I went deep into its forest,
cutting down the best cedar
    and cypress trees.
[25]I dried up every stream
    in the land of Egypt,
and I drank water
    from wells I had dug."

[26]Sennacherib, now listen
    to me, the LORD.

---

[e]**37.9** *Ethiopia:* See the note at 11.11. [f]**37.16** *winged creatures:* Two winged creatures made of gold were on the top of the sacred chest and were symbols of the LORD's throne on earth (see Exodus 25.18; 2 Samuel 6.2). [g]**37.21,22** *Hezekiah, you prayed . . . Assyria:* One possible meaning for the difficult Hebrew text.

I planned all of this long ago.
And you don't even know
    that I alone am the one
who decided that you
    would do these things.
I let you make ruins
    of fortified cities.
²⁷ Their people became weak,
    terribly confused.
They were like wild flowers
or like tender young grass
    growing on a flat roof
or like a field of grain
    before it matures.ʰ

²⁸ I know all about you,
    even how fiercely angry
    you are with me.
²⁹ I have seen your pride
and the tremendous hatred
    you have for me.
Now I will put a hook
    in your nose,
    a bit in your mouth,ⁱ
then I will send you back
    to where you came from.

³⁰Hezekiah, I will tell you what's going to happen. This year you will eat crops that grow on their own, and the next year you will eat whatever springs up where those crops grew. But the third year, you will plant grain and vineyards, and you will eat what you harvest. ³¹Those who survive in Judah will be like a vine that puts down deep roots and bears fruit. ³²I, the LORD All-Powerful, will see to it that some who live in Jerusalem will survive.

³³I promise that the king of Assyria won't get into Jerusalem, or shoot an arrow into the city, or even surround it and prepare to attack. ³⁴As surely as I am the LORD, he will return by the way he came and will never enter Jerusalem. ³⁵I will protect it for the sake of my own honor and because of the promise I made to my servant David.

The Death of King Sennacherib
(2 Kings 19.35-37)

³⁶The LORD sent an angel to the camp of the Assyrians, and he killed one hundred eighty-five thousand of them all in one night. The next morning, the camp was full

of dead bodies. ³⁷After this, King Sennacherib went back to Assyria and lived in the city of Nineveh. ³⁸One day he was worshiping in the temple of his god Nisroch, when his sons, Adrammelech and Sharezer, killed him with their swords. They escaped to the land of Ararat, and his son Esarhaddon became king.ʲ

Hezekiah Gets Sick and Almost Dies
(2 Kings 20.1-11; 2 Chronicles 32.24-26)

38 About this time, Hezekiah got sick and was almost dead. So I went in and told him, "The LORD says you won't ever get well. You are going to die, and so you had better start doing what needs to be done."

²Hezekiah turned toward the wall and prayed, ³"Don't forget that I have been faithful to you, LORD. I have obeyed you with all my heart, and I do whatever you say is right." After this, he cried hard.

⁴Then the LORD sent me ⁵with this message for Hezekiah:

I am the LORD God, who was worshiped by your ancestor David. I heard you pray, and I saw you cry. I will let you live fifteen years more, ⁶while I protect you and your city from the king of Assyria.

⁷Now I will prove to you that I will keep my promise. ⁸Do you see the shadow made by the setting sun on the stairway built for King Ahaz? I will make the shadow go back ten steps. Then the shadow went back ten steps.ᵏ

King Hezekiah's Song of Praise

⁹This is what Hezekiah wrote after he got well:

¹⁰ I thought I would die
    during my best years

ʰ**37.27** *tender young grass . . . matures*: The Standard Hebrew Text; the Dead Sea Scrolls and some Hebrew manuscripts "tender young grass, growing on a flat roof and scorched by the heat." Many of the houses had roofs made of packed earth. Grass would sometimes grow on the roof, but it would die quickly because of the sun and hot winds. ⁱ**37.29** *I will put . . . your mouth*: This is how the Assyrians treated their prisoners, and now the LORD will treat Sennacherib the same way. ʲ**37.38** *Esarhaddon became king*: He ruled Assyria 681-669 B.C. ᵏ**38.8** *steps*: One possible meaning for the difficult Hebrew text of verse 8.

and stay as a prisoner forever
in the world of the dead.
[11] I thought I would never again
see you, my LORD,
or any of the people
who live on this earth.

> *Praise God every day.*
> *Think of five new things*
> *to thank God for. You'll*
> *never run out of ideas,*
> *because God will keep*
> *supplying new ones!*
> ELIZABETH CODY NEWENHUYSE

[12] My life was taken from me
like the tent that a shepherd
pulls up and moves.
You cut me off like thread
from a weaver's loom;
you make a wreck of me
day and night.

[13] Until morning came, I thought
you would crush my bones
just like a hungry lion;
both night and day
you make a wreck of me.[l]
[14] I cry like a swallow;
I mourn like a dove.
My eyes are red
from looking to you, LORD.
I am terribly abused.
Please come and help me.[m]
[15] There's nothing I can say
in answer to you,
since you are the one
who has done this to me.[n]
My life has turned sour;
I will limp until I die.

[16] Your words and your deeds
bring life to everyone,
including me.[o]
Please make me healthy
and strong again.
[17] It was for my own good
that I had such hard times.

But your love protected me
from doom in the deep pit,[p]
and you turned your eyes
away from my sins.

[18] No one in the world of the dead
can thank you or praise you;
none of those in the deep pit
can hope for you to show them
how faithful you are.
[19] Only the living can thank you,
as I am doing today.
Each generation tells the next
about your faithfulness.[q]

[20] You, LORD, will save me,
and every day that we live
we will sing in your temple
to the music
of stringed instruments.

Isaiah's Advice to Hezekiah

[21] I had told King Hezekiah's servants to put some mashed figs on the king's open sore, and he would get well. [22] Then Hezekiah asked for proof that he would again worship in the LORD's temple.

Isaiah Speaks the LORD's Message to Hezekiah
(2 Kings 20.12-19)

39 Merodach Baladan, the son of Baladan, was now king of Babylonia. And when he learned that Hezekiah was well, he sent messengers with letters and a gift for him. [2] Hezekiah welcomed the messengers and showed them all the silver, the gold, the spices, and the fine oils that were in his storehouse. He even showed them where he kept his weapons. Nothing in his palace or in his entire kingdom was kept hidden from them.

[3] I asked Hezekiah, "Where did these men come from? What did they want?"

"They came all the way from Babylonia," Hezekiah answered.

---

[l]**38.13** *of me:* One possible meaning for the difficult Hebrew text of verse 13.   [m]**38.14** *help me:* One possible meaning for the difficult Hebrew text of verse 14.   [n]**38.15** *There's . . . me:* One possible meaning for the difficult Hebrew text.   [o]**38.16** *Your . . . me:* One possible meaning for the difficult Hebrew text.   [p]**38.17** *deep pit:* The world of the dead, as in verse 18.   [q]**38.19** *about your faithfulness:* One possible meaning for the difficult Hebrew text.

⁴"What did you show them?" I asked.
Hezekiah answered, "I showed them everything in my kingdom."

⁵Then I told Hezekiah:

I have a message for you from the LORD All-Powerful. ⁶One day everything you and your ancestors have stored up will be taken to Babylonia. The LORD has promised that nothing will be left. ⁷Some of your own sons will be taken to Babylonia, where they will be disgraced and made to serve in the king's palace.

⁸Hezekiah thought, "At least our nation will be at peace for a while." So he told me, "The message you brought from the LORD is good."

Encourage God's People

40 Our God has said:
"Encourage my people!
    Give them comfort.
²Speak kindly to Jerusalem
    and announce:
Your slavery is past;
    your punishment is over.
I, the LORD, made you pay
    double for your sins."

³Someone is shouting:
"Clear a path in the desert!
    Make a straight road
    for the LORD our God.
⁴Fill in the valleys;
flatten every hill
    and mountain.
Level the rough
    and rugged ground.
⁵Then the glory of the LORD
    will appear for all to see.
The LORD has promised this!"

⁶Someone told me to shout,
    and I asked,
    "What should I shout?"
We humans are merely grass,
    and we last no longer
    than wild flowers.
⁷At the LORD's command,
flowers and grass disappear,
    and so do we.
⁸Flowers and grass fade away,
    but what our God has said
    will never change.

Your God Is Here!

⁹There is good news
    for the city of Zion.
Shout it as loud as you can^r
    from the highest mountain.
Don't be afraid to shout
to the towns of Judah,
    "Your God is here!"
¹⁰Look! The powerful LORD God
    is coming to rule
    with his mighty arm.
He brings with him
what he has taken in war,
    and he rewards his people.
¹¹The LORD cares for his nation,
just as shepherds care
    for their flocks.
He carries the lambs
    in his arms,
while gently leading
    the mother sheep.

Who Compares with God?

¹²Did any of you measure
    the ocean by yourself
or stretch out the sky
    with your own hands?
Did you put the soil
    of the earth in a bucket
or weigh the hills and mountains
    on balance scales?

¹³Has anyone told the LORD^s
    what he must do
    or given him advice?
¹⁴Did the LORD ask anyone
    to teach him wisdom
    and justice?
Who gave him knowledge
    and understanding?
¹⁵To the LORD, all nations
    are merely a drop in a bucket
    or dust on balance scales;
all of the islands
    are but a handful of sand.
¹⁶The cattle
    on Lebanon's mountains
would not be enough to offer
    as a sacrifice to God,
and the trees would not
    be enough for the fire.

---

^r40.9 *There . . . can:* Or "City of Jerusalem, you have good news. Shout it as loud as you can." ^s40.13 *the* LORD: Or "the LORD's Spirit."

¹⁷ God thinks of the nations
as far less than nothing.

¹⁸ Who compares with God?
Is anything like him?
¹⁹ Is an idol at all like God?
It is made of bronze
with a thin layer of gold,
and decorated with silver.
²⁰ Or special wood may be chosen^t
because it doesn't rot—
then skilled hands
take care to make an idol
that won't fall on its face.

God Rules the Whole Earth

²¹ Don't you know?
Haven't you heard?
Isn't it clear that God
created the world?^u
²² God is the one who rules
the whole earth,
and we that live here
are merely insects.
He spread out the heavens
like a curtain or an open tent.

²³ God brings down rulers
and turns them into nothing.
²⁴ They are like flowers
freshly sprung up
and starting to grow.

But when God blows on them,
they wilt and are carried off
like straw in a storm.

²⁵ The holy God asks,
"Who compares with me?
Is anyone my equal?"

²⁶ Look at the evening sky!
Who created the stars?
Who gave them each a name?
Who leads them like an army?
The LORD is so powerful
that none of the stars
are ever missing.

The LORD Gives Strength

²⁷ You people of Israel, say,
"God pays no attention to us!
He doesn't care if we
are treated unjustly."

But how can you say that?
²⁸ Don't you know?
Haven't you heard?

---

^t**40.20** *Or . . . chosen*: One possible meaning for the
difficult Hebrew text. Two kinds of idols seem to be
described: bronze idols covered with gold (verse 19)
and wooden idols (verse 20).   ^u**40.21** *Isn't . . . world*:
Or "Hasn't it been clear since the time of creation?"

SingleLife—How can I feel whole when the world sees me as half?
(Isaiah 40.21-31)

Remember, God gives you freedom to soar.
While the Bible talks about marriage as a gift from God, nowhere does it tell us marriage
is a requirement for a happy, godly life. Yet single Christians, especially single women, are
often treated as "works in progress," not quite ready to contribute to God's kingdom.
What a mistake!

When the gifts of single women are ignored, we all lose out on God's amazing wisdom
in using all kinds of people—young, old, wise, foolish, married, and single—to reach out
to the world. God uses the life situations of each of us to his full advantage. Even when
we don't understand why our life is the way it is, we can be assured that God will give
us energy and inner freedom to soar—as if on eagles' wings. It's what he's promised
(40.29-31).

Trusting in God's wisdom is easier said than done. But as we use the gifts God has given
us, we discover that God uses each of us in a unique way—no matter what our marital
status. (See also Psalm 23; Philippians 1.12-30.)

Words To Remember: *But those who trust the LORD will find new strength. They
will be strong like eagles soaring upward on wings; they will walk and run without getting
tired.—Isaiah 40.31*

The LORD is the eternal God,
    Creator of the earth.
He never gets weary or tired;
    his wisdom cannot be measured.

²⁹ The LORD gives strength
    to those who are weary.
³⁰ Even young people get tired,
    then stumble and fall.
³¹ But those who trust the LORD
    will find new strength.
They will be strong like eagles
    soaring upward on wings;
they will walk and run
    without getting tired.

The LORD Controls Human Events

41 Be silent and listen,
    every island in the sea.
Have courage and come near,
    every one of you nations.
Let's settle this matter!
² Who appointed this ruler
    from the east?^v
Who puts nations and kings
    in his power?^w
His sword and his arrows
turn them to dust
    blown by the wind.
³ He goes after them so quickly
that his feet
    barely touch the ground—
he doesn't even get hurt.

⁴ Who makes these things happen?
Who controls human events?
    I do! I am the LORD.
I was there at the beginning;
    I will be there at the end.
⁵ Islands and foreign nations
saw what I did and trembled
    as they came near.

What Can Idols Do?

⁶ Worshipers of idols
comfort each other,
    saying, "Don't worry!"
⁷ Woodcarvers, goldsmiths,
    and other workers^x
encourage one another and say,
    "We've done a great job!"
Then they nail the idol down,
    so it won't fall over.

The LORD's Chosen Servant

⁸ Israel, you are my servant.
I chose you, the family
    of my friend Abraham.
⁹ From far across the earth
    I brought you here and said,
"You are my chosen servant.
    I haven't forgotten you."

One day I clearly heard God calling me into the ministry. I began to argue, <u>God, I only have a little strength. I'm inadequate. I can't do it.</u> But God didn't accept my excuses. He seemed to respond, <u>Anne, you are weak, but I am strong. You are inadequate, but I am sufficient. Make yourself available to me for service.</u>

ANNE GRAHAM LOTZ

¹⁰ Don't be afraid. I am with you.
    Don't tremble with fear.
    I am your God.
I will make you strong,
    as I protect you with my arm
    and give you victories.
¹¹ Everyone who hates you
    will be terribly disgraced;
those who attack
    will vanish into thin air.
¹² You will look around
    for those brutal enemies,
but you won't find them
    because they will be gone.

¹³ I am the LORD your God.
I am holding your hand,

---

^v **41.2** *ruler from the east*: Probably Cyrus (see 44.28; 45.1; 48.14).   ^w **41.2** *Who puts . . . power*: One possible meaning for the difficult Hebrew text.   ^x **41.7** *and other workers*: One possible meaning for the difficult Hebrew text.

so don't be afraid.
I am here to help you.

¹⁴ People of Israel, don't worry,
though others may say,
   "Israel is only a worm!"
I am the holy God of Israel,
who saves and protects you.
¹⁵ I will let you be like a log
covered with sharp spikes.ʸ
You will grind and crush
every mountain and hillᶻ
   until they turn to dust.
¹⁶ A strong wind will scatter them
in all directions.
Then you will celebrate
and praise me, your LORD,
   the holy God of Israel.

The LORD Helps the Poor

¹⁷ When the poor and needy
are dying of thirst
   and cannot find water,
I, the LORD God of Israel,
will come to their rescue.
I won't forget them.
¹⁸ I will make rivers flow
on mountain peaks.
I will send streams
to fill the valleys.
Dry and barren land
will flow with springs
and become a lake.
¹⁹ I will fill the desert
with all kinds of trees—
cedars, acacias, and myrtles;
olive and cypress trees;
   fir trees and pines.
²⁰ Everyone will see this
and know that I,
the holy LORD God of Israel,
   created it all.

Idols Are Useless

²¹ I am the LORD,
the King of Israel!
Come argue your case with me.
   Present your evidence.
²² Come near me, you idols.ᵃ
Tell us about the past,
and we will think about it.
Tell us about the future,
so we will know
   what is going to happen.

²³ Prove that you are gods
by making your predictions
   come true.
Do something good or evil,
so we can be amazed
   and terrified.ᵇ
²⁴ You idols are nothing,
and you are powerless.ᶜ
To worship you
   would be disgusting.

²⁵ I, the LORD, appointed a ruler
in the north;
now he comes from the east
to honor my name.
He tramplesᵈ kings like mud,
as potters trample clay.ᵉ
²⁶ Did any of you idols predict
what would happen?
Did any of you get it right?
None of you told about this
or even spoke a word.
²⁷ I was the first to tell
the people of Jerusalem,
   "Look, it's happening!"ᶠ
I was the one who announced
this good news to Zion.

²⁸ None of these idols
are able to give advice
   or answer questions.
²⁹ They are nothing,ᵍ
and they can do nothing—
they are less
   than a passing breeze.

The LORD's Servant

42 Here is my servant!
   I have made him strong.
He is my chosen one;
   I am pleased with him.
I have given him my Spirit,

ʸ**41.15** *I will let . . . sharp spikes*: In ancient times a heavy
object was sometimes dragged over wheat or barley to
separate the grain from the husk. This was called
threshing.   ᶻ**41.15** *mountain and hill*: These stand for
the power and pride of Israel's enemies.   ᵃ**41.22** *Come
near . . . idols*: One possible meaning for the difficult
Hebrew text.   ᵇ**41.23** *and terrified*: Or "when we
see it."   ᶜ**41.24** *powerless*: One possible meaning for
the difficult Hebrew text.   ᵈ**41.25** *tramples*: One
possible meaning for the difficult Hebrew text.
ᵉ**41.25** *trample clay*: This was done to soften the
clay and make it easier to shape.   ᶠ**41.27** *Look . . .
happening*: One possible meaning for the difficult
Hebrew text.   ᵍ**41.29** *nothing*: One possible meaning
for the difficult Hebrew text.

and he will bring justice
  to the nations.
² He won't shout or yell
  or call out in the streets.
³ He won't break off a bent reed
  or put out a dying flame,
but he will make sure
  that justice is done.
⁴ He won't quit or give up
until he brings justice
  everywhere on earth,
and people in foreign nations
  long for his teaching.

⁵ I am the LORD God.
I created the heavens
  like an open tent above.
I made the earth and everything
  that grows on it.
I am the source of life
for all who live on this earth,
  so listen to what I say.
⁶ I chose you to bring justice,
  and I am here at your side.
I selected and sent you*h*
  to bring light
and my promise of hope
  to the nations.
⁷ You will give sight
  to the blind;
you will set prisoners free
  from dark dungeons.

⁸ My name is the LORD!
I won't let idols or humans
  share my glory and praise.
⁹ Everything has happened
  just as I said it would;
now I will announce
  what will happen next.

Sing Praises to the LORD

¹⁰ Tell the whole world to sing
  a new song to the LORD!
Tell those who sail the ocean
and those who live far away
  to join in the praise.
¹¹ Tell the tribes of the desert
and everyone in the mountains*i*
  to celebrate and sing.
¹² Let them announce
  his praises everywhere.
¹³ The LORD is marching out
  like an angry soldier,

shouting with all his might
  while attacking his enemies.

The LORD Will Help His People

¹⁴ For a long time, I, the LORD,
  have held my temper;
now I will scream and groan
  like a woman giving birth.
¹⁵ I will destroy the mountains
  and what grows on them;
I will dry up rivers and ponds.

¹⁶ I will lead the blind on roads
  they have never known;
I will guide them on paths
  they have never traveled.
Their road is dark and rough,
  but I will give light
to keep them from stumbling.
  This is my solemn promise.

¹⁷ Everyone who worships idols
as though they were gods
  will be terribly ashamed.

God's People Won't Obey

¹⁸ You people are deaf and blind,
  but the LORD commands you
  to listen and to see.
¹⁹ No one is as blind or deaf
as his messenger,
  his chosen servant,
²⁰ who sees and hears so much,
  but pays no attention.

²¹ The LORD always does right,
  and so he wanted his Law
  to be greatly praised.*j*
²² But his people were trapped
  and imprisoned in holes
  with no one to rescue them.
All they owned had been taken,
  and no one was willing
  to give it back.
²³ Why won't his people
  ever learn to listen?

²⁴ Israel sinned and refused
  to obey the LORD

---

*h**42.6** I selected . . . you: One possible meaning for the difficult Hebrew text.   *i**42.11** desert . . . mountains: The Hebrew text includes the place names of Kedar in the desert and Sela in the mountains.   *j**42.21** greatly praised: One possible meaning for the difficult Hebrew text of verse 21.

or follow his instructions.
So the LORD let them be robbed
   of everything they owned.
25 He was furious with them
   and punished their nation
   with the fires of war.
Still they paid no attention.
   They didn't even care
when they were surrounded
   and scorched by flames.

The LORD Has Rescued His People

43 Descendants of Jacob,
   I, the LORD, created you
      and formed your nation.
Israel, don't be afraid.
   I have rescued you.
I have called you by name;
   now you belong to me.

*Our purpose as
a family is to provide a
safe environment for children
and grown-ups alike,
to learn more about loving
and serving Jesus through
the act of learning
how to love and
serve each other.*

KAREN SCALF LINAMEN

2 When you cross deep rivers,
   I will be with you,
      and you won't drown.
When you walk through fire,
   you won't be burned
      or scorched by the flames.

3 I am the LORD, your God,
   the Holy One of Israel,
      the God who saves you.
I gave up Egypt, Ethiopia,*k*
and the region of Seba*l*
   in exchange for you.
4 To me, you are very dear,
   and I love you.

That's why I gave up nations
   and people to rescue you.

5 Don't be afraid! I am with you.
From both east and west
   I will bring you together.
6 I will say to the north
   and to the south,
"Free my sons and daughters!
Let them return
   from distant lands.
7 They are my people—
I created each of them
   to bring honor to me."

The LORD Alone Is God

The LORD said:

8 Bring my people together.
They have eyes and ears,
   but they can't see or hear.
9 Tell everyone of every nation
   to gather around.
None of them can honestly say,
   "We told you so!"
If someone heard them say this,
   then tell us about it now.

10 My people, you are my witnesses
   and my chosen servant.
I want you to know me,
   to trust me, and understand
      that I alone am God.
I have always been God;
   there can be no others.
11 I alone am the LORD;
   only I can rescue you.
12 I promised to save you,
   and I kept my promise.
You are my witnesses
   that no other god did this.
      I, the LORD, have spoken.
13 I am God now and forever.
No one can snatch you from me
   or stand in my way.

The LORD Will Prepare the Way

14 I, the LORD, will rescue you!
   I am Israel's holy God,

---

*k*43.3 *Ethiopia:* See the note at 11.11.   *l*43.3 *Seba:* A region in southwest Arabia. Egypt, Ethiopia, and Seba probably stood for all that was known of Africa in biblical times.

and this is my promise:
For your sake, I will send
    an army against Babylon
to drag its people away,
    crying as they go.[m]

15 I am the LORD, your holy God,
    Israel's Creator and King.
16 I am the one who cut a path
    through the mighty ocean.
17 I sent an army to chase you
    with chariots and horses;
now they lie dead,
    unable to move.
They are like an oil lamp
    with the flame snuffed out.

Forget the Past

The LORD said:

18 Forget what happened long ago!
    Don't think about the past.
19 I am creating something new.
    There it is! Do you see it?
I have put roads in deserts,
    streams[n] in thirsty lands.
20 Every wild animal honors me,
    even jackals[o] and owls.
I provide water in deserts—
streams in thirsty lands
    for my chosen people.

21 I made them my own nation,
    so they would praise me.

22 I, the LORD, said to Israel:
You have become weary,
    but not from worshiping me.
23 You have not honored me
by sacrificing sheep
    or other animals.
And I have not burdened you
with demands for sacrifices
    or sweet-smelling incense.

24 You have not brought
    delicious spices for me
or given me the best part
    of your sacrificed animals.
Instead, you burden me down
    with your terrible sins.
25 But I wipe away your sins
    because of who I am.
And so, I will forget
    the wrongs you have done.

26 Meet me in court!
State your case and prove
    that you are right.

---

[m]43.14 *crying as they go:* Or "in their glorious ships."
[n]43.19 *streams:* The Standard Hebrew Text; the Dead Sea Scrolls "paths." [o]43.20 *jackals:* Desert animals related to wolves, but smaller.

Friendship—How can I encourage a friend who is going through a divorce?
(Isaiah 43.2-4)

Encourage her with God's words.

You've just heard that your good friend is going through a divorce. You're in shock. What do you do? Is there any way to soothe the hurt? Should you help out with housework, financial resources, a place to stay, a listening ear? And what's worse, what do you say when you first see her?

Sometimes the best thing we can humanly do is just be there and not say anything. Maybe a hug or a night out without talking about the divorce will give your friend the breather she needs to regroup. Let your friend know that you cherish *her* and her friendship—and that God loves her. And in her times of greatest grief and upheaval, be ready with words of comfort from the Bible. These words of Isaiah are perfect for such times. They make it clear that God's heart is tender toward us (43.4), that he will protect us and never leave us (43.2).

Share these verses with your friend in a "Thinking about you" card or in person. They just might be the heavenly hug your friend needs today! (See also Job 13.5-15; Isaiah 61.1-3; 2 Corinthians 1.3-7.)

Words To Remember: *When you cross deep rivers, I will be with you, and you won't drown. When you walk through fire, you won't be burned or scorched by the flames . . . . To me, you are very dear, and I love you.*—Isaiah 43.2,4

²⁷ Your earliest ancestor^p
and all of your leaders^q
    rebelled against me.
²⁸ That's why I don't allow
    your priests to serve me;
I let Israel be destroyed
    and your people disgraced.

The LORD's Promise to Israel

44 People of Israel,
    I have chosen you
        as my servant.
² I am your Creator.
You were in my care
    even before you were born.
Israel, don't be terrified!
You are my chosen servant,
    my very favorite.^r

³ I will bless the thirsty land
    by sending streams of water;
I will bless your descendants
    by giving them my Spirit.
⁴ They will spring up like grass^s
or like willow trees
    near flowing streams.
⁵ They will worship me
    and become my people.
They will write my name
    on the back of their hands.^t

⁶ I am the LORD All-Powerful,
the first and the last,
    the one and only God.
Israel, I have rescued you!
    I am your King.
⁷ Can anyone compare with me?
If so, let them speak up
    and tell me now.
Let them say what has happened
since I made my nation
    long ago,
and let them tell
    what is going to happen.^u
⁸ Don't tremble with fear!
Didn't I tell you long ago?
    Didn't you hear me?
I alone am God—
    no one else is a mighty rock.^v

Idols Can't Do a Thing

The LORD said:

⁹ Those people who make idols
    are nothing themselves,

and the idols they treasure
    are just as worthless.
Worshipers of idols are blind,
    stupid, and foolish.
¹⁰ Why make an idol or an image
    that can't do a thing?
¹¹ Everyone who makes idols
and all who worship them
    are mere humans,
who will end up
    sadly disappointed.
Let them face me in court
    and be terrified.

Idols and Firewood

¹² A metalworker shapes an idol
by using a hammer^w
    and heat from the fire.
In his powerful hand
    he holds a hammer,
as he pounds the metal
    into the proper shape.
But he gets hungry and thirsty
    and loses his strength.

¹³ Some woodcarver measures
a piece of wood,
    then draws an outline.
The idol is carefully carved
    with each detail exact.
At last it looks like a person
    and is placed in a temple.
¹⁴ Either cedar, cypress, oak,
or any tree from the forest
    may be chosen.
Or even a pine tree planted
by the woodcarver
    and watered by the rain.

¹⁵ Some of the wood is used
to make a fire for heating
    or for cooking.
One piece is made into an idol,
then the woodcarver bows down
    and worships it.

---

^p43.27 *earliest ancestor*: Jacob, also known as Israel.
^q43.27 *leaders*: Probably prophets, but perhaps also
priests and kings.   ^r44.2 *my very favorite*: Or
"Jeshurun."   ^s44.4 *like grass*: One possible meaning for
the difficult Hebrew text.   ^t44.5 *write . . . hands*: To
show that they belong to the LORD and to Israel.
^u44.7 *Let them say . . . happen*: One possible meaning
for the difficult Hebrew text.   ^v44.8 *mighty rock*: See
the note at 17.10.   ^w44.12 *by using a hammer*: One
possible meaning for the difficult Hebrew text.

¹⁶ He enjoys the warm fire
and the meat that was roasted
over the burning coals.
¹⁷ Afterwards, he bows down
to worship the wooden idol.
"Protect me!" he says.
"You are my god."

¹⁸Those who worship idols are stupid and blind! ¹⁹They don't have enough sense to say to themselves, "I made a fire with half of the wood and cooked my bread and meat on it. Then I made something worthless with the other half. Why worship a block of wood?"

²⁰How can anyone be stupid enough to trust something that can be burned to ashes?^x No one can save themselves like that. Don't they realize that the idols they hold in their hands are not really gods?

The LORD Won't Forget His People

²¹ People of Israel,
you are my servant,
so remember all of this.
Israel, I created you,
and you are my servant.
I won't forget you.^y

> *I continually need to*
> *remind myself that if I*
> *refuse to forgive myself, I*
> *give no glory to God.*
>
> CAROL EVERETT

²² Turn back to me!
I have rescued you
and swept away your sins
as though they were clouds.

Sing Praises to the LORD

²³ Tell the heavens and the earth
to start singing!
Tell the mountains
and every tree in the forest
to join in the song!
The LORD has rescued his people;
now they will worship him.

The LORD Created Everything

²⁴ Israel, I am your LORD.
I am your source of life,
and I have rescued you.
I created everything
from the sky above
to the earth below.

²⁵ I make liars of false prophets
and fools of fortunetellers.
I take human wisdom
and turn it into nonsense.
²⁶ I will make the message
of my prophets come true.
They are saying, "Jerusalem
will be filled with people,
and the LORD will rebuild
the towns of Judah."

²⁷ I am the one who commands
the sea and its streams
to run dry.
²⁸ I am also the one who says,
"Cyrus will lead my people
and obey my orders.
Jerusalem and the temple
will be rebuilt."

Cyrus Obeys the LORD's Commands

45 The LORD said to Cyrus,
his chosen one:
I have taken hold
of your right hand
to help you capture nations
and remove kings from power.
City gates will open for you;
not one will stay closed.
² As I lead you,
I will level mountains^z
and break the iron bars
on bronze gates of cities.

³ I will give you treasures
hidden in dark
and secret places.
Then you will know that I,
the LORD God of Israel,
have called you by name.
⁴ Cyrus, you don't even know me!

---

^x**44.20** *How . . . ashes*: One possible meaning for the difficult Hebrew text. ^y**44.21** *I won't forget you*: One possible meaning for the difficult Hebrew text.
^z**45.2** *mountains*: The Dead Sea Scrolls and one ancient translation; the Standard Hebrew Text "rising waves."

But I have called you by name
and highly honored you[a]
because of Israel,
my chosen servant.

⁵ Only I am the LORD!
There are no other gods.
I have made you strong,
though you don't know me.
⁶ Now everyone from east to west
will learn that I am the LORD.
No other gods are real.
⁷ I create light and darkness,
happiness and sorrow.
I, the LORD, do all of this.

⁸ Tell the heavens
to send down justice
like showers of rain.
Prepare the earth
for my saving power
to sprout and produce justice
that I, the LORD, create.[b]

The LORD's Mighty Power

The LORD said:
⁹ Israel, you have no right
to argue with your Creator.
You are merely a clay pot
shaped by a potter.
The clay doesn't ask,
"Why did you make me this way?
Where are the handles?"
¹⁰ Children don't have the right
to demand of their parents,
"What have you done
to make us what we are?"

¹¹ I am the LORD, the Creator,
the holy God of Israel.
Do you dare question me
about my own nation
or about what I have done?
¹² I created the world
and covered it with people;
I stretched out the sky
and filled it with stars.
¹³ I have done the right thing
by placing Cyrus in power,
and I will make the roads easy
for him to follow.
I am the LORD All-Powerful!
Cyrus will rebuild my city
and set my people free

without being paid a thing.
I, the LORD, have spoken.

The LORD Alone Can Save

¹⁴ My people, I, the LORD, promise
that the riches of Egypt
and the treasures of Ethiopia[c]
will belong to you.
You will force into slavery
those tall people of Seba.[d]

They will bow down and say,
"The only true God is with you;
there are no other gods."
¹⁵ People of Israel,
your God is a mystery,
though he alone can save.
¹⁶ Anyone who makes idols
will be confused
and terribly disgraced.
¹⁷ But Israel, I, the LORD,
will always keep you safe
and free from shame.

Everyone Is Invited

¹⁸ The LORD alone is God!
He created the heavens
and made a world
where people can live,
instead of creating
an empty desert.
The LORD alone is God;
there are no others.
¹⁹ The LORD did not speak
in a dark secret place
or command Jacob's descendants
to search for him in vain.

The LORD speaks the truth,
and this is what he says
²⁰ to every survivor
from every nation:
"Gather around me!
Learn how senseless it is
to worship wooden idols
or pray to helpless gods.

²¹ "Why don't you get together
and meet me in court?

---

[a]45.4 *But . . . you:* One possible meaning for the
difficult Hebrew text.   [b]45.8 *Prepare . . . create:*
One possible meaning for the difficult Hebrew text.
[c]45.14 *Ethiopia:* See the note at 11.11.   [d]45.14 *Seba:*
See the note at 43.3.

Didn't I tell you long ago
    what would happen?
I am the only God!
    There are no others.
I bring about justice,
    and have the power to save.

²² "I invite the whole world
    to turn to me and be saved.
I alone am God!
    No others are real.
²³ I have made a solemn promise,
    one that won't be broken:
Everyone will bow down
    and worship me.
²⁴ They will admit that I alone
    can bring about justice.
Everyone who is angry with me
will be terribly ashamed
    and will turn to me.
²⁵ I, the LORD, will give
victory and great honor
    to the people of Israel."

Babylonia's Gods Are Helpless

The LORD said:

46

The gods Bel and Nebo[e]
    are down on their knees,
    as wooden images of them
are carried away
    on weary animals.[f]
² They are down on their knees
    to rescue the heavy load,
but the images are still taken
    to a foreign country.

³ You survivors in Israel,
    listen to me, the LORD.
Since the day you were born,
    I have carried you along.
⁴ I will still be the same
when you are old and gray,
    and I will take care of you.
I created you. I will carry you
    and always keep you safe.

⁵ Can anyone compare with me?
    Is anyone my equal?
⁶ Some people hire a goldsmith
    and give silver and gold
to be formed into an idol
    for them to worship.
⁷ They carry the idol
    on their shoulders,

then put it on a stand,
    but it cannot move.

They call out to the idol
    when they are in trouble,
but it doesn't answer,
    and it cannot help.
⁸ Now keep this in mind,[g]
you sinful people.
    And don't ever forget it.

The LORD Alone Is God

⁹ I alone am God!
    There are no other gods;
    no one is like me.
Think about what happened
    many years ago.
¹⁰ From the very beginning,
    I told what would happen
    long before it took place.

I kept my word ¹¹ and brought
someone from a distant land
    to do what I wanted.
He attacked from the east,
    like a hawk swooping down.
Now I will keep my promise
    and do what I planned.

¹² You people are stubborn
    and far from being safe,
    so listen to me.
¹³ I will soon come to save you.
I am not far away
    and will waste no time;
I take pride in Israel
    and will save Jerusalem.

Babylon Will Fall

The LORD said:

47

City of Babylon,
You are delicate
    and untouched,
    but that will change.
Surrender your royal power
    and sit in the dirt.
² Start grinding grain!
    Take off your veil.

---

^e**46.1** *Bel and Nebo:* Bel was another name for Marduk, the chief god of the Babylonians. Nebo was the son of Marduk and also an important god. ^f**46.1** *as . . . animals:* One possible meaning for the difficult Hebrew text. ^g**46.8** *Now . . . mind:* One possible meaning for the difficult Hebrew text.

Strip off your fancy clothes
    and cross over rivers.[h]
[3] You will suffer the shame
    of going naked,
because I will take revenge,
    and no one can escape.[i]
[4] I am the LORD All-Powerful,
    the holy God of Israel.
    I am their Savior.

[5] Babylon, be silent!
    Sit in the dark.
No longer will nations
    accept you as their queen.
[6] I was angry with my people.
So I let you take their land
    and bring disgrace on them.
You showed them no mercy,
but were especially cruel
    to those who were old.
[7] You thought that you
    would be queen forever.
You didn't care what you did;
it never entered your mind
    that you might get caught.

[8] You think that you alone
    are all-powerful,
that you won't be a widow
    or lose your children.
All you care about is pleasure,
    but listen to what I say.
[9] Your magic powers and charms
    will suddenly fail,
then you will be a widow
    and lose your children.

[10] You hid behind evil
like a shield and said,
    "No one can see me!"
You were fooled by your wisdom
    and your knowledge;
you felt sure that you alone
    were in full control.
[11] But without warning,
    disaster will strike—
and your magic charms
    won't help at all.

[12] Keep using your magic powers
    and your charms
        as you have always done.
Maybe—just maybe—
    you will frighten somebody!
[13] You have worn yourself out,

asking for advice
from those who study the stars
and tell the future
    month after month.
Go ask them how to be saved
    from what will happen.
[14] People who trust the stars
are as helpless as straw
    in a flaming fire.
No one can even keep warm,[j]
sitting by a fire
    that feeds only on straw.
[15] These are the fortunetellers
you have done business with
    all of your life.
But they don't know
where they are going,
    and they can't save you.

The LORD Corrects His People

48 People of Israel,
    you come from Jacob's family
        and the tribe[k] of Judah.
You claim to worship me,
    the LORD God of Israel,
        but you are lying.
[2] You call Jerusalem your home
    and say you depend on me,
the LORD All-Powerful,
    the God of Israel.

[3] Long ago I announced
    what was going to be,
then without warning,
    I made it happen.
[4] I knew you were stubborn
    and hardheaded.
[5] And I told you these things,
so that when they happened
    you would not say,
"The idols we worship did this."

[6] You heard what I said,
and you have seen it happen.
    Now admit that it's true!
I will show you secrets
    you have never known.
[7] Today I am doing something new,

---

[h]**47.2** *Strip . . . rivers*: This may be a command to get
ready for work that requires wading in the river, or it
may be a warning that they are going to be taken
away as slaves.   [i]**47.3** *escape*: Or "oppose me."
[j]**47.14** *keep warm*: Or "cook food."   [k]**48.1** *tribe*:
Hebrew "waters."

something you cannot say
you have heard before.
⁸You have never been willing
to listen to what I say;
from the moment of your birth,
I knew you would rebel.

The LORD Warns Israel

⁹I, the LORD, am true to myself;
I will be praised for not punishing
and destroying you.
¹⁰I tested you in hard times
just as silver is refined
in a heated furnace.ˡ
¹¹I did this because of who I am.
I refuse to be dishonoredᵐ
or share my praise
with any other god.

¹²Israel, my chosen people,
listen to me.
I alone am the LORD,
the first and the last.
¹³With my own hand
I created the earth
and stretched out the sky.
They obey my every command.

The LORD Speaks to the Nations

¹⁴Gather around me, all of you!
Listen to what I say.
Did any of your idols
predict this would happen?
Did they say that my friendⁿ
would do what I want done
to Babylonia?ᵒ
¹⁵I was the one who chose him.
I have brought him this far,
and he will be successful.
¹⁶Come closer and listen!
I have never kept secret
the things I have said,
and I was here
before time began.

It Is Best To Obey the LORD

By the power of his Spirit
the LORD God has sent me
¹⁷ with this message:
People of Israel,
I am the holy LORD God,
the one who rescues you.
For your own good,
I teach you, and I lead you
along the right path.

¹⁸How I wish that you
had obeyed my commands!
Your success and good fortune
would then have overflowed
like a flooding river.
¹⁹Your nation would be blessed
with more people
than there are grains of sand
along the seashore.
And I would never have let
your country be destroyed.

²⁰Now leave Babylon!
Celebrate as you go.
Be happy and shout
for everyone to hear,
"The LORD has rescued
his servant Israel!
²¹He led us through the desert
and made water flow from a rock
to satisfy our thirst.
²²But the LORD has promised
that none who are evil
will live in peace."

The Work of the LORD's Servant

49 Everyone, listen,
even you foreign nations
across the sea.
The LORD chose me
and gave me a name
before I was born.
²He made my words pierce
like a sharp sword
or a pointed arrow;
he kept me safely hidden
in the palm of his hand.
³The LORD said to me,
"Israel, you are my servant;
and because of you
I will be highly honored."

⁴I said to myself,
"I'm completely worn out;
my time has been wasted.
But I did it for the LORD God,
and he will reward me."

ˡ**48.10** *furnace:* One possible meaning for the difficult Hebrew text of verse 10.   ᵐ**48.11** *I refuse to be dishonored:* One possible meaning for the difficult Hebrew text.   ⁿ**48.14** *my friend:* Probably Cyrus (see 44.28; 45.1).   ᵒ**48.14** *Babylonia:* One possible meaning for the difficult Hebrew text of verse 14.

5 Even before I was born,
the LORD God chose me
to serve him and to lead back
the people of Israel.
So the LORD has honored me
and made me strong.

6 Now the LORD says to me,
"It isn't enough for you
to be merely my servant.
You must do more than lead back
survivors from the tribes
of Israel.
I have placed you here as a light
for other nations;
you must take my saving power
to everyone on earth."

The LORD Will Rescue His People

7 Israel, I am the holy LORD God,
the one who rescues you.
You are slaves of rulers
and of a nation
who despises you.[p]
Now this is what I promise:
Kings and rulers will honor you
by kneeling at your feet.
You can trust me! I am your LORD,
the holy God of Israel,
and you are my chosen ones.

The LORD Will Lead His People Home

8 This is what the LORD says:
I will answer your prayers
because I have set a time
when I will help
by coming to save you.
I have chosen you
to take my promise of hope
to other nations.[q]
You will rebuild the country
from its ruins,
then people will come
and settle there.
9 You will set prisoners free
from dark dungeons
to see the light of day.

On their way home,
they will find plenty to eat,
even on barren hills.
10 They won't go hungry
or get thirsty;
they won't be bothered
by the scorching sun
or hot desert winds.
I will be merciful
while leading them along
to streams of water.
11 I will level the mountains
and make roads.
12 Then my people will return
from distant lands
in the north and the west
and from the city of Syene.[r]

The LORD's Mercy

13 Tell the heavens and the earth
to celebrate and sing;
command every mountain
to join in the song.
The LORD's people have suffered,
but he has shown mercy
and given them comfort.

14 The people of Zion said,
"The LORD has turned away
and forgotten us."

15 The LORD answered,
"Could a mother forget a child
who nurses at her breast?
Could she fail to love an infant
who came from her own body?
Even if a mother could forget,
I will never forget you.
16 A picture of your city
is drawn on my hand.
You are always in my thoughts!

17 "Your city will be built faster
than it was destroyed[s]—
those who attacked it
will retreat and leave.
18 Look around! You will see
your people coming home.
As surely as I live,
I, the LORD, promise
that your city with its people
will be as lovely as a bride
wearing her jewelry."

---

[p]**49.7** *You . . . you*: One possible meaning for the difficult Hebrew text. [q]**49.8** *my . . . nations*: One possible meaning for the difficult Hebrew text. [r]**49.12** *Syene*: The Dead Sea Scrolls; the Standard Hebrew Text "Sinim." The reference may be to modern Aswan, a city in southern Egypt. [s]**49.17** *Your city . . . destroyed*: One possible meaning for the difficult Hebrew text.

Jerusalem's Bright Future

¹⁹ Jerusalem is now in ruins!
    Nothing is left of the city.
But it will be rebuilt
    and soon overcrowded;
its cruel enemies
    will be gone far away.

²⁰ Jerusalem is a woman
    whose children were born
while she was in deep sorrow*
    over the loss of her husband.
Now those children
    will come and seek room
    in the crowded city,
²¹ and Jerusalem will ask,
    "Am I really their mother?
How could I have given birth
    when I was still mourning
    in a foreign land?
Who raised these children?
    Where have they come from?"

²² The LORD God says:
"I will soon give a signal
    for the nations
to return your sons
    and your daughters
    to the arms of Jerusalem.
²³ The kings and queens
    of those nations
where they were raised
    will come and bow down.
They will take care of you
just like a slave
    taking care of a child.
Then you will know
    that I am the LORD.
You won't be disappointed
    if you trust me."

The LORD Is on Our Side

²⁴ Is it possible to rescue victims
    from someone strong
    and cruel?*
²⁵ But the LORD has promised
    to fight on our side
and to rescue our children
    from those strong
    and violent enemies.
²⁶ He will make those cruel people
    dine on their own flesh
and get drunk from drinking
    their own blood.

Then everyone will know
    that the LORD is our Savior;
the powerful God of Israel
    has rescued his people.

The LORD's Power To Punish

50 The LORD says, "Children,
    I didn't divorce your mother
        or sell you to pay debts;
I divorced her and sold you
    because of your sins.
² I came and called out,
    but you didn't answer.
Have I lost my power
    to rescue and save?
At my command oceans and rivers
    turn into deserts;
fish rot and stink
    for lack of water.
³ I make the sky turn dark
like the sackcloth
    you wear at funerals."

God's Servant Must Suffer

⁴ The LORD God gives me
    the right words
        to encourage the weary.
Each morning he awakens me
    eager to learn his teaching;
⁵ he made me willing to listen
    and not rebel or run away.

⁶ I let them beat my back
    and pull out my beard.
I didn't turn aside
when they insulted me
    and spit in my face.
⁷ But the LORD God keeps me
    from being disgraced.
So I refuse to give up,
because I know
    God will never let me down.

⁸ My protector is nearby;
no one can stand here
    to accuse me of wrong.

---

*49.20 *whose children . . . sorrow:* These "children" are Jews who were born in foreign countries during the time that Jerusalem was in ruins. Jerusalem probably stands for all the cities in Judah that were destroyed by the Babylonians.   *49.24 *cruel:* The Dead Sea Scrolls and two ancient translations; the Standard Hebrew Text "good."

9 The LORD God will help me
and prove I am innocent.
My accusers will wear out
like moth-eaten clothes.

> *"I have confidence in God"
> is what laughter—despite
> difficult circumstances—
> communicates. I love that!*
>
> VALERIE BELL

10 None of you respect the LORD
or obey his servant.
You walk in the dark
instead of the light;
you don't trust the name
of the LORD your God.[v]
11 Go ahead and walk in the light
of the fires you have set.[w]
But with his own hand,
the LORD will punish you
and make you suffer.

The LORD Will Bring Comfort

51 If you want to do right
and obey the LORD,
follow Abraham's example.
He was the rock from which
you were chipped.
2 God chose Abraham and Sarah
to be your ancestors.
The LORD blessed Abraham,
and from that one man
came many descendants.

3 Though Zion is in ruins,
the LORD will bring comfort,
and the city will be as lovely
as the garden of Eden
that he provided.
Then Zion will celebrate;
it will be thankful
and sing joyful songs.

The LORD's Victory Will Last

4 The LORD says:
You are my people and nation!
So pay attention to me.

My teaching will cause justice
to shine like a light
for every nation.
5 Those who live across the sea
are eagerly waiting
for me to rescue them.
I am strong and ready;
soon I will come to save
and to rule all nations.

6 Look closely at the sky!
Stare at the earth.
The sky will vanish like smoke;
the earth will wear out
like clothes.
Everyone on this earth
will die like flies.
But my victory will last;
my saving power never ends.

7 If you want to do right
and to obey my teaching
with all your heart,
then pay close attention.
Don't be discouraged
when others insult you
and say hurtful things.
8 They will be eaten away
like a moth-eaten coat.
But my victory will last;
my saving power
will never end.

A Prayer for the LORD's Help

9 Wake up! Do something, LORD.
Be strong and ready.
Wake up! Do what you did
for our people long ago.
Didn't you chop up
Rahab[x] the monster?
10 Didn't you dry up the deep sea
and make a road for your people
to follow safely across?
11 Now those you have rescued
will return to Jerusalem,
singing on their way.
They will be crowned
with great happiness,
never again to be burdened
with sadness and sorrow.

---

v**50.10** *God:* One possible meaning for the difficult
Hebrew text of verse 10. w**50.11** *Go . . . set:* One
possible meaning for the difficult Hebrew text.
x**51.9** *Rahab:* This may refer to Egypt at the time of
the exodus.

The LORD Gives Hope

¹² I am the LORD, the one
   who encourages you.
Why are you afraid
   of mere humans?
They dry up and die like grass.

¹³ I spread out the heavens
  and laid foundations
   for the earth.
But you have forgotten me,
  your LORD and Creator.
All day long you were afraid
of those who were angry
  and hoped to abuse you.
Where are they now?

¹⁴ Everyone crying out in pain
  will be quickly set free;
they will be rescued
from the power of death
  and never go hungry.
¹⁵ I will help them
  because I am your God,
the LORD All-Powerful,
  who makes the ocean roar.

¹⁶ I have told you what to say,
and I will keep you safe
  in the palm of my hand.
I spread out the heavens
and laid foundations
  for the earth.
Now I say, "Jerusalem,
  your people are mine."

A Warning to Jerusalem

¹⁷ Jerusalem, wake up! Stand up!
You've drunk too much
  from the cup filled
  with the LORD's anger.
You have swallowed every drop,
  and you can't walk straight.
¹⁸ Not one of your many children
  is there to guide you
  or to offer a helping hand.
¹⁹ You have been destroyed
  by war and by famine;
   I cannot comfort you.^y
²⁰ The LORD your God is angry,
  and on every street corner
your children lie helpless,
  like deer trapped in nets.

²¹ You are in trouble and drunk,
  but not from wine.
So pay close attention
²² to the LORD your God,
  who defends you and says,
"I have taken from your hands
the cup filled with my anger
  that made you drunk.
You will never be forced
  to drink it again.
²³ Instead I will give it
  to your brutal enemies,
who treated you like dirt
  and walked all over you."

---

^y**51.19** I . . . you: One possible meaning for the difficult Hebrew text.

SingleLife—As a single mom, is it all right for me to date? Should I wait until my children are grown? (Isaiah 51.12-16)

Put your fears in God's hand.

Is there anything scarier than a first date? It doesn't matter if you're sixteen or sixty; venturing into a new relationship is one of life's riskier endeavors. And when there are children in the picture, well, it's enough to scare any woman into permanent seclusion.

    Fortunately, we've got a God who cares deeply about us and wants to walk alongside us in everything we do—including dating. That means we can let our fears and anxieties about dating fade, and replace them with hope and confidence. After all, God wants what's best for us. If we patiently look to him for help and guidance, we'll sense his loving hand moving us back into the dating world when the time is right. (See also Daniel 12; 2 Thessalonians 2.13-17.)

    Words To Remember: *I have told you what to say, and I will keep you safe in the palm of my hand.*—Isaiah 51.16

Jerusalem Can Celebrate

52 Jerusalem, wake up!
        Stand up and be strong.
Holy city of Zion,
        dress in your best clothes.
Those foreigners who ruined
your sacred city
        won't bother you again.
² Zion, rise from the dirt!
Free yourself from the rope
        around your neck.

Suffering Will End

³ The LORD says:
My people, you were sold,
        but not for money;
now you will be set free,
        but not for a payment.
⁴ Long ago you went to Egypt
where you lived
        as foreigners.
Then Assyria was cruel to you,
⁵   and now another nation^z
has taken you prisoner
        for no reason at all.
Your leaders groan with pain,^a
and day after day
        my own name is cursed.
⁶ My people, you will learn
who I am and who is speaking
        because I am here.

A Message of Hope for Jerusalem

⁷ What a beautiful sight!
On the mountains a messenger
        announces to Jerusalem,
"Good news! You're saved.
There will be peace.
        Your God is now King."
⁸ Everyone on guard duty,
        sing and celebrate!
Look! You can see the LORD
        returning to Zion.
⁹ Jerusalem, rise from the ruins!
        Join in the singing.
The LORD has given comfort
to his people;
        he comes to your rescue.
¹⁰ The LORD has shown all nations
        his mighty strength;
now everyone will see
        the saving power of our God.

A Command To Leave Babylon

¹¹ Leave the city of Babylon!
        Don't touch anything filthy.
Wash yourselves. Be ready
to carry back everything sacred
        that belongs to the LORD.
¹² You won't need to run.
        No one is chasing you.
The LORD God of Israel
will lead and protect you
        from enemy attacks.

The Suffering Servant

¹³ The LORD says:
        My servant will succeed!
He will be given great praise
        and the highest honors.
¹⁴ Many were horrified
        at what happened to him.^b
But everyone who saw him
        was even more horrified
because he suffered until
        he no longer looked human.^c
¹⁵ My servant will make
nations worthy to worship me;^d
        kings will be silent
        as they bow in wonder.^e
They will see and think about
things they have never seen
        or thought about before.

What God's Servant Did for Us

53 Has anyone believed us
        or seen the mighty power
        of the LORD in action?
² Like a young plant or a root
        that sprouts in dry ground,
the servant grew up
        obeying the LORD.
He wasn't some handsome king.
Nothing about the way he looked
        made him attractive to us.
³ He was hated and rejected;
his life was filled with sorrow
        and terrible suffering.
No one wanted to look at him.

---

^z**52.5** *another nation*: Babylonia.   ^a**52.5** *groan with pain*:
One possible meaning for the difficult Hebrew text.
^b**52.14** *him*: One ancient translation; Hebrew "you."
^c**52.14** *human*: One possible meaning for the difficult
Hebrew text of verse 14.   ^d**52.15** *My . . . me*: Hebrew;
one ancient translation "The nations will be amazed
at him."   ^e**52.15** *kings . . . wonder*: One possible
meaning for the difficult Hebrew text.

We despised him and said,
"He is a nobody!"

[4] He suffered and endured
    great pain for us,
but we thought his suffering
    was punishment from God.
[5] He was wounded and crushed
    because of our sins;
by taking our punishment,
    he made us completely well.
[6] All of us were like sheep
    that had wandered off.
We had each gone our own way,
but the LORD gave him
    the punishment we deserved.

[7] He was painfully abused,
    but he did not complain.
He was silent like a lamb
    being led to the butcher,
as quiet as a sheep
    having its wool cut off.

[8] He was condemned to death
    without a fair trial.
Who could have imagined
    what would happen to him?
His life was taken away
because of the sinful things
    my people[f] had done.
[9] He wasn't dishonest or violent,

but he was buried in a tomb
    of cruel and rich people.[g]

[10] The LORD decided his servant
    would suffer as a sacrifice
to take away the sin
    and guilt of others.
Now the servant will live
    to see his own descendants.[h]
He did everything
    the LORD had planned.

[11] By suffering, the servant
will learn the true meaning
    of obeying the LORD.
Although he is innocent,
he will take the punishment
    for the sins of others,
so that many of them
    will no longer be guilty.
[12] The LORD will reward him
with honor and power
    for sacrificing his life.
Others thought he was a sinner,
but he suffered for our sins
    and asked God to forgive us.

---

[f]**53.8** *my people:* Or "his people."   [g]**53.9** *but he . . . people:* One possible meaning for the difficult Hebrew text.   [h]**53.10** *The LORD . . . descendants:* One possible meaning of the difficult Hebrew text.

Friendship—How can I show my friend that Christ is the only way to God?
(*Isaiah 53*)

Show her the straight path.

Let's say you're carpooling with a friend who always takes the long way home. Winding through the countryside might be nice on a sunny autumn day; but when you really want to get somewhere, it seems ridiculous not to take the most direct route.

Yet that's how many of us approach salvation. We try everything possible to earn God's favor, seemingly forgetting that God has already provided us with the straightest path to salvation. Try as we might to find another way to heaven, it's Jesus Christ, the Son of God, who saves us from our sins.

God mapped out the straight road to salvation long before Jesus actually arrived on earth. The book of Isaiah lays out God's plan, explaining how Jesus would come to take the punishment that should have been ours—and take it willingly (53.6,7). That act, and that alone, will bring us the eternal life with God we long for.

So why knock ourselves out trying to find another way? There's only one road to everlasting life—and it's a route that's been mapped out for generations. (See also Isaiah 7.10-17; Mark 16.1-8; John 14.1-14.)

Words To Remember: *He was wounded and crushed because of our sins; by taking our punishment, he made us completely well.—Isaiah 53.5*

A Promise of the LORD's Protection

54 Sing and shout,
even though you have never
    had children!
The LORD has promised that you
  will have more children
than someone married
  for a long time.
[2] Make your tents larger!
Spread out the tent pegs;
  fasten them firmly.
[3] You and your descendants
will take over the land
  of other nations.
You will settle in towns
  that are now in ruins.

[4] Don't be afraid or ashamed
and don't be discouraged.
  You won't be disappointed.
Forget how sinful you were
  when you were young;
stop feeling ashamed
  for being left a widow.
[5] The LORD All-Powerful,
the Holy God of Israel,
  rules all the earth.
He is your Creator and husband,
  and he will rescue you.

[6] You were like a young wife,
  brokenhearted and crying
because her husband
  had divorced her.
But the LORD your God says,
  "I am taking you back!
[7] I rejected you for a while,
but with love and tenderness
  I will embrace you again.
[8] For a while, I turned away
  in furious anger.
Now I will have mercy
  and love you forever!
I, your protector and LORD,
  make this promise."

The LORD Promises Lasting Peace

[9] I once promised Noah that I
would never again destroy
  the earth by a flood.
Now I have promised that I
will never again get angry
  and punish you.

[10] Every mountain and hill
  may disappear.
But I will always be kind
  and merciful to you;
I won't break my agreement
  to give your nation peace.

*If we look for common
ground—our faith in Jesus
Christ and desire to serve
him—we can experience
peace with others.*

JANE JOHNSON STRUCK

The New Jerusalem

[11] Jerusalem, you are sad
and discouraged,
  tossed around in a storm.
But I, the LORD,
will rebuild your city
  with precious stones;[i]
for your foundation
  I will use blue sapphires.
[12] Your fortresses[j]
  will be built of rubies,
your gates of jewels,
  and your walls of gems.
[13] I will teach your children
  and make them successful.

[14] You will be built on fairness
  with no fears of injustice;
every one of your worries
  will be taken far from you.
[15] I will never send anyone
  to attack your city,
and you will make prisoners
  of those who do attack.
[16] Don't forget that I created
metalworkers who make weapons
  over burning coals.
I also created armies
  that can bring destruction.
[17] Weapons made to attack you
  won't be successful;

---

[i] **54.11** *with precious stones*: One possible meaning for
the difficult Hebrew text. [j] **54.12** *fortresses*: One
possible meaning for the difficult Hebrew text.

words spoken against you
  won't hurt at all.

My servants, Jerusalem is yours!
I, the LORD, promise
  to bless you with victory.

The LORD's Invitation

55 If you are thirsty,
  come and drink water!
If you don't have any money,
  come, eat what you want!
Drink wine and milk
  without paying a cent.
[2] Why waste your money
  on what really isn't food?
Why work hard for something
  that doesn't satisfy?
Listen carefully to me,
and you will enjoy
  the very best foods.

[3] Pay close attention!
  Come to me and live.
I will promise you
the eternal love and loyalty
  that I promised David.
[4] I made him the leader and ruler
of the nations;
  he was my witness to them.

[5] You will call out to nations
  you have never known.
And they have never known you,
but they will come running
  because I am the LORD,
the holy God of Israel,
  and I have honored you.

God's Words Are Powerful

[6] Turn to the LORD!
He can still be found.
  Call out to God! He is near.
[7] Give up your crooked ways
  and your evil thoughts.
Return to the LORD our God.
He will be merciful
  and forgive your sins.

[8] The LORD says:
"My thoughts and my ways
  are not like yours.
[9] Just as the heavens
  are higher than the earth,
my thoughts and my ways
  are higher than yours.

[10] "Rain and snow fall from the sky.
But they don't return
  without watering the earth

WORK—How can I find satisfaction with my life outside of work? *(Isaiah 55.1-5)*

Accept God's invitation.
As we've gotten smarter about the role diet plays in living a healthy life, more and more nutrition experts are telling us to give in to our cravings. It wasn't long ago that we were told to resist temptation: When we want chocolate chip cookies, eat carrot sticks. But now, we're encouraged to satisfy that urge for chocolate—in moderation. The reason for the change in thinking? Diet experts finally got a handle on basic human nature.

When we want something, we want *that thing* and that thing only. Nothing else will satisfy us. In our efforts to stick to a diet, we eat around our cravings, munching on everything else we can find, only to end up eating the thing we really wanted anyway. We consume more fat and calories than we would have if we'd just had a couple of cookies in the first place.

The same holds for other areas of our life. We want to satisfy our desires, but we resist the obvious source of satisfaction: God. Instead of turning to him, we fill our time with activities that do little to quench our thirst for a truly fulfilling life. But God promises that those who follow him will be more than satisfied. God's people will experience the best life has to offer. (See also Deuteronomy 8.10-20; Ecclesiastes 3.1-14.)

Words To Remember: *If you are thirsty, come and drink water! If you don't have any money, come, eat what you want! Drink wine and milk without paying a cent. Why waste your money on what really isn't food? Why work hard for something that doesn't satisfy? Listen carefully to me, and you will enjoy the very best foods.—Isaiah 55.1,2*

that produces seeds to plant
and grain to eat.
¹¹ That's how it is with my words.
They don't return to me
without doing everything
I send them to do."

God's People Will Celebrate

¹² When you are set free,
you will celebrate
and travel home in peace.
Mountains and hills will sing
as you pass by,
and trees will clap.
¹³ Cypress and myrtle trees
will grow in fields
once covered by thorns.
And then those trees will stand
as a lasting witness
to the glory of the LORD.

All Nations Will Be Part of God's People

56 The LORD said:
Be honest and fair!
Soon I will come to save you;
my saving power will be seen
everywhere on earth.

² I will bless everyone
who respects the Sabbath
and refuses to do wrong.

³ Foreigners who worship me
must not say,
"The LORD won't let us
be part of his people."
Men who are unable
to become fathers
must no longer say,
"We are dried-up trees."

⁴ To them, I, the LORD, say:
Respect the Sabbath,
obey me completely,
and keep our agreement.
⁵ Then I will set up monuments
in my temple with your names
written on them.
This will be much better
than having children,
because these monuments
will stand there forever.

⁶ Foreigners will follow me.
They will love me and worship
in my name;
they will respect the Sabbath
and keep our agreement.

---

*Spiritual*Life—**If I've turned away from God, is it possible to come back? How?** (Isaiah 55.6-13)

Join the celebration.

There are more than a few Scripture passages that tell of God's great joy when one of his children turns away from a life of sin and comes back to life with God. Many of the stories Jesus told revolve around the theme of the lost being found (for example, the stories of the lost son and the lost coin in Luke 15). But here in Isaiah, we find one of the Bible's most vivid images of God's delight in welcoming back his people.

When we turn away from God, we often do so because we don't feel his presence in our life, or because we're plagued with doubts about his power to act on our behalf. When we finally feel ready to come back to God, we wonder if he'll take us in. We wonder what our punishment will be for rejecting God.

But this passage reminds us that God is not only willing to take us back, he is *waiting* for us to return to him (55.6). And when we do, all of creation celebrates our return (55.12). What a beautiful picture of God's love for us! We find mercy where we expected punishment, joy where we expected anger, and freedom where we expected judgment. When we return our broken life to God, he is more than ready to make us whole again. (See also Lamentations 3.31-40; Ezekiel 37.1-14; Hosea 3; Joel 2.25-27; 1 John 1.8—2.2.)

Words To Remember: *When you are set free, you will celebrate and travel home in peace. Mountains and hills will sing as you pass by, and trees will clap.*—Isaiah 55.12

⁷I will bring them
　　to my holy mountain,
where they will celebrate
　　in my house of worship.
Their sacrifices and offerings
will always be welcome
　　on my altar.
Then my house will be known
as a house of worship
　　for all nations.
⁸I, the LORD, promise
to bring together my people
　　who were taken away,
and let them join the others.

---

*All can be anointed with
God's love. It is there, available
for you. God's love is all
around. Love cannot be
forced, cannot be coaxed or
teased. It comes down from
heaven—unasked and
unsought; may it not
be unreceived.*

BARBARA JOHNSON

God Promises To Punish Israel's Leaders

⁹Come from the forest,
　　you wild animals!
Attack and gobble down
　　your victims.
¹⁰You leaders of Israel
　　should be watchdogs,
　　　　protecting my people.
But you can't see a thing,
　　and you never warn them.
Dozing and daydreaming
　　are all you ever do.
¹¹You stupid leaders are a pack
　　of hungry and greedy dogs
　　　　that never get enough.
You are shepherds
who mistreat your own sheep
　　for selfish gain.
¹²You say to each other,
"Let's drink till we're drunk!

Tomorrow we'll do it again.
We'll really enjoy ourselves."

God's Faithful People Suffer

57 God's faithful people
　　are dragged off and killed,
　　　　and no one even cares.
Evil sweeps them away,
²but in death they find peace
　　for obeying God.ᵏ

The LORD Condemns Idolatry

³You people are unfaithful!
You go to fortunetellers,
　　and you worship idols.
Now pay close attention!
⁴Who are you making fun of?
　　Who are you sneering at?
Look how your sins
　　have made fools of you.

⁵All you think about is sex
under those green trees
　　where idols are worshiped.
You sacrifice your children
on altars built in valleys
　　under rocky slopes.
⁶You have chosen to worship
　　idols made of stone;ˡ
you have given them offerings
of wine and grain.
　　Should I be pleased?

⁷You have spread out your beds
　　on the tops of high mountains,
　　　　where you sacrifice to idols.
⁸Even in your homes
you have placed pagan symbols
　　all around your huge beds.
Yes, you have rejected me,
sold yourselves to your lovers,
　　and gone to bed with them.ᵐ

⁹You smear on olive oil
and all kinds of perfume
　　to worship the god Molech.ⁿ
You even seek advice
　　from spirits of the dead.
¹⁰Though you tired yourself out

ᵏ57.1,2 *Evil . . . God:* One possible meaning for the
difficult Hebrew text.   ˡ57.6 *You have . . . stone:* One
possible meaning for the difficult Hebrew text.
ᵐ57.8 *them:* One possible meaning for the difficult
Hebrew text of verse 8.   ⁿ57.9 *the god Molech:* Or "the
king." In Hebrew "Molech" and "king" sound alike.

by running after idols,
    you refused to stop.
Your desires were so strong
    that they kept you going.

[11] Did you forget about me
    and become unfaithful
because you were more afraid
    of someone else?
Have I been silent so long[o]
    that you no longer fear me?
[12] You think you're so good,
    but I'll point out the truth.
[13] Ask your idols to save you
    when you are in trouble.
Be careful though—
    it takes only a faint breath
    to blow them over.
But if you come to me
    for protection,
this land and my holy mountain
    will always belong to you.

The LORD Helps the Helpless

[14] The LORD says,
"Clear the road!
    Get it ready for my people."

*The Bible is full of God's
promises—from his covenant
with Noah to hold back
world-destroying floodwaters
to his ultimate promise of
salvation through Christ.*

MARIAN V. LIAUTAUD

[15] Our holy God lives forever
in the highest heavens,
    and this is what he says:
Though I live high above
    in the holy place,
I am here to help those
who are humble
    and depend only on me.

[16] My people, I won't stay angry
    and keep on accusing you.

After all, I am your Creator.
I don't want you to give up
    in complete despair.
[17] Your greed made me furious.
That's why I punished you
    and refused to be found,
while you kept returning
    to your old sinful ways.

[18] I know what you are like!
But I will heal you, lead you,
    and give you comfort,
until those who are mourning
[19]   start singing my praises.[p]
No matter where you are,
I, the LORD, will heal you[q]
    and give you peace.

[20] The wicked are a restless sea
    tossing up mud.
[21] But I, the LORD, have promised
that none who are evil
    will live in peace.

True Religion

58 Shout the message!
    Don't hold back.
    Say to my people Israel:
You've sinned! You've turned
    against the LORD.
[2] Day after day, you worship him
and seem eager to learn
    his teachings.
You act like a nation
that wants to do right
    by obeying his laws.
You ask him about justice,
and say you enjoy
    worshiping the LORD.

[3] You wonder why the LORD
    pays no attention
when you go without eating
    and act humble.
But on those same days
    that you give up eating,
you think only of yourselves[r]
    and abuse your workers.

---

[o]**57.11** *so long*: One possible meaning for the difficult
Hebrew text. [p]**57.18,19** *until . . . praises*: One possible
meaning for the difficult Hebrew text. [q]**57.19** *heal you*:
One possible meaning for the difficult Hebrew text.
[r]**58.3** *you think . . . yourselves*: One possible meaning
for the difficult Hebrew text.

⁴You even get angry
    and ready to fight.
No wonder God won't listen
    to your prayers!

⁵Do you think the LORD
    wants you to give up eating
and to act as humble
    as a bent-over bush?
Or to dress in sackcloth
    and sit in ashes?
Is this really what he wants
    on a day of worship?

⁶I'll tell you
what it really means
    to worship the LORD.
Remove the chains of prisoners
    who are chained unjustly.
Free those who are abused!
⁷Share your food with everyone
    who is hungry;
share your home
    with the poor and homeless.
Give clothes to those in need;
    don't turn away your relatives.

⁸Then your light will shine
like the dawning sun, and you
    will quickly be healed.
Your honesty⁵ will protect you
    as you advance,
and the glory of the LORD
    will defend you from behind.
⁹When you beg the LORD for help,
    he will answer, "Here I am!"

Don't mistreat others
or falsely accuse them
    or say something cruel.
¹⁰Give your food to the hungry
    and care for the homeless.
Then your light will shine
    in the dark;
your darkest hour will be
    like the noonday sun.

¹¹The LORD will always guide you
    and provide good things to eat
        when you are in the desert.
He will make you healthy.
You will be like a garden
    that has plenty of water
or like a stream
    that never runs dry.

¹²You will rebuild those houses
    left in ruins for years;
you will be known
    as a builder and repairer
    of city walls and streets.

¹³But first, you must start
    respecting the Sabbath
        as a joyful day of worship.
You must stop doing and saying
    whatever you please
        on this special day.
¹⁴Then you will truly enjoy
    knowing the LORD.
He will let you rule
    from the highest mountains
and bless you with the land
    of your ancestor Jacob.
The LORD has spoken!

Social Injustice Is Condemned

59 The LORD hasn't lost
        his powerful strength;
    he can still hear
        and answer prayers.
²Your sins are the roadblock
    between you and your God.
That's why he doesn't answer
    your prayers
or let you see his face.

³Your talk is filled with lies
    and plans for violence;
every finger on your hands
    is covered with blood.
⁴You falsely accuse others
    and tell lies in court;
sin and trouble are the names
    of your children.
⁵You eat the deadly eggs
    of poisonous snakes,
and more snakes crawl out
    from the eggs left to hatch.
You weave spider webs,
⁶but you can't make clothes
    with those webs
    or hide behind them.

You're sinful and brutal.
⁷You hurry off to do wrong
    or murder innocent victims.
All you think about is sin;

---

⁵58.8 *honesty*: Or "honest leader."

you leave ruin and destruction
   wherever you go.
⁸You don't know how
to live in peace
   or to be fair with others.
The roads you make are crooked;
your followers cannot find peace.

The People Confess Their Sins

⁹No one has come to defend us
   or to bring about justice.
We hoped for a day of sunshine,
but all we found
   was a dark, gloomy night.
¹⁰We feel our way along,
   as if we were blind;
we stumble at noon,
   as if it were night.
We can see no better
   than someone dead.ᵗ

¹¹We growl like bears
   and mourn like doves.
We hope for justice and victory,
   but they escape us.
¹²How often have we sinned
and turned against you,
   the LORD God?
Our sins condemn us!
   We have done wrong.
¹³We have rebelled and refused
   to follow you.
Our hearts were deceitful,
   and so we lied;
we planned to abuse others
   and turn our backs on you.

*He who made us knows just
how much we can take.
He never overloads us.*

RUTH BELL GRAHAM

¹⁴Injustice is everywhere;
   justice seems far away.
Truth is chased out of court;
   honesty is shoved aside.
¹⁵Everyone tells lies;

those who turn from crime
   end up ruined.

The LORD Will Rescue His People

When the LORD noticed
that justice had disappeared,
   he became very displeased.
¹⁶It disgusted him even more
to learn that no one
   would do a thing about it.
So with his own powerful arm,
   he won victories for truth.
¹⁷Justice was the LORD's armor;
   saving power was his helmet;
anger and revenge
   were his clothes.

¹⁸Now the LORD will get furious
   and do to his enemies,
both near and far,
   what they did to his people.
¹⁹He will attack like a flood
   in a mighty windstorm.
Nations in the west and the east
will then honor and praise
   his wonderful name.
²⁰The LORD has promised to rescue
   the city of Zion
and Jacob's descendants
   who turn from sin.

²¹The LORD says: "My people,
I promise to give you my Spirit
   and my message.
These will be my gifts to you
   and your families forever.
I, the LORD, have spoken."

A New Day for Jerusalem

60 Jerusalem, stand up! Shine!
   Your new day is dawning.
The glory of the LORD
   shines brightly on you.
²The earth and its people
   are covered with darkness,
but the glory of the LORD
   is shining upon you.
³Nations and kings
will come to the light
   of your dawning day.

ᵗ**59.10** *We can . . . dead:* One possible meaning for the difficult Hebrew text.

Crowds Are Coming to Jerusalem

The LORD said:

⁴Open your eyes! Look around!
  Crowds are coming.
Your sons are on their way
  from distant lands;
your daughters are being carried
  like little children.
⁵When you see this,
  your faces will glow;
your hearts will pound
  and swell with pride.ᵘ
Treasures from across the sea
and the wealth of nations
  will be brought to you.
⁶Your country will be covered
with caravans of young camels
  from Midian and Ephah.ᵛ
The people of Shebaʷ
will bring gold and spices
  in praise of me, the LORD.
⁷Every sheep of Kedar
  will come to you;
rams from Nebaiothˣ
  will be yours as well.
I will accept them as offerings
  and bring honor to my temple.

⁸What is that sailing by
like clouds
  or like doves flying home?
⁹On those distant islands
your people are waiting
  for me, the LORD.ʸ
Seagoing shipsᶻ lead the way
to bring them home
  with their silver and gold.
I, the holy LORD God of Israel,
do this to honor your people,
  so they will honor me.

Jerusalem Will Be Rebuilt

The LORD said:

¹⁰Jerusalem, your city walls
  will be rebuilt by foreigners;
their rulers will become
  your slaves.
I punished you in my anger;
now I will be kind
  and treat you with mercy.

¹¹Your gates will be open
  day and night

to let the rulers of nations
lead their people to you
  with all their treasures.
¹²Any nation or kingdom
that refuses to serve you
  will be wiped out.
¹³Wood from Lebanon's best trees
will be brought to you—
  the pines, the firs,
  and the cypress trees.
It will be used in my temple
to make beautiful the place
  where I rest my feet.

¹⁴The descendants of enemies
who hated and mistreated you
  will kneel at your feet.
They will say, "You are Zion,
the city of the LORD,
  the holy God of Israel."

¹⁵You were hated and deserted,
  rejected by everyone.
But I will make you beautiful,
a city to be proud of
  for all time to come.
¹⁶You will drain the wealth
  of kings and foreign nations.
You will know that I,
the mighty LORD God of Israel,
  have saved and rescued you.

¹⁷I will bring bronze and iron
  in place of wood and stone;
in place of bronze and iron,
  I will bring gold and silver.
I will appoint peace and justice
  as your rulers and leaders.
¹⁸Violence, destruction, and ruin
will never again be heard of
  within your borders.
"Victory" will be the name
  you give to your walls;
"Praise" will be the name
  you give to your gates.

ᵘ**60.5** *swell with pride*: One possible meaning for the
difficult Hebrew text. ᵛ**60.6** *Midian . . . Ephah*: Midian
was the ancestor of a nomadic tribe of the Arabian
desert, east of the Gulf of Aqaba. Ephah was
a clan within the tribe of Midian. ʷ**60.6** *Sheba*:
Perhaps a place in what is now southwest Arabia.
The Queen of Sheba brought gifts to Solomon
(1 Kings 10.1-13). ˣ**60.7** *Kedar . . . Nebaioth*:
Regions in northern Arabia. ʸ**60.9** *On . . . LORD*:
One possible meaning for the difficult Hebrew text.
ᶻ**60.9** *Seagoing ships*: See the note at 2.16.

[19] You won't need the light
   of the sun or the moon.
I, the LORD your God,
will be your eternal light
   and bring you honor.
[20] Your sun will never set
   or your moon go down.
I, the LORD, will be
   your everlasting light,
and your days of sorrow
   will come to an end.
[21] Your people will live right
   and always own the land;
they are the trees I planted
   to bring praise to me.
[22] Even the smallest family
   will be a powerful nation.
I am the LORD,
and when the time comes,
   I will quickly do all this.

The Good News of Victory

61

The Spirit of the LORD God
   has taken control of me!
The LORD has chosen
   and sent me
to tell the oppressed
   the good news,
to heal the brokenhearted,
and to announce freedom
   for prisoners and captives.
[2] This is the year
   when the LORD God

will show kindness to us
   and punish our enemies.

The LORD has sent me
to comfort those who mourn,
[3] especially in Jerusalem.
He sent me to give them flowers
   in place of their sorrow,
olive oil in place of tears,
and joyous praise
   in place of broken hearts.
They will be called
   "Trees of Justice,"
planted by the LORD
   to honor his name.
[4] Then they will rebuild cities
that have been in ruins
   for many generations.

[5] They will hire foreigners
to take care of their sheep
   and their vineyards.
[6] But they themselves will be
priests and servants
   of the LORD our God.
The treasures of the nations
will belong to them,
   and they will be famous.[a]
[7] They were terribly insulted
   and horribly mistreated;

---

[a]**61.6** *and . . . famous*: One possible meaning for the difficult Hebrew text.

Friendship—How can I encourage a friend who is going through a divorce?
Isaiah 61.1-3

Point to the God of hope.

Remember when you were young and you dreamed about being an adult? Everything in the adult world seemed better, easier, more fun. But when we eventually reach adulthood, we realize (often painfully) that being a grown-up has its price. Adult life can bring crumbling dreams and unbearable heartache. As we struggle to get through the rough spots, we often lose track of the hope we felt as children—the hope that one day, things will get better.

For many people, the hope for a life without seemingly endless struggles is long gone. But for Christians, hope is not only on the horizon, it's within our reach. God promises healing, comfort, and joy to his people—no matter what we've been through. Where the world sees only suffering, we can envision the bright glimmer of a life safe in God's loving care.

When our friends are suffering, we can point them to God, helping them rest in his promise for better days to come. (See also Job 13.5-15; Isaiah 43.2-4; 2 Corinthians 1.3-7.)

Words To Remember: *He sent me to give them flowers in place of their sorrow, olive oil in place of tears, and joyous praise in place of broken hearts.*—Isaiah 61.3

now they will be greatly blessed
and joyful forever.

The LORD Loves Justice

[8] I, the LORD, love justice!
But I hate robbery
and injustice.[b]
My people, I solemnly promise
to reward you
with an eternal agreement.
[9] Your descendants will be known
in every nation.
All who see them will realize
that they have been blessed,
by me, the LORD.

Celebrate and Shout

[10] I celebrate and shout
because of my LORD God.
His saving power and justice
are the very clothes I wear.
They are more beautiful
than the jewelry worn
by a bride or a groom.
[11] The LORD will bring about
justice and praise
in every nation on earth,
like flowers blooming
in a garden.

Jerusalem Will Be Saved

62 Jerusalem, I will speak up
for your good.
I will never be silent
till you are safe and secure,
sparkling like a flame.
[2] Your great victory will be seen
by every nation and king;
the LORD will even give you
a new name.
[3] You will be a glorious crown,
a royal headband,
for the LORD your God.

[4] Your name will no longer be
"Deserted and Childless,"
but "Happily Married."
You will please the LORD;
your country
will be his bride.
[5] Your people will take the land,[c]
just as a young man
takes a bride.
The LORD will be pleased
because of you,

just as a husband is pleased
with his bride.

*Even if you don't have any
"secret sins," you still have
a tremendous story to tell —
that "Yes, against the odds,
I was able to keep myself pure"
or "The Lord protected me
from some real trouble."*

STAR PARKER

[6] Jerusalem, on your walls
I have stationed guards,
whose duty it is
to speak out day and night,
without resting.
They must remind the LORD
[7]　and not let him rest
till he makes Jerusalem strong
and famous everywhere.

[8] The LORD has given his word
and made this promise:
"Never again will I give
to your enemies
the grain and grapes
for which you struggled.
[9] As surely as you harvest
your grain and grapes,
you will eat your bread
with thankful hearts,
and you will drink your wine
in my temple."

[10] People of Jerusalem,
open your gates!
Repair the road to the city
and clear it of stones;
raise a banner to help
the nations find their way.
[11] Here is what the LORD has said
for all the earth to hear:

---

[b]**61.8** *But . . . injustice:* One possible meaning for the
difficult Hebrew text. [c]**62.5** *Your . . . land:* One
possible meaning for the difficult Hebrew text.

"Soon I will come to save
the city of Zion,
and to reward you.
[12] Then you will be called,
'The LORD's Own People,
The Ones He Rescued!'
Your city will be known
as a good place to live
and a city full of people."

The LORD's Victory over the Nations

63 Who is this coming
from Bozrah[d] in Edom
with clothes stained red?
Who is this hero marching
in his glorious uniform?

"It's me, the LORD!
I have won the battle,
and I can save you!"

[2] What are those red spots?
Your clothes look stained
from stomping on grapes.[e]

[3] "I alone stomped the grapes!
None of the nations helped.
I stomped nations in my anger
and stained my clothes
with their blood.
[4] I did this because I wanted
to take revenge—
the time had come
to rescue my people.
[5] No one was there to help me
or to give support;
my mighty arm won the battle,
strengthened by my anger.
[6] In my fury I stomped on nations
and made them drunk;
their blood poured out
everywhere on earth."

The LORD's Goodness to His People

[7] I will tell about the kind deeds
the LORD has done.
They deserve praise!
The LORD has shown mercy
to the people of Israel;
he has been kind and good.

[8] The LORD rescued his people,
and said, "They are mine.
They won't betray me."
[9] It troubled the LORD

to see them in trouble,
and his angel saved them.[f]
The LORD was truly merciful,
so he rescued his people.
He took them in his arms
and carried them all those years.

[10] Then the LORD's people
turned against him and made
his Holy Spirit sad.
So he became their enemy
and attacked them.
[11] But his people remembered
what had happened
during the time of Moses.[g]
Didn't the LORD[h] bring them
and their leaders
safely through the sea?
Didn't he[i] give them
his Holy Spirit?
[12] The glorious power of the LORD
marched beside Moses.
The LORD will be praised forever
for dividing the sea.
[13] He led his people across
like horses running wild
without stumbling.
[14] His Spirit gave them rest,
just as cattle find rest
when led into a valley.[j]
The name of the LORD was praised
for doing these things.

A Prayer for Mercy and Help

[15] Please, LORD, look down
from your holy and glorious
home in the heavens
and see what's going on.
Have you lost interest?
Where is your power?
Show that you care about us[k]
and have mercy!
[16] Our ancestors Abraham and Jacob
have both rejected us.
But you are still our Father;

---

[d]**63.1** *Bozrah*: The main city of Edom.   [e]**63.2** *stomping on grapes*: This is one way that grapes were crushed to make them into juice.   [f]**63.9** *It . . . them*: One possible meaning for the difficult Hebrew text.   [g]**63.11** *But . . . Moses*: One possible meaning for the difficult Hebrew text.   [h]**63.11** *the LORD*: Or "Moses."   [i]**63.11** *he*: Or "Moses."   [j]**63.14** *His . . . valley*: One possible meaning for the difficult Hebrew text.   [k]**63.15** *us*: Hebrew "me."

you have been our protector
  since ancient times.

[17] Why did you make us turn away
    from you, our LORD?
Why did you make us want
  to disobey you?
Please change your mind!
We are your servants,
  your very own people.
[18] For a little while,
    your temple belonged to us;[l]
and now our enemies
  have torn it down.
[19] We act as though you
  had never ruled us
    or called us your people.

64

Rip the heavens apart!
Come down, LORD;
  make the
    mountains tremble.
[2] Be a spark that starts a fire
  causing water to boil.[m]
Then your enemies will know
  who you are;
all nations will tremble
  because you are nearby.

[3] Your fearsome deeds
    have completely amazed us;
even the mountains shake
  when you come down.
[4] You are the only God
    ever seen or heard of
who works miracles
  for his followers.

[5] You help all who gladly obey
and do what you want,
  but sin makes you angry.
Only by your help
  can we ever be saved.[n]
[6] We are unfit to worship you;
each of our good deeds
  is merely a filthy rag.
We dry up like leaves;
  our sins are storm winds
    sweeping us away.
[7] No one worships in your name
  or remains faithful.
You have turned your back on us
and let our sins melt us away.[o]

[8] You, LORD, are our Father.
  We are nothing but clay,
but you are the potter
  who molded us.
[9] Don't be so furious
  or keep our sins
    in your thoughts forever!
Remember that all of us
  are your people.
[10] Every one of your towns
  has turned into a desert,
    especially Jerusalem.
[11] Zion's glorious and holy temple
  where our ancestors praised you
    has been destroyed by fire.
Our beautiful buildings
  are now a pile of ruins.
[12] When you see these things,
  how can you just sit there
    and make us suffer more?

The LORD Will Punish the Guilty

65

I, the LORD, was ready
to answer even those
  who were not asking
and to be found by those
  who were not searching.
To a nation that refused
to worship me,[p]
  I said, "Here I am!"

[2] All day long I have reached out
  to stubborn and sinful people
    going their own way.
[3] They keep making me angry
    by sneering at me,
while offering sacrifices
  to idols in gardens
and burning incense
  to them on bricks.
[4] They spend their nights
    hiding in burial caves;
they eat the meat of pigs,[q]
cooked in sauces
  made of stuff unfit to eat.

---

[l]**63.18** *For . . . us:* One possible meaning for the difficult Hebrew text. [m]**64.2** *Be . . . boil:* One possible meaning for the difficult Hebrew text. [n]**64.5** *saved:* One possible meaning for the difficult Hebrew text of verse 5. [o]**64.7** *and let . . . away:* One possible meaning for the difficult Hebrew text. [p]**65.1** *refused . . . me:* One possible meaning for the difficult Hebrew text. [q]**65.4** *burial . . . pigs:* Coming in contact with the dead or eating the meat of pigs made a person unacceptable to God.

⁵And then they say to others,
  "Don't come near us!
    We're dedicated to God."
Such people are like smoke,
  irritating my nose all day.
⁶I have written this down;
  I won't keep silent.
I'll pay them back
  just as their sins deserve.
⁷I, the LORD, will make them pay
for their sins and for those
  of their ancestors—
they have disgraced me
by burning incense
  on mountains.

⁸Here is what the LORD says:
  A cluster of grapes
  that produces wine
    is worth keeping!
So, because of my servants,
  I won't destroy everyone.
⁹I have chosen the people
  of Israel and Judah,
and I will bless them
  with many descendants.
They will settle here
in this land of mountains,
  and it will be theirs.
¹⁰My people will worship me.
Then the coastlands of Sharon
  and the land as far
  as Achor Valleyʳ
will turn into pastureland
where cattle and sheep
  will feed and rest.

¹¹What will I, the LORD, do
if any of you reject me
  and my holy mountain?
What will happen to you
  for offering food and wine
to the gods you call
  "Good Luck" and "Fate"?
¹²Your luck will end!
I will see to it that you
  are slaughtered with swords.
You refused to answer
  when I called out;
you paid no attention
  to my instructions.
Instead, you did what I hated,
  knowing it was wrong.

¹³I, the LORD God, will give
food and drink to my servants,
  and they will celebrate.
But all of you sinners
will go hungry and thirsty,
  overcome with disgrace.
¹⁴My servants will laugh and sing,
  but you will be sad
  and cry out in pain.
¹⁵I, the LORD God, promise
  to see that you are killed
and that my chosen servants use
  your names as curse words.
But I will give new namesˢ
  to my servants.ᵗ
¹⁶I am God! I can be trusted.
Your past troubles are gone;
  I no longer think of them.
When you pray for someone
  to receive a blessing,
or when you make a promise,
  you must do it in my name.
I alone am the God
  who can be trusted.

The LORD's New Creation

¹⁷I am creating new heavens
  and a new earth;
everything of the past
  will be forgotten.
¹⁸Celebrate and be glad forever!
  I am creating a Jerusalem,
  full of happy people.
¹⁹I will celebrate with Jerusalem
  and all of its people;
there will be no more crying
  or sorrow in that city.

²⁰No child will die in infancy;
  everyone will live
  to a ripe old age.
Anyone a hundred years old
  will be considered young,
and to die younger than that
  will be considered a curse.

²¹My people will live
  in the houses they build;

ʳ**65.10** *coastlands of Sharon . . . Achor Valley:* Sharon is
the coastal plain on the west, and Achor Valley is in the
east near Jericho. These two places stand for the whole
country.   ˢ**65.15** *new names:* The giving of a new name
suggests the beginning of a new life.   ᵗ**65.15** *But
I . . . servants:* One possible meaning for the difficult
Hebrew text.

they will enjoy grapes
   from their own vineyards.
²² No one will take away
   their homes or vineyards.
My chosen people will live
   to be as old as trees,
and they will enjoy
   what they have earned.
²³ Their work won't be wasted,
and their children won't die
   of dreadful diseases.ᵘ
I will bless their children
   and their grandchildren.

*I wonder how many times
I've received from the Lord
what I had asked for—but
just didn't recognize it?*

PATSY CLAIRMONT

²⁴ I will answer their prayers
   before they finish praying.

²⁵ Wolves and lambs
   will graze together;
lions and oxen
   will feed on straw.
Snakes will eat only dirt!
They won't bite or harm anyone
   on my holy mountain.
I, the LORD, have spoken!

True Worship

66 The LORD said:
Heaven is my throne;
   the earth is my footstool.
What kind of house
could you build for me?
   In what place will I rest?
² I have made everything;
   that's how it all came to be.ᵛ
   I, the LORD, have spoken!

The people I treasure most
   are the humble—
they depend only on me
   and tremble when I speak.

³ You sacrifice oxen to me,
   and you commit murder;
you sacrifice lambs to me
   and dogs to other gods;
you offer grain to me
   and pigs' blood to idols;
you burn incense to me
   and praise your idols.ʷ
You have made your own choice
to do these disgusting things
   that you enjoy so much.
⁴ You refused to answer
   when I called out;
you paid no attention
   to my instructions.
Instead, you did what I hated,
   knowing it was wrong.
Now I will punishˣ you
   in a way you dread the most.

The LORD Will Help Jerusalem

⁵ If you tremble
when the LORD speaks,
   listen to what he says:
"Some of your own people hate
and reject you because of me.
   They make fun and say,
'Let the LORD show his power!
Let us see him
   make you truly happy.'ʸ
But those who say these things
   will be terribly ashamed."

⁶ Do you hear that noise
in the city and those shouts
   coming from the temple?
It is the LORD shouting
   as he punishes his enemies.

⁷ Have you ever heard of a woman
   who gave birth to a child
   before having labor pains?
⁸ Who ever heard of such a thing
   or imagined it could happen?

ᵘ**65.23** *their children . . . diseases:* One possible meaning
for the difficult Hebrew text.   ᵛ**66.2** *that's . . . be:*
One possible meaning for the difficult Hebrew text.
ʷ**66.3** *You sacrifice oxen . . . idols:* Or "Sacrificing oxen to
me is the same as murder; sacrificing lambs to me is the
same as sacrificing dogs to other gods; offering grain to
me is the same as offering pigs' blood to idols; and
burning incense to me is the same as praising idols."
ˣ**66.4** *punish:* One possible meaning for the difficult
Hebrew text.   ʸ**66.5** *Some . . . happy:* One possible
meaning for the difficult Hebrew text.

Can a nation be born in a day
   or come to life in a second?
Jerusalem is like a mother
who gave birth to her children
   as soon as she was in labor.
⁹The LORD is the one
   who makes birth possible.
And he will see that Zion
has many more children.
   The LORD has spoken.

¹⁰If you love Jerusalem,
   celebrate and shout!
If you were in sorrow
because of the city,
   you can now be glad.
¹¹She will nurse and comfort you,
just like your own mother,
   until you are satisfied.
You will fully enjoy
   her wonderful glory.

¹²The LORD has promised:
   "I will flood Jerusalem
with the wealth of nations
   and make the city prosper.
Zion will nurse you at her breast,
carry you in her arms,
   and hold you in her lap.
¹³I will comfort you there
like a mother
   comforting her child."

¹⁴When you see this happen,
   you will celebrate;
your strength will return
   faster than grass can sprout.
Then everyone will know
that the LORD is present
   with his servants,
but he is angry
   with his enemies.
¹⁵The LORD will come down
like a whirlwind
   with his flaming chariots.
He will be terribly furious
and punish his enemies
   with fire.
¹⁶The LORD's fiery sword
   will bring justice

everywhere on this earth
   and execute many people.

A Threat and a Promise

¹⁷Some of you get yourselves ready and go to a garden to worship a foreign goddess.ᶻ You eat the meat of pigs, lizards, and mice. But I, the LORD, will destroy you for this. ¹⁸I know everything you do and think! The time has now comeᵃ to bring together the people of every language and nation and to show them my glory ¹⁹by proving what I can do.ᵇ I will send the survivors to Tarshish, Pul,ᶜ Lud, Meshech,ᵈ Tubal, Javan,ᵉ and to the distant islands. I will send them to announce my wonderful glory to nations that have never heard about me.

²⁰They will bring your relatives from the nations as an offering to me, the LORD. They will come on horses, chariots, wagons, mules, and camelsᶠ to Jerusalem, my holy mountain. It will be like the people of Israel bringing the right offering to my temple. ²¹I promise that some of them will be priests and others will be helpers in my temple. I, the LORD, have spoken.

²²I also promise that you will always have descendants and will never be forgotten, just as the new heavens and the new earth that I create will last forever. ²³On the first day of each month and on each Sabbath, everyone will worship me. I, the LORD, have spoken.

²⁴My people will go out and look at the dead bodies of those who turned against me. The worms there never die, the fire never stops burning, and the sight of those bodies will be disgusting to everyone.

ᶻ**66.17** *Some . . . goddess*: One possible meaning for the difficult Hebrew text. ᵃ**66.18** *I . . . come*: One possible meaning for the difficult Hebrew text. ᵇ**66.19** *by . . . do*: One possible meaning for the difficult Hebrew text. ᶜ**66.19** *Pul*: Hebrew; one ancient translation "Put," a country in Africa, but neither the location of Pul or Put is known for certain. ᵈ**66.19** *Meshech*: One ancient translation; Hebrew "those who use bows and arrows." ᵉ**66.19** *Tarshish . . . Javan*: Tarshish may have been a Phoenician city in Spain; Put (see note on Pul) and Lud were African people; Meshech and Tubal were regions south or southeast of the Black Sea; the Javan were people of Asia Minor and the Greek islands. ᶠ**66.20** *camels*: One possible meaning for the difficult Hebrew text.

Jeremiah Faith in the Dark

How does it feel to be rejected by someone you love? In the book of Jeremiah, we discover what rejection felt like to an ancient man named Jeremiah—and to God.

First, much of the book is a vivid description of how God felt about his people rejecting him to follow other gods. Judah belonged to him; the nation was his bride, but like an unfaithful wife the people left him for other gods. In sorrowful anger, God, through the prophet Jeremiah, warned his people that he'd punish them for their sins.

Second, we see how Jeremiah felt when he was rejected by his people. Jeremiah lived during the darkest days of Judah's history. He prophesied under the reigns of five kings and the destruction of Jerusalem in 586 B.C. Called to his ministry when he was just a youth—possibly not even twenty years old—he was given a message from God that no one wanted to hear. Just as the people had rejected God, so also they rejected Jeremiah. His enemies accused him of being a traitor for telling the people they should surrender to Babylon; they tried to kill him and had him jailed for many years. In the end, he was carried off to Egypt where he died in exile.

The book of Jeremiah is unusual in that it reveals not only the prophet's words, but also the prophet's thoughts and feelings. Jeremiah faithfully obeyed God's will despite incredible obstacles, yet he wasn't always happy about his task. So he complained to God about his problems, fears, and feelings (see 11.18-23; 12.1-6; 15.10,11,15-21; 17.14-18; 18.19-23; 20.7-18).

In this book we not only see how God felt about his people and their sin, and how he intervened in the affairs of nations, we also see how he cared for a prophet who remained faithful in the face of a most difficult calling. Just as God was faithful to keep his promise to Jeremiah (1.8), so God will faithfully restore his people under a new agreement (33.14-26). In Jeremiah we find that there is hope even in the midst of the greatest darkness—because God is faithful.

Jeremiah at a Glance

1. God calls Jeremiah to be a prophet (1)
2. God's judgment against Judah; Jeremiah's personal struggles, confessions, and prayers (2–25)
3. Jeremiah contests the false prophets (26–29)
4. God's promises of hope and restoration for his people (30–33)
5. Encounters between Jeremiah and the kings of Judah (34–38)
6. Jeremiah's ministry after the fall of Jerusalem (39–45)
7. Prophecies against heathen nations (46–51)
8. Historical appendix on the fall of Jerusalem and deportations to Babylon (52)

1 My name is Jeremiah. I am a priest, and my father Hilkiah and everyone else in my family are from Anathoth in the territory of the Benjamin tribe. This book contains the things that the LORD told me to say. [2]The LORD first spoke to me in the thirteenth year that Josiah[a] was king of Judah, [3]and he continued to speak to me during the rule of Josiah's son Jehoiakim.[b] The last time the LORD spoke to me was in the fifth month[c] of the eleventh year that Josiah's son Zedekiah[d] was king. That was also when the people of Jerusalem were taken away as prisoners.

The LORD Chooses Jeremiah

[4]The LORD said:

[5] "Jeremiah, I am your Creator,
    and before you were born,
I chose you to speak for me
    to the nations."

[6]I replied, "I'm not a good speaker, LORD, and I'm too young."

[7]"Don't say you're too young," the LORD answered. "If I tell you to go and speak to someone, then go! And when I tell you what to say, don't leave out a word! [8]I promise to be with you and keep you safe, so don't be afraid."

[9]The LORD reached out his hand, then he touched my mouth and said, "I am giving you the words to say, [10]and I am sending you with authority to speak to the nations for me. You will tell them of doom and destruction, and of rising and rebuilding again."

[11]The LORD showed me something in a vision. Then he asked, "What do you see, Jeremiah?"

I answered, "A branch of almonds that ripen early."

[12]"That's right," the LORD replied, "and I always rise early[e] to keep a promise."

[13]Then the LORD showed me something else and asked, "What do you see now?"

I answered, "I see a pot of boiling water in the north, and it's about to spill out toward us."

[14]The LORD said:

I will pour out destruction
    all over the land.
[15]Just watch while I send
    for the kings of the north.
They will attack and capture
    Jerusalem and other towns,

---

[a]1.2 *Josiah*: Ruled 640-609 B.C.   [b]1.3 *Jehoiakim*: Ruled 609-598 B.C.   [c]1.3 *fifth month*: Ab, the fifth month of the Hebrew calendar, from about mid-July to mid-August.   [d]1.3 *Zedekiah*: Ruled 598-586 B.C.
[e]1.11,12 *almonds . . . rise early*: In Hebrew "almonds that ripen early" sounds like "always rise early."

---

*Spiritual*Life—What does God expect of me? *(Jeremiah 1.4-19)*

Speak up when he asks you to.

Has your local video store added an X-rated film section? Did you catch someone stealing on the job? Have you seen someone taking advantage of a poor or homeless person? Did a friend admit to you she cheated on her taxes?

None of these situations—or other situations you may have faced—are easy to handle. You wonder, *What can I do to make a difference in the world?* And if you know the person involved, you may ask yourself, *And how will my honesty with this person affect our relationship?*

Jeremiah, too, was in a tough position. The Lord was asking him to reveal to the Jewish people their sin. Understandably, Jeremiah was hesitant. He came up with two good excuses: "I'm not a good speaker, LORD, and I'm too young" (1.6). But what was the Lord's response? He first asked Jeremiah to obey, and then gave him a promise.

When God calls us to speak for him today, he asks us to obey, no matter how difficult (or unpleasant) we think the task is (1.7). But he doesn't leave us high and dry, with no help. He follows up his command with these comforting, encouraging words: "I promise to be with you and keep you safe, so don't be afraid" (1.8)! (See also Exodus 20.1-17; Judges 5.1-11; Micah 6.6-8; Romans 8.1-17; 1 Corinthians 6.12-20.)

Words To Remember: *If I tell you to go and speak to someone, then go! . . . I promise to be with you and keep you safe, so don't be afraid.—Jeremiah 1.7,8*

then set up their thrones
   at the gates of Jerusalem.

¹⁶I will punish my people,
   because they are guilty
of turning from me
   to worship idols.

¹⁷Jeremiah, get ready!
   Go and tell the people
     what I command you to say.
Don't be frightened by them,
   or I will make you terrified
     while they watch.

¹⁸My power will make you strong
   like a fortress
   or a column of iron
   or a wall of bronze.
You will oppose all of Judah,
including its kings and leaders,
   its priests and people.
¹⁹They will fight back,
   but they won't win.
I, the LORD, give my word—
   I won't let them harm you.

Israel's Unfaithfulness

2 The LORD told me ²to go to Jerusalem
and tell everyone that he had said:

When you were my young bride,
you loved me and followed me
   through the barren desert.
³You belonged to me alone,
like the first part of the harvest,
   and I severely punished
   those who mistreated you.

⁴Listen, people of Israel,^f
⁵ and I, the LORD, will speak.
I was never unfair
   to your ancestors,
but they left me
and became worthless
   by following worthless idols.
⁶Your ancestors refused
   to ask for my help,
though I had rescued them
   from Egypt
and led them through
a treacherous, barren desert,
   where no one lives
   or dares to travel.

⁷I brought you here to my land,
   where food is abundant,
but you made my land filthy
   with your sins.
⁸The priests who teach my laws
   don't care to know me.
Your leaders rebel against me;
your prophets
   give messages from Baal
   and worship false gods.

*Doing the Word of God
activates faith and helps it
to grow. When we put our
faith into action, we allow
God to move in our life.*

KELSEY D. MENEHAN

The LORD Accuses His People

⁹I will take you to court
and accuse you
   and your descendants
*¹⁰of a crime that no nation
   has ever committed before.
Just ask anyone, anywhere,
from the eastern deserts
   to the islands in the west.
¹¹You will find that no nation
   has ever abandoned its gods
     even though they were false.
I am the true and glorious God,
   but you have rejected me
   to worship idols.
¹²Tell the heavens
   to tremble with fear!
¹³You, my people, have sinned
   in two ways—
you have rejected me, the source
   of life-giving water,
and you've tried to collect water

---

f **2.4** *Israel:* After the nation was divided, the northern
kingdom was called "Israel," and the southern kingdom
was called "Judah" (see 1 Kings 12.1-20). In 722 B.C.
the Assyrians conquered the northern kingdom, and
Judah was all that was left. And so in the book of
Jeremiah the name "Israel" is most often used of the
southern kingdom.

in cracked and leaking pits
   dug in the ground.

¹⁴ People of Israel,
   you weren't born slaves;
      you were captured in war.
¹⁵ Enemies roared like lions
   and destroyed your land;
      towns lie burned and empty.
¹⁶ Soldiers from the Egyptian towns
   of Memphis and Tahpanhes
      have cracked your skulls.
¹⁷ It's all your own fault!
   You stopped following me,
      the LORD your God,
¹⁸ and you trusted the power
   of Egypt and Assyria.ᵍ
¹⁹ Your own sins will punish you,
   because it was a bitter mistake
      for you to reject me
         without fear of punishment.
   I, the LORD All-Powerful,
      have spoken.

²⁰ Long ago you left me
   and broke all ties between us,
      refusing to be my servant.
   Now you worship other gods
      by having sex
   on hilltops or in the shade
      of large trees.ʰ
²¹ You were a choice grapevine,
   but now you produce nothing
      but small, rotten grapes.

Israel Is Stained with Guilt

²² The LORD said:

People of Israel,
   you are stained with guilt,
and no soap or bleach
   can wash it away.
²³ You deny your sins
   and say, "We aren't unclean.
      We haven't worshiped Baal."ⁱ
But think about what you do
   in Hinnom Valley.ʲ
And you run back and forth
   like young camels,
as you rush to worship one idol
   after another.
²⁴ You are a female donkey
   sniffing the desert air,
      wanting to mate

with just anyone.
   You are an easy catch!
²⁵ Your shoes are worn out,
   and your throat is parched
from running here and there
   to worship foreign gods.
"Stop!" I shouted,
but you replied, "No!
   I love those gods too much."

²⁶ You and your leaders
   are more disgraceful
      than thieves—
you and your kings,
   your priests and prophets
²⁷ worship stone idols
   and sacred poles
as if they had created you
   and had given you life.
You have rejected me,
   but when you're in trouble,
      you cry to me for help.
²⁸ Go cry to the gods you made!
   There should be enough of them
      to save you,
because Judah has as many gods
   as it has towns.

Israel Rebels against the LORD

²⁹ The LORD said to Israel:

You accuse me of not saving you,
   but I say you have rebelled.
³⁰ I tried punishing you,
   but you refused
      to come back to me,
and like fierce lions
   you killed my prophets.

³¹ Now listen to what I say!
   Did I abandon you in the desert
      or surround you with darkness?
   You are my people,
      yet you have told me,

ᵍ2.18 *trusted . . . Assyria*: Hebrew "went to Egypt and
drank from the Shihor River, and you went to Assyria
and drank from the Euphrates River." ʰ2.20 *having
sex . . . trees*: In some Canaanite religions, worshipers
had sex with temple prostitutes, who represented their
gods; many of the Canaanite places of worship were on
hilltops or under large trees. ⁱ2.23 *Baal*: The Hebrew
text has "the Baals," probably because the god Baal was
believed to be present in different forms at different
places of worship. ʲ2.23 *Hinnom Valley*: Hebrew "the
valley" (see 7.31, 32; 19.1-6).

"We'll do what we want,
and we refuse
to worship you!"
³²A bride could not forget
to wear her jewelry
to her wedding,
but you have forgotten me
day after day.
³³You are so clever
at finding lovers
that you could give lessons
to a prostitute.
³⁴You killed innocent people
for no reason at all.
And even though their blood
can be seen on your clothes,
³⁵you claim to be innocent,
and you want me to stop
being angry with you.
So I'll take you to court,
and we'll see who is right.

³⁶When Assyria let you down,
you ran to Egypt,
but you'll find no help there,
³⁷and you will leave
in great sadness.ᵏ
I won't let you find help
from those you trust.

Sin and Shame

3 The LORD said to the people of Israel:

If a divorced woman marries,
can her first husband
ever marry her again?
No, because this
would pollute the land.
But you have more gods
than a prostitute has lovers.
Why should I take you back?
²Just try to find one hilltop
where you haven't gone
to worship other gods
by having sex.ˡ
You sat beside the road
like a robber in ambush,
except you offered yourself
to every passerby.
Your sins of unfaithfulness
have polluted the land.
³So I, the LORD, refused
to let the spring rains fall.
But just like a prostitute,

you still have no shame
for what you have done.
⁴You call me your father
or your long-lost friend;
⁵you beg me to stop being angry,
but you won't stop sinning.

The LORD Asks Israel To Come Back to Him

⁶When Josiahᵐ was king, the LORD said:
Jeremiah, the kingdom of Israelⁿ was like
an unfaithful wife who became a prostitute
on the hilltops and in the shade of large
trees.ᵒ ⁷⁻⁸I knew that the kingdom of Israel
had been unfaithful and committed many
sins, yet I still hoped she might come back
to me. But she didn't, so I divorced her and
sent her away.

Her sister, the kingdom of Judah, saw
what happened, but she wasn't worried in
the least, and I watched her become unfaithful like her sister. ⁹The kingdom of Judah wasn't sorry for being a prostitute, and
she didn't care that she had made both herself and the land unclean by worshiping
idols of stone and wood. ¹⁰And worst of all,
the people of Judah pretended to come back
to me. ¹¹Even the people of Israel were honest enough not to pretend.
¹²Jeremiah, shout toward the north:

Israel, I am your LORD—
come back to me!
You were unfaithful
and made me furious,
but I am merciful,
and so I will forgive you.
¹³Just admit that you rebelled
and worshiped foreign gods
under large trees everywhere.
¹⁴You are unfaithful children,
but you belong to me.
Come home!
I'll take one or two of you
from each town and clan
and bring you to Zion.
¹⁵Then I'll appoint wise rulers
who will obey me,
and they will care for you
like shepherds.

ᵏ2.37 *in great sadness:* Or "as prisoners."
ˡ3.2 *hilltop . . . sex:* See the note at 2.20. ᵐ3.6 *Josiah:*
Ruled 640-609 B.C. ⁿ3.6 *Israel:* The northern kingdom
(see the note at 2.4). ᵒ3.6 *prostitute . . . trees:* See the
note at 2.20.

¹⁶You will increase in numbers,
and there will be no need
to remember the sacred chest
or to make a new one.^p
¹⁷The whole city of Jerusalem
will be my throne.^q
All nations will come here
to worship me,
and they will no longer follow
their stubborn, evil hearts.

*As our Father and Creator,
God longs for us to draw
near to him.*

RAMONA CRAMER TUCKER

¹⁸Then, in countries to the north,
you people of Judah and Israel
will be reunited,
and you will return to the land
I gave your ancestors.
¹⁹I have always wanted
to treat you as my children
and give you the best land,
the most beautiful on earth.
I wanted you to call me "Father"
and not turn from me.
²⁰But instead, you are like a wife
who broke her wedding vows.
You have been unfaithful to me.
I, the LORD, have spoken.

The People Confess Their Sins

The LORD said:

²¹Listen to the noise
on the hilltops!
It's the people of Israel,
weeping and begging me
to answer their prayers.
They forgot about me
and chose the wrong path.
²²I will tell them, "Come back,
and I will cure you
of your unfaithfulness."

They will answer,
"We will come back, because you
are the LORD our God.

²³On hilltops, we worshiped idols
and made loud noises,
but it was all for nothing—
only you can save us.
²⁴Since the days of our ancestors
when our nation was young,
that shameful god Baal^r has taken
our crops and livestock,
our sons and daughters.
²⁵We have rebelled against you
just like our ancestors,
and we are ashamed of our sins."

How Israel Can Return to the LORD

4 The LORD said:

Israel, if you really want
to come back to me, get rid
of those disgusting idols.
²Make promises only in my name,
and do what you promise!
Then all nations will praise me,
and I will bless them.
³People of Jerusalem and Judah,
don't be so stubborn!
Your hearts have become hard,
like unplowed ground
where thornbushes grow.
⁴With all your hearts,
keep the agreement
I made with you.
But if you are stubborn
and keep on sinning,
my anger will burn like a fire
that cannot be put out.

Disaster Is Coming

The LORD said:

*⁵"Sound the trumpets, my people.
Warn the people of Judah,^s
'Run for your lives!
⁶Head for Jerusalem
or another walled town!'

"Jeremiah, tell them I'm sending
disaster from the north.

---

^p3.16 *make a new one*: The sacred chest was probably destroyed or taken away by the Babylonians when they captured Jerusalem in 586 B.C. ^q3.16,17 *sacred chest . . . throne*: The sacred chest was thought to be God's throne on earth. ^r3.24 *that shameful god Baal*: The Hebrew text has "The Shame," which was sometimes used as a way of making fun of the Canaanite god Baal. ^s4.5 *Judah*: Hebrew "Judah and Jerusalem."

⁷An army will come out,
    like a lion from its den.
It will destroy nations
and leave your towns empty
    and in ruins."

⁸Then I said
    to the people of Israel,
"Put on sackcloth!ᵗ
    Mourn and cry out,
'The LORD is still angry
    with us.' "

⁹The LORD said,

"When all this happens,
    the king and his officials,
the prophets and the priests
    will be shocked and terrified."

¹⁰I said, "You are the LORD God. So why have you fooled everyone, especially the people of Jerusalem? Why did you promise peace, when a knife is at our throats?"

The Coming Disaster

¹¹⁻¹²When disaster comes, the LORD will tell you people of Jerusalem,

"I am sending a windstorm
from the desert—
    not a welcome breeze.ᵘ
And it will sweep you away
    as punishment for your sins.
¹³Look! The enemy army
    swoops down like an eagle;
their cavalry and chariots
race faster than storm clouds
    blown by the wind."

Then you will answer,
    "We are doomed!"

¹⁴But Jerusalem, there is still time
    for you to be saved.
Wash the evil from your hearts
    and stop making sinful plans,
¹⁵before a message of disaster
arrives from the hills of Ephraim
    and the town of Dan.ᵛ

¹⁶⁻¹⁷The LORD said,

"Tell the nations that my people
    have rebelled against me.

And so an army will come
    from far away
to surround Jerusalem
    and the towns of Judah.
I, the LORD, have spoken.

¹⁸"People of Judah,
    your hearts will be in pain,
but it's your own fault
    that you will be punished."

**Jeremiah's Vision
of the Coming Punishment**

¹⁹I can't stand the pain!
My heart pounds,
    as I twist and turn in agony.
I hear the signal trumpet
and the battle cry of the enemy,
    and I cannot be silent.
²⁰I see the enemy defeating us
time after time,
    leaving everything in ruins.
Even my own home
    is destroyed in a moment.
²¹How long will I see enemy flags
    and hear their trumpets?

²²I heard the LORD say,
    "My people ignore me.
They are foolish children
who do not understand
    that they will be punished.
All they know is how to sin."

²³After this, I looked around.
The earth was barren,
    with no form of life.
The sun, moon, and stars
    had disappeared.
²⁴The mountains were shaking;
²⁵no people could be seen,
    and all the birds
    had flown away.

ᵗ4.8 *sackcloth*: A rough, dark-colored cloth made from goat or camel hair and used to make grain sacks. It was worn in times of trouble or sorrow.
ᵘ4.11,12 *a welcome breeze*: Hebrew "a wind to blow away the husks." Farmers used a special shovel to pitch grain and husks into the air. Wind would blow away the light husks, and the grain would fall back to the ground, where it could be gathered up.
ᵛ4.15 *Ephraim . . . Dan*: The hills of Ephraim were to the north of Jerusalem, and Dan was even farther north. They would be reached by the invading army first.

²⁶ Farmland had become a desert,
  and towns were in ruins.
The LORD's fierce anger
  had done all of this.

The Death of Jerusalem

²⁷⁻²⁸The LORD said:

I have made my decision,
  and I won't change my mind.
This land will be destroyed,
  although not completely.
The sky will turn dark,
  and the earth will mourn.

²⁹ Enemy cavalry and archers
  shout their battle cry.
People run for their lives
and try to find safety
  among trees and rocks.
Every town is empty.

³⁰ Jerusalem, your land
  has been wiped out.
But you act like a prostitute
and try to win back your lovers,
  who now hate you.
You can put on a red dress,
gold jewelry, and eye shadow,
  but it's no use—
your lovers are out to kill you!

³¹ I heard groaning and crying.
Was it a woman giving birth
  to her first child?
No, it was Jerusalem.
She was gasping for breath
  and begging for help.
"I'm dying!" she said.
  "They have murdered me."

Is Anyone Honest and Faithful?

The LORD said to me:

5 "Search Jerusalem
  for honest people
    who try to be faithful.
If you can find even one,
  I'll forgive the whole city.
² Everyone breaks promises
  made in my name."

³ I answered, "I know
  that you look for truth.

You punished your people
  for their lies,
but in spite of the pain,
  they became more stubborn
and refused to turn back
  to you."

*Faith is meant to be
lived moment by moment.
It isn't some broad, general
outline—it's a long walk
with a real Person.*

JONI EARECKSON TADA

⁴ Then I thought to myself,
  "These common people
    act like fools,
and they have never learned
what the LORD their God
  demands of them.
⁵ I'll go and talk to the leaders.
They know what God demands."
  But even they had decided
    not to obey the LORD.

⁶ The people have rebelled
and rejected the LORD
  too many times.
So enemies will attack
like lions from the forest
  or wolves from the desert.
Those enemies will watch
  the towns of Judah,
and like leopards
they will tear to pieces
  whoever goes outside.

Enemies Will Punish Judah

The LORD said:

⁷ People of Judah,
  how can I forgive you?
I gave you everything,
but you abandoned me
  and worshiped idols.
You men go to prostitutes
and are unfaithful
  to your wives.

⁸You are no better than animals,
    and you always want sex
        with someone else's wife.

⁹Why shouldn't I punish
    the people of Judah?
¹⁰I will tell their enemies,
    "Go through my vineyard.
Don't destroy the vines,
    but cut off the branches,
because they are the people
    who don't belong to me."

¹¹In every way, Judah and Israel
    have been unfaithful to me.
*¹²Their prophets lie and say,
    "The LORD won't punish us.
We will have peace
    and plenty of food."
¹³They tell these lies in my name,
    so now they will be killed in war
        or starve to death.

¹⁴I am the LORD God All-Powerful.
    Jeremiah, I will tell you
        exactly what to say.
Your words will be a fire;
    Israel and Judah
        will be the fuel.

¹⁵People of Israel,
    I have made my decision.
An army from a distant country
    will attack you.
I've chosen an ancient nation,
    and you won't understand
        their language.
¹⁶All of them are warriors,
    and their arrows bring death.
¹⁷This nation will eat your crops
    and livestock;
they will leave no fruit
    on your vines or trees.
And although you feel safe
    behind thick walls,
your towns will be destroyed
    and your children killed.

Israel Refused To Worship the LORD

¹⁸The LORD said:
Jeremiah, the enemy army won't kill everyone in Judah. ¹⁹And the people who survive will ask, "Why did the LORD our God do such terrible things to us?" Then tell them:

I am the LORD,
    but you abandoned me
and worshiped other gods
    in your own land.
Now you will be slaves
    in a foreign country.
²⁰Tell these things to each other,
    you people of Judah,
        you descendants of Jacob.

²¹You fools! Why don't you listen
    when I speak?
Why can't you understand
²²that you should worship me
    with fear and trembling?
I'm the one who made the shore
    to hold back the ocean.
Waves may crash on the beach,
    but they can come no farther.
²³You stubborn people have rebelled
    and turned your backs on me.
²⁴You refuse to say,
    "Let's worship the LORD!
He's the one who sends rain
    in spring and autumn
        and gives us a good harvest."
²⁵That's why I cannot bless you!

*²⁶A hunter traps birds
    and puts them in a cage,
but some of you trap humans
    and make them your slaves.
²⁷You are evil, and you lie and cheat
    to make yourselves rich.
You are powerful
²⁸   and prosperous,
but you refuse to help^w the poor
    get the justice they deserve.
²⁹You need to be punished,
    and so I will take revenge.
³⁰Look at the terrible things
    going on in this country.
        I am shocked!
³¹Prophets give their messages
    in the name of a false god,^x
my priests don't want
    to serve me,^y
and you—my own people—
    like it this way!
But on the day of disaster,
    where will you turn for help?

---

^w5.28 *refuse to help:* One possible meaning for the difficult Hebrew text.   ^x5.31 *give . . . god:* Or "tell lies."
^y5.31 *don't . . . me:* Or "don't care what I want."

A Warning for the People of Jerusalem

The LORD said:

6 Run for your lives,
  people of Benjamin.
    Get out of Jerusalem.
Sound a trumpet in Tekoa
and light a signal fire
  in Beth-Haccherem.
Soon you will be struck
  by disaster from the north.
*²Jerusalem is a lovely pasture,
  but shepherds will surround it
    and divide it up,
³then let their flocks
  eat all the grass.ᶻ
⁴Kings will tell their troops,
  "If we reach Jerusalem
in the morning,
  we'll attack at noon.
But if we arrive later,
⁵we'll attack after dark
  and destroy its fortresses."

⁶I am the LORD All-Powerful,
and I will command these armies
  to chop down trees
and build a ramp up to the walls
  of Jerusalem.

People of Jerusalem,
I must punish you
  for your injustice.
⁷Evil pours from your city
  like water from a spring.
Sounds of violent crimes
  echo within your walls;
victims are everywhere,
  wounded and dying.

⁸Listen to me,
you people of Jerusalem
  and Judah.
I will abandon you,
and your land will become
  an empty desert.
⁹I will tell your enemies
to leave your nation bare
  like a vine stripped of grapes.
I, the LORD All-Powerful,
  have spoken.

Jeremiah's Anger

¹⁰I have told the people
that you, LORD,
will punish them,
but they just laugh
  and refuse to listen.
¹¹Your anger against Judah
  flames up inside me,
and I can't hold it in
  much longer.

The LORD's Anger Will Sweep Everyone Away

The LORD answered:

Don't hold back my anger!
Let it sweep away everyone—
  the children at play
and all adults,
  young and old alike.
¹²I'll punish the people of Judah
  and give to others
their houses and fields,
  as well as their wives.
I, the LORD, have spoken.

¹³Everyone is greedy and dishonest,
  whether poor or rich.
Even the prophets and priests
  cannot be trusted.
¹⁴All they ever offer
to my deeply wounded people
  are empty hopes for peace.
¹⁵They should be ashamed
of their disgusting sins,
  but they don't even blush.
And so, when I punish Judah,
they will end up on the ground,
  dead like everyone else.
I, the LORD, have spoken.

The People of Judah Rejected God's Way of Life

¹⁶The LORD said:

My people, when you stood
  at the crossroads,
I told you, "Follow the road
  your ancestors took,
and you will find peace."
  But you refused.
¹⁷I also sent prophets
  to warn you of danger,
but when they sounded the alarm,
  you paid no attention.

ᶻ**6.2,3** *Jerusalem . . . grass:* One possible meaning for the difficult Hebrew text.

*[18]So I tell all nations on earth,
    "Watch what I will do!
[19]My people ignored me
    and rejected my laws.
They planned to do evil,
    and now the evil they planned
      will happen to them."

[20]People of Judah,
    you bring me incense from Sheba
      and spices from distant lands.
You offer sacrifices of all kinds.
    But why bother?
    I hate these gifts of yours!
[21]So I will put stumbling blocks
    in your path,
and everyone will die,
including parents and children,
    neighbors and friends.

An Army from the North

[22]The LORD said,

"Look toward the north,
where a powerful nation
    has prepared for war.
[23]Its well-armed troops are cruel
    and never show mercy.
Their galloping horses sound
like ocean waves
    pounding on the shore.
This army will attack you,
    lovely Jerusalem."

It's okay to hurt. Pain is not all bad. With pain comes change. And some pain may be necessary in our lives in order to grow.

JAN DRAVECKY

[24]Then the people said,

"Just hearing about them
    makes us tremble with fear,
and we twist and turn in pain
    like a woman giving birth."

[25]The LORD said,

"Don't work in your fields
    or walk along the roads.
It's too dangerous.
The enemy is well armed
[26]   and attacks without warning.
So mourn, my people, as though
    your only child had died.
Wear clothes made of sackcloth[a]
    and roll in the ash pile."

The LORD's People Must Be Tested

The LORD said:

[27]Jeremiah, test my people
    as though they were metal.
[28]And you'll find they are hard
    like bronze and iron.
They are stubborn rebels,
    always spreading lies.
*[29]Silver can be purified
    in a fiery furnace,
[30]but my people are too wicked
    to be made pure,
and so I have rejected them.

Jeremiah Speaks in the Temple
(*Jeremiah 26.1-6*)

7 [1-3]The LORD told me to stand by the gate of the temple[b] and to tell the people who were going in that the LORD All-Powerful, the God of Israel, had said:

Pay attention, people of Judah! Change your ways and start living right, then I will let you keep on living in your own country.[c] [4]Don't fool yourselves! My temple is here in Jerusalem, but that doesn't mean I will protect you. [5]I will keep you safe only if you change your ways. Be fair and honest with each other. [6]Stop taking advantage of foreigners, orphans, and widows. Don't kill innocent people. And stop worshiping other gods. [7]Then I will let you enjoy a long life in this land I gave your ancestors.

[8]But just look at what is happening! You put your trust in worthless lies. [9]You steal and murder; you lie in court and are unfaithful in marriage. You worship idols and offer incense to Baal, when these gods have

---

[a]*6.26 sackcloth:* See the note at 4.8.   [b]*7.1-3 temple:* The Hebrew text has "house of the LORD," another name for the temple.   [c]*7.1-3 let you . . . own country:* Or "live here with you."

never done anything for you. [10]And then you come into my temple and worship me! Do you think I will protect you so that you can go on sinning? [11]You are thieves, and you have made my temple your hideout. But I've seen everything you have done.

[12]Go to Shiloh, where my sacred tent once stood. Take a look at what I did there. My people Israel sinned, and so I destroyed Shiloh!

[13]While you have been sinning, I have been trying to talk to you, but you refuse to listen. [14]Don't think this temple will protect you. Long ago I told your ancestors to build it and worship me here, but now I have decided to tear it down, just as I destroyed Shiloh. [15]And as for you, people of Judah, I'm going to send you away from my land, just as I sent away the people of Ephraim and the other northern tribes.

Punishment for Worshiping Other Gods

[16]Jeremiah, don't pray for these people! I, the LORD, would refuse to listen. [17]Do you see what the people of Judah are doing in their towns and in the streets of Jerusalem? [18]Children gather firewood, their fathers build fires, and their mothers mix dough to bake bread for the goddess they call the Queen of Heaven.[d] They even offer wine sacrifices to other gods, just to insult me. [19]But they are not only insulting me; they are also insulting themselves by doing these shameful things.

[20]And now, I, the LORD All-Powerful, will flood Judah with my fiery anger until nothing is left—no people or animals, no trees or crops.

It Is Useless To Offer Sacrifices

[21]The LORD told me to say to the people of Judah:

I am the LORD All-Powerful, the God of Israel, but I won't accept sacrifices from you. So don't even bother bringing them to me. You might as well just cook the meat for yourselves.

[22]At the time I brought your ancestors out of Egypt, I didn't command them to offer sacrifices to me. [23]Instead, I told them, "If you listen to me and do what I tell you, I will be your God, you will be my people, and all will go well for you." [24]But your ancestors refused to listen. They were stubborn, and whenever I wanted them to go

one way, they always went the other. [25]Ever since your ancestors left Egypt, I have been sending my servants the prophets to speak for me. [26]But you have ignored me and become even more stubborn and sinful than your ancestors ever were!

Slaughter Valley

The LORD said:

[27]Jeremiah, no matter what you do, the people won't listen. [28]So you must say to them:

People of Judah, I am the LORD your God, but you have refused to obey me, and you didn't change when I punished you. And now, you no longer even pretend to be faithful to me.

[29] Shave your head bald
 and throw away the hair.
 Sing a funeral song
 on top of a barren hill.
 You people have made me angry,
 and I have abandoned you.

[30]You have disobeyed me by putting your disgusting idols in my temple, and now the temple itself is disgusting to me. [31]At Topheth in Hinnom Valley you have built altars where you kill your children and burn them as sacrifices to other gods. I would never think of telling you to do this. [32]So watch out! Someday that place will no longer be called Topheth or Hinnom Valley. It will be called Slaughter Valley, because you will bury your dead there until you run out of room, [33]and then bodies will lie scattered on the ground. Birds and wild animals will come and eat, and no one will be around to scare them off. [34]When I am finished with your land, there will be deathly silence in the empty ruins of Jerusalem and the towns of Judah—no happy voices, no sounds of parties or wedding celebrations.

8 Then the bones of the dead kings of Judah and their officials will be dug up, along with the bones of the priests, the prophets, and everyone else in Jerusalem [2]who loved and worshiped the sun, moon, and stars. These bones will be scattered and left lying on the ground like

---

[d]7.18 *Queen of Heaven:* Probably another name for the goddess Astarte.

trash, where the sun and moon and stars can shine on them.

³Some of you people of Judah will be left alive, but I will force you to go to foreign countries, and you will wish you were dead. I, the LORD God All-Powerful, have spoken.

The People Took the Wrong Road

⁴The LORD said:

People of Jerusalem,
when you stumble and fall,
    you get back up,
and if you take a wrong road,
    you turn around and go back.ᵉ
⁵So why do you refuse
    to come back to me?
Why do you hold so tightly
    to your false gods?

⁶I listen carefully,
but none of you admit
    that you've done wrong.
Without a second thought,
you run down the wrong roadᶠ
    like cavalry troops
    charging into battle.

⁷Storks, doves, swallows,
and thrushes
    all know when it's time
to fly away for the winter
    and when to come back.
But you, my people,
    don't know what I demand.
⁸You say, "We are wise
because we have the teachings
    and laws of the LORD."
But I say that your teachers
have turned my words
    into lies!
⁹Your wise men
have rejected what I say,
    and so they have no wisdom.
Now they will be trapped
and put to shame;
    they won't know what to do.
¹⁰I'll give their wives and fields
    to strangers.

Everyone is greedy and dishonest,
    whether poor or rich.
Even the prophets and priests
    cannot be trusted.

¹¹All they ever offer
to my deeply wounded people
    are empty hopes for peace.
¹²They should be ashamed
of their disgusting sins,
    but they don't even blush.
And so, when I punish Judah,
they will end up on the ground,
    dead like everyone else.
¹³I will wipe them out.ᵍ
They are vines without grapes;
    fig trees without figs or leaves.
They have not done a thing
    that I told them!ʰ
I, the LORD, have spoken.

The People and Their Punishment

¹⁴The people of Judah
    say to each other,
"What are we waiting for?
Let's run to a town with walls
    and die there.
We rebelled against the LORD,
and we were sentenced to die
    by drinking poison.
¹⁵We had hoped for peace
and a time of healing,
    but all we got was terror.
¹⁶Our enemies have reached
    the town of Dan in the north,
and the snorting of their horses
    makes us tremble with fear.
The enemy will destroy Jerusalem
and our entire nation.
    No one will survive."

¹⁷"Watch out!" the LORD says.
"I'm sending poisonous snakes
    to attack you,
and no one can stop them."

Jeremiah Mourns for His People

¹⁸I'm burdened with sorrow
    and feel like giving up.
¹⁹In a foreign land
    my people are crying.
Listen! You'll hear them say,

ᵉ8.4 *if you take . . . go back*: One possible meaning for the difficult Hebrew text. ᶠ8.6 *you run down the wrong road*: One possible meaning for the difficult Hebrew text. ᵍ8.13 *I will wipe them out*: One possible meaning for the difficult Hebrew text. ʰ8.13 *They have not . . . them*: One possible meaning for the difficult Hebrew text.

"Has the LORD deserted Zion?
    Is he no longer its king?"

I hear the LORD reply,
"Why did you make me angry
    by worshiping useless idols?"

²⁰The people complain,
"Spring and summer
    have come and gone,
but still the LORD
    hasn't rescued us."

²¹My people are crushed,
    and so is my heart.
        I am horrified and mourn.
²²If medicine and doctors
may be found in Gilead,
    why aren't my people healed?

9 I wish that my eyes
        were fountains of tears,
    so I could cry day and night
for my people
    who were killed.
²I wish I could go into the desert
    and find a hiding place
from all who are treacherous
    and unfaithful to God.

The LORD Answers Jeremiah

³The LORD replied:

Lies come from the mouths
of my people,
    like arrows from a bow.
With each dishonest deed
    their power increases,
and not one of them will admit
    that I am God.

⁴Jeremiah, all your friends
    and relatives
tell lies about you,
    so don't trust them.
⁵They wear themselves out,
    always looking for a new way
        to cheat their friends.
⁶Everyone takes advantage
    of everyone else,
and no one will admit
    that I am God.

⁷And so I will purify
    the hearts of my people

just as gold is purified
    in a furnace.
        I have no other choice.
⁸They say they want peace,
    but this lie is deadly,
like an arrow that strikes
    when you least expect it.
⁹Give me one good reason
    not to punish them
        as they deserve.
I, the LORD All-Powerful,
    have spoken.

Jeremiah Weeps for His People

¹⁰I weep for the pastureland
    in the hill country.
It's so barren and scorched
    that no one travels there.
No cattle can be found there,
and birds and wild animals
    have all disappeared.

¹¹I heard the LORD reply,
    "When I am finished,
Jerusalem and the towns of Judah
will be piles of ruins
    where only jackalsⁱ live."

Why the Land Was Destroyed

¹²I said to the LORD, "None of us can understand why the land has become like an uncrossable desert. Won't you explain why?" ¹³The LORD said:

I destroyed the land because the people disobeyed me and rejected my laws and teachings. ¹⁴They were stubborn and worshiped Baal,^j just as their ancestors did. ¹⁵So I, the LORD All-Powerful, the God of Israel, promise them poison to eat and drink.^k ¹⁶I'll scatter them in foreign countries that they and their ancestors have never even heard of. Finally, I will send enemy soldiers to kill every last one of them.

The Women Who Are Paid To Weep

¹⁷The LORD All-Powerful said,
    "Send for the women

ⁱ**9.11** *jackals*: Desert animals related to wolves, but smaller. ^j**9.14** *Baal*: See the note at 2.23.
^k**9.15** *poison to eat and drink*: Or "bitter disappointment to eat, and tears to drink."

who are paid to weep
   at funerals,[l]
especially the women
   who can cry the loudest."

[18] The people answered,
"Let them come quickly
   and cry for us,
until our own eyes
   are flooded with tears.
[19] Now those of us on Zion cry,
'We are ruined!
   We can't stand the shame.
Our homes have been destroyed,
   and we must leave our land.'

[20] "We ask you women
to pay attention
   to what the LORD says.
We will teach you a funeral song
that you can teach
   your daughters and friends:
[21] 'We were in our fortress,
but death sneaked in
   through our windows.
It even struck down
children at play
   and our strongest young men.'

[22] "The LORD has told us
the ground will be covered
   with dead bodies,
like stalks of ungathered grain
   or like manure."

*We need to praise God by
being who he created us to be.*

KATHY PEEL

What the LORD Likes Best

[23] The LORD says:

Don't brag about your wisdom
   or strength or wealth.
[24] If you feel you must brag,
   then have enough sense
to brag about worshiping me,
   the LORD.
What I like best
   is showing kindness,

justice, and mercy
   to everyone on earth.

[25-26] Someday I will punish the nations of
Egypt, Edom, Ammon, and Moab, and the
tribes of the desert.[m] The men of these nations are circumcised, but they don't worship me. And it's the same with you people
of Judah. Your bodies are circumcised, but
your hearts are unchanged.

The LORD Talks about Idols

10 *[1] The LORD said:

Listen to me,
   you people of Israel.
[2] Don't follow the customs
   of those nations
who become frightened
when they see something strange
   happen in the sky.
[3] Their religion is worthless!
They chop down a tree,
   carve the wood into an idol,
[4] cover it with silver and gold,
and then nail it down
   so it won't fall over.

[5] An idol is no better
   than a scarecrow.
It can't speak,
and it has to be carried,
   because it can't walk.
Why worship an idol
   that can't help or harm you?

Jeremiah Praises the LORD

[6] Our LORD, great and powerful,
   you alone are God.
[7] You are King of the nations.
   Everyone should worship you.
No human anywhere on earth
   is wiser than you.
[8] Idols are worthless,
and anyone who worships them
   is a fool!
[9] Idols are made by humans.
   A carver shapes the wood.

---

[l] **9.17** *women . . . weep at funerals:* Or "the women who
weep for Baal"; the god Baal was believed to have died
and come back to life, and some women would go to
places of worship and weep over the death of Baal.
[m] **9.25,26** *the tribes of the desert:* One possible meaning
for the difficult Hebrew text.

A metalworker hammers out
a covering of gold from Uphaz
or of silver from Tarshish.
Then the idol is dressed
in blue and purple clothes.

[10] You, LORD, are the only true
and living God.
You will rule for all time.
When you are angry
the earth shakes,
and nations are destroyed.

[11] You told me to say
that idols did not create
the heavens and the earth,
and that you, the LORD,
will destroy every idol.

[12] With your wisdom and power
you created the earth
and spread out the heavens.
[13] The waters in the heavens roar
at your command.
You make clouds appear—
you send the winds
from your storehouse
and make lightning flash
in the rain.

[14] People who make idols
are so stupid!
They will be disappointed,
because their false gods
are not alive.
[15] Idols are merely a joke,
and when the time is right,
they will be destroyed.

[16] But you, Israel's God,
created all things,
and you chose Israel
to be your very own.
Your name is the LORD
All-Powerful.

Judah Will Be Thrown from Its Land

[17] I said to the people of Judah,
"Gather your things;
you are surrounded."
[18] The LORD said these troubles
will lead to your capture,
and he will throw you
from this land
like a rock from a sling."[n]

[19] The people answered,
"We are wounded
and doomed to die.
Why did we say
we could stand the pain?
[20] Our homes are destroyed;
our children are dead.
No one is left
to help us find shelter."

[21] But I told them,
"Our leaders were stupid failures,
because they refused
to listen to the LORD.
And so we've been scattered
like sheep.

[22] "Sounds of destruction
rumble from the north
like distant thunder.
Soon our towns will be ruins
where jackals[o] live."

Jeremiah Prays

[23] I know, LORD, that we humans
are not in control
of our own lives.
[24] Correct me, as I deserve,
but not in your anger,
or I will be dead.
[25] Our enemies refuse
to admit that you are God
or to worship you.
They have wiped out our people
and left our nation
lying in ruins.
So get angry
and sweep them away!

Judah Has Broken the LORD's Agreement

11 [1-3] The LORD God told me to say to the people of Judah and Jerusalem:
I, the LORD, am warning you that I will put a curse on anyone who doesn't keep the agreement I made with Israel. So pay attention to what it says. [4] My commands haven't changed since I brought your ancestors out of Egypt, a nation that seemed like a blazing furnace where iron ore is

melted. I told your ancestors that if
they obeyed my commands, I would
be their God, and they would be my
people. 5Then I did what I had promised and gave them this wonderful
land, where you now live.
"Yes, LORD," I replied, "that's true."
6Then the LORD told me to say to everyone on the streets of Jerusalem and in the
towns of Judah:

Pay attention to the commands in
my agreement with you. 7Ever since I
brought your ancestors out of Egypt, I
have been telling your people to obey
me. But you and your ancestors 8have
always been stubborn. You have refused to listen, and instead you have
done whatever your sinful hearts have
desired.

You have not kept the agreement
we made, so I will make you suffer
every curse that goes with it.
9The LORD said to me:

Jeremiah, the people of Judah and
Jerusalem are plotting against me.
10They have sinned in the same way
their ancestors did, by turning from
me and worshiping other gods. The
northern kingdom of Israel broke the
agreement I made with your ancestors,
and now the southern kingdom of
Judah[p] has done the same.

11Here is what I've decided to do. I
will bring suffering on the people of
Judah and Jerusalem, and no one will
escape. They will beg me to help, but I
won't listen to their prayers. 12-13Then
they will offer sacrifices to their other
gods and ask them for help. After all,
the people of Judah have more gods
than towns, and more altars for Baal
than there are streets in Jerusalem. But
those gods won't be able to rescue the
people of Judah from disaster.
14Jeremiah, don't pray for these
people or beg me to rescue them. If
you do, I won't listen, and I certainly
won't listen if they pray!
15Then the LORD told me to say to the
people of Judah:

You are my chosen people,
but you have no right
to be here in my temple,
doing such terrible things.
The sacrifices you offer me
won't protect you from disaster,
so stop celebrating.[q]
16 Once you were like an olive tree
covered with fruit.
But soon I will send a noisy mob
to break off your branches
and set you on fire.

17I am the LORD All-Powerful. You people
of Judah were like a tree that I had planted,
but you have made me angry by offering
sacrifices to Baal, just as the northern kingdom did. And now I'm going to pull you up
by the roots.

The Plot To Kill Jeremiah

*18 Some people plotted to kill me.
And like a lamb
being led to the butcher,
I knew nothing
about their plans.
19 But then the LORD told me
that they had planned
to chop me down like a tree—
fruit and all—
so that no one would ever
remember me again.
20 I prayed, "LORD All-Powerful,
you always do what is right,
and you know every thought.
So I trust you to help me
and to take revenge."

21Then the LORD said:

Jeremiah, some men from Ana-
thoth[r] say they will kill you, if you keep
on speaking for me. 22But I will punish
them. Their young men will die in
battle, and their children will starve to
death. 23And when I am finished, no
one from their families will be left
alive.

Jeremiah Complains to the LORD

12 Whenever I complain
to you, LORD,
you are always fair.
But now I have questions
about your justice.

---

p11.10 *Israel . . . Judah:* See the note at 2.4.
q11.15 *celebrating:* One possible meaning for the difficult Hebrew text of verse 15.
r11.21 *Anathoth:* Jeremiah's hometown (see 1.1).

Why is life easy for sinners?
Why are they successful?

> *It may look like the ones who*
> *are dishonest are winning,*
> *but that's a short-term view.*
> *When we do what Jesus*
> *would do, we ultimately win.*
>
> MARY WHELCHEL

[2] You plant them like trees;
you let them prosper
and produce fruit.
Yet even when they praise you,
they don't mean it.

[3] But you know, LORD,
how faithful I've always been,
even in my thoughts.
So drag my enemies away
and butcher them like sheep!

[4] How long will the ground be dry
and the pasturelands parched?
The birds and animals
are dead and gone.
And all of this happened because
the people are so sinful.
They even brag, "God can't see
the sins we commit."[s]

The LORD Answers Jeremiah

[5] Jeremiah, if you get tired
in a race against people,
how can you possibly run
against horses?
If you fall in open fields,
what will happen in the forest
along the Jordan River?
[6] Even your own family
has turned against you.
They act friendly,
but don't trust them.
They're out to get you,
and so is everyone else.

The LORD Is Furious with His People

[7] I loved my people and chose them
as my very own.

But now I will reject them
and hand them over
to their enemies.
[8] My people have turned against me
and roar at me like lions.
That's why I hate them.

[9] My people are like a hawk
surrounded and attacked
by other hawks.[t]
Tell the wild animals
to come and eat their fill.
[10] My beautiful land is ruined
like a field or a vineyard
trampled by shepherds
and stripped bare
by their flocks.
[11] Every field I see lies barren,
and no one cares.

[12] A destroying army
marches along desert roads
and attacks everywhere.
They are my deadly sword;
no one is safe from them.

[13] My people, you planted wheat,
but because I was furious,
I let only weeds grow.
You wore yourselves out
for nothing!

The LORD Will Have Pity on Other Nations

[14] The LORD said:
I gave this land to my people Israel, but enemies around it have attacked and robbed it. So I will uproot them from their own countries just as I will uproot Judah from its land. [15] But later, I will have pity on these nations and bring them back to their own lands. [16] They once taught my people to worship Baal. But if they admit I am the only true God, and if they let my people teach them how to worship me, these nations will also become my people. [17] However, if they don't listen to me, I will uproot them from their lands and completely destroy them. I, the LORD, have spoken.

---

[s] **12.4** *God can't see the sins we commit:* Or "Jeremiah won't live to see what happens to us." [t] **12.9** *My people . . . other hawks:* Or "My land has become a hyena's den with vultures circling above."

Jeremiah's Linen Shorts

13 The LORD told me, "Go and buy a pair of linen shorts. Wear them for a while, but don't wash them." ²So I bought a pair of shorts and put them on.

³Then the LORD said, ⁴"Take off the shorts. Go to Parah*ᵘ* and hide the shorts in a crack between some large rocks." ⁵And that's what I did.

⁶Some time later the LORD said, "Go back and get the shorts." ⁷I went back and dug the shorts out of their hiding place, but the cloth had rotted, and the shorts were ruined.

⁸Then the LORD said:

⁹Jeremiah, I will use Babylonia to*ᵛ* destroy the pride of the people of Judah and Jerusalem. ¹⁰The people of Judah are evil and stubborn. So instead of listening to me, they do whatever they want and even worship other gods. When I am finished with these people, they will be good for nothing, just like this pair of shorts. ¹¹These shorts were tight around your waist, and that's how tightly I held onto the kingdoms of Israel and Judah. I wanted them to be my people. I wanted to make them famous, so that other nations would praise and honor me, but they refused to obey me.

Wine Jars

The LORD said:

¹²Jeremiah, tell the people of Judah, "The LORD God of Israel orders you to fill your wine jars with wine."

They will answer, "Of course we fill our wine jars with wine! Why are you telling us something we already know?"

¹³Then say to them:

I am the LORD, and what I'm going to do will make everyone in Judah and Jerusalem appear to be full of wine. And the worst ones will be the kings of David's family and the priests and the prophets. ¹⁴Then I will smash them against each other like jars. I will have no pity on the young or the old, and they will all be destroyed. I, the LORD, have spoken.

The People of Judah Will Be Taken Away

¹⁵People of Judah,
don't be too proud to listen
    to what the LORD has said.
¹⁶You hope for light,
    but God is sending darkness.
Evening shadows already deepen
    in the hills.
So return to God
and confess your sins to him
    before you trip and fall.
¹⁷If you are too proud to listen,
    I will weep alone.
Tears will stream from my eyes
when the LORD's people
    are taken away as prisoners.

¹⁸The LORD told me to tell you
that your king and his mother*ʷ*
    must surrender their thrones
    and remove their crowns.*ˣ*
¹⁹The cities in the Southern Desert
are surrounded;
    no one can get in or out.
Everyone in Judah
    will be taken away.
²⁰Jerusalem, you were so proud
of ruling the people of Judah.
    But where are they now?

Look north, and you will see
    your enemies approaching.
²¹You once trusted them to help,
but now I'll let them rule you.*ʸ*
    What do you say about that?
You will be in pain
    like a woman giving birth.

²²Do you know why
your clothes were torn off
    and you were abused?
It was because
    of your terrible sins.
²³Can you ever change
    and do what's right?
Can people change the color
    of their skin,

---

*ᵘ***13.4** *Parah:* Or "the Euphrates River." Parah was a village about five and a half miles northeast of Jerusalem.   *ᵛ***13.9** *I will use Babylonia to:* Or "that's how I'm going to."   *ʷ***13.18** *mother:* The king's mother usually had an important position in the royal court.   *ˣ***13.18** *and remove their crowns:* One possible meaning for the difficult Hebrew text.   *ʸ***13.21** *You once . . . rule you:* One possible meaning for the difficult Hebrew text.

or can a leopard
>   remove its spots?
If so, then maybe you can change
>   and learn to do right.

²⁴I will scatter you,
>   just as the desert wind
blows husks from grain
>   tossed in the air.
²⁵I won't change my mind.
>   I, the LORD, have spoken.

You rejected me
>   and worshiped false gods.
* ²⁶You were married to me,
>   but you were unfaithful.
You even became a prostitute^z
by worshiping disgusting gods
>   on hilltops and in fields.
²⁷So I'll rip off your clothes
and leave you naked and ashamed
>   for everyone to see.
You are doomed!
Will you ever be worthy
>   to worship me again?

The Land Dries Up

14 When there had been no rain for
a long time, the LORD told me to
say to the people:

²Judah and Jerusalem weep
>   as the land dries up.
³Rulers send their servants
>   to the storage pits for water.^a
But there's none to be found;
they return in despair
>   with their jars still empty.

⁴There has been no rain,
>   and farmers feel sick
as they watch cracks appear
>   in the dry ground.^b

⁵A deer gives birth in a field,
then abandons her newborn fawn
>   and leaves in search of grass.
⁶Wild donkeys go blind
>   from starvation.
So they stand on barren hilltops
>   and sniff the air,^c
hoping to smell green grass.

The LORD's People Pray

⁷Our terrible sins may demand
>   that we be punished.
But if you rescue us, LORD,
everyone will see
>   how great you are.
⁸You're our only hope;
>   you alone can save us now.
You help us one day,
>   but you're gone the next.
⁹Did this disaster
>   take you by surprise?
Are you a warrior
>   with your hands tied?
You have chosen us,
and your temple is here.
>   Don't abandon us!

The LORD's Answer

¹⁰My people,
>   you love to wander away;
you don't even try
>   to stay close to me.
So now I will reject you
and punish you for your sins.
>   I, the LORD, have spoken.

Lying Prophets

¹¹The LORD said, "Jeremiah, don't ask
me to help these people. ¹²They may even
go without eating^d and offer sacrifices to
please me^e and to give thanks.^f But when
they cry out for my help, I won't listen, and
I won't accept their sacrifices. Instead, I'll
send war, starvation, and disease to wipe
them out."

¹³I replied, "The other prophets keep

---

^z**13.26** *prostitute:* See the note at 2.20.
^a**14.3** *storage pits for water:* Since water was scarce,
pits were dug into solid rock for collecting and
storing rainwater. These pits were called "cisterns."
^b**14.4** *cracks . . . ground:* One possible meaning for the
difficult Hebrew text.   ^c**14.6** *sniff the air:* The Hebrew
text has "sniff the air, like jackals" (see the note
at 9.11).   ^d**14.12** *go without eating:* The people of
Israel sometimes went without eating to show sorrow
for their sins.   ^e**14.12** *sacrifices to please me:* These
sacrifices have traditionally been called "whole burnt
offerings" because the whole animal was burned on the
altar. A main purpose of such sacrifices was to please
the LORD with the smell of the sacrifice, and so in the
CEV they are sometimes called "sacrifices to please
the LORD."   ^f**14.12** *sacrifices . . . to give thanks:* These
sacrifices have traditionally been called "grain offerings."
A main purpose of such sacrifices was to thank the
LORD with a gift of grain, and so in the CEV they
are sometimes called "sacrifices to give thanks to
the LORD."

telling everyone that you won't send starvation or war, and that you're going to give us peace."

¹⁴The LORD answered:

They claim to speak for me, but they're lying! I didn't even speak to them, much less choose them to be my prophets. Their messages come from worthless dreams, useless fortunetelling, and their own imaginations. ¹⁵Those lying prophets say there will be peace and plenty of food. But I say that those same prophets will die from war and hunger. ¹⁶And everyone who listens to them will be killed, just as they deserve. Their dead bodies will be thrown out into the streets of Jerusalem, because their families will also be dead, and no one will be left to bury them.^g

¹⁷Jeremiah, go and tell the people how you feel about all this.
So I told them:

"Tears will flood my eyes
    both day and night,
because my nation suffers
    from a deadly wound.
¹⁸ In the fields I see the bodies
    of those killed in battle.
And in the towns I see crowds
    dying of hunger.
But the prophets and priests
    go about their business,
without understanding
    what has happened."^h

Jeremiah Prays to the LORD

¹⁹ Have you rejected Judah, LORD?
    Do you hate Jerusalem?
Why did you strike down Judah
    with a fatal wound?
We had hoped for peace
    and a time of healing,
    but all we got was terror.
²⁰ We and our ancestors are guilty
    of rebelling against you.
²¹ If you save us, it will show
    how great you are.
Don't let our enemies
    disgrace your temple,
    your beautiful throne.
Don't forget that you promised
    to rescue us.
²² Idols can't send rain,

and showers don't fall
    by themselves.
Only you control the rain,
so we put our trust in you,
    the LORD our God.

The People of Judah Will Die

15 The LORD said to me:
Even if Moses and Samuel were here, praying with you, I wouldn't change my mind. So send the people of Judah away. ²And when they ask where they are going, tell them that I, the LORD, have said:

Some of you are going to die
    of horrible diseases.
Others are going to die in war
    or from starvation.
The rest will be led away
    to a foreign country.
³ I will punish you
    in four different ways:
You will be killed in war
and your bodies dragged off
    by dogs,
your flesh will be eaten by birds,
and your bones will be chewed on
    by wild animals.
⁴ This punishment will happen
because of the horrible thingsⁱ
    your King Manasseh^j did.
And you will be disgusting
    to all nations on earth.
⁵ People of Jerusalem,
    who will feel sorry for you?
Will anyone bother
    to ask if you are well?

⁶ My people, you abandoned me
    and walked away.
I am tired of showing mercy;
    that's why I'll destroy you
⁷ by scattering you like straw
    blown by the wind.
I will punish you with sorrow
    and death,
because you refuse
    to change your ways.

---

^g**14.16** *dead bodies . . . bury them*: A proper burial was considered very important. ^h**14.18** *go about . . . has happened*: One possible meaning for the difficult Hebrew text. ⁱ**15.4** *the horrible things*: See 2 Kings 21.1-16. ^j**15.4** *Manasseh*: Hebrew "Manasseh son of Hezekiah"; he ruled 687-642 B.C.

[8] There will be more widows
    in Judah
than grains of sand on a beach.

A surprise attack at noon!
And the mothers in Jerusalem
    mourn for their children.
[9] A mother is in deep despair
    and struggles for breath.
Her daylight has turned
    to darkness—
she has suffered the loss
    of her seven sons.

I will kill anyone who survives.
    I, the LORD, have spoken.

Jeremiah Complains

[10] I wish I had never been born!
I'm always in trouble
    with everyone in Judah.
I never lend or borrow money,
but everyone curses me
    just the same.

[11] Then the LORD replied,
    "I promise to protect you,
    and when disaster comes,
even your enemies
    will beg you for help."[k]

The Enemy Cannot Be Defeated

The LORD told me to say:
[12] People of Judah,
    just as you can't break iron
        mixed with bronze,
    you can't defeat the enemies
        that will attack
        from the north.
[13] I will give them
        everything you own,
    because you have sinned
        everywhere in your country.
[14] My anger is a fire
        that cannot be put out,[l]
    so I will make you slaves
    of your enemies
        in a foreign land.[m]

Jeremiah Complains Again

[15] You can see how I suffer
    insult after insult,
        all because of you, LORD.

Don't be so patient
    with my enemies;
take revenge on them
    before they kill me.

[16] When you spoke to me,
    I was glad to obey,
because I belong to you,
    the LORD All-Powerful.

*I study the Scriptures
to better know Christ
and to open myself to the
Holy Spirit's guidance.*

PATRICIA FUNDERBURK WARE

[17] I don't go to parties
    and have a good time.
Instead, I keep to myself,
because you have filled me
    with your anger.

[18] I am badly injured
    and in constant pain.
Are you going to disappoint me,
like a stream that goes dry
    in the heat of summer?

The LORD Replies

[19] Then the LORD told me:
    Stop talking like a fool!
If you turn back to me
    and speak my message,
I will let you be my prophet
    once again.
I hope the people of Judah
    will accept what you say.
But you can ignore their threats,
*[20] because I am making you strong,
    like a bronze wall.
They are evil and violent,
    but when they attack,

---

[k] **15.11** *help:* One possible meaning for the difficult
Hebrew text of verse 11.   [l] **15.14** *that cannot be put out:*
Some Hebrew manuscripts; most Hebrew manuscripts
"against you."   [m] **15.14** *I will make . . . land:* Many
Hebrew manuscripts; most Hebrew manuscripts "I will
make your enemies go through to a land you don't
know about."

²¹I will be there to rescue you.
 I, the LORD, have spoken.

Jeremiah Must Live His Message

16 The LORD said to me: ²Jeremiah, don't get married and have children—Judah is no place to raise a family. ³I'll tell you what's going to happen to children and their parents here. ⁴They will die of horrible diseases and of war and starvation. No one will give them a funeral or bury them, and their bodies will be food for the birds and wild animals. And what's left will lie on the ground like manure.

⁵When someone dies, don't visit the family or show any sorrow. I will no longer love or bless or have any pity on the people of Judah. ⁶Rich and poor alike will die and be left unburied. No one will mourn and show their sorrow by cutting themselves or shaving their heads.ⁿ ⁷No one will bring food and wine to help comfort those who are mourning the death of their father or mother.

⁸Don't even set foot in a house where there is eating and drinking and celebrating. ⁹Warn the people of Judah that I, the LORD All-Powerful, will put an end to all their parties and wedding celebrations. ¹⁰They will ask, "Why has the LORD our God threatened us with so many disasters? Have we done something wrong or sinned against him?"

¹¹Then tell them I have said:

People of Judah, your ancestors turned away from me; they rejected my laws and teachings and started worshiping other gods. ¹²And you have done even worse! You are stubborn, and instead of obeying me, you do whatever evil comes to your mind. ¹³So I will throw you into a land that you and your ancestors know nothing about, a place where you will have to worship other gods both day and night. And I won't feel the least bit sorry for you.

¹⁴A time will come when you will again worship me. But you will no longer call me the Living God who rescued Israel from Egypt. ¹⁵Instead, you will call me the Living God who rescued you from that country in the north and from the other countries where I had forced you to go.

Someday I will bring you back to this land that I gave your ancestors. ¹⁶But for now, I am sending enemies who will catch you like fish and hunt you down like wild animals in the hills and the caves.

¹⁷I can see everything you are doing, even if you try to hide your sins from me. ¹⁸I will punish you double for your sins, because you have made my own land disgusting. You have filled it with lifeless idols that remind me of dead bodies.

The LORD Gives Strength

I prayed to the LORD:

¹⁹Our LORD, you are the one
 who gives me strength
 and protects me like a fortress
 when I am in trouble.
People will come to you
 from distant nations and say,
"Our ancestors worshiped
 false and useless gods,
²⁰worthless idols
 made by human hands."

²¹Then the LORD replied,
 "That's why I will teach them
 about my power,
and they will know
 that I am the true God."

The LORD Will Punish Judah

The LORD said:

17 People of Judah,
 your sins cannot be erased.
 They are written on your hearts
 like words chiseled in stone
or carved on the corners
 of your altars.ᵒ
*²One generation after another
 has set up pagan altars
 and worshiped the goddess Asherah

ⁿ**16.6** *mourn and show their sorrow by cutting themselves or shaving their heads:* A custom in some Canaanite religions.   ᵒ**17.1** *carved on the corners of your altars:* When sacrifices were offered to the LORD to ask him to forgive sins, some of the blood was smeared on the corners of the altar (see Leviticus 4.7, 18-20, 25, 26, 30, 31, 34, 35; 16.18). But now the LORD refuses to accept these sacrifices.

everywhere in your country—
on hills and mountains,
and under large trees.
³ So I'll take everything you own,
including your altars,
and give it all
to your enemies.ᵖ
⁴ You will loseᑫ the land
that I gave you,
and I will make you slaves
in a foreign country,
because you have made my anger
blaze up like a fire
that won't stop burning.

Trust the LORD

⁵ I, the LORD, have put a curse
on those who turn from me
and trust in human strength.
⁶ They will dry up like a bush
in salty desert soil,
where nothing can grow.

⁷ But I will bless those
who trust me.

> *Whatever we do, we need
> to do it with excellence.*
>
> KAY COLES JAMES

⁸ They will be like trees
growing beside a stream—
trees with roots that reach
down to the water,
and with leaves
that are always green.
They bear fruit every year
and are never worried
by a lack of rain.

⁹ You people of Judah
are so deceitful
that you even fool yourselves,
and you can't change.
¹⁰ But I know your deeds
and your thoughts,
and I will make sure
you get what you deserve.
¹¹ You cheated others,
but everything you gained

will fly away, like birds
hatched from stolen eggs.
Then you will discover
what fools you are.

Jeremiah Prays to the LORD

¹² Our LORD, your temple
is a glorious throne
that has stood on a mountain
from the beginning.
¹³ You are a spring of water
giving Israel life and hope.
But if the people reject
what you have told me,
they will be swept away
like words written in dust.ʳ

¹⁴ You, LORD, are the one I praise.
So heal me and rescue me!
Then I will be completely well
and perfectly safe.

¹⁵ The people of Judah say to me,
"Jeremiah, you claimed to tell us
what the LORD has said.
So why hasn't it come true?"

¹⁶ Our LORD, you chose me
to care for your people,
and that's what I have done.
You know everything I have said,
and I have never once
asked you to punish them.ˢ
¹⁷ I trust you for protection
in times of trouble,
so don't frighten me.
¹⁸ Keep me from failure
and disgrace,
but make my enemies fail
and be disgraced.
Send destruction to make
their worst fears come true.

Resting on the Sabbath

¹⁹⁻²⁰ The LORD said:
Jeremiah, stand at each city gate in Jerusalem, including the one the king uses, and

---

ᵖ**17.3** *enemies:* One possible meaning for the difficult
Hebrew text of verses 2, 3.   ᑫ**17.4** *You will lose:* One
possible meaning for the difficult Hebrew text.
ʳ**17.13** *reject . . . dust:* One possible meaning for
the difficult Hebrew text.   ˢ**17.16** *you chose . . .
punish them:* One possible meaning for the difficult
Hebrew text.

speak to him and everyone else. Tell them I have said:

I am the LORD, so pay attention. ²¹⁻²⁴If you value your lives, don't do any work on the Sabbath. Don't carry anything through the city gates or through the door of your house, or anywhere else. Keep the Sabbath day sacred!

I gave this command to your ancestors, but they were stubborn and refused to obey or to be corrected. But if you obey, ²⁵then Judah and Jerusalem will always be ruled by kings from David's family. The king and his officials will ride through these gates on horses or in chariots, and the people of Judah and Jerusalem will be with them. There will always be people living in Jerusalem, ²⁶and others will come here from the nearby villages, from the towns of Judah and Benjamin,[t] from the hill country and the foothills to the west, and from the Southern Desert. They will bring sacrifices to please me and to give me thanks,[u] as well as offerings of grain and incense.

²⁷But if you keep on carrying things through the city gates on the Sabbath and keep treating it as any other day, I will set fire to these gates and burn down the whole city, including the fortresses.

Jeremiah Goes to the Pottery Shop

18 The LORD told me, ²"Go to the pottery shop, and when you get there, I will tell you what to say to the people."

³I went there and saw the potter making clay pots on his pottery wheel. ⁴And whenever the clay would not take the shape he wanted, he would change his mind and form it into some other shape.

⁵Then the LORD told me to say:

⁶People of Israel, I, the LORD, have power over you, just as a potter has power over clay. ⁷If I threaten to uproot and shatter an evil nation ⁸and that nation turns from its evil, I will change my mind.

⁹If I promise to make a nation strong, ¹⁰but its people start disobeying me and doing evil, then I will change my mind and not help them at all.

¹¹So listen to me, people of Judah and Jerusalem! I have decided to strike you with disaster, and I won't change my mind unless you stop sinning and start living right.

¹²But I know you won't listen. You might as well answer, "We don't care what you say. We have made plans to sin, and we are going to be stubborn and do what we want!"

¹³So I, the LORD, command you to ask the nations, and find out if they have ever heard of such a horrible sin as what you have done.

¹⁴The snow
on Lebanon's mountains
  never melts away,
and the streams there
  never run dry.[v]
¹⁵But you, my people,
  have turned from me
to burn incense
  to worthless idols.
You have left the ancient road
to follow an unknown path
  where you stumble over idols.

¹⁶Your land will be ruined,
  and every passerby
will look at it with horror
  and make insulting remarks.
¹⁷When your enemies attack,
I will scatter you like dust
  blown by an eastern wind.
Then, on that day of disaster,
  I will turn my back on you.

The Plot against Jeremiah

¹⁸Some of the people said, "Let's get rid of Jeremiah! We will always have priests to teach us God's laws, as well as wise people to give us advice, and prophets to speak the LORD's messages. So, instead of listening to Jeremiah any longer, let's accuse him of a crime."

Jeremiah Prays about His Enemies

¹⁹Please, LORD, answer my prayer.
Make my enemies stop
  accusing me of evil.

---

[t]**17.26** *Judah and Benjamin*: These two tribes made up the southern kingdom of Judah.   [u]**17.26** *sacrifices to please me and to give me thanks*: See the notes at 14.12.   [v]**18.14** *dry*: One possible meaning for the difficult Hebrew text of verse 14.

²⁰ I tried to help them,
   but they are paying me back
      by digging a pit to trap me.
   I even begged you
      not to punish them.
²¹ But now I am asking you
   to let their children starve
      or be killed in war.
   Let women lose
      their husbands and sons
         to disease and violence.
²² These people have dug pits
      and set traps for me, LORD.
   Make them scream in fear
   when you send enemy troops
      to attack their homes.
²³ You know they plan to kill me.
   So get angry and punish them!
   Don't ever forgive
      their terrible crimes.

Jeremiah and the Clay Jar

19 The LORD said:
Jeremiah, go to the pottery shop and buy a clay jar. Then take along some of the city officials and leading priests ² and go to Hinnom Valley, just outside Potsherd^w Gate. Tell the people that I have said:

³ I am the LORD All-Powerful, the God of Israel, and you kings of Judah and you people of Jerusalem had better pay attention. I am going to bring so much trouble on this valley that everyone who hears about it will be shocked. ⁴⁻⁵ The people of Judah stopped worshiping me and made this valley into a place of worship for Baal and other gods that have never helped them or their ancestors or their kings. And they have committed murder here, burning their young, innocent children as sacrifices to Baal. I have never even thought of telling you to do that. ⁶ So watch out! Someday this place will no longer be called Topheth or Hinnom Valley. It will be called Slaughter Valley!

⁷ You people of Judah and Jerusalem may have big plans, but here in this valley I'll ruin^x those plans. I'll let your enemies kill you, and I'll tell the birds and wild animals to eat your dead bodies. ⁸ I will turn Jerusalem into a pile of rubble, and every pass-

erby will be shocked and horrified and will make insulting remarks. ⁹ And while your enemies are trying to break through your city walls to kill you, the food supply will run out. You will become so hungry that you will eat the flesh of your friends and even of your own children.

¹⁰ Jeremiah, as soon as you have said this, smash the jar while the people are watching. ¹¹ Then tell them that I have also said:

I am the LORD All-Powerful, and I warn you that I will shatter Judah and Jerusalem just like this jar that is broken beyond repair. You will bury your dead here in Topheth, but so many of you will die that there won't be enough room.

¹²⁻¹³ I will make Jerusalem as unclean as Topheth, by filling the city with your dead bodies. I will do this because you and your kings have gone up to the roofs of your houses and burned incense to the stars in the sky, as though they were gods. And you have given sacrifices of wine to foreign gods.

Jeremiah Speaks in the Temple Courtyard

¹⁴ I went to Topheth, where I told the people what the LORD had said. Then I went to the temple courtyard and shouted to the people, ¹⁵ "Listen, everyone! Some time ago, the LORD All-Powerful, the God of Israel, warned you that he would bring disaster on Jerusalem and all nearby villages. But you were stubborn and refused to listen. Now the LORD is going to bring the disaster he promised."

Pashhur Arrests Jeremiah

20 Pashhur son of Immer was a priest and the chief of temple security. He heard what I had said, ² and so he hit me.^y Then he had me arrested and put in chains^z at the Benjamin Gate in the LORD's temple.^a ³ The next day, when

---

^w**19.2** *Potsherd:* A piece of broken pottery.   ^x**19.7** *ruin:* In Hebrew "ruin" sounds like "jar" (see verse 1).
^y**20.2** *hit me:* Or "beat me up" or "had me beaten up."
^z**20.2** *in chains:* Or "in the stocks" (a wooden frame with holes for the hands, neck, or feet of a prisoner) or "in a prison cell."   ^a**20.2** *the Benjamin Gate in the LORD's temple:* The Hebrew text has "the upper Benjamin Gate in the temple"; the lower Benjamin Gate may have been the city gate of that name.

Pashhur let me go free, I told him that the LORD had said:

No longer will I call you Pashhur. Instead, I will call you Afraid-of-Everything.[b] [4]You will be afraid, and you will bring fear to your friends as well. You will see enemies kill them in battle. Then I will have the king of Babylonia take everyone in Judah prisoner, killing some and dragging the rest away to Babylonia. [5]He will clean out the royal treasury and take everything else of value from Jerusalem.

[6]Pashhur, you are guilty of telling lies and claiming they were messages from me. That's why I will have the Babylonians take you, your family, and your friends as prisoners to Babylonia, where you will all die and be buried.

Jeremiah Complains to the LORD

[7]You tricked me, LORD,
   and I was really fooled.
You are stronger than I am,
   and you have defeated me.
People never stop sneering
   and insulting me.
[8]You have let me announce
   only destruction and death.
Your message has brought me
nothing but insults
   and trouble.
[9]Sometimes I tell myself
not to think about you, LORD,
   or even mention your name.

But your message burns
in my heart and bones,
   and I cannot keep silent.

[10]I heard the crowds whisper,
   "Everyone is afraid.
Now's our chance
   to accuse Jeremiah!"
All of my so-called friends
are just waiting
   for me to make a mistake.
They say, "Maybe Jeremiah
   can be tricked.
Then we can overpower him
   and get even at last."

[11]But you, LORD,
are a mighty soldier,
   standing at my side.
Those troublemakers
will fall down and fail—
   terribly embarrassed,
   forever ashamed.

[12]LORD All-Powerful,
   you test those who do right,
and you know every heart
   and mind.
I have told you my complaints,
so let me watch you
   take revenge on my enemies.
[13]I sing praises to you, LORD.

[b]20.3 *Afraid-of-Everything*: Hebrew "Magor-Missabib."

SingleLife—What if I'm longing for children? *(Jeremiah 20.7-18)*

God can handle your strongest emotions.
Why does God give us such a strong longing for a husband and children, yet not always fulfill it? If you are struggling with disappointment and frustration, you have two choices: You can turn away from God in bitterness, or turn toward him and pour out your heart.

Jeremiah wasn't happy with the task God had given him and he told God so in the strongest language. He accused God of tricking him, of overpowering him (20.7). He admitted the times he thought of turning his back on God (20.9). He cursed the day he was born (20.14-18). But God didn't rebuke Jeremiah for his feelings, and he won't rebuke you. Go ahead and tell God your frustrations. You can be honest with God.

But never forget that God ultimately is in control. Remember that he is "LORD All-Powerful" (20.12). Trust in God's wisdom and his timing for your life. (See also Daniel 10.2-19; Matthew 18.5.)

Words To Remember: *LORD All-Powerful, you test those who do right, and you know every heart and mind. I have told you my complaints, so let me watch you take revenge on my enemies.—Jeremiah 20.12*

You rescue the oppressed
  from the wicked.

¹⁴Put a curse on the day I was born!
  Don't bless my mother.
¹⁵Put a curse on the man
  who told my father, "Good news!
  You have a son."
¹⁶May that man be like the towns
  you destroyed without pity.
Let him hear shouts of alarm
  in the morning
  and battle cries at noon.
¹⁷He deserves to die
  for not killing me
  before I was born.
Then my mother's body
  would have been my grave.
¹⁸Why did I have to be born?
  Was it just to suffer
  and die in shame?

The LORD Will Fight against Jerusalem

21 King Zedekiah^c of Judah sent for Pashhur son of Malchiah and for a priest named Zephaniah son of Maaseiah. Then he told them, "Talk with Jeremiah for me."

So they came to me and said, ²"King Nebuchadnezzar^d of Babylonia has attacked Judah. Please ask the LORD to work miracles for our people, as he has done in the past, so that Nebuchadnezzar will leave us alone."

³⁻⁷I told them that the LORD God of Israel had told me to say to King Zedekiah:

The Babylonians have surrounded Jerusalem and want to kill you and your people. You are asking me to save you, but you have made me furious. So I will stretch out my mighty arm and fight against you myself. Your army is using spears and swords to fight the Babylonians, but I will make your own weapons turn and attack you. I will send a horrible disease to kill many of the people and animals in Jerusalem, and there will be nothing left to eat. Finally, I will let King Nebuchadnezzar and his army fight their way to the center of Jerusalem and capture everyone who is left alive, including you and your officials. But

---

^{c}**21.1** *Zedekiah:* See the note at 1.3.
^{d}**21.2** *Nebuchadnezzar:* Ruled 605-562 B.C.

---

*Spiritual*Life—Does prayer really make a difference? (*Jeremiah 21.1-10*)

Prayer prepares us for God's answer, even when it's a "no."
Have you ever noticed how often we ask God to make life easier for ourselves or others in some way? We pray for healing for the sick, wisdom in our parenting (so our children will turn out well), direction in life (so we'll succeed), and various needs to be fulfilled. There's nothing wrong with such prayers. But we need to remember that sometimes God's answer to our prayers is "no."
  The people of Judah were terrified when King Nebuchadnezzar attacked them. They came to Jeremiah with a natural, heartfelt request: "Please ask the LORD to work miracles for our people, as he has done in the past, so that Nebuchadnezzar will leave us alone" (21.2). You might even say they were praying biblically—they called on God's past actions, as we often do when we pray.
  But God said "no" to their request. He had a bigger plan, and their comfort now wasn't part of it. He did, however, offer them a way of escape: If they surrendered to King Nebuchadnezzar, they would live (21.8,9). Although God intended to deny their original request and even punish them, he gave the people a choice between life or death. God's "no" was tempered by mercy.
  Don't mistake a negative result for proof that God doesn't hear your prayers. "No" may be part of his bigger plan. Trust that God does hear and answer, and that answer is part of his ultimately good plan. (See also 2 Chronicles 20.1-30; Matthew 7.7-12; Luke 18.1-8; 2 Corinthians 12.6-10.)

Words To Remember: *People of Jerusalem, I, the LORD, give you the choice of life or death.—Jeremiah 21.8*

Nebuchadnezzar won't be kind or show any mercy—he will have you killed! I, the LORD, have spoken. [8]Then I told them that the LORD had said:

People of Jerusalem, I, the LORD, give you the choice of life or death. [9]The Babylonian army has surrounded Jerusalem, so if you want to live, you must go out and surrender to them. But if you want to die because of hunger, disease, or war, then stay here in the city. [10]I have decided not to rescue Jerusalem. Instead, I am going to let the king of Babylonia burn it to the ground. I, the LORD, have spoken.

The LORD Warns the King of Judah

*[11]Pay attention, you that belong
    to the royal family.
[12]Each new day, make sure
    that justice is done,
and rescue those
    who are being robbed.
Or else my anger will flame up
like a fire that never goes out.

[13]Jerusalem,
    from your mountaintop
you look out over the valleys[e]
    and think you are safe.
But I, the LORD, am angry,
[14]and I will punish you
    as you deserve.
I'll set your palace[f] on fire,
    and everything around you
    will go up in smoke.

The LORD Will Punish the King of Judah

22 [1-3]The LORD sent me to the palace of the king of Judah to speak to the king, his officials, and everyone else who was there. The LORD told me to say:

I am the LORD, so pay attention! You have been allowing people to cheat, rob, and take advantage of widows, orphans, and foreigners who live here. Innocent people have become victims of violence, and some of them have even been killed. But now I command you to do what is right and see that justice is done. Rescue everyone who has suffered from injustice.

[4]If you obey me, the kings from David's family will continue to rule Judah from this palace. They and their officials will ride in and out on their horses or in their chariots. [5]But if you ignore me, I promise in my own name that this palace will lie in ruins. [6]Listen to what I think about it:

The palace of Judah's king
is as glorious as Gilead
    or Lebanon's highest peaks.
But it will be as empty
as a ghost-town
    when I'm through with it.
[7]I'll send troops to tear it apart,
    and its beautiful cedar beams
    will be used for firewood.

[8]People from different nations will pass by and ask, "Why did the LORD do this to such a great city as Jerusalem?" [9]Others will answer, "It's because the people worshiped foreign gods and broke the agreement that the LORD their God had made with them."

King Jehoahaz

The LORD said:

[10]King Josiah is dead,
    so don't cry for him.[g]
Instead, cry for his son
    King Jehoahaz,[h]
dragged off to another country,
    never to return.

[11-12]Jehoahaz[i] became king of Judah after his father King Josiah died. But Jehoahaz was taken as a prisoner to a foreign country. Now I, the LORD, promise that he will die there without ever seeing his own land again.

King Jehoiakim

The LORD told me to say:

*[13]King Jehoiakim,[j] you are doomed!
    You built a palace

---

[e]21.13 *Jerusalem . . . valleys:* One possible meaning for the difficult Hebrew text. [f]21.14 *your palace:* The Hebrew text has "the forest"; the largest room in the king's palace was known as Forest Hall (see 1 Kings 7.2, 3). [g]22.10 *King Josiah . . . him:* The Hebrew text has "don't cry for the dead one," meaning King Josiah, who ruled 640-609 B.C. [h]22.10 *his son, King Jehoahaz . . . country:* The Hebrew text has "the one who was dragged off to another country," meaning King Jehoahaz, who ruled for three months in 609 B.C. [i]22.11,12 *Jehoahaz:* The Hebrew text has "Shallum," another name for Jehoahaz. [j]22.13 *Jehoiakim:* See the note at 1.3.

with large rooms upstairs.
[14] You put in big windows
and used cedar paneling
and red paint.
But you were unfair
and forced the builders to work
without pay.

*[15] More cedar in your palace
doesn't make you a better king
than your father Josiah.
He always did right—
he gave justice to the poor
and was honest.
[16] That's what it means
to truly know me.
So he lived a comfortable life
and always had enough
to eat and drink.

[17] But all you think about
is how to cheat
or abuse or murder
some innocent victim.
[18] Jehoiakim, no one will cry
at your funeral.
They won't turn to each other
and ask,
"Why did our great king
have to die?"
[19] You will be given a burial
fit for a donkey;
your body will be dragged
outside the city gates
and tossed in the dirt.
I, the LORD, have spoken.

King Jehoiachin and the People of Jerusalem

The LORD told me to say:

[20] People of Jerusalem,
the nations[k] you trusted
have been crushed.
Go to Lebanon and weep;
cry in the land of Bashan
and in Moab.
[21] When times were good,
I warned you.
But you ignored me,
just as you have done
since Israel was young.
[22] Now you will be disgraced
because of your sins.

Your leaders will be swept away
by the wind,
and the nations you trusted
will be captured and dragged
to a foreign country.
[23] Those who live in the palace
paneled with cedar[l]
will groan with pain
like women giving birth.

[24] King Jehoiachin,[m] son of Jehoiakim,[n] even if you were the ring I wear as the sign of my royal power, I would still pull you from my finger. [25] I would hand you over to the enemy you fear, to King Nebuchadnezzar[o] and his army, who want to kill you. [26] You and your mother[p] were born in Judah, but I will throw both of you into a foreign country, where you will die, [27] longing to return home.

[28] Jehoiachin, you are unwanted
like a broken clay pot.
So you and your children
will be thrown into a country
you know nothing about.

[29] Land of Judah, I am the LORD.
Now listen to what I say!
[30] Erase the names
of Jehoiachin's children
from the royal records.
He is a complete failure,
and so none of them
will ever be king.
I, the LORD, have spoken.

A Message of Hope

The LORD said:

23 You leaders of my people are like shepherds that kill and scatter the sheep. [2] You were supposed to take care of my people, but instead you chased them away. So now I'll really take

---

k**22.20** *nations:* Or "gods." l**22.23** *who live in the palace paneled with cedar:* The Hebrew text has "who live in Lebanon and who nest among the cedars," which probably means Forest Hall in the royal palace at Jerusalem, which was paneled with cedar and had cedar columns and a cedar ceiling, all from Lebanon (see 1 Kings 7.2, 3). m**22.24** *Jehoiachin:* The Hebrew text has "Coniah," another form of Jehoiachin's name; he ruled for three months in 598 B.C. n**22.24** *Jehoiakim:* See the note at 1.3. o**22.25** *Nebuchadnezzar:* See the note at 21.2. p**22.26** *mother:* See the note at 13.18.

care of you, and believe me, you will pay for your crimes!

³I will bring the rest of my people home from the lands where I have scattered them, and they will grow into a mighty nation. ⁴I promise to choose leaders who will care for them like real shepherds. All of my people will be there, and they will never again be frightened.

⁵Someday I will appoint
an honest king
    from the family of David,
a king who will be wise
    and rule with justice.
⁶As long as he is king,
Israel will have peace,
    and Judah will be safe.
The name of this king will be
    "The LORD Gives Justice."

⁷A time will come when you will again worship me. But you will no longer call me the Living God who rescued Israel from Egypt. ⁸Instead, you will call me the Living God who rescued you from the land in the north and from all the other countries where I had forced you to go. And you will once again live in your own land.

Jeremiah Thinks about Unfaithful Prophets

⁹When I think of the prophets,
I am shocked, and I tremble^q
    like someone drunk,
because of the LORD
    and his sacred words.
¹⁰Those unfaithful prophets
misuse their power
    all over the country.
So God turned the pasturelands
    into scorching deserts.^r

The LORD Will Punish Unfaithful Prophets

¹¹The LORD told me to say:

You prophets and priests
think so little of me, the LORD,
    that you even sin
    in my own temple!
¹²Now I will punish you
with disaster,
    and you will slip and fall

in the darkness.
I, the LORD, have spoken.

¹³The prophets in Samaria
    were disgusting to me,
because they preached
in the name of Baal
    and led my people astray.
¹⁴And you prophets in Jerusalem
    are even worse.
You're unfaithful in marriage^s
    and never tell the truth.^t
You even lead others to sin
instead of helping them
    turn back to me.
You and the people of Jerusalem
are evil like Sodom
    and Gomorrah.^u
¹⁵You prophets in Jerusalem
    have spread evil everywhere.
That's why I, the LORD, promise
to give you bitter poison
    to eat and drink.

The LORD Gives a Warning

The LORD said:

¹⁶Don't listen to the lies
of these false prophets,
    you people of Judah!
The message they preach
    is something they imagined;
it did not come from me,
    the LORD All-Powerful.
¹⁷These prophets go to people
    who refuse to respect me
and who are stubborn
    and do whatever they want.
The prophets tell them,
"The LORD has promised
    everything will be fine."

¹⁸But I, the LORD, tell you
    that these prophets
have never attended a meeting
    of my council in heaven^v

---

^q**23.9** *tremble:* Or "become weak." ^r**23.10** *deserts:* One possible meaning for the difficult Hebrew text of verse 10. ^s**23.14** *in marriage:* Or "to me." ^t**23.14** *never tell the truth:* Or "worship other gods." ^u**23.14** *Sodom and Gomorrah:* Two cities that the LORD destroyed because their people were so evil (see Genesis 18.16—19.29). ^v**23.18** *a meeting of my council in heaven:* Sometimes, prophets had visions of the LORD meeting with his angels (see 1 Kings 22.19-23).

or heard me speak.
¹⁹They are evil! So in my anger
I will strike them
like a violent storm.
²⁰I won't calm down,
until I have finished
what I have decided to do.
Someday you will understand
exactly what I mean.
²¹I did not send these prophets
or speak to them,
but they ran to find you
and to preach their message.
²²If they had been in a meeting
of my council in heaven,
they would have told
you people of Judah
to give up your sins
and come back to me.

²³I am everywhere—
both near and far,
²⁴   in heaven and on earth.
There are no secret places
where you can hide from me.

²⁵These unfaithful prophets claim that I
have given them a dream or a vision, and
then they tell lies in my name. ²⁶But everything they say comes from their own twisted
minds. How long can this go on? ²⁷They tell
each other their dreams and try to get my
people to reject me, just as their ancestors
left me and worshiped Baal. ²⁸Their dreams
and my truth are as different as straw and

wheat. But when prophets speak for me,
they must say only what I have told them.
²⁹My words are a powerful fire; they are a
hammer that shatters rocks.

³⁰⁻³²These unfaithful prophets claim I
give them their dreams, but it isn't true. I
didn't choose them to be my prophets, and
yet they babble on and on, speaking in my
name, while stealing words from each other.
And when my people hear these liars, they
are led astray instead of being helped. So I
warn you that I am now the enemy of these
prophets. I, the LORD, have spoken.

News and Nuisance

The LORD said to me:

³³Jeremiah, when a prophet or a priest or
anyone else comes to you and asks, "Does
the LORD have news for us?" tell them, "You
people are a nuisanceʷ to the LORD, and heˣ
will get rid of you."

³⁴If any of you say, "Here is news from
the LORD," I will punish you and your families, even if you are a prophet or a priest.
³⁵Instead, you must ask your friends and relatives, "What answer did the LORD give?" or
"What has the LORD said?" ³⁶It seems that
you each have your own news! So if you say,

ʷ**23.33** *news . . . nuisance:* The Hebrew word for "news"
in verses 33-38 is the same as "nuisance" and is related
to "pick up" in verse 39.   ˣ**23.33** *You people are a
nuisance to the LORD, and he:* Two ancient translations;
Hebrew "Does the LORD have news for us? He."

---

*Spiritual*Life—**How can I handle my doubts about God?** *(Jeremiah 23.16-32)*

Consider the source.
Sometimes it's hard to believe in God. Doubts about God, his reality, his work in your life
or in the world, even doubts about his goodness assail you when you're faced with the pain
and contradictions of life. At such times, it's important not to ignore your doubts but to
examine them carefully. Where are the doubts coming from? On what are you focusing?
Are these sources more reliable than God's Word? What does God's Word say about
whatever it is you doubt?

The people of Jeremiah's time were deceived by false prophets who told them what they
wanted to hear. But God said those prophets' words were the product of their own twisted
minds—not his words of truth. When you doubt, the best thing to do is seek God's
perspective on the issue through his Word. Ultimately the Bible is the only source of truth.
As you seek him, he'll see you through your doubts and strengthen your faith. (See also
Job 1; Psalm 136; Romans 4.13-25; Colossians 2.6-19.)

Words To Remember: *My words are a powerful fire; they are a hammer that
shatters rocks.—Jeremiah 23.29*

"Here is news from the LORD," you are twisting my words into a lie. Remember that I am your God, the LORD All-Powerful.

[37]If you go to a prophet, it's all right to ask, "What answer did the LORD give to my question?" or "What has the LORD said?" [38]But if you disobey me and say, "Here is news from the LORD," [39]I will pick you up[y] and throw you far away. And I will abandon this city of Jerusalem that I gave to your ancestors. [40]You will never be free from your shame and disgrace.

Jeremiah Has a Vision of Two Baskets of Figs

24 The LORD spoke to me in a vision after King Nebuchadnezzar[z] of Babylonia had come to Judah and taken King Jehoiachin,[d] his officials, and all the skilled workers back to Babylonia. In this vision I saw two baskets of figs in front of the LORD's temple. [2]One basket was full of very good figs that ripened early, and the other was full of rotten figs that were not fit to eat.

[3]"Jeremiah," the LORD asked, "what do you see?"

"Figs," I said. "Some are very good, but the others are too rotten to eat."

[4]Then the LORD told me to say:

[5]People of Judah, the good figs stand for those of you I sent away as exiles to Babylonia, [6]where I am watching over them. Then someday I will bring them back to this land. I will plant them, instead of uprooting them, and I will build them up, rather than tearing them down. [7]I will give them a desire to know me and to be my people. They will want me to be their God, and they will turn back to me with all their heart.

[8]The rotten figs stand for King Zedekiah[h] of Judah, his officials, and all the others who were not taken away to Babylonia, whether they stayed here in Judah or went to live in Egypt. [9]I will punish them with a terrible disaster, and everyone on earth will tremble when they hear about it. I will force the people of Judah to go to foreign countries, where they will be cursed and insulted. [10]War and hunger and disease will strike them, until they finally disappear from the land that I gave them and their ancestors.

Seventy Years of Exile

25 [1-2]In the fourth year that Jehoiakim was king of Judah,[c] which was the first year that Nebuchadnezzar[d] was king of Babylonia, the LORD told me to speak to the people of Judah and Jerusalem. So I told them:

[3]For twenty-three years now, ever since the thirteenth year that Josiah[e] was king, I have been telling you what the LORD has told me. But you have not listened.

[4]The LORD has sent prophets to you time after time, but you refused to listen. [5]They told you that the LORD had said:

Change your ways! If you stop doing evil, I will let you stay forever in this land that I gave your ancestors. [6]I don't want to harm you. So don't make me angry by worshiping idols and other gods.

[7]But you refused to listen to my prophets. So I, the LORD, say that you have made me angry by worshiping idols, and you are the ones who were hurt by what you did. [8]You refused to listen to me, [9]and now I will let you be attacked by nations from the north, and especially by my servant, King Nebuchadnezzar of Babylonia. You and other nearby nations will be destroyed and left in ruins forever. Everyone who sees what has happened will be shocked, but they will still make fun of you. [10]I will put an end to your parties and wedding celebrations; no one will grind grain or be here to light the lamps at night. [11]This country will be as empty as a desert, because I will make all of you the slaves of the king of Babylonia for seventy years.

[12]When that time is up, I will punish the king of Babylonia and his people for everything they have done wrong, and I will turn that country into a wasteland forever. [13]My servant

---

[y]23.39 *pick you up*: A few Hebrew manuscripts and three ancient translations; most Hebrew manuscripts "forget you completely." [z]24.1 *Nebuchadnezzar*: See the note at 21.2. [d]24.1 *Jehoiachin*: The Hebrew text has "Jeconiah," another form of Jehoiachin's name; he ruled for three months in 598 B.C. [b]24.8 *Zedekiah*: Ruled 598-586 B.C. [c]25.1,2 *Jehoiakim . . . Judah*: See the note at 1.3. [d]25.1,2 *Nebuchadnezzar*: See the note at 21.2. [e]25.3 *Josiah*: Hebrew "Josiah son of Amon"; Josiah ruled 640-609 B.C.

Jeremiah has told you what I said I will do to Babylonia and to the other nations, and he wrote it all down in this book. I will do everything I threatened. [14]I will pay back the Babylonians for every wrong they have done. Great kings from many other nations will conquer the Babylonians and force them to be slaves.

The Cup Full of God's Anger

[15]The LORD God of Israel showed me a vision in which he said, "Jeremiah, here is a cup filled with the wine of my anger. Take it and make every nation drink some. [16]They will vomit and act crazy, because of the war this cup of anger will bring to them."

[17]I took the cup from the LORD's hand, and I went to the kings of the nations and made each of them drink some. [18]I started with Jerusalem and the towns of Judah, and the king and his officials were removed from power in disgrace. Everyone still makes insulting jokes about them and uses their names as curse words. [19]The second place I went was Egypt, where everyone had to drink from the cup, including the king and his officials, the other government workers, the rest of the Egyptians, [20]and all the foreigners who lived in the country.

Next I went to the king of Uz, and then to the four kings of Philistia, who ruled from Ashkelon, Gaza, Ekron, and what was left of Ashdod.[f] [21]Then I went to the kings of Edom, Moab, Ammon, [22]and to the kings of Tyre, Sidon, and their colonies across the sea. [23-24]After this, I went to the kings of Dedan, Tema, Buz, the tribes of the Arabian Desert,[g] [25]Zimri, Elam, Media, [26]and the countries in the north, both near and far.

I went to all the countries on earth, one after another, and finally to Babylonia.[h] [27]The LORD had said to tell each king, "The LORD All-Powerful, the God of Israel, commands you to drink from this cup that is full of the wine of his anger. It will make you so drunk that you will vomit. And when the LORD sends war against the nations, you will be completely defeated."

[28]The LORD told me that if any of them refused to drink from the cup, I must tell them that he had said, "I, the LORD All-Powerful, command you to drink. [29]Starting with my own city of Jerusalem, everyone on

earth will suffer from war. So there is no way I will let you escape unharmed."

[30]The LORD told me to say:

From my sacred temple
    I will roar like thunder,
while I trample my people
    and everyone else
      as though they were grapes.
[31]My voice will be heard
    everywhere on earth,
accusing nations of their crimes
    and sentencing the guilty
      to death.

Disaster Is Coming

[32]The LORD All-Powerful says:

You can see disaster spreading
    from far across the earth,
from nation to nation
    like a horrible storm.

[33]When it strikes, I will kill so many people that their bodies will cover the ground like manure. No one will be left to bury them or to mourn.

The Leaders of Judah Will Be Punished

[34]The LORD's people are his flock,
    and you leaders
      were the shepherds.
But now it's your turn
    to be butchered like sheep.
You'll shatter like fine pottery
    dropped on the floor.[i]
So roll on the ground,
    crying and mourning.
[35]You have nowhere to run,
    nowhere to hide.

*[36]Listen to the cries
    of the shepherds,
[37]as the LORD's burning anger
    turns[j] peaceful meadows
      into barren deserts.

---

[f]25.20 *what was left of Ashdod*: It was defeated by the king of Egypt after being surrounded for twenty-nine years. [g]25.23,24 *the tribes of the Arabian Desert*: One possible meaning for the difficult Hebrew text. [h]25.26 *Babylonia*: The Hebrew text has "Sheshach," a secret way of writing "Babylonia." [i]25.34 *You'll shatter . . . floor*: One possible meaning for the difficult Hebrew text. [j]25.37 *anger turns*: Or "anger and enemy armies turn."

³⁸The LORD has abandoned
his people[k]
like a lion leaving its den.

Jeremiah's Message in the Temple
(Jeremiah 7.1-15)

26 Soon after Jehoiakim[l] became
king of Judah, the LORD said:
²Jeremiah, I have a message
for everyone who comes from the towns of
Judah to worship in my temple. Go to the
temple courtyard and speak every word that
I tell you. ³Maybe the people will listen this
time. And if they stop doing wrong, I will
change my mind and not punish them for
their sins. ⁴Tell them that I have said:

You have refused to listen to me
and to obey my laws and teachings.
⁵Again and again I have sent my servants the prophets to preach to you,
but you ignored them as well. Now I
am warning you that if you don't start
obeying me right away, ⁶I will destroy
this temple, just as I destroyed the
town of Shiloh.[m] Then everyone on
earth will use the name "Jerusalem" as
a curse word.

Jeremiah on Trial

⁷The prophets, the priests, and everyone
else in the temple heard what I said, ⁸⁻⁹and
as soon as I finished, they all crowded
around me and started shouting, "Why did
you preach that the LORD will destroy this
temple, just as he destroyed Shiloh? Why
did you say that Jerusalem will be empty
and lie in ruins? You ought to be put to
death for saying such things in the LORD's
name!" Then they had me arrested.
¹⁰The royal officers heard what had happened, and they came from the palace to the
new gate of the temple to be the judges at
my trial.[n] ¹¹While they listened, the priests
and the prophets said to the crowd, "All of
you have heard Jeremiah prophesy that Jerusalem will be destroyed. He deserves the
death penalty."
¹²⁻¹³Then I told the judges and everyone
else:

The LORD himself sent me to tell
you about the terrible things he will do
to you, to Jerusalem, and to the temple. But if you change your ways and
start obeying the LORD, he will change
his mind.

¹⁴You must decide what to do with
me. Just do whatever you think is
right. ¹⁵But if you put me to death, you
and everyone else in Jerusalem will be
guilty of murdering an innocent man,
because everything I preached came
from the LORD.

*Anything that stretches you,
expands your world, or
helps you share yourself
with others will foster
contentment and give you a
fresh perspective on your life.*

ELIZABETH CODY NEWENHUYSE

¹⁶The judges and the other people told
the priests and prophets, "Since Jeremiah
only told us what the LORD our God had
said, we don't think he deserves to die."
¹⁷Then some of the leaders from other
towns stepped forward. They told the
crowd that ¹⁸years ago when Hezekiah[o] was
king of Judah, a prophet named Micah from
the town of Moresheth had said:

"I, the LORD All-Powerful, say
Jerusalem will be plowed under
and left in ruins.
Thorns will cover the mountain
where the temple
now stands."[p]

¹⁹Then the leaders continued:
No one put Micah to death for saying that. Instead, King Hezekiah
prayed to the LORD with fear and trembling and asked him to have mercy.
Then the LORD decided not to destroy

[k]25.38 *The LORD has . . . people:* Or "And his people
leave their homes." [l]26.1 *Jehoiakim:* See the note
at 1.3. [m]26.6 *Shiloh:* The sacred tent had once stood
at Shiloh. [n]26.10 *new gate . . . trial:* Public trials were
often held in an open area at a gate of a city, palace,
or temple. [o]26.18 *Hezekiah:* Ruled 716-687 B.C.
[p]26.18 *Jerusalem . . . stands:* See Micah 3.12.

Jerusalem, even though he had already said he would.

People of Judah, if Jeremiah is killed, we will bring a terrible disaster on ourselves.

20-24After these leaders finished speaking, an important man named Ahikam son of Shaphan spoke up for me as well. And so, I wasn't handed over to the crowd to be killed.

Uriah the Prophet

While Jehoiakim[q] was still king of Judah, a man named Uriah son of Shemaiah left his hometown of Kiriath-Jearim and came to Jerusalem. Uriah was one of the LORD's prophets, and he was saying the same things about Judah and Jerusalem that I had been saying. And when Jehoiakim and his officials and military officers heard what Uriah said, they tried to arrest him, but he escaped to Egypt. So Jehoiakim sent Elnathan son of Achbor and some other men after Uriah, and they brought him back. Then Jehoiakim had Uriah killed and his body dumped in a common burial pit.

Slaves of Nebuchadnezzar

27 1-2Not long after Zedekiah became king of Judah,[r] the LORD told me:

Jeremiah, make a wooden yoke[s] with leather straps, and place it on your neck. 3Then send a message to the kings of Edom, Moab, Ammon, Tyre, and Sidon. Some officials from these countries are in Jerusalem, meeting with Zedekiah. 4So have them tell their kings that I have said:

I am the All-Powerful LORD God of Israel, 5and with my power I created the earth, its people, and all animals. I decide who will rule the earth, 6-7and I have chosen my servant King Nebuchadnezzar[t] of Babylonia to rule all nations, including yours. I will even let him rule the wild animals. All nations will be slaves of Nebuchadnezzar, his son, and his grandson. Then many nations will join together, and their kings will be powerful enough to make slaves of the Babylonians.

8This yoke stands for the power of King Nebuchadnezzar, and I will destroy any nation that refuses to obey him. Nebuchadnezzar will attack, and many will die in battle or from hunger and disease. 9You might have people in your kingdom who claim they can tell the future by magic or by talking with the dead or by dreams or messages from a god. But don't pay attention if any of them tell you not to obey Nebuchadnezzar. 10If you listen to such lies, I will have you dragged far from your country and killed. 11But if you and your nation are willing to obey Nebuchadnezzar, I will let you stay in your country, and your people will continue to live and work on their farms.

12After I had spoken to the officials from the nearby kingdoms, I went to King Zedekiah and told him the same thing. Then I said:

Zedekiah, if you and the people of Judah want to stay alive, you must obey Nebuchadnezzar and the Babylonians. 13But if you refuse, then you and your people will die from war, hunger, and disease, just as the LORD has warned. 14Your prophets have told you that you don't need to obey Nebuchadnezzar, but don't listen to their lies. 15Those prophets claim to be speaking for the LORD, but he didn't send them. They are lying! If you do what they say, he will have both you and them dragged off to another country and killed. The LORD has spoken.

16When I finished talking to the king, I went to the priests and told them that the LORD had said:

Don't listen to the prophets when they say that very soon the Babylonians will return the things they took from my temple. Those prophets are lying! 17If you choose to obey the king of Babylonia, you will live. But if you listen to those prophets, this whole city will be nothing but a pile of rubble.

18If I really had spoken to those

---

q26.20-24 *Jehoiakim*: See the note at 1.3.
r27.1,2 *Not long after Zedekiah became king of Judah*: A few manuscripts and one ancient translation; most Hebrew manuscripts "Not long after Jehoiakim became king of Judah"; most manuscripts of another ancient translation do not have these words. Jehoiakim ruled 609-598 B.C., and Zedekiah ruled 598-586 B.C.
s27.1,2 *yoke*: A wooden collar that fits around the neck of an ox, so the ox can be made to pull a plow or a cart.
t27.6,7 *Nebuchadnezzar*: See the note at 21.2.

prophets, they would know what I am going to do. Then they would be begging me not to let everything else be taken from the temple and the king's palace and the rest of Jerusalem. [19-21]After all, when Nebuchadnezzar took King Jehoiachin[u] to Babylonia as a prisoner, he didn't take everything of value from Jerusalem. He left the bronze pillars, the huge bronze bowl called the Sea, and the movable bronze stands in the temple, and he left a lot of other valuable things in the palace and in the rest of Jerusalem.

But now I, the LORD All-Powerful, the God of Israel, say that all these things [22]will be taken to Babylonia, where they will remain until I decide to bring them back to Jerusalem. I, the LORD, have spoken.

Jeremiah Accuses Hananiah of Being a False Prophet

28 Later that same year, in the fifth month of the fourth year that Zedekiah[y] was king,[w] the prophet Hananiah son of Azzur from Gibeon came up to me in the temple. And while the priests and others in the temple were listening, [2]he told me that the LORD had said:

I am the LORD All-Powerful, the God of Israel, and I will smash the yoke[x] that Nebuchadnezzar[y] put on the necks of the nations to make them his slaves. [3]And within two years, I will bring back to Jerusalem everything that he took from my temple and carried off to Babylonia. [4]King Jehoiachin[z] and the other people who were taken from Judah to Babylonia will be allowed to come back here as well. All this will happen because I will smash the power of the king of Babylonia!

[5]The priests and the others were still standing there, so I said:

[6]Hananiah, I hope the LORD will do exactly what you said. I hope he does bring back everything the Babylonians took from the temple, and that our people who were taken to Babylonia will be allowed to return home. [7]But let me remind you and everyone else [8]that long before we were born, prophets were saying powerful kingdoms would be struck by war, disaster, and

disease. [9]Now you are saying we will have peace. We will just have to wait and see if that is really what the LORD has said.[a]

[10]Hananiah grabbed the wooden yoke from my neck and smashed it. [11]Then he said, "The LORD says this is the way he will smash the power Nebuchadnezzar has over the nations, and it will happen in less than two years."

I left the temple, [12]and a little while later, the LORD told me [13-14]to go back and say to Hananiah:

I am the LORD All-Powerful, the God of Israel. You smashed a wooden yoke, but I will replace it with one made of iron. I will put iron yokes on all the nations, and they will have to do what King Nebuchadnezzar commands. I will even let him rule the wild animals.

[15-16]Hananiah, I have never sent you to speak for me. And yet you have talked my people into believing your lies and rebelling against me. So now I will send you—I'll send you right off the face of the earth! You will die before this year is over.

[17]Two months later, Hananiah died.

Jeremiah's Letter to the People of Judah in Babylonia

29 [1-2]I had been left in Jerusalem when King Nebuchadnezzar[b] took many of the people of Jerusalem and Judah to Babylonia as prisoners, including King Jehoiachin,[c] his mother, his officials, and the metal workers and others in Jerusalem who were skilled in making things. So I wrote a letter to the prophets, the priests, the leaders, and the rest of our people in Babylonia. [3]I gave the letter to Elasah and Gemariah,[d] two men that King Zedekiah[e] of Judah was sending to Babylon

---

[u]27.19-21 *Jehoiachin:* Hebrew "Jeconiah" (see the note at 24.1).   [v]28.1 *Zedekiah:* See the note at 1.3.   [w]28.1 *Later . . . king:* One possible meaning for the difficult Hebrew text.   [x]28.2 *yoke:* See the note at 27.1, 2.   [y]28.2 *Nebuchadnezzar:* See the note at 21.2.   [z]28.4 *Jehoiachin:* Hebrew "Jeconiah" (see the note at 24.1).   [a]28.9 *We will . . . said:* See Deuteronomy 18.21, 22.   [b]29.1,2 *Nebuchadnezzar:* See the note at 21.2.   [c]29.1,2 *Jehoiachin:* Hebrew "Jeconiah" (see the note at 24.1).   [d]29.3 *Elasah and Gemariah:* Hebrew "Elasah son of Shaphan and Gemariah son of Hilkiah."   [e]29.3 *Zedekiah:* See the note at 1.3.

to talk with Nebuchadnezzar. In the letter, I wrote [4]that the LORD All-Powerful, the God of Israel, had said:

I had you taken from Jerusalem to Babylonia. Now I tell you [5]to settle there and build houses. Plant gardens and eat what you grow in them. [6]Get married and have children, then help your sons find wives and help your daughters find husbands, so they can have children as well. I want your numbers to grow, not to get smaller.

[7]Pray for peace in Babylonia and work hard to make it prosperous. The more successful that nation is, the better off you will be.

[8-9]Some of your people there in Babylonia are fortunetellers, and you have asked them to tell you what will happen in the future. But they will only lead you astray. And don't let the prophets fool you, either. They speak in my name, but they are liars. I have not spoken to them.

[10]After Babylonia has been the strongest nation for seventy years, I will be kind and bring you back to Jerusalem, just as I have promised. [11]I will bless you with a future filled with hope—a future of success, not of suffering. [12]You will turn back to me and ask for help, and I will answer your prayers. [13]You will worship me with all your heart, and I will be with you [14]and accept your worship. Then I will gather you from all the nations where I scattered you, and you will return to Jerusalem.

[15]You feel secure, because you think I have sent prophets to speak for me in Babylonia.

[16-19]But I have been sending prophets to the people of Judah for a long time, and the king from David's family and the people who are left in Jerusalem and Judah still don't obey me. So I, the LORD All-Powerful, will keep attacking them with war and hunger and disease, until they are as useless as rotten figs. I will force them to leave the land, and all nations will be disgusted and shocked at what happens to them. The nations will sneer and make fun of them and use the names "Judah" and "Jerusalem" as curse words.

And you have not obeyed me, even though [20]I had you taken from Jerusalem to Babylonia. But you had better listen to me now. [21-23]You think Ahab son of Kolaiah and Zedekiah son of Maaseiah are prophets because they claim to speak for me. But they are lying! I haven't told them anything.

SingleLife—Sometimes I really want to be married. How can I deal with those times? *(Jeremiah 29.10-14)*

Remember that God holds your future in his hands.
Sometimes God allows us to go through difficult times, times when we don't get what we want. In this passage, God allowed his people to be carried off to Babylonia and remain captive for seventy years. But God had a plan, a plan for restoration and blessing. Even the captivity was part of that plan—in their case, he wanted them to turn from their sin and acknowledge that he, and he only, is God.

If you're single, you may wonder what God has in mind for you for the future. Will you get married? Will you have children? Maybe, unlike the Israelites, you've led a pure and godly life and yet you still don't have your heart's longing: a Christian man.

When you're tempted to doubt the goodness of your situation, tell God about it. Turn to him and ask for help (29.12). God understands, and he's eager to answer your prayers. He knows what your future holds, and he promises it will be good. Work through your feelings before God, knowing he'll take care of you now and forever. Trust his timing. (See also Psalm 84; 1 Peter 3.13-18.)

Words To Remember: *I will bless you with a future filled with hope—a future of success, not of suffering. You will turn back to me and ask for help, and I will answer your prayers.—Jeremiah 29.11,12*

They are also committing other horrible sins in your community, such as sleeping with the wives of their friends. So I will hand them over to King Nebuchadnezzar, who will put them to death while the rest of you watch. And in the future, when you want to put a curse on someone, you will say, "I pray that the LORD will kill you in the same way the king of Babylonia burned Zedekiah and Ahab to death!"

A Message for Shemaiah

24-25The LORD All-Powerful, the God of Israel, told me what would happen to Shemaiah,[j] who was one of our people in Babylonia. After my letter reached Babylonia, Shemaiah wrote letters to the people of Jerusalem, including the priest Zephaniah son of Maaseiah, and the other priests. The letter to Zephaniah said:

26After the death of Jehoiada the priest, the LORD chose you to be the priest in charge of the temple security force. You know that anyone who acts crazy and pretends to be a prophet should be arrested and put in chains[g] and iron collars. 27Jeremiah from the town of Anathoth is pretending to be a prophet there in Jerusalem, so why haven't you punished him? 28He even wrote a letter to the people here in Babylonia, saying we would be here a long time. He told us to build homes and to plant gardens and grow our own food.

29When Zephaniah received Shemaiah's letter, he read it to me. 30Then the LORD told me what to write in a second letter 31to the people of Judah who had been taken to Babylonia. In this letter, I wrote that the LORD had said:

I, the LORD, have not chosen Shemaiah to be one of my prophets, and he has misled you by telling lies in my name. 32He has even talked you into disobeying me. So I will punish Shemaiah. He and his descendants won't live to see the good things I will do for my people. I, the LORD, have spoken.

The LORD Will Rescue Israel and Judah

30 1-2The LORD God of Israel said, "Jeremiah, get a scroll[h] and write down everything I have told you.

3Someday I will let my people from both Israel[i] and Judah return to the land I gave their ancestors."

4-5Then the LORD told me to say to Israel and Judah:

I, the LORD, hear screams
of terror,
   and there is no peace.
6Can men give birth?
Then why do I see them
   looking so pale
and clutching their stomachs
   like women in labor?
7My people, soon you will suffer
worse than ever before,
   but I will save you.

8Now you are slaves
   of other nations,
but I will break the chains
and smash the yokes[j]
   that keep you in slavery.
9Then you will be my servants,
and I will choose a king for you
   from the family of David.

*10Israel,[k] you belong to me,
   so don't be afraid.
You deserved to be punished;
that's why I scattered you
   in distant nations.
But I am with you,
and someday I will destroy
   those nations.
11Then I will bring you
and your descendants
   back to your land,
where I will protect you
   and give you peace.
Then your fears will be gone.
   I, the LORD, have spoken.

The LORD Will Heal Israel and Judah

12The LORD said:

My people, you are wounded
   and near death.

---

j29.24,25 Shemaiah: Hebrew "Shemaiah, who came from the town of Nehelam." g29.26 in chains: See the note at 20.2. h30.1,2 scroll: A roll of paper or special leather used for writing on. i30.3 Israel: The northern kingdom. j30.8 yokes: See the note at 27.1, 2. k30.10 Israel: The people of the northern and southern kingdoms.

¹³You are accused of a crime
   with no one to defend you,
and you are covered with sores
   that no medicine can cure.
*¹⁴Your friends have forgotten you;
   they don't care anymore.
Even I have acted like an enemy.
And because your sins
   are horrible and countless,
I will be cruel
   as I punish you.
¹⁵So don't bother to cry out
   for relief from your pain.

¹⁶But if your enemies try to rob
   or destroy you,
I will rob and destroy them,
and they will be led as captives
   to foreign lands.
¹⁷No one wants you as a friend
   or cares what happens to you.
But I will heal your injuries,
   and you will get well.

The LORD Will Rescue Israel and Judah

¹⁸The LORD said:

Israel, I will be kind to you
   and let you come home.
Jerusalem now lies in ruins,
but you will rebuild it,
   complete with a new palace.ˡ
¹⁹Other nations will respect
   and honor you.
Your homes will be filled
   with children,
and you will celebrate,
   singing praises to me.

²⁰It will be just like old times.
Your nation will worship me,
   and I will punish anyone
   who abuses you.
²¹One of your own people
   will become your ruler.
And when I invite him
   to come near me
at the place of worship,
   he will do so.
No one would dare to come near
   without being invited.
²²You will be my people,
   and I will be your God.
   I, the LORD, have spoken.

²³I am furious!
And like a violent storm
   I will strike those
   who do wrong.
²⁴I won't calm down
until I have finished
   what I have decided to do.
Someday, you will understand
   what I mean.

Israel Will Return to God

31 The LORD said:

Israel, I promise
   that someday all your tribes
will again be my people,
   and I will be your God.
²In the desert I was kind
   to those who escaped death.
I gave them peace,
   and when the time is right,
I'll do the same for you.ᵐ
   I, the LORD, have spoken.

> *God's evaluation of you is not
> dependent on the currently
> popular body type, but on
> his unchangeable standard
> of unconditional love.*
>
> MARY ANN MAYO

The LORD Will Rebuild Israel

³Some time ago, the LORD appeared to
meⁿ and told me to say:

Israel, I will always love you;
   that's why I've been so patient
   and kind.
⁴You are precious to me,
   and so I will rebuild
   your nation.

ˡ**30.18** *Jerusalem . . . palace:* Or "Your towns lie in ruins,
but you will rebuild them, and your homes will be
where they were before."   ᵐ**31.2** *In the desert . . .
same for you:* One possible meaning for the difficult
Hebrew text.   ⁿ**31.3** *Some time . . . me:* Or "The LORD
appeared to me from far away."

Once again you will dance for joy
and play your tambourines.
5 You will plant vineyards
on the hills of Samaria
and enjoy the grapes.
6 Someday those who guard
the hill country of Ephraim
will shout, "Let's go to Zion
and worship the LORD our God."

Israel Will Return to Its Own Land

7 The LORD says:

Celebrate and sing for Israel,
the greatest of nations.
Offer praises and shout,
"Come and rescue
your people, LORD!
Save what's left of Israel."

8 I, the LORD, will bring
my people back from Babylonia[o]
and everywhere else on earth.
The blind and the lame
will be there.
Expectant mothers
and women about to give birth
will come and be part
of that great crowd.
9 They will weep and pray
as I bring them home.
I will lead them
to streams of water.
They will walk on a level[p] road
and not stumble.
I am a father to Israel,[q]
my favorite children.

10 Listen to me, you nations
nearby or across the sea.
I scattered the people of Israel,
but I will gather them again.
I will protect them like a shepherd
guarding a flock;
11 I will rescue them from enemies
who could overpower them.
12 My people will come
to Mount Zion
and celebrate;
their faces will glow
because of my blessings.
I'll give them grain, grapes,
and olive oil,
as well as sheep and cattle.
Israel will be prosperous
and grow like a garden
with plenty of water.
13 Young women and young men,
together with the elderly,
will celebrate and dance,
because I will comfort them
and turn their sorrow
into happiness.
14 I will bless my people
with more food
than they need,
and the priests will enjoy
the choice cuts of meat.
I, the LORD, have spoken.

The LORD Offers Hope

15 In Ramah[r] a voice is heard,
crying and weeping loudly.
Rachel mourns for her children[s]
and refuses to be comforted,
because they are dead.
*16 But I, the LORD, say
to dry your tears.
Someday your children
will come home
from the enemy's land.
Then all you have done for them
will be greatly rewarded.
17 So don't lose hope.
I, the LORD, have spoken.

18 The people of Israel[t] moan
and say to me,
"We were like wild bulls,
but you, LORD, broke us,
and we learned to obey.
You are our God—
please let us come home.
19 When we were young,
we strayed and sinned,
but then we realized
what we had done.
We are ashamed and disgraced
and want to return to you."

---

[o] **31.8** *Babylonia*: The Hebrew text has "that country in the north," referring to Babylonia. [p] **31.9** *level*: Or "straight." [q] **31.9** *Israel*: The Hebrew text also has "Ephraim," the leading tribe of the northern kingdom of Israel, which sometimes stands for the whole northern kingdom. [r] **31.15** *In Ramah*: Or "In the hills." [s] **31.15** *Rachel . . . children*: Rachel was one of the wives of Jacob, the ancestor of the nation of Israel. She was the mother of Joseph and Benjamin. Joseph's two sons Ephraim and Manasseh were the ancestors of the leading tribes of the northern kingdom of Israel. [t] **31.18** *Israel*: Hebrew "Ephraim" (see the note at 31.9).

²⁰People of Israel,
you are my own dear children.
Don't I love you best of all?
Though I often make threats,
I want you to be near me,
so I will have mercy on you.
I, the LORD, have spoken.

²¹With rock piles and signposts,
mark the way home,
my dear people.
It is the same road
by which you left.
²²Will you ever decide
to be faithful?
I will make sure that someday
things will be different,
as different as a woman
protecting a man.^u

The LORD Will Bring Judah Home

²³The LORD All-Powerful, the God of Israel, said:

I promise to set the people of Judah free and to lead them back to their hometowns. And when I do, they will once again say,

"We pray that the LORD
will bless his home,
the sacred hill in Jerusalem
where his temple stands."

²⁴The people will live in Jerusalem and in the towns of Judah. Some will be farmers, and others will be shepherds. ²⁵Those who feel tired and worn out will find new life and energy, ²⁶and when they sleep, they will wake up refreshed.^v
²⁷Someday, Israel and Judah will be my field where my people and their livestock will grow. ²⁸In the past, I took care to uproot them, to tear them down, and to destroy them. But when that day comes, I will take care to plant them and help them grow. ²⁹No longer will anyone go around saying,

"Sour grapes eaten by parents
leave a sour taste in the mouths
of their children."

³⁰When that day comes, only those who eat sour grapes will get the sour taste, and only those who sin will be put to death.

The New Agreement with Israel and Judah

³¹The LORD said:

The time will surely come when I will make a new agreement with the people of Israel and Judah. ³²It will be different from the agreement I made with their ancestors when I led them out of Egypt. Although I was their God, they broke that agreement.
³³Here is the new agreement that I, the LORD, will make with the people of Israel:

"I will write my laws
on their hearts and minds.
I will be their God,
and they will be my people.

³⁴"No longer will they have to teach one another to obey me. I, the LORD, promise that all of them will obey me, ordinary people and rulers alike. I will forgive their sins and forget the evil things they have done."

³⁵I am the LORD All-Powerful.
I command the sun
to give light each day,
the moon and stars
to shine at night,
and ocean waves to roar.
³⁶I will never forget
to give those commands,
and I will never let Israel
stop being a nation.
I, the LORD, have spoken.

³⁷Can you measure the heavens?
Can you explore
the depths of the earth?
That's how hard it would be
for me to reject Israel forever,
even though they have sinned.
I, the LORD, have spoken.

Jerusalem Will Be Rebuilt

³⁸The LORD said:

Someday, Jerusalem will truly belong to me. It will be rebuilt with a boundary line running from Hananel Tower to Corner Gate. ³⁹From there, the boundary will go in a straight line to Gareb Hill, then turn toward Goah. ⁴⁰Even that disgusting Hinnom

---

^u**31.22** *I will make sure . . . a woman protecting a man*: One possible meaning for the difficult Hebrew text.
^v**31.26** *and when they sleep . . . refreshed*: One possible meaning for the difficult Hebrew text.

Valley[w] will be sacred to me, and so will the eastern slopes that go down from Horse Gate into Kidron Valley. Jerusalem will never again be destroyed.

Jeremiah Buys a Field

32 The LORD spoke to me in the tenth year that Zedekiah[x] was king of Judah, which was the eighteenth year that Nebuchadnezzar[y] was king of Babylonia. [2]At that time, the Babylonian army had surrounded Jerusalem, and I was in the prison at the courtyard of the palace guards. [3]Zedekiah had ordered me to be held there because I told everyone that the LORD had said:

I am the LORD, and I am about to let the king of Babylonia conquer Jerusalem. [4]King Zedekiah will be captured and taken to King Nebuchadnezzar, who will speak with him face to face. [5]Then Zedekiah will be led away to Babylonia, where he will stay until I am finished with him. So, if you people of Judah fight against the Babylonians, you will lose. I, the LORD, have spoken.

[6]Later, when I was in prison, the LORD said:

[7]Jeremiah, your cousin Hanamel, the son of your uncle Shallum, will visit you. He must sell his field near the town of Anathoth, and because you are his nearest relative, you have the right and the responsibility to buy it and keep it in the family.[z]

[8]Hanamel came, just as the LORD had promised. And he said, "Please buy my field near Anathoth in the territory of the Benjamin tribe. You have the right to buy it, and if you do, it will stay in our family."

The LORD had told me to buy it [9]from Hanamel, and so I did. The price was seventeen pieces of silver, and I weighed out the full amount on a scale. [10-11]I had two copies of the bill of sale written out, each containing all the details of our agreement. Some witnesses and I signed the official copy, which was folded and tied, before being sealed shut with hot wax.[a] Then I gave Hanamel the silver. [12]And while he, the witnesses, and all the other Jews sitting in the courtyard were still watching, I gave both copies to Baruch son of Neriah.[b]

[13-14]I told Baruch that the LORD had said:

Take both copies of this bill of sale, one sealed shut and the other open, and put them in a clay jar so they will last a long time. [15]I am the LORD All-Powerful, the God of Israel, and I promise you that people will once again buy and sell houses, farms, and vineyards in this country.

Jeremiah Questions the LORD

[16]Then I prayed:

[17]LORD God, you stretched out your mighty arm and made the sky and the earth. You can do anything. [18]You show kindness for a thousand generations,[c] but you also punish people for the sins of their parents. You are the LORD All-Powerful. [19]With great wisdom you make plans, and with your great power you do all the mighty things you planned. Nothing we do is hidden from your eyes, and you reward or punish us as we deserve.

[20]You are famous because you worked miracles in Egypt, and you are still working them in Israel and in the rest of the world as well. [21]You terrified the Egyptians with your miracles, and you reached out your mighty arm and rescued your people Israel from Egypt. [22]Then you gave Israel this land rich with milk and honey, just as you had promised our ancestors.

[23]But when our ancestors took over the land, they did not obey you. And now you have punished Israel with disaster. [24]Jerusalem is under attack, and we suffer from hunger and disease. The Babylonians have already built dirt ramps up to the city walls, and you can see that Jerusalem will be captured just as you said. [25]So why did you tell me to get some wit-

---

w**31.40** *that disgusting Hinnom Valley*: The Hebrew text has "the whole valley of the dead bodies and of the fatty ashes," which probably refers to Hinnom Valley, just southwest of Jerusalem, where human sacrifices had been offered to foreign gods. x**32.1** *Zedekiah*: See the note at 1.3. y**32.1** *Nebuchadnezzar*: See the note at 21.2. z**32.7** *you have the right . . . in the family*: See Leviticus 25.25-32. a**32.10,11** *signed the official copy, which was folded and tied, before being sealed shut with hot wax*: The signing was actually done by pressing a carved clay stamp (called a "seal") into the hot wax, leaving the design in the wax. b**32.12** *Baruch son of Neriah*: Hebrew "Baruch son of Neriah and grandson of Mahseiah." c**32.18** *for a thousand generations*: Or "to thousands of people."

nesses and buy a field with my silver, when Jerusalem is about to be captured by the Babylonians?

The LORD Explains about the Field

²⁶The LORD explained:

²⁷Jeremiah, I am the LORD God. I rule the world, and I can do anything!

²⁸It is true that I am going to let King Nebuchadnezzar^d of Babylonia capture Jerusalem. ²⁹The Babylonian army is already attacking, and they will capture the city and set it on fire. The people of Jerusalem have made me angry by going up to the flat roofs of their houses and burning incense to Baal and offering wine sacrifices to other gods. Now these houses will be burned to the ground!

³⁰⁻³³The kings and the officials, the priests and the prophets, and everyone else in Israel and Judah have turned from me and made me angry by worshiping idols. Again and again I have tried to teach my people to obey me, but they refuse to be corrected.

I am going to get rid of Jerusalem, because its people have done nothing but evil. ³⁴They have set up disgusting idols in my temple, and now it isn't a fit place to worship me. ³⁵And they led Judah into sin by building places to worship Baal in Hinnom Valley, where they also sacrificed their sons and daughters to the god Molech. I have never even thought of telling them to commit such disgusting sins.

³⁶Jeremiah, what you said is true. The people of Jerusalem are suffering from hunger and disease, and so the king of Babylonia will be able to capture Jerusalem.

³⁷I am angry at the people of Jerusalem, and I will scatter them in foreign countries. But someday I will bring them back here and let them live in safety. ³⁸They will be my people, and I will be their God. ³⁹⁻⁴¹I will make their thoughts and desires pure. Then they will realize that, for their own good and the good of their children, they must worship only me. They will even be afraid to turn away from me. I will make an agreement with them that will never end, and I won't ever stop doing good things for them. With all my heart I promise that they will be planted in this land once again. ⁴²Even though I have brought disaster on the people, I will someday do all these good things for them.

⁴³Jeremiah, when you bought the field, you showed that fields will someday be

^d**32.28** *Nebuchadnezzar*: See the note at 21.2.

WORK—How can I be a good supervisor? *(Jeremiah 32.26-44)*

Lead by example.

If you want to make an impact on those you supervise, let your actions speak louder than your words. While your words are important, your actions punctuate your words. Lead by example. Don't, for instance, ask your employees to do anything you're not willing to do yourself.

God knew that Jeremiah's actions would have a greater impact on the people than what he said. So he instructed Jeremiah to buy a plot of land, even though that land was about to be captured by Babylon. God used Jeremiah as an example to show that someday, when God restored their land, property would again be bought and sold. During the years of captivity that followed, that example stayed rooted in their minds, giving them hope.

You may never know exactly how your example will affect others. But as you seek to do the right thing and to follow God, he will use you in surprising ways. (See also Exodus 18; 1 Kings 3.5-15; 4.29-34; Ezra 5.1—6.12; John 21.15-25; 2 Timothy 1.1-7; Philemon 8-16; Philemon 15-25.)

Words To Remember: *I will make their thoughts and desires pure. Then they will realize that, for their own good and the good of their children, they must worship only me. They will even be afraid to turn away from me. I will make an agreement with them that will never end, and I won't ever stop doing good things for them.* —Jeremiah 32.39-41

bought and sold again. You say that this land has been conquered by the Babylonians and has become a desert, emptied of people and animals. 44But someday, people will again spend their silver to buy fields everywhere—in the territory of Benjamin, the region around Jerusalem and the towns of Judah, and in the hill country, the foothills to the west, and the Southern Desert. Buyers and sellers and witnesses will sign and seal the bills of sale for the fields. It will happen, because I will give this land back to my people. I, the LORD, have spoken.

The LORD Promises To Give the Land Back to His People

33 1-2I was still being held prisoner in the courtyard of the palace guards when the LORD told me:
I am the LORD, and I created the whole world.c 3Ask me, and I will tell you things that you don't know and can't find out.

4-5Many of the houses in Jerusalem and some of the buildings at the royal palace have been torn down to be used in repairing the walls to keep out the Babylonian attackers.f Now there are empty spaces where the buildings once stood. But I am furious, and these spaces will be filled with the bodies of the people I kill. The people of Jerusalem will cry out to me for help, but they are evil, and I will ignore their prayers.

6Then someday, I will heal this place and my people as well, and let them enjoy unending peace.g 7I will give this land to Israel and Judah once again, and I will make them as strong as they were before. 8They sinned and rebelled against me, but I will forgive them and take away their guilt. 9When that happens, all nations on earth will see the good things I have done for Jerusalem, and how I have given it complete peace. The nations will celebrate and praise and honor me, but they will also tremble with fear.

10Jeremiah, you say that this land is a desert without people or animals, and for now, you are right. The towns of Judah and the streets of Jerusalem are deserted, and people and animals are nowhere to be seen. But someday you will hear 11happy voices and the sounds of parties and wedding celebrations. And when people come to my temple to offer sacrifices to thank me, you will hear them say:

> "We praise you,
>   LORD All-Powerful!
> You are good to us,
>   and your love never fails."

---

c33.1,2 the whole world: One ancient translation; Hebrew "it." f33.4,5 have been torn down . . . Babylonian attackers: One possible meaning for the difficult Hebrew text. g33.6 let them enjoy unending peace: One possible meaning for the difficult Hebrew text.

MARRIAGE—How can I learn to forgive my husband even when he doesn't apologize? (Jeremiah 33.1-9)

Choose to forgive.

In Jeremiah 33.1-9, the Lord modeled what grace and forgiveness was—and what it wasn't. First, forgiveness didn't mean pretending a wrong had not been done. The Lord said the people were evil, he was furious at their sin and rebellion, and he had to punish them (33.4,5). Sin had broken their relationship. In our relationships, sometimes we, too, have to name the sin, confront in love, and explain its consequences.

But then we can choose forgiveness, as God did. "They sinned and rebelled against me, but I will forgive them and take away their guilt," says the Lord (33.8). The Lord chose to forgive, and he himself took away the guilt of sin. He chose to forgive, heal, and bless his people even before they repented. So, too, we must choose to forgive, knowing God has taken away the guilt of sin at a great price—the death of his Son.

God's ability to forgive is rooted in his character. When we find it hard to forgive our husband, it might help to focus on God and how he forgives us, rather than on the wrong done to us. Once we fully grasp grace as displayed by God himself, it's easier to forgive another person. (See also Ephesians 2.14-18; 1 Peter 3.8-15.)

Words To Remember: *I am the LORD, and I created the whole world. Ask me, and I will tell you things that you don't know and can't find out.—Jeremiah 33.1-3*

The land will once again be productive. [12-13]Now it is empty, without people or animals. But when that time comes, shepherds will take care of their flocks in pastures near every town in the hill country, in the foothills to the west, in the Southern Desert, in the land of the Benjamin tribe, and around Jerusalem and the towns of Judah.

I, the LORD, have spoken.

The LORD's Wonderful Promise

[14]The LORD said:

I made a wonderful promise to Israel and Judah,[h] and the days are coming when I will keep it.

[15]I promise that the time will come
    when I will appoint a king
       from the family of David,
    a king who will be honest
       and rule with justice.
[16]In those days,
       Judah will be safe;
    Jerusalem will have peace
    and will be named,
       "The LORD Gives Justice."

[17]The king of Israel will be one of David's descendants, [18]and there will always be priests from the Levi tribe serving at my altar and offering sacrifices to please me and to give thanks.[i]

[19]Then the LORD told me:

[20]I, the LORD, have an agreement with day and night, so they always come at the right time. You can't break the agreement I made with them, [21]and you can't break the agreements I have made with David's family and with the priests from the Levi tribe who serve at my altar. A descendant of David will always rule as king of Israel, [22]and there will be more descendants of David and of the priests from the Levi tribe than stars in the sky or grains of sand on the beach.

[23]The LORD also said:

[24]You've heard foreigners insult my people by saying, "The LORD chose Israel and Judah, but now he has rejected them, and they are no longer a nation."

[25]Jeremiah, I will never break my agreement with the day and the night or let the sky and the earth stop obeying my commands. [26]In the same way, I will never reject the descendants of Abraham, Isaac, and Jacob or break my promise that they will al-

ways have a descendant of David as their king. I will be kind to my people Israel, and they will be successful again.

Jeremiah Warns Zedekiah

34 King Nebuchadnezzar[j] had a large army made up of people from every kingdom in his empire. He and his army were attacking Jerusalem and all the nearby towns, when the LORD told me [2]to say to King Zedekiah:[k]

I am the LORD, and I am going to let Nebuchadnezzar capture this city and burn it down. [3]You will be taken prisoner and brought to Nebuchadnezzar, and he will speak with you face to face. Then you will be led away to Babylonia.

[4]Zedekiah, I promise that you won't die in battle. [5]You will die a peaceful death. People will mourn when you die, and they will light bonfires in your honor, just as they did for your ancestors, the kings who ruled before you.

[6]I went to Zedekiah and told him what the LORD had said. [7]Meanwhile, the king of Babylonia was trying to break through the walls of Lachish, Azekah, and Jerusalem, the only three towns of Judah that had not been captured.

The People Break a Promise

[8-10]King Zedekiah,[k] his officials, and everyone else in Jerusalem made an agreement to free all Hebrew[l] men and women who were slaves. No Jew would keep another as a slave. And so, all the Jewish slaves were given their freedom.

[11]But those slave owners changed their minds and forced their former slaves back into slavery. [12]That's when the LORD told me to say to the people:

[13]I am the LORD God of Israel, and I made an agreement with your ancestors when I brought them out of Egypt, where they had been slaves. [14]As part of this agreement, you must let a Hebrew slave go free after six years of service.

---

[h]33.14 *Israel and Judah*: See the note at 2.4.
[i]33.18 *sacrifices to please me and to give thanks*: See the notes at 14.12. [j]34.1 *Nebuchadnezzar*: See the note at 21.2. [k]34.2,8-10 *Zedekiah*: See the note at 1.3.
[l]34.8-10 *Hebrew*: An earlier term for Israelite and Jewish.

Your ancestors did not obey me, [15-16]but you decided to obey me and do the right thing by setting your Hebrew slaves completely free. You even went to my temple, and in my name you made an agreement to set them free. But you have abused my name, because you broke your agreement and forced your former slaves back into slavery.

[17]You have disobeyed me by not giving your slaves their freedom. So I will give you freedom—the freedom to die in battle or from disease or hunger. I will make you disgusting to all other nations on earth.

[18]You asked me to be a witness when you made the agreement to set your slaves free. And as part of the ceremony you cut a calf into two parts, then walked between the parts. But you people of Jerusalem have broken that agreement as well as my agreement with Israel. So I will do to you what you did to that calf. [19-20]I will let your enemies take all of you prisoner, including the leaders of Judah and Jerusalem, the royal officials, the priests, and everyone else who walked between the two parts of the calf. These enemies will kill you and leave your bodies lying on the ground as food for birds and wild animals.

[21-22]These enemies are King Nebuchadnezzar[m] of Babylonia and his army. They have stopped attacking Jerusalem, but they want to kill King Zedekiah and his high officials. So I will command them to return and attack again. This time they will conquer the city and burn it down, and they will capture Zedekiah and his officials. I will also let them destroy the towns of Judah, so that no one can live there any longer.

Learn a Lesson from the Rechabites

35 When Jehoiakim[n] was king of Judah, the LORD told me, [2]"Go to the Rechabite clan and invite them to meet you in one of the side rooms[o] of the temple. When they arrive, offer them a drink of wine."

[3]So I went to Jaazaniah,[p] the leader of the clan, and I invited him and all the men of his clan. [4]I brought them into the temple courtyard and took them upstairs to a room belonging to the prophets who were followers of Hanan son of Igdaliah. It was next to a room belonging to some of the officials, and that room was over the one belonging to

Maaseiah, a priest who was one of the high officials in the temple.[q]

[5]I set out some large bowls full of wine together with some cups, and then I said to the Rechabites, "Have some wine!"

[6]But they answered:

No! The ancestor of our clan, Jonadab son of Rechab,[r] made a rule that we must obey. He said, "Don't ever drink wine [7]or build houses or plant crops and vineyards. Instead, you must always live in tents and move from place to place. If you obey this command, you will live a long time."

[8-10]Our clan has always obeyed Jonadab's command. To this very day, we and our wives and sons and daughters don't drink wine or build houses or plant vineyards or crops. And we have lived in tents, [11]except now we have to live inside Jerusalem because Nebuchadnezzar[s] has taken over the countryside with his army from Babylonia and Syria.

[12-13]Then the LORD told me to say to the people of Judah and Jerusalem:

I, the LORD All-Powerful, the God of Israel, want you to learn a lesson [14]from the Rechabite clan. Their ancestor Jonadab told his descendants never to drink wine, and to this very day they have obeyed him. But I have spoken to you over and over, and you haven't obeyed me! [15]You refused to listen to my prophets, who kept telling you, "Stop doing evil and worshiping other gods! Start obeying the LORD, and he will let you live in this land he gave your ancestors."

[16]The Rechabites have obeyed the command of their ancestor Jonadab, but you have not obeyed me, [17]your God. I am the LORD All-Powerful, and I warned you about the terrible things

---

[m]**34.21,22** *Nebuchadnezzar*: See the note at 21.2.
[n]**35.1** *Jehoiakim*: See the note at 1.3. [o]**35.2** *side rooms*: Probably a room with walls on three sides, and open to the courtyard on the fourth side. [p]**35.3** *Jaazaniah*: The Hebrew text has "Jaazaniah son of Jeremiah son of Habazziniah"; this is a different Jeremiah than the author of the book. [q]**35.4** *Maaseiah . . . temple*: Hebrew "Maaseiah son of Shallum, the keeper of the temple door." [r]**35.6** *Jonadab son of Rechab*: See 2 Kings 10.15-23. In the Hebrew of this chapter, "Jonadab" is sometimes spelled "Jehonadab." [s]**35.11** *Nebuchadnezzar*: See the note at 21.2.

that would happen to you if you did not listen to me. You have ignored me, so now disaster will strike you. I, the LORD, have spoken.

The LORD Makes a Promise to the Rechabites

[18]Then the LORD told me to say to the Rechabite clan:

I am the LORD All-Powerful, the God of Israel. You have obeyed your ancestor Jonadab, [19]so I promise that your clan will be my servants and will never die out.

King Jehoiakim Burns Jeremiah's First Scroll

36 During the fourth year that Jehoiakim[f] son of Josiah[u] was king of Judah, the LORD said to me, "Jeremiah, [2]since the time Josiah was king, I have been speaking to you about Israel, Judah, and the other nations. Now, get a scroll[v] and write down everything I have told you, [3]then read it to the people of Judah. Maybe they will stop sinning when they hear what terrible things I plan for them. And if they turn to me, I will forgive them."

[4]I sent for Baruch son of Neriah and asked him to help me. I repeated everything the LORD had told me, and Baruch wrote it all down on a scroll. [5]Then I said,

Baruch, the officials refuse to let me go into the LORD's temple, [6]so you must go instead. Wait for the next holy day when the people of Judah come to the temple to pray and to go without eating.[w] Then take this scroll to the temple and read it aloud. [7]The LORD is furious, and if the people hear how he is going to punish them, maybe they will ask to be forgiven.

[8-10]In the ninth month[x] of the fifth year that Jehoiakim was king, the leaders set a day when everyone who lived in Jerusalem or who was visiting here had to pray and go without eating. So Baruch took the scroll to the upper courtyard of the temple. He went over to the side of the courtyard and stood in a covered area near New Gate, where he read the scroll aloud.

This covered area belonged to Gemariah,[y] one of the king's highest officials. [11]Gemariah's son Micaiah was there and heard Baruch read what the LORD had said. [12]When Baruch finished reading, Micaiah went down to the palace. His father

Gemariah was in the officials' room, meeting with the rest of the king's officials, including Elishama, Delaiah, Elnathan, and Zedekiah.[z] [13]Micaiah told them what he had heard Baruch reading to the people. [14]Then the officials sent Jehudi and Shelemiah[a] to tell Baruch, "Bring us that scroll."

When Baruch arrived with the scroll, [15]the officials said, "Please sit down and read it to us," which he did. [16]After they heard what was written on the scroll, they were worried and said to each other, "The king needs to hear this!" Turning to Baruch, they asked, [17]"Did someone tell you what to write on this scroll?"

[18]"Yes, Jeremiah did," Baruch replied. "I wrote down just what he told me."

[19]The officials said, "You and Jeremiah must go into hiding, and don't tell anyone where you are."

[20-22]The officials put the scroll in Elishama's room and went to see the king, who was in one of the rooms where he lived and worked during the winter. It was the ninth month[b] of the year, so there was a fire burning in the fireplace,[c] and the king was sitting nearby. After the officials told the king about the scroll, he sent Jehudi to get it. Then Jehudi started reading the scroll to the king and his officials. [23-25]But every time Jehudi finished reading three or four columns, the king would tell him to cut them off with his penknife and throw them in the fire. Elnathan, Delaiah, and Gemariah begged the king not to burn the scroll, but he ignored them, and soon there was nothing left of it.

The king and his servants listened to what was written on the scroll, but they were not afraid, and they did not tear their clothes in sorrow.[d]

---

[f]36.1 *Jehoiakim*: See the note at 1.3.   [u]36.1 *Josiah*: See the note at 3.6.   [v]36.2 *scroll*: See the note at 30.1, 2.
[w]36.6 *to go without eating*: As a way of asking for God's help.   [x]36.8-10 *ninth month*: Chislev, the ninth month of the Hebrew calendar, from about mid-November to mid-December.   [y]36.8-10 *Gemariah*: Hebrew "Gemariah son of Shaphan"; Gemariah's brother Ahikam had earlier protected Jeremiah (see 26.20-24).
[z]36.12 *Delaiah, Elnathan, and Zedekiah*: Hebrew "Delaiah son of Shemaiah, Elnathan son of Achbor, and Zedekiah son of Hananiah."   [a]36.14 *Jehudi and Shelemiah*: Hebrew "Jehudi son of Nethaniah and Shelemiah son of Cushi."   [b]36.20-22 *ninth month*: See the note at 36.8-10.   [c]36.20-22 *fireplace*: Probably a large metal or clay pot on a movable stand, with the fire burning inside.   [d]36.23-25 *they did not tear their clothes in sorrow*: Such actions would have shown that they were sorry for disobeying the LORD and were turning back to him.

[26]The king told his son Jerahmeel to take Seraiah and Shelemiah[e] and to go arrest Baruch and me.[f] But the LORD kept them from finding us.

Jeremiah's Second Scroll

[27]I had told Baruch what to write on that first scroll,[g] but King Jehoiakim[h] had burned it. So the LORD told me [28]to get another scroll and write down everything that had been on the first one. [29]Then he told me to say to King Jehoiakim:

Not only did you burn Jeremiah's scroll, you had the nerve to ask why he had written that the king of Babylonia would attack and ruin the land, killing all the people and even the animals. [30]So I, the LORD, promise that you will be killed and your body thrown out on the ground. The sun will beat down on it during the day, and the frost will settle on it at night. And none of your descendants will ever be king of Judah. [31]You, your children, and your servants are evil, and I will punish all of you. I warned you and the people of Judah and Jerusalem that I would bring disaster, but none of you have listened. So now you are doomed!

[32]After the LORD finished speaking to me, I got another scroll and gave it to Baruch. Then I told him what to write, so this second scroll would contain even more than was on the scroll Jehoiakim had burned.

King Zedekiah Asks Jeremiah To Pray

37 King Nebuchadnezzar[i] of Babylonia had removed Jehoiachin[j] son of Jehoiakim[k] from being the king of Judah and had made Josiah's[l] son Zedekiah[m] king instead.[n] [2]But Zedekiah, his officials, and everyone else in Judah ignored everything the LORD had told me.

[3-5]Later, the Babylonian army attacked Jerusalem, but they left after learning that the Egyptian army[o] was headed in this direction.

One day, Zedekiah sent Jehucal and the priest Zephaniah[p] to talk with me. At that time, I was free to go wherever I wanted, because I had not yet been put in prison. Jehucal and Zephaniah said, "Jeremiah, please pray to the LORD our God for us."

[6-7]Then the LORD told me to send them back to Zedekiah with this message:

Zedekiah, you wanted Jeremiah to ask me, the LORD God of Israel, what is going to happen. So I will tell you. The king of Egypt and his army came to your rescue, but soon they will go back to Egypt. [8]Then the Babylonians will return and attack Jerusalem, and this time they will capture the city and set it on fire. [9]Don't fool yourselves into thinking that the Babylonians will leave as they did before. [10]Even if you could defeat their entire army, their wounded survivors would still be able to leave their tents and set Jerusalem on fire.

Jeremiah Is Put in Prison

[11]The Babylonian army had left because the Egyptian army was on its way to help us. [12]So I decided to leave Jerusalem and go to the territory of the Benjamin tribe to claim my share of my family's land. [13]I was leaving Jerusalem through Benjamin Gate, when I was stopped by Irijah,[q] the officer in charge of the soldiers at the gate. He said, "Jeremiah, you're under arrest for trying to join the Babylonians."

[14]"I'm not trying to join them!" I answered. But Irijah wouldn't listen, and he took me to the king's officials. [15-16]They were angry and ordered the soldiers to beat me. Then I was taken to the house that belonged to Jonathan, one of the king's officials. It had been turned into a prison, and I was kept in a basement room.

After I had spent a long time there, [17]King Zedekiah secretly had me brought to his palace, where he asked, "Is there any message for us from the LORD?"

"Yes, there is, Your Majesty," I replied. "The LORD is going to let the king of Babylonia capture you."

---

[e]**36.26** *Seraiah and Shelemiah*: Hebrew "Seraiah son of Azriel and Shelemiah son of Abdeel." [f]**36.26** *me*: Jeremiah. [g]**36.27** *scroll*: See the note at 30.1, 2. [h]**36.27** *Jehoiakim*: See the note at 1.3. [i]**37.1** *Nebuchadnezzar*: See the note at 21.2. [j]**37.1** *Jehoiachin*: Hebrew "Coniah" (see the note at 22.24). [k]**37.1** *Jehoiakim*: See the note at 1.3. [l]**37.1** *Josiah's*: Josiah was the father of both Jehoiakim and Zedekiah. Josiah ruled 640-609 B.C. [m]**37.1** *Zedekiah*: See the note at 1.3. [n]**37.1** *King Nebuchadnezzar . . . instead*: See 2 Kings 24.10-17. [o]**37.3-5** *Egyptian army*: Led by King Apries, also known as Hophra. [p]**37.3-5** *Jehucal and the priest Zephaniah*: Hebrew "Jehucal son of Shelemiah, and the priest Zephaniah son of Maaseiah." [q]**37.13** *Irijah*: Hebrew "Irijah son of Shelemiah and grandson of Hananiah."

[18]Then I continued, "Your Majesty, why have you put me in prison? Have I committed a crime against you or your officials or the nation? [19]Have you locked up the prophets who lied to you and said that the king of Babylonia would never attack Jerusalem? [20]Please, don't send me back to that prison at Jonathan's house. If you do, I will die."

[21]King Zedekiah had me taken to the prison cells in the courtyard of the palace guards. He told the soldiers to give me a loaf of bread[r] from one of the bakeries every day until the city ran out of grain.

Jeremiah Is Held Prisoner in a Dry Well

38 One day, Shephatiah, Gedaliah, Jehucal,[s] and Pashhur[t] heard me tell the people of Judah [2-3]that the LORD had said, "If you stay here in Jerusalem, you will die in battle or from disease or hunger, and the Babylonian army will capture the city anyway. But if you surrender to the Babylonians, they will let you live."

[4]So the four of them went to the king and said, "You should put Jeremiah to death, because he is making the soldiers and everyone else lose hope. He isn't trying to help our people; he's trying to harm them."

[5]Zedekiah replied, "Do what you want with him. I can't stop you."

[6]Then they took me back to the courtyard of the palace guards and let me down with ropes into the well that belonged to Malchiah, the king's son. There was no water in the well, and I sank down in the mud.

[7-8]Ebedmelech from Ethiopia[u] was an official at the palace, and he heard what they had done to me. So he went to speak with King Zedekiah, who was holding court at Benjamin Gate. [9]Ebedmelech said, "Your Majesty, Jeremiah is a prophet, and those men were wrong to throw him into a well. And when Jerusalem runs out of food, Jeremiah will starve to death down there."

[10]Zedekiah answered, "Take thirty[v] of my soldiers and pull Jeremiah out before he dies."

[11]Ebedmelech and the soldiers went to the palace and got some rags from the room under the treasury. He used ropes to lower them into the well. [12]Then he said, "Put these rags under your arms so the ropes won't hurt you." After I did, [13]the men pulled me out. And from then on, I was kept in the courtyard of the palace guards.

King Zedekiah Questions Jeremiah

[14]King Zedekiah[w] had me brought to his private entrance[x] to the temple, and he said, "I'm going to ask you something, and I want to know the truth."

[15]"Why?" I replied. "You won't listen, and you might even have me killed!"

[16]He said, "I swear in the name of the living LORD our Creator that I won't have you killed. No one else can hear what we say, and I won't let anyone kill you."

[17]Then I told him that the LORD had said: "Zedekiah, I am the LORD God All-Powerful, the God of Israel. I promise that if you surrender to King Nebuchadnezzar's[y] officers, you and your family won't be killed, and Jerusalem won't be burned down. [18]But if you don't surrender, I will let the Babylonian army capture Jerusalem and burn it down, and you will be taken prisoner."

[19]Zedekiah answered, "I can't surrender to the Babylonians. I'm too afraid of the Jews that have already joined them. The Babylonians might hand me over to those Jews, and they would torture me."

[20]I said, "If you will just obey the LORD, the Babylonians won't hand you over to those Jews. You will be allowed to live, and all will go well for you. [21]But the LORD has shown me that if you refuse to obey, [22]then the women of your palace will be taken prisoner by Nebuchadnezzar's officials. And those women will say to you:

Friends you trusted led you astray.
　Now you're trapped in mud,
and those friends you trusted
　have all turned away.

---

[r]37.21 *a loaf of bread*: Bread was the main food of the Israelites. During this time of emergency in Jerusalem, everyone probably received the same amount each day. [s]38.1 *Jehucal*: The Hebrew text has "Jucal," another form of the name. [t]38.1 *Shephatiah, Gedaliah, Jehucal, and Pashhur*: Hebrew "Shephatiah son of Mattan, Gedaliah son of Pashhur, Jucal son of Shelemiah, and Pashhur son of Malchiah." [u]38.7,8 *Ethiopia*: The Hebrew text has "Cush," a region south of Egypt that included parts of the present countries of Ethiopia and Sudan. [v]38.10 *thirty*: Most Hebrew manuscripts; one Hebrew manuscript "three." [w]38.14 See the note at 1.3. [x]38.14 *his private entrance*: One possible meaning for the difficult Hebrew text. [y]38.17 *Nebuchadnezzar's*: See the note at 21.2.

²³The Babylonian army will take your wives and children captive, you will be taken as a prisoner to the King of Babylonia, and Jerusalem will be burned down."ᶻ

²⁴Zedekiah said, "Jeremiah, if you tell anyone what we have talked about, you might lose your life. ²⁵And I'm sure that if my officials hear about our meeting, they will ask you what we said to each other. They might even threaten to kill you if you don't tell them. ²⁶So if they question you, tell them you were begging me not to send you back to the prison at Jonathan's house, because going back there would kill you."

²⁷The officials did come and question me about my meeting with the king, and I told them exactly what he had ordered me to say. They never spoke to me about the meeting again, since no one had heard us talking.

²⁸I was held in the courtyard of the palace guards until the day Jerusalem was captured.

Jerusalem Is Captured by the Babylonians
(*Jeremiah 52.4-16; 2 Kings 25.1-12*)

39 ¹⁻³In the tenth monthᵃ of the ninth year that Zedekiahᵇ was king of Judah, King Nebuchadnezzarᶜ and the Babylonian army began their attack on Jerusalem. They kept the city surrounded for a year and a half. Then, on the ninth day of the fourth monthᵈ of the eleventh year that Zedekiah was king, they broke through the city walls.

After Jerusalem was captured,ᵉ Nebuchadnezzar's highest officials,ᶠ including Nebo Sarsechimᵍ and Nergal Sharezer from Simmagir,ʰ took their places at Middle Gate to show they were in control of the city.ⁱ

⁴When King Zedekiah and his troops saw that Jerusalem had been captured, they tried to escape from the city that same night. They went to the king's garden, where they slipped through the gate between the two city wallsʲ and headed toward the Jordan River valley. ⁵But the Babylonian troops caught up with them near Jericho. They arrested Zedekiah and took him to the town of Riblah in the land of Hamath, where Nebuchadnezzar put him on trial, then found him guilty ⁶and gave orders for him to be punished. Zedekiah's sons were killed there in front of him, and so were the leaders of Judah's ruling families. ⁷His eyes were

poked out, and he was put in chains, so he could be dragged off to Babylonia.

⁸Meanwhile, the Babylonian army had burned the houses in Jerusalem, includingᵏ the royal palace, and they had broken down the city walls. ⁹Nebuzaradan, the Babylonian officer in charge of the guards, led away everyone from the city as prisoners, even those who had deserted to Nebuchadnezzar. ¹⁰Only the poorest people who owned no land were left behind in Judah, and Nebuzaradan gave them fields and vineyards.

¹¹Nebuchadnezzar had given the following orders to Nebuzaradan: ¹²"Find Jeremiah and keep him safe. Take good care of him and do whatever he asks."

¹³Nebuzaradan, Nebushazban, Nergal Sharezer, and the other officers of King Nebuchadnezzar ¹⁴sent some of their troops to bring me from the courtyard of the royal palace guards. They put me in the care of Gedaliah son of Ahikamˡ and told him to take me to my home. And so I was allowed to stay with the people who remained in Judah.

The LORD Promises To Protect Ebedmelech

¹⁵While I was a prisoner in the courtyard of the palace guard, the LORD told me to say ¹⁶to Ebedmelech from Ethiopia:ᵐ

ᶻ**38.23** *Jerusalem will be burned down*: A few Hebrew manuscripts and three ancient translations; most Hebrew manuscripts "you will burn Jerusalem down"; one ancient translation "he will burn Jerusalem down." ᵃ**39.1-3** *the tenth month*: Tebeth, the tenth month of the Hebrew calendar, from about mid-December to mid-January. ᵇ**39.1-3** *Zedekiah*: See the note at 1.3. ᶜ**39.1-3** *Nebuchadnezzar*: See the note at 21.2. ᵈ**39.1-3** *fourth month*: Tammuz, the fourth month of the Hebrew calendar, from about mid-June to mid-July. ᵉ**39.1-3** *After Jerusalem was captured*: This phrase is from 38.28. ᶠ**39.1-3** *highest officials*: The Hebrew text gives Nergal Sharezer's title as "the Rabmag," and Nebo Sarsechim's title as "the Rabsaris," but the exact meaning of the titles and the duties of these offices are not known. ᵍ**39.1-3** *Nebo Sarsechim*: Probably another form of the name Nebushazban (see verse 13). ʰ**39.1-3** *Nergal Sharezer from Simmagir*: One possible meaning for the difficult Hebrew text. Probably Nebuchadnezzar's son-in-law, who was king of Babylonia 560-556 B.C. It is also possible that the Hebrew text mentions a second official named Nergal Sharezer. ⁱ**39.1-3** *took their places . . . control of the city*: The rulers and leaders often sat in the broad open area at the gate of a city to take care of official business and hold trials. ʲ**39.4** *the gate between the two city walls*: The construction of the city walls at this point is not known. ᵏ**39.8** *the houses in Jerusalem, including*: Or "the temple and." ˡ**39.14** *son of Ahikam*: Hebrew "son of Ahikam and grandson of Shaphan." ᵐ**39.16** *Ethiopia*: See the note at 38.7, 8.

I am the LORD All-Powerful, the God of Israel. I warned everyone that I would bring disaster, not prosperity, to this city. Now very soon I will do what I said, and you will see it happen. [17-18]But because you trusted me,[n] I will protect you from the officials of Judah, and when Judah is struck by disaster, I will rescue you and keep you alive. I, the LORD, have spoken.

Jeremiah Is Set Free

40 I was led away in chains along with the people of Judah and Jerusalem who were being taken to Babylonia. Nebuzaradan was the officer in charge of the guard, and while we were stopped at Ramah, the LORD had him set me free. [2]Nebuzaradan said:

Jeremiah, the LORD your God warned your people that he would bring disaster on this land. [3]But they continued to rebel against him, and now he has punished them just as he threatened.

After seeing God's promises apply to my life and experiencing firsthand his gracious provision, I am more convinced than ever that God keeps his word.

MARIAN V. LIAUTAUD

---

[4]Today I am taking the chains off your wrists and setting you free! If you want to, you can come with me to Babylonia, and I will see that you are taken care of. Or if you decide to stay here, you can go wherever you wish. [5]King Nebuchadnezzar[o] has chosen Gedaliah to rule Judah. You can live near Gedaliah, and he will provide for you, or you can live anywhere else you want.

Nebuzaradan gave me a supply of food, then let me leave. [6]I decided to stay with the people of Judah, and I went to live near Gedaliah in Mizpah.

The Harvest Is Brought In

[7-8]Ishmael the son of Nethaniah, together with Johanan and Jonathan, the two sons of Kareah, had been officers in Judah's army. And so had Seraiah the son of Tanhumeth, the sons of Ephai the Netophathite, and Jezaniah from Maacah. They and their troops had been stationed outside Jerusalem and had not been captured. They heard that Gedaliah had been chosen to rule Judah, and that the poorest men, women, and children had not been taken away to Babylonia. So they went to Mizpah and met with their new ruler.

[9]Gedaliah told them, "There's no need to be afraid of the Babylonians. Everything will be fine, if we live peacefully and obey King Nebuchadnezzar.[o] [10]I will stay here at Mizpah and meet with the Babylonian officials on each of their visits. But you must go back to your towns and bring in the harvest, then store the wine, olive oil, and dried fruit."

[11-12]Earlier, when the Babylonians had invaded Judah, many of the Jews escaped to Moab, Ammon, Edom, and several other countries. But these Jews heard that the king of Babylonia had appointed Gedaliah as ruler of Judah, and that only a few people were left there. So the Jews in these other countries came back to Judah and helped with the grape and fruit harvest, which was especially large that year.

Gedaliah Is Murdered

[13]One day, Johanan got together with some of the other men who had been army officers, and they came to Mizpah and met with Gedaliah. [14]They said, "Gedaliah, we came to warn you that King Baalis of Ammon hired Ishmael to murder you!"

Gedaliah refused to believe them, [15]so Johanan went to Gedaliah privately and said, "Let me kill Ishmael. No one will find out who did it. There are only a few people left in Judah, but they are depending on you. And if you are murdered, they will be scattered or killed."

[16]Gedaliah answered, "Don't kill Ishmael! What you've said about him can't be true."

---

[n]**39.17,18** *you trusted me*: See 38.7-13, where Ebedmelech helped Jeremiah.   [o]**40.5,9** *Nebuchadnezzar*: See the note at 21.2.

41

But in the seventh month,[p] Ishmael[q] came to Mizpah with ten of his soldiers. He had been one of the king's officials and was a member of the royal family. Ishmael and his men were invited to eat with Gedaliah. [2]During the meal, Ishmael and his soldiers killed Gedaliah, the man chosen as ruler of Judah by the king of Babylonia. [3]Then they killed the Jews who were with Gedaliah, and they also killed the Babylonian soldiers who were there.

[4]The next day, the murders had still not been discovered, [5]when eighty men came down the road toward Mizpah from the towns of Shechem, Shiloh, and Samaria. They were on their way to the temple to offer gifts of grain and incense to the LORD. They had shaved off their beards, torn their clothes, and cut themselves, because they were mourning.

[6]Ishmael went out the town gate to meet them. He pretended to be weeping, and he asked them to come into Mizpah to meet with Gedaliah, the ruler of Judah. [7]But after they were inside the town, Ishmael had his soldiers kill them and throw their bodies into a well. [8]He let ten of the men live, because they offered to give him supplies of wheat, barley, olive oil, and honey they had hidden in a field. [9]The well that he filled with bodies had been dug by King Asa[r] of Judah to store rainwater, because he was afraid that King Baasha[s] of Israel might surround Mizpah and keep the people from getting to their water supply.

[10]Nebuzaradan, King Nebuchadnezzar's[t] officer in charge of the guard, had left King Zedekiah's[u] daughters and many other people at Mizpah, and he had put Gedaliah in charge of them. But now Ishmael took them all prisoner and led them toward Ammon, on the other side of the Jordan River.

[11]Johanan and the other army officers heard what Ishmael had done. [12]So they and their troops chased Ishmael and caught up with him at the large pit at Gibeon. [13]When Ishmael's prisoners saw Johanan and the officers, they were happy [14]and turned around and ran toward Johanan. [15]But Ishmael and eight of his men escaped and went to Ammon.

Johanan Decides To Take the People to Egypt

[16]Johanan and the officers had rescued the women, children, and royal officials that

Ishmael had taken prisoner after killing Gedaliah. Johanan led the people from Gibeon [17-18]toward Egypt. They wanted to go there, because they were afraid of what the Babylonians would do when they found out that Ishmael had killed Gedaliah, the ruler appointed by King Nebuchadnezzar.[v]

The People Ask Jeremiah To Pray for Them

On the way to Egypt, we[w] stopped at the town of Geruth Chimham near Bethlehem.

42

[1]Johanan, Jezaniah,[x] the other army officers, and everyone else in the group, came to me [2]and said, "Please pray to the LORD your God for us. Judah used to have many people, but as you can see, only a few of us are left. [3]Ask the LORD to tell us where he wants us to go and what he wants us to do."

[4]"All right," I answered, "I will pray to the LORD your God, and I will tell you everything he says."

[5]They answered, "The LORD himself will be our witness that we promise to do whatever he says, [6]even if it isn't what we want to do. We will obey the LORD so that all will go well for us."

[7]Ten days later, the LORD gave me an answer for [8]Johanan, the officers, and the other people. So I called them together [9]and told them that the LORD God of Israel had said:

You asked Jeremiah to pray and find out what you should do. [10]I am sorry that I had to punish you, and so I now tell you to stay here in Judah, where I will plant you and build you up, instead of tearing you down and uprooting you. [11]Don't be afraid of the King of Babylonia. I will protect you from him, [12]and I will even force him

---

[p]41.1 seventh month: Tishri, also called Ethanim, the seventh month of the Hebrew calendar, from about mid-September to mid-October.   [q]41.1 Ishmael: Hebrew "Ishmael son of Nethaniah and grandson of Elishama."   [r]41.9 Asa: Ruled 911-870 B.C.
[s]41.9 Baasha: Ruled 909-886 B.C.
[t]41.10 Nebuchadnezzar's: See the note at 21.2.
[u]41.10 Zedekiah's: See the note at 1.3.
[v]41.17,18 Nebuchadnezzar: See the note at 21.2.
[w]41.17,18 we: The group of people included Jeremiah, since he had been staying with Gedaliah near Mizpah (see 40.6).   [x]42.1 Jezaniah: Hebrew "Jezaniah son of Hoshaiah"; one ancient translation "Azariah son of Hoshaiah" (see also 43.2 and the note there).

The LORD Will Destroy the People of Judah

44 The LORD told me to speak with the Jews who were living in the towns of Migdol, Tahpanhes, and Memphis in northern Egypt, and also to those living in southern Egypt. He told me to tell them:

²I am the LORD All-Powerful, the God of Israel. You saw how I destroyed Jerusalem and the towns of Judah. They lie empty and in ruins today, ³because the people of Judah made me angry by worshiping gods that had never helped them or their ancestors.

⁴Time after time I sent my servants the prophets to tell the people of Judah how much I hated their disgusting sins. The prophets warned them to stop sinning, ⁵but they refused to listen and would not stop worshiping other gods. ⁶Finally, my anger struck like a raging flood, and today Jerusalem and the towns of Judah are nothing but empty ruins.

⁷Why do you now insist on heading for another disaster? A disaster that will destroy not only you, but also your children and babies. ⁸You have made me angry by worshiping idols and burning incense to other gods after you came here to Egypt. You will die such a disgusting death, that other nations will use the name of Judah as a curse word. ⁹When you were living in Jerusalem and Judah, you followed the example of your ancestors in doing evil things, just like your kings and queens. ¹⁰Even now, your pride keeps you from respecting me and obeying the laws and teachings I gave you and your ancestors.

¹¹I, the LORD All-Powerful, have decided to wipe you out with disasters. ¹²There were only a few of you left in Judah, and you decided to go to Egypt. But you will die such horrible deaths in war or from starvation, that people of other countries will use the name of Judah as a curse word. ¹³I punished Jerusalem with war, hunger, and disease, and that's how I will punish you. ¹⁴None of you will survive. You may hope to return to Judah someday, but only a very few of you will escape death and be able to go back.

The People Refuse To Worship the LORD

¹⁵A large number of Jews from both northern and southern Egypt listened to me as I told them what the LORD had said. Most of the men in the crowd knew that their wives often burned incense to other gods. So they and their wives shouted:

¹⁶Jeremiah, what do we care if you speak in the LORD's name? We refuse to listen! ¹⁷We have promised to worship the goddess Astarte, the Queen of Heaven,ᶜ and that is exactly what we are going to do. We will burn incense and offer sacrifices of wine to her, just as we, our ancestors, our kings, and our leaders did when we lived in Jerusalem and the other towns of Judah. We had plenty of food back then. We were well off, and nothing bad ever happened to us. ¹⁸But since the time we stopped burning incense and offering wine sacrifices to her, we have been dying from war and hunger.

Worship is not something we do. It's a realization of who we are: the almighty Father's children.

RAMONA CRAMER TUCKER

¹⁹Then the women said, "When we lived in Judah, we worshiped the Queen of Heaven and offered sacrifices of wine and special loaves of bread shaped like her. Our husbands knew what we were doing, and they approved of it."

²⁰Then I told the crowd:

²¹Don't you think the LORD knew that you and your ancestors, your leaders and kings, and the rest of the

---

ᶜ**44.17** *the goddess Astarte, the Queen of Heaven*: The Hebrew text has "the queen of heaven," which probably refers to the goddess Astarte.

to have mercy on you and give back your farms.

Faith is present-tense action. It's taking God's promises and acting on them <u>today</u>.

JONI EARECKSON TADA

¹³But you might keep on saying, "We won't stay here in Judah, and we won't obey the LORD our God. ¹⁴We are going to Egypt, where there is plenty of food and no danger of war."

¹⁵People of Judah, you survived when the Babylonian army attacked. Now you are planning to move to Egypt, and if you do go, this is what will happen. ¹⁶⁻¹⁷You are afraid of war, starvation, and disease here in Judah, but they will follow you to Egypt and kill you there. None of you will survive the disasters I will send.

¹⁸I, the LORD, was angry with the people of Jerusalem and punished them. And if you go to Egypt, I will be angry and punish you the same way. You will never again see your homeland. People will be horrified at what I do to you, and they will use the name of your city as a curse word.

Jeremiah Gives a Warning

¹⁹I told the people:

You escaped the disaster that struck Judah, but now the LORD warns you to stay away from Egypt. ²⁰You asked me to pray and find out what the LORD our God wants you to do, and you promised to obey him. But that was a terrible mistake, ²¹because now that I have given you the LORD's answer, you refuse to obey him. ²²And so, you will die in Egypt from war, hunger, and disease.

The People Go to Egypt

43 ¹I told the people everything the LORD had told me. ²But Azariah, Johanan^y and some other arro-

gant men said to me, "You're lying! The LORD didn't tell you to say that we shouldn't go to Egypt. ³Baruch son of Neriah must have told you to say that. He wants the Babylonians to capture us, so they can take us away to Babylonia or even kill us."

⁴Johanan, the other army officers, and everyone else refused to stay in Judah in spite of the LORD's command. ⁵So Johanan and the officers led us away toward Egypt. The group that left Judah included those who had been scattered in other countries and who had then come back to live in Judah. ⁶Baruch and I and others in the group had been staying with Gedaliah, because Nebuzaradan, the Babylonian officer in charge of the guard, had ordered him to take care of the king's daughters and quite a few men, women, and children.

⁷The people disobeyed the LORD and went to Egypt. The group had settled in Tahpanhes, ⁸when the LORD told me:

⁹Jeremiah, carry some large stones to the entrance of the government building in Tahpanhes. Bury the stones underneath the brick pavement^z and be sure the Jews are watching.

¹⁰Then tell them that I, the LORD All-Powerful, the God of Israel, have sent for my servant, Nebuchadnezzar^a of Babylonia. I will bring him here and have him set up his throne and his royal tent over these stones that I told you to bury. ¹¹He will attack Egypt and kill many of its people; others will die of disease or be dragged away as prisoners. ¹²⁻¹³I will have him set Egypt's temples on fire, and he will either burn or carry off their idols. He will destroy the sacred monuments at the temple of the sun-god.^{b} Then Nebuchadnezzar will pick the land clean, just like a shepherd picking the lice off his clothes. And he will return safely home.

---

^{y}**43.2** *Azariah, Johanan:* Hebrew "Azariah son of Hoshaiah, Johanan son of Kareah." ^{z}**43.9** *underneath the brick pavement:* One possible meaning for the difficult Hebrew text. ^{a}**43.10** *Nebuchadnezzar:* See the note at 21.2. ^{b}**43.12,13** *at the temple of the sun-god:* Or "in the city of Heliopolis."

people were burning incense to other gods in Jerusalem and everywhere else in Judah? [22]And when he could no longer put up with your disgusting sins, he placed a curse on your land and turned it into a desert, as it is today. [23]This disaster happened because you worshiped other gods and rebelled against the LORD by refusing to obey him or follow his laws and teachings.

[24-25]Then I told the men and their wives, that the LORD All-Powerful, the God of Israel, had said:

Here in Egypt you still keep your promises to burn incense and offer sacrifices of wine to the so-called Queen of Heaven. [26]Keep these promises! But let me tell you what will happen. As surely as I am the LORD God, I swear that I will never again accept any promises you make in my name. [27]Instead of watching over you, I will watch for chances to harm you. Some of you will die in war, and others will starve to death. [28]Only a few will escape and return to Judah. Then everyone who went to live in Egypt will know that when I say something will happen, it will—no matter what you say.

[29]And here is how you will know that I will keep my threats to punish you in Egypt. [30]I will hand over King Hophra of Egypt to those who want to kill him,[d] just as I handed Zedekiah[e] over to Nebuchadnezzar,[f] who wanted to kill him.

The LORD Will Not Let Baruch Be Killed

45 In the fourth year that Jehoiakim[g] was king of Judah, Baruch wrote down everything I had told him.[h] [2]Then later, the LORD God of Israel told me to say to Baruch:

[3]You are moaning and blaming me, the LORD, for your troubles and sorrow, and for being so tired that you can't even rest. [4]But all over the earth I am tearing down what I built and pulling up what I planted. [5]I am bringing disaster everywhere, so don't even think about making any big plans for yourself. However, I promise that

wherever you go, I will at least protect you from death. I, the LORD, have spoken.

The LORD Speaks about the Nations

46 The LORD often told me what to say about the different nations of the world.

What the LORD Says about Egypt

[2]In the fourth year that Jehoiakim[i] was king of Judah, King Nebuchadnezzar[j] of Babylonia defeated King Neco of Egypt[k] in a battle at the city of Carchemish near the Euphrates River. And here is what the LORD told me to say about the Egyptian army:

[3]It's time to go into battle!
    So grab your shields,
[4]   saddle your horses,
    and polish your spears.
Put on your helmets and armor,
    then take your positions.

[5]I can see the battle now—
    you are defeated
and running away,
    never once looking back.
Terror is all around.
[6]You are strong and run fast,
    but you can't escape.
You fall in battle
    near the Euphrates River.

[7]What nation is this,
    that rises like the Nile River
    overflowing its banks?
[8]It is Egypt, rising with a roar
    like a raging river
    and saying,
"I'll flood the earth,
    destroying cities, and killing
    everyone in them."

---

[d]**44.30** *King Hophra . . . kill him*: Hophra, also known as Apries, ruled Egypt from 589 to 570 B.C., when he was killed by Ahmosis II, who then became king of Egypt and ruled until 526 B.C.   [e]**44.30** *Zedekiah*: See the note at 1.3.   [f]**44.30** *Nebuchadnezzar*: See the note at 21.2.
[g]**45.1** *Jehoiakim*: See the note at 1.3.   [h]**45.1** *Baruch wrote down everything I had told him*: See 36.1-32.
[i]**46.2** *Jehoiakim*: See the note at 1.3.   [j]**46.2** *King Nebuchadnezzar*: Ruled 605-562 B.C. At the time of the battle in 605 B.C., he was crown prince, but his father died a few months later, and he became king.
[k]**46.2** *King Neco of Egypt*: Neco II, ruled 609-594 B.C.

⁹Go ahead, Egypt.
Tell your chariots and cavalry
to attack and fight hard.
Order your troops to march out,
with Ethiopians[l] and Libyans
carrying shields,
and the Lydians[m] armed with bows
and arrows.

¹⁰But the LORD All-Powerful
will win this battle
and take revenge
on his enemies.
His sword will eat them
and drink their blood
until it is full.
They will be killed in the north
near the Euphrates River,
as a sacrifice to the LORD.

¹¹Egypt, no medicine can heal you,
not even the soothing lotion
from Gilead.
¹²All nations have heard you weep;
you are disgraced,
and they know it.
Your troops fall to the ground,
stumbling over each other.

A Warning for Egypt

¹³⁻¹⁴When King Nebuchadnezzar[n] of
Babylonia was on his way to attack Egypt,
the LORD sent me with a warning for every
Egyptian town, but especially for Migdol,
Memphis, and Tahpanhes. He said to tell
them:

Prepare to defend yourselves!
Everywhere in your nation,
people are dying in war.
¹⁵I have struck down
your mighty god Apis[o]
and chased him away.[p]
¹⁶Your soldiers stumble
over each other
and say, "Get up!
The enemy will kill us,
unless we can escape
to our own land."

¹⁷Give the king of Egypt
this new name,
"Talks-Big-Does-Nothing."

¹⁸Egypt, I am the true king,
the LORD All-Powerful,
and as surely as I live,
those enemies who attack
will tower over you
like Mount Tabor among the hills
or Mount Carmel by the sea.
¹⁹You will be led away captive,
so pack a few things
to bring with you.
Your capital, Memphis,
will lie empty and in ruins.

²⁰An enemy from the north
will attack you, beautiful Egypt,
like a fly biting a cow.
²¹The foreign soldiers you hired
will turn and run.
But they are doomed,
like well-fed calves
being led to the butcher.

*²²The enemy army will go forward
like a swarm of locusts.[q]
Your troops will feel helpless,
like a snake in a forest
²³when men with axes
start chopping down trees.
It can only hiss
and try to escape.
²⁴Your people will be disgraced
and captured by the enemy
from the north.

²⁵I am the LORD All-Powerful, the God of
Israel. Soon I will punish the god Amon of
Thebes[r] and the other Egyptian gods, the
Egyptian kings, the people of Egypt, and
everyone who trusts in the Egyptian power.
²⁶I will hand them over to King Nebuchadnezzar and his army. But I also promise that
Egypt will someday have people living here
again, just as it had before. I, the LORD, have
spoken.

---

[l]46.9 *Ethiopians*: See the note at 38.7, 8.
[m]46.9 *Lydians*: Probably hired soldiers from
Lydia, an area in west-central Asia minor.
[n]46.13,14 *Nebuchadnezzar*: See the note at 21.2.
[o]46.15 *Apis*: A sacred bull, kept in a temple at
Memphis, Egypt, and worshiped as a god.
[p]46.15 *I have . . . him away*: One possible meaning
for the difficult Hebrew text.   [q]46.22 *locusts*: A type
of grasshopper that comes in swarms and causes great
damage to plant life.   [r]46.25 *the god Amon of Thebes*:
Amon was the king of the Egyptian gods and was the
special god of the Egyptian kings.

The LORD Will Bring Israel Home

The LORD said:

²⁷ Israel,^s don't be afraid.
Someday I will bring you home
   from foreign lands.
You and your descendants
will live in peace and safety,
   with nothing to fear.
²⁸ So don't be afraid,
even though now
   you deserve to be punished
and have been scattered
   among other nations.
But when I destroy them,
   I will protect you.
I, the LORD, have spoken.

What the LORD Says about the Philistines

47 Before the king of Egypt attacked the town of Gaza,^t the LORD told me to say to the Philistines:

² I, the LORD, tell you
that your land will be flooded
   with an army from the north.
It will destroy your towns
and sweep you away,
   moaning and screaming.
³ When you hear the thunder
of horses and chariots,
   your courage will vanish,
and parents will abandon
   their own children.
⁴ You refugees from Crete,^u
your time has now come,
   and I will destroy you.
None of you will be left
to help the cities
   of Tyre and Sidon.
*⁵ The Anakim who survive^v
   in Gaza and Ashkelon
will mourn for you
by shaving their heads
   and sitting in silence.
⁶ You ask how long will I continue
   to attack you with my sword,
then you tell me to put it away
   and leave you alone.
⁷ But how can my sword rest,
when I have commanded it
   to attack Ashkelon
   and the seacoast?

What the LORD Says about Moab

48 The LORD All-Powerful, the God of Israel, told me to say to the nation of Moab:

The town of Nebo is doomed;
Kiriathaim will be captured
   and disgraced,
and even its fortress
   will be left in ruins.
² No one honors you, Moab.
In Heshbon, enemies make plans
   to end your life.
My sword will leave only silence
   in your town named "Quiet."^w
³ The people of Horonaim
   will cry for help,
as their town is attacked
   and destroyed.

⁴ Moab will be shattered!
   Your children will sob
⁵ and cry on their way up
   to the town of Luhith;
on the road to Horonaim
   they will tell of disasters.

⁶ Run for your lives!
Head into the desert
   like a wild donkey.^x
⁷ You thought you could be saved
   by your power and wealth,
but you will be captured
along with your god Chemosh,
   his priests, and officials.
⁸ Not one of your towns
   will escape destruction.

I have told your enemies,
"Wipe out the valley
   and the flatlands of Moab.

---

^s**46.27** *Israel:* See the note at 30.10, 11.   ^t**47.1** *attacked the town of Gaza:* One of the major Philistine towns; nothing is known about this attack.   ^u**47.4** *Crete:* Hebrew "Caphtor," another name for Crete, the original homeland of the ancestor of the Philistines.   ^v**47.5** *Anakim who survive:* One ancient translation; Hebrew "people in the valley who survive." The Anakim may have been a group of very large people that lived in Palestine before the Israelites (see Numbers 13.33; Deuteronomy 2.10, 11, 20, 21; and Joshua 11.21, 22).   ^w**48.2** *silence . . . Quiet:* In Hebrew the name of the town was "Madmen," which sounds like the word for "silence."   ^x**48.6** *like a wild donkey:* One ancient translation; Hebrew "like (the town of) Aroer" (see verse 19).

⁹ Spread salt on the ground
to kill the crops.[y]
Leave its towns in ruins,
with no one living there.
¹⁰ I want you to kill the Moabites,
and if you let them escape,
I will put a curse on you."

¹¹ Moab, you are like wine
left to settle undisturbed,
never poured from jar to jar.
And so, your nation continues
to prosper and improve.[z]
¹² But now, I will send enemies
to pour out the wine
and smash the jars!
¹³ Then you will be ashamed,
because your god Chemosh
cannot save you,
just as Bethel[a] could not help
the Israelites.

¹⁴ You claim that your soldiers
are strong and brave.
¹⁵ But I am the LORD,
the all-powerful King,
and I promise that enemies
will overpower your towns.
Even your best warriors
will die in the battle.
¹⁶ It won't be long now—
disaster will hit Moab!

¹⁷ I will order the nearby nations
to mourn for you and say,
"Isn't it sad? Moab ruled others,
but now its glorious power
has been shattered."

¹⁸ People in the town of Dibon,[b]
you will be honored no more,
so have a seat in the dust.
Your walls will be torn down
when the enemies attack.

¹⁹ You people of Aroer,[c]
go wait beside the road,
and when refugees run by,
ask them, "What happened?"
²⁰ They will answer,
"Moab has been defeated!
Weep with us in shame.
Tell everyone at the Arnon River
that Moab is destroyed."

*²¹ I will punish every town
that belongs to Moab,
but especially Holon,
Jahzah, Mephaath,
²² Dibon, Nebo,
Beth-Diblathaim, ²³Kiriathaim,
Beth-Gamul, Beth-Meon,
²⁴ Kerioth, and Bozrah.[d]
²⁵ My decision is final—
your army will be crushed,
and your power broken.

²⁶ People of Moab, you claim
to be stronger than I am.
Now I will tell other nations
to make you drunk
and to laugh while you collapse
in your own vomit.
²⁷ You made fun of my people
and treated them like criminals
caught in the act.
²⁸ Now you must leave your towns
and live like doves
in the shelter of cliffs
and canyons.

²⁹ I know about your pride,
and how you strut and boast.
³⁰ But I also know bragging
will never save you.
³¹ So I will cry and mourn
for Moab
and its town of Kir-Heres.

³² People of Sibmah,
you were like a vineyard
heavy with grapes,
and with branches reaching
north to the town of Jazer
and west to the Dead Sea.[e]
But you have been destroyed,
and so I will weep for you,
as the people of Jazer weep
for the vineyards.

---

[y]48.9 *Spread salt . . . crops:* One possible meaning for
the difficult Hebrew text. [z]48.11 *continues . . .
improve:* Or "remains as evil as ever." [a]48.13 *Bethel:* It
may refer to the Phoenician or Canaanite god of that
name; or it may refer to the town where people of the
northern kingdom worshiped at a local shrine (see
1 Kings 12.26-30). [b]48.18 *Dibon:* The capital city
of Moab. [c]48.19 *Aroer:* A Moabite town located just
north of the Arnon River. [d]48.24 *Bozrah:* Not
the same Bozrah as in 49.13. [e]48.32 *reaching
north . . . Dead Sea:* One possible meaning for the
difficult Hebrew text.

³³ Harvest celebrations are gone
from the orchards and farms
    of Moab.
There are no happy shouts
    from people making wine.
³⁴ Weeping from Heshbon
can be heard as far
    as Elealeh and Jahaz;
cries from Zoar are heard
in Horonaim
    and Eglath-Shelishiyah.
And Nimrim Creek has run dry.

³⁵ I will get rid of anyone
who burns incense
    to the gods of Moab
or offers sacrifices
    at their shrines.
I, the LORD, have spoken.

³⁶ In my heart I moan for Moab,
like a funeral song
    played on a flute.
I mourn for the people
of the town of Kir-Heres,
    because their wealth is gone.

*³⁷ The people of Moab
mourn on the rooftops
    and in the streets.
Men cut off their beards,
    people shave their heads;
they make cuts on their hands
    and wear sackcloth.^f
³⁸ And it's all because I, the LORD,
have shattered Moab like a jar
    that no one wants.
³⁹ Moab lies broken!
Listen to its people cry
    as they turn away in shame.
Other nations are horrified
at what happened,
    but still they laugh.

⁴⁰ Moab, an enemy swoops down
like an eagle spreading its wings
    over your land.
⁴¹ Your cities^g and fortresses
    will be captured,
and your warriors
    gripped by fear.^h
⁴² You are finished as a nation,
because you dared oppose me,
    the LORD.

⁴³ Terror, pits, and traps
    are waiting for you.
⁴⁴ If you are terrified and run,
    you will fall into a pit;
and if you crawl out of the pit,
    you'll get caught in a trap.
The time has come
    for you to be punished.

⁴⁵ Near the city of Heshbon,
    where Sihon once ruled,
tired refugees stand in shadows
cast by the flames
    of their burning city.
Soon, the towns on other hilltops,
where those warlike people live,
    will also go up in smoke.

⁴⁶ People of Moab, you worshiped
Chemosh, your god,
    but now you are done for,
and your children are prisoners
    in a foreign country.
⁴⁷ Yet someday, I will bring
    your people back home.
I, the LORD, have spoken.

What the LORD Says about Ammon

49 The LORD has this to say about
the nation of Ammon:

The people of Israel
have plenty of children
    to inherit their lands.
So why have you worshipers
    of the god Milcomⁱ
taken over towns and land
    belonging to the Gad tribe?
² Someday I will send an army
to attack you in Rabbah,
    your capital city.
It will be left in ruins,
and the surrounding villages
    will lie in ashes.
You took some of Israel's land,
but on that day
    Israel will take yours!

---

^f48.37 *sackcloth*: See the note at 4.8.
^g48.41 *Your cities*: Or "Kerioth." ^h48.41 *gripped
by fear*: One possible meaning for the difficult
Hebrew text. ⁱ49.1 *Milcom*: The national god
of Ammon, probably the same as the god Molech
in 32.35.

³Cry, people of Heshbon;^j
your town will become
    a pile of rubble.^k
You will turn here and there,
    but your path will be blocked.^l

Put on sackcloth^m and mourn,
    you citizens of Rabbah,
because the idol you worshipⁿ
will be taken
    to a foreign country,
along with its priests
    and temple officials.
⁴You rebellious Ammonites
trust your wealth and ask,
    "Who could attack us?"
But I warn you not to boast
    when your strength is fading.^o
⁵I, the LORD All-Powerful,
will send neighboring nations
    to strike you with terror.
You will be scattered,
with no one to care
    for your refugees.
⁶Yet someday, I will bring
    your people back home.
I, the LORD, have spoken.

What the LORD Says about Edom

⁷⁻⁸The LORD All-Powerful says about
Edom:

Wisdom and common sense
    have vanished from Teman.^p
I will send disaster to punish
    you descendants of Esau,^q
so anyone from Dedan^r
had better turn around
    and run back home.^s
⁹People who harvest grapes
    leave some for the poor.
Thieves who break in at night
    take only what they want.
¹⁰But I will take everything
    that belongs to you,
        people of Edom,
and I will uncover every place
    where you try to hide.
Then you will die,
and so will your children,
    relatives, and neighbors.
¹¹But I can be trusted
    to care for your orphans
        and widows.

¹²Even those nations that don't deserve
to be punished will have to drink from the
cup of my anger. So how can you possibly
hope to escape? ¹³I, the LORD, swear in my
own name that your city of Bozrah^t and all
your towns will suffer a horrible fate. They
will lie in ruins forever, and people will use
the name "Bozrah" as a curse word.

¹⁴I have sent a messenger
    to command the nations
to prepare for war
    against you people of Edom.
¹⁵Your nation will be small,
    yet hated by other nations.
¹⁶Pride tricks you into thinking
    that other nations
        look at you with fear.^u
You live along the cliffs
and high in the mountains
    like the eagles,
but I am the LORD,
    and I will bring you down.
¹⁷People passing by your country
    will be shocked and horrified
        to see a disaster
¹⁸as bad as the destruction
of Sodom and Gomorrah
    and towns nearby.
The towns of Edom will be empty.

¹⁹I will attack you
    like a lion from the forest,
attacking sheep in a meadow
    along the Jordan.

---

^j**49.3** *Heshbon:* See also 48.45; since Heshbon was near
the border of Moab and Ammon, it was probably ruled
by the country that was stronger at the time.
^k**49.3** *your town will become a pile of rubble:* Or "because
the town of Ai has been destroyed"; referring to an
Ammonite town named Ai, not the town of that name
near Bethel in the land of Israel.   ^l**49.3** *You will turn . . .
blocked:* One possible meaning for the difficult
Hebrew text.   ^m**49.3** *sackcloth:* See the note at 4.8.
ⁿ**49.3** *the idol you worship:* Hebrew "Milcom" (see
verse 1 and the note there).   ^o**49.4** *when . . .
fading:* One possible meaning for the difficult
Hebrew text.   ^p**49.7,8** *Teman:* The name of a town in
Edom, sometimes used as the name of the northern half
of the nation of Edom; here it probably stands for the
whole nation.   ^q**49.7,8** *Esau:* The ancestor of the
nation of Edom.   ^r**49.7,8** *Dedan:* The name of a town
in northwest Arabia, also used of the northwest region
of Arabia along the Red Sea.   ^s**49.7,8** *anyone . . . home:*
One possible meaning for the difficult Hebrew text.
^t**49.13** *Bozrah:* The main city and capital of Edom.
^u**49.16** *Pride . . . fear:* One possible meaning for the
difficult Hebrew text.

In a moment the flock runs,
  and the land is empty.
Who will I choose to attack you?
  I will do it myself!
No one can force me to fight
  or chase me away.
²⁰ Listen to my plans for you,
  people of Edom.ᵛ
Your children will be dragged off
  and your country destroyed.
²¹ The sounds of your destruction
will reach the Red Seaʷ
  and cause the earth to shake.
²² An enemy will swoop down
  to attack you,
like an eagle spreading its wings
  and circling over Bozrah.
Your warriors will be gripped
  by fear.ˣ

What the LORD Says about Damascus

²³The LORD says about Damascus:

The towns of Hamath and Arpadʸ
  have heard your bad news.
They have lost hope,
  and worries roll over them
  like ocean waves.ᶻ
²⁴ You people of Damascus
  have lost your courage,
and in panic you turn to run,
  gripped by fear and pain.ᵃ

²⁵ I once was pleased
  with your famous city.
But now I warn you, "Escape
  while you still can!"ᵇ
²⁶ Soon, even your best soldiers
  will lie dead in your streets.
I, the LORD All-Powerful,
  have spoken.

²⁷ I will set fire to your city walls
and burn down the fortresses
  King Benhadad built.

Nebuchadnezzar and the People of the Desert

²⁸Here is what the LORD says about the Kedar tribe and the desert villagesᶜ that were conquered by King Nebuchadnezzarᵈ of Babylonia:

Listen, you people of Kedar
  and the other tribes

of the eastern desert.
I have told Nebuchadnezzar
  to attack and destroy you.
²⁹ His fearsome army
  will surround you,
taking your tents and possessions,
  your sheep and camels.

³⁰ Run and hide,
you people of the desert
  who live in villages!ᵉ
Nebuchadnezzar has big plans
  for you.
³¹ You have no city walls
  and no neighbors to help,
yet you think you're safe—
  so I told him to attack.
³² Then your camels
and large herds
  will be yours no longer.

People of the Arabian Desert,ᶠ
  disaster will strike you
  from every side,
and you will be scattered
  everywhere on earth.
³³ Only jackalsᵍ will live
where your villagesʰ once stood.
  I, the LORD, have spoken.

What the LORD Says about Elam

³⁴⁻³⁵Not long after Zedekiahⁱ became king of Judah, the LORD told me to say:

ᵛ**49.20** *Edom*: The Hebrew text also uses the name "Teman" (see the note at verses 7, 8). ʷ**49.21** *Red Sea*: Hebrew *yam suph*, here referring to the Gulf of Aqaba, since the term is extended to include the northeastern arm of the Red Sea (see also the note at Exodus 13.18). ˣ**49.22** *will be gripped by fear*: One possible meaning for the difficult Hebrew text. ʸ**49.23** *Hamath and Arpad*: Two towns in Syria that had been the capitals of small kingdoms allied with the more powerful kingdom whose capital was Damascus. ᶻ**49.23** *worries . . . waves*: One possible meaning for the difficult Hebrew text. ᵃ**49.24** *gripped by fear and pain*: One possible meaning for the difficult Hebrew text. ᵇ**49.25** *can*: One possible meaning for the difficult Hebrew text of verse 25. ᶜ**49.28** *desert villages*: The Hebrew text has "kingdoms of Hazor," which probably refers to several kingdoms of desert peoples who were not nomads, but who lived in small villages. ᵈ**49.28** *Nebuchadnezzar*: See the note at 21.2. ᵉ**49.30** *villages*: See the note at 49.28. ᶠ**49.32** *People of the Arabian Desert*: One possible meaning for the difficult Hebrew text. ᵍ**49.33** *jackals*: See the note at 9.11. ʰ**49.33** *villages*: See the note at 49.28. ⁱ**49.34,35** *Zedekiah*: See the note at 1.3.

People of Elam,[j]
    I, the LORD All-Powerful,
will kill the archers
    who make your army strong.
[36] Enemies will attack
    from all directions,
and you will be led captive
    to every nation on earth.
[37] Their armies will crush
    and kill you,
and you will face the disaster
    that my anger brings.
[38] Your king and his officials
    will die, and I will rule
    in their place.
I, the LORD, have spoken.

[39] But I promise that someday
I will bring your people
    back to their land.

Babylon Will Be Captured

50 [*1] The LORD told me to say:

    Announce what will happen
and don't leave anything out.
[2]   Raise the signal flags;
shout so all nations can hear—
    Babylon will be captured!

Marduk,[k] Babylon's god,
    will be ashamed and terrified,
    and his idols broken.
[3] The attack on the Babylonians
    will come from the north;
they and their animals will run,
    leaving the land empty.

Israel and Judah Will Return to Their Land

[4] The LORD said:

People of Israel and Judah,
    when these things happen
        you will weep, and together
you will return to your land
and worship me,
    the LORD your God.
[5] You will ask the way to Zion
and then come and join with me
    in making an agreement
    you won't break or forget.

[6] My people, you are lost sheep
    abandoned by their shepherds
    in the mountains.

You don't even remember
    your resting place.
[7] I am your true pastureland,
    the one who gave hope
    to your ancestors.
But you abandoned me,
so when your enemies found you,
    they felt no guilt
    as they gobbled you down.

If you read through the Bible with an eye toward unearthing God's promises, you'll discover how they hold true, even today— and your faith will increase immeasurably.

MARIAN V. LIAUTAUD

[8] Escape from Babylonia,
    my people.
Get out of that country!
    Don't wait for anyone else.
[9] In the north I am bringing
    great nations together.
They will attack Babylon
    and capture it.
The arrows they shoot
are like the best soldiers,[l]
    always finding their target.
[10] Babylonia will be conquered,
and its enemies will carry off
    everything they want.

Babylon Will Be Disgraced

The LORD said:

[11] People of Babylonia,
    you were glad
    to rob my people.

---

[j] **49.34,35** *Elam:* A nation east of Babylonia,
attacked by Nebuchadnezzar about 596 B.C.
[k] **50.2** *Marduk:* The Hebrew text has "Bel" and
"Marduk," two names for the same god.
[l] **50.9** *the best soldiers:* Some Hebrew manuscripts
and two ancient translations; most Hebrew manuscripts
"soldiers that kill children."

You had a good time,
making more noise
    than horses
and jumping around
    like calves threshing grain.[m]
[12] The city of Babylon
    was like a mother to you.
But it will be disgraced
and become nothing
    but a barren desert.
[13] My anger will destroy Babylon,
    and no one will live there.
Everyone who passes by
will be shocked to see
    what has happened.

[14] Babylon has rebelled against me.
    Archers, take your places.
Shoot all your arrows at Babylon.
[15]   Attack from every side!

Babylon surrenders!
The enemy tears down
    its walls and towers.
I am taking my revenge
by doing to Babylon what it did
    to other cities.
[16] There is no one in Babylonia
    to plant or harvest crops.
Even foreigners who lived there
have left for their homelands,
    afraid of the enemy armies.

[17] Israel is a flock of sheep
    scattered by hungry lions.
The king of Assyria[n]
    first gobbled Israel down.
Then Nebuchadnezzar,[o]
king of Babylonia,
    crunched on Israel's bones.
[18] I, the LORD All-Powerful,
    the God of Israel,
    punished the king of Assyria,
and I will also punish
    the king of Babylonia.
[19] But I will bring Israel
    back to its own land.
The people will be like sheep
    eating their fill
on Mount Carmel
    and in Bashan,
in the hill country of Ephraim
    and in Gilead.
[20] I will rescue a few people
    from Israel and Judah.

I will forgive them so completely
that their sin and guilt
    will disappear,
    never to be found.

The LORD's Commands
to the Enemies of Babylonia

[21] The LORD said:

I have told
    the enemies of Babylonia,
"Attack the people of Merathaim
    and Pekod.[p]
Kill them all!
    Destroy their possessions!"

[22] Sounds of war
and the noise of destruction
    can be heard.
[23] Babylonia was a hammer
pounding every country,
    but now it lies broken.
What a shock to the nations
    of the world!

[24] Babylonia challenged me,
    the LORD God All-Powerful,
but that nation doesn't know
it is caught in a trap
    that I set.
[25] I've brought out my weapons,
and with them I will put a curse
    on Babylonia.

[26] Come from far away,
    you enemies of Babylon!
Pile up the grain
    from its storehouses,
and destroy it completely,
    along with everything else.
[27] Kill the soldiers of Babylonia,
because the time has come
    for them to be punished.

---

[m]**50.11** *threshing grain*: Hebrew; two ancient translations "in a pasture." [n]**50.17** *king of Assyria*: Either Shalmaneser V, who ruled 726-722 B.C., conquered most of the northern kingdom, and surrounded its capital city Samaria; or Sargon II, who ruled 721-705 B.C. and took thousands of prisoners back to Assyria. [o]**50.17** *Nebuchadnezzar*: See the note at 21.2. [p]**50.21** *Merathaim . . . Pekod*: Hebrew forms of two Babylonian names that refer to the land of Babylonia. Merathaim probably referred to lagoons near the mouth of the Tigris and Euphrates rivers or to the Persian Gulf, but in Hebrew it means "Twice as Rebellious." Pekod referred to a tribe of southeastern Babylonia, but in Hebrew it means "Punishment."

28 The Babylonian army
   destroyed my temple,
      but soon I will take revenge.
   Then refugees from Babylon
      will tell about it in Zion.

29 Attack Babylon, enemy archers;
   set up camp around the city,
      and don't let anyone escape.
   It challenged me, the holy God,
   so do to it
      what it did to other cities.

Proud Babylon Will Fall

30 People of Babylon,
      I, the LORD, promise
   that even your best soldiers
      will lie dead in the streets.

31 Babylon, you should be named,
      "The Proud One."
   But the time has come when I,
   the LORD All-Powerful,
      will punish you.
32 You are proud,
   but you will stumble and fall,
      and no one will help you up.
   I will set your villages on fire,
   and everything around you
      will go up in flames.

33 You Babylonians were cruel
      to Israel and Judah.
   You took them captive, and now
      you refuse to let them go.
34 But I, the LORD All-Powerful,
      will rescue and protect them.
   I will bring peace to their land
      and trouble to yours.
35 I have declared war on you,
      your officials, and advisors.
36 This war will prove
   that your prophets
      are liars and fools.
   And it will frighten
      your warriors.
37 Then your chariot horses
   and the foreigners in your army
      will refuse to go into battle,
   and the enemy will carry away
      everything you treasure.
38 Your rivers and canals
      will dry up.

All of this will happen,
   because your land
      is full of idols,
   and they have made fools
      of you.
39 Never again will people live
      in your land—
   only desert animals, jackals,[q]
      and unclean birds.
40 I destroyed Sodom and Gomorrah
      and the nearby towns,
   and I will destroy Babylon
      just as completely.
   No one will live there again.

Babylonia Is Invaded

The LORD said:
41 Far to the north,
   a nation and its allies
      have been awakened.
   They are powerful
      and ready for war.
42 Bows and arrows and swords
      are in their hands.
   The soldiers are cruel
      and show no pity.
   The hoofbeats of their horses
   echo like ocean waves
      crashing against the shore.
   The army has lined up for battle
   and is coming to attack you,
      people of Babylonia!

43 Ever since your king heard
      about this army,
   he has been weak with fear;
   he twists and turns in pain
      like a woman giving birth.
44 Babylonia, I will attack you
      like a lion from the forest,
   attacking sheep in a meadow
      along the Jordan.
   In a moment the flock runs,
      and the land is empty.
   Who will I choose to attack you?
      I will do it myself!
   No one can force me to fight
      or chase me away.
45 Listen to my plans for you,
      people of Babylonia.

---

q 50.39 *jackals:* See the note at 9.11.

Your children will be dragged off,
and your country destroyed.
⁴⁶ The sounds of your destruction
will be heard among the nations,
and the earth will shake.

Babylon Will Be Destroyed

51 I, the LORD, am sending
a wind[r] to destroy
the people of Babylonia[s]
and Babylon, its capital.
² Foreign soldiers will come
from every direction,
and when the disaster is over,
Babylonia will be empty
and worthless.
³ I will tell these soldiers,
"Attack quickly,
before the Babylonians
can string their bows
or put on their armor.[t]
Kill their best soldiers
and destroy their army!"
⁴ Their troops will fall wounded
in the streets of Babylon.

⁵ Everyone in Israel and Judah
is guilty.
But I, the LORD All-Powerful,
their holy God,
have not abandoned them.

⁶ Get out of Babylon!
Run for your lives!
If you stay, you will be killed
when I take revenge on the city
and punish it for its sins.

⁷ Babylon was my golden cup,
filled with the wine
of my anger.
The nations of the world
got drunk on this wine
and went insane.
⁸ But suddenly, Babylon will fall
and be destroyed.

I, the LORD, told the foreigners[u]
who lived there,
"Weep for the city!
Get medicine for its wounds;
maybe they will heal."

⁹ The foreigners answered,
"We have already tried

to treat Babylon's wounds,
but they would not heal.
Come on, let's all go home
to our own countries.
Nothing is left in Babylonia;
everything is destroyed."

¹⁰ The people of Israel said,
"Tell everyone in Zion!
The LORD has taken revenge
for what Babylon did to us."

The LORD Wants Babylon Destroyed

¹¹ I, the LORD,
want Babylon destroyed,
because its army
destroyed my temple.
So, you kings of Media,[v]
sharpen your arrows
and pick up your shields.

*We have to stand firm
on biblical truths.*

JANE JOHNSON STRUCK

¹² Raise the signal flag
and attack the city walls.
Post more guards.
Have soldiers watch the city
and set up ambushes.
I have made plans
to destroy Babylon,
and nothing will stop me.

¹³ People of Babylon, you live
along the Euphrates River
and are surrounded by canals.
You are rich,
but now the time has come
for you to die.[w]

---

[r]**51.1** *wind:* Or "spirit." [s]**51.1** *Babylonia:* The Hebrew
text has "Leb-Qamai," a secret way of writing
"Babylonia." [t]**51.3** *I will tell . . . armor:* Or "Attack
quickly! String your bows and put on your armor."
[u]**51.8** *the foreigners:* Or "my people." [v]**51.11** *kings of
Media:* Probably kings of smaller kingdoms that were
part of the Median Empire (see also verse 27 and the
note there). [w]**51.13** *for you to die:* One possible
meaning for the difficult Hebrew text.

¹⁴ I, the LORD All-Powerful,
    swear by my own life
that enemy soldiers
will fill your streets
    like a swarm of locusts.^x
They will shout
    and celebrate their victory.

A Hymn of Praise
(Jeremiah 10.12-16)

¹⁵ God used his wisdom and power
    to create the earth
    and spread out the heavens.
¹⁶ The waters in the heavens roar
    at his command.
He makes clouds appear;
he sends the wind
    from his storehouse
and makes lightning flash
    in the rain.

¹⁷ People who make idols
    are stupid!
They will be disappointed,
because their false gods
    cannot breathe.
¹⁸ Idols are merely a joke,
and when the time is right,
    they will be destroyed.
¹⁹ But the LORD, Israel's God,
    is all-powerful.
He created everything,
and he chose Israel
    to be his very own.

God's Hammer

The LORD said:

²⁰ Babylonia, you were my hammer;
I used you to pound nations
    and break kingdoms,
²¹ to shatter cavalry and chariots,
²² as well as men and women,
    young and old,
²³ shepherds and their flocks,
farmers and their oxen,
    and governors and leaders.

²⁴ But now, my people will watch,
while I repay you
    for what you did to Zion.

²⁵ You destroyed the nations
and seem strong as a mountain,
    but I am your enemy.

I might even grab you
    and roll you off a cliff.
When I am finished,
you'll only be a pile
    of scorched bricks.
²⁶ Your stone blocks won't be reused
for cornerstones
    or foundations,
and I promise that forever
    you will be a desert.
I, the LORD, have spoken.

The Nations Will Attack Babylon

The LORD said:

²⁷ Signal the nations
    to get ready to attack.
Raise a flag and blow a trumpet.
Send for the armies of Ararat,
    Minni, and Ashkenaz.^y
Choose a commander;
let the cavalry attack
    like a swarm of locusts.
²⁸ Tell the kings and governors,
    the leaders and the people
of the kingdoms of the Medes
    to prepare for war!

²⁹ The earth twists and turns
    in torment,
because I have decided
to make Babylonia a desert
    where no one can live,
and I won't change my mind.

³⁰ The Babylonian soldiers
have lost their strength
    and courage.^z
They stay in their fortresses,
    unable to fight,
while the enemy breaks through
the city gates,
    then sets their homes on fire.
³¹ One messenger after another
    announces to the king,
"Babylon has been captured!
³² The enemy now controls
    the river crossings!

---

^x**51.14** *locusts:* See the note at 46.22, 23.
^y**51.27** *Ararat, Minni, and Ashkenaz:* Kingdoms to the north of Babylonia that were part of the Median Empire (see also verse 28).   ^z**51.30** *have lost their strength and courage:* Hebrew "have lost their strength and have become like women."

The marshes*a* are on fire!
Your army has panicked!"

³³ I am the LORD All-Powerful,
the God of Israel,
and I make this promise—
"Soon Babylon will be leveled
and packed down
like a threshing place
at harvest time."*b*

Babylonia Will Pay!

³⁴ The people of Jerusalem say,
"King Nebuchadnezzar*c*
made us panic.
That monster stuffed himself
with us and our treasures,
leaving us empty—
he gobbled down
what he wanted
and spit out the rest.
³⁵ The people of Babylonia
harmed some of us*d*
and killed others.
Now, LORD, make them pay!"

The LORD Will Take Revenge on Babylon

³⁶ My people, I am on your side,
and I will take revenge
on Babylon.
I will cut off its water supply,
and its stream*e* will dry up.
³⁷ Babylon will be a pile of rubble
where only jackals*f* live.
People will laugh,
but they will be afraid
to walk among the ruins.
³⁸ The Babylonians roar and growl
like young lions.
³⁹ And since they are hungry,
I will give them a banquet.
They will celebrate, get drunk,
then fall asleep,
never to wake up!
⁴⁰ I will lead them away to die,
like sheep, lambs, and goats
being led to the butcher.
⁴¹ All nations now praise Babylon,*g*
but when it is captured,
those same nations
will be horrified.
⁴² Babylon's enemies will rise
like ocean waves
and flood the city.

⁴³ Horrible destruction will strike
the nearby towns.
The land will become
a barren desert,
where no one can live
or even travel.
⁴⁴ I will punish Marduk,*h*
the god of Babylon,
and make him vomit up
everything he gobbled down.
Then nations will no longer
bring him gifts,
and Babylon's walls will crumble.

*Our ultimate value will be
that we were not only created,
compiled, and, as it were,
written by the Author. Our
true value will rest in the
fact that we have been
autographed by the Author.
And that gives us hope, no
matter the circumstances.*

RUTH BELL GRAHAM

The LORD Offers Hope to His People

⁴⁵ Get out of Babylon, my people,
and run for your lives,
before I strike the city
in my anger!
⁴⁶ Don't be afraid or lose hope,
though year after year
there are rumors
of leaders fighting for control
in the city of Babylon.

*a*51.32 *marshes:* The tall grass in the marshes could
have provided hiding places for people trying to escape
from Babylon.   *b*51.33 *leveled . . . harvest time:* A
threshing place with a dirt surface had to be leveled
and packed down before it could be used.
*c*51.34 *Nebuchadnezzar:* See the note at 21.2.
*d*51.35 *harmed some of us:* One possible meaning for the
difficult Hebrew text.   *e*51.36 *stream:* Probably the
Euphrates River.   *f*51.37 *jackals:* See the note at 9.11.
*g*51.41 *Babylon:* The Hebrew text has "Sheshach,"
a secret way of writing the name "Babylon."
*h*51.44 *Marduk:* Hebrew "Bel" (see the note at 50.2).

⁴⁷The time will come
    when I will punish
        Babylon's false gods.
    Everyone there will die,
    and the whole nation
        will be disgraced,
⁴⁸when an army attacks
    from the north
        and brings destruction.
    Then the earth and the heavens
    and everything in them
        will celebrate.
⁴⁹Babylon must be overthrown,
    because it slaughtered
    the people of Israel
        and of many other nations.

⁵⁰My people, you escaped death
    when Jerusalem fell.
    Now you live far from home,
    but you should trust me
        and think about Jerusalem.
    Leave Babylon! Don't stay!

⁵¹You feel ashamed and disgraced,
    because foreigners have entered
        my sacred temple.
⁵²Soon I will send a war
    to punish Babylon's idols
    and leave its wounded people
        moaning everywhere.
⁵³Although Babylon's walls
    reach to the sky,
    the army I send
        will destroy that city.
    I, the LORD, have spoken.

Babylon Will Be Destroyed

The LORD said:

⁵⁴Listen to the cries for help
    coming from Babylon.
    Everywhere in the country
    the sounds of destruction
        can be heard.
⁵⁵The shouts of the enemy,
    like crashing ocean waves,
    will drown out Babylon's cries
        as I level the city.

⁵⁶An enemy will attack
    and destroy Babylon.
    Its soldiers will be captured
        and their weapons broken,
    because I am a God

who takes revenge against nations
    for what they do.
⁵⁷I, the LORD All-Powerful,
    the true King, promise
    that the officials and advisors,
    the governors and leaders
        and the soldiers of Babylon
    will get drunk, fall asleep,
        and never wake up.
⁵⁸The thick walls of that city
    will be torn down,
        and its huge gates burned.
    Everything that nation
    worked so hard to gain
        will go up in smoke.

Jeremiah Gives Seraiah a Scroll

⁵⁹During Zedekiah's[i] fourth year as king of Judah, he went to Babylon. And Baruch's brother Seraiah[j] went along as the officer in charge of arranging for places to stay overnight.[k] ⁶⁰Before they left, I wrote on a scroll[l] all the terrible things that would happen to Babylon. ⁶¹I gave the scroll to Seraiah and said:

When you get to Babylon, read this scroll aloud, ⁶²then pray, "Our LORD, you promised to destroy this place and make it into a desert where no people or animals will ever live."

⁶³When you finish praying, tie the scroll to a rock and throw it in the Euphrates River. Then say, ⁶⁴"This is how Babylon will sink when the LORD destroys it. Everyone in the city will die, and it won't have the strength to rise again."

The End of Jeremiah's Writing

Jeremiah's writing ends here.

Jerusalem Is Captured
(2 Kings 24.18—25.30; 2 Chronicles 36.11-21)

52 Zedekiah was twenty-one years old when he was appointed king of Judah,[m] and he ruled from

---

ⁱ51.59 *Zedekiah's*: See the note at 1.3.   ʲ51.59 *Baruch's brother Seraiah*: Hebrew "Seraiah son of Neriah and grandson of Mahseiah"; Baruch helped Jeremiah write down his messages (see 32.12; 36.4-10).
ᵏ51.59 *arranging for places to stay overnight*: Hebrew and one ancient translation; two ancient translations, "the tax money."   ˡ51.60 *scroll*: See the note at 30.1, 2.
ᵐ52.1 *appointed king of Judah*: By Nebuchadnezzar (see 37.1).

Jerusalem for eleven years.[n] His mother Hamutal was the daughter of Jeremiah from the town of Libnah.[o] [2]Zedekiah disobeyed the LORD, just as Jehoiakim had done, [3]and it was Zedekiah who finally rebelled against Nebuchadnezzar.[p]

The people of Judah and Jerusalem had made the LORD so angry that he finally turned his back on them. That's why horrible things were happening.

[4]In Zedekiah's ninth year as king, on the tenth day of the tenth month,[q] King Nebuchadnezzar of Babylonia led his entire army to attack Jerusalem. The troops set up camp outside the city and built ramps up to the city walls.

[5-6]After a year and a half,[r] all the food in Jerusalem was gone. Then on the ninth day of the fourth month,[s] [7]the Babylonian troops broke through the city wall. That same night, Zedekiah and his soldiers tried to escape through the gate near the royal garden, even though they knew the enemy had the city surrounded. They headed toward the Jordan River valley, [8]but the Babylonian troops caught up with them near Jericho. The Babylonians arrested Zedekiah, but his soldiers scattered in every direction. [9]Zedekiah was taken to Riblah in the land of Hamath, where Nebuchadnezzar put him on trial and found him guilty. [10]Zedekiah's sons and the officials of Judah were killed while he watched, [11]then his eyes were poked out. He was put in chains, then dragged off to Babylon and kept in prison until he died.

[12]Jerusalem was captured during Nebuchadnezzar's nineteenth year as king of Babylonia.

About a month later,[t] Nebuchadnezzar's officer in charge of the guards arrived in Jerusalem. His name was Nebuzaradan, [13]and he burned down the LORD's temple, the king's palace, and every important building in the city, as well as all the houses. [14]Then he ordered the Babylonian soldiers to break down the walls around Jerusalem. [15]He led away the people left in the city, including everyone who had become loyal to Nebuchadnezzar, the rest of the skilled workers,[u] and even some of the poor people of Judah. [16]Only the very poorest were left behind to work the vineyards and the fields.

[17-20]Nebuzaradan ordered his soldiers to go to the temple and take everything made of gold or silver, including bowls, fire pans, sprinkling bowls, pans, lampstands, dishes for incense, and the cups for wine offerings. The Babylonian soldiers took all the bronze things used for worship at the temple, including the pans for hot ashes, and the shovels, lamp snuffers, sprinkling bowls, and dishes for incense. The soldiers also took everything else made of bronze, including the two columns that stood in front of the temple, the large bowl called the Sea, the twelve bulls that held it up, and the movable stands.[v] The soldiers broke these things into pieces so they could take them to Babylonia. There was so much bronze that it could not be weighed. [21]For example, the columns were about twenty-seven feet high and eighteen feet around. They were hollow, but the bronze was about three inches thick. [22]Each column had a bronze cap over seven feet high that was decorated with bronze designs. Some of these designs were like chains and others were like pomegranates.[w] [23]There were ninety-six pomegranates evenly spaced[x] around each column, and a total of one hundred pomegranates were located above the chains.

[24]Next, Nebuzaradan arrested Seraiah the chief priest, Zephaniah his assistant, and three temple officials. [25]Then he arrested one of the army commanders, seven of King Zedekiah's personal advisors, and the officer in charge of gathering the troops for battle. He also found sixty more soldiers who were still in Jerusalem. [26-27]Nebuzaradan led them to Riblah in the land of Hamath, where Nebuchadnezzar had them killed.

---

[n]**52.1** *he ruled . . . years:* Ruled 598-586 B.C.
[o]**52.1** *Jeremiah from the town of Libnah:* Not the same Jeremiah as the author of this book (see 1.1).
[p]**52.3** *Nebuchadnezzar:* See the note at 21.2.
[q]**52.4** *tenth month:* See the note at 39.1-3.
[r]**52.5,6** *After a year and a half:* Jerusalem was captured in 586 B.C.   [s]**52.5,6** *fourth month:* See the note at 39.1-3.   [t]**52.12** *About a month later:* Hebrew "On the seventh day of the fifth month."   [u]**52.15** *the rest of the skilled workers:* Nebuchadnezzar had taken away some of the skilled workers eleven years before (see 2 Kings 24.14-16).   [v]**52.17-20** *the large bowl called the Sea, the twelve bulls that held it up, and the movable stands:* One ancient translation; Hebrew "the large bowl called the Sea, and the twelve bulls under the movable stands."   [w]**52.22** *pomegranates:* A small red fruit that looks like an apple.   [x]**52.23** *evenly spaced:* One possible meaning for the difficult Hebrew text.

The people of Judah no longer lived in their own country.

People of Judah Taken Prisoner

28-30Here is a list of the number of the people of Judah that Nebuchadnezzar[y] took to Babylonia as prisoners:

In his seventh year as king, he took 3,023 people.
In his eighteenth year as king, he took 832 from Jerusalem.
In his twenty-third year as king, his officer Nebuzaradan took 745 people.

So, Nebuchadnezzar took a total of 4,600 people from Judah to Babylonia.

Jehoiachin Is Set Free
(2 Kings 25.27-30)

31Jehoiachin was a prisoner in Babylon for thirty-seven years. Then Evil Merodach[z] became king of Babylonia, and in the first year of his rule, on the twenty-fifth day of the twelfth month,[a] he let Jehoiachin out of prison. 32Evil Merodach was kind to Jehoiachin and honored him more than any of the other kings held prisoner there. 33Jehoiachin was allowed to wear regular clothes instead of a prison uniform, and he even ate at the king's table every day. 34As long as Jehoiachin lived, he was paid a daily allowance to buy whatever he needed.

---

[y]52.28-30 Nebuchadnezzar: See the note at 21.2.
[z]52.31 Evil Merodach: The son of Nebuchadnezzar who ruled Babylonia from 562-560 B.C. [a]52.31 twelfth month: Adar, the twelfth month of the Hebrew calendar, from about mid-February to mid-March.

Lamentations

Poems of Grief and Pain

Tragedy and misfortune strike even God's people. When they do, we might feel bruised, dazed, angry, or even abandoned by God. How do we work through our grief when terrible things happen to us or to those we love? The book of Lamentations offers us a model of what it means to grieve without losing faith or hope.

The writer, possibly the prophet Jeremiah, witnessed the siege and fall of Jerusalem and its temple in 586 B.C. The book is comprised of five chapters—each one a poem—which fully express the author's grief and the grief of his people. The first four poems are written in the form of an acrostic. The poems are presented as though the city of Jerusalem and the writer are speaking. The verses catalog the horrors and suffering of the prophet and the people, vividly describing the consequences of the people's sin as they experience God's judgment.

These poems provide us with an example of how to handle grief—whether our own or the grief of others. First, notice that the author does not deny his pain, his questions about God, or his desire for revenge on his enemies. He even accuses the Lord of being "cruel" and an "enemy" (2.5,20). He describes in detail what he sees, hears, and feels. He models for us how to fully enter the pain of our grief—the only way to healing.

But the author of Lamentations also finds hope. In the very center of the book, quite deliberately, the writer remembers God's character. He knows God's kindness and mercy will eventually overcome his judgment. Whatever we experience, we can choose to focus on God's unchanging character. We can depend on God because his very nature is kindness and mercy. He may send suffering for a reason, but he's also ready to heal and restore because of his great love (3.22-33).

Lamentations at a Glance

1. First Lament: Jerusalem suffers (1)
2. Second Lament: God's anger is poured out (2)
3. Third Lament: God is merciful (3)
4. Fourth Lament: The horrors of judgment (4)
5. Fifth Lament: A plea for mercy (5)

Lonely Jerusalem

The Prophet Speaks:

1 Jerusalem, once so crowded,
    lies deserted and lonely.
This city that was known
all over the world
    is now like a widow.
This queen of the nations
    has been made a slave.
² Each night, bitter tears
    flood her cheeks.
None of her former lovers
    are there to offer comfort;
her friends[a] have betrayed her
    and are now her enemies.

³ The people of Judah are slaves,
suffering in a foreign land,
    with no rest from sorrow.
Their enemies captured them
    and were terribly cruel.[b]
⁴ The roads to Zion mourn
because no one travels there
    to celebrate the festivals.
The city gates are deserted;
    priests are weeping.
Young women are raped;[c]
    Zion is in sorrow!
⁵ Enemies now rule the city
    and live as they please.
The LORD has punished Jerusalem
    because of her awful sins;
he has let her people
    be dragged away.

⁶ Zion's glory has disappeared.
Her leaders are like deer
    that cannot find pasture;
they are hunted down
    till their strength is gone.
⁷ Her people recall the good life
    that once was theirs;
now they suffer
    and are scattered.
No one was there to protect them
from their enemies who sneered
    when their city was taken.

⁸ Jerusalem's horrible sins
    have made the city a joke.
Those who once admired her
    now hate her instead—
she has been disgraced;
    she groans and turns away.

⁹ Her sins had made her filthy,
but she wasn't worried
    about what could happen.
And when Jerusalem fell,
    it was so tragic.
No one gave her comfort
    when she cried out,
"Help! I'm in trouble, LORD!
    The enemy has won."

¹⁰ Zion's treasures were stolen.
Jerusalem saw foreigners
    enter her place of worship,
though the LORD
had forbidden them
    to belong to his people.[d]
¹¹ Everyone in the city groans
    while searching for food;
they trade their valuables
    for barely enough scraps
    to stay alive.

Jerusalem Speaks:

Jerusalem shouts to the LORD,
"Please look and see
    how miserable I am!"
¹² No passerby even cares.[e]
Why doesn't someone notice
    my terrible sufferings?
You were fiercely angry, LORD,
and you punished me
    worst of all.
¹³ From heaven you sent a fire
    that burned in my bones;
you set a trap for my feet
    and made me turn back.
All day long you leave me
    in shock from constant pain.
¹⁴ You have tied my sins
    around my neck,[f]
and they weigh so heavily
    that my strength is gone.
You have put me in the power
    of enemies too strong for me.

---

[a]**1.2** *lovers . . . friends:* Israel's former allies.
[b]**1.3** *Their . . . cruel:* One possible meaning for
the difficult Hebrew text.   [c]**1.4** *raped:* One
possible meaning for the difficult Hebrew text.
[d]**1.10** *to . . . people:* Or "to enter his temple."
[e]**1.12** *No . . . cares:* One possible meaning for the
difficult Hebrew text.   [f]**1.14** *You . . . neck:* One
possible meaning for the difficult Hebrew text.

¹⁵You, LORD, have turned back
   my warriors and crushed
      my young heroes.
Judah was a woman untouched,
   but you let her be trampled
      like grapes in a wine pit.
¹⁶Because of this, I mourn,
   and tears flood my eyes.
No one is here to comfort
   or to encourage me;
we have lost the war—
   my people are suffering.

The Prophet Speaks:

¹⁷Zion reaches out her hands,
   but no one offers comfort.
The LORD has turned
   the neighboring nations
      against Jacob's descendants.
Jerusalem is merely a filthy rag
   to her neighbors.

Jerusalem Speaks:

¹⁸The LORD was right,
   but I refused to obey him.
Now I ask all of you to look
   at my sufferings—
even my young people
   have been dragged away.
¹⁹I called out to my lovers,
   but they betrayed me.
My priests and my leaders died
while searching the city
   for scraps of food.

²⁰Won't you look and see
   how upset I am, our LORD?
My stomach is in knots,
and my heart is broken
   because I betrayed you.
In the streets and at home,
   my people are slaughtered.

²¹Everyone heard my groaning,
   but no one offered comfort.
My enemies know of the trouble
that you have brought on me,
   and it makes them glad.
Hurry and punish them,
   as you have promised.
²²Don't let their evil deeds
   escape your sight.
Punish them as much
   as you have punished me
      because of my sins.

I never stop groaning—
   I've lost all hope!

*He laid down his own
dear Son that we might
be cleansed and forgiven.*

VIRELLE KIDDER

The LORD Was Like an Enemy

The Prophet Speaks:

2 The Lord was angry!
   So he disgraced[g] Zion
though it was Israel's pride
   and his own place of rest.
In his anger he threw Zion down
   from heaven to earth.
²The LORD had no mercy!
He destroyed the homes
   of Jacob's descendants.
In his anger he tore down
   every walled city in Judah;
he toppled the nation
together with its leaders,
   leaving them in shame.

³The Lord was so furiously angry
that he wiped out
   the whole army[h] of Israel
by not supporting them
   when the enemy attacked.
He was like a raging fire
that swallowed up
   the descendants of Jacob.
⁴He attacked like an enemy
with a bow and arrows,
   killing our loved ones.
He has burned to the ground
   the homes on Mount Zion.[i]

⁵The Lord was like an enemy!
   He left Israel in ruins
with its palaces
   and fortresses destroyed,

ᵍ**2.1** *disgraced:* One possible meaning for the difficult
Hebrew text.   ʰ**2.3** *army:* The Hebrew text has "horn,"
which refers to the horn of a bull, one of the most
powerful animals in ancient Palestine.   ⁱ**2.4** *the homes
on Mount Zion:* Or "the temple on Mount Zion."

and with everyone in Judah
  moaning and weeping.
⁶He shattered his temple
  like a hut in a garden;ʲ
he completely wiped out
  his meeting place,
and did away with festivals
and Sabbaths
  in the city of Zion.
In his fierce anger he rejected
  our king and priests.

⁷The Lord abandoned his altar
  and his temple;
he let Zion's enemies
  capture her fortresses.
Noisy shouts were heard
  from the temple,
as if it were a time
  of celebration.

⁸The LORD had decided
to tear down the walls of Zion
  stone by stone.
So he started destroying
  and did not stop
until walls and fortresses
  mourned and trembled.
⁹Zion's gates have fallen
  facedown on the ground;
the bars that locked the gates
  are smashed to pieces.
Her king and royal family
  are prisoners
  in foreign lands.
Her priests don't teach,

and her prophets don't have
  a message from the LORD.

¹⁰Zion's leaders are silent.
  They just sit on the ground,
tossing dirt on their heads
  and wearing sackcloth.
Her young women can do nothing
  but stare at the ground.

¹¹My eyes are red from crying,
  my stomach is in knots,
  and I feel sick all over.
My people are being wiped out,
and children lie helpless
  in the streets of the city.
¹²A child begs its mother
  for food and drink,
then blacks out
like a wounded soldier
  lying in the street.
The child slowly dies
  in its mother's arms.

¹³Zion, how can I comfort you?
  How great is your pain?ᵏ
Lovely city of Jerusalem,
how can I heal your wounds,
  gaping as wide as the sea?
¹⁴Your prophets deceived you
  with false visions
  and lying messages—

ʲ2.6 He . . . garden: Or "He shattered the temple
walls, as if they were the walls of a garden."
ᵏ2.13 How great . . . pain: Or "What are you really like?"
or "What can I say about you?"

ᴄᴿᴸ SpiritualLife—How can I reach out to a needy world? (Lamentations 2.11-13)

Start with compassion.

When we hear of war or famine, the need and suffering seems so great, it's hard to know what we can do. How can we enter the pain of real people who are suffering?

If nothing else, we can pray—and Lamentations can help us do that. It paints a graphic picture of suffering that can move us to feel compassion and help us to pray in a more heartfelt, specific way. Imagine what it's like for children to beg their mother for food and drink, and the mother is unable to give them anything. Then the child passes out from hunger and dehydration and dies in its helpless mother's arms.

This is what many people in the world suffer. As you picture it, feel it, and grieve for their suffering, you'll be better able to pray in a way that touches the heart of God. (See also 2 Samuel 9; Nehemiah 5.1-13; Jonah 4.5-11; Zechariah 7.7-13; Matthew 6.1-4; Luke 9.10-17.)

ᴄᴿᴸ Words To Remember: *Zion, how can I comfort you? How great is your pain?* —Lamentations 2.13

they should have warned you
to leave your sins
   and be saved from disaster.
[15] Those who pass by
shake their heads and sneer
   as they make fun and shout,
"What a lovely city you were,
the happiest on earth,
   but look at you now!"

[16] Zion, your enemies curse you
and snarl like wild animals,
   while shouting,
"This is the day
we've waited for!
   At last, we've got you!"

[17] The LORD has done everything
that he had planned
   and threatened long ago.
He destroyed you without mercy
and let your enemies boast about
   their powerful forces.[l]

[18] Zion, deep in your heart
   you cried out to the Lord.
Now let your tears overflow
   your walls day and night.
Don't ever lose hope
   or let your tears stop.
[19] Get up and pray for help
   all through the night.
Pour out your feelings
   to the Lord,
as you would pour water
   out of a jug.
Beg him to save your people,
who are starving to death
   at every street crossing.

Jerusalem Speaks:

[20] Think about it, LORD!
Have you ever been this cruel
   to anyone before?
Is it right for mothers
   to eat their children,
or for priests and prophets
   to be killed in your temple?
[21] My people, both young and old,
   lie dead in the streets.
Because you were angry,
my young men and women
   were brutally slaughtered.
[22] When you were angry, LORD,

you invited my enemies
   like guests for a party.
No one survived that day;
enemies killed my children,
   my own little ones.

There Is Still Hope

The Prophet Speaks:

3 I have suffered much
   because God was angry.
[2] He chased me into a dark place,
   where no light could enter.
[3] I am the only one he punishes
over and over again,
   without ever stopping.
[4] God caused my skin and flesh
to waste away,
   and he crushed my bones.
[5] He attacked and surrounded me
   with hardships and trouble;
[6] he forced me to sit in the dark
   like someone long dead.

[7] God built a fence around me
that I cannot climb over,
   and he chained me down.
[8] Even when I shouted
and prayed for help,
   he refused to listen.
[9] God put big rocks in my way
and made me follow
   a crooked path.
[10] God was like a bear or a lion
   waiting in ambush for me;
[11] he dragged me from the road,
   then tore me to shreds.[m]
[12] God took careful aim
and shot his arrows
[13]   straight through my heart.

[14] I am a joke to everyone—
no one ever stops
   making fun of me.
[15] God has turned my life sour.
[16] He made me eat gravel
   and rubbed me in the dirt.
[17] I cannot find peace
   or remember happiness.

---

[l] **2.17** *powerful forces:* The Hebrew text has "horn,"
which refers to the horn of a bull, one of the most
powerful animals in ancient Palestine.   [m] **3.11** *shreds:*
One possible meaning for the difficult Hebrew text of
verse 11.

¹⁸ I tell myself, "I am finished!
I can't count on the LORD
to do anything for me."
¹⁹ Just thinking of my troubles
and my lonely wandering
makes me miserable.
²⁰ That's all I ever think about,
and I am depressed.ⁿ
²¹ Then I remember something
that fills me with hope.
²² The LORD's kindness never fails!
If he had not been merciful,
we would have been destroyed.^o
²³ The LORD can always be trusted
to show mercy each morning.
²⁴ Deep in my heart I say,
"The LORD is all I need;
I can depend on him!"

²⁵ The LORD is kind to everyone
who trusts and obeys him.
²⁶ It is good to wait patiently
for the LORD to save us.
²⁷ When we are young,
it is good to struggle hard
²⁸ and to sit silently alone,
if this is what
the LORD intends.
²⁹ Being rubbed in the dirt
can teach us a lesson;^p
³⁰ we can also learn from insults
and hard knocks.

³¹ The Lord won't always reject us!
³²   He causes a lot of suffering,

but he also has pity
because of his great love.
³³ The Lord doesn't enjoy
sending grief or pain.

³⁴ Don't trample prisoners
under your feet
³⁵ or cheat anyone out of
what is rightfully theirs.
God Most High sees everything,
³⁶ and he knows when you refuse
to give someone a fair trial.
³⁷ No one can do anything
without the Lord's approval.
³⁸ Good and bad each happen
at the command
of God Most High.
³⁹ We're still alive!
We shouldn't complain
when we are being punished
for our sins.
⁴⁰ Instead, we should think
about the way we are living,
and turn back to the LORD.

⁴¹ When we lift our hands
in prayer to God in heaven,
we should offer him our hearts
and say, ⁴² "We've sinned!

ⁿ**3.20** *I am depressed*: One possible meaning for the difficult Hebrew text. ^o**3.22** *destroyed*: One possible meaning for the difficult Hebrew text of verse 22. ^p**3.29** *lesson*: One possible meaning for the difficult Hebrew text of verse 29.

---

*Spiritual*Life—If I've turned away from God, is it possible to come back? How? *(Lamentations 3.31-40)*

Yes, because God always wants us back.
When we try to live apart from God, we run into many problems. This passage suggests that God allows those problems because they may cause us to take a second look at how we're living and change our ways.

What will happen if, after turning away from God, you desire to come back? God won't reject you; he'll welcome you. He doesn't enjoy seeing you suffer the consequences of your sin; he loves you deeply. He'll receive you if you return to him, tell him how sorry you are for turning away from him, and ask him for a new life. This is a healthy fear of the Lord: to realize that nothing escapes his attention, that no one can truly live apart from him, and to turn to him for forgiveness. (See also Isaiah 55.6-13; Ezekiel 37.1-14; Hosea 3; Joel 2.25-27; 1 John 1.8—2.2.)

Words To Remember: *We should think about the way we are living, and turn back to the LORD.*—Lamentations 3.40

We've rebelled against you,
and you haven't forgiven us!
43 Anger is written all over you,
as you pursue and slaughter us
without showing pity.
44 You are behind a wall of clouds
that blocks out our prayers.
45 You allowed nations
to treat us like garbage;
46 our enemies curse us.
47 We are terrified and trapped,
caught and crushed."

48 My people are destroyed!
Tears flood my eyes,
49 and they won't stop
50 until the LORD looks down
from heaven and helps.
51 I am horrified when I see
what enemies have done
to the young women of our city.

52 No one had reason to hate me,
but I was hunted down
like a bird.
53 Then they tried to kill me
by tossing me into a pit
and throwing stones at me.
54 Water covered my head—
I thought I was gone.

55 From the bottom of the pit,
I prayed to you, LORD.
56 I begged you to listen.
"Help!" I shouted. "Save me!"
You answered my prayer
57 and came when I was in need.
You told me, "Don't worry!"
58 You rescued me
and saved my life.
59 You saw them abuse me, LORD,
so make things right.
60 You know every plot
they have made against me.
61 Yes, you know their insults
and their evil plans.
62 All day long they attack
with words and whispers.
63 No matter what they are doing,
they keep on mocking me.

64 Pay them back for everything
they have done, LORD!
65 Put your curse on them
and make them suffer.[q]
66 Get angry and go after them
until not a trace is left
under the heavens.

The Punishment of Jerusalem

The Prophet Speaks:

4 The purest gold is ruined
and has lost its shine;
jewels from the temple
lie scattered in the streets.
2 These are Zion's people,
worth more than purest gold;
yet they are counted worthless
like dishes of clay.

3 Even jackals[r] nurse their young,
but my people are like ostriches
that abandon their own.
4 Babies are so thirsty
that their tongues are stuck
to the roof of the mouth.
Children go begging for food,
but no one gives them any.
5 All who ate expensive foods
lie starving in the streets;
those who grew up in luxury
now sit on trash heaps.

6 My nation was punished worse
than the people of Sodom,
whose city was destroyed
in a flash without the help
of human hands.[s]
7 The leaders of Jerusalem
were purer than snow
and whiter than milk;
their bodies were healthy
and glowed like jewels.[t]
8 Now they are blacker than tar,
and no one recognizes them;
their skin clings to their bones
and is drier than firewood.
9 Being killed with a sword
is better than slowly
starving to death.
10 Life in the city is so bad

---

[q] **3.65** *make them suffer*: One possible meaning for the difficult Hebrew text. [r] **4.3** *jackals*: Desert animals related to wolves, but smaller. [s] **4.6** *hands*: One possible meaning for the difficult Hebrew text of verse 6. [t] **4.7** *jewels*: One possible meaning for the difficult Hebrew text of verse 7.

that loving mothers have boiled
and eaten their own children.

> *Does God get angry over sin*
> *in the world? Of course—*
> *because he's righteous. But*
> *he doesn't stop there. He*
> *offers us forgiveness and*
> *a new life with him.*
> RAMONA CRAMER TUCKER

[11] The LORD was so fiercely angry
that he burned the city of Zion
to the ground.
[12] Not a king on this earth
or the people of any nation
believed enemies could break
through her gates.

[13] Jerusalem was punished because
her prophets and her priests
had sinned and caused the death
of innocent victims.
[14] Yes, her prophets and priests
were covered with blood;
no one would come near them,
as they wandered
from street to street.
[15] Instead, everyone shouted,
"Go away! Don't touch us!
You're filthy and unfit
to belong to God's people!"

So they had to leave
and become refugees.
But foreign nations told them,
"You can't stay here!"[u]
[16] The LORD is the one
who sent them scattering,
and he has forgotten them.
No respect or kindness
will be shown
to the priests or leaders.
[17] Our eyes became weary,
hopelessly looking
for help from a nation[v]
that could not save us.

[18] Enemies hunted us down
on every public street.
Our time was up;
our doom was near.
[19] They swooped down faster
than eagles from the sky.
They hunted for us in the hills
and set traps to catch us
out in the desert.
[20] The LORD's chosen leader[w]
was our hope for survival!
We thought he would keep us safe
somewhere among the nations,
but even he was caught
in one of their traps.

[21] You people of Edom
can celebrate now!
But your time will come
to suffer and stagger
around naked.
[22] The people of Zion
have paid for their sins,
and the Lord will soon
let them return home.
But, people of Edom,
you will be punished,
and your sins exposed.

A Prayer for Mercy

The People of Jerusalem Pray:[x]

5 Our LORD, don't forget
how we have suffered
and been disgraced.
[2] Foreigners and strangers
have taken our land
and our homes.
[3] We are like children
whose mothers are widows.
[4] The water we drink
and the wood we burn
cost far too much.
[5] We are terribly mistreated;[y]
we are worn out
and can find no rest.
[6] We had to surrender

---

[u] **4.15** *here:* One possible meaning for the difficult
Hebrew text of verse 15.   [v] **4.17** *nation:* Egypt, a
former ally of Judah.   [w] **4.20** *chosen leader:* Probably
Zedekiah, the last king of Judah, taken away to
Babylonia in 586 B.C.   [x] **5.1** *The People of Jerusalem Pray:*
Or "The Prophet Prays."   [y] **5.5** *We . . . mistreated:* One
possible meaning for the difficult Hebrew text.

to² Egypt and Assyria
    because we were hungry.

⁷Our ancestors sinned,
    but they are dead,
and we are left to pay
    for their sins.
⁸Slaves are now our rulers,
    and there is no one
    to set us free.
⁹We are in danger
    from brutal desert tribes;
we must risk our lives
    just to bring in our crops.ᵃ
¹⁰Our skin is scorched
    from fever and hunger.

¹¹On Zion and everywhere in Judah
    our wives and daughters
    are being raped.
¹²Our rulers are strung up
    by their arms,
and our nation's advisors
    are treated shamefully.
¹³Young men are forced
    to do the work of slaves;
boys must carry
    heavy loads of wood.

¹⁴Our leaders are not allowed
    to decide cases in court,
and young people
    no longer play music.

¹⁵Our hearts are sad;
instead of dancing,
    we mourn.
¹⁶Zion's glory has disappeared!
And we are doomed
    because of our sins.
¹⁷We feel sick all over
    and can't even see straight;
¹⁸our city is in ruins,
    overrun by wild dogs.

¹⁹You will rule forever, LORD!
    You are King for all time.
²⁰Why have you forgotten us
    for so long?
²¹Bring us back to you!
    Give us a fresh start.
²²Or do you despise us so much
    that you don't want us?

---

²5.6 *surrender to:* Or "make treaties with."
ᵃ5.9 *crops:* One possible meaning for the difficult
Hebrew text of verse 9.

☙

*Spiritual*Life—How should I pray? *(Lamentations 5)*

Pour out your heart to God.
How do you pray when your heart is breaking? How do you pray when you've been
betrayed? How do you pray when your worst fears come to pass? How do you pray when
tragedy strikes?

The answer, according to the Bible, is to tell God about it. Tell him *all* about it, every
detail about what you feel, think, and fear. Sometimes we think we can't come to God
unless we believe perfectly. But the Bible gives us many examples of people who poured out
their grief, bitterness, confusion, pain, sorrow, depression. In this passage, the people of
Jerusalem described what it was like to be conquered by their enemies. The writer detailed
the difficulties: economic hardships; physical pain and weariness; humiliation; injustice;
dangers and sicknesses; the sadness and desolation of having no leaders, no future, no
music in their lives, literally or figuratively.

Not until the last few verses did the author focus on God's nature and cry out for help.
When you pray, don't be too quick to gloss over your feelings before you concentrate on
God. It's difficult to focus properly on God until you've outlined your experience before
him, so pour out your heart. God wants you to be honest. (See also 2 Samuel 7.18-29;
2 Kings 19.14-19; 2 Chronicles 6,7; Nehemiah 1; Psalm 85; Matthew 6.5-15; Acts
4.23-31.)

☙**Words To Remember:** *You will rule forever, LORD! You are King for all time. . . .
Bring us back to you! Give us a fresh start.—Lamentations 5.19,21*

Ezekiel
A Holy God and a Sinful People

Have you ever had to be responsible for someone who was absolutely intent on not heeding any of your warnings? Caring for a two-year-old child who has just learned the meaning of "no" will give you that experience. So will dealing with a drug-addicted teenager.

Ezekiel experienced this frustration on a national scale. Among the Jewish people taken to Babylon with King Jehoiachin in 597 B.C., Ezekiel lived in Babylon throughout the events of his book. Ezekiel lived a trying life—but one full of challenge and direct encounter with the living God.

Ezekiel is one of the few people of the Bible who saw the glory of God. And what images he saw—overwhelming light, wheels within wheels, and strange "living creatures" (1.5)! Once "the LORD God suddenly took control" (8.1) of him and carried him in a vision to Jerusalem seven hundred miles away. There he saw the spiritual leaders of his people hiding in the temple and performing acts of idolatry and pagan worship. Ezekiel then *saw* the glory of the Lord leave his holy temple. Ezekiel's job was to warn them of God's anger.

But not all of Ezekiel is God's judgment and wrath. After Jerusalem was leveled in 586 B.C., God revealed to Ezekiel comforting pictures of the future. He even said, "I will be their shepherd" (34.13) and that he would give his people "a new heart and a desire to be faithful" (36.26). He showed Ezekiel a valley of dry human bones and told Ezekiel to say to the wind, "The LORD God commands you to blow from every direction and to breathe life into these dead bodies" (37.9). Ezekiel saw the bones take shape and move as a strong army. God even showed Ezekiel a

new temple—as glorious as the one they lost and a new city of Jerusalem with a new name: "The-LORD-Is-Herd!" (48.35).

Ezekiel is one of the most forceful, visual books of the Bible. More than fifty times the phrase, "Then you will know that I am the LORD," is repeated. The readers of Ezekiel will hardly forget that message.

Ezekiel at a Glance

1. Ezekiel sees God's glory and is assigned to be a watchman over the people of Israel (1–5)
2. Ezekiel sees a vision of horrible sins in Jerusalem; God's glory leaves the temple (6–11)
3. Ezekiel uses symbols, drama, and direct pleas to warn Jerusalem that God will bring destruction; Ezekiel's wife dies as a symbol of devastating loss (12–24)
4. Ezekiel warns nations surrounding Israel that God will also judge them (25–32)
5. A refugee escapes from Jerusalem and tells Ezekiel that Jerusalem has fallen; God gives Ezekiel a new message of hope (33–37)
6. Ezekiel looks into the distant future and sees an ugly battle, a beautiful temple, holy worship, land divided among all twelve tribes, the return of God's glory to the temple, and a city named "The-LORD-Is-Here!" (38–48)

Ezekiel Sees the LORD's Glory

1 1-3I am Ezekiel—a priest and the son of Buzi.[a]

Five years after King Jehoiachin of Judah had been led away as a prisoner to Babylonia, I was living near the Chebar River among those who had been taken there with him. Then on the fifth day of the fourth month[b] of the thirtieth year,[c] the heavens suddenly opened. The LORD placed his hand upon me[d] and showed me some visions.

4I saw a windstorm blowing in from the north. Lightning flashed from a huge cloud and lit up the whole sky with a dazzling brightness. The fiery center of the cloud was as shiny as polished metal, 5and in that center I saw what looked like four living creatures. They were somewhat like humans, 6except that each one had four faces and four wings. 7Their legs were straight, but their feet looked like the hoofs of calves and sparkled like bronze. 8Under each of their wings, these creatures had a human hand. 9The four creatures were standing back to back with the tips of their wings touching. They moved together in every direction, without turning their bodies.

10Each creature had the face of a human in front, the face of a lion on the right side, the face of a bull on the left, and the face of an eagle in back. 11Two wings[e] of each creature were spread out and touched the wings of the creatures on either side. The other two wings of each creature were folded against its body.

12Wherever the four living creatures went, they moved together without turning their bodies, because each creature faced straight ahead. 13The creatures were glowing like hot coals, and I saw something like a flaming torch moving back and forth among them. Lightning flashed from the torch every time its flame blazed up.[f] 14The creatures themselves moved as quickly as sparks jumping from a fire.[g]

15I then noticed that on the ground beside each of the four living creatures was a wheel,[h] 16shining like chrysolite.[i] Each wheel was exactly the same and had a second wheel that cut through the middle of it,[j] 17so that they could move in any direction without turning. 18The rims of the wheels were large and had eyes all the way

around them.[k] 19-21The creatures controlled when and where the wheels moved—the wheels went wherever the four creatures went and stopped whenever they stopped. Even when the creatures flew in the air, the wheels were beside them.

22-23Above the living creatures, I saw something that was sparkling like ice, and it reminded me of a dome. Each creature had two of its wings stretched out toward the creatures on either side, with the other two wings folded against its body. 24Whenever the creatures flew, their wings roared like an ocean or a large army or even the voice of God All-Powerful. And whenever the creatures stopped, they folded their wings against their bodies.

> *Kneel before God's awesome majesty—after all, he is the King of the universe.*
>
> JONI EARECKSON TADA

25When the creatures stopped flapping their wings, I heard a sound coming from above the dome. 26I then saw what looked like a throne made of sapphire,[l] and sitting on the throne was a figure in the shape of a human. 27From the waist up, it was glowing like metal in a hot furnace, and from the waist down it looked like the flames of a fire. The figure was surrounded by a bright light, 28as colorful as a rainbow that appears after a storm.

---

[a]1.1-3 *a priest and the son of Buzi*: Or "the son of Buzi the priest." [b]1.1-3 *Five years . . . prisoner . . . fourth month*: Probably July of 593 B.C. [c]1.1-3 *thirtieth year*: The event from which this date is figured is unknown. [d]1.1-3 *The LORD placed his hand upon me*: This was a sign that the LORD had chosen Ezekiel to be his prophet. [e]1.11 *Two wings*: One possible meaning for the difficult Hebrew text. [f]1.13 *up*: One possible meaning for the difficult Hebrew text of verse 13. [g]1.14 *as sparks jumping from a fire*: Or "as flashes of lightning." [h]1.15 *wheel*: One possible meaning for the difficult Hebrew text of verse 15. [i]1.16 *chrysolite*: A precious stone that has an olive green color. [j]1.16 *a second wheel that cut through the middle of it*: Or "a smaller wheel inside it." [k]1.18 *them*: One possible meaning for the difficult Hebrew text of verse 18. [l]1.26 *sapphire*: A precious stone that has a blue color.

I realized I was seeing the brightness of the LORD's glory! So I bowed with my face to the ground, and just then I heard a voice speaking to me.

The LORD Chooses Ezekiel

2 The LORD[m] said, "Ezekiel, son of man," I want you to stand up and listen." [2]After he said this, his Spirit took control of me and lifted me to my feet. Then the LORD said:

[3]Ezekiel, I am sending you to the people of Israel. They are just like their ancestors who rebelled against me and refused to stop. [4]They are stubborn and hardheaded. But I, the LORD God, have chosen you to tell them what I say. [5]Those rebels may not even listen, but at least they will know that a prophet has come to them.

[6]Don't be afraid of them or of anything they say. You may think you're in the middle of a thorn patch or a bunch of scorpions. But be brave [7]and preach my message to them, whether they choose to listen or not. [8]Ezekiel, don't rebel against me, as they have done. Instead, listen to everything I tell you.

And now, Ezekiel, open your mouth and eat what I am going to give you.

[9]Just then, I saw a hand stretched out toward me. And in it was a scroll.[o] [10]The hand opened the scroll, and both sides of it were filled with words of sadness, mourning, and grief.

3 The LORD said, "Ezekiel, son of man, after you eat this scroll, go speak to the people of Israel."

[2-3]He handed me the scroll and said, "Eat this and fill up on it." So I ate the scroll, and it tasted sweet as honey.

[4]The LORD said:

Ezekiel, I am sending you to your own people. [5-6]They are Israelites, not some strangers who speak a foreign language you can't understand. If I were to send you to foreign nations, they would listen to you. [7]But the people of Israel will refuse to listen, be-

---

[m]2.1 *The LORD*: Hebrew "The voice." [n]2.1 *Ezekiel, son of man*: The Hebrew text has "Son of man," which is often used in this book when the LORD speaks directly to Ezekiel. It means that Ezekiel is a mere human, yet he is the one the LORD has chosen to be his prophet who speaks for him to the people of Israel. [o]2.9 *scroll*: A roll of paper or special leather used for writing on.

Friendship—Sometimes I feel God is asking me to befriend someone I naturally dislike or who annoys me. How can I overcome my natural inclination to avoid that friendship? (*Ezekiel 2.1-7*)

Remember that God doesn't limit himself to nice people.

It's easy to spot a person who just doesn't fit in. She may be the young woman with stringy hair who tells long stories about her hardships and can't seem to hold a job. She may be the older woman who talks too loudly about her grandchildren and doesn't seem to notice if you edge away. Or she may be the intense woman with bad breath who always whispers something about her health directly into your face.

Few of us *really like* spending time with people who lack social skills. Sometimes they aren't even honest, responsible, or, well, *nice*. Becoming friends with women like these is like putting yourself into "the middle of a thorn patch or a bunch of scorpions" (2.6).

But God is not just the God of nice people. He chooses to befriend all kinds of people not likely to enhance your social standing or even give you an afternoon of comfortable conversation. God called Ezekiel to be his messenger to the Israelites deported to Babylon. God could have abandoned his people there (they had done everything possible to make themselves unacceptable to him). But he didn't. God sent Ezekiel to be his representative.

God may also ask you to represent him to someone few people would befriend. If so, know that you carry with you the friendship of God. (See also Zechariah 4.1-10; Mark 2.13-17; 1 Corinthians 10.31—11.1.)

Words To Remember: *[The Lord said:] "Ezekiel, I am sending you to the people of Israel. . . . Be brave and preach my message to them, whether they choose to listen or not."*—Ezekiel 2.3,6,7

cause they have refused to listen to me. All of them are stubborn and hardheaded, ⁸so I will make you as stubborn as they are. ⁹You will be so determined to speak my message that nothing will stop you. I will make you hard like a diamond, and you'll have no reason to be afraid of those arrogant rebels.

Being focused on God is a life attitude of remaining open to the Holy Spirit's nudges.

MADALENE HARRIS

¹⁰Listen carefully to everything I say and then think about it. ¹¹Then go to the people who were brought here to Babylonia with you and tell them you have a message from me, the LORD God. Do this, whether they listen to you or not.

¹²The Spirit*ᵖ* lifted me up, and as the glory of the LORD started to leave,*q* I heard a loud, thundering noise behind me. ¹³It was the sound made by the creatures' wings as they brushed against each other, and by the rumble of the wheels beside them. ¹⁴Then the Spirit carried me away.

The LORD's power had taken complete control of me, and I was both annoyed and angry.

¹⁵When I was back with the others living at Abib Hill near the Chebar River, I sat among them for seven days, shocked at what had happened to me.

The LORD Appoints Ezekiel To Stand Watch
(Ezekiel 33.1-9)

¹⁶Seven days after I had seen the brightness of the LORD's glory, the LORD said:

¹⁷Ezekiel, son of man, I have appointed you to stand watch for the people of Israel. So listen to what I say, then warn them for me. ¹⁸When I tell wicked people they will die because of their sins, you must warn them to turn from their sinful ways so they won't be

punished. If you refuse, you are responsible for their death. ¹⁹However, if you do warn them, and they keep on sinning, they will die because of their sins, and you will be innocent.

²⁰Now suppose faithful people start sinning, and I decide to put stumbling blocks in their paths to make them fall. They deserve to die because of their sins. So if you refuse to warn them, I will forget about the times they were faithful, and I will hold you responsible for their death. ²¹But if you do warn them, and they listen to you and stop sinning, I will let them live. And you will be innocent.

Ezekiel Cannot Talk

²²The LORD took control of me and said, "Stand up! Go into the valley, and I will talk with you there."

²³I immediately went to the valley, where I saw the brightness of the LORD's glory, just as I had seen near the Chebar River, and I bowed with my face to the ground. ²⁴His Spirit took control of me and lifted me to my feet. Then the LORD said:

As Christians, our calling is to learn how to love God and trust him. We are to be walking advertisements for his incredible power and attributes.

MICHELE HALSEIDE

Go back and lock yourself in your house! ²⁵You will be tied up to keep you inside, ²⁶and I will make you unable to talk or to warn those who have rebelled against me. ²⁷But the time will come, when I will tell you what to say, and you will again be able to speak my message.*r* Some of them will listen;

*p*3.12 *The Spirit:* Or "A wind." *q*3.12 *as the glory of the LORD started to leave:* One possible meaning for the difficult Hebrew text. *r*3.27 *again . . . speak my message:* See 33.21, 22.

others will be stubborn and refuse to listen.

Ezekiel Acts Out an Attack on Jerusalem

The LORD said:

4 Ezekiel, son of man, find a brick and sketch a picture of Jerusalem on it. ²Then prepare to attack the brick as if it were a real city. Build a dirt mound and a ramp up to the top and surround the brick with enemy camps. On every side put large wooden poles as though you were going to break down the gate to the city. ³Set up an iron pan like a wall between you and the brick. All this will be a warning for the people of Israel.

⁴⁻⁵After that, lie down on your left side and stay there for three hundred ninety days as a sign of Israel's punishment*ˢ*—one day for each year of its suffering. ⁶Then turn over and lie on your right side forty more days. That will be a sign of Judah's punishment—one day for each year of its suffering.

⁷The brick stands for Jerusalem, so attack it! Stare at it and shout angry warnings. ⁸I will tie you up, so you can't leave until your attack has ended.

⁹Get a large bowl. Then mix together wheat, barley, beans, lentils, and millet, and make some bread. This is what you will eat for the three hundred ninety days you are lying down. ¹⁰Eat only a small loaf of bread each day ¹¹and drink only two large cups of water. ¹²Use dried human waste to start a fire, then bake the bread on the coals where everyone can watch you. ¹³When I scatter the people of Israel among the nations, they will also have to eat food that is unclean, just as you must do.*ᵗ*

¹⁴I said, "LORD God, please don't make me do that! Never in my life have I eaten food that would make me unacceptable to you. I've never eaten anything that died a natural death or was killed by a wild animal or that you said was unclean."

¹⁵The LORD replied, "Instead of human waste, I will let you bake your bread on a fire

made from cow manure. ¹⁶Ezekiel, the people of Jerusalem will starve. They will have so little food and water that they will be afraid and hopeless. ¹⁷Everyone will be shocked at what is happening, and, because of their sins, they will die a slow death."

Jerusalem's Coming Destruction

The LORD said:

5 Ezekiel, son of man, get a sharp sword and use it to cut off your hair and beard. Weigh the hair and divide it into three equal piles. ²After you attack the brick that stands for Jerusalem, burn one pile of your hair on the brick. Chop up the second pile and let the small pieces of hair fall around the brick. Throw the third pile into the wind, and I will strike it with my own sword.

³Keep a few of the hairs and wrap them in the hem of your clothes. ⁴Then pull out a few of those hairs and throw them in the fire, so they will also burn. This fire will spread, destroying everyone in Israel.

⁵I am the LORD God, and I have made Jerusalem the most important place in the world, and all other nations admire it. ⁶But the people of Jerusalem rebelled and refuse to obey me. They ignored my laws and have become even more sinful than the nations around them.

⁷So tell the people of Jerusalem:

I am the LORD God! You have refused to obey my laws and teachings, and instead you have obeyed the laws of the surrounding nations. You have become more rebellious than any of them! ⁸Now all those nations will watch as I turn against you and punish you ⁹for your sins. Your punishment will be more horrible than anything I've ever done or will ever do again. ¹⁰Parents will be so desperate for food that they will eat their own children, and children will eat their parents.

---

*ˢ***4.4,5** *Israel's punishment:* Israel here refers to the northern kingdom that was destroyed in 722 B.C.
*ᵗ***4.13** *have to eat food that is unclean, just as you must do:* The LORD had forbidden the people of Israel to mix certain things (see Deuteronomy 22.9-11), and so the people would not have been allowed to eat this bread under normal conditions. It is used here to show that when a city is under attack, people eat whatever food is left, even if the LORD had said it was unclean.

Those who survive this horror will be scattered in every direction. [11]Your disgusting sins have made my temple unfit as a place to worship me. So I swear by my own life that I will turn my back on you and show you no pity. [12]A third of you will die here in Jerusalem from disease or starvation. Another third will be killed in war. And I will scatter the last third of you in every direction, then track you down and kill you.

[13]You will feel my fierce anger until I have finished taking revenge. Then you will know that I, the LORD, was furious because of your disobedience. [14]Every passerby will laugh at your destruction. Foreign nations [15]will insult you and make fun of you, but they will also be shocked and terrified at what I did in my anger. [16]I will destroy your crops until you starve to death, and disasters will strike you like arrows. [17]Starvation and wild animals will kill your children. I'll punish you with horrible diseases, and your enemies will strike you down with their swords. I, the LORD, have spoken.

Israel Is Doomed

6 The LORD God said:

[2]Ezekiel, son of man, face the hills of Israel and tell them:

[3]Listen, you mountains and hills, and every valley and gorge! I, the LORD, am about to turn against you and crush all the places where foreign gods are worshiped. [4]Every altar will be smashed, and in front of the idols I will put to death the people who worship them. [5]Dead bodies and bones will be lying around the idols and the altars. [6]Every town in Israel will be destroyed to make sure that each shrine, idol, and altar is smashed—everything the Israelites made will be a pile of ruins. [7]All over the country, your people will die. And those who survive will know that I, the LORD, did these things. [8]I will let some of the people live through this punishment, but I will scatter them among the nations, [9]where they will be prisoners. And when they think of me, they will realize that they disgraced me by rebelling

and by worshiping idols. They will hate themselves for the evil things they did, [10]and they will know that I am the LORD and that my warnings must be taken seriously.

[11]The LORD God then said:

Ezekiel, beat your fists together and stomp your feet in despair! Moan in sorrow, because the people of Israel have done disgusting things and now will be killed by enemy troops, or they will die from starvation and disease. [12]Those who live far away will be struck with deadly diseases. Those who live nearby will be killed in war. And the ones who are left will starve to death. I will let loose my anger on them! [13]These people used to offer incense to idols at altars built on hills and mountaintops and in the shade of large oak trees. But when they see dead bodies lying around those altars, they will know that I am the LORD. [14]I will make their country a barren wasteland, from the Southern Desert to the town of Diblah in the north. Then they will know that I, the LORD, have done these things.

Disaster Is Near

7 The LORD God said:

[2]Ezekiel, son of man, tell the people of Israel that I am saying:

Israel will soon come to an end! Your whole country is about to be destroyed [3]as punishment for your disgusting sins. I, the LORD, am so angry [4]that I will show no pity. I will punish you for the evil you've done, and you will know that I am the LORD.

[5]There's never been anything like the coming disaster." [6]And when it comes, your life will be over. [7]You people of Israel are doomed! Soon there will be panic on the mountaintops instead of celebration." [8]I will let loose my anger and punish you for the evil things you've done. You'll get what you deserve. [9]Your sins are so terrible, that you'll get no mercy from me.

"**7.5** *disaster*: One possible meaning for the difficult Hebrew text of verse 5. "**7.7** *celebration*: One possible meaning for the difficult Hebrew text of verse 7.

Then you will know that I, the LORD, have punished you.

¹⁰Disaster is near! Injustice and arrogance are everywhere, ¹¹and violent criminals run free. None of you will survive the disaster, and everything you own and value will be shattered.ʷ ¹²The time is coming when everyone will be ruined. Buying and selling will stop, ¹³and people who sell property will never get it back, because all of you must be punished for your sins. And I won't change my mind!ˣ

¹⁴A signal has been blown on the trumpet, and weapons are prepared for battle. But no one goes to war, because in my anger I will strike down everyone in Israel.

Israel Is Surrounded

The LORD said to the people of Israel:

¹⁵War, disease, and starvation are everywhere! People who live in the countryside will be killed in battle, and those who live in towns will die from starvation or deadly diseases. ¹⁶Anyone who survives will escape into the hills, like doves who leave the valleys to find safety.

All of you will moanʸ because of your sins. ¹⁷Your hands will tremble, and your knees will go limp. ¹⁸You will put on sackclothᶻ to show your sorrow, but terror will overpower you. Shame will be written all over your faces, and you will shave your heads in despair. ¹⁹Your silver and gold will be thrown into the streets like garbage, because those are the two things that led you into sin, and now they cannot save you from my anger. They are not even worth enough to buy food. ²⁰You took great pride in using your beautiful jewelry to make disgusting idols of foreign gods. So I will make your jewelry worthless.

²¹Wicked foreigners will rob and disgrace you. ²²They will break into my templeᵃ and leave it unfit as a place to worship me, but I will look away and let it happen.

²³Your whole country is in confusion!ᵇ Murder and violence are everywhere in Israel, ²⁴so I will tell the most wicked nations to come and take over your homes. They will put an end to the pride you have in your strong army, and they will make your places of worship unfit to use. ²⁵You will be terrified and will desperately look for peace— but there will be no peace. ²⁶One tragedy will follow another, and you'll hear only bad news. People will beg prophets to give them a message from me. Priests will stop teaching my Law, and wise leaders won't be able to give advice. ²⁷Even your king and his officials will lose hope and cry in despair. Your hands will tremble with fear.

God isn't Santa, he's Savior. What he saves us from isn't only death, but from ourselves and our foolish, selfish desires.
LIZ CURTIS HIGGS

I will punish you for your sins and treat you the same way you have treated others. Then you will know that I am the LORD.

Ezekiel Sees the Terrible Sins of Jerusalem

8 Six years after King Jehoiachin and the rest of us had been led away as prisoners to Babylonia, the leaders of Judah were meeting with me in my house. On the fifth day of the sixth month,ᶜ the LORD God suddenly took control of me, ²and I saw something in the shape of a human.ᵈ This figure was like fire from the waist down, and it was bright as polished metal from the waist up. ³It reached out what seemed to be

ʷ**7.11** *shattered*: One possible meaning for the difficult Hebrew text of verses 10, 11. ˣ**7.13** *mind*: One possible meaning for the difficult Hebrew text of verse 13. ʸ**7.16** *will moan*: Hebrew; two ancient translations "will die." ᶻ**7.18** *sackcloth*: A rough, dark-colored cloth made from goat or camel hair and used to make grain sacks. It was worn in times of trouble or sorrow. ᵃ**7.22** *my temple*: The Hebrew text has "my treasure," which may refer to the temple, to Jerusalem, or to Israel itself. ᵇ**7.23** *Your whole country is in confusion*: One ancient translation; Hebrew "Get chains ready to drag away the dead bodies of your people." ᶜ**8.1** *Six years . . . sixth month*: Probably September of 592 B.C. ᵈ**8.2** *a human*: One ancient translation; Hebrew "a fiery figure."

a hand and grabbed my hair. Then in my vision the LORD's Spirit lifted me into the sky and carried me to Jerusalem.

The Spirit took me to the north gate of the temple's inner courtyard, where there was an idol that disgusted the LORD and made him furious. ⁴Then I saw the brightness of the glory of the God of Israel, just as I had seen it near the Chebar River.

⁵God said to me, "Ezekiel, son of man, look north." And when I did, I saw that disgusting idol by the altar near the gate.

⁶God then said, "Do you see the terrible sins of the people of Israel? Their sins are making my holy temple unfit as a place to worship me. Yet you will see even worse things than this."

⁷Next, I was taken to the entrance of the courtyard, where I saw a hole in the wall.
⁸God said, "Make this hole bigger." And when I did, I realized it was a doorway. ⁹"Go in," God said, "and see what horrible and evil things the people are doing."

¹⁰Inside, I saw that the walls were covered with pictures of reptiles and disgusting, unclean animals,ᵉ as well as with idols that the Israelites were worshiping. ¹¹Seventy Israelite leaders were standing there, including Jaazaniah son of Shaphan. Each of these leaders was holding an incense burner, and the smell of incense filled the room.

¹²God said, "Ezekiel, do you see what horrible things Israel's leaders are doing in secret? They have filled their rooms with idols. And they say I can't see them, because they think I have already deserted Israel. ¹³But I will show you something even worse than this."

¹⁴He took me to the north gate of the temple, where I saw women mourning for the god Tammuz.ᶠ ¹⁵God asked me, "Can you believe what these women are doing? But now I want to show you something worse."

¹⁶I was then led into the temple's inner courtyard, where I saw about twenty-five men standing near the entrance, between the porch and the altar. Their backs were to the LORD's temple, and they were bowing down to the rising sun.

¹⁷God said, "Ezekiel, it's bad enough that the people of Judah are doing these disgusting things. But they have also spread violence and injustice everywhere in Israel and have made me very angry. They have

disgraced and insulted me in the worst possible way.ᵍ ¹⁸So in my fierce anger, I will punish them without mercy and refuse to help them when they cry out to me."

The LORD Gives the Command To Punish Jerusalem

9 After that, I heard the LORD shout, "Come to Jerusalem, you men chosen to destroy the city. And bring your weapons!"

²I saw six men come through the north gate of the temple, each one holding a deadly weapon. A seventh man dressed in a linen robe was with them, and he was carrying things to write with. The men went into the temple and stood by the bronze altar.

³The brightness of God's glory then left its place above the statues of the winged creaturesʰ inside the temple and moved to the entrance. The LORD said to the man in the linen robe, ⁴"Walk through the city of Jerusalem and mark the forehead of anyone who is truly upset and sad about the disgusting things that are being done here."

⁵⁻⁶He turned to the other six men and said, "Follow him and put to death everyone who doesn't have a mark on their forehead. Show no mercy or pity! Kill men and women, parents and children. Begin here at my temple and be sure not to harm those who are marked."

The men immediately killed the leaders who were standing there.

⁷Then the LORD said, "Pollute the temple by piling the dead bodies in the courtyards. Now get busy!" They left and started killing the people of Jerusalem.

⁸I was then alone, so I bowed down and cried out to the LORD, "Why are you doing this? Are you so angry at the people of Jerusalem that everyone must die?"

⁹The LORD answered, "The people of Israel and Judah have done horrible things. Their country is filled with murderers, and

---

ᵉ8.10 *disgusting, unclean animals*: See, for example, Leviticus 11.9-19. ᶠ8.14 *the god Tammuz*: A god of vegetation who was thought to die in the dry season. During the Hebrew month of Tammuz (from about mid-June to mid-July), women mourned the death of this god, hoping to bring him back to life. ᵍ8.17 *disgraced and insulted me . . . way*: One possible meaning for the difficult Hebrew text. ʰ9.3 *the statues of the winged creatures*: These were symbols of the LORD's throne on earth (see Exodus 25.18-22; 1 Kings 6.23-28).

Jerusalem itself is filled with violence. They think that I have deserted them, and that I can't see what they are doing. [10]And so I will not have pity on them or forgive them. They will be punished for what they have done."

[11]Just then, the man in the linen robe returned and said, "I have done what you commanded."

The LORD's Glory Leaves the Temple

10 I saw the dome that was above the four winged creatures,[i] and on it was the sapphire[j] throne.[k] [2]The LORD said to the man in the linen robe, "Walk among the four wheels beside the creatures and pick up as many hot coals as you can carry. Then scatter them over the city of Jerusalem." I watched him as he followed the LORD's instructions.

[3]The winged creatures were standing south of the temple when the man walked among them. A cloud filled the inner courtyard, [4]and the brightness of the LORD's glory moved from above the creatures and stopped at the entrance of the temple. The entire temple was filled with his glory, and the courtyard was dazzling bright. [5]The sound of the creatures' wings was as loud as the voice of God All-Powerful and could even be heard in the outer courtyard.

[6]The man in the robe was now standing beside a wheel. [7]One of the four creatures reached its hand into the fire among them and gave him some of the hot coals. The man took the coals and left.

[8]I noticed again that each of the four winged creatures had what looked like human hands under their wings, [9]and I saw the four wheels near the creatures. These wheels were shining like chrysolite.[l] [10]Each wheel was exactly the same and had a second wheel that cut through the middle of it,[m] [11]so that they could move in any direction without turning. The wheels moved together whenever the creatures moved. [12]I also noticed that the wheels and the creatures' bodies, including their backs, their hands, and their wings, were covered with eyes. [13]And I heard a voice calling these "the wheels that spin."

[14]Each of the winged creatures had four

---

[i]10.1 *winged creatures*: See the note at 9.3.
[j]10.1 *sapphire*: See the note at 1.26. [k]10.1 *dome . . . creatures . . . throne*: See 1.22-26. [l]10.9 *chrysolite*: See the note at 1.16. [m]10.10 *a second wheel that cut through the middle of it*: See the note at 1.16.

---

*Spiritual*Life—How can I make God's presence real in my life? *(Ezekiel 10)*

Realize that even when you don't "feel" God's presence, he's there.
The Bible tells us that God is everywhere at all times, so we know, with our intellect, that God is always with us. Sometimes we're especially aware of his presence—like when a truck almost hits our skidding car or when we're worshiping him intently with his people.

Other times, perhaps for long periods, we seem unable to *feel* God's presence. We search our heart for sin and confess what we find. But God seems absent. We continue in regular worship and prayer. Still, God seems absent. At times, God may bring this sense of his absence to teach us not to depend on what we do and what we feel, but on God himself. As we endure this dark time, trusting God even when we can't feel him, we know that eventually we'll again enjoy feelings of his love.

Is it possible to offend God so completely that he refuses to make himself available to you? Yes, because this is what the people of Jerusalem did in Ezekiel's era. Chapter 8 records a horrifying picture of spiritual leaders using God's holy temple to worship pagan gods. Then, in one of the most tragic scenes of Ezekiel, we see the Lord's glory lift from that temple and depart.

This passage teaches us that we should never take God's presence for granted (as if we can turn him on or off). We must value that holy presence—whether or not we can feel it at that moment in time. (See also 2 Chronicles 29.20-36; Romans 15.14-21; Ephesians 3.14-21; Colossians 3.10,11.)

Words To Remember: *Then I watched the brightness of the LORD's glory move from the entrance of the temple and stop above the winged creatures. They spread their wings and flew into the air with the wheels at their side.—Ezekiel 10.18,19*

faces: the face of a bull,[n] the face of a human, the face of a lion, and the face of an eagle. [15-17]These were the same creatures I had seen near the Chebar River. They controlled when and where the wheels moved—the wheels went wherever the creatures went and stopped whenever they stopped. Even when the creatures flew in the air, the wheels stayed beside them.

[18]Then I watched the brightness of the LORD's glory move from the entrance of the temple and stop above the winged creatures. [19]They spread their wings and flew into the air with the wheels at their side. They stopped at the east gate of the temple, and the LORD's glory was above them.

[20]I knew for sure that these were the same creatures I had seen beneath the LORD's glory near the Chebar River. [21-22]They had four wings with hands beneath them, and they had the same four faces as those near the River. Each creature moved straight ahead without turning.

Ezekiel Condemns Jerusalem's Wicked Leaders

11 The LORD's Spirit[o] lifted me up and took me to the east gate of the temple, where I saw twenty-five men, including the two leaders, Jaazaniah son of Azzur and Pelatiah son of Benaiah. [2]The LORD said, "Ezekiel, son of man, these men are making evil plans and giving dangerous advice to the people of Jerusalem. [3]They say things like, 'Let's build more houses.[p] This city is like a cooking pot over a fire, and we are the meat, but at least the pot keeps us from being burned in the fire.'[q] [4]So, Ezekiel, condemn them!"

[5]The LORD's Spirit took control of me and told me to tell these leaders:

I, the LORD God, know what you leaders are saying. [6]You have murdered so many people that the city is filled with dead bodies! [7]This city is indeed a cooking pot, but the bodies of those you killed are the meat. And so I will force you to leave Jerusalem, [8]and I'll send armies to attack you, just as you fear. [9]Then you will be captured and punished by foreign enemies.[r] [10]You will be killed in your own country, but not before you realize that I, the LORD, have done these things.

[11]You leaders claim to be meat in a cooking pot, but you won't be protected by this city. No, you will die at the border of Israel. [12]You will realize that while you were following the laws of nearby nations, you were disobeying my laws and teachings. And I am the LORD!

[13]Before I finished speaking, Pelatiah dropped dead. I bowed down and cried out, "Please, LORD God, don't kill everyone left in Israel."

A Promise of Hope

[14]The LORD replied:

[15]Ezekiel, son of man, the people living in Jerusalem claim that you and the other Israelites who were taken to Babylonia are too far away to worship me. They also claim that the land of Israel now belongs only to them. [16]But here is what I want you to tell the Israelites in Babylonia:

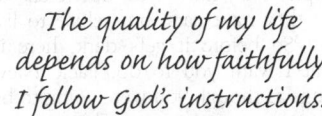

The quality of my life depends on how faithfully I follow God's instructions.

MAYO MATHERS

It's true that I, the LORD God, have forced you out of your own country and made you live among foreign nations. But for now, I will be with you wherever you are, so that you can worship me. [17]And someday, I will gather you from the nations where you are scattered and let you live in Israel again. [18]When that happens, I want you to clear the land of all disgusting idols. [19]Then I will take away your stubbornness and make you eager to be completely faithful to me. You will

---

[n]10.14 *a bull:* The Hebrew text has "a winged creature," but see 1.10. [o]11.1 *The LORD's Spirit:* Or "A wind." [p]11.3 *Let's . . . houses:* One possible meaning for the difficult Hebrew text. [q]11.3 *the pot keeps us from being burned in the fire:* These leaders were trying to convince the people of Jerusalem that they were secure, and that their future was bright. [r]11.9 *foreign enemies:* That is, the Babylonians.

want to obey me [20]and all my laws and teachings. You will be my people, and I will be your God. [21]But those who worship idols will be punished and get what they deserve. I, the LORD God, have spoken.

The LORD's Glory Leaves Jerusalem

[22]After the LORD had finished speaking, the winged creatures spread their wings and flew into the air, and the wheels were beside them. The brightness of the LORD's glory above them [23]left Jerusalem and stopped at a hill east of the city.

[24]Then in my vision, the LORD's Spirit[s] lifted me up and carried me back to the other exiles in Babylonia. The vision faded away, [25]and I told them everything the LORD had shown me.

Ezekiel Acts Out Israel's Captivity

12 The LORD said:
[2]Ezekiel, son of man, you are living among rebellious people. They have eyes, but refuse to see; they have ears, but refuse to listen. [3]So before it gets dark, here is what I want you to do. Pack a few things as though you were going to be taken away as a prisoner. Then go outside where everyone can see you and walk around from place to place. Maybe as they watch, they will realize what rebels they are. [4]After you have done this, return to your house.

Later that evening leave your house as if you were going into exile. [5]Dig through the wall of your house[t] and crawl out, carrying the bag with you. Make sure everyone is watching. [6]Lift the bag to your shoulders, and with your face covered, take it into the darkness, so that you cannot see the land you are leaving. All of this will be a warning for the people of Israel.

[7]I did everything the LORD had said. I packed a few things. Then as the sun was going down, and while everyone was watching, I dug a hole through one of the walls of my house. I pulled out my bag, then lifted it to my shoulders and left in the darkness.

[8]The next morning, the LORD [9]reminded me that those rebellious people didn't even ask what I was doing. [10]So he sent me back to tell them:

The LORD God has a message for the leader of Jerusalem and everyone living there!

[11]I have done these things to show them what will happen when they are taken away as prisoners.

[12]The leader of Jerusalem will lift his own bag to his shoulders at sunset and leave through a hole that the others have dug in the wall of his house. He will cover his face, so he can't see the land he is leaving. [13]The LORD will spread out a net and trap him as he leaves Jerusalem. He will then be led away to the city of Babylon, but will never see that place,[u] even though he will die there. [14]His own officials and troops will scatter in every direction, and the LORD will track them down and put them to death.

[15]The LORD will force the rest of the people in Jerusalem to live in foreign nations, where they will realize that he has done all these things. [16]Some of them will survive the war, the starvation, and the deadly diseases. That way, they will be able to tell foreigners how disgusting their sins were, and that it was the LORD who punished them in this way.

A Sign of Fear

[17]The LORD said:
[18]Ezekiel, son of man, shake with fear when you eat, and tremble when you drink. [19]Tell the people of Israel that I, the LORD, say that someday everyone in Jerusalem will shake when they eat and tremble when they drink. Their country will be destroyed and left empty, because they have been cruel and violent. [20]Every town will lie in ruins, and the land will be a barren desert. Then they will know that I am the LORD.

The Words of the LORD Will Come True

[21]The LORD said:
[22]Ezekiel, son of man, you've heard peo-

---

[s]11.24 the LORD's Spirit: See the note at 11.1.
[t]12.5 Dig through the wall of your house: The walls of most houses in Babylonia were made of mud bricks that had been dried in the sun. A hole could easily have been dug through these bricks.   [u]12.13 He will then be led away . . . that place: According to 2 Kings 25.6, 7, King Zedekiah of Judah was blinded before he was taken to Babylon.

ple in Israel use the saying, "Time passes, and prophets are proved wrong." [23]Now tell the people that I, the LORD, am going to prove that saying wrong. No one will ever be able to use it again in Israel, because very soon everything I have said will come true! [24]The people will hear no more useless warnings and false messages. [25]I will give them my message, and what I say will certainly happen. Warn those rebels that the time has come for them to be punished. I, the LORD, make this promise.

[26-27]Ezekiel, the people of Israel are also saying that your visions and messages are only about things in the future. [28]So tell them that my words will soon come true, just as I have warned. I, the LORD, have spoken.

Lying Prophets

13 The LORD said: [2]Ezekiel, son of man, condemn the prophets of Israel who say they speak in my name, but who preach messages that come from their own imagination. Tell them it's time to hear my message.

[3]I, the LORD God, say those lying prophets are doomed! They don't see visions— they make up their own messages! [4]Israel's prophets are no better than jackals[v] that hunt for food among the ruins of a city. [5]They don't warn the people about coming trouble or tell them how dangerous it is to sin against me. [6]Those prophets lie by claiming they speak for me, but I have not even chosen them to be my prophets. And they still think their words will come true. [7]They say they're preaching my messages, but they are full of lies—I did not speak to them!

[8]So I am going to punish those lying prophets for deceiving the people of Israel with false messages. [9]I will turn against them and no longer let them belong to my people. They will not be allowed to call themselves Israelites or even to set foot in Israel. Then they will realize that I am the LORD God.

[10]Those prophets refuse to be honest. They tell my people there will be peace, even though there's no peace to be found. They are like workers who think they can fix a shaky wall by covering it with paint. [11]But when I send rainstorms, hailstones, and

strong winds, the wall will surely collapse. [12]People will then ask the workers why the paint didn't hold it up.

[13]That wall is the city of Jerusalem. And I, the LORD God, am so angry that I will send strong winds, rainstorms, and hailstones to destroy it. [14]The lying prophets have tried to cover up the evil in Jerusalem, but I will tear down the city, all the way to its foundations. And when it collapses, those prophets will be killed, and everyone will know that I have done these things.

[15]The city of Jerusalem and its lying prophets will feel my fierce anger. Then I will announce that the city has fallen and that the lying prophets are dead, [16]because they promised my people peace, when there was no peace. I, the LORD God, have spoken.

Women Who Wear Magic Charms

The LORD said:

[17]Ezekiel, son of man, now condemn the women of Israel who preach messages that come from their own imagination. [18]Tell them they're doomed! They wear magic charms on their wrists and scarves on their heads, then trick others into believing they can predict the future.[w] They won't get away with telling those lies. [19]They charge my people a few handfuls of barley and a couple pieces of bread, and then give messages that are insulting to me. They use lies to sentence the innocent to death and to help the guilty go free. And my people believe them!

[20]I hate the magic charms they use to trick people into believing their lies. I will rip those charms from their wrists and set free the people they have trapped like birds.[x] [21]I will tear the scarves from their heads and rescue my people from their power once and for all. Then they will know that I am the LORD God.

[22]They do things I would never do. They lie to good people and encourage them to do wrong, and they convince the wicked to keep sinning and ruin their lives. [23]I will no longer let these women give false messages

---

[v]13.4 *jackals:* Desert animals related to wolves, but smaller.   [w]13.18 *They wear . . . the future:* One possible meaning for the difficult Hebrew text.
[x]13.20 *like birds:* One possible meaning for the difficult Hebrew text.

and use magic, and I will free my people from their control. Then they will know that I, the LORD, have done these things.

Ezekiel Encourages the People To Turn Back to the LORD

14 One day, some of Israel's leaders came to me and asked for a message from the LORD. [2]While they were there, the LORD said:

[3]Ezekiel, son of man, these men have started worshiping idols, though they know it will cause them to sin even more. So I refuse to give them a message!

[4]Tell the people of Israel that if they sin by worshiping idols and then go to a prophet to find out what I say, I will give them the answer their sins deserve. [5]When they hear my message, maybe they will see that they need to turn back to me and stop worshiping those idols.

[6]Now, Ezekiel, tell everyone in Israel:

I am the LORD God. Stop worshiping your disgusting idols and come back to me.

[7]Suppose one of you Israelites or a foreigner living in Israel rejects me and starts worshiping idols. If you then go to a prophet to find out what I say, I will answer [8]by turning against you. I will make you a warning to anyone who might think of doing the same thing, and you will no longer belong to my people. Then you will know that I am the LORD and that you have sinned against me.

[9]If a prophet gives a false message, I am the one who caused that prophet to lie. But I will still reject him and cut him off from my people, [10]and anyone who goes to that prophet for a message will be punished in the same way. [11]I will do this, so that you will come back to me and stop destroying yourselves with these disgusting sins. So turn back to me! Then I will be your God, and you will be my people. I, the LORD God, make this promise.

Judgment on a Sinful Nation

[12]The LORD God said:

[13]Ezekiel, son of man, suppose an entire nation sins against me, and I punish it by destroying the crops and letting its people and livestock starve to death. [14]Even if Noah, Daniel,[y] and Job were living in that nation, their faithfulness would not save anyone but themselves.

[15]Or suppose I punish a nation by sending wild animals to eat people and scare away every passerby, so that the land becomes a barren desert. [16]As surely as I live, I promise that even if these three men lived in that nation, their own children would not be spared. The three men would live, but the land would be an empty desert.

[17]Or suppose I send an enemy to attack a sinful nation and kill its people and livestock. [18]If these three men were in that nation when I punished it, not even their children would be spared. Only the three men would live.

[19]And suppose I am so angry that I send a deadly disease to wipe out the people and livestock of a sinful nation. [20]Again, even if Noah, Daniel, and Job were living there, I, the LORD, promise that the children of these faithful men would also die. Only the three of them would be spared.

[21]I am the LORD God, and I promise to punish Jerusalem severely. I will send war, starvation, wild animals, and deadly disease to slaughter its people and livestock. [22]And those who survive will be taken from their country and led here to Babylonia. Ezekiel, when you see how sinful they are, you will know why I did all these things to Jerusalem. [23]You will be convinced that I, the LORD God, was right in doing what I did.

Jerusalem Is a Useless Vine

15 Some time later, the LORD said:
[2]Ezekiel, son of man, what happens to the wood of a grapevine after the grapes have been picked? It isn't like other trees in the forest, [3]because the wood of a grapevine can't be used to make anything, not even a small peg to hang things on. [4]It can only be used as firewood. But after its ends are burnt and its middle is charred, it can't be used for anything. [5]The wood is useless before it is burned, and afterwards it is completely worthless.

[6]I, the LORD God, promise that just as the wood of a grapevine is burned as firewood, [7]I will punish the people of Jerusalem with fire. Some of them have escaped one

---

[y]**14.14** *Daniel:* Or "Danel," possibly a well-known hero or wise man.

destruction, but soon they will be completely burned. And when that happens, you, Ezekiel, will know that I am the LORD. [8]I will make their country an empty wasteland, because they have not been loyal to me. I, the LORD God, have spoken.

Jerusalem Is Unfaithful

16 The LORD said: [2]Ezekiel, son of man, remind the people of Jerusalem of their disgusting sins [3]and tell them that I, the LORD God, am saying:

Jerusalem, you were born in the country where Canaanites lived. Your father was an Amorite, and your mother was a Hittite.[z] [4]When you were born, no one cut you loose from your mother or washed your body. No one rubbed your skin with salt and olive oil,[a] and wrapped you in warm blankets. [5]Not one person loved you enough to do any of these things, and no one even felt sorry for you. You were despised, thrown into a field, and forgotten.

[6]I saw you lying there, rolling around in your own blood, and I couldn't let you die. [7]I took care of you, like someone caring for a tender, young plant. You grew up to be a beautiful young woman with perfect breasts and long hair, but you were still naked.

[8]When I saw you again, you were old enough to have sex. So I covered your naked body with my own robe.[b] Then I solemnly promised that you would belong to me and that I, the LORD God, would take care of you.

[9]I washed the blood off you and rubbed your skin with olive oil. [10]I gave you the finest clothes and the most expensive robes,[c] as well as sandals made from the best leather. [11]I gave you bracelets, a necklace, [12]a ring for your nose, some earrings, and a beautiful crown. [13]Your jewelry was gold and silver, and your clothes were made of only the finest material and embroidered linen. Your bread was baked from fine flour, and you ate honey and olive oil. You were as beautiful as a queen, [14]and everyone on earth knew it. I, the LORD God, had helped you become a lovely young woman.

[15]You learned that you were attractive enough to have any man you wanted, so you offered yourself to every passerby.[d] [16]You made shrines for yourself and decorated them with some of your clothes. That's

where you took your visitors to have sex with them. These things should never have happened![e] [17]You made idols out of the gold and silver jewelry I gave you, then you sinned by worshiping those idols. [18]You dressed them in the clothes you got from me, and you offered them the olive oil and incense I gave you. [19]I supplied you with fine flour, olive oil, and honey, but you sacrificed it all as offerings to please those idols. I, the LORD God, watched this happen.

> *Thank God daily for the body he crafted for you while you were yet in your mother's womb, for your health, for the balance of your days here on earth, and, finally, for the opportunity to serve him with a glad heart.*
>
> KAREN SCALF LINAMEN

[20]But you did something even worse than that—you sacrificed your own children to those idols! [21]You slaughtered my children, so you could offer them as sacrifices. [22]You were so busy sinning and being a prostitute that you refused to think about the days when you were young and were rolling around naked in your own blood.

[23]Now I, the LORD God, say you are doomed! Not only did you do these evil things, [24]but you also built places on every street corner [25]where you disgraced yourself by having sex with anyone who walked by.

---

[z]**16.3** *Amorite . . . Hittite*: People who lived in Canaan before the Israelites and who worshiped idols. [a]**16.4** *rubbed your skin with salt and olive oil*: People believed this toughened the skin of the babies. [b]**16.8** *I covered your naked body with my own robe*: To show that he would protect and take care of her. [c]**16.10** *most expensive robes*: One possible meaning for the difficult Hebrew text. [d]**16.15** *so you offered yourself to every passerby*: One possible meaning for the difficult Hebrew text. [e]**16.16** *These things should never have happened*: One possible meaning for the difficult Hebrew text.

And you did that more and more every day! ²⁶To make me angry, you even offered yourself to Egyptians, who were always ready to sleep with you.

²⁷So I punished you by letting those greedy Philistine enemies take over some of your territory. But even they were offended by your disgusting behavior.

²⁸You couldn't get enough sex, so you chased after Assyrians and slept with them. You still weren't satisfied, ²⁹so you went after Babylonians. But those merchants could not satisfy you either.

³⁰I, the LORD God, say that you were so disgusting that you would have done anything to get what you wanted.^f ³¹You had sex on every street corner, and when you finished, you refused to accept money. That's worse than being a prostitute! ³²You are nothing but an unfaithful wife who would rather have sex with strangers than with your own husband. ³³Prostitutes accept money for having sex, but you bribe men from everywhere to have sex with you. ³⁴You're not like other prostitutes. Men don't ask you for sex—you offer to pay them!

Jerusalem Must Be Punished

The LORD said:

³⁵Jerusalem, you prostitute, listen to me. ³⁶You chased after lovers, then took off your clothes and had sex. You even worshiped disgusting idols and sacrificed your own children as offerings to them. ³⁷So I, the LORD God, will gather every one of your lovers, those you liked and those you hated. They will stand around you, and I will rip off your clothes and let all of those lovers stare at your nakedness. ³⁸I will find you guilty of being an unfaithful wife and a murderer, and in my fierce anger I will sentence you to death! ³⁹Then I will hand you over to your lovers, who will tear down the places where you had sex. They will take your clothes and jewelry, leaving you naked and empty-handed. ⁴⁰Your lovers and an angry mob will stone you to death; they will cut your dead body into pieces ⁴¹and burn down your houses. Other women will watch these terrible things happen to you. I promise to stop you from being a prostitute and paying your lovers for sex.

⁴²Only then will I calm down and stop being angry and jealous. ⁴³You made me furious by doing all these disgusting things and by forgetting how I took care of you when you were young. Then you made things worse by acting like a prostitute. You must be punished! I, the LORD God, have spoken.

Jerusalem's Two Sisters

The LORD said:

⁴⁴People will use this saying about you, Jerusalem: "If the mother is bad, so is her daughter." ⁴⁵You are just like your mother, who hated her husband and her own children. You are also like your sisters, who hated their husbands and children. Your father was an Amorite, and your mother was a Hittite.^g ⁴⁶Your older sister was Samaria, that city to your north with her nearby villages. Your younger sister was Sodom, that city to your south with her nearby villages. ⁴⁷You followed their way of life and their wicked customs, and soon you were more disgusting than they were.

⁴⁸As surely as I am the living LORD God, the people of Sodom and its nearby villages were never as sinful as you. ⁴⁹They were arrogant and spoiled; they had everything they needed and still refused to help the poor and needy. ⁵⁰They thought they were better than everyone else, and they did things I hate. And so I destroyed them.

⁵¹You people of Jerusalem have sinned twice as much as the people of Samaria. In fact, your evil ways have made both Sodom and Samaria look innocent. ⁵²So their punishment will seem light compared to yours. You will be disgraced and put to shame because of your disgusting sins.

Jerusalem Will Be Ashamed

The LORD said to Jerusalem:

⁵³Someday I will bless Sodom and Samaria and their nearby villages. I will also bless you, Jerusalem. ⁵⁴Then you will be ashamed of how you've acted, and Sodom and Samaria will be relieved that they weren't as sinful as you. ⁵⁵When that day

---

^f**16.30** *wanted:* One possible meaning for the difficult Hebrew text of verse 30. ^g**16.45** *Amorite . . . Hittite:* See the note at 16.3.

comes, you and Sodom and Samaria will once again be well-off, and all nearby villages will be restored.

⁵⁶Jerusalem, you were so arrogant that you sneered at Sodom. ⁵⁷But now everyone has learned how wicked you really are. The countries of Syria and Philistia, as well as your other neighbors, hate you and make insulting remarks. ⁵⁸You must pay for all the vulgar and disgusting things you have done. I, the LORD, have spoken.

The LORD Makes a Promise to Jerusalem

The LORD said:

⁵⁹Jerusalem, you deserve to be punished, because you broke your promises and ignored our agreement. ⁶⁰But I remember the agreement I made with you when you were young,ʰ and so I will make you a promise that will last forever. ⁶¹When you think about how you acted, you will be ashamed, especially when I return your sistersⁱ to you as daughters, even though this was not part of our agreement.ʲ ⁶²I will keep this solemn promise, and you will know that I am the LORD. ⁶³I will forgive you, but you will think about your sins and be too ashamed to say a word. I, the LORD God, have spoken.

A Story about Two Eagles and a Vine

17 The LORD said:
²Ezekiel, son of man, tell the people of Israel the following story, ³so they will understand what I am saying to them:

A large eagle with strong wings and beautiful feathers once flew to Lebanon. It broke the top branch off a cedar tree, ⁴then carried it to a nation of merchants and left it in one of their cities. ⁵The eagle also took seed from Israel and planted it in a fertile field with plenty of water, like a willow tree beside a stream.ᵏ ⁶The seed sprouted and grew into a grapevine that spread over the ground. It had lots of leaves and strong, deep roots, and its branches grew upward toward the eagle.

⁷There was another eagle with strong wings and thick feathers. The roots and branches of the grapevine soon turned toward this eagle, hoping it would bring water for the soil. ⁸But the vine was already growing in fertile soil, where there was plenty of

water to produce healthy leaves and large grapes.

⁹Now tell me, Ezekiel, do you think this grapevine will live? Or will the first eagle pull it up by its roots and pluck off the grapes and let its new leaves die? The eagle could easily kill it without the help of a large and powerful army. ¹⁰The grapevine is strong and healthy, but as soon as the scorching desert wind blows, it will quickly wither.

The LORD Explains the Story

¹¹The LORD said:
¹²Ezekiel, ask the rebellious people of Israel if they know what this story means.

Tell them that the king of Babylonia came to Jerusalem, then he captured the king of Judahˡ and his officials, and took them back to Babylon as prisoners. ¹³He chose someone from the family of Judah's kingᵐ and signed a treaty with him, then made him swear to be loyal. He also led away other important citizens, ¹⁴so that the rest of the people of Judah would obey only him and never gain control of their own country again.

¹⁵But this new king of Judah later rebelled against Babylonia and sent officials to Egypt to get horses and troops. Will this king be successful in breaking the treaty with Babylonia? Or will he be punished for what he's done? ¹⁶As surely as I am the living LORD God, I swear that the king of Judah will die in Babylon, because he broke the treaty with the king of Babylonia, who appointed him king. ¹⁷Even the king of Egypt and his powerful army will be useless to Judah when the Babylonians attack and build dirt ramps to invade the cities of Judah and kill its people. ¹⁸The king of Judah broke his own promises and ignored the treaty with Babylonia. And so he will be punished!

¹⁹He made a promise in my name and swore to honor the treaty. And now that he

---

ʰ**16.60** *the agreement . . . when you were young:* See verse 8. ⁱ**16.61** *sisters:* Sodom and Samaria (see verses 44-52). ʲ**16.61** *even though this was not part of our agreement:* One possible meaning for the difficult Hebrew text. ᵏ**17.5** *like a willow tree beside a stream:* One possible meaning for the difficult Hebrew text. ˡ**17.12** *king of Judah:* Probably King Jehoiachin (see 2 Kings 24.10-12, 15, 16). ᵐ**17.13** *someone from the family of Judah's king:* Probably King Zedekiah (see 2 Kings 24.17).

has broken that promise, my name is disgraced. He must pay for what he's done. ²⁰I will spread out a net to trap him. Then I will drag him to Babylon and see that he is punished for his unfaithfulness to me. ²¹His best troops[n] will be killed in battle, and the survivors will be scattered in every direction. I, the LORD, have spoken.

*²²Someday, I, the LORD,
   will cut a tender twig
      from the top of a cedar tree,
   then plant it on the peak
      of Israel's tallest mountain,
   where it will grow
   strong branches
      and produce large fruit.
²³All kinds of birds will find
      shelter under the tree,
   and they will rest in the shade
      of its branches.
²⁴Every tree in the forest
      will know that I, the LORD,
   can bring down tall trees
      and help short ones grow.
   I dry up green trees
      and make dry ones green.
   I, the LORD, have spoken,
      and I will keep my word.

Those Who Sin Will Die

18 The LORD said:
²Ezekiel, I hear the people of Israel using the old saying,

"Sour grapes eaten by parents
   leave a sour taste in the mouths
      of their children."

³Now tell them that I am the LORD God, and as surely as I live, that saying will no longer be used in Israel. ⁴The lives of all people belong to me—parents as well as children. Only those who sin will be put to death.

⁵Suppose there is a truly good man who always does what is fair and right. ⁶He refuses to eat meat sacrificed to foreign gods at local shrines or to worship Israel's idols. He doesn't have sex with someone else's wife or with a woman having her monthly period. ⁷He never cheats or robs anyone and always returns anything taken as security for a loan; he gives food and clothes to the poor ⁸and doesn't charge interest when lending

---

[n]17.21 *best troops:* Two ancient translations; Hebrew "troops that ran away."

PARENTING&*family*—What advice, if any, should I give my twentysomething child? *(Ezekiel 18.1-20)*

Remember that each of us is accountable to God.
Family patterns can have a huge impact on us. Either they fit us as comfortably as old bedroom slippers, or they irritate us like burrs stuck between our toes. In matters of faith, it's tempting to credit (or blame) our parents, whatever our current condition.

That won't wash, according to Ezekiel. He makes startling statements about individual responsibility before God. Chapter 18 describes several situations: a godly parent whose child does not follow God; a sinful parent whose child turns to God. The chapter goes on to describe changes within a single person: an evil person who turns to God; a good person who turns to sin. This emphasizes that we are capable of breaking out of family molds. We are even capable of breaking our own molds. But God holds us individually accountable for what we do.

Twentysomethings are flying their own wings of independence. We can hope that they follow what we did right and avoid what we did wrong. While family members do indeed suffer for each other's wrongdoings, when it comes to our relationship with God, he looks at our individual faith—or lack of it. (See also Ecclesiastes 11.1—12.1; Amos 5.6-27; Matthew 14.24-33; 1 Timothy 4.6-16.)

Words To Remember: *Only those who sin will be put to death. Children won't suffer for the sins of their parents, and parents won't suffer for the sins of their children. Good people will be rewarded for what they do, and evil people will be punished for what they do.*—Ezekiel 18.20

money. He refuses to do anything evil; he is fair to everyone 9and faithfully obeys my laws and teachings. This man is good, and I promise he will live.

10But suppose this good man has an evil son who is violent and commits sins 11his father never did. He eats meat at local shrines, has sex with someone else's wife, 12cheats the poor, and robs people. He keeps what is given to him as security for a loan. He worships idols, does disgusting things, 13and charges high interest when lending money. An evil man like that will certainly not live. He is the one who has done these horrible sins, so it's his own fault that he will be put to death.

14But suppose this evil man has a son who sees his father do these things and refuses to act like him. 15He doesn't eat meat at local shrines or worship Israel's idols, and he doesn't have sex with someone else's wife. 16He never cheats or robs anyone and doesn't even demand security for a loan. He gives food and clothes to the poor 17and refuses to do anything evil[o] or to charge interest. And he obeys all my laws and teachings. Such a man will live. His own father sinned, but this good man will not be put to death for the sins of his father. 18It is his father who will die for cheating and robbing and doing evil.

19You may wonder why a son isn't punished for the sins of his father. It is because the son does what is right and obeys my laws. 20Only those who sin will be put to death. Children won't suffer for the sins of their parents, and parents won't suffer for the sins of their children. Good people will be rewarded for what they do, and evil people will be punished for what they do.

21Suppose wicked people stop sinning and start obeying my laws and doing right. They won't be put to death. 22All their sins will be forgiven, and they will live because they did right. 23I, the LORD God, don't like to see wicked people die. I enjoy seeing them turn from their sins and live.

24But when good people start sinning and doing disgusting things, will they live? No! All their good deeds will be forgotten, and they will be put to death because of their sins.

25You people of Israel accuse me of being unfair! But listen—I'm not unfair; you are! 26If good people start doing evil, they must be put to death, because they have sinned. 27And if wicked people start doing right, they will save themselves from punishment. 28They will think about what they've done and stop sinning, and so they won't be put to death. 29But you still say that I am unfair. You are the ones who have done wrong and are unfair!

30I will judge each of you for what you've done. So stop sinning, or else you will certainly be punished. 31Give up your evil ways and start thinking pure thoughts. And be faithful to me! Do you really want to be put to death for your sins? 32I, the LORD God, don't want to see that happen to anyone. So stop sinning and live!

A Funeral Song for Israel's Leaders

The LORD said:

19 Ezekiel, sing a funeral song for two of Israel's leaders:[p]

2 Your mother was a brave lioness
who raised her cubs
among lions.
3 She taught one of them to hunt,
and he learned to eat people.
4 When the nations heard of him,
they trapped him in a pit,
then they used hooks
to drag him to Egypt.

5 His mother waited
for him to return.
But soon she lost all hope
and raised another cub,
who also became fierce.
6 He hunted with other lions
and learned to eat people.
7 He destroyed fortresses[q]
and ruined towns;
his mighty roar
terrified everyone.
8 Nations plotted to kill him,
and people came from all over
to spread out a net
and catch him in a trap.

---

[o] **18.17** *evil*: One ancient translation; Hebrew "for the poor." [p] **19.1** *two of Israel's leaders*: Probably Jehoahaz (ruled three months in 609 B.C.) and Jehoiachin (ruled three months in 598 B.C.) or Zedekiah (598-586 B.C.). [q] **19.7** *He destroyed fortresses*: One possible meaning for the difficult Hebrew text.

⁹They put him in a cage
    and took him to Babylonia.
The lion was locked away,
    so that his mighty roar
would never again be heard
    on Israel's hills.

¹⁰Your mother was a vine^r
    growing near a stream.
There was plenty of water,
so she was filled with branches
    and with lots of fruit.
¹¹Her strong branches
    became symbols of authority,
and she was taller
    than all other trees—
everyone could see how strong
    and healthy she was.
¹²But in anger, I pulled her up
    by the roots
and threw her to the ground,
where the scorching desert wind
    dried out her fruit.
Her strong branches wilted
    and burned up.
¹³Then she was planted
    in a hot, dry desert,
¹⁴where her stem caught fire,
    and flames burned
        her branches and fruit.
Not one strong branch is left;
    she is stripped bare.

This funeral song must be sung with sorrow.

Israel Keeps On Rebelling

20 Seven years after King Jehoiachin and the rest of us had been led away as prisoners to Babylonia, some of Israel's leaders came to me on the tenth day of the fifth month.^s They sat down and asked for a message from the LORD. ²Just then, the LORD God said:

³Ezekiel, son of man, these leaders have come to find out what I want them to do. As surely as I live, I will not give them an answer of any kind.

⁴Are you willing to warn them, Ezekiel? Then remind them of the disgusting sins of their ancestors.

⁵Tell them that long ago I, the LORD God, chose Israel to be my own. I appeared to their ancestors in Egypt and made a solemn promise that I would be their God and the God of their descendants. ⁶I swore that I would rescue them from Egypt and lead them to a land I had already chosen. This land was rich with milk and honey and was the most splendid land of all. ⁷I told them to get rid of their disgusting idols and not to sin by worshiping the gods of Egypt. I reminded them that I was the LORD their God, ⁸but they still rebelled against me. They refused to listen and kept on worshiping their idols and foreign gods.

In my anger, I decided to punish the Israelites in Egypt. ⁹But that would have made me look like a liar, because I had already promised in front of everyone that I would lead them out of Egypt. ¹⁰So I brought them out and led them into the desert. ¹¹I gave them my laws and teachings, so they would know how to live right. ¹²And I commanded them to respect the Sabbath as a way of showing that they were holy and belonged to me. ¹³But the Israelites rebelled against me in the desert. They refused to obey my laws and teachings, and they treated the Sabbath like any other day.

Then in my anger, I decided to destroy the Israelites in the desert once and for all. ¹⁴But that would have disgraced me, because many other nations had seen me bring the Israelites out of Egypt. ¹⁵Instead, I told them in the desert that I would not lead them into the beautiful, fertile land I had promised. ¹⁶I said this because they had not only ignored my laws and teachings, but had disgraced my Sabbath and worshiped idols.

¹⁷Yet, I felt sorry for them and could not let them die in the desert. ¹⁸So I warned the children not to act like their parents or follow their evil ways or worship their idols. ¹⁹I reminded them that I was the LORD their God and that they should obey my laws and teachings. ²⁰I told them to respect my Sabbath to show that they were my people and that I was the LORD their God. ²¹But the children also rebelled against me. They refused to obey my laws and teachings, and they treated the Sabbath as any other day.

I became angry and decided to punish them in the desert. ²²But I did not. That

---

^r19.10 *Your mother was a vine*: One possible meaning for the difficult Hebrew text.   ^s20.1 *Seven years . . . fifth month*: Probably August of 591 B.C.

would have disgraced me in front of the nations that had seen me bring the Israelites out of Egypt. ²³So I solemnly swore that I would scatter the people of Israel across the nations, ²⁴because they had disobeyed my laws and ignored my teachings; they had disgraced my Sabbath and worshiped the idols their ancestors had made. ²⁵I gave them laws that bring punishment instead of life, ²⁶and I let them offer me unacceptable sacrifices, including their first-born sons. I did this to horrify them and to let them know that I, the LORD, was punishing them.

I'm thankful for a God who cares so much about his children that he sends the Holy Spirit to guide us not only through the big decisions of life, but the most ordinary, everyday circumstances as well.

LEIGH WILKINS

²⁷Ezekiel, tell the people of Israel that their ancestors also rejected and insulted me ²⁸by offering sacrifices, incense, and wine to gods on every hill and under every large tree. I was very angry, because they did these things in the land I had given them! ²⁹I asked them where they went to worship those gods, and they answered, "At the local shrines."^t And those places of worship are still called shrines.

³⁰Then ask the Israelites why they are following the example of their wicked ancestors ³¹by worshiping idols and by sacrificing their own children as offerings. They commit these sins and still think they can ask me for a message. As surely as I am the living LORD God, I will give them no answer. ³²They may think they can be like other nations and get away with worshiping idols made of wood and stone. But that will never happen!

The LORD Promises To Restore Israel

The LORD said to the people of Israel:

³³As surely as I am the living LORD God, I will rule over you with my powerful arm. You will feel my fierce anger ³⁴and my power, when I gather you from the places where you are scattered ³⁵and lead you into a desert surrounded by nations. I will meet you there face to face. Then I will pass judgment on you ³⁶and punish you, just as I punished your ancestors in the desert near Egypt.^u ³⁷I will force each of you to obey the regulations of our solemn agreement. ³⁸I will separate the sinful rebels from the rest of you, and even though I will bring them from the nations where they live in exile, they won't be allowed to return to Israel. Then you will know that I am the LORD.

³⁹Go ahead and worship your idols for now, you Israelites, because soon I will no longer let you dishonor me by offering gifts to them. You will have no choice but to obey me!^v ⁴⁰When that day comes, everyone in Israel will worship me on Mount Zion, my holy mountain in Jerusalem. I will once again call you my own, and I will accept your sacred offerings and sacrifices. ⁴¹When I bring you home from the places where you are now scattered, I will be pleased with you, just as I am pleased with the smell of the smoke from your sacrifices. Every nation on earth will see that I am holy, ⁴²and you will know that I, the LORD, am the one who brought you back to Israel, the land I promised your ancestors. ⁴³Then you will remember your wicked sins, and you will hate yourselves for doing such horrible things. They have made you unacceptable to me, ⁴⁴so you deserve to be punished. But I will treat you in a way that will bring honor to my name, and you will know that I am the LORD God.

Fire from the South

⁴⁵The LORD said, ⁴⁶"Ezekiel, son of man, turn toward the south and warn the forests ⁴⁷that I, the LORD God, will start a fire that will burn up every tree, whether green or

---

^t**20.29** *where they went to worship those gods . . . local shrines*: In Hebrew "where they went" sounds like "local shrines." These were places to worship foreign gods. ^u**20.36** *the desert near Egypt*: The Sinai Desert. ^v**20.39** *me*: One possible meaning for the difficult Hebrew text of verse 39.

dry. Nothing will be able to put out the blaze of that fire as it spreads to the north and burns everything in its path. [48]Everyone will know that I started it, and that it cannot be stopped."

[49]But I complained, "LORD God, I don't want to do that! People already say I confuse them with my messages."

The LORD Will Punish Jerusalem

21 The LORD said:
[2]Ezekiel, son of man, condemn the places in Jerusalem where people worship. Warn everyone in Israel [3]that I am about to punish them. I will pull out my sword and have it ready to kill everyone, whether good or evil. [4]From south to north, people will die, [5]knowing that my sword will never be put away.

[6]Ezekiel, groan in sorrow and despair so that everyone can hear you. [7]When they ask why you are groaning, tell them you have terrifying news that will make them faint and tremble in fear and lose all courage. These things will happen soon. I, the LORD God, make this promise!

A Sword Is Ready To Attack Israel

[8]The LORD said:
[9-10]Ezekiel, son of man, tell the people of Jerusalem:

I have sharpened my sword
　　to slaughter you;
it is shiny and will flash
　　like lightning!
Don't celebrate—
　　punishment is coming,
because everyone has ignored
　　my warnings.[w]
[11]My sword has been polished;
　　it's sharp and ready to kill.

[12]Groan in sorrow, Ezekiel;
　　the sword is drawn against
　　　my people and their leaders.
They will die!
　　So give up all hope.
[13]I am testing my people,
　　and they can do nothing
　　　to stop me.[x]
I, the LORD, have spoken.

[14]Ezekiel, warn my people,
　　then celebrate my victory

by clapping your hands.
My vicious sword will attack
　　again and again,
killing my people
　　with every stroke.
[15]They will lose all courage
　　and stumble with fear.
My slaughtering sword
　　is waiting at every gate,
　　　flashing and ready to kill.[y]
[16]It will slash right and left,
　　wherever the blade is pointed.
[17]Then I will stop being angry,
　　and I will clap my hands
　　　in victory.
I, the LORD, have spoken.

The King of Babylonia and His Sword

[18]The LORD said:
[19]Ezekiel, son of man, mark two roads for the king of Babylonia to follow when he comes with his sword. The roads will begin at the same place, but be sure to put up a signpost where the two roads separate and go in different directions. [20]Clearly mark where the two roads lead. One goes to Rabbah, the capital of Ammon, and the other goes to Jerusalem, the fortified capital of Judah. [21]When the Babylonian king stands at that signpost, he will decide which way to go by shaking his arrows, by asking his idols, and by carefully looking at the liver of a sacrificed animal.[z] [22]His right hand will pull out the arrow marked "Jerusalem." Then he will immediately give the signal to shout the battle cry, to build dirt ramps to the top of the city walls, to break down its walls and gates with large wooden poles, and to kill the people. [23]Everyone in Jerusalem had promised to be loyal to Babylonia, and so none of them will believe that this could happen to them. But Babylonia's king will remind them of their sinful ways and warn them of their coming captivity.

[24]Ezekiel, tell the people of Jerusalem and their ruler that I, the LORD God, am saying:

---

[w]**21.9,10** *Don't celebrate . . . my warnings:* One possible meaning for the difficult Hebrew text.　[x]**21.13** *I am testing . . . me:* One possible meaning for the difficult Hebrew text.　[y]**21.15** *My slaughtering sword . . . ready to kill:* One possible meaning for the difficult Hebrew text.　[z]**21.21** *shaking . . . animal:* These were ways the Babylonians found out what their gods wanted them to do.

Everything you do is wicked and shows how sinful you are. You are guilty and will be taken away as prisoners.

²⁵And now, you evil and wicked ruler of Israel, your day of final punishment is almost here. ²⁶I, the LORD God, command you to take off your royal turban and your crown, because everything will be different. Those who had no power will be put in charge, and those who now rule will become nobodies. ²⁷I will leave Jerusalem in ruins when my chosen one comes to punish this city.

Judgment against Ammon

²⁸The LORD God said:

Ezekiel, son of man, the Ammonites have insulted Israel, so condemn them and tell them I am saying:

A sword is drawn,
    ready to slaughter;
it is polished and prepared
    to kill as fast as lightning.

²⁹You wicked Ammonites see false visions and believe untrue messages. But your day of punishment is coming soon, and my sword will slaughter you! ³⁰Your days to punish others are over, so put your swords away.ᵃ You will be punished in the land of your birth. ³¹My furious anger will scorch you like fire, and I will hand you over to cruel men who are experts in killing. ³²You will be burned and will die in your own land. Then you will be forgotten forever. I, the LORD, have spoken.

Jerusalem Is Condemned

22 Some time later, the LORD said: ²Ezekiel, son of man, are you ready to condemn Jerusalem? That city is filled with murderers, so remind the people of their sins ³and tell them I am saying:

Jerusalem, you have murdered many of your own people and have worshiped idols. You will soon be punished! ⁴Those crimes have made you guilty, and the idols have made you unacceptable to me. So your final punishment is near. Other nations will laugh at you and make insulting remarks, ⁵and people far and near will make fun of your misery.

⁶Your own leaders use their power to murder. ⁷None of you honor your parents, and you cheat foreigners, orphans, and widows. ⁸You show no respect for my sacred places and treat the Sabbath just like any other day. ⁹Some of your own people tell lies, so that others will be put to death. Some of you eat meat sacrificed to idols at local shrines, and others never stop doing vulgar things. ¹⁰Men have sex with their father's wife or with women who are having their monthly period ¹¹or with someone else's wife. Some men even sleep with their own daughter-in-law or half sister. ¹²Others of you accept money to murder someone. Your own people charge high interest when making a loan to other Israelites, and they get rich by cheating. Worst of all, you have forgotten me, the LORD God.

¹³I will shake my fist in anger at your violent crimes. ¹⁴When I'm finished with you, your courage will disappear, and you will be so weak that you won't be able to lift your hands. I, the LORD, have spoken and will not change my mind. ¹⁵I will scatter you throughout every nation on earth and put a stop to your sinful ways. ¹⁶Youᵇ will be humiliated in the eyes of other nations. Then you will know that I, the LORD God, have done these things.

Jerusalem Must Be Purified

¹⁷The LORD said:

¹⁸Ezekiel, son of man, I consider the people of Israel as worthless as the leftover metal in a furnace after silver has been purified. ¹⁹So I am going to bring them together in Jerusalem. ²⁰⁻²¹I will be like a metalworker who collects that metal from the furnace and melts it down. I will collect the Israelites and blow on them with my fiery anger. They will melt inside the city of Jerusalem ²²like silver in a furnace. Then they will know that I, the LORD, have punished them in my anger.

Everyone in Jerusalem Is Guilty

²³The LORD said:

²⁴Ezekiel, son of man, tell the people of Israel that their country is full of sin, and that I, the LORD, am furious! ²⁵Their leaders

---

ᵃ**21.30** *Your days . . . put your swords away:* One possible meaning for the difficult Hebrew text.   ᵇ**22.16** *You:* Hebrew; two ancient translations "Because of you, I."

are like[c] roaring lions, tearing apart their victims. They put people to death, then steal everything of value. Husbands are killed, and many women are left as widows.

[26]The priests of Israel ignore my Law! Not only do they refuse to respect any of my sacred things, but they don't even teach the difference between what is sacred and what is ordinary, or between what is clean and what is unclean. They treat my Sabbath like any other day, and so my own people no longer honor me.

[27]Israel's officials are like ferocious wolves, ripping their victims apart. They make a dishonest living by injuring and killing people.

[28]And then the prophets in Israel cover up these sins by giving false visions. I have never spoken to them, but they lie and say they have a message from me. [29]The people themselves cheat and rob; they abuse the poor and take advantage of foreigners.

[30]I looked for someone to defend the city and to protect it from my anger, as well as to stop me from destroying it. But I found no one. [31]So in my fierce anger, I will punish the Israelites for what they have done, and they will know that I am furious. I, the LORD, have spoken.

Two Sinful Sisters

23 The LORD said: [2]Ezekiel, son of man, listen to this story about two sisters. [3]While they were young and living in Egypt, they became prostitutes. [4]The older one was named Oholah, which stands for Samaria; the younger one was Oholibah, which stands for Jerusalem.[d] They became my wives and gave birth to my children.

[5]Even though Oholah was my wife, she continued to be a prostitute and chased after Assyrian lovers. [6]She offered herself to soldiers in purple uniforms, to every handsome, high-ranking officer, and to cavalry troops. [7]She had sex with all the important Assyrian officials and even worshiped their disgusting idols. [8]Once she started doing these things in Egypt, she never stopped. Men slept with her, and she was always ready for sex.

[9]So I gave Oholah to the Assyrian lovers she wanted so badly. [10]They ripped off her clothes, then captured her children and killed her. Women everywhere talked about what had happened to Oholah.

[11]Oholibah saw all this, but she was more sinful and wanted sex more than her sister Oholah ever did. [12]Oholibah also chased after good-looking Assyrian officers, uniformed soldiers, and cavalry troops. [13]Just like her sister, she did vulgar things.

[14]But Oholibah behaved worse than her sister. Oholibah saw images of Babylonian men carved into walls and painted red. [15]They had belts around their waists and large turbans on their heads, and they reminded her of Babylonian cavalry officers. [16]As soon as she looked at them, she wanted to have sex with them. And so, she sent messengers to bring them to her. [17]Men from Babylonia came and had sex with her so many times that she got disgusted with them. [18]She let everyone see her naked body and didn't care if they knew she was a prostitute. That's why I turned my back on her, just as I had done with her older sister.

[19]Oholibah didn't stop there, but became even more immoral and acted as she had back in Egypt. [20]She eagerly wanted to go to bed with Egyptian men, who were famous for their sexual powers. [21]And she longed for the days when she was a young prostitute, when men enjoyed having sex with her.

The LORD Will Punish Oholibah

[22]The LORD God said:

Oholibah,[e] though you no longer want to be around your lovers, they will surround you like enemies, when I turn them against you. [23]I will gather all the handsome young officials and the high-ranking cavalry officers from Babylonia and Assyria, as well as from the Chaldean tribes of Pekod, Shoa, and Koa. [24]Their large armies will come from the north[f] with chariots and wagons carrying weapons. They will wear shields and helmets and will surround you, and I will let

---

[c]**22.25** *Their leaders are like:* One ancient translation; Hebrew "Their prophets are like herds of."
[d]**23.4** *Samaria . . . Jerusalem:* After the nation of Israel was divided, the northern kingdom was called "Israel," and the southern kingdom was called "Judah." Samaria was the capital of the northern kingdom, and Jerusalem was the capital of the southern kingdom.
[e]**23.22** *Oholibah:* That is, Jerusalem (see verse 4).
[f]**23.24** *from the north:* One ancient translation; Hebrew "with weapons."

them judge and sentence you according to their own laws. ²⁵I am angry with you, so I will let them be very cruel. They will cut off your nose and ears; they will kill your children and put to death anyone in your family who is still alive. ²⁶Your clothes and jewelry will be torn off. ²⁷I will stop your wickedness and the prostitution you started back in Egypt. You will never want to think about those days again.

²⁸I, the LORD God, am ready to hand you over to those hateful enemies that you find so disgusting. ²⁹They will cruelly take away everything you have worked for and strip you naked. Then everyone will see you for the prostitute you really are. Your own vulgar sins ³⁰have led to this. You were the one determined to have sex with men from other nations and to worship their idols. ³¹You have turned out no better than your older sister, and now you must drink from the cup filled with my anger.

³²I, the LORD God, gave your sister a large, deep cup filled with my anger. And when you drink from that cup, you will be mocked and insulted. ³³You will end up drunk and devastated, because that cup is filled with horror and ruin. ³⁴But you must drink every drop! Then smash the cup to pieces and use them to cut your breasts in sorrow. I, the LORD God, have spoken.

³⁵You have completely rejected me, and so I promise that you will be punished for the disgusting things you did as a prostitute.

The Two Sisters Are Condemned

³⁶The LORD said:

Ezekiel, son of man, it's time for you to tell Oholah and Oholibah⁸ that they are guilty. Remind them of their evil ways! ³⁷They have been unfaithful by worshiping idols, and they have committed murder by sacrificing my own children as offerings to idols. ³⁸⁻³⁹They came into my temple that same day, and that made it unfit as a place to worship me. They have even stopped respecting the Sabbath.

⁴⁰They sent messengers to attract men from far away. When those men arrived, the two sisters took baths and put on eye shadow and jewelry. ⁴¹They sat on a fancy couch, and in front of them was a table for the olive oil and incense that had belonged to me. ⁴²Their room was always filled with a noisy crowd of drunkards brought in from the

desert. These men gave the women bracelets and beautiful crowns, ⁴³and I noticed that the men were eager to have sex with these women, though they were exhausted from being prostitutes.ʰ ⁴⁴In fact, the men had sex over and over with Oholah and Oholibah, the two sinful sisters. ⁴⁵But good men will someday accuse those two of murder and of being unfaithful, because they are certainly guilty.

⁴⁶So I, the LORD God, now say to these sisters:

I will call together an angry mob that will abuse and rob you. ⁴⁷They will stone you to death and cut you to pieces; they will kill your children and burn down your houses. ⁴⁸I will get rid of sinful prostitution in this country, so that women everywhere will be warned not to act as you have. ⁴⁹You will be punished for becoming prostitutes and for worshiping idols, and you will know that I am the LORD God.

A Cooking Pot

24 Nine years after King Jehoiachin and the rest of us had been led away as prisoners to Babylonia, the LORD spoke to me on the tenth day of the tenth month.ⁱ He said:

²Ezekiel, son of man, write down today's date, because the king of Babylonia has just begun attacking the city of Jerusalem. ³Then tell my rebellious people:

"Pour water in a cooking pot
and set it over a fire.
*⁴Throw in the legs and shoulders
of your finest sheep
and put in the juicy bones.
⁵ "Pile woodʲ underneath the pot,
and let the meat and bones
boil until they are done."

⁶These words mean that Jerusalem is doomed! The city is filled with murderers and is like an old, rusty pot. The meat is taken out piece by piece, and no one cares

---

ᵍ23.36 *Oholah and Oholibah*: That is, Samaria and Jerusalem (see verse 4). ʰ23.43 *prostitutes*: One possible meaning for the difficult Hebrew text of verse 43. ⁱ24.1 *Nine years . . . tenth month*: Probably January of 588 B.C. ʲ24.5 *Pile wood*: Or "Stack the bones."

what happens to it.[k] [7]The people of Jerusalem murdered innocent people in the city and didn't even try to cover up the blood that flowed out on the hard ground. [8]But I have seen that blood, and it cries out for me to take revenge.

[9]I, the LORD God, will punish that city of violence! I will make a huge pile of firewood, [10]so bring more wood and light it. Cook the meat and boil away the broth[l] to let the bones scorch. [11]Then set the empty pot over the hot coals until it is red-hot. That will clean the pot and burn off the rust. [12]I've tried everything else. Now the rust must be burned away.[m]

[13]Jerusalem is so full of sin and evil that I can't get it clean, even though I have tried. It will stay filthy until I let loose my fierce anger against it. [14]That time will certainly come! And when it does, I won't show the people of Jerusalem any pity or change my mind. They must be punished for the evil they have done. I, the LORD God, have spoken.

Ezekiel's Wife Dies

[15]The LORD said, [16]"Ezekiel, son of man, I will suddenly take the life of the person you love most. But I don't want you to complain or cry. [17]Mourn in silence and don't show that you are grieving. Don't remove your turban or take off your sandals; don't cover your face to show your sorrow, or eat the food that mourners eat."[n]

[18]One morning, I was talking with the people as usual, and by sunset my wife was dead. The next day I did what the LORD told me, [19]and when people saw me, they asked, "Why aren't you mourning for your wife?"

[20]I answered:

The LORD God says [21]he is ready to destroy the temple in which you take such pride and which makes you feel so safe. Your children who now live in Jerusalem will be killed. [22]Then you will do the same things I have done. You will leave your face uncovered and refuse to eat the food that mourners usually eat. [23]You won't take off your turbans and your sandals.[o] You won't cry or mourn, but all day long you will go around groaning because of your sins.

[24]I am a warning sign—everything I have done, you will also do. And

then you will know the LORD God has made these things happen.

We will never grow in our relationship with God if we don't have the gumption to become single-minded, bent on pleasing God—and God only.
MICHELE HALSEIDE

[25]The LORD said, "Ezekiel, I will soon destroy the temple that makes everyone feel proud and safe, and I will take away their children as well. [26]On that same day, someone will escape from the city and come to tell you what has happened. [27]Then you will be able to speak again,[p] and the two of you will talk. You will be a warning sign to the people, and they will know that I am the LORD."

Judgment on Ammon

25

The LORD God said:
[2]Ezekiel, son of man, condemn the people of Ammon [3]and tell them:

You celebrated when my temple was destroyed, when Israel was defeated, and when my people were taken away as prisoners. [4]Now I am going to let you be conquered by tribes from the eastern desert. They will set up their camps in your land and eat your fruit and drink your milk. [5]Your capital city of Rabbah will be nothing but pas-

---

[k]24.6 *and no one cares what happens to it:* One possible meaning for the difficult Hebrew text. [l]24.10 *boil away the broth:* One ancient translation; Hebrew "mix the spices." [m]24.12 *away:* One possible meaning for the difficult Hebrew text of verse 12. [n]24.17 *Don't remove your turban . . . take off your sandals . . . cover your face . . . eat the food that mourners eat:* The usual way people mourned was to remove anything worn on the head, to go barefoot, to cover their faces, and to eat special food to show they were grieving. [o]24.22,23 *You will leave your face uncovered . . . refuse to eat the food . . . won't take off your turbans and your sandals:* See the note at 24.17. [p]24.27 *you will be able to speak again:* See 3.25-27; 33.21, 22.

tureland for camels, and the rest of the country will be pastures for sheep. Then you will know that I am the LORD God.

⁶You hated Israel so much that you clapped and shouted and celebrated. ⁷And so I will hand you over to enemies who will rob you. I will completely destroy you. There won't be enough of your people left to be a nation ever again, and you will know that I, the LORD, have done these things.

Judgment on Moab

⁸The LORD God said, "The people of Moab*ᵈ* thought Judah was no different from any other nation. ⁹So I will let Moab's fortress towns along its border be attacked, including Beth-Jeshimoth, Baal-Meon, and Kiriathaim. ¹⁰The same eastern desert tribes that invade Ammon will invade Moab, and just as Ammon will be forgotten forever, ¹¹Moab will be punished. Then the people there will know that I am the LORD."

Judgment on Edom

¹²The LORD God then said, "The people of Edom are guilty of taking revenge on Judah. ¹³So I will punish Edom by killing all its people and livestock. It will be an empty wasteland all the way from Teman to Dedan. ¹⁴I will send my own people to take revenge on the Edomites by making them feel my fierce anger. And when I punish them, they will know that I am the LORD God."

Judgment on Philistia

¹⁵The LORD God said, "The cruel Philistines have taken revenge on their enemies over and over and have tried to destroy them. ¹⁶Now it's my turn to treat the Philistines as my enemies and to kill everyone*ᵉ* living in their towns along the seacoast. ¹⁷In my fierce anger, I will take revenge on them. And when I punish them, they will know that I am the LORD."

Judgment on the City of Tyre

26 Eleven years*ˢ* after King Jehoiachin and the rest of us had been led away as prisoners to Babylonia, the LORD spoke to me on the first day of the month. He said:

²Ezekiel, son of man, the people of the city of Tyre*ᵗ* have celebrated Jerusalem's defeat by singing,

"Jerusalem has fallen!
It used to be powerful,
    a center of trade.
Now the city is shattered,
    and we will take its place."

³Because the people of Tyre have sung that song, I have the following warning for them: I am the LORD God, and I am now your enemy! I will send nations to attack you, like waves crashing against the shore. ⁴They will tear down your city walls and defense towers. I will sweep away the ruins until all that's left of you is a bare rock, ⁵where fishermen can dry their nets along the coast. I promise that you will be robbed ⁶and that the people who live in your towns along the coast will be killed. Then you will know that I am the LORD.

⁷King Nebuchadnezzar of Babylonia is the world's most powerful king, and I will send him to attack you. He will march from the north with a powerful army, including horses and chariots and cavalry troops. ⁸First, he will attack your towns along the coast and kill the people who live there. Then he will build dirt ramps up to the top of your city walls and set up rows of shields around you. ⁹He will command some of his troops to use large wooden poles to beat down your walls, while others use iron rods to knock down your watchtowers. ¹⁰He will have so many horses that the dust they stir up will seem like a thick fog. And as his chariots and cavalry approach, even the walls will shake, especially when he proudly enters your ruined city. ¹¹His troops will ride through your streets, killing people left and right, and your strong columns will crumble to the ground. ¹²The troops will steal your valuable possessions; they will break down your walls, and crush your expensive houses. Then the stones and wood and all the remains will be dumped into the sea. ¹³You will have no reason to sing or play

---

ᵈ25.8 Moab: One ancient translation; Hebrew "Moab and Edom." *ᵉ25.16 kill everyone:* The Hebrew text also has the name "Cherethites," which was a group of people that lived just southeast of Philistia, and was often identified with the Philistines. *ˢ26.1 Eleven years:* Probably late in 587 B.C. *ᵗ26.2 Tyre:* One of the two major cities of Phoenicia; Sidon was the other.

music on harps, [14]because I will turn you into a bare rock where fishermen can dry their nets. And you will never rebuild your city. I, the LORD God, make this promise.

[15]The people of the nations up and down the coast will shudder when they hear your screams and moans of death. [16]The kings will step down from their thrones, then take off their royal robes and fancy clothes, and sit on the ground, trembling. They will be so shocked at the news of your defeat that they will shake in fear [17]and sing this funeral song:

"The great city beside the sea
    is destroyed![u]
Its people once ruled the coast
    and terrified everyone there.
[18]But now Tyre is in ruins,
    and the people on the coast
        stare at it in horror
        and tremble in fear."

[19]I, the LORD God, will turn you into a ghost-town. The ocean depths will rise over you [20]and carry you down to the world of the dead, where you will join people of ancient times and towns ruined long ago. You will stay there and never again be a city filled with people.[v] [21]You will die a horrible death! People will come looking for your city, but it will never be found. I, the LORD, have spoken.

A Funeral Song for Tyre

27 The LORD said:
    [2]Ezekiel, son of man, sing a funeral song for Tyre,[w] [3]the city that is built along the sea and that trades with nations along the coast. Tell the people of Tyre that the following message is from me:

Tyre, you brag about
    your perfect beauty,
[4]   and your control of the sea.[x]

You are a ship
    built to perfection.
[5]Builders used cypress trees
    from Mount Hermon
        to make your planks
    and a cedar tree from Lebanon
        for your tall mast.

[6]Oak trees from Bashan
    were shaped into oars;
pine trees from Cyprus[y]
    were cut for your deck,
which was then decorated
    with strips of ivory.
[7]The builders used fancy linen
    from Egypt for your sails,
        so everyone could see you.
Blue and purple cloth
    from Cyprus was used
        to shade your deck.
[8]Men from Sidon and Arvad
    did the rowing,
and your own skilled workers
    were the captains.
[9]Experienced men from Byblos
    repaired any damages.
Sailors from all over
    shopped at the stores
        in your port.

[10]Brave soldiers from Persia,
    Lydia, and Libya
        served in your navy,
    protecting you with shields
    and helmets,
        and making you famous.
[11]Your guards came from
    Arvad and Cilicia,
    and men from Gamad
        stood watch in your towers.
    With their weapons
    hung on your walls,
        your beauty was complete.

[12]Merchants from southern Spain[z] traded silver, iron, tin, and lead for your products. [13]The people of Greece, Tubal, and Meshech traded slaves and things made of bronze, [14]and those from Beth-Togarmah traded work horses, war horses, and mules. [15]You also did business with people from Rhodes,[a] and people from nations along the coast gave you ivory and ebony[b] in exchange for

[u]26.17 *The great city . . . is destroyed*: One possible meaning for the difficult Hebrew text. [v]26.20 *You will stay there . . . with people*: One possible meaning for the difficult Hebrew text. [w]27.2 *Tyre*: See the note at 26.2. [x]27.4 *and your control of the sea*: One possible meaning for the difficult Hebrew text. [y]27.6 *pine trees from Cyprus*: One possible meaning for the difficult Hebrew text. [z]27.12 *southern Spain*: The Hebrew text has "Tarshish," which may have been a Phoenician city in southern Spain. [a]27.15 *Rhodes*: One ancient translation; Hebrew "Dedan." [b]27.15 *ebony*: A valuable black wood.

your goods. [16]Edom[c] traded emeralds, purple cloth, embroidery, fine linen, coral, and rubies. [17]Judah and Israel gave you their finest wheat, fancy figs,[d] honey, olive oil, and spices in exchange for your merchandise. [18]The people of Damascus saw what you had to offer and brought you wine from Helbon and wool from Zahar. [19]Vedan and Javan near Uzal[e] traded you iron and spices. [20]The people of Dedan supplied you with saddle blankets, [21]while people from Arabia and the rulers of Kedar traded lambs, sheep, and goats. [22]Merchants from Sheba and Raamah gave you excellent spices, precious stones, and gold in exchange for your products. [23]You also did business with merchants from the cities of Haran, Canneh, Eden, Sheba, Asshur, and Chilmad, [24]and they gave you expensive clothing, purple and embroidered cloth, brightly colored rugs, and strong rope. [25]Large, seagoing ships[f] carried your goods wherever they needed to go.

You were like a ship
loaded with heavy cargo
[26]   and sailing across the sea,
but you were wrecked
    by strong eastern winds.
[27]Everything on board was lost—
    your valuable cargo,
    your sailors and carpenters,
    merchants and soldiers.
[28]The shouts of your drowning crew
    were heard on the shore.

[29]Every ship is deserted;
rowers and sailors and captains
    all stand on shore,
[30]   mourning for you.
They show their sorrow
by putting dust on their heads
    and rolling in ashes;
[31]they shave their heads
    and dress in sackcloth[g]
    as they cry in despair.
[32]In their grief they sing
    a funeral song for you:
"Tyre, you were greater
    than all other cities.
But now you lie in silence
    at the bottom of the sea.[h]

[33]"Nations that received
    your merchandise
    were always pleased;

kings everywhere got rich
    from your costly goods.
[34]But now you are wrecked
    in the deep sea,
with your cargo and crew
    scattered everywhere.
[35]People living along the coast
    are shocked at the news.
Their rulers are horrified,
    and terror is written
    across their faces.
[36]The merchants of the world
    can't believe what happened.
Your death was gruesome,
    and you are gone forever."

Judgment on the King of Tyre

28 The LORD God said: [2]Ezekiel, son of man, tell the king of Tyre[i] that I am saying:
You are so arrogant that you think you're a god and that the city of Tyre is your throne. You may claim to be a god, though you're nothing but a mere human. [3]You think you're wiser than Daniel[j] and know everything.[k]

[4]Your wisdom has certainly made you rich, because you have storehouses filled with gold and silver. [5]You're a clever businessman and are extremely wealthy, but your wealth has led to arrogance!

[6]You compared yourself to a god, so now I, the LORD God, [7]will make you the victim of cruel enemies. They will destroy all the possessions you've worked so hard to get. [8]Your enemies will brutally kill you, and the sea will be your only grave.

[9]When you face your enemies, will you still claim to be a god? They will attack, and you will suffer like any

---

[c]**27.16** *Edom*: Some Hebrew manuscripts and one ancient translation; most Hebrew manuscripts "Syria." [d]**27.17** *their finest wheat, fancy figs*: One possible meaning for the difficult Hebrew text. [e]**27.19** *Vedan and Javan near Uzal*: One possible meaning for the difficult Hebrew text. [f]**27.25** *Large, seagoing ships*: The Hebrew text has "Ships of Tarshish," which may have been a Phoenician city in Spain. "Ships of Tarshish" probably means large, seagoing ships. [g]**27.31** *sackcloth*: See the note at 7.18. [h]**27.32** *Tyre, you were greater . . . the bottom of the sea*: One possible meaning for the difficult Hebrew text. [i]**28.2** *Tyre*: See the note at 26.2. [j]**28.3** *Daniel*: See the note at 14.14. [k]**28.3** *and know everything*: One possible meaning for the difficult Hebrew text.

other human. ¹⁰Foreigners will kill you, and you will die the death of those who don't worship me. I, the LORD, have spoken.

A Funeral Song for the King of Tyre

¹¹The LORD said:

¹²Ezekiel, son of man, sing a funeral song for the king of Tyre^l and tell him I am saying:

At one time, you were perfect,^m intelligent, and good-looking. ¹³You lived in the garden of Eden and wore jewelry made of brightly colored gems and precious stones. They were all set in goldⁿ and were ready for you on the day you were born. ¹⁴I appointed a winged creature to guard your home^o on my holy mountain, where you walked among gems that dazzled like fire.

¹⁵You were truly good from the time of your birth, but later you started doing wicked things. ¹⁶You traded with other nations and became more and more cruel and evil. So I forced you to leave my mountain, and the creature that had been your protector now chased you away from the gems.

¹⁷It was your good looks that made you arrogant, and you were so famous that you started acting like a fool. That's why I threw you to the ground and let other kings sneer at you. ¹⁸You have cheated so many other merchants that your places of worship are corrupt. So I set your city on fire and burned it down. Now everyone sees only ashes where your city once stood, ¹⁹and the people of other nations are shocked. Your punishment was horrible, and you are gone forever.

Judgment on Sidon and Peace for Israel

²⁰The LORD said:

²¹Ezekiel, son of man, condemn the city of Sidon^p ²²and tell its people:

I, the LORD God, am your enemy! People will praise me when I punish you, and they will see that I am holy. ²³I will send deadly diseases to wipe you out, and I will send enemies to invade and surround you. Your people will be killed, and you will know that I am the LORD.

²⁴When that happens, the people

of Israel will no longer have cruel neighbors that abuse them and make them feel as though they are in a field of thorns and briers. And the Israelites will know that I, the LORD God, have done these things.

No matter what surrounds us, we're always safe with God because he's holy—and he has control of all circumstances.

LAURETTA PATTERSON

A Blessing for Israel

²⁵The LORD God said:

Someday I will gather the people of Israel from the nations where they are now scattered, and every nation will see that I am holy. The Israelites will once again live in the land I gave to my servant Jacob. ²⁶They will be safe and will build houses and plant vineyards. They will no longer be in danger, because I will punish their hateful neighbors. Israel will know that I am the LORD their God.

Judgment on the King of Egypt

29 Ten years after King Jehoiachin and the rest of us had been led away as prisoners to Babylonia, the LORD spoke to me on the twelfth day of the tenth month.^q He said:

²Ezekiel, son of man, condemn the king of Egypt. Tell him and his people ³that I am saying:

King of Egypt, you were like a giant crocodile lying in a river. You acted as though you owned the Nile and made

---

^l28.12 *Tyre:* See the note at 26.2.   ^m28.12 *you were perfect:* One possible meaning for the difficult Hebrew text.   ⁿ28.13 *They were all set in gold:* One possible meaning for the difficult Hebrew text. ^o28.14 *I appointed a winged creature to guard your home:* One possible meaning for the difficult Hebrew text. ^p28.21 *Sidon:* See the note at 26.2.   ^q29.1 *Ten years . . . tenth month:* Probably January of 587 B.C.

it for yourself. But now I, the LORD God, am your enemy! [4]I will put a hook in your jaw and pull you out of the water, and all the fish in your river will stick to your scaly body.[r] [5]I'll throw you and the fish into the desert, and your body will fall on the hard ground. You will be left unburied,[s] and wild animals and birds will eat your flesh. [6]Then everyone in Egypt will know that I am the LORD.

You and your nation refused to help the people of Israel and were nothing more than a broken stick. [7]When they reached out to you for support, you broke in half, cutting their arms and making them fall.[t]

[8]So I, the LORD God, will send troops to attack you, king of Egypt. They will kill your people and live-stock, [9]until your land is a barren desert. Then you will know that I have done these things.

You claimed that you made the Nile River and control it. [10]Now I am turning against you and your river. Your nation will be nothing but an empty wasteland all the way from the town of Migdol in the north to Aswan in the south, and as far as the border of Ethiopia.[u] [11]No human or animal will even dare travel through Egypt, be-cause no sign of life will be found there for forty years. [12]It will be the most barren place on earth. Every city in Egypt will lie in ruins during those forty years, and I will scatter your peo-ple throughout the nations of the world.

[13]Then after those forty years have passed, I will bring your people back from the places where I scattered them. [14]They will once again live in their homeland in southern Egypt. But they will be a weak kingdom [15]and won't ever be strong enough to rule nations, as they did in the past. [16]My own people Israel will never again depend on your nation. In fact, when the Israelites remember what hap-pened to you Egyptians, they will real-ize how wrong they were to turn to you for help. Then the Israelites will know that I, the LORD God, did these things.

King Nebuchadnezzar of Babylonia Will Conquer Egypt

[17]Twenty-seven years after King Jehoia-chin and the rest of us had been led away as prisoners to Babylonia, the LORD spoke to me on the first day of the first month.[v] He said:

[18]King Nebuchadnezzar of Babylo-nia has attacked the city of Tyre. He forced his soldiers to carry so many heavy loads that their heads were rubbed bald, and their shoulders were red and sore. Nebuchadnezzar and his army still could not capture the city. [19]So now I will hand over the nation of Egypt to him. He will take Egypt's valuable treasures and give them to his own troops. [20]Egypt will be his reward, because he and his army have been following my orders. I, the LORD God, have spoken.

[21]Ezekiel, when Egypt is defeated, I will make the people of Israel strong, and I will give you the power to speak to them. Then they will know that I, the LORD, have done these things.

Egypt Will Be a Barren Desert

30 The LORD said:
[2]Ezekiel, son of man, tell the people of Egypt that I am saying:

Cry out in despair,
[3]because you will soon
be punished!
That will be a time
of darkness and doom
for all nations.
[4]Your own nation of Egypt
will be attacked,
and Ethiopia[w] will suffer.
You will be killed in battle,

---

[r]**29.4** *all the fish in your river will stick to your scaly body*: All the king's officials will be removed from power and destroyed along with the king himself. [s]**29.5** *You will be left unburied*: A proper burial in a royal tomb was extremely important to Egyptian kings, because they often thought of themselves as gods. [t]**29.7** *making them fall*: One possible meaning for the difficult Hebrew text. [u]**29.10** *Ethiopia*: The Hebrew text has "Cush," which was a region south of Egypt that included parts of the present countries of Ethiopia and Sudan. [v]**29.17** *Twenty-seven . . . first month*: Probably March of 571 B.C. [w]**30.4** *Ethiopia*: See the note at 29.10.

and your land will be robbed
and left in ruins.

⁵Soldiers hired from Ethiopia, Libya, Lydia, Arabia, Kub, as well as from Israel,ˣ will die in that battle. ⁶All of your allies will be killed, and your proud strength will crumble. People will die from Migdol in the north to Aswan in the south. I, the LORD, have spoken.

⁷Your nation of Egypt will be the most deserted place on earth, and its cities will lie in complete ruin. ⁸I will set fire to your land, and anyone who defended your nation will die. Then you will know that I am the LORD.

⁹On the same day I destroy Egypt, I will send messengers to the Ethiopians to announce their coming destruction. They think they are safe, but they will be terrified.

¹⁰Your Egyptian army is very strong, but I will send King Nebuchadnezzar of Babylonia to completely defeat that army. ¹¹He and his cruel troops will invade and destroy your land and leave your dead bodies piled everywhere.

¹²I will dry up the Nile River, then sell the land to evil buyers. I will send foreigners to turn your entire nation into a barren desert. I, the LORD, have spoken.

Egypt's Proud Cities Will Lie in Ruins

The LORD said to the people of Egypt:

¹³All the idols and images you Egyptians worship in the city of Memphisʸ will be smashed. No one will be left to rule your nation, and terror will fill the land. ¹⁴The city of Pathros will be left in ruins, and Zoan will be burned to the ground. Thebes,ᶻ your capital city, will also be destroyed! ¹⁵The fortress city of Pelusium will feel my fierce anger, and all the troops stationed at Thebes will be slaughtered.

¹⁶I will set fire to your nation of Egypt! The city of Pelusium will be in anguish. Thebes will fall, and the people of Memphis will live in constant fear.ᵃ ¹⁷The young soldiers in the cities of Heliopolis and Bubastisᵇ will die in battle, and the rest of the people will be taken prisoner. ¹⁸You were so proud of your nation's power, but when I crush that power and kill that pride, darkness will fall over the city of Tahpanhes. A dark, gloomy cloud will cover the land as you are

being led away into captivity. ¹⁹When I'm through punishing Egypt, you will know that I am the LORD.

Egypt's King Is Powerless

²⁰Eleven years after King Jehoiachin and the rest of us had been led away as prisoners to Babylonia, the LORD spoke to me on the seventh day of the first month.ᶜ He said:

²¹Ezekiel, son of man, I, the LORD, have defeated the king of Egypt! I broke his arm, and no one has wrapped it or put it in a sling, so that it could heal and get strong enough to hold a sword. ²²So tell him that I am now his worst enemy. I will break both his arms—the good one and the broken one! His sword will drop from his hand forever, ²³and I will scatter the Egyptians all over the world.

²⁴⁻²⁵I will strengthen the power of Babylonia's king and give him my sword to use against Egypt. I will also make the wounded king of Egypt powerless, and he will moan in pain and die in front of the Babylonian king. Then everyone on earth will know that I am the LORD. ²⁶I will force the Egyptians to live as prisoners in foreign nations, and they will know that I, the LORD, have punished them.

Egypt's King Will Be Chopped Down like a Cedar Tree

31 Eleven years after King Jehoiachin and the rest of us had been led away as prisoners to Babylonia, the LORD spoke to me on the first day of the third month.ᵈ He said:

²Ezekiel, son of man, tell the king of Egypt and his people that I am saying:

You are more powerful
than anyone on earth.
Now listen to this.
³ There was once a cedar tree
in Lebanon

ˣ**30.5** *as well as from Israel:* One possible meaning for the difficult Hebrew text. ʸ**30.13** *Memphis:* Hebrew "Noph." ᶻ**30.14** *Thebes:* Hebrew "No." ᵃ**30.16** *the people of Memphis . . . constant fear:* One possible meaning for the difficult Hebrew text. ᵇ**30.17** *Heliopolis and Bubastis:* Hebrew "On and Pi-Beseth." ᶜ**30.20** *Eleven years . . . first month:* Probably March of 587 B.C. ᵈ**31.1** *Eleven years . . . third month:* Probably May of 587 B.C.

with large, strong branches
  reaching to the sky.*
4 This tree had plenty of water
  to help it grow tall,
and nearby streams watered
  the other trees
    in the forest.
5 But this tree towered over
  those other trees,
and its branches
  grew long and thick.
6 Birds built nests
  in its branches,
and animals were born
  beneath it.
People from all nations
  lived in the shade
    of this strong tree.

7 It had beautiful,
  long branches,
and its roots found water
  deep in the soil.
8 None of the cedar trees
  in my garden of Eden
were as beautiful
  as this tree;
no tree of any kind
  had such long branches.
9 I, the LORD, gave this tree
  its beauty,
and I helped the branches
  grow strong.
All other trees in Eden
  wanted to be just like it.

10 King of Egypt, now listen to what I, the LORD God, am saying about that tree:

The tree grew so tall that it reached the sky* and became very proud and arrogant. 11 So I, the LORD God, will reject the tree and hand it over to a foreign ruler, who will punish it for its wickedness. 12 Cruel foreigners will chop it down and leave it wherever it falls. Branches and broken limbs will be scattered over the mountains and in the valleys. The people living in the shade of those branches will go somewhere else. 13 Birds will then nest on the stump of the fallen tree, and wild animals will trample its branches.

14 Never again will any tree dare to grow as tall as this tree, no matter how much water it has. Every tree must die, just as humans die and go down to the world of the dead.

15 On the day this tree dies and goes to the world below, I, the LORD God, will command rivers and streams to mourn its death. Every underground spring of water and every river will stop flowing.* The mountains in Lebanon will be covered with darkness as a sign of their sorrow, and all the trees in the forest will wither. 16 This tree will crash to the ground, and I will send it to the world below. Then the nations of the earth will tremble.

The trees from Eden and the choice trees from Lebanon are now in the world of the dead, and they will be comforted when this tree falls. 17 Those people who found protection in its shade will also be sent to the world below, where they will join the dead.*

18 King of Egypt, all these things will happen to you and your people! You were like this tree at one time—taller and stronger than anyone on earth. But now you will be chopped down, just as every tree in the garden of Eden must die. You will be sent down to the world of the dead, where you will join the godless and the other victims of violent death. I, the LORD God, have spoken.

A Funeral Song for the King of Egypt

32 Twelve years after King Jehoiachin and the rest of us had been led away as prisoners to Babylonia, the LORD spoke to me on the first day of the twelfth month.* He said:
2 Ezekiel, son of man, condemn the king of Egypt and tell him I am saying:

You act like a lion
  roaming the earth;
but you are nothing more than
  a crocodile in a river,

*31.3 sky: One possible meaning for the difficult Hebrew text of verse 3. *31.10 the sky: One ancient translation; Hebrew "over the thick branches." *31.15 rivers and streams . . . stop flowing: One possible meaning for the difficult Hebrew text. *31.17 dead: One possible meaning for the difficult Hebrew text of verse 17. *32.1 Twelve years . . . twelfth month: Probably February of 585 B.C.

churning up muddy water
   with your feet.

[3]King of Egypt, listen to me. I, the LORD
God, will catch you in my net and let a
crowd of foreigners drag you to shore. [4]I will
throw you into an open field, where birds
and animals will come to feed on your body.
[5]I will spread your rotting flesh[j] over the
mountains and in the valleys, [6]and your
blood will flow throughout the land and fill
up the streams. [7]I will cover the whole sky
and every star with thick clouds, so that the
sun and moon will stop shining. [8]The heavens will become black, leaving your country
in total darkness. I, the LORD, have spoken.

[9]Foreign nations you have never heard of
will be shocked when I tell them how I destroyed you.[k] [10]They will be horrified, and
when I flash my sword in victory on the day
of your death, their kings will tremble in the
fear of what could happen to them.

[11]The king of Babylonia is coming to attack you, king of Egypt! [12]Your soldiers will
be killed by the cruelest army in the world,
and everything you take pride in will be
crushed. [13]I will slaughter your cattle that
graze by the river,[l] and no people or livestock will be left to muddy its water. [14]The
water will be clear, and streams will be calm.
I, the LORD God, have spoken.

[15]Egypt will become a barren wasteland,
and no living thing will ever survive there.
Then you and your people will know that I
am the LORD.

[16]This is your warning, and it will be
used as a funeral song by foreign women to
mourn the death of your people. I, the LORD
God, have spoken.

A Sad Ending for Egypt

[17]On the fifteenth day of that same
month,[m] the LORD said:
[18]Ezekiel, son of man, mourn for the
Egyptians and condemn them to the world
of the dead, where they will be buried alongside the people of other powerful nations.[n]
[19]Say to them:

You may be more beautiful
  than the people
    of other nations,
but you will also die
  and join the godless
    in the world below.

[20]You cannot escape! The enemy's sword
is ready to slaughter every one of you.[o]
[21]Brave military leaders killed in battle will
gladly welcome you and your allies into the
world of the dead.

[22-23]The graves of soldiers from Assyria
are there. They once terrified people, but
they were killed in battle and now lie deep
in the world of the dead.[p]

[24-25]The graves of soldiers from Elam are
there. The very sight of those godless soldiers once terrified their enemies and made
them panic. But now they are disgraced and
ashamed as they lie in the world of the dead,
alongside others who were killed in battle.

[26]The graves of soldiers from Meshech
and Tubal are there. These godless soldiers
who terrified people were all killed in battle.
[27]They were not given a proper burial like
the heroes of long ago,[q] who were buried
with their swords under their heads and
with their shields[r] over their bodies. These
were the heroes who made their enemies
panic.

[28]You Egyptians will be cruelly defeated,
and you will be buried alongside these other
godless soldiers who died in battle.

[29]The graves of kings and leaders from
Edom are there. They were powerful at one
time. Now they are buried in the world of
the dead with other godless soldiers killed
in battle.

[30]The graves of the rulers of the north[s]
are there, as well as those of the Sidonians.
Their powerful armies once terrified enemies. Now they lie buried in the world of
the dead, where they are disgraced like other soldiers killed in battle.

[31]The LORD God says:

  When your king of Egypt sees all of
these graves, he and his soldiers will
be glad they are not the only ones suf-

---

[j]**32.5** *rotting flesh*: One possible meaning for the difficult
Hebrew text.   [k]**32.9** *when I tell them how I destroyed you*:
Hebrew; one ancient translation "when I scatter you like
prisoners among them."   [l]**32.13** *the river*: This possibly
refers to the Nile River.   [m]**32.17** *that same month*: See
verse 1.   [n]**32.18** *where they will be buried . . . powerful
nations*: One possible meaning for the difficult
Hebrew text.   [o]**32.20** *The enemy's sword . . . you*: One
possible meaning for the difficult Hebrew text.
[p]**32.22,23** *deep in the world of the dead*: The place of
greatest dishonor.   [q]**32.27** *heroes of long ago*: One
ancient translation; Hebrew "godless heroes."
[r]**32.27** *shields*: One possible meaning for the difficult
Hebrew text.   [s]**32.30** *the rulers of the north*: Probably
the Phoenicians.

fering. [32]I sent him to terrify people all over the earth. But he and his army will be killed and buried alongside other godless soldiers in the world of the dead. I, the LORD God, have spoken.

The LORD Appoints Ezekiel To Stand Watch
(Ezekiel 3.16-21)

33 The LORD said:
    [2]Ezekiel, son of man, warn your people by saying:
Someday, I, the LORD, may send an enemy to invade a country. And suppose its people choose someone to stand watch [3]and to sound a warning signal when the enemy is seen coming. [4-5]If any of these people hear the signal and ignore it, they will be killed in battle. But it will be their own fault, because they could have escaped if they had paid attention.

[6]But suppose the person watching fails to sound the warning signal. The enemy will attack and kill some of the sinful people in that country, and I, the LORD, will hold that person responsible for their death.

[7]Ezekiel, I have appointed you to stand watch for the people of Israel. So listen to what I say, then warn them for me. [8]When I tell wicked people they will die because of their sins, you must warn them to turn from their sinful ways. But if you refuse to warn them, you are responsible for their death. [9]If you do warn them, and they keep sinning, they will die because of their sins, and you will be innocent.

The LORD Is Always Fair
(Ezekiel 18.21-30)

[10]The LORD said:
Ezekiel, son of man, the people of Israel are complaining that the punishment for their sins is more than they can stand. They have lost all hope for survival, and they blame me. [11]Tell them that as surely as I am the living LORD God, I don't like to see wicked people die. I enjoy seeing them turn from their sins and live. So if the Israelites want to live, they must stop sinning and turn back to me.

[12]Tell them that when good people start sinning, all the good they did in the past cannot save them from being punished.

And remind them that when wicked people stop sinning, their past sins will be completely forgiven, and they won't be punished.

[13]Suppose I promise good people that they will live, then later they start sinning and believe they will be saved by the good they did in the past. These people will certainly be put to death because of their sins. Their good deeds will be forgotten.

[14]Suppose I warn wicked people that they will die because of their sins, and they stop sinning and start doing right. [15]For example, they need to return anything they have taken as security for a loan and anything they have stolen. Then if they stop doing evil and start obeying my Law, they will live. [16]Their past sins will be forgiven, and they will live because they have done right.

[17]Ezekiel, your people accuse me of being unfair. But they are the ones who are unfair. [18]If good people start doing evil, they will be put to death, because they have sinned. [19]And if wicked people stop sinning and start doing right, they will save themselves from punishment. [20]But the Israelites still think I am unfair. So warn them that they will be punished for what they have done.

The News of Jerusalem's Fall

[21]Twelve years after King Jehoiachin and the rest of us had been led away as prisoners to Babylonia, a refugee who had escaped from Jerusalem came to me on the fifth day of the tenth month.[t] He told me that the city had fallen.

[22]The evening before this man arrived at my house, the LORD had taken control of me. So when the man came to me the next morning, I could once again speak.[u]

What Will Happen to Those Left in Israel?

[23]Then the LORD said:
[24]Ezekiel, son of man, the people living in the ruined cities of Israel are saying, "Abraham was just one man, and the LORD gave him this whole land of Israel. There are many of us, and so this land must be ours."
[25]So, Ezekiel, tell them I am saying:

---

[t]33.21 *Twelve years . . . tenth month:* Probably December of 586 B.C.   [u]33.22 *I could once again speak:* See 3.27.

How can you think the land is still yours? You eat meat with blood in it and worship idols. You commit murder ²⁶and spread violence throughout the land. Everything you do is wicked; you are even unfaithful in marriage. And you claim the land is yours!

²⁷As surely as I am the living LORD God, you people in the ruined cities will be killed in battle. Those of you living in the countryside will be eaten by wild animals, and those hiding in caves and on rocky cliffs will die from deadly diseases. ²⁸I will make the whole country an empty wasteland and crush the power in which you take such pride. Even the mountains will be bare, and no one will try to cross them. ²⁹I will punish you because of your sins, and I will turn your nation into a barren desert. Then you will know that I am the LORD.

The People Listen, but Don't Change

The LORD said:

³⁰Ezekiel, son of man, the people with you in Babylonia talk about you when they meet by the city walls or in the doorways of their houses. They say, "Let's ask Ezekiel what the LORD has said today." ³¹So they all come and listen to you, but they refuse to do what you tell them. They claim to be faithful, but they are forever trying to cheat others out of their money. ³²They treat you as though you were merely singing love songs or playing music. They listen, but don't do anything you say.

³³Soon they will be punished, just as you warned, and they will know that a prophet has been among them.

Israel's Leaders Are Worthless Shepherds

34 The LORD God said:
²Ezekiel, son of man, Israel's leaders are like shepherds taking care of my sheep, the people of Israel. But I want you to condemn these leaders and tell them:

I, the LORD God, say you shepherds of Israel are doomed! You take care of yourselves while ignoring my sheep. ³You drink their milk and use their wool to make your clothes. Then you butcher the best ones for food.

But you don't take care of the flock! ⁴You have never protected the weak ones or healed the sick ones or bandaged those that get hurt. You let them wander off and never look for those that get lost. You are cruel and mean to my sheep. ⁵They strayed in every direction, and because there was no shepherd to watch them, they were attacked and eaten by wild animals. ⁶So my sheep were scattered across the earth. They roamed on hills and mountains, without anyone even bothering to look for them.

⁷⁻⁸Now listen to what I, the living LORD God, am saying to you shepherds. My sheep have been attacked and eaten by wild animals, because you refused to watch them. You never went looking for the lost ones, and you fed yourselves without feeding my sheep. ⁹⁻¹⁰So I, the LORD, will punish you! I will rescue my sheep from you and never let you be their shepherd again or butcher them for food. I, the LORD, have spoken.

The LORD Is the Good Shepherd

¹¹The LORD God then said:

I will look for my sheep and take care of them myself, ¹²just as a shepherd looks for lost sheep. My sheep have been lost since that dark and miserable day when they were scattered throughout the nations.ᵛ But I will rescue them ¹³and bring them back from the foreign nations where they now live. I will be their shepherd and will let them graze on Israel's mountains and in the valleys and fertile fields. ¹⁴They will be safe as they feed on grassy meadows and green hills. ¹⁵I promise to take care of them and keep them safe, ¹⁶to look for those that are lost and bring back the ones that wander off, to bandage those that are hurt and protect the ones that are weak. I will also slaughterʷ those that are fat and strong, because I always do right.

Judgment on the Strong Sheep

¹⁷The LORD God said to his sheep, the people of Israel:

ᵛ**34.12** *dark and miserable day . . . nations:* That is, the day the Babylonians defeated Jerusalem and led its people away as prisoners. ʷ**34.16** *slaughter:* Hebrew; three ancient translations "take care of."

I will carefully watch each one of you to decide which ones are the strong sheep and which ones are weak. [18]Some of you eat the greenest grass, then trample down what's left when you finish. Others drink clean water, then step in the water to make the rest of it muddy. [19]That means my other sheep have nothing fit to eat or drink.

[20]So I, the LORD God, will separate you strong sheep from the weak. [21]You strong ones have used your powerful horns to chase off those that are weak, [22]but I will rescue them and no longer let them be mistreated. I will separate the good from the bad.

[23]After that, I will give you a shepherd from the family of my servant King David. All of you, both strong and weak, will have the same shepherd, and he will take good care of you. [24]He will be your leader, and I will be your God. I, the LORD, have spoken.

A Bright Future for the LORD's Sheep

The LORD God said:

[25]The people of Israel are my sheep, and I solemnly promise that they will live in peace. I will chase away every wild animal from the desert and the forest, so my sheep will not be afraid. [26]They will live around my holy mountain,[x] and I will bless them by sending more than enough rain [27]to make their trees produce fruit and their crops to grow. I will set them free from slavery and let them live safely in their own land. Then they will know that I am the LORD. [28]Foreign nations will never again rob them, and wild animals will no longer kill and eat them. They will have nothing to fear. [29]I will make their fields produce large amounts of crops, so they will never again go hungry or be laughed at by foreigners. [30]Then everyone will know that I protect my people Israel. I, the LORD, make this promise. [31]They are my sheep; I am their God, and I take care of them.

Edom Will Be a Wasteland

35 The LORD said:
[2]Ezekiel, son of man, condemn the people of Edom[y] [3]and say to them:

I, the LORD God,
    am now your enemy!

And I will turn your nation
into an empty wasteland,
[4]   leaving your towns in ruins.
Your land will be a desert,
and then you will know
    that I am the LORD.

[5]People of Edom, not only have you been Israel's longtime enemy, you simply watched when disaster wiped out its people as punishment for their sins. [6]And so, as surely as I am the living LORD God, you are guilty of murder and must be put to death. [7]I will destroy your nation and kill anyone who travels through it. [8]Dead bodies will cover your mountains and fill up your valleys, [9]and your land will lie in ruins forever. No one will live in your towns ever again. You will know that I am the LORD.

[10]You thought the nations of Judah and Israel belonged to you, and that you could take over their territory. But I am their God, [11]and as surely as I live, I will punish you for treating my people with anger and hatred. Then they will know that I, the LORD, am punishing you! [12]And you will finally realize that I heard you laugh at their destruction and say their land was yours to take. [13]You even insulted me, but I heard it all.

[14]Everyone on earth will celebrate when I destroy you, [15]just as you celebrated when Israel was destroyed. Your nation of Edom will be nothing but a wasteland. Then everyone will know that I am the LORD.

A Message for Israel's Mountains

36 The LORD said:
Ezekiel, son of man, tell the mountains of Israel [2]that I, the LORD God, am saying:
Your enemies sneered and said that you mountains belonged to them. [3]They ruined and crushed you from every side, and foreign nations captured and made fun of you. [4]So all you mountains and hills, streams and valleys, listen to what I will do. Your towns may now lie in ruins, and nations may laugh and insult you. [5]But in my fierce anger, I will turn against those nations, and especially the Edomites, because they laughed at you

---

[x]**34.26** *my holy mountain:* That is, Mount Zion in Jerusalem.   [y]**35.2** *Edom:* The Hebrew text has "Mount Seir," another name for Edom.

the loudest and took over your pasture-lands. [6]You have suffered long enough, and, I, the LORD God, am very angry! Nations have insulted you, [7]so I will now insult and disgrace them. That is my solemn promise.

[8]Trees will grow on you mountains of Israel and produce fruit for my people, because they will soon come home. [9]I will take care of you by plowing your soil and planting crops on your fertile slopes. [10]The people of Israel will return and rebuild your ruined towns and live in them. [11]Children will be born, and animals will give birth to their young. You will no longer be deserted as you are now, but you will be covered with people and treated better than ever. Then you will know that I am the LORD.

[12]I will bring my people Israel home, and they will live on you mountains, because you belong to them, and your fertile slopes will never again let them starve. [13]It's true that you have been accused of not producing enough food and of letting your people starve. [14-15]But I, the LORD, promise that you won't hear other nations laugh and sneer at you ever again. From now on, you will always produce plenty of food for your people. I, the LORD God, have spoken.

The LORD Will Be Honored

[16]The LORD said:

[17]Ezekiel, son of man, when the people of Israel were living in their own country, they made the land unclean by the way they behaved, just as a woman's monthly period makes her unclean. [18]They committed murders and worshiped idols, which made the land even worse. So in my anger, I punished my people [19]and scattered them throughout the nations, just as they deserved. [20]Wherever they went, my name was disgraced, because foreigners insulted my people by saying I had forced them out of their own land.

[21]I care what those foreigners think of me, [22]so tell the Israelites that I am saying:

You have disgraced my holy name among the nations where you now live. So you don't deserve what I'm going to do for you. I will lead you home to bring honor to my name [23]and to show foreign nations that I am holy. Then they will know that I am the LORD God. I have spoken.

[24]I will gather you from the foreign nations and bring you home. [25]I will sprinkle you with clean water, and you will be clean and acceptable to me. I will wash away everything that makes you unclean, and I will remove your disgusting idols. [26]I will take away your stubborn heart and give you a new heart and a desire to be faithful. You will have only pure thoughts, [27]because I will put my Spirit in you and make you eager to obey my laws and teachings. [28]You will once again live in the land I gave your ancestors; you will be my people, and I will be your God.

> When other factors in a marriage are weak, this one—a mutual love for God and desire to serve him—can keep two people determined to work toward a relationship that reflects God's love and power.
>
> CAROLE MAYHALL

[29]I will protect you from anything that makes you unclean. Your fields will overflow with grain, and no one will starve. [30]Your trees will be filled with fruit, and crops will grow in your fields, so that you will never again feel ashamed for not having enough food. [31]You will remember your evil ways and hate yourselves for what you've done. [32]People of Israel, I'm not doing these things for your sake. You sinned against me, and you must suffer shame and disgrace for what you have done. I, the LORD God, have spoken.

[33]After I have made you clean, I will let you rebuild your ruined towns and let you live in them. [34]Your land will be plowed again, and nobody will be able to see that it was once barren. [35]Instead, they will say that it looks as beautiful as the garden of Eden. They

won't see towns lying in ruins, but they will see your strong cities filled with people. ³⁶Then the nearby nations that survive will know that I am the one who rebuilt the ruined places and replanted the barren fields. I, the LORD, make this promise.

³⁷I will once again answer your prayers, and I will let your nation grow until you are like a large flock of sheep. ³⁸The towns that now lie in ruins will be filled with people, just as Jerusalem was once filled with sheep to be offered as sacrifices during a festival. Then you will know that I am the LORD.

Dry Bones Live Again

37 Some time later, I felt the LORD's power take control of me, and his Spirit carried me to a valley full of bones. ²The LORD showed me all around, and everywhere I looked I saw bones that were dried out. ³He said, "Ezekiel, son of man, can these bones come back to life?"

I replied, "LORD God, only you can answer that."

⁴He then told me to say:

Dry bones, listen to what the LORD is saying to you, ⁵"I, the LORD God, will put breath in you, and once again you will live. ⁶I will wrap you with muscles and skin and breathe life into you. Then you will know that I am the LORD."

⁷I did what the LORD said, but before I finished speaking, I heard a rattling noise. The bones were coming together! ⁸I saw muscles and skin cover the bones, but they had no life in them.

⁹The LORD said:

Ezekiel, now say to the wind,ᶻ "The LORD God commands you to blow from every direction and to breathe life into these dead bodies, so they can live again."

¹⁰As soon as I said this, the wind blew among the bodies, and they came back to life! They all stood up, and there were enough to make a large army.

¹¹The LORD said:

Ezekiel, the people of Israel are like dead bones. They complain that they are dried up and that they have no

---

ᶻ**37.9** *wind:* Or "breath." The Hebrew word may mean either.

---

*Spiritual*Life—**If I've turned away from God, is it possible to come back? How?** *(Ezekiel 37.1-14)*

Ask God, who can bring you back to life.

It can be a gradual drifting. Slowly you become aware that you haven't prayed for weeks. You misplaced your Bible some time back; you're not sure where. You meant to find a church after that last move, but you never did. Now when you try to pray, you wonder if God hears you. You've drifted away from God, and your relationship with him now seems hollow, lifeless—you're as spiritually dead as dry bones.

Sometimes turning away from God is more sudden. A tragedy has you saying in grief and anger, "If God could allow that, I want nothing to do with him!" Maybe temptation gets the best of you: "I just don't want to live the Christian life any longer, and I'm sick of trying." Or doubts crowd out whatever faith you've claimed, and you say, "How can I keep on believing that the Bible is God's Word when scholars still fight over what makes a valid text? Besides, why would a loving God allow genocide in Africa?"

The causes of spiritual death are limitless, but they are real—with deadly results. But Ezekiel's valley of dry bones can bring us hope. The Lord said, "I am the LORD. My Spirit will give you breath, and you will live again" (37.13,14). What is more alive than the breath of God?

Ask God for new life. And live. (See also Isaiah 55.6-13; Lamentations 3.31-40; Hosea 3; Joel 2.25-27; 1 John 1.8—2.2.)

Words To Remember: *I, the LORD God, will put breath in you, and once again you will live.—Ezekiel 37.5*

hope for the future. ¹²So tell them, "I, the LORD God, promise to open your graves and set you free. I will bring you back to Israel, ¹³and when that happens, you will realize that I am the LORD. ¹⁴My Spirit will give you breath, and you will live again. I will bring you home, and you will know that I have kept my promise. I, the LORD, have spoken."

Judah and Israel Together Again

¹⁵The LORD said:
¹⁶Ezekiel, son of man, get a stick and write on it, "The kingdom of Judah." Then get another stick and write on it, "The kingdom of Israel."ᵃ ¹⁷Hold these two sticks end to end, so they look like one stick. ¹⁸And when your people ask you what this means, ¹⁹tell them that I, the LORD, will join together the stick of Israel and the stick of Judah. I will hold them in my hand, and they will become one.

²⁰Hold these two sticks where they can be seen by everyone ²¹and then say:

I, the LORD God, will gather the people of Israel and bring them home from the foreign nations where they now live. ²²I will make them into one nation and let them once again live in the land of Israel. Only one king will rule them, and they will never again be divided into two nations. ²³They will no longer worship idols and do things that make them unacceptable to me. I will wash away their sin and make them clean, and I will protect them from everything that makes them unclean. They will be my people, and I will be their God.

²⁴⁻²⁵Their king will always come from the family of my servant King David and will care for them like a shepherd. The people of Israel will faithfully obey my laws. They and their descendants will live in the land I gave my servant Jacob, just as their ancestors did. ²⁶I solemnly promise to bless the people of Israel with unending peace. I will protect them and let them become a powerful nation. My temple will stand in Israel for all time, ²⁷and I will live among my people and be their God. ²⁸Every nation on earth will know that my temple is in Israel and that I have chosen the Israelites to be my people.

Gog Invades Israel

38 The LORD said:
²Ezekiel, son of man, condemn Gog, that wicked ruler of the kingdoms of Meshech and Tubal in the land of Magog. Tell him:

³I, the LORD God, am your enemy, ⁴and I will make you powerless! I will put a hook in your jaw and drag away both you and your large army. You command cavalry troops that wear heavy armor and carry shields and swords. ⁵Your army includes soldiers from Persia, Ethiopia,ᵇ and Libya, ⁶as well as from Gomer and Beth-Togarmah in the north. Your army is enormous!

⁷So keep your troops prepared to fight, ⁸because in a few years, I will command you to invade Israel, a country that was ruined by war. It was deserted for a long time, but its people have returned from the foreign nations where they once lived. The Israelites now live in peace in the mountains of their own land. ⁹But you and your army will attack them like a fierce thunderstorm and surround them like a cloud.

¹⁰When that day comes, I know that you will have an evil plan ¹¹to take advantage of Israel, that weak and peaceful country where people live safely inside towns that have no walls or gates or locks. ¹²You will rob the people in towns that were once a pile of rubble. These people lived as prisoners in foreign nations, but they have returned to Israel, the most important place in the world, and they own livestock and property. ¹³The people of Sheba and Dedan, along with merchants from villages inᶜ southern Spain,ᵈ will be your allies. They will want some of the silver and gold, as

---

ᵃ**37.16** *Israel:* The Hebrew text has "Joseph, that is, Ephraim," the leading tribe in the northern kingdom. ᵇ**38.5** *Ethiopia:* See the note at 29.10. ᶜ**38.13** *from villages in:* One ancient translation; Hebrew "and soldiers from." ᵈ**38.13** *southern Spain:* See the note at 27.12.

well as the livestock and property that your army takes from Israel.

[14]I, the LORD God, know that when you see[e] my people Israel living in peace, [15]you will lead your powerful cavalry from your kingdom in the north. [16]You will attack my people like a storm-cloud that covers their land. I will let you invade my country Israel, so that every nation on earth will know that I, the LORD, am holy.

Judgment on Gog

[17]The LORD said to Gog:

Long ago, I had my prophets warn the people of Israel that someday I would send an enemy to attack them. You, Gog, are that enemy, and that day is coming. [18]When you invade Israel, I will become furious, [19]and in my anger I will send a terrible earthquake to shake Israel. [20]Every living thing on earth will tremble in fear of me—every fish and bird, every wild animal and reptile, and every human. Mountains will crumble, cliffs will fall, and cities will collapse. [21]I, the LORD, will make the mountains of Israel turn against you.[f] Your troops will be so terrified that they will attack each other. [22]I will strike you with diseases and punish you with death. You and your army will be pounded with rainstorms, hailstones, and burning sulfur. [23]I will do these things to show the world that I, the LORD, am holy.

Gog Is Defeated

The LORD said:

39 Ezekiel, son of man, condemn Gog and tell him:

You are the ruler of Meshech and Tubal, but I, the LORD, am your enemy! [2]I will turn you around and drag you from the north until you reach the mountains of Israel. [3]I will knock the bow out of your left hand and the arrows out of your right hand, [4]and you and your army will die on those mountains. Then birds and wild animals will eat the flesh [5]of your dead bodies left lying in open fields. I, the LORD, have spoken.

[6]I will set fire to the land of Magog and to those nations along the seacoast that think they are so secure, and they will know that I am the LORD.

[7]My people Israel will know me, and

they will no longer disgrace my holy name. Everyone on earth will know that I am the holy LORD God of Israel. [8]The day is coming when these things will happen, just as I have promised.

[9]When that day comes, the people in the towns of Israel will collect the weapons of their dead enemies. They will use these shields, bows and arrows, spears, and clubs as firewood, and there will be enough to last for seven years. [10]They will burn these weapons instead of gathering sticks or chopping down trees. That's how the Israelites will take revenge on those who robbed and abused them. I, the LORD, have spoken.

The Burial of Gog

The LORD said:

[11]After Gog has been destroyed, I will bury him and his army in Israel, in Travelers'[g] Valley, east of the Dead Sea. That graveyard will be so large that it will block the way of anyone who tries to walk through the valley,[h] which will then be known as "The Valley of Gog's Army."[i] [12]The Israelites will spend seven months burying dead bodies and cleaning up their land. [13]Everyone will help with the burial, and they will be honored for this on the day the brightness of my glory is seen. [14]After those seven months, the people will appoint a group of men to look for any dead bodies left unburied. This must be done for seven months to make sure that the land is no longer unclean. [15]Whenever they find a human bone, they will set up a marker next to it. Then the gravediggers will bury it in "The Valley of Gog's Army" [16]near the town of "Gog's Army." After that, the land will be pure again.

[17]Ezekiel, son of man, I am going to hold a feast on Israel's mountains and offer sacrifices there. So invite all the birds and wild animals to come from every direction and eat the meat of sacrifices and drink the blood. The birds and animals [18]will feast on the bodies of warriors and foreign rulers that

I will sacrifice like sheep, goats, and bulls. [19]I want the birds and animals to eat until they are full and drink until they are drunk. [20]They will come to my table and stuff themselves with the flesh of horses and warriors of every kind. I, the LORD God, have spoken.

Israel Will Be Restored

The LORD said:

[21]When I punish the nations of the earth, they will see the brightness of my glory. [22]The people of Israel will know from then on that I am the LORD their God. [23]Foreign nations will realize that the Israelites were forced to leave their own land because they sinned against me. I turned my back on my people and let enemies attack and kill them. [24]Their lives were wicked and corrupt, and they deserved to be punished.

[25]Now I will show mercy to the people of Israel and bring them back from the nations where they are living. They are Jacob's descendants, so I will bless them and show that I am holy. [26]They will live safely in their own land, but will be ashamed when they remember their evil ways and how they disgraced me.[j] [27]Foreign nations will watch as I take the Israelites from enemy lands and bring them back home, and those nations will see that I am holy.

> *God's Word tells us we*
> *believers have two*
> *Intercessors—Christ at*
> *the right hand of God,*
> *and the Holy Spirit*
> *dwelling in us.*
>
> EVELYN CHRISTENSON

[28]My people will realize that I, the LORD their God, sent them away as prisoners and now will bring them back to their own land. [29]Never again will I turn my back on the people of Israel, and my Spirit will live in them. I, the LORD, have spoken.

Ezekiel Sees the Future Temple in Jerusalem

40 [1-2]Twenty-five years after King Jehoiachin and the rest of us had been led away as prisoners to Babylonia, and fourteen years after the Babylonians had captured Jerusalem, the LORD's power took control of me on the tenth day of the first month.[k] The LORD showed me some visions in which I was carried to the top of a high mountain in Jerusalem. I looked to the south and saw what looked like a city full of buildings. [3]In my vision the LORD took me closer, and I saw a man who was sparkling like polished bronze. He was standing near one of the gates and was holding a tape measure in one hand and a measuring stick in the other. [4]The man said, "Ezekiel, son of man, pay close attention to everything I'm going to show you—that's why you've been brought here. Listen carefully, because you must tell the people of Israel what you see."

The East Gate

[5]The first thing I saw was an outer wall that completely surrounded the temple area. The man took his measuring stick, which was ten feet long, and measured the wall; it was ten feet high and ten feet thick. [6-7]Then he went to the east gate, where he walked up steps that led to a long passageway. On each side of this passageway were three guardrooms, which were ten feet square, and they were separated by walls over eight feet thick. The man measured the distance between the opening of the gate and the first guardroom, and it was ten feet, the thickness of the outer wall.

At the far end of this passageway, I saw an entrance room that faced the courtyard of the temple itself. There was also a distance of ten feet between the last guardroom and the entrance room [8-9]at the end of the passageway. The man measured this room: It was thirteen feet from the doorway to the opposite wall, and the distance from the doorway to the wall on either side was three feet. [10]The three guardrooms on each side of the passageway were the same size, and the

---

[j]39.26 *me:* One possible meaning for the difficult Hebrew text of verse 26. [k]40.1,2 *Twenty-five years . . . first month:* Probably March of 573 B.C.

walls that separated them were the same thickness.

[11]Next, the man measured the width of the passageway, and it was twenty-two feet, but the two doors of the gate were only sixteen feet wide.[l] [12]In front of the guardrooms, which were ten feet square, was a railing about twenty inches high and twenty inches thick. [13]The man measured the distance from the back wall[m] of one of these rooms to the same spot in the room directly across the passageway, and it was forty-two feet. [14]He measured the entrance room at the far end of the passageway, and it was thirty-four feet wide.[n] [15]Finally, he measured the total length of the passageway, from the outer wall to the entrance room, and it was eighty-five feet. [16]The three walls in the guardrooms had small windows in them, just like the ones in the entrance room.[o] The walls along the passageway were decorated with carvings of palm trees.

The Outer Courtyard

[17]The man then led me through the passageway and into the outer courtyard of the temple, where I saw thirty rooms built around the outside of the courtyard.[p] These side rooms were built against the outer wall, and in front of them was a sidewalk that circled the courtyard. [18]This was known as the lower sidewalk, and it was eighty-five feet wide.

[19]I saw the gates that led to the inner courtyard of the temple and noticed that they were higher than those leading to the outer courtyard. The man measured the distance between the outer and inner gates, and it was one hundred seventy feet.[q]

The North Gate

[20]Next, the man measured the north gate that led to the outer courtyard. [21]This gate also had three guardrooms on each side of a passageway. The measurements of these rooms, the walls between them, and the entrance room at the far end of the passageway were exactly the same as those of the east gate. The north gate was also eighty-five feet long and forty-two feet wide, [22]and the windows, the entrance room, and the carvings of palm trees were just like those in the east gate. The entrance room also faced the courtyard of the temple and had seven steps leading up to it. [23]Directly across the outer

courtyard was a gate that led to the inner courtyard, just as there was for the east gate. The man measured the distance between the outer and inner gate, and it was one hundred seventy feet.

The South Gate

[24]The man then took me to the south gate. He measured the walls and the entrance room of this gate, and the measurements were exactly the same as those of the other two gates. [25]There were windows in the guardrooms of this gate and in the entrance room, just like the others, and this gate was also eighty-five feet long and forty-two feet wide. [26]Seven steps led up to the gate; the entrance room was at the far end of the passageway and faced the courtyard of the temple. Carvings of palm trees decorated the walls along the passageway. [27]And directly across the outer courtyard was a gate on the south side of the inner courtyard. The man measured the distance between the outer and inner gate, and it was also one hundred seventy feet.

The Gates Leading to the Inner Courtyard

[28]We then went into the inner courtyard, through the gate on the south side of the temple. The man measured the gate, and it was the same size as the gates in the outer wall. [29-30]In fact, everything along the passageway was also the same size, including the guardrooms, the walls separating them, the entrance room at the far end, and the windows. This gate, like the others, was eighty-five feet long and forty-two feet wide. [31]The entrance room of this gate faced the outer courtyard, and carvings of palm trees decorated the walls of the passageway. Eight steps led up to this gate.

[32]Next, we went through the east gate to the inner courtyard. The man measured this

[l]40.11 the width of the passageway... twenty-two feet... the two doors of the gate... sixteen feet wide: The doors themselves probably were hung on stone sockets, which could explain the six-foot difference in width between the passageway and the doors. [m]40.13 back wall: One ancient translation; Hebrew "roof." [n]40.14 wide: One possible meaning for the difficult Hebrew text of verse 14. [o]40.16 just like the ones in the entrance room: One possible meaning for the difficult Hebrew text. [p]40.17 thirty rooms built around the outside of the courtyard: These were probably used by worshipers as places to meet and share sacrificial meals (see, for example, Jeremiah 35.2). [q]40.19 feet: The Hebrew text adds "the east and the north."

gate, and it was the same size as the others. [33]The guardrooms, the walls separating them, and its entrance room had the same measurements as the other gates. The guardrooms and the entrance room had windows, and the gate was eighty-five feet long and forty-two feet wide. [34]The entrance room faced the outer courtyard, and the walls in the passageway were decorated with carvings of palm trees. Eight steps also led up to this gate.

[35]Then the man took me to the north gate. He measured it, and it was the same size as the others, [36]including the guardrooms, the walls separating them, and the entrance room. There were also windows in this gate. It was eighty-five feet long and forty-two feet wide, [37]and like the other inner gates, its entrance room faced the outer courtyard, and its walls were decorated with carvings of palm trees. Eight steps also led up to this gate.

The Rooms for Sacrificing Animals

[38-39]Inside the entrance room of the north gate, I saw four tables, two on each side of the room, where the animals to be sacrificed were killed. Just outside[r] this room was a small building used for washing the animals before they were offered as sacrifices to please the LORD[s] or sacrifices for sin[t] or sacrifices to make things right.[u] [40]Four more tables were in the outer courtyard, two on each side of the steps leading into the entrance room. [41]So there was a total of eight tables, four inside and four outside, where the animals were killed, [42-43]and where the meat was placed until it was sacrificed on the altar.[v]

Next to the tables in the entrance room were four stone tables twenty inches high and thirty inches square; the equipment used for killing the animals was kept on top of these tables. All around the walls of this room was a three inch shelf.[w]

The Rooms Belonging to the Priests

[44]The man then took me to the inner courtyard, where I saw two buildings, one beside the inner gate on the north and the other beside the inner gate on the south.[x] [45]He said, "The building beside the north gate belongs to the priests who serve in the temple, [46]and the building beside the south gate belongs to those who serve at the altar.

All of them are descendants of Zadok and are the only Levites allowed to serve as the LORD's priests."

The Inner Courtyard and the Temple

[47]Now the man measured the inner courtyard; it was one hundred seventy feet square. I also saw an altar in front of the temple.

[48]We walked to the porch of the temple, and the man measured the doorway of the porch: It was twenty-four feet long,[y] eight feet wide, and the distance from the doorway to the wall on either side was five feet. [49]The porch itself was thirty-four feet by twenty[z] feet, with steps[a] leading up to it. There was a column on each side of these steps.

41 Next we went into the main room of the temple. The man measured the doorway of this room: It was ten feet wide,[b] [2]seventeen feet long, and the distance from the doorway to the wall on either side was eight feet. The main room itself was sixty-eight feet by thirty-four feet.

[3-4]Then the man walked to the far end of the temple's main room and said, "Beyond this doorway is the most holy place." He first measured the doorway: It was three feet wide, ten feet long, and the distance from the doorway to the wall on either side was twelve feet. Then he measured the most holy place, and it was thirty-four feet square.

The Storage Rooms of the Temple

[5]The man measured the wall of the temple, and it was ten feet thick. Storage rooms

---

[r]**40.38,39** *Just outside:* Or "Inside."
[s]**40.38,39** *sacrifices to please the* LORD: These sacrifices have traditionally been called "whole burnt offerings" because the whole animal was burned on the altar. A main purpose of such sacrifices was to please the LORD with the smell of the sacrifice, and so in the CEV they are often called "sacrifices to please the LORD."
[t]**40.38,39** *sacrifices for sin:* See Leviticus 4.1, 2; 6.24-30. [u]**40.38,39** *sacrifices to make things right:* See Leviticus 5.14-19; 7.1-10. [v]**40.42,43** *where the meat . . . altar:* One possible meaning for the difficult Hebrew text. [w]**40.42,43** *was a three inch shelf:* Or "were three inch pegs." [x]**40.44** *south:* One possible meaning for the difficult Hebrew text of verse 44. [y]**40.48** *twenty-four feet long:* One ancient translation; these words are not in the Hebrew text of this verse. [z]**40.49** *twenty:* One ancient translation; Hebrew "eighteen." [a]**40.49** *steps:* Hebrew; one ancient translation "ten steps." [b]**41.1** *It was ten feet wide:* One possible meaning for the difficult Hebrew text.

seven feet wide were built against the outside of the wall. [6]There were three levels of rooms, with thirty rooms on each level, and they rested on ledges that were attached to the temple walls, so that nothing was built into the walls. [7]The walls of the temple were thicker at the bottom than at the top, which meant that the storage rooms on the top level were wider than those on the bottom level.[c] Steps led from the bottom level, through the middle level, and into the top level.

[8]The temple rested on a stone base ten feet high, which also served as the foundation for the storage rooms. [9]The outside walls of the storage rooms were eight feet thick; there was nothing between these walls [10]and the nearest buildings thirty-four feet away. [11]One door led into the storage rooms on the north side of the temple, and another door led to those on the south side. The stone base extended eight feet beyond the outside wall of the storage rooms.

The West Building and the Measurements of the Temple

[12]I noticed another building: It faced the west end of the temple and was one hundred seventeen feet wide, one hundred fifty feet long, and had walls over eight feet thick. [13]The man measured the length of the temple, and it was one hundred seventy feet. He then measured from the back wall of the temple, across the open space behind the temple, to the back wall of the west building; it was one hundred seventy feet. [14]The distance across the front of the temple, including the open space on either side, was also one hundred seventy feet.

[15]Finally, the man measured the length of the west building, including the side rooms on each end, and it was also one hundred seventy feet.

The Inside of the Temple

The inside walls of the temple's porch and main room[d] [16]were paneled with wood all the way from the floor to the windows, while the doorways, the small windows, and the three side rooms were trimmed in wood.[e] [17]The paneling stopped just above the doorway. These walls were decorated[f] [18-20]with carvings of winged creatures and had a carving of a palm tree between the creatures. Each winged creature had two

faces: A human face looking at the palm tree on one side, and a lion's face looking at the palm tree on the other side. These designs were carved into the paneling all the way around the two rooms.

[21]The doorframe to the temple's main room was in the shape of a rectangle.

The Wooden Altar

In front of the doorway to the most holy place was something that looked like [22]a wooden altar. It was five feet high and four feet square,[g] and its corners, its base,[h] and its sides were made of wood. The man said, "This is a reminder that the LORD is constantly watching over his temple."

The Doors in the Temple

[23]Both the doorway to the main room of the temple and the doorway to the most holy place had two doors, [24]and each door had two sections that could fold open. [25]The doors to the main room were decorated with carvings of winged creatures and palm trees just like those on the walls, and there was a wooden covering over the porch just outside these doors. [26]The walls on each side of this porch had small windows and were also decorated with carvings of palm trees.

The Sacred Rooms for the Priests

42 [1-2]After the man and I left the temple and walked back to the outer courtyard, he showed me a set of rooms on the north side of the west building.[i] This set of rooms was one hundred seventy feet long and eighty-five feet wide. [3]On one side of them was the thirty-four feet of open space that ran alongside the temple,[j] and on the other side was the sidewalk that circled the outer courtyard.[k]

---

[c]**41.7** *which meant that . . . on the bottom level*: One possible meaning for the difficult Hebrew text.
[d]**41.15** *The inside walls of the temple's porch and main room*: One possible meaning for the difficult Hebrew text. [e]**41.16** *were trimmed in wood*: One possible meaning for the difficult Hebrew text.
[f]**41.17** *decorated*: One possible meaning for the difficult Hebrew text of verse 17. [g]**41.22** *four feet square*: One ancient translation; Hebrew "four feet wide."
[h]**41.22** *base*: One ancient translation; Hebrew "length." [i]**42.1,2** *he showed me . . . the west building*: One possible meaning for the difficult Hebrew text.
[j]**42.3** *the thirty-four feet of open space . . . the temple*: See 41.10. [k]**42.3** *the sidewalk that circled the outer courtyard*: See 40.17.

The rooms were arranged in three levels [4]with doors that opened toward the north, and in front of them was a walkway seventeen feet wide and one hundred seventy feet long.[l] [5]The rooms on the top level were narrower than those on the middle level, and the rooms on the middle level were narrower than those on the bottom level. [6]The rooms on the bottom level supported those on the two upper levels, and so these rooms did not have columns like other buildings in the courtyard. [7-8]To the north was a privacy wall eighty-five feet long,[m] [9-10]and at the east end of this wall was the door leading from the courtyard to these rooms.

There was also a set of rooms on the south[n] side of the west building. [11]These rooms were exactly like those on the north side, and they also had a walkway in front of them. [12]The door to these rooms was at the east end of the wall that stood in front of them.

[13]The man then said to me:

These rooms on the north and south sides of the temple are the sacred rooms where the LORD's priests will eat the most holy offerings. These offerings include the grain sacrifices, the sacrifices for sin, and the sacrifices to make things right. [14]When the priests are ready to leave the temple, they must go through these rooms before they return to the outer courtyard. They must leave their sacred clothes in these rooms and put on regular clothes before going anywhere near other people.

The Size of the Temple Area

[15]After the man had finished measuring the buildings inside the temple area, he took me back through the east gate and measured the wall around this area. [16]He used his measuring stick to measure the east side of this wall; it was eight hundred forty feet long. [17-19]Then he measured the north side, the south side, and the west side of the wall, and they were each eight hundred forty feet long, [20]and so the temple area was a perfect square. The wall around this area separated what was sacred from what was ordinary.

---

[l]**42.4** *one hundred seventy feet long*: Two ancient translations; Hebrew "twenty inches long."
[m]**42.7,8** *long*: One possible meaning for the difficult Hebrew text of verses 5-8. [n]**42.9,10** *south*: One ancient translation; Hebrew "east."

---

*Spiritual*Life—Why is it important for me to go to church? *(Ezekiel 43.1-5)*

You can see God's glory there.
Maybe you had a bad experience in a church where God's people did not live up to their names, or the fact your family holds differing beliefs makes the choice of a church difficult. Perhaps you live a high-pressure life that begs for Sunday morning in bed, or you feel uneasy walking into a building and sitting in a crowd of people where you don't know a soul and don't know when to stand, sit, kneel, or sing. Church just doesn't address where you are in your life—and besides, you don't like the music. Is it worth overcoming these obstacles to go? Yes.

Every church is flawed (it is, after all, made up of mere humans). But in a mysterious sense, a body of Christian believers gathered to worship God makes up the present-day version of God's temple (see 1 Corinthians 3.16). Near the end of his book, Ezekiel was blessed with a vision of a new temple not yet built. But he saw the glory of God return and fill that temple.

God's glory fills a gathering of his people in a way that isn't possible in us individually. It's one of the wonderful mysteries of God. In church, if we open our spiritual eyes, we just might see his glory. (See also Acts 2.1-13,41-47; Romans 12.3-8; 1 Corinthians 3.10-17; Ephesians 2.11-22.)

Words To Remember: *The LORD's Spirit lifted me to my feet and carried me to the inner courtyard, where I saw that the LORD's glory had filled the temple.*
—Ezekiel 43.5

The LORD's Glory Returns to the Temple

43

The man took me back to the east gate of the temple, [2]where I saw the brightness of the glory of Israel's God coming from the east. The sound I heard was as loud as ocean waves, and everything around was shining with the dazzling brightness of his glory. [3]This vision was like the one I had seen when God came to destroy Jerusalem and like the one I had seen near the Chebar River.

I immediately bowed with my face to the ground, [4]and the LORD's glory came through the east gate and into the temple.[o] [5]The LORD's Spirit lifted me to my feet and carried me to the inner courtyard, where I saw that the LORD's glory had filled the temple.

[6]The man was standing beside me, and I heard the LORD[p] say from inside the temple: [7]Ezekiel, son of man, this temple is my throne on earth. I will live here among the people of Israel forever. They and their kings will never again disgrace me by worshiping idols at local shrines or by setting up memorials to their dead kings.[q] [8]Israel's kings built their palaces so close to my holy temple that only a wall separated them from me. Then these kings disgraced me with their evil ways, and in my fierce anger I destroyed them. [9]But if the people and their kings stop worshiping other gods and tear down those memorials, I will live among them forever.

[10]The people of Israel must suffer shame for sinning against me, so tell them about my holy temple. Let them think about it, [11]then if they are truly sorry, describe for them the design and shape of the temple, the gates, the measurements, and how the buildings are arranged. Explain the regulations about worshiping there, then write down these things, so they can study and obey them.

[12]The temple area on my holy mountain must be kept sacred! This is the most important law about the temple.

The Altar

[13]According to the official standards, the altar in the temple had the following mea-

surements: Around the bottom of the altar was a gutter twenty inches wide and twenty inches deep, with a ten inch ledge on the outer rim. [14-17]The altar rested on a base and had three sections, each one of them square. The bottom section was twenty-seven feet on each side and three feet high. The middle section was twenty-four feet on each side and seven feet high, and it had a ten inch rim around its outer edge. The top section, which was twenty feet on each side and seven feet high, was the place where sacrifices were burned, and the four corners of the top section looked like the horns of a bull. The steps leading up to the altar were on the east side.

The Dedication of the Altar

[18]The LORD God said:

Ezekiel, son of man, after the altar is built, it must be dedicated by offering sacrifices on it and by splattering it with blood. Here is what you must do: [19]The priests of the Levi tribe from the family of Zadok the priest are the only ones who may serve in my temple—this is my law. So give them a young bull to slaughter as a sacrifice for sin. [20]Take some of the animal's blood and smear it on the four corners of the altar, some on the corners of the middle section, and some more on the rim around its edge. That will purify the altar and make it fit for offering sacrifices to me. [21]Then take the body of the bull outside the temple area and burn it at the special place.

[22]The next day, a goat[r] that has nothing wrong with it must be offered as a sacrifice for sin. Purify the altar with its blood, just as you did with the blood of the bull. [23]Then choose a young bull and a young ram that have nothing wrong with them, [24]and bring them to my temple. The priests will sprinkle salt on them[s] and offer them as sacrifices to please me.[t]

[25]Each day for the next seven days, you must offer a goat and a bull and a ram as

---

o43.4 the LORD's glory . . . temple: This was the same gate the LORD's glory went through when it left Jerusalem (see 10.19 and 11.22, 23). p43.6 the LORD: Hebrew "a voice." q43.7 by setting up memorials to their dead kings: One possible meaning for the difficult Hebrew text. r43.22 goat: Hebrew "male goat." s43.24 The priests will sprinkle salt on them: See Leviticus 2.13. t43.24 sacrifices to please me: See the note at 40.38, 39.

sacrifices for sin. These animals must have nothing wrong with them. ²⁶The priests will purify the altar during those days, so that it will be acceptable to me and ready to use. ²⁷From then on, the priests will use this altar to offer sacrifices to please me and sacrifices to ask my blessing." Then I will be pleased with the people of Israel. I, the LORD God, have spoken.

The East Gate Must Remain Closed

44 The man took me back to the outer courtyard, near the east gate of the temple area. I saw that the doors to this gate were closed. ²The LORD said:

I, the LORD God of Israel, came through this gate, so it must remain closed forever! No one must ever use it. ³The ruler of Israel may come here to eat a sacrificial meal that has been offered to me, but he must use only the entrance room of this gate.

People Who Are Not Allowed in the Temple

⁴Then the man took me through the north gate to the front of the temple. I saw that the brightness of the LORD's glory had filled the temple, and I immediately bowed with my face to the ground.

If ever there was a "how-to" book on life, the Bible is it. I'm glad God took the time to publish it.

MARIAN V. LIAUTAUD

⁵The LORD said:
Ezekiel, son of man, I am going to give you the laws for my temple. So pay attention and listen carefully to what kind of people are allowed to come in the temple, and what kind are not. ⁶Tell those rebellious people of Israel:

I, the LORD God, command you to stop your evil ways! ⁷My temple has been disgraced, because you have let godless, stubborn foreigners come here when sacrifices are being offered

to me. You have sinned and have broken our solemn agreement. ⁸Instead of following the proper ways to worship me, you have put foreigners in charge of worship at my temple.

⁹And so I, the LORD God, say that no godless foreigner who disobeys me will be allowed in my temple. This includes any foreigner living in Israel.

The Levites Are Punished

The LORD said:

¹⁰Some of the Levites turned their backs on me and joined the other people of Israel in worshiping idols. So these Levites must be punished! ¹¹They will still be allowed to serve me as temple workers by guarding the gates and by killing the animals to be sacrificed and by helping the worshipers. ¹²But because these Levites served the people of Israel when they worshiped idols, I, the LORD God, promise that the Levites will be punished. They did not stop the Israelites from sinning, ¹³and now I will no longer let the Levites serve as my priests or come near anything sacred to me. They must suffer shame and disgrace for their disgusting sins. ¹⁴They will be responsible for all the hard work that must be done in the temple.

Rules for Priests

The LORD said:

¹⁵The priests of the Levi tribe who are descendants of Zadok the priest were faithful to me, even when the rest of the Israelites turned away. And so, these priests will continue to serve as my priests and to offer the fat and the blood of sacrifices. ¹⁶They will come into my temple, where they will offer sacrifices at my altar and lead others in worship. ¹⁷When they come to the inner courtyard, they must wear their linen priestly clothes. My priests must never wear anything made of wool when they are on duty

---

ᵘ**43.27** *sacrifices to ask my blessing:* These sacrifices have traditionally been called "peace offerings" or "offerings of well-being." A main purpose was to ask for the LORD's blessing, and so in the CEV they are sometimes called "sacrifices to ask the LORD's blessing."

in this courtyard or in the temple. [18]Even their turbans and underwear must be made of linen to keep my priests from sweating when they work. [19]And before they leave to join the other people in the outer courtyard, they must take off their priestly clothes, then place them in the sacred rooms and put on their regular clothes.[v] That way, no one will touch their sacred clothes and be harmed.[w]

[20]Priests must never shave their heads when they are mourning. But they must keep their hair properly trimmed and not let it grow too long. [21]They must not drink wine before going to the inner courtyard.

[22]A priest must not marry a divorced woman; he can marry only a virgin from Israel or the widow of another priest.

[23]Priests must teach my people the difference between what is sacred and what is ordinary, and between what is clean and what is unclean. [24]They will make decisions in difficult legal cases, according to my own laws. They must also observe the religious festivals my Law requires and must always respect the Sabbath.

[25]Touching a dead body will make a person unclean. So a priest must not go near a dead body, unless it is one of his parents or children, or his brother or unmarried sister. [26]If a priest touches a dead body, he is unclean and must go through a ceremony to make himself clean. Then seven days later, [27]he must go to the inner courtyard of the temple and offer a sacrifice for sin. After that, he may once again serve as my priest. I, the LORD God, have spoken.

[28]I myself will provide for my priests, and so they won't receive any land of their own. [29]Instead, they will receive part of the grain sacrifices, as well as part of the sacrifices for sin and sacrifices to make things right. They will also be given everything in Israel that has been completely dedicated to me.[x] [30]The first part of every harvest will belong to the priests. They will also receive part of all special gifts and offerings the Israelites bring to me. And whenever any of my people bake bread, they will give their first loaf as an offering to the priests, and I will bless the homes of the people when they do this.

[31]Priests must not eat any bird or animal that dies a natural death or that has been killed by a wild animal.

The LORD's Sacred Land

The LORD said:

45 When the land of Israel is divided among the twelve tribes, you must set aside an area that will belong to me. This sacred area will be eight miles long and six[y] miles wide. [2]The temple will be on a piece of land eight hundred forty feet square, and the temple will be completely surrounded by an open space eighty-four feet wide.

[3-4]I will give half of my sacred land, a section eight miles long and three miles wide, to the priests who serve in the temple. Their houses will be in this half, as well as my temple, which is the most sacred place of all.

[5]I will give the other half of my land to the Levites who work in my temple, and the towns[z] where they will live will be there.

[6]Next to my sacred land will be an area eight miles long and two miles wide. This will belong to the people of Israel and will include the city of Jerusalem.

Land for Israel's Ruler

The LORD said:

[7-8]The regions west and east of my sacred land and the city of Jerusalem will belong to the ruler of Israel. He will be given the region between the western edge of my land and the Mediterranean Sea, and between the eastern edge of my land and the Jordan River. This will mean that the length of his property will be the same as the sections of land given to the tribes.

This property will belong to every ruler of Israel, so they will always be fair to my people and will let them live peacefully in the land given to their tribes.

---

[v]**44.19** *take off their priestly clothes . . . put on their regular clothes:* See 42.14.   [w]**44.19** *no one will touch . . . and be harmed:* Ordinary people were forbidden to touch anything that was sacred. If they did, it was believed they would somehow be harmed.   [x]**44.29** *that has been completely dedicated to me:* This translates a Hebrew word that describes property and things that were taken away from humans and given to God. In the early history of Israel, such things often had to be destroyed (see Joshua 6.15-19).   [y]**45.1** *six:* One ancient translation; Hebrew "three."   [z]**45.5** *the towns:* One ancient translation; Hebrew "the twenty rooms."

Israel's Rulers Must Be Honest

⁹The LORD God said:

You leaders of Israel have robbed and cheated my people long enough! I want you to stop sinning and start doing what is right and fair. You must never again force my people off their own land. I, the LORD, have spoken.

¹⁰So from now on, you must use honest weights and measures. ¹¹The *ephah* will be the standard dry measure, and the *bath* will be the standard liquid measure. Their size will be based on the *homer*, which will equal ten *ephahs* or ten *baths*.ᵃ

¹²The standard unit of weight will be the *shekel*.ᵇ One *shekel* will equal twenty *gerahs*, and sixty *shekels* will equal one *mina*.

¹³Leaders of Israel, the people must bring you one sixtieth of their grain harvests as offerings to me. ¹⁴They will also bring one percent of their olive oil. These things will be measured according to the *bath*, and ten *baths* is the same as one *homer* or one *cor*. ¹⁵Finally, they must bring one sheep out of every two hundred from their flocks.

These offerings will be used as grain sacrifices, as well as sacrifices to please meᶜ and those to ask my blessing.ᵈ I, the LORD, will be pleased with these sacrifices and will forgive the sins of my people.

¹⁶The people of Israel will bring you these offerings. ¹⁷But during New Moon Festivals, Sabbath celebrations, and other religious feasts, you leaders will be responsible for providing animals for the sacrifices, as well as the grain and wine. All these will be used for the sacrifices for sin, the grain sacrifices, the sacrifices to please me, and those to ask my blessing. I will be pleased and will forgive the sins of my people.

The Festivals
(Exodus 12.1-20; Leviticus 23.33-43)

¹⁸The LORD God said:

On the first day of the first month,ᵉ a young bull that has nothing wrong with it must be offered as a sacrifice to purify the temple. ¹⁹The priest will take some blood from this sacrifice and smear it on the doorposts of the temple, as well as on the four corners of the altar and on the doorposts of the gates that lead into the inner courtyard. ²⁰The same ceremony must also be done on the seventh day of the month, so that anyone who sins accidentally or without knowing it will be forgiven, and so that my temple will remain holy.

²¹Beginning on the fourteenth day of the first month, and continuing for seven days, everyone will celebrate Passover and eat bread made without yeast. ²²On the first day, the ruler will bring a bull to offer as a sacrifice for his sins and for the sins of the people. ²³Each day of the festival he is to bring seven bulls and seven rams as sacrifices to please me,ᶠ and he must bring a goatᵍ as a sacrifice for sin. These animals must have nothing wrong with them. ²⁴He will also provide twenty pounds of grain and four quarts of olive oil to be offered with each bull and each ram.

²⁵The Festival of Shelters will begin on the fifteenth day of the seventh monthʰ and will continue for seven days. On each day of this festival, the ruler will provide the same number of animals that he did each day during Passover, as well as the same amount of grain and olive oil for the sacrifices.

Various Laws for the Ruler and the People

46 The LORD said:

The east gate of the inner courtyard must remain closed during the six working days of each week. But on the Sabbath and on the first day of the month, this gate will be opened. ²Israel's ruler will go from the outer courtyard into the entrance room of this gate and stand in the doorway while the priest offers sacrifices to ask my blessingⁱ and sacrifices to please me.ʲ The ruler will bow with his face to the ground to show that he has worshiped me.

ᵃ**45.11** *the homer . . . ten ephahs . . . ten baths:* A homer was either a dry or a liquid measure and equaled about five bushels or fifty-five gallons; an *ephah* would be about a half bushel, and a *bath* would be about five and a half gallons.   ᵇ**45.12** *the shekel:* The *shekel* was about four-tenths of an ounce.   ᶜ**45.15** *sacrifices to please me:* See the note at 40.38, 39.   ᵈ**45.15** *sacrifices . . . to ask my blessing:* See the note at 43.27.   ᵉ**45.18** *the first month:* Abib (also called Nisan), the first month of the Hebrew calendar, from about mid-March to mid-April.   ᶠ**45.23** *sacrifices to please me:* See the note at 40.38, 39.   ᵍ**45.23** *goat:* See the note at 43.22.   ʰ**45.25** *seventh month:* Tishri (also called Ethanim), the seventh month of the Hebrew calendar, from about mid-September to mid-October.   ⁱ**46.2** *sacrifices to ask my blessing:* See the note at 43.27.   ʲ**46.2** *sacrifices to please me:* See the note at 40.38, 39.

Then he will leave, and the gate will remain open until evening.

³Each Sabbath and on the first day of each month, the people of Israel must also come to the east gate and worship me. ⁴On the Sabbath, the ruler will bring six lambs and one ram to be offered as sacrifices to please me. There must be nothing wrong with any of these animals. ⁵With the ram, he is to offer twenty pounds of grain, and with each of the lambs, he can offer as much as he wants. He must also offer four quarts of olive oil with every twenty pounds of grain.

⁶The ruler is to bring six lambs, a bull, and a ram to be offered as sacrifices at the New Moon Festival. There must be nothing wrong with any of these animals. ⁷With the bull and the ram, he is to offer twenty pounds of grain, and with each of the lambs, he can offer as much as he wants. He must also offer four quarts of olive oil with every twenty pounds of grain. ⁸The ruler must come through the entrance room of the east gate and leave the same way.

⁹When my people come to worship me during any festival, they must always leave by the opposite gate from which they came: Those who come in the north gate must leave by the south gate, and those who come in the south gate must leave by the north gate. ¹⁰Their ruler will come in at the same time they do and leave at the same time they leave.

¹¹At all other festivals and celebrations, twenty pounds of grain will be offered with a bull, and twenty pounds will be offered with a ram. The worshipers can offer as much grain as they want with each lamb. Four quarts of olive oil must be offered with every twenty pounds of grain.

¹²If the ruler voluntarily offers a sacrifice to please me or to ask my blessing, the east gate of the inner courtyard will be opened for him. He will offer his sacrifices just as he does on each Sabbath; then he will leave, and the gate will be closed.

¹³Each morning a year-old lamb that has nothing wrong with it must be offered as a sacrifice to please me. ¹⁴Along with it, three pounds of fine flour mixed with a quart of olive oil must be offered as a grain sacrifice. This law will never change—¹⁵the lamb, the flour, and the olive oil will be offered to me every morning for all time.

Laws about the Ruler's Land

¹⁶The LORD God said:

If the ruler of Israel gives some of his land to one of his children, it will belong to the ruler's child as part of the family property. ¹⁷But if the ruler gives some of his land to one of his servants, the land will belong to the servant until the Year of Celebration, when it will be returned to the ruler.ᵏ Only the ruler's children can keep what is given to them.

¹⁸The ruler must never abuse my people by taking land from them. Any land he gives his children must already belong to him.

The Sacred Kitchens

¹⁹The man who was showing me the templeˡ then took me back to the inner courtyard. We walked to the south side of the courtyard and stopped at the door to the sacred rooms that belonged to the priests. He showed me more rooms at the western edge of the courtyard ²⁰and said, "These are the kitchens where the priests must boil the meat to be offered as sacrifices to make things rightᵐ and as sacrifices for sin.ⁿ They will also bake the grain for sacrifices in these kitchens. That way, these sacred offerings won't have to be carried through the outer courtyard, where someone could accidentally touch them and be harmed."ᵒ

²¹We went back to the outer courtyard and walked past the four corners. ²²At each corner I saw a smaller courtyard, sixty-eight feet long and fifty feet wide. ²³Around the inside of these smaller courtyards was a low wall of stones, and against the wall were places to build fires.ᵖ ²⁴The man said, "These are the kitchens where the temple workers will boil the meat that worshipers offer as sacrifices."

The Stream Flowing from the Temple

47 The man took me back to the temple, where I saw a stream flowing from under the entrance.

ᵏ46.17 the Year of Celebration . . . to the ruler: This was a sacred year for Israel, traditionally called the "Year of Jubilee." During this year, all property had to go back to its original owner (see Leviticus 25.8-34). ˡ46.19 The man . . . temple: See 40.3. ᵐ46.20 sacrifices to make things right: See the note at 40.38, 39. ⁿ46.20 sacrifices for sin: See the note at 40.38, 39. ᵒ46.20 someone . . . touch them and be harmed: See the note at 44.19. ᵖ46.23 fires: One possible meaning for the difficult Hebrew text of verse 23.

It began in the south part of the temple, where it ran past the altar and continued east through the courtyard.

2We walked out of the temple area through the north gate and went around to the east gate. I saw the small stream of water flowing east from the south side of the gate.

3The man walked east, then took out his measuring stick and measured five hundred sixty yards downstream. He told me to wade through the stream there, and the water came up to my ankles. 4Then he measured another five hundred sixty yards downstream, and told me to wade through it there. The water came up to my knees. Another five hundred sixty yards downstream the water came up to my waist. 5Another five hundred sixty yards downstream, the stream had become a river that could be crossed only by swimming. 6The man said, "Ezekiel, son of man, pay attention to what you've seen."

We walked to the riverbank, 7where I saw dozens of trees on each side. 8The man said:

> This water flows eastward to the Jordan River valley and empties into the Dead Sea, where it turns the salt water into fresh water. 9Wherever this water flows, there will be all kinds of animals and fish, because it will bring life and fresh water to the Dead Sea. 10From En-Gedi to Eneglaim, people will fish in the sea and dry their nets along the coast. There will be as many kinds of fish in the Dead Sea as there are in the Mediterranean Sea. 11But the marshes along the shore will remain salty, so that people can use the salt from them.
>
> 12Fruit trees will grow all along this river and produce fresh fruit every month. The leaves will never dry out, because they will always have water from the stream that flows from the temple, and they will be used for healing people.

The Borders of the Land

13-14The LORD God said to the people of Israel:

When the land is divided among the twelve tribes of Israel, the Joseph tribe[q] will receive two shares. Divide the land equally, because I promised your ancestors that this land would someday belong to their descendants. These are the borders of the land:

15The northern border will begin at the Mediterranean Sea, then continue eastward to Hethlon, to Lebo-Hamath, then across to Zedad, 16Berothah,[r] and Sibraim, which is on the border between the two kingdoms of Damascus and Hamath. The border will end at Hazer-Hatticon, which is on the border of Hauran. 17So the northern border will run between the Mediterranean Sea and Hazar-Enon, which is on the border between Damascus and Hamath.[s]

18The eastern border will begin on the border between the two kingdoms of Hauran and Damascus. It will run south along the Jordan River, which separates the territories of Gilead and Israel, and it will end at the Dead Sea near the town of Tamar.[t]

19The southern border will begin at Tamar, then run southwest to the springs near Meribath-Kadesh. It will continue along the Egyptian Gorge and will end at the Mediterranean Sea.

20The western border will run north along the Mediterranean Sea to a point just west of Lebo-Hamath.

21That is the land to be divided among the tribes of Israel. 22It will belong to the Israelites and to any foreigners living among them whose children were born in Israel. These foreigners must be treated like any other Israelite citizen, and they will receive 23a share of the land given to the tribe where they live. I, the LORD God, have spoken.

The Division of Land among Tribes in the North

The LORD said:

48 1-7Each tribe will receive a section of land that runs from the eastern border of Israel west to the Mediterranean Sea. The northern border of Israel will run along the towns of Hethlon and Lebo-Hamath, and will end at Hazar-

[q]47.13,14 *the Joseph tribe*: That is, the two tribes of Manasseh and Ephraim, Joseph's sons. [r]47.15,16 *to Lebo-Hamath, then across to Zedad, 16Berothah*: One ancient translation; Hebrew "to Lebo-Zedad, 16then across to Hamath, Berothah." [s]47.17 *which is on the border between Damascus and Hamath*: One possible meaning for the difficult Hebrew text. [t]47.18 *near the town of Tamar*: One possible meaning for the difficult Hebrew text.

Enon, which is on the border between the kingdoms of Damascus and Hamath. The tribes will receive their share of land in the following order, from north to south: Dan, Asher, Naphtali, Manasseh, Ephraim, Reuben, and Judah.

The Special Section of Land

The LORD said:

⁸South of Judah's territory will be a special section of land. Its length will be eight miles, and its width will run from the eastern border of Israel west to the Mediterranean Sea. My temple will be located in this section of land.

⁹An area in the center of this land will belong to me. It will be eight miles long and six*ᵘ* miles wide.

¹⁰I, the LORD, will give half of my sacred land to the priests. Their share will be eight miles long and three miles wide, and my temple will be right in the middle. ¹¹Only priests who are descendants of Zadok will receive a share of this sacred land, because they remained faithful to me when the Levites and the rest of the Israelites started sinning. ¹²The land belonging to the priests will be the most sacred area and will lie south of the area that belongs to the Levites.

¹³I will give the other half of my sacred land to the Levites. Their share will also be eight miles long and three miles wide, ¹⁴and they must never sell or trade any of this land—it is the best land and belongs to me.

¹⁵South of my sacred land will be a section eight miles long and two miles wide. It will not be sacred, but will belong to the people of Israel and will include the city of Jerusalem, together with its houses and pastureland. ¹⁶The city will be a square: Each side will be a mile and a half long, ¹⁷and an open area four hundred twenty feet wide will surround the city. ¹⁸The land on the east and west sides of the city limits will be farmland for the people of Jerusalem; both sections will be three miles long and two miles wide. ¹⁹People from the city will farm the land, no matter which tribe they belong to.

²⁰And so the center of this special section of land will be for my sacred land, as well as for the city and its property. The land will be a square, eight miles on each side.

²¹The regions east and west of this square of land will belong to the ruler of Israel. His property will run east to the Jordan River and west to the Mediterranean Sea. In the very center of his property will be my sacred land, as well as the temple, ²²together with the share belonging to the Levites and the city of Jerusalem. The northern border of the ruler's property will be the land that belongs to Judah, and the southern border will be the land that belongs to Benjamin.

The Division of Land among Tribes in the South

The LORD God said:

²³⁻²⁷South of this special section will be the land that belongs to the rest of Israel's tribes. Each tribe will receive a section of land that runs from the eastern border of Israel west to the Mediterranean Sea. The tribes will receive their share of land in the following order, from north to south: Benjamin, Simeon, Issachar, Zebulun, and Gad.

²⁸Gad's southern border is also the southern border of Israel. It will begin at the town of Tamar, then run southwest to the springs near Meribath-Kadesh. It will continue along the Egyptian Gorge and end at the Mediterranean Sea.

²⁹That's how the land of Israel will be divided among the twelve tribes. I, the LORD God, have spoken.

The Gates of Jerusalem

The LORD said:

³⁰⁻³⁴The city of Jerusalem will have twelve gates, three on each of the four sides of the city wall. These gates will be named after the twelve tribes of Israel. The gates of Reuben, Judah, and Levi will be in the north; Joseph, Benjamin, and Dan will be in the east; Simeon, Issachar, and Zebulun will be in the south; Gad, Asher, and Naphtali will be in the west. Each side of the city wall will be a mile and a half long, ³⁵and so the total length of the wall will be six miles. The new name of the city will be "The-LORD-Is-Here!"

ᵘ48.9 *six:* The Hebrew text has "three" (but see 45.1 and the note there).

Daniel

How Big Is God?

The world can be a frightening place, especially for women. We can be afraid of rape, abuse, abandonment, death, childlessness, divorce, harassment, discrimination. If we let ourselves, we can easily give in to our fears, becoming isolated, overly cautious, and untrusting. But a life lived in fear is not much of a life.

Daniel is a book designed to help us get rid of that kind of paralyzing fear. As Daniel tells the story of his imprisonment, persecution, and eventual acceptance by the Babylonian government, he teaches us a valuable lesson: Our God is a big God.

In the background of Daniel's story are his fellow Jews, many of whom, like Daniel, had been snatched from their own country, Judah, by the warring Babylonians. As they lived in exile, their temple and homeland destroyed, they certainly feared the future. No doubt they felt abandoned by God. But Daniel tells his story to encourage his people and to remind them of God's power and faithfulness (2.20-23).

Whether he faced death at the hands of a vain king (2.14-16), the jealousy of the king's officials (6.1-9), or a pit full of hungry lions (6.22,23), Daniel continued to believe that his God, the God of Israel, was big enough to handle anything earthly powers could dish out. As we face the fears that threaten us each day, we can be inspired, like the Jews, by Daniel's unwavering faith in our unfailing God.

Daniel at a Glance

1. A strange place (1)
2. The king's dream (2)
3. A fiery rescue (3)
4. The dream comes true (4)
5. The writing on the wall (5)
6. Daniel faces death—again (6)
7. Daniel's visions (7,8)
8. A prayer for the people (9)
9. The promise of peace (10–12)

Daniel and His Friends

1 In the third year that Jehoiakim was king of Judah,[a] King Nebuchadnezzar of Babylonia attacked Jerusalem. [2]The Lord let Nebuchadnezzar capture Jehoiakim and take away some of the things used in God's temple. And when the king returned to Babylonia,[b] he put these things in the temple of his own god.

[3]One day the king ordered Ashpenaz, his highest palace official, to choose some young men from the royal family of Judah and from other leading Jewish families. [4]The king said, "They must be healthy, handsome, smart, wise, educated, and fit to serve in the royal palace. Teach them how to speak and write our language [5]and give them the same food and wine that I am served. Train them for three years, and then they can become court officials."

[6]Four of the young Jews chosen were Daniel, Hananiah, Mishael, and Azariah, all from the tribe of Judah. [7]But the king's chief official gave them Babylonian names: Daniel became Belteshazzar, Hananiah became Shadrach, Mishael became Meshach, and Azariah became Abednego.

[8]Daniel made up his mind to eat and drink only what God had approved for his people to eat. And he asked the king's chief official for permission not to eat the food and wine served in the royal palace. [9]God had made the official friendly and kind to Daniel. [10]But the man still told him, "The king has decided what you must eat and drink. And I am afraid he will kill me, if you eat something else and end up looking worse than the other young men."

[11]The king's official had put a guard in charge of Daniel and his three friends. So Daniel said to the guard, [12]"For the next ten days, let us have only vegetables and water at mealtime. [13]When the ten days are up, compare how we look with the other young men, and decide what to do with us." [14]The guard agreed to do what Daniel had asked.

[15]Ten days later, Daniel and his friends looked healthier and better than the young men who had been served food from the royal palace. [16]After this, the guard let them eat vegetables instead of the rich food and wine.

[17]God made the four young men smart and wise. They read a lot of books and became well educated. Daniel could also tell the meaning of dreams and visions.

[18]At the end of the three-year period set by King Nebuchadnezzar, his chief palace official brought all the young men to him. [19]The king interviewed them and discovered that none of the others were as outstanding as Daniel, Hananiah, Mishael, and Azariah. So they were given positions in the royal court. [20]From then on, whenever the king asked for advice, he found their wisdom was ten times better than that of any of his other advisors and magicians. [21]Daniel served there until the first year of King Cyrus.[c]

> *The beginning of wisdom is realizing where it comes from— the throne of God.*
>
> JOSIE CRAMER

Nebuchadnezzar's Dream

2 During the second year that Nebuchadnezzar was king, he had such horrible nightmares that he could not sleep. [2]So he called in his counselors, advisors, magicians, and wise men, [3]and said, "I am disturbed by a dream that I don't understand, and I want you to explain it."

[4]They answered in Aramaic,[d] "Your Majesty, we hope you live forever! We are your servants. Please tell us your dream, and we will explain what it means."

[5]But the king replied, "No! I have made up my mind. If you don't tell me both the dream and its meaning, you will be chopped to pieces and your houses will be torn down. [6]However, if you do tell me both the dream and its meaning, you will be greatly rewarded and highly honored. Now tell me the dream and explain what it means."

[7]"Your Majesty," they said, "if you will

---

[a]1.1 *Jehoiakim . . . king of Judah*: Ruled 609-598 B.C.
[b]1.2 *Babylonia*: The Hebrew text has "Shinar," another name for Babylonia. [c]1.21 *first year of King Cyrus*: 539 B.C. [d]2.4 *Aramaic*: Chapter 2.4—7.28 is written in Aramaic, a language closely related to Hebrew.

only tell us your dream, we will interpret it for you."

⁸The king replied, "You're just stalling for time, ⁹because you know what's going to happen if you don't come up with the answer. You've decided to make up a bunch of lies, hoping I might change my mind. Now tell me the dream, and that will prove that you can interpret it."

¹⁰His advisors explained, "Your Majesty, you are demanding the impossible! No king, not even the most famous and powerful, has ever ordered his advisors, magicians, or wise men to do such a thing. ¹¹It can't be done, except by the gods, and they don't live here on earth."

¹²⁻¹³This made the king so angry that he gave orders for every wise man in Babylonia to be put to death, including Daniel and his three friends.

God Tells Nebuchadnezzar's Dream to Daniel

¹⁴Arioch was the king's official in charge of putting the wise men to death. He was on his way to have it done, when Daniel very wisely went to him ¹⁵and asked, "Why did the king give such cruelᶜ orders?" After Arioch explained what had happened, ¹⁶Daniel rushed off and said to the king, "If you will just give me some time, I'll explain your dream."

¹⁷Daniel returned home and told his three friends. ¹⁸Then he said, "Pray that the God who rules from heaven will be merciful and explain this mystery, so that we and the others won't be put to death." ¹⁹In a vision one night, Daniel was shown the dream and its meaning. Then he praised the God who rules from heaven:

²⁰ "Our God, your name
 will be praised
  forever and forever.
You are all-powerful,
  and you know everything.
²¹ You control human events—
 you give rulers their power
  and take it away,
and you are the source
  of wisdom and knowledge.

²² "You explain deep mysteries,
 because even the dark
  is light to you.
²³ You are the God
 who was worshiped
  by my ancestors.
Now I thank you and praise you
  for making me wise

ᶜ**2.15** *cruel:* Or "urgent."

⸎

Personal *Concerns*—How can I learn to be more content with my life?
(*Daniel 2.20,21*)

Realize God is in control of it.
Do you wish you were married? that you had a child? a roommate you really clicked with? Or maybe you'd like a different job—one that uses more of your natural skills and is less tedious. Or perhaps you're in a difficult and rather hostile place, like Daniel (one of the young Israelites who was captured and taken to Babylonia). Maybe your boss is hard on you, for no reason you can figure out; your husband is verbally abusive; or you've just become a single parent.

No matter the situation, Daniel tells us that God is "all-powerful" and knows everything (2.20). God is always in control of human events (2.21). What a great thing to remember when times are tough, and you wish your life were different! Knowing that God is in charge lets us relax and live life a day at a time—instead of becoming stressed about what the future holds.

What should our response be to our great God? To praise him "forever and forever" (2.20), even when we don't know how things will turn out. But God always does.
(See also Psalm 107; Ecclesiastes 6.1-9; 2 Peter 1.3-15.)

⸎**Words To Remember:** *"Our God, your name will be praised forever and forever. You are all-powerful, and you know everything. You control human events."*
—Daniel 2.20,21

and telling me the king's dream, together with its meaning."

Daniel Interprets the Dream

[24]Daniel went back to Arioch, the official in charge of executing the wise men. Daniel said, "Don't kill those men! Take me to the king, and I will explain the meaning of his dream."

[25]Arioch rushed Daniel to the king and announced, "Your Majesty, I have found out that one of the men brought here from Judah can explain your dream."

[26]The king asked Daniel,[f] "Can you tell me my dream and what it means?"

[27]Daniel answered:

Your Majesty, not even the smartest person in all the world can do what you are demanding. [28-29]But the God who rules from heaven can explain mysteries. And while you were sleeping, he showed you what will happen in the future. [30]However, you must realize that these mysteries weren't explained to me because I am smarter than everyone else. Instead, it was done so that you would understand what you have seen.

[31]Your Majesty, what you saw standing in front of you was a huge and terrifying statue, shining brightly. [32]Its head was made of gold, its chest and arms were silver, and from its waist down to its knees, it was bronze. [33]From there to its ankles it was iron, and its feet were a mixture of iron and clay.

[34]As you watched, a stone was cut from a mountain—but not by human hands. The stone struck the feet, completely shattering the iron and clay. [35]Then the iron, the clay, the bronze, the silver, and the gold were crushed and blown away without a trace, like husks of wheat at threshing time. But the stone became a tremendous mountain that covered the entire earth.

[36]That was the dream, and now I'll tell you what it means. [37]Your Majesty, you are the greatest of kings, and God has highly honored you with power [38]over all humans, animals, and birds. You are the head of gold. [39]After you are gone, another kingdom will rule,

but it won't be as strong. Then it will be followed by a kingdom of bronze that will rule the whole world. [40]Next, a kingdom of iron will come to power, crushing and shattering everything.[g]

[41-42]This fourth kingdom will be divided—it will be both strong and brittle, just as you saw that the feet and toes were a mixture of iron and clay. [43]This kingdom will be the result of a marriage between kingdoms, but it will crumble, just as iron and clay don't stick together.

[44-45]During the time of those kings, the God who rules from heaven will set up an eternal kingdom that will never fall. It will be like the stone that was cut from the mountain, but not by human hands—the stone that crushed the iron, bronze, clay, silver, and gold. Your Majesty, in your dream the great God has told you what is going to happen, and you can trust this interpretation.

Daniel Is Promoted

[46]King Nebuchadnezzar bowed low to the ground and worshiped Daniel. Then he gave orders for incense to be burned and a sacrifice of grain to be offered in honor of Daniel. [47]The king said, "Now I know that your God is above all other gods and kings, because he gave you the power to explain this mystery." [48]The king then presented Daniel with a lot of gifts; he promoted him to governor of Babylon Province and put him in charge of the other wise men. [49]At Daniel's request, the king appointed Shadrach, Meshach, and Abednego to high positions in Babylon Province, and he let Daniel stay on as a palace official.

King Nebuchadnezzar's Gold Statue

3 King Nebuchadnezzar ordered a gold statue to be built ninety feet high and nine feet wide. He had it set up in Dura Valley near the city of Babylon, [2]and he commanded his governors, advisors, treasurers, judges, and his other officials to come from everywhere in his kingdom to

---

[f]**2.26** *Daniel*: Aramaic "Daniel whose name was Belteshazzar" (see 1.7). [g]**2.40** *crushing . . . everything*: Three ancient translations; Aramaic adds "and like iron crushing."

the dedication of the statue. ³So all of them came and stood in front of it.

⁴Then an official stood up and announced:

People of every nation and race, now listen to the king's command! ⁵Trumpets, flutes, harps, and all other kinds of musical instruments will soon start playing. When you hear the music, you must bow down and worship the statue that King Nebuchadnezzar has set up. ⁶Anyone who refuses will at once be thrown into a flaming furnace.

⁷As soon as the people heard the music, they bowed down and worshiped the gold statue that the king had set up.

⁸Some Babylonians used this as a chance to accuse the Jews to King Nebuchadnezzar. ⁹They said, "Your Majesty, we hope you live forever! ¹⁰You commanded everyone to bow down and worship the gold statue when the music played. ¹¹And you said that anyone who did not bow down and worship it would be thrown into a flaming furnace. ¹²Sir, you appointed three men to high positions in Babylon Province, but they have disobeyed you. Those Jews, Shadrach, Meshach, and Abednego, refuse to worship your gods and the statue you have set up."

¹³King Nebuchadnezzar was furious. So he sent for the three young men and said, ¹⁴"I hear that you refuse to worship my gods and the gold statue I have set up. ¹⁵Now I am going to give you one more chance. If you bow down and worship the statue when you hear the music, everything will be all right. But if you don't, you will at once be thrown into a flaming furnace. No god can save you from me."

¹⁶The three men replied, "Your Majesty, we don't need to defend ourselves. ¹⁷The God we worship can save us from you and your flaming furnace. ¹⁸But even if he doesn't, we still won't worship your gods and the gold statue you have set up."

¹⁹Nebuchadnezzar's face twisted with anger at the three men. And he ordered the furnace to be heated seven times hotter than usual. ²⁰Next, he commanded some of his strongest soldiers to tie up the men and throw them into the flaming furnace. ²¹⁻²³The king wanted it done at that very moment. So the soldiers tied up Shadrach, Meshach, and Abednego and threw them into the flaming furnace with all of their clothes still on, including their turbans. The fire was so hot that flames leaped out and killed the soldiers.

> *God doesn't ask me to be a perfect witness, just a willing one. He can be counted on to do the work if we are simply willing to open up our hearts.*
>
> LUCIA ALEXIS GAINER

²⁴Suddenly the king jumped up and shouted, "Weren't only three men tied up and thrown into the fire?"

"Yes, Your Majesty," the people answered.

²⁵"But I see four men walking around in the fire," the king replied. "None of them is tied up or harmed, and the fourth one looks like a god."ʰ

²⁶Nebuchadnezzar went closer to the flaming furnace and said to the three young men, "You servants of the Most High God, come out at once!"

They came out, ²⁷and the king's high officials, governors, and advisors all crowded around them. The men were not burned, their hair wasn't scorched, and their clothes didn't even smell like smoke. ²⁸King Nebuchadnezzar said:

Praise their God for sending an angel to rescue his servants! They trusted their God and refused to obey my commands. Yes, they chose to die rather than to worship or serve any god except their own. ²⁹And I won't allow people of any nation or race to say anything against their God. Anyone who does will be chopped up and their houses will be torn down, because no other god has such great power to save.

³⁰After this happened, the king appointed

ʰ3.25 *a god:* Aramaic, "a son of the gods."

Shadrach, Meshach, and Abednego to even higher positions in Babylon Province.

King Nebuchadnezzar's Letter about His Second Dream

4 King Nebuchadnezzar sent the following letter to the people of all nations and races on the earth:

Greetings to all of you!
[2] I am glad to tell about
the wonderful miracles
God Most High
has done for me.
[3] His miracles are mighty
and marvelous.
He will rule forever,
and his kingdom
will never end.

> *Woven through your past is the relentless thread of God's presence. God has been faithful to you.*
>
> KELSEY D. MENEHAN

[4] I was enjoying a time of peace and prosperity, [5] when suddenly I had some horrifying dreams and visions. [6] Then I commanded every wise man in Babylonia to appear in my court, so they could explain the meaning of my dream. [7] After they arrived, I told them my dream, but they were not able to say what it meant. [8] Finally, a young man named Daniel came in, and I told him the dream. The holy gods had given him special powers, and I had renamed him Belteshazzar after my own god.

[9] I said, "Belteshazzar, not only are you the wisest of all advisors and counselors, but the holy gods have given you special powers to solve the most difficult mysteries. So listen to what I dreamed and tell me what it means:

[10] In my sleep I saw
a very tall tree
in the center of the world.

[11] It grew stronger and higher,
until it reached to heaven
and could be seen
from anywhere on earth.
[12] It was covered with leaves
and heavy with fruit—
enough for all nations.
Wild animals enjoyed its shade,
birds nested in its branches,
and all creatures on earth
lived on its fruit.

[13] "While I was in bed, having this vision, a holy angel[i] came down from heaven [14] and shouted:

'Chop down the tree
and cut off its branches;
strip off its leaves
and scatter its fruit.
Make the animals leave its shade
and send the birds flying
from its branches.
[15] But leave its stump and roots
in the ground,
surrounded by grass
and held by chains
of iron and bronze.

'Make sure that this ruler
lives like the animals
out in the open fields,
unprotected from the dew.
[16] Give him the mind
of a wild animal
for seven long years.[j]
[17] This punishment is given
at the command
of the holy angels.[k]
It will show to all who live
that God Most High
controls all kingdoms
and chooses for their rulers
persons of humble birth.'

[18] "Daniel,[l] that was the dream that none of the wise men in my kingdom were able to understand. But I am sure that you will understand what it means, because the holy gods have given you some special powers."

---

[i] **4.13** *angel*: The Aramaic text has "watcher," which may be some special class of angel.   [j] **4.16** *long years*: Aramaic "times."   [k] **4.17** *angels*: See the note at 4.13.   [l] **4.18** *Daniel*: See the note at 2.26.

[19]For a while, Daniel[l] was terribly confused and worried by what he was thinking. But I said, "Don't be bothered either by the dream or by what it means."

Daniel replied:

Your Majesty, I wish the dream had been against your enemies. [20]You saw a tree that grew so big and strong that it reached up to heaven and could be seen from anywhere on earth. [21]Its leaves were beautiful, and it produced enough fruit for all living creatures; animals lived in its shade, and birds nested in its branches. [22]Your Majesty, that tree is you. Your glorious reputation has reached heaven, and your kingdom covers the earth.

[23]Then you saw a holy angel[m] come down from heaven and say, "Chop down the tree and destroy it! But leave its stump and roots in the ground, fastened there by a chain of iron and bronze. Let it stay for seven years[n] out in the field with the wild animals, unprotected from the dew."

[24]Your Majesty, God Most High has sent you this message, and it means [25]that you will be forced to live with the wild animals, far away from humans. You will eat grass like a wild animal and live outdoors for seven years,[n] until you learn that God Most High controls all earthly kingdoms and chooses their rulers. [26]But he gave orders not to disturb the stump and roots. This is to show that you will be king once again, after you learn that the God who rules from heaven is in control. [27]Your Majesty, please be willing to do what I say. Turn from your sins and start living right; have mercy on those who are mistreated. Then all will go well with you for a long time.

The Rest of Nebuchadnezzar's Letter about His Second Dream

[28-30]About twelve months later, I was walking on the flat roof of my royal palace and admiring the beautiful city of Babylon, when these things started happening to me. I was saying to myself, "Just look at this wonderful capital city that I have built by my own power and for my own glory!" [31]But before I could finish speaking, a voice from heaven interrupted:

King Nebuchadnezzar, this kingdom is no longer yours. [32]You will be forced to live with the wild animals, away from people. For seven years[n] you will eat grass, as though you were an ox, until you learn that God Most High is in control of all earthly kingdoms and that he is the one who chooses their rulers.

[33]This was no sooner said than done—I was forced to live like a wild animal; I ate grass and was unprotected from the dew. As time went by, my hair grew longer than eagle feathers, and my fingernails looked like the claws of a bird.

[34]Finally, I prayed to God in heaven, and my mind was healed. Then I said:

"I praise and honor
  God Most High.
He lives forever,
  and his kingdom
  will never end.
[35]To him the nations
  are far less than nothing;
God controls the stars in the sky
  and everyone on this earth.
When God does something,
  we cannot change it
  or even ask why."

You can be a "friend" to future generations and make it possible, because of your life, for them to know more of God's lovingkindness.

DEE BRESTIN

[36]At that time my mind was healed, and once again I became the ruler of my glorious kingdom. My advisors and officials returned to me, and I had greater power than ever before. [37]That's why I say:

"Praise and honor the King
who rules from heaven!
Everything he does
is honest and fair,
and he can shatter the power
of those who are proud."

King Belshazzar's Banquet

5 One evening, King Belshazzar gave a great banquet for a thousand of his highest officials, and he drank wine with them. [2]He got drunk and ordered his servants to bring in the gold and silver cups his father Nebuchadnezzar[o] had taken from the temple in Jerusalem. Belshazzar wanted the cups, so that he and all his wives and officials could drink from them.

[3-4]When the gold cups were brought in, everyone at the banquet drank from them and praised their idols made of gold, silver, bronze, iron, wood, and stone.

[5]Suddenly a human hand was seen writing on the plaster wall of the palace. The hand was just behind the lampstand, and the king could see it writing. [6]He was so frightened that his face turned pale, his knees started shaking, and his legs became weak.

[7]The king called in his advisors, who claimed they could talk with the spirits of the dead and understand the meanings found in the stars. He told them, "The man who can read this writing and tell me what it means will become the third most powerful man in my kingdom. He will wear robes of royal purple and a gold chain around his neck."

[8]All of King Belshazzar's highest officials came in, but not one of them could read the writing or tell what it meant, [9]and they were completely puzzled. Now the king was more afraid than ever before, and his face turned white as a ghost.

[10]When the queen heard the king and his officials talking, she came in and said:

Your Majesty, I hope you live forever! Don't be afraid or look so pale. [11]In your kingdom there is a man who has been given special powers by the holy gods. When your father Nebuchadnezzar was king, this man was known to be as smart, intelligent, and wise as the gods themselves. Your father put him in charge of all who claimed they could talk with the spirits or understand the meanings in the stars or tell about the future. [12]He also changed the man's name from Daniel to Belteshazzar. Not only is he wise and intelligent, but he can explain dreams and riddles and solve difficult problems. Send for Daniel, and he will tell you what the writing means.

[13]When Daniel was brought in, the king said:

So you are Daniel, one of the captives my father brought back from Judah! [14]I was told that the gods have given you special powers and that you are intelligent and very wise. [15]Neither my advisors nor the men who talk with the spirits of the dead could read this writing or tell me what it means. [16]But I have been told that you understand everything and that you can solve difficult problems. Now then, if you can read this writing and tell me what it means, you will become the third most powerful man in my kingdom. You will wear royal purple robes and have a gold chain around your neck.

[17]Daniel answered:

Your Majesty, I will read the writing and tell you what it means. But you may keep your gifts or give them to someone else. [18]Sir, the Most High God made your father a great and powerful man and brought him much honor and glory. [19]God did such great things for him that people of all nations and races shook with fear.

Your father had the power of life or death over everyone, and he could honor or ruin anyone he chose. [20]But when he became proud and stubborn, his glorious kingdom was taken from him. [21]His mind became like that of an animal, and he was forced to stay away from people and live with wild donkeys. Your father ate grass like an ox, and he slept outside where his body was soaked with dew. He was forced to do this until he learned that the Most

---

[o]**5.2** *his father Nebuchadnezzar:* Belshazzar was actually the son of King Nabonidus, who was from another family. But in ancient times, it was possible to refer to a previous king as the "father" of the present king.

High God rules all kingdoms on earth and chooses their kings.

²²King Belshazzar, you knew all of this, but you still refused to honor the Lord who rules from heaven. ²³Instead, you turned against him and ordered the cups from his temple to be brought here, so that you and your wives and officials could drink wine from them. You praised idols made of silver, gold, bronze, iron, wood, and stone, even though they cannot see or hear or think. You refused to worship the God who gives you breath and controls everything you do. ²⁴That's why he sent the hand to write this message on the wall.

²⁵⁻²⁸The words written there are *mene*, which means "numbered," *tekel*, which means "weighed," and *parsin*,ᴾ which means "divided." God has numbered the days of your kingdom and has brought it to an end. He has weighed you on his balance scales, and you fall short of what it takes to be king. So God has divided your kingdom between the Medes and the Persians.

²⁹Belshazzar gave a command for Daniel to be made the third most powerful man in his kingdom and to be given a purple robe and a gold chain.

³⁰That same night, the king was killed. ³¹Then Darius the Mede, who was sixty-two years old, took over his kingdom.

Daniel in a Pit of Lions

6 Darius divided his kingdom into a hundred and twenty states and placed a governor in charge of each one. ²In order to make sure that his government was run properly, Darius put three other officials in charge of the governors. One of these officials was Daniel. ³And he did his work so much better than the other governors and officials that the king decided to let him govern the whole kingdom.

⁴The other men tried to find something wrong with the way Daniel did his work for the king. But they could not accuse him of anything wrong, because he was honest and faithful and did everything he was supposed to do. ⁵Finally, they said to one another, "We will never be able to bring any charge against Daniel, unless it has to do with his religion."

⁶They all went to the king and said:

Your Majesty, we hope you live for-

ᴾ**5.25-28** *mene . . . tekel . . . parsin*: In the Aramaic text of verse 25, the words "mene, tekel, parsin," are used, and in verses 26-28 the words "mene, tekel, peres" (the singular of "parsin") are used. "Parsin" means "divided," but "peres" can mean either "divided" or "Persia."

Personal *Concerns*—How should I handle it when I feel rejected or excluded because of my faith? *(Daniel 6)*

Face the lions—with God on your side.

Have you ever wondered how you would respond if you were forced to choose between your life and your faith, as the Christian martyrs had to? Yet each of us is faced with a similar choice every day: Will we follow God, or will we follow the world? With nothing more to lose than the acceptance of friends, many of us crumble under the pressure and choose the world.

But imagine what we might witness if we held on to our faith in those times when we felt pressured to turn away from God. Like Daniel, we might see our faith strengthened as we trust God to stay beside us. We might see the lives of others changed by our willingness to take a stand for Christ. And we might see God work miracles through our faithfulness to him.

When we're faced with the choice between our beliefs and the world, the only choice is to follow our loving, faithful God. (See also John 15.18-27; Hebrews 10.32-39; 1 Peter 4.12-19; Revelation 14.12,13.)

Words To Remember: *He is the living God, the one who lives forever. His power and his kingdom will never end. He rescues people and sets them free by working great miracles.—Daniel 6.26,27*

ever! [7]All of your officials, leaders, advisors, and governors agree that you should make a law forbidding anyone to pray to any god or human except you for the next thirty days. Everyone who disobeys this law must be thrown into a pit of lions. [8]Order this to be written and then sign it, so it cannot be changed, just as no written law of the Medes and Persians can be changed."

[9]So King Darius made the law and had it written down.

[10]Daniel heard about the law, but when he returned home, he went upstairs and prayed in front of the window that faced Jerusalem. In the same way that he had always done, he knelt down in prayer three times a day, giving thanks to God.

[11]The men who had spoken to the king watched Daniel and saw him praying to his God for help. [12]They went back to the king and said, "Didn't you make a law that forbids anyone to pray to any god or human except you for the next thirty days? And doesn't the law say that everyone who disobeys it will be thrown into a pit of lions?"

"Yes, that's the law I made," the king agreed. "And just like all written laws of the Medes and Persians, it cannot be changed."

[13]The men then told the king, "That Jew named Daniel, who was brought here as a captive, refuses to obey you or the law that you ordered to be written. And he still prays to his god three times a day." [14]The king was really upset to hear about this, and for the rest of the day he tried to think how he could save Daniel.

[15]At sunset the men returned and said, "Your Majesty, remember that no written law of the Medes and Persians can be changed, not even by the king."

[16]So Darius ordered Daniel to be brought out and thrown into a pit of lions. But he said to Daniel, "You have been faithful to your God, and I pray that he will rescue you."

[17]A stone was rolled over the pit, and it was sealed. Then Darius and his officials stamped the seal to show that no one should let Daniel out. [18]All night long the king could not sleep. He did not eat anything, and he would not let anyone come in to entertain him.

[19]At daybreak the king got up and ran to the pit. [20]He was anxious and shouted, "Daniel, you were faithful and served your God. Was he able to save you from the lions?"

[21]Daniel answered, "Your Majesty, I hope you live forever! [22]My God knew that I was innocent, and he sent an angel to keep the lions from eating me. Your Majesty, I have never done anything to hurt you."

[23]The king was relieved to hear Daniel's voice, and he gave orders for him to be taken out of the pit. Daniel's faith in his God had kept him from being harmed. [24]And the king ordered the men who had brought charges against Daniel to be thrown into the pit, together with their wives and children. But before they even reached the bottom, the lions ripped them to pieces.

[25]King Darius then sent this message to all people of every nation and race in the world:

"Greetings to all of you!
[26]I command everyone
   in my kingdom
to worship and honor
   the God of Daniel.
He is the living God,
   the one who lives forever.
His power and his kingdom
   will never end.
[27]He rescues people
   and sets them free
by working great miracles.
Daniel's God has rescued him
   from the power of the lions."

[28]All went well for Daniel while Darius was king, and even when Cyrus the Persian ruled.[q]

Daniel's Vision of the Four Beasts

7 [1-2]Daniel wrote:
In the first year of King Belshazzar[r] of Babylonia, I had some dreams and visions while I was asleep one night, and I wrote them down.

The four winds were stirring up the mighty sea, [3]when suddenly four powerful beasts came out of the sea. Each beast was different. [4]The first was like a lion with the wings of an eagle. As I watched, its wings

---

[q]6.28 *Cyrus the Persian ruled*: 539-530 B.C.
[r]7.1,2 *first year of King Belshazzar*: 554 B.C.

were pulled off. Then it was lifted to an upright position and made to stand on two feet, just like a human, and it was given a human mind.

⁵The second beast looked like a bear standing on its hind legs.ˢ It held three ribs in its teeth, and it was told, "Attack! Eat all the flesh you want."

⁶The third beast was like a leopard—except that it had four wings and four heads. It was given authority to rule.

⁷The fourth beast was stronger and more terrifying than the others. Its huge teeth were made of iron, and what it didn't grind with its teeth, it smashed with its feet. It was different from the others, and it had horns on its head—ten of them. ⁸Just as I was thinking about these horns, a smaller horn appeared, and three of the other horns were pulled up by the roots to make room for it. This horn had the eyes of a human and a mouth that spoke with great pride.

Judgment

Daniel wrote:

⁹Thrones were set up
　　while I was watching,
and the Eternal Godᵗ
　　took his place.
His clothing and his hair
　　were white as snow.
His throne was a blazing fire
　　with fiery wheels,
¹⁰and flames were dashing out
　　from all around him.
Countless thousands
were standing there
　　to serve him.
The time of judgment began,
　　and the booksᵘ were opened.

¹¹I watched closely to see what would happen to this smaller horn because of the arrogant things it was saying. Then before my very eyes, the fourth beast was killed and its body destroyed by fire. ¹²The other three beasts had their authority taken from them, but they were allowed to live a while longer.ᵛ ¹³As I continued to watch the vision that night,

I saw what looked like
　　a son of manʷ
coming with the clouds of heaven,

and he was presented
　　to the Eternal God.ˣ

> *Our God is almighty,*
> *all-powerful, all-knowing—*
> *and his kingdom will*
> *last forever. Let us all*
> *bow before him!*
>
> JILL BRISCOE

¹⁴He was crowned king
　　and given power and glory,
so that all people
of every nation and race
　　would serve him.
He will rule forever,
and his kingdom is eternal,
　　never to be destroyed.

The Meaning of Daniel's Vision

¹⁵Daniel wrote:
I was terrified by these visions, and I didn't know what to think. ¹⁶So I asked one of those standing there,ʸ and he explained, ¹⁷"The four beasts are four earthly kingdoms. ¹⁸But God Most High will give his kingdom to his chosen ones, and it will be theirs forever and ever."

¹⁹I wanted to know more about the fourth beast,ᶻ because it was so different and much more terrifying than the others. What was the meaning of its iron teeth and bronze claws and of its feet that smashed what the teeth and claws had not ground and crushed? ²⁰I also wanted to know more about all ten of those horns on its head. I especially wanted to know more about the

---

ˢ**7.5** *standing on its hind legs*: Or "higher on one side than the other" or "with a paw lifted up." ᵗ**7.9** *Eternal God*: Aramaic "Ancient of Days." ᵘ**7.10** *books*: Containing the record of the good and evil that each person has done. ᵛ**7.12** *a while longer*: Aramaic "for a time and a season." ʷ**7.13** *son of man*: Or "human." In Aramaic "son of man" may mean a human or even "oneself" ("I" or "me"). Jesus often used the phrase "the Son of Man" when referring to himself. ˣ**7.13** *Eternal God*: See the note at 7.9. ʸ**7.16** *one of those standing there*: Possibly an angel sent to interpret the visions or one of those thousands mentioned in verse 10. ᶻ**7.19** *fourth beast*: See verses 7, 8.

one that took the place of three of the others—the horn that had eyes and spoke with arrogance and seemed greater than the others. ²¹While I was looking, this horn attacked God's chosen ones and was winning the battle. ²²Then God Most High, the Eternal God,ᵃ came and judged in favor of his chosen ones, because the time had arrived for them to be given the kingdom.

²³Then I was told
     by the one standing there:
"The fourth beast
will be a fourth kingdom
     to appear on earth.
It will be different
     from all the others—
it will trample the earth
     and crush it to pieces.
²⁴All ten of those horns are kings
who will come from this kingdom,
     and one more will follow.
This horn will be different
     from the others,
and it will conquer
     three other kings.

²⁵"This king will speak evil
     of God Most High,
and he will be cruel
     to God's chosen ones.
He will try to change God's Law
     and the sacred seasons.
And he will be able to do this
for a time, two times,
     and half a time.ᵇ
²⁶But he will finally be judged,
and his kingdom
     completely destroyed.

²⁷"Then the greatest kingdom of all
will be given to the chosen ones
     of God Most High.
His kingdom will be eternal,
and all others will serve
     and obey him."

²⁸That was what I saw and heard. I turned pale with fear and kept it all to myself.

Vision of a Ram and a Goat

8 Daniel wrote:
     In the third year of King Belshazzar of Babylonia,ᶜ I had a second vision ²in which I was in Susa, the chief city of Babylonia's Elam Province. I was beside the Ulai River,ᵈ ³when I looked up and saw a ram standing there with two horns on its head—both of them were long, but the second one was longer than the first. ⁴The ram went charging toward the west, the north, and the south. No other animals were strong enough to oppose him, and nothing could save them from his power. So he did as he pleased and became even more powerful.

⁵I kept on watching and saw a goat come from the west and charge across the entire earth, without even touching the ground. Between his eyes was a powerful horn,ᵉ ⁶and with tremendous anger the goat started toward the ram that I had seen beside the river.ᶠ ⁷The goat was so fierce that its attack broke both horns of the ram, leaving him powerless. Then the goat stomped on the ram, and no one could do anything to help. ⁸After this, the goat became even more powerful. But at the peak of his power, his mighty horn was broken, and four other mighty horns took its place—one pointing to the north and one to the east, one to the south and one to the west.

⁹A little horn came from one of these, and its power reached to the south, the east, and even to the holy land.ᵍ ¹⁰It became so strong that it attacked the stars in the sky, which were heaven's army.ʰ Then it threw some of them down to the earth and stomped on them. ¹¹⁻¹²It humiliated heaven's army and dishonored its leaderⁱ by keeping him from offering the daily sacrifices. In fact, it was so terrible that it even disgraced the temple and wiped out true worship. It also did everything else it wanted to do.

¹³Then one of the holy angels asked another, "When will the daily sacrifices be offered again? What about this horrible rebellion? When will the temple and heaven's army no longer be trampled in the dust?"

ᵃ**7.22** *Eternal God:* See the note at 7.9.
ᵇ**7.25** *for . . . time:* Or "for a year, two years, and half a year."   ᶜ**8.1** *third year . . . Babylonia:* 552 B.C., two years after the first vision (see 7.1, 2).   ᵈ**8.2** *River:* Or "Gate."   ᵉ**8.5** *powerful horn:* Hebrew "horn of vision."   ᶠ**8.6** *river:* See the note at 8.2.   ᵍ**8.9** *holy land:* Hebrew "the lovely land."   ʰ**8.10** *heaven's army:* In verses 10-13 the Hebrew word translated "heaven's army" may also mean "God's people."   ⁱ**8.11,12** *leader:* Hebrew "prince."

[14]The other answered, "It will be two thousand three hundred evenings and mornings before the temple is dedicated and in use again."

Gabriel Interprets the Vision

[15]Daniel wrote:

I was trying to figure out the meaning of the vision, when someone suddenly appeared there beside me. [16]And from beside the Ulai River,[j] a voice like that of a human said, "Gabriel, help him understand the vision."

[17]Gabriel came over, and I fell to the ground in fear. Then he said, "You are merely a human, but you need to understand that this vision is about the end of time."

[18]While he was speaking, I fell facedown in a deep sleep. But he lifted me to my feet [19]and said:

Listen, and I will tell you what will happen at the end of time, when God has chosen to show his anger. [20]The two horns of the ram are the kings of Media and Persia, [21]the goat is the kingdom of Greece, and the powerful horn between his eyes is the first of its kings. [22]After this horn is broken, four other kingdoms will appear, but they won't be as strong.

[23]When these rulers have become as evil as possible, their power will end, and then a king who is dangerous and cannot be trusted will appear. [24]He will gain strength, but not on his own, and he will cause terrible destruction. He will wipe out powerful leaders and God's people as well. [25]His deceitful lies will make him so successful, that he will think he is really great. Suddenly he will kill many people, and he will even attack God, the Supreme Ruler. But God will crush him!

[26]This vision about the evenings and mornings is true, but these things won't happen for a long time, so don't tell it to others.

[27]After this, I was so worn out and weak that it was several days before I could get out of bed and go about my duties for the king. I was disturbed by this vision that made no sense to me.

Daniel Prays for the People

9
[1-2]Daniel wrote:

Some years later, Darius the Mede,[k] who was the son of Xerxes,[l] had become king of Babylonia. And during his first year as king, I found out from studying the writings of the prophets that the LORD had said to Jeremiah, "Jerusalem will lie in ruins for seventy years."[m] [3-4]Then, to show my sorrow, I went without eating and dressed in sackcloth[n] and sat in ashes. I confessed my sins and earnestly prayed to the LORD my God:

Our Lord, you are a great and fearsome God, and you faithfully keep your agreement with those who love and obey you. [5]But we have sinned terribly by rebelling against you and rejecting your laws and teachings. [6]We have ignored the message your servants the prophets spoke to our kings, our leaders, our ancestors, and everyone else.

I'm so glad that when I confess my transgressions, God forgives them— unconditionally—and helps me grow deeper spiritual roots.

LIZ CURTIS HIGGS

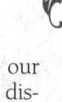

[7]Everything you do is right, our Lord. But still we suffer public disgrace because we have been unfaithful and have sinned against you. This includes all of us, both far and near— the people of Judah, Jerusalem, and Israel, as well as those you dragged away to foreign lands, [8]and even our

---

[j]8.16 *River*: See the note at 8.2.   [k]9.1,2 *Darius the Mede*: See 5.31.   [l]9.1,2 *Xerxes*: Hebrew "Ahasuerus."   [m]9.1,2 *seventy years*: See Jeremiah 25.11-13; 29,10.   [n]9.3,4 *sackcloth*: A rough, dark-colored cloth made from goat or camel hair and used to make grain sacks. It was worn in times of trouble or sorrow.

kings, our officials, and our ancestors. [9]LORD God, you are merciful and forgiving, even though we have rebelled against you [10]and rejected your teachings that came to us from your servants the prophets.

[11]Everyone in Israel has stubbornly refused to obey your laws, and so those curses written by your servant Moses have fallen upon us. [12]You warned us and our leaders that Jerusalem would suffer the worst disaster in human history, and you did exactly as you had threatened. [13]We have not escaped any of the terrible curses written by Moses, and yet we have refused to beg you for mercy and to remind ourselves of how faithful you have always been. [14]And when you finally punished us with this horrible disaster, that was also the right thing to do, because we deserved it so much.

[15]Our Lord God, with your own mighty arm you rescued us from Egypt and made yourself famous to this very day, but we have sinned terribly. [16]In the past, you treated us with such kindness, that we now beg you to stop being so terribly angry with Jerusalem. After all, it is your chosen city built on your holy mountain, even though it has suffered public disgrace because of our sins and those of our ancestors.

[17]I am your servant, Lord God, and I beg you to answer my prayers and bring honor to yourself by having pity on your temple that lies in ruins. [18]Please show mercy to your chosen city, not because we deserve it, but because of your great kindness. [19]Forgive us! Hurry and do something, not only for your city and your chosen people, but to bring honor to yourself.

The Seventy Weeks

Daniel wrote:

[20]I was still confessing my sins and those of all Israel to the LORD my God, and I was praying for the good of his holy mountain,[o] [21]when Gabriel suddenly came flying in at the time of the evening sacrifice. This was the same Gabriel I had seen in my vision, [22]and he explained:

Daniel, I am here to help you understand the vision. [23]God thinks highly of you, and at the very moment you started praying, I was sent to give you the answer. [24]God has decided that for seventy weeks,[p] your people and your holy city must suffer as the price of their sins. Then evil will disappear, and justice will rule forever; the visions and words of the prophets will come true, and a most holy place will be dedicated.[q]

[25]You need to realize that from the command to rebuild Jerusalem until the coming of the Chosen Leader,[r] it will be seven weeks and another sixty-two weeks.[s] Streets will be built in Jerusalem, and a trench will be dug around the city for protection, but these will be difficult times.[t] [26]At the end of the sixty-two weeks,[u] the Chosen Leader[v] will be killed and left with nothing.[w]

A foreign ruler and his army will sweep down like a mighty flood, leaving both the city and the temple in ruins, and war and destruction will continue until the end, just as God has decided. [27]For one week[x] this foreigner[y] will make a firm agreement with many people, and halfway through this week,[z] he will end all sacrifices and offerings. Then the "Horrible Thing" that causes destruction will be put there. And it will stay there until the time God has decided to destroy this one who destroys.

[o]9.20 *holy mountain*: Jerusalem (see verse 16) or the temple. [p]9.24 *seventy weeks*: Or "seventy times seven years." [q]9.24 *a most holy place will be dedicated*: Or "God's Holy One will appear." [r]9.25 *the Chosen Leader*: Or "a chosen leader." In Hebrew the word "chosen" means "to pour oil (on someone's head)." In Old Testament times it was the custom to pour oil on a person's head when that person was chosen to be a priest or a king. [s]9.25 *seven weeks and another sixty-two weeks*: Or "seven times seven years and another sixty-two times seven years." [t]9.25 *it will be seven . . . difficult times*: Or "it will be seven weeks. Then streets will be built in Jerusalem, and a trench will be dug around the city for protection. But Jerusalem will have difficult times for sixty-two weeks." [u]9.26 *sixty-two weeks*: Or "sixty-two times seven years." [v]9.26 *the Chosen Leader*: See the note at 9.25. [w]9.26 *left with nothing*: Or "no one will take his place." [x]9.27 *one week*: Or "seven years." [y]9.27 *this foreigner*: Or "the Chosen Leader." [z]9.27 *halfway through this week*: Or "for half of this week of seven years."

Daniel's Vision beside the Tigris River

10 In the third year[a] of Cyrus the king of Persia, a message came to Daniel[b] from God, and it was explained in a vision. The message was about a horrible war, and it was true. [2]Daniel wrote:

For three weeks I was in sorrow. [3]I ate no fancy food or meat, I drank no wine, and I put no olive oil on my face or hair.[c] [4]Then, on the twenty-fourth day of the first month,[d] I was standing on the banks of the great Tigris River, [5]when I looked up and saw someone dressed in linen and wearing a solid gold belt.[e] [6]His body was like a precious stone,[f] his face like lightning, his eyes like flaming fires, his arms and legs like polished bronze, and his voice like the roar of a crowd. [7]Although the people who were with me did not see the vision, they became so frightened that they scattered and hid. [8]Only I saw this great vision. I became weak and pale, [9]and at the sound of his voice, I fell facedown in a deep sleep.

[10]He raised me to my hands and knees [11]and then said, "Daniel, your God thinks highly of you, and he has sent me. So stand up and pay close attention." I stood trembling, while the angel said:

[12]Daniel, don't be afraid! God has listened to your prayers since the first day you humbly asked for understanding, and he has sent me here. [13]But the guardian angel[g] of Persia opposed me for twenty-one days. Then Michael, who is one of the strongest guardian angels,[h] came to rescue me from the kings of Persia.[i] [14]Now I have come here to give you another vision about what will happen to your people in the future.

[15]While this angel was speaking to me, I stared at the ground, speechless. [16]Then he appeared in human form and touched my lips. I said, "Sir, this vision has brought me great pain and has drained my strength. [17]I am merely your servant. How can I possibly speak with someone so powerful, when I am almost too weak to get my breath?"

[18-19]The angel touched me a second time and said, "Don't be frightened! God thinks highly of you, and he intends this for your good, so be brave and strong."

At this, I regained my strength and re-

---

[a]**10.1** *third year:* 536 B.C.   [b]**10.1** *Daniel:* See the note at 2.26.   [c]**10.3** *olive oil . . . hair:* On special occasions, it was the custom to put olive oil on one's face and hair.   [d]**10.4** *first month:* Nisan (also known as Abib), the first month of the Hebrew calendar, from about mid-March to mid-April.   [e]**10.5** *solid gold belt:* Hebrew "belt of gold from Uphaz."   [f]**10.6** *a precious stone:* The Hebrew text has "beryl," which is green or bluish-green.   [g]**10.13** *guardian angel:* Hebrew "prince."   [h]**10.13** *one of the strongest guardian angels:* Hebrew "chief prince."   [i]**10.13** *came . . . Persia:* One possible meaning for the difficult Hebrew text.

SingleLife—What if I'm longing for children? (Daniel 10.2-19)

God hears your prayers.
For many women, the desire to have a child can be almost overwhelming. And it's a feeling made even more intense when there seems to be no husband on the horizon. As the years tick by, the fear that being single will also mean being childless can lead to tremendous grief and depression. In the midst of it all, it's easy to wonder why God allows us to feel so much pain.

But just as God reassures Daniel that his prayers were heard, God listens to your prayers as well (10.12). He knows your heart. He assures you that he listens as you pour out all your grief and sorrow to him. And he promises repeatedly that his plan for you is good (10.18,19).

Although we can't foresee the future, God promises to walk with us into what he's mapped out for us. And when we get there, it will be God whom we praise for guiding us so wisely. (See also Jeremiah 20.7-18; Matthew 18.5.)

Words To Remember: *The angel touched me a second time and said, "Don't be frightened! God thinks highly of you, and he intends this for your good, so be brave and strong."—Daniel 10.18,19*

plied, "Please speak! You have already made me feel much better."

²⁰Then the angel said:

Now do you understand why I have come? Soon I must leave to fight against the guardian angel of Persia. Then after I have defeated him, the guardian angel of Greece will attack me. ²¹I will tell you what is written in *The Book of Truth*. But first, you must realize that no one except Michael, the guardian angel of Israel, is on my side.

11 ¹You also need to know that I protected and helped Darius the Mede[j] in his first year as king.

The Angel's Message to Daniel

Part One: The Four Kings and their Successors

²What I am going to tell you is certain to happen. Four kings will rule Persia, one after the other, but the fourth one will become much richer than the others. In fact, his wealth will make him so powerful that he will turn everyone against the kingdom of Greece. ³Then a mighty king will come to power and will be able to do whatever he pleases. ⁴But suddenly his kingdom will be crushed and scattered to the four corners of the earth, where four more kingdoms will rise. But these won't be ruled by his descendants or be as powerful as his kingdom.

⁵The king of the south will grow powerful. Then one of his generals will rebel and take over most of the kingdom. ⁶Years later the southern kingdom and the northern kingdom will make a treaty, and the daughter of the king of the south will marry the king of the north. But she will lose her power. Then she, her husband, their child,[k] and the servants who came with her will all be killed.

After this, ⁷one of her relatives will become the ruler of the southern kingdom. He will attack the army of the northern kingdom and capture its fortresses. ⁸Then he will carry their idols to Egypt, together with their precious treasures of silver and gold, but it will be a long time before he attacks the northern kingdom again. Some years later ⁹the king of the north will invade the southern kingdom, but he will be forced back to his own country.

¹⁰The sons of the king of the north will gather a huge army that will sweep down like a roaring flood, reaching all the way to the fortress of the southern kingdom. ¹¹But this will make the king of the south angry, and he will defeat this large army from the north. ¹²The king of the south will feel proud because of the many thousands he has killed. But his victories won't last long, ¹³because the king of the north will gather a larger and more powerful army than ever before. Then in a few years, he will start invading other countries.

¹⁴At this time many of your own people will try to make this vision come true by rebelling against the king of the south, but their rebellion will fail. ¹⁵Then the army from the north will surround and capture a fortress in the south, and not even the most experienced troops of the southern kingdom will be able to make them retreat. ¹⁶The king who invaded from the north will do as he pleases, and he will even capture and destroy the holy land.[l] ¹⁷In fact, he will decide to invade the south with his entire army. Then he will attempt to make peace by giving the king of the south a bride from the northern kingdom, but this won't be successful.

¹⁸Afterwards, this proud king of the north will invade and conquer many of the nations along the coast, but a military leader will defeat him and make him lose his pride. ¹⁹He will retreat to his fortresses in his own country, but on the way he will be defeated and never again be seen. ²⁰The next king of the north will try to collect taxes for the glory of his kingdom. However, he will come to a sudden end in some mysterious way, instead of in battle or because of someone's anger.

Part Two: The Evil King from the North

²¹The successor of this king of the north will be a worthless nobody, who doesn't come from a royal family. He will suddenly appear and gain control of the kingdom by treachery. ²²Then he will destroy armies and remove God's chosen high priest. ²³He will make a treaty, but he will be deceitful and break it, even though he has only a few

---

[j]11.1 *Darius the Mede*: See 5.30.   [k]11.6 *their child*: One Hebrew manuscript and two ancient translations; most Hebrew manuscripts "her father."   [l]11.16 *the holy land*: See the note at 8.9.

followers. ²⁴Without warning, he will successfully invade a wealthy province, which is something his ancestors never did. Then he will divide among his followers all of its treasures and property. But none of this will last very long.

²⁵He will gather a large and powerful army, and with great courage he will attack the king of the south. The king of the south will meet him with a much stronger army, but he will lose the battle, because he will be betrayed ²⁶by members of the royal court. He will be ruined, and most of his army will be slaughtered.

²⁷The two kings will meet around a table and tell evil lies to each other. But their plans will fail, because God has already decided what will happen. ²⁸Then the king of the north will return to his country with great treasures. But on the way, he will attack the religion of God's people and do whatever else he pleases.

²⁹At the time God has decided, the king of the north will invade the southern kingdom again, but this time, things will be different. ³⁰Ships from the west will come to attack him, and he will be discouraged. Then he will start back to his own country and take out his anger on the religion of God's faithful people, while showing kindness to those who are unfaithful. ³¹He will send troops to pollute the temple and the fortress, and he will stop the daily sacrifices. Then he will set up that "Horrible Thing" that causes destruction. ³²The king will use deceit to win followers from those who are unfaithful to God, but those who remain faithful will do everything possible to oppose him.

³³Wise leaders will instruct many of the people. But for a while, some of these leaders will either be killed with swords or burned alive, or else robbed of their possessions and thrown into prison. ³⁴They will receive only a little help in their time of trouble, and many of their followers will be treacherous. ³⁵Some of those who are wise will suffer, so that God will make them pure and acceptable until the end, which will still come at the time he has decided.

³⁶This king will do as he pleases. He will proudly claim to be greater than any god and will insult the only true God. Indeed, he will be successful until God is no longer angry with his people. ³⁷This king will reject

the gods his ancestors worshiped and the god preferred by women.ᵐ In fact, he will put himself above all gods ³⁸and worship only the so-called god of fortresses, who was unknown to his ancestors. And he will honor it with gold, silver, precious stones, and other costly gifts. ³⁹With the help of this foreign god, he will capture the strongest fortresses. Everyone who worships this god will be put in a position of power and rewarded with wealth and land.

> We may feel like failures as Christians, but our shepherd lifts us close to him with tenderness and compassion—until we're ready to walk alongside in perfect confidence.
>
> LAURETTA PATTERSON

Part Three: The Time of the End

⁴⁰At the time of the end, the king of the south will attack the kingdom of the north. But its king will rush out like a storm with war chariots, cavalry, and many ships. Indeed, his forces will flood one country after another, ⁴¹and when they reach the holy land,ⁿ tens of thousands will be killed. But the countries of Edom and Moab and the ruler of Ammonᵒ will escape.

⁴²The king of the north will invade many countries, including Egypt, ⁴³and he will take its rich treasures of gold and silver. He will also conquer Libya and Ethiopia.ᵖ ⁴⁴But he will be alarmed by news from the east and the north, and he will become furious and cause great destruction. ⁴⁵After this, he

---

ᵐ11.37 *god preferred by women:* Perhaps Tammuz or Adonis, which were popular among the women of that time.   ⁿ11.41 *the holy land:* See the note at 8.9.   ᵒ11.41 *the ruler of Ammon:* Or "what is left of Ammon."   ᵖ11.43 *Ethiopia:* The Hebrew text has "Cush," which was a region south of Egypt that included parts of the present countries of Ethiopia and Sudan.

will set up camp between the Mediterranean Sea and Mount Zion. Then he will be destroyed, and no one will be able to save him.

Part Four: The Dead Will Rise to Life

12

Michael, the chief of the angels, is the protector of your people, and he will come at a time of terrible suffering, the worst in all of history. And your people who have their names written in *The Book*[q] will be protected. [2]Many of those who lie dead in the ground will rise from death. Some of them will be given eternal life, and others will receive nothing but eternal shame and disgrace. [3]Everyone who has been wise will shine as bright as the sky above, and everyone who has led others to please God will shine like the stars.

[4]Daniel, I now command you to keep the message of this book secret until the end of time, even though many people will go everywhere, searching for the knowledge to be found in it.[r]

The End of Time

[5]Daniel wrote:

I looked around and saw two other people—one on this side of the river and one on the other side. [6]The angel who had spoken to me was dressed in

linen and was standing upstream from them.[s] So one of the two beside the river asked him, "How long before these amazing things happen?"

[7]The angel then raised both hands toward heaven and said, "In the name of the God who lives forever, I solemnly promise that it will be a time, two times, and half a time.[t] Everything will be over, when the suffering of God's holy people comes to an end."

[8]I heard what the angel said, but I didn't understand. So I asked, "Sir, how will it all end?"

The angel in my vision then replied:

[9]Daniel, go about your business, because the meaning of this message will remain secret until the end of time. [10]Many people will have their hearts and lives made pure and clean, but those who are evil will keep on being evil and never understand. Only the wise will understand. [11]There will

---

[q]**12.1** *The Book*: Either the book with the names of God's people in it or the book with the record of the good and evil that people have done.   [r]**12.4** *even though . . . in it*: One possible meaning for the difficult Hebrew text.   [s]**12.6** *angel . . . upstream from them*: See 10.4-6.   [t]**12.7** *a time, two times, and half a time*: Or "a year, two years, and half a year," that is, about 1260 days.

SingleLife—As a single mom, is it all right for me to date? Should I wait until my children are grown? *(Daniel 12)*

Consider the end result.

Life sure would be a lot easier if we could see the results of our daily decisions before we make them. And dating decisions are no exception. Who hasn't thought, *If I'd known he was so boring/selfish/cheap/fill-in-the-blank, I'd never have wasted my time with him.* As they say, hindsight is 20/20.

But the results of those daily decisions are less important than the results of our decision to follow God. While we can't predict what will happen in our life, we do know this: If we faithfully live for God, we will be rewarded with eternal life.

So what about those daily decisions, like the ones we make about dating? More often than not, there is no "right" choice. In the end, we can only pray about our decisions and trust God to give us the wisdom to make choices that honor him. When we do, we can hold on to the promise made to Daniel (12.13) and be assured that God will be with us, blessing our desires to follow him in every aspect of life, including dating. (See also Isaiah 51.12-16; 2 Thessalonians 2.13-17.)

Words To Remember: *Everyone who has been wise will shine as bright as the sky above, and everyone who has led others to please God will shine like the stars.* —Daniel 12.3

be one thousand two hundred ninety days from the time that the daily sacrifices are stopped, until someone sets up the "Horrible Thing" that causes destruction. [12]God will bless everyone who patiently waits until one thousand three hundred thirty-five days have gone by.

[13]So, Daniel, be faithful until the end! You will rest, and at the end of time, you will rise from death to receive your reward.

Hosea

How God Responds to Rejection

"Unfaithful Wife Flaunts Lovers in Front of Husband." Sounds like a headline in a tabloid newspaper, doesn't it? That's how the book of Hosea begins, but it doesn't end the way the tabloid might—with the husband killing his wife and her lover.

Hosea married Gomer, an unfaithful woman, and struggled to help her come around. Hosea's pain and his faithfulness to her, no matter what, create a picture of God's tough and tender love for Israel. The story of Hosea and Gomer is actually an object lesson, acted out in high drama. It represents God, the faithful spouse, and Israel, who turned her back on God to worship idols.

The book of Hosea, then, is a study in how God behaves when he's rejected. Rejection angers God and results in punishment (5,8–10,12,13); sinful behavior brings on its own destruction (4,6,7,12). Yet God also weeps for those who reject him (11) and offers opportunities to restore them (14). This book portrays God as one who pursues us relentlessly, always coming up with new fences of thorns (2.6) to keep us from wandering off, drawing us with promises of the peace and prosperity found in him alone.

One of the best things about the book of Hosea is that we get a glimpse at the whole heart of God: his severe judgment of Israel ("War will visit their cities, and their plans will fail," 11.6) and his tender desire for Israel to repent ("I just can't do it. My feelings for you are much too strong," 11.8). When we doubt that God loves us, the passionate tenderness of this book swoops down and washes over us to say that we are genuinely, desperately loved.

Hosea lived in the northern nation of Israel during very difficult times. The long reign of King Jeroboam II was prosperous, yet idolatrous, with much social injustice and immorality. Because of their military strength, Israel recovered large areas of land earlier lost to their neighboring enemies. The fortified capital of Samaria gave added security and national pride.

The worship of two golden calves (one at Dan, the other at Bethel), begun at the time of the split into two nations, was prominent. Also, Canaanite fertility religion led to immorality and the breakdown of the family, including child sacrifice. Hosea's dramatic life was an attempt to confront this extreme decadence with toughness and tenderness.

Hosea at a Glance

1. Hosea's faithfulness to Gomer (1–3)
2. Israel commits adultery against God (4,5)
3. Israel's punishment (6–10)
4. God's love for Israel (11)
5. Israel's unfaithfulness to God (12)
6. God's anger with Israel (13)
7. God's forgiveness and offer to restore Israel (14)

1 I am Hosea son of Beeri. When Uzziah, Jotham, Ahaz, and Hezekiah were the kings of Judah, and when Jeroboam son of Jehoash*d* was king of Israel,*b* the LORD spoke this message to me.

Hosea's Family

²The LORD said, "Hosea, Israel has betrayed me like an unfaithful wife.*c* Marry such a woman and have children by her." ³So I married Gomer the daughter of Diblaim, and we had a son.

⁴Then the LORD said, "Hosea, name your son Jezreel,*d* because I will soon punish the descendants of King Jehu of Israel for the murders he committed in Jezreel Valley.*e* I will destroy his kingdom, ⁵and in Jezreel Valley I will break the power of Israel."

⁶Later, Gomer had a daughter, and the LORD said, "Name her Lo-Ruhamah,*f* because I will no longer have mercy and forgive Israel. ⁷But I am the LORD God of Judah, and I will have mercy and save Judah by my own power—not by wars and arrows or swords and cavalry."

⁸After Gomer had stopped nursing Lo-Ruhamah, she had another son. ⁹Then the LORD said, "Name him Lo-Ammi,*g* because these people are not mine, and I am not their God."

Hope for Israel

¹⁰Someday it will be impossible to count the people of Israel, because there will be as many of them as there are grains of sand along the seashore. They are now called "Not My People," but in the future they will be called "Children of the Living God." ¹¹Israel and Judah will unite and choose one leader. Then they will take back their land,

2 and this will be a great day for Jezreel.*h* ¹So let your brothers be called "My People" and your sisters be called "Shown Mercy."*i*

The LORD Promises To Punish Israel

²Accuse! Accuse your mother!
She is no longer my wife,
and now I, the LORD,
am not her husband.
Beg her to give up prostitution
and stop being unfaithful,*j*
³or I will strip her naked
like the day she was born.

I will make her barren
like a desert,
and she will die of thirst.
⁴You children are the result
of her unfaithfulness,
and I'll show you no pity.
⁵Your mother was unfaithful.
She was disgraceful and said,
"I'll run after my lovers.
Everything comes from them—
my food and drink,
my linen and wool,
my olive oil and wine."

⁶I, the LORD, will build
a fence of thorns
to block her path.
⁷She will run after her lovers,
but not catch them;
she will search,
but not find them.
Then she will say, "I'll return
to my first husband.
Life was better then."
⁸She didn't know that her grain,
wine, and olive oil
were gifts from me,
as were the gold and silver
she used in worshiping Baal.*k*

⁹So I'll hold back the harvest
of grain and grapes.

*a*1.1 *Jehoash:* The Hebrew text has "Joash," another spelling of the name. *b*1.1 *kings of Judah . . . king of Israel:* Uzziah (781-740 B.C.), Jotham (740-736), Ahaz (736-716), Hezekiah (716-687), and Jeroboam II (783-743). *c*1.2 *unfaithful wife:* In some Canaanite religions of Old Testament times, young women were expected to have sex with the worshipers of their god before marriage. Such women were called "temple prostitutes." Many of the Israelite women did this same thing, and Hosea is told to marry one of them to show that the nation has turned from the LORD to worship idols. *d*1.4 *Jezreel:* In Hebrew "Jezreel" means "God scatters (seed)." Here the name is used as a threat (meaning the LORD will punish Israel by scattering its people), while in verse 11 it is used as a promise (meaning the LORD will bless Israel by giving their nation many people, just as a big harvest comes when many seeds are scattered in a field). *e*1.4 *murders . . . Valley:* Jehu murdered the wife and relatives of King Ahab (see 2 Kings 9.15—10.14). *f*1.6 *Lo-Ruhamah:* In Hebrew "Lo-Ruhamah" means "No Mercy." *g*1.9 *Lo-Ammi:* In Hebrew "Lo-Ammi" means "Not My People." *h*1.11 *Jezreel:* See the note at verse 4. *i*2.1 *My People . . . Shown Mercy:* In Hebrew "My People" is "Ammi" and "Shown Mercy" is "Ruhamah" (see Lo-Ruhamah in 1.6 and Lo-Ammi in 1.9). *j*2.2 *prostitution . . . unfaithful:* See the note at 1.2. *k*2.8 *Baal:* A Canaanite god of fertility.

I'll take back
my wool and my linen
    that cover her body.
[10] Then I'll strip her naked
in the sight of her lovers.[l]
    No one can rescue her.

[11] I'll stop Israel's celebrations—
no more New Moon Festivals,
    Sabbaths, or other feasts.
[12] She said, "My lovers gave me
vineyards and fig trees
    as payment[m] for sex."

Now I, the LORD, will ruin
her vineyards and fig trees;
they will become clumps of weeds
    eaten by wild animals.

[13] I'll punish her for the days
she worshiped Baal
    and burned incense to him.
I'll punish her for the times
    she forgot about me
and wore jewelry and rings
to attract her lovers.
    I, the LORD, have spoken!

The LORD Will Help Israel

[14] Israel, I, the LORD,
will lure you into the desert
    and speak gently to you.
[15] I will return your vineyards,
and then Trouble Valley[n]
    will become Hopeful Valley.
You will say "Yes" to me
as you did in your youth,
    when leaving Egypt.

[16] I promise that from that day on, you will call me your husband instead of your master.[o] [17] I will no longer even let you mention the names of those pagan gods that you called "Master." [18] And I will agree to let you live in peace—you will no longer be attacked by wild animals and birds or by weapons of war. [19] I will accept you as my wife forever, and instead of a bride price[p] I will give you justice, fairness, love, kindness, [20] and faithfulness. Then you will truly know who I am.
[21] I will command the sky to send rain on the earth, [22] and it will produce grain, grapes, and olives in Jezreel Valley. [23] I will scatter the seeds and show mercy to Lo-

Ruhamah.[q] I will say to Lo-Ammi,[r] "You are my people," and they will answer, "You are our God."

God's Love Offers Hope

3 Once again the LORD spoke to me. And this time he said, "Hosea, fall in love with an unfaithful woman[s] who has a lover. Do this to show that I love the people of Israel, even though they worship idols and enjoy the offering cakes made with fruit."
[2] So I paid fifteen pieces of silver and about ten bushels of grain for such a woman. [3] Then I said, "Now you are mine! You will have to remain faithful to me, though it will be a long time before we sleep together."
[4] It will also be a long time before Israel has a king or before sacrifices are offered at the temple or before there is any way to get guidance from God. [5] But later, Israel will turn back to the LORD their God and to David their king. At that time they will come to the LORD with fear and trembling, and he will be good to them.

---

[l]**2.10** *I'll strip . . . lovers:* Or "I'll show her lovers how disgusting she is." [m]**2.12** *fig trees . . . payment:* Hosea uses an unusual word for "fig tree," which is spelled something like the word for "payment." [n]**2.15** *Trouble Valley:* Or "Achor Valley." The exact location of the valley is unknown, but in Hebrew "Achor" sounds like "Achan," who brought trouble on Israel by disobeying the Lord (see Joshua 7.24-26). [o]**2.16** *husband . . . master:* In Hebrew the word "master" is the same as the name of the god Baal. But the LORD promises that his people will have a deep personal relationship with him (like a devoted wife and husband) rather than merely a legal tie (like a wife and her "master"). [p]**2.19** *bride price:* It was the custom for the husband to pay his wife's parents a bride price. Instead of money, the LORD will give much better benefits to Israel. [q]**2.23** *Lo-Ruhamah:* See the note at 1.6. [r]**2.23** *Lo-Ammi:* See the note at 1.9. [s]**3.1** *unfaithful woman:* This may refer to Gomer, the woman Hosea married (see 1.3), or it may refer to another woman.

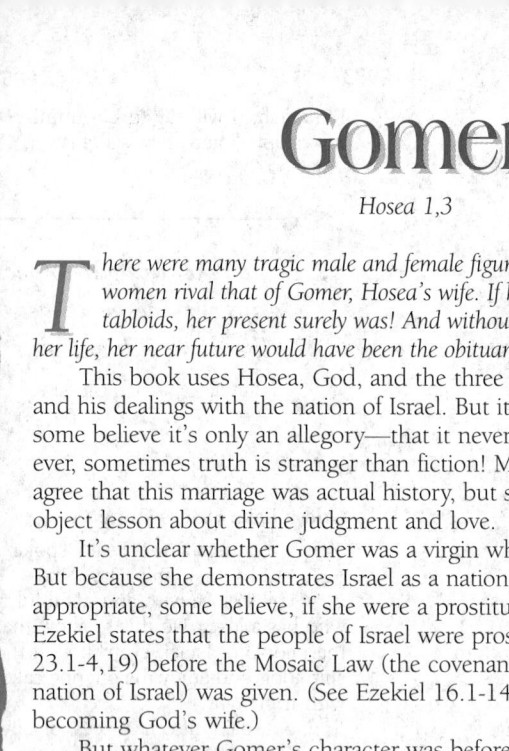

Gomer

Hosea 1,3

*T*here were many tragic male and female figures in the Scriptures, but few women rival that of Gomer, Hosea's wife. If her past were not for the tabloids, her present surely was! And without the intervention of God in her life, her near future would have been the obituary column.

This book uses Hosea, God, and the three children to represent God and his dealings with the nation of Israel. But it's written so adeptly that some believe it's only an allegory—that it never really happened. However, sometimes truth is stranger than fiction! Most scholars now strongly agree that this marriage was actual history, but see it used by God as an object lesson about divine judgment and love.

It's unclear whether Gomer was a virgin when she married Hosea. But because she demonstrates Israel as a nation, it would be more appropriate, some believe, if she were a prostitute when they married. Ezekiel states that the people of Israel were prostitutes in Egypt (Ezekiel 23.1-4,19) before the Mosaic Law (the covenant of God's marriage to the nation of Israel) was given. (See Ezekiel 16.1-14 for the imagery of Israel becoming God's wife.)

But whatever Gomer's character was before her wedding day, it fell apart soon afterwards; so Gomer is a picture of the nation of Israel. Like myriad idol worshipers, Gomer thought that earth's bounties came from the idols of wood and stone (2.8). She didn't realize how much her husband loved her (neither did the people of Israel understand God's love). She apparently sold herself into slavery as a prostitute (3.3)—most likely a religious one in the various fertility temples of the day. (Israel, too, had walked away from God.) But Hosea bought her back, showing what God would do with Israel after their idolatry and immorality because of his deep love.

The last time we see Gomer, Hosea is stating his intentions to reconcile with her (3.3). We leave her standing at that pivotal place in her life, facing a golden opportunity. As a woman who has made wrong choices about her behavior in the past, what will she do now? (And will Israel come back to God?)

Each time we face a moral decision today, we, like Gomer and the nation of Israel, stand at a crossroad. At such crucial moments, we need to ask ourselves: Will I choose the path of integrity, of morality, of faithfulness, of honorable behavior? What if I see that immoral or dishonorable behavior could buy me success or gratification? Will I obey, even though the moral path lacks the glitter of the world, the attention of people I admire? Will things really work for good if I make the right choice and trust God to satisfy my needs?

The choice is up to us. But God is watching, longing for us to choose his way. If we choose righteousness, he offers us this promise (14.9): "If you are wise, you will know and understand what I mean. I am the LORD, and I lead you along the right path. If you obey me, we will walk together."

Israel Is Unfaithful

4 Israel, listen
as the LORD accuses
everyone in the land!
No one is faithful or loyal
or truly cares about God.
[2] Cursing, dishonesty, murder,
robbery, unfaithfulness—
these happen all the time.
Violence is everywhere.
[3] And so your land is a desert.
Every living creature is dying—
people and wild animals,
birds and fish.

The LORD Warns the Priests

[4] Don't accuse just anyone!
Not everyone is at fault.
My case is against you,
the priests.[t]
[5] You and the prophets
will stumble day and night;
I'll silence your mothers.
[6] You priests have rejected me,
and my people are destroyed
by refusing to obey.
Now I'll reject you and forget
your children, because you
have forgotten my Law.

[7] By adding more of you priests,
you multiply the number
of people who sin.
Now I'll change your pride
into shame.
[8] You encourage others to sin,
so you can stuff yourselves
on their sin offerings.

[9] That's why I will punish
the people for their deeds,
just as I will punish
you priests.
[10] Their food won't satisfy,
and having sex at pagan shrines
won't produce children.
My people have rebelled
[11] and have been unfaithful
to me, their LORD.

God Condemns Israel's Idolatry

My people, you are foolish
because of too much pleasure
and too much wine.
[12] You expect wooden idols

---

[t]4.4 *priests*: One possible meaning for the difficult
Hebrew text of verse 4. Hosea may have had in mind
only one priest, possibly the chief priest.

---

*Spiritual*Life—If I've turned away from God, is it possible to come back? How? *(Hosea 3)*

Yes, because God keeps coming back.
God is persistent. He doesn't just wait around for us to come back to him. He keeps
pursuing us. He loves us passionately and goes to great lengths to help us see our situation
with clarity and wisdom: Without him, we're in trouble. We need the love of God. So we
have every reason to come back!

Hosea dramatically presents God's loving heart and persistent nature. And as we read
this passage today, we can be certain that God will come and find us in our worst moments. Then he'll offer to buy us back out of whatever "slavery" (whether it's a love of
money that leads to overspending on our credit cards or workaholism that keeps us
separated from home and family) we've involved ourselves in. Hosea's words "Now you
are mine!" (3.3) are the words we can hear from God.

So don't get sidetracked by Satan's whispers that you have to be "good enough" to
come back. God doesn't wait to buy us back until we become faithful—Hosea bought back
the unfaithful woman. God helps us where we are. Even when the way back to him fills us
with fear and trembling over our mistakes, God gently moves us along. (See also Isaiah
55.6-13; Lamentations 3.31-40; Ezekiel 37.1-14; Joel 2.25-27; 1 John 1.8—2.2.)

Words To Remember: *Israel will turn back to the LORD their God and to David
their king. At that time they will come to the LORD with fear and trembling, and he will be
good to them.—Hosea 3.5*

and other objects of wood
   to give you advice.
Lusting for sex at pagan shrines
has made you unfaithful
   to me, your God.
[13] You offer sacrifices
   on mountaintops and hills,
under oak trees, and wherever
   good shade is found.

Your own daughters
and daughters-in-law
   sell themselves for sex.
[14] But I won't punish them.
   You men are to blame,
because you go to prostitutes
and offer sacrifices with them
   at pagan shrines.
Your own foolishness
   will lead to your ruin.
[15] Israel, you are unfaithful,
   but don't lead Judah to sin.
Stop worshiping at Gilgal
   or at sinful Bethel.[u]
And quit making promises
in my name—the name
   of the living LORD.
[16] You are nothing more
   than a stubborn cow—
so stubborn that I, the LORD,
cannot feed you like lambs
   in an open pasture.

[17] You people of Israel[v]
are charmed by[w] idols.
   Leave them alone!
[18] You get drunk, then sleep
   with prostitutes;
you would rather be vulgar
   than lead a decent life.[x]
[19] And so you will be swept away
   in a whirlwind
   for sacrificing to idols.

Israel and Judah Will Be Judged

The LORD said:

5 Listen, you priests!
   Pay attention, Israel![y]
Listen, you members
   of the royal family.
Justice was your duty.
But[z] at Mizpah and Mount Tabor
   you trapped the people.
[2] At the place of worship

you were a treacherous pit,[a]
   and I will punish you.

[3] Israel, I know all about you,
and because of your unfaithfulness,
   I find you unacceptable.
[4] Your evil deeds are the reason
you won't return to me,
   your LORD God.
And your constant craving for sex
   keeps you from knowing me.

[5] Israel, your pride
   testifies to your guilt;
it makes you stumble,
   and Judah stumbles too.
[6] You offer sheep and cattle
   as sacrifices to me,
but I have turned away
   and refuse to be found.
[7] You have been unfaithful
   to me, your LORD;
you have had children
   by prostitutes.[b]
So at the New Moon Festival,
you and your crops
   will be destroyed.[c]

The LORD Warns Israel and Judah

[8] Give a warning on the trumpet!
Let it be heard in Gibeah,
   Ramah, and sinful Bethel.[d]
Benjamin, watch out![e]
[9] I, the LORD, will punish
   and wipe out Israel.
This is my solemn promise
   to every tribe of Israel.
[10] Judah's leaders are like crooks
   who move boundary markers;

---

[u]**4.15** *sinful Bethel:* The Hebrew text has "Beth-Aven," which means "house of sin" or "house of nothing," referring to "Bethel," which means "house of God." [v]**4.17** *Israel:* The Hebrew text has "Ephraim," the leading tribe of the northern kingdom of Israel, which sometimes stands for the whole kingdom. [w]**4.17** *charmed by:* Or "joined to." [x]**4.18** *life:* One possible meaning for the difficult Hebrew text of verse 18. [y]**5.1** *Israel:* Probably meaning the tribal leaders of Israel. [z]**5.1** *Justice . . . duty. But:* Or "You are doomed, because." [a]**5.2** *At . . . pit:* One possible meaning for the difficult Hebrew text. [b]**5.7** *prostitutes:* See 4.14, and the note at 1.2. [c]**5.7** *So . . . destroyed:* One possible meaning for the difficult Hebrew text. [d]**5.8** *sinful Bethel:* See the note at 4.15. Gibeah is three miles north of Jerusalem, Ramah is five miles north, and Bethel is eleven miles north. The attack comes from the south, and all the land of Benjamin (belonging to Israel) is in danger. [e]**5.8** *watch out:* Or "lead the way."

that's why I will flood them
    with my anger.

[11] Israel was brutally crushed.
    They got what they deserved
        for worshiping useless idols.[j]
[12] Now I, the LORD,
    will fill Israel with maggots
    and make Judah rot.
[13] When Israel and Judah saw
    their sickness and wounds,
    Israel asked help from Assyria
    and its mighty king.[g]

But the king cannot cure them
    or heal their wounds.
[14] So I'll become a fierce lion
    attacking Israel and Judah.
    I'll snatch and carry off
    what I want,
    and no one can stop me.
[15] Then I'll return to my temple
    until they confess their guilt
    and worship me,
    until they are desperate
    and beg for my help.

The LORD's People Speak

6 Let's return to the LORD.
    He has torn us to shreds,
but he will bandage our wounds
    and make us well.
[2] In two or three days
    he will heal us
and restore our strength
    that we may live with him.
[3] Let's do our best
    to know the LORD.
His coming is as certain
    as the morning sun;
he will refresh us like rain
renewing the earth
    in the springtime.

The LORD Speaks to Israel and Judah

[4] People of Israel and Judah,
    what can I do with you?
Your love for me disappears
    more quickly than mist
    or dew at sunrise.
[5] That's why I slaughtered you
    with the words
    of my prophets.
That's why my judgments blazed
    like the dawning sun.[h]

[6] I'd rather for you to be faithful
    and to know me
    than to offer sacrifices.

[7] At a place named Adam,
    you[i] betrayed me
    by breaking our agreement.
[8] Everyone in Gilead is evil;
    your hands are stained
    with the blood of victims.[j]
[9] You priests are like a gang
    of robbers in ambush.[k]
On the road to Shechem[l]
    you murder and commit
    other horrible crimes.
[10] I have seen a terrible thing
    in Israel—
you are unfaithful
    and unfit to worship me.
[11] People of Judah,
    your time is coming too.

The LORD Wants To Help Israel

7 I, the LORD, would like to make
my nation prosper again
    and to heal its wounds.
But then I see the crimes
    in Israel[m] and Samaria.
Everyone is deceitful;
    robbers roam the streets.
[2] No one realizes
    that I have seen their sins
    surround them like a flood.

[3] The king and his officials
    take great pleasure
    in their sin and deceit.
[4] Everyone burns with desire—
    they are like coals in an oven,
    ready to burst into flames.
[5] On the day their king
    was crowned,
    his officials got him drunk,

---

[j]**5.11** *for . . . idols:* One possible meaning for the difficult Hebrew text. [g]**5.13** *and . . . king:* One possible meaning for the difficult Hebrew text. [h]**6.5** *That's why my . . . sun:* One possible meaning for the difficult Hebrew text. [i]**6.7** *At . . . you:* Or "Like Adam, you" or "Each one of you." [j]**6.8** *your hands . . . victims:* This may refer to child sacrifice. [k]**6.9** *You . . . ambush:* One possible meaning for the difficult Hebrew text. [l]**6.9** *Shechem:* This was one of the towns where people could run for safety, if they had accidentally killed someone (see Joshua 20.1-9). [m]**7.1** *Israel:* See the note at 4.17. Samaria was the capital city of Israel.

and he joined
in their foolishness.[n]

[6] Their anger is a fire
that smolders all night,
then flares up at dawn.
[7] They are flames
destroying their leaders.
And their kings are powerless;
none of them trust me.

[8] The people of Israel[o]
have mixed with foreigners;
they are a thin piece of bread
scorched on one side.
[9] They don't seem to realize
how weak and feeble they are;
their hair has turned gray,
while foreigners rule.
[10] I am the LORD, their God,
but in all of their troubles
their pride keeps them
from returning to me.

No Help from Foreign Nations

The LORD said:

[11] Israel[o] is a senseless bird,
fluttering back and forth
between Egypt and Assyria.
[12] But I will catch them in a net
as hunters trap birds;
I threatened to punish them,
and indeed I will.[p]
[13] Trouble and destruction
will be their reward
for rejecting me.
I would have rescued them,
but they told me lies.

[14] They don't really pray to me;
they just howl in their beds.
They have rejected me for Baal
and slashed themselves,[q]
in the hope that Baal
will bless their crops.
[15] I taught them what they know,
and I made them strong.
Now they plot against me
[16]   and refuse to obey.[r]
They are more useless
than a crooked arrow.
Their leaders will die in war
for saying foolish things.
Egyptians will laugh at them.

Israel Rejects the LORD

The LORD said:

8 Sound a warning!
Israel, you broke our agreement
and ignored my teaching.
Now an eagle is swooping down
to attack my land.
[2] Israel, you say, "We claim you,
the LORD, as our God."
[3] But your enemies
will chase you for rejecting
our good agreement.[s]

[4] You chose kings and leaders
without consulting me;
you made silver and gold idols
that led to your downfall.
[5] City of Samaria, I'm angry
because of your idol
in the shape of a calf.
When will you ever
be innocent again?
[6] Someone from Israel built
that idol for you,
but only I am God.
And so it will be smashed
to pieces.[t]

[7] If you scatter wind
instead of wheat,
you will harvest a whirlwind
and have no wheat.
Even if you harvest grain,
enemies will steal it all.

[8] Israel, you are ruined,
and now the nations
consider you worthless.
[9] You are like a wild donkey
that goes its own way.
You've run off to Assyria
and hired them as allies.

---

[n] **7.5** *foolishness:* One possible meaning for the difficult
Hebrew text of verse 5.   [o] **7.8,11** *Israel:* Hebrew
"Ephraim" (see the note at 4.17).   [p] **7.12** *I threatened
. . . will:* One possible meaning for the difficult
Hebrew text.   [q] **7.14** *slashed themselves:* One ancient
translation and some Hebrew manuscripts; other
Hebrew manuscripts "gather together." Slashing
themselves was one way of worshiping Baal (see 1 Kings
18.28).   [r] **7.16** *and . . . obey:* One possible meaning for
the difficult Hebrew text.   [s] **8.3** *our good agreement:* Or
"me, the Good One" (referring to God).   [t] **8.6** *smashed
to pieces:* Or "destroyed by fire."

¹⁰You can bargain with nations,
    but I'll catch you anyway.
Soon you will suffer abuse
    by kings and rulers.

¹¹Israel, you have built
many altars where you offer
    sacrifices for sin.
But these altars have become
    places for sin.
¹²My instructions for sacrifices
    were written in detail,
    but you ignored them.
¹³You sacrifice your best animals
    and eat the sacrificial meals,^u
but I, the LORD,
    refuse your offerings.
I will remember your sins
    and punish you.
Then you will return to Egypt.^v

¹⁴Israel, I created you,
    but you forgot me.
You and Judah built palaces
    and many strong cities.^w
Now I will send fire to destroy
    your towns and fortresses.

Israel Will Be Punished

9 Israel, don't celebrate
    or make noisy shouts^x
        like other nations.
You have been unfaithful
    to your God.
Wherever grain is threshed,
    you behave like prostitutes
because you enjoy
    the money you receive.^y
²But you will run short
    of grain and wine,
³and you will have to leave
    the land of the LORD.
Some of you will go to Egypt;
    others will go to Assyria
        and eat unclean food.

⁴You won't be able to offer
    sacrifices of wine
        to the LORD.
None of your sacrifices
    will please him—
they will be unclean
    like food offered to the dead.
Your food will only be used
    to satisfy your hunger;

none of it will be brought
    to the LORD's temple.
⁵You will no longer be able
    to celebrate the festival
        of the LORD.^z
⁶Even if you escape alive,
    you will end up in Egypt
        and be buried in Memphis.^a
Your silver treasures
    will be lost among weeds;^b
thorns will sprout in your tents.

⁷Israel, the time has come.
You will get what you deserve,
    and you will know it.
"Prophets are fools," you say.
"And God's messengers
    are crazy."
Your terrible guilt
    has filled you with hatred.

⁸Israel, the LORD sent me
    to look after you.^c
But you trap his prophets
and flood his temple
    with your hatred.
⁹You are brutal and corrupt,
    as were the men of Gibeah.^d
But God remembers your sin,
    and you will be punished.

Sin's Terrible Results

¹⁰Israel, when I, the LORD,
    found you long ago
it was like finding

---

^u**8.13** *sacrifice . . . sacrificial meals:* One possible meaning for the difficult Hebrew text. Two kinds of sacrifices are referred to: Those in which the whole animal is burned on the altar ("whole burnt offerings" in traditional translations) and those in which part is eaten by the worshipers ("fellowship offerings" in traditional translations).   ^v**8.13** *return to Egypt:* Either as slaves or to find help against Assyria.   ^w**8.14** *built palaces . . . cities:* They did this because they no longer trusted the LORD to protect them. "Palaces" may also mean "temples."   ^x**9.1** *or . . . shouts:* One possible meaning for the difficult Hebrew text. ^y**9.1** *Wherever . . . receive:* Grain was threshed on hills or other places where the wind could blow away the husks. People also met at these places to worship Baal, the god they thought had given them the grain harvest.   ^z**9.5** *festival of the LORD:* Probably the Festival of Shelters.   ^a**9.6** *Memphis:* An Egyptian city with a famous cemetery.   ^b**9.6** *Your silver . . . weeds:* One possible meaning for the difficult Hebrew text. ^c**9.8** *Israel . . . you:* One possible meaning for the difficult Hebrew text.   ^d**9.9** *the men of Gibeah:* They raped and murdered a woman (see Judges 19).

grapes in a barren desert
  or tender young figs.
Then you worshiped Baal Peor,
  that disgusting idol,
and you became as disgusting
  as the idol you loved.

11 And so, Israel, your glory
  will fly away like birds—
your women will no longer
  be able to give birth.
12 Even if you do have children,
  I will take them all
    and leave you to mourn.
I will turn away,
  and you will sink down
    in deep trouble.
13 Israel, when I first met you,
  I thought of you as palm trees
    growing in fertile ground.ᶜ
Now you lead your people out,
  only to be slaughtered.

Hosea's Advice

14 Our LORD, do just one thing
  for your people—
make their women unable
  to have children
    or to nurse their babies.

The LORD's Judgment on Israel

15 Israel, I first began
  to hate you because
    you did evil at Gilgal.ᶠ
Now I will chase you
  out of my house.
No longer will I love you;
  your leaders betrayed me.
16 Israel, you are a vine
  with dried-up roots
    and fruitless branches.
Even if you had more children
  and loved them dearly,
    I would slaughter them all.

Hosea Warns Israel

17 Israel, you disobeyed my God.
  Now he will force you to roam
    from nation to nation.

10
You were a healthy vine
  covered with grapes.
But the more grapes you grew,
  the more altars you built;
the better off you became,

the better shrines you set up
  for pagan gods.
2 You are deceitful and disloyal.
So you will pay
  for your sins,
because the LORD will destroy
  your altars and images.

3 "We don't have a king,"
  you will say.
"We don't fear the LORD.
  And what good are kings?"
4 Israel, you break treaties
  and don't keep promises;
you turn justice
  into poisonous weeds
where healthy plants should grow.ᵍ

5 All who live in Samaria tremble
with concern for the idolsʰ
  at sinful Bethel.ⁱ
The idol there was the pride
  of the priests,
but it has been put to shame;
  now everyone will cry.
6 It will be taken to Assyria
  and given to the great king.
Then Israel will be disgraced
  for worshiping that idol.

7 Like a twig in a stream,
the king of Samaria
  will be swept away.
8 The altars at sinful Bethel
will be destroyed
  for causing Israel to sin;
they will be grown over
  with thorns and thistles.
Then everyone will beg
the mountains and hills
  to cover and protect them.

The LORD Promises To Punish Israel

9 Israel, you have never
stopped sinningʲ
  since that time at Gibeah.ᵏ

ᶜ9.13 *Israel, when . . . ground*: One possible meaning for the difficult Hebrew text. ᶠ9.15 *Gilgal*: See 4.15. ᵍ10.4 *you turn . . . grow*: One possible meaning for the difficult Hebrew text. ʰ10.5 *idols*: The Hebrew text has "calves," referring to the idols made in the shape of calves. ⁱ10.5 *sinful Bethel*: See the note at 4.15. ʲ10.9 *never stopped sinning*: One possible meaning for the difficult Hebrew text. ᵏ10.9 *Gibeah*: See the note at 9.9.

That's why you
    will be attacked at Gibeah.[l]
[10] Your sins have doubled,
    and you are rebellious.
Now I have decided
    to send nations to attack
    and put you in chains.

[11] Once you were obedient
    like a calf
        that loved to thresh grain.
But I will put a harness
    on your powerful neck;
you and Judah must plow
    and cultivate the ground.

---

*There's a part of me that craves
the consistency and support
of a husband. I will love to have
someone to share the many
beautiful places and wonderful
things I've experienced in
my music ministry. But my
challenge is to enjoy what God's
doing in my life now—to
keep my eyes focused on
the plans God has for me.*

PAM THUM

---

[12] Plow your fields,
    scatter seeds of justice,
        and harvest faithfulness.
    Worship me, the LORD,
    and I will send my saving power
        down like rain.
[13] You have planted evil,
    harvested injustice, and eaten
        the fruit of your lies.
    You trusted your own strength
        and your powerful forces.
[14] So war will break out,
    and your fortresses
        will be destroyed.
    Your enemies will do to you
    what Shalman[m] did to the people
        of Beth-Arbel—

mothers and their children
    will be beaten to death
        against rocks.
[15] Bethel, this will be your fate
    because of your evil.
Israel, at dawn your king
    will be killed.

God's Love for His People

11 When Israel was a child,
    I loved him, and I called
        my son out of Egypt.
[2] But as the saying goes,
"The more they were called,
    the more they rebelled."[n]
They never stopped offering
incense and sacrifices
    to the idols of Baal.

[3] I took Israel by the arm
    and taught them to walk.
But they would not admit
    that I was the one
        who had healed them.
[4] I led them with kindness
    and with love,
        not with ropes.
I held them close to me;[o]
    I bent down to feed them.

[5] But they trusted Egypt
    instead of returning to me;
        now Assyria will rule them.
[6] War will visit their cities,
    and their plans will fail.[p]
[7] My people are determined
    to reject me for a god
        they think is stronger,
        but he can't help.[q]

[8] Israel, I can't let you go.
    I can't give you up.
How could I possibly destroy you
    as I did the towns of Admah
        and Zeboiim?[r]

---

[l]10.9 *That's why . . . Gibeah*: One possible meaning for
the difficult Hebrew text.   [m]10.14 *Shalman*: Perhaps a
Moabite king, also known as Salamanu.   [n]11.2 *But . . .
rebelled*: One possible meaning for the difficult Hebrew
text.   [o]11.4 *I held . . . to me*: One possible meaning for
the difficult Hebrew text.   [p]11.6 *fail*: One possible
meaning for the difficult Hebrew text of verse 6.
[q]11.7 *help*: One possible meaning for the difficult
Hebrew text of verse 7.   [r]11.8 *Admah and Zeboiim*:
When the LORD destroyed Sodom and Gomorrah, he also
destroyed these two towns (see Deuteronomy 29.23).

I just can't do it.
My feelings for you
   are much too strong.
⁹ Israel, I won't lose my temper
   and destroy you again.
I am the Holy God—
not merely some human,
   and I won't stay angry.

¹⁰ I, the LORD, will roar like a lion,
and my children will return,
   trembling from the west.
¹¹ They will come back,
fluttering like birds from Egypt
   or like doves from Assyria.
Then I will bring them
back to their homes.
   I, the LORD, have spoken!

Israel and Judah Compared

¹² Israel is deceitful to me,
   their loyal and holy God;
they surround me with lies,
and Judah worships
   other gods.ˢ

12

All day long Israel chases
wind from the desert;
deceit and violence
are found everywhere.
Treaties are made with Assyria;
olive oil is taken to Egypt.

Israel and Judah Condemned

² The LORD also brings charges
against the people of Judah,
   the descendants of Jacob.
He will punish them
   for what they have done.
³ Even before Jacob was born,
   he cheated his brother,ᵗ
and when he grew up,
   he fought against God.ᵘ

⁴ At Bethel, Jacob wrestled
   with an angel and won;
then with tears in his eyes,
he asked for a blessing,
   and God spoke to usᵛ there.
⁵ God's name is the LORD,
   the LORD God All-Powerful.
⁶ So return to your God.
Patiently trust him,
   and show love and justice.

⁷ Israel, you enjoy cheating
and taking advantage
   of others.
⁸ You say to yourself, "I'm rich!
I earned it all on my own,
   without committing a sin."ʷ

The LORD Is Still the God of Israel

⁹ Israel, I, the LORD,
am still your God,
   just as I have been
since the time
   you were in Egypt.
Now I will force you
to live in tents once again,
   as you did in the desert.ˣ
¹⁰ I spoke to the prophets—
   often I spoke in visions.
And so, I will send my prophets
   with messages of doom.
¹¹ Gilead is terribly sinful
   and will end up ruined.
Bulls are sacrificed in Gilgal
   on altars made of stones,
but those stones will be scattered
   in every field.
¹² Jacobʸ escaped to Syriaᶻ
where he tended sheep
   to earn himself a wife.
¹³ I sent the prophet Moses
to lead Israel from Egypt
   and to keep them safe.
¹⁴ Israel, I will make you pay
for your terrible sins
   and for insulting me.

ˢ11.12 *and Judah worships other gods*: Or "but Judah remains faithful."   ᵗ12.3 *Jacob . . . cheated . . . brother*: In Hebrew "Jacob" sounds like "cheat" and also like "heel." Jacob grabbed his twin brother Esau by the heel at the time of their birth (see Genesis 25.26). Later he cheated him out of his rights and blessings as the first-born son (see Genesis 25.29-34; 27.1-40).   ᵘ12.3 *fought against God*: See Genesis 32.22-32.   ᵛ12.4 *us*: Hebrew; two ancient translations "him."   ʷ12.8 *without . . . sin*: One possible meaning for the difficult Hebrew text.   ˣ12.9 *as . . . desert*: One possible meaning for the difficult Hebrew text. This probably refers to the forty years of wandering through the desert after leaving Egypt, though it could refer to the "tents" (or "shelters") in which the Israelites lived during the Festival of Shelters (see 9.5, 6).   ʸ12.12 *Jacob*: His name was later changed to Israel (see Genesis 32.28), and he became the ancestor of the nation by that name.   ᶻ12.12 *Syria*: The Hebrew text has "Aram," probably referring to northern Syria in the region of Haran.

Israel Is Doomed

The LORD said:

13

When your leaders[a] spoke,
    everyone in Israel trembled
        and showed great respect.
But you sinned by worshiping Baal,
    and you were destroyed.
[2] Now you continue to sin
    by designing and making
idols of silver
    in the shape of calves.
You are told to sacrifice
to these idols[b]—
    yes, even to kiss them.
[3] And so, all of you will vanish
like the mist or the dew
    of early morning,
or husks of grain in the wind
    or smoke from a chimney.

[4] I, the LORD, have been your God
since the time
    you were in Egypt.
I am the only God you know,
    the only one who can save.
[5] I took care of you
    in a thirsty desert.[c]
[6] I fed you till you were satisfied,
    then you became proud
        and forgot about me.
[7] Now I will attack like a lion,
    ambush you like a leopard,
[8] and rip you apart like a bear
    robbed of her cubs.
I will gnaw on your bones,
as though I were a lion
    or some other wild animal.
[9] Israel, you are done for.
    Don't expect help from me.[d]
[10] You wanted a king and rulers.
Where is your king now?
    What cities have rulers?
[11] In my anger, I gave you a king;
    in my fury, I took him away.

Israel's Terrible Fate

The LORD said:

[12] Israel, your terrible sins
    are written down
        and stored away.
[13] You are like a senseless child
who refuses to be born
    at the proper time.

[14] Should I, the LORD, rescue you
    from death and the grave?
No! I call death and the grave
    to strike you like a plague.
    I refuse to show mercy.

[15] No matter how much you prosper
    more than the other tribes,[e]
I, the LORD, will wipe you out,
just as a scorching desert wind
    dries up streams of water.
I will take away
    your precious treasures.
[16] Samaria[f] will be punished
    for turning against me.
It will be destroyed in war—
    children will be beaten
        against rocks,
and pregnant women
    will be ripped open.

Turn Back to the LORD

14

Israel, return! Come back
to the LORD, your God.
    Sin has made you fall.
[2] Return to the LORD and say,
    "Please forgive our sins.
Accept our good sacrifices
    of praise instead of bulls.[g]
[3] Assyria can't save us,
    and chariots can't help.
So we will no longer worship
    the idols we have made.
Our LORD, you show mercy
    to orphans."

The LORD Promises To Forgive

[4] Israel, you have rejected me,
    but my anger is gone;
I will heal you and love you
    without limit.
[5] I will be like the dew—
    then you will blossom like lilies

---

[a]**13.1** *your leaders:* The Hebrew text has "Ephraim," here meaning Mount Ephraim, where the royal palace of Samaria (capital of the northern kingdom of Israel) was located.   [b]**13.2** *You are told . . . idols:* One possible meaning for the difficult Hebrew text.   [c]**13.5** *thirsty desert:* The forty years that Israel wandered through the desert, after leaving Egypt.   [d]**13.9** *Don't . . . me:* Or "You are against me, the one who helps you."   [e]**13.15** *more . . . tribes:* One possible meaning for the difficult Hebrew text.   [f]**13.16** *Samaria:* The capital of the northern kingdom of Israel.   [g]**14.2** *Accept . . . bulls:* One possible meaning for the difficult Hebrew text.

and have roots like a tree.[h]
[6] Your branches will spread
with the beauty
of an olive tree
and with the aroma
of Lebanon Forest.
[7] You will rest in my shade,
and your grain will grow.
You will blossom
like a vineyard
and be famous as the wine
from Lebanon.

[8] Israel, give up your idols!
I will answer your prayers
and take care of you.[i]
I am that glorious tree,
the source of your fruit.[j]

[9] If you are wise, you will know
and understand what I mean.
I am the LORD, and I lead you
along the right path.
If you obey me,
we will walk together,
but if you are wicked,
you will stumble.

---

[h]**14.5** *like a tree*: The Hebrew text has "like Lebanon," probably referring to the famous cedar trees on Mount Lebanon. [i]**14.8** *Israel . . . you*: One possible meaning for the difficult Hebrew text. [j]**14.8** *I am . . . fruit*: This is the only place in the Old Testament where the LORD is compared to a tree. Hosea reminds the people that it is the LORD who is the source of life, rather than the Canaanite gods and goddesses that are worshiped under trees at the local shrines.

MARRIAGE—What does a healthy, successful marriage look like? *(Hosea 14.4-8)*

It mirrors the love of God.

For many people, the word *commitment* has such drudgery attached to it. They picture someone saying, "I'm staying in this marriage whether I like it or not!"

But the book of Hosea shows us a different kind of commitment. God's commitment is proactive. Even though he was rejected by Israel, God took the first step to heal the breach. What a combination of initiative and gentleness! When you disagree with your husband, it may be difficult to be the first to let go of the anger and offer reconciliation. But this is how relationships survive and thrive—someone takes the first step, approaches the other, pulls the relationship out of a standstill, and moves forward.

And God didn't stop with just the approach. He also promised rewards if the people would turn back to him: that they would blossom like lilies, spread with the span of an olive tree, relax in his shade, enjoy the blossoms in a vineyard. Committed love pays attention to the rewards of married life—the beauty of brief words well said, the colorful depth of passion, the easy side-by-side of sitting on the porch at night, the sharing of a vivid sunset.

A healthy, successful marriage mirrors the full-service love of God. It searches out the loved one—and finds joy in the details of living together as a couple. **(See also Genesis 2.18-23; Exodus 32.11-14; Song of Songs 8.5-7; Acts 18; Hebrews 13.4.)**

Words To Remember: *You have rejected me, but my anger is gone; I will heal you and love you without limit.*—Hosea 14.4

Joel
Locusts and Last Days

Have you ever felt your life stripped bare as if locusts had eaten away every green leaf—and what was left is dry and brittle and terribly fragile? Or maybe you've watched disaster footage on TV of some poor woman huddling in the doorway of her earthquake-shattered home or trudging down a dirt path in Africa with sickly children clinging to her ragged skirts. You've prayed, "God, have mercy," then shuddered, and thought, *What if that were me?*

The prophet Joel describes a plague of locusts that left behind those kinds of scenes. No friendly, garden-variety grasshoppers, these were millions of locusts capable of darkening the sky for miles and stripping a tree bare in fifteen minutes. Joel opens his short book with an account of their devastation of his country. Against this backdrop, he tells the people about God—and God's plans for their future.

"Locusts" can make us feel as though we have no future—or that we don't want the future we have. Joel uses the example of locusts to show what the coming "judgment day of the LORD" will be like (2.1). But through Joel, God says, "It isn't too late." The people can still return to him with all their hearts (2.12).

As if assuming the people would return, Joel looks ahead to wonderful blessings. He promises autumn and spring rains, bountiful harvests, and jars filled with wine and olive oil (2.23,24). Then Joel looks even further ahead to another time (our own) when God's Spirit is poured out on *all* his people: sons, daughters, old, young, men, women. What a wonderful privilege to be among those receiving the fulfillment of that prophecy!

Joel glimpses one notch further yet in time. He speaks of a time when "the sun will turn dark, and the moon will be as red as blood," a "great and terrible day" (2.31). He speaks of war when people will "make swords out of plows and spears out of garden tools" (3.10), a "judgment day of the LORD" (3.14). People who'd survived locusts would know that this time is terrible indeed. But even here there is reassurance: "Then the LORD will save everyone who faithfully worships him" (2.32).

Locust-type events can drive us to despair—or point us to God. As for the future, God knows it already. We can walk through it with him. The book of Joel gives us that confidence.

Joel at a Glance
1. Locusts eat everything in sight (1.1-12)
2. Return to God (1.13-20)
3. God's judgment day will be worse than locusts (2.1-11)
4. God's invitation to return to him (2.12-17)
5. God's promise to make up for the losses (2.18-27)
6. Young people will prophesy (2.28-32)
7. War as God's judgment (3.1-16)
8. Peace at last (3.17-21)

1

I am Joel the son of Pethuel.
And this is the message
the LORD gave to me.

Locusts Cover the Land

2 Listen, you leaders
and everyone else
in the land.
Has anything like this
ever happened before?
3 Tell our children!
Let it be told
to our grandchildren
and their children too.

4 Swarm after swarm of locusts*a*
has attacked our crops,
eating everything in sight.
5 Sober up, you drunkards!
Cry long and loud;
your wine supply is gone.
6 A powerful nation*b*
with countless troops
has invaded our land.
They have the teeth and jaws
of powerful lions.
7 Our grapevines and fig trees
are stripped bare;
only naked branches remain.

8 Grieve like a young woman
mourning for the man
she was to marry.
9 Offerings of grain and wine
are no longer brought
to the LORD's temple.
His servants, the priests,
are deep in sorrow.
10 Barren fields mourn;
grain, grapes, and olives
are scorched and shriveled.

11 Mourn for our farms
and our vineyards!
There's no wheat or barley
growing in our fields.
12 Grapevines have dried up
and so has every tree—
figs and pomegranates,*c*
date palms and apples.
All happiness has faded away.

Return to God

13 Mourn, you priests who serve
at the altar of my God.

Spend your days and nights
wearing sackcloth.*d*
Offerings of grain and wine
are no longer brought
to the LORD's temple.

14 Tell the leaders and people
to come together
at the temple.
Order them to go without eating*e*
and to pray sincerely.
15 We are in for trouble!
Soon the LORD All-Powerful
will bring disaster.
16 Our food is already gone;
there's no more celebrating
at the temple of our God.

17 Seeds dry up in the ground;*f*
no harvest is possible.
Our barns are in bad shape,
with no grain
to store in them.
18 Our cattle wander aimlessly,
moaning for lack of pasture,
and sheep are suffering.*g*

---

*Believing in the Lord gives
us an assurance of eternal life,
but it also offers us a strength
beyond our own for this world.*

MARIAN V. LIAUTAUD

---

19 I cry out to you, LORD.
Grasslands and forests are eaten
by the scorching heat.

---

*a*1.4 *Swarm . . . locusts*: The Hebrew text lists either four
kinds of locusts or locusts in four stages of their
development. Locusts are a type of grasshopper that
comes in swarms and causes great damage to plant life.
*b*1.6 *A powerful nation*: The swarms of locusts.
*c*1.12 *pomegranates*: A bright red fruit that looks like
an apple.   *d*1.13 *sackcloth*: A rough, dark-colored
cloth made from goat or camel hair and used to make
grain sacks. It was worn in times of trouble or sorrow.
*e*1.14 *go without eating*: As a way of showing sorrow for
their sins.   *f*1.17 *Seeds . . . ground*: One possible
meaning for the difficult Hebrew text.   *g*1.18 *sheep
are suffering*: One possible meaning for the difficult
Hebrew text.

²⁰ Wild animals have no water
  because of you;
rivers and streams are dry,
  and pastures are parched.

Locusts and an Enemy Army

2 Sound the trumpet on Zion,
  the LORD's sacred hill.
Warn everyone to tremble!
The judgment day of the LORD
is coming soon.
² It will be dark and gloomy
  with storm clouds overhead.
Troops will cover the mountains
  like thunderclouds.
No army this powerful
has ever been gathered before
  or will ever be again.
³ Fiery flames surround them;
  no one escapes.
Before they invaded,
  the land was like Eden;
  now only a desert remains.

⁴ They look like horses
  and charge like cavalry.
⁵ They roar over mountains
  like noisy chariots,
  or a mighty army
  ready for battle.

They are a forest fire
  that feasts on straw.
⁶ The very sight of them
  is frightening.^h
⁷ They climb over walls
  like warriors;
they march in columns
  and never turn aside.
⁸ They charge straight ahead,
  without pushing each other;
even arrows and spears
  cannot make them retreat.
⁹ They swarm over city walls
  and enter our homes;
they crawl in through windows,
  just like thieves.

¹⁰ They make the earth tremble
  and the heavens shake;
the sun and moon turn dark,
  and stars stop shining.
¹¹ The LORD God leads this army
  of countless troops,
  and they obey his commands.
The day of his judgment
is so terrible
  that no one can stand it.

---

^h**2.6** *The very . . . frightening:* One possible meaning for the difficult Hebrew text.

Personal *Concerns*—When a poor decision on my part has damaged my reputation as a Christian, what can I do? *(Joel 2.12-17)*

Return to God with all your heart.

Damage to a Christian's reputation comes in small and large packages. Maybe you made a hasty decision at work that hurt someone's feelings or shared a friend's secret without her permission. Perhaps you told a "white lie" to get yourself out of trouble and got caught. Or maybe you gave in to temptation one night and had sex out of wedlock; now you're pregnant. When such things happen, you might wonder, *Can I ever look another Christian in the eye? Can I ever walk into church again? Can I ever again use the name of Christ as my own?*

Good news! Yes, you can. But returning to God isn't merely saying, "Oops, I guess I goofed." According to Joel, returning to God involves a heart change, even a broken heart (2.13). We must reject what we've done as the evil rebellion against God that it is, make appropriate restitution, and commit to a new and holy way of living. Instead of just being sorry that we were caught, we must invite God to clean us up from the inside out. Joel reassures us that it's God himself who invites us. He says, "I am merciful, kind, and caring. . . . I am the LORD your God" (2.13,14). (See also Jonah 2,3; Micah 7.18,19; Zechariah 10.6-12; Luke 7.36-50; Galatians 1.11-24.)

Words To Remember: *The LORD said: It isn't too late. You can still return to me with all your heart.—Joel 2.12*

The LORD's Invitation

¹²The LORD said:

It isn't too late.
You can still return to me
    with all your heart.
Start crying and mourning!
    Go without eating.
¹³Don't rip your clothes
    to show your sorrow.
Instead, turn back to me
    with broken hearts.
I am merciful, kind, and caring.
I don't easily lose my temper,
    and I don't like to punish.

¹⁴I am the LORD your God.
Perhaps I will change my mind
    and treat you with mercy.
Then you will be blessed
with enough grain and wine
    for offering sacrifices to me.

¹⁵Sound the trumpet on Zion!
    Call the people together.
Show your sorrow
    by going without food.

¹⁶Make sure that everyone
    is fit to worship me.ⁱ
Bring adults, children, babies,
and even bring newlyweds
    from their festivities.

¹⁷Tell my servants, the priests,
    to cry inside the temple
and to offer this prayer
    near the altar:ʲ
"Save your people, LORD God!
Don't let foreign nations
    make jokes about us.
Don't let them laugh and ask,
    'Where is your God?' "

The LORD Will Bless the Land

¹⁸The LORD was deeply concerned
    about his land
    and had pity on his people.
¹⁹In answer to their prayers
    he said,
    "I will give you enough grain,

ⁱ**2.16** *fit to worship me:* This required going through certain kinds of ceremonies.   ʲ**2.17** *inside . . . altar:* The Hebrew text has "between the porch and the altar," which is the place where the priests usually prayed for the people.

---

*Spiritual*Life—If I've turned away from God, is it possible to come back? How? (Joel 2.25-27)

God can make up for wasted years.

Do you ever wish you could just turn back the clock? Go back to that time just before you began to turn away from God. What about the career decision or marriage choice that might have been different if you'd been willing to pray about it? What about the time spent "having fun"—except that the aftermath wasn't much fun at all? Whether it was last week or decades ago, a sense of wasted time is one of the many losses we feel when we decide to walk away from God.

But God can make it up if we repent! The locusts of Joel's first chapter had eaten everything in sight—including the long-growing grapevines and pastures. It would take years, maybe decades, to get back to normal. But God used the locusts to bring his people back to himself—as he can use our own losses. And at their return God promised, "I, the LORD your God, will make up for the losses" (2.25).

We can't turn back the clock. But God can make up for wasted years. God closed his invitation to Joel's people by saying that he (the Lord God), was the only God and that he would never again let them be put to shame (2.27). He offers the same to us, if we but ask him for forgiveness and begin to walk on a godly path. (See also Isaiah 55.6-13; Lamentations 3.31-40; Ezekiel 37.1-14; Hosea 3; 1 John 1.8—2.2.)

Words To Remember: *I, the LORD your God, will make up for the losses caused by those swarms and swarms of locusts I sent to attack you. . . . Then you will praise me for the wonderful things I have done. Never again will you be put to shame.* —Joel 2.25,26

wine, and olive oil
    to satisfy your needs.
No longer will I let you
    be insulted by the nations.
²⁰ An army attacked from the north,
    but I will chase it
        into a scorching desert.
There it will rot and stink
from the Dead Sea
    to the Mediterranean."

The LORD works wonders
²¹   and does great things.
So tell the soil to celebrate
²² and wild animals
    to stop being afraid.
Grasslands are green again;
fruit trees and fig trees
    are loaded with fruit.
Grapevines are covered
    with grapes.

²³ People of Zion,^k
    celebrate in honor
        of the LORD your God!
He is generous and has sent
the autumn and spring rains
    in the proper seasons.^l

²⁴ Grain will cover
    your threshing places;
jars will overflow
    with wine and olive oil.

The LORD Will Rescue His People

²⁵ I, the LORD your God,
    will make up for the losses
        caused by those swarms
and swarms of locusts^m
    I sent to attack you.
²⁶ My people, you will eat
    until you are satisfied.
Then you will praise me
for the wonderful things
    I have done.
Never again will you
    be put to shame.

²⁷ Israel, you will know
    that I stand at your side.
I am the LORD your God—
    there are no other gods.
Never again will you
    be put to shame.

---

^k**2.23** *Zion:* Jerusalem. ^l**2.23** *in . . . seasons:* Or "as he used to do." ^m**2.25** *swarms . . . locusts:* See the note at 1.4.

PARENTING&*family*—How can I know what's best for my elderly parents? (*Joel 2.28-32*)

Respect their dreams.
It's a strange feeling the first time one of your parents asks you for advice. "Does this dress really look all right?" "What do you think I should do about that problem at work?" But as parents grow older, their questions grow more serious. "Should I sell the house?" "Should I have the operation if it might buy more time?" Some parents don't ask. They just need help. Month by month, they grow slower and more hesitant.
    It's tempting to just step in, make whatever decisions are needed, and get the job done. But that would discount what God might be doing in the lives of our parents. In a beautiful description of the work of God's Spirit, Joel speaks of a day (our day) when God would pour out his Spirit on *all* his people: men, women, young, and old. Specifically, he says, "Your old men will have dreams" (2.28). It's important to listen to what our parents say— even when they're old, maybe *especially* when they're old—because we can learn a lot from them. And listening helps us respect their wishes in the decisions we make for them. Young or old, every Christian has God's Spirit inside them; that Spirit will guide us toward wisdom, if we listen. As Peter notes in his sermon at Pentecost (Acts 2), this prophecy is fulfilled with the outpouring of the Holy Spirit to people of all ages. (See also Psalm 25; Proverbs 23.22-25; 1 Corinthians 15.35-58; 1 Timothy 5.1-7.)

    Words To Remember: *I will give my Spirit to everyone. Your sons and daughters will prophesy. Your old men will have dreams, and your young men will see visions. In those days I will even give my Spirit to my servants, both men and women.*—Joel 2.28,29

The LORD Will Work Wonders

The LORD said:

28 Later, I will give my Spirit
to everyone.
Your sons and daughters
will prophesy.
Your old men
will have dreams,
and your young men
will see visions.
29 In those days I will even give
my Spirit to my servants,
both men and women.

30 I will work wonders
in the sky above
and on the earth below.
There will be blood and fire
and clouds of smoke.
31 The sun will turn dark,
and the moon
will be as red as blood
before that great
and terrible day
when I appear.

32 Then the LORD will save everyone who faithfully worships him. He has promised there will be survivors on Mount Zion and in Jerusalem, and among them will be his chosen ones.

The LORD Will Judge the Nations

3 At that time I, the LORD, will make
Judah and Jerusalem prosperous
again. 2 Then in Judgment Valley[n] I
will bring together the nations that scattered
my people Israel everywhere in the world,
and I will bring charges against those nations. They divided up my land 3 and
gambled to see who would get my people;
they sold boys and girls to pay for prostitutes and wine.
4 You people of Tyre and Sidon[o] and you
Philistines, why are you doing this? Are you
trying to get even with me? I'll strike back
before you know what's happened. 5 You've
taken my prized possessions, including my
silver and gold, and carried them off to your
temples.[p] 6 You have dragged the people of
Judah and Jerusalem from their land and
sold them to the Greeks.
7 But I'll make the people of Judah determined to come home, and what happened
to them will happen to you. 8 I'll hand over
your sons and daughters to the people of
Judah, and they will sell them to the
Sabeans,[q] who live far away. I, the LORD,
have spoken!

Judgment in Judgment Valley

9 Say to the nations:

"Get ready for war!
Be eager to fight.
Line up for battle
and prepare to attack.
10 Make swords out of plows
and spears out of garden tools.
Strengthen every weakling."

11 Hurry, all you nations!
Come quickly.
Ask the LORD to bring
his warriors along.[r]
12 You must come now
to Judgment Valley,[s]
where the LORD will judge
the surrounding nations.

13 They are a field of ripe crops.
Bring in the harvest!
They are grapes piled high.
Start trampling them now![t]
If our enemy's sins were wine,
every jar would overflow.
14 Crowds fill Decision Valley.
The judgment day of the LORD
will soon be here—
15 no light from the sun or moon,
and stars no longer shine.
16 From the heart of Jerusalem
the LORD roars like a lion,
shaking the earth and sky.
But the LORD is a fortress,
a place of safety
for his people Israel.

[n] 3.2 *Judgment Valley*: The Hebrew text has "Jehoshaphat Valley," which means "Valley of the LORD's Judgment." This valley is mentioned here and in verse 12, but nowhere else in the Bible. [o] 3.4 *Tyre and Sidon*: Two Phoenician coastal cities. [p] 3.5 *temples*: Or "palaces." [q] 3.8 *Sabeans*: The people of Seba, a region in southwest Arabia. [r] 3.11 *Ask . . . along*: One possible meaning for the difficult Hebrew text. [s] 3.12 *Judgment Valley*: See the note at 3.2. [t] 3.13 *grapes . . . now*: People trampled grapes with their bare feet to squeeze out the juice.

God Will Bless His People

¹⁷ I am the LORD your God.
And you will know I live on Zion,
    my sacred hill,
because Jerusalem will be sacred,
    untouched by foreign troops.

> *When we acknowledge*
> *that the Lord our God is*
> *the one and only God, he*
> *will become our refuge*
> *through any storm.*
>
> CAROLE MAYHALL

¹⁸ On that day, fruitful vineyards
    will cover the mountains.

And your cattle and goats
    that graze on the hills
    will produce a lot of milk.
Streams in Judah
    will never run dry;
a stream from my house
    will flow in Acacia Valley.ᵘ

¹⁹ Egypt and Edom were cruel
and brutal to Judah,
    without a reason.
Now their countries will become
    a barren desert,
²⁰ but Judah and Jerusalem
    will always have people.
²¹ I, the LORD, live on Mount Zion.
I will punish the guilty
    and defend the innocent.ᵛ

ᵘ**3.18** *Acacia Valley*: In the plains of Moab, northeast of the Dead Sea.   ᵛ**3.21** *I will . . . innocent*: One possible meaning for the difficult Hebrew text.

Amos

Let Justice Flow like a River

Amos was a shepherd and fig tree cultivator (7.14) whom God called to leave Tekoa in Judah (1.1) and travel north with a message from God to sister nation, Israel. There were "professional" prophets in Amos's day, but these prophets, along with the other leaders, were busy enjoying the prosperity that had come to Israel (5.10-12; 6.4-6). Neighboring Egypt and Assyria were preoccupied with their concerns, which allowed Israel to spend its resources on itself rather than defend its borders. And because of its location, Israel was a center for economic trade. Not since David's day had God's people enjoyed such abundance.

But instead of acknowledging God for their good fortune and being a righteous example to their pagan neighbors (3.2), people who were already rich thought only of getting richer, often at the expense of the weak—widows, poor people, slaves (2.6-8; 8.4-6). What was worse, the happy Hebrew prophets, judges, and politicians believed that God had given them their luxurious lifestyle simply for being his people and for going through the motions of faith (5.21-23)! God had something to give his people all right, but blessing was the last thing on his mind. He was about to give them punishment (5.18-20).

The book of Amos reminds us that God isn't impressed with just outward piety, like going to church or saying grace before meals. Instead, the real follower of God cares for others (5.14,15,24). She's honest in her business deals, opens her home to the homeless, and stands up for those who can't defend themselves.

Amos also reveals why God wants us to be totally devoted to him: because all other devotion (such as "worshiping" our career, our children, or our looks) ruins us.

Because of Israel's dangerous pre-occupation with prosperity, the book of Amos has often been known as God's plea for social justice. Here, God says, "Let justice and fairness flow like a river that never runs dry" (5.24). Amos probably spoke his warning around 750 B.C. However, the Israelites didn't repent, so God allowed them to be captured by the Assyrians in 722 B.C. Still, Amos ends his book with hope for those willing to return whole-heartedly to him: "I'll plant your roots deep in the land I have given you, and you won't ever be uprooted again. I, the LORD God, have spoken!" (9.15).

Amos at a Glance

1. God is the Judge of all nations (1.1—2.3)
2. God is the Judge of Judah and Israel (2.4-16)
3. Israel and Samaria will be destroyed by their faithlessness (3—6)
4. Five visions of God's punishment of Israel (7.1—9.10)
5. God will save a humbled Israel and bless her future (9.11-15)

1 I am Amos. And I raised sheep near the town of Tekoa[a] when Uzziah was king of Judah and Jeroboam[b] son of Jehoash[c] was king of Israel.

Two years before the earthquake,[d] the LORD gave me several messages[e] about Israel, [2]and I said:

> When the LORD roars
>   from Jerusalem,
> pasturelands and Mount Carmel
>   dry up and turn brown.

Judgment on Syria

[3]The LORD said:

> I will punish Syria[f]
> for countless crimes,
>   and I won't change my mind.
> They dragged logs with spikes[g]
>   over the people of Gilead.
> [4]Now I will burn down the palaces
> and fortresses of King Hazael
>   and of King Benhadad.[h]
> [5]I will break through
>   the gates of Damascus.
> I will destroy the people[i]
> of Wicked Valley[j]
>   and the ruler of Beth-Eden.[k]
> Then the Syrians will be dragged
>   as prisoners to Kir.[l]
> I, the LORD, have spoken!

Judgment on Philistia

[6]The LORD said:

> I will punish Philistia[m]
> for countless crimes,
>   and I won't change my mind.
> They dragged off my people[n]
>   from town after town
> to sell them as slaves
>   to the Edomites.
> [7]That's why I will burn down
> the walls and fortresses
>   of the city of Gaza.
> [8]I will destroy the king[o] of Ashdod
>   and the ruler of Ashkelon.
> I will strike down Ekron,[p]
> and that will be the end
>   of the Philistines.
> I, the LORD, have spoken!

Judgment on Phoenicia

[9]The LORD said:

> I will punish Phoenicia[q]
> for countless crimes,
>   and I won't change my mind.
> They broke their treaty
> and dragged off my people[r]
>   from town after town
> to sell them as slaves
>   to the Edomites.
> [10]That's why I will send flames
> to burn down the city of Tyre
>   along with its fortresses.

Judgment on Edom

[11]The LORD said:

> I will punish Edom
> for countless crimes,
>   and I won't change my mind.
> They killed their own relatives[s]
> and were so terribly furious
>   that they showed no mercy.
> [12]Now I will send fire to wipe out
> the fortresses of Teman
>   and Bozrah.[t]

---

[a]**1.1** *Tekoa*: In the hill country of Judah about five miles south of Bethlehem. [b]**1.1** *Uzziah . . . Jeroboam*: Uzziah was king of Judah 781-740 B.C., and Jeroboam II was king of Israel 783-743 B.C. [c]**1.1** *Jehoash*: The Hebrew text has "Joash," another spelling of the name. [d]**1.1** *Two years . . . earthquake*: Possibly the earthquake of 760 B.C., which seems to have been especially violent. [e]**1.1** *messages*: Or "visions." [f]**1.3** *Syria*: The Hebrew text has "Damascus," the leading city of Syria. [g]**1.3** *logs with spikes*: These were dragged over grain to thresh it. [h]**1.4** *Hazael . . . Benhadad*: Two Syrian kings. [i]**1.5** *people*: Or "king." [j]**1.5** *Wicked Valley*: The Hebrew text has "Aven Valley," probably the fertile valley between the Lebanon and the anti-Lebanon mountains. [k]**1.5** *I will . . . Beth-Eden*: Or "I will destroy the people of Wicked Valley and the king who rules from Beth-Eden." Beth-Eden was a city-state on the banks of the Euphrates River. [l]**1.5** *Kir*: The exact location of this country is not known; in 9.7 Amos refers to Kir as the original home of the Syrians, and so the verse probably means that the Syrians will lose everything they have gained as a people. [m]**1.6** *Philistia*: The Hebrew text has "Gaza," one of the main Philistine cities. [n]**1.6** *my people*: The people of Israel. [o]**1.8** *king*: Or "people." [p]**1.8** *Ashdod . . . Ashkelon . . . Ekron*: Philistine cities. [q]**1.9** *Phoenicia*: The Hebrew text has "Tyre," which was one of the two Phoenician cities; the other was Sidon, which is not mentioned by Amos. [r]**1.9** *my people*: See the note at 1.6. [s]**1.11** *their own relatives*: The Edomites were descendants of Esau, the brother of Jacob, the ancestor of the Israelites. [t]**1.12** *Teman and Bozrah*: These stand for all of Edom; Teman may have been a city or a district. Bozrah, the chief city of northern Edom, was thirty miles southeast of the Dead Sea.

Judgment on Ammon

[13]The LORD said:

I will punish Ammon
for countless crimes,
    and I won't change my mind.
In Gilead they ripped open
pregnant women,
    just to take the land.

[14] Now I will send fire to destroy
the walls and fortresses
    of Rabbah.[u]
Enemies will shout and attack
like a whirlwind.
[15] Ammon's king and leaders
will be dragged away.
I, the LORD, have spoken!

Judgment on Moab

2 The LORD said:

I will punish Moab
for countless crimes,
    and I won't change my mind.
They made lime from the bones[v]
of the king of Edom.
[2] Now I will send fire to destroy
the fortresses of Kerioth.[w]
Battle shouts and trumpet blasts
will be heard as I destroy Moab

[3]   with its king and leaders.
I, the LORD, have spoken!

Judgment on Judah

[4]The LORD said:

I will punish Judah
for countless crimes,
    and I won't change my mind.
They have rejected my teachings
    and refused to obey me.
They were led astray
by the same false gods
    their ancestors worshiped.
[5] Now I will send fire on Judah
and destroy the fortresses
of Jerusalem.

Judgment on Israel

[6]The LORD said:

I will punish Israel
for countless crimes,
    and I won't change my mind.
They sell honest people for money,

---

[u]1.14 *Rabbah*: The capital city of Ammon.
[v]2.1 *They . . . bones*: They dug up the bodies of kings
and made lime out of them to use as whitewash on their
houses and walls.   [w]2.2 *Kerioth*: A leading city of Moab
and a center for the worship of Chemosh, the chief god
of Moab.

WORK—How can I deal with a dishonest coworker? *(Amos 2)*

Honor God in the way *you* do business.

Money sometimes equals power. Power isn't necessarily a bad thing in itself. In the right hands, power can produce tremendous joy and freedom; but in the wrong hands, it brings much misery and pain. The people to whom God sent Amos made particular use of their power to oppress the needy. They sold poor people for the price of sandals (2.6). If a poor person needed money, they provided a "loan" in exchange for the person's cloak—his only way of keeping warm at night. Clearly, they weren't using their power or their money to honor God.

What do you do when the power abuser is your boss? If you confront him or her, you could lose your job. If you keep silent, you could lose the chance to remedy the situation—not to mention regain your self-respect.

Try to approach the situation in a way that honors God. Pick your battles wisely, but when the well-being of the needy is at stake, you ought to speak up. That person may be prompted to change because you had the courage to confront. No matter what the immediate result, God will honor your desire for justice to those in need. Amos followed God's call to expose the power abusers in Israel, but then left their fate to God. You can do the same. (See also Psalm 26; Proverbs 28.11-26; Habakkuk 2.4-17.)

Words To Remember: *I chose some of you to be prophets. . . . I, the LORD, have spoken!*—Amos 2.11

and the needy are sold
    for the price of sandals.
[7] They smear the poor in the dirt
and push aside
    those who are helpless.

My holy name is dishonored,
because fathers and sons sleep
    with the same young women.
[8] They lie down beside altars
on clothes taken
    as security for loans.
And they drink wine in my temple,
wine bought with the money
    they received from fines.

[9] Israel, the Amorites[x] were there
    when you entered Canaan.
They were tall as cedars
    and strong as oaks.
But I wiped them out—
I destroyed their branches
    and their roots.
[10] I had rescued you from Egypt,
and for forty years I had led you
    through the desert.
Then I gave you the land
    of the Amorites.

[11] I chose some of you
to be prophets
    and others to be Nazirites.[y]
People of Israel,
    you know this is true.
    I, the LORD, have spoken!
[12] But you commanded the prophets
    not to speak their message,
and you pressured the Nazirites
    into drinking wine.

[13] And so I will crush you,
just as a wagon full of grain
    crushes the ground.[z]
[14] No matter how fast you run,
    you won't escape.
No matter how strong you are,
you will lose your strength
    and your life.
[15] Even if you are an expert
with a bow and arrow,
    you will retreat.
And you won't get away alive,
not even if you run fast
    or ride a horse.
[16] You may be brave and strong,

but you will run away,
    stripped naked.
I, the LORD, have spoken!

3

People of Israel,
    I rescued you from Egypt.
Now listen to my judgment
    against you.
[2] Of all nations on earth,
you are the only one
    I have chosen.
That's why I will punish you
    because of your sins.

The Work of a Prophet

[3] Can two people walk together
    without agreeing to meet?
[4] Does a lion roar in the forest
unless it has caught
    a victim?
Does it growl in its den
    unless it is eating?
[5] How can anyone catch a bird
    without using a net?
Does a trap spring shut
    unless something is caught?

[6] Isn't the whole city frightened
when the trumpet
    signals an attack?
Isn't it the LORD who brings
    disaster on a city?
[7] Whatever the LORD God
    plans to do,
he tells his servants,
    the prophets.
[8] Everyone is terrified
    when a lion roars—
and ordinary people
become prophets
    when the LORD God speaks.

Samaria Is Doomed

[9] Here is a message
for the leaders
    of Philistia[d] and Egypt—

---

[x]**2.9** *Amorites*: This word is used for all the people
who lived in Canaan at the time Israel took over
the land.   [y]**2.11** *Nazirites*: People who promised the
LORD that they would never drink wine or cut their hair
or come in contact with a dead body.   [z]**2.13** *ground*:
One possible meaning for the difficult Hebrew text of
verse 13.   [d]**3.9** *Philistia*: The Hebrew text has
"Ashdod," one of the leading cities of Philistia.

tell everyone to come together
　　on the hills of Samaria.
Let them see the injustice
and the lawlessness
　　in that city.
¹⁰ The LORD has said
　　that they don't even know how
　　　to do right.
They have become rich
　　from violence and robbery.
¹¹ And so the LORD God has sworn
　　that they will be surrounded.
Enemies will break through
their defenses
　　and steal their treasures.

¹² The LORD has promised
　　that only a few from Samaria
　　　will escape with their lives
and with some broken pieces
　　of their beds and couches.ᵇ
It will be like when a shepherd
　　rescues two leg bones
and part of a sheep's ear
　　from the jaws of a lion.ᶜ

The Altars at Bethel

¹³ The LORD God All-Powerful
　　told me to speak this message
　　against Jacob's descendants:
¹⁴ When I, the LORD, punish Israel
　　for their sins,
I will destroy the altars
　　at Bethel.
Even the corners of the altarᵈ
　　will be left in the dirt.
¹⁵ I will tear down winter homes
　　and summer homes.
Houses decorated with ivory
and all other mansions
　　will be gone forever.
I, the LORD, have spoken!

The Women of Samaria

The LORD said:

4 You women of Samaria
　　are fat cows!ᵉ
You mistreat and abuse
　　the poor and needy,
then you say to your husbands,
　　"Bring us more drinks!"
² I, the LORD God, have sworn
　　by my own name
　　that your time is coming.

Not one of you will be left—
you will be taken away
　　by sharp hooks.ᶠ
³ You will be dragged through holes
　　in your city walls,
and you will be thrown
　　toward Harmon.ᵍ
I, the LORD, have spoken!

Israel Refuses To Obey

The LORD said:

⁴ Come to Bethel and Gilgal.ʰ
　　Sin all you want!
Offer sacrifices the next morning
and bring a tenth of your crops
　　on the third day.ⁱ
⁵ Bring offerings to show me
　　how thankful you are.
Gladly bring more offerings
than I have demanded.
　　You really love to do this.
I, the LORD God, have spoken!

How the LORD Warned Israel

⁶ I, the LORD, took away the food
　　from every town and village,
　　but still you rejected me.
⁷ Three months before harvest,
　　I kept back the rain.
Sometimes I would let it fall
　　on one town or field
but not on another,
　　and pastures dried up.
⁸ People from two or three towns
　　would go to a town

ᵇ**3.12** *some . . . couches:* One possible meaning for the difficult Hebrew text.　ᶜ**3.12** *lion:* When a wild animal attacked and killed a sheep, the shepherd had to rescue part of the sheep and take it to the owner as proof that it had been killed by an animal. Otherwise, the shepherd had to pay the owner the cost of the sheep.　ᵈ**3.14** *altar:* Altars were places of worship but also places of protection. People whose lives were in danger could grab hold of the corners of an altar, and no one was allowed to kill them.　ᵉ**4.1** *fat cows:* The Hebrew text has "cows of Bashan," a fertile plain famous for its rich pastures and well-fed cattle.　ᶠ**4.2** *taken . . . hooks:* One possible meaning for the difficult Hebrew text.　ᵍ**4.3** *Harmon:* Hebrew; some manuscripts of one ancient translation "Mount Hermon," a mountain in the north of Palestine, on the way to Assyria.　ʰ**4.4** *Bethel and Gilgal:* These were two of the most important centers of worship in northern Israel. Amos mentions these together again in 5.5.　ⁱ**4.4** *Offer . . . day:* Or "Offer sacrifices each morning and bring a tenth of your crops every three days." In verses 4, 5 God is condemning the people for meaningless acts of worship.

that still had water,
  but it wasn't enough.
Even then you rejected me.
  I, the LORD, have spoken!

9 I dried up your grain fields;
your gardens and vineyards
  turned brown.
Locusts[j] ate your fig trees
  and olive orchards,
but even then you rejected me.
  I, the LORD, have spoken!

10 I did terrible things to you,
  just as I did to Egypt—
I killed your young men in war;
  I let your horses be stolen,
and I made your camp stink
  with dead bodies.
Even then you rejected me.
  I, the LORD, have spoken!

11 I destroyed many of you,
just as I did the cities
  of Sodom and Gomorrah.
You were a burning stick
  I rescued from the fire.
Even then you rejected me.
  I, the LORD, have spoken!

12 Now, Israel, I myself
will deal with you.
  Get ready to face your God!

*Not only is God my El Elyon,
who oversees the entire world,
but my Abba Father, who
loves me fiercely, personally.*
MAYO MATHERS

13 I created the mountains
  and the wind.
I let humans know
  what I am thinking.[k]
I bring darkness at dawn
  and step over hills.
I am the LORD God All-Powerful!

Turn Back to the LORD

5 Listen, nation of Israel,
  to my mournful message:
2 You, dearest Israel, have fallen,
  never to rise again—
you lie deserted in your own land,
  with no one to help you up.

3 The LORD God has warned,
"From every ten soldiers
  only one will be left;
from a thousand troops,
  only a hundred will survive."

4 The LORD keeps saying,
"Israel, turn back to me
  and you will live!
5 Don't go to Gilgal or Bethel
  or even to Beersheba.[l]
Gilgal will be dragged away,
and Bethel will end up
  as nothing."[m]

6 Turn back to the LORD,
you descendants of Joseph,[n]
  and you will live.
If you don't, the LORD
  will attack like fire.
Bethel will burn to the ground,
  and no one can save it.
7 You people are doomed!
You twist the truth
  and stomp on justice.

8 But the LORD created the stars
  and put them in place.[o]
He turns darkness to dawn
  and daylight to darkness;

---

[j]**4.9** *Locusts:* A type of grasshopper that comes in swarms and causes great damage to plant life.
[k]**4.13** *I let . . . thinking:* Or "No one's secret thoughts are hidden from me."   [l]**5.5** *Gilgal . . . Bethel . . . Beersheba:* These were ancient places of worship, but the LORD had warned his people to stay away from them.
[m]**5.5** *Gilgal . . . nothing:* In Hebrew "Gilgal" and "dragged away" sound something alike. Bethel (meaning "house of God") is sometimes called "house of nothing" or "house of sin" by the prophets (see Hosea 4.15; 5.8; 10.5-8).   [n]**5.6** *descendants of Joseph:* Another name for the people of the northern kingdom of Israel.
[o]**5.8** *the stars . . . place:* The Hebrew text mentions two groups of stars, Pleiades and Orion. Since the LORD is the Creator of the stars, he controls the seasons that are signaled by the different positions of the stars. Moreover, the stars are created objects and should not be worshiped.

he scoops up the ocean
and empties it on the earth.
9 God destroys mighty soldiers
and strong fortresses.

Choose Good Instead of Evil!

The LORD said:

10 You people hate judges
and honest witnesses;
11 you abuse the poor and demand
heavy taxes from them.
You have built expensive homes,
but you won't enjoy them;
you have planted vineyards,
but you will get no wine.
12 I am the LORD, and I know
your terrible sins.
You cheat honest people
and take bribes;
you rob the poor of justice.
13 Times are so evil
that anyone with good sense
will keep quiet.

14 If you really want to live,
you must stop doing wrong
and start doing right.
I, the LORD God All-Powerful,
will then be on your side,
just as you claim I am.
15 Choose good instead of evil!
See that justice is done.
Maybe I, the LORD All-Powerful,
will be kind to what's left
of your people.[p]

Judgment Is Coming

16 This is what the LORD has sworn:

Noisy crying will be heard
in every town and street.
Even farmers will be told
to mourn for the dead,
together with those
who are paid to mourn.[q]
17 Your vineyards will be filled
with crying and weeping,[r]
because I will punish you.
I, the LORD, have spoken!

When the LORD Judges

18 You look forward to the day
when the LORD comes to judge.

---

[p] **5.15** *your people*: Hebrew "Joseph's descendants" (see the note at verse 6). [q] **5.16** *paid to mourn*: In ancient times some people were paid to mourn and make loud cries at funerals. [r] **5.17** *Your vineyards . . . weeping*: Instead of happy celebrations that were often held in vineyards after the harvest.

PARENTING&*family*—What advice, if any, should I give my twentysomething child? *(Amos 5.6-27)*

Choose good instead of evil; see that justice is done.
What we think and do really matters. It matters to God and to all who know us, because we are either a good or a bad influence on them. Remind your child (who's old enough to have had plenty of firsthand experience with this) that there are consequences to his or her actions: reward for doing what's right, and punishment for doing what's wrong. That's the way God made the world, and it's actually for our own good.

You can tell them that owning a hot sports car, dating the best-looking guy on campus, or volunteering at a local charity so people think you're a caring person are shallow pursuits (5.21). God made us to want more out of life, to know his love, and to share it with others. That's where real satisfaction and purpose come from. Then it doesn't matter what we look like or who our friends are or what people think of us, because God accepts us the way we are—and makes us more like him!

Our years on earth are precious and few, so show your son or daughter by the way you serve God that his opinion is worth far more than anyone else's. Encourage your adult child to stand up for other people's rights—and lay down his or her own. Then pray that God will help your son or daughter do what's right (see 5.14,15). (See also Ecclesiastes 11.1—12.1; Ezekiel 18.1-20; Matthew 14.24-33; 1 Timothy 4.6-16.)

Words To Remember: *Choose good instead of evil! See that justice is done.* —Amos 5.15

But you are in for trouble!
It won't be a time of sunshine;
all will be darkness.
¹⁹You will run from a lion,
only to meet a bear.
You will escape to your house,
rest your hand on the wall,
and be bitten by a snake.
²⁰The day when the LORD judges
will be dark, very dark,
without a ray of light.

What the LORD Demands

²¹I, the LORD, hate and despise
your religious celebrations
and your times of worship.
²²I won't accept your offerings
or animal sacrifices—
not even your very best.
²³No more of your noisy songs!
I won't listen
when you play your harps.
²⁴But let justice and fairness
flow like a river
that never runs dry.

²⁵Israel, for forty years
you wandered in the desert,
without bringing offerings
or sacrifices to me.

²⁶Now you will have to carry
the two idols you made—
Sakkuth, the one you call king,
and Kaiwan, the one you built
in the shape of a star.*
²⁷I will force you to march
as captives beyond Damascus.
I, the LORD God All-Powerful,
have spoken!†

Israel Will Be Punished

6 Do you rulers in Jerusalem
and in the city of Samaria
feel safe and at ease?
Everyone bows down to you,
and you think you are better
than any other nation.
But you are in for trouble!
²Look what happened
to the cities of Calneh,
powerful Hamath,

---

*5.26 *star*: One possible meaning for the difficult Hebrew text of verse 26. †5.27 *I, the LORD . . . spoken*: Israel did not offer sacrifices and gifts to the LORD during the time they wandered through the desert. But now they have made idols to carry during their ceremonies. So the LORD warns that he will make them "march" away as captives beyond Damascus, where Israel had extended its borders by victories in war (see 2 Kings 14.28).

Personal *Concerns*—**When it comes to material things, how can I know what's enough and what's too much?** (Amos 6.1-7)

Prayerfully consider what to buy and how to help others.
Who doesn't want nice things or a comfortable life? The trick is not to make them our life's focus. Sometimes materialism is subtle, and we rationalize our secret devotion to it. *If I bought my dream car, I could donate that clunky station wagon to the church.* If you want to know what's really important to you, ask family, friends, and neighbors what your lifestyle says about your values. Then weigh what you find against what Scripture says is truly valuable.

God called Amos to denounce Israel's perverted worship and flagrant preoccupation with pleasure. Israel boasted that no city in her region compared with Israel's material success (6.2). But God said the people of Israel were fools to take pride in their possessions because they worshiped the gift and forgot about the Giver.

If God has given you more than you need, he may want you to help someone who has less, support a missionary, or feed a hungry child. Don't assume that God intends you to indulge yourself. Prayerfully consider what you buy and how to help those in need. (If in doubt, consider taking the courage to err on the side of giving too much.) (See also Leviticus 25.8-28; Deuteronomy 24.19-22; Philippians 3.7-16; 1 Timothy 6.17-19.)

Words To Remember: *Do you . . . feel safe and at ease? Everyone bows down to you, and you think you are better than any other nation. But you are in for trouble!* —Amos 6.1

and Gath[u] in Philistia.
Are you greater than any
    of those kingdoms?
[3] You are cruel, and you forget
    the coming day of judgment.

[4] You rich people lounge around
    on beds with ivory posts,
while dining on the meat
    of your lambs and calves.
[5] You sing foolish songs
    to the music of harps,
and you make up new tunes,
    just as David used to do.
[6] You drink all the wine you want
    and wear expensive perfume,
but you don't care about
    the ruin of your nation.[y]
[7] So you will be the first
to be dragged off as captives;
    your good times will end.

[8] The LORD God All-Powerful
    has sworn by his own name:
"You descendants of Jacob
make me angry by your pride,
    and I hate your fortresses.
And so I will surrender your city
and possessions
    to your enemies."

[9] If only ten of you survive
by hiding in a house
    you will still die.
[10] As you carry out a corpse
    to prepare it for burial,[w]
your relative in the house
will ask, "Are there others?"
    You will answer, "No!"
Then your relative will reply,
"Be quiet! Don't dare mention
    the name of the LORD."[x]
[11] At the LORD's command,
houses great and small
    will be smashed to pieces.

[12] Horses can't gallop on rocks;
    oceans[y] can't be plowed.
But you have turned justice
and fairness
    into bitter poison.
[13] You celebrate the defeat
    of Lo-Debar and Karnaim,[z]
and you boast by saying,
    "We did it on our own."

[14] But the LORD God All-Powerful
will send a nation to attack
    you people of Israel.
They will capture Lebo-Hamath
    in the north,
Arabah Creek[a] in the south,
    and everything in between.

A Vision of Locusts

7 The LORD God showed me that he is going to send locusts[b] to attack your crops. It will happen after the king has already been given his share of the grain and before the rest of the grain has been harvested.[c] [2] In my vision the locusts ate every crop in the land, and I said to the LORD, "Forgive me for asking, but how can the nation survive? It's so weak."

[3] Then the LORD felt sorry and answered, "I won't let it be destroyed."

A Vision of Fire

[4] The LORD showed me that he is going to send a ball of fire to burn up everything on earth, including the ocean. [5] Then I said, "Won't you please stop? How can our weak nation survive?"

[6] Again the LORD felt sorry and answered, "I won't let it be destroyed."

A Vision of a Measuring Line

[7] The LORD showed me a vision of himself standing beside a wall and holding a string with a weight tied to the end of it. The string and weight had been used to measure

---

[u]6.2 *Calneh . . . Hamath . . . Gath*: City-states captured by the Assyrians: Calneh in 738 B.C., Hamath in 720, and Gath in 711.   [v]6.6 *your nation*: Hebrew "Joseph's descendants" (see the note at 5.6).   [w]6.10 *prepare . . . burial*: Or "burn it" or "burn incense for it."   [x]6.10 *the name of the LORD*: Two relatives seem to be carrying out corpses for burial. One of them warns the other to be careful not even to say "Thank the LORD!" for fear that the mention of his name may cause something worse to happen.   [y]6.12 *oceans*: Or "rocks."   [z]6.13 *Lo-Debar and Karnaim*: Two cities east of the Jordan River that were captured by Jeroboam II (see 2 Kings 14.25). In Hebrew "Lo-Debar" can mean "nothing," and "Karnaim" means "two horns (of a bull)." Horns were symbols of strength, and the people are bragging about their military power (defeat of "two horns"), which Amos says is "nothing" (Lo-Debar).   [a]6.14 *Lebo-Hamath . . . Arabah Creek*: The northern and southern boundaries of the northern kingdom.   [b]7.1 *locusts*: See the note at 4.9.   [c]7.1 *harvested*: This would have been an especially bad time for a locust attack. The non-grain crops such as vegetables and onions were just beginning to sprout, and the grain crops were almost ready to be harvested.

the straightness of the wall. ⁸Then he asked, "Amos, what do you see?"

"A measuring line," I answered.

The LORD said, "I'm using this measuring line to show that my people Israel don't measure up, and I won't forgive them any more. ⁹Their sacred places will be destroyed, and I will send war against the nation of King Jeroboam."ᵈ

Amos and Amaziah

¹⁰Amaziah the priest at Bethel sent this message to King Jeroboam of Israel, "Amos is plotting against you in the very heart of Israel. Our nation cannot put up with his message for very long. ¹¹Here is what he is saying:

'Jeroboam will be put to death,
and the people will be taken
to a foreign country.' "

¹²Then Amaziah told me, "Amos, take your visions and get out! Go back to Judah and earn your living there as a prophet. ¹³Don't do any more preaching at Bethel. The king worships here at our national temple."

¹⁴I answered:

I'm not a prophet! And I wasn't trained to be a prophet. I am a shepherd, and I take care of fig trees. ¹⁵But the LORD told me to leave my herds and preach to the people of Israel. ¹⁶And here you are, telling me not to preach! ¹⁷Now, listen to what the LORD says about you:

Your wife will become
a prostitute in the city,
your sons and daughters
will be killed in war,
and your land will be divided
among others.
You will die in a country
of foreigners,
and the people of Israel
will be dragged
from their homeland.

A Basket of Fruit

8 The LORD God showed me a basket of ripe fruit ²and asked, "Amos, what do you see?"

"A basket of ripe fruit," I replied. Then he said,

"This is the endᵉ
for my people Israel.
I won't forgive them again.
³Instead of singing
in the temple,
they will cry and weep.
Dead bodies will be everywhere.
So keep silent!
I, the LORD, have spoken!"

Israel Is Doomed

The LORD said:

⁴You people crush those in need
and wipe out the poor.
⁵You say to yourselves,
"How much longer before the end
of the New Moon Festival?
When will the Sabbathᶠ be over?
Our wheat is ready,
and we want to sell it now.
We can't wait to cheat
and charge high prices
for the grain we sell.
We will use dishonest scales
⁶   and mix dust in the grain.
Those who are needy and poor
don't have any money.
We will make them our slaves
for the price
of a pair of sandals."

⁷I, the LORD, won't forget
any of this,
though you take great pride
in your ancestor Jacob.ᵍ
⁸Your country will tremble,
and you will mourn.
It will be like the Nile River
that rises and overflows,
then sinks back down.

⁹On that day, I, the LORD God,
will make the sun
go down at noon,

ᵈ7.9 *Jeroboam:* Jeroboam II, who ruled Israel 783-743 B.C.   ᵉ8.2 *end:* In Hebrew "ripe fruit" and "end" sound alike.   ᶠ8.5 *New Moon Festival . . . Sabbath:* Selling grain at these times was forbidden by the Law of Moses.   ᵍ8.7 *though . . . Jacob:* Or "though I am the God that Jacob proudly worshiped."

and I will turn daylight
    into darkness.
¹⁰ Your festivals and joyful singing
    will turn into sorrow.
You will wear sackcloth[h]
    and shave your heads,
as you would at the death
    of your only son.
    It will be a horrible day.

---

*It isn't the ones who die
with the most toys who win.
It's those who've loved their
families well and know the joy
of having that love returned.
It's those who've known what
it is to spend their lives for a
purpose greater than
themselves. It's those who've
known their God and look
forward to eternity with him.*

RUTH HALEY BARTON

---

¹¹ I, the LORD, also promise you
    a terrible shortage,
    but not of food and water.
You will hunger and thirst
    to hear my message.
¹² You will search everywhere—
    from north to south,
    from east to west.
You will go all over the earth,
    seeking a message
from me, the LORD.
    But you won't find one.

¹³ Your beautiful young women
    and your young men
    will faint from thirst.
¹⁴ You made promises
    in the name of Ashimah,
    the goddess of Samaria.
And you made vows in my name
    at the shrines
    of Dan and Beersheba.[i]

But you will fall
    and never get up.

Judgment on Israel

9 I saw a vision of the LORD
    standing by the temple altar,[j]
    and he said,
"Shake the columns
until the tops fall loose,
    and the doorposts crumble.
Then make the pieces fall
    on the people below.
I will take a sword and kill
    anyone who escapes.

² "If they dig deep into the earth
    or climb to the sky,
    I'll reach out and get them.
³ If they escape to the peaks
    of Mount Carmel,
    I'll search and find them.
And if they hide from me
    at the bottom of the ocean,
I'll command a sea monster
    to bite them.
⁴ I'll send a sword to kill them,
    wherever their enemies
    drag them off as captives.
I'm determined to hurt them,
    not to help them."

His Name Is the LORD

⁵ When the LORD God All-Powerful
    touches the earth, it melts,
    and its people mourn.
God makes the earth rise
    and then fall,
    just like the Nile River.
⁶ He built his palace in the heavens
    and let its foundations
    rest on the earth.[k]
He scoops up the ocean
    and empties it on the earth.
    His name is the LORD.

---

[h]8.10 *sackcloth:* A rough, dark-colored cloth made from goat or camel hair and used to make grain sacks. It was worn in times of trouble or sorrow.   [i]8.14 *You made . . . Beersheba:* Or "You made promises to the goddess Ashimah at Samaria, and you made vows in the names of other gods at the shrines of Dan and Beersheba."   [j]9.1 *the temple altar:* The one at Bethel.   [k]9.6 *He built . . . earth:* One possible meaning for the difficult Hebrew text.

The LORD Is God

7 Israel, I am the LORD God,
and the Ethiopians[l]
are no less important to me
than you are.
I brought you out of Egypt,
but I also brought
the Philistines from Crete[m]
and the Arameans from Kir.[n]
8 My eyes have seen
what a sinful nation you are,
and I'll wipe you out.
But I will leave a few
of Jacob's descendants.
I, the LORD, have spoken!

9 At my command, all of you
will be sifted like grain.
Israelites who remain faithful
will be scattered
among the nations.
And the others will be trapped
like trash in a sifter.
10 Some of you are evil,
and you deny
that you will ever get caught.
But you will be killed.

The LORD's Promise to Israel

11 In the future, I will rebuild
David's fallen kingdom.
I will build it from its ruins
and set it up again,
just as it used to be.

12 Then you will capture Edom
and the other nations
that are mine.
I, the LORD, have spoken,
and my words will come true.

13 You will have such a harvest
that you won't be able
to bring in all of your wheat
before plowing time.
You will have grapes left over
from season to season;
your fruitful vineyards
will cover the mountains.

14 I'll make Israel prosper again.
You will rebuild your towns
and live in them.
You will drink wine
from your own vineyards
and eat the fruit you grow.
15 I'll plant your roots deep
in the land I have given you,
and you won't ever
be uprooted again.
I, the LORD God, have spoken!

[l]**9.7** *Ethiopians:* The Hebrew text has "people of Cush," which was a region south of Egypt that included parts of the present countries of Ethiopia and Sudan. [m]**9.7** *Crete:* Hebrew "Caphtor." [n]**9.7** *Philistines . . . Arameans from Kir:* The Philistines were Israel's enemies to the west, and the Arameans were enemies to the northeast. For Kir, see the note at 1.5.

Obadiah

Family Feuds

Family feuds can cast long shadows. The sibling rivalry between twin brothers Jacob and Esau didn't end with their deaths. Jacob's descendants, the Israelites, continued to be at odds with Esau's descendants, the Edomites. When the Israelites in the southern kingdom of Judah fell captive to Babylon, Edom gloated. Worse, they ambushed the refugees and went on savage looting raids.

The prophet Obadiah made it clear what God thought of such cruelty. But unlike most parents, the Lord doesn't have to sort through claims of "He started it!" or "It was her fault!" (He always knows what *really* happened.) No one reading the story of Israel throughout the Old Testament could imagine Israel to be blameless. But Israel belonged to God. God knew his own people, and he took care of any injustice against them.

Edom's hatred was so persistent that it became a symbol of the hostility of the unbelieving world toward God's people. Obadiah (and other prophets as well) warned of the punishment such enemies of God ultimately would face (Isaiah 11.14; 34.5,6; Ezekiel 35.5; Amos 9.12).

In a world in which ethnic cleansing, domestic violence, and child abuse are topics on the nightly news, justice sometimes seems a long time in coming. As we become increasingly aware of the persecution of Christians around the world, it may seem as if the Edoms of today are winning. But the prophecy of Obadiah assures us that justice will prevail. We have God's word on it.

The book of Obadiah is the shortest in the Old Testament—so short that it wasn't divided into chapters. We know nothing about the prophet who wrote it except his name, which means "servant or worshiper of the Lord."

Obadiah at a Glance

1. The Lord warns prideful Edom of its destruction (1-9)
2. Edom's cruelty (10-14)
3. The Lord will pay back the wicked and reward his people (15-21)

Edom's Pride and Punishment

The LORD God gave Obadiah
a message[a] about Edom,
  and this is what we heard:
"I, the LORD, have sent
  a messenger
with orders for the nations
  to attack Edom."

[2] The LORD said to Edom:
I will make you the weakest
  and most despised nation.
[3] You live in a mountain fortress,[b]
  because your pride
makes you feel safe from attack,
  but you are mistaken.
[4] I will still bring you down,
even if you fly higher
  than an eagle
or nest among the stars.
  I, the LORD, have spoken!

[5] If thieves break in at night,
they steal
  only what they want.
And people who harvest grapes
  always leave some unpicked.
But, Edom, you are doomed!
[6] Everything you treasure most
  will be taken from you.
[7] Your allies can't be trusted.
They will force you out
  of your own country.
Your best friends

will trick and trap you,
  even before you know it.

[8] Edom, when this happens,
I, the LORD, will destroy
  all your marvelous wisdom.
[9] Warriors from the city of Teman[c]
  will be terrified,
and you descendants of Esau[d]
  will be wiped out.

The LORD Condemns Edom's Cruelty

[10] You were cruel to your relatives,
  the descendants of Jacob.[e]
Now you will be destroyed,
  disgraced forever.
[11] You stood there and watched
as foreigners entered Jerusalem
  and took what they wanted.
In fact, you were no better
  than those foreigners.

[12] Why did you celebrate
when such a dreadful disaster
  struck your relatives?
Why were you so pleased

---

[a]1 *message*: Or "vision."   [b]3 *mountain fortress*: The
Hebrew text has "rocky cliff," which sounds like "Sela,"
the capital of Edom, a fortress city built on a mountain.
[c]9 *Teman*: A famous city in Edom.   [d]9 *descendants of
Esau*: The people of Edom were descendants of Esau,
the brother of Jacob (Israel).   [e]10 *descendants of Jacob*:
Jacob and Esau were brothers (see the note on Esau at
verse 9).

Personal *Concerns*—Should I maintain friendships with non-Christians?
If so, how can I keep from compromising my faith? *(Obadiah 10-14)*

Be supportive, not condemning, when your non-Christian friends face hard times.
God has no use for those who gloat over the misfortunes of others. The Edomites, who
stood by and watched Israel's sufferings without trying to help—or worse, took advantage
of them when they were down—earned God's wrath.

When our non-Christian friends face tough times, it can be tempting to use their
troubles as an object lesson about the consequences of living apart from God, especially if
some of their difficulties arise from their own decisions and behaviors. Like the Edomites,
you might want to stand back and say, "I told you so," or let your silence speak as
eloquently as any words might do.

But instead of imitating the Edomites' behavior, imitate God's compassion. Support
your friends, and help them to find their hope in God. (See also Matthew 22.34-40;
Romans 3.9-20.)

Words To Remember: *They are my people, and you were cruel to them. . . .
The day is coming when I, the LORD, will judge.—Obadiah 13,15*

when everyone in Judah
was suffering?
[13] They are my people,
and you were cruel to them.
You went through their towns,
sneering and stealing
whatever was left.
[14] In their time of torment,
you ambushed refugees
and handed them over
to their attackers.

The LORD Will Judge the Nations

[15] The day is coming
when I, the LORD,
will judge the nations.
And, Edom, you will pay in full
for what you have done.

[16] I forced the people of Judah[f]
to drink the wine of my anger
on my sacred mountain.
Soon the neighboring nations
must drink their fill—
then vanish without a trace.

Victory for Israel

[17] The LORD's people who escape
will go to Mount Zion,
and it will be holy.
Then Jacob's descendants
will capture the land of those
who took their land.
[18] Israel[g] will be a fire,

and Edom will be straw
going up in flames.
The LORD has spoken!

[19] The people of Israel
who live in the Southern Desert
will take the land of Edom.
Those who live in the hills
will capture Philistia,
Ephraim, and Samaria.
And the tribe of Benjamin
will conquer Gilead.

[20] Those who return from captivity
will control Phoenicia
as far as Zarephath.[h]
Captives from Jerusalem
who were taken to Sepharad[i]
will capture the towns
of the Southern Desert.
[21] Those the LORD has saved
will live on Mount Zion
and rule over Edom.[j]
Then the kingdom will belong
to the LORD.

---

[f]16 *I forced . . . Judah*: Or "I will force the people of
Edom."   [g]18 *Israel*: Hebrew "The descendants of Jacob
and of Joseph."   [h]20 *Those who return . . . Zarephath*:
One possible meaning for the difficult Hebrew text.
[i]20 *Sepharad*: Possibly the city of Sardis, the capital of
Lydia, a country north and west of Media. This would
refer to those captives from Judah who had been taken
beyond the kingdom of Babylonia.   [j]21 *Those the
LORD . . . Edom*: Or "Leaders on (from) Mount Zion will
save the people and rule over Edom."

Jonah
God's Runaway

Life was good for Jonah. He was a prophet to God's people in Israel (the ten tribes known to us today as the "northern kingdom"). Israel's main enemy was Assyria, whose capital city was Nineveh, some six hundred miles to the northeast. Not only were they powerful, but they were known for their intense cruelty in taking prisoners. In the midst of this, Jonah had a grand message from God. Israel would be expanding its borders (2 Kings 14.25). That expansion was already happening. King Jeroboam was a great military success, but the nation was very idolatrous.

So God gave Jonah a job: to go to Nineveh and tell them about God. Jonah did what every patriotic, strong-minded hero would do: He ran the other way!

What follows is one of the most captivating stories in Scripture. We can see ourselves at almost every turn. Have you ever wished that, just for a while, you could get away from your responsibilities as a Christian? Maybe if you stay away from his people and go where nobody knows you, God will forget you for a bit? (He doesn't.) Have you ever felt that you don't have time to pray, don't feel inclined to anyway, and maybe God doesn't care? (How about spending three days tucked inside a God-prepared great fish?) Have you ever wished someone would get the divine wrath he deserves and at a place where you could stand back and watch? (Jonah did, but God chose mercy instead of wrath.) Have you ever been so disappointed with life that you wanted to die?

(Jonah was, and God brought him a comforting vine and quiet conversation.)

Jonah is so human that we find ourselves smiling all the way through the book—because we recognize ourselves. But it's Jonah's God who shines through the pages. He's a God of great mercy, a wealth of kindness, and persistent love.

Jonah at a Glance
1. God calls, and Jonah runs away (1)
2. Jonah apologizes to God—from inside a fish (2)
3. Jonah preaches to Nineveh; the people repent (3)
4. Jonah sets up watch, hoping to see God destroy Nineveh (4.1-5)
5. A vine, a worm, a wind, and a talk with God (4.6-11)

Jonah Runs from the LORD

1 One day the LORD told Jonah, the son of Amittai, ²to go to the great city of Nineveh*a* and say to the people, "The LORD has seen your terrible sins. You are doomed!"

³Instead, Jonah ran from the LORD. He went to the seaport of Joppa and bought a ticket on a ship that was going to Spain. Then he got on the ship and sailed away to escape.

⁴But the LORD made a strong wind blow, and such a bad storm came up that the ship was about to be broken to pieces. ⁵The sailors were frightened, and they all started praying to their gods. They even threw the ship's cargo overboard to make the ship lighter.

All this time, Jonah was down below deck, sound asleep. ⁶The ship's captain went to him and said, "How can you sleep at a time like this? Get up and pray to your God! Maybe he will have pity on us and keep us from drowning."

⁷Finally, the sailors got together and said, "Let's ask our gods to show us*b* who caused all this trouble." It turned out to be Jonah.

⁸They started asking him, "Are you the one who brought all this trouble on us? What business are you in? Where do you come from? What is your country? Who are your people?"

⁹Jonah answered, "I'm a Hebrew, and I worship the LORD God of heaven, who made the sea and the dry land."

¹⁰When the sailors heard this, they were frightened, because Jonah had already told them he was running from the LORD. Then they said, "Do you know what you have done?"

¹¹The storm kept getting worse, until finally the sailors asked him, "What should we do with you to make the sea calm down?"

¹²Jonah told them, "Throw me into the sea, and it will calm down. I'm the cause of this terrible storm."

¹³The sailors tried their best to row to the shore. But they could not do it, and the

---

*a*1.2 *Nineveh:* Capital city of Assyria, a hated enemy of Israel. *b*1.7 *ask . . . show us:* The Hebrew text has "cast lots," which were pieces of wood or stone used to find out how and when to do something. In this case, the lots would show who was the guilty person.

PARENTING&*family*—How can I raise a child to be kind and considerate of others? (*Jonah 1*)

Remind your child that God cares about everyone.
Babies are born self-centered. It's a matter of survival. If they don't cry, no one knows they're hungry. If no one feeds them, they don't live. God made babies that way, but he doesn't intend for them to stay selfish for a lifetime. So he gave us an example: himself.

Jonah saw that example firsthand. It started out as a rather unattractive message. God told him to go to Nineveh and say, "The LORD has seen your terrible sins. You are doomed!" But Jonah saw the motivation underneath that message. God cared about the people of Nineveh. The only problem was, Jonah didn't. As far as Jonah was concerned, he hoped God would doom them soon and forever. He worried that if the people of Nineveh heard a message from the real, true God, maybe they'd believe him and repent. And what would his kind, compassionate God do then? Jonah didn't want to take that risk.

So Jonah ran away. In a wonderful twist of God's humor, Jonah wound up having a bunch of frightened, pagan sailors beg him to tell them about his God. So he did—as appropriately as possible in the middle of a ship-shattering storm. The sailors believed and immediately "prayed to the LORD" (1.14).

God led Jonah into a place where he could share his faith, whether he wanted to or not. Part of your children's growing up is learning to share things, including toys, time, money, and the good news of God's love. You can teach your child each of these at the appropriate stages, keeping in mind God himself as the example. (See also Matthew 5.43-48; Luke 10.25-37; 3 John 4-11.)

Words To Remember: *Jonah answered, "I'm a Hebrew, and I worship the LORD God of heaven, who made the sea and the dry land."*—Jonah 1.9

storm kept getting worse every minute. ¹⁴So
they prayed to the LORD, "Please don't let us
drown for taking this man's life. Don't hold
us guilty for killing an innocent man. All of
this happened because you wanted it to."
¹⁵Then they threw Jonah overboard, and the
sea calmed down. ¹⁶The sailors were so terrified that they offered a sacrifice to the LORD
and made all kinds of promises.

¹⁷The LORD sent a big fish to swallow Jonah, and Jonah was inside the fish for three
days and three nights.

Jonah's Prayer

2 From inside the fish, Jonah prayed to
the LORD his God:

²When I was in trouble, LORD,
I prayed to you,
    and you listened to me.
From deep in the world
    of the dead,
I begged for your help,
    and you answered my prayer.

³You threw me down
    to the bottom of the sea.
The water was churning
    all around;

I was completely covered
    by your mighty waves.
⁴I thought I was swept away
    from your sight,
never again to see
    your holy temple.

⁵I was almost drowned
by the swirling waters
    that surrounded me.
Seaweed had wrapped
    around my head.
⁶I had sunk down below
    the underwater mountains;
I knew that forever,
    I would be a prisoner there.

But, you, LORD God,
    rescued me from that pit.
⁷When my life was slipping away,
    I remembered you—
and in your holy temple
    you heard my prayer.

⁸All who worship worthless idols
turn from the God
    who offers them mercy.
⁹But with shouts of praise,
I will offer a sacrifice
    to you, my LORD.

Personal *Concerns*—**When a poor decision on my part has damaged my reputation as a Christian, what can I do?** *(Jonah 2,3)*

Remember, God is a God of second chances.
Your reputation may be hard to reclaim with people, but not with God—if you make reclaiming your relationship with him your top priority. The book of Jonah is full of God's second chances. First, Jonah nearly drowned, as he must have thought he would. After all, it was his idea that the sailors throw him overboard (1.12). He said that seaweed had wrapped around his head, and he had "sunk down below the underwater mountains." He expected to be a prisoner there forever (2.5,6). But God gave him a second chance at life—in the form of a large fish.

Jonah also got a second chance to worship God. Prior to his rescue by means of a fish, Jonah had been running from God. But three days confined in tight quarters gave him plenty of time to pray. By the end of his prayer, Jonah was ready to go back to work—and God gave him a second chance to go to Nineveh. This time Jonah went.

But God's second chances were not just for Jonah. After hearing Jonah's message, the king of Nineveh said to his people, "You must also pray to the LORD God with all your heart and stop being sinful and cruel" (3.7-9). Once again God offered a second chance—this time to the people of Nineveh. God will do the same for you, if you ask him. (See also Joel 2.12-17; Micah 7.18,19; Zechariah 10.6-12; Luke 7.36-50; Galatians 1.11-24.)

Words To Remember: *When I was in trouble, LORD, I prayed to you, and you listened to me. . . . I begged for your help, and you answered my prayer.—Jonah 2.2*

I will keep my promise,
because you are the one
with power to save.

¹⁰The LORD commanded the fish to vomit up Jonah on the shore. And it did.

Jonah Goes to Nineveh

3 Once again the LORD told Jonah ²to go to that great city of Nineveh and preach his message of doom.

³Jonah obeyed the LORD and went to Nineveh. The city was so big that it took three days just to walk through it. ⁴After walking for a day, Jonah warned the people, "Forty days from now, Nineveh will be destroyed!"

⁵They believed God's message and set a time when they would go without eating to show their sorrow. Then everyone in the city, no matter who they were, dressed in sackcloth.

⁶When the king of Nineveh heard what was happening, he also dressed in sackcloth; he left the royal palace and sat in dust.ᶜ ⁷⁻⁹Then he and his officials sent out an order for everyone in the city to obey. It said:

None of you or your animals may eat or drink a thing. Each of you must wear sackcloth, and you must even put sackcloth on your animals.

> *God has assigned the right timing for every event in your life.*
> KAY MARSHALL STROM

You must also pray to the LORD God with all your heart and stop being sinful and cruel. Maybe God will change his mind and have mercy on us, so we won't be destroyed.

¹⁰When God saw that the people had stopped doing evil things, he had pity and did not destroy them as he had planned.

ᶜ**3.5,6** *dressed in sackcloth . . . sat in dust:* Sackcloth was a rough, dark-colored cloth made from goat or camel hair and used to make grain sacks. Sometimes people wore sackcloth and sat in dust to show how sorry they were for their sins.

Personal *Concerns*—Sometimes I'm jealous of others. How can I get out of the jealousy/envy trap? *(Jonah 4)*

Practice contentment instead of anger.

Envy is a restless disease. It's what happens when you walk into a friend's lovely home and instead of enjoying it as one of God's kind gifts to her, you mentally grouse, *After this, how can I go back to my own cracker-box house?* Or, you enter church alone (as usual) and see a three-generation family side-by-side. Instead of whispering a prayer of thanks to God for his work in their lives, you grumble, *My family is so split up, we can't even sit together at the dinner table, let alone church.* Envy breeds discontent and anger.

The closing chapter of this book finds Jonah full of anger. He had no reason for envy; God had been most generous in giving him second chances. But Jonah didn't want that same blessing for the people of Nineveh. In fact, he was so angry about God's kindness to Nineveh that three times he said, "I wish I were dead!" (4.8). Jonah might have been down in the city celebrating the wonderful forgiveness of God and nurturing the faith of new believers into maturity. But Jonah preferred that God not extend his grace to foreigners. His anger led him to devalue life itself.

Envy is like that. It causes us to forget about the good God has brought us and eventually to hate our own life. Don't get caught in that trap. Contentment with thanksgiving is the antidote for envy. (See also 1 Samuel 20; Psalm 73.1-20; James 3.1-12.)

Words To Remember: *You are a kind and merciful God, and you are very patient. You always show love.*—Jonah 4.2

Jonah Gets Angry at the LORD

4 Jonah was really upset and angry. [2]So he prayed:

Our LORD, I knew from the very beginning that you wouldn't destroy Nineveh. That's why I left my own country and headed for Spain. You are a kind and merciful God, and you are very patient. You always show love, and you don't like to punish anyone, not even foreigners.

[3]Now let me die! I'd be better off dead.

[4]The LORD replied, "What right do you have to be angry?"

[5]Jonah then left through the east gate of the city and made a shelter to protect himself from the sun. He sat under the shelter, waiting to see what would happen to Nineveh.

[6]The LORD made a vine grow up to shade Jonah's head and protect him from the sun. Jonah was very happy to have the vine, [7]but early the next morning the LORD sent a worm to chew on the vine, and the vine dried up. [8]During the day the LORD sent a scorching wind, and the sun beat down on Jonah's head, making him feel faint. Jonah was ready to die, and he shouted, "I wish I were dead!"

[9]But the LORD asked, "Jonah, do you have the right to be angry about the vine?"

"Yes, I do," he answered, "and I'm angry enough to die."

[10]But the LORD said:

You are concerned about a vine that you did not plant or take care of, a vine that grew up in one night and died the next. [11]In that city of Nineveh there are more than a hundred twenty thousand people who cannot tell right from wrong, and many cattle are also there. Don't you think I should be concerned about that big city?

---

*Spiritual*Life—How can I reach out to a needy world? (*Jonah 4.5-11*)

Try to see the world through God's eyes.

A speaker at your church urges people to cook dinner once a month for a local homeless shelter. Habitat for Humanity wants to build four low-cost homes in your neighborhood. Your daughter wants to spend next summer helping AIDS patients in Rwanda. You have the opportunity to vote for or against a candidate who will cut services to legal and illegal aliens. What will you consider as you respond to these issues?

We all have a strong sense of self-protection. Peel away the surface layers of polite good behavior and underneath we find the question, "What's in it for me?" Or, conversely, "Could I be hurt by this?" We want to laugh at Jonah sulking in the shade of his God-provided vine. But Jonah had every reason to ask those self-protective questions. He could definitely be hurt by God's kindness to this capital city. In fact, years later in 722 B.C., Assyria flooded Israel with troops, conquered the nation, deported the people, and resettled the land with aliens. Jonah may have had those fears in mind as he watched Nineveh and hoped for God's judgment.

But God saw it differently. He saw a body of people who couldn't tell right from wrong but had called on him for mercy. Jonah needed that same view, and so do we.
(See also 2 Samuel 9; Nehemiah 5.1-13; Lamentations 2.11-13; Zechariah 7.7-13; Matthew 6.1-4; Luke 9.10-17.)

Words To Remember: *But the LORD said: . . . In that city of Nineveh there are more than a hundred twenty thousand people who cannot tell right from wrong, and many cattle are also there. Don't you think I should be concerned about that big city?* —Jonah 4.10,11

Micah

Do Justice, Show Mercy, and Walk Humbly with Your God

"The LORD God has told us what is right and what he demands: 'See that justice is done, let mercy be your first concern, and humbly obey your God'" (6.8). In this well-known verse from Micah we discover the heart of the book: *Doing* right is more important to God than talking about it. In Micah's day, believers would worship, then blatantly hurt people immediately afterward. They must have thought being God's people covered them—but bad behavior is bad, no matter who chooses it.

The book of Micah switches among several speakers: God's prophet Micah, God, and the people. But all encourage the reader to choose God's radically refreshing lifestyle. They focus on honoring God rather than doing the standard religious thing. They give us advice: to refuse greed, embrace justice, have mercy, and humbly obey God.

Micah was first addressed to Samaria, the capital city of Israel, and to Jerusalem, the capital citiy of Judah (1.1). The leadership of these religious and national centers had led people to cheat the poor and worship pagan gods rather than honor the Lord. Micah's words prompted hearers to let God settle arguments, pound swords and spears into rakes and shovels, make war extinct, and find rest beneath their own trees (4.3,4).

Long reigns by Jeroboam II in the nation of Israel and by Uzziah in Judah brought great wealth and security, but mainly for the powerful and rich. Greed, hypocrisy, and injustice had destroyed the people from the inside out. Micah placed more emphasis on Judah than Israel as shown by the kings noted (1.1) and was undoubtedly a younger contemporary of Isaiah.

How does Micah apply to us today?

It brings both God's judgment and hope—but each prompts us toward good. Although Micah's words aren't easy to swallow, they produce a wonderful aftertaste. He urges devoted-to-God living (6.8), foretells universal peace (4.1-4), and perhaps most exciting of all, foresees the birthplace of Jesus (5.2). Micah, a hard-hitting but compassionate servant, decided to "always follow the LORD our God" (4.5) in whatever he did—and you can, too.

Micah at a Glance

1. God punishes cruel behavior, even by believers (1.1—2.11)
2. Hope remains, because punishment is meant to restore us to God (2.12,13)
3. God uncovers evil and lies (3.1-11)
4. Belief doesn't offer protection (3.11,12)
5. Peace, led by God, will come (4)
6. Bethlehem hosts the birth of God's ruler (5.1-4)
7. God promises judgment on Israel's enemies (5.5-15)
8. God finds Israel guilty because of her disloyal choices (6.1—7.7)
9. A look ahead to the time when God's people will turn back to him and honor him (7.8-20)

1 I am Micah from Moresheth.*a* And this is the message about Samaria and Jerusalem*b* that the LORD gave to me when Jotham, Ahaz, and Hezekiah*c* were the kings of Judah.

Judgment on Samaria

2 Listen, all of you!
Earth and everything on it,
   pay close attention.
The LORD God accuses you
   from his holy temple.*d*
3 And he will come down
to crush underfoot
   every pagan altar.

In prayer, we are coming to Almighty God, the Creator of the universe, the King of kings and Lord of lords. He is also our Father.

RUTH BELL GRAHAM

4 Mountains will melt
beneath his feet
   like wax beside a fire.
Valleys will vanish like water
   rushing down a ravine.
5 This will happen because of
the terrible sins of Israel,
   the descendants of Jacob.
Samaria has led Israel to sin,
and pagan altars at Jerusalem
   have made Judah sin.

6 So the LORD will leave Samaria
   in ruins—
merely an empty field
   where vineyards are planted.
He will scatter its stones
   and destroy its foundations.
7 Samaria's idols will be smashed,
   and the wages
of temple prostitutes*e*
   will be destroyed by fire.
Silver and gold from those idols
will then be used by foreigners
   as payment for prostitutes.

Judah Is Doomed

8 Because of this tragedy,*f*
   I go barefoot and naked.
My crying and weeping
sound like howling wolves
   or ostriches.
9 The nation is fatally wounded.
Judah is doomed.
   Jerusalem will fall.

10 Don't tell it in Gath!
   Don't even cry.
Instead, roll in the dust
   at Beth-Leaphrah.*g*
11 Depart naked and ashamed,
   you people of Shaphir.*h*
The town of Bethezel*i* mourns
because no one from Zaanan*j*
   went out to help.*k*
12 Everyone in Maroth*l*
   hoped for the best,
but the LORD sent disaster
   down on Jerusalem.

13 Get the war chariots ready,
   you people of Lachish.*m*
You led Jerusalem into sin,

---

*a*1.1 *Moresheth*: A town in southern Judah not far from Gath. In verse 14 it is called Moresheth-Gath. *b*1.1 *Samaria and Jerusalem*: Samaria was the capital of the northern kingdom (Israel), and Jerusalem was the capital of the southern kingdom (Judah). *c*1.1 *Jotham, Ahaz, and Hezekiah*: Jotham, the son of Uzziah, ruled Judah 740-736 B.C.; Ahaz, the son of Jotham, ruled 736-716 B.C.; Hezekiah, the son of Ahaz, ruled 716-687 B.C. *d*1.2 *holy temple*: Possibly the one in heaven, though it may be the Jerusalem temple. *e*1.7 *wages of temple prostitutes*: At pagan temples, people had sex with prostitutes as a way of worshiping the idols, and the money earned in this way was used to support the pagan religion. *f*1.8 *this tragedy*: Either the destruction of Samaria (verses 6, 7) or the coming destruction of Judah and Jerusalem. *g*1.10 *Gath . . . Beth-Leaphrah*: Gath was a Philistine city; Beth-Leaphrah is unknown, but in Hebrew it sounds like "House of Dust." *h*1.11 *Shaphir*: Mentioned only here in the Old Testament; in Hebrew "Shaphir" means "beautiful." *i*1.11 *Bethezel*: Mentioned only here in the Old Testament; in Hebrew "Bethezel" means "house next door." *j*1.11 *Zaanan*: Mentioned only here in the Old Testament; in Hebrew "Zaanan" means "one who goes out." *k*1.11 *The town . . . help*: Or "No one from Zaanan refused to desert their town, and Bethezel mourns because it is left undefended." *l*1.12 *Maroth*: Mentioned only here in the Old Testament; in Hebrew "Maroth" means "bitter." *m*1.13 *Lachish*: The chief city of southwest Judah, about thirty miles from Jerusalem.

just as Israel did.^{n}
^{14}Now you will have to give
a going-away gift^o
to Moresheth.^{p}
Israel's kings will discover
that they cannot trust
the town of Achzib.^{q}

^{15}People of Mareshah,^{r}
the LORD will send someone
to capture your town.
Then Israel's glorious king
will be forced to hide
in Adullam Cave.^{s}
^{16}Judah, shave your head
as bald as a buzzard
and start mourning.
Your precious children^t
will be dragged off
to a foreign country.

Punishment for Those Who Abuse Their Power

2 Doomed! You're doomed!
At night you lie in bed,
making evil plans.
And when morning comes,
you do what you've planned
because you have the power.
^{2}You grab any field or house
that you want;
you cheat families
out of homes and land.

^{3}But here is what the LORD says:
"I am planning trouble for you.
Your necks will be caught
in a noose,
and you will be disgraced
in this time of disaster."

^{4}When that happens,
this sorrowful song
will be sung about you:
"Ruined! Completely ruined!
The LORD has taken our land
and given it to traitors."^{u}
^{5}And so you will never again
own property
among the LORD's people.

^{6}"Enough of your preaching!"
That's what you tell me.
"We won't be disgraced,
so stop preaching!"

^{7}Descendants of Jacob,
is it right for you to claim
that the LORD did what he did
because he was angry?
Doesn't he always bless
those who do right?
^{8}My people, you have even stolen
clothes right off the backs
of your unsuspecting soldiers
returning home from battle.
^{9}You take over lovely homes
that belong to the women
of my nation.
Then you cheat their children
out of the inheritance
that comes from the LORD.^{v}

^{10}Get out of here, you crooks!
You'll find no rest here.
You're not fit to belong
to the LORD's people,
and you will be destroyed.^{w}
^{11}The only prophet you want
is a liar who will say,
"Drink and get drunk!"

A Promise of Hope

^{12}I, the LORD, promise
to bring together
the people of Israel
who have survived.
I will gather them,

---

^{n}**1.13** *led . . . sin . . . did:* Or "You led Jerusalem and Israel into sin." In Hebrew "Lachish" sounds like "a team of horses (that pulls a war chariot)." And the sin may be that Lachish led the nation to trust the power of war chariots instead of the LORD. But the sin could be idolatry or some false teachings that were brought in from Egypt by way of Lachish. ^{o}**1.14** *going-away gift:* The gift (dowry) that a bride's father gave her when she left the home of her parents to live with the family of her husband. In Hebrew the word for "bride" or "fiancee" sounds like "Moresheth." ^{p}**1.14** *Moresheth:* Hebrew "Moresheth-Gath"; the home of Micah (see verse 1). ^{q}**1.14** *Achzib:* Meaning "lie" or "deception" was near Adullam Cave (verse 15), where David hid from King Saul (see 1 Samuel 22.1, 2). Micah probably means that the people of Israel (including their king) will have to run for their lives, but will find that all hope for escape is merely a "lie" (see verse 15). ^{r}**1.15** *Mareshah:* Sounds something like the Hebrew word for "conqueror" and was only a few miles northeast of Lachish. ^{s}**1.15** *Adullam Cave:* See the note at 1.14. ^{t}**1.16** *precious children:* The towns mentioned in verses 10-15. ^{u}**2.4** *The LORD . . . traitors:* One possible meaning for the difficult Hebrew text. ^{v}**2.9** *inheritance . . . LORD:* The Hebrew text has "my glory," which refers to the inheritance of land that the LORD had promised his people. ^{w}**2.10** *destroyed:* One possible meaning for the difficult Hebrew text.

just as a shepherd
brings sheep together,
    and there will be many.
[13] I will break down the gate
and lead them out—
    then I will be their king.

Evil Rulers and Lying Prophets

3 Listen to me,
        you rulers of Israel!
    You know right from wrong,
[2] but you prefer to do evil
        instead of what is right.
You skin my people alive.
You strip off their flesh,
[3]   break their bones,
        cook it all in a pot,
        and gulp it down.

[4] Someday you will beg the LORD
        to help you,
    but he will turn away
        because of your sins.

[5] You lying prophets promise
security for anyone
    who gives you food,
but disaster for anyone
    who refuses to feed you.
Here is what the LORD says
    to you prophets:
[6] "You will live in the dark,
far from the sight of the sun,
    with no message from me.
[7] You prophets and fortunetellers
will all be disgraced,
    with no message from me."

[8] But the LORD has filled me
    with power and his Spirit.
I have been given the courage
    to speak about justice
and to tell you people of Israel
    that you have sinned.
[9] So listen to my message,
    you rulers of Israel!
You hate justice
    and twist the truth.
[10] You make cruelty and murder
    a way of life in Jerusalem.
[11] You leaders accept bribes
    for dishonest decisions.
You priests and prophets
teach and preach,
    but only for money.

Then you say,
"The LORD is on our side.
    No harm will come to us."
[12] And so, because of you,
Jerusalem will be plowed under
    and left in ruins.

*God is just, which means
"righteous." It's a word that
is pure and established on
unchanging truth and
ultimately serves our
highest interest.*

PATSY CLAIRMONT

Thorns will cover the mountain
    where the temple now stands.

Peace and Prosperity

4 In the future, the mountain
    with the LORD's temple
        will be the highest of all.
It will reach above the hills,
and every nation
    will rush to it.
[2] People of many nations
    will come and say,
"Let's go up to the mountain
of the LORD God of Jacob
    and worship in his temple."

The LORD will teach us his Law
from Jerusalem,
    and we will obey him.
[3] He will settle arguments
between distant
    and powerful nations.
They will pound their swords
and their spears
    into rakes and shovels;
they will never again make war
    or attack one another.
[4] Everyone will find rest
beneath their own fig trees
    or grape vines,
and they will live in peace.
This is a solemn promise
    of the LORD All-Powerful.

⁵Others may follow their gods,
but we will always follow
the LORD our God.

The LORD Will Lead His People Home

⁶The LORD said:
At that time
I will gather my people—
the lame and the outcasts,
and all into whose lives
I have brought sorrow.
⁷Then the lame and the outcasts
will belong to my people
and become a strong nation.
I, the LORD, will rule them
from Mount Zion forever.
⁸Mount Zion in Jerusalem,
guardian of my people,
you will rule again.

⁹Jerusalem, why are you crying?
Don't you have a king?
Have your advisors gone?
Are you suffering
like a woman in childbirth?
¹⁰Keep on groaning with pain,
you people of Jerusalem!
If you escape from your city
to the countryside,
you will still be taken
as prisoners to Babylonia.

But later I will rescue you
from your enemies.

¹¹Zion, because of your sins
you are surrounded
by many nations who say,
"We can hardly wait
to see you disgraced."ˣ
¹²But they don't know
that I, the LORD,
have gathered them here
to grind them like grain.
¹³Smash them to pieces, Zion!
I'll let you be like a bull
with iron horns
and bronze hoofs.
Crush those nations
and bring their wealth to me,
the LORD of the earth.

A Promised Ruler

5 Jerusalem, enemy troops
have surrounded you;ʸ
they have struck Israel's ruler
in the face with a stick.

ˣ**4.11** *We . . . disgraced*: Or "We'll pull up your skirt and expose your nakedness!" ʸ**5.1** *Jerusalem . . . you*: Or "Jerusalem, you are slashing yourself in sorrow, because of the enemy troops."

Personal *Concerns*—How can I handle even difficult times positively?
(*Micah* 4.1-5)

Realize your story's not over yet.
This world is unfair. Sad and horrible things happen. Sweet children die, and beloved spouses get sick. God neither likes nor blesses these scenes. But he will bring a happy ending to them. In a good novel you have to keep reading to get to the end. Similarly, in life we have to keep walking through the mud and muck, the joy and delight. Keep a good attitude through both, an attitude based on God's power. Neither whine nor fake it. Instead look forward to the future when God's rule will be obvious.

In the future, people of many nations will worship God. They'll let God teach them. God will settle arguments. He'll guide them to reshape war instruments into farming tools since no one will have any need for war. Each person will find security under his or her own tree. There'll be peace at last.

So even when times are tough, keep turning the pages of life. And no matter what choices anyone else makes, always follow the Lord, your God. Through the muck and the majesty, he'll be your foundation and light. And one day, one very definite day, fairness and peace will reign. (See also Leviticus 26.1-13; Job 23; Nahum 1.2-7,15; Romans 8.18-30; Ephesians 1.7-23.)

Words To Remember: *Everyone will find rest . . . and they will live in peace. This is a solemn promise of the LORD All-Powerful.*—Micah 4.4

²Bethlehem Ephrath,
you are one of the smallest towns
in the nation of Judah.
But the LORD will choose
one of your people
to rule the nation—
someone whose family
goes back to ancient times.^z
³The LORD will abandon Israel
only until this ruler is born,
and the rest of his family
returns to Israel.
⁴Like a shepherd
taking care of his sheep,
this ruler will lead
and care for his people
by the power and glorious name
of the LORD his God.
His people will live securely,
and the whole earth will know
his true greatness,
⁵because he will bring peace.

Assyria Will Be Defeated

Let Assyria attack our country
and our palaces.
We will counterattack,
led by a number of rulers
⁶whose strong army will defeat
the nation of Assyria.^a

Yes, our leaders will rescue us,
if those Assyrians
dare to invade our land.

The Survivors Will Be Safe

⁷A few of Jacob's descendants
survived and are scattered
among the nations.
But the LORD will let them
cover the earth like dew and rain
that refreshes the soil.
⁸At present they are scattered,
but later they will attack,
as though they were fierce lions
pouncing on sheep.
Their enemies will be torn
to shreds,
with no one to save them;
⁹they will be helpless,
completely destroyed.

Idols Will Be Destroyed in Israel

¹⁰The LORD said:
At that time I will wipe out
your cavalry and chariots,

---

^z**5.2** *family . . . times*: Or "kingdom is eternal."
^a**5.6** *the nation of Assyria*: The Hebrew text uses both "land of Assyria" and "land of Nimrod," which was a poetic name for Assyria.

Personal *Concerns*—How can I overcome my tendency to worry and instead gain confidence about the future? *(Micah 5.2-5)*

Know what's been and watch for what's coming.
Worry isn't always bad; you simply have to let it lead you to action. If you don't spend some time thinking about what bothers you, you won't find out what God wants you to do about it.

Perhaps you worry about insignificance. You wonder if your actions in your little corner of the world make any difference. Remember, Jesus was born in a humanly insignificant town named Bethlehem. But by God's standards it was very significant because he chose to be born there. And one day, this same Jesus will come again to personally take you to heaven!

Let Micah 5.2 remind you that your smallest action frequently carries eternal significance. Your care for your family members, students, or coworkers will impact the way they treat others, which impacts the way those others treat their families, students, and coworkers. You can change this world for or against Jesus through small-by-this-world actions that carry eternal-by-God's-Word significance. (See also Joshua 23.14-16; Psalm 91; Habakkuk 3.16-19; Matthew 6.25-34; Philippians 4.4-9.)

Words To Remember: *Like a shepherd taking care of his sheep, this ruler will lead and care for his people by the power and glorious name of the LORD his God. His people will live securely, and the whole earth will know his true greatness, because he will bring peace.—Micah 5.4,5*

Miriam

Exodus 2.1-10; 15.19-21; Numbers 12; 20.1; Deuteronomy 24.8,9;
1 Chronicles 6.3; Micah 6.4

*A*lthough Miriam appears mostly in earlier books of the Bible, it's intriguing that many hundreds of years later, Micah used her position and importance to get a point across to the people. Miriam was a member of the trio who worked together to lead God's people from Egyptian slavery. The Lord said that he "sent Moses, Aaron, and Miriam" to lead his people from slavery in Egypt (Micah 6.4). Miriam's younger brothers were Aaron, the first high priest, and the great Moses.

The Bible's record of Miriam began with her watching over her baby brother Moses. Jewish babies in Egypt were being systematically killed when Miriam helped save Moses' life. Their mother had hidden Moses until he could be hidden no longer; then she placed him in a basket in the Nile River and asked Miriam to watch him. Pharaoh's daughter found the baby floating in the river and decided to raise him as her own. In those days before formula, Miriam slyly volunteered to find a wet nurse to feed the baby. Moses' own mother became the one who fed him daily.

In the company of two well-known brothers who were great servants of God (which could have intimidated her), Miriam is a beautiful example of the value of behind-the-scenes discipleship. If as a child she had not worked within God's plan, Moses might have died as an infant. Because Miriam cared for her brother, Moses grew to be a man, discovered his Hebrew heritage, and answered God's appointment to lead the Hebrews away from slavery. For nearly four hundred years, the Hebrews had prayed for release. Moses, Aaron, and Miriam became the answer to those prayers. Exodus 15.19-21 records Miriam's leading the Hebrew women in a victory dance over their new freedom.

But Miriam wasn't perfect. Like many people, Miriam could be too quick to speak. She and Aaron criticized Moses for the woman he married. Why? They said it was the woman's race—but actually it was jealousy against Moses (see Numbers 12.2). Moses was the youngest, yet he got more attention than the older siblings. God was so angry at this attitude that he struck Miriam with leprosy, a horrible skin disease. Showing his humble character, Moses begged God to heal her. God did, but only after making Miriam an example.

Miriam died while journeying through the desert toward the Promised Land. During her life she showed her ability to solve problems, celebrate God's action, and work as a team with her brothers. She also too quickly spoke wrong opinions. How does God want you to be like—and different from—Miriam?

¹¹ as well as your cities
    and your fortresses.
¹² I will stop you
    from telling fortunes
    and practicing witchcraft.
¹³ You will no longer worship
    the idols or stone images
        you have made—
    I will destroy them,
¹⁴ together with the sacred poles*ᵇ*
    and even your towns.
¹⁵ I will become furious
    and take revenge on the nations
    that refuse to obey me.

The LORD's Challenge to His People

6 The LORD said to his people:
    Come and present your case
        to the hills and mountains.
² Israel, I am bringing charges
        against you—
    I call upon the mountains
    and the earth's firm foundation
        to be my witnesses.

³ My people, have I wronged you
    in any way at all?
    Please tell me.

⁴ I rescued you from Egypt,
    where you were slaves.
    I sent Moses, Aaron, and Miriam
        to be your leaders.
⁵ Don't forget the evil plans
    of King Balak of Moab
    or what Balaam son of Beor*ᶜ*
        said to him.
    Remember how I, the LORD,
        saved you many times
    on your way from Acacia
        to Gilgal.*ᵈ*

True Obedience

⁶ What offering should I bring
    when I bow down to worship
        the LORD God Most High?
    Should I try to please him*ᵉ*
    by sacrificing
        calves a year old?

---

*ᵇ***5.14** *sacred poles*: Used in the worship of Asherah,
the fertility goddess.   *ᶜ***6.5** *Balak . . . Beor*: See
Numbers 22–24.   *ᵈ***6.5** *Acacia to Gilgal*: Acacia was
where the Israelites camped after the experience with
Balaam (see Numbers 25.1; Joshua 2.1; 3.1); Gilgal was
where they camped while waiting to attack Jericho (see
Joshua 4.19—5.12).   *ᵉ***6.6** *try to please him*: This refers
to what are traditionally called "burnt sacrifices," which
were offered as a way of pleasing the LORD.

---

*Spiritual*Life—**What does God expect of me?** *(Micah 6.6-8)*

Be truly devoted, not outwardly religious.
If a little is good, more must be better, reasoned the prophet Micah, tongue-in-cheek. If
God wanted sacrifices, let's give him more and bigger ones. Lots of calves. Thousands of
sheep. Rivers of oil. Why, we could even give him our first-born children to show that we
really love him!

But as Micah knew, none of this outward giving really shows what's inside. Anyone can
go to church or tithe large portions of their income to God. But that person could have
absolutely no care for God.

People might be impressed at such dramatic displays, but God isn't. The three actions
that show true devotion to God are justice, mercy, and humble obedience. These aren't
easy actions, but they can change the course of history. What would happen if every person
chose to be fair and honest? What would happen in marriages and families if every person
mercifully forgave while expecting excellence? Who would doubt God's existence if
believers quietly did right in God's name? Conversely, what damage is done when believers
cheat, hold grudges, and insist on a showy display of religiosity?

God expects three things of you: to see that justice is done; to let mercy be your first
concern; and to humbly obey your God. (See also Exodus 20.1-17; Judges 5.1-11;
Jeremiah 1.4-19; Romans 8.1-17; 1 Corinthians 6.12-20.)

Words To Remember: *God has told us what is right and what he demands: "See
that justice is done, let mercy be your first concern, and humbly obey your God."*
—**Micah 6.8**

⁷Will thousands of sheep
  or rivers of olive oil
    make God satisfied with me?
Should I sacrifice to the LORD
my first-born child as payment
    for my terrible sins?
⁸The LORD God has told us
what is right
  and what he demands:
"See that justice is done,
let mercy be your first concern,
    and humbly obey your God."

Cheating and Violence

⁹I am the LORD,
and it makes sense to respect
    my power to punish.
So listen to my message
  for the city of Jerusalem:*ʲ*
¹⁰You store up stolen treasures
  and use dishonest scales.*ᵍ*
¹¹But I, the LORD, will punish you
for cheating with weights
  and with measures.
¹²You rich people are violent,
  and everyone tells lies.

¹³Because of your sins,
I will wound you and leave you
  ruined and defenseless.
¹⁴You will eat,
  but still be hungry;
you will store up goods,
  but lose everything—
I, the LORD, will let it all
  be captured in war.
¹⁵You won't harvest what you plant
or use the oil
  from your olive trees
or drink the wine
  from grapes you grow.

¹⁶Jerusalem, this will happen
  because you followed
the sinful example
  of kings Omri and Ahab.*ʰ*
Now I will destroy you
  and your property.
Then the people of every nation
  will make fun and insult you.

Israel Is Corrupt

7 I feel so empty inside—
like someone starving
   for grapes or figs,

after the vines and trees
  have all been picked clean.
²No one is loyal to God;
  no one does right.
Everyone is brutal
and eager to deceive
  everyone else.
³People cooperate to commit crime.
Judges and leaders demand bribes,
  and rulers cheat in court.*ⁱ*
⁴The most honest of them
  is worse than a thorn patch.

Your doom has come!
Lookouts sound the warning,
  and everyone panics.
⁵Don't trust anyone,
  not even your best friend,
and be careful what you say
  to the one you love.

⁶Sons refuse to respect
  their own fathers,
daughters rebel against
  their own mothers,
and daughters-in-law despise
  their mothers-in-law.
Your family is now your enemy.
⁷But I trust the LORD God
  to save me,
and I will wait for him
  to answer my prayer.

The Nation Turns to God

⁸My enemies, don't be glad
  because of my troubles!
I may have fallen,
  but I will get up;
I may be sitting in the dark,
  but the LORD is my light.
⁹I have sinned against the LORD.
And so I must endure his anger,
  until he comes to my defense.
But I know that I will see him

---

*ʲ*6.9 *Jerusalem*: One possible meaning for the difficult Hebrew text of verse 9. *ᵍ*6.10 *scales*: One possible meaning for the difficult Hebrew text of verse 10. *ʰ*6.16 *Omri and Ahab*: King Ahab was the son of Omri and the husband of the evil Jezebel. Almost two centuries before Micah, the prophet Elijah had spoken against the idolatry and the other sinful practices that Ahab had encouraged in Israel (see 1 Kings 16.21-34; 18.1-18; 21.1-26). *ⁱ*7.3 *court*: One possible meaning for the difficult Hebrew text of verse 3.

making things right for me
and leading me to the light.

[10] You, my enemies, said,
"The LORD God is helpless."
Now each of you
will be disgraced
and put to shame.
I will see you trampled
like mud in the street.

A Bright Future

[11] Towns of Judah, the day is coming
when your walls will be rebuilt,
and your boundaries enlarged.
[12] People will flock to you
from Assyria and Egypt,
from Babylonia[j]
and everywhere else.
[13] Those nations will suffer disaster
because of what they did.

Micah's Prayer and the LORD's Answer

[14] Lead your people, LORD!
Come and be our shepherd.
Grasslands surround us,
but we live in a forest.
So lead us to Bashan and Gilead,[k]

and let us find pasture
as we did long ago.

[15] I, the LORD, will work miracles
just as I did when I led you
out of Egypt.
[16] Nations will see this
and be ashamed because
of their helpless armies.
They will be in shock,
unable to speak or hear,
[17] because of their fear of me,
your LORD and God.
Then they will come trembling,
crawling out of their fortresses
like insects or snakes,
lapping up the dust.

No One Is Like God

The people said:

[18] Our God, no one is like you.
We are all that is left
of your chosen people,

---

[j]**7.12** *Babylonia*: The Hebrew text has "the river,"
meaning the Euphrates River, which stood for Babylonia.
[k]**7.14** *Bashan and Gilead*: Two regions east of the Jordan
River, known for their fertile pasturelands.

Personal *Concerns*—When a poor decision on my part has damaged my reputation as a Christian, what can I do? *(Micah 7.18,19)*

Realize you can't change the past, but you can change the present.
God gets rid of our sins forever. That's both freeing and hard to believe. How can God forgive you when you've done such terrible things? He forgives because he loves you. You matter more than anything you've done or refused to do. God's forgiveness says more about him than about what you've done. God forgives so you can make loving decisions from this point forward. He forgives to free you to do the good he wants you to do. He then equips you to make those good choices.

Receive God's forgiveness not because you deserve it, but because you need it. Obey God not because you'll lose his love without obedience, but because you want to please the one who loves you.

Even though God gets rid of our sins forever, people might not forget. That's the rough and painful part. But before you write off the person who's angry with you, see things from her viewpoint. Perhaps you broke a treasured trust. Tell her how you feel: "I've let you down. I'd be really upset with me if I were you. Please know I don't take this lightly. Let's work together to heal this. You're important to me." Then find a way to show that your repentance has led to changed behavior. It takes time to rebuild trust, but do right consistently—no matter how long it takes. (See also Joel 2.12-17; Jonah 2,3; Zechariah 10.6-12; Luke 7.36-50; Galatians 1.11-24.)

Words To Remember: *God, no one is like you. . . . You freely forgive our sin and guilt. . . . You will trample on our sins and throw them in the sea.*—Micah 7.18,19

and you freely forgive
  our sin and guilt.
You don't stay angry forever;
  you're glad to have pity
[19]   and pleased to be merciful.
You will trample on our sins

and throw them in the sea.
[20] You will keep your word
  and be faithful to Jacob
    and to Abraham,
  as you promised our ancestors
    many years ago.

Nahum

Doom to the Crime Capital

Two high-school girls stood outside a public library as they prepared for a youth group meeting. As part of their planned program, they videotaped people's response to the question, "What do you look for in a friend?" Almost without exception, their respondents—male and female, young, old, and middle-aged—mentioned loyalty.

It's comforting *and* surely biblical to know that God is a friend who's always faithful. But sometimes we forget that God demands loyalty from us as well (1.2). God's friends demonstrate their relationship to him by living in trusting dependence on him. Those who are not loyal to God are not his friends.

The people of Nineveh, the capital of Assyria, were not God's friends. In this book, the prophet Nahum declared God's anger against Nineveh in language that makes us quake. Such open talk of revenge might make us uncomfortable, but Nahum reminds us, "The LORD is powerful, yet patient" (1.3). Nineveh had had its warning: The prophet Jonah came to them years before with a message of judgment unless they repented. Even then, Nineveh represented such brutality that Jonah longed for their destruction, not their repentance. The Ninevites did stop their wickedness for a while, and God withheld his judgment on them (Jonah 3.10).

But by the time of Nahum's prophecy (probably about one hundred years after Jonah's message), Nineveh and the rest of Assyria had turned from God and against God's people. They destroyed the capital of Israel in 722 B.C. They attempted to destroy Jerusalem. They were idolaters and the "crime capital" of the Near East (3.1). The Lord God had been patient, but at last God's enemies were going to get what they deserved. In 612 B.C. Nineveh was destroyed by Babylonian invaders.

The book of Nahum reminds us that the God who is our faithful, merciful friend is also an avenging power against those who reject him. They who underestimate God's justice are foolish: "The LORD is good. He protects those who trust him in times of trouble. But like a roaring flood, the LORD chases his enemies into dark places and destroys them. So don't plot against the LORD!" (1.7-9).

Nahum at a Glance

1. God's complete power to punish or protect (1)
2. The punishment facing Nineveh (2)
3. The reasons for Nineveh's punishment (3)

1 I am Nahum from Elkosh.[a] And this is the message[b] that I wrote down about Nineveh.[c]

The Fierce Anger of the LORD

2 The LORD God demands loyalty.
In his anger, he takes revenge
  on his enemies.
3 The LORD is powerful,
  yet patient;
he makes sure that the guilty
  are always punished.
He can be seen in storms
  and in whirlwinds;
clouds are the dust from his feet.

4 At the LORD's command,
  oceans and rivers dry up.
Bashan, Mount Carmel,
and Lebanon[d] wither,
  and their flowers fade.
5 At the sight of the LORD,
  mountains and hills
  tremble and melt;
the earth and its people
  shudder and shake.
6 Who can stand the heat
  of his furious anger?
It flashes out like fire
  and shatters stones.

The Power of Assyria Will Be Broken

7 The LORD is good.
He protects those who trust him
  in times of trouble.
8 But like a roaring flood,

the LORD chases his enemies
  into dark places
  and destroys them.
9 So don't plot against the LORD!
He wipes out his enemies,
  and they never revive.
10 They are like drunkards
  overcome by wine,
or like dry thornbushes
  burning in a fire.[e]
11 Assyria, one of your rulers
has made evil plans
  against the LORD.

12 But the LORD says, "Assyria,
  no matter how strong you are,
  you are doomed!
My people Judah,
I have troubled you before,
  but I won't do it again.
13 I'll snap your chains
  and set you free
  from the Assyrians."

14 Assyria, this is what else
  the LORD says to you:
"Your name will be forgotten.
I will destroy every idol
  in your temple,

---

[a]1.1 *Elkosh:* The location of Elkosh is not known.
[b]1.1 *message:* Or "vision."   [c]1.1 *Nineveh:* The capital of Assyria, the hated enemy of Israel.   [d]1.4 *Bashan, Mount Carmel, and Lebanon:* Three regions noted for their trees and flowers.   [e]1.10 *fire:* One possible meaning for the difficult Hebrew text of verse 10.

Personal *Concerns*—How can I handle even difficult times positively?
(Nahum 1.2-7,15)

Don't dwell on revenge.

Nothing eats away at us like dwelling on the wrongs others have done to us. The more we focus on how unfairly we've been treated, the more angry we get at the world, and the more self-pitying we become. If you've ever been around someone obsessed with getting even, you know just how unhappy—and unpleasant to be with—she is.

God can free you from worrying about what punishments are due to others. He takes full responsibility for rewarding the faithful and punishing the guilty. You don't have to give it a second thought! Instead, build a more positive outlook by celebrating the good news of God's peace (1.15). (See also Leviticus 26.1-13; Job 23; Micah 4.1-5; Romans 8.18-30; Ephesians 1.7-23.)

Words To Remember: *The LORD is powerful, yet patient; he makes sure that the guilty are always punished. He can be seen in storms and in whirlwinds; clouds are the dust from his feet.—Nahum 1.3*

and I will send you to the grave,
because you are worthless."

15 Look toward the mountains,
people of Judah!
Here comes a messenger
with good news of peace.
Celebrate your festivals.
Keep your promises to God.
Your evil enemies are destroyed
and will never again
invade your country.

Nineveh Will Fall

2 Nineveh, someone is coming
to attack and scatter you.
Guard your fortresses!
Watch the road! Be brave!
Prepare for battle!
2 Judah and Israel are like trees
with branches broken
by their enemies.
But the LORD is going to restore
their power and glory.

> *We do not understand joy
> until we face sorrow, faith
> until it is tested, peace until
> faced with conflict, love
> until it is lost, hope until
> confronted with doubts.*
>
> BARBARA JOHNSON

*3 Nineveh, on this day of attack,
your enemies' shields are red;
their uniforms are crimson.
4 Their horses[f] prance,
and their armored[g] chariots
dart around like lightning
or flaming torches.
5 An officer gives a command.
But his soldiers stumble,
as they hasten to build
a shelter to protect themselves
against rocks thrown down
from the city wall.

6 The river gates[h] fly open,
and panic floods the palace.
7 Nineveh is disgraced.
The queen is dragged off.
Her servant women mourn;
they sound like doves,
and they beat their breasts
in sorrow.[i]
8 Nineveh is like a pond
with leaking water.
Shouts of "Stop! Don't go!"
can be heard everywhere.
But everyone is leaving.

9 Enemy soldiers shout,
"The city is full of treasure
and all kinds of wealth.
Steal her silver! Grab her gold!"

10 Nineveh is doomed! Destroyed!
Her people tremble with fear;
their faces turn pale.[j]
11 What happened to this city?
They were safer there
than powerful lions in a den,
with no one to disturb them.
12 These are the same lions
that ferociously attacked
their victims,
then dragged away the flesh
to feed their young.

13 The LORD All-Powerful
is against you, Nineveh.
God will burn your chariots
and send an army to kill
those young lions of yours.
You will never again
make victims of others
or send messengers to threaten
everyone on this earth.

Punishment for Nineveh

The LORD said:

3 Doom to the crime capital!
Nineveh, city of murder
and treachery,

---

f **2.4** *horses:* Two ancient translations; Hebrew "spears."
g **2.4** *armored:* One possible meaning for the difficult
Hebrew text.   *h* **2.6** *river gates:* Nineveh was protected
by a moat filled with water from the nearby Tigris River.
i **2.7** *sorrow:* One possible meaning for the difficult
Hebrew text of verse 7.   *j* **2.10** *faces turn pale:* Or "ashes
cover their faces."

2 here is your fate—
cracking whips,
  churning wheels;
galloping horses,
  roaring chariots;
3 cavalry attacking,
  swords and spears flashing;
soldiers stumbling
  over piles of dead bodies.
4 You were nothing more
  than a prostitute
using your magical charms
and witchcraft
  to attract and trap nations.

5 But I, the LORD All-Powerful,
  am now your enemy.
I will pull up your skirt
and let nations and kingdoms
  stare at your nakedness.
6 I will cover you with garbage,
  treat you like trash,
  and rub you in the dirt.
7 Everyone who sees you
  will turn away and shout,
"Nineveh is done for!
Is anyone willing to mourn
  or to give her comfort?"

Nineveh's Fate Is Sealed

8 Nineveh, do you feel safer
  than the city of Thebes?[k]
The Nile River
  was its wall of defense.[l]
9 Thebes trusted the mighty power
  of Ethiopia[m] and Egypt;
the nations of Put[n] and Libya
  were her allies.
10 But she was captured and taken
  to a foreign country.
Her children were murdered
  at every street corner.
The members of her royal family
  were auctioned off,
and her high officials
  were bound in chains.

11 Nineveh, now it's your turn!
  You will get drunk and try to hide
    from your enemy.
12 Your fortresses are fig trees
  with ripe figs.
Merely shake the trees,
  and fruit will fall
    into every open mouth.

13 Your army is weak.
Fire has destroyed the crossbars
  on your city gates;
now they stand wide open
  to your enemy.

14 Your city is under attack.
Haul in extra water!
  Strengthen your defenses!
Start making bricks!
  Stir the mortar!
15 You will still go up in flames
  and be cut down by swords
that will wipe you out like wheat
  attacked by grasshoppers.
So, go ahead and increase
  like a swarm of locusts![o]

16 More merchants are in your city
  than there are stars
    in the sky—
but they are like locusts
  that eat everything,
    then fly away.
17 Your guards and your officials
  are swarms of locusts.
On a chilly day
  they settle on a fence,
but when the sun comes out,
they take off
  to who-knows-where.

18 King of Assyria,
  your officials and leaders
    sleep the eternal sleep,
while your people are scattered
  in the mountains.
Yes, your people are sheep
  without a shepherd.
19 You're fatally wounded.
  There's no hope for you.
But everyone claps
  when they hear this news,
because your constant cruelty
  has caused them pain.

---

k3.8 *Thebes*: In 663 B.C., the Assyrian King Ashurbanipal captured this Egyptian city, which seems to have been built with protection similar to that of Nineveh.
l3.8 *was its . . . defense*: One possible meaning for the difficult Hebrew text. m3.9 *Ethiopia*: The Hebrew text has "Cush," which was a region south of Egypt that included parts of the present countries of Ethiopia and Sudan. n3.9 *Put*: A region in Africa, possibly part of the present country of Libya. o3.15 *locusts*: A type of grasshopper that comes in swarms and causes great damage to plant life.

Habakkuk

Trust During Chaos

Why do the righteous suffer? Why do the evil prosper? God must hear these questions millions of times. They are asked not just by students of theology, philosophy, and ethics, but even by your next-door neighbor, who wonders why the drug dealer down the street drives a better car than she does.

They are also Habakkuk's questions, which he presented (appropriately) to God. Habakkuk was a prophet to the people of Judah, yet he saw evil all around him. He complained because he felt the Lord was not listening to his pleas for help. He also felt the legal system was faulty—that honest people could never win their cases (1.2,4). Judah must have been a difficult place for a prophet of the living God.

What did Habakkuk expect? He must have hoped God would say, "I'm going to stop all this nonsense. I'll get these bad guys locked up so the rest of you can live in peace. And while I'm about it, I'll get rid of those nasty neighbors of yours, the Babylonians. I wouldn't want you to worry about having them run you over some day."

God's answer must have startled Habakkuk as much as it would have startled us. God's time of patient endurance with his wayward people was running out. He would *use* the Babylonians not only to destroy the evil people among the Israelites, but also to destroy the whole land.

What follows is a conversation between this godly prophet and his Lord. Habakkuk's closing hymn of faith is an inspiration to anyone who has suffered deep loss and wonders if it's still possible to trust God. When devastation weighs us down so heavily that it's hard to get out of bed, let alone stand up and do our normal work, we can remember the final lines of Habakkuk's prayer in 3.19: "He makes my feet as sure as those of a deer, and he helps me stand on the mountains."

Habakkuk at a Glance

1. Habakkuk asks God why he allows evil to continue in his nation (1.1-4)
2. God answers that he'll send the Babylonians to wipe out the nation—and the evil (1.5-11)
3. Habakkuk argues that the Babylonians are even more evil than the Israelites (1.12-17)
4. God answers, "You're doomed," to four kinds of evil people (2.1-17)
5. A contrast between idols and the living God (2.18-20)
6. Habakkuk's prayer of praise and trust (3)

1

I am Habakkuk the prophet. And this is the message*a* that the LORD gave me.

Habakkuk Complains to the LORD

2 Our LORD, how long must I beg
for your help
before you listen?
How long before you save us
from all this violence?
3 Why do you make me watch
such terrible injustice?
Why do you allow violence,
lawlessness, crime, and cruelty
to spread everywhere?
4 Laws cannot be enforced;
justice is always the loser;
criminals crowd out honest people
and twist the laws around.

The LORD Answers Habakkuk

5 Look and be amazed
at what's happening
among the nations!
Even if you were told,
you would never believe
what's taking place now.
6 I am sending the Babylonians.
They are fierce and cruel—
marching across the land,
conquering cities and towns.

7 How fearsome and frightening.
Their only laws and rules
are the ones they make up.
8 Their cavalry troops are faster
than leopards,
more ferocious than wolves
hunting at sunset,
and swifter than hungry eagles
suddenly swooping down.

9 They are eager to destroy,*b*
and they gather captives
like handfuls of sand.
10 They make fun of rulers
and laugh at fortresses,
while building dirt mounds
so they can capture cities.*c*
11 Then suddenly they disappear
like a gust of wind—
those sinful people who worship
their own strength.

---

*a***1.1** *message:* Or "vision."   *b***1.9** *eager to destroy:*
One possible meaning for the difficult Hebrew text.
*c***1.10** *dirt mounds . . . cities:* Attacking armies often
build dirt mounds against city walls to make it
easier for them to climb the wall and capture
the city.

---

*Spiritual*Life—Is it okay to be angry at God? *(Habakkuk 1.2-5)*

Be angry at what angers God.
Habakkuk's world gave him much to be angry about. His nation had existed some four
hundred years, three hundred years since the civil war that separated it from the northern
kingdom. But recent years had seen ever-increasing evil in the land. Manasseh had been the
most wicked king in their history—and he led the people in the same direction. Josiah had
discovered *The Book of God's Law* hidden in the temple and had instituted reforms toward
godliness, but that ended with his sudden death. Kings (his three sons and one grandson)
following him didn't last long. After the biblical record of each came the terse words that
each one disobeyed the Lord (see 2 Kings 23.32,37; 24.9,19).

So Habakkuk complained to God. He used words like *violence, terrible injustice, lawlessness, crime, cruelty.* He complained that laws could not be enforced; that justice was always
the loser; and that criminals twisted the laws to their own advantage (Habakkuk 1.4). He
knew that these conditions offended God even more than they offended him. He knew that
God already joined him in his anger.

When we see evil and injustice around us, it's perfectly appropriate to feel anger and to
express that anger to God. God is holy, and he has all power. God may choose to honor our
prayers by taking action against these wrongs, but we must await his timing. **(See also**
Numbers 20.1-13; Job 19; Psalm 10.)

Words To Remember: *Our LORD, how long must I beg for your help before you
listen? How long before you save us from all this violence?*—Habakkuk 1.2

Habakkuk Complains Again

[12] Holy LORD God, mighty rock,[d]
you are eternal,
    and we[e] are safe from death.
You are using those Babylonians
    to judge and punish others.[f]
[13] But you can't stand sin or wrong.
So don't sit by in silence
    while they gobble down people
who are better than they are.

[14] The people you put on this earth
are like fish or reptiles
    without a leader.
[15] Then an enemy comes along
and takes them captive
    with hooks and nets.
It makes him so happy
[16] that he offers sacrifices
    to his fishing nets,
because they make him rich
    and provide choice foods.
[17] Will he keep hauling in his nets
and destroying nations
    without showing mercy?

The LORD Answers Habakkuk Again

2 While standing guard
    on the watchtower,
  I waited for the LORD's answer,
before explaining the reason
    for my complaint.[g]
[2] Then the LORD told me:
"I will give you my message
    in the form of a vision.
Write it clearly enough
    to be read at a glance.
[3] At the time I have decided,
    my words will come true.
You can trust what I say
    about the future.
It may take a long time,
but keep on waiting—
    it will happen!

[4] "I, the LORD, refuse to accept
anyone who is proud.
Only those who live by faith
    are acceptable to me."[h]

Trouble for Evil People

[5] Wine[i] is treacherous,
and arrogant people
    are never satisfied.

They are no less greedy
    than death itself—
they open their mouths as wide
as the world of the dead
    and swallow everyone.

[6] But they will be mocked
with these words:
    You're doomed!
You stored up stolen goods
and cheated others
    of what belonged to them.
[7] But without warning,
those you owe
    will demand payment.
Then you will become
    a frightened victim.
[8] You robbed cities and nations
everywhere on earth
    and murdered their people.
Now those who survived
    will be as cruel to you.

[9] You're doomed!
You made your family rich
    at the expense of others.
You even said to yourself,
    "I'm above the law."
[10] But you will bring shame
    on your family
and ruin to yourself
    for what you did to others.
[11] The very stones and wood
in your home
    will testify against you.

[12] You're doomed! You built a city
    on crime and violence.
[13] But the LORD All-Powerful
    sends up in flames
what nations and people
    work so hard to gain.

[14] Just as water fills the sea,
    the land will be filled

---

[d]**1.12** *mighty rock*: The Hebrew text has "rock," which is sometimes used in poetry to compare the LORD to a mountain where his people can run for protection from their enemies.   [e]**1.12** *we*: Hebrew; one ancient Jewish tradition "you."   [f]**1.12** *You . . . others*: Or "You will judge and punish those Babylonians."
[g]**2.1** *I . . . complaint*: One possible meaning for the difficult Hebrew text.   [h]**2.4** *Only . . . me*: Or "But those who are acceptable to me will live because of their faithfulness."   [i]**2.5** *Wine*: The Standard Hebrew Text; the Dead Sea Scrolls "Wealth."

with people who know
and honor the LORD.

¹⁵You're doomed!
You get your friends drunk,
just to see them naked.
¹⁶Now you will be disgraced
instead of praised.
The LORD will make you drunk,
and when others see you naked,
you will lose their respect.
¹⁷You destroyed trees and animals
on Mount Lebanon;
you were ruthless to towns
and people everywhere.
Now you will be terrorized.

Idolatry Is Foolish

¹⁸What is an idol worth?
It's merely a false god.
Why trust a speechless image
made from wood or metal
by human hands?
¹⁹What can you learn from idols
covered with silver or gold?
They can't even breathe.
Pity anyone who says to an idol
of wood or stone,
"Get up and do something!"

²⁰Let all the world be silent—
the LORD is present
in his holy temple.

Habakkuk's Prayer

3 This is my prayer:ʲ
²I know your reputation, LORD,
and I am amazed
at what you have done.
Please turn from your anger
and be merciful;
do for us what you did
for our ancestors.

³You are the same Holy God
who came from Teman
and Paranᵏ to help us.
The brightness of your glory
covered the heavens,

ʲ3.1 *prayer*: The Hebrew text adds "according to the shigionoth," which may mean a prayer of request or a prayer to be accompanied by a special musical instrument. ᵏ3.3 *Teman . . . Paran*: Teman is a district in Edom, but the name is sometimes used of the whole country of Edom; Paran is the hill country along the western border of the Gulf of Aqaba. In Judges 5.4, the LORD is said to have marched from Edom to help his people; in Deuteronomy 33.2, Paran is mentioned in connection with the LORD's appearance at Sinai.

WORK—How can I deal with a dishonest coworker? (Habakkuk 2.4-17)

Remember, dishonesty often brings its own punishment.
Your friend at work constantly comes in late—and fakes her time sheet. A coworker in your department takes home office supplies. Your boss suggests you cut projected expenses when you present your proposal next week so it's more likely to be accepted. A colleague charges personal lunches on her corporate credit card or makes long-distance personal calls on company phones.

Honest work is an ongoing challenge. You can't be an honesty cop for every person in your company; but if the occasion and the relationship warrant it, it won't hurt to point out possible results of dishonesty: "Somebody might notice that office supplies are missing when they do inventory at the end of the year." "I thought you might want to know that the boss carefully checks the telephone charges."

When your own supervisor suggests dishonesty, the situation is more personal—and more difficult. It may help to describe potential results of the dishonesty in a way that shows your boss how it might backfire. "Our bottom line might suffer" or, "Additional expenses will be hard to explain after the project is finished and may jeopardize future projects."

God hates dishonesty. His prophecy to Habakkuk shows that dishonesty brings its own disaster. Be impeccably honest at work. Perhaps your coworkers will follow your example. (See also Psalm 26; Proverbs 28.11-26; Amos 2.)

Words To Remember: *Only those who live by faith are acceptable to me.*
—Habakkuk 2.4

and your praises were heard
    everywhere on earth.
[4]Your glory shone like the sun,
    and light flashed from your hands,
        hiding your mighty power.
[5]Dreadful diseases and plagues
    marched in front
        and followed behind.
[6]When you stopped,
    the earth shook;
when you stared,
    nations trembled;
when you walked
    along your ancient paths,
eternal mountains and hills
    crumbled and collapsed.
[7]The tents of desert tribes
    in Cushan and Midian[l]
        were ripped apart.

[8]Our LORD, were you angry
    with the monsters
        of the deep?[m]
You attacked in your chariot
    and wiped them out.
[9]Your arrows were ready
    and obeyed your commands.[n]

You split the earth apart
    with rivers and streams;
[10]mountains trembled
    at the sight of you;
rain poured from the clouds;
    ocean waves roared and rose.
[11]The sun and moon stood still,
    while your arrows and spears
        flashed like lightning.

[12]In your furious anger,
    you trampled on nations
[13]to rescue your people
    and save your chosen one.[o]
You crushed a nation's ruler
    and stripped his evil kingdom
        of its power.[p]
[14]His troops had come like a storm,

[l]**3.7** *Cushan and Midian*: Tribes of the Arabian desert who were enemies of Israel.   [m]**3.8** *monsters of the deep*: The Hebrew text has "rivers and oceans," which may stand for the powerful monsters that were thought to have lived there before the LORD defeated them. [n]**3.9** *obeyed your commands*: One possible meaning for the difficult Hebrew text.   [o]**3.13** *chosen one*: Or "chosen ones."   [p]**3.13** *You crushed . . . power*: One possible meaning for the difficult Hebrew text.

Personal *Concerns*—How can I overcome my tendency to worry and instead gain confidence about the future? *(Habakkuk 3.16-19)*

Trust God to give you strength.
If you're a chronic worrier, you probably use a lot of tricks to keep from getting buried in fear. One trick may be to ask, "What is the worst-case scenario in this particular situation?" With that image fresh in your mind, you plot how you would deal with the outcome. After that, any lesser harm seems simple. But it's still worrisome. Chronic worriers have a hard time actually letting go of their worries.

Habakkuk's message from God was not just a worry, it was a promise—from God. His country was going to be destroyed. Habakkuk pictured how his country would look: the barren fields, the dead trees, the empty animal stalls. He might have waved his arms and cried, "I can't take it; let me die before this happens." But he didn't.

Instead, Habakkuk sang a prayer of praise to God. He recounted God's past goodness in rescuing his people (3.12). He told God how his fears made him feel: "My bones seemed to melt, and I stumbled around" (3.16). Then he described the worst-case scenario—and sang of his committed trust in God.

Worriers, take heart. Even when the worst happens, God will give you strength.
(See also Joshua 23.14-16; Psalm 91; Micah 5.2-5; Matthew 6.25-34; Philippians 4.4-9.)

Words To Remember: *Fig trees may no longer bloom, or vineyards produce grapes; olive trees may be fruitless, and harvest time a failure; sheep pens may be empty, and cattle stalls vacant—but I will still celebrate because the LORD God saves me. The LORD gives me strength. He makes my feet as sure as those of a deer, and he helps me stand on the mountains.*—Habakkuk 3.17-19

hoping to scatter us
  and glad to gobble us down.
To them we were refugees
  in hiding—
but you smashed their heads
  with their own weapons.*q*
¹⁵ Then your chariots churned
  the waters of the sea.

Habakkuk's Response to God's Message

¹⁶ When I heard this message,*r*
I felt weak from fear,
  and my lips quivered.
My bones seemed to melt,
  and I stumbled around.
But I will patiently wait.
Someday those vicious enemies
  will be struck by disaster.*s*

Trust in a Time of Trouble

¹⁷ Fig trees may no longer bloom,
  or vineyards produce grapes;

olive trees may be fruitless,
  and harvest time a failure;
sheep pens may be empty,
  and cattle stalls vacant—
¹⁸ but I will still celebrate
because the LORD God
  saves me.
¹⁹ The LORD gives me strength.
He makes my feet as sure
  as those of a deer,
and he helps me stand
  on the mountains.*t*

To the music director:
Use stringed instruments.

---

*q***3.14** *but you . . . weapons:* One possible meaning for the difficult Hebrew text.   *r***3.16** *heard this message:* Or "saw this vision."   *s***3.16** *I will . . . disaster:* One possible meaning for the difficult Hebrew text.   *t***3.19** *stand on the mountains:* One possible meaning for the difficult Hebrew text.

Zephaniah God's Singing

History repeats itself, or perhaps human nature just doesn't learn from the past. Certainly the history of God's people seems to follow a familiar pattern: times of faith followed by disobedience and judgment, then faith again. It was true of Israel, and now in Zephaniah's day it appeared that Judah would follow in Israel's steps: judgment before renewal.

Like Israel, Judah had become spiritually bankrupt (3.1-4,7). Rather than being a light to the nations, Judah adopted the pagan worship of her neighbors. So God prepared to take Judah to court, so to speak, for not living up to her end of the covenant between them. Evidence for his case was everywhere. For example, pagan astral religions were so popular (1.4,5) that God's people erected altars to worship the stars—even granting official protection to those who practiced magic arts! Clearly God's people had forsaken him. Now God was coming as the primary witness, prosecutor, and judge in the case of the people of Judah vs. the Creator of the heavens—the sun, the moon, and the stars.

Zephaniah was the man God chose to subpoena Judah (1.1). This prophet was possibly the great-great-grandson of godly King Hezekiah. God called Zephaniah to rebuke the people's faithlessness and warn them that "the great day of the LORD" was coming (1.14-17).

Have you ever thought the God of the Old Testament and the God of the New seem like two different Gods: one of wrath and one of love? Then hear Zephaniah's closing words about how willing God is to forgive those who turn from their sin (3.15,17): "Zion, your punishment is over. The LORD has forced your enemies to turn and retreat. Your LORD is King of Israel and stands at your side; you don't have to worry about any more troubles. . . . He celebrates and sings because of you, and he will refresh your life with his love."

Perhaps God is allowing you to experience a difficult time. You can take comfort in the knowledge that God walks with you in those times—as he walked with Judah. God guards your wholehearted devotion the way a loving husband guards his wife's affection and attention.

Zephaniah probably delivered his message about forty years before the destruction of Jerusalem in 586 B.C. All three chapters are poetry. As you read, note the graphic imagery meant to move listeners to repentance. In ancient cultures with oral traditions, poetry was a respected form of communication. It was easy to memorize and pass on to future generations. God spoke through Zephaniah with poetry so his appeal for them to turn back to him would echo in their hearts.

ॐ

Zephaniah at a Glance

1 I am Zephaniah, the son of Cushi, the grandson of Gedaliah, the great-grandson of Amariah, and the great-great-grandson of Hezekiah.[a]

When Josiah son of Amon was king of Judah,[b] the LORD gave me this message.

Judgment on Judah

[2] I, the LORD, now promise
to destroy everything
on this earth—
[3] people and animals,
birds and fish.
Everyone who is evil
will crash to the ground,[c]
and I will wipe out
the entire human race.
[4] I will reach out to punish
Judah and Jerusalem—
nothing will remain
of the god Baal;[d]
nothing will be remembered
of his pagan priests.
[5] Not a trace will be found
of those who worship stars
from their rooftops,
or bow down to the god Milcom,[e]
while claiming loyalty
to me, the LORD.
[6] Nothing will remain of anyone
who has turned away
and rejected me.

[7] Be silent! I am the LORD God,
and the time is near.
I am preparing
to sacrifice my people
and to invite my guests.
[8] On that day I will punish
national leaders
and sons of the king,
along with all who follow
foreign customs.[f]
[9] I will punish worshipers
of pagan gods[g]

and cruel palace officials
who abuse their power.

[10] I, the LORD, promise
that on that day
noisy crying will be heard
from Fish Gate, New Town,
and Upper Hills.
[11] Everyone in Lower Hollow[h]
will mourn loudly,
because merchants
and moneychangers
will be wiped out.
[12] I'll search Jerusalem with lamps
and punish those people
who sit there unworried
while thinking,
"The LORD won't do anything,
good or bad."
[13] Their possessions will be taken,
their homes left in ruins.
They won't get to live
in the houses they build,
or drink wine from the grapes
in their own vineyards.

A Terrible Day

[14] The great day of the LORD
is coming soon, very soon.
On that terrible day,
fearsome shouts of warriors
will be heard everywhere.

---

[a]**1.1** *Hezekiah:* Ruled 716-687 B.C.   [b]**1.1** *Josiah . . . king of Judah:* Ruled 640-609 B.C.   [c]**1.3** *Everyone . . . ground:* One possible meaning for the difficult Hebrew text.   [d]**1.4** *Baal:* A Caananite fertility god.   [e]**1.5** *Milcom:* An Ammonite fertility god.   [f]**1.8** *follow foreign customs:* Hebrew "wear foreign clothes."   [g]**1.9** *worshipers . . . gods:* The Hebrew text has "all who jump over the threshold," which was a Philistine religious practice (see 1 Samuel 5.5).   [h]**1.10,11** *Fish Gate, New Town, and Upper Hills . . . Lower Hollow:* Names for different sections of Jerusalem: Fish Gate was probably the main gate on the north side of the city; New Town was a newer section; Upper Hills may have been a suburb north of the city; Lower Hollow was probably on the southern edge of town.

15 It will be a time of anger—
    of trouble and torment,
of disaster and destruction,
    of darkness and despair,
of storm clouds and shadows,
16 of trumpet calls
    and battle cries
against fortified cities
    and mighty fortresses.

17 The LORD warns everyone
    who has sinned against him,
"I'll strike you blind!
Then your blood and your insides
    will gush out like vomit.
18 Not even your silver or gold
can save you on that day
    when I, the LORD, am angry.
My anger will flare up
    like a furious fire
scorching the earth
    and everyone on it."

Turn to the LORD

2 You disgraceful nation,
    gather around,
2   before it's too late.
The LORD has set a time
    when his fierce anger
will strike like a storm
    and sweep you away.

3 If you humbly obey the LORD,
    then come and worship him.
If you do right and are humble,
    perhaps you will be safe
on that day when the LORD
    turns loose his anger.

*Understanding God's will
for us isn't always easy.
But believing he is in
charge and has a plan
for our life makes the
journey worth traveling.*

MARIAN V. LIAUTAUD

Judgment on Philistia

4 Gaza and Ashkelon
will be deserted
    and left in ruins.
Ashdod will be emptied
in broad daylight,

---

*Spiritual*Life—Will God really condemn people who don't accept Christ as their Savior? *(Zephaniah 1.14-18)*

Only those who believe in him will be saved.
War is bloody, and there are always casualties. In God's holy war, sin is the enemy that must be completely wiped out. Sin destroys its host the way cancer devours a body. Because God is the author of life, he hates sin and the death it brings with a passion we can only imagine. That's why Zephaniah's imagery is so graphic; the stakes are very high. Nations fight over boundary lines and political ideologies, but God wages war over people's eternal destinies.

Heaven and hell are real places, and we each will spend eternity in one or the other. But God has made it possible for us to be washed clean; he sent Christ to serve the death sentence in our place. The sad fact is that every person is full of sin; there's no possible human way to "fix" ourselves, and we must one day stand before God to account for our thoughts and actions. Faith in Christ is the only way anyone can face God—because only his sacrifice was great enough to match the magnitude of our sin.

God sent Zephaniah to warn the people of Judah. God gives us a similar warning about human sinful nature—and the gift of God's grace. He wants us to share it with others who need to know. (See also Deuteronomy 30; John 3.16-18; John 6.60-69; Romans 10.5-21.)

Words To Remember: *The great day of the LORD is coming soon, very soon.*
—Zephaniah 1.14

and Ekron[i] uprooted.
[5] To you people of Philistia[j]
who live along the coast,
    the LORD has this to say:
"I am now your enemy,
    and I'll wipe you out!"

[6] Your seacoast will be changed
into pastureland
    and sheep pens.[k]
[7] The LORD God hasn't forgotten
those survivors in Judah,
    and he will help them—
his people will take your land
    to use for pasture.
And when evening comes,
they will rest
    in houses at Ashkelon.[l]

Judgment on Moab and Ammon

*[8] The LORD All-Powerful,
    the God of Israel, said:
I've heard Moab and Ammon
insult my people
    and threaten their nation.[m]
[9] And so, I swear by my very life
that Moab and Ammon will end up
    like Sodom and Gomorrah—
covered with thornbushes
    and salt pits forever.
Then my people who survive
    will take their land.
[10] This is how Moab and Ammon
will at last be repaid
    for their pride—
and for sneering at the nation
that belongs to me,
    the LORD All-Powerful.
[11] I will fiercely attack.
Then every god on this earth
    will shrink to nothing,
and everyone of every nation
will bow down to me,
    right where they are.

Judgment on Ethiopia

[12] People of Ethiopia,[n]
    the sword of the LORD
    will slaughter you!

Judgment on Assyria

[13] The LORD will reach to the north
    to crush Assyria
    and overthrow Nineveh.[o]

[14] Herds of wild animals
    will live in its rubble;
all kinds of desert owls
will perch on its stones
    and hoot in the windows.
Noisy ravens will be heard
inside its buildings,
    stripped bare of cedar.[p]
[15] This is the glorious city
that felt secure and said,
    "I am the only one!"
Now it's merely ruins,
    a home for wild animals.
Every passerby simply sneers
and makes vulgar signs.

Sinful Jerusalem

3 Too bad for that disgusting,
        corrupt, and lawless city!
[2] Forever rebellious
        and rejecting correction,
Jerusalem refuses to trust
    or obey the LORD God.
[3] Its officials are roaring lions,
    its judges are wolves;
in the evening they attack,
    by morning nothing is left.
[4] Jerusalem's prophets are proud
    and not to be trusted.
The priests have disgraced
the place of worship
    and abused God's Law.
[5] All who do evil are shameless,
but the LORD does right
    and is always fair.
With the dawn of each day,
    God brings about justice.

[6] The LORD wiped out nations
and left fortresses
    crumbling in the dirt.

---

[i]2.4 *Gaza . . . Ekron*: Gaza, Ashkelon, Ashdod, Ekron, and Gath (not mentioned because it was already destroyed) were the five major Philistine towns. [j]2.5 *people of Philistia*: The Hebrew text also mentions "Canaan" and "Cherethites," which are other ways of referring to the Philistines.   [k]2.6 *pens*: One possible meaning for the difficult Hebrew text of verse 6. [l]2.7 *Ashkelon*: A Philistine town; see the note at 2.4. [m]2.8 *threaten their nation*: Or "boast about their own nation."   [n]2.12 *Ethiopia*: The Hebrew text has "Cush," which was a region south of Egypt that included parts of the present countries of Ethiopia and Sudan.   [o]2.13 *Nineveh*: The capital of Assyria; Nineveh was protected by a moat filled with water from the nearby Tigris River.   [p]2.14 *stripped . . . cedar*: One possible meaning for the difficult Hebrew text.

1047   ZEPHANIAH 3.15

Their streets and towns
were reduced to ruins
    and emptied of people.
[7] God felt certain that Jerusalem
would learn to respect
    and obey him.
Then he would hold back
from punishing the city
    and not wipe it out.
But everyone there was eager
    to start sinning again.

Nations Will Turn to the LORD

[8] The LORD said:
Just wait for the day
    when I accuse you nations.
I have decided on a day,
    when I will bring together
every nation and kingdom
and punish them all
    in my fiery anger.
I will become furious
    and destroy the earth.

[9] I will purify each language
and make those languages
    acceptable for praising me.[q]
Then, with hearts united,
everyone will serve
    only me, the LORD.
[10] From across the rivers
    of Ethiopia,[r]

my scattered people,
my true worshipers,
    will bring offerings to me.

[11] When that time comes,
you won't rebel against me
    and be put to shame.
I'll do away with those
    who are proud and arrogant.
Never will any of them
strut around
    on my holy mountain.
[12] But I, the LORD, won't destroy
    any of your people
who are truly humble
    and turn to me for safety.
[13] The people of Israel who survive
will live right
    and refuse to tell lies.
They will eat and rest
    with nothing to fear.

A Song of Celebration

[14] Everyone in Jerusalem and Judah,
    celebrate and shout
        with all your heart!
[15] Zion, your punishment is over.
    The LORD has forced your enemies

---

[q]3.9 *I will . . . praising me*: Or "I will change the
hearts of all people and make them fit for praising me."
[r]3.10 *Ethiopia*: See the note at 2.12.

MARRIAGE—My husband is emotionally distant. How can I feel closer to him? *(Zephaniah 3.16,17)*

Keep trusting in God's power and goodness.

Few things are as painful or discouraging as an unhappy marriage. All other friendships and creative activities you set up for yourself cannot feed your hunger for intimacy with your husband. But what can you do when you feel as though you're living with a stranger? How do you keep from feeling rejected or resentful, or even looking to another man to meet your needs?

Remember who your God is! The same God who healed the rift between us and him can also bring you and your husband closer together. Zephaniah reminded Judah that God wouldn't let their sin keep them separated from him (3.15). And God wants you to see your sadness about your relationship with your husband by the same light. Don't be discouraged. God can bring victory over sin (3.13), and he can use your marriage for good purposes because he loves you and knows what you're going through. Keep trusting in God's power and goodness so you can be the wife God has called you to be—and let God take care of your husband. (See also Proverbs 3.27-35; Ephesians 4.14-16.)

Words To Remember: *The LORD your God wins victory after victory and is always with you. He celebrates and sings because of you, and he will refresh your life with his love.*—Zephaniah 3.17

to turn and retreat.
Your LORD is King of Israel
and stands at your side;
you don't have to worry
about any more troubles.

[16] Jerusalem, the time is coming,
when it will be said to you:
"Don't be discouraged
or grow weak from fear!
[17] The LORD your God
wins victory after victory
and is always with you.
He celebrates and sings
because of you,
and he will refresh your life
with his love."[s]

The LORD's Promise to His People

[18] The LORD has promised:
Your sorrow has ended,

and you can celebrate.[t]
[19] I will punish those
who mistreat you.
I will bring together the lame
and the outcasts,
then they will be praised,
instead of despised,
in every country on earth.
[20] I will lead you home,
and with your own eyes
you will see me bless you
with all you once owned.
Then you will be famous
everywhere on this earth.
I, the LORD, have spoken!

---

[s]**3.17** *refresh . . . love:* Two ancient translations; Hebrew "silently show you his love." [t]**3.18** *celebrate:* One possible meaning for the difficult Hebrew text of verse 18.

Haggai

The Right Time To Serve God

Today's women, we are told, can have it all—education, career, and family—if we choose. Funny how, when we have it all, there's still never enough. Not enough time between corporate meetings and business trips, or carpooling the kids from school to soccer to music lessons. Not enough money in the retirement account, college fund, or checkbook. And not enough energy after juggling work (paid or unpaid), relationships, and day-to-day responsibilities. When you don't have enough (time, money, energy), what do you let slide?

The Jews who had come back to Jerusalem after their long captivity in Babylon put God's temple toward the bottom of their to-do list. It wasn't the right time, they thought, to finish rebuilding the temple. They didn't have enough resources; their energy was taken up with getting themselves resettled in the land.

The prophet Haggai spoke clearly to the situation. This book doesn't sound like other prophecies. Haggai offers no visions, no poetic metaphors, no drama or threats—just the straightforward warning that it's always the right time for God's people to embrace God's priorities.

The temple was supposed to be a priority in Haggai's day. Besides serving as a place of worship, it stood as tangible evidence of the Lord's presence. Where the Lord is present, his people are blessed. Where his presence isn't acknowledged, nothing succeeds for long. How is God's presence seen in your life? What priority do you give to the places and activities that make you conscious of God's presence?

Haggai preached his message of warning and motivation in 520 B.C., more than fifteen years after work first started on the temple. Unlike most prophets, he had the satisfaction of seeing the results of his ministry: The temple was completed just four years later.

Haggai at a Glance

1. The Lord calls the people to rebuild the temple (1)
2. The Lord promises to fill the new temple with his glory (2.1-9)
3. The Lord promises to bless the people (2.10-19)
4. The Lord promises to be with Zerubbabel, governor of Judah (2.20-23)

Rebuild the Temple

1 On the first day of the sixth month of the second year that Darius was king of Persia,[a] the LORD told Haggai the prophet to speak his message to the governor of Judah and to the high priest.

So Haggai told Governor Zerubbabel and High Priest Joshua[b] [2-5]that the LORD All-Powerful had said to them and to the people:

You say this isn't the right time to build a temple for me. But is it right for you to live in expensive houses,[c] while my temple is a pile of ruins? Just look at what's happening. [6]You harvest less than you plant, you never have enough to eat or drink, your clothes don't keep you warm, and your wages are stored in bags full of holes.

[7]Think about what I have said! [8]But first, go to the hills and get wood for my temple, so I can take pride in it and be worshiped there. [9]You expected much, but received only a little. And when you brought it home, I made that little disappear. Why have I done this? It's because you hurry off to build your own houses, while my temple is still in ruins. [10]That's also why the dew doesn't fall and your harvest fails. [11]And so, at my command everything will become barren—your farmland and pastures, your vineyards and olive trees, your animals and you yourselves. All your hard work will be for nothing.

[12]Zerubbabel and Joshua, together with the others who had returned from exile in Babylonia, obeyed the LORD's message spoken by his prophet Haggai, and they started showing proper respect for the LORD. [13]Haggai then told them that the LORD had promised to be with them. [14]So the LORD God All-Powerful made everyone eager to work on his temple, especially Zerubbabel and Joshua. [15]And the work began on the twenty-fourth day of that same month.

The Glorious New Temple

2 [1-2]On the twenty-first day of the next month,[d] the LORD told Haggai the prophet to speak this message to Governor Zerubbabel, High Priest Joshua, and everyone else:

[3]Does anyone remember how glorious this temple used to be? Now it looks like nothing. [4]But cheer up! Because I, the LORD All-Powerful, will be here to help you with the work, [5]just as I promised your ancestors when I brought them out of Egypt.

---

[a]**1.1** *sixth month . . . king of Persia*: Elul, the sixth month of the Hebrew calendar, from about mid-August to mid-September; the second year of the rule of Darius was 520 B.C. [b]**1.1** *Governor . . . Joshua*: Hebrew "Governor Zerubbabel son of Shealtiel and High Priest Joshua son of Jehozadak." [c]**1.2-5** *expensive houses*: Either houses with paneled interiors or with roofs; the temple was not yet completely rebuilt at this time. [d]**2.1,2** *the next month*: Tishri (also called Ethanim), the seventh month of the Hebrew calendar, from about mid-September to mid-October (see the note at 1.1).

---

*Spiritual*Life—How can I show my devotion to God? *(Haggai 1.1-11)*

Use some of your money for God's purposes.

If you wait until you have "enough" before you start giving money for God's work, you'll never have enough. The people of Haggai's time found that out the hard way, and it's still true today. If there's any of your paycheck left over after taking care of the mortgage, groceries, car insurance, and the gas bill, you want to put some away for retirement, upcoming orthodontist bills, or the kids' college tuition.

God doesn't frown on responsible financial planning. But he makes it clear that trust in a well-drawn budget is trust misplaced. He wants you to trust him and to demonstrate it by giving some of your hard-earned money for his work upfront, not out of what's left at the end of the month. That's one very practical way to show your devotion to God. **(See also** 1 Kings 18; 1 Chronicles 29.1-20; Acts 4.32—5.11; 1 Corinthians 13.11-13.)

Words To Remember: *You say this isn't the right time to build a temple for me. But is it right for you to live in expensive houses, while my temple is a pile of ruins?* —Haggai 1.2-5

Don't worry. My Spirit is[c] right here with you.

[6]Soon I will again shake the heavens and the earth, the sea and the dry land. [7]I will shake the nations, and their treasures[f] will be brought here. Then the brightness of my glory will fill this temple. [8]All silver and gold belong to me, [9]and I promise that this new temple will be more glorious than the first one. I will also bless this city[g] with peace.

The Past and the Future

[10]On the twenty-fourth day of the ninth month,[h] the LORD God All-Powerful told the prophet Haggai [11]to ask the priests for their opinion on the following matter:

[12]Suppose meat ready to be sacrificed to God is being carried in the folds of someone's clothing, and the clothing rubs against some bread or stew or wine or olive oil or any other food. Would those foods that were touched then become acceptable for sacrifice?

"Of course not," the priests answered.

[13]Then Haggai said, "Suppose someone has touched a dead body and is considered unacceptable to worship God. If that person touches these foods, would they become unclean?"

"Of course they would," the priests answered.

[14]So the LORD told Haggai to say:

That's how it is with this entire nation. Everything you do and every sacrifice you offer is unacceptable to me. [15]But from now on, things will get better. Before you started laying the foundation for the temple, [16]you recalled what life was like in the past.[i] When you wanted twenty bushels of wheat, there were only ten, and when you wanted fifty jars of wine, there were only twenty. [17]I made all of your hard work useless by sending mildew, mold, and hail—but you still did not return to me, your LORD.

[18]Today you have completed the foundation for my temple, so listen to what your future will be like. [19]Although you have not yet harvested any grain, grapes, figs, pomegranates,[j] or olives, I will richly bless you in the days ahead.

God's Promise to Zerubbabel

[20]That same day the LORD spoke to Haggai again and said:

[21]Tell Governor Zerubbabel of Judah

---

[c]2.5 My Spirit is: Or "I am." [f]2.7 their treasures: Hebrew "what they most desire." [g]2.9 city: Or "temple." [h]2.10 ninth month: Chislev, the ninth month of the Hebrew calendar, from about mid-November to mid-December. [i]2.16 you recalled . . . past: One possible meaning for the difficult Hebrew text. [j]2.19 pomegranates: A bright red fruit that looks like an apple.

Personal Concerns—How can I learn to set priorities? (Haggai 2.6-9)

Share the Lord's priority: his glory.

What an incredible picture Haggai paints here! All the powerful political rulers with their accomplishments, all the seemingly constant forces of nature, will be caught up in the Lord's grasp. As he shakes them, whatever is worthwhile—the "treasures" that kings and presidents lay claim to—will fall like change from a turned-out pocket. But their glitter will be dimmed by the brightness that fills the temple: the brightness of the glory of the Lord.

What competes for top billing in your list of priorities? Money? "All silver and gold belong to me," says the Lord (2.8). Power? Accomplishment? God is going to shake that all out. But the result will be better than anything that has come before: The result will be the Lord's glory and blessing and peace (2.9).

What can you do to contribute to the Lord's glory? Make that a priority. (See also Genesis 22.1-19; 1 Samuel 15.10-35; Luke 10.38-42; Revelation 2.1-7.)

Words To Remember: I will shake the nations, and their treasures will be brought here. Then the brightness of my glory will fill this temple.—Haggai 2.7

that I am going to shake the heavens and the earth ²²and wipe out kings and their kingdoms. I will overturn war chariots, and then cavalry troops will start slaughtering each other. ²³But tell my servant Zerubbabel that I, the LORD All-Powerful, have chosen him, and he will rule in my name.*k*

---

*k***2.23** *rule in my name*: The Hebrew text has "be my signet ring," which signified authority.

Zechariah

The Lord Will Have His Day

If you've ever moved to a new community, started a new job, or entered into a new relationship with high hopes, only to discover that the new venture doesn't live up to your expectations, you can identify with the people who first heard Zechariah's message.

The former captives who returned to Jerusalem from Babylon came with high expectations. But things didn't work out as they'd hoped. They ran into all kinds of trouble rebuilding the temple. Even if they did manage to finish it, the new temple would be disappointingly small and plain compared to the temple that had been destroyed.

In this time of disappointment, God sent Zechariah with a message of encouragement and promise. In the first part of this book (1–8), Zechariah recounts eight visions that poetically describe how the Lord will restore his people and punish their enemies. The last section of the book (9–14) speaks beautifully and hauntingly of a time to come when "the LORD will have his day. . . . Then there will be only one LORD who rules as King and whose name is worshiped everywhere on earth" (14.1,9).

Later, the gospel writers realized that Jesus was the fulfillment of Zechariah's prophecy in 9.9: "Your king has won a victory, and he is coming to you. He is humble and rides on a donkey; he comes on the colt of a donkey."

Both Matthew (Matthew 21.5) and John (John 12.15) quote this.

Because of that King's first coming,

we, too, can look forward to being a part of the wonderful time when the Lord has his day.

Zechariah began his ministry in 520 B.C. and was a contemporary of Haggai.

Zechariah at a Glance

1. First vision: Horses and riders (1.1-17)
2. Second vision: Animal horns (1.18-21)
3. Third vision: A measuring line (2)
4. Fourth vision: The high priest and Satan (3)
5. Fifth vision: A lampstand and olive trees (4)
6. Sixth vision: A flying scroll (5.1-4)
7. Seventh vision: A woman in a basket (5.5-11)
8. Eighth vision: Four chariots (6.1-8)
9. How the Lord wants to be worshiped (6.9—8.23)
10. The Lord will send a king (9.1—11.3)
11. The people reject the good shepherd (11.4-17)
12. Repentance and a return to the Lord (12,13)
13. The Lord will have his day (14)

Turn to the LORD

1 I am the prophet Zechariah, the son of Berechiah and the grandson of Iddo.

In the eighth month of the second year that Darius was king of Persia,[a] the LORD told me to say:

[2-3]Israel, I, the LORD All-Powerful, was very angry with your ancestors. But if you people will return to me, I will turn and help you. [4]Don't be stubborn like your ancestors. They were warned by the earlier prophets[b] to give up their evil and turn back to me, but they paid no attention.

[5]Where are your ancestors now? Not even prophets live forever. [6]But my warnings and my words spoken by the prophets caught up with your ancestors. So they turned back to me and said, "LORD All-Powerful, you have punished us for our sins, just as you had planned."

First Vision: Horses and Riders

[7-8]On the twenty-fourth day of Shebat,[c] which was the eleventh month of that same year,[d] the LORD spoke to me in a vision during the night: In a valley among myrtle trees,[e] I saw someone on a red horse, with riders on red, brown, and white horses behind him. [9]An angel was there to explain things to me, and I asked, "Sir, who are these riders?"

"I'll tell you," the angel answered.

[10]Right away, the man standing among the myrtle trees said, "These are the ones the LORD has sent to find out what's happening on earth."

[11]Then the riders spoke to the LORD's angel, who was standing among the myrtle trees, and they said, "We have gone everywhere and have discovered that the whole world is at peace."

[12]At this, the angel said, "LORD All-Powerful, for seventy years you have been angry with Jerusalem and the towns of Judah. When are you ever going to have mercy on them?"

[13]The LORD's answer was kind and comforting. [14]So the angel told me to announce:

I, the LORD All-Powerful, am very protective of Jerusalem. [15]For a while I was angry at the nations, but now I am furious, because they have made things worse for Jerusalem and are not the least bit concerned. [16]And so, I will have pity on Jerusalem. The city will be completely rebuilt, and my temple will stand again. [17]I also promise that my towns will prosper—Jerusalem will once again be my chosen city, and I will comfort the people of Zion.

Second Vision: Animal Horns

[18]Next, I saw four animal horns.[f] [19-21]The angel who was sent to explain was there, and so I asked, "What do these mean?"

His answer was, "These horns are the nations that scattered the people of Judah, Israel, and Jerusalem, and took away their freedom."

Then the LORD showed me four blacksmiths, and I asked, "What are they going to do?"

He replied, "They are going to terrify and crush those horns."

Third Vision: A Measuring Line

2 This time I saw someone holding a measuring line, [2]and I asked, "Where are you going?"

"To measure Jerusalem," was the answer. "To find out how wide and long it is."

[3]The angel who had spoken to me was leaving, when another angel came up to him [4]and said, "Hurry! Tell that man with the measuring line that Jerusalem won't have any boundaries. It will be too full of people and animals even to have a wall. [5]The LORD himself has promised to be a protective wall of fire surrounding Jerusalem, and he will be its shining glory in the heart of the city."

A Call to Action

[6]The LORD says to his people, "Run! Escape from the land in the north, where I

---

[a]1.1 *eighth month . . . second year . . . king of Persia:* Bul, the eighth month of the Hebrew calendar, from about mid-October to mid-November; the second year of the rule of Darius was 520 B.C. [b]1.4 *the earlier prophets:* Those who preached before the fall of Jerusalem in either 587 or 586 B.C. [c]1.7,8 *Shebat:* The eleventh month of the Hebrew calendar, from about mid-January to mid-February. [d]1.7,8 *that same year:* See verse 1 and the note there. [e]1.7,8 *myrtle trees:* Evergreen shrubs, which in ancient times were symbols of fertility and renewal. [f]1.18 *animal horns:* Horns, especially those of a bull, were symbols of power in ancient times. The number "four" would signal completeness, one representing each of the four directions.

scattered you to the four winds. [7]Leave Babylonia and hurry back to Zion."

[8]Then the glorious LORD All-Powerful ordered me to say to the nations that had raided and robbed Zion:

Zion is as precious to the LORD as are his eyes. Whatever you do to Zion, you do to him. [9]And so, he will put you in the power of your slaves, and they will raid and rob you. Then you will know that I am a prophet of the LORD All-Powerful.

[10]City of Zion, sing and celebrate! The LORD has promised to come and live with you. [11]When he does, many nations will turn to him and become his people. At that time you will know that I am a prophet of the LORD All-Powerful. [12]Then Judah will be his part of the holy land, and Jerusalem will again be his chosen city.

[13]Everyone, be silent!
The LORD is present
and moving about
in his holy place.

Fourth Vision: Joshua and Satan

3 I was given another vision. This time Joshua the high priest was standing in front of the LORD's angel. And there was Satan, standing at Joshua's right side, ready to accuse him. [2]But the LORD said, "Satan, you are wrong. Jerusalem is my chosen city, and this man was rescued like a stick from a flaming fire."

The Lord's already filled my heart with his love and grace. Now it's up to me to not let the sins of my flesh get in the way of the desire of my heart, which is to glorify him.

LIZ CURTIS HIGGS

[3]Joshua's clothes were filthy. [4]So the angel told some of the people to remove Joshua's filthy clothes. Then he said to Josh-

ua, "This means you are forgiven. Now I will dress you in priestly clothes."

[5]I spoke up and said, "Also put a clean priestly turban on his head." Then they dressed him in priestly clothes and put the turban on him, while the LORD's angel stood there watching.

[6]After this, the angel encouraged Joshua by telling him that the LORD All-Powerful had promised:

[7]If you truly obey me, I will put you in charge of my temple, including the courtyard around it, and you will be allowed to speak at any time with the angels standing beside me.[g] [8]Listen carefully, High Priest Joshua and all of you other priests. You are a sign of things to come, because I am going to bring back my servant, the Chosen King.[h]

[9]Joshua, I have placed in front of you a stone with seven sides. I will engrave something on that stone, and in a single day I will forgive this guilty country. [10]Then each of you will live at peace and entertain your friends in your own vineyard and under your own fig trees.

Fifth Vision: A Lampstand and Olive Trees

4 The angel who explained the visions woke me from what seemed like sleep. [2]Then he asked, "What do you see?"

"A solid gold lampstand with an oil container above it," I answered. "On the stand are seven lamps, each with seven flames. [3]One olive tree is on the right side and another on the left of the oil container. [4]But, sir, what do these mean?"

[5]Then he asked, "Don't you know?"

"No sir," I replied.

[6]So the angel explained that it was the following message of the LORD to Zerubbabel:[i]

I am the LORD All-Powerful. So don't depend on your own power or strength, but on my Spirit. [7]Zerubbabel, that mountain in front of you will be leveled to the ground. Then you

---

[g]**3.7** *with the angels . . . me:* Or "with me." The angels are members of God's Council, who stand beside the throne of God in heaven and are allowed to speak with him and for him.　[h]**3.8** *Chosen King:* The Hebrew text has "Sprout" or "Branch," a term used of royalty (see Isaiah 11.1).　[i]**4.6** *Zerubbabel:* Governor of Judah (see Haggai 1.1).

will bring out the temple's most important stone and shout, "God has been very kind."[j]

[8]The LORD spoke to me again and said:

[9]Zerubbabel laid the foundation for the temple, and he will complete it. Then everyone will know that you were sent by me, the LORD All-Powerful. [10]Those who have made fun of this day of small beginnings will celebrate when they see Zerubbabel holding this important stone.[k]

Those seven lamps represent my eyes—the eyes of the LORD—and they see everything on this earth.

[11]Then I asked the angel, "What about the olive trees on each side of the lampstand? What do they represent? [12]And what is the meaning of the two branches from which golden olive oil[l] flows through the two gold pipes?"

[13]"Don't you know?" he asked.

"No sir, I don't," was my answer.

[14]Then he told me, "These branches are the two chosen leaders[m] who stand beside the Lord of all the earth."

Sixth Vision: A Flying Scroll

5 When I looked the next time, I saw a flying scroll,[n] [2]and the angel asked, "What do you see?"

"A flying scroll," I answered. "About thirty feet long and fifteen feet wide."

[3]Then he told me:

This scroll puts a curse on everyone in the land who steals or tells lies. The writing on one side tells about the destruction of those who steal, while the writing on the other side tells about the destruction of those who lie.

[4]The LORD All-Powerful has said, "I am sending this scroll into the house of everyone who is a robber or tells lies in my name, and it will remain there until every piece of wood and stone in that house crumbles."

Seventh Vision: A Woman in a Basket

[5]Now the angel who was there to explain the visions came over and said, "Look up and tell me what you see coming."

[6]"I don't know what it is," was my reply.

"It's a big basket," he said. "And it shows what everyone in the land has in mind."[o]

[7]The lead cover of the basket was

---

[j]4.7 *God . . . kind*: Or "What a beautiful stone." [k]4.10 *important stone*: Or "measuring line (with a stone attached to the end)." [l]4.12 *golden olive oil*: The Hebrew text has "gold," which possibly refers to the color of the olive oil as it flows through the gold pipe. [m]4.14 *chosen leaders*: The Hebrew text has "people of oil." In ancient times prophets, priests, and kings had olive oil poured over their heads to show that they had been chosen (see 1 Samuel 10.1; 16.13). [n]5.1 *scroll*: A roll of paper or special leather used for writing on. [o]5.6 *what . . . mind*: Hebrew; one ancient translation "the sin of everyone in the land."

Friendship—Sometimes I feel God is asking me to befriend someone I naturally dislike or who annoys me. How can I overcome my natural inclination to avoid that friendship? (*Zechariah 4.1-10*)

Depend on God's Spirit, not your own strength.

The thought of building a friendship with someone you naturally dislike seems overwhelming. You can't imagine having phone conversations, chats over coffee, or doing the shared activities that go into making a friendship work. But you can face the thought of inviting this person for coffee once. And with God's help, you can take the next step after that.

When Zerubbabel laid the foundation for the temple in Jerusalem, he might have wondered what he'd gotten himself into. For an overview of just some of the obstacles he faced, read the books of Ezra and Nehemiah. But the Lord promised Zerubbabel that his small beginnings would be capped by the temple's most important stone. How? Not by Zerubbabel's power or strength, but by the strength of the Lord's Spirit—a Spirit powerful enough to flatten any mountains that get in the way. That powerful Spirit will also help you take the first step of friendship. (See also Ezekiel 2.1-7; Mark 2.13-17; 1 Corinthians 10.31—11.1.)

Words To Remember: *I am the LORD All-Powerful. So don't depend on your own power or strength, but on my Spirit.*—Zechariah 4.6

opened, and in the basket was a woman. [8]"This woman represents evil," the angel explained. Then he threw her back into the basket and slammed the heavy cover down tight.

[9]Right after this I saw two women coming through the sky like storks with wings outstretched in the wind. Suddenly they lifted the basket into the air, [10]and I asked the angel, "Where are they taking the basket?"

[11]"To Babylonia,"[p] he answered, "where they will build a house for the basket and set it down inside."

Eighth Vision: Four Chariots

6 Finally, I looked up and saw four chariots coming from between two bronze mountains. [2]The first chariot was pulled by red horses, and the second by black horses; [3]the third chariot was pulled by white horses, and the fourth by spotted gray horses.

[4]"Sir," I asked the angel. "What do these stand for?"

[5]Then he explained, "These are the four winds[q] of heaven, and now they are going out, after presenting themselves to the Lord of all the earth. [6]The chariot with black horses goes toward the north, the chariot with white horses goes toward the west,[r] and the one with spotted horses goes toward the south."

[7]The horses came out eager to patrol the earth, and the angel told them, "Start patrolling the earth."

When they had gone on their way, [8]he shouted to me, "Those that have gone to the country in the north will do what the LORD's Spirit[s] wants them to do there."

The Chosen Leader

[9]The LORD said to me:

[10-11]Heldai, Tobijah, and Jedaiah have returned from Babylonia. Collect enough silver and gold from them to make a crown.[t] Then go with them to the house of Josiah son of Zephaniah and put the crown on the head of the high priest Joshua son of Jehozadak.[u] [12-13]Tell him that I, the LORD All-Powerful, say, "Someone will reach out from here like a branch and build a temple for me. I will name him 'Branch,' and he will rule with royal honors. A priest will stand beside his throne,[v] and the

two of them will be good friends. [14]This crown will be kept in my temple as a reminder and will be taken care of by Heldai,[w] Tobijah, Jedaiah, and Josiah."[x]

> *God created us with an overwhelming desire to soar. He designed us to be tremendously productive and to "mount up with wings like eagles," realistically dreaming of what he can do with our potential.*
>
> CAROL KENT

[15]When people from distant lands come and help build the temple of the LORD All-Powerful, you will know that the LORD is the one who sent me. And this will happen, if you truly obey the LORD your God.

A Question about Going without Eating

7 On the fourth day of Chislev, the ninth month of the fourth year that Darius was king of Persia,[y] the LORD again spoke to me. [2-3]It happened after the people of Bethel had sent Sharezer with Regem-Melech and his men to ask the priests in the LORD's temple and the prophets to

---

[p]5.11 *Babylonia*: The Hebrew text has "Shinar," an ancient name for Babylonia.   [q]6.5 *winds*: Or "spirits." The Hebrew word may mean either.   [r]6.6 *goes toward the west*: Or "follows behind."   [s]6.8 *LORD's Spirit*: Or "LORD."   [t]6.10,11 *a crown*: Two ancient translations; Hebrew "some crowns."   [u]6.10,11 *Heldai . . . Jehozadak*: Or "Go to the house of Josiah son of Zephaniah, where you will find Heldai, Tobijah, and Jedaiah, who have returned from Babylonia. Collect enough silver and gold from them to make a crown. Then put it on the head of the high priest Joshua son of Jehozadak."   [v]6.12,13 *stand beside his throne*: Or "sit on a throne."   [w]6.14 *Heldai*: One ancient translation; Hebrew "Helem."   [x]6.14 *Josiah*: One ancient translation; Hebrew "Hen."
[y]7.1 *Chislev . . . fourth year . . . king of Persia*: Chislev, the ninth month of the Hebrew calendar, from about mid-November to mid-December; the fourth year of the rule of Darius was 518 B.C.

pray for them. So they prayed, "Should we mourn and go without eating during the fifth month,[z] as we have done for many years?"

⁴⁻⁵It was then that the LORD All-Powerful told me to say to everyone in the country, including the priests:

For seventy years you have gone without eating during the fifth and seventh months of the year. But did you really do it for me? ⁶And when you eat and drink, isn't it for your own enjoyment? ⁷My message today is the same one I commanded the earlier prophets[a] to speak to Jerusalem and its villages when they were prosperous, and when all of Judah, including the Southern Desert and the hill country, was filled with people.

⁸⁻⁹So once again, I, the LORD All-Powerful, tell you, "See that justice is done and be kind and merciful to one another! ¹⁰Don't mistreat widows or orphans or foreigners or anyone who is poor, and stop making plans to hurt each other."

¹¹⁻¹²But everyone who heard those prophets, stubbornly refused to obey. Instead, they turned their backs on everything my Spirit[b] had commanded the earlier prophets to preach. So I,

the LORD, became angry ¹³and said, "You people paid no attention when I called out to you, and now I'll pay no attention when you call out to me."

¹⁴That's why I came with a whirlwind and scattered them among foreign nations, leaving their lovely country empty of people and in ruins.

The LORD's Promises to Zion

8 The LORD All-Powerful said to me: ²I love Zion so much that her enemies make me angry. ³I will return to Jerusalem and live there on Mount Zion. Then Jerusalem will be known as my faithful city, and Zion will be known as my holy mountain.

⁴Very old people with walking sticks will once again sit around in Jerusalem, ⁵while boys and girls play in the streets. ⁶This may seem impossible for my people who are left, but it isn't impossible for me, the LORD All-Powerful. ⁷I will save those who were taken to lands in the east and the west,

---

[z]7.2,3 *fifth month*: Ab, the fifth month of the Hebrew calendar, from about mid-July to mid-August. The temple was destroyed by the Babylonians in the year 587 or 586 B.C.   [a]7.7 *the earlier prophets*: See the note at 1.4.   [b]7.11,12 *my Spirit*: Or "I."

---

*Spiritual*Life—How can I reach out to a needy world? *(Zechariah 7.7-13)*

Give help to the powerless.
Ever since the Babylonians had overrun Jerusalem and burned the temple in 586 B.C., the Jews had commemorated that event by mourning during the month that the destruction occurred (see Jeremiah 52.12,13). For seventy years, this act of commemoration had been an important part of their religious identity.

Imagine how earthshaking it was for the Jews to hear that these religious acts weren't the Lord's main concern at all. In fact, when they asked the Lord about them, he changed the subject. "My message today is the same one I commanded the earlier prophets" (7.7), the Lord said. "See that justice is done and be kind and merciful to one another! Don't mistreat widows or orphans or foreigners or anyone who is poor, and stop making plans to hurt each other" (7.8-10).

Our forms of worship may change, but the Lord's message to us stays the same: We need to seek justice and care for the poor and make a home for the homeless. God continues to speak that message to us in the New Testament: "Religion that pleases God the Father must be pure and spotless. You must help needy orphans and widows and not let this world make you evil" (James 1.27). (See also 2 Samuel 9; Nehemiah 5.1-13; Lamentations 2.11-13; Jonah 4.5-11; Matthew 6.1-4; Luke 9.10-17.)

Words To Remember: *I, the LORD All-Powerful, tell you, "See that justice is done and be kind and merciful to one another!"—Zechariah 7.8,9*

[8]and I will bring them to live in Jerusalem. They will be my people, and I will be their God, faithful to bring about justice.

> *Faith is putting our*
> *complete trust in God—*
> *because he is the only*
> *truly Faithful One.*
>
> BARBARA JOHNSON

[9]I am the LORD All-Powerful! So don't give up. Think about the message my prophets spoke when the foundation of my temple was laid. [10]Before that time, neither people nor animals were rewarded for their work, and no one was safe anywhere, because I had turned them against each other.

[11]My people, only a few of you are left, and I promise not to punish you as I did before. [12]Instead, I will make sure that your crops are planted in peace and your vineyards are fruitful, that your fields are fertile and the dew falls from the sky. [13]People of Judah and Israel, you have been a curse to the nations, but I will save you and make you a blessing to them. So don't be afraid or lose courage.

[14]When your ancestors made me angry, I decided to punish you with disasters, and I didn't hold back. [15]Now you no longer need to be afraid. I have decided to treat Jerusalem and Judah with kindness. [16]But you must be truthful with each other, and in court you must give fair decisions that lead to peace. [17]Don't ever plan evil things against others or tell lies under oath. I, the LORD, hate such things.

A Time of Celebration

[18]The LORD All-Powerful told me to say:
[19]People of Judah, I, the LORD, demand that whenever you go without food as a way of worshiping me, it should become a time of celebration.

No matter if it's the fourth month, the fifth month, the seventh month, or the tenth month, you should have a joyful festival. So love truth and live at peace.

[20]I tell you that people will come here from cities everywhere. [21]Those of one town will go to another and say, "We're going to ask the LORD All-Powerful to treat us with kindness. Come and join us."

[22]Many people from strong nations will come to Jerusalem to worship me and to ask me to treat them with kindness. [23]When this happens, ten people from nations with different languages will grab a Jew by his clothes and say, "Let us go with you. We've heard that God is on your side." I, the LORD All-Powerful, have spoken!

Israel's Enemies Will Be Punished

9 This is a message
      from the LORD:
His eyes are on everyone,
especially the tribes
      of Israel.[c]
So he pronounces judgment
against the cities
      of Hadrach and Damascus.[d]
[2]Judgment will also fall
on the nearby city
      of Hamath,
as well as on Tyre and Sidon,[e]
      whose people are clever.
[3]Tyre has built a fortress
      and piled up silver and gold,
as though they were dust
      or mud from the streets.
[4]Now the Lord will punish Tyre
      with poverty;
he will sink its ships
      and send it up in flames.

[5]Both Ashkelon and Gaza
will tremble with fear;
      Ekron will lose all hope.
Gaza's king will be killed,
and Ashkelon emptied
      of its people.

---

[c]9.1 *His . . . Israel:* One possible meaning for the difficult Hebrew text.   [d]9.1 *Hadrach and Damascus:* Hadrach was north of both Damascus (the main city of Syria) and Hamath (verse 2).   [e]9.2 *Tyre and Sidon:* Phoenician cities.

⁶A mob of half-breeds
　　will settle in Ashdod,[f]
and the Lord himself
　　will rob Philistia of pride.

⁷No longer will the Philistines
eat meat with blood in it
　　or any unclean food.[g]
They will become part
of the people of our God
　　from the tribe of Judah.
And God will accept
the people of Ekron,
　　as he did the Jebusites.[h]

⁸God says, "I will stand guard
to protect my temple from those
　　who come to attack.
I know what's happening,
and no one will mistreat
　　my people ever again."

The LORD Tells about the Coming King

⁹Everyone in Jerusalem,
　　celebrate and shout!
Your king has won a victory,
　　and he is coming to you.
He is humble
and rides on a donkey;
he comes on the colt
　　of a donkey.
¹⁰I, the LORD, will take away
war chariots and horses
　　from Israel[i] and Jerusalem.
Bows that were made for battle
　　will be broken.
I will bring peace to nations,
and your king will rule
　　from sea to sea.
His kingdom will reach
from the Euphrates River
　　across the earth.

The LORD Promises To Rescue Captives

¹¹When I made a sacred agreement
with you, my people,
　　we sealed it with blood.[j]
Now some of you are captives
　　in waterless pits,
but I will come to your rescue
¹²　　and offer you hope.
Return to your fortress,
because today I will reward you
　　with twice what you had.

¹³I will use Judah as my bow
　　and Israel[k] as my arrow.
I will take the people of Zion
as my sword
　　and attack the Greeks.

The LORD Will Protect His People

¹⁴Like a cloud, the LORD God
　　will appear over his people,
and his arrows will flash
　　like lightning.
God will sound his trumpet
and attack in a whirlwind
　　from the south.
¹⁵The LORD All-Powerful
　　will protect his people,
and they will trample down
the sharpshooters
　　and their slingshots.
They will drink and get rowdy;
they will be as full as a bowl
　　at the time of sacrifice.

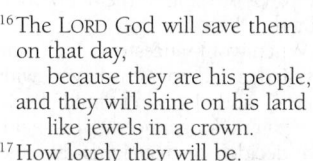

*Faith is allowing God to
work within us so that we
become sparkling jewels
that beautify his kingdom.*

BARBARA JOHNSON

¹⁶The LORD God will save them
on that day,
　　because they are his people,
and they will shine on his land
　　like jewels in a crown.
¹⁷How lovely they will be.

---

[f]9.5,6 *Ashkelon and Gaza . . . Ekron . . . Ashdod:*
Philistine cities.　[g]9.7 *eat . . . food:* The Philistines will
become part of Judah and no longer eat meat with
blood in it (see Genesis 9.4) or any other forbidden
foods (see Leviticus 11.1-23; Deuteronomy 14.3-21).
[h]9.7 *Jebusites:* The original people of Canaan, who lived
in Jerusalem before it was captured by David (see
2 Samuel 5.6-10) and were later accepted as part of
Israel.　[i]9.10 *Israel:* The Hebrew text has "Ephraim,"
the leading tribe of the northern kingdom of Israel,
which sometimes stands for the whole kingdom.
[j]9.11 *an agreement . . . blood:* The agreement at Mount
Sinai (see Exodus 24.7, 8).　[k]9.13 *Israel:* Hebrew
"Ephraim" (see the note at 9.10).

Young people will grow there
   like grain in a field
   or grapes in a vineyard.

A Bright Future for Judah and Israel

10 I, the LORD, am the one
          who sends storm clouds
       and showers of rain
          to make fields produce.
So when the crops need rain,
   you should pray to me.

² You can't believe idols
      and fortunetellers,
   or depend on the hope
you receive from witchcraft
      and interpreters of dreams.
But you have tried all of these,
and now you are like sheep
      without a shepherd.

³ I, the LORD All-Powerful,
      am fiercely angry
with you leaders,
      and I will punish you.
I care for my people,
   the nation of Judah,
and I will change
this flock of sheep
   into charging war horses.

⁴ From this flock will come leaders
   who will be strong

like cornerstones and tent pegs
   and weapons of war.
⁵ They will join in the fighting,
and together they will trample
   their enemies like mud.
They will fight,
because I, the LORD,
   will be on their side.
And they will crush
   the enemy cavalry.

⁶ I will strengthen
   the kingdoms of Judah
      and Israel.*l*
And I will show mercy
   because I am the LORD,
      their God.
I will answer their prayers
   and bring them home.
Then it will seem as though
   I had never rejected them.
⁷ Israel*m* will be like
a tribe of warriors
   celebrating with wine.
When their children see this,
they will also be happy
   because of me, the LORD.

---

*l***10.6** *Israel*: The Hebrew text has "family of Joseph," the ancestor of Ephraim and Manasseh, the leading tribes of the northern kingdom (Israel).   *m***10.7** *Israel*: Hebrew "Ephraim" (see the note at 9.10).

Personal *Concerns*—When a poor decision on my part has damaged my reputation as a Christian, what can I do? *(Zechariah 10.6-12)*

Let God's forgiveness help you start afresh.
Just when you think you're beginning to make an impact on your unbelieving neighbor, you make a bad decision that causes you to wonder whether your witness as a Christian is worth anything. Now what?

That's how Israel, Judah, and King David felt (2 Samuel 11,12). Over and over, God's people had fallen away from their commitments. And over and over, God had wiped the slate clean. After all the times that Israel and Judah abandoned the Lord God in favor of idols, God still promised to show them mercy, answer their prayers, and bring them home because he was "the LORD, their God" (Zechariah 10.6).

When your decisions compromise your reputation, turn to the one who specializes in new beginnings. Then you can acknowledge your failings to your non-Christian friends, but also point them to the God who makes all things new. After all, ultimately what counts in your witness is not who you are, but who God is. (See also Joel 2.12-17; Jonah 2,3; Micah 7.18,19; Luke 7.36-50; Galatians 1.11-24.)

Words To Remember: *I'll strengthen my people because of who I am, and they will follow me. I, the LORD, have spoken!—Zechariah 10.12*

⁸I will give a signal
  for them to come together
    because I have rescued them.
  And there will be as many
    as ever before.
⁹Although I scattered my people
  in distant countries,
    they won't forget me.
  Once their children are raised,ⁿ
    they will return—
¹⁰I will bring them home
  from Egypt and Assyria,
    then let them settle
  as far as Gilead and Lebanon,
  until the land overflows
    with them.
¹¹My people will go through
  an ocean of troubles,
  but I will overcome the waves
  and dry up the deepest part
    of the Nile.
  Assyria's great pride
    will be put down,
  and the power of Egypt
    will disappear.
¹²I'll strengthen my people
  because of who I am,
    and they will follow me.
  I, the LORD, have spoken!

Trouble for Israel's Enemies

11 Lebanon, open your gates!
  Let the fire come in
    to destroy your cedar trees.
²Cry, you cyprus trees!
  The glorious cedars have fallen
    and are rotting.
  Cry, you oak trees of Bashan!
  The dense forest
    has been chopped down.
³Listen! Shepherds are crying.
  Their glorious pastures
    have been ruined.
  Listen! Lions are roaring.
  The forests of the Jordan Valley
    are no more to be found.

Worthless Shepherds

⁴The LORD my God said to me:
  Tend those sheep doomed for
slaughter! ⁵The people who buy and
butcher them go unpunished, while
everyone who sells them says, "Praise
the LORD! I'm rich." Not even their
shepherds have pity on them.

⁶Tend those sheep because I, the
LORD, will no longer have pity on the
people of this earth. I'll turn neighbor
against neighbor and make them
slaves of a king. They will bring disaster on the earth, and I'll do nothing to
rescue any of them.

⁷So I became a shepherd of those sheep
doomed to be slaughtered by the sheep
dealers.ᵒ And I gave names to the two sticks
I used for tending the sheep: One of them
was named "Mercy" and the other "Unity."
⁸In less than a month, I became impatient
with three shepherds who didn't like me,
and I got rid of them. ⁹Then I said, "I refuse
to be your shepherd. Let the sheep that are
going to die, go on and die, and those that
are going to be destroyed, go on and be destroyed. Then let the others eat one another
alive."

¹⁰On that same day, I broke the stick
named "Mercy" to show that the LORD had
canceled his agreement with all people.
¹¹The sheep dealers who saw me knew right
away that this was a message from the LORD.
¹²⁻¹³I told them, "Pay me my wages, if you
think you should; otherwise, forget it." So
they handed me my wages, a measly thirty
pieces of silver.

Then the LORD said, "Throw the money
into the treasury."ᵖ So I threw the money
into the treasury at the LORD's temple.
¹⁴Then I broke the stick named "Unity"
and canceled the ties between Judah and
Israel.

¹⁵Next, the LORD said to me, "Act like a
shepherd again—this time a worthless
shepherd. ¹⁶Once more I am going to let a
worthless nobody rule the land—one who
won't care for the strays or search for the
young or heal the sick or feed the healthy.
He will just dine on the fattest sheep, leaving nothing but a few bones."

¹⁷You worthless shepherd,
  deserting the sheep!
  I hope a sword
  will cripple your arm
    and blind your right eye.

ⁿ10.9 *Once . . . raised*: One possible meaning for the
difficult Hebrew text.   ᵒ11.7 *by the sheep dealers*:
One ancient translation; Hebrew "especially the
weak ones."   ᵖ11.12,13 *Throw . . . treasury*: Hebrew
"Throw the money to the potter."

Victory for Jerusalem

12 This is a message from the LORD
about Israel:
I am the LORD! I stretched
out the heavens; I put the earth on its
foundations and gave breath to humans. 2I have decided that Jerusalem
will become a bowl of wine that makes
the neighboring nations drunk. And
when Jerusalem is attacked, Judah will
also be attacked.[q] 3But I will turn
Jerusalem into a heavy stone that
crushes anyone who tries to lift it.
When all nations on earth surround Jerusalem, 4I will make every
horse panic and every rider confused.
But at the same time, I will watch over
Judah. 5Then every clan in Judah will
realize that I, the LORD All-Powerful,
am their God, and that I am the source
of their strength.
6At that time I will let the clans of
Judah be like a ball of fire in a wood
pile or a fiery torch in a hay stack.
Then Judah will send the surrounding
nations up in smoke. And once again
the city of Jerusalem will be filled with
people.
7But I will first give victory to
Judah, so the kingdom of David and
the city of Jerusalem in all of their
glory won't be thought of more highly
than Judah itself. 8I, the LORD God,
will protect Jerusalem. Even the weakest person there will be as strong as
David, and David's kingdom will rule
as though my very own angel were its
leader. 9I am determined to wipe out
every nation that attacks Jerusalem.

Mourning for the One Pierced with a Spear

10I, the LORD, will make the descendants
of David and the people of Jerusalem feel
deep sorrow and pray when they see the one
they pierced with a spear. They will mourn
and weep for him, as parents weep over the
death of their only child or their first-born.
11On that day the people of Jerusalem will
mourn as much as everyone did for Hadad
Rimmon[r] on the flatlands near Megiddo.
12Everyone of each family in the land will
mourn, and the men will mourn separately
from the women. This includes those from
the family of David, and the families of Nathan, 13Levi, Shimei,[s] 14and all other families
as well.

> *Over and over, God has proven faithful—even when things have happened to shake my world.*
>
> CAROL KENT

Getting Rid of Idols and False Prophets

13 In the future there will be a fountain, where David's descendants
and the people of Jerusalem can
wash away their sin and guilt.
2The LORD All-Powerful says:
When that time comes, I will get
rid of every idol in the country, and
they will be forgotten forever. I will
also do away with their prophets and
those evil spirits that control them. 3If
any such prophets ever appear again,
their own parents must warn them
that they will die for telling lies in my
name—the name of the LORD. If those
prophets don't stop speaking, their
parents must then kill them with a
sword.
4Those prophets will be ashamed
of their so-called visions, and they
won't deceive anyone by dressing like
a true prophet. 5Instead, they will say,
"I'm no prophet. I've been a farmer all
my life."[t]
6And if any of them are asked why
they are wounded,[u] they will answer,
"It happened at the house of some
friends."

---

[q]**12.2** *Judah . . . attacked*: One possible meaning for the difficult Hebrew text. [r]**12.11** *Hadad Rimmon*: Not mentioned elsewhere in the Old Testament. [s]**12.13** *Shimei*: A descendant of Gershon son of Levi (see Numbers 3.18). [t]**13.5** *I've . . . my life*: One possible meaning for the difficult Hebrew text. [u]**13.6** *wounded*: Probably from slashing themselves in the worship of a false god (see 1 Kings 18.28).

A Wounded Shepherd and Scattered Sheep

[7]The LORD All-Powerful said:

My sword, wake up! Attack
   my shepherd and friend.
Strike down the shepherd!
Scatter the little sheep,
   and I will destroy them.
[8]Nowhere in the land
will more than a third of them
   be left alive.

*I've had numerous occasions
to ponder why God doesn't
always answer the way I've
asked him to. I still don't
have a solution. All I
know is that he wants us
to keep talking to him and
that we do not pray to air.*
SANDRA P. ALDRICH

[9]Then I will purify them
   and put them to the test,
just as gold and silver
   are purified and tested.
They will pray in my name,
   and I will answer them.
I will say, "You are my people,"
   and they will reply,
   "You, LORD, are our God!"

War and Victory

14 The LORD will have his day. And when it comes, everything that was ever taken from Jerusalem will be returned and divided among its people. [2]But first, he will bring many nations to attack Jerusalem—homes will be robbed, women raped, and half of the population dragged off, though the others will be allowed to remain.

[3]The LORD will attack those nations like a warrior fighting in battle. [4]He will take his stand on the Mount of Olives east of Jerusa-

lem, and the mountain will split in half, forming a wide valley that runs from east to west. [5]Then you people will escape from the LORD's mountain, through this valley, which reaches to Azal.[v] You will run in all directions, just as everyone did when the earthquake struck[w] in the time of King Uzziah of Judah. Afterwards, the LORD my God will appear with his holy angels.

[6]It will be a bright day that won't turn cloudy.[x] [7]And the LORD has decided when it will happen—this time of unending day.

[8]In both summer and winter, life-giving streams will flow from Jerusalem, half of them to the Dead Sea in the east and half to the Mediterranean Sea in the west. [9]Then there will be only one LORD who rules as King and whose name is worshiped everywhere on earth.

[10-11]From Geba down to Rimmon[y] south of Jerusalem, the entire country will be turned into flatlands, with Jerusalem still towering above. Then the city will be full of people, from Benjamin Gate, Old Gate Place, and Hananel Tower in the northeast part of the city over to Corner Gate in the northwest and down to King's Wine Press in the south. Jerusalem will always be secure and will never again be destroyed.

[12]Here is what the LORD will do to those who attack Jerusalem: While they are standing there, he will make their flesh rot and their eyes fall from their sockets and their tongues drop out. [13]The LORD will make them go into a frenzy and start attacking each other, [14-15]until even the people of Judah turn against those in Jerusalem.[z] This same terrible disaster will also strike every animal nearby, including horses, mules, camels, and donkeys. Finally, everything of value in the surrounding nations will be collected and brought to Jerusalem—gold, silver, and piles of clothing.

[16]Afterwards, the survivors from those

[v]**14.5** *to Azal:* One possible meaning for the difficult Hebrew text. The location of Azal is unknown.
[w]**14.5** *earthquake struck:* See Amos 1.1.
[x]**14.6** *a bright . . . cloudy:* One possible meaning for the difficult Hebrew text. [y]**14.10,11** *From Geba down to Rimmon:* Approximately the northern and southern borders of Judah before the exile (see 2 Kings 23.8); Geba is about ten miles north of Jerusalem, and Rimmon is about ten miles north of Beersheba.
[z]**14.13-15** *each other . . . Jerusalem:* Or "each other." **14.13-15**But the people of Judah will fight on the side of Jerusalem."

nations that attacked Jerusalem will go there each year to worship the King, the LORD All-Powerful, and to celebrate the Festival of Shelters. [17]No rain will fall on the land of anyone in any country who refuses to go to Jerusalem to worship the King, the LORD All-Powerful. [18-19]This horrible disaster will strike the Egyptians and everyone else who refuses to go there for the celebration.

[20-21]At that time the words "Dedicated to the LORD" will be engraved on the bells worn by horses. In fact, every ordinary cooking pot in Jerusalem will be just as sacred to the LORD All-Powerful as the bowls used at the altar. Any one of them will be acceptable for boiling the meat of sacrificed animals, and there will no longer be a need to sell special pots and bowls.[a]

---

[a]**14.20,21** *special pots and bowls*: Since all pots and bowls will be considered acceptable for use in the temple, there will be no more need for merchants to sell special ones to those people who come to offer sacrifices.

Malachi

Faith While You Wait

How would you respond if someone told you that although your present circumstances were difficult, your future would be bright? What if many years passed without your seeing any indication that this was true—and not only were you not prospering, but the people who didn't follow God were doing just great (3.14,15)? How would you react? It's possible that this scenario could tempt you to switch sides, to live by sight, rather than faith. It's easy to let circumstances shape what we believe about God.

In Malachi's day, the Israelites had returned from exile almost a century ago with the hope of rebuilding the temple and enjoying the prosperity that Isaiah, Jeremiah, and Ezekiel had all promised. Instead, they'd found that their land was under Persia's thumb and plagued by drought and locusts (3.10,11). Even their temple was not nearly as grand as the one destroyed during their captivity (Ezra 3.12). Nothing indicated that their circumstances were improving with time, so God's people lost heart—not to mention faith. If God really loved them (1.2-5), why didn't he show it? What was the use of following God if other people prospered more without him?

If you're tempted to excuse half-hearted devotion to God (1.7,8), or to become greedy and dishonest (3.5), or to cheat on your husband (2.11-15), read Malachi's message. He pointed out that the going-through-the-motions religion of Israel's priests and the people's complaints against God were part of the reason God didn't bless them; their own behavior showed their lack of faith (3.7-12). During difficulties there are still evidences of God's love, even if we must look hard to see them. Ultimately God will reward those who are faithful and punish those who are not (3.16—4.6), although for now it seems just the opposite.

During our waiting times, we can allow Malachi's words from God in 3.17,18 to strengthen our faith: "Then the LORD All-Powerful said: You people are precious to me, and when I come to bring justice, I will protect you, just as parents protect an obedient child. Then everyone will once again see the difference between those who obey me by doing right and those who reject me by doing wrong."

Malachi was the last of the Old Testament prophets. He probably gave his message around 450 B.C. After Malachi spoke, there were more than four hundred years of prophetic silence in Israel until John the Baptist cried out from the wilderness.

Malachi at a Glance

1. God confirms his covenant love for Israel (1.1-5)
2. The priests and people show their faithlessness by immoral behavior (1.6—2.16)
3. God is coming to judge the disobedient and ungrateful (2.17—3.5)
4. Repent, in light of the Lord's coming (3.6-15)
5. God will reward faith and punish wickedness (3.16—4.6)

1 I am Malachi. And this is the message that the LORD gave me for Israel.

The LORD's Love for Israel

²Israel, I, the LORD, have loved you. And yet you ask in what way have I loved you. Don't forget that Esau was the brother of your ancestor Jacob, but I chose Jacob ³instead of Esau. And I turned Esau's hill country into a barren desert where jackals*a* roam. ⁴Esau's descendants may say, "Although our nation Edom is in ruins, we will rebuild."

But I, the LORD All-Powerful, promise to tear down whatever they build. Then everyone will know that I will never stop being angry with them as long as they are so sinful.

⁵Israel, when you see this, you will shout, "The LORD's great reputation reaches beyond our borders."

Judgment against Priests

⁶I, the LORD All-Powerful, have something to say to you priests. Children respect their fathers, and servants respect their masters. I am your father and your master, so why don't you respect me? You priests have insulted me, and now you ask, "How did we insult you?"

⁷You embarrass me by offering worthless food on my altar. Then you ask, "How have we embarrassed you?" You have done it by saying, "What's so great about the LORD's altar?"

*a***1.3** *jackals:* Desert animals related to wolves, but smaller.

MARRIAGE—What does God think about divorce? *(Malachi 2.13-16)*

Divorce is cruel.

Whether you're a divorce survivor or you know someone who's gone through a divorce, you know that divorce is cruel. Children who have seen their parents split know that cruelty as well. No one enters marriage full of candlelight and promises planning to divorce. Nor do we anticipate the traumatic (and sometimes unexpected) events that lead to that decision. But divorce, unfortunately, does happen. How does God view this?

God takes marriage seriously: "Didn't God create you to become like one person with your wife?" (2.15). Then Malachi addressed the value of raising children to know God. He railed against unfaithfulness ("Don't ever be unfaithful to your wife," 2.15). Just prior to that, Malachi had spoken of the hypocrisy of people who would "flood the LORD's altar with . . . tears" (2.13), yet be unfaithful in their marriage. They then wondered why God wasn't pleased with them and wouldn't accept their offerings. It seems that how we treat our marriage relationship does indeed impact our relationship with God—and how (or whether) he chooses to respond to our prayers.

But God also hates violence or cruelty, as this passage implies. In a human world where much goes wrong, women sometimes have to choose between a marriage that has become violent and the cruelty of divorce. In that situation, for her own safety and the safety of her children, she may have to seek God's wisdom and trust in his mercy. (See also Matthew 19.1-9; 1 Corinthians 7.10-16; Ephesians 4.1-6.)

Words To Remember: *The LORD God All-Powerful of Israel hates anyone who is cruel enough to divorce his wife. So take care never to be unfaithful!—Malachi 2.16*

[8]But isn't it wrong to offer animals that are blind, crippled, or sick? Just try giving those animals to your governor. That certainly wouldn't please him or make him want to help you. [9]I am the LORD God All-Powerful, and you had better try to please me. You have sinned. Now see if I will have mercy on any of you.

[10]I wish someone would lock the doors of my temple, so you would stop wasting time building fires on my altar. I am not pleased with you priests, and I refuse to accept any more of your offerings. [11]From dawn until dusk my name is praised by every nation on this earth, as they burn incense and offer the proper sacrifices to me. [12]But even you priests insult me by saying, "There's nothing special about the LORD's altar, and these sacrifices are worthless."

[13]You get so disgusted that you even make vulgar signs at me.[b] And for an offering, you bring stolen[c] animals or those that are crippled or sick. Should I accept these? [14]Instead of offering the acceptable animals you have promised, you bring me those that are unhealthy. I will punish you for this, because I am the great King, the LORD All-Powerful, and I am worshiped by nations everywhere.

True and False Priests

2 I, the LORD All-Powerful, have something else to say to you priests. [2]You had better take seriously the need to honor my name. Otherwise, when you give a blessing, I will turn it into a curse. In fact, I have already done this, because you haven't taken to heart your duties as priests. [3]I will punish your descendants and rub your faces in the manure from your animal sacrifices, and then be done with you.[d]

[4]I am telling you this, so I can continue to keep my agreement with your ancestor Levi. [5]I blessed him with a full life, as I had promised, and he kept his part of the agreement by honoring me and respecting my name. [6]He taught the truth and never told lies, and he led a lot of people to turn from sin, because he obeyed me and lived right.

[7]You priests should be eager to spread knowledge, and everyone should come to you for instruction, because you speak for me, the LORD All-Powerful. [8]But you have turned your backs on me. Your teachings have led others to do sinful things, and you

have broken the agreement I made with your ancestor Levi. [9]So I caused everyone to hate and despise you, because you disobeyed me and failed to treat all people alike.

A Broken Agreement

[10]Don't you know that we all have God as our Father? Didn't the one God create each of us? Then why do you cheat each other by breaking the agreement God made with your ancestors? [11]You people in Judah and Jerusalem have been unfaithful to the LORD. You have disgraced the temple that he loves, and you have committed the disgusting sin of worshiping other gods.[e] [12]I pray that the LORD will no longer let those who are guilty belong to his people, even if they eagerly decide to offer the LORD a gift.[f]

[13]And what else are you doing? You cry noisily and flood the LORD's altar with your tears, because he isn't pleased with your offerings and refuses to accept them. [14]And why isn't God pleased? It's because he knows that each of you men has been unfaithful to the wife you married when you were young. You promised that she would be your partner, but now you have broken that promise. [15]Didn't God create you to become like one person with your wife?[g] And why did he do this? It was so you would have children, and then lead them to become God's people. Don't ever be unfaithful to your wife. [16]The LORD God All-Powerful of Israel hates anyone who is cruel enough to divorce his wife. So take care never to be unfaithful!

[17]You have worn out the LORD with your words. And yet, you ask, "How did we do that?"

You did it by saying, "The LORD is pleased with evil and doesn't care about justice."

The Promised Messenger

3 I, the LORD All-Powerful,
   will send my messenger
      to prepare the way for me.

---

[b]1.13 me: Or "the altar." [c]1.13 stolen: Or "injured." [d]2.3 and then be done with you: One possible meaning for the difficult Hebrew text. [e]2.11 worshiping other gods: Or "marrying the worshipers of other gods." [f]2.12 even if . . . gift: One possible meaning for the difficult Hebrew text. [g]2.15 Didn't . . . wife: One possible meaning for the difficult Hebrew text.

Then suddenly the Lord
you are looking for
   will appear in his temple.
The messenger you desire
is coming with my promise,
   and he is on his way.

A Day of Change

²On the day the Lord comes, he will be like a furnace that purifies silver or like strong soap in a washbasin. No one will be able to stand up to him. ³The LORD will purify the descendants of Levi,ʰ as though they were gold or silver. Then they will bring the proper offerings to the LORD, ⁴and the offerings of the people of Judah and Jerusalem will please him, just as they did in the past.

Don't Cheat God

⁵The LORD All-Powerful said:
I'm now on my way to judge you. And I will quickly condemn all who practice witchcraft or cheat in marriage or tell lies in court or rob workers of their pay or mistreat widows and orphans or steal the property of foreigners or refuse to respect me.

⁶Descendants of Jacob, I am the LORD All-Powerful, and I never change. That's why you haven't been wiped out, ⁷even though you have ignored and disobeyed my laws ever

since the time of your ancestors. But if you return to me, I will return to you.
And yet you ask, "How can we return?"

⁸You people are robbing me, your God. And, here you are, asking, "How are we robbing you?"

You are robbing me of the offerings and of the ten percent that belongs to me.ⁱ ⁹That's why your whole nation is under a curse. ¹⁰I am the LORD All-Powerful, and I challenge you to put me to the test. Bring the entire ten percent into the storehouse, so there will be food in my house. Then I will open the windows of heaven and flood you with blessing after blessing.ʲ ¹¹I will also stop locustsᵏ from destroying your crops and keeping your vineyards from producing. ¹²Everyone of every nation will talk about how I have blessed you and about your wonderful land. I, the LORD All-Powerful, have spoken!

ʰ**3.3** *descendants of Levi:* The priests. ⁱ**3.8** *the ten percent . . . to me:* The people of Israel were supposed to give a tenth of their harvests and of their flocks and herds to the LORD (see Leviticus 27.30-33; Deuteronomy 14.22-29). ʲ**3.10** *open the windows . . . blessing:* This may refer to rain, since there seems to have been a terrible drought at this time. ᵏ**3.11** *locusts:* A kind of grasshopper that comes in swarms and causes great damage to plant life.

MARRIAGE—How can we prevent financial issues from becoming stumbling blocks in our marriage? *(Malachi 3.8-12)*

Make giving to God your top priority.

When you receive something from someone you love, doesn't it make you want to turn around and give that person something in return? That's how giving to God should be: a way to recognize and appreciate his goodness to you. Everything God asks of you should be seen within the context of his love for you. God said to the Hebrews, "You people are robbing me, your God" (3.8). It might have helped them (and us) to focus on the fact that all our belongings (and talents and opportunities) come from God in the first place.

In your giving, watch out for any so-called Christian magic formula. God doesn't promise to make you rich if you give. He says he'll bless you for your faithfulness (3.10,11), and his blessing can take many forms, including a deepening faith. God challenges us to test his faithfulness (3.10), so take that first step toward *true* financial freedom by giving enthusiastically to him! (See also Psalm 49.16-20; Matthew 6.19-24; 1 Timothy 6.6-10; Hebrews 13.5,6.)

Words To Remember: *I am the LORD All-Powerful, and I challenge you to put me to the test. Bring the entire ten percent into the storehouse, so there will be food in my house. Then I will open the windows of heaven and flood you with blessing after blessing.* **—Malachi 3.10**

¹³You have said horrible things about me, and yet you ask, "What have we said?"

¹⁴Here is what you have said: "It's foolish to serve the LORD God All-Powerful. What do we get for obeying him and from going around looking sad? ¹⁵See how happy those arrogant people are. Everyone who does wrong is successful, and when they put God to the test, they always get away with it."

Faithfulness Is Rewarded

¹⁶All those who truly respected the LORD and honored his name started discussing these things, and when God saw what was happening, he had their names*ʲ* written as a reminder in his book.

¹⁷Then the LORD All-Powerful said:

You people are precious to me, and when I come to bring justice, I will protect you, just as parents protect an obedient child. ¹⁸Then everyone will once again see the difference between those who obey me by doing right and those who reject me by doing wrong.

The Day of Judgment

The LORD said:

4 The day of judgment is certain to come. And it will be like a red-hot furnace with flames that burn up proud and sinful people, as though they were straw. Not a branch or a root will be left. I, the LORD All-Powerful, have spoken! ²But for you that honor my name, victory will shine like the sun with healing in its rays, and you will jump around like calves at play. ³When I come to bring justice, you will trample those who are evil, as though they were ashes under your feet. I, the LORD All-Powerful, have spoken!

Never let a single day pass without saying an encouraging word to each child. Particularly wherever you have noticed any—even the slightest—improvement.

RUTH BELL GRAHAM

⁴Don't ever forget the laws and teachings I gave my servant Moses on Mount Sinai.*ᵐ*

⁵I, the LORD, promise to send the prophet Elijah before that great and terrible day comes. ⁶He will lead children and parents to love each other more, so that when I come, I won't bring doom to the land.

ʲ**3.16** *names:* Or "deeds."   ᵐ**4.4** *Sinai:* Hebrew "Horeb."

SingleLife—How can God use me as a single woman? *(Malachi 3.16-18)*

Ask God how you can serve him!

If you're single, God has given you that freedom for a purpose. Although it's easy to indulge in the grass-is-greener kind of thinking, looks can be deceiving (that mom of two might be constantly exhausted; or your newly married friend may be enduring abuse). So trust that God knows what he's doing with your life, and don't waste your time wishing you were someone you aren't right now. In 1 Corinthians 7.7,8, Paul said that singleness is a gift from God—and he lived what he said!

But realize that you, like those who are married, need built-in support for your decision to live for God. So choose a few people you trust and begin to cultivate relationships that will keep you following after God when times get hard (3.16). If you make God your focus, he will honor you beyond your imagination. And remember: You're utterly precious to him! (See also Exodus 15.19-21; Judges 6,7; 2 Samuel 20.14-22.)

Words To Remember: *God . . . had their names written as a reminder in his book. Then the LORD All-Powerful said: You people are precious to me.*—Malachi 3.16,17

New
Testament

About the New Testament

The New Testament is a collection of 27 books and letters written in Greek. They are arranged in four groups:

(1) *Gospels and Acts*. This group contains the four Gospels, which are Matthew, Mark, Luke, and John. The term "Gospel" means "good news," and these four Gospels tell how the good news spread in the years after Jesus died and was raised from death.

(2) *Letters of Paul*. This group is made up of Romans, 1 and 2 Corinthians, Galatians, Ephesians, Philippians, Colossians, 1 and 2 Thessalonians, 1 and 2 Timothy, Titus, and Philemon. These letters have traditionally been called the "epistles," and each one is named for the group or person that it was written to.

(3) *Other Letters*. This group contains letters written by people other than Paul. It contains Hebrews, James, 1 and 2 Peter, 1, 2, and 3 John, and Jude. The Letter to the Hebrews doesn't give its author's name, but each of the other letters is named for the person who wrote it.

(4) *Revelation*. This book is quite different from the other New Testament books, because it is a book of visions and prophecies.

Matthew

A Gospel to the Jews

It had been a long time since the Jewish people had heard direct words from God—about four hundred years. Then a baby was born, and with that child the whole New Testament opens. This time, instead of speaking through prophets, God sent himself: Jesus.

Appropriately, the book of Matthew speaks primarily to Jews; it forms a bridge between the Old and New Testaments. In fact, of all the New Testament books, Matthew quotes the Old Testament more. Over and over this story of the life of Jesus shows him as the long-promised Jewish Messiah. The book is fashioned around five sermons or lengthy teachings that Jesus gave to his followers. They are a great help to us as well.

For example, when we worry that a friend might be angry at us, Jesus tells us in the Sermon on the Mount that we must reconcile before we worship: "Leave your gift there in front of the altar. Make peace with that person, then come back and offer your gift to God" (5.24). When we're afraid we're not worth much, Jesus reminds us in his sermon to twelve missionaries: "Even the hairs on your head are counted. So don't be afraid!" (10.30,31). If we wonder whether trying to understand the Bible is worth the effort, we can read Christ's words in his sermon of seven stories: "I have explained the secrets about the kingdom of heaven to you" (13.11). If we fret that day after day of childcare must be a waste of our skills, we can read Jesus' words in his sermon about the kingdom of heaven:

"When you welcome one of these children because of me, you welcome me" (18.5).

This Gospel, introducing Jesus Christ as the long-awaited Jewish Messiah, is a treasure to all who know him and to those who want to know him better. It was probably written by Matthew, a Jewish tax collector who became a disciple to Jesus and listened to him throughout his three years of public teaching.

Matthew at a Glance

1. Ancestry and early life of Jesus (1–4)
2. Sermon on the Mount and several healings (5–9)
3. A sermon to twelve missionaries (10)
4. Jesus is Messiah (11,12)
5. A sermon of seven stories (13)
6. Revelations of Christ's power (14–17)
7. A sermon about the kingdom of heaven (18)
8. Teachings along the road to Jerusalem (19,20)
9. Holy Week begins (21–23)
10. A sermon about the end of time (24,25)
11. Arrest, trial, crucifixion, resurrection, commission (26–28)

The Ancestors of Jesus
(Luke 3.23-38)

1 Jesus Christ came from the family of King David and also from the family of Abraham. And this is a list of his ancestors. [2-6a]From Abraham to King David, his ancestors were:

While making a difference in the lives of the kids who visit your home may seem overwhelming, the impact of small gestures is multiplied powerfully by God.

VALERIE BELL

Abraham, Isaac, Jacob, Judah and his brothers (Judah's sons were Perez and Zerah, and their mother was Tamar), Hezron;

Ram, Amminadab, Nahshon, Salmon, Boaz (his mother was Rahab), Obed (his mother was Ruth), Jesse, and King David.

[6b-11]From David to the time of the exile in Babylonia, the ancestors of Jesus were:

David, Solomon (his mother had been Uriah's wife), Rehoboam, Abijah, Asa, Jehoshaphat, Jehoram;

Uzziah, Jotham, Ahaz, Hezekiah, Manasseh, Amon, Josiah, and Jehoiachin and his brothers.

[12-16]From the exile to the birth of Jesus, his ancestors were:

Jehoiachin, Shealtiel, Zerubbabel, Abiud, Eliakim, Azor, Zadok, Achim;

Eliud, Eleazar, Matthan, Jacob, and Joseph, the husband of Mary, the mother of Jesus, who is called the Messiah.

[17]There were fourteen generations from Abraham to David. There were also fourteen from David to the exile in Babylonia and fourteen more to the birth of the Messiah.

The Birth of Jesus
(Luke 2.1-7)

[18]This is how Jesus Christ was born. A young woman named Mary was engaged to Joseph from King David's family. But before they were married, she learned that she was going to have a baby by God's Holy Spirit. [19]Joseph was a good man[a] and did not want to embarrass Mary in front of everyone. So he decided to quietly call off the wedding.

[20]While Joseph was thinking about this, an angel from the Lord came to him in a dream. The angel said, "Joseph, the baby that Mary will have is from the Holy Spirit. Go ahead and marry her. [21]Then after her baby is born, name him Jesus,[b] because he will save his people from their sins."

[22]So the Lord's promise came true, just as the prophet had said, [23]"A virgin will have a baby boy, and he will be called Immanuel," which means "God is with us."

The mystery of Immanuel, God with us, is that he already is with us—he has paid the price and chosen us as his children—and we can call him "Abba," Daddy. There is no behavioral hoop we need to jump through in order to snuggle in his arms.

LAURETTA PATTERSON

[24]After Joseph woke up, he and Mary were soon married, just as the Lord's angel had told him to do. [25]But they did not sleep together before her baby was born. Then Joseph named him Jesus.

The Wise Men

2 When Jesus was born in the village of Bethlehem in Judea, Herod was king. During this time some wise men[c] from the east came to Jerusalem [2]and said,

---

[a]**1.19** *good man:* Or "kind man," or "man who always did the right thing." [b]**1.21** *name him Jesus:* In Hebrew the name "Jesus" means "the Lord saves." [c]**2.1** *wise men:* People famous for studying the stars.

"Where is the child born to be king of the Jews? We saw his star in the east[d] and have come to worship him."

[3]When King Herod heard about this, he was worried, and so was everyone else in Jerusalem. [4]Herod brought together the chief priests and the teachers of the Law of Moses and asked them, "Where will the Messiah be born?"

[5]They told him, "He will be born in Bethlehem, just as the prophet wrote,

> [6] 'Bethlehem in the land
>   of Judea,
>   you are very important
>   among the towns of Judea.
>   From your town
>   will come a leader,
>   who will be like a shepherd
>   for my people Israel.' "

[7]Herod secretly called in the wise men and asked them when they had first seen the star. [8]He told them, "Go to Bethlehem and search carefully for the child. As soon as you find him, let me know. I want to go and worship him too."

[9]The wise men listened to what the king said and then left. And the star they had seen in the east went on ahead of them until it stopped over the place where the child was. [10]They were thrilled and excited to see the star.

It is a joy to meet Christians who indulge themselves with delight in the Lord until they are full to overflowing with spiritual refreshment!

RUTH BELL GRAHAM

[11]When the men went into the house and saw the child with Mary, his mother, they knelt down and worshiped him. They took out their gifts of gold, frankincense, and myrrh[e] and gave them to him. [12]Later they were warned in a dream not to return to Herod, and they went back home by another road.

The Escape to Egypt

[13]After the wise men had gone, an angel from the Lord appeared to Joseph in a dream and said, "Get up! Hurry and take the child and his mother to Egypt! Stay there until I tell you to return, because Herod is looking for the child and wants to kill him."

[14]That night, Joseph got up and took his wife and the child to Egypt, [15]where they stayed until Herod died. So the Lord's promise came true, just as the prophet had said, "I called my son out of Egypt."

The Killing of the Children

[16]When Herod found out that the wise men from the east had tricked him, he was very angry. He gave orders for his men to kill all the boys who lived in or near Bethlehem and were two years old and younger. This was based on what he had learned from the wise men.

[17]So the Lord's promise came true, just as the prophet Jeremiah had said,

> [18] "In Ramah a voice was heard
>   crying and weeping loudly.
>   Rachel was mourning
>   for her children,
>   and she refused
>   to be comforted,
>   because they were dead."

The Return from Egypt

[19]After King Herod died, an angel from the Lord appeared in a dream to Joseph while he was still in Egypt. [20]The angel said, "Get up and take the child and his mother back to Israel. The people who wanted to kill him are now dead."

[21]Joseph got up and left with them for Israel. [22]But when he heard that Herod's son Archelaus was now ruler of Judea, he was afraid to go there. Then in a dream he was told to go to Galilee, [23]and they went to live there in the town of Nazareth. So the Lord's

---

[d]2.2 *his star in the east:* Or "his star rise."
[e]2.11 *frankincense, and myrrh:* Frankincense was a valuable powder that was burned to make a sweet smell. Myrrh was a valuable sweet-smelling powder often used in perfume.

promise came true, just as the prophet had said, "He will be called a Nazarene."*f*

The Preaching of John the Baptist
(Mark 1.1-8; Luke 3.1-18; John 1.19-28)

3 Years later, John the Baptist started preaching in the desert of Judea. [2]He said, "Turn back to God! The kingdom of heaven*g* will soon be here."*h*

[3]John was the one the prophet Isaiah was talking about, when he said,

> "In the desert someone
>   is shouting,
> 'Get the road ready
>   for the Lord!
> Make a straight path
>   for him.' "

> *Set your heart on*
> *pilgrimage toward God.*
> MICHELE HALSEIDE

[4]John wore clothes made of camel's hair. He had a leather strap around his waist and ate grasshoppers and wild honey. [5]From Jerusalem and all Judea and from the Jordan River Valley crowds of people went to John. [6]They told how sorry they were for their sins, and he baptized them in the river.

[7]Many Pharisees and Sadducees also came to be baptized. But John said to them: You bunch of snakes! Who warned you to run from the coming judgment? [8]Do something to show that you have really given up your sins. [9]And don't start telling yourselves that you belong to Abraham's family. I tell you that God can turn these stones into children for Abraham. [10]An ax is ready to cut the trees down at their roots. Any tree that doesn't produce good fruit will be chopped down and thrown into a fire.

[11]I baptize you with water so that you will give up your sins.*i* But someone more powerful is going to come, and I am not good enough even to carry his sandals.*j* He will baptize you

with the Holy Spirit and with fire. [12]His threshing fork is in his hand, and he is ready to separate the wheat from the husks.*k* He will store the wheat in a barn and burn the husks in a fire that never goes out.

The Baptism of Jesus
(Mark 1.9-11; Luke 3.21, 22)

[13]Jesus left Galilee and went to the Jordan River to be baptized by John. [14]But John kept objecting and said, "I ought to be baptized by you. Why have you come to me?" [15]Jesus answered, "For now this is how it should be, because we must do all that God wants us to do." Then John agreed.

[16]So Jesus was baptized. And as soon as he came out of the water, the sky opened, and he saw the Spirit of God coming down on him like a dove. [17]Then a voice from heaven said, "This is my own dear Son, and I am pleased with him."

Jesus and the Devil
(Mark 1.12, 13; Luke 4.1-13)

4 The Holy Spirit led Jesus into the desert, so that the devil could test him. [2]After Jesus had gone without eating*l* for forty days and nights, he was very hungry. [3]Then the devil came to him and said, "If you are God's Son, tell these stones to turn into bread."

[4]Jesus answered, "The Scriptures say:

> 'No one can live only on food.
> People need every word
>   that God has spoken.' "

[5]Next, the devil took Jesus to the holy city and had him stand on the highest part

---

*f***2.23** *He will be called a Nazarene*: The prophet who said this is not known.   *g***3.2** *kingdom of heaven*: In the Gospel of Matthew "kingdom of heaven" is used with the same meaning as "God's kingdom" in Mark and Luke.   *h***3.2** *will soon be here*: Or "is already here."   *i***3.11** *so that you will give up your sins*: Or "because you have given up your sins."   *j***3.11** *carry his sandals*: This was one of the duties of a slave.   *k***3.12** *His threshing fork is in his hand, and he is ready to separate the wheat from the husks*: After Jewish farmers had trampled out the grain, they used a large fork to pitch the grain and the husks into the air. Wind would blow away the light husks, and the grain would fall back to the ground, where it could be gathered up.   *l***4.2** *without eating*: The Jewish people sometimes went without eating (also called "fasting") to show their love for God or to show sorrow for their sins.

of the temple. ⁶The devil said, "If you are God's Son, jump off. The Scriptures say:

> 'God will give his angels
>   orders about you.
> They will catch you
>   in their arms,
> and you won't hurt
>   your feet on the stones.' "

⁷Jesus answered, "The Scriptures also say, 'Don't try to test the Lord your God!' "
⁸Finally, the devil took Jesus up on a very high mountain and showed him all the kingdoms on earth and their power. ⁹The devil said to him, "I will give all this to you, if you will bow down and worship me."
¹⁰Jesus answered, "Go away Satan! The Scriptures say:

> 'Worship the Lord your God
>   and serve only him.' "

¹¹Then the devil left Jesus, and angels came to help him.

Jesus Begins His Work
(Mark 1.14, 15; Luke 4.14, 15)

¹²When Jesus heard that John had been put in prison, he went to Galilee. ¹³But instead of staying in Nazareth, Jesus moved to Capernaum. This town was beside Lake Galilee in the territory of Zebulun and Naphtali.ᵐ ¹⁴So God's promise came true, just as the prophet Isaiah had said,

> ¹⁵ "Listen, lands of Zebulun
>   and Naphtali,
> lands along the road
> to the sea and east
>   of the Jordan!
> Listen Galilee,
>   land of the Gentiles!
> ¹⁶ Although your people
>   live in darkness,
> they will see
>   a bright light.

ᵐ**4.13** *Zebulun and Naphtali:* In Old Testament times these tribes were in northern Palestine, and in New Testament times many Gentiles lived where these tribes had once been.

WORK—Can I do the "Lord's work" in a secular job? If so, how?
(Matthew 4.18-22)

Listen for God's voice.

Did you ever notice that when Jesus chose disciples, he didn't choose people in religious occupations? Not one of the twelve disciples was a Pharisee or member of the Sanhedrin. The apostle Paul was a Pharisee, but even after he became a missionary, he continued making tents (which helped him befriend Priscilla and Aquila, who became his partners in ministry). Jesus' choices seem to indicate that God uses people in ordinary occupations who daily interact with all kinds of people.

The most important issue in who is chosen to do the "Lord's work" isn't just vocation, but sensitivity to the Lord's voice. Andrew, for example, was a seeker—as evidenced by his having been a disciple of John the Baptist already—but he was still a fisherman (John 1.35-40). What all the people Jesus chose had in common was that they recognized Jesus' voice as the voice of the Messiah and did as he asked them to do. Later, when he asked them to change vocations—"Feed my sheep"—they did that, too.

To recognize God's voice, we need to be good at asking God questions and good at waiting for his answers. We need to be familiar with God's compassion and justice and willing to hear difficult things. Whatever vocation we're in, we need to develop the skill of recognizing God's voice in the midst of our secular work. (See also 1 Samuel 14.1-15; Ecclesiastes 2.24-26; Matthew 15.10-20.)

Words To Remember: *Jesus said to them, "Come with me! I will teach you how to bring in people instead of fish." Right then the two brothers dropped their nets and went with him.—Matthew 4.19,20*

Although they live
   in the shadow of death,
a light will shine
   on them."

[17]Then Jesus started preaching, "Turn back to God! The kingdom of heaven will soon be here."[n]

Jesus Chooses Four Fishermen
(Mark 1.16-20; Luke 5.1-11)

[18]While Jesus was walking along the shore of Lake Galilee, he saw two brothers. One was Simon, also known as Peter, and the other was Andrew. They were fishermen, and they were casting their net into the lake. [19]Jesus said to them, "Come with me! I will teach you how to bring in people instead of fish." [20]Right then the two brothers dropped their nets and went with him.
[21]Jesus walked on until he saw James and John, the sons of Zebedee. They were in a boat with their father, mending their nets. Jesus asked them to come with him too. [22]Right away they left the boat and their father and went with Jesus.

Jesus Teaches, Preaches, and Heals
(Luke 6.17-19)

[23]Jesus went all over Galilee, teaching in the Jewish meeting places and preaching the good news about God's kingdom. He also healed every kind of disease and sickness. [24]News about him spread all over Syria, and people with every kind of sickness or disease were brought to him. Some of them had a lot of demons in them, others were thought to be crazy,[o] and still others could not walk. But Jesus healed them all.
[25]Large crowds followed Jesus from Galilee and the region around the ten cities known as Decapolis.[p] They also came from Jerusalem, Judea, and from across the Jordan River.

The Sermon on the Mount

5 When Jesus saw the crowds, he went up on the side of a mountain and sat down.[q]

Blessings
(Luke 6.20-23)

Jesus' disciples gathered around him, [2]and he taught them:

[3]God blesses those people
   who depend only on him.
They belong to the kingdom
   of heaven![r]

---

[n]4.17 The kingdom of heaven will soon be here: See the two notes at 3.2. [o]4.24 thought to be crazy: In ancient times people with epilepsy were thought to be crazy. [p]4.25 the ten cities known as Decapolis: A group of ten cities east of Samaria and Galilee, where the people followed the Greek way of life. [q]5.1 sat down: Teachers in the ancient world, including Jewish teachers, usually sat down when they taught. [r]5.3 They belong to the kingdom of heaven: Or "The kingdom of heaven belongs to them."

Friendship—How can I repair a broken friendship? (Matthew 5.21-26)

Ask yourself some difficult questions.
When a friendship breaks down, we spend a lot of time figuring out what went wrong— but mostly what she did wrong. We may be obsessed over what she said and what she may have meant. It becomes nearly impossible to be objective and ask, What is my part in this? What did I do to evoke that response? Did I offend her in some way?
   Our goal should be to "make friends with the person who has accused you" (5.25) rather than to place blame. When we set aside our rationalizations and hurt, we can ponder, What's in this person's heart? How can I meet a need in her life?
   Although this sounds as if you're losing the upper hand, you aren't. Impaired relationships plague us and occupy our thoughts. As we resolve these situations (which may take awhile), we become freer to enjoy our relationship with God. (See also Leviticus 19.17,18; Matthew 18.15-20; Luke 6.37-42.)

Words To Remember: So if you are about to place your gift on the altar and remember that someone is angry with you, leave your gift there in front of the altar. Make peace with that person, then come back and offer your gift to God.—Matthew 5.23,24

⁴God blesses those people
who grieve.
  They will find comfort!
⁵God blesses those people
who are humble.
  The earth will belong
  to them!
⁶God blesses those people
who want to obey him⁵
  more than to eat or drink.
  They will be given
  what they want!
⁷God blesses those people
who are merciful.
  They will be treated
  with mercy!
⁸God blesses those people
whose hearts are pure.
  They will see him!
⁹God blesses those people
who make peace.
  They will be called
  his children!
¹⁰God blesses those people
who are treated badly
  for doing right.
  They belong to the kingdom
  of heaven.ᵗ

¹¹God will bless you when people insult you, mistreat you, and tell all kinds of evil lies about you because of me. ¹²Be happy and excited! You will have a great reward in heaven. People did these same things to the prophets who lived long ago.

Salt and Light
(Mark 9.50; Luke 14.34, 35)

¹³You are like salt for everyone on earth. But if salt no longer tastes like salt, how can it make food salty? All it is good for is to be thrown out and walked on. ¹⁴You are like light for the whole world. A city built on top of a hill cannot be hidden, ¹⁵and no one would light a lamp and put it under a clay pot. A lamp is placed on a lampstand, where it can give light to everyone in the house. ¹⁶Make your light shine, so that others will see the good that you do and will praise your Father in heaven.

The Law of Moses

¹⁷Don't suppose that I came to do away with the Law and the Prophets.ᵘ I did not come to do away with them, but to give them their full meaning. ¹⁸Heaven and earth may disappear. But I promise you that not even a period or comma will ever disappear from the Law. Everything written in it must happen. ¹⁹If you reject even the least important command in the Law and teach others to do the same, you will be the least important person in the kingdom of heaven. But if you obey and teach others its commands, you will have an important place in the kingdom. ²⁰You must obey God's commands better than the Pharisees and the teachers of the Law obey them. If you don't, I promise you that you will never get into the kingdom of heaven.

Anger

²¹You know that our ancestors were told, "Do not murder" and "A murderer must be brought to trial." ²²But I promise you that if you are angry with someone,ᵛ you will have to stand trial. If you call someone a fool, you will be taken to court. And if you say that someone is worthless, you will be in danger of the fires of hell.

²³So if you are about to place your gift on the altar and remember that someone is angry with you, ²⁴leave your gift there in front of the altar. Make peace with that person, then come back and offer your gift to God.

²⁵Before you are dragged into court, make friends with the person who has accused you of doing wrong. If you don't, you will be handed over to the judge and then to the officer who will put you in jail. ²⁶I promise you that you will not get out until you have paid the last cent you owe.

ˢ5.6 who want to obey him: Or "who want to do right" or "who want everyone to be treated right."   ᵗ5.10 They belong to the kingdom of heaven: See the note at 5.3.
ᵘ5.17 the Law and the Prophets: The Jewish Scriptures, that is, the Old Testament.   ᵛ5.22 someone: In verses 22-24 the Greek text has "brother," which may refer to people in general or to other followers.

Marriage

²⁷You know the commandment which says, "Be faithful in marriage." ²⁸But I tell you that if you look at another woman and want her, you are already unfaithful in your thoughts. ²⁹If your right eye causes you to sin, poke it out and throw it away. It is better to lose one part of your body, than for your whole body to end up in hell. ³⁰If your right hand causes you to sin, chop it off and throw it away! It is better to lose one part of your body, than for your whole body to be thrown into hell.

Divorce
(Matthew 19.9; Mark 10.11, 12; Luke 16.18)

³¹You have been taught that a man who divorces his wife must write out divorce papers for her.ʷ ³²But I tell you not to divorce your wife unless she has committed some terrible sexual sin.ˣ If you divorce her, you will cause her to be unfaithful, just as any man who marries her is guilty of taking another man's wife.

Promises

³³You know that our ancestors were told, "Don't use the Lord's name to make a promise unless you are going to keep it." ³⁴But I tell you not to swear by anything when you make a promise! Heaven is God's throne, so don't swear by heaven. ³⁵The earth is God's footstool, so don't swear by the earth. Jerusalem is the city of the great king, so don't swear by it. ³⁶Don't swear by your own head. You cannot make one hair white or black. ³⁷When you make a promise, say only "Yes" or "No." Anything else comes from the devil.

Revenge
(Luke 6.29, 30)

³⁸You know that you have been taught, "An eye for an eye and a tooth for a tooth." ³⁹But I tell you not to try to get even with a person who has done something to you. When someone slaps your right cheek,ʸ turn and let that person slap your other cheek. ⁴⁰If someone sues you for your shirt,

---

ʷ**5.31** *write out divorce papers for her*: Jewish men could divorce their wives, but the women could not divorce their husbands. The purpose of writing these papers was to make it harder for a man to divorce his wife. Before this law was made, all a man had to do was to send his wife away and say that she was no longer his wife. ˣ**5.32** *some terrible sexual sin*: This probably refers to the laws about the wrong kinds of marriages that are forbidden in Leviticus 18.6-18 or to some serious sexual sin. ʸ**5.39** *right cheek*: A slap on the right cheek was a bad insult.

PARENTING*&family*—How can I raise a child to be kind and considerate of others? *(Matthew 5.43-48)*

Pray for people you don't get along with.

What a dilemma! Your child complains to you about the neighbor child who picks on her, and all you can think of is, *Yes, let's tie her to a chair and stash her in a closet*. The people who make life difficult for our children are often not our favorite people. The teacher who has taken a dislike to your child needs to grow up! Somehow we're supposed to teach our children to "love their enemies," but we struggle with that ourselves.

To be honest, loving enemies is not only unreachable, but unthinkable. But Scripture suggests that we pray for them. Prayer reorders our hearts as we ask that these "problem" people get the love and positive attention they desire. As our hearts soften toward these troublemakers, we can offer a more gentle attitude toward them to our own children—and even pray with our children for them.

You might begin by asking your child what this person needs, then pray for her needs with your child. As you pray, admit that this child is someone God loves as he loves you. Then pray that God's love would live in you and your child. (See also Jonah 1; Luke 10.25-37; 3 John 4-11.)

Words To Remember: *But I tell you to love your enemies and pray for anyone who mistreats you.—Matthew 5.44*

give up your coat as well. [41]If a soldier forces you to carry his pack one mile, carry it two miles.[z] [42]When people ask you for something, give it to them. When they want to borrow money, lend it to them.

Love

(Luke 6.27, 28, 32-36)

[43]You have heard people say, "Love your neighbors and hate your enemies." [44]But I tell you to love your enemies and pray for anyone who mistreats you. [45]Then you will be acting like your Father in heaven. He makes the sun rise on both good and bad people. And he sends rain for the ones who do right and for the ones who do wrong. [46]If you love only those people who love you, will God reward you for that? Even tax collectors[a] love their friends. [47]If you greet only your friends, what's so great about that? Don't even unbelievers do that? [48]But you must always act like your Father in heaven.

Giving

6 When you do good deeds, don't try to show off. If you do, you won't get a reward from your Father in heaven.

[2]When you give to the poor, don't

blow a loud horn. That's what show-offs do in the meeting places and on the street corners, because they are always looking for praise. I can assure you that they already have their reward.

[3]When you give to the poor, don't let anyone know about it.[b] [4]Then your gift will be given in secret. Your Father knows what is done in secret, and he will reward you.

Prayer

(Luke 11.2-4)

[5]When you pray, don't be like those show-offs who love to stand up and pray in the meeting places and on the street corners. They do this just to look good. I can assure you that they already have their reward.

[6]When you pray, go into a room alone and close the door. Pray to your Father in private. He knows what is done in private, and he will reward you.

---

[z]**5.41** *two miles*: A Roman soldier had the right to force a person to carry his pack as far as one mile. [a]**5.46** *tax collectors*: These were usually Jewish people who paid the Romans for the right to collect taxes. They were hated by other Jews who thought of them as traitors to their country and to their religion. [b]**6.3** *don't let anyone know about it*: The Greek text has, "Don't let your left hand know what your right hand is doing."

---

*Spiritual*Life—**How can I reach out to a needy world?** *(Matthew 6.1-4)*

Enjoy little secrets with God.

Let's say someone who appears to be in need is standing in front of the grocery store where you shop. Suppose he asks you to buy him a loaf of bread while you're inside, and you do it. What goes on inside you after that? It could be easy to feel self-congratulatory—*See what I did for a needy person!* Soon that self-admiration might cause us to casually mention what we did to someone. Helping someone else is difficult not only because it forces us out of our self-preoccupation, but also because we face the temptation of congratulating ourselves.

This passage challenges us to consider our giving to be a little secret between us and God. God spoke (through the voice of this needy person); I heard; I gave. Only God and I know what truly happened. In order to do this, it's important to talk to God about the situation after giving to someone. We can pray for God's guidance in their life, maybe even asking God if there's something more we need to do. Giving to the poor is God's business, and we should keep him at the center of it all. (See also 2 Samuel 9; Nehemiah 5.1-13; Lamentations 2.11-13; Jonah 4.5-11; Zechariah 7.7-13; Luke 9.10-17.)

Words To Remember: *When you give to the poor, don't let anyone know about it. Then your gift will be given in secret. Your Father knows what is done in secret, and he will reward you.*—Matthew 6.3,4

[7]When you pray, don't talk on and on as people do who don't know God. They think God likes to hear long prayers. [8]Don't be like them. Your Father knows what you need before you ask.

[9]You should pray like this:

Our Father in heaven,
help us to honor
your name.
[10]Come and set up
your kingdom,
so that everyone on earth
will obey you,
as you are obeyed
in heaven.
[11]Give us our food for today.[c]
[12]Forgive us for doing wrong,
as we forgive others.
[13]Keep us from being tempted
and protect us from evil.[d]

[14]If you forgive others for the wrongs they do to you, your Father in heaven will forgive you. [15]But if you don't forgive others, your Father will not forgive your sins.

Worshiping God by Going without Eating

[16]When you go without eating,[e] don't try to look gloomy as those show-offs do when they go without eating. I can assure you that they already have their reward. [17]Instead, comb your hair and wash your face. [18]Then others won't know that you are going without eating. But your Father sees what is done in private, and he will reward you.

Treasures in Heaven
(Luke 12.33, 34)

[19]Don't store up treasures on earth! Moths and rust can destroy them, and thieves can break in and steal them. [20]Instead, store up your treasures in heaven, where moths and rust cannot destroy them, and thieves cannot

---

[c]**6.11** *our food for today*: Or "the food that we need" or "our food for the coming day."   [d]**6.13** *evil*: Or "the evil one," that is, the devil. Some manuscripts add, "The kingdom, the power, and the glory are yours forever. Amen."   [e]**6.16** *without eating*: See the note at 4.2.

🐿

*Spiritual*Life—How should I pray? *(Matthew 6.5-15)*

Forget about appearances.
Have you ever prayed, What *must* I do about a certain situation? What *should* my attitude be toward this person? What do I *have to* pray to make this right? You're trying so hard to do everything right that it becomes difficult to speak from the heart. Perhaps you're afraid of how you appear to God and to yourself. And in group prayer you may worry about repeating what someone else said or about bungling a name.

This self-consciousness can keep you from relating to God. No conversation is natural if you're constantly worried about "getting it right." That's why it's important to lose this preoccupation with appearances before God.

What you say to God is private. It's as if you're in a secret place where it's safe to say anything. You can tell God *anything*, including the less-than-admirable things you've done in private. You can reveal your disgusting attitudes to God and ask him to change you. You can tell him about the difficult people in your life and ask him to give you a heart for them. In the safety of that conversation, you can ponder the "shoulds," asking God to work in you in ways you could never achieve on your own. (See also 2 Samuel 7.18-29; 2 Kings 19.14-19; 2 Chronicles 6,7; Nehemiah 1; Psalm 85; Lamentations 5; Acts 4.23-31.)

🐿 **Words To Remember:** *You should pray like this: Our Father in heaven, help us to honor your name. Come and set up your kingdom, so that everyone on earth will obey you, as you are obeyed in heaven.—Matthew 6.9,10*

break in and steal them. ²¹Your heart will always be where your treasure is.

Light
(Luke 11.34-36)

²²Your eyes are like a window for your body. When they are good, you have all the light you need. ²³But when your eyes are bad, everything is dark. If the light inside you is dark, you surely are in the dark.

Money
(Luke 16.13)

²⁴You cannot be the slave of two masters! You will like one more than the other or be more loyal to one than the other. You cannot serve both God and money.

Worry
(Luke 12.22-31)

²⁵I tell you not to worry about your life. Don't worry about having something to eat, drink, or wear. Isn't life more than food or clothing? ²⁶Look at the birds in the sky! They don't plant or harvest. They don't even store grain in barns. Yet your Father in heaven takes care of them. Aren't you worth more than birds?

²⁷Can worry make you live longer?ʲ ²⁸Why worry about clothes? Look how the wild flowers grow. They don't work hard to make their clothes. ²⁹But I tell you that Solomon with all his wealthᵍ wasn't as well clothed as one of them. ³⁰God gives such beauty to everything that grows in the fields, even though it is here today and thrown into a fire tomorrow. He will surely do even more for you! Why do you have such little faith?

³¹Don't worry and ask yourselves, "Will we have anything to eat? Will we have anything to drink? Will we have any clothes to wear?" ³²Only people who don't know God are always worrying about such things. Your Father in heaven knows that you need all of these. ³³But more than anything else, put God's work first and do what he wants. Then the other things will be yours as well.

³⁴Don't worry about tomorrow. It will take care of itself. You have enough to worry about today.

ʲ6.27 *live longer:* Or "grow taller." ᵍ6.29 *Solomon with all his wealth:* The Jewish people thought that Solomon was the richest person who had ever lived.

MARRIAGE—How can we prevent financial issues from becoming stumbling blocks in our marriage? *(Matthew 6.19-24)*

Treasure your husband.

There you are in the department store—face-to-face with an unbeatable sale! Yet you know the money in your purse is allocated for dry cleaning and that you agreed not to charge anything on your credit card. Still, you *need* this blouse, and it normally sells for twice as much. If you buy it, what will you tell your husband?

Financial accountability in marriage either can be a burdensome obligation or a sweet gesture of unification. When you and your spouse agree on spending limits, treasure him so much that you won't violate your agreement.

Of course, some days you won't *feel* like treasuring him, especially when he violates spending agreements. That's why your marriage vows made before God help. On those days, you can ask God for a willingness to honor agreements with your spouse.

Money issues often pose tough questions: Do I serve God and treasure my spouse, or do I serve my desires to own more things and spend more money? Too often, these questions are dismissed lightly with words such as, *Look at how much I saved!* But there's a deeper issue involved. Who do you serve? Who do you treasure? (See also Psalm 49.16-20; Malachi 3.8-12; 1 Timothy 6.6-10; Hebrews 13.5,6.)

Words To Remember: *Your heart will always be where your treasure is. . . . You cannot serve both God and money.—Matthew 6.21,24*

Judging Others
(Luke 6.37, 38, 41, 42)

7 Don't condemn others, and God won't condemn you. ²God will be as hard on you as you are on others! He will treat you exactly as you treat them.

³You can see the speck in your friend's eye, but you don't notice the log in your own eye. ⁴How can you say, "My friend, let me take the speck out of your eye," when you don't see the log in your own eye? ⁵You're nothing but show-offs! First, take the log out of your own eye. Then you can see how to take the speck out of your friend's eye.

⁶Don't give to dogs what belongs to God. They will only turn and attack you. Don't throw pearls down in front of pigs. They will trample all over them.

Ask, Search, Knock
(Luke 11.9-13)

⁷Ask, and you will receive. Search, and you will find. Knock, and the door will be opened for you. ⁸Everyone who asks will receive. Everyone who searches will find. And the door will be opened for everyone who knocks. ⁹Would any of you give your hungry child a stone, if the child asked for some bread? ¹⁰Would you give your child a snake if the child asked for a fish? ¹¹As bad as you are, you still know how to give good gifts to your children. But your heavenly Father is even more ready to give good things to people who ask.

¹²Treat others as you want them to treat you. This is what the Law and the Prophets[h] are all about.

The Narrow Gate
(Luke 13.24)

¹³Go in through the narrow gate. The gate to destruction is wide, and the road that leads there is easy to follow. A lot of people go through that gate. ¹⁴But the gate to life is very narrow. The road that leads there is so hard to follow that only a few people find it.

A Tree and Its Fruit
(Luke 6.43-45)

¹⁵Watch out for false prophets! They dress up like sheep, but inside they are wolves who have come to attack you. ¹⁶You can tell what they are by what they do. No one picks grapes

---

[h]7.12 the Law and the Prophets: See the note at 5.17.

Personal Concerns—How can I overcome my tendency to worry and instead gain confidence about the future? (Matthew 6.25-34)

Do what you can in a single day.

Have you ever felt as if worrying about something really did help? Maybe you feel as if it earns you a positive outcome to a difficult situation. After all, you worked hard by worrying, so it should turn out well. Or you're a Murphy's Law buff and think that if you always plan for the worst, it won't happen.

But worrying not only ties us up emotionally, it hurts our relationship with God. By worrying, we're saying we're in control of circumstances, that we can manipulate the situation with our worry. In truth, God's in charge. While it can be hard to trust him to work for our good, trust is hard work that pays off. We'll experience a peace in difficult situations that equips us to respond better.

Trusting God also helps to limit our "worry" to what can be done today. Maybe all that can be done today is to greet someone civilly, eat a healthy dinner, or pay the one bill you do have money for. Figure out what you can do today and do it; then turn the rest over to God. (See also Joshua 23.14-16; Psalm 91; Micah 5.2-5; Habakkuk 3.16-19; Philippians 4.4-9.)

Words To Remember: *Don't worry about tomorrow. It will take care of itself. You have enough to worry about today.—Matthew 6.34*

or figs from thornbushes. [17]A good tree produces good fruit, and a bad tree produces bad fruit. [18]A good tree cannot produce bad fruit, and a bad tree cannot produce good fruit. [19]Every tree that produces bad fruit will be chopped down and burned. [20]You can tell who the false prophets are by their deeds.

A Warning
(Luke 13.26, 27)

[21]Not everyone who calls me their Lord will get into the kingdom of heaven. Only the ones who obey my Father in heaven will get in. [22]On the day of judgment many will call me their Lord. They will say, "We preached in your name, and in your name we forced out demons and worked many miracles." [23]But I will tell them, "I will have nothing to do with you! Get out of my sight, you evil people!"

Two Builders
(Luke 6.47-49)

[24]Anyone who hears and obeys these teachings of mine is like a wise person who built a house on solid rock. [25]Rain poured down, rivers flooded, and winds beat against that house. But it did not fall, because it was built on solid rock.

[26]Anyone who hears my teachings and doesn't obey them is like a foolish person who built a house on sand. [27]The rain poured down, the rivers flooded, and the winds blew and beat against that house. Finally, it fell with a crash.

[28]When Jesus finished speaking, the crowds were surprised at his teaching. [29]He taught them like someone with authority, and not like their teachers of the Law of Moses.

Jesus Heals a Man
(Mark 1.40-45; Luke 5.12-16)

8 As Jesus came down the mountain, he was followed by large crowds. [2]Suddenly a man with leprosy[i] came and knelt in front of Jesus. He said, "Lord, you have the power to make me well, if only you wanted to."

[3]Jesus put his hand on the man and said, "I want to! Now you are well." At once the man's leprosy disappeared. [4]Jesus told him, "Don't tell anyone about this, but go and show the priest that you are well.

---

[i]**8.2** *leprosy:* In biblical times the word "leprosy" was used for many different kinds of skin diseases.

Personal *Concerns*—How can I forgive someone who has broken my trust? *(Matthew 7.1-5)*

Use compassionate standards.
Most people break trust because they find themselves in a difficult situation. Maybe their loyalties are divided—should they help you or someone else? Or they perceive that they need something you cannot give (affirmation, money, attention, time).

God usually asks us to focus on right and wrong. But, in this case, God seems to ask us to focus on something else: Are we sure, given the same situation, we wouldn't have done the same? Plan on this: As soon as we become holier-than-thou about someone's behavior, we'll violate the same principle in some way. We can justify our actions, but then so can they. We're all fellow-travelers with similar flaws.

So instead of putting others down only to find ourselves doing the same thing, we need to be compassionate from the start. Sure, this person may have goofed, but so have we in some ways. Yes, this person deserves consequences, but we know that consequences hurt. Yes, this person did some things wrong, but because of Jesus Christ there's hope for her and for our relationship. (See also Numbers 14.11-25; 1 Samuel 24; Matthew 18.21-35; Luke 6.27-36.)

Words To Remember: *First, take the log out of your own eye. Then you can see how to take the speck out of your friend's eye.*—Matthew 7.5

Then take a gift to the temple just as Moses commanded, and everyone will know that you have been healed."[j]

Jesus Heals an Army Officer's Servant
(Luke 7.1-10; John 4.43-54)

[5]When Jesus was going into the town of Capernaum, an army officer came up to him and said, [6]"Lord, my servant is at home in such terrible pain that he can't even move."

[7]"I will go and heal him," Jesus replied.

[8]But the officer said, "Lord, I'm not good enough for you to come into my house. Just give the order, and my servant will get well. [9]I have officers who give orders to me, and I have soldiers who take orders from me. I can say to one of them, 'Go!' and he goes. I can say to another, 'Come!' and he comes. I can say to my servant, 'Do this!' and he will do it."

[10]When Jesus heard this, he was so surprised that he turned and said to the crowd following him, "I tell you that in all of Israel I've never found anyone with this much faith! [11]Many people will come from everywhere to enjoy the feast in the kingdom of heaven with Abraham, Isaac, and Jacob. [12]But the ones who should have been in the kingdom will be thrown out into the dark. They will cry and grit their teeth in pain."

[13]Then Jesus said to the officer, "You may go home now. Your faith has made it happen."

Right then his servant was healed.

Jesus Heals Many People
(Mark 1.29-34; Luke 4.38-41)

[14]Jesus went to the home of Peter, where he found that Peter's mother-in-law was sick in bed with fever. [15]He took her by the hand, and the fever left her. Then she got up and served Jesus a meal.

[16]That evening many people with demons in them were brought to Jesus. And with only a word he forced out the evil spirits and healed everyone who was sick. [17]So God's promise came true, just as the prophet Isaiah had said,

> "He healed our diseases
> and made us well."

Some Who Wanted To Go with Jesus
(Luke 9.57-62)

[18]When Jesus saw the crowd,[k] he went across Lake Galilee. [19]A teacher of the Law

---

[j]8.4 everyone will know that you have been healed: People with leprosy had to be examined by a priest and told that they were well (that is "clean") before they could once again live a normal life in the Jewish community. The gift that Moses commanded was the sacrifice of some lambs together with flour mixed with olive oil.
[k]8.18 saw the crowd: Some manuscripts have "large crowd." Others have "large crowds."

SpiritualLife—Does prayer really make a difference? (Matthew 7.7-12)

Prayer cultivates a searching heart.

Prayer not only makes *a* difference, but it makes *many* differences. We pray hoping for a certain outcome, but all kinds of changes go on within us when we have a conversation with God. We show him we want to connect with him. We become someone who asks, seeks, and knocks. We're not asking for more from ourselves, but from God. We're not seeking a great fortune, but we're seeking the one who loves us. We're not knocking on the door of opportunity, but we're gaining entrance to the Father's heart.

What we receive may not be the exact thing we asked for—it may be better. We long for a nicer home, but we gain satisfaction with the home we have. We long for a new friend, and while we wait, we learn a little more about being a friend of God. We long to walk through doors of greater achievement, but in the meantime, we shift our goals to God's purpose for our lives.

Meanwhile, God is changing the hearts of others, too. To our surprise, other people change their attitude toward us. People offer us opportunities that surprise us. The people we worked to know come instead to know us. Prayer really does make a difference.

(See also 2 Chronicles 20.1-30; Jeremiah 21.1-10; Luke 18.1-8; 2 Corinthians 12.6-10.)

Words To Remember: *Everyone who asks will receive. Everyone who searches will find. And the door will be opened for everyone who knocks.*—Matthew 7.8

of Moses came up to him and said, "Teacher, I'll go anywhere with you!"

²⁰Jesus replied, "Foxes have dens, and birds have nests. But the Son of Man doesn't have a place to call his own."

²¹Another disciple said to Jesus, "Lord, let me wait till I bury my father."

²²Jesus answered, "Come with me, and let the dead bury their dead."[l]

God uses the life stories I'm least proud of to force me to my greatest growth.

MARLENE D. LEFEVER

A Storm
(Mark 4.35-41; Luke 8.22-25)

²³After Jesus left in a boat with his disciples, ²⁴a terrible storm suddenly struck the lake, and waves started splashing into their boat.

Jesus was sound asleep, ²⁵so the disciples went over to him and woke him up. They said, "Lord, save us! We're going to drown!"

²⁶But Jesus replied, "Why are you so afraid? You surely don't have much faith." Then he got up and ordered the wind and the waves to calm down. And everything was calm.

²⁷The men in the boat were amazed and said, "Who is this? Even the wind and the waves obey him."

Two Men with Demons in Them
(Mark 5.1-20; Luke 8.26-39)

²⁸After Jesus had crossed the lake, he came to shore near the town of Gadara[m] and started down the road. Two men with demons in them came to him from the tombs.[n] They were so fierce that no one could travel that way. ²⁹Suddenly they shouted, "Jesus, Son of God, what do you want with us? Have you come to punish us before our time?"

³⁰Not far from there a large herd of pigs was feeding. ³¹So the demons begged Jesus, "If you force us out, please send us into those pigs!" ³²Jesus told them to go, and

they went out of the men and into the pigs. All at once the pigs rushed down the steep bank into the lake and drowned.

³³The people taking care of the pigs ran to the town and told everything, especially what had happened to the two men. ³⁴Everyone in town came out to meet Jesus. When they saw him, they begged him to leave their part of the country.

Jesus Heals a Crippled Man
(Mark 2.1-12; Luke 5.17-26)

9 Jesus got into a boat and crossed back over to the town where he lived.[o] ²Some people soon brought to him a crippled man lying on a mat. When Jesus saw how much faith they had, he said to the crippled man, "My friend, don't worry! Your sins are forgiven."

³Some teachers of the Law of Moses said to themselves, "Jesus must think he is God!"

⁴But Jesus knew what was in their minds, and he said, "Why are you thinking such evil things? ⁵Is it easier for me to tell this crippled man that his sins are forgiven or to tell him to get up and walk? ⁶But I will show you that the Son of Man has the right to forgive sins here on earth." So Jesus said to the man, "Get up! Pick up your mat and go on home." ⁷The man got up and went home. ⁸When the crowds saw this, they were afraid[p] and praised God for giving such authority to people.

Jesus Chooses Matthew
(Mark 2.13-17; Luke 5.27-32)

⁹As Jesus was leaving, he saw a tax collector[q] named Matthew sitting at the place for paying taxes. Jesus said to him, "Come with me." Matthew got up and went with him.

¹⁰Later, Jesus and his disciples were having dinner at Matthew's house.[r] Many tax collectors and other sinners were also there.

---

[l]**8.22** *let the dead bury their dead*: For the Jewish people a proper burial of their dead was a very important duty. But Jesus teaches that following him is even more important.   [m]**8.28** *Gadara*: Some manuscripts have "Gergesa." Others have "Gerasa."   [n]**8.28** *tombs*: It was thought that demons and evil spirits lived in tombs and in caves that were used for burying the dead. [o]**9.1** *where he lived*: Capernaum (see 4.13).   [p]**9.8** *afraid*: Some manuscripts have "amazed."   [q]**9.9** *tax collector*: See the note at 5.46.   [r]**9.10** *Matthew's house*: Or "Jesus' house."

¹¹Some Pharisees asked Jesus' disciples, "Why does your teacher eat with tax collectors and other sinners?"

¹²Jesus heard them and answered, "Healthy people don't need a doctor, but sick people do. ¹³Go and learn what the Scriptures mean when they say, 'Instead of offering sacrifices to me, I want you to be merciful to others.' I didn't come to invite good people to be my followers. I came to invite sinners."

People Ask about Going without Eating
(Mark 2.18-22; Luke 5.33-39)

¹⁴One day some followers of John the Baptist came and asked Jesus, "Why do we and the Pharisees often go without eating,ˢ while your disciples never do?"

¹⁵Jesus answered:

The friends of a bridegroom don't go without eating while he is still with them. But the time will come when he will be taken from them. Then they will go without eating.

¹⁶No one uses a new piece of cloth to patch old clothes. The patch would shrink and tear a bigger hole.

¹⁷No one pours new wine into old wineskins. The wine would swell and burst the old skins.ᵗ Then the wine would be lost, and the skins would be ruined. New wine must be put into new wineskins. Both the skins and the wine will then be safe.

A Dying Girl and a Sick Woman
(Mark 5.21-43; Luke 8.40-56)

¹⁸While Jesus was still speaking, an official came and knelt in front of him. The man said, "My daughter has just now died! Please come and place your hand on her. Then she will live again."

¹⁹Jesus and his disciples got up and went with the man.

²⁰A woman who had been bleeding for twelve years came up behind Jesus and barely touched his clothes. ²¹She had said to herself, "If I can just touch his clothes, I will get well."

²²Jesus turned. He saw the woman and said, "Don't worry! You are now well because of your faith." At that moment she was healed.

²³When Jesus went into the home of the official and saw the musicians and the crowd of mourners,ᵘ ²⁴he said, "Get out of here! The little girl isn't dead. She is just asleep." Everyone started laughing at Jesus. ²⁵But after the crowd had been sent out of the house, Jesus went to the girl's bedside. He took her by the hand and helped her up. ²⁶News about this spread all over that part of the country.

Jesus Heals Two Blind Men

²⁷As Jesus was walking along, two blind men began following him and shouting, "Son of David,ᵛ have pity on us!" ²⁸After Jesus had gone indoors, the two blind men came up to him. He asked them, "Do you believe I can make you well?"

"Yes, Lord," they answered.

²⁹Jesus touched their eyes and said, "Because of your faith, you will be healed." ³⁰They were able to see, and Jesus strictly warned them not to tell anyone about him. ³¹But they left and talked about him to everyone in that part of the country.

Jesus Heals a Man Who Could Not Talk

³²As Jesus and his disciples were on their way, some people brought to him a man who could not talk because a demon was in him. ³³After Jesus had forced the demon out, the man started talking. The crowds were so amazed that they began saying, "Nothing like this has ever happened in Israel!"

³⁴But the Pharisees said, "The leader of the demons gives him the power to force out demons."

Jesus Has Pity on People

³⁵Jesus went to every town and village. He taught in their meeting places and preached the good news about God's kingdom. Jesus also healed every kind of disease and sickness. ³⁶When he saw the crowds, he felt sorry for them. They were confused and helpless, like sheep without a shepherd.

ˢ**9.14** *without eating:* See the note at 4.2. ᵗ**9.17** *swell and burst the old skins:* While the juice from grapes was becoming wine, it would swell and stretch the skins in which it had been stored. If the skins were old and stiff, they would burst. ᵘ**9.23** *the crowd of mourners:* The Jewish people often hired mourners for funerals.
ᵛ**9.27** *Son of David:* The Jewish people expected the Messiah to be from the family of King David, and for this reason the Messiah was often called the "Son of David."

³⁷He said to his disciples, "A large crop is in the fields, but there are only a few workers. ³⁸Ask the Lord in charge of the harvest to send out workers to bring it in."

Jesus Chooses His Twelve Apostles
(Mark 3.13-19; Luke 6.12-16)

10 Jesus called together his twelve disciples. He gave them the power to force out evil spirits and to heal every kind of disease and sickness. ²The first of the twelve apostles was Simon, better known as Peter. His brother Andrew was an apostle, and so were James and John, the two sons of Zebedee. ³Philip, Bartholomew, Thomas, Matthew the tax collector,ʷ James the son of Alphaeus, and Thaddaeus were also apostles. ⁴The others were Simon, known as the Eager One,ˣ and Judas Iscariot,ʸ who later betrayed Jesus.

Instructions for the Twelve Apostles
(Mark 6.7-13; Luke 9.1-6)

⁵Jesus sent out the twelve apostles with these instructions:

Stay away from the Gentiles and don't go to any Samaritan town. ⁶Go only to the people of Israel, because they are like a flock of lost sheep. ⁷As you go, announce that the kingdom of heaven will soon be here.ᶻ ⁸Heal the sick, raise the dead to life, heal people who have leprosy,ᵃ and force out demons. You received without paying, now give without being paid. ⁹Don't take along any gold, silver, or copper coins. ¹⁰And don't carryᵇ a traveling bag or an extra shirt or sandals or a walking stick.

Workers deserve their food. ¹¹So when you go to a town or a village, find someone worthy enough to have you as their guest and stay with them until you leave. ¹²When you go to a home, give it your blessing of peace. ¹³If the home is deserving, let your blessing remain with them. But if the home isn't deserving, take back your blessing of peace. ¹⁴If someone won't welcome you or listen to your message, leave their home or town. And shake the dust from your feet at them.ᶜ ¹⁵I promise you that the day of judgment will be easier for the towns of Sodom and Gomorrahᵈ than for that town.

Warning about Trouble
(Mark 13.9-13; Luke 21.12-17)

¹⁶I am sending you like lambs into a pack of wolves. So be as wise as snakes and as innocent as doves. ¹⁷Watch out for people who will take you to court and have you beaten in their meeting places. ¹⁸Because of me, you will be dragged before rulers and kings to tell them and the Gentiles about your faith. ¹⁹But when someone arrests you, don't worry about what you will say or how you will say it. At that time you will be given the words to say. ²⁰But you will not really be the one speaking. The Spirit from your Father will tell you what to say.

²¹Brothers and sisters will betray one another and have each other put to death. Parents will betray their own children, and children will turn against their parents and have them killed. ²²Everyone will hate you because of me. But if you remain faithful until the end, you will be saved. ²³When people mistreat you in one town, hurry to another one. I promise you that before you have gone to all the towns of Israel, the Son of Man will come.

²⁴Disciples are not better than their teacher, and slaves are not better than their master. ²⁵It is enough for disciples to be like their teacher and for slaves to be like their master. If people call the head of the family Satan, what will they say about the rest of the family?

ʷ10.3 *tax collector*: See the note at 5.46.   ˣ10.4 *known as the Eager One*: The Greek text has "Cananaean," which probably comes from a Hebrew word meaning "zealous" (see Luke 6.15). "Zealot" was the name later given to the members of a Jewish group that resisted and fought against the Romans.   ʸ10.4 *Iscariot*: This may mean "a man from Kerioth" (a place in Judea). But more probably it means "a man who was a liar" or "a man who was a betrayer."   ᶻ10.7 *will soon be here*: Or "is already here."   ᵃ10.8 *leprosy*: See the note at 8.2.   ᵇ10.9,10 *Don't take along . . . don't carry*: Or "Don't accept . . . don't accept."   ᶜ10.14 *shake the dust from your feet at them*: This was a way of showing rejection (see Acts 13.51).   ᵈ10.15 *Sodom and Gomorrah*: During the time of Abraham the Lord destroyed these towns because the people there were so evil.

The One To Fear
(Luke 12.2-7)

²⁶Don't be afraid of anyone! Everything that is hidden will be found out, and every secret will be known. ²⁷Whatever I say to you in the dark, you must tell in the light. And you must announce from the housetops whatever I have whispered to you. ²⁸Don't be afraid of people. They can kill you, but they cannot harm your soul. Instead, you should fear God who can destroy both your body and your soul in hell. ²⁹Aren't two sparrows sold for only a penny? But your Father knows when any one of them falls to the ground. ³⁰Even the hairs on your head are counted. ³¹So don't be afraid! You are worth much more than many sparrows.

Telling Others about Christ
(Luke 12.8, 9)

³²If you tell others that you belong to me, I will tell my Father in heaven that you are my followers. ³³But if you reject me, I will tell my Father in heaven that you don't belong to me.

Not Peace, but Trouble
(Luke 12.51-53; 14.26, 27)

³⁴Don't think that I came to bring peace to the earth! I came to bring trouble, not peace. ³⁵I came to turn sons against their fathers, daughters against their mothers, and daughters-in-law against their mothers-in-law. ³⁶Your worst enemies will be in your own family.

³⁷If you love your father or mother or even your sons and daughters more than me, you are not fit to be my disciples. ³⁸And unless you are willing to take up your cross and come with me, you are not fit to be my disciples. ³⁹If you try to save your life, you will lose it. But if you give it up for me, you will surely find it.

Rewards
(Mark 9.41)

⁴⁰Anyone who welcomes you welcomes me. And anyone who welcomes me also welcomes the one who sent me. ⁴¹Anyone who welcomes a prophet, just because that person is a prophet, will be given the same reward as a prophet. Anyone who welcomes a good person, just because that person is good, will be given the same reward as a good person. ⁴²And anyone who gives one of my most humble followers a cup of cool water, just because that person is my follower, will surely be rewarded.

There are people all around us who need to know Christ. Instead of looking for something "big" to do, begin today to invest your gifts and talents in one person.

BABBIE MASON

John the Baptist
(Luke 7.18-35)

11 After Jesus had finished instructing his twelve disciples, he left and began teaching and preaching in the towns.ᵉ

²John was in prison when he heard what Christ was doing. So John sent some of his followers ³to ask Jesus, "Are you the one we should be looking for? Or must we wait for someone else?"

⁴Jesus answered, "Go and tell John what you have heard and seen. ⁵The blind are now able to see, and the lame can walk. People with leprosyᶠ are being healed, and the deaf can hear. The dead are raised to life, and the poor are hearing the good news. ⁶God will bless everyone who doesn't reject me because of what I do."

⁷As John's followers were going away, Jesus spoke to the crowds about John:

What sort of person did you go out into the desert to see? Was he like tall

---

ᵉ**11.1** *the towns:* The Greek text has "their towns," which may refer to the towns of Galilee or to the towns where Jesus' disciples had lived.   ᶠ**11.5** *leprosy:* See the note at 8.2.

grass blown about by the wind? [8]What kind of man did you go out to see? Was he someone dressed in fine clothes? People who dress like that live in the king's palace. [9]What did you really go out to see? Was he a prophet? He certainly was. I tell you that he was more than a prophet. [10]In the Scriptures God says about him, "I am sending my messenger ahead of you to get things ready for you." [11]I tell you that no one ever born on this earth is greater than John the Baptist. But whoever is least in the kingdom of heaven is greater than John.

[12]From the time of John the Baptist until now, violent people have been trying to take over the kingdom of heaven by force. [13]All the Books of the Prophets and the Law of Moses[g] told what was going to happen up to the time of John. [14]And if you believe them, John is Elijah, the prophet you are waiting for. [15]If you have ears, pay attention!

[16]You people are like children sitting in the market and shouting to each other,

[17]"We played the flute,
    but you would not dance!

We sang a funeral song,
    but you would not mourn!"

[18]John the Baptist did not go around eating and drinking, and you said, "That man has a demon in him!" [19]But the Son of Man goes around eating and drinking, and you say, "That man eats and drinks too much! He is even a friend of tax collectors[h] and sinners." Yet Wisdom is shown to be right by what it does.

The Unbelieving Towns
(Luke 10.13-15)

[20]In the towns where Jesus had worked most of his miracles, the people refused to turn to God. So Jesus was upset with them and said:

[21]You people of Chorazin are in for trouble! You people of Bethsaida are in for trouble too! If the miracles that took place in your towns had happened in Tyre and Sidon, the people there would have turned to God long ago. They would have dressed in

---

[g]11.13 *the Books of the Prophets and the Law of Moses*: The Jewish Scriptures, that is, the Old Testament.
[h]11.19 *tax collectors*: See the note at 5.46.

PARENTING&*family*—Sometimes I get upset and angry with my kids. How can I maintain a loving attitude when I'm about to explode?
(Matthew 11.25-29)

Set aside distractions.
Kids operate at a different level from adults. You may have just hung up the telephone, troubled by what someone said to you, but your kids don't notice your furrowed brow. From their perspective, they want to know *when* you're going to take them to the park. Lost in confusion and dismay, you snap at them that you don't know *when!*

Children don't understand that you're upset with the person on the telephone, so if you're wise, you'll make a space for yourself to turn this troubling encounter over to God. Otherwise, you'll take it with you and take it out on children who don't understand what they've done wrong.

Within that space, release the troublesome situation and accept God's rest. Sometimes you can retreat to the bathroom; other times, to a backyard swing. Still other times, scoop up that child; hold her on your lap while you ponder and pray. It's easy to think you're too busy or too strong to need to do this. And maybe that's true. But at the first sign of frustration, your children need you to dump your burdens on God—not on them. (See also Proverbs 15.1-4,18; Titus 3.3-8.)

Words To Remember: *If you are tired from carrying heavy burdens, come to me and I will give you rest.—Matthew 11.28*

sackcloth and put ashes on their heads.[i] [22]I tell you that on the day of judgment the people of Tyre and Sidon will get off easier than you will.

[23]People of Capernaum, do you think you will be honored in heaven? You will go down to hell! If the miracles that took place in your town had happened in Sodom, that town would still be standing. [24]So I tell you that on the day of judgment the people of Sodom will get off easier than you.

Come to Me and Rest
(Luke 10.21, 22)

[25]At that moment Jesus said:

My Father, Lord of heaven and earth, I am grateful that you hid all this from wise and educated people and showed it to ordinary people. [26]Yes, Father, that is what pleased you.

[27]My Father has given me everything, and he is the only one who knows the Son. The only one who truly knows the Father is the Son. But the Son wants to tell others about the Father, so that they can know him too.

[28]If you are tired from carrying heavy burdens, come to me and I will give you rest. [29]Take the yoke[j] I give you. Put it on your shoulders and learn from me. I am gentle and humble, and you will find rest. [30]This yoke is easy to bear, and this burden is light.

A Question about the Sabbath
(Mark 2.23-28; Luke 6.1-5)

12 One Sabbath, Jesus and his disciples were walking through some wheat fields.[k] His disciples were hungry and began picking and eating grains of wheat. [2]Some Pharisees noticed this and said to Jesus, "Why are your disciples picking grain on the Sabbath? They are not supposed to do that!"

[3]Jesus answered:

You surely must have read what David did when he and his followers were hungry. [4]He went into the house of God, and then they ate the sacred loaves of bread that only priests are supposed to eat. [5]Haven't you read in the Law of Moses that the priests are allowed to work in the temple on the Sabbath? But no one says that they are guilty of breaking the law of the Sabbath. [6]I tell you that there is something here greater than the temple. [7]Don't you know what the Scriptures mean when they say, "Instead of offering sacrifices to me, I want you to be merciful to others?" If you knew what this means, you would not condemn these innocent disciples of mine. [8]So the Son of Man is Lord over the Sabbath.

A Man with a Crippled Hand
(Mark 3.1-6; Luke 6.6-11)

[9]Jesus left and went into one of the Jewish meeting places, [10]where there was a man whose hand was crippled. Some Pharisees wanted to accuse Jesus of doing something wrong, and they asked him, "Is it right to heal someone on the Sabbath?"

[11]Jesus answered, "If you had a sheep that fell into a ditch on the Sabbath, wouldn't you lift it out? [12]People are worth much more than sheep, and so it is right to do good on the Sabbath." [13]Then Jesus told the man, "Hold out your hand." The man did, and it became as healthy as the other one.

[14]The Pharisees left and started making plans to kill Jesus.

God's Chosen Servant

[15]When Jesus found out what was happening, he left there and large crowds followed him. He healed all of their sick, [16]but warned them not to tell anyone about him. [17]So God's promise came true, just as Isaiah the prophet had said,

[18]"Here is my chosen servant!
  I love him,
    and he pleases me.
  I will give him my Spirit,
    and he will bring justice
      to the nations.
[19]He won't shout or yell
    or call out in the streets.

---

[i]**11.21** *sackcloth . . . ashes on their heads*: This was one way that people showed how sorry they were for their sins. [j]**11.29** *yoke*: Yokes were put on the necks of animals, so that they could pull a plow or wagon. A yoke was a symbol of obedience and hard work. [k]**12.1** *walking through some wheat fields*: It was the custom to let hungry travelers pick grains of wheat.

²⁰ He won't break off a bent reed
    or put out a dying flame,
  but he will make sure
    that justice is done.
²¹ All nations will place
    their hope in him."

*After I became a parent, it
was easier for me to grasp the
concept of God's love. As I
went through the triumphs
and traumas of parenting
and found myself still
constantly loving my son,
only then did I begin to
understand God's ability to
love me unconditionally.*

MAYO MATHERS

Jesus and the Ruler of the Demons
(Mark 3.20-30; Luke 11.14-23; 12.10)

²²Some people brought to Jesus a man who was blind and could not talk because he had a demon in him. Jesus healed the man, and then he was able to talk and see. ²³The crowds were so amazed that they asked, "Could Jesus be the Son of David?"ˡ

²⁴When the Pharisees heard this, they said, "He forces out demons by the power of Beelzebul, the ruler of the demons!"

²⁵Jesus knew what they were thinking, and he said to them:

Any kingdom where people fight each other will end up ruined. And a town or family that fights will soon destroy itself. ²⁶So if Satan fights against himself, how can his kingdom last? ²⁷If I use the power of Beelzebul to force out demons, whose power do your own followers use to force them out? Your followers are the ones who will judge you. ²⁸But when I force out demons by the power of God's Spirit, it proves that God's kingdom has already come to you. ²⁹How can anyone

break into a strong man's house and steal his things, unless he first ties up the strong man? Then he can take everything.

³⁰If you are not on my side, you are against me. If you don't gather in the harvest with me, you scatter it. ³¹⁻³²I tell you that any sinful thing you do or say can be forgiven. Even if you speak against the Son of Man, you can be forgiven. But if you speak against the Holy Spirit, you can never be forgiven, either in this life or in the life to come.

A Tree and Its Fruit
(Luke 6.43-45)

³³A good tree produces only good fruit, and a bad tree produces bad fruit. You can tell what a tree is like by the fruit it produces. ³⁴You are a bunch of evil snakes, so how can you say anything good? Your words show what is in your hearts. ³⁵Good people bring good things out of their hearts, but evil people bring evil things out of their hearts. ³⁶I promise you that on the day of judgment, everyone will have to account for every careless word they have spoken. ³⁷On that day they will be told that they are either innocent or guilty because of the things they have said.

A Sign from Heaven
(Mark 8.11, 12; Luke 11.29-32)

³⁸Some Pharisees and teachers of the Law of Moses said, "Teacher, we want you to show us a sign from heaven."

³⁹But Jesus replied:

You want a sign because you are evil and won't believe! But the only sign you will get is the sign of the prophet Jonah. ⁴⁰He was in the stomach of a big fish for three days and nights, just as the Son of Man will be deep in the earth for three days and nights. ⁴¹On the day of judgment the people of Ninevehᵐ will stand there

---

ˡ12.23 *Could Jesus be the Son of David:* Or "Does Jesus think he is the Son of David?" See the note at 9.27.
ᵐ12.41 *Nineveh:* During the time of Jonah this city was the capital of the Assyrian Empire, which was Israel's worst enemy. But Jonah was sent there to preach, so that the people would turn to the Lord and be saved.

with you and condemn you. They turned to God when Jonah preached, and yet here is something far greater than Jonah. [42]The Queen of the South[n] will also stand there with you and condemn you. She traveled a long way to hear Solomon's wisdom, and yet here is something much greater than Solomon.

Return of an Evil Spirit
(Luke 11.24-26)

[43]When an evil spirit leaves a person, it travels through the desert, looking for a place to rest. But when the demon doesn't find a place, [44]it says, "I will go back to the home I left." When it gets there and finds the place empty, clean, and fixed up, [45]it goes off and finds seven other evil spirits even worse than itself. They all come and make their home there, and the person ends up in worse shape than before. That's how it will be with you evil people of today.

Jesus' Mother and Brothers
(Mark 3.31-35; Luke 8.19-21)

[46]While Jesus was still speaking to the crowds, his mother and brothers came and stood outside because they wanted to talk with him. [47]Someone told Jesus, "Your mother and brothers are standing outside and want to talk with you."[o]

[48]Jesus answered, "Who is my mother and who are my brothers?" [49]Then he pointed to his disciples and said, "These are my mother and my brothers! [50]Anyone who obeys my Father in heaven is my brother or sister or mother."

A Story about a Farmer
(Mark 4.1-9; Luke 8.4-8)

13 That same day Jesus left the house and went out beside Lake Galilee, where he sat down to teach.[p] [2]Such large crowds gathered around him that he had to sit in a boat, while the people stood on the shore. [3]Then he taught them many things by using stories. He said:

A farmer went out to scatter seed in a field. [4]While the farmer was scattering the seed, some of it fell along the road and was eaten by birds. [5]Other seeds fell on thin, rocky ground and quickly started growing because the soil wasn't very deep. [6]But when the sun came up, the plants were scorched and dried up, because they did not have enough roots. [7]Some other seeds fell where thornbushes grew up and choked the plants. [8]But a few seeds did fall on good ground where the plants produced a hundred or sixty or thirty times as much as was scattered. [9]If you have ears, pay attention!

Why Jesus Used Stories
(Mark 4.10-12; Luke 8.9, 10)

[10]Jesus' disciples came to him and asked, "Why do you use nothing but stories when you speak to the people?"

[11]Jesus answered:

I have explained the secrets about the kingdom of heaven to you, but not to others. [12]Everyone who has something will be given more. But people who don't have anything will lose even what little they have. [13]I use stories when I speak to them because when they look, they cannot see, and when they listen, they cannot hear or understand. [14]So God's promise came true, just as the prophet Isaiah had said,

"These people will listen
and listen,
    but never understand.
They will look and look,
    but never see.
[15]All of them have
    stubborn minds!
Their ears are stopped up,
    and their eyes are covered.
They cannot see or hear
    or understand.
If they could,
they would turn to me,
    and I would heal them."

[16]But God has blessed you, because your eyes can see and your ears can hear! [17]Many prophets and good

---

[n]**12.42** *Queen of the South:* Sheba, probably a country in southern Arabia. [o]**12.47** *with you:* Some manuscripts do not have verse 47. [p]**13.1** *sat down to teach:* See the note at 5.1.

people were eager to see what you see and to hear what you hear. But I tell you that they did not see or hear.

Jesus conveyed truth through both tough and tender talk. The tough words pierced the conscience and exposed the content of the heart. The tender words penetrated pain and produced peace.

PATSY CLAIRMONT

Jesus Explains the Story about the Farmer
(Mark 4.13-20; Luke 8.11-15)

[18]Now listen to the meaning of the story about the farmer:

[19]The seeds that fell along the road are the people who hear the message about the kingdom, but don't understand it. Then the evil one comes and snatches the message from their hearts. [20]The seeds that fell on rocky ground are the people who gladly hear the message and accept it right away. [21]But they don't have deep roots, and they don't last very long. As soon as life gets hard or the message gets them in trouble, they give up. [22]The seeds that fell among the thornbushes are also people who hear the message. But they start worrying about the needs of this life and are fooled by the desire to get rich. So the message gets choked out, and they never produce anything. [23]The seeds that fell on good ground are the people who hear and understand the message. They produce as much as a hundred or sixty or thirty times what was planted.

Weeds among the Wheat

[24]Jesus then told them this story:

The kingdom of heaven is like what happened when a farmer scattered good seed in a field. [25]But while everyone was sleeping, an enemy came and scattered weed seeds in the field and then left.

[26]When the plants came up and began to ripen, the farmer's servants could see the weeds. [27]The servants came and asked, "Sir, didn't you scatter good seed in your field? Where did these weeds come from?"

[28]"An enemy did this," he replied.

His servants then asked, "Do you want us to go out and pull up the weeds?"

[29]"No!" he answered. "You might also pull up the wheat. [30]Leave the weeds alone until harvest time. Then I'll tell my workers to gather the weeds and tie them up and burn them. But I'll have them store the wheat in my barn."

Stories about a Mustard Seed and Yeast
(Mark 4.30-32; Luke 13.18-21)

[31]Jesus told them another story:

The kingdom of heaven is like what happens when a farmer plants a mustard seed in a field. [32]Although it is the smallest of all seeds, it grows larger than any garden plant and becomes a tree. Birds even come and nest on its branches.

[33]Jesus also said:

The kingdom of heaven is like what happens when a woman mixes a little yeast into three big batches of flour. Finally, all the dough rises.

The Reason for Teaching with Stories
(Mark 4.33, 34)

[34]Jesus used stories when he spoke to the people. In fact, he did not tell them anything without using stories. [35]So God's promise came true, just as the prophet[d] had said,

"I will use stories
    to speak my message
and to explain things
    that have been hidden
since the creation
    of the world."

---

[d]13.35 *the prophet*: Some manuscripts have "the prophet Isaiah."

Jesus Explains the Story about the Weeds

³⁶After Jesus left the crowd and went inside,ʳ his disciples came to him and said, "Explain to us the story about the weeds in the wheat field."

³⁷Jesus answered:

The one who scattered the good seed is the Son of Man. ³⁸The field is the world, and the good seeds are the people who belong to the kingdom. The weed seeds are those who belong to the evil one, ³⁹and the one who scattered them is the devil. The harvest is the end of time, and angels are the ones who bring in the harvest.

⁴⁰Weeds are gathered and burned. That's how it will be at the end of time. ⁴¹The Son of Man will send out his angels, and they will gather from his kingdom everyone who does wrong or causes others to sin. ⁴²Then he will throw them into a flaming furnace, where people will cry and grit their teeth in pain. ⁴³But everyone who has done right will shine like the sun in their Father's kingdom. If you have ears, pay attention!

A Hidden Treasure

⁴⁴The kingdom of heaven is like what happens when someone finds treasure hidden in a field and buries it again. A person like that is happy and goes and sells everything in order to buy that field.

A Valuable Pearl

⁴⁵The kingdom of heaven is like what happens when a shop owner is looking for fine pearls. ⁴⁶After finding a very valuable one, the owner goes and sells everything in order to buy that pearl.

A Fish Net

⁴⁷The kingdom of heaven is like what happens when a net is thrown into a lake and catches all kinds of fish. ⁴⁸When the net is full, it is dragged to the shore, and the fishermen sit down to separate the fish. They keep the good ones, but throw the bad ones away. ⁴⁹That's how it will be at the end of time. Angels will come and separate the evil people from the ones who have done right. ⁵⁰Then those evil people will be thrown into a flaming furnace, where they will cry and grit their teeth in pain.

New and Old Treasures

⁵¹Jesus asked his disciples if they understood all these things. They said, "Yes, we do."

⁵²So he told them, "Every student of the Scriptures who becomes a disciple in the kingdom of heaven is like someone who brings out new and old treasures from the storeroom."

The People of Nazareth Turn against Jesus
(Mark 6.1-6; Luke 4.16-30)

⁵³When Jesus had finished telling these stories, he left ⁵⁴and went to his hometown. He taught in their meeting place, and the people were so amazed that they asked, "Where does he get all this wisdom and the power to work these miracles? ⁵⁵Isn't he the son of the carpenter? Isn't Mary his mother, and aren't James, Joseph, Simon, and Judas his brothers? ⁵⁶Don't his sisters still live here in our town? How can he do all this?" ⁵⁷So the people were very unhappy because of what he was doing.

But Jesus said, "Prophets are honored by everyone, except the people of their hometown and their own family." ⁵⁸And because the people did not have any faith, Jesus did not work many miracles there.

The Death of John the Baptist
(Mark 6.14-29; Luke 9.7-9)

14 About this time Herod the rulerˢ heard the news about Jesus ²and told his officials, "This is John the Baptist! He has come back from death, and that's why he has the power to work these miracles."

³⁻⁴Herod had earlier arrested John and had him chained and put in prison. He did this because John had told him, "It isn't right for you to take Herodias, the wife of your brother Philip." ⁵Herod wanted to kill John. But the people thought John was a

---

ʳ13.36 went inside: Or "went home."   ˢ14.1 Herod the ruler: Herod Antipas, the son of Herod the Great (see 2.1).

prophet, and Herod was afraid of what they might do.

⁶When Herod's birthday came, the daughter of Herodias danced for the guests. She pleased Herod ⁷so much that he swore to give her whatever she wanted. ⁸But the girl's mother told her to say, "Here on a platter I want the head of John the Baptist!"

⁹The king was sorry for what he had said. But he did not want to break the promise he had made in front of his guests. So he ordered a guard ¹⁰to go to the prison and cut off John's head. ¹¹It was taken on a platter to the girl, and she gave it to her mother. ¹²John's followers took his body and buried it. Then they told Jesus what had happened.

Jesus Feeds Five Thousand
(Mark 6.30-44; Luke 9.10-17; John 6.1-14)

¹³After Jesus heard about John, he crossed Lake Galilee*ᵗ* to go to some place where he could be alone. But the crowds found out and followed him on foot from the towns. ¹⁴When Jesus got out of the boat, he saw the large crowd. He felt sorry for them and healed everyone who was sick.

¹⁵That evening the disciples came to Jesus and said, "This place is like a desert, and it is already late. Let the crowds leave, so they can go to the villages and buy some food."

¹⁶Jesus replied, "They don't have to

leave. Why don't you give them something to eat?"

¹⁷But they said, "We have only five small loaves of bread*ᵘ* and two fish." ¹⁸Jesus asked his disciples to bring the food to him, ¹⁹and he told the crowd to sit down on the grass. Jesus took the five loaves and the two fish. He looked up toward heaven and blessed the food. Then he broke the bread and handed it to his disciples, and they gave it to the people.

²⁰After everyone had eaten all they wanted, Jesus' disciples picked up twelve large baskets of leftovers.

²¹There were about five thousand men who ate, not counting the women and children.

Jesus Walks on the Water
(Mark 6.45-52; John 6.15-21)

²²Right away, Jesus made his disciples get into a boat and start back across the lake.*ᵛ* But he stayed until he had sent the crowds away. ²³Then he went up on a mountain where he could be alone and pray. Later that evening, he was still there.

²⁴By this time the boat was a long way

ᵗ**14.13** *crossed Lake Galilee:* To the east side.
ᵘ**14.17** *small loaves of bread:* These would have been flat and round or in the shape of a bun.   ᵛ**14.22** *back across the lake:* To the west side.

WORK—How can I balance the competing demands of home and work?
(Matthew 14.22,23)

Plan a getaway.
Getting away can seem selfish. *If I'm mature enough, why should I have to get away for an afternoon and go for a walk? For an evening to sit and stare in a coffee shop? For a weekend to enjoy leisure with my girlfriends or husband?* Yet the Son of God needed getaways and took them freely.

In the competing demands of home and work, you can forget who you are, what you want, and whom you care about. But within the "downtime" of a getaway, you can spend time with God thinking about what's really important in life. Sometimes a distraction—such as watching a sporting event or visiting an art museum—allows God to work on your heart so you can right those mixed-up feelings and motives. Other times a walk allows you to rant and rave about who did what and why they make you crazy. The release of it all lightens the load!

It's amazing how clear everything can look when you return from a getaway. Your home, however humble, is familiar and inviting. Your rowdy children are dear to you. Your routine seems just right. (See also Exodus 23.10-13; Deuteronomy 6.1-9; 2 Samuel 1.)

Words To Remember: *Then he went up on a mountain where he could be alone and pray.*—Matthew 14.23

Herodias

Matthew 14.1-12; Mark 6.14-29

When someone criticizes you, how do you respond? Do you "welcome critics as God's messengers"? Or do you mentally argue with them (*I'll just tell her . . .*) or even plot to destroy their credibility? Through the person of Herodias, the Bible shows us clearly what not to do so that we'll do the Christlike thing: the reverse of what she did.

Herodias, one of the New Testament's few fearless bad girls, had a critic to respond to, but unlike us, she was of royal lineage. She was the granddaughter of Herod the Great, who at Jesus' birth pretended to want to know about the Messiah but then ordered babies born at the same time as Jesus to be murdered. Herodias evidently craved this royal power because she stayed in the royal family by marrying relatives. First, she married Philip, who was her half uncle. (He and her father had the same father, but a different mother.) It isn't clear how or why, but she left him and married Herod Antipas—also her half uncle.

Enter John the Baptist, who publicly criticized Herodias and Herod for their promiscuous and quasi-incestuous behavior. Even though they were married, John publicly reproved them, quoting Old Testament law (Leviticus 18.16; 20.20,21). The only recorded reaction from the couple is that they wanted to kill John (Matthew 14.5; Mark 6.19). Herod at least feared John and protected him (Mark 6.19,20), but Herodias had no fear at all.

Herodias managed to overpower Herod and his fear. Herod adored the dancing of her daughter so much that he promised the girl anything she liked. At her mother's prompting, this young woman asked for the head of John the Baptist on a plate. Even though Herod was distressed, he gave in because "he did not want to break the promise he had made in front of his guests" (Matthew 14.9). What a study in contradictions—concern about keeping his oath, yet willingness to kill. We wonder how Herodias, having executed John, her arch-critic, felt when the man's head was presented to her at the dinner hour. Was she satisfied? Was that enough revenge? Was she glad to have brought her daughter into an above-the-law execution?

According to Josephus, the ambition of Herodias ruined Herod Antipas. She became jealous of Agrippa her brother and induced Herod to demand the title of king from Caligula, the Roman emperor. Agrippa managed to thwart this, and Herod was banished to Spain. Herodias, who went with Herod, died there.

from the shore. It was going against the wind and was being tossed around by the waves. ²⁵A little while before morning, Jesus came walking on the water toward his disciples. ²⁶When they saw him, they thought he was a ghost. They were terrified and started screaming.

²⁷At once, Jesus said to them, "Don't worry! I am Jesus. Don't be afraid."

²⁸Peter replied, "Lord, if it is really you, tell me to come to you on the water."

²⁹"Come on!" Jesus said. Peter then got out of the boat and started walking on the water toward him.

³⁰But when Peter saw how strong the wind was, he was afraid and started sinking. "Save me, Lord!" he shouted.

³¹Right away, Jesus reached out his hand. He helped Peter up and said, "You surely don't have much faith. Why do you doubt?"

³²When Jesus and Peter got into the boat, the wind died down. ³³The men in the boat worshiped Jesus and said, "You really are the Son of God!"

Jesus Heals Sick People in Gennesaret
(Mark 6.53-56)

³⁴Jesus and his disciples crossed the lake and came to shore near the town of Gennesaret. ³⁵The people found out that he was there, and they sent word to everyone who lived in that part of the country. So they brought all the sick people to Jesus. ³⁶They begged him just to let them touch his clothes, and everyone who did was healed.

The Teaching of the Ancestors
(Mark 7.1-13)

15 About this time some Pharisees and teachers of the Law of Moses came from Jerusalem. They asked Jesus, ²"Why don't your disciples obey what our ancestors taught us to do? They don't even wash their hands[w] before they eat."

³Jesus answered:

Why do you disobey God and follow your own teaching? ⁴Didn't God command you to respect your father and mother? Didn't he tell you to put to death all who curse their parents? ⁵But you let people get by without helping their parents when they should. You let them say that what they have has been offered to God.[x] ⁶Is this any way to show respect to your parents? You ignore God's commands in order to follow your own teaching.

ᵂ15.2 *wash their hands*: The Jewish people had strict laws about washing their hands before eating, especially if they had been out in public. ˣ15.5 *has been offered to God*: According to Jewish custom, when people said something was offered to God, it belonged to him and could not be used for anyone else, not even for their own parents.

PARENTING&*family*—What advice, if any, should I give to my twentysomething child? (Matthew 14.24-33)

Aim for independence.
The twentysomething person looks at the world and wants to take a crack at all kinds of opportunities. But you're afraid the world's opportunities will crack your child into pieces. How can you help her avoid the mistakes you made? How can you save him the grief you've suffered?

You can't, because through those mistakes, your twentysomething will learn and become as wise as you—or even wiser. If your son or daughter wants to leave the nest, let them move away from you peaceably. If you hold on to your children too tightly, they won't feel free to come back to you if a problem arises. They'll be afraid that if they reach for your hand, you'll never let go again, or you'll scold them for leaving.

You might try a little advice now and then, but don't alienate your child. He or she needs you too badly as a friend. So give yourself about three seconds and check: Is she listening? Has he tuned you out? Should you just laugh and say, "Let me know what you decide"? (See also Ecclesiastes 11.1—12.1; Ezekiel 18.1-20; Amos 5.6-27; 1 Timothy 4.6-16.)

Words To Remember: *"Don't worry! I am Jesus. Don't be afraid."*
—Matthew 14.27

[7]And you are nothing but show-offs! Isaiah the prophet was right when he wrote that God had said,

[8] "All of you praise me
     with your words,
   but you never really
     think about me.
[9] It is useless for you
     to worship me,
   when you teach rules
     made up by humans."

What Really Makes People Unclean
(Mark 7.14-23)

[10]Jesus called the crowd together and said, "Pay attention and try to understand what I mean. [11]The food that you put into your mouth doesn't make you unclean and unfit to worship God. The bad words that come out of your mouth are what make you unclean."

[12]Then his disciples came over to him and asked, "Do you know that you insulted the Pharisees by what you said?"

[13]Jesus answered, "Every plant that my Father in heaven did not plant will be pulled up by the roots. [14]Stay away from those Pharisees! They are like blind people leading other blind people, and all of them will fall into a ditch."

[15]Peter replied, "What did you mean when you talked about the things that make people unclean?"

[16]Jesus then said:

Don't any of you know what I am talking about by now? [17]Don't you know that the food you put into your mouth goes into your stomach and then out of your body? [18]But the words that come out of your mouth come from your heart. And they are what make you unfit to worship God. [19]Out of your heart come evil thoughts, murder, unfaithfulness in marriage, vulgar deeds, stealing, telling lies, and insulting others. [20]These are what make you unclean. Eating without washing your hands will not make you unfit to worship God.

A Woman's Faith
(Mark 7.24-30)

[21]Jesus left and went to the territory near the cities of Tyre and Sidon. [22]Suddenly a Canaanite woman[y] from there came out shouting, "Lord and Son of David,[z] have pity on me! My daughter is full of demons." [23]Jesus did not say a word. But the woman kept following along and shouting, so his disciples came up and asked him to send her away.

[24]Jesus said, "I was sent only to the people of Israel! They are like a flock of lost sheep."

---

[y]15.22 Canaanite woman: This woman was not Jewish.
[z]15.22 Son of David: See the note at 9.27.

WORK—Can I do the "Lord's work" in a secular job? If so, how?
(Matthew 15.10-20)

Let God work from the inside out.
Any task you have to do—whether it's conducting a meeting, invoicing an order, cleaning someone's bathroom, or taking a patient's blood pressure—can be done with many different attitudes: *What's in it for me? When do I get to go home? How can I help the other person?* The outward words and actions matter, but not as much as what's in your heart.

It helps to be aware of what we are here on earth to do: to make peace between God and other people, to bring them together, to reconcile the world to God (2 Corinthians 5.18,19). As we work in any kind of job, we need to ask ourselves how we can help someone get a clearer picture of God's love. And we can enjoy God's company while doing the task. It's not so much the specific task we do as the heart with which we do it. A peacemaking, reconciling heart doesn't give itself easily to evil thoughts, lies, and insults. Instead it makes peace, and puts forth what is right, in a loving way. (See also 1 Samuel 14.1-15; Ecclesiastes 2.24-26; Matthew 4.18-22.)

Words To Remember: *The words that come out of your mouth come from your heart.*—Matthew 15.18

²⁵The woman came closer. Then she knelt down and begged, "Please help me, Lord!"

²⁶Jesus replied, "It isn't right to take food away from children and feed it to dogs."ᵃ

²⁷"Lord, that's true," the woman said, "but even dogs get the crumbs that fall from their owner's table."

²⁸Jesus answered, "Dear woman, you really do have a lot of faith, and you will be given what you want." At that moment her daughter was healed.

Jesus Heals Many People

²⁹From there, Jesus went along Lake Galilee. Then he climbed a hill and sat down. ³⁰Large crowds came and brought many people who were crippled or blind or lame or unable to talk. They placed them, and many others, in front of Jesus, and he healed them all. ³¹Everyone was amazed at what they saw and heard. People who had never spoken could now speak. The lame were healed, the crippled could walk, and the blind were able to see. Everyone was praising the God of Israel.

Jesus Feeds Four Thousand
(Mark 8.1-10)

³²Jesus called his disciples together and told them, "I feel sorry for these people. They have been with me for three days, and they don't have anything to eat. I don't want to send them away hungry. They might faint on their way home."

³³His disciples said, "This place is like a desert. Where can we find enough food to feed such a crowd?"

³⁴Jesus asked them how much food they had. They replied, "Seven small loaves of breadᵇ and a few little fish."

³⁵After Jesus had told the people to sit down, ³⁶he took the seven loaves of bread and the fish and gave thanks. He then broke them and handed them to his disciples, who passed them around to the crowds.

³⁷Everyone ate all they wanted, and the leftovers filled seven large baskets.

³⁸There were four thousand men who ate, not counting the women and children.

³⁹After Jesus had sent the crowds away, he got into a boat and sailed across the lake. He came to shore near the town of Magadan.ᶜ

A Demand for a Sign from Heaven
(Mark 8.11-13; Luke 12.54-56)

16 The Pharisees and Sadducees came to Jesus and tried to test him by asking for a sign from heaven. ²He told them:

If the sky is red in the evening, you say the weather will be good. ³But if the sky is red and gloomy in the morning, you say it is going to rain. You can tell what the weather will be like by looking at the sky. But you don't understand what is happening now.ᵈ ⁴You want a sign because you are evil and won't believe! But the only sign you will be given is what happened to Jonah.ᵉ

Then Jesus left.

The Yeast of the Pharisees and Sadducees
(Mark 8.14-21)

⁵The disciples had forgotten to bring any bread when they crossed the lake.ᶠ ⁶Jesus then warned them, "Watch out! Guard against the yeast of the Pharisees and Sadducees."

⁷The disciples talked this over and said to each other, "He must be saying this because we didn't bring along any bread."

⁸Jesus knew what they were thinking and said:

You surely don't have much faith! Why are you talking about not having any bread? ⁹Don't you understand? Have you forgotten about the five thousand people and all those baskets of leftovers from just five loaves of bread? ¹⁰And what about the four thousand people and all those baskets of leftovers from only seven loaves of bread? ¹¹Don't you know by now that I am not talking to you about bread? Watch out for the yeast of the Pharisees and Sadducees!

¹²Finally, the disciples understood that

ᵃ**15.26** *feed it to dogs:* The Jewish people sometimes referred to Gentiles as dogs. ᵇ**15.34** *small loaves of bread:* See the note at 14.17. ᶜ**15.39** *Magadan:* The location is unknown. ᵈ**16.2,3** *If the sky is red . . . what is happening now:* The words of Jesus in verses 2 and 3 are not in some manuscripts. ᵉ**16.4** *what happened to Jonah:* Jonah was in the stomach of a big fish for three days and nights (see 12.40). ᶠ**16.5** *crossed the lake:* To the east side.

Jesus wasn't talking about the yeast used to make bread, but about the teaching of the Pharisees and Sadducees.

Who Is Jesus?
(Mark 8.27-30; Luke 9.18-21)

¹³When Jesus and his disciples were near the town of Caesarea Philippi, he asked them, "What do people say about the Son of Man?"

¹⁴The disciples answered, "Some people say you are John the Baptist or maybe Elijah[g] or Jeremiah or some other prophet."

> *Who do you say Christ is? The Son of God? Just a good man? Your response will determine how you live your life—and where you spend eternity.*
>
> RUTH BELL GRAHAM

¹⁵Then Jesus asked them, "But who do you say I am?"

¹⁶Simon Peter spoke up, "You are the Messiah, the Son of the living God."

¹⁷Jesus told him:

Simon, son of Jonah, you are blessed! You didn't discover this on your own. It was shown to you by my Father in heaven. ¹⁸So I will call you Peter, which means "a rock." On this rock I will build my church, and death itself will not have any power over it. ¹⁹I will give you the keys to the kingdom of heaven, and God in heaven will allow whatever you allow on earth. But he will not allow anything that you don't allow.

²⁰Jesus told his disciples not to tell anyone that he was the Messiah.

Jesus Speaks about His Suffering and Death
(Mark 8.31—9.1; Luke 9.22-27)

²¹From then on, Jesus began telling his disciples what would happen to him. He said, "I must go to Jerusalem. There the nation's leaders, the chief priests, and the teachers of the Law of Moses will make me suffer terribly. I will be killed, but three days later I will rise to life."

²²Peter took Jesus aside and told him to stop talking like that. He said, "God would never let this happen to you, Lord!"

²³Jesus turned to Peter and said, "Satan, get away from me! You're in my way because you think like everyone else and not like God."

²⁴Then Jesus said to his disciples:

If any of you want to be my followers, you must forget about yourself. You must take up your cross and follow me. ²⁵If you want to save your life,[h] you will destroy it. But if you give up your life for me, you will find it. ²⁶What will you gain, if you own the whole world but destroy yourself? What would you give to get back your soul?

²⁷The Son of Man will soon come in the glory of his Father and with his angels to reward all people for what they have done. ²⁸I promise you that some of those standing here will not die before they see the Son of Man coming with his kingdom.

The True Glory of Jesus
(Mark 9.2-13; Luke 9.28-36)

17 Six days later Jesus took Peter and the brothers James and John with him. They went up on a very high mountain where they could be alone. ²There in front of the disciples, Jesus was completely changed. His face was shining like the sun, and his clothes became white as light.

³All at once Moses and Elijah were there talking with Jesus. ⁴So Peter said to him, "Lord, it is good for us to be here! Let us make three shelters, one for you, one for Moses, and one for Elijah."

⁵While Peter was still speaking, the shadow of a bright cloud passed over them.

---

g16.14 *Elijah:* Many of the Jewish people expected the prophet Elijah to come and prepare the way for the Messiah.   h16.25 *life:* In verses 25 and 26 the same Greek word is translated "life," "yourself," and "soul."

From the cloud a voice said, "This is my own dear Son, and I am pleased with him. Listen to what he says!" [6]When the disciples heard the voice, they were so afraid that they fell flat on the ground. [7]But Jesus came over and touched them. He said, "Get up and don't be afraid!" [8]When they opened their eyes, they saw only Jesus.

[9]On their way down from the mountain, Jesus warned his disciples not to tell anyone what they had seen until after the Son of Man had been raised from death.

[10]The disciples asked Jesus, "Don't the teachers of the Law of Moses say that Elijah must come before the Messiah does?"

[11]Jesus told them, "Elijah certainly will come and get everything ready. [12]In fact, he has already come. But the people did not recognize him and treated him just as they wanted to. They will soon make the Son of Man suffer in the same way." [13]Then the disciples understood that Jesus was talking to them about John the Baptist.

Jesus Heals a Boy
(Mark 9.14-29; Luke 9.37-43a)

[14]Jesus and his disciples returned to the crowd. A man knelt in front of him [15]and said, "Lord, have pity on my son! He has a bad case of epilepsy and often falls into a fire or into water. [16]I brought him to your disciples, but none of them could heal him."

[17]Jesus said, "You people are too stub-born to have any faith! How much longer must I be with you? Why do I have to put up with you? Bring the boy here." [18]Then Jesus spoke sternly to the demon. It went out of the boy, and right then he was healed.

[19]Later the disciples went to Jesus in private and asked him, "Why couldn't we force out the demon?"

[20-21]Jesus replied:

It is because you don't have enough faith! But I can promise you this. If you had faith no larger than a mustard seed, you could tell this mountain to move from here to there. And it would. Everything would be possible for you.[i]

Jesus Again Speaks about His Death
(Mark 9.30-32; Luke 9.43b-45)

[22]While Jesus and his disciples were going from place to place in Galilee, he told them, "The Son of Man will be handed over to people [23]who will kill him. But three days later he will rise to life." All of this made the disciples very sad.

Paying the Temple Tax

[24]When Jesus and the others arrived in Capernaum, the collectors for the temple

---

[i]17.20,21 *for you:* Some manuscripts add, "But the only way to force out that kind of demon is by praying and going without eating."

∽⅏∽ ──────────────

SpiritualLife—How can I know good spiritual leaders? *(Matthew 17.1-13)*

They shine with the light of Jesus.
Maybe she's the one who introduced you to the faith. Or he's the pastor who's preached in your church for ten years. Or they're the couple who leads your Bible study. You trust their wisdom, and you've learned to count on their friendship. Why? Because they shine with the light of Jesus.

Just as Jesus reflected the glory of God to Peter, James, and John, on the high mountain (17.2), good spiritual leaders visibly reflect Christ in everything they do. They encourage, challenge, inspire, and yes, even rebuke when needed. They're your friends, your leaders, your coworkers, and your counselors. But above all, they shine with the love of Jesus. They serve humbly, rather than acting self-important. And they point the way to the most important person of all—our great and mighty God.

So for a true test of a good spiritual leader, check their habits and attitudes. Do they reflect Jesus? (See also 1 Kings 12.1-20; Ezra 7; Jude 3-7.)

∽⅏∽ **Words To Remember:** *There in front of the disciples, Jesus was completely changed. His face was shining like the sun, and his clothes became white as light.*
—**Matthew 17.2**

tax came to Peter and asked, "Does your teacher pay the temple tax?"

²⁵"Yes, he does," Peter answered.

After they had returned home, Jesus went up to Peter and asked him, "Simon, what do you think? Do the kings of this earth collect taxes and fees from their own people or from foreigners?"ʲ

²⁶Peter answered, "From foreigners."

Jesus replied, "Then their own peopleᵏ don't have to pay. ²⁷But we don't want to cause trouble. So go cast a line into the lake and pull out the first fish you hook. Open its mouth, and you will find a coin. Use it to pay your taxes and mine."

Who Is the Greatest?
(Mark 9.33-37; Luke 9.46-48)

18 About this time the disciples came to Jesus and asked him who would be the greatest in the kingdom of heaven. ²Jesus called a child over and had the child stand near him. ³Then he said:

I promise you this. If you don't change and become like a child, you will never get into the kingdom of heaven. ⁴But if you are as humble as this child, you are the greatest in the kingdom of heaven. ⁵And when you welcome one of these children because of me, you welcome me.

Temptations To Sin
(Mark 9.42-48; Luke 17.1, 2)

⁶It will be terrible for people who cause even one of my little followers to sin. Those people would be better off thrown into the deepest part of the ocean with a heavy stone tied around their necks! ⁷The world is in for trouble because of the way it causes people to sin. There will always be something to cause people to sin, but anyone who does this will be in for trouble.

⁸If your hand or foot causes you to sin, chop it off and throw it away! You would be better off to go into life crippled or lame than to have two hands or two feet and be thrown into the fire that never goes out. ⁹If your eye causes you to sin, poke it out and get rid of it. You would be better off to go into life with only one eye than to have two eyes and be thrown into the fires of hell.

The Lost Sheep
(Luke 15.3-7)

¹⁰⁻¹¹Don't be cruel to any of these little ones! I promise you that their

---

ʲ17.25 *from their own people or from foreigners*: Or "from their children or from others." ᵏ17.26 *From foreigners . . . their own people*: Or "From other people . . . their children."

SingleLife—What if I'm longing for children? *(Matthew 18.5)*

For now, welcome and love the children you encounter.
The longing for children can be so powerful that it hurts. But if you turn it over to God, he'll reveal to you ways to fulfill that longing—for now. There are plenty of children in today's world who need nurturing! The tough part is finding ways to connect. Try these ABCs to get you started:

[A]unting—be an interested relative to actual nieces and nephews, or to children of friends. Every child needs a nonparent adult who cares about the details in his or her life. Invite parents to let you babysit while they go off for a date. Take these children to the zoo, bake cookies together, or do other things you long for in parenting.

[B]ible study teacher—volunteer to teach Sunday school or a midweek Bible study provided by your church. As you guide preschoolers, children, or teens to talk about the Scripture, they'll learn how to live it. This is nurture at its best.

[C]onsider adoption—single parenting is a real possibility, especially to special-needs children. Call a Christian adoption agency for details.

The parent longing is the longing to nurture. Find the children God wants you to love—and do just that! (See also Jeremiah 20.7-18; Daniel 10.2-19.)

Words To Remember: *And when you welcome one of these children because of me, you welcome me.*—Matthew 18.5

angels are always with my Father in heaven.[l] [12]Let me ask you this. What would you do if you had a hundred sheep and one of them wandered off? Wouldn't you leave the ninety-nine on the hillside and go look for the one that had wandered away? [13]I am sure that finding it would make you happier than having the ninety-nine that never wandered off. [14]That's how it is with your Father in heaven. He doesn't want any of these little ones to be lost.

When Someone Sins
(Luke 17.3)

[15]If one of my followers[m] sins against you, go and point out what was wrong. But do it in private, just between the two of you. If that person listens, you have won back a follower. [16]But if that one refuses to listen, take along one or two others. The Scriptures teach that every complaint must be proven true by two or more witnesses. [17]If the follower refuses to listen to them, report the matter to the church. Anyone who refuses to listen to the church must be treated like an unbeliever or a tax collector.[n]

Allowing and Not Allowing

[18]I promise you that God in heaven will allow whatever you allow on earth, but he will not allow anything you don't allow. [19]I promise that when any two of you on earth agree about something you are praying for, my Father in heaven will do it for you. [20]Whenever two or three of you come together in my name,[o] I am there with you.

An Official Who Refused To Forgive

[21]Peter came up to the Lord and asked, "How many times should I forgive someone[p] who does something wrong to me? Is seven times enough?"

[22]Jesus answered:

Not just seven times, but seventy-seven times![q] [23]This story will show you what the kingdom of heaven is like:

One day a king decided to call in his officials and ask them to give an account of what they owed him. [24]As he was doing this, one official was brought in who owed him fifty million silver coins. [25]But he didn't have any money to pay what he owed. The king ordered him to be sold, along with his

---

[l]18.10,11 in heaven: Some manuscripts add, "The Son of Man came to save people who are lost."
[m]18.15 followers: The Greek text has "brother," which is used here and elsewhere in this chapter to refer to a follower of Christ. [n]18.17 tax collector: See the note at 5.46. [o]18.20 in my name: Or "as my followers." [p]18.21 someone: Or "a follower." See the note at 18.15. [q]18.22 seventy-seven times: Or "seventy times seven." The large number means that one follower should never stop forgiving another.

Friendship—How can I repair a broken friendship? (Matthew 18.15-20)

If possible, keep the matter private between you.
What's your first response when a friend has hurt you? Get her back? Pretend that nothing's wrong? Ask the advice of another friend? These all are perfectly natural responses. And, according to Jesus, all of them are wrong. As hard and embarrassing as it may seem, the first response is to go to that person privately, admit you've been hurt, and try to sort it out—just between the two of you. It doesn't always work, but if it does, you've gained a friend, and no one else need ever know about the problem.

But Jesus was a realist. He knew that not all relational problems are so easily solved, so he prescribed further steps toward reconciliation: Enlist the help of one or two others, perhaps even your church. If serious sin is involved and there's still no repentance after those steps, it may be best to separate. Perhaps the separation will cause your friend to miss relationships with other believers, turn away from her sin, and come back to the people of God. (See also Leviticus 19.17,18; Matthew 5.21-26; Luke 6.37-42.)

Words To Remember: *If one of my followers sins against you, go and point out what was wrong. But do it in private, just between the two of you. If that person listens, you have won back a follower.—Matthew 18.15*

wife and children and all he owned, in order to pay the debt.

²⁶The official got down on his knees and began begging, "Have pity on me, and I will pay you every cent I owe!" ²⁷The king felt sorry for him and let him go free. He even told the official that he did not have to pay back the money.

²⁸As the official was leaving, he happened to meet another official, who owed him a hundred silver coins. So he grabbed the man by the throat. He started choking him and said, "Pay me what you owe!"

²⁹The man got down on his knees and began begging, "Have pity on me, and I will pay you back." ³⁰But the first official refused to have pity. Instead, he went and had the other official put in jail until he could pay what he owed.

³¹When some other officials found out what had happened, they felt sorry for the man who had been put in jail. Then they told the king what had happened. ³²The king called the first official back in and said, "You're an evil man! When you begged for mercy, I said you did not have to pay back a cent. ³³Don't you think you should show pity to someone else, as I did to you?" ³⁴The king was so angry that he ordered the official to be tortured until

he could pay back everything he owed. ³⁵That is how my Father in heaven will treat you, if you don't forgive each of my followers with all your heart.

Teaching about Divorce
(Mark 10.1-12)

19 When Jesus finished teaching, he left Galilee and went to the part of Judea that is east of the Jordan River. ²Large crowds followed him, and he healed their sick people.

³Some Pharisees wanted to test Jesus. They came up to him and asked, "Is it right for a man to divorce his wife for just any reason?"

⁴Jesus answered, "Don't you know that in the beginning the Creator made a man and a woman? ⁵That's why a man leaves his father and mother and gets married. He becomes like one person with his wife. ⁶Then they are no longer two people, but one. And no one should separate a couple that God has joined together."

⁷The Pharisees asked Jesus, "Why did Moses say that a man could write out divorce papers and send his wife away?"

⁸Jesus replied, "You are so heartless! That's why Moses allowed you to divorce your wife. But from the beginning God did not intend it to be that way. ⁹I say that if your wife has not committed some terrible

---

Personal *Concerns*—How can I forgive someone who has broken my trust? *(Matthew 18.21-35)*

Pass on God's love.
Has someone ever been really good to you, and you felt "eternally grateful"? Maybe she even said to you, "You don't have to thank me. Just pass the good deed on to someone else."

That seems to be what God says to us. Yes, God has forgiven us a great deal, and he wants us to thank him. But he also asks us to ponder the huge debt of love we owe him—to the extent that we are willing to pass it on to someone as undeserving as we.

This is such a handy thing for us because we simply cannot forgive on our own. We have no power—only the power comes with being forgiven. It's as if that forgiveness has not only paid our debt to God, but put forgiveness into a savings account from which we can pay the debts of others. We pay off their debt with warm smiles and gentle conversations that flow from a heart that wants to forgive. (See also Numbers 14.11-25; 1 Samuel 24; Matthew 7.1-5; Luke 6.27-36.)

Words To Remember: *"Don't you think you should show pity to someone else, as I did to you?"*—Matthew 18.33

sexual sin,ʳ you must not divorce her to marry someone else. If you do, you are unfaithful."

¹⁰The disciples said, "If that's how it is between a man and a woman, it's better not to get married."

¹¹Jesus told them, "Only those people who have been given the gift of staying single can accept this teaching. ¹²Some people are unable to marry because of birth defects or because of what someone has done to their bodies. Others stay single for the sake of the kingdom of heaven. Anyone who can accept this teaching should do so."

Jesus Blesses Little Children
(Mark 10.13-16; Luke 18.15-17)

¹³Some people brought their children to Jesus, so that he could place his hands on them and pray for them. His disciples told the people to stop bothering him. ¹⁴But Jesus said, "Let the children come to me, and don't try to stop them! People who are like these children belong to God's kingdom."ˢ ¹⁵After Jesus had placed his hands on the children, he left.

A Rich Young Man
(Mark 10.17-31; Luke 18.18-30)

¹⁶A man came to Jesus and asked, "Teacher, what good thing must I do to have eternal life?"

¹⁷Jesus said to him, "Why do you ask me about what is good? Only God is good. If you want to have eternal life, you must obey his commandments."

¹⁸"Which ones?" the man asked.

Jesus answered, "Do not murder. Be faithful in marriage. Do not steal. Do not tell lies about others. ¹⁹Respect your father and mother. And love others as much as you love yourself." ²⁰The young man said, "I have obeyed all of these. What else must I do?"

²¹Jesus replied, "If you want to be perfect, go sell everything you own! Give the money to the poor, and you will have riches in heaven. Then come and be my follower." ²²When the young man heard this, he was sad, because he was very rich.

²³Jesus said to his disciples, "It's terribly hard for rich people to get into the kingdom of heaven! ²⁴In fact, it's easier for a camel to go through the eye of a needle than for a rich person to get into God's kingdom."

²⁵When the disciples heard this, they were greatly surprised and asked, "How can anyone ever be saved?"

²⁶Jesus looked straight at them and said,

ʳ**19.9** *some terrible sexual sin:* See the note at 5.32.
ˢ**19.14** *People who are like these children belong to God's kingdom:* Or "God's kingdom belongs to people who are like these children."

MARRIAGE—What does God think about divorce? *(Matthew 19.1-9)*

God's original design is for marriage—for a lifetime.
Have you ever asked someone a simple question—then she gave you a long answer explaining her philosophy on the whole subject? That's what Jesus did on the question of divorce. The Pharisees asked him if they could divorce someone and still be okay with God.

Jesus dealt instead with God's original design for marriage: that two people become so much a part of each other that the marriage cannot be broken without doing them harm. That means that two people do whatever work is required to stay married. (Note: However, this does not mean that a woman should put up with violence.) When questioned again, Jesus responded, "You are so heartless!" (19.8). It takes *work* to truly have a heart for someone else. We see only *our* side, so it becomes difficult to crawl into the other person's skin and understand his perspective. But Christ calls us to nurture our marriage, even when we don't feel like it.

These then are Christ's commands to us regarding marriage: Understand the sacredness of it (and expect to be ripped apart if the marriage ends); push away the heartlessness that kills a relationship. These are serious issues to consider whether you're single, dating, married, or divorced. (See also Malachi 2.13-16; 1 Corinthians 7.10-16; Ephesians 4.1-6.)

Words To Remember: *They are no longer two people, but one. And no one should separate a couple that God has joined together.—Matthew 19.6*

"There are some things that people cannot do, but God can do anything."

²⁷Peter replied, "Remember, we have left everything to be your followers! What will we get?"

²⁸Jesus answered:

Yes, all of you have become my followers. And so in the future world, when the Son of Man sits on his glorious throne, I promise that you will sit on twelve thrones to judge the twelve tribes of Israel. ²⁹All who have given up home or brothers and sisters or father and mother or children or land for me will be given a hundred times as much. They will also have eternal life. ³⁰But many who are now first will be last, and many who are last will be first.

Workers in a Vineyard

20 As Jesus was telling what the kingdom of heaven would be like, he said:

Early one morning a man went out to hire some workers for his vineyard. ²After he had agreed to pay them the usual amount for a day's work, he sent them off to his vineyard.

³About nine that morning, the man saw some other people standing in the market with nothing to do. ⁴He said he would pay them what was fair, if they would work in his vineyard. ⁵So they went.

At noon and again about three in the afternoon he returned to the market. And each time he made the same agreement with others who were loafing around with nothing to do.

⁶Finally, about five in the afternoon the man went back and found some others standing there. He asked them, "Why have you been standing here all day long doing nothing?"

⁷"Because no one has hired us," they answered. Then he told them to go work in his vineyard.

⁸That evening the owner of the vineyard told the man in charge of the workers to call them in and give them their money. He also told the man to begin with the ones who were hired last. ⁹When the workers arrived, the ones who had been hired at five in the afternoon were given a full day's pay.

¹⁰The workers who had been hired first thought they would be given more than the others. But when they were given the same, ¹¹they began complaining to the owner of the vineyard. ¹²They said, "The ones who were hired last worked for only one hour. But you paid them the same that you did us. And we worked in the hot sun all day long!"

¹³The owner answered one of them, "Friend, I didn't cheat you. I paid you exactly what we agreed on. ¹⁴Take your money now and go! What business is it of yours if I want to pay them the same that I paid you? ¹⁵Don't I have the right to do what I want with my own money? Why should you be jealous, if I want to be generous?"

¹⁶Jesus then said, "So it is. Everyone who is now first will be last, and everyone who is last will be first."

Jesus Again Tells about His Death
(Mark 10.32-34; Luke 18.31-34)

¹⁷As Jesus was on his way to Jerusalem, he took his twelve disciples aside and told them in private:

¹⁸We are now on our way to Jerusalem, where the Son of Man will be handed over to the chief priests and the teachers of the Law of Moses. They will sentence him to death, ¹⁹and then they will hand him over to foreigners[t] who will make fun of him. They will beat him and nail him to a cross. But on the third day he will rise from death.

A Mother's Request
(Mark 10.35-45)

²⁰The mother of James and John[u] came to Jesus with her two sons. She knelt down and started begging him to do something for her. ²¹Jesus asked her what she wanted, and she said, "When you come into your kingdom, please let one of my sons sit at your right side and the other at your left."[v]

---

[t]**20.19** *foreigners:* The Romans, who ruled Judea at this time.   [u]**20.20** *mother of James and John:* The Greek text has "mother of the sons of Zebedee" (see 26.37).
[v]**20.21** *right side . . . left:* The most powerful people in a kingdom sat at the right and left side of the king.

²²Jesus answered, "Not one of you knows what you are asking. Are you able to drink from the cup^w that I must soon drink from?"

James and John said, "Yes, we are!"

²³Jesus replied, "You certainly will drink from my cup! But it isn't for me to say who will sit at my right side and at my left. That is for my Father to say."

²⁴When the ten other disciples heard this, they were angry with the two brothers. ²⁵But Jesus called the disciples together and said:

You know that foreign rulers like to order their people around. And their great leaders have full power over everyone they rule. ²⁶But don't act like them. If you want to be great, you must be the servant of all the others. ²⁷And if you want to be first, you must be the slave of the rest. ²⁸The Son of Man did not come to be a slave master, but a slave who will give his life to rescue^x many people.

Jesus Heals Two Blind Men
(Mark 10.46-52; Luke 18.35-43)

²⁹Jesus was followed by a large crowd as he and his disciples were leaving Jericho. ³⁰Two blind men were sitting beside the road. And when they heard that Jesus was coming their way, they shouted, "Lord and Son of David,^y have pity on us!"

³¹The crowd told them to be quiet, but they shouted even louder, "Lord and Son of David, have pity on us!"

³²When Jesus heard them, he stopped and asked, "What do you want me to do for you?"

³³They answered, "Lord, we want to see!"

³⁴Jesus felt sorry for them and touched their eyes. Right away they could see, and they became his followers.

Jesus Enters Jerusalem
(Mark 11.1-11; Luke 19.28-38; John 12.12-19)

21 When Jesus and his disciples came near Jerusalem, he went to Bethphage on the Mount of Olives and sent two of them on ahead. ²He told them, "Go into the next village, where you will at once find a donkey and her colt. Untie the two donkeys and bring them to me. ³If anyone asks why you are doing that,

---

^w**20.22** *drink from the cup*: In the Scriptures a cup is sometimes used as a symbol of suffering. To "drink from the cup" is to suffer. ^x**20.28** *rescue*: The Greek word often, though not always, means the payment of a price to free a slave or a prisoner. ^y**20.30** *Son of David*: See the note at 9.27.

WORK—How can I rise above office politics? *(Matthew 20.20-28)*

Remember who you are.
One coworker negotiates for this perk, another one wheels and deals for additional compensatory days off, and you're left in their dust. Maybe you've heard the phrase, "Fight fire with fire!" and you're ready to do it. You almost forget you're a Christian, a reconciler, a woman who fights fire with water.

It's difficult to maintain godly values when others around you are being greedy and malicious, doing whatever it takes to get ahead. The disciples fell into that trap, but Jesus told them that even though other people were on power trips, "Don't act like them" (20.26). Christ's strong words confirm that God's people are called to be radically different from the world. We are to stand out by being salt and light in our surroundings.

That means that gossip doesn't interest us because our goal is to care for the person being gossiped about, not to make a spectacle of her. That means we can see past popularity scales and talk with the person who's often left out. It means we pray for each of our coworkers and ask God to show us how to have a heart for them—even for those who play the politics game. **(See also Deuteronomy 5.20,21; Esther 7.1-6; Galatians 5.13-16; Colossians 3.22—4.1; James 3.5-18.)**

Words To Remember: *If you want to be great, you must be the servant of all the others.*—Matthew 20.26

just say, 'The Lord[z] needs them.' Right away he will let you have the donkeys."

[4]So God's promise came true, just as the prophet had said,

> [5]"Announce to the people
>   of Jerusalem:
> 'Your king is coming to you!
> He is humble
>   and rides on a donkey.
> He comes on the colt
>   of a donkey.' "

[6]The disciples left and did what Jesus had told them to do. [7]They brought the donkey and its colt and laid some clothes on their backs. Then Jesus got on.

[8]Many people spread clothes in the road, while others put down branches[a] which they had cut from trees. [9]Some people walked ahead of Jesus and others followed behind. They were all shouting,

> "Hooray[b] for the Son of David![c]
> God bless the one who comes
>   in the name of the Lord.
> Hooray for God
>   in heaven above!"

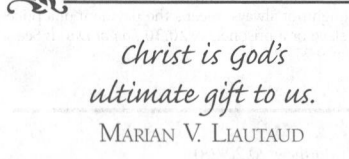

*Christ is God's
ultimate gift to us.*

MARIAN V. LIAUTAUD

[10]When Jesus came to Jerusalem, everyone in the city was excited and asked, "Who can this be?"

[11]The crowd answered, "This is Jesus, the prophet from Nazareth in Galilee."

Jesus in the Temple
(Mark 11.15-19; Luke 19.45-48; John 2.13-22)

[12]Jesus went into the temple and chased out everyone who was selling or buying. He turned over the tables of the money-changers and the benches of the ones who were selling doves. [13]He told them, "The Scriptures say, 'My house should be called a place of worship.' But you have turned it into a place where robbers hide."

[14]Blind and lame people came to Jesus in the temple, and he healed them. [15]But the chief priests and the teachers of the Law of Moses were angry when they saw his miracles and heard the children shouting praises to the Son of David.[c] [16]The men said to Jesus, "Don't you hear what those children are saying?"

"Yes, I do!" Jesus answered. "Don't you know that the Scriptures say, 'Children and infants will sing praises'?" [17]Then Jesus left the city and went out to the village of Bethany, where he spent the night.

Jesus Puts a Curse on a Fig Tree
(Mark 11.12-14, 20-24)

[18]When Jesus got up the next morning, he was hungry. He started out for the city, [19]and along the way he saw a fig tree. But when he came to it, he found only leaves and no figs. So he told the tree, "You will never again grow any fruit!" Right then the fig tree dried up.

[20]The disciples were shocked when they saw how quickly the tree had dried up. [21]But Jesus said to them, "If you have faith and don't doubt, I promise that you can do what I did to this tree. And you will be able to do even more. You can tell this mountain to get up and jump into the sea, and it will. [22]If you have faith when you pray, you will be given whatever you ask for."

A Question about Jesus' Authority
(Mark 11.27-33; Luke 20.1-8)

[23]Jesus had gone into the temple and was teaching when the chief priests and the leaders of the people came up to him. They asked, "What right do you have to do these things? Who gave you this authority?"

[24]Jesus answered, "I have just one question to ask you. If you answer it, I will tell you where I got the right to do these things. [25]Who gave John the right to baptize? Was it God in heaven or merely some human being?"

They thought it over and said to each other, "We can't say that God gave John this

---

[z]**21.3** *The Lord:* Or "The master of the donkeys." [a]**21.8** *spread clothes . . . put down branches:* This was one way that the Jewish people welcomed a famous person. [b]**21.9** *Hooray:* This translates a word that can mean "please save us." But it is most often used as a shout of praise to God. [c]**21.9,15** *Son of David:* See the note at 9.27.

right. Jesus will ask us why we didn't believe John. ²⁶On the other hand, these people think that John was a prophet, and we are afraid of what they might do to us. That's why we can't say that it was merely some human who gave John the right to baptize." ²⁷So they told Jesus, "We don't know."

Jesus said, "Then I won't tell you who gave me the right to do what I do."

A Story about Two Sons

²⁸Jesus said:

I will tell you a story about a man who had two sons. Then you can tell me what you think. The father went to the older son and said, "Go work in the vineyard today!" ²⁹His son told him that he would not do it, but later he changed his mind and went. ³⁰The man then told his younger son to go work in the vineyard. The boy said he would, but he didn't go. ³¹Which one of the sons obeyed his father?

"The older one," the chief priests and leaders answered.

Then Jesus told them:

You can be sure that tax collectors^d and prostitutes will get into the kingdom of God before you ever will! ³²When John the Baptist showed you how to do right, you would not believe him. But these evil people did believe. And even when you saw what they did, you still would not change your minds and believe.

Renters of a Vineyard

(Mark 12.1-12; Luke 20.9-19)

³³Jesus told the chief priests and leaders to listen to this story:

A land owner once planted a vineyard. He built a wall around it and dug a pit to crush the grapes in. He also built a lookout tower. Then he rented out his vineyard and left the country. ³⁴When it was harvest time, the owner sent some servants to get his share of the grapes. ³⁵But the renters grabbed those servants. They beat up one, killed one, and stoned one of them to death. ³⁶He then sent more servants than he did the first time. But the renters treated them in the same way.

³⁷Finally, the owner sent his own son to the renters, because he thought they would respect him. ³⁸But when they saw the man's son, they said, "Someday he will own the vineyard. Let's kill him! Then we can have it all for ourselves." ³⁹So they grabbed him, threw him out of the vineyard, and killed him.

⁴⁰Jesus asked, "When the owner of that vineyard comes, what do you suppose he will do to those renters?"

⁴¹The chief priests and leaders answered, "He will kill them in some horrible way. Then he will rent out his vineyard to people who will give him his share of grapes at harvest time."

⁴²Jesus replied, "You surely know that the Scriptures say,

'The stone that the builders
    tossed aside
is now the most important
    stone of all.
This is something
the Lord has done,
    and it is amazing to us.'

⁴³I tell you that God's kingdom will be taken from you and given to people who will do what he demands. ⁴⁴Anyone who stumbles over this stone will be crushed, and anyone it falls on will be smashed to pieces."^e

⁴⁵When the chief priests and the Pharisees heard these stories, they knew that Jesus was talking about them. ⁴⁶So they looked for a way to arrest Jesus. But they were afraid to, because the people thought he was a prophet.

The Great Banquet

(Luke 14.15-24)

22 Once again Jesus used stories to teach the people:

²The kingdom of heaven is like what happened when a king gave a wedding banquet for his son. ³The king sent some servants to tell the invited guests to come to the banquet, but the guests refused. ⁴He sent other servants to say to the guests, "The banquet is ready! My cattle and prize

---

^d**21.31** *tax collectors*: See the note at 5.46.
^e**21.44** *pieces*: Verse 44 is not in some manuscripts.

calves have all been prepared. Everything is ready. Come to the banquet!"

⁵But the guests did not pay any attention. Some of them left for their farms, and some went to their places of business. ⁶Others grabbed the servants, then beat them up and killed them.

⁷This made the king so furious that he sent an army to kill those murderers and burn down their city. ⁸Then he said to the servants, "It is time for the wedding banquet, and the invited guests don't deserve to come. ⁹Go out to the street corners and tell everyone you meet to come to the banquet." ¹⁰They went out on the streets and brought in everyone they could find, good and bad alike. And the banquet room was filled with guests.

¹¹When the king went in to meet the guests, he found that one of them wasn't wearing the right kind of clothes for the wedding. ¹²The king asked, "Friend, why didn't you wear proper clothes for the wedding?" But the guest had no excuse. ¹³So the king gave orders for that person to be tied hand and foot and to be thrown outside into the dark. That's where people will cry and grit their teeth in pain. ¹⁴Many are invited, but only a few are chosen.

Paying Taxes
(Mark 12.13-17; Luke 20.20-26)

¹⁵The Pharisees got together and planned how they could trick Jesus into saying something wrong. ¹⁶They sent some of their followers and some of Herod's followers⁄ to say to him, "Teacher, we know that you are honest. You teach the truth about what God wants people to do. And you treat everyone with the same respect, no matter who they are. ¹⁷Tell us what you think! Should we pay taxes to the Emperor or not?"

¹⁸Jesus knew their evil thoughts and said, "Why are you trying to test me? You show-offs! ¹⁹Let me see one of the coins used for paying taxes." They brought him a silver coin, ²⁰and he asked, "Whose picture and name are on it?"

²¹"The Emperor's," they answered.

Then Jesus told them, "Give the Emperor what belongs to him and give God

what belongs to God." ²²His answer surprised them so much that they walked away.

Life in the Future World
(Mark 12.18-27; Luke 20.27-40)

²³The Sadducees did not believe that people would rise to life after death. So that same day some of the Sadducees came to Jesus and said:

²⁴Teacher, Moses wrote that if a married man dies and has no children, his brother should marry the widow. Their first son would then be thought of as the son of the dead brother.

²⁵Once there were seven brothers who lived here. The first one married, but died without having any children. So his wife was left to his brother. ²⁶The same thing happened to the second and third brothers and finally to all seven of them. ²⁷At last the woman died. ²⁸When God raises people from death, whose wife will this woman be? She had been married to all seven brothers.

²⁹Jesus answered:

You are completely wrong! You don't know what the Scriptures teach. And you don't know anything about the power of God. ³⁰When God raises people to life, they won't marry. They will be like the angels in heaven. ³¹And as for people being raised to life, God was speaking to you when he said, ³²"I am the God worshiped by Abraham, Isaac, and Jacob."ᵍ He isn't the God of the dead, but of the living.

³³The crowds were surprised to hear what Jesus was teaching.

The Most Important Commandment
(Mark 12.28-34; Luke 10.25-28)

³⁴After Jesus had made the Sadducees look foolish, the Pharisees heard about it and got together. ³⁵One of them was an expert in the Jewish Law. So he tried to test Jesus by asking, ³⁶"Teacher, what is the most important commandment in the Law?"

⁄22.16 Herod's followers: People who were political followers of the family of Herod the Great (see 2.1) and his son Herod Antipas (see 14.1), and who wanted Herod to be king in Jerusalem. ᵍ22.32 I am the God worshiped by Abraham, Isaac, and Jacob: Jesus argues that if God is worshiped by these three, they must still be alive, because he is the God of the living.

³⁷Jesus answered:

Love the Lord your God with all your heart, soul, and mind. ³⁸This is the first and most important commandment. ³⁹The second most important commandment is like this one. And it is, "Love others as much as you love yourself." ⁴⁰All the Law of Moses and the Books of the Prophets[h] are based on these two commandments.

About David's Son
(Mark 12.35-37; Luke 20.41-44)

⁴¹While the Pharisees were still there, Jesus asked them, ⁴²"What do you think about the Messiah? Whose family will he come from?"

They answered, "He will be a son of King David."[i]

⁴³Jesus replied, "How then could the Spirit lead David to call the Messiah his Lord? David said,

⁴⁴ 'The Lord said to my Lord:
    Sit at my right side[j]
until I make your enemies
    into a footstool for you.'

⁴⁵If David called the Messiah his Lord, how can the Messiah be a son of King David?" ⁴⁶No one was able to give Jesus an answer, and from that day on, no one dared ask him any more questions.

Jesus Condemns the Pharisees and the Teachers of the Law of Moses
(Mark 12.38-40; Luke 11.37-52; 20.45-47)

23 Jesus said to the crowds and to his disciples:

²The Pharisees and the teachers of the Law are experts in the Law of Moses. ³So obey everything they teach you, but don't do as they do. After all, they say one thing and do something else.

⁴They pile heavy burdens on people's shoulders and won't lift a finger to help. ⁵Everything they do is just to show off in front of others. They even make a big show of wearing Scripture verses on their foreheads and arms, and they wear big tassels[k] for

---

[h]**22.40** *the Law of Moses and the Books of the Prophets*: The Jewish Scriptures, that is, the Old Testament.
[i]**22.42** *son of King David*: See the note at 9.27.
[j]**22.44** *right side*: The place of power and honor.
[k]**23.5** *wearing Scripture verses on their foreheads and arms . . . tassels*: As a sign of their love for the Lord and his teachings, the Jewish people had started wearing Scripture verses in small leather boxes. But the Pharisees tried to show off by making the boxes bigger than necessary. The Jewish people were also taught to wear tassels on the four corners of their robes to show their love for God.

Personal *Concerns*—Should I maintain friendships with non-Christians? If so, how can I keep from compromising my faith? *(Matthew 22.34-40)*

Love your neighbor—but love God first.

As women in today's busy culture, we're often stretched to our limits time-wise and relationship-wise. Friends sometimes are put on the back burner (unless we see them as a regular part of our schedule). As Christians, most likely we spend the majority of our time with other Christians—and that's good, because they keep us accountable and help us grow in the faith.

But what about spending time with non-Christians? For some of us, that means we have to be *intentional* about our friendships. It means we say hello to the woman in the park who jogs there every Tuesday; we invite a new coworker out to lunch; we knock on a neighbor's door and offer fresh-baked cookies.

Jesus loved people, and so should we: "Love others as much as you love yourself" (22.39). But he also made clear what our top priority should be as Christians: To "love the Lord your God with all your heart, soul, and mind" (22.37). Thus, when we meet non-Christians, our goal should be not only to "love" and befriend them, but to introduce them to the best friend they could ever have—Jesus! (See also Obadiah 10-14; Romans 3.9-20.)

Words To Remember: *"Love the Lord your God with all your heart, soul, and mind. . . . Love others as much as you love yourself."*—Matthew 22.37,39

everyone to see. [6]They love the best seats at banquets and the front seats in the meeting places. [7]And when they are in the market, they like to have people greet them as their teachers.

[8]But none of you should be called a teacher. You have only one teacher, and all of you are like brothers and sisters. [9]Don't call anyone on earth your father. All of you have the same Father in heaven. [10]None of you should be called the leader. The Messiah is your only leader. [11]Whoever is the greatest should be the servant of the others. [12]If you put yourself above others, you will be put down. But if you humble yourself, you will be honored.

[13-14]You Pharisees and teachers of the Law of Moses are in for trouble! You're nothing but show-offs. You lock people out of the kingdom of heaven. You won't go in yourselves, and you keep others from going in.[l]

[15]You Pharisees and teachers of the Law of Moses are in for trouble! You're nothing but show-offs. You travel over land and sea to win one follower. And when you have done so, you make that person twice as fit for hell as you are.

[16]You are in for trouble! You are supposed to lead others, but you are blind. You teach that it doesn't matter if a person swears by the temple. But you say that it does matter if someone swears by the gold in the temple. [17]You blind fools! Which is greater, the gold or the temple that makes the gold sacred?

[18]You also teach that it doesn't matter if a person swears by the altar. But you say that it does matter if someone swears by the gift on the altar. [19]Are you blind? Which is more important, the gift or the altar that makes the gift sacred? [20]Anyone who swears by the altar also swears by everything on it. [21]And anyone who swears by the temple also swears by God, who lives there. [22]To swear by heaven is the same as swearing by God's throne and by the one who sits on that throne.

[23]You Pharisees and teachers are show-offs, and you're in for trouble! You give God a tenth of the spices from your garden, such as mint, dill, and cumin. Yet you neglect the more important matters of the Law, such as justice, mercy, and faithfulness. These are the important things you should have done, though you should not have left the others undone either. [24]You blind leaders! You strain out a small fly but swallow a camel.

[25]You Pharisees and teachers are show-offs, and you're in for trouble! You wash the outside of your cups and dishes, while inside there is nothing but greed and selfishness. [26]You blind Pharisee! First clean the inside of a cup, and then the outside will also be clean.

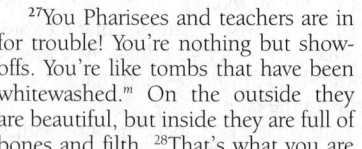

What we need to remember is this: The Bible says man looks at the outward appearance, but the Lord looks at the heart. Your outward appearance is never as important as your heart. That's what's eternally significant.

Dr. Lori Hansen

[27]You Pharisees and teachers are in for trouble! You're nothing but show-offs. You're like tombs that have been whitewashed.[m] On the outside they are beautiful, but inside they are full of bones and filth. [28]That's what you are like. Outside you look good, but in-

---

[l]**23.13,14** *from going in:* Some manuscripts add, "You Pharisees and teachers are in for trouble! And you're nothing but show-offs! You cheat widows out of their homes and then pray long prayers just to show off. So you will be punished most of all."
[m]**23.27** *whitewashed:* Tombs were whitewashed to keep anyone from accidentally touching them. A person who touched a dead body or a tomb was considered unclean and could not worship with the rest of the Jewish people.

side you are evil and only pretend to be good.

[29]You Pharisees and teachers are nothing but show-offs, and you're in for trouble! You build monuments for the prophets and decorate the tombs of good people. [30]And you claim that you would not have taken part with your ancestors in killing the prophets. [31]But you prove that you really are the relatives of the ones who killed the prophets. [32]So keep on doing everything they did. [33]You are nothing but snakes and the children of snakes! How can you escape going to hell?

[34]I will send prophets and wise people and experts in the Law of Moses to you. But you will kill them or nail them to a cross or beat them in your meeting places or chase them from town to town. [35]That's why you will be held guilty for the murder of every good person, beginning with the good man Abel. This also includes Barachiah's son Zechariah,[n] the man you murdered between the temple and the altar. [36]I can promise that you people living today will be punished for all these things!

Jesus Loves Jerusalem
(Luke 13.34, 35)

[37]Jerusalem, Jerusalem! Your people have killed the prophets and have stoned the messengers who were sent to you. I have often wanted to gather your people, as a hen gathers her chicks under her wings. But you wouldn't let me. [38]And now your temple will be deserted. [39]You won't see me again until you say,

"Blessed is the one who comes
in the name of the Lord."

The Temple Will Be Destroyed
(Mark 13.1, 2; Luke 21.5, 6)

24 After Jesus left the temple, his disciples came over and said, "Look at all these buildings!" [2]Jesus replied, "Do you see these buildings? They will certainly be torn down! Not one stone will be left in place."

Warning about Trouble
(Mark 13.3-13; Luke 21.7-19)

[3]Later, as Jesus was sitting on the Mount of Olives, his disciples came to him in private and asked, "When will this happen? What will be the sign of your coming and of the end of the world?"

[4]Jesus answered:

Don't let anyone fool you. [5]Many will come and claim to be me. They will say that they are the Messiah, and they will fool many people.

[6]You will soon hear about wars and threats of wars, but don't be afraid. These things will have to happen first, but that isn't the end. [7]Nations and kingdoms will go to war against each other. People will starve to death, and in some places there will be earthquakes. [8]But this is just the beginning of troubles.

[9]You will be arrested, punished, and even killed. Because of me, you will be hated by people of all nations. [10]Many will give up and will betray and hate each other. [11]Many false prophets will come and fool a lot of people. [12]Evil will spread and cause many people to stop loving others. [13]But if you keep on being faithful right to the end, you will be saved. [14]When the good news about the kingdom has been preached all over the world and told to all nations, the end will come.

The Horrible Thing
(Mark 13.14-23; Luke 21.20-24)

[15]Someday you will see that "Horrible Thing" in the holy place, just as the prophet Daniel said. Everyone who reads this must try to understand! [16]If you are living in Judea at that time, run to the mountains. [17]If you are on the roof[o] of your house, don't go inside to get anything. [18]If you are out in the field, don't go back for your coat. [19]It will be a terrible time

---

[n]23.35 *Zechariah*: Genesis is the first book in the Jewish Scriptures, and it tells that Abel was the first person to be murdered. Second Chronicles is the last book in the Jewish Scriptures, and the last murder that it tells about is that of Zechariah.   [o]24.17 *roof*: In Palestine the houses usually had a flat roof. Stairs on the outside led up to the roof, which was made of beams and boards covered with packed earth.

for women who are expecting babies or nursing young children. [20]And pray that you won't have to escape in winter or on a Sabbath.[p] [21]This will be the worst time of suffering since the beginning of the world, and nothing this terrible will ever happen again. [22]If God doesn't make the time shorter, no one will be left alive. But because of God's chosen ones, he will make the time shorter.

[23]Someone may say, "Here is the Messiah!" or "There he is!" But don't believe it. [24]False messiahs and false prophets will come and work great miracles and signs. They will even try to fool God's chosen ones. [25]But I have warned you ahead of time. [26]If you are told that the Messiah is out in the desert, don't go there! And if you are told that he is in some secret place, don't believe it! [27]The coming of the Son of Man will be like lightning that can be seen from east to west. [28]Where there is a corpse, there will always be buzzards.[q]

When the Son of Man Appears
(Mark 13.24-27; Luke 21.25-28)

[29]Right after those days of suffering,

> "The sun will become dark,
>   and the moon
>   will no longer shine.
> The stars will fall,
>   and the powers in the sky[r]
>   will be shaken."

[30]Then a sign will appear in the sky. And there will be the Son of Man.[s] All nations on earth will weep when they see the Son of Man coming on the clouds of heaven with power and great glory. [31]At the sound of a loud trumpet, he will send his angels to bring his chosen ones together from all over the earth.

A Lesson from a Fig Tree
(Mark 13.28-31; Luke 21.29-33)

[32]Learn a lesson from a fig tree. When its branches sprout and start

putting out leaves, you know that summer is near. [33]So when you see all these things happening, you will know that the time has almost come.[t] [34]I can promise you that some of the people of this generation will still be alive when all this happens. [35]The sky and the earth won't last forever, but my words will.

No One Knows the Day or Time
(Mark 13.32-37; Luke 17.26-30, 34-36)

[36]No one knows the day or hour. The angels in heaven don't know, and the Son himself doesn't know.[u] Only the Father knows. [37]When the Son of Man appears, things will be just as they were when Noah lived. [38]People were eating, drinking, and getting married right up to the day that the flood came and Noah went into the big boat. [39]They didn't know anything was happening until the flood came and swept them all away. That is how it will be when the Son of Man appears.

[40]Two men will be in the same field, but only one will be taken. The other will be left. [41]Two women will be together grinding grain, but only one will be taken. The other will be left. [42]So be on your guard! You don't know when your Lord will come. [43]Homeowners never know when a thief is coming, and they are always on guard to keep one from breaking in. [44]Always be ready! You don't know when the Son of Man will come.

---

[p]24.20 *in winter or on a Sabbath*: In Palestine the winters are cold and rainy and make travel difficult. The Jewish people were not allowed to travel much more than half a mile on the Sabbath. For these reasons it was hard for them to escape from their enemies in the winter or on a Sabbath.   [q]24.28 *Where there is a corpse, there will always be buzzards*: This saying may mean that when anything important happens, people soon know about it. Or the saying may mean that whenever something bad happens, curious people gather around and stare. But the word translated "buzzard" also means "eagle" and may refer to the Roman army, which had an eagle as its symbol.   [r]24.29 *the powers in the sky*: In ancient times people thought that the stars were spiritual powers.   [s]24.30 *And there will be the Son of Man*: Or "And it will be the Son of Man."   [t]24.33 *the time has almost come*: Or "he (that is, the Son of Man) will soon be here."   [u]24.36 *and the Son himself doesn't know*: These words are not in some manuscripts.

Faithful and Unfaithful Servants
(Luke 12.35-48)

⁴⁵Who are faithful and wise servants? Who are the ones the master will put in charge of giving the other servants their food supplies at the proper time? ⁴⁶Servants are fortunate if their master comes and finds them doing their job. ⁴⁷You may be sure that a servant who is always faithful will be put in charge of everything the master owns. ⁴⁸But suppose one of the servants thinks that the master won't return until late. ⁴⁹Suppose that evil servant starts beating the other servants and eats and drinks with people who are drunk. ⁵⁰If that happens, the master will surely come on a day and at a time when the servant least expects him. ⁵¹That servant will then be punished and thrown out with the ones who only pretended to serve their master. There they will cry and grit their teeth in pain.

A Story about Ten Girls

25 The kingdom of heaven is like what happened one night when ten girls took their oil lamps and went to a wedding to meet the groom.ᵛ ²Five of the girls were foolish and five were wise. ³The foolish ones took their lamps, but no extra oil. ⁴The ones who were wise took along extra oil for their lamps.

⁵The groom was late arriving, and the girls became drowsy and fell asleep. ⁶Then in the middle of the night someone shouted, "Here's the groom! Come to meet him!"

⁷When the girls got up and started getting their lamps ready, ⁸the foolish ones said to the others, "Let us have some of your oil! Our lamps are going out."

⁹The girls who were wise answered, "There's not enough oil for all of us! Go and buy some for yourselves."

¹⁰While the foolish girls were on their way to get some oil, the groom arrived. The girls who were ready went into the wedding, and the doors were closed. ¹¹Later the other girls returned and shouted, "Sir, sir! Open the door for us!"

¹²But the groom replied, "I don't even know you!"

¹³So, my disciples, always be ready! You don't know the day or the time when all this will happen.

A Story about Three Servants
(Luke 19.11-27)

¹⁴The kingdom is also like what happened when a man went away and put his three servants in charge of all he owned. ¹⁵The man knew what each servant could do. So he handed five thousand coins to the first servant, two thousand to the second, and one thousand to the third. Then he left the country.

¹⁶As soon as the man had gone, the servant with the five thousand coins used them to earn five thousand more. ¹⁷The servant who had two thousand coins did the same with his money and earned two thousand more. ¹⁸But the servant with one thousand coins dug a hole and hid his master's money in the ground.

¹⁹Some time later the master of those servants returned. He called them in and asked what they had done with his money. ²⁰The servant who had been given five thousand coins brought them in with the five thousand that he had earned. He said, "Sir, you gave me five thousand coins, and I have earned five thousand more."

²¹"Wonderful!" his master replied. "You are a good and faithful servant. I left you in charge of only a little, but now I will put you in charge of much more. Come and share in my happiness!"

²²Next, the servant who had been given two thousand coins came in and said, "Sir, you gave me two thousand coins, and I have earned two thousand more."

ᵛ**25.1** *to meet the groom:* Some manuscripts add "and the bride." It was the custom for the groom to go to the home of the bride's parents to get his bride. Young girls and other guests would then go with them to the home of the groom's parents, where the wedding feast would take place.

²³"Wonderful!" his master replied. "You are a good and faithful servant. I left you in charge of only a little, but now I will put you in charge of much more. Come and share in my happiness!"

²⁴The servant who had been given one thousand coins then came in and said, "Sir, I know that you are hard to get along with. You harvest what you don't plant and gather crops where you haven't scattered seed. ²⁵I was frightened and went out and hid your money in the ground. Here is every single coin!"

²⁶The master of the servant told him, "You are lazy and good-for-nothing! You know that I harvest what I don't plant and gather crops where I haven't scattered seed. ²⁷You could have at least put my money in the bank, so that I could have earned interest on it."

²⁸Then the master said, "Now your money will be taken away and given to the servant with ten thousand coins! ²⁹Everyone who has something will be given more, and they will have more than enough. But everything will be taken from those who don't have anything. ³⁰You are a worthless servant, and you will be thrown out into the dark where people will cry and grit their teeth in pain."

The Final Judgment

³¹When the Son of Man comes in his glory with all of his angels, he will sit on his royal throne. ³²The people of all nations will be brought before him, and he will separate them, as shepherds separate their sheep from their goats.

³³He will place the sheep on his right and the goats on his left. ³⁴Then the king will say to those on his right, "My father has blessed you! Come and receive the kingdom that was prepared for you before the world was created. ³⁵When I was hungry, you gave me something to eat, and when I was thirsty, you gave me something to drink. When I was a stranger, you welcomed me, ³⁶and when I was naked, you gave me clothes to wear. When I was sick, you took care of me, and when I was in jail, you visited me."

³⁷Then the ones who pleased the Lord will ask, "When did we give you something to eat or drink? ³⁸When did we welcome you as a stranger or give you clothes to wear ³⁹or visit you while you were sick or in jail?"

⁴⁰The king will answer, "Whenever you did it for any of my people, no matter how unimportant they seemed, you did it for me."

⁴¹Then the king will say to those on

---

*Spiritual*Life—How can I keep my life centered on God? *(Matthew 25.31-46)*

Serve others with your eye on God.

Think of some people who are charming or who obviously like you. It's easy to be nice to them, isn't it? But when we try to behave compassionately toward a hungry person halfway around the world, a friend who's chronically sick, or a family member who's made a few trips to jail, God has to be in it. There's just not enough goodness within us to do anything about it.

But if we want God at the center of all we think and do, first he requires us to look at life through *his* eyes. God loves all humans and wants them to know his love and come to him. Will we be a part of that? Second, we have to maintain constant contact with God, or our compassion will fade and we'll become cynical. Third, we need to get a taste of being the hands and feet of Christ by doing the work he did here on this earth. Through our service to others, we partner with God. We talk with him about his purposes and our attitudes. (See also Genesis 12.1-7; Acts 13.1-5; Galatians 5.16-26; 2 Timothy 2.14-26; 2 John.)

Words To Remember: *"Whenever you did it for any of my people, no matter how unimportant they seemed, you did it for me."*—Matthew 25.40

his left, "Get away from me! You are under God's curse. Go into the everlasting fire prepared for the devil and his angels! [42]I was hungry, but you did not give me anything to eat, and I was thirsty, but you did not give me anything to drink. [43]I was a stranger, but you did not welcome me, and I was naked, but you did not give me any clothes to wear. I was sick and in jail, but you did not take care of me."

[44]Then the people will ask, "Lord, when did we fail to help you when you were hungry or thirsty or a stranger or naked or sick or in jail?"

[45]The king will say to them, "Whenever you failed to help any of my people, no matter how unimportant they seemed, you failed to do it for me."

[46]Then Jesus said, "Those people will be punished forever. But the ones who pleased God will have eternal life."

The Plot To Kill Jesus
(Mark 14.1, 2; Luke 22.1, 2; John 11.45-53)

26 When Jesus had finished teaching, he told his disciples, [2]"You know that two days from now will be Passover. That is when the Son of Man will be handed over to his enemies and nailed to a cross."

[3]At that time the chief priests and the nation's leaders were meeting at the home of Caiaphas the high priest. [4]They planned how they could sneak around and have Jesus arrested and put to death. [5]But they said, "We must not do it during Passover, because the people will riot."

At Bethany
(Mark 14.3-9; John 12.1-8)

[6]Jesus was in the town of Bethany, eating at the home of Simon, who had leprosy.[w] [7]A woman came in with a bottle of expensive perfume and poured it on Jesus' head. [8]But when his disciples saw this, they became angry and complained, "Why such a waste? [9]We could have sold this perfume for a lot of money and given it to the poor."

[10]Jesus knew what they were thinking, and he said:

Why are you bothering this woman? She has done a beautiful thing for

me. [11]You will always have the poor with you, but you won't always have me. [12]She has poured perfume on my body to prepare it for burial.[x] [13]You may be sure that wherever the good news is told all over the world, people will remember what she has done. And they will tell others.

Judas and the Chief Priests
(Mark 14.10, 11; Luke 22.3-6)

[14]Judas Iscariot[y] was one of the twelve disciples. He went to the chief priests [15]and asked, "How much will you give me if I help you arrest Jesus?" They paid Judas thirty silver coins, [16]and from then on he started looking for a good chance to betray Jesus.

Jesus Eats the Passover Meal with His Disciples
(Mark 14.12-21; Luke 22.7-13; John 13.21-30)

[17]On the first day of the Festival of Thin Bread, Jesus' disciples came to him and asked, "Where do you want us to prepare the Passover meal?"

[18]Jesus told them to go to a certain man in the city and tell him, "Our teacher says, 'My time has come! I want to eat the Passover meal with my disciples in your home.' " [19]They did as Jesus told them and prepared the meal.

[20-21]When Jesus was eating with his twelve disciples that evening, he said, "One of you will surely hand me over to my enemies."

[22]The disciples were very sad, and each one said to Jesus, "Lord, you can't mean me!"

[23]He answered, "One of you men who has eaten with me from this dish will betray me. [24]The Son of Man will die, as the Scriptures say. But it's going to be terrible for the one who betrays me! That man would be better off if he had never been born."

[25]Judas said, "Teacher, you surely don't mean me!"

"That's what you say!" Jesus replied. But later, Judas did betray him.

---

w**26.6** *leprosy:* See the note at 8.2.   x**26.12** *poured perfume on my body to prepare it for burial:* The Jewish people taught that giving someone a proper burial was even more important than helping the poor. y**26.14** *Iscariot:* See the note at 10.4.

The Lord's Supper
(Mark 14.22-26; Luke 22.14-23;
1 Corinthians 11.23-25)

²⁶During the meal Jesus took some bread in his hands. He blessed the bread and broke it. Then he gave it to his disciples and said, "Take this and eat it. This is my body."

²⁷Jesus picked up a cup of wine and gave thanks to God. He then gave it to his disciples and said, "Take this and drink it. ²⁸This is my blood, and with it God makes his agreement with you. It will be poured out, so that many people will have their sins forgiven. ²⁹From now on I am not going to drink any wine, until I drink new wine with you in my Father's kingdom." ³⁰Then they sang a hymn and went out to the Mount of Olives.

Peter's Promise
(Mark 14.27-31; Luke 22.31-34; John 13.36-38)

³¹Jesus said to his disciples, "During this very night, all of you will reject me, as the Scriptures say,

'I will strike down
   the shepherd,
and the sheep
   will be scattered.'

³²But after I am raised to life, I will go to Galilee ahead of you."

³³Peter spoke up, "Even if all the others reject you, I never will!"

³⁴Jesus replied, "I promise you that before a rooster crows tonight, you will say three times that you don't know me." ³⁵But Peter said, "Even if I have to die with you, I will never say I don't know you."

All the others said the same thing.

Jesus Prays
(Mark 14.32-42; Luke 22.39-46)

³⁶Jesus went with his disciples to a place called Gethsemane. When they got there, he told them, "Sit here while I go over there and pray."

³⁷Jesus took along Peter and the two brothers, James and John.^z He was very sad and troubled, ³⁸and he said to them, "I am so sad that I feel as if I am dying. Stay here and keep awake with me."

³⁹Jesus walked on a little way. Then he knelt with his face to the ground and prayed, "My Father, if it is possible, don't make me suffer by having me drink from this cup.^a But do what you want, and not what I want."

⁴⁰He came back and found his disciples sleeping. So he said to Peter, "Can't any of you stay awake with me for just one hour? ⁴¹Stay awake and pray that you won't be tested. You want to do what is right, but you are weak."

⁴²Again Jesus went to pray and said, "My Father, if there is no other way, and I must suffer, I will still do what you want."

⁴³Jesus came back and found them sleeping again. They simply could not keep their eyes open. ⁴⁴He left them and prayed the same prayer once more.

⁴⁵Finally, Jesus returned to his disciples and said, "Are you still sleeping and resting?^b The time has come for the Son of Man to be handed over to sinners. ⁴⁶Get up! Let's go. The one who will betray me is already here."

Jesus Is Arrested
(Mark 14.43-50; Luke 22.47-53; John 18.3-12)

⁴⁷Jesus was still speaking, when Judas the betrayer came up. He was one of the twelve disciples, and a large mob armed with swords and clubs was with him. They had been sent by the chief priests and the nation's leaders. ⁴⁸Judas had told them ahead of time, "Arrest the man I greet with a kiss."^c

⁴⁹Judas walked right up to Jesus and said, "Hello, teacher." Then Judas kissed him.

⁵⁰Jesus replied, "My friend, why are you here?"^d

The men grabbed Jesus and arrested him. ⁵¹One of Jesus' followers pulled out a sword. He struck the servant of the high priest and cut off his ear.

⁵²But Jesus told him, "Put your sword away. Anyone who lives by fighting will die by fighting. ⁵³Don't you know that I could

---

^z**26.37** *the two brothers, James and John:* The Greek text has "the two sons of Zebedee" (see 27.56). ^a**26.39** *having me drink from this cup:* In the Scriptures "to drink from a cup" sometimes means to suffer (see the note at 20.22). ^b**26.45** *Are you still sleeping and resting:* Or "You may as well keep on sleeping and resting." ^c**26.48** *the man I greet with a kiss:* It was the custom for people to greet each other with a kiss on the cheek. ^d**26.50** *why are you here:* Or "do what you came for."

ask my Father, and right away he would send me more than twelve armies of angels? [54]But then, how could the words of the Scriptures come true, which say that this must happen?"

[55]Jesus said to the mob, "Why do you come with swords and clubs to arrest me like a criminal? Day after day I sat and taught in the temple, and you didn't arrest me. [56]But all this happened, so that what the prophets wrote would come true."

All of Jesus' disciples left him and ran away.

Jesus Is Questioned by the Council
(Mark 14.53-65; Luke 22.54, 55, 63-71; John 18.13, 14, 19-24)

[57]After Jesus had been arrested, he was led off to the house of Caiaphas the high priest. The nation's leaders and the teachers of the Law of Moses were meeting there. [58]But Peter followed along at a distance and came to the courtyard of the high priest's palace. He went in and sat down with the guards to see what was going to happen.

[59]The chief priests and the whole council wanted to put Jesus to death. So they tried to find some people who would tell lies about him in court.[e] [60]But they could not find any, even though many did come and tell lies. At last, two men came forward [61]and said, "This man claimed that he

would tear down God's temple and build it again in three days."

[62]The high priest stood up and asked Jesus, "Why don't you say something in your own defense? Don't you hear the charges they are making against you?" [63]But Jesus did not answer. So the high priest said, "With the living God looking on, you must tell the truth. Tell us, are you the Messiah, the Son of God?"[f]

[64]"That is what you say!" Jesus answered. "But I tell all of you,

'Soon you will see
    the Son of Man
sitting at the right side[g]
    of God All-Powerful
and coming on the clouds
    of heaven.' "

[65]The high priest then tore his robe and said, "This man claims to be God! We don't need any more witnesses! You have heard what he said. [66]What do you think?"

They answered, "He is guilty and deserves to die!" [67]Then they spit in his face

---

[e]**26.59** *some people who would tell lies about him in court:* The Law of Moses taught that two witnesses were necessary before a person could be put to death (see verse 60). [f]**26.63** *Son of God:* One of the titles used for the kings of Israel. [g]**26.64** *right side:* See the note at 22.44.

SingleLife—How can I overcome my feelings of loneliness? (Matthew 26.36-46)

Realize that loneliness is common to all humans.
Even if you do everything right—behave perfectly in friendships, have a heart for others, keep your life straight—the bad news is, you'll be lonely sometimes. (Even if you marry the "right person," you'll still have times of intense loneliness.) How do we know that? Jesus, at the worst moment of his life, was abandoned by the people he'd poured his life into. Jesus made it clear, while he was praying in Gethsemane, that he needed them: "I am so sad that I feel as if I am dying." He expressed exactly what he wanted from them: "Stay here and keep awake with me" (26.38). But his three special friends fell asleep; not even one stayed awake.

In the rawest edges of life, it's God, and God alone, who sustains us. Everyone we know will desert us at some time. Some will willingly leave our physical presence; others will quit our companionship; still others will die. But, "The Lord has promised that he will not leave us or desert us" (Hebrews 13.5).

Jesus sympathizes with us in our loneliness. He knows what it feels like to be abandoned, and he can comfort us. (See also Psalm 22; Psalm 68.4-6; 2 Timothy 4.16-18; Revelation 3.20-22.)

Words To Remember: *"I am so sad that I feel as if I am dying. Stay here and keep awake with me."*—Matthew 26.38

and hit him with their fists. Others slapped him [68]and said, "You think you are the Messiah! So tell us who hit you!"

Peter Says He Doesn't Know Jesus
(Mark 14.66-72; Luke 22.56-62;
John 18.15-18, 25-27)

[69]While Peter was sitting out in the courtyard, a servant girl came up to him and said, "You were with Jesus from Galilee."

[70]But in front of everyone Peter said, "That isn't so! I don't know what you are talking about!"

[71]When Peter had gone out to the gate, another servant girl saw him and said to some people there, "This man was with Jesus from Nazareth."

[72]Again Peter denied it, and this time he swore, "I don't even know that man!"

[73]A little while later some people standing there walked over to Peter and said, "We know that you are one of them. We can tell it because you talk like someone from Galilee."

[74]Peter began to curse and swear, "I don't know that man!"

Right then a rooster crowed, [75]and Peter remembered that Jesus had said, "Before a rooster crows, you will say three times that you don't know me." Then Peter went out and cried hard.

Jesus Is Taken to Pilate
(Mark 15.1; Luke 23.1, 2; John 18.28-32)

27 Early the next morning all the chief priests and the nation's leaders met and decided that Jesus should be put to death. [2]They tied him up and led him away to Pilate the governor.

The Death of Judas
(Acts 1.18, 19)

[3]Judas had betrayed Jesus, but when he learned that Jesus had been sentenced to death, he was sorry for what he had done. He returned the thirty silver coins to the chief priests and leaders [4]and said, "I have sinned by betraying a man who has never done anything wrong."

"So what? That's your problem," they replied. [5]Judas threw the money into the temple and then went out and hanged himself.

[6]The chief priests picked up the money and said, "This money was paid to have a man killed. We can't put it in the temple treasury." [7]Then they had a meeting and decided to buy a field that belonged to someone who made clay pots. They wanted to use it as a graveyard for foreigners. [8]That's why people still call that place "Field of Blood." [9]So the words of the prophet Jeremiah came true,

"They took
    the thirty silver coins,
the price of a person
    among the people of Israel.
[10]They paid it
    for a potter's field,[h]
as the Lord
    had commanded me."

Pilate Questions Jesus
(Mark 15.2-5; Luke 23.3-5; John 18.33-38)

[11]Jesus was brought before Pilate the governor, who asked him, "Are you the king of the Jews?"

"Those are your words!" Jesus answered. [12]And when the chief priests and leaders brought their charges against him, he did not say a thing.

[13]Pilate asked him, "Don't you hear what crimes they say you have done?" [14]But Jesus did not say anything, and the governor was greatly amazed.

The Death Sentence
(Mark 15.6-15; Luke 23.13-26; John 18.39—19.16)

[15]During Passover the governor always freed a prisoner chosen by the people. [16]At that time a well-known terrorist named Jesus Barabbas[i] was in jail. [17]So when the crowd came together, Pilate asked them, "Which prisoner do you want me to set free? Do you want Jesus Barabbas or Jesus who is called the Messiah?" [18]Pilate knew that the leaders had brought Jesus to him because they were jealous.

[19]While Pilate was judging the case, his wife sent him a message. It said, "Don't have anything to do with that innocent man. I have had nightmares because of him."

[20]But the chief priests and the leaders

---

[h]**27.10** *a potter's field*: Perhaps a field owned by someone who made clay pots. But it may have been a field where potters came to get clay or to make pots or to throw away their broken pieces of pottery.
[i]**27.16** *Jesus Barabbas*: Here and in verse 17 many manuscripts have "Barabbas."

convinced the crowds to ask for Barabbas to be set free and for Jesus to be killed. [21]Pilate asked the crowd again, "Which of these two men do you want me to set free?"

"Barabbas!" they replied.

[22]Pilate asked them, "What am I to do with Jesus, who is called the Messiah?"

They all yelled, "Nail him to a cross!"

[23]Pilate answered, "But what crime has he done?"

"Nail him to a cross!" they yelled even louder.

[24]Pilate saw that there was nothing he could do and that the people were starting to riot. So he took some water and washed his hands[j] in front of them and said, "I won't have any-thing to do with killing this man. You are the ones doing it!"

[25]Everyone answered, "We and our own families will take the blame for his death!"

[26]Pilate set Barabbas free. Then he ordered his soldiers to beat Jesus with a whip and nail him to a cross.

Soldiers Make Fun of Jesus
(Mark 15.16-21; John 19.2, 3)

[27]The governor's soldiers led Jesus into the fortress[k] and brought together the rest of the troops. [28]They stripped off Jesus' clothes and put a scarlet robe[l] on him. [29]They made a crown out of thorn branches and placed it on his head, and they put a stick in his right hand. The soldiers knelt down and pretended to worship him. They made fun of him and shouted, "Hey, you king of the Jews!" [30]Then they spit on him. They took the stick from him and beat him on the head with it.

Jesus Is Nailed to a Cross
(Mark 15.22-32; Luke 23.27-43; John 19.17-27)

[31]When the soldiers had finished making fun of Jesus, they took off the robe. They put his own clothes back on him and led him off to be nailed to a cross. [32]On the way they met a man from Cyrene named Simon, and they forced him to carry Jesus' cross.

[33]They came to a place named Golgotha, which means "Place of a Skull."[m] [34]There they gave Jesus some wine mixed with a drug to ease the pain. But when Jesus tasted what it was, he refused to drink it.

[35]The soldiers nailed Jesus to a cross and gambled to see who would get his clothes. [36]Then they sat down to guard him. [37]Above his head they put a sign that told why he

was nailed there. It read, "This is Jesus, the King of the Jews." [38]The soldiers also nailed two criminals on crosses, one to the right of Jesus and the other to his left.

> *We might assume that a pure and polished reputation is obviously God's will. But Jesus' reputation was mocked and slandered. What God wants instead is a pure heart.*
>
> JONI EARECKSON TADA

[39]People who passed by said terrible things about Jesus. They shook their heads and [40]shouted, "So you're the one who claimed you could tear down the temple and build it again in three days! If you are God's Son, save yourself and come down from the cross!"

[41]The chief priests, the leaders, and the teachers of the Law of Moses also made fun of Jesus. They said, [42]"He saved others, but he can't save himself. If he is the king of Israel, he should come down from the cross! Then we will believe him. [43]He trusted God, so let God save him, if he wants to. He even said he was God's Son." [44]The two criminals also said cruel things to Jesus.

The Death of Jesus
(Mark 15.33-41; Luke 23.44-49; John 19.28-30)

[45]At noon the sky turned dark and stayed that way until three o'clock. [46]Then about that time Jesus shouted, "Eli, Eli, lema sabachthani?"[n] which means, "My God, my God, why have you deserted me?"

[47]Some of the people standing there

---

[j]27.24 *washed his hands*: To show that he was innocent. [k]27.27 *fortress*: The place where the Roman governor stayed. It was probably at Herod's palace west of Jerusalem, though it may have been Fortress Antonia north of the temple, where the Roman troops were stationed. [l]27.28 *scarlet robe*: This was probably a Roman soldier's robe. [m]27.33 *Place of a Skull*: The place was probably given this name because it was near a large rock in the shape of a human skull. [n]27.46 *Eli . . . sabachthani*: These words are in Hebrew.

heard Jesus and said, "He's calling for Elijah."[o] [48]One of them at once ran and grabbed a sponge. He soaked it in wine, then put it on a stick and held it up to Jesus.

[49]Others said, "Wait! Let's see if Elijah will come[p] and save him." [50]Once again Jesus shouted, and then he died.

[51]At once the curtain in the temple[q] was torn in two from top to bottom. The earth shook, and rocks split apart. [52]Graves opened, and many of God's people were raised to life. [53]Then after Jesus had risen to life, they came out of their graves and went into the holy city, where they were seen by many people.

[54]The officer and the soldiers guarding Jesus felt the earthquake and saw everything else that happened. They were frightened and said, "This man really was God's Son!"

[55]Many women had come with Jesus from Galilee to be of help to him, and they were there, looking on at a distance. [56]Mary Magdalene, Mary the mother of James and Joseph, and the mother of James and John[r] were some of these women.

Jesus Is Buried

(Mark 15.42-47; Luke 23.50-56; John 19.38-42)

[57]That evening a rich disciple named Joseph from the town of Arimathea [58]went and asked for Jesus' body. Pilate gave orders for it to be given to Joseph, [59]who took the body and wrapped it in a clean linen cloth. [60]Then Joseph put the body in his own tomb that had been cut into solid rock[s] and had never been used. He rolled a big stone against the entrance to the tomb and went away.

[61]All this time Mary Magdalene and the other Mary were sitting across from the tomb.

[62]On the next day, which was a Sabbath, the chief priests and the Pharisees went together to Pilate. [63]They said, "Sir, we remember what that liar said while he was still alive. He claimed that in three days he would come back from death. [64]So please order the tomb to be carefully guarded for three days. If you don't, his disciples may come and steal his body. They will tell the people that he has been raised to life, and this last lie will be worse than the first one."[t]

[65]Pilate said to them, "All right, take some of your soldiers and guard the tomb as well as you know how." [66]So they sealed it tight and placed soldiers there to guard it.

Jesus Is Alive

(Mark 16.1-8; Luke 24.1-12; John 20.1-10)

28 The Sabbath was over, and it was almost daybreak on Sunday when Mary Magdalene and the other Mary went to see the tomb. [2]Suddenly a strong earthquake struck, and the Lord's angel came down from heaven. He rolled away the stone and sat on it. [3]The angel looked as bright as lightning, and his clothes were white as snow. [4]The guards shook from fear and fell down, as though they were dead.

[5]The angel said to the women, "Don't be afraid! I know you are looking for Jesus, who was nailed to a cross. [6]He isn't here! God has raised him to life, just as Jesus said he would. Come, see the place where his body was lying. [7]Now hurry! Tell his disciples that he has been raised to life and is on his way to Galilee. Go there, and you will see him. That is what I came to tell you."

[8]The women were frightened and yet very happy, as they hurried from the tomb and ran to tell his disciples. [9]Suddenly Jesus met them and greeted them. They went near him, held on to his feet, and worshiped him. [10]Then Jesus said, "Don't be afraid! Tell my followers to go to Galilee. They will see me there."

Report of the Guard

[11]While the women were on their way, some soldiers who had been guarding the tomb went into the city. They told the chief priests everything that had happened. [12]So the chief priests met with the leaders and decided to bribe the soldiers with a lot of money. [13]They said to the soldiers, "Tell everyone that Jesus' disciples came during

---

[o]**27.47** *Elijah*: In Aramaic the name "Elijah" sounds like "Eli," which means "my God." [p]**27.49** *Elijah will come*: See the note at 16.14. [q]**27.51** *curtain in the temple*: There were two curtains in the temple. One was at the entrance, and the other separated the holy place from the most holy place that the Jewish people thought of as God's home on earth. The second curtain is probably the one that is meant. [r]**27.56** *of James and John*: The Greek text has "of Zebedee's sons" (see 26.37). [s]**27.60** *tomb . . . solid rock*: Some of the Jewish people buried their dead in rooms carved into solid rock. A heavy stone was rolled against the entrance. [t]**27.64** *the first one*: Probably the belief that Jesus is the Messiah.

the night and stole his body while you were asleep. [14]If the governor[u] hears about this, we will talk to him. You won't have anything to worry about." [15]The soldiers took the money and did what they were told. The Jewish people still tell each other this story.

> *I know becoming a Christian was the right thing to do—but I never dreamed it could be fun! I love telling others about Jesus.*
>
> LIZ CURTIS HIGGS

What Jesus' Followers Must Do
(Mark 16.14-18; Luke 24.36-49; John 20.19-23; Acts 1.6-8)

[16]Jesus' eleven disciples went to a mountain in Galilee, where Jesus had told them to meet him. [17]They saw him and worshiped him, but some of them doubted.

[18]Jesus came to them and said:

I have been given all authority in heaven and on earth! [19]Go to the people of all nations and make them my disciples. Baptize them in the name of the Father, the Son, and the Holy Spirit, [20]and teach them to do everything I have told you. I will be with you always, even until the end of the world.

---

[u]**28.14** *governor:* Pontius Pilate.

Mark — Good News in a Nutshell

Four Bible books tell the story of Jesus: Matthew, Mark, Luke, and John. Each book shares the name of the one who recorded God's words. Each has unique features and a unique perspective. Mark is known for its brevity. You'll delight in the events Mark chose, and the pithy way he presented God's truth. Cutting directly to the heart of each story, Mark focused on the main events that showed Jesus as the slave of God (10.45). His brief writing has provided room for you to discover more about Jesus, discoveries that can fill a lifetime of adventure shared with God.

Mark's interest was in highlighting public group reaction to Jesus—their amazement and astonishment at his person and actions. Mark began with Isaiah, an Old Testament prophet who foresaw Jesus and wrote of someone who would teach about Jesus. This someone was John the Baptist, the first of many persons who personally encountered Jesus. Through these people, Mark's own experience, and the words and actions of Jesus himself, Mark shows us Jesus and his authority over illness, the spirit world, sin, and the material world. Mark's book paints a powerful picture of Jesus that's especially good for new believers. Mark's Gospel is also a delightful refresher to those who have known God a long time.

Three of Jesus' miracles appear in Mark's very first chapter. Miracles show Jesus' power, his love for individual people, and the undisputed fact that he is God. God has come to earth in the person Jesus to show us just what he's like and just how much he loves us. He died for us, conquered sin for us, and conquered death for us. As you read Mark, you'll want to love and imitate Jesus even more.

Mark at a Glance

1. Isaiah's prophecy and John the Baptist (1.1-8)
2. Beginnings for Jesus: baptism, temptation, followers (1.9-20)
3. Jesus in Galilee: healings and teachings (1.21—9.50)
4. Jesus heads for Jerusalem: childlikeness, real riches, and true greatness (10)
5. Jesus in Jerusalem: welcome, rejection, and illustrations (11–13)
6. Jesus closes his earthly ministry: plots, farewells, and unfair trials (14.1—15.15)
7. Jesus dies and lives again: dying, rising, and appearing to people (15.16—16.20)

The Preaching of John the Baptist
(Matthew 3.1-12; Luke 3.1-18; John 1.19-28)

1 This is the good news about Jesus Christ, the Son of God.[a] [2]It began just as God had said in the book written by Isaiah the prophet,

"I am sending my messenger
to get the way ready
for you.
[3]In the desert
someone is shouting,
'Get the road ready
for the Lord!
Make a straight path
for him.' "

[4]So John the Baptist showed up in the desert and told everyone, "Turn back to God and be baptized! Then your sins will be forgiven."
[5]From all Judea and Jerusalem crowds of people went to John. They told how sorry they were for their sins, and he baptized them in the Jordan River.
[6]John wore clothes made of camel's hair. He had a leather strap around his waist and ate grasshoppers and wild honey.
[7]John also told the people, "Someone more powerful is going to come. And I am not good enough even to stoop down and untie his sandals.[b] [8]I baptize you with water, but he will baptize you with the Holy Spirit!"

The Baptism of Jesus
(Matthew 3.13-17; Luke 3.21, 22)

[9]About that time Jesus came from Nazareth in Galilee, and John baptized him in the Jordan River. [10]As soon as Jesus came out of the water, he saw the sky open and the Holy Spirit coming down to him like a dove. [11]A voice from heaven said, "You are my own dear Son, and I am pleased with you."

Jesus and Satan
(Matthew 4.1-11; Luke 4.1-13)

[12]Right away God's Spirit made Jesus go into the desert. [13]He stayed there for forty days while Satan tested him. Jesus was with the wild animals, but angels took care of him.

Jesus Begins His Work
(Matthew 4.12-17; Luke 4.14, 15)

[14]After John was arrested, Jesus went to Galilee and told the good news that comes from God.[c] [15]He said, "The time has come! God's kingdom will soon be here.[d] Turn back to God and believe the good news!"

Jesus Chooses Four Fishermen
(Matthew 4.18-22; Luke 5.1-11)

[16]As Jesus was walking along the shore of Lake Galilee, he saw Simon and his brother Andrew. They were fishermen and were casting their nets into the lake. [17]Jesus said to them, "Come with me! I will teach you how to bring in people instead of fish." [18]Right then the two brothers dropped their nets and went with him.
[19]Jesus walked on and soon saw James and John, the sons of Zebedee. They were in a boat, mending their nets. [20]At once Jesus asked them to come with him. They left their father in the boat with the hired workers and went with him.

A Man with an Evil Spirit
(Luke 4.31-37)

[21]Jesus and his disciples went to the town of Capernaum. Then on the next Sabbath he went into the Jewish meeting place and started teaching. [22]Everyone was amazed at his teaching. He taught with authority, and not like the teachers of the Law of Moses. [23]Suddenly a man with an evil spirit[e] in him entered the meeting place and yelled, [24]"Jesus from Nazareth, what do you want with us? Have you come to destroy us? I know who you are! You are God's Holy One."
[25]Jesus told the evil spirit, "Be quiet and come out of the man!" [26]The spirit shook him. Then it gave a loud shout and left.
[27]Everyone was completely surprised and kept saying to each other, "What is this? It must be some new kind of powerful teaching! Even the evil spirits obey him." [28]News about Jesus quickly spread all over Galilee.

---

[a]**1.1** *the Son of God*: These words are not in some manuscripts.   [b]**1.7** *untie his sandals*: This was the duty of a slave.   [c]**1.14** *that comes from God*: Or "that is about God."   [d]**1.15** *will soon be here*: Or "is already here."   [e]**1.23** *evil spirit*: A Jewish person who had an evil spirit was considered "unclean" and was not allowed to eat or worship with other Jewish people.

Jesus Heals Many People
(Matthew 8.14-17; Luke 4.38-41)

²⁹As soon as Jesus left the meeting place with James and John, they went home with Simon and Andrew. ³⁰When they got there, Jesus was told that Simon's mother-in-law was sick in bed with fever. ³¹Jesus went to her. He took hold of her hand and helped her up. The fever left her, and she served them a meal.

³²That evening after sunset,ᶠ all who were sick or had demons in them were brought to Jesus. ³³In fact, the whole town gathered around the door of the house. ³⁴Jesus healed all kinds of terrible diseases and forced out a lot of demons. But the demons knew who he was, and he did not let them speak.

> *We can read all the books of prayer or listen to the greatest intercessors in the world, but none of that means a thing if we don't just jump in and start talking to God.*
>
> SANDRA P. ALDRICH

³⁵Very early the next morning, Jesus got up and went to a place where he could be alone and pray. ³⁶Simon and the others started looking for him. ³⁷And when they found him, they said, "Everyone is looking for you!"

³⁸Jesus replied, "We must go to the nearby towns, so that I can tell the good news to those people. This is why I have come." ³⁹Then Jesus went to Jewish meeting places everywhere in Galilee, where he preached and forced out demons.

Jesus Heals a Man
(Matthew 8.1-4; Luke 5.12-16)

⁴⁰A man with leprosyᵍ came to Jesus and knelt down.ʰ He begged, "You have the power to make me well, if only you wanted to."

⁴¹Jesus felt sorry forⁱ the man. So he put his hand on him and said, "I want to! Now you are well." ⁴²At once the man's leprosy disappeared, and he was well.

⁴³After Jesus strictly warned the man, he sent him on his way. ⁴⁴He said, "Don't tell anyone about this. Just go and show the priest that you are well. Then take a gift to the temple as Moses commanded, and everyone will know that you have been healed."ʲ

⁴⁵The man talked about it so much and told so many people, that Jesus could no longer go openly into a town. He had to stay away from the towns, but people still came to him from everywhere.

Jesus Heals a Crippled Man
(Matthew 9.1-8; Luke 5.17-26)

2 Jesus went back to Capernaum, and a few days later people heard that he was at home.ᵏ ²Then so many of them came to the house that there wasn't even standing room left in front of the door.

Jesus was still teaching ³when four people came up, carrying a crippled man on a mat. ⁴But because of the crowd, they could not get him to Jesus. So they made a hole in the roofˡ above him and let the man down in front of everyone.

⁵When Jesus saw how much faith they had, he said to the crippled man, "My friend, your sins are forgiven."

⁶Some of the teachers of the Law of Moses were sitting there. They started wondering, ⁷"Why would he say such a thing? He must think he is God! Only God can forgive sins."

⁸Right away, Jesus knew what they were thinking, and he said, "Why are you thinking such things? ⁹Is it easier for me to tell

---

ʲ**1.32** *after sunset:* The Sabbath was over, and a new day began at sunset. ᵍ**1.40** *leprosy:* In biblical times the word "leprosy" was used for many different kinds of skin diseases. ʰ**1.40** *and knelt down:* These words are not in some manuscripts. ⁱ**1.41** *felt sorry for:* Some manuscripts have "was angry with." ʲ**1.44** *everyone will know that you have been healed:* People with leprosy had to be examined by a priest and told that they were well (that is, "clean") before they could once again live a normal life in the Jewish community. The gift that Moses commanded was the sacrifice of some lambs together with flour mixed with olive oil. ᵏ**2.1** *at home:* Or "in the house" (perhaps Simon Peter's home). ˡ**2.4** *roof:* In Palestine the houses usually had a flat roof. Stairs on the outside led up to the roof that was made of beams and boards covered with packed earth.

this crippled man that his sins are forgiven or to tell him to get up and pick up his mat and go on home? [10]I will show you that the Son of Man has the right to forgive sins here on earth." So Jesus said to the man, [11]"Get up! Pick up your mat and go on home."

[12]The man got right up. He picked up his mat and went out while everyone watched in amazement. They praised God and said, "We have never seen anything like this!"

Jesus Chooses Levi
(Matthew 9.9-13; Luke 5.27-32)

[13]Once again, Jesus went to the shore of Lake Galilee. A large crowd gathered around him, and he taught them. [14]As he walked along, he saw Levi, the son of Alphaeus. Levi was sitting at the place for paying taxes, and Jesus said to him, "Come with me!" So he got up and went with Jesus.

[15]Later, Jesus and his disciples were having dinner at Levi's house.[m] Many tax collectors[n] and other sinners had become followers of Jesus, and they were also guests at the dinner.

[16]Some of the teachers of the Law of Moses were Pharisees, and they saw that Jesus was eating with sinners and tax collectors. So they asked his disciples, "Why does he eat with tax collectors and sinners?"

[17]Jesus heard them and answered,

"Healthy people don't need a doctor, but sick people do. I didn't come to invite good people to be my followers. I came to invite sinners."

People Ask about Going without Eating
(Matthew 9.14-17; Luke 5.33-39)

[18]The followers of John the Baptist and the Pharisees often went without eating.[o] Some people came and asked Jesus, "Why do the followers of John and those of the Pharisees often go without eating, while your disciples never do?"

[19]Jesus answered:

The friends of a bridegroom don't go without eating while he is still with them. [20]But the time will come when he will be taken from them. Then they will go without eating.

[21]No one patches old clothes by sewing on a piece of new cloth. The new piece would shrink and tear a bigger hole.

---

[m]**2.15** *Levi's house:* Or "Jesus' house." [n]**2.15** *tax collectors:* These were usually Jewish people who paid the Romans for the right to collect taxes. They were hated by other Jews who thought of them as traitors to their country and to their religion. [o]**2.18** *without eating:* The Jewish people sometimes went without eating (also called "fasting") to show their love for God or to show sorrow for their sins.

Friendship—Sometimes I feel God is asking me to befriend someone I naturally dislike or who annoys me. How can I overcome my natural inclination to avoid that friendship? *(Mark 2.13-17)*

Focus on that person's potential to follow Jesus.

If Jesus prods you to befriend someone you don't click with, it's not unusual to buck it. That's okay. The important thing is to move past your initial reaction and take deliberate action, such as smiling when you encounter that person, or initiating a conversation. While it feels forced at first, it will become natural with time and prayer.

During this process, give yourself a break. Rather than beat yourself up emotionally because it's hard to befriend someone, recognize that it's normal to not get along with everyone. But we serve a supernatural God; we serve Jesus, who crossed barriers to see the real person. Jesus befriended tax collectors who cheated those they taxed. He ate dinner with people who had done obvious wrong. And in the process, people who had made bad choices started to make good ones.

We can't transform a person like Jesus did. But we *can* offer the friendship that opens that person to the Lord we serve. Action by deliberate action, choose the care that overcomes barriers. (See also Ezekiel 2.1-7; Zechariah 4.1-10; 1 Corinthians 10.31—11.1.)

Words To Remember: *[Jesus said,] "I didn't come to invite good people to be my followers. I came to invite sinners."*—Mark 2.17

[22]No one pours new wine into old wineskins. The wine would swell and burst the old skins.[p] Then the wine would be lost, and the skins would be ruined. New wine must be put into new wineskins.

A Question about the Sabbath

(Matthew 12.1-8; Luke 6.1-5)

[23]One Sabbath Jesus and his disciples were walking through some wheat fields. His disciples were picking grains of wheat as they went along.[q] [24]Some Pharisees asked Jesus, "Why are your disciples picking grain on the Sabbath? They are not supposed to do that!"

[25]Jesus answered, "Haven't you read what David did when he and his followers were hungry and in need? [26]It was during the time of Abiathar the high priest. David went into the house of God and ate the sacred loaves of bread that only priests are allowed to eat. He also gave some to his followers."

[27]Jesus finished by saying, "People were not made for the good of the Sabbath. The Sabbath was made for the good of people. [28]So the Son of Man is Lord over the Sabbath."

A Man with a Crippled Hand

(Matthew 12.9-14; Luke 6.6-11)

3 The next time that Jesus went into the meeting place, a man with a crippled hand was there. [2]The Pharisees[r] wanted to accuse Jesus of doing something wrong, and they kept watching to see if Jesus would heal him on the Sabbath.

[3]Jesus told the man to stand up where everyone could see him. [4]Then he asked, "On the Sabbath should we do good deeds or evil deeds? Should we save someone's life or destroy it?" But no one said a word.

[5]Jesus was angry as he looked around at the people. Yet he felt sorry for them because they were so stubborn. Then he told the man, "Stretch out your hand." He did, and his bad hand was healed.

[6]The Pharisees left. And right away they started making plans with Herod's followers[s] to kill Jesus.

Large Crowds Come to Jesus

[7]Jesus led his disciples down to the shore of the lake. Large crowds followed him from Galilee, Judea, [8]and Jerusalem. People came from Idumea, as well as other places east of the Jordan River. They also came from the region around the cities of Tyre and Sidon. All of these crowds came because they had heard what Jesus was doing. [9]He even had to tell his disciples to get a boat ready to keep him from being crushed by the crowds.

[10]After Jesus had healed many people, the other sick people begged him to let them touch him. [11]And whenever any evil spirits saw Jesus, they would fall to the ground and shout, "You are the Son of God!" [12]But Jesus warned the spirits not to tell who he was.

Jesus Chooses His Twelve Apostles

(Matthew 10.1-4; Luke 6.12-16)

[13]Jesus decided to ask some of his disciples to go up on a mountain with him, and they went. [14]Then he chose twelve of them to be his apostles,[t] so that they could be with him. He also wanted to send them out to preach [15]and to force out demons. [16]Simon was one of the twelve, and Jesus named him Peter. [17]There were also James and John, the two sons of Zebedee. Jesus called them Boanerges, which means "Thunderbolts." [18]Andrew, Philip, Bartholomew, Matthew, Thomas, James son of Alphaeus, and Thaddaeus were also apostles. The others were Simon, known as the Eager One,[u] [19]and Judas Iscariot,[v] who later betrayed Jesus.

Jesus and the Ruler of Demons

(Matthew 12.22-32; Luke 11.14-23; 12.10)

[20]Jesus went back home,[w] and once again such a large crowd gathered that there was

---

[p]**2.22** *swell and burst the old skins*: While the juice from grapes was becoming wine, it would swell and stretch the skins in which it had been stored. If the skins were old and stiff, they would burst. [q]**2.23** *went along*: It was the custom to let hungry travelers pick grains of wheat. [r]**3.2** *Pharisees*: The Greek text has "they" (but see verse 6). [s]**3.6** *Herod's followers*: People who were political followers of the family of Herod the Great and his son Herod Antipas. [t]**3.14** *to be his apostles*: These words are not in some manuscripts. [u]**3.18** *known as the Eager One*: The Greek text has "Cananaean," which probably comes from a Hebrew word meaning "zealous" (see Luke 6.15). "Zealot" was the name later given to the members of a Jewish group that resisted and fought against the Romans. [v]**3.19** *Iscariot*: This may mean "a man from Kerioth" (a place in Judea). But more probably it means "a man who was a liar" or "a man who was a betrayer." [w]**3.20** *went back home*: Or "entered a house" (perhaps the home of Simon Peter).

no chance even to eat. [21]When Jesus' family heard what he was doing, they thought he was crazy and went to get him under control.

[22]Some teachers of the Law of Moses came from Jerusalem and said, "This man is under the power of Beelzebul, the ruler of demons! He is even forcing out demons with the help of Beelzebul."

[23]Jesus told the people to gather around him. Then he spoke to them in riddles and said:

How can Satan force himself out? [24]A nation whose people fight each other won't last very long. [25]And a family that fights won't last long either. [26]So if Satan fights against himself, that will be the end of him.

[27]How can anyone break into the house of a strong man and steal his things, unless he first ties up the strong man? Then he can take everything.

[28]I promise you that any of the sinful things you say or do can be forgiven, no matter how terrible those things are. [29]But if you speak against the Holy Spirit, you can never be forgiven. That sin will be held against you forever.

[30]Jesus said this because the people were saying that he had an evil spirit in him.

Jesus' Mother and Brothers
(Matthew 12.46-50; Luke 8.19-21)

[31]Jesus' mother and brothers came and stood outside. Then they sent someone with a message for him to come out to them. [32]The crowd that was sitting around Jesus told him, "Your mother and your brothers and sisters[x] are outside and want to see you."

[33]Jesus asked, "Who is my mother and who are my brothers?" [34]Then he looked at the people sitting around him and said, "Here are my mother and my brothers. [35]Anyone who obeys God is my brother or sister or mother."

A Story about a Farmer
(Matthew 13.1-9; Luke 8.4-8)

4 The next time Jesus taught beside Lake Galilee, a big crowd gathered. It was so large that he had to sit in a boat out on the lake, while the people stood on the shore. [2]He used stories to teach them many things, and this is part of what he taught:

[3]Now listen! A farmer went out to scatter seed in a field. [4]While the farmer was scattering the seed, some of it fell along the road and was eaten by birds. [5]Other seeds fell on thin, rocky ground and quickly started growing because the soil wasn't very deep. [6]But when the sun came up, the plants were scorched and dried up, because they did not have enough roots. [7]Some other seeds fell where thornbushes grew up and choked out the plants. So they did not produce any grain. [8]But a few seeds did fall on good ground where the plants grew and produced thirty or sixty or even a hundred times as much as was scattered.

[9]Then Jesus said, "If you have ears, pay attention."

Why Jesus Used Stories
(Matthew 13.10-17; Luke 8.9, 10)

[10]When Jesus was alone with the twelve apostles and some others, they asked him about these stories. [11]He answered:

I have explained the secret about God's kingdom to you, but for others I can use only stories. [12]The reason is,

"These people will look
    and look, but never see.
They will listen and listen,
    but never understand.
If they did,
they would turn to God,
    and he would forgive them."

Jesus Explains the Story about the Farmer
(Matthew 13.18-23; Luke 8.11-15)

[13]Jesus told them:

If you don't understand this story, you won't understand any others. [14]What the farmer is spreading is really the message about the kingdom. [15]The seeds that fell along the road are the people who hear the message. But Satan soon comes and snatches it away from them. [16]The seeds that fell

---

x3.32 and sisters: These words are not in some manuscripts.

on rocky ground are the people who gladly hear the message and accept it right away. [17]But they don't have any roots, and they don't last very long. As soon as life gets hard or the message gets them in trouble, they give up.

[18]The seeds that fell among the thornbushes are also people who hear the message. [19]But they start worrying about the needs of this life. They are fooled by the desire to get rich and to have all kinds of other things. So the message gets choked out, and they never produce anything. [20]The seeds that fell on good ground are the people who hear and welcome the message. They produce thirty or sixty or even a hundred times as much as was planted.

Light
(Luke 8.16-18)

[21]Jesus also said:

You don't light a lamp and put it under a clay pot or under a bed. Don't you put a lamp on a lampstand? [22]There is nothing hidden that will not be made public. There is no secret that will not be well known. [23]If you have ears, pay attention!

[24]Listen carefully to what you hear! The way you treat others will be the way you will be treated—and even worse. [25]Everyone who has something will be given more. But people who don't have anything will lose what little they have.

Another Story about Seeds

[26]Again Jesus said:

God's kingdom is like what happens when a farmer scatters seed in a field. [27]The farmer sleeps at night and is up and around during the day. Yet the seeds keep sprouting and growing, and he doesn't understand how. [28]It is the ground that makes the seeds sprout and grow into plants that produce grain. [29]Then when harvest season comes and the grain is ripe, the farmer cuts it with a sickle.[y]

A Mustard Seed
(Matthew 13.31, 32; Luke 13.18, 19)

[30]Finally, Jesus said:

What is God's kingdom like? What

story can I use to explain it? [31]It is like what happens when a mustard seed is planted in the ground. It is the smallest seed in all the world. [32]But once it is planted, it grows larger than any garden plant. It even puts out branches that are big enough for birds to nest in its shade.

The Reason for Teaching with Stories
(Matthew 13.34, 35)

[33]Jesus used many other stories when he spoke to the people, and he taught them as much as they could understand. [34]He did not tell them anything without using stories. But when he was alone with his disciples, he explained everything to them.

A Storm
(Matthew 8.23-27; Luke 8.22-25)

[35]That evening, Jesus said to his disciples, "Let's cross to the east side." [36]So they left the crowd, and his disciples started across the lake with him in the boat. Some other boats followed along. [37]Suddenly a windstorm struck the lake. Waves started splashing into the boat, and it was about to sink.

[38]Jesus was in the back of the boat with his head on a pillow, and he was asleep. His disciples woke him and said, "Teacher, don't you care that we're about to drown?"

[39]Jesus got up and ordered the wind and the waves to be quiet. The wind stopped, and everything was calm.

[40]Jesus asked his disciples, "Why were you afraid? Don't you have any faith?"

[41]Now they were more afraid than ever and said to each other, "Who is this? Even the wind and the waves obey him!"

A Man with Evil Spirits
(Matthew 8.28-34; Luke 8.26-39)

5 Jesus and his disciples crossed Lake Galilee and came to shore near the town of Gerasa.[z] [2]When he was getting out of the boat, a man with an evil spirit quickly ran to him [3]from the graveyard[a]

---

[y]**4.29** *sickle:* A knife with a long curved blade, used to cut grain and other crops.   [z]**5.1** *Gerasa:* Some manuscripts have "Gadara," and others have "Gergesa." [a]**5.3** *graveyard:* It was thought that demons and evil spirits lived in graveyards.

where he had been living. No one was able to tie the man up anymore, not even with a chain. [4]He had often been put in chains and leg irons, but he broke the chains and smashed the leg irons. No one could control him. [5]Night and day he was in the graveyard or on the hills, yelling and cutting himself with stones.

[6]When the man saw Jesus in the distance, he ran up to him and knelt down. [7]He shouted, "Jesus, Son of God in heaven, what do you want with me? Promise me in God's name that you won't torture me!" [8]The man said this because Jesus had already told the evil spirit to come out of him.

[9]Jesus asked, "What is your name?"

The man answered, "My name is Lots, because I have 'lots' of evil spirits." [10]He then begged Jesus not to send them away.

[11]Over on the hillside a large herd of pigs was feeding. [12]So the evil spirits begged Jesus, "Send us into those pigs! Let us go into them." [13]Jesus let them go, and they went out of the man and into the pigs. The whole herd of about two thousand pigs rushed down the steep bank into the lake and drowned.

> Whenever I tell my story—including what God has done in my life—I know it helps others get on that path of freedom for themselves. And in the process, I'm also healed.
>
> STAR PARKER

[14]The men taking care of the pigs ran to the town and the farms to spread the news. Then the people came out to see what had happened. [15]When they came to Jesus, they saw the man who had once been full of demons. He was sitting there with his clothes on and in his right mind, and they were terrified. [16]Everyone who had seen what had happened told about the man and the pigs.

[17]Then the people started begging Jesus to leave their part of the country.

[18]When Jesus was getting into the boat, the man begged to go with him. [19]But Jesus would not let him. Instead, he said, "Go home to your family and tell them how much the Lord has done for you and how good he has been to you."

[20]The man went away into the region near the ten cities known as Decapolis[b] and began telling everyone how much Jesus had done for him. Everyone who heard what had happened was amazed.

A Dying Girl and a Sick Woman
(Matthew 9.18-26; Luke 8.40-56)

[21]Once again Jesus got into the boat and crossed Lake Galilee.[c] Then as he stood on the shore, a large crowd gathered around him. [22]The person in charge of the Jewish meeting place was also there. His name was Jairus, and when he saw Jesus, he went over to him. He knelt at Jesus' feet [23]and started begging him for help. He said, "My daughter is about to die! Please come and touch her, so she will get well and live." [24]Jesus went with Jairus. Many people followed along and kept crowding around.

[25]In the crowd was a woman who had been bleeding for twelve years. [26]She had gone to many doctors, and they had not done anything except cause her a lot of pain. She had paid them all the money she had. But instead of getting better, she only got worse.

[27]The woman had heard about Jesus, so she came up behind him in the crowd and barely touched his clothes. [28]She had said to herself, "If I can just touch his clothes, I will get well." [29]As soon as she touched them, her bleeding stopped, and she knew she was well.

[30]At that moment Jesus felt power go out from him. He turned to the crowd and asked, "Who touched my clothes?"

[31]His disciples said to him, "Look at all these people crowding around you! How can you ask who touched you?" [32]But Jesus turned to see who had touched him.

[33]The woman knew what had happened

---

[b]**5.20** *the ten cities known as Decapolis:* A group of ten cities east of Samaria and Galilee, where the people followed the Greek way of life.   [c]**5.21** *crossed Lake Galilee:* To the west side.

to her. She came shaking with fear and knelt down in front of Jesus. Then she told him the whole story.

³⁴Jesus said to the woman, "You are now well because of your faith. May God give you peace! You are healed, and you will no longer be in pain."

³⁵While Jesus was still speaking, some men came from Jairus' home and said, "Your daughter has died! Why bother the teacher anymore?"

³⁶Jesus heard[d] what they said, and he said to Jairus, "Don't worry. Just have faith!"

³⁷Jesus did not let anyone go with him except Peter and the two brothers, James and John. ³⁸They went home with Jairus and saw the people crying and making a lot of noise.[e] ³⁹Then Jesus went inside and said to them, "Why are you crying and carrying on like this? The child isn't dead. She is just asleep." ⁴⁰But the people laughed at him.

After Jesus had sent them all out of the house, he took the girl's father and mother and his three disciples and went to where she was. ⁴¹⁻⁴²He took the twelve-year-old girl by the hand and said, "Talitha, koum!"[f] which means, "Little girl, get up!" The girl got right up and started walking around.

Everyone was greatly surprised. ⁴³But Jesus ordered them not to tell anyone what had happened. Then he said, "Give her something to eat."

The People of Nazareth Turn against Jesus

(Matthew 13.53-58; Luke 4.16-30)

6 Jesus left and returned to his hometown[g] with his disciples. ²The next Sabbath he taught in the Jewish meeting place. Many of the people who heard him were amazed and asked, "How can he do all this? Where did he get such wisdom and the power to work these miracles? ³Isn't he the carpenter,[h] the son of Mary? Aren't James, Joseph, Judas, and Simon his brothers? Don't his sisters still live here in our town?" The people were very unhappy because of what he was doing.

⁴But Jesus said, "Prophets are honored by everyone, except the people of their hometown and their relatives and their own family." ⁵Jesus could not work any miracles there, except to heal a few sick people by placing his hands on them. ⁶He was surprised that the people did not have any faith.

Instructions for the Twelve Apostles

(Matthew 10.5-15; Luke 9.1-6)

Jesus taught in all the neighboring villages. ⁷Then he called together his twelve apostles and sent them out two by two with power over evil spirits. ⁸He told them, "You may take along a walking stick. But don't carry food or a traveling bag or any money. ⁹It's all right to wear sandals, but don't take along a change of clothes. ¹⁰When you are welcomed into a home, stay there until you leave that town. ¹¹If any place won't welcome you or listen to your message, leave and shake the dust from your feet[i] as a warning to them."

¹²The apostles left and started telling everyone to turn to God. ¹³They forced out many demons and healed a lot of sick people by putting olive oil[j] on them.

The Death of John the Baptist

(Matthew 14.1-12; Luke 9.7-9)

¹⁴Jesus became so well-known that Herod the ruler[k] heard about him. Some people thought he was John the Baptist, who had come back to life with the power to work miracles. ¹⁵Others thought he was Elijah[l] or some other prophet who had lived long ago. ¹⁶But when Herod heard about Jesus, he said, "This must be John! I had his head cut off, and now he has come back to life."

¹⁷⁻¹⁸Herod had earlier married Herodias, the wife of his brother Philip. But John had told him, "It isn't right for you to take your brother's wife!" So, in order to please Herodias, Herod arrested John and put him in prison.

¹⁹Herodias had a grudge against John and wanted to kill him. But she could not do it ²⁰because Herod was afraid of John and

---

[d]**5.36** *heard:* Or "ignored."   [e]**5.38** *crying and making a lot of noise:* The Jewish people often hired mourners for funerals.   [f]**5.41,42** *Talitha, koum:* These words are in Aramaic, a language spoken in Palestine during the time of Jesus.   [g]**6.1** *hometown:* Nazareth.   [h]**6.3** *carpenter:* The Greek word may also mean someone who builds or works with stone or brick.   [i]**6.11** *shake the dust from your feet:* This was a way of showing rejection. [j]**6.13** *olive oil:* The Jewish people used olive oil as a way of healing people. Sometimes olive oil is a symbol for healing by means of a miracle (see James 5.14). [k]**6.14** *Herod the ruler:* Herod Antipas, the son of Herod the Great.   [l]**6.15** *Elijah:* Many of the Jewish people expected the prophet Elijah to come and prepare the way for the Messiah.

protected him. He knew that John was a good and holy man. Even though Herod was confused by what John said,[m] he was glad to listen to him. And he often did.

²¹Finally, Herodias got her chance when Herod gave a great birthday celebration for himself and invited his officials, his army officers, and the leaders of Galilee. ²²The daughter of Herodias[n] came in and danced for Herod and his guests. She pleased them so much that Herod said, "Ask for anything, and it's yours! ²³I swear that I will give you as much as half of my kingdom, if you want it."

²⁴The girl left and asked her mother, "What do you think I should ask for?"

Her mother answered, "The head of John the Baptist!"

²⁵The girl hurried back and told Herod, "Right now on a platter I want the head of John the Baptist!"

²⁶The king was very sorry for what he had said. But he did not want to break the promise he had made in front of his guests. ²⁷At once he ordered a guard to cut off John's head there in prison. ²⁸The guard put the head on a platter and took it to the girl. Then she gave it to her mother.

²⁹When John's followers learned that he had been killed, they took his body and put it in a tomb.

Jesus Feeds Five Thousand
(Matthew 14.13-21; Luke 9.10-17; John 6.1-14)

³⁰After the apostles returned to Jesus,[o] they told him everything they had done and taught. ³¹But so many people were coming and going that Jesus and the apostles did not even have a chance to eat. Then Jesus said, "Let's go to a place[p] where we can be alone and get some rest." ³²They left in a boat for a place where they could be alone. ³³But many people saw them leave and figured out where they were going. So people from every town ran on ahead and got there first.

³⁴When Jesus got out of the boat, he saw the large crowd that was like sheep without a shepherd. He felt sorry for the people and started teaching them many things.

³⁵That evening the disciples came to Jesus and said, "This place is like a desert, and it is already late. ³⁶Let the crowds leave, so they can go to the farms and villages near here and buy something to eat."

³⁷Jesus replied, "You give them something to eat."

But they asked him, "Don't you know that it would take almost a year's wages[q] to buy all of these people something to eat?"

³⁸Then Jesus said, "How much bread do you have? Go and see!"

They found out and answered, "We have five small loaves of bread[r] and two fish." ³⁹Jesus told his disciples to have the people sit down on the green grass. ⁴⁰They sat down in groups of a hundred and groups of fifty.

⁴¹Jesus took the five loaves and the two fish. He looked up toward heaven and blessed the food. Then he broke the bread and handed it to his disciples to give to the people. He also divided the two fish, so that everyone could have some.

⁴²After everyone had eaten all they wanted, ⁴³Jesus' disciples picked up twelve large baskets of leftover bread and fish. ⁴⁴There were five thousand men who ate the food.

You're not a bad wife,
friend, mother, or employee
for taking alone time.
Friends and family will
appreciate a rejuvenated you.

JUDITH COUCHMAN

Jesus Walks on the Water
(Matthew 14.22-33; John 6.15-21)

⁴⁵Right away, Jesus made his disciples get into the boat and start back across to Bethsaida. But he stayed until he had sent the crowds away. ⁴⁶Then he told them good-by

---

[m]**6.20** *was confused by what John said*: Some manuscripts have "did many things because of what John said."
[n]**6.22** *Herodias*: Some manuscripts have "Herod."
[o]**6.30** *the apostles returned to Jesus*: From the mission on which he had sent them (see 6.7, 12, 13).
[p]**6.31** *a place*: This was probably northeast of Lake Galilee (see verse 45).   [q]**6.37** *almost a year's wages*: The Greek text has "two hundred silver coins." Each coin was the average day's wage for a worker.   [r]**6.38** *small loaves of bread*: These would have been flat and round or in the shape of a bun.

and went up on the side of a mountain to pray. ⁴⁷Later that evening he was still there by himself, and the boat was somewhere in the middle of the lake. ⁴⁸He could see that the disciples were struggling hard, because they were rowing against the wind. Not long before morning, Jesus came toward them. He was walking on the water and was about to pass the boat.

⁴⁹When the disciples saw Jesus walking on the water, they thought he was a ghost, and they started screaming. ⁵⁰All of them saw him and were terrified. But at that same time he said, "Don't worry! I am Jesus. Don't be afraid." ⁵¹He then got into the boat with them, and the wind died down. The disciples were completely confused. ⁵²Their minds were closed, and they could not understand the true meaning of the loaves of bread.

Jesus Heals Sick People in Gennesaret
(Matthew 14.34-36)

⁵³Jesus and his disciples crossed the lake and brought the boat to shore near the town of Gennesaret. ⁵⁴As soon as they got out of the boat, the people recognized Jesus. ⁵⁵So they ran all over that part of the country to bring their sick people to him on mats. They brought them each time they heard where he was. ⁵⁶In every village or farm or marketplace where Jesus went, the people brought their sick to him. They begged him to let them just touch his clothes, and everyone who did was healed.

The Teaching of the Ancestors
(Matthew 15.1-9)

7 Some Pharisees and several teachers of the Law of Moses from Jerusalem came and gathered around Jesus. ²They noticed that some of his disciples ate without first washing their hands.ˢ

³The Pharisees and many other Jewish people obey the teachings of their ancestors. They always wash their hands in the proper wayᵗ before eating. ⁴None of them will eat anything they buy in the market until it is washed. They also follow a lot of other teachings, such as washing cups, pitchers, and bowls.ᵘ

⁵The Pharisees and teachers asked Jesus, "Why don't your disciples obey what our

ancestors taught us to do? Why do they eat without washing their hands?"

⁶Jesus replied:
You are nothing but show-offs! The prophet Isaiah was right when he wrote that God had said,

"All of you praise me
     with your words,
but you never really
     think about me.
⁷It is useless for you
     to worship me,
when you teach rules
     made up by humans."

⁸You disobey God's commands in order to obey what humans have taught. ⁹You are good at rejecting God's commands so that you can follow your own teachings! ¹⁰Didn't Moses command you to respect your father and mother? Didn't he tell you to put to death all who curse their parents? ¹¹But you let people get by without helping their parents when they should. You let them say that what they own has been offered to God.ᵛ ¹²You won't let those people help their parents. ¹³And you ignore God's commands in order to follow your own teaching. You do a lot of other things that are just as bad.

What Really Makes People Unclean
(Matthew 15.10-20)

¹⁴Jesus called the crowd together again and said, "Pay attention and try to understand what I mean. ¹⁵⁻¹⁶The food that you put into your mouth doesn't make you unclean and unfit to worship God. The bad words that come out of your mouth are what make you unclean."ʷ

¹⁷After Jesus and his disciples had left the crowd and had gone into the house,

---

ˢ**7.2** *without first washing their hands:* The Jewish people had strict laws about washing their hands before eating, especially if they had been out in public.   ᵗ**7.3** *in the proper way:* The Greek text has "with the fist," but the exact meaning is not clear. It could mean "to the wrist" or "to the elbow."   ᵘ**7.4** *bowls:* Some manuscripts add "and sleeping mats."   ᵛ**7.11** *has been offered to God:* According to Jewish custom, when anything was offered to God, it could not be used for anyone else, not even for a person's parents.   ʷ**7.15,16** *unclean:* Some manuscripts add, "If you have ears, pay attention."

they asked him what these sayings meant. [18]He answered, "Don't you know what I am talking about by now? You surely know that the food you put into your mouth cannot make you unclean. [19]It doesn't go into your heart, but into your stomach, and then out of your body." By saying this, Jesus meant that all foods were fit to eat.

[20]Then Jesus said:

What comes from your heart is what makes you unclean. [21]Out of your heart come evil thoughts, vulgar deeds, stealing, murder, [22]unfaithfulness in marriage, greed, meanness, deceit, indecency, envy, insults, pride, and foolishness. [23]All of these come from your heart, and they are what make you unfit to worship God.

A Woman's Faith
(Matthew 15.21-28)

[24]Jesus left and went to the region near the city of Tyre, where he stayed in someone's home. He did not want people to know he was there, but they found out anyway. [25]A woman whose daughter had an evil spirit in her heard where Jesus was. And right away she came and knelt down at his feet. [26]The woman was Greek and had been born in the part of Syria known as Phoenicia. She begged Jesus to force the demon out of her daughter. [27]But Jesus said, "The children must first be fed! It isn't right to take away their food and feed it to dogs."[x]

[28]The woman replied, "Lord, even dogs eat the crumbs that children drop from the table."

[29]Jesus answered, "That's true! You may go now. The demon has left your daughter." [30]When the woman got back home, she found her child lying on the bed. The demon had gone.

Jesus Heals a Man Who Was Deaf and Could Hardly Talk

[31]Jesus left the region around Tyre and went by way of Sidon toward Lake Galilee. He went through the land near the ten cities known as Decapolis.[y] [32]Some people brought to him a man who was deaf and could hardly talk. They begged Jesus just to touch him.

[33]After Jesus had taken him aside from the crowd, he stuck his fingers in the man's ears. Then he spit and put it on the man's tongue. [34]Jesus looked up toward heaven, and with a groan he said, "Effatha!"[z] which means "Open up!" [35]At once the man could hear, and he had no more trouble talking clearly.

[36]Jesus told the people not to say anything about what he had done. But the more he told them, the more they talked about it. [37]They were completely amazed and said, "Everything he does is good! He even heals people who cannot hear or talk."

Jesus Feeds Four Thousand
(Matthew 15.32-39)

8 One day another large crowd gathered around Jesus. They had not brought along anything to eat. So Jesus called his disciples together and said, [2]"I feel sorry for these people. They have been with me for three days, and they don't have anything to eat. [3]Some of them live a long way from here. If I send them away hungry, they might faint on their way home."

[4]The disciples said, "This place is like a desert. Where can we find enough food to feed such a crowd?"

[5]Jesus asked them how much food they had. They replied, "Seven small loaves of bread."[a]

[6]After Jesus told the crowd to sit down, he took the seven loaves and blessed them. He then broke the loaves and handed them to his disciples, who passed them out to the crowd. [7]They also had a few little fish, and after Jesus had blessed these, he told the disciples to pass them around.

[8-9]The crowd of about four thousand people ate all they wanted, and the leftovers filled seven large baskets.

As soon as Jesus had sent the people away, [10]he got into the boat with the disciples and crossed to the territory near Dalmanutha.[b]

A Sign from Heaven
(Matthew 16.1-4)

[11]The Pharisees came out and started an argument with Jesus. They wanted to test

---

x7.27 feed it to dogs: The Jewish people often referred to Gentiles as dogs.   y7.31 the ten cities known as Decapolis: See the note at 5.20.   z7.34 Effatha: This word is in Aramaic, a language spoken in Palestine during the time of Jesus.   a8.5 small loaves of bread: See the note at 6.38.   b8.10 Dalmanutha: The place is unknown.

A Phoenician Woman

Matthew 15.21-28; Mark 7.24-30

*T*he power of persistence. The unnamed woman (who was not a Jew and thus, in the Jews' eyes, a lesser human) knew, used, and benefited from persistence. Any mom can identify with this woman's desperate longing to help her daughter. Her confidence in Jesus' power over demons fueled her determination. Even though her initial request to Jesus was met with silence, she kept asking for help. The disciples grew aggravated and wanted to send her away, but Jesus responded with a proverb about food that referred to minority groups. In those days, the Jews often saw the Gentiles as dogs, which explains why the Phoenician woman (who understood what Jesus was really saying with his proverb) responded, "Lord, even dogs eat the crumbs that children drop from the table" (Mark 7.28).

Why did Jesus initially turn down this mother's request for her daughter's healing? Because she didn't deserve it? Not at all. Jesus demonstrates in other encounters that he values people independent of family, religion, rank, or race. He passionately works to draw each person to him. So Jesus' character showed no desire or need to push this woman away. Instead, the tender words with which Jesus concluded their discussion show he was pleased to see her demonstrate persistence and faith—no matter how frequently she was questioned. Here are his words: "Dear woman, you really do have a lot of faith, and you will be given what you want." Here are his actions: At that moment, her daughter was healed (Matthew 15.28).

Will you show persistent faith? It's easy to honor God at church when people around you say and do holy things. But what if the person next to you is grouchy? Do you choose to respond with a positive attitude? What if you've been sick with the flu and your children have cabin fever? Will you creatively find activities that keep them busy while you rest? What if finances are tight and you want to purchase something specific? Can you faithfully wait, without self-pity or self-righteousness until you save the money? These are marks of faithfulness—the ability to persistently show Christlikeness even when you don't feel like it, and even when people or circumstances make it hard.

When you choose to persistently honor Jesus, your actions will bring healing to relationships. They'll turn your worry to peace—and your sadness to joy!

him by asking for a sign from heaven. [12]Jesus groaned and said, "Why are you always looking for a sign? I can promise you that you will not be given one!" [13]Then he left them. He again got into a boat and crossed over to the other side of the lake.

The Yeast of the Pharisees and of Herod
(Matthew 16.5-12)

[14]The disciples had forgotten to bring any bread, and they had only one loaf with them in the boat. [15]Jesus warned them, "Watch out! Guard against the yeast of the Pharisees and of Herod."[c]

[16]The disciples talked this over and said to each other, "He must be saying this because we don't have any bread."

[17]Jesus knew what they were thinking and asked, "Why are you talking about not having any bread? Don't you understand? Are your minds still closed? [18]Are your eyes blind and your ears deaf? Don't you remember [19]how many baskets of leftovers you picked up when I fed those five thousand people with only five small loaves of bread?"

"Yes," the disciples answered. "There were twelve baskets."

[20]Jesus then asked, "And how many baskets of leftovers did you pick up when I broke seven small loaves of bread for those four thousand people?"

"Seven," they answered.

[21]"Don't you know what I am talking about by now?" Jesus asked.

Jesus Heals a Blind Man at Bethsaida

[22]As Jesus and his disciples were going into Bethsaida, some people brought a blind man to him and begged him to touch the man. [23]Jesus took him by the hand and led him out of the village, where he spit into the man's eyes. He placed his hands on the blind man and asked him if he could see anything. [24]The man looked up and said, "I see people, but they look like trees walking around."

[25]Once again Jesus placed his hands on the man's eyes, and this time the man stared. His eyes were healed, and he saw everything clearly. [26]Jesus said to him, "You may return home now, but don't go into the village."

Who Is Jesus?
(Matthew 16.13-20; Luke 9.18-21)

[27]Jesus and his disciples went to the villages near the town of Caesarea Philippi. As they were walking along, he asked them, "What do people say about me?"

[28]The disciples answered, "Some say you are John the Baptist or maybe Elijah.[d] Others say you are one of the prophets."

---

[c]8.15 *Herod*: Herod Antipas, the son of Herod the Great.   [d]8.28 *Elijah*: See the note at 6.15.

SingleLife—How can I tell the difference between good ambition and self-centeredness? (Mark 8.34-38)

Shift your thinking to an eternal perspective.

Selfishness is frequently the most destructive of sins. But an eternal perspective can help you decide what's worth going after, and what's self-centered. Following Jesus impacts everyday life. You have God's power to solve every situation, so there's no room for whining or selfish pouting.

When your coworker dumps work on you, an eternal perspective helps you find the energy to address the problem. List solutions with your coworker and agree on deadlines, then follow through with your commitments. If your daughter speaks to you with ugly words and attitudes, insist that she make her requests known kindly or lose thirty minutes of computer time; then monitor her to make sure she knows you mean it. And if a church member expects too much of you, an eternal perspective helps you explain to her that as much as you'd like to take on three jobs, one is all you can do well. Agree on exactly what that job includes, then do it well without guilt. No whining. No self-pity. Just Jesus-centered problem-solving. (See also Genesis 11.1-9; Hebrews 4.12,13.)

Words To Remember: *If you give up your life for me and for the good news, you will save it. What will you gain, if you own the whole world but destroy yourself?* —Mark 8.35,36

²⁹Then Jesus asked them, "But who do you say I am?"

"You are the Messiah!" Peter replied.

³⁰Jesus warned the disciples not to tell anyone about him.

Jesus Speaks about His Suffering and Death

(Matthew 16.21-28; Luke 9.22-27)

³¹Jesus began telling his disciples what would happen to him. He said, "The nation's leaders, the chief priests, and the teachers of the Law of Moses will make the Son of Man suffer terribly. He will be rejected and killed, but three days later he will rise to life." ³²Then Jesus explained clearly what he meant.

Peter took Jesus aside and told him to stop talking like that. ³³But when Jesus turned and saw the disciples, he corrected Peter. He said to him, "Satan, get away from me! You are thinking like everyone else and not like God."

³⁴Jesus then told the crowd and the disciples to come closer, and he said:

If any of you want to be my followers, you must forget about yourself. You must take up your cross and follow me. ³⁵If you want to save your life,ᵉ you will destroy it. But if you give up your life for me and for the good news, you will save it. ³⁶What will you gain, if you own the whole world but destroy yourself? ³⁷What could you give to get back your soul?

³⁸Don't be ashamed of me and my message among these unfaithful and sinful people! If you are, the Son of Man will be ashamed of you when he comes in the glory of his Father with the holy angels.

9 I can assure you that some of the people standing here will not die before they see God's kingdom come with power.

The True Glory of Jesus

(Matthew 17.1-13; Luke 9.28-36)

²Six days later Jesus took Peter, James, and John with him. They went up on a high mountain, where they could be alone. There in front of the disciples, Jesus was completely changed. ³And his clothes became much whiter than any bleach on earth could

make them. ⁴Then Moses and Elijah were there talking with Jesus.

⁵Peter said to Jesus, "Teacher, it is good for us to be here! Let us make three shelters, one for you, one for Moses, and one for Elijah." ⁶But Peter and the others were terribly frightened, and he did not know what he was talking about.

⁷The shadow of a cloud passed over and covered them. From the cloud a voice said, "This is my Son, and I love him. Listen to what he says!" ⁸At once the disciples looked around, but they saw only Jesus.

⁹As Jesus and his disciples were coming down the mountain, he told them not to say a word about what they had seen, until the Son of Man had been raised from death. ¹⁰So they kept it to themselves. But they wondered what he meant by the words "raised from death."

¹¹The disciples asked Jesus, "Don't the teachers of the Law of Moses say that Elijah must come before the Messiah does?"

¹²Jesus answered:

Elijah certainly will comeʲ to get everything ready. But don't the Scriptures also say that the Son of Man must suffer terribly and be rejected? ¹³I can assure you that Elijah has already come. And people treated him just as they wanted to, as the Scriptures say they would.

Jesus Heals a Boy

(Matthew 17.14-20; Luke 9.37-43a)

¹⁴When Jesus and his three disciples came back down, they saw a large crowd around the other disciples. The teachers of the Law of Moses were arguing with them. ¹⁵The crowd was really surprised to see Jesus, and everyone hurried over to greet him.

¹⁶Jesus asked, "What are you arguing about?"

¹⁷Someone from the crowd answered, "Teacher, I brought my son to you. A demon keeps him from talking. ¹⁸Whenever the demon attacks my son, it throws him to the ground and makes him foam at the mouth and grit his teeth in pain. Then he becomes

---

ᵉ**8.35** *life:* In verses 35-37 the same Greek word is translated "life," "yourself," and "soul."
ʲ**9.12** *Elijah certainly will come:* See the note at 6.15.

stiff. I asked your disciples to force out the demon, but they couldn't do it."

¹⁹Jesus said, "You people don't have any faith! How much longer must I be with you? Why do I have to put up with you? Bring the boy to me."

²⁰They brought the boy, and as soon as the demon saw Jesus, it made the boy shake all over. He fell down and began rolling on the ground and foaming at the mouth.

²¹Jesus asked the boy's father, "How long has he been like this?"

The man answered, "Ever since he was a child. ²²The demon has often tried to kill him by throwing him into a fire or into water. Please have pity and help us if you can!"

²³Jesus replied, "Why do you say 'if you can'? Anything is possible for someone who has faith!"

²⁴Right away the boy's father shouted, "I do have faith! Please help me to have even more."

²⁵When Jesus saw that a crowd was gathering fast, he spoke sternly to the evil spirit that had kept the boy from speaking or hearing. He said, "I order you to come out of the boy! Don't ever bother him again."

²⁶The spirit screamed and made the boy shake all over. Then it went out of him. The boy looked dead, and almost everyone said he was. ²⁷But Jesus took hold of his hand and helped him stand up.

²⁸After Jesus and the disciples had gone back home and were alone, they asked him, "Why couldn't we force out that demon?"

²⁹Jesus answered, "Only prayer can force out that kind of demon."

Jesus Again Speaks about His Death
(Matthew 17.22, 23; Luke 9.43b-45)

³⁰Jesus left with his disciples and started through Galilee. He did not want anyone to know about it, ³¹because he was teaching the disciples that the Son of Man would be handed over to people who would kill him. But three days later he would rise to life. ³²The disciples did not understand what Jesus meant, and they were afraid to ask.

Who Is the Greatest?
(Matthew 18.1-5; Luke 9.46-48)

³³Jesus and his disciples went to his home in Capernaum. After they were inside the house, Jesus asked them, "What were you arguing about along the way?" ³⁴They

had been arguing about which one of them was the greatest, and so they did not answer.

³⁵After Jesus sat down and told the twelve disciples to gather around him, he said, "If you want the place of honor, you must become a slave and serve others!"

³⁶Then Jesus had a child stand near him. He put his arm around the child and said, ³⁷"When you welcome even a child because of me, you welcome me. And when you welcome me, you welcome the one who sent me."

For or against Jesus
(Luke 9.49, 50)

³⁸John said, "Teacher, we saw a man using your name to force demons out of people. But he wasn't one of us, and we told him to stop."

How compassionate God is to bring ministry out of brokenness. He's brought purpose to my pain— and he's thrown in some surprises, too.

DONNA RICE HUGHES

³⁹Jesus said to his disciples:

Don't stop him! No one who works miracles in my name will soon turn and say something bad about me. ⁴⁰Anyone who isn't against us is for us. ⁴¹And anyone who gives you a cup of water in my name, just because you belong to me, will surely be rewarded.

Temptations To Sin
(Matthew 18.6-9; Luke 17.1, 2)

⁴²It will be terrible for people who cause even one of my little followers to sin. Those people would be better off thrown into the ocean with a heavy stone tied around their necks. ⁴³⁻⁴⁴So if your hand causes you to sin, cut it off! You would be better off to go into life crippled than to have two hands and be thrown into the fires of hell that

never go out.[g] [45-46]If your foot causes you to sin, chop it off. You would be better off to go into life lame than to have two feet and be thrown into hell.[h]

[47]If your eye causes you to sin, get rid of it. You would be better off to go into God's kingdom with only one eye than to have two eyes and be thrown into hell. [48]The worms there never die, and the fire never stops burning.

[49]Everyone must be salted with fire.[i]

[50]Salt is good. But if it no longer tastes like salt, how can it be made salty again? Have salt among you and live at peace with each other.[j]

Teaching about Divorce
(Matthew 19.1-12; Luke 16.18)

10 After Jesus left, he went to Judea and then on to the other side of the Jordan River. Once again large crowds came to him, and as usual, he taught them.

[2]Some Pharisees wanted to test Jesus. So they came up to him and asked if it was right for a man to divorce his wife. [3]Jesus asked them, "What does the Law of Moses say about that?"

[4]They answered, "Moses allows a man to write out divorce papers and send his wife away."

[5]Jesus replied, "Moses gave you this law because you are so heartless. [6]But in the beginning God made a man and a woman. [7]That's why a man leaves his father and mother and gets married. [8]He becomes like one person with his wife. Then they are no longer two people, but one. [9]And no one should separate a couple that God has joined together."

[10]When Jesus and his disciples were back in the house, they asked him about what he had done. [11]He told them, "A man who divorces his wife and marries someone else is unfaithful to his wife. [12]A woman who divorces her husband[k] and marries again is also unfaithful."

Jesus Blesses Little Children
(Matthew 19.13-15; Luke 18.15-17)

[13]Some people brought their children to Jesus so that he could bless them by placing his hands on them. But his disciples told the people to stop bothering him.

[14]When Jesus saw this, he became angry and said, "Let the children come to me! Don't try to stop them. People who are like these little children belong to the kingdom of God.[l] [15]I promise you that you cannot get into God's kingdom, unless you accept it the way a child does." [16]Then Jesus took the children in his arms and blessed them by placing his hands on them.

A Rich Man
(Matthew 19.16-30; Luke 18.18-30)

[17]As Jesus was walking down a road, a man ran up to him. He knelt down, and asked, "Good teacher, what can I do to have eternal life?"

[18]Jesus replied, "Why do you call me good? Only God is good. [19]You know the commandments. 'Do not murder. Be faithful in marriage. Do not steal. Do not tell lies about others. Do not cheat. Respect your father and mother.' "

[20]The man answered, "Teacher, I have obeyed all these commandments since I was a young man."

[21]Jesus looked closely at the man. He liked him and said, "There's one thing you still need to do. Go sell everything you own. Give the money to the poor, and you will have riches in heaven. Then come with me."

[22]When the man heard Jesus say this, he went away gloomy and sad because he was very rich.

[23]Jesus looked around and said to his disciples, "It's hard for rich people to get into God's kingdom!" [24]The disciples were shocked to hear this. So Jesus told them again, "It's terribly hard[m] to get into God's kingdom! [25]In fact, it's easier for a camel to

---

[g]**9.43,44** *never go out*: Some manuscripts add, "The worms there never die, and the fire never stops burning." [h]**9.45,46** *thrown into hell*: Some manuscripts add, "The worms there never die, and the fire never stops burning." [i]**9.49** *salted with fire*: Some manuscripts add "and every sacrifice will be seasoned with salt." The verse may mean that Christ's followers must suffer because of their faith. [j]**9.50** *Have salt among you and live at peace with each other*: This may mean that when Christ's followers have to suffer because of their faith, they must still try to live at peace with each other. [k]**10.12** *A woman who divorces her husband*: Roman law let a woman divorce her husband, but Jewish law did not let a woman do this. [l]**10.14** *People who are like these little children belong to the kingdom of God*: Or "The kingdom of God belongs to people who are like these little children." [m]**10.24** *hard*: Some manuscripts add "for people who trust in their wealth." Others add "for the rich."

go through the eye of a needle than for a rich person to get into God's kingdom."

²⁶Jesus' disciples were even more amazed. They asked each other, "How can anyone ever be saved?"

²⁷Jesus looked at them and said, "There are some things that people cannot do, but God can do anything."

²⁸Peter replied, "Remember, we left everything to be your followers!"

²⁹Jesus told him:

You can be sure that anyone who gives up home or brothers or sisters or mother or father or children or land for me and for the good news ³⁰will be rewarded. In this world they will be given a hundred times as many houses and brothers and sisters and mothers and children and pieces of land, though they will also be mistreated. And in the world to come, they will have eternal life. ³¹But many who are now first will be last, and many who are now last will be first.

Jesus Again Tells about His Death
(Matthew 20.17-19; Luke 18.31-34)

³²The disciples were confused as Jesus led them toward Jerusalem, and his other followers were afraid. Once again, Jesus took the twelve disciples aside and told them what was going to happen to him. He said:

³³We are now on our way to Jerusalem where the Son of Man will be handed over to the chief priests and the teachers of the Law of Moses. They will sentence him to death and hand him over to foreigners,ⁿ ³⁴who will make fun of him and spit on him. They will beat him and kill him. But three days later he will rise to life.

The Request of James and John
(Matthew 20.20-28)

³⁵James and John, the sons of Zebedee, came up to Jesus and asked, "Teacher, will you do us a favor?"

³⁶Jesus asked them what they wanted, ³⁷and they answered, "When you come into your glory, please let one of us sit at your right side and the other at your left."ᵒ

³⁸Jesus told them, "You don't really

ⁿ**10.33** *foreigners:* The Romans who ruled Judea at this time. ᵒ**10.37** *right side . . . left:* The most powerful people in a kingdom sat at the right and left side of the king.

Friendship—How can I keep from comparing myself with my friends?
(Mark 10.29-31,35-45)

Remember that earthly position is just that—earthly.
Have you ever felt just the least bit jealous of a friend? Maybe she's a fit-and-trim aerobics instructor, and you're having trouble with those last ten pounds you'd like to lose. Every time you see her in her leotards, you grimace inwardly and wish you looked like her. Or perhaps your single friend just got the job of her dreams, and you're a stay-at-home mom who's trapped in a tiny house with three kids for the summer. Or your friend who became a Christian three months ago is growing rapidly in her faith—and yours seems to be going nowhere.

It's easy to compare yourself (and your life) with others. But let's face it. No one person has everything (looks, talent, spiritual growth, and so on). In this passage, Mark sets the record straight. Instead of looking for what other people have, especially those friends who seem to have more than we do (a bigger house, better looks, a nicer family), we need to remember that looks are just that—looks. Jesus says that, in the long run, "many who are now first will be last, and many who are now last will be first" (10.31). He also reminds us that, in order to be great in God's kingdom, we must serve others (10.43).

That means that, instead of comparing ourselves to others, we accept our talents, looks, and financial status as gifts from God. Then we focus on loving our friends as Christ would. (See also Numbers 6.22-27; 1 Samuel 16.1-13.)

Words To Remember: *If you want to be great, you must be the servant of all the others.—Mark 10.43*

know what you're asking! Are you able to drink from the cup[p] that I must soon drink from or be baptized as I must be baptized?"[q]

³⁹"Yes, we are!" James and John answered.

Then Jesus replied, "You certainly will drink from the cup from which I must drink. And you will be baptized just as I must! ⁴⁰But it isn't for me to say who will sit at my right side and at my left. That is for God to decide."

⁴¹When the ten other disciples heard this, they were angry with James and John. ⁴²But Jesus called the disciples together and said:

You know that those foreigners who call themselves kings like to order their people around. And their great leaders have full power over the people they rule. ⁴³But don't act like them. If you want to be great, you must be the servant of all the others. ⁴⁴And if you want to be first, you must be everyone's slave. ⁴⁵The Son of Man did not come to be a slave master, but a slave who will give his life to rescue[r] many people.

Jesus Heals Blind Bartimaeus
(Matthew 20.29-34; Luke 18.35-43)

⁴⁶Jesus and his disciples went to Jericho. And as they were leaving, they were followed by a large crowd. A blind beggar by the name of Bartimaeus son of Timaeus was sitting beside the road. ⁴⁷When he heard that it was Jesus from Nazareth, he shouted, "Jesus, Son of David,[s] have pity on me!" ⁴⁸Many people told the man to stop, but he shouted even louder, "Son of David, have pity on me!"

⁴⁹Jesus stopped and said, "Call him over!"

They called out to the blind man and said, "Don't be afraid! Come on! He is calling for you." ⁵⁰The man threw off his coat as he jumped up and ran to Jesus.

⁵¹Jesus asked, "What do you want me to do for you?"

The blind man answered, "Master,[t] I want to see!"

⁵²Jesus told him, "You may go. Your eyes are healed because of your faith."

Right away the man could see, and he went down the road with Jesus.

Jesus Enters Jerusalem
(Matthew 21.1-11; Luke 19.28-40; John 12.12-19)

11 Jesus and his disciples reached Bethphage and Bethany near the Mount of Olives. When they were getting close to Jerusalem, Jesus sent two of them on ahead. ²He told them, "Go into the next village. As soon as you enter it, you will find a young donkey that has never been ridden. Untie the donkey and bring it here. ³If anyone asks why you are doing that, say, 'The Lord[u] needs it and will soon bring it back.' "

⁴The disciples left and found the donkey tied near a door that faced the street. While they were untying it, ⁵some of the people standing there asked, "Why are you untying the donkey?" ⁶They told them what Jesus had said, and the people let them take it.

⁷The disciples led the donkey to Jesus. They put some of their clothes on its back, and Jesus got on. ⁸Many people spread clothes on the road, while others went to cut branches from the fields.[v]

⁹In front of Jesus and behind him, people went along shouting,

"Hooray![w]
God bless the one who comes
    in the name of the Lord!
¹⁰God bless the coming kingdom
    of our ancestor David.
Hooray for God
    in heaven above!"

¹¹After Jesus had gone to Jerusalem, he went into the temple and looked around at everything. But since it was already late in the day, he went back to Bethany with the twelve disciples.

---

[p]10.38 drink from the cup: In the Scriptures a "cup" is sometimes used as a symbol of suffering. To "drink from the cup" would be to suffer.   [q]10.38 as I must be baptized: Baptism is used with the same meaning that "cup" has in this verse.   [r]10.45 rescue: The Greek word often, though not always, means the payment of a price to free a slave or a prisoner.   [s]10.47 Son of David: The Jewish people expected the Messiah to be from the family of King David, and for this reason the Messiah was often called the "Son of David."   [t]10.51 Master: A Hebrew word that may also mean "Teacher."   [u]11.3 The Lord: Or "The master of the donkey."   [v]11.8 spread . . . branches from the fields: This was one way that the Jewish people welcomed a famous person.   [w]11.9 Hooray: This translates a word that can mean "please save us." But it is most often used as a shout of praise to God.

Jesus Puts a Curse on a Fig Tree
(Matthew 21.18, 19)

¹²When Jesus and his disciples left Bethany the next morning, he was hungry. ¹³From a distance Jesus saw a fig tree covered with leaves, and he went to see if there were any figs on the tree. But there were not any, because it wasn't the season for figs. ¹⁴So Jesus said to the tree, "Never again will anyone eat fruit from this tree!" The disciples heard him say this.

Jesus in the Temple
(Matthew 21.12-17; Luke 19.45-48; John 2.13-22)

¹⁵After Jesus and his disciples reached Jerusalem, he went into the temple and began chasing out everyone who was selling and buying. He turned over the tables of the moneychangers and the benches of those who were selling doves. ¹⁶Jesus would not let anyone carry things through the temple. ¹⁷Then he taught the people and said, "The Scriptures say, 'My house should be called a place of worship for all nations.' But you have made it a place where robbers hide!"

¹⁸The chief priests and the teachers of the Law of Moses heard what Jesus said, and they started looking for a way to kill him. They were afraid of him, because the crowds were completely amazed at his teaching.

¹⁹That evening, Jesus and the disciples went outside the city.

A Lesson from the Fig Tree
(Matthew 21.20-22)

²⁰As the disciples walked past the fig tree the next morning, they noticed that it was completely dried up, roots and all. ²¹Peter remembered what Jesus had said to the tree. Then Peter said, "Teacher, look! The tree you put a curse on has dried up."

²²Jesus told his disciples:

Have faith in God! ²³If you have faith in God and don't doubt, you can tell this mountain to get up and jump into the sea, and it will. ²⁴Everything you ask for in prayer will be yours, if you only have faith.

²⁵⁻²⁶Whenever you stand up to pray, you must forgive what others have done to you. Then your Father in heaven will forgive your sins.ˣ

A Question about Jesus' Authority
(Matthew 21.23-27; Luke 20.1-8)

²⁷Jesus and his disciples returned to Jerusalem. And as he was walking through the temple, the chief priests, the nation's leaders, and the teachers of the Law of Moses came over to him. ²⁸They asked, "What right do you have to do these things? Who gave you this authority?"

> *God is "jealous" for us, desiring that our whole heart, mind, body, and soul be focused on him.*
>
> LIZ CURTIS HIGGS

²⁹Jesus answered, "I have just one question to ask you. If you answer it, I will tell you where I got the right to do these things. ³⁰Who gave John the right to baptize? Was it God in heaven or merely some human being?"

³¹They thought it over and said to each other, "We can't say that God gave John this right. Jesus will ask us why we didn't believe John. ³²On the other hand, these people think that John was a prophet. So we can't say that it was merely some human who gave John the right to baptize."

They were afraid of the crowd ³³and told Jesus, "We don't know."

Jesus replied, "Then I won't tell you who gave me the right to do what I do."

Renters of a Vineyard
(Matthew 21.33-46; Luke 20.9-19)

12 Jesus then told them this story: A farmer once planted a vineyard. He built a wall around it and dug a pit to crush the grapes in. He also built a lookout tower. Then he rented out his vineyard and left the country.

ˣ**11.25,26** *your sins:* Some manuscripts add, "But if you do not forgive others, God will not forgive you."

²When it was harvest time, he sent a servant to get his share of the grapes. ³The renters grabbed the servant. They beat him up and sent him away without a thing.

⁴The owner sent another servant, but the renters beat him on the head and insulted him terribly. ⁵Then the man sent another servant, and they killed him. He kept sending servant after servant. They beat some of them and killed others.

⁶The owner had a son he loved very much. Finally, he sent his son to the renters because he thought they would respect him. ⁷But they said to themselves, "Someday he will own this vineyard. Let's kill him! That way we can have it all for ourselves." ⁸So they grabbed the owner's son and killed him. Then they threw his body out of the vineyard.

⁹Jesus asked, "What do you think the owner of the vineyard will do? He will come and kill those renters and let someone else have his vineyard. ¹⁰You surely know that the Scriptures say,

'The stone that the builders
    tossed aside
is now the most important
    stone of all.
¹¹This is something
    the Lord has done,
    and it is amazing to us.' "

¹²The leaders knew that Jesus was really talking about them, and they wanted to arrest him. But because they were afraid of the crowd, they let him alone and left.

Paying Taxes
(Matthew 22.15-22; Luke 20.20-26)

¹³The Pharisees got together with Herod's followers.ʸ Then they sent some men to trick Jesus into saying something wrong. ¹⁴They went to him and said, "Teacher, we know that you are honest. You treat everyone with the same respect, no matter who they are. And you teach the truth about what God wants people to do. Tell us, should we pay taxes to the Emperor or not?"

¹⁵Jesus knew what they were up to, and

he said, "Why are you trying to test me? Show me a coin!"

¹⁶They brought him a silver coin, and he asked, "Whose picture and name are on it?"

"The Emperor's," they answered.

¹⁷Then Jesus told them, "Give the Emperor what belongs to him and give God what belongs to God." The men were amazed at Jesus.

Life in the Future World
(Matthew 22.23-33; Luke 20.27-40)

¹⁸The Sadducees did not believe that people would rise to life after death. So some of them came to Jesus and said:

¹⁹Teacher, Moses wrote that if a married man dies and has no children, his brother should marry the widow. Their first son would then be thought of as the son of the dead brother. ²⁰There were once seven brothers. The first one married, but died without having any children. ²¹The second brother married his brother's widow, and he also died without having children. The same thing happened to the third brother, ²²and finally to all seven brothers. At last the woman died. ²³When God raises people from death, whose wife will this woman be? After all, she had been married to all seven brothers.

²⁴Jesus answered:

You are completely wrong! You don't know what the Scriptures teach. And you don't know anything about the power of God. ²⁵When God raises people to life, they won't marry. They will be like the angels in heaven. ²⁶You surely know about people being raised to life. You know that in the story about Moses and the burning bush, God said, "I am the God worshiped by Abraham, Isaac, and Jacob."ᶻ ²⁷He isn't the God of the dead, but of the living. You Sadducees are all wrong.

The Most Important Commandment
(Matthew 22.34-40; Luke 10.25-28)

²⁸One of the teachers of the Law of Moses came up while Jesus and the Sadducees were arguing. When he heard Jesus give a good answer, he asked him, "What is the most important commandment?"

> *See yourself as in process,*
> *not as a finished product.*
> KAY MARSHALL STROM

²⁹Jesus answered, "The most important one says: 'People of Israel, you have only one Lord and God. ³⁰You must love him with all your heart, soul, mind, and strength.' ³¹The second most important commandment says: 'Love others as much as you love yourself.' No other commandment is more important than these."

³²The man replied, "Teacher, you are certainly right to say there is only one God. ³³It is also true that we must love God with all our heart, mind, and strength, and that we must love others as much as we love ourselves. These commandments are more important than all the sacrifices and offerings that we could possibly make."

³⁴When Jesus saw that the man had given a sensible answer, he told him, "You are not far from God's kingdom." After this, no one dared ask Jesus any more questions.

About David's Son
(Matthew 22.41-46; Luke 20.41-44)

³⁵As Jesus was teaching in the temple, he said, "How can the teachers of the Law of Moses say that the Messiah will come from the family of King David? ³⁶The Holy Spirit led David to say,

> 'The Lord said to my Lord:
>   Sit at my right side[a]
> until I make your enemies
>   into a footstool for you.'

³⁷If David called the Messiah his Lord, how can the Messiah be his son?"[b]

The large crowd enjoyed listening to Jesus teach.

Jesus Condemns the Pharisees and the Teachers of the Law of Moses
(Matthew 23.1-36; Luke 20.45-47)

³⁸As Jesus was teaching, he said:

Guard against the teachers of the Law of Moses! They love to walk around in long robes and be greeted in the market. ³⁹They like the front seats in the meeting places and the best seats at banquets. ⁴⁰But they cheat widows out of their homes and pray long prayers just to show off. They will be punished most of all.

A Widow's Offering
(Luke 21.1-4)

⁴¹Jesus was sitting in the temple near the offering box and watching people put in their gifts. He noticed that many rich people were giving a lot of money. ⁴²Finally, a poor widow came up and put in two coins that were worth only a few pennies. ⁴³Jesus told his disciples to gather around him. Then he said:

I tell you that this poor widow has put in more than all the others. ⁴⁴Everyone else gave what they didn't need. But she is very poor and gave everything she had. Now she doesn't have a cent to live on.

The Temple Will Be Destroyed
(Matthew 24.1, 2; Luke 21.5, 6)

13 As Jesus was leaving the temple, one of his disciples said to him, "Teacher, look at these beautiful stones and wonderful buildings!"

²Jesus replied, "Do you see these huge buildings? They will certainly be torn down! Not one stone will be left in place."

Warning about Trouble
(Matthew 24.3-14; Luke 21.7-19)

³Later, as Jesus was sitting on the Mount of Olives across from the temple, Peter, James, John, and Andrew came to him in private. ⁴They asked, "When will these things happen? What will be the sign that they are about to take place?"

---

[a]**12.36** *right side:* The place of power and honor.
[b]**12.37** *David . . . his son:* See the note at 10.47.

⁵Jesus answered:

Watch out and don't let anyone fool you! ⁶Many will come and claim to be me. They will use my name and fool many people.

⁷When you hear about wars and threats of wars, don't be afraid. These things will have to happen first, but that isn't the end. ⁸Nations and kingdoms will go to war against each other. There will be earthquakes in many places, and people will starve to death. But this is just the beginning of troubles.

⁹Be on your guard! You will be taken to courts and beaten with whips in their meeting places. And because of me, you will have to stand before rulers and kings to tell about your faith. ¹⁰But before the end comes, the good news must be preached to all nations.

¹¹When you are arrested, don't worry about what you will say. You will be given the right words when the time comes. But you will not really be the ones speaking. Your words will come from the Holy Spirit.

¹²Brothers and sisters will betray each other and have each other put to death. Parents will betray their own children, and children will turn against their parents and have them killed. ¹³Everyone will hate you be-cause of me. But if you keep on being faithful right to the end, you will be saved.

The Horrible Thing
(Matthew 24.15-21; Luke 21.20-24)

¹⁴Someday you will see that "Horrible Thing" where it should not be.ᶜ Everyone who reads this must try to understand! If you are living in Judea at that time, run to the mountains. ¹⁵If you are on the roofᵈ of your house, don't go inside to get anything. ¹⁶If you are out in the field, don't go back for your coat. ¹⁷It will be an awful time for women who are expecting babies or nursing young children. ¹⁸Pray that it won't happen in winter.ᵉ ¹⁹This will be the worst time of suffering since God created the world, and nothing this terrible will ever happen again. ²⁰If the Lord doesn't make the time shorter, no one will be left alive. But because of his chosen and special ones, he will make the time shorter.

²¹If someone should say, "Here is the Messiah!" or "There he is!" don't believe it. ²²False messiahs and false

---

ᶜ**13.14** *where it should not be*: Probably the holy place in the temple.   ᵈ**13.15** *roof*: See the note at 2.4.
ᵉ**13.18** *in winter*: In Palestine the winters are cold and rainy and make travel difficult.

---

*Spiritual*Life—I'm so busy! How can I find time for God? *(Mark 13.32-37)*

Make God the companion of your schedule.

If you ask most Christians how to spend time with God, they'll respond: "Go to church, read your Bible, and pray." But these critical communication times are only a portion of your time with God. He's the foundation for your day, the companion of your schedule. As Mark 13.32-37 illustrates, let every action and every minute be one you'd be proud for Jesus to see. Why? He's coming back at a time only God knows.

Not only is Jesus coming back, but he's here with you now in the Holy Spirit. Please him with your every word, attitude, and choice. Learn how to do this by spending time in the Bible. While no one has unlimited time, you can squeeze minutes here and there with the following strategies: Read a chapter before you get in the car for work, then think about it all the way there; purchase Scripture on cassette and listen to it in the car (ditto for praise songs that quote Scripture word-for-word); read a verse before you go on break at work, then pray it through as you walk to the break room or converse with your coworkers. (See also 1 Thessalonians 4.13-18; Titus 3.4-7,14.)

Words To Remember: *Be alert! You don't know when the master of the house will come back. It could be in the evening or at midnight or before dawn or in the morning. . . . Don't let him find you asleep.—Mark 13.35,36*

prophets will come and work miracles and signs. They will even try to fool God's chosen ones. ²³But be on your guard! That's why I am telling you these things now.

When the Son of Man Appears
(Matthew 24.29-31; Luke 21.25-28)

²⁴In those days, right after that time of suffering,

"The sun will become dark,
and the moon
will no longer shine.
²⁵ The stars will fall,
and the powers in the sky*ʲ*
will be shaken."

²⁶Then the Son of Man will be seen coming in the clouds with great power and glory. ²⁷He will send his angels to gather his chosen ones from all over the earth.

A Lesson from a Fig Tree
(Matthew 24.32-35; Luke 21.29-33)

²⁸Learn a lesson from a fig tree. When its branches sprout and start putting out leaves, you know summer is near. ²⁹So when you see all these things happening, you will know that the time has almost come.*ᵍ* ³⁰You can be sure that some of the people of this generation will still be alive when all this happens. ³¹The sky and the earth will not last forever, but my words will.

No One Knows the Day or Time
(Matthew 24.36-44)

³²No one knows the day or the time. The angels in heaven don't know, and the Son himself doesn't know. Only the Father knows. ³³So watch out and be ready! You don't know when the time will come. ³⁴It is like what happens when a man goes away for a while and places his servants in charge of everything. He tells each of them what to do, and he orders the guard to keep alert. ³⁵So be alert! You don't know when the master of the house will come back. It could be in the evening or at midnight or before dawn or in the morning. ³⁶But if he comes suddenly, don't let him find

you asleep. ³⁷I tell everyone just what I have told you. Be alert!

A Plot To Kill Jesus
(Matthew 26.1-5; Luke 22.1, 2; John 11.45-53)

14 It was now two days before Passover and the Festival of Thin Bread. The chief priests and the teachers of the Law of Moses were planning how they could sneak around and have Jesus arrested and put to death. ²They were saying, "We must not do it during the festival, because the people will riot."

At Bethany
(Matthew 26.6-13; John 12.1-8)

³Jesus was eating in Bethany at the home of Simon, who once had leprosy,*ʰ* when a woman came in with a very expensive bottle of sweet-smelling perfume.*ⁱ* After breaking it open, she poured the perfume on Jesus' head. ⁴This made some of the guests angry, and they complained, "Why such a waste? ⁵We could have sold this perfume for more than three hundred silver coins and given the money to the poor!" So they started saying cruel things to the woman.

⁶But Jesus said:

Leave her alone! Why are you bothering her? She has done a beautiful thing for me. ⁷You will always have the poor with you. And whenever you want to, you can give to them. But you won't always have me here with you. ⁸She has done all she could by pouring perfume on my body to prepare it for burial. ⁹You may be sure that wherever the good news is told all over the world, people will remember what she has done. And they will tell others.

Judas and the Chief Priests
(Matthew 26.14-16; Luke 22.3-6)

¹⁰Judas Iscariot*ʲ* was one of the twelve disciples. He went to the chief priests and offered to help them arrest Jesus. ¹¹They

---

*ʲ***13.25** *the powers in the sky:* In ancient times people thought that the stars were spiritual powers.
*ᵍ***13.29** *the time has almost come:* Or "he (that is, the Son of Man) will soon be here." *ʰ***14.3** *leprosy:* In biblical times the word "leprosy" was used for many different skin diseases. *ⁱ***14.3** *sweet-smelling perfume:* The Greek text has "perfume made of pure spikenard," a plant used to make perfume. *ʲ***14.10** *Iscariot:* See the note at 3.19.

were glad to hear this, and they promised to pay him. So Judas started looking for a good chance to betray Jesus.

Jesus Eats with His Disciples
(Matthew 26.17-25; Luke 22.7-14, 21-23; John 13.21-30)

¹²It was the first day of the Festival of Thin Bread, and the Passover lambs were being killed. Jesus' disciples asked him, "Where do you want us to prepare the Passover meal?"

¹³Jesus said to two of the disciples, "Go into the city, where you will meet a man carrying a jar of water.ᵏ Follow him, ¹⁴and when he goes into a house, say to the owner, 'Our teacher wants to know if you have a room where he can eat the Passover meal with his disciples.' ¹⁵The owner will take you upstairs and show you a large room furnished and ready for you to use. Prepare the meal there."

¹⁶The two disciples went into the city and found everything just as Jesus had told them. So they prepared the Passover meal.

¹⁷⁻¹⁸While Jesus and the twelve disciples were eating together that evening, he said, "The one who will betray me is now eating with me."

¹⁹This made the disciples sad, and one after another they said to Jesus, "You surely don't mean me!"

²⁰He answered, "It is one of you twelve men who is eating from this dish with me. ²¹The Son of Man will die, just as the Scriptures say. But it is going to be terrible for the one who betrays me. That man would be better off if he had never been born."

The Lord's Supper
(Matthew 26.26-30; Luke 22.14-23; 1 Corinthians 11.23-25)

²²During the meal Jesus took some bread in his hands. He blessed the bread and broke it. Then he gave it to his disciples and said, "Take this. It is my body."

²³Jesus picked up a cup of wine and gave thanks to God. He gave it to his disciples, and they all drank some. ²⁴Then he said, "This is my blood, which is poured out for many people, and with it God makes his agreement. ²⁵From now on I will not drink any wine, until I drink new wine in God's kingdom." ²⁶Then they sang a hymn and went out to the Mount of Olives.

ᵏ**14.13** *a man carrying a jar of water:* A male slave carrying water could mean that the family was rich.

Personal *Concerns*—How can I accept my body as it is? *(Mark 14.3-9)*

Remember, beauty is more than skin deep.
Am I too fat? Do my arms look flabby? Have I passed the age when people see me as young and vibrant? When you wonder about your looks (as we all do, especially as we age), it's good to put beauty into perspective. God looks at the heart—and so do most people. When you show love and care to the people around you, they see the beauty of your spirit, not your body. They recognize you as gorgeous, no matter what your physical features or background.

In this passage we meet Simon and "the unnamed woman." Simon once had had leprosy, a dreaded and ugly skin disease. Victims frequently experienced patches on the skin, running sores, even loss of fingers and toes. People avoided lepers because the disease was so contagious, and because they believed it rendered them unclean. But Jesus embraced lepers as friends, healed many lepers, and ate in Simon's home.

Jesus also welcomed the generous unnamed woman. Although we have no physical description of her in these verses, it's clear from her actions that she didn't care how she looked to others. She was focused on one thing only: serving Jesus.

By eating with Simon and accepting the woman's act of love, Jesus showed he cares much more about the actions and attitudes of people than about their appearance. Do we? (See also Psalm 104; Psalm 139.13-16.)

Words To Remember: *Jesus said: ". . . She has done a beautiful thing for me. . . . You may be sure that wherever the good news is told all over the world, people will remember what she has done. And they will tell others."—Mark 14.6,9*

Peter's Promise

(Matthew 26.31-35; Luke 22.31-34; John 13.36-38)

[27]Jesus said to his disciples, "All of you will reject me, as the Scriptures say,

> 'I will strike down
>   the shepherd,
> and the sheep
>   will be scattered.'

[28]But after I am raised to life, I will go ahead of you to Galilee."

[29]Peter spoke up, "Even if all the others reject you, I never will!"

[30]Jesus replied, "This very night before a rooster crows twice, you will say three times that you don't know me."

[31]But Peter was so sure of himself that he said, "Even if I have to die with you, I will never say that I don't know you!"

All the others said the same thing.

Jesus Prays

(Matthew 26.36-46; Luke 22.39-46)

[32]Jesus went with his disciples to a place called Gethsemane, and he told them, "Sit here while I pray."

[33]Jesus took along Peter, James, and John. He was sad and troubled and [34]told them, "I am so sad that I feel as if I am dying. Stay here and keep awake with me."

[35-36]Jesus walked on a little way. Then he knelt down on the ground and prayed, "Father,[l] if it is possible, don't let this happen to me! Father, you can do anything. Don't make me suffer by having me drink from this cup.[m] But do what you want, and not what I want."

[37]When Jesus came back and found the disciples sleeping, he said to Simon Peter, "Are you asleep? Can't you stay awake for just one hour? [38]Stay awake and pray that you won't be tested. You want to do what is right, but you are weak."

[39]Jesus went back and prayed the same prayer. [40]But when he returned to the disciples, he found them sleeping again. They simply could not keep their eyes open, and they did not know what to say.

[41]When Jesus returned to the disciples the third time, he said, "Are you still sleeping and resting?[n] Enough of that! The time has come for the Son of Man to be handed over to sinners. [42]Get up! Let's go. The one who will betray me is already here."

Jesus Is Arrested

(Matthew 26.47-56; Luke 22.47-53; John 18.3-12)

[43]Jesus was still speaking, when Judas the betrayer came up. He was one of the twelve disciples, and a mob of men armed with swords and clubs were with him. They had been sent by the chief priests, the nation's leaders, and the teachers of the Law of Moses. [44]Judas had told them ahead of time, "Arrest the man I greet with a kiss.[o] Tie him up tight and lead him away."

[45]Judas walked right up to Jesus and said, "Teacher!" Then Judas kissed him, [46]and the men grabbed Jesus and arrested him.

[47]Someone standing there pulled out a sword. He struck the servant of the high priest and cut off his ear.

[48]Jesus said to the mob, "Why do you come with swords and clubs to arrest me like a criminal? [49]Day after day I was with you and taught in the temple, and you didn't arrest me. But what the Scriptures say must come true."

[50]All of Jesus' disciples ran off and left him. [51]One of them was a young man who was wearing only a linen cloth. And when the men grabbed him, [52]he left the cloth behind and ran away naked.

Jesus Is Questioned by the Council

(Matthew 26.57-68; Luke 22.54, 55, 63-71; John 18.13, 14, 19-24)

[53]Jesus was led off to the high priest. Then the chief priests, the nation's leaders, and the teachers of the Law of Moses all met together. [54]Peter had followed at a distance. And when he reached the courtyard of the high priest's house, he sat down with the guards to warm himself beside a fire.

[55]The chief priests and the whole council tried to find someone to accuse Jesus of a crime, so they could put him to death. But they could not find anyone to accuse him. [56]Many people did tell lies against Jesus, but

---

[l]**14.35,36** *Father:* The Greek text has "Abba," which is an Aramaic word meaning "father."   [m]**14.35,36** *by having me drink from this cup:* See the note at 10.38.
[n]**14.41** *Are you still sleeping and resting:* Or "You may as well keep on sleeping and resting."   [o]**14.44** *greet with a kiss:* It was the custom for people to greet each other with a kiss on the cheek.

they did not agree on what they said. [57]Finally, some men stood up and lied about him. They said, [58]"We heard him say he would tear down this temple that we built. He also claimed that in three days he would build another one without any help." [59]But even then they did not agree on what they said.

[60]The high priest stood up in the council and asked Jesus, "Why don't you say something in your own defense? Don't you hear the charges they are making against you?" [61]But Jesus kept quiet and did not say a word. The high priest asked him another question, "Are you the Messiah, the Son of the glorious God?"[p]

[62]"Yes, I am!" Jesus answered.

"Soon you will see
    the Son of Man
sitting at the right side[q]
    of God All-Powerful,
and coming with the clouds
    of heaven."

[63]At once the high priest ripped his robe apart and shouted, "Why do we need more witnesses? [64]You heard him claim to be God! What is your decision?" They all agreed that he should be put to death.

[65]Some of the people started spitting on Jesus. They blindfolded him, hit him with their fists, and said, "Tell us who hit you!" Then the guards took charge of Jesus and beat him.

Peter Says He Doesn't Know Jesus
(Matthew 26.69-75; Luke 22.56-62;
John 18.15-18, 25-27)

[66]While Peter was still in the courtyard, a servant girl of the high priest came up [67]and saw Peter warming himself by the fire. She stared at him and said, "You were with Jesus from Nazareth!"

[68]Peter replied, "That isn't true! I don't know what you're talking about. I don't have any idea what you mean." He went out to the gate, and a rooster crowed.[r]

[69]The servant girl saw Peter again and said to the people standing there, "This man is one of them!"

[70]"No, I'm not!" Peter replied.

A little while later some of the people said to Peter, "You certainly are one of them. You're a Galilean!"

[71]This time Peter began to curse and swear, "I don't even know the man you're talking about!"

[72]Right away the rooster crowed a second time. Then Peter remembered that Jesus had told him, "Before a rooster crows twice, you will say three times that you don't know me." So Peter started crying.

Pilate Questions Jesus
(Matthew 27.1, 2, 11-14; Luke 23.1-5;
John 18.28-38)

15 Early the next morning the chief priests, the nation's leaders, and the teachers of the Law of Moses met together with the whole Jewish council. They tied up Jesus and led him off to Pilate. [2]He asked Jesus, "Are you the king of the Jews?"

"Those are your words," Jesus answered.

[3]The chief priests brought many charges against Jesus. [4]Then Pilate questioned him again, "Don't you have anything to say? Don't you hear what crimes they say you have done?" [5]But Jesus did not answer, and Pilate was amazed.

The Death Sentence
(Matthew 27.15-26; Luke 23.13-25;
John 18.39—19.16)

[6]During Passover, Pilate always freed one prisoner chosen by the people. [7]And at that time there was a prisoner named Barabbas. He and some others had been arrested for murder during a riot. [8]The crowd now came and asked Pilate to set a prisoner free, just as he usually did.

[9]Pilate asked them, "Do you want me to free the king of the Jews?" [10]Pilate knew that the chief priests had brought Jesus to him because they were jealous.

[11]But the chief priests told the crowd to ask Pilate to free Barabbas.

[12]Then Pilate asked the crowd, "What do you want me to do with this man you say is[s] the king of the Jews?"

[13]They yelled, "Nail him to a cross!"

[14]Pilate asked, "But what crime has he done?"

---

[p]14.61 *Son of the glorious God*: "Son of God" was one of the titles used for the kings of Israel.   [q]14.62 *right side*: See the note at 12.36.   [r]14.68 *a rooster crowed*: These words are not in some manuscripts.   [s]15.12 *this man you say is*: These words are not in some manuscripts.

"Nail him to a cross!" they yelled even louder.

[15]Pilate wanted to please the crowd. So he set Barabbas free. Then he ordered his soldiers to beat Jesus with a whip and nail him to a cross.

Soldiers Make Fun of Jesus
(*Matthew 27.27-30; John 19.2, 3*)

[16]The soldiers led Jesus inside the courtyard of the fortress[t] and called together the rest of the troops. [17]They put a purple robe[u] on him, and on his head they placed a crown that they had made out of thorn branches. [18]They made fun of Jesus and shouted, "Hey, you king of the Jews!" [19]Then they beat him on the head with a stick. They spit on him and knelt down and pretended to worship him.

[20]When the soldiers had finished making fun of Jesus, they took off the purple robe. They put his own clothes back on him and led him off to be nailed to a cross. [21]Simon from Cyrene happened to be coming in from a farm, and they forced him to carry Jesus' cross. Simon was the father of Alexander and Rufus.

Jesus Is Nailed to a Cross
(*Matthew 27.31-44; Luke 23.27-43; John 19.17-27*)

[22]The soldiers took Jesus to Golgotha, which means "Place of a Skull."[v] [23]There they gave him some wine mixed with a drug to ease the pain, but he refused to drink it.

[24]They nailed Jesus to a cross and gambled to see who would get his clothes. [25]It was about nine o'clock in the morning when they nailed him to the cross. [26]On it was a sign that told why he was nailed there. It read, "This is the King of the Jews."

[27-28]The soldiers also nailed two criminals on crosses, one to the right of Jesus and the other to his left.[w]

[29]People who passed by said terrible things about Jesus. They shook their heads and shouted, "Ha! So you're the one who claimed you could tear down the temple and build it again in three days. [30]Save yourself and come down from the cross!"

[31]The chief priests and the teachers of the Law of Moses also made fun of Jesus. They said to each other, "He saved others, but he can't save himself. [32]If he is the Messiah, the king of Israel, let him come down from the cross! Then we will see and be-

lieve." The two criminals also said cruel things to Jesus.

The Death of Jesus
(*Matthew 27.45-56; Luke 23.44-49; John 19.28-30*)

[33]About noon the sky turned dark and stayed that way until around three o'clock. [34]Then about that time Jesus shouted, "Eloi, Eloi, lema sabachthani?"[x] which means, "My God, my God, why have you deserted me?"

> *Because Jesus lived and died on earth, he knows our pain. He stands beside us and endures every hardship with us.*
>
> MARIAN V. LIAUTAUD

[35]Some of the people standing there heard Jesus and said, "He is calling for Elijah."[y] [36]One of them ran and grabbed a sponge. After he had soaked it in wine, he put it on a stick and held it up to Jesus. He said, "Let's wait and see if Elijah will come[z] and take him down!" [37]Jesus shouted and then died.

[38]At once the curtain in the temple[a] tore in two from top to bottom.

[39]A Roman army officer was standing in front of Jesus. When the officer saw how Jesus died, he said, "This man really was the Son of God!"

---

[t]15.16 *fortress*: The place where the Roman governor stayed. It was probably at Herod's palace west of Jerusalem, though it may have been Fortress Antonia, north of the temple, where the Roman troops were stationed.   [u]15.17 *purple robe*: This was probably a Roman soldier's robe.   [v]15.22 *Place of a Skull*: The place was probably given this name because it was near a large rock in the shape of a human skull. [w]15.27,28 *left*: Some manuscripts add, "So the Scriptures came true which say, 'He was accused of being a criminal.' "   [x]15.34 *Eloi . . . sabachthani*: These words are in Hebrew.   [y]15.35 *Elijah*: The name "Elijah" sounds something like "Eloi," which means "my God." [z]15.36 *see if Elijah will come*: See the note at 6.15. [a]15.38 *curtain in the temple*: There were two curtains in the temple. One was at the entrance, and the other separated the holy place from the most holy place that the Jewish people thought of as God's home on earth. The second curtain is probably the one which is meant.

⁴⁰⁻⁴¹Some women were looking on from a distance. They had come with Jesus to Jerusalem. But even before this they had been his followers and had helped him while he was in Galilee. Mary Magdalene and Mary the mother of the younger James and of Joseph were two of these women. Salome was also one of them.

Jesus Is Buried
(Matthew 27.57-61; Luke 23.50-56; John 19.38-42)

⁴²It was now the evening before the Sabbath, and the Jewish people were getting ready for that sacred day. ⁴³A man named Joseph from Arimathea was brave enough to ask Pilate for the body of Jesus. Joseph was a highly respected member of the Jewish council, and he was also waiting for God's kingdom to come.

⁴⁴Pilate was surprised to hear that Jesus was already dead, and he called in the army officer to find out if Jesus had been dead very long. ⁴⁵After the officer told him, Pilate let Joseph have Jesus' body.

⁴⁶Joseph bought a linen cloth and took the body down from the cross. He had it wrapped in the cloth, and he put it in a tomb that had been cut into solid rock. Then he rolled a big stone against the entrance to the tomb.

⁴⁷Mary Magdalene and Mary the mother of Joseph were watching and saw where the body was placed.

Jesus Is Alive
(Matthew 28.1-8; Luke 24.1-12; John 20.1-10)

16 After the Sabbath, Mary Magdalene, Salome, and Mary the mother of James bought some spices to put on Jesus' body. ²Very early on Sunday morning, just as the sun was coming up, they went to the tomb. ³On their way, they were asking one another, "Who will roll the stone away from the entrance for us?" ⁴But when they looked, they saw that the stone had already been rolled away. And it was a huge stone!

⁵The women went into the tomb, and on the right side they saw a young man in a white robe sitting there. They were alarmed. ⁶The man said, "Don't be alarmed! You are looking for Jesus from Nazareth, who was nailed to a cross. God has raised him to life, and he isn't here. You can see the place where they put his body. ⁷Now go and tell his disciples, and especially Peter, that he will go ahead of you to Galilee. You will see him there, just as he told you."

⁸When the women ran from the tomb, they were confused and shaking all over.

Friendship—How can I show my friend that Christ is the only way to God?
Mark 16.1-8

Point out that only Jesus rose from death never to die again.
The way to God is not a competition between religions. It's the discovery of truth. How do we know Jesus is the only way to God? Because Jesus is God and he says he is. Only Jesus rose from death never to die again. Other religious leaders might teach truth, but they don't embody Truth. Many people have near-death experiences, but they die again. Jesus did not. Jesus' resurrection is indisputable evidence that he is indeed God. Only God can conquer death.

If a friend responds with "That's okay for you, but I choose another way," encourage her to get to know Jesus for herself. Suggest she read the Gospel of Mark, talk with Jesus each day, and invite Jesus to know her. Stress knowing God, not knowing about God. The Almighty God cared enough about each of us to come to us as a person. He came to earth and lived as a human being. He demonstrated how to treat people (Mark 6.34-41; 9.33-37), how to respond to troubles (Mark 14.32-38,60-62), and much more. He was both fully God and fully human—something our mind has trouble comprehending but our heart can embrace. (See also Isaiah 7.10-17; Isaiah 53; John 14.1-14.)

Words To Remember: *"Don't be alarmed! You are looking for Jesus from Nazareth, who was nailed to a cross. God has raised him to life, and he isn't here. You can see the place where they put his body. . . . He will go ahead of you to Galilee. You will see him there, just as he told you."*—Mark 16.6,7

They were too afraid to tell anyone what had happened.

ONE OLD ENDING TO MARK'S GOSPEL[b]

Jesus Appears to Mary Magdalene
(Matthew 28.9, 10; John 20.11-18)

⁹Very early on the first day of the week, after Jesus had risen to life, he appeared to Mary Magdalene. Earlier he had forced seven demons out of her. ¹⁰She left and told his friends, who were crying and mourning. ¹¹Even though they heard that Jesus was alive and that Mary had seen him, they would not believe it.

Jesus Appears to Two Disciples
(Luke 24.13-35)

¹²Later, Jesus appeared in another form to two disciples, as they were on their way out of the city. ¹³But when these disciples told what had happened, the others would not believe.

What Jesus' Followers Must Do
(Matthew 28.16-20; Luke 24.36-49; John 20.19-23; Acts 1.6-8)

¹⁴Afterwards, Jesus appeared to his eleven disciples as they were eating. He scolded them because they were too stubborn to believe the ones who had seen him after he had been raised to life. ¹⁵Then he told them:

Go and preach the good news to everyone in the world. ¹⁶Anyone who believes me and is baptized will be saved. But anyone who refuses to believe me will be condemned. ¹⁷Everyone who believes me will be able to do wonderful things. By using my name they will force out demons, and they will speak new languages. ¹⁸They will handle snakes and will drink poison and not be hurt. They will also heal sick people by placing their hands on them.

Jesus Returns to Heaven
(Luke 24.50-53; Acts 1.9-11)

¹⁹After the Lord Jesus had said these things to the disciples, he was taken back up to heaven where he sat down at the right side[c] of God. ²⁰Then the disciples left and preached everywhere. The Lord was with them, and the miracles they worked proved that their message was true.

ANOTHER OLD ENDING TO MARK'S GOSPEL[d]

⁹⁻¹⁰The women quickly told Peter and his friends what had happened. Later, Jesus sent the disciples to the east and to the west with his sacred and everlasting message of how people can be saved forever.

---

[b]**16.9** *One Old Ending to Mark's Gospel:* Verses 9-20 are not in some manuscripts. [c]**16.19** *right side:* See the note at 12.36. [d]**16.9,10** *Another Old Ending to Mark's Gospel:* Some manuscripts and early translations have both this shorter ending and the longer one (verses 9-20).

Luke — Good News for All People

Luke is a book you can hardly read sitting down. It starts with songs of praise—Mary's song (1.46-56), Zechariah's song (1.67-79), Simeon's song (2.29-32), even the angels' hallelujah ("Praise God") chorus (2.14)—and overflows with the joy of people whose lives have been changed by Jesus Christ. People such as Zacchaeus, who climbed down from his tree to welcome the Savior into his home and into his life. The book concludes with Jesus' followers constantly praising God at the temple.

Luke is apparently the only non-Jewish author in the New Testament, and his book reflects strongly the truth that salvation is for all people (including the poor and racial, religious, and gender minorities), not just for Jews. In fact, Luke emphasizes Jesus as the Son of Man, who "came to look for and to save people who are lost" (19.10). Of the four Gospel writers, only Luke records the angel's joyful shout, "I have good news for you, which will make *everyone* happy" (2.10).

Much of Luke's material shows his concern for the downcast or the outcast. Luke alone gives us the story of the good Samaritan (10.25-37) and the beggar Lazarus (16.19-31). Tax collectors and sinners, as well as Gentiles, are among those pictured as Jesus' followers.

Luke also gives special attention to women and family relationships. His narration of the births of John the Baptist and Jesus are rich with detail, and Luke gives us the only account of Jesus' childhood. He writes of the friction between sisters Mary and Martha (10.38-42) and records Jesus' wonderful parable about the wayward son and his return home (15.11-32). He enriches our understanding of women prominent in the Gospel stories (Mary, the mother of Jesus, and Elizabeth, John the Baptist's mother) and brings to our attention less familiar names: Anna (2.36-38), Mary Magdalene, Joanna, and Susanna (8.2,3). He gives us the only accounts of women whose names we may never know: the widow who lost her only son (7.11-15), the sinful woman who washed Jesus' feet with her tears (7.36-50), the woman so crippled she couldn't stand up straight (13.10-13).

But Luke's Gospel isn't ultimately about women or any of the other groups of people who were held in low esteem in the first century. It's about Jesus and the joy of knowing him.

Luke at a Glance

1. Luke's reason for writing this Gospel (1.1-4)
2. Two amazing conceptions and births: John the Baptist and Jesus (1.5—2.52)
3. John the Baptist prepares the way for Jesus (3.1-20)

4. Jesus receives baptism and overcomes temptation (3.21—4.13)
5. Jesus preaches, teaches, and heals throughout Galilee (4.14—9.50)
6. Jesus goes from Galilee to Jerusalem (9.51—19.27)

7. Jesus' last week in Jerusalem ends in his death (19.28—23.56)
8. Jesus is alive! (24.1-12)
9. Jesus' final appearances and his return to heaven (24.13-53)

1 Many people have tried to tell the story of what God has done among us. ²They wrote what we had been told by the ones who were there in the beginning and saw what happened. ³So I made a careful study[a] of everything and then decided to write and tell you exactly what took place. Honorable Theophilus, ⁴I have done this to let you know the truth about what you have heard.

An Angel Tells about the Birth of John

⁵When Herod was king of Judea, there was a priest by the name of Zechariah from the priestly group of Abijah. His wife Elizabeth was from the family of Aaron.[b] ⁶Both of them were good people and pleased the Lord God by obeying all that he had commanded. ⁷But they did not have children. Elizabeth could not have any, and both Zechariah and Elizabeth were already old.

⁸One day Zechariah's group of priests were on duty, and he was serving God as a priest. ⁹According to the custom of the priests, he had been chosen to go into the Lord's temple that day and to burn incense,[c] ¹⁰while the people stood outside praying.

¹¹All at once an angel from the Lord appeared to Zechariah at the right side of the altar. ¹²Zechariah was confused and afraid when he saw the angel. ¹³But the angel told him:

Don't be afraid, Zechariah! God has heard your prayers. Your wife Elizabeth will have a son, and you must name him John. ¹⁴His birth will make you very happy, and many people will be glad. ¹⁵Your son will be a great servant of the Lord. He must never drink wine or beer, and the power of the Holy Spirit will be with him from the time he is born.
¹⁶John will lead many people in Israel to turn back to the Lord their God. ¹⁷He will go ahead of the Lord with the same power and spirit that Elijah[d] had. And because of John, par-

ents will be more thoughtful of their children. And people who now disobey God will begin to think as they ought to. That is how John will get people ready for the Lord.

¹⁸Zechariah said to the angel, "How will I know this is going to happen? My wife and I are both very old."

¹⁹The angel answered, "I am Gabriel, God's servant, and I was sent to tell you this good news. ²⁰You have not believed what I have said. So you will not be able to say a thing until all this happens. But everything will take place when it is supposed to."

²¹The crowd was waiting for Zechariah and kept wondering why he was staying so long in the temple. ²²When he did come out, he could not speak, and they knew he had seen a vision. He motioned to them with his hands, but did not say a thing.

²³When Zechariah's time of service in the temple was over, he went home. ²⁴Soon after that, his wife was expecting a baby, and for five months she did not leave the house. She said to herself, ²⁵"What the Lord has done for me will keep people from looking down on me."[e]

An Angel Tells about the Birth of Jesus

²⁶One month later God sent the angel Gabriel to the town of Nazareth in Galilee ²⁷with a message for a virgin named Mary. She was engaged to Joseph from the family of King David. ²⁸The angel greeted Mary and said, "You are truly blessed! The Lord is with you."

²⁹Mary was confused by the angel's words and wondered what they meant.

---

[a]**1.3** *a careful study:* Or "a study from the beginning."
[b]**1.5** *Aaron:* The brother of Moses and the first priest.
[c]**1.9** *burn incense:* This was done twice a day, once in the morning and again in the late afternoon.
[d]**1.17** *Elijah:* The prophet Elijah was known for his power to work miracles. [e]**1.25** *keep people from looking down on me:* When a married woman could not have children, it was thought that the Lord was punishing her.

Elizabeth

Luke 1.1-80

Have you ever felt as though life has passed you by? That the hopes and dreams you once had have failed to materialize? Then you can probably identify with Elizabeth.

While her husband, Zechariah, found fulfillment in a meaningful vocation as a priest, Elizabeth was denied the primary calling of women in her time: bearing and rearing children. As a result, even though she came from an enviable family background (she was a descendant of Aaron, the first high priest [1.5]), she felt that people looked down on her (1.25).

When we first meet Elizabeth, she was "very old" (1.7,18). She knew that all hope of having children was lost to her forever. While we can imagine that Elizabeth must have felt deeply disappointed in the way her life had turned out, we have no indication that she was bitter or had turned against God. Rather, we are told that she "pleased the Lord God by obeying all that he had commanded" (1.6).

Then, amazingly, God intervened. His angel told Zechariah that Elizabeth would have a baby—and not just any baby! Her child would be "a great servant of the Lord" (1.15) with "the same power and spirit that Elijah had" (1.17).

Zechariah couldn't believe it, and as a result was struck dumb before he could even tell his wife the incredible news. We don't know whether he managed to convey the angel's message to Elizabeth or not, but we do know that when she conceived she immediately acknowledged her pregnancy as a wonderful gift from the Lord (1.25).

Suddenly Elizabeth's whole life was turned around. Formerly barren and looked down on, she was now the talk of the town (1.65,66). No longer merely the wife of a respected priest, now it was Elizabeth on whom the Holy Spirit fell (1.41). While Zechariah remained mute, it was Elizabeth who spoke out boldly the name God had chosen for her son (1.60).

The secret to Elizabeth's fulfillment lay deeper than simply having a child. Her life was changed because the Lord acted on her behalf (1.25), poured out his Holy Spirit on her (1.41), and gave her a role in the coming of God's kingdom.

The barrenness in our life may be different from that Elizabeth faced. But the path to fulfillment is the same. We, too, know that the Lord has done great things for us on the cross. We, too, have received the Holy Spirit. And each of us has been called to serve in our own way. Even when life seems to have passed us by, we can find fulfillment in God, for "nothing is impossible for God!" (1.37).

³⁰Then the angel told Mary, "Don't be afraid! God is pleased with you, ³¹and you will have a son. His name will be Jesus. ³²He will be great and will be called the Son of God Most High. The Lord God will make him king, as his ancestor David was. ³³He will rule the people of Israel forever, and his kingdom will never end."

³⁴Mary asked the angel, "How can this happen? I am not married!"

³⁵The angel answered, "The Holy Spirit will come down to you, and God's power will come over you. So your child will be called the holy Son of God. ³⁶Your relative Elizabeth is also going to have a son, even though she is old. No one thought she could ever have a baby, but in three months she will have a son. ³⁷Nothing is impossible for God!"

³⁸Mary said, "I am the Lord's servant! Let it happen as you have said." And the angel left her.

Mary Visits Elizabeth

³⁹A short time later Mary hurried to a town in the hill country of Judea. ⁴⁰She went into Zechariah's home, where she greeted Elizabeth. ⁴¹When Elizabeth heard Mary's greeting, her baby moved within her.

The Holy Spirit came upon Elizabeth. ⁴²Then in a loud voice she said to Mary:

God has blessed you more than any other woman! He has also blessed the child you will have. ⁴³Why should the mother of my Lord come to me? ⁴⁴As soon as I heard your greeting, my baby became happy and moved within me. ⁴⁵The Lord has blessed you because you believed that he will keep his promise.

Mary's Song of Praise

⁴⁶Mary said:

With all my heart
    I praise the Lord,
⁴⁷and I am glad
    because of God my Savior.
⁴⁸He cares for me,
    his humble servant.
From now on,
all people will say
    God has blessed me.
⁴⁹God All-Powerful has done

great things for me,
    and his name is holy.
⁵⁰He always shows mercy
to everyone
    who worships him.
⁵¹The Lord has used
    his powerful arm
to scatter those
    who are proud.
⁵²He drags strong rulers
    from their thrones
and puts humble people
    in places of power.
⁵³God gives the hungry
    good things to eat,
and sends the rich away
    with nothing.
⁵⁴He helps his servant Israel
and is always merciful
    to his people.
⁵⁵The Lord made this promise
    to our ancestors,
to Abraham and his family
    forever!

⁵⁶Mary stayed with Elizabeth about three months. Then she went back home.

The Birth of John the Baptist

⁵⁷When Elizabeth's son was born, ⁵⁸her neighbors and relatives heard how kind the Lord had been to her, and they too were glad.

⁵⁹Eight days later they did for the child what the Law of Moses commands.ʲ They were going to name him Zechariah, after his father. ⁶⁰But Elizabeth said, "No! His name is John."

⁶¹The people argued, "No one in your family has ever been named John." ⁶²So they motioned to Zechariah to find out what he wanted to name his son.

⁶³Zechariah asked for a writing tablet. Then he wrote, "His name is John." Everyone was amazed. ⁶⁴Right away, Zechariah started speaking and praising God.

⁶⁵All the neighbors were frightened because of what had happened, and everywhere in the hill country people kept

ʲ1.59 *what the Law of Moses commands*: This refers to circumcision. It is the cutting off of skin from the private part of Jewish boys eight days after birth to show that they belong to the Lord.

Mary, Mother of Jesus

Matthew 1.16—2.23; Mark 6.1-6; Luke 1.26-56; 2.1-52;
John 2.1-12; 19.25-27; Acts 1.12-14

I magine that you're a young woman looking forward to being married soon. Suddenly you learn you're about to become pregnant—but not by your fiancé or any other man. What is your response?

Mary's response, "I am the Lord's servant! Let it happen as you have said" (Luke 1.38), stands in dramatic contrast to the response of Zechariah, recorded just a few verses earlier. Although Zechariah was a priest who had spent his life serving God, he couldn't believe the angel's promise of a child to him and Elizabeth (Luke 1.18,19). Mary, however, not only believed, she rejoiced, despite the fact that an unwed pregnancy was likely to have unpleasant consequences. (Her fiancé, Joseph, had to be persuaded by a divine dream to stand by Mary [Matthew 1.18-25].)

When we look at Mary's calm acceptance of God's will for her life, it's tempting to imagine her as wiser and more perceptive than we are. Yet Mary's faith wasn't based on some privileged information about God's plan. In fact, Mary's reaction throughout much of her life as Jesus' mother seems to have been one of surprise and bewilderment. When the angel made his startling announcement, Mary was "confused" and wondered what he meant (Luke 1.29). When the shepherds told Mary and Joseph what the angel had said about Jesus at his birth, Mary was again "surprised. . . . wondering what it meant" (Luke 2.18,19). When Simeon proclaimed Jesus to be the promised Christ, Mary was "surprised" yet again (Luke 2.33). Twelve years later, when Mary found Jesus talking with the teachers in the temple, she was still "amazed" and "did not understand" (Luke 2.46-50).

Clearly, Mary's act of submission to God's will in her life was an act of faith, not a reasoned response to a heavenly blueprint outlining future events and consequences. We see trust and faith, combined with plain motherly pride, when she nudged Jesus to perform his first miracle, changing water into wine at a wedding feast (John 2.3-5). We see her faithfulness, combined with the pain only a mother can feel, when she stood at the foot of the cross (John 19.25). And we see her faith, combined at last with a true understanding of who Jesus was, when she met to pray regularly with the apostles and other believers after Jesus' ascension (Acts 1.14).

We, like Mary, often find ourselves surprised and confused as we try to submit to God's will in our life. We can respond like Zechariah—skeptical and demanding explanations—or we can respond like Mary, singing, "With all my heart I praise the Lord, and I am glad because of God my Savior. God cares for me, his humble servant" (Luke 1.46-48).

talking about these things. ⁶⁶Everyone who heard about this wondered what this child would grow up to be. They knew that the Lord was with him.

Zechariah Praises the Lord

⁶⁷The Holy Spirit came upon Zechariah, and he began to speak:

⁶⁸ Praise the Lord,
　　the God of Israel!
He has come
　　to save his people.
⁶⁹ Our God has given us
　　a mighty Saviorᵍ
from the family
　　of David his servant.
⁷⁰ Long ago the Lord promised
　　by the words
　　of his holy prophets
⁷¹ to save us from our enemies
　　and from everyone
　　who hates us.
⁷² God said he would be kind
　　to our people and keep
　　his sacred promise.
⁷³ He told our ancestor Abraham
⁷⁴ that he would rescue us
　　from our enemies.
Then we could serve him
　　without fear,
⁷⁵ by being holy and good
　　as long as we live.

⁷⁶ You, my son, will be called
　　a prophet of God
　　in heaven above.
You will go ahead of the Lord
　　to get everything ready
　　for him.
⁷⁷ You will tell his people
　　that they can be saved
when their sins
　　are forgiven.
⁷⁸ God's love and kindness
　　will shine upon us
like the sun that rises
　　in the sky.ʰ
⁷⁹ On us who live
　　in the dark shadow
　　of death
this light will shine
to guide us
　　into a life of peace.

⁸⁰As John grew up, God's Spirit gave him great power. John lived in the desert until the time he was sent to the people of Israel.

The Birth of Jesus
(Matthew 1.18-25)

2 About that time Emperor Augustus gave orders for the names of all the people to be listed in record books.ⁱ ²These first records were made when Quirinius was governor of Syria.ʲ ³Everyone had to go to their own hometown to be listed. ⁴So Joseph had to leave Nazareth in Galilee and go to Bethlehem in Judea. Long ago Bethlehem had been King David's hometown, and Joseph went there because he was from David's family. ⁵Mary was engaged to Joseph and traveled with him to Bethlehem. She was soon going to have a baby, ⁶and while they were there, ⁷she gave birth to her first-bornᵏ son. She dressed him in baby clothesˡ and laid him on a bed of hay, because there was no room for them in the inn.

The Shepherds

⁸That night in the fields near Bethlehem some shepherds were guarding their sheep. ⁹All at once an angel came down to them from the Lord, and the brightness of the Lord's glory flashed around them. The shepherds were frightened. ¹⁰But the angel said, "Don't be afraid! I have good news for you, which will make everyone happy. ¹¹This very day in King David's hometown a Savior was born for you. He is Christ the Lord. ¹²You will know who he is, because you will find him dressed in baby clothes and lying on a bed of hay." ¹³Suddenly many other angels came down from heaven and joined in praising God. They said:

ᵍ**1.69** *a mighty Savior:* The Greek text has "a horn of salvation." In the Scriptures animal horns are often a symbol of great strength.　ʰ**1.78** *like the sun that rises in the sky:* Or "like the Messiah coming from heaven."　ⁱ**2.1** *names . . . listed in record books:* This was done so that everyone could be made to pay taxes to the Emperor.　ʲ**2.2** *Quirinius was governor of Syria:* It is known that Quirinius made a record of the people in A.D. 6 or 7. But the exact date of the record taking that Luke mentions is not known.　ᵏ**2.7** *first-born:* The Jewish people said that the first-born son in each of their families belonged to the Lord.　ˡ**2.7** *dressed him in baby clothes:* The Greek text has "wrapped him in wide strips of cloth," which was how young babies were dressed.

Anna

Luke 2.36-38

S ometimes a quiet life makes an impact that lasts a long, long time. We know nothing more about Anna than what we read in these three verses in Luke. Yet her brief appearance was significant enough to warrant mention in the Holy Bible, and to guarantee that millions of people would read about her.

Anna seems to have led a quiet life. Her life was centered on the temple, where she served God night and day. Undoubtedly she was present for the communal ceremonies in the temple, but she also devoted herself to the private disciplines of prayer and fasting.

The meeting between Anna and Mary in the temple that day must have been poignant. One woman was old, widowed most of her life, set apart by God's Spirit for uncommon service in uncommon ways. Her life revolved around the quiet disciplines of prayer and fasting. The other was young, newly married, but also set apart by God's Spirit for uncommon service. Her service would be characterized by diapers, feedings, and all that's ordinary.

Anna, near the end of her life, saw the beginning of all she'd hoped for. She almost certainly didn't live long enough to see Christ's ministry, death, resurrection, and ascension. But she didn't need to see those things to know whom it was she saw in the infant before her. She praised God for sending Jesus, and she talked to "everyone who hoped" about Jesus (2.38). Did she also speak to Mary? What conversation would have passed between these two servants of the Lord, one at the end of her life and the other just starting?

What about Anna warrants her appearance in the Bible? Why is this short episode so significant that God preserved it for us to read? Perhaps simply this: Anna was a woman who served God night and day. She lived a disciplined, devotional life. She praised God. And she spoke to everyone about Jesus. We would do well if the same is said of us.

14 "Praise God in heaven!
    Peace on earth to everyone
      who pleases God."

15After the angels had left and gone back to heaven, the shepherds said to each other, "Let's go to Bethlehem and see what the Lord has told us about." 16They hurried off and found Mary and Joseph, and they saw the baby lying on a bed of hay.

17When the shepherds saw Jesus, they told his parents what the angel had said about him. 18Everyone listened and was surprised. 19But Mary kept thinking about all this and wondering what it meant.

20As the shepherds returned to their sheep, they were praising God and saying wonderful things about him. Everything they had seen and heard was just as the angel had said.

21Eight days later Jesus' parents did for him what the Law of Moses commands.m And they named him Jesus, just as the angel had told Mary when he promised she would have a baby.

Simeon Praises the Lord

22The time came for Mary and Joseph to do what the Law of Moses says a mother is supposed to do after her baby is born.n

They took Jesus to the temple in Jerusalem and presented him to the Lord, 23just as the Law of the Lord says, "Each first-borno baby boy belongs to the Lord." 24The Law of the Lord also says that parents have to offer a sacrifice, giving at least a pair of doves or two young pigeons. So that is what Mary and Joseph did.

25At this time a man named Simeon was living in Jerusalem. Simeon was a good man. He loved God and was waiting for God to save the people of Israel. God's Spirit came to him 26and told him that he would not die until he had seen Christ the Lord.

27When Mary and Joseph brought Jesus to the temple to do what the Law of Moses says should be done for a new baby, the Spirit told Simeon to go into the temple. 28Simeon took the baby Jesus in his arms and praised God,

29 "Lord, I am your servant,
    and now I can die in peace,
  because you have kept
    your promise to me.

30With my own eyes I have seen
  what you have done
    to save your people,
31and foreign nations
  will also see this.
32Your mighty power is a light
  for all nations,
and it will bring honor
  to your people Israel."

33Jesus' parents were surprised at what Simeon had said. 34Then he blessed them and told Mary, "This child of yours will cause many people in Israel to fall and others to stand. The child will be like a warning sign. Many people will reject him, 35and you, Mary, will suffer as though you had been stabbed by a dagger. But all this will show what people are really thinking."

Anna Speaks about the Child Jesus

36The prophet Anna was also there in the temple. She was the daughter of Phanuel from the tribe of Asher, and she was very old. In her youth she had been married for seven years, but her husband died. 37And now she was eighty-four years old.p Night and day she served God in the temple by praying and often going without eating.q

38At that time Anna came in and praised God. She spoke about the child Jesus to everyone who hoped for Jerusalem to be set free.

The Return to Nazareth

39After Joseph and Mary had done everything that the Law of the Lord commands, they returned home to Nazareth in Galilee. 40The child Jesus grew. He became strong and wise, and God blessed him.

The Boy Jesus in the Temple

41Every year Jesus' parents went to Jerusalem for Passover. 42And when Jesus was

---

m2.21 *what the Law of Moses commands:* See the note at 1.59. n2.22 *after her baby is born:* After a Jewish mother gave birth to a son, she was considered "unclean" and had to stay home until he was circumcised (see the note at 1.59). Then she had to stay home for another 33 days, before offering a sacrifice to the Lord. o2.23 *first-born:* See the note at 2.7. p2.37 *And now she was eighty-four years old:* Or "And now she had been a widow for eighty-four years." q2.37 *without eating:* The Jewish people sometimes went without eating (also called "fasting") to show their love for God or to show sorrow for their sins.

twelve years old, they all went there as usual for the celebration. ⁴³After Passover his parents left, but they did not know that Jesus had stayed on in the city. ⁴⁴They thought he was traveling with some other people, and they went a whole day before they started looking for him. ⁴⁵When they could not find him with their relatives and friends, they went back to Jerusalem and started looking for him there.

⁴⁶Three days later they found Jesus sitting in the temple, listening to the teachers and asking them questions. ⁴⁷Everyone who heard him was surprised at how much he knew and at the answers he gave.

⁴⁸When his parents found him, they were amazed. His mother said, "Son, why have you done this to us? Your father and I have been very worried, and we have been searching for you!"

⁴⁹Jesus answered, "Why did you have to look for me? Didn't you know that I would be in my Father's house?"ʳ ⁵⁰But they did not understand what he meant.

⁵¹Jesus went back to Nazareth with his parents and obeyed them. His mother kept on thinking about all that had happened.

⁵²Jesus became wise, and he grew strong. God was pleased with him and so were the people.

The Preaching of John the Baptist
(Matthew 3.1-12; Mark 1.1-8; John 1.19-28)

3 For fifteen yearsˢ Emperor Tiberius had ruled that part of the world. Pontius Pilate was governor of Judea, and Herodᵗ was the ruler of Galilee. Herod's brother, Philip, was the ruler in the countries of Iturea and Trachonitis, and Lysanias was the ruler of Abilene. ²Annas and Caiaphas were the Jewish high priests.ᵘ

At that time God spoke to Zechariah's son John, who was living in the desert. ³So John went along the Jordan Valley, telling the people, "Turn back to God and be baptized! Then your sins will be forgiven." ⁴Isaiah the prophet wrote about John when he said,

> "In the desert
>   someone is shouting,
> 'Get the road ready
>   for the Lord!

ʳ**2.49** *in my Father's house:* Or "doing my Father's work." ˢ**3.1** *For fifteen years:* This was either A.D. 28 or 29, and Jesus was about thirty years old (see 3.23). ᵗ**3.1** *Herod:* Herod Antipas, the son of Herod the Great. ᵘ**3.2** *Annas and Caiaphas . . . high priests:* Annas was high priest from A.D. 6 until 15. His son-in-law Caiaphas was high priest from A.D. 18 until 37.

PARENTING&*family*—How can I tell if I'm doing a good job as a mother?
(Luke 2.41-52)

Remember that God always knows what's best for your children.
"Why have you done this to us? Your father and I have been very worried . . . !" (2.48).

What mother hasn't echoed those words of Mary's? Sometimes our children baffle us, dismay us, or even exasperate us. We wonder about the best possible way to handle emotional swings, academic challenges, developmental issues, and discipline. We want so badly to rear children who will love God and serve their neighbors. But frankly, we often feel inadequate to the task.

Imagine how Mary must have felt, knowing she was charged with rearing God's Son! When she accepted the task, she may have thought that perhaps God would give her some detailed instructions. But, like us, she had to get by with on-the-job training.

But no matter how much in the dark we may feel about what's best for our children, God knows. Nothing about our children is hidden from him. Even before they were born, God had written their days in his book (Psalm 139.15,16).

With the heavenly Father involved in our parenting, we can relax and be assured that he'll use our faithful efforts to do what's best for our children. (See also Ephesians 6.1-4; Hebrews 12.5-13.)

Words To Remember: *Jesus became wise, and he grew strong. God was pleased with him and so were the people.—Luke 2.52*

Make a straight path
   for him.
⁵Fill up every valley
   and level every mountain
     and hill.
Straighten the crooked paths
   and smooth out
     the rough roads.
⁶Then everyone will see
   the saving power of God.' "

⁷Crowds of people came out to be baptized, but John said to them, "You bunch of snakes! Who warned you to run from the coming judgment? ⁸Do something to show that you really have given up your sins. Don't start saying that you belong to Abraham's family. God can turn these stones into children for Abraham.ᵛ ⁹An ax is ready to cut the trees down at their roots. Any tree that doesn't produce good fruit will be cut down and thrown into a fire."

¹⁰The crowds asked John, "What should we do?"

¹¹John told them, "If you have two coats, give one to someone who doesn't have any. If you have food, share it with someone else."

¹²When tax collectorsʷ came to be baptized, they asked John, "Teacher, what should we do?"

¹³John told them, "Don't make people pay more than they owe."

¹⁴Some soldiers asked him, "And what about us? What do we have to do?"

John told them, "Don't force people to pay money to make you leave them alone. Be satisfied with your pay."

¹⁵Everyone became excited and wondered, "Could John be the Messiah?"

¹⁶John said, "I am just baptizing with water. But someone more powerful is going to come, and I am not good enough even to untie his sandals.ˣ He will baptize you with the Holy Spirit and with fire. ¹⁷His threshing forkʸ is in his hand, and he is ready to separate the wheat from the husks. He will store the wheat in his barn and burn the husks with a fire that never goes out."

¹⁸In many different ways John preached the good news to the people. ¹⁹But to Herod the ruler, he said, "It was wrong for you to take Herodias, your brother's wife." John also said that Herod had done many other

---

ᵛ**3.8** *children for Abraham*: The Jewish people thought they were God's chosen people because of God's promises to their ancestor Abraham. ʷ**3.12** *tax collectors*: These were usually Jewish people who paid the Romans for the right to collect taxes. They were hated by other Jews who thought of them as traitors to their country and to their religion. ˣ**3.16** *untie his sandals*: This was the duty of a slave. ʸ**3.17** *threshing fork*: After Jewish farmers had trampled out the grain, they used a large fork to pitch the grain and the husks into the air. Wind would blow away the light husks, and the grain would fall back to the ground, where it could be gathered up.

WORK—My husband is sometimes threatened by my career. How should I respond? *(Luke 3.7-20)*

Focus on Christ's power, not your own.
People naturally tend to rank others by the relative value they perceive in their work, and may feel threatened when they think their value is diminished by someone else's position. Even John the Baptist, whose sole purpose was to point to the coming Messiah, discovered that people were just as interested in John's status—"Could John be the Messiah?" (3.15)—as in his message.

In marriage we sometimes forget that we're all ultimately working as servants of God. Instead of seeing ourselves and each other in relationship to Christ, we focus on the status we perceive our careers give us. But if we communicate to our spouse that we don't consider ourselves or our career to be of the greatest importance, we demonstrate the truth that Christ is more powerful than any CEO or high-powered executive. Together husbands and wives can work for Christ in the careers he has given each of them. (See also Numbers 12; 1 Corinthians 12.1-11.)

   Words To Remember: *John said, "I am just baptizing with water. But someone more powerful is going to come, and I am not good enough even to untie his sandals. He will baptize you with the Holy Spirit and with fire."—Luke 3.16*

bad things. ²⁰Finally, Herod put John in jail, and this was the worst thing he had done.

The Baptism of Jesus
(Matthew 3.13-17; Mark 1.9-11)

²¹While everyone else was being baptized, Jesus himself was baptized. Then as he prayed, the sky opened up, ²²and the Holy Spirit came down upon him in the form of a dove. A voice from heaven said, "You are my own dear Son, and I am pleased with you."

The Ancestors of Jesus
(Matthew 1.1-17)

²³When Jesus began to preach, he was about thirty years old. Everyone thought he was the son of Joseph. But his family went back through Heli, ²⁴Matthat, Levi, Melchi, Jannai, Joseph, ²⁵Mattathias, Amos, Nahum, Esli, Naggai, ²⁶Maath, Mattathias, Semein, Josech, Joda; ²⁷Joanan, Rhesa, Zerubbabel, Shealtiel, Neri, ²⁸Melchi, Addi, Cosam, Elmadam, Er, ²⁹Joshua, Eliezer, Jorim, Matthat, Levi; ³⁰Simeon, Judah, Joseph, Jonam, Eliakim, ³¹Melea, Menna, Mattatha, Nathan, David, ³²Jesse, Obed, Boaz, Salmon, Nahshon; ³³Amminadab, Admin, Arni, Hezron, Perez, Judah, ³⁴Jacob, Isaac, Abraham, Terah, Nahor, ³⁵Serug, Reu, Peleg, Eber, Shelah; ³⁶Cainan, Arphaxad, Shem, Noah, Lamech, ³⁷Methuselah, Enoch, Jared, Mahalaleel, Kenan, ³⁸Enosh, and Seth. The family of Jesus went all the way back to Adam and then to God.

Jesus and the Devil
(Matthew 4.1-11; Mark 1.12, 13)

4 When Jesus returned from the Jordan River, the power of the Holy Spirit was with him, and the Spirit led him into the desert. ²For forty days Jesus was tested by the devil, and during that time he went without eating.ᶻ When it was all over, he was hungry.

³The devil said to Jesus, "If you are God's Son, tell this stone to turn into bread."

⁴Jesus answered, "The Scriptures say, 'No one can live only on food.' "

⁵Then the devil led Jesus up to a high place and quickly showed him all the nations on earth. ⁶The devil said, "I will give all this power and glory to you. It has been given to me, and I can give it to anyone I want to. ⁷Just worship me, and you can have it all."

⁸Jesus answered, "The Scriptures say:

'Worship the Lord your God
   and serve only him!' "

⁹Finally, the devil took Jesus to Jerusalem and had him stand on top of the temple. The devil said, "If you are God's Son, jump off. ¹⁰⁻¹¹The Scriptures say:

'God will tell his angels
   to take care of you.
They will catch you
   in their arms,
and you will not hurt
   your feet on the stones.' "

¹²Jesus answered, "The Scriptures also say, 'Don't try to test the Lord your God!' "

¹³After the devil had finished testing Jesus in every way possible, he left him for a while.

Jesus Begins His Work
(Matthew 4.12-17; Mark 1.14, 15)

¹⁴Jesus returned to Galilee with the power of the Spirit. News about him spread everywhere. ¹⁵He taught in the Jewish meeting places, and everyone praised him.

The People of Nazareth Turn against Jesus
(Matthew 13.53-58; Mark 6.1-6)

¹⁶Jesus went back to Nazareth, where he had been brought up, and as usual he went to the meeting place on the Sabbath. When he stood up to read from the Scriptures, ¹⁷he was given the book of Isaiah the prophet. He opened it and read,

¹⁸ "The Lord's Spirit
      has come to me,
   because he has chosen me
   to tell the good news
      to the poor.
   The Lord has sent me
   to announce freedom
      for prisoners,

ᶻ4.2 *went without eating:* See the note at 2.37.

to give sight to the blind,
to free everyone
    who suffers,
[19] and to say, 'This is the year
    the Lord has chosen.' "

> *Do you have scars? Jesus understands—and he's willing to turn them into something beautiful.*
>
> MARY ELLEN TON

[20]Jesus closed the book, then handed it back to the man in charge and sat down. Everyone in the meeting place looked straight at Jesus.

[21]Then Jesus said to them, "What you have just heard me read has come true today."

[22]All the people started talking about Jesus and were amazed at the wonderful things he said. They kept on asking, "Isn't he Joseph's son?"

[23]Jesus answered:

You will certainly want to tell me this saying, "Doctor, first make yourself well." You will tell me to do the same things here in my own hometown that you heard I did in Capernaum. [24]But you can be sure that no prophets are liked by the people of their own hometown.

[25]Once during the time of Elijah there was no rain for three and a half years, and people everywhere were starving. There were many widows in Israel, [26]but Elijah was sent only to a widow in the town of Zarephath near the city of Sidon. [27]During the time of the prophet Elisha, many men in Israel had leprosy.[a] But no one was healed, except Naaman who lived in Syria.

[28]When the people in the meeting place heard Jesus say this, they became so angry [29]that they got up and threw him out of town. They dragged him to the edge of the cliff on which the town was built, because they wanted to throw him down from there. [30]But Jesus slipped through the crowd and got away.

A Man with an Evil Spirit
(Mark 1.21-28)

[31]Jesus went to the town of Capernaum in Galilee and taught the people on the Sabbath. [32]His teaching amazed them because he spoke with power. [33]There in the Jewish meeting place was a man with an evil spirit. He yelled out, [34]"Hey, Jesus of Nazareth, what do you want with us? Are you here to get rid of us? I know who you are! You are God's Holy One."

[35]Jesus ordered the evil spirit to be quiet and come out. The demon threw the man to the ground in front of everyone and left without harming him.

[36]They all were amazed and kept saying to each other, "What kind of teaching is this? He has power to order evil spirits out of people!" [37]News about Jesus spread all over that part of the country.

Jesus Heals Many People
(Matthew 8.14-17; Mark 1.29-34)

[38]Jesus left the meeting place and went to Simon's home. When Jesus got there, he was told that Simon's mother-in-law was sick with a high fever. [39]So Jesus went over to her and ordered the fever to go away. Right then she was able to get up and serve them a meal.

[40]After the sun had set, people with all kinds of diseases were brought to Jesus. He put his hands on each one of them and healed them. [41]Demons went out of many people and shouted, "You are the Son of God!" But Jesus ordered the demons not to speak because they knew he was the Messiah.

[42]The next morning Jesus went out to a place where he could be alone, and crowds came looking for him. When they found him, they tried to stop him from leaving. [43]But Jesus said, "People in other towns must hear the good news about God's kingdom. That's why I was sent." [44]So he kept on preaching in the Jewish meeting places in Judea.[b]

---

[a]**4.27** *leprosy:* In biblical times the word "leprosy" was used for many different kinds of skin diseases.
[b]**4.44** *Judea:* Some manuscripts have "Galilee."

Jesus Chooses His First Disciples
(Matthew 4.18-22; Mark 1.16-20)

5 Jesus was standing on the shore of Lake Gennesaret,[c] teaching the people as they crowded around him to hear God's message. [2]Near the shore he saw two boats left there by some fishermen who had gone to wash their nets. [3]Jesus got into the boat that belonged to Simon and asked him to row it out a little way from the shore. Then Jesus sat down[d] in the boat to teach the crowd.

[4]When Jesus had finished speaking, he told Simon, "Row the boat out into the deep water and let your nets down to catch some fish."

[5]"Master," Simon answered, "we have worked hard all night long and have not caught a thing. But if you tell me to, I will let the nets down." [6]They did it and caught so many fish that their nets began ripping apart. [7]Then they signaled for their partners in the other boat to come and help them. The men came, and together they filled the two boats so full that they both began to sink.

[8]When Simon Peter saw this happen, he knelt down in front of Jesus and said, "Lord, don't come near me! I am a sinner." [9]Peter and everyone with him were completely surprised at all the fish they had caught. [10]His partners James and John, the sons of Zebedee, were surprised too.

Jesus told Simon, "Don't be afraid! From now on you will bring in people instead of fish." [11]The men pulled their boats up on the shore. Then they left everything and went with Jesus.

Jesus Heals a Man
(Matthew 8.1-4; Mark 1.40-45)

[12]Jesus came to a town where there was a man who had leprosy.[e] When the man saw Jesus, he knelt down to the ground in front of Jesus and begged, "Lord, you have the power to make me well, if only you wanted to."

[13]Jesus put his hand on him and said, "I want to! Now you are well." At once the man's leprosy disappeared. [14]Jesus told him, "Don't tell anyone about this, but go and show yourself to the priest. Offer a gift to the priest, just as Moses commanded, and everyone will know that you have been healed."[f]

[15]News about Jesus kept spreading. Large crowds came to listen to him teach and to be healed of their diseases. [16]But Jesus would often go to some place where he could be alone and pray.

Jesus Heals a Crippled Man
(Matthew 9.1-8; Mark 2.1-12)

[17]One day some Pharisees and experts in the Law of Moses sat listening to Jesus teach. They had come from every village in Galilee and Judea and from Jerusalem.

God had given Jesus the power to heal the sick, [18]and some people came carrying a crippled man on a mat. They tried to take him inside the house and put him in front of Jesus. [19]But because of the crowd, they could not get him to Jesus. So they went up on the roof,[g] where they removed some tiles and let the mat down in the middle of the room.

[20]When Jesus saw how much faith they had, he said to the crippled man, "My friend, your sins are forgiven."

[21]The Pharisees and the experts began arguing, "Jesus must think he is God! Only God can forgive sins."

[22]Jesus knew what they were thinking, and he said, "Why are you thinking that? [23]Is it easier for me to tell this crippled man that his sins are forgiven or to tell him to get up and walk? [24]But now you will see that the Son of Man has the right to forgive sins here on earth." Jesus then said to the man, "Get up! Pick up your mat and walk home."

[25]At once the man stood up in front of everyone. He picked up his mat and went home, giving thanks to God. [26]Everyone was amazed and praised God. What they saw surprised them, and they said, "We have seen a great miracle today!"

---

[c]**5.1** *Lake Gennesaret:* Another name for Lake Galilee. [d]**5.3** *sat down:* Teachers in the ancient world, including Jewish teachers, usually sat down when they taught. [e]**5.12** *leprosy:* See the note at 4.27. [f]**5.14** *everyone will know that you have been healed:* People with leprosy had to be examined by a priest and told that they were well (that is, "clean") before they could once again live a normal life in the Jewish community. The gift that Moses commanded was the sacrifice of some lambs together with flour mixed with olive oil. [g]**5.19** *roof:* In Palestine the houses usually had a flat roof. Stairs on the outside led up to the roof, which was made of beams and boards covered with packed earth. Luke says that the roof was made of (clay) tiles, which were also used for making roofs in New Testament times.

Jesus Chooses Levi
(Matthew 9.9-13; Mark 2.13-17)

²⁷Later, Jesus went out and saw a tax collector[h] named Levi sitting at the place for paying taxes. Jesus said to him, "Come with me." ²⁸Levi left everything and went with Jesus.

²⁹In his home Levi gave a big dinner for Jesus. Many tax collectors and other guests were also there.

³⁰The Pharisees and some of their teachers of the Law of Moses grumbled to Jesus' disciples, "Why do you eat and drink with those tax collectors and other sinners?"

³¹Jesus answered, "Healthy people don't need a doctor, but sick people do. ³²I didn't come to invite good people to turn to God. I came to invite sinners."

People Ask about Going without Eating
(Matthew 9.14-17; Mark 2.18-22)

³³Some people said to Jesus, "John's followers often pray and go without eating,[i] and so do the followers of the Pharisees. But your disciples never go without eating or drinking."

³⁴Jesus told them, "The friends of a bridegroom don't go without eating while he is still with them. ³⁵But the time will come when he will be taken from them. Then they will go without eating."

³⁶Jesus then told them these sayings:

No one uses a new piece of cloth to patch old clothes. The patch would shrink and make the hole even bigger.

³⁷No one pours new wine into old wineskins. The new wine would swell and burst the old skins.[j] Then the wine would be lost, and the skins would be ruined. ³⁸New wine must be put only into new wineskins.

³⁹No one wants new wine after drinking old wine. They say, "The old wine is better."

A Question about the Sabbath
(Matthew 12.1-8; Mark 2.23-28)

6 One Sabbath when Jesus and his disciples were walking through some wheat fields,[k] the disciples picked some wheat. They rubbed the husks off with their hands and started eating the grain.

²Some Pharisees said, "Why are you picking grain on the Sabbath? You're not supposed to do that!"

³Jesus answered, "You surely have read what David did when he and his followers were hungry. ⁴He went into the house of God and took the sacred loaves of bread that only priests were supposed to eat. He not only ate some himself, but even gave some to his followers."

⁵Jesus finished by saying, "The Son of Man is Lord over the Sabbath."

A Man with a Crippled Hand
(Matthew 12.9-14; Mark 3.1-6)

⁶On another Sabbath[l] Jesus was teaching in a Jewish meeting place, and a man with a crippled right hand was there. ⁷Some Pharisees and teachers of the Law of Moses kept watching Jesus to see if he would heal the man. They did this because they wanted to accuse Jesus of doing something wrong.

⁸Jesus knew what they were thinking. So he told the man to stand up where everyone could see him. And the man stood up. ⁹Then Jesus asked, "On the Sabbath should we do good deeds or evil deeds? Should we save someone's life or destroy it?"

¹⁰After he had looked around at everyone, he told the man, "Stretch out your hand." He did, and his bad hand became completely well.

¹¹The teachers and the Pharisees were furious and started saying to each other, "What can we do about Jesus?"

Jesus Chooses His Twelve Apostles
(Matthew 10.1-4; Mark 3.13-19)

¹²About that time Jesus went off to a mountain to pray, and he spent the whole night there. ¹³The next morning he called his disciples together and chose twelve of them to be his apostles. ¹⁴One was Simon, and Jesus named him Peter. Another was Andrew, Peter's brother. There were also James, John, Philip, Bartholomew, ¹⁵Mat-

---

h**5.27** *tax collector*: See the note at 3.12. i**5.33** *without eating*: See the note at 2.37. j**5.37** *swell and burst the old skins*: While the juice from grapes was becoming wine, it would swell and stretch the skins in which it had been stored. If the skins were old and stiff, they would burst. k**6.1** *walking through some wheat fields*: It was the custom to let hungry travelers pick grains of wheat. l**6.6** *On another Sabbath*: Some manuscripts have a reading which may mean "the Sabbath after the next."

thew, Thomas, and James the son of Alphaeus. The rest of the apostles were Simon, known as the Eager One,^{m} ^{16}Jude, who was the son of James, and Judas Iscariot,^{n} who later betrayed Jesus.

Jesus Teaches, Preaches, and Heals
(Matthew 4.23-25)

^{17}Jesus and his apostles went down from the mountain and came to some flat, level ground. Many other disciples were there to meet him. Large crowds of people from all over Judea, Jerusalem, and the coastal cities of Tyre and Sidon were there too. ^{18}These people had come to listen to Jesus and to be healed of their diseases. All who were troubled by evil spirits were also healed. ^{19}Everyone was trying to touch Jesus, because power was going out from him and healing them all.

Blessings and Troubles
(Matthew 5.1-12)

^{20}Jesus looked at his disciples and said:

God will bless you people
who are poor.
His kingdom belongs to you!
^{21}God will bless
you hungry people.
You will have plenty
to eat!

God will bless you people
who are crying.
You will laugh!

^{22}God will bless you when others hate you and won't have anything to do with you. God will bless you when people insult you and say cruel things about you, all because you are a follower of the Son of Man. ^{23}Long ago your own people did these same things to the prophets. So when this happens to you, be happy and jump for joy! You will have a great reward in heaven.

^{24}But you rich people
are in for trouble.
You have already had
an easy life!
^{25}You well-fed people
are in for trouble.
You will go hungry!
You people

---

^{m}**6.15** *known as the Eager One:* The word "eager" translates the Greek word "zealot," which was a name later given to the members of a Jewish group that resisted and fought against the Romans.
^{n}**6.16** *Iscariot:* This may mean "a man from Kerioth" (a place in Judea). But more probably it means "a man who was a liar" or "a man who was a betrayer."

Personal *Concerns*—How can I forgive someone who has broken my trust? *(Luke 6.27-36)*

Model yourself on your heavenly Father.
When someone betrays you, the natural response is to remember that betrayal and keep your distance. Why open yourself up to potential hurt again?

But God doesn't call us to do what comes naturally. He calls us to treat others the way he treats us. When you're battling thoughts of bitterness or even revenge, try this: Make a list of all the ways you've broken faith with God in word, thought, or action. Compare what God has forgiven you with what you need to forgive in another person. Does it put things in a new perspective?

Then take the very practical action step given in this passage: "Pray for everyone who is cruel to you" (6.28). Don't only pray for yourself, "God, help *me* to forgive." Also pray for the person: "God, give _____ what she needs today." It's almost impossible to stay angry with someone you're truly praying for!

God wants us to treat others as kindly as he treats us. Nothing pleases our Father in heaven more than to see his children following in his footsteps. (See also Numbers 14.11-25; 1 Samuel 24; Matthew 7.1-5; Matthew 18.21-35.)

Words To Remember: *Love your enemies and be good to them. . . . Then you will get a great reward, and you will be the true children of God in heaven.—Luke 6.35*

who are laughing now
    are in for trouble.
You are going to cry
    and weep!

²⁶You are in for trouble when everyone says good things about you. That is what your own people said about those prophets who told lies.

Love for Enemies
(Matthew 5.38-48; 7.12a)

²⁷This is what I say to all who will listen to me:
    Love your enemies, and be good to everyone who hates you. ²⁸Ask God to bless anyone who curses you, and pray for everyone who is cruel to you. ²⁹If someone slaps you on one cheek, don't stop that person from slapping you on the other cheek. If someone wants to take your coat, don't try to keep back your shirt. ³⁰Give to everyone who asks and don't ask people to return what they have taken from you. ³¹Treat others just as you want to be treated.
    ³²If you love only someone who loves you, will God praise you for that? Even sinners love people who love them. ³³If you are kind only to someone who is kind to you, will God be pleased with you for that? Even sinners are kind to people who are kind to them. ³⁴If you lend money only to someone you think will pay you back, will God be pleased with you for that? Even sinners lend to sinners because they think they will get it all back.
    ³⁵But love your enemies and be good to them. Lend without expecting to be paid back.ᵒ Then you will get a great reward, and you will be the true children of God in heaven. He is good even to people who are unthankful and cruel. ³⁶Have pity on others, just as your Father has pity on you.

Judging Others
(Matthew 7.1-5)

³⁷Jesus said:
    Don't judge others, and God won't judge you. Don't be hard on others, and God won't be hard on you. Forgive others, and God will forgive you. ³⁸If you give to others, you will be given a full amount in return. It will be packed down, shaken together, and spilling over into your lap. The way

---

ᵒ6.35 *without expecting to be paid back*: Some manuscripts have "without giving up on anyone."

Friendship—How can I repair a broken friendship? *(Luke 6.37-42)*

See your own contribution to the rift in your relationship.
When a friendship goes sour, it hurts. So we often respond to that hurt by trying to find someone—anyone other than ourselves—to blame. A friend's casual comment becomes, in memory, a malicious attack. A forgotten appointment symbolizes a callous disregard for our feelings.
    Jesus warns us to stop finding fault with our friends and take a good, hard look at our own shortcomings first. Not only is Jesus' advice spiritually healthy, it's also eminently practical.
    Imagine that you go to your friend to "take the speck out of [her] eye" (6.42) by offering to "help" her fix the faults you so generously point out. How is she likely to respond? Now imagine that you go to your friend acknowledging the "log in your own eye" (6.41). You admit your share of the problem and try to fix it first, maybe even asking for your friend's help. How is she likely to respond now?
    Jesus reminds us that when we look at our own failings realistically, we'll have a much better perspective on the perceived failings of our friends. For better friendships, be a better friend. (See also Leviticus 19.17,18; Matthew 5.21-26; Matthew 18.15-20.)

    Words To Remember: *Don't judge others, and God won't judge you. Don't be hard on others, and God won't be hard on you. Forgive others, and God will forgive you.*
—Luke 6.37

you treat others is the way you will be treated.

³⁹Jesus also used some sayings as he spoke to the people. He said:

Can one blind person lead another blind person? Won't they both fall into a ditch? ⁴⁰Are students better than their teacher? But when they are fully trained, they will be like their teacher.

⁴¹You can see the speck in your friend's eye. But you don't notice the log in your own eye. ⁴²How can you say, "My friend, let me take the speck out of your eye," when you don't see the log in your own eye? You show-offs! First, get the log out of your own eye. Then you can see how to take the speck out of your friend's eye.

A Tree and Its Fruit
(Matthew 7.17-20; 12.34b, 35)

⁴³A good tree cannot produce bad fruit, and a bad tree cannot produce good fruit. ⁴⁴You can tell what a tree is like by the fruit it produces. You cannot pick figs or grapes from thornbushes. ⁴⁵Good people do good things because of the good in their hearts. Bad people do bad things because of the evil in their hearts. Your words show what is in your heart.

Two Builders
(Matthew 7.24-27)

⁴⁶Why do you keep on saying that I am your Lord, when you refuse to do what I say? ⁴⁷Anyone who comes and listens to me and obeys me ⁴⁸is like someone who dug down deep and built a house on solid rock. When the flood came and the river rushed against the house, it was built so well that it didn't even shake. ⁴⁹But anyone who hears what I say and doesn't obey me is like someone whose house wasn't built on solid rock. As soon as the river rushed against that house, it was smashed to pieces!

Jesus Heals an Army Officer's Servant
(Matthew 8.5-13; John 4.43-54)

7 After Jesus had finished teaching the people, he went to Capernaum. ²In that town an army officer's servant was sick and about to die. The officer liked this servant very much. ³And when he heard about Jesus, he sent some Jewish leaders to ask him to come and heal the servant.

⁴The leaders went to Jesus and begged him to do something. They said, "This man deserves your help! ⁵He loves our nation and even built us a meeting place." ⁶So Jesus went with them.

When Jesus wasn't far from the house, the officer sent some friends to tell him, "Lord, don't go to any trouble for me! I am not good enough for you to come into my house. ⁷And I am certainly not worthy to come to you. Just say the word, and my servant will get well. ⁸I have officers who give orders to me, and I have soldiers who take orders from me. I can say to one of them, 'Go!' and he goes. I can say to another, 'Come!' and he comes. I can say to my servant, 'Do this!' and he will do it."

⁹When Jesus heard this, he was so surprised that he turned and said to the crowd following him, "In all of Israel I've never found anyone with this much faith!"

¹⁰The officer's friends returned and found the servant well.

A Widow's Son

¹¹Soon Jesus and his disciples were on their way to the town of Nain, and a big crowd was going along with them. ¹²As they came near the gate of the town, they saw people carrying out the body of a widow's only son. Many people from the town were walking along with her.

¹³When the Lord saw the woman, he felt sorry for her and said, "Don't cry!"

¹⁴Jesus went over and touched the stretcher on which the people were carrying the dead boy. They stopped, and Jesus said, "Young man, get up!" ¹⁵The boy sat up and began to speak. Jesus then gave him back to his mother.

¹⁶Everyone was frightened and praised God. They said, "A great prophet is here with us! God has come to his people."

¹⁷News about Jesus spread all over Judea and everywhere else in that part of the country.

John the Baptist
(Matthew 11.1-19)

¹⁸⁻¹⁹John's followers told John everything that was being said about Jesus. So he sent

two of them to ask the Lord, "Are you the
one we should be looking for? Or must we
wait for someone else?"
20When these messengers came to Jesus,
they said, "John the Baptist sent us to ask,
'Are you the one we should be looking for?
Or are we supposed to wait for someone
else?' "
21At that time Jesus was healing many
people who were sick or in pain or were
troubled by evil spirits, and he was giving
sight to a lot of blind people. 22Jesus said to
the messengers sent by John, "Go and tell
John what you have seen and heard. Blind
people are now able to see, and the lame can
walk. People who have leprosy[p] are being
healed, and the deaf can now hear. The dead
are raised to life, and the poor are hearing
the good news. 23God will bless everyone
who doesn't reject me because of what
I do."
24After John's messengers had gone,
Jesus began speaking to the crowds about
John:

What kind of person did you go
out to the desert to see? Was he like
tall grass blown about by the wind?
25What kind of man did you really go
out to see? Was he someone dressed in
fine clothes? People who wear expensive clothes and live in luxury are in
the king's palace. 26What then did you
go out to see? Was he a prophet? He
certainly was! I tell you that he was
more than a prophet. 27In the Scriptures, God calls John his messenger
and says, "I am sending my messenger
ahead of you to get things ready for
you." 28No one ever born on this earth
is greater than John. But whoever is
least important in God's kingdom is
greater than John.

29Everyone had been listening to John.
Even the tax collectors[q] had obeyed God
and had done what was right by letting John
baptize them. 30But the Pharisees and the
experts in the Law of Moses refused to obey
God and be baptized by John.
31Jesus went on to say:

What are you people like? What
kind of people are you? 32You are like
children sitting in the market and
shouting to each other,

"We played the flute,
 but you would not dance!
We sang a funeral song,
 but you would not cry!"

33John the Baptist did not go around
eating and drinking, and you said,
"John has a demon in him!" 34But because the Son of Man goes around
eating and drinking, you say, "Jesus
eats and drinks too much! He is even a
friend of tax collectors and sinners."
35Yet Wisdom is shown to be right by
what its followers do.

---

p7.22 *leprosy*: See the note at 4.27. q7.29 *tax collectors*: See the note at 3.12.

Personal *Concerns*—**When a poor decision on my part has damaged my reputation as a Christian, what can I do?** *(Luke 7.36-50)*

Serve others.

Many are quick to point the finger at you if you've taken a wrong turn in your Christian walk. Facing such people requires courage; they may doubt your sincerity when you try to rebuild your reputation as a Christian.

But Jesus knows your heart. When you respond to him in love, you demonstrate that his forgiveness is real in your life. The "sinful woman" in this passage didn't waste her time trying to convince Simon and the other Pharisees of her devotion to Jesus. She concentrated on serving Jesus himself. And Jesus gave her peace (7.50).

Let your loving service demonstrate your desire to start fresh. And Jesus will give you peace. (See also Joel 2.12-17; Jonah 2,3; Micah 7.18,19; Zechariah 10.6-12; Galatians 1.11-24.)

Words To Remember: ***But Jesus told the woman, "Because of your faith, you are now saved. May God give you peace!"*****—Luke 7.50**

A Sinful Woman

Luke 7.36-50

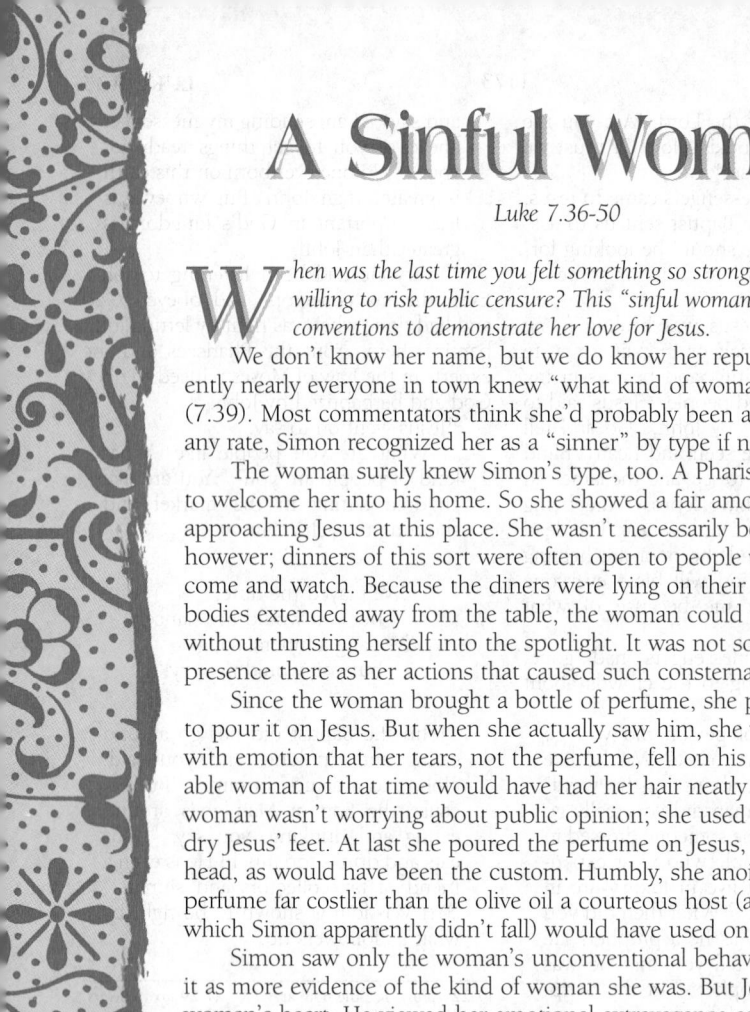

When was the last time you felt something so strongly that you were willing to risk public censure? This "sinful woman" broke all sorts of conventions to demonstrate her love for Jesus.

We don't know her name, but we do know her reputation. Apparently nearly everyone in town knew "what kind of woman" she was (7.39). Most commentators think she'd probably been a prostitute. At any rate, Simon recognized her as a "sinner" by type if not by name.

The woman surely knew Simon's type, too. A Pharisee was not likely to welcome her into his home. So she showed a fair amount of courage in approaching Jesus at this place. She wasn't necessarily being pushy, however; dinners of this sort were often open to people who wanted to come and watch. Because the diners were lying on their sides with their bodies extended away from the table, the woman could reach Jesus' feet without thrusting herself into the spotlight. It was not so much her presence there as her actions that caused such consternation to the host.

Since the woman brought a bottle of perfume, she probably intended to pour it on Jesus. But when she actually saw him, she was so overcome with emotion that her tears, not the perfume, fell on his feet. A respectable woman of that time would have had her hair neatly bound, but this woman wasn't worrying about public opinion; she used her loose hair to dry Jesus' feet. At last she poured the perfume on Jesus, but not on his head, as would have been the custom. Humbly, she anointed his feet with perfume far costlier than the olive oil a courteous host (a category into which Simon apparently didn't fall) would have used on his guest's head.

Simon saw only the woman's unconventional behavior and counted it as more evidence of the kind of woman she was. But Jesus saw the woman's heart. He viewed her emotional extravagance as a gesture of love and gratitude for what Jesus had done for her. He explained, "I tell you that all her sins are forgiven, and that is why she has shown great love" (7.47).

Imagine the impact if all of us who've had our sins forgiven would demonstrate our love for Jesus with the same courage, passion, and extravagance as this "sinful woman"!

Simon the Pharisee

36A Pharisee invited Jesus to have dinner with him. So Jesus went to the Pharisee's home and got ready to eat.*r*

37When a sinful woman in that town found out that Jesus was there, she bought an expensive bottle of perfume. **38**Then she came and stood behind Jesus. She cried and started washing his feet with her tears and drying them with her hair. The woman kissed his feet and poured the perfume on them.

39The Pharisee who had invited Jesus saw this and said to himself, "If this man really were a prophet, he would know what kind of woman is touching him! He would know that she is a sinner."

40Jesus said to the Pharisee, "Simon, I have something to say to you."

"Teacher, what is it?" Simon replied.

41Jesus told him, "Two people were in debt to a moneylender. One of them owed him five hundred silver coins, and the other owed him fifty. **42**Since neither of them could pay him back, the moneylender said that they didn't have to pay him anything. Which one of them will like him more?"

43Simon answered, "I suppose it would be the one who had owed more and didn't have to pay it back."

"You are right," Jesus said.

44He turned toward the woman and said to Simon, "Have you noticed this woman? When I came into your home, you didn't give me any water so I could wash my feet. But she has washed my feet with her tears and dried them with her hair. **45**You didn't greet me with a kiss, but from the time I came in, she has not stopped kissing my feet. **46**You didn't even pour olive oil on my head,*s* but she has poured expensive perfume on my feet. **47**So I tell you that all her sins are forgiven, and that is why she has shown great love. But anyone who has been forgiven for only a little will show only a little love."

48Then Jesus said to the woman, "Your sins are forgiven."

49Some other guests started saying to one another, "Who is this who dares to forgive sins?"

50But Jesus told the woman, "Because of your faith, you are now saved.*t* May God give you peace!"

Women Who Helped Jesus

8 Soon after this, Jesus was going through towns and villages, telling the good news about God's kingdom. His twelve apostles were with him, **2**and so were some women who had been healed of evil spirits and all sorts of diseases. One of the women was Mary Magdalene,*u* who once had seven demons in her. **3**Joanna, Susanna, and many others had also used what they owned to help Jesus*v* and his disciples. Joanna's husband Chuza was one of Herod's officials.*w*

A Story about a Farmer
(Matthew 13.1-9; Mark 4.1-9)

4When a large crowd from several towns had gathered around Jesus, he told them this story:

5A farmer went out to scatter seed in a field. While the farmer was doing it, some of the seeds fell along the road and were stepped on or eaten by birds. **6**Other seeds fell on rocky ground and started growing. But the plants did not have enough water and soon dried up. **7**Some other seeds fell where thorn-bushes grew up and choked the plants. **8**The rest of the seeds fell on good ground where they grew and produced a hundred times as many seeds.

When Jesus had finished speaking, he said, "If you have ears, pay attention!"

---

*r***7.36** *got ready to eat:* On special occasions the Jewish people often followed the Greek and Roman custom of lying down on their left side and leaning on their left elbow, while eating with their right hand. This is how the woman could come up behind Jesus and wash his feet (see verse 38). *s***7.44-46** *washed my feet . . . greet me with a kiss . . . pour olive oil on my head:* Guests in a home were usually offered water so they could wash their feet, because most people either went barefoot or wore sandals and would come in the house with very dusty feet. Guests were also greeted with a kiss on the cheek, and special ones often had sweet-smelling olive oil poured on their head. *t***7.50** *saved:* Or "healed." The Greek word may have either meaning. *u***8.2** *Magdalene:* Meaning "from Magdala," a small town on the western shore of Lake Galilee. There is no hint that she is the sinful woman in 7.36-50. *v***8.3** *used what they owned to help Jesus:* Women often helped Jewish teachers by giving them money. *w***8.3** *Herod's officials:* Herod Antipas, the son of Herod the Great.

Why Jesus Used Stories
(Matthew 13.10-17; Mark 4.10-12)

⁹Jesus' disciples asked him what the story meant. ¹⁰So he answered:

I have explained the secrets about God's kingdom to you, but for others I can only use stories. These people look, but they don't see, and they hear, but they don't understand.

Jesus Explains the Story about a Farmer
(Matthew 13.18-23; Mark 4.13-20)

¹¹This is what the story means: The seed is God's message, ¹²and the seeds that fell along the road are the people who hear the message. But the devil comes and snatches the message out of their hearts, so that they will not believe and be saved. ¹³The seeds that fell on rocky ground are the people who gladly hear the message and accept it. But they don't have deep roots, and they believe only for a little while. As soon as life gets hard, they give up. ¹⁴The seeds that fell among the thornbushes are also people who hear the message. But they are so eager for riches and pleasures that they never produce anything. ¹⁵Those seeds that fell on good ground are the people who listen to the message and keep it in good and honest hearts. They last and produce a harvest.

> *You must see light with your heart when all your eyes see is darkness.*
>
> BARBARA JOHNSON

Light
(Mark 4.21-25)

¹⁶No one lights a lamp and puts it under a bowl or under a bed. A lamp is always put on a lampstand, so that people who come into a house will see the light. ¹⁷There is nothing hidden that will not be found. There is no secret that will not be well known. ¹⁸Pay attention to how you listen! Everyone who has something will be given more, but people who have nothing will lose what little they think they have.

Jesus' Mother and Brothers
(Matthew 12.46-50; Mark 3.31-35)

¹⁹Jesus' mother and brothers went to see him, but because of the crowd they could not get near him. ²⁰Someone told Jesus, "Your mother and brothers are standing outside and want to see you."

²¹Jesus answered, "My mother and my brothers are those people who hear and obey God's message."

A Storm
(Matthew 8.23-27; Mark 4.35-41)

²²One day, Jesus and his disciples got into a boat, and he said, "Let's cross the lake."ˣ They started out, ²³and while they were sailing across, he went to sleep.

Suddenly a windstorm struck the lake, and the boat started sinking. They were in danger. ²⁴So they went to Jesus and woke him up, "Master, Master! We are about to drown!"

Jesus got up and ordered the wind and waves to stop. They obeyed, and everything was calm. ²⁵Then Jesus asked the disciples, "Don't you have any faith?"

But they were frightened and amazed. They said to each other, "Who is this? He can give orders to the wind and the waves, and they obey him!"

A Man with Demons in Him
(Matthew 8.28-34; Mark 5.1-20)

²⁶Jesus and his disciples sailed across Lake Galilee and came to shore near the town of Gerasa.ʸ ²⁷As Jesus was getting out of the boat, he was met by a man from that town. The man had demons in him. He had gone naked for a long time and no longer lived in a house, but in the graveyard.ᶻ

²⁸The man saw Jesus and screamed. He knelt down in front of him and shouted, "Jesus, Son of God in heaven, what do you

---

ˣ**8.22** *cross the lake*: To the eastern shore of Lake Galilee, where most of the people were not Jewish. ʸ**8.26** *Gerasa*: Some manuscripts have "Gergesa." ᶻ**8.27** *graveyard*: It was thought that demons and evil spirits lived in graveyards.

want with me? I beg you not to torture me!" [29]He said this because Jesus had already told the evil spirit to go out of him.

The man had often been attacked by the demon. And even though he had been bound with chains and leg irons and kept under guard, he smashed whatever bound him. Then the demon would force him out into lonely places.

[30]Jesus asked the man, "What is your name?"

He answered, "My name is Lots." He said this because there were 'lots' of demons in him. [31]They begged Jesus not to send them to the deep pit,[a] where they would be punished.

[32]A large herd of pigs was feeding there on the hillside. So the demons begged Jesus to let them go into the pigs, and Jesus let them go. [33]Then the demons left the man and went into the pigs. The whole herd rushed down the steep bank into the lake and drowned.

[34]When the men taking care of the pigs saw this, they ran to spread the news in the town and on the farms. [35]The people went out to see what had happened, and when they came to Jesus, they also found the man. The demons had gone out of him, and he was sitting there at the feet of Jesus. He had clothes on and was in his right mind. But the people were terrified.

[36]Then all who had seen the man healed told about it. [37]Everyone from around Gerasa[b] begged Jesus to leave, because they were so frightened.

When Jesus got into the boat to start back, [38]the man who had been healed begged to go with him. But Jesus sent him off and said, [39]"Go back home and tell everyone how much God has done for you." The man then went all over town, telling everything that Jesus had done for him.

A Dying Girl and a Sick Woman
(Matthew 9.18-26; Mark 5.21-43)

[40]Everyone had been waiting for Jesus, and when he came back, a crowd was there to welcome him. [41]Just then the man in charge of the Jewish meeting place came and knelt down in front of Jesus. His name was Jairus, and he begged Jesus to come to his home [42]because his twelve-year-old child was dying. She was his only daughter.

While Jesus was on his way, people were crowding all around him. [43]In the crowd was a woman who had been bleeding for twelve years. She had spent everything she had on doctors,[c] but none of them could make her well.

[44]As soon as she came up behind Jesus and barely touched his clothes, her bleeding stopped.

[45]"Who touched me?" Jesus asked.

While everyone was denying it, Peter said, "Master, people are crowding all around and pushing you from every side."[d]

[46]But Jesus answered, "Someone touched me, because I felt power going out from me." [47]The woman knew that she could not hide, so she came trembling and knelt down in front of Jesus. She told everyone why she had touched him and that she had been healed right away.

[48]Jesus said to the woman, "You are now well because of your faith. May God give you peace!"

[49]While Jesus was speaking, someone came from Jairus' home and said, "Your daughter has died! Why bother the teacher anymore?"

[50]When Jesus heard this, he told Jairus, "Don't worry! Have faith, and your daughter will get well."

[51]Jesus went into the house, but he did not let anyone else go with him, except Peter, John, James, and the girl's father and mother. [52]Everyone was crying and weeping for the girl. But Jesus said, "The child isn't dead. She is just asleep." [53]The people laughed at him because they knew she was dead.

[54]Jesus took hold of the girl's hand and said, "Child, get up!" [55]She came back to life and got right up. Jesus told them to give her something to eat. [56]Her parents were surprised, but Jesus ordered them not to tell anyone what had happened.

Instructions for the Twelve Apostles
(Matthew 10.5-15; Mark 6.7-13)

9 Jesus called together his twelve apostles and gave them complete power over all demons and diseases. [2]Then

---

[a]**8.31** *deep pit*: The place where evil spirits are kept and punished. [b]**8.37** *Gerasa*: See the note at 8.26. [c]**8.43** *She had spent everything she had on doctors*: Some manuscripts do not have these words. [d]**8.45** *from every side*: Some manuscripts add "and you ask, 'Who touched me?' "

he sent them to tell about God's kingdom and to heal the sick. [3]He told them, "Don't take anything with you! Don't take a walking stick or a traveling bag or food or money or even a change of clothes. [4]When you are welcomed into a home, stay there until you leave that town. [5]If people won't welcome you, leave the town and shake the dust from your feet[e] as a warning to them."

[6]The apostles left and went from village to village, telling the good news and healing people everywhere.

Herod Is Worried
(Matthew 14.1-12; Mark 6.14-29)

[7]Herod[f] the ruler heard about all that was happening, and he was worried. Some people were saying that John the Baptist had come back to life. [8]Others were saying that Elijah had come[g] or that one of the prophets from long ago had come back to life. [9]But Herod said, "I had John's head cut off! Who is this I hear so much about?" Herod was eager to meet Jesus.

Jesus Feeds Five Thousand
(Matthew 14.13-21; Mark 6.30-44; John 6.1-14)

[10]The apostles came back and told Jesus everything they had done. He then took them with him to the village of Bethsaida, where they could be alone. [11]But a lot of people found out about this and followed

him. Jesus welcomed them. He spoke to them about God's kingdom and healed everyone who was sick. [12]Late in the afternoon the twelve apostles came to Jesus and said, "Send the crowd to the villages and farms around here. They need to find a place to stay and something to eat. There is nothing in this place. It is like a desert!"

[13]Jesus answered, "You give them something to eat."

But they replied, "We have only five small loaves of bread[h] and two fish. If we are going to feed all these people, we will have to go and buy food." [14]There were about five thousand men in the crowd.

Jesus said to his disciples, "Have the people sit in groups of fifty." [15]They did this, and all the people sat down. [16]Jesus took the five loaves and the two fish. He looked up toward heaven and blessed the food. Then he broke the bread and fish and handed them to his disciples to give to the people.

[17]Everyone ate all they wanted. What was left over filled twelve baskets.

---

[e]**9.5** *shake the dust from your feet*: This was a way of showing rejection.　[f]**9.7** *Herod*: Herod Antipas, the son of Herod the Great.　[g]**9.8** *Elijah had come*: Many of the Jewish people expected the prophet Elijah to come and prepare the way for the Messiah.　[h]**9.13** *small loaves of bread*: These would have been flat and round or in the shape of a bun.

---

*Spiritual*Life—How can I reach out to a needy world? *(Luke 9.10-17)*

Realize Jesus has the power to use even our smallest efforts.
The apostles had been with Jesus long enough to know that he wanted them to be concerned for people's physical as well as spiritual needs. So when Jesus showed signs of preaching right through the dinner hour, the apostles gently reminded him that crowds don't live by sermons alone. They suggested Jesus send the people away so they could get some food.

But Jesus had a bigger plan. In essence, he said, "You're on the right track to be thinking about food and shelter. But don't stop with noticing the need. *You* feed them."

Jesus says the same thing to us. "Don't just send the hungry to the welfare office. Don't leave affordable housing up to the government. Contribute to a food pantry. Volunteer at a homeless shelter. *You* feed them."

By ourselves, we can't feed the needy of this world. By themselves, the apostles couldn't feed the crowd. But Jesus doesn't ask us to estimate our limitations; he tells us to get busy giving. He'll do the rest. (See also 2 Samuel 9; Nehemiah 5.1-13; Lamentations 2.11-13; Jonah 4.5-11; Zechariah 7.7-13; Matthew 6.1-4.)

Words To Remember: *Jesus answered, "You give them something to eat."*
—Luke 9.13

Who Is Jesus?

(Matthew 16.13-19; Mark 8.27-29)

¹⁸When Jesus was alone praying, his disciples came to him, and he asked them, "What do people say about me?"

¹⁹They answered, "Some say that you are John the Baptist or Elijah[i] or a prophet from long ago who has come back to life."

²⁰Jesus then asked them, "But who do you say I am?"

Peter answered, "You are the Messiah sent from God."

²¹Jesus strictly warned his disciples not to tell anyone about this.

Jesus Speaks about His Suffering and Death

(Matthew 16.20-28; Mark 8.30—9.1)

²²Jesus told his disciples, "The nation's leaders, the chief priests, and the teachers of the Law of Moses will make the Son of Man suffer terribly. They will reject him and kill him, but three days later he will rise to life."

²³Then Jesus said to all the people:

If any of you want to be my followers, you must forget about yourself. You must take up your cross each day and follow me. ²⁴If you want to save your life,[j] you will destroy it. But if you give up your life for me, you will save it. ²⁵What will you gain, if you own the whole world but destroy yourself or waste your life? ²⁶If you are ashamed of me and my message, the Son of Man will be ashamed of you when he comes in his glory and in the glory of his Father and the holy angels. ²⁷You can be sure that some of the people standing here will not die before they see God's kingdom.

The True Glory of Jesus

(Matthew 17.1-8; Mark 9.2-8)

²⁸About eight days later Jesus took Peter, John, and James with him and went up on a mountain to pray. ²⁹While he was praying, his face changed, and his clothes became shining white. ³⁰Suddenly Moses and Elijah were there speaking with him. ³¹They appeared in heavenly glory and talked about all that Jesus' death[k] in Jerusalem would mean.

³²Peter and the other two disciples had been sound asleep. All at once they woke up and saw how glorious Jesus was. They also saw the two men who were with him.

³³Moses and Elijah were about to leave, when Peter said to Jesus, "Master, it is good for us to be here! Let us make three shelters, one for you, one for Moses, and one for Elijah." But Peter did not know what he was talking about.

³⁴While Peter was still speaking, a shadow from a cloud passed over them, and they were frightened as the cloud covered them. ³⁵From the cloud a voice spoke, "This is my chosen Son. Listen to what he says!"

³⁶After the voice had spoken, Peter, John, and James saw only Jesus. For some time they kept quiet and did not say anything about what they had seen.

Jesus Heals a Boy

(Matthew 17.14-18; Mark 9.14-27)

³⁷The next day Jesus and his three disciples came down from the mountain and were met by a large crowd. ³⁸Just then someone in the crowd shouted, "Teacher, please do something for my son! He is my only child! ³⁹A demon often attacks him and makes him scream. It shakes him until he foams at the mouth, and it won't leave him until it has completely worn the boy out. ⁴⁰I begged your disciples to force out the demon, but they couldn't do it."

⁴¹Jesus said to them, "You people are stubborn and don't have any faith! How much longer must I be with you? Why do I have to put up with you?"

Then Jesus said to the man, "Bring your son to me." ⁴²While the boy was being brought, the demon attacked him and made him shake all over. Jesus ordered the demon to stop. Then he healed the boy and gave him back to his father. ⁴³Everyone was amazed at God's great power.

Jesus Again Speaks about His Death

(Matthew 17.22, 23; Mark 9.30-32)

While everyone was still amazed at what Jesus was doing, he said to his disciples, ⁴⁴"Pay close attention to what I am telling you! The Son of Man will be handed over to

---

ⁱ**9.19** *Elijah:* See the note at 9.8. ^j**9.24** *life:* In verses 24, 25 a Greek word which often means "soul" is translated "life" and "yourself." ^k**9.31** *Jesus' death:* In Greek this is "his departure," which probably includes his rising to life and his return to heaven.

his enemies." [45]But the disciples did not know what he meant. The meaning was hidden from them. They could not understand it, and they were afraid to ask.

Who Is the Greatest?
(Matthew 18.1-5; Mark 9.33-37)

[46]Jesus' disciples were arguing about which one of them was the greatest. [47]Jesus knew what they were thinking, and he had a child stand there beside him. [48]Then he said to his disciples, "When you welcome even a child because of me, you welcome me. And when you welcome me, you welcome the one who sent me. Whichever one of you is the most humble is the greatest."

For or against Jesus
(Mark 9.38-40)

[49]John said, "Master, we saw a man using your name to force demons out of people. But we told him to stop, because he isn't one of us."

[50]"Don't stop him!" Jesus said. "Anyone who isn't against you is for you."

A Samaritan Village Refuses To Receive Jesus

[51]Not long before it was time for Jesus to be taken up to heaven, he made up his mind to go to Jerusalem. [52]He sent some messengers on ahead to a Samaritan village to get things ready for him. [53]But he was on his way to Jerusalem, so the people there refused to welcome him. [54]When the disciples James and John saw what was happening, they asked, "Lord, do you want us to call down fire from heaven to destroy these people?"[l] [55]But Jesus turned and corrected them for what they had said.[m] [56]Then they all went on to another village.

Three People Who Wanted To Be Followers
(Matthew 8.19-22)

[57]Along the way someone said to Jesus, "I'll go anywhere with you!"

[58]Jesus said, "Foxes have dens, and birds have nests, but the Son of Man doesn't have a place to call his own."

[59]Jesus told someone else to come with him. But the man said, "Lord, let me wait until I bury my father."[n]

[60]Jesus answered, "Let the dead take care of the dead, while you go and tell about God's kingdom."

[61]Then someone said to Jesus, "I want to go with you, Lord, but first let me go back and take care of things at home."

[62]Jesus answered, "Anyone who starts plowing and keeps looking back isn't worth a thing to God's kingdom!"

The Work of the Seventy-Two Followers

10 Later the Lord chose seventy-two[o] other followers and sent them out two by two to every town and village where he was about to go. [2]He said to them:

A large crop is in the fields, but there are only a few workers. Ask the Lord in charge of the harvest to send out workers to bring it in. [3]Now go, but remember, I am sending you like lambs into a pack of wolves. [4]Don't take along a moneybag or a traveling bag or sandals. And don't waste time greeting people on the road.[p] [5]As soon as you enter a home, say, "God bless this home with peace." [6]If the people living there are peace-loving, your prayer for peace will bless them. But if they are not peace-loving, your prayer will return to you. [7]Stay with the same family, eating and drinking whatever they give you, because workers are worth what they earn. Don't move around from house to house.

[8]If the people of a town welcome you, eat whatever they offer. [9]Heal their sick and say, "God's kingdom will soon be here!"[q]

[10]But if the people of a town refuse to welcome you, go out into the street and say, [11]"We are shaking the dust from our feet[r] as a warning to you. And

---

[l]**9.54** *to destroy these people*: Some manuscripts add "as Elijah did." [m]**9.55** *what they had said*: Some manuscripts add, "and said, 'Don't you know what spirit you belong to? The Son of Man did not come to destroy people's lives, but to save them.'" [n]**9.59** *bury my father*: The Jewish people taught that giving someone a proper burial was even more important than helping the poor. [o]**10.1** *seventy-two*: Some manuscripts have "seventy." According to Jewish tradition, there were seventy nations on earth. But the ancient Greek translation of the Old Testament has "seventy-two" in place of "seventy." Jesus probably chose this number of followers to show that his message was for everyone in the world. [p]**10.4** *waste time greeting people on the road*: In those days a polite greeting could take a long time. [q]**10.9** *will soon be here*: Or "is already here." [r]**10.11** *shaking the dust from our feet*: This was a way of showing rejection.

you can be sure that God's kingdom will soon be here!"[s] [12]I tell you that on the day of judgment the people of Sodom will get off easier than the people of that town!

The Unbelieving Towns
(Matthew 11.20-24)

[13]You people of Chorazin are in for trouble! You people of Bethsaida are also in for trouble! If the miracles that took place in your towns had happened in Tyre and Sidon, the people there would have turned to God long ago. They would have dressed in sackcloth and put ashes on their heads.[t] [14]On the day of judgment the people of Tyre and Sidon will get off easier than you will. [15]People of Capernaum, do you think you will be honored in heaven? Well, you will go down to hell!

[16]My followers, whoever listens to you is listening to me. Anyone who says "No" to you is saying "No" to me. And anyone who says "No" to me is really saying "No" to the one who sent me.

The Return of the Seventy-Two

[17]When the seventy-two[u] followers returned, they were excited and said, "Lord, even the demons obeyed when we spoke in your name!"

[18]Jesus told them:

I saw Satan fall from heaven like a flash of lightning. [19]I have given you the power to trample on snakes and scorpions and to defeat the power of your enemy Satan. Nothing can harm you. [20]But don't be happy because evil spirits obey you. Be happy that your names are written in heaven!

Jesus Thanks His Father
(Matthew 11.25-27; 13.16, 17)

[21]At that same time, Jesus felt the joy that comes from the Holy Spirit,[v] and he said:

My Father, Lord of heaven and

---

[s]**10.11** *will soon be here:* Or "is already here."
[t]**10.13** *dressed in sackcloth . . . ashes on their heads:* This was one way that people showed how sorry they were for their sins.   [u]**10.17** *seventy-two:* See the note at 10.1.
[v]**10.21** *the Holy Spirit:* Some manuscripts have "his spirit."

PARENTING&family—How can I raise a child to be kind and considerate of others? (Luke 10.25-37)

Help your child see others in a new way.
Have you ever noticed how easily children tune out direct commands? "Share your toys." "Don't pester your brother." "Let somebody else go first." Good instructions, yet they're rarely as effective as we'd like them to be!

But children quickly tune in to stories—especially stories about themselves or characters they can identify with. Jesus knew that we not only listen to, but learn from stories. So he told a Jewish audience a story about someone just like themselves: a Jerusalem resident making a trip. He knew his listeners would identify with the main character, would get caught up in the drama and suspense, and would be shocked out of their complacency when the hero of the story was revealed as none other than a member of a despised ethnic group.

In this story, Jesus not only taught that race is no barrier to the love God calls us to, he also showed how to bring that message home with real impact. Tell stories. Let your children discover the good in others through accounts that grip their imagination rather than commands on how they should act and feel. (See also Jonah 1; Matthew 5.43-48; 3 John 4-11.)

Words To Remember: *Then Jesus asked, "Which one of these three people was a real neighbor to the man who was beaten up by robbers?"*
The teacher answered, "The one who showed pity."
Jesus said, "Go and do the same!"—Luke 10.36,37

earth, I am grateful that you hid all this from wise and educated people and showed it to ordinary people. Yes, Father, that is what pleased you.

²²My Father has given me everything, and he is the only one who knows the Son. The only one who really knows the Father is the Son. But the Son wants to tell others about the Father, so that they can know him too.

²³Jesus then turned to his disciples and said to them in private, "You are really blessed to see what you see! ²⁴Many prophets and kings were eager to see what you see and to hear what you hear. But I tell you that they did not see or hear."

The Good Samaritan

²⁵An expert in the Law of Moses stood up and asked Jesus a question to see what he would say. "Teacher," he asked, "what must I do to have eternal life?"

²⁶Jesus answered, "What is written in the Scriptures? How do you understand them?"

²⁷The man replied, "The Scriptures say, 'Love the Lord your God with all your heart, soul, strength, and mind.' They also say,

'Love your neighbors as much as you love yourself.' "

²⁸Jesus said, "You have given the right answer. If you do this, you will have eternal life."

²⁹But the man wanted to show that he knew what he was talking about. So he asked Jesus, "Who are my neighbors?"

³⁰Jesus replied:

As a man was going down from Jerusalem to Jericho, robbers attacked him and grabbed everything he had. They beat him up and ran off, leaving him half dead.

³¹A priest happened to be going down the same road. But when he saw the man, he walked by on the other side. ³²Later a temple helper^w came to the same place. But when he saw the man who had been beaten up, he also went by on the other side.

³³A man from Samaria then came traveling along that road. When he saw the man, he felt sorry for him ³⁴and went over to him. He treated his

---

^w10.32 *temple helper*: A man from the tribe of Levi, whose job it was to work around the temple.

Personal *Concerns*—How can I learn to set priorities? *(Luke 10.38-42)*

Make time to spend with God, no matter how busy you are.

Martin Luther is reported to have said that he was "too busy not to pray." Unfortunately, for most of us, when our agenda gets too full, time in prayer and God's Word are among the first to go.

Most of us can identify with Martha—at least sometimes. After all, the work has to be done, whether it's meal preparation, planning for tomorrow's meeting, or taking the kids in for their checkups. Even church volunteer work can make us feel "too busy to pray."

Jesus didn't tell Martha that preparing for guests and accomplishing her daily chores was wrong. But he did point out that her extreme busyness, stressful running around, and frustration with her sister Mary wasn't good for her. It affected her personal relationships. If she had to choose between spending her hours on making a gourmet dinner or spending time with her Lord, who was only there for a short time, she'd better not spend all her time in the kitchen.

Choosing to make time to spend with God in prayer and personal devotions is a risk. You might risk criticism about how you spend your time. You might risk leaving something undone that you think is important. But what's more important than time with Jesus, your Savior?

What time will you choose to spend with him today? (See also Genesis 22.1-19; 1 Samuel 15.10-35; Haggai 2.6-9; Revelation 2.1-7.)

Words To Remember: *The Lord answered, "Martha, Martha! You are worried and upset about so many things, but only one thing is necessary. Mary has chosen what is best, and it will not be taken away from her."*—Luke 10.41,42

wounds with olive oil and wine[x] and bandaged them. Then he put him on his own donkey and took him to an inn, where he took care of him. [35]The next morning he gave the innkeeper two silver coins and said, "Please take care of the man. If you spend more than this on him, I will pay you when I return."

[36]Then Jesus asked, "Which one of these three people was a real neighbor to the man who was beaten up by robbers?"

[37]The teacher answered, "The one who showed pity."

Jesus said, "Go and do the same!"

Martha and Mary

[38]The Lord and his disciples were traveling along and came to a village. When they got there, a woman named Martha welcomed him into her home. [39]She had a sister named Mary, who sat down in front of the Lord and was listening to what he said. [40]Martha was worried about all that had to be done. Finally, she went to Jesus and said, "Lord, doesn't it bother you that my sister has left me to do all the work by myself? Tell her to come and help me!"

[41]The Lord answered, "Martha, Martha! You are worried and upset about so many things, [42]but only one thing is necessary. Mary has chosen what is best, and it will not be taken away from her."

Prayer
(Matthew 6.9-13; 7.7-11)

11 When Jesus had finished praying, one of his disciples said to him, "Lord, teach us to pray, just as John taught his followers to pray."

[2]So Jesus told them, "Pray in this way:

'Father, help us
    to honor your name.
Come and set up
    your kingdom.
[3] Give us each day
    the food we need.[y]
[4] Forgive our sins,
    as we forgive everyone
        who has done wrong to us.
And keep us
    from being tempted.' "

[5]Then Jesus went on to say:

Suppose one of you goes to a friend in the middle of the night and says, "Let me borrow three loaves of bread. [6]A friend of mine has dropped in, and I don't have a thing for him to eat." [7]And suppose your friend answers, "Don't bother me! The door is bolted, and my children and I are in bed. I cannot get up to give you something."

[8]He may not get up and give you the bread, just because you are his friend. But he will get up and give you as much as you need, simply because you are not ashamed to keep on asking.

Prayer is cooperation with God, not getting what I want, but learning what he wants.

ELISABETH ELLIOT

[9]So I tell you to ask and you will receive, search and you will find, knock and the door will be opened for you. [10]Everyone who asks will receive, everyone who searches will find, and the door will be opened for everyone who knocks. [11]Which one of you fathers would give your hungry child a snake if the child asked for a fish? [12]Which one of you would give your child a scorpion if the child asked for an egg? [13]As bad as you are, you still know how to give good gifts to your children. But your heavenly Father is even more ready to give the Holy Spirit to anyone who asks.

Jesus and the Ruler of Demons
(Matthew 12.22-30; Mark 3.20-27)

[14]Jesus forced a demon out of a man who could not talk. And after the demon had

---

x10.34 *olive oil and wine*: In New Testament times these were used as medicine. Sometimes olive oil is a symbol for healing by means of a miracle (see James 5.14).
y11.3 *the food we need*: Or "food for today" or "food for the coming day."

gone out, the man started speaking, and the crowds were amazed. [15]But some people said, "He forces out demons by the power of Beelzebul, the ruler of the demons!"

[16]Others wanted to put Jesus to the test. So they asked him to show them a sign from God. [17]Jesus knew what they were thinking, and he said:

A kingdom where people fight each other will end up in ruin. And a family that fights will break up. [18]If Satan fights against himself, how can his kingdom last? Yet you say that I force out demons by the power of Beelzebul. [19]If I use his power to force out demons, whose power do your own followers use to force them out? They are the ones who will judge you. [20]But if I use God's power to force out demons, it proves that God's kingdom has already come to you.

[21]When a strong man arms himself and guards his home, everything he owns is safe. [22]But if a stronger man comes and defeats him, he will carry off the weapons in which the strong man trusted. Then he will divide with others what he has taken. [23]If you are not on my side, you are against me. If you don't gather in the crop with me, you scatter it.

Return of an Evil Spirit
(Matthew 12.43-45)

[24]When an evil spirit leaves a person, it travels through the desert, looking for a place to rest. But when it doesn't find a place, it says, "I will go back to the home I left." [25]When it gets there and finds the place clean and fixed up, [26]it goes off and finds seven other evil spirits even worse than itself. They all come and make their home there, and that person ends up in worse shape than before.

Being Really Blessed

[27]While Jesus was still talking, a woman in the crowd spoke up, "The woman who gave birth to you and nursed you is blessed!"

[28]Jesus replied, "That's true, but the people who are really blessed are the ones who hear and obey God's message!"[z]

A Sign from God
(Matthew 12.38-42; Mark 8.12)

[29]As crowds were gathering around Jesus, he said:

You people of today are evil! You keep looking for a sign from God. But what happened to Jonah[a] is the only sign you will be given. [30]Just as Jonah was a sign to the people of Nineveh, the Son of Man will be a sign to the people of today. [31]When the judgment comes, the Queen of the South[b] will stand there with you and condemn you. She traveled a long way to hear Solomon's wisdom, and yet here is something far greater than Solomon. [32]The people of Nineveh will also stand there with you and condemn you. They turned to God when Jonah preached, and yet here is something far greater than Jonah.

Light
(Matthew 5.15; 6.22, 23)

[33]No one lights a lamp and then hides it or puts it under a clay pot. A lamp is put on a lampstand, so that everyone who comes into the house can see the light. [34]Your eyes are the lamp for your body. When your eyes are good, you have all the light you need. But when your eyes are bad, everything is dark. [35]So be sure that your light isn't darkness. [36]If you have light, and nothing is dark, then light will be everywhere, as when a lamp shines brightly on you.

Jesus Condemns the Pharisees and Teachers of the Law of Moses
(Matthew 23.1-36; Mark 12.38-40; Luke 20.45-47)

[37]When Jesus finished speaking, a Pharisee invited him home for a meal. Jesus went and sat down to eat.[c] [38]The Pharisee was surprised that he did not wash his hands[d] before eating. [39]So the Lord said to him:

---

[z]**11.28** "That's true, but the people who are really blessed . . . message": Or " 'That's not true, the people who are blessed . . . message.' " [a]**11.29** what happened to Jonah: Jonah was in the stomach of a big fish for three days and nights (see Matthew 12.40). [b]**11.31** Queen of the South: Sheba, probably a country in southern Arabia. [c]**11.37** sat down to eat: See the note at 7.36. [d]**11.38** did not wash his hands: The Jewish people had strict laws about washing their hands before eating, especially if they had been out in public.

You Pharisees clean the outside of cups and dishes, but on the inside you are greedy and evil. [40]You fools! Didn't God make both the outside and the inside?[e] [41]If you would only give what you have to the poor, everything you do would please God.

[42]You Pharisees are in for trouble! You give God a tenth of the spices from your gardens, such as mint and rue. But you cheat people, and you don't love God. You should be fair and kind to others and still give a tenth to God.

[43]You Pharisees are in for trouble! You love the front seats in the meeting places, and you like to be greeted with honor in the market. [44]But you are in for trouble! You are like unmarked graves[f] that people walk on without even knowing it.

[45]A teacher of the Law of Moses spoke up, "Teacher, you said cruel things about us."

[46]Jesus replied:

You teachers are also in for trouble! You load people down with heavy burdens, but you won't lift a finger to help them carry the loads. [47]Yes, you are really in for trouble. You build monuments to honor the prophets your own people murdered long ago. [48]You must think that was the right thing for your people to do, or else you would not have built monuments for the prophets they murdered.

[49]Because of your evil deeds, the Wisdom of God said, "I will send prophets and apostles to you. But you will murder some and mistreat others." [50]You people living today will be punished for all the prophets who have been murdered since the beginning of the world. [51]This includes every prophet from the time of Abel to the time of Zechariah,[g] who was murdered between the altar and the temple. You people will certainly be punished for all of this.

[52]You teachers of the Law of Moses are really in for trouble! You carry the keys to the door of knowledge about God. But you never go in, and you keep others from going in.

[53]Jesus was about to leave, but the teach-

ers and the Pharisees wanted to get even with him. They tried to make him say what he thought about other things, [54]so that they could catch him saying something wrong.

Warnings

12 As thousands of people crowded around Jesus and were stepping on each other, he told his disciples:

Be sure to guard against the dishonest teaching[h] of the Pharisees! It is their way of fooling people. [2]Everything that is hidden will be found out, and every secret will be known. [3]Whatever you say in the dark will be heard when it is day. Whatever you whisper in a closed room will be shouted from the housetops.

The One To Fear
(Matthew 10.28-31)

[4]My friends, don't be afraid of people. They can kill you, but after that, there is nothing else they can do. [5]God is the one you must fear. Not only can he take your life, but he can throw you into hell. God is certainly the one you should fear!

[6]Five sparrows are sold for just two pennies, but God doesn't forget a one of them. [7]Even the hairs on your head are counted. So don't be afraid! You are worth much more than many sparrows.

Telling Others about Christ
(Matthew 10.32, 33; 12.32; 10.19, 20)

[8]If you tell others that you belong to me, the Son of Man will tell God's angels that you are my followers. [9]But

---

[e]**11.40** *Didn't God make both the outside and the inside:* Or "Doesn't the person who washes the outside always wash the inside too?" [f]**11.44** *unmarked graves:* Tombs were whitewashed to keep anyone from accidentally touching them. A person who touched a dead body or a tomb was considered unclean and could not worship with other Jewish people. [g]**11.51** *from the time of Abel . . . Zechariah:* Genesis is the first book in the Jewish Scriptures, and it tells that Abel was the first person to be murdered. Second Chronicles is the last book in the Jewish Scriptures, and the last murder that it tells about is that of Zechariah. [h]**12.1** *dishonest teaching:* The Greek text has "yeast," which is used here of a teaching that is not true (see Matthew 16.6, 12).

if you reject me, you will be rejected in front of them. [10]If you speak against the Son of Man, you can be forgiven, but if you speak against the Holy Spirit, you cannot be forgiven.

[11]When you are brought to trial in the Jewish meeting places or before rulers or officials, don't worry about how you will defend yourselves or what you will say. [12]At that time the Holy Spirit will tell you what to say.

A Rich Fool

[13]A man in a crowd said to Jesus, "Teacher, tell my brother to give me my share of what our father left us when he died."

[14]Jesus answered, "Who gave me the right to settle arguments between you and your brother?"

[15]Then he said to the crowd, "Don't be greedy! Owning a lot of things won't make your life safe."

[16]So Jesus told them this story:

A rich man's farm produced a big crop, [17]and he said to himself, "What can I do? I don't have a place large enough to store everything."

[18]Later, he said, "Now I know what I'll do. I'll tear down my barns and build bigger ones, where I can store all my grain and other goods. [19]Then I'll say to myself, 'You have stored up enough good things to last for years to come. Live it up! Eat, drink, and enjoy yourself.' "

[20]But God said to him, "You fool! Tonight you will die. Then who will get what you have stored up?"

[21]"This is what happens to people who store up everything for themselves, but are poor in the sight of God."

Worry
(Matthew 6.25-34)

[22]Jesus said to his disciples:

I tell you not to worry about your life! Don't worry about having something to eat or wear. [23]Life is more than food or clothing. [24]Look at the crows! They don't plant or harvest, and they don't have storehouses or barns. But God takes care of them. You are much more important than any birds. [25]Can worry make you live longer?[i] [26]If you

don't have power over small things, why worry about everything else?

[27]Look how the wild flowers grow! They don't work hard to make their clothes. But I tell you that Solomon with all his wealth[j] wasn't as well clothed as one of these flowers. [28]God gives such beauty to everything that grows in the fields, even though it is here today and thrown into a fire tomorrow. Won't he do even more for you? You have such little faith!

We will never completely eradicate anxiety from our lives, but we can learn not to live with it as a daily experience.

ELIZABETH SKOGLUND

[29]Don't keep worrying about having something to eat or drink. [30]Only people who don't know God are always worrying about such things. Your Father knows what you need. [31]But put God's work first, and these things will be yours as well.

Treasures in Heaven
(Matthew 6.19-21)

[32]My little group of disciples, don't be afraid! Your Father wants to give you the kingdom. [33]Sell what you have and give the money to the poor. Make yourselves moneybags that never wear out. Make sure your treasure is safe in heaven, where thieves cannot steal it and moths cannot destroy it. [34]Your heart will always be where your treasure is.

Faithful and Unfaithful Servants
(Matthew 24.45-51)

[35]Be ready and keep your lamps burning [36]just like those servants who

---

[i]**12.25** *live longer:* Or "grow taller." [j]**12.27** *Solomon with all his wealth:* The Jewish people thought that Solomon was the richest person who had ever lived.

wait up for their master to return from a wedding feast. As soon as he comes and knocks, they open the door for him. [37]Servants are fortunate if their master finds them awake and ready when he comes! I promise you that he will get ready and have his servants sit down so he can serve them. [38]Those servants are really fortunate if their master finds them ready, even though he comes late at night or early in the morning. [39]You would surely not let a thief break into your home, if you knew when the thief was coming. [40]So always be ready! You don't know when the Son of Man will come.

[41]Peter asked Jesus, "Did you say this just for us or for everyone?"

[42]The Lord answered:

Who are faithful and wise servants? Who are the ones the master will put in charge of giving the other servants their food supplies at the proper time? [43]Servants are fortunate if their master comes and finds them doing their job. [44]A servant who is always faithful will surely be put in charge of everything the master owns.

[45]But suppose one of the servants thinks that the master won't return until late. Suppose that servant starts beating all the other servants and eats and drinks and gets drunk. [46]If that happens, the master will come on a day and at a time when the servant least expects him. That servant will then be punished and thrown out with the servants who cannot be trusted.

[47]If servants are not ready or willing to do what their master wants them to do, they will be beaten hard. [48]But servants who don't know what their master wants them to do will not be beaten so hard for doing wrong. If God has been generous with you, he will expect you to serve him well. But if he has been more than generous, he will expect you to serve him even better.

Not Peace, but Trouble
(Matthew 10.34-36)

[49]I came to set fire to the earth, and I wish it were already on fire! [50]I am going to be put to a hard test. And I will have to suffer a lot of pain until it is over. [51]Do you think that I came to bring peace to earth? No indeed! I came to make people choose sides. [52]A family of five will be divided, with two of them against the other three. [53]Fathers and sons will turn against one another, and mothers and daughters will do the same. Mothers-in-law and daughters-in-law will also turn against each other.

Knowing What To Do
(Matthew 16.2, 3; 5.25, 26)

[54]Jesus said to all the people:

As soon as you see a cloud coming up in the west, you say, "It's going to rain," and it does. [55]When the south wind blows, you say, "It's going to get hot," and it does. [56]Are you trying to fool someone? You can predict the weather by looking at the earth and sky, but you don't really know what's going on right now. [57]Why don't you understand the right thing to do? [58]When someone accuses you of something, try to settle things before you are taken to court. If you don't, you will be dragged before the judge. Then the judge will hand you over to the jailer, and you will be locked up. [59]You won't get out until you have paid the last cent you owe.

Turn Back to God

13 About this same time Jesus was told that Pilate had given orders for some people from Galilee to be killed while they were offering sacrifices. [2]Jesus replied:

Do you think that these people were worse sinners than everyone else in Galilee just because of what happened to them? [3]Not at all! But you can be sure that if you don't turn back to God, every one of you will also be killed. [4]What about those eighteen people who died when the tower in Siloam fell on them? Do you think they were worse than everyone else in Jerusalem? [5]Not at all! But you can be sure that if you don't turn back to God, every one of you will also die.

A Story about a Fig Tree

[6]Jesus then told them this story:

A man had a fig tree growing in his vineyard. One day he went out to pick some figs, but he didn't find any. [7]So he said to the gardener, "For three years I have come looking for figs on this tree, and I haven't found any yet. Chop it down! Why should it take up space?"

[8]The gardener answered, "Master, leave it for another year. I'll dig around it and put some manure on it to make it grow. [9]Maybe it will have figs on it next year. If it doesn't, you can have it cut down."

Healing a Woman on the Sabbath

[10]One Sabbath, Jesus was teaching in a Jewish meeting place, [11]and a woman was there who had been crippled by an evil spirit for eighteen years. She was completely bent over and could not straighten up. [12]When Jesus saw the woman, he called her over and said, "You are now well." [13]He placed his hands on her, and right away she stood up straight and praised God.

[14]The man in charge of the meeting place was angry because Jesus had healed someone on the Sabbath. So he said to the people, "Each week has six days when we can work. Come and be healed on one of those days, but not on the Sabbath."

[15]The Lord replied, "Are you trying to fool someone? Won't any one of you untie your ox or donkey and lead it out to drink on a Sabbath? [16]This woman belongs to the family of Abraham, but Satan has kept her bound for eighteen years. Isn't it right to set her free on the Sabbath?" [17]Jesus' words made his enemies ashamed. But everyone else in the crowd was happy about the wonderful things he was doing.

A Mustard Seed and Yeast
(Matthew 13.31-33; Mark 4.30-32)

[18]Jesus said, "What is God's kingdom like? What can I compare it with? [19]It is like what happens when someone plants a mustard seed in a garden. The seed grows as big as a tree, and birds nest in its branches."

[20]Then Jesus said, "What can I compare God's kingdom with? [21]It is like what happens when a woman mixes yeast into three batches of flour. Finally, all the dough rises."

The Narrow Door
(Matthew 7.13, 14, 21-23)

[22]As Jesus was on his way to Jerusalem, he taught the people in the towns and villages. [23]Someone asked him, "Lord, are only a few people going to be saved?"

Jesus answered:

[24]Do all you can to go in by the narrow door! A lot of people will try to get in, but will not be able to. [25]Once the owner of the house gets up and locks the door, you will be left standing outside. You will knock on the door and say, "Sir, open the door for us!"

But the owner will answer, "I don't know a thing about you!"

[26]Then you will start saying, "We dined with you, and you taught in our streets."

[27]But he will say, "I really don't know who you are! Get away from me, you evil people!"

[28]Then when you have been thrown outside, you will weep and grit your teeth because you will see Abraham, Isaac, Jacob, and all the prophets in God's kingdom. [29]People will come from all directions and sit down to feast in God's kingdom. [30]There the ones who are now least important will be the most important, and those who are now most important will be least important.

Jesus and Herod

[31]At that time some Pharisees came to Jesus and said, "You had better get away from here! Herod[k] wants to kill you."

[32]Jesus said to them:

Go tell that fox, "I am going to force out demons and heal people today and tomorrow, and three days later I'll be through." [33]But I am going on my way today and tomorrow and the next day. After all, Jerusalem is the place where prophets are killed.

---

[k]13.31 *Herod*: Herod Antipas, the son of Herod the Great.

Jesus Loves Jerusalem
(Matthew 23.37-39)

[34]Jerusalem, Jerusalem! Your people have killed the prophets and have stoned the messengers who were sent to you. I have often wanted to gather your people, as a hen gathers her chicks under her wings. But you wouldn't let me. [35]Now your temple will be deserted. You won't see me again until the time when you say,

"Blessed is the one who comes
in the name of the Lord."

Jesus Heals a Sick Man

14 One Sabbath, Jesus was having dinner in the home of an important Pharisee, and everyone was carefully watching Jesus. [2]All of a sudden a man with swollen legs stood up in front of him. [3]Jesus turned and asked the Pharisees and the teachers of the Law of Moses, "Is it right to heal on the Sabbath?" [4]But they did not say a word.

Jesus took hold of the man. Then he healed him and sent him away. [5]Afterwards, Jesus asked the people, "If your son or ox falls into a well, wouldn't you pull him out right away, even on the Sabbath?" [6]There was nothing they could say.

How To Be a Guest

[7]Jesus saw how the guests had tried to take the best seats. So he told them:

[8]When you are invited to a wedding feast, don't sit in the best place. Someone more important may have been invited. [9]Then the one who invited you will come and say, "Give your place to this other guest!" You will be embarrassed and will have to sit in the worst place.

[10]When you are invited to be a guest, go and sit in the worst place. Then the one who invited you may come and say, "My friend, take a better seat!" You will then be honored in front of all the other guests. [11]If you put yourself above others, you will be put down. But if you humble yourself, you will be honored.

[12]Then Jesus said to the man who had invited him:

When you give a dinner or a banquet, don't invite your friends and family and relatives and rich neighbors. If you do, they will invite you in return, and you will be paid back. [13]When you give a feast, invite the poor, the crippled, the lame, and the blind. [14]They cannot pay you back. But God will bless you and reward you when his people rise from death.

The Great Banquet
(Matthew 22.1-10)

[15]After Jesus had finished speaking, one of the guests said, "The greatest blessing of all is to be at the banquet in God's kingdom!"

[16]Jesus told him:

A man once gave a great banquet and invited a lot of guests. [17]When the banquet was ready, he sent a servant to tell the guests, "Everything is ready! Please come."

[18]One guest after another started making excuses. The first one said, "I bought some land, and I've got to look it over. Please excuse me."

[19]Another guest said, "I bought five teams of oxen, and I need to try them out. Please excuse me."

[20]Still another guest said, "I have just gotten married, and I can't be there."

[21]The servant told his master what happened, and the master became so angry that he said, "Go as fast as you can to every street and alley in town! Bring in everyone who is poor or crippled or blind or lame."

[22]When the servant returned, he said, "Master, I've done what you told me, and there is still plenty of room for more people."

[23]His master then told him, "Go out along the back roads and fence rows and make people come in, so that my house will be full. [24]Not one of the guests I first invited will get even a bite of my food!"

Being a Disciple
(Matthew 10.37, 38)

[25]Large crowds were walking along with Jesus, when he turned and said:

[26]You cannot be my disciple, unless

you love me more than you love your father and mother, your wife and children, and your brothers and sisters. You cannot come with me unless you love me more than you love your own life.

27You cannot be my disciple unless you carry your own cross and come with me.

28Suppose one of you wants to build a tower. What is the first thing you will do? Won't you sit down and figure out how much it will cost and if you have enough money to pay for it? 29Otherwise, you will start building the tower, but not be able to finish. Then everyone who sees what is happening will laugh at you. 30They will say, "You started building, but could not finish the job."

31What will a king do if he has only ten thousand soldiers to defend himself against a king who is about to attack him with twenty thousand soldiers? Before he goes out to battle, won't he first sit down and decide if he can win? 32If he thinks he won't be able to defend himself, he will send messengers and ask for peace while the other king is still a long way off. 33So then, you cannot be my disciple unless you give away everything you own.

Salt and Light
(Matthew 5.13; Mark 9.50)

34Salt is good, but if it no longer tastes like salt, how can it be made to taste salty again? 35It is no longer good for the soil or even for the manure pile. People simply throw it out. If you have ears, pay attention!

One Sheep
(Matthew 18.12-14)

15 Tax collectors[l] and sinners were all crowding around to listen to Jesus. 2So the Pharisees and the teachers of the Law of Moses started grumbling, "This man is friendly with sinners. He even eats with them."

3Then Jesus told them this story:

4If any of you has a hundred sheep, and one of them gets lost, what will you do? Won't you leave the ninety-nine in the field and go look for the lost sheep until you find it? 5And when you find it, you will be so glad that you will put it on your shoulder 6and carry it home. Then you will call in your friends and neighbors and say, "Let's celebrate! I've found my lost sheep."

7Jesus said, "In the same way there is more happiness in heaven because of one sinner who turns to God than over ninety-nine good people who don't need to."

One Coin

8Jesus told the people another story:

What will a woman do if she has ten silver coins and loses one of them? Won't she light a lamp, sweep the floor, and look carefully until she finds it? 9Then she will call in her friends and neighbors and say, "Let's celebrate! I've found the coin I lost."

10Jesus said, "In the same way God's angels are happy when even one person turns to him."

Two Sons

11Jesus also told them another story:

Once a man had two sons. 12The younger son said to his father, "Give me my share of the property." So the father divided his property between his two sons.

13Not long after that, the younger son packed up everything he owned and left for a foreign country, where he wasted all his money in wild living. 14He had spent everything, when a bad famine spread through that whole land. Soon he had nothing to eat.

15He went to work for a man in that country, and the man sent him out to take care of his pigs.[m] 16He would have been glad to eat what the pigs were eating,[n] but no one gave him a thing.

---

[l]15.1 *Tax collectors*: See the note at 3.12.
[m]15.15 *pigs*: The Jewish religion taught that pigs were not fit to eat or even to touch. A Jewish man would have felt terribly insulted if he had to feed pigs, much less eat with them. [n]15.16 *what the pigs were eating*: The Greek text has "(bean) pods," which came from a tree in Palestine. These were used to feed animals. Poor people sometimes ate them too.

¹⁷Finally, he came to his senses and said, "My father's workers have plenty to eat, and here I am, starving to death! ¹⁸I will go to my father and say to him, 'Father, I have sinned against God in heaven and against you. ¹⁹I am no longer good enough to be called your son. Treat me like one of your workers.'"

²⁰The younger son got up and started back to his father. But when he was still a long way off, his father saw him and felt sorry for him. He ran to his son and hugged and kissed him.

²¹The son said, "Father, I have sinned against God in heaven and against you. I am no longer good enough to be called your son."

²²But his father said to the servants, "Hurry and bring the best clothes and put them on him. Give him a ring for his finger and sandals° for his feet. ²³Get the best calf and prepare it, so we can eat and celebrate. ²⁴This son of mine was dead, but has now come back to life. He was lost and has now been found." And they began to celebrate.

²⁵The older son had been out in the field. But when he came near the house, he heard the music and dancing. ²⁶So he called one of the servants over and asked, "What's going on here?"

²⁷The servant answered, "Your brother has come home safe and sound, and your father ordered us to kill the best calf." ²⁸The older brother got so angry that he would not even go into the house.

His father came out and begged him to go in. ²⁹But he said to his father, "For years I have worked for you like a slave and have always obeyed you. But you have never even given me a little goat, so that I could give a dinner for my friends. ³⁰This other son of yours wasted your money on prostitutes. And now that he has come home, you ordered the best calf to be killed for a feast."

³¹His father replied, "My son, you are always with me, and everything I have is yours. ³²But we should be glad and celebrate! Your brother was dead, but he is now alive. He was lost and has now been found."

A Dishonest Manager

16 Jesus said to his disciples: A rich man once had a manager to take care of his

---

°**15.22** *ring . . . sandals:* These show that the young man's father fully accepted him as his son. A ring was a sign of high position in the family. Sandals showed that he was a son instead of a slave, since slaves did not usually wear sandals.

PARENTING&*family*—How can I nurture my child's self-worth?
(*Luke 15.11-32*)

Show your children unconditional love.
Human love usually comes with strings attached. Friends can be fickle, dates can lose interest, and popularity can evaporate overnight. A teacher's approval seems to be based on grades, and a coach's praise is tied to performance. No wonder a child who occasionally fails feels like a failure all the way through.

Your children—of whatever age—need to know that you love them no matter what. No matter what grades they get. No matter whether they make the team or not. No matter how badly they misbehave. No matter what stupid or immoral choices they make.

Too much to ask? You bet! On our own, we parents can never give that kind of love. But we're not on our own. We're on the receiving end of that very same unconditional love, flowing directly from our Father in heaven. So pass it on! (See also 1 Samuel 17.24-54; Psalm 139; Ephesians 1.3-14; 2 Thessalonians 3.6-15.)

Words To Remember: *The younger son got up and started back to his father. But when he was still a long way off, his father saw him and felt sorry for him. He ran to his son and hugged and kissed him.—Luke 15.20*

business. But he was told that his manager was wasting money. [2]So the rich man called him in and said, "What is this I hear about you? Tell me what you have done! You are no longer going to work for me."

[3]The manager said to himself, "What shall I do now that my master is going to fire me? I can't dig ditches, and I'm ashamed to beg. [4]I know what I'll do, so that people will welcome me into their homes after I've lost my job."

[5]Then one by one he called in the people who were in debt to his master. He asked the first one, "How much do you owe my master?"

[6]"A hundred barrels of olive oil," the man answered.

So the manager said, "Take your bill and sit down and quickly write 'fifty'."

[7]The manager asked someone else who was in debt to his master, "How much do you owe?"

"A thousand bushels[p] of wheat," the man replied.

The manager said, "Take your bill and write 'eight hundred'."

[8]The master praised his dishonest manager for looking out for himself so well. That's how it is! The people of this world look out for themselves better than the people who belong to the light.

[9]My disciples, I tell you to use wicked wealth to make friends for yourselves. Then when it is gone, you will be welcomed into an eternal home. [10]Anyone who can be trusted in little matters can also be trusted in important matters. But anyone who is dishonest in little matters will be dishonest in important matters. [11]If you cannot be trusted with this wicked wealth, who will trust you with true wealth? [12]And if you cannot be trusted with what belongs to someone else, who will give you something that will be your own? [13]You cannot be the slave of two masters. You will like one more than the other or be more loyal to one than to the other. You cannot serve God and money.

Some Sayings of Jesus

(Matthew 11.12, 13; 5.31, 32; Mark 10.11, 12)

[14]The Pharisees really loved money. So when they heard what Jesus said, they made fun of him. [15]But Jesus told them:

You are always making yourselves look good, but God sees what is in your heart. The things that most people think are important are worthless as far as God is concerned.

[16]Until the time of John the Baptist, people had to obey the Law of Moses and the Books of the Prophets.[q] But since God's kingdom has been preached, everyone is trying hard to get in. [17]Heaven and earth will disappear before the smallest letter of the Law does.

[18]It is a terrible sin[r] for a man to divorce his wife and marry another woman. It is also a terrible sin for a man to marry a divorced woman.

Lazarus and the Rich Man

[19]There was once a rich man who wore expensive clothes and every day ate the best food. [20]But a poor beggar named Lazarus was brought to the gate of the rich man's house. [21]He was happy just to eat the scraps that fell from the rich man's table. His body was covered with sores, and dogs kept coming up to lick them. [22]The poor man died, and angels took him to the place of honor next to Abraham.[s]

The rich man also died and was buried. [23]He went to hell[t] and was suffering terribly. When he looked up and saw Abraham far off and Lazarus at his side, [24]he said to Abraham, "Have pity on me! Send Lazarus to dip his finger in water and touch my tongue. I'm suffering terribly in this fire."

---

[p]**16.7** *A thousand bushels*: The Greek text has "A hundred measures," and each measure is about ten or twelve bushels. [q]**16.16** *the Law of Moses and the Books of the Prophets*: The Jewish Scriptures, that is, the Old Testament. [r]**16.18** *a terrible sin*: The Greek text uses a word that means the sin of being unfaithful in marriage. [s]**16.22** *the place of honor next to Abraham*: The Jewish people thought that heaven would be a banquet that God would give for them. Abraham would be the most important person there, and the guest of honor would sit next to him. [t]**16.23** *hell*: The Greek text has "hades," which the Jewish people often thought of as the place where the dead wait for the final judgment.

²⁵Abraham answered, "My friend, remember that while you lived, you had everything good, and Lazarus had everything bad. Now he is happy, and you are in pain. ²⁶And besides, there is a deep ditch between us, and no one from either side can cross over."

²⁷But the rich man said, "Abraham, then please send Lazarus to my father's home. ²⁸Let him warn my five brothers, so they won't come to this horrible place."

²⁹Abraham answered, "Your brothers can read what Moses and the prophets[u] wrote. They should pay attention to that."

³⁰Then the rich man said, "No, that's not enough! If only someone from the dead would go to them, they would listen and turn to God."

³¹So Abraham said, "If they won't pay attention to Moses and the prophets, they won't listen even to someone who comes back from the dead."

Faith and Service
(Matthew 18.6, 7, 21, 22; Mark 9.42)

17 Jesus said to his disciples:
There will always be something that causes people to sin. But anyone who causes them to sin is in for trouble. A person who causes even one of my little followers to sin ²would be better off thrown into the ocean with a heavy stone tied around their neck. ³So be careful what you do.

Forgiveness usually isn't a one-time experience. It's an ongoing process. You have to work at it.
ELISA MORGAN

Correct any followers[v] of mine who sin, and forgive the ones who say they are sorry. ⁴Even if one of them mistreats you seven times in one day and says, "I am sorry," you should still forgive that person.

⁵The apostles said to the Lord, "Make our faith stronger!"

⁶Jesus replied:
If you had faith no bigger than a tiny mustard seed, you could tell this mulberry tree to pull itself up, roots and all, and to plant itself in the ocean. And it would!

⁷If your servant comes in from plowing or from taking care of the sheep, would you say, "Welcome! Come on in and have something to eat"? ⁸No, you wouldn't say that. You would say, "Fix me something to eat. Get ready to serve me, so I can have my meal. Then later on you can eat and drink." ⁹Servants don't deserve special thanks for doing what they are supposed to do. ¹⁰And that's how it should be with you. When you've done all you should, then say, "We are merely servants, and we have simply done our duty."

Ten Men with Leprosy

¹¹On his way to Jerusalem, Jesus went along the border between Samaria and Galilee. ¹²As he was going into a village, ten men with leprosy[w] came toward him. They stood at a distance ¹³and shouted, "Jesus, Master, have pity on us!"

¹⁴Jesus looked at them and said, "Go show yourselves to the priests."[x]

On their way they were healed. ¹⁵When one of them discovered that he was healed, he came back, shouting praises to God. ¹⁶He bowed down at the feet of Jesus and thanked him. The man was from the country of Samaria.

¹⁷Jesus asked, "Weren't ten men healed? Where are the other nine? ¹⁸Why was this foreigner the only one who came back to thank God?" ¹⁹Then Jesus told the man, "You may get up and go. Your faith has made you well."

God's Kingdom
(Matthew 24.23-28, 37-41)

²⁰Some Pharisees asked Jesus when God's kingdom would come. He answered,

[u]**16.29** *Moses and the prophets*: The Jewish Scriptures, that is, the Old Testament.   [v]**17.3** *followers*: The Greek text has "brothers," which is often used in the New Testament for followers of Jesus.   [w]**17.12** *leprosy*: See the note at 4.27.   [x]**17.14** *show yourselves to the priests*: See the note at 5.14.

"God's kingdom isn't something you can see. [21]There is no use saying, 'Look! Here it is' or 'Look! There it is.' God's kingdom is here with you.'"[y]

[22]Jesus said to his disciples:

The time will come when you will long to see one of the days of the Son of Man, but you will not. [23]When people say to you, "Look there," or "Look here," don't go looking for him. [24]The day of the Son of Man will be like lightning flashing across the sky. [25]But first he must suffer terribly and be rejected by the people of today. [26]When the Son of Man comes, things will be just as they were when Noah lived. [27]People were eating, drinking, and getting married right up to the day when Noah went into the big boat. Then the flood came and drowned everyone on earth.

[28]When Lot[z] lived, people were also eating and drinking. They were buying, selling, planting, and building. [29]But on the very day Lot left Sodom, fiery flames poured down from the sky and killed everyone. [30]The same will happen on the day when the Son of Man appears.

[31]At that time no one on a rooftop[a] should go down into the house to get anything. No one in a field should go back to the house for anything. [32]Remember what happened to Lot's wife.[b]

[33]People who try to save their lives will lose them, and those who lose their lives will save them. [34]On that night two people will be sleeping in the same bed, but only one will be taken. The other will be left. [35-36]Two women will be together grinding wheat, but only one will be taken. The other will be left.[c]

[37]Then Jesus' disciples spoke up, "But where will this happen, Lord?"

Jesus said, "Where there is a corpse, there will always be buzzards."[d]

---

[y]**17.21** *here with you:* Or "in your hearts."
[z]**17.27,28** *Noah . . . Lot:* When God destroyed the earth by a flood, he saved Noah and his family. And when God destroyed the cities of Sodom and Gomorrah and the evil people who lived there, he rescued Lot and his family (see Genesis 19.1-29). [a]**17.31** *rooftop:* See the note at 5.19. [b]**17.32** *what happened to Lot's wife:* She turned into a block of salt when she disobeyed God (see Genesis 19.26). [c]**17.35,36** *will be left:* Some manuscripts add, "Two men will be in the same field, but only one will be taken. The other will be left." [d]**17.37** *Where there is a corpse, there will always be buzzards:* This saying may mean that when anything important happens, people soon know about it. Or the saying may mean that whenever something bad happens, curious people gather around and stare. But the word translated "buzzard" also means "eagle" and may refer to the Roman army, which had an eagle as its symbol.

---

*Spiritual*Life—Does prayer really make a difference? *(Luke 18.1-8)*

Prayer both demonstrates and strengthens our faith.

Many people who take a pass on writing their governmental representatives about key issues say they do so because writing "won't do any good, anyway." We don't want to waste our time when we're sure we won't get a response. Silence is, in effect, a vote of no confidence.

The widow in Jesus' story, however, felt confident that pleading her cause persistently would get her a hearing. And, Jesus pointed out, if an unjust judge responded to petitioning, how much more would our loving Father respond to us? Prayer is a vote of confidence in the relationship we have with God, a confidence that God listens and cares.

But prayer is much more than a one-sided affirmation of our faith. Prayer is communication with our heavenly Father. Just as ongoing communication between earthly parents and children strengthens their relationship, so daily prayer strengthens our relationship with God.

Jesus asked, "When the Son of Man comes, will he find on this earth anyone with faith?" (18.8). In other words, will he find praying people? What about you? (See also 2 Chronicles 20.1-30; Jeremiah 21.1-10; Matthew 7.7-12; 2 Corinthians 12.6-10.)

Words To Remember: *Won't God protect his chosen ones who pray to him day and night? Won't he be concerned for them? He will surely hurry and help them.*
—Luke 18.7,8

A Widow and a Judge

18 Jesus told his disciples a story about how they should keep on praying and never give up:
²In a town there was once a judge who didn't fear God or care about people. ³In that same town there was a widow who kept going to the judge and saying, "Make sure that I get fair treatment in court."

⁴For a while the judge refused to do anything. Finally, he said to himself, "Even though I don't fear God or care about people, ⁵I will help this widow because she keeps on bothering me. If I don't help her, she will wear me out."
⁶The Lord said:

Think about what that crooked judge said. ⁷Won't God protect his chosen ones who pray to him day and night? Won't he be concerned for them? ⁸He will surely hurry and help them. But when the Son of Man comes, will he find on this earth anyone with faith?

A Pharisee and a Tax Collector

⁹Jesus told a story to some people who thought they were better than others and who looked down on everyone else:
¹⁰Two men went into the temple to pray.ᵉ One was a Pharisee and the other a tax collector.ᶠ ¹¹The Pharisee stood over by himself and prayed,ᵍ "God, I thank you that I am not greedy, dishonest, and unfaithful in marriage like other people. And I am really glad that I am not like that tax collector over there. ¹²I go without eatingʰ for two days a week, and I give you one tenth of all I earn."

¹³The tax collector stood off at a distance and did not think he was good enough even to look up toward heaven. He was so sorry for what he had done that he pounded his chest and prayed, "God, have pity on me! I am such a sinner."

¹⁴Then Jesus said, "When the two men went home, it was the tax collector and not the Pharisee who was pleasing to God. If you put yourself above others, you will be put down. But if you humble yourself, you will be honored."

Jesus Blesses Little Children
(Matthew 19.13-15; Mark 10.13-16)

¹⁵Some people brought their little children for Jesus to bless. But when his disciples saw them doing this, they told the people to stop bothering him. ¹⁶So Jesus called the children over to him and said, "Let the children come to me! Don't try to stop them. People who are like these children belong to God's kingdom.ⁱ ¹⁷You will never get into God's kingdom unless you enter it like a child!"

A Rich and Important Man
(Matthew 19.16-30; Mark 10.17-31)

¹⁸An important man asked Jesus, "Good Teacher, what must I do to have eternal life?"
¹⁹Jesus said, "Why do you call me good? Only God is good. ²⁰You know the commandments: 'Be faithful in marriage. Do not murder. Do not steal. Do not tell lies about others. Respect your father and mother.' "
²¹He told Jesus, "I have obeyed all these commandments since I was a young man."
²²When Jesus heard this, he said, "There is one thing you still need to do. Go and sell everything you own! Give the money to the poor, and you will have riches in heaven. Then come and be my follower." ²³When the man heard this, he was sad, because he was very rich.
²⁴Jesus saw how sad the man was. So he said, "It's terribly hard for rich people to get into God's kingdom! ²⁵In fact, it's easier for a camel to go through the eye of a needle than for a rich person to get into God's kingdom."
²⁶When the crowd heard this, they asked, "How can anyone ever be saved?"
²⁷Jesus replied, "There are some things that people cannot do, but God can do anything."
²⁸Peter said, "Remember, we left everything to be your followers!"
²⁹Jesus answered, "You can be sure that anyone who gives up home or wife or brothers

---

ᵉ**18.10** *into the temple to pray:* Jewish people usually prayed there early in the morning and late in the afternoon.   ᶠ**18.10** *tax collector:* See the note at 3.12.
ᵍ**18.11** *stood over by himself and prayed:* Some manuscripts have "stood up and prayed to himself."
ʰ**18.12** *without eating:* See the note at 2.37.
ⁱ**18.16** *People who are like these children belong to God's kingdom:* Or "God's kingdom belongs to people who are like these children."

or family or children because of God's kingdom [30]will be given much more in this life. And in the future world they will have eternal life."

Jesus Again Tells about His Death
(Matthew 20.17-19; Mark 10.32-34)

[31]Jesus took the twelve apostles aside and said:

We are now on our way to Jerusalem. Everything that the prophets wrote about the Son of Man will happen there. [32]He will be handed over to foreigners,[j] who will make fun of him, mistreat him, and spit on him. [33]They will beat him and kill him, but three days later he will rise to life.

[34]The apostles did not understand what Jesus was talking about. They could not understand, because the meaning of what he said was hidden from them.

Jesus Heals a Blind Beggar
(Matthew 20.29-34; Mark 10.46-52)

[35]When Jesus was coming close to Jericho, a blind man sat begging beside the road. [36]The man heard the crowd walking by and asked what was happening. [37]Some people told him that Jesus from Nazareth was passing by. [38]So the blind man shouted, "Jesus, Son of David,[k] have pity on me!" [39]The people who were going along with Jesus told the man to be quiet. But he shouted even louder, "Son of David, have pity on me!"

[40]Jesus stopped and told some people to bring the blind man over to him. When the blind man was getting near, Jesus asked, [41]"What do you want me to do for you?"

"Lord, I want to see!" he answered.

[42]Jesus replied, "Look and you will see! Your eyes are healed because of your faith." [43]Right away the man could see, and he went with Jesus and started thanking God. When the crowds saw what happened, they praised God.

Zacchaeus

19 Jesus was going through Jericho, [2]where a man named Zacchaeus lived. He was in charge of collecting taxes[l] and was very rich. [3-4]Jesus was heading his way, and Zacchaeus wanted to see what he was like. But Zacchaeus was a short man and could not see over the crowd. So he ran ahead and climbed up into a sycamore tree.

[5]When Jesus got there, he looked up and said, "Zacchaeus, hurry down! I want to stay with you today." [6]Zacchaeus hurried down and gladly welcomed Jesus.

[7]Everyone who saw this started grumbling, "This man Zacchaeus is a sinner! And Jesus is going home to eat with him."

[8]Later that day Zacchaeus stood up and said to the Lord, "I will give half of my

---

[j]18.32 foreigners: The Romans, who ruled Judea at this time. [k]18.38 Son of David: The Jewish people expected the Messiah to be from the family of King David, and for this reason the Messiah was often called the "Son of David." [l]19.2 in charge of collecting taxes: See the note at 3.12.

Personal Concerns—What can I do when I've hurt someone? (Luke 19.1-10)

Be willing to go the extra mile to make amends.

In the story of Zacchaeus, we see what repentance is really all about. Zacchaeus not only undid the damage he inflicted, but repaid four times over the people he'd wronged.

People who've been wronged aren't always quick to accept an apology. Taxpayers probably slammed the door in Zacchaeus's face the first time he came by with a refund, and the person you've hurt may try to shut you out, too. But ultimately it's hard to doubt the sincerity of someone willing to back up her words with the kind of action Zacchaeus took. If you're willing to more than make up for the wrong you've done, the other person will eventually be willing to let the wound heal.

How do you get the courage and persistence to make amends? The same way Zacchaeus did: by knowing that Jesus has come to stay with you. (See also Psalm 51; Luke 22.54-62.)

Words To Remember: Later that day Zacchaeus stood up and said to the Lord, "I will give half of my property to the poor. And I will now pay back four times as much to everyone I have ever cheated."—Luke 19.8

property to the poor. And I will now pay back four times as much[m] to everyone I have ever cheated."

[9]Jesus said to Zacchaeus, "Today you and your family have been saved,[n] because you are a true son of Abraham.[o] [10]The Son of Man came to look for and to save people who are lost."

A Story about Ten Servants
(Matthew 25.14-30)

[11]The crowd was still listening to Jesus as he was getting close to Jerusalem. Many of them thought that God's kingdom would soon appear, [12]and Jesus told them this story:

A prince once went to a foreign country to be crowned king and then to return. [13]But before leaving, he called in ten servants and gave each of them some money. He told them, "Use this to earn more money until I get back."

[14]But the people of his country hated him, and they sent messengers to the foreign country to say, "We don't want this man to be our king."

[15]After the prince had been made king, he returned and called in his servants. He asked them how much they had earned with the money they had been given.

[16]The first servant came and said, "Sir, with the money you gave me I have earned ten times as much."

[17]"That's fine, my good servant!" the king said. "Since you have shown that you can be trusted with a small amount, you will be given ten cities to rule."

[18]The second one came and said, "Sir, with the money you gave me, I have earned five times as much."

[19]The king said, "You will be given five cities."

[20]Another servant came and said, "Sir, here is your money. I kept it safe in a handkerchief. [21]You are a hard man, and I was afraid of you. You take what isn't yours, and you harvest crops you didn't plant."

[22]"You worthless servant!" the king told him. "You have condemned yourself by what you have just said. You knew that I am a hard man, taking what isn't mine and harvesting what I've not planted. [23]Why didn't you put my money in the bank? On my return, I could have had the money together with interest."

[24]Then he said to some other servants standing there, "Take the money away from him and give it to the servant who earned ten times as much."

[25]But they said, "Sir, he already has ten times as much!"

[26]The king replied, "Those who have something will be given more. But everything will be taken away from those who don't have anything. [27]Now bring me the enemies who didn't want me to be their king. Kill them while I watch!"

Jesus Enters Jerusalem
(Matthew 21.1-11; Mark 11.1-11; John 12.12-19)

[28]When Jesus had finished saying all this, he went on toward Jerusalem. [29]As he was getting near Bethphage and Bethany on the Mount of Olives, he sent two of his disciples on ahead. [30]He told them, "Go into the next village, where you will find a young donkey that has never been ridden. Untie the donkey and bring it here. [31]If anyone asks why you are doing that, just say, 'The Lord[p] needs it.'"

[32]They went off and found everything just as Jesus had said. [33]While they were untying the donkey, its owners asked, "Why are you doing that?"

[34]They answered, "The Lord[p] needs it."

[35]Then they led the donkey to Jesus. They put some of their clothes on its back and helped Jesus get on. [36]And as he rode along, the people spread clothes on the road[q] in front of him. [37]When Jesus was starting down the Mount of Olives, his large crowd of disciples were happy and praised God because of all the miracles they had seen. [38]They shouted,

---

[m]**19.8** *pay back four times as much:* Both Jewish and Roman law said that a person must pay back four times the amount that was taken.   [n]**19.9** *saved:* Zacchaeus was Jewish, but it is only now that he is rescued from sin and placed under God's care.   [o]**19.9** *son of Abraham:* As used in this verse, the words mean that Zacchaeus is truly one of God's special people. [p]**19.31,34** *The Lord:* Or "The master of the donkey." [q]**19.36** *spread clothes on the road:* This was one way that the Jewish people welcomed a famous person.

"Blessed is the king who comes
  in the name of the Lord!
Peace in heaven
  and glory to God."

³⁹Some Pharisees in the crowd said to
Jesus, "Teacher, make your disciples stop
shouting!"
⁴⁰But Jesus answered, "If they keep
quiet, these stones will start shouting."
⁴¹When Jesus came closer and could see
Jerusalem, he cried ⁴²and said:
    It is too bad that today your people
don't know what will bring them
peace! Now it is hidden from them.
⁴³Jerusalem, the time will come when
your enemies will build walls around
you to attack you. Armies will surround you and close in on you from
every side. ⁴⁴They will level you to the
ground and kill your people. Not one
stone in your buildings will be left on
top of another. This will happen because you did not see that God had
come to save you.ᵗ

Jesus in the Temple
(Matthew 21.12-17; Mark 11.15-19; John 2.13-22)

⁴⁵When Jesus entered the temple, he
started chasing out the people who were
selling things. ⁴⁶He told them, "The Scriptures say, 'My house should be a place of
worship.' But you have made it a place
where robbers hide!"
⁴⁷Each day, Jesus kept on teaching in the
temple. So the chief priests, the teachers of
the Law of Moses, and some other impor-
tant people tried to have him killed. ⁴⁸But
they could not find a way to do it, because
everyone else was eager to listen to him.

A Question about Jesus' Authority
(Matthew 21.23-27; Mark 11.27-33)

20 One day, Jesus was teaching in
the temple and telling the good
news. So the chief priests, the
teachers, and the nation's leaders ²asked
him, "What right do you have to do these
things? Who gave you this authority?"
³Jesus replied, "I want to ask you a ques-
tion. ⁴Who gave John the right to baptize?
Was it God in heaven or merely some hu-
man being?"
⁵They talked this over and said to each
other, "We can't say that God gave John this

right. Jesus will ask us why we didn't believe
John. ⁶And we can't say that it was merely
some human who gave John the right to
baptize. The crowd will stone us to death,
because they think John was a prophet."
⁷So they told Jesus, "We don't know who
gave John the right to baptize."
⁸Jesus replied, "Then I won't tell you
who gave me the right to do what I do."

Renters of a Vineyard
(Matthew 21.33-46; Mark 12.1-12)

⁹Jesus told the people this story:
    A man once planted a vineyard and
rented it out. Then he left the country
for a long time. ¹⁰When it was time to
harvest the crop, he sent a servant to
ask the renters for his share of the
grapes. But they beat up the servant
and sent him away without anything.
¹¹So the owner sent another servant.
The renters also beat him up. They insulted him terribly and sent him away
without a thing. ¹²The owner sent a
third servant. He was also beaten terribly and thrown out of the vineyard.
¹³The owner then said to himself,
"What am I going to do? I know what.
I'll send my son, the one I love so
much. They will surely respect him!"
¹⁴When the renters saw the
owner's son, they said to one another,
"Someday he will own the vineyard.
Let's kill him! Then we can have it all
for ourselves." ¹⁵So they threw him out
of the vineyard and killed him.
Jesus asked, "What do you think the
owner of the vineyard will do? ¹⁶I'll tell you
what. He will come and kill those renters
and let someone else have his vineyard."
When the people heard this, they said,
"This must never happen!"
¹⁷But Jesus looked straight at them and
said, "Then what do the Scriptures mean
when they say, 'The stone that the builders
tossed aside is now the most important
stone of all'? ¹⁸Anyone who stumbles over
this stone will get hurt, and anyone it falls
on will be smashed to pieces."
¹⁹The chief priests and the teachers of

ᵗ**19.44** *that God had come to save you:* The Jewish people
looked for the time when God would come and rescue
them from their enemies. But when Jesus came, many
of them refused to obey him.

the Law of Moses knew that Jesus was talking about them when he was telling this story. They wanted to arrest him right then, but they were afraid of the people.

Paying Taxes
(Matthew 22.15-22; Mark 12.13-17)

²⁰Jesus' enemies kept watching him closely, because they wanted to hand him over to the Roman governor. So they sent some men who pretended to be good. But they were really spies trying to catch Jesus saying something wrong. ²¹The spies said to him, "Teacher, we know that you teach the truth about what God wants people to do. And you treat everyone with the same respect, no matter who they are. ²²Tell us, should we pay taxes to the Emperor or not?"

²³Jesus knew that they were trying to trick him. So he told them, ²⁴"Show me a coin." Then he asked, "Whose picture and name are on it?"

"The Emperor's," they answered.

²⁵Then he told them, "Give the Emperor what belongs to him and give God what belongs to God." ²⁶Jesus' enemies could not catch him saying anything wrong there in front of the people. They were amazed at his answer and kept quiet.

Life in the Future World
(Matthew 22.23-33; Mark 12.18-27)

²⁷The Sadducees did not believe that people would rise to life after death. So some of them came to Jesus ²⁸and said:

Teacher, Moses wrote that if a married man dies and has no children, his brother should marry the widow. Their first son would then be thought of as the son of the dead brother. ²⁹There were once seven brothers. The first one married, but died without having any children. ³⁰The second one married his brother's widow, and he also died without having any children. ³¹The same thing happened to the third one. Finally, all seven brothers married that woman and died without having any children. ³²At last the woman died. ³³When God raises people from death, whose wife will this woman be? All seven brothers had married her.

³⁴Jesus answered:

The people in this world get mar-

ried. ³⁵But in the future world no one who is worthy to rise from death will either marry ³⁶or die. They will be like the angels and will be God's children, because they have been raised to life.

³⁷In the story about the burning bush, Moses clearly shows that people will live again. He said, "The Lord is the God worshiped by Abraham, Isaac, and Jacob."ˢ ³⁸So the Lord isn't the God of the dead, but of the living. This means that everyone is alive as far as God is concerned.

³⁹Some of the teachers of the Law of Moses said, "Teacher, you have given a good answer!" ⁴⁰From then on, no one dared to ask Jesus any questions.

About David's Son
(Matthew 22.41-46; Mark 12.35-37)

⁴¹Jesus asked, "Why do people say that the Messiah will be the son of King David?ᵗ ⁴²In the book of Psalms, David himself says,

'The Lord said to my Lord,
  Sit at my right sideᵘ
⁴³ until I make your enemies
  into a footstool for you.'

⁴⁴David spoke of the Messiah as his Lord, so how can the Messiah be his son?"

Jesus and the Teachers of the Law of Moses
(Matthew 23.1-36; Mark 12.38-40; Luke 11.37-54)

⁴⁵While everyone was listening to Jesus, he said to his disciples:

⁴⁶Guard against the teachers of the Law of Moses! They love to walk around in long robes, and they like to be greeted in the market. They want the front seats in the meeting places and the best seats at banquets. ⁴⁷But they cheat widows out of their homes and then pray long prayers just to show off. These teachers will be punished most of all.

ˢ**20.37** *"The Lord is the God worshiped by Abraham, Isaac, and Jacob"*: Jesus argues that if God is worshiped by these three, they must be alive, because he is the God of the living. ᵗ**20.41** *the son of King David*: See the note at 18.38. ᵘ**20.42** *right side*: The place of power and honor.

A Widow's Offering
(Mark 12.41-44)

21 Jesus looked up and saw some rich people tossing their gifts into the offering box. ²He also saw a poor widow putting in two pennies. ³And he said, "I tell you that this poor woman has put in more than all the others. ⁴Everyone else gave what they didn't need. But she is very poor and gave everything she had."

Believe God and give thanks to him for all things.

MICHELE HALSEIDE

The Temple Will Be Destroyed
(Matthew 24.1, 2; Mark 13.1, 2)

⁵Some people were talking about the beautiful stones used to build the temple and about the gifts that had been placed in it. Jesus said, ⁶"Do you see these stones? The time is coming when not one of them will be left in place. They will all be knocked down."

Warning about Trouble
(Matthew 24.3-14; Mark 13.3-13)

⁷Some people asked, "Teacher, when will all this happen? How can we know when these things are about to take place?"

⁸Jesus replied:

Don't be fooled by those who will come and claim to be me. They will say, "I am Christ!" and "Now is the time!" But don't follow them. ⁹When you hear about wars and riots, don't be afraid. These things will have to happen first, but that isn't the end. ¹⁰Nations will go to war against one another, and kingdoms will attack each other. ¹¹There will be great earthquakes, and in many places people will starve to death and suffer terrible diseases. All sorts of frightening things will be seen in the sky.

¹²Before all this happens, you will be arrested and punished. You will be tried in your meeting places and put in jail. Because of me you will be placed on trial before kings and governors. ¹³But this will be your chance to tell about your faith.

¹⁴Don't worry about what you will say to defend yourselves. ¹⁵I will give you the wisdom to know what to say. None of your enemies will be able to oppose you or to say that you are wrong. ¹⁶You will be betrayed by your own parents, brothers, family, and friends. Some of you will even be killed. ¹⁷Because of me, you will be hated by everyone. ¹⁸But don't worry!ᵛ ¹⁹You will be saved by being faithful to me.

Jerusalem Will Be Destroyed
(Matthew 24.15-21; Mark 13.14-19)

²⁰When you see Jerusalem surrounded by soldiers, you will know that it will soon be destroyed. ²¹If you are living in Judea at that time, run to the mountains. If you are in the city, leave it. And if you are out in the country, don't go back into the city. ²²This time of punishment is what is written about in the Scriptures. ²³It will be an awful time for women who are expecting babies or nursing young children! Everywhere in the land people will suffer horribly and be punished. ²⁴Some of them will be killed by swords. Others will be carried off to foreign countries. Jerusalem will be overrun by foreign nations until their time comes to an end.

When the Son of Man Appears
(Matthew 24.29-31; Mark 13.24-27)

²⁵Strange things will happen to the sun, moon, and stars. The nations on earth will be afraid of the roaring sea and tides, and they won't know what to do. ²⁶People will be so frightened that they will faint because of what is happening to the world. Every power in the sky will be shaken.ʷ ²⁷Then the

---

ᵛ**21.18** *But don't worry:* The Greek text has "Not a hair of your head will be lost," which means, "There's no need to worry." ʷ**21.26** *Every power in the sky will be shaken:* In ancient times people thought that the stars were spiritual powers.

Son of Man will be seen, coming in a cloud with great power and glory. [28]When all of this starts happening, stand up straight and be brave. You will soon be set free.

A Lesson from a Fig Tree
(Matthew 24.32-35; Mark 13.28-31)

[29]Then Jesus told them a story:

When you see a fig tree or any other tree [30]putting out leaves, you know that summer will soon come. [31]So, when you see these things happening, you know that God's kingdom will soon be here. [32]You can be sure that some of the people of this generation will still be alive when all of this takes place. [33]The sky and the earth won't last forever, but my words will.

A Warning

[34]Don't spend all of your time thinking about eating or drinking or worrying about life. If you do, the final day will suddenly catch you [35]like a trap. That day will surprise everyone on earth. [36]Watch out and keep praying that you can escape all that is going to happen and that the Son of Man will be pleased with you.

[37]Jesus taught in the temple each day, and he spent each night on the Mount of Olives. [38]Everyone got up early and came to the temple to hear him teach.

A Plot To Kill Jesus
(Matthew 26.1-5, 14, 16; Mark 14.1, 2, 10, 11; John 11.45-53)

22 The Festival of Thin Bread, also called Passover, was near. [2]The chief priests and the teachers of the Law of Moses were looking for a way to get rid of Jesus, because they were afraid of what the people might do. [3]Then Satan entered the heart of Judas Iscariot,[x] who was one of the twelve apostles.

[4]Judas went to talk with the chief priests and the officers of the temple police about how he could help them arrest Jesus. [5]They were very pleased and offered to pay Judas some money. [6]He agreed and started looking for a good chance to betray Jesus when the crowds were not around.

Jesus Eats with His Disciples
(Matthew 26.17-25; Mark 14.12-21; John 13.21-30)

[7]The day had come for the Festival of Thin Bread, and it was time to kill the Passover lambs. [8]So Jesus said to Peter and John, "Go and prepare the Passover meal for us to eat."

[9]But they asked, "Where do you want us to prepare it?"

[10]Jesus told them, "As you go into the city, you will meet a man carrying a jar of water.[y] Follow him into the house [11]and say to the owner, 'Our teacher wants to know where he can eat the Passover meal with his disciples.' [12]The owner will take you upstairs and show you a large room ready for you to use. Prepare the meal there."

[13]Peter and John left. They found everything just as Jesus had told them, and they prepared the Passover meal.

The Lord's Supper
(Matthew 26.26-30; Mark 14.22-26; 1 Corinthians 11.23-25)

[14]When the time came for Jesus and the apostles to eat, [15]he said to them, "I have very much wanted to eat this Passover meal with you before I suffer. [16]I tell you that I will not eat another Passover meal until it is finally eaten in God's kingdom."

[17]Jesus took a cup of wine in his hands and gave thanks to God. Then he told the apostles, "Take this wine and share it with each other. [18]I tell you that I will not drink any more wine until God's kingdom comes."

[19]Jesus took some bread in his hands and gave thanks for it. He broke the bread and handed it to his apostles. Then he said, "This is my body, which is given for you. Eat this as a way of remembering me!"

[20]After the meal he took another cup of wine in his hands. Then he said, "This is my blood. It is poured out for you, and with it God makes his new agreement. [21]The one who will betray me is here at the table with me! [22]The Son of Man will die in the way that has been decided for him, but it will be terrible for the one who betrays him!"

[23]Then the apostles started arguing about who would ever do such a thing.

[x]22.3 Iscariot: See the note at 6.16. [y]22.10 a man carrying a jar of water: A male slave carrying water would probably mean that the family was rich.

An Argument about Greatness

²⁴The apostles got into an argument about which one of them was the greatest. ²⁵So Jesus told them:

Foreign kings order their people around, and powerful rulers call themselves everyone's friends.ᶻ ²⁶But don't be like them. The most important one of you should be like the least important, and your leader should be like a servant. ²⁷Who do people think is the greatest, a person who is served or one who serves? Isn't it the one who is served? But I have been with you as a servant.

²⁸You have stayed with me in all my troubles. ²⁹So I will give you the right to rule as kings, just as my Father has given me the right to rule as a king. ³⁰You will eat and drink with me in my kingdom, and you will each sit on a throne to judge the twelve tribes of Israel.

Jesus' Disciples Will Be Tested

(Matthew 26.31-35; Mark 14.27-31; John 13.36-38)

³¹Jesus said, "Simon, listen to me! Satan has demanded the right to test each one of you, as a farmer does when he separates wheat from the husks.ᵃ ³²But Simon, I have prayed that your faith will be strong. And when you have come back to me, help the others."

³³Peter said, "Lord, I am ready to go with you to jail and even to die with you."

³⁴Jesus replied, "Peter, I tell you that before a rooster crows tomorrow morning, you will say three times that you don't know me."

Moneybags, Traveling Bags, and Swords

³⁵Jesus asked his disciples, "When I sent you out without a moneybag or a traveling bag or sandals, did you need anything?"

"No!" they answered.

³⁶Jesus told them, "But now, if you have a moneybag, take it with you. Also take a traveling bag, and if you don't have a sword,ᵇ sell some of your clothes and buy one. ³⁷Do this because the Scriptures say, 'He was considered a criminal.' This was written about me, and it will soon come true."

³⁸The disciples said, "Lord, here are two swords!"

"Enough of that!" Jesus replied.

Jesus Prays

(Matthew 26.36-46; Mark 14.32-42)

³⁹Jesus went out to the Mount of Olives, as he often did, and his disciples went with him. ⁴⁰When they got there, he told them, "Pray that you won't be tested."

⁴¹Jesus walked on a little way before he knelt down and prayed, ⁴²"Father, if you will, please don't make me suffer by having me drink from this cup.ᶜ But do what you want, and not what I want."

⁴³Then an angel from heaven came to help him. ⁴⁴Jesus was in great pain and prayed so sincerely that his sweat fell to the ground like drops of blood.ᵈ

⁴⁵Jesus got up from praying and went over to his disciples. They were asleep and worn out from being so sad. ⁴⁶He said to them, "Why are you asleep? Wake up and pray that you won't be tested."

Jesus Is Arrested

(Matthew 26.47-56; Mark 14.43-50; John 18.3-11)

⁴⁷While Jesus was still speaking, a crowd came up. It was led by Judas, one of the twelve apostles. He went over to Jesus and greeted him with a kiss.ᵉ

⁴⁸Jesus asked Judas, "Are you betraying the Son of Man with a kiss?"

⁴⁹When Jesus' disciples saw what was about to happen, they asked, "Lord, should we attack them with a sword?" ⁵⁰One of the disciples even struck at the high priest's servant with his sword and cut off the servant's right ear.

⁵¹"Enough of that!" Jesus said. Then he touched the servant's ear and healed it.

⁵²Jesus spoke to the chief priests, the

ᶻ**22.25** *everyone's friends:* This translates a Greek word that rulers sometimes used as a title for themselves or for special friends.　ᵃ**22.31** *separates wheat from the husks:* See the note at 3.17.　ᵇ**22.36** *moneybag . . . traveling bag . . . sword:* These were things that someone would take on a dangerous journey. Jesus was telling his disciples to be ready for anything that might happen. They seem to have understood what he meant (see 22.49-51).　ᶜ**22.42** *having me drink from this cup:* In the Scriptures "to drink from a cup" sometimes means to suffer.　ᵈ**22.43,44** *Then an angel . . . like drops of blood:* Verses 43, 44 are not in some manuscripts.　ᵉ**22.47** *greeted him with a kiss:* It was the custom for people to greet each other with a kiss on the cheek.

temple police, and the leaders who had come to arrest him. He said, "Why do you come out with swords and clubs and treat me like a criminal? 53I was with you every day in the temple, and you didn't arrest me. But this is your time, and darkness[f] is in control."

Peter Says He Doesn't Know Jesus
(Matthew 26.57, 58, 67-75; Mark 14.53, 54, 66-72; John 18.12-18, 25-27)

54Jesus was arrested and led away to the house of the high priest, while Peter followed at a distance. 55Some people built a fire in the middle of the courtyard and were sitting around it. Peter sat there with them, 56and a servant girl saw him. Then after she had looked at him carefully, she said, "This man was with Jesus!"

57Peter said, "Woman, I don't even know that man!"

58A little later someone else saw Peter and said, "You are one of them!"

"No, I'm not!" Peter replied.

59About an hour later another man insisted, "This man must have been with Jesus. They both come from Galilee."

60Peter replied, "I don't know what you are talking about!" Right then, while Peter was still speaking, a rooster crowed. 61The Lord turned and looked at Peter. And Peter remembered that the Lord had said, "Before a rooster crows tomorrow morning, you will say three times that you don't know me." 62Then Peter went out and cried hard.

63The men who were guarding Jesus made fun of him and beat him. 64They put a blindfold on him and said, "Tell us who struck you!" 65They kept on insulting Jesus in many other ways.

Jesus Is Questioned by the Council
(Matthew 26.59-66; Mark 14.55-64; John 18.19-24)

66At daybreak the nation's leaders, the chief priests, and the teachers of the Law of Moses got together and brought Jesus before their council. 67They said, "Tell us! Are you the Messiah?"

Jesus replied, "If I said so, you wouldn't believe me. 68And if I asked you a question, you wouldn't answer. 69But from now on, the Son of Man will be seated at the right side of God All-Powerful."

70Then they asked, "Are you the Son of God?"[g]

Jesus answered, "You say I am!"[h]

71They replied, "Why do we need more witnesses? He said it himself!"

---

[f]22.53 *darkness*: Darkness stands for the power of the devil. [g]22.70 *Son of God*: This was one of the titles used for the kings of Israel. [h]22.70 *You say I am*: Or "That's what you say."

Personal *Concerns*—What can I do when I've hurt someone? *(Luke 22.54-62)*

Let the other person see your genuine sorrow.
The account of Peter's denial of Jesus is one of the most poignant in the Bible. But imagine how different the story would be if Peter, instead of breaking down in remorse, had gotten defensive. Suppose, instead of weeping, he had blustered, "What are you looking at me like that for? Anybody else would have done the same thing. And besides, I didn't really mean it."

Some of us have difficulty admitting when we're wrong. If we feel wretched over what we've done, we cover it up; we don't want to make ourselves vulnerable, especially to someone who might be out for revenge. But self-protection won't heal the hurts we cause, and defensiveness only puts up more walls.

If you're truly sick at heart over hurting someone, let the person see your grief. You will have taken the first step to restoring a healthy relationship. (See also Psalm 51; Luke 19.1-10.)

Words To Remember: *Peter remembered that the Lord had said, "Before a rooster crows tomorrow morning, you will say three times that you don't know me." Then Peter went out and cried hard.*—Luke 22.61,62

Pilate Questions Jesus

(Matthew 27.1, 2, 11-14; Mark 15.1-5; John 18.28-38)

23 Everyone in the council got up and led Jesus off to Pilate. ²They started accusing him and said, "We caught this man trying to get our people to riot and to stop paying taxes to the Emperor. He also claims that he is the Messiah, our king."

³Pilate asked Jesus, "Are you the king of the Jews?"

"Those are your words," Jesus answered.

⁴Pilate told the chief priests and the crowd, "I don't find him guilty of anything."

⁵But they all kept on saying, "He has been teaching and causing trouble all over Judea. He started in Galilee and has now come all the way here."

Jesus Is Brought before Herod

⁶When Pilate heard this, he asked, "Is this man from Galilee?" ⁷After Pilate learned that Jesus came from the region ruled by Herod,ⁱ he sent him to Herod, who was in Jerusalem at that time.

⁸For a long time Herod had wanted to see Jesus and was very happy because he finally had this chance. He had heard many things about Jesus and hoped to see him work a miracle.

⁹Herod asked him a lot of questions, but Jesus did not answer. ¹⁰Then the chief priests and the teachers of the Law of Moses stood up and accused him of all kinds of bad things.

¹¹Herod and his soldiers made fun of Jesus and insulted him. They put a fine robe on him and sent him back to Pilate. ¹²That same day Herod and Pilate became friends, even though they had been enemies before this.

The Death Sentence

(Matthew 27.15-26; Mark 15.6-15; John 18.39—19.16)

¹³Pilate called together the chief priests, the leaders, and the people. ¹⁴He told them, "You brought Jesus to me and said he was a troublemaker. But I have questioned him here in front of you, and I have not found him guilty of anything that you say he has done. ¹⁵Herod didn't find him guilty either and sent him back. This man doesn't de-serve to be put to death! ¹⁶⁻¹⁷I will just have him beaten with a whip and set free."ʲ

¹⁸But the whole crowd shouted, "Kill Jesus! Give us Barabbas!" ¹⁹Now Barabbas was in jail because he had started a riot in the city and had murdered someone.

²⁰Pilate wanted to set Jesus free, so he spoke again to the crowds. ²¹But they kept shouting, "Nail him to a cross! Nail him to a cross!"

²²Pilate spoke to them a third time, "But what crime has he done? I have not found him guilty of anything for which he should be put to death. I will have him beaten with a whip and set free."

²³The people kept on shouting as loud as they could for Jesus to be put to death. ²⁴Finally, Pilate gave in. ²⁵He freed the man who was in jail for rioting and murder, because he was the one the crowd wanted to be set free. Then Pilate handed Jesus over for them to do what they wanted with him.

Jesus Is Nailed to a Cross

(Matthew 27.31-44; Mark 15.21-32; John 19.17-27)

²⁶As Jesus was being led away, some soldiers grabbed hold of a man from Cyrene named Simon. He was coming in from the fields, but they put the cross on him and made him carry it behind Jesus.

²⁷A large crowd was following Jesus, and in the crowd a lot of women were crying and weeping for him. ²⁸Jesus turned to the women and said:

Women of Jerusalem, don't cry for me! Cry for yourselves and for your children. ²⁹Someday people will say, "Women who never had children are really fortunate!" ³⁰At that time everyone will say to the mountains, "Fall on us!" They will say to the hills, "Hide us!" ³¹If this can happen when the wood is green, what do you think will happen when it is dry?ᵏ

³²Two criminals were led out to be put to death with Jesus. ³³When the soldiers came

---

ⁱ**23.7** *Herod:* Herod Antipas, the son of Herod the Great.   ʲ**23.16,17** *set free:* Some manuscripts add, "Pilate said this, because at every Passover he was supposed to set one prisoner free for the Jewish people."   ᵏ**23.31** *If this can happen when the wood is green, what do you think will happen when it is dry:* This saying probably means, "If this can happen to an innocent person, what do you think will happen to one who is guilty?"

to the place called "The Skull,"[l] they nailed Jesus to a cross. They also nailed the two criminals to crosses, one on each side of Jesus.

[34-35]Jesus said, "Father, forgive these people! They don't know what they're doing."[m]

While the crowd stood there watching Jesus, the soldiers gambled for his clothes. The leaders insulted him by saying, "He saved others. Now he should save himself, if he really is God's chosen Messiah!"

[36]The soldiers made fun of Jesus and brought him some wine. [37]They said, "If you are the king of the Jews, save yourself!"

[38]Above him was a sign that said, "This is the King of the Jews."

Love God enough to recognize your value in his eyes.

KAY MARSHALL STROM

[39]One of the criminals hanging there also insulted Jesus by saying, "Aren't you the Messiah? Save yourself and save us!"

[40]But the other criminal told the first one off, "Don't you fear God? Aren't you getting the same punishment as this man? [41]We got what was coming to us, but he didn't do anything wrong." [42]Then he said to Jesus, "Remember me when you come into power!"

[43]Jesus replied, "I promise that today you will be with me in paradise."[n]

The Death of Jesus

(Matthew 27.45-56; Mark 15.33-41; John 19.28-30)

[44]Around noon the sky turned dark and stayed that way until the middle of the afternoon. [45]The sun stopped shining, and the curtain in the temple[o] split down the middle. [46]Jesus shouted, "Father, I put myself in your hands!" Then he died.

[47]When the Roman officer saw what had happened, he praised God and said, "Jesus must really have been a good man!"

[48]A crowd had gathered to see the terrible sight. Then after they had seen it, they felt brokenhearted and went home. [49]All of Jesus' close friends and the women who had

come with him from Galilee stood at a distance and watched.

Jesus Is Buried

(Matthew 27.57-61; Mark 15.42-47; John 19.38-42)

[50-51]There was a man named Joseph, who was from Arimathea in Judea. Joseph was a good and honest man, and he was eager for God's kingdom to come. He was also a member of the council, but he did not agree with what they had decided.

[52]Joseph went to Pilate and asked for Jesus' body. [53]He took the body down from the cross and wrapped it in fine cloth. Then he put it in a tomb that had been cut out of solid rock and had never been used. [54]It was Friday, and the Sabbath was about to begin.[p]

[55]The women who had come with Jesus from Galilee followed Joseph and watched how Jesus' body was placed in the tomb. [56]Then they went to prepare some sweet-smelling spices for his burial. But on the Sabbath they rested, as the Law of Moses commands.

Jesus Is Alive

(Matthew 28.1-10; Mark 16.1-8; John 20.1-10)

24 Very early on Sunday morning the women went to the tomb, carrying the spices that they had prepared. [2]When they found the stone rolled away from the entrance, [3]they went in. But they did not find the body of the Lord[q] Jesus, [4]and they did not know what to think.

Suddenly two men in shining white clothes stood beside them. [5]The women were afraid and bowed to the ground. But the men said, "Why are you looking in the place of the dead for someone who is alive?

---

[l]**23.33** *"The Skull"*: The place was probably given this name because it was near a large rock in the shape of a human skull.   [m]**23.34,35** *Jesus said, "Father, forgive these people! They don't know what they're doing."*: These words are not in some manuscripts.   [n]**23.43** *paradise*: In the Greek translation of the Old Testament, this word is used for the Garden of Eden. In New Testament times it was sometimes used for the place where God's people are happy and at rest, as they wait for the final judgment.   [o]**23.45** *curtain in the temple*: There were two curtains in the temple. One was at the entrance, and the other separated the holy place from the most holy place that the Jewish people thought of as God's home on earth. The second curtain is probably the one which is meant.   [p]**23.54** *the Sabbath was about to begin*: The Sabbath begins at sunset on Friday.   [q]**24.3** *the Lord*: These words are not in some manuscripts.

⁶Jesus isn't here! He has been raised from death. Remember that while he was still in Galilee, he told you, ⁷'The Son of Man will be handed over to sinners who will nail him to a cross. But three days later he will rise to life.' " ⁸Then they remembered what Jesus had said.

⁹⁻¹⁰Mary Magdalene, Joanna, Mary the mother of James, and some other women were the ones who had gone to the tomb. When they returned, they told the eleven apostles and the others what had happened. ¹¹The apostles thought it was all nonsense, and they would not believe.

¹²But Peter ran to the tomb. And when he stooped down and looked in, he saw only the burial clothes. Then he returned, wondering what had happened.ʳ

Jesus Appears to Two Disciples
(Mark 16.12, 13)

¹³That same day two of Jesus' disciples were going to the village of Emmaus, which was about seven miles from Jerusalem. ¹⁴As they were talking and thinking about what had happened, ¹⁵Jesus came near and started walking along beside them. ¹⁶But they did not know who he was.

> *Anywhere, at any time, we may turn to him. Talk to him. Hear his voice. Feel his hand. And catch — even if just for a moment — the fragrance of heaven.*
>
> JONI EARECKSON TADA

¹⁷Jesus asked them, "What were you talking about as you walked along?"

The two of them stood there looking sad and gloomy. ¹⁸Then the one named Cleopas asked Jesus, "Are you the only person from Jerusalem who didn't know what was happening there these last few days?"

¹⁹"What do you mean?" Jesus asked.

They answered:

Those things that happened to Jesus from Nazareth. By what he did and said he showed that he was a powerful prophet, who pleased God and all the people. ²⁰Then the chief priests and our leaders had him arrested and sentenced to die on a cross. ²¹We had hoped that he would be the one to set Israel free! But it has already been three days since all this happened.

²²Some women in our group surprised us. They had gone to the tomb early in the morning, ²³but did not find the body of Jesus. They came back, saying that they had seen a vision of angels who told them that he is alive. ²⁴Some men from our group went to the tomb and found it just as the women had said. But they didn't see Jesus either.

²⁵Then Jesus asked the two disciples, "Why can't you understand? How can you be so slow to believe all that the prophets said? ²⁶Didn't you know that the Messiah would have to suffer before he was given his glory?" ²⁷Jesus then explained everything written about himself in the Scriptures, beginning with the Law of Moses and the Books of the Prophets.ˢ

²⁸When the two of them came near the village where they were going, Jesus seemed to be going farther. ²⁹They begged him, "Stay with us! It's already late, and the sun is going down." So Jesus went into the house to stay with them.

³⁰After Jesus sat down to eat, he took some bread. He blessed it and broke it. Then he gave it to them. ³¹At once they knew who he was, but he disappeared. ³²They said to each other, "When he talked with us along the road and explained the Scriptures to us, didn't it warm our hearts?" ³³So they got right up and returned to Jerusalem.

The two disciples found the eleven apostles and the others gathered together. ³⁴And they learned from the group that the Lord was really alive and had appeared to Peter. ³⁵Then the disciples from Emmaus told what happened on the road and how they knew he was the Lord when he broke the bread.

ʳ**24.12** *what had happened*: Verse 12 is not in some manuscripts. ˢ**24.27** *the Law of Moses and the Books of the Prophets*: See the note at 16.16.

What Jesus' Followers Must Do

(Matthew 28.16-20; Mark 16.14-18; John 20.19-23; Acts 1.6-8)

³⁶While Jesus' disciples were talking about what had happened, Jesus appeared and greeted them. ³⁷They were frightened and terrified because they thought they were seeing a ghost.

³⁸But Jesus said, "Why are you so frightened? Why do you doubt? ³⁹Look at my hands and my feet and see who I am! Touch me and find out for yourselves. Ghosts don't have flesh and bones as you see I have."

⁴⁰After Jesus said this, he showed them his hands and his feet. ⁴¹The disciples were so glad and amazed that they could not believe it. Jesus then asked them, "Do you have something to eat?" ⁴²They gave him a piece of baked fish. ⁴³He took it and ate it as they watched.

⁴⁴Jesus said to them, "While I was still with you, I told you that everything written about me in the Law of Moses, the Books of the Prophets, and in the Psalms*t* had to happen."

⁴⁵Then he helped them understand the Scriptures. ⁴⁶He told them:

The Scriptures say that the Messiah must suffer, then three days later he will rise from death. ⁴⁷They also say that all people of every nation must be told in my name to turn to God, in order to be forgiven. So beginning in Jerusalem, ⁴⁸you must tell everything that has happened. ⁴⁹I will send you the one my Father has promised,*u* but you must stay in the city until you are given power from heaven.

Jesus Returns to Heaven

(Mark 16.19, 20; Acts 1.9-11)

⁵⁰Jesus led his disciples out to Bethany, where he raised his hands and blessed them. ⁵¹As he was doing this, he left and was taken up to heaven.*v* ⁵²After his disciples had worshiped him,*w* they returned to Jerusalem and were very happy. ⁵³They spent their time in the temple, praising God.

---

*t***24.44** *Psalms:* The Jewish Scriptures were made up of three parts: (1) the Law of Moses, (2) the Books of the Prophets, (3) and the Writings, which included the Psalms. Sometimes the Scriptures were just called the Law or the Law (of Moses) and the Books of the Prophets.   *u***24.49** *the one my Father has promised:* Jesus means the Holy Spirit.   *v***24.51** *and was taken up to heaven:* These words are not in some manuscripts. *w***24.52** *After his disciples had worshiped him:* These words are not in some manuscripts.

John
You Are My Friends

Do you remember what it was like when you were first getting to know a new friend? Can you recall how, over time, you shared parts of yourself, waiting to see how those were received before sharing a little more? Were you aware that your friend was probably doing the same thing, looking for signs that it was safe for her to be a little bit more vulnerable with you? This is how a friendship develops—it may feel a little awkward at first but soon there's a level of caring, commitment, and comfort in being together.

The Gospel of John is about just such a relationship—the developing love between Jesus, who is God in the flesh, and people like you and me with whom he greatly desires to become friends. The first chapter of John tells us that God initiated a loving relationship with us by communicating through the Word, Jesus Christ. God sent Jesus as a very personal revelation of divine truth. He isn't merely a communicator, but the communication itself. He didn't merely tell God's truth. He *is* the truth (14.6).

The Gospel of John, written by Jesus' favorite disciple of the same name, is the most personal and intimate of the Gospels. There is almost a plaintive quality to Christ's words as he seeks to communicate who he is, his relationship with his Father, and his reason for being on the earth. His longing to be received by those to whom he's ministering is palpable; he moves among his disciples and others with an open heart, inviting them into intimate relationship with himself.

John's Gospel records some of Jesus' more lengthy conversations with individuals, such as Nicodemus, the woman at the well, Mary and Martha, and Peter. From these we can see how Jesus interacted with others. Through John's record of Jesus'

miracles, we can sense how deeply he cared for people in distress. Whether it was the embarrassment of a host running out of wine at a party, a son's illness, physical hunger, the disciples' fear of strong winds that rocked their boat, or the grief of losing a friend—all were human experiences that Christ entered into and blessed.

John wrote this book so we could get to know Jesus and then put our faith in him (20.31). Here we find a Savior who speaks to us as his friends (15.15).

John at a Glance
1. God communicates through the Word (1.1-18)
2. Jesus begins his public ministry (1.19-51)
3. Miracles and conversations that show how much Jesus cares (2–12)
4. Jesus prepares his disciples for his departure (13–16)
5. A passionate prayer (17)
6. Jesus' betrayal, death, and burial (18,19)
7. He's alive! (20)
8. Jesus reestablishes contact with those he loves (21)

The Word of Life

1 In the beginning was the one
who is called the Word.
The Word was with God
and was truly God.
² From the very beginning
the Word was with God.

³ And with this Word,
God created all things.
Nothing was made
without the Word.
Everything that was created
⁴ received its life from him,
and his life gave light
to everyone.
⁵ The light keeps shining
in the dark,
and darkness has never
put it out.ᵃ
⁶ God sent a man named John,
⁷ who came to tell
about the light
and to lead all people
to have faith.
⁸ John wasn't that light.
He came only to tell
about the light.

⁹ The true light that shines
on everyone
was coming into the world.

---

*The biggest impact in my life
was the personal love I felt
from the Lord. I'd always
felt my achievements gained
me acceptance, but when
I came to know Christ, he
loved me just the way I was.*

PATRICIA FUNDERBURK WARE

---

¹⁰ The Word was in the world,
but no one knew him,
though God had made the world
with his Word.

¹¹ He came into his own world,
but his own nation
did not welcome him.
¹² Yet some people accepted him
and put their faith in him.
So he gave them the right
to be the children of God.
¹³ They were not God's children
by nature or because
of any human desires.
God himself was the one
who made them his children.

¹⁴ The Word became
a human being
and lived here with us.
We saw his true glory,
the glory of the only Son
of the Father.
From him all the kindness
and all the truth of God
have come down to us.

¹⁵ John spoke about him and shouted, "This is the one I told you would come! He is greater than I am, because he was alive before I was born."

¹⁶ Because of all that the Son is, we have been given one blessing after another.ᵇ ¹⁷ The Law was given by Moses, but Jesus Christ brought us undeserved kindness and truth. ¹⁸ No one has ever seen God. The only Son, who is truly God and is closest to the Father, has shown us what God is like.

John the Baptist Tells about Jesus
(Matthew 3.1-12; Mark 1.1-8; Luke 3.15-17)

¹⁹⁻²⁰ The Jewish leaders in Jerusalem sent priests and temple helpers to ask John who he was. He told them plainly, "I am not the Messiah." ²¹ Then when they asked him if he were Elijah, he said, "No, I am not!" And when they asked if he were the Prophet,ᶜ he also said "No!"

²² Finally, they said, "Who are you then? We have to give an answer to the ones who sent us. Tell us who you are!"

²³ John answered in the words of the prophet Isaiah, "I am only someone shout-

---

ᵃ1.5 *put it out*: Or "understood it." ᵇ1.16 *one blessing after another*: Or "one blessing in place of another." ᶜ1.21 *the Prophet*: Many of the Jewish people expected God to send them a prophet who would be like Moses, but with even greater power (see Deuteronomy 18.15, 18).

ing in the desert, 'Get the road ready for the Lord!' "

24Some Pharisees had also been sent to John. 25They asked him, "Why are you baptizing people, if you are not the Messiah or Elijah or the Prophet?"

26John told them, "I use water to baptize people. But here with you is someone you don't know. 27Even though I came first, I am not good enough to untie his sandals." 28John said this as he was baptizing east of the Jordan River in Bethany.d

The Lamb of God

29The next day, John saw Jesus coming toward him and said:

Here is the Lamb of God who takes away the sin of the world! 30He is the one I told you about when I said, "Someone else will come. He is greater than I am, because he was alive before I was born." 31I didn't know who he was. But I came to baptize you with water, so that everyone in Israel would see him.

32I was there and saw the Spirit come down on him like a dove from heaven. And the Spirit stayed on him. 33Before this I didn't know who he was. But the one who sent me to baptize with water had told me, "You will see the Spirit come down and stay on someone. Then you will know that he is the one who will baptize with the Holy Spirit." 34I saw this happen, and I tell you that he is the Son of God.

The First Disciples of Jesus

35The next day, John was there again, and two of his followers were with him. 36When he saw Jesus walking by, he said, "Here is the Lamb of God!" 37John's two followers heard him, and they went with Jesus.

38When Jesus turned and saw them, he asked, "What do you want?"

They answered, "Rabbi, where do you live?" The Hebrew word "Rabbi" means "Teacher."

39Jesus replied, "Come and see!" It was already about four o'clock in the afternoon when they went with him and saw where he lived. So they stayed on for the rest of the day.

40One of the two men who had heard John and had gone with Jesus was Andrew, the brother of Simon Peter. 41The first thing Andrew did was to find his brother and tell him, "We have found the Messiah!" The Hebrew word "Messiah" means the same as the Greek word "Christ."

42Andrew brought his brother to Jesus. And when Jesus saw him, he said, "Simon son of John, you will be called Cephas." This name can be translated as "Peter."e

Jesus Chooses Philip and Nathanael

43-44The next day Jesus decided to go to Galilee. There he met Philip, who was from Bethsaida, the hometown of Andrew and Peter. Jesus said to Philip, "Come with me."

45Philip then found Nathanael and said, "We have found the one that Moses and the Prophetsf wrote about. He is Jesus, the son of Joseph from Nazareth."

46Nathanael asked, "Can anything good come from Nazareth?"

Philip answered, "Come and see."

47When Jesus saw Nathanael coming toward him, he said, "Here is a true descendant of our ancestor Israel. And he isn't deceitful."g

48"How do you know me?" Nathanael asked.

Jesus answered, "Before Philip called you, I saw you under the fig tree."

49Nathanael said, "Rabbi, you are the Son of God and the King of Israel!"

50Jesus answered, "Did you believe me just because I said that I saw you under the fig tree? You will see something even greater. 51I tell you for certain that you will see heaven open and God's angels going up and coming down on the Son of Man."h

Jesus at a Wedding in Cana

2 Three days later Mary, the mother of Jesus, was at a wedding feast in the village of Cana in Galilee. 2Jesus and his

---

d1.28 Bethany: An unknown village east of the Jordan with the same name as the village near Jerusalem. e1.42 Peter: The Aramaic name "Cephas" and the Greek name "Peter" each mean "rock." f1.45 Moses and the Prophets: The Jewish Scriptures, that is, the Old Testament. g1.47 Israel . . . isn't deceitful: Israel (meaning "a man who wrestled with God" or "a prince of God") was the name that the Lord gave to Jacob (meaning "cheater" or "deceiver"), the famous ancestor of the Jewish people. h1.51 going up and coming down on the Son of Man: When Jacob (see the note at verse 47) was running from his brother Esau, he had a dream in which he saw angels going up and down on a ladder from earth to heaven (see Genesis 32.22-32).

disciples had also been invited and were there.

[3]When the wine was all gone, Mary said to Jesus, "They don't have any more wine."

[4]Jesus replied, "Mother, my time hasn't yet come![i] You must not tell me what to do."

[5]Mary then said to the servants, "Do whatever Jesus tells you to do."

[6]At the feast there were six stone water jars that were used by the people for washing themselves in the way that their religion said they must. Each jar held about twenty or thirty gallons. [7]Jesus told the servants to fill them to the top with water. Then after the jars had been filled, [8]he said, "Now take some water and give it to the man in charge of the feast."

The servants did as Jesus told them, [9]and the man in charge drank some of the water that had now turned into wine. He did not know where the wine had come from, but the servants did. He called the bridegroom over [10]and said, "The best wine is always served first. Then after the guests have had plenty, the other wine is served. But you have kept the best until last!"

[11]This was Jesus' first miracle,[j] and he did it in the village of Cana in Galilee. There Jesus showed his glory, and his disciples put their faith in him. [12]After this, he went with his mother, his brothers, and his disciples to the town of Capernaum, where they stayed for a few days.

Jesus in the Temple

(Matthew 21.12, 13; Mark 11.15-17; Luke 19.45, 46)

[13]Not long before the Jewish festival of Passover, Jesus went to Jerusalem. [14]There he found people selling cattle, sheep, and doves in the temple. He also saw moneychangers sitting at their tables. [15]So he took some rope and made a whip. Then he chased everyone out of the temple, together with their sheep and cattle. He turned over the tables of the moneychangers and scattered their coins.

[16]Jesus said to the people who had been selling doves, "Get those doves out of here! Don't make my Father's house a marketplace."

[17]The disciples then remembered that the Scriptures say, "My love for your house burns in me like a fire."

[18]The Jewish leaders asked Jesus, "What miracle[j] will you work to show us why you have done this?"

[19]"Destroy this temple," Jesus answered, "and in three days I will build it again!"

[20]The leaders replied, "It took forty-six years to build this temple. What makes you think you can rebuild it in three days?"

[21]But Jesus was talking about his body as a temple. [22]And when he was raised from death, his disciples remembered what he had told them. Then they believed the Scriptures and the words of Jesus.

Jesus Knows What People Are Like

[23]In Jerusalem during Passover many people put their faith in Jesus, because they saw him work miracles.[j] [24]But Jesus knew what was in their hearts, and he would not let them have power over him. [25]No one had to tell him what people were like. He already knew.

Jesus and Nicodemus

3 There was a man named Nicodemus who was a Pharisee and a Jewish leader. [2]One night he went to Jesus and said, "Sir, we know that God has sent you to teach us. You could not work these miracles, unless God were with you."

[3]Jesus replied, "I tell you for certain that you must be born from above[k] before you can see God's kingdom!"

[4]Nicodemus asked, "How can a grown man ever be born a second time?"

[5]Jesus answered:

I tell you for certain that before you can get into God's kingdom, you must be born not only by water, but by the Spirit. [6]Humans give life to their children. Yet only God's Spirit can change you into a child of God. [7]Don't be surprised when I say that you must be born from above. [8]Only God's Spirit gives new life. The Spirit is like the wind that blows wherever it wants to.

---

[i]**2.4** *my time hasn't yet come*: The time when the true glory of Jesus would be seen, and he would be recognized as God's Son (see 12.23).
[j]**2.11,18,23** *miracle(s)*: The Greek text has "sign." In the Gospel of John the word "sign" is used for the miracle itself and as a way of pointing to Jesus as the Son of God. [k]**3.3** *from above*: Or "in a new way." The same Greek word is used in verses 7, 31.

You can hear the wind, but you don't know where it comes from or where it is going.

[9]"How can this be?" Nicodemus asked.

[10]Jesus replied:

How can you be a teacher of Israel and not know these things? [11]I tell you for certain that we know what we are talking about because we have seen it ourselves. But none of you will accept what we say. [12]If you don't believe when I talk to you about things on earth, how can you possibly believe if I talk to you about things in heaven?

[13]No one has gone up to heaven except the Son of Man, who came down from there. [14]And the Son of Man must be lifted up, just as that metal snake was lifted up by Moses in the desert.[l] [15]Then everyone who has faith in the Son of Man will have eternal life.

[16]God loved the people of this world so much that he gave his only Son, so that everyone who has faith in him will have eternal life and never really die. [17]God did not send his Son into the world to condemn its people. He sent him to save them! [18]No one who has faith in God's Son will be condemned. But everyone who doesn't have faith in him has already been condemned for not having faith in God's only Son.

[19]The light has come into the world, and people who do evil things are judged guilty because they love the dark more than the light. [20]People who do evil hate the light and won't come to the light, because it clearly shows what they have done. [21]But everyone who lives by the truth will come to the light, because they want others to know that God is really the one doing what they do.

Jesus and John the Baptist

[22]Later, Jesus and his disciples went to Judea, where he stayed with them for a while and was baptizing people.

[23-24]John had not yet been put in jail. He was at Aenon near Salim, where there was a lot of water, and people were coming there for John to baptize them.

[25]John's followers got into an argument with a Jewish man[m] about a ceremony of

---

[l]**3.14** *just as that metal snake was lifted up by Moses in the desert*: When the Lord punished the people of Israel by sending snakes to bite them, he told Moses to hold a metal snake up on a pole. Everyone who looked at the snake was cured of the snake bites (see Numbers 21.4-9). [m]**3.25** *a Jewish man*: Some manuscripts have "some Jewish men."

PARENTING&*family*—How can I best relate to my adult child? (*John 3.1-21*)

Pray that your child will decide where he or she is heading—eternally.

Your son goes off to college. Your daughter calls at midnight to say, "Guess what, Mom? I'm getting married!" Your son shares with you that he's beginning to doubt his Christian faith—or that he's renounced his faith. Or maybe your child has never really accepted Christ, and you see her headed down the wrong road.

It isn't always easy to do what the well-known bumper sticker says: "Let go, and let God." Sometimes we'd rather take back the reins of control that we had over our children when they were little. We want to guard them from mistakes—and the resulting unhappiness—and yet we know we can't always be physically present.

This passage offers hope for any parent who has to "let go" of her child into the adult world and isn't sure where her child stands with God. If Nicodemus, a Pharisee and "grown man" (3.4), can come to Christ, we can pray for our children to do the same—or to rediscover the godly path of their childhood! As Jesus says, "Humans give life to their children. Yet only God's Spirit can change you into a child of God" (3.6). Ask God today to make his presence real to your children so that they, too, will want to walk with him—toward eternity. (See also Genesis 13,14; Ruth 3.)

Words To Remember: *Humans give life to their children. Yet only God's Spirit can change you into a child of God.—John 3.6*

washing.ⁿ ²⁶They went to John and said, "Rabbi, you spoke about a man when you were with him east of the Jordan. He is now baptizing people, and everyone is going to him."

²⁷John replied:

No one can do anything unless God in heaven allows it. ²⁸You surely remember how I told you that I am not the Messiah. I am only the one sent ahead of him.

²⁹At a wedding the groom is the one who gets married. The best man is glad just to be there and to hear the groom's voice. That's why I am so glad. ³⁰Jesus must become more important, while I become less important.

The One Who Comes from Heaven

³¹God's Son comes from heaven and is above all others. Everyone who comes from the earth belongs to the earth and speaks about earthly things. The one who comes from heaven is above all others. ³²He speaks about what he has seen and heard, and yet no one believes him. ³³But everyone who does believe him has shown that God is truthful. ³⁴The Son was sent to speak God's message, and he has been given the full power of God's Spirit.

³⁵The Father loves the Son and has given him everything. ³⁶Everyone who has faith in the Son has eternal life. But no one who rejects him will ever share in that life, and God will be angry with them forever.

4 Jesus knew that the Pharisees had heard that he was winning and baptizing more followers than John was. ²But Jesus' disciples were really the ones doing the baptizing, and not Jesus himself.

Jesus and the Samaritan Woman

³Jesus left Judea and started for Galilee again. ⁴This time he had to go through Samaria, ⁵and on his way he came to the town of Sychar. It was near the field that Jacob had long ago given to his son Joseph. ⁶⁻⁸The well that Jacob had dug was still there, and Jesus sat down beside it because he was tired from traveling. It was noon, and after Jesus' disciples had gone into town to buy some food, a Samaritan woman came to draw water from the well.

Jesus asked her, "Would you please give me a drink of water?"

⁹"You are a Jew," she replied, "and I am a Samaritan woman. How can you ask me for a drink of water when Jews and Samaritans won't have anything to do with each other?"ᵒ

ⁿ**3.25** *about a ceremony of washing*: The Jewish people had many rules about washing themselves and their dishes, in order to make themselves fit to worship God. ᵒ**4.9** *won't have anything to do with each other*: Or "won't use the same cups." The Samaritans lived in the land between Judea and Galilee. They worshiped God differently from the Jews and did not get along with them.

---

*Spiritual*Life—Will God really condemn people who don't accept Christ as their Savior? *(John 3.16-18)*

Those who don't receive Christ remain in the condemned state in which they were born.

The overwhelming message of the Gospel of John in general and of this passage in particular is the message that God loves us. Jesus is the ultimate expression of God's love, not God's judgment. This passage makes it very clear that "God did not send his Son into the world to condemn its people. He sent him to save them!" (3.17).

However, those who don't respond to God's expression of love by putting their faith in Christ remain in the state of condemnation in which they were born. Unless we turn to God, we're on our way to eternal death. But once we belong to Christ, we no longer have to be concerned about punishment or condemnation. Christ took our punishment when he died for us—so we could have eternal life. (See also Deuteronomy 30; Zephaniah 1.14-18; John 6.60-69; Romans 10.5-21.)

Words To Remember: *God did not send his Son into the world to condemn its people. He sent him to save them!—John 3.17*

¹⁰Jesus answered, "You don't know what God wants to give you, and you don't know who is asking you for a drink. If you did, you would ask me for the water that gives life."

¹¹"Sir," the woman said, "you don't even have a bucket, and the well is deep. Where are you going to get this life-giving water? ¹²Our ancestor Jacob dug this well for us, and his family and animals got water from it. Are you greater than Jacob?"

¹³Jesus answered, "Everyone who drinks this water will get thirsty again. ¹⁴But no one who drinks the water I give will ever be thirsty again. The water I give is like a flowing fountain that gives eternal life."

¹⁵The woman replied, "Sir, please give me a drink of that water! Then I won't get thirsty and have to come to this well again."

¹⁶Jesus told her, "Go and bring your husband."

¹⁷⁻¹⁸The woman answered, "I don't have a husband."

"That's right," Jesus replied, "you're telling the truth. You don't have a husband. You have already been married five times, and the man you are now living with isn't your husband."

¹⁹The woman said, "Sir, I can see that you are a prophet. ²⁰My ancestors worshiped on this mountain,ᵖ but you Jews say Jerusalem is the only place to worship."

²¹Jesus said to her:

Believe me, the time is coming when you won't worship the Father either on this mountain or in Jerusalem. ²²You Samaritans don't really know the one you worship. But we Jews do know the God we worship, and by using us, God will save the world. ²³But a time is coming, and it is already here! Even now the true worshipers are being led by the Spirit to worship the Father according to the truth. These are the ones the Father is seeking to worship him. ²⁴God is Spirit, and those who worship God must be led by the Spirit to worship him according to the truth.

²⁵The woman said, "I know that the Messiah will come. He is the one we call Christ. When he comes, he will explain everything to us."

²⁶"I am that one," Jesus told her, "and I am speaking to you now."

²⁷The disciples returned about this time and were surprised to find Jesus talking with a woman. But none of them asked him what he wanted or why he was talking with her.

²⁸The woman left her water jar and ran back into town. She said to the people, ²⁹"Come and see a man who told me everything I have ever done! Could he be the Messiah?" ³⁰Everyone in town went out to see Jesus.

³¹While this was happening, Jesus' disciples were saying to him, "Teacher, please eat something."

³²But Jesus told them, "I have food that you don't know anything about."

³³His disciples started asking each other,

ᵖ4.20 *this mountain:* Mount Gerizim, near the city of Shechem.

PARENTING&*family*—How can I encourage my child's faith to grow?
(*John 3.16-21*)

Explain the simple message of God's love.
All humans share a deep need for love. As babies and children we first begin to sense whether or not we are loved. If we feel loved, we begin to trust in the goodness of God, and it becomes increasingly natural to put our life in his hands. It is, after all, much easier to trust someone once we're sure he loves us and has our best interests at heart.

Because we want our children to develop a deep trust in the fact that God loves them and wants to work out his best in their life, in addition, we can't tell them too often how greatly they're loved by God. By drawing attention to God's love, as expressed through Christ and the myriad other ways he blesses them daily, we create an atmosphere in which faith is likely to blossom. (See also Joshua 4; 1 Chronicles 22; Ezra 3; Proverbs 2.1-15.)

Words To Remember: *God loved the people of this world so much that he gave his only Son.*—John 3.16

"Has someone brought him something to eat?"

³⁴Jesus said:

My food is to do what God wants! He is the one who sent me, and I must finish the work that he gave me to do. ³⁵You may say that there are still four months until harvest time. But I tell you to look, and you will see that the fields are ripe and ready to harvest. ³⁶Even now the harvest workers are receiving their reward by gathering a harvest that brings eternal life. Then everyone who planted the seed and everyone who harvests the crop will celebrate together. ³⁷So the saying proves true, "Some plant the seed, and others harvest the crop." ³⁸I am sending you to harvest crops in fields where others have done all the hard work.

³⁹A lot of Samaritans in that town put their faith in Jesus because the woman had said, "This man told me everything I have ever done." ⁴⁰They came and asked him to stay in their town, and he stayed on for two days. ⁴¹Many more Samaritans put their faith in Jesus because of what they heard him say. ⁴²They told the woman, "We no longer have faith in Jesus just because of what you told us. We have heard him ourselves, and we are certain that he is the Savior of the world!"

Jesus Heals an Official's Son
(Matthew 8.5-13; Luke 7.1-10)

⁴³⁻⁴⁴Jesus had said, "Prophets are honored everywhere, except in their own country." Then two days later he left ⁴⁵and went to Galilee. The people there welcomed him, because they had gone to the festival in Jerusalem and had seen everything he had done.

⁴⁶While Jesus was in Galilee, he returned to the village of Cana, where he had turned the water into wine. There was an official in Capernaum whose son was sick. ⁴⁷And when the man heard that Jesus had come from Judea, he went and begged him to keep his son from dying.

⁴⁸Jesus told the official, "You won't have faith unless you see miracles and wonders!"

⁴⁹The man replied, "Lord, please come before my son dies!"

⁵⁰Jesus then said, "Your son will live. Go on home to him." The man believed Jesus and started back home.

⁵¹Some of the official's servants met him along the road and told him, "Your son is better!" ⁵²He asked them when the boy got

---

Friendship—How can I reach out to people who differ from me in habits, faith, culture, or race? *(John 4.4-26)*

Be respectful, listen, and share yourself.

Relating effectively to people we view as different from ourselves doesn't always come naturally. The categories humans have created (based on gender, race, economic status, age, and personality) often obscure the things we share in common. Instead of being enriched by diversity, it might make us uneasy.

We can look at Jesus' conversation with the Samaritan woman as a prototype for our own interactions with those we perceive as being different from ourselves. First, Jesus initiated the interaction rather than waiting for the Samaritan woman to speak with him (4.8). He didn't allow the differences in gender, race, marital status, or spiritual condition to be a deterrent. And he responded to her questions and comments with respect (4.9-26).

Rather than judging by her outward circumstances, Jesus looked into her heart (4.19-24). And he revealed important aspects of himself so she also could get to know him. When the disciples offered him lunch, he affirmed her value by saying, in effect, that talking with his new friend was more important to him than eating (4.34).

If we follow Christ's example in being open to a variety of individuals, we may be surprised by the unity we experience—and enriched by the diversity they bring. (See also Romans 3.21-31; 2 Corinthians 5.16-21; Galatians 3.26-29; Colossians 4.2-6.)

Words To Remember: *God is Spirit, and those who worship God must be led by the Spirit to worship him according to the truth.*—John 4.24

Woman of Sychar

John 4.1-42

When the woman of Sychar went to draw water from the well on the day she met Christ, she had many reasons to believe she wasn't worth much. Not only was she of the lesser sex (as women were viewed in that culture), she was also of the lesser race (Jews despised Samaritans because they were "half-breeds"). Besides, she was known for her blatant immorality. She'd had five husbands, and at the time she met Christ, she was living with a man to whom she was not married.

The fact that she chose to draw water in the heat of the day rather than the cool of the morning suggests that perhaps she was so depressed and ostracized that she avoided contact with those who might demean her. But Christ demonstrated he had no such damaging favoritism. Just by beginning an intelligent conversation with her and treating her as an equal, Jesus communicated her significance. He didn't treat her as though she were beneath him or as someone who needed to be pulled out of the gutter and saved. Rather, he affirmed her ability to grasp spiritual truth by discussing religion with her and revealing truth that was, as far as we can tell, unknown to anyone else, including the disciples (4.21-26). Jesus saw beyond her exterior to the deep spiritual hunger that characterized her heart. And he valued her even though he knew about her failings.

What an amazing first this encounter must have been for her, and how life-changing it was! Entering into a personal relationship with Christ that day helped her to see that it was not romantic relationships with men that defined her. Yet, Christ did encourage a realistic assessment of herself when he gave her the opportunity to face her sin and her failure to relate with men in a healthy fashion (4.16-18). But then he pointed out that the true source of her identity was her pursuit of truth in her relationship with God (4.23,24). No longer would she be defined by gender, race, marital status, or desirability to men. Once she placed her faith in Jesus, realizing that he was the Messiah for whom she had been waiting, she received a spiritual identity that transcended all other roles and relationships.

Later that same day, the woman of Sychar shared her experience of Christ with the people of her community. Many came to hear him speak, and they, too, believed in Jesus—making the woman of Sychar one of the earliest evangelists in the New Testament (4.41,42).

better, and they answered, "The fever left
him yesterday at one o'clock."
53 The boy's father realized that at one
o'clock the day before, Jesus had told him,
"Your son will live!" So the man and everyone in his family put their faith in Jesus.
54 This was the second miracle[q] that Jesus
worked after he left Judea and went to
Galilee.

Jesus Heals a Sick Man

5 Later, Jesus went to Jerusalem for another Jewish festival.[r] 2 In the city near
the sheep gate was a pool with five
porches, and its name in Hebrew was
Bethzatha.[s]
3-4 Many sick, blind, lame, and crippled
people were lying close to the pool.[t]
5 Beside the pool was a man who had
been sick for thirty-eight years. 6 When Jesus
saw the man and realized that he had been
crippled for a long time, he asked him, "Do
you want to be healed?"
7 The man answered, "Lord, I don't have
anyone to put me in the pool when the water is stirred up. I try to get in, but someone
else always gets there first."
8 Jesus told him, "Pick up your mat and
walk!" 9 Right then the man was healed. He
picked up his mat and started walking
around. The day on which this happened
was a Sabbath.
10 When the Jewish leaders saw the man
carrying his mat, they said to him, "This is
the Sabbath! No one is allowed to carry a
mat on the Sabbath."
11 But he replied, "The man who healed
me told me to pick up my mat and walk."
12 They asked him, "Who is this man that
told you to pick up your mat and walk?"
13 But he did not know who Jesus was, and
Jesus had left because of the crowd.
14 Later, Jesus met the man in the temple
and told him, "You are now well. But don't
sin anymore or something worse might happen to you." 15 The man left and told the
leaders that Jesus was the one who had
healed him. 16 They started making a lot of
trouble for Jesus because he did things like
this on the Sabbath.
17 But Jesus said, "My Father has never
stopped working, and that is why I keep on
working." 18 Now the leaders wanted to kill
Jesus for two reasons. First, he had broken
the law of the Sabbath. But even worse, he
had said that God was his Father, which
made him equal with God.

The Son's Authority

19 Jesus told the people:
I tell you for certain that the Son
cannot do anything on his own. He
can do only what he sees the Father
doing, and he does exactly what he
sees the Father do. 20 The Father loves
the Son and has shown him everything he does. The Father will show
him even greater things, and you will
be amazed. 21 Just as the Father raises
the dead and gives life, so the Son
gives life to anyone he wants to.

> *I not only want to show God's love and mercy to those I meet, but to introduce them to Jesus Christ, the only one who totally knows and understands us.*
>
> RAMONA CRAMER TUCKER

22 The Father doesn't judge anyone,
but he has made his Son the judge of
everyone. 23 The Father wants all people to honor the Son as much as they
honor him. When anyone refuses to
honor the Son, that is the same as refusing to honor the Father who sent
him. 24 I tell you for certain that everyone who hears my message and has
faith in the one who sent me has eternal life and will never be condemned.
They have already gone from death to
life.

---

[q] **4.54** *miracle*: See the note at 2.11. [r] **5.1** *another Jewish festival*: Either the Festival of Shelters or Passover. [s] **5.2** *Bethzatha*: Some manuscripts have "Bethesda" and others have "Bethsaida." [t] **5.3,4** *pool*: Some manuscripts add, "They were waiting for the water to be stirred, because an angel from the Lord would sometimes come down and stir it. The first person to get into the pool after that would be healed."

²⁵I tell you for certain that the time will come, and it is already here, when all of the dead will hear the voice of the Son of God. And those who listen to it will live! ²⁶The Father has the power to give life, and he has given that same power to the Son. ²⁷And he has given his Son the right to judge everyone, because he is the Son of Man.

²⁸Don't be surprised! The time will come when all of the dead will hear the voice of the Son of Man, ²⁹and they will come out of their graves. Everyone who has done good things will rise to life, but everyone who has done evil things will rise and be condemned.

³⁰I cannot do anything on my own. The Father sent me, and he is the one who told me how to judge. I judge with fairness, because I obey him, and I don't just try to please myself.

Witnesses to Jesus

³¹If I speak for myself, there is no way to prove I am telling the truth. ³²But there is someone else who speaks for me, and I know what he says is true. ³³You sent messengers to John, and he told them the truth. ³⁴I don't depend on what people say about me, but I tell you these things so that you may be saved. ³⁵John was a lamp that gave a lot of light, and you were glad to enjoy his light for a while.

³⁶But something more important than John speaks for me. I mean the things that the Father has given me to do! All of these speak for me and prove that the Father sent me.

³⁷The Father who sent me also speaks for me, but you have never heard his voice or seen him face to face. ³⁸You have not believed his message, because you refused to have faith in the one he sent.

³⁹You search the Scriptures, because you think you will find eternal life in them. The Scriptures tell about me, ⁴⁰but you refuse to come to me for eternal life.

⁴¹I don't care about human praise, ⁴²but I do know that none of you love God. ⁴³I have come with my Father's authority, and you have not welcomed me. But you will welcome people who

come on their own. ⁴⁴How could you possibly believe? You like to have your friends praise you, and you don't care about praise that the only God can give!

⁴⁵Don't think that I will be the one to accuse you to the Father. You have put your hope in Moses, yet he is the very one who will accuse you. ⁴⁶Moses wrote about me, and if you had believed Moses, you would have believed me. ⁴⁷But if you don't believe what Moses wrote, how can you believe what I say?

Feeding Five Thousand
(Matthew 14.13-21; Mark 6.30-44; Luke 9.10-17)

6 Jesus crossed Lake Galilee, which was also known as Lake Tiberias. ²A large crowd had seen him work miracles to heal the sick, and those people went with him. ³⁻⁴It was almost time for the Jewish festival of Passover, and Jesus went up on a mountain with his disciples and sat down.ᵘ

⁵When Jesus saw the large crowd coming toward him, he asked Philip, "Where will we get enough food to feed all these people?" ⁶He said this to test Philip, since he already knew what he was going to do.

⁷Philip answered, "Don't you know that it would take almost a year's wagesᵛ just to buy only a little bread for each of these people?"

⁸Andrew, the brother of Simon Peter, was one of the disciples. He spoke up and said, ⁹"There is a boy here who has five small loavesʷ of barley bread and two fish. But what good is that with all these people?"

¹⁰The ground was covered with grass, and Jesus told his disciples to have everyone sit down. About five thousand men were in the crowd. ¹¹Jesus took the bread in his hands and gave thanks to God. Then he passed the bread to the people, and he did the same with the fish, until everyone had plenty to eat.

¹²The people ate all they wanted, and Jesus told his disciples to gather up the left-

---

ᵘ6.3,4 sat down: Possibly to teach. Teachers in the ancient world, including Jewish teachers, usually sat down to teach.   ᵛ6.7 almost a year's wages: The Greek text has "two hundred silver coins." Each coin was worth the average day's wages for a worker.   ʷ6.9 small loaves: These would have been flat and round or in the shape of a bun.

overs, so that nothing would be wasted. [13]The disciples gathered them up and filled twelve large baskets with what was left over from the five barley loaves.

[14]After the people had seen Jesus work this miracle,[x] they began saying, "This must be the Prophet[y] who is to come into the world!" [15]Jesus realized that they would try to force him to be their king. So he went up on a mountain, where he could be alone.

Jesus Walks on the Water
(Matthew 14.22-27; Mark 6.45-52)

[16]That evening, Jesus' disciples went down to the lake. [17]They got into a boat and started across for Capernaum. Later that evening Jesus had still not come to them, [18]and a strong wind was making the water rough.

[19]When the disciples had rowed for three or four miles, they saw Jesus walking on the water. He kept coming closer to the boat, and they were terrified. [20]But he said, "I am Jesus![z] Don't be afraid!" [21]The disciples wanted to take him into the boat, but suddenly the boat reached the shore where they were headed.

The Bread That Gives Life

[22]The people who had stayed on the east side of the lake knew that only one boat had been there. They also knew that Jesus had not left in it with his disciples. But the next day [23]some boats from Tiberias sailed near the place where the crowd had eaten the bread for which the Lord had given thanks. [24]They saw that Jesus and his disciples had left. Then they got into the boats and went to Capernaum to look for Jesus. [25]They found him on the west side of the lake and asked, "Rabbi, when did you get here?"

[26]Jesus answered, "I tell you for certain that you are not looking for me because you saw the miracles,[a] but because you ate all the food you wanted. [27]Don't work for food that spoils. Work for food that gives eternal life. The Son of Man will give you this food, because God the Father has given him the right to do so."

[28]"What exactly does God want us to do?" the people asked.

[29]Jesus answered, "God wants you to have faith in the one he sent."

[30]They replied, "What miracle will you work, so that we can have faith in you?

What will you do? [31]For example, when our ancestors were in the desert, they were given manna[b] to eat. It happened just as the Scriptures say, 'God gave them bread from heaven to eat.' "

[32]Jesus then told them, "I tell you for certain that Moses wasn't the one who gave you bread from heaven. My Father is the one who gives you the true bread from heaven. [33]And the bread that God gives is the one who came down from heaven to give life to the world."

[34]The people said, "Lord, give us this bread and don't ever stop!"

[35]Jesus replied:

I am the bread that gives life! No one who comes to me will ever be hungry. No one who has faith in me will ever be thirsty. [36]I have told you already that you have seen me and still do not have faith in me. [37]Everything and everyone that the Father has given me will come to me, and I won't turn any of them away.

[38]I didn't come from heaven to do what I want! I came to do what the Father wants me to do. He sent me, [39]and he wants to make certain that none of the ones he has given me will be lost. Instead, he wants me to raise them to life on the last day.[c] [40]My Father wants everyone who sees the Son to have faith in him and to have eternal life. Then I will raise them to life on the last day.

[41]The people started grumbling because Jesus had said he was the bread that had come down from heaven. [42]They were asking each other, "Isn't he Jesus, the son of Joseph? Don't we know his father and mother? How can he say that he has come down from heaven?"

[43]Jesus told them:

Stop grumbling! [44]No one can come to me, unless the Father who

---

[x]**6.14** *miracle*: See the note at 2.11.   [y]**6.14** *the Prophet*: See the note at 1.21.   [z]**6.20** *I am Jesus*: The Greek text has "I am" (see the note at 8.24).   [a]**6.26** *miracles*: The Greek text has "signs" here and "sign" in verse 30 (see the note at 2.11).   [b]**6.31** *manna*: When the people of Israel were wandering through the desert, the Lord gave them a special kind of food to eat. It tasted like a wafer and was called "manna," which in Hebrew means, "What is this?"   [c]**6.39** *the last day*: When God will judge all people.

sent me makes them want to come. But if they do come, I will raise them to life on the last day. [45]One of the prophets wrote, "God will teach all of them." And so everyone who listens to the Father and learns from him will come to me.

[46]The only one who has seen the Father is the one who has come from him. No one else has ever seen the Father. [47]I tell you for certain that everyone who has faith in me has eternal life.

[48]I am the bread that gives life! [49]Your ancestors ate manna[d] in the desert, and later they died. [50]But the bread from heaven has come down, so that no one who eats it will ever die. [51]I am that bread from heaven! Everyone who eats it will live forever. My flesh is the life-giving bread that I give to the people of this world.

[52]They started arguing with each other and asked, "How can he give us his flesh to eat?"

[53]Jesus answered:

I tell you for certain that you won't live unless you eat the flesh and drink the blood of the Son of Man. [54]But if you do eat my flesh and drink my blood, you will have eternal life, and I will raise you to life on the last day. [55]My flesh is the true food, and my blood is the true drink. [56]If you eat my

flesh and drink my blood, you are one with me, and I am one with you.

[57]The living Father sent me, and I have life because of him. Now everyone who eats my flesh will live because of me. [58]The bread that comes down from heaven isn't like what your ancestors ate. They died, but whoever eats this bread will live forever.

[59]Jesus was teaching in a Jewish place of worship in Capernaum when he said these things.

The Words of Eternal Life

[60]Many of Jesus' disciples heard him and said, "This is too hard for anyone to understand."

[61]Jesus knew that his disciples were grumbling. So he asked, "Does this bother you? [62]What if you should see the Son of Man go up to heaven where he came from? [63]The Spirit is the one who gives life! Human strength can do nothing. The words that I have spoken to you are from that life-giving Spirit. [64]But some of you refuse to have faith in me." Jesus said this, because from the beginning he knew who would have faith in him. He also knew which one would betray him.

[65]Then Jesus said, "You cannot come to me, unless the Father makes you want to

---

[d]**6.49** *manna*: See the note at 6.31.

 ᔑ

*Spiritual*Life—Will God really condemn people who don't accept Christ as their Savior? *(John 6.60-69)*

God invites people to Christ, but they need to accept the invitation.
Sometimes we think of God as one who sits in judgment on us, waiting for his next opportunity to punish us for something we've done wrong. Perhaps our parents treated us that way, so we project that image onto God. But nothing could be further from the truth!

In the Gospel of John, Jesus told us that God's greatest desire was to draw people to his Son so we could find life. In fact, Jesus went so far as to say that no one comes to him unless God draws him first. But even when God draws us, we may still fight against that invitation. Just as Jesus invited Judas to come to him (even though Judas would later betray him) so God draws us to life-giving faith in Christ.

God begs us to respond by first accepting his offer of forgiveness and grace and then following him. As we turn our lives over to Jesus, this demonstrates whether we are saved or condemned. And life without Christ is spiritual death. (See also Deuteronomy 30; Zephaniah 1.14-18; John 3.16-18; Romans 10.5-21.)

 ᔒ **Words To Remember:** *"Lord, there is no one else that we can go to! Your words give eternal life."*—John 6.68

come. That is why I have told these things to all of you."

⁶⁶Because of what Jesus said, many of his disciples turned their backs on him and stopped following him. ⁶⁷Jesus then asked his twelve disciples if they were going to leave him. ⁶⁸Simon Peter answered, "Lord, there is no one else that we can go to! Your words give eternal life. ⁶⁹We have faith in you, and we are sure that you are God's Holy One."

⁷⁰Jesus told his disciples, "I chose all twelve of you, but one of you is a demon!" ⁷¹Jesus was talking about Judas, the son of Simon Iscariot.ᶜ He would later betray Jesus, even though he was one of the twelve disciples.

Jesus' Brothers Don't Have Faith in Him

7 Jesus decided to leave Judea and to start going through Galilee because the Jewish leaders wanted to kill him. ²It was almost time for the Festival of Shelters, ³and Jesus' brothers said to him, "Why don't you go to Judea? Then your disciples can see what you are doing. ⁴No one does anything in secret, if they want others to know about them. So let the world know what you are doing!" ⁵Even Jesus' own brothers had not yet become his followers.

⁶Jesus answered, "My time hasn't yet come,ᶠ but your time is always here. ⁷The people of this world cannot hate you. They hate me, because I tell them that they do evil things. ⁸Go on to the festival. My time hasn't yet come, and I am not going." ⁹Jesus said this and stayed on in Galilee.

Jesus at the Festival of Shelters

¹⁰After Jesus' brothers had gone to the festival, he went secretly, without telling anyone. ¹¹During the festival the Jewish leaders looked for Jesus and asked, "Where is he?" ¹²The crowds even got into an argument about him. Some were saying, "Jesus is a good man," while others were saying, "He is lying to everyone." ¹³But the people were afraid of their leaders, and none of them talked in public about him.

¹⁴When the festival was about half over, Jesus went into the temple and started teaching. ¹⁵The leaders were surprised and said, "How does this man know so much? He has never been taught!"

¹⁶Jesus replied:

I am not teaching something that I thought up. What I teach comes from the one who sent me. ¹⁷If you really want to obey God, you will know if what I teach comes from God or from me. ¹⁸If I wanted to bring honor to myself, I would speak for myself. But I want to honor the one who sent me. That is why I tell the truth and not a lie. ¹⁹Didn't Moses give you the Law? Yet none of you obey it! So why do you want to kill me?

²⁰The crowd replied, "You're crazy! What makes you think someone wants to kill you?"

> *Unfortunately, we can become obsessed about anything, whether it be appearance, diet, or clothing. What I want to do for my patients is help them focus on their unique, God-given beauty.*
>
> DR. LORI HANSEN

²¹Jesus answered:

I worked one miracle,ᵍ and it amazed you. ²²Moses commanded you to circumcise your sons. But it wasn't really Moses who gave you this command. It was your ancestors, and even on the Sabbath you circumcise your sons ²³in order to obey the Law of Moses. Why are you angry with me for making someone completely well on the Sabbath? ²⁴Don't judge by appearances. Judge by what is right.

ᶜ**6.71** *Iscariot:* This may mean "a man from Kerioth" (a place in Judea). But more probably it means "a man who was a liar" or "a man who was a betrayer."
ᶠ**7.6** *My time hasn't yet come:* See the note at 2.4.
ᵍ**7.21** *one miracle:* The healing of the lame man (5.1-18; see also the note at 2.11).

[25]Some of the people from Jerusalem were saying, "Isn't this the man they want to kill? [26]Yet here he is, speaking for everyone to hear. And no one is arguing with him. Do you suppose the authorities know that he is the Messiah? [27]But how could that be? No one knows where the Messiah will come from, but we know where this man comes from."

[28]As Jesus was teaching in the temple, he shouted, "Do you really think you know me and where I came from? I didn't come on my own! The one who sent me is truthful, and you don't know him. [29]But I know the one who sent me, because I came from him."

[30]Some of the people wanted to arrest Jesus right then. But no one even laid a hand on him, because his time had not yet come.[h] [31]A lot of people in the crowd put their faith in him and said, "When the Messiah comes, he surely won't perform more miracles[i] than this man has done!"

Officers Sent To Arrest Jesus

[32]When the Pharisees heard the crowd arguing about Jesus, they got together with the chief priests and sent some temple police to arrest him. [33]But Jesus told them, "I will be with you a little while longer, and then I will return to the one who sent me. [34]You will look for me, but you won't find me. You cannot go where I am going."

[35]The Jewish leaders asked each other, "Where can he go to keep us from finding him? Is he going to some foreign country where our people live? Is he going there to teach the Greeks?[j] [36]What did he mean by saying that we will look for him, but won't find him? Why can't we go where he is going?"

Streams of Life-Giving Water

[37]On the last and most important day of the festival, Jesus stood up and shouted, "If you are thirsty, come to me and drink! [38]Have faith in me, and you will have life-giving water flowing from deep inside you, just as the Scriptures say." [39]Jesus was talking about the Holy Spirit, who would be given to everyone that had faith in him. The Spirit had not yet been given to anyone, since Jesus had not yet been given his full glory.[k]

The People Take Sides

[40]When the crowd heard Jesus say this, some of them said, "He must be the Prophet!"[l] [41]Others said, "He is the Messiah!" Others even said, "Can the Messiah come from Galilee? [42]The Scriptures say that the Messiah will come from the family of King David. Doesn't this mean that he will be born in David's hometown of Bethlehem?" [43]The people started taking sides against each other because of Jesus. [44]Some of them wanted to arrest him, but no one laid a hand on him.

The Leaders Refuse To Have Faith in Jesus

[45]When the temple police returned to the chief priests and Pharisees, they were asked, "Why didn't you bring Jesus here?"

[46]They answered, "No one has ever spoken like that man!"

[47]The Pharisees said to them, "Have you also been fooled? [48]Not one of the chief priests or the Pharisees has faith in him. [49]And these people who don't know the Law are under God's curse anyway."

[50]Nicodemus was there at the time. He was a member of the council, and was the same one who had earlier come to see Jesus.[m] He said, [51]"Our Law doesn't let us condemn people before we hear what they have to say. We cannot judge them before we know what they have done."

[52]Then they said, "Nicodemus, you must be from Galilee! Read the Scriptures, and you will find that no prophet is to come from Galilee."

A Woman Caught in Sin

8 [53]Everyone else went home, [1]but Jesus walked out to the Mount of Olives. [2]Then early the next morning he went to the temple. The people came to him, and he sat down[n] and started teaching them.

[3]The Pharisees and the teachers of the Law of Moses brought in a woman who had

been caught in bed with a man who wasn't her husband. They made her stand in the middle of the crowd. [4]Then they said, "Teacher, this woman was caught sleeping with a man who isn't her husband. [5]The Law of Moses teaches that a woman like this should be stoned to death! What do you say?"

[6]They asked Jesus this question, because they wanted to test him and bring some charge against him. But Jesus simply bent over and started writing on the ground with his finger.

[7]They kept on asking Jesus about the woman. Finally, he stood up and said, "If any of you have never sinned, then go ahead and throw the first stone at her!" [8]Once again he bent over and began writing on the ground. [9]The people left one by one, beginning with the oldest. Finally, Jesus and the woman were there alone.

[10]Jesus stood up and asked her, "Where is everyone? Isn't there anyone left to accuse you?"

[11]"No sir," the woman answered.

Then Jesus told her, "I am not going to accuse you either. You may go now, but don't sin anymore."[o]

Jesus Is the Light for the World

[12]Once again Jesus spoke to the people. This time he said, "I am the light for the world! Follow me, and you won't be walking in the dark. You will have the light that gives life."

[13]The Pharisees objected, "You are the only one speaking for yourself, and what you say isn't true!"

[14]Jesus replied:

Even if I do speak for myself, what I say is true! I know where I came from and where I am going. But you don't know where I am from or where I am going. [15]You judge in the same way that everyone else does, but I don't judge anyone. [16]If I did judge, I would judge fairly, because I would not be doing it alone. The Father who sent me is here with me. [17]Your Law requires two witnesses to prove that something is true. [18]I am one of my witnesses, and the Father who sent me is the other one.

[19]"Where is your Father?" they asked.

"You don't know me or my Father!"

Jesus answered. "If you knew me, you would know my Father."

[20]Jesus said this while he was still teaching in the place where the temple treasures were stored. But no one arrested him, because his time had not yet come.[p]

You Cannot Go Where I Am Going

[21]Jesus also told them, "I am going away, and you will look for me. But you cannot go where I am going, and you will die with your sins unforgiven."

[22]The Jewish leaders asked, "Does he intend to kill himself? Is that what he means by saying we cannot go where he is going?"

[23]Jesus answered, "You are from below, but I am from above. You belong to this world, but I don't. [24]That is why I said you will die with your sins unforgiven. If you don't have faith in me for who I am,[q] you will die, and your sins will not be forgiven."

[25]"Who are you?" they asked Jesus.

Jesus answered, "I am exactly who I told you at the beginning. [26]There is a lot more I could say to condemn you. But the one who sent me is truthful, and I tell the people of this world only what I have heard from him."

[27]No one understood that Jesus was talking to them about the Father.

[28]Jesus went on to say, "When you have lifted up the Son of Man,[r] you will know who I am. You will also know that I don't do anything on my own. I say only what my Father taught me. [29]The one who sent me is with me. I always do what pleases him, and he will never leave me."

[30]After Jesus said this, many of the people put their faith in him.

The Truth Will Set You Free

[31]Jesus told the people who had faith in him, "If you keep on obeying what I have said, you truly are my disciples. [32]You will know the truth, and the truth will set you free."

[33]They answered, "We are Abraham's

---

[o]8.11 *don't sin anymore*: Verses 1-11 are not in some manuscripts. In other manuscripts these verses are placed after 7.36 or after 21.25 or after Luke 21.38, with some differences in the text.   [p]8.20 *his time had not yet come*: See the note at 2.4.   [q]8.24 *I am*: For the Jewish people the most holy name of God is "Yahweh," which may be translated "I am." In the Gospel of John "I am" is sometimes used by Jesus to show that he is that one.   [r]8.28 *lifted up the Son of Man*: See the note at 7.39.

children! We have never been anyone's slaves. How can you say we will be set free?" [34]Jesus replied:

I tell you for certain that anyone who sins is a slave of sin! [35]And slaves don't stay in the family forever, though the Son will always remain in the family. [36]If the Son gives you freedom, you are free! [37]I know that you are from Abraham's family. Yet you want to kill me, because my message isn't really in your hearts. [38]I am telling you what my Father has shown me, just as you are doing what your father has taught you.

Your Father Is the Devil

[39]The people said to Jesus, "Abraham is our father!"

Jesus replied, "If you were Abraham's children, you would do what Abraham did. [40]Instead, you want to kill me for telling you the truth that God gave me. Abraham never did anything like that. [41]But you are doing exactly what your father does."

"Don't accuse us of having someone else as our father!" they said. "We just have one father, and he is God."

[42]Jesus answered:

If God were your Father, you would love me, because I came from God and only from him. He sent me. I did not come on my own. [43]Why can't you understand what I am talking about? Can't you stand to hear what I am saying? [44]Your father is the devil, and you do exactly what he wants. He has always been a murderer and a liar. There is nothing truthful about him. He speaks on his own, and everything he says is a lie. Not only is he a liar himself, but he is also the father of all lies. [45]Everything I have told you is true, and you still refuse to have faith in me. [46]Can any of you accuse me of sin? If you cannot, why won't you have faith in me? After all, I am telling you the truth. [47]Anyone who belongs to God will listen to his message. But you refuse to listen, because you don't belong to God.

Jesus and Abraham

[48]The people told Jesus, "We were right to say that you are a Samaritan[s] and that you have a demon in you!"

[49]Jesus answered, "I don't have a demon in me. I honor my Father, and you refuse to honor me. [50]I don't want honor for myself. But there is one who wants me to be honored, and he is also the one who judges. [51]I tell you for certain that if you obey my words, you will never die."

[52]Then the people said, "Now we are sure that you have a demon. Abraham is dead, and so are the prophets. How can you say that no one who obeys your words will ever die? [53]Are you greater than our father Abraham? He died, and so did the prophets. Who do you think you are?"

[54]Jesus replied, "If I honored myself, it would mean nothing. My Father is the one who honors me. You claim that he is your God, [55]even though you don't really know him. If I said I didn't know him, I would be a liar, just like all of you. But I know him, and I do what he says. [56]Your father Abraham was really glad to see me."

[57]"You are not even fifty years old!" they said. "How could you have seen Abraham?"

[58]Jesus answered, "I tell you for certain that even before Abraham was, I was, and I am."[t] [59]The people picked up stones to kill Jesus, but he hid and left the temple.

Jesus Heals a Man Born Blind

9 As Jesus walked along, he saw a man who had been blind since birth. [2]Jesus' disciples asked, "Teacher, why was this man born blind? Was it because he or his parents sinned?"

[3]"No, it wasn't!" Jesus answered. "But because of his blindness, you will see God work a miracle for him. [4]As long as it is day, we must do what the one who sent me wants me to do. When night comes, no one can work. [5]While I am in the world, I am the light for the world."

[6]After Jesus said this, he spit on the ground. He made some mud and smeared it on the man's eyes. [7]Then he said, "Go and wash off the mud in Siloam Pool." The man went and washed in Siloam, which means "One Who Is Sent." When he had washed off the mud, he could see.

[8]The man's neighbors and the people who had seen him begging wondered if he really could be the same man. [9]Some of

---

[s]8.48 *Samaritan*: See 4.9 and the note there.
[t]8.58 *I am*: See the note at 8.24.

them said he was the same beggar, while others said he only looked like him. But he told them, "I am that man."

¹⁰"Then how can you see?" they asked.

¹¹He answered, "Someone named Jesus made some mud and smeared it on my eyes. He told me to go and wash it off in Siloam Pool. When I did, I could see."

¹²"Where is he now?" they asked.

"I don't know," he answered.

The Pharisees Try To Find Out What Happened

¹³⁻¹⁴The day when Jesus made the mud and healed the man was a Sabbath. So the people took the man to the Pharisees. ¹⁵They asked him how he was able to see, and he answered, "Jesus made some mud and smeared it on my eyes. Then after I washed it off, I could see."

¹⁶Some of the Pharisees said, "This man Jesus doesn't come from God. If he did, he would not break the law of the Sabbath."

Others asked, "How could someone who is a sinner work such a miracle?"ᵘ

Since the Pharisees could not agree among themselves, ¹⁷they asked the man, "What do you say about this one who healed your eyes?"

"He is a prophet!" the man told them.

¹⁸But the Jewish leaders would not believe that the man had once been blind. They sent for his parents ¹⁹and asked them, "Is this the son that you said was born blind? How can he now see?"

²⁰The man's parents answered, "We are certain that he is our son, and we know that he was born blind. ²¹But we don't know how he got his sight or who gave it to him. Ask him! He is old enough to speak for himself."

²²⁻²³The man's parents said this because they were afraid of the Jewish leaders. The leaders had already agreed that no one was to have anything to do with anyone who said Jesus was the Messiah.

²⁴The leaders called the man back and said, "Swear by God to tell the truth! We know that Jesus is a sinner."

²⁵The man replied, "I don't know if he is a sinner or not. All I know is that I used to be blind, but now I can see!"

²⁶"What did he do to you?" the Jewish leaders asked. "How did he heal your eyes?"

²⁷The man answered, "I have already told you once, and you refused to listen. Why do you want me to tell you again? Do you also want to become his disciples?"

²⁸The leaders insulted the man and said, "You are his follower! We are followers of Moses. ²⁹We are sure that God spoke to Moses, but we don't even know where Jesus comes from."

³⁰"How strange!" the man replied. "He healed my eyes, and yet you don't know where he comes from. ³¹We know that God listens only to people who love and obey him. God doesn't listen to sinners. ³²And this is the first time in history that anyone has ever given sight to someone born blind. ³³Jesus could not do anything unless he came from God."

³⁴The leaders told the man, "You have been a sinner since the day you were born! Do you think you can teach us anything?" Then they said, "You can never come back into any of our meeting places!"

³⁵When Jesus heard what had happened, he went and found the man. Then Jesus asked, "Do you have faith in the Son of Man?"

³⁶He replied, "Sir, if you will tell me who he is, I will put my faith in him."

³⁷"You have already seen him," Jesus answered, "and right now he is talking with you."

³⁸The man said, "Lord, I put my faith in you!" Then he worshiped Jesus.

³⁹Jesus told him, "I came to judge the people of this world. I am here to give sight to the blind and to make blind everyone who can see."

⁴⁰When the Pharisees heard Jesus say this, they asked, "Are we blind?"

⁴¹Jesus answered, "If you were blind, you would not be guilty. But now that you claim to see, you will keep on being guilty."

A Story about Sheep

10 Jesus said:
I tell you for certain that only thieves and robbers climb over the fence instead of going in through the gate to the sheep pen. ²⁻³But the gatekeeper opens the gate for the shepherd, and he goes in through it. The sheep know their

---

ᵘ**9.16** *miracle*: See the note at 2.11.

shepherd's voice. He calls each of them by name and leads them out.

[4]When he has led out all of his sheep, he walks in front of them, and they follow, because they know his voice. [5]The sheep will not follow strangers. They don't recognize a stranger's voice, and they run away. [6]Jesus told the people this story. But they did not understand what he was talking about.

Jesus Is the Good Shepherd

[7]Jesus said:

I tell you for certain that I am the gate for the sheep. [8]Everyone who came before me was a thief or a robber, and the sheep did not listen to any of them. [9]I am the gate. All who come in through me will be saved. Through me they will come and go and find pasture.

Learning what I'm gifted in has led me to heartfelt yeses—and the liberating sense of finding my specific niche in God's kingdom. Learning what I'm not gifted in has led to wonderfully guilt-free nos (most days)!

RUTH E. VAN REKEN

---

[10]A thief comes only to rob, kill, and destroy. I came so that everyone would have life, and have it in its fullest. [11]I am the good shepherd, and the good shepherd gives up his life for his sheep. [12]Hired workers are not like the shepherd. They don't own the sheep, and when they see a wolf coming, they run off and leave the sheep. Then the wolf attacks and scatters the flock. [13]Hired workers run away because they don't care about the sheep.

[14]I am the good shepherd. I know my sheep, and they know me. [15]Just as the Father knows me, I know the Father, and I give up my life for my sheep. [16]I have other sheep that are not in this sheep pen. I must bring them together too, when they hear my voice. Then there will be one flock of sheep and one shepherd.

[17]The Father loves me, because I give up my life, so that I may receive it back again. [18]No one takes my life from me. I give it up willingly! I have the power to give it up and the power to receive it back again, just as my Father commanded me to do.

[19]The people took sides because of what Jesus had told them. [20]Many of them said, "He has a demon in him! He is crazy! Why listen to him?"

[21]But others said, "How could anyone with a demon in him say these things? No one like that could give sight to a blind person!"

Jesus Is Rejected

[22]That winter, Jesus was in Jerusalem for the Temple Festival. [23]One day he was walking in that part of the temple known as Solomon's Porch,[v] [24]and the people gathered all around him. They said, "How long are you going to keep us guessing? If you are the Messiah, tell us plainly!"

[25]Jesus answered:

I have told you, and you refused to believe me. The things I do by my Father's authority show who I am. [26]But since you are not my sheep, you don't believe me. [27]My sheep know my voice, and I know them. They follow me, [28]and I give them eternal life, so that they will never be lost. No one can snatch them out of my hand. [29]My Father gave them to me, and he is greater than all others.[w] No one can snatch them from his hands, [30]and I am one with the Father.

[31]Once again the Jewish leaders picked up stones in order to kill Jesus. [32]But he said, "I have shown you many good things that my Father sent me to do. Which one are you going to stone me for?"

---

[v]**10.23** *Solomon's Porch:* A public place with tall columns along the east side of the temple.   [w]**10.29** *he is greater than all others:* Some manuscripts have "they are greater than all others."

[33]They answered, "We are not stoning you because of any good thing you did. We are stoning you because you did a terrible thing. You are just a man, and here you are claiming to be God!"

[34]Jesus replied:

In your Scriptures doesn't God say, "You are gods"? [35]You can't argue with the Scriptures, and God spoke to those people and called them gods. [36]So why do you accuse me of a terrible sin for saying that I am the Son of God? After all, it is the Father who prepared me for this work. He is also the one who sent me into the world. [37]If I don't do as my Father does, you should not believe me. [38]But if I do what my Father does, you should believe because of that, even if you don't have faith in me. Then you will know for certain that the Father is one with me, and I am one with the Father.

[39]Again they wanted to arrest Jesus. But he escaped [40]and crossed the Jordan to the place where John had earlier been baptizing. While Jesus was there, [41]many people came to him. They were saying, "John didn't work any miracles, but everything he said about Jesus is true." [42]A lot of those people also put their faith in Jesus.

The Death of Lazarus

11 [1-2]A man by the name of Lazarus was sick in the village of Bethany. He had two sisters, Mary and Martha. This was the same Mary who later poured perfume on the Lord's head and wiped his feet with her hair. [3]The sisters sent a message to the Lord and told him that his good friend Lazarus was sick.

[4]When Jesus heard this, he said, "His sickness won't end in death. It will bring glory to God and his Son."

[5]Jesus loved Martha and her sister and brother. [6]But he stayed where he was for two more days. [7]Then he said to his disciples, "Now we will go back to Judea."

[8]"Teacher," they said, "the people there want to stone you to death! Why do you want to go back?"

[9]Jesus answered, "Aren't there twelve hours in each day? If you walk during the day, you will have light from the sun, and you won't stumble. [10]But if you walk during the night, you will stumble, because you

don't have any light." [11]Then he told them, "Our friend Lazarus is asleep, and I am going there to wake him up."

[12]They replied, "Lord, if he is asleep, he will get better." [13]Jesus really meant that Lazarus was dead, but they thought he was talking only about sleep.

[14]Then Jesus told them plainly, "Lazarus is dead! [15]I am glad that I wasn't there, because now you will have a chance to put your faith in me. Let's go to him."

[16]Thomas, whose nickname was "Twin," said to the other disciples, "Come on. Let's go, so we can die with him."

Jesus Brings Lazarus to Life

[17]When Jesus got to Bethany, he found that Lazarus had already been in the tomb four days. [18]Bethany was only about two miles from Jerusalem, [19]and many people had come from the city to comfort Martha and Mary because their brother had died.

[20]When Martha heard that Jesus had arrived, she went out to meet him, but Mary stayed in the house. [21]Martha said to Jesus, "Lord, if you had been here, my brother would not have died. [22]Yet even now I know that God will do anything you ask."

[23]Jesus told her, "Your brother will live again!"

[24]Martha answered, "I know that he will be raised to life on the last day,[x] when all the dead are raised."

[25]Jesus then said, "I am the one who raises the dead to life! Everyone who has faith in me will live, even if they die. [26]And everyone who lives because of faith in me will never really die. Do you believe this?"

[27]"Yes, Lord!" she replied. "I believe that you are Christ, the Son of God. You are the one we hoped would come into the world."

[28]After Martha said this, she went and privately said to her sister Mary, "The Teacher is here, and he wants to see you." [29]As soon as Mary heard this, she got up and went out to Jesus. [30]He was still outside the village where Martha had gone to meet him. [31]Many people had come to comfort Mary, and when they saw her quickly leave the house, they thought she was going out to the tomb to cry. So they followed her.

[32]Mary went to where Jesus was. Then as

---

[x]11.24 *the last day:* When God will judge all people.

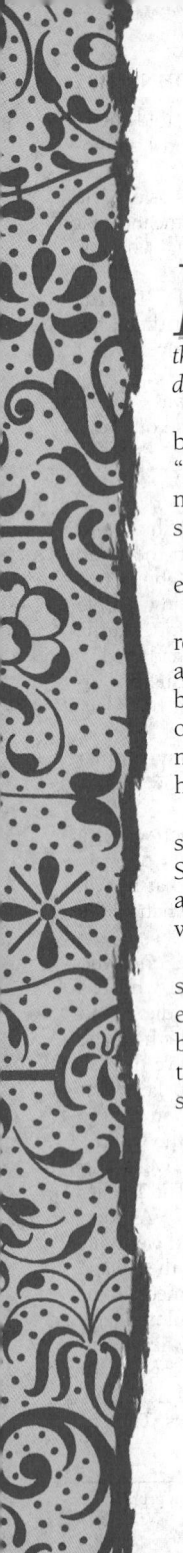

Mary and Martha

Luke 10.38-42; John 11.1—12.8

Mary and Martha were sisters with different personalities, interests, and skills. But they shared a common love for Jesus. They met Jesus when he was traveling through the town of Bethany where they lived with their brother, Lazarus. Martha welcomed Jesus into their home, and a friendship developed that was a blessing to all of them.

During Jesus' initial visit, Mary and Martha both attended to Jesus—but in different ways. Martha felt responsible for all the preparations and "worried about all that had to be done" (Luke 10.40). Mary, in the meantime, "sat down in front of the Lord and was listening to what he said" (Luke 10.39).

Mary's "inaction" bothered Martha. She rebuked Jesus and demanded that he tell Mary to come and help her.

But Jesus understood the state of Martha's soul, for he replied to her rebuke with gentleness: "Martha, Martha! You are worried and upset about so many things. . . . Mary has chosen what is best, and it will not be taken away from her" (Luke 10.41,42). Jesus wasn't judging Martha or making unflattering comparisons; rather, he was telling her that she needed to let go of her worries and the extreme expectations she had for her hospitality skills.

While Mary seemed to be the quieter of the two sisters, Martha spoke her mind very strongly with Jesus (Luke 10.40; John 11.21-28,39). She had great spiritual insight as exhibited in her conversation with Jesus after Lazarus's death (John 11.17-44). And she struggled with balance as we all do.

The last time we see Martha in Scripture (John 12.1-8), she's still serving, but this time she's not worried and upset. She allows Mary to express her love for Jesus in her own way—by pouring an expensive bottle of perfume on his feet and wiping them with her hair. At the same time, Martha seems comfortable with her own expression of love through service. And there is peace.

soon as she saw him, she knelt at his feet and said, "Lord, if you had been here, my brother would not have died."

[33]When Jesus saw that Mary and the people with her were crying, he was terribly upset [34]and asked, "Where have you put his body?"

They replied, "Lord, come and you will see."

[35]Jesus started crying, [36]and the people said, "See how much he loved Lazarus."

[37]Some of them said, "He gives sight to the blind. Why couldn't he have kept Lazarus from dying?"

[38]Jesus was still terribly upset. So he went to the tomb, which was a cave with a stone rolled against the entrance. [39]Then he told the people to roll the stone away. But Martha said, "Lord, you know that Lazarus has been dead four days, and there will be a bad smell."

[40]Jesus replied, "Didn't I tell you that if you had faith, you would see the glory of God?"

[41]After the stone had been rolled aside, Jesus looked up toward heaven and prayed, "Father, I thank you for answering my prayer. [42]I know that you always answer my prayers. But I said this, so that the people here would believe that you sent me."

[43]When Jesus had finished praying, he shouted, "Lazarus, come out!" [44]The man who had been dead came out. His hands and feet were wrapped with strips of burial cloth, and a cloth covered his face.

Jesus then told the people, "Untie him and let him go."

The Plot To Kill Jesus
(Matthew 26.1-5; Mark 14.1, 2; Luke 22.1, 2)

[45]Many of the people who had come to visit Mary saw the things that Jesus did, and they put their faith in him. [46]Others went to the Pharisees and told what Jesus had done. [47]Then the chief priests and the Pharisees called the council together and said, "What should we do? This man is working a lot of miracles.[y] [48]If we don't stop him now, everyone will put their faith in him. Then the Romans will come and destroy our temple and our nation."[z]

[49]One of the council members was Caiaphas, who was also high priest that year. He spoke up and said, "You people don't have any sense at all! [50]Don't you know it is better for one person to die for the people than for the whole nation to be destroyed?" [51]Caiaphas did not say this on his own. As high priest that year, he was prophesying that Jesus would die for the nation. [52]Yet Jesus would not die just for the Jewish nation. He would die to bring together all of God's scattered people. [53]From that day on, the council started making plans to put Jesus to death.

[54]Because of this plot against him, Jesus stopped going around in public. He went to the town of Ephraim, which was near the desert, and he stayed there with his disciples.

[55]It was almost time for Passover. Many of the Jewish people who lived out in the country had come to Jerusalem to get themselves ready[a] for the festival. [56]They looked around for Jesus. Then when they were in the temple, they asked each other, "You don't think he will come here for Passover, do you?"

[57]The chief priests and the Pharisees told the people to let them know if any of them saw Jesus. That is how they hoped to arrest him.

At Bethany
(Matthew 26.6-13; Mark 14.3-9)

12 Six days before Passover Jesus went back to Bethany, where he had raised Lazarus from death. [2]A meal had been prepared for Jesus. Martha was doing the serving, and Lazarus himself was there.

[3]Mary took a very expensive bottle of perfume[b] and poured it on Jesus' feet. She wiped them with her hair, and the sweet smell of the perfume filled the house.

[4]A disciple named Judas Iscariot[c] was there. He was the one who was going to betray Jesus, and he asked, [5]"Why wasn't this perfume sold for three hundred silver coins and the money given to the poor?" [6]Judas did not really care about the poor. He asked

---

[y]**11.47** *miracles:* See the note at 2.11.   [z]**11.48** *destroy our temple and our nation:* The Jewish leaders were afraid that Jesus would lead his followers to rebel against Rome and that the Roman army would then destroy their nation.   [a]**11.55** *get themselves ready:* The Jewish people had to do certain things to prepare themselves to worship God.   [b]**12.3** *very expensive bottle of perfume:* The Greek text has "expensive perfume made of pure spikenard," a plant used to make perfume.   [c]**12.4** *Iscariot:* See the note at 6.71.

this because he carried the moneybag and sometimes would steal from it.

> *God doesn't wait for us to "arrive" before he can use us. He sees us not only as we are now, but as we will be.*
>
> JUNKO CHENG

[7]Jesus replied, "Leave her alone! She has kept this perfume for the day of my burial. [8]You will always have the poor with you, but you won't always have me."

A Plot To Kill Lazarus

[9]A lot of people came when they heard that Jesus was there. They also wanted to see Lazarus, because Jesus had raised him from death. [10]So the chief priests made plans to kill Lazarus. [11]He was the reason that many of the Jewish people were turning from them and putting their faith in Jesus.

Jesus Enters Jerusalem

(Matthew 21.1-11; Mark 11.1-11; Luke 19.28-40)

[12]The next day a large crowd was in Jerusalem for Passover. When they heard that Jesus was coming for the festival, [13]they took palm branches and went out to greet him.[d] They shouted,

> "Hooray![e]
> God bless the one who comes
>   in the name of the Lord!
> God bless the King
>   of Israel!"

[14]Jesus found a donkey and rode on it, just as the Scriptures say,

> [15]"People of Jerusalem,
>   don't be afraid!
> Your King is now coming,
>   and he is riding
>   on a donkey."

[16]At first, Jesus' disciples did not understand. But after he had been given his glory,[f] they remembered all this. Everything had happened exactly as the Scriptures said it would.

[17-18]A crowd had come to meet Jesus because they had seen him call Lazarus out of the tomb. They kept talking about him and this miracle.[g] [19]But the Pharisees said to each other, "There is nothing that can be done! Everyone in the world is following Jesus."

Some Greeks Want To Meet Jesus

[20]Some Greeks[h] had gone to Jerusalem to worship during Passover. [21]Philip from Bethsaida in Galilee was there too. So they went to him and said, "Sir, we would like to meet Jesus." [22]Philip told Andrew. Then the two of them went to Jesus and told him.

The Son of Man Must Be Lifted Up

[23]Jesus said:

The time has come for the Son of Man to be given his glory.[i] [24]I tell you for certain that a grain of wheat that falls on the ground will never be more than one grain unless it dies. But if it dies, it will produce lots of wheat. [25]If you love your life, you will lose it. If you give it up in this world, you will be given eternal life. [26]If you serve me, you must go with me. My servants will be with me wherever I am. If you serve me, my Father will honor you.

[27]Now I am deeply troubled, and I don't know what to say. But I must not ask my Father to keep me from this time of suffering. In fact, I came into the world to suffer. [28]So Father, bring glory to yourself.

A voice from heaven then said, "I have already brought glory to myself, and I will do it again!" [29]When the crowd heard the voice, some of them thought it was thunder. Others thought an angel had spoken to Jesus.

[30]Then Jesus told the crowd, "That voice spoke to help you, not me. [31]This world's

---

[d]**12.13** *took palm branches and went out to greet him*: This was one way that the Jewish people welcomed a famous person.   [e]**12.13** *Hooray*: This translates a word that can mean "please save us." But it is most often used as a shout of praise to God.   [f]**12.16** *had been given his glory*: See the note at 7.39.   [g]**12.17,18** *miracle*: See the note at 2.11.   [h]**12.20** *Greeks*: Perhaps Gentiles who worshiped with the Jews. See the note at 7.35.   [i]**12.23** *be given his glory*: See the note at 7.39.

people are now being judged, and the ruler of this world[j] is already being thrown out! [32]If I am lifted up above the earth, I will make everyone want to come to me." [33]Jesus was talking about the way he would be put to death.

[34]The crowd said to Jesus, "The Scriptures teach that the Messiah will live forever. How can you say that the Son of Man must be lifted up? Who is this Son of Man?"

[35]Jesus answered, "The light will be with you for only a little longer. Walk in the light while you can. Then you won't be caught walking blindly in the dark. [36]Have faith in the light while it is with you, and you will be children of the light."

The People Refuse To Have Faith in Jesus

After Jesus had said these things, he left and went into hiding. [37]He had worked a lot of miracles[k] among the people, but they were still not willing to have faith in him. [38]This happened so that what the prophet Isaiah had said would come true,

> "Lord, who has believed
>   our message?
> And who has seen
>   your mighty strength?"

[39]The people could not have faith in Jesus, because Isaiah had also said,

> [40]"The Lord has blinded
>   the eyes of the people,
> and he has made
>   the people stubborn.
> He did this so that they
>   could not see
>   or understand,
> and so that they
>   would not turn to the Lord
>   and be healed."

[41]Isaiah said this, because he saw the glory of Jesus and spoke about him.[l] [42]Even then, many of the leaders put their faith in Jesus, but they did not tell anyone about it. The Pharisees had already given orders for the people not to have anything to do with anyone who had faith in Jesus. [43]And besides, the leaders liked praise from others more than they liked praise from God.

Jesus Came To Save the World

[44]In a loud voice Jesus said:

Everyone who has faith in me also has faith in the one who sent me. [45]And everyone who has seen me has seen the one who sent me. [46]I am the light that has come into the world. No one who has faith in me will stay in the dark.

[47]I am not the one who will judge those who refuse to obey my teachings. I came to save the people of this world, not to be their judge. [48]But everyone who rejects me and my teachings will be judged on the last day[m] by what I have said. [49]I don't speak on my own. I say only what the Father who sent me has told me to say. [50]I know that his commands will bring eternal life. That is why I tell you exactly what the Father has told me.

Jesus Washes the Feet of His Disciples

13 It was before Passover, and Jesus knew that the time had come for him to leave this world and to return to the Father. He had always loved his followers in this world, and he loved them to the very end.

[2]Even before the evening meal started, the devil had made Judas, the son of Simon Iscariot,[n] decide to betray Jesus. [3]Jesus knew that he had come from God and would go back to God. He also knew that the Father had given him complete power. [4]So during the meal Jesus got up, removed his outer garment, and wrapped a towel around his waist. [5]He put some water into a large bowl. Then he began washing his disciples' feet and drying them with the towel he was wearing.

[6]But when he came to Simon Peter, that disciple asked, "Lord, are you going to wash my feet?"

[7]Jesus answered, "You don't really know what I am doing, but later you will understand."

---

[j]**12.31** *world:* In the Gospel of John "world" sometimes refers to the people who live in this world and to the evil forces that control their lives.   [k]**12.37** *miracles:* See the note at 2.11.   [l]**12.41** *he saw the glory of Jesus and spoke about him:* Or "he saw the glory of God and spoke about Jesus."   [m]**12.48** *the last day:* See the note at 6.39.   [n]**13.2** *Iscariot:* See the note at 6.71.

⁸"You will never wash my feet!" Peter replied.

"If I don't wash you," Jesus told him, "you don't really belong to me."

⁹Peter said, "Lord, don't wash just my feet. Wash my hands and my head."

¹⁰Jesus answered, "People who have bathed and are clean all over need to wash just their feet. And you, my disciples, are clean, except for one of you." ¹¹Jesus knew who would betray him. That is why he said, "except for one of you."

¹²After Jesus had washed his disciples' feet and had put his outer garment back on, he sat down again.ᵒ Then he said:

Do you understand what I have done? ¹³You call me your teacher and Lord, and you should, because that is who I am. ¹⁴And if your Lord and teacher has washed your feet, you should do the same for each other. ¹⁵I have set the example, and you should do for each other exactly what I have done for you. ¹⁶I tell you for certain that servants are not greater than their master, and messengers are not greater than the one who sent them. ¹⁷You

know these things, and God will bless you, if you do them.

¹⁸I am not talking about all of you. I know the ones I have chosen. But what the Scriptures say must come true. And they say, "The man who ate with me has turned against me!" ¹⁹I am telling you this before it all happens. Then when it does happen, you will believe who I am.ᵖ ²⁰I tell you for certain that anyone who welcomes my messengers also welcomes me, and anyone who welcomes me welcomes the one who sent me.

Jesus Tells What Will Happen to Him
(Matthew 26.20-25; Mark 14.17-21; Luke 22.21-23)

²¹After Jesus had said these things, he was deeply troubled and told his disciples, "I tell you for certain that one of you will

---

ᵒ**13.12** *sat down again*: On special occasions the Jewish people followed the Greek and Roman custom of lying down on their left side and leaning on their left elbow, while eating with their right hand.   ᵖ**13.19** *I am*: See the note at 8.24.

⌐꠸꠸ᒪ

MARRIAGE—How can I lead my unbelieving husband to Christ without offending him? *(John 13.1-17)*

Show your husband grace, humility, and unconditional love.

When Christ wanted to teach his disciples how to treat each other, he realized that *experiencing* something is more life-changing than words alone. So Jesus got up from the meal, took off his outer garments, and began washing their dusty feet—a service usually relegated to the lowliest servant. Then, based on the powerful experience they'd just shared, he taught his disciples about serving each other.

In the same way, an unbelieving husband may need to *experience* Christ's love through another human being before he can believe it's real. The Christian wife who consistently demonstrates Christ's love by serving her husband appropriately gives him the opportunity to experience Christ's love in a way that goes beyond mere words and religious talk.

If her husband is receptive, she can link her service with an explanation that she's following Christ's example. Christ didn't intend to become a perpetual doormat. He said, "You call me your teacher and Lord, and you should, because that is who I am" (13.13). But he explained that this ceremony modeled the attitude of service that ought to develop among his disciples (13.12-20). In the same way, a wife's service to her husband models Christ's love—so that her husband will be drawn to faith. Her service also provides an example of the servant attitude that should eventually characterize both husband and wife. (See also Genesis 39; 41.39; Song of Songs 2.16—3.4; 1 Peter 3.1-6; Revelation 21.9—22.21.)

⌐꠸ᒪ **Words To Remember:** *I have set the example, and you should do for each other exactly what I have done for you.*—**John 13.15**

betray me." ²²They were confused about what he meant. And they just stared at each other.

²³Jesus' favorite disciple was sitting next to him at the meal, ²⁴and Simon motioned for that disciple to find out which one Jesus meant. ²⁵So the disciple leaned toward Jesus and asked, "Lord, which one of us are you talking about?"

²⁶Jesus answered, "I will dip this piece of bread in the sauce and give it to the one I was talking about."

Then Jesus dipped the bread and gave it to Judas, the son of Simon Iscariot.⁹ ²⁷Right then Satan took control of Judas.

Jesus said, "Judas, go quickly and do what you have to do." ²⁸No one at the meal understood what Jesus meant. ²⁹But because Judas was in charge of the money, some of them thought that Jesus had told him to buy something they needed for the festival. Others thought that Jesus had told him to give some money to the poor. ³⁰Judas took the piece of bread and went out.

It was already night.

The New Command

³¹After Judas had gone, Jesus said:
Now the Son of Man will be given

glory, and he will bring glory to God. ³²Then, after God is given glory because of him, God will bring glory to him, and God will do it very soon.

³³My children, I will be with you for a little while longer. Then you will look for me, but you won't find me. I tell you just as I told the people, "You cannot go where I am going." ³⁴But I am giving you a new command. You must love each other, just as I have loved you. ³⁵If you love each other, everyone will know that you are my disciples.

Peter's Promise

(Matthew 26.31-35; Mark 14.27-31; Luke 22.31-34)

³⁶Simon Peter asked, "Lord, where are you going?"

Jesus answered, "You can't go with me now, but later on you will."

³⁷Peter asked, "Lord, why can't I go with you now? I would die for you!"

³⁸"Would you really die for me?" Jesus asked. "I tell you for certain that before a rooster crows, you will say three times that you don't even know me."

---

⁹13.26 Iscariot: See the note at 6.71.

Friendship—If I'm naturally introverted and independent, why should I go out of my way to make friends? (John 13.18-35)

To live out God's command to "love each other."
Friendships take time and effort—even for those gregarious souls to whom it comes naturally. But if you are naturally introverted, friendship presents an even greater challenge. You may wonder if any relationship is worth the risk.

Jesus had every reason to wonder if friendship was worth it. He invested a great deal of time, energy, and love into twelve special friends only to have one of them betray him by turning him over to religious leaders who wanted to kill him. Jesus knew all along that this would happen, yet he maintained an open heart and continued to include Judas in his circle of friends.

One would think that after Judas left to betray him (13.31), Jesus might have sat the rest of the disciples down and said, "This is how you protect yourself from people who want to use and abuse you." But no. Jesus used Judas's betrayal as an opportunity to *encourage* them to keep loving each other—because this would be the way that the world would know they were his followers.

God is love. When we allow ourselves to become a conduit of that love in our friendships with others, we identify ourselves as Christ-followers, and others are drawn to him. (See also Ecclesiastes 4.9-12; Hebrews 13.1,2.)

Words To Remember: *If you love each other, everyone will know that you are my disciples.*—John 13.35

Jesus Is the Way to the Father

14 Jesus said to his disciples, "Don't be worried! Have faith in God and have faith in me.ʳ ²There are many rooms in my Father's house. I wouldn't tell you this, unless it was true. I am going there to prepare a place for each of you. ³After I have done this, I will come back and take you with me. Then we will be together. ⁴You know the way to where I am going."

⁵Thomas said, "Lord, we don't even know where you are going! How can we know the way?"

⁶"I am the way, the truth, and the life!" Jesus answered. "Without me, no one can go to the Father. ⁷If you had known me, you would have known the Father. But from now on, you do know him, and you have seen him."

⁸Philip said, "Lord, show us the Father. That is all we need."

⁹Jesus replied:

Philip, I have been with you for a long time. Don't you know who I am? If you have seen me, you have seen the Father. How can you ask me to show you the Father? ¹⁰Don't you believe that I am one with the Father and that the Father is one with me? What I say isn't said on my own. The Father who lives in me does these things.

¹¹Have faith in me when I say that the Father is one with me and that I am one with the Father. Or else have faith in me simply because of the things I do. ¹²I tell you for certain that if you have faith in me, you will do the same things that I am doing. You will do even greater things, now that I am going back to the Father. ¹³Ask me, and I will do whatever you ask. This way the Son will bring honor to the Father. ¹⁴I will do whatever you ask me to do.

The Holy Spirit Is Promised

¹⁵Jesus said to his disciples:

If you love me, you will do as I command. ¹⁶Then I will ask the Father to send you the Holy Spirit who will helpˢ you and always be with you. ¹⁷The Spirit will show you what is true. The people of this world cannot accept the Spirit, because they don't see or know him. But you know the Spirit, who is with you and will keep on living in you.

¹⁸I won't leave you like orphans. I will come back to you. ¹⁹In a little

---

ʳ14.1 *Have faith in God and have faith in me:* Or "You have faith in God, so have faith in me." ˢ14.16 *help:* The Greek word may mean "comfort," "encourage," or "defend."

Friendship—How can I show my friend that Christ is the only way to God?
(*John 14.1-14*)

Encourage her to get to know Jesus.

We live in an image-conscious, media-driven culture in which it can be quite challenging to get beneath the surface and find out who people really are. Even where Christ is concerned, it's hard to differentiate between facts and feelings.

In John 14, the disciples wrestled with faith issues similar to the ones facing spiritual seekers today. They might well have been asking Jesus, "Who are you? What's your relationship to God? Where are you going? How can we know how to get there, too?" Jesus' answer then and now is to allow seekers to be with him and get to know him as a real person.

By spending time getting to know Christ through Scripture, prayer, and the ministry of the Holy Spirit, the spiritual seeker begins to know deep in his or her heart that Jesus is the way, the truth, and the life. This kind of knowing goes beyond our so-very-human feelings. As a friend who cares about another friend's faith, you can rest in the fact that as you encourage her to get to know Christ, he will show her that he's the only way to God—just as he did for his disciples. (See also Isaiah 7.10-17; Isaiah 53; Mark 16.1-8.)

Words To Remember: *"I am the way, the truth, and the life!" Jesus answered. "Without me, no one can go to the Father."*—John 14.6

while the people of this world won't be able to see me, but you will see me. And because I live, you will live. [20]Then you will know that I am one with the Father. You will know that you are one with me, and I am one with you. [21]If you love me, you will do what I have said, and my Father will love you. I will also love you and show you what I am like.

[22]The other Judas, not Judas Iscariot,[t] then spoke up and asked, "Lord, what do you mean by saying that you will show us what you are like, but you will not show the people of this world?"

[23]Jesus replied:

If anyone loves me, they will obey me. Then my Father will love them, and we will come to them and live in them. [24]But anyone who doesn't love me, won't obey me. What they have heard me say doesn't really come from me, but from the Father who sent me.

[25]I have told you these things while I am still with you. [26]But the Holy Spirit will come and help[u] you, because the Father will send the Spirit to take my place. The Spirit will teach you everything and will remind you of what I said while I was with you.

[27]I give you peace, the kind of peace that only I can give. It isn't like the peace that this world can give. So don't be worried or afraid.

[28]You have already heard me say that I am going and that I will also come back to you. If you really love me, you should be glad that I am going back to the Father, because he is greater than I am.

[29]I am telling you this before I leave, so that when it does happen, you will have faith in me. [30]I cannot speak with you much longer, because the ruler of this world is coming. But he has no power over me. [31]I obey my Father, so that everyone in the world might know that I love him.

It is time for us to go now.

Jesus Is the True Vine

15 Jesus said to his disciples:
I am the true vine, and my Father is the gardener. [2]He cuts away every branch of mine that doesn't produce fruit. But he trims clean every branch that does produce fruit, so that it will produce even more fruit. [3]You are already clean because of what I have said to you.

[4]Stay joined to me, and I will stay joined to you. Just as a branch cannot produce fruit unless it stays joined to the vine, you cannot produce fruit unless you stay joined to me. [5]I am the vine, and you are the branches. If you stay joined to me, and I stay joined to you, then you will produce lots of fruit. But you cannot do anything without me. [6]If you don't stay joined to me, you will be thrown away. You will be like dry branches that are gathered up and burned in a fire.

[7]Stay joined to me and let my teachings become part of you. Then you can pray for whatever you want, and your prayer will be answered. [8]When you become fruitful disciples of mine, my Father will be honored. [9]I have loved you, just as my Father has loved me. So remain faithful to my love for you. [10]If you obey me, I will keep loving you, just as my Father keeps loving me, because I have obeyed him.

[11]I have told you this to make you as completely happy as I am. [12]Now I tell you to love each other, as I have loved you. [13]The greatest way to show love for friends is to die for them. [14]And you are my friends, if you obey me. [15]Servants don't know what their master is doing, and so I don't speak to you as my servants. I speak to you as my friends, and I have told you everything that my Father has told me.

[16]You did not choose me. I chose you and sent you out to produce fruit, the kind of fruit that will last. Then my Father will give you whatever you ask for in my name.[v] [17]So I command you to love each other.

The World's Hatred

[18]If the people of this world[w] hate you, just remember that they hated me

---

[t]**14.22** *Iscariot:* See the note at 6.71.   [u]**14.26** *help:* See the note at 14.16.   [v]**15.16** *in my name:* Or "because you are my followers."   [w]**15.18** *world:* See the note at 12.31.

first. ¹⁹If you belonged to the world, its people would love you. But you don't belong to the world. I have chosen you to leave the world behind, and that is why its people hate you. ²⁰Remember how I told you that servants are not greater than their master. So if people mistreat me, they will mistreat you. If they do what I say, they will do what you say.

²¹People will do to you exactly what they did to me. They will do it because you belong to me, and they don't know the one who sent me. ²²If I had not come and spoken to them, they would not be guilty of sin. But now they have no excuse for their sin.

²³Everyone who hates me also hates my Father. ²⁴I have done things that no one else has ever done. If they had not seen me do these things, they would not be guilty. But they did see me do these things, and they still hate me and my Father too. ²⁵That is why the Scriptures are true when they say, "People hated me for no reason."

²⁶I will send you the Spirit who comes from the Father and shows what is true. The Spirit will help^x you and will tell you about me. ²⁷Then you will also tell others about me, because you have been with me from the beginning.

16

I am telling you this to keep you from being afraid. ²You will be chased out of the Jewish meeting places. And the time will come when people will kill you and think they are doing God a favor. ³They will do these things because they don't know either the Father or me. ⁴I am saying this to you now, so that when the time comes, you will remember what I have said.

The Work of the Holy Spirit

I was with you at the first, and so I didn't tell you these things. ⁵But now I am going back to the Father who sent me, and none of you asks me where I am going. ⁶You are very sad from hearing all of this. ⁷But I tell you that I am going to do what is best for you. That is why I am going away. The Holy Spirit cannot come to help^x you until I leave. But after I am gone, I will send the Spirit to you.

⁸The Spirit will come and show the people of this world the truth about sin and God's justice and the judgment. ⁹The Spirit will show them that

---

^{x}**15.26; 16.7** *help:* See the note at 14.16.

Personal *Concerns*—How should I handle it when I feel rejected or excluded because of my faith? *(John 15.18-27)*

Be comforted by the fact that Jesus was also hated.
Have you ever extended kindness to someone only to have that person take it the wrong way and explode with anger? This happened to Jesus many times during his time on this earth. He came to bring the message of God's love, but was often rejected and excluded.

We're tempted to think that if only we communicated differently, loved better, behaved more perfectly, we'd be spared the pain of rejection, and people would easily receive our message. The truth is that Jesus loved perfectly, never sinned, and communicated with divine insight and grace. Still, people responded to him with hatred. Why? Because his message upset their neat categories. The love to which he called people was radical indeed.

Jesus wants us to know that we won't be spared the pain of hatred and rejection as we live out our faith. We can, however, be encouraged by several truths: We are in good company; we are not alone because we can rely on the Holy Spirit to teach us and comfort us; and love conquers all. When Jesus died on the cross, God's love conquered death. His love is the only force that can conquer the hatred that's in the world. (See also Daniel 6; Hebrews 10.32-39; 1 Peter 4.12-19; Revelation 14.12,13.)

Words To Remember: *Servants are not greater than their master. So if people mistreat me, they will mistreat you.—John 15.20*

they are wrong about sin, because they didn't have faith in me. ¹⁰They are wrong about God's justice, because I am going to the Father, and you won't see me again. ¹¹And they are wrong about the judgment, because God has already judged the ruler of this world.

¹²I have much more to say to you, but right now it would be more than you could understand. ¹³The Spirit shows what is true and will come and guide you into the full truth. The Spirit doesn't speak on his own. He will tell you only what he has heard from me, and he will let you know what is going to happen. ¹⁴The Spirit will bring glory to me by taking my message and telling it to you. ¹⁵Everything that the Father has is mine. That is why I have said that the Spirit takes my message and tells it to you.

Sorrow Will Turn into Joy

¹⁶Jesus told his disciples, "For a little while you won't see me, but after a while you will see me."

¹⁷They said to each other, "What does Jesus mean by saying that for a little while we won't see him, but after a while we will see him? What does he mean by saying that he is going to the Father? ¹⁸What is this 'little while' that he is talking about? We don't know what he means."

¹⁹Jesus knew that they had some questions, so he said:

You are wondering what I meant when I said that for a little while you won't see me, but after a while you will see me. ²⁰I tell you for certain that you will cry and be sad, but the world will be happy. You will be sad, but later you will be happy.

²¹When a woman is about to give birth, she is in great pain. But after it is all over, she forgets the pain and is happy, because she has brought a child into the world. ²²You are now very sad. But later I will see you, and you will be so happy that no one will be able to change the way you feel. ²³When that time comes, you won't have to ask me about anything. I tell you for certain that the Father will give you whatever you ask for in my name. ²⁴You have not asked for anything in

this way before, but now you must ask in my name.ʸ Then it will be given to you, so that you will be completely happy.

²⁵I have used examples to explain to you what I have been talking about. But the time will come when I will speak to you plainly about the Father and will no longer use examples like these. ²⁶You will ask the Father in my name,ᶻ and I won't have to ask him for you. ²⁷God the Father loves you because you love me, and you believe that I have come from him. ²⁸I came from the Father into the world, but I am leaving the world and returning to the Father.

²⁹The disciples said, "Now you are speaking plainly to us! You are not using examples. ³⁰At last we know that you understand everything, and we don't have any more questions. Now we believe that you truly have come from God."

³¹Jesus replied:

Do you really believe me? ³²The time will come and is already here when all of you will be scattered. Each of you will go back home and leave me by myself. But the Father will be with me, and I won't be alone. ³³I have told you this, so that you might have peace in your hearts because of me. While you are in the world, you will have to suffer. But cheer up! I have defeated the world.ᵃ

Jesus Prays

17 After Jesus had finished speaking to his disciples, he looked up toward heaven and prayed:

Father, the time has come for you to bring glory to your Son, in order that he may bring glory to you. ²And you gave him power over all people, so that he would give eternal life to everyone you give him. ³Eternal life is to know you, the only true God, and to know Jesus Christ, the one you sent. ⁴I have brought glory to you here on earth by doing everything you gave me

ʸ16.23,24 *in my name . . . in my name*: Or "as my disciples . . . as my disciples." ᶻ16.26 *in my name*: Or "because you are my followers." ᵃ16.33 *world*: See the note at 12.31.

to do. ⁵Now, Father, give me back the glory that I had with you before the world was created.

⁶You have given me some followers from this world, and I have shown them what you are like. They were yours, but you gave them to me, and they have obeyed you. ⁷They know that you gave me everything I have. ⁸I told my followers what you told me, and they accepted it. They know that I came from you, and they believe that you are the one who sent me. ⁹I am praying for them, but not for those who belong to this world.ᵃ My followers belong to you, and I am praying for them. ¹⁰All that I have is yours, and all that you have is mine, and they will bring glory to me.

¹¹Holy Father, I am no longer in the world. I am coming to you, but my followers are still in the world. So keep them safe by the power of the name that you have given me. Then they will be one with each other, just as you and I are one. ¹²While I was with them, I kept them safe by the power you have given me. I guarded them, and not one of them was lost, except the one who had to be lost. This happened so that what the Scriptures say would come true.

¹³I am on my way to you. But I say these things while I am still in the world, so that my followers will have the same complete joy that I do. ¹⁴I have told them your message. But the people of this world hate them, because they don't belong to this world, just as I don't.

¹⁵Father, I don't ask you to take my followers out of the world, but keep them safe from the evil one. ¹⁶They don't belong to this world, and neither do I. ¹⁷Your word is the truth. So let this truth make them completely yours. ¹⁸I am sending them into the world, just as you sent me. ¹⁹I have given myself completely for their sake, so that they may belong completely to the truth.

²⁰I am not praying just for these followers. I am also praying for everyone else who will have faith because of what my followers will say about me.

²¹I want all of them to be one with each other, just as I am one with you and you are one with me. I also want them to be one with us. Then the people of this world will believe that you sent me.

> *Knowing we've all been created by the same heavenly Father puts our differences in the proper perspective.*
>
> EVANGELINE SCHOCK

²¹I have honored my followers in the same way that you honored me, in order that they may be one with each other, just as we are one. ²³I am one with them, and you are one with me, so that they may become completely one. Then this world's people will know that you sent me. They will know that you love my followers as much as you love me.

²⁴Father, I want everyone you have given me to be with me, wherever I am. Then they will see the glory that you have given me, because you loved me before the world was created. ²⁵Good Father, the people of this world don't know you. But I know you, and my followers know that you sent me. ²⁶I told them what you are like, and I will tell them even more. Then the love that you have for me will become part of them, and I will be one with them.

Jesus Is Betrayed and Arrested
(Matthew 26.47-56; Mark 14.43-50; Luke 22.47-53)

18 When Jesus had finished praying, he and his disciples crossed the Kidron Valley and went into a garden.ᵇ ²Jesus had often met there with his

---

ᵃ17.9 *world:* See the note at 12.31.   ᵇ18.1 *garden:* The Greek word is usually translated "garden," but probably referred to an olive orchard.

disciples, and Judas knew where the place was.

[3-5]Judas had promised to betray Jesus. So he went to the garden with some Roman soldiers and temple police, who had been sent by the chief priests and the Pharisees. They carried torches, lanterns, and weapons. Jesus already knew everything that was going to happen, but he asked, "Who are you looking for?"

They answered, "We are looking for Jesus from Nazareth!"

Jesus told them, "I am Jesus!"[c] [6]At once they all backed away and fell to the ground.

[7]Jesus again asked, "Who are you looking for?"

"We are looking for Jesus from Nazareth," they answered.

[8]This time Jesus replied, "I have already told you that I am Jesus. If I am the one you are looking for, let these others go. [9]Then everything will happen, just as I said, 'I did not lose anyone you gave me.' "

[10]Simon Peter had brought along a sword. He now pulled it out and struck at the servant of the high priest. The servant's name was Malchus, and Peter cut off his right ear. [11]Jesus told Peter, "Put your sword away. I must drink from the cup[d] that the Father has given me."

Jesus Is Brought to Annas
(Matthew 26.57, 58; Mark 14.53, 54; Luke 22.54)

[12]The Roman officer and his men, together with the temple police, arrested Jesus and tied him up. [13]They took him first to Annas, who was the father-in-law of Caiaphas, the high priest that year. [14]This was the same Caiaphas who had told the Jewish leaders, "It is better if one person dies for the people."

Peter Says He Doesn't Know Jesus
(Matthew 26.69, 70; Mark 14.66-68; Luke 22.55-57)

[15]Simon Peter and another disciple followed Jesus. That disciple knew the high priest, and he followed Jesus into the courtyard of the high priest's house. [16]Peter stayed outside near the gate. But the other disciple came back out and spoke to the girl at the gate. She let Peter go in, [17]but asked him, "Aren't you one of that man's followers?"

"No, I am not!" Peter answered.

[18]It was cold, and the servants and temple police had made a charcoal fire. They were warming themselves around it, when Peter went over and stood near the fire to warm himself.

Jesus Is Questioned by the High Priest
(Matthew 26.59-66; Mark 14.55-64; Luke 22.66-71)

[19]The high priest questioned Jesus about his followers and his teaching. [20]But Jesus told him, "I have spoken freely in front of everyone. And I have always taught in our meeting places and in the temple, where all of our people come together. I have not said anything in secret. [21]Why are you questioning me? Why don't you ask the people who heard me? They know what I have said."

[22]As soon as Jesus said this, one of the temple police hit him and said, "That's no way to talk to the high priest!"

[23]Jesus answered, "If I have done something wrong, say so. But if not, why did you hit me?" [24]Jesus was still tied up, and Annas sent him to Caiaphas the high priest.

Peter Again Denies that He Knows Jesus
(Matthew 26.71-75; Mark 14.69-72; Luke 22.58-62)

[25]While Simon Peter was standing there warming himself, someone asked him, "Aren't you one of Jesus' followers?"

Again Peter denied it and said, "No, I am not!"

[26]One of the high priest's servants was there. He was a relative of the servant whose ear Peter had cut off, and he asked, "Didn't I see you in the garden with that man?"

[27]Once more Peter denied it, and right then a rooster crowed.

Jesus Is Tried by Pilate
(Matthew 27.1, 2, 11-14; Mark 15.1-5; Luke 23.1-5)

[28]It was early in the morning when Jesus was taken from Caiaphas to the building where the Roman governor stayed. But the crowd waited outside. Any of them who had gone inside would have become unclean

---

[c]**18.3-5** *I am Jesus:* The Greek text has "I am" (see the note at 8.24).   [d]**18.11** *drink from the cup:* In the Scriptures a cup is sometimes used as a symbol of suffering. To "drink from the cup" is to suffer.

and would not be allowed to eat the Passover meal.[e]

²⁹Pilate came out and asked, "What charges are you bringing against this man?"

³⁰They answered, "He is a criminal! That's why we brought him to you."

³¹Pilate told them, "Take him and judge him by your own laws."

The crowd replied, "We are not allowed to put anyone to death." ³²And so what Jesus said about his death[f] would soon come true.

³³Pilate then went back inside. He called Jesus over and asked, "Are you the king of the Jews?"

³⁴Jesus answered, "Are you asking this on your own or did someone tell you about me?"

³⁵"You know I'm not a Jew!" Pilate said. "Your own people and the chief priests brought you to me. What have you done?"

³⁶Jesus answered, "My kingdom doesn't belong to this world. If it did, my followers would have fought to keep me from being handed over to the Jewish leaders. No, my kingdom doesn't belong to this world."

³⁷"So you are a king," Pilate replied.

"You are saying that I am a king," Jesus told him. "I was born into this world to tell about the truth. And everyone who belongs to the truth knows my voice."

³⁸Pilate asked Jesus, "What is truth?"

Jesus Is Sentenced to Death

(Matthew 27.15-31; Mark 15.6-20; Luke 23.13-25)

Pilate went back out and said, "I don't find this man guilty of anything! ³⁹And since I usually set a prisoner free for you at Passover, would you like for me to set free the king of the Jews?"

⁴⁰They shouted, "No, not him! We want Barabbas." Now Barabbas was a terrorist.[g]

19 Pilate gave orders for Jesus to be beaten with a whip. ²The soldiers made a crown out of thorn branches and put it on Jesus. Then they put a purple robe on him. ³They came up to him and said, "Hey, you king of the Jews!" They also hit him with their fists.

⁴Once again Pilate went out. This time he said, "I will have Jesus brought out to you again. Then you can see for yourselves that I have not found him guilty."

⁵Jesus came out, wearing the crown of thorns and the purple robe. Pilate said, "Here is the man!"[h]

⁶When the chief priests and the temple police saw him, they yelled, "Nail him to a cross! Nail him to a cross!"

Pilate told them, "You take him and nail him to a cross! I don't find him guilty of anything."

⁷The crowd replied, "He claimed to be the Son of God! Our Jewish Law says that he must be put to death."

⁸When Pilate heard this, he was terrified. ⁹He went back inside and asked Jesus, "Where are you from?" But Jesus did not answer.

¹⁰"Why won't you answer my question?" Pilate asked. "Don't you know that I have the power to let you go free or to nail you to a cross?"

¹¹Jesus replied, "If God had not given you the power, you couldn't do anything at all to me. But the one who handed me over to you did something even worse."

¹²Then Pilate wanted to set Jesus free. But the crowd again yelled, "If you set this man free, you are no friend of the Emperor! Anyone who claims to be a king is an enemy of the Emperor."

¹³When Pilate heard this, he brought Jesus out. Then he sat down on the judge's bench at the place known as "The Stone Pavement." In Aramaic this pavement is called "Gabbatha." ¹⁴It was about noon on the day before Passover, and Pilate said to the crowd, "Look at your king!"

¹⁵"Kill him! Kill him!" they yelled. "Nail him to a cross!"

"So you want me to nail your king to a cross?" Pilate asked.

The chief priests replied, "The Emperor is our king!" ¹⁶Then Pilate handed Jesus over to be nailed to a cross.

---

[e]18.28 would have become unclean and would not be allowed to eat the Passover meal: Jewish people who came in close contact with foreigners right before Passover were not allowed to eat the Passover meal. [f]18.32 about his death: Jesus had said that he would die by being "lifted up," which meant that he would die on a cross. The Romans killed criminals by nailing them on a cross, but they did not let the Jews kill anyone in this way. [g]18.40 terrorist: Someone who stirred up trouble against the Romans in the hope of gaining freedom for the Jewish people. [h]19.5 "Here is the man!": Or "Look at the man!"

Jesus Is Nailed to a Cross

(Matthew 27.32-44; Mark 15.21-32; Luke 23.26-43)

Jesus was taken away, [17]and he carried his cross to a place known as "The Skull."[i] In Aramaic this place is called "Golgotha." [18]There Jesus was nailed to the cross, and on each side of him a man was also nailed to a cross.

[19]Pilate ordered the charge against Jesus to be written on a board and put above the cross. It read, "Jesus of Nazareth, King of the Jews." [20]The words were written in Hebrew, Latin, and Greek.

The place where Jesus was taken wasn't far from the city, and many of the Jewish people read the charge against him. [21]So the chief priests went to Pilate and said, "Why did you write that he is King of the Jews? You should have written, 'He claimed to be King of the Jews.' "

[22]But Pilate told them, "What is written will not be changed!"

[23]After the soldiers had nailed Jesus to the cross, they divided up his clothes into four parts, one for each of them. But his outer garment was made from a single piece of cloth, and it did not have any seams. [24]The soldiers said to each other, "Let's not rip it apart. We will gamble to see who gets it." This happened so that the Scriptures would come true, which say,

"They divided up my clothes
and gambled
for my garments."

The soldiers then did what they had decided.

[25]Jesus' mother stood beside his cross with her sister and Mary the wife of Clopas. Mary Magdalene was standing there too.[j] [26]When Jesus saw his mother and his favorite disciple with her, he said to his mother, "This man is now your son." [27]Then he said to the disciple, "She is now your mother." From then on, that disciple took her into his own home.

The Death of Jesus

(Matthew 27.45-56; Mark 15.33-41; Luke 23.44-49)

[28]Jesus knew that he had now finished his work. And in order to make the Scrip-

tures come true, he said, "I am thirsty!" [29]A jar of cheap wine was there. Someone then soaked a sponge with the wine and held it up to Jesus' mouth on the stem of a hyssop plant. [30]After Jesus drank the wine, he said, "Everything is done!" He bowed his head and died.

A Spear Is Stuck in Jesus' Side

[31]The next day would be both a Sabbath and the Passover. It was a special day for the Jewish people,[k] and they did not want the bodies to stay on the crosses during that day. So they asked Pilate to break the men's legs[l] and take their bodies down. [32]The soldiers first broke the legs of the other two men who were nailed there. [33]But when they came to Jesus, they saw that he was already dead, and they did not break his legs.

[34]One of the soldiers stuck his spear into Jesus' side, and blood and water came out. [35]We know this is true, because it was told by someone who saw it happen. Now you can have faith too. [36]All this happened so that the Scriptures would come true, which say, "No bone of his body will be broken" [37]and, "They will see the one in whose side they stuck a spear."

Jesus Is Buried

(Matthew 27.57-61; Mark 15.42-47; Luke 23.50-56)

[38]Joseph from Arimathea was one of Jesus' disciples. He had kept it secret though, because he was afraid of the Jewish leaders. But now he asked Pilate to let him have Jesus' body. Pilate gave him permission, and Joseph took it down from the cross.

---

[i]**19.17** *The Skull*: The place was probably given this name because it was near a large rock in the shape of a human skull. [j]**19.25** *Jesus' mother stood beside his cross with her sister and Mary the wife of Clopas. Mary Magdalene was standing there too*: The Greek text may also be understood to include only three women ("Jesus' mother stood beside the cross with her sister, Mary the mother of Clopas. Mary Magdalene was standing there too.") or merely two women ("Jesus' mother was standing there with her sister Mary of Clopas, that is, Mary Magdalene."). "Of Clopas" may mean "daughter of" or "mother of." [k]**19.31** *a special day for the Jewish people*: Passover could be any day of the week. But according to the Gospel of John, Passover was on a Sabbath in the year that Jesus was nailed to a cross. [l]**19.31** *break the men's legs*: This was the way that the Romans sometimes speeded up the death of a person who had been nailed to a cross.

Mary Magdalene

Matthew 27.55—28.10; Mark 15.40—16.11; Luke 8.1-3; 24.9-12;
John 19.25-27; 20.11-18

*O*ne of the most intriguing aspects of Jesus' life on this earth was his friendship with women. Although women were not highly regarded in that culture, Jesus always had women as his faithful followers and close friends. In fact, there was a group of women who traveled with him and the disciples and supported them financially (Luke 8.1-3). One of these was Mary Magdalene, out of whom Jesus had cast seven demons. Not wanting to be far from this man who treated her with such love and respect, Mary Magdalene traveled with him and helped to care for his material needs.

Mary Magdalene became one of Jesus' most faithful friends, standing by him at the cross while he died (John 19.25), watching as he was buried (Matthew 27.61), and returning to the tomb early Sunday morning to bring spices for his body (Mark 16.1). When Mary arrived at the tomb and discovered that the stone had been rolled away, she feared the worst: that thieves had come, desecrated the tomb, and stolen Jesus' body. Never in all her wildest dreams could she have imagined the joy that awaited her. Jesus had risen from the dead! And he chose to appear to her before appearing to anyone else.

At first she didn't know him; perhaps Jesus' appearance had changed, or maybe she couldn't see him well in the early morning light. But when Jesus tenderly called her by name, she recognized her Savior and friend. Mary responded with tenderness and love, calling him "Rabboni," or Teacher. In her joy, Mary must have reached out to embrace Jesus, for he said, "Don't hold on to me!" (John 20.17). Perhaps this signified that she and the other disciples would need to become less attached to Jesus' physical presence now that he'd be going back to heaven. But Jesus also had a job for her to do. As the first one to see the risen Christ, it was now her responsibility to proclaim the good news to the rest of the disciples. And what a joyful task it was!

That Christ would choose a woman to deliver such an important message in a culture that didn't validate women as official witnesses speaks to the value Christ placed on Mary. From Mary we learn that we can give ourselves completely to Christ in love, friendship, and service—for Jesus will always value us and will never disappoint us.

³⁹Nicodemus also came with about seventy-five pounds of spices made from myrrh and aloes. This was the same Nicodemus who had visited Jesus one night.^m ⁴⁰The two men wrapped the body in a linen cloth, together with the spices, which was how the Jewish people buried their dead. ⁴¹In the place where Jesus had been nailed to a cross, there was a garden with a tomb that had never been used. ⁴²The tomb was nearby, and since it was the time to prepare for the Sabbath, they were in a hurry to put Jesus' body there.

Jesus Is Alive

(Matthew 28.1-10; Mark 16.1-8; Luke 24.1-12)

20 On Sunday morning while it was still dark, Mary Magdalene went to the tomb and saw that the stone had been rolled away from the entrance. ²She ran to Simon Peter and to Jesus' favorite disciple and said, "They have taken the Lord from the tomb! We don't know where they have put him."

³Peter and the other disciple started for the tomb. ⁴They ran side by side, until the other disciple ran faster than Peter and got there first. ⁵He bent over and saw the strips of linen cloth lying inside the tomb, but he did not go in.

⁶When Simon Peter got there, he went into the tomb and saw the strips of cloth. ⁷He also saw the piece of cloth that had been used to cover Jesus' face. It was rolled up and in a place by itself. ⁸The disciple who got there first then went into the tomb, and when he saw it, he believed. ⁹At that time Peter and the other disciple did not know that the Scriptures said Jesus would rise to life. ¹⁰So the two of them went back to the other disciples.

Jesus Appears to Mary Magdalene

(Mark 16.9-11)

¹¹Mary Magdalene stood crying outside the tomb. She was still weeping, when she stooped down ¹²and saw two angels inside. They were dressed in white and were sitting where Jesus' body had been. One was at the head and the other was at the foot. ¹³The angels asked Mary, "Why are you crying?"

She answered, "They have taken away my Lord's body! I don't know where they have put him."

¹⁴As soon as Mary said this, she turned around and saw Jesus standing there. But she did not know who he was. ¹⁵Jesus asked her, "Why are you crying? Who are you looking for?"

She thought he was the gardener and said, "Sir, if you have taken his body away, please tell me, so I can go and get him."

> *Worship and worry cannot*
> *live in the same heart.*
> *They are mutually exclusive.*
> RUTH BELL GRAHAM

¹⁶Then Jesus said to her, "Mary!"

She turned and said to him, "Rabboni." The Aramaic word "Rabboni" means "Teacher."

¹⁷Jesus told her, "Don't hold on to me! I have not yet gone to the Father. But tell my disciples that I am going to the one who is my Father and my God, as well as your Father and your God." ¹⁸Mary Magdalene then went and told the disciples that she had seen the Lord. She also told them what he had said to her.

Jesus Appears to His Disciples

(Matthew 28.16-20; Mark 16.14-18;
Luke 24.36-49)

¹⁹The disciples were afraid of the Jewish leaders, and on the evening of that same Sunday they locked themselves in a room. Suddenly, Jesus appeared in the middle of the group. He greeted them ²⁰and showed them his hands and his side. When the disciples saw the Lord, they became very happy.

²¹After Jesus had greeted them again, he said, "I am sending you, just as the Father has sent me." ²²Then he breathed on them and said, "Receive the Holy Spirit. ²³If you forgive anyone's sins, they will be forgiven. But if you don't forgive their sins, they will not be forgiven."

---

^m**19.39** *Nicodemus who had visited Jesus one night:* See 3.1-21.

Jesus and Thomas

²⁴Although Thomas the Twin was one of the twelve disciples, he wasn't with the others when Jesus appeared to them. ²⁵So they told him, "We have seen the Lord!"

But Thomas said, "First, I must see the nail scars in his hands and touch them with my finger. I must put my hand where the spear went into his side. I won't believe unless I do this!"

²⁶A week later the disciples were together again. This time, Thomas was with them. Jesus came in while the doors were still locked and stood in the middle of the group. He greeted his disciples ²⁷and said to Thomas, "Put your finger here and look at my hands! Put your hand into my side. Stop doubting and have faith!"

²⁸Thomas replied, "You are my Lord and my God!"

²⁹Jesus said, "Thomas, do you have faith because you have seen me? The people who have faith in me without seeing me are the ones who are really blessed!"

Why John Wrote His Book

³⁰Jesus worked many other miracles[n] for his disciples, and not all of them are written in this book. ³¹But these are written so that you will put your faith in Jesus as the Messiah and the Son of God. If you have faith in[o] him, you will have true life.

Jesus Appears to Seven Disciples

21 Jesus later appeared to his disciples along the shore of Lake Tiberias. ²Simon Peter, Thomas the Twin, Nathanael from Cana in Galilee, and the brothers James and John,[p] were there, together with two other disciples. ³Simon Peter said, "I'm going fishing!"

The others said, "We will go with you." They went out in their boat. But they didn't catch a thing that night.

⁴Early the next morning Jesus stood on the shore, but the disciples did not realize who he was. ⁵Jesus shouted, "Friends, have you caught anything?"

"No!" they answered.

⁶So he told them, "Let your net down on the right side of your boat, and you will catch some fish."

---

[n]**20.30** *miracles:* See the note at 2.11. [o]**20.31** *put your faith in . . . have faith in:* Some manuscripts have "keep on having faith in . . . keep on having faith in."
[p]**21.2** *the brothers James and John:* Greek "the two sons of Zebedee."

WORK—How can I be a good supervisor? *(John 21.15-25)*

Be gracious about the imperfections of others.
Peter must have had tremendously mixed feelings after Jesus' resurrection. On the one hand, it was a joy to know he'd see his Savior again! But on the other hand, he knew he'd failed Jesus miserably. How he must have revisited those shameful moments by the courtyard fire before Jesus' death (John 18.15-27), wishing he could change his three betrayals into courageous affirmations.

But Jesus gave Peter a second chance. While sitting by a fire on the beach with the other disciples, Jesus asked Peter three times, "Do you love me?" It was no accident that after three betrayals Jesus now provided three opportunities for Peter to affirm his love and commitment. In addition, Jesus' comment "When you are old . . . others will wrap your belt around you and lead you where you don't want to go" (21.18) predicted that Peter would have opportunity to bring honor to God by dying a martyr's death.

Leaders and supervisors who are patient about mistakes, offering people a chance to redeem themselves, bring out the best in their workers. When workers don't fear judgment and harsh penalties, they're free to try new things, make mistakes, and learn from them. As long as we remember our own humanity and our ability to make mistakes, it'll be natural for us to offer this grace to others. (See also Exodus 18; 1 Kings 3.5-15; 4.29-34; Ezra 5.1—6.12; Jeremiah 32.26-44; 2 Timothy 1.1-7; Philemon 8-16; Philemon 15-25.)

Words To Remember: *"Simon son of John, do you love me . . . ?"*
"Yes, Lord, you know I do!"—John 21.15

They did, and the net was so full of fish that they could not drag it up into the boat.

7Jesus' favorite disciple told Peter, "It's the Lord!" When Simon heard that it was the Lord, he put on the clothes that he had taken off while he was working. Then he jumped into the water. 8The boat was only about a hundred yards from shore. So the other disciples stayed in the boat and dragged in the net full of fish.

9When the disciples got out of the boat, they saw some bread and a charcoal fire with fish on it. 10Jesus told his disciples, "Bring some of the fish you just caught." 11Simon Peter got back into the boat and dragged the net to shore. In it were one hundred fifty-three large fish, but still the net did not rip.

12Jesus said, "Come and eat!" But none of the disciples dared ask who he was. They knew he was the Lord. 13Jesus took the bread in his hands and gave some of it to his disciples. He did the same with the fish. 14This was the third time that Jesus appeared to his disciples after he was raised from death.

Jesus and Peter

15When Jesus and his disciples had finished eating, he asked, "Simon son of John, do you love me more than the others do?"q

Simon Peter answered, "Yes, Lord, you know I do!"

"Then feed my lambs," Jesus said.

16Jesus asked a second time, "Simon son of John, do you love me?"

Peter answered, "Yes, Lord, you know I love you!"

"Then take care of my sheep," Jesus told him.

17Jesus asked a third time, "Simon son of John, do you love me?"

Peter was hurt because Jesus had asked him three times if he loved him. So he told Jesus, "Lord, you know everything. You know I love you."

Jesus replied, "Feed my sheep. 18I tell you for certain that when you were a young man, you dressed yourself and went wherever you wanted to go. But when you are old, you will hold out your hands. Then others will wrap your belt around you and lead you where you don't want to go."

19Jesus said this to tell how Peter would die and bring honor to God. Then he said to Peter, "Follow me!"

Jesus and His Favorite Disciple

20Peter turned and saw Jesus' favorite disciple following them. He was the same one who had sat next to Jesus at the meal and had asked, "Lord, who is going to betray you?" 21When Peter saw that disciple, he asked Jesus, "Lord, what about him?"

22Jesus answered, "What is it to you, if I want him to live until I return? You must follow me." 23So the rumor spread among the other disciples that this disciple would not die. But Jesus did not say he would not die. He simply said, "What is it to you, if I want him to live until I return?"

24This disciple is the one who told all of this. He wrote it, and we know he is telling the truth.

25Jesus did many other things. If they were all written in books, I don't suppose there would be room enough in the whole world for all the books.

---

q21.15 more than the others do: Or "more than you love these things?"

Acts
A Church Is Born

Have you ever listened to someone who was present at the start of a business, the founding of a church, the birth of a child? There's a certain shine in that person's eyes as she recounts all the steps that led to the big event and all the stages of growth that followed. Hindsight shows the importance of each seemingly small incident.

The book of Acts recounts the birth of the Christian church after the death and the resurrection of Jesus Christ. The opening chapter reports that in the "forty days after he had suffered and died, he proved in many ways that he had been raised from death." He also appeared to his apostles and told them to wait in Jerusalem for his promised Holy Spirit. So, not knowing what to expect, they waited—together.

By the end of the book, some thirty years later, a mother church had been founded. Dozens of satellite churches sprang up in cities as far as a thousand miles away with the gospel infiltrating the community of each. Leaders hammered out basic elements of the Christian faith and ethical behavior based on the teachings of Jesus. Christians endured intense persecution, even death. Still, they believed and told the good news of Jesus to their neighbors.

As with any beginning, heroes dot the story. We hear of church leaders Peter and James, deacons Stephen and Philip, the great missionary Paul and his travel companions Barnabas, Silas, Mark, Timothy—and peeking between the lines, author Luke. We meet a prophet named Agabus, a businesswoman named Lydia, and the husband-and-wife team Aquila and Priscilla. But threading through every chapter is God himself (in the person of the Holy Spirit), nourishing, protecting, em-powering, exploding this new church. This is the heritage of today's Christian. The history of the early church is our own.

Acts at a Glance

1. The Holy Spirit descends (1,2)
2. Peter and John heal, preach, and go to jail (3,4)
3. Ananias and Sapphira lie to God about money—and die (5)
4. The church chooses seven deacons to help the poor (6)
5. Deacon Stephen preaches a sermon and gets stoned to death (7)
6. Deacon Philip copes with a power-grabbing magician, then leads an Ethiopian official to Christ (8)
7. Saul persecutes Christians, meets Jesus, and becomes a Christian himself (9)
8. Can people who are not Jews become Christians? (10,11)
9. King Herod murders Christians—and dies (12)
10. The church sends Paul (Saul) on three missionary journeys (13–20)
11. Paul gets arrested in Jerusalem (21)
12. Paul preaches and receives a murder threat (22,23)
13. Paul defends himself in a Roman court, but Governor Felix waits for a bribe (24)

14. Governor Festus invites King Agrippa to hear Paul's story (25,26)
15. Paul sails for Rome and is shipwrecked (27)
16. Paul spends the winter on the island of Malta, then enters Rome under house arrest (28)

Theophilus, I first wrote to you[a] about all that Jesus did and taught from the very first [2]until he was taken up to heaven. But before he was taken up, he gave orders to the apostles he had chosen with the help of the Holy Spirit.

[3]For forty days after Jesus had suffered and died, he proved in many ways that he had been raised from death. He appeared to his apostles and spoke to them about God's kingdom. [4]While he was still with them, he said:

Don't leave Jerusalem yet. Wait here for the Father to give you the Holy Spirit, just as I told you he has promised to do. [5]John baptized with water, but in a few days you will be baptized with the Holy Spirit.

Jesus Is Taken to Heaven

[6]While the apostles were still with Jesus, they asked him, "Lord, are you now going to give Israel its own king again?"[b]

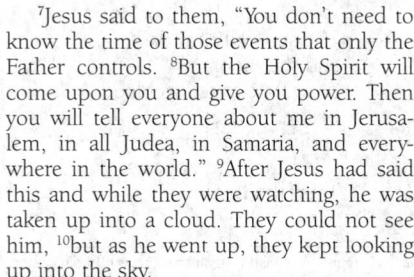

The proof of the love of God within you is the love you show to others. You are Christ's witness to the world.

KAY MARSHALL STROM

[7]Jesus said to them, "You don't need to know the time of those events that only the Father controls. [8]But the Holy Spirit will come upon you and give you power. Then you will tell everyone about me in Jerusalem, in all Judea, in Samaria, and everywhere in the world." [9]After Jesus had said this and while they were watching, he was taken up into a cloud. They could not see him, [10]but as he went up, they kept looking up into the sky.

Suddenly two men dressed in white clothes were standing there beside them.

[11]They said, "Why are you men from Galilee standing here and looking up into the sky? Jesus has been taken to heaven. But he will come back in the same way that you have seen him go."

Someone To Take the Place of Judas

[12-13]The Mount of Olives was about half a mile from Jerusalem. The apostles who had gone there were Peter, John, James, Andrew, Philip, Thomas, Bartholomew, Matthew, James the son of Alphaeus, Simon, known as the Eager One,[c] and Judas the son of James.

After the apostles returned to the city, they went upstairs to the room where they had been staying.

[14]The apostles often met together and prayed with a single purpose in mind.[d] The women and Mary the mother of Jesus would meet with them, and so would his brothers. [15]One day there were about one hundred twenty of the Lord's followers meeting together, and Peter stood up to speak to them. [16-17]He said:

My friends, long ago by the power of the Holy Spirit, David said something about Judas, and what he said has now happened. Judas was one of us and had worked with us, but he brought the mob to arrest Jesus. [18]Then Judas bought some land with the money he was given for doing that evil thing. He fell headfirst into the field. His body burst open, and all his insides came out. [19]When the people of Jerusalem found out about this, they called the place Akeldama, which in the local language means "Field of Blood."

[20]In the book of Psalms it says,

---

[a]**1.1** *I first wrote to you:* The Gospel of Luke.
[b]**1.6** *are you now going to give Israel its own king again:* Or "Are you now going to rule Israel as its king?"
[c]**1.12,13** *known as the Eager One:* The Greek text has "Zealot," a name later given to the members of a Jewish group that resisted and fought against the Romans.
[d]**1.14** *met together and prayed with a single purpose in mind:* Or "met together in a special place for prayer."

"Leave his house empty,
and don't let anyone
live there."

It also says,

"Let someone else
have his job."

²¹⁻²²So we need someone else to help us tell others that Jesus has been raised from death. He must also be one of the men who was with us from the very beginning. He must have been with us from the time the Lord Jesus was baptized by John until the day he was taken to heaven. ²³Two men were suggested: One of them was Joseph Barsabbas, known as Justus, and the other was Matthias. ²⁴Then they all prayed, "Lord, you know what everyone is like! Show us the one you have chosen ²⁵to be an apostle and to serve in place of Judas, who got what he deserved." ²⁶They drew names, and Matthias was chosen to join the group of the eleven apostles.

The Coming of the Holy Spirit

2 On the day of Pentecost^e all the Lord's followers were together in one place. ²Suddenly there was a noise from heaven like the sound of a mighty wind! It filled the house where they were meeting. ³Then they saw what looked like fiery tongues moving in all directions, and a tongue came and settled on each person there. ⁴The Holy Spirit took control of everyone, and they began speaking whatever languages the Spirit let them speak.

⁵Many religious Jews from every country in the world were living in Jerusalem. ⁶And when they heard this noise, a crowd gathered. But they were surprised, because they were hearing everything in their own languages. ⁷They were excited and amazed, and said:

Don't all these who are speaking come from Galilee? ⁸Then why do we hear them speaking our very own languages? ⁹Some of us are from Parthia, Media, and Elam. Others are from Mesopotamia, Judea, Cappadocia, Pontus, Asia, ¹⁰Phrygia, Pamphylia, Egypt, parts of Libya near Cyrene, Rome, ¹¹Crete, and Arabia. Some of us

were born Jews, and others of us have chosen to be Jews. Yet we all hear them using our own languages to tell the wonderful things God has done. ¹²Everyone was excited and confused. Some of them even kept asking each other, "What does all this mean?" ¹³Others made fun of the Lord's followers and said, "They are drunk."

Peter Speaks to the Crowd

¹⁴Peter stood with the eleven apostles and spoke in a loud and clear voice to the crowd:

Friends and everyone else living in Jerusalem, listen carefully to what I have to say! ¹⁵You are wrong to think that these people are drunk. After all, it is only nine o'clock in the morning. ¹⁶But this is what God had the prophet Joel say,

¹⁷ "When the last days come,
I will give my Spirit
to everyone.
Your sons and daughters
will prophesy.
Your young men
will see visions,
and your old men
will have dreams.
¹⁸ In those days I will give
my Spirit to my servants,
both men and women,
and they will prophesy.

¹⁹ I will work miracles
in the sky above
and wonders
on the earth below.
There will be blood and fire
and clouds of smoke.
²⁰ The sun will turn dark,
and the moon
will be as red as blood
before the great
and wonderful day
of the Lord appears.
²¹ Then the Lord

---

^e2.1 *Pentecost*: A Jewish festival that came fifty days after Passover and celebrated the wheat harvest. Jews later celebrated Pentecost as the time when they were given the Law of Moses.

will save everyone
  who asks for his help."

²²Now, listen to what I have to say about Jesus from Nazareth. God proved that he sent Jesus to you by having him work miracles, wonders, and signs. All of you know this. ²³God had already planned and decided that Jesus would be handed over to you. So you took him and had evil men put him to death on a cross. ²⁴But God set him free from death and raised him to life. Death could not hold him in its power. ²⁵What David said are really the words of Jesus,

"I always see the Lord
    near me,
  and I will not be afraid
    with him at my right side.
²⁶Because of this,
    my heart will be glad,
  my words will be joyful,
    and I will live in hope.
²⁷The Lord won't leave me
    in the grave.
  I am his holy one,
  and he won't let
    my body decay.

²⁸He has shown me
    the path to life,
  and he makes me glad
    by being near me."

²⁹My friends, it is right for me to speak to you about our ancestor David. He died and was buried, and his tomb is still here. ³⁰But David was a prophet, and he knew that God had made a promise he would not break. He had told David that someone from his own family would someday be king.
³¹David knew this would happen, and so he told us that Christ would be raised to life. He said that God would not leave him in the grave or let his body decay. ³²All of us can tell you that God has raised Jesus to life!
³³Jesus was taken up to sit at the right side* of God, and he was given the Holy Spirit, just as the Father had promised. Jesus is also the one who has given the Spirit to us, and that is what you are now seeing and hearing.
³⁴David didn't go up to heaven. So he wasn't talking about himself when

---

2.33 right side: The place of honor and power.

---

*Spiritual*Life—Why is it important for me to go to church? (Acts 2.1-13,41-47)

The Christian faith is best practiced among other believers.
Individuality is a trait prized by Americans. We admire the rugged lone cowboy. We respect the strong businesswoman who stands alone against greedy corporate power. Even some of our missionaries must "raise their own support." It's not surprising that many of us think we can follow the Christian faith alone, that it's a personal faith best expressed between "me and God." Many argue that they can worship God just as well alone on a nature trail or from their own living-room sofa as in any church.

But individualism isn't a biblical concept. The earliest teachings of the Christian faith emphasized its group qualities. The Lord's followers waited together (2.1). Three thousand believed and were baptized at one time (2.41). They ate together, learned together, prayed together (2.42). Even the sacrament of communion begun by Christ himself was a *group* meal. God's people belonged to the church. It started out that way in Acts and continued throughout the rest of the New Testament.

It's tempting to be a lone Christian—no responsibilities, no accountability, no flawed people to annoy us. But that's not what Christianity is. In Christ, we're a family. Church expresses that relationship. (See also Ezekiel 43.1-5; Romans 12.3-8; 1 Corinthians 3.10-17; Ephesians 2.11-22.)

Words To Remember: *They spent their time learning from the apostles, and they were like family to each other. They also broke bread and prayed together.—Acts 2.42*

he said, "The Lord told my Lord to sit at his right side, [35]until he made my Lord's enemies into a footstool for him." [36]Everyone in Israel should then know for certain that God has made Jesus both Lord and Christ, even though you put him to death on a cross.

[37]When the people heard this, they were very upset. They asked Peter and the other apostles, "Friends, what shall we do?"

[38]Peter said, "Turn back to God! Be baptized in the name of Jesus Christ, so that your sins will be forgiven. Then you will be given the Holy Spirit. [39]This promise is for you and your children. It is for everyone our Lord God will choose, no matter where they live."

[40]Peter told them many other things as well. Then he said, "I beg you to save yourselves from what will happen to all these evil people." [41]On that day about three thousand believed his message and were baptized. [42]They spent their time learning from the apostles, and they were like family to each other. They also broke bread[g] and prayed together.

Life among the Lord's Followers

[43]Everyone was amazed by the many miracles and wonders that the apostles worked. [44]All the Lord's followers often met together, and they shared everything they had. [45]They would sell their property and possessions and give the money to whoever needed it. [46]Day after day they met together in the temple. They broke bread[g] together in different homes and shared their food happily and freely, [47]while praising God. Everyone liked them, and each day the Lord added to their group others who were being saved.

Peter and John Heal a Lame Man

3 The time of prayer[h] was about three o'clock in the afternoon, and Peter and John were going into the temple. [2]A man who had been born lame was being carried to the temple door. Each day he was placed beside this door, known as the Beautiful Gate. He sat there and begged from the people who were going in.

[3]The man saw Peter and John entering the temple, and he asked them for money.

[4]But they looked straight at him and said, "Look up at us!"

[5]The man stared at them and thought he was going to get something. [6]But Peter said, "I don't have any silver or gold! But I will give you what I do have. In the name of Jesus Christ from Nazareth, get up and start walking." [7]Peter then took him by the right hand and helped him up.

It's not so much <u>what</u> we do; it's if we do it in the Lord's name.

DR. LORI HANSEN

At once the man's feet and ankles became strong, [8]and he jumped up and started walking. He went with Peter and John into the temple, walking and jumping and praising God. [9]Everyone saw him walking around and praising God. [10]They knew that he was the beggar who had been lying beside the Beautiful Gate, and they were completely surprised. They could not imagine what had happened to the man.

Peter Speaks in the Temple

[11]While the man kept holding on to Peter and John, the whole crowd ran to them in amazement at the place known as Solomon's Porch.[i] [12]Peter saw that a crowd had gathered, and he said:

Friends, why are you surprised at what has happened? Why are you staring at us? Do you think we have some power of our own? Do you think we were able to make this man walk because we are so religious? [13]The God that Abraham, Isaac, Jacob, and our other ancestors worshiped has brought honor to his Servant[j] Jesus. He is the one you betrayed. You turned

---

[g]**2.42,46** *broke bread*: They ate together and celebrated the Lord's Supper. [h]**3.1** *The time of prayer*: Many of the Jewish people prayed in their homes at regular times each day (see Daniel 6.11), and on special occasions they prayed in the temple. [i]**3.11** *Solomon's Porch*: A public place with tall columns along the east side of the temple. [j]**3.13** *Servant*: Or "Son."

against him when he was being tried by Pilate, even though Pilate wanted to set him free.

[14]You rejected Jesus, who was holy and good. You asked for a murderer to be set free, [15]and you killed the one who leads people to life. But God raised him from death, and all of us can tell you what he has done. [16]You see this man, and you know him. He put his faith in the name of Jesus and was made strong. Faith in Jesus made this man completely well while everyone was watching.

[17]My friends, I am sure that you and your leaders didn't know what you were doing. [18]But God had his prophets tell that his Messiah would suffer, and now he has kept that promise. [19]So turn to God! Give up your sins, and you will be forgiven. [20]Then that time will come when the Lord will give you fresh strength. He will send you Jesus, his chosen Messiah. [21]But Jesus must stay in heaven until God makes all things new, just as his holy prophets promised long ago.

[22]Moses said, "The Lord your God will choose one of your own people to be a prophet, just as he chose me. Listen to everything he tells you. [23]No one who disobeys that prophet will be one of God's people any longer."

[24]Samuel and all the other prophets who came later also spoke about what is now happening. [25]You are really the ones God told his prophets to speak to. And you were given the promise that God made to your ancestors. He said to Abraham, "All nations on earth will be blessed because of someone from your family." [26]God sent his chosen Son[k] to you first, because God wanted to bless you and make each one of you turn away from your sins.

Peter and John Are Brought in Front of the Council

4 The apostles were still talking to the people, when some priests, the captain of the temple guard, and some Sadducees arrived. [2]These men were angry because the apostles were teaching the people that the dead would be raised from death, just as Jesus had been raised from death. [3]It was already late in the afternoon, and they arrested Peter and John and put them in jail for the night. [4]But a lot of people who had heard the message believed it. So by now there were about five thousand followers of the Lord.

[5]The next morning the leaders, the elders, and the teachers of the Law of Moses met in Jerusalem. [6]The high priest Annas was there, as well as Caiaphas, John, Alexander, and other members of the high priest's family. [7]They brought in Peter and John and made them stand in the middle while they questioned them. They asked, "By what power and in whose name have you done this?"

[8]Peter was filled with the Holy Spirit and told the nation's leaders and the elders:

[9]You are questioning us today about a kind deed in which a crippled man was healed. [10]But there is something we must tell you and everyone else in Israel. This man is standing here completely well because of the power of Jesus Christ from Nazareth. You put Jesus to death on a cross, but God raised him to life. [11]He is the stone that you builders thought was worthless, and now he is the most important stone of all. [12]Only Jesus has the power to save! His name is the only one in all the world that can save anyone.

[13]The officials were amazed to see how brave Peter and John were, and they knew that these two apostles were only ordinary men and not well educated. The officials were certain that these men had been with Jesus. [14]But they could not deny what had happened. The man who had been healed was standing there with the apostles.

[15]The officials commanded them to leave the council room. Then the officials said to each other, [16]"What can we do with these men? Everyone in Jerusalem knows about this miracle, and we cannot say it didn't happen. [17]But to keep this thing from spreading, we will warn them never again to speak to anyone about the name of Jesus." [18]So they called the two apostles back in and told them that they must never, for any reason, teach anything about the name of Jesus.

---

[k]3.26 *Son:* Or "Servant."

[19]Peter and John answered, "Do you think God wants us to obey you or to obey him? [20]We cannot keep quiet about what we have seen and heard."

[21-22]The officials could not find any reason to punish Peter and John. So they threatened them and let them go. The man who was healed by this miracle was more than forty years old, and everyone was praising God for what had happened.

Peter and Others Pray for Courage

[23]As soon as Peter and John had been set free, they went back and told the others everything that the chief priests and the leaders had said to them. [24]When the rest of the Lord's followers heard this, they prayed together and said:

Master, you created heaven and earth, the sea, and everything in them. [25]And by the Holy Spirit you spoke to our ancestor David. He was your servant, and you told him to say:

"Why are all the Gentiles so furious?

Why do people make foolish plans?
[26]The kings of earth prepare for war, and the rulers join together against the Lord and his Messiah."

[27]Here in Jerusalem, Herod[l] and Pontius Pilate got together with the Gentiles and the people of Israel. Then they turned against your holy Servant[m] Jesus, your chosen Messiah. [28]They did what you in your power and wisdom had already decided would happen.

[29]Lord, listen to their threats! We are your servants. So make us brave enough to speak your message. [30]Show your mighty power, as we heal people and work miracles and wonders in the name of your holy Servant[m] Jesus.

---

[l]**4.27** *Herod:* Herod Antipas, the son of Herod the Great. [m]**4.27,30** *Servant:* See the note at 3.13.

---

*Spiritual*Life—How should I pray? (Acts 4.23-31)

Ask God for courage.

When you face a fearsome situation, what's your first prayer? "Lord, protect me. Lord, keep me out of trouble. Lord, please calm my churning stomach."

If anyone had reason to pray that kind of prayer, it was Peter and John. They'd just been hauled before the highest religious court of their land: elders, teachers of the Law, the high priest, even the family of the high priest. This court of their superiors roundly lectured them for stirring up trouble. (Peter and John had healed a lame man and then used the occasion of an assembled crowd to preach about Jesus.) The conclusion of the court was to threaten them with the warning that "they must never, for any reason, teach anything about the name of Jesus" (4.18).

As soon as they were free, Peter and John joined with other believers and prayed. Their outline for prayer is one we can use in our own fearsome situations. They praised God as Master of heaven and earth. They recited his work in history. They reminded God of what had just happened to them and acknowledged that this, too, was under his power. Then they asked God for courage. Not safety, not peace, not health. Courage. When they finished praying, "the meeting place shook" and "they were all filled with the Holy Spirit and bravely spoke God's message" (4.31).

Sometimes when what we most *want* is peace, health, and safety, what we *need* is bravery. In these cases, we should pray for courage—and get on with the job. (See also 2 Samuel 7.18-29; 2 Kings 19.14-19; 2 Chronicles 6,7; Nehemiah 1; Psalm 85; Lamentations 5; Matthew 6.5-15.)

Words To Remember: *Lord, listen to their threats! We are your servants. So make us brave enough to speak your message.*—Acts 4.29

³¹After they had prayed, the meeting place shook. They were all filled with the Holy Spirit and bravely spoke God's message.

Sharing Possessions

³²The group of followers all felt the same way about everything. None of them claimed that their possessions were their own, and they shared everything they had with each other. ³³In a powerful way the apostles told everyone that the Lord Jesus was now alive. God greatly blessed his followers,ⁿ ³⁴and no one went in need of anything. Everyone who owned land or houses would sell them and bring the money ³⁵to the apostles. Then they would give the money to anyone who needed it.

³⁶⁻³⁷Joseph was one of the followers who had sold a piece of property and brought the money to the apostles. He was a Levite from Cyprus, and the apostles called him Barnabas, which means "one who encourages others."

Peter Condemns Ananias and Sapphira

5 Ananias and his wife Sapphira also sold a piece of property. ²But they agreed to cheat and keep some of the money for themselves.

So when Ananias took the rest of the money to the apostles, ³Peter said, "Why has Satan made you keep back some of the money from the sale of the property? Why have you lied to the Holy Spirit? ⁴The property was yours before you sold it, and even after you sold it, the money was still yours. What made you do such a thing? You didn't lie to people. You lied to God!"

⁵As soon as Ananias heard this, he dropped dead, and everyone who heard about it was frightened. ⁶Some young men came in and wrapped up his body. Then they took it out and buried it.

⁷Three hours later Sapphira came in, but she did not know what had happened to her husband. ⁸Peter asked her, "Tell me, did you sell the property for this amount?"

"Yes," she answered, "that's the amount."

⁹Then Peter said, "Why did the two of you agree to test the Lord's Spirit? The men who buried Ananias are by the door, and they will carry you out!" ¹⁰At once she fell at Peter's feet and died.

When the young men came back in, they found Sapphira lying there dead. So they carried her out and buried her beside her husband. ¹¹The church members were afraid, and so was everyone else who heard what had happened.

ⁿ4.33 *God greatly blessed his followers*: Or "Everyone highly respected his followers."

SpiritualLife—How can I show my devotion to God? (Acts 4.32—5.11)

Follow God's standards.

Ananias and his wife Sapphira looked like good Christians—at least on the outside. Like the other followers of Jesus, they agreed to sell their land and bring the money to the apostles (who would then pass it on to anyone who needed it).

But Ananias and Sapphira didn't follow God's standards for honesty. They figured they could keep back some of the money for themselves. The problem wasn't that they decided to keep some of the money (they could have been honest and told the other Christians they needed to keep some of the profits for their own purposes); rather, it was that they *lied* about giving it all to the church. They wanted to look like "good Christians" to others. But they forgot that God sees and knows everything.

How different the story could have been for them if they'd followed God's standards for honesty! The next time you're tempted to shade the truth "just a little," think of Ananias and Sapphira. By being honest in all things, you'll show your utmost devotion to God. (See also 1 Kings 18; 1 Chronicles 29.1-20; Haggai 1.1-11; 1 Corinthians 13.11-13.)

Words To Remember: *They shared everything they had with each other. In a powerful way the apostles told everyone that the Lord Jesus was now alive.* —Acts 4.32,33

Peter's Unusual Power

¹²The apostles worked many miracles and wonders among the people. All of the Lord's followers often met in the part of the temple known as Solomon's Porch.ᵒ ¹³No one outside their group dared join them, even though everyone liked them very much.

¹⁴Many men and women started having faith in the Lord. ¹⁵Then sick people were brought out to the road and placed on cots and mats. It was hoped that Peter would walk by, and his shadow would fall on them and heal them. ¹⁶A lot of people living in the towns near Jerusalem brought those who were sick or troubled by evil spirits, and they were all healed.

Trouble for the Apostles

¹⁷The high priest and all the other Sadducees who were with him became jealous. ¹⁸They arrested the apostles and put them in the city jail. ¹⁹But that night an angel from the Lord opened the doors of the jail and led the apostles out. The angel said, ²⁰"Go to the temple and tell the people everything about this new life." ²¹So they went into the temple before sunrise and started teaching.

The high priest and his men called together their council, which included all of Israel's leaders. Then they ordered the apostles to be brought to them from the jail. ²²The temple police who were sent to the jail did not find the apostles. They returned and said, ²³"We found the jail locked tight and the guards standing at the doors. But when we opened the doors and went in, we didn't find anyone there." ²⁴The captain of the temple police and the chief priests listened to their report, but they did not know what to think about it.

²⁵Just then someone came in and said, "Right now those men you put in jail are in the temple, teaching the people!" ²⁶The captain went with some of the temple police and brought the apostles back. But they did not use force. They were afraid that the people might start throwing stones at them.

²⁷When the apostles were brought before the council, the high priest said to them, ²⁸"We told you plainly not to teach in the name of Jesus. But look what you have done! You have been teaching all over Jerusalem, and you are trying to blame us for his death."

²⁹Peter and the apostles replied:

We don't obey people. We obey God. ³⁰You killed Jesus by nailing him to a cross. But the God our ancestors worshiped raised him to life ³¹and made him our Leader and Savior. Then God gave him a place at his right side,ᵖ so that the people of Israel would turn back to him and be forgiven. ³²We are here to tell you about all this, and so is the Holy Spirit, who is God's gift to everyone who obeys God.

³³When the council members heard this, they became so angry that they wanted to kill the apostles. ³⁴But one of the members was the Pharisee Gamaliel, a highly respected teacher. He ordered the apostles to be taken out of the room for a little while. ³⁵Then he said to the council:

People of Israel, be careful what you do with these men. ³⁶Not long ago Theudas claimed to be someone important, and about four hundred men joined him. But he was killed. All his followers were scattered, and that was the end of that.

³⁷Later, when the people of our nation were being counted, Judas from Galilee showed up. A lot of people followed him, but he was killed, and all his followers were scattered.

³⁸So I advise you to stay away from these men. Leave them alone. If what they are planning is something of their own doing, it will fail. ³⁹But if God is behind it, you cannot stop it anyway, unless you want to fight against God.

The council members agreed with what he said, ⁴⁰and they called the apostles back in. They had them beaten with a whip and warned them not to speak in the name of Jesus. Then they let them go.

⁴¹The apostles left the council and were happy, because God had considered them worthy to suffer for the sake of Jesus. ⁴²Every day they spent time in the temple and in one home after another. They never stopped teaching and telling the good news that Jesus is the Messiah.

ᵒ5.12 *Solomon's Porch*: See the note at 3.11.
ᵖ5.31 *right side*: See the note at 2.33.

Seven Leaders for the Church

6 A lot of people were now becoming followers of the Lord. But some of the ones who spoke Greek started complaining about the ones who spoke Aramaic. They complained that the Greek-speaking widows were not given their share when the food supplies were handed out each day.

2The twelve apostles called the whole group of followers together and said, "We should not give up preaching God's message in order to serve at tables.[q] 3My friends, choose seven men who are respected and wise and filled with God's Spirit. We will put them in charge of these things. 4We can spend our time praying and serving God by preaching."

5This suggestion pleased everyone, and they began by choosing Stephen. He had great faith and was filled with the Holy Spirit. Then they chose Philip, Prochorus, Nicanor, Timon, Parmenas, and also Nicolaus, who worshiped with the Jewish people[r] in Antioch. 6These men were brought to the apostles. Then the apostles prayed and placed their hands on the men to show that they had been chosen to do this work. 7God's message spread, and many more people in Jerusalem became followers. Even a large number of priests put their faith in the Lord.

Stephen Is Arrested

8God gave Stephen the power to work great miracles and wonders among the people. 9But some Jews from Cyrene and Alexandria were members of a group who called themselves "Free Men."[s] They started arguing with Stephen. Some others from Cilicia and Asia also argued with him. 10But they were no match for Stephen, who spoke with the great wisdom that the Spirit gave him. 11So they talked some men into saying, "We heard Stephen say terrible things against Moses and God!"

12They turned the people and their leaders and the teachers of the Law of Moses against Stephen. Then they all grabbed Stephen and dragged him in front of the council.

13Some men agreed to tell lies about Stephen, and they said, "This man keeps on saying terrible things about this holy temple and the Law of Moses. 14We have heard him claim that Jesus from Nazareth will destroy this place and change the customs that Moses gave us." 15Then all the council members stared at Stephen. They saw that his face looked like the face of an angel.

Stephen's Speech

7 The high priest asked Stephen, "Are they telling the truth about you?"

2Stephen answered:

Friends, listen to me. Our glorious God appeared to our ancestor Abraham while he was still in Mesopotamia, before he had moved to Haran. 3God told him, "Leave your country and your relatives and go to a land that I will show you." 4Then Abraham left the land of the Chaldeans and settled in Haran.

After his father died, Abraham came and settled in this land where you now live. 5God didn't give him any part of it, not even a square foot. But God did promise to give it to him and his family forever, even though Abraham didn't have any children. 6God said that Abraham's descendants would live for a while in a foreign land. There they would be slaves and would be mistreated four hundred years. 7But he also said, "I will punish the nation that makes them slaves. Then later they will come and worship me in this place."

8God said to Abraham, "Every son in each family must be circumcised to show that you have kept your agreement with me." So when Isaac was eight days old, Abraham circumcised him. Later, Isaac circumcised his son Jacob, and Jacob circumcised his twelve sons. 9These men were our ancestors.

Joseph was also one of our famous ancestors. His brothers were jealous of him and sold him as a slave to be taken to Egypt. But God was with him

---

[q] **6.2** *to serve at tables*: This may mean either that they were in charge of handing out food to the widows or that they were in charge of the money, since the Greek word "table" may also mean "bank." [r] **6.5** *worshiped with the Jewish people*: This translates the Greek word "proselyte" that means a Gentile who had accepted the Jewish religion. [s] **6.9** *Free Men*: A group of Jewish men who had once been slaves, but had been freed.

¹⁰and rescued him from all his troubles. God made him so wise that the Egyptian king Pharaoh[f] thought highly of him. The king even made Joseph governor over Egypt and put him in charge of everything he owned.

¹¹Everywhere in Egypt and Canaan the grain crops failed. There was terrible suffering, and our ancestors could not find enough to eat. ¹²But when Jacob heard that there was grain in Egypt, he sent our ancestors there for the first time. ¹³It was on their second trip that Joseph told his brothers who he was, and Pharaoh learned about Joseph's family.

¹⁴Joseph sent for his father and his relatives. In all, there were seventy-five of them. ¹⁵His father went to Egypt and died there, just as our ancestors did. ¹⁶Later their bodies were taken back to Shechem and placed in the tomb that Abraham had bought from the sons of Hamor.

¹⁷Finally, the time came for God to do what he had promised Abraham. By then the number of our people in Egypt had greatly increased. ¹⁸Another king was ruling Egypt, and he didn't know anything about Joseph. ¹⁹He tricked our ancestors and was cruel to them. He even made them leave their babies outside, so they would die.

²⁰During this time Moses was born. He was a very beautiful child, and for three months his parents took care of him in their home. ²¹Then when they were forced to leave him outside, the king's daughter found him and raised him as her own son. ²²Moses was given the best education in Egypt. He was a strong man and a powerful speaker.

²³When Moses was forty years old, he wanted to help the Israelites because they were his own people. ²⁴One day he saw an Egyptian mistreating one of them. So he rescued the man and killed the Egyptian. ²⁵Moses thought the rest of his people would realize that God was going to use him to set them free. But they didn't understand.

²⁶The next day Moses saw two of his own people fighting, and he tried to make them stop. He said, "Men, you are both Israelites. Why are you so cruel to each other?"

²⁷But the man who had started the fight pushed Moses aside and asked, "Who made you our ruler and judge? ²⁸Are you going to kill me, just as you killed that Egyptian yesterday?" ²⁹When Moses heard this, he ran away to live in the country of Midian. His two sons were born there.

> It isn't until you realize who God is—a loving, powerful, eternal God who yet allows finite man to make his own choices—that you can move on with life, even when it doesn't seem fair.
>
> LEE EZELL

³⁰Forty years later, an angel appeared to Moses from a burning bush in the desert near Mount Sinai. ³¹Moses was surprised by what he saw. He went closer to get a better look, and the Lord said, ³²"I am the God who was worshiped by your ancestors, Abraham, Isaac, and Jacob." Moses started shaking all over and didn't dare to look at the bush.

³³The Lord said to him, "Take off your sandals. The place where you are standing is holy. ³⁴With my own eyes I have seen the suffering of my people in Egypt. I have heard their groans and have come down to rescue them. Now I am sending you back to Egypt."

³⁵This was the same Moses that the people rejected by saying, "Who made you our leader and judge?" God's angel had spoken to Moses from the

---

[f]7.10 *Pharaoh*: a Hebrew word sometimes used for the title of the King of Egypt.

bush. And God had even sent the angel to help Moses rescue the people and be their leader.

³⁶In Egypt and at the Red Sea[u] and in the desert, Moses rescued the people by working miracles and wonders for forty years. ³⁷Moses is the one who told the people of Israel, "God will choose one of your people to be a prophet, just as he chose me." ³⁸Moses brought our people together in the desert, and the angel spoke to him on Mount Sinai. There he was given these life-giving words to pass on to us. ³⁹But our ancestors refused to obey Moses. They rejected him and wanted to go back to Egypt.

⁴⁰The people said to Aaron, "Make some gods to lead us! Moses led us out of Egypt, but we don't know what's happened to him now." ⁴¹Then they made an idol in the shape of a calf. They offered sacrifices to the idol and were pleased with what they had done.

⁴²God turned his back on his people and left them. Then they worshiped the stars in the sky, just as it says in the Book of the Prophets, "People of Israel, you didn't offer sacrifices and offerings to me during those forty years in the desert. ⁴³Instead, you carried the tent where the god Molech is worshiped, and you took along the star of your god Rephan. You made those idols and worshiped them. So now I will have you carried off beyond Babylonia."

⁴⁴The tent where our ancestors worshiped God was with them in the desert. This was the same tent that God had commanded Moses to make. And it was made like the model that Moses had seen. ⁴⁵Later it was given to our ancestors, and they took it with them when they went with Joshua. They carried the tent along as they took over the land from those people that God had chased out for them. Our ancestors used this tent until the time of King David. ⁴⁶He pleased God and asked him if he could build a house of worship for the people[v] of Israel. ⁴⁷And it was finally King Solomon who built a house for God.[w]

⁴⁸But the Most High God doesn't live in houses made by humans. It is just as the prophet said, when he spoke for the Lord,

⁴⁹"Heaven is my throne,
　and the earth
　　is my footstool.
What kind of house
　will you build for me?
In what place will I rest?
⁵⁰　I have made everything."

⁵¹You stubborn and hardheaded people! You are always fighting against the Holy Spirit, just as your ancestors did. ⁵²Is there one prophet that your ancestors didn't mistreat? They killed the prophets who told about the coming of the One Who Obeys God.[x] And now you have turned against him and killed him. ⁵³Angels gave you God's Law, but you still don't obey it.

Stephen Is Stoned to Death

⁵⁴When the council members heard Stephen's speech, they were angry and furious. ⁵⁵But Stephen was filled with the Holy Spirit. He looked toward heaven, where he saw our glorious God and Jesus standing at his right side.[y] ⁵⁶Then Stephen said, "I see heaven open and the Son of Man standing at the right side of God!"

⁵⁷The council members shouted and covered their ears. At once they all attacked Stephen ⁵⁸and dragged him out of the city. Then they started throwing stones at him. The men who had brought charges against him put their coats at the feet of a young man named Saul.[z]

⁵⁹As Stephen was being stoned to death, he called out, "Lord Jesus, please welcome

---

u7.36 *Red Sea*: This name comes from the Bible of the early Christians, a translation made into Greek about 200 B.C. It refers to the body of water that the Israelites crossed and was one of the marshes or fresh water lakes near the eastern part of the Nile Delta, where they lived and where the towns of Exodus 13.17—14.9 were located. v7.46 *the people*: Some manuscripts have "God." w7.47 *God*: Or "the people." x7.52 *One Who Obeys God*: That is, Jesus. y7.55 *standing at his right side*: The "right side" is the place of honor and power. "Standing" may mean that Jesus is welcoming Stephen (see verse 59). z7.58 *Saul*: Better known as Paul, who became a famous follower of Jesus.

me!" [60]He knelt down and shouted, "Lord, don't blame them for what they have done." Then he died.

8 [1-2]Saul approved the stoning of Stephen. Some faithful followers of the Lord buried Stephen and mourned very much for him.

Saul Makes Trouble for the Church

At that time the church in Jerusalem suffered terribly. All of the Lord's followers, except the apostles, were scattered everywhere in Judea and Samaria. [3]Saul started making a lot of trouble for the church. He went from house to house, arresting men and women and putting them in jail.

The Good News Is Preached in Samaria

[4]The Lord's followers who had been scattered went from place to place, telling the good news. [5]Philip went to the city of Samaria and told the people about Christ. [6]They crowded around Philip because they were eager to hear what he was saying and to see him work miracles. [7]Many people with evil spirits were healed, and the spirits went out of them with a shout. A lot of crippled and lame people were also healed. [8]Everyone in that city was very glad because of what was happening.

[9]For some time a man named Simon had lived in the city of Samaria and had amazed the people. He practiced witchcraft and claimed to be somebody great. [10]Everyone, rich and poor, crowded around him. They said, "This man is the power of God called 'The Great Power.' "

[11]For a long time, Simon had used witchcraft to amaze the people, and they kept crowding around him. [12]But when they believed what Philip was saying about God's kingdom and about the name of Jesus Christ, they were all baptized. [13]Even Simon believed and was baptized. He stayed close to Philip, because he marveled at all the miracles and wonders.

[14]The apostles in Jerusalem heard that some people in Samaria had accepted God's message, and they sent Peter and John. [15]When the two apostles arrived, they prayed that the people would be given the Holy Spirit. [16]Before this, the Holy Spirit had not been given to anyone in Samaria, though some of them had been baptized in the name of the Lord Jesus. [17]Peter and John then placed their hands on everyone who had faith in the Lord, and they were given the Holy Spirit.

[18]Simon noticed that the Spirit was given only when the apostles placed their hands on the people. So he brought money [19]and said to Peter and John, "Let me have this power too! Then anyone I place my hands on will also be given the Holy Spirit."

[20]Peter said to him, "You and your money will both end up in hell if you think you can buy God's gift! [21]You don't have any part in this, and God sees that your heart isn't right. [22]Get rid of these evil thoughts and ask God to forgive you. [23]I can see that you are jealous and bound by your evil ways."

[24]Simon said, "Please pray to the Lord, so that what you said won't happen to me."

[25]After Peter and John had preached about the Lord, they returned to Jerusalem. On their way they told the good news in many villages of Samaria.

Philip and an Ethiopian Official

[26]The Lord's angel said to Philip, "Go south[a] along the desert road that leads from Jerusalem to Gaza."[b] [27]So Philip left.

An important Ethiopian official happened to be going along that road in his chariot. He was the chief treasurer for Candace, the Queen of Ethiopia. The official had gone to Jerusalem to worship [28]and was now on his way home. He was sitting in his chariot, reading the book of the prophet Isaiah.

[29]The Spirit told Philip to catch up with the chariot. [30]Philip ran up close and heard the man reading aloud from the book of Isaiah. Philip asked him, "Do you understand what you are reading?"

[31]The official answered, "How can I understand unless someone helps me?" He then invited Philip to come up and sit beside him.

[32]The man was reading the passage that said,

> "He was led like a sheep
>   on its way to be killed.
> He was silent as a lamb

---

[a]**8.26** *Go south*: Or "About noon go." [b]**8.26** *the desert road that leads from Jerusalem to Gaza*: Or "the road that leads from Jerusalem to Gaza in the desert."

whose wool
  is being cut off,
and he did not say
  a word.
[33] He was treated like a nobody
and did not receive
  a fair trial.
How can he have children,
if his life
  is snatched away?"

[34] The official said to Philip, "Tell me, was the prophet talking about himself or about someone else?" [35] So Philip began at this place in the Scriptures and explained the good news about Jesus.

[36-37] As they were going along the road, they came to a place where there was some water. The official said, "Look! Here is some water. Why can't I be baptized?"[c] [38] He ordered the chariot to stop. Then they both went down into the water, and Philip baptized him.

[39] After they had come out of the water, the Lord's Spirit took Philip away. The official never saw him again, but he was very happy as he went on his way.

[40] Philip later appeared in Azotus. He went from town to town, all the way to Caesarea, telling people about Jesus.

Saul Becomes a Follower of the Lord
(Acts 22.6-16; 26.12-18)

9 Saul kept on threatening to kill the Lord's followers. He even went to the high priest [2] and asked for letters to the Jewish leaders in Damascus. He did this because he wanted to arrest and take to Jerusalem any man or woman who had accepted the Lord's Way.[d] [3] When Saul had almost reached Damascus, a bright light from heaven suddenly flashed around him. [4] He fell to the ground and heard a voice that said, "Saul! Saul! Why are you so cruel to me?"

[5] "Who are you?" Saul asked.

"I am Jesus," the Lord answered. "I am the one you are so cruel to. [6] Now get up and go into the city, where you will be told what to do."

[7] The men with Saul stood there speechless. They had heard the voice, but they had not seen anyone. [8] Saul got up from the ground, and when he opened his eyes, he could not see a thing. Someone then led

him by the hand to Damascus, [9] and for three days he was blind and did not eat or drink.

[10] A follower named Ananias lived in Damascus, and the Lord spoke to him in a vision. Ananias answered, "Lord, here I am."

[11] The Lord said to him, "Get up and go to the house of Judas on Straight Street. When you get there, you will find a man named Saul from the city of Tarsus. Saul is praying, [12] and he has seen a vision. He saw a man named Ananias coming to him and putting his hands on him, so that he could see again."

[13] Ananias replied, "Lord, a lot of people have told me about the terrible things this man has done to your followers in Jerusalem. [14] Now the chief priests have given him the power to come here and arrest anyone who worships in your name."

[15] The Lord said to Ananias, "Go! I have chosen him to tell foreigners, kings, and the people of Israel about me. [16] I will show him how much he must suffer for worshiping in my name."

[17] Ananias left and went into the house where Saul was staying. Ananias placed his hands on him and said, "Saul, the Lord Jesus has sent me. He is the same one who appeared to you along the road. He wants you to be able to see and to be filled with the Holy Spirit."

[18] Suddenly something like fish scales fell from Saul's eyes, and he could see. He got up and was baptized. [19] Then he ate and felt much better.

Saul Preaches in Damascus

For several days Saul stayed with the Lord's followers in Damascus. [20] Soon he went to the Jewish meeting places and started telling people that Jesus is the Son of God. [21] Everyone who heard Saul was amazed and said, "Isn't this the man who caused so much trouble for those people in Jerusalem who worship in the name of Jesus? Didn't he come here to arrest them and take them to the chief priests?"

[22] Saul preached with such power that he

---

[c] **8.36,37** *Why can't I be baptized:* Some manuscripts add, "Philip replied, 'You can, if you believe with all your heart.' The official answered, 'I believe that Jesus Christ is the Son of God.' " [d] **9.2** *accepted the Lord's Way:* In the book of Acts, this means to become a follower of the Lord Jesus.

completely confused the Jewish people in Damascus, as he tried to show them that Jesus is the Messiah.

²³Later some of them made plans to kill Saul, ²⁴but he found out about it. He learned that they were guarding the gates of the city day and night in order to kill him. ²⁵Then one night his followers let him down over the city wall in a large basket.

> *In the aftermath of the scandal, when I prayed, God I wish you were here to talk to me, to put your arms around me, to wipe my tears away, it dawned on me he was doing that—through the Christians around me. That's when I began to understand church isn't a building; it's the body of Christ. In the middle of my pain, God gave me Christian friends who taught me about love and forgiveness.*
>
> DONNA RICE HUGHES

Saul in Jerusalem

²⁶When Saul arrived in Jerusalem, he tried to join the followers. But they were all afraid of him, because they did not believe he was a true follower. ²⁷Then Barnabas helped him by taking him to the apostles. He explained how Saul had seen the Lord and how the Lord had spoken to him. Barnabas also said that when Saul was in Damascus, he had spoken bravely in the name of Jesus.

²⁸Saul moved about freely with the followers in Jerusalem and told everyone about the Lord. ²⁹He was always arguing with the Jews who spoke Greek, and so they tried to kill him. ³⁰But the followers found out about

this and took Saul to Caesarea. From there they sent him to the city of Tarsus.

³¹The church in Judea, Galilee, and Samaria now had a time of peace and kept on worshiping the Lord. The church became stronger, as the Holy Spirit encouraged it and helped it grow.

Peter Heals Aeneas

³²While Peter was traveling from place to place, he visited the Lord's followers who lived in the town of Lydda. ³³There he met a man named Aeneas, who for eight years had been sick in bed and could not move. ³⁴Peter said to Aeneas, "Jesus Christ has healed you! Get up and make up your bed."ᵉ Right away he stood up.

³⁵Many people in the towns of Lydda and Sharon saw Aeneas and became followers of the Lord.

Peter Brings Dorcas Back to Life

³⁶In Joppa there was a follower named Tabitha. Her Greek name was Dorcas, which means "deer." She was always doing good things for people and had given much to the poor. ³⁷But she got sick and died, and her body was washed and placed in an upstairs room. ³⁸Joppa wasn't far from Lydda, and the followers heard that Peter was there. They sent two men to say to him, "Please come with us as quickly as you can!" ³⁹Right away, Peter went with them.

The men took Peter upstairs into the room. Many widows were there crying. They showed him the coats and clothes that Dorcas had made while she was still alive.

⁴⁰After Peter had sent everyone out of the room, he knelt down and prayed. Then he turned to the body of Dorcas and said, "Tabitha, get up!" The woman opened her eyes, and when she saw Peter, she sat up. ⁴¹He took her by the hand and helped her to her feet.

Peter called in the widows and the other followers and showed them that Dorcas had been raised from death. ⁴²Everyone in Joppa heard what had happened, and many of them put their faith in the Lord. ⁴³Peter stayed on for a while in Joppa in the house of a man named Simon, who made leather.

ᵉ9.34 *and make up your bed:* Or "and fix something to eat."

Peter and Cornelius

10 In Caesarea there was a man named Cornelius, who was the captain of a group of soldiers called "The Italian Unit." [2]Cornelius was a very religious man. He worshiped God, and so did everyone else who lived in his house. He had given a lot of money to the poor and was always praying to God.

[3]One afternoon at about three o'clock,[j] Cornelius had a vision. He saw an angel from God coming to him and calling him by name. [4]Cornelius was surprised and stared at the angel. Then he asked, "What is this all about?"

The angel answered, "God has heard your prayers and knows about your gifts to the poor. [5]Now send some men to Joppa for a man named Simon Peter. [6]He is visiting with Simon the leather maker, who lives in a house near the sea." [7]After saying this, the angel left.

Cornelius called in two of his servants and one of his soldiers who worshiped God. [8]He explained everything to them and sent them off to Joppa.

[9]The next day about noon these men were coming near Joppa. Peter went up on the roof[g] of the house to pray [10]and became very hungry. While the food was being prepared, he fell sound asleep and had a vision. [11]He saw heaven open, and something came down like a huge sheet held up by its four corners. [12]In it were all kinds of animals, snakes, and birds. [13]A voice said to him, "Peter, get up! Kill these and eat them."

[14]But Peter said, "Lord, I can't do that! I've never eaten anything that is unclean and not fit to eat."[h]

[15]The voice spoke to him again, "When God says that something can be used for food, don't say it isn't fit to eat."

[16]This happened three times before the sheet was suddenly taken back to heaven.

[17]Peter was still wondering what all of this meant, when the men sent by Cornelius came and stood at the gate. They had found their way to Simon's house [18]and were asking if Simon Peter was staying there.

[19]While Peter was still thinking about the vision, the Holy Spirit said to him, "Three[i] men are here looking for you. [20]Hurry down and go with them. Don't worry, I sent them."

[21]Peter went down and said to the men, "I am the one you are looking for. Why have you come?"

[22]They answered, "Captain Cornelius sent us. He is a good man who worships God and is liked by the Jewish people. One of God's holy angels told Cornelius to send for you, so he could hear what you have to say." [23]Peter invited them to spend the night.

> *Racial prejudice breaks down when young moms of all races do babysitting co-ops together, when women invite coworkers or neighbors out to lunch, or strike up conversations in the grocery store or on the playground. We don't always have to have "a plan"—we just need to be friendly and open to the people we meet.*
>
> JUNKO CHENG

The next morning, Peter and some of the Lord's followers in Joppa left with the men who had come from Cornelius. [24]The next day they arrived in Caesarea where Cornelius was waiting for them. He had also invited his relatives and close friends.

[25]When Peter arrived, Cornelius greeted him. Then he knelt at Peter's feet and started worshiping him. [26]But Peter took hold of him and said, "Stand up! I am nothing more than a human."

---

[j]**10.3** *at about three o'clock*: Probably while he was praying (see 3.1 and the note there). [g]**10.9** *roof*: In Palestine the houses usually had a flat roof. Stairs on the outside led up to the roof, which was made of beams and boards covered with packed earth. [h]**10.14** *unclean and not fit to eat*: The Law of Moses taught that some foods were not fit to eat. [i]**10.19** *Three*: One manuscript has "two;" some manuscripts have "some."

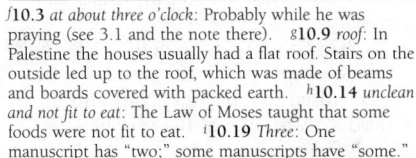

²⁷As Peter entered the house, he was still talking with Cornelius. Many people were there, ²⁸and Peter said to them, "You know that we Jews are not allowed to have anything to do with other people. But God has shown me that he doesn't think anyone is unclean or unfit. ²⁹I agreed to come here, but I want to know why you sent for me."

³⁰Cornelius answered:

Four days ago at about three o'clock in the afternoon I was praying at home. Suddenly a man in bright clothes stood in front of me. ³¹He said, "Cornelius, God has heard your prayers, and he knows about your gifts to the poor. ³²Now send to Joppa for Simon Peter. He is visiting in the home of Simon the leather maker, who lives near the sea."

³³I sent for you right away, and you have been good enough to come. All of us are here in the presence of the Lord God, so that we can hear what he has to say.

³⁴Peter then said:

Now I am certain that God treats all people alike. ³⁵God is pleased with everyone who worships him and does right, no matter what nation they come from. ³⁶This is the same message that God gave to the people of Israel, when he sent Jesus Christ, the Lord of all, to offer peace to them.

³⁷You surely know what happened[j] everywhere in Judea. It all began in Galilee after John had told everyone to be baptized. ³⁸God gave the Holy Spirit and power to Jesus from Nazareth. He was with Jesus, as he went around doing good and healing everyone who was under the power of the devil. ³⁹We all saw what Jesus did both in Israel and in the city of Jerusalem. Jesus was put to death on a cross. ⁴⁰But three days later, God raised him to life and let him be seen. ⁴¹Not everyone saw him. He was seen only by us, who ate and drank with him after he was raised from death. We were the ones God chose to tell others about him.

⁴²God told us to announce clearly to the people that Jesus is the one he has chosen to judge the living and the dead. ⁴³Every one of the prophets has said that all who have faith in Jesus will have their sins forgiven in his name.

⁴⁴While Peter was still speaking, the Holy Spirit took control of everyone who was listening. ⁴⁵Some Jewish followers of the Lord had come with Peter, and they were surprised that the Holy Spirit had been given to Gentiles. ⁴⁶Now they were hearing Gentiles speaking unknown languages and praising God.

Peter said, ⁴⁷"These Gentiles have been given the Holy Spirit, just as we have! I am certain that no one would dare stop us from baptizing them." ⁴⁸Peter ordered them to be baptized in the name of Jesus Christ, and they asked him to stay on for a few days.

Peter Reports to the Church in Jerusalem

11 The apostles and the followers in Judea heard that Gentiles had accepted God's message. ²So when Peter came to Jerusalem, some of the Jewish followers started arguing with him. They wanted Gentile followers to be circumcised, and ³they said, "You stayed in the homes of Gentiles, and you even ate with them!"

⁴Then Peter told them exactly what had happened:

⁵I was in the town of Joppa and was praying when I fell sound asleep and had a vision. I saw heaven open, and something like a huge sheet held by its four corners came down to me. ⁶When I looked in it, I saw animals, wild beasts, snakes, and birds. ⁷I heard a voice saying to me, "Peter, get up! Kill these and eat them."

⁸But I said, "Lord, I can't do that! I've never taken a bite of anything that is unclean and not fit to eat."[k]

⁹The voice from heaven spoke to me again, "When God says that something can be used for food, don't say it isn't fit to eat." ¹⁰This happened three times before it was all taken back into heaven.

¹¹Suddenly three men from Caesarea stood in front of the house where I was staying. ¹²The Holy Spirit told me to go with them and not to worry. Then six of the Lord's followers went with me to the home of a man ¹³who

---

[j]10.37 *what happened:* Or "the message that went."
[k]11.8 *unclean and not fit to eat:* See the note at 10.14.

told us that an angel had appeared to him. The angel had ordered him to send to Joppa for someone named Simon Peter. [14]Then Peter would tell him how he and everyone in his house could be saved.

[15]After I started speaking, the Holy Spirit was given to them, just as the Spirit had been given to us at the beginning. [16]I remembered that the Lord had said, "John baptized with water, but you will be baptized with the Holy Spirit." [17]God gave those Gentiles the same gift that he gave us when we put our faith in the Lord Jesus Christ. So how could I have gone against God?

[18]When they heard Peter say this, they stopped arguing and started praising God. They said, "God has now let Gentiles turn to him, and he has given life to them!"

The Church in Antioch

[19]Some of the Lord's followers had been scattered because of the terrible trouble that started when Stephen was killed. They went as far as Phoenicia, Cyprus, and Antioch, but they told the message only to the Jews.

[20]Some of the followers from Cyprus and Cyrene went to Antioch and started telling Gentiles[l] the good news about the Lord Jesus. [21]The Lord's power was with them, and many people turned to the Lord and put their faith in him. [22]News of what was happening reached the church in Jerusalem. Then they sent Barnabas to Antioch.

[23]When Barnabas got there and saw what God had been kind enough to do for them, he was very glad. So he begged them to remain faithful to the Lord with all their hearts. [24]Barnabas was a good man of great faith, and he was filled with the Holy Spirit. Many more people turned to the Lord.

[25]Barnabas went to Tarsus to look for Saul. [26]He found Saul and brought him to Antioch, where they met with the church for a whole year and taught many of its people. There in Antioch the Lord's followers were first called Christians.

[27]During this time some prophets from Jerusalem came to Antioch. [28]One of them was Agabus. Then with the help of the Spirit, he told that there would be a terrible famine everywhere in the world. And it happened when Claudius was Emperor.[m] [29]The followers in Antioch decided to send what-

ever help they could to the followers in Judea. [30]So they had Barnabas and Saul take their gifts to the church leaders in Jerusalem.

Herod Causes Trouble for the Church

12 At that time King Herod[n] caused terrible suffering for some members of the church. [2]He ordered soldiers to cut off the head of James, the brother of John. [3]When Herod saw that this pleased the Jewish people, he had Peter arrested during the Festival of Thin Bread. [4]He put Peter in jail and ordered four squads of soldiers to guard him. Herod planned to put him on trial in public after the festival.

[5]While Peter was being kept in jail, the church never stopped praying to God for him.

We don't have to know the future when we pray. All we have to do is trust the one who does.

SANDRA P. ALDRICH

Peter Is Rescued

[6]The night before Peter was to be put on trial, he was asleep and bound by two chains. A soldier was guarding him on each side, and two other soldiers were guarding the entrance to the jail. [7]Suddenly an angel from the Lord appeared, and light flashed around in the cell. The angel poked Peter in the side and woke him up. Then he said, "Quick! Get up!"

The chains fell off his hands, [8]and the angel said, "Get dressed and put on your sandals." Peter did what he was told. Then the angel said, "Now put on your coat and follow me." [9]Peter left with the angel, but he

---

[l]11.20 *Gentiles*: This translates a Greek word that may mean "people who speak Greek" or "people who live as Greeks do." Here the word seems to mean "people who are not Jews." Some manuscripts have "Greeks," which also seems to mean "people who are not Jews." [m]11.28 *when Claudius was Emperor*: A.D. 41-54. [n]12.1 *Herod*: Herod Agrippa I, the grandson of Herod the Great.

thought everything was only a dream. [10]They went past the two groups of soldiers, and when they came to the iron gate to the city, it opened by itself. They went out and were going along the street, when all at once the angel disappeared.

[11]Peter now realized what had happened, and he said, "I am certain that the Lord sent his angel to rescue me from Herod and from everything the Jewish leaders planned to do to me." [12]Then Peter went to the house of Mary the mother of John whose other name was Mark. Many of the Lord's followers had come together there and were praying.

[13]Peter knocked on the gate, and a servant named Rhoda came to answer. [14]When she heard Peter's voice, she was too excited to open the gate. She ran back into the house and said that Peter was standing there.

[15]"You are crazy!" everyone told her. But she kept saying that it was Peter. Then they said, "It must be his angel."[o] [16]But Peter kept on knocking, until finally they opened the gate. They saw him and were completely amazed.

[17]Peter motioned for them to keep quiet. Then he told how the Lord had led him out of jail. He also said, "Tell James[p] and the others what has happened." After that, he left and went somewhere else.

[18]The next morning the soldiers who had been on guard were terribly worried and wondered what had happened to Peter. [19]Herod ordered his own soldiers to search for him, but they could not find him. Then he questioned the guards and had them put to death. After this, Herod left Judea to stay in Caesarea for a while.

Herod Dies

[20]Herod and the people of Tyre and Sidon were very angry with each other. But their country got its food supply from the region that he ruled. So a group of them went to see Blastus, who was one of Herod's high officials. They convinced Blastus that they wanted to make peace between their cities and Herod, [21]and a day was set for them to meet with him.

Herod came dressed in his royal robes. He sat down on his throne and made a speech. [22]The people shouted, "You speak more like a god than a man!" [23]At once an angel from the Lord struck him down be-

cause he took the honor that belonged to God. Later, Herod was eaten by worms and died.

[24]God's message kept spreading. [25]And after Barnabas and Saul had done the work they were sent to do, they went back to Jerusalem[q] with John, whose other name was Mark.

Barnabas and Saul Are Chosen and Sent

13 The church at Antioch had several prophets and teachers. They were Barnabas, Simeon, also called Niger, Lucius from Cyrene, Manaen, who was Herod's[r] close friend, and Saul. [2]While they were worshiping the Lord and going without eating,[s] the Holy Spirit told them, "Appoint Barnabas and Saul to do the work for which I have chosen them." [3]Everyone prayed and went without eating for a while longer. Next, they placed their hands on Barnabas and Saul to show that they had been appointed to do this work. Then everyone sent them on their way.

Barnabas and Saul in Cyprus

[4]After Barnabas and Saul had been sent by the Holy Spirit, they went to Seleucia. From there they sailed to the island of Cyprus. [5]They arrived at Salamis and began to preach God's message in the Jewish meeting places. They also had John[t] as a helper.

[6]Barnabas and Saul went all the way to the city of Paphos on the other end of the island, where they met a Jewish man named Bar-Jesus. He practiced witchcraft and was a false prophet. [7]He also worked for Sergius Paulus, who was very smart and was the governor of the island. Sergius Paulus wanted to hear God's message, and he sent for Barnabas and Saul. [8]But Bar-Jesus, whose other name was Elymas, was against them. He even tried to keep the governor from having faith in the Lord.

[9]Then Saul, better known as Paul, was

---

[o]12.15 his angel: Probably meaning "his guardian angel." [p]12.17 James: The brother of the Lord. [q]12.25 went back to Jerusalem: Some manuscripts have "left Jerusalem," and others have "went to Antioch." [r]13.1 Herod's: Herod Antipas, the son of Herod the Great. [s]13.2 going without eating: The Jews often went without eating as a way of showing how much they loved God. This is also called "fasting." [t]13.5 John: Whose other name was Mark (see 12.12, 25).

filled with the Holy Spirit. He looked straight at Elymas [10]and said, "You son of the devil! You are a liar, a crook, and an enemy of everything that is right. When will you stop speaking against the true ways of the Lord? [11]The Lord is going to punish you by making you completely blind for a while."

Suddenly the man's eyes were covered by a dark mist, and he went around trying to get someone to lead him by the hand. [12]When the governor saw what had happened, he was amazed at this teaching about the Lord. So he put his faith in the Lord.

Paul and Barnabas in Antioch of Pisidia

[13]Paul and the others left Paphos and sailed to Perga in Pamphylia. But John[t] left them and went back to Jerusalem. [14]The rest of them went on from Perga to Antioch in Pisidia. Then on the Sabbath they went to the Jewish meeting place and sat down.

[15]After the reading of the Law and the Prophets,[u] the leaders sent someone over to tell Paul and Barnabas, "Friends, if you have anything to say that will help the people, please say it."

[16]Paul got up. He motioned with his hand and said:

People of Israel, and everyone else who worships God, listen! [17]The God of Israel chose our ancestors, and he let our people prosper while they were living in Egypt. Then with his mighty power he led them out, [18]and for about forty years he took care of[v] them in the desert. [19]He destroyed seven nations in the land of Canaan and gave their land to our people. [20]All this happened in about 450 years.

Then God gave our people judges until the time of the prophet Samuel, [21]but the people demanded a king. So for forty years God gave them King Saul, the son of Kish from the tribe of Benjamin. [22]Later, God removed Saul and let David rule in his place. God said about him, "David the son of Jesse is the kind of person who pleases me most! He does everything I want him to do."

---

[t]**13.13** *John:* Whose other name was Mark (see 12.12, 25). [u]**13.15** *the Law and the Prophets:* The Jewish Scriptures, that is, the Old Testament. [v]**13.18** *took care of:* Some manuscripts have "put up with."

---

*Spiritual*Life—How can I keep my life centered on God? *(Acts 13.1-5)*

Invite help from other believers.

Centering your life on God is a noble task, but not an easy one. It means shutting out distractions and self-centered priorities, and searching out personal hidden motives. It means studying to know the true meaning of Scripture—and being willing to live by what it teaches. It may mean giving up favorite goals in order to follow a path that God has set out. Centering your life on God isn't a task you should attempt alone; that's why God gave us the church.

These five verses in Acts 13 show us a picture of how people in the early church helped each other keep centered on God. Even the names reveal a wide diversity of social position, race, and vocation. But they were united in the church. They prayed together with such intensity that they voluntarily went without food for hours. In that context it became clear to them that God had a special assignment for Saul (Paul) and Barnabas. As a symbol of God's special call to these two men "they placed their hands on Barnabas and Saul" and "sent them on their way" (13.3).

Many Christians today continue these ancient practices of praying together, fasting, and laying on hands. Through these and other means we can grow together to become more and more God-centered as we accomplish the work he gives us to do. (See also Genesis 12.1-7; Matthew 25.31-46; Galatians 5.16-26; 2 Timothy 2.14-26; 2 John.)

Words To Remember: *Everyone prayed and went without eating. . . . Next, they placed their hands on Barnabas and Saul to show that they had been appointed to do this work. Then everyone sent them on their way.—Acts 13.3*

²³God promised that someone from David's family would come to save the people of Israel, and that one is Jesus. ²⁴But before Jesus came, John was telling everyone in Israel to turn back to God and be baptized. ²⁵Then, when John's work was almost done, he said, "Who do you people think I am? Do you think I am the Promised One? He will come later, and I am not good enough to untie his sandals."

²⁶Now listen, you descendants of Abraham! Pay attention, all of you Gentiles who are here to worship God! Listen to this message about how to be saved, because it is for everyone. ²⁷The people of Jerusalem and their leaders didn't realize who Jesus was. And they didn't understand the words of the prophets that they read each Sabbath. So they condemned Jesus just as the prophets had said. ²⁸⁻²⁹They did exactly what the Scriptures said they would. Even though they couldn't find any reason to put Jesus to death, they still asked Pilate to have him killed.

After Jesus had been put to death, he was taken down from the cross^w and placed in a tomb. ³⁰But God raised him from death! ³¹Then for many days Jesus appeared to his followers who had gone with him from Galilee to Jerusalem. Now they are telling our people about him.

³²God made a promise to our ancestors. And we are here to tell you the good news ³³that he has kept this promise to us. It is just as the second Psalm says about Jesus,

"You are my son because today
I have become your Father."

³⁴God raised Jesus from death and will never let his body decay. It is just as God said,

"I will make to you
the same holy promise
that I made to David."

³⁵And in another psalm it says, "God will never let the body of his Holy One decay."

³⁶When David was alive, he obeyed God. Then after he died, he was buried in the family grave, and his body decayed. ³⁷But God raised Jesus from death, and his body did not decay.

³⁸My friends, the message is that Jesus can forgive your sins! The Law of Moses could not set you free from all your sins. ³⁹But everyone who has faith in Jesus is set free. ⁴⁰Make sure that what the prophets have said doesn't happen to you. They said,

⁴¹ "Look, you people
    who make fun of God!
Be amazed
    and disappear.
I will do something today
    that you won't believe,
even if someone
    tells you about it!"

⁴²As Paul and Barnabas were leaving the meeting, the people begged them to say more about these same things on the next Sabbath. ⁴³After the service, many Jews and a lot of Gentiles who worshiped God went with them. Paul and Barnabas begged them all to remain faithful to God, who had been so kind to them.

⁴⁴The next Sabbath almost everyone in town came to hear the message about the Lord.^x ⁴⁵When the Jewish people saw the crowds, they were very jealous. They insulted Paul and spoke against everything he said.

⁴⁶But Paul and Barnabas bravely said:

We had to tell God's message to you before we told it to anyone else. But you rejected the message! This proves that you don't deserve eternal life. Now we are going to the Gentiles. ⁴⁷The Lord has given us this command,

"I have placed you here
    as a light
        for the Gentiles.
You are to take
    the saving power of God
    to people everywhere on earth."

---

^w13.28,29 *cross:* This translates a Greek word that means "wood," "pole," or "tree." ^x13.44 *the Lord:* Some manuscripts have "God."

[48]This message made the Gentiles glad, and they praised what they had heard about the Lord.[x] Everyone who had been chosen for eternal life then put their faith in the Lord.

[49]The message about the Lord spread all over that region. [50]But the Jewish leaders went to some of the important men in the town and to some respected women who were religious. They turned them against Paul and Barnabas and started making trouble for them. They even chased them out of that part of the country.

[51]Paul and Barnabas shook the dust from that place off their feet[y] and went on to the city of Iconium.

[52]But the Lord's followers in Antioch were very happy and were filled with the Holy Spirit.

Paul and Barnabas in Iconium

14 Paul and Barnabas spoke in the Jewish meeting place in Iconium, just as they had done at Antioch, and many Jews and Gentiles[z] put their faith in the Lord. [2]But the Jews who did not have faith in him made the other Gentiles angry and turned them against the Lord's followers.

[3]Paul and Barnabas stayed there for a while, having faith in the Lord and bravely speaking his message. The Lord gave them the power to work miracles and wonders, and he showed that their message about his great kindness was true.

[4]The people of Iconium did not know what to think. Some of them believed the Jewish group, and others believed the apostles. [5]Finally, some Gentiles and Jews, together with their leaders, decided to make trouble for Paul and Barnabas and to stone them to death.

[6-7]But when the two apostles found out what was happening, they escaped to the region of Lycaonia. They preached the good news there in the towns of Lystra and Derbe and in the nearby countryside.

Paul and Barnabas in Lystra

[8]In Lystra there was a man who had been born with crippled feet and had never been able to walk. [9]The man was listening to Paul speak, when Paul saw that he had faith in Jesus and could be healed. So he looked straight at the man [10]and shouted, "Stand up!" The man jumped up and started walking around.

[11]When the crowd saw what Paul had done, they yelled out in the language of Lycaonia, "The gods have turned into humans and have come down to us!" [12]The people then gave Barnabas the name Zeus, and they gave Paul the name Hermes,[a] because he did the talking.

[13]The temple of Zeus was near the entrance to the city. Its priest and the crowds wanted to offer a sacrifice to Barnabas and Paul. So the priest brought some bulls and flowers to the city gates. [14]When the two apostles found out about this, they tore their clothes in horror and ran to the crowd, shouting:

[15]Why are you doing this? We are humans just like you. Please give up all this foolishness. Turn to the living God, who made the sky, the earth, the sea, and everything in them. [16]In times past, God let each nation go its own way. [17]But he showed that he was there by the good things he did. God sends rain from heaven and makes your crops grow. He gives food to you and makes your hearts glad.

[18]Even after Paul and Barnabas had said all this, they could hardly keep the people from offering a sacrifice to them.

[19]Some Jewish leaders from Antioch and Iconium came and turned the crowds against Paul. They hit him with stones and dragged him out of the city, thinking he was dead. [20]But when the Lord's followers gathered around Paul, he stood up and went back into the city. The next day he and Barnabas went to Derbe.

Paul and Barnabas Return to Antioch in Syria

[21]Paul and Barnabas preached the good news in Derbe and won some people to the Lord. Then they went back to Lystra, Iconium, and Antioch in Pisidia. [22]They encouraged the followers and begged them to

---

[x]**13.48** *the Lord:* Some manuscripts have "God." [y]**13.51** *shook the dust from that place off their feet:* This was a way of showing rejection. [z]**14.1** *Gentiles:* The Greek text has "Greeks," which probably means people who were not Jews. But it may mean Gentiles who worshiped with the Jews. [a]**14.12** *Hermes:* The Greeks thought of Hermes as the messenger of the other gods, especially of Zeus, their chief god.

remain faithful. They told them, "We have to suffer a lot before we can get into God's kingdom." [23]Paul and Barnabas chose some leaders for each of the churches. Then they went without eating[b] and prayed that the Lord would take good care of these leaders.

[24]Paul and Barnabas went on through Pisidia to Pamphylia, [25]where they preached in the town of Perga. Then they went down to Attalia [26]and sailed to Antioch in Syria. It was there that they had been placed in God's care for the work they had now completed.[c]

[27]After arriving in Antioch, they called the church together. They told the people what God had helped them do and how he had made it possible for the Gentiles to believe. [28]Then they stayed there with the followers for a long time.

15 Some people came from Judea and started teaching the Lord's followers that they could not be saved, unless they were circumcised as Moses had taught. [2]This caused trouble, and Paul and Barnabas argued with them about this teaching. So it was decided to send Paul and Barnabas and a few others to Jerusalem to discuss this problem with the apostles and the church leaders.

> *I want to bring to others,
> to love them where they're at,
> to point them to Jesus. That's
> really what life is all about.*
>
> PAM THUM

The Church Leaders Meet in Jerusalem

[3]The men who were sent by the church went through Phoenicia and Samaria, telling how the Gentiles had turned to God. This news made the Lord's followers very happy. [4]When the men arrived in Jerusalem, they were welcomed by the church, including the apostles and the leaders. They told them everything God had helped them do. [5]But some Pharisees had become followers of the Lord. They stood up and said, "Gentiles who have faith in the Lord must be circumcised and told to obey the Law of Moses."

[6]The apostles and church leaders met to discuss this problem about Gentiles. [7]They had talked it over for a long time, when Peter got up and said:

My friends, you know that God decided long ago to let me be the one from your group to preach the good news to the Gentiles. God did this so that they would hear and obey him. [8]He knows what is in everyone's heart. And he showed that he had chosen the Gentiles, when he gave them the Holy Spirit, just as he had given his Spirit to us. [9]God treated them in the same way that he treated us. They put their faith in him, and he made their hearts pure.

[10]Now why are you trying to make God angry by placing a heavy burden on these followers? This burden was too heavy for us or our ancestors. [11]But our Lord Jesus was kind to us, and we are saved by faith in him, just as the Gentiles are.

[12]Everyone kept quiet and listened as Barnabas and Paul told how God had given them the power to work a lot of miracles and wonders for the Gentiles.

[13]After they had finished speaking, James[d] said:

My friends, listen to me! [14]Simon Peter[e] has told how God first came to the Gentiles and made some of them his own people. [15]This agrees with what the prophets wrote,

[16] "I, the Lord, will return
and rebuild
David's fallen house.
I will build it from its ruins
and set it up again.
[17] Then other nations
will turn to me
and be my chosen ones.
I, the Lord, say this.
[18]   I promised it long ago."

---

[b]**14.23** *went without eating*: See the note at 13.2.
[c]**14.26** *the work they had now completed*: See 13.1-3.
[d]**15.13** *James*: The Lord's brother.   [e]**15.14** *Simon Peter*: The Greek text has "Simeon," which is another form of the name "Simon." The apostle Peter is meant.

[19]And so, my friends, I don't think we should place burdens on the Gentiles who are turning to God. [20]We should simply write and tell them not to eat anything that has been offered to idols. They should be told not to eat the meat of any animal that has been strangled or that still has blood in it. They must also not commit any terrible sexual sins.[f]

[21]We must remember that the Law of Moses has been preached in city after city for many years, and every Sabbath it is read when we Jews meet.

A Letter to Gentiles Who Had Faith in the Lord

[22]The apostles, the leaders, and all the church members decided to send some men to Antioch along with Paul and Barnabas. They chose Silas and Judas Barsabbas,[g] who were two leaders of the Lord's followers. [23]They wrote a letter that said:

We apostles and leaders send friendly greetings to all of you Gentiles who are followers of the Lord in Antioch, Syria, and Cilicia.

[24]We have heard that some people from here have terribly upset you by what they said. But we did not send them! [25]So we met together and decided to choose some men and to send them to you along with our good friends Barnabas and Paul. [26]These men have risked their lives for our Lord Jesus Christ. [27]We are also sending Judas and Silas, who will tell you in person the same things that we are writing.

[28]The Holy Spirit has shown us that we should not place any extra burden on you. [29]But you should not eat anything offered to idols. You should not eat any meat that still has the blood in it or any meat of any animal that has been strangled. You must also not commit any terrible sexual sins. If you follow these instructions, you will do well.

We send our best wishes.

[30]The four men left Jerusalem and went to Antioch. Then they called the church members together and gave them the letter. [31]When the letter was read, everyone was pleased and greatly encouraged. [32]Judas and Silas were prophets, and they spoke a long time, encouraging and helping the Lord's followers.

[33]The men from Jerusalem stayed on in Antioch for a while. And when they left to return to the ones who had sent them, the followers wished them well. [34-35]But Paul and Barnabas stayed on in Antioch, where they and many others taught and preached about the Lord.[h]

Paul and Barnabas Go Their Separate Ways

[36]Sometime later Paul said to Barnabas, "Let's go back and visit the Lord's followers in the cities where we preached his message. Then we will know how they are doing." [37]Barnabas wanted to take along John, whose other name was Mark. [38]But Paul did not want to, because Mark had left them in Pamphylia and had stopped working with them.

[39]Paul and Barnabas argued, then each of them went his own way. Barnabas took Mark and sailed to Cyprus, [40]but Paul took Silas and left after the followers had placed them in God's care. [41]They traveled through Syria and Cilicia, encouraging the churches.

Timothy Works with Paul and Silas

16 Paul and Silas went back to Derbe and Lystra, where there was a follower named Timothy. His mother was also a follower. She was Jewish, and his father was Greek. [2]The Lord's followers in Lystra and Iconium said good things about Timothy, [3]and Paul wanted him to go with them. But Paul first had him circumcised, because all the Jewish people around there knew that Timothy's father was Greek.[i]

[4]As Paul and the others went from city to city, they told the followers what the apostles and leaders in Jerusalem had decided, and they urged them to follow these instructions. [5]The churches became stronger in

---

[f]**15.20** *not commit any terrible sexual sins:* This probably refers to the laws about the wrong kind of marriages that are forbidden in Leviticus 18.6-18 or to some serious sexual sin.   [g]**15.22** *Judas Barsabbas:* He may have been a brother of Joseph Barsabbas (see 1.23), but the name "Barsabbas" was often used by the Jewish people.   [h]**15.34,35** Verse 34, which says that Silas decided to stay on in Antioch, is not in some manuscripts.   [i]**16.3** *had him circumcised . . . Timothy's father was Greek:* Timothy would not have been acceptable to the Jews unless he had been circumcised, and Greeks did not circumcise their sons.

Lydia

Acts 16.6-15

What would you do if you lived where no church existed? Be thankful for serious relief to your schedule? Worship God independently? Start a church?

Lydia had lived in Thyatira where there was a large Jewish population. Scripture describes her as a "worshiper of the Lord God" (16.14), a term often used for Gentile converts to Judaism. But Lydia didn't stay in Thyatira. She moved, probably for business reasons, more than two hundred miles to the Roman city of Philippi. Not many Jews lived there. There was no synagogue. In fact, it seems likely that there weren't even ten practicing Jewish men in the whole town. (Traditionally, it took ten men to create a synagogue and hold official worship.) What should Lydia do about practicing her adopted Jewish faith?

Lydia found other Jews (mostly women), and they met together to pray—which is how they met Paul and his band of traveling missionaries. It must have been a confusing trip for Paul because every time he decided to go one direction, God's Spirit pointed somewhere else. Every time he wanted to stop and preach, the Holy Spirit said "not here." So Paul kept moving, mouth closed, until one night he saw a vision with a person begging, "Come over to Macedonia and help us!" (16.9). Paul went.

When he got to Philippi he followed his usual Sabbath custom and looked up the Jews so he could worship with them. What he found was Lydia and her band of women pray-ers. As usual, Paul talked about the good news: that Jesus Christ is the long-promised Jewish Messiah, that Jesus died for the sins of his people, that he came back to life and ascended into heaven, that he invites us to believe in him and come into God's family. Scripture says, "[God] made [Lydia] willing to accept what Paul was saying" (16.14).

This successful businesswoman wasted no time in acting on her newfound faith. She and her family were baptized, and she invited Paul and his party to stay in her home. This later step turned out to be potentially dangerous. Paul healed a fortune-telling slave girl of her "gift" of seeing the future. This irritated her owner, who was used to pocketing her profits. He incited an angry crowd saying, "These Jews are upsetting our city!" (16.20). And Paul wound up in jail.

But God brought even more converts to Christianity from the affair. Paul protected the Jews (now Christian Jews) from blame by claiming his rights as a Roman citizen, and so won an official apology. By then a Christian church was meeting in Lydia's home (16.40).

Lydia was a hard-working businesswoman. She carried all the traits that made her business a success into her practice of faith. She exerted effort to find other believers and meet with them for prayer. She made quick, informed decisions and acted on them. She took calculated risks, sharing her home with Paul's group. In so doing, Lydia became a founding mother of the Christian church in Europe.

their faith, and each day more people put their faith in the Lord.

Paul's Vision in Troas

[6]Paul and his friends went through Phrygia and Galatia, but the Holy Spirit would not let them preach in Asia. [7]After they arrived in Mysia, they tried to go into Bithynia, but the Spirit of Jesus would not let them. [8]So they went on through[j] Mysia until they came to Troas.

[9]During the night, Paul had a vision of someone from Macedonia who was standing there and begging him, "Come over to Macedonia and help us!" [10]After Paul had seen the vision, we began looking for a way to go to Macedonia. We were sure that God had called us to preach the good news there.

Lydia Becomes a Follower of the Lord

[11]We sailed straight from Troas to Samothrace, and the next day we arrived in Neapolis. [12]From there we went to Philippi, which is a Roman colony in the first district of Macedonia.[k]

We spent several days in Philippi. [13]Then on the Sabbath we went outside the city gate to a place by the river, where we thought there would be a Jewish meeting place for prayer. We sat down and talked with the women who came. [14]One of them was Lydia, who was from the city of Thyatira and sold expensive purple cloth. She was a worshiper of the Lord God, and he made her willing to accept what Paul was saying. [15]Then after she and her family were baptized, she kept on begging us, "If you think I really do have faith in the Lord, come stay in my home." Finally, we accepted her invitation.

Paul and Silas Are Put in Jail

[16]One day on our way to the place of prayer, we were met by a slave girl. She had a spirit in her that gave her the power to tell the future. By doing this she made a lot of money for her owners. [17]The girl followed Paul and the rest of us and kept yelling, "These men are servants of the Most High God! They are telling you how to be saved."

[18]This went on for several days. Finally, Paul got so upset that he turned and said to the spirit, "In the name of Jesus Christ, I or-

der you to leave this girl alone!" At once the evil spirit left her.

[19]When the girl's owners realized that they had lost all chances for making more money, they grabbed Paul and Silas and dragged them into court. [20]They told the officials, "These Jews are upsetting our city! [21]They are telling us to do things we Romans are not allowed to do."

[22]The crowd joined in the attack on Paul and Silas. Then the officials tore the clothes off the two men and ordered them to be beaten with a whip. [23]After they had been badly beaten, they were put in jail, and the jailer was told to guard them carefully. [24]The jailer did as he was told. He put them deep inside the jail and chained their feet to heavy blocks of wood.

[25]About midnight Paul and Silas were praying and singing praises to God, while the other prisoners listened. [26]Suddenly a strong earthquake shook the jail to its foundations. The doors opened, and the chains fell from all the prisoners.

[27]When the jailer woke up and saw that the doors were open, he thought that the prisoners had escaped. He pulled out his sword and was about to kill himself. [28]But Paul shouted, "Don't harm yourself! No one has escaped."

[29]The jailer asked for a torch and went into the jail. He was shaking all over as he knelt down in front of Paul and Silas. [30]After he had led them out of the jail, he asked, "What must I do to be saved?"

[31]They replied, "Have faith in the Lord Jesus and you will be saved! This is also true for everyone who lives in your home."

[32]Then Paul and Silas told him and everyone else in his house about the Lord. [33]While it was still night, the jailer took them to a place where he could wash their cuts and bruises. Then he and everyone in his home were baptized. [34]They were very glad that they had put their faith in God. After this, the jailer took Paul and Silas to his home and gave them something to eat.

[35]The next morning the officials sent some police with orders for the jailer to let Paul and Silas go. [36]The jailer told Paul, "The

---

[j]16.8 *went on through:* Or *"passed by."* [k]16.12 *in the first district of Macedonia:* Some manuscripts have "and the leading city of Macedonia."

officials have ordered me to set you free. Now you can leave in peace."

[37]But Paul told the police, "We are Roman citizens,[l] and the Roman officials had us beaten in public without giving us a trial. They threw us into jail. Now do they think they can secretly send us away? No, they cannot! They will have to come here themselves and let us out."

[38]When the police told the officials that Paul and Silas were Roman citizens, the officials were afraid. [39]So they came and apologized. They led them out of the jail and asked them to please leave town. [40]But Paul and Silas went straight to the home of Lydia, where they saw the Lord's followers and encouraged them. Then they left.

Trouble in Thessalonica

17 After Paul and his friends had traveled through Amphipolis and Apollonia, they went on to Thessalonica. A Jewish meeting place was in that city. [2]So as usual, Paul went there to worship, and on three Sabbaths he spoke to the people. He used the Scriptures [3]to show them that the Messiah had to suffer, but that he would rise from death. Paul also told them that Jesus is the Messiah he was preaching about. [4]Some of them believed what Paul had said, and they became followers with Paul and Silas. Some Gentiles[m] and many important women also believed the message.

[5]The Jewish leaders were jealous and got some worthless bums who hung around the marketplace to start a riot in the city. They wanted to drag Paul and Silas out to the mob, and so they went straight to Jason's home. [6]But when they did not find them there, they dragged out Jason and some of the Lord's followers. They took them to the city authorities and shouted, "Paul and Silas have been upsetting things everywhere. Now they have come here, [7]and Jason has welcomed them into his home. All of them break the laws of the Roman Emperor by claiming that someone named Jesus is king."

[8]The officials and the people were upset when they heard this. [9]So they made Jason and the other followers pay bail before letting them go.

People in Berea Welcome the Message

[10]That same night the Lord's followers sent Paul and Silas on to Berea, and after they arrived, they went to the Jewish meeting place. [11]The people in Berea were much nicer than those in Thessalonica, and they gladly accepted the message. Day after day they studied the Scriptures to see if these things were true. [12]Many of them put their faith in the Lord, including some important Greek women and several men.

[13]When the Jewish leaders in Thessalonica heard that Paul had been preaching God's message in Berea, they went there and caused trouble by turning the crowds against Paul.

[14]Right away the followers sent Paul down to the coast, but Silas and Timothy stayed in Berea. [15]Some men went with Paul as far as Athens, and then returned with instructions for Silas and Timothy to join him as soon as possible.

Paul in Athens

[16]While Paul was waiting in Athens, he was upset to see all the idols in the city. [17]He went to the Jewish meeting place to speak to the Jews and to anyone who worshiped with them. Day after day he also spoke to everyone he met in the market. [18]Some of them were Epicureans[n] and some were Stoics,[o] and they started arguing with him.

People were asking, "What is this know-it-all trying to say?"

Some even said, "Paul must be preaching about foreign gods! That's what he means when he talks about Jesus and about people rising from death."[p]

[19]They brought Paul before a council called the Areopagus, and said, "Tell us what your new teaching is all about. [20]We have heard you say some strange things, and we want to know what you mean."

[21]More than anything else the people of Athens and the foreigners living there loved to hear and to talk about anything new. [22]So Paul stood up in front of the council and said:

People of Athens, I see that you are

---

[l]**16.37** *Roman citizens*: Only a small number of the people living in the Roman Empire were citizens, and they had special rights and privileges.   [m]**17.4** *Gentiles*: See the note at 14.1.   [n]**17.18** *Epicureans*: People who followed the teaching of a man named Epicurus, who taught that happiness should be the main goal in life.   [o]**17.18** *Stoics*: Followers of a man named Zeno, who taught that people should learn self-control and be guided by their consciences.   [p]**17.18** *people rising from death*: Or "a goddess named 'Rising from Death.'"

very religious. 23As I was going
through your city and looking at the
things you worship, I found an altar
with the words, "To an Unknown
God." You worship this God, but you
don't really know him. So I want to tell
you about him. 24This God made the
world and everything in it. He is Lord
of heaven and earth, and he doesn't
live in temples built by human hands.
25He doesn't need help from anyone.
He gives life, breath, and everything
else to all people. 26From one person
God made all nations who live on
earth, and he decided when and where
every nation would be.

> *I want to be impacted by contact and communion with God. May I become more astute at hearing God's voice and seeing things not just from a human perspective but from God's perspective.*
>
> VALERIE BELL

27God has done all this, so that we
will look for him and reach out and
find him. He isn't far from any of us,
28and he gives us the power to live, to
move, and to be who we are. "We are
his children," just as some of your po-
ets have said.

29Since we are God's children, we
must not think that he is like an idol
made out of gold or silver or stone. He
isn't like anything that humans have
thought up and made. 30In the past,
God forgave all this because people
did not know what they were doing.
But now he says that everyone everywhere must turn to him. 31He has set a
day when he will judge the world's
people with fairness. And he has chosen the man Jesus to do the judging
for him. God has given proof of this to
all of us by raising Jesus from death.

32As soon as the people heard Paul say
that a man had been raised from death,
some of them started laughing. Others said,
"We will hear you talk about this some other
time." 33When Paul left the council meeting,
34some of the men put their faith in the Lord
and went with Paul. One of them was a
council member named Dionysius. A woman
named Damaris and several others also put
their faith in the Lord.

Paul in Corinth

18 Paul left Athens and went to Corinth, 2where he met Aquila, a
Jewish man from Pontus. Not
long before this, Aquila had come from Italy
with his wife Priscilla, because Emperor
Claudius had ordered the Jewish people to
leave Rome.[q] Paul went to see Aquila and
Priscilla 3and found out that they were tent
makers. Paul was a tent maker too. So he
stayed with them, and they worked together.

4Every Sabbath, Paul went to the Jewish
meeting place. He spoke to Jews and
Gentiles[r] and tried to win them over. 5But
after Silas and Timothy came from Macedonia, he spent all his time preaching to the
Jews about Jesus the Messiah. 6Finally, they
turned against him and insulted him. So he
shook the dust from his clothes[s] and told
them, "Whatever happens to you will be
your own fault! I am not to blame. From
now on I am going to preach to the Gentiles."

7Paul then moved into the house of a
man named Titius Justus, who worshiped
God and lived next door to the Jewish meeting place. 8Crispus was the leader of the
meeting place. He and everyone in his family put their faith in the Lord. Many others
in Corinth also heard the message, and all
the people who had faith in the Lord were
baptized.

9One night, Paul had a vision, and in it
the Lord said, "Don't be afraid to keep on
preaching. Don't stop! 10I am with you, and

---

[q] **18.2** *Emperor Claudius had ordered the Jewish people to leave Rome*: Probably A.D. 49, though it may have been A.D. 41. [r] **18.4** *Gentiles*: Here the word is "Greeks." But see the note at 14.1. [s] **18.6** *shook the dust from his clothes*: This means the same as shaking dust from the feet (see the note at 13.51).

you won't be harmed. Many people in this city belong to me." ¹¹Paul stayed on in Corinth for a year and a half, teaching God's message to the people.

¹²While Gallio was governor of Achaia, some of the Jewish leaders got together and grabbed Paul. They brought him into court ¹³and said, "This man is trying to make our people worship God in a way that is against our Law!"

¹⁴Even before Paul could speak, Gallio said, "If you were charging this man with a crime or some other wrong, I would have to listen to you. ¹⁵But since this concerns only words, names, and your own law, you will have to take care of it. I refuse to judge such matters." ¹⁶Then he sent them out of the court. ¹⁷The crowd grabbed Sosthenes, the Jewish leader, and beat him up in front of the court. But none of this mattered to Gallio.

Paul Returns to Antioch in Syria

¹⁸After Paul had stayed for a while with the Lord's followers in Corinth, he told them good-by and sailed on to Syria with Aquila and Priscilla. But before he left, he had his head shaved[t] at Cenchreae because he had made a promise to God.

¹⁹The three of them arrived in Ephesus, where Paul left Priscilla and Aquila. He then went into the Jewish meeting place to talk with the people there. ²⁰They asked him to stay longer, but he refused. ²¹He told them good-by and said, "If God lets me, I will come back."

²²Paul sailed to Caesarea, where he greeted the church. Then he went on to Antioch. ²³After staying there for a while, he left and visited several places in Galatia and Phrygia. He helped the followers there to become stronger in their faith.

Apollos in Ephesus

²⁴A Jewish man named Apollos came to Ephesus. Apollos had been born in the city of Alexandria. He was a very good speaker and knew a lot about the Scriptures. ²⁵He also knew much about the Lord's Way,[u] and

---

[t]18.18 *he had his head shaved:* Paul had promised to be a "Nazirite" for a while. This meant that for the time of the promise, he could not cut his hair or drink wine. When the time was over, he would have to cut his hair and offer a sacrifice to God.   [u]18.25 *the Lord's Way:* See the note at 9.2.

MARRIAGE—What does a healthy, successful marriage look like? *(Acts 18)*

It's a team effort.
Is your marriage near perfect? Less than ideal? Disastrous? Or has it been all those at one time or another? Whatever the current quality of your marriage, you can benefit by observing a healthy marriage in action. Priscilla and Aquila give us one of those pictures.

Though their story threads through much of Paul's mission work, Scripture hardly mentions Priscilla without Aquila. They worked together, traveled together, and taught together. We don't even know the individual strengths of either person. As far as the biblical account is concerned, they were a team.

In real life, we know our friends better than that. We may know an outgoing, fun-loving husband with a quiet, thoughtful wife who gets things done behind the scenes. We know a brisk, skillful surgeon who is paired with a sensitive pastor-husband. We see homemaker dads linked to executive moms—and also the opposite pattern. In spite of these unlikely pairings, a healthy Christian marriage pools individual strengths to make a powerful team.

Of course, opposite qualities can make for war, not teamwork. If your marriage is heading toward war, try to spot a healthy marriage or two among your friends. Spend time with them. Watch their teamwork: how they treat each other, how they resolve differences, what they do about each other's weaknesses. Then come up with your own ideas on how you can improve the health of your marriage—and try one this week! (See also Genesis 2.18-23; Exodus 32.11-14; Song of Songs 8.5-7; Hosea 14.4-8; Hebrews 13.4.)

Words To Remember: *Apollos started speaking bravely in the Jewish meeting place. But when Priscilla and Aquila heard him, they took him to their home and helped him understand God's Way even better.—Acts 18.26*

he spoke about it with great excitement. What he taught about Jesus was right, but all he knew was John's message about baptism.

²⁶Apollos started speaking bravely in the Jewish meeting place. But when Priscilla and Aquila heard him, they took him to their home and helped him understand God's Way even better.

²⁷Apollos decided to travel through Achaia. So the Lord's followers wrote letters, encouraging the followers there to welcome him. After Apollos arrived in Achaia, he was a great help to everyone who had put their faith in the Lord Jesus because of God's kindness. ²⁸He got into fierce arguments with the Jewish people, and in public he used the Scriptures to prove that Jesus is the Messiah.

Paul in Ephesus

19 While Apollos was in Corinth, Paul traveled across the hill country to Ephesus, where he met some of the Lord's followers. ²He asked them, "When you put your faith in Jesus, were you given the Holy Spirit?"

"No!" they answered. "We have never even heard of the Holy Spirit."

³"Then why were you baptized?" Paul asked.

They answered, "Because of what John taught."ᵛ

⁴Paul replied, "John baptized people so that they would turn to God. But he also told them that someone else was coming, and that they should put their faith in him. Jesus is the one that John was talking about." ⁵After the people heard Paul say this, they were baptized in the name of the Lord Jesus. ⁶Then Paul placed his hands on them. The Holy Spirit was given to them, and they spoke unknown languages and prophesied. ⁷There were about twelve men in this group.

⁸For three months Paul went to the Jewish meeting place and talked bravely with the people about God's kingdom. He tried to win them over, ⁹but some of them were stubborn and refused to believe. In front of everyone they said terrible things about God's Way. Paul left and took the followers with him to the lecture hall of Tyrannus. He spoke there every day ¹⁰for two years, until every Jew and Gentileʷ in Asia had heard the Lord's message.

The Sons of Sceva

¹¹God gave Paul the power to work great miracles. ¹²People even took handkerchiefs and aprons that had touched Paul's body, and they carried them to everyone who was sick. All of the sick people were healed, and the evil spirits went out.

¹³Some Jewish men started going around trying to force out evil spirits by using the name of the Lord Jesus. They said to the spirits, "Come out in the name of that same Jesus that Paul preaches about!"

¹⁴Seven sons of a Jewish high priest named Sceva were doing this, ¹⁵when an evil spirit said to them, "I know Jesus! And I have heard about Paul. But who are you?" ¹⁶Then the man with the evil spirit jumped on them and beat them up. They ran out of the house, naked and bruised.

¹⁷When the Jews and Gentilesʷ in Ephesus heard about this, they were so frightened that they praised the name of the Lord Jesus. ¹⁸Many who were followers now started telling everyone about the evil things they had been doing. ¹⁹Some who had been practicing witchcraft even brought their books and burned them in public. These books were worth about fifty thousand silver coins. ²⁰So the Lord's message spread and became even more powerful.

The Riot in Ephesus

²¹After all of this had happened, Paul decidedˣ to visit Macedonia and Achaia on his way to Jerusalem. Paul had said, "From there I will go on to Rome." ²²So he sent his two helpers, Timothy and Erastus, to Macedonia. But he stayed on in Asia for a while.

²³At that time there was serious trouble because of the Lord's Way.ʸ ²⁴A silversmith named Demetrius had a business that made silver models of the temple of the goddess Artemis. Those who worked for him earned a lot of money. ²⁵Demetrius brought together everyone who was in the same business and said:

Friends, you know that we make a good living at this. ²⁶But you have

---

ᵛ**19.3** *Then why were you baptized? . . . Because of what John taught:* Or "In whose name were you baptized? . . . We were baptized in John's name." ʷ**19.10,17** *Gentile(s):* The text has "Greek(s)" (see the note at 14.1). ˣ**19.21** *Paul decided:* Or "Paul was led by the Holy Spirit." ʸ**19.23** *the Lord's Way:* See the note at 9.2.

surely seen and heard how this man Paul is upsetting a lot of people, not only in Ephesus, but almost everywhere in Asia. He claims that the gods we humans make are not really gods at all. ²⁷Everyone will start saying terrible things about our business. They will stop respecting the temple of the goddess Artemis, who is worshiped in Asia and all over the world. Our great goddess will be forgotten!

²⁸When the workers heard this, they got angry and started shouting, "Great is Artemis, the goddess of the Ephesians!" ²⁹Soon the whole city was in a riot, and some men grabbed Gaius and Aristarchus, who had come from Macedonia with Paul. Then everyone in the crowd rushed to the place where the town meetings were held.

³⁰Paul wanted to go out and speak to the people, but the Lord's followers would not let him. ³¹A few of the local officials were friendly to Paul, and they sent someone to warn him not to go.

³²Some of the people in the meeting were shouting one thing, and others were shouting something else. Everyone was completely confused, and most of them did not even know why they were there.

³³Several of the Jewish leaders pushed a man named Alexander to the front of the crowd and started telling him what to say. He motioned with his hand and tried to explain what was going on. ³⁴But when the crowd saw that he was Jewish, they all shouted for two hours, "Great is Artemis, the goddess of the Ephesians!"

³⁵Finally, a town official made the crowd be quiet. Then he said:

People of Ephesus, who in the world doesn't know that our city is the center for worshiping the great goddess Artemis? Who doesn't know that her image which fell from heaven is right here? ³⁶No one can deny this, and so you should calm down and not do anything foolish. ³⁷You have brought men in here who have not robbed temples or spoken against our goddess.

³⁸If Demetrius and his workers have a case against these men, we have courts and judges. Let them take their complaints there. ³⁹But if you want to do more than that, the matter will

have to be brought before the city council. ⁴⁰We could easily be accused of starting a riot today. There is no excuse for it! We cannot even give a reason for this uproar.

⁴¹After saying this, he told the people to leave.

Paul Goes through Macedonia and Greece

20 When the riot was over, Paul sent for the followers and encouraged them. He then told them good-by and left for Macedonia. ²As he traveled from place to place, he encouraged the followers with many messages. Finally, he went to Greece^z ³and stayed there for three months.

Paul was about to sail to Syria. But some of the Jewish leaders plotted against him, so he decided to return by way of Macedonia. ⁴With him were Sopater, son of Pyrrhus from Berea, and Aristarchus and Secundus from Thessalonica. Gaius from Derbe was also with him, and so were Timothy and the two Asians, Tychicus and Trophimus. ⁵They went on ahead to Troas and waited for us there. ⁶After the Festival of Thin Bread, we sailed from Philippi. Five days later we met them in Troas and stayed there for a week.

Paul's Last Visit to Troas

⁷On the first day of the week^d we met to break bread together.^b Paul spoke to the people until midnight because he was leaving the next morning. ⁸In the upstairs room where we were meeting, there were a lot of lamps. ⁹A young man by the name of Eutychus was sitting on a window sill. While Paul was speaking, the young man got very sleepy. Finally, he went to sleep and fell three floors all the way down to the ground. When they picked him up, he was dead.

¹⁰Paul went down and bent over Eutychus. He took him in his arms and said, "Don't worry! He's alive." ¹¹After Paul had gone back upstairs, he broke bread, and ate with us. He then spoke until dawn and left. ¹²Then the followers took the young man home alive and were very happy.

---

^z**20.2** *Greece:* Probably Corinth.   ^d**20.7** *On the first day of the week:* Since the Jewish day began at sunset, the meeting would have begun in the evening.   ^b**20.7** *break bread together:* See the note at 2.46.

The Voyage from Troas to Miletus

[13]Paul decided to travel by land to Assos. The rest of us went on ahead by ship, and we were to take him aboard there. [14]When he met us in Assos, he came aboard, and we sailed on to Mitylene. [15]The next day we came to a place near Chios, and the following day we reached Samos. The day after that we sailed to Miletus. [16]Paul had decided to sail on past Ephesus, because he did not want to spend too much time in Asia. He was in a hurry and wanted to be in Jerusalem in time for Pentecost.[c]

Paul Says Good-By
to the Church Leaders of Ephesus

[17]From Miletus, Paul sent a message for the church leaders at Ephesus to come and meet with him. [18]When they got there, he said:

You know everything I did during the time I was with you when I first came to Asia. [19]Some of the Jews plotted against me and caused me a lot of sorrow and trouble. But I served the Lord and was humble. [20]When I preached in public or taught in your homes, I didn't hold back from telling anything that would help you. [21]I told Jews and Gentiles to turn to God and have faith in our Lord Jesus.

God says he has a unique purpose for my life, and he created me with everything I need to fulfill it. If I'm missing particular gifts— like artistic skills or organizational genius— I won't need them to accomplish what God has in mind for me.

RUTH E. VAN REKEN

[22]I don't know what will happen to me in Jerusalem, but I must obey God's Spirit and go there. [23]In every city I visit, I am told by the Holy Spirit that I will be put in jail and will be in trouble in Jerusalem. [24]But I don't care what happens to me, as long as I finish the work that the Lord Jesus gave me to do. And that work is to tell the good news about God's great kindness.

[25]I have gone from place to place, preaching to you about God's kingdom, but now I know that none of you will ever see me again. [26]I tell you today that I am no longer responsible for any of you! [27]I have told you everything God wants you to know. [28]Look after yourselves and everyone the Holy Spirit has placed in your care. Be like shepherds to God's church. It is the flock that he bought with the blood of his own Son.[d]

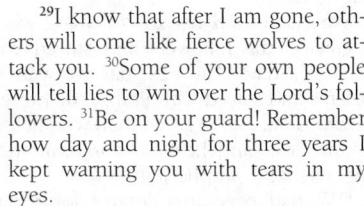

In God's economy, whether he is making a flower or a human soul, nothing ever comes to nothing. The losses are his way of accomplishing the gains.

ELISABETH ELLIOT

[29]I know that after I am gone, others will come like fierce wolves to attack you. [30]Some of your own people will tell lies to win over the Lord's followers. [31]Be on your guard! Remember how day and night for three years I kept warning you with tears in my eyes.

[32]I now place you in God's care. Remember the message about his great kindness! This message can help you and give you what belongs to you

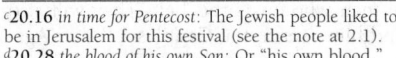

[c]**20.16** *in time for Pentecost:* The Jewish people liked to be in Jerusalem for this festival (see the note at 2.1). [d]**20.28** *the blood of his own Son:* Or "his own blood."

as God's people. ³³I have never wanted anyone's money or clothes. ³⁴You know how I have worked with my own hands to make a living for myself and my friends. ³⁵By everything I did, I showed how you should work to help everyone who is weak. Remember that our Lord Jesus said, "More blessings come from giving than from receiving."

³⁶After Paul had finished speaking, he knelt down with all of them and prayed. ³⁷Everyone cried and hugged and kissed him. ³⁸They were especially sad because Paul had told them, "You will never see me again."

Then they went with him to the ship.

Paul Goes to Jerusalem

21 After saying good-by, we sailed straight to Cos. The next day we reached Rhodes and from there sailed on to Patara. ²We found a ship going to Phoenicia, so we got on board and sailed off.

³We came within sight of Cyprus and then sailed south of it on to the port of Tyre in Syria, where the ship was going to unload its cargo. ⁴We looked up the Lord's followers and stayed with them for a week. The Holy Spirit had told them to warn Paul not to go on to Jerusalem. ⁵But when the week was over, we started on our way again. All the men, together with their wives and children, walked with us from the town to the seashore. We knelt on the beach and prayed. ⁶Then after saying good-by to each other, we got into the ship, and they went back home.

⁷We sailed from Tyre to Ptolemais, where we greeted the followers and stayed with them for a day. ⁸The next day we went to Caesarea and stayed with Philip, the preacher. He was one of the seven men who helped the apostles, ⁹and he had four unmarried[e] daughters who prophesied.

¹⁰We had been in Caesarea for several days, when the prophet Agabus came to us from Judea. ¹¹He took Paul's belt, and with it he tied up his own hands and feet. Then he told us, "The Holy Spirit says that some of the Jewish leaders in Jerusalem will tie up the man who owns this belt. They will also hand him over to the Gentiles." ¹²After Agabus said this, we and the followers living

there begged Paul not to go to Jerusalem. ¹³But Paul answered, "Why are you crying and breaking my heart? I am not only willing to be put in jail for the Lord Jesus, I am even willing to die for him in Jerusalem!"

¹⁴Since we could not get Paul to change his mind, we gave up and prayed, "Lord, please make us willing to do what you want."

¹⁵Then we got ready to go to Jerusalem. ¹⁶Some of the followers from Caesarea went with us and took us to stay in the home of Mnason. He was from Cyprus and had been a follower from the beginning.

Paul Visits James

¹⁷When we arrived in Jerusalem, the Lord's followers gladly welcomed us. ¹⁸Paul went with us to see James[f] the next day, and all the church leaders were present. ¹⁹Paul greeted them and told how God had used him to help the Gentiles. ²⁰Everyone who heard this praised God and said to Paul:

My friend, you can see how many tens of thousands of the Jewish people have become followers! And all of them are eager to obey the Law of Moses. ²¹But they have been told that you are teaching those who live among the Gentiles to disobey this Law. They claim that you are telling them not to circumcise their sons or to follow Jewish customs.

²²What should we do now that our people have heard that you are here? ²³Please do what we ask, because four of our men have made special promises to God. ²⁴Join with them and prepare yourself for the ceremony that goes with the promises. Pay the cost for their heads to be shaved. Then everyone will learn that the reports about you are not true. They will know that you do obey the Law of Moses.

²⁵Some while ago we told the Gentile followers what we think they should do. We instructed them not to eat anything offered to idols. They were told not to eat any meat with blood still in it or the meat of an animal that has been strangled. They

---

ᵉ21.9 *unmarried:* Or "virgin."   ᶠ21.18 *James:* The Lord's brother.

were also told not to commit any terrible sexual sins.[g]

26The next day Paul took the four men with him and got himself ready at the same time they did. Then he went into the temple and told when the final ceremony would take place and when an offering would be made for each of them.

Paul Is Arrested

27When the period of seven days for the ceremony was almost over, some of the Jewish people from Asia saw Paul in the temple. They got a large crowd together and started attacking him. 28They were shouting, "Friends, help us! This man goes around everywhere, saying bad things about our nation and about the Law of Moses and about this temple. He has even brought shame to this holy temple by bringing in Gentiles." 29Some of them thought that Paul had brought Trophimus from Ephesus into the temple, because they had seen them together in the city.

30The whole city was in an uproar, and the people turned into a mob. They grabbed Paul and dragged him out of the temple. Then suddenly the doors were shut. 31The people were about to kill Paul when the Roman army commander heard that all Jerusalem was starting to riot. 32So he quickly took some soldiers and officers and ran to where the crowd had gathered.

As soon as the mob saw the commander and soldiers, they stopped beating Paul. 33The army commander went over and arrested him and had him bound with two chains. Then he tried to find out who Paul was and what he had done. 34Part of the crowd shouted one thing, and part of them shouted something else. But they were making so much noise that the commander could not find out a thing. Then he ordered Paul to be taken into the fortress. 35As they reached the steps, the crowd became so wild that the soldiers had to lift Paul up and carry him. 36The crowd followed and kept shouting, "Kill him! Kill him!"

Paul Speaks to the Crowd

37When Paul was about to be taken into the fortress, he asked the commander, "Can I say something to you?"

"How do you know Greek?" the commander asked. 38"Aren't you that Egyptian who started a riot not long ago and led four thousand terrorists into the desert?"

39"No!" Paul replied. "I am a Jew from Tarsus, an important city in Cilicia. Please let me speak to the crowd."

40The commander told him he could speak, so Paul stood on the steps and motioned to the people. When they were quiet, he spoke to them in Aramaic:

22 "My friends and leaders of our nation, listen as I explain what happened!" 2When the crowd heard Paul speak to them in Aramaic, they became even quieter. Then Paul said:

3I am a Jew, born and raised in the city of Tarsus in Cilicia. I was a student of Gamaliel and was taught to follow every single law of our ancestors. In fact, I was just as eager to obey God as any of you are today.

4I made trouble for everyone who followed the Lord's Way,[h] and I even had some of them killed. I had others arrested and put in jail. I didn't care if they were men or women. 5The high priest and all the council members can tell you that this is true. They even gave me letters to the Jewish leaders in Damascus, so that I could arrest people there and bring them to Jerusalem to be punished.

6One day about noon I was getting close to Damascus, when a bright light from heaven suddenly flashed around me. 7I fell to the ground and heard a voice asking, "Saul, Saul, why are you so cruel to me?"

8"Who are you?" I answered.

The Lord replied, "I am Jesus from Nazareth! I am the one you are so cruel to." 9The men who were traveling with me saw the light, but did not hear the voice.

10I asked, "Lord, what do you want me to do?"

Then he told me, "Get up and go to Damascus. When you get there, you will be told what to do." 11The light had been so bright that I couldn't see. And the other men had to lead me by the hand to Damascus.

g21.25 not to commit any terrible sexual sins: See the note at 15.20. h22.4 followed the Lord's Way: See the note at 9.2.

¹²In that city there was a man named Ananias, who faithfully obeyed the Law of Moses and was well liked by all the Jewish people living there. ¹³He came to me and said, "Saul, my friend, you can now see again!"

At once I could see. ¹⁴Then Ananias told me, "The God that our ancestors worshiped has chosen you to know what he wants done. He has chosen you to see the One Who Obeys God[i] and to hear his voice. ¹⁵You must tell everyone what you have seen and heard. ¹⁶What are you waiting for? Get up! Be baptized, and wash away your sins by praying to the Lord."

¹⁷After this I returned to Jerusalem and went to the temple to pray. There I had a vision ¹⁸of the Lord who said to me, "Hurry and leave Jerusalem! The people won't listen to what you say about me."

¹⁹I replied, "Lord, they know that in many of our meeting places I arrested and beat people who had faith in you. ²⁰Stephen was killed because he spoke for you, and I stood there and cheered them on. I even guarded the clothes of the men who murdered him."

²¹But the Lord told me to go, and he promised to send me far away to the Gentiles.

²²The crowd listened until Paul said this. Then they started shouting, "Get rid of this man! He doesn't deserve to live." ²³They kept shouting. They waved their clothes around and threw dust into the air.

Paul and the Roman Army Commander

²⁴The Roman commander ordered Paul to be taken into the fortress and beaten with a whip. He did this to find out why the people were screaming at Paul.

²⁵While the soldiers were tying Paul up to be beaten, he asked the officer standing there, "Is it legal to beat a Roman citizen before he has been tried in court?"

²⁶When the officer heard this, he went to the commander and said, "What are you doing? This man is a Roman citizen!"

²⁷The commander went to Paul and asked, "Tell me, are you a Roman citizen?"

"Yes," Paul answered.

²⁸The commander then said, "I paid a lot of money to become a Roman citizen."[j]

But Paul replied, "I was born a Roman citizen."

²⁹The men who were about to beat and question Paul quickly backed off. And the commander himself was frightened when he realized that he had put a Roman citizen in chains.

Paul Is Tried by the Council

³⁰The next day the commander wanted to know the real reason why the Jewish leaders had brought charges against Paul. So he had Paul's chains removed, and he ordered the chief priests and the whole council to meet. Then he had Paul led in and made him stand in front of them.

23 Paul looked straight at the council members and said, "My friends, to this day I have served God with a clear conscience!"

²Then Ananias the high priest ordered the men standing beside Paul to hit him on the mouth. ³Paul turned to the high priest and said, "You whitewashed wall![k] God will hit you. You sit there to judge me by the Law of Moses. But at the same time you order men to break the Law by hitting me."

⁴The men standing beside Paul asked, "Don't you know you are insulting God's high priest?"

⁵Paul replied, "Oh! I didn't know he was the high priest. The Scriptures do tell us not to speak evil about a leader of our people."

⁶When Paul saw that some of the council members were Sadducees and others were Pharisees, he shouted, "My friends, I am a Pharisee and the son of a Pharisee. I am on trial simply because I believe that the dead will be raised to life."

⁷As soon as Paul said this, the Pharisees and the Sadducees got into a big argument, and the council members started taking sides. ⁸The Sadducees do not believe in angels or spirits or that the dead will rise to life. But the Pharisees believe in all of these, ⁹and so there was a lot of shouting. Some of the teachers of the Law of Moses were Pharisees. Finally, they became angry and said,

---

ⁱ22.14 *One Who Obeys God:* See the note at 7.52.
ʲ22.28 *Roman citizen:* See the note at 16.37.
ᵏ23.3 *whitewashed wall:* Someone who pretends to be good, but really isn't.

"We don't find anything wrong with this man. Maybe a spirit or an angel really did speak to him."

[10]The argument became fierce, and the commander was afraid that Paul would be pulled apart. So he ordered the soldiers to go in and rescue Paul. Then they took him back into the fortress.

[11]That night the Lord stood beside Paul and said, "Don't worry! Just as you have told others about me in Jerusalem, you must also tell about me in Rome."

A Plot To Kill Paul

[12-13]The next morning more than forty Jewish men got together and vowed that they would not eat or drink anything until they had killed Paul. [14]Then some of them went to the chief priests and the nation's leaders and said, "We have promised God that we would not eat a thing until we have killed Paul. [15]You and everyone in the council must go to the commander and pretend that you want to find out more about the charges against Paul. Ask for him to be brought before your court. Meanwhile, we will be waiting to kill him before he gets there."

[16]When Paul's nephew heard about the plot, he went to the fortress and told Paul about it. [17]So Paul said to one of the army officers, "Take this young man to the commander. He has something to tell him."

[18]The officer took him to the commander and said, "The prisoner named Paul asked me to bring this young man to you, because he has something to tell you."

[19]The commander took the young man aside and asked him in private, "What do you want to tell me?"

[20]He answered, "Some men are planning to ask you to bring Paul down to the Jewish council tomorrow. They will claim that they want to find out more about him. [21]But please don't do what they say. More than forty men are going to attack Paul. They have made a vow not to eat or drink anything until they have killed him. Even now they are waiting to hear what you decide."

[22]The commander sent the young man away after saying to him, "Don't let anyone know that you told me this."

Paul Is Sent to Felix the Governor

[23]The commander called in two of his officers and told them, "By nine o'clock to-night have two hundred soldiers ready to go to Caesarea. Take along seventy men on horseback and two hundred foot soldiers with spears. [24]Get a horse ready for Paul and make sure that he gets safely through to Felix the governor."

[25]The commander wrote a letter that said:

[26]Greetings from Claudius Lysias to the Honorable Governor Felix:

[27]Some Jews grabbed this man and were about to kill him. But when I found out that he was a Roman citizen, I took some soldiers and rescued him.

[28]I wanted to find out what they had against him. So I brought him before their council [29]and learned that the charges concern only their religious laws. This man isn't guilty of anything for which he should die or even be put in jail.

[30]As soon as I learned that there was a plot against him, I sent him to you and told their leaders to bring charges against him in your court.

[31]The soldiers obeyed the commander's orders, and that same night they took Paul to the city of Antipatris. [32]The next day the foot soldiers returned to the fortress and let the soldiers on horseback take him the rest of the way. [33]When they came to Caesarea, they gave the letter to the governor and handed Paul over to him.

[34]The governor read the letter. Then he asked Paul and found out that he was from Cilicia. [35]The governor said, "I will listen to your case as soon as the people come to bring their charges against you." After saying this, he gave orders for Paul to be kept as a prisoner in Herod's palace.[l]

Paul Is Accused in the Court of Felix

24 Five days later Ananias the high priest, together with some of their leaders and a lawyer named Tertullus, went to the governor to present their case against Paul. [2]So Paul was called in, and Tertullus stated the case against him:[m]

---

[l]23.35 *Herod's palace:* The palace built by Herod the Great and used by the Roman governors of Palestine.
[m]24.2 *Paul was called in, and Tertullus stated the case against him:* Or "Tertullus was called in and stated the case against Paul."

Honorable Felix, you have brought our people a long period of peace, and because of your concern our nation is much better off. [3]All of us are always grateful for what you have done. [4]I don't want to bother you, but please be patient with us and listen to me for just a few minutes.

[5]This man has been found to be a real pest and troublemaker for Jews all over the world. He is also a leader of a group called Nazarenes. [6-8]When he tried to disgrace the temple, we arrested him.[n] If you question him, you will find out for yourself that our charges are true.

[9]The Jewish crowd spoke up and agreed with what Tertullus had said.

Paul Defends Himself

[10]The governor motioned for Paul to speak, and he began:

I know that you have judged the people of our nation for many years, and I am glad to defend myself in your court.

[11]It was no more than twelve days ago that I went to worship in Jerusalem. You can find this out easily enough. [12]Never once did the Jews find me arguing with anyone in the temple. I didn't cause trouble in the Jewish meeting places or in the city itself. [13]There is no way that they can prove these charges that they are now bringing against me.

[14]I admit that their leaders think that the Lord's Way[o] which I follow is based on wrong beliefs. But I still worship the same God that my ancestors worshiped. And I believe everything written in the Law of Moses and in the Prophets.[p] [15]I am just as sure as these people are that God will raise from death everyone who is good or evil. [16]And because I am sure, I try my best to have a clear conscience in whatever I do for God or for people.

[17]After being away for several years, I returned here to bring gifts for the poor people of my nation and to offer sacrifices. [18]This is what I was doing when I was found going through a ceremony in the temple. I wasn't with a crowd, and there was no uproar.

[19]Some Jews from Asia were there at that time, and if they have anything to say against me, they should be here now. [20]Or ask the ones who are here. They can tell you that they didn't find me guilty of anything when I was tried by their own council. [21]The only charge they can bring against me is what I shouted out in court, when I said, "I am on trial today because I believe that the dead will be raised to life!"

[22]Felix knew a lot about the Lord's Way.[q] But he brought the trial to an end and said, "I will make my decision after Lysias the commander arrives." [23]He then ordered the army officer to keep Paul under guard, but not to lock him up or to stop his friends from helping him.

Paul Is Kept under Guard

[24]Several days later Felix and his wife Drusilla, who was Jewish, went to the place where Paul was kept under guard. They sent for Paul and listened while he spoke to them about having faith in Christ Jesus. [25]But Felix was frightened when Paul started talking to them about doing right, about self-control, and about the coming judgment. So he said to Paul, "That's enough for now. You may go. But when I have time I will send for you." [26]After this, Felix often sent for Paul and talked with him, because he hoped that Paul would offer him a bribe.

[27]Two years later Porcius Festus became governor in place of Felix. But since Felix wanted to do the Jewish leaders a favor, he kept Paul in jail.

Paul Asks To Be Tried
by the Roman Emperor

25 Three days after Festus had become governor, he went from Caesarea to Jerusalem. [2]There the chief priests and some Jewish leaders told him about their charges against Paul. They also asked Festus [3]if he would be willing to bring Paul to Jerusalem. They begged

---

[n]24.6-8 *we arrested him*: Some manuscripts add, "We wanted to judge him by our own laws. But Lysias the commander took him away from us by force. Then Lysias ordered us to bring our charges against this man in your court." [o]24.14 *the Lord's Way*: See the note at 9.2. [p]24.14 *Law of Moses . . . the Prophets*: The Jewish Scriptures, that is, the Old Testament. [q]24.22 *the Lord's Way*: See the note at 9.2.

him to do this because they were planning to attack and kill Paul on the way. ⁴But Festus told them, "Paul will be kept in Caesarea, and I am soon going there myself. ⁵If he has done anything wrong, let your leaders go with me and bring charges against him there."

⁶Festus stayed in Jerusalem for eight or ten more days before going to Caesarea. Then the next day he took his place as judge and had Paul brought into court. ⁷As soon as Paul came in, the Jewish leaders from Jerusalem crowded around him and said he was guilty of many serious crimes. But they could not prove anything. ⁸Then Paul spoke in his own defense, "I have not broken the Law of my people. And I have not done anything against either the temple or the Emperor."

⁹Festus wanted to please the leaders. So he asked Paul, "Are you willing to go to Jerusalem and be tried by me on these charges?"

¹⁰Paul replied, "I am on trial in the Emperor's court, and that's where I should be tried. You know very well that I have not done anything to harm the Jewish nation. ¹¹If I had done something deserving death, I would not ask to escape the death penalty. But I am not guilty of any of these crimes, and no one has the right to hand me over to these people. I now ask to be tried by the Emperor himself."

¹²After Festus had talked this over with members of his council, he told Paul, "You have asked to be tried by the Emperor, and to the Emperor you will go!"

Paul Speaks to Agrippa and Bernice

¹³A few days later King Agrippa and Bernice came to Caesarea to visit Festus. ¹⁴They had been there for several days, when Festus told the king about the charges against Paul. He said:

Felix left a man here in jail, ¹⁵and when I went to Jerusalem, the chief priests and the Jewish leaders came and asked me to find him guilty. ¹⁶I told them that it isn't the Roman custom to hand a man over to people who are bringing charges against him. He must first have the chance to meet them face to face and to defend himself against their charges.

¹⁷So when they came here with me, I wasted no time. On the very next day

I took my place on the judge's bench and ordered him to be brought in. ¹⁸But when the men stood up to make their charges against him, they did not accuse him of any of the crimes that I thought they would. ¹⁹Instead, they argued with him about some of their beliefs and about a dead man named Jesus, who Paul said was alive.

²⁰Since I did not know how to find out the truth about all this, I asked Paul if he would be willing to go to Jerusalem and be put on trial there. ²¹But Paul asked to be kept in jail until the Emperor could decide his case. So I ordered him to be kept here until I could send him to the Emperor.

²²Then Agrippa said to Festus, "I would also like to hear what this man has to say." Festus answered, "You can hear him tomorrow."

²³The next day Agrippa and Bernice made a big show as they came into the meeting room. High ranking army officers and leading citizens of the town were also there. Festus then ordered Paul to be brought in ²⁴and said:

King Agrippa and other guests, look at this man! Every Jew from Jerusalem and Caesarea has come to me, demanding for him to be put to death. ²⁵I have not found him guilty of any crime deserving death. But because he has asked to be judged by the Emperor, I have decided to send him to Rome.

²⁶I have to write some facts about this man to the Emperor. So I have brought him before all of you, but especially before you, King Agrippa. After we have talked about his case, I will then have something to write. ²⁷It makes no sense to send a prisoner to the Emperor without stating the charges against him.

Paul's Defense before Agrippa

26 Agrippa told Paul, "You may now speak for yourself."

Paul stretched out his hand and said:

²King Agrippa, I am glad for this chance to defend myself before you today on all these charges that my own people have brought against me. ³You

know a lot about our religious customs and the beliefs that divide us. So I ask you to listen patiently to me.

⁴⁻⁵All the Jews have known me since I was a child. They know what kind of life I have lived in my own country and in Jerusalem. And if they were willing, they could tell you that I was a Pharisee, a member of a group that is stricter than any other. ⁶Now I am on trial because I believe the promise God made to our people long ago.

⁷Day and night our twelve tribes have earnestly served God, waiting for his promised blessings. King Agrippa, because of this hope, the Jewish leaders have brought charges against me. ⁸Why should any of you doubt that God raises the dead to life?

⁹I once thought that I should do everything I could to oppose Jesus from Nazareth. ¹⁰I did this first in Jerusalem, and with the authority of the chief priests I put many of God's people in jail. I even voted for them to be killed. ¹¹I often had them punished in our meeting places, and I tried to make them give up their faith. In fact, I was so angry with them, that I went looking for them in foreign cities.

¹²King Agrippa, one day I was on my way to Damascus with the authority and permission of the chief priests. ¹³About noon I saw a light brighter than the sun. It flashed from heaven on me and on everyone traveling with me. ¹⁴We all fell to the ground. Then I heard a voice say to me in Aramaic, "Saul, Saul, why are you so cruel to me? It's foolish to fight against me!"

¹⁵"Who are you?" I asked.

Then the Lord answered, "I am Jesus! I am the one you are so cruel to. ¹⁶Now stand up. I have appeared to you, because I have chosen you to be my servant. You are to tell others what you have learned about me and what I will show you later."

¹⁷The Lord also said, "I will protect you from the Jews and from the Gentiles that I am sending you to. ¹⁸I want you to open their eyes, so that they will turn from darkness to light and from the power of Satan to God. Then their sins will be forgiven, and by faith in me they will become part of God's holy people."

¹⁹King Agrippa, I obeyed this vision from heaven. ²⁰First I preached to the people in Damascus, and then I went to Jerusalem and all over Judea. Finally, I went to the Gentiles and said, "Stop sinning and turn to God! Then prove what you have done by the way you live."

²¹That is why some men grabbed me in the temple and tried to kill me. ²²But all this time God has helped me, and I have preached both to the rich and to the poor. I have told them only what the prophets and Moses said would happen. ²³I told them how the Messiah would suffer and be the first to be raised from death, so that he could bring light to his own people and to the Gentiles.

²⁴Before Paul finished defending himself, Festus shouted, "Paul, you're crazy! Too much learning has driven you out of your mind."

²⁵But Paul replied, "Honorable Festus, I am not crazy. What I am saying is true, and it makes sense. ²⁶None of these things happened off in a corner somewhere. I am sure that King Agrippa knows what I am talking about. That's why I can speak so plainly to him."

²⁷Then Paul said to Agrippa, "Do you believe what the prophets said? I know you do."

²⁸Agrippa asked Paul, "In such a short time do you think you can talk me into being a Christian?"

²⁹Paul answered, "Whether it takes a short time or a long time, I wish you and everyone else who hears me today would become just like me! Except, of course, for these chains."

³⁰Then King Agrippa, Governor Festus, Bernice, and everyone who was with them got up. ³¹But before they left, they said, "This man isn't guilty of anything. He doesn't deserve to die or to be put in jail."

³²Agrippa told Festus, "Paul could have been set free, if he had not asked to be tried by the Roman Emperor."

Romans
Faith Connects to Real Life

"I am sure that nothing can separate us from God's love—not life or death, not angels or spirits, not the present or the future, and not powers above or powers below. Nothing in all creation can separate us from God's love for us in Christ Jesus our Lord!" (8.38,39). These strong words come from Paul's letter to the Christians in Rome. Security in Jesus is a certainty every Christian can count on. Because of this security, we can live for God without fear of his abandoning us. God's certain love gives us the confidence to do right, no matter how hard it is. God's steady care helps us know that no matter what we face, we're never alone—and better days are coming. How can we please this God we adore so deeply? The book of Romans shows us.

Romans is a faith manual. Its early chapters define much better than any other book of the Bible what the Christian faith really is. In a no-nonsense manner, Romans assures you of your security in Christ. Then in later chapters, it demonstrates how to respond with equally loyal love. To begin your walk as a Christian, simply accept Jesus Christ by faith. Then express your security in him by allowing Jesus to work in you. No matter what your background, you need God. He has shown his love for you by coming in Jesus Christ. He died to conquer sin and death for you. In response, let him conquer the selfishness so common in today's world.

Romans shows the adventure of the Christian life. There's the adventure of understanding God and his nature (1–6). There's the continual battle to overcome self-centeredness (7.1—8.2). There's the delightful journey of accepting that God really loves us, warts and all (8–11). There's the discovery of new life that comes with each decision to honor God (12). There's the balance of doing right without rules, while needing rules to show us how to do right (13–16). The Christian walk is a lifetime of discovery and ever-deepening devotion.

Embark on the adventure of faith. Let God be your tour guide and companion as you discover ways to walk in the light of Jesus Christ.

Romans at a Glance

1. Those who respond to God in faith will live (1.1-17)
2. Everybody does wrong (1.18—3.31)
3. Faith is a choice (4)
4. Each event can go deeper (5.1-11)
5. Adam brought death; Jesus brings life (5.12—6.14)
6. We battle sin with God's power (6.15—8.17)
7. Present suffering will end and we will make it through (8.18-39)
8. Coming into God's family (9–11)

¹⁷Three days after we got there, Paul called together some of the Jewish leaders and said:

My friends, I have never done anything to hurt our people, and I have never gone against the customs of our ancestors. But in Jerusalem I was handed over as a prisoner to the Romans. ¹⁸They looked into the charges against me and wanted to release me. They found that I had not done anything deserving death. ¹⁹The Jewish leaders disagreed, so I asked to be tried by the Emperor.

But I don't have anything to say against my own nation. ²⁰I am bound by these chains because of what we people of Israel hope for. That's why I have called you here to talk about this hope of ours.

²¹The leaders replied, "No one from Judea has written us a letter about you. And not one of them has come here to report on you or to say anything against you. ²²But we would like to hear what you have to say. We understand that people everywhere are against this new group."

²³They agreed on a time to meet with Paul, and many of them came to his house. From early morning until late in the afternoon, Paul talked to them about God's kingdom. He used the Law of Moses and the Books of the Prophetsᵘ to try to win them over to Jesus.

²⁴Some of the leaders agreed with what Paul said, but others did not. ²⁵Since they could not agree among themselves, they started leaving. But Paul said, "The Holy Spirit said the right thing when he sent Isaiah the prophet ²⁶to tell our ancestors,

'Go to these people
    and tell them:
You will listen and listen,
    but never understand.
You will look and look,
    but never see.

²⁷All of you
    have stubborn hearts.
Your ears are stopped up,
    and your eyes are covered.
You cannot see or hear
    or understand.
If you could,
you would turn to me,
    and I would heal you.' "

> *sharing the gospel isn't so much what you know as* **whom** *you know. If you know the Savior and are surrounded by friends and family who haven't met him yet, then who better to handle the introductions than you?*
>
> LIZ CURTIS HIGGS

²⁸⁻²⁹Paul said, "You may be sure that God wants to save the Gentiles! And they will listen."ᵛ

³⁰For two years Paul stayed in a rented house and welcomed everyone who came to see him. ³¹He bravely preached about God's kingdom and taught about the Lord Jesus Christ, and no one tried to stop him.

ᵘ**28.23** *Law of Moses and the Books of the Prophets:* The Jewish Bible, that is, the Old Testament.
ᵛ**28.28,29** *And they will listen:* Some manuscripts add, "After Paul said this, the people left, but they got into a fierce argument among themselves."

[30]The sailors wanted to escape from the ship. So they lowered the lifeboat into the water, pretending that they were letting down an anchor from the front of the ship. [31]But Paul said to Captain Julius and the soldiers, "If the sailors don't stay on the ship, you won't have any chance to save your lives." [32]The soldiers then cut the ropes that held the lifeboat and let it fall into the sea.

[33]Just before daylight Paul begged the people to eat something. He told them, "For fourteen days you have been so worried that you haven't eaten a thing. [34]I beg you to eat something. Your lives depend on it. Do this and not one of you will be hurt."

[35]After Paul had said this, he took a piece of bread and gave thanks to God. Then in front of everyone, he broke the bread and ate some. [36]They all felt encouraged, and each of them ate something. [37]There were 276 people on the ship, [38]and after everyone had eaten, they threw the cargo of wheat into the sea to make the ship lighter.

The Shipwreck

[39]Morning came, and the ship's crew saw a coast that they did not recognize. But they did see a cove with a beach. So they decided to try to run the ship aground on the beach. [40]They cut the anchors loose and let them sink into the sea. At the same time they untied the ropes that were holding the rudders. Next, they raised the sail at the front of the ship and let the wind carry the ship toward the beach. [41]But it ran aground on a sandbank. The front of the ship stuck firmly in the sand, and the rear was being smashed by the force of the waves.

[42]The soldiers decided to kill the prisoners to keep them from swimming away and escaping. [43]But Captain Julius wanted to save Paul's life, and he did not let the soldiers do what they had planned. Instead, he ordered everyone who could swim to dive into the water and head for shore. [44]Then he told the others to hold on to planks of wood or parts of the ship. At last, everyone safely reached shore.

On the Island of Malta

28 When we came ashore, we learned that the island was called Malta. [2]The local people were very friendly, and they welcomed us by building a fire, because it was rainy and cold.

[3]After Paul had gathered some wood and had put it on the fire, the heat caused a snake to crawl out, and it bit him on the hand. [4]When the local people saw the snake hanging from Paul's hand, they said to each other, "This man must be a murderer! He didn't drown in the sea, but the goddess of justice will kill him anyway."

[5]Paul shook the snake off into the fire and wasn't harmed. [6]The people kept thinking that Paul would either swell up or suddenly drop dead. They watched him for a long time, and when nothing happened to him, they changed their minds and said, "This man is a god."

[7]The governor of the island was named Publius, and he owned some of the land around there. Publius was very friendly and welcomed us into his home for three days. [8]His father was in bed, sick with fever and stomach trouble, and Paul went to visit him. Paul healed the man by praying and placing his hands on him.

[9]After this happened, everyone on the island brought their sick people to Paul, and they were all healed. [10]The people were very respectful to us, and when we sailed, they gave us everything we needed.

From Malta to Rome

[11]Three months later we sailed in a ship that had been docked at Malta for the winter. The ship was from Alexandria in Egypt and was known as "The Twin Gods."[t] [12]We arrived in Syracuse and stayed for three days. [13]From there we sailed to Rhegium. The next day a south wind began to blow, and two days later we arrived in Puteoli. [14]There we found some of the Lord's followers, who begged us to stay with them. A week later we left for the city of Rome.

[15]Some of the followers in Rome heard about us and came to meet us at the Market of Appius and at the Three Inns. When Paul saw them, he thanked God and was encouraged.

Paul in Rome

[16]We arrived in Rome, and Paul was allowed to live in a house by himself with a soldier to guard him.

---

[t]**28.11** *known as "The Twin Gods":* Or "carried on its bow a wooden carving of the Twin Gods." These gods were Castor and Pollux, two of the favorite gods among sailors.

Paul Is Taken to Rome

27 When it was time for us to sail to Rome, Captain Julius from the Emperor's special troops was put in charge of Paul and the other prisoners. [2]We went aboard a ship from Adramyttium that was about to sail to some ports along the coast of Asia. Aristarchus from Thessalonica in Macedonia sailed on the ship with us.

[3]The next day we came to shore at Sidon. Captain Julius was very kind to Paul. He even let him visit his friends, so they could give him whatever he needed. [4]When we left Sidon, the winds were blowing against us, and we sailed close to the island of Cyprus to be safe from the wind. [5]Then we sailed south of Cilicia and Pamphylia until we came to the port of Myra in Lycia. [6]There the army captain found a ship from Alexandria that was going to Italy. So he ordered us to board that ship.

[7]We sailed along slowly for several days and had a hard time reaching Cnidus. The wind would not let us go any farther in that direction, so we sailed past Cape Salmone, where the island of Crete would protect us from the wind. [8]We went slowly along the coast and finally reached a place called Fair Havens, not far from the town of Lasea.

[9]By now we had already lost a lot of time, and sailing was no longer safe. In fact, even the Great Day of Forgiveness[r] was past. [10]Then Paul spoke to the crew of the ship, "Men, listen to me! If we sail now, our ship and its cargo will be badly damaged, and many lives will be lost." [11]But Julius listened to the captain of the ship and its owner, rather than to Paul.

[12]The harbor at Fair Havens wasn't a good place to spend the winter. Because of this, almost everyone agreed that we should at least try to sail along the coast of Crete as far as Phoenix. It had a harbor that opened toward the southwest and northwest,[s] and we could spend the winter there.

The Storm at Sea

[13]When a gentle wind from the south started blowing, the men thought it was a good time to do what they had planned. So they pulled up the anchor, and we sailed along the coast of Crete. [14]But soon a strong wind called "The Northeaster" blew against

us from the island. [15]The wind struck the ship, and we could not sail against it. So we let the wind carry the ship.

[16]We went along the island of Cauda on the side that was protected from the wind. We had a hard time holding the lifeboat in place, [17]but finally we got it where it belonged. Then the sailors wrapped ropes around the ship to hold it together. They lowered the sail and let the ship drift along, because they were afraid it might hit the sandbanks in the gulf of Syrtis.

[18]The storm was so fierce that the next day they threw some of the ship's cargo overboard. [19]Then on the third day, with their bare hands they threw overboard some of the ship's gear. [20]For several days we could not see either the sun or the stars. A strong wind kept blowing, and we finally gave up all hope of being saved.

[21]Since none of us had eaten anything for a long time, Paul stood up and told the men:

You should have listened to me! If you had stayed on in Crete, you would not have had this damage and loss. [22]But now I beg you to cheer up, because you will be safe. Only the ship will be lost.

[23]I belong to God, and I worship him. Last night he sent an angel [24]to tell me, "Paul, don't be afraid! You will stand trial before the Emperor. And because of you, God will save the lives of everyone on the ship." [25]Cheer up! I am sure that God will do exactly what he promised. [26]But we will first be shipwrecked on some island.

[27]For fourteen days and nights we had been blown around over the Mediterranean Sea. But about midnight the sailors realized that we were getting near land. [28]They measured and found that the water was about one hundred twenty feet deep. A little later they measured again and found it was only about ninety feet. [29]The sailors were afraid that we might hit some rocks, and they let down four anchors from the back of the ship. Then they prayed for daylight.

---

[r]**27.9** *Great Day of Forgiveness:* This Jewish festival took place near the end of September. The sailing season was dangerous after the middle of September, and it was stopped completely between the middle of November and the middle of March. [s]**27.12** *southwest and northwest:* Or "northeast and southeast."

9. Fresh life and happy relationships come as you imitate Jesus (12,13)

10. Christians with differing opinions can get along (14,15)

11. Every person matters (16)

---

1 From Paul, a servant of Christ Jesus. God chose me to be an apostle, and he appointed me to preach the good news [2]that he promised long ago by what his prophets said in the holy Scriptures. [3-4]This good news is about his Son, our Lord Jesus Christ! As a human, he was from the family of David. But the Holy Spirit[a] proved that Jesus is the powerful Son of God,[b] because he was raised from death.

[5]Jesus was kind to me and chose me to be an apostle,[c] so that people of all nations would obey and have faith. [6]You are some of those people chosen by Jesus Christ.

[7]This letter is to all of you in Rome. God loves you and has chosen you to be his very own people.

I pray that God our Father and our Lord Jesus Christ will be kind to you and will bless you with peace!

A Prayer of Thanks

[8]First, I thank God in the name of Jesus Christ for all of you. I do this because people everywhere in the world are talking about your faith. [9]God has seen how I never stop praying for you, while I serve him with all my heart and tell the good news about his Son.

[10]In all my prayers, I ask God to make it possible for me to visit you. [11]I want to see you and share with you the same blessings that God's Spirit has given me. Then you will grow stronger in your faith. [12]What I am saying is that we can encourage each other by the faith that is ours.

[13]My friends, I want you to know that I have often planned to come for a visit. But something has always kept me from doing it. I want to win followers to Christ in Rome, as I have done in many other places. [14-15]It doesn't matter if people are civilized and educated, or if they are uncivilized and uneducated. I must tell the good news to everyone. That's why I am eager to visit all of you in Rome.

The Power of the Good News

[16]I am proud of the good news! It is God's powerful way of saving all people who have faith, whether they are Jews or Gentiles. [17]The good news tells how God accepts everyone who has faith, but only those who have faith.[d] It is just as the Scriptures say, "The people God accepts because of their faith will live."[e]

> *While I was in Nigeria, I was challenged by the African believers' walk with God. They own so very little, so possessions don't get in the way of their relationship with God. They've learned to trust him literally for their daily bread.*
>
> BABBIE MASON

Everyone Is Guilty

[18]From heaven God shows how angry he is with all the wicked and evil things that sinful people do to crush the truth. [19]They know everything that can be known about God, because God has shown it all to them. [20]God's eternal power and character cannot be seen. But from the beginning of creation, God has shown what these are like by all he has made. That's why those people don't have any excuse. [21]They know about God, but they don't honor him or even thank him. Their thoughts are useless, and their stupid minds are in the dark. [22]They claim to be wise, but they are fools. [23]They don't

---

[a]**1.3,4** *the Holy Spirit*: Or "his own spirit of holiness."
[b]**1.3,4** *proved that Jesus is the powerful Son of God*: Or "proved in a powerful way that Jesus is the Son of God." [c]**1.5** *Jesus was kind to me and chose me to be an apostle*: Or "Jesus was kind to us and chose us to be his apostles." [d]**1.17** *but only those who have faith*: Or "and faith is all that matters." [e]**1.17** *The people God accepts because of their faith will live*: Or "The people God accepts will live because of their faith."

worship the glorious and eternal God. Instead, they worship idols that are made to look like humans who cannot live forever, and like birds, animals, and reptiles.

²⁴So God let these people go their own way. They did what they wanted to do, and their filthy thoughts made them do shameful things with their bodies. ²⁵They gave up the truth about God for a lie, and they worshiped God's creation instead of God, who will be praised forever. Amen.

²⁶God let them follow their own evil desires. Women no longer wanted to have sex in a natural way, and they did things with each other that were not natural. ²⁷Men behaved in the same way. They stopped wanting to have sex with women and had strong desires for sex with other men. They did shameful things with each other, and what has happened to them is punishment for their foolish deeds.

²⁸Since these people refused even to think about God, he let their useless minds rule over them. That's why they do all sorts of indecent things. ²⁹They are evil, wicked, and greedy, as well as mean in every possible way. They want what others have, and they murder, argue, cheat, and are hard to get along with. They gossip, ³⁰say cruel things about others, and hate God. They are proud, conceited, and boastful, always thinking up new ways to do evil.

These people don't respect their parents. ³¹They are stupid, unreliable, and don't have any love or pity for others. ³²They know God has said that anyone who acts this way deserves to die. But they keep on doing evil things, and they even encourage others to do them.

God's Judgment Is Fair

2 Some of you accuse others of doing wrong. But there is no excuse for what you do. When you judge others, you condemn yourselves, because you are guilty of doing the very same things. ²We know that God is right to judge everyone who behaves in this way. ³Do you really think God won't punish you, when you behave exactly like the people you accuse? ⁴You surely don't think much of God's wonderful goodness or of his patience and willingness to put up with you. Don't you know that the reason God is good to you is because he wants you to turn to him?

⁵But you are stubborn and refuse to turn to God. So you are making things even worse for yourselves on that day when he will show how angry he is and will judge the world with fairness. ⁶God will reward each of us for what we have done. ⁷He will give eternal life to everyone who has patiently done what is good in the hope of receiving glory, honor, and life that lasts forever. ⁸But he will show how angry and furious he can be with every selfish person who rejects the truth and wants to do evil. ⁹All who are wicked will be punished with trouble and suffering. It doesn't matter if they are Jews or Gentiles. ¹⁰But all who do right will be rewarded with glory, honor, and peace, whether they are Jews or Gentiles. ¹¹God doesn't have any favorites!

¹²Those people who don't know about God's Law will still be punished for what they do wrong. And the Law will be used to judge everyone who knows what it says. ¹³God accepts those who obey his Law, but not those who simply hear it.

¹⁴Some people naturally obey the Law's commands, even though they don't have the Law. ¹⁵This proves that the conscience is like a law written in the human heart. And it will show whether we are forgiven or condemned, ¹⁶when God appoints Jesus Christ to judge everyone's secret thoughts, just as my message says.

The Jews and the Law

¹⁷Some of you call yourselves Jews. You trust in the Law and take pride in God. ¹⁸By reading the Scriptures you learn how God wants you to behave, and you discover what is right. ¹⁹You are sure that you are a guide for the blind and a light for all who are in the dark. ²⁰And since there is knowledge and truth in God's Law, you think you can instruct fools and teach young people.

²¹But how can you teach others when you refuse to learn? You preach that it is wrong to steal. But do you steal? ²²You say people should be faithful in marriage. But are you faithful? You hate idols, yet you rob their temples. ²³You take pride in the Law, but you disobey the Law and bring shame to God. ²⁴It is just as the Scriptures tell us, "You have made foreigners say insulting things about God."

²⁵Being circumcised is worthwhile, if you obey the Law. But if you don't obey the Law,

you are no better off than people who are not circumcised. ²⁶In fact, if they obey the Law, they are as good as anyone who is circumcised. ²⁷So everyone who obeys the Law, but has never been circumcised, will condemn you. Even though you are circumcised and have the Law, you still don't obey its teachings.

²⁸Just because you live like a Jew and are circumcised doesn't make you a real Jew. ²⁹To be a real Jew you must obey the Law. True circumcision is something that happens deep in your heart, not something done to your body. And besides, you should want praise from God and not from humans.

3 What good is it to be a Jew? What good is it to be circumcised? ²It is good in a lot of ways! First of all, God's messages were spoken to the Jews. ³It is true that some of them did not believe the message. But does this mean that God cannot be trusted, just because they did not have faith? ⁴No, indeed! God tells the truth, even if everyone else is a liar. The Scriptures say about God,

"Your words
    will be proven true,
and in court
    you will win your case."

⁵If our evil deeds show how right God is, then what can we say? Is it wrong for God to become angry and punish us? What a foolish thing to ask. ⁶But the answer is, "No." Otherwise, how could God judge the world? ⁷Since your lies bring great honor to God by showing how truthful he is, you may ask why God still says you are a sinner. ⁸You might as well say, "Let's do something evil, so that something good will come of it!" Some people even claim that we are saying this. But God is fair and will judge them as well.

No One Is Good

⁹What does all this mean? Does it mean that we Jews are better offᶠ than the Gentiles? No, it doesn't! Jews, as well as Gentiles, are ruled by sin, just as I have said. ¹⁰The Scriptures tell us,

"No one is acceptable to God!
¹¹ Not one of them understands
    or even searches for God.
¹² They have all turned away
    and are worthless.
There isn't one person
    who does right.
¹³ Their words are like
    an open pit,

ᶠ**3.9** *better off*: Or "worse off."

Personal *Concerns*—Should I maintain friendships with non-Christians? If so, how can I keep from compromising my faith? *(Romans 3.9-20)*

Keep a balance of Christian and non-Christian friends.

In the eternal scheme of things, before you aligned yourself to Jesus Christ, you and your non-Christian friend were the same. It's only through God's grace that you received forgiveness and salvation, so beware of communicating an aura of superiority when dealing with your friend. Instead, show her the impact following Christ has on your life.

Your friend will see faith in action when you discreetly refuse to gossip. She'll see the value of God when you tenderly care for each person and genuinely work hard at your endeavors. By sharing your life with a non-believer, you give a picture of Christianity she'll want to imitate.

Even when you know this, you may be tempted to water down your Christian beliefs when around non-Christians. If you give in, your friend will notice. Compromised faith is deeply destructive. So continue also to maintain friendships with Christians who encourage you to do right in honorable and humble ways. And let your closest relationships—dating and marriage—be with believers who will hold you accountable. **(See also Obadiah 10-14; Matthew 22.34-40.)**

Words To Remember: *Not one of them understands or even searches for God. They have all turned away and are worthless. There isn't one person who does right.* —Romans 3.11,12

and their tongues are good
    only for telling lies.
Each word is as deadly
    as the fangs of a snake,
¹⁴and they say nothing
    but bitter curses.
¹⁵These people quickly
    become violent.
¹⁶Wherever they go,
    they leave ruin
    and destruction.
¹⁷They don't know how
    to live in peace.
¹⁸   They don't even fear God."

¹⁹We know that everything in the Law was written for those who are under its power. The Law says these things to stop anyone from making excuses and to let God show that the whole world is guilty. ²⁰God doesn't accept people simply because they obey the Law. No, indeed! All the Law does is to point out our sin.

God's Way of Accepting People

²¹Now we see how God does make us acceptable to him. The Law and the Prophets[g] tell how we become acceptable, and it isn't by obeying the Law of Moses. ²²God treats everyone alike. He accepts people only because they have faith in Jesus Christ. ²³All of us have sinned and fallen short of God's glory. ²⁴But God treats us much better than we deserve,[h] and because of Christ Jesus, he freely accepts us and sets us free from our sins. ²⁵⁻²⁶God sent Christ to be our sacrifice. Christ offered his life's blood, so that by faith in him we could come to God. And God did this to show that in the past he was right to be patient and forgive sinners. This also shows that God is right when he accepts people who have faith in Jesus.

²⁷What is left for us to brag about? Not a thing! Is it because we obeyed some law? No! It is because of faith. ²⁸We see that people are acceptable to God because they have faith, and not because they obey the Law. ²⁹Does God belong only to the Jews? Isn't he also the God of the Gentiles? Yes, he is! ³⁰There is only one God, and he accepts Gentiles as well as Jews, simply because of their faith. ³¹Do we destroy the Law by our faith? Not at all! We make it even more powerful.

g3.21 The Law and the Prophets: The Jewish Scriptures, that is, the Old Testament. *h3.24 treats us much better than we deserve*: The Greek word *charis*, traditionally rendered "grace," is translated here and other places in the CEV to express the overwhelming kindness of God.

Friendship—How can I reach out to people who differ from me in habits, faith, culture, or race? *(Romans 3.21-31)*

See the need for salvation as the great unifier.

Most people feel most comfortable with people who are most like them. It's not easy to bridge differences in habits, faith, culture, or race. But God's love shows powerfully when friendships form between dissimilar persons. And each difference can enhance our understanding of what it means to serve God and love people.

Certainly differences can rub us the wrong way. As an early-to-bed-and-early-to-rise person, you may see a late sleeper as lazy. Yet that person may accomplish more after your bedtime than you do in your whole day. Talk long enough to find out. Invite her to tell you how she spends her day. Rejoice inwardly when you find that though you sleep in different time zones, you both make and complete lists. Build on those commonalities with phrases like, "As someone who likes to make the most of her day, isn't it neat Jesus wants to make the most of our lives? How have you seen this happen?"

Perhaps most valuable in bridging relationships is a refusal to categorize anyone. Recognize each person as God's one-of-a-kind creation who's worth knowing. Rather than define a person by race or denomination, recognize a kindred spirit with skin on. Call each person by name rather than category. Asking his or her name is a good start. (See also John 4.4-26; 2 Corinthians 5.16-21; Galatians 3.26-29; Colossians 4.2-6.)

Words To Remember: *God treats everyone alike.*—Romans 3.22

The Example of Abraham

4 Well then, what can we say about our ancestor Abraham? [2]If he became acceptable to God because of what he did, then he would have something to brag about. But he would never be able to brag about it to God. [3]The Scriptures say, "God accepted Abraham because Abraham had faith in him."

[4]Money paid to workers isn't a gift. It is something they earn by working. [5]But you cannot make God accept you because of something you do. God accepts sinners only because they have faith in him. [6]In the Scriptures David talks about the blessings that come to people who are acceptable to God, even though they don't do anything to deserve these blessings. David says,

[7] "God blesses people
   whose sins are forgiven
and whose evil deeds
   are forgotten.
[8] The Lord blesses people
   whose sins are erased
   from his book."

[9]Are these blessings meant for circumcised people or for those who are not circumcised? Well, the Scriptures say that God accepted Abraham because Abraham had faith in him. [10]But when did this happen? Was it before or after Abraham was circumcised? Of course, it was before. [11]Abraham let himself be circumcised to show that he had been accepted because of his faith even before he was circumcised. This makes Abraham the father of all who are acceptable to God because of their faith, even though they are not circumcised. [12]This also makes Abraham the father of everyone who is circumcised and has faith in God, as Abraham did before he was circumcised.

The Promise Is for All Who Have Faith

[13]God promised Abraham and his descendants that he would give them the world. This promise wasn't made because Abraham had obeyed a law, but because his faith in God made him acceptable. [14]If Abraham and his descendants were given this promise because they had obeyed a law, then faith would mean nothing, and the promise would be worthless.

[15]God becomes angry when his Law is broken. But where there isn't a law, it cannot be broken. [16]Everything depends on having faith in God, so that God's promise is assured by his great kindness. This promise isn't only for Abraham's descendants who have the Law. It is for all who are Abraham's descendants because they have faith, just as he did. Abraham is the ancestor of us all. [17]The Scriptures say that Abraham would become the ancestor of many nations. This promise was made to Abraham because he had faith in God, who raises the dead to life and creates new things.

[18]God promised Abraham a lot of descendants. And when it all seemed hopeless, Abraham still had faith in God and

---

♦♦♦

*Spiritual*Life—How can I handle my doubts about God? *(Romans 4.13-25)*

Let your doubts lead to deeper discovery.
Every great believer has struggled in some way with doubt. Even Abraham (whose faith in God's promise is celebrated in this passage) at one point wondered how long it would take God to deliver the heir he had promised (Genesis 17.17,18).

What did this spiritual giant do? After trying to do things his way for a while, he took his doubts to God—and God gave Abraham evidence and encouragement he needed to move forward. His questions led to the discovery of truth and a firmer foundation of faith. Abraham kept believing God's promise, then rejoiced in the birth of Isaac.

So quit squelching doubt. Doubts are troublesome when they become hidden reasons to refuse to obey God. But if you bring them out of hiding and place them before God, they can become the building material for actions of faith. (See also Job 1; Psalm 136; Jeremiah 23.16-32; Colossians 2.6-19.)

♦♦**Words To Remember:** *God's promise is assured by his great kindness.*
—**Romans 4.16**

Sarah

Genesis 11.29—23.20; 24.34-38; 24.66—25.11; 49.29-33; Isaiah 51.1,2;
Romans 4.18-25; 9.6-9

*L*aughter. That's how Sarah, formerly called Sarai, responded when God told her she'd become a mother at age ninety. Her husband Abraham was ninety-nine. Sarah's laughter appeared to be based both in delight and amazement. There's nothing wrong with laughter, but Sarah denied that she laughed (Genesis 18.12-15). The direct approach works much better with God.

Sarah had much to learn about the direct approach. She and her husband Abraham had received a promise from God that they'd bear a son. The tricky part was they had to wait many years for that promise to come true. Already past childbearing age, they'd waited years after God's promise—and still no baby. Fearing time was running out, they devised their own plan. It was customary to offer a servant if a wife couldn't conceive, so Sarah proposed this plan, offering her servant Hagar. Legally the child would be Sarah's. But this plan backfired. Hagar boasted about her pregnancy, Sarah rejected the child Ishmael, and he and Hagar were eventually banished from the family (Genesis 16.4-16; 21.9-14; 25.12-18).

Eventually, the promised child arrived to Abraham and Sarah. They named him Isaac, which means "laughter" (Genesis 21.1-8). Sarah and Isaac grew quite close, shown by the intense grief Isaac felt after Sarah's death (Genesis 24.67). Isaac became the father of Jacob and thus the ancestor of the twelve men for whom the twelve tribes of Israel were named. From these twelve tribes came the whole Israelite nation, God's chosen people (Genesis 25.1-11; 49.29-33; Isaiah 51.1,2). (In the New Testament, all Christians, by faith, become his people—Romans 4.15-17.)

But even this happy ending couldn't erase the damage caused by Sarah and Abraham's impatience. The descendants of Hagar's child Ishmael, the Arabs, still fight with the descendants of Sarah's child, the Israelites.

Abraham and Sarah failed to trust God in other instances also. At sixty-five Sarah left her home to travel with her seventy-five-year-old husband to Canaan (Genesis 12.4,5). Their resettling included a time in Egypt. While there, Abraham begged Sarah to claim to be his sister so the Egyptians wouldn't kill him to get her. When the king took her as his wife, his household was struck with horrible diseases. Abraham got in big trouble for this lie. But he didn't learn his lesson. Later he did it again with King Abimelech in Gerar (Genesis 20.1-18).

Even with all these mistakes, the book of Romans describes Abraham and Sarah in glowing terms: "Abraham's faith never became weak" and "Abraham never doubted or questioned God's promise" (Romans 4.19,20). Over their lifetime, Abraham and Sarah apparently learned to trust God. Sarah, Abraham, and Isaac demonstrate that God will keep his promises in his own good timing (Romans 4.18-25; 9.6-9). Instead of inflicting the consequences of our impatience on coming generations, we, too, can learn to wait on and obey God.

became the ancestor of many nations. [19]Abraham's faith never became weak, not even when he was nearly a hundred years old. He knew that he was almost dead and that his wife Sarah could not have children. [20]But Abraham never doubted or questioned God's promise. His faith made him strong, and he gave all the credit to God.

[21]Abraham was certain that God could do what he had promised. [22]So God accepted him, [23]just as we read in the Scriptures. But these words were not written only for Abraham. [24]They were written for us, since we will also be accepted because of our faith in God, who raised our Lord Jesus to life. [25]God gave Jesus to die for our sins, and he raised him to life, so that we would be made acceptable to God.

What It Means To Be Acceptable to God

5 By faith we have been made acceptable to God. And now, because of our Lord Jesus Christ, we live at peace[i] with God. [2]Christ has also introduced us[j] to God's undeserved kindness on which we take our stand. So we are happy, as we look forward to sharing in the glory of God. [3]But that's not all! We gladly suffer,[k] because we know that suffering helps us to endure. [4]And endurance builds character, which gives us a hope [5]that will never disappoint us. All of this happens because God has given us the Holy Spirit, who fills our hearts with his love.

> God knows all about us and he _still_ chooses to embrace us—even when we don't deserve it.
> SUSAN ASHTON

[6]Christ died for us at a time when we were helpless and sinful. [7]No one is really willing to die for an honest person, though someone might be willing to die for a truly good person. [8]But God showed how much he loved us by having Christ die for us, even though we were sinful.

[9]But there is more! Now that God has accepted us because Christ sacrificed his life's blood, we will also be kept safe from God's anger. [10]Even when we were God's enemies, he made peace with us, because his Son died for us. Yet something even greater than friendship is ours. Now that we are at peace with God, we will be saved by his Son's life. [11]And in addition to everything else, we are happy because God sent our Lord Jesus Christ to make peace with us.

Adam and Christ

[12]Adam sinned, and that sin brought death into the world. Now everyone has sinned, and so everyone must die. [13]Sin was in the world before the Law came. But no record of sin was kept, because there was no Law. [14]Yet death still had power over all who lived from the time of Adam to the time of Moses. This happened, though not everyone disobeyed a direct command from God, as Adam did.

In some ways Adam is like Christ who came later. [15]But the gift that God was kind enough to give was very different from Adam's sin. That one sin brought death to many others. Yet in an even greater way, Jesus Christ alone brought God's gift of kindness to many people.

[16]There is a lot of difference between Adam's sin and God's gift. That one sin led to punishment. But God's gift made it possible for us to be acceptable to him, even though we have sinned many times. [17]Death ruled like a king because Adam had sinned. But that cannot compare with what Jesus Christ has done. God has been so kind to us, and he has accepted us because of Jesus. And so we will live and rule like kings.

[18]Everyone was going to be punished because Adam sinned. But because of the good thing that Christ has done, God accepts us and gives us the gift of life. [19]Adam disobeyed God and caused many others to be sinners. But Jesus obeyed him and will make many people acceptable to God.

[20]The Law came, so that the full power of sin could be seen. Yet where sin was powerful, God's kindness was even more

---

[i]**5.1** _we live at peace_: Some manuscripts have "let us live at peace." [j]**5.2** _introduced us_: Some manuscripts add "by faith." [k]**5.3** _We gladly suffer_: Or "Let us gladly suffer."

powerful. [21]Sin ruled by means of death. But God's kindness now rules, and God has accepted us because of Jesus Christ our Lord. This means that we will have eternal life.

Dead to Sin but Alive because of Christ

6 What should we say? Should we keep on sinning, so that God's wonderful kindness will show up even better? [2]No, we should not! If we are dead to sin, how can we go on sinning? [3]Don't you know that all who share in Christ Jesus by being baptized also share in his death? [4]When we were baptized, we died and were buried with Christ. We were baptized, so that we would live a new life, as Christ was raised to life by the glory of God the Father.

[5]If we shared in Jesus' death by being baptized, we will be raised to life with him. [6]We know that the persons we used to be were nailed to the cross with Jesus. This was done, so that our sinful bodies would no longer be the slaves of sin. [7]We know that sin doesn't have power over dead people.

[8]As surely as we died with Christ, we believe we will also live with him. [9]We know that death no longer has any power over Christ. He died and was raised to life, never again to die. [10]When Christ died, he died for sin once and for all. But now he is alive, and he lives only for God. [11]In the same way, you must think of yourselves as dead to the power of sin. But Christ Jesus has given life to you, and you live for God.

[12]Don't let sin rule your body. After all, your body is bound to die, so don't obey its desires [13]or let any part of it become a slave of evil. Give yourselves to God, as people who have been raised from death to life. Make every part of your body a slave that pleases God. [14]Don't let sin keep ruling your lives. You are ruled by God's kindness and not by the Law.

Slaves Who Do What Pleases God

[15]What does all this mean? Does it mean we are free to sin, because we are ruled by God's wonderful kindness and not by the Law? Certainly not! [16]Don't you know that you are slaves of anyone you obey? You can be slaves of sin and die, or you can be obedient slaves of God and be acceptable to him. [17]You used to be slaves of sin. But I thank God that with all your heart you obeyed the teaching you received from me. [18]Now you

are set free from sin and are slaves who please God.

[19]I am using these everyday examples, because in some ways you are still weak. You used to let the different parts of your body be slaves of your evil thoughts. But now you must make every part of your body serve God, so that you will belong completely to him.

[20]When you were slaves of sin, you didn't have to please God. [21]But what good did you receive from the things you did? All you have to show for them is your shame, and they lead to death. [22]Now you have been set free from sin, and you are God's slaves. This will make you holy and will lead you to eternal life. [23]Sin pays off with death. But God's gift is eternal life given by Jesus Christ our Lord.

An Example from Marriage

7 My friends, you surely understand enough about law to know that laws only have power over people who are alive. [2]For example, the Law says that a man's wife must remain his wife as long as he lives. But once her husband is dead, she is free [3]to marry someone else. However, if she goes off with another man while her husband is still alive, she is said to be unfaithful.

[4]That is how it is with you, my friends. You are now part of the body of Christ and are dead to the power of the Law. You are free to belong to Christ, who was raised to life so that we could serve God. [5]When we thought only of ourselves, the Law made us have sinful desires. It made every part of our bodies into slaves who are doomed to die. [6]But the Law no longer rules over us. We are like dead people, and it cannot have any power over us. Now we can serve God in a new way by obeying his Spirit, and not in the old way by obeying the written Law.

The Battle with Sin

[7]Does this mean that the Law is sinful? Certainly not! But if it had not been for the Law, I would not have known what sin is really like. For example, I would not have known what it means to want something that belongs to someone else, unless the Law had told me not to do that. [8]It was sin

that used this command as a way of making me have all kinds of desires. But without the Law, sin is dead.

⁹Before I knew about the Law, I was alive. But as soon as I heard that command, sin came to life, ¹⁰and I died. The very command that was supposed to bring life to me, instead brought death. ¹¹Sin used this command to trick me, and because of it I died. ¹²Still, the Law and its commands are holy and correct and good.

¹³Am I saying that something good caused my death? Certainly not! It was sin that killed me by using something good. Now we can see how terrible and evil sin really is. ¹⁴We know that the Law is spiritual. But I am merely a human, and I have been sold as a slave to sin. ¹⁵In fact, I don't understand why I act the way I do. I don't do what I know is right. I do the things I hate. ¹⁶Although I don't do what I know is right, I agree that the Law is good. ¹⁷So I am not the one doing these evil things. The sin that lives in me is what does them.

¹⁸I know that my selfish desires won't let me do anything that is good. Even when I want to do right, I cannot. ¹⁹Instead of doing what I know is right, I do wrong. ²⁰And so, if I don't do what I know is right, I am no longer the one doing these evil things. The sin that lives in me is what does them.

²¹The Law has shown me that something in me keeps me from doing what I know is right. ²²With my whole heart I agree with the Law of God. ²³But in every part of me I discover something fighting against my mind, and it makes me a prisoner of sin that controls everything I do. ²⁴What a miserable person I am. Who will rescue me from this body that is doomed to die? ²⁵Thank God! Jesus Christ will rescue me.

So with my mind I serve the Law of God, although my selfish desires make me serve the law of sin.

Living by the Power of God's Spirit

8 If you belong to Christ Jesus, you won't be punished. ²The Holy Spirit will give you life that comes from Christ Jesus and will set you¹ free from sin and death. ³The Law of Moses cannot do this, because our selfish desires make the Law weak. But God set you free when he sent his own Son to be like us sinners and to be a sacrifice for our sin. God used Christ's

¹8.2 *you:* Some manuscripts have "me."

Friendship—How can I forgive a friend who has greatly wronged or disappointed me? *(Romans 7.21—8.5)*

Make grace a state where you live.
Has a friend deliberately hurt you and shown no regret? Or maybe she's remorseful, but your wounds are deep? Admit it: Forgiveness is never easy. But you can make it a bit easier by recognizing that every Christian (even you) struggles with sin (7,8). Some struggles are more obvious, but we all fight to do right. The Bible says we do the evil we want to avoid; we don't do the good we aspire to. Realizing we're comrades in this battle makes it easier to show grace—undeserved love—to our brother and sister soldiers.

There's a mistaken belief we have to forget in order to forgive. But only God can do that. Rather than struggle to forgive or forget the wrong, move to the state of grace. Whatever your friend did wrong, she doesn't deserve your love. She doesn't deserve your forgiveness. But quite honestly, you don't deserve God's forgiveness either; yet he loves you anyway. If you allow him to, God will work with both of you to free you from the separation sin causes. Forgiveness isn't a feeling but an action. So express God's grace through deliberately showing care to your friend.

With God to empower you, you can choose to treat your friend as forgiven, even when you don't feel like it. Then freedom comes to you both. (See also Ephesians 2.1-10; Colossians 3.12-14.)

Words To Remember: *God set you free when he sent his own Son to be like us sinners and to be a sacrifice for our sin. . . . He did this, so that we would do what the Law commands by obeying the Spirit instead of our own desires.—Romans 8.3,4*

body to condemn sin. [4]He did this, so that we would do what the Law commands by obeying the Spirit instead of our own desires.

[5]People who are ruled by their desires think only of themselves. Everyone who is ruled by the Holy Spirit thinks about spiritual things. [6]If our minds are ruled by our desires, we will die. But if our minds are ruled by the Spirit, we will have life and peace. [7]Our desires fight against God, because they do not and cannot obey God's laws. [8]If we follow our desires, we cannot please God.

[9]You are no longer ruled by your desires, but by God's Spirit, who lives in you. People who don't have the Spirit of Christ in them don't belong to him. [10]But Christ lives in you. So you are alive because God has accepted you, even though your bodies must die because of your sins. [11]Yet God raised Jesus to life! God's Spirit now lives in you, and he will raise you to life by his Spirit.

[12]My dear friends, we must not live to satisfy our desires. [13]If you do, you will die. But you will live, if by the help of God's Spirit you say "No" to your desires. [14]Only those people who are led by God's Spirit are his children. [15]God's Spirit doesn't make us slaves who are afraid of him. Instead, we become his children and call him our Father.[m] [16]God's Spirit makes us sure that we are his children. [17]His Spirit lets us know that together with Christ we will be given what God has promised. We will also share in the glory of Christ, because we have suffered with him.

A Wonderful Future for God's People

[18]I am sure that what we are suffering now cannot compare with the glory that will be shown to us. [19]In fact, all creation is eagerly waiting for God to show who his children are. [20]Meanwhile, creation is confused, but not because it wants to be confused. God made it this way in the hope [21]that creation would be set free from decay and would share in the glorious freedom of his children. [22]We know that all creation is still groaning and is in pain, like a woman about to give birth.

[23]The Spirit makes us sure about what we will be in the future. But now we groan silently, while we wait for God to show that we are his children.[n] This means that our bodies will also be set free. [24]And this hope is what saves us. But if we already have what we hope for, there is no need to keep on hoping. [25]However, we hope for something we have not yet seen, and we patiently wait for it.

[26]In certain ways we are weak, but the Spirit is here to help us. For example, when we don't know what to pray for, the Spirit prays for us in ways that cannot be put into words. [27]All of our thoughts are known to God. He can understand what is in the

[m]8.15 our Father: The Greek text uses the Aramaic word "Abba" (meaning "father"), which shows the close relation between the children and their father. [n]8.23 to show that we are his children: These words are not in some manuscripts. The translation of the remainder of the verse would then read, "while we wait for God to set our bodies free."

SpiritualLife—What does God expect of me? *(Romans 8.1-17)*

Live by the power of his Spirit.

If a friend hurt your feelings, what would you do? Pretend it never happened? Get angry and ignore her? Or approach her with gentleness and let her know that what she did upset you? Humanly, we'd probably want to do one of the first two. But although those options may seem easier now, they'll cause problems in your friendship down the line.

In this passage, Paul tells us that when we belong to Christ Jesus, we will no longer think only of ourselves (and the consequences). Instead, he says, "You are no longer ruled by your desires, but by God's Spirit, who lives in you" (8.9).

No matter what we face in life, we can count on the power of God's Spirit to lead us to the godly response—if we listen. After all, "we become his children and call him our Father" (8.15). And our heavenly Father always knows what's best for us. (See also Exodus 20.1-17; Judges 5.1-11; Jeremiah 1.4-19; Micah 6.6-8; 1 Corinthians 6.12-20.)

Words To Remember: *You are no longer ruled by your desires, but by God's Spirit, who lives in you.—Romans 8.9*

> *Saturate yourself with God's*
> *Word so that when you*
> *awaken in the middle of*
> *the night with anxiety*
> *symptoms, you will hear the*
> *voice of God whisper to you,*
> *"My child, this will all*
> *work out for good because*
> *you love me and are*
> *called to my purpose."*
>
> BARBARA JOHNSON

so that his Son would be the first of many children. ³⁰God then accepted the people he had already decided to choose, and he has shared his glory with them.

God's Love

³¹What can we say about all this? If God is on our side, can anyone be against us? ³²God did not keep back his own Son, but he gave him for us. If God did this, won't he freely give us everything else? ³³If God says his chosen ones are acceptable to him, can anyone bring charges against them? ³⁴Or can anyone condemn them? No indeed! Christ died and was raised to life, and now he is at God's right side,ᵖ speaking to him for us. ³⁵Can anything separate us from the love of Christ? Can trouble, suffering, and hard times, or hunger and nakedness, or danger and death? ³⁶It is exactly as the Scriptures say,

> "For you we face death
>   all day long.

mind of the Spirit, as the Spirit prays for God's people. ²⁸We know that God is always at work for the good of everyone who loves him.ᵒ They are the ones God has chosen for his purpose, ²⁹and he has always known who his chosen ones would be. He had decided to let them become like his own Son,

ᵒ**8.28** *God is always at work for the good of everyone who loves him:* Or "All things work for the good of everyone who loves God" or "God's Spirit always works for the good of everyone who loves God." ᵖ**8.34** *right side:* The place of power and honor.

Personal *Concerns*—How can I handle even difficult times positively?
(*Romans 8.18-30*)

Be confident about the future—even if you can't always smile.
In today's culture of "don't worry, be happy," it's not easy to suffer honestly. When a loved one dies, visitors seem in awe of family members who "keep it together" and don't cry during the funeral. Yet, those family members may be going through such grief that they're literally aching in lonely silence. And it doesn't help when well-meaning observers say things, such as, "It was her time to go home" or "You wouldn't have wanted him to live like that, so it's best he died now."

But saying such things is a gross misapplication of what Paul says here in Romans. We all will suffer and "groan silently" (8.23) at one time or another, Paul says. It's okay, even holy, to cry and mourn over sad events. Yet, even in our deepest despair, the Holy Spirit is there to assure us that God works through the bad to bring about good.

How do we suffer positively? We invite the Holy Spirit to show us how. We let him express our prayers in "ways that cannot be put into words" (8.26). We recognize that bad events are side effects of this imperfect world we live in, a world eagerly waiting for God (8.18-22). And we invite people to cry with us so we can go on to find the good God persistently gives (8.28)—as we hope and wait for it. (See also Leviticus 26.1-13; Job 23; Micah 4.1-5; Nahum 1.2-7,15; Ephesians 1.7-23.)

Words To Remember: *We know that God is always at work for the good of everyone who loves him.*—**Romans 8.28**

We are like sheep
on their way
    to be butchered."

[37]In everything we have won more than a victory because of Christ who loves us. [38]I am sure that nothing can separate us from God's love—not life or death, not angels or spirits, not the present or the future, [39]and not powers above or powers below. Nothing in all creation can separate us from God's love for us in Christ Jesus our Lord!

God's Choice of Israel

9 I am a follower of Christ, and the Holy Spirit is a witness to my conscience. So I tell the truth and I am not lying when I say [2]my heart is broken and I am in great sorrow. [3]I would gladly be placed under God's curse and be separated from Christ for the good of my own people. [4]They are the descendants of Israel, and they are also God's chosen people. God showed them his glory. He made agreements with them and gave them his Law. The temple is theirs and so are the promises that God made to them. [5]They have those famous ancestors, who were also the ancestors of Jesus Christ. I pray that God, who rules over all, will be praised forever![q] Amen.

[6]It cannot be said that God broke his promise. After all, not all of the people of Israel are the true people of God. [7-8]In fact, when God made the promise to Abraham, he meant only Abraham's descendants by his son Isaac. God was talking only about Isaac when he promised [9]Sarah, "At this time next year I will return, and you will already have a son."

[10]Don't forget what happened to the twin sons of Isaac and Rebekah. [11-12]Even before they were born or had done anything good or bad, the Lord told Rebekah that her older son would serve the younger one. The Lord said this to show that he makes his own choices and that it wasn't because of anything either of them had done. [13]That's why the Scriptures say that the Lord liked Jacob more than Esau.

[14]Are we saying that God is unfair? Certainly not! [15]The Lord told Moses that he has pity and mercy on anyone he wants to. [16]Everything then depends on God's mercy and not on what people want or do. [17]In the Scriptures the Lord says to Pharaoh of Egypt, "I let you become king, so that I could show you my power and be praised by all people on earth." [18]Everything depends on what God decides to do, and he can either have pity on people or make them stubborn.

God's Anger and Mercy

[19]Someone may ask, "How can God blame us, if he makes us behave in the way he wants us to?" [20]But, my friend, I ask, "Who do you think you are to question God? Does the clay have the right to ask the potter why he shaped it the way he did? [21]Doesn't a potter have the right to make a fancy bowl and a plain bowl out of the same lump of clay?"

[22]God wanted to show his anger and reveal his power against everyone who deserved to be destroyed. But instead, he patiently put up with them. [23]He did this by showing how glorious he is when he has pity on the people he has chosen to share in his glory. [24]Whether Jews or Gentiles, we are those chosen ones, [25]just as the Lord says in the book of Hosea,

"Although they are not
my people,
    I will make them my people.
I will treat with love
those nations
    that have never been loved.

[26]"Once they were told,
    'You are not my people.'
But in that very place
they will be called
    children of the living God."

[27]And this is what the prophet Isaiah said about the people of Israel,

"The people of Israel
    are as many
as the grains of sand
    along the beach.
But only a few who are left
    will be saved.

[q]9.5 Christ. I pray that God, who rules over all, will be praised forever: Or "Christ, who rules over all. I pray that God will be praised forever" or "Christ. And I pray that Christ, who is God and rules over all, will be praised forever."

[28] The Lord will be quick
and sure to do on earth
what he has warned
he will do."

[29] Isaiah also said,

"If the Lord All-Powerful
had not spared some
of our descendants,
we would have been destroyed
like the cities of Sodom
and Gomorrah."[r]

Israel and the Good News

[30] What does all of this mean? It means that the Gentiles were not trying to be acceptable to God, but they found that he would accept them if they had faith. [31-32] It also means that the people of Israel were not acceptable to God. And why not? It was because they were trying[s] to be acceptable by obeying the Law instead of by having faith in God. The people of Israel fell over the stone that makes people stumble, [33] just as God says in the Scriptures,

"Look! I am placing in Zion
a stone to make people
stumble and fall.
But those who have faith

in that one will never
be disappointed."

10 Dear friends, my greatest wish and my prayer to God is for the people of Israel to be saved. [2] I know they love God, but they don't understand [3] what makes people acceptable to him. So they refuse to trust God, and they try to be acceptable by obeying the Law. [4] But Christ makes the Law no longer necessary[t] for those who become acceptable to God by faith.

Anyone Can Be Saved

[5] Moses said that a person could become acceptable to God by obeying the Law. He did this when he wrote, "If you want to live, you must do all that the Law commands." [6] But people whose faith makes them acceptable to God will never ask, "Who will go up to heaven to bring Christ down?" [7] Neither will they ask, "Who will go down into the world of the dead to raise him to life?"

---

[r] **9.29** *Sodom and Gomorrah*: During the time of Abraham the Lord destroyed these two cities because their people were so sinful. [s] **9.31,32** *because they were trying*: Or "while they were trying" or "even though they were trying." [t] **10.4** *But Christ makes the Law no longer necessary*: Or "But Christ gives the full meaning to the Law."

---

*Spiritual*Life—Will God really condemn people who don't accept Christ as their Savior? *(Romans 10.5-21)*

God condemns no one. People choose to reject God.
God has been tirelessly seeking to reach people since time began. He has used the wonders of creation, his laws, his prophets, his sinless son, Jesus Christ, and the Bible to express his love and desire to relate to each person. Faith in Jesus Christ is the only way to salvation because he is the redeemer who died for our sins. Jesus is the ultimate communication between God and people; God became a person so we could know and understand him face-to-face. Rejection of Jesus is a rejection of God himself.

The search for faith is not a popularity contest or a vote. It's the discovery of truth—from a very real, ever-present God who's always working to show himself to every person. Some people come to God first and then understand Jesus; others come to Jesus first and then understand God. But in both cases "the message is as near as your mouth or your heart" (10.8). God doesn't penalize people for what they don't know; he continues to find ways to reveal himself to them. The one thing God won't do is force response. If people choose to reject him, he allows them to do so, clearly recognizing that a forced love is no love at all. (See also Deuteronomy 30; Zephaniah 1.14-18; John 3.16-18; John 6.60-69.)

Words To Remember: *All who call out to the Lord will be saved.*
—**Romans 10.13**

⁸All who are acceptable because of their faith simply say, "The message is as near as your mouth or your heart." And this is the same message we preach about faith. ⁹So you will be saved, if you honestly say, "Jesus is Lord," and if you believe with all your heart that God raised him from death. ¹⁰God will accept you and save you, if you truly believe this and tell it to others.

¹¹The Scriptures say that no one who has faith will be disappointed, ¹²no matter if that person is a Jew or a Gentile. There is only one Lord, and he is generous to everyone who asks for his help. ¹³All who call out to the Lord will be saved.

¹⁴How can people have faith in the Lord and ask him to save them, if they have never heard about him? And how can they hear, unless someone tells them? ¹⁵And how can anyone tell them without being sent by the Lord? The Scriptures say it is a beautiful sight to see even the feet of someone coming to preach the good news. ¹⁶Yet not everyone has believed the message. For example, the prophet Isaiah asked, "Lord, has anyone believed what we said?"

¹⁷No one can have faith without hearing the message about Christ. ¹⁸But am I saying that the people of Israel did not hear? No, I am not! The Scriptures say,

> "The message was told
>   everywhere on earth.
> It was announced
>   all over the world."

¹⁹Did the people of Israel understand or not? Moses answered this question when he told that the Lord had said,

> "I will make Israel jealous
>   of people
> who are a nation
>   of nobodies.
> I will make them angry
>   at people
> who don't understand
>   a thing."

²⁰Isaiah was fearless enough to tell that the Lord had said,

> "I was found by people
>   who were not looking
>   for me.

> I appeared to the ones
>   who were not asking
>   about me."

²¹And Isaiah said about the people of Israel,

> "All day long the Lord
>   has reached out
> to people who are stubborn
>   and refuse to obey."

God Has Not Rejected His People

11 Am I saying that God has turned his back on his people? Certainly not! I am one of the people of Israel, and I myself am a descendant of Abraham from the tribe of Benjamin. ²God did not turn his back on his chosen people. Don't you remember reading in the Scriptures how Elijah complained to God about the people of Israel? ³He said, "Lord, they killed your prophets and destroyed your altars. I am the only one left, and now they want to kill me."

⁴But the Lord told Elijah, "I still have seven thousand followers who have not worshiped Baal." ⁵It is the same way now. God was kind to the people of Israel, and so a few of them are still his followers. ⁶This happened because of God's undeserved kindness and not because of anything they have done. It could not have happened except for God's kindness.

⁷This means that only a chosen few of the people of Israel found what all of them were searching for. And the rest of them were stubborn, ⁸just as the Scriptures say,

> "God made them so stupid
>   that their eyes are blind,
> and their ears
>   are still deaf."

⁹Then David said,

> "Turn their meals
>   into bait for a trap,
> so that they will stumble
> and be given
>   what they deserve.
> ¹⁰Blindfold their eyes!
>   Don't let them see.
> Bend their backs
> beneath a burden
>   that will never be lifted."

Gentiles Will Be Saved

[11]Do I mean that the people of Israel fell, never to get up again? Certainly not! Their failure made it possible for the Gentiles to be saved, and this will make the people of Israel jealous. [12]But if the rest of the world's people were helped so much by Israel's sin and loss, they will be helped even more by their full return.

[13]I am now speaking to you Gentiles, and as long as I am an apostle to you, I will take pride in my work. [14]I hope in this way to make some of my own people jealous enough to be saved. [15]When Israel rejected God,[u] the rest of the people in the world were able to turn to him. So when God makes friends with Israel, it will be like bringing the dead back to life. [16]If part of a batch of dough is made holy by being offered to God, then all of the dough is holy. If the roots of a tree are holy, the rest of the tree is holy too.

[17]You Gentiles are like branches of a wild olive tree that were made to be part of a cultivated olive tree. You have taken the place of some branches that were cut away from it. And because of this, you enjoy the blessings that come from being part of that cultivated tree. [18]But don't think you are better than the branches that were cut away. Just remember that you are not supporting the roots of that tree. Its roots are supporting you.

[19]Maybe you think those branches were cut away, so that you could be put in their place. [20]That's true enough. But they were cut away because they did not have faith, and you are where you are because you do have faith. So don't be proud, but be afraid. [21]If God cut away those natural branches, couldn't he do the same to you?

[22]Now you see both how kind and how hard God can be. He was hard on those who fell, but he was kind to you. And he will keep on being kind to you, if you keep on trusting in his kindness. Otherwise, you will be cut away too.

[23]If those other branches will start having faith, they will be made a part of that tree again. God has the power to put them back. [24]After all, it wasn't natural for branches to be cut from a wild olive tree and to be made part of a cultivated olive tree. So it is much more likely that God will join the natural branches back to the cultivated olive tree.

The People of Israel Will Be Brought Back

[25]My friends, I don't want you Gentiles to be too proud of yourselves. So I will explain the mystery of what has happened to the people of Israel. Some of them have become stubborn, and they will stay like that until the complete number of you Gentiles has come in. [26]In this way all of Israel will be saved, as the Scriptures say,

> "From Zion someone will come
>   to rescue us.
> Then Jacob's descendants
>   will stop being evil.
> [27]This is what the Lord
>   has promised to do
> when he forgives their sins."

[28]The people of Israel are treated as God's enemies, so that the good news can come to you Gentiles. But they are still the chosen ones, and God loves them because of their famous ancestors. [29]God doesn't take back the gifts he has given or forget about the people he has chosen.

Our God is so trustworthy that we are to throw our confidence on him, not leaning on our own limited understanding. If God's mind was small enough for me to understand, he wouldn't be God!

JONI EARECKSON TADA

[30]At one time you Gentiles rejected God. But now Israel has rejected God, and you have been shown mercy. [31]And because of the mercy shown to you, they will also be

---

[u]11.15 *When Israel rejected God:* Or "When Israel was rejected."

shown mercy. ³²All people have disobeyed God, and that's why he treats them as prisoners. But he does this, so that he can have mercy on all of them.

³³Who can measure the wealth and wisdom and knowledge of God? Who can understand his decisions or explain what he does?

³⁴"Has anyone known
the thoughts of the Lord
or given him advice?
³⁵Has anyone loaned
something to the Lord
that must be repaid?"

³⁶Everything comes from the Lord. All things were made because of him and will return to him. Praise the Lord forever! Amen.

Christ Brings New Life

12 Dear friends, God is good. So I beg you to offer your bodies to him as a living sacrifice, pure and pleasing. That's the most sensible way to serve God. ²Don't be like the people of this world, but let God change the way you think. Then you will know how to do everything that is good and pleasing to him.

³I realize how kind God has been to me, and so I tell each of you not to think you are better than you really are. Use good sense and measure yourself by the amount of faith that God has given you. ⁴A body is made up of many parts, and each of them has its own use. ⁵That's how it is with us. There are many of us, but we each are part of the body of Christ, as well as part of one another.

⁶God has also given each of us different gifts to use. If we can prophesy, we should do it according to the amount of faith we have. ⁷If we can serve others, we should serve. If we can teach, we should teach. ⁸If we can encourage others, we should encourage them. If we can give, we should be generous. If we are leaders, we should do our best. If we are good to others, we should do it cheerfully.

Rules for Christian Living

⁹Be sincere in your love for others. Hate everything that is evil and hold tight to everything that is good. ¹⁰Love each other as brothers and sisters and honor others more than you do yourself. ¹¹Never give up. Eagerly follow the Holy Spirit and serve the Lord. ¹²Let your hope make you glad. Be patient in time of trouble and never stop praying. ¹³Take care of God's needy people and welcome strangers into your home.

¹⁴Ask God to bless everyone who mistreats you. Ask him to bless them and not to curse them. ¹⁵When others are happy, be

---

*Spiritual*Life—Why is it important for me to go to church? *(Romans 12.3-8)*

You need people; people need you.
God is everywhere, and you can honor him at any time. But when you're at church, other people have the opportunity to encourage and strengthen you. And, equally important, you can encourage and strengthen other believers. God made us like puzzle pieces who fit together with other believers to complete the total picture of his people.

Like in a puzzle, pieces are not interchangeable. Another believer cannot fill the spot God specifically created for you. Maybe you're the one who smiles at a timid child and makes him feel a part of things. No one else has quite your sensitivity to the quiet ones. Maybe you're the one who sees persons with mental handicaps as ministers rather than projects. You find ways for them to serve in church rather than just attend Bible study. No one else had respected them before you facilitated the connections.

Whatever your sensitivity and gifts, the church needs you. Learn to express your gifts in church as you invite others to express theirs. When believers work together, we can present a caring unity that invites others to join with Jesus. (See also Ezekiel 43.1-5; Acts 2.1-13, 41-47; 1 Corinthians 3.10-17; Ephesians 2.11-22.)

Words To Remember: *A body is made up of many parts, and each of them has its own use. That's how it is with us. There are many of us, but we each are part of the body of Christ, as well as part of one another.—Romans 12.4,5*

happy with them, and when they are sad, be sad. ¹⁶Be friendly with everyone. Don't be proud and feel that you are smarter than others. Make friends with ordinary people.ᵛ ¹⁷Don't mistreat someone who has mistreated you. But try to earn the respect of others, ¹⁸and do your best to live at peace with everyone.

¹⁹Dear friends, don't try to get even. Let God take revenge. In the Scriptures the Lord says,

> "I am the one to take revenge
>   and pay them back."

²⁰The Scriptures also say,

> "If your enemies are hungry,
>   give them something to eat.
> And if they are thirsty,
> give them something
>   to drink.
> This will be the same
> as piling burning coals
>   on their heads."

²¹Don't let evil defeat you, but defeat evil with good.

Obey Rulers

13 Obey the rulers who have authority over you. Only God can give authority to anyone, and he puts these rulers in their places of power. ²People who oppose the authorities are opposing what God has done, and they will be punished. ³Rulers are a threat to evil people, not to good people. There is no need to be afraid of the authorities. Just do right, and they will praise you for it. ⁴After all, they are God's servants, and it is their duty to help you.

If you do something wrong, you ought to be afraid, because these rulers have the right to punish you. They are God's servants who punish criminals to show how angry God is. ⁵But you should obey the rulers because you know it is the right thing to do, and not just because of God's anger.

⁶You must also pay your taxes. The authorities are God's servants, and it is their duty to take care of these matters. ⁷Pay all that you owe, whether it is taxes and fees or respect and honor.

ᵛ**12.16** *Make friends with ordinary people*: Or "Do ordinary jobs."

WORK—How can I have healthy relationships with the men I work with?
(Romans 12.9-18)

Treat male coworkers as brothers.
Anytime individuals get together, there is opportunity for problems. But when one person is male, and the other is female, the potential for trouble can increase. Yet togetherness also provides an excellent opportunity for you to show just what God meant friendship between the sexes to be! You can demonstrate the encouragement, teamwork, and support that promote a happy workplace.

Start by following Romans 12.9-18: Hate evil and hold on to good. It's unfortunate, but Hollywood makes attraction between unmarried persons look good, not evil. Movies imply that males and females cannot work together without losing control sexually. Sad things seldom happen in movie affairs; but in real life, damage always comes to those who express attraction outside of marriage. Hate this evil, and love the purity of friendship.

Aim to grow solid, caring *friendships* with your male coworkers. Refuse to compete with or mistreat each other. Always act in ways that invite respect, and give yourself boundaries that make certain you never act flirtatiously toward an office mate. Even the strongest Christian must avoid going places alone with an opposite-gender coworker or giving too much emotional support. Make it your rule to avoid all appearance of evil. Then you can "live at peace with everyone" (12.18). (See also Esther 4; Proverbs 5; Galatians 6.1-10.)

Words To Remember: *Love each other as brothers and sisters and honor others more than you do yourself.—Romans 12.10*

Love

[8]Let love be your only debt! If you love others, you have done all that the Law demands. [9]In the Law there are many commands, such as, "Be faithful in marriage. Do not murder. Do not steal. Do not want what belongs to others." But all of these are summed up in the command that says, "Love others as much as you love yourself." [10]No one who loves others will harm them. So love is all that the Law demands.

Nothing trains and teaches so powerfully as love. Love attracts; it does not coerce.

ELISABETH ELLIOT

The Day When Christ Returns

[11]You know what sort of times we live in, and so you should live properly. It is time to wake up. You know that the day when we will be saved is nearer now than when we first put our faith in the Lord. [12]Night is almost over, and day will soon appear. We must stop behaving as people do in the dark and be ready to live in the light. [13]So behave properly, as people do in the day. Don't go to wild parties or get drunk or be vulgar or indecent. Don't quarrel or be jealous. [14]Let the Lord Jesus Christ be as near to you as the clothes you wear. Then you won't try to satisfy your selfish desires.

Don't Criticize Others

14 Welcome all the Lord's followers, even those whose faith is weak. Don't criticize them for having beliefs that are different from yours. [2]Some think it is all right to eat anything, while those whose faith is weak will eat only vegetables. [3]But you should not criticize others for eating or for not eating. After all, God welcomes everyone. [4]What right do you have to criticize someone else's servants? Only their Lord can decide if they are doing right, and the Lord will make sure that they do right.

[5]Some of the Lord's followers think one day is more important than another. Others think all days are the same. But each of you should make up your own mind. [6]Any followers who count one day more important than another day do it to honor their Lord. And any followers who eat meat give thanks to God, just like the ones who don't eat meat.

[7]Whether we live or die, it must be for God, rather than for ourselves. [8]Whether we live or die, it must be for the Lord. Alive or dead, we still belong to the Lord. [9]This is

SingleLife—I like being single. Is that normal? *(Romans 14.1-12)*

God wants you to humbly enjoy your life.
It's perfectly normal! Contentment has less to do with being single or married than with having an attitude of gratitude toward God. So go ahead and enjoy your life. Your delight in life will be contagious.

Beware of the temptation to make others exactly like you, however. You may wonder why other single people focus on finding a mate. Or you may grow frustrated with the whining of your single *and* married friends who refuse to appreciate the good in their lives. Keep in mind that someone already has the job of helping them change—the Holy Spirit. Let him show you what to say so neither your attitude (a too-happy attitude toward your own singleness may wound a friend who's currently hurting over her singleness) nor words hinder his convicting, refining process. At the same time invite God's Spirit to refine you, so that you're living for him—whether you stay single or get married. **(See also Numbers 11; Nehemiah 4; 6.15,16; 1 Corinthians 7.29-35.)**

Words To Remember: *Whether we live or die, it must be for God, rather than for ourselves. . . . Each of us must give an account to God for what we do.*
—Romans 14.7,12

because Christ died and rose to life, so that he would be the Lord of the dead and of the living. [10]Why do you criticize other followers of the Lord? Why do you look down on them? The day is coming when God will judge all of us. [11]In the Scriptures God says,

"I swear by my very life
that everyone will kneel down
and praise my name!"

[12]And so, each of us must give an account to God for what we do.

Don't Cause Problems for Others

[13]We must stop judging others. We must also make up our minds not to upset anyone's faith. [14]The Lord Jesus has made it clear to me that God considers all foods fit to eat. But if you think some foods are unfit to eat, then for you they are not fit.

[15]If you are hurting others by the foods you eat, you are not guided by love. Don't let your appetite destroy someone Christ died for. [16]Don't let your right to eat bring shame to Christ. [17]God's kingdom isn't about eating and drinking. It is about pleasing God, about living in peace, and about true happiness. All this comes from the Holy Spirit. [18]If you serve Christ in this way, you will please God and be respected by

people. [19]We should try[w] to live at peace and help each other have a strong faith.

[20]Don't let your appetite destroy what God has done. All foods are fit to eat, but it is wrong to cause problems for others by what you eat. [21]It is best not to eat meat or drink wine or do anything else that causes problems for other followers of the Lord. [22]What you believe about these things should be kept between you and God. You are fortunate, if your actions don't make you have doubts. [23]But if you do have doubts about what you eat, you are going against your beliefs. And you know that is wrong, because anything you do against your beliefs is sin.

Please Others and Not Yourself

15 If our faith is strong, we should be patient with the Lord's followers whose faith is weak. We should try to please them instead of ourselves. [2]We should think of their good and try to help them by doing what pleases them. [3]Even Christ did not try to please himself. But as the Scriptures say, "The people who insulted you also insulted me." [4]And the Scriptures were written to teach and encourage us by giving us hope. [5]God is the one who

---

[w]14.19 *We should try*: Some manuscripts have "We try."

∽

WORK—Sometimes I think it's okay to work while my kids are young; other times I'm not sure. How can I be certain I'm making the best decision for my family? *(Romans 14.13-23)*

Seek God's wisdom in your decision.
No matter where you turn, you can find advice on the work-versus-stay-at-home decision. And each person will tell you with personal certainty what's right and what's wrong. Filter out the money aspect; you can usually live on less. Filter out the career aspect; you may find ways to work from home and still stay on track with your chosen vocation. Filter out social pressure; you can build support on both sides of the argument.

Because only God can determine what's right and wrong, let him be your main guide. Call on his Holy Spirit to help you focus on what's best for your children. How can you best give the attention and structure your children need? What values are you teaching by going to work outside the home or by working within your home? How will you provide a parent presence—will your husband be at home while you work, and you at home while he works? How are you portioning your energy and why? God himself will help you answer these questions and make your decision. (See also Proverbs 16.1-3; Titus 2.3-8.)

Words To Remember: *God's kingdom ... is about pleasing God, about living in peace, and about true happiness. All this comes from the Holy Spirit. If you serve Christ in this way, you will please God and be respected by people.—Romans 14.17,18*

makes us patient and cheerful. I pray that he will help you live at peace with each other, as you follow Christ. ⁶Then all of you together will praise God, the Father of our Lord Jesus Christ.

The Good News Is for Jews and Gentiles

⁷Honor God by accepting each other, as Christ has accepted you. ⁸I tell you that Christ came as a servant of the Jews to show that God has kept the promises he made to their famous ancestors. Christ also came, ⁹so that the Gentiles would praise God for being kind to them. It is just as the Scriptures say,

"I will tell the nations
    about you,
and I will sing praises
    to your name."

¹⁰The Scriptures also say to the Gentiles, "Come and celebrate with God's people."
¹¹Again the Scriptures say,

"Praise the Lord,
    all you Gentiles.
All you nations, come
    and worship him."

¹²Isaiah says,

"Someone from David's family
    will come to power.

He will rule the nations,
    and they will put their hope
        in him."

¹³I pray that God, who gives hope, will bless you with complete happiness and peace because of your faith. And may the power of the Holy Spirit fill you with hope.

Paul's Work as a Missionary

¹⁴My friends, I am sure that you are very good and that you have all the knowledge you need to teach each other. ¹⁵But I have spoken to you plainly and have tried to remind you of some things. God was so kind to me! ¹⁶He chose me to be a servant of Christ Jesus for the Gentiles and to do the work of a priest in the service of his good news. God did this so that the Holy Spirit could make the Gentiles into a holy offering, pleasing to him. ¹⁷Because of Christ Jesus, I can take pride in my service for God. ¹⁸In fact, all I will talk about is how Christ let me speak and work, so that the Gentiles would obey him. ¹⁹Indeed, I will tell how Christ worked miracles and wonders by the power of the Holy Spirit. I have preached the good news about him all the way from Jerusalem to Illyricum. ²⁰But I have always tried to preach where people have never heard about Christ. I am like a builder who doesn't build on anyone else's foundation. ²¹It is just as the Scriptures say,

SingleLife—How can I best relate to my married friends? *(Romans 15.1-6)*

Realize you have plenty to offer in any relationship.
"Singles ministry." What an annoying term! On first reading it seems to imply ministry *to* singles. But when you stop to think about it, it's exactly the right phrase: singles are the ministers as well as those ministered to. Every church member—married or single—both gives and receives. This is the same balance that feeds healthy relationships with all your friends. And when a friend gets married, she still needs your perspective—and you need hers—for a richer, more fulfilling life.

So work toward mutuality with your married friend, instead of one of you always giving and the other one always receiving. Share your work, church, struggles, and victories. Encourage each other to honor God in each area of life. Weep together. Laugh together.

Just like any two friends, you'll struggle to find time together that fits both your schedules. You'll need to honor each other's commitments. But maintaining your friendship is possible with patience, commitment, and God (instead of your married or non-married state) as your foundation! (See also Ephesians 5.1-5; 1 John 4.7-12.)

Words To Remember: *God is the one who makes us patient and cheerful. I pray that he will help you live at peace with each other, as you follow Christ.—Romans 15.5*

"All who haven't been told
about him
　　will see him,
and those who haven't heard
about him
　　will understand."

Paul's Plan To Visit Rome

²²My work has always kept me from coming to see you. ²³Now there is nothing left for me to do in this part of the world, and for years I have wanted to visit you. ²⁴So I plan to stop off on my way to Spain. Then after a short, but refreshing, visit with you, I hope you will quickly send me on.

²⁵⁻²⁶I am now on my way to Jerusalem to deliver the money that the Lord's followers in Macedonia and Achaia collected for God's needy people. ²⁷This is something they really wanted to do. But sharing their money with the Jews was also like paying back a debt, because the Jews had already shared their spiritual blessings with the Gentiles. ²⁸After I have safely delivered this money, I will visit you and then go on to Spain. ²⁹And when I do arrive in Rome, I know it will be with the full blessings of Christ.

³⁰My friends, by the power of the Lord Jesus Christ and by the love that comes from the Holy Spirit, I beg you to pray sincerely with me and for me. ³¹Pray that God will protect me from the unbelievers in Judea, and that his people in Jerusalem will be pleased with what I am doing. ³²Ask God to let me come to you and have a pleasant and refreshing visit. ³³I pray that God, who gives peace, will be with all of you. Amen.

Personal Greetings

16 I have good things to say about Phoebe, who is a leader in the church at Cenchreae. ²Welcome her in a way that is proper for someone who has faith in the Lord and is one of God's own people. Help her in any way you can. After all, she has proved to be a respected leader for many others, including me.

³Give my greetings to Priscilla and Aquila. They have not only served Christ Jesus together with me, ⁴but they have even risked their lives for me. I am grateful for them and so are all the Gentile churches. ⁵Greet the church that meets in their home.

Greet my dear friend Epaenetus, who was the first person in Asia to have faith in Christ.

⁶Greet Mary, who has worked so hard for you.

⁷Greet my relativesˣ Andronicus and Junias,ʸ who were in jail with me. They are

---

ˣ16.7 *relatives*: Or "Jewish friends."   ʸ16.7 *Junias*: Or Junia. Some manuscripts have Julia.

---

*Spiritual*Life—How can I make God's presence real in my life?
(*Romans 15.14-21*)

It's already real; just tune in!
Radio signals project whether or not anyone tunes in. In a much greater sense, God is with you right now. He knows what you're doing, even when you don't pay attention. So rather than try to "make" his presence real, tune into the very real presence that's already there. God isn't present only when we feel him most; he's present all the time and in every place.

One of the best ways to get clear reception of God's presence is to serve others both in formal and casual ways. Formal service may include teaching a Sunday School class or working in the church kitchen. Informal service recognizes that your every action is a way to make Jesus obvious. Each time you bend on your knee to hear a child's story, you show that God cares about the details of life. Every time you make certain a son or daughter follows the rules, you show the value of doing the right thing. Each time you show a person consideration, you highlight the value of loving others as much as you love yourself. And as you serve others, you'll see God's transforming power at work in others *and* in you.
(See also 2 Chronicles 29.20-36; Ezekiel 10; Ephesians 3.14-21; Colossians 3.10,11.)

Words To Remember: *It is just as the Scriptures say, "All who haven't been told about him will see him, and those who haven't heard about him will understand."*
—**Romans 15.21**

highly respected by the apostles and were followers of Christ before I was.

⁸Greet Ampliatus, my dear friend whose faith is in the Lord.

⁹Greet Urbanus, who serves Christ along with us.

Greet my dear friend Stachys.

¹⁰Greet Apelles, a faithful servant of Christ.

Greet Aristobulus and his family.

¹¹Greet Herodion, who is a relative* of mine.

Greet Narcissus and the others in his family, who have faith in the Lord.

¹²Greet Tryphaena and Tryphosa, who work hard for the Lord.

Greet my dear friend Persis. She also works hard for the Lord.

¹³Greet Rufus, that special servant of the Lord, and greet his mother, who has been like a mother to me.

¹⁴Greet Asyncritus, Phlegon, Hermes, Patrobas, and Hermas, as well as our friends who are with them.

¹⁵Greet Philologus, Julia, Nereus and his sister, and Olympas, and all of God's people who are with them.

> *I hope that when Jesus looks into my eyes, he sees my obedience, and the presence of God's Spirit.*
>
> MICHELE HALSEIDE

¹⁶Be sure to give each other a warm greeting.

All of Christ's churches greet you.

¹⁷My friends, I beg you to watch out for anyone who causes trouble and divides the church by refusing to do what all of you were taught. Stay away from them! ¹⁸They want to serve themselves and not Christ the Lord. Their flattery and fancy talk fool people who don't know any better. ¹⁹I am glad that everyone knows how well you obey the Lord. But still, I want you to understand what is good and not have anything to do with evil. ²⁰Then God, who gives peace, will soon crush Satan under your feet. I pray that our Lord Jesus will be kind to you.

²¹Timothy, who works with me, sends his greetings, and so do my relatives,* Lucius, Jason, and Sosipater.

²²I, Tertius, also send my greetings. I am a follower of the Lord, and I wrote this letter.ᵃ

²³⁻²⁴Gaius welcomes me and the whole church into his home, and he sends his greetings.

Erastus, the city treasurer, and our dear friend Quartus send their greetings too.ᵇ

Paul's Closing Prayer

²⁵Praise God! He can make you strong by means of my good news, which is the message aboutᶜ Jesus Christ. For ages and ages this message was kept secret, ²⁶but now at last it has been told. The eternal God commanded his prophets to write about the good news, so that all nations would obey and have faith. ²⁷And now, because of Jesus Christ, we can praise the only wise God forever! Amen.ᵈ

---

*16.11,21 *relative(s)*: See the note at 16.7.
ᵃ16.22 *I wrote this letter*: Paul probably dictated this letter to Tertius.   ᵇ16.23,24 *send their greetings too*: Some manuscripts add, "I pray that our Lord Jesus Christ will always be kind to you. Amen."
ᶜ16.25 *about*: Or "from."   ᵈ16.27 *Amen*: Some manuscripts have verses 25-27 after 14.23. Others have the verses here and after 14.23, and one manuscript has them after 15.33.

1 Corinthians

The Growing Young Church

Paul loved the Christians of the Corinthian church, but he was also concerned about the way they treated one another—there was much arguing and division (1.10—4.21). The Corinthian church was a church filled with believers who had been Christians for only a few years. This was a *young* church—full of energy, full of God's Holy Spirit, but a little short on wisdom, love, and common sense. Their friend, the apostle Paul, had founded the church during an eighteen-month visit to Corinth a few years back. Now they needed his stabilizing advice in all sorts of areas, and they received it in this letter.

Today we all can still benefit from Paul's wise counsel. If your taste in worship music is different from other people's in your church, check out what Paul says about taking sides in chapter one. If you've had to sit through a church battle on the budget, Paul's counsel in chapter four may settle some dust. If a friend thinks today's sexual practices are more to his taste than the prudish customs of some previous century, chapter five may help you figure out how to respond. If you're wondering what to do with the Christian construction worker who's cheated you and are considering small claims court, read chapter six for a better plan. If a friend's unbelieving husband has walked out on her, chapter seven outlines her options. If you worry about death, or grieve for someone you've lost, find comfort, even joy, in chapter fifteen. And if you wonder what a Spirit-filled church looks like, you'll find the Spirit's presence throughout the book.

In the centuries since Paul wrote this letter, God has used the wise, practical counsel found here to lead his people toward spiritual maturity. He can do the same for us.

1 Corinthians at a Glance

1. Paul's greeting and prayer for his friends in the church at Corinth (1.1-9)
2. Don't fight! Work together (1.10—4.21)
3. Confront your relationship problems— and settle them (5,6)
4. Questions about marriage, divorce, and sex (7)
5. What's right? What's wrong? And how does it impact your Christian friend? (8–10)
6. Worshiping God together (11,12)
7. What is love? (13)
8. More on worship and using your spiritual gifts for the good of everyone else (14)
9. Jesus is alive! We don't need to fear death (15)
10. Collect money for the Jerusalem church; I'm coming for a visit (16.1-12)
11. Personal notes about friends (16.13-24)

1 From Paul, chosen by God to be an apostle of Christ Jesus, and from Sosthenes, who is also a follower.

²To God's church in Corinth. Christ Jesus chose you to be his very own people, and you worship in his name, as we and all others do who call him Lord.

³My prayer is that God our Father and the Lord Jesus Christ will be kind to you and will bless you with peace!

⁴I never stop thanking my God for being kind enough to give you Christ Jesus, ⁵who helps you speak and understand so well. ⁶Now you are certain that everything we told you about our Lord Christ Jesus is true. ⁷You are not missing out on any blessings, as you wait for him to return. ⁸And until the day Christ does return, he will keep you completely innocent. ⁹God can be trusted, and he chose you to be partners with his Son, our Lord Jesus Christ.

Taking Sides

¹⁰My dear friends, as a follower of our Lord Jesus Christ, I beg you to get along with each other. Don't take sides. Always try to agree in what you think. ¹¹Several people from Chloe's family[a] have already reported to me that you keep arguing with each other. ¹²They have said that some of you claim to follow me, while others claim to follow Apollos or Peter[b] or Christ.

¹³Has Christ been divided up? Was I nailed to a cross for you? Were you baptized in my name? ¹⁴I thank God[c] that I didn't baptize any of you except Crispus and Gaius. ¹⁵Not one of you can say that you were baptized in my name. ¹⁶I did baptize the family[d] of Stephanas, but I don't remember if I baptized anyone else. ¹⁷Christ did not send me to baptize. He sent me to tell the good news without using big words that would make the cross of Christ lose its power.

Christ Is God's Power and Wisdom

¹⁸The message about the cross doesn't make any sense to lost people. But for those of us who are being saved, it is God's power at work. ¹⁹As God says in the Scriptures,

"I will destroy the wisdom
of all who claim
    to be wise.
I will confuse those
who think they know
    so much."

²⁰What happened to those wise people? What happened to those experts in the Scriptures? What happened to the ones who think they have all the answers? Didn't God show that the wisdom of this world is foolish? ²¹God was wise and decided not to let the people of this world use their wisdom to learn about him.

Instead, God chose to save only those who believe the foolish message we preach. ²²Jews ask for miracles, and Greeks want something that sounds wise. ²³But we preach that Christ was nailed to a cross. Most Jews have problems with this, and most Gentiles think it is foolish. ²⁴Our message is God's power and wisdom for the Jews and the Greeks that he has chosen. ²⁵Even when God is foolish, he is wiser than everyone else, and even when God is weak, he is stronger than everyone else.

> *No matter what happens,*
> *God is the most wise, loving*
> *Father anyone could have.*
> VIRELLE KIDDER

²⁶My dear friends, remember what you were when God chose you. The people of this world didn't think that many of you were wise. Only a few of you were in places of power, and not many of you came from important families. ²⁷But God chose the foolish things of this world to put the wise to shame. He chose the weak things of this world to put the powerful to shame. ²⁸What the world thinks is worthless, useless, and nothing at all is what God has used to destroy what the world considers important. ²⁹God did all this to keep anyone

---

[a]1.11 *family:* Family members and possibly slaves and others who may have lived in the house.   [b]1.12 *Peter:* The Greek text has "Cephas," which is an Aramaic name meaning "rock." Peter is the Greek name with the same meaning.   [c]1.14 *I thank God:* Some manuscripts have "I thank my God."   [d]1.16 *family:* See the note at 1.11.

from bragging to him. [30]You are God's children. He sent Christ Jesus to save us and to make us wise, acceptable, and holy. [31]So if you want to brag, do what the Scriptures say and brag about the Lord.

Telling about Christ and the Cross

2 Friends, when I came and told you the mystery[e] that God had shared with us, I didn't use big words or try to sound wise. [2]In fact, while I was with you, I made up my mind to speak only about Jesus Christ, who had been nailed to a cross.

[3]At first, I was weak and trembling with fear. [4]When I talked with you or preached, I didn't try to prove anything by sounding wise. I simply let God's Spirit show his power. [5]That way you would have faith because of God's power and not because of human wisdom.

[6]We do use wisdom when speaking to people who are mature in their faith. But it isn't the wisdom of this world or of its rulers, who will soon disappear. [7]We speak of God's hidden and mysterious wisdom that God decided to use for our glory long before the world began. [8]The rulers of this world didn't know anything about this wisdom. If they had known about it, they would not have nailed the glorious Lord to a cross. [9]But it is just as the Scriptures say,

"What God has planned
    for people who love him
is more than eyes have seen
    or ears have heard.
It has never even
    entered our minds!"

[10]God's Spirit has shown you everything. His Spirit finds out everything, even what is deep in the mind of God. [11]You are the only one who knows what is in your own mind, and God's Spirit is the only one who knows what is in God's mind. [12]But God has given us his Spirit. That's why we don't think the same way that the people of this world think. That's also why we can recognize the blessings that God has given us.

[13]Every word we speak was taught to us by God's Spirit, not by human wisdom. And this same Spirit helps us teach spiritual things to spiritual people.[f] [14]That's why only someone who has God's Spirit can understand spiritual blessings. Anyone who

doesn't have God's Spirit thinks these blessings are foolish. [15]People who are guided by the Spirit can make all kinds of judgments, but they cannot be judged by others. [16]The Scriptures ask,

"Has anyone ever known
    the thoughts of the Lord
    or given him advice?"

But we understand what Christ is thinking.[g]

Working Together for God

3 My friends, you are acting like the people of this world. That's why I could not speak to you as spiritual people. You are like babies as far as your faith in Christ is concerned. [2]So I had to treat you like babies and feed you milk. You could not take solid food, and you still cannot, [3]because you are not yet spiritual. You are jealous and argue with each other. This proves that you are not spiritual and that you are acting like the people of this world.

[4]Some of you say that you follow me, and others claim to follow Apollos. Isn't that how ordinary people behave? [5]Apollos and I are merely servants who helped you to have faith. It was the Lord who made it all happen. [6]I planted the seeds, Apollos watered them, but God made them sprout and grow. [7]What matters isn't those who planted or watered, but God who made the plants grow. [8]The one who plants is just as important as the one who waters. And each one will be paid for what they do. [9]Apollos and I work together for God, and you are God's garden and God's building.

Only One Foundation

[10]God was kind and let me become an expert builder. I laid a foundation on which others have built. But we must each be careful how we build, [11]because Christ is the only foundation. [12-13]Whatever we build on that foundation will be tested by fire on the day of judgment. Then everyone will find out if we have used gold, silver, and precious stones, or wood, hay, and straw. [14]We will be

---

[e]2.1 *mystery:* Some manuscripts have "testimony."
[f]2.13 *teach spiritual things to spiritual people:* Or "compare spiritual things with spiritual things."
[g]2.16 *we understand what Christ is thinking:* Or "we think as Christ does."

rewarded if our building is left standing. [15]But if it is destroyed by the fire, we will lose everything. Yet we ourselves will be saved, like someone escaping from flames.

[16]All of you surely know that you are God's temple and that his Spirit lives in you. [17]Together you are God's holy temple, and God will destroy anyone who destroys his temple.

[18]Don't fool yourselves! If any of you think you are wise in the things of this world, you will have to become foolish before you can be truly wise. [19]This is because God considers the wisdom of this world to be foolish. It is just as the Scriptures say, "God catches the wise when they try to outsmart him." [20]The Scriptures also say, "The Lord knows that the plans made by wise people are useless." [21-22]So stop bragging about what anyone has done. Paul and Apollos and Peter[h] all belong to you. In fact, everything is yours, including the world, life, death, the present, and the future. Everything belongs to you, [23]and you belong to Christ, and Christ belongs to God.

The Work of the Apostles

4 Think of us as servants of Christ who have been given the work of explaining God's mysterious ways. [2]And since our first duty is to be faithful to the one we work for, [3]it doesn't matter to me if I am judged by you or even by a court of law. In fact, I don't judge myself. [4]I don't know of anything against me, but that doesn't prove that I am right. The Lord is my judge. [5]So don't judge anyone until the Lord returns. He will show what is hidden in the dark and what is in everyone's heart. Then God will be the one who praises each of us.

[6]Friends, I have used Apollos and myself as examples to teach you the meaning of the saying, "Follow the rules." I want you to stop saying that one of us is better than the other. [7]What is so special about you? What do you have that you were not given? And if it was given to you, how can you brag? [8]Are you already satisfied? Are you now rich? Have you become kings while we are still

---

[h]**3.21,22** *Peter:* See the note at 1.12.

---

*Spiritual*Life—Why is it important for me to go to church?
(*1 Corinthians 3.10-17*)

The people of a church make up God's temple.

There are many excuses people use for not going to church, among them:

"I don't like the hard pews."
"I don't like the kind of music."
"I don't get anything out of the service."
"The people there are a bunch of hypocrites."

But in this passage, Paul gives us the best reason of all for attending church: "Together you are God's holy temple" (3.17). What did he mean by that? In the Old Testament, the temple was the most important building in the nation. It was holy, because God's people had built it for him, and they went to worship him there. In the New Testament, God's temple is something altogether different. It's not a building at all. God's temple is *the people* who belong to him. Thus, when we meet together with fellow believers as a church, God is present—in the same special way God inhabited the holy temple of the Old Testament.

In addition, we need each other for encouragement and challenge. As Paul said, "I laid a foundation on which others have built. But we must each be careful how we build, because Christ is the only foundation" (3.10,11). If you're having a tough time at home, it helps to be able to talk and pray with a fellow believer. And if a friend in the church is doubting her faith, she may need your wisdom to help her sort through her life issues. Together, as God's temple, we are safe. For God promises us that he "will destroy anyone who destroys his temple" (3.17). That's a nice surety in this upside-down world! (See also Ezekiel 43.1-5; Acts 2.1-13,41-47; Romans 12.3-8; Ephesians 2.11-22.)

Words To Remember: *All of you surely know that you are God's temple and that his Spirit lives in you. Together you are God's holy temple.*—1 Corinthians 3.16,17

nobodies? I wish you were kings. Then we could have a share in your kingdom.

> *It's so important in this life that we integrate the principles of God's Word in everything we do—the kind of people we hang out with, the places we go, the words we say.*
>
> BABBIE MASON

[9]It seems to me that God has put us apostles in the worst possible place. We are like prisoners on their way to death. Angels and the people of this world just laugh at us. [10]Because of Christ we are thought of as fools, but Christ has made you wise. We are weak and hated, but you are powerful and respected. [11]Even today we go hungry and thirsty and don't have anything to wear except rags. We are mistreated and don't have a place to live. [12]We work hard with our own hands, and when people abuse us, we wish them well. When we suffer, we are patient. [13]When someone curses us, we answer with kind words. Until now we are thought of as nothing more than the trash and garbage of this world.

[14]I am not writing to embarrass you. I want to help you, just as parents help their own dear children. [15]Ten thousand people may teach you about Christ, but I am your only father. You became my children when I told you about Christ Jesus, [16]and I want you to be like me. [17]That's why I sent Timothy to you. I love him like a son, and he is a faithful servant of the Lord. Timothy will tell you what I do to follow Christ and how it agrees with what I always teach about Christ in every church.

[18]Some of you think I am not coming for a visit, and so you are bragging. [19]But if the Lord lets me come, I will soon be there. Then I will find out if the ones who are doing all this bragging really have any power. [20]God's kingdom isn't just a lot of words. It is power. [21]What do you want me to do when I arrive? Do you want me to be hard on you or to be kind and gentle?

Immoral Followers

5 I have heard terrible things about some of you. In fact, you are behaving worse than the Gentiles. A man is even sleeping with his own stepmother.[i] [2]You are proud, when you ought to feel bad enough to chase away anyone who acts like that.

[3-4]I am with you only in my thoughts. But in the name of our Lord Jesus I have already judged this man, as though I were with you in person. So when you meet together and the power of the Lord Jesus is with you, I will be there too. [5]You must then hand that man over to Satan. His body will be destroyed, but his spirit will be saved when the Lord Jesus returns.

[6]Stop being proud! Don't you know how a little yeast can spread through the whole batch of dough? [7]Get rid of the old yeast! Then you will be like fresh bread made without yeast, and that is what you are. Our Passover lamb is Christ, who has already been sacrificed. [8]So don't celebrate the festival by being evil and sinful, which is like serving bread made with yeast. Be pure and truthful and celebrate by using bread made without yeast.

[9]In my other letter[j] I told you not to have anything to do with immoral people. [10]But I wasn't talking about the people of this world. You would have to leave this world to get away from everyone who is immoral or greedy or who cheats or worships idols. [11]I was talking about your own people who are immoral or greedy or worship idols or curse others or get drunk or cheat. Don't even eat with them! [12]Why should I judge outsiders? Aren't we supposed to judge only church members? [13]God judges everyone else. The Scriptures say, "Chase away any of your own people who are evil."

Taking Each Other to Court

6 When one of you has a complaint against another, do you take your complaint to a court of sinners? Or do

---

[i]5.1 *is even sleeping with his own stepmother*: Or "has even married his own stepmother." [j]5.9 *other letter*: An unknown letter that Paul wrote to the Christians at Corinth before he wrote this one.

you take it to God's people? ²Don't you know that God's people will judge the world? And if you are going to judge the world, can't you settle small problems? ³Don't you know that we will judge angels? And if that is so, we can surely judge everyday matters. ⁴Why do you take everyday complaints to judges who are not respected by the church? ⁵I say this to your shame. Aren't any of you wise enough to act as a judge between one follower and another? ⁶Why should one of you take another to be tried by unbelievers?

⁷When one of you takes another to court, all of you lose. It would be better to let yourselves be cheated and robbed. ⁸But instead, you cheat and rob other followers.

⁹Don't you know that evil people won't have a share in the blessings of God's kingdom? Don't fool yourselves! No one who is immoral or worships idols or is unfaithful in marriage or is a pervert or behaves like a homosexual ¹⁰will share in God's kingdom. Neither will any thief or greedy person or drunkard or anyone who curses and cheats others. ¹¹Some of you used to be like that. But now the name of our Lord Jesus Christ and the power of God's Spirit have washed you and made you holy and acceptable to God.

Honor God with Your Body

¹²Some of you say, "We can do anything we want to." But I tell you that not everything is good for us. So I refuse to let anything have power over me. ¹³You also say, "Food is meant for our bodies, and our bodies are meant for food." But I tell you that God will destroy them both. We are not supposed to do indecent things with our bodies. We are to use them for the Lord who is in charge of our bodies. ¹⁴God will raise us from death by the same power that he used when he raised our Lord to life.

¹⁵Don't you know that your bodies are part of the body of Christ? Is it right for me to join part of the body of Christ to a prostitute? No, it isn't! ¹⁶Don't you know that a man who does that becomes part of her body? The Scriptures say, "The two of them will be like one person." ¹⁷But anyone who is joined to the Lord is one in spirit with him.

¹⁸Don't be immoral in matters of sex. That is a sin against your own body in a way that no other sin is. ¹⁹You surely know that your body is a temple where the Holy Spirit lives. The Spirit is in you and is a gift from God. You are no longer your own. ²⁰God paid a great price for you. So use your body to honor God.

---

*Spiritual*Life—What does God expect of me? *(1 Corinthians 6.12-20)*

Honor God with your body.

We are complex beings. We are body *and* soul. One of the heresies that plagued the early church was that mind and spirit were the important parts of a human being. The body was separate and unimportant, so God didn't care what we did with our bodies. With this viewpoint, a person could overeat or starve herself—with no harmful spiritual effect. It didn't matter what one did about sex, since sexual acts were purely physical and therefore unimportant. People express the same opinion today. They say, "If it feels good, do it. It's just physical fun."

Paul says this view is all wrong: "We are to use [our bodies] for the Lord who is in charge of our bodies" (6.13). He points out that since we are linked to Christ, what we do about sex becomes terribly important. We don't have the right to give our bodies first to one person and then to another. Our bodies already belong to Christ. His Holy Spirit lives inside our bodies (6.19). God expects us to enjoy sex, but only according to his design: in the context of marriage.

But appropriate sexual behavior isn't the only issue here. How about appropriate eating, appropriate exercise, appropriate medical care—and using our bodies to perform actions that please our Lord? Our bodies belong to him. (See also Exodus 20.1-17; Judges 5.1-11; Jeremiah 1.4-19; Micah 6.6-8; Romans 8.1-17.)

Words To Remember: *God paid a great price for you. So use your body to honor God.—1 Corinthians 6.20*

Questions about Marriage

7 Now I will answer the questions that you asked in your letter. You asked, "Is it best for people not to marry?"[k] ²Well, having your own husband or wife should keep you from doing something immoral. ³Husbands and wives should be fair with each other about having sex. ⁴A wife belongs to her husband instead of to herself, and a husband belongs to his wife instead of to himself. ⁵So don't refuse sex to each other, unless you agree not to have sex for a little while, in order to spend time in prayer. Then Satan won't be able to tempt you because of your lack of self-control. ⁶In my opinion that is what should be done, though I don't know of anything the Lord said about this matter. ⁷I wish that all of you were like me, but God has given different gifts to each of us.

⁸Here is my advice for people who have never been married and for widows. You should stay single, just as I am. ⁹But if you don't have enough self-control, then go ahead and get married. After all, it is better to marry than to burn with desire.[l]

¹⁰I instruct married couples to stay together, and this is exactly what the Lord himself taught. A wife who leaves her husband ¹¹should either stay single or go back to her husband. And a husband should not leave his wife.

¹²I don't know of anything else the Lord said about marriage. All I can do is to give you my own advice. If your wife isn't a follower of the Lord, but is willing to stay with you, don't divorce her. ¹³If your husband isn't a follower, but is willing to stay with you, don't divorce him. ¹⁴Your husband or wife who isn't a follower is made holy by having you as a mate. This also makes your children holy and keeps them from being unclean in God's sight.

¹⁵If your husband or wife isn't a follower of the Lord and decides to divorce you, then you should agree to it. You are no longer bound to that person. After all, God chose you and wants you to live at peace. ¹⁶And besides, how do you know if you will be able to save your husband or wife who isn't a follower?

Obeying the Lord at All Times

¹⁷In every church I tell the people to stay as they were when the Lord Jesus chose them and God called them to be his own. Now I say the same thing to you. ¹⁸If you are

---

[k]7.1 *people not to marry*: Or "married couples not to have sex." [l]7.9 *with desire*: Or "in the flames of hell."

MARRIAGE—What's essential for a healthy, rewarding sex life?
(1 Corinthians 7.1-5)

Keep practicing. Keep talking.

Sex isn't something one person does to another. It's a shared gift. But that sharing requires a giving up of personal freedom. According to Paul in verse 4, "A wife belongs to her husband"—not at all a surprise in that era. But Paul went on to say, "A husband belongs to his wife." This must have come as a terrible shock to men who viewed a wife as personal property.

This principle has far-reaching results. How often will we have sex? Who initiates it? What sexual practices will we choose? If a husband and wife belong to each other, these decisions are mutually agreed upon, with the goal of giving and receiving pleasure from each other.

That means talking—about sex. For many couples, that isn't easy because of their background, beliefs, or communication style. But we can't really know what our spouse wants without occasionally talking about sex, even the "when" and "how" parts. And once that discussion begins, be ready for a few surprises. Then listen, talk, and adjust. Remember—you belong to each other! (See also Genesis 1.27-31; Song of Songs 5.10-16.)

Words To Remember: *Husbands and wives should be fair with each other about having sex. A wife belongs to her husband instead of to herself, and a husband belongs to his wife instead of to himself.*—1 Corinthians 7.3,4

already circumcised, don't try to change it. If you are not circumcised, don't get circumcised. [19]Being circumcised or uncircumcised isn't really what matters. The important thing is to obey God's commands. [20]So don't try to change what you were when God chose you. [21]Are you a slave? Don't let that bother you. But if you can win your freedom, you should. [22]When the Lord chooses slaves, they become his free people. And when he chooses free people, they become slaves of Christ. [23]God paid a great price for you. So don't become slaves of anyone else. [24]Stay what you were when God chose you.

Unmarried People

[25]I don't know of anything that the Lord said about people who have never been married.[m] But I will tell you what I think. And you can trust me, because the Lord has treated me with kindness. [26]We are now going through hard times, and I think it is best for you to stay as you are. [27]If you are married, stay married. If you are not married, don't try to get married. [28]It isn't wrong to marry, even if you have never been married before. But those who marry will have a lot

of trouble, and I want to protect you from that.

[29]My friends, what I mean is that the Lord will soon come,[n] and it won't matter if you are married or not. [30]It will be all the same if you are crying or laughing, or if you are buying or are completely broke. [31]It won't make any difference how much good you are getting from this world or how much you like it. This world as we know it is now passing away.

[32]I want all of you to be free from worry. An unmarried man worries about how to please the Lord. [33]But a married man has more worries. He must worry about the things of this world, because he wants to please his wife. [34]So he is pulled in two directions. Unmarried women and women who have never been married[o] worry only about pleasing the Lord, and they keep their bodies and minds pure. But a married woman worries about the things of this world, because she wants to please her hus-

---

[m]**7.25** *people who have never been married:* Or "virgins."
[n]**7.29** *the Lord will soon come:* Or "there's not much time left" or "the time for decision comes quickly."
[o]**7.34** *women who have never been married:* Or "virgins."

MARRIAGE—What does God think about divorce? *(1 Corinthians 7.10-16)*

God wants us to be at peace with each other.

Corinth was a young church, full of new Christians. And, as in many marriages today, both partners in a marriage didn't always become Christians at the same time—or even at all. Newfound faith put a strain on marriages. The unbelieving partner saw an intense change in the person he or she had married. The believer, on the other hand, felt more compatibility with fellow believers in church. So they asked the question, "Should we divorce?"

In a mixed marriage between believer and unbeliever, Paul puts the responsibility for generosity on the Christian. If your partner wants to stay married, stay married. Paul even describes a spiritual value to that decision: "Your husband or wife who isn't a follower is made holy by having you as a mate" (7.14). But Paul doesn't advocate permanent marriage ties if the unbeliever deserted. In that case, says Paul, "You are no longer bound to that person" (7.15).

Paul's next pronouncement brings comfort to a woman distraught by the prospect of divorce and abandoned by the person who once filled her life with love: "God chose you and wants you to live at peace" (7.15).

What if the couple are both Christians? Paul teaches that they should stay together, that the husband should not leave the wife, and that a wife who leaves her husband should either stay single or go back to him (7.10,11). These strong words echo the traditional marriage blessing: "What God has joined together, let no man break asunder." (See also Malachi 2.13-16; Matthew 19.1-9; Ephesians 4.1-6.)

Words To Remember: *God chose you and wants you to live at peace.*
—1 Corinthians 7.15

band. ³⁵What I am saying is for your own good—it isn't to limit your freedom. I want to help you to live right and to love the Lord above all else.

³⁶But suppose you are engaged to someone old enough to be married, and you want her so much that all you can think about is getting married. Then go ahead and marry.^p There is nothing wrong with that. ³⁷But it is better to have self-control and to make up your mind not to marry. ³⁸It is perfectly all right to marry, but it is better not to get married at all.

³⁹A wife should stay married to her husband until he dies. Then she is free to marry again, but only to a man who is a follower of the Lord. ⁴⁰However, I think I am obeying God's Spirit when I say she would be happier to stay single.

Food Offered to Idols

8 In your letter you asked me about food offered to idols. All of us know something about this subject. But knowledge makes us proud of ourselves, while love makes us helpful to others. ²In fact, people who think they know so much don't know anything at all. ³But God has no doubts about who loves him.

⁴Even though food is offered to idols, we know that none of the idols in this world are alive. After all, there is only one God. ⁵Many things in heaven and on earth are called gods and lords, but none of them really are gods or lords. ⁶We have only one God, and he is the Father. He created everything, and we live for him. Jesus Christ is our only Lord. Everything was made by him, and by him life was given to us.

The Creator of the universe became human for us so that we might experience a relationship with him.

RAMONA CRAMER TUCKER

p7.36 But suppose you are engaged . . . go ahead and marry: Verses 36-38 may also be translated: ³⁶"If you feel that you are not treating your grown daughter right by keeping her from getting married, then let her marry. You won't be doing anything wrong. ³⁷But it is better to have self-control and make up your mind not to let your daughter get married. ³⁸It is all right for you to let her marry. But it is better if you don't let her marry at all."

SingleLife—I like being single. Is that normal? *(1 Corinthians 7.29-35)*

Sure, Paul liked it, too.
There's a certain freedom to singleness. Who else could run out late at night for a quart of pistachio ice cream—no questions asked? Or drop everything and spend six weeks in Africa on a medical service project? Or wake up in the morning without the immediate worry about the whereabouts of five or six family members?

Many single women miss the love and responsibility that come with family life. But some have adapted to what's missing and focus instead on the freedom that singleness offers. Paul spoke particularly about the freedom from worry that the single life offers. He had good reason to do so. Christians were already experiencing persecution—and much more persecution was to come. Christians would be hunted, tortured, and killed for their faith. Marriage brought greater cause for worry (and caution) than did singleness. Marriage limited what a person could do and bear for the cause of Christ. Besides, Paul pointed out, "the Lord will soon come" (7.29).

Paul couldn't know that "soon" was at least two thousand years away. But he did give us perspective on the temporariness of life. In the eternal perspective, neither marriage nor singleness is terribly important. Most important, as Paul said, is "to live right and to love the Lord above all else" (7.35). **(See also Numbers 11; Nehemiah 4; 6.15,16; Romans 14.1-12.)**

Words To Remember: *I want all of you to be free from worry. . . . Unmarried women and women who have never been married worry only about pleasing the Lord, and they keep their bodies and minds pure.—1 Corinthians 7.32,34*

[7]Not everyone knows these things. In fact, many people have grown up with the belief that idols have life in them. So when they eat meat offered to idols, they are bothered by a weak conscience. [8]But food doesn't bring us any closer to God. We are no worse off if we don't eat, and we are no better off if we do.

[9]Don't cause problems for someone with a weak conscience, just because you have the right to eat anything. [10]You know all this, and so it doesn't bother you to eat in the temple of an idol. But suppose a person with a weak conscience sees you and decides to eat food that has been offered to idols. [11]Then what you know has destroyed someone Christ died for. [12]When you sin by hurting a follower with a weak conscience, you sin against Christ. [13]So if I hurt one of the Lord's followers by what I eat, I will never eat meat as long as I live.

The Rights of an Apostle

9 I am free. I am an apostle. I have seen the Lord Jesus and have led you to have faith in him. [2]Others may think that I am not an apostle, but you are proof that I am an apostle to you.

[3]When people question me, I tell them [4]that Barnabas and I have the right to our food and drink. [5]We each have the right to marry one of the Lord's followers and to take her along with us, just as the other apostles and the Lord's brothers and Peter[q] do. [6]Are we the only ones who have to support ourselves by working at another job? [7]Do soldiers pay their own salaries? Don't people who raise grapes eat some of what they grow? Don't shepherds get milk from their own goats?

[8-9]I am not saying this on my own authority. The Law of Moses tells us not to muzzle an ox when it is grinding grain. But was God concerned only about an ox? [10]No, he wasn't! He was talking about us. This was written in the Scriptures so that all who plow and all who grind the grain will look forward to sharing in the harvest.

[11]When we told the message to you, it was like planting spiritual seed. So we have the right to accept material things as our harvest from you. [12]If others have the right to do this, we have an even greater right. But we haven't used this right of ours. We are willing to put up with anything to keep from causing trouble for the message about Christ.

[13]Don't you know that people who work in the temple make their living from what is brought to the temple? Don't you know that a person who serves at the altar is given part of what is offered? [14]In the same way, the Lord wants everyone who preaches the good news to make a living from preaching this message.

[15]But I have never used these privileges of mine, and I am not writing this because I want to start now. I would rather die than have someone rob me of the right to take pride in this. [16]I don't have any reason to brag about preaching the good news. Preaching is something God told me to do, and if I don't do it, I am doomed. [17]If I preach because I want to, I will be paid. But even if I don't want to, it is still something God has sent me to do. [18]What pay am I given? It is the chance to preach the good news free of charge and not to use the privileges that are mine because I am a preacher.

> *The continual devastation of lives from sexual misconduct would overwhelm me if it weren't for my faith in Christ. It's a battle, but if even one person changes because I've stayed faithful to Christ, it's worth it.*
>
> PATRICIA FUNDERBURK WARE

[19]I am not anyone's slave. But I have become a slave to everyone, so that I can win as many people as possible. [20]When I am with the Jews, I live like a Jew to win Jews. They are ruled by the Law of Moses, and I am not. But I live by the Law to win them. [21]And when I am with people who are not ruled by the Law, I forget about the Law to

---

[q]9.5 *Peter:* See the note at 1.12.

win them. Of course, I never really forget about the law of God. In fact, I am ruled by the law of Christ. ²²When I am with people whose faith is weak, I live as they do to win them. I do everything I can to win everyone I possibly can. ²³I do all this for the good news, because I want to share in its blessings.

A Race and a Fight

²⁴You know that many runners enter a race, and only one of them wins the prize. So run to win! ²⁵Athletes work hard to win a crown that cannot last, but we do it for a crown that will last forever. ²⁶I don't run without a goal. And I don't box by beating my fists in the air. ²⁷I keep my body under control and make it my slave, so I won't lose out after telling the good news to others.

Don't Worship Idols

10 Friends, I want to remind you that all of our ancestors walked under the cloud and went through the sea. ²This was like being baptized and becoming followers of Moses. ³All of them also ate the same spiritual food ⁴and drank the same spiritual drink, which flowed from the spiritual rock that followed them. That rock was Christ. ⁵But most of them did not please God. So they died, and their bodies were scattered all over the desert.

⁶What happened to them is a warning to keep us from wanting to do the same evil things. ⁷They worshiped idols, just as the Scriptures say, "The people sat down to eat and drink. Then they got up to dance around." So don't worship idols. ⁸Some of those people did shameful things, and in a single day about twenty-three thousand of them died. Don't do shameful things as they did. ⁹And don't try to test Christ,ʳ as some of them did and were later bitten by poisonous snakes. ¹⁰Don't even grumble, as some of them did and were killed by the destroying angel. ¹¹These things happened to them as a warning to us. All this was written in the Scriptures to teach us who live in these last days.

¹²Even if you think you can stand up to temptation, be careful not to fall. ¹³You are tempted in the same way that everyone else is tempted. But God can be trusted not to let you be tempted too much, and he will

---

ʳ10.9 *Christ*: Some manuscripts have "the Lord."

Friendship—Sometimes I feel God is asking me to befriend someone I naturally dislike or who annoys me. How can I overcome my natural inclination to avoid that friendship? (*1 Corinthians 10.31—11.1*)

Follow the example of Christ.

She drops by your home several times a week and wants you to drop everything so you can chat; she's stuck like glue to your side at every church function; she phones you every day at work with a question or concern; she's always down in the dumps. You feel smothered, and no wonder. You feel like disconnecting your phone and moving to a desert island—or strangling her. But that wouldn't be very Christian, would it?

In these verses, Paul tells us that no matter what we do (whether it's eating or drinking, as the previous verses talk about, or befriending someone), we should "always do it to honor God" (10.31). In situations of friendship (or anything else for that matter), honoring God with our actions is sometimes tough. The last thing we want to do is smile (and mean it) and take some of our precious time with someone who drives us crazy.

Then Paul hits us with a zinger, the second reason for befriending someone we naturally dislike: "I always try to please others instead of myself, in the hope that many of them will be saved" (10.33). That puts annoying, frustrating people in an eternal perspective, doesn't it?

Will you, like Paul, "follow the example of Christ"? (See also Ezekiel 2.1-7; Zechariah 4.1-10; Mark 2.13-17.)

Words To Remember: *You must follow my example, as I follow the example of Christ.*—1 Corinthians 11.1

show you how to escape from your temptations.

¹⁴My friends, you must keep away from idols. ¹⁵I am speaking to you as people who have enough sense to know what I am talking about. ¹⁶When we drink from the cup that we ask God to bless, isn't that sharing in the blood of Christ? When we eat the bread that we break, isn't that sharing in the body of Christ? ¹⁷By sharing in the same loaf of bread, we become one body, even though there are many of us.

¹⁸Aren't the people of Israel sharing in the worship when they gather around the altar and eat the sacrifices offered there? ¹⁹Am I saying that either the idols or the food sacrificed to them is anything at all? ²⁰No, I am not! That food is really sacrificed to demons and not to God. I don't want you to have anything to do with demons. ²¹You cannot drink from the cup of demons and still drink from the Lord's cup. You cannot eat at the table of demons and still eat at the Lord's table. ²²We would make the Lord jealous if we did that. And we are not stronger than the Lord.

Always Honor God

²³Some of you say, "We can do whatever we want to!" But I tell you that not everything may be good or helpful. ²⁴We should think about others and not about ourselves. ²⁵However, when you buy meat in the market, go ahead and eat it. Keep your conscience clear by not asking where the meat came from. ²⁶The Scriptures say, "The earth and everything in it belong to the Lord."

²⁷If an unbeliever invites you to dinner, and you want to go, then go. Eat whatever you are served. Don't cause a problem for someone's conscience by asking where the food came from. ²⁸⁻²⁹But if you are told that it has been sacrificed to idols, don't cause a problem by eating it. I don't mean a problem for yourself, but for the one who told you. Why should my freedom be limited by someone else's conscience? ³⁰If I give thanks for what I eat, why should anyone accuse me of doing wrong?

³¹When you eat or drink or do anything else, always do it to honor God. ³²Don't cause problems for Jews or Greeks or anyone else who belongs to God's church. ³³I always try to please others instead of myself, in the hope that many of them will be saved.

11

¹You must follow my example, as I follow the example of Christ.

Rules for Worship

²I am proud of you, because you always remember me and obey the teachings I gave you. ³Now I want you to know that Christ is the head over all men, and a man is the head over a woman. But God is the head over Christ. ⁴This means that any man who prays or prophesies with something on his head brings shame to his head.

> *It is unrealistic to ask the Lord to do in someone else's life that which we are unwilling for him to do in ours.*
>
> RUTH BELL GRAHAM

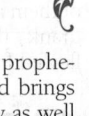

⁵But any woman who prays or prophesies without something on her head brings shame to her head. In fact, she may as well shave her head.ˢ ⁶A woman should wear something on her head. It is a disgrace for a woman to shave her head or cut her hair. But if she refuses to wear something on her head, let her cut off her hair.

⁷Men were created to be like God and to bring honor to God. This means that a man should not wear anything on his head. Women were created to bring honor to men. ⁸It was the woman who was made from a man, and not the man who was made from a woman. ⁹He wasn't created for her. She was created for him. ¹⁰And so, because of this, and also because of the angels, a woman ought to wear something on her head, as a sign of her authority.ᵗ

¹¹As far as the Lord is concerned, men and women need each other. ¹²It is true that

---

ˢ11.5 *she may as well shave her head*: A woman's hair was a mark of beauty, and it was shameful for a woman to cut her hair short or to shave her head, so that she looked like a man. ᵗ11.10 *as a sign of her authority*: Or "as a sign that she is under someone's authority."

the first woman came from a man, but all other men have been given birth by women. Yet God is the one who created everything. [13]Ask yourselves if it is proper for a woman to pray without something on her head. [14]Isn't it unnatural and disgraceful for men to have long hair? [15]But long hair is a beautiful way for a woman to cover her head. [16]This is how things are done in all of God's churches,[u] and that's why none of you should argue about what I have said.

Rules for the Lord's Supper

[17]Your worship services do you more harm than good. I am certainly not going to praise you for this. [18]I am told that you can't get along with each other when you worship, and I am sure that some of what I have heard is true. [19]You are bound to argue with each other, but it is easy to see which of you have God's approval.

[20]When you meet together, you don't really celebrate the Lord's Supper. [21]You even start eating before everyone gets to the meeting, and some of you go hungry, while others get drunk. [22]Don't you have homes where you can eat and drink? Do you hate God's church? Do you want to embarrass people who don't have anything? What can I say to you? I certainly cannot praise you.

The Lord's Supper
(Matthew 26.26-29; Mark 14.22-25; Luke 22.14-20)

[23]I have already told you what the Lord Jesus did on the night he was betrayed. And it came from the Lord himself.

He took some bread in his hands. [24]Then after he had given thanks, he broke it and said, "This is my body, which is given for you. Eat this and remember me."

[25]After the meal, Jesus took a cup of wine in his hands and said, "This is my blood, and with it God makes his new agreement with you. Drink this and remember me."

[26]The Lord meant that when you eat this bread and drink from this cup, you tell about his death until he comes.

[27]But if you eat the bread and drink the wine in a way that isn't worthy of the Lord, you sin against his body and blood. [28]That's why you must examine the way you eat and drink. [29]If you fail to understand that you

are the body of the Lord, you will condemn yourselves by the way you eat and drink. [30]That's why many of you are sick and weak and why a lot of others have died. [31]If we carefully judge ourselves, we won't be punished. [32]But when the Lord judges and punishes us, he does it to keep us from being condemned with the rest of the world.

[33]My dear friends, you should wait until everyone gets there before you start eating. [34]If you really are hungry, you can eat at home. Then you won't condemn yourselves when you meet together.

After I arrive, I will instruct you about the other matters.

Spiritual Gifts

12 My friends, you asked me about spiritual gifts. [2]I want you to remember that before you became followers of the Lord, you were led in all the wrong ways by idols that cannot even talk. [3]Now I want you to know that if you are led by God's Spirit, you will say that Jesus is Lord, and you will never curse Jesus.

[4]There are different kinds of spiritual gifts, but they all come from the same Spirit. [5]There are different ways to serve the same Lord, [6]and we can each do different things. Yet the same God works in all of us and helps us in everything we do.

[7]The Spirit has given each of us a special way of serving others. [8]Some of us can speak with wisdom, while others can speak with knowledge, but these gifts come from the same Spirit. [9]To others the Spirit has given great faith or the power to heal the sick [10]or the power to work mighty miracles. Some of us are prophets, and some of us recognize when God's Spirit is present.[v] Others can speak different kinds of languages, and still others can tell what these languages mean. [11]But it is the Spirit who does all this and decides which gifts to give to each of us.

One Body with Many Parts

[12]The body of Christ has many different parts, just as any other body does. [13]Some of

---

[u]*11.16 This is how things are done in all of God's churches:* Or "There is no set rule for this in any of God's churches." [v]*12.10 and some of us . . . present:* Or "and some of us recognize the difference between God's Spirit and other spirits."

us are Jews, and others are Gentiles. Some of us are slaves, and others are free. But God's Spirit baptized each of us and made us part of the body of Christ. Now we each drink from that same Spirit.[w]

[14]Our bodies don't have just one part. They have many parts. [15]Suppose a foot says, "I'm not a hand, and so I'm not part of the body." Wouldn't the foot still belong to the body? [16]Or suppose an ear says, "I'm not an eye, and so I'm not part of the body." Wouldn't the ear still belong to the body? [17]If our bodies were only an eye, we couldn't hear a thing. And if they were only an ear, we couldn't smell a thing. [18]But God has put all parts of our body together in the way that he decided is best.

[19]A body isn't really a body, unless there is more than one part. [20]It takes many parts to make a single body. [21]That's why the eyes cannot say they don't need the hands. That's also why the head cannot say it doesn't need the feet. [22]In fact, we cannot get along without the parts of the body that seem to be the weakest. [23]We take special care to dress up some parts of our bodies. We are modest about our personal parts, [24]but we don't have to be modest about other parts.

God put our bodies together in such a way that even the parts that seem the least important are valuable. [25]He did this to make all parts of the body work together smoothly, with each part caring about the others. [26]If one part of our body hurts, we hurt all over. If one part of our body is honored, the whole body will be happy.

[27]Together you are the body of Christ. Each one of you is part of his body. [28]First, God chose some people to be apostles and prophets and teachers for the church. But he also chose some to work miracles or heal the sick or help others or be leaders or speak different kinds of languages. [29]Not everyone is an apostle. Not everyone is a prophet. Not everyone is a teacher. Not everyone can work miracles. [30]Not everyone can heal the sick. Not everyone can speak different kinds of languages. Not everyone can tell what these languages mean. [31]I want you to desire the best gifts.[x] So I will show you a much better way.

---

[w]**12.13** *Some of us are Jews . . . that same Spirit*: Verse 13 may also be translated, "God's Spirit is inside each of us, and all around us as well. So it doesn't matter that some of us are Jews and others are Gentiles and that some are slaves and others are free. Together we are one body." [x]**12.31** *I want you to desire the best gifts*: Or "You desire the best gifts."

WORK—My husband is sometimes threatened by my career. How should I respond? *(1 Corinthians 12.1-11)*

Respect your own and your husband's skills as gifts from God.

Feeling threatened by someone else's career probably is normal in the sense that personal shortcomings are routine in a world full of imperfection. But it's not the way God designed Christians to relate to each other in the church—or in marriage.

God created his people to be individuals, not so they could fight and make each other jealous, but so they could benefit from each other's skills and gifts. The Christian church needs all sorts of talents. Paul listed wisdom, knowledge, faith, and the power to heal the sick, prophesy, work miracles, speak in languages, and interpret them. His point was not that we should tally up our skills and have contests about who's most important. His point was that we should share these spiritual gifts with each other—because they are *all* gifts from God.

The same is true in marriage. We are a gift from God to each other—and that includes our skills on and off the job. We should use these gifts for the well-being of other people, including our family and coworkers, and to serve God. At the same time, we should do all we can to respect and support our husband's skills as a gift from God. (See also Numbers 12; Luke 3.7-20.)

Words To Remember: *There are different ways to serve the same Lord, and we can each do different things. Yet the same God works in all of us and helps us in everything we do.—1 Corinthians 12.5,6*

Love

13 What if I could speak
all languages of humans
and of angels?
If I did not love others,
I would be nothing more
than a noisy gong
or a clanging cymbal.
2 What if I could prophesy
and understand all secrets
and all knowledge?
And what if I had faith
that moved mountains?
I would be nothing,
unless I loved others.
3 What if I gave away all
that I owned
and let myself
be burned alive?[y]
I would gain nothing,
unless I loved others.
4 Love is kind and patient,
never jealous, boastful,
proud, or 5rude.
Love isn't selfish
or quick tempered.
It doesn't keep a record
of wrongs that others do.

6 Love rejoices in the truth,
but not in evil.
7 Love is always supportive,
loyal, hopeful,
and trusting.
8 Love never fails!

Everyone who prophesies
will stop,
and unknown languages
will no longer
be spoken.
All that we know
will be forgotten.
9 We don't know everything,
and our prophecies
are not complete.
10 But what is perfect
will someday appear,
and what isn't perfect
will then disappear.

11 When we were children,
we thought and reasoned
as children do.

---

[y]13.3 *and let myself be burned alive*: Some manuscripts have "so that I could brag."

MARRIAGE—What does it really mean to "become one" with my husband?
(1 Corinthians 12.12-31)

You feel each other's pain and joy.
What happens if you accidentally nick your finger with a kitchen knife? Your back stiffens, your voice says "ouch," your eyes water, and your feet head for the medicine cabinet. What happens when you see your son make his first home run? Your legs suddenly put you in a standing position, your voice yells, your hands clap—and maybe your eyes water again. Joy and pain are *whole body* experiences.

It's supposed to be that way in a church, too. In his beautiful metaphor of the body of Christ, Paul talks about how various people make up the feet, hands, eyes, and head. He even talks about body parts (people) who are "least important" (12.24). His point is that it takes *all* these varied people to make up a church. Since they're really one body, if one hurts, the others should say "ouch." If one is honored, they should all be smiling. That's the way a single body works.

The same is true in a marriage. In marriage you "become one" with your husband. When he hurts, you're sad. When he's honored, you're joyful. If you're both Christians, the one body that the two of you have become symbolizes the body of Christ. In the next week, try each day to find a new way to express a "one-body" relationship with your husband. You'll be surprised what you learn—and you'll have some fun along the way, too! (See also Genesis 2.18-25; Ruth 1.15-18.)

Words To Remember: *If one part of our body hurts, we hurt all over. If one part of our body is honored, the whole body will be happy. Together you are the body of Christ.*—1 Corinthians 12.26,27

But when we grew up,
  we quit our childish ways.
¹²Now all we can see of God
  is like a cloudy picture
  in a mirror.
Later we will see him
  face to face.
We don't know everything,
  but then we will,
just as God completely
  understands us.
¹³For now there are faith,
  hope, and love.
But of these three,
  the greatest is love.

**Speaking Unknown Languages
and Prophesying**

14 Love should be your guide. Be eager to have the gifts that come from the Holy Spirit, especially the gift of prophecy. ²If you speak languages that others don't know, God will understand what you are saying, though no one else will know what you mean. You will be talking about mysteries that only the Spirit understands. ³But when you prophesy, you will be understood, and others will be

helped. They will be encouraged and made to feel better.

⁴By speaking languages that others don't know, you help only yourself. But by prophesying you help everyone in the church. ⁵I am glad for you to speak unknown languages, although I had rather for you to prophesy. In fact, prophesying does much more good than speaking unknown languages, unless someone can help the church by explaining what you mean.

⁶My friends, what good would it do, if I came and spoke unknown languages to you and didn't explain what I meant? How would I help you, unless I told you what God had shown me or gave you some knowledge or prophecy or teaching? ⁷If all musical instruments sounded alike, how would you know the difference between a flute and a harp? ⁸If a bugle call isn't clear, how would you know to get ready for battle?

⁹That's how it is when you speak unknown languages. If no one can understand what you are talking about, you will only be talking to the wind. ¹⁰There are many different languages in this world, and all of them make sense. ¹¹But if I don't understand the language that someone is using, we will be like foreigners to each other. ¹²If you really

---

SingleLife—What should I look for in a future spouse? *(1 Corinthians 13)*

Look for someone who's able to give and receive love—long term.
Love as a ticklish, cushy feeling is vastly overrated. It feels good when you're falling into it—but by the time you've gotten through a wedding and honeymoon, it may have been replaced by, "Who's going to make the coffee this morning?" and, "No, you can't take the paper to work with you; I want to read it, too." Even so, twinkle-eyed couples in their eighties testify that they still get those "I love you" feelings.

Tucked between two chapters on spiritual gifts in the church is a description of *real* love. Paul interrupted himself with the words, "I want you to desire the best gifts. So I will show you a much better way" (12.31). Then he explained how love is more than a feeling; he spoke of what love does and doesn't do, what it endures, how it lasts.

If you want the best definition of love in the world, study this poem (13.4-8). In today's world, some people seem incapable of receiving love; others have trouble giving it. Still others have a history that says, *I love for awhile, then I move on.* (If you're currently dating, a few inquiries about his family relationships and friendships will give you clues about the staying power of his love.) Meanwhile, cultivate your own ability to love as you relate to your own friends and family members.

No one is able to love this way all the time, but it's a great goal. If you find a man who seems capable of this kind of love, you may be looking at a potential husband. Only time will tell. (See also Genesis 24; Song of Songs 1; Ephesians 5.21-33.)

Words To Remember: *Love is always supportive, loyal, hopeful, and trusting. Love never fails!*—1 Corinthians 13.7,8

want spiritual gifts, choose the ones that will be most helpful to the church.

[13]When we speak languages that others don't know, we should pray for the power to explain what we mean. [14]For example, if I use an unknown language in my prayers, my spirit prays but my mind is useless. [15]Then what should I do? There are times when I should pray with my spirit, and times when I should pray with my mind. Sometimes I should sing with my spirit, and at other times I should sing with my mind.

[16]Suppose some strangers are in your worship service, when you are praising God with your spirit. If they don't understand you, how will they know to say, "Amen"? [17]You may be worshiping God in a wonderful way, but no one else will be helped. [18]I thank God that I speak unknown languages more than any of you. [19]But words that make sense can help the church. That's why in church I had rather speak five words that make sense than to speak ten thousand words in a language that others don't know.

[20]My friends, stop thinking like children. Think like mature people and be as innocent as tiny babies. [21]In the Scriptures the Lord says,

"I will use strangers
who speak unknown languages
    to talk to my people.
They will speak to them
    in foreign languages,
but still my people
    won't listen to me."

[22]Languages that others don't know may mean something to unbelievers, but not to the Lord's followers. Prophecy, on the other hand, is for followers, not for unbelievers. [23]Suppose everyone in your worship service started speaking unknown languages, and some outsiders or some unbelievers come in. Won't they think you are crazy? [24]But suppose all of you are prophesying when those unbelievers and outsiders come in. They will realize that they are sinners, and they will want to change their ways because of what you are saying. [25]They will tell what is hidden in their hearts. Then they will kneel down and say to God, "We are certain that you are with these people."

Worship Must Be Orderly

[26]My friends, when you meet to worship, you must do everything for the good of

---

Friendship—What are the marks of a good friendship? *(1 Corinthians 13.4-8)*

That you love one another.

How can you tell if someone is a good friend? You know that she's always there for you, and that she loves you—no matter what. Maybe she stayed up all night to type your term paper on the computer when you got sick. Or she listened and empathized when your date stood you up. Perhaps she's the one who drove you home after you got your wisdom teeth pulled. Or she's the one who rushed you to the hospital when you were going into labor and your husband was out of town on business. She's the one who prays with you, gives you gentle advice when you ask for it, and points out kindly when you're wrong.

Now that's a friend to be trusted—the kind of loving friend that the apostle Paul talks about in these verses.

If you want to health-test your relationship with a friend, try reading verses 4-8 aloud, inserting your friend's name in place of each mention of the word *love*. Is this true about your friend? Is his or her concept of friendship at least similar to what's in this passage? Then try inserting your own name. How do you measure up in your practice of friendship love toward him or her? Where do you need to improve? In what areas are you doing well?

If you want to have godly, healthy friendships, memorize these words. They'll help you—and your friend—become better friends! (See also Ruth 1–4; Proverbs 17.17; 18.24; Proverbs 27.17-19; James 5.13-20.)

Words To Remember: *Love is kind and patient, never jealous, boastful, proud, or rude. Love isn't selfish or quick tempered. It doesn't keep a record of wrongs that others do. Love rejoices in the truth, but not in evil. Love is always supportive, loyal, hopeful, and trusting. Love never fails!*—1 Corinthians 13.4-8

everyone there. That's how it should be when someone sings or teaches or tells what God has said or speaks an unknown language or explains what the language means. ²⁷No more than two or three of you should speak unknown languages during the meeting. You must take turns, and someone should always be there to explain what you mean. ²⁸If no one can explain, you must keep silent in church and speak only to yourself and to God.

²⁹Two or three persons may prophesy, and everyone else must listen carefully. ³⁰If someone sitting there receives a message from God, the speaker must stop and let the other person speak. ³¹Let only one person speak at a time, then all of you will learn something and be encouraged. ³²A prophet should be willing to stop and let someone else speak. ³³God wants everything to be done peacefully and in order.

When God's people meet in church, ³⁴the women must not be allowed to speak. They must keep quiet and listen, as the Law of Moses teaches. ³⁵If there is something they want to know, they can ask their husbands when they get home. It is disgraceful for women to speak in church. ³⁶God's message did not start with you people, and you are not the only ones it has reached.

³⁷If you think of yourself as a prophet or a spiritual person, you will know that I am writing only what the Lord has commanded. ³⁸So don't pay attention to anyone who ignores what I am writing. ³⁹My friends, be eager to prophesy and don't stop anyone from speaking languages that others don't know. ⁴⁰But do everything properly and in order.

Christ Was Raised to Life

15 My friends, I want you to remember the message that I preached and that you believed and trusted. ²You will be saved by this message, if you hold firmly to it. But if you don't, your faith was all for nothing.

³I told you the most important part of the message exactly as it was told to me. That part is:

Christ died for our sins,
  as the Scriptures say.
⁴He was buried,
  and three days later
he was raised to life,
  as the Scriptures say.
⁵Christ appeared to Peter,ᶻ
  then to the twelve.
⁶After this, he appeared
  to more than five hundred

ᶻ**15.5** *Peter:* See the note at 1.12.

---

*Spiritual*Life—**How can I show my devotion to God?** *(1 Corinthians 13.11-13)*

Show faith, hope, and love.

When things are going well, it's relatively easy (unless we forget because life is so good) to praise God. But when little or big events make life difficult (your refrigerator goes on the blink in the middle of summer; a truck runs a stoplight—and into your car; a close friend's child is hospitalized; a parent dies), sometimes we wonder if God is still there, and if he cares.

It's interesting that, within the context of the famous "Love passage," 1 Corinthians 13, Paul includes these verses. He points out that, on earth, we won't always know the whats, hows, and whys: "Now all we can see of God is like a cloudy picture in a mirror" and "We don't know everything" (13.12).

Not knowing why a life event is happening can be terribly frustrating. But we can use the opportunity either to turn away from God or to turn toward him. If we really want to show our devotion to God, it must be unconditional, as God's love for us is. If we just have "faith, hope, and love" (13.13), Paul promises that someday we'll see God face-to-face. Then we'll know and understand everything! **(See also 1 Kings 18; 1 Chronicles 29.1-20; Haggai 1.1-11; Acts 4.32—5.11.)**

Words To Remember: *We don't know everything, but then we will, just as God completely understands us. For now there are faith, hope, and love. But of these three, the greatest is love.—1 Corinthians 13.12,13*

other followers.
Most of them are still alive,
but some have died.
[7] He also appeared to James,
and then to all
of the apostles.

[8] Finally, he appeared to me, even though I am like someone who was born at the wrong time.[a]
[9] I am the least important of all the apostles. In fact, I caused so much trouble for God's church that I don't even deserve to be called an apostle. [10] But God was kind! He made me what I am, and his wonderful kindness wasn't wasted. I worked much harder than any of the other apostles, although it was really God's kindness at work and not me. [11] But it doesn't matter if I preached or if they preached. All of you believed the message just the same.

God's People Will Be Raised to Life

[12] If we preach that Christ was raised from death, how can some of you say that the dead will not be raised to life? [13] If they won't be raised to life, Christ himself wasn't raised to life. [14] And if Christ wasn't raised to life, our message is worthless, and so is your faith. [15] If the dead won't be raised to life, we have told lies about God by saying that he raised Christ to life, when he really did not. [16] So if the dead won't be raised to life, Christ wasn't raised to life. [17] Unless Christ was raised to life, your faith is useless, and you are still living in your sins. [18] And those people who died after putting their faith in him are completely lost. [19] If our hope in Christ is good only for this life, we are worse off than anyone else.

[20] But Christ has been raised to life! And he makes us certain that others will also be raised to life. [21] Just as we will die because of Adam, we will be raised to life because of Christ. [22] Adam brought death to all of us, and Christ will bring life to all of us. [23] But we must each wait our turn. Christ was the first to be raised to life, and his people will be raised to life when he returns. [24] Then after Christ has destroyed all powers and forces, the end will come, and he will give the kingdom to God the Father.

[25] Christ will rule until he puts all his

---

[a]15.8 *who was born at the wrong time:* The meaning of these words in Greek is not clear.

---

*Spiritual*Life—How can I learn to appreciate and use the talents and gifts God has given me? *(1 Corinthians 14.1-25)*

Point others to God.

Take stock of your skills. Are you good at baking? Are you a crack typist? Maybe accounting is your forte. How about gardening, listening to someone's emotional needs, understanding Scripture, lovingly caring for children, talking with the elderly, or reading aloud? Chances are you could use any one of these skills for the well-being of someone else and in the process point that person toward Jesus Christ.

It seemed that Christians at Corinth appreciated their own skills and gifts—but they were tempted to showcase some gifts as more important than others. In this chapter Paul talks especially about the spiritual gifts of prophesying and speaking unknown languages, both regarded as spectacular gifts from God. Slowly, carefully, Paul continued his theme present throughout the book: How can you use your skills for the good of the whole church (14.12)? Then he added another note: How can you use your skills in a way that invites others to know Jesus Christ (14.16)?

Every skill or ability we have (whether or not it rates as a "spiritual gift") comes as a present from God. We can thank him for it—and use it for his glory. (See also 1 Samuel 16.14-23; 1 Chronicles 15.1—16.3.)

Words To Remember: *But suppose all of you are prophesying when those unbelievers and outsiders come in. They will realize that they are sinners, and they will want to change their ways because of what you are saying. They will tell what is hidden in their hearts. Then they will kneel down and say to God, "We are certain that you are with these people."*—1 Corinthians 14.24,25

enemies under his power, [26]and the last enemy he destroys will be death. [27]When the Scriptures say that he will put everything under his power, they don't include God. It was God who put everything under the power of Christ. [28]After everything is under the power of God's Son, he will put himself under the power of God, who put everything under his Son's power. Then God will mean everything to everyone.

[29]If the dead are not going to be raised to life, what will people do who are being baptized for them? Why are they being baptized for those dead people? [30]And why do we always risk our lives [31]and face death every day? The pride that I have in you because of Christ Jesus our Lord is what makes me say this. [32]What do you think I gained by fighting wild animals in Ephesus? If the dead are not raised to life,

> "Let's eat and drink.
>   Tomorrow we die."

[33]Don't fool yourselves. Bad friends will destroy you. [34]Be sensible and stop sinning. You should be embarrassed that some people still don't know about God.

What Our Bodies Will Be Like

[35]Some of you have asked, "How will the dead be raised to life? What kind of bodies will they have?" [36]Don't be foolish. A seed must die before it can sprout from the ground. [37]Wheat seeds and all other seeds look different from the sprouts that come up. [38]This is because God gives everything the kind of body he wants it to have. [39]People, animals, birds, and fish are each made of flesh, but none of them are alike. [40]Everything in the heavens has a body, and so does everything on earth. But each one is very different from all the others. [41]The sun isn't like the moon, the moon isn't like the stars, and each star is different.

[42]That's how it will be when our bodies are raised to life. These bodies will die, but the bodies that are raised will live forever. [43]These ugly and weak bodies will become beautiful and strong. [44]As surely as there are physical bodies, there are spiritual bodies. And our physical bodies will be changed into spiritual bodies.

[45]The first man was named Adam, and the Scriptures tell us that he was a living person. But Jesus, who may be called the last Adam, is a life-giving spirit. [46]We see that

---

PARENTING&family—How can I know what's best for my elderly parents? *(1 Corinthians 15.35-58)*

Accept the aging process—even death.

Try to see the disabilities of aging through the eyes of your parents: Arthritis eats at your joints. Teeth go bad. You can't hear or see as well as you used to. Mysterious pains play hide-and-seek throughout your frame. Even your mind gets foggy and at the most embarrassing moments. You look in the mirror and think, *Who is that old lady looking back at me?* A trip to the grocery store becomes an expedition requiring most of your energy for the day. Yet you remember when groceries were something you took care of between one kid's soccer practice and the other's trumpet lesson. Worst of all, you know your physical failings will get worse before they get better.

Help your parents accept their limitations with creativity and humor—and even prepare for death. Then focus on the "better." First Corinthians 15 offers a triumphant picture of victory over death. "Christ has been raised to life! And he makes us certain that others will also be raised to life" (15.20). Paul described the hope of healthy new bodies, fit for eternity with Jesus. If we can help our parents accept that physical disabilities are temporary and even death a brief (if fearsome) interlude aimed toward eternity, we can help them age with dignity, grace, and hope. (See also Psalm 25; Proverbs 23.22-25; Joel 2.28-32; 1 Timothy 5.1-7.)

Words To Remember: *These bodies will die, but the bodies that are raised will live forever. These ugly and weak bodies will become beautiful and strong. . . . Then the Scriptures will come true, "Death has lost the battle! Where is its victory? Where is its sting?"*—1 Corinthians 15.42,43,54,55

the one with a spiritual body did not come first. He came after the one who had a physical body. ⁴⁷The first man was made from the dust of the earth, but the second man came from heaven. ⁴⁸Everyone on earth has a body like the body of the one who was made from the dust of the earth. And everyone in heaven has a body like the body of the one who came from heaven. ⁴⁹Just as we are like the one who was made out of earth, we will be like the one who came from heaven.

⁵⁰My friends, I want you to know that our bodies of flesh and blood will decay. This means that they cannot share in God's kingdom, which lasts forever. ⁵¹I will explain a mystery to you. Not every one of us will die, but we will all be changed. ⁵²It will happen suddenly, quicker than the blink of an eye. At the sound of the last trumpet the dead will be raised. We will all be changed, so that we will never die again. ⁵³Our dead and decaying bodies will be changed into bodies that won't die or decay. ⁵⁴The bodies we now have are weak and can die. But they will be changed into bodies that are eternal. Then the Scriptures will come true,

> "Death has lost the battle!
> ⁵⁵Where is its victory?
>   Where is its sting?"

⁵⁶Sin is what gives death its sting, and the Law is the power behind sin. ⁵⁷But thank God for letting our Lord Jesus Christ give us the victory!

⁵⁸My dear friends, stand firm and don't be shaken. Always keep busy working for the Lord. You know that everything you do for him is worthwhile.

A Collection for God's People

16 When you collect money for God's people, I want you to do exactly what I told the churches in Galatia to do. ²That is, each Sunday each of you must put aside part of what you have earned. If you do this, you won't have to take up a collection when I come. ³Choose some followers to take the money to Jerusalem. I will send them on with the money and with letters which show that you approve of them. ⁴If you think I should go along, they can go with me.

Paul's Travel Plans

⁵After I have gone through Macedonia, I hope to see you ⁶and visit with you for a while. I may even stay all winter, so that you can help me on my way to wherever I will be going next. ⁷If the Lord lets me, I would rather come later for a longer visit than to stop off now for only a short visit. ⁸I will stay in Ephesus until Pentecost, ⁹because there is a wonderful opportunity for me to do some work here. But there are also many people who are against me.

¹⁰When Timothy arrives, give him a friendly welcome. He is doing the Lord's work, just as I am. ¹¹Don't let anyone mistreat him. I am looking for him to return to me together with the other followers. So when he leaves, send him off with your blessings.

¹²I have tried hard to get our friend Apollos to visit you with the other followers. He doesn't want to come just now, but he will come when he can.

Personal Concerns and Greetings

¹³Keep alert. Be firm in your faith. Stay brave and strong. ¹⁴Show love in everything you do.

¹⁵You know that Stephanas and his family were the first in Achaia to have faith in the Lord. They have done all they can for God's people. My friends, I ask you ¹⁶to obey leaders like them and to do the same for all others who work hard with you.

¹⁷I was glad to see Stephanas and Fortunatus and Achaicus. Having them here was like having you. ¹⁸They made me feel much better, just as they made you feel better. You should appreciate people like them.

¹⁹Greetings from the churches in Asia.

Aquila and Priscilla, together with the church that meets in their house, send greetings in the name of the Lord.

²⁰All of the Lord's followers send their greetings.

Give each other a warm greeting.

²¹I am signing this letter myself: PAUL.

²²I pray that God will put a curse on everyone who doesn't love the Lord. And may the Lord come soon.

²³I pray that the Lord Jesus will be kind to you.

²⁴I love everyone who belongs to Christ Jesus.

Priscilla

Acts 18; Romans 16.1-5; 1 Corinthians 16.19,20

What can happen if a woman uses her home as a center for work, hospitality, and ministry? What can happen if that woman is a gifted teacher—as is her husband? This is Priscilla's story.

We first read of Priscilla and Aquila in Acts 18. As Jews, they had just arrived in Corinth as exiles from Rome. In Corinth, they set up their tentmaking business and soon became acquainted with another tentmaker named Paul, whom they invited into their home. Their house guest stayed for a year and a half! We can only imagine the conversations of these three early Christians as they sat around the fire late at night. Inspired by God, they sharpened each other's thinking in a way that helped Paul in his extensive Christian missionary work.

When Paul left Corinth, Priscilla and Aquila left with him—but went only as far as Ephesus, while Paul went back to Jerusalem. They stayed in Ephesus, established a church in their home, and prepared people there for Paul's return. Meanwhile a learned and fervent speaker named Apollos arrived from Egypt. Priscilla and Aquila invited him to their home and "helped him understand God's Way even better" (Acts 18.26). Apollos continued his trip, a more capable missionary than ever. By the time Paul returned to Ephesus, Priscilla and Aquila were back at Rome and had a church meeting in their home.

Two of Paul's letters speak of Priscilla and Aquila. He says that they risked their lives for him and that they "served Christ Jesus together with me" (Romans 16.3). Priscilla didn't see her home as her own private space. She saw it as a center for ministry. Whether Priscilla was instructing a fiery but misguided missionary, putting up with the mess from church meetings, making tents, or moving on to a new home where she would do the same again, she used her home for the cause of Christ. And through it all, she and Aquila, her husband, were side by side. They were a team.

What can we learn from Priscilla's story? We can imitate her by holding loosely to our possessions. Whether "home" is an estate, a dorm room, or a two-room apartment, we can share what is ours with God's people and with those who need to hear about him. When we're tempted to think of our time as even more valuable than our possessions, we can share that, too. And when we must move on because we're needed elsewhere, we can pack up what we need, leave the rest, and go where the next assignment takes us.

2 Corinthians

Spring Cleaning for the Soul

At the top of Acro-Corinthus, a mountain that rose over 1,800 feet to the south of Corinth, stood the temple of Aphrodite, goddess of love—a fitting idol for the city! With Corinth's general reputation as a sensual playground, we can see why the young church there struggled with difficult issues about appropriate behavior for followers of Christ. But Corinth was also a hub for commerce and communication; anything that caught on there was sure to spread. Paul recognized how strategic Corinth was for the cause of the gospel, so he went there to preach Christ crucified for our sins, then promised to come back as soon as he could.

A few years later, Paul was ready to return. But having heard about some serious problems in the church, he wrote ahead to address the issues head-on. Second Corinthians is the most personal of all his letters. That's because here he makes an autobiographical case for being a true apostle of Jesus Christ (12.12). Certain false teachers (5.12; 11.13) accused Paul of being an impostor (10.2) who was simply pocketing the money collected for impoverished believers in Jerusalem (2.17; 7.1,2). Paul wrote to rebuke such notions and to give the church time to do some spiritual house cleaning before he arrived (13.10).

With this letter, you can do a little spiritual "spring cleaning" of your own. Are people questioning your calling to serve the church as a leader? You'll appreciate knowing from where Paul derived his identity and confidence (1.1,12; 3.4-6). Have you been falsely accused or your motives questioned? Paul's perspective on his circumstances (4.17,18; 6.3-11) and his deep love for God's people (1.3-5;

1.23—2.4) will encourage (and challenge!) you. Are you suffering because you follow Jesus? Paul testified that God helps his children stand firm in faith and continue to obey him (4.7-16). Are you sad? Paul promised, "The Father is a merciful God, who always gives us comfort" (1.3).

As you read 2 Corinthians, keep two things in mind. First, epistles should be read just as you read your personal mail, from beginning to end in one sitting. Their message only makes sense when viewed as a whole. Second, a text cannot mean what it could not have meant to its author or readers. We all tend to read into Scripture our own experience, upbringing, or church tradition. But if you look for what Paul meant to say to the particular readers of his era, you won't be tempted to impose your assumptions on the passage.

2 Corinthians at a Glance

1. The value of suffering and God's deliverance (1.1-11)

2. Why Paul changed his plans (1.12—2.17)
3. The difference between the ministry of the Law and the ministry of the Spirit (3)
4. God can turn our weakness into his strength (4)
5. Life in the new age (5.1-18)
6. Paul's apostolic ministry abroad and in Corinth (5.19—9.15)
7. Paul's case for being an apostle and his warning to all self-appointed apostles (10–13)

---

1 From Paul, chosen by God to be an apostle of Jesus Christ, and from Timothy, who is also a follower.
To God's church in Corinth and to all of God's people in Achaia.
²I pray that God our Father and the Lord Jesus Christ will be kind to you and will bless you with peace!

Paul Gives Thanks

³Praise God, the Father of our Lord Jesus Christ! The Father is a merciful God, who always gives us comfort. ⁴He comforts us when we are in trouble, so that we can share that same comfort with others in trouble. ⁵We share in the terrible sufferings of Christ, but also in the wonderful comfort he gives. ⁶We suffer in the hope that you will be comforted and saved. And because we are comforted, you will also be comforted, as you patiently endure suffering like ours. ⁷You never disappoint us. You suffered as much as we did, and we know that you will be comforted as we were.

⁸My friends, I want you to know what a hard time we had in Asia. Our sufferings were so horrible and so unbearable that death seemed certain. ⁹In fact, we felt sure that we were going to die. But this made us stop trusting in ourselves and start trusting God, who raises the dead to life. ¹⁰God saved us from the threat of death,ᵃ and we are sure that he will do it again and again. ¹¹Please help us by praying for us. Then many people will give thanks for the blessings we receive in answer to all these prayers.

ᵃ1.10 *the threat of death*: Some manuscripts have "many threats of death."

Friendship—How can I encourage a friend who is going through a divorce?
(2 Corinthians 1.3-7)

Draw on the comfort God has given you.
Divorce can bring grief so intense that it resembles the grief of a family death. (Some women who have gone through both insist that divorce is worse.) You'll need to draw on your own times of sorrow, whether it's sorrow over past sin or over losses you've suffered. Try to remember how God and his followers comforted you. Then pass on the comfort you received.

There's nothing like having come through a dark time to give confidence to a friend who's in the middle of one. Listen respectfully to any doubts she expresses about God, any sorrow she feels, or her fears for the future. As you do this, you demonstrate how God still loves her and will walk with her through her time of trouble (1.3,4).

Sometimes the most comforting thing you can do for a friend is simply to be available and to let her express her pain and fear without judgment. She's going through a time when tunnel vision may take over, and her perspective may be temporarily lost. So listen with one ear tuned to wisdom from God. As you offer comfort, expect God to continue to bring new levels of meaning and healing to your own experiences with suffering. (See also Job 13.5-15; Isaiah 43.2-4; Isaiah 61.1-3.)

Words To Remember: *Praise God, the Father of our Lord Jesus Christ! The Father is a merciful God, who always gives us comfort. He comforts us when we are in trouble, so that we can share that same comfort with others in trouble.*
—2 Corinthians 1.3,4

Paul's Change of Plans

[12]We can be proud of our clear conscience. We have always lived honestly and sincerely, especially when we were with you. And we were guided by God's wonderful kindness instead of by the wisdom of this world. [13]I am not writing anything you cannot read and understand. I hope you will understand it completely, [14]just as you already partly understand us. Then when our Lord Jesus returns, you can be as proud of us as we are of you.

[15]I was so sure of your pride in us that I had planned to visit you first of all. In this way you would have the blessing of two visits from me. [16]Once on my way to Macedonia and again on my return from there. Then you could send me on to Judea. [17]Do you think I couldn't make up my mind about what to do? Or do I seem like someone who says "Yes" or "No" simply to please others? [18]God can be trusted, and so can I, when I say that our answer to you has always been "Yes" and never "No." [19]This is because Jesus Christ the Son of God is always "Yes" and never "No." And he is the one that Silas,[b] Timothy, and I told you about.

[20]Christ says "Yes" to all of God's promises. That's why we have Christ to say "Amen"[c] for us to the glory of God. [21]And so God makes it possible for you and us to stand firmly together with Christ. God is also the one who chose us [22]and put his Spirit in our hearts to show that we belong only to him.

[23]God is my witness that I stayed away from Corinth, just to keep from being hard on you. [24]We are not bosses who tell you what to believe. We are working with you to make you glad, because your faith is strong.

2 I have decided not to make my next visit with you so painful. [2]If I make you feel bad, who would be left to cheer me up, except the people I had made to feel bad? [3]The reason I want to be happy is to make you happy. I wrote as I did because I didn't want to visit you and be made to feel bad, when you should make me feel happy. [4]At the time I wrote, I was suffering terribly. My eyes were full of tears, and my heart was broken. But I didn't want to make you feel bad. I only wanted to let you know how much I cared for you.

---

[b]1.19 Silas: The Greek text has "Silvanus," which is another form of the name Silas. [c]1.20 Amen: The word "amen" is used here with the meaning of "yes."

Friendship—What's the best way to find friends? (2 Corinthians 2.14-17)

Look for people who are "being saved."

For many people, coming to Christ is a gradual process. They hear a few words about Jesus and like what they hear. They read a brief passage of Scripture, and it "rings true" to them. They meet a person who is a Christian and long for that added *something* to their life. What happens after that?

In this section of his letter to the church at Corinth, Paul said Christians are like perfume (2.15,16). But not everyone likes that scent. Some people even think it stinks. But for those who are "being saved," the fragrance of Christian faith is like a magnet. These people are ready for a Christian friend whom God can use to continue to draw that person into his family.

We all tend to gravitate toward people who are like us (similar educational, economic, and religious backgrounds), but such a narrow understanding of relationship isn't what Paul had in mind. He saw Christians as people who lead others "to a better life" (2.15).

Are you living your life in open gratitude to God in front of the checkout person, your coworker, your son's baseball coach? If you are, you'll be the sweet smell of perfume that God intends you to be. And those whom God is calling to faith will be drawn to you because of your example—the best basis for friendship anyway! (See also 1 Kings 19.1-21; Revelation 7.9-12.)

Words To Remember: *God thinks of us as a perfume that brings Christ to everyone. For people who are being saved, this perfume has a sweet smell and leads them to a better life.*—2 Corinthians 2.15,16

Forgiveness

⁵I don't want to be hard on you. But if one of you has made someone feel bad, I am not really the one who has been made to feel bad. Some of you are the ones. ⁶Most of you have already pointed out the wrong that person did, and that is punishment enough for what was done.

⁷When people sin, you should forgive and comfort them, so they won't give up in despair. ⁸You should make them sure of your love for them.

⁹I also wrote because I wanted to test you and find out if you would follow my instructions. ¹⁰I will forgive anyone you forgive. Yes, for your sake and with Christ as my witness, I have forgiven whatever needed to be forgiven. ¹¹I have done this to keep Satan from getting the better of us. We all know what goes on in his mind.

¹²When I went to Troas to preach the good news about Christ, I found that the Lord had already prepared the way. ¹³But I was worried when I didn't find my friend Titus there. So I left the other followers and went on to Macedonia.

¹⁴I am grateful that God always makes it possible for Christ to lead us to victory. God also helps us spread the knowledge about Christ everywhere, and this knowledge is like the smell of perfume. ¹⁵-¹⁶In fact, God thinks of us as a perfume that brings Christ to everyone. For people who are being saved, this perfume has a sweet smell and leads them to a better life. But for people who are lost, it has a bad smell and leads them to a horrible death.

No one really has what it takes to do this work. ¹⁷A lot of people try to get rich from preaching God's message. But we are God's sincere messengers, and by the power of Christ we speak our message with God as our witness.

God's New Agreement

3 Are we once again bragging about ourselves? Do we need letters to you or from you to tell others about us? Some people do need letters that tell about them. ²But you are our letter, and you are in our*ᵈ* hearts for everyone to read and understand. ³You are like a letter written by Christ and delivered by us. But you are not written with pen and ink or on tablets made of stone. You are written in our hearts by the Spirit of the living God.

⁴We are sure about all this. Christ makes us sure in the very presence of God. ⁵We don't have the right to claim that we have done anything on our own. God gives us what it takes to do all that we do. ⁶He makes us worthy to be the servants of his new agreement that comes from the Holy Spirit and not from a written Law. After all, the Law brings death, but the Spirit brings life.

⁷The Law of Moses brought only the promise of death, even though it was carved on stones and given in a wonderful way. Still the Law made Moses' face shine so brightly that the people of Israel could not look at it, even though it was a fading glory. ⁸So won't the agreement that the Spirit brings to us be even more wonderful? ⁹If something that brings the death sentence is glorious, won't something that makes us acceptable to God be even more glorious? ¹⁰In fact, the new agreement is so wonderful that the Law is no longer glorious at all. ¹¹The Law was given with a glory that faded away. But the glory of the new agreement is much greater, because it will never fade away.

> *I'm convinced the more we become like Jesus and raise our children to be like Jesus, the better influence we'll be in our community, country, and the world.*
>
> KARYN HENLEY

¹²This wonderful hope makes us feel like speaking freely. ¹³We are not like Moses. His face was shining, but he covered it to keep the people of Israel from seeing the brightness fade away. ¹⁴The people were stubborn, and something still keeps them from seeing the truth when the Law is read. Only Christ can take away the covering that keeps them from seeing.

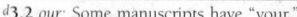

*ᵈ*3.2 *our:* Some manuscripts have "your."

¹⁵When the Law of Moses is read, they have their minds covered over ¹⁶with a covering that is removed only for those who turn to the Lord. ¹⁷The Lord and the Spirit are one and the same, and the Lord's Spirit sets us free. ¹⁸So our faces are not covered. They show the bright glory of the Lord, as the Lord's Spirit makes us more and more like our glorious Lord.

Treasure in Clay Jars

4 God has been kind enough to trust us with this work. That's why we never give up. ²We don't do shameful things that must be kept secret. And we don't try to fool anyone or twist God's message around. God is our witness that we speak only the truth, so others will be sure that we can be trusted. ³If there is anything hidden about our message, it is hidden only to someone who is lost.

⁴The god who rules this world has blinded the minds of unbelievers. They cannot see the light, which is the good news about our glorious Christ, who shows what God is like. ⁵We are not preaching about ourselves. Our message is that Jesus Christ is Lord. He also sent us to be your servants. ⁶The Scriptures say, "God commanded light to shine in the dark." Now God is shining in our hearts to let you know that his glory is seen in Jesus Christ.

⁷We are like clay jars in which this treasure is stored. The real power comes from God and not from us. ⁸We often suffer, but we are never crushed. Even when we don't know what to do, we never give up. ⁹In times of trouble, God is with us, and when we are knocked down, we get up again. ¹⁰⁻¹¹We face death every day because of Jesus. Our bodies show what his death was like, so that his life can also be seen in us. ¹²This means that death is working in us, but life is working in you.

¹³In the Scriptures it says, "I spoke because I had faith." We have that same kind of faith. So we speak ¹⁴because we know that God raised the Lord Jesus to life. And just as God raised Jesus, he will also raise us to life. Then he will bring us into his presence together with you. ¹⁵All of this has been done for you, so that more and more people will know how kind God is and will praise and honor him.

Faith in the Lord

¹⁶We never give up. Our bodies are gradually dying, but we ourselves are being

---

WORK—What's a good way for me to share my faith at work?
(2 Corinthians 4.1-15)

Remember you are a clay jar—with treasure inside.
It's easy to get caught up with the idea that when we share our faith, we're really sharing ourselves. In other words, if I'm not perfect (or nearly so), I'd better keep my mouth shut. And work has a way of bringing out our imperfections. Paul's epistle helps us with that problem. He says in essence, "You are no big showpiece; you are only a clay jar." "But," he continues, "you have treasure inside!" (4.7). It's the treasure of Jesus Christ that we are to share.

On the surface, Paul's formula for evangelism sounds easy: Point people to Christ. But there's a catch. We are to model the same willingness to suffer and serve that Christ showed us (4.11). Those around us will know God is real because transformed sinners like us are living proof! True discipleship is costly, but it's worth every penny.

Do you pray for your boss or coworkers to know Christ? Have you spent time getting to know them personally so you can better understand why they've not yet trusted him? Depending on your situation, you might invite someone to church, start a weekly Bible study, or let a particular coworker know you've been praying for that difficult situation she told you about weeks ago. You don't need to be "spiritual" or share anything flashy—just offer genuine, humble caring, for Christ's sake. (See also 1 Thessalonians 4.9-12; 1 Timothy 5.17—6.2; 2 Timothy 1.6-14.)

Words To Remember: *We are like clay jars in which this treasure is stored. The real power comes from God and not from us.*—2 Corinthians 4.7

made stronger each day. [17]These little troubles are getting us ready for an eternal glory that will make all our troubles seem like nothing. [18]Things that are seen don't last forever, but things that are not seen are eternal. That's why we keep our minds on the things that cannot be seen.

5 Our bodies are like tents that we live in here on earth. But when these tents are destroyed, we know that God will give each of us a place to live. These homes will not be buildings that someone has made, but they are in heaven and will last forever. [2]While we are here on earth, we sigh because we want to live in that heavenly home. [3]We want to put it on like clothes and not be naked.

[4]These tents we now live in are like a heavy burden, and we groan. But we don't do this just because we want to leave these bodies that will die. It is because we want to change them for bodies that will never die. [5]God is the one who makes all of this possible. He has given us his Spirit to make us certain that he will do it. [6]So always be cheerful!

As long as we are in these bodies, we are away from the Lord. [7]But we live by faith, not by what we see. [8]We should be cheerful, because we would rather leave these bodies and be at home with the Lord. [9]But whether we are at home with the Lord or away from him, we still try our best to please him. [10]Af-

ter all, Christ will judge each of us for the good or the bad that we do while living in these bodies.

Bringing People to God

[11]We know what it means to respect the Lord, and we encourage everyone to turn to him. God himself knows what we are like, and I hope you also know what kind of people we are. [12]We are not trying once more to brag about ourselves. But we want you to be proud of us, when you are with those who are not sincere and brag about what others think of them.

[13]If we seem out of our minds, it is between God and us. But if we are in our right minds, it is for your good. [14]We are ruled by Christ's love for us. We are certain that if one person died for everyone else, then all of us have died. [15]And Christ did die for all of us. He died so we would no longer live for ourselves, but for the one who died and was raised to life for us.

[16]We are careful not to judge people by what they seem to be, though we once judged Christ in that way. [17]Anyone who belongs to Christ is a new person. The past is forgotten, and everything is new. [18]God has done it all! He sent Christ to make peace between himself and us, and he has given us the work of making peace between himself and others.

[19]What we mean is that God was in

Friendship—How can I reach out to people who differ from me in habits, faith, culture, or race? *(2 Corinthians 5.16-21)*

Focus on what you have in common—a need for Christ.

What Christ accomplished on the cross not only affects our relationship with God, but also our relationships with other people. Paul says, "We are careful not to judge people by what they seem to be" (5.16). The transformation that took place in us at conversion was something like spiritual eye surgery. The fog is lifted! Because Christ forgives us, we're able to view others with generosity instead of judgment. Further, God gives us the mission of "making peace between himself and others" (5.18). That peace comes through relationship with Jesus Christ.

And if Christ reached out to you (despite your different culture and race, not to mention your sin), you shouldn't feel threatened by different kinds of people (5.19). You at least have sin in common—the profound leveler of all human differences! If you reach out to people with the understanding of what you have in common (a need for God's forgiveness), the differences will seem far less daunting. (See also John 4.4-26; Romans 3.21-31; Galatians 3.26-29; Colossians 4.2-6.)

Words To Remember: *Anyone who belongs to Christ is a new person. The past is forgotten, and everything is new.*—2 Corinthians 5.17

Christ, offering peace and forgiveness to the people of this world. And he has given us the work of sharing his message about peace. [20]We were sent to speak for Christ, and God is begging you to listen to our message. We speak for Christ and sincerely ask you to make peace with God. [21]Christ never sinned! But God treated him as a sinner, so that Christ could make us acceptable to God.

6 We work together with God, and we beg you to make good use of God's kindness to you. [2]In the Scriptures God says,

"When the time came,
　　I listened to you,
and when you needed help,
　　I came to save you."

That time has come. This is the day for you to be saved.

[3]We don't want anyone to find fault with our work, and so we try hard not to cause problems. [4]But in everything and in every way we show that we truly are God's servants. We have always been patient, though we have had a lot of trouble, suffering, and hard times. [5]We have been beaten, put in jail, and hurt in riots. We have worked hard and have gone without sleep or food. [6]But we have kept ourselves pure and have been understanding, patient, and kind. The Holy Spirit has been with us, and our love has

been real. [7]We have spoken the truth, and God's power has worked in us. In all our struggles we have said and done only what is right.

[8]Whether we were honored or dishonored or praised or cursed, we always told the truth about ourselves. But some people said we did not. [9]We are unknown to others, but well known to you. We seem to be dying, and yet we are still alive. We have been punished, but never killed, [10]and we are always happy, even in times of suffering. Although we are poor, we have made many people rich. And though we own nothing, everything is ours.

[11]Friends in Corinth, we are telling the truth when we say that there is room in our hearts for you. [12]We are not holding back on our love for you, but you are holding back on your love for us. [13]I speak to you as I would speak to my own children. Please make room in your hearts for us.

The Temple of the Living God

[14]Stay away from people who are not followers of the Lord! Can someone who is good get along with someone who is evil? Are light and darkness the same? [15]Is Christ a friend of Satan?[e] Can people who follow

---

[e]**6.15** *Satan*: The Greek text has "Beliar," which is another form of the Hebrew word "Belial," meaning "wicked" or "useless." The Jewish people sometimes used this as a name for Satan.

Friendship—How can I tell if a friendship is unhealthy? *(2 Corinthians 6.14-18)*

By looking at your commitment to Christ.
Having just talked about the "ministry of reconciliation" we have as Christ's ambassadors (5.11—6.10), Paul now sets certain limits on our relationships with unbelievers. Paul doesn't name specific issues such as marriage; the Bible addresses that concern elsewhere. He does say that, as a general rule, you must decide whether certain alliances and experiences with unbelievers will weaken your commitment to Christ.

In Corinth, idol worship was a fundamental part of life. Since Christ lived in the Corinthian believers, they had to make a complete break with their culture. Paul's language is strong because the stakes are high (5.15). Do certain friendships, relatives, or jobs cause you to dishonor God or compromise your commitment to him? Prayerfully consider who and what you're involved in. Ask advice from wise, believing friends for perspective and support. God promises to bless you for honoring him above all others. That blessing comes in this life—and the next. (See also Psalm 1; Proverbs 4.14,15; Proverbs 22.24,25.)

Words To Remember: *Stay away from people who are not followers of the Lord! Can someone who is good get along with someone who is evil? Are light and darkness the same? . . . We are the temple of the living God.*—2 Corinthians 6.14,16

the Lord have anything in common with those who don't? [16]Do idols belong in the temple of God? We are the temple of the living God, as God himself says,

> "I will live with these people
> and walk among them.
> I will be their God,
> and they will be
> my people."

[17]The Lord also says,

> "Leave them and stay away!
> Don't touch anything
> that isn't clean.
> Then I will welcome you
> [18]   and be your Father.
> You will be my sons
> and my daughters,
> as surely as I am God,
> the All-Powerful."

7 My friends, God has made us these promises. So we should stay away from everything that keeps our bodies and spirits from being clean. We should honor God and try to be completely like him.

The Church Makes Paul Happy

[2]Make a place for us in your hearts! We haven't mistreated or hurt anyone. We haven't cheated anyone. [3]I am not saying this to be hard on you. But, as I have said before, you will always be in our thoughts, whether we live or die. [4]I trust you completely.[j] I am always proud of you, and I am greatly encouraged. In all my trouble I am still very happy.

[5]After we came to Macedonia, we didn't have any chance to rest. We were faced with all kinds of problems. We were troubled by enemies and troubled by fears. [6]But God cheers up people in need, and that is what he did when he sent Titus to us. [7]Of course, we were glad to see Titus, but what really made us glad is the way you cheered him up. He told how sorry you were and how concerned you were about me. And this made me even happier.

[8]I don't feel bad anymore, even though my letter[g] hurt your feelings. I did feel bad at first, but I don't now. I know that the letter hurt you for a while. [9]Now I am happy, but

not because I hurt your feelings. It is because God used your hurt feelings to make you turn back to him, and none of you were harmed by us. [10]When God makes you feel sorry enough to turn to him and be saved, you don't have anything to feel bad about. But when this world makes you feel sorry, it can cause your death.

[11]Just look what God has done by making you feel sorry! You sincerely want to prove that you are innocent. You are angry. You are shocked. You are eager to see that justice is done. You have proved that you were completely right in this matter. [12]When I wrote you, it wasn't to accuse the one who was wrong or to take up for the one who was hurt. I wrote, so that God would show you how much you do care for us. [13]And we were greatly encouraged.

Although we were encouraged, we felt even better when we saw how happy Titus was, because you had shown that he had nothing to worry about. [14]We had told him how much we thought of you, and you did not disappoint us. Just as we have always told you the truth, so everything we told him about you has also proved to be true. [15]Titus loves all of you very much, especially when he remembers how you obeyed him and how you trembled with fear when you welcomed him. [16]It makes me really glad to know that I can depend on you.

Generous Giving

8 My friends, we want you to know that the churches in Macedonia[h] have shown others how kind God is. [2]Although they were going through hard times and were very poor, they were glad to give generously. [3]They gave as much as they could afford and even more, simply because they wanted to. [4]They even asked and begged us to let them have the joy of giving their money for God's people. [5]And they did more than we had hoped. They gave themselves first to the Lord and then to us, just as God wanted them to do.

[6]Titus was the one who got you started

---

[j]7.4 *I trust you completely*: Or "I have always spoken the truth to you" or "I can speak freely to you."   [g]7.8 *my letter*: There is no copy of this letter that Paul wrote to the church at Corinth.   [h]8.1 *churches in Macedonia*: The churches that Paul had started in Philippi and Thessalonica. The church in Berea is probably also meant.

doing this good thing, so we begged him to have you finish what you had begun. [7]You do everything better than anyone else. You have stronger faith. You speak better and know more. You are eager to give, and you love us better.[i] Now you must give more generously than anyone else.

[8]I am not ordering you to do this. I am simply testing how real your love is by comparing it with the concern that others have shown. [9]You know that our Lord Jesus Christ was kind enough to give up all his riches and become poor, so that you could become rich.

[10]A year ago you were the first ones to give, and you gave because you wanted to. So listen to my advice. [11]I think you should finish what you started. If you give according to what you have, you will prove that you are as eager to give as you were to think about giving. [12]It doesn't matter how much you have. What matters is how much you are willing to give from what you have.

[13]I am not trying to make life easier for others by making life harder for you. But it is only fair [14]for you to share with them when you have so much, and they have so little. Later, when they have more than enough, and you are in need, they can share with you. Then everyone will have a fair share, [15]just as the Scriptures say,

> "Those who gathered
> too much
>   had nothing left.
> Those who gathered
> only a little
>   had all they needed."

Titus and His Friends

[16]I am grateful that God made Titus care as much about you as we do. [17]When we begged Titus to visit you, he said he would. He wanted to because he cared so much for you. [18]With Titus we are also sending one of the Lord's followers who is well known in every church for spreading the good news. [19]The churches chose this follower to travel with us while we carry this gift that will bring praise to the Lord and show how much we hope to help. [20]We don't want anyone to find fault with the way we handle your generous gift. [21]But we want to do what pleases the Lord and what people think is right.

[22]We are also sending someone else with Titus and the other follower. We approve of this man. In fact, he has already shown us many times that he wants to help. And now he wants to help even more than ever, because he trusts you so much. [23]Titus is my partner, who works with me to serve you. The other two followers are sent by the churches, and they bring honor to Christ. [24]Treat them in such a way that the churches will see your love and will know why we bragged about you.

The Money for God's People

9 I don't need to write you about the money you plan to give for God's people. [2]I know how eager you are to give. And I have proudly told the Lord's followers in Macedonia that you people in Achaia have been ready for a whole year. Now your desire to give has made them want to give. [3]That's why I am sending Titus and the two others to you. I want you to be ready, just as I promised. This will prove that we were not wrong to brag about you.

[4]Some followers from Macedonia may come with me, and I want them to find that you have the money ready. If you don't, I would be embarrassed for trusting you to do this. But you would be embarrassed even more. [5]So I have decided to ask Titus and the others to spend some time with you before I arrive. This way they can arrange to collect the money you have promised. Then you will have the chance to give because you want to, and not because you feel forced to.

[6]Remember this saying,

> "A few seeds make
>   a small harvest,
> but a lot of seeds make
>   a big harvest."

[7]Each of you must make up your own mind about how much to give. But don't feel sorry that you must give and don't feel that you are forced to give. God loves people who love to give. [8]God can bless you with everything you need, and you will always have more than enough to do all kinds of good things for others. [9]The Scriptures say,

---

[i]**8.7** *you love us better*: Some manuscripts have "we love you better."

"God freely gives his gifts
to the poor,
        and always does right."

[10]God gives seed to farmers and provides everyone with food. He will increase what you have, so that you can give even more to those in need. [11]You will be blessed in every way, and you will be able to keep on being generous. Then many people will thank God when we deliver your gift.

[12]What you are doing is much more than a service that supplies God's people with what they need. It is something that will make many others thank God. [13]The way in which you have proved yourselves by this service will bring honor and praise to God. You believed the message about Christ, and you obeyed it by sharing generously with God's people and with everyone else. [14]Now they are praying for you and want to see you, because God used you to bless them so very much. [15]Thank God for his gift that is too wonderful for words!

Paul Defends His Work for Christ

10 Do you think I am a coward when I am with you and brave when I am far away? Well, I ask you to listen, because Christ himself was humble and gentle. [2]Some people have said that we act like the people of this world. So when I arrive, I expect I will have to be firm and forceful in what I say to them. Please don't make me treat you that way. [3]We live in this world, but we don't act like its people [4]or fight our battles with the weapons of this world. Instead, we use God's power that can destroy fortresses. We destroy arguments [5]and every bit of pride that keeps anyone from knowing God. We capture people's thoughts and make them obey Christ. [6]And when you completely obey him, we will punish anyone who refuses to obey.

[7]You judge by appearances.[j] If any of you think you are the only ones who belong to Christ, then think again. We belong to Christ as much as you do. [8]Maybe I brag a little too much about the authority that the Lord gave me to help you and not to hurt you. Yet I am not embarrassed to brag. [9]And I am not trying to scare you with my letters. [10]Some of you are saying, "Paul's letters are harsh and powerful. But in person, he is a weakling and has nothing worth saying."

[11]Those people had better understand that when I am with you, I will do exactly what I say in my letters.

Nothing would please me more than knowing I'd seriously thwarted the destructive plans of the Evil One. I want there to be no doubt about which side benefited from my loyalties.

VALERIE BELL

[12]We won't dare compare ourselves with those who think so much of themselves. But they are foolish to compare themselves with themselves. [13]We won't brag about something we don't have a right to brag about. We will only brag about the work that God has sent us to do, and you are part of that work. [14]We are not bragging more than we should. After all, we did bring the message about Christ to you.

[15]We don't brag about what others have done, as if we had done those things ourselves. But I hope that as you become stronger in your faith, we will be able to reach many more of the people around you.[k] That has always been our goal. [16]Then we will be able to preach the good news in other lands where we cannot take credit for work someone else has already done. [17]The Scriptures say, "If you want to brag, then brag about the Lord." [18]You may brag about yourself, but the only approval that counts is the Lord's approval.

Paul and the False Apostles

11 Please put up with a little of my foolishness. [2]I am as concerned about you as God is. You were like a virgin bride I had chosen only for Christ. ³But now I fear that you will be tricked, just as Eve was tricked by that lying snake. I am afraid that you might stop thinking about Christ in an honest and sincere way. ⁴We told you about Jesus, and you received the Holy Spirit and accepted our message. But you let some people tell you about another Jesus. Now you are ready to receive another spirit and accept a different message. ⁵I think I am as good as any of those super apostles. ⁶I may not speak as well as they do, but I know as much. And this has already been made perfectly clear to you.

⁷Was it wrong for me to lower myself and honor you by preaching God's message free of charge? ⁸I robbed other churches by taking money from them to serve you. ⁹Even when I was in need, I still didn't bother you. In fact, some of the Lord's followers from Macedonia brought me what I needed. I have not been a burden to you in the past, and I will never be a burden. ¹⁰As surely as I speak the truth about Christ, no one in Achaia can stop me from bragging about this. ¹¹And it isn't because I don't love you. God himself knows how much I do love you.

¹²I plan to go on doing just what I have always done. Then those people won't be able to brag about doing the same things we are doing. ¹³Anyway, they are no more than false apostles and dishonest workers. They only pretend to be apostles of Christ. ¹⁴And it is no wonder. Even Satan tries to make himself look like an angel of light. ¹⁵So why does it seem strange for Satan's servants to pretend to do what is right? Someday they will get exactly what they deserve.

Paul's Sufferings for Christ

¹⁶I don't want any of you to think that I am a fool. But if you do, then let me be a fool and brag a little. ¹⁷When I do all this bragging, I do it as a fool and not for the Lord. ¹⁸Yet if others want to brag about what they have done, so will I. ¹⁹And since you are so smart, you will gladly put up with a fool. ²⁰In fact, you let people make slaves of you and cheat you and steal from you. Why, you even let them strut around and slap you in the face. ²¹I am ashamed to say that we are too weak to behave in such a way.

If they can brag, so can I, but it is a fool-ish thing to do. ²²Are they Hebrews? So am I. Are they Jews? So am I. Are they from the family of Abraham? Well, so am I. ²³Are they servants of Christ? I am a fool to talk this way, but I serve him better than they do. I have worked harder and have been put in jail more times. I have been beaten with whips more and have been in danger of death more often.

²⁴Five times the Jews gave me thirty-nine lashes with a whip. ²⁵Three times the Romans beat me with a big stick, and once my enemies stoned me. I have been ship-wrecked three times, and I even had to spend a night and a day in the sea. ²⁶During my many travels, I have been in danger from rivers, robbers, my own people, and foreigners. My life has been in danger in cities, in deserts, at sea, and with people who only pretended to be the Lord's followers.

²⁷I have worked and struggled and spent many sleepless nights. I have gone hungry and thirsty and often had nothing to eat. I have been cold from not having enough clothes to keep me warm. ²⁸Besides everything else, each day I am burdened down, worrying about all the churches. ²⁹When others are weak, I am weak too. When others are tricked into sin, I get angry.[1]

³⁰If I have to brag, I will brag about how weak I am. ³¹God, the Father of our Lord Jesus, knows I am not lying. And God is to be praised forever! ³²The governor of Damascus at the time of King Aretas had the city gates guarded, so that he could capture me. ³³But I escaped by being let down in a basket through a window in the city wall.

Visions from the Lord

12 I have to brag. There is nothing to be gained by it, but I must brag about the visions and other things that the Lord has shown me. ²I know about one of Christ's followers who was taken up into the third heaven fourteen years ago. I don't know if the man was still in his body when it happened, but God certainly knows.

³As I said, only God really knows if this man was in his body at the time. ⁴But he

---

[1] **11.29** *When others are tricked into sin, I get angry:* Or "When others stumble into sin, I hurt for them."

was taken up into paradise,[m] where he heard things that are too wonderful to tell. [5]I will brag about that man, but not about myself, except to say how weak I am.

[6]Yet even if I did brag, I would not be foolish. I would simply be speaking the truth. But I will try not to say too much. That way, none of you will think more highly of me than you should because of what you have seen me do and say. [7]Of course, I am now referring to the wonderful things I saw. One of Satan's angels was sent to make me suffer terribly, so that I would not feel too proud.[n]

[8]Three times I begged the Lord to make this suffering go away. [9]But he replied, "My kindness is all you need. My power is strongest when you are weak." So if Christ keeps giving me his power, I will gladly brag about how weak I am. [10]Yes, I am glad to be weak or insulted or mistreated or to have troubles and sufferings, if it is for Christ. Because when I am weak, I am strong.

Paul's Concern for the Lord's Followers at Corinth

[11]I have been making a fool of myself. But you forced me to do it, when you should have been speaking up for me. I may be nothing at all, but I am as good as those super apostles. [12]When I was with you, I was patient and worked all the powerful miracles and signs and wonders of a true apostle. [13]You missed out on only one blessing that the other churches received. That is, you didn't have to support me. Forgive me for doing you wrong.

[14]I am planning to visit you for the third time. But I still won't make a burden of myself. What I really want is you, and not what you have. Children are not supposed to save up for their parents, but parents are supposed to take care of their children. [15]So I will gladly give all that I have and all that I am. Will you love me less for loving you too much? [16]You agree that I wasn't a burden to you. Maybe that's because I was trying to catch you off guard and trick you. [17]Were you cheated by any of those I sent to you? [18]I urged Titus to visit you, and I sent another follower with him. But Titus didn't cheat you, and we felt and behaved the same way he did.

[19]Have you been thinking all along that we have been defending ourselves to you? Actually, we have been speaking to God as

---

[m]12.4 *paradise*: In the Greek translation of the Old Testament, this word is used for the Garden of Eden. In New Testament times it was sometimes used for the place where God's people are happy and at rest, as they wait for the final judgment.   [n]12.7 *Of course . . . too proud*: Or "Because of the wonderful things that I saw, one of Satan's angels was sent to make me suffer terribly, so that I would not feel too proud."

SpiritualLife—Does prayer really make a difference? (2 Corinthians 12.6-10)

God always responds to our requests.
Have you ever prayed and prayed and prayed for something you were sure you needed—only to feel as if God were looking the other way? This happened to Paul.

Paul suffered terribly from some malady, a "gift" from one of Satan's angels, so he prayed to God to relieve his suffering. We don't know the type of suffering, but it must have been quite difficult. Paul was no stranger to hardship, yet he kept asking God to take *this* suffering away. But through his experience of praying and trusting, Paul came to a deeper appreciation of God's sovereign care over every aspect of his life (12.8-10). He was even able to accept this weakness because it revealed God's power.

Prayer makes all the difference in this world. It gives us the chance to put ourselves and our circumstances into God's capable hands. There is no such thing as "unanswered prayer." God responds to all our requests with a "yes," a "not yet," or a "no, that wouldn't be good for you." He's our loving and wise Father; we can trust him to give what's best—even when we don't know what that is. Prayer doesn't change God; it changes the one who is praying. (See also 2 Chronicles 20.1-30; Jeremiah 21.1-10; Matthew 7.7-12; Luke 18.1-8.)

Words To Remember: [God] replied, "My kindness is all you need. My power is strongest when you are weak."—2 Corinthians 12.9

followers of Christ. But, my friends, we did it all for your good.

²⁰I am afraid that when I come, we won't be pleased with each other. I fear that some of you may be arguing or jealous or angry or selfish or gossiping or insulting each other. I even fear that you may be proud and acting like a mob. ²¹I am afraid God will make me ashamed when I visit you again. I will feel like crying because many of you have never given up your old sins. You are still doing things that are immoral, indecent, and shameful.

Final Warnings and Greetings

13 I am on my way to visit you for the third time. And as the Scriptures say, "Any charges must be proved true by at least two or three witnesses." ²During my second visit I warned you that I would punish you and anyone else who doesn't stop sinning. I am far away from you now, but I give you the same warning. ³This should prove to you that I am speaking for Christ. When he corrects you, he won't be weak. He will be powerful! ⁴Although he was weak when he was nailed to the cross, he now lives by the power of God. We are weak, just as Christ was. But you will see that we will live by the power of God, just as Christ does.

⁵Test yourselves and find out if you really are true to your faith. If you pass the test, you will discover that Christ is living in you. But if Christ isn't living in you, you have failed. ⁶I hope you will discover that we have not failed. ⁷We pray that you will stop doing evil things. We don't pray like this to make ourselves look good, but to get you to do right, even if we are failures.

⁸All we can do is to follow the truth and not fight against it. ⁹Even though we are weak, we are glad that you are strong, and we pray that you will do even better. ¹⁰I am writing these things to you before I arrive. This way I won't have to be hard on you when I use the authority that the Lord has given me. I was given this authority, so that I could help you and not destroy you.

> After twenty-five years of trial and error, I have to say my best efforts and the well-intentioned advice of self-help books have educated, not perfected, me. God is the only one who can do that. And fortunately, along the way, he never <u>condemns</u> and <u>always</u> forgives.
>
> KATHY PEEL

¹¹Good-by, my friends. Do better and pay attention to what I have said. Try to get along and live peacefully with each other.

Now I pray that God, who gives love and peace, will be with you. ¹²Give each other a warm greeting. All of God's people send their greetings.

¹³I pray that the Lord Jesus Christ will bless you and be kind to you! May God bless you with his love, and may the Holy Spirit join all your hearts together.

Galatians

Faith Is the Only Way

None of us likes to feel that we have to defend ourselves to our friends or colleagues. Yet this is the position in which Paul found himself when he wrote the book of Galatians. Not only was it necessary for him to defend himself as a true apostle (1.11—2.21), but he also had to defend the message God had given him: that faith alone makes us right with God (3.1-14).

The book of Galatians is a letter written to the churches in Galatia in which so-called experts were casting doubts on Paul's apostleship and his message. It shocked and disappointed Paul that the Galatians would turn so quickly from the one true message. He feared that these friends, whom he had nurtured in the faith, would be led back into the bondage of a works-based religion.

There's a strong belief in our culture (and probably in the culture of the early church) that you can't get something for nothing. That's why the truth of God's undeserved kindness toward us is so hard to accept; deep down we, too, are tempted to believe there must be something we can do to bring about a right relationship with God. So we need the message contained in the book of Galatians—that faith is the only way to be saved—as much as those to whom this letter was originally written.

This message of grace impacts not only our relationship with God, but also our relationship with others. When we know deep in our heart that there is nothing we can do to earn God's favor, and that he freely gives his love and kindness, we are free to extend grace to others. We also begin to understand that outward distinctions, such as gender, race, and class, are inappropriate categories for governing how we should relate to one another (3.28). Then we can live in the freedom of knowing we are all equally sinful and equally redeemed to love and serve Christ and each other. Paul's practical message to us is that we are to use the freedom God gives us not to satisfy our own selfish desires, but to serve each other with love (5.13).

Galatians at a Glance

1. Paul defends himself and his message (1.1-12)
2. Paul describes his calling as a true apostle (1.13—2.10)
3. Paul confronts Peter regarding discriminatory behavior (2.11-21)
4. A discussion of faith vs. works (3,4)
5. Living as free persons (5.1—6.10)
6. A personal note (6.11-18)

1 [1-2]From the apostle Paul and from all the Lord's followers with me.

I was chosen to be an apostle by Jesus Christ and by God the Father, who raised him from death. No mere human chose or appointed me to this work.

To the churches in Galatia.

[3]I pray that God the Father and our Lord Jesus Christ will be kind to you and will bless you with peace! [4]Christ obeyed God our Father and gave himself as a sacrifice for our sins to rescue us from this evil world. [5]God will be given glory forever and ever. Amen.

The Only True Message

[6]I am shocked that you have so quickly turned from God, who chose you because of his wonderful kindness.[a] You have believed another message, [7]when there is really only one true message. But some people are causing you trouble and want to make you turn away from the good news about Christ. [8]I pray that God will punish anyone who preaches anything different from our message to you! It doesn't matter if that person is one of us or an angel from heaven. [9]I have said it before, and I will say it again. I hope God will punish anyone who preaches any-

thing different from what you have already believed.

[10]I am not trying to please people. I want to please God. Do you think I am trying to please people? If I were doing that, I would not be a servant of Christ.

How Paul Became an Apostle

[11]My friends, I want you to know that no one made up the message I preach. [12]It wasn't given or taught to me by some mere human. My message came directly from Jesus Christ when he appeared to me.

[13]You know how I used to live as a Jew. I was cruel to God's church and even tried to destroy it. [14]I was a much better Jew than anyone else my own age, and I obeyed every law that our ancestors had given us. [15]But even before I was born, God had chosen me. He was kind and had decided [16]to show me his Son, so that I would announce his message to the Gentiles. I didn't talk this over with anyone. [17]I didn't say a word, not even to the men in Jerusalem who were apostles before I was. Instead, I went at once to Arabia, and afterwards I returned to Damascus.

---

[a]1.6 his wonderful kindness: Some manuscripts have "the wonderful kindness of Christ."

Personal *Concerns*—When a poor decision on my part has damaged my reputation as a Christian, what can I do? *(Galatians 1.11-24)*

Realize God can use even our failures for his good purposes.
Few of us have past failures that are as devastating as the apostle Paul's. In his zeal as a devout Jew he'd been cruel to the church of God and even tried to destroy it (1.13). Luke, in writing the book of Acts, was unflinching in describing the trouble that Paul (then called Saul) caused as he went from house to house arresting Christ's followers and having them thrown into jail (Acts 8.3). With Paul's approval, Stephen, one of the church's Spirit-filled leaders, was stoned to death for preaching the truth (Acts 7.57—8.2).

These were painful memories for Paul, and he must have wondered how God could ever use him. But Paul found that God really can redeem even our worst mistakes. He points out in Galatians 1.24 that his conversion from a persecutor of Christ's followers to a Christ follower himself was a powerful testimony to others. It was upon hearing of Paul's transformation that the people in Judea in particular began to praise God.

From Paul we can learn that it's best to be honest about our mistakes. Such honesty expresses appropriate humility—and also allows God's strength and power to shine in our lives. (See also Joel 2.12-17; Jonah 2,3; Micah 7.18,19; Zechariah 10.6-12; Luke 7.36-50.)

Words To Remember: *They . . . heard that the one who had been cruel to them was now preaching the message that he had once tried to destroy. And because of me, they praised God.*—Galatians 1.23,24

¹⁸Three years later I went to visit Peter*b* in Jerusalem and stayed with him for fifteen days. ¹⁹The only other apostle I saw was James, the Lord's brother. ²⁰And in the presence of God I swear I am telling the truth.

²¹Later, I went to the regions of Syria and Cilicia. ²²But no one who belonged to Christ's churches in Judea had ever seen me in person. ²³They had only heard that the one who had been cruel to them was now preaching the message that he had once tried to destroy. ²⁴And because of me, they praised God.

2 Fourteen years later I went to Jerusalem with Barnabas. I also took along Titus. ²But I went there because God had told me to go, and I explained the good news that I had been preaching to the Gentiles. Then I met privately with the ones who seemed to be the most important leaders. I wanted to make sure that my work in the past and my future work would not be for nothing.

³Titus went to Jerusalem with me. He was a Greek, but still he wasn't forced to be circumcised. ⁴We went there because of those who pretended to be followers and had sneaked in among us as spies. They had come to take away the freedom that Christ Jesus had given us, and they were trying to make us their slaves. ⁵But we wanted you to have the true message. That's why we didn't give in to them, not even for a second.

⁶Some of them were supposed to be important leaders, but I didn't care who they were. God doesn't have any favorites! None of these so-called special leaders added anything to my message. ⁷They realized that God had sent me with the good news for Gentiles, and that he had sent Peter with the same message for Jews. ⁸God, who had sent Peter on a mission to the Jews, was now using me to preach to the Gentiles.

⁹James, Peter,*b* and John realized that God had given me the message about his undeserved kindness. And these men are supposed to be the backbone of the church. They even gave Barnabas and me a friendly handshake. This was to show that we would work with Gentiles and that they would work with Jews. ¹⁰They only asked us to remember the poor, and that was something I had always been eager to do.

Paul Corrects Peter at Antioch

¹¹When Peter came to Antioch, I told him face to face that he was wrong. ¹²He used to eat with Gentile followers of the Lord, until James sent some Jewish followers. Peter was afraid of the Jews and soon stopped eating with Gentiles. ¹³He and the other Jews hid their true feelings so well that even Barnabas was fooled. ¹⁴But when I saw that they were not really obeying the truth that is in the good news, I corrected Peter in front of everyone and said:

Peter, you are a Jew, but you live like a Gentile. So how can you force Gentiles to live like Jews?

¹⁵We are Jews by birth and are not sinners like Gentiles. ¹⁶But we know that God accepts only those who have faith in Jesus Christ. No one can please God by simply obeying the Law. So we put our faith in Christ Jesus, and God accepted us because of our faith.

If you want to understand love, then look at the way it behaves—not the way it feels.
RAMONA CRAMER TUCKER

¹⁷When we Jews started looking for a way to please God, we discovered that we are sinners too. Does this mean that Christ is the one who makes us sinners? No, it doesn't! ¹⁸But if I tear down something and then build it again, I prove that I was wrong at first. ¹⁹It was the Law itself that killed me and freed me from its power, so that I could live for God.

I have been nailed to the cross with Christ. ²⁰I have died, but Christ lives in me. And I now live by faith in the Son of God, who loved me and gave his life for me. ²¹I don't turn my back

---

*b*1.18; 2.9 *Peter:* The Greek text has "Cephas," which is an Aramaic name meaning "rock." Peter is the Greek name with the same meaning.

on God's undeserved kindness. If we can be acceptable to God by obeying the Law, it was useless for Christ to die.

Faith Is the Only Way

3 You stupid Galatians! I told you exactly how Jesus Christ was nailed to a cross. Has someone now put an evil spell on you? [2]I want to know only one thing. How were you given God's Spirit? Was it by obeying the Law of Moses or by hearing about Christ and having faith in him? [3]How can you be so stupid? Do you think that by yourself you can complete what God's Spirit started in you? [4]Have you gone through all of this for nothing? Is it all really for nothing? [5]God gives you his Spirit and works miracles in you. But does he do this because you obey the Law of Moses or because you have heard about Christ and have faith in him?

[6]The Scriptures say that God accepted Abraham because Abraham had faith. [7]And so, you should understand that everyone who has faith is a child of Abraham.[c] [8]Long ago the Scriptures said that God would accept the Gentiles because of their faith. That's why God told Abraham the good news that all nations would be blessed because of him. [9]This means that everyone who has faith will share in the blessings that were given to Abraham because of his faith.

[10]Anyone who tries to please God by obeying the Law is under a curse. The Scriptures say, "Everyone who doesn't obey everything in the Law is under a curse." [11]No one can please God by obeying the Law. The Scriptures also say, "The people God accepts because of their faith will live."[d] [12]The Law isn't based on faith. It promises life only to people who obey its commands. [13]But Christ rescued us from the Law's curse, when he became a curse in our place. This is because the Scriptures say that anyone who is nailed to a tree is under a curse. [14]And because of what Jesus Christ has done, the blessing that was promised to Abraham was taken to the Gentiles. This happened so that by faith we would be given the promised Holy Spirit.

The Law and the Promise

[15]My friends, I will use an everyday example to explain what I mean. Once

---

[c]3.7 *a child of Abraham*: God chose Abraham, and so it was believed that anyone who was a child of Abraham was also a child of God (see the note at 3.29).   [d]3.11 *The people God accepts because of their faith will live*: Or "The people God accepts will live because of their faith."

🐚

Friendship—How can I reach out to people who differ from me in habits, faith, culture, or race? *(Galatians 3.26-29)*

Realize believers are all one in Christ.
It's a human tendency to put people in categories and then classify the people in those categories as being very different from each other. The result is stereotyping. The problem with stereotyping is that it causes us to prejudge and even limit others because of our own preconceived notions, rather than relate to them as unique individuals created by God in his image.

In Galatians 3.26-29, Paul dealt with three ways in which we often tend to categorize each other: race, class, and gender. Paul declared, "Faith in Christ Jesus is what makes each of you equal with each other" (3.28). How does this belief in equality play itself out in real relationships?

It fosters a respectful attitude that recognizes the uniqueness, mystery, and potential of every human being. And it reminds us that no matter what differences we observe, we hold the most important things in common: our relationship as sisters and brothers in God's family. (See also John 4.4-26; Romans 3.21-31; 2 Corinthians 5.16-21; Colossians 4.2-6.)

🐚 **Words To Remember:** *Faith in Christ Jesus is what makes each of you equal with each other, whether you are a Jew or a Greek, a slave or a free person, a man or a woman.—Galatians 3.28*

someone agrees to something, no one else can change or cancel the agreement.[e] [16]That is how it is with the promises God made to Abraham and his descendant.[f] The promises were not made to many descendants, but only to one, and that one is Christ. [17]What I am saying is that the Law cannot change or cancel God's promise that was made 430 years before the Law was given. [18]If we have to obey the Law in order to receive God's blessings, those blessings don't really come to us because of God's promise. But God was kind to Abraham and made him a promise.

[19]What is the use of the Law? It was given later to show that we sin. But it was only supposed to last until the coming of that descendant[g] who was given the promise. In fact, angels gave the Law to Moses, and he gave it to the people. [20]There is only one God, and the Law did not come directly from him.

Slaves and Children

[21]Does the Law disagree with God's promises? No, it doesn't! If any law could give life to us, we could become acceptable to God by obeying that law. [22]But the Scriptures say that sin controls everyone, so that God's promises will be for anyone who has faith in Jesus Christ.

[23]The Law controlled us and kept us under its power until the time came when we would have faith. [24]In fact, the Law was our teacher. It was supposed to teach us until we had faith and were acceptable to God. [25]But once a person has learned to have faith, there is no more need to have the Law as a teacher.

[26]All of you are God's children because of your faith in Christ Jesus. [27]And when you were baptized, it was as though you had put on Christ in the same way you put on new clothes. [28]Faith in Christ Jesus is what makes each of you equal with each other, whether you are a Jew or a Greek, a slave or a free person, a man or a woman. [29]So if you belong to Christ, you are now part of Abraham's family,[h] and you will be given what God has promised. [1]Children who are under age are no better off than slaves, even though everything their parents own will someday be theirs. [2]This is because children are placed in the care of guardians and teachers until the time their parents have set. [3]That is how it was with us. We were like children ruled by the powers of this world.

[4]But when the time was right, God sent

---

[e]3.15 *Once someone . . . cancel the agreement*: Or "Once a person makes out a will, no one can change or cancel it." [f]3.16 *descendant*: The Greek text has "seed," which may mean one or many descendants. In this verse Paul says it means Christ. [g]3.19 *that descendant*: Jesus. [h]3.29 *you are now part of Abraham's family*: Paul tells the Galatians that faith in Jesus Christ is what makes someone a true child of Abraham and of God (see the note at 3.7).

WORK—How can I rise above office politics? *(Galatians 5.13-16)*

Realize you're free—to respond with love.

Love is the only force that can help us rise above the pettiness, competition, and gossip that occasionally occurs in the workplace. Sometimes people who spend their working hours embroiled in office politics merely lack constructive ways to handle situations that come up at work. Instead, they "eat each other alive" and stress clutches at their insides. The old adage is true: Any time we attack others, we destroy them—and ourselves. And we put ourselves in bondage.

Freedom, on the other hand, is the ability to respond with love, no matter what's going on around us. The best way to rise above office politics is to allow love to guide us. We can continually ask God, "How can I show love to those involved in this situation?" Then act on whatever insight we gain. When we sense that no one can take away our choice to do what is loving, then we know we are free indeed! (See also Deuteronomy 5.20,21; Esther 7.1-6; Matthew 20.20-28; Colossians 3.22—4.1; James 3.5-18.)

Words To Remember: *My friends, you were chosen to be free. So don't use your freedom as an excuse to do anything you want. Use it as an opportunity to serve each other with love.—Galatians 5.13*

his Son, and a woman gave birth to him. His Son obeyed the Law, ⁵so he could set us free from the Law, and we could become God's children. ⁶Now that we are his children, God has sent the Spirit of his Son into our hearts. And his Spirit tells us that God is our Father. ⁷You are no longer slaves. You are God's children, and you will be given what he has promised.

> *Worship is a beautiful outward display of your inward relationship with your heavenly Father.*
>
> BABBIE MASON

Paul's Concern for the Galatians

⁸Before you knew God, you were slaves of gods that are not real. ⁹But now you know God, or better still, God knows you. How can you turn back and become the slaves of those weak and pitiful powers?ⁱ ¹⁰You even celebrate certain days, months, seasons, and years. ¹¹I am afraid I have wasted my time working with you.

¹²My friends, I beg you to be like me, just as I once tried to be like you. Did you mistreat me ¹³when I first preached to you? No you didn't, even though you knew I had come there because I was sick. ¹⁴My illness must have caused you some trouble, but you didn't hate me or turn me away because of it. You welcomed me as though I were one of God's angels or even Christ Jesus himself. ¹⁵Where is that good feeling now? I am sure that if it had been possible, you would have taken out your own eyes and given them to me. ¹⁶Am I now your enemy, just because I told you the truth?

¹⁷Those people may be paying you a lot of attention, but it isn't for your good. They only want to keep you away from me, so you will pay them a lot of attention. ¹⁸It is always good to give your attention to something worthwhile, even when I am not with you. ¹⁹My children, I am in terrible pain until Christ may be seen living in you. ²⁰I wish I were with you now. Then I would not have to talk this way. You really have me puzzled.

Hagar and Sarah

²¹Some of you would like to be under the rule of the Law of Moses. But do you know what the Law says? ²²In the Scriptures we

---

ⁱ4.9 *powers:* Spirits were thought to control human lives and were believed to be connected with the movements of the stars.

*Spiritual*Life—How can I keep my life centered on God? (*Galatians 5.16-26*)

Stay open to the presence and influence of the Holy Spirit.
One of the most enigmatic realities of the Christian life is the presence and influence of the Holy Spirit. We try to capture the nature of the Holy Spirit in words and images such as wind, breath, fire, or life-giving force, but we're still left with a limited view of how the Spirit works in our lives.

One of the ways we can better "see" the reality of the Spirit in us is when we discover we're no longer compelled to fulfill our selfish desires (the results of which Paul aptly describes in Galatians 5.19-21). Instead, the presence of the Spirit produces in us love, joy, peace, patience, and many other life-giving qualities, qualities we can't create through our own efforts. The Bible says that the Spirit is like the wind that blows where it chooses (John 3.8). We cannot control the Spirit any more than we can control the wind. We can, however, open our hearts to God's Spirit through silence and prayer, expectantly inviting him to move through our lives and transform us. (See also Genesis 12.1-7; Matthew 25.31-46; Acts 13.1-5; 2 Timothy 2.14-26; 2 John.)

Words To Remember: *God's Spirit has given us life, and so we should follow the Spirit.—*Galatians 5.25

learn that Abraham had two sons. The mother of one of them was a slave, while the mother of the other one had always been free. [23]The son of the slave woman was born in the usual way. But the son of the free woman was born because of God's promise.

[24]All of this has another meaning as well. Each of the two women stands for one of the agreements God made with his people. Hagar, the slave woman, stands for the agreement that was made at Mount Sinai. Everyone born into her family is a slave. [25]Hagar also stands for Mount Sinai in Arabia[j] and for the present city of Jerusalem. She[k] and her children are slaves.

[26]But our mother is the city of Jerusalem in heaven above, and she isn't a slave. [27]The Scriptures say about her,

> "You have never had children,
>   but now you can be glad.
> You have never given birth,
>   but now you can shout.
> Once you had no children,
>   but now you will have
> more children than a woman
> who has been married
>   for a long time."

[28]My friends, you were born because of this promise, just as Isaac was. [29]But the child who was born in the natural way made trouble for the child who was born because of the Spirit. The same thing is happening today. [30]The Scriptures say, "Get rid of the slave woman and her son! He won't be given anything. The son of the free woman will receive everything." [31]My friends, we are children of the free woman and not of the slave.

Christ Gives Freedom

5 Christ has set us free! This means we are really free. Now hold on to your freedom and don't ever become slaves of the Law again.

[2]I, Paul, promise you that Christ won't do you any good if you get circumcised. [3]If you do, you must obey the whole Law. [4]And if you try to please God by obeying the Law, you have cut yourself off from Christ and his wonderful kindness. [5]But the Spirit makes us sure that God will accept us because of our faith in Christ. [6]If you are a follower of Christ Jesus, it makes no difference whether you are circumcised or not. All that matters is your faith that makes you love others.

[7]You were doing so well until someone made you turn from the truth. [8]And that

---

[j]4.25 *Hagar also stands for Mount Sinai in Arabia:* Some manuscripts have "Sinai is a mountain in Arabia." This sentence would then be translated: "Sinai is a mountain in Arabia, and Hagar stands for the present city of Jerusalem." [k]4.25 *She:* "Hagar" or "Jerusalem."

MARRIAGE—How can my husband and I grow spiritually as a couple?
(Galatians 6.1-3)

Support each other as you grow together.
One of the great things about marriage is that a husband and wife have the opportunity to walk a spiritual journey together. There will be many times when both of you are strong spiritually and feel as though you are progressing down the road with ease. However, there will also be times when one of you is strong and the other is weak. It's during those times that the beauty of God's plan for marriage is clearly seen: the one who's strong helps the one who's weak—and the marriage is strengthened as a result.

It's important that the one offering help do so with an attitude of love and acceptance, realizing that at some point he or she may need similar assistance. Paul warns us about thinking we're somehow better than someone else just because we're strong at a particular moment. Our moment of need will come soon enough!

When husband and wife understand that neither is better nor "more spiritual" than the other and that both have strength to offer, they can give and receive this assistance in a way that isn't threatening, but comforting. (See also Hebrews 5.11—6.3; 1 Peter 4.8-11.)

Words To Remember: *You obey the law of Christ when you offer each other a helping hand.—Galatians 6.2*

person was certainly not sent by the one who chose you. [9]A little yeast can change a whole batch of dough, [10]but you belong to the Lord. That makes me certain that you will do what I say, instead of what someone else tells you to do. Whoever is causing trouble for you will be punished.

[11]My friends, if I still preach that people need to be circumcised, why am I in so much trouble? The message about the cross would no longer be a problem, if I told people to be circumcised. [12]I wish that everyone who is upsetting you would not only get circumcised, but would cut off much more!

[13]My friends, you were chosen to be free. So don't use your freedom as an excuse to do anything you want. Use it as an opportunity to serve each other with love. [14]All that the Law says can be summed up in the command to love others as much as you love yourself. [15]But if you keep attacking each other like wild animals, you had better watch out or you will destroy yourselves.

God's Spirit and Our Own Desires

[16]If you are guided by the Spirit, you won't obey your selfish desires. [17]The Spirit and your desires are enemies of each other. They are always fighting each other and keeping you from doing what you feel you

should. [18]But if you obey the Spirit, the Law of Moses has no control over you.

[19]People's desires make them give in to immoral ways, filthy thoughts, and shameful deeds. [20]They worship idols, practice witchcraft, hate others, and are hard to get along with. People become jealous, angry, and selfish. They not only argue and cause trouble, but they are [21]envious. They get drunk, carry on at wild parties, and do other evil things as well. I told you before, and I am telling you again: No one who does these things will share in the blessings of God's kingdom.

[22]God's Spirit makes us loving, happy, peaceful, patient, kind, good, faithful, [23]gentle, and self-controlled. There is no law against behaving in any of these ways. [24]And because we belong to Christ Jesus, we have killed our selfish feelings and desires. [25]God's Spirit has given us life, and so we should follow the Spirit. [26]But don't be conceited or make others jealous by claiming to be better than they are.

Help Each Other

6 My friends, you are spiritual. So if someone is trapped in sin, you should gently lead that person back to the right path. But watch out, and don't be

---

WORK—How can I have healthy relationships with the men I work with?
(Galatians 6.1-10)

Help each other live by God's purposes.
Relationships between men and women are still fraught with a great deal of confusion and misunderstanding. The focus in recent years on differing leadership and communication styles, gender discrimination, and sexual harassment highlights the fact that our culture is still struggling to figure out how men and women can work together effectively.

In this passage, Paul sets forth some wonderfully simple ideas for getting along together which, when applied to relationships between men and women, can be quite transforming. First, those of us who are trying to live according to spiritual values need to do what we can to help others (6.1). We can help men by being loving but not seductive in the way we dress and act around them. Second, it's important to do our work well (6.4,5). When men see us being competent and able to carry our own weight on the job, they'll respect us and enjoy having us as their coworkers.

One thing is for sure: We harvest what we plant (6.7). If we "plant" seductive behavior, selfishness, and poor working habits, we'll reap predictable results. If, on the other hand, we're appropriate, generous, and competent in relationships with male coworkers, eventually we'll be rewarded with their respect and friendship. (See also Esther 4; Proverbs 5; Romans 12.9-18.)

Words To Remember: *Don't get tired of helping others. You will be rewarded when the time is right, if you don't give up.—Galatians 6.9*

tempted yourself. [2]You obey the law of Christ when you offer each other a helping hand.

[3]If you think you are better than others, when you really aren't, you are wrong. [4]Do your own work well, and then you will have something to be proud of. But don't compare yourself with others. [5]We each must carry our own load.

[6]Share every good thing you have with anyone who teaches you what God has said.

[7]You cannot fool God, so don't make a fool of yourself! You will harvest what you plant. [8]If you follow your selfish desires, you will harvest destruction, but if you follow the Spirit, you will harvest eternal life. [9]Don't get tired of helping others. You will be rewarded when the time is right, if you don't give up. [10]We should help people whenever we can, especially if they are followers of the Lord.

Final Warnings

[11]You can see what big letters I make when I write with my own hand.

[12]Those people who are telling you to get circumcised are only trying to show how important they are. And they don't want to get into trouble for preaching about the cross of Christ. [13]They are circumcised, but they don't obey the Law of Moses. All they want is to brag about having you circumcised. [14]But I will never brag about anything except the cross of our Lord Jesus Christ. Because of his cross, the world is dead as far as I am concerned, and I am dead as far as the world is concerned.

[15]It doesn't matter if you are circumcised or not. All that matters is that you are a new person. [16]If you follow this rule, you will belong to God's true people. God will treat you with undeserved kindness and will bless you with peace.

[17]On my own body are scars that prove I belong to Christ Jesus. So I don't want anyone to bother me anymore.

[18]My friends, I pray that the Lord Jesus Christ will be kind to you! Amen.

Ephesians

Living Toward Eternity

After a long trip, it's natural to reflect on how far you've come and what you've seen. In the midst of traveling, you think mostly about the day-to-day details: what to eat, where to stop, when to rest. But when you finally arrive at your destination, it's satisfying to look up from the speedometer and be reminded of how your trip fits into a much larger journey—the journey of life.

Paul was coming to the end of his earthly journey when he wrote Ephesians. Sitting in his Roman prison cell, he had plenty of time to think about his life. As he recalled all the miracles and prayers and changed lives God had allowed him to see and be a part of, he couldn't keep from praising God (1.3; 3.20,21)—an amazing response considering he'd been beaten, shipwrecked, flogged, and stoned for telling people about Jesus Christ! Paul also couldn't help feeling a twinge of concern for the churches he'd helped start (1.18; 4.1-3). How could he keep them growing in their devotion to Christ after he was gone? He would show them how to see their struggles and concerns in light of everything they are in Christ. That was all they'd need.

Do you get so weighed down with tensions at work that you forget for whom you actually work? Let the CEO of the universe promote you to a level where you can see things from his perspective (5.1-16). Does one day of motherhood seem to blur into the next, leaving you questioning your purpose in life? God is in control of every season of your life, so find your identity in Christ; it's his grace, not what you do, that saves you (1,2). Is the Holy Spirit showing you ways you subtly look down on Christians who don't work or act exactly like you? Remember that believers are like the various parts of a body, each performing a necessary function for the total well-being of the body. Only together can Christians fully represent the body of Christ (4.14-16).

When Paul wrote Ephesians, he probably intended it to be circulated throughout Asia Minor, leaving the destination in verse 1 blank so the messenger could fill it in (as "in Ephesus" appears to have been). When you read his letter, pause over the images Paul used to describe all that you are in Christ. They are glorious truths for you to feed on.

Ephesians at a Glance

1. God's purpose in time and eternity (1.1-14)
2. The church's life in Christ (1.15—3.21)
3. The church's life in society (4.1—6.9)
4. The spiritual battle of all Christians (6.10-20)
5. Paul's personal remarks (6.21-24)

1 From Paul, chosen by God to be an apostle of Christ Jesus.

To God's people who live in Ephesus and[a] are faithful followers of Christ Jesus.

[2]I pray that God our Father and our Lord Jesus Christ will be kind to you and will bless you with peace!

Christ Brings Spiritual Blessings

[3]Praise the God and Father of our Lord Jesus Christ for the spiritual blessings that Christ has brought us from heaven! [4]Before the world was created, God had Christ choose us to live with him and to be his holy and innocent and loving people. [5]God was kind[b] and decided that Christ would choose us to be God's own adopted children. [6]God was very kind to us because of the Son he dearly loves, and so we should praise God.

[7-8]Christ sacrificed his life's blood to set us free, which means that our sins are now forgiven. Christ did this because God was so kind to us. God has great wisdom and understanding, [9]and by what Christ has done, God has shown us his own mysterious ways. [10]Then when the time is right, God will do all that he has planned, and Christ will bring together everything in heaven and on earth.

[11]God always does what he plans, and that's why he appointed Christ to choose us. [12]He did this so that we Jews would bring honor to him and be the first ones to have hope because of him. [13]Christ also brought you the truth, which is the good news about how you can be saved. You put your faith in Christ and were given the promised Holy Spirit to show that you belong to God. [14]The Spirit also makes us sure that we will be given what God has stored up for his people. Then we will be set free, and God will be honored and praised.

Paul's Prayer

[15]I have heard about your faith in the Lord Jesus and your love for all of God's people. [16]So I never stop being grateful for you, as I mention you in my prayers. [17]I ask the glorious Father and God of our Lord Jesus Christ to give you his Spirit. The Spirit will make you wise and let you understand what it means to know God. [18]My prayer is that light will flood your hearts and that you will understand the hope that was given to you when God chose you. Then you will discover the glorious blessings that will be yours together with all of God's people.

[19]I want you to know about the great and mighty power that God has for us followers. It is the same wonderful power he used [20]when he raised Christ from death and let

---

[a]1.1 *live in Ephesus and:* Some manuscripts do not have these words. [b]1.4,5 *holy and innocent and loving people.* [5]*God was kind:* Or "holy and innocent people. God was loving [5]and kind."

PARENTING&*family*—How can I nurture my child's self-worth?
(*Ephesians 1.3-14*)

Set an example of healthy self-worth.
It's part of human nature to seek out our identity in anything but God, so you won't have to help your children exercise that muscle. What you *can* do is make a point of showing them in everyday events how glad you are that God is your loving heavenly Father. As your children see your faith in action, it will be easier for them to understand God's sovereign care over their lives as well (1.4).

You have the great privilege, as well as responsibility, of representing God to your children. As you train them to ask for forgiveness when they do something wrong, show a humble and teachable heart when the problem lies with you. And, just as God didn't wait for you to get your act together but made the first move toward reconciliation (2.4,5), offer that same gracious, unconditional love to your kids. Raising your children to see and know the depth of God's mercy is the strongest foundation upon which to build healthy self-worth in your children. (See also 1 Samuel 17.24-54; Psalm 139; Luke 15.11-32; 2 Thessalonians 3.6-15.)

Words To Remember: *God was kind and decided that Christ would choose us to be God's own adopted children.—Ephesians 1.5*

him sit at his right side[c] in heaven. [21]There Christ rules over all forces, authorities, powers, and rulers. He rules over all beings in this world and will rule in the future world as well. [22]God has put all things under the power of Christ, and for the good of the church he has made him the head of everything. [23]The church is Christ's body and is filled with Christ who completely fills everything.[d]

From Death to Life

2 In the past you were dead because you sinned and fought against God. [2]You followed the ways of this world and obeyed the devil. He rules the world, and

---

[c]**1.20** *right side:* The place of power and honor.
[d]**1.23** *and is filled with Christ who completely fills everything:* Or "which completely fills Christ and fully completes his work."

Personal *Concerns*—How can I handle even difficult times positively?
(Ephesians 1.7-23)

Trust that God knows what he's doing in your life.
It's the invisible qualities—such as love, forgiveness, joy—that give life meaning. Yet we often spend much of our time interpreting our experiences by what we can see, taste, and touch: *I am a successful businesswoman; therefore, I must be important. My son has decided not to live for God; therefore, I must be a bad mother.* Like a baby who cries when her mother leaves to go to the next room, we feel as though God periodically abandons us because we can't see how very near he is to us.

Life is often hard, certainly more than a "positive mental attitude" can bear. But thank God that he gives us real reasons to be hopeful, even when we're struggling (1.7). We are his, and nothing can separate us from him. Even our difficult circumstances can be turned into joys when we let them remind us of God's truths (1.11). Even during times of emotional famine, we can feed on God's eternal truths. (See also Leviticus 26.1-13; Job 23; Micah 4.1-5; Nahum 1.2-7,15; Romans 8.18-30.)

Words To Remember: *My prayer is that light will flood your hearts and that you will understand the hope that was given to you when God chose you. Then you will discover the glorious blessings that will be yours together with all of God's people.* —Ephesians 1.18

Friendship—How can I forgive a friend who has greatly wronged or disappointed me? *(Ephesians 2.1-10)*

Remember you, too, are a sinner saved by grace.
You thought she was your friend—until she shared a secret about your past with some of the women in your Bible study group. Now you feel uncomfortable attending the group. She's greatly wronged you, and you don't know if you can ever forgive her.

Or maybe your friend has disappointed you. You've talked with her time and time again regarding her behavior around men (she tends to be flirty), and now you've discovered she's having an affair with a married man. What should you do?

Friends are only human—too human sometimes. But so are we. In this passage, the writer reminds us that all of us are sinners. If we're Christians, we've been saved by grace because of God's mercy and love (2.4,5). Just as God "treats us much better than we deserve" (2.8), so we should treat our friends that way—even when they hurt us.

So when you think you just can't forgive a friend for what she's done, reflect on these verses—and remember what Christ has done for you. (See also Romans 7.21—8.5; Colossians 3.12-14.)

Words To Remember: *You were saved by faith in God, who treats us much better than we deserve. This is God's gift to you, and not anything you have done on your own.*—Ephesians 2.8

his spirit has power over everyone who doesn't obey God. ³Once we were also ruled by the selfish desires of our bodies and minds. We had made God angry, and we were going to be punished like everyone else.

⁴⁻⁵But God was merciful! We were dead because of our sins, but God loved us so much that he made us alive with Christ, and God's wonderful kindness is what saves you. ⁶God raised us from death to life with Christ Jesus, and he has given us a place beside Christ in heaven. ⁷God did this so that in the future world he could show how truly good and kind he is to us because of what Christ Jesus has done. ⁸You were saved by faith in God, who treats us much better than we deserve.ᵉ This is God's gift to you, and not anything you have done on your own. ⁹It isn't something you have earned, so there is nothing you can brag about. ¹⁰God planned for us to do good things and to live as he has always wanted us to live. That's why he sent Christ to make us what we are.

United by Christ

¹¹Don't forget that you are Gentiles. In fact, you used to be called "uncircumcised" by those who take pride in being circumcised. ¹²At that time you did not know about Christ. You were foreigners to the people of Israel, and you had no part in the promises that God had made to them. You were living in this world without hope and without God, ¹³and you were far from God. But Christ offered his life's blood as a sacrifice and brought you near God.

¹⁴Christ has made peace between Jews and Gentiles, and he has united us by breaking down the wall of hatred that separated us. Christ gave his own body ¹⁵to destroy the Law of Moses with all its rules and commands. He even brought Jews and Gentiles together as though we were only one person, when he united us in peace. ¹⁶On the cross Christ did away with our hatred for each other. He also made peaceᶠ between us and God by uniting Jews and Gentiles in one body. ¹⁷Christ came and preached peace to you Gentiles, who were far from God, and peace to us Jews, who were near God. ¹⁸And because of Christ, all of us can come to the Father by the same Spirit.

¹⁹You Gentiles are no longer strangers and foreigners. You are citizens with everyone else who belongs to the family of God. ²⁰You are like a building with the apostles and prophets as the foundation and with Christ as the most important stone. ²¹Christ is the one who holds the building together and makes it grow into a holy temple for the Lord. ²²And you are part of that building Christ has built as a place for God's own Spirit to live.

ᵉ**2.8** *treats us much better than we deserve:* The Greek word *charis,* traditionally rendered "grace," is translated here and other places in the CEV to express the overwhelming kindness of God. ᶠ**2.16** *He also made peace:* Or "The cross also made peace."

SpiritualLife—Why is it important for me to go to church? *(Ephesians 2.11-22)*

The church shows Christ's transforming power to the world.
Have you ever visited a foreign country, only to be faced with the culture shock that comes from being surrounded by a different language and different customs? You suddenly gain an appreciation for what it means to be an outsider, to be a stranger who doesn't fit in.

So much of our world is polarized by racial and political differences. Yet in Christ, all barriers of race and culture have been torn down—a remarkable and transforming fact. Now Jews and Gentiles (2.12,13), blacks and whites, women and men, rich and poor, educated and uneducated are the same in Christ. It's a miracle! It's a privilege to be part of Christ's body, so don't let your need for independence, a difference of opinion on some nonessential doctrine, or some *more important* time commitment keep you from offering your time and talents to a local church. God has made you with the need to fellowship with other believers and to use your gifts for their spiritual benefit. (See also Ezekiel 43.1-5; Acts 2.1-13,41-47; Romans 12.3-8; 1 Corinthians 3.10-17.)

Words To Remember: *And you are part of that building Christ has built as a place for God's own Spirit to live.—Ephesians 2.22*

Paul's Mission to the Gentiles

3 Christ Jesus made me his prisoner, so that I could help you Gentiles. [2]You have surely heard about God's kindness in choosing me to help you. [3]In fact, this letter tells you a little about how God has shown me his mysterious ways. [4]As you read the letter, you will also find out how well I really do understand the mystery about Christ. [5]No one knew about this mystery until God's Spirit told it to his holy apostles and prophets. [6]And the mystery is this: Because of Christ Jesus, the good news has given the Gentiles a share in the promises that God gave to the Jews. God has also let the Gentiles be part of the same body.

[7]God treated me with kindness. His power worked in me, and it became my job to spread the good news. [8]I am the least important of all God's people. But God was kind and chose me to tell the Gentiles that because of Christ there are blessings that cannot be measured. [9]God, who created everything, wanted me to help everyone understand the mysterious plan that had always been hidden in his mind. [10]Then God

MARRIAGE—How can I learn to forgive my husband even when he doesn't apologize? *(Ephesians 2.14-18)*

Let Jesus help you tear down walls of discord.

Did you know that God thinks of you as his bride? Throughout Scripture, especially the Old Testament, God used the analogy of marriage to describe the intimate covenant he made between him and his people.

And just as God didn't wait for you to come to him before he forgave your sins, you can forgive your husband even before he's truly sorry for hurting you. God knew your sin wouldn't allow you to turn to him first, so he graciously took the initiative. When you're struggling to find room in your heart to forgive your unrepentant husband, think about all God has done to forgive you. He let his own Son die in your place so you could be saved by his grace (2.14,15). What is human forgiveness when compared with that sacrifice? (See also Jeremiah 33.1-9; 1 Peter 3.8-15.)

Words To Remember: *On the cross Christ did away with our hatred for each other. He also made peace between us and God.*—Ephesians 2.16

*Spiritual*Life—How can I make God's presence real in my life? *(Ephesians 3.14-21)*

Kneel before him.

If you long to grow closer to God, to make his presence real in your life, you're not alone. A recent survey done by *Today's Christian Woman* magazine reveals that women list growing closer to God—and feeling his love—as #1 on their wish list.

Paul offers us some help in this passage on Christ's love for us. If you're desiring more of Christ's presence on a daily basis, try these steps:

1. Kneel in prayer before the Father and acknowledge who he is.
2. Ask Christ to live in your heart.
3. Pray to become a strong follower.
4. Stand firm.
5. Love God—and others.
6. Believe God can do anything!

God longs for you to get to know him better. If you persevere in your search for him and become "deeply rooted in his love" (3.17), he gives you this glorious promise: "His power at work in us can do far more than we dare ask or imagine" (3.20,21)! (See also 2 Chronicles 29.20-36; Ezekiel 10; Romans 15.14-21; Colossians 3.10,11.)

Words To Remember: *I kneel in prayer to the Father. All beings in heaven and on earth receive their life from him.*—Ephesians 3.14,15

would use the church to show the powers and authorities in the spiritual world that he has many different kinds of wisdom.

¹¹God did this according to his eternal plan. And he was able to do what he had planned because of all that Christ Jesus our Lord had done. ¹²Christ now gives us courage and confidence, so that we can come to God by faith. ¹³That's why you should not be discouraged when I suffer for you. After all, it will bring honor to you.

Christ's Love for Us

¹⁴I kneel in prayer to the Father. ¹⁵All beings in heaven and on earth receive their life from him.ᵍ ¹⁶God is wonderful and glorious. I pray that his Spirit will make you become strong followers ¹⁷and that Christ will live in your hearts because of your faith. Stand firm

---

ᵍ3.15 *receive their life from him*: Or "know who they really are because of him."

MARRIAGE—What does God think about divorce? *(Ephesians 4.1-6)*

God emphasizes unity.

Paul spent the first half of Ephesians describing God's relationship with his people, the very body of Christ. In the second half, he applied those lofty realities in some very practical areas: family life, tensions at work, and the exercise of gifts and discipline in the church. All of what Paul said in the second half of his letter can be summed up this way: Be all that God has made you to be.

God has made husbands and wives to be one flesh. Paul used the words *same* and *one* seven times in this passage to bring home the importance of the concept of oneness in Christ (4.4-6). Christian couples are to love one another in a way that's worthy of Christ's sacrifice on their behalf. When there's unity in your marriage it shows that you both understand what God has done for you. If you and your husband are struggling to stay married, God can give you what you need to work out your problems. If you are able, pray together that God will keep you as *one*. (See also Malachi 2.13-16; Matthew 19.1-9; 1 Corinthians 7.10-16.)

Words To Remember: *Live in a way that is worthy of the people God has chosen to be his own. Always be humble and gentle. Patiently put up with each other and love each other.*—Ephesians 4.1,2

MARRIAGE—My husband is emotionally distant. How can I feel closer to him? *(Ephesians 4.14-16)*

Tell him the truth with love.

Marriage is the most intimate relationship humans can have. But sometimes you can feel more empty or lonely being married than you did when you were single. You have the context for closeness, but not the substance. Do you wish your husband showed more interest in you? Do you wonder whether he really understands you? There are all sorts of ways you can tell him, but some are better than others.

Paul said that, as Christians, we have been anchored in truth by Christ's work on the cross so we don't need to resort to the world's tactics of manipulation, jealousy, and rivalry in our relationships with others (4.17-19). God wants you to avoid anger, resentment, and guile in your relationship with your husband. Because God didn't force you to love him, even though God longed for you to know his love, you need to respect your husband's right to choose to remain distant from you. Pray that God will give you the strength to love your husband the way God loves you—unconditionally. (See also Proverbs 3.27-35; Zephaniah 3.16,17.)

Words To Remember: *Love should always make us tell the truth. Then we will grow in every way and be more like Christ, the head of the body.*—Ephesians 4.15,16

and be deeply rooted in his love. [18]I pray that you and all of God's people will understand what is called wide or long or high or deep.[h] [19]I want you to know all about Christ's love, although it is too wonderful to be measured. Then your lives will be filled with all that God is.

[20-21]I pray that Christ Jesus and the church will forever bring praise to God. His power at work in us can do far more than we dare ask or imagine. Amen.

Unity with Christ

4 As a prisoner of the Lord, I beg you to live in a way that is worthy of the people God has chosen to be his own. [2]Always be humble and gentle. Patiently put up with each other and love each other. [3]Try your best to let God's Spirit keep your hearts united. Do this by living at peace. [4]All of you are part of the same body. There is only one Spirit of God, just as you were given one hope when you were chosen to be God's people. [5]We have only one Lord, one faith, and one baptism. [6]There is one God who is the Father of all people. Not only is God above all others, but he works by using all of us, and he lives in all of us.

[7]Christ has generously divided out his gifts to us. [8]As the Scriptures say,

"When he went up
    to the highest place,

he led away many prisoners
    and gave gifts to people."

[9]When it says, "he went up," it means that Christ had been deep in the earth. [10]This also means that the one who went deep into the earth is the same one who went into the highest heaven, so that he would fill the whole universe. [11]Christ chose some of us to be apostles, prophets, missionaries, pastors, and teachers, [12]so that his people would learn to serve and his body would grow strong. [13]This will continue until we are united by our faith and by our understanding of the Son of God. Then we will be mature, just as Christ is, and we will be completely like him.[i]

[14]We must stop acting like children. We must not let deceitful people trick us by their false teachings, which are like winds that toss us around from place to place. [15]Love should always make us tell the truth. Then we will grow in every way and be more like Christ, the head [16]of the body. Christ holds it together and makes all of its parts work perfectly, as it grows and becomes strong because of love.

---

[h]3.18 *what is called wide or long or high or deep*: This may refer to the heavenly Jerusalem or to God's love or wisdom or to the meaning of the cross.   [i]4.13 *and we will be completely like him*: Or "and he is completely perfect."

Friendship—How can I speak the truth in love and still maintain a friendship? *(Ephesians 4.25—5.2)*

Let go of your anger and resentment.

Anger itself is not a sin. Jesus got extremely upset at God's people for turning the temple into a virtual mall. And Paul, in his warning not to let anger turn into an opportunity for the devil, assumed that anger sometimes is warranted (4.26,27). So if someone has wronged you, it's not wrong to feel angry. What you *do* with your anger is the issue. Either you hold on to your anger so it festers and grows (4.31), or you address the issue that caused it in a way that honors Christ (4.32).

One of the evidences of true faith is the way we handle difficult situations. Most people lack the personal integrity or courage to face challenges with honesty, humility, and truth. But Jesus has set the example through his love and sacrifice (5.1,2). A tree can be identified by the kind of fruit it bears. What kind of fruit are you bearing by the way you handle this strain in your friendship? Perhaps God has something to teach you about his mercy toward you and his power to heal the wounds of a friend. (See also Job 42.7-9; Proverbs 27.6; James 1.5-8.)

Words To Remember: *We are part of the same body. . . . Start telling each other the truth. Don't get so angry that you sin.—Ephesians 4.25,26*

The Old Life and the New Life

¹⁷As a follower of the Lord, I order you to stop living like stupid, godless people. ¹⁸Their minds are in the dark, and they are stubborn and ignorant and have missed out on the life that comes from God. They no longer have any feelings about what is right, ¹⁹and they are so greedy that they do all kinds of indecent things.

²⁰⁻²¹But that isn't what you were taught about Jesus Christ. He is the truth, and you heard about him and learned about him. ²²You were told that your foolish desires will destroy you and that you must give up your old way of life with all its bad habits. ²³Let the Spirit change your way of thinking ²⁴and make you into a new person. You were created to be like God, and so you must please him and be truly holy.

Rules for the New Life

²⁵We are part of the same body. Stop lying and start telling each other the truth. ²⁶Don't get so angry that you sin. Don't go to bed angry ²⁷and don't give the devil a chance.

²⁸If you are a thief, quit stealing. Be honest and work hard, so you will have something to give to people in need.

²⁹Stop all your dirty talk. Say the right thing at the right time and help others by what you say.

³⁰Don't make God's Spirit sad. The Spirit makes you sure that someday you will be free from your sins.

³¹Stop being bitter and angry and mad at others. Don't yell at one another or curse each other or ever be rude. ³²Instead, be kind and merciful, and forgive others, just as God forgave you because of Christ.

5 Do as God does. After all, you are his dear children. ²Let love be your guide. Christ loved us ʲ and offered his life for us as a sacrifice that pleases God.

³You are God's people, so don't let it be said that any of you are immoral or indecent or greedy. ⁴Don't use dirty or foolish or filthy words. Instead, say how thankful you are. ⁵Being greedy, indecent, or immoral is just another way of worshiping idols. You can be sure that people who behave in this way will never be part of the kingdom that belongs to Christ and to God.

ʲ5.2 *us:* Some manuscripts have "you."

SingleLife—How can I best relate to my married friends? *(Ephesians 5.1-5)*

Don't flirt with a friend's husband, for any reason.

Paul's command goes against everything our culture tells us on TV, in magazines, over the radio, and in the classroom: Don't even hint at immoral things, let alone practice them (5.3,4). For single Christian women that's a tall order—especially given the tremendous cultural pressure to be sexually promiscuous. That's not to suggest you shouldn't spend time with married men; you'd have to leave the planet if that were the case! But you're not to follow the example of women in television sitcoms and fashion magazines who intentionally say suggestive things or wear provocative clothing to attract men's attention. Such behavior is not the way of love Christ has shown you.

How do you treat your friend's husband? A good test is to ask yourself if you treat him the way you'd want other women to treat your husband, if you were married. In today's world, most people think it's no big deal if you send a few mixed messages or even if you're unfaithful. But the Bible says that everything we do matters to God—he wants us to reflect his standards in the way we conduct all our relationships.

A good thing to remember is that, even though you are single, you are married—to Christ! He has shown you a love so pure and true (5.1,2) that the experience of it should leave you wanting to please him, in all areas of your life. (See also Romans 15.1-6; 1 John 4.7-12.)

 Words To Remember: *Do as God does. After all, you are his dear children. Let love be your guide. . . . Don't let it be said that any of you are immoral or indecent or greedy.—Ephesians 5.1-3*

Living as People of Light

⁶Don't let anyone trick you with foolish talk. God punishes everyone who disobeys him and says[k] foolish things. ⁷So don't have anything to do with anyone like that.

⁸You used to be like people living in the dark, but now you are people of the light because you belong to the Lord. So act like people of the light ⁹and make your light shine. Be good and honest and truthful, ¹⁰as you try to please the Lord. ¹¹Don't take part in doing those worthless things that are done in the dark. Instead, show how wrong they are. ¹²It is disgusting even to talk about what is done in the dark. ¹³But the light will show what these things are really like.

_____

[k]**5.6** *says:* Or "does."

WORK—Sometimes my male colleagues don't take me seriously. How can a Christian woman be assertive at work without being offensive? (*Ephesians 5.6-21*)

Demonstrate your talents with integrity and humility.

Some of the greatest challenges to our faith come from our daily interactions with unbelievers. Sometimes you may feel as if you come from a different planet! In a sense you do: Christians live in the world of light, and unbelievers live in the world of darkness (5.8). Paul reminded his readers about all they are in Christ (1–3) and how believers are to relate to each other (4). Here in chapter 5, he laid the groundwork for how to conduct yourself with unbelievers.

How can Paul's warnings not to let unbelievers deceive you and not to associate with such people (5.6,7) help you relate to certain chauvinistic men at work? God has called you to be a light in your world (5.8). Men who treat you poorly because you are a woman and a Christian may see the foolishness of their behavior when you respond with charity instead of hostility and vindictiveness (5.13). Are you having trouble being kind to those who don't deserve it? It may help to remember that you, too, were once in the darkness until Christ brought you into the light of day. (See also Genesis 50.15-21; Judges 4.4-15; Isaiah 11.1-9.)

Words To Remember: *Make your light shine. Be good and honest and truthful, as you try to please the Lord.*—Ephesians 5.9,10

MARRIAGE—Why does the Bible talk about submission in marriage? What does God mean by it? (*Ephesians 5.21-33*)

Submission is an issue for both husbands and wives.

Submitting to your husband's leadership in marriage isn't hard if you marry the right kind of man. If you trust that your husband has your best interests in mind and lays aside his own needs to love you sacrificially—the way Christ loved the church—why would you not submit to him? This is God's ideal: you and your husband, both committed to putting the other one first in love. A wife is to think of her husband's needs first, and a husband is to model Christ's sacrificial love by serving his wife.

If your marriage is less than ideal and your husband doesn't always love you with sacrificial love, remember you are also married to Jesus Christ; he is your first love. Jesus laid aside his rights as God to become human so he could bear the penalty of sin in your place. Just as Christ loves us even when we don't show our gratitude for what he did, we are still called to put husband first, even when his love is not so perfect. Love covers a multitude of sins, and some days it may be your husband who's loving his not-so-grateful wife. (See also Proverbs 17.1; Philippians 2.1-11.)

Words To Remember: *Honor Christ and put others first.*— Ephesians 5.21

[14]Light shows up everything,[l] just as the Scriptures say,

> "Wake up from your sleep
> and rise from death.
> Then Christ will shine on you."

[15]Act like people with good sense and not like fools. [16]These are evil times, so make every minute count. [17]Don't be stupid. Instead, find out what the Lord wants you to do. [18]Don't destroy yourself by getting drunk, but let the Spirit fill your life. [19]When you meet together, sing psalms, hymns, and spiritual songs, as you praise the Lord with all your heart. [20]Always use the name of our Lord Jesus Christ to thank God the Father for everything.

Wives and Husbands

[21]Honor Christ and put others first. [22]A wife should put her husband first, as she does the Lord. [23]A husband is the head of his wife, as Christ is the head and the Savior of the church, which is his own body. [24]Wives should always put their husbands first, as the church puts Christ first.

[25]A husband should love his wife as much as Christ loved the church and gave his life for it. [26]He made the church holy by the power of his word, and he made it pure by washing it with water. [27]Christ did this, so that he would have a glorious and holy church, without faults or spots or wrinkles or any other flaws.

[28]In the same way, a husband should love his wife as much as he loves himself. A husband who loves his wife shows that he loves himself. [29]None of us hate our own bodies. We provide for them and take good care of them, just as Christ does for the church, [30]because we are each part of his body. [31]As the Scriptures say, "A man leaves his father and mother to get married, and he becomes like one person with his wife." [32]This is a great mystery, but I understand it to mean Christ and his church. [33]So each husband should love his wife as much as he loves himself, and each wife should respect her husband.

Children and Parents

6 Children, you belong to the Lord, and you do the right thing when you obey your parents. The first commandment with a promise says, [2]"Obey your father and your mother, [3]and you will have a long and happy life."

[4]Parents, don't be hard on your children. Raise them properly. Teach them and instruct them about the Lord.

---

[l]**5.14** *Light shows up everything*: Or "Everything that is seen in the light becomes light itself."

~~~

SingleLife—What should I look for in a future spouse? *(Ephesians 5.21-33)*

Look for a man who's sacrificial.
No man is going to be a perfect husband. Knights in shining armor make great myths and movies, but real-life men are fallen like the rest of us. So if you want to develop a realistic perspective on marriage, don't look to the latest blockbuster movie or romance novel. Scripture clearly tells you what God wants husbands to be: selfless, faithful servants who appreciate what Christ has done for them (5.25-29).

Where do you find a man like that? He's already out serving people because of his love for God. He's volunteering at the local homeless shelter, being a big brother to a boy who has no father, or serving as an elder in the church. This is the kind of man who'll be praying to meet a godly wife, one who is already out serving people because *she* loves God. So get about the business of serving God in the ways he has gifted you—and leave the rest to God! (See also Genesis 24; Song of Songs 1; 1 Corinthians 13.)

Words To Remember: *A husband should love his wife as much as he loves himself. A husband who loves his wife shows that he loves himself. None of us hate our own bodies. We provide for them and take good care of them, just as Christ does for the church.*—Ephesians 5.28,29

Slaves and Masters

⁵Slaves, you must obey your earthly masters. Show them great respect and be as loyal to them as you are to Christ. ⁶Try to please them at all times, and not just when you think they are watching. You are slaves of Christ, so with your whole heart you must do what God wants you to do. ⁷Gladly serve your masters, as though they were the Lord himself, and not simply people. ⁸You know that you will be rewarded for any good things you do, whether you are slaves or free.

⁹Slave owners, you must treat your slaves with this same respect. Don't threaten them. They have the same Master in heaven that you do, and he doesn't have any favorites.

PARENTING&*family*—How can I tell if I'm doing a good job as a mother?
(Ephesians 6.1-4)

Teach your children who they *really* belong to.

Mounting piles of diapers, socks, and underwear. Flute lessons. Staying up all night with a newborn—or waiting for a rebellious teen to come home. Scout meetings. Sunday school and church activities. Bake sales that are announced at the last minute. All of these things stack up to an awful lot for moms to do. It's no wonder they get tired!

When you're feeling overwhelmed with things to do, this passage offers relief. It states some straightforward ways you can tell if you're being a godly mom (6.4):

1. Don't be hard on your kids. That means not taking your stress or busyness out on them.

2. Raise them properly. You can raise your kids to be kind to others; provide for their physical needs (such as food, clothing, shelter), their emotional needs (for love and discipline), their mental needs (for schooling), and, most of all, for their spiritual needs (where they're heading for eternity).

3. Teach them and instruct them about the Lord. Take them to Sunday school and church. Read Bible stories to them at home. And, above all, live out the truths of Scripture in *your* daily life! (See also Luke 2.41-52; Hebrews 12.5-13.)

Words To Remember: *Parents, don't be hard on your children. Raise them properly. Teach them and instruct them about the Lord.*—Ephesians 6.4

SingleLife—How can I resist the pressure to be sexually active?
(Ephesians 6.10-20)

Be wise, and look for friends to support you.

As a single woman, sex outside the sanction of marriage is a real and powerful temptation, no matter how long you've been a Christian. It's such a common part of most people's lives in our world today that honoring God with your body requires serious effort on your part. What can you do to stay sexually pure?

You should by all means pray (6.18) that God will protect you from sexual sin. Your prayers, however, must be coupled with wise choices. If certain men, movies, or social settings tempt you to sin, avoid them out of devotion to God. You are God's temple, after all, and there are spiritual forces at work in your life that will tempt you in subtle ways to compromise your faith (6.12). Be choosy about whom you date. Respect your weaknesses and surround yourself with people who promise to pray for you to be sexually pure. This is how you arm yourself against the weapons of the devil (6.13). (See also Joshua 7; Psalm 103; James 1.12-18; 2 Peter 2.7-9.)

Words To Remember: *Let the mighty strength of the Lord make you strong.*
—Ephesians 6.10

The Fight against Evil

[10]Finally, let the mighty strength of the Lord make you strong. [11]Put on all the armor that God gives, so you can defend yourself against the devil's tricks. [12]We are not fighting against humans. We are fighting against forces and authorities and against rulers of darkness and powers in the spiritual world. [13]So put on all the armor that God gives. Then when that evil day[m] comes, you will be able to defend yourself. And when the battle is over, you will still be standing firm.

[14]Be ready! Let the truth be like a belt around your waist, and let God's justice protect you like armor. [15]Your desire to tell the good news about peace should be like shoes on your feet. [16]Let your faith be like a shield, and you will be able to stop all the flaming arrows of the evil one. [17]Let God's saving power be like a helmet, and for a sword use God's message that comes from the Spirit.

[18]Never stop praying, especially for others. Always pray by the power of the Spirit. Stay alert and keep praying for God's people. [19]Pray that I will be given the message to speak and that I may fearlessly explain the mystery about the good news. [20]I was sent to do this work, and that's the reason I am in jail. So pray that I will be brave and will speak as I should.

Final Greetings

[21-22]I want you to know how I am getting along and what I am doing. That's why I am sending Tychicus to you. He is a dear friend, as well as a faithful servant of the Lord. He will tell you how I am doing, and he will cheer you up.

[23]I pray that God the Father and the Lord Jesus Christ will give peace, love, and faith to every follower! [24]May God be kind to everyone who keeps on loving our Lord Jesus Christ.

---

[m]6.13 *that evil day*: Either the present (see 5.16) or "the day of death" or "the day of judgment."

Philippians
Letter of Joy

"Because you belong to Christ Jesus, God will bless you with peace that no one can completely understand. And this peace will control the way you think and feel" (4.7).

Many people find it easy to show happiness, but few express the relaxed peace that is joy. They either put on a fake smile and hide their pain behind it or grumble at the tiniest of struggles. Paul demonstrates in Philippians how to *choose* joy—the persistence of well-being through the best and the worst of times. And he provides a variety of ways through which we can let God give us joy: through gratitude, community, unity, obedience, peaceful living, assurance of salvation, helpfulness, friendliness to other believers, and more. Joy is more an action than a feeling, more a commitment than a reward.

Joy begins with the certainty that the bad we go through here is temporary, that God uses this time to complete his work in us (1.6). Joy continues as we choose to express a Christlike attitude during both the good and bad of life (2.1-11). Joy grows deeper as we press on toward the goal of righteousness (3.12,13). Joy reaches maturity as we learn through God's power what action to take to manage our own lives, and to meet needs in the lives of others (4.13,19). Some of us find it hard to be joyful during struggles. Oddly, others find it hard to be joyful when things go well. But in both circumstances, joy testifies to God's provision.

Paul originally addressed the book of Philippians to Christians in the city of Philippi, but his words apply to our lives as well. Paul expressed joy and appreciation for help from the Philippian believers—and we can pass on our own expressions of appreciation. Paul encouraged them in their faith and witness—and his words encourage us in the same. Familiar passages from Philippians include a description of Christ's attitude (2.1-11) and the promise of God's strength (4.13,19). Let the wisdom in Philippians guide you to choose joy.

Philippians at a Glance

1. Paul's prayer for the Philippian church (1.1-11)
2. Paul's focus on Christ even during tough times (1.12-30)
3. Call to imitate Jesus Christ (2.1-11)
4. Believers need to be a light to the world (2.12-30)
5. Keep pressing toward the goal (3.1—4.1)
6. Admonition to help other believers (4.2,3)
7. Change worry into prayerful action (4.4-20)
8. Final greetings (4.21-23)

1 From Paul and Timothy, servants of Christ Jesus.

To all of God's people who belong to Christ Jesus at Philippi and to all of your church officials and officers.*

²I pray that God our Father and the Lord Jesus Christ will be kind to you and will bless you with peace!

Paul's Prayer for the Church in Philippi

³Every time I think of you, I thank my God. ⁴And whenever I mention you in my prayers, it makes me happy. ⁵This is because you have taken part with me in spreading the good news from the first day you heard about it. ⁶God is the one who began this good work in you, and I am certain that he won't stop before it is complete on the day that Christ Jesus returns.

⁷You have a special place in my heart. So it is only natural for me to feel the way I do. All of you have helped in the work that God has given me, as I defend the good news and tell about it here in jail. ⁸God himself knows how much I want to see you. He knows that I care for you in the same way that Christ Jesus does.

⁹I pray that your love will keep on growing and that you will fully know and understand ¹⁰how to make the right choices. Then you will still be pure and innocent when Christ returns. And until that day, ¹¹Jesus Christ will keep you busy doing good deeds that bring glory and praise to God.

What Life Means to Paul

¹²My dear friends, I want you to know that what has happened to me has helped to spread the good news. ¹³The Roman guards and all the others know that I am here in jail because I serve Christ. ¹⁴Now most of the Lord's followers have become brave and are fearlessly telling the message.ᵇ

¹⁵Some are preaching about Christ because they are jealous and envious of us.

ᵃ**1.1** *church officials and officers:* Or "bishops and deacons." ᵇ**1.14** *the message:* Some manuscripts have "the Lord's message," and others have "God's message."

SingleLife—How can I feel whole when the world sees me as half?
(Philippians 1.12-30)

Hang out with people who can manage bad press.
There's a lot of misinformation circulating about being single. Many times, people have preset expectations of what it's like; and instead of finding out how things really are, they impose their expectations on you. So what can you do to clear up any misperceptions? Look to the example of Paul.

He was unfairly imprisoned, but rather than whine away his time, he got in contact with people who cared. He did things for those people who honored God. One of these "doings" was his letter to the Philippians.

Not everything was happy for Paul. He faced the very real possibility of being put to death (1.23-25). But despite his tough circumstances, Paul persisted in helping others. If you feel imprisoned by a preconception that says everyone gets married—or ought to—remember, as a Christian, you are a whole person fully capable of caring in Jesus' name, whether married *or* single. Respond to your struggle with four actions:

1. Find reasons to be glad (1.12-18).
2. Let God enable you to choose honorable actions. Refuse premarital affairs and other temptations that sprout from loneliness (1.19,20).
3. Address your struggles directly (1.21-26).
4. Talk to and treat people in ways that bring attention to God. Be so caring that people will understand God's love simply by being around you (1.27-30).
(See also Psalm 23; Isaiah 40.21-31.)

Words To Remember: *I will keep on being glad, because I know that your prayers and the help that comes from the Spirit of Christ Jesus will keep me safe. I honestly expect and hope that I will never do anything to be ashamed of. Whether I live or die, I always want to . . . bring honor to Christ.*—Philippians 1.18-20

Others are preaching because they want to help. [16]They love Christ and know that I am here to defend the good news about him. [17]But the ones who are jealous of us are not sincere. They just want to cause trouble for me while I am in jail. [18]But that doesn't matter. All that matters is that people are telling about Christ, whether they are sincere or not. That is what makes me glad.

I will keep on being glad, [19]because I know that your prayers and the help that comes from the Spirit of Christ Jesus will keep me safe. [20]I honestly expect and hope that I will never do anything to be ashamed of. Whether I live or die, I always want to be as brave as I am now and bring honor to Christ.

[21]If I live, it will be for Christ, and if I die, I will gain even more. [22]I don't know what to choose. I could keep on living and doing something useful. [23]It is a hard choice to make. I want to die and be with Christ, because that would be much better. [24-25]But I know that all of you still need me. That's why I am sure I will stay on to help you grow and be happy in your faith. [26]Then, when I visit you again, you will have good reason to take great pride in Christ Jesus because of me.[c]

[27]Above all else, you must live in a way that brings honor to the good news about Christ. Then, whether I visit you or not, I will hear that all of you think alike. I will know that you are working together and that you are struggling side by side to get others to believe the good news.

[28]Be brave when you face your enemies. Your courage will show them that they are going to be destroyed, and it will show you that you will be saved. God will make all of this happen, [29]and he has blessed you. Not only do you have faith in Christ, but you suffer for him. [30]You saw me suffer, and you still hear about my troubles. Now you must suffer in the same way.

True Humility

2 Christ encourages you, and his love comforts you. God's Spirit unites you, and you are concerned for others. [2]Now make me completely happy! Live in harmony by showing love for each other. Be united in what you think, as if you were only one person. [3]Don't be jealous or proud, but be humble and consider others more important than yourselves. [4]Care about them as much as you care about yourselves [5]and think the same way that Christ Jesus thought:[d]

[6]Christ was truly God.
But he did not try to remain[e]
equal with God.

---

[c]**1.26** take great pride in Christ Jesus because of me: Or "take great pride in me because of Christ Jesus." [d]**2.5** think the same way that Christ Jesus thought: Or "think the way you should because you belong to Christ Jesus." [e]**2.6** remain: Or "become."

MARRIAGE—Why does the Bible talk about submission in marriage? What does God mean by it? (Philippians 2.1-11)

What's most important is doing what's best for each other.
Being "one unit" shouldn't mean one member of a marriage does all the thinking and the other blindly agrees. Ideally both husband and wife give their best to the mix of marriage to create something better than either could do alone. And submission means working to bring out the best in the other. Submission is perfected as each partner imitates Christ, but jealousy, pride, and selfishness can get in submission's way. Rather than show jealousy, act out genuine joy for your husband's accomplishment. And when you've messed up, admit your wrongs—then make an effort to do better next time.

Jesus voluntarily submitted to his Father. If each partner follows Christ's example of humility toward the other, submission in marriage isn't oppressive at all. It's beautiful—and freeing. (See also Proverbs 17.1; Ephesians 5.21-33.)

Words To Remember: *Be united in what you think, as if you were only one person. Don't be jealous or proud, but be humble and consider others more important than yourselves. Care about them as much as you care about yourselves and think the same way that Christ Jesus thought.*—Philippians 2.2-4

Euodia
and Syntyche

Philippians 2.1-8; 3.20—4.9

"*E*uodia and Syntyche, you belong to the Lord, so I beg you to stop arguing with each other" (4.2).

Sometimes, Christians have trouble getting along with each other—just as non-Christians do! The difference is, we have the option of calling on God's power and the help of other believers. Euodia and Syntyche were two church leaders who refused this option. While we don't know the nature of their arguments or the reason they argued so persistently, we can learn much from them on how *not* to handle disputes.

Their arguments were probably not petty, at least to them. Maybe there was a conviction at stake. Maybe one had hurt the other and the retaliation continued. Perhaps one had something the other longed for, or they simply rubbed each other the wrong way. Maybe they'd begun fighting so long ago, they'd almost forgotten why. But they chose to keep the argument going until no one could win. Their private war became a sore spot in the church.

These two women were Christians who had worked together with Paul's mission team to spread the good news about Jesus. But somehow they had lost sight of Jesus' example—at least where their relationship was concerned. Paul's letter to their church was meant to help these two women leaders and the church as a whole remember the character of Jesus. Chapter 2 tells us that "Christ encourages you, and his love comforts you" (2.1). Then in one of the most beautiful sections in Scripture, he reminds us that though Christ was truly God, he did not try to remain equal with God. In fact, "he gave up everything and became a slave" (2.7). Jesus was humble; he obeyed his Father; he even gave up life itself (2.8). It's hard to keep on bickering with that kind of example to follow.

We don't know if Euodia and Syntyche ever found harmony. We do know that Paul asked another believer in the church to help them. This, too, is an example to us. If we can't resolve a difference with another Christian, we shouldn't just let the dispute fester and eventually infect others. Instead, we should ask for help.

In any disagreement, the Philippians 2.1-8 prescription is helpful: Let Christ encourage you both; let his love give you the comfort you need to talk calmly; let God's Spirit unite you and equip you to show concern for the other. Replace jealousy and pride with humility. Care about the other person with the same deep love you hold for yourself. In so doing, let Jesus show you how to think, talk, and act.

⁷Instead he gave up everything[f]
  and became a slave,
when he became
  like one of us.

⁸Christ was humble.
He obeyed God and even died
  on a cross.
⁹Then God gave Christ
  the highest place
and honored his name
  above all others.

¹⁰So at the name of Jesus
  everyone will bow down,
those in heaven, on earth,
  and under the earth.
¹¹And to the glory
  of God the Father
everyone will openly agree,
  "Jesus Christ is Lord!"

Lights in the World

¹²My dear friends, you always obeyed when I was with you. Now that I am away, you should obey even more. So work with fear and trembling to discover what it really means to be saved. ¹³God is working in you to make you willing and able to obey him.

¹⁴Do everything without grumbling or arguing. ¹⁵Then you will be the pure and innocent children of God. You live among people who are crooked and evil, but you must not do anything that they can say is wrong. Try to shine as lights among the people of this world, ¹⁶as you hold firmly to[g] the message that gives life. Then on the day when Christ returns, I can take pride in you. I can also know that my work and efforts were not useless.

¹⁷Your faith in the Lord and your service are like a sacrifice offered to him. And my own blood may have to be poured out with the sacrifice.[h] If this happens, I will be glad and rejoice with you. ¹⁸In the same way, you should be glad and rejoice with me.

Timothy and Epaphroditus

¹⁹I want to be encouraged by news about you. So I hope the Lord Jesus will soon let me send Timothy to you. ²⁰I don't have anyone else who cares about you as much as he

---

[f]**2.7** *He gave up everything:* Greek, "He emptied himself."
[g]**2.16** *hold firmly to:* Or "offer them." [h]**2.17** *my own blood may have to be poured out with the sacrifice:* Offerings of water or wine were sometimes poured out when animals were sacrificed on the altar.

Personal *Concerns*—When it comes to material things, how can I know what's enough and what's too much? *(Philippians 3.7-16)*

Keep things in their proper perspective.
The dress you saw in the mall (it's the perfect color for you, but beyond your budget). Your friend's refurbished kitchen, complete with island and built-in microwave. The neighbor's new car. Another friend's state-of-the-art computer system.

Sometimes looking at what others have can be frustrating when we don't—and can't—have those things, too. This passage can help: "But Christ has shown me that what I once thought was valuable is worthless. Nothing is as wonderful as knowing Christ Jesus my Lord" (3.7,8). That puts things in their proper perspective, doesn't it?

When you're tempted to buy more, borrow more, own more, reread these verses. Reaching for a heavenly perspective doesn't mean that we won't still struggle with "how much is too much" in earthly possessions; however, we can "forget what is behind" and "struggle for what is ahead" (3.13) Our ultimate goal, as Christians, should be to become more godly and to point our feet toward what's important in eternity. That doesn't mean that we can't buy or own things; just that we should carefully evaluate what to buy and not buy—for the kingdom of God's sake. (See also Leviticus 25.8-28; Deuteronomy 24.19-22; Amos 6.1-7; 1 Timothy 6.17-19.)

Words To Remember: *But Christ has shown me that what I once thought was valuable is worthless. Nothing is as wonderful as knowing Christ Jesus my Lord.*
—Philippians 3.7,8

does. ²¹The others think only about what interests them and not about what concerns Christ Jesus. ²²But you know what kind of person Timothy is. He has worked with me like a son in spreading the good news. ²³I hope to send him to you, as soon as I find out what is going to happen to me. ²⁴And I feel sure that the Lord will also let me come soon.

²⁵I think I ought to send my dear friend Epaphroditus back to you. He is a follower and a worker and a soldier of the Lord, just as I am. You sent him to look after me, ²⁶but now he is eager to see you. He is worried, because you heard he was sick. ²⁷In fact, he was very sick and almost died. But God was kind to him, and also to me, and he kept me from being burdened down with sorrow.

²⁸Now I am more eager than ever to send Epaphroditus back again. You will be glad to see him, and I won't have to worry any longer. ²⁹Be sure to give him a cheerful welcome, just as people who serve the Lord deserve. ³⁰He almost died working for Christ, and he risked his own life to do for me what you could not.

Being Acceptable to God

3 Finally, my dear friends, be glad that you belong to the Lord. It doesn't bother me to write the same things to you that I have written before. In fact, it is for your own good.

²Watch out for those people who behave like dogs! They are evil and want to do more than just circumcise you. ³But we are the ones who are truly circumcised, because we worship by the power of God's Spirit[i] and take pride in Christ Jesus. We don't brag about what we have done, ⁴although I could. Others may brag about themselves, but I have more reason to brag than anyone else. ⁵I was circumcised when I was eight days old,[j] and I am from the nation of Israel and the tribe of Benjamin. I am a true Hebrew. As a Pharisee, I strictly obeyed the Law of Moses. ⁶And I was so eager that I even made trouble for the church. I did everything the Law demands in order to please God.

---

[i]**3.3** *by the power of God's Spirit*: Some manuscripts have "sincerely."   [j]**3.5** *when I was eight days old*: Jewish boys are circumcised eight days after birth.

Personal *Concerns*—How can I overcome my tendency to worry and instead gain confidence about the future? *(Philippians 4.4-9)*

Turn your worries into conversation with God.
For many of us, being told "Don't worry" is easier said than done! Worry is one way we express our concern. While it's hard to keep worry from coming to our door, we can transform it into prayer instead of inviting it in. Philippians 4.4-9 gives the elements of this transformation process:

1. Focus on gladness. Because of Jesus, there's always something to be glad about (4.4).

2. Let people be your priority. What action will bring good to others both now and in the future? Choose that gentle and future-looking action (4.5).

3. Recognize worry. It's a concern that goes pointlessly round and round. Stop the cycle by pointing your concern toward God (4.6).

4. Let Jesus show you what to do about your worry—and give you the peace "that no one can completely understand" (4.7).

When your loved one has cancer, you don't just sit and pray; you pray as you seek the best medical treatment available—medical treatment God himself has provided. Then you relax, knowing God has directed you to the resources that will fight the illness. It's a peace that can "control the way you think and feel" (4.7). (See also Joshua 23.14-16; Psalm 91; Micah 5.2-5; Habakkuk 3.16-19; Matthew 6.25-34.)

Words To Remember: *With thankful hearts offer up your prayers and requests to God. Then, because you belong to Christ Jesus, God will bless you with peace that no one can completely understand. And this peace will control the way you think and feel.* —Philippians 4.6,7

7But Christ has shown me that what I once thought was valuable is worthless. 8Nothing is as wonderful as knowing Christ Jesus my Lord. I have given up everything else and count it all as garbage. All I want is Christ 9and to know that I belong to him. I could not make myself acceptable to God by obeying the Law of Moses. God accepted me simply because of my faith in Christ. 10All I want is to know Christ and the power that raised him to life. I want to suffer and die as he did, 11so that somehow I also may be raised to life.

Running toward the Goal

12I have not yet reached my goal, and I am not perfect. But Christ has taken hold of me. So I keep on running and struggling to take hold of the prize. 13My friends, I don't feel that I have already arrived. But I forget what is behind, and I struggle for what is ahead. 14I run toward the goal, so that I can win the prize of being called to heaven. This is the prize that God offers because of what Christ Jesus has done. 15All of us who are mature should think in this same way. And if any of you think differently, God will make it clear to you. 16But we must keep going in the direction that we are now headed.

17My friends, I want you to follow my ex-ample and learn from others who closely fol-low the example we set for you. 18I often warned you that many people are living as enemies of the cross of Christ. And now with tears in my eyes, I warn you again 19that they are headed for hell! They worship their stomachs and brag about the disgust-ing things they do. All they can think about are the things of this world.

20But we are citizens of heaven and are eagerly waiting for our Savior to come from there. Our Lord Jesus Christ 21has power over everything, and he will make these poor bodies of ours like his own glorious body.

4 Dear friends, I love you and long to see you. Please keep on being faithful to the Lord. You are my pride and joy.

Paul Encourages the Lord's Followers

2Euodia and Syntyche, you belong to the Lord, so I beg you to stop arguing with each other. 3And, my true partner,k I ask you to help them. These women have worked to-gether with me and with Clement and with the others in spreading the good news. Their names are now written in the book of life.l

---

k4.3 partner: Or "Syzygus," a person's name. l4.3 the book of life: A book in which the names of God's people are written.

PARENTING&family—How can I deal with the challenges of being a single parent? (Philippians 4.10-20)

Invite help from people around you, and give your help to them.
No doubt about it, single parenting is tough because you have no consistent partner with which to share things. There's no one else in your house to exclaim over the delightful antics of your child. There's no one to share decision making or to contribute energy to the tiring but fulfilling privilege of parenting. But you're far from alone. You have a huge extended family from which to draw acclamation, decision making, and energy. This is your church family. Invite their support while you give them yours.

Inviting support from your church family won't necessarily come instantly or easily, however. It's similar to marriage in that you need to make others aware of your needs. A friend at church won't know you want to brag about your child unless you do! Nor will she know you need encouragement during a tiring week unless you let her know you're weary. Find one or two same-sex friends you can trust and risk telling them what you need. At the same time, be a friend who's willing to give what other parents need. You'll be energized through both giving and receiving. And in the process, you'll all show each other the love of Christ. You'll be the vehicle through whom Jesus meets needs (4.19). **(See also 1 Kings 17.8-16; Psalm 71.1-6; Psalm 138.)**

Words To Remember: *The Lord has made me very grateful that at last you have thought about me once again. Actually, you were thinking about me all along, but you didn't have any chance to show it.*—Philippians 4.10

[4]Always be glad because of the Lord! I will say it again: Be glad. [5]Always be gentle with others. The Lord will soon be here. [6]Don't worry about anything, but pray about everything. With thankful hearts offer up your prayers and requests to God. [7]Then, because you belong to Christ Jesus, God will bless you with peace that no one can completely understand. And this peace will control the way you think and feel.

[8]Finally, my friends, keep your minds on whatever is true, pure, right, holy, friendly, and proper. Don't ever stop thinking about what is truly worthwhile and worthy of praise. [9]You know the teachings I gave you, and you know what you heard me say and saw me do. So follow my example. And God, who gives peace, will be with you.

Paul Gives Thanks for the Gifts He Was Given

[10]The Lord has made me very grateful that at last you have thought about me once again. Actually, you were thinking about me all along, but you didn't have any chance to show it. [11]I am not complaining about having too little. I have learned to be satisfied with[m] whatever I have. [12]I know what it is to be poor or to have plenty, and I have lived under all kinds of conditions. I know what it means to be full or to be hungry, to have too much or too little. [13]Christ gives me the strength to face anything.

[14]It was good of you to help me when I was having such a hard time. [15]My friends at Philippi, you remember what it was like when I started preaching the good news in Macedonia.[n] After I left there, you were the only church that became my partner by giving blessings and by receiving them in return. [16]Even when I was in Thessalonica, you helped me more than once. [17]I am not trying to get something from you, but I want you to receive the blessings that come from giving.

[18]I have been paid back everything, and with interest. I am completely satisfied with the gifts that you had Epaphroditus bring me. They are like a sweet-smelling offering or like the right kind of sacrifice that pleases God. [19]I pray that God will take care of all your needs with the wonderful blessings that come from Christ Jesus! [20]May God our Father be praised forever and ever. Amen.

Final Greetings

[21]Give my greetings to all who are God's people because of Christ Jesus.

The Lord's followers here with me send you their greetings.

[22]All of God's people send their greetings, especially those in the service of the Emperor.

[23]I pray that our Lord Jesus Christ will be kind to you and will bless your life!

---

[m]4.11 *be satisfied with*: Or "get by on." [n]4.15 *when I started preaching the good news in Macedonia*: Paul is talking about his first visit to Philippi (see Acts 16.12-40).

Colossians

Christ, Who Is Fully God

The book of Colossians was originally a letter from the apostle Paul in prison to the Christians at Colossae. In his letter Paul corrected false teachings believers had been hearing. Though Paul didn't outline specifics, he presented truth in basic terms so believers, then and now, could identify deviations from true Christianity. Apparently the teachings encountered by the Colossians were similar to today's "Any religion is okay as long as you're sincere." That teaching is dangerously wrong. Jesus is true, unique, and superior. He's the only way to the Father and God in the flesh ("God lives fully in Christ," 2.9).

The truths in the book of Colossians continue to help us distinguish true faith from today's counterfeit cults. No imitation can compete with the fact that God dwells completely in Jesus. Only Jesus is God. Jesus reveals everything we need for faith and life. He's superior to any prophet, any leader, any religion. In fact, Christianity is more a relationship than a religion—we come into direct contact with the real God through the person Jesus Christ. He is sufficient for our entire existence. We relate to him more fully and better understand him with each act of obedience.

One of the most awesome things about our God is that he came to earth to live. As Jesus Christ he obeyed his own rules and succeeded in living on earth. Imitating him means we, too, can find the joy that God intended for us right here and now. While we wait for the perfection of heaven, we can experience the goodness that transcends present imperfections.

Delve into Colossians with the goal of discovering how to grow in unity with Christ. Chapter 3 provides actions to begin your venture. The chapters around it give the reasons to do these actions and grow these attitudes. As this book shows repeatedly, we need no elaborate scheme to get to God; we relate to him directly through Jesus. Faith is as simple and as complicated as imitating Jesus. We imitate him because we love God—not because God will "get us" if we don't. Our relationship with Jesus leads to choosing good based on love, not just on following rules. It's a direct, pure, and delightful unity with God that grows deeper and wider forever.

Colossians at a Glance

1. Paul's greeting to the believers (1.1,2)
2. Hope comes with real faith (1.3-8)
3. Christ's preeminence established (1.9-14)
4. Believers are redeemed through Christ's work (1.15-20)
5. Reconciliation is found through Christ (1.21-29)
6. Beware of deceivers (2.1-5)
7. Stay rooted in Christ (2.6-23)
8. The right focus for life this side of heaven (3.1-4)
9. The character of the believer (3.5—4.6)
10. Final greetings for real believers (4.7-18)

1 From Paul, chosen by God to be an apostle of Christ Jesus, and from Timothy, who is also a follower. ²To God's people who live in Colossae and are faithful followers of Christ.

I pray that God our Father will be kind to you and will bless you with peace!

A Prayer of Thanks

³Each time we pray for you, we thank God, the Father of our Lord Jesus Christ. ⁴We have heard of your faith in Christ and of your love for all of God's people, ⁵because what you hope for is kept safe for you in heaven. You first heard about this hope when you believed the true message, which is the good news.

> *While we can't see the full picture, God can. Knowing Christ and relying on him will help you get through the tough times.*
>
> MARY JOE FERNANDEZ

⁶The good news is spreading all over the world with great success. It has spread in that same way among you, ever since the first day you learned the truth about God's wonderful kindness ⁷from our good friend Epaphras. He works together with us for Christ and is a faithful worker for you.ᵃ ⁸He is also the one who told us about the love that God's Spirit has given you.

The Person and Work of Christ

⁹We have not stopped praying for you since the first day we heard about you. In fact, we always pray that God will show you everything he wants you to do and that you may have all the wisdom and understanding that his Spirit gives. ¹⁰Then you will live a life that honors the Lord, and you will always please him by doing good deeds. You will come to know God even better. ¹¹His glorious power will make you patient and strong enough to endure anything, and you will be truly happy.

¹²I pray that you will be grateful to God for letting youᵃ have part in what he has promised his people in the kingdom of light. ¹³God rescued us from the dark power of Satan and brought us into the kingdom of his dear Son, ¹⁴who forgives our sins and sets us free.

¹⁵Christ is exactly like God,
    who cannot be seen.
He is the first-born Son,
    superior to all creation.
¹⁶Everything was created by him,
    everything in heaven
        and on earth,
    everything seen and unseen,
    including all forces
        and powers,
    and all rulers
        and authorities.
All things were created
    by God's Son,
and everything was made
    for him.

¹⁷God's Son was before all else,
    and by him everything
        is held together.
¹⁸He is the head of his body,
    which is the church.
He is the very beginning,
    the first to be raised
        from death,
    so that he would be
        above all others.

¹⁹God himself was pleased
    to live fully in his Son.
²⁰And God was pleased
    for him to make peace
by sacrificing his blood
    on the cross,
so that all beings in heaven
    and on earth
would be brought back to God.

²¹You used to be far from God. Your thoughts made you his enemies, and you did evil things. ²²But his Son became a human and died. So God made peace with you, and now he lets you stand in his presence as people who are holy and faultless

---

ᵃ1.7,12 *you:* Some manuscripts have "us."

and innocent. ²³But you must stay deeply rooted and firm in your faith. You must not give up the hope you received when you heard the good news. It was preached to everyone on earth, and I myself have become a servant of this message.

Paul's Service to the Church

²⁴I am glad that I can suffer for you. I am pleased also that in my own body I can continue[b] the suffering of Christ for his body, the church. ²⁵God's plan was to make me a servant of his church and to send me to preach his complete message to you. ²⁶For ages and ages this message was kept secret from everyone, but now it has been explained to God's people. ²⁷God did this because he wanted you Gentiles to understand his wonderful and glorious mystery. And the mystery is that Christ lives in you, and he is your hope of sharing in God's glory.

²⁸We announce the message about Christ, and we use all our wisdom to warn and teach everyone, so that all of Christ's followers will grow and become mature. ²⁹That's why I work so hard and use the mighty power he gives me.

2 I want you to know what a struggle I am going through for you, for God's people at Laodicea, and for all of those followers who have never met me. ²I do it to encourage them. Then as their hearts are joined together in love, they will be wonderfully blessed with complete understanding. And they will truly know Christ. Not only is he the key to God's mystery, ³but all wisdom and knowledge are hidden away in him. ⁴I tell you these things to keep you from being fooled by fancy talk. ⁵Even though I am not with you, I keep thinking about you. I am glad to know that you are living as you should and that your faith in Christ is strong.

Christ Brings Real Life

⁶You have accepted Christ Jesus as your Lord. Now keep on following him. ⁷Plant your roots in Christ and let him be the foundation for your life. Be strong in your faith, just as you were taught. And be grateful.

⁸Don't let anyone fool you by using senseless arguments. These arguments may sound wise, but they are only human teachings. They come from the powers of this world[c] and not from Christ.

⁹God lives fully in Christ. ¹⁰And you are fully grown because you belong to Christ, who is over every power and authority. ¹¹Christ has also taken away your selfish desires, just as circumcision removes flesh

---

[b]1.24 *continue:* Or "complete." [c]2.8 *powers of this world:* Spirits and unseen forces were thought to control human lives and were believed to be connected with the movements of the stars.

SpiritualLife—How can I handle my doubts about God? (*Colossians 2.6-19*)

Plant your roots in Christ, and let them grow deeper.
Doubts tend to come during crisis times. *Why did this terrible thing happen? What should I really be doing with my life? How can I guide my child to turn from this path she's chosen? How will I handle this injustice?* Crises can feel like gale force winds against your seedling tree of faith.

Because you've accepted Jesus, you can bend without breaking. To do this, let each action, attitude, and choice show your confidence that obeying God is the right way to go. Each good choice shoots out another root of stability. Each caring response helps you grow taller and more mature. Each recognition and refusal of evil puts forth a branch that draws in God's light and power. The growth you build will give you the assurance that nothing can shake you from security in Jesus when a crisis hits. And you'll discover that troubles are more an encounter with this imperfect world than anything God brings. Doubt will fade as you find resources and strength from the hand of Jesus. (See also Job 1; Psalm 136; Jeremiah 23.16-32; Romans 4.13-25.)

Words To Remember: *You have accepted Christ Jesus as your Lord. Now keep on following him. Plant your roots in Christ and let him be the foundation for your life. Be strong in your faith, just as you were taught.*—Colossians 2.6

from the body. [12]And when you were baptized, it was the same as being buried with Christ. Then you were raised to life because you had faith in the power of God, who raised Christ from death. [13]You were dead, because you were sinful and were not God's people. But God let Christ make you[d] alive, when he forgave all our sins.

[14]God wiped out the charges that were against us for disobeying the Law of Moses. He took them away and nailed them to the cross. [15]There Christ defeated all powers and forces. He let the whole world see them being led away as prisoners when he celebrated his victory.

[16]Don't let anyone tell you what you must eat or drink. Don't let them say that you must celebrate the New Moon festival, the Sabbath, or any other festival. [17]These

---

[d]2.13 *you:* See the note at 1.7.

SpiritualLife—How can I make God's presence real in my life?
(*Colossians 3.10,11*)

Treat others with respect and compassion.
One of the best ways to experience God's presence in your life is to act as he acts. Because God values each person, you can do the same. In so doing, you'll see the beauty of each person, the unique ways she contributes to life, her hidden gifts that don't come out until someone notices them.

You'll discover that each believer is a new person with unique actions to contribute to God's kingdom. Not everyone will be talkative and interested in large groups. Several will thrive in smaller groups or will welcome people behind the scenes. Rather than try to make believers over in your image, notice the way God has already shaped and grown them. As you see what they have that you don't have, you'll understand more facets of the Creator who has made us all and is helping us become more like him. Then work in harmony to let Christ give "meaning to your life" (3.4). (See also 2 Chronicles 29.20-36; Ezekiel 10; Romans 15.14-21; Ephesians 3.14-21.)

 Words To Remember: *Each of you is now a new person. You are becoming more and more like your Creator, and you will understand him better.*—Colossians 3.10

Friendship—How can I forgive a friend who has greatly wronged or disappointed me? (*Colossians 3.12-14*)

Ask God to give you the power to forgive.
One of the most amazing features of our God is that he empowers us to follow him. For example, it's hard to forgive. But when we feel that forgiveness simply isn't within our resources, we can call on God to forgive. Through him, we can choose to stay in relationship with the friend who's wronged us, remove the barriers of grudge-holding and hurt and keep building the friendship despite being wronged. That's forgiveness.

Forgiveness doesn't mean thinking the hurt was okay or that you deserved to be wronged. It does mean your friend is more important than her actions. You forgive because you know God has forgiven you.

What if your friend continues to relate to you in hurtful ways? Do you still have to forgive? Yes, but you don't have to continue in close relationship. Still you can choose to "be gentle, kind, humble, meek, and patient" (3.12) toward that person. Find friends who will care for you with gentleness, kindness, humility, meekness, and patience. Through them, God will give you the power to forgive the ones who do not. (See also Romans 7.21—8.5; Ephesians 2.1-10.)

Words To Remember: *Be gentle, kind, humble, meek, and patient. Put up with each other.*—Colossians 3.12,13

things are only a shadow of what was to come. But Christ is real!

¹⁸Don't be cheated by people who make a show of acting humble and who worship angels.*ᵉ They brag about seeing visions. But it is all nonsense, because their minds are filled with selfish desires. ¹⁹They are no longer part of Christ, who is the head of the whole body. Christ gives the body its strength, and he uses its joints and muscles to hold it together, as it grows by the power of God.

Christ Brings New Life

²⁰You died with Christ. Now the forces of the universe*ᶠ don't have any power over you. Why do you live as if you had to obey such rules as, ²¹"Don't handle this. Don't taste that. Don't touch this."? ²²After these things are used, they are no longer good for anything. So why be bothered with the rules that humans have made up? ²³Obeying these rules may seem to be the smart thing to do. They appear to make you love God more and to be very humble and to have control over your body. But they don't really have any power over our desires.

3 You have been raised to life with Christ. Now set your heart on what is in heaven, where Christ rules at God's right side.*ᵍ ²Think about what is up there, not about what is here on earth. ³You died, which means that your life is hidden with Christ, who sits beside God. ⁴Christ gives meaning to your*ʰ life, and when he appears, you will also appear with him in glory.

⁵Don't be controlled by your body. Kill every desire for the wrong kind of sex. Don't be immoral or indecent or have evil thoughts. Don't be greedy, which is the same as worshiping idols. ⁶God is angry with people who disobey him by doing*ⁱ these things. ⁷And that is exactly what you did, when you lived among people who behaved in this way. ⁸But now you must stop doing such things. You must quit being angry, hateful, and evil. You must no longer say insulting or cruel things about others.

---

*ᵉ**2.18** *worship angels:* Or "worship with angels (in visions of heaven)."   *ᶠ**2.20** *forces of the universe:* See the note at 2.8.   *ᵍ**3.1** *right side:* The place of power and honor.   *ʰ**3.4** *your:* Some manuscripts have "our."   *ⁱ**3.6** *people who disobey him by doing:* Some manuscripts do not have these words.

MARRIAGE—How does God define my role as a wife? *(Colossians 3.15-19)*

To think of your husband before yourself.

Marriage is a two-way love street. Your husband depends on you for attention, encouragement, ideas, and opportunities to serve you, and you depend on him for the same. The tough part is that each person has the freedom to choose to take these actions. Choose for yourself—then make it easy for your husband also to encourage, give, and serve. Ways to do this include:

1. Be appreciative. Few people can resist giving to someone who appreciates them. Thank your husband for the money he earns, the attention he gives you, the understanding you share, and much more (3.16,17).

2. Be wise. Time what you say and do. Don't interrupt when your husband has a critical need to talk. Don't hold back crucial advice at decision time. Let God show you what to say, the tone to use, and the time to say it (3.16).

3. Work for the peace of Christ. Peace is not giving in, but confidently doing the right thing. Find places to build peace (3.15,16).

4. Remember your connection to God. You and your husband are two parts of the body of Jesus Christ. Treat your husband the way you'd treat Jesus (3.15).

If Jesus would do it, you do it. And if you'd be pleased to put Jesus' name with this action or attitude, it's likely a good choice. (See also Proverbs 31.10-31; Ecclesiastes 7.11-14.)

Words To Remember: *Each one of you is part of the body of Christ, and you were chosen to live together in peace. . . . Whatever you say or do should be done in the name of the Lord Jesus.—Colossians 3.15,17*

⁹And stop lying to each other. You have given up your old way of life with its habits. ¹⁰Each of you is now a new person. You are becoming more and more like your Creator, and you will understand him better. ¹¹It doesn't matter if you are a Greek or a Jew, or if you are circumcised or not. You may even be a barbarian or a Scythian,ʲ and you may be a slave or a free person. Yet Christ is all that matters, and he lives in all of us.

¹²God loves you and has chosen you as his own special people. So be gentle, kind, humble, meek, and patient. ¹³Put up with each other, and forgive anyone who does you wrong, just as Christ has forgiven you. ¹⁴Love is more important than anything else. It is what ties everything completely together.

¹⁵Each one of you is part of the body of Christ, and you were chosen to live together in peace. So let the peace that comes from Christ control your thoughts. And be grateful. ¹⁶Let the message about Christ completely fill your lives, while you use all your wisdom to teach and instruct each other. With thankful hearts, sing psalms, hymns, and spiritual songs to God. ¹⁷Whatever you say or do should be done in the name of the Lord Jesus, as you give thanks to God the Father because of him.

Some Rules for Christian Living

¹⁸A wife must put her husband first. This is her duty as a follower of the Lord. ¹⁹A husband must love his wife and not abuse her. ²⁰Children must always obey their parents. This pleases the Lord. ²¹Parents, don't be hard on your children. If you are, they might give up. ²²Slaves, you must always obey your earthly masters. Try to please them at all times, and not just when you think they are watching. Honor the Lord and serve your masters with your whole heart. ²³Do your work willingly, as though you were serving the Lord himself, and not just your earthly master. ²⁴In fact, the Lord Christ is the one you are really serving, and you know that he will reward you. ²⁵But Christ has no favorites! He will punish evil people, just as they deserve.

4 Slave owners, be fair and honest with your slaves. Don't forget that you have a Master in heaven. ²Never give up praying. And when you

---

ʲ3.11 *a barbarian or a Scythian*: Barbarians were people who could not speak Greek and would be in the lower class of society. Scythians were people who were known for their cruelty.

WORK—How can I rise above office politics? *(Colossians 3.22—4.1)*

Recognize that your master is God.
No one is immune from the temptation to play office politics. We may discover—to our dismay—how easy it can be to shade the truth or paint our actions in a pretty light. Then we may find ourselves excusing our wrong motives with the-end-justifies-the-means thinking.

Office politics are especially tempting because selfishness is hard for others to detect. How can a person outside you know whether you said something to get your way—or because it was the right thing for the team? But while your office mates may not recognize when you play the politics game, God does. So run from politics like a deadly disease. Remember that whether you're a supervisor or under supervision, your true master is God. You are no better than anyone else; you take priority over no one else. All of us are equal at the foot of the cross.

You're a valuable human being loved by God and created to do his good. You're in relationship with coworkers who are also valuable human beings loved by God. Treat others this way—even if you're the only one in the office who does it. (See also Deuteronomy 5.20,21; Esther 7.1-6; Matthew 20.20-28; Galatians 5.13-16; James 3.5-18.)

Words To Remember: *Do your work willingly, as though you were serving the Lord himself, and not just your earthly master. In fact, the Lord Christ is the one you are really serving, and you know that he will reward you.—Colossians 3.23,24*

us from speaking his message to the Gentiles and from leading them to be saved. The Jews have always gone too far with their sins. Now God has finally become angry and will punish them.

Paul Wants To Visit the Church Again

[17]My friends, we were kept from coming to you for a while, but we never stopped thinking about you. We were eager to see you and tried our best to visit you in person. [18]We really wanted to come. I myself tried several times, but Satan always stopped us. [19]After all, when the Lord Jesus appears, who else but you will give us hope and joy and be like a glorious crown for us? [20]You alone are our glory and joy!

3 Finally, we couldn't stand it any longer. We decided to stay in Athens by ourselves [2]and send our friend Timothy to you. He works with us as God's servant and preaches the good news about Christ. We wanted him to make you strong in your faith and to encourage you. [3]We didn't want any of you to be discouraged by all these troubles. You knew we would have to suffer, [4]because when we were with you, we told you this would happen. And we did suffer, as you well know. [5]At last, when I could not wait any longer, I sent Timothy to find out about your faith. I hoped that Satan

had not tempted you and made all our work useless.

[6]Timothy has come back from his visit with you and has told us about your faith and love. He also said that you always have happy memories of us and that you want to see us as much as we want to see you.

[7]My friends, even though we have a lot of trouble and suffering, your faith makes us feel better about you. [8]Your strong faith in the Lord is like a breath of new life. [9]How can we possibly thank God enough for all the happiness you have brought us? [10]Day and night we sincerely pray that we will see you again and help you to have an even stronger faith.

[11]We pray that God our Father and our Lord Jesus will let us visit you. [12]May the Lord make your love for each other and for everyone else grow by leaps and bounds. That's how our love for you has grown. [13]And when our Lord comes with all of his people, I pray that he will make your hearts pure and innocent in the sight of God the Father.

A Life That Pleases God

4 Finally, my dear friends, since you belong to the Lord Jesus, we beg and urge you to live as we taught you. Then you will please God. You are already living that way, but try even harder. [2]Re-

Friendship—How can I have healthy friendships with men?
(1 Thessalonians 4.1-8)

Remember that wrong use of sex cheats people—and God.
Sexual temptation is powerful, and being a Christian doesn't make you immune. Few Christians enter an unmarried relationship planning a sexual encounter. But all Christians can keep it from happening. We can learn how to resist. First, call on the power of almighty God. Second, recognize that everyone is vulnerable. Third, steer clear of any circumstance that would make sexual encounters possible. Take meals and business trips in trios, not duos. Refuse to meet in hotel rooms. Let any meetings be conducted in public with the door open. Fourth, back off when you sense an emotional attachment forming, even in safe settings. You can't stop initial attraction, but you can squash its growth.
Paul wrote, "You must not cheat any of the Lord's followers in matters of sex." So refuse to cheat your brother in Christ. Learn to control yourself. Be honorable. Refuse to take advantage of your brother. It's never God's will to become sexually involved, physically or mentally, outside of marriage. So focus on friendship and focus on work. With God's help, you can do it. (See also 1 Samuel 25; 2 Kings 4.1-7.)

Words To Remember: *God wants you to be holy, so don't be immoral in matters of sex. . . . You must not cheat any of the Lord's followers in matters of sex.*—1 Thessalonians 4.3,6

---

pray, keep alert and be thankful. [3]Be sure to pray that God will make a way for us to spread his message and explain the mystery about Christ, even though I am in jail for doing this. [4]Please pray that I will make the message as clear as possible.

[5]When you are with unbelievers, always make good use of the time. [6]Be pleasant and hold their interest when you speak the message. Choose your words carefully and be ready to give answers to anyone who asks questions.

Final Greetings

[7]Tychicus is the dear friend, who faithfully works and serves the Lord with us, and he will give you the news about me. [8]I am sending him to cheer you up by telling you how we are getting along. [9]Onesimus, that dear and faithful follower from your own group, is coming with him. The two of them will tell you everything that has happened here.

[10]Aristarchus is in jail with me. He sends greetings to you, and so does Mark, the cousin of Barnabas. You have already been told to welcome Mark, if he visits you. [11]Jesus, who is known as Justus, sends his

greetings. These three men are the only Jewish followers who have worked with me for the kingdom of God. They have given me much comfort.

[12]Your own Epaphras, who serves Christ Jesus, sends his greetings. He always prays hard that you may fully know what the Lord wants you to do and that you may do it completely. [13]I have seen how much trouble he has gone through for you and for the followers in Laodicea and Hierapolis.

[14]Our dear doctor Luke sends you his greetings, and so does Demas.

[15]Give my greetings to the followers at Laodicea, especially to Nympha and the church that meets in her home.

[16]After this letter has been read to your people, be sure to have it read in the church at Laodicea. And you should read the letter that I have sent to them.[k]

[17]Remind Archippus to do the work that the Lord has given him to do.

[18]I am signing this letter myself: PAUL.
Don't forget that I am in jail.
I pray that God will be kind to you.

---

[k]**4.16** *the letter that I have sent to them:* This is the only mention of the letter to the church at Laodicea.

Friendship—How can I reach out to people who differ from me in habits, faith, culture, or race? (Colossians 4.2-6)

Remember that Christianity is about turning "outsiders" into insiders.
Have you ever felt like an outsider? Maybe it's the first day of school, and you're more nervous than your child. You wonder what the other moms will be like. Or you're learning how to play tennis—and everybody seems to know more about the sport than you. Or you visit a different church and have a difficult time following their order of service (but the others seem to be enjoying it).
Being "on the outside" is rarely fun—and this is particularly true of us women, since God has created us to be relational. But once you've been an outsider, you have more empathy for others who feel as you have. In this passage, Paul gives some tips for how to reach out to those who differ from you:
1. Keep alert and be thankful for opportunities (4.2)
2. Pray that God will make a way (4.3)
3. Make your message as clear as possible (4.4)
4. Make good use of the time (4.5)
5. Be pleasant and hold their interest (4.6)
And, above all, Paul says that we need to be open to telling others about him and ready to give answers to anyone who asks questions. Does this mean we need to know all the answers to share our faith? No. We just need to be ready and willing to reach out. (See also John 4.4-26; Romans 3.21-31; 2 Corinthians 5.16-21; Galatians 3.26-29.)

Words To Remember: *Choose your words carefully and be ready to give answers to anyone who asks questions.*—Colossians 4.6

1 Thessalonians

Anticipating the Future

"We beg and urge you to live . . . [to] please God" (4.1). The Christians in Thessalonica were intensely interested in the second coming of Jesus Christ. To help them understand it, the apostle Paul devoted a large portion of both Thessalonian letters to Christ's return. But Paul balanced their passion for the future with a focus on the present. He urged attention to immediate worries, questions, and problems. He showed the Thessalonian believers (and us) how Jesus helps with hostilities toward faith, grief over dead loved ones, pressures to conform to the world's values, deceptive prophecies, and lazy people who don't do their share of work.

The Thessalonians also had a leadership crisis. Paul and Silas had started the church at Thessalonica while on Paul's second missionary journey. Because the Jews and Romans were jealous of this enthusiastic church, Paul had been forced to leave Thessalonica shortly afterward (Acts 17.1-15). Timothy returned to help. In addition to sending Timothy, Paul also wrote letters to the Thessalonians during his travels.

A swift return of Jesus would have solved all the Thessalonians' problems—and it would solve ours as well. But that wasn't God's plan for the Thessalonians, and if you are reading this introduction, it hasn't been God's plan for you, either. Rather than let excitement about Jesus' return distract you from God's present purposes, express your excitement through living daily for Jesus.

Like the Thessalonians, you may wonder how to live as a Christian when things aren't going well. You may wonder about the second coming of Jesus Christ. Will he come in your lifetime? What

should you do until he gets here? One of the best ways to express your eagerness for Christ's return is to live each moment in a way that would please him. Live for him now. You'll not only find help for the future, but also help for the present. The first Thessalonian letter provides principles that equip you to learn from and live for Jesus. It might be subtitled "Living Until Jesus Comes."

1 Thessalonians at a Glance

1. Persistent relationships with believers (1.1-3)
2. Confident knowledge of your security in Jesus (1.4-6)
3. Steady examples of faithfulness (1.7-10)
4. Honest communication of God's message (2.1-16)
5. Eager desire to encourage (2.17—3.13)
6. Please God in the way you treat people (4.1-12)
7. Grieve with hope (4.13-18)
8. Expectantly await Christ's return (5)

1 From Paul, Silas,[a] and Timothy.
To the church in Thessalonica, the people of God the Father and of the Lord Jesus Christ.
I pray that God will be kind to you and will bless you with peace!
[2]We thank God for you and always mention you in our prayers. Each time we pray, [3]we tell God our Father about your faith and loving work and about your firm hope in our Lord Jesus Christ.

The Thessalonians' Faith and Example

[4]My dear friends, God loves you, and we know he has chosen you to be his people. [5]When we told you the good news, it was with the power and assurance that come from the Holy Spirit, and not simply with words. You knew what kind of people we were and how we helped you. [6]So, when you accepted the message, you followed our example and the example of the Lord. You suffered, but the Holy Spirit made you glad. [7]You became an example for all the Lord's followers in Macedonia and Achaia. [8]And because of you, the Lord's message has spread everywhere in those regions. Now the news of your faith in God is known all over the world, and we don't have to say a thing about it. [9]Everyone is talking about how you welcomed us and how you turned away from idols to serve the true and living God. [10]They also tell how you are waiting for his Son Jesus to come from heaven. God raised him from death, and on the day of judgment Jesus will save us from God's anger.

Paul's Work in Thessalonica

2 My friends, you know that our time with you wasn't wasted. [2]As you remember, we had been mistreated and insulted at Philippi. But God gave us the courage to tell you the good news about him, even though many people caused us trouble. [3]We didn't have any hidden motives when we won you over, and we didn't try to fool or trick anyone. [4]God was pleased to trust us with his message. We didn't speak to please people, but to please God who knows our motives.
[5]You also know that we didn't try to flatter anyone. God himself knows that what we did wasn't a cover-up for greed. [6]We were not trying to get you or anyone else to praise

us. [7]But as apostles, we could have demanded help from you. After all, Christ is the one who sent us. We chose to be like children or like a mother[b] nursing her baby. [8]We cared so much for you, and you became so dear to us, that we were willing to give our lives for you when we gave you God's message.

> *I'm convinced sharing your faith simply requires caring enough about someone else to let that person know how Christ has changed your life.*
>
> LIZ CURTIS HIGGS

[9]My dear friends, you surely haven't forgotten our hard work and hardships. You remember how night and day we struggled to make a living, so that we could tell you God's message without being a burden to anyone. [10]Both you and God are witnesses that we were pure and honest and innocent in our dealings with you. [11]You also know we did everything for the Lord. [11]You also know we did everything for you that parents would do for their own children. [12]We begged, encouraged, and urged each of you to live in a way that would honor God. He is the one who chose you to share in his own kingdom and glory.
[13]We always thank God that you believed the message we preached. It came from him, and it isn't something made up by humans. You accepted it as God's message, and now he is working in you. [14]My friends, you did just like God's churches in Judea and like the other followers of Christ Jesus there. And so, you were mistreated by your own people, in the same way they were mistreated by their people.
[15]Those Jews killed the Lord Jesus and the prophets, and they even chased us away. God doesn't like what they do and neither does anyone else. [16]They keep

[a]1.1 *Silas:* The Greek text has "Silvanus," another form of the name Silas. [b]2.7 *like children or like a mother:* Some manuscripts have "as gentle as a mother."

member the instructions we gave you as followers of the Lord Jesus. ³God wants you to be holy, so don't be immoral in matters of sex. ⁴Respect and honor your wife.ᶜ ⁵Don't be a slave of your desires or live like people who don't know God. ⁶You must not cheat any of the Lord's followers in matters of sex.ᵈ Remember, we warned you that he punishes everyone who does such things. ⁷God didn't choose you to be filthy, but to be pure. ⁸So if you don't obey these rules, you are not really disobeying us. You are disobeying God, who gives you his Holy Spirit.

⁹We don't have to write you about the need to love each other. God has taught you to do this, ¹⁰and you already have shown your love for all of his people in Macedonia. But, my dear friends, we ask you to do even more. ¹¹Try your best to live quietly, to mind your own business, and to work hard, just as we taught you to do. ¹²Then you will be respected by people who are not followers of the Lord, and you won't have to depend on anyone.

The Lord's Coming

¹³My friends, we want you to understand how it will be for those followers who have already died. Then you won't grieve over them and be like people who don't have any hope. ¹⁴We believe that Jesus died and was raised to life. We also believe that when God brings Jesus back again, he will bring with him all who had faith in Jesus before they died. ¹⁵Our Lord Jesus told us that when he comes, we won't go up to meet him ahead of his followers who have already died.

¹⁶With a loud command and with the shout of the chief angel and a blast of God's trumpet, the Lord will return from heaven. Then those who had faith in Christ before they died will be raised to life. ¹⁷Next, all of us who are still alive will be taken up into the clouds together with them to meet the Lord in the sky. From that time on we will all be with the Lord forever. ¹⁸Encourage each other with these words.

5 I don't need to write you about the time or date when all this will happen. ²You surely know that the Lord's returnᵉ will be as a thief coming at night. ³People will think they are safe and secure. But destruction will suddenly strike them like the pains of a woman about to give birth. And they won't escape.

⁴My dear friends, you don't live in

ᶜ**4.4** *your wife*: Or "your body."   ᵈ**4.6** *in matters of sex*: Or "in business."   ᵉ**5.2** *the Lord's return*: The Greek text has "the day of the Lord."

WORK—What's a good way for me to share my faith at work?
(1 Thessalonians 4.9-12)

Earn the respect of your coworkers.
Hard work implies selflessness, dedication, problem-solving, and concern for coworkers. All these qualities demonstrate faith in God. Hard work invites respect, even from those who have no faith of their own. Sure you'll find coworkers who respect no one, no matter how hard they work. You'll also find coworkers who will try to dump their work on you because you work hard. But most recognize selfless work as a good quality.

Hard work—coupled with quiet living and a respect for others—is a way to demonstrate that each person belongs to a team. It invites cooperation and recognizes and appreciates the efforts of others. These qualities show you care less about who gets the credit than that the job is well done.

In all these ways, you can give testimony to your Lord. When people ask you why you're so diligent, you can explain you do it to honor God. You can invite them to become part of God's team where everyone has a place and a job to do. But even if no one ever speaks to you about your work, you'll still be giving a picture of God and what God designed work to be. (See also 2 Corinthians 4.1-15; 1 Timothy 5.17—6.2; 2 Timothy 1.6-14.)

Words To Remember: *Try your best to live quietly, to mind your own business, and to work hard, just as we taught you to do. Then you will be respected by people who are not followers of the Lord.*—1 Thessalonians 4.11,12

darkness, and so that day won't surprise you like a thief. [5]You belong to the light and live in the day. We don't live in the night or belong to the dark. [6]Others may sleep, but we should stay awake and be alert. [7]People sleep during the night, and some even get drunk. [8]But we belong to the day. So we must stay sober and let our faith and love be like a suit of armor. Our firm hope that we will be saved is our helmet.

[9]God doesn't intend to punish us, but wants us to be saved by our Lord Jesus Christ. [10]Christ died for us, so that we could live with him, whether we are alive or dead when he comes. [11]That's why you must encourage and help each other, just as you are already doing.

Final Instructions and Greetings

[12]My friends, we ask you to be thoughtful of your leaders who work hard and tell you how to live for the Lord. [13]Show them great respect and love because of their work. Try to get along with each other. [14]My friends, we beg you to warn anyone who isn't living right. Encourage anyone who feels left out, help all who are weak, and be patient with everyone. [15]Don't be hateful to people, just because they are hateful to you. Rather, be good to each other and to everyone else.

[16]Always be joyful [17]and never stop praying. [18]Whatever happens, keep thanking God because of Jesus Christ. This is what God wants you to do.

[19]Don't turn away God's Spirit [20]or ignore prophecies. [21]Put everything to the test. Accept what is good [22]and don't have anything to do with evil.

[23]I pray that God, who gives peace, will make you completely holy. And may your spirit, soul, and body be kept healthy and faultless until our Lord Jesus Christ returns. [24]The one who chose you can be trusted, and he will do this.

[25]Friends, please pray for us. [26]Give the Lord's followers a warm greeting.

[27]In the name of the Lord I beg you to read this letter to all his followers.

[28]I pray that our Lord Jesus Christ will be kind to you!

---

*Spiritual*Life—I'm so busy! How can I find time for God?
(1 Thessalonians 4.13-18)

Make every moment count.
Jesus will return—unexpectedly. No matter what you do and no matter where you are, act in such a way that you'd be pleased to have Jesus appear. In this way every minute of your life belongs to God. Your whole day becomes time with God, a continuous worship.

To discover ways to live out this continual contact with God, sift through the portions of your day. As you rise with your family, what thoughtful words can you say to encourage family members for the challenges ahead? As you begin the day's tasks, how can you plan to make the most of every minute? How can you spend lunchtime to bring glory to God—by preparing your Sunday school lesson or befriending someone? With what attitude will you manage the end-of-the-day crazies? How will you close the day with the people you hold dear?

Your life in its entirety belongs to God; make every moment count. (See also Mark 13.32-37; Titus 3.4-7,14.)

Words To Remember: *We believe that Jesus died and was raised to life. We also believe that when God brings Jesus back again, he will bring with him all who had faith in Jesus before they died.*—1 Thessalonians 4.14

2 Thessalonians

Direction for the Toughest of Times

"God our Father loves us. He is kind and has given us eternal comfort and a wonderful hope. We pray that our Lord Jesus Christ and God our Father will encourage you and help you always to do and say the right thing" (2.16,17). No matter how bad things get, a happy ending is coming—even if it's not until after death. And despite how many things go wrong, God will walk with you to show you just what to do and say in circumstances. These comforts are the heart of Paul's second letter to the Thessalonians.

The young Thessalonian Christians faced non-Christians who misunderstood and ridiculed them. Jealous Jews continued to stir up controversy and trouble. Someone even claimed to have a letter from Paul saying Jesus had already returned. Because of these and other problems, the Thessalonans worried that they were no longer worthy to be part of God's kingdom.

Even in all their worries and fears, the Thessalonians continued to express faith, love, and persistence; this delighted Paul. But they also struggled and grew discouraged; this concerned Paul. So he wrote to help with both. Paul wrote this second letter about six months after 1 Thessalonians.

In both letters to the Thessalonians, Paul suggested ways to respond to persecution, assured the believers that they were secure in Jesus, repeated that Jesus would definitely come back, encouraged steady spiritual growth, and promoted daily work. The first letter has a warm, friendly tone; the second is a bit more formal, driving home points the Thessalonians didn't catch the first time. For example, in 1 Thessalonians 4.11 and 5.6, Paul suggested hard work and alertness. In 2 Thessalonians 3.10-12, Paul more firmly named don't-work-don't-eat as the cure for laziness.

Like the Thessalonians, persevere when things don't go well, confident that the story isn't over yet. Jesus will win in the end. Look forward to Christ's return with eagerness, and don't become distracted. Show your anticipation by letting Jesus give your daily routine meaning and purpose. Even the simple things, like the way you greet family members upon waking, are ways to show that Jesus is alive and caring. Learn from, live for, and grow closer to Jesus in the journey called discipleship. Second Thessalonians is one of the best books to guide your discipleship journey.

2 Thessalonians at a Glance

1 From Paul, Silas,[a] and Timothy.
To the church in Thessalonica, the people of God our Father and of the Lord Jesus Christ.

[2]I pray that God our Father and the Lord Jesus Christ will be kind to you and will bless you with peace!

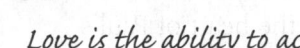

Love is the ability to act in such a way that we build up others and ourselves.

JILL BRISCOE

When Christ Returns

[3]My dear friends, we always have good reason to thank God for you, because your faith in God and your love for each other keep growing all the time. [4]That's why we brag about you to all of God's churches. We tell them how patient you are and how you keep on having faith, even though you are going through a lot of trouble and suffering.

[5]All of this shows that God judges fairly and that he is making you fit to share in his kingdom for which you are suffering. [6]It is only right for God to punish everyone who is causing you trouble, [7]but he will give you relief from your troubles. He will do the same for us, when the Lord Jesus comes from heaven with his powerful angels [8]and with a flaming fire.

Our Lord Jesus will punish anyone who doesn't know God and won't obey his message. [9]Their punishment will be eternal destruction, and they will be kept far from the presence of our Lord and his glorious strength. [10]This will happen on that day when the Lord returns to be praised and honored by all who have faith in him and

belong to him. This includes you, because you believed what we said.

[11]God chose you, and we keep praying that God will make you worthy of being his people. We pray for God's power to help you do all the good things that you hope to do and that your faith makes you want to do. [12]Then, because God and our Lord Jesus Christ are so kind, you will bring honor to the name of our Lord Jesus, and he will bring honor to you.

The Lord's Return

2 When our Lord Jesus returns, we will be gathered up to meet him. So I ask you, my friends, [2]not to be easily upset or disturbed by people who claim that the Lord[b] has already come. They may say that they heard this directly from the Holy Spirit, or from someone else, or even that they read it in one of our letters. [3]But don't be fooled! People will rebel against God. Then before the Lord returns, the wicked[c] one who is doomed to be destroyed will appear. [4]He will brag and oppose everything that is holy or sacred. He will even sit in God's temple and claim to be God. [5]Don't you remember that I told you this while I was still with you?

[6]You already know what is holding this wicked one back until it is time for him to come. [7]His mysterious power is already at work, but someone is holding him back. And the wicked one won't appear until that someone is out of the way. [8]Then he will appear, but the Lord Jesus will kill him simply by breathing on him. He will even sit in completely destroyed by the Lord's glorious return.

[9]When the wicked one appears, Satan will pretend to work all kinds of miracles,

---

[a]**1.1** *Silas*: The Greek text has "Silvanus," which is another form of the name Silas. [b]**2.2** *Lord*: The Greek text has "day of the Lord." [c]**2.3** *wicked*: Some manuscripts have "sinful."

wonders, and signs. [10]Lost people will be fooled by his evil deeds. They could be saved, but they will refuse to love the truth and accept it. [11]So God will make sure that they are fooled into believing a lie. [12]All of them will be punished, because they would rather do evil than believe the truth.

Be Faithful

[13]My friends, the Lord loves you, and it is only natural for us to thank God for you. God chose you to be the first ones to be saved.[d] His Spirit made you holy, and you put your faith in the truth. [14]God used our preaching as his way of inviting you to share in the glory of our Lord Jesus Christ. [15]My friends, that's why you must remain faithful and follow closely what we taught you in person and by our letters.

[16]God our Father loves us. He is kind and has given us eternal comfort and a wonderful hope. We pray that our Lord Jesus Christ and God our Father [17]will encourage you and help you always to do and say the right thing.

Pray for Us

3 Finally, our friends, please pray for us. This will help the message about the Lord to spread quickly, and others will respect it, just as you do. [2]Pray that we may be kept safe from worthless and evil people. After all, not everyone has faith. [3]But the Lord can be trusted to make you strong and protect you from harm. [4]He has made us sure that you are obeying what we taught you and that you will keep on obeying. [5]I pray that the Lord will guide you to be as loving as God and as patient as Christ.

Warnings against Laziness

[6]My dear friends, in the name of[e] the Lord Jesus, I beg you not to have anything to do with any of your people who loaf around and refuse to obey the instructions we gave you. [7]You surely know that you should follow our example. We didn't waste our time loafing, [8]and we didn't accept food from anyone without paying for it. We didn't want to be a burden to any of you, so night and day we worked as hard as we could.

[9]We had the right not to work, but we wanted to set an example for you. [10]We also gave you the rule that if you don't work, you don't eat. [11]Now we learn that some of you

---

[d]**2.13** *God chose you to be the first ones to be saved:* Some manuscripts have "From the beginning God chose you to be saved."   [e]**3.6** *in the name of:* Or "as a follower of."

SingleLife—As a single mom, is it all right for me to date? Should I wait until my children are grown? *(2 Thessalonians 2.13-17)*

Let love for God and your children determine your choices.
If you're thinking of dating (or you're currently dating), consider that the person(s) you choose to date can influence you and your children for better or for worse, and that impact can be far-reaching. So search 2 Thessalonians 2.13-17 for a description of the kind of relationship God wants for you: Can you "thank God" for this person? Does he show that he is "holy" and that your relationship is "holy," which means set apart for use by God? Do your actions with this person "share in the glory of our Lord Jesus Christ," which means bringing positive attention to God for God's purposes? Can you "remain faithful" to God while with this person? Does your time with this person show that "God our Father loves us"?

That's a lot of questions. But they help you evaluate the health of a dating relationship. Before children, dating is a trio; after you have children, it's a quartet: you, God, your date, and your children. Make sure any dating relationship moves in harmony with your relationship to God and your children, and brings positive attention to God. (See also Isaiah 51.12-16; Daniel 12.)

Words To Remember: *God our Father loves us. He is kind and has given us eternal comfort and a wonderful hope. We pray that our Lord Jesus Christ and God our Father will encourage you and help you always to do and say the right thing.*
—2 Thessalonians 2.16,17

just loaf around and won't do any work, except the work of a busybody. [12]So, for the sake of our Lord Jesus Christ, we ask and beg these people to settle down and start working for a living. [13]Dear friends, you must never become tired of doing right.

[14]Be on your guard against any followers who refuse to obey what we have written in this letter. Put them to shame by not having anything to do with them. [15]Don't consider them your enemies, but speak kindly to them as you would to any other follower.

Final Prayer

[16]I pray that the Lord, who gives peace, will always bless you with peace. May the Lord be with all of you.

[17]I always sign my letters as I am now doing: PAUL.

[18]I pray that our Lord Jesus Christ will be kind to all of you.

PARENTING&*family*—How can I nurture my child's self-worth?
(2 Thessalonians 3.6-15)

Give your child age-appropriate work to do.
Self-worth is based in the fact that God created us. We demonstrate self-worth when we honor God in daily living, and one of these areas is work. Far from being a burden, work demonstrates that every believer has a critical role in the kingdom of God. Give your child this privilege throughout life by assigning age-appropriate tasks.

As you assign tasks, insure success by insisting that your child follow through. Your toddler will find it great fun to take her laundry to the laundry basket. But when involved with her toys, she won't want to stop. When you hold her toys until she finishes, you give her success. You also demonstrate self-discipline—a skill that will enable her to accomplish great things for God. Later you'll withhold computer games until she finishes homework, or keep the car keys until the lawn is mowed. As children get more independent, create schedules of household responsibilities, such as laundry, cleaning, yardwork, cooking, and cleanup. Many parents excuse lack of follow-through with "my kids just won't do it," or "they won't do it as well as I could." But these parents may themselves be taking the lazy path described in 2 Thessalonians 3.6-13.

When we teach a child to work, we teach a child to become a responsible adult, able to work together with her family and world with competence and confidence. (See also 1 Samuel 17.24-54; Psalm 139; Luke 15.11-32; Ephesians 1.3-14.)

Words To Remember: *We didn't want to be a burden to any of you, so night and day we worked as hard as we could. . . . Dear friends, you must never become tired of doing right.*—2 Thessalonians 3.8,13

1 Timothy

How To Be a Church

Church is not something you go to; it's something you become. Not by yourself, of course. You join with other believers, and together you make up a church. But how? Paul's letter to his dear friend Timothy gives us help.

Scholars are a little uncertain about the circumstances of this writing. We read about Paul's life in the book of Acts, but this letter doesn't fit comfortably into the events there which end with Paul in prison at Rome. It seems likely that Paul was later released from prison, that he sent Timothy to strengthen the church in Ephesus, and that he traveled to assist the churches he'd founded in Macedonia (1.3). This letter advised Timothy, whom he considered a spiritual son, how to help the Christians in Ephesus be a church.

How can Paul's first letter to Timothy help us do the same? Do you wonder if anyone is checking on old Mrs. Brown who hasn't been to church for a month—or whether anyone in church will care when you are eighty-five and absent? Paul commanded the church, "Take care of any widow who is really in need" (5.3). Do you suspect that money carries the right to make major decisions for the church? Paul wrote, "Warn the rich people . . . not to be proud or to trust in wealth that is easily lost" (6.17). Is it time to elect church officers and you want to vote for someone who supports your own favorite cause? Paul wrote a whole list of spiritual qualifications for those who lead the church—and said nothing at all about favorite causes (3.1-13; 5.17-22). Do you

wonder whether your church is teaching what's true? Paul shared your concern. An emphasis on truth pervades the letter, as well as a host of clues about how to spot what's false. Do you think everyone in your church is different from you? Paul expected it—and tells you how to respect and honor each other (5.1-3). Becoming a church is complex, but it's worth the effort. This book shows us how.

1 Timothy at a Glance

1. Greetings and blessings from Paul to Timothy (1.1,2)
2. Get rid of wrong teachings in the church (1.3-11)
3. Jesus came to the world to save sinners (1.12-20)
4. How to pray and behave in church (2)
5. What makes a good church leader? (3.1-13)
6. Keep teaching what's true—and resisting what's false (3.14—4.16)
7. Relating to others in the church (5.1—6.2)
8. Right and wrong beliefs about money (6.2-10)
9. Guard your own faith (6.11-21)

1

From Paul.

God our Savior and Christ Jesus commanded me to be an apostle of Christ Jesus, who gives us hope.

[2]Timothy, because of our faith, you are like a son to me. I pray that God our Father and our Lord Jesus Christ will be kind and merciful to you. May they bless you with peace!

Warning against False Teaching

[3]When I was leaving for Macedonia, I asked you to stay on in Ephesus and warn certain people there to stop spreading their false teachings. [4]You needed to warn them to stop wasting their time on senseless stories and endless lists of ancestors. Such things only cause arguments. They don't help anyone to do God's work that can only be done by faith.

[5]You must teach people to have genuine love, as well as a good conscience and true faith. [6]There are some who have given up these for nothing but empty talk. [7]They want to be teachers of the Law of Moses. But they don't know what they are talking about, even though they think they do.

> *If we haven't filled ourselves with his Word, how can we possibly recognize his presence in our lives?*
>
> LAURETTA PATTERSON

[8]We know that the Law is good, if it is used in the right way. [9]We also understand that it wasn't given to control people who please God, but to control lawbreakers, criminals, godless people, and sinners. It is for wicked and evil people, and for murderers, who would even kill their own parents. [10]The Law was written for people who are sexual perverts or who live as homosexuals or are kidnappers or liars or won't tell the truth in court. It is for anything else that opposes the correct teaching [11]of the good news that the glorious and wonderful God has given me.

Being Thankful for God's Kindness

[12]I thank Christ Jesus our Lord. He has given me the strength for my work because he knew that he could trust me. [13]I used to say terrible and insulting things about him, and I was cruel. But he had mercy on me because I didn't know what I was doing, and I had not yet put my faith in him. [14]Christ Jesus our Lord was very kind to me. He has greatly blessed my life with faith and love just like his own.

[15]"Christ Jesus came into the world to save sinners." This saying is true, and it can be trusted. I was the worst sinner of all! [16]But since I was worse than anyone else, God had mercy on me and let me be an example of the endless patience of Christ Jesus. He did this so that others would put their faith in Christ and have eternal life. [17]I pray that honor and glory will always be given to the only God, who lives forever and is the invisible and eternal King! Amen.

[18]Timothy, my son, the instructions I am giving you are based on what some prophets[a] once said about you. If you follow these instructions, you will fight like a good soldier. [19]You will be faithful and have a clear conscience. Some people have made a mess of their faith because they didn't listen to their consciences. [20]Two of them are Hymenaeus and Alexander. I have given these men over to the power of Satan, so they will learn not to oppose God.

How To Pray

2

First of all, I ask you to pray for everyone. Ask God to help and bless them all, and tell God how thankful you are for each of them. [2]Pray for kings and others in power, so that we may live quiet and peaceful lives as we worship and honor God. [3]This kind of prayer is good, and it pleases God our Savior. [4]God wants everyone to be saved and to know the whole truth, which is,

[5]There is only one God,
and Christ Jesus
    is the only one
who can bring us
    to God.

---

[a]1.18 *prophets:* Probably the Christian prophets referred to in 4.14.

Jesus was truly human,
and he gave himself
to rescue all of us.
[6] God showed us this
at the right time.

[7] This is why God chose me to be a preacher and an apostle of the good news. I am telling the truth. I am not lying. God sent me to teach the Gentiles about faith and truth.

[8] I want everyone everywhere to lift innocent hands toward heaven and pray, without being angry or arguing with each other. [9] I would like for women to wear modest and sensible clothes. They should not have fancy hairdos, or wear expensive clothes, or put on jewelry made of gold or pearls. [10] Women who claim to love God should do helpful things for others, [11] and they should learn by being quiet and paying attention. [12] They should be silent and not be allowed to teach or to tell men what to do. [13] After all, Adam was created before Eve, [14] and the man Adam wasn't the one who was fooled. It was the woman Eve who was completely fooled and sinned. [15] But women will be saved by having children,[b] if they stay faithful, loving, holy, and modest.

Church Officials

3 It is true that[c] anyone who desires to be a church official[d] wants to be something worthwhile. [2] That's why officials must have a good reputation and be faithful in marriage.[e] They must be self-controlled, sensible, well-behaved, friendly to strangers, and able to teach. [3] They must not be heavy drinkers or troublemakers. Instead, they must be kind and gentle and not love money.

[4] Church officials must be in control of their own families, and they must see that their children are obedient and always respectful. [5] If they don't know how to control their own families, how can they look after God's people?

[6] They must not be new followers of the Lord. If they are, they might become proud and be doomed along with the devil. [7] Finally, they must be well-respected by people who are not followers. Then they won't be trapped and disgraced by the devil.

Church Officers

[8] Church officers[f] should be serious. They must not be liars, heavy drinkers, or greedy for money. [9] And they must have a clear conscience and hold firmly to what God has shown us about our faith. [10] They must first prove themselves. Then if no one has anything against them, they can serve as officers.

[11] Women[g] must also be serious. They must not gossip or be heavy drinkers, and they must be faithful in everything they do. [12] Church officers must be faithful in marriage.[h] They must be in full control of their children and everyone else in their home. [13] Those who serve well as officers will earn a good reputation and will be highly respected for their faith in Christ Jesus.

The Mystery of Our Religion

[14] I hope to visit you soon. But I am writing these instructions, [15] so that if I am delayed, you will know how everyone who belongs to God's family ought to behave. After all, the church of the living God is the strong foundation of truth.

[16] Here is the great mystery of our religion:

*I'm convinced that giving
away and saving money are
the antidotes for overspending.
They produce a lasting feeling
of well-being and satisfaction
that spending money can
never satisfy long-term.*

MARY HUNT

[b]**2.15** *saved by having children*: Or "brought safely through childbirth" or "saved by the birth of a child" (that is, by the birth of Jesus) or "saved by being good mothers." [c]**3.1** *It is true that*: These words may be taken with 2.15. If so, that verse would be translated: "It is true that women will be saved . . . holy, and modest." And 3.1 would be translated, "Anyone who desires . . . something worthwhile." [d]**3.1** *church official*: Or "bishop." [e]**3.2** *be faithful in marriage*: Or "be the husband of only one wife" or "have never been divorced." [f]**3.8** *Church officers*: Or "Deacons." [g]**3.11** *Women*: Either church officers or the wives of church officers. [h]**3.12** *be faithful in marriage*: See the note at 3.2.

Christ[i] came as a human.
The Spirit proved
        that he pleased God,
and he was seen by angels.

Christ was preached
        to the nations.
People in this world
        put their faith in him,
and he was taken up to glory.

People Will Turn from Their Faith

4 God's Spirit clearly says that in the last days many people will turn from their faith. They will be fooled by evil spirits and by teachings that come from demons. [2]They will also be fooled by the false claims of liars whose consciences have lost all feeling. These liars [3]will forbid people to marry or to eat certain foods. But God created these foods to be eaten with thankful hearts by his followers who know the truth. [4]Everything God created is good. And if you give thanks, you may eat anything. [5]What God has said and your prayer will make it fit to eat.

Paul's Advice to Timothy

[6]If you teach these things to other followers, you will be a good servant of Christ Jesus. You will show that you have grown up

on the teachings about our faith and on the good instructions you have obeyed. [7]Don't have anything to do with worthless, senseless stories. Work hard to be truly religious. [8-9]As the saying goes,

"Exercise is good
        for your body,
but religion helps you
        in every way.
It promises life
        now and forever."

These words are worthwhile and should not be forgotten. [10]We have put our hope in the living God, who is the Savior of everyone, but especially of those who have faith. That's why we work and struggle so hard.[j]
[11]Teach these things and tell everyone to do what you say. [12]Don't let anyone make fun of you, just because you are young. Set an example for other followers by what you say and do, as well as by your love, faith, and purity.
[13]Until I arrive, be sure to keep on reading the Scriptures in worship, and don't

---

[i]3.16 *Christ:* The Greek text has "he," probably meaning "Christ." Some manuscripts have "God."
[j]4.10 *struggle so hard:* Some manuscripts have "are treated so badly."

PARENTING&family—What advice, if any, should I give to my twentysomething child? (1 Timothy 4.6-16)

Keep the faith.

Twentysomethings have to spread their wings. This is true in matters of work, money, location—and faith. This last item may be the hardest on a Christian mom. It's difficult to see the young adult you raised as a Christian turn to some other religion or none at all. Even the church across town looks like a poor second to one you hoped your child would stay in all of his life. You ache when you see a three-generation family sitting in front of you in church, and you suspect that your own twentysomething is attending "the church of the open sheets."

But faith, if it's real, must become our own. It won't do to spend a lifetime piggybacked on the faith of mom and dad. A twentysomething has to appropriate faith for himself. The transition from family faith to personal faith may mean a time of separation before the young adult can settle into his own path. It's a time when moms can pray, but probably should keep mum. However, when the occasion warrants it, simply saying "Keep the faith" isn't bad advice. (See also Ecclesiastes 11.1—12.1; Ezekiel 18.1-20; Amos 5.6-27; Matthew 14.24-33.)

Words To Remember: *If you teach these things to other followers, you will be a good servant of Christ Jesus. You will show that you have grown up on the teachings about our faith and on the good instructions you have obeyed.*—1 Timothy 4.6

stop preaching and teaching. ¹⁴Use the gift you were given when the prophets spoke and the group of church leaders[k] blessed you by placing their hands on you. ¹⁵Remember these things and think about them, so everyone can see how well you are doing. ¹⁶Be careful about the way you live and about what you teach. Keep on doing this, and you will save not only yourself, but the people who hear you.

How To Act toward Others

5 Don't correct an older man. Encourage him, as you would your own father. Treat younger men as you would your own brother, ²and treat older women as you would your own mother. Show the same respect to younger women that you would to your sister.

³Take care of any widow who is really in need. ⁴But if a widow has children or grandchildren, they should learn to serve God by taking care of her, as she once took care of them. This is what God wants them to do. ⁵A widow who is really in need is one who doesn't have any relatives. She has faith in God, and she keeps praying to him night and day, asking for his help.

⁶A widow who thinks only about having a good time is already dead, even though she is still alive.

⁷Tell all of this to everyone, so they will do the right thing. ⁸People who don't take care of their relatives, and especially their own families, have given up their faith. They are worse than someone who doesn't have faith in the Lord.

⁹For a widow to be put on the list of widows, she must be at least sixty years old, and she must have been faithful in marriage.[l] ¹⁰She must also be well-known for doing all sorts of good things, such as raising children, giving food to strangers, welcoming God's people into her home,[m] helping people in need, and always making herself useful.

¹¹Don't put young widows on the list. They may later have a strong desire to get married. Then they will turn away from Christ ¹²and become guilty of breaking their promise to him. ¹³Besides, they will become lazy and get into the habit of going from

---

[k]**4.14** *group of church leaders:* Or "group of elders" or "group of presbyters" or "group of priests." This translates one Greek word, and it is related to the one used in 5.17, 19. [l]**5.9** *been faithful in marriage:* Or "been the wife of only one husband" or "never been divorced." [m]**5.10** *welcoming God's people into her home:* The Greek text has "washing the feet of God's people." In New Testament times most people either went barefoot or wore sandals, and a host would often wash the feet of special guests.

PARENTING&*family*—How can I know what's best for my elderly parents? *(1 Timothy 5.1-7)*

Take care of them.

In Paul's era, the church was a Christian's social service agency. If you had needs, the church would help. You certainly couldn't count on the Roman government, which was likely to use you for lion bait. In 1 Timothy, Paul also pointed to the family as a resource to meet those needs. It was the responsibility of children and grandchildren to care for aging family members. Paul used strong words: "People who don't take care of their relatives, and especially their own families, have given up their faith. They are worse than someone who doesn't have faith in the Lord" (5.8). Paul didn't suggest we give time to serve our parents *instead* of serving God. He said that caring for our parents *is* serving God.

Of course we hope that our parents make financial arrangements for their own support during old age. And we draw on available government and community services. We encourage our parents to be as independent as they can for as long as they can. But in the end, caring for parents is a family responsibility.

What do our parents need? Us. (See also Psalm 25; Proverbs 23.22-25; Joel 2.28-32; 1 Corinthians 15.35-58.)

Words To Remember: *If a widow has children or grandchildren, they should learn to serve God by taking care of her, as she once took care of them. This is what God wants them to do.—1 Timothy 5.4*

house to house. Next, they will start gossiping and become busybodies, talking about things that are none of their business.

[14]I would prefer that young widows get married, have children, and look after their families. Then the enemy won't have any reason to say insulting things about us. [15]Look what's already happened to some of the young widows! They have turned away to follow Satan.

[16]If a woman who is a follower has any widows in her family, she[n] should help them. This will keep the church from having that burden, and then the church can help widows who are really in need.

Church Leaders

[17]Church leaders[o] who do their job well deserve to be paid[p] twice as much, especially if they work hard at preaching and teaching. [18]It is just as the Scriptures say, "Don't muzzle an ox when you are using it to grind grain." You also know the saying, "Workers are worth their pay."

[19]Don't listen to any charge against a church leader, unless at least two or three people bring the same charges. [20]But if any of the leaders should keep on sinning, they must be corrected in front of the whole group, as a warning to everyone else.

[21]In the presence of God and Christ Jesus and their chosen angels, I order you to follow my instructions! Be fair with everyone, and don't have any favorites.

[22]Don't be too quick to accept people into the service of the Lord[q] by placing your hands on them.

Don't sin because others do, but stay close to God.

[23]Stop drinking only water. Take a little wine to help your stomach trouble and the other illnesses you always have.

[24]Some people get caught in their sins right away, even before the time of judgment. But other people's sins don't show up until later. [25]It is the same with good deeds. Some are easily seen, but none of them can be hidden.

6 If you are a slave, you should respect and honor your owner. This will keep people from saying bad things about

---

[n]**5.16** *woman . . . she:* Some manuscripts have "man or woman . . . that person." [o]**5.17** *leaders:* Or "elders" or "presbyters" or "priests." [p]**5.17** *paid:* Or "honored" or "respected." [q]**5.22** *to accept people into the service of the Lord:* Or "to forgive people."

WORK—What's a good way for me to share my faith at work?
(1 Timothy 5.17—6.2)

Be honest, respectful, and fair—just as if you were in church.
Are you a slave at work? Many of us would say yes, though we know that employment and slavery are quite different. Even so, some of the same spiritual principles apply. In the early Christian church, slaves and slave owners worshiped side by side. It must have been a challenge as they looked at each other out of the corners of their eyes, each knowing that on Monday, it would all be different. But in church they were brothers and sisters. Paul's epistle tells us to spread that brother/sister relationship into the workplace.

Many of Paul's other principles about relating to each other within the church transfer well to work. In this section of his letter to Timothy he said, "Workers are worth their pay" (5.18). So *earn* your pay. (No cheating on time and effort!) And if you're in charge of money, pay what the workers earn. Paul added, "Don't listen to any charge . . . unless at least two or three people bring the same charges" (5.19). At work, we shouldn't jump to conclusions without hard evidence. We shouldn't encourage gossip. Paul also said, "Be fair with everyone, and don't have any favorites" (5.21). Good advice for employers and workers as well.

How can we share our faith at work? By taking our faith to work and living it out—right on the job. (See also 2 Corinthians 4.1-15; 1 Thessalonians 4.9-12; 2 Timothy 1.6-14.)

Words To Remember: *Be fair with everyone, and don't have any favorites. . . . If you are a slave, you should respect and honor your owner. This will keep people from saying bad things about God and about our teaching.*—1 Timothy 5.21; 6.1

God and about our teaching. ²If any of you slaves have owners who are followers, you should show them respect. After all, they are also followers of Christ, and he loves them. So you should serve and help them the best you can.

False Teaching and True Wealth

These are the things you must teach and tell the people to do. ³Anyone who teaches something different disagrees with the correct and godly teaching of our Lord Jesus Christ. ⁴Those people who disagree are proud of themselves, but they don't really know a thing. Their minds are sick, and they like to argue over words. They cause jealousy, disagreements, unkind words, evil suspicions, ⁵and nasty quarrels. They have wicked minds and have missed out on the truth.

These people think religion is supposed to make you rich. ⁶And religion does make your life rich, by making you content with what you have. ⁷We didn't bring anything into this world, and we won't^r take anything with us when we leave. ⁸So we should be satisfied just to have food and clothes. ⁹People who want to be rich fall into all sorts of temptations and traps. They are caught by foolish and harmful desires that drag them down and destroy them. ¹⁰The love of money causes all kinds of trouble. Some people want money so much that they have given up their faith and caused themselves a lot of pain.

Fighting a Good Fight for the Faith

¹¹Timothy, you belong to God, so keep away from all these evil things. Try your best to please God and to be like him. Be faithful, loving, dependable, and gentle. ¹²Fight a good fight for the faith and claim eternal life. God offered it to you when you clearly told about your faith, while so many people listened. ¹³Now I ask you to make a promise. Make it in the presence of God, who gives life to all, and in the presence of Jesus Christ, who openly told Pontius Pilate about his faith. ¹⁴Promise to obey completely and fully all that you have been told until our Lord Jesus Christ returns.

> ¹⁵The glorious God
>   is the only Ruler,
>   the King of kings
>   and Lord of lords.
> At the time that God
>   has already decided,
> he will send Jesus Christ
>   back again.

---

^r6.7 *we won't*: Some manuscripts have "we surely won't."

MARRIAGE—How can we prevent financial issues from becoming stumbling blocks in our marriage? *(1 Timothy 6.6-10)*

Don't focus too much on finances.
Money problems are a leading cause of divorce, so it's not enough to say, "Don't pay attention to money." Married couples *have* to pay attention to money. They have to learn to plan its use together, to talk about their differences, and learn to recover from financial emergencies.

But don't spend too much time on money; it's simply not worth it. In his letter, Paul said, "We didn't bring anything into this world, and we won't take anything with us when we leave. So we should be satisfied just to have food and clothes" (6.7,8). One way to keep money from hurting your marriage is to keep money in its proper place. Learn to use it wisely, but know that money itself will never bring you contentment. That comes from God alone.

Learn to enjoy together what God gives you—whether it's a sunset or the comfort of an old sweater. Most of what is truly important can never be bought with cash. (See also Psalm 49.16-20; Malachi 3.8-12; Matthew 6.19-24; Hebrews 13.5,6.)

Words To Remember: *[Be] content with what you have. We didn't bring anything into this world, and we won't take anything with us when we leave. So we should be satisfied.*—1 Timothy 6.6-8

¹⁶Only God lives forever!
And he lives in light
   that no one can come near.
No human has ever seen God
   or ever can see him.
God will be honored,
and his power
   will last forever. Amen.

¹⁷Warn the rich people of this world not to be proud or to trust in wealth that is easily lost. Tell them to have faith in God, who is rich and blesses us with everything we need to enjoy life. ¹⁸Instruct them to do as many good deeds as they can and to help everyone. Remind the rich to be generous and share what they have. ¹⁹This will lay a solid foundation for the future, so that they will know what true life is like.

²⁰Timothy, guard what God has placed in your care! Don't pay any attention to that godless and stupid talk that sounds smart but really isn't. ²¹Some people have even lost their faith by believing this talk.

I pray that the Lord will be kind to all of you!

Personal *Concerns*—When it comes to material things, how can I know what's enough and what's too much? *(1 Timothy 6.17-19)*

Focus your attention on God, instead of stuff.
It's not the amount of "things" that is too much; it's how we feel about them. Paul told Timothy to *warn* rich people. This must have been a rather daunting task. People who are rich are used to taking care of themselves and may not take kindly to warnings—especially about how they use their money. Even so, Paul thought this message important enough to alert Timothy, his young representative in the church at Ephesus.

Paul knew the temptation to trust in ourselves once we have earned enough money to feel secure. It's at that point that danger lurks. Paul invited the wealthy to turn their attention to God, whom he described, incidentally, as "rich." Instead of being proud of our own accomplishments, we should recognize that it is God who "blesses us with everything we need to enjoy life" (6.17). Paul was quick to add that the blessing of wealth brings its own responsibility. He said that we are to do "good deeds," "help everyone," "be generous," and "share" what we have (6.18).

It's easy to assume that only people in a higher earning bracket than our own are "the rich." But in a global sense, anyone who has a home or apartment, several changes of clothing, two or three meals a day, and regular medical care are among the wealthy of the world. (See also Leviticus 25.8-28; Deuteronomy 24.19-22; Amos 6.1-7; Philippians 3.7-16.)

 Words To Remember: *Warn the rich people of this world not to be proud or to trust in wealth that is easily lost. Tell them to have faith in God, who is rich and blesses us with everything we need to enjoy life.—1 Timothy 6.17*

2 Timothy
Last Words

"Timothy, you are like a dear child to me" (2 Timothy 1.2). Think of someone to whom you would say such affectionate words. Then imagine you expect to die soon and have one more chance to say something to that person. What would you say? Now add these complicating circumstances: You're in prison many miles from that loved person, a letter is your only way to communicate, and there may not be time for the other person to reply. What final words would you write?

That's the situation in which the apostle Paul, imprisoned in Rome, wrote this letter to the young pastor, Timothy, in Ephesus. Paul fully expected to die soon (4.6). He hoped Timothy would be able to see him, but he couldn't be sure there was time for Timothy to get there.

The two of them had so much history together! Paul had taken Timothy under his wing, mentored him, traveled with him to spread the good news of Christ, and gone to jail with him. He loved Timothy like a son. Paul had left this young man in a demanding position of leadership in the church at Ephesus.

Naturally Paul cared deeply about how things were going with Timothy. But there wasn't time for two-way correspondence. Paul had to wrap up everything he longed to say to Timothy and send it off before it was too late. So this final letter contains all we would expect it to contain: affection, encouragement, warnings, remembrance, instructions, news, and a plea to come for a visit.

This second letter to Timothy is an open door into Paul's heart. It shows that Paul cared for more than theology or right living. He loved people. Stressed to the limit at the end of his life, Paul reached for the certainty of heaven—and for simple human affection.

2 Timothy at a Glance

1. Paul's affectionate greetings to Timothy (1.1-7)
2. Paul expresses confidence despite his situation in prison (1.8-18)
3. Encouragement to Timothy to stay focused on Christ (2.1-13)
4. The plea to avoid arguments and temptations (2.14-26)
5. Warnings against devious people (3.1-9)
6. Paul gives his final charge to Timothy (3.10—4.8)
7. Personal notes (4.9-22)

1 From Paul, an apostle of Christ Jesus. God himself chose me to be an apostle, and he gave me the promised life that Jesus Christ makes possible.

²Timothy, you are like a dear child to me. I pray that God our Father and our Lord Christ Jesus will be kind and merciful to you and will bless you with peace!

Do Not Be Ashamed of the Lord

³Night and day I mention you in my prayers. I am always grateful for you, as I pray to the God my ancestors and I have served with a clear conscience. ⁴I remember how you cried, and I want to see you, because that will make me truly happy. ⁵I also remember the genuine faith of your mother Eunice. Your grandmother Lois had the same sort of faith, and I am sure that you have it as well. ⁶So I ask you to make full use of the gift that God gave you when I placed my hands on you.*ᵃ* Use it well. ⁷God's Spirit*ᵇ* doesn't make cowards out of us. The Spirit gives us power, love, and self-control.

⁸Don't be ashamed to speak for our Lord. And don't be ashamed of me, just because I am in jail for serving him. Use the power that comes from God and join with me in suffering for telling the good news.

⁹God saved us and chose us
  to be his holy people.
We did nothing
  to deserve this,
but God planned it
  because he is so kind.
Even before time began
God planned for Christ Jesus
  to show kindness to us.

¹⁰Now Christ Jesus has come
to show us the kindness
  of God.
Christ our Savior defeated death
and brought us
  the good news.
It shines like a light
and offers life
  that never ends.

---

*ᵃ*1.6 *when I placed my hands on you:* Church leaders placed their hands on people who were being appointed to preach or teach (see 1 Timothy 4.14). *ᵇ*1.7 *God's Spirit:* Or "God."

WORK—How can I be a good supervisor? *(2 Timothy 1.1-7)*

Help other people flourish.

If you're in a supervisory role (of any kind, whether it's at home, at work, at church, in your community), you already know something about "getting ahead"—because of your position. But sometimes people in supervisory roles don't know, don't care, or forget about helping *others* get ahead.

A good supervisor brings other people along in the growth process. Paul did that with Timothy. He handpicked Timothy as his helper, but wasn't content to let Timothy stay in a subordinate role. Paul saw Timothy's potential as a future leader, so he spent time and energy encouraging the younger man's gifts. Their relationship wasn't one of aloof manager to employee, but more like father and son, till at the end of his life Paul could write to Timothy, "You are like a dear child to me" (1.2).

In the person of Timothy, Paul was developing a Christian minister. While you may not be developing a Christian leader in your supervisory role at work, you still can bring out the best in your coworkers. (And if your work is supervising children at home, you *are* helping them develop into Christ followers!) With the right attitude, you can help your fellow workers be even more than they think they can be.

Concentrate on guiding and teaching employees who are less experienced. Ask God to help you look beneath the surface to see the potential of the people he created. Then do all you can to help that potential emerge. (See also Exodus 18; 1 Kings 3.5-15; 4.29-34; Ezra 5.1—6.12; Jeremiah 32.26-44; John 21.15-25; Philemon 8-16; Philemon 15-25.)

Words To Remember: *So I ask you to make full use of the gift that God gave you when I placed my hands on you. Use it well.—2 Timothy 1.6*

[11]My work is to be a preacher, an apostle, and a teacher.[c] [12]That's why I am suffering now. But I am not ashamed! I know the one I have faith in, and I am sure that he can guard until the last day what he has trusted me with.[d] [13]Now follow the example of the correct teaching I gave you, and let the faith and love of Christ Jesus be your model. [14]You have been trusted with a wonderful treasure. Guard it with the help of the Holy Spirit, who lives within you.

[15]You know that everyone in Asia has turned against me, especially Phygelus and Hermogenes.

[16]I pray that the Lord will be kind to the family of Onesiphorus. He often cheered me up and wasn't ashamed of me when I was put in jail. [17]Then after he arrived in Rome, he searched everywhere until he found me. [18]I pray that the Lord Jesus will ask God to show mercy to Onesiphorus on the day of judgment. You know how much he helped me in Ephesus.

A Good Soldier of Christ Jesus

2 Timothy, my child, Christ Jesus is kind, and you must let him make you strong. [2]You have often heard me teach. Now I want you to tell these same things to followers who can be trusted to tell others.

[3]As a good soldier of Christ Jesus you must endure your share of suffering. [4]Soldiers on duty don't work at outside jobs. They try only to please their commanding officer. [5]No one wins an athletic contest without obeying the rules. [6]And farmers who work hard are the first to eat what grows in their field. [7]If you keep in mind what I have told you, the Lord will help you understand completely.

[8]Keep your mind on Jesus Christ! He was from the family of David and was raised from death, just as my good news says. [9]And because of this message, I am locked up in jail and treated like a criminal. But God's good news isn't locked in jail, [10]and so I am willing to put up with anything. Then God's special people will be saved. They will be given eternal glory because they belong to Christ Jesus. [11]Here is a true message:

[c]**1.11** *teacher*: Some manuscripts add "of the Gentiles."
[d]**1.12** *what he has trusted me with*: Or "what I have trusted him with."

WORK—What's a good way for me to share my faith at work? *(2 Timothy 1.6-14)*

Bring your faith up naturally when it's appropriate.
"I don't want to be pushy." "I might offend somebody." "Maybe they aren't ready to listen." "If I talk about Jesus at work, I'll get in trouble with my supervisor."

No doubt you've grappled with these typical concerns when you think about sharing your faith with your coworkers—and each one is legitimate. We've heard enough stories about Christians who do the hard sell and turn off everybody around them. You may even hear stories like that in your own workplace, stories about somebody who used to work there. Certainly you don't want to be a repeat offender.

On the other hand, don't let your fear of being pushy shut your mouth entirely. If you're *that* conscious of offending people, listen carefully to your own words, and you won't trample on others' feelings.

Paul encouraged Timothy, "Don't be ashamed to speak for our Lord" (1.8). Be alert to the Holy Spirit's promptings to take advantage of openings that come up naturally in conversation. Just be scrupulous not to steal time from your employer—God put you in that place to do a job, and your faithfulness to it is an important part of your witness. If you talk to your coworker and she's not interested in hearing about the Lord, respect her feelings. Your wise restraint may later open a door through which you can move boldly. (See also 2 Corinthians 4.1-15; 1 Thessalonians 4.9-12; 1 Timothy 5.17—6.2.)

Words To Remember: *God's Spirit doesn't make cowards out of us. The Spirit gives us power, love, and self-control.... Do your best to win God's approval as a worker who doesn't need to be ashamed and who teaches only the true message.*
—2 Timothy 1.7; 2.15

Lois and Eunice

2 Timothy 1.1-7

Paul first met his young protégé Timothy in the area of the cities of Derbe and Lystra, in what is now Turkey (Acts 16.1-3). Timothy was already a follower of Christ. His father was Greek; nothing is said in the Bible about his father's religious faith. Much is made, however, of the faith of Timothy's mother Eunice and grandmother Lois. They were Jewish Christians who first taught Timothy about Christ.

How did the mixed marriage of Eunice and her Gentile husband happen? How did the family wind up in Asia Minor? Perhaps Eunice grew up in Lystra, the child of exiled Jewish parents. Perhaps Timothy's father lived for a time in Palestine and met Eunice there. Perhaps the tide turned against the family in Palestine so Timothy's father wanted to go home to Gentile territory, and when they left, Eunice's widowed mother Lois came with them.

In any case, Paul made it clear Timothy's mother and grandmother were believers; they were the ones who taught Timothy the Christian faith. His Greek father appears to have been uninvolved in any religious instruction.

What does it take to be the only believer in your marriage? Apparently that was Eunice's situation. She had to be strong enough to hold on to her own beliefs and teach them to her son without apology. We can presume she made some necessary compromises, since Timothy had not been circumcised as all Jewish boy babies were (Acts 16.3).

From being around the family, Paul became very aware of the influence Timothy's mother and grandmother had exercised on him. He wanted Timothy to remember to give them credit. "After all," he reminded his young friend later in this letter, "you know who taught you these things. Since childhood, you have known the Holy Scriptures that are able to make you wise enough to have faith in Christ Jesus and be saved" (2 Timothy 3.14,15). At a time when men were usually the literate ones, Eunice and Lois did their own studying of God's Word (which then was only the Old Testament). They knew the Scriptures, or they never could have taught Timothy from childhood.

This mother and daughter had the kind of faith we all long for. Paul called it "genuine faith" (2 Timothy 1.5). They didn't rely on superficial good feelings or empty ritual. Their faith was embedded in their souls. It countered family indifference, perhaps even family opposition, and it reached out to multiply itself.

Earlier Paul told Timothy not to let anyone disregard him because he was young (1 Timothy 4.12). In praising Lois and Eunice (2 Timothy 1.5), Paul also implied we shouldn't look down on anyone because she's older. These two women were infinitely valuable in Timothy's life, and they continue as striking examples of Christian faithfulness for us today.

"If we died with Christ,
  we will live with him.
¹²If we don't give up,
  we will rule with him.
If we deny
  that we know him,
he will deny
  that he knows us.
¹³If we are not faithful,
  he will still be faithful.
Christ cannot deny
  who he is."

An Approved Worker

¹⁴Don't let anyone forget these things. And with God*ᵉ* as your witness, you must warn them not to argue about words. These arguments don't help anyone. In fact, they ruin everyone who listens to them. ¹⁵Do your best to win God's approval as a worker who doesn't need to be ashamed and who teaches only the true message.

¹⁶Keep away from worthless and useless talk. It only leads people farther away from God. ¹⁷That sort of talk is like a sore that won't heal. And Hymenaeus and Philetus have been talking this way ¹⁸by teaching that the dead have already been raised to life. This is far from the truth, and it is destroying the faith of some people.

¹⁹But the foundation that God has laid is solid. On it is written, "The Lord knows who his people are. So everyone who worships the Lord must turn away from evil."

²⁰In a large house some dishes are made of gold or silver, while others are made of wood or clay. Some of these are special, and others are not. ²¹That's also how it is with people. The ones who stop doing evil and make themselves pure will become special. Their lives will be holy and pleasing to their Master, and they will be able to do all kinds of good deeds.

²²Run from temptations that capture young people. Always do the right thing. Be faithful, loving, and easy to get along with. Worship with people whose hearts are pure. ²³Stay away from stupid and senseless arguments. These only lead to trouble, ²⁴and God's servants must not be troublemakers. They must be kind to everyone, and they must be good teachers and very patient. ²⁵Be humble when you correct people who oppose you. Maybe God will lead them to turn to him and learn the truth. ²⁶They have been trapped by the devil, and he makes them obey him, but God may help them escape.

What People Will Be Like in the Last Days

3 You can be certain that in the last days there will be some very hard times. ²People will love only themselves and money. They will be proud, stuck-up, rude, and disobedient to their parents. They will also be ungrateful, godless, ³heartless, and hateful. Their words will be cruel, and they

---

ᵉ**2.14** *God*: Some manuscripts have "the Lord," and others have "Christ."

SpiritualLife—How can I keep my life centered on God? (*2 Timothy 2.14-26*)

Make the right choices along the way.

It's easy to let life "just happen." You go along doing the most convenient thing without thinking about its consequences. One painless choice leads to another painless choice. Life stays comfortable for a while, but before long, you wake up to realize that you're in a bad situation. Too late you discover your circumstance is the result of a long series of decisions that led you toward compromise and away from God.

Paul kept reminding Timothy to stay aware of what he was doing and watch the choices he was making. He peppers this part of his letter with advice like "Keep away . . ." (2.16); "Run from . . ." (2.22); "Be faithful . . ." (2.22); "Stay away from . . ." (2.23); "Be humble . . ." (2.25). Paul was reminding Timothy—and us today—to make the right choices, because our choices do have lasting consequences. (See also Genesis 12.1-7; Matthew 25.31-46; Acts 13.1-5; Galatians 5.16-26; 2 John.)

Words To Remember: *The ones who stop doing evil and make themselves pure will become special. Their lives will be holy and pleasing to their Master, and they will be able to do all kinds of good deeds.*—2 Timothy 2.21

will have no self-control or pity. These people will hate everything that is good. [4]They will be sneaky, reckless, and puffed up with pride. Instead of loving God, they will love pleasure. [5]Even though they will make a show of being religious, their religion won't be real. Don't have anything to do with such people.

[6]Some men fool whole families, just to get power over those women who are slaves of sin and are controlled by all sorts of desires. [7]These women always want to learn something new, but they never can discover the truth. [8]Just as Jannes and Jambres[f] opposed Moses, these people are enemies of the truth. Their minds are sick, and their faith isn't real. [9]But they won't get very far with their foolishness. Soon everyone will know the truth about them, just as Jannes and Jambres were found out.

Paul's Last Instructions to Timothy

[10]Timothy, you know what I teach and how I live. You know what I want to do and what I believe. You have seen how patient and loving I am, and how in the past I put up with [11]trouble and suffering in the cities of Antioch, Iconium, and Lystra. Yet the Lord rescued me from all those terrible troubles. [12]Anyone who belongs to Christ Jesus and wants to live right will have trouble

from others. [13]But evil people who pretend to be what they are not will become worse than ever, as they fool others and are fooled themselves.

The thing I love about being a Christian is that the ground is level at the foot of the cross. God equips all of us for service.

JILL BRISCOE

[14]Keep on being faithful to what you were taught and to what you believed. After all, you know who taught you these things. [15]Since childhood, you have known the Holy Scriptures that are able to make you wise enough to have faith in Christ Jesus

---

f3.8 *Jannes and Jambres*: These names are not found in the Old Testament. But many believe these were the names of the two Egyptian magicians who opposed Moses when he wanted to lead the people of Israel out of Egypt (see Exodus 7.11, 22).

SingleLife—How can I overcome my feelings of loneliness? *(2 Timothy 4.16-18)*

Focus on the one who never leaves us.
Loneliness. When we're feeling it deeply, it hurts to even see the word. We want to tell somebody how lonely we are, but we're afraid to voice it. If we tell her and she doesn't understand or care, we'll only feel more lonely. People might even wonder what's wrong with us if we don't have lots of friends who care.

Human friendship and love can be fickle. Even our most loyal friends get distracted by their own concerns and neglect us. But God has promised he'll never leave us. In Christ he has committed himself to us forever. His Spirit lives with us and is even *in* us. We may not always have the comfort of a human presence, but we have the assurance of God's presence always.

Allow God to comfort you in your loneliness. Admit your feelings and trust yourself, physically and emotionally, to him. Give up any bitterness toward people who have neglected you. Paul mercifully said of the people who deserted him, "I hope it won't be held against them" (4.16). Talk honestly with God and listen to him, for as long as it takes, until his comfort fills your lonely places. **(See also Psalm 22; Psalm 68.4-6; Matthew 26.36-46; Revelation 3.20-22.)**

Words To Remember: *When I was first put on trial, no one helped me. In fact, everyone deserted me. . . . But the Lord stood beside me. . . . Praise him forever and ever!*
—2 Timothy 4.16-18

and be saved. [16]Everything in the Scriptures is God's Word. All of it is useful for teaching and helping people and for correcting them and showing them how to live. [17]The Scriptures train God's servants to do all kinds of good deeds.

4 When Christ Jesus comes as king, he will be the judge of everyone, whether they are living or dead. So with God and Christ as witnesses, I command you [2]to preach God's message. Do it willingly, even if it isn't the popular thing to do. You must correct people and point out their sins. But also cheer them up, and when you instruct them, always be patient. [3]The time is coming when people won't listen to good teaching. Instead, they will look for teachers who will please them by telling them only what they are itching to hear. [4]They will turn from the truth and eagerly listen to senseless stories. [5]But you must stay calm and be willing to suffer. You must work hard to tell the good news and to do your job well.

[6]Now the time has come for me to die. My life is like a drink offering[g] being poured out on the altar. [7]I have fought well. I have finished the race, and I have been faithful. [8]So a crown will be given to me for pleasing the Lord. He judges fairly, and on the day of judgment he will give a crown to me and to everyone else who wants him to appear with power.

Personal Instructions

[9]Come to see me as soon as you can. [10]Demas loves the things of this world so much that he left me and went to Thessalonica. Crescens has gone to Galatia, and Titus has gone to Dalmatia. [11]Only Luke has stayed with me.

Mark can be very helpful to me, so please find him and bring him with you. [12]I sent Tychicus to Ephesus.

[13]When you come, bring the coat I left at Troas with Carpus. Don't forget to bring the scrolls, especially the ones made of leather.[h]

[14]Alexander, the metalworker, has hurt me in many ways. But the Lord will pay him back for what he has done. [15]Alexander opposes what we preach. You had better watch out for him.

[16]When I was first put on trial, no one helped me. In fact, everyone deserted me. I hope it won't be held against them. [17]But the Lord stood beside me. He gave me the strength to tell his full message, so that all Gentiles would hear it. And I was kept safe from hungry lions. [18]The Lord will always keep me from being harmed by evil, and he will bring me safely into his heavenly kingdom. Praise him forever and ever! Amen.

Final Greetings

[19]Give my greetings to Priscilla and Aquila and to the family of Onesiphorus.

[20]Erastus stayed at Corinth.

Trophimus was sick when I left him at Miletus.

[21]Do your best to come before winter.

Eubulus, Pudens, Linus, and Claudia send you their greetings, and so do the rest of the Lord's followers.

[22]I pray that the Lord will bless your life and will be kind to you.

---

[g]4.6 *drink offering*: Water or wine was sometimes poured out as an offering when an animal sacrifice was made. [h]4.13 *the ones made of leather*: A scroll was a kind of rolled up book, and it could be made out of paper (called "papyrus") or leather (that is, animal skin) or even copper.

Titus
Instructions for a Young Leader

Relationships. Paul covers them all in this letter to Titus, his young protégé to whom he gave the responsibility of straightening out problems at the church in Crete. Paul freely admitted that the Cretans were a tough bunch—greedy, deceitful, and lazy like wild animals (1.12). They needed effective leaders to help them grow. Titus was to appoint these leaders according to some very specific guidelines.

Christians at Crete also needed basic, hard-nosed teaching about how to conduct their relationships; Titus was to leave no stone unturned. Whether they were young or old, male or female, in the church, in the family, or in the community, there was to be instruction for everyone.

Paul's tone in this book was fatherly because Titus was like a son to him in the faith. Paul offered him pointers about how to be a good leader in a tough situation. He pointed out that a good part of his success would have to do with Titus's own integrity and exemplary behavior.

Paul said at the end of the book that teachings such as these "are useful and helpful for everyone" (3.8). All of us have opportunities to lead and to train new leaders—even if those new leaders are our own children. Paul's letter to Titus will help us cultivate relationships that are God-honoring. In this way we demonstrate that we've been given spiritual new birth and a fresh beginning.

Titus at a Glance

1. Greetings to a special friend (1.1-4)
2. The task of appointing leaders in Crete (1.5-16)
3. Maintaining healthy relationships in God's family (2)
4. A reminder about God's transforming power (3.1-7)
5. Hints for making the most of our time (3.8-15)

1 From Paul, a servant of God and an apostle of Jesus Christ.
I encourage God's own people to have more faith and to understand the truth about religion. [2]Then they will have the hope of eternal life that God promised long ago. And God never tells a lie! [3]So, at the proper time, God our Savior gave this message and told me to announce what he had said.

As my relationship with God matures—and I trust him with more of my deepest feelings—my intimacy with him increases.

MAYO MATHERS

[4]Titus, because of our faith, you are like a son to me. I pray that God our Father and Christ Jesus our Savior will be kind to you and will bless you with peace!

What Titus Was To Do in Crete

[5]I left you in Crete to do what had been left undone and to appoint leaders[a] for the churches in each town. As I told you, [6]they must have a good reputation and be faithful in marriage.[b] Their children must be followers of the Lord and not have a reputation for being wild and disobedient.

[7]Church officials[c] are in charge of God's work, and so they must also have a good reputation. They must not be bossy, quick-tempered, heavy drinkers, bullies, or dishonest in business. [8]Instead, they must be friendly to strangers and enjoy doing good things. They must also be sensible, fair, pure, and self-controlled. [9]They must stick to the true message they were taught, so that their good teaching can help others and correct everyone who opposes it.

[10]There are many who don't respect authority, and they fool others by talking nonsense. This is especially true of some Jewish followers. [11]But you must make them be quiet. They are after money, and they upset

_____
[a]1.5 *leaders*: Or "elders" or "presbyters" or "priests."
[b]1.6 *be faithful in marriage*: Or "be the husband of only one wife" or "have never been divorced." [c]1.7 *Church officials*: Or "Bishops."

WORK—Sometimes I think it's okay to work while my kids are young; other times I'm not sure. How can I be certain I'm making the best decision for my family? (*Titus 2.3-8*)

Make sure your priorities align with Scripture.
To work or not to work—it's definitely one of the biggest, toughest decisions women face. It's a choice that affects not only us, but our whole family. We wonder, *Will my children be all right without me around? Will I be satisfied as a stay-at-home mom? Can we make it on one income?*

This passage of Scripture can help. It clearly states what godly priorities should be for all women, whether older or younger. Older women are "to behave as those who love the Lord" (2.3) and "they must teach what is proper, so the younger women will be loving wives and mothers" (2.3,4). Younger women "must be sensible and kind, as well as a good homemaker, who puts her own husband first. Then no one can say insulting things about God's message" (2.5).

No matter what choice we make (whether to work full-time, part-time, or stay at home), we need to make sure that our priorities are in line with Scripture: God first; family second; whatever else we do third. This may mean staying home with our kids—or it may mean that if we choose to work, we say no to community work, more schooling, extra church commitments, or long hours at work. Above all, our priority must be to honor God—and to obey what his Holy Spirit prompts us to do. (See also Proverbs 16.1-3; Romans 14.13-23.)

Words To Remember: *Always set a good example for others.*—Titus 2.7

whole families by teaching what they should not. ¹²It is like one of their own prophets once said,

"The people of Crete
    always tell lies.
They are greedy and lazy
    like wild animals."

¹³That surely is a true saying. And you should be hard on such people, so you can help them grow stronger in their faith. ¹⁴Don't pay any attention to any of those senseless Jewish stories and human commands. These are made up by people who won't obey the truth.

¹⁵Everything is pure for someone whose heart is pure. But nothing is pure for an unbeliever with a dirty mind. That person's mind and conscience are destroyed. ¹⁶Such people claim to know God, but their actions prove that they really don't. They are disgusting. They won't obey God, and they are too worthless to do anything good.

Instructions for Different Groups of People

2 Titus, you must teach only what is correct. ²Tell the older men to have self-control and to be serious and sensible. Their faith, love, and patience must never fail.

³Tell the older women to behave as those who love the Lord should. They must not gossip about others or be slaves of wine. They must teach what is proper, ⁴so the younger women will be loving wives and mothers. ⁵Each of the younger women must be sensible and kind, as well as a good homemaker, who puts her own husband first. Then no one can say insulting things about God's message.

⁶Tell the young men to have self-control in everything. ⁷Always set a good example for others. Be sincere and serious when you teach. ⁸Use clean language that no one can criticize. Do this, and your enemies will be too ashamed to say anything against you.

⁹Tell slaves always to please their owners by obeying them in everything. Slaves must not talk back to their owners ¹⁰or steal from them. They must be completely honest and trustworthy. Then everyone will show great respect for what is taught about God our Savior.

God's Kindness and the New Life

¹¹God has shown us how kind he is by coming to save all people. ¹²He taught us to give up our wicked ways and our worldly desires and to live decent and honest lives in this world. ¹³We are filled with hope, as we wait for the glorious return of our great God

---

PARENTING&*family*—Sometimes I get upset and angry with my kids. How can I maintain a loving attitude when I'm about to explode? *(Titus 3.3-8)*

Remember how much God's love and patience means to you.
Parenting is probably the most challenging task you'll ever undertake. Many times your children can take you to the limits of your wisdom, patience, love, and understanding. Parenting is stressful! It helps if you remember God's compassion toward you in those moments when you feel as though you are being pushed to your limit.

When you remember how God extends compassion rather than judgment to you, you'll be more able to extend that grace to your children when they need it. If necessary, in the most stressful moments, slow down, breathe deeply, and ask yourself what you really want to demonstrate in that moment. Then you can make a choice to respond in a way that's consistent with who you are in Christ.

Self-control isn't a discipline imposed from outside yourself, but a strong choice you make from within to behave in ways that are consistent with God's best. By quieting yourself, experiencing God's compassion, and inviting the Holy Spirit to flood your being, you'll be more able to respond to your children with love. (See also Proverbs 15.1-4,18; Matthew 11.25-29.)

Words To Remember: *God our Savior showed us how good and kind he is.* —Titus 3.4

and Savior Jesus Christ.[d] [14]He gave himself to rescue us from everything that is evil and to make our hearts pure. He wanted us to be his own people and to be eager to do right.

[15]Teach these things, as you use your full authority to encourage and correct people. Make sure you earn everyone's respect.

Doing Helpful Things

3 Remind your people to obey the rulers and authorities and not to be rebellious. They must always be ready to do something helpful [2]and not say cruel things or argue. They should be gentle and kind to everyone. [3]We used to be stupid, disobedient, and foolish, as well as slaves of all sorts of desires and pleasures. We were evil and jealous. Everyone hated us, and we hated everyone.

[4]God our Savior showed us
how good and kind he is.
[5]He saved us because
of his mercy,
and not because
of any good things
that we have done.

God washed us by the power
of the Holy Spirit.

He gave us new birth
and a fresh beginning.
[6]God sent Jesus Christ
our Savior
to give us his Spirit.

[7]Jesus treated us much better
than we deserve.
He made us acceptable to God
and gave us the hope
of eternal life.

[8]This message is certainly true.

These teachings are useful and helpful for everyone. I want you to insist that the people follow them, so that all who have faith in God will be sure to do good deeds. [9]But don't have anything to do with stupid arguments about ancestors. And stay away from disagreements and quarrels about the Law of Moses. Such arguments are useless and senseless.

[10]Warn troublemakers once or twice. Then don't have anything else to do with them. [11]You know that their minds are

---

[d]**2.13** *the glorious return of our great God and Savior Jesus Christ*: Or "the glorious return of our great God and our Savior Jesus Christ" or "the return of Jesus Christ, who is the glory of our great God and Savior."

---

*Spiritual*Life—I'm so busy! How can I find time for God? *(Titus 3.4-7,14)*

Filter out activities that don't have lasting value.

Carpooling. Serving on church or community committees. Keeping up with friends and family. Watching television. Taking kids to the doctor, to soccer practice, to music lessons. Working long hours to finish a project. Let's face it—most of us are incredibly busy. And when we're busy, finding time for God can feel like just one more thing in an already overloaded schedule.

Titus reminds us in this passage that although we need to do helpful things, we must keep our focus on what's most important: our relationship with Jesus Christ. In fact, he says bluntly, "He saved us because of his mercy, and not because of any good things that we have done" (3.5). This doesn't mean we shouldn't do good things for others, but that we should evaluate what's "useful and worthwhile" (3.14).

It's so easy to let others' desires pull us in many directions. When we allow that to happen, we can feel as if we have no control over our lives. But that isn't the case. Teach your kids not to interrupt you during your quiet time. Spend your lunch hour, your baby's feeding, or your preschooler's nap time in praising God. Go on a women's retreat. Or use a long commute to pray. There are many creative ways to maintain spiritual priorities in the midst of your busy life. Your challenge is to say "no" to lesser things so you can say "yes" to what really matters. (See also Mark 13.32-37; 1 Thessalonians 4.13-18.)

Words To Remember: *Our people should learn to spend their time doing something useful and worthwhile.—Titus 3.14*

twisted, and their own sins show how guilty they are.

Personal Instructions and Greetings

[12]I plan to send Artemas or Tychicus to you. After he arrives, please try your best to meet me at Nicopolis. I have decided to spend the winter there.

[13]When Zenas the lawyer and Apollos get ready to leave, help them as much as you can, so they won't have need of anything.

[14]Our people should learn to spend their time doing something useful and worthwhile.

[15]Greetings to you from everyone here. Greet all of our friends who share in our faith.

I pray that the Lord will be kind to all of you!

Philemon
A Plea for Reconciliation

Have you ever taken a stand for someone in trouble? It was probably a scary thing to do. You stuck your neck out and risked the wrath of other people just because you cared about somebody. And you had nothing to gain from it except the satisfaction of helping an underdog.

In the culture of the Roman Empire in Paul's time, slaves were the underdogs, and a runaway slave who had stolen from the master was less than an underdog—he was subject to severe punishment, even execution.

Onesimus was a slave in a wealthy household in the Gentile city of Colossae. He ran from his master and apparently sought refuge in the anonymity of Rome. Somehow he met up with Paul in prison—maybe while doing time in prison himself, or after being brought there by Paul's friends. We only know that Paul, while imprisoned, led Onesimus to faith in Christ. The two established such a warm relationship that Paul said, "He is like a son to me" (10).

But there was a serious complication. At some point Paul discovered that Onesimus was not only a runaway slave, but that he was the legal property of Paul's Christian friend Philemon. Even worse, Onesimus seems to have helped himself to some of Philemon's property when he escaped. We don't know who brought up the uncomfortable subject first, but it had to come up: Would Onesimus go back to his master and make things right? Paul must have been torn between wanting to do right by Philemon and wanting to protect Onesimus.

Finally the decision was reached. Onesimus would travel back to Colossae, but symbolically he'd take Paul with him in the form of a letter asking Philemon to show mercy. The letter would be skillful, diplomatic, and daring. It would do far more than ask Philemon to refrain from punishing Onesimus. It would ask Philemon to accept his guilty slave as an equal, as a fellow believer, a brother in Christ! Paul was so willing to identify himself with this fugitive slave that he told Philemon, "Welcome Onesimus as you would welcome me" (17).

What an appeal! Paul's request turned the conventions of Roman society upside down—or right side up. Paul was saying that in Christ, everyone is equal because everyone is equally loved and equally forgiven. Social status and past sins have no part to play in the new possibilities of fellowship. All that matters is oneness in Jesus Christ.

Philemon at a Glance

1. Paul's greetings to an old friend (1-3)
2. Prayers for Philemon (4-7)
3. A request for mercy for Onesimus (8-14)
4. Paul stands up for Onesimus (15-20)
5. Closing messages (21-25)

¹From Paul, who is in jail for serving Christ Jesus, and from Timothy, who is like a brother because of our faith.

Philemon, you work with us and are very dear to us. This letter is to you ²and to the church that meets in your home. It is also to our dear friend Apphia and to Archippus, who serves the Lord as we do.

³I pray that God our Father and our Lord Jesus Christ will be kind to you and will bless you with peace!

Philemon's Love and Faith

⁴Philemon, each time I mention you in my prayers, I thank God. ⁵I hear about your faith in our Lord Jesus and about your love for all of God's people. ⁶As you share your faith with others, I pray that they may come to know all the blessings Christ has given us. ⁷My friend, your love has made me happy and has greatly encouraged me. It has also cheered the hearts of God's people.

Paul Speaks to Philemon about Onesimus

⁸Christ gives me the courage to tell you what to do. ⁹But I would rather ask you to do it simply because of love. Yes, as someone*ᵃ* in jail for Christ, ¹⁰I beg you to

help Onesimus!*ᵇ* He is like a son to me because I led him to Christ here in jail. ¹¹Before this, he was useless to you, but now he is useful both to you and to me.

¹²Sending Onesimus back to you makes me very sad. ¹³I would like to keep him here with me, where he could take your place in helping me while I am here in prison for preaching the good news. ¹⁴But I won't do anything unless you agree to it first. I want your act of kindness to come from your heart, and not be something you feel forced to do.

¹⁵Perhaps Onesimus was taken from you for a little while so that you could have him back for good, ¹⁶but not as a slave. Onesimus is much more than a slave. To me he is a dear friend, but to you he is even more, both as a person and as a follower of the Lord.

¹⁷If you consider me a friend because of Christ, then welcome Onesimus as you would welcome me. ¹⁸If he has cheated you or owes you anything, charge it to my account. ¹⁹With my own hand I write: I, PAUL, WILL PAY YOU BACK. But don't forget that you owe me your life. ²⁰My dear

---

*ᵃ*9 *someone:* Greek "a messenger" or "an old man."
*ᵇ*10 *Onesimus:* In Greek this name means "useful."

WORK—How can I be a good supervisor? *(Philemon 8-16)*

Correct the mistake; forgive the person.

Employees make mistakes for all kinds of reasons. They're coming down with the flu or have a splitting headache. They need a little more instruction for the job they're doing, or they're distracted by enormous personal problems. Or possibly they just don't care much about their work.

When mistakes happen, any supervisor is tempted to blow up or pull rank. After all, errors by employees make the boss look bad.

When you're picking up the pieces after somebody has goofed, remember that a failing employee is still a beloved creation of God with an eternal soul and perhaps a fragile sense of worth. Now isn't the time to trample on that person's feelings. Try to find out why the error happened and how the person can avoid making the same mistake again. If the person is really incompetent or poses a danger, you will have to deal firmly with that. But even in such an extreme case, as much as possible, affirm the worth of that employee as a human being.

The slave Onesimus had made major mistakes. Paul took Onesimus's part and tried to build a bridge between him and his employer (actually his owner) Philemon. Paul asked for mercy, not because Onesimus was such a good person, but because Christ is merciful. (See also Exodus 18; 1 Kings 3.5-15; 4.29-34; Ezra 5.1—6.12; Jeremiah 32.26-44; John 21.15-25; 2 Timothy 1.1-7; Philemon 15-25.)

Words To Remember: *I want your act of kindness to come from your heart, and not be something you feel forced to do.—Philemon 14*

friend and follower of Christ our Lord, please cheer me up by doing this for me.

²¹I am sure you will do all I have asked, and even more. ²²Please get a room ready for me. I hope your prayers will be answered, and I can visit you.

²³Epaphras is also here in jail for being a follower of Christ Jesus. He sends his greetings, ²⁴and so do Mark, Aristarchus, Demas, and Luke, who work together with me.

²⁵I pray that the Lord Jesus Christ will be kind to you!

WORK—How can I be a good supervisor? (Philemon 15-25)

Don't let position go to your head.

It's one thing to go to church with fellow Christians; it can be something else entirely to have to work with them. Sunday-morning politeness quickly evaporates into Monday-morning bossiness.

If we're in a supervisory position, God has given us a sphere of authority over certain people for the good of that workplace and everyone in it. But a person's relative position at work has nothing to do with his or her position in Christ. The person you stand next to in choir may be far below you on the business ladder, but she may chair a church committee where you're the newest and most naive member. God seems to enjoy mixing up place and position like that!

Christians who work together should still think of each other as brothers and sisters in Christ not just on Sunday, but during the rest of the week as well. We're all equals before him and each other. A supervisory role gives us no license to lord it over other Christians—or anyone else for that matter—at work. (See also Exodus 18; 1 Kings 3.5-15; 4.29-34; Ezra 5.1—6.12; Jeremiah 32.26-44; John 21.15-25; 2 Timothy 1.1-7; Philemon 8-16.)

Words To Remember: *Onesimus is much more than a slave. To me he is a dear friend, but to you he is even more, both as a person and as a follower of the Lord.* —Philemon 16

Hebrews

A Race to the Finish

Imagine yourself taking on a monumental task, like running the Boston Marathon, climbing Mt. Everest, or just trying to get through next week without losing your sanity. Will you have the stamina, the inner strength to make it to the end of your trek? Will you be strong enough to push past the "wall" of pain and exhaustion to finish what you've started?

Anyone who's ever challenged herself to do something difficult knows the hardest part is getting past that wall. That's where we come up with all the excuses: "It's too hard." "I'm not good enough." "I just can't do it anymore." That's where we give up.

And it's that understanding of human nature that stands behind the book of Hebrews. The early Christians had a major transition to make. As they moved from their Jewish faith to a faith based on the saving power of Christ, they naturally had some big questions. Were they really willing to move past their Jewish traditions and trust in God's grace? Were they really prepared to let go of their time-honored belief in a lofty, judging God and see him as loving and forgiving, a God who came to earth in the person of Jesus Christ? Was this whole "Christianity" business all it was cracked up to be? In the middle of the monumental task of living as Christ's followers, they were hitting the wall.

And so the writer of Hebrews offers this pep talk of sorts to get those early Christians past the wall. As it recounts God's endless mercies, Hebrews builds us up, too, reminding us of God's tremendous love for us and encouraging us to "run the race that is ahead of us" (12.1).

As we take on life's monumental tasks—whether it's running a marathon or trying to live a life that honors God—we can trust fully in the promises we find in Hebrews. We can be encouraged that when we keep our focus on Jesus, we will finish life's race with flying colors.

Hebrews at a Glance

1. The greatness of Jesus (1.1-4)
2. Jesus is greater than the angels (1.5—2.18)
3. Jesus is greater than Moses and Joshua (3.1—4.13)
4. Jesus is the true High Priest (4.14—5.10)
5. The next steps of faith (5.11—6.20)
6. The new promises of God (7.1—9.22)
7. Jesus' lasting sacrifice (9.23—10.31)
8. A history of faith (11)
9. The example of Jesus (12.1—13.19)
10. Final prayers and greetings (13.20-25)

1 Long ago in many ways and at many times God's prophets spoke his message to our ancestors. [2]But now at last, God sent his Son to bring his message to us. God created the universe by his Son, and everything will someday belong to the Son. [3]God's Son has all the brightness of God's own glory and is like him in every way. By his own mighty word, he holds the universe together.

After the Son had washed away our sins, he sat down at the right side[a] of the glorious God in heaven. [4]He had become much greater than the angels, and the name he was given is far greater than any of theirs.

God's Son Is Greater than Angels

[5]God has never said
to any of the angels,
"You are my Son, because today
I have become your Father!"
Neither has God said
to any of them,
"I will be his Father,
and he will be my Son!"

[6]When God brings his first-born Son[b] into the world, he commands all of his angels to worship him. [7]And when God speaks about the angels, he says,

"I change my angels into wind
and my servants
into flaming fire."

[8]But God says about his Son,

"You are God,
and you will rule
as King forever!
Your[c] royal power
brings about justice.
[9]You loved justice
and hated evil,
and so I, your God,
have chosen you.
I appointed you
and made you happier
than any of your friends."

[10]The Scriptures also say,

"In the beginning, Lord,
you were the one

who laid the foundation
of the earth
and created the heavens.
[11]They will all disappear
and wear out like clothes,
but you will last forever.
[12]You will roll them up
like a robe
and change them
like a garment.
But you are always the same,
and you will live forever."

[13]God never said to any
of the angels,
"Sit at my right side
until I make your enemies
into a footstool for you!"

[14]Angels are merely spirits sent to serve people who are going to be saved.

This Great Way of Being Saved

2 We must give our full attention to what we were told, so that we won't drift away. [2]The message spoken by angels proved to be true, and all who disobeyed or rejected it were punished as they deserved. [3]So if we refuse this great way of being saved, how can we hope to escape? The Lord himself was the first to tell about it, and people who heard the message proved to us that it was true. [4]God himself showed that his message was true by working all kinds of powerful miracles and wonders. He also gave his Holy Spirit to anyone he chose to.

The One Who Leads Us To Be Saved

[5]We know that God did not put the future world under the power of angels. [6]Somewhere in the Scriptures someone says to God,

"What makes you care
about us humans?
Why are you concerned
for weaklings such as we?
[7]You made us lower

---

[a]**1.3** *right side*: The place of honor and power.
[b]**1.6** *first-born Son*: The first son born into a family had certain privileges that the other children did not have. In 12.23 "first-born" refers to God's special people.
[c]**1.8** *Your*: Some manuscripts have "His."

than the angels
for a while.
Yet you have crowned us
with glory and honor.[d]
⁸And you have put everything
under our power!"

God has put everything under our power
and has not left anything out of our power.
But we still don't see it all under our power.
⁹What we do see is Jesus, who for a little
while was made lower than the angels. Because of God's wonderful kindness, Jesus
died for everyone. And now that Jesus has
suffered and died, he is crowned with glory
and honor!
¹⁰Everything belongs to God, and all
things were created by his power. So God
did the right thing when he made Jesus perfect by suffering, as Jesus led many of God's
children to be saved and to share in his
glory. ¹¹Jesus and the people he makes holy
all belong to the same family. That is why he
isn't ashamed to call them his brothers and
sisters. ¹²He even said to God,

"I will tell them your name
and sing your praises
when they come together
to worship."

¹³He also said,

"I will trust God."

Then he said,

"Here I am with the children
God has given me."

*For every nudge we feel
from Satan to give in to
temptation, God stands
ready with an escape route.*

MARIAN V. LIAUTAUD

¹⁴We are people of flesh and blood. That
is why Jesus became one of us. He died to

destroy the devil, who had power over
death. ¹⁵But he also died to rescue all of us
who live each day in fear of dying. ¹⁶Jesus
clearly did not come to help angels, but he
did come to help Abraham's descendants.
¹⁷He had to be one of us, so that he could
serve God as our merciful and faithful high
priest and sacrifice himself for the forgiveness of our sins. ¹⁸And now that Jesus has
suffered and was tempted, he can help anyone else who is tempted.

Jesus Is Greater than Moses

3 My friends, God has chosen you to be
his holy people. So think about Jesus,
the one we call our apostle and high
priest! ²Jesus was faithful to God, who appointed him, just as Moses was faithful in
serving all of[e] God's people. ³But Jesus deserves more honor than Moses, just as the
builder of a house deserves more honor
than the house. ⁴Of course, every house is
built by someone, and God is really the one
who built everything.
⁵Moses was a faithful servant and told
God's people what would be said in the future. ⁶But Christ is the Son in charge of
God's people. And we are those people, if
we keep on being brave and don't lose hope.

A Rest for God's People

⁷It is just as the Holy Spirit says,

"If you hear God's voice today,
⁸   don't be stubborn!
Don't rebel like those people
who were tested
in the desert.
*⁹For forty years your ancestors
tested God and saw
the things he did.

¹⁰"Then God got tired of them
and said,
'You people never
show good sense,
and you don't understand
what I want you to do.'
¹¹God became angry
and told the people,

---

d2.7 *and honor*: Some manuscripts add "and you have
placed us in charge of all you created." e3.2 *all of*:
Some manuscripts do not have these words.

'You will never enter
    my place of rest!' "

¹²My friends, watch out! Don't let evil thoughts or doubts make any of you turn from the living God. ¹³You must encourage one another each day. And you must keep on while there is still a time that can be called "today." If you don't, then sin may fool some of you and make you stubborn. ¹⁴We were sure about Christ when we first became his people. So let's hold tightly to our faith until the end. ¹⁵The Scriptures say,

"If you hear his voice today,
    don't be stubborn
        like those who rebelled."

> We pass on our faith by being and doing. We have to integrate the principles of God's Word in everything we do—including the kind of people we hang out with, the places we go, the words we say, the songs we sing, the clothes we wear and don't wear, the language we use.
>
> BABBIE MASON

¹⁶Who were those people that heard God's voice and rebelled? Weren't they the same ones that came out of Egypt with Moses? ¹⁷Who were the people that made God angry for forty years? Weren't they the ones that sinned and died in the desert? ¹⁸And who did God say would never enter his place of rest? Weren't they the ones that disobeyed him? ¹⁹We see that those people did not enter the place of rest because they did not have faith.

4 The promise to enter the place of rest is still good, and we must take care that none of you miss out. ²We have heard the message, just as they did. But they failed to believe what they heard, and the message did not do them any good. ³Only people who have faith will enter the place of rest. It is just as the Scriptures say,

"God became angry
    and told the people,
'You will never enter
    my place of rest!' "

God said this, even though everything has been ready from the time of creation. ⁴In fact, somewhere the Scriptures say that by the seventh day, God had finished his work, and so he rested. ⁵We also read that he later said, "You people will never enter my place of rest!" ⁶This means that the promise to enter is still good, because those who first heard about it disobeyed and did not enter. ⁷Much later God told David to make the promise again, just as I have already said,

"If you hear his voice today,
    don't be stubborn!"

⁸If Joshua had really given the people rest, there would not be any need for God to talk about another day of rest. ⁹But God has promised us a Sabbath when we will rest, even though it has not yet come. ¹⁰On that day God's people will rest from their work, just as God rested from his work.

¹¹We should do our best to enter that place of rest, so that none of us will disobey and miss going there, as they did. ¹²What God has said isn't only alive and active! It is sharper than any double-edged sword. His word can cut through our spirits and souls and through our joints and marrow, until it discovers the desires and thoughts of our hearts. ¹³Nothing is hidden from God! He sees through everything, and we will have to tell him the truth.

Jesus Is the Great High Priest

¹⁴We have a great high priest, who has gone into heaven, and he is Jesus the Son of God. That is why we must hold on to what we have said about him. ¹⁵Jesus understands every weakness of ours, because he was tempted in every way that we are. But he did not sin! ¹⁶So whenever we are in need, we should come bravely before the throne of our merciful God. There we will

be treated with undeserved kindness, and we will find help.

5 Every high priest is appointed to help others by offering gifts and sacrifices to God because of their sins. ²A high priest has weaknesses of his own, and he feels sorry for foolish and sinful people. ³That is why he must offer sacrifices for his own sins and for the sins of others. ⁴But no one can have the honor of being a high priest simply by wanting to be one. Only God can choose a priest, and God is the one who chose Aaron.

⁵That is how it was with Christ. He became a high priest, but not just because he wanted the honor of being one. It was God who told him,

"You are my Son, because today
    I have become your Father!"

⁶In another place, God says,

"You are a priest forever
    just like Melchizedek."ᶠ

⁷God had the power to save Jesus from death. And while Jesus was on earth, he begged God with loud crying and tears to save him. He truly worshiped God, and God listened to his prayers. ⁸Jesus is God's own Son, but still he had to suffer before he could learn what it really means to obey God. ⁹Suffering made Jesus perfect, and now he can save forever all who obey him. ¹⁰This is because God chose him to be a high priest like Melchizedek.

Warning against Turning Away

¹¹Much more could be said about this subject. But it is hard to explain, and all of you are slow to understand. ¹²By now you should have been teachers, but once again you need to be taught the simplest things about what God has said. You need milk instead of solid food. ¹³People who live on milk are like babies who don't really know what is right. ¹⁴Solid food is for mature people who have been trained to know right from wrong.

6 We must try to become mature and start thinking about more than just the basic things we were taught about Christ. We shouldn't need to keep talking about why we ought to turn from deeds that bring death and why we ought to have faith in God. ²And we shouldn't need to keep

---

ᶠ5.6 *Melchizedek*: When Melchizedek is mentioned in the Old Testament, he is described as a priest who lived before Aaron. Nothing is said about his ancestors or his death (see 7.3 and Genesis 14.17-20).

SingleLife—How can I tell the difference between good ambition and self-centeredness? *(Hebrews 4.12,13)*

Use Scripture as a check.

Are you considering switching jobs? Asking your current supervisor for more pay? Are you wishing you had a roommate who cared more about the cleanliness of your apartment, like you do? Do you wonder why it seems that you always get passed over on that church committee?

God has some wisdom for any decision we may need to make—or any thoughts or emotions that are stirring around in our head. In fact, this passage tells us that if we read and study his Word, God will help us discover "the desires and thoughts of our hearts" (4.12). Nothing is hidden from God—our good days, our bad days; our happy thoughts, our jealous or angry thoughts. We can fool some people, and we can sometimes rationalize and convince ourselves that we're doing the right thing. But we can never fool God. As the Scripture here says, "He sees through everything, and we will have to tell him the truth" (4.13). What a relief—and a privilege—that our great God knows us so well, and loves us anyway! (See also Genesis 11.1-9; Mark 8.34-38.)

Words To Remember: *What God has said isn't only alive and active! It is sharper than any double-edged sword. His word can cut through our spirits and souls and through our joints and marrow, until it discovers the desires and thoughts of our hearts.*—Hebrews 4.12

teaching about baptisms[g] or about the laying on of hands[h] or about people being raised from death and the future judgment. [3]Let's grow up, if God is willing.

[4-6]But what about people who turn away after they have already seen the light and have received the gift from heaven and have shared in the Holy Spirit? What about those who turn away after they have received the good message of God and the powers of the future world? There is no way to bring them back. What they are doing is the same as nailing the Son of God to a cross and insulting him in public!

[7]A field is useful to farmers, if there is enough rain to make good crops grow. In fact, God will bless that field. [8]But land that produces only thornbushes is worthless. It is likely to fall under God's curse, and in the end it will be set on fire.

[9]My friends, we are talking this way. But we are sure that you are doing those really good things that people do when they are being saved. [10]God is always fair. He will remember how you helped his people in the past and how you are still helping them. You belong to God, and he won't forget the love you have shown his people. [11]We wish that each of you would always be eager to show how strong and lasting your hope really is.

[12]Then you would never be lazy. You would be following the example of those who had faith and were patient until God kept his promise to them.

God's Promise Is Sure

[13]No one is greater than God. So he made a promise in his own name when he said to Abraham, [14]"I, the Lord, will bless you with many descendants!" [15]Then after Abraham had been very patient, he was given what God had promised. [16]When anyone wants to settle an argument, they make a vow by using the name of someone or something greater than themselves. [17]So when God wanted to prove for certain that his promise to his people could not be broken, he made a vow. [18]God cannot tell lies! And so his promises and vows are two things that can never be changed.

We have run to God for safety. Now his promises should greatly encourage us to take hold of the hope that is right in front of us. [19]This hope is like a firm and steady anchor for our souls. In fact, hope reaches

[g]**6.2** *baptisms:* Or "ceremonies of washing."
[h]**6.2** *laying on of hands:* This was a ceremony in which church leaders and others put their hands on people to show that those people were chosen to do some special kind of work.

MARRIAGE—How can my husband and I grow spiritually as a couple?
(Hebrews 5.11—6.3)

Learn to grow deeper.
Think back to the early days of your relationship with your husband. Everything you did together seemed romantic, fun, and special. But as you learned more about each other, and eventually settled into a routine, those giddy feelings that marked the beginning stages of love probably turned to something much deeper. You and your husband moved beyond the "young love" stage and into a more mature, lasting kind of love.

The same needs to be true in our spiritual life. As exciting as newfound faith feels, eventually it must become something more mature. As this passage tells us, we need to move beyond the questions that marked our faith when it was new and start living as mature Christians so others can learn from us (6.1).

You and your husband can encourage each other to grow into a mature faith. Think about how the two of you can better serve your community and church. Consider developing a "mission statement" as a couple, focusing on ways you'd like to reach out to others. Share your own moments of spiritual growth with your husband and encourage him to do the same. Together, you can move toward a faith that will grow stronger every day. (See also Galatians 6.1-3; 1 Peter 4.8-11.)

Words To Remember: *We must try to become mature and start thinking about more than just the basic things we were taught about Christ. . . . Let's grow up, if God is willing.—Hebrews 6.1,3*

behind the curtain[i] and into the most holy place. [20]Jesus has gone there ahead of us, and he is our high priest forever, just like Melchizedek.[j]

The Priestly Family of Melchizedek

7 Melchizedek was both king of Salem and priest of God Most High. He was the one who went out and gave Abraham his blessing, when Abraham returned from killing the kings. [2]Then Abraham gave him a tenth of everything he had.

The meaning of the name Melchizedek is "King of Justice." But since Salem means "peace," he is also "King of Peace." [3]We are not told that he had a father or mother or ancestors or beginning or end. He is like the Son of God and will be a priest forever.[k]

[4]Notice how great Melchizedek is! Our famous ancestor Abraham gave him a tenth of what he had taken from his enemies. [5]The Law teaches that even Abraham's descendants must give a tenth of what they possess. And they are to give this to their own relatives, who are the descendants of Levi and are priests. [6]Although Melchizedek wasn't a descendant of Levi, Abraham gave him a tenth of what he had. Then Melchizedek blessed Abraham, who had been given God's promise. [7]Everyone agrees that a person who gives a blessing is greater than the one who receives the blessing.

[8]Priests are given a tenth of what people earn. But all priests die, except Melchizedek, and the Scriptures teach that he is alive. [9]Levi's descendants are now the ones who receive a tenth from people. We could even say that when Abraham gave Melchizedek a tenth, Levi also gave him a tenth. [10]This is because Levi was born later into the family of Abraham, who gave a tenth to Melchizedek.

[11]Even though the Law of Moses says that the priests must be descendants of Levi, those priests cannot make anyone perfect. So there needs to be a priest like Melchizedek, rather than one from the priestly family of Aaron.[l] [12]And when the rules for selecting a priest are changed, the Law must also be changed.

[13]The person we are talking about is our Lord, who came from a tribe that had never had anyone to serve as a priest at the altar. [14]Everyone knows he came from the tribe of Judah, and Moses never said that priests would come from that tribe.

[15]All of this becomes clearer, when someone who is like Melchizedek is appointed to be a priest. [16]That person wasn't appointed because of his ancestors, but because his life can never end. [17]The Scriptures say about him,

> "You are a priest forever,
> just like Melchizedek."

[18]In this way a weak and useless command was put aside, [19]because the Law cannot make anything perfect. At the same time, we are given a much better hope, and it can bring us close to God.

[20-21]God himself made a promise when this priest was appointed. But he did not make a promise like this when the other priests were appointed. The promise he made is,

> "I, the Lord, promise that you
> will be a priest forever!
> And I will never
> change my mind!"

[22]This means that Jesus guarantees us a better agreement with God. [23]There have been a lot of other priests, and all of them have died. [24]But Jesus will never die, and so he will be a priest forever! [25]He is forever able to save[m] the people he leads to God, because he always lives to speak to God for them.

[26]Jesus is the high priest we need. He is holy and innocent and faultless, and not at all like us sinners. Jesus is honored above all beings in heaven, [27]and he is better than any other high priest. Jesus doesn't need to offer sacrifices each day for his own sins and then for the sins of the people. He offered a sacrifice once for all, when he gave himself. [28]The Law appoints priests who have weaknesses. But God's promise, which came later than

---

[i]6.19 *behind the curtain*: In the tent that was used for worship, a curtain separated the "holy place" from the "most holy place," which only the high priest could enter. [j]6.20 *Melchizedek*: See the note at 5.6.
[k]7.3 *will be a priest forever*: See the note at 5.6.
[l]7.11 *descendants of Levi . . . from the priestly family of Aaron*: Levi was the ancestor of the tribe from which priests and their helpers (called "Levites") were chosen. Aaron was the first high priest. [m]7.25 *forever able to save*: Or "able to save forever."

the Law, appoints his Son. And he is the perfect high priest forever.

A Better Promise

8 What I mean is that we have a high priest who sits at the right side[n] of God's great throne in heaven. [2]He also serves as the priest in the most holy place[o] inside the real tent there in heaven. This tent of worship was set up by the Lord, not by humans.

[3]Since all priests must offer gifts and sacrifices, Christ also needed to have something to offer. [4]If he were here on earth, he would not be a priest at all, because here the Law appoints other priests to offer sacrifices. [5]But the tent where they serve is just a copy and a shadow of the real one in heaven. Before Moses made the tent, he was told, "Be sure to make it exactly like the pattern you were shown on the mountain!" [6]Now Christ has been appointed to serve as a priest in a much better way, and he has given us much assurance of a better agreement.

[7]If the first agreement with God had been all right, there would not have been any need for another one. [8]But the Lord found fault with it and said,

> *Help us never to forget,*
> *whatever else, Lord,*
> *you're about, you have not*
> *finished with us—yet.*
>
> RUTH BELL GRAHAM

"I tell you the time will come,
when I will make
a new agreement
with the people of Israel
and the people of Judah.
[9]It won't be like the agreement
that I made
with their ancestors,
when I took them by the hand
and led them out of Egypt.
They broke their agreement
with me,

and I stopped caring
about them!

[10]"But now I tell the people
of Israel
this is my new agreement:
'The time will come
when I, the Lord,
will write my laws
on their minds and hearts.
I will be their God,
and they will be
my people.
[11]Not one of them
will have to teach another
to know me, their Lord.'

"All of them will know me,
no matter who they are.
[12]I will treat them with kindness,
even though they are wicked.
I will forget their sins."

[13]When the Lord talks about a new agreement, he means that the first one is out of date. And anything that is old and useless will soon disappear.

The Tent in Heaven

9 The first promise that was made included rules for worship and a tent for worship here on earth. [2]The first part of the tent was called the holy place, and a lampstand, a table, and the sacred loaves of bread were kept there.

[3]Behind the curtain was the most holy place. [4]The gold altar that was used for burning incense was in this holy place. The gold-covered sacred chest was also there, and inside it were three things. First, there was a gold jar filled with manna.[p] Then there was Aaron's walking stick that sprouted.[q] Finally, there were the flat stones with the Ten Commandments written on them. [5]On top of the chest were the glorious creatures

---

[n]8.1 *right side*: See the note at 1.3.   [o]8.2 *most holy place*: See the note at 6.19.   [p]9.4 *manna*: When the people of Israel were wandering through the desert, the Lord provided them with food that could be made into thin wafers. This food was called manna, which in Hebrew means "What is it?"   [q]9.4 *Aaron's walking stick that sprouted*: According to Numbers 17.1-11, Aaron's walking stick sprouted and produced almonds to show that the Lord was pleased with him and Moses.

with wings[r] opened out above the place of mercy.[s]

Now isn't the time to go into detail about these things. [6]But this is how everything was when the priests went each day into the first part of the tent to do their duties. [7]However, only the high priest could go into the second part of the tent, and he went in only once a year. Each time he carried blood to offer for his sins and for any sins that the people had committed without meaning to.

[8]All of this is the Holy Spirit's way of saying that no one could enter the most holy place while the tent was still the place of worship. [9]This also has a meaning for today. It shows that we cannot make our consciences clear by offering gifts and sacrifices. [10]These rules are merely about such things as eating and drinking and ceremonies for washing ourselves. And rules about physical things will last only until the time comes to change them for something better.

[11]Christ came as the high priest of the good things that are now here.[t] He also went into a much better tent that wasn't made by humans and that doesn't belong to this world. [12]Then Christ went once for all into the most holy place and freed us from sin forever. He did this by offering his own blood instead of the blood of goats and bulls.

[13]According to the Law of Moses, those people who become unclean are not fit to worship God. Yet they will be considered clean, if they are sprinkled with the blood of goats and bulls and with the ashes of a sacrificed calf. [14]But Christ was sinless, and he offered himself as an eternal and spiritual sacrifice to God. That's why his blood is much more powerful and makes our[u] consciences clear. Now we can serve the living God and no longer do things that lead to death.

[15]Christ died to rescue those who had sinned and broken the old agreement. Now he brings his chosen ones a new agreement with its guarantee of God's eternal blessings! [16]In fact, making an agreement of this kind is like writing a will. This is because the one who makes the will must die before it is of any use. [17]In other words, a will doesn't go into effect as long as the one who made it is still alive. [18]Blood was also used[v] to put the first

agreement into effect. [19]Moses told the people all that the Law said they must do. Then he used red wool and a hyssop plant to sprinkle the people and the book of the Law with the blood of bulls and goats[w] and with water. [20]He told the people, "With this blood God makes his agreement with you." [21]Moses also sprinkled blood on the tent and on everything else that was used in worship. [22]The Law says that almost everything must be sprinkled with blood, and no sins can be forgiven unless blood is offered.

Christ's Great Sacrifice

[23]These things are only copies of what is in heaven, and so they had to be made holy by these ceremonies. But the real things in heaven must be made holy by something better. [24]This is why Christ did not go into a tent that had been made by humans and was only a copy of the real one. Instead, he went into heaven and is now there with God to help us.

[25]Christ did not have to offer himself many times. He wasn't like a high priest who goes into the most holy place each year to offer the blood of an animal. [26]If he had offered himself every year, he would have suffered many times since the creation of the world. But instead, near the end of time he offered himself once and for all, so that he could be a sacrifice that does away with sin. [27]We die only once, and then we are judged. [28]So Christ died only once to take away the sins of many people. But when he comes again, it will not be to take away sin. He will come to save everyone who is waiting for him.

10 The Law of Moses is like a shadow of the good things to come. This shadow isn't the good things themselves, because it cannot free people from sin by the sacrifices that are offered year after year. [2]If there were worshipers who already have their sins washed away and

---

[r]9.5 *glorious creatures with wings*: Two of these creatures (called "cherubim" in Hebrew and Greek) with outspread wings were on top of the sacred chest and were symbols of God's throne.   [s]9.5 *place of mercy*: The lid of the sacred chest, which was thought to be God's throne on earth.   [t]9.14 *that are now here*: Some manuscripts have "that were coming."   [u]9.14 *our*: Some manuscripts have "your," and others have "their."   [v]9.18 *Blood was also used*: Or "There also had to be a death."   [w]9.19 *blood of bulls and goats*: Some manuscripts do not have "and goats."

their consciences made clear, there would not be any need to go on offering sacrifices. ³⁻⁴But the blood of bulls and goats cannot take away sins. It only reminds people of their sins from one year to the next.

⁵When Christ came into the world, he said to God,

> "Sacrifices and offerings
>   are not what you want,
> but you have given me
>   my body.
> ⁶ No, you are not pleased
>   with animal sacrifices
>   and offerings for sin."

⁷Then Christ said,

> "And so, my God,
>   I have come to do
> what you want,
>   as the Scriptures say."

⁸The Law teaches that offerings and sacrifices must be made because of sin. But why did Christ mention these things and say that God did not want them? ⁹Well, it was to do away with offerings and sacrifices and to replace them. That is what he meant by saying to God, "I have come to do what you want." ¹⁰So we are made holy because Christ obeyed God and offered himself once for all.

¹¹The priests do their work each day, and they keep on offering sacrifices that can never take away sins. ¹²But Christ offered himself as a sacrifice that is good forever. Now he is sitting at God's right side,ˣ ¹³and he will stay there until his enemies are put under his power. ¹⁴By his one sacrifice he has forever set free from sin the people he brings to God.

¹⁵The Holy Spirit also speaks of this by telling us that the Lord said,

> ¹⁶ "When the time comes,
>   I will make an agreement
>   with them.
>   I will write my laws
>   on their minds and hearts.
> ¹⁷ Then I will forget
>   about their sins
>   and no longer remember
>   their evil deeds."

¹⁸When sins are forgiven, there is no more need to offer sacrifices.

Encouragement and Warning

¹⁹My friends, the blood of Jesus gives us courage to enter the most holy place ²⁰by a new way that leads to life! And this way

---

ˣ**10.12** *right side:* See the note at 1.3.

Personal *Concerns*—How should I handle it when I feel rejected or excluded because of my faith? *(Hebrews 10.32-39)*

Stand firm.
There's no doubt about it; rejection hurts. But as odd as it may sound, rejection could be a compliment to Christians. It might mean we're doing things right.

Throughout the New Testament, we're reminded that being a Christian means living a countercultural life. It means paying attention to the people the world rejects, people like the poor. It means loving God and his people more than we love our possessions. It means following a man (who's actually the Son of God) who broke some of the rules of his own day and ushered in a new kind of world order.

When we truly follow Christ, when we're faithful to his calling, the book of Hebrews tells us to *expect* rejection, to *expect* suffering. Instead of letting this response to our faith discourage us, we can take heart as we follow Jesus that we're on the right track.

It'll never be easy to be a Christian in a non-Christian world. But God has a tremendous reward waiting for us—an everlasting life with him. (See also Daniel 6; John 15.18-27; 1 Peter 4.12-19; Revelation 14.12,13.)

Words To Remember: *Keep on being brave! It will bring you great rewards.* —Hebrews 10.35

takes us through the curtain that is Christ himself.

²¹We have a great high priest who is in charge of God's house. ²²So let's come near God with pure hearts and a confidence that comes from having faith. Let's keep our hearts pure, our consciences free from evil, and our bodies washed with clean water. ²³We must hold tightly to the hope that we say is ours. After all, we can trust the one who made the agreement with us. ²⁴We should keep on encouraging each other to be thoughtful and to do helpful things. ²⁵Some people have gotten out of the habit of meeting for worship, but we must not do that. We should keep on encouraging each other, especially since you know that the day of the Lord's coming is getting closer.

²⁶No sacrifices can be made for people who decide to sin after they find out about the truth. ²⁷They are God's enemies, and all they can look forward to is a terrible judgment and a furious fire. ²⁸If two or more witnesses accused someone of breaking the Law of Moses, that person could be put to death. ²⁹But it is much worse to dishonor God's Son and to disgrace the blood of the promise that made us holy. And it is just as bad to insult the Holy Spirit, who shows us mercy. ³⁰We know that God has said he will punish and take revenge. We also know that the Scriptures say the Lord will judge his people. ³¹It is a terrible thing to fall into the hands of the living God!

³²Don't forget all the hard times you went through when you first received the light. ³³Sometimes you were abused and mistreated in public, and at other times you shared in the sufferings of others. ³⁴You were kind to people in jail. And you gladly let your possessions be taken away, because you knew you had something better, something that would last forever.

³⁵Keep on being brave! It will bring you great rewards. ³⁶Learn to be patient, so that you will please God and be given what he has promised. ³⁷As the Scriptures say,

"God is coming soon!
    It won't be very long.
³⁸ The people God accepts
    will live because
        of their faith.ʸ
But he isn't pleased

with anyone
    who turns back."

³⁹We are not like those people who turn back and get destroyed. We will keep on having faith until we are saved.

The Great Faith of God's People

11 Faith makes us sure of what we hope for and gives us proof of what we cannot see. ²It was their faith that made our ancestors pleasing to God.

³Because of our faith, we know that the world was made at God's command. We also know that what can be seen was made out of what cannot be seen.

⁴Because Abel had faith, he offered God a better sacrifice than Cain did. God was pleased with him and his gift, and even though Abel is now dead, his faith still speaks for him.

⁵Enoch had faith and did not die. He pleased God, and God took him up to heaven. That's why his body was never found. ⁶But without faith no one can please God. We must believe that God is real and that he rewards everyone who searches for him.

It's hard to change the way you live. I know—I've been there. But God, in his mercy and grace, has taken my mistakes and turned them into a life lesson for others to learn from.

MARY HUNT

---

⁷Because Noah had faith, he was warned about something that had not yet happened. He obeyed and built a boat that saved him and his family. In this way the people of the world were judged, and Noah

---

ʸ10.38 *The people God accepts will live because of their faith:* Or "The people God accepts because of their faith will live."

was given the blessings that come to everyone who pleases God.

⁸Abraham had faith and obeyed God. He was told to go to the land that God had said would be his, and he left for a country he had never seen. ⁹Because Abraham had faith, he lived as a stranger in the promised land. He lived there in a tent, and so did Isaac and Jacob, who were later given the same promise. ¹⁰Abraham did this, because he was waiting for the eternal city that God had planned and built.

¹¹Even when Sarah was too old to have children, she had faith that God would do what he had promised, and she had a son. ¹²Her husband Abraham was almost dead, but he became the ancestor of many people. In fact, there are as many of them as there are stars in the sky or grains of sand along the beach.

¹³Every one of those people died. But they still had faith, even though they had not received what they had been promised. They were glad just to see these things from far away, and they agreed that they were only strangers and foreigners on this earth. ¹⁴When people talk this way, it is clear that they are looking for a place to call their own. ¹⁵If they had been talking about the land where they had once lived, they could have gone back at any time. ¹⁶But they were looking forward to a better home in heaven. That's why God wasn't ashamed for them to call him their God. He even built a city for them.

¹⁷⁻¹⁸Abraham had been promised that Isaac, his only son,ᶻ would continue his family. But when Abraham was tested, he had faith and was willing to sacrifice Isaac, ¹⁹because he was sure that God could raise people to life. This was just like getting Isaac back from death.

²⁰Isaac had faith, and he promised blessings to Jacob and Esau. ²¹Later, when Jacob was about to die, he leaned on his walking stick and worshiped. Then because of his faith he blessed each of Joseph's sons. ²²And right before Joseph died, he had faith that God would lead the people of Israel out of Egypt. So he told them to take his bones with them.

²³Because Moses' parents had faith, they kept him hidden until he was three months old. They saw that he was a beautiful child, and they were not afraid to disobey the king's orders.ᵃ ²⁴Then after Moses grew up, his faith made him refuse to be called Pharaoh's grandson. ²⁵He chose to be mistreated with God's people instead of having the good time that sin could bring for a little while. ²⁶Moses knew that the treasures of Egypt were not as wonderful as what he would receive from suffering for the Messiah,ᵇ and he looked forward to his reward.

²⁷Because of his faith, Moses left Egypt. Moses had seen the invisible God and wasn't afraid of the king's anger. ²⁸His faith also made him celebrate Passover. He sprinkled the blood of animals on the doorposts, so that the first-born sons of the people of Israel would not be killed by the destroying angel.

²⁹Because of their faith, the people walked through the Red Seaᶜ on dry land. But when the Egyptians tried to do it, they were drowned.

³⁰God's people had faith, and when they had walked around the city of Jericho for seven days, its walls fell down.

³¹Rahab had been a prostitute, but she had faith and welcomed the spies. So she wasn't killed with the people who disobeyed.

³²What else can I say? There isn't enough time to tell about Gideon, Barak, Samson, Jephthah, David, Samuel, and the prophets. ³³Their faith helped them conquer kingdoms, and because they did right, God made promises to them. They closed the jaws of lions ³⁴and put out raging fires and escaped from the swords of their enemies. Although they were weak, they were given the strength and power to chase foreign armies away.

³⁵Some women received their loved ones back from death. Many of these people were tortured, but they refused to be released.

ᶻ11.17,18 *his only son*: Although Abraham had a son by a slave woman, his son Isaac was considered his only son, because he was born as a result of God's promise to Abraham. ᵃ11.23 *the king's orders*: The king of Egypt ordered all Israelite baby boys to be left outside of their homes, so they would die or be killed. ᵇ11.26 *the Messiah*: Or "Christ." ᶜ11.29 *Red Sea*: This name comes from the Bible of the early Christians, a translation made into Greek about 200 B.C. It refers to the body of water that the Israelites crossed and was one of the marshes or fresh water lakes near the eastern part of the Nile Delta, where they lived and where the towns of Exodus 13.17—14.9 were located.

They were sure that they would get a better reward when the dead are raised to life. ³⁶Others were made fun of and beaten with whips, and some were chained in jail. ³⁷Still others were stoned to death or sawed in two*d* or killed with swords. Some had nothing but sheep skins or goat skins to wear. They were poor, mistreated, and tortured. ³⁸The world did not deserve these good people, who had to wander in deserts and on mountains and had to live in caves and holes in the ground.

³⁹All of them pleased God because of their faith! But still they died without being given what had been promised. ⁴⁰This was because God had something better in store for us. And he did not want them to reach the goal of their faith without us.

A Large Crowd of Witnesses

12 Such a large crowd of witnesses is all around us! So we must get rid of everything that slows us down, especially the sin that just won't let go. And we must be determined to run the race that is ahead of us. ²We must keep our eyes on Jesus, who leads us and makes our faith complete. He endured the shame of being nailed to a cross, because he knew that later on he would be glad he did. Now he is seated at the right side*e* of God's throne! ³So keep your mind on Jesus, who put up with many insults from sinners. Then you won't get discouraged and give up.

⁴None of you have yet been hurt*f* in your battle against sin. ⁵But you have forgotten that the Scriptures say to God's children,

"When the Lord punishes you,
    don't make light of it,
and when he corrects you,
    don't be discouraged.
⁶ The Lord corrects the people
    he loves
and disciplines those
    he calls his own."

⁷Be patient when you are being corrected! This is how God treats his children. Don't all parents correct their children? ⁸God corrects all of his children, and if he doesn't correct you, then you don't really belong to him. ⁹Our earthly fathers correct us, and we still respect them. Isn't it even better to be given true life by letting our spiritual Father correct us?

¹⁰Our human fathers correct us for a short time, and they do it as they think best. But God corrects us for our own good, because he wants us to be holy, as he is. ¹¹It is never fun to be corrected. In fact, at the time it is always painful. But if we learn to obey by being corrected, we will do right and live at peace.

¹²Now stand up straight! Stop your knees from shaking ¹³and walk a straight

---

*d*11.37 *sawed in two*: Some manuscripts have "tested" or "tempted."   *e*12.2 *right side*: See the note at 1.3.   *f*12.4 *hurt*: Or "killed."

PARENTING&*family*—How can I tell if I'm doing a good job as a mother?
(Hebrews 12.5-13)

Practice the art of discipline.
One of parenting's biggest challenges is finding the balance between being tough and being loving. We know we need to love our children unconditionally, and we know we need to discipline them when they do something wrong. But loving our kids is usually a lot easier than disciplining them.

So how can parents find the balance between tough and tender? We need only look to God for a beautiful example of a loving parent who also gently corrects his children when they make mistakes. God corrects us *because* he loves us. God wants us to learn the right way of doing things so we can live the life he wants for us (12.11).

We can do the same with our children. When we think of discipline as a way of guiding them, it no longer clashes with our desire to show them love. Gentle correction and loving guidance are crucial parts of good parenting. (See also Luke 2.41-52; Ephesians 6.1-4.)

Words To Remember: *"The Lord corrects the people he loves and disciplines those he calls his own."*—Hebrews 12.6

path. Then lame people will be healed, instead of getting worse.

Warning against Turning from God

[14]Try to live at peace with everyone! Live a clean life. If you don't, you will never see the Lord. [15]Make sure that no one misses out on God's wonderful kindness. Don't let anyone become bitter and cause trouble for the rest of you. [16]Watch out for immoral and ungodly people like Esau, who sold his future blessing[g] for only one meal. [17]You know how he later wanted it back. But there was nothing he could do to change things, even though he begged his father and cried.

[18]You have not come to a place like Mount Sinai[h] that can be seen and touched. There is no flaming fire or dark cloud or storm [19]or trumpet sound. The people of Israel heard a voice speak. But they begged it to stop, [20]because they could not obey its commands. They were even told to kill any animal that touched the mountain. [21]The sight was so frightening that Moses said he shook with fear.

[22]You have now come to Mount Zion and to the heavenly Jerusalem. This is the city of the living God, where thousands and thousands of angels have come to celebrate. [23]Here you will find all of God's dearest children,[i] whose names are written in heaven. And you will find God himself, who judges everyone. Here also are the spirits of those good people who have been made perfect. [24]And Jesus is here! He is the one who makes God's new agreement with us, and his sprinkled blood says much better things than the blood of Abel.[j]

[25]Make sure that you obey the one who speaks to you. The people did not escape, when they refused to obey the one who spoke to them at Mount Sinai. Do you think you can possibly escape, if you refuse to obey the one who speaks to you from heaven? [26]When God spoke the first time, his voice shook only the earth. This time he has promised to shake the earth once again, and heaven too.

[27]The words "once again" mean that these created things will someday be shaken and removed. Then what cannot be shaken will last. [28]We should be grateful that we were given a kingdom that cannot be

---

[g]**12.16** *sold his future blessing:* As the first-born son, Esau had certain privileges that were known as a "birthright." [h]**12.18** *a place like Mount Sinai:* The Greek text has "a place," but the writer is referring to the time that the Lord spoke to the people of Israel from Mount Sinai (see Exodus 19.16-25). [i]**12.23** *all of God's dearest children:* The Greek text has "the gathering of the first-born children" (see the note at 1.6). [j]**12.24** *blood of Abel:* Cain and Abel were the two sons of Adam and Eve. Cain murdered Abel (see Genesis 4.1-16).

Friendship—If I'm naturally introverted and independent, why should I go out of my way to make friends? *(Hebrews 13.1,2)*

Because God tells us to "welcome" others.
The doorbell rings. It's your next-door neighbor—again. She pops over several times a week. By the time you get home from work, you're so exhausted from all the hubbub that you'd rather be by yourself—or just with your immediate family.

But what does it mean to be "concerned about each other" (13.1)? Does it mean you have to be the perfect hostess, with a four-course meal, decorated table, and picked-up living room? Certainly not. What's more important is the spirit of hospitality—that we care more about the person we invited into our home than how our home looks or whether or not the person's arrival is convenient for us.

As Scripture says (13.2), we never know whom we might be influencing by our welcome attitude—maybe a future CEO, the head of a woman's organization, an overseas missionary, a stay-at-home mom. So invite your new coworker out to lunch, open your door to your neighbor, have a church visitor over for lunch—and you'll be fulfilling God's Word and pleasing him, not to mention bringing joy to others! (See also Ecclesiastes 4.9-12; John 13.18-35.)

Words To Remember: *Keep being concerned about each other as the Lord's followers should. Be sure to welcome strangers into your home.*—Hebrews 13.1,2

shaken. And in this kingdom we please God by worshiping him and by showing him great honor and respect. [29]Our God is like a destructive fire!

Service That Pleases God

13 Keep being concerned about each other as the Lord's followers should.

[2]Be sure to welcome strangers into your home. By doing this, some people have welcomed angels as guests, without even knowing it.

[3]Remember the Lord's people who are in jail and be concerned for them. Don't forget those who are suffering, but imagine that you are there with them.

[4]Have respect for marriage. Always be faithful to your partner, because God will punish anyone who is immoral or unfaithful in marriage.

[5]Don't fall in love with money. Be satisfied with what you have. The Lord has promised that he will not leave us or desert us. [6]That should make you feel like saying,

> "The Lord helps me!
> Why should I be afraid
> of what people
> can do to me?"

[7]Don't forget about your leaders who taught you God's message. Remember what kind of lives they lived and try to have faith like theirs.

[8]Jesus Christ never changes! He is the same yesterday, today, and forever. [9]Don't be fooled by any kind of strange teachings. It is better to receive strength from God's undeserved kindness than to depend on certain foods. After all, these foods don't really help the people who eat them. [10]But we have an altar where even the priests who serve in the place of worship have no right to eat.

[11]After the high priest offers the blood of animals as a sin offering, the bodies of those animals are burned outside the camp. [12]Jesus himself suffered outside the city gate, so that his blood would make people holy. [13]That's why we should go outside the camp to Jesus and share in his disgrace. [14]On this earth we don't have a city that lasts forever, but we are waiting for such a city.

[15]Our sacrifice is to keep offering praise to God in the name of Jesus. [16]But don't forget to help others and to share your possessions with them. This too is like offering a sacrifice that pleases God.

[17]Obey your leaders and do what they say. They are watching over you, and they must answer to God. So don't make them sad as they do their work. Make them happy. Otherwise, they won't be able to help you at all.

[18]Pray for us. Our consciences are clear,

MARRIAGE—What does a healthy, successful marriage look like? *(Hebrews 13.4)*

It's focused and committed.

There are times in every marriage when one partner wonders if there is any love left in the relationship. She might start thinking about the ways her marriage failed to meet her expectations, or the times her husband disappointed her. She might start thinking that there isn't much left to hold onto in a relationship that seems to be dying.

But for many couples, such times are only the low point in the cycle of changing seasons that mark a lifetime together. While we'd like to think it's the norm, the idea of a marriage that's consistently filled with unending love is unrealistic. After all, men and women are human beings, complete with changing moods, feelings, and desires. It's natural for our relationships to be affected by those changes.

By focusing on the commitment they've made before God, couples can weather the times in their marriage when love seems to fade. By building a marriage that's based on a respect for that commitment, the institution of marriage itself, a husband and wife can be assured that they'll survive the times when love isn't quite enough. (See also Genesis 2.18-23; Exodus 32.11-14; Song of Songs 8.5-7; Hosea 14.4-8; Acts 18.)

Words To Remember: *Have respect for marriage. Always be faithful to your partner.—Hebrews 13.4*

and we always try to live right. [19]I especially want you to pray that I can visit you again soon.

Final Prayers and Greetings

[20]God gives peace, and he raised our Lord Jesus Christ from death. Now Jesus is like a Great Shepherd whose blood was used to make God's eternal agreement with his flock.[k] [21]I pray that God will make you ready to obey him and that you will always be eager to do right. May Jesus help you do what pleases God. To Jesus Christ be glory forever and ever! Amen.

[22]My friends, I have written only a short letter to encourage you, and I beg you to pay close attention to what I have said.

[23]By now you surely must know that our friend Timothy is out of jail. If he gets here in time, I will bring him with me when I come to visit you.

[24]Please give my greetings to your leaders and to the rest of the Lord's people.

His followers from Italy send you their greetings.

[25]I pray that God will be kind to all of you![l]

---

[k]13.20 *whose blood was used to make God's eternal agreement with his flock:* See 9.18-22.   [l]13.25 *to all of you:* Some manuscripts add "Amen."

MARRIAGE—How can we prevent financial issues from becoming stumbling blocks in our marriage? (Hebrews 13.5,6)

Don't fall in love with money.

How many times have you said to yourself, *If I only had more money, more stuff, everything would be fine.* It seems we're never quite satisfied with what we have. No matter how much money or stuff we have, we could always use a little more.

But when we do get more, we still find ourselves unsatisfied. When will it ever be enough? According to Hebrews, the answer is never. Why? Because money and stuff are only temporary. They can be taken away at any time. To pin our hopes for happiness on material possessions is to ask to be dissatisfied.

But there's a remedy to the vicious cycle of wanting more and more. We can look to God, who promises to fulfill us forever. By putting our hopes in God, we no longer need to worry about having enough money, enough stuff. In God, our every need is satisfied—and satisfied for eternity. (See also Psalm 49.16-20; Malachi 3.8-12; Matthew 6.19-24; 1 Timothy 6.6-10.)

Words To Remember: *Don't fall in love with money. Be satisfied with what you have. The Lord has promised that he will not leave us or desert us.*—Hebrews 13.5

James
The Picture Book

Have you ever bought a cookbook filled with gorgeous pictures of tantalizing food, only to get it home and discover that the recipes are faulty? Isn't it incredibly frustrating to see the end results and have no idea how to achieve them?

Sometimes, living our faith can be as frustrating as that cookbook. We know the end result is a life that honors God. But *how* do we make it happen? What does the Christian life really look like?

That's where James comes in. One of the most practical books in the Bible, the book of James is packed with real things real Christians should be doing to live out their faith. With no patience for hypocrisy and inaction, James gets right to the point and offers clear instructions on watching our words, reaching out to the poor, and keeping our eyes fixed on Jesus—not on the world.

James's emphasis on action has caused some problems in the past. Martin Luther was so concerned that James contradicted Paul's message of free grace that he wanted the entire book thrown out of the Bible. But since James was likely written before any of Paul's letters, most biblical scholars look at Paul and James as focusing on different sides of the

same coin. While it's Christ's death and resurrection that saves us, we are to respond to God's grace with action.

To say we have faith is one thing; to live that way is another. That's why James stresses the practical side of faith. As we work to bring the good news of the gospel to others, our life may speak much louder than our words. By emphasizing the *how* of our faith, James helps us make our Christian life easy to read.

James at a Glance
1. Greetings (1.1)
2. A life of faith (1.2-18)
3. Obeying God's commands (1.19-27)
4. Don't favor the rich (2.1-13)
5. Faith and works (2.14-26)
6. Wisdom and words (3)
7. Watch out for the world (4.1—5.6)
8. Patience, kindness, and prayer (5.7-20)

1

From James, a servant of God and of our Lord Jesus Christ.
Greetings to the twelve tribes scattered all over the world.[a]

Faith and Wisdom

[2]My friends, be glad, even if you have a lot of trouble. [3]You know that you learn to endure by having your faith tested. [4]But you must learn to endure everything, so that you will be completely mature and not lacking in anything.

[5]If any of you need wisdom, you should ask God, and it will be given to you. God is generous and won't correct you for asking. [6]But when you ask for something, you must have faith and not doubt. Anyone who doubts is like an ocean wave tossed around in a storm. [7-8]If you are that kind of person, you can't make up your mind, and you surely can't be trusted. So don't expect the Lord to give you anything at all.

Poor People and Rich People

[9]Any of God's people who are poor should be glad that he thinks so highly of them. [10]But any who are rich should be glad when God makes them humble. Rich people will disappear like wild flowers [11]scorched by the burning heat of the sun. The flowers lose their blossoms, and their beauty is destroyed. That is how the rich will disappear, as they go about their business.

Trials and Temptations

[12]God will bless you, if you don't give up when your faith is being tested. He will reward you with a glorious life,[b] just as he rewards everyone who loves him.

[13]Don't blame God when you are tempted! God cannot be tempted by evil, and he doesn't use evil to tempt others. [14]We are tempted by our own desires that drag us off and trap us. [15]Our desires make us sin, and when sin is finished with us, it leaves us dead.

[16]Don't be fooled, my dear friends. [17]Every good and perfect gift comes down from the Father who created all the lights in the heavens. He is always the same and never makes dark shadows by changing. [18]He wanted us to be his own special people,[c] and so he sent the true message to give us new birth.

Hearing and Obeying

[19]My dear friends, you should be quick to listen and slow to speak or to get angry.

---

[a]1.1 *twelve tribes scattered all over the world*: James is saying that the Lord's followers are like the tribes of Israel that were scattered everywhere by their enemies. [b]1.12 *a glorious life*: The Greek text has "the crown of life." In ancient times an athlete who had won a contest was rewarded with a crown of flowers as a sign of victory. [c]1.18 *his own special people*: The Greek text has "the first of his creatures." The Law of Moses taught that the first-born of all animals and the first part of the harvest were special and belonged to the Lord.

Friendship—How can I speak the truth in love and still maintain a friendship? *(James 1.5-8)*

Ask God for wisdom.

You're close friends. You've listened to one another, cried with one another, even advised each other. You've shared your deepest fears, toughest questions, and most painful struggles. You have a great relationship, and you're certain that your "sisterly" bond could get you through any difficult moment.

Until now. Now your friend doesn't seem to want to hear the truth from you, and you're not sure how to approach her.

James offers the best source of help: God. When we need wisdom that's far beyond our own, he says, "Ask God, and it will be given to you" (1.5). What a marvelous promise, in any situation! God is ready to listen to *any* struggles we might be going through. All he asks is that we "have faith and not doubt" (1.6).

What do you need him to help you with today? (See also Job 42.7-9; Proverbs 27.6; Ephesians 4.25—5.2.)

 Words To Remember: *If any of you need wisdom, you should ask God, and it will be given to you.—James 1.5*

²⁰If you are angry, you cannot do any of the good things that God wants done. ²¹You must stop doing anything immoral or evil. Instead be humble and accept the message that is planted in you to save you.

²²Obey God's message! Don't fool yourselves by just listening to it. ²³If you hear the message and don't obey it, you are like people who stare at themselves in a mirror ²⁴and forget what they look like as soon as they leave. ²⁵But you must never stop looking at the perfect law that sets you free. God will bless you in everything you do, if you listen and obey, and don't just hear and forget.

²⁶If you think you are being religious, but can't control your tongue, you are fooling yourself, and everything you do is useless. ²⁷Religion that pleases God the Father must be pure and spotless. You must help needy orphans and widows and not let this world make you evil.

Warning against Having Favorites

2 My friends, if you have faith in our glorious Lord Jesus Christ, you won't treat some people better than others. ²Suppose a rich person wearing fancy clothes and a gold ring comes to one of your meetings. And suppose a poor person dressed in worn-out clothes also comes.

³You must not give the best seat to the one in fancy clothes and tell the one who is poor to stand at the side or sit on the floor. ⁴That is the same as saying that some people are better than others, and you would be acting like a crooked judge.

⁵My dear friends, pay attention. God has given a lot of faith to the poor people in this world. He has also promised them a share in his kingdom that he will give to everyone who loves him. ⁶You mistreat the poor. But isn't it the rich who boss you around and drag you off to court? ⁷Aren't they the ones who make fun of your Lord?

We need to be as patient with each other as God is with us.

SUSAN ASHTON

⁸You will do all right, if you obey the most important law*d* in the Scriptures. It is

---

*d*2.8 *most important law:* The Greek text has "royal law," meaning the one given by the king (that is, God).

SingleLife—How can I resist the pressure to be sexually active? *(James 1.12-18)*

Respect God's good gift.

If you believe what you see and hear in magazines, on television, in books and movies, you might just think that casual sex is one of the greatest things in life—something wonderful you're missing out on because of your beliefs. But those images only show you half the picture.

What you rarely see in those movies and books are the damaged self-images, the struggling marriages, the emotional pain, and the physical disease caused by sex that strays from God's intentions. As passionate and satisfying as premarital sex appears, it's a ticket to misery and heartache.

That's why God intended sex as a unique bond between two people committed to each other for life. Without the commitment of marriage, sex leaves people feeling used, cheated, and insecure. And those kinds of feelings are far from what God wants for us.

When you're feeling tempted by sex, remember that God wants you to wait, not so he can test your strength, but so that you can experience the gift of sex as God intended it: a pure, holy, and loving expression of lifelong commitment. (See also Joshua 7; Psalm 103; Ephesians 6.10-20; 2 Peter 2.7-9.)

Words To Remember: *God will bless you, if you don't give up when your faith is being tested. He will reward you with a glorious life, just as he rewards everyone who loves him.—James 1.12*

the law that commands us to love others as much as we love ourselves. ⁹But if you treat some people better than others, you have done wrong, and the Scriptures teach that you have sinned.

¹⁰If you obey every law except one, you are still guilty of breaking them all. ¹¹The same God who told us to be faithful in marriage also told us not to murder. So even if you are faithful in marriage, but murder someone, you still have broken God's Law.

¹²Speak and act like people who will be judged by the law that sets us free. ¹³Do this, because on the day of judgment there will be no pity for those who have not had pity on others. But even in judgment, God is merciful!ᵉ

Faith and Works

¹⁴My friends, what good is it to say you have faith, when you don't do anything to show that you really do have faith? Can that kind of faith save you? ¹⁵If you know someone who doesn't have any clothes or food, ¹⁶you shouldn't just say, "I hope all goes well for you. I hope you will be warm and have plenty to eat." What good is it to say this, unless you do something to help? ¹⁷Faith that doesn't lead us to do good deeds is all alone and dead!

¹⁸Suppose someone disagrees and says, "It is possible to have faith without doing kind deeds."

I would answer, "Prove that you have faith without doing kind deeds, and I will prove that I have faith by doing them." ¹⁹You surely believe there is only one God. That's fine. Even demons believe this, and it makes them shake with fear.

²⁰Does some stupid person want proof that faith without deeds is useless? ²¹Well, our ancestor Abraham pleased God by putting his son Isaac on the altar to sacrifice him. ²²Now you see how Abraham's faith and deeds worked together. He proved that his faith was real by what he did. ²³This is what the Scriptures mean by saying, "Abraham had faith in God, and God was pleased with him." That's how Abraham became God's friend.

²⁴You can now see that we please God by what we do and not only by what we believe. ²⁵For example, Rahab had been a prostitute. But she pleased God when she welcomed the spies and sent them home by another way.

²⁶Anyone who doesn't breathe is dead, and faith that doesn't do anything is just as dead!

ᵉ2.13 *But even in judgment, God is merciful*: Or "So be merciful, and you will be shown mercy on the day of judgment."

Personal *Concerns*—Sometimes I'm jealous of others. How can I get out of the jealousy/envy trap? *(James 3.1-12)*

Watch your mind—and your tongue.
Since many of us struggle with our self-image, it's no surprise we often feel pangs of envy when we meet someone thinner, smarter, prettier, or richer. Occasionally those pangs turn into full-blown resentments based in petty jealousies.

In some ways, jealousy seems like a victimless crime. When the Bible warns against jealousy, it usually reminds us that jealousy is a sin because it affects our relationship with God. But jealousy damages much more than that. When we let jealousy into our head and heart, it's bound to leak out through our mouth.

This passage in James couldn't be clearer about the damage we do when we let envy lead to lies, gossip, and bitter words. It compares our hateful words to a forest fire that consumes and destroys everything it touches (3.5,6). It's pretty obvious that jealousy—depicted with such a powerful image—affects more lives than just our own.

As we struggle to rein in our feelings of envy, we need to remember to watch not only what's filling up our heart, but what's flowing out of our mouth as well. (See also 1 Samuel 20; Psalm 73.1-20; Jonah 4.)

Words To Remember: *All of us do many wrong things. But if you can control your tongue, you are mature and able to control your whole body.—James 3.2*

The Tongue

3 My friends, we should not all try to become teachers. In fact, teachers will be judged more strictly than others. ²All of us do many wrong things. But if you can control your tongue, you are mature and able to control your whole body.

³By putting a bit into the mouth of a horse, we can turn the horse in different directions. ⁴It takes strong winds to move a large sailing ship, but the captain uses only a small rudder to make it go in any direction. ⁵Our tongues are small too, and yet they brag about big things.

It takes only a spark to start a forest fire! ⁶The tongue is like a spark. It is an evil power that dirties the rest of the body and sets a person's entire life on fire with flames that come from hell itself. ⁷All kinds of animals, birds, reptiles, and sea creatures can be tamed and have been tamed. ⁸But our tongues get out of control. They are restless and evil, and always spreading deadly poison.

⁹⁻¹⁰My dear friends, with our tongues we speak both praises and curses. We praise our Lord and Father, and we curse people who were created to be like God, and this isn't right. ¹¹Can clean water and dirty water both flow from the same spring? ¹²Can a fig tree produce olives or a grapevine produce figs? Does fresh water come from a well full of salt water?

Wisdom from Above

¹³Are any of you wise or sensible? Then show it by living right and by being humble and wise in everything you do. ¹⁴But if your heart is full of bitter jealousy and selfishness, don't brag or lie to cover up the truth. ¹⁵That kind of wisdom doesn't come from above. It is earthly and selfish and comes from the devil himself. ¹⁶Whenever people are jealous or selfish, they cause trouble and do all sorts of cruel things. ¹⁷But the wisdom that comes from above leads us to be pure, friendly, gentle, sensible, kind, helpful, genuine, and sincere. ¹⁸When peacemakers plant seeds of peace, they will harvest justice.

Friendship with the World

4 Why do you fight and argue with each other? Isn't it because you are full of selfish desires that fight to control your body? ²You want something you don't have, and you will do anything to get it. You will even kill! But you still cannot get what you want, and you won't get it by fighting and arguing. You should pray for it. ³Yet even when you do pray, your prayers are not answered, because you pray just for selfish reasons.

⁴You people aren't faithful to God! Don't you know that if you love the world, you are God's enemies? And if you decide to be a

---

WORK—How can I rise above office politics? *(James 3.5-18)*

Don't overrate the in-crowd.
Think back to your high-school days. Remember how hard it was to stand apart from the crowd, to be your own person? The rule in most schools seemed to be "fit in or get out." There wasn't much room for individuals.

Unfortunately, the workplace can be strangely similar to high school. Everyone wants to be liked, everyone wants to please, and everyone wants to fit in. And while you're not likely to become an outcast for being your own person at the office, there's still not much room for individuals. Especially when it comes to office politics.

Like high school, the office atmosphere often encourages you to be ruthless, backstabbing, or cruel to get ahead. But as Christians, we know there's a better way. God's way is to treat others with kindness, gentleness, and respect. You may not become CEO by following God's path, but your eternal reward will be well worth the sacrifice. (See also Deuteronomy 5.20,21; Esther 7.1-6; Matthew 20.20-28; Galatians 5.13-16; Colossians 3.22—4.1.)

Words To Remember: *But the wisdom that comes from above leads us to be pure, friendly, gentle, sensible, kind, helpful, genuine, and sincere. When peacemakers plant seeds of peace, they will harvest justice.*—James 3.17,18

friend of the world, you make yourself an enemy of God. [5]Do you doubt the Scriptures that say, "God truly cares about the Spirit he has put in us"?[f] [6]In fact, God treats us with even greater kindness, just as the Scriptures say,

"God opposes everyone
    who is proud,
but he is kind to everyone
    who is humble."

*How grateful we can
be that God has no
answering service.*

RUTH BELL GRAHAM

[7]Surrender to God! Resist the devil, and he will run from you. [8]Come near to God, and he will come near to you. Clean up your lives, you sinners. Purify your hearts, you people who can't make up your mind. [9]Be sad and sorry and weep. Stop laughing and start crying. Be gloomy instead of glad. [10]Be humble in the Lord's presence, and he will honor you.

Saying Cruel Things about Others

[11]My friends, don't say cruel things about others! If you do, or if you condemn others, you are condemning God's Law. And if you condemn the Law, you put yourself above the Law and refuse to obey either it [12]or God who gave it. God is our judge, and he can save or destroy us. What right do you have to condemn anyone?

Warning against Bragging

[13]You should know better than to say, "Today or tomorrow we will go to the city. We will do business there for a year and make a lot of money!" [14]What do you know about tomorrow? How can you be so sure about your life? It is nothing more than mist that appears for only a little while before it disappears. [15]You should say, "If the Lord

---

[f]4.5 *God truly cares about the Spirit he has put in us:* One possible meaning for the difficult Greek text; other translations are possible, such as, "the Spirit that God put in us truly cares."

MARRIAGE—My husband doesn't share my passion for spiritual things. How can I deal with my frustration and sadness? *(James 5.7-11)*

Practice patience.

In a manual for marriage, the first chapter could be titled, "You Can't Change Another Person." Many people could have avoided a lot of the frustration and strife in their marriage if they'd realized from the get-go that their partner wasn't likely to be any closer to their design after ten years of marriage than he was on their wedding day. Instead of feeling they'd been sold a false bill of goods, they'd have had a realistic expectation of the kind of man who would be sharing their life.

Unfortunately, the fact that we can't make other people change is a lesson we don't easily learn. So does that mean you just have to learn to live with the things about your spouse you wish you could alter? Well, yes. But you don't have to give up praying for a new attitude toward your husband—an attitude of patience.

The book of James reminds us of one of the Bible's great role models of patience: Job. As you strive to be more patient with your partner, remember Job's lasting hope in the face of his suffering. He never doubted that God would eventually change his situation. In the end, God helped him. He'll do the same in your life. (See also Job 6.14-21; Revelation 21.1-4.)

Words To Remember: *We praise the ones who endured the most. You remember how patient Job was and how the Lord finally helped him. The Lord did this because he is so merciful and kind.—James 5.11*

lets us live, we will do these things." [16]Yet you are stupid enough to brag, and it is wrong to be so proud. [17]If you don't do what you know is right, you have sinned.

Warning to the Rich

5 You rich people should cry and weep! Terrible things are going to happen to you. [2]Your treasures have already rotted, and moths have eaten your clothes. [3]Your money has rusted, and the rust will be evidence against you, as it burns your body like fire. Yet you keep on storing up wealth in these last days. [4]You refused to pay the people who worked in your fields, and now their unpaid wages are shouting out against you. The Lord All-Powerful has surely heard the cries of the workers who harvested your crops.

[5]While here on earth, you have thought only of filling your own stomachs and having a good time. But now you are like fat cattle on their way to be butchered. [6]You have condemned and murdered innocent people, who couldn't even fight back.

Be Patient and Kind

[7]My friends, be patient until the Lord returns. Think of farmers who wait patiently for the spring and summer rains to make their valuable crops grow. [8]Be patient like those farmers and don't give up. The Lord will soon be here! [9]Don't grumble about each other or you will be judged, and the judge is right outside the door.

[10]My friends, follow the example of the prophets who spoke for the Lord. They were patient, even when they had to suffer. [11]In fact, we praise the ones who endured the most. You remember how patient Job was and how the Lord finally helped him. The Lord did this because he is so merciful and kind.

[12]My friends, above all else, don't take an oath. You must not swear by heaven or by earth or by anything else. "Yes" or "No" is all you need to say. If you say anything more, you will be condemned.

[13]If you are having trouble, you should pray. And if you are feeling good, you should sing praises. [14]If you are sick, ask the church leaders[g] to come and pray for you. Ask them to put olive oil[h] on you in the name of the Lord. [15]If you have faith when you pray for sick people, they will get well. The Lord will heal them, and if they have sinned, he will forgive them.

[16]If you have sinned, you should tell each other what you have done. Then you can pray for one another and be healed. The

---

[g]5.14 *church leaders*: Or "elders" or "presbyters" or "priests." [h]5.14 *olive oil*: The Jewish people used olive oil for healing.

Friendship—**What are the marks of a good friendship?** (*James* 5.13-20)

That you're able to lean on each other.

The English poet John Donne wrote this famous quote: "No man is an island." As we watch the old-fashioned friendliness of small-town life transform into the anonymity of urban life, we're starting to discover just how true that statement is. We *need* other people in our life. Not just a few family members or a select group of friends, but neighbors, coworkers, and the people we run into on the streets of our community. God designed us to be social beings (Genesis 2.18).

Our need for others is especially strong in the church. When the first followers of Christ found themselves persecuted by society, they banded together, finding strength and encouragement in each other. In James, we see that our need to have friends extends to our daily Christian walk as well. Strong Christian friendships are marked by shared times of worship, joy, suffering, prayer, confession, and accountability. Without friends who will share the ups and downs of life, we are stuck on a very lonely island indeed. (See also Ruth 1–4; Proverbs 17.17; 18.24; Proverbs 27.17-19; 1 Corinthians 13.4-8.)

Words To Remember: *My friends, if any followers have wandered away from the truth, you should try to lead them back. If you turn sinners from the wrong way, you will save them from death, and many of their sins will be forgiven.*—**James 5.19,20**

prayer of an innocent person is powerful, and it can help a lot. [17]Elijah was just as human as we are, and for three and a half years his prayers kept the rain from falling. [18]But when he did pray for rain, it fell from the skies and made the crops grow.

[19]My friends, if any followers have wandered away from the truth, you should try to lead them back. [20]If you turn sinners from the wrong way, you will save them from death, and many of their sins will be forgiven.

1 Peter
Courage for Hard Times

Have you ever wondered if something major is about to go wrong? Peter had more than a hunch. He *knew* that Christians were about to enter a period of intense suffering. They would be harassed. They'd lose their jobs. They'd be deported and scattered. Their homes would be burned. Their leaders (including Peter) would be tortured and murdered.

How ought Christians to prepare? How would you prepare? Would you freeze in panic? Would you keep a low profile so no one would know you were a Christian? Would you gather your family and hide in the mountains? Would you live with reckless abandon, because comfortable life would soon end? Would you collect weapons and learn to use them? Or would you check out of the soon-to-be persecuted Christian faith?

In the face of such a traumatic future, Peter's advice was amazingly ordinary. He reminded Christians that Jesus led the way: he suffered and died. But he also rose from the dead. Peter says, "God is so good, and by raising Jesus from death, he has given us new life and a hope that lives on" (1.3). Peter went on to advise routine holy living: "Be alert and think straight. . . . Don't let your lives be controlled by your desires. . . . Sincerely love each other" (1.13,14,22). While Peter gave brief instructions on how to approach the dangerous political scene ("Honor God and respect the Emperor," 2.17), he focused much more on the everyday important relationships: people at work, home, and in the church. In these, he told his read-

ers to fulfill their own responsibilities and at the same time submit to each other out of love, consideration, and loyalty. In other words, as disaster approaches, keep on living the normal Christian life.

Peter's counsel can help us as well—especially when our darkest fears bear down upon us. Peter reminds us that life here is only a small part of God's big scene. He closes his letter by saying, "You will suffer for a while, but God will make you complete, steady, strong, and firm. God will be in control forever! Amen" (5.10,11). Now that's a hope we can hang on to!

1 Peter at a Glance

1. Greetings to God's family (1.1,2)
2. Hope—because Jesus is alive (1.3-12)
3. Holy living (1.13—2.3)
4. God chose you (2.4-12)
5. Submission at work and at home (2.13—3.7)
6. The good side of suffering (3.8—4.19)
7. Responsibilities of elders and young men (5.1-11)
8. Final notes from friends (5.12-14)

1 From Peter, an apostle of Jesus Christ. To God's people who are scattered like foreigners in Pontus, Galatia, Cappadocia, Asia, and Bithynia.

[2]God the Father decided to choose you as his people, and his Spirit has made you holy. You have obeyed Jesus Christ and are sprinkled with his blood.[a]

I pray that God will be kind to you and will keep on giving you peace!

A Real Reason for Hope

[3]Praise God, the Father of our Lord Jesus Christ. God is so good, and by raising Jesus from death, he has given us new life and a hope that lives on. [4]God has something stored up for you in heaven, where it will never decay or be ruined or disappear.

[5]You have faith in God, whose power will protect you until the last day.[b] Then he will save you, just as he has always planned to do. [6]On that day you will be glad, even if you have to go through many hard trials for a while. [7]Your faith will be like gold that has been tested in a fire. And these trials will prove that your faith is worth much more than gold that can be destroyed. They will show that you will be given praise and honor and glory when Jesus Christ returns.

> *If we don't share what we're learning through a bad situation, part of the good God wants to bring out of it is lost.*
>
> TWILA PARIS

[8]You have never seen Jesus, and you don't see him now. But still you love him and have faith in him, and no words can tell how glad and happy [9]you are to be saved. That's why you have faith.

[10]Some prophets told how kind God would be to you, and they searched hard to find out more about the way you would be saved. [11]The Spirit of Christ was in them and was telling them how Christ would suffer and would then be given great honor. So they searched to find out exactly who Christ

would be and when this would happen. [12]But they were told that they were serving you and not themselves. They preached to you by the power of the Holy Spirit, who was sent from heaven. And their message was only for you, even though angels would like to know more about it.

Chosen To Live a Holy Life

[13]Be alert and think straight. Put all your hope in how kind God will be to you when Jesus Christ appears. [14]Behave like obedient children. Don't let your lives be controlled by your desires, as they used to be. [15]Always live as God's holy people should, because God is the one who chose you, and he is holy. [16]That's why the Scriptures say, "I am the holy God, and you must be holy too."

[17]You say that God is your Father, but God doesn't have favorites! He judges all people by what they do. So you must honor God while you live as strangers here on earth. [18]You were rescued[c] from the useless way of life that you learned from your ancestors. But you know that you were not rescued by such things as silver or gold that don't last forever. [19]You were rescued by the precious blood of Christ, that spotless and innocent lamb. [20]Christ was chosen even before the world was created, but because of you, he did not come until these last days. [21]And when he did come, it was to lead you to have faith in God, who raised him from death and honored him in a glorious way. That's why you have put your faith and hope in God.

[22]You obeyed the truth,[d] and your souls were made pure. Now you sincerely love each other. But you must keep on loving with all your heart. [23]Do this because God has given you new birth by his message that lives on forever. [24]The Scriptures say,

> "Humans wither like grass,
> and their glory fades
> like wild flowers.

---

[a]**1.2** *sprinkled with his blood:* According to Exodus 24.3-8 the people of Israel were sprinkled with the blood of cows to show they would keep their agreement with God. Peter says that it is the blood of Jesus that seals the agreement between God and his people (see Hebrews 9.18-21). [b]**1.5** *the last day:* When God will judge all people. [c]**1.18** *rescued:* The Greek word often, though not always, means payment of a price to free a slave or prisoner. [d]**1.22** *You obeyed the truth:* Some manuscripts add "by the power of the Spirit."

Grass dries up,
and flowers fall
    to the ground.
[25] But what the Lord has said
    will stand forever."

Our good news to you is what the Lord
has said.

A Living Stone and a Holy Nation

2 Stop being hateful! Quit trying to fool
people, and start being sincere. Don't
be jealous or say cruel things about
others. [2] Be like newborn babies who are
thirsty for the pure spiritual milk that will
help you grow and be saved. [3] You have already found out how good the Lord really is.
[4] Come to Jesus Christ. He is the living
stone that people have rejected, but which
God has chosen and highly honored. [5] And
now you are living stones that are being
used to build a spiritual house. You are also
a group of holy priests, and with the help of
Jesus Christ you will offer sacrifices that
please God. [6] It is just as God says in the
Scriptures,

"Look! I am placing in Zion
a choice and precious
    cornerstone.
No one who has faith
in that one
    will be disappointed."

> I want the virtues
> of Jesus—his purity,
> humility, mercy, and
> kindness—to be such a
> part of my character
> that when people look
> in my eyes or hear my voice,
> they see or hear Jesus.
>
> KATHY TROCCOLI

[7] You are followers of the Lord, and that
stone is precious to you. But it isn't precious

to those who refuse to follow him. They are
the builders who tossed aside the stone that
turned out to be the most important one of
all. [8] They disobeyed the message and stumbled and fell over that stone, because they
were doomed.
[9] But you are God's chosen and special
people. You are a group of royal priests and a
holy nation. God has brought you out of
darkness into his marvelous light. Now you
must tell all the wonderful things that he
has done. The Scriptures say,

[10] "Once you were nobody.
    Now you are God's people.
At one time no one
    had pity on you.
Now God has treated you
    with kindness.

Live as God's Servants Should

[11] Dear friends, you are foreigners and
strangers on this earth. So I beg you not to
surrender to those desires that fight against
you. [12] Always let others see you behaving
properly, even though they may still accuse
you of doing wrong. Then on the day of
judgment, they will honor God by telling
the good things they saw you do.
[13] The Lord wants you to obey all human
authorities, especially the Emperor, who
rules over everyone. [14] You must also obey
governors, because they are sent by the Emperor to punish criminals and to praise good
citizens. [15] God wants you to silence stupid
and ignorant people by doing right. [16] You
are free, but still you are God's servants, and
you must not use your freedom as an excuse
for doing wrong. [17] Respect everyone and
show special love for God's people. Honor
God and respect the Emperor.

The Example of Christ's Suffering

[18] Servants, you must obey your masters
and always show respect to them. Do this,
not only to those who are kind and thoughtful, but also to those who are cruel. [19] God
will bless you, even if others treat you unfairly for being loyal to him. [20] You don't gain
anything by being punished for some wrong
you have done. But God will bless you, if
you have to suffer for doing something
good. [21] After all, God chose you to suffer as
you follow in the footsteps of Christ, who
set an example by suffering for you.

²²Christ did not sin
    or ever tell a lie.
²³Although he was abused,
    he never tried to get even.
And when he suffered,
    he made no threats.
Instead, he had faith in God,
    who judges fairly.
²⁴Christ carried the burden
    of our sins.
He was nailed to the cross,
    so that we would stop sinning
    and start living right.
By his cuts and bruises
    you are healed.
²⁵You had wandered away
    like sheep.
Now you have returned
    to the one
who is your shepherd
    and protector.

Wives and Husbands

3 If you are a wife, you must put your husband first. Even if he opposes our message, you will win him over by what you do. No one else will have to say anything to him, ²because he will see how you honor God and live a pure life. ³Don't depend on things like fancy hairdos or gold jewelry or expensive clothes to make you look beautiful. ⁴Be beautiful in your heart by being gentle and quiet. This kind of beauty will last, and God considers it very special.

⁵Long ago those women who worshiped God and put their hope in him made themselves beautiful by putting their husbands first. ⁶For example, Sarah obeyed Abraham and called him her master. You are her true children, if you do right and don't let anything frighten you.

⁷If you are a husband, you should be thoughtful of your wife. Treat her with honor, because she isn't as strong as you are, and she shares with you in the gift of life. Then nothing will stand in the way of your prayers.

Suffering for Doing Right

⁸Finally, all of you should agree and have concern and love for each other. You should also be kind and humble. ⁹Don't be hateful and insult people just because they are hateful and insult you. Instead, treat everyone

---

MARRIAGE—How can I lead my unbelieving husband to Christ without offending him? *(1 Peter 3.1-6)*

Win him over by what you do.

Words are powerful tools. But when you're married to an unbeliever, words can get tiresome, especially if your husband remains unconvinced of the Christian faith. The apostle Peter suggested a different route: actions.

What kind of actions? Peter wasn't specific (which may be just as well for us who live some two thousand years later). But whatever you do, your husband should be able to "see how you honor God and live a pure life" (3.2). Peter's next statements about hair, jewelry, and clothes are confusing. Some Christian women take these instructions literally and practice personal grooming accordingly. Others assume Peter was teaching about a difference in emphasis rather than giving exact instructions. But whatever your interpretation, we are to develop *inner* Christian character. Verse 2 contrasts with verse 4: "Be beautiful in your heart." It's the same emphasis Jesus made when he complained to religious leaders, "You Pharisees clean the outside of cups and dishes, but on the inside you are greedy and evil" (Luke 11.39).

How can a Christian wife put her husband first (without pulling herself into sin)? Focus on his favorites: favorite foods, favorite vacation place, favorite clothes, favorite way to spend free time, favorite place to live. Of course, it's important for you to convey your preferences as well—so that he can express his own love for you. But when you "put your husband first," you are honoring him—and God. (See also Genesis 39; 41.39; Song of Songs 2.16—3.4; John 13.1-17; Revelation 21.9—22.21.)

Words To Remember: *Put your husband first. Even if he opposes our message, you will win him over by what you do.*—1 Peter 3.1

with kindness. You are God's chosen ones, and he will bless you. The Scriptures say,

[10] "Do you really love life?
    Do you want to be happy?
Then stop saying cruel things
    and quit telling lies.
[11] Give up your evil ways
    and do right,
as you find and follow
    the road that leads
    to peace.
[12] The Lord watches over
    everyone who obeys him,
and he listens
    to their prayers.
But he opposes everyone
    who does evil."

[13] Can anyone really harm you for being eager to do good deeds? [14] Even if you have to suffer for doing good things, God will bless you. So stop being afraid and don't worry about what people might do. [15] Honor Christ and let him be the Lord of your life.

Always be ready to give an answer when someone asks you about your hope. [16] Give a kind and respectful answer and keep your conscience clear. This way you will make people ashamed for saying bad things about your good conduct as a follower of Christ.

[17] You are better off to obey God and suffer for doing right than to suffer for doing wrong.

[18] Christ died once for our sins.
    An innocent person died
    for those who are guilty.
Christ did this
    to bring you to God,
when his body
    was put to death
and his spirit
    was made alive.

[19] Christ then preached to the spirits that were being kept in prison. [20] They had disobeyed God while Noah was building the boat, but God had been patient with them. Eight people went into that boat and were brought safely through the flood. [21] Those flood waters were like baptism that now saves you. But baptism is more than just washing your body. It means turning to God with a clear conscience, because Jesus Christ was raised from death. [22] Christ is now in heaven, where he sits at the right side[c] of God. All angels, authorities, and powers are under his control.

---

[c]3.22 *right side*: The place of honor and power.

◦◦◦ ━━━━━━━━━━━━━━━━━━━━━━━━━━━━━━━━

MARRIAGE—How can I learn to forgive my husband even when he doesn't apologize? *(1 Peter 3.8-15)*

Remember that your feelings matter to God.
Peter's letter is about suffering. Some sections seem like rules for ordinary Christian living. But Peter keeps coming back to his main theme: how to live during suffering.

Living with a husband who doesn't admit his mistakes isn't quite as painful as being a human torch for one of Nero's garden parties. But it's suffering all the same. Peter's instructions apply for both: "Have concern and love for each other"; "Be kind and humble"; "Treat everyone with kindness" (3.8,9); "Stop being afraid and don't worry about what people might do" (3.14). And then there's the undergirding statement that helps us forgive, even when it's hard: "Honor Christ and let him be the Lord of your life" (3.15).

One of the responsibilities of a wife is to let your husband know, as tactfully as you can, when he's hurt you. Even when you do this, an apology may not be forthcoming. Living with a husband who doesn't ask for forgiveness can take a terrible toll on your self-esteem. You may feel unworthy of an apology or think that your feelings don't matter—at least to your husband. But you *do* matter to God. Christ is your Lord. You are one of "God's chosen ones" (3.9). With that confidence, you can begin to forgive your husband—even if he doesn't ask. (See also Jeremiah 33.1-9; Ephesians 2.14-18.)

◦◦◦ **Words To Remember:** *The Lord watches over everyone who obeys him, and he listens to their prayers.*—1 Peter 3.12

Being Faithful to God

4 Christ suffered here on earth. Now you must be ready to suffer as he did, because suffering shows that you have stopped sinning. ²It means you have turned from your own desires and want to obey God for the rest of your life. ³You have already lived long enough like people who don't know God. You were immoral and followed your evil desires. You went around drinking and partying and carrying on. In fact, you even worshiped disgusting idols. ⁴Now your former friends wonder why you have stopped running around with them, and they curse you for it. ⁵But they will have to answer to God, who judges the living and the dead. ⁶The good news has even been preached to the dead,ᶠ so that after they have been judged for what they have done in this life, their spirits will live with God.

⁷Everything will soon come to an end. So be serious and be sensible enough to pray.

⁸Most important of all, you must sincerely love each other, because love wipes away many sins.

⁹Welcome people into your home and don't grumble about it.

¹⁰Each of you has been blessed with one of God's many wonderful gifts to be used in the service of others. So use your gift well. ¹¹If you have the gift of speaking, preach God's message. If you have the gift of helping others, do it with the strength that God supplies. Everything should be done in a way that will bring honor to God because of Jesus Christ, who is glorious and powerful forever. Amen.

Suffering for Being a Christian

¹²Dear friends, don't be surprised or shocked that you are going through testing that is like walking through fire. ¹³Be glad for the chance to suffer as Christ suffered. It will prepare you for even greater happiness when he makes his glorious return.

¹⁴Count it a blessing when you suffer for being a Christian. This shows that God's glorious Spirit is with you. ¹⁵But you deserve to suffer if you are a murderer,

---

ᶠ4.6 *the dead*: Either people who died after becoming followers of Christ or the people of Noah's day (see 3.19).

SingleLife—Sometimes I really want to be married. How can I deal with those times? *(1 Peter 3.13-18)*

Consider your current status a sacrifice for your faith.
Let's face it. There are more Christian women out there than men. Take a look at any church service on Sunday morning or any Christian singles group on Saturday night and the statistics are undeniable: You've got a lot better chance of finding a spouse there if you are male than if you are female. Sociologists write textbooks to explain this phenomena, but that's not much comfort to a Christian woman edging into her thirties—unaccompanied.

A woman in this category has several choices. She can explore romance with a non-Christian. Or she can start getting used to the possibility that she *may* be single for the rest of her life. It's not an easy choice. If she begins to consider non-Christians, she goes against Paul's specific instructions to Christians: "Stay away from people who are not followers of the Lord! . . . Can people who follow the Lord have anything in common with those who don't?" (2 Corinthians 6.14,15). The New King James Version says: "Do not be unequally yoked together with unbelievers." Paul wisely warns that in this kind of marriage, the husband and wife will find little in common.

But for the Christian woman who intensely desires marriage, the alternative of remaining single seems harsh indeed. She is in fact suffering for her faith—and her choice to obey God's teachings. But Peter's letter is full of comfort for those who suffer for their faith. In this passage, he points to the example of Christ, who also suffered for us (3.18). And because of Jesus, he also speaks of blessing and hope, even during suffering (3.14,15). (See also Psalm 84; Jeremiah 29.10-14.)

Words To Remember: *You are better off to obey God and suffer for doing right than to suffer for doing wrong.—1 Peter 3.17*

a thief, a crook, or a busybody. ¹⁶Don't be ashamed to suffer for being a Christian. Praise God that you belong to him. ¹⁷God has already begun judging his own people. And if his judgment begins with us, imagine how terrible it will be for those who refuse to obey his message. The Scriptures say,

¹⁸ "If good people barely escape,
    what will happen to sinners
  and to others
    who don't respect God?"

¹⁹If you suffer for obeying God, you must have complete faith in your faithful Creator and keep on doing right.

PARENTING&family—How can I effectively balance my roles as parent and wife? (1 Peter 4.1-8)

Love each other.
Parents face some of the same pressures that suffering Christians did in Peter's era. There was the fear of what might happen next (4.1). There was the nagging guilt of past mistakes (4.3). And there was the constant pressure of work that needed to be done (4.9-11). Peter's counsel to suffering Christians is also practical for today's busy parents. He points them to basics: prayer and love.

"Everything will soon come to an end," said Peter (4.7). He probably meant Christ's return and the end of this world. But parents can benefit from the reminder that childhood also comes to an end—although anyone with a two year old will have trouble believing this! But soon enough, that important, yet limited, year of life ends. Remembering Peter's words will help you put your parenting efforts in perspective. And while you are in the endurance phase, "be serious and be sensible enough to pray" (4.7).

What doesn't end, if we do it right, is marriage. Peter instructed his readers to endure suffering by loving each other. Parents, too, need to focus on each other. So take time to keep on developing your love. Long after the children have graduated to adulthood, you'll still be looking at the same husband across the kitchen table. (See also Deuteronomy 8.1-10; Job 38.1—40.5.)

Words To Remember: *Everything will soon come to an end. So be serious and be sensible enough to pray. Most important of all, you must sincerely love each other, because love wipes away many sins.—1 Peter 4.7,8*

MARRIAGE—How can my husband and I grow spiritually as a couple?
(1 Peter 4.8-11)

Enjoy and use your God-given differences.
Marriage has a way of revealing sins in yourself and your husband that you never knew you had. The way to get rid of sin is to confess it and then stop doing it. With confession comes forgiveness. Forgiveness is hard, but love (offered first by God to you and then from you to your husband) can wipe away those sins as deftly as crumbs swept from the kitchen table.

But this passage doesn't stay focused on sin. It moves quickly to service. God has given you special skills that he didn't give your husband. He has also given your husband talents and interests that aren't your own. These differences can lead to competition or a power struggle. But that's not the way toward spiritual growth. Enjoy your differences; glory in them. Practice saying, "My husband is good at . . ." Then use your varied skills to serve others and to "bring honor to God" (4.11). (See also Galatians 6.1-3; Hebrews 5.11—6.3.)

Words To Remember: *Each of you has been blessed with one of God's many wonderful gifts to be used in the service of others. So use your gift well.—1 Peter 4.10*

Personal *Concerns*—How should I handle it when I feel rejected or excluded because of my faith? *(1 Peter 4.12-19)*

Feel included—among the ranks of Christians.

Being rejected hurts. We may turn that pain outward and lash out at the people who reject us, which usually makes matters worse. Or we may turn inward with fretful questions such as, *What's wrong with me?*

It doesn't hurt to do a little soul-searching after rejection. Ask questions like: *Have I been insensitive or offensive in something I said? Did I fail to listen? Does my manner suggest coldness or disinterest?* We could all improve our sensitivity to others, and these questions may alert us to our shortcomings—and help us correct them.

But occasionally, rejection has nothing at all to do with personal faults. We are rejected simply because of our Christian faith. In more restrictive societies (such as Peter's time and place), Christians could expect social rejection, job discrimination, political persecution, and even death. Peter's words to his friends offer us support for our own rejections: "Dear friends, don't be surprised or shocked" (4.12). "It will prepare you for even greater happiness when he [Christ] makes his glorious return" (4.13). "This shows that God's glorious Spirit is with you" (4.14). "Keep on doing right" (4.19).

Christians in all eras have suffered (and are still suffering), so we may occasionally join their ranks. Peter's words can help us endure with confidence. (See also Daniel 6; John 15.18-27; Hebrews 10.32-39; Revelation 14.12,13.)

Words To Remember: *Don't be ashamed to suffer for being a Christian. Praise God that you belong to him.*—1 Peter 4.16

PARENTING&*family*—How can I protect my kids from negative cultural influences? *(1 Peter 5.2-11)*

Be their shepherd.

Parenting is a huge responsibility. Sometimes we want to build a glass bubble around our children and keep them encapsulated until they're twenty-one. But we can't. And even if we could, it wouldn't be good for them. They'd simply emerge at age twenty-one with the coping skills of the average preschooler. Somehow parents have to allow kids enough freedom to explore and learn from their mistakes, protecting them from serious harm—like a shepherd protects his sheep.

Peter's instructions to Christian leaders serve as excellent guidance for parents. We are to "watch over" our children (5.2). We are not to be "bossy," but instead "set an example for them" (5.3). We are to "be humble" (5.6). We are to "be on [our] guard and stay awake" (5.8)—advice familiar to parents of infants and teens alike. We are assured that God will make us "complete, steady, strong, and firm" (5.10)—important qualities for any parent.

In the family, parents *are* the spiritual leaders; God expects us to "watch over" our children. It's appropriate to guard against negative cultural influences. Some parents refuse to own a television, or they keep it in a closet and bring it out only for special occasions. Some parents frequently invite their children's friends into their homes. In that way the parents influence (and protect) their children—and their guests. But wise parents also allow certain freedoms so their children can learn to deal with cultural influences and make wise choices for themselves. (See also Ezra 8.21-34; Psalm 119.97-105; Proverbs 4.10-27; Song of Songs 8.8,9.)

Words To Remember: *Just as shepherds watch over their sheep, you must watch over everyone God has placed in your care. . . . God cares for you, so turn your worries over to him.*—1 Peter 5.2,7

Helping Christian Leaders

5 Church leaders,[g] I am writing to encourage you. I too am a leader, as well as a witness to Christ's suffering, and I will share in his glory when it is shown to us. [2]Just as shepherds watch over their sheep, you must watch over everyone God has placed in your care. Do it willingly in order to please God, and not simply because you think you must. Let it be something you want to do, instead of something you do merely to make money. [3]Don't be bossy to those people who are in your care, but set an example for them. [4]Then when Christ the Chief Shepherd returns, you will be given a crown that will never lose its glory.

[5]All of you young people should obey your elders. In fact, everyone should be humble toward everyone else. The Scriptures say,

"God opposes proud people,
    but he helps everyone
        who is humble."

[6]Be humble in the presence of God's mighty power, and he will honor you when the time comes. [7]God cares for you, so turn all your worries over to him.

[8]Be on your guard and stay awake. Your enemy, the devil, is like a roaring lion, sneaking around to find someone to attack. [9]But you must resist the devil and stay strong in your faith. You know that all over the world the Lord's followers are suffering just as you are. [10]But God shows undeserved kindness to everyone. That's why he appointed Christ Jesus to choose you to share in his eternal glory. You will suffer for a while, but God will make you complete, steady, strong, and firm. [11]God will be in control forever! Amen.

Final Greetings

[12]Silvanus helped me write this short letter, and I consider him a faithful follower of the Lord. I wanted to encourage you and tell you how kind God really is, so that you will keep on having faith in him.

[13]Greetings from the Lord's followers in Babylon.[h] They are God's chosen ones.

Mark, who is like a son to me, sends his greetings too.

[14]Give each other a warm greeting. I pray that God will give peace to everyone who belongs to Christ.[i]

---

[g]5.1 *Church leaders*: Or "Elders" or "Presbyters" or "Priests." [h]5.13 *Babylon*: This may be a secret name for the city of Rome. [i]5.14 *Christ*: Some manuscripts add "Amen."

2 Peter — Living as God's Followers Now—and Forever

Have you ever heard a speech that stopped you in your tracks? A sermon that convicted you? Had a conversation with a friend that changed your perspective on an issue or relationship? Talked with an older person whose wise words affected you so much you're still thinking about them—even years later?

Godly men and women who've had a lot of life experience are intriguing. They've faced good times and bad times—and thrived through both. They have an unshakeable faith in God and his goodness that overcomes any obstacles. They're encouraging, yet challenging. So no wonder we listen with even more rapt attention to their perspectives when they've reached the end of their careers and the fall of their lives. It's at such times of maturity that we're able to ask them honestly how they've thought through their decisions, relationships, and other life issues. And they can share with us openly either the regret or joy for the way they've lived.

The apostle Peter is one of the most intriguing of Jesus' apostles. Yes, he shared the hopes and experiences of his comrades in the apostolic group, but he was different in many ways. Peter's life was filled with joyful "firsts." He was one of the first to follow Jesus, and often was the first to respond to a question or a challenging issue or event. Partway through Jesus' ministry, he was one of three in Jesus' inner circle. And by the festival of Pentecost (following Jesus' ascension), he was the leader of the newly formed church.

But Peter also had some regretful firsts. He was often impetuous, acting before he thought through reasons or consequences (the night Jesus was arrested,

he pulled out his sword and cut off the ear of a servant of the high priest—John 18.10,11). And he was the first to openly deny his association with the Lord (John 18.15-27) not only once, but three times. Yet, toward the end of his life, he could say with confidence, "Praise Jesus now and forever! Amen" (2 Peter 3.18).

In this epistle Peter anticipates the return of the Lord and the consequent need for spiritual character building: "Let the wonderful kindness and the understanding that come from our Lord and Savior Jesus Christ help you to keep on growing" (3.18). What does it mean to be a follower of Christ—in today's culture? How can we know that God is powerful and that Jesus is truly his Son? How can we balance being Christians with living in this sinful world? And, most important, how can we know for certain that the Lord is coming again?

The book of 2 Peter offers answers to all these questions. And what's more, it gives us the glorious promise of Christ's return that takes us beyond today's problems and shows us our eternal hope!

2 Peter at a Glance

1. Opening greetings to Christians (1.1,2)
2. Peter encourages Christians to live consistently (1.3-15)

1 From Simon Peter, a servant and an apostle of Jesus Christ.
To everyone who shares with us in the privilege of believing that our God and Savior Jesus Christ will do what is just and fair.[a]

²I pray that God will be kind to you and will let you live in perfect peace! May you keep learning more and more about God and our Lord Jesus.

Living as the Lord's Followers

³We have everything we need to live a life that pleases God. It was all given to us by God's own power, when we learned that he had invited us to share in his wonderful goodness. ⁴God made great and marvelous promises, so that his nature would become part of us. Then we could escape our evil desires and the corrupt influences of this world.

⁵Do your best to improve your faith. You can do this by adding goodness, under-

standing, ⁶self-control, patience, devotion to God, ⁷concern for others, and love. ⁸If you keep growing in this way, it will show that what you know about our Lord Jesus Christ has made your lives useful and meaningful. ⁹But if you don't grow, you are like someone who is nearsighted or blind, and you have forgotten that your past sins are forgiven.

¹⁰My friends, you must do all you can to show that God has really chosen and selected you. If you keep on doing this, you won't stumble and fall. ¹¹Then our Lord and Savior Jesus Christ will give you a glorious welcome into his kingdom that will last forever.

¹²You are holding firmly to the truth that you were given. But I am still going to remind you of these things. ¹³In fact, I think I should keep on reminding you until I leave

---

a1.1 *To everyone who . . . just and fair*: Or "To everyone whose faith in the justice and fairness of our God and Savior Jesus Christ is as precious as our own faith."

Personal *Concerns*—How can I learn to be more content with my life?
(2 Peter 1.3-15)

Fill up on more of the right things.
More. That's what our consumer society tells us we have to have all the time—more goods, more power, more status, more leisure, more excitement, more freedom. No wonder most of us fight chronic feelings of discontent! Everything around us tells us to be dissatisfied with what we have.

Interestingly enough, this passage encourages us to keep adding more to our lives. The difference is, what should we be adding? "Goodness, understanding, self-control, patience, devotion to God, concern for others, and love" (1.5-7) are qualities Peter said we should keep expanding.

Ironically, Peter also assures us that we already have these things because God has given them to us. But we can always make fuller use of everything God gives us for our spiritual health and ministry to others.

As we love God and minister to other people, we'll feel less restless. We'll be more content with our place in life because we'll find purpose in doing what God gives us to do. (See also Psalm 107; Ecclesiastes 6.1-9; Daniel 2.20,21.)

Words To Remember: *We have everything we need to live a life that pleases God. It was all given to us by God's own power, when we learned that he had invited us to share in his wonderful goodness.*—2 Peter 1.3

this body. ¹⁴And our Lord Jesus Christ has already told me that I will soon leave it behind. ¹⁵That is why I am doing my best to make sure that each of you remembers all of this after I am gone.

The Message about the Glory of Christ

¹⁶When we told you about the power and the return of our Lord Jesus Christ, we were not telling clever stories that someone had made up. But with our own eyes we saw his true greatness. ¹⁷God, our great and wonderful Father, truly honored him by saying, "This is my own dear Son, and I am pleased with him." ¹⁸We were there with Jesus on the holy mountain and heard this voice speak from heaven.

¹⁹All of this makes us even more certain that what the prophets said is true. So you should pay close attention to their message, as you would to a lamp shining in some dark place. You must keep on paying attention until daylight comes and the morning star rises in your hearts. ²⁰But you need to realize that no one alone can understand any of the prophecies in the Scriptures. ²¹The prophets did not think these things up on their own, but they were guided by the Spirit of God.

False Prophets and Teachers

2 Sometimes false prophets spoke to the people of Israel. False teachers will also sneak in and speak harmful lies to

you. But these teachers don't really belong to the Master who paid a great price for them, and they will quickly destroy themselves. ²Many people will follow their evil ways and cause others to tell lies about the true way. ³They will be greedy and cheat you with smooth talk. But long ago God decided to punish them, and God doesn't sleep.

⁴God did not have pity on the angels that sinned. He had them tied up and thrown into the dark pits of hell until the time of judgment. ⁵And during Noah's time, God did not have pity on the ungodly people of the world. He destroyed them with a flood, though he did save eight people, including Noah, who preached the truth.

⁶God punished the cities of Sodom and Gomorrah*ᵇ* by burning them to ashes, and this is a warning to anyone else who wants to sin.

⁷⁻⁸Lot lived right and was greatly troubled by the terrible way those wicked people were living. He was a good man, and day after day he suffered because of the evil things he saw and heard. So the Lord rescued him. ⁹This shows that the Lord knows how to rescue godly people from their sufferings and to punish evil people while they wait for the day of judgment.

¹⁰The Lord is especially hard on people

---

*ᵇ***2.6** *Sodom and Gomorrah*: During the time of Abraham the Lord destroyed these cities because the people there were so evil (see Genesis 19.24).

SingleLife—**How can I resist the pressure to be sexually active?** *(2 Peter 2.7-9)*

Remember that God rewards righteousness.
With all the sexy billboards, sex-laced television shows and movies, clothing catalogs (not to mention all the conversations you have with friends or overhear), it's impossible to bury your head in the sand and not think about sex as a single.

God has created us as sexual beings, with sex drives. But he also makes it clear that we need to choose the godly path—sex only within marriage. When others tell us, "Do what feels right," or "You're marrying him anyway," or make fun of our virginity, we can say "no" because God has called us to be righteous—even when it's tough to do so in today's world.

Second Peter tells the story of Lot and says that he "lived right and was greatly troubled by the terrible way those wicked people were living. He was a good man" (2.7,8). Even in the midst of an evil generation, Lot didn't give in to the temptations of his day—and neither should we. Then we, like Lot, will receive our reward. The Lord will rescue us (2.9) and proclaim us righteous. (See also Joshua 7; Psalm 103; Ephesians 6.10-20; James 1.12-18.)

Words To Remember: *Lot lived right. . . . He was a good man, and day after day he suffered because of the evil things he saw and heard. So the Lord rescued him.* —2 Peter 2.7,8

who disobey him and don't think of anything except their own filthy desires. They are reckless and proud and are not afraid of cursing the glorious beings in heaven. [11]Although angels are more powerful than these evil beings,[c] even the angels don't dare to accuse them to the Lord.

[12]These people are no better than senseless animals that live by their feelings and are born to be caught and killed. They speak evil of things they don't know anything about. But their own corrupt deeds will destroy them. [13]They have done evil, and they will be rewarded with evil.

They think it is fun to have wild parties during the day. They are immoral, and the meals they eat with you are spoiled by the shameful and selfish way they carry on.[d] [14]All they think about is having sex with someone else's husband or wife. There is no end to their wicked deeds. They trick people who are easily fooled, and their minds are filled with greedy thoughts. But they are headed for trouble!

[15]They have left the true road and have gone down the wrong path by following the example of the prophet Balaam. He was the son of Beor and loved what he got from being a crook. [16]But a donkey corrected him for this evil deed. It spoke to him with a human voice and made him stop his foolishness.

[17]These people are like dried up water holes and clouds blown by a windstorm. The darkest part of hell is waiting for them. [18]They brag out loud about their stupid nonsense. And by being vulgar and crude, they trap people who have barely escaped from living the wrong kind of life. [19]They promise freedom to everyone. But they are merely slaves of filthy living, because people are slaves of whatever controls them.

[20]When they learned about our Lord and Savior Jesus Christ, they escaped from the filthy things of this world. But they are again caught up and controlled by these filthy things, and now they are in worse shape than they were at first. [21]They would have been better off if they had never known about the right way. Even after they knew what was right, they turned their backs on the holy commandments that they were given. [22]What happened to them is just like the true saying,

"A dog will come back
  to lick up its own vomit.
A pig that has been washed
  will roll in the mud."

The Lord Will Return

3 My dear friends, this is the second letter I have written to encourage you to do some honest thinking. I don't want you to forget [2]what God's prophets said would happen. You must never forget what the holy prophets taught in the past. And you must remember what the apostles told you our Lord and Savior has commanded us to do.

[3]But first you must realize that in the last days some people won't think about anything except their own selfish desires. They will make fun of you [4]and say, "Didn't your Lord promise to come back? Yet the first leaders have already died, and the world hasn't changed a bit."

[5]They will say this because they want to forget that long ago the heavens and the earth were made at God's command. The earth came out of water and was made from water. [6]Later it was destroyed by the waters of a mighty flood. [7]But God has commanded the present heavens and earth to remain until the day of judgment. Then they will be set on fire, and ungodly people will be destroyed.

[8]Dear friends, don't forget that for the Lord one day is the same as a thousand years, and a thousand years is the same as one day. [9]The Lord isn't slow about keeping his promises, as some people think he is. In fact, God is patient, because he wants everyone to turn from sin and no one to be lost.

[10]The day of the Lord's return will surprise us like a thief. The heavens will disappear with a loud noise, and the heat will melt the whole universe.[e] Then the earth and everything on it will be seen for what they are.[f]

[11]Everything will be destroyed. So you

---

[c]2.11 *evil beings*: Or "evil teachers." [d]2.13 *and the meals they eat with you are spoiled by the shameful and selfish way they carry on*: Some manuscripts have "and the meals they eat with you are spoiled by the shameful way they carry on during your feasts of Christian love." [e]3.10 *the whole universe*: Probably the sun, moon, and stars, or the elements that everything in the universe is made of. [f]3.10 *will be seen for what they are*: Some manuscripts have "will go up in flames."

should serve and honor God by the way you live. [12]You should look forward to the day when God judges everyone, and you should try to make it come soon.[g] On that day the heavens will be destroyed by fire, and everything else will melt in the heat. [13]But God has promised us a new heaven and a new earth, where justice will rule. We are really looking forward to that!

[14]My friends, while you are waiting, you should make certain that the Lord finds you pure, spotless, and living at peace. [15]Don't forget that the Lord is patient because he wants people to be saved. This is also what our dear friend Paul said when he wrote you with the wisdom that God had given him. [16]Paul talks about these same things in all his letters, but part of what he says is hard to understand. Some ignorant and unsteady people even destroy themselves by twisting what he said. They do the same thing with other Scriptures too.

[17]My dear friends, you have been warned ahead of time! So don't let the errors of evil people lead you down the wrong path and make you lose your balance. [18]Let the wonderful kindness and the understanding that come from our Lord and Savior Jesus Christ help you to keep on growing. Praise Jesus now and forever! Amen.[h]

---

[g]**3.12** *and you should try to make it come soon:* Or "and you should eagerly desire for that day to come."
[h]**3.18** *Amen:* Some manuscripts do not have "Amen."

1 John

The Secrets of a Victorious Christian Life

In his Gospel, John wrote to show that Jesus *is* the Christ. Now, in this letter written as a companion to his Gospel, the apostle John reminded his readers that he actually heard, saw, and touched Jesus! Since Jesus is the Messiah, the Son of God, the question he addressed is: *Believing that, how should we live once we believe?* John gives us the secrets to living victoriously. We women will be particularly interested in John's themes, for he stressed relationships with God and with each other. He also tells us the secret to building confidence.

The first secret is to stay in the light—and if we walk out of the light, to confess it and get back in (1.5-9)! Do you want to experience the power of the Holy Spirit in your life? Then practice walking in the light!

The second secret is love. A child of the light loves her brothers and sisters (2.10). Our fellowship with God impacts our fellowship with each other. John gave the example of Cain (3.12), whose walk into the darkness led to murdering his brother. Often when a problem exists in our relationship with a family member or a friend, the real problem began with one of us walking away from the light of God. To begin healing, we must walk back into the light.

Do you worry, as many women do, whether you're valuable and loved by God? Are there times when you doubt your salvation? Do you long for the peace of God to calm your worries? Learning how to walk in light and love will also set your heart at rest in God's presence (3.19).

John also warns us about those who can rob us of our victory and joy (4.1). As believers, we're called not only to guard our own hearts, but the hearts of our children and the hearts of less-mature believers. Not only are we to be on guard against cults, but also against the lies that find their way into our lives through mass media, schools, and people who don't follow Christ.

We *can* live a victorious life (5.4), we *can* know we have eternal life (5.13), and we *can* experience answers to our prayers (5.14). First John tells us the secrets!

1 John at a Glance

1. God is light, so walk in the light (1)
2. If we know God, we will obey him (2)
3. God is love, so walk in love (3)
4. Watch out for error (4)
5. You can have victory and confidence! (5)

1
The Word that gives life
was from the beginning,
and this is the one
our message is about.

Our ears have heard,
our own eyes have seen,
and our hands touched
this Word.

[2]The one who gives life appeared! We saw it happen, and we are witnesses to what we have seen. Now we are telling you about this eternal life that was with the Father and appeared to us. [3]We are telling you what we have seen and heard, so that you may share in this life with us. And we share in it with the Father and with his Son Jesus Christ. [4]We are writing to tell you these things, because this makes us[a] truly happy.

God Is Light

[5]Jesus told us that God is light and doesn't have any darkness in him. Now we are telling you.
[6]If we say that we share in life with God and keep on living in the dark, we are lying and are not living by the truth. [7]But if we live in the light, as God does, we share in life with each other. And the blood of his Son Jesus washes all our sins away. [8]If we say that we have not sinned, we are fooling ourselves, and the truth isn't in our hearts. [9]But if we confess our sins to God, he can always be trusted to forgive us and take our sins away.

[10]If we say that we have not sinned, we make God a liar, and his message isn't in our hearts.[b]

Christ Helps Us

2
My children, I am writing this so that you won't sin. But if you do sin, Jesus Christ always does the right thing, and he will speak to the Father for us. [2]Christ is the sacrifice that takes away our sins and the sins of all the world's people.
[3]When we obey God, we are sure that we know him. [4]But if we claim to know him and don't obey him, we are lying and the truth isn't in our hearts. [5]We truly love God only when we obey him as we should, and then we know that we belong to him. [6]If we say we are his, we must follow the example of Christ.

The New Commandment

[7]My dear friends, I am not writing to give you a new commandment. It is the same one that you were first given, and it is the message you heard. [8]But it really is a new commandment, and you know its true meaning, just as Christ does. You can see the darkness fading away and the true light already shining.
[9]If we claim to be in the light and hate someone, we are still in the dark. [10]But if we love others, we are in the light, and we don't

---

[a]1.4 *us:* Some manuscripts have "you."   [b]1.10 *and his message isn't in our hearts:* Or "because we have not accepted his message."

---

*Spiritual*Life—If I've turned away from God, is it possible to come back? How? *(1 John 1.8—2.2)*

Trust God to forgive you.

Many Christian women have trouble receiving God's forgiveness—especially for sexual sins. One woman said: "How I wish I'd been a virgin on my wedding night. It's been twenty years, but my past still haunts our marriage bed."

But when we refuse to receive the forgiveness Christ offers us, it not only keeps us from experiencing his joy, it can lead us into other sin. For example, in the experience above, this woman's inability to trust that God could cleanse her was still affecting her husband, her marriage, and herself. It's far better to admit sin and repent than to try to justify it. Jesus paid a high price for our sins. Who are we to reject his offer of cleansing? He offers his tender forgiveness. All we have to do is ask. (See also Isaiah 55.6-13; Lamentations 3.31-40; Ezekiel 37.1-14; Hosea 3; Joel 2.25-27.)

Words To Remember: *But if we confess our sins to God, he can always be trusted to forgive us and take our sins away.*—1 John 1.9

cause problems for them.[c] [11]If we hate others, we are living and walking in the dark. We don't know where we are going, because we can't see in the dark.

[12]Children, I am writing you,
　because your sins
have been forgiven
　in the name of Christ.
[13]Parents, I am writing you,
　because you have known
the one who was there
　from the beginning.
Young people, I am writing you,
　because you have defeated
the evil one.
[14]Children, I am writing you,
　because you have known
the Father.
Parents, I am writing you,
　because you have known
the one who was there
　from the beginning.
Young people, I am writing you,
　because you are strong.
God's message is firm
　in your hearts,
and you have defeated
　the evil one.

[15]Don't love the world or anything that belongs to the world. If you love the world, you cannot love the Father. [16]Our foolish pride comes from this world, and so do our selfish desires and our desire to have everything we see. None of this comes from the Father. [17]The world and the desires it causes are disappearing. But if we obey God, we will live forever.

The Enemy of Christ

[18]Children, this is the last hour. You heard that the enemy of Christ would appear at this time, and many of Christ's enemies have already appeared. So we know that the last hour is here. [19]These people came from our own group, yet they were not part of us. If they had been part of us, they would have stayed with us. But they left, which proves that they did not belong to our group.

[20]Christ, the Holy One,[d] has blessed[e] you, and now all of you understand.[f] [21]I did not need to write you about the truth, since you already know it. You also know that liars

do not belong to the truth. [22]And a liar is anyone who says that Jesus isn't truly Christ. Anyone who says this is an enemy of Christ and rejects both the Father and the Son. [23]If we reject the Son, we reject the Father. But if we say that we accept the Son, we have the Father. [24]Keep thinking about the message you first heard, and you will always be one in your heart with the Son and with the Father. [25]The Son[g] has promised us[h] eternal life.

[26]I am writing to warn you about those people who are misleading you. [27]But Christ has blessed you with the Holy Spirit.[i] Now the Spirit stays in you, and you don't need any teachers. The Spirit is truthful and teaches you everything. So stay one in your heart with Christ, just as the Spirit has taught you to do.

Children of God

[28]Children, stay one in your hearts with Christ. Then when he returns, we will have confidence and won't have to hide in shame. [29]You know that Christ always does right and that everyone who does right is a child of God.

3 Think how much the Father loves us. He loves us so much that he lets us be called his children, as we truly are. But since the people of this world did not know who Christ[j] is, they don't know who we are. [2]My dear friends, we are already God's children, though what we will be hasn't yet been seen. But we do know that when Christ returns, we will be like him, because

---

[c]2.10 *and we don't cause problems for them:* Or "and we can see anything that might make us fall."
[d]2.20 *Christ, the Holy One:* The Greek text has "the Holy One" which may refer either to Christ or to God the Father. [e]2.20 *blessed:* This translates a word which means "to pour olive oil on (someone's head)." In Old Testament times it was the custom to pour olive oil on a person's head when that person was chosen to be a priest or a king. Here the meaning is not clear. It may refer to the ceremony of pouring olive oil on the followers of the Lord right before they were baptized or it may refer to the gift of the Holy Spirit which they were given at baptism (see verse 27). [f]2.20 *now all of you understand:* Some manuscripts have "you understand all things." [g]2.25 *The Son:* The Greek text has "he" and may refer to God the Father. [h]2.25 *us:* Some manuscripts have "you." [i]2.27 *Christ has blessed you with the Holy Spirit:* The Greek text has "You received a pouring on of olive oil from him" (see verse 20). The "pouring on of olive oil" is here taken to refer to the gift of the Holy Spirit, and "he" may refer either to Christ or to the Father. [j]3.1 *Christ:* The Greek text has "he" and may refer to God.

we will see him as he truly is. ³This hope makes us keep ourselves holy, just as Christ* is holy.

⁴Everyone who sins breaks God's law, because sin is the same as breaking God's law. ⁵You know that Christ came to take away sins. He isn't sinful, ⁶and people who stay one in their hearts with him won't keep on sinning. If they do keep on sinning, they don't know Christ, and they have never seen him.

⁷Children, don't be fooled. Anyone who does right is good, just like Christ himself. ⁸Anyone who keeps on sinning belongs to the devil. He has sinned from the beginning, but the Son of God came to destroy all that he has done. ⁹God's children cannot keep on being sinful. His life-giving power' lives in them and makes them his children, so that they cannot keep on sinning. ¹⁰You can tell God's children from the devil's children, because those who belong to the devil refuse to do right or to love each other.

Love Each Other

¹¹From the beginning you were told that we must love each other. ¹²Don't be like Cain, who belonged to the devil and murdered his own brother. Why did he murder him? He did it because his brother was good, and he was evil. ¹³My friends, don't be surprised if the people of this world hate you. ¹⁴Our love for each other proves that we have gone from death to life. But if you don't love each other, you are still under the power of death.

¹⁵If you hate each other, you are murderers, and we know that murderers do not have eternal life. ¹⁶We know what love is because Jesus gave his life for us. That's why we must give our lives for each other. ¹⁷If we have all we need and see one of our own people in need, we must have pity on that person, or else we cannot say we love God. ¹⁸Children, you show love for others by truly helping them, and not merely by talking about it.

¹⁹When we love others, we know that we belong to the truth, and we feel at ease in the presence of God. ²⁰But even if we don't feel at ease, God is greater than our feelings, and he knows everything. ²¹Dear friends, if we feel at ease in the presence of God, we will have the courage to come near him. ²²He will give us whatever we ask, because we obey him and do what pleases him. ²³God wants us to have faith in his Son Jesus Christ and to love each other. This is also what Jesus taught us to do. ²⁴If we obey God's commandments, we will stay one in

---

*k*3.3 *Christ:* The Greek text has "that one" and may refer to God.   *l*3.9 *His life-giving power:* The Greek text has "his seed."

WORK—How can I be more confident about my work?   *(1 John 3.19-24)*

Obedience to God leads to confidence.

Do you wish you were more confident about your work? Maybe everyone in your office just got new computers, and you look at yours and get intimidated by all the new procedures you'll have to learn. Or you're beginning a daycare in your home and after doing all the legal paperwork and signing up your first "little clients," you wonder if you can really handle four toddlers running around your house all day. Or you have a supervisor who always seems grumpy, no matter how nice you are or how much you get done.

Whether your work is in the home, mothering your children (or other children), or on a job site, John tells us a vital secret concerning our confidence: Obedience to God leads to confidence. The more you obey God in loving your children, treating your coworkers with kindness, or giving your employer the best performance possible, the more your confidence in your relationship with God will grow. When you don't feel confident, remember that God is greater than your feelings (3.20) and that he's in control. And, as your confidence in your relationship with God grows, the more ready you'll be to ask him for help—and the more apt you are to see God at work in your job! (See also Deuteronomy 31.1-6; Joshua 1.1-9; Psalm 73.21-28; Psalm 108.)

Words To Remember: *When we love others, we know that we belong to the truth, and we feel at ease in the presence of God.*—1 John 3.19

our hearts with him, and he will stay one with us. The Spirit that he has given us is proof that we are one with him.

God Is Love

4 Dear friends, don't believe everyone who claims to have the Spirit of God. Test them all to find out if they really do come from God. Many false prophets have already gone out into the world, ²and you can know which ones come from God. His Spirit says that Jesus Christ had a truly human body. ³But when someone doesn't say this about Jesus, you know that person has a spirit that doesn't come from God and is the enemy of Christ. You knew that this enemy was coming into the world and now is already here.

⁴Children, you belong to God, and you have defeated these enemies. God's Spirit ᵐ is in you and is more powerful than the one that is in the world. ⁵These enemies belong to this world, and the world listens to them, because they speak its language. ⁶We belong to God, and everyone who knows God will listen to us. But the people who don't know God won't listen to us. That is how we can tell the Spirit that speaks the truth from the one that tells lies.

⁷My dear friends, we must love each other. Love comes from God, and when we love each other, it shows that we have been given new life. We are now God's children,

and we know him. ⁸God is love, and anyone who doesn't love others has never known him. ⁹God showed his love for us when he sent his only Son into the world to give us life. ¹⁰Real love isn't our love for God, but his love for us. God sent his Son to be the sacrifice by which our sins are forgiven. ¹¹Dear friends, since God loved us this much, we must love each other.

¹²No one has ever seen God. But if we love each other, God lives in us, and his love is truly in our hearts.

¹³God has given us his Spirit. That is how we know that we are one with him, just as he is one with us. ¹⁴God sent his Son to be the Savior of the world. We saw his Son and are now telling others about him. ¹⁵God stays one with everyone who openly says that Jesus is the Son of God. That's how we stay one with God ¹⁶and are sure that God loves us.

God is love. If we keep on loving others, we will stay one in our hearts with God, and he will stay one with us. ¹⁷If we truly love others and live as Christ did in this world, we won't be worried about the day of judgment. ¹⁸A real love for others will chase those worries away. The thought of being punished is what makes us afraid. It shows that we have not really learned to love.

ᵐ**4.4** *God's Spirit*: The Greek text has "he" and may refer to the Spirit or to God or to Jesus.

SingleLife—How can I best relate to my married friends? *(1 John 4.7-12)*

Remember that envy builds walls; love breaks them down.

It takes effort to cross the boundaries of race, social class, age, and marital status. But if we belong to God, we are sisters, and we should make the loving effort to cross over those boundaries and "love each other" (4.7). Envy builds walls. But here we see that love tears them down and "shows that we have been given new life." Just as the love of God broke down the wall between him and us, so can our love for our sisters break down any walls of division.

But in real life, that can be easier said than done. When a friend gets married, sometimes we can't help it—we do feel envious, wondering what life is like "on the other side." However, part of loving others is being content with our life. Then we can relate to others without envy, focusing on what we have in common. We can take the initiative and open up to our married friends about our work, our joys or struggles in our spiritual journey, or ways we've seen God at work in mutual friends' lives. And we can listen to what they're discovering about God, too! (See also Romans 15.1-6; Ephesians 5.1-5.)

Words To Remember: *My dear friends, we must love each other. Love comes from God, and when we love each other, it shows that we have been given new life.* —1 John 4.7

[19]We love because God loved us first. [20]But if we say we love God and don't love each other, we are liars. We cannot see God. So how can we love God, if we don't love the people we can see? [21]The commandment that God has given us is: "Love God and love each other!"

Victory over the World

5 If we believe that Jesus is truly Christ, we are God's children. Everyone who loves the Father will also love his children. [2]If we love and obey God, we know that we will love his children. [3]We show our love for God by obeying his commandments, and they are not hard to follow.

[4]Every child of God can defeat the world, and our faith is what gives us this victory. [5]No one can defeat the world without having faith in Jesus as the Son of God.

Who Jesus Is

[6]Water and blood came out from the side of Jesus Christ. It wasn't just water, but water and blood.[n] The Spirit tells about this, because the Spirit is truthful. [7]In fact, there are three who tell about it. [8]They are the Spirit, the water, and the blood, and they all agree.

[9]We believe what people tell us. But we can trust what God says even more, and God is the one who has spoken about his Son. [10]If we have faith in God's Son, we have believed what God has said. But if we don't believe what God has said about his Son, it is the same as calling God a liar. [11]God has also said that he gave us eternal life and that this life comes to us from his Son. [12]And so, if we have God's Son, we have this life. But if we don't have the Son, we don't have this life.

Knowing about Eternal Life

[13]All of you have faith in the Son of God, and I have written to let you know that you have eternal life. [14]We are certain that God will hear our prayers when we ask for what pleases him. [15]And if we know that God listens when we pray, we are sure that our prayers have already been answered.

Don't just pray when you feel like it. Make an appointment with God, and don't let anything stop you.

RAMONA CRAMER TUCKER

[16]Suppose you see one of our people commit a sin that isn't a deadly sin. You can pray, and that person will be given eternal life. But the sin must not be one that is deadly. [17]Everything that is wrong is sin, but not all sins are deadly.

[18]We are sure that God's children do not keep on sinning. God's own Son protects them, and the devil cannot harm them. [19]We are certain that we come from God and that the rest of the world is under the power of the devil. [20]We know that Jesus Christ the Son of God has come and has shown us the true God. And because of Jesus, we now belong to the true God who gives eternal life. [21]Children, you must stay away from idols.

---

[n]**5.6** *Water and blood came out from the side of Jesus Christ. It wasn't just water, but water and blood:* See John 19.34. It is also possible to translate, "Jesus Christ came by the water of baptism and by the blood of his death! He was not only baptized, but he bled and died." The purpose of the verse is to tell that Jesus was truly human and that he really died.

2 John
Walking in the Truth

Like the book of 1 John, which refers to the church as children and family, 2 John uses "family" terms—"the special woman and her children"—in its address. That's how we know that this letter from John is a note to a local church over which he had authority and where he might personally have preached and thus known the individual members and situations. In any case, it gives us a glimpse of a Christian fellowship in which the young members were raised in the truth and were obeying the truth. Seeing this made John joyful, and he longed for them to continue walking in the truth.

Therefore he cautions them to be on their guard against deception, because "many liars have gone out into the world" (7). Theirs was a hospitable fellowship, so John warned them not to be hospitable to false teachers (10). This does not mean we are to be rude to the occasional cult member who comes to our church, but we should be on guard. The main heresy John addressed concerned the denial that Jesus is God incarnate. In John's day some taught that Jesus didn't have a human body (7). Today it's also common for various religious movements or cults to explicitly or implicitly deny Jesus is God in the flesh. (Some cults say Jesus is a god but that we are all gods or becoming gods; others say that Jesus was just a good teacher.) Spiritual error is not confined to cult members, but has multiplied through the mass media, which typically welcomes all religions *but* uniquely rejects Christ and ridicules those who speak on his behalf. Those of us who are Christians have a responsibility to protect our homes and churches against false teaching and to refuse to be hospitable to spiritual lies (10,11). God has called us to be on guard! If we fail, we not only are taking part in their evil deeds mentioned in verse 11, but we may endanger other Christians' ability to walk in the truth.

2 John at a Glance
1. Greetings (1-3)
2. Encouragement: Keep on loving and obeying! (4-6)
3. Warning: Don't be hospitable to lies. (7-11)
4. Final Greetings (12,13)

[1]From the church leader.[a]

To a very special woman and her children.[b] I truly love all of you, and so does everyone else who knows the truth. [2]We love you because the truth is now in our hearts, and it will be there forever.

[3]I pray that God the Father and Jesus Christ his Son will be kind and merciful to us! May they give us peace and truth and love.

Truth and Love

[4]I was very glad to learn that some of your children are obeying the truth, as the Father told us to do. [5]Dear friend, I am not writing to tell you and your children to do something you have not done before. I am writing to tell you to love each other, which is the first thing you were told to do. [6]Love means that we do what God tells us. And from the beginning, he told you to love him. [7]Many liars have gone out into the world. These deceitful liars are saying that Jesus Christ did not have a truly human body. But they are liars and the enemies of Christ. [8]So be sure not to lose what we[c] have worked for. If you do, you won't be given your full reward. [9]Don't keep changing what you were taught about Christ, or else God will no longer be with you. But if you hold firmly to what you were taught, both the Father and the Son will be with you. [10]If people won't agree to this teaching, don't welcome them into your home or even greet them. [11]Greeting them is the same as taking part in their evil deeds.

Final Greetings

[12]I have much more to tell you, but I don't want to write it with pen and ink. I want to come and talk to you in person, because that will make us[d] really happy.

[13]Greetings from the children of your very special sister.[e]

---

[a]**1** *church leader:* Or "elder" or "presbyter" or "priest."
[b]**1** *very special woman and her children:* A group of the Lord's followers who met together for worship. "The children of your . . . sister" (see verse 13) is another group of followers. "Very special" (here and verse 13) probably means "chosen (by the Lord)." [c]**8** *we:* Some manuscripts have "you." [d]**12** *us:* Some manuscripts have "you." [e]**13** *sister:* See the note at verse 1.

*Spiritual*Life—How can I keep my life centered on God? *(2 John)*

Get to know who Christ Jesus, his Son, really is.
Spirituality is cropping up everywhere these days—through angel-on-your-shoulder pins, music, books, magazines, and psychic readings. With such an emphasis on "religion" in today's world, how can we tell what's really Christian from what's not?

The answer is a Person—Jesus Christ—for what we believe about Jesus Christ makes an eternal difference. If we think he's merely a good man, a moral role model, then he can be lumped together with the leaders of Buddhism, Mormonism, etc. But if we believe he truly is the Son of God, that he was sent from God himself to live on earth in human form, that he died a sacrificial death on the cross for our sins, then we have to *choose* whether to accept this sacrifice personally or not.

Second John makes it clear that life as a Christian won't be easy. We'll be bombarded with all sorts of lies: "Many liars have gone out into the world" (7). But we don't have to fall for their spiels. We can check out their words and philosophies against the truth of the Bible and "hold firmly" to "what [we] were taught" (9).

What do *you* believe about Jesus Christ? (See also Genesis 12.1-7; Matthew 25.31-46; Acts 13.1-5; Galatians 5.16-26; 2 Timothy 2.14-26.)

Words To Remember: *Don't keep changing what you were taught about Christ, or else God will no longer be with you. But if you hold firmly to what you were taught, both the Father and the Son will be with you.—2 John 9*

3 John
A Hospitable and an Inhospitable Heart

This writing from John was a personal letter to Gaius, who serves as a wonderful example of a hospitable heart. Gaius was spiritually strong (2) and lived an obedient life (3). He was hospitable to missionaries he'd never met, and they came back and told John about his love (6). Jesus exhorted us to be hospitable not only to friends and family, which even the pagans do, but to open our homes to those in need (Luke 14.13). Gaius was a living example of this.

When we're truly generous to fellow believers, we take part in their ministry (6-8)! As women, we especially have unique opportunities to help the kingdom of God grow through the ministry of hospitality. In addition to missionaries, there are many other coworkers in the kingdom who receive little encouragement. How much it would mean to your child's Sunday school teacher or church custodian to receive a note of encouragement, a plate of cookies, or an invitation to dinner! There are also women in your life who can benefit by being invited into your home where they can see, firsthand, how to live a godly life. And consider how you can love the children in your neighborhood into the family of Jesus! A spiritually healthy heart, like the heart of Gaius, is a hospitable heart.

Some church workers are motivated not by love of God, but by the applause of people. Diotrephes was an example of this (9). He refused to open his heart or his home to missionaries and discouraged other believers from being hospitable to them by putting them out of the church (10)! Here was a man with power who was working against God's kingdom—but he's forever recorded as a negative example. When our life is motivated by earning people's approval instead of God's, we won't have people to our house until our home looks like a photo from *Better Homes and Gardens*. But if we're concerned with pleasing God, we'll begin inviting—not necessarily for a prime rib dinner, but maybe for popcorn and praise choruses!

Hospitality means opening your home to people, but it goes beyond that. A hospitable heart is one that draws others into conversation, that affirms, that encourages, that prays for coworkers in the truth. We must follow the example of those who have hospitable hearts. If we aren't doing these things, according to John, it reveals a heart that doesn't love God (11).

3 John at a Glance
1. Greetings to Gaius (1-4)
2. Gaius, an example of a hospitable heart (5-8)
3. Diotrephes, an example of an inhospitable heart (9-11)
4. A word about Demetrius (12)
5. Final greetings (13-15)

[1]From the church leader.[a]

To my dear friend Gaius.

I love you because we follow the truth, [2]dear friend, and I pray that all goes well for you. I hope that you are as strong in body, as I know you are in spirit. [3]It makes me very happy when the Lord's followers come by and speak openly of how you obey the truth. [4]Nothing brings me greater happiness than to hear that my children[b] are obeying the truth.

Working Together

[5]Dear friend, you have always been faithful in helping other followers of the Lord, even the ones you didn't know before. [6]They have told the church about your love. They say you were good enough to welcome them and to send them on their mission in a way that God's servants deserve. [7]When they left to tell others about the Lord, they decided not to accept help from anyone who wasn't a follower. [8]We must support people like them, so that we can take part in what they are doing to spread the truth.

[9]I wrote to the church. But Diotrephes likes to be the number-one leader, and he won't pay any attention to us. [10]So if I come, I will remind him of how he has been attacking us with gossip. Not only has he been doing this, but he refuses to welcome any of the Lord's followers who come by. And when other church members want to welcome them, he puts them out of the church.

[11]Dear friend, don't copy the evil deeds of others! Follow the example of people who do kind deeds. They are God's children, but those who are always doing evil have never seen God.

[12]Everyone speaks well of Demetrius, and so does the true message that he teaches. I also speak well of him, and you know what I say is true.

Final Greetings

[13]I have much more to say to you, but I don't want to write it with pen and ink. [14]I hope to see you soon, and then we can talk in person.

[15]I pray that God will bless you with peace!

Your friends send their greetings. Please give a personal greeting to each of our friends.

---

[a]1 *church leader*: Or "elder" or "presbyter" or "priest."
[b]4 *children*: Probably persons that the leader had led to be followers of the Lord.

PARENTING&*family*—How can I raise a child to be kind and considerate of others? *(3 John 4-11)*

Be hospitable yourself.

If you want your child to be kind and considerate of others, you have a perfect setting in which to teach them: your home! You can encourage your children to share toys with visiting children and to speak respectfully to adults. You can involve them in making and decorating cookies for a sick friend, and then let them have the joy of taking the treats to her.

You can also show them what Gaius exemplified in this passage—true hospitality. The difference between entertaining and hospitality is this: when you entertain, you're concerned about how beautiful your table is or how clean your house is because you want to make a good impression; when you're hospitable, your focus is on the person. You seek to minister, to meet that person's needs.

It's always easier to "minister" to someone you know—and that's good. But Gaius took hospitality a step further. He was hospitable to followers of the Lord whom he didn't even know (5)! The result? These followers were encouraged, and they told of his love, which strengthened others' faith in Jesus (6). (See also Jonah 1; Matthew 5.43-48; Luke 10.25-37.)

Words To Remember: *Dear friend, you have always been faithful in helping other followers of the Lord, even the ones you didn't know before.*—3 John 5

Jude
Blunt Warnings

You're on your way out the door to run an important errand when you hear the phone ring. For a moment you debate whether to go back and answer it—it's probably nothing—but something tells you to turn back and grab it. When you do, you have to sit down. The call brings frightening news. Someone you love is in terrible danger and needs you right away. That errand you were on your way to do seems trivial now. All that matters is saving the person you love.

Jude was getting ready to write a letter to his fellow Christians about "God's saving power at work in our lives" (3). All indications are that it would have been a vibrant, valuable letter. We'd love to have it, but we'll never know what Jude planned to say. At the last minute the alarm bell rang. Jude found out that the Christian community had been infiltrated by some outright frauds.

The hypocrites were masquerading as sincere teachers of the Christian way. They didn't care about Christ or the welfare of believers; they were in this game for themselves. The errors they spread went beyond trivial matters to cut the heart out of Christian morality and Christ's right to be master of Christians' lives.

Immediately Jude went to work with his pen, warning Christians to watch out for these dangerous people. He exposed the impostors and made no apologies for his strong language. Politeness was not an issue when alerting his sisters and brothers about liars among them.

The tone of Jude's letter did turn gentle as he encouraged the believers to stay strong. He was filled with as much kindness and concern for them as he was filled with anger and urgency about the fake teachers.

False teachers and false ideas are still with us. Some of the same ones found in the early church are still around. When we find them, tolerance is not an option; we have to expose them and warn other believers.

Jude at a Glance

1. Opening greetings (1,2)
2. An interrupted letter (3,4)
3. Warnings about what happened to immoral people and even angels (5-7)
4. Jude unapologetically condemns false teachers (8-19)
5. A positive note: stay true to Christ and rescue those you can (20-23)
6. Benediction (24,25)

¹From Jude, a servant of Jesus Christ and the brother of James.

To all who are chosen and loved by God the Father and are kept safe by Jesus Christ. ²I pray that God will greatly bless you with kindness, peace, and love!

False Teachers

³My dear friends, I really wanted to write you about God's saving power at work in our lives. But instead, I must write and ask you to defend the faith that God has once for all given to his people. ⁴Some godless people have sneaked in among us and are saying, "God treats us much better than we deserve, and so it is all right to be immoral." They even deny that we must obey Jesus Christ as our only Master and Lord. But long ago the Scriptures warned that these godless people were doomed.

⁵Don't forget what happened to those people that the Lord rescued from Egypt. Some of them did not have faith, and he later destroyed them. ⁶You also know about the angels[d] who didn't do their work and left their proper places. God chained them with everlasting chains and is now keeping them in dark pits until the great day of judgment. ⁷We should also be warned by what happened to the cities of Sodom and Gomorrah[b] and the nearby towns. Their

people became immoral and did all sorts of sexual sins. Then God made an example of them and punished them with eternal fire.

⁸The people I am talking about are behaving just like those dreamers who destroyed their own bodies. They reject all authority and insult angels. ⁹Even Michael, the chief angel, didn't dare to insult the devil, when the two of them were arguing about the body of Moses.[c] All Michael said was, "The Lord will punish you!"

¹⁰But these people insult powers they don't know anything about. They are like senseless animals that end up getting destroyed, because they live only by their feelings. ¹¹Now they are in for real trouble. They have followed Cain's example[d] and have made the same mistake that Balaam[e] did by

---

[a]**6** *angels*: This may refer to the angels who liked the women on earth so much that they came down and married them (see Genesis 6.2).   [b]**7** *Sodom and Gomorrah*: During the time of Abraham the Lord destroyed these cities because the people there were so evil.   [c]**9** *Michael . . . the body of Moses*: This refers to what was said in an ancient Jewish book about Moses.   [d]**11** *Cain's example*: Cain murdered his brother Abel.   [e]**11** *Balaam*: According to the biblical account, Balaam refused to curse the people of Israel for profit (see Numbers 22.18; 24.13), though he led them to be unfaithful to the Lord (see Numbers 25.1-3; 31.16). But by New Testament times, some Jewish teachers taught that Balaam was greedy and did accept money to curse them.

---

*Spiritual*Life—How can I know good spiritual leaders? *(Jude 3-7)*

They preach God's righteousness.

Have you ever heard a spiritual leader say something like, "God loves us too much to judge us. He'll overlook what we do wrong. He understands that we're fallible and that we all make mistakes"?

The most effective lies are the ones that are almost true. God does love us, and he went to great lengths to keep from condemning us for our sins. He understands our weaknesses. As we stumble through life he shows us mercy every day, even every minute.

But God is not a congenial do-gooder who goes around dispensing favors like lollipops. He is holy and perfect. He sees sin and hates it because it violates his nature. The only reason we receive mercy from God is that Christ entered this world and offered his own life to pay for our sins. God is not "nice"; he is merciful, and his mercy cost him the ultimate.

So watch out for spiritual teachers who emphasize God's big-hearted love but downplay his righteousness. When we accept Christ as Savior, we commit ourselves to following him by living in new, holy ways. Christ's love is never an excuse for sin. (See also 1 Kings 12.1-20; Ezra 7; Matthew 17.1-13.)

Words To Remember: *Some godless people have sneaked in among us and are saying, "God treats us much better than we deserve, and so it is all right to be immoral." They even deny that we must obey Jesus Christ as our only Master and Lord. But long ago the Scriptures warned that these godless people were doomed.—Jude 4*

caring only for money. They have also rebelled against God, just as Korah did.[j] Because of all this, they will be destroyed.

[12]These people are filthy minded, and by
their shameful and selfish actions they spoil
the meals you eat together. They are like
clouds blown along by the wind, but never
bringing any rain. They are like leafless
trees, uprooted and dead, and unable to
produce fruit. [13]Their shameful deeds show
up like foam on wild ocean waves. They are
like wandering stars forever doomed to the
darkest pits of hell.

[14]Enoch was the seventh person after
Adam, and he was talking about these people when he said:

Look! The Lord is coming with
thousands and thousands of holy angels [15]to judge everyone. He will punish all those ungodly people for all the
evil things they have done. The Lord
will surely punish those ungodly sinners for every evil thing they have ever
said about him.

[16]These people grumble and complain
and live by their own selfish desires. They
brag about themselves and flatter others to
get what they want.

More Warnings

[17]My dear friends, remember the warning you were given by the apostles of our
Lord Jesus Christ. [18]They told you that near
the end of time, selfish and godless people
would start making fun of God. [19]And now
these people are already making you turn
against each other. They think only about
this life, and they don't have God's Spirit.

[20]Dear friends, keep building on the
foundation of your most holy faith, as the
Holy Spirit helps you to pray. [21]And keep in
step with God's love, as you wait for our
Lord Jesus Christ to show how kind he is by
giving you eternal life. [22]Be helpful to[g] all
who may have doubts. [23]Rescue any who
need to be saved, as you would rescue
someone from a fire. Then with fear in your
own hearts, have mercy on everyone who
needs it. But hate even the clothes of those
who have been made dirty by their filthy
deeds.

Final Prayer

[24-25]Offer praise to God our Savior because of our Lord Jesus Christ! Only God
can keep you from falling and make you
pure and joyful in his glorious presence. Before time began and now and forevermore,
God is worthy of glory, honor, power, and
authority. Amen.

---

[j]11 *just as Korah did*: Together with Dathan and Abiram,
Korah led a rebellion against Moses and Aaron (see
Numbers 16.1-35; 26.9, 10).   [g]22 *Be helpful to*: Some
manuscripts have "Correct."

Revelation
Joy in the End

Revelation is the most hopeful book in the Bible. That's because it gives us a sneak preview of how the world ends. And Jesus wins! His people are already on the winning side! This was wonderful news to the people in the early church. Christians were suffering for their faith—sometimes hunted like national criminals. Domitian, one of the Roman emperors, declared himself *Dominus et Deus noster* ("our Lord and God"). Since Christians could never call a human king by that title, they were charged with treason.

The apostle John had been exiled to the Island of Patmos for speaking up for his faith. There he saw Jesus with pictures so vivid that it seemed John actually stepped into scenes of cosmic battles and future triumphs. We see a "shameless prostitute who sits on many oceans" (17.1) and a horrible battle between the forces of good and evil so violent that blood "was . . . almost deep enough to cover a horse" (14.20). But we also watch vibrant scenes of heaven where living creatures with six wings sing day and night: "Holy, holy, holy is the Lord, the all-powerful God, who was and is and is coming!" (4.8). We view Christians who have suffered on earth enter heaven where the Lamb (Jesus) leads them to streams of life-giving water, and "God will wipe all tears from their eyes" (7.17). Near the end we glimpse "a new heaven and a new earth" (21.1), populated by God's people, "a large crowd with more people than could be counted . . . from every race, tribe, nation, and language" (7.9).

For those who belong to Jesus, no matter what our current disappointments, the book of Revelation brings a smile to our lips and hope for our future. We will be there! Our side has already won! John opened his book with a blessing: "God will bless everyone who reads this prophecy to others, and he will bless everyone who hears and obeys it. The time is almost here" (1.3). Alleluia!

Revelation at a Glance

1. A revealing letter from John (1.1-8)
2. Jesus standing among seven churches (1.9-20)
3. Seven letters from Jesus to seven churches (2,3)
4. An open door reveals worship in heaven (4,5)
5. Opened seals bring plagues to the earth (6)
6. God wipes away tears (7)
7. A seventh seal, silence, and seven trumpets with judgments and rewards (8–11)
8. War between good and evil—with blood as high as a horse (12–14)
9. Seven angels bring seven terrible troubles (15,16)
10. An evil city that ruined the earth is destroyed (17.1—19.4)
11. A wedding supper for Jesus (19.5-10)

12. Christ captures Satan and locks him up for a thousand years (19.11—20.6)
13. Satan is thrown into a lake of fire forever (20.7-10)
14. A final judgment for the living and the dead—Is your name in the book of life? (20.11-15)
15. A new heaven and a new earth (21.1—22.5)
16. Jesus will come soon (22.6-21)

---

1 This is what God showed to Jesus Christ, so that he could tell his servants what must happen soon. Christ then sent his angel with the message to his servant John. ²And John told everything that he had seen about God's message and about what Jesus Christ had said and done.

³God will bless everyone who reads this prophecy to others,ᵃ and he will bless everyone who hears and obeys it. The time is almost here.

⁴From John to the seven churches in Asia.ᵇ

> I pray that you
>   will be blessed
> with kindness and peace
> from God, who is and was
>   and is coming.
> May you receive
>   kindness and peace
> from the seven spirits
>   before the throne of God.
> ⁵May kindness and peace
>   be yours
> from Jesus Christ,
>   the faithful witness.

God is ultimately faithful to his promises.

RAMONA CRAMER TUCKER

> Jesus was the first
>   to conquer death,
> and he is the ruler
>   of all earthly kings.
> Christ loves us,
>   and by his blood
> he set us free
>   from our sins.
> ⁶He lets us rule as kings

and serve God his Father
    as priests.
To him be glory and power
    forever and ever! Amen.
⁷Look! He is coming
    with the clouds.
Everyone will see him,
even the ones who stuck
    a sword through him.
All people on earth
will weep because of him.
    Yes, it will happen! Amen.

⁸The Lord God says, "I am Alpha and Omega,ᶜ the one who is and was and is coming. I am God All-Powerful!"

A Vision of the Risen Lord

⁹I am John, a follower together with all of you. We suffer because Jesus is our king, but he gives us the strength to endure. I was sent to Patmos Island,ᵈ because I had preached God's message and had told about Jesus. ¹⁰On the Lord's day the Spirit took control of me, and behind me I heard a loud voice that sounded like a trumpet. ¹¹The voice said, "Write in a book what you see. Then send it to the seven churches in Ephesus, Smyrna, Pergamum, Thyatira, Sardis, Philadelphia, and Laodicea."ᵉ

¹²When I turned to see who was speaking to me, I saw seven gold lampstands. ¹³There with the lampstands was someone who seemed to be the Son of Man.ᶠ He was wearing a robe that reached down to his feet, and a gold cloth was wrapped around his chest. ¹⁴His head and his hair were white

---

ᵃ1.3 *who reads this prophecy to others*: A public reading, in a worship service. ᵇ1.4 *Asia*: The section 1.4—3.22 is in the form of a letter. Asia was in the eastern part of the Roman Empire and is present day Turkey. ᶜ1.8 *Alpha and Omega*: The first and last letters of the Greek alphabet, which sometimes mean "first" and "last." ᵈ1.9 *Patmos Island*: A small island where prisoners were sometimes kept by the Romans. ᵉ1.11 *Ephesus . . . Laodicea*: Ephesus was in the center with the six other cities forming a half-circle around it. ᶠ1.13 *Son of Man*: That is, Jesus.

as wool or snow, and his eyes looked like flames of fire. [15]His feet were glowing like bronze being heated in a furnace, and his voice sounded like the roar of a waterfall. [16]He held seven stars in his right hand, and a sharp double-edged sword was coming from his mouth. His face was shining as bright as the sun at noon.

[17]When I saw him, I fell at his feet like a dead person. But he put his right hand on me and said:

Don't be afraid! I am the first, the last, [18]and the living one. I died, but now I am alive forevermore, and I have the keys to death and the world of the dead.[g] [19]Write what you have seen and what is and what will happen after these things. [20]I will explain the mystery of the seven stars that you saw at my right side and the seven gold lampstands. The seven stars are the angels[h] of the seven churches, and the lampstands are the seven churches.

The Letter to Ephesus

2 This is what you must write to the angel of the church in Ephesus:

I am the one who holds the seven stars in my right hand, and I walk among the seven gold lampstands. Listen to what I say.

[2]I know everything you have done, including your hard work and how you have endured. I know you won't put up with anyone who is evil. When some people pretended to be apostles, you tested them and found out that they were liars. [3]You have endured and gone through hard times because of me, and you have not given up.

[4]But I do have something against you! And it is this: You don't have as much love as you used to. [5]Think about where you have fallen from, and then turn back and do as you did at first. If you don't turn back, I will come and take away your lampstand. [6]But there is one thing you are doing right. You hate what the Nicolaitans[i] are doing, and so do I.

---

[g]1.18 *keys to death and the world of the dead*: That is, power over death and the world of the dead.
[h]1.20 *angels*: Perhaps guardian angels that represent the churches, or they may be church leaders or messengers sent to the churches.   [i]2.6 *Nicolaitans*: Nothing else is known about these people, though it is possible that they claimed to be followers of Nicolaus from Antioch (see Acts 6.5).

Personal *Concerns*—How can I learn to set priorities? *(Revelation 2.1-7)*

Don't put work ahead of love.

How do you decide how you'll spend your time, money, energy? We all set priorities all day every day. Most of the time we don't even think about it. We just do what needs to be done when it comes up. But sometimes *what* we do isn't nearly as important as *why* we do it. Christ's message to the church at Ephesus bears that out.

Jesus had all kinds of good things to say about that church. The people worked hard; they got rid of evil in their midst; when teachers came to them they checked them out before swallowing everything they said; they endured hard times because of their faith. All this was good. In fact, it was outstanding. But one thing was lacking: love. They used to love God and each other, but somehow that love had cooled.

This can happen to us, too. We can check off every item on the "to do" list and fling supper on the table as if we were feeding ducks at a local park. We can teach every point on the Sunday school lesson and mutter something about "little brats" under our breath. We can pray each morning and night—and feel as if we were paying dues to God. Jesus invited the church of Ephesus to return to its first love, "turn back and do as you did at first" (2.5). He invites us to do the same. (See also Genesis 22.1-19; 1 Samuel 15.10-35; Haggai 2.6-9; Luke 10.38-42.)

Words To Remember: *I know everything you have done, including your hard work and how you have endured. . . . You don't have as much love as you used to. Think about where you have fallen from, and then turn back and do as you did at first.*
—Revelation 2.2,4,5

[7]If you have ears, listen to what the Spirit says to the churches. I will let everyone who wins the victory eat from the life-giving tree in God's wonderful garden.

The Letter to Smyrna

[8]This is what you must write to the angel of the church in Smyrna:

I am the first and the last. I died, but now I am alive! Listen to what I say. [9]I know how much you suffer and how poor you are, but you are rich. I also know the cruel things being said about you by people who claim to be Jews. But they are not really Jews. They are a group that belongs to Satan. [10]Don't worry about what you will suffer. The devil will throw some of you into jail, and you will be tested and made to suffer for ten days. But if you are faithful until you die, I will reward you with a glorious life.[j]

[11]If you have ears, listen to what the Spirit says to the churches. Whoever wins the victory will not be hurt by the second death.[k]

The Letter to Pergamum

[12]This is what you must write to the angel of the church in Pergamum:

I am the one who has the sharp double-edged sword! Listen to what I say. [13]I know that you live where Satan has his throne.[l] But you have kept true to my name. Right there where Satan lives, my faithful witness Antipas[m] was taken from you and put to death. Even then you did not give up your faith in me. [14]I do have a few things against you. Some of you are following the teaching of Balaam.[n] Long ago he told Balak to teach the people of Israel to eat food that had been offered to idols and to be immoral. [15]Now some of you are following the teaching of the Nicolaitans.[o] [16]Turn back! If you don't, I will come quickly and fight against these people. And my words will cut like a sword.

[17]If you have ears, listen to what the Spirit says to the churches. To everyone who wins the victory, I will give some of the hidden food.[p] I will also give each one a white stone[q] with a new name[r] written on it. No one will know that name except the one who is given the stone.

The Letter to Thyatira

[18]This is what you must write to the angel of the church in Thyatira:

I am the Son of God! My eyes are like flames of fire, and my feet are like bronze. Listen to what I say. [19]I know everything about you, including your love, your faith, your service, and how you have endured. I know that you are doing more now than you have ever done before. [20]But I still have something against you because of that woman Jezebel.[s] She calls herself a prophet, and you let her teach and mislead my servants to do immoral things and to eat food offered to idols. [21]I gave her a chance to turn from her sins, but she did not want to stop doing these immoral things.

[22]I am going to strike down Jezebel. Everyone who does these immoral things with her will also be punished,

---

[j]**2.10** *a glorious life*: The Greek text has "a crown of life." In ancient times an athlete who had won a contest was rewarded with a crown of flowers as a sign of victory. [k]**2.11** *second death*: The first death is physical death, and the "second death" is eternal death. [l]**2.13** *where Satan has his throne*: The meaning is uncertain, but it may refer to the city as a center of pagan worship or of Emperor worship. [m]**2.13** *Antipas*: Nothing else is known about this man, who is mentioned only here in the New Testament. [n]**2.14** *Balaam*: According to Numbers 22–24, Balaam refused to disobey the Lord. But in other books of the Old Testament, he is spoken of as evil (see Deuteronomy 23.4, 5; Joshua 13.22; 24.9, 10; Nehemiah 13.2). [o]**2.15** *Nicolaitans*: See the note at 2.6. [p]**2.17** *hidden food*: When the people of Israel were going through the desert, the Lord provided a special food for them. Some of this was placed in a jar and stored in the sacred chest (see Exodus 16). According to later Jewish teaching, the prophet Jeremiah rescued the sacred chest when the temple was destroyed by the Babylonians. He hid the chest in a cave, where it would stay until God came to save his people. [q]**2.17** *white stone*: The meaning of this is uncertain, though it may be the same as a ticket that lets a person into God's banquet where the "hidden food" is eaten. Or it may be a symbol of victory. [r]**2.17** *a new name*: Either the name of Christ or God or the name of the follower who is given the stone. [s]**2.20** *Jezebel*: Nothing else is known about her. This may have been her real name or a name that was given to her because she was like Queen Jezebel, who opposed the Lord (see 1 Kings 19.1, 2; 21.1-26).

if they don't stop. ²³I will even kill her followers.ᵗ Then all the churches will see that I know everyone's thoughts and feelings. I will treat each of you as you deserve.

²⁴Some of you in Thyatira don't follow Jezebel's teaching. You don't know anything about what her followers call the "deep secrets of Satan." So I won't burden you down with any other commands. ²⁵But until I come, you must hold firmly to the teaching you have.

²⁶I will give power over the nations to everyone who wins the victory and keeps on obeying me until the end. ²⁷⁻²⁸I will give each of them the same power that my Father has given me. They will rule the nations with an iron rod and smash those nations to pieces like clay pots. I will also give them the morning star.ᵘ

²⁹If you have ears, listen to what the Spirit says to the churches.

The Letter to Sardis

3 This is what you must write to the angel of the church in Sardis:

I have the seven spirits of God and the seven stars. Listen to what I say.

I know what you are doing. Everyone may think you are alive, but you are dead. ²Wake up! You have only a little strength left, and it is almost gone. So try to become stronger. I have found that you are not completely obeying God. ³Remember the teaching that you were given and that you heard. Hold firmly to it and turn from your sins. If you don't wake up, I will come when you least expect it, just as a thief does.

⁴A few of you in Sardis have not dirtied your clothes with sin. You will walk with me in white clothes, because you are worthy. ⁵Everyone who wins the victory will wear white clothes. Their names will not be erased from the book of life,ᵛ and I will tell my Father and his angels that they are my followers.

⁶If you have ears, listen to what the Spirit says to the churches.

The Letter to Philadelphia

⁷This is what you must write to the angel of the church in Philadelphia:

I am the one who is holy and true, and I have the keys that belonged to David.ʷ When I open a door, no one can close it. And when I close a door, no one can open it. Listen to what I say.

⁸I know everything you have done. And I have placed before you an open door that no one can close. You were not very strong, but you obeyed my message and did not deny that you are my followers.ˣ ⁹Now you will see what I will do with those people who belong to Satan's group. They claim to be Jews, but they are liars. I will make them come and kneel down at your feet. Then they will know that I love you.

¹⁰You obeyed my message and endured. So I will protect you from the time of testing that everyone in all the world must go through. ¹¹I am coming soon. So hold firmly to what you have, and no one will take away the crown that you will be given as your reward.

¹²Everyone who wins the victory will be made into a pillar in the temple of my God, and they will stay there forever. I will write on each of them the name of my God and the name of his city. It is the new Jerusalem that my God will send down from heaven. I will also write on them my own new name.

¹³If you have ears, listen to what the Spirit says to the churches.

The Letter to Laodicea

¹⁴This is what you must write to the angel of the church in Laodicea:

I am the one called Amen!ʸ I am the faithful and true witness and the

---

ᵗ**2.23** *her followers:* Or "her children." ᵘ**2.27,28** *the morning star:* Probably thought of as the star that signals the end of night and the beginning of day. In 22.16 Christ is called the "morning star." ᵛ**3.5** *book of life:* The book in which the names of God's people are written. ʷ**3.7** *the keys that belonged to David:* The keys stand for authority over David's kingdom. ˣ**3.8** *did not deny that you are my followers:* Or "did not say evil things about me." ʸ**3.14** *Amen:* Meaning "Trustworthy."

source[z] of God's creation. Listen to what I say.

[15]I know everything you have done, and you are not cold or hot. I wish you were either one or the other. [16]But since you are lukewarm and neither cold nor hot, I will spit you out of my mouth. [17]You claim to be rich and successful and to have everything you need. But you don't know how bad off you are. You are pitiful, poor, blind, and naked.

[18]Buy your gold from me. It has been refined in a fire, and it will make you rich. Buy white clothes from me. Wear them and you can cover up your shameful nakedness. Buy medicine for your eyes, so that you will be able to see.

[19]I correct and punish everyone I love. So make up your minds to turn away from your sins. [20]Listen! I am standing and knocking at your door. If you hear my voice and open the door, I will come in and we will eat together. [21]Everyone who wins the victory will sit with me on my throne, just as I won the victory and sat with my Father on his throne.

[22]If you have ears, listen to what the Spirit says to the churches.

Worship in Heaven

4 After this, I looked and saw a door that opened into heaven. Then the voice that had spoken to me at first and that sounded like a trumpet said, "Come up here! I will show you what must happen next." [2]Right then the Spirit took control of me, and there in heaven I saw a throne and someone sitting on it. [3]The one who was sitting there sparkled like precious stones of jasper[a] and carnelian.[b] A rainbow that looked like an emerald[c] surrounded the throne.

[4]Twenty-four other thrones were in a circle around that throne. And on each of these thrones there was an elder dressed in white clothes and wearing a gold crown. [5]Flashes of lightning and roars of thunder came out from the throne in the center of the circle. Seven torches, which are the seven spirits of God, were burning in front of the throne. [6]Also in front of the throne was something that looked like a glass sea, clear as crystal.

Around the throne in the center were four living creatures covered front and back

[z]3.14 source: Or "beginning." [a]4.3 jasper: Usually green or clear. [b]4.3 carnelian: Usually deep-red or reddish-white. [c]4.3 emerald: A precious stone, usually green.

SingleLife—How can I overcome my feelings of loneliness? (Revelation 3.20-22)

Enjoy the company of Christ.

Singleness can be lonely at times. Sure, you can fill your day with friends, activities, work, and family members, but by eleven o'clock at night, when other women are snuggling into bed with a husband, you turn off the lights alone. Breakfast is a place setting for one, and holidays find you heading back to your childhood home. But you always get the roll-away cot on the porch because there's *only one* of you. Vacations are organized group affairs, or you skip them altogether. You're beginning to think about retirement—alone.

But it doesn't have to be that way. Jesus invites himself for supper! "Listen!" he says, "I am standing and knocking at your door. If you hear my voice and open the door, I will come in and we will eat together." Jesus wants to get close to you, to talk with you, to keep you company. So when you're feeling extra lonely, invite him as a dinner guest—or anytime guest!

Inviting Jesus through the door of your life won't relieve all the loneliness of singleness—especially the need for human relationships. But in a spiritual sense, you need never be alone again. You'll always have the company of Jesus. (See also Psalm 22; Psalm 68.4-6; Matthew 26.36-46; 2 Timothy 4.16-18.)

Words To Remember: *Listen! I am standing and knocking at your door. If you hear my voice and open the door, I will come in and we will eat together.*
—Revelation 3.20

with eyes. [7]The first creature was like a lion, the second one was like a bull, the third one had the face of a human, and the fourth was like a flying eagle. [8]Each of the four living creatures had six wings, and their bodies were covered with eyes. Day and night they never stopped singing,

"Holy, holy, holy is the Lord,
    the all-powerful God,
who was and is
    and is coming!"

[9]The living creatures kept praising, honoring, and thanking the one who sits on the throne and who lives forever and ever. [10]At the same time the twenty-four elders knelt down before the one sitting on the throne. And as they worshiped the one who lives forever, they placed their crowns in front of the throne and said,

[11]"Our Lord and God,
    you are worthy
to receive glory,
    honor, and power.
You created all things,
    and by your decision they are
        and were created."

When Jesus said he could give me an abundant life, he meant it. It's a lot more fun being who God created me to be instead of trying to be someone else!

RUTH E. VAN REKEN

The Scroll and the Lamb

5 In the right hand of the one sitting on the throne I saw a scroll[d] that had writing on the inside and on the outside. And it was sealed in seven places. [2]I saw a mighty angel ask with a loud voice, "Who is worthy to open the scroll and break its seals?" [3]No one in heaven or on earth or under the earth was able to open the scroll or see inside it.

[4]I cried hard because no one was found worthy to open the scroll or see inside it. [5]Then one of the elders said to me, "Stop crying and look! The one who is called both the 'Lion from the Tribe of Judah'[e] and 'King David's Great Descendant'[f] has won the victory. He will open the book and its seven seals."

[6]Then I looked and saw a Lamb standing in the center of the throne that was surrounded by the four living creatures and the elders. The Lamb looked as if it had once been killed. It had seven horns and seven eyes, which are the seven spirits[g] of God, sent out to all the earth.

[7]The Lamb went over and took the scroll from the right hand of the one who sat on the throne. [8]After he had taken it, the four living creatures and the twenty-four elders knelt down before him. Each of them had a harp and a gold bowl full of incense,[h] which are the prayers of God's people. [9]Then they sang a new song,

"You are worthy
    to receive the scroll
and open its seals,
    because you were killed.
And with your own blood
    you bought for God
people from every tribe,
    language, nation, and race.
[10]You let them become kings
    and serve God as priests,
    and they will rule on earth."

[11]As I looked, I heard the voices of a lot of angels around the throne and the voices of the living creatures and of the elders. There were millions and millions of them, [12]and they were saying in a loud voice,

"The Lamb who was killed
    is worthy to receive power,

---

[d]**5.1** *scroll:* A roll of paper or special leather used for writing on. Sometimes a scroll would be sealed on the outside with one or more pieces of wax.   [e]**5.5** *'Lion from the Tribe of Judah':* In Genesis 49.9 the tribe of Judah is called a young lion, and King David was from Judah.   [f]**5.5** *'King David's Great Descendant':* The Greek text has "the root of David" which is a title for the Messiah based on Isaiah 11.1, 10.   [g]**5.6** *the seven spirits:* Some manuscripts have "the spirits."   [h]**5.8** *incense:* A material that produces a sweet smell when burned. Sometimes it is a symbol for the prayers of God's people.

riches, wisdom, strength,
>honor, glory, and praise."

¹³Then I heard all beings in heaven and on the earth and under the earth and in the sea offer praise. Together, all of them were saying,

>"Praise, honor, glory,
>and strength
>>forever and ever
>to the one who sits
>on the throne
>>and to the Lamb!"

¹⁴The four living creatures said "Amen," while the elders knelt down and worshiped.

Opening the Seven Seals

6 At the same time that I saw the Lamb open the first of the seven seals, I heard one of the four living creatures shout with a voice like thunder. It said, "Come out!" ²Then I saw a white horse. Its rider carried a bow and was given a crown. He had already won some victories, and he went out to win more.

³When the Lamb opened the second seal, I heard the second living creature say, "Come out!" ⁴Then another horse came out. It was fiery red. And its rider was given the power to take away all peace from the earth, so that people would slaughter one another. He was also given a big sword.

⁵When the Lamb opened the third seal, I heard the third living creature say, "Come out!" Then I saw a black horse, and its rider had a balance scale in one hand. ⁶I heard what sounded like a voice from somewhere among the four living creatures. It said, "A quart of wheat will cost you a whole day's wages! Three quarts of barley will cost you a day's wages too. But don't ruin the olive oil or the wine."

⁷When the Lamb opened the fourth seal, I heard the voice of the fourth living creature say, "Come out!" ⁸Then I saw a pale green horse. Its rider was named Death, and Death's Kingdom followed behind. They were given power over one fourth of the earth, and they could kill its people with swords, famines, diseases, and wild animals.

⁹When the Lamb opened the fifth seal, I saw under the altar the souls of everyone who had been killed for speaking God's message and telling about their faith. ¹⁰They shouted, "Master, you are holy and faithful! How long will it be before you judge and punish the people of this earth who killed us?"

¹¹Then each of those who had been killed was given a white robe and told to rest for a little while. They had to wait until the complete number of the Lord's other servants and followers would be killed.

¹²When I saw the Lamb open the sixth seal, I looked and saw a great earthquake. The sun turned as dark as sackcloth,ⁱ and the moon became as red as blood. ¹³The stars in the sky fell to earth, just like figs shaken loose by a windstorm. ¹⁴Then the sky was rolled up like a scroll,ʲ and all mountains and islands were moved from their places.

¹⁵The kings of the earth, its famous people, and its military leaders hid in caves or behind rocks on the mountains. They hid there together with the rich and the powerful and with all the slaves and free people. ¹⁶Then they shouted to the mountains and the rocks, "Fall on us! Hide us from the one who sits on the throne and from the anger of the Lamb. ¹⁷That terrible day has come! God and the Lamb will show their anger, and who can face it?"

The 144,000 Are Marked for God

7 ¹⁻²After this I saw four angels. Each one was standing on one of the earth's four corners. The angels held back the four winds, so that no wind would blow on the earth or on the sea or on any tree. These angels had also been given the power to harm the earth and the sea. Then I saw another angel come up from where the sun rises in the east, and he was ready to put the mark of the living God on people. He shouted to the four angels, ³"Don't harm the earth or the sea or any tree! Wait until I have marked the foreheads of the servants of our God."

⁴Then I heard how many people had been marked on the forehead. There were

---

ⁱ**6.12** *sackcloth*: A rough, dark-colored cloth made from goat or camel hair and used to make grain sacks. It was worn in times of trouble or sorrow. ʲ**6.14** *scroll*: See the note at 5.1.

one hundred forty-four thousand, and they came from every tribe of Israel:

⁵12,000 from Judah,
 12,000 from Reuben,
 12,000 from Gad,
⁶12,000 from Asher,
 12,000 from Naphtali,
 12,000 from Manasseh,
⁷12,000 from Simeon,
 12,000 from Levi,
 12,000 from Issachar,
⁸12,000 from Zebulun,
 12,000 from Joseph, and
 12,000 from Benjamin.

People from Every Nation

⁹After this, I saw a large crowd with more people than could be counted. They were from every race, tribe, nation, and language, and they stood before the throne and before the Lamb. They wore white robes and held palm branches in their hands, ¹⁰as they shouted,

"Our God, who sits
    upon the throne,
has the power

to save his people,
    and so does the Lamb."

¹¹The angels who stood around the throne knelt in front of it with their faces to the ground. The elders and the four living creatures knelt there with them. Then they all worshiped God ¹²and said,

"Amen! Praise, glory, wisdom,
    thanks, honor, power,
and strength belong to our God
    forever and ever! Amen!"

¹³One of the elders asked me, "Do you know who these people are that are dressed in white robes? Do you know where they come from?"

¹⁴"Sir," I answered, "you must know." Then he told me:

"These are the ones
who have gone through
    the great suffering.
They have washed their robes
    in the blood of the Lamb
    and have made them white.
¹⁵And so they stand
    before the throne of God

Friendship—What's the best way to find friends? *(Revelation 7.9-12)*

Enjoy the diversity of God's people.

Good friends are like comfortable old shoes. They mold to the shape of our feet. They are *like* us. So it's tempting to look for friends who are similar to us in surface ways. We look for someone who's about the same age, not too much richer or poorer, who lives near us, who has common interests. It helps if her kids are at the same stage as ours. She should have fun doing the same things we like. And of course she should speak the same language!

But a scene from heaven might help us rethink those requirements for friendship. Jesus allowed John a glimpse into heaven. And what he found there was astounding. First, he saw people from every tribe of Israel. But after that he saw an even larger crowd, "more people than could be counted" (7.9). "They were from every race, tribe, nation, and language" (7.9). They were all wearing white robes. (Their sins had been washed away.) And they were all doing the same thing—praising God. Even the angels and the heavenly elders knelt down and joined in their praise.

If we will be part of such a diverse body in heaven (and we will), we may as well get started on it now. The rich diversity of God's people will enrich our own life and prepare us for eternity. (See also 1 Kings 19.1-21; 2 Corinthians 2.14-17.)

Words To Remember: *After this, I saw a large crowd with more people than could be counted. They were from every race, tribe, nation, and language, and they stood before the throne and before the Lamb. They wore white robes and held palm branches in their hands.*—Revelation 7.9

and worship him in his temple
  day and night.
The one who sits on the throne
will spread his tent
  over them.
[16]They will never hunger
  or thirst again,
and they won't be troubled
by the sun
  or any scorching heat.

[17]The Lamb in the center
of the throne
  will be their shepherd.
He will lead them to streams
  of life-giving water,
and God will wipe all tears
  from their eyes."

The Seventh Seal Is Opened

8 When the Lamb opened the seventh
seal, there was silence in heaven for
about half an hour. [2]I noticed that the
seven angels who stood before God were
each given a trumpet.

[3]Another angel, who had a gold container for incense,[k] came and stood at the
altar. This one was given a lot of incense to
offer with the prayers of God's people on
the gold altar in front of the throne. [4]Then
the smoke of the incense, together with the
prayers of God's people, went up to God
from the hand of the angel.

[5]After this, the angel filled the incense
container with fire from the altar and threw
it on the earth. Thunder roared, lightning
flashed, and the earth shook.

The Trumpets

[6]The seven angels now got ready to blow
their trumpets.

[7]When the first angel blew his trumpet,
hail and fire mixed with blood were thrown
down on the earth. A third of the earth, a
third of the trees, and a third of all green
plants were burned.

[8]When the second angel blew his trumpet, something like a great fiery mountain
was thrown into the sea. A third of the sea
turned to blood, [9]a third of the living creatures in the sea died, and a third of the ships
were destroyed.

[10]When the third angel blew his trumpet, a great star fell from heaven. It was
burning like a torch, and it fell on a third of
the rivers and on a third of the springs of
water. [11]The name of the star was Bitter, and
a third of the water turned bitter. Many people died because the water was so bitter.

[12]When the fourth angel blew his trumpet, a third of the sun, a third of the moon,
and a third of the stars were struck. They
each lost a third of their light. So during a
third of the day there was no light, and a
third of the night was also without light.

[13]Then I looked and saw a lone eagle flying across the sky. It was shouting, "Trouble, trouble, trouble to everyone who lives
on earth! The other three angels are now
going to blow their trumpets."

9 When the fifth angel blew his trumpet, I saw a star[l] fall from the sky to
earth. It was given the key to the tunnel that leads down to the deep pit. [2]As it
opened the tunnel, smoke poured out like
the smoke of a great furnace. The sun and
the air turned dark because of the smoke.
[3]Locusts[m] came out of the smoke and covered the earth. They were given the same
power that scorpions have.

[4]The locusts were told not to harm the
grass on the earth or any plant or any tree.
They were to punish only those people who
did not have God's mark on their foreheads.
[5]The locusts were allowed to make them
suffer for five months, but not to kill them.
The suffering they caused was like the sting
of a scorpion. [6]In those days people will
want to die, but they will not be able to.
They will hope for death, but it will escape
from them.

[7]These locusts looked like horses ready
for battle. On their heads they wore something like gold crowns, and they had human
faces. [8]Their hair was like a woman's long
hair, and their teeth were like those of a lion.
[9]On their chests they wore armor made of
iron. Their wings roared like an army of
horse-drawn chariots rushing into battle.
[10]Their tails were like a scorpion's tail with a
stinger that had the power to hurt someone
for five months. [11]Their king was the angel
in charge of the deep pit. In Hebrew his

---

[k]**8.3** *incense:* See the note at 5.8. [l]**9.1** *star:* In the
ancient world, stars were often thought of as living
beings, such as angels. [m]**9.3** *Locusts:* A type of
grasshopper that comes in swarms and causes great
damage to crops.

name was Abaddon, and in Greek it was Apollyon.[n]

[12]The first horrible thing has now happened! But wait. Two more horrible things will happen soon.

[13]Then the sixth angel blew his trumpet. I heard a voice speak from the four corners of the gold altar that stands in the presence of God. [14]The voice spoke to this angel and said, "Release the four angels who are tied up beside the great Euphrates River." [15]The four angels had been prepared for this very hour and day and month and year. Now they were set free to kill a third of all people.

[16]By listening, I could tell there were more than two hundred million of these war horses. [17]In my vision their riders wore fiery-red, dark-blue, and yellow armor on their chests. The heads of the horses looked like lions, with fire and smoke and sulfur coming out of their mouths. [18]One-third of all people were killed by the three terrible troubles caused by the fire, the smoke, and the sulfur. [19]The horses had powerful mouths, and their tails were like poisonous snakes that bite and hurt.

[20]The people who lived through these terrible troubles did not turn away from the idols they had made, and they did not stop worshiping demons. They kept on worshiping idols that were made of gold, silver, bronze, stone, and wood. Not one of these idols could see, hear, or walk. [21]No one stopped murdering or practicing witchcraft or being immoral or stealing.

The Angel and the Little Scroll

10 I saw another powerful angel come down from heaven. This one was covered with a cloud, and a rainbow was over his head. His face was like the sun, his legs were like columns of fire, [2]and with his hand he held a little scroll[o] that had been unrolled. He stood there with his right foot on the sea and his left foot on the land. [3]Then he shouted with a voice that sounded like a growling lion. Thunder roared seven times.

[4]After the thunder stopped, I was about to write what it had said. But a voice from heaven shouted, "Keep it secret! Don't write these things."

[5]The angel I had seen standing on the sea and the land then held his right hand up toward heaven. [6]He made a promise in the

name of God who lives forever and who created heaven, earth, the sea, and every living creature. The angel said, "You won't have to wait any longer. [7]God told his secret plans to his servants the prophets, and it will all happen by the time the seventh angel sounds his trumpet."

[8]Once again the voice from heaven spoke to me. It said, "Go and take the open scroll from the hand of the angel standing on the sea and the land."

[9]When I went over to ask the angel for the little scroll, the angel said, "Take the scroll and eat it! Your stomach will turn sour, but the taste in your mouth will be as sweet as honey." [10]I took the little scroll from the hand of the angel and ate it. The taste was as sweet as honey, but my stomach turned sour.

[11]Then some voices said, "Keep on telling what will happen to the people of many nations, races, and languages, and also to kings."

The Two Witnesses

11 An angel gave me a measuring stick and said:
Measure around God's temple. Be sure to include the altar and everyone worshiping there. [2]But don't measure the courtyard outside the temple building. Leave it out. It has been given to those people who don't know God, and they will trample all over the holy city for forty-two months. [3]My two witnesses will wear sackcloth,[p] while I let them preach for one thousand two hundred sixty days.

[4]These two witnesses are the two olive trees and the two lampstands that stand in the presence of the Lord who rules the earth. [5]Any enemy who tries to harm them will be destroyed by the fire that comes out of their mouths. [6]They have the power to lock up the sky and to keep rain from falling while they are prophesying. And whenever they want to, they can turn water to blood and cause all kinds of terrible troubles on earth.

[7]After the two witnesses have finished

---

[n]**9.11** *Abaddon . . . Apollyon:* The Hebrew word "Abaddon" and the Greek word "Apollyon" each mean "destruction." [o]**10.2** *scroll:* See the note at 5.1. [p]**11.3** *sackcloth:* See the note at 6.12.

preaching God's message, the beast that lives in the deep pit will come up and fight against them. It will win the battle and kill them. [8]Their bodies will be left lying in the streets of the same great city where their Lord was nailed to a cross. And that city is spiritually like the city of Sodom or the country of Egypt.

[9]For three and a half days the people of every nation, tribe, language, and race will stare at the bodies of these two witnesses and refuse to let them be buried. [10]Everyone on earth will celebrate and be happy. They will give gifts to each other, because of what happened to the two prophets who caused them so much trouble. [11]But three and a half days later, God will breathe life into their bodies. They will stand up, and everyone who sees them will be terrified.

[12]The witnesses then heard a loud voice from heaven, saying, "Come up here." And while their enemies were watching, they were taken up to heaven in a cloud. [13]At that same moment there was a terrible earthquake that destroyed a tenth of the city. Seven thousand people were killed, and the rest were frightened and praised the God who rules in heaven.

[14]The second horrible thing has now happened! But the third one will be here soon.

The Seventh Trumpet

[15]At the sound of the seventh trumpet, loud voices were heard in heaven. They said,

> "Now the kingdom
>   of this world
> belongs to our Lord
>   and to his Chosen One!
> And he will rule
>   forever and ever!"

[16]Then the twenty-four elders, who were seated on thrones in God's presence, knelt down and worshiped him. [17]They said,

> "Lord God All-Powerful,
> you are and you were,
>   and we thank you.
> You used your great power
>   and started ruling.
> [18]When the nations got angry,
>   you became angry too!

> Now the time has come
> for the dead
>   to be judged.
> It is time for you to reward
>   your servants the prophets
> and all of your people
> who honor your name,
>   no matter who they are.
> It is time to destroy everyone
> who has destroyed
>   the earth."

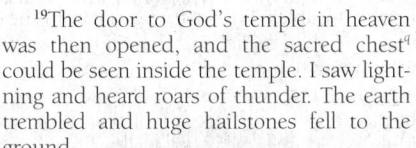

We must give thanks to God in all circumstances and reverence his name. He, and he alone, is ultimately worthy of our praise.

LAURETTA PATTERSON

[19]The door to God's temple in heaven was then opened, and the sacred chest[d] could be seen inside the temple. I saw lightning and heard roars of thunder. The earth trembled and huge hailstones fell to the ground.

The Woman and the Dragon

12 Something important appeared in the sky. It was a woman whose clothes were the sun. The moon was under her feet, and a crown made of twelve stars was on her head. [2]She was about to give birth, and she was crying because of the great pain.

[3]Something else appeared in the sky. It was a huge red dragon with seven heads and ten horns, and a crown on each of its seven heads. [4]With its tail, it dragged a third of the stars from the sky and threw them down to the earth. Then the dragon turned toward the woman, because it wanted to eat her child as soon as it was born.

---

[d]**11.19** *sacred chest:* In Old Testament times the sacred chest was kept in the tent used for worship. It was the symbol of God's presence with his people and also of his agreement with them.

⁵The woman gave birth to a son, who would rule all nations with an iron rod. The boy was snatched away. He was taken to God and placed on his throne. ⁶The woman ran into the desert to a place that God had prepared for her. There she would be taken care of for one thousand two hundred sixty days.

Michael Fights the Dragon

⁷A war broke out in heaven. Michael and his angels were fighting against the dragon and its angels. ⁸But the dragon lost the battle. It and its angels were forced out of their places in heaven ⁹and were thrown down to the earth. Yes, that old snake and his angels were thrown out of heaven! That snake, who fools everyone on earth, is known as the devil and Satan. ¹⁰Then I heard a voice from heaven shout,

"Our God has shown
his saving power,
and his kingdom has come!
God's own Chosen One
has shown his authority.
Satan accused our people
in the presence of God
day and night.
Now he has been thrown out!

¹¹ Our people defeated Satan
because of the blood^r
of the Lamb
and the message of God.
They were willing
to give up their lives.

¹² The heavens should rejoice,
together with everyone
who lives there.
But pity the earth
and the sea,
because the devil
was thrown down
to the earth.
He knows his time is short,
and he is very angry."

¹³When the dragon realized that it had been thrown down to the earth, it tried to make trouble for the woman who had given birth to a son. ¹⁴But the woman was given two wings like those of a huge eagle, so that she could fly into the desert. There she would escape from the snake and be taken care of for a time, two times, and half a time. ¹⁵The snake then spewed out water like a river to sweep the woman away. ¹⁶But the earth helped her and swallowed the water that had come from the dragon's mouth. ¹⁷This made the dragon terribly angry with the woman. So it started a war against the rest of her children. They are the people who obey God and are faithful to what Jesus did and taught. ¹⁸The dragon^s stood on the beach beside the sea.

The Two Beasts

13 I looked and saw a beast coming up from the sea. This one had ten horns and seven heads, and a crown was on each of its ten horns. On each of its heads were names that were an insult to God. ²The beast that I saw had the body of a leopard, the feet of a bear, and the mouth of a lion. The dragon handed over its own power and throne and great authority to this beast. ³One of its heads seemed to have been fatally wounded, but now it was well. Everyone on earth marveled at this beast, ⁴and they worshiped the dragon who had given its authority to the beast. They also worshiped the beast and said, "No one is like this beast! No one can fight against it."

⁵The beast was allowed to brag and claim to be God, and for forty-two months it was allowed to rule. ⁶The beast cursed God, and it cursed the name of God. It even cursed the place where God lives, as well as everyone who lives in heaven with God. ⁷It was allowed to fight against God's people and defeat them. It was also given authority over the people of every tribe, nation, language, and race. ⁸The beast was worshiped by everyone whose name wasn't written before the time of creation in the book of the Lamb who was killed.^t

⁹ If you have ears,
then listen!
¹⁰ If you are doomed
to be captured,
you will be captured.

---

^r 12.11 *blood:* Or "death." ^s 12.18 *The dragon:* The text has "he," and some manuscripts have "I." ^t 13.8 *wasn't written . . . was killed:* Or "not written in the book of the Lamb who was killed before the time of creation."

If you are doomed
     to be killed by a sword,
you will be killed
     by a sword.

This means that God's people must learn to endure and be faithful!

[11]I now saw another beast. This one came out of the ground. It had two horns like a lamb, but spoke like a dragon. [12]It worked for the beast whose fatal wound had been healed. And it used all its authority to force the earth and its people to worship that beast. [13]It worked mighty miracles, and while people watched, it even made fire come down from the sky.

[14]This second beast fooled people on earth by working miracles for the first one. Then it talked them into making an idol in the form of the beast that did not die after being wounded by a sword. [15]It was allowed to put breath into the idol, so that it could speak. Everyone who refused to worship the idol of the beast was put to death. [16]All people were forced to put a mark on their right hand or forehead. Whether they were powerful or weak, rich or poor, free people or slaves, [17]they all had to have this mark, or else they could not buy or sell anything. This mark stood for the name of the beast and for the number of its name.

[18]You need wisdom to understand the number of the beast! But if you are smart enough, you can figure this out. Its number is six hundred sixty-six, and it stands for a person.

The Lamb and His 144,000 Followers

14 I looked and saw the Lamb standing on Mount Zion![u] With him were a hundred forty-four thousand, who had his name and his Father's name written on their foreheads. [2]Then I heard a sound from heaven that was like a roaring flood or loud thunder or even like the music of harps. [3]And a new song was being sung in front of God's throne and in front of the four living creatures and the elders. No one could learn that song, except the one hundred forty-four thousand who had been rescued from the earth. [4]All of these are pure virgins, and they follow the Lamb wherever he leads. They have been rescued to be presented to God and the Lamb as the most precious people[v] on

earth. [5]They never tell lies, and they are innocent.

The Messages of the Three Angels

[6]I saw another angel. This one was flying across the sky and had the eternal good news to announce to the people of every race, tribe, language, and nation on earth. [7]The angel shouted, "Worship and honor God! The time has come for him to judge everyone. Kneel down before the one who created heaven and earth, the oceans, and every stream."

[8]A second angel followed and said, "The great city of Babylon has fallen! This is the city that made all nations drunk and immoral. Now God is angry, and Babylon has fallen."

[9]Finally, a third angel came and shouted:
     Here is what will happen if you worship the beast and the idol and have the mark of the beast on your hand or forehead. [10]You will have to drink the wine that God gives to everyone who makes him angry. You will feel his mighty anger, and you will be tortured with fire and burning sulfur, while the holy angels and the Lamb look on.
     [11]If you worship the beast and the idol and accept the mark of its name, you will be tortured day and night. The smoke from your torture will go up forever and ever, and you will never be able to rest.
     [12]God's people must learn to endure. They must also obey his commands and have faith in Jesus.

[13]Then I heard a voice from heaven say, "Put this in writing. From now on, the Lord will bless everyone who has faith in him when they die."

The Spirit answered, "Yes, they will rest from their hard work, and they will be rewarded for what they have done."

The Earth Is Harvested

[14]I looked and saw a bright cloud, and someone who seemed to be the Son of Man[w] was sitting on the cloud. He wore a gold

---

[u]**14.1** *Mount Zion:* Another name for Jerusalem.
[v]**14.4** *the most precious people:* The Greek text has "the first people." The Law of Moses taught that the first-born of all animals and the first part of the harvest were special and belonged to the Lord.   [w]**14.14** *Son of Man:* See the note at 1.13.

crown on his head and held a sharp sickle[x] in his hand. [15]An angel came out of the temple and shouted, "Start cutting with your sickle! Harvest season is here, and all crops on earth are ripe." [16]The one on the cloud swung his sickle and harvested the crops.

[17]Another angel with a sharp sickle then came out of the temple in heaven. [18]After this, an angel with power over fire came from the altar and shouted to the angel who had the sickle. He said, "All grapes on earth are ripe! Harvest them with your sharp sickle." [19]The angel swung his sickle on earth and cut off its grapes. He threw them into a pit[y] where they were trampled on as a sign of God's anger. [20]The pit was outside the city, and when the grapes were mashed, blood flowed out. The blood turned into a river that was about two hundred miles long and almost deep enough to cover a horse.

The Last of the Terrible Troubles

15 After this, I looked at the sky and saw something else that was strange and important. Seven angels were bringing the last seven terrible troubles. When these are ended, God will no longer be angry.

[2]Then I saw something that looked like a glass sea mixed with fire, and people were

> *Revelation fills us with hope because it tells us one day Jesus will set all the wrong right, truth will prevail over lies, and love will win over hate. God himself will wipe away all the tears—there will be no more depression. Regardless of the past or present, we can be confident of a glorious future because it belongs to him!*
>
> ANNE GRAHAM LOTZ

[x]**14.14** *sickle:* A knife with a long curved blade, used to cut grain and other crops. [y]**14.19** *pit:* It was the custom to put grapes in a pit (called a wine press) and stomp on them to make juice that would later turn to wine.

Personal *Concerns*—How should I handle it when I feel rejected or excluded because of my faith? *(Revelation 14.12,13)*

Learn to endure.

We Christians have to make a choice. Will we claim the name of Christ no matter what, or will we be Christians of convenience? In a society that tolerates almost any form of belief or unbelief, this is rarely an issue. But that hasn't always been the case—nor will the Christian life always be so placid. At almost any moment, Christians somewhere in the world are dying for their faith.

John was shown a "last call" scene of what it means to endure in the Christian faith. Angels flew across the sky announcing, "Worship and honor God! The time has come for him to judge everyone" (14.7). Yet Babylon, with its prostitute queen and her dragon, was in power and had many followers (you lived longer that way). But living long on earth wasn't the most important issue: worshiping God was. In this context, an angel shouted, "God's people must learn to endure" (14.12). The angel made no mention of rescue. In fact, he spoke of death. But after that the Holy Spirit promised, "They will rest from their hard work, and they will be rewarded for what they have done" (14.13).

Christians today may suffer minor slights—or major ones. The message from God is the same: Endure. (See also Daniel 6; John 15.18-27; Hebrews 10.32-39; 1 Peter 4.12-19.)

Words To Remember: *God's people must learn to endure.... The Spirit answered, "Yes, they will rest from their hard work, and they will be rewarded for what they have done."*—Revelation 14.12,13

standing on it. They were the ones who had defeated the beast and the idol and the number that tells the name of the beast. God had given them harps, [3]and they were singing the song that his servant Moses and the Lamb had sung. They were singing,

"Lord God All-Powerful,
you have done great
   and marvelous things.
You are the ruler
   of all nations,
and you do what is
   right and fair.
[4]Lord, who doesn't honor
   and praise your name?
You alone are holy,
and all nations will come
   and worship you,
because you have shown
that you judge
   with fairness."

[5]After this, I noticed something else in heaven. The sacred tent used for a temple was open. [6]And the seven angels who were bringing the terrible troubles were coming out of it. They were dressed in robes of pure white linen and wore belts made of pure gold. [7]One of the four living creatures gave each of the seven angels a bowl made of gold. These bowls were filled with the anger of God who lives forever and ever. [8]The temple quickly filled with smoke from the glory and power of God. No one could enter it until the seven angels had finished pouring out the seven last troubles.

The Bowls of God's Anger

16 From the temple I heard a voice shout to the seven angels, "Go and empty the seven bowls of God's anger on the earth."

[2]The first angel emptied his bowl on the earth. At once ugly and painful sores broke out on everyone who had the mark of the beast and worshiped the idol.

[3]The second angel emptied his bowl on the sea. Right away the sea turned into blood like that of a dead person, and every living thing in the sea died.

[4]The third angel emptied his bowl into the rivers and streams. At once they turned to blood. [5]Then I heard the angel, who has power over water, say,

"You have always been,
and you always will be
   the holy God.
You had the right
   to judge in this way.
[6]They poured out the blood[z]
of your people
   and your prophets.
So you gave them blood
   to drink, as they deserve!"
[7]After this, I heard
   the altar shout,
"Yes, Lord God All-Powerful,
your judgments are honest
   and fair."

[8]The fourth angel emptied his bowl on the sun, and it began to scorch people like fire. [9]Everyone was scorched by its great heat, and all of them cursed the name of God who had power over these terrible troubles. But no one turned to God and praised him.

[10]The fifth angel emptied his bowl on the throne of the beast. At once darkness covered its kingdom, and its people began biting their tongues in pain. [11]And because of their painful sores, they cursed the God who rules in heaven. But still they did not stop doing evil things.

[12]The sixth angel emptied his bowl on the great Euphrates River, and it completely dried up to make a road for the kings from the east. [13]An evil spirit that looked like a frog came out of the mouth of the dragon. One also came out of the mouth of the beast, and another out of the mouth of the false prophet. [14]These evil spirits had the power to work miracles. They went to every king on earth, to bring them together for a war against God All-Powerful. But that will be the day of God's great victory.

[15]Remember that Christ says, "When I come, it will surprise you like a thief! But God will bless you, if you are awake and ready. Then you won't have to walk around naked and be ashamed."

[16]Those armies came together in a place that in Hebrew is called Armagedon.[a]

[17]As soon as the seventh angel emptied

---

[z]**16.6** *They poured out the blood*: A way of saying, "They murdered."   [a]**16.16** *Armagedon*: The Hebrew form of the name would be "Har Megiddo," meaning "Hill of Megiddo," where many battles were fought in ancient times (see Judges 5.19; 2 Kings 23.29, 30).

his bowl in the air, a loud voice from the throne in the temple shouted, "It's done!" [18]There were flashes of lightning, roars of thunder, and the worst earthquake in all history. [19]The great city of Babylon split into three parts, and the cities of other nations fell. So God made Babylon drink from the wine cup that was filled with his anger. [20]Every island ran away, and the mountains disappeared. [21]Hailstones, weighing about a hundred pounds each, fell from the sky on people. Finally, the people cursed God, because the hail was so terrible.

The Prostitute and the Beast

17One of the seven angels who had emptied the bowls came over and said to me, "Come on! I will show you how God will punish that shameless prostitute who sits on many oceans. [2]Every king on earth has slept with her, and her shameless ways are like wine that has made everyone on earth drunk."

[3]With the help of the Spirit, the angel took me into the desert, where I saw a woman sitting on a red beast. The beast was covered with names that were an insult to God, and it had seven heads and ten horns. [4]The woman was dressed in purple and scarlet robes, and she wore jewelry made of gold, precious stones, and pearls. In her hand she held a gold cup filled with the filthy and nasty things she had done. [5]On her forehead a mysterious name was written:

I AM THE GREAT CITY OF BABYLON,
THE MOTHER OF EVERY IMMORAL
AND FILTHY THING ON EARTH.

[6]I could tell that the woman was drunk on the blood of God's people who had given their lives for Jesus. This surprising sight amazed me, [7]and the angel said:

Why are you so amazed? I will explain the mystery about this woman and about the beast she is sitting on, with its seven heads and ten horns. [8]The beast you saw is one that used to be and no longer is. It will come back from the deep pit, but only to be destroyed. Everyone on earth whose names were not written in the book of life[b] before the time of creation will be amazed. They will see this beast that used to be and no longer is, but will be once more.

[9]Anyone with wisdom can figure this out. The seven heads that the woman is sitting on stand for seven hills. These heads are also seven kings. [10]Five of the kings are dead. One is ruling now, and the other one has not yet come. But when he does, he will rule for only a little while.

[11]You also saw a beast that used to be and no longer is. That beast is one of the seven kings who will return as the eighth king, but only to be destroyed.

[12]The ten horns that you saw are ten more kings, who have not yet come into power, and they will rule with the beast for only a short time. [13]They all think alike and will give their power and authority to the beast. [14]These kings will go to war against the Lamb. But he will defeat them, because he is Lord over all lords and King over all kings. His followers are chosen and special and faithful.

[15]The oceans that you saw the prostitute sitting on are crowds of people from all races and languages. [16]The ten horns and the beast will start hating the shameless woman. They will strip off her clothes and leave her naked. Then they will eat her flesh and throw the rest of her body into a fire. [17]God is the one who made these kings all think alike and decide to give their power to the beast. And they will do this until what God has said comes true.

[18]The woman you saw is the great city that rules over all kings on earth.

The Fall of Babylon

18I saw another angel come from heaven. This one had great power, and the earth was bright because of his glory. [2]The angel shouted,

"Fallen! Powerful Babylon
     has fallen
and is now the home
     of demons.
It is the den
     of every filthy spirit

---

[b]**17.8** *book of life:* See the note at 3.5.

and of all unclean birds,
  and every dirty
    and hated animal.
³Babylon's evil and immoral wine
    has made all nations drunk.
Every king on earth
    has slept with her,
and every merchant on earth
is rich because of
    her evil desires."

⁴Then I heard another voice
    from heaven shout,
"My people, you must escape
    from Babylon.
Don't take part in her sins
    and share her punishment.
⁵Her sins are piled
    as high as heaven.
God has remembered the evil
    she has done.
⁶Treat her as she
    has treated others.
Make her pay double
    for what she has done.
Make her drink twice as much
of what she mixed
    for others.
⁷That woman honored herself
    with a life of luxury.
Reward her now
    with suffering and pain.

"Deep in her heart
Babylon said,
  'I am the queen!
Never will I be a widow
or know what it means
  to be sad.'
⁸And so, in a single day
she will suffer the pain
    of sorrow, hunger, and death.
Fire will destroy
    her dead body,
because her judge
    is the powerful Lord God."

⁹Every king on earth who slept with her
and shared in her luxury will mourn. They
will weep, when they see the smoke from
that fire. ¹⁰Her sufferings will frighten them,
and they will stand at a distance and say,

"Pity that great
    and powerful city!

Pity Babylon!
In a single hour
    her judgment has come."

¹¹Every merchant on earth will mourn,
because there is no one to buy their goods.
¹²There won't be anyone to buy their gold,
silver, jewels, pearls, fine linen, purple cloth,
silk, scarlet cloth, sweet-smelling wood,
fancy carvings of ivory and wood, as well as
things made of bronze, iron, or marble. ¹³No
one will buy their cinnamon, spices, incense, myrrh, frankincense,ᶜ wine, olive oil,
fine flour, wheat, cattle, sheep, horses, chariots, slaves, and other humans.

¹⁴Babylon, the things
    your heart desired
have all escaped
    from you.
Every luxury
and all your glory
    will be lost forever.
You will never
    get them back.

¹⁵The merchants had become rich because of her. But when they saw her sufferings, they were terrified. They stood at a
distance, crying and mourning. ¹⁶Then they
shouted,

"Pity the great city
    of Babylon!
She dressed in fine linen
and wore purple
    and scarlet cloth.
She had jewelry
    made of gold
and precious stones
    and pearls.
¹⁷Yet in a single hour
    her riches disappeared."

Every ship captain and passenger and
sailor stood at a distance, together with
everyone who does business by traveling on
the sea. ¹⁸When they saw the smoke from
her fire, they shouted, "This was the greatest
city ever!"

ᶜ18.13 *myrrh, frankincense*: Myrrh was a valuable sweet-
smelling powder often used in perfume. Frankincense
was a valuable powder that was burned to make a
sweet smell.

¹⁹They cried loudly, and in their sorrow they threw dust on their heads, as they said,

"Pity the great city
of Babylon!
Everyone who sailed the seas
became rich
from her treasures.
But in a single hour
the city was destroyed.
²⁰The heavens should be happy
with God's people
and apostles and prophets.
God has punished her
for them."

²¹A powerful angel then picked up a huge stone and threw it into the sea. The angel said,

"This is how the great city
of Babylon
will be thrown down,
never to rise again.
²²The music of harps and singers
and of flutes and trumpets
will no longer be heard.
No workers will ever
set up shop in that city,
and the sound
of grinding grain
will be silenced forever.
²³Lamps will no longer shine
anywhere in Babylon,
and couples will never again
say wedding vows there.
Her merchants ruled
the earth,
and by her witchcraft
she fooled all nations.
²⁴On the streets of Babylon
is found the blood
of God's people
and of his prophets,
and everyone else."

19 After this, I heard what sounded like a lot of voices in heaven, and they were shouting,

"Praise the Lord!
To our God belongs
the glorious power to save,
²because his judgments
are honest and fair.

That filthy prostitute
ruined the earth
with shameful deeds.
But God has judged her
and made her pay
the price for murdering
his servants."

³Then the crowd shouted,

"Praise the Lord!
Smoke will never stop rising
from her burning body."

⁴After this, the twenty-four elders and the four living creatures all knelt before the throne of God and worshiped him. They said, "Amen! Praise the Lord!"

The Marriage Supper of the Lamb

⁵From the throne a voice said,

"If you worship
and fear our God,
give praise to him,
no matter who you are."

*On this earth, your body's
a tremendous gift that's
meant to be cherished and
taken care of—but in the
end, its significance pales
in the light of the health
and well-being of your soul.*

KAREN SCALF LINAMEN

⁶Then I heard what seemed to be a large crowd that sounded like a roaring flood and loud thunder all mixed together. They were saying,

"Praise the Lord!
Our Lord God All-Powerful
now rules as king.
⁷So we will be glad and happy
and give him praise.

The wedding day of the Lamb
is here,
    and his bride is ready.
[8]She will be given
    a wedding dress
made of pure
    and shining linen.
This linen stands for
the good things
    God's people have done."

[9]Then the angel told me, "Put this in writing. God will bless everyone who is invited to the wedding feast of the Lamb." The angel also said, "These things that God has said are true."

[10]I knelt at the feet of the angel and began to worship him. But the angel said, "Don't do that! I am a servant, just like you and everyone else who tells about Jesus. Don't worship anyone but God. Everyone who tells about Jesus does it by the power of the Spirit."

The Rider on the White Horse

[11]I looked and saw that heaven was open, and a white horse was there. Its rider was called Faithful and True, and he is always fair when he judges or goes to war. [12]He had eyes like flames of fire, and he was wearing a lot of crowns. His name was written on him, but he was the only one who knew what the name meant. [13]The rider wore a robe that was covered with[d] blood, and he was known as "The Word of God." [14]He was followed by armies from heaven that rode on horses and were dressed in pure white linen. [15]From his mouth a sharp sword went out to attack the nations. He will rule them with an iron rod and will show the fierce anger of God All-Powerful by trampling the grapes in the pit where wine is made. [16]On the part of the robe that covered his thigh was written, "KING OF KINGS AND LORD OF LORDS."

[17]I then saw an angel standing on the sun, and he shouted to all the birds flying in the sky, "Come and join in God's great feast! [18]You can eat the flesh of kings, rulers, leaders, horses, riders, free people, slaves, important people, and everyone else."

[19]I also saw the beast and all kings of the earth come together. They fought against the rider on the white horse and against his army. [20]But the beast was captured and so was the false prophet. This is the same prophet who had worked miracles for the beast, so that he could fool everyone who had the mark of the beast and worshiped the idol. The beast and the false prophet were thrown alive into a lake of burning sulfur. [21]But the rest of their army was killed by the sword that came from the mouth of the rider on the horse. Then birds stuffed themselves on the dead bodies.

The Thousand Years

20 I saw an angel come down from heaven, carrying the key to the deep pit and a big chain. [2]He chained the dragon for a thousand years. It is that old snake, who is also known as the devil and Satan. [3]Then the angel threw the dragon into the pit. He locked and sealed it, so that a thousand years would go by before the dragon could fool the nations again. But after that, it would have to be set free for a little while.

[4]I saw thrones, and sitting on those thrones were the ones who had been given the right to judge. I also saw the souls of the people who had their heads cut off because they had told about Jesus and preached God's message. They were the same ones who had not worshiped the beast or the idol, and they had refused to let its mark be put on their hands or foreheads. They will come to life and rule with Christ for a thousand years.

[5-6]These people are the first to be raised to life, and they are especially blessed and holy. The second death[e] has no power over them. They will be priests for God and Christ and will rule with them for a thousand years.

No other dead people were raised to life until a thousand years later.

Satan Is Defeated

[7]At the end of the thousand years, Satan will be set free. [8]He will fool the countries of Gog and Magog, which are at the far ends of the earth, and their people will follow him into battle. They will have as many followers

---

[d]**19.13** *covered with:* Some manuscripts have "sprinkled with."   [e]**20.5,6** *second death:* See the note at 2.11.

as there are grains of sand along the beach, [9]and they will march all the way across the earth. They will surround the camp of God's people and the city that his people love. But fire will come down from heaven and destroy the whole army. [10]Then the devil who fooled them will be thrown into the lake of fire and burning sulfur. He will be there with the beast and the false prophet, and they will be in pain day and night forever and ever.

The Judgment at the Great White Throne

[11]I saw a great white throne with someone sitting on it. Earth and heaven tried to run away, but there was no place for them to go. [12]I also saw all the dead people standing in front of that throne. Every one of them was there, no matter who they had once been. Several books were opened, and then the book of life[f] was opened. The dead were judged by what those books said they had done. [13]The sea gave up the dead people who were in it, and death and its kingdom also gave up their dead. Then everyone was judged by what they had done. [14]Afterwards, death and its kingdom were thrown into the lake of fire. This is the second death.[g] [15]Anyone whose name wasn't written in the book of life was thrown into the lake of fire.

The New Heaven and the New Earth

21 I saw a new heaven and a new earth. The first heaven and the first earth had disappeared, and so had the sea. [2]Then I saw New Jerusalem, that holy city, coming down from God in heaven. It was like a bride dressed in her wedding gown and ready to meet her husband.

[3]I heard a loud voice shout from the throne:

God's home is now with his people. He will live with them, and they will be his own. Yes, God will make his home among his people. [4]He will wipe all tears from their eyes, and there will be no more death, suffering, crying, or pain. These things of the past are gone forever.

[5]Then the one sitting on the throne said:

I am making everything new. Write down what I have said. My words are true and can be trusted. [6]Everything is finished! I am Alpha and Omega,[h] the beginning and the end. I will freely

---

[f]**20.12** *book of life*: See the note at 3.5.
[g]**20.14** *second death*: See the note at 2.11.
[h]**21.6** *Alpha and Omega*: See the note at 1.8.

MARRIAGE—My husband doesn't share my passion for spiritual things. How can I deal with my frustration and sadness? *(Revelation 21.1-4)*

Remember that God himself will wipe away your tears.
All things here come to an end—even our pain. But God and his people live forever. If your husband is a Christian, God will someday heal him of his lack of passion. By the time you are living in the new heaven and new earth, your husband will know with full intensity the grace of God. And you'll be able to worship God together, joining all the creatures of heaven. If your husband is not yet a Christian, you can continue to pray that God will draw him to himself so you can share that day.

Meanwhile, you'll feel the loss of all that could be but is not. When it seems appropriate, mention this sense of loss to your husband in a way that expresses your love and your longing to share such an important part of your life with the most important person in your life.

Continue to talk to God about your feelings. God can make all things new. He will make a new heaven and a new earth and a new city of Jerusalem. And he can even bring new faith to your husband. (See also Job 6.14-21; James 5.7-11.)

Words To Remember: *God will make his home among his people. He will wipe all tears from their eyes, and there will be no more death, suffering, crying, or pain. These things of the past are gone forever.—Revelation 21.3,4*

give water from the life-giving fountain to everyone who is thirsty. [7]All who win the victory will be given these blessings. I will be their God, and they will be my people.

[8]But I will tell you what will happen to cowards and to everyone who is unfaithful or dirty-minded or who murders or is sexually immoral or uses witchcraft or worships idols or tells lies. They will be thrown into that lake of fire and burning sulfur. This is the second death.[i]

The New Jerusalem

[9]I saw one of the seven angels who had the bowls filled with the seven last terrible troubles. The angel came to me and said, "Come on! I will show you the one who will be the bride and wife of the Lamb." [10]Then with the help of the Spirit, he took me to the top of a very high mountain. There he showed me the holy city of Jerusalem coming down from God in heaven.

[11]The glory of God made the city bright. It was dazzling and crystal clear like a pre-

cious jasper stone. [12]The city had a high and thick wall with twelve gates, and each one of them was guarded by an angel. On each of the gates was written the name of one of the twelve tribes of Israel. [13]Three of these gates were on the east, three were on the north, three more were on the south, and the other three were on the west. [14]The city was built on twelve foundation stones. On each of the stones was written the name of one of the Lamb's twelve apostles.

[15]The angel who spoke to me had a gold measuring stick to measure the city and its gates and its walls. [16]The city was shaped like a cube, because it was just as high as it was wide. When the angel measured the city, it was about fifteen hundred miles high and fifteen hundred miles wide. [17]Then the angel measured the wall, and by our measurements it was about two hundred sixteen feet high.

[18]The wall was built of jasper, and the city was made of pure gold, clear as crystal. [19]Each of the twelve foundations was a pre-

---

[i]21.8 *second death*: See the note at 2.11.

MARRIAGE—How can I lead my unbelieving husband to Christ without offending him? *(Revelation 21.9—22.21)*

Show him your hope of eternity.

It's hard to want the faith of someone who's full of fear. The book of Revelation offers the best cure for fear. It admits that life here can be awful, that it ends in death. But then the good news begins. Death, for the Christian, isn't the end; it's only the beginning. God will make a new heaven and a new earth—both exquisitely beautiful. He'll fill it with his believers. And life with him will never end.

This hope of eternity can take the edge off many of our fears. We spend much of our time trying to avoid discomfort and death. While we need to be prudent about such things, the book of Revelation shows us that our hope goes far beyond the small things of our current existence. Allow this hope, this perspective, to pervade your life, especially as you relate to your husband.

When it seems appropriate, explain to him your faith in Jesus who is "the first and the last, the beginning and the end" (22.13). Because Christ is eternal, you, too, can take the long view that includes eternity in heaven with him. Continue to pray that your husband will accept Christ's invitation to real life. (See also Genesis 39; 41.39; Song of Songs 2.16—3.4; John 13.1-17; 1 Peter 3.1-6.)

Words To Remember: *Only those whose names are written in the Lamb's book of life will be in the city.*
The Spirit and the bride say, "Come!"
Everyone who hears this should say, "Come!"
If you are thirsty, come! If you want life-giving water, come and take it. It's free!
—Revelation 21.27; 22.17

cious stone. The first was jasper,[j] the second was sapphire, the third was agate, the fourth was emerald, [20]the fifth was onyx, the sixth was carnelian, the seventh was chrysolite, the eighth was beryl, the ninth was topaz, the tenth was chrysoprase, the eleventh was jacinth, and the twelfth was amethyst. [21]Each of the twelve gates was a solid pearl. The streets of the city were made of pure gold, clear as crystal.

[22]I did not see a temple there. The Lord God All-Powerful and the Lamb were its temple. [23]And the city did not need the sun or the moon. The glory of God was shining on it, and the Lamb was its light.

[24]Nations will walk by the light of that city, and kings will bring their riches there. [25]Its gates are always open during the day, and night never comes. [26]The glorious treasures of nations will be brought into the city. [27]But nothing unworthy will be allowed to enter. No one who is dirty-minded or who tells lies will be there. Only those whose names are written in the Lamb's book of life[k] will be in the city.

22 The angel showed me a river that was crystal clear, and its waters gave life. The river came from the throne where God and the Lamb were seated. [2]Then it flowed down the middle of the city's main street. On each side of the river are trees[l] that grow a different kind of fruit each month of the year. The fruit gives life, and the leaves are used as medicine to heal the nations.

I used to think God would use me to heal. But now I realize my job is to let him heal. There's so much that's out of my control, but all healing is in his hand.

Dr. Lori Hansen

[3]God's curse will no longer be on the people of that city. He and the Lamb will be seated there on their thrones, and its people will worship God [4]and will see him face to face. God's name will be written on the foreheads of the people. [5]Never again will night appear, and no one who lives there will ever need a lamp or the sun. The Lord God will be their light, and they will rule forever.

The Coming of Christ

[6]Then I was told:

These words are true and can be trusted. The Lord God controls the spirits of his prophets, and he is the one who sent his angel to show his servants what must happen right away. [7]Remember, I am coming soon! God will bless everyone who pays attention to the message of this book.

[8]My name is John, and I am the one who heard and saw these things. Then after I had heard and seen all this, I knelt down and began to worship at the feet of the angel who had shown it to me.

[9]But the angel said,

Don't do that! I am a servant, just like you. I am the same as a follower or a prophet or anyone else who obeys what is written in this book. God is the one you should worship.

[10]Don't keep the prophecies in this book a secret. These things will happen soon.

[11]Evil people will keep on being evil, and everyone who is dirty-minded will still be dirty-minded. But good people will keep on doing right, and God's people will always be holy.

[12]Then I was told:

I am coming soon! And when I come, I will reward everyone for what they have done. [13]I am Alpha and Omega,[m] the first and the last, the beginning and the end.

[14]God will bless all who have washed their robes. They will each have the right to eat fruit from the tree

---

[j]**21.19** *jasper:* The precious and semi-precious stones mentioned in verses 19, 20 are of different colors. *Jasper* is usually green or clear; *sapphire* is blue; *agate* has circles of brown and white; *emerald* is green; *onyx* has different bands of color; *carnelian* is deep-red or reddish-white; *chrysolite* is olive-green; *beryl* is green or bluish-green; *topaz* is yellow; *chrysoprase* is apple-green; *jacinth* is reddish-orange; and *amethyst* is deep purple. [k]**21.27** *book of life:* See the note at 3.5. [l]**22.2** *trees:* The Greek has "tree," which is used in a collective sense of trees on both sides of the heavenly river. [m]**22.13** *Alpha and Omega:* See the note at 1.8.

that gives life, and they can enter the gates of the city. [15]But outside the city will be dogs, witches, immoral people, murderers, idol worshipers, and everyone who loves to tell lies and do wrong.

[16]I am Jesus! And I am the one who sent my angel to tell all of you these things for the churches. I am David's Great Descendant,[n] and I am also the bright morning star.[o]

[17]The Spirit and the bride say, "Come!" Everyone who hears this[p] should say, "Come!"

If you are thirsty, come! If you want life-giving water, come and take it. It's free!

[18]Here is my warning for everyone who hears the prophecies in this book:

If you add anything to them, God will make you suffer all the terrible troubles written in this book. [19]If you take anything away from these prophecies, God will not let you have part in the life-giving tree and in the holy city described in this book.

[20]The one who has spoken these things says, "I am coming soon!"

So, Lord Jesus, please come soon! [21]I pray that the Lord Jesus will be kind to all of you.

---

[n]22.16 *David's Great Descendant*: See the note at 5.5. [o]22.16 *the bright morning star*: Probably thought of as the brightest star (see 2.27, 28). [p]22.17 *who hears this*: The reading of the book of Revelation in a service of worship.

Index to Words To Remember

Want to carry God's words with you on an index card? Or memorize a verse a day or one per week? This listing, in Bible book order, will help.

✺OLD TESTAMENT✺

GENESIS

So God created humans to be like himself; he made men and women.
—GENESIS 1.27

The LORD God said, "It isn't good for the man to live alone. I need to make a suitable partner for him."
—GENESIS 2.18

That's why a man will leave his own father and mother. He marries a woman, and the two of them become like one person.
—GENESIS 2.24

They said: Let's build a city with a tower that reaches to the sky! . . . We'll become famous.
—GENESIS 11.3,4

The LORD said to Abram: . . . I will bless you and make your descendants into a great nation. You will become famous and be a blessing to others.
—GENESIS 12.1,2

Abram said to Lot, "We are close relatives. We shouldn't argue, and our men shouldn't be fighting one another. There is plenty of land for you to choose from. Let's separate. If you go north, I'll go south; if you go south, I'll go north."
—GENESIS 13.8,9

"Don't hurt the boy or harm him in any way!" the angel said. "Now I know that you truly obey God, because you were willing to offer him your only son."
—GENESIS 22.12

Isaac took Rebekah into the tent where his mother had lived before she died, and Rebekah became his wife. He loved her and was comforted over the loss of his mother.
—GENESIS 24.67

The king told Joseph, "God is the one who has shown you these things. No one else is as wise as you are or knows as much as you do."
—GENESIS 41.39

"You tried to harm me, but God made it turn out for the best, so that he could save all these people, as he is now doing."
—GENESIS 50.20

EXODUS

Miriam the sister of Aaron was a prophet.
—EXODUS 15.20

Having them to share the load will make your work easier.
—EXODUS 18.22

I am the LORD your God, and I demand all your love.
—EXODUS 20.5

Work the first six days of the week, but rest and relax on the seventh day.
—EXODUS 23.12

So even though the LORD had threatened to destroy the people, he changed his mind and let them live.
—EXODUS 32.14

LEVITICUS

Stop being angry and don't try to take revenge. I am the LORD, and I command you to love others as much as you love yourself.
—LEVITICUS 19.18

[The land] all belongs to me—it isn't your land, and you only live there for a little while.
—LEVITICUS 25.23

I have set you free; now walk with your heads held high.
—LEVITICUS 26.13

NUMBERS

I pray that the LORD will bless and protect you, and that he will show you mercy and kindness. May the LORD be good to you and give you peace.
—NUMBERS 6.24-26

The LORD answered, "I can do anything! Watch and you'll see my words come true."
—NUMBERS 11.23

He [the Lord] said, "My servant Moses is the leader of my people. He sees me face to face, and everything I say to him is perfectly clear. You have no right to criticize my servant Moses."
—NUMBERS 12.6-8

Show us your great power, LORD. You promised that you love to show mercy and kindness.
—NUMBERS 14.17,18

The Israelites had complained against the LORD, and he had shown them his holy power by giving them water to drink.
—NUMBERS 20.13

DEUTERONOMY

Do not tell lies about others. Do not want anything that belongs to someone else.
—DEUTERONOMY 5.20,21

Listen, Israel! The LORD our God is the only true God! So love the LORD your God with all your heart, soul, and strength.
—DEUTERONOMY 6.4,5

After you eat and are full, give praise to the LORD your God.
—DEUTERONOMY 8.10

When you become successful, don't say, "I'm rich, and I've earned it all myself." Instead, remember that the LORD your God gives you the strength to make a living.
—DEUTERONOMY 8.17,18

If you forget to bring in a stack of harvested grain, don't go back in the field to get it. Leave it for the poor, including foreigners, orphans, and widows, and the LORD will make you successful in everything you do.
—DEUTERONOMY 24.19

Be completely faithful to the LORD your God, love him, and do whatever he tells you. The LORD is the only one who can give life.
—DEUTERONOMY 30.20

Be brave and strong! Don't be afraid of the nations on the other side of the Jordan. The LORD your God will always be at your side, and he will never abandon you.
—DEUTERONOMY 31.6

JOSHUA

Be strong and brave. Don't ever be afraid or discouraged! I am the LORD your God, and I will be there to help you wherever you go.
—JOSHUA 1.9

Someday your children will ask, "Why are these rocks here?" Then you can tell them . . . what happened here today.
—JOSHUA 4.6,7

I cannot help you anymore until you do exactly what I have said.
—JOSHUA 7.12

Yes, when the LORD makes a promise, he does what he has promised.
—JOSHUA 23.15,16

JUDGES

Deborah the wife of Lappidoth was a prophet and a leader of Israel.
—JUDGES 4.4

Even those who carry water to the animals will tell you, "The LORD has won victories, and so has Israel."
—JUDGES 5.11

Then the LORD himself said, "Gideon, you will be strong, because I am giving you the power to rescue Israel from the Midianites."
—JUDGES 6.14

RUTH

Ruth answered, "I will go where you go, I will live where you live; your people will be my people, your God will be my God."
—RUTH 1.16

Ruth answered, "I'll do whatever you say." She went out to the place where Boaz was working and did what Naomi had told her.
—RUTH 3.5,6

He will make you happy and take care of you in your old age, because he is the son of your daughter-in-law. And she loves you more than seven sons of your own would love you.
—RUTH 4.15

1 SAMUEL

"Follow me! The LORD is going to let us win."
—1 SAMUEL 14.11,12

"Does the LORD really want sacrifices and offerings? No! He doesn't want your sacrifices. He wants you to obey him."
—1 SAMUEL 15.22

"People judge others by what they look like, but I judge people by what is in their hearts."
—1 SAMUEL 16.7

"Find me someone who is good at playing the harp and bring him here. . . . The LORD is with him."
—1 SAMUEL 16.17,18

David answered [Goliath], "You've come out to fight me with a sword and a spear and a dagger. But I've come out to fight you in the name of the LORD All-Powerful. . . . The LORD always wins his battles, and he will help us defeat you."
—1 SAMUEL 17.45,47

I pray that the LORD will bless you.
—1 SAMUEL 20.13

I'll let the LORD decide which one of us has done right.
—1 SAMUEL 24.12

I pray that you won't ever do anything evil as long as you live. The LORD your God will keep you safe.
—1 SAMUEL 25.28,29

2 SAMUEL

Jonathan, I miss you most! I loved you like a brother.
—2 SAMUEL 1.26

LORD All-Powerful, you are God. You have promised me some very good things, and you can be trusted to do what you promise.
—2 SAMUEL 7.28

David said, "Don't be afraid. I'll be kind to you."
—2 SAMUEL 9.7

A wise woman shouted from the top of the wall, "Listen to me! Listen to me!"
—2 SAMUEL 20.16

1 KINGS

Please make me wise and teach me the difference between right and wrong.
—1 KINGS 3.9

When the people [of Israel] realized that Rehoboam would not listen to them, they shouted: ". . . Let's go home! Rehoboam can rule his own people."
—1 KINGS 12.15

The LORD kept the promise that his prophet Elijah had made, and she did not run out of flour or oil.
—1 KINGS 17.16

Elijah said, "I'm a servant of the living LORD All-Powerful, and I swear in his name that I will meet with Ahab today."
—1 KINGS 18.15

The LORD asked, "Elijah, why are you here?" Elijah answered, "LORD God All-Powerful, I've always done my best to obey you."
—1 KINGS 19.13,14

2 KINGS

"Maybe there's something I can do to help," Elisha said.
—2 KINGS 4.2

Then everyone in every kingdom on earth will know that you are the only God.
—2 KINGS 19.19

1 CHRONICLES

While the sacred chest was being carried into Jerusalem, everyone was celebrating by shouting and playing music on horns, trumpets, cymbals, harps, and other stringed instruments.
—1 CHRONICLES 15.28

Solomon, my son, I now pray that the LORD your God will be with you. . . . May he give you wisdom and knowledge.
—1 CHRONICLES 22.11,12

But why should we be happy that we have
given you these gifts? They belong to you, and
we have only given back what is already yours.
—1 CHRONICLES 29.14

2 CHRONICLES

If my own people will humbly pray and turn
back to me and stop sinning, then I will answer
them from heaven. I will forgive them and
make their land fertile once again.
—2 CHRONICLES 7.14

You won't even have to fight. Just take your
positions and watch the LORD rescue you from
your enemy. Don't be afraid. Just do as you're
told. And as you march out tomorrow, the
LORD will be there with you.
—2 CHRONICLES 20.17

They bowed down and joyfully sang praises to
the LORD.
—2 CHRONICLES 29.30

EZRA

They praised the LORD and gave thanks as
they took turns singing: "The LORD is good!
His faithful love for Israel will last forever."
—EZRA 3.11

So Zerubbabel the governor and Joshua the
priest urged the people to start working on the
temple again.
—EZRA 5.2

Ezra had spent his entire life studying and
obeying the Law of the LORD and teaching it
to others.
—EZRA 7.10

We humbled ourselves and asked God to bring
us and our children safely to Jerusalem with all
of our possessions.
—EZRA 8.21

NEHEMIAH

LORD God of heaven, you are great and
fearsome. And you faithfully keep your
promises to everyone who loves you and obeys
your commands.
—NEHEMIAH 1.5

But we kept on praying to our God, and we
also stationed guards day and night.
—NEHEMIAH 4.9

I continued, "What you have done is wrong!
We must honor our God by the way we live, so
the Gentiles can't find fault with us."
—NEHEMIAH 5.9

"Stand and shout praises to your LORD, the
eternal God! Praise his wonderful name,
though he is greater than words can express."
—NEHEMIAH 9.5

God had made the people very happy, and so
on that day they celebrated and offered many
sacrifices. The women and children joined in
the festivities, and joyful shouts could be heard
far from the city of Jerusalem.
—NEHEMIAH 12.43

ESTHER

[Mordecai said to Esther,] "It could be that you
were made queen for a time like this!"
—ESTHER 4.14

Esther answered, "Your Majesty, if you really
care for me and are willing to help, you can
save me and my people."
—ESTHER 7.3

JOB

[Job] said: "We bring nothing at birth; we take
nothing with us at death. The LORD alone
gives and takes. Praise the name of the LORD!"
—JOB 1.21

My friends, I am desperate, and you should
help me. . . . I am like a caravan, lost in the
desert while searching for water.
—JOB 6.14,18

The wisest thing you can do is to keep quiet
and listen to my argument.
—JOB 13.5,6

I wish that my words could be written down or
chiseled into rock. I know that my Savior lives,
and at the end he will stand on this earth. My
flesh may be destroyed, yet from this body I will
see God. Yes, I will see him for myself, and I
long for that moment.
—JOB 19.23-27

God is always at work, though I never see him.
But he knows what I am doing, and when he
tests me, I will be pure as gold.
—JOB 23.9,10

When the ocean was born, I set its boundaries
and wrapped it in blankets of thickest fog. . . .
I am the LORD All-Powerful.
—JOB 38.8,9; 40.1

Job said: "No one can oppose you, because you
have the power to do what you want. . . . I
have talked about things that are far beyond
my understanding.
—JOB 42.1-3

The LORD said to Eliphaz: What my servant
Job has said about me is true, but I am angry at
you and your two friends for not telling the truth.
—JOB 42.7

PSALMS

They are like trees growing beside a stream,
trees that produce fruit in season and always
have leaves. Those people succeed in everything
they do.
—PSALM 1.3

You listen to the longings of those who suffer.
You offer them hope, and you pay attention to
their cries for help.
—PSALM 10.17

When I cried out, he listened and did not turn
away.
—PSALM 22.24

You treat me to a feast, while my enemies
watch. You honor me as your guest, and you
fill my cup until it overflows.
—PSALM 23.5

You will show the right path to all who worship
you.
—PSALM 25.12

Show that I am right, LORD! I stay true to
myself, and I have trusted you without
doubting. Test my thoughts and find out what I
am like. I never forget your kindness, and I am
always faithful to you.
—PSALM 26.1-3

In my heart, I am thirsty for you, the living
God. When will I see your face?
—PSALM 42.2

Don't let it bother you when others get rich
and live in luxury.
—PSALM 49.16

You are kind, God! Please have pity on me. You
are always merciful! Please wipe away my sins.
—PSALM 51.1

You find families for those who are lonely.
—PSALM 68.6

I have relied on you from the day I was
born. . . . Let me tell future generations about
your mighty power. Your deeds of kindness are
known in the heavens. No one is like you!
—PSALM 71.6,18,19

God is truly good to Israel, especially to
everyone with a pure heart.
—PSALM 73.1

My body and mind may fail, but you are my
strength and my choice forever.
—PSALM 73.26

LORD God All-Powerful, my King and my
God, . . . you bless everyone who lives in your
house, and they sing your praises.
—PSALM 84.3,4

You are ready to rescue everyone who worships
you, so that you will live with us in all of your
glory. Love and loyalty will come together;
goodness and peace will unite.
—PSALM 85.9,10

Live under the protection of God Most High
and stay in the shadow of God All-Powerful.
—PSALM 91.1

Each day that we live, he provides for our needs
and gives us the strength of a young eagle.
—PSALM 103.5

I hope my thoughts will please you, because
you are the one who makes me glad.
—PSALM 104.34

You should praise the LORD for his love and for
the wonderful things he does for all of us.
—PSALM 107.8

Your love reaches higher than the heavens, and
your loyalty extends beyond the clouds.
—PSALM 108.4

Your word is a lamp that gives light wherever I
walk.
—PSALM 119.105

Only God works great miracles. God's love
never fails.
—PSALM 136.4

When I asked for your help, you answered my
prayer and gave me courage. . . . You, LORD,
will always treat me with kindness. Your love
never fails.
—PSALM 138.3,8

You are the one who put me together inside my
mother's body, and I praise you because of the
wonderful way you created me.
—PSALM 139.13,14

I was secretly woven together deep in the earth
below, but with your own eyes you saw my body
being formed.
—PSALM 139.15,16

PROVERBS

My child, you must follow and treasure my
teachings and my instructions.
—PROVERBS 2.1

Do all you can for everyone who deserves your
help. . . . You will be praised if you are wise.
—PROVERBS 3.27,35

Don't follow the bad example of cruel and evil
people. Turn aside and keep going. Stay away
from them.
—PROVERBS 4.14,15

The lifestyle of good people is like sunlight at
dawn that keeps getting brighter until broad
daylight.
—PROVERBS 4.18

The LORD sees everything, and he watches us
closely.
—PROVERBS 5.21

Kind words are good medicine.
—PROVERBS 15.4

Share your plans with the LORD, and you will
succeed.
—PROVERBS 16.3

A dry crust of bread eaten in peace and quiet is
better than a feast eaten where everyone
argues.
—PROVERBS 17.1

A friend is always a friend.
—PROVERBS 17.17

Don't make friends with anyone who has a bad
temper. You might turn out like them and get
caught in a trap.
—PROVERBS 22.24,25

Pay attention to your father, and don't neglect
your mother when she grows old.
—PROVERBS 23.22

You can trust a friend who corrects you, but
kisses from an enemy are nothing but lies.
—PROVERBS 27.6

Just as iron sharpens iron, friends sharpen the
minds of each other. . . . You see your face in a
mirror and your thoughts in the minds of
others.
—PROVERBS 27.17,19

Honest correction is appreciated more than
flattery.
—PROVERBS 28.23

Charm can be deceiving, and beauty fades
away, but a woman who honors the LORD
deserves to be praised.
—PROVERBS 31.30

ECCLESIASTES

The best thing we can do is to enjoy eating,
drinking, and working. I believe these are
God's gifts to us.
—ECCLESIASTES 2.24

Everything on earth has its own time and its
own season.
—ECCLESIASTES 3.1

A rope made from three strands of cord is hard
to break.
—ECCLESIASTES 4.12

It's better to enjoy what we have than to
always want something else, because that
makes no more sense than chasing the wind.
—ECCLESIASTES 6.9

Having wisdom is better than an inheritance.
Wisdom will protect you just like money;
knowledge with good sense will lead you to life.
Think of what God has done!
—ECCLESIASTES 7.11-13

*Keep your Creator in mind while you are
young!*
—ECCLESIASTES 12.1

SONG OF SONGS

*My darling, you are lovely, so very lovely—
your eyes are those of a dove.*
—SONG OF SONGS 1.15

*While in bed at night, I reached for the one I
love with heart and soul.*
—SONG OF SONGS 3.1

*His kisses are sweet. I desire him so much! . . .
He is my lover and friend.*
—SONG OF SONGS 5.16

*The passion of love bursting into flame is more
powerful than death, stronger than the grave.*
—SONG OF SONGS 8.6

*She isn't a wall that we can defend behind a
silver shield. Neither is she a room that we can
protect behind a wooden door.*
—SONG OF SONGS 8.9

ISAIAH

*But the LORD will still give you proof. A virgin
is pregnant; she will have a son and will name
him Immanuel.*
—ISAIAH 7.14

*The Spirit of the LORD will be with him to give
him understanding, wisdom, and insight. He
will be powerful, and he will know and honor
the LORD.*
—ISAIAH 11.2

*But those who trust the LORD will find new
strength. They will be strong like eagles soaring
upward on wings; they will walk and run
without getting tired.*
—ISAIAH 40.31

*When you cross deep rivers, I will be with you,
and you won't drown. When you walk through
fire, you won't be burned or scorched by the
flames. . . . To me, you are very dear, and I
love you.*
—ISAIAH 43.2,4

*I have told you what to say, and I will keep you
safe in the palm of my hand.*
—ISAIAH 51.16

*He was wounded and crushed because of our
sins; by taking our punishment, he made us
completely well.*
—ISAIAH 53.5

*If you are thirsty, come and drink water! If you
don't have any money, come, eat what you
want! Drink wine and milk without paying a
cent. Why waste your money on what really
isn't food? Why work hard for something that
doesn't satisfy? Listen carefully to me, and you
will enjoy the very best foods.*
—ISAIAH 55.1,2

*When you are set free, you will celebrate and
travel home in peace. Mountains and hills will
sing as you pass by, and trees will clap.*
—ISAIAH 55.12

*He sent me to give them flowers in place of
their sorrow, olive oil in place of tears, and
joyous praise in place of broken hearts.*
—ISAIAH 61.3

JEREMIAH

*If I tell you to go and speak to someone, then
go! . . . I promise to be with you and keep you
safe, so don't be afraid.*
—JEREMIAH 1.7,8

*LORD All-Powerful, you test those who do right,
and you know every heart and mind. I have
told you my complaints, so let me watch you
take revenge on my enemies.*
—JEREMIAH 20.12

*People of Jerusalem, I, the LORD, give you the
choice of life or death.*
—JEREMIAH 21.8

*My words are a powerful fire; they are a
hammer that shatters rocks.*
—JEREMIAH 23.29

*I will bless you with a future filled with hope—
a future of success, not of suffering. You will
turn back to me and ask for help, and I will
answer your prayers.*
—JEREMIAH 29.11,12

*I will make their thoughts and desires pure.
Then they will realize that, for their own good
and the good of their children, they must
worship only me. They will even be afraid to
turn away from me. I will make an agreement*

with them that will never end, and I won't ever
stop doing good things for them.
—JEREMIAH 32.39-41

I am the LORD, and I created the whole world.
Ask me, and I will tell you things that you
don't know and can't find out.
—JEREMIAH 33.1-3

LAMENTATIONS
Zion, how can I comfort you? How great is
your pain?
—LAMENTATIONS 2.13

We should think about the way we are living,
and turn back to the LORD.
—LAMENTATIONS 3.40

You will rule forever, LORD! You are King for all
time. . . . Bring us back to you! Give us a fresh
start.
—LAMENTATIONS 5.19,21

EZEKIEL
[The Lord said:] "Ezekiel, I am sending you to
the people of Israel. . . . Be brave and preach
my message to them, whether they choose to
listen or not."
—EZEKIEL 2.3,6,7

Then I watched the brightness of the LORD's
glory move from the entrance of the temple and
stop above the winged creatures. They spread
their wings and flew into the air with the
wheels at their side.
—EZEKIEL 10.18,19

Only those who sin will be put to death.
Children won't suffer for the sins of their
parents, and parents won't suffer for the sins of
their children. Good people will be rewarded
for what they do, and evil people will be
punished for what they do.
—EZEKIEL 18.20

I, the LORD God, will put breath in you, and
once again you will live.
—EZEKIEL 37.5

The LORD's Spirit lifted me to my feet and
carried me to the inner courtyard, where I saw
that the LORD's glory had filled the temple.
—EZEKIEL 43.5

DANIEL
"Our God, your name will be praised forever
and forever. You are all-powerful, and you
know everything. You control human events."
—DANIEL 2.20,21

He is the living God, the one who lives forever.
His power and his kingdom will never end. He
rescues people and sets them free by working
great miracles.
—DANIEL 6.26,27

The angel touched me a second time and said,
"Don't be frightened! God thinks highly of you,
and he intends this for your good, so be brave
and strong."
—DANIEL 10.18,19

Everyone who has been wise will shine as
bright as the sky above, and everyone who has
led others to please God will shine like the
stars.
—DANIEL 12.3

HOSEA
Israel will turn back to the LORD their God
and to David their king. At that time they will
come to the LORD with fear and trembling, and
he will be good to them.
—HOSEA 3.5

You have rejected me, but my anger is gone; I
will heal you and love you without limit.
—HOSEA 14.4

JOEL
The LORD said: It isn't too late. You can still
return to me with all your heart.
—JOEL 2.12

I, the LORD your God, will make up for the
losses caused by those swarms and swarms of
locusts I sent to attack you. . . . Then you will
praise me for the wonderful things I have done.
Never again will you be put to shame.
—JOEL 2.25,26

I will give my Spirit to everyone. Your sons and
daughters will prophesy. Your old men will have
dreams, and your young men will see visions.
In those days I will even give my Spirit to my
servants, both men and women.
—JOEL 2.28,29

AMOS

*I chose some of you to be prophets. . . . I, the
LORD, have spoken!*
—AMOS 2.11

*Choose good instead of evil! See that justice is
done.*
—AMOS 5.15

*Do you . . . feel safe and at ease? Everyone
bows down to you, and you think you are
better than any other nation. But you are in
for trouble!*
—AMOS 6.1

OBADIAH

*They are my people, and you were cruel to
them. . . . The day is coming when I, the
LORD, will judge.*
—OBADIAH 13,15

JONAH

*Jonah answered, "I'm a Hebrew, and I worship
the LORD God of heaven, who made the sea
and the dry land."*
—JONAH 1.9

*When I was in trouble, LORD, I prayed to you,
and you listened to me. . . . I begged for your
help, and you answered my prayer.*
—JONAH 2.2

*You are a kind and merciful God, and you are
very patient. You always show love.*
—JONAH 4.2

*But the LORD said: . . . In that city of Nineveh
there are more than a hundred twenty
thousand people who cannot tell right from
wrong, and many cattle are also there. Don't
you think I should be concerned about that big
city?*
—JONAH 4.10,11

MICAH

*Everyone will find rest . . . and they will live in
peace. This is a solemn promise of the LORD
All-Powerful.*
—Micah 4.4

*Like a shepherd taking care of his sheep, this
ruler will lead and care for his people by the*
*power and glorious name of the LORD his God.
His people will live securely, and the whole
earth will know his true greatness, because he
will bring peace.*
—MICAH 5.4,5

*God has told us what is right and what he
demands: "See that justice is done, let mercy be
your first concern, and humbly obey your God."*
—MICAH 6.8

*God, no one is like you. . . . You freely forgive
our sin and guilt. . . . You will trample on our
sins and throw them in the sea.*
—MICAH 7.18,19

NAHUM

*The LORD is powerful, yet patient; he makes
sure that the guilty are always punished.
He can be seen in storms and in whirlwinds;
clouds are the dust from his feet.*
—NAHUM 1.3

HABAKKUK

*Our LORD, how long must I beg for your help
before you listen? How long before you save us
from all this violence?*
—HABAKKUK 1.2

Only those who live by faith are acceptable to me.
—HABAKKUK 2.4

*Fig trees may no longer bloom, or vineyards
produce grapes; olive trees may be fruitless,
and harvest time a failure; sheep pens may be
empty, and cattle stalls vacant—but I will still
celebrate because the LORD God saves me. The
LORD gives me strength. He makes my feet as
sure as those of a deer, and he helps me stand
on the mountains.*
—HABAKKUK 3.17-19

ZEPHANIAH

*The great day of the LORD is coming soon, very
soon.*
—ZEPHANIAH 1.14

*The LORD your God wins victory after victory
and is always with you. He celebrates and
sings because of you, and he will refresh your
life with his love.*
—ZEPHANIAH 3.17

HAGGAI

You say this isn't the right time to build a temple for me. But is it right for you to live in expensive houses, while my temple is a pile of ruins?
—HAGGAI 1.2-5

I will shake the nations, and their treasures will be brought here. Then the brightness of my glory will fill this temple.
—HAGGAI 2.7

ZECHARIAH

I am the LORD All-Powerful. So don't depend on your own power or strength, but on my Spirit.
—ZECHARIAH 4.6

I, the LORD All-Powerful, tell you, "See that justice is done and be kind and merciful to one another!"
—ZECHARIAH 7.8,9

I'll strengthen my people because of who I am, and they will follow me. I, the LORD, have spoken!
—ZECHARIAH 10.12

MALACHI

The LORD God All-Powerful of Israel hates anyone who is cruel enough to divorce his wife. So take care never to be unfaithful!
—MALACHI 2.16

I am the LORD All-Powerful, and I challenge you to put me to the test. Bring the entire ten percent into the storehouse, so there will be food in my house. Then I will open the windows of heaven and flood you with blessing after blessing.
—MALACHI 3.10

God . . . had their names written as a reminder in his book. Then the LORD All-Powerful said: You people are precious to me.
—MALACHI 3.16,17

ᕙNEW TESTAMENTᕘ

MATTHEW

Jesus said to them, "Come with me! I will teach you how to bring in people instead of fish." Right then the two brothers dropped their nets and went with him.
—MATTHEW 4.19,20

So if you are about to place your gift on the altar and remember that someone is angry with you, leave your gift there in front of the altar. Make peace with that person, then come back and offer your gift to God.
—MATTHEW 5.23,24

But I tell you to love your enemies and pray for anyone who mistreats you.
—MATTHEW 5.44

When you give to the poor, don't let anyone know about it. Then your gift will be given in secret. Your Father knows what is done in secret, and he will reward you.
—MATTHEW 6.3,4

You should pray like this: Our Father in heaven, help us to honor your name. Come

and set up your kingdom, so that everyone on earth will obey you, as you are obeyed in heaven.
—MATTHEW 6.9,10

Your heart will always be where your treasure is. . . . You cannot serve both God and money.
—MATTHEW 6.21,24

Don't worry about tomorrow. It will take care of itself. You have enough to worry about today.
—MATTHEW 6.34

First, take the log out of your own eye. Then you can see how to take the speck out of your friend's eye.
—MATTHEW 7.5

Everyone who asks will receive. Everyone who searches will find. And the door will be opened for everyone who knocks.
—MATTHEW 7.8

If you are tired from carrying heavy burdens, come to me and I will give you rest.
—MATTHEW 11.28

Then he went up on a mountain where he could be alone and pray.
—MATTHEW 14.23

"Don't worry! I am Jesus. Don't be afraid."
—Matthew 14.27

The words that come out of your mouth come from your heart.
—MATTHEW 15.18

There in front of the disciples, Jesus was completely changed. His face was shining like the sun, and his clothes became white as light.
—Matthew 17.2

And when you welcome one of these children because of me, you welcome me.
—MATTHEW 18.5

If one of my followers sins against you, go and point out what was wrong. But do it in private, just between the two of you. If that person listens, you have won back a follower.
—MATTHEW 18.15

"Don't you think you should show pity to someone else, as I did to you?"
—MATTHEW 18.33

They are no longer two people, but one. And no one should separate a couple that God has joined together.
—MATTHEW 19.6

If you want to be great, you must be the servant of all the others.
—MATTHEW 20.26

"Love the Lord your God with all your heart, soul, and mind. . . . Love others as much as you love yourself."
—MATTHEW 22.37,39

"Whenever you did it for any of my people, no matter how unimportant they seemed, you did it for me."
—MATTHEW 25.40

"I am so sad that I feel as if I am dying. Stay here and keep awake with me."
—MATTHEW 26.38

MARK

[Jesus said,] "I didn't come to invite good people to be my followers. I came to invite sinners."
—MARK 2.17

If you give up your life for me and for the good news, you will save it. What will you gain, if you own the whole world but destroy yourself?
—MARK 8.35,36

If you want to be great, you must be the servant of all the others.
—MARK 10.43

Be alert! You don't know when the master of the house will come back. It could be in the evening or at midnight or before dawn or in the morning. . . . Don't let him find you asleep.
—MARK 13.35,36

Jesus said: ". . . She has done a beautiful thing for me. . . . You may be sure that wherever the good news is told all over the world, people will remember what she has done. And they will tell others."
—MARK 14.6,9

"Don't be alarmed! You are looking for Jesus from Nazareth, who was nailed to a cross. God has raised him to life, and he isn't here. You can see the place where they put his body. . . . He will go ahead of you to Galilee. You will see him there, just as he told you."
—MARK 16.6,7

LUKE

Jesus became wise, and he grew strong. God was pleased with him and so were the people.
—LUKE 2.52

John said, "I am just baptizing with water. But someone more powerful is going to come, and I am not good enough even to untie his sandals. He will baptize you with the Holy Spirit and with fire."
—LUKE 3.16

Love your enemies and be good to them. . . . Then you will get a great reward, and you will be the true children of God in heaven.
—LUKE 6.35

Don't judge others, and God won't judge you. Don't be hard on others, and God won't be

hard on you. Forgive others, and God will forgive you.
—LUKE 6.37

But Jesus told the woman, "Because of your faith, you are now saved. May God give you peace!"
—LUKE 7.50

Jesus answered, "You give them something to eat."
—LUKE 9.13

Then Jesus asked, "Which one of these three people was a real neighbor to the man who was beaten up by robbers?"
The teacher answered, "The one who showed pity."
Jesus said, "Go and do the same!"
—LUKE 10.36,37

The Lord answered, "Martha, Martha! You are worried and upset about so many things, but only one thing is necessary. Mary has chosen what is best, and it will not be taken away from her."
—LUKE 10.41,42

The younger son got up and started back to his father. But when he was still a long way off, his father saw him and felt sorry for him. He ran to his son and hugged and kissed him.
—LUKE 15.20

Won't God protect his chosen ones who pray to him day and night? Won't he be concerned for them? He will surely hurry and help them.
—LUKE 18.7,8

Later that day Zacchaeus stood up and said to the Lord, "I will give half of my property to the poor. And I will now pay back four times as much to everyone I have ever cheated."
—LUKE 19.8

Peter remembered that the Lord had said, "Before a rooster crows tomorrow morning, you will say three times that you don't know me." Then Peter went out and cried hard.
—LUKE 22.61,62

JOHN
Humans give life to their children. Yet only God's Spirit can change you into a child of God.
—JOHN 3.6

God loved the people of this world so much that he gave his only Son.
—JOHN 3.16

God did not send his Son into the world to condemn its people. He sent him to save them!
—JOHN 3.17

God is Spirit, and those who worship God must be led by the Spirit to worship him according to the truth.
—JOHN 4.24

"Lord, there is no one else that we can go to! Your words give eternal life."
—JOHN 6.68

I have set the example, and you should do for each other exactly what I have done for you.
—JOHN 13.15

If you love each other, everyone will know that you are my disciples.
—JOHN 13.35

"I am the way, the truth, and the life!" Jesus answered. "Without me, no one can go to the Father."
—JOHN 14.6

Servants are not greater than their master. So if people mistreat me, they will mistreat you.
—JOHN 15.20

"Simon son of John, do you love me . . . ?"
"Yes, Lord, you know I do!"
—JOHN 21.15

ACTS
They spent their time learning from the apostles, and they were like family to each other. They also broke bread and prayed together.
—ACTS 2.42

Lord, listen to their threats! We are your servants. So make us brave enough to speak your message.
—ACTS 4.29

They shared everything they had with each other. In a powerful way the apostles told everyone that the Lord Jesus was now alive.
—ACTS 4.32,33

*Everyone prayed and went without eating. . . .
Next, they placed their hands on Barnabas
and Saul to show that they had been appointed
to do this work. Then everyone sent them on
their way.*
—ACTS 13.3

*Apollos started speaking bravely in the Jewish
meeting place. But when Priscilla and Aquila
heard him, they took him to their home and
helped him understand God's Way even better.*
—ACTS 18.26

ROMANS

*Not one of them understands or even searches
for God. They have all turned away and are
worthless. There isn't one person who does
right.*
—ROMANS 3.11,12

God treats everyone alike.
—ROMANS 3.22

God's promise is assured by his great kindness.
—ROMANS 4.16

*God set you free when he sent his own Son to
be like us sinners and to be a sacrifice for our
sin. . . . He did this, so that we would do what
the Law commands by obeying the Spirit
instead of our own desires.*
—ROMANS 8.3,4

*You are no longer ruled by your desires, but by
God's Spirit, who lives in you.*
—ROMANS 8.9

*We know that God is always at work for the
good of everyone who loves him.*
—ROMANS 8.28

All who call out to the Lord will be saved.
—ROMANS 10.13

*A body is made up of many parts, and each of
them has its own use. That's how it is with us.
There are many of us, but we each are part of
the body of Christ, as well as part of one
another.*
—ROMANS 12.4,5

*Love each other as brothers and sisters and
honor others more than you do yourself.*
—ROMANS 12.10

*Whether we live or die, it must be for God,
rather than for ourselves. . . . Each of us must
give an account to God for what we do.*
—ROMANS 14.7,12

*God's kingdom . . . is about pleasing God,
about living in peace, and about true
happiness. All this comes from the Holy Spirit.
If you serve Christ in this way, you will please
God and be respected by people.*
—ROMANS 14.17,18

*God is the one who makes us patient and
cheerful. I pray that he will help you live at
peace with each other, as you follow Christ.*
—ROMANS 15.5

*It is just as the Scriptures say, "All who haven't
been told about him will see him, and those
who haven't heard about him will understand."*
—ROMANS 15.21

1 CORINTHIANS

*All of you surely know that you are God's
temple and that his Spirit lives in you.
Together you are God's holy temple.*
—1 CORINTHIANS 3.16,17

*God paid a great price for you. So use your
body to honor God.*
—1 CORINTHIANS 6.20

*Husbands and wives should be fair with each
other about having sex. A wife belongs to her
husband instead of to herself, and a husband
belongs to his wife instead of to himself.*
—1 CORINTHIANS 7.3,4

God chose you and wants you to live at peace.
—1 CORINTHIANS 7.15

*I want all of you to be free from worry. . . .
Unmarried women and women who have never
been married worry only about pleasing the
Lord, and they keep their bodies and minds
pure.*
—1 CORINTHIANS 7.32,34

*You must follow my example, as I follow the
example of Christ.*
—1 CORINTHIANS 11.1

*There are different ways to serve the same
Lord, and we can each do different things. Yet*

the same God works in all of us and helps us
in everything we do.
—1 CORINTHIANS 12.5,6

If one part of our body hurts, we hurt all over.
If one part of our body is honored, the whole
body will be happy. Together you are the body
of Christ.
—1 CORINTHIANS 12.26,27

Love is kind and patient, never jealous,
boastful, proud, or rude. Love isn't selfish or
quick tempered. It doesn't keep a record of
wrongs that others do. Love rejoices in the
truth, but not in evil. Love is always supportive, loyal, hopeful, and trusting. Love never
fails!
—1 CORINTHIANS 13.4-8

Love is always supportive, loyal, hopeful, and
trusting. Love never fails!
—1 CORINTHIANS 13.7,8

We don't know everything, but then we will,
just as God completely understands us. For
now there are faith, hope, and love. But of
these three, the greatest is love.
—1 CORINTHIANS 13.12,13

But suppose all of you are prophesying when
those unbelievers and outsiders come in. They
will realize that they are sinners, and they will
want to change their ways because of what you
are saying. They will tell what is hidden in
their hearts. Then they will kneel down and say
to God, "We are certain that you are with
these people."
—1 CORINTHIANS 14.24,25

These bodies will die, but the bodies that are
raised will live forever. These ugly and weak
bodies will become beautiful and strong. . . .
Then the Scriptures will come true, "Death has
lost the battle! Where is its victory? Where is
its sting?"
—1 CORINTHIANS 15.42,43,54,55

2 CORINTHIANS
Praise God, the Father of our Lord Jesus
Christ! The Father is a merciful God, who
always gives us comfort. He comforts us when
we are in trouble, so that we can share that
same comfort with others in trouble.
—2 CORINTHIANS 1.3,4

God thinks of us as a perfume that brings
Christ to everyone. For people who are being
saved, this perfume has a sweet smell and leads
them to a better life.
—2 CORINTHIANS 2.15,16

We are like clay jars in which this treasure is
stored. The real power comes from God and
not from us.
—2 CORINTHIANS 4.7

Anyone who belongs to Christ is a new person.
The past is forgotten, and everything is new.
—2 CORINTHIANS 5.17

Stay away from people who are not followers of
the Lord! Can someone who is good get along
with someone who is evil? Are light and
darkness the same?. . . . We are the temple of
the living God.
—2 CORINTHIANS 6.14,16

[God] replied, "My kindness is all you
need. My power is strongest when you are
weak."
—2 CORINTHIANS 12.9

GALATIANS
They . . . heard that the one who had been
cruel to them was now preaching the message
that he had once tried to destroy. And because
of me, they praised God.
—GALATIANS 1.23,24

Faith in Christ Jesus is what makes each of you
equal with each other, whether you are a Jew or
a Greek, a slave or a free person, a man or a
woman.
—GALATIANS 3.28

My friends, you were chosen to be free. So
don't use your freedom as an excuse to do
anything you want. Use it as an opportunity to
serve each other with love.
—GALATIANS 5.13

God's Spirit has given us life, and so we should
follow the Spirit.
—GALATIANS 5.25

You obey the law of Christ when you offer each
other a helping hand.
—GALATIANS 6.2

Don't get tired of helping others. You will be

rewarded when the time is right, if you don't give up.
—GALATIANS 6.9

EPHESIANS

God was kind and decided that Christ would choose us to be God's own adopted children.
—EPHESIANS 1.5

My prayer is that light will flood your hearts and that you will understand the hope that was given to you when God chose you. Then you will discover the glorious blessings that will be yours together with all of God's people.
—EPHESIANS 1.18

You were saved by faith in God, who treats us much better than we deserve. This is God's gift to you, and not anything you have done on your own.
—EPHESIANS 2.8

On the cross Christ did away with our hatred for each other. He also made peace between us and God.
—EPHESIANS 2.16

And you are part of that building Christ has built as a place for God's own Spirit to live.
—EPHESIANS 2.22

I kneel in prayer to the Father. All beings in heaven and on earth receive their life from him.
—EPHESIANS 3.14,15

Live in a way that is worthy of the people God has chosen to be his own. Always be humble and gentle. Patiently put up with each other and love each other.
—EPHESIANS 4.1,2

Love should always make us tell the truth. Then we will grow in every way and be more like Christ, the head of the body.
—EPHESIANS 4.15,16

We are part of the same body. . . . Start telling each other the truth. Don't get so angry that you sin.
—EPHESIANS 4.25,26

Do as God does. After all, you are his dear children. Let love be your guide. . . . Don't let

it be said that any of you are immoral or indecent or greedy.
—EPHESIANS 5.1-3

Make your light shine. Be good and honest and truthful, as you try to please the Lord.
—EPHESIANS 5.9,10

Honor Christ and put others first.
—EPHESIANS 5.21

A husband should love his wife as much as he loves himself. A husband who loves his wife shows that he loves himself. None of us hate our own bodies. We provide for them and take good care of them, just as Christ does for the church.
—EPHESIANS 5.28,29

Parents, don't be hard on your children. Raise them properly. Teach them and instruct them about the Lord.
—EPHESIANS 6.4

Let the mighty strength of the Lord make you strong.
—EPHESIANS 6.10

PHILIPPIANS

I will keep on being glad, because I know that your prayers and the help that comes from the Spirit of Christ Jesus will keep me safe. I honestly expect and hope that I will never do anything to be ashamed of. Whether I live or die, I always want to . . . bring honor to Christ.
—PHILIPPIANS 1.18-20

Be united in what you think, as if you were only one person. Don't be jealous or proud, but be humble and consider others more important than yourselves. Care about them as much as you care about yourselves and think the same way that Christ Jesus thought.
—PHILIPPIANS 2.2-4

But Christ has shown me that what I once thought was valuable is worthless. Nothing is as wonderful as knowing Christ Jesus my Lord.
—PHILIPPIANS 3.7,8

With thankful hearts offer up your prayers and requests to God. Then, because you belong to Christ Jesus, God will bless you with peace that no one can completely understand. And this

peace will control the way you think and feel.
—PHILIPPIANS 4.6,7

The Lord has made me very grateful that at last you have thought about me once again. Actually, you were thinking about me all along, but you didn't have any chance to show it.
—PHILIPPIANS 4.10

COLOSSIANS

You have accepted Christ Jesus as your Lord. Now keep on following him. Plant your roots in Christ and let him be the foundation for your life. Be strong in your faith, just as you were taught.
—COLOSSIANS 2.6

Each of you is now a new person. You are becoming more and more like your Creator, and you will understand him better.
—COLOSSIANS 3.10

Be gentle, kind, humble, meek, and patient. Put up with each other.
—COLOSSIANS 3.12,13

Each one of you is part of the body of Christ, and you were chosen to live together in peace. . . . Whatever you say or do should be done in the name of the Lord Jesus.
—COLOSSIANS 3.15,17

Do your work willingly, as though you were serving the Lord himself, and not just your earthly master. In fact, the Lord Christ is the one you are really serving, and you know that he will reward you.
—COLOSSIANS 3.23,24

Choose your words carefully and be ready to give answers to anyone who asks questions.
—COLOSSIANS 4.6

1 THESSALONIANS

God wants you to be holy, so don't be immoral in matters of sex. . . . You must not cheat any of the Lord's followers in matters of sex.
—1 THESSALONIANS 4.3,6

Try your best to live quietly, to mind your own business, and to work hard, just as we taught you to do. Then you will be respected by people who are not followers of the Lord.
—1 THESSALONIANS 4.11,12

We believe that Jesus died and was raised to life. We also believe that when God brings Jesus back again, he will bring with him all who had faith in Jesus before they died.
—1 THESSALONIANS 4.14

2 THESSALONIANS

God our Father loves us. He is kind and has given us eternal comfort and a wonderful hope. We pray that our Lord Jesus Christ and God our Father will encourage you and help you always to do and say the right thing.
—2 THESSALONIANS 2.16,17

We didn't want to be a burden to any of you, so night and day we worked as hard as we could. . . . Dear friends, you must never become tired of doing right.
—2 THESSALONIANS 3.8,13

1 TIMOTHY

If you teach these things to other followers, you will be a good servant of Christ Jesus. You will show that you have grown up on the teachings about our faith and on the good instructions you have obeyed.
—1 TIMOTHY 4.6

If a widow has children or grandchildren, they should learn to serve God by taking care of her, as she once took care of them. This is what God wants them to do.
—1 TIMOTHY 5.4

Be fair with everyone, and don't have any favorites. . . . If you are a slave, you should respect and honor your owner. This will keep people from saying bad things about God and about our teaching.
—1 TIMOTHY 5.21; 6.1

[Be] content with what you have. We didn't bring anything into this world, and we won't take anything with us when we leave. So we should be satisfied.
—1 TIMOTHY 6.6-8

Warn the rich people of this world not to be proud or to trust in wealth that is easily lost. Tell them to have faith in God, who is rich and blesses us with everything we need to enjoy life.
—1 TIMOTHY 6.17

2 TIMOTHY

So I ask you to make full use of the gift that God gave you when I placed my hands on you. Use it well.
—2 TIMOTHY 1.6

God's Spirit doesn't make cowards out of us. The Spirit gives us power, love, and self-control. . . . Do your best to win God's approval as a worker who doesn't need to be ashamed and who teaches only the true message.
—2 TIMOTHY 1.7; 2.15

The ones who stop doing evil and make themselves pure will become special. Their lives will be holy and pleasing to their Master, and they will be able to do all kinds of good deeds.
—2 TIMOTHY 2.21

When I was first put on trial, no one helped me. In fact, everyone deserted me. . . . But the Lord stood beside me. . . . Praise him forever and ever!
—2 TIMOTHY 4.16-18

TITUS

Always set a good example for others.
—TITUS 2.7

God our Savior showed us how good and kind he is.
—TITUS 3.4

Our people should learn to spend their time doing something useful and worthwhile.
—TITUS 3.14

PHILEMON

I want your act of kindness to come from your heart, and not be something you feel forced to do.
—PHILEMON 14

Onesimus is much more than a slave. To me he is a dear friend, but to you he is even more, both as a person and as a follower of the Lord.
—PHILEMON 16

HEBREWS

What God has said isn't only alive and active! It is sharper than any double-edged sword. His word can cut through our spirits and souls and through our joints and marrow, until it discovers the desires and thoughts of our hearts.
—HEBREWS 4.12

We must try to become mature and start thinking about more than just the basic things we were taught about Christ. . . . Let's grow up, if God is willing.
—HEBREWS 6.1,3

Keep on being brave! It will bring you great rewards.
—HEBREWS 10.35

"The Lord corrects the people he loves and disciplines those he calls his own."
—HEBREWS 12.6

Keep being concerned about each other as the Lord's followers should. Be sure to welcome strangers into your home.
—HEBREWS 13.1,2

Have respect for marriage. Always be faithful to your partner.
—HEBREWS 13.4

Don't fall in love with money. Be satisfied with what you have. The Lord has promised that he will not leave us or desert us.
—HEBREWS 13.5

JAMES

If any of you need wisdom, you should ask God, and it will be given to you.
—JAMES 1.5

God will bless you, if you don't give up when your faith is being tested. He will reward you with a glorious life, just as he rewards everyone who loves him.
—JAMES 1.12

All of us do many wrong things. But if you can control your tongue, you are mature and able to control your whole body.
—JAMES 3.2

But the wisdom that comes from above leads us to be pure, friendly, gentle, sensible, kind, helpful, genuine, and sincere. When peacemakers plant seeds of peace, they will harvest justice.
—JAMES 3.17,18

We praise the ones who endured the most. You remember how patient Job was and how the Lord finally helped him. The Lord did this because he is so merciful and kind.
—JAMES 5.11

My friends, if any followers have wandered away from the truth, you should try to lead them back. If you turn sinners from the wrong way, you will save them from death, and many of their sins will be forgiven.
—JAMES 5.19,20

1 PETER
Put your husband first. Even if he opposes our message, you will win him over by what you do.
—1 PETER 3.1

The Lord watches over everyone who obeys him, and he listens to their prayers.
—1 PETER 3.12

You are better off to obey God and suffer for doing right than to suffer for doing wrong.
—1 PETER 3.17

Everything will soon come to an end. So be serious and be sensible enough to pray. Most important of all, you must sincerely love each other, because love wipes away many sins.
—1 PETER 4.7,8

Each of you has been blessed with one of God's many wonderful gifts to be used in the service of others. So use your gift well.
—1 PETER 4.10

Don't be ashamed to suffer for being a Christian. Praise God that you belong to him.
—1 PETER 4.16

Just as shepherds watch over their sheep, you must watch over everyone God has placed in your care. . . . God cares for you, so turn your worries over to him.
—1 PETER 5.2,7

2 PETER
We have everything we need to live a life that pleases God. It was all given to us by God's own power, when we learned that he had invited us to share in his wonderful goodness.
—2 PETER 1.3

Lot lived right. . . . He was a good man, and day after day he suffered because of the evil things he saw and heard. So the Lord rescued him.
—2 PETER 2.7,8

1 JOHN
But if we confess our sins to God, he can always be trusted to forgive us and take our sins away.
—1 JOHN 1.9

When we love others, we know that we belong to the truth, and we feel at ease in the presence of God.
—1 JOHN 3.19

My dear friends, we must love each other. Love comes from God, and when we love each other, it shows that we have been given new life.
—1 JOHN 4.7

2 JOHN
Don't keep changing what you were taught about Christ, or else God will no longer be with you. But if you hold firmly to what you were taught, both the Father and the Son will be with you.
—2 JOHN 9

3 JOHN
Dear friend, you have always been faithful in helping other followers of the Lord, even the ones you didn't know before.
—3 JOHN 5

JUDE
Some godless people have sneaked in among us and are saying, "God treats us much better than we deserve, and so it is all right to be immoral." They even deny that we must obey Jesus Christ as our only Master and Lord. But long ago the Scriptures warned that these godless people were doomed.
—JUDE 4

REVELATION
I know everything you have done, including your hard work and how you have endured. . . . You don't have as much love as you used to. Think about where you have fallen from, and then turn back and do as you did at first.
—REVELATION 2.2,4,5

Listen! I am standing and knocking at your door. If you hear my voice and open the door, I will come in and we will eat together.
—REVELATION 3.20

After this, I saw a large crowd with more people than could be counted. They were from every race, tribe, nation, and language, and they stood before the throne and before the Lamb. They wore white robes and held palm branches in their hands.
—Revelation 7.9

God's people must learn to endure. . . .
The Spirit answered, "Yes, they will rest from their hard work, and they will be rewarded for what they have done."
—REVELATION 14.12,13

God will make his home among his people. He will wipe all tears from their eyes, and there will be no more death, suffering, crying, or pain. These things of the past are gone forever.
—REVELATION 21.3,4

Only those whose names are written in the Lamb's book of life will be in the city. . . .
The Spirit and the bride say, "Come!"
Everyone who hears this should say, "Come!"
If you are thirsty, come! If you want life-giving water, come and take it. It's free!
—REVELATION 21.27; 22.17

About the Contributors

(All the women who've served faithfully on this project.)

CARLA BARNHILL has a Master's Degree in English Literature from the University of Edinburgh in Scotland. She has also taken classes toward an M.A. in Theology at Fuller Theological Seminary. Carla is an assistant editor with *Campus Life* magazine and has worked with youth for more than 10 years. She and her husband, Jim, live in the Chicago area with their daughter.

RUTH BARTON is working on an M.Div. from Northern Baptist Theological Seminary. She is the author of four books and numerous articles, and is a frequent speaker and teacher. She has served on a pastoral staff as Director of Women's Ministries and is current president of the Chicago Chapter of Christians for Biblical Equality. She lives in Illinois with her husband, Chris, and three daughters.

SUSAN WISE BAUER was homeschooled and entered college at age seventeen—which she finished in five semesters. She then earned an M.A. in English Language and Literature from the College of William and Mary and an M.Div. from Westminster Theological Seminary. She has written several books, both fiction and nonfiction, and writes regularly for Charles Colson's BreakPoint radio commentary. She also teaches British Literature at William and Mary College. She lives in Virginia with husband, Peter, and their three children.

DEE BRESTIN is best known for her writing and speaking on women's relationships. Among her books are *The Friendships of Women* and *We Are Sisters*, both published by Victor Books. She also has a series of Bible study guides with Victor including *A Woman of Joy* and *A Woman of Insight*. Dee and her husband, Steve, are parents of five children and live in Nebraska.

BARBARA M. CALVERT is Editorial Coordinator for *Today's Christian Woman* and *Marriage Partnership* magazines. She and her husband, Roy, live in the Chicago area and are currently on their tenth year of a "through the Bible in ten years" study. They enjoy Christian history study tours, archaeology conferences, and have found the "empty nest" a time of personal and spiritual growth.

KAREN DOCKREY has an M.Div. from Southern Baptist Theological Seminary and has worked as an educator and a youth minister. She has been writing for youth and families for more than twenty years. She is the author of more than twenty-five books including *Growing a Family Where People Really Like Each Other* (Bethany), *Holman Student Bible Dictionary* (Broadman and Holman), and *When a Hug Won't Fix the Hurt* (Victor) which tells of her daughter's battle with cancer. She and her husband are parents to daughters, Sarah and Emily.

DIANE EBLE has a B.A. from the University of Connecticut. She works as a freelance writer and editor and has written numerous articles. Her work has been published in *Marriage Partnership, Campus Life, Christianity Today, Discipleship Journal,* and other magazines. She is the author of *A Life You Can Love, Men in Search of Work and the Women Who Love Them*, and *Knowing the Voice of God* (all by Zondervan). She and her husband live in the Chicago area with their two children.